World Trade Organization
Dispute Settlement Decisions

Bernan's Annotated Reporter

Volume 67-B
Decisions Reported
March 8–15, 2005

World Trade Organization
Dispute Settlement Decisions

Bernan's Annotated Reporter

Bernan Press
Lanham, Maryland, USA
James J. Patton, Editor

Printed by Automated Graphic Systems, Inc., White Plains, MD, USA, on acid-free paper that meets The American National Standards Institute Z39-48 standard.

BERNAN PRESS
4611-F Assembly Drive
Lanham, MD 20706-4391
(800) 274-4447 (301) 459-2255
Email: info@bernan.com
www.bernanpress.com

ISBN: 1-59888-000-4
ISSN: 1534-7559

TABLE OF CONTENTS

PREFACE

The WORLD TRADE ORGANIZATION DISPUTE SETTLEMENT DECISIONS: BERNAN'S ANNOTATED REPORTER series is intended to provide the user with comprehensive and efficient access to the decisions of the World Trade Organization's Dispute Settlement Body and its activities. Provided herein are the full text cases of all WTO Panels and of the Appellate Body.

Cases are set forth in chronological order, based on the date of the decision being reported. References to the disputes may be limited to the common name (i.e., *Japan – Alcohol*), or the Dispute Settlement reference number (i.e., WT/DS8/AB/R). Before each opinion, several additional features are offered. Each case has a front section that includes:

i. Title of case
ii. Parties
iii. Procedural history
iv. Summary of conclusions
v. Annotations
vi. Table of contents

The annotations recite significant legal determinations made by the Panel or Appellate Body in the course of its ruling. Each such annotation includes a paragraph reference, a principle, and a WTO treaty source document reference. An example follows:

7.70–7.72 **Allocation of quotas** [GATT, Article XIII.2(d)]

This indicates that on paragraphs 7.70–7.72 of the given case, the user will find a ruling or interpretation by the Panel (or Appellate Body) on quota allocation as regulated under the terms of the General Agreements on Tariffs and Trade, Article XIII.2(d). The principles used in reference to GATT provisions are based on the *GATT Guide to Law and Practice*, co-published by the World Trade Organization and Bernan.

Four tables follow the reported cases.

i. Overview of Dispute Settlement Activity
ii. Countries Involved in Disputes
iii. Treaty Provisions Interpreted
iv. BISD and Dispute References

The first two of these tables relate to dispute settlement activity generally under the auspices of the Dispute Settlement Body. Table I provides an update of disputes that have been acted upon during the time period covered within this volume. Noted along with dispute name and reference number are the complainant(s) and a brief description of the action that occurred. Also noted are connections between complaints where the same laws, regulations, or government practices are being disputed by more than one Member. Table II shows the distribution of dispute settlement activity to date by country. Herein, each country is listed with dispute reference citations noted as to whether the country was a complainant or a respondent.

The third and fourth tables refer only to the cases reported in this volume. Table III indicates which WTO agreements have been interpreted by the Panels and Appellate Body in the cases within this volume. Paragraph references are again provided, with the number indicating the location of the analysis of the given provision. Table IV is a table of references within the reports of this volume to other WTO and GATT materials, particularly decisions, protocols, announcements, and reports published in the Basic Instruments and Selected Documents (BISD) and WTO dispute settlement references.

Lastly, each volume includes a topical index. The index also provides reference to the cases by paragraph number.

*****

The goal of producing this series is to increase access to the World Trade Organization's Dispute Settlement system through the conveyance of its decisions in a comprehensive and accessible manner. Please submit any questions or remarks to the address on page iv, or by e-mail to info@bernan.com.

ANNEX B-6

ORAL STATEMENT OF THE EUROPEAN COMMUNITIES SECOND SUBSTANTIVE MEETING

(12 August 2004)

TABLE OF CONTENTS

(a) The exception is "limited"
(b) The exception "takes account" of the interests of the trademark owners and third parties

B. CLAIM 20: REGULATION 2081/92 DOES NOT PROVIDE FOR A PRESUMPTION OF A LIKELIHOOD OF CONFUSION IN THE CASE OF USE OF AN IDENTICAL SIGN FOR IDENTICAL GOODS

C. CLAIMS 21 AND 22: ARTICLE 7(4) OF REGULATION 2081/92 IS INCONSISTENT WITH ARTICLE 16.1 OF THE TRIPS AGREEMENT BECAUSE IT DOES NOT PROVIDE A RIGHT OF OBJECTION

VI. THE EC MEASURE IS CONSISTENT WITH THE OBLIGATION TO PROVIDE PROTECTION TO GEOGRAPHICAL INDICATIONS UNDER ARTICLE 22.2 OF THE TRIPS AGREEMENT

VII. REGULATION 2081/92 IS CONSISTENT WITH OBLIGATIONS UNDER THE TBT AGREEMENT

A. ARTICLE (12)(2) OF REGULATION 2081/92 IS NOT A TECHNICAL REGULATION

B. ARTICLES 4 AND 10 OF REGULATION 2081/92 ARE NOT A TECHNICAL REGULATION

VIII. CONCLUSION

Table of WTO and GATT cases referred to in this statement

Short Title	Full Case Title and Citation of Case
Argentina – Footwear (EC)	Appellate Body Report, *Argentina – Safeguard Measures on Imports of Footwear*, WT/DS121/AB/R, adopted 12 January 2000, DSR 2000:I, 515
EC – Asbestos	Appellate Body Report, *European Communities – Measures Affecting Asbestos and Asbestos-Containing Products*, WT/DS135/AB/R, adopted 5 April 2001
Indonesia – Autos	Panel Report, *Indonesia – Certain Measures Affecting the Automobile Industry*, WT/DS54/R, WT/DS55/R, WT/DS59/R, WT/DS64/R and Corr.1, 2, 3, and 4, adopted 23 July 1998, DSR 1998:VI, 2201
Korea – Dairy	Appellate Body Report, *Korea – Definitive Safeguard Measure on Imports of Certain Dairy Products*, WT/DS98/AB/R, adopted 12 January 2000, DSR 2000:I, 3
Korea – Various Measures on Beef	Appellate Body Report, *Korea – Measures Affecting Imports of Fresh, Chilled and Frozen Beef*, WT/DS161/AB/R, WT/DS169/AB/R, adopted 10 January 2001
US – Section 337	Panel Report, *US – Section 337 of the Tariff Act of 1930*, Report by the Panel adopted on 7 November 1989 (L/6439 – 36S/345)
US – Taxes on Automobiles	Panel Report, *United State – Taxes on Automobiles*, DS31/R, 11 October 1994

GLOSSARY

Commission, EC Commission	Commission of the European Communities
Committee	Committee of representatives of the Member States referred to in Article 15 of Council Regulation 2081/92
Community Trademark Regulation	Council Regulation (EC) No 40/94, of 20 December 1993, on the Community Trademark, as amended
Council, EC Council	Council of the European Union
Court of Justice, European Court of Justice	Court of Justice of the European Communities
DSU	Understanding on Rules and Procedures Governing the Settlement of Disputes
EC	European Communities
GATT	General Agreement on Tariffs and Trade 1994
FOS	First Oral Statement
FWS	First Written Submission
GI	Geographical indication
Member States, EC Member States	Member States of the European Union
Official Journal	Official Journal of the European Union
OHIM	Office for Harmonization in the Internal Market
Paris Convention	Stockholm Act of the Paris Convention for the protection of Industrial property, of 14 July 1967
Regulation 2081/92, Regulation	Council Regulation (EEC) No 2081/92 of 14 July 1992 on the protection of geographical indications and designations of origin for agricultural products and foodstuffs, as amended on the date of establishment of the Panel
SCM Agreement, SCM	Agreement on Subsidies and Countervailing Duties
SWS	Second Written Submission
Trademarks Directive	First Council Directive 89/104, of 20 December, on the Community Trademark, as amended
TBT Agreement, TBT	Agreement on Technical Barriers to Trade

TRIPS Agreement, TRIPS	Agreement on Trade-Related Aspects of Intellectual Property Rights
US	United States
WTO Agreement	Marrakesh Agreement Establishing the World Trade Organization

I. INTRODUCTION

1. The European Communities welcomes this opportunity to submit its views in this dispute. In our statement of this morning we will provide a response to the rebuttal submissions of the complainants. We will follow the same order of claims as in our written submissions.

2. While we have striven to avoid unnecessary repetitions, the large number of claims involved, together with the fact that the complainants often make divergent, if not contradictory arguments under each claim, have prevented us from being as concise as we would have liked at this stage of the proceedings. We trust, however, that the panel will understand that the EC cannot leave without response the numerous new arguments, and in some cases new claims, made by the complainants in their rebuttal submissions.

II. THE OBJECTIVE ASSESSMENT OF THE CONTENT OF REGULATION 2081/92

3. The complainants and the EC disagree about the interpretation which must be given to a number of the provisions of Regulation 2081/92. A central task for the Panel will therefore be to establish the proper meaning of Regulation 2081/92 as a measure of EC domestic law. The Panel must carry out this task in accordance with Article 11 of the DSU, which requires "an objective assessment of the facts of the case."

4. At this stage, the EC does not wish to repeat what it has already said in its previous submissions.[1] However, since this is a horizontal issue of some importance to a number of the claims, and since the complainants persist in interpreting several of the provisions of Regulation 2081/92 in a way which does not correspond to the meaning of the measure, the EC would like to offer some general observations about the objective assessment of Regulation 2081/92.

5. First, and maybe most obviously, it must be recalled that since the interpretation of Regulation 2081/92 is a question of fact, the burden of proof for establishing that Regulation 2081/92 has the meaning which the complainants allege is on the complainants. In their submissions, however, the complainants have repeatedly attempted to shift this burden of proof to the EC, and asked the EC to disprove their claims.[2] This is not admissible. In order to prove their case, the complainants must do more than simply make factual assertions. They must establish that the interpretation of Regulation 2081/92 which they defend is the only correct one, taking into account the wording, objectives and context of the measure in the EC legal order.

6. Second, the assessment of the content of Regulation 2081/92 must be objective. In their submissions, the complainants are systematically defending those interpretations of Regulation 2081/92 which are the least compatible with the EC's WTO obligations. In contrast, the complainants systematically discard those interpretations of Regulation 2081/92 which do not result in a violation of WTO obligations, even where these interpretations are mandated by the wording, objectives and context of the Regulation. It is submitted that such an approach to the interpretation of Regulation 2081/92 does not constitute an objective assessment of the facts.

7. Third, as a measure of EC domestic law, Regulation 2081/92 must be interpreted in accordance with the principles of interpretation applicable in the EC domestic legal order. A particularly important element for the interpretation of Regulation 2081/92 are therefore the international obligations of the European Community, including the WTO Agreements. Contrary to what Australia continues to argue, this has nothing to do with the question of whether WTO law has "direct effect" in the EC legal order, and whether the European Court of Justice can review the legality of EC measures on the basis of their compatibility with WTO obligations.[3]

---

[1] EC Response to the Panel's Question No. 1, para. 1 et seq.; EC SWS, para. 3 et seq.

[2] US Response to Panel's Question No. 1, para. 1.

[3] Australia's SWS, para. 42.

8. The European Court of Justice has held repeatedly that Community law must be interpreted in accordance with the Community's international obligations.[4] This principle is highly relevant to the present case. It seems excluded that when faced with two equally possible interpretations of a provision of Community law, the Court of Justice would simply chose the one which leads to a violation of WTO obligations rather than the one which would not.

9. As one practical example for the way in which the European Court of Justice takes into account WTO law in the interpretation of EC law, the EC has referred to the Court's judgment in the Petrotub case.[5] To the EC's surprise, the United States has found this case not only instructive, but also "worrisome."[6] In the view of the EC, the Petrotub judgment should be reassuring to the complainants, not worrisome. In this judgment, the Court gave effect to a provision of the Anti-Dumping Agreement on the basis that the EC Anti-Dumping Regulation was intended to implement this agreement. The Court of Justice reached this result despite the fact that the AD Regulation did not contain a specific reference to the provision applied, let alone a "without prejudice" clause similar to that contained in Article 12(1) of Regulation 2081/92.[7]

10. The US has also referred to the fact that in the Petrotub case, the Commission had defended a contrary position in the proceedings before the Court of Justice to the one the EC had taken in a response to questions in the WTO AD Committee.[8] The EC does not consider this relevant for the present case. What is relevant is that despite the contrary position of the Commission and the Council, the Court of Justice took account of the international obligations of the Community, and of the statements of the EC in the WTO, and applied these international obligations.

11. In the case of Regulation 2081/92, the case for an interpretation in the light of the EC's WTO commitments is even clearer. Regulation 2081/92 contains clear references to international obligations, particularly in Article 12(1). In the present proceedings, the EC has unambiguously and publicly explained the interpretation to be given to the contentious provisions of the Regulation. On the basis of the case law of the European Court of Justice, there should be no doubt that the Court will take this into due account in its interpretation of the Regulation.

12. In its second submission, the United States has suggested that the explanations offered by the EC should be disregarded because they "lack legal force." Moreover, the United States has raised the concern that the Council, the "25 Member States" or individuals might contest the "Commission's" interpretation.

13. In this respect, the EC would like to recall once again that the explanations given before this Panel are given on behalf of the European Communities, not of any particular Community institution. Secondly, the question before the Panel involves the interpretation of an act of domestic law within the domestic legal order of the Member concerned. There is therefore no need to create new legal obligations, but to establish the proper meaning of the EC measure within the EC legal system. It is not sufficient for the complainants simply to refer to the risk that the interpretation of the Regulation could be contested. In a system based on the rule of law, any legal measure can in principle be contested. However, the question is whether such a challenge would realistically succeed; and this the complainants have failed to show.

---

[4] EC Response to Panel's Question No. 15, para. 32 et seq.; EC, SWS, para. 18 et seq.

[5] EC Response to the Panel's Question No. 15, para. 36.

[6] US SWS, para. 13.

[7] The US has attempted to cast doubt on this fact by pointing out that in the Petrotub judgment, the Court of Justice also referred to Article 253 EC Treaty (former Article 190 EC), which lays down the general duty to state reasons for Community legislative acts (US SWS, para. 17-18). The EC fails to see the relevance of this distinction. Whether the Court applied the EC Anti-Dumping Regulation or Article 253 EC Treaty, the fact is that it interpreted EC law in line with the EC's WTO commitments. The fact that it did this even with respect to a provision of EC primary law should strengthen the confidence of the US, not diminish it.

[8] US SWS, para. 14.

14. In its second submission, the United States has also argued that "if a WTO-consistent interpretation is not possible, the ECJ will apply EC law alone."[9] The EC can agree with this statement. However, in its submission, the US is not applying its own standard correctly. It is not sufficient for the complainants to show that a WTO-inconsistent interpretation is possible; rather, they must show that a WTO-consistent interpretation is impossible. As the EC will show with respect to the individual claims, the complainants do not meet this standard.

III. REGULATION 2081/92 IS COMPATIBLE WITH NATIONAL TREATMENT OBLIGATIONS, AND DOES NOT IMPOSE A REQUIREMENT OF DOMICILE OR ESTABLISHMENT

15. The EC will now address the claims that Regulation 2081/92 constitutes a violation of the national treatment provisions of the TRIPS and the GATT, as well as the prohibition on conditions of domicile and establishment in Article 2.2 of the Paris Convention.

A. NATIONAL TREATMENT UNDER THE TRIPS AGREEMENT (ARTICLE 3.1 TRIPS AND ARTICLE 2.1 TRIPS IN CONJUNCTION WITH ARTICLE 2.1 PARIS CONVENTION)

1. The Meaning and Scope of National Treatment under the TRIPS Agreement

16. Before addressing the individuals claims of the complainants under the national treatment provisions of the TRIPS Agreement, the EC considers it necessary to comment on the following general points:

- TRIPS national treatment concerns the treatment of nationals;
- Regulation 2081/92 does not discriminate between nationals;
- Regulation 2081/92 does not involve *de facto* discrimination between nationals;
- The fact that different legal provisions apply does not prove that there is less favourable treatment.

(a) TRIPS national treatment concerns the treatment of nationals, not of goods, or of residents

17. As the EC has already set out in its previous submissions, unlike Article III:4 GATT, the national treatment provisions of the TRIPS concern discrimination as between <u>nationals</u>, not between goods, or between residents.[10]

18. In their second submission, the complainants continue to contest this essential difference between GATT and TRIPS national treatment.[11] According to the complainants, the fact that different legal provisions apply depending on the location of the area to which the geographical indication is related amounts to discrimination between nationals.[12] In the view of the EC, this interpretation is incompatible with the national treatment provisions of the TRIPS Agreement.

19. Article 3(1) of the TRIPS Agreement—and similarly Article 2(1) of the Paris Convention—requires WTO Members to accord to the <u>nationals</u> of other Members treatment no less favourable than to their own <u>nationals</u>. This reference to nationals in the TRIPS Agreement is intentional, and must be given meaning.

---

[9] US SWS, para. 16.

[10] EC FWS, para. 104 et seq.; EC SWS, para. 28 et seq.

[11] US SWS, para. 25 et seq. ; Australia SWS, para. 182.

[12] The complainants have made similar arguments also as regards the right of objection.

20. In their submissions, the complainants fail to provide a meaningful interpretation of this concept. Their argument is that the Regulation requires foreign nationals to become resident or established in the EC, and that because of this requirement, foreign nationals are required to become "EC nationals."[13] This argument is false in two respects. First, as the EC will set out, the Regulation 2081/92 does not contain any requirement of domicile or establishment. Second, even if a foreign national becomes domiciled or established in the EC, this does not mean he becomes an EC national.

21. Nationality on the one hand, and domicile and establishment on the other, are distinct concepts which cannot simply be equated in the way the complainants suggest. For a natural person, a national is a person who holds the nationality of a country in accordance with the laws of that country. Neither in the EC, nor in the United States or Australia, does a person acquire the nationality simply by being a resident. In the same way, the nationality of legal persons is defined using various criteria other than establishment, most importantly the law of incorporation.

22. The fact that nationality and domicile are separate concepts is also borne out in the TRIPS Agreement itself. Several provisions of the TRIPS Agreement, namely Article 24.4, 40.3 and 40.4, refer to "nationals and domiciliaries" in the alternative. If the drafters of the TRIPS Agreement had wanted to refer to both "nationals and domiciliaries" in Article 3.1 TRIPS Agreement, they could very easily have done so. That they did not indicates that TRIPS national treatment was intended to apply as between nationals, not as between domiciliaries. The same also follows from the specific prohibition of conditions of domicile and establishment in Article 2 (2) of the Paris Convention, which otherwise would have been superfluous.

23. The only text in the TRIPS Agreement to which the United States has pointed in support of its interpretation is footnote 1 to Article 1.3 of the TRIPS Agreement. In its second submission, the United States claims again that this provision "would apply to the EC, among other WTO Members."[14] This is manifestly wrong. Footnote 1 defines the term "national" only for separate customs territories, which are part of another State, and which therefore may not have a "nationality." Footnote 1 would therefore seem to apply, for instance, to Chinese Taipei, Hong Kong, China, or Macao, China. It does not apply to the EC, or to other WTO Members which are not separate customs territories.

24. Accordingly, the Panel should find that Article 3(1) TRIPS Agreement requires national treatment as between <u>nationals</u>, not as between domiciliaries or as between goods.

(b) Regulation 2081/92 does not discriminate between nationals

25. Once Article 3(1) TRIPS Agreement is given its proper scope, it is clear that Regulation 2081/92 does not discriminate between nationals.

26. In support of their claims, the complainants have referred in particular to the fact that Regulation 2081/92 contains separate provisions governing the registration of geographical indications, depending on where the geographical area to which the indication is related is located. The US has argued that there is "a close relationship between the geographical area that gives rise to the GI right and the nationality of the right holder."[15] Moreover, the US has argued that "any legal person producing or obtaining agricultural products and foodstuffs in a country will, as a practical <u>and perhaps a legal matter</u>, become a juridical person of that Member."[16]

---

[13] US SWS, para. 29.

[14] US SWS, para. 27.

[15] US, SWS para. 26.

[16] US, SWS para. 32 (emphasis added). As for Australia, Australia's arguments seem to be limited to noting that 10 headlines in the EC's first submission use the word "national" (cf. Australia's SWS, para. 182). The EC would comment that this is hardly surprising, given that these headlines restated the claims of the complainants.

27. The EC submits that these statements are unsupported by fact. Regulation 2081/92 does not contain any requirements as regards the nationality of producers which produce products bearing a protected name. It is not enough for the US to state that this is "perhaps a legal matter." It should state where, in the measure at issue, namely Regulation 2081/92, there is a requirement as to the nationality of producers.

28. In this context, it may be important to know for the Panel that there are cases where non-EC companies have become producers of products bearing a protected name under Regulation 2081/92. Some examples of which the EC is aware, but which are presumably not exhaustive, are the following:

- In 1996, Sara Lee, a large US multinational, acquired Al Ponte Prosciutti, which produces Prosciutto di Parma (Exhibit EC-61).
- From 1985 to 2003, Kraft Foods, a large US multinational, owned Invernizzi, an Italian company which produces among other products Gorgonzola and Grana Padano (Exhibit EC-62).
- Until 2000, Nestlé, a large Swiss multinational, used to own Vismara, an Italian company which produces among others Prosciutto di Parma (Exhibit EC-63).

29. These cases show clearly that non-EC companies may become producers of products bearing a protected name under Regulation 2081/92. In its second submission, the EC has also shown similar examples from the area of wines and spirits.[17] Whether and to which extent foreign nationals become producers of such products may depend on business interests, and to some extent on coincidence. It has nothing to do with Regulation 2081/92, which is entirely neutral as to the nationality of producers.

30. The complainants might argue that even where a foreign company acquires an EC producer, or establishes itself as a producer, it is likely to do this through a European subsidiary. However, even if, as a practical matter, this were true in certain cases, it is still not attributable to Regulation 2081/92, which is the measure before this Panel.

31. Accordingly, the Panel should find that Regulation 2081/92 does not constitute discrimination between nationals.

(c) Regulation 2081/92 does not involve *de facto* discrimination between nationals

32. The EC would like to emphasize that if Regulation 2081/92 does not involve discrimination of nationals *de jure*, it also does not do so *de facto*.

33. As the EC has set out in its earlier submissions, *de facto* discrimination is a concept which is closely related to preventing circumvention of national treatment obligations.[18] A good complying with the product specifications of a protected geographical indication will originate in the geographical area to which the indication is related. As a consequence, any discrimination on the basis of whether the geographical indication is located in the EC or abroad would be discrimination between foreign and domestic products. The EC sees therefore no reason to extend TRIPS national treatment to a situation which by definition is covered by Article III:4 GATT.

34. In its second submission, the United States has referred to the Panel Report in *US – Section 337*, in which the Panel held that procedures in principle applying to persons can still involve a discrimination of goods of foreign origin.[19] However, this report hardly supports the US view. First, in the present case, the submission

---

[17] EC SWS, para. 46.

[18] EC Response to Panel's Question No. 29, para. 67 et seq; EC SWS, para. 49.

[19] US SWS, para. 38-39.

of the complainants is the reverse of the conclusions in *US – Section 337*, namely that even though covered by Article III:4 GATT, an alleged discrimination between products should also be considered discrimination between nationals. Second, *US – Section 337* was decided under the GATT 1949 at a time when the TRIPS Agreement did not yet exist. Accordingly, the question of how TRIPS and GATT national treatment relate was not an issue before that Panel.

35. In its submission, as an example for a *de facto* violation of TRIPS national treatment, the United States has constructed a case where all patents first filed abroad are subjected to higher fees.[20] Once again, this example does nothing to support the US arguments in the present case. In the US example, the fees for the registration of patents are not related to the origin of products. Accordingly, such a case would not fall under Article III:4 GATT, and a case for a *de facto* application of TRIPS national treatment might possibly be made. This is different from the present case, which clearly falls under Article III:4 GATT.

36. The US has attempted to dismiss the EC's arguments by stating that there is no reason why the national treatment obligations of the GATT and the TRIPS should not apply simultaneously.[21] At a general level, it is of course true that obligations arising under several covered agreements can apply simultaneously. Still, the US argument is too superficial. In particular, the US overlooks Article II:2 of the WTO Agreement, according to which both the TRIPS and the GATT are integral parts of the WTO Agreement, i.e. of one single international agreement. As the Appellate Body has stated repeatedly, the covered agreements must therefore be interpreted as a whole, and "in a way that gives meaning to all of them, harmoniously."[22] For the same reason, the Panel in *Indonesia – Autos* found that there is a presumption against conflict between the covered agreements.[23]

37. The interpretation of the complainants is not in line with these principles. It is not a harmonious interpretation to needlessly enlarge the scope of TRIPS national treatment to overlap with GATT national treatment. In addition, there are important structural differences between the GATT and the TRIPS. For instance, the TRIPS Agreement does not contain any provision corresponding to Article XX GATT. It would not seem appropriate that a measure discriminating between goods which is justified on the basis of Article XX GATT would nonetheless be found incompatible with the covered agreements on the simple basis of a *de facto* application of TRIPS national treatment.[24]

38. Accordingly, the Panel should not find that Regulation 2081/92 involves *de facto* discrimination between nationals.

(d) The fact that different legal provisions apply does not prove that there is less favourable treatment

39. Throughout its submission, the United States has argued that because there are different provisions governing the registration of geographical indications depending on where the geographical area is located, the EC is applying "differential treatment," and has called on the EC to show that, despite such differences, the no

[20] US SWS, para. 40.

[21] US SWS, para. 42.

[22] Appellate Body Report, *Argentina – Footwear (EC)*, para. 81; Appellate Body Report, *Korea – Dairy*, para. 81.

[23] Panel Report, *Indonesia – Autos*, para. 14.28. The US has argued that the report of the Panel in *Indonesia – Autos*, which cautioned against an extensive interpretation of TRIPS national treatment, is not relevant to the present case because it dealt with measure of support not relating to intellectual property (US SWS, para. 43). However, the US overstates the difference between this case and the present. The Panel in *Indonesia – Autos* was concerned with the maintenance of an intellectual property right, namely a trademark. The only difference was that the Panel did not consider specifically the relationship of TRIPS national treatment to Article III:4 GATT, but to other disciplines of the covered agreements. However, in carrying out its analysis, the Panel clearly recognised that the need for a harmonious and coherent interpretation of the covered agreements which required caution with respect to a *de facto* application of Article 3.1 TRIPS.

[24] The EC is not taking a view on the complex legal issue of whether Article XX GATT may be of relevance in connection with the TRIPS Agreement. However, the interpretation of TRIPS national treatment put forward by the complainants inevitably would raise this complex systemic question.

less favourable standard is met.[25] The US has also made similar suggestions with respect to the right of objection.[26]

40. The EC strongly contests this attempt by the United States to shift the burden of proof. In *Korea – Various Measures on Beef*, the Appellate Body stated clearly that a formal difference in treatment is not sufficient to show that there is less favourable treatment.[27] Accordingly, the US must do more than just show that the registration of EC and foreign geographical indications is dealt with in different provisions. It must show that there is a substantive difference between these provisions, and that this difference entails less favourable treatment of foreign nationals.

41. In support of its statement, the United States[28] has referred to the Panel Report in *US – Section 337*, where the Panel stated that where "different provisions" apply, it is incumbent on the contracting party applying "differential treatment" to show that in spite of such differences, the no less favourable standard is met.[29] However, it does not appear that the Panel in this case meant to say to a formal difference in treatment would entail "differential treatment," and thus entail a reversal of the burden of proof. Moreover, if this is what it meant, then this is certainly not in line with the case law of the Appellate Body, which has not linked such consequences to a formal difference in treatment.[30]

42. It should also be noted that the United States argument is inconsistent with its own submissions on other claims. As a matter of fact, the United States does not want formally equal treatment for foreign geographical indications, but differential treatment. For instance, the United States argues that unlike EC geographical indications, foreign geographical indications should not have to satisfy the requirement of inspection structures. Similarly, the United States argues that unlike for EC geographical indications, requests for the registration of foreign geographical indications should not have to be submitted through the government of the country in which the area is located. Accordingly, the submission of the United States would appear to be that there is formally equal treatment, but that this formally equal treatment nevertheless involves less favourable treatment.

43. Accordingly, the burden of proof that Regulation 2081/92 involves less favourable treatment is on the US, not on the EC.

2. Claim 1: Non-EC nationals are accorded less favorable treatment than EC nationals with respect to the registration of geographical indications through the application of a condition of reciprocity and equivalence

44. We will now turn to the individual claims of the United States and Australia regarding TRIPS national treatment. The first claim is that by subjecting the registration of geographic indications from other WTO members to "conditions of reciprocity and equivalence," Regulation 2081/92 violates the national treatment provisions of Article 3.1 TRIPS and 2.1 Paris Convention.

45. In its submissions to the Panel, the EC has already confirmed that it does not apply such conditions to the registration of geographical indications from other WTO Members.[31] The EC, in particular, has explained that the application of these conditions to WTO Members is in fact excluded by the introductory language of Article 12(1) of Regulation 2081/92, which provides that these conditions apply "without prejudice to

---

[25] US SWS, para. 25, 46, 70, 88.

[26] US SWS, para. 86.

[27] Appellate Body Report, *Korea – Various Measures on Beef*, para. 137.

[28] US SWS, para. 46.

[29] Panel Report, *US – Section 337*, para. 5.11.

[30] It is interesting to note that in *Korea – Various Measures on Beef*, para. 136, the Appellate Body omits from its quotation the last two sentences of para. 5.11 of the Panel Report in *US – Section 337*. It appears that this omission is deliberate.

[31] Cf. in particular EC SWS, para. 51 et seq.

international agreements." The EC has also explained that this reference to international agreements requires in particular that the EC's WTO obligations be taken into account. As the EC has said earlier, this is fully in line with the jurisprudence of the Court of Justice, according to which EC law must be interpreted consistently with international law.

46. In their second submissions, the complainants have not advanced many new arguments which have not already been responded to by the EC. The EC can therefore limit itself to a few additional remarks.

47. In its second submission, the United States has argued that even if Article 12(1) did not apply to WTO Members, the EC could still not register geographical indications from other WTO Members because Article 12a (1) provides for such a registration procedure "in the case provided for in Article (12)(3)."[32] The US has claimed that because of this, "there is no registration procedure at all in the EC GI Regulation for non-WTO Members."[33]

48. These US arguments do not do justice to the content and objectives of Regulation 2081/92. First of all, the US overlooks that the "without prejudice" clause in Article 12(1) applies to the conditions set out in this Article only. It does not exclude the applicability of the registration procedures set out in Article 12a. Obviously, if the conditions of Article 12(1) do not apply because they would prejudice an international agreement, then the consequence cannot be that the registration procedures of Regulation 2081/92 do not apply. This would be a nonsensical result, which would not be in accordance with the requirement to interpret the EC legislation in accordance with WTO obligations. As the EC has already explained in response to the Panel's questions, the reference to the procedure of Article (12)(3) is therefore relevant only where the conditions of Article 12(1) are applicable.[34]

49. In its second submission, Australia has concentrated less on the text of Regulation 2081/92, and more on the various statements that the EC is alleged to have made in the past. However, in its second written submission, the EC has already discussed most of these statements, and has shown that they are not relevant for the interpretation of Article 12(1) of Regulation 2081/92.[35]

50. Finally, it is important for the Panel to be aware that the European Commission has issued a 2nd edition of its Guide to Regulation 2081/92 (Exhibit EC-64).[36] This 2nd edition contains also a specific section on the interpretation of geographical indications related to areas located outside the EC. In this guide, it is explained that the conditions of Article 12(1) do not apply to other WTO Members.[37]

---

[32] US SWS, para. 8, 21.

[33] US SWS, para. 21.

[34] EC Response to Panel's Question No. 7, para. 17.

[35] EC SWS, para. 78 et seq. About the only document on which the EC has not yet commented is the Opinion of the European Parliament's Agriculture and Rural Development Committee, to which Australia refers in its second submission (Australia's SWS, para. 36). In this respect, it should first be recalled that according to the Panel Report in *US – Taxes on Automobiles*, para. 5.12, the assessment of the aim of a legislative act should not be based only on statements of legislators or other preparatory work, but on the wording of the legislation as a whole. Second, the statement in the Committee's report, which concerned Regulation 692/2003, did not concern the "without prejudice" language, in Article 12(1), which was not the subject of the amendment. Third, Australia fails to quote the opinion of the Committee on Legal Affairs and the Internal Market, contained in the same report, which does recall that the conditions of reciprocity and equivalence apply "without prejudice to the international agreements in force" (Exhibit COMP-14, p. 23). Finally, it should be generally noted that individual committees of the Parliament do not represent the opinion of the European Parliament as a whole, and frequently give divergent opinions. Moreover, particularly where the European Parliament is only consulted, they cannot be regarded as giving an authoritative statement of the intention of the legislator.

[36] This new edition replaces the version referred to by the US as Exhibit US-24.

[37] Cf. Exhibit EC-64, p. 18: "However, the conditions in Article 12(1) of Regulation (EEC) no. 2081/92 are without prejudice to international agreements. Relevant international agreements include the WTO Agreements, in particular the TRIPS Agreement. Since under the TRIPS Agreement, WTO Members are obliged to provide protection to geographical indications, the conditions set out in Article 12(1) do not apply to WTO Members. Accordingly, an application for registration of a PGI or PDO relating to an area located in a WTO Member may be made without a prior Commission decision on the basis of Article (12)(3) of Regulation (EEC) no. 2081/92."

51. Accordingly, since the EC does not apply conditions of reciprocity and equivalence to the registration of geographical indications from other WTO Members, the claim should be rejected.

3. Claim 1bis: Regulation 2081/92 violates the national treatment obligations under the TRIPS Agreement by requiring the existence of inspection structures with respect to the specific product for which protection is requested

52. It has become clear that the United States is also claiming that the requirement that inspection structures must exist for each protected name is in violation of TRIPS national treatment obligations. Australia has made no such claim under TRIPS, but has made a similar claim under the GATT.

53. In its second submission, the EC has explained in detail that the requirement of inspection structures represents equal, not unequal treatment; that the requirement of inspection structures does not require "equivalence by another name;" that Regulation 2081/92 does not impose an "EC model" of inspection structures; and that existence of inspection structures is necessary for attaining the objectives of Regulation 2081/92.[38] In its present statement, the EC will therefore only respond to a number of erroneous arguments of the United States, and similarly, by Australia in the context of its claims under the TBT Agreement.

(a) The requirement of inspection structures does not require "equivalence by another name"

54. In its submission, the EC has already explained that the requirement of inspection structures is not "equivalence by another name," but rather is a requirement that is applied on a product-specific basis for each product for which protection is sought.[39]

55. In its second submission, the US continues to submit that the requirement of inspection structures is "a requirement for a broad inspection structure capable of performing this function for all agricultural products and foodstuffs."[40] The EC notes that Australia has explicitly not shared this view of the US.[41]

56. In fact, the United States interpretation is incompatible with both the wording and the application in practice of Regulation 2081/92. Nowhere in the Regulation does it say that when transmitting an application for registration of a geographical indication, a WTO Member must show the existence of "a broad inspection structure capable of performing this function for all agricultural products and foodstuffs." Article 12a(2) merely requires the declaration that the inspection structures by Article (10)(1) are in place.

57. Article 10(1), in turn, requires that the necessary inspection structures exist to ensure that agricultural products and foodstuffs bearing a protected name meet the requirements laid down in the specification. Article (10)(1) refers to "structures" in the plural. Nothing in Article (10)(1) therefore requires one single structure; it is entirely imaginable that in one state, several structures might co-exist. Moreover, Article (10)(1) requires inspection structures only for products "bearing a protected name," not for "all" agricultural products or foodstuffs as the US suggests.

58. Should there have been any doubt left about the interpretation of Regulation 2081/92, the practical application of the Regulation should have dispelled it. The EC has already provided the Panel with the latest publication of the inspection bodies existing in the Member States of the Community.[42] As is obvious from this publication, there is not a single Member State in which one single "broad inspection structure" exists. Rather,

---

[38] EC SWS, para. 91 et seq.

[39] EC SWS, para. 96 et seq.

[40] US SWS, para. 53.

[41] Australia's SWS, para. 216.

[42] Exhibit EC-48.

all Member States have a multitude of inspection bodies showing a considerable variety of designs, and mixing private and public elements.[43]

59. Accordingly, it is clear that the requirement of inspection structures is not "equivalence by another name," but is applied on a product-specific basis.[44]

(b) Regulation 2081/92 does not impose an "EC model" of inspection structures, and is not unduly prescriptive

60. Despite their frequent reference to an "EC model" of inspection structures imposed by the Regulation, the United States and Australia have so far not been able to identify clearly what aspects of the EC requirements they consider objectionable.

61. In its second submission, the United States now argues that the "pertinent issue" is not which aspects of the inspection structures are objectionable, but whether the EC can demand "the establishment of the same particular inspection structure that the EC has chosen for itself."[45] The EC must say that it does not understand how the United States can complain about having to adopt "the same" structures if it is not able to say in which way the structures should be different.

62. Presumably conscious of this contradiction, the US now attempts to identify certain aspects that would be objectionable. In particular, the US complains about the requirement in Article 10 (3) that inspection bodies must permanently "have at their disposal the qualified staff and resources necessary to carry out inspections."[46] A similar argument has also been made by Australia in the context of its claim under the TBT Agreement.[47] Secondly, the US questions why the inspection structure must be independent from the producers which it inspects.[48]

63. As regards the requirement that inspection bodies must permanently have at their disposal the necessary qualified personnel, the EC fails to see what should be objectionable about this. In fact, the EC notes that this requirement corresponds closely to §205.501 of the Regulations of the US Organic Program (Exhibit EC-55), which require that certifying agents "must use a sufficient number of adequately trained personnel." It is obvious that inspections cannot be carried out without qualified personnel. Moreover, the Regulation does not specify how much personnel is necessary, during which periods it should be employed, and whether such employment should for instance be full-time or part-time. All that is required is that the "necessary" personnel is at the disposal of the inspection body. What this means has to be decided for each specific inspection structure in the concrete circumstances. The Regulation is thus not overly prescriptive.[49]

---

[43] This practice has been entirely consistent since the beginning of the implementation of the Regulation. For further information of the Panel, the EC also attaches the first publication of inspection bodies dating from 1996 (Exhibit EC-65).

[44] This is also confirmed by the Guide to Regulation 2081/92 (Exhibit EC-64, p. 23).

[45] US SWS, para. 49 (emphasis added).

[46] US SWS, para. 53.

[47] Australia's SWS.

[48] US SWS, para. 57. The US also claims that inspection bodies must comply with the European standard for inspection bodies (EN 45011—Exhibit EC-2). However, it follows clearly from Article 10 (3) of Regulation 2081/92 that compliance with an equivalent international standard is sufficient. In its first written submission, the EC has already identified ISO/IEC Guide 65: 1996 as such an equivalent standard (EC FWS, para. 54 and Exhibit EC-3).

[49] Australia has argued that it in certain cases, it may not be necessary for inspection bodies to have personnel "permanently" at their disposal, for instance where there is a particular harvest season. Although this is certainly not the rule, the EC does not exclude that there might be products for which the entire production process is confined to a part of the year, and for which therefore the need for inspections arises only or primarily during that time of the year. In this case, the Regulation 2081/92 does not require unnecessary levels of staff to be maintained throughout the year. In fact, since it is presumably not economic to establish and wind down an inspection body every year, in such a case it would be reasonable to entrust the function of inspections to a body which also carries out tasks other than inspections under Regulation 2081/92. In its second submission, the EC has pointed to the existence of private firms which can carry out such tasks (EC SWS para. 107 and Exhibits EC-49 and EC-50).

64. As regards the US argument that inspection bodies should not be required to be independent of producers, the EC finds this wholly unconvincing. If inspection structures are to deserve their name, they have to be objective and impartial as regards producers. It is noteworthy that in the context of its organic program, the US follows exactly the same logic by requiring that certifying agents should prevent conflicts of interest with respect to producers and handlers, and should exclude any person with a conflict of interest from the certification process (§ 205.501 (a) (10) and (11), Exhibit EC-55).

(c) The existence of inspection structures is necessary for attaining the objectives of Regulation 2081/92

65. The real issue before this Panel is therefore not the precise nature of the inspection structures, but that the EC requires such inspection structures at all.

66. In this context, the United States has referred to its system of certification marks and collective marks, and argued that the owner of the private rights are in the best position to ensure that the marks are used in manner consistent with their specifications.[50] This appears somewhat similar to the arguments made by Australia, which has argued that the application of unfair competition law may be sufficient to prevent the misuse of protected geographical indications.[51]

67. At the outset, the EC would remark that this US position contradicts earlier statements made by the US according to which "normally, a private individual is not in the best position" to control the use of a certification mark.[52] The EC finds it therefore surprising, and contrary to US practice, that the United States is now arguing that certification marks and collective marks can be enforced efficiently purely at the initiative of the owner of the mark.[53]

68. Moreover, in response to the arguments of Australia, the EC has already explained that the application of unfair competition law does not provide the same degree of protection and assurance to producers and consumers as the EC system.[54] These arguments apply equally if the United States now argues that geographical indications should be protected purely through the initiative of the owner of the certification mark or collective mark. As in the case of the application of unfair competition law, the enforcement of marks depends on the initiative of the owner of the mark. Accordingly, the control and monitoring is by definition intermittent and varying, and will not provide a full degree of assurance to producers and consumers.

69. The United States has put a certain emphasis on the fact that collective marks and certification marks are private rights. However, whether the rights are private is not the question. Like geographical indications, collective marks and certification marks remain collective rights, and are used by a potentially large number of producers. It cannot simply be assumed that because these collectives rights are "private," their enforcement and protection would necessarily be as efficient as the one provided through Regulation 2081/92.

70. Once again, the EC would like to emphasize that it is not contesting the right of the United States to protect geographical indications in its territory through a system of certification marks or collective marks. However, it seems that it is not the EC which is trying to "impose" its system on the US, but the US and Australia which are trying to impose their system on the EC. By requiring the EC to protect US or Australian geographical indications without requiring inspection structures, the EC would essentially have to lower its level of protection of geographical indications to that of the US and Australia. This would be incompatible with

[50] US SWS, para. 51.

[51] Australia's SWS, para. 220.

[52] Cf. EC FWS, para. 496.

[53] In this context, the EC would like to recall that it has not ruled out that the owner of a certification mark might fulfil the requirements of Article 10 of Regulation 2081/92 (EC Response to Panel's Question No. 59, paras. 130-131. However, whether these requirements are met, and in particular whether the necessary objectivity and impartiality with regard to producers is ensured, would have to be evaluated on a case by case basis.

[54] EC SWS, para. 114 et seq.

Article 1.1 TRIPS Agreement, which allows the EC to provide a higher level of protection to geographical indications than that required by the TRIPS Agreement.

71. Accordingly, this claim should be rejected.

4. Claim 2: Regulation 2081/92 violates the national treatment obligations under the TRIPS and the Paris Convention by requiring that applications must be transmitted by the country in which the geographical area is located

72. In its previous submissions, the EC has responded in detail to the claim that Regulation 2081/92 violates the national treatment obligations under TRIPS and the Paris Convention by requiring that applications must be transmitted by the country in which the geographical area is located. In particular, the EC has explained that this requirement for the involvement of the country to whose territory the geographical indication is related constitutes equal, not unequal treatment, that this involvement is indispensable for the proper implementation of Regulation 2081/92, and that this requirement does not impose any undue burden on third country governments.[55]

73. In its second submission, the United States[56] fails to provide a convincing response to the EC's arguments. The United States continues to argue that the EC's requirements are unwarranted because in the United States, geographical indications are protected through collective marks and certification marks, and because the US government therefore "does not have any specialized knowledge that would render it better qualified than the rightholder or the EC."[57]

74. These arguments are remarkable. The EC would like to recall that according to Article 24.9 TRIPS, the EC is not obliged to protect geographical indications which are not protected in their country of origin. Now, whether a geographical indication relating to US territory is protected in the US is clearly a question of US law. It is not unreasonable for the EC to request the cooperation of the US on such a question of US law. In contrast, it is simply not credible for the United States to pretend that it does not have any greater experience on questions of US law than the EC, and that therefore the EC should resolve these questions for itself.

75. The United States has also argued that it is in no position to make a determination on whether a US geographical indication has a reputation <u>in the EC market</u>.[58] With due respect, this is besides the point. Obviously, the EC does not expect the US to make a determination about reputation in the EC market. However, first of all, the protection of geographical indications is not just based on reputation, but also on whether products have a particular quality or other characteristics attributable to their geographic origin. Since the geographical origin is in the United States, that question should be one which the United States is best placed to evaluate. Second, where the protection is based on reputation of a geographical indication, that reputation must also be based on its geographical origin. Since this origin is in the US, one would normally expect the geographical indication to have a reputation in the US market. This, once again, is a question which the US is best placed to evaluate.

76. Finally, the United States has argued that it protects foreign geographical indications in the US as collective marks or certification marks without the intercession of foreign governments.[59] This argument is without merit. First, whether the United States protects geographical indications as marks irrespective of whether they are protected in their country of origin is a matter for the United States, but irrelevant in the

---

[55] EC SWS, para. 122 et seq.

[56] Australia has made no such claim under the TRIPS Agreement, but has raised similar claims under Article III:4 GATT. In its second submission, however, Australia has not provided any substantive response to the arguments of the EC on this claim (Australia's SWS, para. 177-181). Accordingly, Australia's corresponding claims should also be rejected.

[57] US SWS, para. 73.

[58] US SWS, para. 73.

[59] US SWS, para. 73.

present context. Second, it should be noted that even as regards the registration of marks, Article 6 (A) (a) *quinquies* of the Paris Convention explicitly permits the registering country to request a certificate of registration issued by the country of origin. Finally, at least as regards geographical indications from the EC, which has a specific registration system, the question of whether a geographical indication is protected in the EC is fairly easy to ascertain. As the United States has itself acknowledged, this is not as obvious for US geographical indications, given the absence of a specific system of protection in the US. It is unreasonable for the United States to try to devolve these difficulties on other governments.

77. Accordingly, claim 2 should be rejected.

5. Claim 3: Non-EC nationals are accorded less favorable treatment than EC nationals with respect to the requirement to indicate the country of origin for homonymous geographical indications

78. According to the United States, the requirement in Article 12(2) of Regulation 2081/92 to indicate the country of origin for homonymous geographical indications constitutes a violation of national treatment provisions under TRIPS and the Paris Convention.[60]

79. In its previous submissions, the EC has already explained that Article 12(2) does not apply to all foreign geographical indications, but only to the names in the specific situation of the first subparagraph, and that it requires the indication of the country of origin for both EC and third country names, depending on which geographical indication has been protected earlier. Accordingly, Article 12(2) of the Regulation treats geographical indications from the EC and third countries alike.[61]

80. In its second submission, the United States continues to contest even the first premise of the EC's arguments, namely that Article 12(2) applies only to homonymous geographical indications.[62] The EC is unable to understand the basis for the United States' view. The second subparagraph of Article 12(2) refers clearly to "such names," i.e. the homonymous names referred to in the first subparagraph. There is no ambiguity about this in the Regulation. Indeed, the US view seems to be inspired more by a desire to find fault with the EC measure than by the text of the EC measure.

81. As regards the second element of the EC's response, the EC's interpretation is clearly borne out by the wording of Article 12(2) of Regulation 2081/92, which refers to "protected names" both from the EC and from third countries. As its only counter-argument, the US has argued that Article (12)(2) seems to be "directed at the authorisation of third country GIs." However, there is nothing in the wording of the provision to prevent it from applying to geographical indications from both third countries and from the EC.

82. Interestingly, this point seems to have been recognised by Australia, which has argued that the expression "Community protected name" in Article (12)(2) should be read also to include names from third countries under the GI regulation.[63] This is not the interpretation of the EC. However, if indeed this were the correct interpretation, then surely the expression "protected name of a third country" should similarly be

---

[60] Australia has not made such a claim under TRIPS, but has made a similar claim under Article 2.1 TBT Agreement. In its second submission, apparently unsure of this legal basis, Autralia has now raised such a claim also under Article III:4 GATT, but still not under the TRIPS Agreement (cf. Australia's SWS, para. 179).

[61] EC SWS, para. 143 et seq. This interpretation is also confirmed in the Guide to Regulation 2081/92 (Exhibit EC-64, p. 21).

[62] US SWS, para. 76.

[63] Australia's SWS, para. 65.

interpreted to include names protected in a third country regardless of whether they are from a third country or the EC. In this case, Article (12)(2) once again would not result in any discrimination.[64]

83. Finally, the EC would remark that it does not see in which way a requirement to truthfully indicate the origin of a product constitutes less favourable treatment. In this context, the EC also notes that the complainants have not yet provided any response as to how their claims under the TRIPS Agreement relate to Article IX:1 of the GATT, which explicitly excludes origin marking requirements for imported goods from national treatment obligations. The EC will comment on this question in more detail in response to the complainants' claims under the GATT.

84. In conclusion, this claim should be rejected.

6. Claim 4: Regulation 2081/92 accords less favourable treatment to non-EC nationals by subjecting the right to object to the registration of geographical indications to conditions of reciprocity and equivalence

85. The United States has claimed that only nationals from WTO member countries recognised in accordance with Article 12(3) of Regulation 2081/92 as fulfilling the conditions of reciprocity and equivalence may object to registrations of geographical indications.

86. As the EC has set out in its previous submissions, it is clear from the explicit reference to WTO Members in Article 12d(1) and 12b(2) of the Regulation that WTO Members are not subject to the procedure of Article 12(3) applicable to other third countries.[65] Still, in its second submission, the US argues that the Regulation requires persons to reside in the EC "in order to object under Article 7 objection procedures."[66]

87. This argument is manifestly unfounded. Persons resident or established in the US can object to the registration of EC geographical indications under the procedures of Article 12d(1) or 12b(2). The US has failed to explain in which way this procedure is different from the one available to persons resident or established in the EC. As said earlier, the fact that a different legal provision applies does not show that there is differential treatment.[67] In fact, it is the US which argues that unlike for EC residents, its residents should not be required to have to transmit objections through the US government. Accordingly, it is the US which wants differential treatment, while the EC measure provides equal treatment.

88. Claim 4 is unfounded and should be rejected.

7. Claim 5: Regulation 2081/92 accords less favourable treatment to non-EC nationals by requiring their own country to transmit the objection

89. With claim 5, the complainants have claimed that Regulation 2081/92 accords less favourable treatment to non-EC nationals by requiring their own country to transmit the objection.

---

64 In addition, the complainants have argued that Article 6 (6) of Regulation 2081/92 would be applicable to the registration of a geographical indication from the EC which is homonymous with an already registered geographical indication from a third country. The EC does not agree. However, even if the complainants were right, the results would be not different. As a precondition for the registration of homonymous geographical indications, Article 6(6) requires "a clear distinction in practice." Where two homonymous geographical indications are from different countries, this will require the indication of origin. Accordingly, even if Article 6(6) did apply, there still would be no difference in treatment.

65 EC FWS, para. 140; EC SWS, para. 150 et seq.

66 US SWS, para. 86.

67 In passing, it should be noted that objections to geographical indications from outside the EC are covered by Article 12b(2) both for EC and foreign residents.

90. This claim is equally unfounded. As the EC has already explained, this requirement applies both to persons resident or established in the EC or in third countries and is neither unreasonable nor unduly burdensome for third countries.[68]

91. In their second submissions, the United States and Australia have offered almost no arguments in support of this claim.[69] In particular, they do not acknowledge the difference in the requirements for the transmission and verification of applications for registration, on the one hand, and the transmission of objections, on the other.

92. In fact, the United States seems to suggest that third country governments must verify the admissibility of the statement of objection on the basis of the criteria set out in Article 7(4) of the Regulation.[70] This is not true. In its submissions, the EC has clearly explained that Articles 12b(2) and 12d(1) do not require the third country government to verify the admissibility of the objection.[71]

93. Accordingly, the transmission of objections is, as the US has itself acknowledged,[72] a "purely ministerial act" which should not pose any particular problem to the government of any WTO Member, including the United States and Australia. The only way in which US or Australian residents could be prejudiced would be by the unwillingness of their governments to transmit such objections. However, such a problem would not be attributable to the EC, and can therefore not be argued to constitute less favourable treatment by the EC.

94. Accordingly, claim 5 is equally unfounded.

8. Claim 6: Regulation 2081/92 accords less favourable treatment to non-EC nationals by requiring non-EC national to have a "legitimate interest" to object to the registration of geographical indications

95. In its second submission, the US continues to claim that Article 12d(1) of Regulation 2081/92 accords less favourable treatment to non-EC residents by requiring non-EC residents to have a "legitimate interest" to object to the registration of geographical indications, whereas as regards EC residents, Article 7(3) requires that they be "legitimately concerned."[73]

96. In its submissions, the EC has already shown that there is no substantive difference between the term "legitimate interest" used in Article 12d(1) of Regulation 2081/92 and the term "legitimately concerned" in Article 7(3).[74] The EC would have expected this to be obvious enough, but apparently, for the United States it is not. Therefore, the EC will make two additional remarks.

97. First, it is important to note that Article 12b(2), which concerns objections to registrations of third country geographical indications, and which applies for residents of the EC and WTO Members, also requires a "legitimate interest." If the United States were right, and "legitimate interest" were a more demanding standard than "legitimately concerned," this would mean that EC residents could object to the registration of third country geographical indications under stricter conditions than to the registration of EC geographical indications. This would be an odd result.

---

[68] EC SWS, para. 154 et seq.

[69] Cf. Australia's SWS, which merely refers to a requirement for the "involvement" of another WTO Member without distinguishing between applications and objections, and without answering any of the EC's arguments.

[70] US SWS, para. 66.

[71] EC Response to Panel's Question No. 34, para. 86; EC SWS, para. 155.

[72] US Response to Panel's Question No. 38, para. 74.

[73] US SWS, para. 87-88.

[74] EC FWS, para. 78, 150-152; EC SWS, para. 160 et seq.

98. Second, reference should also be made to the French and Spanish versions of Regulation 2081/92, which are equally authentic. In fact, in the French version, Articles 7(3), 12b(2) and 12d(1) uniformly use the expression "legitimement concerné." The Spanish version in both Articles 7(3) and 12d(1) uses the expression "legítimamente interesada," whereas Article 12b(2) uses, without any difference in meaning, the expression "legítimamente afectada."

99. In conclusion, the difference between "legitimately concerned" and "legitimately interested" is a mere difference of drafting specific to the English text of the Regulation, which does not entail any difference in meaning. Accordingly, the Panel should reject the US claim.

9. Claim 7: Regulation 2081/92 accords less favourable treatment because a non-EC rightholder has no "representative" in the regulatory committee to "speak for him"

100. Australia has argued that Regulation 2081/92 accords less favourable treatment because a non-EC rightholder has no "representative" in the regulatory committee to "speak for him." In its second submission, Australia has provided no further arguments to substantiate its claim.[75] Accordingly, Australia's claim should be dismissed.

10. Claims 8 and 9: A right of objection was available to persons resident or established in an EC Member State that was not available to other WTO Member nationals

101. Australia has claimed that there is a violation of national treatment in the fact that a right of objection was available to persons resident or established in an EC Member State that was not available to other WTO Member nationals in respect of the registration of more than 120 geographical indications under the normal registration process (Claim 8). Australia has also raised a similar claim with respect to the absence of an objection procedure under the simplified procedure which used to be provided for in Article 17 of Regulation 2081/92 (Claim 9).[76]

102. In its prior submissions, the EC has already explained why these claims must fail.[77] First, as regards Regulation 2081/92 itself, the claims relate to a measure which was no longer in force at the time of establishment of the Panel, and which is therefore not within the terms of reference of the Panel. Second, as regards the individual registrations, even if considered to be within the Panel's terms of reference, they are not in violation of national treatment obligations.

103. In its second written submission, Australia has not provided any coherent response to the EC's submissions.[78] In particular, Australia apparently does not appreciate that Regulation 2081/92, on the one hand, and the individual registrations, on the other, are separate measures. Accordingly, Australia does not clearly state whether its claims relate to Regulation 2081/92, or to the individual registrations. However, such a clear

---

[75] Instead, Australia has engaged, over a length of two and a half pages, in a discussion of the EC's "Article 15 decision making process," which culminates in the statement that the EC "has not disproved the factual premise informing Australia's claims" that the Committee/and or the Council "participate in the decision-making process under Regulation 2081/92" (Australia's SWS, para. 59). The EC wonders why it should "disprove" this "factual premise" given that it never contested that the Council and/or the Committee participate under certain conditions in the decision-making process under the Regulation. What the EC did have to correct was the rash statement by Australia that the Committee and/or the Council were somehow the "ultimate decision-maker" under the Regulation (EC FWS, para. 79 et seq). Cf. also EC Response to Panel's Question 40, para. 105-107, and Exhibit EC-28, which shows that only three geographical indications were ever the subject of a Regulation adopted by the Council, whereas all others were registered through Regulations of the Commission.

[76] In its second submission, Australia has occasionally referred to "600 registrations," and occasionally to "120" (Australia's SWS, para. 17, 185). The EC is therefore uncertain to which extent Australia maintains its argument that the simplified procedure was incompatible with national treatment obligations. In any event, as the EC has set out in its previous submissions (EC FWS, para. 170 et seq.; EC SWS, para. 197 et seq.), Claim 9 is unfounded also because first, there was never any right of objection in the context of the simplified procedure, whether for domestic or for foreign residents; and second, because these claims fall outside the temporal scope of the temporal scope of the TRIPS Agreement as defined in Article 70.1 thereof.

[77] EC FWS, para 156 et seq.; EC SWS, para. 168 et seq.

[78] Australia's SWS, para. 15-19, 185.

distinction is essential for an appraisal of whether the measures in question fall within the terms of reference of the Panel, and if they do, whether the measures are in violation of national treatment obligations.

104. As regards Regulation 2081/92, the EC has already shown in its previous submission that Australia's panel request did not clearly refer to historical versions of the Regulation as the "measure at issue" in the present dispute.[79] Even more importantly, it is not up to Australia to enlarge the terms of reference of the Panel contrary to the object and purpose of the DSU. Dispute settlement under the DSU serves the purpose of solving disputes about existing measures. Its purpose is not to provide opinions about historical grievances, in particular where it is not demonstrated what relevance such grievances are still supposed to have. This is why the present Panel, like all WTO Panel before it, should decide on the measure at issue as it existed at the time of the establishment of the Panel.

105. As regards the individual registrations, it is clear that these registrations are still in force. On the basis of the preliminary ruling issued by the Panel, and for the purposes of the present proceedings, the EC therefore bases itself on the assumption that the individual registrations are within the terms of reference of the present Panel.[80]

106. However, the issue regarding the registrations is whether these registrations are in violation of national treatment obligations. So far, Australia has not substantiated its allegations in this respect. Indeed, it has tried to shift the burden of proof to the EC by reproaching the EC for having asserted that the registrations are compatible with national treatment obligations "without any supporting argument."[81] In this context, it appears necessary to recall that the burden of showing that there is a violation is on Australia, not on the EC.

107. The EC submits that Australia has not demonstrated the existence of such a violation. Australia has brought the present claim under the national treatment obligations of the TRIPS. However, Australia fails to explain how the registration of a particular geographical indication can constitute a violation of national treatment obligations.

108. Presumably aware of this weakness, Australia has, in its responses to the Panel's questions, also referred to other WTO provisions as violated by the individual registrations, and in particular to Article 16.1 of the TRIPS Agreement.[82] However, Australia has not offered a scrap of evidence for any such violation. It has acknowledged that it is not able to identify a single Australian trade mark that would be infringed by any geographical indication registered under Regulation 2081/92.[83] Rather it has told the panel that it has "chosen" not to identify specific commercial interests potentially affected by the EC measure.[84] The EC does not know what the reasons for this choice are, but the consequences are clear: Australia has failed to establish its claim, and its claim should be rejected.

109. Australia has also argued that the EC is asking the Panel to find that "short-lived statutory frameworks" are beyond the reach of WTO dispute settlement. In this regard, it is worth pointing out that 11 years passed between the adoption of Regulation 2081/92 and its amendment by Regulation 692/2003. This can hardly be called a "short lived" statutory framework. The EC does not know why Australia did not bring its national treatment claims when Regulation 2081/92 was still in force. However, it cannot now bring these claims against the individual registrations, when it failed to bring them against the measure which allegedly constituted the violation, namely the Regulation itself.

---

[79] EC SWS, para. 174.

[80] The EC reserves the right to raise this issue in the context of a possible appeal.

[81] Australia's SWS, para. 185. Cf. also Australia's Response to Panel's Question No. 93.

[82] Australia's Response to Panel's Question No. 92.

[83] Australia's Response to Panel's Question No. 93.

[84] Australia's SWS, para. 10.

110. In conclusion, the Panel should firmly resist Australia's attempt to revive moot claims in flagrant disregard for the law and practice of the DSU.

B. PROHIBITED REQUIREMENT OF DOMICILE OR ESTABLISHMENT (ARTICLE 2.1 TRIPS IN CONJUNCTION WITH ARTICLE 2.2 PARIS CONVENTION)

111. The US has also raised certain claims under Article 2.1 TRIPS in conjunction with Article 2.2 Paris Convention. The EC considers that these claims under Article 2.2 Paris Convention are not within the Panel's terms of reference. Subsidiarily, the EC will show that these claims are unfounded.

1. The claims based on Article 2(2) Paris Convention are not within the Panel's terms of reference

112. First, the claims based on Article 2.2 of the Paris Convention are outside the Panel's terms of reference.

113. Article 2.2 of the Paris Convention contains a separate prohibition of conditions of domicile or establishment, which is independent of Article 2.1 of the Paris Convention. The complainants have argued that this is not so because the word "however" at the beginning of Article 2.2 establishes a "linkage" between the two provisions.[85] The EC does not agree. The word "however" indicates a contradiction between the provisions; rather than link, it separates. The use of the word "however" therefore clearly indicates that Article 2.2 contains an obligation going beyond Article 2.1 of the Paris Convention.

114. In fact, the US own arguments are based on the assumption that Article 2.2 is a separate legal obligation. In its first written submission, the US argued that conditions of domicile or establishment were "directly" prohibited by Article 2.2.[86] Similarly, in its second written submission, the US speaks of an obligation "under Article 2 (2) not to impose any requirement as to domicile or establishment."[87]

115. However, the US and Australian panel requests did not contain any explicit reference to Article 2(2) of the Paris Convention. Nor did they contain any claim about the application of illicit conditions of domicile or establishment by the EC.

116. In its submission, the only response of the US has been that "the EC was clearly aware of the nature of the US complaint."[88] The EC formally contests this statement. Until the US first written submission, the EC was not aware that the US intended to claim that the EC measure involved illicit conditions of domicile or establishment. Moreover, the EC also notes that the US argument is in contradiction with the United States response to the EC's request for a preliminary ruling, where the United States announced that precisely how Regulation 2081/92 is incompatible with WTO obligations would be the subject of future US submissions.[89]

117. Accordingly, the Panel should find that the claims under Article 2(2) of the Paris Convention are not within its terms of reference.

2. Claim 10: Regulation 2081/92 requires non-EC nationals to become established in the EC as a condition for registering geographical indications

118. The United States has argued that Regulation 2081/92 requires non-EC nationals to become established in the EC as a condition for registering geographical indications. As the EC has set out in previous

[85] US SWS, para. 80; Australia's SWS, para. 27.

[86] US FWS, para. 85.

[87] US SWS, para. 79.

[88] US SWS, para. 83.

[89] Response of the United States of 15 March 2004, para. 36.

submissions,[90] this claim is unfounded because first, geographical indications relating to an area located in a WTO country can be registered under Regulation 2081/92; second, the right to register a geographical indication does not depend on domicile or establishment; and third, Article 2.2 Paris Convention cannot exclude measures which ensure that a product originates in the geographical area to which a protected geographical indication is related.

119. In its second submission, the United States has responded that it is arguing merely that the EC cannot require that the geographical area to which an indication relates be in the EC.[91]

120. However, as the EC has already said earlier in response to Claim 1, Regulation 2081/92 contains no such requirement. Geographical indications relating to an area located in another WTO Member can be registered under Regulation 2081/92. Accordingly, already for this reason, Regulation 2081/92 cannot be said to establish a requirement of domicile.[92]

121. Accordingly, the US claim should be rejected.

3. Claim 11: Regulation 2081/92 requires non-EC nationals to become established in the EC as a condition for objecting

122. In its second submission, the United States continues to argue that Regulation 2081/92 establishes a condition of domicile or establishment because a person "must reside or become established in the EC in order to object under the Article 7 objection procedures."[93]

123. As the EC has already said, this claim is manifestly unfounded. The point is not whether a person can object "under Article 7 objection procedures," but whether a person can object at all. Persons resident or established in WTO countries can object according to Article 12d (1) and 12b (2), and are therefore in exactly the same position as persons resident or established in the EC.

124. Accordingly, the US claim should be rejected.

C. NATIONAL TREATMENT UNDER ARTICLE III:4 GATT

1. The Regulation 2081/92 is not incompatible with Article III:4 GATT (Claims 12–15)

125. The complainants have raised a number of their claims also under Article III:4 GATT, namely with respect to the registration of foreign geographical indications, the requirement of inspection structures, the transmission and verification of applications for registration, the requirement to indicate the country of origin for homonymous geographical indications, and finally the alleged overall bias in decision making.

126. All of these claims involve allegations of less favourable treatment similar to those also made under the TRIPS Agreement. In their second submissions, the complainants have not added any specific new arguments regarding their claims under Article III:4. Accordingly, the EC can refer to what it has said already previously in respect to the complainant's arguments under the TRIPS agreement.

---

[90] EC FWS, para. 176 et seq.

[91] US SWS, para. 85.

[92] Moreover, the EC would recall that regardless of whether EC or foreign geographical indications are concerned, Regulation 2081/92 does not establish any requirements of domicile or establishment. It merely requires that product specifications are established which ensure that the products in question in fact have a specific quality, reputation or characteristics attributable to their geographical origin (cf. EC FWS, para. 183).

[93] US SWS, para. 86.

127. There is, however, one specific aspect arising under the GATT on which the EC would like to comment. It concerns the US claim that the requirement to indicate the country of origin for homonymous geographical indications constitutes a violation of Article III:4 GATT. The EC notes that in their second submissions, both the United States and Australia recognise that Article IX:1 GATT exempts country of origin marking requirements from the national treatment obligations of Article III:4.[94] However, the United States does not offer any convincing explanation of why this exemption would then not also apply to the labelling requirement in Article (12)(2) of Regulation 2081/92, assuming that indeed this requirement was in violation of national treatment obligations.

128. As its only argument, the US has advanced that Regulation 2081/92 is not a "general" marking requirement. However, the word "general" does not appear in Article IX:1 GATT. Article IX:1 simply refers to requirements to mark the country of origin, regardless of whether they apply to all imported products or only to some. The EC also does not understand what would be the logic of a provision that would permit subjecting all imported products to country of origin marking, but not only some of them.

129. The perverse logic of the US claim—and similarly of Australia's corresponding claim under the TBT Agreement—is also illustrated by the practice of the US and Australia with respect to origin marking. Unlike the EC, both the US and Australia require the indication of the country of origin for all imported products.[95] This is a condition for the importation of any product into the United States or Australia, with which compliance is mandatory, and which does not apply to domestic products.

130. It is astonishing that the United States and Australia, while themselves applying discriminatory country of origin marking requirements of the most sweeping nature, would fault the EC for applying a targeted, entirely reasonable and non-discriminatory labelling provision allowing the distinction between two homonymous geographical indications.

131. In the view of the EC, the Panel should resist this attempt to create double standards for WTO Members, and accordingly reject the claim.

2. The measure would be justified under Article XX(d) GATT

132. At a subsidiary level, the EC considers that if the Panel were to find that Regulation 2081/92 does involve less favourable treatment of foreign goods by requiring the existence of inspection structures, the transmission and verification of applications by the third country government, and the indication of the country of origin for homonymous geographical indications, this less favourable treatment would be justified by Article XX(d) GATT.

133. In their second submission, the complainants have argued that the EC has not shown that the alleged inconsistencies would be justified by Article XX(d) GATT.[96] However, in its second submission, the EC has set out in detail why the requirement of inspection structures, the requirement of the transmission and verification of applications by the third country government, and the indication of the country of origin for homonymous geographical indications, are necessary to secure compliance with Regulation 2081/92.[97]

134. The United States and Australia have so far not rebutted these arguments of the EC. They have also not shown that the EC measure is applied in a manner which would constitute an arbitrary or unjustifiable

---

[94] US SWS, para. 99; Australia's SWS, para. 212.

[95] Cf. for the US 19 CFR 134.11 (Exhibit EC-66); for Australia, cf. the Commerce (Trade Descriptions) Act (Exhibit EC-67) and Commerce (Imports) Regulations, Regulation 8 (c) (i) (Exhibit EC-68).

[96] US SWS, para. 100; Australia's SWS, para. 181.

[97] EC SWS, para. 228-242 (incorporating by reference the EC arguments in response to the claims under the national treatment provision of the TRIPS Agreement).

discrimination between countries where the same conditions prevail, or constitute a disguised restriction on international trade.

135. Accordingly, the measures in question are justified by Article XX(d) GATT. As a consequence, the corresponding claims should be rejected.

IV. REGULATION 2081/92 IS COMPATIBLE WITH THE OBLIGATION TO PROVIDE MOST-FAVOURED-NATION TREATMENT

136. The EC will now turn to the US claims that Regulation 2081/92 is incompatible with the obligation to provide most-favoured-nation treatment under Article 4 TRIPS and Article I:1 GATT.

A. ARTICLE 4 TRIPS

1. Claim 16: As among non-EC WTO Members, nationals from WTO Members that satisfy the EC's conditions of reciprocity and equivalency are accorded more favourable treatment than nationals from those WTO Members that do not

137. Originally, the United States claimed that Regulation 2081/92 is incompatible with Article 4 TRIPS Agreement because nationals from WTO Members that satisfy conditions of reciprocity and equivalence are accorded more favourable treatment than nationals from those WTO Members that do not.

138. In its second submission, the United States has enlarged this claim, and is now alleging that three separate aspects of Regulation 2081/92 constitute a violation of most-favoured nation obligations, namely:[98]

- the application of conditions of "reciprocity and equivalence" (**claim 16**);
- the requirement of inspection structures (**claim 16bis**);
- the requirement of "substantial participation" in administering and enforcing the EC Regulation (**claim 16ter**).

139. As regards the first claim, the EC has already confirmed that it does not apply conditions of reciprocity and equivalence to other WTO Members. Already for this reason, the US claim is unfounded. Moreover, the EC has also explained that even if Article 12(1) were applicable to WTO Members, this provision merely sets out the conditions under which Regulation 2081/92 may apply, but does not confer any advantage within the meaning of Article 4 TRIPS Agreement. Finally, the EC has also explained that Regulation 2081/92 does not discriminate on the basis of nationality.[99] For all these reasons, this US claim should be rejected.

140. As regards Claim 16bis, the EC has already set out in detail that the requirement of inspection structures is not "equivalence by another name," but rather is applied on a product-specific basis.[100] This means that the question whether appropriate inspection structures exist must be evaluated for each specific application separately. There is no rule which would imply that for certain countries, inspection structures are automatically deemed to exist, whereas for other countries they are deemed not to exist.

141. This is not just so for applications from third countries, but also for applications from the EC. In fact, each application must contain the indication of the competent inspection body.[101] If no inspection body is

[98] US SWS, para. 104.
[99] Cf. EC FWS, para. 228 et seq.; EC SWS, para. 245 et seq.
[100] EC SWS, para. 96 et seq.; above, para. 54 et seq.
[101] Cf. as examples the applications in Exhibits EC-51 to EC-54, EC-56.

indicated, or if the inspection body indicated is not in compliance with the requirements of Article 10 of Regulation 2081/92, the geographical indication cannot be registered. The requirement of inspection structures is thus applied in a completely non-discriminatory fashion. It involves discrimination neither on the basis of nationality nor on the basis of product origin. Accordingly, Claim 16bis should be rejected.

142. As regards Claim 16ter, which is newly raised by the United States, essentially the same objections apply. There is no rule in the Regulation 2081/92 which would define which WTO members can transmit and verify applications for registration and which cannot. In fact, the United States does not even claim this, but instead argues that some WTO Members "might not be able to prosecute" applications for registration, whereas others might be.[102] This argument is without merit. The Regulation does not require anything that would be outside the scope of any WTO Member with a normally functioning government.

143. In reality, and certainly as regards the United States itself, the issue is not ability, but willingness. The United States has stated clearly that it is unwilling to cooperate in the registration process under Regulation 2081/92. However, this is not a choice which is attributable to the EC. Accordingly, Claim 16ter should equally be rejected.

2. Claim 17: Under Regulation 2081/92, an EC Member State grants more favourable treatment to nationals from other EC Member States than it accords to nationals from non-EC WTO Members

144. The United States has claimed that under Regulation 2081/92, an EC Member State grants more favourable treatment to nationals from other EC Member States than it accords to nationals from non-EC WTO Members.

145. In its written submissions, the EC has already explained that this claim is unfounded.[103] In particular, the EC is an original member of the WTO. Measures with which the EC harmonises the law inside the EC are not measures through which the Member States grant "each other" advantages. Since Regulation 2081/92 is a measure of the EC, the United States has therefore correctly brought its claim against the EC, and not against the Member States.

146. Obvious as this seems, in its second submission, the US persists with its fallacious arguments. In particular, the US argues that the terms of reference of the Panel include also "related implementation and enforcement measures," including measures taken by the Member States. On this basis, the US asks the Panel to "review" whether the measures of the EC Member States are in accordance with MFN obligations.

147. At the outset, the EC would observe that the United States has not indicated what measures of the Member States it is talking about, and in which way such measures are supposed to be in violation of WTO obligations. Accordingly, the United States has not provided sufficient evidence to establish the existence of a violation.

148. Moreover, the EC would remark that the present dispute relates to measures adopted by the EC. That, as in many other areas of EC law, the EC Member States have certain responsibilities in the execution of Regulation 2081/92 is irrelevant. The EC generally does not execute its laws through authorities at the EC level; rather, it has recourse to the authorities of the Member States, which in such a situation act *de facto* as organs of the Community, for which the Community would be responsible under WTO law and international law in general. In this context, it is also interesting to note that the European Court of Justice upheld EC competence for an agreement falling under the common commercial policy while holding that "it was of little importance

[102] US SWS, para. 107.

[103] EC FWS, para. 249 et seq. ; EC SWS, para. 252 et seq.

that the obligations and financial burdens inherent in the execution of the agreement envisaged are borne directly by the Member States."[104]

149. Accordingly, where EC Member States take measures for the execution of Community law, such measures are derived from Community law, fall under the competence of the Community, and it is the Community that is responsible for them, not the Member States. Accordingly, such measures cannot be regarded as the granting of an advantage from one WTO Member to another, or as "avoiding MFN obligations" towards other WTO Members. Moreover, the fact that MFN obligations do not apply does not mean that other WTO obligations, and in particular national treatment obligations, would become inapplicable.

150. The EC would also remark that this US claim has nothing to do specifically with the protection of geographical indications, but is of a horizontal nature. The EC has adopted tens of thousands of acts harmonising the law within the EC. If the United States were right, then presumably the entire body of EC law should be applied to the US, and indeed to any other WTO Member. This cannot be right, and to the knowledge of the EC, no other Member has ever made a similar claim.

151. To conclude this point, this claim is an ill-considered attempt to undermine the integrity of the EC legal system, and the Panel should reject it as such.

B. CLAIM 18: BY SUBJECTING THE REGISTRATION OF THIRD-COUNTRY GEOGRAPHICAL INDICATIONS TO CONDITIONS OF RECIPROCITY AND EQUIVALENCE, THE EC MEASURE IS INCONSISTENT WITH THE MOST-FAVOURED-NATION OBLIGATION UNDER THE ARTICLE I:1 GATT

152. The United States has argued that by subjecting the registration of third-country geographical indications to conditions of reciprocity and equivalence, the EC measure is inconsistent with the most-favoured-nation obligation under Article I:1 GATT.

153. As the EC has already set out in its written submission, Regulation 2081/92 is not incompatible with Article I:1.[105] In its second submission, the United States has not made any specific arguments on Article I:1 GATT, but simply referred to its arguments on Article 4 TRIPS.[106] Accordingly, the EC can also refer to the arguments that it has made earlier in response to the United States claim under Article 4 TRIPS.[107] Accordingly, the claim should be rejected.

V. REGULATION 2081/92 DOES NOT DIMINISH THE LEGAL PROTECTION OF TRADEMARKS

154. In this section of our statement, we will address the complainants' claims under Article 16.1 of the TRIPS Agreement and, in particular, their claims concerning the issue of "co-existence." The complainants have submitted no new arguments with respect to their other claims in their rebuttal submissions. The EC refers, with respect to those claims, to its earlier submissions to the Panel.

---

[104] Opinion 1/75, *Local Cost Standard,* [1975] ECR 1355 (Exhibit EC-69).

[105] EC SWS, para. 259.

[106] US SWS, paras. 114-115.

[107] It is not clear from the US second submission whether the United States considers also that the requirement of inspection procedures and of transmission and verification of applications by the government of the home country of the geographical indication constitutes a violation of Article I:1 GATT. To the extent that the US makes such a claim, the EC can refer to its response to the claims under Article 4 TRIPS. Moreover, subsidiarily, the EC would also consider that these measures would be justified by Article XX(d) GATT, in line with what it has already set out in response to the claims under Article III:4 GATT.

A. CLAIM 19: ARTICLE 14(2) OF REGULATION 2081/92 IS INCONSISTENT WITH ARTICLE 16.1 OF THE TRIPS IN THAT IT ALLOWS THE CO-EXISTENCE OF GEOGRAPHICAL INDICATIONS AND EARLIER TRADEMARKS

1. Article 14(3) of Regulation 2081/92

155. The EC has shown that the co-existence of geographical indications and earlier trademarks provided in Article 14(2) of Regulation 2081/92 would not be inconsistent with Article 16.1 of the TRIPS Agreement, even if the complainants' interpretation of that provision, and of its relationship to Section 3 of Part II, were correct:

- first, the criteria for the registrability of trademarks limit *a priori* the possibility of conflicts between geographical indications and earlier trademarks;
- second, to the extent that any such conflict arises, Article 14(3) of Regulation 2081/92 provides the necessary means to trademark owners in order to oppose or invalidate the registration of *any* confusing geographical indication;
- finally, the provisions of Regulation 2081/92, together with other provisions of EC law and the unfair competition laws of the Member States, provide the necessary means to ensure that, in practice, registered geographical indications are not used in a confusing manner.

(a) Registrability of geographical names as trademarks

156. The EC has set out in detail the criteria for the registrability of trademarks because they define the legal context within which Article 14(3) must be applied. A proper understanding of those criteria is, therefore, essential in order to interpret correctly Article 14(3).

157. Contrary to the complainants' assertions, the EC has never said that "valid registered trademarks cannot incorporate certain geographical elements."[108] Indeed, if so, it would have been unnecessary to include Article 14(3) in Regulation 2081/92. Rather, the EC has explained that, under EC trademark law, terms which are, or which may reasonably qualify in the future, as geographical indications cannot be validly registered as trademarks unless they have acquired distinctiveness (a "secondary meaning") through use. Hence the express reference in Article 14(3) to the criteria that are relevant for measuring such acquired distinctiveness.

158. The facts bear out the EC's position. Neither the complainants nor the third parties have been able to identify even one single geographical indication, of the more than 600 registered by the EC, which gives rise to a likelihood of confusion with an earlier trademark. Instead, the United States cites hypothetical examples involving cheese from the Moon and tropical products from Portugal.

159. Australia argues that the registrability criteria of the Trademark Directive did not apply to trademarks registered before its adoption.[109] Australia has overlooked that, under the Trademark Directive, the grounds for refusing a registration are also grounds for invalidating existing trademarks, including trademarks pre-dating the Trademark Directive, unless the Member States have provided otherwise. Moreover, the Trademark Directive was hardly innovative on this point. Before the adoption of the Trademark Directive, the trademark laws of the Member States provided already similar registrability criteria, just like the laws of most other countries, including those of the complainants.

---

[108] US SWS, para. 169.

[109] Australia's SWS, para. 91.

160. In turn, the Unites States argues that the EC's reasoning would not apply to registered geographical indications which do not consist of a place name.[110] The United States is wrong. The Trademark Directive prohibits the registration of trademarks which consist "of signs or indications which may serve, in trade, to designate ... geographical origin."[111] Terms like "Feta" or "Reblochon" operate as indirect indications of origin and, therefore, fit this description even if they are not place names. In any event, the Trademark Directive also prohibits the registration of terms which serve to designate the "kind," "quality" or "other characteristics" of the goods.[112]

(b) The Complainants have misinterpreted Article 14(3)

161. The EC has shown that, far from being the only reasonable interpretation of Article 14(3), the complainants' reading of that provision is unsupported by the ordinary meaning of its terms. Furthermore, the complainants' interpretation is neither reasonable nor workable in practice and cannot be reconciled with the terms of other provisions of Regulation 2081/92.

162. Australia asserts that "the term misleading establishes a stricter evidentiary standard than confusing."[113] At most, this could be considered one possible reading of "misleading." But Australia has not proved that the EC's own interpretation of "misleading" is less reasonable, or that it is impossible to interpret the term "misleading" consistently with Article 16.1. In fact, Australia's interpretation does not even pass the dictionary test. As acknowledged by Australia, one of the ordinary meanings of "misleading" is "confusing."[114] The same is true of the other linguistic versions of Regulation 2081/92. For example, the term "mislead" has been rendered as "inducir a error" in the Spanish version. According to the Diccionario de la Real Academia Española, one of the ordinary meanings of "error" is "equivocación, confusión."[115] Furthermore, the EC's reading of "misleading" is supported contextually by Article 7 (5) (b) of Regulation 2081/92, which provides that the Commission shall decide on the objections having regard to the "likelihood of confusion."

163. For its part, the United States persists on its misguided theory that Article 14(3) applies only with respect to a certain subset of trademarks. But this is not what Article 14(3) says. Article 14(3) does not say that registration shall be refused where it leads to confusion with a trademark *provided* that such trademark has been used for a long time and *provided* that it enjoys considerable reputation and renown. Instead, Article 14(3) says that registration shall be refused where the proposed name would be misleading "*in the light of* a trademark's reputation and renown and the length of time it has been used." Thus, length of use and reputation/renown are not "threshold pre-requisites" for the application of Article 14(3). They are criteria for assessing whether the geographical indication is misleading. As explained, Article 14(3) mentions expressly those criteria because they will be particularly relevant, given that geographical terms are inherently non-distinctive as trademarks.

164. The United States notes that Article 6*bis* of the Paris Convention and Articles 16.2 and 16.3 of the TRIPS Agreement confer additional protection to so-called "well-known" marks and that reputation, renown and length of use are "factors" generally used in order to establish whether a trademark qualifies as "well known."[116] But from this it does not follow logically that these factors are relevant *only* as "threshold pre-requisites" for the application of the provisions in question. Length of use and reputation/renown are relevant criteria in order to assess the likelihood of confusion with *any* trademark. In particular, regardless of whether a trademark has enough reputation/renown to qualify as a "well-known" mark under Paris Article 6*bis*, its reputation/renown (or the lack thereof) will also be relevant for the purposes of establishing the likelihood of confusion with a sign for similar goods under Article 16.1.

---

[110] US SWS, para. 168.

[111] Cf. Article 3.1(c) of the Trademark Directive.

[112] Ibid.

[113] Australia's SWS, para. 104.

[114] Australia's SWS, para. 104.

[115] Diccionario de la Real Academia Española, 20th Edition, 1984. (Exhibit EC-70).

[116] US SWS, para. 146.

165. The United States also refers[117] to the so-called "anti-dilution" provisions of the Trademark Directive and the Community Trademark Regulation, which confer protection to a trademark, despite the lack of similarity between the goods concerned, "where the trademark has a reputation." In the context of those provisions, "reputation" functions as a "threshold pre-requisite." But, again, this does not mean that, under EC trademark law, reputation is relevant only for that purpose. Nor does it mean that the relatively high level of reputation required by the ECJ[118] and the OHIM[119] when applying those provisions can be extrapolated to Article 14(3). That standard is linked to the far-reaching protection afforded by the "anti-dilution" provisions and would not be justified in a situation involving signs for similar goods.

166. The tenth recital of the Trademark Directive says that the appreciation of likelihood of confusion

> depends on numerous elements and, in particular, on the recognition of the trade mark on the market, of the association which can be made with the used or registered sign, of the degree of similarity between the trade mark and the sign and between the goods or services identified.

167. Interpreting Article 4(1)(b) of the Trademark Directive, which is the equivalent of Article 16.1, the ECJ has said that[120]

> ... the more distinctive the earlier mark, the greater the risk of confusion ... Since protection of a trademark depends, in accordance with Article 4.1(b) of the Directive, on there being a likelihood of confusion, marks with a highly distinctive character, either *per se* or because of the *reputation* they possess in the market, enjoy broader protection than marks with a less distinctive character.

168. This confirms that reputation, in addition to being a "threshold pre-requisite" for the application of certain provisions providing additional protections to highly reputed marks, is also a general criterion for assessing likelihood of confusion with *any* trademark.

169. EC trademark law is by no means unique in this respect.[121] Similar criteria are applied by most other Members.[122] In the United States, the factors to be examined in determining likelihood of confusion in infringement proceedings include the so-called "strength" of the trademark.[123] Trademarks consisting of descriptive terms, such as place names, are deemed inherently "weak" and are protected only to the extent that

---

[117] US SWS, para. 150.

[118] US SWS, para. 151.

[119] US SWS, para. 152.

[120] Case C-39/97, *Canon Kabushiki Kaisha v Metro Goldwyn-Mayer Inc.* , ECR [1998] I-5507, para. 18 (Exhibit EC-71). Emphases added.

[121] According to WIPO's Trademark Manual:

If the infringed trademark is being used, the extent of use can influence the test of confusing similarity. Intensive use increases distinctiveness of the mark, and confusion with well known marks is more likely if the goods on which the infringing mark is used are less similar or if the similarity of the marks is less apparent.

WIPO, *Introduction to Trademark Law & Practice, The Basic Concepts, A WIPO Training Manual*, Geneva 1993, 2nd Ed., at point. 6.2.3 in fine (Exhibit EC-72).

WIPO's Manual distinguishes the relevance of intensive use as a factor that influences the test of confusing similarity from the protection given to well known marks beyond the scope of confusing similarity. (Ibid., at point 6.2.4).

[122] For example, Section 6(5) of Canada's Trade Marks Act (Exhibit EC-73) provides that (emphases added):

In determining whether trade-marks or trade names are confusing, the court or the Registrar, as the case may be, shall have regard to all the surrounding circumstances including: (a) the inherent distinctiveness of the trade-marks or trade names and *the extent to which they have become known*; (b) *the length of time the trade-marks or trade-names have been in use*; (c) the nature of the wares, services or business; (d) the nature of the trade; and (e) the degree of resemblance between the trade-marks or trade names in appearance or sound or in the ideas suggested by them.

[123] See e.g. *Polaroid Corp. v. Polarad Elect. Corp.*, 287 F.2d 492 (2d Cir.) cert. denied, 368 U.S. 820 (1961) (Exhibit EC-74); *E.I. DuPont DeNemours & Co. Application of*, 476 F.2d 1357 (Cust. & Pat. App.1973), 261 (Exhibit EC-75).

"secondary meaning" is shown.[124] In turn, secondary meaning is measured according to criteria such as reputation, renown and length of use.[125]

170. Even less pertinent are the US references to the EC Wine Regulation.[126] Indeed, the Wine Regulation proves the opposite. The differences between Article 14(3) and the corresponding provision of the Wine Regulation underscore that the EC authorities intended to apply a different rule in the context of Regulation 2081/92.

171. The United States alleges that the EC's interpretation of Article 14(3) is a novel one which contradicts previous positions of the EC. Given the tone in which this accusation is made, one would expect that the United States has credible evidence to substantiate it. It does not.

172. The United States cites three pieces of "evidence:"

- The first one is a slide included in a promotional presentation made by a low level Commission official in Tokyo, which, for pedagogical reasons, describes the requirements of Article 14(3) in an oversimplified manner. Needless to say, that slide has no legal authority whatsoever.

- The second one is a passage from the EC Commission's Guide to Regulation 2081/92.[127] The passage in question, however, repeats verbatim the wording of Article 14(3) and, therefore, does not support the US interpretation. The United States makes much of the fact that the passage describes Article 14(3) as "the only circumstance" in which a "conflicting trademark" (i.e. a trademark that engenders one of the situations indicated in Article 13(1)) prevents the registration of the geographical indication. However, the EC's interpretation does not contradict this. Regardless of which is the correct interpretation of Article 14(3), it is beyond dispute that the situation referred to in that Article is the "only circumstance" in which the registration of a geographical indication must be refused. The reference to "other cases" in the passage quoted by the United States is an allusion to the other situations included in Article 13(1) in which a trademark "conflicts" with a geographical indication.

- The third one is a statement of "ministerial reasoning" accompanying Section 45 of Hungary's Law on the Protection of Trademarks and Geographical Indications.[128] Contrary to what is said by the United States, that provision does not implement Regulation 2081/92, which, being a directly applicable Regulation, and not a Directive, need not, and indeed must not, be implemented by the Member States. The provision in question applies to products not covered by Regulation 2081/92, in respect of which the Member States remain competent to adopt their own rules. The EC finds it rather curious that the United States considers more authoritative the interpretation of an EC Regulation made by a minister of a Member State in order to explain an amendment to a law of that Member State which, on that point, does not implement EC law, than the interpretation made by the EC authorities of an EC Regulation which those authorities have drafted and adopted themselves and which they have been interpreting and applying for more than 15 years prior to Hungary's accession to the EC. But then, of course, one should not forget that the United States speaks from the premise that the EC institutions are the only government in the world which is entitled to no deference from panels.[129]

---

[124] See e.g. *AMF Inc. v. Sleekcraft Boats*, 5499 F.2d 341 (9th Cir. 1979) (Exhibit EC-76).

[125] See e.g. *Zatarian's, Inc. v. Oak Grove Smokehouse*, Inc., 698 F.2d 786 (5th Cir. 1983) (Exhibit EC-77).

[126] US SWS, para. 152.

[127] US SWS, para. 155, with reference to Exhibit US-24.

[128] US SWS, para. 148.

[129] US Response to the Panel's Question No. 1, para. 8 and para. 18.

173. The EC has pointed out that the interpretation of Article 14(3) made by the United States would lead to a result which cannot be reconciled with the terms of other provisions of Regulation 2081/92 and, in particular, with Article 7(4).[130] In response, the United States notes that the two provisions apply cumulatively.[131] However, this still does not explain why Article 7(4) allows objections in respect of *any* trademarks, and not just in respect of "well-known" trademarks. It would be pointless to admit an objection on certain grounds if, in any event, it were not possible to reject the objection on such grounds. The United States has no answer for this.

(c) Article 14(3) confers enforceable rights to the trademark owners

174. The United States argues that, even if the EC's reading of Article 14(3) were correct, that provision "merely authorizes the EC to decline registration of a GI"[132], but does not accord rights to the trademark owners.[133]

175. The United States is wrong again. When applying Article 14(3), the EC authorities have a margin of appreciation in order to assess the relevant facts. But once they have determined, as a factual matter, that a proposed geographical indication would be misleading, they are required, and not simply authorized, to refuse the registration of that geographical indication.

176. Furthermore, Article 14(3) confers judicially enforceable rights to the owners of trademarks.

177. In accordance with Article 230 of the EC Treaty, if a trademark owner can show that it is directly and individually concerned by the decision to register a geographical indication, it may bring an action in annulment before the European Court of Justice against that decision on the grounds that it is inconsistent with Article 14(3) of Regulation 2081/92.

178. In any event, trademark owners may raise the invalidity of the registration of a geographical indication before the courts of the Member States in accordance with the procedure provided in Article 234 of the EC Treaty. For example, a trademark owner could bring infringement proceedings under the Community Trademark Regulation and/or under the trademark law of a Member State against the user of a registered geographical indication and argue that the registration of the geographical indication is invalid because it is inconsistent with Article 14(3) of Regulation 2081/92. The national court would then have to request a preliminary ruling on the validity of the registration from the European Court of Justice. That ruling would be binding upon the national court. Unlike the action in annulment, the possibility to request a preliminary ruling is not subject to any time limits.[134]

179. Australia has said that the decisions to register a geographical indication under Regulation 2081/92 are subject to judicial review only "on points of law."[135] This is wrong. The ECJ may review not only points of law but also the factual assessment made by the registering authorities, both in annulment proceedings under Article 230 of the EC Treaty and in the context of a preliminary ruling on the validity of the registration under Article 234 of the EC Treaty.

---

[130] Articles 12b(3) and 12d(2) provide, respectively, that the criteria of Article 7(4) shall apply also with respect to the admissibility of objections to the registration of foreign geographical indications and of objections from outside the EC to EC geographical indications.

[131] US SWS, para. 161.

[132] US FOS, para. 54. See also US Responses to Panel's Questions Nos. 14 (at para. 41) and 67 (at para. 87).

[133] US SWS, para. 136.

[134] US SWS, para. 138.

[135] US SWS, para. 152.

(d) EC law provides means to prevent confusing uses of a registered geographical indication

180. The United States goes on to argue that, even if Article 14(3) prevents the registration of confusing geographical indications, it does not provide means to prevent that a registered geographical indication is used subsequently in a confusing manner.

181. The United States is asking the EC to provide a remedy against the use of a registered geographical indication which is not required by Article 16.1 and which few Members, if any, provide against the use of a registered trademark. The registration of a trademark confers a right to use that sign.[136] For that reason, in most jurisdictions a trademark owner cannot prevent the owner of another registered trademark from using the sign covered by the registration unless it requests and obtains first the cancellation, invalidation or revocation of such registration.[137] Under EC law, the relationship between trademarks and registered geographical indications rests on the same principle. The owner of a trademark may not prevent the right holders of a registered geographical indication from using the registered name on the grounds that such name is confusing. As just explained, however, the trademark owner is entitled to request a judicial ruling to the effect that the registration of the geographical indication is invalid on those grounds.

182. The United States contends that, in practice, questions may arise as to what exactly is encompassed by the "registered name." The same kind of questions, however, may arise in connection with the scope of the registration of a trademark. Whether or not a particular sign falls within the scope of a particular registration is a factual question to be resolved by the courts on a case-by-case basis. In should not, and indeed cannot possibly be decided in the abstract by this Panel.

183. The United States also argues that confusion could arise if the geographical indication is used "in ways that cannot be anticipated, such as in a trademark-like manner."[138] This reflects certain pre-conceived notions as to how trademarks and geographical indications should be used which have no basis in the TRIPS Agreement and which the EC does not share. For example, the EC does not agree that the "pictorial depictions" of the packaging for four EC cheeses included in Exhibit US-52 ("Esrom," "Bra," "Bitto" and "Tomme de Savoie") demonstrate that the geographical indications are used in "trademark-like fashion."[139] Rather, they demonstrate simply that trademarks and geographical indications can be presented in similar fashion. To characterize that fashion as "trademark-like" assumes that trademarks enjoy priority in order to use certain types or styles of presentation.

184. What the United States characterizes as "trademark-like" manner is, in fact, a legitimate, ordinary and predictable manner of using a geographical indication, at least in the EC. EC consumers are familiar with the use of geographical indications for foodstuffs. They value them as much as trademarks when making their purchasing decisions, if not more, and expect them to be used in what the United States calls "trademark-like" fashion. For example, Italian consumers probably care more about whether their cheese is genuine "Bra" (rather than, say, "Bitto") than about whether it has been produced by the firm "Vittorio" or by another cheese maker, in particular since the conditions for using the geographical indication ensure that all Bra cheese has homogenous characteristics, regardless of the brand. In conducting the assessment provided in Article 14(3), the

---

[136] For example, Section 122 of Australia's Trade Marks Act 1995 (Exhibit EC-7) provides that:

In spite of section 120, a person does not infringe a registered trade mark when: [...] (e) the person exercises a right to use a trade mark given to the person under this Act.

Section 120 defines when a trademark is deemed infringed (Exhibit EC-78). Section 23 of Australia's Trade Marks Act 1995 (Exhibit EC-79) further clarifies that:

If trade marks that are substantially identical or deceptively similar have been registered by more than one person (whether in respect of the same or different goods or services), the registered owner of any one of those trademarks does not have the right to prevent the registered owner of any other of those trade marks from using that trade mark except to the extent that the first mentioned owner is authorised to do so under the registration of his or her trade mark.

[137] See e.g. Article 95 of the Community Trademark Regulation.

[138] US SWS, para. 131.

[139] US SWS, para. 133.

EC authorities will assume that the proposed geographical indication will be used in what the United States calls "trademark-like" manner. Accordingly, if the EC authorities reach the conclusion that a geographical indication is not "misleading," it is because they consider that such name is not "misleading" even when used in what the United States calls "trademark-like" fashion.

185. Finally, the EC recalls once again that, while the right holders of a geographical indication have a positive right to use the registered name, this does not mean that they are allowed to use it in any conceivable manner. As explained[140], the use of a name registered as a geographical indication, like the use of name registered as a trademark, is subject to the generally applicable provisions of Directive 2000/13 on the labelling, presentation and advertising of foodstuffs[141], of Directive 84/450 on misleading advertising[142] and of the unfair competition laws of the Member States.[143]

2. Article 24.5 of the TRIPS Agreement

(a) The relationship between Section 3 of Part II and Article 16.1

186. The United States has argued that "it is not necessary for the Panel to even consider Article 24.5 to find a violation of Article 16.1, as Article 24.5 is an exception to GI protection, not trademark protection"[144].

187. As we have shown, this argument is specious. True, Article 24.5 limits "GI protection." But, in turn, the measures taken to implement "GI protection" under Section 3 of Part II limit "trademark protection." Thus, by defining the scope of "GI protection" Article 24.5 defines simultaneously the scope of "trademark protection." In other words, as conceded by Australia[145], together with other provisions of Section 3 of Part II, Article 24.5 defines the boundary between the right to protect geographical indications and the obligation to protect trademarks. The issue before the Panel is whether the co-existence provided in Regulation 2081/92 is within the boundary defined by Article 24.5.

188. Moreover, Article 16.1 must be read together with Article 15.2. In accordance with that provision, Members have a right to refuse (and by implication to invalidate) the registration of trademarks on a variety of grounds relating to the "form" of the trademark. That right, however, is circumscribed by Article 24.5, which provides that, in implementing protection for geographical indications, Members may not invalidate a grandfathered trademark "on the basis that such a trademark is identical with or similar to a geographical indication." Since Article 24.5 limits the right of Members under Section 2 of Part III to invalidate the registration of certain trademarks, it may, at the same time, limit some of the obligations arising from the registration of such trademarks under that section.

(b) The meaning of "the right to use a trademark"

189. By now it has become clear that the key issue before the Panel is the interpretation of the phrase "the right to use a trademark." Australia and the United States have advanced different and contradictory interpretations of that phrase.

---

[140] EC's FWS, para. 319. See also the responses of the EC and its Member States to the review under Article 24.2 of the TRIPS Agreement contained in document IP/C/W/117/Add.10 (Exhibit EC-29).

[141] Exhibit EC–30.

[142] Exhibit EC–31.

[143] References to the relevant laws of the Member States are found in their responses to the review under Article 24.2 of the TRIPS Agreement (Exhibit EC-32).

[144] US SWS, para. 173

[145] Australia's SWS, para. 96.

190. Australia says that the phrase "the right to use a trademark" applies only to the trademarks acquired through use.[146] There are, however, obvious problems with this reading, which Australia has failed to address. First, it cannot be reconciled with the ordinary meaning of the term "trademark," which includes all trademarks. Moreover, as used throughout the TRIPS Agreement, the term "trademark" includes both types of trademarks. When the drafters intended to distinguish between registered trademarks and trademarks acquired through use they did so expressly, like in Article 16.1 or in Article 21.

191. Australia suggests that the phrase "the right to use a trademark" is linked to the reference made in the chapeau of Article 24.5 to the situation where "rights to a trademark have been acquired through use." But, if so, it would have been more logical to say that the implementation of protection for geographical indications "shall not prejudice ... the rights to a trademark acquired through use." Contradicting expressly Australia's position, the United States has said that "'the right to use a trademark' is not specifically linked in the text to trademarks whose rights are acquired through use."[147]

192. Furthermore, by arguing that the phrase "the right to use a trademark" refers exclusively to the trademarks acquired through use, and not contesting that this phrase does not include the right to prevent others from using the trademark, Australia concedes that Article 24.5 provides for the co-existence of geographical indications with earlier trademark acquired through use. Australia suggests that co-existence is justified in the case of non-registered trademarks, because Article 16.1 only requires to grant exclusive rights to the owners of registered trademarks.[148] However, Article 16.1 reserves expressly the right of Members to grant rights on the basis of use, including exclusive rights. Australia does not explain how Article 24.5, which Australia insists is <u>not</u> an exception to Article 16.1, can nevertheless limit the Members' right to protect non-registered trademarks under Article 16.1.

193. In turn, the United States argues that the phrase "the right to use a trademark" means in fact "the right to use a trademark and, in addition, to exclude others from using it." This reading cannot be reconciled with the ordinary meaning of that phrase. Nor with the meaning commonly given to that phrase in the context of trademark law, including in US trademark law. Contradicting expressly the US position, Australia agrees with the EC that the phrase "the right to use a trademark" does not mean the *exclusive* right to use a trademark.[149]

194. The United States attempts to stretch the meaning of the phrase "the right to use the trade mark" by resorting to what it calls a "contextual" interpretation. It is, of course, true that the purpose of a trademark is to distinguish the goods from a certain undertaking. But from this it does not follow logically that "the right to use a trademark" is inherently exclusive. In practice, the right to use a trademark is not always exclusive. Indeed, if so, it would have been superfluous to provide in Article 16.1 that registered trademarks must be exclusive. Also, on the US interpretation, any rights granted to the owners of unregistered trademarks on the basis of use would have to be exclusive. Yet, while this may be generally the case, there is no obligation under the TRIPS Agreement to grant such exclusive rights, as emphasised by Australia.[150]

195. The United States confuses the trademark, which is a sign, with the rights that the law may confer over that sign. That a trademark is a sign, and not a right, is confirmed by the fact that an undertaking may use a sign as a trademark even if it has acquired no rights over it. In most countries, including the majority of EC Member States, the rights over a trademark are acquired only upon registration. In other words, an undertaking has no rights over a trademark, including the right to use it, unless and until it registers it. But there is nothing that prevents an undertaking from using a non-registered trademark in order to distinguish its goods, even if it has no rights over it, provided that it does not infringe the rights of another undertaking. In other countries, including the United States, it is possible to acquire rights over a trademark on the basis of use. But even in

---

[146] Australia's SWS, para. 100.

[147] US Response to the Panel's Question No. 70, para. 105.

[148] Australia's SWS, para. 100.

[149] Australia's SWS, para. 100.

[150] Australia's SWS, para. 100.

those countries it is necessary, before any rights over the trademark are acquired, that the trademark is used for a certain period of time. This confirms that one thing is using a sign as a trademark and another thing having a right to use such trademark, let alone an exclusive right.

(c) The validity of the registration

196. While the two complainants disagree with respect to the meaning of the phrase "the right to use a trademark," both contend that the phrase "shall not prejudice ... the validity of the registration" means that the implementation of protection for geographical indications cannot prejudice the right to exclude others from using the trademark.

197. This reading confuses the registration with the exercise of one the rights that may be conferred by the registration. That the validity of the registration cannot be "prejudiced" means that Members cannot cancel the registration, or limit its scope or its duration. It does not mean that Members are prohibited from adopting any measure that may affect the exercise of the rights of the owner of the registered trademark. Moreover, on the complainants' interpretation, the phrase "the right to use a trademark" would become duplicative and superfluous. If the obligation not to prejudice the exclusive right to use a trademark were already inherent in the obligation not to prejudice the validity of the trademark, it would have been pointless to specify that the implementation of protection for geographical indications shall not prejudice "the right to use a trademark."

198. The complainants suggest[151] that while the right to exclude others is inherent in the "validity" of the registration by virtue of Article 16.1, the "right to use a trademark" is not. However, the right to use a trademark is the most basic right of the owner of a registered trademark. Indeed, even more so than the right to exclude others. Trademarks are generally exclusive, but not inherently so. Hence the obligation provided in Article 16.1. On the other hand, a registered trademark which did not confer the right to use the trademark would be meaningless. The right to use a trademark is implicit in Section 2 of Part III. It is implicit, for example, in Article 16.1. The right to prevent others from using a sign which would result in a likelihood of confusion with the registered trademark presupposes that the owner of the registered trademark can use the trademark himself, since otherwise there could be no possibility of confusion. The right to use a trademark is also implicit in Article 19, which provides that, in order to maintain a registration, Members may require the use of the trademark. It is also implicit in Article 20, which provides that the use of a trademark shall not be unjustifiably encumbered.

199. If the drafters deemed necessary to specify in Article 24.5 that the implementation of protection for geographical indications shall not prejudice the most basic right of the owner of a registered trademark ("the right to use it"), but not the right to exclude others from using it, the clear implication is that they did not intend to prevent Members from limiting the exercise of the latter right in order to allow the use of a geographical indication in co-existence with a grandfathered trademark.

3. Article 24.3 of the TRIPS Agreement

200. The EC has argued that, regardless of whether the co-existence of geographical indications and earlier trademarks is envisaged by Article 24.5, it is required to maintain such co-existence by virtue of the stand-still obligation contained in Article 24.3.[152]

201. The complainants read Article 24.3 as if it were subject to the proviso that Members are exempted from the obligation not to diminish the protection of geographical indications, where such protection would not be consistent with the provisions of Section 2 of Part III.[153] But Article 24.3 contains no such proviso. The

[151] See e.g. Australia's SWS, para. 99.

[152] EC FWS, paras. 312-314.

[153] See e.g. US SWS, paras. 189-190.

United States suggests that Article 24.3 is subject to Article 1.1.[154] But Article 1.1 applies only when a Member decides, voluntarily, to implement more extensive protection. Article 24.3, however, does not simply *permit* Members to implement more extensive protection. It *requires* them to do so. This obligation is not subordinated in any manner to the obligation imposed by Article 16.1. Both have equal rank. Thus, the complainants' reading of Article 24.3 would result in a genuine conflict between that provision and Article 16.1.

202. The distinction drawn by the complainants between the "implementation" of Section 2 and that of Section 3 is fallacious, because the protection of geographical indications with respect to trademarks is an essential and inseparable component of the protection of geographical indications provided in Section 3. Several provisions of Section 3 limit expressly the protection of trademarks under Section 2. There is no reason why Article 24.3 cannot impose an additional limitation.

203. The United States devotes considerable space to argue that the EC's reading of Article 24.3 would have provided "a road map to circumvent the disciplines of the TRIPS Agreement."[155] The US concerns are exaggerated and unconvincing.

204. In the first place, Article 24.3 is not an open ended provision. It applies only with respect to measures that were in force prior to the entry into force of the WTO Agreement. Those measures should have been known to the negotiators. Even if the disciplines of the TRIPS Agreement "were essentially agreed"[156] as of 1991, there was nothing that prevented the participants from reopening the negotiation of Article 24.3, had they considered that other participants were taking advantage of it in order to circumvent their future TRIPS obligations. Furthermore, the conduct described by the United States would have been manifestly contrary to the requirements of the principle of good faith. The interpretation of Article 24.3 cannot be premised on the assumption that the participants in the negotiations would have acted in bad faith.

205. Moreover, the Unites States exaggerates the opportunities for circumvention. The EC's interpretation of Article 24.3 does not extend to measures limiting copyright or patent protection. Section 3 of Part II does not address the relationship between geographical indications and those rights. Therefore, measures limiting those rights cannot be considered as "implementing" Section 3. Moreover, the United States does not explain how a limitation of patent rights or other intellectual property rights could contribute to protect geographical indications. The example provided by the United States with respect to copyrights[157] is so contrived and unrealistic that it undermines rather than supports its argument.

206. Both complainants argue that, in any event, Article 24.3 would apply only with respect to protection provided to individual geographical indications registered prior to the entry into force of the WTO Agreement.[158] The complainants, however, do not address the EC's argument that this would have the consequence that Article 24.3 would impose obligations only upon those Members that protect geographical indications via a system of registration, or another system involving the recognition *ex ante* of geographical indications.

207. Furthermore, if it were considered that, for purposes of Article 24.3, a geographical indication is not "protected" unless and until it has been registered, the same interpretation should apply to Article 24.9. Accordingly, the EC would be entitled to deny protection to any US or Australian geographical indication which has not been registered or otherwise individually recognised in those countries.

---

[154] US SWS, para. 191.

[155] US SWS, para. 192.

[156] US SWS, para. 192.

[157] US SWS, para. 193.

[158] US SWS, paras. 196-197. Australia's SWS, para. 115.

208. Finally, the United States makes much of the fact that the French and the Spanish version of Article 24.3 use the Article *des/las*, respectively, before the term "geographical indication.[159] However, as any French speaker or Spanish speaker struggling to speak English would attest, French and Spanish use liberally determinative articles in contexts where none would be required in English. For example, in Spanish it would be grossly ungrammatical to say "indicaciones geográficas deben ser protegidas," which would be the literal translation of "geographical indications must be protected." Instead, one would have to say "*las* indicaciones geográficas deben ser protegidas," even if the phrase refers to all and not just to certain geographical indications.

4. Article 17 of the TRIPS Agreement

209. The EC has submitted in the alternative that, even if Regulation 2081/92 were found to be *prima facie* inconsistent with Article 16.1 of the TRIPS Agreement, the co-existence of geographical indications and earlier trademarks would be justified under Article 17 of the TRIPS Agreement.[160]

210. At the outset, it is useful to recall the differences between the terms of Article 17 and those of the exceptions provided in Article 13, with respect to copyrights, in Article 26.2, with respect to industrial designs, and in Article 30, with respect to patents. Those three provisions, like Article 17, provide for "limited" exceptions. But the similarities end there:

- unlike Article 13, Article 17 does not require that the exceptions be "confined" to "certain special cases;"

- unlike Articles 13, 26.2 and 30, Article 17 does not require that the exceptions "do no conflict unreasonably with the normal exploitation" of the right; and

- unlike Articles 13, 26.2 and 30, Article 17 does not require that the exceptions "do not unreasonably prejudice the legitimate interests" of the right holder.

211. All that is required by Article 17 is that the exception be "limited" and that it "take account of the legitimate interests of the owner of the trademark and of third parties." The EC has shown that the co-existence provided in Regulation 2081/92 fulfils both conditions.

(a) The exception is "limited"

212. The United States has advanced several arguments to the effect that the exception claimed by the EC is not "limited." All of them are without merit.

213. First, the United States contends that the exception is not "limited" because "there are no limits on the number of potential GI right holders for each individual GI."[161] But the same is true of other place names which do not qualify as geographical indications. Yet the United States concedes that the use of those place names may be permitted by Article 17.[162]

214. The United States argues that, unlike ordinary place names, geographical indications are not "descriptive terms" because they indicate not only the origin of the product but also certain product characteristics attributable to that origin.[163] In other words, the United States appears to be saying that

---

[159] US SWS, para. 196.

[160] EC FWS, paras. 315-319.

[161] US SWS, para. 205.

[162] US SWS, note 194.

[163] US SWS, note 194.

geographical indications are not "descriptive terms" because they are "too descriptive." The United States concedes that a place name is a "descriptive term." And we assume that it would not dispute that a term which describes a product characteristic is also a "descriptive term." Yet, inexplicably, the United States takes the view that a term which indicates both a place name and a product characteristic linked to that place is not "descriptive." The EC does not understand this logic, which would have manifestly absurd consequences. For example, it would mean that the wine makers of the Santa Rita Hills in California would have qualified for an Article 17 exception vis-à-vis the registered trademark "Santa Rita," before the place name "Santa Rita Hills" was recognised as a geographical indication by the US authorities, but would have lost the entitlement to the exception as a result of such recognition.

215. Furthermore, the US reading of the term "descriptive" in Article 17 is in contradiction with the meaning given to that term under US trademark law. The Lanham Act prohibits the registration of terms which are "primarily geographically *descriptive*" except as collective or certification marks.[164] If geographical indications were not "descriptive" terms, they would be registrable as ordinary trademark marks. Yet, as the Panel is aware, the United States purports to protect geographical indications *inter alia* through their registration as certification marks.

216. The United States also argues that the exception is not "limited" because it does not require that the geographical indication be used "otherwise than as mark."[165] However, this is a requirement of US trademark law[166], which is not provided in the trademark laws of many other Members. For example, all that is required by Australia's trademark law is that indications of origin be used "in good faith."[167]

217. As mentioned before, the requirement that geographical indications should not be used "as trademarks," as this term is interpreted by the United States, reflects certain pre-conceived notions as to how trademarks and geographical indications should be used, which have no basis in the TRIPS Agreement and which the EC does not share. When interpreting the notion of "fair use" it is necessary to take account of local factors, such as the consumers' habits and expectations, business practices or even the production and distribution structures prevailing in each country. The United States cannot expect to export its own notions of "fairness" together with its cheese.

218. Furthermore, if geographical indications could not be used "as trademarks," as this term is understood by the United States, the use of a geographical indication could never give rise, by definition, to a likelihood of confusion with a trademark and, therefore, would not need to be justified under Article 17. Indeed, the US courts have construed the US "fair use" exception as requiring that the use of the descriptive term must not cause a likelihood of confusion.[168] As explained in our written submission, importing that interpretation into Article 17 would render it wholly redundant.[169]

(b) The exception "takes account" of the interests of the trademark owners and third parties

219. Contrary to the complainants' assertions, EC law does take account of the legitimate interests of the trademark owners and third parties.

220. First, even if the complainants' interpretation of Article 14(3) were correct and that provision did not prevent the registration of all confusing geographical indications, it would nonetheless prevent registration in

[164] 15 USC 1052(e) (Exhibit EC-6).

[165] US SWS, para. 199.

[166] 15 USC Section 1115(b)(4) (Exhibit EC-6).

[167] Section 122(1)(a) of Australia's Trade Marks Act 1995 (Exhibit EC-7). To mention but another example, Section 95 of New Zealand's Trade Marks Act 2002 (Exhibit EC-80), provides that indications of origin must be used "in accordance with honest practices in industrial or commercial matters."

[168] US Response to the Panel's Question No. 80.

[169] EC SWS, para. 342.

those instances where the likelihood of confusion is greater, because the trademarks are particularly distinctive, and may cause a more significant prejudice to the trademark owner, because of the reputation and renown of the trademark.

221. This may be contrasted with the situation under US law, where the risk of likelihood of confusion with an existing trademark is *never* considered a relevant ground for refusing the recognition of a geographical indication for wines.[170] Hence the recognition of geographical indications such as "Rutherford" or "Santa Rita Hills," despite the existence of virtually identical earlier trademarks such as "Rutherford Vintners" and "Santa Rita," respectively. Once again, EC law is more protective of the rights of trademark owners than US law. Indeed, last week the Supreme Court of California upheld a California statute that prohibits the use of *any* trademarks consisting of or including a recognised geographical indication for wines of a different origin, including the trademarks grandfathered by federal labelling regulations.[171]

222. The United States has described Article 14(3) as a "narrow"[172] exception for "well-known" [173] trademarks. However, the term "well-known" trademarks is not used in Article 14(3). Even if the length of use and renown/reputation of the trademark were "threshold prerequisites"[174] for the application of Article 14(3), rather than criteria for assessing the likelihood of confusion with any trademark, there is no reason why those criteria should be construed "narrowly." Nor has the United States provided any evidence that, in practice, those criteria are being interpreted and applied "narrowly" by the EC authorities.

223. Moreover, contrary to the US assertions, it is not correct that EC law "places no limits on the manner in which a geographical indication can be used."[175]

224. First, the specific concerns with respect to certain particular uses raised by the United States do not relate to the use of the name registered as a geographical indication, but instead to the use of *other* signs in place of or in conjunction with the registered geographical indication. Regulation 2081/92 does no confer a positive right to use those other signs.

225. Furthermore, while the right holders of a geographical indication have a positive right to use the registered name, this does not mean that they are allowed to use that name in any conceivable manner. As explained[176], the use of a name registered as a geographical indication, like the use of a name registered as a trademark, is subject to the requirements of Directive 2000/13 on the labelling, presentation and advertising of foodstuffs[177], and in particular to Article 2(1)(a), which provides that "the labelling and methods used must not be such as could mislead the purchaser to a material degree." This applies *inter alia* with respect to misleading statements concerning the producer or the brand of the goods.[178] The use of registered geographical indications

---

[170] See *Sociedad Anonima Viña Santa Rita v. U.S. Dept. of the Treasury*, 193 F. Supp. 2d 6 (D.D.C 2001) (Exhibit US–48).

[171] Exhibit EC-81.

[172] US SWS, para. 208.

[173] US SWS, para. 208.

[174] US SWS, para. 145.

[175] US SWS, para. 203.

[176] EC FWS, para. 319. See also the responses of the EC and its Member States to the review under Article 24.2 of the TRIPS Agreement contained in document IP/C/W/117/Add10 (Exhibit EC-29).

[177] Exhibit EC-30.

[178] See also Article 3(1) of Directive 2000/13, which requires that labels must state among other things:
(7) the name, or business name and address of the manufacturer or packager, or of a seller established within the Community …
(8) particulars of the place of origin or provenance where failure to give such particulars might mislead the consumer as to the true origin or provenance of the foodstuff.

is subject as well to Directive 84/450 on misleading advertising[179] and the unfair competition laws of the Member States, including both specific legislation and/or case law based on general tort law.[180]

226. The United States has dismissed this legislation as irrelevant[181], but without giving any proper reason. The Directives on labelling and misleading advertising and the laws on unfair competition limit the use of geographical indications in a manner which protects the interests of competitors (including trademark owners) and third parties and are, therefore, relevant for the purposes of Article 17. The United States appears to be suggesting that only those conditions for the use of geographical indications that are provided in Regulation 2081/92 itself or in the EC trademark laws are relevant. But, once again, Article 17 does not prescribe any particular implementation method. Whether the conditions for the use of geographical indications are found in Regulation 2081/92 or in a separate legal instrument is totally irrelevant, as long as the legitimate interests of the trademark owners and of third parties are sufficiently taken into account.

B. CLAIM 20: REGULATION 2081/92 DOES NOT PROVIDE FOR A PRESUMPTION OF A LIKELIHOOD OF CONFUSION IN THE CASE OF USE OF AN IDENTICAL SIGN FOR IDENTICAL GOODS

227. The EC notes that neither Australia nor the United States appear to contest that Members are not required to restate explicitly in their legislation the evidentiary presumption that the use of identical signs for identical goods will result in a likelihood of confusion.[182] Furthermore, Australia takes the view that such presumption may be rebutted.[183]

228. The terms of Article 14(3) do not prevent the EC authorities from applying the presumption. As shown by the EC, in applying Article 14(3) the authorities must take into account not only the criteria mentioned expressly therein, but also the similarity of goods and signs. And the complainants have provided no evidence that, in practice, the EC is not applying the presumption. The Complainants, therefore, have failed to meet their burden of proof with respect to this claim.

C. CLAIMS 21 AND 22: ARTICLE 7(4) OF REGULATION 2081/92 IS INCONSISTENT WITH ARTICLE 16.1 OF THE TRIPS AGREEMENT BECAUSE IT DOES NOT PROVIDE A RIGHT OF OBJECTION

229. The EC has shown that Article 16.1 does not require to make available a right of objection with respect to the registration of another intellectual property right and that, in any event, Regulation 2081/92 does not limit the right of objection in the manner alleged by Australia.

230. Australia argues that "the terms 'jeopardise the existence' used in Article 7(4)[184] establish a far more rigorous standard than a likelihood of confusion."[185] Once again, Australia makes an unwarrantedly narrow interpretation of the terms of the Regulation. Australia's interpretation is, at most, one possible interpretation. But this is not enough to meet Australia's burden of proof. To repeat, Australia must show that the EC's own reading is unreasonable and that it is impossible to read Article 7(4) consistently with Article 16.1. As usual, Australia omits to consider other linguistic versions of the Regulation which shed light on the intention of the

---

[179] Exhibit EC-31. Article 2(2) defines misleading advertising as:

any advertising which in any way, including presentation, deceives or is likely to deceive the person to whom it is addressed or whom it reaches and which, by reason of its deceptive nature, is likely to affect their economic behaviour or which, for those reasons, injures or is likely to injure a competitor

[180] One of the aspects typically covered by such laws is the imitation of labels and packaging in cases where it cannot be addressed as a trademark infringement. See WIPO's *Introduction to Trademark Law & Practice, the Basic Concepts, a WIPO Training Manual*, Geneva 1993, 2nd Edition, pp. 97-100. (Exhibit EC-82).

[181] US SWS, para. 210.

[182] See e.g. Australia's SWS, para. 137.

[183] Australia's SWS, para. 137.

[184] Articles 12b(3) and 12d(2) provide, respectively, that the criteria of Article 7(4) shall apply also with respect to the admissibility of objections to the registration of foreign geographical indications and of objections from outside the EC to EC geographical indications.

[185] Australia's SWS, para. 133.

EC legislator. For example, in the Spanish version the terms "jeopardise the existence" have been rendered as "perjudicar la existencia." In order to show this, it is not necessary to show that "the very being of that trademark would be threatened."[186] Also, Australia fails to take into account the relevant context and in particular Article 7(5)(b), which provides that objections shall be decided having regard to the "likelihood of confusion."[187] In view of this, there would be no good reason to read Article 7(4) as limiting the grounds of objection in the manner asserted by Australia. Furthermore, the EC recalls once again that Australia has submitted no evidence that any Member State or the Commission have ever rejected a statement of objections for the reasons alleged by Australia.

231. The EC would like to clarify that, when it said in its first submission that the decisions of the Member States rejecting a statement of objection are subject to judicial review in accordance with the national law of each Member State, it was referring to the procedural requirements provided by the administrative law of each Member State, and not to the substantive grounds that can be raised before the courts of the Member States, contrary to what appears to be assumed by Australia.[188] Regulation 2081/92 is directly applicable, like all EC regulations. This means that if, for example, the authorities of a Member States reject a statement because they consider that the objecting party has failed to show that the proposed name does not meet the definition of geographical indication in Regulation 2081/92, the national courts are required to apply the relevant provisions of that Regulation, if necessary after requesting a preliminary ruling from the ECJ.

VI. THE EC MEASURE IS CONSISTENT WITH THE OBLIGATION TO PROVIDE PROTECTION TO GEOGRAPHICAL INDICATIONS UNDER ARTICLE 22.2 OF THE TRIPS AGREEMENT

232. The complainants have not submitted any new arguments with respect to their claims under Article 22.2. The EC would like, nevertheless, to correct some incorrect factual assertions by the complainants regarding the relationship between Regulation 2081/92 and the other means of protection of geographical indications provided in EC law.

233. Australia has argued that the Directives on labelling and misleading advertising "are not Community 'law' in the sense of a Regulation with Community level effect in relation to labelling and misleading advertising in any case."[189] Australia goes on to suggest that Regulation 2081/92 would prevail over the measures of the Member States implementing those Directives by virtue of the principle of supremacy of Community law. Australia's arguments evidence once again a crass ignorance of the most basic principles of EC law.

234. First, a Directive is no less "Community law" than a Regulation. Further, there is no hierarchy between a Regulation and a Directive. Second, Community law prevails over the law of the Member States only where there is a conflict between them. Since the laws of the Member States implement the Directives on labelling and misleading advertising, which are themselves Community law, they cannot be said to "conflict" with EC law. To the extent that there was a conflict between the Directives and Regulation 2081/92, *quod non*, it could not be resolved by applying the principle of primacy of Community law, but instead the usual principle that the later law prevails.

235. Australia also suggests that there is a conflict between Regulation 2081/92 and the unfair competition laws of the Member States.[190] But it fails to provide any evidence of such conflict. In the EC, like in most

---

[186] Australia's SWS, para. 133.

[187] Similar language is found in Articles 12b(3) and 12d(3) with regard to the registration of geographical indications from other WTO Members and third countries and to the registration of EC geographical indications, following an objection from outside the EC, respectively.

[188] Australia's SWS, para. 134.

[189] Australia's SWS, para. 146.

[190] Australia's SWS, para. 171.

countries, unfair competition laws complement the legislation on specific intellectual property rights, by providing supplementary protection.[191] Thus, for example, the Community Trademark Regulation contains a declaratory provision clarifying expressly that it applies without prejudice to the laws on unfair competition of the Member States.[192] The same is true of the Trademark Directive and of Regulation 2081/92.

236. For its part, the United States suggests that Article 2(1) of Regulation 2081/92 would exclude the application of the Directives on labelling and misleading advertising.[193] The United States has misunderstood the purpose of Article 2(1), which is to make clear that Members States cannot adopt or maintain their own national systems for protecting *specifically* geographical indications. For example, they cannot create or maintain a register of geographical indications of their own. The Directives on labelling and misleading advertising, however, do not protect geographical indications *qua* geographical indications. They provide protection against any misleading trade description, including any misleading use of indications of source or provenance, regardless of whether they qualify as geographical indications.

VII. REGULATION 2081/92 IS CONSISTENT WITH OBLIGATIONS UNDER THE TBT AGREEMENT

237. Australia has raised two claims under the TBT Agreement:

- that Article (12)(2) of Regulation 2081/92 is incompatible with Article 2.1 of the TBT Agreement (Claim 37);
- and that Articles 4 and 10 of Regulation 2081/92 are incompatible with Article 2.2 of the TBT Agreement (Claim 38).[194]

238. As to the substance of these claims, the EC has already shown that Article (12)(2) of Regulation 2081/92 does not involve any discrimination between goods. As regards the requirement of inspection structures, the EC has also shown that these are indispensable for the attainment of the objectives of Regulation 2081/92. Accordingly, they cannot be considered as unnecessarily trade-restrictive.

239. However, for these questions even to arise under Article 2 TBT Agreement, Australia has to show that the relevant provisions of Regulation 2081/92 are a technical regulation. Australia's claims do not even meet this threshold test.

A. ARTICLE (12)(2) OF REGULATION 2081/92 IS NOT A TECHNICAL REGULATION

240. First of all, as regards Article (12)(2), the core issue is that this provision does not lay down any product characteristics for identifiable products.

241. Australia has not contested that the requirement in Article (12)(2) does not apply to all products covered by the Regulation, but only to a specific class of protected names, namely homonyms.[195] However,

---

[191] See e.g. Article 1(2) of WIPO's *Model Provisions on Protection Against Unfair Competition* (Exhibit AUS-9), which stipulates that those provisions "shall apply independently of, and in addition to, any legislative provisions protecting ... trademarks ... and other intellectual property subject matter." The comment to this Article reads as follows in pertinent part:

Paragraph (2) makes it clear that the availability of ... trademark ... protection does not preclude the application of the provisions against unfair competition.... The protection against unfair competition then constitutes a kind of supplementary protection, additional to the protection of specific intellectual property subject matter...

[192] Cf. Article 14.2:

This Regulation shall not prevent actions concerning a Community trademark being brought under the law of the member States relating in particular to civil liability and unfair competition.

[193] US SWS, para. 216.

[194] Australia's FWS, para. 249 et seq.

[195] Australia's SWS, para. 191.

Australia argues that it is sufficient that the product be "identifiable."[196] It is certainly true that a product need not be explicitly identified in the document.[197] However, the product should at least be identifiable on the basis of the document itself. This is not the case here: as long as no application has been made for the registration of protected homonymous names, it is simply not knowable to which products this requirement will apply.

242. Second, Article (12)(2) does not lay down any product characteristics or labelling requirements. It merely provides that as a condition for the registration of a geographical indication, the indication of the country of origin is necessary. The specific labelling requirements will then be contained, in accordance with Article 4 (2) (h) of the Regulation, in the product specifications. Accordingly, Article (12)(2) is not a technical regulation, but simply a condition for the registration and acquisition of an intellectual property right.

243. Finally, the requirement to indicate the country of origin is also not a labelling requirement as it relates to a "product, process or production method." Contrary to the view of Australia, "origin" is a concept different from "product." Even though the origin can confer certain characteristics on a product, origin as such is not a "product characteristic." For this reason, an origin marking requirement does not fall under the definition of a technical regulation.

244. This interpretation is also required by the need for a harmonious interpretation of the WTO Agreements, which the Appellate Body has repeatedly recognised, and to which the EC has already referred above.[198] Article IX:1 GATT contains specific disciplines on origin marking, which exclude, as Australia has recognised, a national treatment obligation. If origin marking requirements nevertheless fell under Article 2.1 TBT Agreement, the specific rule in Article IX:1 would be devoid of its practical scope.

245. In response to the EC's reference to Article IX:1 GATT, Australia has invoked the general interpretative note to Annex 1 A to the WTO Agreement, and has argued that in case of a conflict, the TBT Agreement should prevail over the GATT.[199] However, the EC does not argue that there is a conflict. Rather, the EC argues that Article 2.1 TBT Agreement and Article IX:1 GATT should be interpreted in such a way as to give meaning to both of them. The natural result of such a harmonious interpretation is that, in line with the wording of the definition of a technical regulation, origin marking requirements do not fall under Article 2.1 TBT Agreement. The EC notes that otherwise, Australia's and the US's own country of origin marking requirements for imported goods would be in violation of Article 2.1 TBT Agreement (cf. Exhibits EC-66 to EC-68).

B. ARTICLES 4 AND 10 OF REGULATION 2081/92 ARE NOT A TECHNICAL REGULATION

246. With respect to the requirement of inspection structures laid down in Articles 4 and 10 of the Regulation, the problem is similarly that these do not lay down product characteristics. Already in its previous submissions, the EC has explained that a requirement of inspection structures would, if anything, have to be regarded as a conformity assessment procedure.[200]

247. In its second submission, Australia has not provided any convincing arguments in response. Australia's only new argument has been that inspection structures might be regarded as "related processes."[201] However, this manifestly wrong. Point 1 of Annex 1 to the TBT Agreement refers to "product characteristics or their related processes." Accordingly, the processes must be "related" to the product characteristics, as would be the case for production processes and methods. If Australia's interpretation were correct, in contrast, then all conformity assessment procedures would automatically also become technical regulations. This would lead to a

---

196 Australia's SWS, para. 192.

197 Appellate Body Report, *EC – Asbestos*, para. 70.

198 Above para. 36.

199 Australia's SWS, para. 213.

200 EC SWS, para. 256.

201 Australia's SWS, para. 202.

systematic overlap between the provisions of the TBT Agreement governing technical regulations and those governing conformity assessment procedures.

248. Accordingly, none of the provisions attacked by Australia can be considered a technical regulation. Australia's claims under the TBT Agreement should accordingly be rejected.

VIII. CONCLUSION

249. For the above reasons, the EC requests the Panel not to consider any claims not within its terms of reference, and to reject all other claims of the complainants.

*

* *

Thank you for your attention. This concludes our statement. We look forward to answering any questions that the Panel may wish to ask.

ANNEX B-7

REPLIES BY THE EUROPEAN COMMUNITIES TO QUESTIONS POSED BY THE PANEL FOLLOWING THE SECOND SUBSTANTIVE MEETING

(26 August 2004)

Table of WTO and GATT Cases Referred to in the Responses

Short Title	Full Case Title and Citation
Canada – Pharmaceutical Patents	Panel Report, *Canada – Patent Protection of Pharmaceutical Products*, WT/DS114/R, adopted 7 April 2000, DSR 2000;V, 2295.
EC – Asbestos	Appellate Body Report, *European Communities – Measures Affecting Asbestos and Asbestos-Containing Products*, WT/DS135/AB/R, adopted 5 April 2001
EEC – Regulation on Imports of Parts and Components	EEC – *Regulation on Imports of Parts and Components*, Report by the Panel adopted on 16 May 1990, L/6657 – 37S/132
Korea – Various Measures on Beef	Appellate Body Report, *Korea – Measures Affecting Imports of Fresh, Chilled and Frozen Beef*, WT/DS161/AB/R, WT/DS169/AB/R, adopted 10 January 2001
US – Section 110(5) Copyright Act	Panel Report, *United States – Section 110(5) of the US Copyright Act*, WT/DS160/R,adopted 27 July 2000, DSR 2000;VIII, 3769

GLOSSARY

Commission, EC Commission	Commission of the European Communities
Committee	Committee of representatives of the Member States referred to in Article 15 of Council Regulation 2081/92
Community Trademark Regulation	Council Regulation (EC) No 40/94, of 20 December 1993, on the Community Trademark, as amended
Council, EC Council	Council of the European Union
Court of Justice, European Court of Justice	Court of Justice of the European Communities
DSU	Understanding on Rules and Procedures Governing the Settlement of Disputes
EC	European Communities
GATT	General Agreement on Tariffs and Trade 1994
FOS	First Oral Statement
FWS	First Written Submission
GI	Geographical indication
Member States, EC Member States	Member States of the European Union
Official Journal	Official Journal of the European Union
Paris Convention	Stockholm Act of the Paris Convention for the protection of Industrial property, of 14 July 1967
Regulation 2081/92, Regulation	Council Regulation (EEC) No 2081/92 of 14 July 1992 on the protection of geographical indications and designations of origin for agricultural products and foodstuffs, as amended on the date of establishment of the Panel
SCM Agreement, SCM	Agreement on Subsidies and Countervailing Duties
Trademarks Directive	First Council Directive 89/104, of 20 December, on the Community Trademark, as amended
TBT Agreement, TBT	Agreement on Technical Barriers to Trade
TRIPS Agreement, TRIPS	Agreement on Trade-Related Aspects of Intellectual Property Rights

US	United States
WTO Agreement	Marrakesh Agreement Establishing the World Trade Organization

Question 94

The Panel takes note that, in the EC's view, the specific conditions contained in Article 12(1) of Regulation (EC) No. 2081/92 do not apply to WTO Members because the introductory phrase "[w]ithout prejudice to international agreements" ensures that the WTO agreements prevail where there is a conflict with the Regulation (EC rebuttal, para. 55). Which precise EC obligations under the WTO agreements would be prejudiced by the application of those specific conditions to other WTO Members? In particular:

(a) would the EC's obligations under Article III:4 of GATT 1994 be prejudiced?

1. Yes.

(b) would the EC's obligations under Article 3.1 of the TRIPS Agreement be prejudiced? If not, please explain the relevance of your reference to the fact that the TRIPS Agreement obliges WTO Members to provide protection to GIs in accordance with Section 3 of Part II and the general provisions and basic principles of the TRIPS Agreement (EC first written submission, paras. 65-66).

2. No. As the EC has already explained, Regulation 2081/92 does not involve any discrimination between nationals.[1]

3. The fact that WTO Members are obliged under the TRIPS Agreement to provide protection to geographical indications is relevant because it means that it is not justified to apply conditions of reciprocity and equivalence to other WTO Members as a precondition for the protection of geographical indications. Should another WTO Member not provide adequate protection to geographical indications, then the appropriate response, in accordance with Article 23.1 of the DSU, would be recourse to dispute settlement under the DSU.

Question 95

Can the EC provide the Panel with any official statement by the Commission or any other EC institution, that the application of conditions of reciprocity and equivalence, such as those under Article 12(1) of Regulation (EC) No. 2081/92, would be inconsistent with the EC's obligations under international agreements, in particular, the WTO Agreement?

4. The EC can refer the Panel to the statement in the TRIPS Council it made on 16 June 2004, and to which it has already referred in response to the Panel's Question No. 16.[2] This EC statement is also reflected in the minutes of the TRIPS Council, which are attached as Exhibit EC-83.[3]

5. Second, the EC can refer the Panel to the 2nd edition of the Guide to Regulation 2081/92, which the EC has provided as Exhibit EC-64. This guide was prepared by the Commission as guidance to the implementation of Regulation 2081/92, and is the most detailed and authoritative document available. The EC notes that the United States has also variously referred to this guide in support of its submissions before the Panel.[4]

6. Finally, the statements made on behalf of the EC before the Panel in the present proceedings are also official statements of the EC, and confirm that the EC does not apply conditions of reciprocity and equivalence.

[1] EC FWS, paras. 110–111; SWS, para. 53 et seq.; EC SOS, para. 17 et seq.

[2] EC Response to Panel's Question 16, para. 39.

[3] IP/C/M/44, 19 July 2004 (para. 62–63). This should alleviate the concerns expressed by Australia "that there may not even be an official record of the EC's statement" (Australia's SWS, footnote 29).

[4] US FOS, para. 53; US SWS, para. 155.

Question 96

The EC has provided a revised Guide to Regulation (EC) No. 2081/92, dated August 2004 (Exhibit EC-64). Was this new version prepared in connection with this Panel proceeding? How is it relevant to the Panel's work if the Commission assumes no liability for its contents (see its cover page)? A new paragraph in the introduction (page 5) indicates that "the Commission reserves the right to amend procedures" and indicates the possibility of further possible revisions. Does this mean that the Guide could be changed back to the old version?

7. The revised edition was prepared in response to the increased interest from other WTO Members in the registration of geographical indications under Regulation 2081/92. This increased interest from other WTO countries has made it desirable to include a specific section in the guide providing guidance to interested governments and applicants. The guide was not prepared in connection with the Panel proceedings. However, the EC does not exclude that the increased interest is partially caused by awareness on the part of other WTO Members of the ongoing Panel proceedings.

8. The note on the cover page, according to which "the Commission does not assume any liability for its contents," is a standard liability disclaimer, which can be found in numerous similar publications.[5] The intention of this disclaimer is to ensure that the extra-contractual liability of the Community cannot be invoked as regards the contents of the guide. However, it is clear that the guide, like similar such publications, is prepared with utmost care, and that its contents are highly relevant for the application and interpretation of Regulation 2081/92 by all EC institutions.

9. In fact, according to the constant case law of the European Court of Justice, where an institution has adopted rules which are not legally binding, it may nevertheless not depart from such rules without giving the reasons which have led it to do so. Otherwise, the institution would infringe the principles of equality of treatment or the protection of legitimate expectations.[6]

10. The final paragraph of the introduction to the guide merely states that in the light of administrative need and experience in managing applications, the Commission may modify certain practical aspects of the guide. Similarly, the Commission may also have to modify the guide if the rules contained in the basic legislative texts, and in particular Regulation 2081/92, are amended. In contrast, the Commission could not amend the guide in a way contrary to the basic legislative acts applicable.

11. There is therefore no conceivable reason why the Commission should change the Guide back to the old version. Moreover, since Regulation 2081/92 does in any event allow the registration of geographical indications from other WTO Members, such a change would not affect the possibility of such registrations under Regulation 2081/92.

---

[5] For examples for such disclaimers, see Exhibit EC-84 and Exhibit EC-85.

[6] Case 148/73, *Louwage*, [1974] ECR 81, para. 12 (Exhibit EC-86); Case T-15/89, *Chemie Linz*, [1992] ECR II-1275, para. 53 (Exhibit EC-87).

Question 97

The Panel takes note of the EC's responses to Panel questions nos. 16 and 17 and the EC's rebuttal, paras. 79-86 Please explain in detail how the Commission's interpretation that Article 12(1) of Regulation (EC) No. 2081/92 does not apply to WTO Members is consistent with the statements in the EC responses in the TRIPS Council review of legislation to question No. 4 posed by New Zealand and the follow-up question posed by India on page 24 in IP/Q2/EEC/1 (cited in Australia's rebuttal, para. 33, fn. 23).

12. In response to the question posed by New Zealand, the EC gave the following response in the above-mentioned document:[7]

> As for the protection of geographical indications of WTO Members, it is necessary to distinguish the following situations:
>
> 1. The protection pursuant to Article 22 of the TRIPS Agreement, which is guaranteed by the Member States' application of Council Directive 79/112/EEC concerning labelling (prohibition to mislead the public). In the event of a problem relating to a geographical indication of a WTO Member, the EC Member States must also ensure the possibility for the operators concerned to take legal action in their courts.
>
> 2. The ex officio protection pursuant to the above-mentioned Regulation 2081/92, for which either:
>
>   – the procedure followed by Community producers as outlined above must be followed, in accordance with the principle of national treatment; or
>
>   – a bilateral agreement should be concluded as envisaged in Article 12, when the system of protection is equivalent to the Community regime.

13. The EC considers that this response is fully compatible with its submissions in the present proceedings. As regards protection under Regulation 2081/92, the EC's response distinguishes two possible alternatives for the protection of geographical indications of WTO Members: either the normal procedure for registration to be followed on a product-specific basis, or the conclusion of a bilateral agreement where the system of protection is equivalent to the Community regime. The reference to a bilateral agreement was clearly mentioned as an alternative, not as the only possibility for the protection of geographical indications from WTO Members.

14. In response to the Question from India, the EC confirmed essentially the same, namely that bilateral agreements were an alternative, not the only route to protection of geographical indications from other WTO Members under Regulation 2081/92:[8]

> It is important to stress that, in general, conditions provided in Article 12 of Regulation 2081/92/EEC are only required when a bilateral agreement is concluded between the EC and a WTO Member. This means that it only occurs when two parties voluntarily wish higher level of protection ("ex officio") than this provided under the TRIPS Agreement. So, this is not a compulsory condition but another option that can be used when systems are equivalent, in particular conditions under Article 4 (specifications) and Article 10 (inspection).

---

[7] IP/Q2/EEC1, p. 4.

[8] IP/Q2/EEC1, p. 23.

15. In response to the follow-up questions from India, which concerned particularly the requirement of inspection structures, the EC once again confirmed that there were no conditions of equivalence or reciprocity, but that the EC simply applied the conditions for registration contained in Regulation 2081/92 on a non-discriminatory basis:[9]

> (b) The inspection of the conformity for the products whose geographical name has been registered as a protected designation of origin (PDO) or a protected geographical indication (PGI) is essential to ensure the credibility of the system for the consumers. This is an essential element of the Regulation. In order to obtain the same protection (Article 13 of the Regulation), if it must be complied with by the producers established in the EC, it must also be complied with by the third country nationals, to avoid discrimination.
>
> (c) Article 12 of Council Regulation 2081/92/EEC provides for the same protection in respect of products from third countries which meet those requirements. Therefore, nationals from other WTO Members are afforded treatment "no less favourable" than Community nationals, as required by Article 3 of the TRIPS Agreement.
>
> (d) Under Council Regulation 2081/92/EEC, the advantage of registration is available to the nationals of all WTO Members without any distinction. Accordingly, Council Regulation 2081/92/EEC is fully consistent with the requirements of Article 4 of the TRIPS Agreement.

16. In conclusion, the EC considers that the above statements are fully consistent with its submissions in the present proceedings.

Question 98

Is it the EC's submission that the conditions in Article 12(1) of Regulation (EC) No. 2081/92 do not apply to WTO Members so that:

> *(a) WTO Member nationals may obtain GIs for areas located in all countries; or*

17. No. The conditions for the registration of geographical indications in Regulation 2081/92 do not depend on nationality. Inversely, nationality as such does not confer the right to register geographical indications in any particular country.

> *(b) persons from all countries may obtain GIs for areas located in all WTO Members?*

18. Yes. Since the registration of geographical indications under Regulation 2081/92 does not depend on nationality, registration of a geographical indication in another WTO Member may be obtained by any group or person that complies with the requirements of Article 5 (1) and (2) of Regulation 2081/92,[10] regardless of nationality. Similarly, regardless of nationality, any person may use a geographical indication from another WTO Member protected under Regulation 2081/92, provided that the products are in accordance with the product specifications.

---

[9] IP/Q2/EEC1, p. 24.

[10] On these requirements, and notably on the fact that they do not involve a requirement of nationality, see already EC Response to Panel's Question No. 22.

Question 99

The EC has referred to other Community legal acts in relation to the meaning of the phrase "without prejudice to international agreements" (EC rebuttal, paras. 62-66). Please also refer to Regulation (EC) No. 2082/92 on certificates of specific character for agricultural products and foodstuffs, which was adopted with the Regulation at issue in this dispute. To what international agreements does the phrase "[w]ithout prejudice to international agreements" refer as used in Article 16 of that Regulation?

19. As in the case of Article 12(1) of Regulation 2081/92,[11] the phrase "without prejudice to international agreements" used in Article 16 of Regulation 2082/92 refers to any international agreement concluded by the EC, including both multilateral and bilateral agreements. In the case of Regulation 2082/92, such agreements would include in particular the GATT.

Question 100

In Regulation (EC) No. 753/2002 on wine (set out in Exhibit US-35), Articles 34-36 refer to "third countries," apparently to refer to both WTO and non-WTO Members. It expressly states wherever a "third country" is limited to, or excludes, WTO Members. Why was Regulation (EC) No. 2081/92 drafted in such a way that the meaning of "third country" in Articles 12 through 12d is not clearer each time it was used? Does the use of "WTO Member" together with "third country" in certain instances in Articles 12 through 12d of Regulation (EC) No. 2081/92 not suggest that the term "third country" excludes WTO Members in those articles?

20. Regulation 753/2002 and Regulation 2081/92 are separate legal acts and were drafted at different times. The fact that there may be differences in terminology or legal drafting between Community legislative acts is an inevitable result of complex legislative procedures, and is not something that is peculiar to the EC.

21. As concerns the drafting of Regulation 2081/92, it should be recalled that several of its provisions were also drafted at different points in time. In particular, Articles 12a to 12d were inserted only in 2003. The fact that they did not use the "without prejudice language" but instead distinguished specifically between WTO Members and other third countries may be due to the heightened awareness of the concerns of WTO Members at that time. However, this does not mean that the "without prejudice" language which was included in Article 12(1) in 1992 should be ignored and deprived of its useful meaning.[12]

Question 101

The Panel takes note of the parties' respective views on the meaning of "nationals" under the TRIPS Agreement and the Paris Convention. Without prejudice to those views, please explain in detail <u>which nationals should be compared</u> for the purposes of the TRIPS national treatment obligations, based on the text of the agreement.

Please refer to the quadrant in the third party submission of Chinese Taipei (para. 9). Both the EC and the US compare an EC national with rights to a GI located in the EC. On the US view, that national should be compared with a US national with rights to a GI located in the US. But on the EC view, that national should be compared with a US national with rights to a GI located in the EC. Would it be appropriate instead to compare <u>all EC nationals</u> with rights to GIs who might wish to register them under Regulation (EC) No. 2081/92, wherever the geographical areas are located, and compare them with <u>all US nationals</u> with rights to GIs who might wish to register them under the Regulation, wherever the geographical areas are located?

---

[11] EC SWS, para. 68.

[12] See also EC Responses to Panel's Questions 8 and 9.

More generally, is there a principle in the TRIPS Agreement that all nationals of one WTO Member with rights to a particular category of intellectual property, such as GIs, should be compared with all nationals of other WTO Members with rights to the same category of intellectual property, unless the text of the agreement indicates that with respect to particular types of products or other sub-categories, they require particular treatment?

22. The EC does not consider that the present case requires any comparison between nationals.

23. As the EC has already explained, Regulation 2081/92 does not contain any discrimination on the basis of nationality. For this reason, the quadrant prepared by Chinese Taipei in its third party submission is not pertinent. There are no two "columns" depending on the nationality of the applicant or producer. The only relevant element to which the Regulation refers is the location of the area to which the geographical indication is related. Accordingly, the present case may require a comparison in the treatment of goods originating in the EC, in the US, or in Australia. It does not require a comparison between nationals.

Question 102

Is it safe to assume that persons resident or established in one country to produce agricultural products or foodstuffs will be considered "nationals" of that country for the purposes of TRIPS? Why is it, or is it not, safe to assume that applicants for GIs under Regulation (EC) No. 2081/92 are "nationals" of the country where their GI is located, for the purposes of TRIPS?

24. It is not safe to assume that persons resident or established in one country to produce agricultural products or foodstuffs will be considered "nationals" of that country for the purposes of TRIPS. As the EC has already set out, the TRIPS Agreement, and in particular Article 3.1 thereof, uses the term "national." It requires national treatment as between nationals, not between "domiciliaries," "persons resident or established," or "products."[13]

25. Moreover, the EC sees no basis for the assumption apparently made by the US[14] that somehow, the definition of "national" might be different when agricultural products are concerned. Agricultural products are also products with an identifiable origin, which is not linked to the nationality of the producer.[15] Like any other product, agricultural products are subject to the disciplines of the GATT. The same also applies for foodstuffs.

26. In contrast, the TRIPS Agreement does not contain any different definition of the term "national" for agricultural products. The EC can therefore not agree that different disciplines should apply under the TRIPS Agreement to intellectual property rights depending on whether they relate to agricultural products, foodstuffs, or to other products.

---

[13] EC FWS, para. 104 et seq.; SWS, para. 28 et seq.; SOS, para. 17 et seq.

[14] US SOS, para. 14.

[15] Cf. also Article 2 of the Agreement on Agriculture, which defines the term "agricultural product" for the purposes of that agreement.

Question 103

The Panel takes note that the EC does not exclude entirely that "under certain circumstances, measures which are neutral on their face may nonetheless constitute less favourable treatment of foreign nationals" and that the EC believes that national treatment under TRIPS should not overlap with GATT 1994 (EC response to Panel question No. 29, paras. 71 and 74). What other considerations are relevant to the assessment of de facto discrimination under TRIPS? What is the relevance, if any, of the fact that the TRIPS Agreement does not contain a general exceptions provision analogous to Article XX of GATT 1994?

27. So far, Article 3.1 TRIPS Agreement has never been applied on a *de facto* basis. In particular, unlike under Article III:4 GATT, there is no accepted definition of what constitutes "less favourable treatment" of nationals with regard to the protection of intellectual property rights.

28. Under Article III:4 GATT, it is accepted that "treatment no less favourable" means "according conditions of competition no less favourable to the imported product than to the like domestic product."[16] However, in the view of the EC, this definition is not easily transposable to Article 3.1 TRIPS.

29. First, it cannot be assumed that nationals necessarily "compete" with respect to the protection of intellectual property rights. For instance, Article 3.1 TRIPS would require that the conditions for the protection of a patent for a pharmaceutical product of a foreign national are no less favourable than the conditions for the protection of a patent for an appliance to be fitted on a motor vehicle of a domestic national. However, it does not appear that the domestic and the foreign national are in any kind of "competitive relationship." Similarly, their products are not "like products," and are therefore also not in any relationship of competition.

30. Second, it should be noted that the objective of national treatment under the GATT and the TRIPS Agreement is not identical. According to Article III:1 GATT, the overarching objective of GATT national treatment is to prevent that internal measures are applied so as "to afford protection to domestic production." As the Appellate Body has stated in *EC – Asbestos*, this objective also inspires the interpretation of Article III:4 GATT.[17]

31. It cannot be assumed that this same objective also underlies Article 3.1 TRIPS Agreement. Rather, the objectives of TRIPS national treatment would seem to be related to the first paragraph of the Preamble to the TRIPS Agreement, which refers to the desire "to reduce distortions and impediments to international trade, and taking into account the need to promote effective and adequate protection of intellectual property rights, and to ensure that measures and procedures to enforce intellectual property rights do not themselves become barriers to legitimate trade."

32. In the view of the EC, the complainants have made no effort to show in which way Regulation 2081/92 discriminate between nationals. Instead, they have simply referred to alleged discriminations on the basis of the area to which the geographical area is related, i.e. on the basis of the origin of the good.[18] However, whereas the origin of the good may be a relevant starting point for examining whether the conditions of competition between domestic and foreign goods are altered to the detriment of foreign goods, it is not a relevant starting point for examining whether there is discrimination between nationals.

33. In the view of the EC, the Panel should therefore not simply transpose the jurisprudence on *de facto* discrimination under Article III:4 GATT to Article 3.1 TRIPS Agreement. Rather, the definition of less favourable treatment of nationals in the context of Article 3.1 TRIPS Agreement would have to be based on the wording and context of the provision, including the broader objectives of the TRIPS Agreement.

---

[16] Appellate Body Report, *Korea – Various Measures on Beef*, para. 229 (emphasis original).

[17] Appellate Body Report, *EC – Asbestos*, para. 94.

[18] Cf. most recently US SOS, para. 7 et seq.

34. In the view of the EC, there is no need for the Panel to address this complex question in the present dispute. However, if the Panel wishes to address the issue of *de facto* discrimination under the TRIPS Agreement, it should also take into account the fact that both the TRIPS and the GATT are an integral part of the WTO Agreements, and the need for a harmonious interpretation between the two. As the EC has already set out, this means that the Panel should not interpret TRIPS national treatment in such a way as to create an unnecessary potential for conflict with the GATT.[19]

35. This potential for conflict is particularly evident with respect to Article XX of the GATT. As the EC has already said, it consider that a number of the challenged aspects of Regulation 2081/92, if they were held to constitute less favourable treatment, would nonetheless be justified by Article XX(d) GATT. The complainants have contested the EC's submissions in this respect, but they have not contested that Article XX(d) GATT is a possible defense to their claims under the GATT. However, they have not indicated what the relevance of Article XX GATT is with respect to their analogous claims under the TRIPS.

36. In the view of the EC, it would not be in line with a harmonious interpretation that a *de facto* application of the TRIPS Agreement would render inapplicable defenses which are available to otherwise entirely identical claims under the GATT. Therefore, should the Panel consider that Regulation 2081/92 involves *de facto* discrimination, the Panel would have to resolve the issue of what is the relevance of Article XX(d) GATT with respect to those claims under the TRIPS Agreement.[20]

Question 104

Please provide your interpretation of the term "separate customs territory" as used in footnote 1 to Article 1.3 of the TRIPS Agreement in accordance with the customary rules of treaty interpretation. What relevance can be drawn from the fact that the same term is used in Article XXVI of GATT 1994?

37. In accordance with the customary rules of treaty interpretation as reflected in Article 31 of the Vienna Convention on the Law of Treaties, the term "separate customs territory" in footnote 1 to Article 1.3 of the TRIPS Agreement must be interpreted in accordance with the ordinary meaning to be given to the terms of the treaty in its context and in the light of its object and purpose.

38. The term "customs territory" is defined in Article XXIV.2 of the GATT to mean "any territory with respect to which separate tariffs or other regulation of commerce are maintained for a substantial part of the trade of such territory with other territories." There is no doubt that the EC, like the US or Australia, has a "customs territory" within the meaning of Article XXIV.2 of the GATT.

39. However, footnote 1 to Article 1.3 of the TRIPS Agreement does not just refer to "customs territories," but to "<u>separate</u> customs territories." The term "separate" is an essential part of the expression used, and must be given meaning. The adjective "separate" is defined as "separated, solitary, secluded, detached, set apart, not incorporated or joined."[21] In other words, the "separate customs territory" must be "separated" from something else.

40. However, it cannot be sufficient for it simply to be "separate" from the customs territory of other Members, since otherwise, any "customs territory" would also be a "separate customs territory." Rather, a separate customs territory is only a territory which otherwise constitutes part of another territory, and in particular another state, or for which another state has international responsibility. Accordingly, the term "separate customs territories" applies to territories such as Hong Kong, Macao, Chinese Taipei, or certain overseas dependencies of a number of WTO Members.[22]

---

[19] See EC SOS, para. 36–37.

[20] See EC SOS, para. 37.

[21] The New Shorter Oxford English Dictionary, vol. 2, 1993, p. 2779.

[22] EC SOS, para. 23.

41. This interpretation is also confirmed by the objective of footnote 1. Separate customs territories which are a part of another state frequently may not have a concept of "nationality" which could be applied for the purposes of the TRIPS Agreement. The definition in footnote 1 therefore serves as a substitute for the definition of "national" in such cases. This definition is not relevant to the EC, which has a nationality.[23]

42. The EC's interpretation is also confirmed by the context of the provision, and notably by the use of the term "separate customs territory" in the GATT. As the Panel has rightly pointed out, Article XXVI (5) (a) GATT refers to "other territories for which [a Member] has international responsibility, except such separate customs territories as it shall notify [...]." In a similar sense, Article XXXIII also refers to "a government acting on behalf of a separate customs territory." It follows clearly that "separate customs territories" are territories for which another State has international responsibility, be it because they are part of its territory, or because they are in some other way dependent on it.

43. It is clear from these considerations that the EC cannot be considered a "separate customs territory." The EC has a customs territory which includes the territory of all its Member States. However, there is no other State which is responsible in international law for the EC, nor is the EC part of any other State. Accordingly, the EC cannot be said to be any more of a "separate customs territory" than the US or Australia.

Question 105

The Panel takes note of the EC's view that it is not a separate customs territory Member of the WTO within the meaning of footnote 1 to Article 1.3 of the TRIPS Agreement (EC rebuttal, para. 35).

> *(a) Which natural persons does the EC consider EC nationals for the purposes of TRIPS? Are they also nationals of EC member States?*

44. Article 17 (1) of the EC Treaty establishes the Citizenship of the Union, and provides that "every person holding the nationality of a Member States shall be a citizen of the Union." Accordingly, any person which is a national of a Member State is a national of the EC.

> *(b) Which legal persons does the EC consider EC nationals for the purposes of TRIPS? Are they also nationals of EC member States? **EC***

45. The nationality of legal persons in international law and in domestic law is a highly complex question.[24] Like the domestic law of most other WTO Members, EC law does not contain a specific definition of nationality for legal persons. However, Article 17 (1) of the EC Treaty is relevant by analogy. Accordingly, any legal person which is considered a national under the laws of a Member States would also be an EC national.

46. However, like the law of most other WTO Members, the law of the Member States may not contain a general definition of nationality of legal persons, but rather define nationality only for certain specific purposes. Moreover, the criteria used by Member States in this context may vary, and include criteria such as the law of incorporation, or the seat of the company, the nationality of shareholders, or a combination of such criteria.[25]

47. Moreover, it should be noted that where the nationality of legal persons is relevant for the application of Community law, Community law itself may define the relevant criteria. An example for this is Article 48 (2)

---

[23] EC SWS, para. 27; SOS, para. 23. See also EC response to the following question.

[24] As background on this issue, see A.A. Fatourous, *National Legal Persons in International Law*, Encyclopaedia of Public International, vol. 3, p. 495–501 (1997) (Exhibit EC-88).

[25] Cf. the overview in A.A. Fatourous, *National Legal Persons in International Law*, Encyclopaedia of Public International, vol. 3, p. 495–496 (1997) (Exhibit EC-88).

of the EC Treaty, which provides that for the purposes of the freedom of establishment "companies and firms formed in accordance with the law of a Member States and having their registered office, central administration or principal place of business within the Community shall, for the purposes of this Chapter, be treated in the same way as natural persons who are nationals of Member States." However, no such definition exists for the purposes of the application of Regulation 2081/92, since nationality is not a relevant element for the application of that Regulation.

48. Moreover, the EC would like to remark that the difficulty of establishing criteria for the nationality of legal persons cannot be an excuse for substituting other definitions, such as residence or establishment, for nationality, where nationality is in fact irrelevant for the purposes of the measure in question.

Question 106

What are the nationalities of the applicants for GIs registered under Regulation (EC) No. 2081/92? Have there been any applicants who were not nationals of the EC member State in which the relevant GI was located? Please supply details of any that were not, and the relevant GIs. To the extent that you are aware of the nationality of persons other than the applicants who use a GI in accordance with its registration, please supply the same information.

49. At the outset, the EC would like to clarify that the notion of "applicant" is of limited relevance in the context of the present dispute. According to Article 5 (1) of Regulation 2081/92, a group, or under certain conditions a natural person,[26] may apply for the registration of a geographical indication. However, the applicant is not identical with the rightholder. Since a geographical indication is a collective right, any person producing in accordance with the product specifications may use the geographical indication. The conditions for applicants are a procedural modality of the application process. They do not imply that the applicant becomes a rightholder.

50. As the EC has already said, Regulation 2081/92 does not contain any requirement as to the nationality of the applicant.[27] More importantly still, Regulation 2081/92 does not contain any requirement as regards the nationality of persons who use a protected name. Any person producing in accordance with the product specifications, regardless of nationality, may use the protected name.

51. Since nationality is not a relevant criterion under Regulation 2081/92, the EC does not request any information on the nationality of applicants or producers when an application for the registration is submitted. Similarly, the EC does not monitor the nationality of the producers of a product using a geographical indication.

52. Moreover, the EC would like to recall that the burden of proof for showing that Regulation 2081/92 involves discrimination on the basis of nationality is on the complainants, and not on the EC.

53. For these reasons, the EC is not able, and should not be expected to be able, to give detailed information about the nationality of producers of products using names protected under Regulation 2081/92. In fact, such information is not any more available to the EC than it is to the United States and Australia.

54. Without prejudice to these remarks, and beyond the examples of non-EC producers already referred to in previous EC submissions,[28] the EC can refer the Panel to at least two examples where a producer of a product using a protected name comes from a different Member State than the one where the geographical area is located:

[26] These conditions are set out in Article 1 of Commission Regulation 2037/93 (Exhibit COMP-2).

[27] See EC Response to Panel's Question No. 22.

[28] EC SOS, para. 28.

- Lactalis, a French-based dairy group, owns Locatelli and Invernizzi, which produce among others Gorgonzola and Grana Padano (Exhibit EC-62).

- Stella Artois, a Belgian Brewery, used to produce "Kölsch" beer, a protected name for beer from the Cologne area in Germany (Exhibit EC-89).

Question 107

The Panel takes note of the examples of foreigners and foreign companies which have invested in Europe (EC rebuttal, para. 46 and Exhibits EC-36 to EC-39; EC second oral statement, para. 28 and Exhibits EC-61 to EC-63). Is the Larsen firm a French company? Have Suntory Limited, E & J Gallo and the Robert Mondavi family formed subsidiaries, joint ventures or other entities under the laws of France and Italy to invest in those wine estates? Did Sara Lee, Kraft Foods and Nestlé purchase companies formed under the law of an EC member State?

The Panel takes note that the EC argues that the possibility that these foreign nationals formed legal persons under the laws of an EC member State is not attributable to Regulation (EC) No. 2081/92 (EC second oral statement, para. 30). Is it appropriate to exclude such other factors from an examination of the WTO-consistency of the Regulation? Does the EC submit that the Panel should "pierce the corporate veil" and refer to ownership and control to determine nationality for the purposes of TRIPS?

55. It appears from the information available on the website of Larsen Cognac that today, Larsen Cognac is a Société anonyme incorporated under French law. From the information contained in Exhibit EC-61, it appears that Al Ponte Prosciutti, an Italian limited liability company, was purchased by Sara Lee Personal Products S.p.A., an Italian cooporation. It also appears that Al Ponte Prosciutti is controlled by Aoste Holding, SA, a French Cooperation, which in turn was purchased by Sara Lee Charcuterie SA, a French cooperation belonging to the Sara Lee Group. The EC does not have specific information on the ownership situation in the other cases.

56. In the view of the EC, the measure at issue is exclusively Regulation 2081/92, which does not involve any discrimination on the basis of nationality. If, for practical considerations related for instance to taxation or labour law, a person producing in conformity with a product specification chooses to set up a legal entity in the area where the geographical indication is located, this is not related to Regulation 2081/92.

57. It is simply a practical consequence of the fact that products have to be produced in accordance with the product specifications, which may require that an important part of the production process takes place in the geographical area concerned. If the submission of the complainants were correct, then any discrimination on the basis of the origin of goods would *de facto* also always be a discrimination between nationals. The EC does not consider that such an interpretation would be an appropriate interpretation of the national treatment provisions of the TRIPS and the GATT.

58. Finally, the EC does not submit that the Panel should "pierce the corporate veil" and refer to ownership and control to determine the nationality for the purposes of the TRIPS. In the view of the EC, the nationality of the legal person involved, if and where relevant, should be determined on the basis of the municipal law of the Member concerned.[29]

[29] Cf. also EC Response to Panel's Question No. 105.

Question 110

Does the EC contest that, to the extent that Regulation (EC) No. 2081/92 provides GI protection for EC nationals and is a law affecting EC products, GI protection for other WTO Member nationals and imported products solely through other laws, such as labelling and unfair competition, would be less favourable treatment?

59. No. However, as regards nationals, rather than products, the EC would like to recall that Regulation 2081/92 does not provide protection on the basis of nationality.

Question 111

Does the EC contest that national treatment and MFN obligations under TRIPS apply to TRIPS-plus protection, and apply to Regulation (EC) No. 2081/92 even to the extent that it does not merely implement the EC's obligations under Article 22?

60. The EC does not contest that national treatment and MFN obligations under TRIPS applies to more extensive protection granted in respect to intellectual property rights addressed in the TRIPS Agreement. However, the EC contests that Regulation 2081/92 involves discrimination on the basis of nationality.

Question 112

The Panel takes note that the Commission has not recognized any country under Article 12(3) of Regulation (EC) No. 2081/92 (EC response to Panel question No. 10, para. 22). Is the Commission obliged to recognize any country that satisfies the conditions set out in Article 12(1)?

61. If the conditions of Article 12(1) are fulfilled, the Commission will normally recognise the country in question. However, Article 12(1) does not create any legal "obligation" as against the third country. This follows from the wording "this Regulation may apply" in Article 12(1) of Regulation 2081/92. Moreover, the EC would like to recall that the conditions of Article 12(1) do not apply to WTO Members.

Question 113

The EC argues that there must be a substantive difference between two provisions governing the registration of GIs in order for one to entail less favourable treatment (EC second oral statement, para. 40). What is a "substantive" difference in this sense? Does the EC allege that there is a de minimis standard for less favourable treatment under TRIPS or GATT 1994? Is a simple difference in language insufficient to establish different treatment?

62. For the purposes of Article III:4 GATT, it follows from the case law of the Appellate Body that a "substantive difference of treatment" is a difference in treatment which modifies the conditions of competition to the disadvantage of imported goods.[30]

63. As the EC has also explained, the definition of "less favourable treatment" for the purposes of Article 3.1 TRIPS is less clear, and cannot be assumed to be identical with that of Article III:4 GATT.[31] However, it would appear that in order to constitute a violation of Article 3.1 TRIPS, a measure would have to modify the conditions regarding the protection of intellectual property rights within the meaning of the TRIPS to the detriment of foreign nationals.

---

[30] Appellate Body Report, *Korea – Various Measures on Beef*, para. 229. Cf. also above, para. 28.

[31] Cf. above para. 28 et seq.

64. The EC does not believe that there is a *de minimis* standard for less favourable treatment under the GATT or under the TRIPS Agreement. However, as the Appellate Body has held, a formal difference in language, which does not modify the conditions of competition, cannot be held to constitute less favourable treatment under Article III:4 GATT.[32] Similarly, a simple difference in language which does not modify the conditions for the protection of intellectual property could not be held to constitute less favourable treatment under Article 3.1 TRIPS. This is not the application of a *de minimis* standard, but simply the application of the requirements of Article III:4 GATT and Article 3.1 TRIPS.

Question 114

With respect to registration applications under Article 12a(2) of Regulation (EC) No. 2081/92, a third country must verify that the requirements of the Regulation are satisfied before it transmits the application:

> *(a) to what extent is this designed to confirm the protection of the GI in its country of origin in accordance with Article 24.9 of the TRIPS Agreement, and to what extent does it respond to other objectives?*

65. The verification envisaged in Article 12a(2) of Regulation is intended to confirm that the requirements of the Regulation for the registration of the geographical indication are fulfilled. This means in particular that the application must contain a product specification in accordance with Article 4(2) of the Regulation. As can be seen from Article 4(2)(a) to (f), the details contained in the product specification permit to confirm that the name for which protection is sought corresponds to the definition of a geographical indication in Article 2 of Regulation 2081/92. Moreover, Article 12a(2)(b) of the Regulation also requires the third country to verify that the inspection structures required by Article 10 are established.

66. In addition, Article 12a(2)(a) of Regulation 2081/92 requires also "a description of the legal provisions and the usage and the usage on the basis of which the designation of origin or the geographical indication is protected or established in the country." The purpose of this requirement is to ensure, in accordance with Article 24.9 TRIPS Agreement, that the geographical indication for which protection is sought in the EC is also protected in its country of origin.

> *(b) is this additional to the requirement that a registration application transmitted to the Commission must be accompanied by a description of the matters set out in Article 12a(2)(a)?*

67. The protection in the country of origin is a requirement for the registration of geographical indications from third countries, which is in accordance with Article 24.9 TRIPS Agreement. As regards geographical indications from within the EC, for which protection is obtained in accordance with Regulation 2081/92, this requirement can by definition not apply.

68. However, it should also be noted that the requirement that the geographical indication is protected in its country of origin, and the other conditions of the Regulation, are closely related and will tend to overlap. If a geographical indication is protected in its country of origin, this means that according to the country of origin, the geographical indication falls under the definition of Article 22.1 TRIPS, i.e. identifies goods as originating in the territory of a Member, or a region or locality in that territory, where a given quality, reputation, or other characteristics are essentially attributable to its geographical origin. Accordingly, if a geographical indication is protected in the country of origin, this should normally also facilitate the examination of whether the name fulfils the conditions for protection under Regulation 2081/92.

---

[32] Appellate Body, *Korea – Various Measures on Beef*, para. 137; cf. on this also EC SOS, para. 39 et seq.

(c) *Does the Commission also examine whether the application satisfies the conditions for protection under Article 12b(1)(a)? How is this examination different from the verification by the third country?*

69. When deciding on the registration of a geographical indication from a third country, the Commission must verify whether the conditions for the registration set out in Regulation 2081/92 are met. However, in making this evaluation, the Commission will rely on the factual assessment provided by the country of origin. In fact, only on the basis of this information can the Commission verify whether the conditions for registration are fulfilled.

70. As regards the requirement that the geographical indications must be protected or established in its country of origin, this question regards the law of a third country. The Commission will therefore have to rely on the assessment provided by the third country.

Question 115

With respect to objections under Article 12b(2)(a) of Regulation (EC) No. 2081/92, what is an objection that "comes from a WTO Member"? With respect to objections under Article 12d(1) of the Regulation, what is the meaning of a person who "is from a WTO Member"? Do they both refer to the place of residence or establishment of the person who wishes to object? Must objections under both provisions be sent to the country in which the person resides or is established?

71. In both Article 12b(2)(a) and in Article 12(d)(1), a person that "is from a WTO Member country" is a person resident or established in the WTO Member country.

72. In both cases, objections must be sent to the country in which the person resides or is established. In the case of Article 12b(2)(a), this follows from the reference to Article 12d.

Question 116

To the extent that certain responsibilities under Articles 12a and 12d(1) of Regulation (EC) No. 2081/92 are borne by non-EC WTO Members:

(a) *how is the EC satisfied that every other WTO Member has the authorization to carry them out? (Please refer to Brazil's response to Panel third party question No. 1) (EC second oral statement, paras. 72-77).*

73. The EC does not consider that any specific "authorization" is needed to carry out the responsibilities in Articles 12a and 12d(1).

74. As regards the confirmation that the geographical indication is protected or established in its country of origin required by Article 12a(2)(a) of Regulation 2081/92, the EC would like to recall that a) all WTO Members are obliged to provide protection to geographical indications in accordance with Article 22 TRIPS Agreement, and b) that the EC is not obliged to provide protection to geographical indications not protected in their country of origin, in accordance with Article 24.9 TRIPS Agreement. Accordingly, any WTO Member should be able to state whether it protects a geographical indication for which protection is sought in the EC. A WTO Member can therefore not argue that it does not have "authority" to state whether a geographical indication is protected in its territory, and at the same time claim that this geographical indication should be protected in the EC.

75. As regards the verification of the further requirements in Article 12a(2)(a), and notably the verification of the product specifications, this is a primarily factual verification carried out at the request of the applicant. The EC does not see why a specific "authorization" would be required for this purpose. Moreover, the EC

would like to remark that the requirements of the product specifications closely reflect the requirements of Article 22.1 TRIPS Agreement. Since any WTO Member is obliged protection of geographical indications as defined in Article 22.1 TRIPS, it cannot be argued that a WTO Member "has no authority" to carry out such examinations.

76. As regards finally the transmission of the statement of objections required by Article 12d(1), this is, as the US has itself acknowledged,[33] a "purely ministerial act" of a kind routinely carried out by governments in many contexts.[34] The EC does not see why a specific "authorization" would be needed.

> *(b) if other WTO Member governments lack authorization to carry them out, can they be carried out by the EC instead?*

77. No. The EC cannot make findings as to whether a geographical indication is protected under the law of a third country. Second, as regards the other requirements of Regulation 2081/92, these relate to a geographical area located in a third country, and may involve inspections and verifications in the third country. The EC does not consider that it could carry out such inspections verifications in a third country without the consent of that country. Moreover, as the EC has also explained, the verifications require intimate knowledge of the conditions in the geographical area concerned, which the EC does not have.[35]

> *(c) to what extent does the EC itself accord no less favourable treatment to the nationals of other Members, and to what extent do other WTO Members share the implementation of that obligation? Can a Member delegate the implementation of WTO obligations to other Members with or without their prior consent?*

78. As the EC has explained in response to subquestion (a) and (b), where the registration of a geographical indication from another WTO Member is sought in the EC, that WTO Member must cooperate with the EC in two respects:

- it must enable the EC to evaluate whether the geographical indication is in accordance with the requirements of the Regulation, which reflect Article 22.1 TRIPS Agreement;
- it must confirm that the geographical indication is protected or established in its territory.

79. If the third country does not cooperate with the EC on these aspects, then the registration cannot be carried out. In this case, the failure to register would not be attributable to an act of the EC, but to the failure of the country of origin of the geographical indication to assume those tasks which fall within its sphere of responsibility. To this extent, it can indeed be said that with respect to the registration of geographical indications abroad, the country of origin and the country of registration share obligations.

80. The EC does not consider that it can delegate the implementation of WTO obligations to other Members without their prior consent. However, the EC considers that it can require the cooperation of other WTO Members where this is indispensable for the proper implementation of provisions of the WTO agreements, such as Article 22.1, 22.2, and 24.9 TRIPS Agreement.

> *(d) to what extent has the EC accorded certain treatment to the nationals of other WTO Members rather than to the governments of those other WTO Members?*

81. Regulation 2081/92 does not accord any treatment to nationals, but to products. It also does not accord any treatment to governments. Rather, whether a government assumes its responsibilities with respect to the

---

[33] US Response to Panel's Question No. 38, para. 74.

[34] Cf. the examples given in EC Response to Panel's Question No. 37.

[35] See EC Response to Panel's Question No. 33, para. 81.

registration of a geographical indication relating to its territory can only be ascertained with respect to the specific application, not with respect to the third government overall.

Question 117

The Panel takes note of the EC's response to Panel question No. 8 concerning the meaning of "third country" and seeks clarification as to whether "third country" as used in Article 12(2) of Regulation (EC) No. 2081/92, includes WTO Members. If so, why does the "without prejudice" clause in Article 12(1) form part of the context of Articles 12(1) and (3) but not Article 12(2)? If not, where does the Regulation cover identical GIs from the EC and other WTO Members?

82. The reference to names "of a third country" refers to any name which has been protected under the Regulation, or for which protection is sought. Therefore, it can include names both from WTO Members and from other third countries recognized in accordance with Article 12(3).

83. The "without prejudice" clause in Article 12(1) is relevant for Article 12(3) because Article 12(3) sets out the procedure for establishing whether the conditions in Article 12(1) are met. Article 12(2) has no such specific link with Article 12(1). The fact that it is included in Article 12, and not for instance in Article 12a, is simply due to the fact that it was already contained in the original version of Regulation 2081/92.

Question 118

The Panel takes note that, in Australia's view, the identical GI labelling requirement would not be inconsistent with Article 2.1 of the TBT Agreement if it was applied to both EC and imported products according to date of registration, not origin. (Australia's response to Panel question No. 53). Even if Article 12(2) does not apply to EC products as well as imported products, does the Commission have the discretion to apply the same requirement according to the date of registration to EC products under Article 6(6) in order to ensure that the identical labelling requirement is applied to the later GI irrespective of the origin of the products?

84. Yes. As the EC has already set out, where the identical names are from different countries, the clear distinction in practice would normally require the indication of the country of origin.[36]

Question 119

What is the difference, if any, in the meaning of the word "homonymous" as used in Article 6(6) of Regulation (EC) No. 2081/92 and "identical" as used in Article 12(2)? Why does the EC consider that homonyms are covered by the word "identical" in Article 12(2) (EC response to Panel question No. 43)?

85. There is no difference. "Homonym" is defined as "a person or thing having the same name as another, a namesake."[37] In other words, "identical name" is a synonymous expression for "homonym."

86. Moreover, the French and the Spanish version of Regulation 2081/92 both use the same expression ("dénomination homonyme"/"denominación homónima") in both Articles 6(6) and 12(2) of Regulation 2081/92.

---

[36] EC FWS, para. 479.

[37] The New Shorter Oxford English Dictionary, vol. 1, 1993, p. 1254.

Question 120

The Panel takes note of Australia's confirmation that the only less favourable treatment under the identical GIs labelling requirement is relabelling costs (Australia's response to Panel question No. 52). Would imported products have to be relabelled? Would existing marks of origin satisfy this requirement? What does "clearly and visibly indicated" mean?

87. Imported products would not necessarily have to be relabeled. It the country of origin is already clearly and visibly indicated on the label, then this will be sufficient. Existing marks of origin may therefore be sufficient to the extent that the country of origin is clearly and visibly indicated. To the extent that the country of origin is not indicated, the affixation of an additional label clearly and visibly indicating the country of origin would also be sufficient.

88. What "clearly and visibly indicated" means must be evaluated in each specific case from the point of view of a normal consumer. The country of origin will be clearly and visibly indicated if a normally attentive consumer can easily notice the indication, and will therefore not be induced in error as to the origin of the product concerned.

Question 122

Please refer to the phrase "labelling requirements as they apply to a product" as used in the definition of "technical regulation" in Annex 1.1 of the TBT Agreement.

> *(a) The EC argues that the "origin of a product is different from the product itself" (EC response to Panel question No. 50). However, as the EC acknowledges, the origin of a product may confer specific characteristics on it. This is consistent with the definitions of designation of origin and geographical indication in Article 2 of Regulation (EC) No. 2081/92, which provide that "the quality or characteristics of the product ... are essentially or exclusively due to a particular geographical environment ..." and that the product "possesses a specific quality, reputation or other characteristics attributable to that geographical origin ...." How then is the origin of a product entitled to bear a registered GI different from the product itself?*

89. The origin of a product is the place where the product originates. It can be a country, or a region or place in a country. The origin of a product is therefore different from the product itself.

90. Moreover, the origin of a product is also not necessarily linked to product characteristics. Where the origin does confer specific characteristics, then this may justify the protection of a geographical indication, as foreseen in the TRIPS Agreement. However, there are many cases, particularly in the case of industrial products, where the origin as such does not confer any characteristics on the product.

91. The concept of "origin" of a product is also the subject of regulation outside the TBT Agreement. Qualifying the origin of a product as a product characteristic within the meaning of the definition of a technical regulation in Point 1 of Annex 1 to the TBT Agreement would therefore risk creating unnecessary overlap and conflict between the TBT Agreement and other covered agreements.

92. One example is origin marking, which is already regulated in Article IX GATT. Another example are geographical indications, which are dealt with in the TRIPS Agreement. A third example would be Article XI:1 of the GATT, which prohibits quantitative restrictions on imports, including import bans on foreign products. If origin were a product characteristic, then an import ban could be interpreted as a technical regulation laying down that products must be of domestic origin. However, the EC sees no justification for applying Article 2.1 or 2.2 TBT Agreement to import bans, when such restrictions are already satisfactorily dealt with in the GATT.

93. Finally, the Agreement on Rules of Origin must also be mentioned in this context. According to Article 1.2 of the Agreement on Rules of Origin, the Agreement defines rules of origin in particular with respect to numerous provisions of the GATT, including explicitly Article IX GATT on marks of origin. In contrast, no mention is made of the TBT Agreement. If the TBT Agreement applied to marks of origin, however, then it would be hard to explain why Article 1.2 of the Agreement on Rules of Origin only mentions Article IX of the GATT, but not the TBT Agreement.

> (b) *What is the meaning of the words "as they apply to" as used in this part of the definition? Do they refer to the application of labelling requirements to the characteristics of a product, or to the product itself, or both?*

94. The second sentence of Point 1 of Annex 1 to the TBT Agreement refers to "marking or labeling requirements as they apply to a product, process or production method." The EC would remark that a mark or a label cannot be applied to a process or production method as such. Rather, it would appear that the process and production method would be the content of the labeling requirement. Accordingly, it seems to the EC that the words "as they apply to" are meant to refer to the application of labeling requirements to characteristics of a product, process or production method.

Question 123

Does the requirement to display a country of origin on a label under Article 12(2) of Regulation (EC) No. 2081/92 constitute a mark of origin covered by Article IX of GATT 1994?

95. Yes.[38]

Question 124

The definition of "technical regulation" in Annex 1.1 of the TBT Agreement expressly encompasses "marking or labelling requirements as they apply to a product, process or production method." Are marks of origin and labels of origin covered by Article IX of GATT 1994 excluded from the scope of the TBT Agreement? Why did the negotiators not explicitly carve them out of its scope? Can a line be drawn between marks of origin that fall under the TBT Agreement and those that do not? What are the systemic consequences for marks of origin if they all fall within the scope of the TBT Agreement?

96. As the EC has already explained in response to the Panel's Question 122, origin marking requirements are not a technical regulation within the meaning of the TBT Agreement, and therefore do not fall within the scope of the TBT Agreement.

97. There was no need for the drafters of the TBT Agreement to specifically exclude origin marks from the scope of the agreement if the negotiators considered that origin marking did not fall under the definition of a technical regulation.

98. In the view of the EC, it is not possible to distinguish origin marks which fall under the TBT Agreement and such which do not. The US has suggested that Article IX:1 GATT might cover only "general origin marking requirements," but not origin marking requirements covering only specific products.[39] As the EC has already explained, there no textual basis for such a distinction in Article IX:1 GATT.[40] Similarly, there is also no basis for this distinction in the definition of a technical regulation in Point 1 of Annex 1 to the TBT Agreement, which does not distinguish as to whether a technical regulation relates to many products or only to a

---

[38] As to the US argument to the contrary, see EC SOS, para. 128 and below para. 98.

[39] US SWS, para. 77.

[40] EC SOS, para. 128.

few. Moreover, as the EC has also said, there is simply no logic to the proposition that an origin marking maybe imposed on all imported products, but not just on some.

99. As regards the systemic consequences of the complainants' interpretation, if marks of origin fell under the TBT Agreement, this would mean that any such marking requirements which apply only to imported products would be incompatible with Article 2.1 of the TBT Agreement. As a consequence, Article XI:1 GATT, which exempts origin marking from national treatment obligations would be obsolete. Similarly, origin marking requirements would be subject to Article 2.2 TBT Agreement, which would make the specific provisions of Article IX:2 to IX:6 GATT largely redundant.

Question 125

To what extent would any less favourable treatment under Article 2.1 of the TBT Agreement have to be determined in light of the regulatory objective a Member is trying to pursue under Article 2.2?

100. As evidenced by the 6th paragraph of the Preamble to the TBT Agreement, the TBT Agreement does not prejudice the right of WTO Members to pursue legitimate regulatory goals. However, frequently, the pursuit of such regulatory goals may make it necessary to discriminate between products even if consumers consider them as like, for instance on account of environmental hazards that they pose.

101. Therefore, the EC considers that the legitimate regulatory objectives of the Member concerned must be taken into account in the application of both Article 2.1 and 2.2 TBT Agreement. Alternatively, the Panel would have to consider whether Article XX of the GATT is applicable within the context of the TBT Agreement.

Question 126

With respect to Article 10(3) of Regulation (EC) No. 2081/92:

> *(a) the first indent sets out certain requirements for designated inspection authorities and/or approved private bodies. Do these apply to all countries whose GIs are protected under the Regulation, including non-EC member States?*

102. Yes.

> *(b) the fifth indent appears to refer only to EC member States and third countries recognized pursuant to Article 12(3). Where does the Regulation refer to the applicable standard for WTO Members not recognized pursuant to Article 12(3), whose requirements private bodies must fulfil for approval purposes?*

103. As the EC has set out earlier, the reference to the procedure in Article 12(3) is relevant only where the conditions of Article 12(1) are applicable.[41] Accordingly, the last subparagraph of Article 10(3) of Regulation 2081/92 applies also to WTO Members.

> *(c) the fifth indent refers to "[t]he equivalent standard or the applicable version of the equivalent standard." What equivalent standard has been established for GIs for areas located in WTO Members which do not satisfy the conditions of equivalence and reciprocity in Article 12(1)? What are the criteria for establishing that standard? Is it a matter of determining what is "equivalent" to standard EN 45011? Or is it a matter of determining what standard would fulfil the objectives of the Regulation in the light of each third country's own circumstances and conditions?*

[41] EC Response to Panel's Question No. 8; EC SOS, para. 48.

104. No standard has been established so far. Therefore, as long as no specific standard has been established, compliance with any equivalent standard to standard EN 45011 is sufficient. In its earlier submissions, the EC has referred to ISO Standard 65:1996 as such an equivalent standard.[42]

105. The EC would like to note that the situation is the same for EC Member States. Although the fourth subparagraph also provides a legal basis for establishing "the standard or the applicable version of standard EN 45011," no such standard or version has so far been established. In the absence of any decision on the basis of the fourth subparagraph of Article 10 (3) of Regulation 2081/92, standard EN 45011 continues to be applied.

Question 127

Article 12a(2)(b) requires a declaration by a third country government that the structures provided for in Article 10 are established on its territory. Article 10(2) refers to inspection authorities and/or private bodies approved for that person by the Member State and Article 10(3) provides that where they outsource they continue to be responsible vis-à-vis the Member State for all inspections. What is the exact nature of the role that third country governments must play in the creation and maintenance of the inspection structures that are called for under Article 10?

106. When a Member State or a third country approve an inspection structure, they must ascertain that the inspection structure is capable of fulfilling its functions in accordance with Article 10 (1), and that it meets the requirements of Article 10 (3) of the Regulation. Moreover, the Member State or the third country is also responsible for ensuring that the inspection body, as long as it is approved to carry out inspections, continues to comply with the requirements of Article 10 of the Regulation. How exactly the Member State or third country carries out this continued monitoring, i.e. through occasional on-the-spot checks, audits, or reporting requirements, is for each Member State or third country to decide.

Question 131

Which EC Directives govern conformity assessment to EC technical regulations in the goods area? To what extent do those Directives require foreign governmental involvement in the designation/approval of conformity assessment bodies, when mutual recognition agreements in the conformity assessment area do not already exist?

107. EC Directives governing conformity assessment to EC technical regulations in the goods area are extremely numerous, so that no exhaustive list can be given.

108. However, Council Decision 93/465/EEC concerning the modules for the various phases of the conformity assessment procedures and the rules for the affixing and use of the CE conformity marking, which are intended to be used in the technical harmonization directives (Exhibit EC-90) defines certain general principles for EC conformity assessment relevant in the present context. In particular, Point A (k) of the Annex to Decision 93/465 provides as follows:

> for the purposes of operating the modules, Member States must notify on their own responsibility bodies under their jurisdiction which they have chosen from the technically competent bodies complying with the requirements of the directives. This responsibility involves the obligation for the Member States to ensure that the notified bodies permanently have the technical qualifications required by the directives and that the latter keep their competent national authorities informed of the performance of their tasks. Where a Member State withdraws its notification of a body, it must take appropriate steps to ensure that the dossiers are processed by another notified body to ensure continuity;

[42] EC FWS, para. 54 and Exhibit EC-3.

109. Since conformity assessment bodies must be under the jurisdiction of the Member State, they must be located on the territory of that Member State. The reason for this rule is that only with respect to bodies under its jurisdiction can the Member States effectively ensure that the body properly exercises its functions. In principle, a Member State can therefore not designate a conformity assessment body located in a third country. Accordingly, the question of third country governmental involvement does not pose itself.

110. It should also be noted that the TBT Agreement explicitly foresees the possibility of Members to apply conformity assessment procedures to imported products. No provision of the TBT Agreement obliges Members to simply accept conformity assessment carried out by bodies of another Member. In fact, Article 6.1 TBT Agreement obliges Member to accept conformity assessment in other Members only under specific conditions, in particular if they are satisfied that procedures offer an assurance of conformity with applicable technical regulations or standards equivalent to their own procedures. Article 6.1 TBT Agreement moreover recognises that prior consultations may be necessary to arrive at a mutually satisfactory understanding, and Article 6.2 encourages Members to enter into negotiations for the mutual recognition of conformity assessment procedures.

111. In addition, Article 6.4 TBT Agreement "encourages" Members to permit participation of conformity assessment bodies located in the territories of other Members in their conformity assessment procedures. However, it is clear from the word "encourage" that there is no legal obligation in the TBT Agreement to permit such participation. The reason for this is that the participation of a conformity assessment requires that certain guarantees for the technical competence and capacity of the conformity assessment to be fulfilled, and that fulfilment of these criteria may be difficult to guarantee for a body located in a third country, in particular in the absence of cooperation of the government of that country.

112. The EC notes that its practice in this respect is not unique. For instance, United States regulations foresee that the United States Federal Communications commission may designate telecommunication certification bodies to approve telecommunications equipment. According to 47 CFR 68.160 (b), the Federal Communications Commission shall designate such bodies located <u>in the United States</u> (Exhibit EC-91).[43] According to 47 CFR 68.160 (c), bodies outside the United States shall be permitted to authorize equipment only "in accordance with the terms of an effective bilateral or multilateral recognition agreement or arrangement to which the United States is a party" (Exhibit EC-91).

113. It is before this background that the EC, the US and Australia have concluded mutual recognition agreements under which they agree to recognize the results of conformity assessment carried out by bodies designated by the other party.[44] On this basis, numerous conformity assessment bodies have been recognized under the Sectoral Annexes to the EC-US and EC-Australia MRAs.[45]

114. As a consequence, bodies designated by the United States and Australia can carry out conformity assessment with respect to the EC's standards, and vice versa. Accordingly, such bodies are in exactly the same situation as inspection bodies approved by the United States or Australia to carry out inspections under Regulation 2081/92. The EC considers it odd that the complainants consider themselves disadvantaged by the possibility to approve inspection structures for the purposes of Regulation 2081/92, when this possibility to directly designate conformity assessment bodies for the covered sectors was in fact the main objective of the mutual recognition agreements between the parties.

---

[43] It appears that indeed all telecommunication certification bodies designated under this provision are located in the US (Exhibit EC-92).

[44] Cf. Exhibits EC-23 and EC-24. Telecommunications terminal equipment is one of the sectors covered by these agreements.

[45] Lists of approved conformity assessment bodies are available under http://europa.eu.int/comm/enterprise/international/indexb1.htm#listsapprovedcabs.

Question 132

The Panel takes note of the EC's examples of flexibility in the design of inspections structures (EC rebuttal, para. 104 and Exhibit EC-48). Do these examples all relate to the nature of the inspecting authority? Who determines what constitutes an appropriate inspection for each product, and on the basis of what criteria?

115. The examples given relate to the nature of the inspection body, i.e. whether this body is public or private, local, regional, or national, focusing only on geographical indications or not, commercial or non-profit.

116. Regulation 2081/92 does not define what constitutes an appropriate inspection for each product. Accordingly, it is in principle for each designated inspection structure to define the concrete modalities of inspections for the products in question, for instance with respect to the place, time, frequency, and other modalities of the inspections. In accordance with Article 10(1) of the Regulation, the basic criterion is that the inspections must effectively ensure that product bearing a protected name comply with the products specifications.

Question 133

The Panel takes note that Australia argues that the product specification requirements set out in Article 4(2) of Regulation (EC) No. 2081/92 include "product characteristics," in particular subparagraphs (b) and (e). (Australia's rebuttal, paras. 197 and 204) If the inspection structures are designed to ensure that the product specifications under Article 4 of the Regulation are fulfilled, how can they be a technical regulation and not a conformity assessment procedure?

117. In the view of the EC, they cannot be both a technical regulation and a conformity assessment procedure.[46]

Question 134

The Panel takes note of the EC's response to Panel question No. 61, in particular regarding the Panel's terms of reference. However, does the EC contest that a "conformity assessment procedure" within the meaning of the TBT Agreement assesses conformity with a "technical regulation" or "standard" within the meaning of the TBT Agreement? If not, then can the EC complete its analysis and explain whether the inspection structures of Regulation (EC) No. 2081/92 assess conformity with each individual product specification referred to in Article 4 of the Regulation for a registered name, and that those specifications therefore would constitute a "technical regulation" within the meaning of the TBT Agreement?

118. The EC does not contest that a conformity assessment procedure assesses conformity with a technical regulation or a standard as defined in Point 3 of Annex 1 to the TBT Agreement.

119. However, since Australia has not made any claim under the provision of the TBT Agreement concerning inspection structures, the EC does not consider that the Panel needs to decide whether the inspection structures are indeed conformity assessment procedures or not. Since Australia has brought its claims exclusively under Article 2 TBT Agreement, the essential question which the Panel needs to decide is whether these structures by themselves are a technical regulation. According to Point 1 of Annex 1 to the TBT Agreement, this in turn depends on whether they lay down product characteristics. The EC has raised the aspect of conformity assessment merely to illustrate its argument that structures which "ensure conformity" with requirements regarding product characteristics (whatever their legal quality may be) are not "laying down product characteristics."

---

[46] EC SWS, para. 404 et seq.; EC SOS, para. 246 et seq.

120. For this reason, the EC also does not consider that this Panel should examine the question of whether the product specifications are a technical regulation, a standard, or something else. Australia has not formulated any claim regarding the specifications for any particular product or name under the TBT Agreement. Accordingly, the question whether the product specifications can be considered a technical regulation, or a standard, is outside the scope of the present Panel.

121. In addition, the EC would note that this question is highly complicated and involves complex issues regarding the relationship between the TRIPS Agreement and the TBT Agreement. Moreover, such issues could arise not just in respect to geographical indications, but also to patents, designs, copyrights, plant variety rights, or other intellectual property rights which involve the definition of product characteristics.

Question 135

The EC invokes Article XX(d) of GATT 1994 as a defence to the national treatment and MFN claims with respect to third country governments' verification and transmittal of applications, the identical GIs labelling requirement and inspection structures requirement. The EC alleges that these requirements are "necessary" to secure compliance with Regulation (EC) No. 2081/92 or to attain the legitimate objectives of the Regulation (EC rebuttal, paras. 228-242, paras. 263-265; EC second oral statement, paras. 132-135):

(a) *what is the "measure" necessary to secure compliance with laws or regulations within the meaning of Article XX(d) in each case? What are the laws and regulations with which each one secures compliance? Are the "measures" separate from the laws or regulations?*

122. The "measure necessary to secure compliance with laws and regulations" are the provisions of Regulation 2081/92 which foresee the requirements of inspection structures, the verification and transmission of applications for the registration of geographical indications by the government of the country of origin, and the indication of the country of origin for homonymous geographical indications. The "laws and regulations" with which compliance is secured within the meaning of Article XX(d) of GATT are equally provisions of Regulation 2081/92. It should be noted that Article XX(d) does not exclude that the "measures necessary to secure compliance" and the "laws and regulations" may be part of the same legal act.

(b) *can a measure that secures compliance with the "objectives" of a regulation, rather than a regulation itself, satisfy Article XX(d)?*

123. Article XX(d) GATT refers to measures necessary to "secure compliance with laws and regulations." Accordingly, the measure to be justified must secure compliance with the provisions of the law or regulation in question.[47] However, the objectives of a regulation may be relevant for establishing the meaning of the provisions with which compliance is secured.

(c) *in what sense does each of these measures "secure compliance" with laws or regulations? Are they enforcement mechanisms?*

124. According to Article 4(1) of Regulation 2081/92, to be eligible to use a protected designation of origin or a protected geographical indication, an agricultural product or foodstuff <u>must comply with a product specification</u>. Article 8 of Regulation 2081/92 provides that the indications "protected designation of origin," "protected geographical indication" or equivalent indications <u>may appear only on agricultural products and foodstuffs that comply with the Regulation</u>. Accordingly, both provisions contain clear obligations with which compliance must be secured.

125. According to Article 4(2)(g), the product specifications must contain details of the inspection structures foreseen in Article 10 of the Regulation. In accordance with Article 10 (3), the function of inspection

[47] Cf. GATT Panel Report, *EEC – Regulation on Imports of Parts and Components*, paras. 5.17-5.18.

structures is to ensure that "agricultural products and foodstuffs bearing a protected name meet the requirements laid down in the specifications." Accordingly, the function of inspection structures is to secure compliance with the requirement in Article 4(1) that products bearing a protected name must comply with a product specification. Similarly, the requirement of inspections structures also secures compliance with the requirement in Article 8 of the Regulation that the indications "protected designation of origin," "protected geographical indication" or equivalent indications may appear only on agricultural products and foodstuffs that comply with the Regulation.

126. In accordance with Article 12a(2) of the Regulation, the verification (and incidentally also the transmission) of the application by the government of the country of origin of the geographical indication serves the purpose of establishing whether the requirements of the Regulation for the registration of geographical indications are satisfied. Among these requirements are that the indication in question corresponds to the definition of a geographical indication in Article 2 of the Regulation, that the product specifications comply with Article 4(2) of the Regulation, that the geographical indication is protected or established in its country of origin, and that the required inspection structures are established. Accordingly, the verification of the application by the government of country of origin of the geographical indication secures compliance with the requirement in Article 8 of the Regulation that the indications "protected designation of origin," "protected geographical indication" or equivalent indications may appear only on agricultural products and foodstuffs that comply with the Regulation.

127. According to the first subparagraph of Article 12(2), if a protected name of a third country is identical to a Community protected name, registration shall be granted with due regard for local and traditional usage and the practical risks of confusion. According to the second subparagraph, use of such names shall only be authorised if the country of origin of the product is clearly and visibly indicated on the label. In this way, the second subparagraph secures compliance with the first. At the same time, the second subparagraph of Article 12(2) also secures compliance with the requirement in Article 8 of the Regulation that the indications "protected designation of origin," "protected geographical indication" or equivalent indications may appear only on agricultural products and foodstuffs that comply with the Regulation.

128. The EC is not entirely sure what is understood by "enforcement mechanisms." If enforcement mechanisms are understood as mechanisms which secure compliance with the regulation *ex post*, i.e. after the registration of a particular geographical indication has taken place, then the inspection structures would qualify as "enforcement mechanisms," but possibly not the verification and transmission of applications for the registration of geographical indications by the government of the country of origin, and the indication of the country of origin for homonymous geographical indications.

129. However, the EC notes that Article XX(d) GATT does not speak of "enforcement mechanisms," but of "measures necessary to ensure compliance," including those relating to "the protection of patents, trade marks and copyrights, and the prevention of deceptive practices." There is no indication in Article XX(d) GATT that only "*ex post*" enforcement could qualify under Article XX(d) GATT. Rather, measures which secure compliance at other stages, for instance through appropriate safeguards in the registration process, may also be regarded as measures to "secure compliance." Accordingly, the verification and transmission of applications for the registration of geographical indications by the government of the country of origin, and the indication of the country of origin for homonymous geographical indications should also be regarded as "measures necessary to secure compliance" within the meaning of Article XX(d) GATT.

(d) how are the laws and regulations with which each measure secures compliance not inconsistent with the GATT 1994?

130. Regulation 2081/92 is a measure which provides protection to geographical indications. It implements Section 3 of Part II of the TRIPS Agreement, which obliges WTO Members to provide protection to geographical indications. It does so in providing, in accordance with Article 1.1 of the TRIPS Agreement, a

higher degree of protection than that required by Article 22 TRIPS Agreement. Accordingly, Regulation 2081/29 is a measure which is not inconsistent with the GATT 1994.

Question 136

With respect to the issue whether the measures are necessary to secure compliance, and without prejudice to the WTO-consistency of any alternative measures:

> *(a) is the requirement that a third country government verify applications "necessary" to secure compliance in cases where an applicant itself is able to prove that a GI is protected in its country of origin, for example, by submitting an authenticated copy of a registration certificate?*

131. As the EC has set out above in Response to the Panel's Question 114, the verification to be carried out by the third country government does not only concern the question whether the geographical indication is protected in its country of origin, but also whether the other requirements for the registration of the geographical indication are fulfilled, namely whether the name complies with the definition of a geographical indication, whether the product specifications are in accordance with Article 4 (2) of the Regulation, and whether the necessary inspection structures are established.

132. As the EC has said in its previous submissions,[48] the verification of these conditions requires knowledge of local factors specific to the territory of the country of origin of the geographical indication, which typically only the country of origin will have. Moreover, the verification may also require on-site checks and verifications in the territory of the country of origin, which the EC could not carry out without the express consent of the country of origin. Accordingly, the verification of applications by the country of origin is necessary to secure compliance with the Regulation already for these aspects.

133. As regards the requirement that the geographical indication is protected in the country of origin, a certificate of registration of the geographical indication authenticated by the country of origin of the indication would normally provide sufficient evidence that the indication is protected in its country of origin. However, the EC considers that this question is hypothetical in the context of the present case. Many WTO Members, and in particular the United States and Australia, do not have specific registration systems for the protection of geographical indications. Therefore, the submission of an authenticated certificate of registration does not appear to be an option for a US or Australian geographical indication.

134. The EC would also like to recall that according to the Appellate Body, the evaluation of whether a measure is "necessary" within the meaning of Article XX(d) GATT requires "a process of weighing and balancing a series of factors which prominently include the contribution made by the compliance measure to the enforcement of the law or regulation at issue, the importance of the common interests or values protected by that law or regulation, and the accompanying impact of the law or regulation on imports or exports."[49] In the case of a country which does have a dedicated registration system for the protection of geographical indications, the preparation of an authenticated certificate would not pose any difficulties. Similarly, the transmission of this certificate together with the other documents required by Article 12a(2) would not seem burdensome. Accordingly, the impact on exports of this requirement in Article 12a(2) should be extremely small.

---

[48] EC Response to Panel's Question No. 33; EC SWS, para. 124 et seq.

[49] Appellate Body Report, *Korea – Various Measures on Beef*, para. 164.

(b) is the requirement that a third country government verify applications "necessary" to secure compliance in cases where the third country has no registration system for GIs or where determinations that a GI is protected under unfair competition laws are only made by the judicial branch of government after litigation?

135. Yes. In fact, the requirement of verification by the country of origin is particularly necessary in this case. The EC appreciates that in the absence of a specific registration system, the evaluation of whether a geographical indication is protected in its country of origin may be more difficult. However, this does not create an exemption from Article 24.9 TRIPS, according to which there is no obligation to protect geographical indications which are not protected in their country of origin. Moreover, the question whether the geographical indication is protected in the country of origin remains a question of the law of the third country. Accordingly, the absence of a specific registration system makes the involvement of the country of origin more necessary, not less.

136. The United States has claimed that "the US government does not have any specialized knowledge or expertise that would render it better qualified than the right holder, or indeed, the EC."[50] As the EC has already explained, the EC does not find this argument credible.[51] The United States and Australia cannot claim protection of geographical indications which are not protected in their country.

137. The question which branch of government in the United States or Australia is responsible for the protection of geographical indications is not relevant. Under Article 24.9 TRIPS Agreement, the United States and Australia as WTO Members cannot claim protection for geographical indications which are not protected in their country. This is entirely independent of which branch of government assures this protection in the US and Australia. It is for the United States and Australia to decide which branch of government will be entitled to establish whether a geographical indication is protected in their country in accordance with Article 24.9 TRIPS Agreement.

138. The EC would also remark that if the US or Australian executive branch did not have authority, within the US or Australian legal system, to make such findings, the EC hardly sees how the EU institutions could be expected to make them.

(c) is the requirement that a third country government transmit applications "necessary" to secure compliance in cases where an applicant itself is able to send an application to the Commission?

139. The transmission of the application is an integral part of the application process, which reflects the necessary involvement of the government of the country of origin in the verification of the application. By transmitting the application, the government of the country of origin certifies that it deems the requirements of Article 12a(2) to be fulfilled. For this reason, the EC submits that the requirement that the application should be transmitted by the country of origin should not be considered in isolation, but in the context of the application and verification process.

140. The United States has also indicated that it considered that the transmission of applications or objections was a "purely ministerial act" which as such would not pose particular difficulties.[52] In the process of weighing and balancing as required by the Appellate Body in the context of Article XX(d) GATT, it therefore would not appear that the requirement that the application be transmitted by the country of origin could be regarded as having a significant impact on imports.

141. The EC also notes that in its second oral statement, Australia has indicated that the EC could "ask for the cooperation of another WTO Member after an application has been lodged should such cooperation be

---

[50] US SWS, para. 73.

[51] EC SWS, para. 134; EC SOS, para. 76.

[52] US Response to Panel's Question No. 38, para. 74.

necessary to assess an application."[53] As the EC has set out above, cooperation between the country of origin and the country of registration is necessary. What remains therefore of the Australian submission seems to be that rather than asking for the cooperation before the application is filed, the EC should ask for it after it is filed. However, this is purely an issue of timing and sequencing of the application process. The EC does not see why it should make a difference whether the necessary cooperation occurs before the application is filed, or after.

> *(d) why does a third country government need to verify whether the person objecting is resident or established in the third country? Why does the Commission need consult with the third country if the statement of objection is admissible? (EC response to Panel question No. 34).*

142. First, the EC would like to note that the complainants have formulated their claims regarding the right of objection only under the TRIPS Agreement, not under the GATT.

143. Second, as the United States has indicated, the transmission of applications or objections is a "purely ministerial act" which as such would not pose particular difficulties.[54] This is why the EC has submitted that the transmission of applications by the government of the country of origin cannot be regarded as constituting less favorable treatment.[55]

144. Finally, as the EC has also indicated in response to subquestion c) above, in a process of weighing and balancing as required by Article XX(d) GATT, the pure transmission of an objection does not have any significant impact on trade in goods. Accordingly, should the Panel consider that Article XX(d) GATT is available as a defense to the complainants' claims under the TRIPS, it should find that the measure is necessary within the meaning of Article XX(d) GATT.

> *(e) is the identical GIs labelling requirement "necessary" to secure compliance in cases where there is already a clear distinction in practice in the usual presentation of the relevant products without clearly and visibly displaying the country of origin?*

145. Article 12(2) is based on the assumption that the protected names are homonyms. In such a situation, if the two homonyms are from different countries, the indication of the country appears as the most obvious distinguishing element. Accordingly, the EC considers it unlikely that an equivalent clear distinction could be achieved without the indication of the country of origin.

> *(f) is the requirement that a third country government designate inspection authorities "necessary" to secure compliance in cases where the Commission could designate them in third countries (see US second oral statement, para. 53)?*

146. The EC could not simply designate an inspection body in a third country. As the EC has explained, the designation of an inspection body may require on-site inspections and audits. Similarly, such on-site inspections and audits are also necessary at periodic intervals for the continued monitoring of the inspection body. The EC does not consider that it could carry out such inspections and audits without the agreement of the country in which the body is located.

147. In this context, the EC would like to note that certain provisions in the covered agreements give WTO Members under certain conditions the right to carry out inspections in the territory of another WTO Member. This is the case for instance for Article 6.7 AD Agreement and Article 12.6 CVD Agreement. Even here, the inspection may only be carried out, however, in accordance with the provisions of the annexes to these agreements, and if the importing Member does not object. Similar provisions implying a right to conduct

---

[53] Australia's SOS, para. 68.

[54] US Response to Panel's Question No. 38, para. 74.

[55] EC SWS, para. 158.

investigations in another WTO Member can also be found in Article 6.3 of the SPS Agreement and in Point 2 of Annex C to the SPS Agreement.

148. However, similar provisions do not apply in the present case. The EC can therefore not simply assume that it may carry out such inspections in respect of inspection bodies for geographical indications in a third country. The designation by the third country is therefore necessary also out of respect for the territorial sovereignty of the third country.

149. This is also fully compatible with the practice of the parties in the field of conformity assessment, as explained by the EC in response to the Panel's Question No. 127. Accordingly, the designation of the inspection body by the country of origin is necessary within the meaning of Article XX(d) GATT.

> *(g) is the requirement that a third country government declare that inspection structures are established on its territory "necessary" to secure compliance in cases where an applicant could arrange for independent inspection structures to be put in place in respect of a specific product (see US second oral statement, para. 53)?*

150. As the EC has explained, inspection bodies can be public or private.[56] However, as the EC has also explained, inspection bodies are required by Article 10 (3) to offer adequate guarantees of objectivity and impartiality with respect to producers or processors.[57]

151. This reflects the fact that independently of whether they are public or private, inspection bodies fulfill a function both towards producers and to consumers. This is why the Regulation requires that inspection bodies, even if private, must be responsible to the public authorities of the territory in which they are located. Only through some form of public oversight can it be ensured that the inspection body will at all times carry out its functions duly and appropriately in accordance with the requirements of the Regulation. This is also necessary to secure equal treatment between EC and third country geographical indications, which have to comply with the same requirements.

152. Accordingly, the declaration by the government in which the inspection body is located is necessary to secure compliance with the Regulation.

> *(h) how is the requirement that a private inspection body continues to be responsible vis-à-vis a third country government "necessary" to secure compliance in cases where the EC could conduct its own inspections of foreign GIs (see US second oral statement, para. 53)?*

153. The EC cannot itself conduct inspections of foreign geographical indications. First of all, the EC does not itself have inspection bodies. Rather, for EC geographical indications, inspections bodies are carried out through a multitude of public or private bodies in the individual Member States.[58] Second, the carrying out of inspections typically requires a presence in or near the geographical area to which the indication is related. Finally, the EC would remark that according to Article 10(7) of Regulation 2081/92, the cost of inspections must be borne by the producers using the protected name. Accordingly, if the EC carried out such inspections for foreign geographical indications, this would result in less favourable treatment for EC geographical indications.

---

[56] EC SWS, para. 103.

[57] EC SOS, para. 64.

[58] Cf. EC SWS, para. 104 and Exhibit EC-48.

(i) how is the requirement that the inspection authorities and/or private bodies have permanently at their disposal staff and resources necessary to ensure that all products bearing GIs comply with the product specifications in their registrations? (see Australia's rebuttal submission, para. 217).

154. At the outset, the EC would like to clarify that this requirement does not apply to "all products bearing GIs." First, a particular inspection structure is only responsible, and its staff need must be determined with regard to, the specific product for which it has been designated. Second, there is no requirements that an inspection structure must examine "all" products in a physical sense. Rather, it is up to the inspection structure to decide the place, time and frequency of inspections. Obviously, such inspections may involve sampling or random checks.[59]

155. As regards the requirement to an inspection body must "permanently" have staff and resources at its disposal, Australia has argued that this may not be necessary in certain cases, for instance where there is a particular harvest season. Although this is not the rule for most protected products, the EC does not exclude that there might be products for which the entire production process is confined to a part of the year, and for which therefore the need for inspections arises only or primarily during that time of the year. In this case, Regulation 2081/92 does not require unnecessary levels of staff to be maintained throughout the year. In fact, since it is presumably not economic to establish and wind down an inspection body every year, in such a case it would be reasonable to entrust the function of inspections to a body which also carries out tasks other than inspections under Regulation 2081/92. In its second submission, the EC has pointed to the existence of private firms which can carry out such tasks.[60]

Question 137

The Panel takes note of the EC's view that Article 14(3) of Regulation (EC) No. 2081/92 allows its authorities to refuse or invalidate the registration of any confusing GIs (EC first written submission, para. 286; EC rebuttal, para. 270). The complainants do not agree (US second written submission, para. 166 and Australia's second written submission, para. 109). The following examples have been referred to in this proceeding:

(a) BAYERISCHES BIER and BAVARIA and HØKER BAJER?

(b) BUDEJOVICKÉ PIVO and BUDWEISER?

(c) GORGONZOLA and CAMBOZOLA?

Could these GIs be used in accordance with their registrations in a way that results in a likelihood of confusion with the respective trademark(s)?

156. At the outset, the EC would note that, of the three "examples," only the first one is relevant to this dispute.

157. The EC would recall, once again, that the names "Budějovické pivo," "Českobudějovické pivo" and "Budějovický měšt'anský var" were registered several months after the date of the requests for the establishment of this Panel and are, therefore, outside the Panel's terms of reference.[61] In any event, the EC understands that the United States does not argue that any of those names gives rise to a likelihood of confusion with the name "Budweiser." The US concerns appear to be limited to the use of some translations of those names to other languages.

---

[59] Cf. above Response to Panels' Question No. 132.

[60] EC SWS para. 107 and Exhibits EC-49 and EC-50.

[61] EC FWS, paras. 21-25.

158. In the Cambozola case[62], the right holders of the geographical indication "Gorgonzola" alleged that the use of the trademark "Cambozola" engendered one of the situations mentioned in Article 13(1) of Regulation 2081/92.[63] To the best of the EC's knowledge, the owner of the trademark "Cambozola" never claimed that the use of the geographical indication "Gorgonzola" gave rise to a likelihood of confusion with its trademark or that the registration of the geographical indication Gorgonzola should have been refused in accordance with Article 14(3) of Regulation 2081/92. The two issues are different and should not be confused.

159. In principle, a name which has been found not to be confusing *per se* following the assessment required by Article 14(3) should not give rise to confusion when used subsequently. The EC would submit that, in practice, this may happen only where the registered name is used together with other signs (whether verbal or figurative), or as part of a combination of signs. If those other signs, or the combination thereof, are themselves the subject of trademark rights, the trademark owner retains the right to prevent their use in a confusing manner. Even if they are not covered by trademark rights, the confusing use of those other signs, or of the combination including the geographical indication, could still be prevented under the laws on unfair competition or on misleading labelling or advertising.

160. The United States has argued that, in practice, a name registered as a geographical indication, even if not confusing *per se*, could be confusing when used in translation.[64] But, as already explained by the EC, the registration does no cover translations.

161. The United States also has argued that a name registered as a geographical indication which is not confusing *per se* may be confusing when used "as a trademark."[65] By this, apparently, the United States means that the use of a geographical indication may be confusing if displayed in a prominent way, or at least more prominently than the trademark. As explained by the EC, this reflects pre-conceived notions regarding the respective uses of trademarks and geographical indications which assume a priority of trademarks over geographical indications. The EC does not share those notions, which have no basis in the TRIPS Agreement. In making the assessment required by Article 14(3) of Regulation 2081/92, the EC authorities will assume that the geographical indication will be used in what the United States calls "trademark-like" fashion. Accordingly, the EC authorities will refuse a proposed geographical indication it if is anticipated that, when used in what the United States calls "trademark-like fashion," it will result in a likelihood of confusion with an earlier trademark.

162. Finally, the United States has argued that the use of a registered geographical indication may be confusing when the registered name is deformed, mutilated or otherwise manipulated so as to imitate a trademark.[66] However, as already explained by the EC, a court could consider that, in such case, the used sign is different from the registered name.[67]

163. As noted by the EC, the complainants are requesting the EC to provide a remedy against the confusing use of a registered geographical indications which many Members do not provide with respect to the infringement of a registered trademark by a latter registered trademark. Indeed, as discussed below, in many Members the use of registered trademark is deemed not to be an infringement of an earlier trademark, subject to the possibility to invalidate the registration of the latter trademark on the grounds that it is confusing. (See below the response to Question 139). Upholding the complainants' claims would have necessarily the implication that the trademark laws of those Members are also in violation of Article 16.1 TRIPS.

---

[62] Case C-87/97, *Consorzio per la tutela del frommagio Gorgonzola v Käserai Champignon Hofmeister GmbH & Co Kg,* [1999] ECR I-1301 (Exhibit EC-32).

[63] EC Response to the Panel's Question No. 66.

[64] US SWS, para. 134.

[65] US SWS, para. 133.

[66] US FOS, para. 54.

[67] EC SWS, para. 302.

Question 138

What is the meaning of the phrase "[w]ith due regard to Community law" in Article 14(2) of Regulation (EC) No. 2081/92? Which aspects of "Community law" are relevant?

164. The phrase "with due regard to Community law" clarifies that the right to use the trademark conferred by Article 14(2) of Regulation 2081/92 is not unqualified, but must be exercised in accordance with all other applicable provisions of EC law. Those provisions include not only the Community Trademark Regulation and the Trademark Directive but also, for example, the laws on labeling and unfair competition or the antitrust laws.

What is the meaning of the phrase "shall not affect [Regulation No. 2081/92] ... and in particular Article 14 thereof" in Article 142 of Regulation (EC) No. 40/94 on the Community trade mark?

165. It means that the relationship between Community trademarks and geographical indications registered under Regulation 2081/92 is controlled by the latter, and in particular by Article 14.

Question 139

The Panel takes note of the EC's view that the owner of a trademark may not prevent the right holders of a registered GI from using the registered name on the grounds that such name is confusing (EC second oral statement, para. 181). Please confirm that as long as a GI remains registered and is used in accordance with its registration, a trademark owner may not enforce his trademark rights against that use either under the Regulation on the Community trademark or the national trademark laws of the member States.

166. The EC can confirm that a trademark owner cannot prevent the holders of a registered geographical indication from using the name or names registered under Regulation 2081/92 on the grounds that the use of such name or names is confusing *per se* with an earlier trademark.

167. As explained, however, this does not mean that the right holders of a geographical indication have an unqualified right to use the registered name in any conceivable manner. First, the right to use the registered name does not confer a right to use other names not covered by the registration, or to use the registered name together with other signs or as part of a combination of signs. Furthermore, the registered name must be used in accordance with other generally applicable laws, including in particular with the laws on labeling, misleading advertising and unfair competition.

What legal provisions prevent the trademark owners exercising their rights against persons using a GI in accordance with its registration?

168. Regulation 2081/92 does not contain any provision which prohibits expressly the trademark owners from exercising their rights with respect to a registered geographical indication. However, the protection provided by Regulation 2081/92 would become meaningless if a trademark owner could prevent the use of the registered name by the right holders of a geographical indication on the grounds that the use of such name is confusing *per se* with an earlier trademark.

169. The registration of a name under Regulation 2081/92 establishes a legal presumption that the use of that name as a geographical indication does not give rise *per se* to a likelihood of confusion with an earlier trademark, because otherwise the registration should have been refused in accordance with Article 14(3). In order to be able to exercise its trademark rights, the trademark owner must rebut first that legal presumption by invalidating the registration of the geographical indication.

170. The EC would note that, by the same token, under the trademarks laws of many Members, the use of a registered trademark is deemed not to constitute an infringement of an earlier trademark, subject to the possibility to invalidate the latter trademark on those grounds.[68]

Question 140

Under what provision of Regulation (EC) No. 2081/92 does the registration of a GI give the right holder a positive right to use the GI?

171. Regulation 2081/92 does not include any provision which confers expressly a positive right to use the registered name. But that right is implicit in several provisions, for example:

- Article 4(1), which provides that:

  > ... to be eligible to use a protected designation (PDO) or a protected geographical indication (PGI) an agricultural product or foodstuff must comply with a specification.

- Article 8, which provides that:

  > The indications PDO, PGI or equivalent traditional national indications may appear only on agricultural products and foodstuffs that comply with this Regulation.

- Article 13(1)(a), which states that registered names shall be protected against

  > any direct or indirect commercial use of a name registered in respect of products not covered by the registration ...

---

[68] For example, Section 19 of Canada's Trade Marks Law (Exhibit EC-93) provides that:
the registration of a trade-mark in respect of any wares or services, unless shown to be invalid, gives to the owner of the trade-mark the exclusive right to the use throughout Canada of the trade-mark in respect of those wares or services.
Section 20 (1) (Exhibit EC-93) goes on to provide that the right of the owner of a registered trade-mark to its exclusive use is not deemed to be infringed by a person "entitled to its use under this Act."
Section 19(2) of Hong Kong's Trade Marks Ordinance (Exhibit EC-94) provides that:
A registered trademark is not infringed by the use of another registered trademark in relation to goods or services for which the latter is registered (but see section 53(9) for the effect of a declaration of invalidity of registration).
Section 30(2) of India's Trade Marks Act (Exhibit EC-95) provides that:
A registered trademark is not infringed where--... (e) the use of a registered trade mark, being one of two or more registered under this Act which are identical or nearly resemble each other, in exercise of the right to use that trade mark given by registration under this Act.
Section 93 of New Zealand's Trade Marks Act 2002 (Exhibit EC-96) provides that:
A registered trade mark is not infringed by the use of another registered trademark in relation to any goods or services for which that other trademark is registered.
Section 28 of Singapore's Trade Marks Act (Exhibit EC-97) provides that:
... a registered trademark is not infringed by the use of another registered trademark in relation to goods or services for which the latter is registered.
Section 34(2) of South Africa's Trade Marks Act (Exhibit EC-98) provides that:
A registered trade mark is not infringed by—.... (g) the use of any identical or confusingly or deceptively similar trade mark which is registered.
Section 11(1) of the United Kingdom's Trade Marks Act 1994 (Exhibit US-50) provides that:
A trademark is not infringed by the use of another registered trademark in relation to goods or services for which the latter is registered (but see section 47(6))(effect of declaration of invalidity of registration).
Finally, Section 122 of Australia's Trade Marks Act 1995 (Exhibit EC-7) provides that:
In spite of section 120, a person does not infringe a registered trade mark when: [...] (e) the person exercises a right to use a trade mark given to the person under this Act.

172. Moreover, once again, if the right holders of a geographical indication did not have a positive right to use the name, the protection provided under the Regulation against other uses would be meaningless.

How is that right delimited? Does it include translations of the protected term?

173. The positive right to use a registered geographical indication extends to the name or names that have been entered into the "Register of protected designations of origin and protected geographical indications." The registered name or names are specified in the annex to the regulation providing for the registration of each name and are added to the annex to Regulation 2400/96[69], in the case of applications under Article 6, or the annex to Regulation 1107/96[70], in the case of applications under former Article 17.

174. The registered name must be used in accordance with the approved specifications, including the labeling details.

175. Subject to any restrictions provided in the specifications, the registered name may be used together with other signs (verbal or figurative) or as part of a combination of signs. But the registration under Regulation 2081/92 does not confer a positive right to use any such other signs or combination of signs. To the extent that those signs or combinations of signs are the same as, or confusingly similar to, a sign covered by a trademark right, the trademark owner is entitled to prevent their use. Even when they are not covered by trademarks rights, their use may be prevented under the laws on labeling, advertising or unfair competition.

176. The positive right extends only to the linguistic versions that have been entered into the register. Thus, for example, Commission Regulation (EC) No 865/2003 provided for the registration of both the Spanish name "Cítricos Valencianos" and the Catalan name "Citrics Valencians."[71]

For example, what uses do the registrations of the four cheese GIs referred to in Exhibit US-52 permit?

177. The EC is providing herewith the approved specifications for the four products concerned (Exhibits EC-99, EC-100, EC-101, EC-102).

178. As regards labeling details, the specifications provide the following:

- Bitto: the product must be marketed with a distinguishing mark consisting of the designation of origin with the accompanying logo. The trademark and the logo are reproduced in an annex to the Italian decree recognizing the geographical indication.

- Tomme de Savoie: the specifications state the following:

  L'identification du produit, conformément aux Réglements Techniques « Tomme de Savoie" 78 RA 01 et 89 RA 01 est realisé :

  – Par un étiquetage en conformité avec la réglementation générale francaise et européenne.

  – Par un étiquetage propre au "Label Regional Savoie"

  * soit une vignette reproduisant le sigle de la Marque Savoie [reproduced in the specifications] + sigle I.G.P

[69] Exhibit COMP-4 a.

[70] Exhibit COMP-3 a.

[71] Exhibit COMP-4bi.

   * *soit sur l'étiquette commerciale de l'enterprise*

   - impression rouge sur fond blanc de l'appellation « TOMME DE SAVOIE »

   - % de MG

   - le logo de la "Marque Collective Savoie" + sigle I.G.P.

   - la mention de l'Organisme Certificateur.

- Esrom: the label must contain the mention "Esrom (45 + or 60 +)" followed by the mention "Beskyttet Oprindelses-Betignese" or "BOB" [PDO in Danish] in all Community official languages.

- Bra: the product must be marketed with the label of the relevant manufacturers' consortium.

How far does that positive right extend before it can be challenged under labelling and misleading advertising laws?

179. It is difficult to define *a priori* which particular uses of a registered geographical indication may violate the provisions of the Directives on labelling and misleading advertising and/or the laws on unfair competition. This question requires necessarily a case-by-case analysis and cannot be responded in the abstract. Nevertheless, the EC will attempt to set out here below some indications.

180. The use of a geographical indication in what the United States calls "trademark- like fashion" is not sufficient to consider that it is inconsistent with those laws. Indeed, the United States appears to consider that a geographical indication is used "as a trademark" whenever it is displayed prominently, or at least more prominently than the trademark. The EC does not share this view, which assumes that trademarks enjoy priority over geographical indications. As explained, EC consumers are familiar with the use of geographical indications for foodstuffs, value them as much as trademarks, if not more, and expect them to be used in ways which the United States would like to reserve for trademarks. EC consumers are unlikely to mistake a geographical indication for foodstuff for a trademark simply because it is displayed in the label in relatively big sized letters or in attractive colours or typography.

181. On the other hand, if the holder of a geographical indication which has a right to use a certain name (say "Bayerisches Bier") were to use it in a manner which imitates the label or the packaging of the products of a trademark ("Bavaria"), this could be considered as a breach of the laws on labelling and unfair competition, even if the constituent elements of the label or the packaging, other than the trademark itself, were not covered by any intellectual property rights.

182. To mention but another example, the laws on labelling and unfair competition could be violated if the name of the geographical indication were used together with other signs or statements that suggested or indicated that the geographical indication is in fact the trademark of a producer, rather than a geographical indication. For example, if the geographical indication were used under, or close to, the terms "produced by." Or if it were used together with a sign (e.g. a Dutch flag or emblem, a map of The Netherlands, or a Dutch windmill) which suggested that the product is of the origin generally associated with the products of a co-existing trademark, rather than with that indicated by the geographical indication.

Question 141

What is the legal basis for an action to invalidate a registration under Regulation (EC) No. 2081/92 on the grounds of confusion with a trademark?

183. Article 14(3) of Regulation 2081/92.

Is there any basis for an action to invalidate a GI registration in Regulation (EC) No. 40/94 on the Community trade mark?

184. No.

Question 142

The Panel takes note of the EC's view that the owner of a concurrent trademark could challenge a decision to register a GI inconsistently with Article 14(3) of Regulation (EC) No. 2081/92 even after the GI has been formally registered (EC response to Panel question No. 67; EC rebuttal paras. 270 and 296). If a trademark owner applied to invalidate a GI registration under Article 14(3):

(a) is this a precondition to a trademark infringement action?

185. As explained[72], the trademark owner may raise the invalidity of the registration of the geographical indication in accordance with the procedure laid down in Article 234 of the EC Treaty in the context of a trademark infringement action brought before a court of a Member State.

(b) is there any time-limit on such an invalidation action?

186. Applications in annulment under Article 230 of the EC Treaty must be filed within a two-month time limit. The possibility to raise the invalidity of the registration of the geographical indication under Article 234 of the EC Treaty is not subject to any time limit.

(c) is this possibility available where the GI is registered pursuant to an Act of Accession or otherwise without the normal application procedures?

187. So-called "fast track" registrations made pursuant to a request under former Article 17 of Regulation 2081/92 can be annulled pursuant to an action brought in accordance with Article 230 of the EC Treaty or invalidated in accordance with Article 234 of the EC Treaty under the same conditions as the registrations made pursuant to an ordinary application under Article 6 of Regulation 2081/92.

188. Contrary to what has been suggested by the United States, the registration of a geographical indication pursuant to an Act of Accession is not a frequent occurrence. In fact, of the more than 600 registrations, only one has been made pursuant to an Act of Accession: that of the names "Budějovické pivo," "Českobudějovické pivo" and "Budějovický měšťanský var." As explained, this registration is not within the terms of reference of the Panel.[73] This registration is unique also in that it provides that it applies "without prejudice to any beer trademark or other rights existing in the European Union on the date of accession."

---

[72] EC SOS, para. 178.

[73] EC FWS, paras. 21-25.

(d) how would such an application for invalidation relate to the cancellation procedure in Article 11a of the Regulation? Are the grounds for cancellation in Article 11a exhaustive?

189. The cancellation procedure presupposes that the registration is valid and produces effects *ex nunc*. The grounds for cancellation mentioned in Articles11 and 11a are exhaustive.

Question 143

The Panel takes note that the Council Decision to register BAYERISCHES BIER as a GI states that "[i]n view of the facts and information available, it was, however, considered that registration of [that name] was not liable to mislead the consumer as to the true identity of the product" (Exhibit EC-9, para. (3), cited in EC rebuttal, para. 287). Please detail what were the facts and information to which the Council referred in that Decision and how they were evaluated so that the Panel can see how the criteria in Article 14(3) were applied in that case.

190. The Council's decision took account of the submissions made by the interested parties and by some Member States, as well as of the discussions which took place within the Committee.

191. The main facts taken into consideration were: the similarity of the signs; the similarity of the products, having regard to the production methods and organoleptic properties; the date of registration of the trademark; the recognition of the trademark in the different Member States, having regard in particular to the level of exports; and the labeling practices of the trademark and the proposed geographical indication.

192. In essence, it was concluded that, although the products were similar, the signs were not sufficiently similar to mislead the public, having regard to the degree of recognition of the trademark in the different Member States.

Question 144

The Panel takes note that Commission Regulation (EC) No. 1107/96 (set out in Exhibit COMP-3a), which effected the registration of many individual GIs, recites Article 14(2) and (3) of Regulation (EC) No. 2081/92. How were Article 14(2) and (3) taken into account in the registration of those GIs?

193. As already explained, Article 14(2) is not applied by the registering authority (see EC response to Question 66). It is for the courts to decide whether a trademark falls within one of the situations mentioned in Article 13(1) and, if so, whether the trademark is entitled to co-exist in accordance with Article 14(2) or should be invalidated or revoked in accordance with the Trademark Directive and the Community Trademark Directive.

194. Regulation 1107/96 provides for the registration of names notified by the Member States in accordance under former Article 17 of Regulation 2081/92. In the context of that procedure, the EC authorities conducted the assessment provided in Article 14(3) where, because of the concerns raised directly by interested parties or by the Member States, they became aware of the existence of a potentially conflicting trademark.

195. The recital mentioned in the question is an implicit reference to the Bayerische Bier case. Because of the concerns raised by the owners of the trademarks at issue and by some Member States, the EC institutions could not reach a decision with respect to that name as of the time of the adoption of Regulation 1107/96. Therefore, that name continued to be protected at national level in accordance with the second paragraph of Article 1 of Regulation 1107/96.

Question 145

Please refer to Article 24.5 of the TRIPS Agreement and comment on the suggestion that:

(a) the phrase "shall not prejudice eligibility for or the validity of the registration of a trademark" merely creates an exception to the obligations in Articles 22.3 and 23.2 to refuse or invalidate the registration of trademarks; and

(b) the phrase "shall not prejudice ... the right to use a trademark" merely creates an exception to the obligations in Articles 22.2 and 23.1 to provide the legal means to prevent certain uses and does not create any positive right.

196. Article 24.5 is not a "mere exception" to the obligations stipulated in the provisions of Section 3 of Part II of the TRIPS Agreement mentioned in the question. The suggestion made in the question is mistaken in two fundamental respects.

197. First, Article 24.5 applies with respect to "any measures adopted to implement this section," and not just with respect to the provisions cited in the question. In accordance with Article 1.1 TRIPS, Members may implement more extensive protection of geographical indications than is required by the provisions of Section 3 of Part II cited in the question, provided that such protection does not contravene other provisions of the TRIPS Agreement. Any such additional protection is subject to the rule contained in Article 24.5, just like the minimum protection required by the provisions of Section 3 of Part II cited in the question

198. Second, Article 24.5 is drafted in mandatory terms, unlike the genuine exceptions in Articles 24.4, 24.6, 24.7 and 24.8. As a result, by limiting the obligations to protect geographical indications in Articles 22 and 23, Article 24.5 imposes simultaneously upon Members correlative obligations with respect to the protection of trademarks that go beyond those provided in Section 2 of Part II.

199. The following two examples may illustrate this:

- assume that a Member's trademark law provides that a trademark including or consisting of a geographical indication shall not be registered or, if registered, shall be invalidated.[74] This goes beyond the obligation stipulated in Article 22.3. Nevertheless, there is nothing in Section 2 of Part II and, more specifically, in Article 15.2, which would prevent a Member from enacting such additional protection of geographical indications. Yet, if a trademark has been registered, or applied for, before either of the two dates mentioned in Article 24.5, the Member in question would be prohibited by virtue of Article 24.5 from invalidating that trademark on the ground that such trademark is identical or similar to a geographical indication. This obligation not to invalidate certain trademarks does not result from Section 2 of Part II, or from Article 22.3, but exclusively from Article 24.5.

- assume that a Member's trademark law prohibits the use of any trademark acquired by use which is identical or similar to a subsequently recognized geographical indication. This prohibition goes beyond the obligation provided in Article 22.2. Nevertheless, it would be fully consistent with Section 2 of Part II, which provides for the "possibility"[75] to grant trademark rights on the basis of use, but imposes no obligation to do so. Therefore, Members are free to grant, limit or withdraw such rights at will. Yet, if the rights to the trademark in question had been acquired before either of the dates mentioned in Article 24.5, the Member concerned would be prevented from

---

[74] The example is not hypothetical. In practice, many Members prohibit the registration of trademarks including or consisting of geographical indications. For example, Section 61 of Australia's Trade Marks Act 1995 (Exhibit EC-103) allows to oppose the registration of a sign that contains or consists of a geographical indication.

[75] Cf. Article 16.1 of the TRIPS Agreement.

prohibiting the use of that trademark by virtue of Article 24.5. Again, this obligation does no result from Section 2 of Part II, or from Article 22.2, but exclusively from Article 24.5.

200. As shown by the above two examples, Article 24.5 imposes self-standing obligations with respect to the protection of trademarks that go beyond the obligations provided in Section 2 of Part II. Therefore, it would be manifestly incorrect to characterize Article 24.5 as a "mere exception" to the obligations provided in other provisions of Section 3. "Exceptions" exempt from an obligation stipulated in another provision.[76] They do not impose positive obligations by themselves.

201. For the above reasons, Article 24.5 is not an "exception." Rather, Article 24.5 lays down a positive rule which defines in a comprehensive manner the boundary between the protection that Members *must* (in accordance with Articles 22 and 23) or *may* (in accordance with Article 1.1) afford to geographical indications and the protection which Members *must* (in accordance with Section 2 of Part II) or *may* (in accordance with Article 1.1) provide to the sub-category of "grandfathered" trademarks, as defined in Article 24.5. That rule stipulates rights and obligations which are different from, and apply in place of, those provided in Section 2, including in Article 16.1, and elsewhere in Section 3, with respect to other trademarks.

202. The special rule for grandfathered trademarks established in Article 24.5 purports to establish a compromise between the protection of trademarks and the protection of geographical indications and must be interpreted in the light of that objective. On the one hand, Article 24.5 limits the Members' right under Section 2 of Part II to refuse and invalidate the registration of a trademark on the grounds that it is identical or similar to a geographical indication. At the same time, however, Article 24.5 limits the obligations that would normally follow from the registration of one such trademark under Article 16.1, by providing that the trademark owner shall have "the right to use the trademark," but not the right to prevent the use of the trademark by the right holders of the geographical indication. This limitation, however, does not represent a real restriction of the protection of trademarks provided in Article 16.1, because it applies only within the limits of the additional protection provided in Article 24.5 with respect to "grandfathered" trademarks, which goes beyond that required by Section 2 of Part II.

Question 146

The Panel takes note of the respective views of the EC and US on simultaneous exercise of rights with respect to use (EC rebuttal, para. 309 and US rebuttal, para. 119). Without prejudice to the EC's views on Article 24.5, would there be any <u>practical</u> conflict between the rights to prevent certain uses conferred under Articles 16.1 and 22.2 of TRIPS? Under what circumstances is it impossible for, simultaneously:

> *(a) a trademark owner to prevent <u>uses</u> of a sign where such use would result in a likelihood of confusion (under Article 16.1), and*
>
> *(b) a right holder in a GI to prevent <u>uses</u> of an indication that are misleading with respect to the geographical origin of the product or which constitute unfair competition (under Article 22.2) except on the basis that the trademark is identical with, or similar to, the GI (under Article 24.5)?*

203. The EC has not argued that there is a "conflict" between the rights conferred by Article 16.1 and by Article 22.2 (or 23.1) because it is "impossible" to exercise both of them simultaneously.

204. Rather, the EC has noted that the simultaneous exercise of those two rights would lead to a situation where neither the trademark owner nor the right holders of the geographical indications could use the sign which is the subject matter of their respective right.

---

[76] See US SWS, para. 171.

205. Although neither Article 16.1 nor Article 22.2 (or Article 23.1) confer expressly a positive right to use a trademark or to use a geographical indication, respectively, that right is implicit in the protection conferred by those provisions. The right to exclude others from using a sign, whether as a trademark or as a geographical indication, would be meaningless unless the holders of that right were entitled to use the sign themselves.

206. The simultaneous exercise of the rights conferred by Articles 16.1 and 22.2 (and 23.1) would prevent both rights from fulfilling the purpose for which they are granted and deprive them of their *raison d'être*, which is to ensure that the right holder can enjoy the right to use the sign exclusively. By doing so, the simultaneous exercise of Articles 16.1 and 22.2 gives rise to a genuine "conflict" in substance, if not in the form. That "conflict" is resolved by Article 22.3 (and 23.2), which provides for the invalidation of the trademark, thereby effectively giving priority to the geographical indication. This "rule of conflict," however, does not apply to "grandfathered trademarks," as defined in Article 24.5, which are subject to a different rule, as explained in the response to the preceding question.

Question 147

Article 24.5 as finally agreed contains the phrase "measures adopted to implement this Section shall not prejudice eligibility for or the validity of the registration of a trademark, or the right to use a trademark." Please comment on the suggestion that during the Uruguay Round negotiations there was a disagreement as to whether the predecessor to this provision in the Brussels Draft should be made permissive rather than mandatory, and that the choice of this language was part of an effort to reach agreement on the issue of the mandatory / permissive nature of the provision.

207. As suggested in the question, some participants in the negotiations were of the view that Article 24.5, like the other exceptions included in Article 24, should be permissive, rather than mandatory. Among other reasons, because a "mandatory exception" would have the anomalous result of imposing upon Members obligations with respect to the protection of trademarks that go beyond those agreed as part of Section 2 of Part II.

208. Also, as suggested in the question, the wording of Article 24.5 embodies a compromise. The EC and other participants agreed to make the "exception" mandatory on the understanding that the trademark owners would have "the right to use the trademark," as specified expressly in Article 24.5, but not the right to exclude the use of the trademark by the right holders of the geographical indication.

Question 148

What is the meaning of the phrase "where such use would result in a likelihood of confusion" as used in Article 16.1 of the TRIPS Agreement?

209. The phrase "where such use would result in a likelihood of confusion" must be read in the context of Article 15.1. The purpose of a trademark is to distinguish the products of a given undertaking from those of other undertakings. Accordingly, there is a "likelihood of confusion" where the use of a sign gives rise to a likelihood that the public will not be able to distinguish the products of the owner of the registered trademark from the products of other undertakings bearing the sign in question.

How should such likelihood of confusion be assessed?

210. The TRIPS Agreement does not provide any specific guidance to assess the likelihood of confusion. In practice, most Members use similar criteria.

211. Canada's trademark law, which is one of the few to specify the criteria to assess the likelihood of confusion, provides that[77]

> In determining whether trade-marks or trade names are confusing, the court or the Registrar, as the case may be, shall have regard to all the surrounding circumstances including
>
> (a) the inherent distinctiveness of the trade-marks or trade names and *the extent to which they have become known*;
>
> (b) *the length of time the trade-marks or trade-names have been in use*;
>
> (c) the nature of the wares, services or business;
>
> (d) the nature of the trade; and
>
> (e) the degree of resemblance between the trade-marks or trade names in appearance or sound or in the ideas suggested by them.

212. The tenth recital of the EC's Trademark Directive says that the appreciation of likelihood of confusion

> depends on numerous elements and, in particular, on the recognition of the trade mark on the market, of the association which can be made with the used or registered sign, of the degree of similarity between the trade mark and the sign and between the goods or services identified.

213. Interpreting Article 4(1)(b) of the Trademark Directive, which is the equivalent of Article 16.1, the ECJ has held that[78]

> The likelihood of confusion on the part of the public … must be appreciated globally, taking into account all factors relevant to the circumstances of the case …
>
> A global assessment of the likelihood of confusion implies some interdependence between the relevant factors, and in particular a similarity between the trademarks and between these goods or services. Accordingly, a lesser degree of similarity between these goods or services may be offset by a greater degree of similarity between the marks, and vice-versa …
>
> Furthermore, … the more distinctive the earlier mark, the greater the risk of confusion … Since protection of a trademark depends, in accordance with Article 4.1(b) of the Directive, on there being a likelihood of confusion, marks with a highly distinctive character, either *per se* or because of the *reputation* they possess in the market, enjoy broader protection than marks with a less distinctive character.

214. In the United States, the courts have considered that the following factors may be relevant for a determination of likelihood of confusion:[79]

> (1) The similarity or dissimilarity of the marks in their entireties as to appearance, sound, connotation and commercial impression.

---

[77] Section 6(5) of Canada's Trade-marks Act (Exhibit EC-73). Emphases added.

[78] Case C-39/97, *Canon Kabushiki Kaisha v Metro Goldwyn-Mayer Inc.*, [1998] ECR I-5507, para. 16 *et seq.* (Exhibit EC-71). Emphases added.

[79] *E.I. Du Pont De Nemours & Co., Application of*, 476 F. 2d 1357 (Cust. & Pat. App. 1973), 26 (Exhibit EC-73). Emphases added.

(2) The similarity or dissimilarity of and nature of the goods or services as described in an application or registration or in connection with which a prior mark is in use.

(3) The similarity or dissimilarity of established, likely-to-continue trade channels.

(4) The conditions under which and buyers to whom sales are made, i.e. "impulse" vs. careful, sophisticated purchasing.

(5) *The fame of the prior mark (sales, advertising, length of use).*

(6) The number and nature of similar marks in use on similar goods.

(7) The nature and extent of any actual confusion.

(8) *The length of time during and conditions under which there has been concurrent use without evidence of actual confusion.*

(9) The variety of goods on which a mark is or is not used (house mark, "family" mark, product mark).

(10) The market interface between applicant and the owner of a prior mark:

(a) a mere "consent" to register or use.

(b) agreement provisions designed to preclude confusion, i.e. limitations on continued use of the marks by each party.

(c) assignment of mark, application, registration and good will of the related business.

(d) laches and estoppel attributable to owner of prior mark and indicative of lack of confusion.

(11) The extent to which applicant has a right to exclude others from use of its mark on its goods.

(12) The extent of potential confusion, i.e., whether *de minimis* or substantial.

(13) Any other established fact probative of the effect of use.

How does the assessment differ from that under Article 14(3) of Regulation (EC) No. 2081/92?

215. The assessment made by the EC authorities under Article 14(3) is analogous to the assessment carried out by the EC trademark authorities in order to establish whether the use of a later trademark will give rise to likelihood of confusion with an earlier trademark. When applying Article 14(3), the registering authorities, or the courts, as applicable, must take into account all relevant factors, including in particular the similarity of goods and signs. As explained, length of use, reputation and renown are mentioned expressly in Article 14(3) because geographical indications, when used as trademarks, are primarily descriptive and non-distinctive.

In particular:

(a) how should the likelihood of confusion, and the liability to mislead the consumer, be assessed with respect to a mark to which rights have not been acquired on the basis of use?

216. In principle, the criteria for assessing likelihood of confusion/liability to mislead are the same irrespective of whether the earlier trademark has been acquired through registration or through use.

(b) as of what time should the likelihood of confusion, and the liability to mislead the consumer, be assessed?

217. The "likelihood of confusion" is assessed as of the time of registration of the later trademark and/or at the time of the infringement, depending on the type of procedure in the framework of which it is alleged and of the peculiarities of each legal system for the protection of trademarks.

218. The "liability to mislead" for purposes of Article 14(3) is assessed as of the time of the registration of the geographical indication. But if a trademark owner raises the invalidity of the registration subsequently, it could rely on any relevant intervening circumstances, such as, for example, cases of actual confusion, in order to show that the initial assessment was flawed.

(c) are the trademark's reputation and renown and the length of time it has been used necessarily relevant to both analyses?

219. Yes, these criteria are relevant in all cases. However, this is not saying that they will have the same weight in all cases. As emphasized by the European Court of Justice, the criteria for assessing the likelihood of confusion are "interdependent."[80] In general, the more similar the signs, the less important will be these criteria. On the other hand, the "weaker" (i.e. the less inherently distinctive) the trademark, the more important will become these criteria. Terms which qualify, or which may reasonably qualify as geographical indications, are primarily descriptive and non-distinctive as trademarks. Indeed, the registration of those terms as trademarks should be permitted only to the extent that they have acquired distinctiveness through use. For that reason, the public is unlikely to confuse a geographical indication with a trademark consisting of that geographical indication if the trademark has never been used and enjoys no recognition.

220. For example, assume that the name Australia, which Australia claims is a geographical indication for wine, had been registered in the EC as a trademark for wine, but that such trademark had never been used. The EC public would be unlikely to mistake wine bearing the geographical indication "Australia" for wine of the totally unknown trademark "Australia," despite the identity of the names.

Question 149

What are the differences between "confusion" and "misleads" as used in Articles 16.1 and 22.2 of the TRIPS Agreement, respectively? Do they have any bearing on the misleading standard under Article 14(3) of Regulation (EC) No. 2081/92?

221. The meaning of the term "mislead" in TRIPS Article 22.2 (and 22.3) does not prejudge of the meaning of the term "misleading" in Article 14(3) in Regulation 2081/92.

222. In the first place, Article 14(3) must be interpreted in the context of Regulation 2081/92, including in particular Articles 7(4) and 7(5)(b), and in accordance with the rules and principles of interpretation of EC law.

---

[80] Case C-39/97, *Canon Kabushiki Kaisha v Metro Goldwyn-Mayer Inc.*, [1998] ECR I-5507, para. 16 *et seq.* (Exhibit EC-71).

223. Moreover, Article 14(3) of Regulation 2081/92 and Article 22.2 (and 22.3) TRIPS is concerned each with a different issue. The purpose of Article 14(3) is to prevent the use of a geographical indication where it may cause an error with respect to the "identity of the product." In other words, to avoid that the public confuses the products bearing the geographical indication with the products of a given undertaking bearing an earlier trademark. This is the same type of error addressed by Article 16.1 TRIPS. In contrast, Articles 22.2 and 22.3 address the situation where the use of a sign in connection with a product may cause an error as to the geographical origin of that product.

224. Even assuming that Article 22.2 TRIPS were relevant for the interpretation of Article 14(3), from the mere fact that TRIPS Article 16.1 and Article 22.2 (and 22.3) use different terminology, it does not follow that they purport to establish substantially different standards, let alone that Article 22.2 (and 22.3) imposes a more rigorous standard, contrary to what is asserted by Australia.

225. As acknowledged by Australia, one of the ordinary meanings of "misleading" is "confusing."[81] That the two terms may be used interchangeably in ordinary speech, as well as in the specific context of trademark law is illustrated, for example, by the following passage of WIPO's Trademark Manual, which explains the notion of "likelihood of confusion" by saying that[82]

> A trademark is confusingly similar to a prior trademark if it is used for similar goods and so closely resembles the prior mark that there is a likelihood of consumers being *misled* as to the origin of the goods.

226. Australia argues that a misleading use is a use "which *positively* provokes an error."[83] However, Australia does not explain what it means by "positively." Articles 22.2 and 22.3 do not require an "intent" to mislead on the part of the infringer. As made clear by Article 22.3, all that is required is that the use be "of such a nature as to" mislead, i.e. objectively capable of causing an error.

227. The use of different terms in Article 16.1 and in Article 22.2 (and 22.3) reflects the fact that they are concerned each with a different type of error. Article 16.1 addresses the situation where the use of two similar signs for similar goods by two different undertakings has the consequence that the public cannot distinguish between the two signs and makes the error of mistaking the goods of one of the undertakings for those of the other. In contrast, Articles 22.2 and 22.3 address the situation where the use of one sign in connection with one product leads the public to make an error with respect to the geographical origin of *that* product. The term "confusion" would not be appropriate to describe the type of error addressed in Articles 22.2 and 22.3, because that error does not involve the impossibility of distinguishing between two signs for goods of two different undertakings.

Question 151

Please comment on the suggestion that Article 24.3 of the TRIPS Agreement was inserted in the draft text in November 1991 to make it clear that the exceptions provisions in Section 3 of Part II could not be used as a justification for diminishing a Member's pre-existing protection of GIs.

228. Assuming that the suggestion made in the question were correct, and assuming further that the complainants' interpretation of Article 24.5 were also correct, Article 24.5 would be one of the "exceptions provisions in Section 3." Accordingly, Members could not rely upon Article 24.5 as a "justification" to diminish the re-existing protection of geographical indications.

---

[81] Australia's SWS, para. 104.

[82] WIPO, *Introduction to Trademark Law and Practice, The Basic Concepts, a WIPO Training Manual*, Geneva 1993, para. 6.2.2 (Exhibit EC-108). Emphasis added.

[83] Australia's SWS, para. 104.

Question 152

If a Member is obliged to diminish the pre-existing protection of GIs in order to allow trademark owners to exercise their rights under Article 16.1 as against GIs, does that obligation not arise under Article 16.1 rather than "[i]n implementing this Section," as used in Article 24.3?

229. No. On the complainants' own interpretation of Article 24.5, the obligation to diminish protection would arise from the obligation imposed by Article 24.5 and not from Article 16.1. But for Article 24.5, Members would be entitled to invalidate and prohibit the use of "grandfathered" trademarks, as defined in Article 24.5, on the basis that they are identical or similar to a geographical indication, just like they are entitled to refuse or invalidate other trademarks on those grounds.

Question 153

Without prejudice to the EC's view that a GI confusingly similar to a trademark will not be registered, if one were registered nevertheless, in what way would this exception be "limited"? In particular, could the rights of the GI owner be limited in such a way as to minimize the likelihood of confusion?

230. The exception is "limited" because it allows the use of the registered name only in relation to goods that originate in the area designated by the geographical indication and which, furthermore, comply will all the relevant requirements provided in the approved specifications. The trademark owner retains the right to prevent the use of the name by *any* person in relation to *any* goods which originate in a different geographical area or which do not comply with the specifications.

231. As explained by the EC[84], the potential universe of uses covered by the exception claimed by the EC is narrower than the potential universe of uses of other descriptive terms, such as an indication of source which does not qualify as a geographical indication or a term used to describe a product characteristic. Yet, both Australia and the United States appear to concede that the use of those terms would qualify for an exception under Article 17.

232. Article 17 contains no requirement to the effect that the "likelihood of confusion" must be "minimized." Indeed, such a requirement would pre-empt the balancing of conflicting interests required by the second condition of Article 17. If the term "limited" required to confine the likelihood of confusion to the strictly necessary, it would be unnecessary to "take account," as a separate condition, of the interests of the trademark owner and of third parties.

233. In any event, the exception claimed by the EC limits the likelihood of confusion in two different ways.

234. First, even if the complainants' reading of Article 14(3) were correct and that provision did not prevent the registration of all geographical indications that give rise to a likelihood of confusion with an earlier trademark, it would remain that Article 14(3) would prevent registration in those cases where the likelihood of confusion would be greater, because of the recognition enjoyed by the trademark.

235. Second, the use of the geographical indication is subject to the requirements of Directive 2000/13 on the labelling, presentation and advertising of foodstuffs[85], and in particular to Article 2(1)(a), which provides that "the labelling and methods used must not be such as could mislead the purchaser to a material degree." This applies *inter alia* with respect to any misleading statements concerning the producer or the brand of the goods.

236. Moreover, Article 3(1) of Directive 2000/13 requires that labels must state among other things:

---

[84] EC SWS, para. 338. EC SOS, paras. 213-218.

[85] Exhibit EC-30.

(7) the name, or business name and address of the manufacturer or packager, or of a seller established within the Community ...

(8) particulars of the place of origin or provenance where failure to give such particulars might mislead the consumer as to the true origin or provenance of the foodstuff.

237. The requirement to state these particulars in the label limits the risk that the geographical indication may be mistaken for the brand name of the products.[86]

238. In addition, the use of registered geographical indications is subject to Directive 84/450 on misleading advertising.[87]

239. Finally, the use of registered geographical indications is subject to the unfair competition laws of the Member States, including both specific legislation and/or case law based on general tort law. One of the aspects typically covered by such laws is the imitation of labels and packaging in cases where it cannot be addressed as a trademark infringement.[88]

240. The requirement to use the registered geographical indications in accordance with the Directives on labeling and on misleading advertising and with the laws on unfair competition is equivalent to and, in practice, achieves the same effect as the requirements usually stipulated in the exceptions provided in the trademark laws of many Members with respect to the use of descriptive terms, including those used to indicate geographical origin. For example:

- Section 122(1)(b)(i) of Australia's Trade Marks Act 1995[89] provides that a person does not infringe a registered trademark when

  The person uses a sign in good faith to indicate the ... geographical origin ... of the goods ...

- Section 19(3) of Hong Kong's Trade Marks Ordinance[90] provides that:

  A registered trade mark is not infringed by—....(c) the use of signs which serve to designate the ... geographical origin ... of goods ... provided the use is in accordance with honest practices in industrial or commercial matters.

- Section 95 of New Zealand's Trade Marks Act 2002[91] provides that

  A person does not infringe a registered trademark if, in accordance with honest practices in industrial or commercial matters, the persons uses -.... c) a sign to indicate—(i) ... the geographical origin...

---

86 In *Sociedad Anónima Viña Santa Rita v. U.S. Dept. of the Treasury*, 193 F. Supp. 2d 6 (D.D.C 2001) (Exhibit EC-48), the ATF argued, and the court accepted, that:

... the fact that domestic products are required to indicate name and address of the bottler or packer minimizes the likelihood of confusion between a "Santa Rita Hills" wine and a product of Santa Rita in Chile or any other place.

87 Exhibit EC-31. Article 2(2) defines misleading advertising as:

any advertising which in any way, including presentation, deceives or is likely to deceive the person to whom it is addressed or whom it reaches and which, by reason of its deceptive nature, is likely to affect their economic behaviour or which, for those reasons, injures or is likely to injure a competitor.

88 See WIPO's *Introduction to Trademark Law & Practice, the Basic Concepts, a WIPO Training Manual*, Geneva 1993, 2nd Edition, pp. 97-100. (Exhibit EC-82).

89 Exhibit EC-7.

90 Exhibit EC-94.

91 Exhibit EC-80.

- Section 28 of Singapore's Trade Marks Act[92] provides that:

  ... a person does not infringe a registered trade mark when: ...(b) he uses a sign to indicate (i) the ... geographical origin ... of goods or services ... and such use is in accordance with honest practices in industrial or commercial matters.

- Section 34(1) of South Africa's Trade Marks Act[93] provides that:

  A registered trade mark is not infringed by ... (b) the use by any person of any *bona fide* description or indication of the ... geographical origin ... of his goods ... [p]rovided that the use contemplated in paragraph (b).... is consistent with fair practice.

- Section 30(2) of India's Trade Marks Act 1999[94] provides that:

  A registered trademark is not infringed where—(a) the use in relation to goods ... indicates the ... geographical origin ....

- Section 26(1) of Japan's Trademark Law[95] provides that:

  The effects of the trademark right shall not extend to the following trademarks ... (i) trademarks indicating, in a common way, the ... origin [of] of the designated goods or goods similar thereto ...

- Section 38 of Romania's Trade Marks Act[96] provides that:

  The owner of a mark may not request that other persons be prohibited from using in the course of trade ... (b) indications concerning ... geographical origin .... with the proviso that [they] are used in accordance with honest practice.

- Section 6 of Iceland's Trade Marks Act[97] provides that:

  Provided that the use is in accordance with honest business practice, the proprietor of a trade mark may not prohibit others from using in trade or business; .... 2. descriptions of ... [the] ... origin ... of the goods or services.

241. The above exceptions provide no requirements for using an indication of origin in co-existence with a registered trademark other than that such use must be "in good faith" or in accordance with "honest," "fair" or "proper" business or trade practices or "in a common way" and, therefore, would have to be deemed inconsistent with Article 17 if the complainants' narrow reading of that provision were upheld by the Panel.

242. The EC's own Trademark Directive[98] provides that:

---

[92] Exhibit EC-97.
[93] Exhibit EC-98.
[94] Exhibit EC-95.
[95] Exhibit EC-104.
[96] Exhibit EC-105.
[97] Exhibit EC-106.
[98] Cf. Article 6.1(b).

> The trademark shall not entitle the proprietor to prohibit a third party from using, in the course of trade, ... (b) indications concerning the... geographical origin...of goods ... provided he uses them in accordance with honest practices in industrial or commercial matters.

243. Similarly, Article 12(b) of the Community Trademark Regulation provides that:

> The trademark shall not entitle the proprietor to prohibit a third party from using, in the course of trade, ... (b) indications concerning the ... geographical origin ... of goods ... provided he uses them in accordance with honest practices in industrial or commercial matters.[99]

244. It follows that, even if trademark owners were permitted to enforce their rights under the Trademark Directive or the Community Trademark Directive with respect to the confusing use of a registered geographical indication, as demanded by the complainants, the trademark owners could still not prevent such use if it is "in accordance with honest practices in industrial or commercial matters."

Question 154

What, specifically, are "the legitimate interests of the owner of the trademark and of third parties" within the meaning of Article 17?

245. Trademark owners have an interest in preserving the economic "value" of their rights.[100] That value is a function of the recognition enjoyed by the trademark, which in turn is related to the length of use and the reputation/renown acquired as a result. A trademark which has never been used or which is virtually unknown has little intrinsic value and could be easily replaced without significant prejudice to the owner.

246. The "legitimate interest" of the trademark owner must not be equated with the full enjoyment of the exclusivity rights granted by Article 16.1. There are circumstances in which the exercise of those rights may not be "legitimate," having regard to the purposes for which trademark rights are granted and/or having regard to the legitimate interests of other parties.

247. Thus, in *Canada – Pharmaceutical Patents*, the Panel rejected an argument to the effect that the patent owner had a "legitimate interest" in "the full enjoyment of its patent rights." The Panel noted, among other things that[101]

> ... a definition equating "legitimate interests" with legal interests makes no sense at all when applied to the final phrase of Article 30 referring to the "legitimate interests" of third parties. Third parties are by definition parties who have no legal right at all in being able to perform the tasks excluded by Article 28 patent rights. An exceptions clause permitting them to take account of such third party legal interests would be permitting them to take account of nothing. And third, reading the third condition as further protection of legal rights would render it essentially redundant in light of the very similar protection of legal rights in the first condition of Article 30 ("limited exception").

248. The panel went on to conclude that:[102]

> To make sense of the term legitimate interests in this context, the term must be defined in the way that is often used in legal discourse—as a normative claim calling for protection of

[99] See the Judgement of the ECJ of 7 January 2004 in the Case C-100/02, *Gerolsteiner Brunnen GmbH & Co. v. Putsch GmbH*, which illustrates the application of Article 6(1)(b) of the Trademark Direcxtive with respect to geographical indications (Exhibit EC-107).

[100] Panel Report, *United States – Section 110(5)*, para. 6.227.

[101] Panel Report, *Canada – Pharmaceutical Products*, para. 7.68.

[102] Panel Report, *Canada – Pharmaceutical Products*, para. 7.69.

> interests that are justifiable in the sense that they are supported by relevant public policies or other social norms.

249. The "legitimate interests of third parties" include the commercial interest of other parties that produce or sell goods originating in a certain area to which a given reputation or characteristic is associated in using the term which designates that area in order to describe their products. As explained in the US Restatement of Unfair Competition[103]

> That a watch is Swiss, that a wine is from California, that maple syrup is from Vermont, or that a dress has been designed in New York or Paris, are facts in which consumers are interested and which sellers therefore wish to disclose in a prominent manner.

250. The "legitimate interests of third parties" include also the interest of consumers in being informed about the geographical origin and the product characteristics associated to that origin. As noted by WIPO,[104]

> The legal recognition and protection of indications of source and appellations of origin are in the general interest. They convey very important information to consumers on the geographical origin of goods and services and, indirectly, on their inherent quality and characteristics. Therefore, if properly used, geographical indications can help the public in its purchasing decisions and frequently exercise a strong influence thereon.

251. The fact that the use of a geographical indication may give rise to some degree of *likelihood* of confusion does not necessarily mean that it is incapable of performing this important informative function. In particular, where the finding of likelihood of confusion is based on the presumption provided in Article 16.1, or where the geographical indication enjoys more recognition than the trademark.

How can legitimate interests be taken into account under Article 17 where they conflict with other relevant interests?

252. Article 17 calls for a balancing of the different interests in conflict. Members enjoy a wide margin of discretion in making such a balancing. Indeed, all that is required by Article 17 is that Members "take account of" the different interests at issue. Furthermore, Article 17 puts on an equal level all the interests involved. In contrast, Articles 26.2 and 30 distinguish between the interests of the right holder, which must not be "unreasonably prejudiced," and the interests of third parties, which must simply be "taken into account."

253. In balancing the interests of the trademark owners and other parties in the case at hand, the following considerations are relevant and have been taken into account by the EC:

- trademarks are much easier to create than geographical indications. Trademarks can be acquired almost instantaneously, simply by an "intent to use" or by the mere lodging of an application with a registration system. In contrast, the creation of a geographical indication requires to establish first a "link" between the name and certain product characteristics, which may require years. Indeed, as is often the case in the EC, such link is the result of centuries of tradition. For this reason, the strict application of the first-in-time rule would privilege trademark owners and be inequitable to the holders of a geographical indication;

- trademarks are arbitrary, with the consequence that there is a virtually unlimited choice of trademarks. By choosing deliberately a geographical name as a trademark, an undertaking accepts the risk that the same sign may be used concurrently as a geographical indication. In contrast,

---

[103] *Restatement (Third) of Unfair Competition*, para. 14 cmt. D (1995). Cited in In *Sociedad Anónima Viña Santa Rita v. U.S. Dept. of the Treasury*, 193 F. Supp. 2d 6 (D.D.C 2001) (Exhibit EC-48).

[104] WIPO (Ed.) *Introduction to Intellectual Property, Theory and Practice*, Geneva 1997, para. 1.55. (Exhibit EC-109).

geographical indications are "necessary" in the sense that the range of names used to designate a certain geographical is limited *a priori* by well established usage. Right holders of geographical indications may not easily change the name given by the public to the geographical area where they are located. For that reason, it is much more difficult to find an alternative geographical indication than it is to find an alternative trademark;

- geographical indications are collective rights, the use of which is available to any person who produces or sells goods which have the origin designated by the geographical indication and meet the relevant specifications. It would be inequitable to deprive that collectivity from the right to use a geographical indication for the exclusive benefit of an individual trademark owner, who may or may not have contributed to the development of the geographical indication, simply because he happened to register that name first as a trademark;

- geographical indications serve to inform consumers that the product originates in a certain area and has certain characteristics linked to that origin. In contrast, trademarks only guarantee the identity of the undertaking that markets the product. Thus, in addition to having a commercial function, geographical indications serve a public interest, which deserves additional protection.

254. Having regard to the above considerations, EC law allows in principle the use of a geographical indication in co-existence with earlier trademarks. Nevertheless, in order to take account of the legitimate interests of the trademark owners, such use is subject to the following restrictions:

- first, even on the complainants' interpretation of Article 14(3) of Regulation 2081/92, that provision would prevent the registration of geographical indications in those circumstances where the trademark owner would suffer a more significant economic prejudice, because of the reputation acquired by the trademark. As mentioned, a trademark which has not been used, or which is hardly known, has little intrinsic value and could be easily replaced with a more distinctive sign. In those circumstances, co-existence does not cause an unreasonable prejudice to the trademark owner;

- second, again, even if the complainants' reading of Article 14(3) were correct and that provision did not prevent the registration of all geographical indications that give rise to a likelihood of confusion with an earlier trademark, it would remain that Article 14(3) would prevent the registration in those cases where the likelihood of confusion would be greater, because of the recognition enjoyed by the trademark;

- third, as explained above, the Directives on labelling and misleading advertising and the laws on unfair competition ensure that geographical indications are used in a fair and honest manner, thereby reducing the likelihood of confusion and the ensuing prejudice to the interests of the trademark owner.

Question 156

Why do the requirements in Article 17 differ from those in Articles 13, 26.2 and 30 of the TRIPS Agreement? How should their interpretation reflect those differences?

255. The differences between the conditions of Article 17 and those of the other provisions cited in the question reflect, among other things, the different function of each type of intellectual property right, the nature and the extent of the obligations imposed by the TRIPS Agreement with respect to each of them, and the previous practice of Members in granting exceptions.

256. More specifically, and without purporting to be exhaustive, the EC would point to the following differences:

- unlike patents, copyrights or the rights over industrial designs, trademark rights do not reward an invention or a creative effort. Rather, they are an instrument of fair competition;[105]

- unlike inventions, artistic works or industrial designs, trademarks do not have to be novel or original, but merely distinctive. Trademarks are relatively easy to conceive and to register. For the same reason, trademarks have little intrinsic value. Whatever value they may have is a function of their recognition by the public and is acquired through use;

- unlike patents, copyrights or industrial designs, which all have a limited duration, trademarks may have an indefinite validity, or at least may be renewed without any limitation. This makes it more necessary to allow for exceptions, so as to avoid permanent monopolies;

- the WIPO conventions do not guarantee the exclusivity of trademarks. The TRIPS Agreement is the first multilateral agreement to recognize such right. It is only natural that the participants wished to reserve for themselves a wider discretion in granting exceptions with respect to trademarks than with respect to other intellectual property rights where international harmonization was more advanced;

- prior to the TRIPS Agreement, the trademark laws of most Members provided relatively broad exceptions, including in particular with respect to the use of descriptive terms.[106] The wording used in other exceptions clauses would not have accommodated many of the existing "descriptive terms" exceptions.

257. Irrespective of the reasons, it is beyond dispute that the requirements of Article 17 are substantially less stringent than those of the other provisions cited in the question. Alone among all the exceptions clauses, Article 17 does not require that the exceptions "do not prejudice unreasonably" the legitimate interests of the right holder, but merely that those interests be taken into account. Likewise, alone among all the exceptions provisions, Article 17 does not require that the exceptions "do not unreasonably conflict with a normal exploitation of the patent."[107] These differences must be given meaning. It would be contrary to the drafters' intention and to basic rules of treaty interpretation if these differences were ignored and Article 17 were interpreted as imposing, in practice, the same requirements as the other exceptions clauses.

Question 159

May protection for designations of origin and geographical indications now be afforded in the EC <u>only</u> within the framework laid down by Regulation (EC) No. 2081/92?

258. No. Regulation 2081/92 and the other measures mentioned by the EC in its first submission apply cumulatively. The other measures afford protection to any indication of source, including those that qualify as designations of origin or geographical indications under Regulation 2081/92.

---

[105] WIPO has noted that, in the case of trademarks,

... the aspect of intellectual creations –although existent- is less prominent, but what counts here is that the object of industrial property typically consists of signs transmitting information to consumers, in particular as regards products and services offered on the market, and that protection is directed against unauthorized use of such signs which is likely to mislead consumers, and misleading practices in general.

WIPO (Ed.) *Introduction to Intellectual Property, Theory and Practice*, Geneva 1997, para. 1.9. (Exhibit EC-110).

[106] See the examples cited above in the response to Question No. 155.

[107] At the second meeting with the Panel, Australia seemed to argue that trademarks are not "exploited" but "used." Even so, this would not explain why Article 17 does not prescribe that the exceptions shall not "unreasonably conflict with the normal *use* of the trademark."

To what extent does the EC implement its obligations under Article 22.2 of the TRIPS Agreement through Regulation (EC) No. 2081/92 and to what extent through other measures (see EC first written submission, paras. 433 and 434)?

259. As explained, Regulation 2081/92 and the other measures apply cumulatively. The other measures afford protection to all indications of source, including all geographical indications as defined in Article 22.1 of the TRIPS Agreement. Regulation 2081/92 provides additional protection to those geographical indications that qualify as designations of origin or geographical indications within the meaning of that Regulation.

Are the other measures cited by the EC alone sufficient to fulfil its obligations under Article 22.2?

260. Yes. The EC refers to the responses provided by the EC and its Member States, as part of the review under Article 24.2 of the TRIPS Agreement, which have been submitted by the EC as Exhibit EC-29.

261. The EC understands that the complainants do not contest that the other measures cited by the EC are sufficient to fulfill the EC's obligations under Article 22.2. Indeed, they could hardly do so since the complainants purport to implement their obligations under Article 22.2 through the application of similar measures.

262. Instead, the United States appears to argue, mistakenly, that Regulation 2081/92 excludes the application of the other measures to designations of origin and geographical indications as defined in that Regulation.[108]

263. In turn, as far as the EC understands, Australia's claim under Article 22.2 is that the additional protection afforded to the registered geographical indications under Article 13(1) of Regulation 2081/92 (or the subsequent use thereof made by the holders of a geographical indication) could be an "act of unfair competition" within the meaning of Article 22.2, against which EC law provides no remedy, and not that the other measures cited by the EC are not sufficient to protect geographical indications that have not been registered under Regulation 2081/92.

Question 160

To what extent does the EC implement its obligations under Article 22.2 of the TRIPS Agreement through Regulation (EC) No. 2081/92 and to what extent through other measures?

264. See above the response to Question 159.

Does the EC believe that the complainants should prove a negative, i.e. that no legal means required under Article 22.2 are available? Can a respondent simply argue that other measures, outside the Panel's terms of reference, fulfil an obligation, without proof of how those other measures fulfil that obligation?

265. The complainants were well aware of the existence of the other measures cited by the EC in its first submission. Indeed, those measures had been identified in the response of the EC and its Member States in the review under Article 24.2 TRIPS among the means provided by them to comply with Article 22.2 TRIPS. Had the complainants been of the view that those measures are not sufficient to comply with Article 22.2, they could and should have mentioned them in their panel requests. A complaining party should not be allowed to shift the burden of proof to the respondent simply by asserting that the respondent provides no means to comply with Article 22.2, or by deliberately omitting to mention some of the means which the respondent has previously identified under the relevant WTO procedures among those implementing its obligations under Article 22.2.

[108] See EC SOS, para. 236.

266. In any event, assuming that the other measures in question were within the Panel's terms of reference, and assuming further that the complainants' mere assertion that the EC does not provide the necessary means to comply with Article 22.2 were sufficient to establish a *prima facie* case, the EC submits that the explanations provided by the EC in its previous submissions to the Panel, as well as in the responses of the EC and its Member States to the review under Article 24.2, which are part of the EC's submissions, would be sufficient to rebut that *prima facie* case.

267. It would then be for the complainants to make specific claims (or arguments) in order to show why the other measures identified by the EC are not consistent with Article 22.2, despite the explanations provided by the EC. The complainants, however, have not made any such claim or argument. The EC cannot be reasonably expected to identify and formulate each and every conceivable claim and arguments to the effect that its own measures fail to comply with Article 22.2 and then rebut them.

Question 163

The Panel takes note of Australia's and the EC's respective views on the applicability of Article 70.1 of the TRIPS Agreement to individual GI registrations (Australia's response to Panel question No. 90; EC rebuttal, para. 202). On 31 December 1995, at what stage of the procedure under the former Article 15 were the GIs later registered under Article 17? Did any individual GIs registered under Article 6 have an objection period that expired prior to 1 January 1996?

268. The draft regulation to register a first list of names under the simplified procedure under Article 17 was distributed to the Member States in the 7th meeting of the regulatory committee on 22 September 1995 and was discussed at every meeting until the end of 1995, the last of which was the 11th meeting (22 November 1995). The vote took place on 19 January 1996 and the matter was transferred to the Council later on.

269. Logically, if an objection procedure is provided for, then the decision-making process regarding the registration, including the consultation of the regulatory committee, cannot take place before the period for objections has expired. This is also the case under the normal procedure provided for in Article 6 and 7 of Regulation 2081/92. Accordingly, by the time the file was referred to the regulatory committee, the time at which an objection procedure should have been foreseen, had it indeed been necessary, had passed.

270. The EC notes that in its second oral statement, Australia continues to insist that the relevant point in time is the registration of the geographical indications under the simplified procedure.[109] However, Australia forgets that it has brought a claim under the national treatment provisions of the TRIPS Agreement. In Australia's submission, the EC has violated its national treatment obligations by <u>not providing </u>for a possibility for objections. Accordingly, the alleged violation stems not from the <u>act</u> of registering the indications in question, but from the <u>omission</u> to provide a right of objection. However, this omission clearly occurred before 1 January 1996, i.e. the date of application of the TRIPS Agreement to the EC.

271. Moreover, the EC would like to recall that as a matter of fact, no objection procedure applied under the simplified procedure regardless of whether EC residents or foreign residents were involved.[110] There was therefore no violation of national treatment. Accordingly, the question "at which time" the national treatment violation may have occurred has a rather speculative character.

272. No application under Article 6 of Regulation 2081/92 had a period of objections which expired prior to 1 January 1996.

---

[109] Australia's SOS, para. 78.

[110] EC FWS, para. 91 et seq.

Question 164

In what way are the objectives and principles set out in Articles 7 and 8 of the TRIPS Agreement, and the considerations recited in the first paragraph of its preamble, relevant to the interpretation of the provisions of that agreement at issue in this dispute?

273. Regulation 2081/92 protects products which have a special quality, reputation, or other characteristics attributable to their geographical origin. As can be seen from Article 2 of the Regulation 2081/29, these characteristics must be due to a particular geographical environment with its inherent natural and human facts, which also may include traditional knowledge, processes, and working methods. Whereas Regulation 2081/92 does not primarily focus on technological innovation as referred to in Article 7 of the TRIPS Agreement, the human factor may include some such elements. Overall, however, Article 7 seems to be of limited relevance for the present case.

274. As stated in the Preamble to Regulation 2081/92, the production of agricultural products and foodstuffs has a vital role for the Community economy. The protection of geographical indications in Regulation 2081/92 is important for the development of this sector by encouraging diversification into high-value production. Accordingly, Regulation 2081/92 is a measure which promotes the public interest in a sector of vital importance to the EC's socio-economic and technological development as referred to in Article 8.1 TRIPS Agreement, and which is consistent with the provisions of the Agreement.

275. The considerations recited in the first paragraph of the Preamble to the TRIPS Agreement are relevant for interpreting the provisions of the TRIPS Agreement in accordance with the customary rules of interpretation of international law.[111]

---

[111] Cf. also above, Response to Panel's Question No. 103, para. 31.

ANNEX B-8

REPLIES BY THE EUROPEAN COMMUNITIES TO QUESTIONS POSED BY AUSTRALIA FOLLOWING THE SECOND SUBSTANTIVE MEETING

Question 1

Can the EC provide any official statement predating its first written submission that expressly states that names of geographical areas located in WTO Members could be registered under regulation 2081?92 without satisfying its equivalence and reciprocity conditions?

1. The EC refers Australia to the EC's responses to the Panel's questions Nos. 16 and 95.

Question 2

The decision of the Court of First Instance in the "Canard" judgement held that Regulation 2081/92 "does not establish specific procedural safeguards for individuals," and for that reason a person who has made an objection against a proposed regulation "is not individually concerned by the contested [registration] within the meaning of the fourth paragraph of Article 230 of the EC Treaty.

In this light, can the EC say that a trademark holder will certainly be able to commence procedures under Article 230 of the EC Treaty to contest the registration of a GI under Regulation 2081/92.

2. The fourth paragraph of Article 230 of the EC treaty provides that

> Any natural or legal person may, under the same conditions, institute proceedings against a decision addressed to that person or against a decision which, although in the form of a regulation or a decision addressed to another person, is of direct and individual concern to the former

3. The decision to register a geographical indication under Regulation 2081/92 takes the form of a Council or Commission regulation. Accordingly, a trademark holder will be able to bring an action in annulment under Article 230 against the registration of a geographical indication if he can show that the registration, although in the form of a regulation, is of direct and individual concern to him.

4. According to well-established case law of the European Court of Justice[1],

> a provision which by virtue of its nature and scope is of legislative nature, may be of individual concern to natural or legal persons where it affects them by reason of certain attributes which are peculiar to them or by reason of circumstances in which they are differentiated from all other persons and by virtue of those factors distinguishes them individually just as in the case of the addressee of a decision …

5. <u>One</u> of the situations in which regulations have been found to be of individual concern to an economic operator is where the regulation has been adopted pursuant to a procedure that affords certain procedural safeguards specifically to that operator.[2] For example, the ECJ held in the *Timex* case that regulations imposing

---

[1] See e.g. Case T-215/00, *SCEA La Conqueste v. Commission,* [2001] ECR II-181, para. 34 (Exhibit COMP-12).

[2] This case law originated in Case 191/82 *EEC Seed Crushers' and Oil Processors' Federation (Fediol) v. Commission* [1983] ECR 2913, which concerned a complaint under the EC Basic Anti-subsidy Regulation.

anti-dumping measures may be challenged under Article 230 by the person who filed the complaint.[3] Subsequently, the ECJ has recognised standing to the investigated producers or exporters[4] and to their related importers[5], but not, in principle, to the independent importers.[6]

6. However, contrary to what appears to be Australia's understanding, the situation described in the above paragraph is not the only situation where an economic operator may be found to be individually concerned for the purposes of Article 230. In particular, the ECJ has held that a regulation may be of individual concern to an operator where it adversely affects that operator's *specific* rights. Thus, in the *Codorniu* case[7], the ECJ held that the applicant had standing to challenge a regulation concerning the use of a designation for sparkling wine ("crémant"), because as a result it was prevented from using a graphic mark which it had registered and used for a long time before the adoption of the contested regulation, so that it was distinguished from all the other economic operators.

7. In the *La Conqueste* case[8], the applicant was a producer of *canard à foie gras* of the area designated by the geographical indication who had objected to the specifications approved by the Commission. The applicant argued that the application was admissible on two different grounds: first, referring to the *Codorniu* judgement, because the measures affected adversely his specific rights; and second, referring to the *Timex* case law, because Regulation 2081/92 afforded him certain procedural guarantees.

8. The Court of First Instance rejected both arguments and held the application inadmissible. First, the court distinguished, on the facts, the situation of the applicant from the situation in *Codorniu*.[9] Second, the court held that, unlike the EC Basic Anti-dumping Regulation, Regulation 2081/92 does not establish specific procedural safeguards, at Community level, for individuals.[10]

9. The court's finding that Regulation 2081/92 does not establish specific procedural safeguards, at Community level, for individuals would prevent a trademark holder from invoking the *Timex* case law in order to establish that it is individually concerned. However, this does not mean necessarily that a trademark holder will never be able to show that it is individually concerned. In particular, a trademark holder could seek to rely on the *Codorniu* case law. Whether or not a trademark holder will be able to show that the registration of a give geographical indication affects adversely its "specific" substantive trademark rights will depend upon the factual circumstances of each case.

Question 3

Will a trademark holder, even if he or she can not show direct and individual concern and/or even if he or she does not commence proceedings within 2 months of the decision being made, certainly be able to take advantage of the procedure for obtaining a preliminary opinion under Article 234 of the EC Treaty to have the ECJ review the validity of the registration of a GI under regulation 2081/92.

10. The fact that an operator is not individually and directly concerned by a Community regulation is *never* an obstacle for raising the invalidity of that measure in accordance with the procedure provided in Article 234 of the EC Treaty.

---

[3] Case 264/82, *Timex v. Council and Commission* [1985] ECR 849 (Exhibit EC-112).

[4] See e.g. Case C-156/87 *Gestetner Holdings plc v. Council and Commission* [1990] ECR I-781.

[5] See e.g. Case T-164/94 *Ferchimex SA v. Council* [1995] ECR II-2681.

[6] See e.g. Case 205/87 *Nuova Cream Srl v. Commission* [1987] ECR 4427.

[7] Case C-309/89, *Codorniu v. Council* [1194] ECR I-1853 (Exhibit EC-111).

[8] Case T-215/00, *SCEA La Conqueste v. Commission,* [2001] ECR II-181 (Exhibit COMP-12).

[9] Ibid., para. 28.

[10] Ibid., para. 47. Australia's question misquotes the paragraph of the judgement which it cites by omitting the crucial words "at Community level."

11. Contrary to what has been said by the United States[11], there is no general rule to the effect that if a person could have brought a direct action under Article 230, but fails to do so within the two month time limit, it is precluded from raising the invalidity of the measure under Article 234.

12. The case law cited by the United States[12] applies only in very specific situations where the applicant is "fully aware of [the measure] and of the fact that it could *without any doubt* have challenged it under Article [230]."[13]

13. So far, the ECJ has found that these conditions were present in a case involving the beneficiary of a state aid[14] and a in a case concerning a related importer in an anti-dumping investigation.[15] In both cases, there was well-established and clear case law recognising generally the standing of any individual in the same procedural position as the applicant to bring a direct action under Article 230.[16]

14. In contrast, as explained in the response to the previous question, whether or not a trademark holder will have standing to bring an action under Article 230 against a regulation registering a geographical indication will depend on the appreciation of the particular circumstances of each case by the court, something which cannot be predicted in advance "without any doubt" by the trademark holder.

15. Moreover, the concern expressed by the United States is that a registered geographical indication which is not confusing *per se* may be used in a confusing manner after the two month time limit.[17] However, since in that case the circumstances that could, arguably, justify a finding of individual concern for the purposes of Article 230 would not have been present during the two month period, the applicant could not have been "fully aware" during that period that it could "without any doubt" bring a direct action.

16. As a final remark, it should be noted that the Court of Justice has stressed repeatedly the principle that all Community legal acts must be subject to effective judicial review:[18]

> 29. ... individuals are entitled to effective judicial protection of the rights they derive from the Community legal order, and the right to such protection is one of the general principles of law stemming from the constitutional traditions of the member States. That right has also been enshrined in Articles 6 and 13 of the [European Convention on Human Rights] ...
>
> 30. By Articles 230 EC and 241 EC, on the one hand, and by Articles 234, on the other, the Treaty has established a complete system of legal remedies and procedures designed to

---

[11] US SOS, para. 78.

[12] Ibid.

[13] Case C-188/92, *TWD Textielwerke Deggendorf v. Bundesrepublik Deutschland* [1994], ECR, I-833, point 24 [emphasis added] (Exhibit US-78).

[14] Case C-188/92, *TWD Textielwerke Deggendorf v. Bundesrepublik Deutschland* [1994], ECR, I-833 (Exhibit US-78).
The ECJ took pains to distinguish this case from a previous case (Case 216/82, *Universität Hamburg v. Hauptzollamt Hamburg-Kehrwieder*, [1983] ECR 2771). The ECJ noted that in that case the ECJ had declared the request for a preliminary ruling admissible on the grounds that (Id. at para. 23, emphasis added):
the rejection of the application by national authority was the only measure directly addressed to the person concerned of which it had been necessarily informed in good time and *which it could challenge in the courts without encountering any difficulty in demonstrating its interest in bringing proceedings.*

[15] Case C-239/99, *Nachi Europe GmbH v. Hauptzollamt Krefeld* [2001] ECR I-1197, para. 37 (Exhibit US-78).
The court emphasised that the applicant "could *undoubtedly* have sought its annulment under Article 230 of the EC Treaty" (Id., para. 370) [emphasis added].

[16] As regards the standing of a complainant in an anti-dumping proceeding, see above the Timex case. As regards the standing of the beneficiary of a state aid, see Case C-730/79 *Philip Morris v. Commission* [1980] ECR 2671.

[17] US SOS, para. 78.

[18] Judgement of the European Court of Justice of 1 April 2004, Case C-263/02, *Commission v. Jégo-Quéré & Cie. SA* [not published yet in the ECR] (Exhibit EC-113).

ensure review of the legality of acts of the institutions and has entrusted such review to the Community Courts. Under that system, where natural or legal persons cannot, by reason of the conditions for admissibility laid down in the fourth paragraph of Article 230 EC, directly challenge Community measures of general application, they are able, depending on the case, either indirectly to plead the invalidity of such acts before the Community Courts under Article 241 EC or to do so before the national courts and ask them, since they have no jurisdiction themselves to declare those measures invalid, to make a reference to the Court of Justice for a preliminary ruling on validity....

31. Thus it is for the Member States to establish a system of legal remedies and procedures which ensure respect for the right to effective judicial protection ....

32. In that context, in accordance with the principle of sincere cooperation laid down in Article 10 EC, national courts are required, so far as possible, to interpret and apply national procedural rules governing the exercise of rights of action in a way that enables natural and legal persons to challenge before the courts the legality of any decision or other national measure relative to the application to them of a Community act of general application, by pleading the invalidity of such an act.

ANNEX B-9

COMMENTS OF THE EUROPEAN COMMUNITIES TO AUSTRALIA'S AND THE UNITED STATES' REPLIES TO QUESTIONS POSED BY THE PANEL FOLLOWING THE SECOND SUBSTANTIVE MEETING

(2 September 2004)

1. In its present submission, the EC provides its comments on the responses of the complainants to the Questions of the Panel after the second substantive meeting. Given the advanced stage of the proceedings, the EC will, in the present submission, focus on arguments which are made for the first time in the responses of the complainants. The fact that the EC does not comment on a particular response does not imply that the EC agrees with the response. To the extent that the complainants reiterate arguments to which the EC has already responded in earlier submissions, the EC refers to its earlier submissions.

Question 101

2. As the EC has already stated in its response to Question 101, the EC considers that the quadrant provided in the third party submission of Chinese Taipei is not pertinent, since Regulation 2081/92 does not involve any discrimination on the basis of nationality.

3. In their responses, the complainants are relying on this quadrant to demonstrate that the EC measure involves discrimination between nationals. However, the arguments of the complainants have no basis in the text of Regulation 2081/92, and in addition are logically inconsistent. For ease of reference, the table in question is reproduced below:

GI: EC National: EC 1	GI: Non-EC National: EC 3
2 GI: EC National: Non-EC	4 GI: Non-EC National: Non-EC

4. An examination of whether the EC measure violates the national treatment obligation of Article 3.1 TRIPS would require a comparison of the treatment it accords to domestic nationals and to foreign nationals. Logically, the comparison of treatment should therefore take place between quadrants 1 and 2, and between quadrants 3 and 4. In the case of Regulation 2081/92, this examination would confirm that there is no difference in treatment on the grounds of nationality. This is why the EC has submitted that the only relevant comparison is between the treatment accorded to domestic geographical indications, and to foreign geographical indications.[1]

5. Interestingly, in their responses, the complainants do not allege any difference in treatment between quadrants 1 and 2, or between quadrants 3 and 4. The complainants do not attempt to show, either, that there is any difference between quadrants 1 and 3, or between quadrants 2 and 4. Rather, they argue that the comparison

[1] EC Response to Panel's Question No. 101, para. 23.

should take place between quadrants 1 and 4.[2] In support of this view, the United States claims that quadrant 1 is the sole "benchmark," against which both quadrants 2 and 4 should be measured. As for quadrant 3, the US argues that "it does not matter whether some EC nationals (...) are also treated less favourably than the EC nationals in quadrant 1."[3]

6. In the view of the EC, these arguments simply disregard the content of Regulation 2081/92. The EC has pointed out repeatedly that Regulation 2081/92 treats EC and foreign nationals exactly alike as regards the protection of geographical indications relating to areas in the EC. Similarly, the EC has pointed out that Regulation 2081/92 treats EC and foreign nationals exactly alike as regards the registration of geographical indications relating to areas outside the EC. The complainants cannot respond to this by arguing that the treatment accorded by Regulation 2081/92 in quadrants 2 and 3 should simply be ignored. Such an approach to the interpretation of Regulation 2081/92 would clearly be incompatible with Article 11 of the DSU, which requires an objective assessment of the facts.

7. The EC also finds the complainants' arguments logically inconsistent. If the complainants accept that the quadrant prepared by Chinese Taipei constitutes a correct description of the possible constellations for comparison of favourable treatment of nationals and goods in respect of geographical indications, then the complainants must accept this analytical tool in its entirety. They cannot simply ignore half of the possible constellations and base their argument purely on a comparison of those constellations which suit them. Such a selective reasoning does not do justice to the national treatment obligations of the TRIPS Agreement.

Question 102

8. In its response to Question No. 102, the United States argues that "it is not critical for the Panel to make a factual assumption that all persons producing GI products in a country are nationals of that country." The United States goes on to argue that "[i]ndeed, it is undisputed that the EC GI Regulation on its face provides for different treatment of persons depending on which quadrant set out in response to question 101 they fall in."[4]

9. Already these premises are false. The EC does not see how the US can submit that the Panel should make a finding that Regulation 2081/92 involves discrimination between nationals and at the same time claim that the Panel need not come to any conclusion on whether in fact there is any link between nationality and the protection of geographical indications under Regulation 2081/92.

10. The EC is also astonished that the US would claim that "it is undisputed" that Regulation 2081/92 provides for different treatment of persons "depending on which quadrant set out in response to question 101 they fall in." As the EC has repeatedly confirmed, Regulation 2081/92 treats EC and foreign nationals exactly alike as regards the protection of geographical indications relating to areas in the EC. Similarly, the EC has pointed out that Regulation 2081/92 treats EC and foreign nationals exactly alike as regards the registration of geographical indications relating to areas outside the EC. Accordingly, the treatment accorded by quadrant 1 is the same as that accorded by quadrant 2, and the treatment accorded by quadrant 3 is the same as that accorded by quadrant 4.

11. In its further attempts to show that there is discrimination on the basis of nationality, the United states argues that "in order to produce agricultural foodstuffs in accordance with the product specifications for a protected name, persons "will be established in that area" and "will have to set up a legal person under the laws

[2] US Response to Panel's Question No. 101, para. 2; Australia's Response to Panel's Question No. 101, para. 2.

[3] US Response to Panel's Question No. 101, para. 4.

[4] US Response to Panel's Question No. 102, para. 9.

of the country in which they are established."[5] The US goes on to argue that "it will generally follow that those established [...] are nationals of that Member" and that this "also generally follows as a practical matter."[6]

12. In the view of the EC, these US arguments are mere speculation without any supporting proof. Regulation 2081/92 does not require any form of establishment, nor does it require the setting up of legal persons. Similarly, even where a natural or legal person is resident or established in a particular country, this does not mean it becomes a national of that country.

13. The EC notes also that the United States has not provided the Panel with any information as to what legal persons it considers to be its nationals. In this context, the EC would refer to the definition of "enterprises of a Party" in the North American Free Trade Agreement (NAFTA), which reads as follows: "enterprise of a Party means an enterprise constituted or organized under the law of a Party."[7] It is interesting to note that NAFTA, to which the US is a party, does not in fact define the nationality of enterprises on the basis of establishment.[8]

14. It seems to the EC that the complainants are attempting to impose a definition of nationality on the EC which has no basis in the EC measure in question, does not reflect the national treatment provisions of the TRIPS Agreement, and runs counter to international practice.

15. The EC notes that the United States also points out that "US agricultural land is held almost exclusively by US nationals."[9] The EC does not consider this statement relevant for the present case, nor does it wish to speculate on why the percentage of foreign ownership in the US might be so low. The EC notes also that the United States has not shown that the same is also true for EC agricultural land. Finally, the United States has not shown that there is no foreign ownership in the food-producing sector, which is equally concerned by Regulation 2081/92.

Question 103

16. In its response to the Panel's questions, the EC has emphasized that Article 3.1 TRIPS requires that the conditions for the acquisition of intellectual property rights are modified to the detriment of foreign nationals.[10] The EC has also shown that the interpretation of TRIPS national treatment is a complex question, which cannot simply be resolved by transposing the jurisprudence under Article III:4 GATT to the TRIPS Agreement.[11]

17. In their response, the complainants make very little effort to interpret the specific terms of Article 3.1 TRIPS Agreement. Rather, the United States repeats its argument according to which "there is a close connection between geographical indications, geographic regions, and the persons established in those regions."[12] The EC is unsure what exactly the United States means by "close connection," and what is the relevance of this "close connection" for the purposes of TRIPS national treatment.

18. Whatever the precise meaning the US attaches to these terms, it seems to the EC that with the same justification it could be argued that there is a "close connection" between the place where any product is produced and the persons who produce it. However, the EC does not think that this can mean that any person

---

[5] US Response to Panel's Question No. 102, para. 10.

[6] US Response to Panel's Question No. 102, para. 12.

[7] NAFTA Article 201.1 (Exhibit EC-111).

[8] Another relevant example would be Article XXVIII (m) (i) of the GATT, which defines a "juridical person of another Member "as a juridical person which is "constituted or otherwise organized under the law of that other Member, and is engaged in substantive business operations in the territory of that Member or any other Member."

[9] US Response to Panel's Question No. 102, para. 12.

[10] EC Response to Panel's Question No. 113, para. 63.

[11] EC Response to Panel's Question No. 103, para. 27.

[12] US Response to Panel's Question No. 103, para. 16 (3).

producing a product must therefore necessarily have the nationality of the place where the product is produced. Otherwise, any discrimination on the basis of the origin of a product would also be discrimination on the basis of nationality.

19. In its response, the United States has attempted to dismiss the examples of foreign involvement by characterizing them as examples of "EC nationals with some non-EC connections." This response misses the point of the EC's examples. First, the EC's examples show clearly that Regulation 2081/92 contains no legal obstacle to foreign nationals taking advantage of EC geographical indications. Second, that they may do so, "as a practical matter" and for reasons unrelated to Regulation 2081/92, by setting up a legal entity under EC law or by acquiring such an entity, does not show that Regulation 2081/92 involves discrimination on the basis of nationality. Finally, the EC finds it misleading to characterize cases where a US multinational acquires 100% of an EC producer of protected products as a case of an EC national with "some non-EC connections."

20. As regards the relevance of Article XX GATT, the complainants argue that this provision is not applicable in the context of the TRIPS Agreement, and that the non-inclusion of a similar provision in the TRIPS Agreement is deliberate.[13] However, the complainants fail to acknowledge that the limitation of TRIPS national treatment to nationals is equally deliberate. Moreover, the fact that the TRIPS Agreement contains not provision corresponding to Article XX GATT must be seen before the background that the TRIPS Agreement, and TRIPS national treatment in particular, is concerned primarily with nationals, not with the treatment of goods. The complainant's expansive interpretation of TRIPS national treatment has the effect of rendering ineffective defenses which would otherwise be available under Article XX GATT. The EC considers such an interpretation incompatible with the principles of a harmonious interpretation of the WTO Agreements.

Question 104

21. In its response to Question No 104, the United States persists in arguing that the EC is a "separate customs territory" within the meaning of footnote 1 to Article 1.3 of the TRIPS Agreement.

22. In support of its argument, the US is referring to Article XII:1 of the WTO Agreement, according to which "any State or separate customs territory possessing full autonomy in the conduct of its external commercial relations" may accede to this Agreement. In the submission of the United States, this provision proves that there are two categories of WTO Members, namely States and separate customs territories; therefore, in the view of the United States, since the EC is not a State, it must be a separate customs territory.[14]

23. This view is incorrect. Article XII:1 WTO Agreement does not apply to the EC. Rather, as the United States notes itself, the EC became an Original Member of the WTO under Article XI:1 WTO Agreement, which provides for the Membership of the "contracting parties to the GATT 1947 [...] and the European Communities."[15] In other words, the WTO Agreement refers to the EC neither as a state nor as a separate customs territory, but instead refers to it individually as a specific case.

24. The US has attempted to explain this drafting by arguing that "the EC could be identified by name as the sole original WTO Member that was not a GATT contracting party."[16] However, the US fails to explain why such a specific reference to the EC was then not made in footnote 1 to Article 1.3 of the TRIPS Agreement, if indeed the intention had been that this footnote should apply to the EC.

25. In fact, it is noted that there are also other provisions which refer specifically to the EC. For instance, Article IX:1 WTO Agreement defines the voting rights of the European Communities. This shows that where a specific provision was necessary to take account of the specific nature of the EC, a specific provision was

[13] US Response to Panel's Question No. 103, para. 18; Australia's Response to Panel's Question No. 103, paras. 13-14.

[14] US Response to Panels' Question No. 104, paras. 24-27.

[15] US Response to Panel's Question No. 104, para. 28.

[16] EC Response to Panel's Question No. 104, para. 28.

included. The fact that no such provision concerning the EC was included in the TRIPS Agreement means that the general provisions applicable to all Members should apply to the EC.

26. It should also be noted that the US interpretation would deprive the word "separate" in the expression "separate customs territory" of its useful purpose. As the US has acknowledged, "separateness" is an intrinsic feature of a "customs territory."[17] However, by arguing that the EC is a "separate customs territory Member of the WTO," the US is effectively removing the word "separate" from the definition in footnote 1. In fact, if the US interpretation were correct, the United States, Australia, or in fact all other WTO would also have to be considered a "separate customs territory Member of the WTO."

27. The US has also argued that footnote 1 should apply to the EC because the EC "has no nationals."[18] As the EC has already explained in response to Panel's Question No. 105, this is patently wrong. Moreover, as the EC has also explained, the fact that the definition of nationality for legal persons is a complex question does not mean that the EC "has no nationals." In this context, it is also useful to refer to Brownlie's International Law, which fully confirms the EC's view:[19]

> The attribution of legal persons (personnes morales) to a particular state for the purpose of applying a rule of domestic or international law is commonly based upon the concept of nationality. The borrowing of a concept developed in relation to individuals as awkward in some respects but is now well established. A major point of distinction is the absence of legislative provisions in municipal law systems which create a national status for corporations: domestic nationality laws do not concern themselves with corporations. The consequences of this are twofold. First, the nationality must be derived either from the fact of incorporation, i.e. creation as a legal person, within the given system of domestic law, or from various links including the centre of administration (siège social) and the national basis of ownership and control. Secondly, the content of the nationality tends to depend on the context of the particular rule of law involved: nationality appears more as a functional attribution or tracing and less as a formal and general status of the kind relating to individuals.

28. The US has also referred to the drafting history of the TRIPS Agreement. In particular, the United States has noted that an earlier version of footnote one referred specifically to Hong Kong.[20] This footnote, which was contained in the Brussels draft of the TRIPS Agreement, read as follows:[21]

> When the term "national" is used in this Agreement, it shall be deemed, in the case of Hong Kong, to mean persons, natural or legal, who are domiciled or who have a real and effective industrial or commercial establishment in Hong Kong.

29. The only significant different between this version and the final version of footnote 1 is that the reference to "Hong Kong" has been replaced by a reference to a "separate customs territory Member of the WTO." In other words, the specific reference to Hong Kong was replaced by a generic reference to the category of Member to which Hong Kong belongs. The drafting history therefore confirms the EC's submission that footnote 1 was intended to cover cases of territories such as for instance Hong Kong or Macao, but not the EC.

30. In addition, the US also refers to an "Informal Note by the Secretariat" dated 7 December 1992. Unfortunately, the US does not provide a copy of this "Informal Note," which is not available to the EC, as an Exhibit. Accordingly, the EC cannot comment on the US arguments in this respect. The EC requests the United States to provide a copy of the informal note to the Panel and the other Parties. Moreover, the EC should be

---

[17] US Response to Panel's Question No. 104, para. 23.

[18] US Response to Panel's Question No. 104, para. 33.

[19] Ian Brownlie, *Principles of Public International Law*, 5th edition (1998), p. 425–426 (Exhibit EC-112). Emphases added.

[20] US Response to Panel's Question No. 104, para 34.

[21] Cf. Daniel Gervais, *The TRIPS Agreement: Drafting History and Analysis*, 2nd edition (2003), para. 2.15.

given an occasion to comment on the note once it has been provided by the United States. As long as the EC has not had an occasion to comment, the Panel should not take into account the arguments made by the US in respect of the informal note of 7 December 1992.

31. Australia, for its part, has referred to the fact that competence for the matters covered by the TRIPS Agreement is shared between the EC and its Member States, and has argued that for this reason, "there may be occasions in relation to matters covered by the TRIPS Agreement when the customs territories of its Member States may be distinct from the customs territory of the EC itself."[22] This is entirely wrong. The fact that competence for matters falling under the TRIPS Agreement is shared between the EC and its Member States is due to the fact that the TRIPS Agreement also concerns the harmonisation of intellectual property law.[23] The fact that certain areas of intellectual property law may not be harmonised within the EC has nothing to do with the customs territory of the EC. The EC has exclusive competence for trade in goods, and it has only one customs territory; this also applies for the purposes of the TRIPS Agreement.[24]

Question 108

32. The EC fails to see the relevance of the discussion of the ECJ's case law concerning Article 13(1) of Regulation 2081/92 included in Australia's response to this question, given that Australia confirms that it is not making any claim under GATT Article III:4 to the effect that Article 13(1) provides less favourable treatment to imported products.[25]

33. In view of the above, the EC does not consider it necessary to address all the errors made in Australia's response. The EC would like, nevertheless, to correct Australia's mistaken reading of the findings of the ECJ in the Case C-66/00, *Dante Bigi*[26] (which Australia calls the "Parmesan judgement").

34. Australia says that the use of the word "parmesan" is banned in the EC "on the basis that the ECJ found 'it is far from clear that the designation 'Parmesan' has become generic'" in that case.[27] This is incorrect. The question whether the term "parmesan" is generic was not before the ECJ and was not decided in that case. The Italian court had raised a number of questions regarding the interpretation of Regulation 2081/92, but not the question whether "parmesan" was a generic term. The German Government, which intervened as a third party, raised the preliminary objection that the reference was not admissible because the questions put by the Italian court were not relevant, given that in any event "parmesan" was a generic term which could not be protected under Regulation 2081/92.

35. The ECJ first recalled that, in principle, it is for the national courts to decide whether the reference to the ECJ is necessary:[28]

> It is settled case-law that, in the context of the cooperation between the Court of Justice and the national courts established by Article 234 EC, it is solely for the national court before which the dispute has been brought, and which must assume responsibility for the subsequent judicial decision, to determine in the light of the particular circumstances of the case both the need for a preliminary ruling in order to enable it to deliver judgment and the relevance of the questions which it submits to the Court. Consequently, where the questions submitted by the

22 Australia's Response to Panel's Question No. 104, para. 16.

23 See Opinion 1/94, *Accession to the WTO*, [1994] ECR I-5389, para. 58 (Exhibit Aus-13).

24 This is confirmed in Opinion 1/94, *Accession to the WTO*, [1994] ECR I-5389, para. 55 (Exhibit Aus-13), where the Court of Justice confirmed that the provisions of the TRIPS Agreement on the enforcement of intellectual property rights at the border, which are carried out by the customs authorities, fall under exclusive Community competence for the commercial policy.

25 Australia's Response to Panel's Question No. 18, para. 27.

26 Exhibit AUS-16.

27 Australia's Response to Panel's Question No. 18, para. 26.

28 Exhibit AUS-16, para. 18.

> national court concern the interpretation of Community law, the Court of Justice is, in principle, bound to give a ruling (see, for example, Case C-415/93 Bosman [1995] ECR I-4921, paragraph 59).

36. The ECJ then went on to recall that, in exceptional cases, the ECJ may refuse to rule on a question referred by a national court where it is obvious that the question is unrelated to the dispute before that court:[29]

> However, the Court has also stated that, in exceptional circumstances, it can examine the conditions in which the case was referred to it by the national court, in order to assess whether it has jurisdiction. The Court may refuse to rule on a question referred for a preliminary ruling by a national court only where it is quite obvious that the interpretation of Community law that is sought bears no relation to the actual facts of the main action or its purpose, where the problem is hypothetical, or where the Court does not have before it the factual or legal material necessary to give a useful answer to the questions submitted to it (see, for example, Case C-390/99 Canal Satélite Digital [2002] I-607, paragraph 19).

37. The German Government had argued that the questions raised by the Italian court were irrelevant because "parmesan" was in any event generic, with the consequence that Regulation 2081/92 was inapplicable. The ECJ, nevertheless, concluded that it was far from clear that "parmesan" was generic and, therefore, the questions raised by the Italian court were not so obviously irrelevant as to be inadmissible:[30]

> However, in the present case it is far from clear that the designation parmesan has become generic. It is contended by all the governments which have submitted written observations in this case, apart from the German Government and, to a certain extent, the Austrian Government, and by the Commission that the French designation parmesan is the correct translation of the PDO Parmigiano Reggiano.
>
> Against that background it cannot be argued that it is clear that the questions raised by the referring court are covered by one of the situations listed in the case-law cited at paragraph 19 of this judgment. It follows that the reference for a preliminary ruling is admissible.

38. In sum, in the *Dante Bigi* Case, the ECJ was not asked to rule, and did not rule, on the question whether the term "parmesan" is generic. The ECJ considered that question only in order to resolve a preliminary procedural objection to the effect that *other* questions raised by the Italian court were obviously irrelevant and inadmissible.

39. As noted by Australia[31], the EC Commission is of the view that "parmesan" is not a generic term. Germany, however, takes a different view. For that reason, the EC Commission has brought infringement proceedings under Article 226 of the EC Treaty against Germany. It will be for the ECJ, in the context of those proceedings, to decide whether or not "parmesan" is a generic term. The EC fails to see what is so intrinsically objectionable about the fact that the application of Article 13(1) of Regulation 2081/92 to a particular set of facts may give rise to doubts and that different interested parties may take different views, with the consequence that it is necessary for the courts to resolve the disagreement. Or is it that in Australia the federal government and the states never disagree about the interpretation of federal law?

40. Contrary to what Australia says at paragraph 23, Article 13(1) of Regulation 2081/92 does not prejudge the question of whether "the owner of a registered trademark would be able to prevent confusingly similar or identical use of a sign for similar or identical goods." Australia confuses two different issues: the scope of the *negative* right of the holders of a registered geographical indication to prevent certain uses, which

---

[29] Exhibit AUS-16, para. 19.

[30] Exhibit AUS-16, paras. 20-21.

[31] Australia's Response to Panel's Question No. 108, para. 21.

is defined in Article 13(1), and the scope of the *positive* right to use a registered geographical indication, which is circumscribed to the registered sign (see below the comments to Australia's response to Question 137).

41. Australia concludes this response by saying that:

> the uncertainties created by the practical operation of Article 13.1 of Regulation No. 2081/92 and its application in situations involving generic terms partially inform Australia's claims concerning Articles 22.2 and Paris Articles 10*bis*(1) and 10*ter*(1) in respect of the registration of an EC-defined GI. Australia has not been able to identify any means within the EC's legal order why which a legitimately interested person –whether natural or legal, or a national of the EC or of another WTO Member—is assured of access to a court empowered to consider substantively an act of unfair competition contrary to honest practices in industrial or commercial matters, including in international trade, in respect of the registration of an EC-defined GI.

42. The EC would note, first of all, that the above passage appears to contradict Australia's response to Question No. 161, where Australia explains that the "EC measure" is inconsistent with Paris Article 10*bis*(1), because it "diminishes the legal protection of trademarks." The EC fails to see the connection between Australia's concerns about the use of generic terms and the protection of trademarks.

43. Second, the EC has provided a thorough rebuttal to Australia's suggestion to the effect that the registration of a name which is not generic in the EC but may be generic in "international trade" may be an "act of unfair competition."[32] Australia has not responded to the EC's arguments. Instead, at the second meeting with the Panel, Australia denied that it was making such a claim [33]

> Australia has not said that registration of a term as an EC-defined GI in territory A could be deemed misleading simply because the term has become generic in territory B

44. Australia then reformulated its claim as follows:[34]

> What is clear, however, is that the EC has an obligation to provide the legal means by which interested parties can seek to test such issues in relation to the registration of an EC-defined GI.

45. This amounts to saying that a Member may not adopt any legislation or regulations that specify which types of uses may or may not be deemed an "act of unfair competition," but instead must leave exclusively to the courts to define what constitutes an "act of unfair competition." The EC disagrees with that proposition, which is manifestly contrary to the fundamental principle enshrined in the last sentence of Article 1.1 TRIPS. Article 22.2 does not impose an obligation to provide means to "test" any conceivable allegations of "unfair competition," no matter how frivolous. Rather, Article 22.2 requires to provide the means to prevent uses that constitute genuine "acts of unfair competition." If a use is not an "act of unfair competition," there is no obligation to provide any means to prevent it. Accordingly, in order to establish a violation of Article 22.2, the plaintiff must establish, first, that a certain type of use would constitute an "act of unfair competition" within the meaning of Paris Article 10*bis*(1) and, second, that the respondent does not provide the necessary means to prevent that type of uses.

46. Finally, the EC has clarified repeatedly that, in any event, Regulation 2081/92 does not exclude the application of the Directives on labelling and misleading advertising and of the laws on unfair competition of the Member States with respect to the use of registered geographical indications. Australia seems to concede

---

[32] EC SWS, paras. 381-393.

[33] Australia's SOS, para. 82.

[34] Australia's SOS, para. 85.

that those Directives and laws are sufficient to comply with TRIPS Article 22.2 and Paris Articles 10*bis*(1) and 10*ter*(1) with respect to the use of non-registered geographical indications. At the very least, Australia has submitted no argument or evidence to the effect that the provisions of those Directives and laws in question are not sufficient *per se* to comply with those provisions. Since, contrary to Australia's mistaken assumption, the same Directives and laws apply also with respect to the use of registered geographical indications, Australia's concerns are unfounded. Yet, apparently, Australia takes the view that, in respect of registered geographical indications, the EC should replace those Directives and laws by an EC Regulation. However, there is no obligation under the TRIPS Agreement to provide the required protection at any given territorial level. Australia's claims represent an unfounded and unacceptable attempt to interfere with the constitutional allocation of powers between the EC and its Member States.

Question 112

47. The EC notes that in its response to the Panel's Question, the United States appears to argue that Article 12(3) contains a legal obligation towards the third country concerned.[35] As the EC has explained in its response, this is not the case.[36] The EC notes that its view is shared by Australia, which offers an interpretation contrary to that of the United States.[37]

Question 120

48. In its response to the Panel's Question No. 120, the United States argues that the requirement to indicate the country of origin for homonymous geographical indications "is not simply a labelling cost issue," but that the labelling requirement "is in the nature of a qualifier that detracts from the value of the GI," implying that the foreign GI "is something other than a 'true' GI."[38]

49. At the outset, the EC notes that these arguments of the United States are contradictory with those of Australia, which has clearly stated that it does not allege that Article 12(2) of Regulation 2081/92 entails less favourable treatment other than with regard to labelling costs.[39]

50. In addition, the US response is without any basis in Regulation 2081/92. Article 12(2) of the Regulation requires simply that in the case of two homonymous names from the EC and from a third country, the country of origin be indicated for the name which is registered later. As the EC has already explained, the objective of this rule is to inform the consumer about the true origin of the product concerned.[40] In the case of two homonymous geographical indications, this is an entirely legitimate policy objective. The truthful indication of the country of origin does not in any way detract from the value of the geographical indication, nor is there any implication in the requirement of Article 12(2) that the geographical indication to which the requirement is applied is somehow "of a different stature" or "something other than a true GI."

51. Finally, the US is also incorrect to argue "the EC-based GI will be known purely by that GI, while the non-EC product's homonymous GI will be qualified by a country of origin."[41] As the EC has already explained repeatedly, the labelling requirement of Article 12(2) will apply to whichever of the names is registered later, regardless of whether this is the EC or the foreign name.[42]

---

[35] US Response to Panel's Question No. 112, para. 45.

[36] EC Response to Panel's Question No. 112, para. 61.

[37] Australia's Response to Panel's Question No. 112, para. 33 – 34.

[38] US Response to Panel's Question No. 120, para. 47.

[39] Australia's Response to Panel's Question No. 52.

[40] See EC Response to Panel's Question No. 54, para. 126.

[41] US Response to Panel's Question No. 120, para. 47.

[42] See most recently EC SOS, para. 145.

Question 123

52. In its response to Question No. 123, the United States persists in its argument that Article 12(2) of Regulation 2081/92 is "not a general country of origin marking requirement," but is "above and beyond any other general country of origin marking requirement that may apply to all agricultural products and foodstuffs."[43]

53. As the EC has already explained in its responses, there is simply no basis for arguing that Article IX GATT applies only to "general" origin marking requirements, but not to an origin marking requirement such as the one contained in Article 12(2).[44]

54. The full absurdity of the US argument becomes apparent when considering once again the United States' own practice as regards origin marking. Under US law, "every article of foreign origin [...] imported into the United States shall be marked in a conspicuous place as legibly, indelibly, and permanently as the nature of the article will permit in such manner as to indicated to an ultimate purchaser in the United States the English name of the country of origin of the article."[45]

55. It is fair to say that this origin marking requirement of the United States for imported products is, if anything, more restrictive and burdensome than the EC requirement contained in Article 12(2) of Regulation 2081/92. The fact that the United States, like Australia, applies this discriminatory country of origin marking to all products rather then just to some can hardly be a mitigating factor. It seems therefore that if the United States were right, and Article 12(2) constituted a violation of national treatment obligations, then the origin marking requirements of the United States and Australia are also in violation of national treatment obligations.

56. The United States has also claimed that the EC has not argued that "any existing origin marking requirements in the EC" would meet the requirement of Article 12(2) of Regulation 2081/92.[46] This argument is besides the point. Since the EC does not have country of origin marking requirements, requirements "in the EC" are obviously not relevant. However, as the EC has already said, it is very well possible that marks of origin affixed pursuant to the requirements of other countries, such as the United States, might fulfil the requirements of Article 12(2) of the Regulation.[47]

57. In any event, the main point of the EC is that the United States has for many years, presumably because it considered that national treatment obligations do not apply to country of origin marking requirements, applied discriminatory marking requirements. The US claim is therefore in stark contrast with the United States' own practice, and the Panel should not disregard this fact in evaluating the US claim.

58. In addition, the EC would also draw the attention of the Panel to the logical conclusion of the United States argument: if really Article IX:1 GATT covered only "general," but not product-specific marking requirements, the EC could easily remedy any eventual finding of a violation by introducing a general origin marking requirement similar to the one of the United States and Australia. In other words, Article IX:1 GATT would encourage the adoption of more rather than less restrictive requirements. This is hardly an interpretation in line with the objectives of the GATT.

[43] US Response to Panel's Question No. 123, para. 48.

[44] EC Response to Panel's Question No. 124, para. 98.

[45] 19 US 1304 (a) (Exhibit EC-113). Exhibit EC-66, which the EC provided earlier, contains only an indirect reference to this provision; for ease of reference of the Panel, the EC also provides the immediate source.

[46] US Response to Panel's Question No. 122, para. 47; US Response to Panel's Question No. 123, para. 48.

[47] EC Response to Panel's Question No. 120, para. 87.

Question 124

59. In its Response to Question No. 124, the United States argues that the US claim "does not present the systemic questions posed in the Panel's question." As the EC has just explained, this US view is based on a highly artificial and self-serving interpretation of Article IX:1 GATT. Accordingly, the United States' attempts to isolate its claim regarding Article 12(2) of Regulation 2081/92 from the general question of origin marking must fail.

60. In addition, the United States argues that the requirement of Article 12(2) to indicate the country of origin "is all the more confusing since geographical indications by their very nature concern indicating the particular geographical origin of products." The truthful indication of the country of origin gives the consumer more information, rather than less. The EC does therefore not see how the truthful indication of the country of origin, in which the geographical area is located, could be confusing for the consumer. Moreover, if the US arguments were correct, then the application of the US country or origin marking requirements to EC products bearing a name protected under Regulation 2081/92 would equally have to be regarded as confusing for the consumer, and as detracting from the value of the geographical indication.

Question 128

61. In their responses to the Panel's Question No. 128, both the United States and Australia fail to explain why they consider the requirement of government involvement in the approval of inspection structures problematic. Since they have no satisfactory answer to this question, they instead choose to mischaracterise the requirements of Regulation 2081/92 by arguing that the Regulation imposes "a requirement on sovereign WTO Members to put in place certain inspection structures dictated by the EC,"[48] or involves the "imposition of EC-mandate inspection structures on other WTO Members."[49]

62. As the EC has already explained a number of times, the requirement of inspection structures is applied and evaluated purely with respect to the specific product for which protection is sought.[50] Accordingly, contrary to the arguments of the United States and Australia, it is not "equivalence by another name." Regulation 2081/92 does not concern the question of how the complainants protect geographical indications within their own territory, and in particular whether they require the existence of inspection structures for this purpose or not. The objective of the Regulation is purely to ensure that in order to be protected in the EC, geographical indications from third countries fulfil the same conditions as geographical indications from the EC.

63. As the EC has explained, since the inspection bodies will be located on the territory of the country of origin of the geographical indication, an involvement of the home country of the geographical indication is indispensable for the designation and continued monitoring of such inspection structures.[51] As the EC has also said, this possibility to have inspection bodies approved by their home country should in fact constitute an advantage rather than a disadvantage for applicants and producers from the US or Australia.[52]

64. In its response, the United States is contesting this argument by claiming that the EC "does not allow the United States to make its own determination as to the sufficiency of the inspection structures."[53] This is misleading. Article 12a (2) (b) of Regulation 2081/92 requires a declaration by the country of origin "that the structures provided for in Article 10 are established on its territory." Obviously, the Community institution responsible for deciding on an application for protection under Regulation 2081/92 must make sure that all the requirements of the Regulation are met. However, as the EC has already said, in doing so, the Community

[48] US Response to Panel's Question No. 128, para. 53.

[49] Australia's Response to Panel's Question No. 128, para. 51.

[50] EC SOS, para. 54 et seq.; EC SWS, para. 96 et seq.

[51] EC Response to Panel's Question No. 136, para. 146.

[52] EC Response to Panel's Question No. 131, para. 114.

[53] US Response to Panel's Question No. 128, para. 57.

institutions will have to rely to a considerable extent on the information provided by the country of origin.[54] Contrary to the US' suggestion, the declaration of the country of origin is therefore of considerable importance, and will be given due weight by the Community institutions in the registration process.

Question 130

65. The EC notes that in their responses, the US and Australia fail to identify any aspect of the requirement of inspection structures beyond the involvement of their governments that they consider objectionable.[55] Accordingly, the EC understands that the claims of the United States and Australia are therefore now limited to the requirement of government involvement in the designation of inspection structures.

Question 137

<u>US Response</u>

66. The United States complains that it "does not have access to the product specifications for any of the GIs cited by the Panel." This complaint is unwarranted.[56] The specifications of any registered geographical indication, including those mentioned in the question, can be obtained upon request from the EC Commission or from the competent authorities of the Member States.

67. With respect to the argument made at paragraph 67, the terms used by the EC are "not very qualified." The EC used those terms in order to make clear that whether a "used" sign is the same or different from the sign covered by the registration can only be decided on a case-by-case basis. The EC does not see how the complainants could disagree with this.

68. With respect to the issue of translations[57], the EC has explained repeatedly that the registration confers a positive right to use the registered name, to the exclusion of any other sign. A "translation" is not necessarily a different sign, something which appears to be overlooked by the United States. For example, the translation of the name "Gorgonzola" into Spanish, English and French is in all cases "Gorgonzola." For that reason, it would be not be correct to say that the registered term cannot be used in "translation." Moreover, in some cases a registration may cover different linguistic versions (e.g. "Cítricos Valencianos" and "Citrics Valencians").[58] For those reasons, the relevant issue is not whether the registration allows the use of a name "in translation," but rather whether it gives a positive right to use a different sign, a question which has been answered by the EC in an unequivocal manner.

69. As explained by the EC in its response to Questions 2 and 3 from Australia, the assertion made by the United States in footnote 38 is based on a misunderstanding of the relevant EC law.

70. At paragraph 69 the United States asserts that:

> Under Article 16.1, rather than seeking rejection or cancellation of a GI registration on an EC wide basis, the owner of an identical or similar valid trademark registered in the EC is entitled to prevent particular "uses" of the GI that confuse consumers in that state.

71. The EC submits that, in accordance with the last sentence of Article 1.1 TRIPS, it is for each Member to decide whether or not the sign should be invalidated first. As explained by the EC[59], in many Members the

---

[54] EC Response to Panel's Question No. 114, para. 69.

[55] US Response to Panel's Question No. 130, para. 62; Australia's Response to Panel's Question No. 130, para. 53.

[56] US Response to Panel's Question No. 137, para 65.

[57] US Response to Panel's Question No. 137, para. 68.

[58] See EC Response to Panel's Question No. 140, para. 176.

[59] See EC Response to Panel's Question No. 138, para. 170.

owner of a registered trademark cannot be prevented from using it, even where it results in a likelihood of confusion with an earlier trademark, unless the registration is invalidated first. The interpretation advanced by the United States would imply that the trademark laws of all those Members are inconsistent with Article 16.1 TRIPS.

72. At paragraph 70, the United States refers to a decision of a South African court, according to which the use of the trademark "Budějovické Budvar" would give rise to a likelihood of confusion with the trademarks "Budweiser" and "Bud." In the first place, the EC recalls, once again, that the registration of the names "Budějovické pivo," "Českobudějovické pivo" and "Budějovický měšt'anský" is not before this Panel[60], as well as the fact that such registration is unique in that it is the only registration under Regulation 2081/92 which is subject to the proviso that it applies "without prejudice to any beer trademark or other rights existing in the Eureopean Union as of the date of accession." Moreover, the names "Budějovické Budvar" and "Bud" are not among the names registered under Regulation 2081/92. In any event, as stressed by the United States elsewhere, a determination of likelihood of confusion must take account of "the consumers' perception in a given territory."[61]

73. The United States also refers[62] to a decision of an Italian court enjoining a Czech producer of beer from using the names "Bud" and "Budweiser" because they give rise to a likelihood of confusion with the trademarks "Budweiser" and "Bud." However, once again, the names "Bud" and "Budweiser" are not among those registered under Regulation 2081/92.

74. Moreover, the EC understands that the decision of the South African court was adopted in response to an application for the registration of a trademark by the Czech producer and not in the context of infringement proceedings involving two registered trademarks. Therefore, it is totally irrelevant in connection with the issue raised in the Panel's question, which is whether a validly registered sign which is not confusing *per se* may, nevertheless, be used subsequently in a confusing manner. Similarly, the EC understands that the Italian case involves the infringement of a registered trademark by a non-registered trademark and is, therefore, irrelevant for the same reasons.

75. Finally, the EC would note the United States is misleadingly selective when citing examples of "likelihood of confusion" involving the trademarks "Bud" and "Budweiser." The Panel should be aware that the courts of other countries, including, for example, Australia and New Zealand, have found that there was no likelihood of confusion between the names which it cites in its response.[63]

Australia's Response

76. Australia says that[64]

> Even within the Member States where the trademarks "Bavaria," "Hoker Bajer" and "Budweiser" are registered, the protection afforded by Regulation No. 2081—in particular Article 13.1—makes clear that the owner of a registered trademark would not be able to prevent confusingly similar or identical use of a sign or identical goods …

77. Australia is confusing two different issues. Article 13(1) of Regulation 2081/92 defines the scope of the *negative* right of the right holders of a registered geographical indication to prevent certain uses, including as trademarks. It does not prejudice the answer to the distinct and previous question of whether the registration

---

[60] EC FWS, paras. 21-25.

[61] US Response to Panel's Question No. 137, para. 64.

[62] US Response to Panel's Question No. 137, para. 70.

[63] See Exhibit EC-114 and Exhibit EC-115.

[64] Australia's Response to Panel's Question No. 137, para. 59.

of a geographical indication must be refused in accordance with Article 14(3). Nor does it prejudge the answer to the distinct question of what is the scope of the *positive* right to use a geographical indication[65], and more specifically of whether that right includes the right to use a geographical indication in a manner that is contrary to the labelling Directive and the laws on unfair competition.

78. Australia also says that:[66]

> Even where those trademarks are not registered in other EC Member States, each could still enjoy a reputation in the territories of those other States –particularly in adjoining States- which the EC-defined GI right holders could exploit through confusingly similar use of translations of the EC-defined GIs. The EC has not explained how, in such situations, the owners of those trademarks would be assured of the rights of a registered trademark owner to initiate infringement action, or of the standing to initiate legal action under other legal provisions, such as labelling, misleading advertising or unfair competition laws.

79. The relevance of this argument in the context of Australia's claims is unclear to the EC. As emphasised by Australia throughout these proceedings, trademark rights are territorial. The registration of a trademark in Member State A confers no exclusive rights in Member State B, just like the registration of a trademark in the United States confers no exclusive rights in Australia (subject to what is provided in Article 16.2 TRIPS, which Australia has not invoked in this dispute). Indeed, it is precisely for that reason that the EC institutions adopted the Regulation creating the Community Trademark.

80. On the other hand, the EC can confirm, once again, that there is nothing that prevents the owner of a trademark registered in Member State A from bringing an action in Member State B against the use of a geographical indication in a manner which is contrary to the Directive on labelling or to the unfair competition laws of Member State B, even if the trademark concerned is not registered in Member State B.

Question 145

81. The EC notes that the responses of the United States and Australia are contradictory and irreconcilable. While the United States persists in the mistaken theory that Article 24.5 is an "exception" to Articles 22 and 23[67], Australia agrees with the EC that Article 24.5 is not a "mere exception"[68] and that it creates "positive rights."[69] Further, Australia agrees with the EC that Article 24.5 "defines the boundary between a Member's right to implement measures relating to TRIPS-defined GIs and its obligation to afford protection to pre-existing trademarks."[70] Nevertheless, Australia, fails to draw the appropriate conclusion from this.

82. If, as Australia and the EC agree, Article 24.5 is not an "exception" but rather defines the "boundary" between the right to implement protection for geographical indications and the obligation to protect grandfathered trademarks, it would follow that a Member which acts consistently with its rights and obligations under Article 24.5 could not violate Article 16.1. Yet, both Australia and the United States have made a point of not raising any claim, even in the alternative, to the effect that Article 14(2) of Regulation 2081/92 is inconsistent with Article 24.5. Their claims concerning the issue of co-existence are based on Article 16.1 exclusively.

---

[65] By the same token, the fact that a registered trademark confers the *negative* right to prevent the use of confusingly similar signs does not mean that the owner of the trademark has a *positive* right to use the confusingly similar signs himself.

[66] Australia's Response to Panel's Question No. 137, para. 59.

[67] US Response to Panel's Question No. 145, para. 72.

[68] Australia's Response to Panel's Question No. 145, para. 61.

[69] Ibid.

[70] Australia's Response to Panel's Question No. 145, para. 61.

83. The EC, therefore, submits that, if the Panel agrees with the definition of the relationship between Articles 24.5 and Article 16.1 put forward by Australia and the EC, it should reject the complainants' claim under Article 16.1 with respect to the issue of co-existence, without it being necessary for the Panel to consider whether Article 14(2) of Regulation 2081/92 is inconsistent with Article 24.5, given that the complainants have not submitted any claim to that effect.

84. The United States takes advantage of the response to this question in order to elaborate upon its interpretation of the phrase "shall not prejudice ... the validity of the registration."[71] As explained by the EC, the United States fails to distinguish between the "validity" of the registration and the exercise of the rights conferred by the registration. Moreover, the US interpretation would render duplicative and superfluous the reference to "the right to use a trademark." That right is the most fundamental right of the owner of any trademark, whether or not it is registered. If the drafters of Article 24.5 specified that the measures to implement protection of geographical indications shall not prejudice the right to use a trademark, but not the right to exclude others from using the trademark, it is because they did not intend to limit the Members' right to do so. The US interpretation reads an obligation to preserve the right to exclude others, where Article 24.5 provides none.

85. Furthermore, the US interpretation is clearly contradicted by the Spanish and the French versions of Article 24.5, which read as follows:[72]

> Cuando una marca de fábrica o de comercio haya sido solicitada o registrada de buena fe, o cuando los derechos a una marca de fábrica o de comercio se hayan adquirido mediante su uso de buena fe:
>
> a) antes de la fecha de aplicación de estas disposiciones en ese Miembro, según lo establecido en la Parte VI; o
>
> b) antes de que la indicación geográfica estuviera protegida en su país de origen;
>
> las medidas adoptadas para aplicar esta Sección no **prejuzgarán** la posibilidad de registro ni la validez del registro de una marca de fábrica o de comercio, ni el derecho a hacer uso de dicha marca, por el motivo de que ésta es idéntica o similar a una indicación geográfica.
>
> Dans les cas où une marque de fabrique ou de commerce a été déposée ou enregistrée de bonne foi, ou dans les cas où les droits à une marque de fabrique ou de commerce ont été acquis par un usage de bonne foi:
>
> a) avant la date d'application des présentes dispositions dans ce Membre telle qu'elle est définie dans la Partie VI, ou
>
> b) avant que l'indication géographique ne soit protégée dans son pays d'origine,
>
> les mesures adoptées pour mettre en oeuvre la présente section ne **préjugeront** pas la recevabilité ou la validité de l'enregistrement d'une marque de fabrique ou de commerce, ou le droit de faire usage d'une marque de fabrique ou de commerce, au motif que cette marque est identique ou similaire à une indication géographique.

86. The Spanish term "prejuzgarán" and the French term "préjugeront" do not have the ordinary meaning which the United States attributes to the English word "prejudice," i.e. to cause "injury, damage, harm."[73] The

---

[71] US Response to Panel's Question No. 145, para. 74.

[72] Emphases added.

dictionary definition of "prejuzgar"is "juzgar de las cosas antes del tiempo oportuno, o sin tener de ellas cabal conocimiento." [74]

87. In turn, the dictionary definition of "préjuger"[75] is

> I. 1. *Vx ou littér.* porter un jugement prématuré sur (qqch.). *Je ne veux point préjuger la question.*—Prévoir au moyen des indices dont on dispose. *Autant qu'on peut le préjuger; a ce qu'on peut préjuger*. 2 *Dr.* prendre un décision provisoire sur (qqch.) en laissant prévoir le jugement définitif.

88. The above definitions are similar to one of the ordinary meanings of the English term "prejudice," which is to "judge beforehand."[76]

89. Article 24.5 may be contrasted with other provisions of the TRIPS Agreement, such as Articles 13, 16.1, 26.2 or 30 where the English term "prejudice" has been rendered as "perjuicio" in the Spanish version and as "préjudice" in the French one. Unlike the terms "prejuzgar" and "préjuger" those terms mean "harm, injury, damage." This difference confirms that the terms "prejuzgarán" and "préjugeront" were chosen deliberately in order to convey a different meaning from that which the United States attributes to the English term "prejudice."

90. The French and the Spanish versions of Article 24.5 make it clear that, contrary to the US view, the phrase "shall not prejudice … the validity of the registration" does not mean that a Member is prevented from taking any measure that may affect negatively the exercise of the rights conferred by the registration. Instead, it means that Members cannot invalidate the trademark merely on the basis that it is identical or similar to a geographical indication, *without prejudice* to the possibility to invalidate it on other grounds, such as that the trademark is not distinctive or is deemed misleading for other reasons. By the same token, the phrase "shall not prejudice … the right to use the trademark" means that Members may not deny the right to use a trademark on the basis that it is the same or similar as a geographical indication, without prejudice to the possibility to do so on other grounds (e.g. because it would result in a likelihood of confusion with an earlier trademark).

Question 148

91. The United States persists in obfuscating unnecessarily the discussion by confusing two issues which are clearly distinct under the TRIPS Agreement and under the trademark laws of both the United States and the EC.

92. The fact that Article 16.3 TRIPS and the anti-dilution provisions of the EC Trademark Directive and the Community Trademark Regulation afford additional protection to trademarks which enjoy reputation does not mean that reputation is irrelevant in order to establish a likelihood of confusion between signs for similar goods. The EC has shown that this is an uncontroversial proposition under both EC law and US law.[77]

93. The United States mischaracterizes the EC position. The EC has not said that a finding of likelihood of confusion for the purposes of Article 16.1 TRIPS requires *always* a finding that the earlier trademark enjoys reputation, regardless of the inherent "strength" (distinctiveness) of the trademark. Rather the EC has noted the following:

---

[73] US Response to Panel's Question No. 76, para. 99.

[74] Diccionario de la Real Academia Española, 20th Edition, 1984.

[75] Le Nouveau Petit Robert, 1993.

[76] The New Shorter Oxford English Dictionary, Ed. Lesley Brown, Clarendon Press, Oxford 1993.

[77] EC SOS, paras. 166-169.

- first, terms which are, or which may reasonably qualify, as geographical indications for a certain product are "descriptive" terms and, hence, primarily "non-distinctive." As such, they may be validly registered only to the extent that they have acquired distinctiveness (secondary meaning).

- second, the "strength" or degree of distinctiveness of a trademark (whether inherent or acquired) is a relevant criterion for assessing the "likelihood of confusion;"

- third, length of use, reputation and renown are the basic criteria for measuring the degree of acquired distinctiveness of a trademark. Therefore, those criteria are particularly relevant when assessing the likelihood of confusion with trademarks which are primarily non-distinctive because they consist of descriptive terms, such as a geographical indication.

94. For the above reasons, Article 14(3) of Regulation 2081/92 directs expressly the authorities to consider length of use, reputation and renown. But this does not mean that other criteria are irrelevant. Nor that the criteria mentioned in Article 14(3) are necessarily dispositive. As explained by the EC[78], if Article 14(3) does not mention the similarity of signs and goods is because such criteria are necessarily relevant for any determination of likelihood of confusion. Indeed, as also explained by the EC[79], the criteria mentioned in Article 14(3) could not be meaningfully applied without taken into account the similarity of goods and signs.

95. For the above reasons, the decisions of the OHIM, of the ECJ and of Member State courts cited by the United States[80] are irrelevant. Indeed, as far as the EC can see, none of them concerns a situation involving a situation which can be considered as similar to that addressed by Article 14(3) of Regulation 2081/92, i.e. a situation requiring the assessment of the likelihood of confusion between a geographical indication or another descriptive sign and a registered trademark which consists of such sign.

Question 149

96. The EC notes that the United States appears to concede[81] that Article 22.2 TRIPS is not relevant for the interpretation of Article 14(3) of Regulation 2081/92, given that Article 14(3) does not purport to implement that provision, but instead Article 16.1 TRIPS.

97. The United States, nevertheless, goes on to argue that:[82]

> The word "mislead" appears to be used throughout the EC GI Regulation in the sense of affirmatively leading the public to believe something about the product that this is not true …

98. Similarly, Australia contends that:[83]

> the word "misleading" is used throughout the Regulation—in Articles 3.2, 6.6, 13.1(c), 13.1(d) and 14.3—in the sense of an action which positively provokes an error on the part of the consumer.

---

78 EC Response to Panel's Question No. 68.

79 Ibid.

80 US Response to Panel's Question No. 148, para. 98.

81 US Response to Panel's Question No. 149, para. 102.

82 Australia's Response to Panel's Question No. 149, para. 104.

83 Australia's Response to Panel's Question No. 149, para. 77.

99. However, neither Australia nor the United States explain what they mean by "positively" or "affirmatively," respectively. Nor do they explain how the text of the provisions which they cite support that conclusion.

100. Both Australia and the United States contend that the French version of the provisions which they cite would confirm their reading. But they limit themselves to copy the text of those provisions, without explaining how it supports their interpretation.[84] As explained by the EC[85], one of the ordinary meanings of the Spanish term "error," and of its equivalents in other romance languages (e.g. "erreur," "errore") is "confusión" ("confusion," "confusione"). The complainants do not address this argument.

101. The complainants' assertions fall short of a proper contextual interpretation. They limit themselves to note the obvious fact that different terms are used in different provisions, but make not attempt to read them in a coherent manner.

102. As explained by the EC, Article 14(3) of Regulation 2081/912 must be read together with Articles 7(4) and 7(5)(b)[86]. Article 7(4) allows trademark owners to object to the registration of a proposed name *inter alia* on the grounds that the registration would give rise to the situation described in Article 14(3). Article 7(5)(b) then provides that the authorities must resolve that objection having regard to the "likelihood of confusion." It would give rise to an internal contradiction within the Regulation if the standard for deciding an objection under Article 7(5)(b) were different from and more rigorous than the standard of Article 14(3).

103. Additional guidance is provided by Article 13(1)(d), which provides that registered names shall be protected against "any other practice liable to mislead the public as to the true origin of the product." The term "other" implies that the practices previously described in letters a) b) and c) are also "liable to mislead." Yet, those letters do not provide for a more rigorous standard than that of "likelihood of confusion" within the meaning of Article 16.1 TRIPS, but rather the opposite.

Question 150

104. In answering this question the United States concedes that the exceptions provided in Article 6.1(b) of the Trademark Directive and Article 12(b) of the Community Trademark Directive are consistent with Article 17 TRIPS. Indeed, the United States could hardly contest this given that many other Members have similar exceptions in their statute books.[87]

105. Yet, as explained by the EC[88], the requirement to use a registered geographical indication in accordance with the Directives on labelling and misleading advertising and with the laws on unfair competition is equivalent to the condition that they must be used "in accordance with honest practices in industrial or commercial matters."

106. Thus, in definitive, what the United States appears to consider objectionable is the mere fact that the limitations on the use of a registered geographical indication are not provided in the EC's trademarks laws but instead in different legal instruments. However, neither Article 16.1 TRIPS nor any other provision of the TRIPS Agreement contains any requirement to that effect. To the contrary, Article 1.1 provides that "Members shall be free to determine the appropriate method of implementing the provisions of this Agreement within their own legal system and practice."

---

[84] US Response to Panel's Question No. 149, para. 104 and Australia's Response to Panel's Question No. 149, para. 78.

[85] EC SOS, para. 162.

[86] See also the equivalent provisions in Articles 12b(3), 12d(2) and 12d(3).

[87] See EC Response to Panel's Question No. 153, para. 240.

[88] EC Response to Panel's Question No. 153, paras. 242-244.

Question 151

107. The United States says that it agrees with the proposition made in the question that "Article 24.3 is an exception to Part II, Section 3."[89]

108. The EC does not read the suggestion made in the question as meaning that Article 24.3 is an "exception," but rather the opposite. As the EC understands it, the suggestion made in the question is that the obligation provided in Article 24.3 applies only with respect to the "exceptions" provided in *other* paragraphs of Article 24. If Article 24.3 were also an "exception," it could not impose upon Members the obligation not to rely upon those exceptions as a justification for diminishing pre-existing protection.

Question 154

109. The EC takes issue with the US suggestion[90] that the "legitimate interests" of consumers are necessarily the same as those of the trademark owner. Consumers, and in particular the EC consumers of foodstuffs, are often more interested in being informed about the origin of the products, and the characteristics associated thereto, than about the identity of the undertaking which is the source of the goods, in particular where that undertaking has no special reputation.[91]

110. In this connection, it is important to recall that, even if the complainants' narrow interpretation of Article 14(3) of Regulation 2081/92 were correct, that provision would prevent the registration of a geographical indication where it leads to confusion with a trademark that has been used for a certain period of time and enjoys some reputation or renown. Thus, on the complainants' own interpretation of Article 14(3), Article 14(2) would provide for the co-existence of geographical indications only with trademarks that have been used for a short period of time and/or enjoy little reputation/renown, if at all.

111. Both complainants attempt to read into the conditions of Article 17 a narrow "necessity" test, whereby the use of indications of origin would be permitted only to the extent strictly necessary to inform consumers about the origin of the products.[92]

112. This interpretation is not supported by the text of Article 17. All that is required by Article 17 is that the exception be "limited" and that the interests of the trademark owner and of third parties be "taken into account." Reading the condition that the exception must be "limited" as imposing a strict "necessity" test would pre-empt the balancing of interests provided in the second condition of Article 17. In turn, the condition to "take account of the legitimate interests of the trademark owner and third parties" does not establish any hierarchy between the relevant interests and affords a margin of discretion to Members in order to find a proper balance between them.

113. Moreover, the "necessity" test advanced by the complainants would render irrelevant the exception provided in Article 17 with respect to the fair use of descriptive terms. The holders of a geographical indication have a legitimate interest in informing consumers about the origin of their products, and the characteristics associated thereto, in a manner which can be easily recognised by the public. One could, of course, argue that all that is "necessary" in order to inform consumers that a product is of a certain geographical indication is to mention it in small print at the bottom of a back label, somewhere between the ingredients list and the expiry

---

[89] US Response to Panel's Question No. 151, para. 108.

[90] US Response to Panel's Question 154, paras. 113 and 119.

[91] While US consumers may not be as familiar yet with geographical indications, there is a growing awareness. For example, as explained by the EC, the State of California has enacted legislation which prohibits the use of *any* trademark including or consisting of a recognised geographical indication for wine, including earlier trademarks grandfathered by Article 25.4, and regardless of whether they are subject to invalidation as being misleading. This statute, which has been recently upheld by California's Supreme Court (Exhibit EC-81) purports to protect not only the interests of the wine makers concerned but also those of the Californian consumers. This suggests that the State of California does not agree with the views expressed by the USTR in this dispute.

[92] See e.g. US Response to Panel's Question No. 154, paras 119-120; Australia's Response to Panel's Question No. 154, para. 84.

date. That use, however, would not give rise to a "likelihood of confusion" and would not need to be justified under Article 17. The exception provided in Article 17 with respect to the "fair use" of descriptive terms only becomes necessary to extent that geographical indications are used in what the United States calls misleadingly "trademark-like" fashion.

114. Finally, as shown by the EC, the "necessity" test devised by the complainants cannot be reconciled with the terms of the exceptions clauses included in the trademark laws of a large number of Members, which do not require that the use be "necessary," but instead that it be "in good faith," or in accordance with "honest," "fair" or "proper" business or trade practices.[93]

115. By way of conclusion, the Unites States asserts that:[94]

> Under the EC's interpretation of TRIPS Article 17, all uses of a registered GI are automatically entitled to the "fair use" exception, no matter what the facts of particular case at hand (i.e. whether the use is fair, the term is descriptive, or the legitimate interests of the trademark owner are considered) by simple virtue of registration alone.

116. This is a gross mischaracterization of the EC's position:

- first, the EC does not claim an exception with respect to terms that are not "descriptive." The EC argues that geographical indications, like all other indications of source, are *per se* descriptive terms;

- second, the EC has explained that the interests of the trademark owners are taken into account in several ways.[95] The United States does not address the EC's arguments in its response.

- third, the EC has explained that registered geographical indications must be used in accordance with the requirements of the Directives on labelling and misleading advertising and the laws on unfair competition. This reduces the likelihood of confusion and ensures that the use of the geographical indications is "fair."[96] Again, the US does not address this argument in its response.

Question 155

117. The EC agrees with both complainants that "trademarks are not merely descriptive and cannot be considered 'descriptive terms' within the meaning of Article 17."[97]

118. As pointed out by Australia[98], the reason why trademarks are not "descriptive" is that, in accordance with Article 15.1 TRIPS, they must be "distinctive," i.e. they must be capable of distinguishing the products of *one* undertaking from those of other undertakings. A "descriptive" term is inherently not "distinctive" and, therefore, incapable of being a trademark. A geographical term (except where it is fanciful because it cannot be reasonably associated to the products concerned) is primarily descriptive of the origin of the products and, hence, non-distinctive. For that reason, geographical terms are generally not registrable as trademarks, unless they have acquired distinctiveness through use.

---

[93] EC Response to Panel's Question No. 153, para. 240.

[94] EC Response to Panel's Question No. 154, para. 120.

[95] EC Response to Panel's Question No. 154, para. 254.

[96] See e.g. EC Response to Panel's Question No. 153, paras. 234-244.

[97] See e.g. US Response to Panel's Question No. 155, para. 123; US Response to Panel's Question No. 156, para. 130; and Australia's Response to Panel's Question No. 155, para. 92.

[98] Australia's Response to Panel's Question No. 155, para. 89.

119. Having explained correctly that trademarks are not "descriptive" terms because they must be "distinctive" within the meaning of Article 15.1 TRIPS, Australia goes on to assert that[99]

> In the same way, and for the same reasons, use of a GI cannot be said to be merely use of an indication of source within the meaning of the Paris Convention or to be use of a descriptive term within the meaning of TRIPS Article 17.

120. This is incorrect. The analysis made by Australia with respect to trademarks cannot be extrapolated to geographical indications. Australia disregards that there is a fundamental difference between trademarks and geographical indications. Unlike trademarks, geographical indications are not "distinctive" within the meaning of Article 15.1, because they do not serve to distinguish the products of *one* undertaking from those of other undertakings. Rather, the purpose of a geographical indication is to identify the geographical area in which a product originates, where certain characteristics are associated to that origin, regardless of the undertaking which produces or markets that product.

121. Australia is also wrong when it says that geographical indications are not indications of source within the meaning of the Paris Convention.[100] Geographical indications are a subset of indications of source. The name "Australia" is always an indication of source, regardless of whether it may qualify as well as a geographical indication with respect to certain products, as claimed by Australia outside these proceedings. Commenting upon Article 1(2) of the Paris Convention, Bodenhausen says that[101]

> Appellations of origin are now considered to be a *species* of the *genus* 'indications of source', characterized by their relationship with quality or characteristics derived from the source.

122. Geographical indications differ from simple indications of source in that, in addition to describing the origin of the products, they describe certain product characteristics that are attributable to that origin. But this does not make them "distinctive" within the meaning of Article 15.1.

123. Australia also says that "if geographical indications were purely descriptive there would not be any need –or indeed any basis- for an intellectual property right."[102] The EC does not understand this argument, which appears to be based on the erroneous notion that intellectual property rights must necessarily be owned by individuals. As explained, descriptive terms cannot be the subject of trademark rights because trademarks must be "distinctive." On the other hand, there is no reason why a descriptive term cannot be the subject of other intellectual property rights owned collectively by all the producers of goods conforming to the relevant description. Indeed, Article 1(2) of the Paris Convention provides expressly that "the protection of industrial property has as its object," among other things, "indications of source," which Australia does not dispute are "purely descriptive."

124. Finally, even if geographical indications were not "descriptive terms" within the meaning of Article 17, the complainants have not given any good reason why fair use of a geographical indication should not qualify for an exception under Article 17. The exception provided in Article 17 with respect to the fair use of descriptive terms is just an example. The potential universe of uses of an indication of source is not more "limited" than that of a geographical indication. And the interest in using a geographical indication is no less "legitimate" than the interest in using an indication of source. Nor is there any reason why the use of a geographical indication should be more confusing *per se* or more prejudicial to the interests of the trademark owner. Australia has said that it is "reasonable and fair for people to be able to say … 'made in Australia'."[103]

---

[99] Australia's Response to Panel's Question No. 155, para. 92.

[100] Australia's Response to Panel's Question No. 157, para. 92.

[101] G.H.C. Bodenhausen, *Guide to the Application of the Paris Convention for the Protection of Industrial Property*, BIRPI Geneva 1968, p. 23.

[102] Australia's Response to Panel's Question No. 157.

[103] Australia's Response to Panel's Question No. 154, para. 86.

The EC agrees. The EC would add, however, that it is reasonable and fair for people to be able to say that their products are made in Australia, irrespective of whether "Australia" is an indication of source or a geographical indication for the goods concerned (as Australia claims with respect to wine, for example). It would be absurd if only the producers of goods originating in an area which qualifies as a geographical indication were prevented from indicating the origin of their goods.

Question 156

125. The United States makes a remarkable argument to the effect that the exception provided in Article 17 is narrower than the exceptions in Articles 13, 26.3 and 30 because it is subject to *less* conditions.

126. Even more remarkable is the US argument to the effect that the "take account" standard of Article 17 is in fact more protective of the interests of the right holder than the "unreasonably prejudice" standard of Articles 13, 26.3 and 30, even though Articles 26.3 and 30 distinguish expressly between the two standards and reserve the "take account" standard for the interests of third parties.

127. In essence, the United States argues that Article 17 does not include the "normal exploitation" and the "unreasonable prejudice" conditions because any limitation of the exclusive rights of the trademark owner would necessarily fail to meet those conditions.[104] However, from the fact that Article 17 does not include those conditions it cannot be inferred that it purports to provide even stricter standards which are not reflected in the wording of the text. Rather, the logical inference is that the drafters mean to provide for more lenient standards.

128. The United States confuses the "legitimate interests" of the trademark owner with the full enjoyment of its legal rights, despite the clear distinction drawn by the Panel in *Canada – Pharmaceutical Patents*.[105]

129. Moreover, even where legal rights rather than legitimate interests are taken into account, the co-existence of a trademark with another trademark or with a geographical indication is far from being so "abnormal" or "unreasonable" as the United States pretends. It is envisaged by several provisions of Sections 2 and 3 of Part III, even where it may lead to some confusion. For example:

- Article 16.1 provides for the co-existence of registered trademarks with existing prior rights;

- Article 23.2 allows co-existence of a geographical indication for wines or spirits and a trademark consisting or including such geographical indication if used for wines and spirits originating in the area to which the geographical indication relates. *A priori*, the risk that consumers may confuse that geographical indication with the trademark may be the same as when the products covered by the trademark do not originate in that area. Nevertheless, co-existence is allowed because it does not mislead consumers as to the true geographical origin of the products;

- co-existence may arise as well from Article 24.3, when the protection of geographical indications existing before the date of entry into force of the WTO Agreement provided for such co-existence;

- co-existence is envisaged also by Article 24.4, which provides that a Member may allow "continued and similar" use of a geographical indication[106] for wines or spirits of another Member by its nationals or domiciliaries who have used it before 1 April 1994 in good faith or for at least 10 years preceding that date, regardless of whether this gives rise to confusion with the products of the other Member that are entitled to use that geographical indication.

---

[104] US Response to Panel's Question No. 156, para. 130.

[105] Panel Report, *Canada – Pharmaceutical Patents*, paras. 7-68-7.69.

[106] The EC recalls that the United States has argued that Article 24.4 applies also with respect to the use of geographical indications as trademarks, including trademarks which are not grandfathered by virtue of Article 24.5.

130. Finally, there is nothing in the TRIPS Agreement that prevents Members from providing for the co-existence of non-registered trademarks and other trademarks, including latter registered trademarks, or geographical indications. In particular, as conceded by Australia, Article 24.5 allows co-existence with respect to non-registered grandfathered trademarks even on the complainants' reading of that provision.

Question 157

131. Contrary to the US assertions,[107] it is simply not true that the EC has left "unspecified" the other measures which it applies in order to comply with Article 22.2 TRIPS, in addition to Regulation 2081/92. The EC mentioned those measures in its first written submission.[108] Furthermore, the EC referred the Panel and the other parties to the responses of the EC and of its Member States to the review under Article 24.2 TRIPS, where those measures were further specified and explained. The EC has provided as Exhibit EC-22 copies of those responses, which must therefore be deemed part of the EC's submissions to the Panel.

132. The EC noted in its first written submission that the complainants were well aware of the existence of those other measures, as well as of the EC's position that those measures implement its obligations under Article 22.2. The complainants have not denied this. Yet, neither of them mentioned those measures in their panel requests. Furthermore, even after the EC confirmed in the course of these proceedings that, as explained in its responses to the review under Article 24.2 TRIPS, it applies other measures in order to implement Article 22.2, the United States and Australia failed to submit any argument or evidence in order to show that, contrary to what is explained in the responses, those measures are not sufficient to comply with Article 22.2.

133. The US suggestion[109] that the EC declined to provide information requested by the Panel is also untrue. At the first meeting with the Panel, the EC confirmed its willingness to provide any information requested by the Panel. The EC, nevertheless, pointed out that in makings its requests for information the Panel should be careful not to shift the burden on proof from the complainants to the EC. This was a legitimate concern which the EC believes the Panel has properly taken into account in formulating its questions to the parties.

---

107 US Response to Panel's Question No. 157, para. 134.

108 See EC FWS, para. 434.

109 US Response to Panel's Question No. 157, para. 134.

ANNEX B-10

COMMENTS OF THE EUROPEAN COMMUNITIES ON THE REPLY OF THE INTERNATIONAL BUREAU OF WIPO TO THE PANEL'S LETTER OF 9 JULY 2004

(28 September 2004)

The EC is referring to your letter of 14 September 2004, in which you are requesting comments on the factual information provided by the International Bureau of WIPO.

The EC notes that in its letter to WIPO, the Panel requested information in particular as regards the meaning of the term "national" in Article 2 of the Paris Convention.

In the view of the EC, the drafting materials of the Paris Convention provided by the International Bureau of WIPO confirm the view which the EC has expressed throughout the proceedings, namely that the word "national" is a distinct term which cannot be equated with persons "domiciled or established" in the territory of a particular member.[1]

In particular, the EC notes that until the Act of the Hague, 1925, Article 2 of the Paris Convention referred to "subjects or citizens," instead of nationals. The terms "subject or citizen" clearly refer to a specific status conferred on persons under the law of the State in question. The terms "subjects or citizens" were subsequently replaced by the single expression "nationals" (French: ressortissants) for reasons of simplification.[2] There was clearly no intention to enlarge the meaning of "nationals" to all persons domiciled or established in the territory of a party.

The same is also demonstrated by the drafting history of Article 3 of the Paris Convention. In the Materials of the Paris Conference of 1880, it is clarified « que la Convention sera applicable, non pas à tous les étrangers, sans distinction, mais à ceux qui seraient domiciliés ou établis dans l'un des Etats de l'Union ». It follows clearly from this that a person which does not possess the nationality of a Member is not a "national" of that Member only because it is domiciled or established on the territory of the Member.

Accordingly, the drafting history of Articles 2 and 3 of the Paris Convention illustrate that contrary to the views of the complainants, "nationality" is a different concept from domicile or establishment. In the view of the EC, the same also applies for the similarly worded provision of Article 3(1) of the TRIPS Agreement.

The EC would like to thank the Panel for this occasion to comment on the information provided by WIPO.

---

[1] Cf. EC Second Oral Statement, paras. 20–21.

[2] Cf. for instance the discussions in the Actes de la conférence de Paris de 1880, neuvième séance, p. 125.

EUROPEAN COMMUNITIES – PROTECTION OF TRADEMARKS AND GEOGRAPHICAL INDICATIONS FOR AGRICULTURAL PRODUCTS AND FOODSTUFFS

COMPLAINT BY THE UNITED STATES

WT/DS174/R/ADD.3
REPORT OF THE PANEL

Addendum

This addendum contains Annexes C and D to the Report of the Panel to be found in document WT/DS174/R. Annex A can be found in Add.1 and Annex B can be found in Add.2.

ANNEX C

ARGUMENTS OF THE THIRD PARTIES

TABLE OF CONTENTS

1. This Annex reflects the arguments made by third parties. It has been prepared by the Panel based on the written submissions, oral statements and responses to questions received from the third parties.

A. ARGENTINA

1. Introduction

2. Argentina has a general systemic interest in the proper implementation and interpretation by WTO Members of the rights provided for in the TRIPS Agreement. However, as a major agro-exporter, Argentina also has a specific interest in the proper implementation of multilateral rules, to ensure that they are not implemented in such a way as to constitute or become obstacles to food trade. Firstly, Argentina wishes to make it quite clear that it does not object to the European Communities having, nor does it consider that the European Communities does not have, a legitimate right to develop or maintain a unified geographical indication registration and protection system in its territory. Neither does Argentina question the system chosen by the European Communities to establish such protection, given that the TRIPS Agreement itself authorizes Members to implement the Agreement within their own legal system and practice. Nonetheless, Argentina does agree with the complainants' comments on the importance of Members providing protection, in accordance with the TRIPS Agreement, for both trademarks and geographical indications, without either one being to the detriment of the other.

2. The EC Regulation in the light of the TRIPS Agreement

(a) The concept of a geographical indication

3. The definition given in Article 2 of the EC Regulation differs from that established in Article 22 of the TRIPS Agreement. Article 2(1) of the EC Regulation protects designations of origin and geographical indications of agricultural products and foodstuffs. Article 2(2) establishes two concepts for ensuring such protection, namely, "designations of origin" and "geographical indications." Argentina believes that there is a substantial difference between the definition laid down in Article 22 of the TRIPS Agreement and that established in Article 2.2(a) and (b) of the EC Regulation, namely the requirement that production and/or processing and/or preparation take place in the defined geographical area. Additionally, the EC Regulation in turn includes in Article 2(3) a sub-classification pursuant to which "[c]ertain traditional geographical or non-

geographical names designating an agricultural product or a foodstuff originating in a region or a specific place, which fulfil the conditions referred to in the second indent of paragraph 2(a) shall also be considered as designations of origin." In this regard, Argentina draws attention to the fact that, in the case of "traditional names," the EC Regulation affords the possibility of protection being granted to non-geographical names, in stark contrast to the practice of WTO Members and the spirit of the TRIPS Agreement. This tendency of the European Communities to provide for protection other than that envisaged by the TRIPS Agreement is reinforced by Article 2(4) of the EC Regulation, according to which, under certain circumstances, certain geographical designations shall be treated as designations of origin where the raw materials of the products concerned come from a geographical area larger than or different from the processing area.

4. Argentina points out that, under Article 2(2) of the EC Regulation, protection is extended by allowing a degree of independence in the concept of a geographical indication from a geographical area (Article 2(3)), and by including certain raw materials from a geographical area larger than or different from the processing area, subject to three restrictions (Article 2(4)). Argentina is of the opinion that this is inconsistent with Article 22 of the TRIPS Agreement.

(b) Coexistence of protection systems

5. One protection system may not prevail at the expense of or to the detriment of the other, given that this would create a conflict of predominance between Sections 2 (Trademarks) and 3 (Geographical indications), both of which are found in Part II of the TRIPS Agreement. However, the obligations set out in these two sections are not mutually exclusive: each category must be granted the degree of protection conferred by the provisions of the Agreement. In other words, Members must ensure that protection is afforded both to trademarks, under Article 16.1, and to geographical indications, under Article 22.2, without, in so doing, undermining in any way the protection granted under the other Article. By providing for the coexistence of a trademark with a geographical indication or designation of origin and making such coexistence conditional upon a given temporal relationship, the EC Regulation violates Article 16.1 of the TRIPS Agreement (which provides for the exclusive right to use a trademark, so the possibility of coexistence restricts the right of the owner of the trademark), Article 22.3 (which neither provides for coexistence, nor establishes a specific cut-off date, as is the case of the EC Regulation), and Article 24.4 (which provides for a critical time different from the cut-off date established in the Regulation).

6. Article 24.5, in addition to establishing a different cut-off date from that laid down in the Regulation, prejudices eligibility for and the validity of the registration of a trademark, and the right to use a trademark, on the basis that such a trademark is identical with, or similar to a geographical indication. Moreover, Article 24.5 does not provide for the possibility of restricting the right of a trademark owner, as is the case in the Regulation, which provides for coexistence. Strictly speaking, it is Article 24.5 which determines the confines of the alternatives available to WTO Members with regard to the application of measures related to the protection of geographical indications and their interrelation with trademarks.

(c) The registration procedure is inconsistent with the TRIPS Agreement

7. Argentina considers it important that particular reference be made to the registration procedure established in the Regulation in the light of the obligations laid down in the TRIPS Agreement. To this end, there follows an objective description of each of the various steps involved, together with comments on their inconsistency with the TRIPS Agreement, as deemed appropriate.

(i) Application for registration / Compliance with specifications

8. Article 4 of the Regulation provides that "to be eligible to use" a protected designation of origin (PDO) or a protected geographical indication (PGI), an agricultural product or foodstuff must "*comply with a specification.*" In this respect, the Regulation gives rise to great uncertainty, given that, while it sets forth a

series of nine elements—Article 4.2(a), (b), (c), (d), (e), (f), (g), (h) and (i)—with which compliance is mandatory, it is precisely subparagraph (i) which allows for the possibility of other requirements being "*laid down by Community and/or national provisions*." Such uncertainty is related to the familiarity with or identification of the relevant Community and/or national provisions in order to comply with the registration requirement, and the means for complying with the requirement laid down in subparagraph (i), bearing in mind the above-mentioned difficulty in identifying pertinent legislation. Knowledge of Community and/or national legislation is obviously even more complicated for a foreign applicant.

9. Furthermore, by mentioning "Community and/or national provisions" without stating whether this refers to regulations specifically related to the protection of geographical indications, the said provision expands yet further the legislative universe with which a potential applicant must comply and could act as a market-access restriction on a product applying for effective protection by means of a PGI / PDO. That is to say that, while the requirements of subparagraphs (a) to (h) are binding upon applicants, this does not mean that the list of requirements is exhaustive, given that, by virtue of subparagraph (i), it can be extended by means of a series of conditions which can be provided for in Community and/or national legislation and compliance with which is also—in principle—mandatory.: It should be recalled at this point that, pursuant to Article 12 of the Regulation, the third country shall be able to give guarantees identical or equivalent to those referred to in Article 4, extending it to the requirement laid down in Article 10.

10. Argentina also makes a further comment on requirements relating to Article 4(h), which refers to the inspection structure(s) provided for in Article 10. The question here is what the criteria for identifying these inspection structures would be in the case of a foreign applicant.: It should be noted that, for a foreign applicant and with regard to this stage, Article 12 provides that "the third country concerned has inspection arrangements (...) equivalent to those laid down in this Regulation." This creates an obstacle which is altogether immune to any decision by a foreign natural or legal person to "accept" the Article 4 requirement, given that the decision to create the inspection bodies referred to in Article 10 is restricted to State level. Provision is not made for inspection structures in all third countries and, even supposing that they were provided for, such structures could fail to meet the equivalence requirement under Articles 10 and 12 of the Regulation.

(ii) Application for registration at the national level (of a member State) / Transitional protection at the national level

11. Pursuant to Article 5(4) of the Regulation, applications shall be sent to the member State in which the geographical area is located. The member State is then responsible for checking that the application is "justified" and, "if it considers that it satisfies the requirements of this Regulation," it forwards the application, including the product specification and other documents on which it has based its decision, to the Commission. That member State may then grant transitional protection at the national level. Such protection ceases when protection is granted at Community level. Furthermore, it is incumbent on the member State to consult another member State or a third country if the application concerns a name designating a border geographical area or a traditional name connected to that area, regardless of whether it is situated in another member State or in a third country.

(iii) Role of the Commission / Examination of applications / Publication of applications/Objections

12. At this stage, it falls to the Commission to conduct, within a period of six months, a formal investigation to verify whether the registration application includes all the particulars provided for in Article 4. The Commission shall inform the member State of its findings and publish the registration applications and their filing dates. The purpose of publication is to permit the notification of statements of objection. Three possibilities exist, (a) No statement of objections is notified and the name is entered in the Register of Protected Designations of Origin and Protected Geographical Indications, as published in the Official Journal of the European Communities; (b) there are objections to the registration—Article 7—within six months of the date of publication in the Official Journal of the European Communities; and (c) the Commission concludes that the

geographical indication does not qualify for protection and decides not to proceed with publication. The Commission may in all cases request the opinion of the Committee on Designations of Origin and Geographical Indications—Article 15—prior to publication.

(iv) Amendment of a specification

13. Article 9 authorizes any member State to request the amendment of a specification to take account of developments in scientific and technical knowledge or to redefine the geographical area.

(v) Failure to comply with specifications / Right of complaint / Intervention of the Commission / Cancellation of registration

14. Any member State may submit that a condition laid down in the product specification has not been met—pursuant to Article 11—by making its submission to the member State concerned. The member State concerned shall examine the complaint and inform the other member State of its findings and of any measures taken. The Commission will have to intervene in the event of repeated irregularities. If the member States concerned fail to come to an agreement and file a duly substantiated application, the Commission will examine the application by consulting the member States concerned and, where appropriate, having consulted the specific committee and considering it pertinent, will take the necessary steps, including cancellation of the registration. Article 11*bis* establishes the cases in which the registration may be cancelled.

15. To sum up, Argentina emphasizes the uncertainty with regard to: (a) the possible implementation of these provisions in the case of non-Community countries, and (b) their consistency with the characterization of intellectual property rights in the TRIPS Agreement, by requiring that States manage the registration of geographical indications instead of their legitimate owners, persons under private law (not to mention what appears yet more serious: the covert subordination, established by the Regulation, of governments of non-member states vis-à-vis EC institutions). Therefore, and contrary to the assertions of the European Communities, the EC Regulation does indeed make a distinction on the basis of nationality. Evidence for this are the provisions under Articles 5, 6, 7 and 10.

16. In short, the reciprocity and equivalence requirements laid down in Council Regulation (EEC) No. 2081/92 are inconsistent with the national treatment clause in Article 3 of the TRIPS Agreement.

(d) Applicability of equivalence and reciprocity criteria to WTO Members

17. Argentina observes the European Communities' attempt to reduce the entire issue raised by the complainants to a mere question of the interpretation of the relevant Community legislation. To this end, Argentina submits a brief interpretation to demonstrate that the Regulation provides for a method inconsistent with the European Communities' obligations in the WTO in the light of the TRIPS Agreement. In Argentina's opinion, the explanation by the European Communities in its first written submission of the application of reciprocity and equivalence criteria is not convincing. Had the intention been to make a distinction not only between EC member States and non-Community countries but also, as the European Communities maintains, between WTO Members and third countries, the distinction could have been made more explicitly. However, even a simple amendment to that effect would not resolve the substantive issues previously raised regarding the application of this regulation to non-Community countries, given that the only registration and objection procedures provided for are through the intermediary of member States and that the requirements are laid down for the establishment of inspection structures which are not binding on any country other than EC member States. The requirements mentioned above clearly deviate from the national treatment obligation in Article 3 of the TRIPS Agreement.

3. Points raised in response to the Panel's questions

18. Argentina is not aware of any group or person ever having filed with its authorities either an application for or an objection to a registration pursuant to the EC Regulation. As to the question whether Argentina would be willing or able to transmit such applications, without prejudice to its willingness to cooperate in any procedural aspect involving the transmission of an application for registration, on behalf of any domestic group or person, that eventually the Government of Argentina could hypothetically show at any point in time, Argentina would like the Panel to note that, as a non-EC member, it has never delegated any sovereign right to the supranational institutions of the European Union. Hence, there would be no legal obligation for the Argentine State to fulfil any requirement imposed by the EC legislation, even less in a case like the one in question, which involves a private right, as established in the preamble of the TRIPS Agreement. Argentina's legislation allows direct access by GI applicants to the national authority irrespective of nationality.

19. Argentina's domestic law establishes the exceptions to trademark rights provided for in Article 17 of the TRIPS Agreement, under the conditions and with the scope provided therein. Argentina is not aware of any GIs registered under the EC Regulation that are identical or confusingly similar to Community protected trademarks owned by nationals of Argentina. It notes, however, that this should not be interpreted as saying that this would never happen, as the EC Regulation provides for the possibility of broadening the applicability of the Regulation, by making products which are not currently included in the list of products covered by this Regulation, subject to it in the future.

20. Argentina believes that there is—in principle—no conflict between Articles 16.1 and 22.3 of TRIPS Agreement. However, given the broad discretion given by the TRIPS Agreement to the Members in implementing its provisions (Article 1.1 of the TRIPS Agreement), such a conflict could arise as a consequence of the way a Member chooses to implement it. In other words, there is no contradiction arising from the textual reading of either provision, but for those that could eventually arise during, or as a consequence of its implementation.

21. Argentina is of the view that the EC Regulation is challengeable under the TRIPS Agreement, due its mandatory nature.

B. BRAZIL

1. Introduction

22. Brazil has a systemic interest in the matter subject to this dispute. Brazil has no geographical indications ("GIs") as yet registered in the EC under the procedure set out in the measure at issue, but private parties in the country have demonstrated increasing awareness of the implications stemming from the development of a culture fostering the registration of Brazilian GIs, both in Brazil and elsewhere.

2. Reciprocity and equivalence requirements in the registration of, and objection to, a GI

23. Both Australia and the United States claim that Article 12(1) of the EC Regulation fails to comply with the national treatment obligation provided for by Article 3 of the TRIPS Agreement and Article III:4 of GATT 1994 since, in order to benefit from the Regulation, it requires that WTO Members meet certain conditions, such as reciprocity and equivalence. Brazil supports this understanding. In fact, the requirements set forth in Article 12(1) of the EC Regulation, despite assertions to the contrary by the European Communities, clearly establish "extra hurdles" for WTO Members. The several requirements spread throughout Article 12 create a bias against third countries and violate national treatment obligations. As a matter of fact, these inconsistent requirements pervade most of the Regulation and taint its practical operation to the detriment of other WTO Members. In a nutshell, and as abundantly argued by the complainants and other third parties, WTO Members, before they can apply for protection under Article 12(1), must adopt an internal system for GI protection that

guarantees equivalence to the EC Regulation and that must also provide reciprocity to "corresponding" EC products. These requirements, if they do not amount to something close to "extra-territoriality," certainly collide with the essence of the national treatment obligations enshrined in Article III of GATT 1994 and Article 3.1 of the TRIPS Agreement.

24. As graphically shown by New Zealand in the exhibits to its submission, nationals from WTO Members are at a disadvantage with regard to EC nationals. The GATT and WTO underlying principle of national treatment would be completely voided of any meaning if it were made conditional on requirements of reciprocity and adoption of equivalent legislation. The European Communities in its first submission argues that the proviso in Article 12(1)—"without prejudice to international agreements"—excludes WTO Members from the scope and requirements of Article 12. Brazil welcomes this novel and official interpretation by the European Communities to the effect that "international agreements" include the WTO agreements and that consequentially Articles 12(1) and 12(3) of the Regulation do not apply to WTO Members. Irrespective, however, of this interpretation by the Commission, which would not necessarily withstand scrutiny by a judicial body, it would seem unlikely that provisions in the EC Regulation that refer to "third countries" would have been drafted only with a handful of non-WTO Members in mind. Furthermore, the utilization of the terms "third countries" and "Community" in Article 12(2) suggests that, in this opposition, "third countries" mean all those countries which are not EC member States. If, on any account, one were to accept the EC's arguments about the proviso, i.e. that it excludes WTO Members, it could, *a contrario senso*, indicate a recognition by the European Communities that the reciprocity and equivalence requirements in Article 12 violate national treatment obligations in the GATT 1994 and TRIPS Agreement. Brazil takes note, however, of the use in the Regulation of the terms "WTO members" and "third countries" in Articles 12b(2)(a) and (b) and 12d(1), something that could indicate that third countries are confined to those non-WTO Members. Therefore, Brazil is of the view that the language of Article 12(1) should clearly specify that WTO Members are exempt from offering reciprocity and equivalence in order to be in compliance with the national treatment obligation.

25. As regards the issue of objection procedures to registration of GIs, Brazil is equally concerned with the fact that the procedures, set forth in Article 12d(1), can be subject to the same inconsistent requirements of reciprocity and equivalence applicable to the registration procedure as explained above.

3. Aspects of the registration and objection procedures for GIs

26. Brazil also calls the attention of the Panel to two specific procedural aspects of both the registration and the objection procedures as stated in Articles 12a(1) and (2) and 12d(1), which appear to be inconsistent with the agreed multilateral rules.

27. These provisions require that WTO Members "pre-approve" the application for registration of geographical areas located in their territories before they forward it to the European Commission. WTO Member national authorities must first analyse and deem that the requirements of the EC Regulation are satisfied. Brazil opines that, if this requirement applies to WTO Members, it is in striking violation of the national treatment obligation under Article 3 of the TRIPS Agreement and Article III:4 of GATT 1994. The inconsistencies appear to be twofold: first, that an additional national procedure is introduced, whereas in the EC, the application sent to an EC member State by an EC applicant is tantamount to a mere formality (Article 5(5) of the Regulation); second, and most disturbing, the analysis by the national authority in the WTO Member must be undertaken according to the EC Regulation, and not to its own domestic rules—Article 12a(2) of the Regulation. In this situation, assuming that the State concerned will likely have its own standards to assess the adequacy of the application *vis-à-vis* the EC Regulation, it is only fair to assume that more often than not, the Commission, in its turn, will not deem appropriate the evaluation carried out by the WTO Member, which could then lead to further procedural delays. Thus, a more balanced treatment of the issue would be to grant applicants from WTO Members direct access to the Commission for registration purposes. This direct access by the applicant to the national authority, irrespective of nationality, is provided, for example, by the Brazilian legislation. In sum, even if in formal terms the treatment given to applications from EC member States

and WTO Members is similar, the effects that are produced by such procedure are clearly different and detrimental to interested parties located in the latter.

28. Article 12d(1) of Regulation 2081/92 requires that, whenever a natural or legal person from a WTO Member wishes to object to the registration of a geographical indication submitted by an EC member State, it should do so by sending a duly substantiated statement to the country in which it resides. Brazil is of the opinion that this requirement establishes an "unnecessarily complicated or costly" procedure concerning the enforcement of intellectual property rights, in breach of Article 41.2 of the TRIPS Agreement. Brazil sees no "necessity" that would justify preventing private parties from addressing their objections directly to the European Commission. Many countries, like Brazil, have domestic legislations that allow for direct access by foreigners in order to object to registration procedures. The EC has not provided convincing reasons to deny interested parties direct access to the EC bodies. If, according to its Article 12d(2), the Regulation already determines that the "Commission shall examine the admissibility of objections," Brazil fails to see the need for requiring prior submission of the objection to the WTO Member in which the objector resides or is established.

4. Remarks on the coexistence of trademarks and GIs

29. While Brazil recognizes that both trademarks and GIs are "signs" that represent products or services, one cannot overlook the fact that geographical indications that are identical to trademarks are likely to create confusion and, consequently, may affect the value of trademarks. Brazil recalls that Article 16.1 of the TRIPS Agreement protects the owner of a registered trademark from the use by third parties of identical or similar signs for goods or services identical or similar to those in respect of which the trademark is registered, where such use would result in a likelihood of confusion. Therefore, what seems clear is that the protection the TRIPS Agreement mandates countries to offer to owners of trademark comprehends the use of any sign (and not only that of a trademark) that might cause confusion. In Brazil's view, Article 16.1 of the TRIPS Agreement deals with trademarks in general, and not only with those referred to in the narrow terms of Article 14(3) of the Regulation, which establishes that a geographical indication shall not be registered where, "in the light of a trademark's reputation and renown and the length of time it has been used, registration is liable to mislead the consumer as to the true identity of the product."

30. Despite a theoretical hypothesis of coexistence between a trademark and a geographical indication in terms of Articles 24.5 and 16.1 of the TRIPS Agreement, when read in conjunction, Brazil believes that without disregarding the peculiar features surrounding the use of a geographical indication and the need to protect it, one must not do so at the expense of both the trademark owners and the consumers. Otherwise, the commercial value of a trademark may be undermined, which runs contrary to the "exclusive rights" of a trademark owner provided for in Article 16.1 of the TRIPS Agreement. It should also be noted that pursuant to Article 16.1, in cases of the use of an identical sign for identical goods or services, "a likelihood of confusion shall be presumed." Regulation 2081/92 does not have any provision incorporating such a presumption. Brazil does not agree with the EC's argument that there was no need to "reproduce explicitly" this presumption, on the grounds that it would suffice that domestic law grants the registering authority or to the courts the adequate level of discretion to apply this provision. Brazil submits that even if domestic law incorporated the presumption in each EC member State, this would not mean automatically that Community-level registration, regulated by Regulation 2081/92, would have also provided for its incorporation. Therefore, the European measure would still remain inconsistent with the TRIPS Agreement.

31. Brazil also highlights another possible imbalance between the protection of EC nationals and WTO Member nationals as regards the effective use of the protection mechanism of Article 22.3 of the TRIPS Agreement in that, through the use of the EC Regulation, the EC national would much more rapidly and efficiently protect a GI to the detriment of a previous registered trademark, than would a WTO Member national be in a position to defend trademark owner rights *vis-à-vis* the application for registration of a new GI.

5. Points raised in response to the Panel's questions

32. Brazil is not aware of any group or person ever having filed with its authorities either an application for, or an objection to, a registration pursuant to the EC Regulation. As to the question whether Brazil would be willing or able to transmit such applications, it states that, the issue here is not simply a matter of mechanistic, bureaucratic "transmittal" of applications. Article 12a(2) of the EC Regulation requires from authorities of third countries a thorough analysis of the applications in light of that Regulation before transmitting them to the Commission. Brazil also recalls that there is no legal provision in Brazilian law establishing the need for Government intervention in the registration of GIs in foreign countries. Moreover, the Brazilian authorities would be devoid of legal competence to perform the analysis of the application as required by the EC Regulation, especially in light of the principle of legality, enshrined in Article 37 of the Brazilian Constitution.

33. Brazil calls the Panel's attention to the existence of the Patent Cooperation Treaty ("PCT"). This Agreement imposes that requests for international search and preliminary examination of private parties' patent applications be transmitted to the Office of the PCT by national governments. The European Communities, through Regulation 2081/92—rather than through an internationally agreed mechanism—seeks to impose unilaterally its own rules and parameters on all other countries, something which would amount to extra-territoriality. Harmonization of rules or standards on intellectual property rights can only be obtained through multilateral or bilateral cooperation agreements. The European Communities' stance, if taken *ad absurdum*, could allow a situation where other countries would also issue their own strict legislation and procedures and would request that all other countries analyse applications for registration in accordance with those unilaterally-fixed rules.

34. Brazil understands that the interpretation of "nationals" as used in Articles 1.3 (including its footnote 1), 3.1 and 4 of the TRIPS Agreement and Article 2 of the Paris Convention, depends on how a national legal system defines the "nationality" of a legal person. Due to particular features pertaining to geographical indications—which are necessarily bound to a given territorial basis—it is reasonable to assume that the legal person holding the right over their use, will be a group or association established in the territory of the Member in which the GI is located, without prejudice to the provision of Article 2(2) of the Paris Convention. This is tantamount to saying that the geographical area from which a geographical indication originates determines the nationality of the interested parties seeking to register it and that the parties applying for registration of non-EC GIs will most likely be legal persons that are "nationals" of non-EC countries. The European Communities concedes that Regulation 2081/92 provides for different treatment regarding "geographical areas."[1] Thus, in most cases, discriminating between geographical areas is equivalent to discriminating between nationals. In other words, the area in which a geographical indication is located is actually linked to the nationality of the applicant.

35. : Brazil agrees that the words "country of the Union" in Article 2(1) of the Paris Convention (1967), as incorporated in the TRIPS Agreement by its Article 2.1, should be read *mutatis mutandis* to refer to "WTO Member." This reasoning is in accordance with the understanding of the Appellate Body in *US – Section 211 Appropriations Act*.[2]

36. Brazil's views on the relationship between the national treatment obligation under the TRIPS Agreement and GATT 1994 are threefold. First, Brazil notes that on a theoretical level not all "different treatment" amounts to "less favourable treatment." Second, Brazil understands that a less-favourable-treatment-situation in violation to national treatment obligation arises where a measure "modifie[s] the conditions of competition in the market to the detriment of imported products," which appears to be the case with reference to the EC Regulation at issue. Third, as the Appellate Body stated in *US – Section 211 Appropriations Act*, "[t]he Panel was correct in concluding that, as the language of Article 3.1 of the TRIPS Agreement, in particular, is

---

[1] European Communities' first written submission, para. 125.

[2] Appellate Body Report on *US – Section 211 Appropriations Act*, para. 238.

similar to that of Article III:4 of the GATT 1994, the jurisprudence on Article III:4 of the GATT 1994 may be useful in interpreting the national treatment obligation in the TRIPS Agreement."[3]

37. Brazil is not aware of any GIs registered under the EC Regulation that are identical or confusingly similar to Community protected trademarks owned by Brazilian nationals.

38. Brazils recalls that previous WTO panels and Appellate Body reports have considered that there is a presumption against conflict in public international law, and it quotes two panel reports in this regard.[4] If it can be assumed that there is a presumption against conflicts between international legal instruments, one can also reasonably expect that the same presumption applies to apparent conflicts within the same agreement. Therefore, in addressing the issue of the conflict between Articles 16.1 and 22.3 of the TRIPS Agreement, Brazil submits that Article 22.3 imposes two tests in order to allow a trademark registration to be refused or invalidated. In turn, Article 16.1 grants the trademark owner the exclusive right to prevent third parties from using identical or similar signs for goods or services which are identical or similar to those in respect of which the trademark is registered, where such use would result in a likelihood of confusion. The protection of the distinctiveness of the trademark is thus contingent upon the likelihood of confusion brought about by signs which are identical or similar. One should consider that, without disregarding the peculiar features surrounding the use of a geographical indication and the need to protect it, this must not be done at the expense of both the trademark owners and the consumers. In other words, it means that the approach to the issue should be carried out taking due account of the fact that: a) geographical indications do not *a priori* prevail over registered trademarks; and b) other factors must be borne in mind when deciding whether to allow either the coexistence between trademarks and geographical indications or the predominance of one over the other, such as, for instance, the length of time a given trademark has been used.

39. Brazil's Industrial Property Law (Article 132) sets out exceptions to the exclusive right of a trademark owner. Accordingly, a trademark owner cannot: (a) prohibit retailers or distributors from utilizing distinctive signs pertaining to their businesses along with a product trademark for marketing purposes; (b) prohibit parts manufacturers from utilizing a trademark in order to indicate the product destination, provided fair competition practices are met; and (c) prohibit the mentioning of a trademark in a speech, scientific or literary work or in whatever sort of publication, as long as deprived of commercial meaning and without prejudice to its distinctive character.

40. Brazil notes that in *US – Section 211 Appropriations Act*, a dispute dealing with the interpretation of several TRIPS provisions, the Appellate Body confirmed the Panel's view in *US – 1916 Act* and stated that "a distinction should be made between legislation that mandates WTO-inconsistent behaviour, and legislation that gives rise to executive authority that can be exercised with discretion."[5] On the other hand, the Appellate Body in *US – Corrosion-Resistant Steel Sunset Review*, did not express a view on whether the mandatory/discretionary distinction is a legally appropriate analytical tool for panels to use. It observed that "as with any such analytical tool, the import of the mandatory/discretionary distinction may vary from case to case. For this reason, we also wish to caution against the application of this distinction in a mechanistic fashion."[6] Thus, while the distinction can certainly be applied under the TRIPS Agreement, as a jurisprudential construction, it must be used with caution (*cum granum salis*). Brazil also remarks that the mandatory/discretionary distinction is always centred on a specific measure taken by a Member. As to the issue of "omissions" or "failures" to take certain required actions, Brazil is of the opinion, firstly, that an omission can also be considered a violation of a provision and, secondly, that, by definition, the "mandatory/discretionary" distinction cannot be applicable to instances of failure to take action, i.e. an

[3] *Ibid.*, para. 242.

[4] Panel Report on *Indonesia – Autos*, para. 14.28 and fn. 649; and Panel Report on *Turkey – Textiles*, para. 9.92.

[5] Appellate Body Report on *US – Section 211 Appropriations Act*, para. 259.

[6] Appellate Body Report on *US – Corrosion-Resistant Steel Sunset Review*, para. 93.

omission, for there would be no concrete legislation issued by a Member upon which the distinction could focus.

C. CANADA

1. Introduction

41. Canada has a systemic interest in the interpretation of the national treatment obligations of WTO Members under the TRIPS Agreement, specifically as these apply to the implementation of intellectual property rights for the protection of geographical indications.

42. Canada focuses its views mainly on two issues related to national treatment obligations under the TRIPS Agreement as they are interpreted and applied in the present case. These are:

- the degree to which Articles 2.1 and 3.1 of the TRIPS Agreement prevent a WTO Member from requiring *reciprocity and equivalence* when protecting the intellectual property rights of nationals of other WTO Members, including whether or not such reciprocity and equivalence is in fact required by the EC Regulation; and
- the implications of the reference to *nationals* in Articles 2.1 and 3.1 of the TRIPS Agreement, in particular the degree to which such references permit WTO Members to discriminate in a manner not directly based on *nationality* when protecting intellectual property rights.

2. Reciprocity and equivalence requirements of the EC Regulation

43. The national treatment obligations under the TRIPS Agreement prevent the European Communities from requiring reciprocal and equivalent protection in non-EC WTO Members as a condition for protection in the European Communities of geographical indications originating in the territory of those WTO Members. The national treatment obligations of WTO Members with regard to the protection of intellectual property are contained in two separate provisions of the TRIPS Agreement. First, the earlier national treatment obligations of the Paris Convention are incorporated by reference into Article 2.1 of the TRIPS Agreement. Second, national treatment applies in the TRIPS Agreement more broadly by virtue of the requirement in Article 3.1 that a WTO Member "accord to the nationals of other Members treatment no less favourable than it accords to its own nationals with regard to the protection of intellectual property." These obligations mean that any intellectual property right provided by a WTO Member within its territory must be made available to nationals of all other WTO Members, without regard to the conditions of substantive protection available in those WTO Members. Requiring reciprocal and equivalent treatment—that is, conditioning the protection of rights of foreign nationals in the domestic jurisdiction on equivalent protection being afforded to domestic nationals in the foreign jurisdiction—runs precisely counter to national treatment obligations.

44. All parties to the present case substantially agree on the fundamental importance of the national treatment obligations under the TRIPS Agreement. The main issues of contention are: (i) whether the EC Regulation treats geographical indications originating outside the European Communities less favourably than geographical indications originating within the European Communities; (ii) and whether this less favourable treatment applies also to geographical indications originating in the territory of other WTO Members.

45. The European Communities submits that a significant feature of the EC Regulation is the provision of separate procedures for the registration, and objection to registration, of geographical indications originating from an area *within* the European Communities (in Articles 5, 6 and 7) and the parallel procedures set out for the registration, and objection to registration, of geographical indications originating from areas *outside* the European Communities (in Articles 12, 12a, 12b, 12c and 12d). While the two separate procedures in the EC Regulation do exhibit certain similarities, a significant difference is that Article 12 provides that the EC

Regulation "may" apply to geographical indications originating from the territory of a third country but only if that third country meets certain conditions. One of these conditions is the requirement in Article 12(1) that "the third country concerned is prepared to provide protection *equivalent to that available in the Community* to corresponding agricultural products [or] foodstuffs coming from the Community." Article 12(3) further requires the European Commission to examine the national legislation of the third country to certify that it satisfies the "equivalence conditions" specified in Article 12(1).

46. In other words, applicants for intellectual property protection in the European Communities of geographical indications originating in third countries that do not meet the conditions in Article 12(1) are automatically disqualified from eligibility for such protection simply on the basis of the absence of equivalent protection in their home jurisdiction. This requirement imposes a condition on applicants for geographical indications originating outside the European Communities that does not exist for applicants for geographical indications originating within the European Communities. The EC Regulation therefore accords less favourable treatment to geographical indications from outside European Communities than it accords to geographical indications from within the European Communities. The European Communities in fact admits that Article 12 of the EC Regulation requires reciprocity and equivalence for registration for protection in the European Communities of geographical indications originating from outside the European Communities (see, e.g., recital 9 of EC Regulation No. 692/2003, which says that "[t]he protection provided by registration under Regulation (EEC) No 2081/92 is open to third countries' names by reciprocity and under equivalence conditions as provided for in Article 12 of that Regulation"). If these *de jure* discriminatory provisions were to apply to WTO Members, they would violate the European Communities' national treatment obligations under the TRIPS Agreement.

47. The European Communities contends in its first written submission that the reciprocity and equivalence requirements contained in Articles 12(1) and (3) simply do not apply to WTO Members since these countries already must provide adequate protection for geographical indications by virtue of their obligations under the TRIPS Agreement. To justify this interpretation of Article 12, the European Communities points to the reference in Article 12(1) to "[w]ithout prejudice to international agreements," arguing that this clause preserves the rights of WTO Members to access the EC registration system on a national treatment basis. Heartening as this contention is in principle, when read in the context of Articles 12a, 12b and 12d, Article 12 cannot support the interpretation advanced by the European Communities. The ambiguous reference to "international agreements" in Article 12 is simply insufficient to counter the clear wording of Articles 12, 12a, 12b, and 12d, which, when taken together suggest an interpretation opposite to that offered by the European Communities.

48. First, if the European Communities' interpretation of Article 12(1) and (3) were to be accepted, there would not appear to be an alternative legal basis for an applicant with a geographical indication originating from the territory of a non-EC WTO Member to commence an application for registration in the European Communities. The EC Regulation is drafted in such a way that the only starting point for third countries, WTO Members as well as non-Members, is Article 12 (additionally to Canada it remains unclear why the European Communities argues that these sub-articles operate in this manner whereas Article 12(2) does not). The European Communities response is that the relevant starting point for WTO Members is Article 12a, suggesting that these countries pass immediately to the procedures provided for in that article for registration of geographical indications from third countries. While Article 12a is the operative paragraph governing the *transmission* of an application to the European Communities, this provision does not appear to operate in the manner suggested by the European Communities. Article 12a(1) of the EC Regulation provides that "*[i]n the case provided for in Article 12(3)* ... a group or a natural or legal person ... shall send a registration application to the authorities in the country in which the geographical area is located" [emphasis added]. The underlined portion of that provision suggests that this procedure is only available in the case of those third countries that have already qualified according to the procedure laid out in Article 12(3), which requires meeting the conditions specified in Article 12(1). Even Article 12a(2), which governs the actual transmission of the applications from the third country to the European Communities, depends on the country first being identified

by the procedure in 12a(1). Therefore, Article 12a does not provide an independent basis for a geographical indication originating from a non-EC WTO Member to be registered in the European Communities.

49. Second, the European Communities refers to distinctions made in Articles 12b(2)(a) and (b) (objections to registrations of geographical indications originating from areas outside the European Communities) and 12d(1) (objections to registrations of geographical indications originating within the EC). Those provisions distinguish between a "WTO Member" on the one hand and, respectively, "a third country meeting the equivalence conditions of Article 12(3)" and "a third country recognized under the procedure provided for in Article 12(3)." The European Communities' argument seems to be that the distinction in these latter provisions implies the existence of a distinction between WTO Members and third countries for the purposes of Article 12(1) and (3). However, the European Communities' own argument on a separate but related point supports precisely the opposite conclusion. Specifically, with respect to Article 12d(1) the European Communities argues that the reference to 12(3) only applies to "third countries other than WTO Members." The European Communities continues: "[O]therwise, the specific reference to WTO members [in 12d(1)] would be meaningless." Using the European Communities' own logic, if the *presence* of the reference to "WTO Members" in the context of Article 12b and 12d *meaningfully* suggests differential application of those provisions between WTO Members and other third countries, then the *absence* of a reference to "WTO Members" in the context of Article 12 and 12a must *meaningfully* suggest no differential application of those provisions between WTO Members and other third countries.

50. Thus, notwithstanding the contrary interpretation offered by the European Communities, the clear wording of Article 12 and 12a means that those provisions apply equally to WTO Members and other third countries. The only way for "a group or a natural or legal person" from a WTO Member to apply for registration for a non EC-based geographical indication is for the WTO Member from which the indication originates to qualify according to the "equivalence conditions" of Article 12(1) and 12(3). Moreover, in the September 2002 meeting of the Council for TRIPS, the European Communities provided its views on the application of national treatment in the context of registration systems for geographical indications saying that "[t]he EC believes that registration systems should be primarily aimed at the identification of domestic GIs."[7] Later in the same intervention, the European Communities continued: "[I]t seems to us that the logical conclusion is to *limit the registration system to domestic GIs* and protect foreign GIs via other means." In light of these statements, there is no doubt about the European Communities' intention that Article 12 applies to WTO Members.

3. National treatment of "nationals" of WTO Members under the TRIPS Agreement

51. The reference to *nationals* in the TRIPS Agreement cannot be interpreted so narrowly as to render that term meaningless when it comes to national treatment with regard to the protection of intellectual property rights. This is most importantly the case in the context of the protection of geographical indications, which are tied more closely to the territories from which they originate than to the nationality of the rights holders. The European Communities acknowledges the important, and deliberate, emphasis in the TRIPS Agreement on *nationals*, as opposed to the focus on *products* under the GATT. Since minimum standards for intellectual property protection is about conferring rights, it necessarily follows that *natural and legal persons* are the holders of these rights, and that as a result WTO non-discrimination obligations generally apply as between the *nationals* who hold these rights. However, having acknowledged these important features of the TRIPS Agreement, the European Communities fails to fully appreciate their implications.

52. Specifically, the European Communities submits that even if the two parallel procedures in the EC Regulation operate differently (which the European Communities does not admit), the separate procedures do not distinguish between *nationals*, but simply distinguish between *geographical areas*, that is, geographic indications originating from areas within the European Communities, as opposed to geographic indications

[7] See the minutes of that meeting in document IP/C/M/37/Add.1, at p. 80.

originating from areas outside the European Communities. The European Communities claims that "[w]hether the area to which a geographic indication is related is located inside the European Communities or outside is in no way linked to the question of the nationality of the producers or the product concerned." This statement misinterprets the nature of intellectual property rights generally and the nature of protection of geographical indications specifically. The European Communities ignores the full meaning of Article 3.1 of the TRIPS Agreement, in particular by downplaying the *de facto* effect on nationals of a measure that the European Communities itself admits discriminates on the basis of national territories. The European Communities further underestimates the degree to which Article 3.1 applies to more than just the nationality of a national from a WTO Member, but also to the full availability and scope of the rights sought.

4. *De Facto* discrimination according to nationality

53. The European Communities claims that Articles 5 and 6 operate without distinction as between nationals when it comes to geographical indications originating from within the European Communities, and that Articles 12 and 12a operate in a similarly non-discriminatory fashion when it comes to geographical indications originating from outside the European Communities. This claim ignores the simple and incontestable reality that EC nationals are likely to register for protection of geographical indications originating from within the European Communities, whereas non-EC nationals are likely to register for protection of geographical indications originating from outside of the European Communities. The distinction between geographical areas is illusory if the effect of the EC Regulation is to *de facto* prevent nationals from non-EC WTO Members from registering for protection of the geographical indications from their own territories.

54. As the United States has argued, the principles developed in the context of national treatment with respect to goods are instructive. In particular, in assessing whether the EC Regulation *de facto* affords more favourable treatment to EC nationals than it does to non-EC nationals, this Panel needs to look beyond the literal provisions of the EC Regulation, and examine objectively the structure and overall application of the Regulation, including the underlying criteria used to allow registration of a geographical indication.[8] The structure of the EC Regulation clearly provides two different procedures for the registration of geographical indications. The sole criterion used in determining which procedure an application for registration shall follow is *geographical area*, with the only difference being whether or not the geographical area is within the boundaries of the European Communities. This choice of the boundaries of the European Communities as the only criterion raises significant concerns about the neutrality of the provisions as to the nationality of the applicants. This is particularly the case for geographical indications that, by definition, are tied to the production of goods originating in the area identified by the geographical indication and, by extension, producers in that area. Given this explicit requirement that physical production of the associated good take place in the same area as indicated by the geographical indication, an applicant for a geographical indication that refers to an area within the European Communities will, in all probability, be a national of an EC member State. Conversely, an applicant for a geographical indication referring to an area in a third country will, in all probability, be a national of that third country. As a result, despite the apparently neutral application of the EC Regulation regarding nationality, it is clear that the procedure set aside for geographical indications originating within the European Communities (Articles 5 and 6) *de facto* serves EC nationals, whereas the procedure set aside for geographical indications originating outside the European Communities (Article 12 and 12a) *de facto* serves nationals of third countries, including nationals of other WTO Members.

55. The European Communities claims that caution must be exercised in finding that the EC Regulation provides *de facto* less favourable support to non-EC nationals, citing the Panel report in *Indonesia – Autos*.[9] The Panel in that case failed to find discrimination between nationals on the grounds that the Indonesian National Car Programme (which forced applicants to the programme to choose between the mark of the local programme and their global marks) applied equally to Indonesians and foreigners. The Panel found no discrimination

---

[8] Appellate Body Report on *Japan – Alcoholic Beverages II*, DSR 1996:I, at 120.

[9] Panel Report on *Indonesia – Autos*, paras. 14.271 and 14.273.

between nationals on the basis that both nationals and non-nationals faced the same choice.[10] That is not the case here. The EC Regulation does not require all applicants to choose between registering a foreign geographical indication (or global mark) and an EC-based geographical indication. Rather, the EC Regulation requires all applicants to choose between registering an EC-based geographical indication and not registering a geographical indication at all. Applicants of non-EC nationality are, by definition, not likely to be registering an EC-based geographical indication.

56. The European Communities further cites with favour the finding of that same Panel regarding the application of TRIPS Agreement national treatment obligations to matters not directly related to equal treatment of *nationals*. The Panel found that it would be unreasonable to use the national treatment obligations in relation to intellectual property rights to challenge domestic support measures not involving intellectual property rights, on the grounds that such measures could have the *de facto* effect of giving an advantage to domestic nationals.[11] Once again, that is not the case here. Invoking national treatment concerns against an EC system that *de facto* favours EC nationals, as does the EC Regulation, is not about challenging a non-intellectual property support measure to enforce equal treatment of nationals with regard to intellectual property rights. On the contrary, it is precisely about challenging the operation of an intellectual property measure in order to enforce equal treatment of nationals with regard to that *same* intellectual property measure. The findings of the Panel in *Indonesia – Autos* have no bearing on this case.

5. *De jure* discrimination according on nationality

57. The EC Regulation *de facto* discriminates between EC nationals and non-EC nationals in a manner that violates the national treatment obligations contained in Articles 2.1 and 3.1 of the TRIPS Agreement.

58. Canada submits that the EC Regulation discriminates between nationals of WTO Members as a matter of legal construction. Consider further the example of an inventor seeking patent protection for her invention. In all but the rarest of cases, an invention is also independent of the location of production and the location of eventual patent protection. Further, an inventor could be a natural person with nationality in her country of origin, or an inventor could be a legal person whose nationality, so to speak, will be in the country in which it has such legal personality. In either case, when patent protection is sought in Europe, the nationality of the inventor is usually retained. It is therefore equally important that European patent law not deny the inventor a patent over the invention because of nationality, and of course it cannot.

59. Contrast those two scenarios with the case of an applicant for protection of a geographical indication. First, unlike copyrighted works or patented inventions, which are independent of the location of their creation, geographical indications are by definition tied to the particular location that they represent. Second, determining the nationality of the rights holder of a geographical indication is a different matter than it is for the creator of a copyrighted work or a patented invention. In the specific case of the EC Regulation, the rights holder will only in exceptional cases be a natural person or even an individual producer. Rather, the rights holder will generally be a group or association of local producers, established for the purpose of marketing their similar products, and it is these groups that subsequently authorize individual producers to use the geographical indication. Since these groups are the "interested parties" referred to in provisions on geographical indications in the TRIPS Agreement, it is the nationality of these groups that is relevant for the purposes of national treatment, and not the nationality of individual producers. The nationality of these groups or associations will invariably be in the jurisdiction in which they operate.

60. Combining these two features of geographical indications—a group of local producers (by design) registering a local indication (by definition)—virtually guarantees that the *nationality* of the rights holder will be in the country from which the geographical indication originates. In other words, the geographical area from

[10] Panel Report on *Indonesia – Autos*, para. 14.271.

[11] Panel Report on *Indonesia – Autos*, para. 14.273.

which a geographical indication originates *determines* the nationality of the interested parties seeking to register it. For example, if a Canadian farmer establishes operations in Belgium to produce a product to be marketed with a geographical indication from Belgium, that farmer's nationality will not alter the Belgian nationality of the local group that is the registered rights holder of the geographical indication. As a result, despite the apparently neutral application of the EC Regulation regarding nationality, it is clear that the procedures set aside for geographical indications originating within the European Communities *de jure* serve EC nationals, whereas the procedures set aside for geographical indications originating outside the European Communities *de jure* serve nationals of third countries. Therefore, by discriminating according to geographical area, the parallel procedures in the EC Regulation not only discriminate between nationals of WTO Members as a matter of simple probabilities, they discriminate between nationals of WTO Members as a matter of legal construction.

61. This problem is best illustrated with reference to other branches of intellectual property rights. Consider, for example, an author claiming protection under copyright for a work such as a book. The book can be written anywhere in the world, so the act of creation is independent of the location of production and the location of eventual copyright protection. Further, the author is likely to be a natural person with citizenship in his country of origin, and if he seeks protection in Europe for the book, he is likely to retain his nationality. It is important then that European copyright law not deny him copyright in the book because of his nationality, and of course it cannot.

6. National treatment applies to geographical area

62. While the prohibition on discrimination between *nationals* in the TRIPS Agreement is fundamentally different from the prohibition on discrimination between *products* that is central to national treatment under the GATT, it is possible, as the European Communities has done in its submission, to make too much of that distinction. The reference to nationals in the TRIPS Agreement cannot be divorced from its context in a trade agreement under the WTO. It cannot, for example, be reduced to a source of a general right to be free from discrimination on the basis of nationality (in the sense of citizenship) in the laws and practices of domestic institutions. The European Communities appears to be suggesting that as long as *nationality* is not specifically cited by a WTO Member as the reason for refusing the registration of an intellectual property right, that WTO Member would not be in violation of its national treatment obligations. If Article 3.1 of the TRIPS Agreement referred only to nationality, the European Communities argument might have some merit. However, the TRIPS Agreement provides national treatment to *nationals* "with regard to the protection of intellectual property" and not simply their nationality. "Protection" is further defined in footnote 3 to include "matters affecting the *availability*, acquisition, *scope*, maintenance and enforcement of intellectual property rights as well as those matters affecting the use of intellectual property rights specifically addressed in this Agreement" [emphasis added]. The European Communities notes that non-EC nationals are eligible to *acquire*, without discrimination, intellectual property rights under Articles 5 and 6 of the EC Regulation, as long as the geographical indication for which protection is sought originates within the European Communities. However, the protection of intellectual property rights in geographical indications involves more than just *acquisition*; it also involves, *inter alia*, the *availability* and *scope* of those rights. The full scope of the requirement to provide national treatment to *nationals* of all WTO Members is not restricted to the *nationality* of the party seeking registration, but extends to all facets of the protection of rights. By the European Communities' own admission, Articles 5 and 6 of the EC Regulation limit the *availability* and *scope* of protection available to a non-EC national to rights in geographical indications originating in a narrowly defined geographical area (i.e. within the European Communities). To avail themselves of the full scope of rights over geographical indications, non-EC nationals must turn to Articles 12 and 12a, an avenue that is closed off for nationals of all but a few WTO Members. The requirement to provide national treatment under the TRIPS Agreement to nationals therefore extends beyond the mere nationality of the applicant, and applies to the availability and scope of the rights for which registration is sought. By providing more favourable treatment to geographical indications from a narrow geographical area, the EC Regulation violates Articles 2.1 and 3.1 of the TRIPS Agreement.

63. Canada requests this Panel to find that EC Regulation 2081/92 violates the European Communities' national treatment obligations contained in Articles 2.1 and 3.1 of the TRIPS Agreement. In particular this

Panel should find that the EC Regulation *de jure* accords less favourable treatment to geographical indications originating from outside the European Communities than it does to those originating within the territory of the European Communities, and further that, contrary to the European Communities' interpretation of its own Regulation, this less favourable treatment applies to WTO Members. This Panel should further find that the European Communities may not rely on an artificial distinction between nationality and geographical area to mask what is otherwise *de facto* less favourable treatment in the EC Regulation of non-EC nationals than EC nationals, both with regard to the fact that geographical indications originating from outside the European Communities are sought by non-EC nationals and vice versa, and with regard to the fact that the scope of protection against discrimination in the case of geographical indications extends to include geographical area.

7. The relationship between WTO Members, the EC, EC member States and nationals

64. The EC Regulation, and the European Communities' first written submission in defence of that regulation, confuse the respective rights and responsibilities of these various actors, and as a result improperly imposes burdens on nationals of WTO Members in the name of equal treatment. The TRIPS Agreement requires WTO Members to implement in their domestic laws minimum standards concerning the protection of what are ultimately private rights. WTO Members are also required to ensure that these domestic private rights regimes—whether based on the minimum standards or reflecting more extensive protection—are equally accessible to nationals from other WTO Members. These requirements establish a direct relationship between WTO Members and foreign nationals, a relationship that is independent of any involvement of the government of the foreign nationals. The European Communities disregards this point completely when it claims that it "finds it remarkable that the United States would invoke its own unwillingness to cooperate in the registration process in order to demonstrate a national treatment violation on the part of the EC."[12] In fact, the United States would be entirely justified in invoking any unwillingness to cooperate in the registration process, because the United States is under no obligation to facilitate the acquisition of private rights by its nationals in the European Communities. That obligation falls exclusively on the European Communities. The European Communities cannot then require another WTO Member to assist it in fulfilling its obligation to protect the rights of foreign nationals, regardless of whether or not that assistance would be "burdensome."

65. The European Communities then takes the confusion a step farther by drawing EC member States into the equation. It is not Canada's place to interpret the internal EC rules governing the division of competence between the European Communities and its member States when it comes to the implementation of the TRIPS Agreement—and Canada will not do so here. Instead, Canada relies on the European Communities' own statements that: (i) it has adopted the EC Regulation on the basis of its own competence; (ii) the European Communities is an original Member of the WTO; (iii) it is irrelevant that the EC member States are also Members of the WTO; and (iv) the subject matter of the present dispute falls within the exclusive competence of the European Communities.[13] On the basis of these explanations provided by the European Communities, Canada concludes that the EC Regulation is the equivalent of a national measure, and that any functions carried out by EC member States for the purposes of implementing the EC Regulation are carried out as sub-national units of the European Communities. As a result, Canada is not surprised that the EC Regulation delegates certain functions to EC member States that it cannot delegate to the sovereign governments of third countries. Of particular note, Article 5(6) provides that "EC member States shall introduce the laws, regulations and administrative provisions necessary to comply with this Article." There is no equivalent provision in the sections that set out the procedures that apply to third country governments; nor could there be.

66. However, having established its exclusive competence over the registration of geographical indications within the European Communities, the European Communities then confuses its relationship toward sub-national units of the European Communities with its relationship toward sovereign WTO Members.[14] In

[12] European Communities' first written submission, para. 130.

[13] European Communities' first written submission, paras. 253-255.

[14] European Communities' first written submission, para. 129.

particular, the European Communities seeks to defend the requirement that third country governments, including those of WTO Members, assist applicants to comply with the requirements of the EC Regulation. This position by the European Communities effectively equates the downward delegation of responsibility to sub-national units with the outward delegation of responsibility to sovereign WTO Members. The European Communities apparently considers it "equal treatment" to require nationals of sovereign WTO Members to depend on the action of their governments (over which the European Communities has no authority) in the same way nationals of the European Communities depend on the action of their own governments (in circumstances where European Communities law requires that action). This is not equal treatment; it is less favourable treatment.: The EC Regulation therefore imposes on WTO Members a requirement for reciprocal and equivalent treatment that is in violation of the national treatment obligations contained in Articles 2.1 and 3.1 of the TRIPS Agreement.

8. Points raised in response to Panel's questions

67. Canada interprets the term "nationals," based on the ordinary meaning of this term as used in various provisions of the TRIPS Agreement, to refer to those natural and legal persons that have certain kinds of legal status in a given WTO Member, either through citizenship, in the case of natural persons, or through place of incorporation, in the case of legal persons such as corporations or associations. As such, natural and legal persons will be "nationals" of a WTO Member when they acquire such legal status. Only in the case of separate customs territory Members of the WTO, and in the case of nationals of non-WTO-Members residing or operating in the territories of WTO Members, does domicile or commercial establishment become a relevant factor for determining whether a natural or legal person is eligible for treatment otherwise available to nationals of a WTO Member. This distinction is clear from the provisions of the TRIPS Agreement, and from related provisions in the Paris Convention (1967) and the Berne Convention (1971), incorporated by reference into the TRIPS Agreement. For instance, Article 1.3 of the TRIPS Agreement provides that nationals "shall be understood as those natural or legal persons that would meet the criteria for eligibility for protection provided for in the Paris Convention (1967) [and the] Rome Convention (1971)." Article 3 of the Paris Convention (1967) sets out how to treat nationals from countries that are not members of the Union, and in doing so makes an explicit distinction between natural or legal persons who are "nationals of countries outside the Union who are domiciled or who have real and effective industrial or commercial establishments" in a country of the Union, on the one hand, and "nationals" of a country of the Union on the other. Similarly, Article 3(2) of the Berne Convention (1971) makes an explicit distinction between authors who are "not nationals of one of the countries of the Union but who have their habitual residence" in a country of the Union on the one hand, and "nationals" of a country of the Union on the other. In both these cases, as a result of their domicile, habitual residence, or industrial or commercial establishment, natural or legal persons who are not otherwise nationals of a country of the respective Unions are *accorded treatment similar* to that accorded nationals of a country of one of the Unions. However, they *do not become nationals*, for the purposes of granting rights, of the country in which they reside. Therefore, as a result of the explicit reference to this distinction, the ordinary definition of "nationals" does not "necessarily include" natural persons who are domiciled, and legal persons who have an industrial or commercial establishment in a WTO Member.

68. Canada believes that the words "country of the Union," used in Article 2(1) of the Paris Convention (1967) as incorporated in the TRIPS Agreement by its Article 2.1, should be read *mutatis mutandis* to refer to "WTO Members." The TRIPS Agreement incorporates by reference certain of the substantive provisions (Articles 1 through 12, and Article 19) of the Paris Convention (1967) such that the obligations contained in those provisions apply to WTO Members as if they were all members of the Paris Union. While WTO Members who are *not* a "country of the Union" have no rights under the Paris Convention *per se*, the TRIPS Agreement incorporates these provisions of the Paris Convention (1967) for *all* WTO Members such that the Paris Convention (1967) provisions become WTO provisions. Therefore, for the purpose of the operation of the provisions thus incorporated, the words "country of the Union" are the same as "WTO Members." For example, Article 3 of the Paris Convention operates such that it grants national treatment to certain natural and legal persons for the purposes of the operation of the Convention. As a result of incorporation into the TRIPS Agreement, that provision should be read as: "Nationals of Non-WTO Members who are domiciled or who

have real and effective industrial or commercial establishments in the territory of a WTO Member shall be treated in the same manner as nationals of WTO Members."

69. Canada understands that, in traditional trade disciplines, which are generally prohibitions on trade-distorting discriminatory behaviour, a WTO Member may have a legal measure that is broad enough to be applied by domestic statutory authorities either consistently or inconsistently with that Member's international trade obligations. The question in such a case is whether the fact that the measure *could* be applied in a manner inconsistent with international trade law is sufficient to challenge the measure as such. In the case of intellectual property rights, the TRIPS Agreement establishes minimum standards of the protection. It *requires* WTO Members to implement domestic legislation that grants rights to private rights applicants as long as they meet the minimum criteria for eligibility established by the TRIPS Agreement. While a WTO Member has flexibility in deciding how to protect these rights, all Members must protect the same rights according to at least the minimum standards. Given that it is the specific rights that are prescribed by the TRIPS Agreement, once a Member has decided how it intends to grant those rights, the implementing measure cannot authorize the exercise of discretion other than in a manner consistent with the minimum standards. Otherwise, there would be no minimum standards for rights.

D. CHINA

1. Introduction

70. China submits that a successful resolution of this dispute requires the removal of ambiguity in, and proper interpretation of, the following issues:

- applicability of Article 12 of the EC Regulation to non-EC WTO Members;
- verification and publication affecting non-EC WTO Members; and
- product specifications and inspection structures affecting non-EC WTO Members.

71. The provisions of the EC Regulation of particular concern to China are those relating to non-EC WTO Members. In this respect, ambiguities remain in the EC Regulation. Its frequent references to "third countries," "conditions for protection," etc., are without any express delineation as to whether certain provisions are applicable to a non-EC WTO Member or not. The interpretations and cross-references offered in the European Communities first written submission fail to remove these ambiguities.

2. Applicability of Article 12 of the EC Regulation

72. The European Communities' textual interpretation of Article 12, including the wording "[w]ithout prejudice to international agreements" is not accompanied by any evidentiary support, whether in terms of actual implementation or of judicial deliberation. Nor is there any regulatory language in the provisions to expressly exclude the applicability of these provisions to non-EC WTO Members. While paragraph (10) of the recitals speaks specifically of a right of objection granted to nationals of WTO Member countries on the basis of the "without prejudice" *chapeau*, the preamble of the EC Regulation's amendments does not expressly exclude WTO Members from the Article 12 applicability of the reciprocity and equivalence requirement to third countries. Had the drafters intended that Article 12 would not apply to non-EC WTO Members, a clause to that effect sitting next to the express reference to the right to object in the Preamble would have been inserted.

73. The European Communities itself admits that the EC Regulation *does* require that conditions be met in respect of "specific geographical indications from third countries" which, more likely than not, includes WTO

Members, where it stated that it does require that the product specifications and inspection regimes with regard to specific GIs from third countries meet the conditions of Regulation 2081/92.[15]

74. Immediately after that paragraph, the European Communities continues to argue that, in the event that the above equivalence and reciprocity requirements with respect to product specification and inspection regime were challenged by the complainants in this case, it would not be inconsistent with Article 3.1 of the TRIPS Agreement and Article 2(1) of the Paris Convention.

75. The language of Article 12 does not support the European Communities' interpretation that it was not applicable to WTO Members. That interpretation requires steps in reasoning with precise attention to the WTO TRIPS Agreement. The "without prejudice" *chapeau* is too general to reflect such reasoning.

76. Putting aside the legitimacy of such specification and inspection issues, it is worth noting that the European Communities' reversion to demanding equivalence and reciprocity in respect of certain components of its GI protection regime is particularly significant. It further added complication to the proper interpretation of Article 12 as quoted above. By reintroducing the equivalence and reciprocity requirement for specifications and inspections in relation to specific GIs from WTO Members, the European Communities appears to admit that portions of Article 12, particularly in respect of the whole first indent and the first portion of the second indent of Article 12(1), apply to WTO Members, in contradiction to its earlier argument that the whole Article does not apply.

77. The language of Article 12 does not suggest a split in the applicability of, for example, the registration requirement versus the overall protection regime. The leading sentence "this Regulation may apply to an agricultural product or foodstuff from a third country provided that" appeared to suggest that the overall applicability of the whole Regulation would be available or withheld depending on whether equivalence would be met. The European Communities' split interpretation could only be understood easily if there were a separate set of provisions regarding applicability of this Article to non-EC WTO Members, or if WTO Members are expressly excluded from the definition of third countries in relation to specific indents of this Article.

3. Verification and publication affecting non-EC WTO Members

78. Other provisions pertaining to verification and publication in the EC Regulation did not appear to afford clarity. As the European Communities describes, verification and publication bifurcated to two "parallel" sections of the GI Regulation, Article 6 in relation to GIs from the European Communities, and Article 12b in relation to GIs from third countries. However, in the same portions of its first written submission, the European Communities avoids setting out in detail the different verification and publication procedures as they respectively apply to applications from EC member States and those from third countries, including WTO Members. A closer reading of the two articles reveals that, while parallel in form, they are not the same in substance. If no less favourable treatment is granted to GIs from WTO Members in comparison to those from EC member States, Article 6 should govern both EC member States and WTO Members, and non-WTO third countries should be governed by Article 12b.

79. Under Article 6, within six months of its receipt of an application transmitted from an EC member State, the EC Commission is required to verify and investigate whether the application contained all product specification requirements under Article 4. If the Commission finds "that the name qualifies for protection," publication for objection and ultimate registration would ensue; if the Commission concludes otherwise, the name is not published. Prior to publication, the Commission may request the opinion of a Committee composed of representatives of EC member States; in the event that the Commission differs with the Committee, or if the Committee delivers no opinion, the matter is required to be submitted to the EC Council for final determination on the basis of qualified majority.

---

[15] European Communities' first written submission, para. 118.

80. Article 12b, on the other hand, requires the EC Commission to verify and investigate "whether the registration request sent by the third country [including WTO Members] contains all the necessary elements," a wording different from "whether the application includes all the particulars provided in Article 4" in respect of applications from the European Communities. A transmission from WTO Members, together with non-WTO third countries, is treated as a "registration request" in contrast to an "application" from within EC member States. Such a difference in terminology, albeit slight, is significant as a scrutiny of whether the request contains "all the necessary elements" is wider and more intensive than a verification of whether the application includes all the particulars under Article 4. For verification by the Commission of requests from third countries, including WTO Members, Article 12b does not simply refer to Article 4 particulars. It appears to suggest that a third country, including a WTO Member in transmitting its request, has more to satisfy than a EC member State in transmitting an application. The suggestion is further borne out by the requirement under Article 12a(2) that the third country, including a WTO Member must "deem the requirement of this Regulation to be satisfied" before transmitting in contrast to the Article 5(5) requirement that a EC member State only has to "check that the application is justified."

81. Further indication of the difference and likely extra burden is the Article's reference to "conditions for protection." In place of the parallel requirement that the EC Commission shall make the determination of whether to publish or not based on whether a EC name "qualifies for protection" under Articles 6(2) and 6(5), Article 12b requires that the Commission make the determination of publication by analyzing whether a third country name, including a name from a WTO Member, "satisfies the conditions for protection."

82. The EC Regulation fails to define what "all the necessary elements" and what "the conditions for protection" are. Yet these requirements tend to lead WTO Members to look to the direction of the prior European Communities' insistence upon reciprocity and equivalence requirements, at least in respect of product specifications and inspection regimes.

83. Prior to publication of names from all third countries including WTO Members, the Commission may request the opinion of a Committee composed only of representatives of EC member States. In the event that the Commission differs with the Committee, or if the Committee delivers no opinion, the matter is then required to be submitted to the EC Council for final determination on the basis of qualified majority. This resolution of possible disputes on publication was again available to names from WTO Members, but the process does not invite WTO Members to participate.

4. Product specifications and inspection structures affecting non-EC WTO Members

84. Article 10 contains relatively detailed provisions with respect to the obligations on EC member States to establish inspection structures to ensure quality of EC GIs; the EC Regulation does not contain express parallel provisions for WTO Members in connection with their own GIs. The European Communities insists that its EC Regulation does require that the product specifications and inspection regimes with regard to specific geographical indications from third countries, presumably including WTO Members, meet the conditions of Regulation 2081/92.[16]

85. There is no express definition or cross-reference as to what these conditions are in relation to WTO Members. Article 12a(2) provides that a WTO Member must attach certain documents to its transmitted registration request. The EC Commission, pursuant to its verification and publication powers under Article 12b, determines whether the above attachment transmitted by the WTO Member satisfies the conditions of the EC Regulation. It is not clear that the above requirements are the only conditions for WTO Members to satisfy. Again, in possible cases of doubt, the EC Council would have the final power to make sure a determination, under Article 12b, without participation from other WTO Members.

---

[16] European Communities' first written submission, para. 118.

86. In contrast, the parallel provision of Article 5(4) does not require EC member States to guarantee Article 10 inspection structures, as they are obligated to establish the structure pursuant to the requirements under the Article; nor are EC member States required to describe their domestic GI protection system. Subsequently, EC member States can expect a relatively simple prima facie verification process, involving only a review of whether the application contained all the particulars.

87. A further example of the European Communities' ambiguity under Article 10 is the silence on whether designated inspection authorities in non-EC WTO Members can be readily accepted by the EC Commission and how that acceptance relates to the particulars of its inspection structure which is to be reviewed by the Commission. Under Article 10(2), EC member States, while obligated to establish their respective inspection structures, can reasonably expect no objection by the Commission to accept their designated authorities. With respect to "approved inspection bodies" in third countries, the EC Regulation specifically requires that "third countries recognized pursuant to Article 12(3)" are to comply with "[t]he equivalent standard or the applicable version of the equivalent standard" "to be established or amended in accordance with the procedure laid down in Article 15," a procedure without representation from other third countries. Ambiguity exists as to whether WTO Members are required to comply with this requirement. Again, since the European Communities in its first written submission in interpreting Article 12 admits that WTO Members are required to meet the conditions of the GI Regulation in respect of product specification and inspection structure, it appears that under the GI Regulation, WTO Members are required to establish "equivalent standard" for private inspection bodies and possibly for "designated inspection authorities."

88. No clarification as to what that equivalent standard is was available until the European Communities gave its first written submission. It provides no guidance as to what constituted equivalent standard for WTO Members. It refers to ISO/IEC Guide 65:1996, but only as "an example"[17], and it is also not clear whether that standard has passed the Commission's Article 15 procedure, as required under Article 10(3) of the Regulation below.

89. If the European Communities' interpretation that "third countries recognized pursuant to Article 12(3)" did not include WTO Members for the purpose of awarding right to object[18] is to be acceptable, the EC Regulation is again silent as to what the equivalent standard for private inspection bodies is for WTO Members except for the general statement made in its first written submission that it did require reciprocity and equivalence in respect of inspection structures, or it would be contradicting itself by implying that ISO/IEC Guide 65:1996 applies to WTO Members. Such a contradiction does not assist in the proper interpretation of the EC Regulation.

90. Notwithstanding the above inconsistency, the European Communities insists upon reciprocity and equivalence conditions, both in terms of product specifications and in particular inspection structure, whether appearing in the form of requisite attachments or the outright requirement for equivalence. WTO Members are required to have a prior established set of legal rules for the protection and inspection of GIs, including GIs from the European Communities, before they can expect to transmit registration requests from their nationals to the European Communities for EC GI protection. In making a transmission, no WTO Member would ignore the EC Regulation's "all the necessary elements" and "the conditions for protection" requirement set out by the European Communities under Article 12b(1) or the European Communities' express insistence upon equivalence in product specifications and inspection structures. The safest approach in order to have their respective registration request accepted for publication is to meet the European Communities' equivalence conditions.

---

[17] European Communities' first written submission, para. 54.

[18] European Communities' first written submission, para. 74.

91. In that respect, China believes that product specification and inspection structures are quintessential for the value and quality of GIs, just as the European Communities argued.[19] An overall GI protection system built upon reciprocal and equivalent product specification and inspection from WTO Members can hardly be described as reciprocity and equivalence, neutral for such WTO Members. In arguing that its reciprocity and equivalence conditioning would only be limited to these two components of its GI protection regime and not be applicable to its overall GI regulatory protection system, the European Communities is far from convincing. The essential link between product specification and inspection structure and the overall GI protection cannot be artificially separated.

5. Other points raised in response to the Panel's questions

92. China refers to the example of the Patent Cooperation Treaty ("PCT") as an international arrangement according to which national governments cooperate by acting as agents or intermediaries in the protection of private rights. To the best of China's knowledge, there is no other international arrangement established under the legislation of one of the parties to that arrangement. In the case of international arrangement established under PCT, application requirements and procedures are applied universally and equally among members. If an international arrangement in respect of protection of private rights is to be established under the legislation of one of the parties to the arrangement, such legislation or international arrangements, established thereunder, shall not impose extra burdens with respect to availability, acquisition, scope, maintenance and enforcement of private rights as well as those matters affecting the use of such private rights.

93. China understands that the term "nationals" as used in Article 1.3, including footnote 1, and Articles 3.1 and 4 of the TRIPS Agreement and Article 2 of the Paris Convention (1967) relates to national treatment in this dispute. In the context of protection of intellectual property rights, natural persons who were domiciled, or legal persons who had a real and effective industrial and commercial establishment in a specific member are required under the TRIPS Agreement and Paris Convention (1967) to be treated in the same manner as nationals of that Member. In this regard, China believes that "nationals" as used in Article 1.3, including footnote 1, and Articles 3.1 and 4 of the TRIPS Agreement and Article 2 of the Paris Convention (1967) covered both natural or legal persons holding the nationality of a certain Member of the TRIPS Agreement as well as natural persons who are domiciled, or legal persons who had a real and effective industrial and commercial establishment in that Member.

94. China does not consider that the words "country of the Union," in Article 2(1) of the Paris Convention (1967), as incorporated in the TRIPS Agreement by its Article 2.1, should be read *mutatis mutandis* to refer to "WTO Member" for the following reasons. First, the text of the two international agreements does not support such an inference. According to Article 1(1) of the Paris Convention (1967) the words "country of the Union" refer to a member state of the Paris Convention (1967). In contrast, "WTO Member" means a party to the Agreement Establishing the World Trade Organization. The Paris Convention and the Agreement Establishing the World Trade Organization are two international agreements among different member states. The TRIPS Agreement was one of the series of WTO agreements. The member states of each of these two international agreements promised to take on different obligations and are entitled to different rights under different international agreements of which they are member states. Although certain Articles of the Paris Convention are incorporated by Article 2.1 of the TRIPS Agreement, the two agreements still remain separate and independent international agreements, and both are in force. The incorporation does not affect other existing obligations between other member states under TRIPS and the Paris Convention. Second, the factual member status does not allow such inference. In fact, there are more member states of the Paris Convention than of the WTO; while the Paris Convention has 160 member states, the WTO has 147 Members.

95. China considers that that different treatment of GIs under the EC Regulation would also amount to less favourable treatment of like products. It quotes the view of the Appellate Body in *Korea – Various Measures on*

---

[19] European Communities' first written submission, paras. 48-55 and 121.

Beef that according "treatment no less favourable" means according conditions of competition no less favourable to the imported product than to the like domestic product and that this should be assessed by examining whether a measure modified the conditions of competition in the relevant market to the detriment of imported products.[20] Therefore, in the current case, if different treatment accorded to names by the EC Regulation is found to result in modification of the conditions of competition under which like products, imported products and EC like products, competed in the EC market to the disadvantage of imported products, then the different treatment granted to names would amount to less favourable treatment of like products. China therefore believes that evidence in respect of different treatment of names is relevant to a determination of less favourable treatment of like products.

96. China believes that measures that came into force after this Panel was established are within the terms of reference of this Panel. The complainants had specified the concerned amendments in their request for the establishment of a panel, and those contents accordingly have been properly included in the terms of reference of this panel. The European Communities claims that only measures in force at the time that the Panel was established are within the terms of reference of the Panel. However, there is no requirement in the DSU or in WTO dispute settlement practice for arguments that the Panel's jurisdiction is only limited to measures that had already come into force when the Panel was established. The European Communities does not provide any legal basis for its claim nor could it find support from the functions and the objective of the terms of reference, as explained by the Appellate Body in *Brazil – Desiccated Coconut*. The parties and third parties, therefore, were given sufficient information concerning the claims at issue in the dispute, and were allowed enough opportunity to respond to the complainant's case. It is irrelevant in this respect whether the concerned amendments came into effect before or after this Panel was established. Furthermore, following the European Communities' logic, when a measure was challenged before the DSB, once the respondent had replaced the challenged measure with an amendment before the Panel was established, and that new amendment came into force immediately after the establishment of the Panel, then the Panel would not be able to examine either the old measure or the amendment, because the challenged old measure no longer had any effect by the time of the Panel's establishment, while the new amendment had not yet come into effect.

97. China considers that the mandatory/discretionary distinction in GATT and WTO jurisprudence fully applies under the TRIPS Agreement and that the nature of the concerned obligations under the TRIPS Agreement therefore shall not affect the application of the distinction. It is irrelevant whether the nature of some TRIPS obligations is to prohibit or to oblige Members to take certain actions in respect of the application of the mandatory/discretionary distinction. The nature of the concerned obligations under the TRIPS Agreement therefore shall not affect the application of the distinction. It is established under WTO law that a Member could challenge measures of another Member on a *per se* basis when those measures mandate, in certain circumstances, a violation of its WTO obligations. There is a considerable body of dispute settlement practice concerning the mandatory/discretionary distinction, or *per se* violation rule, as it is more commonly referred to. In the relevant panel and Appellate Body reports addressing the mandatory/discretionary distinction, nowhere is it stated that the nature of the concerned WTO obligations as distinguished by the Panel in this question shall affect the application of the distinction. Furthermore, certain obligations, (e.g. the national treatment principle under TRIPS), *inter alia*, on one hand, that oblige Members to take certain actions, are also prohibitions in nature on the other. The national treatment principle in Article 3.1 of the TRIPS Agreement, prohibits a Member according to the nationals of other Members treatment less favourable than that it accords to its own nationals. Therefore, from the text of this provision, it is clear that the nature of the national treatment principle is an obligation which both obliges each Member to accord to the nationals of other Members treatment no less favourable than that it accords to its own nationals, and prohibits Member from according to the nationals of other Members treatment less favourable than that it accords to its own nationals.

[20] Appellate Body Report on *Korea – Various Measures on Beef*, para. 135.

E. COLOMBIA

1. Introduction

98. Colombia has a systemic interest in this dispute in that it attaches great importance to determining the scope of the obligations assumed by WTO Members under the TRIPS Agreement. As a country that has protected one of its main export products with a trademark, Colombia is interested in ensuring that WTO Member countries continue to be entitled to allow their nationals to decide whether they must choose one of the intellectual property protection instruments or whether they are in fact entitled to combine those instruments according to the specificities of the different markets.

2. Reciprocity and equivalence requirement

99. In response to the argument made by Australia and the United States with respect to the violation of the national treatment provisions for the registration of, or objection to, a geographical indication, the European Communities has stated that the expression "without prejudice to international agreements" included in Article 12(1) and (3) of the EC Regulation ensures that the rights of WTO Members are preserved. According to the European Communities, the WTO membership of the country to which the applicant for registration belongs is a sufficient guarantee that there is protection of geographical indications.[21] If this is the correct interpretation of the legislation, Colombia thinks the Panel should recommend that the European Communities amend its legislation to ensure that the clause in question is given the scope and meaning that the European Communities attributes to it in its submission as such an interpretation cannot be drawn from a simple reading of the clause in its current version.

100. Even if Colombia were to accept, for the sake of discussion, that this is the scope of the clause with respect to international agreements, there is still a point that remains unclear, namely the way in which the third country would transmit the registration application under Article 12a(2). Indeed, Colombia wonders whether the country of origin of the applicant, being required in any case to describe the legal provisions protecting the said designation and the way in which its inspection structures operate, is not subject to a certification or equivalency process. In practice, Colombia sees this requirement as a condition involving an evaluation of protection systems in force in the country of origin of applicants for geographical indications. Consequently, Colombia sees protection as being clearly contingent on the evaluation of the applicant's system, and this is contrary to Article 1.1 of the TRIPS Agreement.

101. Colombia does not agree with the European Communities' argument that drawing a distinction between geographical areas or territories is not a violation of the national treatment principle. Any distinction that in any way identifies the geographical indications of the European Communities as opposed to the others would clearly result in a violation of national treatment commitments.

3. Relationship between trademarks and geographical indications

102. With respect to the relationship between trademarks and geographical indications, Colombia agrees with the argument that the TRIPS Agreement does not establish any supremacy of one instrument of protection over another. This does not mean, however, that the European Communities' regulations can simply ignore the right of the trademark owner under Article 16.1 of the TRIPS Agreement. To do so is a clear violation of the European Communities' WTO commitments.

---

[21] European Communities' first written submission, para. 66.

F. INDIA

1. Points raised in response to the Panel's questions

103. India is not aware of any group or person ever having filed with its authorities either an application for, or an objection to, a registration pursuant to the EC Regulation. If such filing was to occur, India would be willing to transmit such an application to the European Communities. However, the question whether the Government would be able to do so would depend upon what the transmission entails, in particular whether it may involve any procedures or need for any infrastructure for which there may be capacity constraints. India allows direct access by GI applicants to its national authority irrespective of nationality. In respect of applicants who do not have a principal place of business in India, it is necessary to indicate an address for service in India. In case of applicants from other WTO Member countries, it is necessary to include a certificate by the Registry or competent authority of the Geographical Indications Office of the WTO Member country in the application for registration and it is necessary to include the particulars of the geographical indication, the country and date of filing of the first application in the WTO Member country and such other particulars as may be required by the Registrar.

104. India understands that the European Communities has stated that it does not provide less favourable treatment to geographical indications located in other WTO Members.[22] At the same time, it is not very clear to India from the European Communities' statement whether providing no less favourable treatment to nationals of other WTO Members along with providing less favourable treatment to geographical indications located outside the EC member States would satisfy the requirement of national treatment in Article 3.1 of the TRIPS Agreement. It is India's view that the only valid interpretation of the terms "treatment...with regard to the protection" in Article 3.1 is that "no less favourable treatment" to nationals of other WTO Members cannot be provided unless "no less favourable treatment" is also provided to the geographical indications applied for by them, whether located inside the EC member States or located in other WTO Members. The only deviations permitted are the procedural ones, such as those provided in Article 3.2, whereby additional requirement for judicial or administrative procedures can be imposed upon applicants of other WTO Member countries.

105. In India's view, the words "country of the Union" in Article 2(1) of the Paris Convention (1967) as incorporated in the TRIPS Agreement by its Article 2.1, should be read *mutatis mutandis* to refer to "WTO Member."

106. India is not aware of any GIs registered under the EC Regulation that are identical (or confusingly similar) to Community protected trademarks owned by Indian nationals.

107. India sees no apparent conflict between Articles 16.1 and 22.3 of the TRIPS Agreement. Article 16.1 deals with rights of a trademark owner against "third parties" in the context of use of identical or similar signs which may cause confusion. It also provides that these rights shall not prejudice any existing prior rights. Article 22.3 entitles WTO Members to refuse or invalidate the registration of a trademark which consists of or contains geographical indication with respect to the goods not in the territory indicated if such use is of a nature as to mislead the public as to the true place or origin. Any potential conflict would be avoided in India as provisions of Section 25 of the Geographical Indications of Goods (Registration and Protection) Act, 1999 of India provide for refusal or invalidation of registration of trademarks that contain or consist of geographical indications that may cause confusion.

108. Under Section 12 of India's Trade Marks Act of 1999, registration by more than one proprietor of trademarks which are identical or similar may be permitted in the case of honest concurrent use. However, GIs are not covered by that provision. Section 26 of India's Geographical Indications (Registration and Protection) Act of 1999 provides that where a trademark contains or consists of a geographical indication and has been

[22] European Communities' first written submission, para. 125.

applied for or registered in good faith under the law relating to trademarks or where rights to such trademark have been acquired through use in good faith either (a) before the commencement of the Act, or (b) before the date of filing of the application for registration of such geographical indication under the Act, nothing contained in the Act will prejudice the registrability or the validity of the registration of such trademark or the right to use such trademark on the ground that such trademark is identical with, or similar to, such geographical indication. India's Geographical Indication Act does not discriminate between GIs and trademarks of European Communities and non-EC countries.

G. MEXICO

1. Introduction

109. Mexico presents arguments in support of its view that the EC Regulation is inconsistent with the TRIPS Agreement. It addresses the following points which it considers fundamental to this dispute:

- the national treatment obligation;
- the MFN treatment obligation;
- the protection of trademark rights under Articles 16.1 and 24.5 of the TRIPS Agreement; and
- cochineal: a product of Mexican origin.

2. National treatment

110. Like the complaining parties, Mexico submits that Article 12(1) of the Regulation violates the principle of national treatment in that it accords less favourable treatment to third countries than it accords to EC member countries. Under Article 12(1) of the Regulation, foreign countries cannot enjoy the same benefits as EC nationals with respect to the registration of geographical indications unless they meet certain conditions of reciprocity. The language of Article 12(1) of the Regulation is precise and unequivocal: a third country must "give guarantees identical or equivalent" in order to be able to receive the same protection as EC member countries; otherwise, nationals of other WTO Members cannot enjoy the protection accorded by the Regulation. This is clearly contrary to the principle of national treatment contained in Article 3.1 of the TRIPS Agreement. Moreover, the Regulation violates the principle of national treatment by once again imposing conditions of reciprocity and preventing nationals of countries that are not EC members from submitting their objections with respect to applications for the registration of geographical indications directly to the European authorities. Indeed, Article 12d(1) of the Regulation stipulates that objections from WTO Member countries must be submitted first to the government of the country in question, which must then transmit the objection to the European Commission. In other words, unlike the EC member countries, WTO Member countries that do not belong to the European Communities bear the additional burden of first having to address themselves to their national authorities, and then having to delegate to those authorities the task of following up the objection process.

3. MFN treatment

111. The Regulation also represents an infringement of the principle of most-favoured-nation treatment established in Article 4 of the TRIPS Agreement. By limiting intellectual property protection exclusively to third countries that provide equivalent guarantees, the European Communities is denying equal treatment to non-EC member States. Article 12(1) of the Regulation provides for treatment that discriminates between third countries to the detriment of those which fail to comply with the reciprocity conditions laid down in the Regulation. In other words, the advantages, favours and privileges of the Regulation are available to certain

third countries only, and are not accorded immediately and unconditionally to the nationals of all other WTO Members as stipulated in Article 4 of the TRIPS Agreement.

4. Protection of trademark rights under Articles 16.1 and 24.5 of the TRIPS Agreement

112. This dispute touches on the delicate subject of the relationship between trademarks and geographical indications. Indeed, these two forms of protection of intellectual property rights can easily become the subject of conflicts, since they can protect, albeit from different angles, one and the same product with the same distinctive sign. The TRIPS Agreement addresses, and tries to resolve, these possible confusions through Articles 16.1 and 24.5, which establish the rights of trademark and geographical indication owners. In this connection, Mexico notes that the Regulation violates at least two provisions of the TRIPS Agreement, namely Articles 24.5 and 16.1.

113. Article 14(1) of the Regulation clearly violates Article 24.5 of the TRIPS Agreement. Contrary to what is provided for in the TRIPS Agreement, this provision of the Regulation gives clear preference to geographical indications over trademarks that were registered subsequently. This priority for GIs takes as a time reference the day of registration or application of the trademark with the EC authorities and rejects the possibility of a trademark having previously been registered in a non-EC member country. The deliberate failure to recognize prior registrations in third countries violates not only Article 24.5 of the TRIPS Agreement, but also Article 4 of the Paris Convention. In its written submission, the European Communities confirms its position by stating that the only relevant date for the purposes of Article 24.5 is the date of filing of the application before the national authorities, in this case before the EC authorities. This argument clearly does not justify a deviation from Article 24.5 of the TRIPS Agreement.

114. The exclusive right conferred by Article 16.1 is severely impaired by Article 14(2) of the Regulation, which permits coexistence between a previously registered trademark and a subsequent geographical indication. This means that in the European Communities, the fact that a trademark was registered prior to a subsequent geographical indication does not constitute an obstacle to invalidating the registration of the geographical indication. In its first written submission, the European Communities goes so far as stating that the TRIPS Agreement not only permits the coexistence of trademarks and geographical indications, but, in fact, requires such coexistence. In the same submission, the European Communities admits that coexistence of the two types of protection is not the perfect solution, but it is preferable to a rigid application of the "first-in-time" rule. Mexico considers these justifications to be insufficient. By acknowledging that the solution implemented under the Regulation may not be the perfect solution, the European Communities is recognizing the inconsistency of its legislation. Similarly, by ignoring the "first-in-time" approach, the European Communities is violating not only Article 24.5 of the TRIPS Agreement, but also a recognized general principle of law.

5. Cochineal: a product of Mexican origin

115. Mexico considers that "cochineal" should be removed from Annex II of the Regulation. Annexes I and II of the Regulation specifically mention the products falling within the scope of application of the Regulation. Article 1 of the Regulation establishes the relationship between Annexes I and II and the other provisions. The list of products in Annex II includes a product of Mexican origin, "cochineal" (*Coccus Cacti*), a small insect which lives on the nopal cactus, or Mexican cactus, and which produces an intense red colour used as textile dye and food colouring. The use of cochineal in Mexico dates back to the pre-colonial period. The Aztecs used this colouring matter for centuries before Hernán Cortés arrived in Mexico from Spain in 1519. The first export of the product to Spain took place in 1523, a few years after Cortés's invasion of Mexico. Subsequently, cochineal bugs were cultivated in parts of Spain in which the climate and conditions were similar to those of Mexico. Thus, cochineal is now also produced in Spain, specifically in the Canary Islands. Given that the product exists simultaneously in Mexico and the European Communities, registration of cochineal from Mexico in the European Communities would clearly be refused under the Regulation.

116. Mexico submits that, according to the definition of geographical indications in Article 22 of the TRIPS Agreement, the product in question must be of a quality, reputation or other characteristic essentially attributable to its geographical origin. In the case of cochineal, a number of its characteristics can be attributed essentially to the territory of Mexico. The product's history demonstrates that, if there is a country to which the special qualities of cochineal can be attributed for the purposes of intellectual property protection, it is Mexico. Consequently, it would make no sense to register cochineal as a geographical indication in any territory which is not in Mexico. Hence, Mexico requests that the Panel rule that the inclusion of the product "cochineal" as eligible for protection as a geographical indication of the European Communities is illegal.

117. In response to a question from the Panel, Mexico explains that it considers cochineal a product classification which is capable of being registered as a geographical indication under the EC Regulation. The categories of "product classification" and "geographical indication" are not mutually exclusive. The EC Regulation is the "specific measure at issue." Since Annex II is part of such Regulation, it is clearly contained in the "specific measure at issue." Mexico is fully aware that this Panel has standard terms of reference and is, therefore, limited to examining the claims made by Australia and the United States. As a third party, Mexico does not intend to submit, and is not submitting, claims which are different from those raised by the parties. In fact, Mexico is only addressing some of these claims. In this respect, Mexico is providing arguments to support at least two of the three claims made by the parties, namely the violation of the principles of national treatment and MFN treatment and the violation of the TRIPS rules regarding the relationship between trademarks and geographical indications. Mexico brings cochineal as a real-world example of how the EC Regulation violates these rules and it simply intends to support the United States' and Australia's arguments in these respects. From Mexico's perspective, it is clear that Mexican producers of cochineal are required to go through specific procedures which EC nationals (national treatment) or countries which give equivalent guarantees to nationals of the European Communities (MFN treatment) are not. Furthermore, Mexico would observe that the Panel is fully entitled under Article 19.1, second sentence, of the DSU, to suggest ways in which a Member may implement the Panel's own recommendations and rulings. There is no requirement in the DSU that such a request has to be forwarded by a party to the case. In the past, panels have issued suggestions for Members to withdraw their measures which have been found to be WTO-inconsistent.[23] Given that Mexico's interest in cochineal is so specific, Mexico does not request that the Panel suggest that the European Communities repeal its legislation as a whole, but merely to solve Mexico's very specific problem in this way. If the Panel does not deem it appropriate to suggest specifically that the European Communities remove the name of cochineal from Annex II of the Regulation, Mexico would certainly obtain the same result if the Panel suggested that the European Communities comply with its recommendations and rulings by withdrawing the Regulation.

6. Points raised in response to the Panel's questions

118. Mexico is not aware of any group or person ever having filed with its authorities either an application for or an objection to a registration pursuant to the EC Regulation. As to the question whether Mexico would be willing or able to transmit such applications, according to Article 6.III of Mexico's Industrial Property Law (LPI), the Mexican Institute of Industrial Property (IMPI) is the administrative authority in charge of ensuring the protection of appellations of origin. The IMPI, acting through the Ministry of Foreign Affairs, would thus be empowered to request or, where appropriate, to transmit an application for registration of an appellation of origin to any international agency. The use of this procedure, including the submission of an application for registration of a Mexican appellation of origin under the EC Regulation will, however, depend on the findings made by this Panel. Mexico's LPI makes no distinction on the basis of nationality. According to its provisions, the owner of appellations of origin is the Mexican State and authorization to use them is issued by the IMPI to any natural person or legal entity that complies with the requirements and procedures in Articles 169-178 of the LPI.

[23] Panel Report on *Guatemala – Cement I*, para. 9.6; and Panel Report on *US – Offset Act (Byrd Amendment)*, para. 8.6.

119. Mexico submits that foreign GIs are protected under the TRIPS Agreement, the Lisbon Agreement for the Protection of Appellations of Origin and their International Registration, and treaties which Mexico has concluded with other countries. As established in the Paris Convention, the principles of national treatment and of assimilation to nationals imply that, with respect to industrial property, each member State is required to afford nationals of other member States the same treatment as that afforded to its own citizens without conditioning such treatment on reciprocity. Hence, nationals—i.e. both natural persons and legal entities—enjoy the industrial property rights granted by the member State without any requirement as to domicile or establishment. Pursuant to Article 2(3) of the Paris Convention, however, member States may apply the domicile requirement for the purpose of judicial or administrative procedures. Additionally, the fact that Article 2(1) of the Paris Convention is incorporated by reference in Article 2.1 of the TRIPS Agreement, means that WTO Members are required to comply with Articles 1 through 12 and Article 19 of the Paris Convention in respect of geographical indications as regulated in Part II of the Agreement.

120. Mexico is not aware of any GIs registered under the EC Regulation that are identical or confusingly similar to trademarks in the European Communities registered by Mexican nationals. Mexico also considers that Articles 16.1 and 22.3 of the TRIPS Agreement apply to different situations. Article 16.1 of the TRIPS Agreement deals with trademarks, and more specifically with the rights conferred on trademark owners and situations relating to existing prior rights and rights made available on the basis of use. Article 22.3 regulates the protection which WTO Members are required to provide for geographical indications and specifies the circumstances in which registration of a trademark which contains or consists of a geographical indication may be invalidated or refused.

121. Under Mexican law, and specifically the LPI, there are two situations in which registration of a mark is not effective against third parties, as well as exceptions to the use of a mark being classified as an administrative infringement. In the first instance, Article 92.I of the LPI specifies that the owner of a registered mark may not prevent a third party acting in good faith from using the same or a confusingly similar mark for the same or similar products or services, provided that such use is made in good faith and occurred prior to the date of filing the application for registration, or the date of first declared use of the mark. In the second instance, Article 213.X of the LPI provides that, in the case of comparative advertising, a third party may use a registered mark for the purpose of informing the public, provided that the comparison is not tendentious, false or exaggerated within the meaning of the Federal Consumer Protection Law. Application of these two scenarios to geographical indications is governed by the provisions of the TRIPS Agreement and other international instruments to which Mexico is party.

122. Mexico does not believe that previous panel decisions constitute binding jurisprudence for subsequent panel determinations, including previous decisions on the mandatory/discretionary distinction in GATT and WTO. In this sense, Mexico agrees with the statement by the Appellate Body[24] that panel reports bind the parties to the dispute but do not create definitive interpretations of the relevant provisions.

H. NEW ZEALAND

1. Introduction

123. New Zealand has a significant systemic interest in ensuring that the WTO disciplines applicable to intellectual property rights are respected. These disciplines seek to ensure that such rights are adequately and effectively protected while also ensuring that the measures Members adopt to enforce these rights do not of themselves become barriers to legitimate trade. New Zealand has a significant interest in maintaining protection for the intellectual property rights of New Zealand producers who have invested in innovation and in the promotion of their products, and in ensuring that the market access and ability to brand New Zealand products is not precluded. As a major exporter of agricultural products and foodstuffs, New Zealand has an interest in

[24] Appellate Body Report on *Japan – Alcoholic Beverages II*, at pp 13-14.

ensuring that its producers are able to brand and promote their agricultural products in export markets, including the European Communities.

124. In the present case New Zealand brings forward arguments to support the claims of the complainants that the EC Regulation violates the European Communities WTO obligations. New Zealand focuses its arguments on the claims raised by the complainants under Articles 2.1, 3.1, 16.1 and 22.2 of the TRIPS Agreement and Article III:4 of GATT 1994. New Zealand also supports the arguments made by Australia that the EC Regulation is inconsistent with Articles 2.1 and 2.2 of the TBT Agreement but, for the sake of brevity, does not address them in its submissions.

2. The EC Regulation is inconsistent with national treatment obligations under the TRIPS Agreement and GATT 1994

(a) Introduction

125. The national treatment obligation is "a cornerstone of the world trading system that is served by the WTO."[25] In the TRIPS Agreement, this obligation is incorporated into the legal framework for protection of intellectual property rights by way of Article 2.1 (which requires WTO Members to comply with, *inter alia*, Article 2(1) of the Paris Convention) and Article 3.1. By virtue of Article 2.1, the European Communities is obliged to provide nationals of other WTO Members with "the same protection" as its own nationals. Under Article 3.1, the European Communities is obliged to provide "treatment no less favourable than that it accords to its own nationals with regard to the protection of intellectual property." The European Communities is also obliged under Article III:4 of GATT 1994 to accord to imported products of the territory of any contracting party "treatment no less favourable than that accorded to like products of national origin in respect of all laws, regulations and requirements affecting their internal sale." The European Communities does not dispute that these national treatment obligations apply to the EC Regulation.

(b) Interpretation of the EC Regulation

126. The European Communities disputes as a factual matter the complainants' interpretation of Article 12(1) of the EC Regulation on which the national treatment violation arguments are based. The European Communities claims this interpretation "is based on a misunderstanding" of its Regulation.[26] The European Communities argues that Article 12(1) of Regulation 2081/92 clearly applies "without prejudice to international agreements." It goes on to state that such international agreements include the WTO Agreements, and for this reason "Article 12(1) and (3) of Regulation 2081/92 do not apply to WTO Members."[27] Rather, the European Communities continues, WTO Members are to follow the procedures set out in Article 12a and 12b of the EC Regulation. This novel interpretation of the European Communities does not withstand close scrutiny. First, it runs counter to the usual meaning of the phrase "without prejudice to international agreements." Second, it is inconsistent with the wording of the EC Regulation itself. Third, to New Zealand's knowledge, this is the first time that this interpretation has been raised by the European Communities, despite consultations being held on the interpretation of its Regulation.

127. The European Communities interprets the phrase "without prejudice to international agreements" in a manner which acknowledges its obligations under the TRIPS Agreement.[28] It appears to New Zealand that the European Communities is effectively admitting that requiring nationals of WTO Members to follow the procedures set out in Article 12(1) and 12(3) of the EC Regulation would be contrary to its WTO obligations. However, in New Zealand's view there are sufficient internal inconsistencies between the European

---

[25] Appellate Body Report on *US – Section 211 Appropriations Act*, para. 241.

[26] European Communities' first written submission, para. 65.

[27] European Communities' first written submission, para. 66.

[28] European Communities' first written submission, para. 65.

Communities' novel interpretation and the wording of the EC Regulation to doubt whether any reliance can be placed on this interpretation of the EC Regulation in the future. The European Communities notes the distinctions made in Articles 12(b)(2)(a) and (b) and Article 12d(1) between "WTO countries" and "third countries" in support of its interpretation. It also states that the procedure provided for in Article 12(3) does not apply to WTO Members. New Zealand notes, however, that Article 12a is prefaced with the phrase "[i]n the case provided for in Article 12(3)." If Article 12(3) does not apply to WTO Members then, based on the European Communities' own arguments, Article 12(a) would not apply to WTO Members. Taken to its logical conclusion, therefore, the European Communities' argument would mean that there is in fact no application procedure in the EC Regulation under which a national of a WTO Member could apply for GI protection. In that case the Panel must find that the European Communities is in breach of its national treatment obligations under the TRIPS Agreement and GATT 1994 by failing to provide a WTO-consistent application procedure for GI registration for WTO Members. New Zealand does not believe that the European Communities would agree with this consequence of its interpretation. New Zealand notes that this is the first time this interpretation has been raised, despite numerous consultations on the EC Regulation, including under the DSU. As the Appellate Body has indicated, all parties engaged in dispute settlement under the DSU should be fully forthcoming with respect to the facts, and consultations "do much to shape the substance and the scope of subsequent panel proceedings."[29]

128. Essentially, the European Communities' argument that Article 12(1) and 12(3) of the EC Regulation do not apply to WTO Members rests on the claim that the Regulation will indeed be interpreted in the manner the European Communities suggests, that is, in a WTO consistent manner. But the European Communities can offer no basis for assuring WTO Members that this will be so. The European Communities' position is even less credible where the interpretation that the European Communities puts forward is one that is not suggested by the ordinary meaning of the text of the EC Regulation. The alternative interpretation, and one which is consistent with the wording of the EC Regulation, is that adopted by the complainants, namely that Article 12(1) and (3) apply to WTO Members.

(c) Article 2.1 of the TRIPS Agreement (incorporating Article 2(1) of the Paris Convention) and Article 3.1 of the TRIPS Agreement

(i) The EC is obliged to provide no less favourable treatment to other WTO Member nationals than it does to EC nationals

129. Article 2.1 of the TRIPS Agreement requires WTO members to comply with, *inter alia*, Article 2(1) of the Paris Convention. The European Communities is therefore obliged to provide nationals of other WTO Members with "the same protection" as provided to foreign nationals. It is also required to accord to nationals of other WTO Members "treatment no less favourable than that it accords to its own nationals with regard to the protection of intellectual property" under Article 3.1 of the TRIPS Agreement. There are three essential components of the national treatment obligation under Articles 2.1 and 3.1 of the TRIPS Agreement. First, it is the treatment received by "nationals" that is key. Second, the standard for comparison with the treatment received by foreign nationals is the most favourable treatment received by domestic nationals. Third, foreign nationals must receive no less favourable treatment than that accorded to nationals.

130. The national treatment obligations in the TRIPS Agreement are owed to nationals, that is, natural or legal persons (see Article 1.3). In the context of the present case, this means that the standard for comparison is simply with EC nationals, since all EC nationals are potentially eligible to apply for GI registration under the EC Regulation.

131. In the present case, the European Communities has raised a creative but nevertheless erroneous interpretation of "nationals" in an attempt to claim that its conditions for registration and objections do not

[29] Appellate Body Report on *India – Patents (US)*, para. 94.

breach its national treatment obligations. In particular, the European Communities claims that "the conditions and procedures contained in Regulation 2081/92 for the registration of geographical indications do not depend on nationality."[30] New Zealand submits that this interpretation of the national treatment obligation as applying to persons of a particular "nationality" cannot be correct. The WTO Agreements are to be interpreted according to the ordinary meaning of the words in their context, and in light of their object and purpose (see Article 31(1) of the Vienna Convention on the Law of Treaties). In the context of the TRIPS Agreement the term "nationals" clearly has a geographical connotation. Support for this is gleaned from both the TRIPS Agreement and the Paris Convention (incorporated by reference into the TRIPS Agreement). Article 1.3 of the TRIPS Agreement provides that "[M]embers shall accord the treatment provided for in this Agreement to the nationals of other Members. In respect of the relevant intellectual property rights, the nationals of other Members shall be understood as those natural or legal persons *that would meet the criteria for eligibility for protection in the Paris Convention*" (emphasis added). One particular category of natural or legal persons that meet the criteria for eligibility for the same protection as nationals under the Paris Convention are those eligible under Article 3 [Same Treatment for Certain Categories of Persons as for Nationals of Countries of the Union] of the Paris Convention. This provides that "[n]ationals of countries outside the Union who are domiciled or who have real and effective industrial or commercial establishments in the territory of one of the countries of the Union *shall be treated in the same manner as nationals* of the countries of the Union" (emphasis added). The Paris Convention therefore includes not only a "nationality" element to the national treatment obligation, but also includes a "geographical" element relating to the person's place of domicile or establishment. This is further supported by footnote 1 to Article 1.3 of the TRIPS Agreement which also adopts a geographical element to the term "nationals" when used in the relation to separate customs territories.

132. In the geographical context of GIs, therefore, the term "nationals" includes not only natural or legal persons of a particular nationality, but also those who are domiciled or who have a real and effective industrial or commercial establishment in a particular WTO Member. Those legal or natural persons who are domiciled or have an establishment in the third country to which the GI relates are therefore "non-EC nationals" for the purpose of the national treatment obligation under the TRIPS Agreement. As a consequence of its erroneous interpretation of "nationals," the European Communities asserts that it is the area where the GI is located that determines which procedure under the EC Regulation applies in a given case, not the "nationality" of the producers of the product concerned. Therefore, it claims there is no breach of the national treatment obligations. If this argument were correct, it would mean that even if a Regulation provided that only EC GIs could be registered, there would be no violation of the national treatment obligation because in theory the nationals of any country could live in the European Communities and register their GIs. This would gut the TRIPS Agreement of the national treatment obligation with respect to GIs. In any case, the EC Regulation as drafted does not support the European Communities assertion. In particular, New Zealand submits that the plain meaning of the words "a group or a natural or legal person … in a third country" in Article 12a of the EC Regulation is that all persons domiciled or with a real and effective industrial or commercial establishment outside of the European Communities are subject to the procedure in Article 12a of the EC Regulation (provided that the requirements of Article 12(3) have been met). So a person's location is indeed relevant to which application process applies. The EC Regulation, therefore, adopts two different registration procedures—one for EC nationals in respect of GIs located in the EC; and one for nationals "in a third country." The European Communities is obliged by its national treatment obligations to provide a no less favourable application process for nationals "in a third country" than it does for EC nationals.

133. New Zealand supports the complainants arguments that a WTO Member cannot require reciprocity of a higher standard of treatment than that required by the TRIPS Agreement before the right to that higher standard accrues under national treatment. To do otherwise would in effect result in a WTO Member being able secure concessions that it was unable achieve at the negotiating table.

[30] European Communities' first written submission, para. 123.

134. In determining whether a particular measure violates the national treatment obligation, a first line of inquiry is whether there is a difference in treatment in the applicable laws. A difference in applicable law, by itself, is not sufficient to constitute a breach of national treatment.[31] It must be demonstrated that "less favourable treatment" or some disadvantage accruing to the foreign national as a consequence of the difference in treatment has occurred.[32] In terms of what may amount to a disadvantage, the Appellate Body has found that subjecting foreigners to additional procedures constitutes a breach of national treatment. The Appellate Body in *US – Section 211 Appropriations Act* concluded that "even the *possibility* that non-United States successors-in-interest face two hurdles is *inherently less favourable* than the undisputed fact that United States successors-in-interest face only one."[33] Thus an "extra hurdle" faced by foreigners constitutes "less favourable treatment" under Article 3.1 of the TRIPS Agreement. Further, whether or not "less favourable treatment" is accorded to nationals should be assessed "by examining whether a measure modifies the *conditions of competition* in the relevant market."[34] In other words, treatment no less favourable in Article III:4 of GATT 1994 calls for "effective equality of opportunities."[35]

(ii) Registration procedure provides less favourable treatment to WTO Member nationals

135. The complainants have demonstrated that nationals from WTO Members are subject to different registration procedures from those applying to EC nationals. New Zealand has summarized the differences between the registration processes applicable to the European Communities and WTO Member applications.[36] The particular difference at issue between the two registration procedures is the requirements of equivalence and reciprocity in Article 12(1) of the EC Regulation (this argument takes as its premise the fact that Article 12(1) and 12(3) of the EC Regulation apply to WTO Members.). Further, while the requirement to submit all applications through government applies equally to applications from the European Communities and WTO Member nationals, its effect is to disadvantage nationals from WTO Members.

136. New Zealand submits that the effects of the differences in registration process mean that, at worst, the benefits of registration are entirely unavailable to producers from countries outside the European Communities. Indeed, New Zealand is not aware of any successful registration applications from nationals from WTO Members made under the process set out in the EC Regulation, whereas there have been more than 600 successful applications for registration of EC GIs. At best, WTO Member nationals are subject to "extra hurdles" and are as a consequence, disadvantaged under the EC Regulation when compared to EC nationals. An "extra hurdle" exists for WTO Member nationals if WTO Members are required to comply with the equivalence and reciprocity requirements in the EC Regulation. The complainants have shown that before a WTO Member national is eligible to apply for protection under Article 12(1) of EC Regulation, the country of origin of that national must grant *reciprocal* treatment for EC GIs under an *equivalent* system.

137. Not only are these requirements for reciprocity and equivalence a breach in and of themselves of the national treatment obligations, but they also mean that WTO Member nationals do not have the same opportunities to protect their GIs through registration as do EC nationals. In such case, an individual's right to apply for registration under the EC Regulation is conditioned on factors over which the applicant has no control, in other words, whether the applicant's government applies reciprocal and equivalent treatment. New Zealand notes that applications for registration under the EC Regulation are to be submitted by governments, rather than by individuals (Articles 5(5) and 12a(2) of the EC Regulation). The European Communities claims that the "rules relating to the registration of such geographical indications from outside the EC ... closely parallel the

[31] See the GATT Panel Report on *US – Section 337,* cited by the Appellate Body in *US – Section 211 Appropriations Act,* at para. 261.

[32] See the Appellate Body Report on *Korea – Various Measures on Beef,* at para. 135.

[33] Appellate Body Report on *US – Section 211 Appropriations Act,* para. 265.

[34] Appellate Body Report on *Korea – Various Measures on Beef,* para. 137.

[35] GATT Panel Report on *US – Section 337*, para. 5.11.

[36] See Exhibit NZ-1 reproduced at the end of this Annex.

provisions applicable to geographical indications from inside the EC."[37] It is worth recalling, however, that a breach of national treatment may arise from the application of formally identical laws.[38] New Zealand argues that in this case "formally identical legal provisions" (or closely parallel legal provisions) in the EC Regulation do indeed result in less favourable treatment for WTO Member nationals. EC nationals have an enforceable right that applications that satisfy the requirements of the regulation are forwarded to the Commission. This right exists by virtue of Article 5(6) of the EC Regulation. Thus, for an EC national, submission via their member State government becomes essentially a formality. Failure to submit an application may be judiciable according to the member States' applicable national laws. WTO Member nationals have no such enforceable right to ensure that submission occurs. Thus, WTO Member nationals face significant "extra hurdles" in order to obtain protection for their GIs under the EC Regulation and are thus accorded less favourable treatment than an EC national. Furthermore, the Panel should find that the European Communities is in breach of its national treatment obligations by conditioning the receipt of intellectual property protection on provision of reciprocal equivalent treatment.

138. For producers able to register a GI under the EC Regulation, registration grants certain advantages, including: (i) being able to protect GIs from certain conduct set out in Article 13(1) of the EC Regulation; (ii) being able to prevent the GI term from becoming generic under Article 13(3) of the EC Regulation; (iii) being able to obtain such protection of GIs on a Community wide basis; and (iv) according to the EC Regulation's preamble, being able to secure higher incomes as a result of "a growing demand for agricultural products or foodstuffs with an identifiable geographical origin." Accordingly, not being able to register GIs under the EC Regulation results in commercial disadvantage for WTO Member nationals. They are unable to obtain the same level of protection on a Community-wide level as EC nationals and are unable to "secure higher incomes," as claimed by the European Communities to be a consequence of their GI protection. Thus the conditions of competition faced by WTO Member nationals are modified by the operation of the EC Regulation. As a consequence, the EC Regulation effectively operates as a barrier to trade.

(iii) Objections procedure provides less favourable treatment to WTO Member nationals

139. As stated in its preamble, the EC Regulation also provides an objection procedure to enable "any person individually and directly concerned in a member State to exercise his rights by notifying the Commission of his opposition." The objection procedure can potentially result in an application for registration but not for a proceeding. Consequently, not having the right to object is a loss of a valuable right in the arsenal of a producer to protect his or her commercial interests or intellectual property rights. The complainants have demonstrated that nationals from WTO countries are subject to different objection processes from EC nationals. New Zealand has summarized and compared the applicable objection procedures.[39] The process for objections from WTO nationals suffers from the same shortcomings as the process for registrations: namely, objections are subject to reciprocity and equivalence requirements and must be submitted through governments.

140. The European Communities has, however, asserted that the requirements for reciprocity and equivalence do not apply to WTO Members and thus are not preconditions for the admissibility of objections from WTO Members. In particular, the European Communities has argued that "[t]he phrase [in Article 12d(1) 'recognised under the procedure provided for in Article 12(3)' only refers to third countries other than WTO Members."[40] As has been indicated earlier, New Zealand finds the above argument unconvincing. Such an intention (to refer to third countries other than WTO Members) is not clear from the language of the EC Regulation. The fact that the rest of the EC Regulation and, in particular, the application procedure under Articles 12 and 12a, fail to explicitly distinguish between WTO Members and third countries suggests that there is in fact no such distinction. The distinction could have been made clear in Article 12d(1) by inserting a comma

[37] European Communities' first written submission, para. 62.

[38] See the GATT Panel Report on *US – Section 337*, para. 5.11.

[39] See Exhibit NZ-2 reproduced at the end of this Annex.

[40] European Communities' first written submission para. 74.

or words in the phrase to make it apparent that the procedures provided for in Article 12(3) apply only to third countries and not to WTO Members. However, no such distinction is apparent from the face of the EC Regulation. Therefore the conclusion must be drawn that the EC Regulation requires both WTO Members and third countries to be recognized under the Article 12(3). New Zealand submits that the complainants' interpretation of Article 12d(1) is the correct interpretation. WTO Members are required by the EC Regulation to provide equivalent and reciprocal treatment as a precondition to the initiation of the objection procedure by their nationals. Accordingly, the objection procedure breaches the European Communities' national treatment obligations for the same reasons that the registration procedure does. The effect of the differences in objection processes means that, at best, WTO Member nationals are disadvantaged under the EC Regulation when compared to EC nationals. At worst, the benefits of the right to object are entirely unavailable to producers from countries outside the European Communities. As a result, the European Communities has in place a system that virtually guarantees no objections will be received from WTO Member nationals to applications for the registration of EC GIs.

(d) GATT 1994

(i) The EC Regulation is inconsistent with Article III:4

141. New Zealand considers that the complainants have demonstrated that all three elements constituting a violation of Article III:4 of GATT 1994 have been satisfied.[41] First, the European Communities agrees that the EC Regulation is a measure affecting the internal sale of products. Second, the European Communities appears not to raise concerns about whether the products at issue must be "like products." New Zealand notes, in any case, that the United States is correct that for measures of general application the issue is whether the measure makes distinctions between products based solely on origin, rather than whether particular traded products are "like." It follows that the only issue under debate is whether the EC Regulation confers "less favourable treatment" on imported products. As the phrase "less favourable treatment" is the same as that used in Article 3.1 of the TRIPS Agreement, all arguments raised by New Zealand under Articles 2.1 and 3.1 of the TRIPS Agreement apply equally to Article III:4 of GATT 1994 and demonstrate that the EC Regulation also breaches Article III:4 of GATT 1994.

(ii) The EC Regulation cannot be justified under Article XX(d)

142. The European Communities has also claimed that the measure is justified under Article XX(d) of GATT 1994. In particular, the European Communities claims that "the requirements at issue are *necessary* in order to ensure that only those products which conform to the definition of geographical indications contained in Article 2(2) of Regulation 2081/92, which is itself fully consistent with GATT 1994, benefit from the protection afforded to geographical indications by Regulation 2081/92" (emphasis added).[42] New Zealand agrees with the United States that the European Communities' claim cannot be sustained. Whether a measure is "necessary" is assessed against the high standard of whether the measure is the "least-trade restrictive" option available to the party. Hence, if another WTO-consistent alternative can be employed, then a measure will not be justified under Article XX(d).

143. The European Communities claims that it is necessary for all applications to be submitted through government "to ensure that only those products which confirm to the definition of geographical indications contained in Article 2(2) of the EC Regulation ... benefit from the protection afforded to geographical indications." Given that the European Communities itself conducts a six-month investigation into precisely the issue of whether the products conform to the definition of a GI (that is, as set out in the product specification required under Article 4 of the EC Regulation), New Zealand submits that it is not necessary for applications to be passed through a government filter. The European Communities provides no claim with respect to the

[41] See the Appellate Body Report on *Korea – Various Measures on Beef*, para. 133.

[42] European Communities' first written submission, para. 226.

necessity of reciprocity and equivalence requirements imposed on non-EC products. Further, this claim does not apply to objection procedures, which are also transmitted through governments. New Zealand therefore submits that the EC Regulation cannot be justified on the basis of Article XX(d) of GATT 1994. The Panel should find that the EC Regulation violates Article III:4 of GATT 1994 as well as Articles 2.1 and 3.1 of the TRIPS Agreement.

3. The EC Regulation is inconsistent with Article 22.2 of the TRIPS Agreement

144. Article 22.2 of the TRIPS Agreement provides a negative right, or a right to prevent certain actions, rather than a positive right, such as a right to authorize use. Consequently, it is an important legal right for "interested parties" to ensure appropriate use of geographical indications. The complainants have demonstrated that the European Communities has failed to provide this right to nationals of WTO Members by requiring reciprocity and equivalence as preconditions to admissibility of registration applications and objections, and by requiring that all applications be submitted through government. New Zealand raises three points to support the complainants' views.

145. First, New Zealand submits that the phrase "legal means" is used to indicate any laws, rules and regulations through which redress for misleading uses and acts of unfair competition "in respect of geographical indications" can be obtained. Various models of legal means are envisaged under Article 22.2 of the TRIPS Agreement, consistent with the principle that WTO Members are free to determine the most appropriate method of implementation within their own legal system and practices (see Article 1.1 of the TRIPS Agreement). For GI users, registration of their GI under the EC Regulation provides the legal means to prevent a range of uses, including misleading uses and acts of unfair competition under Article 22.2 (see Article 13(1) of the EC Regulation). Once a GI has been registered under the EC Regulation, persons affected by use of that GI have extremely limited options to challenge the use of that registered GI. Indeed, they have no such options under the EC Regulation itself for only repeated failure to comply with the product specification or a request for cancellation by the natural or legal person or group authorized to seek cancellation may result in the registration being cancelled. Thus the right to object to an application for registration of a GI prior to registration occurring is a crucial aspect of the legal means that the European Communities must provide under Article 22.2 of the TRIPS Agreement.

146. Second, New Zealand submits that "interested parties" is a broad term. "Interested" is defined as meaning "having an interest, share, or concern, in something; affected, involved."[43] "Parties" encompasses any legal or natural person, or group of legal or natural persons. In the context of the TRIPS Agreement, "interested parties" has a broad meaning and includes persons with an interest in, or affected by, a GI. The term "interested parties" can be contrasted with specific terms used in other provisions which confer rights on particular groups of people. For example, when setting out the particular rights accruing to persons that have registered a trademark, Article 16.1 of the TRIPS Agreement refers specifically to "the owner of a registered trademark." Likewise, Section 1 of Part II of the TRIPS Agreement refers to "authors" in Article 11, "right holders" in Article 13, and "performers" and "producers of phonograms" in Article 14. The European Communities claims that Article 22.2 "cannot be invoked by a trademark right holder in order to prevent the use of a geographical indication which supposedly infringes its trademark right."[44] This assertion reveals the European Communities' particular bias toward systems of GI protection analogous to its registration model. It fails to acknowledge that WTO Members implement their obligations on GIs under the TRIPS Agreement in a variety of ways, including for example through collective and certification trademarks. Some trademark owners clearly do have a concern or are affected by use of geographical indications. A trademark holder can, and should in particular circumstances, be able to defend use of a trademark under Article 22.2 of the TRIPS Agreement. The European Communities' narrow interpretation of the phrase "interested parties" in Article 22.2 of the TRIPS Agreement cannot be justified.

---

[43] *The New Shorter Oxford English Dictionary*, (4th edition, 1993), Vol. 1, p.1393.

[44] European Communities' first written submission, para. 412.

147. Third, New Zealand submits that the obligation in Article 22.2 to provide a legal means to prevent misleading uses or acts of unfair competition must be read together with the other provisions of the TRIPS Agreement, including in particular the national treatment obligations in Articles 2.1 and 3.1 of the TRIPS Agreement. Thus the European Communities is obliged to provide "the same protection" or "the same legal means" to WTO nationals as it does to EC nationals. The European Communities has argued that there are other means of preventing the acts mentioned in Article 22.2 of the TRIPS Agreement available in the European Communities. However, in failing to provide the opportunity for WTO nationals to register under the EC Regulation at the centre of the present dispute, the European Communities fails to provide the same legal means to WTO nationals as it has to the more than 600 GI users in the European Communities that have had their GIs registered.

4. The EC Regulation is inconsistent with Article 16.1 of the TRIPS Agreement

148. The European Communities is obliged under Article 16.1 of the TRIPS Agreement to give owners of registered trademarks the "exclusive right" to prevent confusing uses of similar or identical signs by "all third parties." This right recognises the utility of trademarks to their owners as marketing tools. While Article 16.1 of the TRIPS Agreement provides an "exclusive right" to registered trademark owners, this is not an *absolute* right to prevent all use of the sign by other parties. The right is subject to certain limitations explicitly set out in the TRIPS Agreement in the same way that the rights to GI protection in Articles 22.2 and 22.3 are also explicitly limited by the terms of Articles 22 and 24 of the TRIPS Agreement. In any given case, for example, a registered trademark owner bringing an infringement claim against a GI user might not succeed under the requirements of Article 16.1 of the TRIPS Agreement. The trademark owner may fail to prove that the GI is identical or similar to the trademark; or that the use of the sign is in respect of goods that are identical or similar; or that use of the GI would result in a likelihood of confusion. Alternatively, the GI user may successfully argue in defence that the trademark misleads the public as to the true place of origin of the goods and should therefore be invalidated under the national law implementing Article 22.3 of the TRIPS Agreement. Article 16.1 does, however, guarantee the entitlement of a trademark owner, whether a national of the European Communities or another WTO Member, to a "day in court" to argue his or her rights against *all* third parties.

(a) Relationship between Articles 16.1 and 22.2 of the TRIPS Agreement

149. New Zealand agrees with the observations of Australia and the United States regarding the relationship between Articles 16.1 and 22.2 of the TRIPS Agreement. Despite appearances of a conflict between the two rights on the face of both provisions due to the "exclusivity" of the rights they both accord, there is a presumption of consistency between international obligations.[45] Further, any exception to an obligation must be explicit in the text of an Agreement.[46] The rights in Articles 16.1 and 22.2 of the TRIPS Agreement must therefore be balanced—each must be read to the fullest extent permissible under the text of the relevant provisions without conflicting with the other right. In other words, the protection of one right cannot be enhanced at the expense of the other. Where the negotiators intended a conflict between two rights to be resolved by compromising this exclusivity, they specifically provided for this in the TRIPS Agreement. Article 24.5 of the TRIPS Agreement is one example of this. In all other cases, upholding the rights granted in both Article 16.1 for trademarks and Article 22.2 for geographical indications is required. To the extent that the EC Regulation compromises the exclusive rights guaranteed to registered trademark owners in ways not foreseen by the TRIPS Agreement, it is inconsistent with Article 16.1 of the TRIPS Agreement.

[45] See the Panel Report on *Indonesia – Autos*, para. 14.28.

[46] See the Appellate Body Report on *EC – Sardines*, paras. 201-208.

(b) The EC Regulation is inconsistent with Article 16.1 of the TRIPS Agreement

150. New Zealand agrees with the complainants that the EC Regulation violates Article 16.1 of the TRIPS Agreement. New Zealand addresses three aspects of the EC Regulation in particular that violate Article 16.1 of the TRIPS Agreement, namely Articles 14(2), 14(3) and 7(4) of the EC Regulation.

151. Article 14(2) of the EC Regulation provides that use of a prior registered trademark that engenders one of the situations prevented by Article 13 of the EC Regulation "may continue notwithstanding the registration" of a GI. The effect of this provision is that under the EC Regulation a registered trademark and a registered GI can "co-exist" despite the existence of a likelihood of confusion between the two. The United States is correct in pointing out that under Article 14(2) of the EC Regulation the best that the owner of a valid prior registered trademark can hope for is the ability to continue using his or her trademark, but without the ability to exclude all others from using a confusingly identical or similar GI. In effect, Article 14(2) of the EC Regulation excludes registered GI users from the scope of the group of "all parties" against whom the owner of a prior registered trademark owner should be entitled under Article 16.1 of the TRIPS Agreement to defend the trademark. This is inconsistent with the exclusive rights of the trademark owner under Article 16.1 of the TRIPS Agreement.

152. Article 14(3) of the EC Regulation provides for an exception to the presumption of coexistence of prior registered trademarks and registered GIs in Article 14(2) of the EC Regulation, taking into account the "reputation, renown and the length of time trademark has been in use." However, just as there is no basis for coexistence under Article 14(3), there is no basis in Article 16.1 of the TRIPS Agreement for conditioning a prior registered trademark owner's right to prevent misleading use on such factors. New Zealand agrees with the United States that the exclusive right in Article 16.1 to prevent confusing use is not limited to owners of trademarks that are longstanding, renowned or reputable. Rather, it is an exclusive right that must be provided to all owners of valid prior registered trademarks, irrespective of how long the trademark has been used, or its reputation and renown.

153. Article 7(4) of the EC Regulation provides the criteria by which the admissibility of a statement of objection to an application for registration of a GI is judged. The criteria in Article 7(4) of the EC Regulation apply to objections from nationals of the European Communities, as well as from nationals of WTO members by virtue of Article 12d(2) of the EC Regulation. One such criterion of admissibility is if the objection "shows that the proposed registration of a name would *jeopardise the existence* of an entirely or partly identical name or of a mark..." (Article 7(4) of the EC Regulation). If the proposed GI registration is identical to the prior registered trademark, however, under Article 16.1 of the TRIPS Agreement there is a presumption of confusion and the trademark owner should have the right to prevent the use of the GI. Consequently, New Zealand agrees with the arguments by Australia that the EC Regulation breaches Article 16.1 of the TRIPS Agreement because the owner of the registered trademark may not be able to successfully object to a proposed GI even if its use would constitute use of an identical or similar sign that would result in a likelihood of confusion.

(i) Article 24.5 of the TRIPS Agreement does not permit "coexistence"

154. The European Communities relies on Article 24.5 of the TRIPS Agreement as envisaging coexistence of GIs and earlier trademarks. The European Communities adopts a flawed interpretation as the basis for its argument that coexistence of GIs and earlier trademarks is envisaged under Article 24.5 of the TRIPS Agreement. It argues that Article 24.5 distinguishes the "right to use" a trademark, which may not be prejudiced, from the right to prevent others from using the trademark sign, which may be prejudiced. New Zealand submits that this interpretation is incorrect for two reasons.

155. First, the purpose of Article 24.5 is to prevent the implementation of new forms of intellectual property resulting from the negotiations of the TRIPS Agreement from prejudicing rights to intellectual property legitimately acquired prior to the entry into force of the TRIPS Agreement. Trademark owners who had registered a trademark or acquired rights to a trademark through use had the rights both to use and to prevent

others from using their trademarks prior to the entry into force of the TRIPS Agreement. New Zealand contends that the TRIPS Agreement was not intended to detrimentally affect the private rights of individuals by removing trademark owners' entitlement to prevent all third parties from using their trademark where its existence pre-dated the TRIPS Agreement.

156. Second, Article 24.5 covers trademark rights acquired by registration as well as trademark rights acquired by use. The rights protected under Article 24.5 are dealt with separately. Thus "where a trademark has been applied for or registered in good faith" GI protection measures "shall not prejudice eligibility for or the validity of the registration of a trademark." And "where rights to a trademark have been acquired through use in good faith" GI protection measures "shall not prejudice the right to use a trademark."

157. The European Communities' reading of Article 24.5 confuses the two concepts of registration and use. It suggests that registered trademarks retain the right to use as well as rights to the continued eligibility for or validity of registration. If this reading were correct, the corollary would also be true, namely that trademark rights acquired by use would continue to be eligible for registration, despite the owner not having submitted an application for registration prior to the entry into force of the TRIPS Agreement. As the purpose of Article 24.5 is to protect private rights existing immediately prior to the entry into force of the TRIPS Agreement, it is clear that it was not intended that unregistered trademark owners would gain the right to registration through use, despite having failed to safeguard their rights through registration prior to the entry into force of the TRIPS Agreement. Thus New Zealand agrees with the complainants that Article 24.5 of the TRIPS Agreement does not permit coexistence of "grandfathered" trademarks and GI registrations.

(ii) The EC is not required to maintain coexistence on the basis of Article 24.3 of the TRIPS Agreement

158. The European Communities goes on to argue that, irrespective of whether coexistence of geographical indications is consistent with Article 24.5, it is required to maintain coexistence under Article 24.3 of the TRIPS Agreement. The purpose of this Article appears to be the same as Article 24.5, namely to prevent the entry into force of the TRIPS Agreement from detrimentally affecting the private rights of individuals. However, despite the EC Regulation having entered into force on 14 July 1993, the first registration of a geographical indication under the regulation did not occur until after the entry into force of the TRIPS Agreement on 1 January 1995. So while the EC Regulation provided for coexistence prior to the entry into force of the TRIPS Agreement, in fact the EC Regulation conferred no rights to individuals at that time. In any case, New Zealand submits that the phrase "[i]n implementing this Section" that prefaces Article 24.3 does not justify a breach of other sections of the TRIPS Agreement, including Section 2 on trademarks.

(iii) Coexistence is not a limited exception under Article 17 of the TRIPS Agreement

159. The European Communities also argues in the alternative that coexistence is justified as a "limited exception to the rights conferred by a trademark" under Article 17 of the TRIPS Agreement. In New Zealand's view the exclusion of an entire group of producers from the parties which a registered trademark owner has the right to prevent from using an identical or similar mark in confusing manner is not a "*limited* exception." Rather, it is a major exception to the rights granted to a registered trademark owner.

5. Points raised in response to the Panel's questions

160. New Zealand has not received any registration applications or objections to registrations pursuant to the EC Regulation from persons or groups in its territory. New Zealand notes that its Government and potential New Zealand applicants and objectors understood the EC Regulation to mean that no applications or objections would be accepted or considered by the European Communities without New Zealand meeting the reciprocity and equivalence requirements. As to the question of what would be New Zealand's position if such filing was to occur, New Zealand notes that this is a hypothetical question and it is difficult to answer in the abstract. Despite no formal procedure for the transmission of applications for registration or objections to registration under the

EC Regulation existing in New Zealand, New Zealand would consider any registration or objection submitted to New Zealand authorities on a case-by-case basis. In any event, the issue before the Panel is the consistency of the EC Regulation with the WTO Agreements, not whether other WTO Members would comply with the requirements of a WTO-inconsistent measure.

161. New Zealand provides the legal means for the protection of geographical indications, as required by Article 22 of the TRIPS Agreement, through its trademarks legislation (including collective trademarks and certification trademarks), and through consumer protection law (Fair Trading Act, common law tort of passing off). These legal means are available to all interested parties irrespective of nationality. A geographical indication (that meets the requirements for registration) may be registered as a trademark through applying, including via the internet, directly to the Intellectual Property Office of New Zealand. An interested party may also apply directly to the Intellectual Property Office to oppose or seek invalidation of the registration of a trademark. For geographical indications other than those registered as trademarks, nationals of any country may take action in New Zealand courts to enforce their rights under the Fair Trading Act 1986, and the common law tort of "passing off." The New Zealand Parliament has enacted a Geographical Indications Act, but this is not in force.

162. New Zealand submits that, by virtue of Article 2.1 of the TRIPS Agreement, all WTO Members must comply with Article 2(1) of the Paris Convention. All WTO Members are therefore "countries of the Union" for the purposes of that Article of the Paris Convention as incorporated in the TRIPS Agreement.

163. New Zealand submits that Article 22.1 of the TRIPS Agreement defines geographical indications as indications that "identify a good as originating in the territory of a Member, or a region or locality in that territory, where a given quality, reputation or other characteristic of the good is essentially attributable to its geographical origin." By definition, therefore, a geographical indication must relate to a particular good. As a consequence, the indication and the good are inextricably linked. The EC Regulation claims that commercial benefits are conferred on goods or products bearing a registered geographical indication. In other words, it claims that the conditions of sale are positively affected by the products bearing registered geographical indications. As a result of the different treatment accorded to EC nationals and nationals of WTO Members, only products bearing a registered EC geographical indication have the opportunity to obtain any commercial benefits which are claimed by the European Communities to ensue from protection under the EC Regulation. The foreign like product does not have this opportunity and therefore receives less favourable treatment. New Zealand considers that evidence of disadvantages accorded to foreigners in applying for and objecting to protection of particular geographical indications is relevant to whether like products receive less favourable treatment.

164. Under New Zealand's trademark legislation, a trademark (including a geographical indication for which registration as a trademark has been sought) that would otherwise be considered identical or similar to a registered trademark may be registered if: (i) the owner of the registered trademark consents to the registration of the later filed trademark; or (ii) the Commissioner of Trade Marks (or Court) considers that a case of honest concurrent use exists or other special circumstances exist, which makes it proper for the trademark to be registered. In making such a determination, the Commissioner of Trade Marks (or Court) will have regard to, *inter alia*, whether confusion is likely to occur, the degree of that confusion, and whether any confusion has in fact been proved. A registered trademark may be used for the purpose of comparative advertising provided that the mark is used in accordance with honest practices in industrial or commercial matters. Use of a sign (including a geographical indication) will not amount to infringement of a registered trademark if, in accordance with honest practices in industrial or commercial matters, the sign is used to indicate, *inter alia*, a person's name, place of business, or the kind, quality, geographical origin or other characteristic of the goods or services. If the use of the trademark is misleading or is likely to cause confusion then its use is unlikely to be considered "in accordance with honest practices"

165. In New Zealand, the concurrent use of geographical indications with prior trademarks would not be permitted where this would result in a breach of the Trade Marks Act, the Fair Trading Act or the common law

tort of "passing off." Confusion is relevant to all three causes of action. Infringement proceedings may be taken under the Trade Marks Act (section 89) for use of a sign that is identical or similar to a registered trademark where such use would be likely to deceive or confuse (note, however that there is a presumption of infringement under the Trade Marks Act where a mark that is identical to a registered trademark is used in respect of identical goods). The Fair Trading Act (section 9) prohibits conduct in trade that is deceptive or misleading or likely to deceive or mislead, while passing off is aimed at preventing misrepresentation that can result from use of a confusingly similar mark. A geographical indication could not be protected as a registered trademark if its use would be likely to deceive or cause confusion, particularly with a prior registered mark (sections 17 and 25 of the Trade Marks Act).

166. New Zealand believes that the mandatory/discretionary distinction has limited application under the TRIPS Agreement. As indicated by the Appellate Body in *US – Section 211 Appropriations Act*, the characterization of legislation as mandatory or discretionary is not the only relevant inquiry for a panel.[47] Nor should a finding that the legislation is discretionary be conclusive as to whether a State has complied with WTO rules. In particular, the "extra hurdles" in the EC Regulation that disadvantage foreigners and breach national treatment apply regardless of whether or not that legislation is deemed "discretionary." Further, the granting of intellectual property rights necessarily involves the exercise of discretion, as does for example the initiation of anti-dumping investigations. The objectives of the TRIPS Agreement would be undermined if the European Communities can be excused from its TRIPS obligations on the basis that its implementing legislation is discretionary. New Zealand notes that obligations prohibiting certain action and obligations requiring certain action, whether in the TRIPS Agreement or in other WTO Agreements, are all binding and mandatory obligations upon WTO Members. Accordingly, New Zealand cannot see that WTO jurisprudence on the mandatory/discretionary distinction should apply differently depending on whether the obligations prohibit certain action, or require certain action.

I. SEPARATE CUSTOMS TERRITORY OF TAIWAN, PENGHU, KINMEN AND MATSU

1. Introduction

167. The Separate Customs Territory of Taiwan, Penghu, Kinmen and Matsu (hereinafter referred to as "Chinese Taipei") has a trade and systemic interest in the proper interpretation of the TRIPS Agreement, specifically, the national treatment requirements contained in the TRIPS Agreement and Paris Convention, the MFN requirement contained in the TRIPS Agreement, and in the relationship between geographical indications ("GIs") and trademarks.

2. National treatment

168. National treatment is a long-standing and fundamental obligation in the multilateral trading system. The European Communities completely ignores the fact that the protection of intellectual property plays a part in the national treatment provisions. By citing the specific paragraph in the Panel Report of *Indonesia – Autos* cautioning against reading extraneous obligations into a provision, the European Communities also seems to suggest that the protection of intellectual property rights is not in fact an objective of the TRIPS Agreement, and that one should not read the protection of intellectual property into Article 3.1 of the TRIPS Agreement. The drafters of Article 3.1 of the TRIPS Agreement and Article 2(1) of the Paris Convention recognize that, in the context of the protection of intellectual property, nationals and the intellectual property rights they hold cannot be divorced from each other. Conceptually, to grant national treatment to nationals who are not holders of intellectual property rights would be illogical. Similarly, intellectual property rights by themselves cannot enforce the requirement of national treatment without their attendant holder-nationals. The two national treatment provisions would simply be incomprehensible if the protection of intellectual property were taken out of the equation. Furthermore, Article 3.1 of the TRIPS Agreement and Article 2(1) of the Paris Convention do

[47] See the Appellate Body Report on *US – Section 211 Appropriations Act*, para. 260.

not specify the origin of the intellectual property being held by the "nationals." The focus of the national treatment provisions is on the nationals who have an intellectual property to register or the rights to enforce, not on the origin of the actual intellectual property. Be it domestic nationals holding domestic intellectual property rights, domestic nationals holding foreign intellectual property rights, foreign nationals holding domestic intellectual property rights, or foreign nationals holding foreign intellectual property rights, national treatment applies in all scenarios in the same manner.

169. In order to demonstrate how the TRIPS Agreement and Paris Convention national treatment obligations apply in this case, Chinese Taipei presents the following chart:

GI EC National EC 1	GI Non EC National EC 3
2 GI EC National Non EC	4 GI Non EC National Non EC

170. The four quadrants represent the four possible scenarios. The European Communities, focusing only on nationals in its interpretation, is essentially arguing that it can establish a separate set of rules for and discriminate against non-EC GIs as it wishes. To the European Communities, quadrants 1 and 2 are completely independent from quadrants 3 and 4. As long as the national in quadrant 2 is treated no less favourably than the national in quadrant 1, and the national in quadrant 4 is treated no less favourably than the national in quadrant 3, the national treatment obligation, according to the European Communities, is satisfied. However, as already presented above, there exists two linked elements in the TRIPS Agreement and Paris Convention national treatment obligations, and the four quadrants need to be examined as a whole. This means that quadrants 2, 3, and 4 all cannot be treated less favourably than quadrant 1. Therefore, the Panel should examine, whether the EC Regulation results in any one of the quadrants 2, 3, or 4 being treated less favourably than quadrant 1. If even one of the quadrants is treated less favourably, the EC Regulation would be inconsistent with the national treatment obligations. Chinese Taipei agrees with the submissions of the United States and Australia in their analyses of how Article 12 of EC Regulation results in less favourable treatment being afforded to non-EC nationals. Since the scenarios in quadrant 2 and 3 in practice happen infrequently, it would suffice to examine only the consistency of the EC Regulation with regard to the scenario under quadrant 4. By applying the same arguments the two complainants made with regard to EC Regulation Article 12, the Panel would be able to see a blatant violation in the scenario represented by quadrant 4.

171. Chinese Taipei also agrees with the United States and Australia that Article 12.1 of the EC Regulation constitutes conditions on WTO Members in exchange for the recognition of GIs from non-EC sources. Such conditions violate Article 3.1 of the TRIPS Agreement and Article 2(1) of the Paris Convention. The European Communities conditions the protection of GIs, an explicit obligation under Article 22 of the TRIPS Agreement, on reciprocity and equivalence. Such requirements do not exist in Part II Section 3 of the TRIPS Agreement which deals with GIs nor anywhere else in the TRIPS Agreement as preconditions to implementing an explicit TRIPS Agreement obligation. Furthermore, Article 12.3 of the EC Regulation provides that, "[t]he Commission shall examine, at the request of the country concerned...whether a third country satisfies the equivalence conditions and offers guarantees within the meaning of paragraph 1 as a result of its national legislation." Therefore, even if a WTO Member deems its GI specifications, inspection arrangements, the right to object and protection of EC GIs to be equivalent, the European Communities still holds the final say on whether the equivalence conditions have been met. The European Communities has yet to give an indication as to what it considers to constitute "equivalence," but the existence of this requirement to gain approval from the Commission suggests that the standard for equivalence is high.

172. In essence, the European Communities is requiring other WTO Members to adopt a system of GI

protection substantially similar to, if not the same as, the European Communities and be prepared to accept automatically all EC GIs. By requiring the reciprocity and equivalency conditions, the European Communities ignores the fact that the second sentence of Article 1.1 of the TRIPS Agreement provides that, "Members shall be free to determine the appropriate method of implementing the provisions of this Agreement within their own legal system and practice," and that Article 22 of the TRIPS Agreement does not specify any particular "legal means" for the protection of GIs. In this connection, Chinese Taipei agrees with the United States that the TRIPS Agreement recognizes more than one acceptable GI protection system. Moreover, reciprocity and equivalency may be better addressed in the context of bilateral or multilateral negotiations, should the European Communities wish to do so. But they cannot constitute conditions on the implementation of an explicit TRIPS Agreement obligation to provide national treatment to foreign producers with regard to intellectual property. Additionally, if a Member such as the European Communities believes that another Member is not granting the proper protection to GIs as stipulated in the TRIPS Agreement, the recourse is the WTO dispute settlement, not the denial of national treatment. As it is, these reciprocity and equivalence conditions are simply extra hurdles to be fulfilled by WTO Members before producers with GIs from their territories can gain protection from the European Communities. These extra hurdles constitute an additional burden on non-EC nationals seeking to register, and enforce non-EC GIs within the European Communities as compared to the requirements on EC nationals. Thus, the EC Regulation violates the national treatment provisions pursuant to Article 3.1 of the TRIPS Agreement and the Article 2(1) of the Paris Convention.

3. MFN treatment

173. Chinese Taipei also shares the view of the United States and Australia that, just as the EC Regulation violates the national treatment obligation under the TRIPS Agreement, the measure also violates the TRIPS Agreement MFN obligation. It should be noted, in light of the arguments presented above on national treatment, that the MFN obligation with regard to nationals should be viewed with respect to the protection of intellectual property, from the perspective of nationals holding intellectual property rights. Similarly, as with TRIPS and Paris Convention national treatment obligations, Article 4 cannot be interpreted as an obligation on nationals alone.

174. The chart presented in the context of national treatment above can be slightly modified to be applied here:

GI approved National approved 1	GI not approved National approved 3
2 GI approved National not approved	4 GI not approved National not approved

175. The above chart sets out how the MFN treatment comparison should be made. With regard to the protection of intellectual property, the MFN treatment in essence requires the Member in question to grant equal treatment to the nationals of all other Members. Therefore, the basic premise of this quadrant is that both the GI and the national are non-EC in origin (Chinese Taipei takes no position with regard to the issue raised by the complainants that the individual members of the European Communities who are also Members of the WTO should be viewed as separate non-EC Members of the WTO under MFN treatment). The term "national" in the table is used in the same manner as the word "nationals" in Article 4 of the TRIPS Agreement, but with the above premise in mind. The terms "approved" and "not approved" relate to the approval scheme in Articles 12(1) and 12(3) of the EC Regulation under which a third country GI may be protected within the European Communities after determination by the EC Commission that the "equivalence conditions" have been satisfied. "Approved" thus means that the GI or national originated from a WTO Member which has been

deemed by the EC Commission to have satisfied the conditions set out in Article 12(1). On the other hand, "not approved" means that the GI or national originated from a WTO Member which has not been deemed by the EC Commission to have satisfied the conditions set out in the Article 12(1). The GI and the national may have different origins, hence the existence of quadrants 2 and 3.

176. Under the MFN treatment, the scenarios under quadrants 2, 3, and 4 must all receive the same treatment from European Communities as the treatment received by quadrant 1, or else the European Communities has violated the obligation. Having granted full protection under the EC Regulation to the nationals of an approved WTO Member holding GIs originating from the territories of that member, the European Communities cannot deny the same "advantage, favour, privilege or immunity" to the nationals of other WTO Members holding GIs originating from other territories. But this is exactly what EC Regulation does. Once again, quadrant 4 shows where the EC Regulation most blatantly violates the MFN treatment obligation.

4. Relationship between GIs and trademarks in the TRIPS Agreement

177. Unlike other types of intellectual property such as patents and copyrights, which tend to be independent concepts and manifest themselves in different forms, trademarks and GIs are closely related. The purpose of both is to inform consumers about the source and indirectly the quality of the product. Because of this purpose, GIs and trademarks can and tend to manifest themselves in similar forms, i.e., as prominent and distinguishing signs. The close relationship between GIs and trademarks and the possible overlap in their physical manifestations and protection are recognized in the TRIPS Agreement. Articles 22.3, 23.2 and 24.5 directly address the relationship between GIs and trademarks. The rights are derived from the need to prevent consumers from being misled about the qualities of the product, and thus the provision in Article 16.1 for trademarks and Article 22.2 for GIs spelling out the extent of the rights.

178. However, the text of these two TRIPS provisions must be given their full scope in a manner that would not cause conflict. This is consistent with the established principle of international treaty interpretation, which requires that the "interpretation must give meaning and effect to all the terms of a treaty." Furthermore, "[a]n interpreter is not free to adopt a meaning that would result in whole clauses or paragraphs of a treaty to redundancy or inutility."[48] An interpretation or implementation of these two provisions that creates conflict would inevitably render one of the provisions inutile. Thus, the Panel in *Indonesia – Autos* concluded that, "in public international law there is a presumption against conflict."[49] However, the EC Regulation creates precisely such a conflict by allowing a later registered GI to be used alongside a prior trademark, even when such use has the potential of resulting in the likelihood of confusion on the part of the consumer. Thus, Article 14(2) of the Regulation negates the right of trademark owners contained in Article 16.1 of the TRIPS Agreement. Likewise, under Article 14(3) of the EC Regulation, a potential GI is only prevented from being registered if the trademark fulfils the conditions of reputation, renown, and length of time, the provision negates the right granted to trademark owners pursuant to Article 16.1 of the TRIPS Agreement. The result of the EC Regulation is the creation of a hierarchy between GIs and trademarks, when the two are equal under the TRIPS Agreement. GIs within the European Communities have a superior status than trademarks, and the protection of GIs is granted at the expense of trademarks. Such a hierarchy is simply not contemplated in the TRIPS Agreement.

5. Points raised in response to Panel's questions

179. Chinese Taipei is not aware of any group or person ever having filed with its authorities either an application for, or an objection to, a registration pursuant to the EC Regulation. In any case, it does not believe that whether its Government is able and/or willing to transmit to the European Communities an application from

[48] Appellate Body Report on *US – Gasoline*, DSR 1996:I, at 21.
[49] Panel Report on *Indonesia – Autos*, para. 14.28.

persons interested in a GI or objection has any bearing on the issues in this dispute. Even if its Government is able and/or willing, the fact remains, that the TRIPS Agreement does not contain any obligation for Members to comply with an internal regulation of the European Communities. The European Communities is free to require its member States to do so, but to require WTO Members to transmit applications for registration or objections to registration when no such obligation exists in the TRIPS Agreement would be to create an additional hurdle for non-EC nationals who wish to register their GIs within the European Communities, thus violating Article 3.1 of the TRIPS Agreement and Article 2 of the Paris Convention.

180. Chinese Taipei's legislation protects trademarks and collective marks of foreign nationals in the same manner as that of domestic nationals, and nothing in its legislation prevents foreign nationals with a potential GI from applying for the registration of a trademark or collective mark.

181. Chinese Taipei believes that footnote 1 of the TRIPS Agreement is meant to apply the term "nationals" to separate customs territory Members of the WTO. The first clause of the footnote makes the application of the definition to the entire Agreement clear with the words "in this Agreement." The definition therefore applies to the European Communities, as a separate customs territory, with regard to Articles 3.1 and 4 of the TRIPS Agreement. There is no logical reason to believe that the term "nationals" in Article 2 of the Paris Convention should be interpreted any differently from the TRIPS Agreement, with respect to the European Communities. It is established jurisprudence that Articles 1 through 12 and Article 19 of the Paris Convention are incorporated into the TRIPS Agreement. Article 3 of the TRIPS Agreement, which is the parallel provision to Article 2 of Paris Convention, makes explicit reference to the applicability of the exceptions in the Paris Convention. If key terms such as "nationals" are interpreted differently in the TRIPS Agreement and the Paris Convention, incorporation and direct applicability of certain provisions would be difficult, if not impossible. Therefore, unless there is an explicit reason to believe otherwise, the term "nationals" in Article 2 of the Paris Convention should be interpreted in the same manner as in the TRIPS Agreement.

182. Chinese Taipei understands that Articles 16.1 and 22.3 of the TRIPS Agreement do not, and should not be, interpreted to conflict. The established principle of international treaty interpretation requires that any interpretation shall give meaning and effect to all terms of a treaty. An interpretation that creates a conflict between two provisions would inevitably render one of the provisions inutile. The third sentence of Article 16.1 states that, "the rights described above shall not prejudice any existing prior rights." Therefore, the "exclusive right" granted to trademarks under Article 16.1 is dependent upon existing prior rights. Similarly, and in a parallel manner, the rights obtained pursuant to GI protection are curtailed by Article 24.5, where the right of a prior trademark owner, which is exclusive, is guaranteed. The combination of Articles 16.1, 22.3 and 24.5 establishes a protection scheme where a prior existing right, be it under trademark or GI, bars any later requests to register trademarks or GIs that would confuse or mislead the public. The EC Regulation creates a conflict between the protection of trademarks and GIs, when no such conflict exists, by disregarding the exclusive right of prior trademarks owners and favouring the right of GI owners. Such a hierarchy is not contemplated by the TRIPS Agreement.

EXHIBIT NZ-1

APPLICATION PROCESS FOR THE REGISTRATION OF A GEOGRAPHICAL INDICATION UNDER EC REGULATION 2081/92

[OMITTED]

EXHIBIT NZ-2

OBJECTION PROCESS DURING THE REGISTRATION OF A GEOGRAPHICAL INDICATION UNDER EC REGULATION 2081/92

[OMITTED]

ANNEX D

MISCELLANEOUS

CONTENTS		PAGE

WORLD TRADE ORGANIZATION

WT/DS174/20
19 August 2003

(03-4330)

Original: English

EUROPEAN COMMUNITIES – PROTECTION OF TRADEMARKS AND GEOGRAPHICAL INDICATIONS FOR AGRICULTURAL PRODUCTS AND FOODSTUFFS

Request for the Establishment of a Panel by the United States

The following communication, dated 18 August 2003, from the Permanent Mission of the United States to the Chairman of the Dispute Settlement Body, is circulated pursuant to Article 6.2 of the DSU.

On 1 June 1999, the United States requested consultations with the European Communities ("EC") pursuant to Article 4 of the *Understanding on Rules and Procedures Governing the Settlement of Disputes* ("DSU") and Article 64 of the *Agreement on Trade-Related Aspects of Intellectual Property Rights* ("TRIPS Agreement") (to the extent that it incorporates by reference Article XXIII of the *General Agreement on Tariffs and Trade 1994* ("GATT 1994")) regarding EC Council Regulation (EEC) No 2081/92 of 14 July 1992 on the protection of geographical indications and designations of origin for agricultural products and foodstuffs, as amended (*European Communities – Protection of Trademarks and Geographical Indications for Agricultural Products and Foodstuffs* (WT/DS174/1)). The United States and the EC held consultations on 9 July 1999, and thereafter, but these consultations failed to resolve the dispute.

On 4 April 2003, the United States supplemented its earlier request with a request for additional consultations with the EC pursuant to Article 4 of the DSU, Article 64 of the TRIPS Agreement and Article XXII of the GATT 1994, regarding the protection of trademarks and geographical indications for agricultural products and foodstuffs in the European Communities pursuant to Regulation 2081/92, as amended, and its related implementing and enforcement measures ("Regulation 2081/92") (*European Communities – Protection of Trademarks and Geographical Indications for Agricultural Products and Foodstuffs* (WT/DS174/1/Add.1)). The United States and the EC held consultations pursuant to this supplemental request on 27 May 2003, but these consultations also failed to resolve the dispute.

Regulation 2081/92 does not provide the same treatment to other nationals and products originating outside the EC that it provides to the EC's own nationals and products, does not accord immediately and unconditionally to the nationals and products of each WTO Member any advantage, favour, privilege or immunity granted to the nationals and products of other WTO Members, diminishes the legal protection for trademarks (including to prevent the use of an identical or similar sign that is likely to confuse and adequate protection against invalidation), does not provide legal means for interested parties to prevent the misleading use of a geographical indication, does not define a geographical indication in a manner that is consistent with the definition provided in the TRIPS Agreement, is not sufficiently transparent, and does not provide adequate enforcement procedures.

Regulation 2081/92 appears to be inconsistent with:

(1) TRIPS Agreement Articles 1.1, 2.1 (incorporating by reference Article 2 of the *Paris Convention for the Protection of Industrial Property* (Paris Convention (1967)), 3.1, 4, 16.1, 20, 22.1, 22.2, 24.5, 41.1, 41.2, 41.4, 42, 44.1, 63.1, 63.3, 65.1; and

(2) Articles I and III:4 of the GATT 1994.

Accordingly, the United States respectfully asks the DSB to establish a panel with standard terms of reference as set out in Article 7.1 of the DSU.

ANNEX D-2

LETTER DATED 9 JULY 2004 FROM THE PANEL TO THE INTERNATIONAL BUREAU OF WIPO

At its meeting on 2 October 2003, the WTO Dispute Settlement Body established the Panel on European Communities – Protection of Trademarks and Geographical Indications for Agricultural Products and Foodstuffs pursuant to the requests by the United States in document WT/DS174/20 and Australia in document WT/DS290/18 (please see the attached documents), in accordance with Article 9 of the Dispute Settlement Understanding. On 23 February 2004, a Panel was composed to examine this complaint (please see the attached document with a dual symbol WT/DS174/21 and WT/DS290/19).

A number of provisions of the Paris Convention have been raised in these proceedings as relevant to the interpretation of the European Communities' obligations under the TRIPS Agreement. Given that the International Bureau of WIPO is responsible for the administration of that Convention, the purpose of this letter is to request, on behalf of the panel, the assistance of the International Bureau of WIPO in the form of any factual information available to it relevant to the interpretation of the provisions in question, in particular as reflected in the materials of diplomatic conferences, subsequent developments in the framework of the Paris Union or other work under the auspices of the WIPO as well as, to the extent available to the International Bureau, on the state practice of the Paris Union members.

The specific provisions of the Paris Convention in regard to which the panel would seek this assistance at this stage are:

– Article 2 of the Stockholm Act of 1967 of the Paris Convention, in particular as regards:

  (a) the national treatment obligation contained in that provision; and
  (b) the intended meaning of the term "national" used therein.

– Any other provisions, of relevance to the categories of intellectual property at issue in this dispute, which set out criteria for the eligibility of natural or legal persons for protection under the Paris Convention (1967).

The Panel may, at a later stage, wish to seek from the International Bureau further such information on other provisions of the Paris Convention (1967) that have been referred to by the parties to the dispute.

It would facilitate the work of the Panel if such information could be made available by Thursday, 29 July 2004.

ANNEX D-3

REPLY FROM THE INTERNATIONAL BUREAU OF WIPO TO THE PANEL'S LETTER DATED 9 JULY 2004, RECEIVED BY THE PANEL AND THE WTO SECRETARIAT ON 14 SEPTEMBER 2004

I refer to your letter of July 9, 2004, addressed to the Director General of the World Intellectual Property Organization (WIPO), relating to the Panel established by the WTO Dispute Settlement Body to examine two ongoing disputes on the basis of the matter referred to in WTO documents WT/DS174/20 and WT/DS290/18.

In response to your request, please find attached a note with five annexes prepared by the International Bureau.

On behalf of WIPO, I wish to reiterate our readiness to provide any further assistance.

List of Materials from Diplomatic Conferences Adopting, Revising and Amending Articles 2 and 3 of the Paris Convention for the Protection of Industrial Property (1967)

General

This note contains a list of the materials that the International Bureau of the World Intellectual Property Organization (WIPO) has compiled following a request for assistance as contained in a letter, dated July 9, 2004, received from Mr. Miguel Rodríguez Mendoza, Chairman of the Panel on European Communities – Protection of Trademarks and Geographical Indications for Agricultural Products and Foodstuffs established by the WTO Dispute Settlement Body.

The Panel has sought the assistance of the International Bureau of WIPO, at this stage, in respect of Article 2 of the Paris Convention for the Protection of Industrial Property (Stockholm Act of 1967) and any other provisions, of relevance to the categories of intellectual property at issue in this dispute, which set out criteria for the eligibility of natural or legal persons for protection under the Paris Convention requesting, as indicated in the letter in question, "the assistance of the International Bureau in the form of any factual information available to it relevant to the interpretation of the provisions in question, in particular as reflected in the materials of diplomatic conferences, subsequent developments in the framework of the Paris Union or other work under the auspices of the WIPO as well as, to the extent available to the International Bureau, on the state practice of the Paris Union members."

The Panel's request would, at this stage, appear to concern:

(i) the national treatment obligation contained in Article 2 of the Paris Convention and the intended meaning of the term "national" used therein; and

(ii) the criteria for determining the eligibility of natural or legal persons to enjoy protection under the Paris Convention.

The materials compiled by the International Bureau in respect of these two items and listed below are confined to Articles 2 and 3 of the Paris Convention. Article 2 refers to what is generally referred to as the "national treatment" obligation. Article 3 provides for the assimilation of certain persons with "nationals" of the Paris Union. Both articles apply generally to all categories of industrial property under the Paris Convention.

The International Bureau understands that the Panel's request for information does not extend to the question of a person's "eligibility" under any specific provision of the Paris Convention resulting from compliance with the particular requirements specified by such provision in addition to the qualification of that person under Articles 2 and 3.

The materials compiled include excerpts from the Official Records of the various Diplomatic Conferences which adopted, amended or revised the provisions currently contained in Articles 2 and 3 of the Paris Convention (Stockholm Act of 1967). These provisions were last changed at the Revision Conference held at The Hague in 1925, and have not been amended since.

The official records of the diplomatic conferences, from which the excerpts listed below have been extracted, are only available in the French language. The English translations of the successive versions of Articles 2 and 3 as included in the abovementioned Acts of the Paris Convention have been prepared by the International Bureau of WIPO and are also attached.

1. Excerpts from the Records of the Paris Diplomatic Conference (1880/1883)

A. Conférence internationale pour la protection de la propriété intellectuelle (1880)

General

Pages 11 to 24 (*Procès-verbal de la première séance*)

Pages 25 to 41 (*Procès-verbal de la deuxième séance)*

Article 2

Pages 42 to 47 (*Procès-verbal de la troisième séance*)

Articles 2 and 3

Pages 123 to 132 (*Procès-verbal de la neuvième séance*)

Article 3

Pages 137 to 138, 147 to 150 (*Procès-verbal de la dixième séance*)

Pages 161 to 167 (*Séance de clôture, Projet de convention et Protocole de clôture)*

B. Conférence internationale pour la protection de la propriété intellectuelle (1883)

General

Pages 3, 51 to 62 (*Convention et Protocole de clôture)*

2. Excerpts from the Records of the Brussels Revision Conference (1897/1900)

Article 2

Pages 89 and 95 to 97 (*Proposition présentée par l'Administration des États-Unis*)

Pages 143 to 144 (*Première annexe au procès-verbal de la Réunion préparatoire du 1er décembre 1897 – Tableau général des propositions, contre-propositions et amendements soumis à la conférence)*

Articles 2 and 3

Pages 163 and 164 (*Proposition présentée par la Délégation française au cours de la réunion préparatoire du 1er décembre 1897*)

Pages 185, 187, 188 (*Procès-verbal de la deuxième séance – 4 décembre 1897)*

Pages 195 to 200 (*Procès-verbal de la troisième séance – 6 décembre 1897)*

Pages 309 to 311 *(Procès-verbal de la neuvième séance – 13 décembre 1897)*

Page 341 (*Premier protocole final - 14 décembre 1897)*

General

Pages 407, 410 to 412 *(Acte additionel du 14 décembre 1900 modifiant la Convention du 20 novembre 1883 ainsi que le Protocole de clôture y annexé)*

3. Excerpts from the Records of the Washington Revision Conference (1911)

Article 2

Pages 42 to 44 and 53 *(Exposé des motifs et propositions préparé par le Bureau international; II. Personnes protégées et étendue de la protection; Juridiction)*

Pages 58 and 59 *(Avant-projet d'une Convention pour la protection de la propriété industrielle)*

Articles 2 and 3

Pages 94, 105, 106, 109 and 110 *(Propositions, contre-propositions et observations présentées par diverses administrations : 2. Administration de la France; 3. Administration de la Grande-Bretagne; 4. Administration des Pays-Bas)*

Pages 183 to 187 *(Procès-verbal de la réunion préparatoire, première annexe : Tableau général des propositions, contre-propositions et amendements soumis à la Conférence)*

Pages 223 and 224 *(Procès-verbal de la réunion préparatoire, deuxième annexe : Propositions présentées au cours de la réunion préparatoire)*

Page 226 *(Procès-verbal de la réunion préparatoire, troisième annexe : Nouvelle rédaction pour les articles 1, 2, 5 à 9, 11, et 16 de l'avant-projet)*

Pages 245 to 247 *(Procès-verbal de la troisième séance)*

Pages 269 to 271 *(Premier rapport présenté au nom de la sous-commission chargée d'examiner les articles 1 et 2 de la Convention)*

Pages 306, 307, 310 to 312 *(Rapport présenté à la commission plénière)*

Page 331 *(Actes adoptés par la Conférence)*

4. Excerpts from the Records of the Hague Revision Conference (1925)

Article 2

Pages 222 to 225 (*Exposé des motifs et propositions; II Principes fondamentaux de la Convention*)

Page 267 (*Avant-projet de la Convention de Paris révisée pour la protection de la propriété industrielle; Texte unique révisé*)

Page 333 (*Propositions, contre-propositions et observations*)

Page 413 to 415 (*Rapport de la première sous-commission*)

Page 517 (*Rapport de la commission générale à la conférence*)

Pages 536 to 537 (*Rapport de la commission de rédaction*)

Page 572 (*Procès-verbal de la deuxième séance plénière*)

Article 3

This provision was not discussed at the Hague Revision Conference.

5. English translations of Articles 2 and 3 as contained in the 1883, 1900, 1911 and 1925 Acts of the Paris Convention

---

EUROPEAN COMMUNITIES – PROTECTION OF TRADEMARKS AND GEOGRAPHICAL INDICATIONS FOR AGRICULTURAL PRODUCTS AND FOODSTUFFS – COMPLAINT BY AUSTRALIA

WT/DS290/R
REPORT OF THE PANEL

Complainant: Australia

Respondent: European Communities

Third Parties: Argentina, Brazil, Canada, China, Colombia, Guatemala, India, Mexico, New Zealand, Chinese Taipei, United States

Reported: March 15, 2005

Procedural History

On 17 April 2003, Australia requested consultations with the European Communities.

Australia and the European Communities held consultations on 27 May 2003, but these consultations failed to resolve the dispute.

On 18 August 2003, Australia requested the Dispute Settlement Body to establish a panel.

On 13 February 2004, the United States (in WT/DS174) and Australia requested the Director-General to determine the composition of the Panel.

On 23 February 2004, the Director-General accordingly composed the Panel.

Argentina, , Brazil, Canada, China, Colombia, Guatemala, India, Mexico, New Zealand, the Separate Customs Territory of Taiwan, Penghu, Kinmen and Matsu (hereinafter referred to as "Chinese Taipei"), Turkey, and United States (in respect of Australia's complaint) reserved their rights to participate in the Panel proceedings as third parties.

The Panel met with the parties on 23-24 June 2004 and on 11-12 August 2004.

The Panel submitted its interim report to the parties on 16 November 2004.

The Panel submitted its final report to the parties on 21 December 2004.

Conclusions

- The Panel rules that Australia's request for establishment of a panel did not fail to identify the specific measures at issue in accordance with Article 6.2 of the DSU.

- On the basis of the facts available, the Panel rules that Australia's request for establishment of a panel did not fail to provide a brief summary of the legal basis of the complaint sufficient to present the problem clearly in accordance with Article 6.2 of the DSU.

- The Panel notes that Australia's other claims (considered in Section VII:E of this report), brought under the provisions discussed in paragraphs 36 and 39 of the preliminary ruling, were not pursued in such detail. The Panel has found no prima facie case or rejected all these claims. This confirms the Panel's assessment that no prejudice has been caused to the rights of the respondent by these claims.

- The Panel notes the distinction between provisions of the Regulation which established procedures, but are no longer in force, and individual registrations affected under them. With respect to the former, the Panel recalls that its mandate to make recommendations in this dispute is found in Article 19.1 of the DSU, which foresees only one type of recommendation, namely, that a Member bring a measure into conformity with a covered agreement. It is obvious that versions of the Regulation cannot be brought into conformity if they have already ceased to exist. Therefore, the Panel will not make any recommendation with respect to prior versions of the Regulation that are no longer in force.

- In the course of its assessment of the matter before it, the Panel will make findings with respect to prior versions of the Regulation where they serve some useful purpose in reaching conclusions with respect to measures within its terms of reference, including individual registrations, which are currently in force. References in this report to the "Regulation" refer to the current version, unless the context indicates otherwise.

- The Panel does not consider it necessary to rule on whether the individual registrations effected after the date of establishment of the Panel fall within the terms of reference in order to secure a positive solution to this dispute.

- The Panel rules that the claims under Article 2(2) of the Paris Convention (1967), as incorporated by Article 2.1 of the TRIPS Agreement, are within the Panel's terms of reference.

- Article 24.5 of the TRIPS Agreement, amounts to a claim under Article 4, which should have been disclosed in the request for establishment of a panel. The inclusion of this claim for the first time in the first written submission took the European Communities by surprise and deprived it of the right to begin preparing its defence to this claim earlier. Therefore, in this respect, the request for establishment of a panel does not satisfy the requirement of Article 6.2 to "provide a brief summary of the legal basis of the complaint sufficient to present the problem clearly." Accordingly, this claim is outside the Panel's terms of reference.

- The claim under Article 41 of the TRIPS Agreement in conjunction with Articles 43, 44, 45, 46, 48 and 49 is outside the Panel's terms of reference.

- The Panel notes that Australia only asks the Panel to address Article 12(2) of the Regulation under Article III:4 of GATT 1994 should the Panel consider that Article 12(2) does not constitute a technical regulation within the meaning of Annex 1.1 of the TBT Agreement. This premise has not been met and further consideration is therefore unnecessary.

- The Panel does not consider that Australia's statement that it endorsed all of the United States' arguments was a sufficient basis for the Panel to consider that Australia's arguments as presented earlier were modified. Nevertheless, the Panel accepts Australia's earlier endorsements of certain comments of the United States, and takes note of the referenced comments.

- The Panel concludes that Australia has made a prima facie case that the equivalence and reciprocity conditions in Article 12(1) of the Regulation apply to the availability of protection for GIs located in third countries, including WTO Members. In other words, the registration procedure in Articles 12a and 12b is not available for GIs located in third countries, including WTO Members, that do not satisfy the conditions in Article 12(1). The European Communities has not succeeded in rebutting that case.

- The Panel finds that the equivalence and reciprocity conditions modify the effective equality of opportunities with respect to the availability of protection to persons who wish to obtain GI protection under the Regulation, to the detriment of those who wish to obtain protection in respect of geographical areas located in third countries, including WTO Members. This is less favourable treatment.

- Australia has not challenged the criteria used by the European Communities to determine nationality. The Panel notes that these criteria appear to be the same as those used in public international law. Therefore, the Panel can use them to determine which persons are "nationals" under Article 3.1 of the TRIPS Agreement.

- The Panel accepts the European Communities' submission that it is not a "separate customs territory Member of the WTO" within the meaning of footnote 1 to the TRIPS Agreement, and finds that its nationals, for the purposes of the TRIPS Agreement, are not defined by that footnote.

- The Panel's preliminary conclusion is that, with respect to the availability of protection, the treatment accorded to the group of nationals of other Members is different from, and less favourable than, that accorded to the European Communities' own nationals.

- With respect to the equivalence and reciprocity conditions, as applicable to the availability of GI protection, the Regulation accords treatment to the nationals of other Members less favourable than that it accords to the European Communities' own nationals, inconsistently with Article 3.1 of the TRIPS Agreement.

- The Panel concludes that, with respect to the availability of protection, the Regulation does not impose a requirement as to domicile or establishment inconsistently with Article 2(2) of the Paris Convention (1967), as incorporated by Article 2.1 of the TRIPS Agreement.

- The Regulation sets down requirements concerning the use of certain names in the presentation for sale of agricultural products and foodstuffs. It is therefore a law or regulation affecting the internal sale and offering for sale of products within the meaning of Article III:4 of GATT 1994. This is not altered by the fact that the Regulation is also an intellectual property measure covered by the TRIPS Agreement since GATT 1994 and the TRIPS Agreement apply cumulatively.

- The Panel concludes that, with respect to the equivalence and reciprocity conditions, as applicable to the availability of protection, the Regulation accords less favourable treatment to imported products, inconsistently with Article III:4 of GATT 1994.

- The Panel concludes that, with respect to the application procedures, insofar as they require examination and transmission of applications by governments, the Regulation accords other WTO Member nationals less favourable treatment than it accords the European Communities' own nationals, inconsistently with Article 3.1 of the TRIPS Agreement.

- The Panel concludes that, with respect to the application procedures, insofar as they require examination and transmission of applications by governments, the Regulation accords less favourable treatment to imported products than domestic products, inconsistently with Article III:4 of GATT 1994.

- The Panel concludes that, with respect to the application procedures, insofar as they require examination and transmission of applications by governments, the Regulation accords less favourable treatment to imported products inconsistently with Article III:4 of GATT 1994, and these requirements are not justified by Article XX(d).

- Persons resident or established in third countries, including other WTO Members, who wish to object to applications for registration under the Regulation do not have a right in the objection procedures that is provided to persons in the European Communities. Objectors in third countries face an "extra hurdle" in ensuring that the authorities in those countries carry out the functions reserved to them under the Regulation, which objectors in EC member States do not face. Consequently, certain objections may not be verified or transmitted. Each of these considerations significantly reduces the opportunities available to other WTO Member nationals in matters affecting the acquisition of rights under the Regulation compared with those available to EC nationals. For this reason, the Regulation accords nationals of other WTO Members "less favourable treatment" within the meaning of Article 3.1 of the TRIPS Agreement.

- The Panel concludes that, with respect to the equivalence and reciprocity conditions, as allegedly applicable to objections, Australia has not made a prima facie case in support of its claims under Article 3.1 of the TRIPS Agreement or Article 2(1) of the Paris Convention (1967) as incorporated by Article 2.1 of the TRIPS Agreement.

- Applicants for GIs that refer to geographical areas located in third countries do not have a right in the availability of protection and application procedures that is provided to applicants for GIs that refer to geographical areas located within the European Communities. Applicants in third countries face an "extra hurdle" in ensuring that the authorities in those countries carry out the functions reserved to them under the Regulation, which applicants in EC member States do not face. Consequently, certain applications may be rejected. This significantly reduces the opportunities available to the nationals of other WTO Members in the availability and acquisition of rights under the Regulation below those available to the European Communities' own nationals. For this reason, the Regulation accords nationals of other WTO Members "less favourable treatment" within the meaning of Article 3.1 of the TRIPS Agreement than it accords the European Communities' own nationals.

- The Panel concludes that, with respect to the labelling requirement, Australia has not made a prima facie case in support of its claim under Article 3.1 of the TRIPS Agreement.

- The Panel considers that the European Communities has not rebutted Australia's prima facie case that Article 14(3) of the Regulation cannot prevent all situations from occurring in which a trademark would be subject to Article 14(2) and, hence, in which the Regulation would limit the rights of the owner of such a trademark.

- The Panel concludes that, under Article 16.1 of the TRIPS Agreement, Members are required to make available to trademark owners a right against certain uses, including uses as a GI. The Regulation limits the availability of that right for the owners of trademarks which are subject to Article 14(2). Article 24.5 of the TRIPS Agreement is inapplicable and does not provide authority to limit that right.

- The Panel interprets the phrase "the protection of geographical indications that existed in that Member immediately prior to the date of entry into force of the WTO Agreement" to mean the state of protection of GIs immediately prior to 1 January 1995, in terms of the individual GIs which were protected at that point in time. In the present dispute, the parties agree that no GIs were registered under the Regulation prior to 1 January 1995. Therefore, Article 24.3 is inapplicable.

- The Panel finds that the Regulation creates a "limited exception" within the meaning of Article 17 of the TRIPS Agreement.

- The Panel considers that the exception created by the Regulation takes account of the legitimate interests of the owner of the trademark within the meaning of Article 17.

- The Panel concludes that, with respect to the coexistence of GIs with prior trademarks, the Regulation is inconsistent with Article 16.1 of the TRIPS Agreement but, on the basis of the evidence presented to the Panel, this is justified by Article 17 of the TRIPS Agreement. Article 24.3 and Article 24.5 of the TRIPS Agreement are inapplicable.

Annotations

7.2 **Request for Establishment** [DSU, Article 6.2]

The Panel considers the ordinary meaning of the terms of the text in Article 6.2 of the DSU, read in their context and in the light of the object and purpose of the provision, to be quite clear. They require that a request for establishment of a panel "identify the specific measures at issue." They do not require the identification of the "specific aspects" of these "specific measures."

7.2 **Request for Establishment** [DSU, Article 6.2]

The Panel considers that the mere listing of provisions of the relevant covered agreements may not satisfy the standard of Article 6.2 of the DSU, for instance, where the listed provisions establish multiple obligations rather than one single, distinct obligation. However, where the multiple obligations are closely related and interlinked, a reference to a common obligation in the specific listed provisions should be sufficient to meet the standard of Article 6.2 of the DSU under certain circumstances in a particular case.

7.2 **Request for Establishment** [DSU, Article 6.2]

Article 6.2 of the DSU calls for sufficient clarity with respect to the legal basis of the complaint so as to enable a defending party to begin preparing its defence.

7.39 **International Negotiations: Exceptions** [TRIPs, Article 24.5]

It is not disputed that Article 24.5 refers to three aspects of the protection of trademarks, one of which is the eligibility of a trademark for registration. This concerns trademark applications. However, in the Panel's view, the reference to protection of trademarks and Article 24.5 does not necessarily concern each and every possible aspect of trademark application procedures. Article 15 of the TRIPS Agreement and numerous distinct obligations under the Paris Convention (1967), including Articles 4, 6, 6*bis*, 6*quinquies* and 7 relate to trademark applications and procedures.

7.183 **"treatment no less favourable"** [GATT, Article III.4]

The words 'treatment no less favourable' in paragraph 4 call for effective equality of opportunities for imported products in respect of the application of laws, regulations and requirements affecting the internal sale, offering for sale, purchase, transportation, distribution or use of products. This clearly sets a minimum permissible standard as a basis.

7.186 **"treatment no less favourable"** [GATT, Article III.4]

The examination of whether a measure involves 'less favourable treatment' of imported products within the meaning of Article III:4 of the GATT 1994 must be grounded in close scrutiny of the fundamental thrust and effect of the measure itself. This examination cannot rest on simple assertion, but must be founded on a careful analysis of the contested measure and of its implications in the marketplace. At the same time, however, the examination need not be based on the *actual effects* of the contested measure in the marketplace.

7.198 **National Treatment** [TRIPs, Article 3.1]

Whilst the TRIPS Agreement does not create obligations for a Member to accord treatment to its own nationals, it does refer to the treatment that each Member accords to its own nationals as the benchmark for its obligation to accord national treatment under Article 3.1, as well as under the other national treatment obligations incorporated by reference, including Article 2 of the Paris Convention (1967). To that extent, the way in which a Member defines its own nationals can also be subject to review for the purposes of determining conformity with its national treatment obligations under the TRIPS Agreement.

7.234 [TRIPs, footnote 1]

The text of the TRIPS Agreement contains a recognition that discrimination according to residence and establishment will be a close substitute for nationality.

7.245-46 **Principles** [TRIPs, Article 8]

Article 8 of the TRIPS Agreement sets out the principles of that agreement. These principles reflect the fact that the TRIPS Agreement does not generally provide for the grant of positive rights to exploit or use certain subject matter, but rather provides for the grant of negative rights to prevent certain acts. This fundamental feature of intellectual property protection inherently grants Members freedom to pursue legitimate public policy objectives since many measures to attain those public policy objectives lie outside the scope of intellectual property rights and do not require an exception under the TRIPS Agreement.

7.248 **National Treatment** [TRIPs, Article 3.1]

The fact that a general exceptions provision analogous to Article XX of GATT 1994 was not included in the TRIPS Agreement has no impact on its analysis of Article 3.1.

7.266 **"treatment no less favourable"** [GATT, Article III.4]

The "less favourable treatment" standard should be assessed under Article III:4 of GATT 1994 by examining whether the measures at issue modify the conditions of competition between domestic and imported products in the relevant market to the detriment of imported products. This examination must closely scrutinize the "fundamental thrust and effect of the measure itself" founded on a careful analysis of the contested measure and of its implications in the marketplace.

7.364 [TRIPs, footnote 3]

Procedures for the filing and examination of *applications* for registration are matters affecting the acquisition of intellectual property rights, within the scope of "protection" of intellectual property as clarified in footnote 3 of the TRIPS Agreement. Procedures for *objections* to such applications are related to the procedures for acquisition. Hence, opposition procedures are also matters "affecting" the acquisition of intellectual property rights which concern the "protection" of intellectual property, as clarified in footnote 3 to the TRIPS Agreement.

7.598 **Standards Concerning the Availability, Scope and Use of Intellectual Property Rights** [TRIPs, Part II]

Part II of the TRIPS Agreement contains minimum standards concerning the availability, scope and use of intellectual property rights. The first seven Sections of Part II contain standards relating to categories of intellectual property rights. Each Section sets out, as a minimum, the *subject matter* which is eligible for protection, the scope of the *rights conferred* by the relevant category of intellectual property and permitted *exceptions* to those rights.

7.602 **Rights Conferred** [TRIPs, Article 16.1]

The text of Article 16.1 stipulates that the right for which it provides is an "exclusive" right. This indicates that the right belongs to the owner of the registered trademark alone, who may exercise it to prevent certain uses by "all third parties" not having the owner's consent.

7.610 **International Negotiations: Exceptions** [TRIPs, Article 24.5]

There is no language in Article 24.5 of the TRIPS Agreement which would provide for the conferral of a right to use a trademark. Instead, it is a saving provision which ensures that "the right to use a trademark" is not prejudiced, or affected, by measures adopted to implement Section 3 of Part II. Irrespective of how the right to use a trademark arises, there is no obligation under Article 24.5 to confer it.

7.615 **International Negotiations: Exceptions** [TRIPs, Article 24.5]

The Panel considers that Article 24.5 creates an exception to GI protection—as reflected in the title of Article 24.

7.619 **International Negotiations: Exceptions** [TRIPs, Article 24.5]

It is inappropriate to imply in Article 24.5 *either* the right to prevent confusing uses *or* a limitation on the right to prevent confusing uses.

7.647-48 **Exceptions** [TRIPs, Article 17]

Article 17 expressly permits Members to provide limited exceptions to the rights conferred by a trademark, which include the right provided for in Article 16.1 of the TRIPS Agreement. Article 17 permits "limited exceptions." It provides an example of a limited exception, and is subject to a proviso that "such exceptions take account of the legitimate interests of the owner of the trademark and of third parties." The ordinary meaning of the terms indicates that an exception must not only be "limited" but must also comply with the proviso in order to satisfy Article 17. The example of "fair use of descriptive terms" is illustrative only, but it can provide interpretative guidance because, *a priori*, it falls within the meaning of a "limited" exception and must be capable of satisfying the proviso in some circumstances.

7.650 **Exceptions** [TRIPs, Article 17]

The meaning of the term "limited exceptions" as used in Article 17 should be equated to a minor derogation, one that does not undercut the body of rules from which it is made" where the exception must be narrow and permit only a small diminution of rights. The fact that the exception may affect only few trademarks or few trademark owners is irrelevant to the question whether it is limited. The issue is whether the exception to the *rights conferred by a trademark* is narrow.

7.662-64 **Exceptions** [TRIPs, Article 17]

The term "legitimate interests" of a trademark owner and third parties in the context of Article 17 must be defined as a normative claim calling for protection of interests that are 'justifiable' in the sense that they are supported by relevant public policies or other social norms. Every trademark owner has a legitimate interest in preserving the distinctiveness, or capacity to distinguish, of its trademark so that it can perform that function. This includes its interest in using its own trademark in connection with the relevant goods and services of its own and authorized undertakings. Taking account of that legitimate interest will also take account of the trademark owner's interest in the economic value of its mark arising from the reputation that it enjoys and the quality that it denotes.

7.676-81 **Exceptions** [TRIPs, Article 17]

Third parties for the purposes of Article 17 include consumers and persons using a GI in accordance with a geographical indication ("GI") registration. Third parties" for the purposes of Article 17 also include trademark licensees, but the legitimate interests of trademark licensees are, to a large extent, identified with those of the trademark owner, and can be taken into account at the same time. It is not clear how their interests could be taken into account as a separate issue.

7.680 **Exceptions** [TRIPs, Article 17]
Protection of Geographical Indications [TRIPs, Article 22.1]

The definition of a GI in Article 22.1 reflects a legitimate interest that a person may have in identifying the source and other characteristics of a good by the name of the place where it is from, if the name would serve that purpose. Nevertheless, as "legitimate interests," the interests of GI users as third parties within the meaning of Article 17 would be different from the legal protection provided for in Articles 22 and 23.

7.681 **Exceptions** [TRIPs, Article 17]

Although GIs are intellectual property rights, and not purely descriptive terms, the function of the terms in the example is analogous to a descriptive function of GIs and provides contextual support for the notion that the interest of GIs users in using a place name to indicate their products is "legitimate."

EUROPEAN COMMUNITIES – PROTECTION OF TRADEMARKS AND GEOGRAPHICAL INDICATIONS FOR AGRICULTURAL PRODUCTS AND FOODSTUFFS – COMPLAINT BY AUSTRALIA

WT/DS290/R
REPORT OF THE PANEL

TABLE OF CONTENTS

LIST OF ANNEXES

ANNEX A

SUBMISSIONS BY AUSTRALIA

ANNEX B

SUBMISSIONS BY THE EUROPEAN COMMUNITIES*

* Annex B is shared with the companion case WT/DS174/R and can be found earlier in this volume.

ANNEX C

ARGUMENTS OF THE THIRD PARTIES[**]

ANNEX D

MISCELLANEOUS[***]

CONTENTS		PAGE

[**] Annex C is shared with the companion case WT/DS174/R and can be found earlier in this volume.
[***] Annex D is shared with the companion case WT/DS174/R and can be found earlier in this volume.

TABLE OF CASES CITED IN THIS REPORT

Short Title	Full Case Title and Citation
Argentina – Footwear (EC)	Appellate Body Report, *Argentina – Safeguard Measures on Imports of Footwear*, WT/DS121/AB/R, adopted 12 January 2000, DSR 2000:I, 515
Australia – Salmon	Appellate Body Report, *Australia – Measures Affecting Importation of Salmon*, WT/DS18/AB/R, adopted 6 November 1998, DSR 1998:VIII, 3327
Brazil – Aircraft	Appellate Body Report, *Brazil – Export Financing Programme for Aircraft*, WT/DS46/AB/R, adopted 20 August 1999, DSR 1999:III, 1161
Canada – Patent Term	Appellate Body Report, *Canada – Term of Patent Protection*, WT/DS170/AB/R, adopted 12 October 2000, DSR 2000:X, 5093
Canada – Periodicals	Appellate Body Report, *Canada – Certain Measures Concerning Periodicals*, WT/DS31/AB/R, adopted 30 July 1997, DSR 1997:I, 449
Canada – Pharmaceutical Patents	Panel Report, *Canada – Patent Protection of Pharmaceutical Products*, WT/DS114/R, adopted 7 April 2000, DSR 2000:V, 2289
EC – Asbestos	Appellate Body Report, *European Communities – Measures Affecting Asbestos and Asbestos-Containing Products*, WT/DS135/AB/R, adopted 5 April 2001, DSR 2001:VII, 3243
EC – Bananas III	Appellate Body Report, *European Communities – Regime for the Importation, Sale and Distribution of Bananas*, WT/DS27/AB/R, adopted 25 September 1997, DSR 1997:II, 591
EC – Bananas III (US)	Panel Report, *European Communities – Regime for the Importation, Sale and Distribution of Bananas – Complaint by the United States*, WT/DS27/R/USA, adopted 25 September 1997, as modified by the Appellate Body Report, WT/DS27/AB/R, DSR 1997:II, 943
EC – Hormones	Appellate Body Report, *EC Measures Concerning Meat and Meat Products (Hormones)*, WT/DS26/AB/R, WT/DS48/AB/R, adopted 13 February 1998, DSR 1998:I, 135
EC – Sardines	Appellate Body Report, *European Communities – Trade Description of Sardines*, WT/DS231/AB/R, adopted 23 October 2002
EC – Tariff Preferences	Appellate Body Report, *European Communities – Conditions for the Granting of Tariff Preferences to Developing Countries*, WT/DS246/AB/R, adopted 20 April 2004.
EEC – Parts and Components	GATT Panel Report, *European Economic Community – Regulation on Imports of Parts and Components*, adopted 16 May 1990, BISD 37S/132
India – Patents (US)	Appellate Body Report, *India – Patent Protection for Pharmaceutical and Agricultural Chemical Products*, WT/DS50/AB/R, adopted 16 January 1998, DSR 1998:I, 9
India – Patents (US)	Panel Report, *India – Patent Protection for Pharmaceutical and Agricultural Chemical Products – Complaint by the United States*, WT/DS50/R, adopted 16 January 1998, as modified by the Appellate Body Report, WT/DS50/AB/R, DSR 1998:I, 41
India – Patents (EC)	Panel Report, *India – Patent Protection for Pharmaceutical and Agricultural Chemical Products – Complaint by the European Communities*, WT/DS79/R, adopted 22 September 1998, DSR 1998:VI, 2661
Indonesia – Autos	Panel Report, *Indonesia – Certain Measures Affecting the Automobile Industry*, WT/DS54/R, WT/DS55/R, WT/DS59/R, WT/DS64/R and Corr.1, 2, 3, and 4, adopted 23 July 1998, DSR 1998:VI, 2201
Japan – Alcoholic Beverages II	Appellate Body Report, *Japan – Taxes on Alcoholic Beverages*, WT/DS8/AB/R, WT/DS10/AB/R, WT/DS11/AB/R, adopted 1 November 1996, DSR 1996:I, 97

Short Title	Full Case Title and Citation
Korea – Dairy	Appellate Body Report, *Korea – Definitive Safeguard Measure on Imports of Certain Dairy Products*, WT/DS98/AB/R, adopted 12 January 2000, DSR 2000:I, 3
Korea – Various Measures on Beef	Appellate Body Report, *Korea – Measures Affecting Imports of Fresh, Chilled and Frozen Beef*, WT/DS161/AB/R, WT/DS169/AB/R, adopted 10 January 2001, DSR 2001:I, 5
Korea – Various Measures on Beef	Panel Report, *Korea – Measures Affecting Imports of Fresh, Chilled and Frozen Beef*, WT/DS161/R, WT/DS169/R, adopted 10 January 2001, as modified by the Appellate Body Report, WT/DS161/AB/R, WT/DS169/AB/R, DSR 2001:I, 59
Thailand – H-Beams	Appellate Body Report, *Thailand – Anti-Dumping Duties on Angles, Shapes and Sections of Iron or Non-Alloy Steel and H-Beams from Poland*, WT/DS122/AB/R, adopted 5 April 2001, DSR 2001:VII, 2701
Turkey – Textiles	Panel Report, *Turkey – Restrictions on Imports of Textile and Clothing Products*, WT/DS34/R, adopted 19 November 1999, as modified by the Appellate Body Report, WT/DS34/AB/R, DSR 1999:VI, 2363
US – 1916 Act	Appellate Body Report, *United States – Anti-Dumping Act of 1916*, WT/DS136/AB/R, WT/DS162/AB/R, adopted 26 September 2000, DSR 2000:X, 4793
US – Carbon Steel	Appellate Body Report, *United States – Countervailing Duties on Certain Corrosion-Resistant Carbon Steel Flat Products from Germany*, WT/DS213/AB/R and Corr.1, adopted 19 December 2002
US – Certain EC Products	Appellate Body Report, *United States – Import Measures on Certain Products from the European Communities*, WT/DS165/AB/R, adopted 10 January 2001, DSR 2001:I, 373
US – Corrosion-Resistant Steel Sunset Review	Appellate Body Report, *United States – Sunset Review of Anti-Dumping Duties on Corrosion-Resistant Carbon Steel Flat Products from Japan*, WT/DS244/AB/R, adopted 9 January 2004
US – FSC (Article 21.5 – EC)	Appellate Body Report, *United States – Tax Treatment for "Foreign Sales Corporations" – Recourse to Article 21.5 of the DSU by the European Communities*, WT/DS108/AB/RW, adopted 29 January 2002
US – Gasoline	Appellate Body Report, *United States – Standards for Reformulated and Conventional Gasoline*, WT/DS2/AB/R, adopted 20 May 1996, DSR 1996:I, 3
US – Section 110(5) Copyright Act	Panel Report, *United States – Section 110(5) of the US Copyright Act*, WT/DS160/R, adopted 27 July 2000, DSR 2000:VIII, 3769
US – Section 211 Appropriations Act	Appellate Body Report, *United States – Section 211 Omnibus Appropriations Act of 1998*, WT/DS176/AB/R, adopted 1 February 2002
US – Section 301 Trade Act	Panel Report, *United States – Sections 301-310 of the Trade Act of 1974*, WT/DS152/R, adopted 27 January 2000, DSR 2000:II, 815
US – Section 337	GATT Panel Report, *United States Section 337 of the Tariff Act of 1930*, adopted 7 November 1989, BISD 36S/345

I. INTRODUCTION

1.1 On 17 April 2003, Australia requested consultations[1] with the European Communities pursuant to Article 4 of the Understanding on Rules and Procedures Governing the Settlement of Disputes ("DSU"), Article XXII of the General Agreement on Tariffs and Trade 1994 ("GATT 1994"), Article 64 of the Agreement on Trade-Related Aspects of Intellectual Property Rights ("TRIPS Agreement") and Article 14 of the Agreement on Technical Barriers to Trade ("TBT Agreement") concerning the protection of trademarks and the registration and protection of geographical indications for foodstuffs and agricultural products in the European Communities. The request was circulated to Members on 23 April 2003 in document WT/DS290/1. Consultations were held on 27 May 2003 but did not lead to a resolution of the dispute.

1.2 On 18 August 2003, Australia requested the Dispute Settlement Body ("DSB") to establish a panel pursuant to Articles 4.7 and 6 of the DSU, Article XXIII:2 of GATT 1994, Article 64 of the TRIPS Agreement and Article 14 of the TBT Agreement.[2] At its meeting on 2 October 2003, the DSB established a single Panel pursuant to the requests of the United States in document WT/DS174/20 and Australia in document WT/DS290/18, in accordance with Article 9 of the DSU (WT/DSB/M/156)[3]. At that meeting, the parties to the dispute also agreed that the Panel should have standard terms of reference. The terms of reference are, therefore, the following:

> To examine, in the light of the relevant provisions of the covered agreements cited by the United States in document WT/DS174/20 and Australia in document WT/DS290/18, the matter referred to the DSB by the United States and Australia in those documents, and to make such findings as will assist the DSB in making the recommendations or in giving the rulings provided for in those agreements.

1.3 On 13 February 2004, the United States and Australia requested the Director-General to determine the composition of the Panel, pursuant to paragraph 7 of Article 8 of the DSU.

1.4 On 23 February 2004, the Director-General accordingly composed the Panel as follows:

Chair: Mr Miguel Rodríguez Mendoza

Members: Prof. Seung Wha Chang
Mr Peter Kam-fai Cheung

1.5 Argentina, Australia (in respect of the United States' complaint), Brazil, Canada, China, Colombia, Guatemala, India, Mexico, New Zealand, the Separate Customs Territory of Taiwan, Penghu, Kinmen and Matsu (hereinafter referred to as "Chinese Taipei"), Turkey and the United States (in respect of Australia's complaint) reserved their rights to participate in the Panel proceedings as third parties.

1.6 The Panel met with the parties on 23-24 June 2004 and on 11-12 August 2004. It met with the third parties on 24 June 2004.

1.7 The Panel submitted its interim report to the parties on 16 November 2004. The Panel submitted its final report to the parties on 21 December 2004.

---

[1] WT/DS290/1.

[2] WT/DS290/18.

[3] WT/DS290/19 and Corr.1.

II. FACTUAL ASPECTS

A. Measure at Issue

2.1 The measure at issue in this dispute is identified in Australia's request for establishment of a panel as Council Regulation (EEC) No. 2081/92 of 14 July 1992 on the protection of geographical indications and designations of origin for agricultural products and foodstuffs, any amendments thereto (including Council Regulation (EC) No. 692/2003 of 8 April 2003, published in the Official Journal of the European Union No. L99 of 17 April 2003), and related implementing and enforcement measures.

B. Procedural History

1. *Preliminary ruling prior to the first written submissions*

2.2 On 24 February 2004, the day after the Panel was composed and prior to the organizational meeting, the European Communities requested that the Panel issue a preliminary ruling that the United States' and Australia's respective requests for establishment of a panel were inconsistent with the requirements of Article 6.2 of the DSU. The European Communities considered it appropriate that the Panel issue a preliminary ruling before the first written submissions of the parties were due.

2.3 At the organizational meeting, the Panel sought the parties' views on appropriate procedures to deal with this request. The complainants did not object to filing written responses to the request for a preliminary ruling prior to their first written submissions but requested additional time for the filing of their first written submissions.

2.4 On 8 March 2004, the Panel adopted its working procedures and timetable, which indicated a date for the United States and Australia to file written responses to the European Communities' request for a preliminary ruling. They submitted their responses accordingly.

2.5 On 5 April 2004, the Panel issued a preliminary ruling, which is set out in full in Section VII:A of this report.

2.6 On 20 April 2004, the European Communities sent a letter to the Panel expressing its regret at the Panel's ruling and "reserving its right to raise issues of law regarding the interpretation of Article 6.2 of the DSU before the Appellate Body." In its letter, the European Communities asked the Panel to clarify the status of its preliminary ruling of 5 April 2004, in particular whether such ruling would be incorporated into the Panel's final reports and whether the findings contained in the ruling would be an integral part of the final reports.

2.7 On 23 April 2004, the Panel responded to the European Communities, advising that its preliminary ruling would be reflected in the Panel's final reports, as appropriate.

2.8 On 26 April 2004, the European Communities sent a second letter to the Panel indicating that it had understood from the Panel's previous response that the findings contained in the preliminary ruling of 5 April 2004 would be incorporated into the Panel's final reports, and could, therefore, be appealed in the same way as any legal interpretation contained in these reports.

2.9 On 28 April 2004, the Panel responded again to the European Communities, advising that it had taken note of the European Communities' letter of 26 April 2004 and reiterating that its preliminary ruling would be reflected in its final reports, as appropriate.

2. *Request for extension of time*

2.10 On 9 March 2004, the European Communities requested that the Panel extend the period for it to submit its first written submission in view of the circumstances that (a) there were two cases brought by two complainants; (b) these cases did not appear to contain identical claims; and (c) these cases raised new and complex issues and involved a large number of claims. It also alleged that the timetable was unbalanced in favour of the complainants.

2.11 On 16 March 2004, the United States and Australia each responded to the European Communities' request, disagreeing with its assertions but not objecting to an extension of the period for the European Communities to submit its first written submission, provided that such extension would not affect the timeframe structure of the remainder of the timetable.

2.12 On 22 March 2004, the Panel revised its timetable, extending the time for the submission of the respondent's first written submission, without affecting the time between any of the subsequent steps as established in the original timetable.

3. Request for separate reports

2.13 On 3 March 2004, after the conclusion of the Panel's organizational meeting, the European Communities filed a request pursuant to Article 9.2 of the DSU that the Panel submit separate reports on the present dispute. On 8 March 2004 the Panel acknowledged receipt of such request. The complainants did not comment on this request.

2.14 On 23 April 2004, the Panel informed the parties that it would submit separate reports on this dispute, as requested by the European Communities.

2.15 At the second substantive meeting with the parties on 11-12 August 2004, the Panel invited the parties to comment on the way in which the Panel should submit separate reports. The Panel took note of the parties' views and confirmed the following facts: (a) the complainants have made similar, but not identical claims in this dispute; (b) the complainants have made separate written submissions and separate oral statements and submitted separate responses to questions, although they did submit 16 common exhibits with their respective first written submissions; (c) the complainants have not collectively endorsed the arguments made in one another's submissions although Australia, in its first oral statement, expressly endorsed certain comments made by the United States[4], and the United States, on occasions, cited information and arguments submitted by Australia in support of its arguments; and (d) although each complainant reserved its right to participate in the Panel proceedings as a third party in respect of the other's complaint, they did not exercise these rights. They both declined the opportunity given to them by the Panel to make a statement as a third party during the session with the third parties.

4. Request for factual information from the International Bureau of WIPO

2.16 On 9 July 2004, the Panel sent a letter to the International Bureau of WIPO requesting its assistance in the form of any factual information available to it relevant to the interpretation of certain provisions of the Paris Convention for the Protection of Industrial Property.[5] The parties were given the opportunity to comment.

2.17 The International Bureau's reply was received by the Panel and the WTO Secretariat on 14 September 2004. The Panel gave the parties an opportunity to submit comments on the reply by 28 September 2004. The parties submitted their comments accordingly.[6]

---

[4] Australia also stated that it endorsed all arguments put forward by the United States in its closing statement at the second substantive meeting. This is considered in paragraphs 7.69-7.82, below.

[5] Attached as Annex D-2 to this report.

[6] The submissions are attached to this report as Annexes A-10 and B-10.

2.18 The factual information provided by the International Bureau consists of a note it prepared and five annexes containing excerpts from the Official Records of the various Diplomatic Conferences which adopted, amended or revised the provisions currently contained in Articles 2 and 3 of the Paris Convention (Stockholm Act of 1967)[7].

III. PARTIES' REQUESTS FOR FINDINGS AND RECOMMENDATIONS

A. Australia

3.1 Australia requests that the Panel find that the measures at issue are inconsistent with the European Communities' obligations under:

(a) Articles 1.1, 1.3, 3.1, 16.1, 22.2, 24.5, 41.1, 41.2, 41.3, 42, and 65.1 of the TRIPS Agreement and Article 2.1 of the TRIPS Agreement, incorporating Articles 2(1) and 2(2), 10*bis*(1) and 10*ter*(1) of the Paris Convention (1967);[8]

(b) Article III:4 of GATT 1994;

(c) Articles 2.1 and 2.2 of the TBT Agreement; and

(d) Article XVI:4 of the WTO Agreement.

3.2 Australia requests that the Panel recommend that the European Communities bring its measures into conformity with its obligations under the WTO Agreement, including in respect of the TRIPS Agreement, GATT 1994 and the TBT Agreement.

B. European Communities

3.3 The European Communities requests that the Panel:

(a) find that certain measures no longer in force or not yet adopted at the time the Panel was established, and Australia's claims "under Articles 43, 44, 45, 46, 47, 48, 49 of the TRIPS Agreement," under Article 2(2) of the Paris Convention (1967) and "under Article 4 of the Paris Convention (1967)" as incorporated by Article 2.1 of the TRIPS Agreement, are outside the Panel's terms of reference; and

(b) reject all claims within the Panel's terms of reference.

IV. ARGUMENTS OF THE PARTIES

4.1 The arguments of the European Communities and Australia, as set out in their submissions (European Communities' request for a preliminary ruling; Australia's response to the European Communities' request for a preliminary ruling, first written submissions, written rebuttals, oral statements, responses to questions; comments on each other's responses; and comments on the factual information from the International Bureau of WIPO), are attached as Annexes A and B.

V. ARGUMENTS OF THE THIRD PARTIES

5.1 The arguments of those third parties that made submissions to the Panel (first written submissions, oral statements and responses to questions) are summarized and attached as Annex C.

---

[7] The International Bureau's Note, but not its annexes, are attached as Annex D-3 to this report.

[8] Australia withdrew a claim made under Article 20 of the TRIPS Agreement as described in paragraph 7.53 below.

VI. INTERIM REVIEW

6.1 On 16 November 2004, the Panel submitted its interim report to the parties. On 30 November 2004, Australia and the European Communities submitted written requests for review of precise aspects of the interim report. On 7 December 2004, Australia and the European Communities submitted written comments on each other's request for interim review.

6.2 The Panel has modified aspects of its report in light of the parties' comments where it considered appropriate, as explained below. The Panel has also made certain revisions and technical corrections for the purposes of clarity and accuracy. References to paragraph numbers and footnotes in this Section VI refer to those in the interim report, except as otherwise noted.

further comments on 5 April 2004 preliminary ruling

6.3 The European Communities requests the deletion of paragraphs 7.3 to 7.7 as the conformity of a panel request with Article 6.2 of the DSU must be evaluated on the face of the panel request. In its view, the references to discussions that take place in other fora, such as the Council for TRIPS, are irrelevant for this purpose.

6.4 Australia responds that nothing in the DSU precludes the Panel noting that subsequent events confirmed the correctness of a particular conclusion.

6.5 The Panel recalls that the European Communities made a request for a preliminary ruling the day after the Panel was composed in which it alleged defects in the panel request and submitted that it was appropriate that the Panel issue a preliminary ruling before the first written submissions of the parties were due. The Panel issued a preliminary ruling accordingly, in which it found that those allegations were unfounded on the face of the panel request and on the basis of the facts available to it at that time. That preliminary ruling sets out part of the basic rationale for the Panel's findings and recommendation in this dispute. Accordingly, in the course of making an objective assessment of the facts, the Panel does not disregard probative evidence relevant to that ruling submitted later in the course of the proceeding, other than the references to what took place during the consultations, which were without prejudice to the rights of the European Communities and other parties in these proceedings, in accordance with Article 4.6 of the DSU. The Panel has modified the relevant paragraphs, numbered 7.3 to 7.9 of the final report, to elaborate on the reasons for their inclusion.

other preliminary rulings

6.6 Australia requests that the Panel elaborate its reasoning in paragraphs 7.35 to 7.39 and 7.42 to 7.45 with a view to reconciling it with that of the Appellate Body in *Korea – Various Measures on Beef.* Australia asserts that at paragraph 88 of its report on that dispute, the Appellate Body held that a panel could validly examine a WTO provision not specified in the panel request for the purposes of determining the consistency of a measure with a provision that was specified in the panel request.

6.7 As a general comment, the European Communities considers that the interim review stage should not serve as an occasion to restate major parts of a party's arguments, nor to relitigate substantial parts of the interim report. Accordingly, the European Communities indicates that it refrains from commenting on all but two of the numerous issues raised by Australia without implying its agreement to the others. Specifically, the European Communities asks the Panel to include the preliminary rulings in these paragraphs in its conclusions at paragraph 8.1.

6.8 The Panel notes that paragraph 7.38, numbered 7.42 in the final report, already explains why the assertion of an inconsistency with Article 4 of the Paris Convention (1967) amounts to a claim, rather than an argument. That distinction is referred to in the passage which Australia cites in its interim review comments.

The Panel has added further detail and quotations of language where Australia in effect asserted its claim and made consequential amendments. The Panel notes that paragraph 39 of the Panel's preliminary ruling set out at paragraph 7.2 of the report already explains the basis on which the Panel accepted that the claim under Article 41 of the TRIPS Agreement was within its terms of reference. The Panel did not rule that Article 41 was within the terms of reference in all respects. This situation is quite different from that of the claims and arguments in the case to which Australia refers.

claims regarding the "EC measure as a whole"

6.9 Australia comments that, apart from one limited aspect relating to the regulatory committee, the Panel has not addressed its claim that the EC measure as a whole accords less favourable treatment to imported products bearing an EC-defined GI than to like domestic products bearing an EC-defined GI, contrary to Article III:4 of GATT 1994. It requests that the Panel address the claim and reflect its finding on the "EC measure as a whole" in the conclusions.

6.10 The Panel notes that Australia made claims regarding the "EC measure as a whole" under both the TRIPS Agreement and GATT 1994. With respect to the claims under the TRIPS Agreement, Australia referred in paragraphs 195 to 205 of its first written submission to five aspects of the Regulation which the Panel dealt with separately in sub-sections B.2, B.1, E.5, B.3 and E.3 of the findings, respectively. With respect to the claims under Article III:4 of GATT 1994, Australia listed eight bullet points at paragraph 177 of its first written submission and referred to their cumulative effect at paragraph 178. The Panel dealt with the third to sixth points in sub-section B.1 of the findings, the seventh point in sub-section B.2 and the eighth point in sub-section B.4. The Panel has added paragraphs 7.274 and 7.275 of the final report to explain why it is unnecessary to consider further the first and second points or the cumulative effect, and revised paragraph 7.66, numbered 7.68 in the final report, with respect to the labelling requirement, which was not mentioned in the first written submission in support of this claim. As for the conclusions, the Panel specifically sought the parties' views on whether they sought separate rulings on the procedural aspects of the Regulation or a ruling on the Regulation as a whole, in Panel question No. 49. In its response, Australia requested "that the Panel's findings be sufficiently detailed so as to facilitate a positive solution to the current dispute." The Panel has identified specific aspects of the Regulation in its conclusions which it has found inconsistent with a covered agreement in order to enable the European Communities to implement the recommendation. The Panel has not added a separate conclusion on the measure as a whole as this would not facilitate a positive solution to this dispute.

endorsement of arguments by co-complainant

6.11 Australia requests that the Panel amend paragraphs 7.67 to 7.75. It comments that it did endorse generally all U.S. arguments, and did not just purport or attempt to endorse the arguments. This is a separate issue from whether the Panel considered any arguments that arose from this general endorsement. Australia recalls that a panel is not bound to accept the arguments of any party and is free to develop its own legal reasoning. Where there is a single panel, but multiple complainants and multiple reports, a panel can use arguments put to it by either party in assessing common claims. In this context, Australia has the right—either on grounds of efficiency or by way of endorsing either similar or alternative arguments—to endorse, in general terms, arguments by the other complainant in this dispute.

6.12 With respect to the timing of the general endorsement, Australia recalls the Appellate Body's comment in *India – Patents (US)* (at para. 88) that arguments—as distinct from claims—"are set out and progressively clarified in the first written submissions, the rebuttal submission and the first and second Panel meetings with the parties as a case proceeds" and asserts that, in this dispute, the timing of the general endorsement can be readily explained when the appropriate context is recalled. At the time of the first opening statement, Australia endorsed U.S. arguments relating to the European Communities' obligations concerning the overlapping claims that Australia and the United States had made with regard to national treatment (under the TRIPS Agreement and GATT 1994) and trademark rights. The rest of Australia's first opening statement covered mainly claims that had not been made by the United States, namely, claims under Article 22.2 of the TRIPS Agreement and under the TBT Agreement. Australia repeated this endorsement at the opening of the second panel hearing. During the second hearing, however, the European Communities sought to make much of the fact that the United States and Australia did not have exactly the same arguments and that this meant that the European Communities' arguments were correct. It was in seeking to reject the European Communities' attempt to make more of the different arguments by the complainants that Australia responded by clarifying that it endorsed all of the United States' arguments.

6.13 Australia accepts that it could have made clearer that its general endorsement was on the basis of endorsing the United States' arguments as alternative arguments wherever these were inconsistent with Australian arguments. However, Australia maintains that any differences between the United States' and Australian arguments are not material to the matter before the Panel. For example, regardless of the interpretation of Article 24.5 of the TRIPS Agreement, both Australia and the United States agree that it does not provide the European Communities with an excuse for its breach of Article 16.1 of the TRIPS Agreement.

6.14 Australia refers to the statement in paragraph 7.72 that the Panel (or the European Communities) should not have to sift through the United States or Australian arguments looking for any inconsistency in order to understand the Australian case (where it intersects with the general endorsement of the United States' arguments). The Panel's comments may indicate that it does not consider a careful sifting of all of the arguments put to it, including Australia's, to be a necessary and integral part of its role. As such a view would be clearly contrary to Article 11 of the DSU, Australia requests that the statement be amended or withdrawn.

6.15 Australia refers to the statement at paragraph 7.74 and asserts that the Panel attributes, without evidence, certain motives to Australia and, as a consequence, impugns Australia's conduct. However, it asserts that the Panel's assessment of Australia's motives is wrong and requests that the statement be withdrawn. While the Panel is right to ensure that a respondent's due process rights are protected, Australia comments that it is also incumbent on the Panel to respect the rights of a complainant and to ensure a fair hearing for all parties to a dispute. The European Communities did not object to a single panel being established by the DSB. Further, the European Communities was given extra time to prepare its first written submission, notwithstanding the largely overlapping nature of the claims by both complainants. In the hearings, the European Communities was allowed to speak as long as it wished, to introduce irrelevant material late in the process, to continuously reiterate immaterial points, and to waste time by asking the complainants a large number of irrelevant questions. This hardly suggests that the European Communities has suffered in any way from the single panel considering, for both reports, all the arguments put to it by either of the complainants. Further, as the European Communities had ample opportunity to counter the United States' arguments, Australia's general endorsement of the United States' arguments did not increase the "case" the European Communities had to answer or that the Panel had to consider.

6.16 The European Communities expresses regret that Australia, in its comments on paragraphs 7.72, 7.74 and 7.75, summarily dismisses arguments made by the European Communities as irrelevant or immaterial.

6.17 The Panel agrees that a complainant can endorse a co-complainant's arguments. However, the Panel does not consider that Australia's comment in its closing statement at the second substantive meeting that "Australia endorses all of the arguments put forward by the United States" was a sufficient basis for the Panel to consider that Australia's arguments as presented earlier were modified, given that there were material differences between those arguments and no information was provided as to how they should be reconciled. Paragraphs 7.71 and 7.72 already explained this point but the Panel has expanded them into paragraphs 7.73 to 7.79 in the final report to illustrate the problem. The Panel has examined the parties' arguments in the course of its objective assessment under Article 11 of the DSU but it does not undertake tasks inconsistent with that function. The Panel has expanded paragraph 7.72, numbered 7.79 in the final report, for the avoidance of doubt.

6.18 The Panel has been mindful of the due process rights of all parties in these proceedings. The European Communities' consent to the establishment of a single panel did not relieve Australia of its burden of making a prima facie case in support of all its claims.

6.19 The Panel takes note of Australia's explanation of the surrounding circumstances. Paragraph 7.74 reflected the oral interventions at the second substantive meeting. If Australia intended to respond to the European Communities' emphasis of differences between the complainants' respective arguments, then the mere assertion that those differences were not material was ineffective, and the endorsement would have transformed differences between the complainants' cases into contradictions within Australia's own case. Australia's interim review comments do not present any circumstances that would justify the Panel taking a different approach but, rather, point out differences between the arguments Australia presented itself and those of the United States. Therefore, the Panel has retained the first and second sentences of paragraph 7.74, numbered 7.81 in the final report, but deleted the following discussion. The Panel has also corrected paragraph 2.15.

<u>the phrase "[w]ithout prejudice to international agreements"</u>

6.20 The European Communities requests the deletion of paragraphs 7.132 to 7.137 because it did not argue that the application of Article 12 of the Regulation would prejudice "<u>the EC's obligations under the TRIPS Agreement</u>." It quotes paragraph 66 of its first written submission and paragraph 43 of its first oral statement and asserts that "[t]hese statements do not contain any indication that the EC consider that its obligations under the TRIPS Agreement would be prejudiced by the application of Article 12 of Regulation 2081/92. Rather, the reference to the obligation to provide protection for geographical indications was clearly intended as a reference to the obligation <u>of other WTO Members</u> to provide protection. This is also what the EC explained in response to the Panel's Question No. 94(b)." The European Communities agrees that it is true that it did not provide an explicit response to Panel question No. 20 but it asserts that it did, however, address this point in response to Panel question No. 94, in which it clarified that whereas the application of these conditions would not prejudice the European Communities' national treatment obligations under the TRIPS Agreement, it would prejudice its national treatment obligations under the GATT. Given this context, it comments that the Panel is wrong to read into the European Communities' submission a statement which the European Communities clearly did not make, and which contradicts the entire logic of the European Communities' submissions. In its view, by attempting to read admissions into the European Communities' submissions, the Panel effectively distorts these submissions. This is not compatible with the task of the Panel under Article 11 of the DSU, which is to make an objective assessment of the facts. The European Communities also requests the deletion of paragraph 7.247 for the same reason and because it is unnecessary to the legal analysis which precedes it.

6.21 Australia responds that, in its view, the Panel's summation of the arguments put forward by the European Communities is accurate. Australia notes that the statements quoted by the European Communities from its first written submission, first oral statement and response to question No. 94, in fact concern what Australia has referred to in this dispute as "TRIPS-defined GIs" of which the "EC-defined GIs" covered by the Regulation are generally a subset. However, the dispute has not concerned the European Communities' implementation of its obligations under the TRIPS Agreement and GATT 1994 concerning TRIPS-defined GIs more generally, it has concerned the European Communities' implementation of its obligations in relation to EC-defined GIs. Australia suggests that the relevance of the European Communities' arguments might be better understood if the Panel were to recall the relevance of the distinction between a "TRIPS-defined GI" and an "EC-defined GI." At the same time, however, Australia is of the view that the Panel's analysis of the arguments put forward by the European Communities is entirely correct. Since the allegedly incorrect nature of the statements was the only basis on which the European Communities requested that paragraphs 7.132 to 7.137 be deleted and paragraph 7.247 be amended, Australia suggests that the paragraphs be retained.

6.22 The Panel takes note of the parties' comments and has carefully reviewed the European Communities' submissions, statements and responses to questions in this dispute, and confirms the following facts: (a) the interim report is consistent with the European Communities' own detailed analysis of the phrase "[w]ithout prejudice to international agreements" in its rebuttal submission; and (b) the European Communities repeatedly emphasized the importance of *its own* obligations in the interpretation of the equivalence and reciprocity conditions but there is no clear explanation on the record of this dispute as to how the obligations of *other* WTO Members would render the equivalence and reciprocity conditions under the European Communities' own Regulation inapplicable and the Panel declines to speculate. Therefore, the Panel has expanded and revised, rather than deleted, the relevant paragraphs, numbered 7.139 to 7.145 in the final report, and deleted the other paragraph without affecting the preceding legal analysis.

6.23 The Panel takes note that, although the European Communities has now requested the deletion of most consideration of its own arguments concerning the phrase "[w]ithout prejudice to international agreements," this point is important to its defence and those arguments have not been withdrawn. Therefore, the Panel considers it important to address them as part of its objective assessment of the matter before it, in accordance with its function under Article 11 of the DSU.

specific definitions of "nationals"

6.24 Australia comments that, in view of the Panel's ruling that it cannot be considered to have endorsed all of the United States' arguments in its closing statement at the second substantive meeting, Australia has not argued that the European Communities is a separate customs territory Member of the WTO within the meaning of footnote 1 to Article 1.3 of the TRIPS Agreement or that, as a consequence, a special regime to determine nationals applies. Notwithstanding that Australia has pointed to some seeming anomalies in the European Communities' responses to the United States' arguments on the issue in Australia's response to Panel question No. 104, Australia's views on the meaning of the term "national" are as set out in its response to Panel question No. 23 (and referred to in paragraph 7.146). It is not contested by Australia that the determination of which persons are EC nationals is generally a matter for determination by the European Communities under its own law.

6.25 The Panel had observed that Australia's views on the meaning of "national," as reflected in the interim report, include references to persons who are domiciled or who have a real and effective industrial or commercial establishment in a separate customs territory Member of the WTO. Consequently, the Panel considered it necessary to address the applicability of that specific definition. However, in light of Australia's confirmation in its interim review comments that it did not argue that the European Communities is a separate customs territory Member of the WTO, the Panel has revised paragraph 7.194, numbered 7.201 in the final report, and deleted the reasoning regarding that issue.

examination of applications for registration

6.26 The European Communities requests the amendment of paragraph 7.307(b) to take account of the requirement in Article 12a(2)(a) of the Regulation that a third country must also transmit "a description of the legal provisions and the usage on the basis of which the designation of origin or the geographical indication is protected or established in the country," which is a question of the law of the third country not Community law. It also comments that paragraph 7.307 should explain how the European Communities can implement Article 24.9 of the TRIPS Agreement with respect to such questions of foreign law, taking into account that the complainants have stated that such questions can be of high complexity and have indicated their unwillingness or inability to cooperate on such issues.

6.27 Australia believes that the Panel's statement at paragraph 7.307 is accurate. It does not preclude information concerning the domestic law of the country of origin being one of the criteria referred to in Article 12a(2)(a) of the Regulation. Consequently, Australia suggests that there is no need for any change to paragraph 7.317. While the Panel may choose to elaborate its reasoning in respect of the consequences of Article 24.9 of the TRIPS Agreement, Australia does not believe such elaboration is necessary to the resolution of the dispute.

6.28 The Panel takes note of the European Communities' request and notes that the description of protection in the country of origin is already included in paragraph 7.307, numbered 7.303 in the final report, which is the logical place for it. The Panel considers it inappropriate to make further findings in the paragraph. The Panel's findings on transmission of applications already apply to all accompanying documents, including the description of protection in the country of origin. Further, this is an "as such" claim but Article 12a(2)(a) of the Regulation does not specify what form of description of protection in the country of origin would be acceptable, nor is there conclusive evidence on this point. In any event, Article 62 of the TRIPS Agreement would appear to be important in framing any recommendation on implementation, but it lies outside the Panel's terms of reference, as explained in paragraph 7.314 of the final report.

6.29 The Panel has also replaced, where appropriate, the word "verification" in relation to applications for registration later in the report in order to be consistent with the use of the word "examination" used in the description of the application procedures and the consideration of the national treatment claim under the TRIPS Agreement.

Article 2.1 of the TBT Agreement

6.30 Australia requests that the Panel review the reasoning set out in paragraphs 7.475 to 7.484, and elaborate its reasoning for the first sentence of paragraph 7.469 and the last sentence of paragraph 7.471. It comments that the Panel's analysis of the "less favourable treatment" elements of this claim seems premised on a misunderstanding of the basis of Australia's claim, which is the fact that Article 12(2) of the Regulation mandates—in the specified circumstances—a labelling requirement for an imported product bearing a GI that is not similarly mandated for a domestically produced product bearing a GI. Further, that mandated differential treatment results in less favourable treatment for an imported product bearing a GI. Australia comments that, as the Panel noted, the challenge is made to the relevant provision "as such." Thus, the fact that the European Communities may have the discretion to impose the same labelling requirement on a domestically produced product in the specified circumstances does not overcome the inconsistency of the labelling requirement set out in Article 12(2) of the Regulation with the European Communities' national treatment obligation under the TBT Agreement. If the Panel concludes that some revisions are necessary, it requests that the Panel complete its analysis of this claim. On the issue of "like products," it requests the insertion in paragraph 7.471 of an example from its arguments.

6.31 The European Communities opposes Australia's request regarding "like products." The example given is one on which no discussion has taken place, and this is an issue on which Australia has made no claims or arguments.

6.32 Regarding marks of origin, the European Communities requests the deletion of point (b) of paragraph 7.469, with which it does not agree. The use of the words "made in" is not a specific requirement for a mark of origin in Article IX:1 of GATT 1994. It comments that it does not understand what is meant by the references in that paragraph to indication "in pictorial matter" nor by indication "alongside the GI" nor how this is relevant. Given the Panel's findings, it considers it unnecessary to reach a conclusion on this issue.

6.33 The Panel notes that the interim report already explains why Australia's argument does not demonstrate any difference in treatment but has made an addition to paragraph 7.469 in the final report. The reasoning in the paragraphs identified by Australia forms the basis for the statements it references in paragraphs 7.465 and 7.467 and the Panel sees no need to elaborate. The Panel has also retained the factual point in the paragraph, numbered 7.461 in the final report, because it is appropriate to explain why the European Communities' defence concerning marks of origin appears to be irrelevant to the preceding legal analysis. However, it has modified the point.

<u>right to prevent the use of translations of registered GIs</u>

6.34 The European Communities considers that it would be useful to recall in paragraph 7.530, for the sake of completeness, that under Article 13(1)(b) of the Regulation, GI holders do have a negative right to prevent the use of the registered name or names in translation.

6.35 The Panel has added a footnote to clarify the scope of the positive right to use a GI with respect to translations and has also clarified the importance of the fact that a trademark may continue to be used under Article 14(2) of the Regulation. However, the Panel declines to amend the referenced paragraph as requested because the protection granted by Article 13 of the Regulation is already addressed elsewhere and it has not been shown to what extent Article 13(1)(b) covers translations.

<u>exceptions in trademark legislation with respect to the use of GIs</u>

6.36 The European Communities comments that the assertion in paragraph 7.569 to the effect that the its trademark legislation provides no exceptions with respect to the use of geographical indications is factually incorrect, and refers to its response to Panel question No. 153 and, specifically, to Article 6.1(b) of the First Trademark Directive and Article 12(b) of the Community Trademark Regulation. Therefore, even where a trademark owner is allowed under the GI Regulation to enforce his rights under the First Trademark Directive or the Community Trademark Regulation with respect to the confusing use of a registered GI, he cannot prevent such use if it is "in accordance with honest practices in industrial or commercial matters."

6.37 Australia notes that the European Communities' comment is premised on the basis that an "indication concerning the ... geographical origin ... of goods" necessarily includes a GI, which is not always the case. In any case, the European Communities' comment intersects with the issue raised by Australia concerning whether a TRIPS-defined GI—and thus an EC-defined GI—can be analogous to "a descriptive term" within the meaning of Article 17 of the TRIPS Agreement.

6.38 The Panel takes note of the European Communities' factual correction and has deleted the paragraph.

<u>scope of a limited exception for GIs in translation</u>

6.39 The European Communities suggests a redraft of paragraph 7.668 for the following reasons: (a) lest it imply that the European Communities agrees with the last sentence of paragraph 7.666; (b) to include all the relevant limitations to the exception in Article 14(2) of the Regulation relied upon by the Panel including "what is undoubtedly the most crucial one, namely that the trademark owner maintains the right to prevent any confusing uses by all parties except the GI holders;" and (c) because a registration under the Regulation may specify more than one linguistic version of the geographical indication and the last part of the second sentence of paragraph 7.668 may suggest otherwise.

6.40 Australia requests that the argument attributed to it in the first sentence of paragraph 7.668 should be referenced or deleted. Should the Panel retain the paragraph, Australia notes that the suggested re-draft by the European Communities eliminates the final point of the second sentence that registration "does not cover the name where rendered differently in another language." In Australia's view, the Panel's finding on this point is an accurate summation of the European Communities' own description of the effect of registration of a term as a GI, and it cites various statements in the European Communities' submissions. Australia suggests that any redraft of the existing second sentence of the paragraph retain the point, given the arguments actually made by the European Communities.

6.41 The Panel has taken careful note of the parties' comments and has amended the paragraph, numbered 7.659 in the final report, to track more closely the wording of the explanations in the European Communities' own submissions, and then made a finding on the basis of the terms of the legislation and those explanations. It has also deleted the reference to Australia, and added references in the succeeding paragraph and elsewhere to the limitation provided by certain directives which the European Communities explained during the proceeding.

descriptive terms

6.42 Australia requests that the Panel elaborate its reasoning at paragraph 7.689 which assumes that a GI is analogous to a descriptive term within the meaning of the example in Article 17, taking account of the arguments put forward by the parties, including those made by Australia in relation to the design and architecture of the TRIPS Agreement.

6.43 The Panel has revised this and the preceding paragraph for clarity and added a reference to certain directives which the European Communities explained during the proceeding that provide further explanation of the legitimacy of certain interests. However, further elaboration on descriptiveness is unnecessary given that the Panel has expressly recognized that GIs are intellectual property rights, has not found that GIs are purely descriptive terms, and has noted the express requirements in Article 2(2) of the Regulation that GIs registered under the Regulation must describe certain matters.

comparison of exceptions provisions

6.44 Australia requests that paragraph 7.679 be substantially revised as it is not possible to consider differences in the language of the various provisos in isolation from the nature of the minimum standards for the intellectual property rights concerned.

6.45 The Panel has interpreted Article 17 in light of the minimum standards of which it forms a part, and has noted differences from rights granted by other forms of intellectual property protection where appropriate elsewhere. The Panel considers an observation of how the text differs from analogous texts in the same agreement to be relevant and does not base its reasoning on that observation alone. The Panel has modified the paragraph, numbered 7.671, in light of the comment received.

Articles 10*bis* and 10*ter* of the Paris Convention (1967)

6.46 Australia comments that the reasoning as currently expressed in paragraphs 7.729 to 7.733 seems to indicate that a responding party's assertion that it does not understand a claim is of itself a sufficient defence to a claim. Australia requests that the Panel review the content of these paragraphs and make appropriate amendments. In Australia's view, the key issue is whether the Panel understood Australia's claim and arguments and, if it did not, the steps it took to undertake an objective assessment. Moreover, it asserts that when the European Communities said it could not understand the claim because it could not see how a situation could arise where there would be an act of unfair competition, that this indicated that the European Communities did understand the claim, but did not agree that a relevant circumstance could arise. This does not affect the relevant obligation under the TRIPS Agreement.

6.47 The Panel takes note of Australia's comments and has expanded and revised the paragraphs, numbered 7.721 to 7.726 in the final report, to remove this impression and to clarify the full extent of the argumentation in support of this claim on which the Panel was called upon to make its assessment.

individual registrations

6.48 Australia requests that the Panel elaborate its reasoning in paragraph 7.753. It seeks clarification whether Australia's failure to specify any individual registrations in respect of which it requires relief affected the Panel's conclusion, and whether the Panel exercises judicial economy concerning ongoing registrations.

6.49 The Panel has reworded its existing reasoning in the paragraph numbered 7.750 in the final report. Australia's failure to specify any particular individual registration effected after the date of establishment of the Panel was relevant to the exercise of judicial economy on the preliminary ruling but not the conclusion on the claim, and this has been clarified in paragraph 7.26 for the avoidance of doubt.

conclusions

6.50 Australia asks whether the Panel exercises judicial economy on the claims under Article 2(1) of the Paris Convention (1967), as incorporated by Article 2.1 of the TRIPS Agreement.

6.51 The Panel has revised paragraph 7.252 to state its reasons for exercising judicial economy in relation to this provision, and reflected this in its conclusions in paragraph 8.1.

suggestion by the Panel on a way to implement its recommendation

6.52 Australia comments that it may assist the resolution of the dispute if the Panel were not to make any recommendation on how the European Communities could bring its measure into conformity. In Australia's view, amending the Regulation to accord with the interpretation that the European Communities submitted to the Panel would not necessarily bring the measure into conformity, even with respect to the reciprocity and equivalence conditions. This is because the European Communities consistently argued that the reciprocity and equivalence conditions of the Regulation were not inconsistent with the European Communities' national treatment obligations under the TRIPS Agreement. In addition, Australia is concerned that a recommendation by the Panel in respect of just one finding could be seen to suggest that the Panel's other findings of inconsistency are of lesser importance.

6.53 The European Communities expresses surprise at Australia's suggestion as it would appear that a clarification that the European Communities does not apply conditions of reciprocity and equivalence would remove the concern expressed by Australia regarding the protection of its GIs under the Regulation. As regards Australia's argument that "the EC consistently argued that the reciprocity and equivalence conditions of the Regulation were not inconsistent with the EC's national treatment obligations under the TRIPS Agreement," the European Communities recalls that it conceded that the application of such conditions would be incompatible with the GATT. Furthermore, the European Communities fails to see the relevance of Australia's comment in the context of the discussion of paragraph 8.5, which concerns an issue of implementation. Finally, as regards Australia's concern that certain of the Panel's findings should not be regarded as being of lesser importance than others, the European Communities fails to see why a suggestion made by a Panel in respect of one of its findings would indicate that this finding is more or less important than other findings. For these reasons, the European Communities requests that paragraph 8.5 not be deleted.

6.54 The Panel has modified its suggestion in paragraph 8.5 but, on the basis of the European Communities' remarks on interim review, considers it helpful to retain it. This suggestion does not imply that the Panel's other findings of inconsistency are of lesser importance.

other requests for review

6.55 Australia also requested deletion of paragraphs 7.64, 7.65 and 7.357 and footnote 526, and modifications to paragraphs 7.194, 7.214, 7.439, 7.473, 7.515 to 7.523, 7.589, 7.621, 7.700 and 8.2 and footnotes 565 and 591. It also makes some clerical observations. The Panel has modified its report in light of those comments.

6.56 The European Communities also requested modification of paragraphs 8.1 and 8.2. The Panel has modified those paragraphs and paragraph 7.758 in light of those comments.

VII. FINDINGS

A. Preliminary Issues

1. *Consistency of panel requests with Article 6.2 of the DSU*

7.1 On 24 February 2004, the day after the Panel was composed and prior to the organizational meeting, the European Communities submitted a detailed request that the Panel issue a preliminary ruling that the United States' and Australia's respective requests for establishment of a panel were inconsistent with the requirements of Article 6.2 of the DSU. In accordance with the Panel's timetable, the United States and Australia submitted responses to the European Communities' request for a preliminary ruling.

7.2 On 5 April 2004, the Panel issued the following preliminary ruling.[9]

(a) Introduction

1. The European Communities is of the view that the requests for establishment of a panel in this matter do not meet the requirements of Article 6.2 of the DSU. It has requested that the Panel issue a preliminary ruling regarding this question.[10]

(...)[11]

3. Australia is of the view that its request for establishment of a panel fully complies with the requirements of Article 6.2 of the DSU. It submits that the substantive basis of the European Communities' request for a preliminary ruling should be denied in full.[12]

4. Article 6.2 of the DSU provides as follows:

> 2. The request for the establishment of a panel shall be made in writing. It shall indicate whether consultations were held, identify the specific measures at issue and provide a brief summary of the legal basis of the complaint sufficient to present the problem clearly. In case the applicant requests the establishment of a panel with other than standard terms of reference, the written request shall include the proposed text of special terms of reference.

5. The European Communities alleges that the requests for establishment of a panel are inconsistent with the following requirements in Article 6.2:

(a) they fail to identify the specific measure at issue; and

(b) they do not provide a brief summary of the legal basis of the complaint sufficient to present the problem clearly.

6. The Panel will examine each of the requests for establishment of a panel as a whole on its face in the light of the parties' respective communications to the Panel to date and the relevant provisions of the covered agreements to assess its compliance with each of these requirements in the sections below.[13]

---

[9] The preliminary ruling is reproduced with minor editorial changes.

[10] *(footnote original)* European Communities' request for a preliminary ruling dated 24 February 2004 ("EC request"), paras. 1, 2, 3 and 5. [Note: that request is attached as Annex B-1 to this final report.]

[11] Note: paragraph 2 of the preliminary ruling dealt with the United States' request for establishment of a panel.

[12] *(footnote original)* Australia's comments on EC request, dated 15 March 2004 ("Australia's response"), paras. 1 and 48. [Note: those comments are attached as Annex A-1 to this final report.]

[13] *(footnote original)* This is consistent with the approach of the Appellate Body in *US – Carbon Steel*.

(...)[14]

(c) Australia's request for establishment of a panel[15]

(i) Identification of the specific measure at issue

23. Australia's request, in its fourth paragraph, identifies the following measures at issue:

> The measure at issue is Council Regulation (EEC) No. 2081/92 of 14 July 1992 *on the protection of geographical indications and designations of origin for agricultural products and foodstuffs*, any amendments thereto (including Council Regulation (EC) No. 692/2003 of 8 April 2003, published in the *Official Journal of the European Union* No. L99 of 17 April 2003), and related implementing and enforcement measures ('the EC measure'). The EC measure lays down and implements rules on the protection of designations of origin and geographical indications for agricultural products and foodstuffs, excluding wines and spirits.

<u>Council Regulation (EEC) No. 2081/92 and any amendments thereto</u>

24. Australia's request identifies a particular regulation by the name of the authority which adopted it, by its number, by its date of adoption and by its full title. It includes amendments of this regulation, including one amendment which is identified by the name of the authority which adopted it, by its number, by its date of adoption, by its full title and by the date and place of its publication. This is a specific measure, [16] and the request has identified it. There is no doubt as to which specific measure is in issue, as the European Communities has itself demonstrated by annexing a consolidated text of the regulation to the request for a preliminary ruling.[17]

25. The European Communities argues that:

> The unspecific reference to Regulation 2081/92 made in the Panel requests does not permit the EC to understand *which specific aspects among those covered by Regulation 2081/92* the complainants intend to raise in the context of the present proceedings. (italics added)

26. The Panel considers the ordinary meaning of the terms of the text in Article 6.2 of the DSU, read in their context and in the light of the object and purpose of the provision, to be quite clear. They require that a request for establishment of a panel "identify the specific measures at issue." They do not require the identification of the "specific aspects" of these "specific measures."

---

[14] Note: paragraphs 7-22 of the preliminary ruling dealt with the United States' request for establishment of a panel.

[15] *(footnote original)* Document WT/DS290/18.

[16] *(footnote original)* In this respect, the Panel notes that the Appellate Body in *EC – Bananas III* (at para. 140 of its report) agreed with the Panel in that case that similar language in the following extract from a panel request sufficiently identified the specific measure at issue in accordance with Article 6.2 of the DSU: "a regime for the importation, sale and distribution of bananas established by Regulation 404/93 [...], and subsequent EC legislation, regulations and administrative measures, including those reflecting the provisions of the Framework Agreement on bananas, which implement, supplement and amend that regime."

[17] *(footnote original)* Exhibit EC-1 annexed to EC request, *supra* at 10. A list containing the names, numbers and dates of the amendments reflected in the consolidated text of the regulation can be found on page 1 of that document.

"related implementing and enforcement measures"

27. Australia's request identifies, in addition to the regulation and any amendments thereto, "related implementing and enforcement measures." This phrase expressly refers to measures which implement and enforce Regulation (EEC) No. 2081/92, as amended. The word "related" is not used in isolation in the request.

28. The Regulation as amended itself expressly provides for the taking of particular types of decisions and actions and the adoption of rules of procedure for applying the Regulation. For example, Article 6 provides for the Commission to verify that registration applications include all the requisite particulars and, if it concludes that the name qualifies for protection, to publish certain details and, if no objection is notified, the name is entered in a register or, if the Commission concludes that the name does not qualify for protection, to decide not to proceed with the publication. Article 11a provides that the Commission may cancel the registration of a name. Article 12 provides for decisions by the Commission as to whether a third country satisfies the equivalence conditions and offers the requisite guarantees. Article 12b provides for the Commission, if it concludes that a name the subject of a registration request sent by a third country satisfies the conditions for protection, to publish certain details or, if it concludes that the name does not satisfy the conditions for protection, to decide not to proceed with publication. Article 16 provides for detailed rules for applying the Regulation to be adopted.[18] Those decisions, actions and rules, among others, implement the Regulation. The European Communities has indicated that the competent judicial and executive authorities enforce the Regulation.[19] In the Panel's view, this does not imply that there is any uncertainty as to which measures taken by those authorities implement and enforce the Regulation and which do not. All of the Regulation's implementing and enforcement measures form a group of specific measures which, although they may be a large group, are identified by Australia's request for establishment of a panel.[20]

29. For these reasons, on the basis of the facts available to us, the Panel rules that Australia's request for establishment of a panel did not fail to identify the specific measures at issue in accordance with Article 6.2 of the DSU.

(ii) A brief summary of the legal basis of the complaint sufficient to present the problem clearly

30. Australia's request, in its fifth paragraph, sets out in eight bullet points alleged inconsistencies with the covered agreements, by providing narrative text quoting or paraphrasing treaty text accompanied by provisions of the covered agreements identified by number. The numbered provisions identify every article of every covered agreement at issue and, in most cases where there are paragraphs within an article, such paragraphs are identified.

31. The European Communities takes issue with Australia's reference to whether Regulation No. 2081/92 is a "technical regulation" within the meaning of Annex 1 to the TBT Agreement because the definition does not impose any obligations which could have been violated.[21]

32. The Panel notes that the definition of "technical regulation" *per se* is not an obligation but rather defines a term used in other provisions of the TBT Agreement set out in Australia's request. The reference to the definition actually presents the problem more, rather than less, clearly because it explains why Australia considers that the measures at issue are subject to the relevant obligations.

---

[18] *(footnote original)* Exhibit EC-1.

[19] *(footnote original)* EC request, *supra* at 10, para. 30.

[20] *(footnote original)* See *supra* at 16.

[21] *(footnote original)* EC request, *supra* at 10, para. 63.

33. The European Communities also takes issue with the reference to Article 2 of the TRIPS Agreement (incorporating by reference Articles 10, 10*bis* and 10*ter* of the Paris Convention). It argues that Articles 10, 10*bis* and 10*ter* are "complex provisions" divided into various paragraphs, and imposing numerous distinct obligations.

34. Australia replies that, irrespective of the accuracy of the European Communities' portrayal of these provisions, its claim is that the measures at issue diminish the legal protection for trademarks under the TRIPS Agreement, contrary to *all* aspects of these cited provisions.[22]

35. The Panel considers that the mere listing of provisions of the relevant covered agreements may not satisfy the standard of Article 6.2 of the DSU, for instance, where the listed provisions establish multiple obligations rather than one single, distinct obligation.[23] However, where the multiple obligations are closely related and interlinked, a reference to a common obligation in the specific listed provisions may be sufficient to meet the standard of Article 6.2 of the DSU under certain circumstances in a particular case.[24]

36. With these considerations in mind, the Panel now examines the articles to which the European Communities has referred in Australia's request for establishment of a panel. The Panel notes that, on their face, the provisions within each of these articles are interlinked and very closely related, and that the separate paragraphs do not necessarily create distinct obligations. In particular:

(a) Article 10 of the Paris Convention (1967) extends the application of the provisions of Article 9, which relates to seizure of goods, to false indications of source. The second paragraph of Article 10 sets out a deeming provision for the purposes of the first paragraph;

(b) Article 10*bis* of the Paris Convention (1967) sets out a single obligation in paragraph (1) regarding unfair competition which is clarified in, and therefore closely related to, paragraphs (2) and (3); and

(c) Article 10*ter* of the Paris Convention (1967) sets out in paragraph (1) an obligation regarding legal remedies to repress all the acts referred to in Articles 9, 10 and 10*bis*, and in paragraph (2) an obligation regarding action to repress the same acts by particular types of legal person.

37. The European Communities also takes issue with the reference to "Articles 41 and/or 42 of the TRIPS Agreement." It submits that Article 41 is a "complex provision" subdivided into a number of paragraphs, which contain a number of different obligations; that Article 42 comprises several sentences establishing distinct obligations; and that it "does not understand the 'and/or' which seems to indicate that Articles 41 and 42 of the TRIPS Agreement are somehow alternative obligations."[25]

38. Australia replies that its reference to the essential elements of the relevant provisions is sufficient in this dispute to shed light on the nature of the obligations at issue in relation to the specific measures at issue. It also states that, in accordance with common usage, the expression "and/or" applies to all of the provisions cited.[26]

---

[22] *(footnote original)* Australia's response, *supra* at 12, para. 25.

[23] *(footnote original)* See the Appellate Body report on *Korea – Dairy*, para. 124.

[24] *(footnote original)* See the Appellate Body report on *Thailand – H-Beams*, para. 93.

[25] *(footnote original)* EC request, *supra* at 10, para. 57.

[26] *(footnote original)* Australia's response, *supra* at 12, paras. 23 and 24.

39. The Panel makes the following observations:

(a) Article 41 of the TRIPS Agreement contains general obligations which relate to acts of infringement of intellectual property rights covered by this Agreement. The accompanying narrative text of Australia's request clarifies that this claim is made because the measure at issue allegedly "diminishes the legal protection for trademarks under the TRIPS Agreement." The general obligations in Article 41 relate to "enforcement procedures as specified in [Part III]." Certain of those enforcement procedures, namely under Article 42, are also raised which clarifies that the general obligations are the subject of a claim in relation to these procedures. In particular, Article 42 is entitled "fair and equitable procedures" which is the subject of an obligation in Article 41.2;

(b) Article 42 of the TRIPS Agreement contains closely related obligations concerning fair and equitable procedures. The accompanying narrative text clarifies that this claim is made in relation to "the legal protection for trademarks under the TRIPS Agreement." The requirements of each sentence in Article 42 are distinct but they all set out specific features of fair and equitable civil judicial procedures concerning the enforcement of intellectual property rights; and

(c) the use of the term "and/or" at the end of a series or list of items connected by commas is a standard means of indicating that all items in that series or list may apply cumulatively or separately.[27] There is nothing in the context of Australia's request for the establishment of a panel that would indicate that it refers only to the last two items in the series. There is nothing which prevents a complainant making claims in the alternative. This puts the respondent on notice that the complainant effectively makes all these claims.

40. The European Communities further contends that it is entitled to know which provision or aspect of Regulation No. 2081/92 is supposed to violate certain obligations and in which way such a violation is deemed to occur. In the Panel's view, the European Communities is seeking the arguments, rather than just the claims, of Australia.[28] That being said, the Panel wishes to assure the European Communities that it is fully entitled to know the arguments of Australia *during the course of the proceedings*. Those arguments must be set out and may be clarified in Australia's submissions.[29] However, Article 6.2 of the DSU does not require those arguments to be set out in the request for establishment of a panel.[30]

41. The Panel notes that Article 6.2 of the DSU calls for sufficient clarity with respect to the legal basis of the complaint so as to enable a defending party to begin preparing its defence.[31] Our examination of Australia's request for establishment of a panel as a whole, in the light of Australia's and the European Communities' respective communications to the Panel to date and the relevant provisions of the covered agreements, leads us to believe that the request for establishment of a panel was sufficiently clear for the European Communities to begin preparing its defence.

---

[27] *(footnote original) The Oxford English Dictionary* defines "and/or" as "a formula denoting that the items joined by it can be taken either together or as alternatives." (*A Supplement to the Oxford English Dictionary*, R.W. Burchfield (ed.) (Clarendon Press, 1972, reprinted, with corrections, 1980, Vol. I).

[28] *(footnote original)* See the Appellate Body reports in *EC – Bananas III*, para. 141; *Korea – Dairy*, para. 139; and *US – Carbon Steel*, para. 173.

[29] *(footnote original)* See *supra* at 24.

[30] *(footnote original)* See the Appellate Body report on *Korea – Dairy*, para. 123.

[31] *(footnote original)* See Appellate Body report on *Thailand – H-Beams*, para. 88.

42. For these reasons, on the basis of the facts available to us, the Panel rules that Australia's request for establishment of a panel did not fail to provide a brief summary of the legal basis of the complaint sufficient to present the problem clearly in accordance with Article 6.2 of the DSU.

(d) Due process

43. The European Communities is also of the view that the "deficiencies" of the requests for establishment of a panel seriously prejudice its due process rights as a defending party, notably, to know the case it has to answer.[32]

44. The Panel recalls once again that Article 6.2 of the DSU calls for sufficient clarity with respect to the legal basis of the complaint so as to enable a defending party to begin preparing its defence.[33] In this respect, the Panel has found that the complainants' requests for establishment of a panel were sufficiently clear for the European Communities to begin preparing its defence.[34] Therefore, the Panel considers that it is not necessary to make a separate ruling on this issue, as presented by the European Communities in its request.[35]

45. The Panel is mindful of the due process rights of all parties in this proceeding. In this regard, it notes that the European Communities had a period of over four months after the establishment of the Panel prior to its constitution plus a period of over seven weeks prior to receipt of the complainants' first written submissions to begin preparing its case, and will have an additional period of four and a half weeks from receipt of the complainants' first written submissions to continue preparation of its own first written submission, which is in excess of the maximum period proposed in Appendix 3 to the DSU.

(e) Timeliness

46. The European Communities submitted its request for a preliminary ruling two days after the composition of the Panel. It also raised its concerns at the DSB meetings at which the requests for establishment of a panel were considered.[36]

47. The Panel therefore considers that the European Communities has raised its concerns in a timely manner.[37]

(f) Conclusion

48. In light of the foregoing, on the basis of the facts available to us, the Panel rules that the measures and claims in Australia's and the United States' respective requests for establishment of a panel did not fail to meet the requirements of Article 6.2 of the DSU that they identify the specific measures at issue and provide a brief summary of the legal basis of the complaint sufficient to present the problem clearly. [End of 5 April 2004 ruling]

---

[32] *(footnote original)* EC request, *supra* at 10, para. 4.

[33] *(footnote original)* See *supra* at 31.

[34] *(footnote original)* See para. 41.

[35] *(footnote original)* The Panel takes note that the European Communities stated that it does not take a position as to whether "the requirement of prejudice in Article 6.2 DSU" constitutes an additional requirement to those set out in Article 6.2 of the DSU: EC request, *supra* at 10, para. 66, fn. 25.

[36] *(footnote original)* See the minutes of those meetings in documents WT/DSB/M/155, para. 75 and M/156, para. 32, reproduced in Exhibits EC-2 and EC-3, respectively. The Panel takes note that the European Communities did not clearly raise any problem concerning the alleged failure of Australia's request to identify the specific measures at issue on those occasions.

[37] *(corrected footnote original)* This does not imply that these issues could not be raised later in the proceedings.

7.3 The Panel stated expressly that its 5 April 2004 preliminary ruling was based on the facts available to it at that time.[38] In this final report, the Panel makes further findings on the sufficiency of the panel request, in light of submissions made later during the course of the panel proceeding. These submissions confirm the Panel's ruling as to the meaning of the words used in the panel request and the Panel's assessment that the ability of the respondent to defend itself was not prejudiced.[39]

7.4 First, the Panel recalls that the European Communities argued, in its request for a preliminary ruling, that:

> The unspecific reference to Regulation 2081/92 made in the Panel requests does not permit the EC to understand which specific aspects among those covered by Regulation 2081/92 the complainants intend to raise in the context of the present proceedings.[40]

7.5 The Panel ruled that Article 6.2 did not require the identification of the "specific aspects" of the specific measures at issue.[41] In any event, after consulting the parties' first written submissions, it is clear that the reference to "Regulation No. 2081/92, as amended" in the request for establishment of a panel did identify certain specific aspects among those covered by the Regulation that the complainant later raised, as follows:

(a) Australia's principal claims concerning national treatment (considered in Section VII:B of this report) are based on the differences between the two sets of registration and objection procedures set out in Regulation (EEC) No. 2081/92 (the "Regulation") in Articles 5 through 7 and 12 through 12d, respectively.[42] This is one of the principal features of the Regulation. It was clear from the request for establishment of a panel that the complainant intended to raise these aspects of the Regulation; and

(b) Australia's principal claim concerning the legal protection for trademarks (considered in Section VII:D of this report) is based on Article 14 of the Regulation. This provision is specifically devoted to that issue. It was clear from the request for establishment of a panel that the complainant intended to raise this article of the Regulation, as the European Communities itself confirmed in its request for a preliminary ruling.[43]

7.6 Second, the Panel recalls that the European Communities submitted in its February 2004 request for a preliminary ruling that:

> In the present case, the ambiguity of the Panel request is such that the EC is, to this date, not sure of the case which the United States and Australia are bringing before the Panel. As a consequence, the EC has been seriously hampered in its efforts to prepare its defence.[44]

7.7 Specifically, with respect to the national treatment claims, it submitted as follows:

---

[38] See paras. 6, 29 and 48 of the preliminary ruling set out above.

[39] This is consistent with the approach of the Appellate Body in *US – Carbon Steel*, para. 127.

[40] Quoted at para. 25 of the preliminary ruling set out above.

[41] See para. 11 of the preliminary ruling set out above.

[42] To the extent that the claims concern the actions of EC member State authorities in the verification and transmission of applications and objections, the European Communities expressly referred to these actions in its request for a preliminary ruling, *supra* at 10, para. 31. It also informed the Panel during this proceeding that Community laws are generally not executed through authorities at Community level but rather through recourse to the authorities of its member States: see para. 7.148 below.

[43] The claim concerned coexistence under Article 14(2), subject to Article 14(3). The European Communities expressly referred to both, as well as Article 7(4), to which it referred in its defence, in its request for a preliminary ruling, *supra* at 10, paras. 47 and 61. The only aspect of the Regulation which it raised in this respect in its request for a preliminary ruling, that it did not later raise in its defence, was Article 14(1): see Section VII:D of this report.

[44] European Communities' request, *supra* at 10, para. 68.

> [T]he US claim is limited to a paraphrasing of the treaty language of [Article 3 TRIPS and Article III:4 GATT]. The US claim does not permit to understand which provision or aspect of Regulation 2081/92 is supposed to violate the national treatment principle, and in which way such a violation is deemed to occur; and
>
> Like the US claims, Australia's claims [regarding *inter alia* national treatment under Article 3.1 TRIPS and Article III:4 GATT] are limited to the restatement of language already contained in treaty provisions, and therefore encounter the same objections.[45]

7.8 The Panel's assessment was that the request for establishment of a panel was sufficiently clear for the European Communities to begin preparing its defence.[46] After consulting the European Communities' first written submission, and information submitted by Australia, the Panel is now aware that prior to the date of the request for establishment of a panel, the European Communities had already presented in the Council for TRIPS in September 2002 a statement that responded specifically to the argument that national treatment under the TRIPS Agreement applied to geographical indications. In that statement, the European Communities quoted the texts of Article 3 of the TRIPS Agreement and Article III:4 of GATT 1994 and argued that "[t]hose entitled to rights under TRIPS are nationals." This is also an important defence set out in the European Communities' first written submission, in which it is argued that "[t]he conditions for the registration of geographical indications do not depend on nationality."[47] This supports the Panel's assessment that the relevant wording of the request for establishment of a panel was sufficiently clear for the European Communities to begin preparing its defence of the first national treatment claim.[48]

7.9 Third, the Panel notes that, in any event, Australia's other claims (considered in Section VII:E of this report), brought under the provisions discussed in paragraphs 36 and 39 of the preliminary ruling, were not pursued in such detail. The Panel has found no prima facie case or rejected all these claims. This confirms the Panel's assessment that no prejudice has been caused to the rights of the respondent by these claims.

2. Measures no longer in force at the date of establishment of the Panel

(a) Main arguments of the parties

7.10 Australia challenges Council Regulation (EEC) No. 2081/92[49], including not only the current version of that Regulation as in force as at the date of establishment of the Panel[50] but also two prior versions of the Regulation as originally adopted in 1992 and as amended in 1997.[51] Australia's claims refer variously to the current version and these two prior versions of the Regulation.

7.11 The European Communities responds that Australia's request for establishment of a panel does not make it clear that Australia intends to challenge several versions of the same measure resulting from subsequent amendments made over time. It also submits that the measure at issue is the Regulation as in force at the time the Panel was established and that an analysis of historical versions is not useful for the purposes of settling the present dispute.[52]

---

[45] *Ibid,*, paras. 44 and 61.

[46] See para. 41 of the preliminary ruling set out above.

[47] European Communities' first written submission, paras. 114 and 123-126.

[48] See also para. 6.5 above.

[49] Australia's first written submission, para. 20.

[50] Amendment effected by Council Regulation (EC) No. 692/2003, set out in Exhibit COMP-1h.

[51] Australia's first written submission, para. 18, defines "Regulation No. 2081/92" "#1," "#2" and "#3."

[52] European Communities' first written submission, paras. 13-20. The European Communities addressed the individual registrations on the basis of the preliminary ruling by the Panel but reserved its right to raise this issue in the context of a possible appeal: see its second oral statement, para. 105 and fn. 80.

(b) *Consideration by the Panel*

7.12 The Panel notes that Australia's request for establishment of a panel specifies the Regulation as well as "any amendments thereto, (including Council Regulation (EC) No. 692/2003 ...)." Whilst this wording can be read to encompass the original version of the Regulation, and a subsequent amended version, which are no longer in force, it is unnecessary to rule on whether those measures are within the Panel's terms of reference, for the reasons given below.

7.13 In its submissions, Australia seeks relief in respect of these prior versions of the Regulation. For example, it claims that registration procedures under versions of Articles 7(4) and 14(1) of the Regulation, which were deleted and replaced in April 2003, were inconsistent with the TRIPS Agreement.[53] Australia expressly seeks "rulings and recommendations" from the Panel in respect of prior versions of the Regulation to the degree necessary to establish the extent to which individual registrations were inconsistent with the covered agreements, and therefore the extent to which those registrations continued the alleged violations. It cites Articles 3.7, 11, 12.7 and 19.1 of the DSU in support of its request.[54]

7.14 The Panel notes the distinction between provisions of the Regulation which established procedures, but are no longer in force, and individual registrations affected under them. With respect to the former, the Panel recalls that its mandate to make recommendations in this dispute is found in Article 19.1 of the DSU, which foresees only one type of recommendation, namely, that a Member bring a measure into conformity with a covered agreement. It is obvious that versions of the Regulation cannot be brought into conformity if they have already ceased to exist.[55] Therefore, the Panel will not make any recommendation with respect to prior versions of the Regulation that are no longer in force.

7.15 However, individual GI registrations effected under prior versions of the Regulation remain in force. There is, in principle, no reason why it should not be possible to challenge them under the TRIPS Agreement. They are measures which may affect the operation of that agreement. Australia's request for establishment of a panel specifically identified "[the Regulation and any amendments thereto] and related implementing ... measures" as part of the measure at issue. Registrations under Articles 6 and 12b of the Regulation, and under the former Article 17, constitute such implementing measures. Therefore, they are within the Panel's terms of reference.[56] Given that they remain in force, the Panel can make a recommendation that the respondent Member bring them into conformity with a covered agreement. Therefore, the Panel may examine these individual registrations as part of the matter before it.

7.16 The Panel wishes to note that, in certain respects, Australia's description of provisions of prior versions of the Regulation assists it in understanding provisions of the current version of the Regulation. For example, the description of Articles 12 and following of the Regulation prior to its amendment in April 2003 assists the Panel in understanding the European Commission's contemporaneous explanations of the Regulation, as discussed in Section VII:B of this report.[57] Moreover, a description of the Regulation as it stood prior to 1 January 1995 would be essential in applying Article 24.3 of the TRIPS Agreement, which refers to a state of affairs "immediately prior to the date of entry into force of the WTO Agreement," according to the European Communities' interpretation of that provision, as discussed in Section VII:D of this report.[58] Further, a description of the simplified registration procedure under the former Article 17 of the Regulation, which has been repealed, demonstrates that there is no evidence that individual registrations effected under that procedure

---

53 Australia's first written submission, paras. 89 and 86, respectively.

54 Australia's first oral statement, paras. 13-14 and its response to Panel question No. 88.

55 This was also the approach of the Appellate Body in *US – Certain EC Products*, at para. 81.

56 This is subject to comments in para. 7.26 concerning individual registrations adopted after the date of establishment of the Panel. See also the Panel's conclusion at para. 7.751 below.

57 Exhibit AUS-4 and documents IP/Q2/EEC/1 and IP/C/M/37/Add.1, para. 142 and Annex.

58 See para. 7.628.

involved a denial of national treatment to persons who wished to object, as discussed in Section VII:E of this report.[59]

7.17 Therefore, in the course of its assessment of the matter before it, the Panel will make findings with respect to prior versions of the Regulation where they serve some useful purpose in reaching conclusions with respect to measures within its terms of reference, including individual registrations, that are currently in force. References in this report to the "Regulation" refer to the current version, unless the context indicates otherwise.

3. Measures adopted after the date of establishment of the Panel

(a) Main arguments of the parties

7.18 Australia and the United States submitted, as an exhibit, a copy of Commission Regulation (EC) No. 2400/96[60], which is effectively the register under Article 6 of Council Regulation (EEC) No. 2081/92. Individual designations of origin and geographical indications are added to the register by amending the Commission Regulation. The exhibit includes amendments made up until the time of the first written submissions in this proceeding, nine of which were adopted after the date of establishment of the Panel. Those nine amendments effected the registrations of 15 individual designations of origin and geographical indications.[61]

7.19 Australia and the United States also submitted, as an exhibit, an unofficial consolidated version of Council Regulation (EEC) No. 2081/92, which included amendments published in the Official Journal of the European Communities up until the date of establishment of the Panel.[62] The latest of these amendments is the Act of Accession of ten new EC member States. They also submitted, as an exhibit, an extract from that Act of Accession which provides for the registration of three Czech beer GIs under Article 17 of the Regulation.[63]

7.20 Australia challenges individual registrations effected under the Regulation and notes that registrations are "ongoing."[64]

7.21 The European Communities responds that these measures did not yet exist at the time the Panel was established and are therefore outside the terms of reference. In particular, it submits that the Act of Accession was subject to ratification, which was not completed on the date of establishment of the Panel, and did not enter into force until 1 May 2004.[65]

(b) Main arguments of third parties

7.22 China argues that the wording of the request for establishment of a panel specified amendments to the Regulation and that, therefore, they are properly included in the Panel's terms of reference. The respondent received notice of the inclusion of amendments and had enough opportunity to respond to the complainant's case. It is irrelevant whether the amendments came into effect before or after the Panel was established.[66]

---

[59] See paras. 7.746 and 7.747.

[60] Exhibit COMP-4.

[61] Exhibit COMP-4b.viii to xvi. The 15 GIs are "Westlandse druif;" "Alcachofa de Benicarló" or "Carxofa de Benicarló;" "Marrone di San Zeno;" "Mantequilla de l'Alt Urgell y la Cerdanya" or "Mantega de l'Alt Urgell i la Cerdanya;" "Thüringer Leberwurst," "Thüringer Rotwurst," "Thüringer Rostbratwurst;" "Spressa delle Giudicarie;" "Fraise du Périgord;" "Queso de Valdeón;" "Ensaimada de Mallorca" or "Ensaimada mallorquina;" "Arbroath Smokies;" "Carciofo di Paestum;" "Farina di Neccio della Garfagnana;" "Agneau de Pauillac" and "Agneau du Poitou-Charentes."

[62] Exhibit COMP-1a.

[63] Exhibit COMP-3c. The Czech beer GIs are "Budějovické pivo," "Českobudějovické pivo" and "Budějovický měšťanský var."

[64] Australia's first written submission, paras. 20 and 33.

[65] European Communities' first written submission, paras. 21-25.

[66] Annex C, para. 96.

(c) Consideration by the Panel

7.23 The Panel begins by noting that Council Regulation (EEC) No. 2081/92 (referred to in this report as the "Regulation") has not been amended in any relevant respects during this panel proceeding. It was last amended in April 2003, prior to the date of the request for establishment of a panel.

7.24 The Panel's terms of reference include not only the Regulation, but also its "related implementing and enforcement measures." The Panel considers that this phrase in the request for establishment of a panel is broad enough to include individual registrations, for the reasons given in paragraph 28 of its preliminary ruling of 5 April 2004, and in paragraph 7.15 above. The individual GIs which are entered in the Register under Articles 6 and 17 of the Regulation are set out in Commission Regulations (EC) No. 2400/96 and No. 1107/96.[67] New registrations take the form of amendments to these Commission Regulations. Certain individual registrations were effected after the date of establishment of the Panel and prior to the date of the complainants' first written submissions[68], and registrations continue to be made after that date.

7.25 Australia's challenge of the individual registrations includes those effected after the date of establishment of the Panel. Each of the individual registrations applies to a different GI, is used by different producers and/or processors and may, in turn, affect rights in different trademarks. They are distinct measures. Those effected after the date of establishment of the Panel have added to the implementing measures as they stood at that date, although they have not affected the essence of the implementing measures vis-à-vis other registrations as they stood at that date.[69]

7.26 However, Australia has not sought particular relief in respect of individual registrations effected after the date of establishment of the Panel[70], as opposed to those effected earlier, and the Panel has found no prima facie case in support of the claims in respect of individual registrations effected at any time.[71] Therefore, the Panel does not consider it necessary to rule on whether the individual registrations effected after the date of establishment of the Panel fall within the terms of reference in order to secure a positive solution to this dispute.

7.27 The Panel wishes to note that individual registrations effected after the date of the request for establishment of a panel can be among the best evidence of the way in which certain provisions of the Regulation itself, which are at issue, are interpreted and applied.[72] The Panel therefore refers to them, as factual evidence, in the course of its assessment of the matter before it.[73] References in this report to the "Regulation" refer to the basic Regulation rather than related and implementing measures, unless the context indicates otherwise.

4. Claims under Article 2(2) of the Paris Convention (1967), as incorporated by Article 2.1 of the TRIPS Agreement

(a) Main arguments of the parties

7.28 Australia claims that the Regulation imposes on other WTO Member nationals a requirement as to domicile or establishment in the European Communities for the enjoyment of rights contrary to Article 2(1) and

---

[67] Set out in Exhibits COMP-4a and 3a, respectively.

[68] See *supra* at 61 and 63 .

[69] This is consistent with the approach of the Appellate Body in *Brazil – Aircraft,* para. 132 and *Chile – Price Band System* at paras. 135-144.

[70] Australia's responses to Panel questions Nos. 91 and 93.

[71] See para. 7.751 below.

[72] In fact, the European Communities itself has included one of these GIs in its exhibits: the 2002 publication of the application to register "Thüringer Leberwurst" is Exhibit EC-54.

[73] The Panel refers to the registration of the Czech beer GIs submitted in an exhibit by the complainants (see para. 7.18 above) as evidence of the operation of Article 14(3) of the Regulation in paras.7.574 and 7.669.

2(2) of the Paris Convention (1967) as incorporated by Article 2.1 of the TRIPS Agreement.[74] In its view, Article 2(2) is an integral aspect of the national treatment obligation under Article 2(1).[75]

7.29 The European Communities responds that these claims are outside the Panel's terms of reference because they relate to Article 2(2) of the Paris Convention (1967) which was not explicitly mentioned in the request for establishment of a panel. Article 2(2) prohibits the imposition of requirements as to domicile or establishment and is therefore different from, and additional to, the obligations resulting from the national treatment provision of Article 2(1).[76]

(b) Consideration by the Panel

7.30 The Panel notes that Australia's request for establishment of a panel adapts the text of the national treatment obligations in Article 3.1 of the TRIPS Agreement and Article III:4 of GATT 1994. Australia's request then cites by number both those articles as well as Article 2 of the TRIPS Agreement "incorporating by reference Article 2 of the Paris Convention (1967)."

7.31 In its submissions to the Panel, Australia claims that certain aspects of the Regulation are inconsistent with both Article 2(1) and 2(2) of the Paris Convention (1967) as incorporated by Article 2.1 of the TRIPS Agreement. The issue for the Panel is whether the reference to national treatment and to Article 2 of the Paris Convention (1967) is sufficient to present the legal basis of the complaint under Article 2(1) and 2(2), or only Article 2(1).

7.32 The Panel considers that the mere listing of provisions of the relevant covered agreements may not satisfy the standard of Article 6.2 of the DSU, for instance, where the listed provisions establish multiple obligations rather than one single, distinct obligation.[77] However, where the multiple obligations are closely related and interlinked, a reference to a common obligation in the specific listed provisions should be sufficient to meet the standard of Article 6.2 of the DSU under certain circumstances in a particular case.[78]

7.33 Paragraph 1 of Article 2 of the Paris Convention (1967) expresses a national treatment obligation. Paragraph 2 prohibits local domicile or establishment requirements as a condition for the enjoyment of any industrial property rights. The texts of paragraphs 1 and 2 are linked by the use of the conjunction "[h]owever" which indicates that paragraph 2 restricts the rule of paragraph 1. Paragraph 2 in effect provides that certain conditions may not be imposed on foreign nationals, even if they are imposed on a country's own nationals.[79] Paragraph 3 also reserves or excepts certain conditions from the national treatment obligation, but by stating certain conditions which may be imposed on foreign nationals, even if they are not imposed on a country's own nationals. Read in context, all three paragraphs either establish a single obligation or are very closely related: paragraph 1 sets out an obligation to provide national treatment and paragraphs 2 and 3 limit that obligation.

7.34 Therefore, in the Panel's view, the references in the request for establishment of a panel to national treatment and to Article 2 of the Paris Convention (1967), which does not specify particular paragraphs, as incorporated by Article 2.1 of the TRIPS Agreement, is sufficient to explain the legal basis of the complaints under both paragraphs 1 and 2 of Article 2. Accordingly, the Panel rules that the claims under Article 2(2) of the

---

[74] Australia's first written submission, paras. 189 and 194.

[75] Australia's first oral statement, para. 16.

[76] European Communities' first written submission, paras. 36-42; second oral statement, paras. 112-117.

[77] See the Appellate Body report on *Korea – Dairy*, para. 124.

[78] See the Appellate Body report on *Thailand – H-Beams*, para. 93.

[79] A leading commentator explains the addition of the word "however" as follows: "Even when the conditions imposed upon nationals of a country include the stipulation that *those nationals* can claim protection of certain industrial property rights only if they are domiciled or established in the country, this same stipulation cannot be imposed upon *nationals of other countries* of the Union." in Bodenhausen, Professor G.H.C., *Guide to the Application of the Paris Convention for the Protection of Industrial Property*, United International Bureaux for the Protection of Intellectual Property (BIRPI) (1969) (reprinted 1991) ("Bodenhausen"), p. 31. [Emphasis in the original]

Paris Convention (1967), as incorporated by Article 2.1 of the TRIPS Agreement, are within the Panel's terms of reference.

5. *Claim under Article 4 of the Paris Convention (1967), as incorporated by Article 2.1 of the TRIPS Agreement and, consequently, under Article 24.5 of the TRIPS Agreement*
(a) *Main arguments of the parties*

7.35 Australia claims that Article 14(1) of the Regulation does not afford the right of priority in respect of trademark applications required to be granted by Article 4 of the Paris Convention (1967), contrary to Article 24.5 of the TRIPS Agreement.[80] In its view, the reference to Article 24.5 of the TRIPS Agreement in its request for establishment of a panel permits the Panel to examine the consistency of the Regulation with Article 4 of the Paris Convention (1967) and, indeed, that examination is necessary for such a determination.[81] It argues that the obligation not to prejudice eligibility for the registration of a trademark is plain on a reading of Article 24.5 and, given the express obligation on the European Communities to comply with Article 4 of the Paris Convention (1967), it was clear that non-compliance with that provision would constitute prejudice to the eligibility for registration of a trademark. Article 6.2 of the DSU should not be interpreted and applied in such a way as to require that a complaining party must have fully developed its argumentation for a dispute before presenting its request for establishment of a panel. [82]

7.36 The European Communities responds that this claim is outside the Panel's terms of reference because Australia's request for establishment of a panel did not refer to Article 4 of the Paris Convention (1967).[83]

(b) *Consideration by the Panel*

7.37 The Panel recalls that Australia's request for establishment of a panel includes the following passage:

Australia is of the view that the EC measure:

- diminishes the legal protection for trademarks under the TRIPS Agreement, contrary to Articles 1, 2 (incorporating by reference Articles 6*quinques*(B), 10, 10*bis* and 10*ter* of the Paris Convention (1967)), 16, 20, 24.5, 41 and/or 42 of the TRIPS Agreement;

7.38 It is not disputed that the Panel's terms of reference include the general issue whether the Regulation diminishes protection for trademarks contrary to Article 16.1 of the TRIPS Agreement, since that is expressly set out in Australia's request for establishment of a panel. The parties' evidence and arguments address in detail the extent to which Article 24.5 prohibits Members from diminishing the protection of trademarks in the course of protecting geographical indications, and the Panel makes detailed findings on this issue in this report. The reference to Article 24.5 in Australia's request for establishment of a panel appears to relate to this issue.

7.39 It is not disputed that Article 24.5 refers to three aspects of the protection of trademarks, one of which is the eligibility of a trademark for registration. This concerns trademark applications. However, in the Panel's view, the reference to protection of trademarks and Article 24.5 does not necessarily concern each and every possible aspect of trademark application procedures. Article 15 of the TRIPS Agreement and numerous distinct obligations under the Paris Convention (1967), including Articles 4, 6, 6*bis*, 6*quinquies* and 7 relate to trademark applications and procedures. If a mere allegation of diminished protection of trademarks contrary to

---

[80] Australia's first written submission, paras. 81-87.

[81] Australia's first oral statement, para. 15.

[82] Australia's response to Panel question No. 162; rebuttal submission, para. 25.

[83] European Communities' first written submission, paras. 28-30; first oral statement, para. 6. The European Communities also submits that Australia has not clarified this claim, despite a request to do so, and that Australia has not identified a single application for a trademark that falls within the situation that Australia alleges in this claim: see European Communities' rebuttal submission, paras. 356-357.

Article 24.5 of the TRIPS Agreement could include the specific obligation to accord priority filing dates for trademark applications, it could conceivably relate to all of these other distinct obligations as well.

7.40 The Panel recalls that Article 6.2 of the DSU requires that a request for establishment of a panel shall "provide a brief summary of the legal basis of the complaint sufficient to present the problem clearly." This calls for sufficient clarity with respect to the legal basis of the complaint so as to enable a defending party to begin preparing its defence.[84] Australia's request for establishment of a panel makes no mention of the right of priority, or Article 4 of the Paris Convention (1967) as incorporated by Article 2.1 of the TRIPS Agreement, or their relationship with prejudice to trademark applications under Article 24.5 of the TRIPS Agreement. In that request, the obligation under Article 4 of the Paris Convention (1967) is not "express" or implied. There was simply no way for the European Communities to know that the right of priority under Article 4 of the Paris Convention (1967) was at issue.

7.41 In its first written submission, Australia described why, in its view, Article 14(1) of the Regulation covered a situation within the meaning of Article 24.5. In order to explain the alleged inconsistency, it addressed Article 4 of the Paris Convention (1967), "and in particular paragraph B of that provision, incorporated by TRIPS Article 2.1" and concluded as follows:

> Article 14.1 of Regulation No. 2081/93#3 does not afford the right of priority in respect of an application for registration of a trademark previously filed in another WTO Member required to be granted by Paris Article 4 where that trademark is identical with or similar to an EC-defined GI which is later registered. By not doing so, Article 14.1 of Regulation No. 2081/93#3 continues to prejudice, or adversely affect, the eligibility for registration of a trademark for which an application has been made in good faith, contrary to TRIPS Article 24.5.

7.42 Australia was not required to disclose its arguments until its first written submission, but its assertion of an inconsistency with Article 4 of the Paris Convention (1967), as incorporated by Article 2.1 of the TRIPS Agreement and, consequently, Article 24.5 of the TRIPS Agreement, amounts to a claim under Article 4, which should have been disclosed in the request for establishment of a panel. The inclusion of this claim for the first time in the first written submission took the European Communities by surprise and deprived it of the right to begin preparing its defence to this claim earlier.

7.43 Therefore, in this respect, the request for establishment of a panel does not satisfy the requirement of Article 6.2 to "provide a brief summary of the legal basis of the complaint sufficient to present the problem clearly." Accordingly, this claim is outside the Panel's terms of reference.

6. Claim under Article 41 in conjunction with Articles 43, 44, 45, 46, 48 and 49 of the TRIPS Agreement

(a) Main arguments of the parties

7.44 Australia argues in its first written submission that the European Communities has not ensured that enforcement procedures as specified in Part III of the TRIPS Agreement are available under its law, contrary to Article 41.1 of the TRIPS Agreement, as a consequence of *inter alia* the fact that the Regulation does not grant the Consultative Committee the authority required by Articles 43, 44, 45, 46 and 48 of the TRIPS Agreement, and does not provide judicial authorities with the authority required by Articles 43, 44, 45, 46, 48 and 49.[85] Australia submits that the reference to Article 41 of the TRIPS Agreement in its request for establishment of a

[84] See the Appellate Body report on *Thailand – H-Beams*, para. 88.

[85] Australia's first written submission, para. 148.

panel permits the Panel to examine the consistency of the Regulation with Articles 43 to 49 respectively and, indeed, that such an examination is necessary for such a determination.[86]

7.45 The European Communities responds that this amounts to a claim under Articles 43 to 49 of the TRIPS Agreement not mentioned in the request for establishment of a panel and is therefore outside the Panel's terms of reference. The reference to Article 41 in the request for establishment of a panel is not sufficient to specify Articles 43 to 49 and, more specifically, Article 41.1 is a purely introductory provision which does not create separate legal obligations.[87]

(b) Consideration by the Panel

7.46 The Panel recalls that Article 6.2 of the DSU requires that a request for establishment of a panel shall "provide a brief summary of the legal basis of the complaint sufficient to present the problem clearly." This calls for sufficient clarity with respect to the legal basis of the complaint so as to enable a defending party to begin preparing its defence.[88]

7.47 The Panel recalls that in its preliminary ruling dated 5 April 2004, reproduced above, it considered the relationship between Article 41, which is specifically identified in the request for establishment of a panel, and the enforcement procedures in Part III of the TRIPS Agreement, in particular, in Article 42, which is also specifically identified in that request. The Panel did not rule that Article 41 was clearly within the terms of reference in all respects. After consulting the parties' first written submissions, it is clear that the relevant references in the request for establishment of a panel did not identify all the claims that Australia subsequently raised. Australia's request for establishment of a panel does not refer to Articles 43, 44, 45, 46, 48 or 49 or the other provisions of Part III. The textual link in the TRIPS Agreement between Article 41 and the other articles of Part III is found in paragraph 1 of Article 41, which provides that "Members shall ensure that enforcement procedures as specified in this Part are available under their law ...". Australia's request for establishment of a panel does not indicate which of these other enforcement procedures are at issue, does not cite this text, nor does it refer specifically to paragraph 1 of Article 41.

7.48 The Panel considers that Article 41.1 imposes an obligation. The language of that provision is expressed in terms of what Members "shall" ensure and is not hortatory. The substance of the provision adds qualitative elements to the procedures specified in Part III through use of terms such as "effective," "expeditious" and "deterrent" and is not redundant. However, it was not possible for the European Communities to know from the request for establishment of a panel that the claim under Article 41 put in issue the procedures required under any of Articles 43 through 49. The inclusion of a claim in Australia's first written submission under Article 41 of the TRIPS Agreement in conjunction with Articles 43, 44, 45, 46, 48 and 49 took the European Communities by surprise and deprived it of the right to begin preparing its defence of this claim earlier.

7.49 Therefore, in this respect, the request for establishment of a panel does not satisfy the requirement of Article 6.2 to "provide a brief summary of the legal basis of the complaint sufficient to present the problem clearly." Accordingly, the claim under Article 41 of the TRIPS Agreement in conjunction with Articles 43, 44, 45, 46, 48 and 49 is outside the Panel's terms of reference.

7.50 In any event, the Panel rejects all of Australia's claims under Articles 41 and 42 of the TRIPS Agreement, for the reason given in paragraph 7.731 of this report, which applies with equal force to all grounds on which these claims were purportedly made.

---

[86] Australia's first oral statement, para. 15.

[87] European Communities' first written submission, paras. 31-35.

[88] See the Appellate Body report on *Thailand – H-Beams*, para. 88.

7. Claim under Article 20 of the TRIPS Agreement

7.51 Australia includes in its request for establishment of a panel a claim that the Regulation diminishes the legal protection of trademarks contrary to Article 20 of the TRIPS Agreement. It presents arguments in support of that claim in its first written submission.[89]

7.52 The European Communities responds that the Regulation is not inconsistent with Article 20 of the TRIPS Agreement.[90]

7.53 In its second oral statement, Australia withdrew its claim under Article 20 of the TRIPS Agreement.[91] Therefore, the Panel does not consider this claim any further.

8. Claims under Article 4 of the TRIPS Agreement, Article I:1 of GATT 1994 and Article 2.1 of the TBT Agreement

7.54 Australia includes in its request for establishment of a panel claims that the Regulation is inconsistent with the MFN treatment obligations in Article 4 of the TRIPS Agreement, Article I:1 of GATT 1994 and Article 2.1 of the TBT Agreement.

7.55 In its first written submission, Australia "reserves the right" to pursue these claims in the event that the European Communities is applying protection under the Regulation to GIs from another WTO Member or begins to do so.[92] Australia did not pursue these claims. Therefore, the Panel does not consider them any further.

9. Claim under Articles 1, 63.1 and 63.3 of the TRIPS Agreement

7.56 Australia includes in its request for establishment of a panel a claim that the Regulation is not applied in a transparent manner contrary to Articles 1, 63.1 and 63.3 of the TRIPS Agreement.

7.57 In its first written submission, Australia "reserves the right" to pursue the claim under Articles 63.1 and 63.3 in the event that the European Communities should in fact have in place criteria and/or guidelines for the purposes of making assessments and/or determinations under "various provisions" of the Regulation.[93] Australia did not pursue the claim regarding transparency under Articles 1, 63.1 or 63.3 of the TRIPS Agreement. Therefore, the Panel does not consider it any further.

10. Claim regarding application procedures under the TRIPS Agreement

7.58 The European Communities submits that Australia has not made a claim concerning the application procedures under the TRIPS Agreement but only under GATT 1994.[94] It does not indicate the reasons for its view.

7.59 Australia replies that it makes its claim in relation to the application procedures under the TRIPS Agreement as well and refers to passages in its first written submission.[95]

---

[89] Australia's first written submission, paras. 108-112.

[90] European Communities' first written submission, paras. 345-351.

[91] Australia's second oral statement, para. 99.

[92] Australia's first written submission, para. 65; noted by the European Communities in its first written submission, para. 227, fn. 108 and para. 239, fn. 112.

[93] Australia's first written submission, para. 66.

[94] European Communities' first written submission, para. 127; and its rebuttal submission, para. 122.

7.60 The Panel has reviewed the passages in Australia's first written submission, to which it refers. They appear under a heading which refers expressly to "national treatment" and specific national treatment provisions of the TRIPS Agreement. They include the following statements:

> 198.However, non-EC nationals seeking to register, and thus protect, an EC-defined GI in respect of a geographical location in the territory of another WTO Member pursuant to Regulation No. 2081/92 are not able to apply directly to the EC (whether to the Commission or another Community level body) to register an EC-defined GI.
>
> (...)
>
> 205. Moreover, notwithstanding any outward appearance of symmetry of treatment, the EC measure accords non-EC nationals less favourable treatment than that accorded to EC nationals in respect of the registration of an EC-defined GI from another WTO Member and in respect of the enforcement of trademark rights concerning the proposed registration of an EC-defined GI. The fact that the EC and its Member States have legally defined rights and obligations in relation to each other and to EC Member State nationals makes the registration and objection processes for EC nationals fundamentally different to those for non-EC nationals. Few other WTO Member governments have such legally defined relationships affecting the maintenance and enforcement of an intellectual property right, a right expressly recognised as a private right by the *TRIPS Agreement.*

7.61 The Panel considers that the claim in respect of the application procedures under the TRIPS Agreement, whilst it could have been expressed more clearly, does appear in these passages in Australia's first written submission. The references to persons seeking to register a GI, or the proposed registration of a GI, include the application procedures. The submission refers expressly to the lack of direct applications for non-EC nationals and the obligations of EC member States in the registration process, which are the basis for this claim. Any doubts which the European Communities had in this respect should have been dispelled by Australia's express confirmation in its first oral statement that it had made this argument in support of its claim that the measure as a whole does not accord national treatment to non-EC nationals. A respondent that chooses not to respond to a claim does so at its own risk.

7.62 The European Communities has suffered no prejudice to its ability to defend itself, because it has responded to overlapping claims presented by Australia based on the same aspects of the application procedures under GATT 1994 and the opposition procedures based on the same obligation under the TRIPS Agreement, as well as the same claim as made by the United States based on the same aspects of the application procedures under GATT 1994.

7.63 For these reasons, the Panel will consider this claim.[96]

11. Claim regarding the labelling requirement under GATT 1994

7.64 Australia claimed in its first written submission that the labelling requirement in Article 12(2) of the Regulation was inconsistent with Article 2.1 of the TBT Agreement, but it did not claim at that time that it was inconsistent with Article III:4 of GATT 1994.[97]

7.65 The European Communities responded to Australia's claim in its first written submission, arguing that Article 12(2) of the Regulation did not constitute a technical regulation within the meaning of Annex 1.1 of the

[95] Australia's first oral statement, para. 34, citing its first written submission, paras. 198-199 and 205.

[96] See paras. 7.276 and following below.

[97] Australia's first written submission, paras. 157-180 and 264.

TBT Agreement and was not otherwise incompatible with Article 2.1 of the TBT Agreement. It responded to the United States' claim that Article 12(2) was inconsistent with Article III:4 of GATT 1994 and noted that Australia did not make such a claim in this regard.[98]

7.66 In its rebuttal, Australia submitted that, should the Panel consider that Article 12(2) of the Regulation did not constitute a technical regulation within the meaning of Annex 1.1 of the TBT Agreement, it nevertheless accorded treatment less favourable to imported products inconsistently with Article III:4 of GATT 1994.[99]

7.67 In its second oral statement, the European Communities maintained that Australia had challenged Article 12(2) of the Regulation under Article 2.1 of the TBT Agreement and that the United States had challenged it under Article III:4 of GATT 1994.[100]

7.68 The Panel notes that Australia only asks the Panel to address Article 12(2) of the Regulation under Article III:4 of GATT 1994 should the Panel consider that Article 12(2) does not constitute a technical regulation within the meaning of Annex 1.1 of the TBT Agreement. This premise has not been met and further consideration is therefore unnecessary.[101]

12. Endorsement of arguments by another complainant

7.69 Australia, in its opening statement at the first substantive meeting with the Panel, formally endorsed certain comments made by the United States. These were "those comments concerning the rights required to be granted in respect of trademarks" and "the comments made by the United States concerning the EC's national treatment obligations under the TRIPS Agreement and GATT 1994." Australia also offered "additional comments" in its first oral statement.[102]

7.70 The Panel understands that these endorsements refer to comments made by the United States in its first opening oral statement. By virtue of these endorsements, the referenced comments of the United States form part of Australia's case. This was confirmed in Australia's opening statement at the second substantive meeting as follows:

> Our case in total would include of course all the material we have submitted to the Panel directly, or via endorsement of arguments made by the US in this dispute.[103]

7.71 However, the next day, in its closing statement, the representative of Australia said the following:

> Australia endorses all of the arguments put forward by the United States. Where there are differences between the complainants, these are a result of different understandings of the flawed measure at issue in this dispute and, in any case, are not material differences.[104]

7.72 The European Communities objected orally during the same meeting. It informed the Panel that it did not know which particular arguments Australia was endorsing because at times the United States' arguments contradicted Australia's arguments. Further, an overall endorsement did not respect its rights of defence.

---

[98] European Communities' first written submission, paras. 437-457, 469-482, 209 and fn. 100.

[99] Australia's rebuttal submission, para. 179.

[100] European Communities' second oral statement, para. 129.

[101] See para. 7.459 below.

[102] Australia's first oral statement, paras. 30 and 33.

[103] Australia's opening statement at the second substantive meeting, para. 2.

[104] Australia's closing statement at the second substantive meeting, second paragraph. In its comments on the descriptive part of this report, it requested that paragraph 2.15 be elaborated to make clear that Australia made this endorsement.

7.73 The Panel notes, by way of illustration, the following examples provided by the European Communities of differences between the arguments presented by Australia and the United States. First, Australia had argued as follows with respect to the interpretation of Article 24.5 of the TRIPS Agreement:

> [T]he right to use a trademark refers to the ongoing ability to use a trademark where rights to a trademark have been acquired through use in good faith.[105]

7.74 In its closing statement, Australia said that it endorsed arguments which include the following:

> '[T]he right to use a trademark' is not specifically limited in the text to trademarks whose rights are acquired through use (although it would appear to include such trademarks). Rather the obligation not to prejudice the right to use a trademark—to harm or damage the permitted or forbidden activity associated with application of a trademark to its purpose—would include an obligation with respect both to registered and non-registered trademarks (...)[106]

7.75 Australia's endorsement in its closing statement does not enable the Panel to ascertain the case that Australia asks it to consider on this key point (considered in Section VII:D of this report).

7.76 Second, when the Panel asked Australia whether it alleged that Article 12(2) of the Regulation provides any less favourable treatment to imported products besides labelling costs, Australia replied "No."[107] In its closing statement, Australia said that it endorsed arguments which included the following:

> The requirement of Article 12(2) that GIs for imported products, but not for domestic products, must be accompanied by a clear and visible indication of country of origin on the label is not simply a labeling cost issue. This requirement provides less favorable treatment to non-EC nationals and products in part because the non-EC GI, unlike the EC GI, is being burdened by an additional labeling requirement that is in the nature of a qualifier that detracts from the value of the GI (...)[108]

7.77 Australia's endorsement in its closing statement does not enable the Panel to ascertain the case that Australia asks it to consider on this point (considered in Section VII:B of this report). By way of further illustration, the Panel notes that the United States has presented arguments in support of its MFN claims which Australia chose not to pursue after the establishment of the Panel (mentioned in Section VII:A of this report).

7.78 Therefore, the Panel does not agree with Australia that there are no material differences between the complainants' respective cases. Australia's endorsement in its closing statement was sweeping and unlimited. More information was required in order to explain how it related to parts of Australia's case as presented prior to the end of the second substantive meeting with the Panel.

7.79 The Panel has examined the parties' arguments in the course of its assessment of the matter before it. However, it is not part of the Panel's function to participate in making a party's case, as this would compromise its duty to make an objective assessment. The Panel should not have to sift Australia's and the United States' respective arguments and make an assessment of where there are possible contradictions, where there is possible support for a claim and where the United States' arguments are irrelevant to Australia's claims, simply in order to establish what case Australia wished to bring. Further, the European Communities, as the respondent, is entitled to know the case that it has to answer from each complainant. It is unable to know with certainty what Australia's case actually is in the final analysis, as regards the endorsement in the closing

---

[105] Australia's response to Panel question No. 76.

[106] United States' response to Panel question No. 76.

[107] Australia's response to Panel question No. 52.

[108] United States' response to Panel question No. 120.

statement. Australia bore the responsibility to make its own case clear and, as regards the arguments covered by this endorsement, it has failed to discharge that responsibility.

7.80 The lateness of this endorsement also raises an issue of due process. Whilst the overlapping nature of the claims presented by the two complainants is a particular feature of this dispute, a respondent may choose to defend certain arguments in support of one claim, but not others. After the enlargement of one complainant's case at the end of the second substantive meeting, the respondent may understandably wish to respond to certain arguments for the first time. However, at that stage, it only has the opportunity to respond to written questions and comment on the other parties' responses, which may provide insufficient opportunity to respond to those arguments. This could compromise the respondent's ability to defend itself against each complainant.

7.81 There are no relevant specific circumstances in this proceeding to take into account. Australia had ample opportunity to make its case. It did not endorse all the United States' arguments earlier when it endorsed specific comments, either at the first substantive meeting or in its opening statement at the second substantive meeting.

7.82 Accordingly, the Panel does not consider that Australia's statement that it endorsed all of the United States' arguments was a sufficient basis for the Panel to consider that Australia's arguments as presented earlier were modified. Nevertheless, the Panel accepts Australia's earlier endorsements of certain comments of the United States, as described in paragraphs 7.69-7.70above, and takes note of the referenced comments.

13. Exhibits containing legislation of other Members

7.83 Australia requests that the Panel reject six exhibits submitted by the European Communities which consist of extracts of legislation of Australia and two third parties. This request is made on the grounds that the exhibits are allegedly not relevant.[109]

7.84 The Panel does not consider it appropriate to remove these exhibits from the record. They form part of the respondent's submission. To the extent that they lack evidentiary worth, they will suffer from that defect and the Panel will disregard them.

14. Request by a third party for a suggestion on ways to implement a recommendation

7.85 Mexico considers that "cochineal" should be removed from the list of products covered by the Regulation set out in its Annex II. As a third party, Mexico does not submit this as a claim, but requests that the Panel make a suggestion to this effect pursuant to the second sentence of Article 19.1 of the DSU. Mexico argues that there is no requirement that a request for such a suggestion must be forwarded by one of the parties. If the Panel does not deem it appropriate to make such a specific suggestion, the same result would be achieved by a suggestion that the European Communities withdraw the Regulation.[110]

7.86 The Panel takes note of Mexico's request. The issue of the product coverage of the Regulation is not challenged by the claims in this dispute and is therefore outside the Panel's terms of reference. However, Mexico's attention is drawn to Article 10.4 of the DSU.

---

[109] Australia's second oral statement, para. 104. Australia also requests that the Panel exclude these and other exhibits submitted by the European Communities consisting of extracts of legislation of other Members, on the grounds that it has failed to establish the meaning of the legal provisions within the legal order of those Members: see Australia's comments on the EC's responses to questions, paras. 2-4. This does not concern the record of the proceedings and can be dealt with, if necessary, in the consideration of the relevant claim.

[110] Annex C, para. 117.

15. Order of analysis of claims

7.87 The claims in this dispute are made under the TRIPS Agreement, GATT 1994 and the TBT Agreement. Certain claims under the TRIPS Agreement and GATT 1994 relate to the same aspects of the measure at issue.[111] There is no hierarchy between these two agreements, which appear in separate annexes to the WTO Agreement. One logical approach would be to begin in each instance with the TRIPS Agreement. The Panel will follow that order of analysis in this report.

7.88 The Panel will consider the claims relevant to each aspect of the measure in turn. The following sections of the findings are organized as follows:

- Section B National treatment claims
- Section C Trade-restrictiveness claim
- Section D Trademark claims
- Section E Other claims

B. National Treatment Claims

1. Availability of protection

(a) Do the conditions in Article 12(1) of the Regulation apply to WTO Members?

(i) main arguments of the parties[112]

7.89 Australia claims that GIs (as defined in the Regulation) located in the territory of a WTO Members outside the European Union can only be registered under the Regulation if the Member government in whose territory the GI is located is able and willing to meet the conditions in Article 12(1), which require it to adopt a system for GI protection that is equivalent to that in the European Communities and provide reciprocal protection to products from the European Communities.[113] It specifically endorses comments made by the United States in its first oral statement concerning the European Communities' national treatment obligations under the TRIPS Agreement and GATT 1994.[114]

7.90 Australia argues that the European Communities had consistently led other WTO Members to believe that Article 12(1) of the Regulation applied to them. It argues that the European Communities' interpretation of the Regulation does not invalidate the meaning of the provisions submitted by Australia, and is not supported by the text of Articles 12 to 12d, which only distinguish between nationals of WTO Members and other third countries where the express language so provides. The Regulation would not be interpreted by the European Court of Justice in light of the European Communities' international obligations because it does not state that it is intended to implement a particular GATT 1947 or WTO obligation.[115] Australia understands that the introductory phrase "[w]ithout prejudice to international agreements" was intended to allow for an international

---

[111] In its rebuttal, Australia also referred to a claim under GATT 1994 as an alternative to one of its claims under the TBT Agreement. The Panel's approach to this issue is discussed in paras. 7.64-7.68.

[112] The Panel's citations of parties' submissions in this report are not exhaustive. At times, parties' positions are elaborated in other submissions and responses to questions which are attached in full in Annexes A and B to this report.

[113] Australia's first written submission, paras. 165-168, 172-173 and 199.

[114] Australia's first oral statement, para. 33. The United States' first oral statement included *inter alia* comments that Article 12(1) does not suggest that WTO Members are excluded from its conditions and Article 12a sets out the sole process under the Regulation for the registration of non-EC GIs. If the conditions in Article 12(1) do not apply to WTO Members, then they may not be recognized under Article 12(3) and the Article 12a procedure is still not available for them.

[115] Australia's first oral statement, paras. 18-23; rebuttal submission, paras. 33-49; second oral statement, paras. 3-9.

agreement—whether bilateral or plurilateral—to incorporate different conditions but it does not, and was not intended to, incorporate the European Communities' obligations under the WTO Agreement.[116]

7.91 Australia argues that the Panel is not bound by the European Communities' interpretation of its own measure to any extent. The Panel's obligation is to appraise whether that interpretation is supported by the text of the Regulation, having regard to all relevant factors including the plain text of the relevant provisions, the European Communities' previous explanations of their meaning, its failure to explain inconsistencies in its new interpretation and the fact that the statements of EC representatives to the Panel do not create new legal obligations in Community law.[117]

7.92 The European Communities responds that the conditions in Article 12(1) of the Regulation do not apply to geographical areas located in WTO Members. The introductory phrase of Article 12(1) provides that it applies "[w]ithout prejudice to international agreements"—which include the WTO agreements. This is made clear by the eighth recital of the April 2003 amending Regulation which took specific account of the provision of the TRIPS Agreement. WTO Members are obliged to provide protection to geographical indications in accordance with Section 3 of Part II and the general provisions and basic principles of the TRIPS Agreement. For this reason, Article 12(1) and 12(3) do not apply to WTO Members. Accordingly, the registration of GIs from other WTO Members is subject to exactly the same conditions as the registration of GIs from the European Communities.[118]

7.93 The European Communities argues that the procedure under Article 12a of the Regulation is not limited to the cases covered by Article 12(3). The term "third country" in Articles 12 through 12d does or does not include WTO Members depending on the wording, context and objectives of each specific provision. The evidence of prior statements by Community officials does not contradict the European Communities' interpretation in this Panel proceeding and more recent statements support it. The statements made by the agents of the European Commission before the Panel commit and engage the European Communities but their intention is not to create new legal obligations in public international or in Community law. They are made on behalf of the European Communities as a whole and not only the Commission. Community legislation must, so far as possible, be interpreted in a manner that is consistent with international law, in particular where its provisions are intended specifically to give effect to an international agreement concluded by the Community, as indicated by the phrase "[w]ithout prejudice to international agreements." An interpretation that limited that phrase to bilateral agreements would largely deprive it of its useful value.[119]

7.94 The European Communities does not consider that the Panel is "bound" by the EC's interpretation of its own measure. However, it submits that the Panel must take due account of the fact that the Regulation is a measure of EC domestic law and establish its meaning as a factual element. This means that: (1) the burden of proof is on the complainant to establish the meaning of the measure. Given that the claim in the present dispute is based on the measure *per se* and not as applied, the complainant must establish "beyond doubt" that the measure entails a violation; (2) in making an objective assessment of the facts and the interpretation of the measure, the Panel should be guided by the rules of interpretation customary in the EC's domestic legal order; and (3) it is the EC's authorities who must interpret and apply the measure and therefore its explanations must be given considerable deference.[120]

---

[116] Australia's response to Panel question No. 6.

[117] Australia's response to Panel question No. 1; rebuttal submission, paras. 69-71.

[118] European Communities' first written submission, paras. 62-67; first oral statement, paras. 41-44; rebuttal submission, para. 52.

[119] European Communities' responses to Panel questions Nos. 7, 8, 15 and 16; rebuttal submission, paras. 11, 58-60 and 71-87; second oral statement, paras. 45 and 50.

[120] European Communities' response to Panel question No. 1; second oral statement, paras. 5-7.

(ii) main arguments of third parties

7.95 Argentina asserts that the conditions of equivalence and reciprocity apply to GIs located in all third countries. It is unconvinced by the European Communities' explanation of its measure. If its intention had been to distinguish between WTO Members and other third countries, it could have done so more explicitly.[121]

7.96 Brazil asserts that the conditions of equivalence and reciprocity apply to GIs located in all third countries. It considers that the European Commission's interpretation of the phrase "without prejudice to international agreements" would not necessarily withstand scrutiny by a judicial body and is unlikely given that the provisions that refer to "third countries" would have been drafted with only a handful of non-WTO Members in mind. The reference in Article 12(2) indicates that third countries means all third countries outside the European Communities, although in Articles 12a(2) and 12d(1) it could mean non-WTO Members. The EC's interpretation could *a contrario* indicate a recognition that the equivalence and reciprocity conditions violate national treatment obligations in GATT 1994 and TRIPS.[122]

7.97 Canada considers that Article 12 of the Regulation, read in context with Articles 12a, 12b and 12d, cannot support the interpretation advanced by the European Communities. The ambiguous reference to "international agreements" is insufficient to counter the clear wording. There would not appear to be an alternative legal basis for filing applications for countries outside the European Communities besides Article 12 due to the wording of Article 12a(1). Articles 12b and 12d refer to "WTO Members" and "third countries" which suggests no differential application to "third countries" in Articles 12 and 12a. The European Communities indicated that Article 12 applied to all WTO Members in a statement in September 2002 to the Council for TRIPS.[123]

7.98 China argues that the European Communities' interpretation is not accompanied by any supporting evidence and that there is no regulatory language in the provisions to exclude expressly the application of these provisions to WTO Members. The preamble to the April 2003 amending Regulation refers specifically to WTO Members in relation to the right of objection, but does not exclude WTO Members from the equivalence and reciprocity conditions. Had the drafters intended that it should not apply, they would have inserted a clause to that effect in the preamble. The European Communities appears to have admitted that portions of Article 12, regarding product specifications and inspection, do apply to WTO Members.[124]

7.99 Colombia submits that, if the European Communities' interpretation of "without prejudice to international agreements" is correct, the Panel should recommend that it modify its legislation in such a way that that phrase acquires the scope and meaning that are assigned to it in the EC's first written submission.[125]

7.100 Mexico submits that the language of Article 12(1) of the Regulation is precise and unequivocal. Third countries must satisfy conditions of equivalence and reciprocity in order to receive the same protection as EC member States.[126]

7.101 New Zealand submits that the European Communities' interpretation of Article 12(1) and (3) and the phrase "without prejudice to international agreements" is novel and does not withstand close scrutiny. It runs counter to the usual meaning of that phrase and effectively admits that requiring nationals of WTO Members to satisfy the procedures in Article 12(1) and (3) would be contrary to WTO obligations. It is inconsistent with the wording of the Regulation itself and, if Article 12(3) does not apply to WTO Members, then the application

[121] Annex C, para. 17.
[122] Annex C, paras. 23-24.
[123] Annex C, paras. 47-50.
[124] Annex C, para. 72.
[125] Annex C, para. 99.
[126] Annex C, para. 110.

procedure in Article 12a would not either. This is the first time that this interpretation has been raised by the European Communities. The alternative interpretation adopted by the complainant is consistent with the wording of the Regulation.[127]

7.102 Chinese Taipei asserts that the conditions of equivalence and reciprocity apply to GIs located in all third countries.[128]

(iii) consideration by the Panel

7.103 The first issue in this dispute concerns the conditions for registration of GIs under the Regulation. It is not disputed that a GI located outside the European Communities has never been registered nor the subject of an application made under the Regulation, and that no attempt has ever been made to file an application to register such a GI under the Regulation.[129] Therefore, the provisions concerning the protection of such GIs have never been applied in a particular instance. However, Australia challenges this aspect of the Regulation "as such."

7.104 The parties agree that the conditions set out in Article 12(1) of the Regulation do not apply to the protection of GIs located within the territory of the European Communities. They disagree as to whether they apply to the protection of GIs located in other WTO Members. Australia claims that they do so apply, and it is not disputed that the European Communities never made a clear statement that these conditions did not so apply prior to this panel proceeding. However, the European Communities responds in its submissions to the Panel that the conditions only apply to third countries that are not WTO Members.

7.105 The European Communities' position, as expressed in its submissions to the Panel, has been welcomed in principle by the complainants and by two third parties.[130] If Australia were satisfied with this position, it would provide a positive solution to many of the national treatment claims in this dispute. However, Australia is not persuaded that the European Communities would be able to implement the position that it has presented to the Panel in light of the terms of the Regulation on its face, allegedly prior inconsistent statements by the European Communities in the Council for TRIPS, the Commission's Guide to the Regulation and elsewhere, and inconsistent statements made during this Panel proceeding by the European Communities.[131] Australia submits that only formal amendments of the provisions of the Regulation could ensure their interpretation in a manner consistent with the European Communities' obligations.[132] Therefore, although the European Communities submits that the Regulation already is in conformity with its obligations, the Panel is obliged to proceed with its assessment of the national treatment claims based on Article 12(1) of the Regulation.

7.106 The fact that this is an "as such" challenge, and that the parties disagree sharply on whether the European Communities' interpretation of its own measure is correct, requires the Panel to conduct a detailed examination of the Regulation. In doing so, the Panel examines the Regulation solely for the purpose of determining its conformity with relevant obligations under the WTO covered agreements.[133] Although the Regulation is part of the European Communities' domestic law, the parties agree that the Panel is not bound by the European Communities' interpretation of its provisions.[134] Rather, the Panel is obliged, in accordance with its mandate, to make an objective assessment of the meaning of the relevant provisions of the Regulation. In this context, the Panel is mindful that, objectively, a Member is normally well placed to explain the meaning of its

[127] Annex C, paras. 126-128.

[128] Annex C, paras. 171-172.

[129] See the parties' respective responses to Panel questions Nos. 11 and 12 and third party comments in Annex C. For the sake of brevity, the Panel refers to a name that refers to a geographical area located in a Member as a GI located in that Member.

[130] See para. 7 of the United States' first oral statement, endorsed by Australia, first oral statement, para. 33, and summaries of arguments of Brazil and Canada, Annex C, paras. 24 and 47.

[131] Australia's first oral statement, para. 19; rebuttal submission, paras. 32-49.

[132] Australia's rebuttal submission, para. 72.

[133] This was the approach of the Appellate Body in *India – Patents (US)*, paras. 65-68.

[134] Parties' respective responses to Panel question No. 1.

own law. To the extent that either party advances a particular interpretation of a provision of the Regulation at issue, it bears the burden of proof that its interpretation is correct.

7.107 Turning to the Regulation, the Panel notes that it applies to the registration of "designations of origin" and "geographical indications," as defined.[135] For ease of reference, and without prejudice to their consistency with the definition of a geographical indication in Article 22.1 of the TRIPS Agreement, we shall refer to them both as "GIs" in this report, except where the context requires otherwise.

7.108 Certain facts are agreed. The parties agree that the Regulation contains two sets of detailed procedures for the registration of GIs for agricultural products and foodstuffs. The first procedure, in Articles 5 through 7, applies to the names of geographical areas located in the European Communities.[136] It has been part of the Regulation since its adoption in 1992, although it has been amended subsequently in certain respects. The second procedure, principally found in Articles 12a and 12b, applies to the names of geographical areas located in third countries outside the European Communities.[137] It was inserted in the Regulation in April 2003. A third procedure for registration of GIs protected under the national law of EC member States was formerly available under Article 17, but was deleted in April 2003. A fourth possibility is registration by means of an international agreement, discussed below.

7.109 The parties disagree as to whether the second of these procedures is subject to additional conditions found in Article 12(1) of the Regulation that do not apply to the first procedure. Article 12(1) provides as follows:

> 1. Without prejudice to international agreements, this Regulation may apply to an agricultural product or foodstuff from a third country provided that:
>
> - the third country is able to give guarantees identical or equivalent to those referred to in Article 4,
>
> - the third country concerned has inspection arrangements and a right to objection equivalent to those laid down in this Regulation,
>
> - the third country concerned is prepared to provide protection equivalent to that available in the Community to corresponding agricultural products or foodstuffs coming from the Community.

7.110 Article 12 has been part of the Regulation since its adoption in 1992, although it was amended in April 2003 by the insertion of the requirement of a right of objection equivalent to those laid down in the Regulation, when Article 12(3) and Articles 12a through 12d, including the second procedure described above, were inserted. It is not in dispute that many WTO Members, including Australia, do *not* satisfy the conditions set out in Article 12(1).

7.111 The factual issue for the Panel to decide is whether the conditions set out in Article 12(1) apply to the availability of protection for GIs located in WTO Members. In other words, the factual issue is whether the

---

[135] The terms "designation of origin" and "geographical indication" are defined in Article 2(2) of the Regulation and they and the abbreviations "PDO" and "PGI" are found in Article 4 of the Regulation (Exhibits COMP-1b and EC-1). Detailed rules of application of the Regulation are found in Commission Regulation (EEC) No. 2037/93 (Exhibit COMP-2).

[136] This is apparent from Article 5(4) of the Regulation which provides that "[t]he application shall be sent to the Member State in which the geographical area is located," and was confirmed by the European Communities in its response to Panel question No. 2. The European Communities also noted that Articles 12a and 12b refer to certain provisions in Articles 5 to 7 as well.

[137] This is apparent from Article 12a(1) of the Regulation which provides that "if a group of a natural or legal person ... in a third country wishes to have a name registered under this Regulation it shall send a registration application to the authorities in the country in which the geographical area is located," and was confirmed by the European Communities in its response to Panel question No. 2.

registration procedure in Articles 12a and 12b is available for GIs located in WTO Members that do not satisfy the conditions in Article 12(1).

7.112 Australia presents two types of evidence. The first is the text of the Regulation and the second consists of the European Communities' own statements concerning the Regulation prior to, and during, this Panel proceeding.

7.113 The Panel begins its analysis by reviewing the measure on its face.[138] The procedure in Articles 12a and 12b of the Regulation begins with the filing of an application under paragraph 1 of Article 12a and continues with its initial examination under paragraph 2. The text of paragraph 1 begins "[i]n the case provided for in Article 12(3)," which immediately limits the availability of the procedure according to the terms of Article 12(3). The text of paragraph 2 of Article 12a begins "[i]f the third country referred to in paragraph 1 deems ..." which confirms that this aspect of the procedure is limited in the same way as paragraph 1. Paragraph 1 of Article 12b sets out the next step in the same procedure and refers to the registration request sent by "the third country," which is the third country described in Article 12b(2).

7.114 Article 12(3) of the Regulation provides as follows:

> 3. The Commission shall examine, at the request of the country concerned, and in accordance with the procedure laid down in Article 15 whether a third country satisfies the equivalence conditions and offers guarantees within the meaning of paragraph 1 as a result of its national legislation. Where the Commission decision is in the affirmative, the procedure set out in Article 12a shall apply.

7.115 The case provided for in this paragraph is clear: it refers to a third country which satisfies the conditions in Article 12(1). The initial clause of Article 12a, as confirmed by the chain of cross-references in Articles 12a(2) and 12b(1), therefore limits the procedure in Articles 12a and 12b to such third countries. No other provision in Article 12a or 12b indicates that that procedure is available for the registration of GIs located in a third country which does not satisfy the conditions in Article 12(1), even if it is a WTO Member. This is consistent with Article 12b(2), which provides for objections in the same procedure, and expressly distinguishes between a "Member State of the European Union or a WTO member" and "a third country meeting the equivalence conditions of Article 12(3)." The implication is that a WTO Member is not necessarily a third country meeting those conditions.[139]

7.116 The only other provision in the Regulation which could indicate the possibility of registration of GIs located in a third country which does *not* satisfy the conditions in Article 12(1) is the introductory phrase of Article 12(1) itself, which prefaces the conditions with the clause "[w]ithout prejudice to international agreements." The European Communities concedes that the application of the conditions in Article 12(1) of the Regulation would prejudice its obligations under Article III:4 of GATT 1994 and submits to the Panel that, as a consequence, it would not apply those conditions to GIs located in WTO Members. Nevertheless, it does not follow that the procedure in Articles 12a and 12b is available for the registration of GIs located in WTO Members. That procedure is limited to third countries which satisfy the conditions in Article 12(1) and there is no other procedure in the Regulation available for WTO Members that do not satisfy those conditions. There is the possibility of protection pursuant to an international agreement, but no existing international agreement either incorporates the procedure under Articles 12a and 12b of the Regulation or contains an application and registration procedure for GIs located in all WTO Members. In particular, neither GATT 1994 nor the TRIPS Agreement contains any such procedure.

---

[138] This was the Appellate Body's approach to an "as such" claim in its report on *US – Corrosion-Resistant Steel Sunset Review*, at para. 168.

[139] The second sentence of Article 12(3) provides that the procedure in Article 12a shall apply to third countries which the Commission decides satisfy the conditions in Article 12(1). This sentence alone does not exclude the possibility that the procedure might apply to other third countries which do not satisfy those conditions, but there is no other provision in the Regulation to that effect.

7.117 Other provisions in the Regulation may also shed light on this issue. Article 12d(1), which provides a right of objection to registration of GIs located in the European Communities, distinguishes twice between persons from "a WTO Member country or a third country recognized under the procedure provided for in Article 12(3)."[140] This expressly grants a right of objection to persons from WTO Members and is a further indication that where the Regulation refers to "a third country recognized under the procedure provided for in Article 12(3)" it does not include a WTO Member unless it has been recognized under that procedure.

7.118 Four other provisions also refer to "a third country recognized under the procedure provided for in Article 12(3)" (or analogous terms) without referring to a WTO Member: Article 5(5) on registration of GIs that straddle the external border of the European Communities, Article 6(6) on homonymous GIs, Article 10(3) on inspection structures and Article 13(5) on the coexistence of registered and unregistered GIs. The European Communities' view of Article 10(3) is that it includes WTO Members[141], and there seems to be no reason why the other three provisions should exclude WTO Members. These provisions seem to confirm that WTO Members are included in the term "third countries" and therefore require recognition under the procedure provided for in Article 12(3).

7.119 The preamble of the Regulation, which has contained the conditions in Article 12(1) more or less in their current form since the original version was adopted in 1992, sets out its justification. The 19th recital reads as follows:

> Whereas provision should be made for trade with third countries offering equivalent guarantees for the issue and inspection of geographical indications or designations of origin granted on their territory;[142]

7.120 The phrase "equivalent guarantees for the issue and inspection" of GIs is a clear reference to the conditions in Article 12(1). There is no recital referring to the possibility of GIs located in any other third countries which do not satisfy these conditions.

7.121 The preamble to the April 2003 amending Regulation, which modified Article 12 and inserted a detailed procedure for applications and objections from third countries in Articles 12a through 12d, sets out the justification for the amendments as follows:

> (8) The Agreement on Trade-Related Aspects of Intellectual Property Rights (TRIPS Agreement 1994, contained in Annex 1C to the Agreement establishing the World Trade Organisation contains detailed provisions on the existence, acquisition, scope, maintenance and enforcement of intellectual property rights.
>
> (9) The protection provided by registration under Regulation (EEC) No 2081/92 is open to third countries' names by reciprocity and under equivalence conditions as provided for in Article 12 of that Regulation. That Article should be supplemented so as to guarantee that the Community registration procedure is available to the countries meeting those conditions.
>
> (10) Article 7 of Regulation (EEC) No 2081/92 specifies how objections are to be made and dealt with. To satisfy the obligation resulting from Article 22 of the TRIPS Agreement it should be made clear that in this matter nationals of WTO member countries are covered

140 This is considered in detail in para. 7.382 below.

141 European Communities' responses to Panel question Nos. 126(a) and (b).

142 Exhibits COMP-1b and EC-1.

> by these arrangements and that the provisions in question apply without prejudice to international agreements, as provided for in Article 12 of the said Regulation. (...)[143]

7.122 Paragraph 8 recalls the subject-matter of the TRIPS Agreement without elaborating on its relevance to the Regulation. This clarifies the reference to Article 22 of the TRIPS Agreement in paragraph 10 but it is not clear whether it also relates to paragraph 9. In any event, on the European Communities' later interpretation, the TRIPS Agreement is not relevant to the WTO-consistency of the conditions provided for in Article 12, as referred to in paragraph 9. Rather, the European Communities submits that GATT 1994 ensures their WTO-consistency. GATT 1994 is not recited in the preamble.

7.123 Paragraph 9 contains no qualifier referring to WTO Members, which appears to confirm the position that the conditions in Article 12(1) apply to the availability of protection of GIs located in third countries and that the registration procedure in Articles 12a and 12b is not available for GIs located in WTO Members that do not satisfy those conditions.

7.124 Paragraph 10 includes the phrase "without prejudice to international agreements, as provided for in Article 12," but it only relates to the right of objection granted to WTO Members' nationals. This is a clear reference to Articles 12b(2) and 12d(1), which were inserted by the amending Regulation. It can be noted that they are the only two provisions in the current version of the Regulation that expressly refer to a "WTO Member," where they also distinguish a WTO Member from a third country recognized under Article 12(3).

7.125 In the Panel's view, the meaning and content of these aspects of the Regulation, together with the amending Regulation, are sufficiently clear on their face for Australia to have discharged its burden of proof of establishing that, under the Regulation "as such," the availability of protection for GIs located in WTO Members is contingent upon satisfaction of the conditions set out in Article 12(1) and recognition by the Commission under Article 12(3).[144]

7.126 There is no supporting evidence of the meaning of these aspects of the Regulation in the form of an interpretation of the relevant provisions by the European Court of Justice or any other domestic court.[145] This is partly explained by the facts that no requests for registration of foreign GIs have been made under the Regulation and that Articles 12a through 12d were inserted only recently, in April 2003.

7.127 Australia also presents evidence consisting of various statements by executive authorities of the European Communities which contain interpretations of the Regulation. The Panel considers that such statements can be useful as, objectively, a WTO Member is normally well placed to explain the meaning of its own domestic law.[146] However, the usefulness of any particular statement will depend on its contents and the circumstances in which it was made. The Panel has weighed the evidence and considers that one statement in particular, in light of the clarity of its contents and the official capacity in which it was delivered, is highly relevant to the issue at hand.

7.128 In a lengthy statement to the Council for TRIPS in September 2002 (prior to the insertion of Articles 12a through 12d), the European Communities specifically responded to the following view expressed by a group of Members, including Australia:

> [U]nder the current EC regulations, the EC does not appear to provide protection for non-EC geographical indications (i.e., place names of other WTO Members), except on the basis of

143 Exhibit COMP-1h.

144 The European Commission has not recognized any other country under this procedure: see European Communities' response to Panel question No. 10. It is not contested that the Commission cannot recognize a third country under Article 12(3) that does not satisfy the equivalence and reciprocity conditions.

145 European Communities' response to Panel question No. 19.

146 See para. 7.106 above.

bilateral agreements, or if the EC has determined that a country has a system for geographical indications that is equivalent to the detailed system of the EC.[147]

7.129 The European Communities introduced the relevant part of its response as follows:

> (...) I would like to address one issue that is raised regarding the fact that the EU register for GIs on foodstuffs does not allow the registration of foreign GI unless it is determined that a third country has an equivalent or reciprocal system of GI protection.[148]

7.130 The Panel notes that the European Communities was emphatic at that time that registration systems should primarily be aimed at domestic GIs and it quoted the legislation of several other WTO Members which allegedly do not register foreign GIs without an international agreement.[149] This statement by the European Communities in September 2002 to the Council for TRIPS therefore appears to support Australia's interpretation of the Regulation on its face.

7.131 The European Communities argues that the interpretation set forth in its September 2002 statement to the Council for TRIPS "is not incompatible with the text of Regulation 2081/92 as in force at the time it was made or with the statements of the EC in the present case." In its view, its intention at that time was not primarily to explain the EC system for the protection of geographical indications and its statement did not take account of amendments made in April 2003.

7.132 In the Panel's view, the European Communities' September 2002 statement was very clear in its interpretation of the relevant point of the Regulation. Further, nothing in the April 2003 amending Regulation appears to render that statement incompatible with the current version of the Regulation. In fact, the Panel's examination of the insertion of Article 12(3) and Articles 12a through 12d confirms that the conditions in Article 12(1) remain applicable on the same terms.

7.133 Australia also refers to the explanation of the amendments given by the European Commission at the time it proposed them, in March 2002. The Panel considers that this evidence corroborates the previous statement because of the clarity of its contents and the capacity in which it was made. In a press release, the Commission explained that, in order to comply with the TRIPS Agreement, it proposed to extend the right of objection to certain other WTO Member country nationals and further stated:

> Beyond mere TRIPS consistency, the Commission proposes important amendments designed to promote the EU system of denominations of origin as a model to the rest of the world. The driving idea behind is the wish to improve protection of European quality products also outside the EU. As the EU cannot force non-EU countries to do so, they would be invited to do so on a 'reciprocal basis'. If a non-EU country introduced an 'equivalent system' including the right of objection for the EU and the commitment to protect EU names on their territory, the EU would offer a specific protection to register their products for the EU market.[150]

The references to a reciprocal basis and an equivalent system are clear references to the conditions in Article 12(1) of the Regulation.

7.134 In its submissions to the Panel, the European Communities rejects that interpretation and submits that, due to the introductory phrase of Article 12(1) of the Regulation, "[w]ithout prejudice to international

---

[147] Communication from Australia, Canada, Guatemala, New Zealand, Paraguay, the Philippines and the United States (IP/C/W/360) para. 4.

[148] See the statement in the Annex to the minutes of that meeting in document IP/C/M/37/Add.1.

[149] *Ibid.*

[150] European Commission: "Food quality: Commission proposes better protection for geographical names" (Press Release Reference: IP/02/422), Brussels, 15 March 2002 set out in Exhibit AUS-4.

agreements," the conditions in Article 12(1) do not apply to the availability of protection for GIs located in WTO Members. It refers to a statement it made to the Council for TRIPS in June 2004 in the days before the first substantive meeting of this Panel[151] and a second edition of the Commission's Guide to the Regulation published in August 2004 in the days prior to the second substantive meeting of this Panel.[152] It advises that "[t]he guide was not prepared in connection with the Panel proceedings."[153]

7.135 The Panel recalls its reasoning in paragraph 7.116 above, and reiterates its view that, even if the phrase "[w]ithout prejudice to international agreements" had the effect of subjecting the conditions in Article 12(1) to the terms of GATT 1994 or the TRIPS Agreement, those agreements do not contain a procedure for applications and registration for GIs located in all WTO Members. WTO Members would still have to satisfy the conditions in Article 12(1) in order for their GIs to gain access to the procedure in Articles 12a and 12b.

7.136 The European Communities admits that this would be a "nonsensical result."[154] However, it is unable to provide a satisfactory explanation as to how this result could be avoided in light of the wording of Article 12a, which begins "[i]n the case provided for in Article 12(3)." The European Communities points out that Article 12(3) refers to the conditions in Article 12(1) and since, in its view, those conditions do not apply to WTO Members, the procedure in Article 12(3) and the reference in Article 12a do not apply to them either.[155]

7.137 The Panel agrees that Article 12(3) provides for a Commission decision on whether a third country satisfies the conditions in Article 12(1) and accepts that, if those conditions do not apply to a third country, there would be no relevant decision under Article 12(3). Yet this does not alter the text of Article 12a which applies "[i]n the case provided for in Article 12(3)." Article 12a does not appear, on its face, to apply to the registration of a GI located in a third country, including a WTO Member, which is not recognized under Article 12(3). For these reasons, the Panel is not persuaded that the European Communities' interpretation is correct.

7.138 It is not necessary for the purposes of this dispute to determine which are the precise international agreements covered by the phrase "[w]ithout prejudice to international agreements." It suffices to note that there is a plausible alternative interpretation that it refers to bilateral agreements under which the European Communities would protect specific GIs.[156] The European Communities does not exclude this, but argues that there is no reason why *only* such specific agreements should be covered.[157] There are currently no such bilateral agreements for agricultural products and foodstuffs, although one has been foreshadowed in a joint declaration with Switzerland.[158]

7.139 In any event, the Panel is not persuaded by the European Communities' explanations during this Panel proceeding of the phrase "[w]ithout prejudice to international agreements" as used in Article 12(1) of the Regulation. At the first substantive meeting, in support of its first defence, it provided the following explanation of that phrase:

---

151 See the minutes of that meeting in IP/C/M/44, paras. 62-63, quoted in the European Communities' response to Panel question No. 16 prior to circulation and also set out in Exhibit EC-83. Responses given by the European Communities to questions posed by two other WTO Members in the TRIPS Council review of its legislation in 1996-1997, before the insertion of Articles 12a through 12d, are inconclusive on this issue as they contain no clear statement that equivalence and reciprocity conditions do not apply to the registration of GIs located outside the European Communities in countries without a bilateral agreement: see European Communities' response to Panel question No. 97.

152 Exhibit EC-64.

153 European Communities' response to Panel question No. 96.

154 European Communities' second oral statement, para. 48.

155 European Communities' response to Panel question No. 7.

156 Australia's response to Panel question No. 6.

157 European Communities' rebuttal submission, para. 69.

158 European Communities' response to Panel question No. 21.

> (...) Such international agreements include the WTO Agreements. This is made clear by the 8th recital of Regulation 692/2003, which amended the procedures for the registration of non-EC geographical indications, and in this context took specific account of the provisions of the TRIPS.
>
> WTO Members are obliged to provide protection to geographical indications in accordance with Section 3 of Part II and the general provisions and basic principles of the TRIPS Agreement. For this reason, Article 12 (1) and (3) of Regulation 2081/92 do not apply to WTO Members. (...)[159]

7.140 This explanation was also reflected in a June 2004 statement that the European Communities made to the Council for TRIPS[160] and the August 2004 edition of the Commission's Guide to the Regulation[161].

7.141 At the same time, the European Communities' second defence was that the conditions in Article 12(1) of the Regulation were not inconsistent with the national treatment obligations in the TRIPS Agreement, essentially because they discriminate according to the location of GIs and not according to the nationality of persons with rights in relation to GIs.[162]

7.142 It was not clear how these two defences could be reconciled. If the first defence implied that the conditions did not apply because they would prejudice the European Communities' national treatment obligations under the TRIPS Agreement, it would have contradicted the second defence that these conditions were not inconsistent with the national treatment obligations in the TRIPS Agreement. The Panel sought clarification from the European Communities by posing the question "does the EC contest that equivalence and reciprocity conditions such as those under Article 12(1) and (3) of Regulation (EC) No. 2081/92, if applied to other WTO Members, would be inconsistent with the national treatment obligations in the TRIPS Agreement and/or Article III:4 of the GATT 1994?." The European Communities declined to give a specific answer to the Panel's question and concluded as follows:

> As regards the specific conditions contained in Article 12 (1) of Regulation 2081/92, the EC has already confirmed that it does not apply these to WTO Members. For this reason, the EC considers that the question whether these conditions are inconsistent with the national treatment obligations of the TRIPS Agreement and the GATT does not arise.[163]

7.143 Australia then submitted that the European Communities had impliedly admitted that the conditions in Article 12(1) of the Regulation were contrary to WTO obligations.[164]

7.144 The Panel again sought clarification at the second substantive meeting, by asking which precise obligations under an international agreement would be prejudiced by the application of the specific conditions in Article 12(1) of the Regulation to WTO Members. The European Communities responded that it was its obligations under Article III:4 of GATT 1994, but not Article 3.1 of the TRIPS Agreement, because the

---

[159] European Communities' first written submission, paras. 65-66. It reiterated this in its first oral statement, at para. 43, and confirmed it in its response to Panel question No. 3 adding as follows:
"At the time that Regulation 2081/92 was adopted, the GATT was one of the agreements to which the 'without prejudice' clause applied. Moreover, at the time that Regulation 2081/92 was adopted, the TRIPS Agreement was in the final phases of its negotiation. It was therefore the objective that the 'without prejudice' clause should also apply to the TRIPS and other WTO agreements resulting from the Uruguay Round."

[160] See the minutes of that meeting in document IP/C/M/44, paras. 62-63, cited in response to Panel questions Nos. 16 and 95 and set out in Exhibit EC-83.

[161] Set out in Exhibit EC-64.

[162] European Communities' first written submission, paras. 123-126; first oral statement, paras. 46-47; rebuttal submission, para. 43.

[163] European Communities' response to Panel question No. 20.

[164] Australia's first oral statement, para. 23; rebuttal submission, para. 177; second oral statement, para. 61.

Regulation did not involve any discrimination between nationals. It later confirmed this in writing.[165] Therefore, to the extent that the European Communities' explanation of the phrase "[w]ithout prejudice to international agreements" as used in Article 12(1) of the Regulation relies on the TRIPS Agreement, the European Communities has expressly denied that the phrase refers to its own obligations and the Panel does not consider that possible explanation further.[166]

7.145 At this time, the European Communities' explanation of the phrase "[w]ithout prejudice to international agreements" as used in Article 12(1) of the Regulation relies on GATT 1994. In light of the European Communities' analysis that this phrase ensures that "should a conflict between the two acts or provisions occur, then the act or provision to which the 'without prejudice' reference is made prevails"[167], it is clear that this explanation depends on the view that the equivalence and reciprocity conditions are inconsistent with the European Communities' obligations under Article III:4 of GATT 1994. However, this is difficult to reconcile with the European Communities' earlier view that the question whether these conditions are inconsistent with the national treatment obligations of GATT does not arise, quoted at paragraph 7.142 above. It was also omitted from the earlier explanation that the conditions did not apply because of obligations under the TRIPS Agreement, quoted at paragraph 7.139 above. Further, the evidence submitted by the European Communities provides no additional support for this explanation, as the amending Regulation recites the TRIPS Agreement but not GATT 1994, and the evidence identified at paragraph 7.140 above also reflects the explanation quoted at paragraph 7.139 above.

7.146 For all these reasons, the Panel is not persuaded by the European Communities' explanations of the phrase "[w]ithout prejudice to international agreements" as used in Article 12(1) of the Regulation.

7.147 The Panel takes note that there are various executive authorities involved in the implementation of the Regulation, including representatives of EC member States. Article 15 of the Regulation provides for a regulatory procedure under which the Commission shall be assisted by a regulatory committee composed of the representatives of the EC member States and chaired by the representative of the Commission, who does not vote.[168]

7.148 The European Communities' delegation to this panel proceeding confirms that the submissions made by agents of the European Commission before the Panel commit and engage the European Communities.[169] It also indicates that Community laws are generally not executed through authorities at Community level but rather through recourse to the authorities of its member States which, in such a situation, "act *de facto* as organs of the Community, for which the Community would be responsible under WTO law and international law in general."[170] The Panel accepts this explanation of what amounts to the European Communities' domestic constitutional arrangements and accepts that the submissions of the European Communities' delegation to this panel proceeding are made on behalf of all the executive authorities of the European Communities.[171]

7.149 The parties have presented evidence with respect to the approach that would be taken by the European Court of Justice if the executive authorities registered a GI that was not the subject of an international

---

[165] European Communities' response to Panel question No. 94.

[166] In the same question, the Panel also sought clarification of the relevance of the reference to the TRIPS Agreement in the European Communities' first written submission, quoted at paragraph 7.139 above. The European Communities' response does not provide a clear explanation of the relationship between the obligations of WTO Members under the TRIPS Agreement and the applicability of the equivalence and reciprocity conditions under the EC's GI Regulation: see its response to question No. 94(b), second paragraph.

[167] European Communities' rebuttal submission, para. 55.

[168] This procedure is described in detail in paras. 7.388 to 7.389 below.

[169] European Communities' responses to Panel questions Nos. 15 and 18.

[170] European Communities' second oral statement, para. 148.

[171] The delegation of the European Communities to the meetings with the Panel was composed of officials of the European Commission and delegates of certain EC member States. The European Communities indicated that its statements to the Panel "commit and engage the European Communities:" see response to Panel question No. 15. The Panel accepts that explanation, for the same reasons as those explained by the Panel in *US – Section 301 Trade Act*, at para. 7.123. See also, in this regard, paras. 7.304, 7.372 and 7.399 of the present report.

agreement and that was located in a third country that did not satisfy the conditions in Article 12(1) of the Regulation. The European Communities submits that, according to the settled case law of the European Court of Justice:

> Community legislation must, so far as possible, be interpreted in a manner that is consistent with international law, in particular where its provisions are intended specifically to give effect to an international agreement concluded by the Community.[172]

7.150 The Panel is not persuaded that it is possible to interpret the relevant aspects of the Regulation in the manner advanced by the European Communities in these proceedings, for the reasons already given. The Panel also notes that the basic Regulation does not indicate that its provisions are intended specifically to give effect to any international agreement concluded by the Community. Whilst the April 2003 amending Regulation recites the TRIPS Agreement, it would only seem to do so to justify extending the right of objection to nationals of WTO Members. In any case, the European Communities' later explanation is that the interpretation must take account of GATT 1994, which is not mentioned at all, rather than the TRIPS Agreement.

7.151 Article 11 of the DSU requires that "a panel should make an objective assessment of the matter before it, including an objective assessment of the facts of the case ...." In our view, our duty to make an *objective* assessment prohibits us from accepting the interpretation of the applicability of the conditions in Article 12(1) of the Regulation presented by the European Communities in this proceeding, for the reasons set out above.

7.152 Therefore, the Panel concludes that Australia has made a prima facie case that the equivalence and reciprocity conditions in Article 12(1) of the Regulation apply to the availability of protection for GIs located in third countries, including WTO Members. In other words, the registration procedure in Articles 12a and 12b is not available for GIs located in third countries, including WTO Members, that do not satisfy the conditions in Article 12(1). The European Communities has not succeeded in rebutting that case.

7.153 The Panel wishes to note that it has evaluated the European Communities' interpretation of the applicability of the equivalence and reciprocity conditions and not found it reflected in the text of the Regulation. Had this interpretation been reflected in the text of the Regulation, the Panel could have reached a different conclusion which would have rendered it unnecessary to continue with an examination of the consistency of those conditions with the provisions of the covered agreements.

(b) National treatment under the TRIPS Agreement

(i) main arguments of the parties

7.154 Australia claims that the Regulation is inconsistent with Article 3.1 of the TRIPS Agreement and Article 2(1) of the Paris Convention (1967), as incorporated by Article 2.1 of the TRIPS Agreement, because it imposes conditions of *reciprocity* and *equivalence* on the availability of protection. Unless the WTO Member government in whose territory the geographical location at issue is situated is able and willing to meet the equivalence and reciprocity conditions, non-EC nationals are not able to access the rights available to EC nationals, including the advantages of registration.[173] Australia, at the first substantive meeting, expressly endorsed the comments made by the United States concerning the EC's national treatment obligations under the TRIPS Agreement.[174]

---

[172] European Communities' response to Panel question No. 15 quoting Case C-341/95, *Bettati*, [1998] ECR I-4355, para. 20; which cited Case C-61/94, *Commission/Germany* [1996] ECR I-4006, para. 52, set out in Exhibits EC-13 and EC-14.

[173] Australia's first written submission, para. 199.

[174] Australia's first oral statement, para. 33. The United States' first oral statement included *inter alia* comments that the distinction between the location of a geographical area and the nationality of the right holder is not meaningful as right holders are overwhelmingly nationals of the place where their respective GIs are located and that there is an obvious link and close relationship between the nationality

7.155 Australia argues that at least one right at issue in this dispute is the right to obtain registration. Under the Regulation, a non-EC *national* seeking to register a GI for an area located outside the EU is treated less favourably than an EC national seeking to register a GI for an area located within the EU. It is not necessary to make assumptions about the population of other categories of nationals and the location of their rights.[175] In its view, a national for the purposes of the TRIPS Agreement, in the case of a natural person, is a person who possesses the nationality of a state in accordance with that state's laws or a person who is domiciled or who has a real and effective industrial or commercial establishment in a separate customs territory, as a proxy for the ordinary notion of nationality. In the case of a legal person, it is a person who is domiciled or who is established in the Member in accordance with whose laws nationality is claimed.[176]

7.156 Australia considers that *less favourable treatment* under Article 3.1 of the TRIPS Agreement does not preclude formally different treatment, and could include disadvantages or costs, whereas Article 2(1) of the Paris Convention (1967) requires the granting of the *same advantages*.[177] It argues that the perceived advantages of registration under the Regulation include protection against a registered name becoming generic, broad-ranging protection, including even against evocation of a registered GI, as well as ex officio Community-wide protection.[178]

7.157 Australia refers to the jurisprudence on Article III:4 of GATT 1994 and considers that "treatment no less favourable" in Article 3.1 of the TRIPS Agreement could be examined in terms of whether the effect of a measure is to modify the conditions of competition in the EC market to the detriment of nationals of other WTO Members with regard to the protection of intellectual property.[179] The effect of the Regulation at issue in this dispute is to accord less favourable treatment to non-EC nationals because the additional requirements for GIs located outside the EC overwhelmingly apply to non-EC nationals, given the reality that persons with an interest in securing the registration of the name of a geographical area will almost always be nationals of the Member in which that geographical area is located.[180]

7.158 Australia considers that an overarching exceptions provision analogous to Article XX of GATT 1994 was unnecessary in the TRIPS Agreement and is irrelevant to the assessment of *de facto* discrimination under that agreement because there were pre-existing multilateral intellectual property conventions already in place; Members may take account of legitimate public policy objectives as recognized in Articles 7 and 8 but then must apply them in accordance with national treatment and MFN treatment; specific exceptions exist in the TRIPS Agreement for separate categories of intellectual property rights.[181]

7.159 Australia also claims that the Regulation imposes a requirement of establishment in the EC inconsistently with Article 2(2) of the Paris Convention (1967).[182]

7.160 The European Communities responds that this claim must fail. Its first defence is that it does not, in fact, apply the conditions in Article 12(1) of the Regulation to geographical areas located in WTO Members. That defence has been considered in the previous sub-section.

---

of the persons who would seek GI protection for agricultural products and foodstuffs and the territory of the Member in which they are growing or producing such products, which is supported by data on the applicants for certification marks in the United States.

175 Australia's response to Panel question No. 101.

176 Australia's response to Panel question No. 23.

177 Australia's response to Panel question No. 31.

178 Australia's first written submission, para. 197.

179 Australia's second oral statement, para. 74; response to Panel question No. 103.

180 Australia's responses to Panel questions Nos. 22, 27 and 102; rebuttal submission, para. 184.

181 Australia's response to Panel question No. 103.

182 Australia's first written submission, paras. 199 and 206.

7.161 The European Communities does not contest that national treatment under the TRIPS Agreement applies to more extensive protection granted in respect of intellectual property rights addressed in the TRIPS Agreement.[183]

7.162 The European Communities argues that the conditions in Article 12(1) of the Regulation do not depend on *nationality*. The Regulation sets out two procedures for registration: one for geographical areas located within the European Communities and one for those located outside the European Communities. Whether the geographical area is located within or outside the European Communities is in no way linked to the question of the nationality of the producers concerned.[184] This may concern the origin of the product but has nothing to do with the nationality of the producer, which is simply of no relevance for the registration of the GI.[185] There are no legal requirements which ensure that applicants for GIs for geographical areas located in the European Communities are always, or usually, EC nationals.[186] There is no reason why a foreign national cannot produce products in accordance with a product specification in a GI registration located in the European Communities, and there are examples of foreign companies which have invested in the European Communities in this way.[187] If an applicant or user sets up a legal entity in the geographical area, that is simply a practical consequence of the fact that products must be produced in accordance with product specifications.[188] Nationality is determined by the laws of each State and is not simply a matter of domicile or establishment, which is highlighted by the specific rules in Article 3 of the Paris Convention (1967) and footnote 1 to the TRIPS Agreement which would otherwise be unnecessary.[189] The European Communities is not a "separate customs territory" within the meaning of footnote 1 to the TRIPS Agreement.[190] The meaning of "interested parties" in Article 10(2) of the Paris Convention (1967) is inapplicable in Article 22 of the TRIPS Agreement.[191] Nationality is not linked to the points of attachment but must be given a uniform meaning for all intellectual property rights.[192] The Regulation does not require any comparison of nationals because it does not contain any discrimination on the basis of nationality.[193]

7.163 The European Communities argues that the existence of different procedures which apply according to location of geographical areas is not sufficient to show *less favourable treatment* but rather there must be a substantive difference between those provisions which entails less favourable treatment. A measure would have to modify the conditions regarding the protection of intellectual property rights within the meaning of the TRIPS Agreement to the detriment of foreign nationals.[194]

7.164 The European Communities argues that the jurisprudence on Article III:2 of GATT 1994 is not relevant to the present dispute because of differences between paragraphs 2 and 4 of Article III and between Article III and Article 3.1 of the TRIPS Agreement. There is no general concept of discrimination common to all WTO agreements. There has never been a *de facto* application of Article 3.1 and the concept of conditions of competition is not easily transposable to the TRIPS Agreement. Whilst it may be possible under certain circumstances that measures which are neutral on their face accord less favourable treatment to nationals, the Panel should take account of the following: (1) the present case relates primarily to the origin of goods which is already dealt with more appropriately in the context of Article III:4 of GATT 1994, not the TRIPS Agreement;

---

[183] European Communities' response to Panel question No. 111.

[184] European Communities' first written submission, paras. 123-126.

[185] European Communities' first oral statement, paras. 46-47; response to Panel question No. 106.

[186] European Communities' response to Panel question No. 22.

[187] European Communities' rebuttal submission, paras. 45-48; second oral statement, paras. 28-30; response to Panel question No. 106.

[188] European Communities' response to Panel question No. 107; second oral statement, paras. 29-30.

[189] European Communities' response to Panel question No. 23; rebuttal submission, paras. 37-40.

[190] European Communities' rebuttal submission, para. 35.

[191] European Communities' response to Panel question No. 24.

[192] European Communities' response to Panel question No. 26.

[193] European Communities' response to Panel question No. 101 and comments on that response.

[194] European Communities' second oral statement, paras. 39-41; response to Panel question No. 113.

(2) *de facto* discrimination is a notion closely related to preventing circumvention of national treatment obligations, which does not exist when the specific issue is dealt with in other national treatment provisions, such as those of GATT; and (3) the national treatment provisions of GATT and the TRIPS Agreement should not systematically overlap. In addition, the TRIPS Agreement does not contain any provision corresponding to Article XX of GATT 1994 and it would not seem appropriate for a measure justified on the basis of Article XX to be found incompatible with the covered agreements on the basis of a *de facto* application of TRIPS national treatment.[195]

(ii) main arguments of third parties

7.165 Brazil submits that the equivalence and reciprocity conditions in the Regulation are inconsistent with national treatment under Article 3.1 of the TRIPS Agreement. In most cases under the Regulation, discrimination according to geographical areas is discrimination between nationals.[196]

7.166 Canada submits that the equivalence and reciprocity conditions in the Regulation are inconsistent with national treatment under Articles 2.1 and 3.1 of the TRIPS Agreement. Discrimination on the basis of geographical area discriminates on the basis of nationality because of the "simple and incontestable" reality that EC nationals are likely to register for protection of GIs located in the European Communities and non-EC nationals are likely to register for protection of GIs located outside the European Communities. The explicit requirement that the physical production of a good that qualifies for a GI take place in the area indicated by the GI, means that an applicant for a GI located in the European Communities will, in all probability be a national of an EC member State. The treatment of "nationals" under the TRIPS Agreement extends *de jure* to geographical area.[197]

7.167 China considers that "nationals" within the meaning of the TRIPS Agreement includes natural persons who are domiciled, or legal persons who have a real and effective industrial and commercial establishment, in that Member.[198]

7.168 Colombia considers that any distinction that in any way identifies the GIs of the European Communities clearly entails a violation of national treatment obligations.[199]

7.169 India considers that the only valid interpretation of "treatment with regard to the protection " in Article 3.1 of the TRIPS Agreement is that no less favourable treatment to nationals of other WTO Members cannot be provided unless no less favourable treatment is also provided to the GIs for which they apply, whether located in the European Communities or in other WTO Members. The only available exceptions are found in Article 3.2.[200]

7.170 Mexico considers that the equivalence and reciprocity conditions prevent nationals of other WTO Members enjoying the protection afforded by the Regulation, which is contrary to the national treatment principle in Article 3.1 of the TRIPS Agreement.[201]

7.171 New Zealand submits that the term "nationals" clearly has a geographical connotation in the context of the TRIPS Agreement. Article 3 of the Paris Convention (1967) sets out a criterion for eligibility for protection

---

[195] European Communities' response to Panel question No. 29; rebuttal submission, para. 49; second oral statement, paras. 33-37; response to Panel question No. 103.

[196] Annex C, paras. 23 and 34.

[197] Annex C, paras. 57-63.

[198] Annex C, para. 93.

[199] Annex C, para. 101.

[200] Annex C, para. 104.

[201] Annex C, para. 110.

to which the definition of "nationals" in Article 1.3 of the TRIPS Agreement refers. Footnote 1 to Article 1.3 of the TRIPS Agreement provides further support. The definition of an applicant in the Regulation includes persons according to their location. The most favourable treatment accorded to EC nationals should be compared with that received by WTO Member nationals. "Less favourable treatment" requires not only a difference in applicable laws but some disadvantage as a result of that difference. At worst, the difference means that the benefits of registration are entirely unavailable. At best, it means that other WTO Member nationals are subject to "extra hurdles" and disadvantaged. As a result, they do not have the same opportunities to protect their GIs through registration as do EC nationals. The individual's right to apply for protection is conditioned on factors over which the applicant has no control. The advantages granted by registration include those under Article 13 and, according to the preamble, higher incomes.[202]

7.172 Chinese Taipei submits that the equivalence and reciprocity conditions violate the national treatment obligation in Article 3.1 of the TRIPS Agreement and Article 2(1) of the Paris Convention (1967). It recalls that national treatment under the TRIPS Agreement applies to "nationals" and that the European Communities compares EC nationals and non-EC nationals with GIs located in the European Communities. It treats them completely independently of EC nationals and non-EC nationals with GIs located outside the European Communities. This essentially is an argument that the European Communities can establish a separate set of rules for, and discriminate against, non-EC GIs as it wishes. Chinese Taipei submits that the Panel should examine whether any person, whether an EC or a non-EC national, with a GI, whether located in the European Communities or outside the European Communities, receives treatment less favourable than that accorded to an EC national with a GI located in the European Communities. Footnote 1 to the TRIPS Agreement applies to the European Communities as a separate customs territory.[203]

(iii) consideration by the Panel

national treatment obligations in the TRIPS Agreement

7.173 These claims are made under two national treatment obligations: one found in Article 3 of the TRIPS Agreement, which forms part of the text of that agreement, and the other found elsewhere, in Article 2 of the Paris Convention (1967) as incorporated by Article 2.1 of the TRIPS Agreement. The Panel will first consider the claim under Article 3 of the TRIPS Agreement.

7.174 Article 3.1 of the TRIPS Agreement provides as follows:

> 1. Each Member shall accord to the nationals of other Members treatment no less favourable than that it accords to its own nationals with regard to the protection of intellectual property, subject to the exceptions already provided in, respectively, the Paris Convention (1967), the Berne Convention (1971), the Rome Convention or the Treaty on Intellectual Property in Respect of Integrated Circuits. ... [footnote 3 omitted]

7.175 Two elements must be satisfied to establish an inconsistency with this obligation: (1) the measure at issue must apply with regard to the protection of intellectual property; and (2) the nationals of other Members must be accorded "less favourable" treatment than the Member's own nationals. The Panel will address each of these elements in turn. The parties do not agree on the meaning of "nationals" for the purposes of this claim. The Panel will therefore address that issue in the course of its consideration of the second element of this claim.

[202] Annex C, paras. 130-132.

[203] Annex C, paras. 168-172.

protection of intellectual property

7.176 The national treatment obligation in Article 3 of the TRIPS Agreement applies "with regard to the protection of intellectual property." Footnote 3 provides an inclusive definition of the term "protection" as used in Articles 3 and 4. It reads as follows:

> For the purposes of Articles 3 and 4, 'protection' shall include matters affecting the availability, acquisition, scope, maintenance and enforcement of intellectual property rights as well as those matters affecting the use of intellectual property rights specifically addressed in this Agreement.

7.177 Article 1.2 explains the term "intellectual property:"

> 2. For the purposes of this Agreement, the term 'intellectual property' refers to all categories of intellectual property that are the subject of Sections 1 through 7 of Part II.

7.178 Turning to the Regulation, Article 12(1) refers to how the Regulation "may apply," which is a reference to the *availability* of intellectual property rights in relation to "designations of origin" and "geographical indications," as defined in the Regulation. It is not disputed that "designations of origin" and "geographical indications," as defined in the Regulation, fall within the category of "geographical indications," the subject of Section 3 of Part II, and therefore part of a category of intellectual property within the meaning of Article 1.2 of the TRIPS Agreement.

7.179 Therefore, this claim concerns the "protection" of intellectual property, as clarified in footnote 3 to the TRIPS Agreement, within the scope of the national treatment obligation in Article 3 of that Agreement.

7.180 It is not necessary to show that the Regulation implements the minimum standards in Part II of the TRIPS Agreement for the purposes of these claims. National treatment is required with regard to the protection of intellectual property, even where measures provide a higher level of protection.

less favourable treatment accorded to the nationals of other Members

less favourable treatment

7.181 The Panel now examines the second element of this claim which is whether the nationals of other Members are accorded less favourable treatment than the European Communities' own nationals. It is useful to recall that Article 3.1 of the TRIPS Agreement combines elements of national treatment both from pre-existing intellectual property agreements and GATT 1994.[204] Like the pre-existing intellectual property conventions, Article 3.1 applies to "nationals," not products. Like GATT 1994, Article 3.1 refers to "no less favourable" treatment, not the advantages or rights that laws now grant or may hereafter grant, but it does not refer to likeness. This combination of elements is reflected in the preamble to the TRIPS Agreement which explains the purpose of the "basic principles" in Articles 3 and 4 (a term highlighted in the title of Part I) as follows:

> *Recognizing*, to this end, the need for new rules and disciplines concerning:
>
> (a) the applicability of the basic principles of GATT 1994 and of relevant international intellectual property agreements or conventions;

[204] Three of these national treatment obligations are incorporated in the TRIPS Agreement itself: Article 2 of the Paris Convention (1967), (considered below at paras. 7.250 and following) Article 5 of the Berne Convention (1971) and Article 5 of the IPIC Treaty, which are incorporated by Articles 2.1, 9.1 and 35 of the TRIPS Agreement, respectively.

7.182 The "no less favourable" treatment standard set out in the first sentence of Article 3.1 of the TRIPS Agreement is subject to certain specific exceptions, some of them found in the pre-existing intellectual property conventions. None of the exceptions in Article 3.1 and 3.2 are relevant to this dispute.[205] Where these exceptions and limitations do not apply, the language of the basic obligation in the first sentence of Article 3 is very broad, referring to treatment that is "no less favourable."

7.183 We recall that the Panel in *US – Section 211 Appropriations Act*, in a finding with which the Appellate Body agreed[206], found that the appropriate standard of examination under Article 3.1 of the TRIPS Agreement is that enunciated by the GATT Panel in *US – Section 337*. That GATT Panel made the following findings on the "no less favourable" treatment standard under Article III:4 of GATT 1947:

> The words 'treatment no less favourable' in paragraph 4 call for effective equality of opportunities for imported products in respect of the application of laws, regulations and requirements affecting the internal sale, offering for sale, purchase, transportation, distribution or use of products. This clearly sets a minimum permissible standard as a basis.[207]

7.184 Therefore, the Panel will examine whether the difference in treatment affects the "effective equality of opportunities" between the nationals of other Members and the European Communities' own nationals with regard to the "protection" of intellectual property rights, to the detriment of nationals of other Members.

7.185 The interpretation of the "no less favourable" treatment standard under other covered agreements may be relevant in interpreting Article 3.1 of the TRIPS Agreement, taking account of its context in each agreement including, in particular, any differences arising from its application to like products or like services and service suppliers, rather than to nationals.[208]

7.186 Under Article III:4 of GATT 1994, the Appellate Body in *US – FSC (Article 21.5 – EC)* has explained its approach to the examination of whether measures affecting the internal sale of *products* accord "treatment no less favourable" as follows:

> The examination of whether a measure involves 'less favourable treatment' of imported products within the meaning of Article III:4 of the GATT 1994 must be grounded in close scrutiny of the 'fundamental thrust and effect of the measure itself'. This examination cannot rest on simple assertion, but must be founded on a careful analysis of the contested measure and of its implications in the marketplace. At the same time, however, the examination need not be based on the *actual effects* of the contested measure in the marketplace.[209]

7.187 Similarly, in the present dispute, the Panel considers it appropriate to base its examination under Article 3.1 of the TRIPS Agreement on the fundamental thrust and effect of the Regulation, including an analysis of its terms and its practical implications. However, as far as the TRIPS Agreement is concerned, the relevant practical implications are those on opportunities with regard to the protection of intellectual property. The implications in the marketplace for the agricultural products and foodstuffs in respect of which GIs may be protected are relevant to the examination under Article III:4 of GATT 1994, considered later in this report.

---

[205] Article 24.9 also provides that there shall be no obligation under this Agreement to protect GIs which are not or cease to be protected in their country of origin or which have fallen into disuse in that country.

[206] See the Panel report on *US – Section 211 Appropriations Act*, at paras. 8.131-8.133, the Appellate Body report, at para. 258. The Appellate Body has also assessed "no less favourable" treatment in the context of trade in goods under Article III:4 of GATT 1994 in terms of whether the measure modifies conditions of competition: see its report in *Korea – Various Measures on Beef*, paras. 137 and 144

[207] GATT Panel report on *US – Section 337*, para. 5.11.

[208] In *US – Section 211 Appropriations Act*, the Panel considered that the jurisprudence on Article III:4 of GATT 1994 may be useful in interpreting Article 3.1 of the TRIPS Agreement due to the similarity of their language: see the Panel report at para. 8.129; Appellate Body report at para. 242.

[209] Appellate Body Report, *US – FSC (Article 21.5 – EC)*, para. 215, quoting reports in *Korea – Various Measures on Beef*, para. 142, and *Japan – Alcoholic Beverages II*, at 110.

7.188 The parties disagree on whether the equivalence and reciprocity conditions in Article 12(1) of the Regulation apply to GIs located in other WTO Members outside the European Communities. The Panel recalls its finding at paragraph 7.152 that they do so apply.

7.189 Although the parties disagree on whether the equivalence and reciprocity conditions in Article 12(1) of the Regulation discriminate in a manner inconsistent with the covered agreements, it is not disputed that those conditions accord less favourable treatment to persons with interests in the *GIs* to which those conditions apply.[210] The Panel considers that those conditions modify the effective equality of opportunities to obtain protection with respect to intellectual property in two ways. First, GI protection is not available under the Regulation in respect of geographical areas located in third countries which the Commission has not recognized under Article 12(3). The European Communities confirms that the Commission has not recognized any third countries. Second, GI protection under the Regulation may become available if the third country in which the GI is located enters into an international agreement or satisfies the conditions in Article 12(1). Both of those requirements represent a significant "extra hurdle" in obtaining protection that does not apply to geographical areas located in the European Communities.[211] The significance of the hurdle is reflected in the fact that currently no third country has entered into such an agreement or satisfied those conditions.

7.190 Accordingly, the Panel finds that the equivalence and reciprocity conditions modify the effective equality of opportunities with respect to the availability of protection to persons who wish to obtain GI protection under the Regulation, to the detriment of those who wish to obtain protection in respect of geographical areas located in third countries, including WTO Members. This is less favourable treatment.

nationals of other Members

7.191 The issue for the Panel is how the less favourable treatment accorded under the Regulation with respect to the availability of protection affects the treatment accorded to the nationals of other Members and that accorded to the European Communities' own nationals for the purposes of Article 3.1 of the TRIPS Agreement. Article 1.3 defines "nationals of other Members" in order to determine the persons to whom Members shall accord treatment, which includes national treatment.[212] It provides as follows:

> 3. Members shall accord the treatment provided for in this Agreement to the nationals of other Members. In respect of the relevant intellectual property right, the nationals of other Members shall be understood as those natural or legal persons that would meet the criteria for eligibility for protection provided for in the Paris Convention (1967), the Berne Convention (1971), the Rome Convention and the Treaty on Intellectual Property in Respect of Integrated Circuits, were all Members of the WTO members of those conventions. (...) [footnote 1 omitted]

7.192 In respect of the intellectual property rights relevant to this dispute, it is not disputed that the criteria for eligibility for protection that apply are those found in the Paris Convention (1967). Articles 2 and 3 of the

---

[210] Australia's first written submission, paras. 196, 199 and 206. Note that the European Communities asserts only that the product specifications and inspection regimes for individual GIs do not constitute less favourable treatment. With respect to the equivalence and reciprocity conditions, it asserts that it does not apply them and that they do not depend on nationality, but *not* that they do not accord less favourable treatment where they apply: see its first written submission, paras. 62-69 and 113-126. It also concedes that they constitute less favourable treatment for the purposes of Article III:4 of GATT 1994, but does not consider that the meaning of the phrase is necessarily the same as in Article 3.1 of the TRIPS Agreement: see its responses to Panel questions Nos. 94(a) and 113.

[211] This was also the approach of the Appellate Body in *US – Section 211 Appropriations Act* to an "extra hurdle" imposed only on foreign nationals: see para. 268 of its report.

[212] This can be contrasted with the detailed definitions in Article XXVIII of GATS of "natural person of another Member," "juridical person of another Member," "juridical person" and a juridical person "owned" or "controlled" by persons of a Member or "affiliated" with another person.

Paris Convention (1967) provide how nationals and persons assimilated to nationals are to be treated. In the Panel's view, these are "criteria for eligibility for protection" for the purposes of the TRIPS Agreement.[213]

7.193 Articles 2 and 3 of the Paris Convention (1967) refer to "nationals" without defining that term. Article 3 of the Paris Convention (1967) provides for the assimilation of certain persons to nationals as follows:

> Nationals of countries outside the Union who are domiciled or who have real and effective industrial or commercial establishments in the territory of one of the countries of the Union shall be treated in the same manner as nationals of the countries of the Union.

7.194 The rule in Article 3 of the Paris Convention (1967) only applies to nationals of countries *outside the Paris Union.* According to Article 1.3 of the TRIPS Agreement, these criteria shall be understood as if "all Members of the WTO" were members of that Convention. Therefore, for the purposes of the TRIPS Agreement, that rule of assimilation only applies to persons that are nationals of a country *that is not a WTO Member*. It does not apply to nationals of other WTO Members, such as Australia. Therefore, it does not mean that all persons who have a domicile or a real and effective industrial and commercial establishment in a WTO Member are necessarily nationals of that WTO Members for the purposes of the TRIPS Agreement.

7.195 Otherwise, the Paris Convention (1967) contains no common rules on the meaning of "nationals." It can be noted that the original Paris Convention of 1883 appeared to use the term "subjects and citizens" and "nationals" interchangeably. The phrase "subjects and citizens" was replaced with "nationals" in Articles 2 and 3 in the Hague Act of 1925 without, apparently, changing the scope of the Convention.[214]

7.196 A leading commentator on the Paris Convention (1967) explains the practice under that Convention as follows:

> With respect to *natural* persons, nationality is a quality accorded or withdrawn by the legislation of the State whose nationality is claimed. Therefore, it is only the legislation of that State which can define the said nationality and which must be applied also in other countries where it is invoked.
>
> "With respect to *legal* persons, the question is more complicated because generally no 'nationality' as such is granted to legal persons by existing legislations. Where these legal persons are the State themselves, or State enterprises, or other bodies of *public status*, it would be logical to accord to them the nationality of their country. With regard to corporate bodies of *private status*, such as companies and associations, the authorities of the countries where application of the Convention is sought will have to decide on the criterion of 'nationality' which they will employ. This 'nationality' can be made dependent upon the law according to which these legal persons have been constituted, or upon the law of their actual headquarters, or even on other criteria. Such law will also decide whether a legal person or entity really exists. [original footnote omitted][215]

---

[213] Article 1.3 of the TRIPS Agreement also refers to the criteria for eligibility for protection in the Berne Convention (1971). It can be observed that the title inserted to facilitate identification of Article 3 of the Berne Convention (1971) which concerns authors who are nationals or assimilated to nationals, also refers to "Criteria of Eligibility for Protection." This is consistent with the Panel's view of the criteria in the Paris Convention (1967) for the purposes of the TRIPS Agreement.

[214] Article 2 originally provided that "subjects and citizens" will enjoy the advantages granted to "nationals." As early as 1897, the Chair of the Brussels Diplomatic Conference commented that, in practice, the rights conferred on physical persons must belong equally to juridical persons and it seemed to be unanimously recognized that this was the scope of the Convention, see *Actes de Paris*, 1897, 3rd session, p. 196. "Subjects and citizens" was replaced with the word "nationals" at the 1925 Hague Diplomatic Conference because, in its brevity, it was considered more comprehensive, and was consistent with the terminology of the Convention: see *Actes de Paris*, 1925, report of drafting committee, p. 538.

[215] See Bodenhausen *supra* at 79, pp. 27-28.

7.197 This is consistent with the position under public international law.[216] With respect to the meaning of "nationals of other Members" for the purposes of the TRIPS Agreement, WTO Members have, through Article 1.3 of the TRIPS Agreement, incorporated the meaning of "nationals" as it was understood in the Paris Convention (1967) and under public international law. With respect to natural persons, they refer first to the law of the Member of which nationality is claimed.[217] With respect to legal persons, each Member first applies its own criteria to determine nationality.

7.198 The meaning of "nationals" under public international law is also relevant to the meaning of a Member's "own nationals." Whilst the TRIPS Agreement does not create obligations for a Member to accord treatment to its own nationals, it does refer to the treatment that each Member accords to its own nationals as the benchmark for its obligation to accord national treatment under Article 3.1, as well as the other national treatment obligations incorporated by reference, including Article 2 of the Paris Convention (1967). To that extent, the way in which a Member defines its own nationals can also be subject to review for the purposes of determining conformity with its national treatment obligations under the TRIPS Agreement.

7.199 The European Communities has explained to the Panel that, with respect to natural persons, under the domestic law of the European Communities, any person who is a national of an EC member State is a citizen of the European Union and, accordingly, an EC national.[218] It has explained that, with respect to legal persons, the domestic law of the European Communities does not contain a specific definition of nationality, but nor does the domestic law of many other WTO Members.[219] However, the European Communities informs the Panel that any legal person considered a national under the laws of an EC member State would also be an EC national. The criteria used by the EC member States to determine the nationality of a legal person may vary and include criteria such as the place of incorporation and the place of the seat of the company or a combination of such criteria.[220]

7.200 Australia has not challenged the criteria used by the European Communities to determine nationality. The Panel notes that these criteria appear to be the same as those used in public international law.[221] Therefore, the Panel can use them to determine which persons are "nationals" under Article 3.1 of the TRIPS Agreement.

7.201 Australia has referred to the specific definition of "nationals" in footnote 1 to the TRIPS Agreement.[222] The Panel notes that that specific definition only applies in the case of a separate customs territory Member of the WTO. The European Communities submits that it is not such a Member and Australia does not assert that it is.[223] Therefore, the Panel does not consider this specific definition further.

---

216 See, for example, A.A. Fatouros, "National Legal Persons in International Law" in R. Bernhardt (ed.), *Encyclopedia of Public International Law,* Volume III (1997) pp. 495-501; and I. Brownlie, *Principles of Public International Law* (5th edition, Oxford, 1998), p. 426, submitted to the Panel by the European Communities in Exhibits EC-88 and EC-115, respectively.

217 With respect to natural persons, the Panel also notes that a State may not be bound to recognize a grant of nationality if it does not represent a genuine connection between the natural person and the State granting the nationality: see the judgement of the International Court of Justice in the *Nottenbohm case (Liechtenstein v Guatemala)* (second phase), ICJ Reports (1955), 4.

218 Article 8 of the EC Treaty.

219 Article 58 of the EC Treaty provides that companies or firms formed in accordance with the law of an EC member State and having their registered office, central administration or principal place of business within the European Community shall, for the purposes of Chapter 2 of the EC Treaty on the right of establishment, be treated in the same way as natural persons who are nationals of EC member States.

220 European Communities' response to Panel question No. 105. It also referred to a criterion based on the nationality of controlling shareholders, but the evidence in support does not appear to indicate that this is of relevance to corporate nationality under the TRIPS Agreement.

221 *Supra* at 216.

222 Australia's response to Panel question No. 23.

223 Australia's response to Panel question No. 104.

7.202 Australia also refers to Article 10(2) of the Paris Convention (1967) which sets out persons who shall be deemed an "interested party" for the purposes of an obligation related to certain false indications. Article 10(2) refers *inter alia* to establishment in the locality or country falsely indicated.

7.203 The Panel accepts that an "interested party" is a person who is entitled to receive protection under Articles 22 and 23 of the TRIPS Agreement. Article 10(2) is a deeming provision for the term "interested party" used in Article 9(3) of the Paris Convention (1967), as made applicable under Article 10(1). Once a person has qualified as a national, Article 10(2) may provide guidance on whether that person may be treated as an interested party for the purposes of Articles 22 and 23 of the TRIPS Agreement. However, Article 10(2) does not set out a criterion for eligibility for protection under the Paris Convention (1967) for the purposes of Article 1.3 of the TRIPS Agreement.

7.204 Therefore, the Panel finds no specific definition of "nationals" applicable in this dispute and confirms its finding at paragraph 7.200 as to the criteria that can be used to determine which persons are "nationals" for the purposes of Article 3.1 of the TRIPS Agreement, for the purposes of this dispute.

7.205 Turning to the Regulation, it is agreed that it does not, on its face, refer to "nationals." It refers to the location of geographical areas, or GIs. In theory, there may be foreign citizens or corporations who are entitled to use GIs located in the European Communities and obtain protection under the Regulation. The issue for the Panel is to determine the treatment accorded to the nationals of other Members and that accorded to the European Communities' own nationals, when such treatment depends on the location of GIs.

formally identical provisions

7.206 On its face, the Regulation contains formally identical provisions vis-à-vis the nationals of different Members, with respect to the availability of GI protection.

7.207 It is well recognized that the concept of "no less favourable" treatment under Article III:4 of GATT 1994 is sufficiently broad to include situations where the application of formally identical legal provisions would in practice accord less favourable treatment. The GATT Panel in *US – Section 337*, which considered an intellectual property enforcement measure prior to the conclusion of the TRIPS Agreement, interpreted the "no less favourable" standard under Article III:4 as follows:

> On the one hand, contracting parties may apply to imported products different formal legal requirements if doing so would accord imported products more favourable treatment. On the other hand, it also has to be recognised that there may be cases where application of formally identical legal provisions would in practice accord less favourable treatment to imported products and a contracting party might thus have to apply different legal provisions to imported products to ensure that the treatment accorded them is in fact no less favourable.[224]

7.208 The Appellate Body in *Korea – Various Measures on Beef*, in a dispute concerning formally different treatment, quoted this passage and drew the conclusion that "[a] formal difference in treatment between imported and like domestic products is thus neither necessary, nor sufficient, to show a violation of Article III:4."[225] It then proceeded to apply the relevant standard of examination.

---

[224] GATT Panel report on *US – Section 337*, para. 5.11.

[225] Appellate Body report on *Korea – Various Measures on Beef*, para. 137. This view is also consistent with the findings of the Appellate Body in its report on *EC – Bananas III* with respect to the phrase "treatment no less favourable" as used in the MFN obligation in relation to trade in services in Article II of GATS, at para. 233.

7.209 The Panel in *Canada – Pharmaceutical Patents* also considered that claims against both formal and practical discrimination are possible under the TRIPS Agreement, although that dispute concerned minimum standards of protection in Part II and not the basic principles in Part I.[226]

7.210 We consider that this reasoning applies with equal force to the no less favourable treatment standard in Article 3.1 of the TRIPS Agreement. In our view, even if the provisions of the Regulation are formally identical in the treatment that they accord to the nationals of other Members and to the European Communities' own nationals, this is not sufficient to demonstrate that there is no violation of Article 3.1 of the TRIPS Agreement. Whether or not the Regulation accords less favourable treatment to the nationals of other Members than it accords to the European Communities' own nationals should be examined instead according to the standard we set out at paragraph 7.184, namely, the "effective equality of opportunities" with regard to the protection of intellectual property rights. In this examination, we will follow the approach that we set out at paragraph 7.187, which focuses on the "fundamental thrust and effect" of the Regulation.

which nationals to compare?

7.211 The text of Article 3.1 expressly calls for a comparison when it provides that "[e]ach Member shall accord to the nationals of other Members treatment no *less* favourable *than* that it accords to its own nationals" (emphasis added). The question arises as to which nationals it is appropriate to compare.

7.212 The Panel finds that the following graphic, based on one set out in Chinese Taipei's third party submission, provides a useful framework for its analysis of this issue.

1. EC national with GI located in the EC	3. EC national with GI located outside the EC
2. Non-EC national with GI located in the EC	4. Non-EC national with GI located outside the EC

Graphic 1

7.213 The graphic depicts the four relevant possible combinations of nationality of persons and the location of a GI, each in a separate numbered quadrant. In terms of this graphic, the Panel's conclusion at paragraph 7.152 is that the conditions of reciprocity and equivalence in Article 12(1) of the Regulation apply to the persons in quadrants 3 and 4 only. There is therefore discrimination between the persons in quadrants 1 and 2, on the one hand, and those in quadrants 3 and 4, on the other hand.

7.214 Australia submits that the Panel should compare the treatment of a hypothetical EC national with a GI located in the European Communities, and the treatment of a hypothetical non-EC national with a GI located outside the European Communities. This is a comparison of a person in quadrant 1 with a person in quadrant 4 in the graphic.

7.215 The Panel recalls that the Regulation contains formally identical provisions vis-à-vis the nationals of different Members. In the absence of less favourable treatment based on a formal criterion of nationality, or a criterion that fully corresponds with nationality, the Panel is reluctant to compare a hypothetical national of one Member with a national of another Member simply because they both claim rights to the same category of

[226] Panel report on *Canada – Pharmaceutical Patents*, at paras. 7.100-7.105.

intellectual property. This is a very low threshold with possibly unforeseen systemic implications for all intellectual property rights covered by the TRIPS Agreement.

7.216 Australia also submits that there is discrimination according to nationality on the basis of a comparison of the group of the European Communities' own nationals who wish to obtain GI protection under the Regulation, with the group of nationals of other WTO Members who wish to obtain GI protection under the Regulation. This is a comparison of the persons in both quadrants 1 and 3 with the persons in both quadrants 2 and 4, in the graphic.

7.217 The Panel recalls that the standard of examination is based on "effective equality of opportunities." It follows that the nationals that are relevant to an examination under Article 3.1 of the TRIPS Agreement should be those who seek opportunities with respect to the same type of intellectual property in comparable situations.[227] On the one hand, this excludes a comparison of opportunities for nationals with respect to different categories of intellectual property, such as GIs and copyright. On the other hand, no reason has been advanced as to why the equality of opportunities should be limited *a priori* to rights with a territorial link to a particular Member.[228]

7.218 The Panel therefore considers it appropriate for the purposes of this claim to compare the effective equality of opportunities for the group of nationals of other Members who may wish to seek GI protection under the Regulation and the group of the European Communities' own nationals who may wish to seek GI protection under the Regulation. On this approach, there is no need to make a factual assumption that every person who wishes to obtain protection for a GI in a particular Member is a national of that Member.[229]

7.219 The European Communities disagrees with this approach. It argues that the concept of *de facto* discrimination should be limited to cases of circumvention of obligations, which is unnecessary in this dispute because of the applicability of the national treatment obligation under GATT 1994.[230]

7.220 The Panel is mindful of the need to ensure a harmonious interpretation of the national treatment obligation within the TRIPS Agreement itself as applied to different intellectual property rights. The fact that circumvention of that obligation may be prevented, uniquely, under GATT 1994 in certain cases concerning geographical indications, does not justify a different interpretation of Article 3.1 of the TRIPS Agreement from that which would be applicable to all other intellectual property rights, which do not have an inherent link to the territorial origin of a product. The Panel's interpretation preserves internal coherence in the interpretation of national treatment under the TRIPS Agreement.

---

[227] The Appellate Body in *EC – Asbestos* adopted an analogous approach to the term "like" products in Article III:4 of GATT 1994, which it interpreted in terms of the competitive relationship between products: see its report at para. 99.

[228] See the European Communities' responses to Panel questions Nos. 25, 101 and 103.

[229] The Panel notes that its approach based on the respective treatment accorded to groups (of nationals) is consistent with an approach based on the respective treatment accorded to groups (of products) contemplated by the Appellate Body in *EC – Asbestos*, in the context of the national treatment obligation in Article III:4 of GATT 1994:

"... A complaining Member must still establish that the measure accords to the group of 'like' *imported* products 'less favourable treatment' than it accords to the group of 'like' *domestic* products. The term 'less favourable treatment' expresses the general principle, in Article III:1, that internal regulations 'should not be applied ... so as to afford protection to domestic production'. If there is 'less favourable treatment' of the group of 'like' imported products, there is, conversely, 'protection' of the group of 'like' domestic products. However, a Member may draw distinctions between products which have been found to be 'like', without, for this reason alone, according to the group of 'like' *imported* products 'less favourable treatment' than that accorded to the group of 'like' *domestic* products. ..." at para. 100.

[230] European Communities' rebuttal submission, para. 49; response to Panel question No. 29.

comparison of treatment accorded to the nationals of other Members and that accorded to the European Communities' own nationals

7.221 Articles 5 through 7 of the Regulation set out a registration procedure for GIs that refer to a geographical area located within the territory of the European Communities.[231] Articles 12a and 12b set out a registration procedure for GIs that refers to a geographical area located in third countries, including WTO Members. The conditions in Article 12(1) only apply to the latter procedures and, hence, only to GIs that refer to geographical areas located in third countries.

7.222 There is a link between the location of a geographical area to which a GI refers and certain persons. Article 5(1) and 5(2) provides that the following persons may apply for registration of a GI:

> 1. Only a group or, subject to certain conditions to be laid down in accordance with the procedure provided for in Article 15[232], a natural or legal person, shall be entitled to apply for registration.
>
> For the purposes of this Article, 'Group' means any association, irrespective of its legal form or composition, of producers and/or processors working with the same agricultural product or foodstuff. Other interested parties may participate in the group.
>
> 2. A group or a natural or legal person may apply for registration only in respect of agricultural products or foodstuffs which it produces or obtains within the meaning of Article 2(2)(a) or (b).

7.223 These definitions of applicants cross-refer to the definitions of designations of origin and geographical indications in the Regulation in Article 2(2)(a) and (b), which provide as follows:

> 2. For the purposes of this Regulation:
>
> (a) *designation of origin*: means the name of a region, a specific place or, in exceptional cases, a country, used to describe an agricultural product or a foodstuff:
>
> – originating in that region, specific place or country, and
>
> – the quality or characteristics of which are essentially or exclusively due to a particular geographical environment with its inherent natural and human factors, and the production, processing and preparation of which take place in the defined geographical area;
>
> (b) *geographical indication*: means the name of a region, a specific place or, in exceptional cases, a country, used to describe an agricultural product or a foodstuff:

[231] This is reflected in the fact that under Article 5(4) an application under the procedures set out in Articles 5 through 7 shall be sent to the EC member State in which the geographical area is located but under Article 12a(1) an application under the procedures set out in Articles 12a and 12b shall be sent to the authorities in the country in which the geographical area is located. This was confirmed by the European Communities in its response to Panel question No. 2.

[232] The European Commission has laid down in Article 1 of Commission Regulation (EEC) No. 2037/93 that applications for registration pursuant to Article 5 of Regulation (EEC) No. 2081/92 may be submitted by a natural or legal person not complying with the definition in the second subparagraph of Article 5(1) in exceptional, duly substantiated cases where the person concerned is the only producer in the geographical area defined at the time the application is submitted.

- originating in that region, specific place or country, and

- which possesses a specific quality, reputation or other characteristics attributable to that geographical origin and the production and/or processing and/or preparation of which take place in the defined geographical area."

7.224 Registration confers certain protection, but only agricultural products or foodstuffs that comply with a specification are eligible to "use" a registered GI. Article 4(2) sets out the minimum requirements which must be included in a product specification, which include *inter alia* "evidence that the agricultural product or the foodstuff originates in the geographical area," "a description of the method of obtaining the agricultural product or foodstuff and, if appropriate, the authentic and unvarying local methods" and "the details bearing out the link with the geographical environment or the geographical origin" (from items (d), (e) and (f), respectively). Any person, and not merely the applicant, that produces or obtains the products in accordance with the specification in the registration is entitled to use the GI.

7.225 These provisions create a link between persons, the territory of a particular Member, and the availability of protection. The definition of a "designation of origin" requires that the applicant and users must produce, process and prepare the products covered by a registration in the relevant geographical area, whilst the definition of a "geographical indication" requires that the applicant and users must carry out at least one, or some combination, of these three activities, in the geographical area, and must do so in accordance with a GI specification.

7.226 Accordingly, insofar as the Regulation discriminates with respect to the availability of protection between GIs located in the European Communities, on the one hand, and those located in third countries, including WTO Members, on the other hand, it formally discriminates between those persons who produce, process and/or prepare a product, in accordance with a specification, in the European Communities, on the one hand, and those persons who produce, process and/or prepare a product, in accordance with a specification, in third countries, including WTO Members, on the other hand.

7.227 The Panel recalls its finding in paragraph 7.218 that it is appropriate for the purposes of this dispute to compare the treatment accorded to the group of nationals of other Members who may wish to seek GI protection under the Regulation, and the group of the European Communities' own nationals who may wish to seek GI protection under the Regulation.

7.228 Australia argues that the reality is that persons with an interest in securing registration of the name of a geographical area as a GI under the Regulation will overwhelmingly be nationals of the WTO Member in which that geographical area is located.[233]

7.229 The European Communities does not deny this. It relies on the fact that the Regulation itself contains no legal obstacle to foreign nationals taking advantage of EC geographical indications and disputes that any person who is producing a product must *necessarily* have the nationality of the place where the product is produced.[234] However, in the Panel's view, that is not dispositive of the issue.

7.230 The Panel agrees that the vast majority of natural and legal persons who produce, process and/or prepare products according to a GI specification within the territory of a WTO Member party to this dispute will be nationals of that Member. The fact that there may be cases where such a person does not qualify as a national—and none has been brought to its attention—does not alter the fact that the distinction made by the Regulation on the basis of the location of a GI will operate in practice to discriminate between the group of

---

[233] Australia's rebuttal submission, para. 184 and response to Panel question No. 102. Brazil and Canada expressed the same view: see Annex C, paras. 24 and 47.

[234] European Communities' comment on US responses to Panel questions Nos. 102 and 103.

nationals of other Members who wish to obtain GI protection, and the group of the European Communities' own nationals who wish to obtain GI protection, to the detriment of the nationals of other Members. This will not occur as a random outcome in a particular case but as a feature of the design and structure of the system. This design is evident in the Regulation's objective characteristics, in particular, the definitions of "designation of origin" and "geographical indication" and the requirements of the product specifications. The structure is evident in the different registration procedures.

7.231 Complete data on the persons who have actually availed themselves of protection under the Regulation is not available. Any person who produces and/or processes and/or prepares products according to the specifications in a GI registration is entitled to use the GI. Data on the persons who have applied for, and obtained, protection under the Regulation and their respective addresses is available but their nationality is not recorded. However, there is no clear evidence that even a single person who has applied for, or is entitled to use, a registered GI is not one of the European Communities' own nationals.

7.232 Whilst certain of the European Communities' own nationals may wish to obtain protection for GIs located outside the European Communities as well, it cannot seriously be contested that the GIs for which nationals of other WTO Members would wish to obtain protection are overwhelmingly located outside the European Communities.

7.233 The European Communities presented evidence intended to show that certain foreign nationals have actually obtained protection under the Regulation. The Panel notes that all its examples consist of a foreign national, or a corporation incorporated under the laws of an EC member State, that acquired another corporation incorporated under the laws of an EC member State, which produces products entitled to GI protection.[235] Those subsidiary corporations obtaining the benefit of protection appear to be the European Communities' own nationals, according to a place of incorporation test. Evidence is not available on the place of their company seat but such cases appear to be rare. This evidence confirms, rather than contradicts, the link between the treatment accorded to GIs located in the European Communities and EC nationality.

7.234 The text of the TRIPS Agreement contains a recognition that discrimination according to residence and establishment will be a close substitute for nationality. The criteria set out in footnote 1 to the TRIPS Agreement, which apply in the case of a separate customs territory Member of the WTO, are clearly intended to provide close substitute criteria to determine nationality where criteria to determine nationality as such are not available in a Member's domestic law. These criteria are "domicile" and "real and effective industrial or commercial establishment." They are taken from the criteria used for the assimilation of nationals in Article 3 of the Paris Convention (1967). It is clear that, in using these terms, the drafters of footnote 1 of the TRIPS Agreement chose terms that were already understood in this pre-existing intellectual property convention. Under Article 3 of the Paris Convention (1967), "domicile" is not generally understood to indicate a legal situation, but rather a more or less permanent residence of a natural person, and an actual headquarters of a legal person. A "real and effective industrial and commercial establishment" is intended to refer to all but a sham or ephemeral establishment.[236]

---

[235] The evidence is as follows: Mr. Jens-Reidar Larsen, a Norwegian national, acquired a French cognac firm in 1928—cognac is not a product covered by the Regulation at issue. Sara Lee Personal Products SpA, an Italian corporation under common control with Sara Lee Charcuterie SA, a French corporation, belonging to the Sara Lee group, acquired Al Ponte Prosciutto SRL, an Italian corporation; Kraft Foods Group, which has an Italian subsidiary, acquired the business of Giovanni Invernizzi, an Italian, and partly sold it to Lactalis, a French dairy company with an Italian subsidiary; Nestlé which sold Vismara, a salami firm, to an Italian company. The persons who acquired GI protection in these three examples may all be the European Communities' own nationals. The European Communities also refers to the website of a private beer label collector who disclaims accuracy but suggests that a Belgian company used to produce a beer with a German GI, possibly before the Regulation entered into force. The Panel considers this example unreliable. See Exhibits EC-36, EC-61, EC-62, EC-63 and EC-89.

[236] Bodenhausen, *supra* at 79, p. 33, citing Ladas, *The International Protection of Industrial Property*, pp. 187-188, and Roubier, *Le Droit de la propriété industrielle I,* pp. 268-269. This is confirmed by the Official Records of the Paris Convention provided to the Panel by the International Bureau of WIPO, and quoted in Bodenhausen, *ibid.*, p. 34.

7.235 The object and purpose of the TRIPS Agreement depends on the obligation in Article 1.3 to accord the treatment provided for in the Agreement to the nationals of other Members, including national treatment under Article 3.1. That object and purpose would be severely undermined if a Member could avoid its obligations by simply according treatment to its own nationals on the basis of close substitute criteria, such as place of production, or establishment, and denying treatment to the nationals of other WTO Members who produce or are established in their own countries.

7.236 Further, the Panel recalls its finding at paragraph 7.218 that it is appropriate for the purposes of this claim under Article 3.1 to compare the effective equality of opportunities for the group of nationals of other Members who may wish to seek GI protection under the Regulation and the group of the European Communities' own nationals who may wish to seek GI protection under the Regulation. An objective assessment of that comparison cannot ignore the difference in treatment between quadrants 1 and 2 and quadrants 3 and 4 in the graphic set out earlier.

7.237 The Panel also notes that the close link between nationality, on the one hand, and residence and establishment, on the other, appears to be recognized in the Regulation itself. Article 12d of the Regulation accords a right of objection to persons, which the European Communities confirms is a reference to persons resident or established outside the European Communities, regardless of their nationality.[237] Yet the April 2003 amending Regulation, which inserted Article 12d, explained that it granted the right of objection to the *nationals* of other WTO Members.[238]

7.238 The European Communities argues that any difference in treatment of the nationals of other Members is not attributable to the Regulation. In its view, if a person sets up a legal entity in the area where the GI is located, "[i]t is simply a practical consequence of the fact that products have to be produced in accordance with the product specification, which may require that an important part of the production process takes place in the geographical area concerned." It argues that if, for practical considerations related for instance to taxation or labour law, a person producing in conformity with a product specification chooses to set up a legal entity in the area where the geographical area is located, this is not related to the Regulation.[239]

7.239 The Panel considers that this constitutes part of the fundamental thrust and effect of the Regulation, including its practical implications, and that therefore it must be taken into account in assessing whether the Regulation accords less favourable treatment. Whilst the Regulation does not prevent a foreign national from producing goods within the territory of the European Communities which would be entitled to use a GI, the implications of its design and structure on the opportunities for protection are such that its different procedures will operate to accord different treatment to the European Communities' own nationals and to the nationals of other Members, to the detriment of the nationals of other Members.[240]

7.240 Accordingly, the Panel's preliminary conclusion is that, with respect to the availability of protection, the treatment accorded to the group of nationals of other Members is different from, and less favourable than, that accorded to the European Communities' own nationals.

---

[237] European Communities' first written submission, para. 142.

[238] See paragraph 10 of the recitals to the April 2003 amending Regulation, set out in para. 7.121.

[239] European Communities' response to Panel question No. 107.

[240] Article 8a of the EC Treaty provides that every citizen of the European Union shall have the right to move and reside freely within the territory of the EC member States. Article 52 (in conjunction with Article 58) provides for the progressive abolition of restrictions on the freedom of establishment of nationals of an EC member State. These provisions remove obstacles to persons who wish to produce products according to a GI specification within the territory of the European Communities, but apply to the European Communities' own nationals only.

defences based on systemic considerations

7.241 The European Communities argues that the interpretation of the national treatment obligations in the TRIPS Agreement and GATT 1994 should not lead to "systematic overlap" between them.

7.242 The Panel notes that the demonstration of less favourable treatment under each agreement remains a distinct exercise since national treatment under Article 3.1 of the TRIPS Agreement ensures effective equality of opportunities for nationals with regard to the protection of intellectual property rights, whereas national treatment under GATT 1994 ensures equality of conditions of competition between products.[241]

7.243 The European Communities also argues that one must take account of the absence in the TRIPS Agreement of a general exceptions provision analogous to Article XX of GATT 1994.

7.244 The Panel notes that there is no hierarchy between the TRIPS Agreement and GATT 1994, which appear in separate annexes to the WTO Agreement. The ordinary meaning of the texts of the TRIPS Agreement and GATT 1994, as well as Article II:2 of the WTO Agreement, taken together, indicates that obligations under the TRIPS Agreement and GATT 1994 can co-exist and that one does not override the other. This is analogous to the finding of the Panel in *Canada – Periodicals,* with which the Appellate Body agreed, concerning the respective scopes of GATS and GATT 1994.[242] Further, a "harmonious interpretation" does not require an interpretation of one that shadows the contours of the other. It is well established that the covered agreements apply cumulatively and that consistency with one does not necessarily imply consistency with them all.[243]

7.245 More specifically, the Panel notes that Article 8 of the TRIPS Agreement sets out the principles of that agreement. Article 8.1 provides as follows:

> 1. Members may, in formulating or amending their laws and regulations, adopt measures necessary to protect public health and nutrition, and to promote the public interest in sectors of vital importance to their socio-economic and technological development, provided that such measures are consistent with the provisions of this Agreement.

7.246 These principles reflect the fact that the agreement does not generally provide for the grant of positive rights to exploit or use certain subject matter, but rather provides for the grant of negative rights to prevent certain acts. This fundamental feature of intellectual property protection inherently grants Members freedom to pursue legitimate public policy objectives since many measures to attain those public policy objectives lie outside the scope of intellectual property rights and do not require an exception under the TRIPS Agreement.

7.247 The scope of the national treatment obligation in Article 3.1 of the TRIPS Agreement also differs from that of the national treatment obligation in Article III:4 of GATT 1994, as it is subject to certain exceptions in Articles 3.1, 3.2 and 5, one of which is inspired by the language of Article XX of GATT 1994.[244] There is also a series of specific exceptions in the provisions relating to the minimum standards in Part II of the TRIPS Agreement and Part VII contains a provision on security exceptions analogous to Article XXI of GATT 1994, but none on general exceptions.

---

241 See the Appellate Body report on *Korea – Various Measures on Beef*, paras. 137 and 144 and the GATT Panel report on *US – Section 337*, para. 5.11.

242 Panel report on *Canada – Periodicals*, at para. 5.17; Appellate Body report on *Canada – Periodicals*, DSR 1997:I, 449, at 465.

243 See, for example, the Appellate Body report on *Argentina – Footwear (EC)*, para. 81; and the Appellate Body report on *Korea – Dairy*, para. 74; and the Panel reports on *EC – Bananas III*, para. 7.160.

244 Article 24.9 of the TRIPS Agreement also provides that there shall be no obligation under the TRIPS Agreement to protect geographical indications which are not or cease to be protected in their country of origin, or which have fallen into disuse in that country.

7.248 For all these reasons, in the Panel's view, the fact that a general exceptions provision analogous to Article XX of GATT 1994 was not included in the TRIPS Agreement has no impact on its analysis of Article 3.1.

conclusion with respect to Article 3.1 of the TRIPS Agreement

7.249 Therefore, the Panel concludes that, with respect to the equivalence and reciprocity conditions, as applicable to the availability of GI protection, the Regulation accords treatment to the nationals of other Members less favourable than that it accords to the European Communities' own nationals, inconsistently with Article 3.1 of the TRIPS Agreement.

Article 2 of the Paris Convention (1967)

7.250 Australia also makes claims under the national treatment obligation set out in Article 2 of the Paris Convention (1967). These claims are made under paragraphs 1 and 2 of that article, which provide as follows:

> (1) Nationals of any country of the Union shall, as regards the protection of industrial property, enjoy in all the other countries of the Union the advantages that their respective laws now grant, or may hereafter grant, to nationals; all without prejudice to the rights specially provided for by this Convention. Consequently, they shall have the same protection as the latter, and the same legal remedy against any infringement of their rights, provided that the conditions and formalities imposed upon nationals are complied with.
>
> (2) However, no requirement as to domicile or establishment in the country where protection is claimed may be imposed upon nationals of countries of the Union for the enjoyment of any industrial property rights.

7.251 The text refers to the "countries of the Union" for the purposes of identifying States which bear the obligation to accord national treatment under that provision. However, Article 2.1 of the TRIPS Agreement obliges WTO Members to comply with Articles 1 through 12, and Article 19, of that Convention.[245] Therefore, as a WTO Member, the European Communities owes obligations under Article 2 of the Paris Convention (1967), as incorporated by Article 2.1 of the TRIPS Agreement.

7.252 With respect to the claim under paragraph 1 of Article 2 of the Paris Convention (1967), as incorporated by Article 2.1 of the TRIPS Agreement, the Panel observes that, unlike Article 3.1 of the TRIPS Agreement, Article 2(1) of the Paris Convention (1967) refers to "the advantages that ... laws now grant, or may hereafter grant" and not to "no less favourable" treatment. Therefore, the Panel has not actually reached a conclusion on this claim. However, further findings on this claim would not provide any additional contribution to a positive solution to this dispute and are therefore unnecessary.

7.253 With respect to the claim under paragraph 2 of Article 2 of the Paris Convention (1967), as incorporated by Article 2.1 of the TRIPS Agreement, the Panel does not consider that the Regulation contains a requirement of domicile or establishment.[246] We have found that the design and structure of the Regulation will operate to ensure that persons who use a protected GI, located in the European Communities, will have a domicile or establishment within the territory of the European Communities. We have also found that the availability of protection for GIs located in third countries, including WTO Members, is dependent on whether the third country in which the GI is located satisfies the conditions of equivalence or reciprocity or enters into an international agreement with the European Communities. It is irrelevant to the protection of a GI located in a

---

[245] The Appellate Body report on *US – Section 211 Appropriations Act* also notes that the obligations of countries of the Paris Union under the Paris Convention (1967) are also obligations of WTO Members by virtue of Article 2.1 of the TRIPS Agreement, para. 125.

[246] The Panel recalls its findings at para. 7.234 above on the meaning of those terms as understood under Article 3 of the Paris Convention (1967).

third country whether or not the person who seeks protection has a domicile or establishment in the European Communities.

7.254 Therefore, the Panel concludes that, with respect to the availability of protection, the Regulation does not impose a requirement as to domicile or establishment inconsistently with Article 2(2) of the Paris Convention (1967), as incorporated by Article 2.1 of the TRIPS Agreement.

(c) National treatment under GATT 1994

(i) main arguments of the parties

7.255 Australia claims the Regulation is inconsistent with Article III:4 of GATT 1994 because it imposes conditions of *reciprocity* and *equivalence* on the availability of protection. The agricultural products and foodstuffs from the European Communities and from third countries for which GIs may be registered under the Regulation are *like products* in the sense of Article III:4. The reciprocity condition in Article 12(1) of the Regulation refers to protection of "corresponding products" from the European Communities which encompasses, at least, *like products*.[247] It argues that the Regulation is a measure *affecting the internal sale and/or offering for sale* of imported products because imported products can only benefit from the Community-wide protection under the Regulation and/or the esteem purportedly attached where they are registered, and imported products may not bear a registered GI even if it is the common name for a product in the country of origin and/or in the course of trade.[248]

7.256 Australia argues that the Regulation accords *less favourable treatment* to imported products because it imposes distinct additional requirements of equivalence and reciprocity for registration to which domestic products are not subject. Those additional requirements significantly modify the conditions of competition for imported products because if another WTO Member is not willing and able to satisfy them, GIs from that Member are unable to be registered and protected for products imported from that Member into the EC market.[249]

7.257 The European Communities responds that the Regulation is fully compatible with Article III:4 of GATT 1994. It does not contest that products from the European Communities and from third countries falling under the scope of the Regulation may be *like products*, although it stresses that this alone does not preclude the European Communities from applying the conditions for registration to individual GIs.[250] It does not contest that the Regulation is a measure *affecting the internal sale* of products.[251]

7.258 The European Communities argues that the Regulation does not accord *less favourable treatment* to imported products because it does not apply the conditions in Article 12(1) to the registration of GIs from other WTO Members.[252] It concedes that the application of those conditions would prejudice its obligations under Article III:4 of GATT 1994.[253]

247 Australia's first written submission, paras. 161-162 and 166-167.

248 Australia's first written submission, para. 164.

249 Australia's first written submission, paras. 168 and 179; response to Panel question No. 32.

250 European Communities' first written submission, paras. 195-197.

251 European Communities' first written submission, para. 194.

252 European Communities' first written submission, para. 203; rebuttal submission, para. 212.

253 European Communities' response to Panel question No. 94.

(ii) main arguments of third parties

7.259 Brazil argues the GATT– and WTO– underlying principle of national treatment would be completely voided of any meaning if it were made conditional on requirements of reciprocity and adoption of equivalent legislation.[254]

7.260 China argues that the different treatment accorded to GIs by the Regulation will amount to less favourable treatment if it is found to modify the conditions of competition under which like imported and EC products compete in the EC market to the disadvantage of imported products.[255]

7.261 New Zealand considers that the complainant has demonstrated all three elements constituting a violation of Article III:4 of GATT 1994. The only issue under debate is whether the Regulation confers "less favourable treatment" on imported products. As the same phrase is used in Article 3.1 of the TRIPS Agreement, all arguments raised in relation to that claim apply equally here.[256]

(iii) consideration by the Panel

7.262 The Panel notes that the European Communities concedes that the conditions of equivalence and reciprocity in Article 12(1) of the Regulation, if applied to WTO Members, are inconsistent with Article III:4 of GATT 1994.[257] Given that the Panel has found that the Regulation "as such" imposes those conditions on the registration of GIs located in other WTO Members, there is no longer any defence before the Panel to the claim that, in this respect, the Regulation is inconsistent with Article III:4 of GATT 1994. It suffices to recall below that the essential elements of an inconsistency with Article III:4 are all met in this claim. These are that the imported and domestic products at issue are "like products;" that the measure at issue is a "law, regulation, or requirement affecting their internal sale, offering for sale, purchase, transportation, distribution, or use;" and that the imported products are accorded "less favourable" treatment than that accorded to like domestic products.[258]

7.263 The Regulation sets down requirements concerning the use of certain names in the presentation for sale of agricultural products and foodstuffs.[259] It is therefore a law or regulation affecting the internal sale and offering for sale of products within the meaning of Article III:4 of GATT 1994. This is not altered by the fact that the Regulation is also an intellectual property measure covered by the TRIPS Agreement since GATT 1994 and the TRIPS Agreement apply cumulatively.[260]

7.264 The Regulation links the protection of the name of a product to the territory of a particular country.[261] In the case of "designations of origin," as defined in Article 2 of the Regulation, this is the place of production, processing and preparation of the product and, in the case of "geographical indications," as defined in Article 2 of the Regulation, this is the place of production, processing and/or preparation. It is not disputed that in most

---

254 Annex C, para. 25.

255 Annex C, para. 95.

256 Annex C, para. 141.

257 European Communities' response to Panel question No. 94(a).

258 These three elements are also set out in the Appellate Body report on *Korea – Various Measures on Beef* at para. 133.

259 Article 1(1) of the Regulation provides that it "lays down rules on the protection of designations of origin and geographical indications of agricultural products ... and of ... foodstuffs ..." and Commission Regulation (EEC) No. 2037/93 sets out detailed rules on the application of the Regulation with respect to use of the PDO and PGI logos in the promotion of products. (see Exhibit COMP-2). Article 13(1) of the Regulation sets out uses against which registered names are protected.

260 The Panel recalls its comment on the order of analysis in para. 7.87 and its findings in para. 7.244, that there is no hierarchy between GATT 1994 and the TRIPS Agreement, which appear in separate annexes to the WTO Agreement. Further, an intellectual property measure was the subject of conclusions under Article III:4 of GATT 1947 in the GATT Panel report on *US – Section 337*. The Panel does not consider that the conclusion of the TRIPS Agreement reduced the scope of application of GATT: see, on the same point with respect to GATS, the Appellate Body report on *Canada – Periodicals*, DSR 1997:I, 449, at 465.

261 Exceptionally, it may extend across a border of more than one country, see Articles 5(5) and 12a(1) of the Regulation.

cases these criteria are sufficient to confer origin on the products. Given that the Panel has found that the protection of names of products from other WTO Members is contingent on satisfaction of certain conditions of equivalence and reciprocity that do not apply to the names of products from the European Communities, the Regulation formally discriminates between imported products and products of European Communities origin within the meaning of Article III:4 of GATT 1994.

7.265 The Regulation applies to the names of a wide class of products described in Article 1(1), which refers to the large number of agricultural products intended for human consumption referred to in Annex 1 to the EC Treaty as well as 13 additional types of agricultural products and foodstuffs listed in the annexes to the Regulation. The European Communities does not contest that there are, among this group, "like products" among the imported products and products of European Communities origin. The European Communities and other WTO Members produce the same types of covered agricultural products and foodstuffs with GIs that may be eligible for protection. Article 13(1)(a) of the Regulation provides that protection is provided against use of a name in respect of products "comparable to the products registered under that name." It is axiomatic that one must compare apples with apples and oranges with oranges. In this dispute, it is not contested that Tasmanian apples may be like *pommes de Savoie*[262] and Florida citrus may be like *cítricos valencianos*[263] for the purposes of Article III:4 of GATT 1994.

7.266 In our analysis of the question of "less favourable treatment," we follow the approach of the Appellate Body in *Korea – Various Measures on Beef* and *US – FSC (Article 21.5 – EC)* that this standard should be assessed under Article III:4 of GATT 1994 by examining whether the measures at issue modify the conditions of competition between domestic and imported products in the relevant market to the detriment of imported products. This examination must closely scrutinize the "fundamental thrust and effect of the measure itself" founded on a careful analysis of the contested measure and of its implications in the marketplace.[264]

7.267 The Regulation provides in Article 13 that registered GIs shall be protected against certain commercial uses and other practices. Registration provides the legal means to prevent the sale and offering for sale of products, including competitive products, where they use, imitate or evoke a registered GI, which is a substantive advantage conferred on products that comply with the GI registration. Registration does not grant a right to exclude competition, or deny the possibility of sale without a registered GI but, where products, including competitive products, bear an indication that falls within the protection granted by registration, they may be removed from sale. This is a substantive advantage that affects the conditions of competition of the relevant products.

7.268 The declared purposes of the Regulation set out in its preamble include the following, which links GIs to demand for products:

> Whereas, moreover, it has been observed in recent years that consumers are tending to attach greater importance to the quality of foodstuffs rather than to quantity; whereas this quest for specific products generates a growing demand for agricultural products or foodstuffs with an identifiable geographical origin;

7.269 Agricultural products and foodstuffs from the European Communities may obtain this advantage where they satisfy the eligibility criteria in the Regulation. Like products imported from WTO Members that the Commission has not decided meet the equivalence and reciprocity conditions in Article 12(1) of the Regulation—which is all of them—are not able to obtain that advantage and, hence, are accorded less favourable treatment. Products from WTO Members which can satisfy the equivalence and reciprocity conditions in Article 12(1) still face an "extra hurdle" in obtaining the advantage of registration since the

---

262 Registered by Commission Regulation (EC) No. 1107/96, p. 13, Exhibit COMP-3a.

263 Registered by Commission Regulation (EC) No. 865/2003, Exhibit COMP-4b.i.

264 See the Appellate Body report on *Korea – Various Measures on Beef*, paras. 137 and 142; and also *US – FSC (Article 21.5 – EC)*, para. 215, quoted at para. 7.186 above.

Commission must decide that their country of origin meets those conditions—a step which is not required of like products from the European Communities. This is also less favourable treatment.

7.270 The European Communities does not contest that these are benefits of protection under the Regulation. It refers to the right to use the designation and logo under Article 8 and the possibility of excluding others from use of the GI under Article 13.[265]

7.271 The Panel also notes that there is the possibility that a WTO Member could conclude an international agreement with the European Communities for the protection of specific GIs for its agricultural products and foodstuffs. It is not in dispute that this possibility would provide less favourable treatment to imported agricultural products and foodstuffs than the procedure for the registration of GIs provides for agricultural products and foodstuffs from the European Communities.

7.272 Therefore, the Panel concludes that, with respect to the equivalence and reciprocity conditions, as applicable to the availability of protection, the Regulation accords less favourable treatment to imported products, inconsistently with Article III:4 of GATT 1994.[266]

7.273 The European Communities has not asserted that, with respect to the availability of protection, the Regulation is justified by Article XX(d) of GATT 1994.[267]

7.274 Australia argues that less favourable treatment is accorded by the European Communities' "inability to state clearly" what is required by Article 12 of the Regulation, or to state the decision-making criteria that would govern the assessments required to be made under Article 12 of the Regulation.[268] However, the Panel notes that, given the European Communities' defence that it did not apply the conditions in Article 12 to WTO Members, there was little discussion of what precisely is required by those conditions. In view of the Panel's conclusion, it is unnecessary to consider this issue further.

7.275 Australia also argues that the disadvantage accorded by the Regulation to imported products bearing a GI located in another Member is "cumulative," by reference to the equivalence and reciprocity conditions, the application procedures, the regulatory committee (considered below) and the two factors in paragraph 7.274.[269] However, given that Australia did not elaborate on how the cumulative effect of these aspects of the Regulation allegedly accords less favourable treatment distinct from that accorded by each of them separately, the Panel does not consider it necessary to consider this issue further.

2. *Application procedures*

(a) *Description of application procedures under Articles 5 and 12a of the Regulation*

7.276 The parties agree on the features of the application procedures under the Regulation. There are separate provisions setting out the procedures for applications for registration of GIs which apply according to the

[265] European Communities' rebuttal submission, para. 118.

[266] This conclusion is without prejudice to the Panel's examination of the inspection structures required for registration, considered later in this report.

[267] See the European Communities' first written submission, paras. 224-225, in which it asserts Article XX(d) as a defence only in relation to Article 12a, in conjunction with Articles 4 and 10, of the Regulation. See also its rebuttal submission, paras. 228-242, and its second oral statement, paras. 132 and 135, in which it assert Article XX(d) as a defence only with respect to inspections, application procedures and the labelling requirement. Despite broader references to the Regulation in its first written submission , para. 190, and first oral statement, para. 73, the European Communities did not provide any specific arguments in defence of the equivalence and reciprocity conditions under Article XX(d).

[268] Australia's first written submission, para. 177.

[269] Australia's first written submission, para. 178; response to Panel question No. 32.

location of the GI.[270] Article 5 applies where it is located in an EC member State. Article 12a applies where the GI is located in a third country.

7.277 Article 5(4) and 5(5) provide, relevantly, as follows:

> 4. The application shall be sent to the Member State in which the geographical area is located.
>
> 5. The Member State shall check that the application is justified and shall forward the application, including the product specification referred to in Article 4 and other documents on which it has based its decision, to the Commission, if it considers that it satisfies the requirements of this Regulation. [...]

7.278 Article 12a(1) and 12a(2) provide, relevantly, as follows:

> 1. In the case provided for in Article 12(3), if a group or a natural or legal person as referred to in Article 5(1) and (2) in a third country wishes to have a name registered under this Regulation it shall send a registration application to the authorities in the country in which the geographical area is located. [...]
>
> 2. If the third country referred to in paragraph 1 deems the requirements of this Regulation to be satisfied it shall transmit the registration application to the Commission accompanied by:
>
> (a) a description of the legal provisions and the usage on the basis of which the designation of origin or the geographical indication is protected or established in the country,
>
> (b) a declaration that the structures provided for in Article 10 are established on its territory, and
>
> (c) other documents on which it has based its assessment.

7.279 After an application is forwarded by an EC member State or a third country, Articles 6(1) and 12b(1) of the Regulation oblige the Commission to verify whether the registration application includes all the requisite particulars and satisfies the conditions for protection. There are differences in the drafting of Articles 6(1) and 12b(1) which relate, respectively, to applications forwarded by EC member States and those transmitted by third countries which Australia has not put in issue.

(b) National treatment under the TRIPS Agreement

(i) main arguments of the parties

7.280 Australia claims that the Regulation is inconsistent with Article 3.1 of the TRIPS Agreement and Article 2 of the Paris Convention (1967), as incorporated by Article 2.1 of the TRIPS Agreement, because non-EC nationals seeking to register a GI located in the territory of another WTO Member are not able to apply for registration directly to the European Communities—whether to the Commission or another Community-level body. Articles 12(3) and 12a of the Regulation, read together, require that another WTO Member in which the GI is located pre-approve every application.[271] The European Communities has an obligation to provide the

---

[270] For the sake of brevity, the Panel refers to a name that refers to a geographical area located in a Member as a GI located in that Member.

[271] Australia's first written submission, paras. 172 and 198; first oral statement, para. 34.

means for intellectual property right holders to exercise their rights without intervention by another government.[272]

7.281 Australia argues that the legally defined rights and obligations between the European Communities and EC member States and EC member State nationals makes the registration process for EC nationals fundamentally different for non-EC nationals.[273] Australia adopts Canada's portrayal of the issues concerning the relationship between WTO Members, the European Communities, the EC member States and nationals. If the subject matter of this dispute lies within the exclusive competence of the European Communities, not EC member States, then any functions carried out by EC member States in implementing the Regulation are carried out as sub-national units of the European Communities. Any outward appearance of symmetry of treatment therefore masks a fundamentally different situation.[274] Australia would transmit an application for registration to the Commission if it became aware of one from within Australia, but it could not state positively that it could meet the equivalence and reciprocity conditions.[275]

7.282 Australia also claims that the Regulation imposes a requirement of establishment in the European Communities inconsistently with Article 2(2) of the Paris Convention (1967).[276]

7.283 The European Communities responds that this claim must fail. Its first defence is that the application procedures do not apply to nationality but according to the location of geographical areas. That defence has been considered above.

7.284 The European Communities argues that the application procedures do not accord *less favourable treatment* because the role of third country governments corresponds exactly to that of EC member States. The transmission of applications by governments in fact ensures equal treatment.[277] The authorities of third countries and EC member States are best placed to evaluate whether a GI fulfils the conditions for protection, which requires familiarity with a host of factors and may require knowledge of the market conditions in the country of origin. The evaluation of whether a GI is protected in the country of origin requires the implication of the authorities of the third country. Verification in a third country calls for respect for its sovereignty. Involvement of third country authorities facilitates cooperation during the registration process and should be of practical benefit to the applicant.[278]

7.285 The European Communities argues that the verification and transmission of an application are not overly burdensome for another WTO Member. Another WTO Member cannot invoke its own unwillingness to cooperate in the registration process in order to demonstrate a national treatment violation on the part of the EC.[279] There are many examples of international cooperation between governments in the protection of private rights including, in the field of intellectual property protection, such as the Madrid Protocol, the Lisbon Agreement and Article 6*quinquies*A(1) of the Paris Convention, and in the fields of certificates of origin, technical standards, conformity assessment, transport, fisheries and judicial cooperation. These examples illustrate that in an increasingly interdependent world, the effective protection of individual rights in cross-border situations inevitably engenders a need for cross-border cooperation.[280]

---

[272] Australia's response to Panel question No. 38.

[273] Australia's first written submission, para. 205; first oral statement, para. 34.

[274] Australia's rebuttal submission, paras. 174-176, citing Canada's third party oral statement; and Australia's second oral statement, para. 77.

[275] Australia's response to Panel question No. 38.

[276] Australia's first written submission, paras. 198 and 206.

[277] European Communities' first written submission, para. 130.

[278] European Communities' response to Panel question No. 33; rebuttal submission, paras. 124-129.

[279] European Communities' first written submission, para. 131.

[280] European Communities' response to Panel question No. 37.

7.286 The European Communities does not want to impose obligations on third countries, but the protection of GIs located in the territory of third countries depends on their cooperation. This is partially mandated by the definition of a GI in Article 22.1 of the TRIPS Agreement, which requires verification of whether certain characteristics of a good are essentially attributable to its geographical origin. This is an obligation for all Members and should normally facilitate the examination of whether the name fulfils the criteria in the Regulation. The description of how a GI is protected in its country of origin reflects the provision in Article 24.9 of the TRIPS Agreement. Even where there is no specific registration system in the country of origin, that is still a TRIPS requirement for the European Communities and a matter of foreign law.[281] The transmission of the application by the same government is not a significant extra burden.[282]

(ii) main arguments of third parties

7.287 Argentina, Brazil, India, Mexico, New Zealand and Chinese Taipei all inform the Panel that they are not aware of any person ever having attempted to file with their respective authorities an application for registration under the Regulation.[283]

7.288 Argentina expresses uncertainty regarding the consistency of the application procedures with the characterization of intellectual property rights under the TRIPS Agreement, in that they require States to manage the registration of a GI instead of right holders who are private persons.[284]

7.289 Brazil argues that the application procedures require WTO Members to "pre-approve" applications before they forward them to the European Commission, which is a striking violation of the national treatment obligation in Article 3.1 of the TRIPS Agreement for two reasons: (1) this is an additional procedure for other WTO Members; and (2) the approval process must be conducted according to EC law, not the law of the other WTO Member. [285]

7.290 China argues that the provisions on verification and publication do not afford clarity. The procedures for EC member States and third countries are in parallel but are not the same in substance. The provisions on verification by, and transmission to, the Commission differ between the procedures which suggests that third countries must satisfy more than an EC member State.

7.291 Colombia expresses uncertainty as to whether the country of origin must in all cases provide a declaration under Article 12a(2) with a description of the legal provisions under which the GI is protected. This is, in practice, a condition which entails an evaluation of the system of GI protection in the country of origin contrary to Article 1.1 of the TRIPS Agreement.[286]

7.292 Mexico refers to cochineal as a practical example of the way in which Mexican producers would be required to go through specific procedures which EC nationals are not.[287]

7.293 New Zealand submits that, although the requirement to submit all applications through government applies equally to applications from EC member States and other WTO Member nationals, its effect is to disadvantage nationals from other WTO Members. EC nationals have an enforceable right that applications that

---

[281] European Communities' rebuttal submission, paras. 131-134; response to Panel question No. 114.

[282] European Communities' rebuttal submission, para. 139.

[283] See their respective responses in Annex C, paras. 18, 32, 103, 118, 160 and 179.

[284] Annex C, paras. 7-15.

[285] Annex C, para. 27.

[286] Annex C, para. 99.

[287] Annex C, paras. 115-117.

satisfy the requirements of the Regulation are forwarded to the Commission. Submission of an application via an EC member State is essentially a formality. Other WTO Member nationals have no such enforceable right.[288]

(iii) consideration by the Panel

7.294 These claims are made under the national treatment obligations in Article 3.1 of the TRIPS Agreement and Article 2 of the Paris Convention (1967), as incorporated by Article 2.1 of the TRIPS Agreement. The Panel will first consider the claim under Article 3.1 of the TRIPS Agreement.

7.295 The Panel recalls that two elements must be satisfied to establish an inconsistency with this obligation: (1) the measure at issue must apply with regard to the protection of intellectual property; and (2) the nationals of other Members must be accorded "less favourable" treatment than the Member's own nationals. The Panel will address each of these elements in turn.

<u>protection of intellectual property</u>

7.296 This claim concerns procedures for filing and examination of applications for registration of "designations of origin" and "geographical indications," as defined in the Regulation. They are referred to in this report, for the sake of brevity, as "application procedures."

7.297 The Panel recalls that the national treatment obligation in Article 3 of the TRIPS Agreement applies to the treatment accorded by a Member "with regard to the protection of intellectual property." Footnote 3 provides an inclusive definition of the term "protection" as used in Articles 3 and 4. It reads as follows:

> For the purposes of Articles 3 and 4, 'protection' shall include matters affecting the availability, acquisition, scope, maintenance and enforcement of intellectual property rights as well as those matters affecting the use of intellectual property rights specifically addressed in this Agreement.

7.298 Turning to the Regulation, procedures for the filing and examination of applications for registration are matters affecting the *acquisition* of intellectual property rights in relation to "designations of origin and "geographical indications," as defined in the Regulation. It is not disputed that "designations of origin" and "geographical indications," as defined in the Regulation, are a subset of "geographical indications," the subject of Section 3 of Part II, and therefore part of a category of intellectual property within the meaning of Article 1.2 of the TRIPS Agreement.

7.299 Therefore, this claim concerns the "protection" of intellectual property, as clarified in footnote 3 to the TRIPS Agreement, within the scope of the national treatment obligation in Article 3.1 of that Agreement.

<u>less favourable treatment accorded to the nationals of other Members</u>

7.300 The Panel recalls its findings:

(a) at paragraphs 7.221 to 7.239 as to the treatment accorded to the "nationals of other Members" under the Regulation by its treatment according to the location of GIs; and

(b) at paragraph 7.184 that under Article 3.1 of the TRIPS Agreement we must examine the "effective equality of opportunities" with regard to the protection of intellectual property rights and, at paragraph 7.187 that in this examination we will focus on the "fundamental thrust and effect" of the Regulation.

---

[288] Annex C, paras. 136-137.

7.301 The parties and third parties who responded to the Panel's question on this point all reported that they were not aware of any application for the registration of a name of an area located in a third country outside the European Communities ever having been filed with the authorities of a third country.[289] However, Australia challenges the Regulation, in this respect, "as such."

7.302 Australia claims that the treatment accorded under the application procedures in Article 12a(1) and (2) is less favourable treatment than that accorded under the applications procedures in Article 5(4) and (5). There is an apparent equivalence in the drafting of these provisions but the question is whether this would imply a modification of the effective equality of opportunities with regard to the protection of intellectual property.

7.303 The Panel notes that the initial steps in the application procedures can be broken down as follows.

(a) as a first step, *all* applicants are required to submit their application to the authorities in the country in which the geographical area is located. These will be authorities of an EC member State or a third country, depending on the case;

(b) as a second step, the authorities who receive an application consider whether the application is justified or satisfies the requirements of the Regulation. This involves a detailed examination of the application in accordance with the criteria in the European Communities' Regulation, not the domestic law of the country where the application is filed; and

(c) as a third step, if the authorities who receive an application consider that the application is justified or satisfies the requirements of the Regulation, they forward or transmit it to the Commission. If the application concerns a geographical area located outside the European Communities, the authorities must also transmit a description of the protection of the GI in its country of origin, as well as a declaration concerning inspection structures.[290]

7.304 We recall the European Communities' explanation of its domestic constitutional arrangements, set out at paragraph 7.148, that Community laws are generally not executed through authorities at Community level but rather through recourse to the authorities of its member States which, in such a situation, "act *de facto* as organs of the Community, for which the Community would be responsible under WTO law and international law in general."[291] It follows that any application relating to a geographical area located in an EC member State is filed directly with a "*de facto* organ of the Community" which also carries out the initial examination. An application relating to a geographical area located in a third country cannot be filed directly, but must be filed with a foreign government. This is a formal difference in treatment.

7.305 Further, Article 5 of the Regulation provides for application procedures for GIs located in the European Communities. Paragraph 6 provides as follows:

> 6. Member States shall introduce the laws, regulations and administrative provisions necessary to comply with this Article.

7.306 An EC member State has an obligation to establish application procedures for the purposes of the Regulation. Under Community law, an EC member State has an obligation to examine an application and

---

[289] However, the United States provided evidence from the Idaho Potato Commission that it could not obtain protection for its US certification mark in the European Union. Its attorneys in three EC member States had advised that there were no steps it could take to stop use of the term "Idaho" by other companies in Europe. The European Communities responds that this is based on a misperception of the content of the Regulation, that it does not contain evidence of an attempt to register a GI under the Regulation, and that it seems to relate more to the protection of trademarks than GIs: see its rebuttal submission, para. 85.

[290] For the purposes of this report, references to examination and transmission of "applications" include examination and transmission of these supporting documents. Inspection structures requirements are considered later in this report.

[291] European Communities' second oral statement, para. 148.

decide whether it is justified and, if it is justified, to forward it to the Commission. A group or person who submits an application in an EC member State may enforce these obligations through recourse to judicial procedures based on the Regulation. In contrast, a third country government has no obligation under Community law or any other law to examine an application or to transmit it or any other document to the Commission. A group or person who submits an application in a third country has no right to such treatment.

7.307 Therefore, applicants for GIs that refer to geographical areas located in third countries do not have a right in the application procedures that is provided to applicants for GIs that refer to geographical areas located in the European Communities. Applicants in third countries face an "extra hurdle" in ensuring that the authorities in those countries carry out the functions reserved to them under the Regulation, which applicants in EC member States do not face. Consequently, certain applications and requisite supporting documents may not be examined or transmitted. Each of these considerations significantly reduces the opportunities available to the nationals of other WTO Members in the acquisition of rights under the Regulation below those available to the European Communities' own nationals.

7.308 The European Communities submits that that "[t]he Regulation does not require anything that would be outside the scope of any WTO Member with a normally functioning government."[292] The Panel notes that, whilst a normally functioning government might have the capacity to carry out the first and third steps, it cannot be assumed that it would have the capacity to carry out the examination according to EC law required by the second step. WTO Members have no obligation to implement a system of protection for geographical indications comparable to that of the European Communities and there is no reason to believe that they would nevertheless have the capacity to carry out examinations of technical issues that involve interpretations of EC law. In this regard, we note that one third party in this Panel proceeding indicates that its authorities would be devoid of legal competence to perform this analysis.[293] Whilst a WTO Member that provided equivalent protection under its domestic law might presumably have the technical capacity, if not the legal competence, to perform this analysis, the provision of such protection forms part of the conditions under Article 12(1) of the Regulation. We have found that requirement, as a precondition to the availability of GI protection, to be inconsistent with the national treatment obligations in the TRIPS Agreement and GATT 1994.

7.309 In any event, even if any normally functioning government could perform these three steps, that would not alter the Panel's conclusion. The obligation to accord national treatment with respect to a measure of the European Communities is the obligation of the European Communities. This is highlighted in the text of Article 3.1 of the TRIPS Agreement under which "[e]ach Member" shall accord to the nationals of other Members no less favourable treatment.

7.310 In accordance with its domestic law, the European Communities is entitled to delegate certain functions under its measure to the authorities of EC member States. However, under the Regulation, the European Communities has purported to delegate part of this obligation to other WTO Members, who must carry out these three steps in the application procedures in order to ensure that no less favourable treatment is accorded to their respective nationals. To that extent, the European Communities fails to accord no less favourable treatment *itself* to the nationals of other Members.

7.311 The Panel notes that the European Commission does not have the discretion to ensure that applications for GIs that refer to geographical areas located in third countries receive no less favourable treatment than those located in the European Communities because it has structured the Regulation in such a way that certain functions are completely outside its control.

---

[292] European Communities' rebuttal submission, para. 141; second oral statement, para. 142.

[293] See comments by Brazil in Annex C, para. 32.

7.312 The European Communities drew the Panel's attention to many examples of international cooperation in the protection of private rights, including in the field of intellectual property protection.[294] The Panel notes that under two of them, the Patent Cooperation Treaty and the Madrid Protocol, the possibility of filing an application with an office in the applicant's own country does not prevent the applicant filing an application directly in the another country. The Panel certainly does not intend to discourage international cooperation. However, in each of these examples, cooperation is provided in the framework of treaties in which contracting parties have voluntarily agreed to participate. In contrast, the Regulation is a domestic law adopted by one Member.

7.313 The Panel also confirms that nothing in these findings purports to diminish the rights of Members under Article 24.9 of the TRIPS Agreement, which provides, in essence, that there is no obligation under this Agreement to protect geographical indications which are not protected in their country of origin.[295]

7.314 The Panel further confirms that the European Communities is entitled, under Article 62.1 of the TRIPS Agreement, to require that applicants comply with reasonable procedures and formalities that are consistent with the Agreement in order to prove that they meet the conditions of protection. However, Article 62 is outside the Panel's terms of reference.

7.315 The Panel recalls its finding at paragraph 7.248 that the fact that a general exceptions provision analogous to Article XX of GATT 1994 was not included in the TRIPS Agreement has no impact on its analysis of Article 3.1.

7.316 For the above reasons, the Panel concludes that, with respect to the application procedures, insofar as they require examination and transmission of applications by governments, the Regulation accords other WTO Member nationals less favourable treatment than it accords the European Communities' own nationals, inconsistently with Article 3.1 of the TRIPS Agreement.

7.317 In view of that conclusion, it is unnecessary to consider the consistency of the Regulation, with respect to the application procedures, with Article 2(1) of the Paris Convention (1967), as incorporated by Article 2.1 of the TRIPS Agreement. With respect to Article 2(2) of the Paris Convention (1967), the Panel recalls its finding at paragraph 7.251 and, for the same reasons, concludes that, with respect to the application procedures, the Regulation does not impose a requirement of domicile or establishment inconsistently with that provision, as incorporated by Article 2.1 of the TRIPS Agreement.

(c) National treatment under GATT 1994

(i) main arguments of the parties

7.318 Australia claims that the Regulation is inconsistent with Article III:4 of GATT 1994 because it requires the WTO Member in whose territory a geographical area is located to pre-approve each and every application for registration. This is a distinct and additional requirement imposed on products imported into the European Communities which significantly modifies the conditions of competition for imported products vis-à-vis domestic like products in the EC market. Any outward appearance of symmetry of treatment therefore masks a fundamentally different situation, for the reasons given earlier.[296]

7.319 Australia argues that the relevant aspects of the application procedures are not justified under Article XX(d) of GATT 1994. They do not satisfy the "necessary" test in paragraph (d) because, as in *Korea – Various Measures on Beef*, alternative measures are reasonably available. The European Communities could leave it to the applicant to provide the required information and/or it could ask for the cooperation of another

---

[294] See European Communities' response to Panel question No. 37, and Exhibits EC-20 through EC-27.

[295] Nothing in these findings purports to diminish the rights of Members under Article 5 of the TRIPS Agreement either.

[296] Australia's first written submission, paras. 172-174.

WTO Member government after an application has been filed should such cooperation be necessary to enable an application to be assessed. They do not satisfy the chapeau of Article XX because if the term is already registered, the applicant could provide a registration certificate as readily as the third country government. As in *US – Shrimp*, the Regulation requires other WTO Members to adopt a regulatory framework that is not merely comparable but essentially the same.[297]

7.320 The European Communities responds that this claim must fail. It reiterates its arguments that the application procedures provide equal treatment, not less favourable treatment.[298]

7.321 The European Communities asserts that verification and transmission of applications by the government of the home country of the GI is justified by Article XX(d) of GATT 1994.[299] It argues that this is necessary to secure compliance with the Regulation itself, in particular, the definition of a GI, the product specifications, protection in the country of origin, establishment of the inspection structures and the requirement that only products that comply with a specification bear the PDO and PGI indications. It argues that the cooperation of the home government is indispensable for the implementation of the Regulation which, in particular, requires the evaluation of factual and legal questions which only the home country of the GI is in a position to carry out. These requirements for cooperation do not go beyond what is necessary for the implementation of the Regulation. The requirement of transmission follows naturally from the required intergovernmental cooperation and is not particularly burdensome for WTO Members. Article XX(d) does not exclude that the measures and the laws and regulations with which they secure compliance may be part of the same legal act. In addition, there is nothing which limits measures which secure compliance to *ex post* enforcement and excludes safeguards in the registration process. The Regulation is not inconsistent with GATT 1994 because it implements an obligation under Article 22 of the TRIPS Agreement and a higher level of protection permitted by Article 1.1. It is applied in a manner consistent with the chapeau of Article XX.[300]

7.322 The European Communities argues that, with respect to verification that the GI is protected in its country of origin, verification requires knowledge of local factors that typically only the country of origin will have and which may also require on-site checks. Submission of a registration certificate authenticated by the country of origin would normally provide sufficient evidence that the indication is protected in the country of origin. However, it is not an option for those Members which do not have a specific register, such as Australia. Verification by third country governments is particularly necessary where they do not have a specific register as evaluation of protection in the country of origin may be more difficult. It is not credible that the Australian government would not be better qualified than the right holder or the European Communities. Transmission of applications by third country governments is an integral part of the application procedure and should not be viewed in isolation. It has no significant impact on trade in goods. It makes no difference whether the European Communities asks for cooperation from a third country government before or after an application is filed.[301]

(ii) main arguments by third parties

7.323 Argentina, Brazil, India, Mexico and Chinese Taipei inform the Panel that direct applications to register GIs located in third countries are possible under their respective national legislation.[302]

7.324 Brazil argues that the application procedures require WTO Members to "pre-approve" applications before they forward them to the European Commission, which is a striking violation of the national treatment obligation in Article 3.1 of the TRIPS Agreement.[303]

---

[297] Australia's second oral statement paras. 66-70.

[298] European Communities' first written submission, para. 207; rebuttal submission, para. 218.

[299] European Communities' rebuttal submission, paras. 237-239.

[300] European Communities' rebuttal submission, paras. 237-239; responses to Panel question Nos. 135(a), (b) and (c) and 136(a).

[301] European Communities' response to Panel question No. 136(b), (c) and (d).

[302] See their respective responses in Annex C at paras. 18, 27, 103, 118 and 180.

7.325 New Zealand considers that, as the same phrase "less favourable treatment" is used in Article III:4 as in Article 3.1 of the TRIPS Agreement, all arguments raised under that claim apply equally here. New Zealand does not consider that the measure can be justified as "necessary" within the meaning of Article XX(d) of GATT 1994. The Commission conducts its own six-month investigation of an application so that it is not necessary for applications to be passed through a third country government filter.[304]

(iii) consideration by the Panel

7.326 This claim concerns procedures for applications for registration under the Regulation. The Panel recalls its findings:

(a) at paragraph 7.263, that the Regulation is a law or regulation affecting the internal sale and offering for sale of products within the meaning of Article III:4 of GATT 1994;

(b) at paragraph 7.264 that the Regulation links the protection of the name of a product to the territory of a particular country and formally discriminates between imported products and products of European Communities origin within the meaning of Article III:4 of GATT 1994;

(c) at paragraph 7.265 that the European Communities does not contest that there are, among the group of products covered by the Regulation, "like products" among the imported products and products of European Communities origin;

(d) at paragraph 7.266, that under Article III:4 of GATT 1994 we must examine whether the measure modifies the conditions of competition between domestic and imported products and that in this examination we will focus on the "fundamental thrust and effect of the measure itself;" and

(e) at paragraphs 7.267 to 7.269 on the substantive advantage provided under Article 13 of the Regulation that affects the conditions of competition of the relevant products;

(f) at paragraphs 7.303 to 7.307 concerning the differences between the application procedures for GIs that refer to geographical areas located in EC member States and those located in third countries. These differences can result in some applications from third countries, including WTO Members, not being transmitted to the Commission; and

(g) at paragraph 7.311 that the European Communities has no discretion in the implementation of the Regulation to ensure that all applications from third countries are transmitted to the Commission.

7.327 A failure to transmit an application would entail non-registration of GIs, which would lead to failure of the products from those third countries to obtain the benefits of registration set out in Article 13 of the Regulation. Therefore, the Panel concludes that, with respect to the application procedures, insofar as they require examination and transmission of applications by governments, the Regulation accords less favourable treatment to imported products than domestic products, inconsistently with Article III:4 of GATT 1994.

7.328 The European Communities asserts that these procedures are justified by Article XX(d) of GATT 1994. As the party invoking this affirmative defence, the European Communities bears the burden of proof that the conditions of the defence are met.

7.329 Article XX provides exceptions for certain measures. The "measures" which the European Communities needs to justify at this point are the requirements of examination and transmission of applications

---

[303] Annex C, para. 27.

[304] Annex C, paras. 141-143.

for registration by governments under the Regulation. These apply to applications from both EC member States and third countries. However, it does not need to justify the less favourable treatment which denies applicants for GIs located in third countries the opportunity to file direct applications.[305]

7.330 Paragraph (d) of Article XX refers to "measures" falling within the following description:

> (*d*) necessary to secure compliance with laws or regulations which are not inconsistent with the provisions of this Agreement, including those relating to customs enforcement, the enforcement of monopolies operated under paragraph 4 of Article II and Article XVII, the protection of patents, trade marks and copyrights, and the prevention of deceptive practices;

7.331 The Panel takes note that paragraph (d) refers to laws or regulations, including those relating to "the protection of patents, trade marks and copyrights, and the prevention of deceptive practices." The Regulation provides for the protection of GIs and is an analogous law or regulation, as the European Communities points out.[306] However, the term "laws or regulations" is qualified by the phrase "not inconsistent with the provisions of this Agreement."

7.332 The European Communities argues that the requirements of examination and transmission of applications by governments secure compliance with the Regulation.[307] However, the Panel has found that the Regulation itself is inconsistent with the provisions of GATT 1994 for the reasons set out in this report. Therefore, the Regulation is not a law or regulation within the meaning of paragraph (d). In response to questions, the European Communities argued that these requirements secure compliance with a provision within the Regulation. However, if that provision could itself be a law or regulation within the meaning of paragraph (d), the European Communities did not demonstrate that it was "not inconsistent" with GATT 1994.[308]

7.333 The Panel also notes the use of the term "necessary" in paragraph (d) of Article XX. We recall the clarification of that term provided by the Appellate Body in *Korea – Various Measures on Beef*, as follows:

> We believe that, as used in the context of Article XX(d), the reach of the word 'necessary' is not limited to that which is 'indispensable' or 'of absolute necessity' or 'inevitable'. Measures which are indispensable or of absolute necessity or inevitable to secure compliance certainly fulfil the requirements of Article XX(d). But other measures, too, may fall within the ambit of this exception. As used in Article XX(d), the term 'necessary' refers, in our view, to a range of degrees of necessity. At one end of this continuum lies 'necessary' understood as 'indispensable'; at the other end, is 'necessary' taken to mean as 'making a contribution to'. We consider that a 'necessary' measure is, in this continuum, located significantly closer to the pole of 'indispensable' than to the opposite pole of simply 'making a contribution to.'[footnote omitted][309]

[305] This is consistent with the approach of the Appellate Body in *US – Gasoline*, according to which one must examine whether the relevant "measure," rather than the legal finding of less favourable treatment, falls within a paragraph of Article XX: see DSR 1996:I, 3, at 15.

[306] European Communities' rebuttal submission, para. 234.

[307] European Communities' first written submission, para. 226; rebuttal submission, para. 238.

[308] The European Communities argued that verification (and incidentally also the transmission) of applications by the government of the country of origin served the purpose of establishing whether the requirements of the Regulation for registration of GIs are satisfied and, accordingly, secured compliance with the requirement in Article 8 that the PDO, PGI and equivalent indications may appear only on products that comply with the Regulation. However, it only explained how the Regulation itself was, in its view, not inconsistent with GATT 1994: see its responses to Panel questions No. 135(a), (c) and (d).

[309] Appellate Body report on *Korea – Various Measures on Beef*, para. 161.

7.334 The Appellate Body summed up its approach to the determination of whether a measure which is not "indispensable" may nevertheless be "necessary" within the meaning of Article XX(d) as a process of weighing and balancing a series of factors. It approved the approach of the GATT Panel in *US – Section 337* as a way in which to apply this process as follows:

> In our view, the weighing and balancing process we have outlined is comprehended in the determination of whether a WTO-consistent alternative measure which the Member concerned could 'reasonably be expected to employ' is available, or whether a less WTO-inconsistent measure is 'reasonably available.'[310]

7.335 The Panel will follow this approach.

7.336 Australia argues that the European Communities could reasonably be expected to allow applicants to file applications directly with its authorities without prior verification by third country governments, and that this is WTO-consistent. Many other WTO Members employ such a procedure.[311] It is not disputed that such a procedure would be WTO-consistent.

7.337 The European Communities submits that the cooperation of the government of the country where the GI is located is indispensable because the registration of GIs requires the evaluation of factual and legal questions which "only the home country of the GI is in a position to carry out."[312]

7.338 The Panel observes that Articles 6(2) and 12b(1) of the Regulation provide that the Commission makes the decision on whether the conditions are satisfied so as to warrant publication. It is not clear why an additional examination of the conditions by other governments is also required. Nor is it clear that a third country government is even able to conduct an examination according to the requirements, not of its own law, but of an EC Regulation. The European Communities has not explained why physical proximity or potential knowledge of certain questions in the country of origin implies a capacity to assess matters of EC law. Therefore, it is not clear to what extent examination by governments, including third country governments, contributes to securing compliance with the conditions for registration.

7.339 With respect to factual and legal questions that, as part of the examination, can be verified in the country of origin, the European Communities does not explain why the Regulation does not permit applicants to provide objective and impartial evidence that may verify their applications nor does it explain why the Commission cannot seek consent to carry out its own verifications. In its responses to the Panel's questions, the European Communities indicates that "typically" only the country of origin has the required knowledge of local factors and that verification "may" require on-site checks which the Commission cannot carry out in third countries without express consent.[313] The Panel considers that these responses constitute an admission that, in some cases, verification by third country governments is not necessary and that, if it sought and obtained consent, the Commission could conduct verifications itself. The European Communities has not demonstrated the factual premise of its defence that only the government of the country of origin is in a position to carry out the evaluation of these factual and legal questions. Therefore, the Panel does not need to consider further the requirement of examination by governments.

7.340 With respect to the transmission of applications, the European Communities is unable to explain why a procedure permitting applicants to file applications directly with its competent authorities would not permit an examination of whether an application for a GI in another WTO Member complies with the conditions in the

---

[310] *Ibid.* para. 166. The Appellate Body also followed this approach to the word "necessary" as used in paragraph (b) of Article XX in *EC – Asbestos*, para. 172.

[311] See comments of Argentina, Brazil, India, Mexico, New Zealand and Chinese Taipei as third parties in Annex C, paras. 18, 28, 103, 118, 161 and 180.

[312] European Communities' rebuttal submission, para. 237.

[313] European Communities' response to Panel question No. 136(a).

Regulation. It submitted that transmission of applications by governments should not be viewed in isolation. Given that it has not established that examination by governments, including third country governments, is necessary, it has not established that transmission by them is necessary either.

7.341 Therefore, the Panel considers that the European Communities has not discharged its burden of proving that examination and transmission of applications by governments are covered by paragraph (d) of Article XX. It is therefore unnecessary to consider the chapeau of Article XX.

7.342 For these reasons, the Panel concludes that, with respect to the application procedures, insofar as they require examination and transmission of applications by governments, the Regulation accords less favourable treatment to imported products inconsistently with Article III:4 of GATT 1994, and these requirements are not justified by Article XX(d).

3. *Objection procedures*

(a) Description of objection procedures under Articles 7, 12b and 12d of the Regulation

7.343 The parties agree on most features of the objection procedures under the Regulation. There are separate provisions setting out the procedures for objections to applications for registration of GIs which apply according to the location of the geographical area and the location of the person who wishes to file an objection. Article 7 applies where the geographical area and the person who wishes to file an objection are both located in EC member States. Article 12b applies where the geographical area is located in a third country. Article 12d applies where the geographical area is located in an EC member State and the person who wishes to file an objection is located in a third country.

7.344 Article 7(1) and 7(3) provide as follows:

> 1. Within six months of the date of publication in the *Official Journal of the European Communities* referred to in Article 6(2), any Member State may object to the registration.
>
> 3. Any legitimately concerned natural or legal person may object to the proposed registration by sending a duly substantiated statement to the competent authority of the Member State in which he resides or is established. The competent authority shall take the necessary measures to consider these comments or objection within the deadline laid down."

7.345 Article 12b(2) provides, relevantly, as follows:

> 2. Within six months of the date of publication as provided for in paragraph 1(a), any natural or legal person with a legitimate interest may object to the application published in accordance with paragraph 1(a) on the following terms:
>
> > (a) where the objection comes from a Member State of the European Union or a WTO Member, Article 7(1), (2) and (3) or Article 12d respectively shall apply;
> >
> > (b) where the objection comes from a third country meeting the equivalence conditions of Article 12(3), a duly substantiated statement of objection shall be addressed to the country in which the abovementioned natural or legal person resides or is established, which shall forward it to the Commission.

7.346 Article 12d(1) provides, relevantly, as follows:

> 1. Within six months of the date of the notice in the *Official Journal of the European Union* specified in Article 6(2) relating to a registration application submitted by a Member State,

> any natural or legal person that has a legitimate interest and is from a WTO member country or a third country recognised under the procedure provided for in Article 12(3) may object to the proposed registration by sending a duly substantiated statement to the country in which it resides or is established, which shall transmit it, made out or translated into a Community language, to the Commission.

7.347 Article 7(4) sets out the grounds for admission of objections. Articles 12b(3) and 12d(2) provide that the Commission shall examine the admissibility of objections in accordance with the criteria laid down in Article 7(4).

(b) National treatment under the TRIPS Agreement
(i) main arguments of the parties

7.348 Australia claims that the Regulation is inconsistent with Article 3.1 of the TRIPS Agreement and Article 2 of the Paris Convention (1967), as incorporated by Article 2.1 of the TRIPS Agreement, because the objection procedures accord less favourable treatment to non-EC nationals.[314]

7.349 Australia argues that a non-EC national resident or established in a third country has no direct means to object to registration but must lodge an objection through the government of the WTO Member in which that person resides or is established.[315] That government is responsible for verification and transmission of the objection. Australia argues that, with respect to objection procedures, as with respect to application procedures, the legally defined rights and obligations between the European Communities and EC member States and EC member State nationals makes the registration process for EC nationals fundamentally different for non-EC nationals.[316] Any outward appearance of symmetry of treatment therefore masks a fundamentally different situation.[317]

7.350 Australia submits that Article 12d of the Regulation limits the persons who may file objections to those resident or established in a country that satisfies the conditions of *equivalence* and *reciprocity*.[318]

7.351 Australia argues that certain individual registrations, which remain in force, were effected under the simplified procedure in Article 17 of the Regulation prior to its deletion in April 2003, without granting a right of objection to WTO Member nationals.[319] It refers to the *Bayerisches Bier* registration (considered in Section VII:D below) and argues that there was a mechanism available to at least some EC trademark right holders to make their objections known.[320]

7.352 Australia also claims that the measure at issue is inconsistent with national treatment obligations under the TRIPS Agreement because certain individual registrations, which remain in force, were effected under Article 6 of the Regulation prior to its amendment by the insertion of Article 12d in April 2003, without granting a right of objection to WTO Member nationals.[321] This claim is dealt with in Section VII:E of this report under the heading "individual registrations."[322]

---

[314] Australia's first written submission, para. 203 and second oral statement, para. 77.

[315] Australia's first written submission, para. 203.

[316] Australia's first written submission, para. 205; first oral statement, para. 34.

[317] Australia's rebuttal submission, paras. 174-176, citing Canada's third party oral statement; and Australia's second oral statement, para. 77.

[318] Australia's first written submission, para. 204.

[319] Australia's first written submission, paras. 190-194.

[320] Australia's comments on EC response to question No. 163.

[321] Australia's first written submission, paras. 184-189.

[322] Australia mentioned Article III:4 of GATT 1994 in response to Panel question No. 92 but has not raised a claim under GATT 1994 in relation to the objection procedures.

7.353 The European Communities responds that these claims must fail. The verification and transmission of an objection by a third country should not be particularly burdensome and does not amount to an "extra hurdle" for third country residents. A third country is not required to conduct a substantive verification under Article 7(4) the Regulation—which is clear from the wording of Article12d(2) that indicates that the criteria must be assessed in relation to the territory of the Community. Rather, the third country verifies whether the person objecting is indeed resident or established there. It could also be useful to have an official contact point if questions arise concerning the territory of the third country, it should be beneficial to the person objecting to deal directly with an authority in the third country and, if the objection is admissible, the third country is to be consulted before the Commission takes its decision on registration.[323]

7.354 The European Communities argues that Article 12d grants a right of objection to persons from WTO Members because the phrase "recognised under the procedure provided for in Article 12(3)" only applies to other third countries. The conditions of equivalence and reciprocity do not apply to WTO Members' right to object. Otherwise, the specific reference to "WTO Members" would be meaningless. This is also clear in Article 12b(2).[324] It also argues that Article 12d does not discriminate according to nationality but according to residence or establishment. It cannot simply be assumed that the reference to "nationals" in Article 3.1 of the TRIPS Agreement and Article 2 of the Paris Convention (1967) also applies to persons who are domiciled or established abroad, regardless of their nationality.[325]

(ii) main arguments of third parties

7.355 Argentina, India, Mexico, New Zealand and Chinese Taipei all inform the Panel that they are not aware of any person ever having attempted to file with their respective authorities an objection to registration under the Regulation.[326]

7.356 Brazil considers that the requirement to file objections with the country in which the objector resides or is established is an "unnecessarily complicated or costly" procedure in breach of Article 41.2 of the TRIPS Agreement. Brazil sees no necessity that would justify preventing private parties forwarding objections directly to the European Commission as many countries, including Brazil, allow for direct access for foreigners to object.[327]

7.357 Mexico argues that the Regulation is inconsistent with national treatment because it imposes conditions of reciprocity and prevents third country nationals filing objections directly with European authorities. Non-EC WTO Member nationals have an additional burden to involve their national authorities and delegate to them the objection process. Mexico refers to cochineal as a practical example of the way in which Mexican producers would be required to go through specific procedures which EC nationals are not.[328]

7.358 New Zealand argues that the objection procedure can potentially result in an application for registration not proceeding. Not having the right to object is a loss of a valuable right of a producer to protect its intellectual property rights. Objections under the Regulation are subject to equivalence and reciprocity requirements: the distinction between WTO Members and other third countries in Article 12d(1) could have been made clear by inserting a comma or other words. Objections must also be submitted through governments. At worst, the benefits of the right to object are entirely unavailable to third country producers. As a result, the

---

[323] European Communities' response to Panel question No. 34; rebuttal submission, paras. 155-159; second oral statement, paras. 89-94.

[324] European Communities' first written submission, paras. 73-75; first oral statement, para. 50; second oral statement, paras. 86-88.

[325] European Communities' first written submission, para. 142; first oral statement, para. 51.

[326] See their respective comments in Annex C in paras. 18, 103, 118, 110 and 179.

[327] Annex C, para. 28.

[328] Annex C, para. 110.

system virtually guarantees that no objections will be received from WTO Member nationals to applications for registration of GIs.[329]

(iii) consideration by the Panel

7.359 These claims concern procedures for filing and examination of objections to applications for registration of "designations of origin" and "geographical indications," as defined in the Regulation. They are referred to in this report, for the sake of brevity, as "opposition procedures."

7.360 These claims relate to two separate issues: (1) regarding verification and transmission of objections by governments; and (2) regarding equivalence and reciprocity conditions.[330] The Panel will address these issues in turn.

verification and transmission

7.361 These claims are made under the national treatment obligations in Article 3.1 of the TRIPS Agreement and Article 2 of the Paris Convention (1967), as incorporated by Article 2.1 of the TRIPS Agreement. The Panel will first consider the claim under Article 3.1 of the TRIPS Agreement.

7.362 The Panel recalls that two elements must be satisfied to establish an inconsistency with this obligation. (1) the measure at issue must apply with regard to the protection of intellectual property; and (2) the nationals of other Members must be accorded "less favourable" treatment than the Member's own nationals. The Panel will address each of these elements in turn.

protection of intellectual property

7.363 The Panel recalls that the national treatment obligation in Article 3 of the TRIPS Agreement applies to the treatment accorded by a Member "with regard to the protection of intellectual property." Footnote 3 provides an inclusive definition of the term "protection" as used in Articles 3 and 4:

> For the purposes of Articles 3 and 4, 'protection' shall include matters affecting the availability, acquisition, scope, maintenance and enforcement of intellectual property rights as well as those matters affecting the use of intellectual property rights specifically addressed in this Agreement.

7.364 The Panel recalls its finding at paragraph 7.299 that procedures for the filing and examination of *applications* for registration are matters affecting the acquisition of intellectual property rights, within the scope of "protection" of intellectual property as clarified in footnote 3 of the TRIPS Agreement. Procedures for *objections* to such applications are related to the procedures for acquisition, as recognized in the fourth paragraph of Article 62 (which uses the word "opposition") and the title of that article. Hence, opposition procedures are also matters "affecting" the acquisition of intellectual property rights which concern the "protection" of intellectual property, as clarified in footnote 3 to the TRIPS Agreement. It is not disputed that "designations of origin" and "geographical indications," as defined in the Regulation, are a subset of geographical indications, the subject of Section 3 of Part II, and therefore part of a category of intellectual property within the meaning of Article 1.2 of the TRIPS Agreement. Therefore, the objection procedures are subject to the national treatment obligation in Article 3.1 of that Agreement.

---

[329] Annex C, paras. 139-140.

[330] Australia also makes a claim with respect to the right of objection under the former Article 17 of the Regulation, which has been repealed. The Panel recalls its decision in paras. 7.14 and 7.17 that it would not make any recommendation with respect to prior versions of the Regulation that are no longer in force but it would make findings with respect to prior versions of the Regulation where they serve some useful purpose in reaching conclusions with respect to measures within its terms of reference, including individual registrations, that are currently in force. The Panel makes certain findings on the right of objection under the former Article 17 for that purpose in para. 7.746.

less favourable treatment accorded to the nationals of other Members

7.365 Australia claims that the procedures relating to verification and transmission of objections are inconsistent with the national treatment obligations under the TRIPS Agreement.

7.366 The Panel notes that, unlike the application procedures, the objection procedures do *not* concern the location of the geographical area to which the GI refers. Rather, they refer to the place where the objector resides or is established. The Panel recalls its findings at paragraphs 7.221 to 7.239 and considers, for the same reasons *a fortiori*, that the treatment accorded by the Regulation to persons resident or established in certain countries will, objectively, translate into treatment of persons with the nationality of those countries.

7.367 The Panel notes once again that the close link between nationality, on the one hand, and residence and establishment, on the other, appears to be recognized in the Regulation itself. Articles 12b(2)(a) and 12d(1) of the Regulation accord a right of objection to persons, which the European Communities confirms refers to persons resident or established outside the European Communities regardless of their nationality.[331] Yet the April 2003 amending Regulation, which inserted these provisions, explained that Article 12d granted the right of objection to the *nationals* of other WTO Members.[332]

7.368 The Panel recalls its finding at paragraph 7.184 that under Article 3.1 of the TRIPS Agreement we must examine the "effective equality of opportunities" with regard to the protection of intellectual property rights and at paragraph 7.187 that in this examination we will focus on the "fundamental thrust and effect" of the Regulation.

7.369 The parties and third parties who responded to the Panel's question on this point all reported that they were not aware of any objections to registration of GIs under the Regulation ever having been filed with the authorities of a third country.[333] However, Australia challenges the Regulation, in this respect, "as such."

7.370 Australia claims that the treatment accorded under the objection procedures in Articles 12b(2) and 12d(1) is less favourable treatment than that accorded under Article 7(3). There is an apparent equivalence in the drafting of these provisions but the question is whether this would imply a modification of the effective equality of opportunities with regard to the protection of intellectual property.

7.371 The Panel notes that the initial steps in the procedures for objections by private persons can be broken down as follows:

(a) as a first step, all objectors are required to submit their objection to the authorities in the country in which they reside or are established. These will be authorities of an EC member State or a third country, depending on the case; and

(b) as a second step, the authorities who receive an objection verify certain formal matters[334] and forward or transmit it to the Commission.

---

[331] European Communities' first written submission, para. 142.

[332] See paragraph 10 of the recitals to the April 2003 amending Regulation, set out in para. 7.121 above.

[333] However, the United States provided evidence from the US Dairy Export Council and the National Milk Producers Federation that US dairy producers and processors had been unable to prevent the registration as protected GIs in the European Union of a number of cheese types that they considered generic prior to registration. The European Communities responds that this is based on a misperception of the content of the Regulation: see its rebuttal submission, para. 85.

[334] The Panel takes note of the European Communities' position that it does not require third country governments to verify whether the objections are admissible, but it agrees that it does require them to verify certain formal matters: see European Communities' rebuttal submission, paras. 155-156.

7.372 We recall the European Communities' explanation of what amounts to its domestic constitutional arrangements, set out at paragraph 7.148, that Community laws are generally not executed through authorities at Community level but rather through recourse to the authorities of its member States which, in such a situation, "act *de facto* as organs of the Community, for which the Community would be responsible under WTO law and international law in general."[335] It follows that any objection from a person in an EC member State is filed directly with a "*de facto* organ of the Community." An objection from a person in a third country cannot be filed directly, but must be filed with a foreign government. This is a formal difference in treatment.

7.373 An EC member State has an obligation under Community law to verify an objection and forward it to the Commission. A group or person who submits an objection in an EC member State may enforce these obligations through recourse to judicial procedures based on the Regulation. In contrast, a third country government has no obligation under Community law or any other law to receive an objection or to transmit it to the Commission. A group or person who submits an objection in a third country has no right to such treatment.

7.374 Therefore, persons resident or established in third countries, including other WTO Members, who wish to object to applications for registration under the Regulation do not have a right in the objection procedures that is provided to persons in the European Communities. Objectors in third countries face an "extra hurdle" in ensuring that the authorities in those countries carry out the functions reserved to them under the Regulation, which objectors in EC member States do not face. Consequently, certain objections may not be verified or transmitted. Each of these considerations significantly reduces the opportunities available to other WTO Member nationals in matters affecting the acquisition of rights under the Regulation compared with those available to EC nationals. For this reason, the Regulation accords nationals of other WTO Members "less favourable treatment" within the meaning of Article 3.1 of the TRIPS Agreement.

7.375 The European Communities submits that the requirement that statements of objection be transmitted by the country where the person is resident or established is not an unreasonable condition and that, if there is no objective reason for the third country government to refuse to cooperate, it is not the European Communities' rules which create an "extra hurdle" for third country residents.[336] The Panel recalls its finding at paragraph 7.309 that the obligation to accord national treatment with respect to a measure of the European Communities is the obligation of the European Communities. For the reason set out in paragraph 7.310 in relation to application procedures, the Panel considers that the European Communities has failed to accord no less favourable treatment *itself* to the nationals of other Members.

7.376 The Panel confirms that the European Communities is entitled, under Article 62.4 of the TRIPS Agreement, to provide for procedures for objections that comply with the general principles in paragraphs 2 and 3 of Article 41. However, Article 62 is outside the Panel's terms of reference.

7.377 The Panel recalls its finding at paragraph 7.248 that the fact that a general exceptions provision along the lines of Article XX of GATT 1994 was not included in the TRIPS Agreement has no impact on its analysis of Article 3.1.

7.378 Therefore, the Panel concludes that, with respect to the objection procedures, insofar as they require the verification and transmission of objections by governments, the Regulation accords less favourable treatment to the nationals of other Members, inconsistently with Article 3.1 of the TRIPS Agreement.

Article 2 of the Paris Convention (1967)

7.379 In view of the conclusion at paragraph 7.378 with respect to the objection procedures, insofar as they require the verification and transmission of objections by governments, it is unnecessary to consider their

---

[335] European Communities' second oral statement, para. 148.

[336] European Communities' rebuttal submission, para. 157.

consistency with Article 2(1) of the Paris Convention (1967), as incorporated by Article 2.1 of the TRIPS Agreement.

7.380 The Panel recalls its finding at paragraph 7.253 and, for the same reasons, concludes that, with respect to the opposition procedures, the Regulation does not impose a requirement of domicile or establishment inconsistently with Article 2(2) of the Paris Convention (1967), as incorporated by Article 2.1 of the TRIPS Agreement.

equivalence and reciprocity conditions

7.381 Australia claims that the right to file an objection under Article 12d(1) of the Regulation is limited to countries that satisfy the equivalence and reciprocity conditions in Article 12(1) based on a reading of the phrase "a WTO member country or a third country recognised under the procedure provided for in Article 12(3)" as if it read "a WTO member country recognised under the procedure provided for in Article 12(3) or a third country recognised under the procedure provided for in Article 12(3)." It is necessary for the Panel to make an objective assessment of the meaning of that phrase in this provision, although solely for the purpose of determining the European Communities' compliance with its WTO obligations.[337]

7.382 The Panel observes that this claim is based entirely on the absence of a comma. A reading of the text of Article 12d(1), set out in full at paragraph 7.346 shows that if there were a comma after the words "a WTO member country," it would be clear that it was separate from the following words "or a third country recognised under the procedure provided for in Article 12(3)." However, in the Panel's view, even without a comma, it is unlikely that the phrase "recognised under the procedure provided for in Article 12(3)" refers to both a "WTO member country" and a "third country" in this context. If that were the correct reading, then there would be no need to specify a "WTO member country" separately because, outside the European Communities, a "WTO member country" is necessarily a third country. There would be no need to refer specifically to a "WTO member country" if it was not distinguished in some way from any other third country. The difference must be that a third country is only included if it is recognized under the procedure provided for in Article 12(3) so that, consequently, this phrase would not apply to a "WTO member country." Indeed, the fact that there is no need for a WTO Member to obtain recognition under Article 12(3) for its residents to object seems to be precisely the reason that it is included.

7.383 This is consistent with the fact that Article 12b(2), in which the format is clearer, creates a right of objection for WTO Member and other third country nationals but clearly indicates that recognition under the procedure in Article 12(3) does not apply to WTO Members in this respect. Further confirmation is provided by the recitals to the April 2003 amending Regulation which explained the justification for the insertion of the right of objection in Articles 12b and 12d in terms of WTO Members, but limited the explanation of the equivalence and reciprocity conditions to the issue of protection provided by registration to foreign names.[338]

7.384 The European Communities confirms that the Panel's interpretation of this aspect of the Regulation is correct and submits undisputed evidence that since the entry into force of Article 12d(1), the publications of all applications for registration of a geographical indication specifically refer to the possibility for residents from WTO countries to object to the application.[339]

7.385 Therefore, based on this understanding of Article 12d(1) of the Regulation, the Panel concludes that with respect to the equivalence and reciprocity conditions, as allegedly applicable to objections, Australia has not made a prima facie case in support of its claims under Article 3.1 of the TRIPS Agreement or Article 2(1) of the Paris Convention (1967) as incorporated by Article 2.1 of the TRIPS Agreement.

---

[337] In this regard, the Panel recalls its comments at para. 7.106 above.

[338] Paragraphs 9 and 10 of the recitals to Council Regulation (EC) No. 692/2003 set out at para. 7.121 above.

[339] European Communities' rebuttal submission, para. 152, attaching as an example the publication of the application to register "Lardo di Colonnata" dated 5 June 2003, set out in Exhibit EC-56.

summary of conclusions regarding objection procedures

7.386 In summary:

(a) with respect to the objection procedures, insofar as they require the verification and transmission of objections by governments, the Regulation accords the nationals of other Members less favourable treatment than the European Communities' own nationals inconsistently with Article 3.1 of the TRIPS Agreement;

(b) with respect to the objection procedures, the Regulation does not impose a requirement of domicile or establishment inconsistently with Article 2(2) of the Paris Convention (1967) as incorporated by Article 2.1 of the TRIPS Agreement; and

(c) Australia has not made a prima facie case in support of its claims with respect to the equivalence and reciprocity conditions, as allegedly applicable to the objection procedures.

4. Regulatory committee
(a) Description of procedure laid down in Article 15 of the Regulation

7.387 The Regulation provides that certain decisions shall be taken by the European Commission "in accordance with the procedure laid down in Article 15." These include decisions *not* to proceed with registration of a GI under Articles 6(5) and 12b(1)(b); decisions whether or not to proceed with registration of a GI where an objection is admissible under Articles 7(5)(b)[340], 12b(3) and 12d(3); decisions to cancel registration of a GI under Article 11a; and decisions whether a third country satisfies the equivalence and reciprocity conditions under Article 12(3).[341] The Regulation provides that the Commission may ask the committee provided for in Article 15 for its opinion prior to taking certain other decisions. These include decisions to proceed with registration of a GI located in a third country under Article 12b(1)(a) and decisions to register a homonym of an already registered GI under Article 6(6).[342]

7.388 Article 15 of the Regulation provides, relevantly, as follows:

> 1. The Commission shall be assisted by a committee.
>
> 2. Where reference is made to this Article, Articles 5 and 7 of Decision 1999/468/EC shall apply. (...)

7.389 Decision 1999/468/EC (the so-called "Comitology Decision") lays down the procedures for the exercise of implementing powers conferred on the Commission.[343] Article 5 of that Decision sets out a regulatory procedure which provides that the Commission shall be assisted by a regulatory committee composed of the representatives of the EC member States and chaired by the representative of the Commission, who does not vote. The representative of the Commission shall submit to the committee a draft of the measures to be taken. The committee shall deliver its opinion on the draft within a time-limit by qualified majority voting. The Commission shall adopt the measures envisaged if they are in accordance with the opinion of the committee. If the measures are not in accordance with the opinion of the committee, or if no opinion is delivered, the Commission shall, without delay, submit to the Council a proposal relating to the measures to be taken and shall inform the European Parliament. The Council may act by qualified majority on the proposal

---

[340] Where no agreement is reached among EC member States.

[341] Under the simplified procedure in the former Article 17 of the Regulation, the Commission was required to register all names in accordance with the procedure laid down in Article 15.

[342] The procedure under Article 15 is also applicable in certain other cases, including Articles 1(1), 2(5) and 5(5).

[343] It is reproduced in full in Exhibit COMP-8.

within three months. If the Council indicates by qualified majority that it opposes the proposal, the Commission shall re-examine it. If the Council neither adopts the proposed measure nor indicates its opposition within three months, the Commission shall adopt the proposed measure.[344]

(b) National treatment under the TRIPS Agreement

(i) main arguments of the parties

7.390 Australia argues that the Regulation is inconsistent with Article 3.1 of the TRIPS Agreement and Article 2.1 of the TRIPS Agreement (incorporating Article 2 of the Paris Convention (1967)) because "a non-EC national trademark right holder does not have a national representative on the Committee to speak for its interests." It set out the procedure that is established under Article 15.[345]

7.391 The European Communities responds that this claim is manifestly unfounded. The decision-maker is the Commission, or exceptionally the Council. The Committee merely assists the Commission but does not take decisions itself. EC member State representatives on the Committee do not speak for particular right holders, but represent the respective EC member State.[346] Australia has not provided arguments to substantiate its claim.[347]

(ii) main arguments of third parties

7.392 China notes the procedure under Article 15 and that the committee is composed only of representatives of EC member States. This procedure for the resolution of possible disputes on publication is available to names from WTO Members, but the process does not invite WTO Members to participate.[348]

(iii) consideration by the Panel

7.393 These claims are made under the national treatment obligations in Article 3.1 of the TRIPS Agreement and Article 2 of the Paris Convention (1967), as incorporated by Article 2.1 of the TRIPS Agreement. The Panel can consider these claims together.

7.394 The parties agree that the regulatory procedure established under Article 15 of the Regulation is as described above. The procedure under Article 15 has been applied to the consideration of particular applications to register GIs located within the European Communities where there was an admissible objection from an EC member State. In several cases the Commission's draft measures were not in accordance with the opinion of the Committee and therefore had to be submitted to the Council of Ministers. In most of these cases the Council did not act and the Commission then adopted the measures.[349] The Council adopted the measures itself in the cases of "Bayerisches Bier," "Aceto Balsamico tradizionale di Modena" and "Aceto Balsamico tradizionale di Reggio Emilia."[350]

---

[344] Article 15 of the Regulation, set out in Exhibits COMP-1b and EC-1, Article 5 of Council Decision (EC) No. 1999/468 set out in Exhibit COMP-8 and the European Communities' first written submission, paras. 81-82. The three month time-limit is set by Article 15 of the Regulation.

[345] Australia's first written submission, paras. 58 and 203. In relation to a claim under Article 41 of the TRIPS Agreement, it also referred to the Committee as the ultimate decision-making body for the enforcement of trademark rights in the circumstances governed by the Regulation: see para. 147.

[346] European Communities' first written submission, para. 154.

[347] European Communities' second oral statement, para. 100.

[348] See Annex C, para. 83.

[349] This included the first registration of "Feta" which was later annulled.

[350] This information was provided by the European Communities in a table of applications for registration on which the Committee established by Article 15 was consulted. See Exhibit EC-28.

7.395 The Panel notes that this regulatory procedure, which is set out in Article 5 of the Comitology Decision, appears to be a standard procedure for the exercise of implementing powers conferred on the European Commission under Community law. However, in the context of this Regulation, the standard regulatory procedure operates in conjunction with the application and objection procedures, which require the EC member States to examine and transmit applications and objections to the Commission.

7.396 Australia's claims rest on the premise that the representatives of the EC member States on the regulatory committee act as representatives of groups who submit an application for registration of a GI located in their respective territories, of persons who wish to object who are resident or established in their respective territories, and of interests in products the subject of an application for registration of a GI located in their respective territories.

7.397 The Panel notes that the regulatory committee must be consulted in cases where the Commission proposes to register a GI and there is an admissible objection. In these cases, the representatives of both the EC member State that forwarded the application and the EC member State that objects participate in the Committee's consideration of the matter, as well as in any action taken by the Council of Ministers. However, according to Article 5(5), the EC member State which transmitted the application has already decided that the application satisfies the requirements of the Regulation and, according to Article 7, the EC member State that objects has already taken the view that there are grounds to do so.

7.398 The Panel notes that the Regulation refers to both persons and EC member States, as well as third countries. With respect to applicants, Article 5 of the Regulation refers to an applicant group but an EC member State checks and forwards the application and, thereafter, the Commission communicates with the "Member State concerned." With respect to objections, Article 7(1) grants only the EC member States the right to raise objections to registration before the Commission, whilst Article 7(3) provides that any legitimately concerned natural or legal person may object to the proposed registration by sending its statement to the EC member State in which he resides or is established. Where an objection is acknowledged to be admissible within the meaning of Article 7(4), Article 7(5) provides that the Commission is to ask the "Member States concerned" to seek agreement among themselves: it makes no provision for any intervention by individuals.[351] Articles 6(1), 9 and 11 also refer to the "Member State(s) concerned" in the procedures under the Regulation.[352]

7.399 The Panel recalls that it has already accepted the European Communities' explanation that Community laws are generally not executed through authorities at Community level but rather through recourse to the authorities of its member States which, in such a situation, "act *de facto* as organs of the Community, for which the Community would be responsible under WTO law and international law in general."[353] We note its explanation that:

> When fulfilling their functions under Regulation 2081/92, a Member State is in no way identified with the applicant or the person raising the objection. In verifying the applications or statements of objection, the Member State must correctly, impartially and objectively apply the terms of the Regulation. Similarly, when exercising its role in the Committee, the Member States must be guided by the terms of the Regulation, and not act as a representative of any individual applicant or objecting person.[354]

7.400 The Panel does not consider that these features of the Regulation "as such" compel any different treatment of different GIs. Under the national treatment obligations of the TRIPS Agreement, evidence is

[351] Confirmed by the Court of First Instance of the European Communities in Case T-215/00, *SCEA La Conqueste v Commission* [2001] ECR II-181, para. 45, reproduced in Exhibit COMP-12.

[352] Article 11 establishes a process for cancellation due to non-compliance with specifications among "Member States concerned." Article 11a also distinguishes between requests for cancellation by persons and the State which submitted the original application.

[353] European Communities' second oral statement, para. 148.

[354] European Communities' response to Panel question No. 39.

required that, in the application of these procedures, the authorities cannot, do not or will not apply the Regulation in the same way to the nationals of other Members and the European Communities' own nationals. Australia has not provided any such evidence.

7.401 Further, Australia's references to procedural fairness, due process and/or transparency in the regulatory committee's decision-making process do not appear to relate to the national treatment obligations, but rather other provisions of the TRIPS Agreement.

7.402 Accordingly, the Panel concludes that Australia has not made a prima facie case in support of its claims with respect to the regulatory committee under Article 3.1 of the TRIPS Agreement and Article 2(1) of the Paris Convention (1967), as incorporated by Article 2.1 of the TRIPS Agreement.

(c) National treatment under GATT 1994

(i) main arguments of the parties

7.403 Australia argues that the Regulation is inconsistent with Article III:4 of GATT 1994 because the outcome of applications for registration are determined through a process, that is, the Committee of EC member State representatives, "in which there is no representative or advocate for the registration of a GI for an imported product and no requirement for procedural fairness, due process and/or transparency concerning that Committee's decision-making process."[355]

7.404 The European Communities responds that Australia's claim to have a representative on the Committee is not reasonable. The public authorities of a WTO Member must be presumed to administer their duties properly and fairly. This is independent of the nationality of the civil servants and employees working for such authorities. There are no "EC representatives" in the public authorities and agencies of Australia.[356]

(ii) consideration by the Panel

7.405 The Panel notes that this claim, like those claims in respect of the regulatory committee brought under the TRIPS Agreement, rests on the premise that the representatives of the EC member States on the regulatory committee act as representatives of groups who submit an application for registration of a GI located in their respective territories, of persons who wish to object who are resident or established in their respective territories, and of interests in products the subject of an application for registration of a GI located in their respective territories.

7.406 The Panel recalls its finding at paragraph 7.400 that the relevant features of the Regulation "as such" do not compel any different treatment of different GIs. Under the national treatment obligation in Article III:4 of GATT 1994, evidence is required that, in the application of these procedures, the authorities cannot, do not or will not apply the Regulation in the same way to imported products and EC products and that this accords less favourable treatment. Australia has not provided any such evidence. Accordingly, the Panel concludes that Australia has not made a prima facie case in support of its claim with respect to the regulatory committee under Article III:4 of GATT 1994.

---

355 Australia's first written submission, para. 177.

356 European Communities' first written submission, para. 155.

5. Labelling requirement

(a) Factual aspects of the labelling requirement in Article 12(2) of the Regulation

(i) text of Article 12(2) of the Regulation

7.407 This claim concerns a labelling requirement in the second indent of Article 12(2) of the Regulation. The parties disagree sharply on the meaning and scope of this provision, read in its context. Therefore, the Panel will begin by quoting Article 12(2) in full before turning to the factual arguments of the parties.

> 2. If a protected name of a third country is identical to a Community protected name, registration shall be granted with due regard for local and traditional usage and the practical risks of confusion.
>
> Use of such names shall be authorized only if the country of origin of the product is clearly and visibly indicated on the label.

(ii) main arguments of the parties

7.408 Australia claims that this labelling requirement applies to the use of GIs from other WTO Members so that use of a GI on a product from another WTO Member can be authorized only if it meets this labelling requirement.[357]

7.409 Australia does not consider that Article 12(2) of the Regulation can apply to the registration of both EC and third country GIs in view of its actual text which expressly relates to a situation where the later registered GI is "a protected name of a third country." As long as it is drafted in that form, the European Communities is not bound to apply the interpretation that it has offered, and the European Court of Justice would enforce the specific terms of the Regulation.[358] Australia also argues that the European Communities' explanation of the country of origin labelling requirement in Article 12(2) is not supported by the actual text of Article 12(2), particularly when read together with Article 6(6), which applies to the registration of a GI located in the European Communities.[359]

7.410 Australia submits that the meaning of "such names" is unclear but understands that it refers to a third country GI protected in that third country and which is identical to a prior GI on the EC register. It submits that the meaning of "protected name of a third country" is ambiguous but, given the context, it assumes that it refers to a third country GI protected in that third country.[360] Later, it argues that the term "Community protected name" refers to a GI already on the register whether from the European Communities or a third country.[361]

7.411 Australia argues that "clearly and visibly indicated" means that the label must be noticeably evident in the same field of vision as the GI and the GI symbol.[362]

7.412 The European Communities responds that the second subparagraph of Article 12(2) only applies to the GIs in the situation referred to in its first subparagraph. It only applies in cases of homonyms and not to third

[357] Australia's first written submission, paras. 220 and 223.

[358] Australia's first oral statement, para. 25; response to Panel question No. 53.

[359] Australia's first written submission, para. 34; first oral statement, para. 26.

[360] Australia's first written submission, paras. 235-236.

[361] Australia's rebuttal submission, para. 65.

[362] Australia's response to Panel question No. 120.

country names in general.[363] It confirms that there have been no cases in which this provision has been applied in practice.[364]

7.413 The European Communities argues that "such names" in the second subparagraph refers to both "a protected name of a third country" and a "Community protected name," so that the requirement to indicate the country of origin can apply to both the third country name and the Community name. In practice, this would mean that whichever indication is registered later would normally be required to indicate the country of origin.[365] In both these terms, "protected" means, in principle, "protected under Regulation 2081/92" but "the provision also applies where protection is sought for a protected name from a third country." "Community protected name" covers only protected names of geographical areas located in the EC.[366] Article 12(2) covers both a situation where a third country GI is a homonym of an EC GI already on the register, as well as an EC GI which is a homonym of a third country GI already on the register.[367] "Such names" is written in the plural which clearly indicates that the requirement can relate to both the EC and third country GIs.[368] Nothing in the wording of the provision prevents it applying to GIs from both third countries and the EC.[369] Even if "Community protected name" referred to EC and third country names already on the register, "protected name of a third country" should be interpreted to include names protected in a third country, whether or not from the European Communities or a third country.[370] In the EC's view, Article 12(2) has no specific link with Article 12(1).[371]

7.414 The European Communities argues that, in cases of homonymous GIs from the European Communities, the last indent of Article 6(6) also requires a clear distinction in practice between them which would normally, in practice, require the indication of the country of origin.[372] The only reason why the last indent of Article 6(6) does not explicitly require the indication of the country of origin is that this provision deals with a wider set of conflicts than Article 12(2).[373] There is no difference between the word "homonymous" in Article 6(6) and "identical" in Article 12(2) as the English definitions of those words are synonymous and the French and Spanish versions use the same term in both provisions.[374] Article 6(6) deals with a wider set of conflicts than Article 12(2), such as homonyms from within the European Communities, homonyms from within the same third country or different third countries.[375] Article 6(6) simply refers to "protected names" from the European Communities and a third country, without specifying which of these is the one the subject of an application and which is already on the register.[376]

7.415 The European Communities argues that "clearly and visibly indicated" must be evaluated in each specific case from the point of view of what a normally attentive consumer can easily notice and not be induced in error as to the origin of the product.[377]

---

[363] European Communities' first written submission, paras. 445-446 and 475-476.

[364] European Communities' response to Panel question No. 44.

[365] European Communities' first written submission, para. 88 and 134-135; rebuttal submission, para. 145.

[366] European Communities' response to Panel question No. 41.

[367] European Communities' response to Panel question No. 43.

[368] European Communities' rebuttal submission, para. 147.

[369] European Communities' second oral statement, para. 81.

[370] European Communities' second oral statement, para. 82.

[371] European Communities' response to Panel question No. 117.

[372] European Communities' first written submission, para. 89; response to Panel question No. 118.

[373] European Communities' first written submission, para. 479.

[374] European Communities' response to Panel question No. 119.

[375] European Communities' response to Panel question No. 42.

[376] European Communities' rebuttal submission, para. 146.

[377] European Communities' response to Panel question No. 120.

(iii) consideration by the Panel

7.416 The Panel begins by noting that the second indent of Article 12(2) of the Regulation expressly sets out a requirement that concerns what is indicated on "the label" of a product. Therefore, for the sake of brevity, the Panel refers to it as "the labelling requirement."[378] The labelling requirement has not been applied in practice. However, Australia challenges this aspect of the Regulation "as such."

7.417 The meaning of the various terms in the second indent of Article 12(2) is essential to a resolution of this claim. Therefore, it is necessary for the Panel to make an objective assessment of the meaning of this provision, although solely for the purpose of determining the European Communities' compliance with its WTO obligations.[379]

7.418 The parties disagree on the scope of the labelling requirement. Australia does not exclude that it may apply to all GIs from third countries, like the wider context in Article 12, which applies to all GIs from third countries that satisfy the conditions in paragraph 1 and are recognized as equivalent under paragraph 3. The European Communities responds that it applies only to identical or homonymous GIs, consistent with the immediate context in paragraph 2 of Article 12.

7.419 The Panel observes that the scope of the labelling requirement is indicated by its subject: "[u]se of such names." "Such" is a demonstrative adjective that refers to something previously specified, which expressly requires an examination of the context. The context indicates that "such names" refers to the subject of the previous indent, which is eligible GIs from third countries that are identical to a Community protected name. This is confirmed by the content of the two indents: the first refers to practical risks of confusion, and the second imposes a requirement that a detail be clearly and visibly indicated, which appears to be a specific requirement that addresses the more general consideration in the first. Whilst it is possible to look back further in the context and read the phrase "[u]se of such names" as referring to the names or GIs in the preceding paragraph 1, such a reading is, in our view, constrained. We note that the position of paragraph 2 near the beginning of Articles 12 through 12d might suggest that it is a more general provision, but its position can perhaps be explained by the fact that it is one of the two original provisions on GIs from third countries that predate the insertion of Articles 12(3) and 12a through 12d. The European Communities has confirmed that "such names" refers to the previous indent, which covers only identical GIs. On the basis of the text of the provision, which has not been applied, the Panel agrees.

7.420 Even though Australia understands that the provision only refers to "identical" GIs[380], the parties disagree on the meaning of "such names." Australia assumes from the context that it refers to the subject of the previous indent, which is "a protected name of a third country" that is identical to a Community protected name. The European Communities responds that it refers not only to "a protected name of a third country" which is identical, but also to the "Community protected name" with which it is identical.

7.421 The Panel considers, once again, that, "such names" refers to the subject of the previous indent, which is eligible GIs from third countries that are identical to a Community protected name. Although the term "a Community protected name" also appears in the previous indent, its registration is not in issue. It appears that the first indent relates only to the registration of GIs from a third country. The second indent attaches a condition to that registration which, logically, only applies to the use of GIs from a third country.

---

[378] The use of this term does not prejudge whether this is a "labelling requirement" as used in Annex 1.1 of the TBT Agreement. That issue is considered at paras. 7.448-7.449.

[379] In this regard, the Panel recalls its comments at para. 7.106.

[380] The Panel notes that, whilst the English version of the Regulation uses the word "identical" in Article 12(2), two other official versions of the Regulation use words corresponding to the English word "homonymous:" these are *homonyme* in the French version and *homónima* in the Spanish version. The Panel assumes that the meaning of the different versions of the text can be reconciled, and uses the word "identical" in relation to Article 12(2) in the English version of this report in such a sense. See further para. 7.467 below.

7.422 This reading is confirmed by the wider context in Articles 12 through 12b which relates only to the registration of GIs from third countries. The registration of GIs located within the European Communities is dealt with in Articles 5 through 7. A provision permitting objections to such registrations from persons in third countries was inserted in Article 12d in April 2003. It would be a very special reading if the second indent of Article 12(2) were the sole provision in the scheme of Articles 12 through 12b that attached a condition to registration of GIs located within the European Communities, which is unlikely, given that context. The Panel takes note that the term "such names" is in the plural, unlike "a protected name of a third country" which is in the singular. However, the qualifier "such names" is linked to "the product" which is in the singular, so that the plural form is not determinative of the issue before us.

7.423 Therefore, the Panel concludes that Article 12(2), including the labelling requirement in the second indent, refers only to the registration and use of a GI from a third country that is identical to a "Community protected name." It appears that this refers to a GI that is already registered under the Regulation, as no party has suggested a reason why it would matter for this requirement where the prior GI was located, as long as it was identical.

7.424 The Panel also notes that the first indent of Article 12(2) contains language almost identical to that found in Article 6(6) of the Regulation. Both refer to registration of names "with due regard for local and traditional usage and the actual risk [or practical risks] of confusion." However, Article 6(6) applies to an application to register a GI located *within the European Communities* which "concerns a homonym of an already registered name from the European Union or a third country recognised in accordance with the procedure in Article 12(3)." Unlike the second indent of Article 12(2), the last tiret of Article 6(6) sets out the following requirement:

> [T]he use of a registered homonymous name shall be subject to there being a clear distinction in practice between the homonym registered subsequently and the name already on the register, having regard to the need to treat the producers concerned in an equitable manner and not to mislead consumers.

7.425 The Panel will revert to the parallel in the construction of the requirements in Articles 12(2) and 6(6) in its consideration of this claim.

(b) National treatment under the TBT Agreement

(i) main arguments of the parties

7.426 Australia claims that the Regulation is inconsistent with Article 2.1 of the TBT Agreement because the labelling requirement in Article 12(2) accords less favourable treatment to imported products.[381] Firstly, it argues that the labelling requirement in Article 12(2) of the Regulation falls within the definition of a "technical regulation" in Annex 1.1 of the TBT Agreement.

7.427 Australia argues that the Regulation applies to an "identifiable group of products" within the meaning of Annex 1.1 of the TBT Agreement because Article 12(2) applies to agricultural products and foodstuffs for which GI protection is sought where the GI is identical to a GI already on the EC register. These are not expressly identified in the Regulation but they are identifiable.[382] Although it applies to GIs, these exist with regard to specific agricultural products or foodstuffs for which the homonymous GIs have been registered.[383]

7.428 Australia argues that the Regulation lays down "product characteristics or their related processes" within the meaning of the definition in Annex 1.1 of the TBT Agreement, in that it sets out a specific labelling

[381] Australia's first written submission, para. 241.

[382] Australia's first written submission, paras. 209-213; rebuttal submission, para. 192.

[383] Australia's rebuttal submission, para. 191.

requirement. It provides that the use of GIs from other WTO Members will only be authorized "if the country of origin of the product is clearly and visibly indicated on the label." To that extent, the Regulation is a document which "include[s] ... labelling requirements as they apply to a product" within the meaning of a technical regulation as defined in Annex 1.1 of the TBT Agreement. If this requirement was not considered to relate to a product, it would render the concept of a label meaningless. The words "as they apply to" refer to a product, as opposed to the characteristics of a product. In any case, the origin of a product is inextricably linked to that product by virtue of the definitions of a "designation of origin" and "geographical indication" in Article 2(2) of the Regulation and inherently involves a product. Australia does not argue that "origin" is product characteristic, but that the labelling requirement itself is a product characteristic.[384]

7.429 Australia argues that the labelling requirement is "mandatory" within the meaning of Annex 1.1 of the TBT Agreement because Article 12(2) uses the term "shall." Australia does not dispute that it is not a precondition for the marketing of a product in the European Communities. However, it is mandatory for trading an imported product in the European Communities with a GI in the same competitive conditions as those afforded to a domestic product in the European Communities with a GI. An imported product does not benefit from the protection against unauthorized use provided by registration, nor from the reputation of superior quality engendered by registration.[385]

7.430 Australia submits that the labelling requirement concerns both imported and domestic products that are "like" within the meaning of Article 2.1 of the TBT Agreement. It is sufficient for the Panel to consider the issues in the context of a general presumption of likeness. GIs are intellectual property rights and do not affect the analysis of likeness of the underlying products. Products bearing a GI from an area that straddles the external border of the European Communities could be exactly the same although some would be imported. Further, GI protection under the Regulation concerns unfair competition between products which normally involves a high degree of similarity or likeness. Jurisprudence on Article III:4 of GATT 1994 can be looked to for clarification of the national treatment obligation in Article 2.1 of the TBT Agreement.[386]

7.431 Australia claims that Article 12(2) provides different treatment to imported products because Article 6(6) does not mandate that corresponding domestic products bear a country of origin label.[387] It alleges that this is less favourable treatment because "there are likely to be situations" where the labelling requirement modifies the conditions of competition to the detriment of imported products.[388] Specifically, it creates costs of additional labelling or re-labelling. It does not allege that it accords any other less favourable treatment. It accepts that in some cases existing labels may, coincidentally, satisfy the labelling requirement. However, where a different, or additional, label is required to be produced and attached to a product, this will create extra expense that can be expected to modify the conditions of competition to the detriment of producers of the imported product.[389] The appropriate standard for determining less favourable treatment is that whether the measure modifies the conditions of competition in the relevant market to the detriment of imported products.[390] The European Communities bears the burden of proving that Article XX of GATT 1994 has any significance in the context of the TBT Agreement but it has not presented any supporting arguments.[391]

7.432 Australia accepts that, if the European Communities were to interpret Article 12(2) of the Regulation according to whichever GI was registered later, that this could be expected to overcome its inconsistency with

---

384 Australia's first written submission, paras. 219-220; response to Panel question No. 122 and comment on EC response to that question.

385 Australia's first written submission, para. 223; rebuttal submission, paras. 195-196.

386 Australia's first written submission, paras. 226, 230-233; rebuttal submission, para. 207.

387 Australia's first written submission, para. 237; rebuttal submission, para. 209.

388 Australia's first written submission, para. 239.

389 Australia's responses to Panel questions Nos. 52, 120 and 121.

390 Australia's response to Panel question No. 125.

391 Australia's comment on EC response to Panel question No. 125.

Article 2.1 of the TBT Agreement.[392] However, in the situation covered by Article 12(2) which is the subject of its claim, Article 6(6) of the Regulation has no relevance.[393] It refers to Article 6(6) only in relation to the factual issue of the proper interpretation of Article 12(2).[394]

7.433 Australia argues that a measure implementing matters concerning intellectual property rights is not necessarily excluded from the scope of the TBT Agreement.[395] The assessment of whether a measure is a technical regulation within the meaning of the TBT Agreement is a threshold issue for the application of that agreement but is not determinative of a violation. WTO obligations are generally cumulative.[396]

7.434 Australia argues that the labelling requirement mandates a means of distinguishing an imported product, rather than functioning as a mark of origin *per se*. Even if it is a mark of origin, Article 12(2) is the means by which the Regulation compulsorily differentiates between GIs on imported and domestic products. Article IX:1 of GATT 1994 is silent on the issue of national treatment and marks of origin. However, even if excludes the application of Article III of GATT 1994, it does not exclude the application of Article 2.1 of the TBT Agreement if the measure is a "technical regulation." Further, even if Article 2.1 did conflict with Article IX, Article 2.1 would prevail in accordance with the General Interpretative Note to Annex 1A to the WTO Agreement.[397]

7.435 The European Communities responds that Article 12(2) of the Regulation is not a technical regulation within the meaning of Annex 1.1 of the TBT Agreement.[398] It is not a labelling requirement but merely sets out the conditions under which a GI will be registered in a situation where there are homonyms from the European Communities and a third country.[399]

7.436 The European Communities argues that Article 12(2) does not apply to identifiable products within the meaning of Annex 1.1 because the Regulation itself does not allow one to identify the products which might be affected by the requirement to indicate the country of origin.[400]

7.437 The European Communities argues that Article 12(2) does not lay down product characteristics within the meaning of Annex 1.1 because it does not contain a specific labelling requirement for any specific product. It is not Article 12(2) itself which imposes a labelling requirement but rather, according to Article 4(2)(h), the product specification for an individual GI, which contains the specific labelling details. Further, it does not relate to a product, process or its production method but merely to a product's geographic origin which is different from the product itself. Origin may confer specific characteristics or a reputation on a product which may entitle it for protection as a GI but those issues are already covered by TRIPS and do not need to be addressed by the TBT Agreement. Origin marking is already covered by Article IX of GATT 1994.[401] In addition, the phrase "labelling requirements as they apply to a product" appears to refer to the application of labelling requirements to characteristics of a product, process or production method.[402]

---

[392] Australia's response to Panel question No. 53.

[393] Australia's response to Panel question No. 118.

[394] Australia's response to Panel question No. 121.

[395] Australia's first oral statement, para. 41.

[396] Australia's rebuttal submission, para. 203.

[397] Australia's rebuttal submission, paras. 212-213; responses to Panel question Nos. 123-124.

[398] European Communities' first written submission, paras. 439 and 457.

[399] European Communities' first written submission, para. 449; response to Panel question No. 50.

[400] European Communities' first written submission, para. 447.

[401] European Communities' first written submission, paras. 448-452; responses to Panel question Nos. 50 and 122.

[402] European Communities' response to Panel question No. 122.

7.438 The European Communities argues that Article 12(2) is not mandatory within the meaning of Annex 1.1 because the possibility to apply for GI protection is a right, not an obligation. GI registration is voluntary and not a precondition for the marketing of products.[403]

7.439 The European Communities argues that Australia has failed to establish that products bearing homonymous GIs from the European Communities covered by Article 6(6) and a product from a third country covered by Article 12(2) would be "like." The comparable situation under Article 6(6) is that of two homonymous GIs from the European Communities, not one from the European Communities and one from a third country. It is therefore unnecessary to resolve the meaning of "like products" in Article 2.1 of the TBT Agreement.[404]

7.440 The European Communities argues that Article 12(2) does not accord less favourable treatment because it applies in a non-discriminatory fashion to European Communities and third country GIs. The requirement applies to homonyms from the European Communities and a third country and will be a condition for the registration of the GI for which protection is sought later. Article 6(6) does not explicitly require the indication of a country of origin because it deals with a wider set of conflicts, in particular, homonyms from the same EC member State, where the country of origin would not make a "clear distinction" in practice." It could also deal with other conflicts not resolved by Article 12(2) such as homonyms from the same third country, or different third countries.[405] An indication of the country of origin of the later registered GI avoids practical risks of confusion because, typically, the prior registered GI will have been marketed longer under that GI and be known by consumers. It also takes into account the fact that the prior registration cannot easily be amended.[406] Imported products would not necessarily have to be re-labelled as the country of origin may already be clearly and visibly indicated on the label. Existing marks of origin may be sufficient. The affixation of an additional label clearly and visibly indicating the country of origin would also be sufficient.[407] The legitimate regulatory objectives of the Member concerned must be taken into account in the application of both Article 2.1 and 2.2 of the TBT Agreement. Alternatively, the Panel would have to consider whether Article XX of GATT 1994 is applicable within the context of the TBT Agreement.[408]

7.441 The European Communities argues that the requirement under Article 12(2) is a mark of origin covered by Article IX of GATT 1994, which excludes national treatment obligations. It is not possible to distinguish marks of origin which fall under the TBT Agreement and those which do not. There is no textual basis for distinguishing general origin marking requirements and those which cover only specific products. If Article 12(2) was considered a technical regulation, Article 2.1 of the TBT Agreement could not apply to origin marking requirements lest it render Article IX:1 useless.[409] The European Communities does not argue that there is a conflict, but rather that Article IX:1 and Article 2.1 should be interpreted in a harmonious way that gives meaning to both of them.[410] Finally, Article 1.2 of the Agreement on Rules of Origin deals *inter alia* with Article IX on marks of origin but makes no mention of the TBT Agreement, which would be hard to explain if the TBT Agreement applied to marks of origin.[411]

---

[403] European Communities' first written submission, paras. 453-456.

[404] European Communities' response to Panel question No. 51.

[405] European Communities' first written submission, paras. 477-479; response to Panel question No. 42.

[406] European Communities' response to Panel question No. 54.

[407] European Communities' response to Panel question No. 120.

[408] European Communities' response to Panel question No. 125.

[409] European Communities' first written submission, para. 481; first oral statement, para. 72; responses to Panel questions Nos. 123 and 124.

[410] European Communities' second oral statement, para. 245.

[411] European Communities' response to Panel question No. 122.

(ii) main arguments of third parties

7.442 New Zealand supports the arguments of Australia in its first written submission that the Regulation is inconsistent with Article 2.1 of the TBT Agreement.[412]

(iii) consideration by the Panel

7.443 This claim concerns Article 12(2) of the Regulation "as such."[413] Article 2.1 provides as follows:

> 2.1 Members shall ensure that in respect of technical regulations, products imported from the territory of any Member shall be accorded treatment no less favourable than that accorded to like products of national origin and to like products originating in any other country.

7.444 The Panel considers that the essential elements of an inconsistency with Article 2.1 of the TBT Agreement are, as a minimum, that the measure at issue is a "technical regulation;" that the imported and domestic products at issue are "like products" within the meaning of that provision; and that the imported products are accorded "less favourable" treatment than that accorded to like domestic products. We will consider these elements below.

<u>technical regulation</u>

7.445 The threshold issue for the Panel to decide is whether the requirement in Article 12(2) of the Regulation is a "technical regulation" within the meaning of the TBT Agreement. If it is not, then Article 2.1 of the TBT Agreement will not be applicable. Annex 1.1 of that agreement provides as follows:

> For the purpose of this Agreement, however, the following definitions shall apply:
>
> *1. Technical regulation*
>
> Document which lays down product characteristics or their related processes and production methods, including the applicable administrative provisions, with which compliance is mandatory. It may also include or deal exclusively with terminology, symbols, packaging, marking or labelling requirements as they apply to a product, process or production method." [Explanatory note omitted]

7.446 The parties refer to the two elements that appear in the text of this definition, namely that a technical regulation is a "[d]ocument which lays down product characteristics or their related processes and production methods, including the applicable administrative provisions" and "with which compliance is mandatory," as well as to the issue that a technical regulation must be applicable to an identifiable product or group of products, explained by the Appellate Body in *EC – Asbestos* and *EC – Sardines*.[414] The Panel will address these in turn.

7.447 The parties disagree as to whether the second indent of Article 12(2) itself *lays down* a labelling detail. In the Panel's view, it clearly does. The text of the second indent of Article 12(2) expressly sets out the condition that the country of origin must be clearly and visibly indicated on the label. Even though the product specifications under Article 4.2(h) lay down the labelling details for products relating to each individual GI as it is registered, this does not alter the terms of Article 12(2).

---

[412] Annex C, para. 124.

[413] In this sub-section will refer to it as the "second indent of Article 12(2)" as the words "labelling requirement" appear in the text of Annex 1.1 of the TBT Agreement.

[414] Australia's first written submission, para. 210, and the European Communities' first written submission, paras. 441-442, both cite the Appellate Body report on *EC – Sardines*, para. 176, which referred to the Appellate Body report on *EC – Asbestos*, paras. 66-70.

7.448 The parties disagree as to whether the second indent of Article 12(2) of the Regulation lays down *a product characteristic*. The Panel notes that it expressly sets out a requirement that concerns what must be indicated on "the label" of a product. That is a labelling requirement.[415] The second sentence of the definition of "technical regulation" in Annex 1.1 of the TBT Agreement expressly refers to "labelling requirements" as an example of a technical regulation.

7.449 The Panel notes that this example in the definition in Annex 1.1 is qualified by the words "as they apply to a product, process or production method." The text does not limit the scope of the example by stating what the labels must indicate in order for them to constitute a technical regulation. Rather, they explain to what the labelling requirements "apply." This simply means that a requirement concerning a product label is a labelling requirement that applies to a product. The context shows that the subject of the second sentence, "[i]t" refers back to the noun "[d]ocument" as qualified by the relative clause beginning "which lays down" and ending with the word "mandatory." Were this not so, the element that "compliance is mandatory," for example, would not apply to the items described in the second sentence, which would be contrary to the object and purpose of the obligations concerning technical regulations. As a result, a document that "deal[s] exclusively with ... labelling requirements as they apply to a product" can be an example of a "[d]ocument that lays down product characteristics." The issue is not whether the content of the label refers to a product characteristic: the label on a product *is* a product characteristic. Therefore, the second indent of Article 12(2) of the Regulation deals exclusively with a labelling requirement "as it applies to a product."

7.450 In any event, the second indent of Article 12(2) requires that the country of origin be clearly and visibly indicated on the label of a product in order to provide a means of identification where two GIs are identical. In the Panel's view, the purpose of this requirement is indicated by the first indent of Article 12(2), namely, that it is a means to avoid the practical risks of confusion. In other words, it is a means of identification. In this respect, the Panel agrees with the view of the Appellate Body in *EC – Asbestos* and *EC – Sardines* that a means of identification is, itself, a product characteristic.[416]

7.451 In summary, a document that lays down a requirement that a product label must contain a particular detail, in fact, lays down a product characteristic. This interpretation is consistent with a Decision of the TBT Committee in which Members agreed as follows:

> In conformity with Article 2.9 of the Agreement, Members are obliged to notify all mandatory labelling requirements that are not based substantially on a relevant international standard and that may have a significant effect on the trade of other Members. That obligation is not dependent upon the kind of information which is provided on the label, whether it is in the nature of a technical specification or not.[417]

7.452 Therefore, the Panel considers that the second indent of Article 12(2) is a "[d]ocument which lays down product characteristics or their related processes and production methods, including the applicable administrative provisions" and a labelling requirement that applies to a product, within the meaning of the definition of "technical regulation."

7.453 The Panel will now consider whether *compliance is mandatory* with the second indent of Article 12(2) of the Regulation. The ordinary meaning of the word "mandatory" can be defined in the case of an action as "obligatory in consequence of a command, compulsory. (Foll. by *upon*)."[418] The second indent uses the word "shall," which indicates that it is mandatory for products subject to Article 12(2) to obtain the benefits of registration under the Regulation.

---

[415] It is not contested that it cannot be a labelling requirement because it only lays down one product characteristic.

[416] Appellate Body reports on *EC – Asbestos*, para. 67, and *EC – Sardines*, para. 191.

[417] "Decisions and Recommendations adopted by the Committee since 1 January 1995," document G/TBT/1/Rev. 8 of 23 May 2003.

[418] *The New Shorter Oxford English Dictionary* (1993).

7.454 As to the European Communities' argument that this is not a mandatory requirement in order to market the relevant products in the European Communities, the Panel notes the approach taken to a similar argument made by the European Communities in a previous dispute. The panel in that dispute recalled that a document may require positively that a product contain certain characteristics or it may require negatively that the product not possess certain characteristics. That panel reasoned that, by requiring the use of a particular type of product under a particular trade description, the measure at issue in effect lay down product characteristics in a negative form, that is, by excluding other products from being marketed under that description.[419]

7.455 In the present dispute, the Panel notes that only products that comply with a product specification in a GI registration may use the indications PDO, PGI or equivalent national indications. Further, agricultural products and foodstuffs bearing an unregistered identical GI may not be marketed in the European Communities under that name where they infringe prior registered GIs which, given that the GI is identical, appears inevitable unless the products are not comparable.

7.456 The second indent of Article 12(2) makes a distinction between those products using a GI identical to a Community protected name that satisfy the labelling requirement, and those which do not. The negative implication that follows from this requirement is that products with a GI identical to a Community protected name that do not satisfy this labelling requirement must *not* use the indications PDO, PGI or equivalent national indications and, to the extent that they fall within the protection granted to a prior identical Community protected name, must *not* be marketed in the European Communities using that GI. Therefore, the second indent of Article 12(2) is an obligatory or mandatory requirement.

7.457 The Panel agrees with the view of the Appellate Body that compliance would be impossible with a technical regulation if it were not applicable to identifiable products.[420] The parties disagree as to whether the second indent of Article 12(2) applies to an identifiable product. It refers to "the product" but does not name any product. However, Article 12(2) forms part of the Regulation which has a defined product coverage described in Article 1(1) as those agricultural products intended for human consumption referred to in Annex I to the EC Treaty, the foodstuffs listed in Annex I to the Regulation and the agricultural products listed in Annex II to the Regulation, subject to certain exceptions for wine-sector products, except wine vinegars or spirit drinks. A procedure is specified for the amendment of the product coverage in Annexes I and II to the Regulation. That is a large, but defined, group of products. Article 12(2) is applicable to them all, although it lays down a specific requirement that is only triggered where a name is identical to a Community protected name. The identical criterion permits identification of the products to which this requirement will apply in a given case. To date, there have not been any.

7.458 Therefore, the Panel considers that compliance is mandatory with the second indent of Article 12(2) of the Regulation, within the meaning of the definition of "technical regulation," and that this requirement applies to identifiable products.

7.459 Accordingly, the Panel's preliminary finding is that the labelling requirement is a "technical regulation" within the meaning of the definition in the TBT Agreement and that Article 2.1 of that agreement may be applicable.

7.460 The European Communities argues that this labelling requirement cannot be subject to the national treatment obligation in Article 2.1 of the TBT Agreement due to the terms of Article IX of GATT 1994 on marks of origin.

7.461 The Panel considers it unnecessary to reach a definitive view on this issue, in view of its findings below on "less favourable treatment." It suffices for the purposes of this dispute to note that the definition of a

---

[419] Panel report on *EC – Sardines,* paras. 7.43-7.45, citing the Appellate Body report on *EC – Asbestos,* para. 69.

[420] "A 'technical regulation' must, of course, be applicable to an *identifiable* product, or group of products. Otherwise, enforcement of the regulation will, in practical terms, be impossible:" Appellate Body report in *EC – Asbestos,* para. 70, cited in *EC – Sardines*, para. 185.

"technical regulation" in Annex 1.1 and the preamble to the TBT Agreement specifically include "marking and labelling requirements" without any indication that marks of origin are excluded.[421] Article 1.4 and 1.5 specifically exclude certain purchasing specifications addressed in the Agreement on Government Procurement and sanitary and phytosanitary measures as defined in the SPS Agreement, but there is no express exclusion for marks of origin.[422] In any event, it has not been shown that Article 12(2) of the Regulation is, in fact, a requirement to display a mark of origin.[423]

7.462 The Panel also recalls the views of the Appellate Body in *EC – Asbestos* and *EC – Sardines* that, when examining whether a measure is a technical regulation, "the proper legal character of the measure at issue cannot be determined unless the measure is examined as a whole."[424] The second indent of Article 12(2) is a small part of the Regulation which applies in a narrow circumstance. Clearly, the Regulation is an intellectual property measure but the parties do not ask the Panel to take a position on whether the product specifications required under Article 4(2) are technical regulations and the inspection structures required under Article 10 are conformity assessment procedures within the meaning of the TBT Agreement.[425] The characterization of the whole measure is therefore a complex issue on which there has been little argument and which the Panel considers unnecessary to decide for the purposes of this claim.

<u>like products</u>

7.463 Article 2.1 of the TBT Agreement refers to "products imported from the territory of any Member" and *inter alia* "like products of national origin." An essential element of a claim under Article 2.1 is the existence of like products. Australia submits that it is sufficient for the Panel to consider the issues in the context of "a general presumption of likeness." The European Communities contests the likeness of products within the meaning of Article 2.1 of the TBT Agreement. The Panel considers it unnecessary to reach any view on this issue, in view of the findings below on "less favourable treatment."

<u>less favourable treatment</u>

7.464 Article 2.1 of the TBT Agreement refers to "treatment no less favourable." An essential element of a claim under Article 2.1 is that, in respect of technical regulations, the treatment accorded to imported products is "less favourable" than that accorded to like products of national origin. The Panel notes the similarity in the terms used in Article 2.1 of the TBT Agreement and Article III:4 of GATT 1994, which also refers to "treatment no less favourable." The preamble to the TBT Agreement expressly sets out the desire "to further the objectives of GATT 1994." However, in view of its findings below, the Panel considers it sufficient for the

---

[421] Many Members, including the parties to this dispute, have notified marks and labels of origin to the TBT Committee. See, for example, G/TBT/Notif.95.155, G/TBT/Notif.95.106, G/TBT/Notif.95.438, G/TBT/Notif.96.42, G/TBT/Notif.96.269, G/TBT/Notif.96.364, G/TBT/Notif.96.450, G/TBT/Notif.97.112, G/TBT/Notif.97.113, G/TBT/Notif.98.206, G/TBT/Notif.98.448, G/TBT/Notif.99.548, G/TBT/Notif.99.668, G/TBT/Notif.00.65, G/TBT/Notif.00.94, G/TBT/Notif.00.289, G/TBT/Notif.00.483, G/TBT/N/ARG/7, G/TBT/N/ARG/9, G/TBT/N/JPN/7, G/TBT/N/JPN/12, G/TBT/N/PER/A, G/TBT/N/CHL/33, G/TBT/N/THA/92, G/TBT/N/THA/94, G/TBT/N/USA/25, G/TBT/N/JPN/78, G/TBT/N/GBR/7, G/TBT/N/JPN/123, G/TBT/N/JPN/124, G/TBT/N/KOR/76, G/TBT/N/ISR/36 and G/TBT/N/ISR/42. Further, there was a general understanding among signatories of the Tokyo Round TBT Agreement, recorded in the 1994 Annual Report of the Committee established under that agreement, that mandatory marking requirements applied in the context of marking the origin of products were covered by the provisions of that agreement, but one signatory (not a party to the current dispute) could not join a consensus on that issue: see GATT document L/7558 of 30 November 1994 in BISD 41S/718 at 719. The Tokyo Round TBT agreement, like the current TBT Agreement, referred to "marking and labelling requirements."

[422] This implies no view as to whether Article IX of GATT 1994, which includes an MFN treatment obligation but no national treatment obligation, impliedly excludes marks of origin from the scope of the obligation in Article III:4 of GATT 1994. That is an issue which need not, and do not, decide.

[423] See, for example, the GATT CONTRACTING PARTIES Recommendation of 21 November 1958 on marks of origin, para. 5, "Countries should accept as a satisfactory marking the indication of the name of the country of origin in the English language introduced by the words 'made in':" BISD 7S/30. That example shows that a mark of origin can be different from the labelling requirement at issue.

[424] Appellate Body reports in *EC – Asbestos,* para. 64, and *EC – Sardines,* paras. 192-193.

[425] See the parties' respective responses to Panel question No. 60 and the European Communities' response to Panel question No. 134.

purposes of this dispute simply to observe that the starting point for this analysis must be whether the measure at issue accords any difference in treatment.

7.465 Australia claims that the treatment accorded under the labelling requirement for GIs located in third countries, including WTO Members, is less favourable than that accorded to GIs located within the European Communities.

7.466 The Panel has found at paragraph 7.423 that the labelling requirement only applies to products bearing GIs from third countries that are identical to a Community protected name. This is a narrow circumstance.

7.467 The Panel notes that Articles 12(2) and 6(6) share almost identical language that indicates that the purpose of each provision is to minimize actual, or practical, risks of confusion between the use of two registered identical or homonymous GIs. An obvious difference in the English version is that Article 12(2) uses the word "identical" and Article 6(6) uses the word "homonymous." However, two other official versions of the Regulation use the same word in both provisions (*homonyme* in French and *homónima* in Spanish). The Panel assumes that the meaning of the different versions of the text can be reconciled, and that, therefore, the words in Articles 12(2) and 6(6) can have the same meaning in English as well.

7.468 Both requirements are mandatory, providing that use "shall" be authorized only if a particular condition is met or "shall" be subject to a particular condition. However, there is a formal difference in that Article 12(2) states the condition expressly by providing that "the country of origin of the product is clearly and visibly indicated on the label." In contrast, Article 6(6) states the condition in terms of factors that "a clear distinction in practice between the homonym registered subsequently and the name already on the register, having regard to the need to treat the producers concerned in an equitable manner and not to mislead consumers."

7.469 The Panel does not consider that the mere fact that imported products and products of European Communities' origin are subject to different legal provisions is in itself conclusive in establishing an inconsistency with the national treatment obligation in Article 2.1 of the TBT Agreement. Nor is it conclusive that the indication of the "country of origin" is both mandatory and express in the Regulation for imported products only, since the Regulation does not mandate that the European Communities must *not* impose the same labelling requirement on domestic products.

7.470 The European Communities explains that the difference in wording of the relevant provisions is due to the fact that Article 6(6) applies to a wider class of GIs. For example, it could apply to identical GIs located in different EC member States, as well as to a GI within the European Communities identical to a GI located in a third country, which Article 12(2) does not.

7.471 The essential point is that nothing in the text appears to prevent the European Communities implementing the two requirements in the same manner where an application is made to register a GI, whether located within the European Communities or in a third country, that is identical to a prior registered GI. It appears that the wording of Article 6(6) of the Regulation permits the European Communities to apply the same condition found in the text of Article 12(2) so that both requirements would be applied to the GI registered later in time, irrespective of the origin of the product or the location of the GI. The European Communities has confirmed to the Panel that the clear distinction in practice would normally require the indication of the country of origin.[426]

7.472 Australia accepts that, if the European Communities were to interpret Article 12(2) of the Regulation according to whichever GI was registered later in time, this could be expected to overcome its inconsistency

426 European Communities' first written submission, para. 479; response to Panel question No. 118.

with Article 2.1 of the TBT Agreement.[427] Although it later argued that Article 6(6) was of no relevance, the Panel does not agree for the reasons set out above.

7.473 Australia has not provided any evidence that the formal difference in the wording of the two requirements leads to any difference in treatment nor that it accords any different treatment to imported products. It has not provided evidence that, where the European Commission applies the same condition under the labelling requirement in Article 12(2) and the last tiret of Article 6(6), that such a practice would not survive a legal challenge before the European Court of Justice.

7.474 The Panel recalls the European Communities' submission that, according to the settled case law of the European Court of Justice, "Community legislation must, so far as possible, be interpreted in a manner that is consistent with international law."[428]

7.475 Therefore, for the above reasons, in particular, the confirmation by the European Communities that the clear distinction in practice under Article 6(6) would normally require the indication of the country of origin, the Panel concludes that Australia has not made a prima facie case in support of this claim.

7.476 Accordingly, it is unnecessary for the Panel to consider whether an assessment of conformity with Article 2.1 of the TBT Agreement requires reference to be had to the regulatory objective pursued by a measure as referred to in Article 2.2 of the TBT agreement, or the absence in the text of the TBT Agreement of a general exceptions provision such as Article XX of GATT 1994.

C. Trade-Restrictiveness Claim

1. Inspection structures

(a) Description of inspection structures (Articles 4.2(g), 10 and 12a of the Regulation)

7.477 The condition in Article 12(1) of the Regulation that a "third country ... has inspection arrangements ... equivalent to those laid down in this Regulation" was considered earlier as one of the equivalence and reciprocity conditions. That is a per-country condition. The condition at issue here concerns the inspection structures required by Article 10 of the Regulation under the procedures for registration of individual GIs. This is, allegedly, a per-product requirement.

7.478 The Panel continues its examination in respect of these particular requirements, bearing in mind the aim of the dispute settlement mechanism, which is to secure a positive solution to a dispute[429], and the views of the Appellate Body in *Australia – Salmon* on the principle of judicial economy.[430] Were the Panel not to examine the claim with respect to the inspection structures requirements within the application procedures, its conclusion on the inspection structures condition in Article 12(1) would not enable the DSB to make sufficiently precise recommendations and rulings so as to allow for prompt compliance in order to ensure effective resolution of this dispute.

7.479 An application for registration of a GI must be accompanied by certain documents. The first is the product specification. Article 5(3) provides as follows with respect to an application to register a GI located within the European Communities:

> 3. The application for registration shall include the product specification referred to in Article 4.

---

[427] Australia's response to Panel question No. 53.

[428] See *supra* at 172.

[429] Article 3.7 of the DSU.

[430] Appellate Body report on *Australia – Salmon,* para. 223.

7.480 Article 12a(1) of the Regulation provides as follows with respect to applications to register GIs located in third countries:

> 1. Applications must be accompanied by the specification referred to in Article 4 for each name.

7.481 With respect to the specification, Article 4 provides as follows:

> 1. To be eligible to use a protected designation of origin (PDO) or a protected geographical indication (PGI) an agricultural product or foodstuff must comply with a specification.
>
> 2. The product specification shall include at least: (...)
>
> (g) details of the inspection structures provided for in Article 10;

7.482 A specification refers to a particular product and the list of items that Article 4 requires to be included in a product specification all appear to be product-specific.

7.483 Applications to register GIs located in third countries must also be accompanied by a declaration by a third country government. Article 12a(2)(b) of the Regulation provides for a third country to transmit to the Commission an application to register a GI located in its territory accompanied by:

> (b) a declaration that the structures provided for in Article 10 are established on its territory.

7.484 This declaration is not required of an EC member State when it transmits to the Commission an application to register a GI located within the European Communities. However, EC member States have an obligation under Article 10 itself to ensure that inspection structures are in place. The European Communities confirms that the requirements are the same for EC member States and third countries.[431]

7.485 Article 10(1) explains that the function of inspection structures is "to ensure that agricultural products and foodstuffs bearing a protected name meet the requirements laid down in the specifications." Article 10(2) provides that an "inspection structure" may comprise one or more "designated inspection authorities and/or private bodies approved for that purpose" by the EC member State. Article 10(3) lays down requirements regarding the characteristics and duties of the inspection authorities and/or private bodies but not the product-specific requirements which appear in product specifications. We highlight the requirements for inspection authorities under Article 10(3) which are relevant to the claims below.

7.486 The characteristics of the inspection authorities and/or private bodies include the following:

> Designated inspection authorities and/or approved private bodies must offer adequate guarantees of objectivity and impartiality with regard to all producers or processors subject to their control and have permanently at their disposal the qualified staff and resources necessary to carry out inspection of agricultural products and foodstuffs bearing a protected name.

7.487 The inspection authorities and/or private bodies may outsource certain functions as follows:

> If an inspection structure uses the services of another body for some inspections, that body must offer the same guarantees. In that event, the designated inspection authorities and/or approved private bodies shall, however, continue to be responsible *vis-à-vis* the Member State for all inspections.

---

[431] European Communities' response to Panel question No. 126(a).

7.488 The applicable standards for private bodies are described as follows:

> As from 1 January 1998, in order to be approved by the Member States for the purpose of this Regulation, private bodies must fulfil the requirements laid down in standard EN 45011 of 26 June 1989.
>
> The standard or the applicable version of standard EN 45011, whose requirements private bodies must fulfil for approval purposes, shall be established or amended in accordance with the procedure laid down in Article 15.
>
> The equivalent standard or the applicable version of the equivalent standard in the case of third countries recognised pursuant to Article 12(3), whose requirements private bodies must fulfil for approval purposes, shall be established or amended in accordance with the procedure laid down in Article 15.

7.489 Standard EN 45011 sets out "General requirements for bodies operating product certification systems." It specifies general requirements that a third party operating a product certification system shall meet if it is to be recognized as competent and reliable. These include requirements relating to the certification body itself and its personnel; changes in the certification requirements; applications for, evaluation of, and decisions on, certification; surveillance; use of licences, certificates and marks of conformity; and complaints to suppliers. It applies for EC member States although the European Communities has not yet established the standard or the applicable version of that standard on the basis of Article 10(3) of the Regulation.

7.490 Standard EN 45011 is a European standard that takes over the text of ISO/IEC Guide 65:1996 prepared by the ISO Committee on Conformity Assessment (CASCO). The European Communities has not established an equivalent standard in the case of third countries, but the European Communities informs the Panel that ISO/IEC Guide 65:1996 is an example of such an equivalent international standard.[432]

7.491 The responsibilities of governments are set out in Article 10(1) and (2).[433] Governments must ensure that inspection structures are in place by designating a public inspection authority and/or approving a private inspection body and then notify them to the Commission. Where the government designates a public inspection authority, it carries out inspections itself. Where the government approves a private inspection body, it must ascertain that the private body is capable of fulfilling its functions in accordance with Article 10(1) and meets the requirements of Article 10(3), set out above. The basic criterion for the approval process is that the private body can effectively ensure that products comply with a specification. After designation and/or approval, the government is responsible for continued monitoring that an approved private body continues to meet the requirements.[434]

(b) Trade-restrictiveness under the TBT Agreement

(i) main arguments of the parties

7.492 Australia claims that the inspection structures required by Articles 4, 10 and 12(1) of the Regulation are inconsistent with Article 2.2 of the TBT Agreement. Article 10 requires that EC member States have in place these inspection structures. Article 12a(2)(b) requires that other WTO Members provide a declaration that the structures provided for in Article 10 are established in its territory.[435]

---

[432] The European Communities supplied copies of EN 45011 and ISO/IEC Guide 65:1996 to the Panel in Exhibits EC-2 and EC-3, respectively. See European Communities' response to Panel question No. 126(c).

[433] Article 10(1) and (2) refers to EC member States but, in conjunction with Article 12a(2)(a), they also apply to the governments of third countries.

[434] Uncontested information provided by the European Communities in its responses to Panel question Nos. 127 and 132.

[435] Australia's first written submission, para. 249.

7.493 Australia argues that the Regulation is a "technical regulation" within the definition in Annex 1.1 of the TBT Agreement because Articles 10 and 4 (in particular Article 4.2(g)) together require inspection structures to check that products using a GI comply with the product specifications in the GI registration. Article 4.2(b) and (e) provide that product specifications include "product characteristics." The process of checking compliance with the specifications is a regular sequence of actions, i.e. a process, and falls within the meaning of "product characteristics or their related processes."[436]

7.494 Australia does not take a position on whether the definitions of "technical regulation" and "standard" and the definition of a "conformity assessment procedure" in Annex 1 are necessarily mutually exclusive, but agrees that a conformity assessment procedure requires at the very least a separate technical regulation or standard against which products are to be assessed.[437] Australia submits that it is irrelevant to this claim whether or not the Regulation is an intellectual property measure and also subject to another WTO covered agreement.[438]

7.495 Australia argues that the inspection structure requirements are mandatory for products that use a registered GI. Therefore, they are mandatory for trading an imported product in the same competitive conditions as those afforded to a domestic product that uses a registered GI. Australia does not dispute that inspection structures, and GI registration, are not a precondition for the marketing of a product in the EC.[439]

7.496 Australia does not contest that the Regulation could pursue legitimate objectives or that it is capable of generally fulfilling those legitimate objectives.[440] It argues that the Regulation is more trade restrictive than necessary to fulfil its legitimate objective, taking account of the risks non-fulfilment would create, contrary to Article 2.2 of the TBT Agreement. Its claim is based on the allegation that the Regulation imposes an "absolute requirement" for an EC model inspection structure as a condition for the registration of a GI, irrespective of the circumstances in the Member in which the GI is located or of the circumstances of the trade in the relevant products.[441]

7.497 Australia argues that the Regulation mandates the type of structure or design for inspection that other WTO Members must have in place. Such a requirement cannot be necessary to fulfil the Regulation's legitimate objective unless the European Communities had determined that no other systems in any WTO Member would in any circumstances provide the same degree of assurance as its own system.[442] Inspection structures in a WTO Member where the good is produced is meaningless where the unauthorized use involving goods from a third country WTO Member occurs in the European Communities.[443]

7.498 Australia does not contest that inspection structures may be required with respect to a specific product for which protection is sought or that some type of compliance verification mechanism may be necessary in most cases. Nor does it consider that government involvement is necessarily problematic.[444] It challenges the fact that the Regulation dictates specific design features: Article 10(3) provides that an inspection structure must have permanently have at its disposal the necessary qualified staff, yet temporary staff may be all that is necessary to provide the required level of assurance[445]; Article 10 does not allow for the possibility that inspection structures might be unnecessary[446]; Article 12a(2)(b) requires a declaration as to the structures

[436] Australia's first written submission, paras. 221-222, 224; rebuttal submission, paras. 201-202; response to Panel question No. 133 and comment on EC response to Panel question No. 134.

[437] Australia's response to Panel question No. 60.

[438] Australia's rebuttal submission, para. 203.

[439] Australia's first written submission, paras. 221-222, 224; rebuttal submission, paras. 195-197.

[440] Australia's first written submission, paras. 247-248.

[441] Australia's response to Panel question No. 58.

[442] Australia's first written submission, paras. 249-254.

[443] Australia's first written submission, para. 256.

[444] Australia's rebuttal submission, para. 219; response to Panel question No. 128.

[445] Australia's rebuttal submission, para. 217

[446] Australia's first written submission, para. 255; rebuttal submission, para. 217.

provided for in Article 10, which excludes alternative measures that are not inspection structures at all, such as systems of laws. However, Australia does not challenge these specific elements, rather it challenges the fact that the Article 10-type inspection structure is imposed on other WTO Members regardless of their existing inspection structures or other systems that would perform the same function.[447]

7.499 Australia argues that alternative measures can achieve the EC's legitimate objectives with the same degree of effectiveness, such as laws against misleading and deceptive commercial practices enforced by an investigating authority, which may operate in conjunction with food labelling laws enforced by a food authority. These authorities could ensure that products comply with their specifications and address any risks created by non-fulfilment. Further alternative measures include the tort of passing off, industry certifications, self-regulation by producers and consumer protection mechanisms.[448]

7.500 The European Communities responds that none of these provisions are a "*technical regulation*" within the meaning of the TBT Agreement. Article 4 does not lay down product characteristics for specific products. These characteristics are contained in the application for registration. Article 4 simply sets out the requirements with which a product specification must comply in order to permit GI registration. The product characteristics are contained in an individual GI application.[449] Inspection structures are not "related processes" within the definition of a technical regulation in Annex 1.1 of the TBT Agreement because they are not related to the product characteristics and, if they were, then all conformity assessment procedures would be technical regulations which would lead to a systematic overlap between the various provisions of the TBT Agreement.[450]

7.501 The European Communities submits that the purpose of Article 4.2(g) in conjunction with Article 10 is to ensure conformity with the product specification, not to lay down product characteristics. The TBT Agreement makes a clear distinction between technical regulations and standards in Articles 2 to 4 and procedures to assess conformity with them in Articles 5 to 9. The dividing line between them is perfectly clear in the definitions in Annex 1. This claim does not fall within Article 2 but appears to fall within Articles 5 to 9 of the TBT Agreement.[451] The inspection structure requirements are not a technical regulation. They cannot be both a technical regulation and a *conformity assessment procedure*.[452] It does not contest that a conformity assessment procedure assesses conformity with a technical regulation or a standard as defined in Annex 1.3 of the TBT Agreement but does not consider it necessary for the Panel to decide whether the inspection structures are indeed conformity assessment procedures. It does not contend that the general requirement that a GI must correspond to certain product specifications constitutes a technical regulation since it is merely a condition for the grant of an intellectual property right. A different question would be whether individual product specifications for individual GIs would be technical regulations but that is an issue which the Panel does not need to address.[453]

7.502 The European Communities argues that Articles 4 and 10 are not *mandatory* because GI protection is voluntary. It is not a precondition for placing products on the market.[454]

7.503 The European Communities argues that the existence of inspection structures is *not more trade-restrictive than necessary* because it is only required with respect to the specific product for which protection is sought; it does not determine the specific design of the inspection structures; and they are necessary to achieve the legitimate objectives of the Regulation. Unfair competition laws might be adequate to implement GI

---

447 Australia's second oral statement, paras. 94-95.

448 Australia's first written submission, paras. 258-260; response to Panel question No. 62; rebuttal submission , para. 219.

449 European Communities' first written submission, paras. 464-465.

450 European Communities' second oral statement paras. 246-247.

451 European Communities' first written submission, paras. 460-463.

452 European Communities' rebuttal submission, para. 406; response to Panel question No. 133.

453 European Communities' second written submission, paras. 407-408.

454 European Communities' first written submission, para. 467.

protection under Article 22.2 of the TRIPS Agreement but Article 1.1 allows Members to implement more extensive protection. This discretion under Article 1.1 cannot be limited on the basis of Article 2.2 of the TBT Agreement.[455] The European Communities refers to its arguments on this point in relation to the claim under national treatment obligations of the TRIPS Agreement.[456]

7.504 The European Communities refers to the conformity assessment procedures foreseen in Article 6 of the TBT Agreement. Nothing in that agreement obliges Members simply to accept conformity assessment carried out by bodies of another Member. While Article 6.1 of the TBT Agreement stipulates that Members ensure, whenever possible, that they accept the results of conformity assessment procedures in other Members, this only applies when certain conditions are fulfilled. Article 6.3 encourages Members to enter into negotiations for the mutual recognition of conformity assessment procedures. Article 6.4 encourages Members to permit participation of conformity assessment bodies located in the territories of other Members in their conformity assessment procedures but it is not a legal obligation to permit such participation. Australia has concluded a mutual recognition agreement which permits bodies designated by those countries to carry out conformity assessment with respect to EC standards and vice versa.[457] Australia has failed to explain why government involvement in designation of inspection bodies is problematic.[458]

(ii) main arguments of third parties

7.505 New Zealand supports the arguments of Australia in its first written submission that the Regulation is inconsistent with Article 2.2 of the TBT Agreement.[459]

(iii) consideration by the Panel

7.506 This claim is made under Article 2.2 of the TBT Agreement, which provides as follows:

> 2.2 Members shall ensure that technical regulations are not prepared, adopted or applied with a view to or with the effect of creating unnecessary obstacles to international trade. For this purpose, technical regulations shall not be more trade-restrictive than necessary to fulfil a legitimate objective, taking account of the risks non-fulfilment would create. Such legitimate objectives are, *inter alia:* national security requirements; the prevention of deceptive practices; protection of human health or safety, animal or plant life or health, or the environment. In assessing such risks, relevant elements of consideration are, *inter alia:* available scientific and technical information, related processing technology or intended end-uses of products.

7.507 The threshold issue for the Panel to decide is whether the inspection structures requirements under Article 10 of the Regulation, read together with the product specifications of Article 4 of the Regulation, are a "technical regulation" within the meaning of the TBT Agreement. We note, once again, that the definition of that term in Annex 1.1 provides as follows:

> For the purpose of this Agreement, however, the following definitions shall apply:
>
> *1. Technical regulation*

---

[455] European Communities' first written submission, paras. 484-501.

[456] European Communities' rebuttal submission, paras. 415.

[457] European Communities' response to Panel question No. 131.

[458] European Communities' comment on Australia's response to Panel question No. 128.

[459] Annex C, para. 124.

> Document which lays down product characteristics or their related processes and production methods, including the applicable administrative provisions, with which compliance is mandatory. It may also include or deal exclusively with terminology, symbols, packaging, marking or labelling requirements as they apply to a product, process or production method." [Explanatory note omitted]

7.508 The Panel will first examine whether Articles 4 and 10, read together, are a "[d]ocument which lays down product characteristics or their related processes and production methods, including the applicable administrative provisions." If they are not, they cannot be a technical regulation within the meaning of this definition and it is unnecessary to examine whether "compliance [with it] is mandatory" or whether it applies to identifiable products.[460]

7.509 Australia claims that the inspection structures requirements lay down a "process" which is related to an identifiable group of products. Whilst it appears that the specification for a particular product described in Article 4 must lay down product characteristics and related production methods, Australia has not pursued a claim in respect of product specifications except insofar as they relate to the inspection structures requirements.

7.510 The Panel must consider whether the inspection structures requirements, read together with Article 4 of the Regulation, are a "process" within the meaning of the definition of a "technical regulation." The ordinary meaning of the term "process" can be defined as follows:

> A thing that goes on or is carried on; a continuous series of actions, events or changes; a course of action, a procedure; *esp.* a continuous and regular action or succession of actions occurring or performed in a definite manner; a systematic series of actions or operations directed to some end, as in manufacturing, printing, photography, etc.[461]

7.511 Inspections of particular product specifications, in a general sense, may correspond to this definition. However, the context of the term "technical regulation" in Annex 1 shows that it is one of a suite of definitions that includes "standard" and "conformity assessment procedures." The terms "technical regulations" and "standards" themselves form part of the definition of the term "conformity assessment procedures," which is defined as follows:

> 3. *Conformity assessment procedures*
>
> Any procedure used, directly or indirectly, to determine that relevant requirements in technical regulations or standards are fulfilled.
>
> *Explanatory note*
>
> Conformity assessment procedures include, *inter alia*, procedures for sampling, testing and inspection; evaluation, verification and assurance of conformity; registration, accreditation and approval as well as their combinations.

7.512 This definition shows that "conformity assessment procedures" assess conformity with "technical regulations" and "standards." This suggests that they are not only distinct from one other, but mutually exclusive. Whilst a single measure can combine both a technical regulation and a procedure to assess conformity with that technical regulation, it would be an odd result if a conformity assessment procedure could fall within the definition of a technical regulation as well.

---

[460] These issues are set out in paras. 7.446 and following in relation to the claim under Article 2.1 of the TBT Agreement.

[461] *The New Shorter Oxford English Dictionary* (1993).

7.513 The object and purpose of the TBT Agreement is, in large part, disclosed by the two main groups of substantive provisions that it contains: one that relates to technical regulations and standards in Articles 2 to 4, and another that relates to conformity assessment procedures in Articles 5 to 9. It is also reflected in the preamble, of which the fifth recital, and also the third and fourth recitals, draw this distinction.[462] If the Panel were to embed measures subject to Articles 5 to 9 in the definition of a technical regulation and thereby subject them to the technical regulations provisions in Articles 2 to 4 as well, it would lead to an unreasonable result. In this respect, we note that the explanatory note refers to "procedures for ... inspection" as an example of conformity assessment procedures. This suggests that a procedure for inspection is not a technical regulation.

7.514 Turning to the Regulation, the Panel notes that the inspection structures provided for in Article 10 of the Regulation do not set out "a continuous series of actions, events or changes" or a "course of action, a procedure" within the ordinary meaning set out at paragraph 7.510 above. It does not set out the steps that are to be undertaken to ensure compliance with a product specification, such as with the product specifications contained in Article 4 of the Regulation. Rather, it merely sets out the requirements for the design of inspection authorities and private bodies. It does not deal with the process by which these inspection authorities and private bodies are to conduct their inspections once they are established. Further, these inspection structures may be excluded *a priori* from the definition of a "technical regulation" under the TBT Agreement, in view of the context of that definition and the object and purpose of the Agreement, as explained at paragraphs 7.511 to 7.513 above. However, it is unnecessary to consider this issue further for the purposes of this dispute.

7.515 Therefore, the Panel concludes that the inspection structures requirements in the Regulation, read together with Article 4 of the Regulation, are not a "technical regulation" within the definition of that term in Annex 1.1 of the TBT Agreement. Accordingly, the Panel concludes that Article 2.2 of the TBT Agreement is inapplicable and rejects Australia's claim.

D. Trademark Claims

1. *The relationship between GIs and prior trademarks*

(a) *Introduction*

7.516 Australia claims that the Regulation is inconsistent with Article 16.1 of the TRIPS Agreement because it denies the owner of a registered trademark the exclusive right to prevent uses of GIs which would result in a likelihood of confusion with a prior trademark.[463] Its claim does not concern conflicts involving the future acquisition of trademark rights and GIs.[464]

7.517 The European Communities responds that this claim is unfounded for several reasons: (1) Article 14(3) of the Regulation, in fact, prevents the registration of GIs, use of which would result in a likelihood of confusion with a prior trademark; (2) Article 24.5 of the TRIPS Agreement provides for the "coexistence" of GIs and prior trademarks; (3) Article 24.3 of the TRIPS Agreement requires the European Communities to maintain "coexistence;" and (4) in any event, Article 14(2) of the Regulation would be justified as a limited exception under Article 17 of the TRIPS Agreement.[465]

7.518 For the sake of brevity, the Panel uses the term "coexistence" in this report to refer to a legal regime under which a GI and a trademark can both be used concurrently to some extent even though the use of one or

---

[462] They provide as follows:
"*Recognizing* the important contribution that *international standards* and *conformity assessment systems* can make in this regard by improving efficiency of production and facilitating the conduct of international trade;
Desiring therefore to encourage the development of such *international standards* and *conformity assessment systems*;
Desiring however to ensure that *technical regulations and standards*, including packaging, marking and labelling requirements, and *procedures for assessment of conformity with technical regulations and standards* do not create unnecessary obstacles to international trade" [emphasis added]

[463] Australia's first written submission, paras. 6, 60 and 102-103.

[464] Australia's rebuttal submission, para. 95.

[465] European Communities' first written submission, paras. 268-273.

both of them would otherwise infringe the rights conferred by the other. The use of this term does not imply any view on whether such a regime is justified.

7.519 The Panel will begin its examination of this claim by describing Article 14(2) of the Regulation and how the Regulation can, in principle, limit the right of the owner of a trademark subject to Article 14(2) against the use of a GI. We will then assess whether Article 14(3) of the Regulation prevents a situation from occurring in which a trademark would be subject to Article 14(2). If Article 14(3) cannot prevent that situation from occurring, we will proceed to examine whether Article 16.1 of the TRIPS Agreement requires Members to make available to trademark owners the right to prevent confusing uses of signs, even where the signs are used as GIs. If it does, we will consider whether Article 24.5 provides authority to limit that right and, if Article 24.5 does not, conclude our examination by assessing whether Article 17 or Article 24.3 of the TRIPS Agreement permits or requires the European Communities to limit that right with respect to uses of signs used as GIs.

(b) Description of Article 14(2) of the Regulation

7.520 Article 13 of the Regulation sets out the protection conferred by registration of a GI under the Regulation. Paragraph 1 provides for the prevention of certain uses of the GI and other practices. These are negative rights to prevent, essentially, uses which are misleading as to the origin of a product or otherwise unfair.

7.521 Under the European Communities' domestic law, it is considered that the Regulation impliedly grants the positive right to use the GI in accordance with the product specification and other terms of its registration to the exclusion of any other sign. The European Communities explains, and Australia does not contest, that under the European Communities' domestic law, this positive right is implicit in several provisions, including Article 4(1), which refers to eligibility to use a protected designation of origin or a protected geographical indication; Article 8, which provides that the indications PDO and PGI and equivalent national indications may appear only on agricultural products and foodstuffs that comply with the Regulation; and Article 13(1)(a) which provides protection for registered names against direct or indirect commercial use on certain conditions. Without this positive right, in the European Communities' view, the protection granted by Article 13 would be "meaningless." Accordingly, under the European Communities' domestic law, that positive right prevails over the rights of trademark owners to prevent the use of a sign that infringes trademarks.[466]

7.522 A registered GI may be used together with other signs or as part of a combination of signs but the registration does not confer a positive right to use any such other signs or combination of signs or to use the name in any linguistic versions not entered in the register.[467] Therefore, the registration does not affect the right of trademark owners to exercise their rights with respect to such uses.[468]

7.523 Article 14 of the Regulation governs the relationship of GIs and trademarks under Community law. Paragraph 1 deals with later trademarks. It provides for the refusal of trademark applications where use of the trademark would infringe the rights in a GI already registered under the Regulation. This, in effect, ensures that a registered *GI prevails over a later trademark.*

7.524 Paragraph 2 of Article 14 deals with prior trademarks. It provides as follows:

---

[466] Confirmed in the European Communities' response to Panel question No. 139.

[467] The European Communities explains that "[t]he positive right extends only to the linguistic versions that have been entered into the register" in its response to Panel question No. 140; see also its rebuttal submission, paras. 288 and 293; response to Panel question No. 137 and comment on US response to that question. A different "linguistic version" means a translation which renders the name differently. Some GIs are registered in more than one linguistic version: see, for example, the second, fourth and eleventh GIs set out *supra* at note 61.

[468] Under Community law, those rights would become meaningless if there was no positive right to use the registered GI. See the European Communities' rebuttal submission, para. 301; responses to Panel questions Nos. 139 and 140 (but contrast its comment on Australia's response to Panel question No. 137).

> 2. With due regard to Community law, a trademark the use of which engenders one of the situations indicated in Article 13 and which has been applied for, registered, or established by use, if that possibility is provided for by the legislation concerned, in good faith within the territory of the Community, before either the date of protection in the country of origin or the date of submission to the Commission of the application for registration of the designation of origin or geographical indication, may continue to be used notwithstanding the registration of a designation of origin or geographical indication, provided that no grounds for its invalidity or revocation exist as specified by Council Directive 89/194/EEC of 21 December 1998 to approximate the laws of the Member States relating to trade marks and/or Council Regulation (EC) No 40/94 of 20 December 1993 on the Community trade mark. [footnotes omitted]

7.525 This is an exception to Article 13, as it provides for the continued use of a prior trademark even though use of that trademark would conflict with the rights conferred by registration of a GI under the Regulation. It prevents the exercise of rights conferred by registration of a GI against the continued use of that particular prior trademark and is an express recognition that, in principle, *a GI and a trademark can coexist* under Community law. It is intended to implement Article 24.5 of the TRIPS Agreement.[469]

7.526 Article 14(2) only applies:

(a) with respect to the GI, where a particular indication satisfies the conditions for protection, including the definitions of a "designation of origin" or a "geographical indication," and is not subject to refusal on any grounds, including those in paragraph 3 of Article 14 (discussed below);

(b) with respect to the trademark, where a particular sign has already been applied for, registered, or established by use in good faith and there are no grounds for its invalidity or revocation; and

(c) where use of that trademark would infringe the GI registration.

7.527 The scope of Article 14(2) is confined temporally to those trademarks applied for, registered or established by use either before the GI is protected in its country of origin or before the date of submission to the Commission of an application for GI registration.

7.528 The text of Article 14(2) begins with the introductory phrase "[w]ith due regard to Community law." This refers, among other things, to the Community Trademark Regulation and the First Trademark Directive[470], both of which provide that trademark registration confers the right to prevent "all third parties" from certain uses of "any sign," including uses where there exists a likelihood of confusion.[471] This corresponds to the right provided for in Article 16.1 of the TRIPS Agreement.

7.529 However, Article 159 of the Community Trademark Regulation, as amended[472], provides as follows:

---

[469] Paragraph 11 of the recitals to the April 2003 amending Regulation explained that the dates referred to in Article 14(2) should be amended in line with Article 24.5 of the TRIPS Agreement: see Exhibit COMP-1h. Article 14(2) has been interpreted once by the European Court of Justice, in Case C-87/97, *Consorzio per la tutela del frommagio Gorgonzola v Käserai Champignon Hofmeister GmbH & Co Kg* [1999] ECR I-1301, concerning the trademark CAMBOZOLA for cheese and the GI "Gorgonzola." The judgement of the Court was submitted by the European Communities' in Exhibit EC-32.

[470] European Communities' response to Panel question No. 138. The "Community Trademark Regulation" refers to Council Regulation (EC) No. 40/94 on the Community trade mark, as amended by Council Regulation (EC) No. 1992/2003 and Council Regulation (EC) No. 422/2004, set out in Exhibit COMP-7. The "First Trademark Directive" refers to the First Council Directive 89/104/EEC to approximate the laws of the member States relating to trade marks, set out in Exhibit COMP-6.

[471] Article 9 of the Community Trademark Regulation and Article 5 of the First Trademark Directive.

[472] Article 142 of the original Council Regulation (EC) No. 40/94 was renumbered Article 159 by Article 156(5) of Council Regulation (EC) No. 1992/2003.

> This Regulation shall not affect Council Regulation (EEC) No. 2081/92 on the protection of geographical indications and designations of origin for agricultural products and foodstuffs of 14 July 1992, and in particular Article 14 thereof. [original footnote omitted]

7.530 This ensures that the rights conferred by a trademark registration against "all third parties" and uses of "any sign" do not prevail over a third party using a registered GI in accordance with its registration. It does not limit the rights conferred by a trademark registration against any other third party.[473] The same applies to trademarks protected under the national laws of the EC member States: due to the principle of the primacy of Community legislation, a trademark owner's rights cannot prevail over a third party using a GI registered under the Regulation in accordance with its registration. The rights conferred by a trademark registration against other third parties are not affected.

7.531 Accordingly, the trademark owner's right provided by trademark legislation in the implementation of Article 16.1 of the TRIPS Agreement, in principle, cannot be exercised against a person who uses a registered GI in accordance with its registration where the trademark is subject to Article 14(2) of the Regulation.

7.532 The phrase "[w]ith due regard to Community law" also refers to other legislation, such as labelling and misleading advertising legislation, which qualify the right to continue use of a trademark under Article 14(2). Conversely, the same legislation allows persons, including trademark owners, to take action against certain uses of a registered GI which are not covered by the GI registration.[474]

7.533 Paragraph 3 of Article 14 provides as follows:

> 3. A designation of origin or geographical indication shall not be registered where, in the light of a trade mark's reputation and renown and the length of time it has been used, registration is liable to mislead the consumer as to the true identity of the product.

7.534 This is a condition for the registration of a GI, as it provides for the refusal of registration of a GI that is liable to mislead the consumer as to the true identity of the product in light of certain factors relevant to a prior trademark. This, in effect, provides that *a prior trademark may prevail* over a later application for GI registration under certain conditions.

7.535 The European Communities argues that Article 14(3) of the Regulation, together with the criteria for registrability of trademarks applied under EC law, prevent the registration of a GI, use of which would result in a likelihood of confusion with a prior trademark. Australia disagrees. The Panel will consider this factual issue below.

(c) Article 14(3) of the Regulation

(i) main arguments of the parties

7.536 Australia argues that Article 14(3) of the Regulation does not concern use that is liable to "confuse" but rather concerns use that is liable to "mislead." "Misleading" is a stricter evidentiary standard than "confusing." The ordinary meaning of "confusing" is "perplexing, bewildering." Although the two words can be synonyms, the context of "mislead" in Article 22.2 and 22.3 of the TRIPS Agreement refers to misleading use which positively provokes an error on the part of a consumer. The standard of confusing established by Article 16.1 is a separate standard. The wording, context and aim of Article 14(3) of the Regulation confirm that its use of "misleading" is similar to that in Article 22.2 and 22.3 of the TRIPS Agreement. Therefore, the express terms of Article 14(3) do not exclude registration of GIs whose use would be confusing but not

---

[473] European Communities' first written submission, para. 317; response to Panel question No. 76; rebuttal submission, para. 336.

[474] European Communities' response to Panel question No. 140.

necessarily misleading.[475] If this were not so, the reference in Article 14(2) to grounds for revocation of a trademark in the Community Trademark Regulation and Trademark Directive would be meaningless because those grounds include liability to "mislead the public ... as to ... geographical origin" and are distinguished from the exclusive right to prevent use where there exists a "likelihood of confusion." The reference to revocation imports that differentiation into the Regulation.[476] The word "confusion" is used in Articles 6.6, 7.5(b), 12.2, 12b(3) and 12d(3) of the Regulation in the sense of wondering about the source of the good, but the word "misleading" is used in Articles 3.2, 6.6, 13.1(c), 13.1(d) and 14.3 in the sense of an action which positively provokes an error on the part of the consumer.[477]

7.537 Australia argues that Article 14(3) requires consideration of a trademark's reputation, renown and the length of time it has been used, which are not required by Article 16.1 of the TRIPS Agreement. Trademark owners cannot exercise their rights against GIs where their use would be misleading for other reasons. Trademarks that do not meet the tests expressly established by Article 14(3) of the Regulation cannot be protected by the right provided for in Article 16.1 of the TRIPS Agreement.[478]

7.538 Australia notes that the right provided for in Article 16.1 of the TRIPS Agreement refers to where "such use would result in a likelihood of confusion." It argues that this implies that there is, or is intended to be, active use of a trademark and that the right encompasses pre-emptive action. The way in which the trademark rights have been acquired does not affect the assessment as it is the prospective use of the second sign that is in issue. Reputation is not a prerequisite and it is possible to cause confusion with a registered trademark even where it has little use and no reputation. The right to prevent confusing use applies both at the time of the application for registration of the later trademark or GI and at later stages of use, including in the case of changed circumstances which would result in a likelihood of confusion on the basis of a likelihood of confusion.[479]

7.539 Australia argues that the only instance in which Article 14(3) has been applied shows that there was no consideration of the issue whether registration of the GI "Bayerisches Bier" would constitute confusing use in relation to the prior trademark "BAVARIA."[480] In response to a question from the Panel, Australia argued that the registered GIs "Bayerisches Bier," "Budejovické pivo" and "Gorgonzola" could be used in accordance with their respective registrations in a way that results in a likelihood of confusion with particular trademarks.[481]

7.540 Australia argues that the protection provided by the Regulation, in particular Article 13.1, makes clear that the owner of a registered trademark would not be able to prevent "confusingly similar or identical use of a sign for similar or identical goods." The right of a trademark owner to initiate an infringement action on the grounds that a GI as used is different from the GI as registered depends on the circumstances of the case. Trademarks registered in particular EC member States only, could still enjoy reputation in other EC member States. The European Communities has not explained how owners of those trademarks would have standing to initiate legal action under labelling, misleading advertising or unfair competition laws.[482]

7.541 Australia notes that Article 7(4) of the Regulation provides that an objection is admissible if it "shows that the registration of the name proposed would jeopardize the existence ... of a mark." This refers to a threat to

---

[475] Australia's rebuttal submission, paras. 104-106; in its second oral statement it referred to the difference between "mislead" and "confuse" as causing a consumer to "mistake" the true identity of a product and to be "puzzled" about the true identity of a product: see para. 15.

[476] Australia's second oral statement, paras. 18-19.

[477] Australia's response to Panel question No. 149.

[478] Australia's rebuttal submission, paras. 107-108.

[479] Australia's response to Panel question No. 148.

[480] Australia's rebuttal submission, para. 110.

[481] Australia's response to Panel question No. 137.

[482] Australia's response to Panel question No. 137.

the very being of the mark which is a far more rigorous standard than a likelihood of confusion. This is also true of the French and Spanish versions of the Regulation.[483]

7.542 Australia denies the allegation that it is requesting a remedy against GI rights that it does not provide with respect to trademark rights under its own law. It submits that the Panel should not consider the provisions of the trademark laws of other Members in isolation. For example, whilst Australia's trademark law excepts certain actions from infringing an earlier trademark right, it applies only where the prior right holder expressly consented to the coexistence or failed to prevent the acquisition of the later trademark right.[484]

7.543 The European Communities argues that, as a factual matter, the risk of registration of a GI confusingly similar to a prior trademark is very limited due to the criteria for registrability of trademarks applied under EC law. Moreover, Article 14(3) of the Regulation, if properly interpreted, is sufficient to prevent the registration of any confusing GIs.[485] The complainant bears the burden of proving that its interpretation of Article 14(3) is the only reasonable one and that the European Communities' interpretation is not reasonable or that the provision is being applied in a manner which results in the registration of confusing GIs.[486]

7.544 The European Communities argues that the criteria for the registrability of trademarks limit *a priori* the possibility of conflicts between GIs and earlier trademarks. Geographical names are primarily non-distinctive and, as such, are not apt for registration as trademarks. Their use may also be deceptive insofar as they are used for goods that do not originate in the location that they designate. Under EC law, they may only be registered as a trademark where the geographical name is not currently associated, and it can reasonably be assumed that it will not be associated in the future, with the product concerned; or where the name has acquired distinctiveness through use.[487]

7.545 The European Commission considers that the criteria listed in Article 14(3) of the Regulation are not exhaustive, so that other relevant criteria may be taken into account in order to assess whether the registration of the GI will result in a likelihood of confusion, such as the similarity between the signs or between the goods concerned. The likelihood of confusion will depend to a large extent on the degree of distinctiveness which the trademark has acquired through use. A trademark consisting of a GI, which has never been used or has no reputation or renown, should not have been registered in the first place because it would lack the required distinctiveness.[488] The length of time a trademark has been used does not limit Article 14(3) to cases where the trademark has been used for a long time as it is conceivable that a trademark which has been used for a relatively short period of time may have become strongly distinctive through other means, e.g. publicity.[489] It asserts that Australia bears the burden of proving that the EC's interpretation of "misleading" is less reasonable or that it is impossible to interpret "misleading" consistently with Article 16.1. One of the ordinary meanings of "misleading" is "confusing."[490]

7.546 The European Communities informs the Panel that the only instance in which Article 14(3) has been applied was the registration of "Bayerisches Bier" as a GI. There was no suggestion that this decision was based on the fact that the trademarks concerned were not famous enough or had not been used for long enough. The complainants have not identified an example of a GI which gives rise to a likelihood of confusion with an earlier trademark. Registration covers only the term in the specification and not its translations into other languages unless the term is the same in translation. The three Czech beer GIs also contain a unique

483 Australia's rebuttal submission, para. 133; second oral statement, paras. 20-21 and 23.

484 Australia's comment on EC responses to Panel question Nos. 137 and 139.

485 European Communities' first written submission, paras. 275-277.

486 European Communities' first written submission, para. 292; rebuttal submission, paras. 271-276.

487 European Communities' first written submission, paras. 278-285; rebuttal submission, para. 270.

488 European Communities' first written submission, paras. 286-291.

489 European Communities' response to Panel question No. 68.

490 European Communities' second oral statement, para. 162.

endorsement that they apply "without prejudice to any beer trademark or other rights existing in the European Union on the date of accession."[491]

7.547 The European Communities argues that Article 14(3) requires the EC authorities to refuse registrations and does not allow for a margin of discretion. It can be invoked before the courts after registration of a GI, including in trademark infringement proceedings brought against a user of a GI. This applies to registrations under the ordinary procedure in Article 6 or the "fast-track" procedure in Article 17. A trademark owner may raise the invalidity of the measure before the courts under the preliminary ruling procedure in Article 234 of the EC Treaty. Depending on the factual circumstances of each case, a trademark owner may also have standing to bring an action in annulment under Article 230 of the EC Treaty, if a GI registration were considered to affect adversely specific substantive trademark rights. A two-month time limit applies to the action in annulment and, in specific circumstances, may also apply to the preliminary ruling procedure.[492] Under both procedures, judicial review is available on points of fact and law. The cancellation procedure is set out in Article 11a of the Regulation and the grounds mentioned in Articles 11 and 11a are exhaustive.[493]

7.548 The European Communities notes that Article 7(4) of the Regulation provides that an objection is admissible if it "shows that the registration of the name proposed would jeopardize the existence ... of a mark." It argues that this language is broad enough to encompass any instance of likelihood of confusion with any mark. Logically, Article 14(3) must permit registration to be refused in such cases. Article 7(5)(b) refers expressly to a decision having regard to the "likelihood of confusion."[494]

7.549 The European Communities argues that Community law provides the means to prevent use of a registered GI in a confusing manner. Failure to comply with the product specifications in the registration may lead to cancellation. The right conferred by registration does not extend to other names or signs not in the registration. Registration does not cover translations. A presentation of a GI in a mutilated or deformed manner may be deemed different from the registered sign and not protected. Use of a GI is subject to the Community directives on labelling, presentation and advertising of foodstuffs and on misleading advertising and the EC member States' unfair competition laws.[495]

7.550 The European Communities argues that few, if any, Members provide a remedy to prevent confusing use of a registered trademark without first obtaining cancellation, invalidation or revocation of the trademark registration. In the same way, Community law does not provide a remedy to prevent use of a registered GI on the grounds that it is confusing, although the trademark owner may request a judicial ruling that the GI registration is invalid on those grounds.[496]

(ii) main arguments of third parties

7.551 Argentina, Brazil, India and Mexico indicated, in response to a question from the Panel, that they were not aware of any GIs registered under the Regulation that were identical or confusingly similar to a trademark owned by their respective nationals and protected in the European Communities.[497]

7.552 Brazil argues that Article 16.1 of the TRIPS Agreement deals with trademarks in general and not only with those referred to in the narrow terms of Article 14(3) of the Regulation, which refers to the trademark's

---

491 European Communities' rebuttal submission, paras. 286-293; response to Panel question No. 142.

492 European Communities' responses to Australia's questions Nos. 2 and 3 after the second substantive meeting.

493 European Communities' responses to Panel questions Nos. 67 and 142; rebuttal submission, paras. 294-297; second oral statement, paras. 174-179.

494 European Communities' first written submission, para. 336; response to Panel question No. 68; rebuttal submission, paras. 282-285.

495 European Communities' response to Panel question No. 63; rebuttal submission, paras. 298-303.

496 European Communities' second oral statement, para. 181; response to Panel question No. 139.

497 See their respective comments in Annex C, see paras. 19, 37, 106 and 120.

reputation, renown, and the length of time it has been used, and its liability to mislead the consumer as to the true identity of the product.[498]

7.553 New Zealand argues that Article 14(3) conditions the rights of a prior registered trademark owner on certain factors, such as reputation, renown and length of time of use, for which there is no basis in Article 16.1 of the TRIPS Agreement.[499]

7.554 Chinese Taipei argues that Article 14(3) of the Regulation only prevents the registration of a trademark if it fulfils the conditions of reputation, renown and length of time of use. This provision negates the right granted to trademark owners pursuant to Article 16.1 of the TRIPS Agreement.[500]

(iii) consideration by the Panel

7.555 Australia does not take issue in this dispute with trademark rights acquired after a GI is registered. Therefore, there is no need to consider Article 14(1) of the Regulation. Moreover, it does not take issue in this dispute with the *dates* for establishing which trademarks are considered earlier than a GI under Article 14(2) of the Regulation. Therefore, there is no need to consider that issue either.

7.556 Australia challenges coexistence under the Regulation "as such." It relies on the fact that Article 14(2) of the Regulation, on its face, can apply to certain trademarks and, when it does, the Regulation will limit the right of the owner of such a trademark against the use of a GI.[501]

7.557 The parties largely agree on the factual implications, in principle, of the application of Article 14(2). It allows the continued use of a trademark on certain conditions but, at the same time, the Regulation confers a positive right to use a GI which prevents the owner of a trademark from exercising the right conferred by that trademark against a person who uses a registered GI in accordance with its registration. The particular right of a trademark owner at issue is the right to prevent uses of a sign that would result in a likelihood of confusion, which is discussed in paragraphs 7.598 to 7.603 below.

7.558 The European Communities' first defence is that Article 14(3) can prevent the registration of any GI which would subject a prior trademark to Article 14(2), where the GI could be used in a manner that would result in a likelihood of confusion. This is a factual issue for the Panel to decide. This involves matters of interpretation of an EC Regulation which forms part of the European Communities' domestic law. It is necessary for the Panel to make an objective assessment of the meaning of this provision, although solely for the purpose of determining the European Communities' compliance with its WTO obligations.[502]

7.559 As a preliminary remark, the Panel does not consider that this defence is necessarily contradicted by the European Communities' other defences that it is fully entitled and even required under the TRIPS Agreement to apply its coexistence regime, regardless of whether a GI would otherwise infringe the rights in a prior trademark. However, given that this is the European Communities' view of its rights and obligations under the TRIPS Agreement, it would seem coincidental if Article 14(3) of the Regulation could operate in a way that a GI would never, in fact, otherwise infringe the rights in a prior trademark.

---

498 Annex C, para. 29.

499 Annex C, paras. 148-152.

500 Annex C, para. 178.

501 Although Article 14(2) of the Regulation is drafted as an exception to GI protection in Article 13, it is not disputed that in most of the situations described in Article 13, in which Article 14(2) applies, the use of the GI would otherwise constitute infringement of the trademark. If Article 14(3) were able to prevent the registration of any GI, use of which could otherwise constitute a trademark infringement, Article 14(2) would be redundant in all of these situations.

502 In this regard, the Panel recalls its comments at para. 7.106.

7.560 Turning to the text of Article 14(3) of the Regulation, the Panel's first observation is that Article 14(3) requires GI registration to be refused where it would be "liable to mislead the consumer as to the true identity of the product." This is limited to liability to mislead as to a single issue, and not with respect to anything else.

7.561 The Panel's second observation is that Article 14(3) specifically prohibits GI registration "in light of a trade mark's reputation and renown and the length of time it has been used." It is clear that these factors must all be taken into account in the application of Article 14(3). It is difficult to imagine how Article 14(3) could be applied without some consideration of the similarity of the signs and goods as well.[503] However, even if these factors are not exhaustive, and even if they do not require strong reputation, wide renown and long use, they indicate that the scope of Article 14(3) is limited to a subset of trademarks which, as a minimum, excludes trademarks with no reputation, renown or use. Otherwise, Article 14(3) does not prevent the registration of a GI, on the basis that its use would affect any prior trademark outside that subset.

7.562 The Panel's third observation on the text of Article 14(3) is that it does not refer to use (of the GI), or to likelihood or to confusion, when other provisions of the Regulation do. Articles 7(5)(b), 12b(3) and 12d(3) permit refusal of a GI registration "having regard to" or "taking account of" factors including the "actual likelihood of confusion" and the "actual risk of confusion."[504] This indicates that the standard in Article 14(3) that registration would "mislead the consumer as to the true identity of the product" is intended to apply in a narrower set of circumstances than the trademark owner's right to prevent use that would result in a likelihood of confusion.[505]

7.563 For these reasons, the Panel considers that Australia has made a prima facie case that Article 14(3) of the Regulation cannot prevent all situations from occurring in which Article 14(2) would, in fact, limit the rights of a trademark owner.

7.564 Consistent with this view, it can be noted that the European Communities specifically rejected a proposal by a Committee of the European Parliament to amend Article 14(2) so as to subject it to the trademark owners' rights when Article 14 was amended in April 2003.[506] This at least suggests that Article 14(3) was considered different from a blanket protection of trademark rights.

7.565 The European Communities has submitted that Australia's interpretation of Article 14(3) would conflict with Article 7(4), which provides that a statement of objection shall be admissible *inter alia* if it shows that the proposed GI registration would jeopardize the existence of a mark. It asserts that this language encompasses any instance of likelihood of confusion between the proposed GI and a prior trademark.[507] It has not explained why the text does not set forth the likelihood of confusion standard, when the following provision of the Regulation in Article 7(5)(b) does. The contrast is marked. Article 7(5)(b) sets out a procedure to reach agreement in cases where an objection is admissible, which appears to indicate that it contains a lower standard than the ground for objection in Article 7(4).

7.566 The European Communities has submitted that the criteria for registrability of a trademark limit *a priori* the risk of GIs being confused with a prior trademark, but it does not submit that they completely eliminate this risk. The evidence shows that signs eligible for protection as GIs can and have been registered as

---

503 Article 14(3) presupposes the applicability of Article 13, which requires a consideration of the similarity of the goods and signs.

504 Articles 7(5)(b) and 12d(3) do not apply to GIs located in third countries. To the extent that they apply to GIs located in the European Communities', they only apply in limited circumstances where there is an admissible objection from an EC member State, other than the one which transmitted the application, or a third country, and they do not provide that the actual likelihood or risk of confusion is an absolute ground for refusal.

505 The TRIPS Agreement does not define the terms "likelihood of confusion" and "mislead the public as to the geographical origin." These terms define the scope of protection provided for in Articles 16.1 and 22.2 of the TRIPS Agreement and apply in a very wide range of factual situations. Therefore, the Panel considers it inappropriate to embark on a detailed interpretation of these or similar terms unless necessary for the purposes of the resolution of the dispute, which is not the case here.

506 The Committee proposal is set out in Exhibit COMP-14.

507 European Communities' response to Panel question No. 68; rebuttal submission, paras. 282-285.

trademarks in the Community.[508] The European Communities has not shown that the criteria for registrability of trademarks can anticipate adequately a situation in which a GI could be used in a way that results in a likelihood of confusion with a trademark, wherever Article 14(3) of the Regulation does not provide for refusal of registration of a GI. Those criteria and Article 14(3) would have to offset each other in every case. However, Article 14(2) and (3) apply to trademarks that are already protected. They cannot apply to signs which do not satisfy the trademark registrability criteria, either because they are geographical names or for whatever other reason, and have been refused registration, are subject to invalidation or are otherwise unprotected. These signs are filtered out before Article 14 of the GI Regulation comes into play. Given that Article 14(3) applies to a subset of protected trademarks, those to which it does *not* apply have by definition already satisfied the trademark registrability criteria.

7.567 There is also the question of how Article 14(3) can protect a trademark owner's right to prevent uses which occur subsequent to GI registration. In response to a question from the Panel as to whether Article 14(3) could be invoked if use of the GI would otherwise infringe the trademark *subsequent* to GI registration, the European Communities submitted that it could.[509] The parties then made various submissions on this point, based on which the Panel makes the following observations:

(a) the Regulation does not refer to invalidation under Article 14(3). It sets out cancellation procedures in Articles 11 and 11a, the grounds for which do not appear to relate to improper application of Article 14(3). If invalidation procedures are possible, it would be as a matter of general Community law under the EC Treaty;

(b) Article 230 of the EC Treaty provides a procedure for a direct challenge to the validity of a Community measure before the Court of First Instance of the European Communities on the condition that the applicant "is directly and individually concerned" by the measure. It is not submitted by any party that all trademark owners can satisfy that condition. Further, this procedure is subject to a two-month time limit which could render it unavailable to certain trademark owners who did satisfy that condition;[510]

(c) Article 234 of the EC Treaty provides a procedure for an indirect challenge to a Community measure under which a court of an EC member State can refer a question to the European Court of Justice for a preliminary ruling. This procedure could be invoked in a trademark infringement proceeding to obtain invalidation of a GI registration. It is not clear in what circumstances this procedure is available to a trademark owner who could have invoked the Article 230 procedure. The procedure under Article 234 would only be available where the court of the EC member State considered the question of validity of the GI necessary to resolve the trademark infringement action. In any case, the decision not to refuse a registration under Article 14(3) of the Regulation would be interpreted in the preliminary ruling as at the time of that decision, and not at the time of the subsequent allegedly infringing use;[511] and

(d) Article 14(3) is apparently not mandatory in all cases as three GIs registered in accordance with the terms of an Act of Accession to the European Union cannot be invalidated on the basis of Article 14(3).[512]

---

[508] For example, the following are registered Community trademarks: CALABRIA for pasta; DERBY for milk and chocolate based products; WIENERWALD for prepared meals, condiments and other goods and services.

[509] European Communities' response to Panel question No. 67; see also rebuttal submission, paras. 270 and 296. The Panel's findings do not imply any view on whether a requirement to seek GI invalidation as a condition precedent to obtaining relief against trademark infringement would be consistent with the enforcement obligations under the TRIPS Agreement.

[510] Australia's comment on EC response to Panel question Nos. 159 and 160; European Communities' second oral statement, para. 177.

[511] Australia's comment on EC responses to Panel question Nos. 159 and 160; European Communities' second oral statement, para. 178.

[512] European Communities' response to Panel question No. 142(c).

7.568 In light of these observations, the Panel considers that there is no evidence to show that it is possible to seek invalidation of a GI registration under Article 14(3) in *all* cases in which use of a GI would otherwise infringe a prior trademark. In those cases where it is not possible, it would be necessary for the owner of a prior trademark to be able to anticipate, at the time of the proposed GI registration, all subsequent uses of the proposed GI that would result in a likelihood of confusion. There is no reason to believe that this is possible. The evidence submitted to the Panel shows that GI registrations under the Regulation simply refer to names without limiting the way in which they are used.

7.569 The European Communities has submitted that the food labelling and misleading advertising directives and unfair competition laws of the EC member States also prevent confusing uses. We understand, and the European Communities does not deny, that this is only possible where the use is not in accordance with the GI registration. In any event, the scope of the directives is narrower than that of the GI Regulation and the standards which they apply are different from the right of a trademark owner to prevent use which would result in a likelihood of confusion, for the following reasons:

(a) the food labelling directive only applies to the labelling of foodstuffs to be delivered as such to the ultimate consumer and certain aspects relating to the presentation and advertising thereof. It provides that "labelling and methods used must not be such as could mislead the purchaser to a material degree, particularly ... as to the characteristics of the foodstuff and, in particular, as to its nature, identity, properties, composition, quantity, durability, origin or provenance, method of manufacture or production"[513]; and

(b) the misleading advertising directive applies to "any advertising which in any way, including presentation, deceives or is likely to deceive the persons to whom it is addressed or whom it reaches and which, by reason of its deceptive nature is likely to affect their economic behaviour or which, for those reasons, injures or is likely to injure a competitor."[514]

7.570 The unfair competition laws of the EC member States apply subject to the terms of registration under the Regulation, due to the primacy of Community law. It is not clear to what extent these laws apply in addition to the Regulation but, to the extent that they do, they use various standards, some of which require deception, which is narrower than confusion, and some of which appear only to apply the misleading standard which is embodied in the Regulation itself.[515]

7.571 Australia also refers to some specific cases in which the Regulation has been applied in support of its claim, as set out in the following paragraphs.

7.572 Article 14(3) of the Regulation has only been applied once. This was the case of "Bayerisches Bier," which was registered as a protected geographical indication in 2001 subject to the proviso that the use of certain prior trademarks, for example, BAVARIA and HØKER BAJER, was permitted to continue under Article 14(2). The GI refers to a beer and the trademarks are registered in respect of beer. The GI and the trademarks are, respectively, the words "Bavaria" or "Bavarian Beer" rendered in the German, English and Danish languages.

[513] Articles 1 and 2(1)(a)(i) of Directive 2000/13/EC of the European Parliament and of the Council on the approximation of the laws of the Member States relating to the labelling, presentation and advertising of foodstuffs, referred to in the European Communities' responses to Panel question No. 63, fn 38, and reproduced in Exhibit EC-30.

[514] Article 2(2) of Council Directive 84/450/EEC relating to the approximation of the laws, regulations and administrative provisions of the Member States concerning misleading advertising, referred to in the European Communities' responses to Panel question No. 63, fn 39, and reproduced in Exhibit EC-31.

[515] See information supplied by the European Communities' and some of its member States to the Council for TRIPS in the review under Article 24.2 of the TRIPS Agreement, document IP/C/W/117/Add.10, reproduced in Exhibit EC-29. The European Communities' did not supply information on the unfair competition laws of its ten new member States.

Upon its registration, the EC Council concluded that the GI would not mislead the public as to the identity of the product, which is the standard embodied in Article 14(3) of the Regulation.[516]

7.573 Australia alleges that the GI "Bayerisches Bier" could be used in a manner that would result in a likelihood of confusion with these prior trademarks.[517] In response to a direct question from the Panel, the European Communities did not deny this specific allegation. It only responded that "in principle" a name registered following the assessment required by Article 14(3) "should not give rise to confusion when used subsequently" and submitted that "in practice" this may happen only when the registered name is used together with other signs or as part of a combination of signs. This was a conspicuous choice of words because in the same response it commented in detail on two other specific cases which it considered irrelevant to the dispute.[518]

7.574 Australia also alleges that three Czech beer GIs, "Budějovické pivo," "Českobudějovické pivo" and "Budějovický měšt'anský var" could be used in a manner that would result in a likelihood of confusion with the prior trademarks BUDWEISER and BUD, registered in respect of beer.[519] In response to a direct question from the Panel, the European Communities did not deny that these GIs could be used in a manner that would result in a likelihood of confusion with these prior trademarks. Instead, it pointed to an endorsement on the three GI registrations that they apply "without prejudice to any beer trademark or other rights existing in the European Union on the date of accession."[520] This might imply that it accepts a likelihood of confusion, but considers that there are other means besides Article 14(3) to deal with that.

7.575 There appears to be an inconsistency between the European Communities' position that Article 14(3) of the Regulation, in practice, prevents the registration of GIs, use of which would result in a likelihood of confusion with a prior trademark, and its decision to avoid contesting that there may be circumstances in which the four specific GIs referred to above could be used which would not result in such a likelihood of confusion with these specific prior trademarks.

7.576 For the above reasons, the Panel considers that the European Communities has not rebutted Australia's prima facie case that Article 14(3) of the Regulation cannot prevent all situations from occurring in which a trademark would be subject to Article 14(2) and, hence, in which the Regulation would limit the rights of the owner of such a trademark.

7.577 The Panel will now proceed to examine whether the TRIPS Agreement requires Members to make available to trademark owners rights against signs when they are used as GIs.

(d) Relationship between protection of GIs and prior trademarks under the TRIPS Agreement

(i) main arguments of the parties

7.578 Australia argues that nothing in the TRIPS Agreement justifies a failure to grant the right provided for in Article 16.1. Had the negotiators intended to permit Members to act inconsistently with this obligation, they

---

516 Council Regulation (EC) No. 1347/2001 reproduced in Exhibit EC-9.

517 See Australia's response to Panel question No. 137.

518 The European Communities submitted twice that the EC Council had concluded that the registration of this GI would not lead to a likelihood of confusion with these prior trademarks but this is different from the EC Council's conclusion as stated in the decision on registration. The European Communities later indicated in response to a question from the Panel that the EC Council's conclusion was that the signs were not sufficiently similar to mislead the public, which is closer to the wording of the conclusion as stated in the decision, but not necessarily a likelihood of confusion: see European Communities' first written submission, fn. 140 to para. 288; rebuttal submission, para. 287; and responses to Panel questions Nos. 137 and 143 and compare Council Regulation (EC) No. 1347/2001 *supra* at 516 and the Commission Guide to the Regulation (August 2004 edition, p. 12) in Exhibit EC-64.

519 The evidence indicates that these trademarks are registered in at least two EC member States and rights to them appear to have been acquired through use in another EC member State: see Exhibits US-53, Section 3.6; US-51, para. 26; and US-82.

520 European Communities' rebuttal submission, paras. 286-293; response to Panel question No. 142.

would have said so explicitly. Article 17 is an express exception to trademarks and nothing in Section 3 of Part II on GI protection could be interpreted in such a way as to create an exception to trademarks.[521]

7.579 Australia does not argue that trademarks must prevail over later GIs.[522] Rather, it argues that Article 24.5, together with Articles 22.3 and 23.2, defines the boundaries of the range of possible actions open to a Member to implement GI protection in relation to trademarks.[523] Article 24.5 does not require or permit any negation or other limitation of the trademark owner's right under Article 16.1.[524] It can only be an exception to the provisions of Section 3 on GI protection in view of its location and title.[525] It also creates a positive right that specified trademark rights cannot be adversely affected.[526]

7.580 Australia argues that the "validity of the registration of a trademark" refers to the ongoing legality of the good faith registration of a trademark. The legal bundle of rights contained in a validly registered trademark includes the exclusive right to prevent confusing use granted under Article 16.1. Measures adopted to implement GI protection cannot undermine that exclusive right. The "right to use a trademark" refers to the ongoing ability to use a trademark to which rights have been acquired through use. Measures adopted to implement GI protection cannot adversely affect such rights.[527] Whatever may have been intended by the phrase the "right to use a trademark," it is separate from, and additional to, the exclusive right to prevent confusing uses required under Article 16.1.[528] It is not required under Section 2 of Part II.[529] Article 24.5 does not refer to the "exclusive" right to use a trademark because trademark rights acquired through use are not always exclusive.[530]

7.581 Australia argues that there is no conflict between Articles 16.1 and 22. With respect to Article 22.2, the only relevance of Article 22.2(a) to trademark rights would be in the context of acquisition of new trademark rights.[531] With respect to Article 22.3, for example, Australian trademark law expressly provides that registration of a trademark may be opposed if it contains or consists of a false GI.[532]

7.582 Australia argues that a complaining party bears the burden of proof where it alleges a breach of obligations pursuant to Article 24.5 but a responding party bears the burden of proof where it relies on Article 24.5 to excuse or justify a measure's inconsistency with another provision. Article 24.5 does not alter the scope of Article 16.1 but confirms the continued applicability of the rights granted under Article 16.1 in the circumstances covered by Article 24.5.[533]

7.583 The European Communities responds that this claim is unfounded.[534] The TRIPS Agreement recognizes trademarks and GIs as intellectual property rights on the same level, and confers no superiority to trademarks over GIs. The provisions of Section 3 of Part II on GI protection are not "exceptions" to the provision of Article 16.1 on trademark rights. The criteria for registrability of trademarks limit *a priori* the possibility of conflicts between GIs and trademarks but conflicts may arise. Article 16.1 does not address this

[521] Australia's first written submission, para. 104.
[522] Australia's rebuttal submission, para. 96.
[523] Australia's first written submission, para. 74.
[524] Australia's first written submission, para. 106; response to Panel question No. 72.
[525] Australia's response to Panel question No. 78; rebuttal submission, para. 93.
[526] Australia's response to Panel question No. 145.
[527] Australia's response to Panel question No. 76; rebuttal submission, para. 100.
[528] Australia's response to Panel question No. 77.
[529] Australia's rebuttal submission, para. 99.
[530] Australia's rebuttal submission, para. 100.
[531] Australia's response to Panel question No. 146.
[532] Australia's response to Panel question No. 79.
[533] Australia's response to Panel question No. 75(a).
[534] European Communities' first written submission, paras. 269-273.

issue. Rather, the boundary between GIs and trademarks is defined by Article 24.5 which provides for coexistence with earlier trademarks. Article 24.5 must be read with Articles 22.3 and 23.2 which also provide protection to GIs vis-à-vis trademarks.[535] Section 2 of Part II cannot be applied without having regard to Section 3.[536]

7.584 The European Communities argues that Article 24.5 has two implications: (1) with respect to grandfathered trademarks (or applications): (a) Members are not allowed to prejudice the validity of the registration (or the eligibility of the application or the right to use the trademark), but (b) Members may prejudice other rights of the trademark owner, including in particular the right to prevent others from using the sign of which the trademark consists; and (2) with respect to other trademarks (or applications), Members may prejudice any right.[537]

7.585 The European Communities argues that the ordinary meaning of the word "prejudice" used in all three official versions includes the notion of "judge beforehand" but only the word in the English version includes the notion of "cause injury, damage or harm."[538] The phrase "validity of the registration" does not necessarily imply that the registration must confer exclusive rights vis-à-vis all third parties. The fact that the owner cannot prevent use of the same or a similar sign by the GI right holder does not mean that the registration is set aside. The phrase "the right to use a trademark" refers to the basic right of the trademark owner to use the trademark, whether it has been acquired through registration or use.[539] It is the right to use a sign, which is different from the right to prevent others from using the same or a similar sign. If that right were inherent in the term "validity of the registration," it would have been superfluous to refer to the "right to use a trademark" as well. If that right had been intended, the drafters would have referred to the "exclusive right to use a trademark." If that right were inherently exclusive, it would have been superfluous to provide in Article 16.1 that the owners of trademarks shall have exclusive rights. The drafting history shows that the Brussels Draft referred to the continued use of a GI as a trademark, which envisaged coexistence, in a separate provision from the predecessor to Article 24.5. Its transfer to Article 24.5 in the final version did not alter its meaning or purpose.[540]

7.586 The European Communities argues that Article 24.5 is drafted in mandatory terms and imposes self-standing obligations which go beyond those in Section 2 of Part II. This may be illustrated by the case of a Member which provides for the refusal or invalidation of registration of a trademark in terms broader than those in Article 22.3, or which prohibits the use of any trademark acquired by use in terms broader than those in Article 22.2. Both would be consistent with Section 2 of Part II but Article 24.5 would prevent either applying to prior trademarks. This would be an obligation arising exclusively under Article 24.5.[541]

7.587 The European Communities argues that if Article 24.5 did not allow coexistence, the protection of GIs provided under Section 3 of Part II would become pointless whenever there is a grandfathered trademark. The phrase "measures adopted to implement this Section" assumes that Members will continue to protect GIs notwithstanding the existence of grandfathered trademarks. Coexistence may not be a perfect solution to resolve conflicts between different types of intellectual property rights but there is no such perfect solution.[542] It is not an unusual solution, since coexistence is envisaged in Articles 23.2 (with respect to a GI and a trademark that is not misleading), 23.3, 24.3 (where pre-existing protection provided for coexistence) 24.4 and 16.1 (vis-à-vis existing prior rights).[543] Article 24.5 embodies a compromise. The European Communities and other

---

535 European Communities' first written submission, paras. 294-300.

536 European Communities' rebuttal submission, paras. 306-307.

537 European Communities' first written submission, para. 301.

538 European Communities' comment on US response to Panel question No. 145.

539 European Communities' first written submission, para. 305; response to Panel question No. 76.

540 European Communities' response to Panel question No. 76; rebuttal submission, paras. 327-328.

541 European Communities' response to Panel question No. 145.

542 European Communities' first written submission, para. 307; response to Panel question No. 77.

543 European Communities' first written submission, para. 308; response to Panel question No. 76.

participants agreed to make it mandatory on the understanding that the trademark owners would have the right to use the trademark but not the right to exclude use by GI right holders.[544]

7.588 The European Communities argues that there is no "conflict" between Articles 16.1 and 22.3 but that there is a potential "conflict" between Articles 16.1 and 22.2(a), and possibly 23.1. Article 22.2 confers on GI right holders the right to prevent certain uses of trademarks, which may conflict with the right of the trademark owner under Article 16.1 to prevent certain uses of signs. The simultaneous exercise of both rights would lead to a situation where neither the trademark owner nor the GI right holders could use the sign in question. Neither would be able to fulfil its purpose. This conflict is resolved by Articles 22.3, 23.2 and 24.5.[545]

7.589 The European Communities argues that only the object and purpose of the treaty as a whole is relevant to the general rule of treaty interpretation. To the extent that the exclusivity of a trademark is an object and purpose of the TRIPS Agreement, it submits that exclusivity is as essential to a GI or even more essential, because the choice of a GI is not arbitrary, unlike a trademark, and the establishment of a GI takes longer than a trademark.[546]

7.590 The European Communities argues that the complainant bears the burden of proof that a measure falls within the scope of the obligations provided in Article 16.1. Article 24.5 is not an exception but defines the boundary between the obligations in Article 16.1 and a Member's right to implement GI protection. It does not provide an exemption from an obligation but places a limit on the measures that Members must or may take when implementing GI protection under Section 3 of Part II. It confers a right to use a trademark, a right which owners of trademarks acquired through use do not have under Article 16.1 because rights the basis of use are optional under Article 16.1. It notes that Australia cited Article 24.5 in its request for establishment of a panel and makes a claim under that provision in its first written submission.[547]

(ii) main arguments of third parties

7.591 Argentina argues that coexistence is inconsistent with Articles 16.1 and 22.3 of the TRIPS Agreement. Article 24.5 sets out a cut-off date different from the one in the Regulation and does not provide for the possibility of limiting the trademark owner's right as the Regulation does. Article 24.4 determines the boundaries for alternatives available to Members in the implementation of measures relating to GI protection and its link to trademarks.[548]

7.592 Brazil argues GIs which are identical to trademarks are likely to create confusion and, consequently, may affect the value of trademarks. Article 16.1 of the TRIPS Agreement provides for a right that covers the use of any sign, and not only that of a trademark, which might cause confusion. The possibility of coexistence between a trademark and a GI is only acceptable in terms of Articles 24.5 and 16.1, read in conjunction, which mean that the use of a GI and the need to protect it must not be at the expense of both trademark owners and consumers, which may undermine the value of a trademark contrary to the "exclusive rights" of a trademark owner under Article 16.1.[549]

---

[544] European Communities' response to Panel question No. 147.

[545] European Communities' rebuttal submission, paras. 308-310; response to Panel question No. 146.

[546] European Communities' response to Panel question No. 76.

[547] European Communities' response to Panel question No. 75; rebuttal submission, paras. 312-315.

[548] Annex C, para. 5.

[549] Annex C, para. 36.

7.593 Colombia argues that, under the TRIPS Agreement, no form of protection is superior to another. Therefore, the Regulation cannot deny the right of the trademark owner under Article 16.1 of the TRIPS Agreement. Such denial constitutes a clear violation of WTO obligations.[550]

7.594 Mexico argues that the exclusive right in Article 16.1 of the TRIPS Agreement is severely nullified by Article 14(2) of the Regulation as it permits coexistence between a prior registered trademark and a later GI. The European Communities' explanation that coexistence is not the perfect solution is an inadequate justification but a recognition of inconsistency. By ignoring the "first in time, first in right" rule, the Regulation not only contravenes Article 24.5 of the TRIPS Agreement but also a recognized general principle of law.[551]

7.595 New Zealand argues that Article 16.1 of the TRIPS Agreement provides for a right against "all third parties." Despite an appearance of conflict between the rights in Articles 16.1 and 22.2, each must be read to the fullest extent permissible without conflicting with the other. Article 24.5 is a provision that resolves conflict by compromising this exclusivity, but in all other cases, the rights provided for in Articles 16.1 and 22.2 must both be upheld. Article 14(2) of the Regulation excludes users of a registered GI from the scope of "all third parties" against whom a trademark owner should be able to exercise rights, and is inconsistent with Article 16.1.[552]

7.596 Chinese Taipei argues that Articles 16.1 and 22.2 of the TRIPS Agreement must be given their full scope in a manner that would not cause conflict. The Regulation creates precisely such a conflict, rendering Article 16.1 inutile, as the right of trademark owners under that article is negated by coexistence under Article 14(2) of the Regulation. The result is the creation of a hierarchy in which GIs have a superior status than trademarks, which is not contemplated by the TRIPS Agreement.[553]

(iii) consideration by the Panel

7.597 The Panel will now proceed to examine whether the TRIPS Agreement requires Members to make available to trademark owners rights against the use of GIs. This involves two steps: first, we examine the right of trademark owners provided for in Article 16.1 of the TRIPS Agreement and then we continue by examining whether Article 24.5 provides authority to limit that right.

Article 16.1 of the TRIPS Agreement

7.598 Part II of the TRIPS Agreement contains minimum standards concerning the availability, scope and use of intellectual property rights. The first seven Sections contain standards relating to categories of intellectual property rights. Each Section sets out, as a minimum, the *subject matter* which is eligible for protection, the scope of the *rights conferred* by the relevant category of intellectual property and permitted *exceptions* to those rights.

7.599 Although each of the Sections in Part II provides for a different category of intellectual property, at times they refer to one another[554], as certain subject matter may be eligible for protection by more than one category of intellectual property. This is particularly apparent in the case of trademarks and GIs, both of which are, in general terms, forms of distinctive signs. The potential for overlap is expressly confirmed by

---

[550] Annex C, para. 102.

[551] Annex C, para. 114.

[552] Annex C, paras. 148-151.

[553] Annex C, para. 178.

[554] For instance, Article 25.2 of the TRIPS Agreement refers to more than one category of intellectual property, as does Article 4 of the IPIC Treaty as incorporated by Article 35 of the TRIPS Agreement.

Articles 22.3 and 23.2, which provide for the refusal or invalidation of the registration of a trademark which contains or consists of a GI.[555]

7.600 Section 2 of Part II provides for the category of trademarks. Article 15.1 sets out the definition of the subject matter which is capable of constituting a trademark. These are signs that satisfy certain criteria. Article 16.1 sets out a right which must be conferred on the owner of a registered trademark, and which may also be acquired on the basis of use, as follows:

> 1. The owner of a registered trademark shall have the exclusive right to prevent all third parties not having the owner's consent from using in the course of trade identical or similar signs for goods or services which are identical or similar to those in respect of which the trademark is registered where such use would result in a likelihood of confusion. In case of the use of an identical sign for identical goods or services, a likelihood of confusion shall be presumed. The rights described above shall not prejudice any existing prior rights, nor shall they affect the possibility of Members making rights available on the basis of use.

7.601 The right which must be conferred on the owner of a registered trademark is set out in the first sentence of the text. There are certain limitations on that right which relate to use in the course of trade, the signs, the goods or services for which the signs are used and those with respect to which they are registered and the likelihood of confusion. The ordinary meaning of the text indicates that, basically, this right applies to use in the course of trade of identical or similar signs, on identical or similar goods, where such use would result in a likelihood of confusion. It does not specifically exclude use of signs protected as GIs.

7.602 The text of Article 16.1 stipulates that the right for which it provides is an "exclusive" right. This must signify more than the fact that it is a right to "exclude" others, since that notion is already captured in the use of the word "prevent." Rather, it indicates that this right belongs to the owner of the registered trademark alone, who may exercise it to prevent certain uses by "all third parties" not having the owner's consent. The last sentence provides for an exception to that right, which is that it shall not prejudice any existing prior rights. Otherwise, the text of Article 16.1 is unqualified.

7.603 Other exceptions to the right under Article 16.1 are provided for in Article 17 and possibly elsewhere in the TRIPS Agreement. However, there is no implied limitation vis-à-vis GIs in the text of Article 16.1 on the exclusive right which Members must make available to the owner of a registered trademark. That right may be exercised against a third party not having the owner's consent on the same terms, whether or not the third party uses the sign in accordance with GI protection, subject to any applicable exception.

<u>Article 24.5 of the TRIPS Agreement</u>

7.604 The parties have referred to Article 24.5 of the TRIPS Agreement. This appears in Section 3 of Part II, which provides for the category of GIs.[556] Article 24.5 provides as follows:

> 5. Where a trademark has been applied for or registered in good faith, or where rights to a trademark have been acquired through use in good faith either:
>
> (a) before the date of application of these provisions in that Member as defined in Part VI; or
>
> (b) before the geographical indication is protected in its country of origin;

---

[555] Articles 22.3 and 23.2, respectively.

[556] Section 3 of Part II consists of three articles: Articles 22, 23 and 24. Article 23 concerns only GIs for wines and spirits, which are not covered by the Regulation. Nevertheless, the meaning of that article is important in understanding Section 3 in general and Article 24 in particular. The Panel therefore refers to it in its examination, where that is helpful.

measures adopted to implement this Section shall not prejudice eligibility for or the validity of the registration of a trademark, or the right to use a trademark, on the basis that such a trademark is identical with, or similar to, a geographical indication.

7.605 The Panel must interpret this provision, like all other provisions of the covered agreements relevant to this dispute, in accordance with the customary rules of interpretation of public international law, as required by Article 3.2 of the DSU. For present purposes, this means the general rule of treaty interpretation contained in Article 31 of the Vienna Convention on the Law of Treaties. This requires an interpretation in good faith in accordance with the ordinary meaning to be given to the terms in their context and in the light of the object and purpose of the agreement. Recourse may be had to supplementary means of interpretation in accordance with Article 32 of that Convention.[557]

7.606 Commencing with the terms of the provision, we observe that Article 24.5 consists of a single sentence, of which the subject is "measures adopted to implement this Section." Article 24.5 appears in Section 3 of Part II of the TRIPS Agreement. Therefore, the reference to "this Section" is a reference to Section 3.

7.607 The principal verb in Article 24.5 is "shall not prejudice." There are various definitions of the verb "prejudice" used in the three authentic language versions of the TRIPS Agreement.[558] The ordinary meaning of the verb "prejudice" in English can be defined as "affect adversely or unfavourably; injure or impair the validity of (a right, claim, etc.)." The latter part of this definition appears particularly apposite in this context since it refers to a right or claim, and the objects of the verb in Article 24.5 are legal rights. However, the European Communities emphasizes that the verbs used in the French and Spanish versions, *préjuger* and *prejuzgar* respectively, correspond to the modern English verb "prejudge." The Panel notes that this is an archaic sense of the English verb "prejudice" now analogous to its use in the phrase "without prejudice." Other usages of the English verb "prejudice" in the TRIPS Agreement outside Article 24 have been rendered differently in the French and Spanish versions, which are equally authentic[559], to capture the sense of adverse effect or injury, so that that sense should not be read into Article 24.5. Nevertheless, the essence of all these definitions is that the provision does not affect certain other rights. The Panel's task in this dispute is to determine the applicability of Article 24.5. For that purpose, it suffices to note that the verb "shall not prejudice" denotes that the measures that are the subject of that provision shall not affect certain other rights.

7.608 The Panel notes that the word "prejudice" is relatively common in all three versions of the TRIPS Agreement and the phrase "shall not prejudice" or "shall in no way prejudice" occurs three other times in the English version, including once in another exception in Article 24, and once in relation to prior rights in Article 16.1 itself.[560] Read in context, "prejudice" simply appears to be a word which the drafters used to indicate that a particular measure shall not affect certain other rights, including prior rights.

7.609 The objects of the principal verb in Article 24.5 are "the eligibility for or the validity of the registration of a trademark" and "the right to use a trademark." The context indicates the relevance of these rights in Article 24.5. The choice of words "the eligibility for or the validity of the registration of a trademark" reflects the fact that these are the aspects of trademark protection which might otherwise be prejudiced by the obligations to "refuse or invalidate the registration of a trademark" and that "registration of a trademark ... shall be refused or invalidated" in Articles 22.3 and 23.2. In the same way, the choice of the words "the right to use a

---

[557] See, for example, the Appellate Body report on *US – Gasoline*, DSR 1996:I, 3, at 16; Appellate Body report on *Japan – Alcoholic Beverages II*, DSR 1996:I, 97, at 104; and Appellate Body report on *India – Patents (US)*, paras. 45-46.

[558] *The New Shorter Oxford English Dictionary* (1993); *Le Nouveau Petit Robert: Dictionnaire de la langue française* (June 2000) and *Diccionario de la Lengua Española*, 21st edition, (1992).

[559] See the final clause of the WTO Agreement.

[560] The phrase "shall in no way prejudice" appears in all three versions in Article 24.8, and "shall not prejudice" appears in Articles 16.1 and 53.2 in the English version. The phrase "without prejudice" appears in Articles 10.2, 40.3, 50.6, 57 and 59, and the word "prejudice" appears in the exception clauses in Articles 13, 26.2 and 30 (and Article 27.2 in the English version), and also in Article 63.4.

trademark" reflects the fact that this is the aspect of trademark protection which would otherwise be prejudiced by the obligations to provide the legal means to prevent certain uses in Articles 22.2 and 23.1.[561]

7.610 The European Communities asserts that the words "the right to use a trademark" provide for an additional positive right to use a trademark. However, in the Panel's view, the verb "shall not prejudice" is not capable of supporting this interpretation. It does not provide for the conferral of new rights on trademark owners or GI holders, but provides that the specifically mentioned rights shall not be affected by the measures that are the subject of the provision. If the drafters had intended to grant a positive right, they would have used positive language. Indeed, Article 14(2) of the Regulation (which was adopted prior to the end of the TRIPS negotiations) expressly provides that "a trademark ... may continue to be used" under certain conditions. In contrast, there is no language in Article 24.5 of the TRIPS Agreement which would provide for the conferral of a right to use a trademark. Instead, it is a saving provision which ensures that "the right to use a trademark" is not prejudiced, or affected, by measures adopted to implement Section 3 of Part II. Irrespective of how the right to use a trademark arises, there is no obligation under Article 24.5 to confer it.[562]

7.611 Even if the TRIPS Agreement does not expressly provide for a "right to use a trademark" elsewhere, this does not mean that a provision that measures "shall not prejudice" that right provides for it instead. The right to use a trademark is a right that Members may provide under national law.[563] This is the right saved by Article 24.5 where it provides that certain measures "shall not prejudice ... the right to use a trademark."[564]

7.612 The context in other paragraphs of Article 24 confirms the Panel's interpretation of "the eligibility for or the validity of the registration of a trademark" and "the right to use a trademark," as used in paragraph 5. Other exceptions in that article also refer to the implications of these two types of protection. Paragraph 4 refers to "continued and similar *use* of a particular [GI] ... identifying wines and spirits;" paragraph 7 refers to "any request made under this Section in connection with the *use* or *registration of a trademark*;" and paragraph 8 refers to "the right of any person to *use*, in the course of trade, that person's name."

7.613 There is no reason to limit the "right to use a trademark" to trademarks acquired through use due to the optical symmetry between, on the one hand, the passive subjects of the first relative clause: "a trademark applied for ... in good faith," "a trademark ... registered in good faith" and "rights to a trademark ... acquired through use in good faith" and, on the other hand, the active objects of the principal verb: "eligibility for ... the registration of a trademark," "the validity of the registration of a trademark" and "the right to use a trademark."

---

[561] The order of these two exceptions in Article 24.5 reverses the order of the types of protection in relation to *uses* and in relation to *registration of a trademark* in Article 22.2 and 22.3 and in Article 23.1 and 23.2. However, it can be observed that the exceptions followed the same order as the corresponding rights in paragraphs 1 and 2 of the GI exceptions provision in the Brussels Draft, which were the predecessors of Article 24.4 and 24.5 in the final version. Draft paragraph 1 referred to a GI that had been "used," "including use as a trademark," and draft paragraph 2 only referred to "action to refuse or invalidate registration of a trademark:" see document MTN.TNC/W/35/Rev.1 dated 3 December 1990 entitled "Draft Final Act Embodying the Results of the Uruguay Round of Multilateral Trade Negotiations—Revision," the so-called "Brussels Draft." The phrase "including use as a trademark" was later deleted from paragraph 1 and prior trademark issues, including the right to use a trademark, were dealt with in Article 24.5 in the final version, in that order.

[562] The European Communities' raises the issue of a Member that provides additional GI protection beyond that which is required by Article 22, in support of its view that Article 24.5 imposes self-standing obligations. It argues that in this situation Article 24.5, not Article 22 nor Section 2, would prohibit that Member from invalidating or denying protection to prior trademarks inconsistent with that additional protection. See the European Communities' response to Panel question No. 145. In the Panel's view, this overlooks the subject of Article 24.5 which is "measures adopted to implement ... Section [3]." To the extent that measures implement GI protection beyond that which is required by Article 22 for products other than wines and spirits they are, by definition, not measures adopted to implement Section 3 and Article 24.5 is irrelevant to them. It has not been argued by any party that the Regulation is not such a measure.

[563] This is confirmed in WIPO publications, including *Introduction to Trademark Law & Practice, The Basic Concepts, A WIPO Training Manual* (1993), pp. 51-52, and *WIPO Intellectual Property Handbook: Policy, Law and Use*, (June 2001) at p. 82, cited by the European Communities' in its rebuttal submission, para. 324 and its response to Panel question No. 76. See, for example, Australia's Trade Marks Act 1995, Section 20(1)(a), reproduced in Exhibit EC-58.

[564] Article 16.1 of the TRIPS Agreement only provides for a negative right to prevent all third parties from using signs in certain circumstances. Article 15.3 permits Members to make registrability depend on use and Article 19.1 permits Members to require use in order to maintain a registration, which might imply a right to use the trademark, but any such right is subject to the general law. Article 20 does not preclude a requirement prescribing the use of a trademark in a certain way.

The operative parallel is between the rights which shall not be prejudiced and the types of GI protection which would otherwise prejudice them.

7.614 Therefore, according to their ordinary meaning read in context, the terms "shall not prejudice," "the eligibility for or the validity of the registration of a trademark" and "the right to use a trademark" as used in paragraph 5 of Article 24 indicate the creation of exceptions to the obligations to provide two types of GI protection in Section 3. Both these types of protection could otherwise affect the rights identified in paragraph 5. Indeed, the refusal or invalidation of the registration of a trademark has no other function but to extinguish the eligibility for or the validity of the registration of a trademark. Paragraph 5 ensures that each of these types of protection shall not affect those rights.

7.615 Accordingly, the Panel considers that Article 24.5 creates an exception to GI protection—as reflected in the title of Article 24.

7.616 Both parties submit that Article 24.5 implies certain things. Australia argues that the term "validity of the registration" impliedly refers to all the rights which flow from registration, including the right to prevent uses that would result in a likelihood of confusion. In contrast, the European Communities argues that the use of the more specific language in Article 24.5 in fact implies a limitation on the trademark owner's right to exclude use.[565]

7.617 As to Australia's argument, the Panel notes the contrast between the use of the specific terms "eligibility for or the validity of the registration" in Article 24.5, rather than simply "existing prior rights," which is the language used in the last sentence of Article 16.1. The use of language such as "existing prior rights" would have clearly preserved the right to prevent certain uses without any need for implication. The more specific language used in Article 24.5 does not, which suggests that Article 24.5 does not impliedly preserve that right. However, this does not mean that Article 24.5 authorizes Members to prejudice that right. Members may prejudice that right if there is another provision that obliges or permits them to do so.

7.618 As to the European Communities' argument, the Panel considers that it is difficult to sustain an argument that a limitation which is allegedly implied can prevail over an obligation in a WTO covered agreement which is express. It is evidently the position under the European Communities' domestic law that an implied positive right to use a registered GI prevails over the negative right of a prior trademark holder to prevent confusing uses.[566] However, such an interpretation of the TRIPS Agreement is not possible without a suitable basis in the treaty text. The text of Article 24.5 expressly preserves the right to use a trademark—which is *not* expressly provided for in the TRIPS Agreement—and is silent as to any limitation on the trademark owner's exclusive right to prevent confusing uses of signs—which *is* expressly provided for in the TRIPS Agreement—when the sign is used as a GI.

7.619 Accordingly, the Panel's preliminary conclusion is that it is inappropriate to imply in Article 24.5 *either* the right to prevent confusing uses *or* a limitation on the right to prevent confusing uses.

7.620 The ordinary meaning of the terms in their context must also be interpreted in light of the object and purpose of the agreement. The object and purpose of the TRIPS Agreement, as indicated by Articles 9 through 62 and 70 and reflected in the preamble, includes the provision of adequate standards and principles concerning the availability, scope, use and enforcement of trade-related intellectual property rights. This confirms that a limitation on the standards for trademark or GI protection should not be implied unless it is supported by the text.

---

[565] European Communities' first written submission, para. 301; response to Panel question No. 147.

[566] That position may be evidenced by, among other things, the express provision in the Community Trademark Regulation that it shall not affect the GI Regulation and, in particular, Article 14 thereof. There is no such provision in Section 2 of Part II of the TRIPS Agreement on trademarks that refers to Section 3 of Part II on GIs.

7.621 The standards of protection in Part II of the Agreement and, hence, the procedures for their enforcement under Part III, could be undermined by systematic conflicts between the standards for different categories of intellectual property available to different parties but applied to the same subject matter. This is particularly apparent in the case of trademarks and GIs due to the similarity of the subject matter eligible for protection by those two categories of intellectual property and the fact that the rights in respect of uses are indifferent as to whether the infringing subject matter is protected by another category of intellectual property. The subject matter eligible for protection overlaps whilst the rights conferred by each category intersect.

7.622 The European Communities submits that this is a conflict resolved by Article 22.3 (and 23.2) by effectively giving priority to the GI.[567] The Panel agrees that Article 22.3 and Article 23.2 can resolve conflicts with *later* trademarks but they do not resolve conflicts with prior trademarks that meet the conditions set out in Article 24.5.

7.623 The European Communities notes that the simultaneous exercise of two negative rights to prevent uses provided for in Articles 16.1 and 22.2 (and 23.1) can lead to a conflict between different private parties who wish to use an individual sign as a trademark and as a GI. It sees this potential for conflict as a matter which should be avoided in the interpretation of the TRIPS Agreement.

7.624 The Panel notes that the parties do not dispute that *Members* may comply simultaneously with both obligations in the TRIPS Agreement. They do not allege that there are conflicting provisions in the treaty itself.[568] The general rule of treaty interpretation requires us to interpret the treaty in accordance with the ordinary meaning to be given to its terms in their context in the light of its object and purpose. The Panel has had recourse to supplementary means of interpretation, in particular a draft text, in order to confirm the meaning resulting from the application of the general rule of treaty interpretation, which has not left the meaning ambiguous or obscure or led to a result which is manifestly absurd or unreasonable. We would not adopt an approach in treaty interpretation that produced a result that might, on one view, further the object and purpose of the Agreement, but which is not supported by the ordinary meaning to be given to its terms in their context. The following statement by the Appellate Body in *EC – Hormones* appears apposite:

> The fundamental rule of treaty interpretation requires a treaty interpreter to read and interpret the words actually used by the agreement under examination, not words the interpreter may feel should have been used.[569]

7.625 Therefore, the Panel concludes that, under Article 16.1 of the TRIPS Agreement, Members are required to make available to trademark owners a right against certain uses, including uses as a GI. The Regulation limits the availability of that right for the owners of trademarks subject to Article 14(2). Article 24.5 of the TRIPS Agreement is inapplicable and does not provide authority to limit that right.

7.626 The European Communities raises two other defences that, in this respect, the Regulation is justified by exceptions found in Articles 24.3 and 17 of the TRIPS Agreement. The Panel will consider each of these in turn.

(e) Article 24.3 of the TRIPS Agreement

(i) main arguments of the parties

7.627 Australia argues that Article 24.3 of the TRIPS Agreement refers to the protection provided by Article 13 of the Regulation, which is subject to the exception in Article 14(2). Removal of the coexistence

[567] European Communities' response to Panel question No. 146.

[568] In this respect, the Panel recalls the findings in the Panel reports on *Indonesia – Autos* at para 14.28; *Turkey – Textiles* at paras. 9.92-9.95; and *EC – Bananas III* at paras. 7.151-7.163.

[569] Appellate Body report on *EC – Hormones*, para. 181.

standard in Article 14(2) of the Regulation would not diminish that protection. Further, Article 24.3 encompasses protection for individual GIs as of 31 December 1994. As of that date, there were no GIs registered under the Regulation, but only GIs registered under the laws of the EC member States. Finally, Article 24.3 relates only to the implementation of Section 3 and not the trademark right under Article 16.1 of the TRIPS Agreement.[570]

7.628 The European Communities argues that it is required to maintain coexistence of GIs and earlier trademarks by Article 24.3 of the TRIPS Agreement, which is a standstill obligation that prohibits Members from diminishing the level of GI protection that existed at the time of entry into force of the WTO Agreement. The Regulation provided for coexistence in Article 14(2) immediately prior to the entry into force of the WTO Agreement. If the European Communities allowed the owners of prior registered trademarks to prevent the use of later GIs, this would diminish the protection of GIs contrary to Article 24.3.[571] The standstill obligation applies to the general level of protection of GIs available in a Member on 1 January 1995 rather than the protection of individual GIs registered or applied for on that date. The relevant verb, "existed," appears in the singular in the French and Spanish versions, which indicates that it refers to the whole phrase "protection of geographical indications" rather than the plural noun "geographical indications." It is an additional obligation, not an exception. It refers to GI protection, which expressly includes protection vis-à-vis trademark rights in Articles 22.3, 23.2 and 24.5. Those provisions limit the trademark obligations under Article 16.1, as does Article 24.3.[572] Article 24.3 applies "[i]n implementing this Section." The Section includes Article 24.5, which prevents Members from invalidating and prohibiting the use of grandfathered trademarks.[573]

(ii) main arguments of third parties

7.629 New Zealand informs the Panel that no GIs were registered under the Regulation prior to the entry into force of the TRIPS Agreement. In any case, Article 24.3 is qualified by the phrase "[i]n implementing this Section" and does not justify a breach of the Section on trademarks.[574]

(iii) consideration by the Panel

7.630 The Panel now considers the European Communities' argument that it is required to maintain coexistence of GIs and earlier trademarks by Article 24.3 of the TRIPS Agreement. That provision reads as follows:

> 3. In implementing this Section, a Member shall not diminish the protection of geographical indications that existed in that Member immediately prior to the date of entry into force of the WTO Agreement.

7.631 Article 24.3 appears in Section 3 of Part II of the TRIPS Agreement. The reference to "this Section" is therefore a reference to Section 3, which sets out standards for the protection of GIs. The "date of entry into force of the WTO Agreement" was 1 January 1995.

7.632 The scope of Article 24.3 is limited by the introductory phrase "[i]n implementing this Section." It does not apply to measures adopted to implement provisions outside Section 3. Trademark owners' rights, which Members must make available in the implementation of Article 16.1, are found in Section 2. Therefore, Article 24.3 is inapplicable.

---

570 Australia's rebuttal submission, paras. 111-117; second oral statement, para. 27.

571 European Communities' first written submission, paras. 272, 312-314.

572 European Communities' response to Panel question No. 74.

573 European Communities' response to Panel question No. 152.

574 Annex C, para. 158.

7.633 Turning to the ordinary meaning of the terms used in the rest of the provision, the principal verb is "shall not diminish." This indicates that this is a standstill provision, and that it is mandatory. The parties do not agree on the meaning of the object of that verb, which is the phrase "the protection of geographical indications" as qualified by the final relative clause. In the English version of the text, that phrase could refer either to "the protection of GIs" as a whole, or to "the protection" of individual GIs. In the French and Spanish versions, which are equally authentic[575], the verb "existed" in the relative clause is in the singular, which indicates that the "protection of geographical indications" must be interpreted as a whole. It is unclear in all three versions whether this refers to the legal framework or system of protection in a Member that existed immediately prior to 1 January 1995, or to the state of GI protection in a Member that existed at that time in terms of the individual rights which were protected.

7.634 If Article 24.3 referred to a system of protection in a Member, this would have two important consequences. First, as a mandatory provision, it would prevent a Member which had a system that granted a higher level of protection than that provided for in the TRIPS Agreement from implementing the same minimum standards of protection as other Members, even if it wished to do so. For example, in the European Communities, Article 14 of the Regulation entered into force in 1993 but was amended in April 2003 in respect of trademark rights acquired through use.[576] To the extent that those amendments diminished the general level of protection of GIs under the European Communities' system, they would be inconsistent with Article 24.3 on its own view.

7.635 Second, a standstill provision for a system of protection would exclude from the scope of Section 3 not only individual rights already in force under that system as at the date of entry into force of the WTO Agreement, but also rights subsequently granted under that system in perpetuity. This would be a sweeping exclusion which would grow, rather than diminish, in importance, as an increasing number of GIs were protected under the prior legislation. The Panel is reluctant to find such an exclusion in the absence of any clear language to that effect, and none has been drawn to its attention. In this respect, it can be noted that the TRIPS Agreement *does* contain an exclusion for a type of system (in respect of phonograms) in Article 14.4 but it is optional, it clearly refers to a "system" and it is subject to a proviso against abuse. Article 24.3 contains none of these features.

7.636 For these reasons, the Panel interprets the phrase "the protection of geographical indications that existed in that Member immediately prior to the date of entry into force of the WTO Agreement" to mean the state of protection of GIs immediately prior to 1 January 1995, in terms of the individual GIs which were protected at that point in time. In the present dispute, the parties agree that no GIs were registered under the Regulation prior to 1 January 1995. Therefore, Article 24.3 is inapplicable.

7.637 For all the reasons set out above, the Panel concludes that Article 24.3 is inapplicable.

(f) Article 17 of the TRIPS Agreement

(i) main arguments of the parties

7.638 Australia argues that the European Communities has not met its burden of proof to establish that the conditions of Article 17 of the TRIPS Agreement are fulfilled. Australia interprets "limited exception" to mean small diminutions to trademark rights. Article 14(2) of the Regulation is not a "limited exception" because it allows coexistence with a pre-existing trademark in every case in which a GI is registered. If Article 17 covered this situation it would render Article 24.5 meaningless. Fair use of descriptive terms does not include use of all descriptive terms, but only such use as is fair. Use of a term in a way with a signifying function, rather than a purely descriptive function, is not "fair use." If a GI was purely descriptive, there would be no need or basis for an intellectual property right and thus, for Section 3 of Part II of the TRIPS Agreement. A trademark does not

[575] See the final clause of the WTO Agreement.

[576] See Council Regulation (EC) No. 692/2003, Article 13, and paragraph 11 of the recitals, set out in Exhibit COMP-1h.

attract the same spectrum of rights as other categories of intellectual property: it attracts only one right, to prevent uses which result in a likelihood of confusion.[577]

7.639 Article 14(2) does not take account of the legitimate interests of the owner of the trademark because it denies the exclusive right to prevent confusingly similar or identical use required by Article 16.1 of the TRIPS Agreement. A legitimate interest of the owner is to maintain the trademark's capacity to distinguish the owner's goods. Article 17 only permits a small diminution of the capacity to distinguish. The third parties would normally include consumers and other traders. Consumers have a legitimate interest in being able to purchase products which they intended to purchase. Other traders have a legitimate interest in being able to use signs that they *need to use*. For this reason, Article 17 gives the example of fair use of descriptive terms. Having regard to the text of Article 17 and the design and architecture of the TRIPS Agreement generally, Article 17 does not permit a general release from a Member's obligation to grant the basic right attached to a registered trademark in the event of acquisition of another type of intellectual property right without some express recognition of that fact.[578]

7.640 The European Communities argues that, in the alternative, the coexistence of GIs and earlier trademarks would be justified under Article 17 of the TRIPS Agreement. It considers that Article 17 is an exception to the obligations in Article 16 and that previous panels have taken the view that the burden of invoking similar exceptions was on the respondent. It accepts that it bears the burden of proof. Article 14(2) of the Regulation is a "limited exception" because it only allows use by those producers who are established in the geographical area on products that comply with the specification. The trademark owner retains the exclusive right to prevent use by any other persons. Coexistence falls within the example of "fair use of descriptive terms" because GIs are descriptive terms, even where they consist of a non-geographical name, and their use to indicate the true origin of goods and the characteristic associated with that origin is "fair."[579]

7.641 The European Communities argues that the legitimate interests of the trademark owner and of third parties are taken into account because Article 14(3) of the Regulation would prevent the most significant cases of confusion, and legislation on labelling, misleading advertising and unfair competition still applies. The legitimate interests of the trademark owner are less than full enjoyment of all exclusive rights under Article 16.1 of the TRIPS Agreement. The legitimate interests of third parties include the interests of producers who use GIs as well as consumers. GIs inform consumers about the origin of products and take account of the interests of third parties in that way. Article 17 of the TRIPS Agreement does not require the avoidance of all likelihood of confusion, otherwise it would be superfluous, nor does it require confusion to be confined to that which is strictly necessary, which would render the example of "fair use of descriptive term" irrelevant. Article 17 calls for a balancing of different interests which, in the present dispute, requires that account should be taken of the fact that trademarks are arbitrary and much easier to create than GIs and GIs are collective rights and also serve a public interest of informing consumers.[580]

(ii) main arguments of third parties

7.642 Argentina, Brazil, India, Mexico and New Zealand indicated, in response to a question from the Panel, that they provide certain exceptions to exclusive trademark rights. Examples included honest concurrent use, prior use in good faith, comparative advertising, uses for spare parts and certain non-commercial fair uses.[581]

---

577 Australia's rebuttal submission, paras. 120-124; responses to Panel question Nos. 154-156.

578 Australia's rebuttal submission, paras. 125-127; response to Panel question No. 154.

579 European Communities' first written submission, paras. 315-318; rebuttal submission, paras. 333-338, 348-350; responses to Panel question No. 75(b).

580 European Communities' first written submission, para. 319; rebuttal submission, paras. 339-347; responses to Panel questions Nos. 153 and 154; comment on US response to Panel question No. 154.

581 See their respective comments in Annex C.

7.643 New Zealand also argues that coexistence is not a "limited" exception within the meaning of Article 17 of the TRIPS Agreement because it excludes an entire group of producers from the trademark owner's right to prevent confusing uses, which is a major exception.[582]

(iii) consideration by the Panel

introduction

7.644 The Panel will now consider the European Communities' argument that its particular regime of coexistence between GIs and prior trademarks is justified under Article 17 of the TRIPS Agreement. The European Communities defends its regime of coexistence "as such," not as applied. Therefore, our consideration of this defence focuses almost entirely on the terms of the measure and its potential effects, rather than any actual effects. Nevertheless, we will refer to the few examples of how the GI Regulation has been applied with respect to prior trademarks, where that is instructive.

7.645 Australia submits that the European Communities, as the party asserting that its measure is covered by the exception in Article 17, bears the burden of proving that assertion. The European Communities does not contest this position.[583] Therefore, the Panel will follow this approach in the present dispute.

7.646 Article 17 provides as follows:

Exceptions

> Members may provide limited exceptions to the rights conferred by a trademark, such as fair use of descriptive terms, provided that such exceptions take account of the legitimate interests of the owner of the trademark and of third parties.

7.647 Article 17 expressly permits Members to provide limited exceptions to the rights conferred by a trademark, which include the right provided for in Article 16.1 of the TRIPS Agreement. The Panel has already found that the Regulation limits the availability of the right provided for in Article 16.1. Therefore, to the extent that it satisfies the conditions in Article 17, this limitation will be permitted under the TRIPS Agreement.

7.648 Article 17 permits "limited exceptions." It provides an example of a limited exception, and is subject to a proviso that "such exceptions take account of the legitimate interests of the owner of the trademark and of third parties." The ordinary meaning of the terms indicates that an exception must not only be "limited" but must also comply with the proviso in order to satisfy Article 17. The example of "fair use of descriptive terms" is illustrative only, but it can provide interpretative guidance because, *a priori*, it falls within the meaning of a "limited" exception and must be capable of satisfying the proviso in some circumstances. Any interpretation of the term "limited" or of the proviso which excluded the example would be manifestly incorrect.

7.649 The structure of Article 17 differs from that of other exceptions provisions to which the parties refer. It can be noted that Articles 13, 26.2 and 30 of the TRIPS Agreement, as well as Article 9(2) of the Berne Convention (1971) as incorporated by Article 9.1 of the TRIPS Agreement, also permit exceptions to

---

[582] Annex C, para. 159.

[583] All parties note that it was the approach of two previous panels to exceptions provisions in Part II of the TRIPS Agreement: see Panel reports on *US – Section 110(5) Copyright Act*, para. 6.239; and *Canada – Pharmaceutical Patents*, para. 7.16. This approach was not contested in those disputes and was adopted without discussion, although the Panel in *Canada – Pharmaceuticals* observed that a respondent cannot demonstrate that no legitimate interest of a patent owner has been prejudiced until it knows what claims of legitimate interests can be made by the complainant. Similarly, the weight of legitimate third party interests cannot be fully appraised until the legitimacy of the patent owner's legitimate interests, if any, are defined: see para. 7.60 of its report. These practical problems also apply in disputes under Article 17. In this regard, the Panel recalls the distinction between the rights and obligations owed by WTO Members to one another under the covered agreements, and the rights conferred by Members on nationals by individual intellectual property rights under the TRIPS Agreement. The burden of proof in WTO dispute settlement between Members relates to the first set of rights and obligations and not to the fact that a provision creates exceptions to the rights to be conferred by Members on the nationals of other Members.

intellectual property rights and all contain, to varying degrees, similar language to Article 17. However, unlike these other provisions, Article 17 contains no reference to "conflict with a [or the] normal exploitation," no reference to "unreasonabl[e] prejudice" to the legitimate interests" of the right holder or owner, and it not only refers to the legitimate interests of third parties but treats them on par with those of the right holder. It is also the only one of these provisions which contains an example. Further, Article 17 permits exceptions to trademark rights, which differ from each of the intellectual property rights to which these other exceptions apply. Therefore, whilst it is instructive to refer to the interpretation by two previous panels of certain shared elements found in Articles 13 and 30, it is important to interpret Article 17 according to its own terms.

limited exceptions

7.650 The first issue to decide is the meaning of the term "limited exceptions" as used in Article 17. Australia interprets this in terms of a small diminution of rights. The European Communities does not disagree with this approach. The Panel agrees with the views of the Panel in *Canada – Pharmaceutical Patents*, which interpreted the identical term in Article 30, that "[t]he word 'exception' by itself connotes a limited derogation, one that does not undercut the body of rules from which it is made."[584] The addition of the word "limited" emphasizes that the exception must be narrow and permit only a small diminution of rights. The limited exceptions apply "to the rights conferred by a trademark." They do not apply to the set of all trademarks or all trademark owners. Accordingly, the fact that it may affect only few trademarks or few trademark owners is irrelevant to the question whether an exception is limited. The issue is whether the exception to the *rights conferred by a trademark* is narrow.

7.651 There is only one right conferred by a trademark at issue in this dispute, namely the exclusive right to prevent certain uses of a sign provided for in Article 16.1. Therefore, it is necessary to examine the exception on an individual "per right" basis. This is a legal assessment of the extent to which the exception curtails that right. There is no indication in the text of Article 17 that this involves an economic assessment, although economic impact can be taken into account in the proviso. In this regard, the Panel notes the absence of any reference to a "normal exploitation" of the trademark in Article 17, and the absence of any reference in Section 2, to which Article 17 permits exceptions, to rights to exclude legitimate competition. Rather, they confer, *inter alia*, the right to prevent uses that would result in a likelihood of confusion, which can lead to the removal of products from sale where they are marketed using particular signs, but without otherwise restraining the manufacture, sale or import of competing goods or services.

7.652 The right provided for in Article 16.1 contains several elements and an exception could, in principle, curtail the right in respect of any of them. The Panel recalls these elements in the text of that provision as follows:

> The owner of a registered trademark shall have the exclusive right to prevent *all third parties* not having the owner's consent from using in the course of trade *identical or similar signs* for *goods or services which are identical or similar* to those in respect of which the trademark is registered where such use would result in *a likelihood of confusion*. [emphasis added]

7.653 In principle, an exception could curtail the right of the owner in respect of the third parties concerned, or with respect to the identity or the similarity of the signs or the goods or services concerned or with respect to the degree of likelihood of confusion, or some combination of these. There may be other possibilities as well. The overriding requirement is that the exception must be "limited" and it must also satisfy the proviso, considered below. These elements provide a useful framework for an assessment of the extent to which an exception curtails the right provided for in Article 16.1.

---

[584] Panel report on *Canada – Pharmaceutical Patents*, para. 7.30.

7.654 The example in the text, "fair use of descriptive terms," provides guidance as to what is considered a "limited exception," although it is illustrative only. Fair use of descriptive terms is inherently limited in terms of the sign which may be used and the degree of likelihood of confusion which may result from its use, as a purely descriptive term on its own is not distinctive and is not protectable as a trademark. Fair use of descriptive terms is *not* limited in terms of the number of third parties who may benefit, nor in terms of the quantity of goods or services with respect to which they use the descriptive terms, although implicitly it only applies to those third parties who would use those terms in the course of trade and to those goods or services which those terms describe. The number of trademarks or trademark owners affected is irrelevant, although implicitly it would only affect those marks which can consist of, or include, signs that can be used in a descriptive manner. According to the text, this is a "limited" exception for the purposes of Article 17.

7.655 Turning to the Regulation, it curtails the trademark owner's right in respect of certain goods but not all goods identical or similar to those in respect of which the trademark is registered. It prevents the trademark owner from exercising the right to prevent confusing uses of a sign for the agricultural product or foodstuff produced in accordance with the product specification in the GI registration. The Panel recalls that, according to Article 2(2) of the Regulation, set out above at paragraph 7.223, those goods must all be produced, processed and/or prepared in the region, specific place or, in exceptional cases, country, the name of which is used to describe them. Goods that are not from that geographical area may not use the GI. Further, according to Article 4 of the Regulation, all products using a GI must comply with a product specification. Products that do not so comply may not use the GI even if they are from the geographical area. The trademark owner's right against all other goods is not curtailed. The Panel notes that there is no limit in terms of the quantity of goods which may benefit from the exception, as long as they conform to the product specification. However, this cannot prevent the limitation on rights of owners of trademarks subject to Article 14(2) from constituting a limited exception for the purposes of Article 17, as fair use of descriptive terms implies no limit in terms of quantity either, and the text indicates that it is a limited exception for the purposes of Article 17. The quantity of goods which benefits from an exception may be related to the curtailment of the rights to prevent the acts of making, selling or importing a product, but these are not rights conferred by a trademark.

7.656 The Regulation curtails the trademark owner's right against certain third parties, but not "all third parties." It prevents the trademark owner from exercising the right to prevent confusing uses against persons using a registered GI on a good in accordance with its registration. This is a limitation on the third parties who may benefit from the exception. The trademark owner's right is not curtailed with respect to any other third parties.

7.657 The Regulation curtails the trademark owner's right in respect of certain signs but not all signs identical or similar to the one protected as a trademark. It prevents the trademark owner from exercising its right to prevent use of an indication registered as a GI in accordance with its registration. The Panel recalls its finding earlier in paragraph 7.522 that the GI registration does not confer a positive right to use any other signs or combinations of signs nor to use the name in any linguistic versions not entered in the register. The trademark owner's right is not curtailed against any such uses. If the GI registration prevented the trademark owner from exercising its rights against these signs, combinations of signs or linguistic versions, which do not appear expressly in the GI registration, it would seriously expand the exception and undermine the limitations on its scope.

7.658 Under the Regulation, once a GI has been registered and a trademark is subject to the coexistence regime under Article 14(2), set out above at paragraph 7.524, the GI may, in principle, be used without regard to the likelihood of confusion that it may cause. However, the Regulation refers to the likelihood or risk of confusion, with a given mark, which would result from use as a GI of an identical or similar sign, in Articles 7(5)(b), 12b(3) and 12d(3) in relation to the decision on whether to register a GI where an objection is admissible. Article 7(4) (and hence Article 12b(3)) provides a ground for objection where registration would jeopardize the existence of a mark, and Article 14(3) provides a ground for refusal of registration which refers to the trademark's reputation and renown and the length of time it has been used. These factors are relevant to the likelihood of confusion which could result from subsequent use of the GI. The Panel recalls its finding in paragraph 7.525 that Article 14(2) is an exception to Article 13, which presupposes a consideration of the similarity of the signs and goods as well. They are essential to an analysis of a likelihood of confusion. Whilst Articles 7(4), 12b(3) and 14(3) do not specifically refer to the concept of likelihood of confusion between a GI and a trademark subject to the exception in Article 14(2), they, together with Articles 7(5)(b), 12b(3) and 12d(3) can ensure that, in cases where the likelihood of confusion is relatively high, the exception simply does not apply.

7.659 The Panel notes that Article 14(2) only expressly provides that the trademark may continue to be used. However, the European Communities has emphasized that the trademark owner retains the right to prevent the use of a name registered as a GI by any person in relation to any goods which originate in a different geographical area or which do not comply with the specifications[585], and that the positive right to use the GI extends only to the linguistic versions that have been entered in the register and not to other names or signs which have not been registered.[586] Accordingly, on the basis of the terms of the GI Regulation and of the Community Trademark Regulation, and the explanation of them provided by the European Communities, the Panel finds that not only may the trademark continue to be used, but that the trademark owner's right to prevent confusing uses is unaffected, except with respect to the use of a GI as entered in the GI register in accordance with its registration.

7.660 Furthermore, the European Communities has explained that the use of a name registered as a GI is subject to the applicable provisions of the food labelling and misleading advertising directives so that the ways in which it may be used are not unlimited.[587]

7.661 For the above reasons, the Panel finds that the Regulation creates a "limited exception" within the meaning of Article 17 of the TRIPS Agreement.

<u>the proviso to Article 17</u>

7.662 Limited exceptions must satisfy the proviso that "such exceptions take account of the legitimate interests of the owner of the trademark and of third parties" in order to benefit from Article 17. The Panel must first establish what are "legitimate interests." Read in context, the "legitimate interests" of the trademark owner are contrasted with the "rights conferred by a trademark," which also belong to the trademark owner. Given that Article 17 creates an exception to the rights conferred by a trademark, the "legitimate interests" of the trademark owner must be something different from full enjoyment of those legal rights. The "legitimate interests" of the trademark owner are also compared with those of "third parties," who have no rights conferred by the trademark. Therefore, the "legitimate interests," at least of third parties, are different from simply the enjoyment of their legal rights. This is confirmed by the use of the verb "take account of," which is less than "protect."

7.663 The Panel agrees with the following view of the Panel in *Canada – Pharmaceutical Patents*, which interpreted the term "legitimate interests" of a patent owner and third parties in the context of Article 30 as follows:

> To make sense of the term 'legitimate interests' in this context, that term must be defined in the way that it is often used in legal discourse—as a normative claim calling for protection of

---

[585] European Communities' first written submission, para. 317; rebuttal submission, para. 336; responses to Panel questions Nos. 76 and 153.

[586] European Communities' rebuttal submission, paras. 288, 293 and 301; responses to Panel questions Nos. 63, 137 and 140; and comment on US response to Panel question No. 137.

[587] *Supra* at note 495 and European Communities' first written submission, para. 319; response to Panel question No. 153.

> interests that are 'justifiable' in the sense that they are supported by relevant public policies or other social norms.[588]

In our view, this is also true of the term "legitimate interests" of a trademark owner and third parties in the context of Article 17.

7.664 The legitimacy of some interest of the trademark owner is assumed because the owner of the trademark is specifically identified in Article 17. The TRIPS Agreement itself sets out a statement of what all WTO Members consider adequate standards and principles concerning trademark protection. Although it sets out standards for legal rights, it also provides guidance as to WTO Members' shared understandings of the policies and norms relevant to trademarks and, hence, what might be the legitimate interests of trademark owners. The function of trademarks can be understood by reference to Article 15.1 as distinguishing goods and services of undertakings in the course of trade. Every trademark owner has a legitimate interest in preserving the distinctiveness, or capacity to distinguish, of its trademark so that it can perform that function. This includes its interest in using its own trademark in connection with the relevant goods and services of its own and authorized undertakings. Taking account of that legitimate interest will also take account of the trademark owner's interest in the economic value of its mark arising from the reputation that it enjoys and the quality that it denotes.

7.665 Turning to the Regulation, the evidence shows that the owner's legitimate interest in preserving the distinctiveness, or capacity to distinguish, of its trademark can be taken into account in various ways. Article 7(4) of the Regulation provides that a statement of objection shall be admissible *inter alia* if it shows that the registration of the proposed GI would "jeopardize the existence ... of a mark." This requires GI registration to be refused.

7.666 Article 14(3) also requires the refusal of GI registration in light of a trademark's reputation and renown and the length of time it has been used, if a particular condition is fulfilled. This addresses the distinctiveness, or capacity to distinguish, of prior trademarks and can ensure that, in cases where trademark owners' legitimate interests would be most likely to be affected, the exception in Article 14(2) simply does not apply.

7.667 In the one instance in which Article 14(3) has been applied, the European Communities informs the Panel that its authorities:

> [T]ook account of the submissions made by the interested parties and by some Member States, as well as of the discussions which took place within the Committee. The main facts taken into consideration were the similarity of the signs; the similarity of the products, having regard to the production methods and organoleptic properties; the date of registration of the trademark; the recognition of the trademark in the different EC member States, having regard in particular to the level of exports; and the labeling practices of the trademark and the proposed geographical indication.[589]

7.668 This indicates to the Panel that Article 14(3) of the Regulation was, in fact, applied to take account *inter alia* of the legitimate interest of the trademark owners to protect the distinctiveness of their respective marks.

7.669 In the other instance to which the parties refer, the registration of the three Czech beer GIs contains an endorsement that they apply "without prejudice to any beer trademark or other rights existing in the European Union on the date of accession."[590] Although the European Communities has confirmed that such an

---

588 Panel report on *Canada – Pharmaceutical Patents*, para. 7.69.

589 European Communities' response to Panel question No. 143. Although there is no supporting evidence, all of the considerations cited by the European Communities correspond to factors set out in Articles 13 and 14(3) of the Regulation.

590 European Communities' rebuttal submission, paras. 286-293; response to Panel question No. 142.

endorsement is unique and it has not explained in what other circumstances such an endorsement might be possible, this example does show that, at least in this case, not only the legitimate interests of trademark owners, but also their rights, have been taken into account.

7.670 Where Articles 7(4) and 14(3) of the Regulation are unavailable, and a trademark is subject to Article 14(2), there remains the possibility that its distinctiveness will be affected by the use of the GI. The Panel does not consider this fatal to the applicability of Article 17 given that, as a provision permitting an exception to the exclusive right to prevent uses that would result in a likelihood of confusion, it presupposes that a certain degree of likelihood of confusion can be permitted. In the light of the provisions of Articles 7(4) and 14(3), we are satisfied that where the likelihood of confusion is relatively high, the exception in Article 14(2) will not apply. In any event, even where the exception does apply, Article 14(2) expressly provides that the trademark may continue to be used, on certain conditions.

7.671 The Panel notes that the proviso to Article 17 requires only that exceptions "take account" of the legitimate interests of the owner of the trademark, and does not refer to "unreasonabl[e] prejudice" to those interests, unlike the provisos in Articles 13, 26.2 and 30 of the TRIPS Agreement and Article 9(2) of the Berne Convention (1971) as incorporated by Article 9.1 of the TRIPS Agreement. This suggests that a lesser standard of regard for the legitimate interests of the owner of the trademark is required.

7.672 The Panel also notes that there may be situations where, in order to take account of the legitimate interests of the owner of a trademark and third parties, practical conditions may be required to distinguish the goods with the trademark from those using the GI and to distinguish the respective undertakings.

7.673 For these reasons, the Panel considers that the exception created by the Regulation takes account of the legitimate interests of the owner of the trademark within the meaning of Article 17. This finding is confirmed by responses to a question from the Panel which revealed that, of over 600 GIs registered under the Regulation over a period of eight years, the complainants and third parties are unable to identify any that, in their view, could be used in a way that would result in a likelihood of confusion with a prior trademark, with four exceptions.[591] Three of these are the Czech beer GIs, the registration of which is subject to the endorsement set out earlier. The only remaining example is "Bayerisches Bier," in respect of which the complainants have not shown an example of actual likelihood of confusion with a prior trademark.

7.674 The Panel will now consider whether the exception created by the Regulation takes account of the legitimate interests of third parties.

7.675 The parties to this dispute agree that "third parties" for the purposes of Article 17 include consumers. The function of a trademark is to distinguish goods and services of undertakings in the course of trade. That function is served not only for the owner, but also for consumers. Accordingly, the relevant third parties include consumers.[592] Consumers have a legitimate interest in being able to distinguish the goods and services of one undertaking from those of another, and to avoid confusion.

7.676 Turning to the Regulation, Article 14(3) expressly addresses consumers, by providing for the refusal of GI registration where "registration is liable to mislead the consumer as to the true identity of the product." In the one instance in which Article 14(3) has been applied, the European Communities informs the Panel that:

---

[591] See responses to Panel question No. 47 and Annex C.

[592] This is confirmed by the reference in Article 16.2 to "the relevant sector of the public," in relation to well-known trademarks.

> In essence, it was concluded that, although the products were similar, the signs were not sufficiently similar to mislead the public, having regard to the degree of recognition of the trademark in the different Member States.[593]

7.677 This indicates to the Panel that Article 14(3) of the Regulation was, in fact, applied to take account *inter alia* of the legitimate interests of consumers.

7.678 The Panel also observes, once again, that a name can only be registered as a GI where it is used to describe an agricultural product or a foodstuff. It is a precondition to GI registration that some consumers do, in fact, understand that the GI refers to the product from that geographical area with particular qualities or characteristics, which means that they do not consider that it indicates the trademark owner's goods.

7.679 The European Communities submits that "third parties" for the purposes of Article 17 include persons using a GI in accordance with a GI registration. The Panel agrees. Article 17 permits an exception to the rights conferred by a trademark which include, according to Article 16.1, a right to prevent "all third parties" from using certain signs. The basis of the complainant's claim is that those third parties include GI users. It is logical that, if GI users are included in the third parties subject to the trademark owner's right, they are also included in the third parties taken into account in assessing the availability of an exception to that right.

7.680 The legitimacy of the interests of GI users is reflected in the TRIPS Agreement itself, to which all WTO Members have subscribed. Under Section 3 of Part II, all WTO Members agree to provide certain protection to GIs, although they remain free to determine the appropriate method of implementing those provisions in accordance with Article 1.1. The definition of a GI in Article 22.1 reflects a legitimate interest that a person may have in identifying the source and other characteristics of a good by the name of the place where it is from, if the name would serve that purpose. Nevertheless, as "legitimate interests," the interests of GI users as third parties within the meaning of Article 17 would be different from the legal protection provided for in Articles 22 and 23.

7.681 The Panel recalls that the example contained in Article 17 itself of "fair use of descriptive terms" provides some guidance as to what may satisfy its proviso. Its use of the word "fair" and the nature of descriptive terms illustrate a public policy concern that certain terms should be available for use under certain conditions. Although GIs are intellectual property rights, and not purely descriptive terms, the function of the terms in the example is analogous to a descriptive function of GIs and provides contextual support for the notion that the interest of GIs users in using a place name to indicate their products is "legitimate."

7.682 Turning to the Regulation, Article 2(2) provides that a "designation of origin" or a "geographical indication" "means the name of a region, a specific place or, in exceptional cases, a country, used to *describe* an agricultural product or a foodstuff ..." (emphasis added). There are additional conditions relevant to the origin and quality, reputation or characteristics of the product. Further, the European Communities has confirmed that use of a GI remains subject to the requirements of the food labelling and misleading advertising directives which prohibit certain misleading and deceptive uses.[594] These considerations support the view that the interests of GI users of which the Regulation takes account are "legitimate."

7.683 Article 13 of the Regulation sets out the protection conferred by GI registration. In providing such protection, the Regulation not only "takes account" of this legitimate interest, it also provides legally enforceable rights.

7.684 For these reasons, the Panel considers that the exception created by the Regulation takes account of the legitimate interests of third parties within the meaning of Article 17.

---

593 European Communities' response to Panel question No. 143.

594 *Supra* at note 495 and European Communities' first written submission, para. 319; response to Panel question No. 153.

7.685 On the basis of the evidence presented to the Panel, which is necessarily limited given that Article 14(3) of the Regulation has only been applied once, and for all of the above reasons, the Panel concludes that the European Communities has succeeded in raising a presumption that the exception created by the Regulation to the trademark owner's right provided for in Article 16.1 of the TRIPS Agreement is justified by Article 17 of the TRIPS Agreement. Australia has not succeeded in rebutting that presumption.

7.686 Therefore, the Panel concludes that with respect to the coexistence of GIs with prior trademarks, the Regulation is inconsistent with Article 16.1 of the TRIPS Agreement but, on the basis of the evidence presented to the Panel, this is justified by Article 17 of the TRIPS Agreement. Articles 24.3 and Article 24.5 of the TRIPS Agreement are inapplicable.

2. Identical signs for identical goods

(a) Presumption of confusion

(i) main arguments of the parties

7.687 Australia claims that the measure at issue is inconsistent with Article 16.1 of the TRIPS Agreement because it does not "provide for" or "implement" the presumption of a likelihood of confusion in the case of use of an identical sign for identical goods.[595] The provisions of the Regulation do not grant to the authorities the necessary discretion to apply that presumption.[596]

7.688 The European Communities refers to its defence to the previous claim and makes some additional comments: Members are not required to reproduce explicitly the presumption of Article 16.1 in their domestic law as long as the authorities have the necessary discretion and comply with the presumption in practice. It is extremely unlikely that this situation will ever present itself in practice in view of the trademark registrability criteria and the GI definitions and product specifications. If the situation should arise, Article 14(3) of the Regulation would permit the authorities to implement the presumption. This claim is purely theoretical as none of the GIs actually registered fall within this situation.[597]

(ii) main arguments of third parties

7.689 Brazil does not agree with the European Communities that there is no need to "reproduce explicitly" the presumption in Article 16.1 of the TRIPS Agreement as long as the registering authority or the courts had adequate discretion to apply it. In Brazil's view, even if the domestic law of each EC member State incorporated the presumption, this would not mean that the Community-level registration under the Regulation also provided for its incorporation.[598]

7.690 New Zealand refers to the second ground for admissibility of objections in Article 7(4) of the Regulation. It agrees with Australia that the Regulation is inconsistent with Article 16.1 of the TRIPS Agreement because the owner of a registered trademark may not be able to object successfully to a proposed GI registration even if its use would constitute use of an identical or similar sign that would result in a likelihood of confusion.[599]

(iii) consideration by the Panel

7.691 Article 16.1 of the TRIPS Agreement, in its first sentence, provides for a right that refers to "identical or similar" "signs" and "goods or services" and depends on a "likelihood of confusion." In its second sentence,

---

[595] Australia's first written submission, para. 93 and subheading.

[596] Australia's rebuttal submission, para. 138.

[597] European Communities' first written submission, paras. 320-324.

[598] Annex C, para. 30.

[599] Annex C, para. 153.

it provides for a presumption of a "likelihood of confusion" with respect to use of an "identical sign for identical goods or services." Therefore, the second sentence clarifies how the first sentence is implemented, in particular circumstances.

7.692 The Panel refers to its conclusion on the previous claim, which is based on the finding that the first sentence of Article 16.1 is applicable, and that the Regulation prevents the exercise of the right that it requires to be conferred. It follows that the presumption in the second sentence, which governs implementation of the first sentence, is also applicable, in the particular circumstances that it sets out.

7.693 Australia has argued that the measure at issue does not "provide for" or "implement" a presumption of a likelihood of confusion in the case of use of an identical sign for identical goods. There is no requirement that the text of the GI Regulation, or its related or implementing measures, should explicitly "provide for" this presumption. As for the discretion granted to authorities under the Regulation, Australia has only demonstrated that the Regulation "as such" does not permit the authorities to implement the presumption in the second sentence only to the extent that it does not permit them to implement the right provided for in the first sentence. Therefore, a finding on this claim will not provide any additional contribution to a positive solution to this dispute and the Panel declines to consider it further.

3. Trademark owners' right to object to GI registration

(a) Admissibility of objections

(i) main arguments of the parties

7.694 Australia claims that the Regulation is inconsistent with Article 16.1 of the TRIPS Agreement because it does not ensure that objections to registration are admissible on the grounds that use of the GI would result in a likelihood of confusion. Article 7(4) of the Regulation provides that objections are only admissible if the GI does not comply with the conditions in the Regulation or registration would "jeopardize the existence" of an entirely or partly identical trademark. This requirement also applies to objections by persons resident or established in other WTO Members by virtue of Articles 12b(3) and 12d(2).[600]

7.695 Australia argues that a right of objection is necessary to allow exercise of the right expressly required by Article 16.1 of the TRIPS Agreement, although a right of objection itself may not be expressly required. An objection procedure is the only means available to a trademark owner to prevent a confusing use. The standard of "jeopardize the existence" is a far more rigorous standard than a "likelihood of confusion."[601]

7.696 The European Communities responds that Article 16.1 of the TRIPS Agreement does not grant a right to object to the registration of trademarks, GIs or other intellectual property rights. Objection procedures in general are addressed in Article 62.4 of the TRIPS Agreement and trademark objection procedures specifically are addressed in Article 15.5. The right to object is not necessary to "exercise" effectively the substantive right provided for in Article 16 if final registration decisions are subject to judicial review in accordance with Article 62.5.[602]

7.697 The European Communities argues that Article 7(4) of the Regulation permits objections if the proposed GI would jeopardize the existence of the mark, regardless of whether it is entirely or partially identical. It refers to the French and Spanish versions of the Regulation and asserts that this ground is broad enough to encompass the likelihood of confusion with the trademark.[603] This is confirmed by the fact that Australia is unable to identify any case in which the grounds of objection were limited in the manner alleged.[604]

---

[600] Australia's first written submission, paras. 88-92.

[601] Australia's rebuttal submission, paras. 131, 133.

[602] European Communities' first written submission, paras. 327-333.

[603] European Communities' first written submission, paras. 334-338.

[604] European Communities' rebuttal submission, para. 353, citing Australia's response to EC question No. 1.

Australia bears the burden of proof and must show that this reading is unreasonable and that it is impossible to read Article 7(4) of the Regulation consistently with Article 16.1 of the TRIPS Agreement.[605]

(ii) main arguments of third parties

7.698 Brazil argues that EC nationals would be able to protect a GI to the detriment of a prior registered trademark much more rapidly and efficiently than another WTO Member national would be able to defend trademark rights vis-à-vis an application for registration.[606]

(iii) consideration by the Panel

7.699 Article 16.1 of the TRIPS Agreement sets out the minimum right which Members must provide to the owners of registered trademarks and which they may also make available on the basis of use. It is a right for trademark owners to prevent certain uses. The Panel takes note that trademark owners are not able to exercise their right to prevent use of a GI after GI registration. However, Australia has not explained why the trademark owner's right to prevent use implies a right to object to GI registration.

7.700 Article 15.5 provides for a right of objection to registration *of a trademark* but there is no corresponding provision in Part II regarding the registration *of a GI*. There are provisions on the acquisition and maintenance of intellectual property rights, including GIs, in Article 62. These specifically refer to related *inter partes* procedures such as opposition, revocation and cancellation, in paragraph 4, which is cross-referenced in paragraph 5. The opportunity or right to object forms part of an opposition procedure. However, Article 62 lies outside the Panel's terms of reference.

7.701 For these reasons, the Panel concludes that Australia has not made a prima facie case in support of this claim.

(b) Consideration of objections

(i) main arguments of the parties

7.702 Australia also claims that the Regulation is inconsistent with Article 16.1 of the TRIPS Agreement because it does not ensure that an objection by the owner of a registered trademark will be considered by the "ultimate decision maker," being the regulatory committee of EC member States. This applies to objections filed by persons resident or established in an EC member State under Article 7(1) of the Regulation and also objections filed by persons resident or established in other WTO Members under Article 12b(2) and 12d(1). Australia argues that consideration of an objection by the regulatory committee is essential to a registered trademark owner being able to exercise the rights required to be conferred by Article 16.1 of the TRIPS Agreement.[607] Australia disagrees with the European Communities' views on estoppel.[608]

7.703 The European Communities refers to its defence to the previous claim. It adds that the Committee established under Article 15 of the Regulation is not the "ultimate decision maker." Further, the authorities of the EC member States are not required to transmit objections to the Commission, but their decisions are not discretionary and may be subject to judicial review based on procedural requirements of their respective administrative laws. Whilst the authorities of other WTO Members enjoy complete discretion in the transmission of objections to the Commission, those Members would be estopped from complaining that the

[605] European Communities' second oral statement, para. 230.

[606] Annex C, para. 31.

[607] Australia's first written submission, paras. 94-99.

[608] Australia's rebuttal submission, paras. 73-83.

refusal of their own authorities to transmit an objection had infringed the trademark rights of their own nationals.[609]

(ii) consideration by the Panel

7.704 The Panel refers to its findings at paragraphs 7.699 and 7.700 and concludes, for the same reasons, that Australia has not made a prima facie case in support of this claim.

E. Other Claims

1. Minimum standards of GI protection

(a) Main arguments of the parties

7.705 Australia claims that the European Communities fails to provide at Community level the legal means for interested parties to prevent uses in respect of a GI registered, or proposed to be registered, under the Regulation, contrary to Article 22.2 of the TRIPS Agreement.[610] It argues that the obligation under Article 22.2 of the TRIPS Agreement creates an obligation "in respect of" GIs which means "as concerns" GIs. The obligation is not limited to actions to protect GIs, but extends to any situation that concerns GIs, including a situation involving the proposed registration of a GI that potentially constitutes an act of unfair competition within the meaning of Article 10*bis* of the Paris Convention (1967).[611]

7.706 Australia argues, by way of example, that it is entirely possible that there are products which, while originally based on a European production process, have been further developed and refined outside the European country of origin and which have subsequently come to represent the "international" trading standard for that product. Registration of that name as a GI—although it may qualify for registration—could well constitute misleading use or an act of unfair competition within the meaning of Article 10*bis* of the Paris Convention (1967).[612] Australia does not challenge any particular GI as contrary to Article 22.2 of the TRIPS Agreement, but argues that the European Communities has failed to provide the legal means by which interested parties can seek to test "such issues" in relation to the registration of a GI under the Regulation.[613]

7.707 Australia argues that the European Communities is not obliged to comply with a particular obligation through a single measure applicable throughout its territory but rather, while it can choose to offer more extensive protection of GIs at the Community level, it must also ensure that it does not breach its TRIPS obligations in doing so. The European Communities has effectively implemented a TRIPS right—at the Community level—without also effectively implementing at the same level the concurrent TRIPS obligations.[614] An assertion that the European Communities complies with Article 22.2 of the TRIPS Agreement under the laws of the EC member States is an admission that the Regulation itself does not comply. The Regulation disturbs what may otherwise be sufficient to meet the European Communities' obligations.[615]

7.708 The European Communities considers that this claim is insufficiently argued but responds as follows: (1) It considers that Article 22.2 of the TRIPS Agreement is concerned exclusively with the protection of GIs. It cannot be invoked by a trademark right holder to prevent the use of a GI; (2) The use of a validly registered GI, which is otherwise consistent with the TRIPS Agreement, cannot mislead the public as to the geographical origin of the goods. Registration of the GI seeks to avoid precisely that; and (3) Registration or use of a GI consistently with domestic law cannot constitute an act of unfair competition within the meaning of Article

609 European Communities' first written submission, paras. 339-344; second oral statement, para. 231.

610 Australia's first written submission, paras. 7 and 61.

611 Australia's first written submission, paras. 154-155.

612 Australia's rebuttal submission, para. 170. See also its response to Panel question No. 24.

613 Australia's second oral statement, para. 85.

614 Australia's responses to Panel questions Nos. 81 and 82.

615 Australia's second oral statement, para. 112.

10*bis* of the Paris Convention (1967). In any event, registered GIs remain subject to EC labelling and misleading advertising legislation and the unfair competition laws of the EC member States. These other measures and the Regulation apply cumulatively. In any event, registration of a GI is not a "use." (4) There is no requirement that protection must be at the Community level.[616]

7.709 The European Communities comments as follows on the example of a product name which has become generic: (a) It does not understand how use of a name which is not generic but is a GI in the country of protection could be misleading; (b) Article 22.2 concerns acts against the holders of GIs as defined in Article 22.1, not other parties; (c) the exercise of a right conferred by a Member to comply with the TRIPS Agreement is not a dishonest practice in international trade; and (d) Article 22.2(a) requires the protection of GIs unless they have become generic in the country of protection, but Australia's example implies that Article 22.2(b) prevents the protection of GIs if they have become generic in another country.[617]

(b) Consideration by the Panel

7.710 The Panel begins its consideration of this claim by noting that Article 22.2 of the TRIPS Agreement provides as follows:

> 2. In respect of geographical indications, Members shall provide the legal means for interested parties to prevent:
>
> > (a) the use of any means in the designation or presentation of a good that indicates or suggests that the good in question originates in a geographical area other than the true place of origin in a manner which misleads the public as to the geographical origin of the good;
> >
> > (b) any use which constitutes an act of unfair competition within the meaning of Article 10*bis* of the Paris Convention (1967)."

7.711 The term "geographical indications" is defined in Article 22.1 of the TRIPS Agreement. It is not disputed that registered "designations of origin" and registered "geographical indications," as defined in the Article 2(2) of the Regulation, are a subset of "geographical indications" as defined in Article 22.1 and therefore relevant to the European Communities' implementation of Article 22.2.

7.712 Article 22.2 creates an obligation that applies "in respect of" geographical indications. The ordinary meaning of the word "respect" as used in that phrase can be defined as "relation, connection, reference, regard. Earliest in *have respect to;* now chiefly in *with respect to, in respect to*."[618]

7.713 This is a very broad phrase. However, in accordance with the general rule of treaty interpretation, the ordinary meaning of the phrase "in respect of" must be interpreted in context and in the light of the object and purpose of the Agreement.

7.714 Article 22.2 is found in Section 3 of Part II of the TRIPS Agreement. Part II sets out minimum standards concerning the availability, scope and use of intellectual property rights, which is one of the objects and purposes of the Agreement, as highlighted in paragraph (b) of the second recital in its preamble. The first seven sections of Part II contain standards relating to categories of intellectual property rights. Each Section provides for a different category of intellectual property, setting out, as a minimum, the subject matter which is eligible for protection, the scope of the rights conferred by the relevant category of intellectual property and

---

616 European Communities' first written submission, paras. 411-415; rebuttal submission, para. 393; response to Panel question No. 159.

617 European Communities' rebuttal submission, paras. 386-392.

618 *The New Shorter Oxford English Dictionary* (1993).

permitted exceptions to those rights. Section 3 contains all these features for the category of GIs, as highlighted in its title, which reads "Protection of Geographical Indications." Article 23.1 expressly provides for protection to prevent use *of* a GI for wines and spirits. Whilst the protection of GIs affects the protection of trademarks, as expressly recognized in Articles 22.3 and 23.2, Section 3 does not provide for trademark protection, except to the extent that trademark systems are used to protect GIs. Therefore, read in context, the obligation in Article 22.2 to provide certain legal means "in respect of" GIs, is an obligation to provide for the protection of GIs.[619] Australia's claim does not appear to concern the protection of GIs, but rather the protection of other subject matter *against* the protection of GIs. Therefore, it does not disclose a cause of action under Article 22.2.

7.715 With respect to the example of product names that may satisfy the conditions for protection in the Member where protection is sought but which have become the international trading standard for a product, it is not entirely clear what Australia means by the term "international trading standard." However, it suffices to note that Article 22.2 applies to geographical indications that satisfy the definition in Article 22.1. Article 22.2 does not apply to generic terms, as confirmed by Article 24.6. Each Member applies the definition of GIs with respect to its own territory so that the question whether the indication is generic or otherwise not entitled to protection in another Member's territory is not relevant, unless the other Member is the country of origin.

7.716 Australia's example does not concern another Member that is the country of origin, and therefore is inapposite to Article 22.2.

7.717 With respect to the suggestion that the European Communities must provide the legal means to test issues such as those in the above example, the Panel notes that Article 22.2 creates an obligation to provide the legal means to prevent certain uses. To the extent that Australia's reference to the testing of issues relates to the right to seek eventual legal relief, it has failed to demonstrate what uses covered by Article 22.2 are permitted by the Regulation without a legal means of prevention.

7.718 For the above reasons, the Panel rejects Australia's claim under Article 22.2 of the TRIPS Agreement.

2. *Articles 10*bis *and 10*ter *of the Paris Convention (1967)*

(a) *Main arguments of the parties*

7.719 Australia claims that the European Communities denies to nationals of other WTO Members effective protection against unfair competition and appropriate legal remedies to repress effectively all acts of unfair competition, contrary to Article 2.1 of the TRIPS Agreement "incorporating Articles 10*bis*(1) and 10*ter*(1) of the Paris Convention (1967)."[620] This claim is based on the argument that the Regulation provides a Community-wide system of registration of GIs that provides effective protection from acts of unfair competition, including in relation to later trademark applications, within the Community, but not a Community-wide system of effective protection of trademarks from acts of unfair competition arising from the later registration of GIs under the Regulation.[621] Australia argues that Article 10*bis*(1) includes the obligation to protect trademarks against unfair competition from a GI and that Article 10*ter*(1) therefore ensures that a Member provides the mechanisms necessary to assure protection against unfair competition "in any guise"[622] and to assure to nationals of other Members effective protection against unfair competition that permits account to be taken of honest practices established in international trade.[623] Australia confirms that it seeks distinct

[619] Consequently, whilst Article 22.4 provides for protection *against* GIs, it only applies to the protection *of* other GIs.

[620] Australia's first written submission, paras. 6 and 60. Australia quotes the text of Articles 10*bis* and 10*ter* and Bodenhausen, see *supra* at 79, p. 144, on the meaning of Article 10*bis*(2), in first written submission, paras. 75 and 76, fns. 32, 33 and 34; and rebuttal submission, para. 144, referring to the same source and WIPO Model Provisions on Protection against Unfair Competition set out in Exhibit AUS-9.

[621] Australia's first written submission, paras. 10, 113-118.

[622] Australia's response to Panel question No. 82.

[623] Australia's rebuttal submission, paras. 144-145.

findings in respect of its claim under Article 10*bis* pursuant to Article 2.1 of the TRIPS Agreement and its claim under Article 22.2(b) of the TRIPS Agreement.[624]

7.720 The European Communities responds that this claim is insufficiently argued and difficult to understand. Australia does not explain how the use of a registered GI, which is otherwise consistent with the TRIPS Agreement and, in particular, Articles 16 and 24.5, could constitute an act of unfair competition within the meaning of Article 10*bis*(1) of the Paris Convention (1967). In any event, the use of a registered GI remains subject to EC legislation on labelling and misleading advertising, as well as the laws of the EC member States on unfair competition, which are outside the Panel's terms of reference. There is no basis in Article 10*bis*(1), or anywhere else in the Paris Convention (1967) for the proposition that the protection against unfair competition must be provided at any given territorial level. The claim under Article 10*ter*(1) of the Paris Convention (1967) is unfounded for the same reasons.[625] The European Communities responded to the claim under Article 2.1 of the TRIPS Agreement separately, and argued that, as a consequence of the other two claims, this claim was also unfounded.[626]

(b) Consideration by the Panel

7.721 The Panel notes that Australia's claims relate to two provisions of the Paris Convention (1967) and the protection of trademarks against acts of unfair competition arising from the later registration of GIs. These claims are based on the assertion that where the European Communities implements "Community-wide" protection for GIs against unfair competition arising from trademark protection, it must also implement Community-wide protection for trademarks against unfair competition arising from GI protection.

7.722 The European Communities indicated that it had difficulty understanding the claims but it responded as set out in paragraph 7.720.

7.723 Australia's response to the European Communities' concerns was that "[i]t is irrelevant that the EC might not understand" how the use of a TRIPS-consistent GI could constitute an act of unfair competition and that "[i]t is also irrelevant" that the use of a registered GI remains subject to legislation on labelling, misleading advertising and unfair competition laws.[627] However, it did provide an additional element to its arguments when it referred to Article 10*bis*(2) and speculated as follows:

> It may be that, having regard to the principle of territoriality and to developments in international trade over time, recognition of a TRIPS-defined GI could constitute an act of unfair competition within the meaning of Paris Article 10*bis*(2).

7.724 The Panel sought clarification from Australia as to the relevance of the fact that a measure is or is not applicable throughout a Member's territory, and whether Australia's claim was related to the fact that the EC member States are also WTO Members. Australia reiterated the assertion in its claim, but added that the European Communities had effectively implemented a "TRIPS right," at Community level, without also effectively implementing at the same level the concurrent "TRIPS obligations."[628] Australia did not explain why, in its view, the right to provide more extensive protection than that required by the minimum standards of the TRIPS Agreement entailed "concurrent" obligations.

7.725 The Panel observed that these claims related to trademark protection and sought clarification from Australia on the need for additional conclusions if there were a conclusion on the claims under Article 16.1 of

---

624 Australia's response to Panel question No. 161.

625 European Communities' first written submission, paras. 398-402.

626 European Communities' first written submission, paras. 403-404.

627 Australia's rebuttal submission, para. 146.

628 Australia's response to Panel question No. 81.

the TRIPS Agreement. Australia reiterated its assertion of an obligation to protect trademarks against unfair competition from a GI, but added that these provisions together ensure that a Member actually provides the mechanisms necessary to ensure protection against unfair competition "in any guise." Australia did not elaborate on why, in its view, the GI Regulation should provide such protection. Its final comments on these claims were as follows:

> The obligations established by Paris Articles 10*bis*(1) and 10*ter*(1) are straightforward, and WTO Members are required to comply with those obligations by the terms of TRIPS Article 2.1. *Australia does not have to explain* how the use of a registered EC-defined GI could constitute an act of unfair competition within the meaning of those provisions of the Paris Convention. That would be determined by the body required to be empowered by the EC to consider such matters in the event that the holder of an industrial property right within the EC considered that such issues may be raised by the registration of an EC-defined GI. [emphasis added]

7.726 The Panel has reviewed Australia's submissions, statements and responses to questions and notes that, whilst Australia has repeatedly stated the obligations with which it alleges inconsistencies, it has not clearly explained the fundamental premise of its claims, which is that the European Communities must provide at Community-level protection for trademarks against unfair competition arising from GIs. Nor has it clearly explained why the measure at issue should provide that protection. The Panel considers that those issues needed to be explained. The Panel itself sought clarification of certain issues and notes that the respondent also raised these matters in its first written submission.

7.727 The Panel cannot relieve Australia of its responsibility to prove its case. Some evidence, although not necessarily specific instances, was required to indicate what uses covered by Article 10*bis* of the Paris Convention (1967) are permitted by the Regulation without a legal means of prevention. Australia's speculative remark "having regard to the principle of territoriality and to developments in international trade over time" restated the nature of the measure at issue and the nature of the obligation at issue without making a clear link between the two. Australia's example of products that have become the "international" trading standard, considered in the previous sub-section in relation to Article 22.2(b) of the TRIPS Agreement, does not appear to relate to the present claim, which relates to the protection of *trademarks* from acts of unfair competition. Consequently, Australia has not demonstrated that legal remedies are required in accordance with Article 10*ter*(1) either.

7.728 Accordingly, the Panel concludes that Australia has not made a prima facie case in support of its claims under Articles 10*bis* and 10*ter* of the Paris Convention (1967) "as incorporated in" the TRIPS Agreement.[629]

3. *Claims under Part III of the TRIPS Agreement*

(a) *Main arguments of the parties*

7.729 Australia claims that the Regulation is inconsistent with Articles 41.1, 41.2, 41.3 and 42 of the TRIPS Agreement because of the provisions concerning objections by a trademark right holder, and the functioning of the regulatory committee.[630]

7.730 The European Communities responds that these claims are unfounded because Part III of the TRIPS Agreement does not apply to the Regulation. The Regulation lays down an administrative procedure for the

---

[629] This does not imply any view as to whether and in what respects Articles 10*bis* and 10*ter* of the Paris Convention (1967) are incorporated by Article 2.1 of the TRIPS Agreement.

[630] Australia's first written submission, paras. 119-148.

acquisition of GIs via a system of registration and does not purport to regulate enforcement procedures, which are the subject of Part III of the TRIPS Agreement.[631]

(b) Consideration by the Panel

7.731 These claims are made under the obligations with respect to enforcement procedures found in Part III of the TRIPS Agreement. The obligations in Part III are applicable to intellectual property rights covered by the Agreement, including geographical indications, by virtue of the definition of "intellectual property" in Article 1.2 and the first sentence of Part III. However, Australia's claims concern an *inter partes* procedure permitting objections which is related to the acquisition of intellectual property rights under the Regulation. As such, it is covered by Part IV of the TRIPS Agreement, not Part III. The general principles in Article 41.2 and 41.3 apply to such *inter partes* procedures, where a Member's law provides for them, by virtue of Article 62.4 of the TRIPS Agreement. However, Article 62.4 is outside the Panel's terms of reference. Accordingly, the Panel rejects these claims.

4. Claims concerning transitional national protection

(a) Main arguments of the parties

7.732 Australia claims that the Regulation does not ensure that decisions by EC member States to grant transitional national protection pursuant to Article 5(5) do not diminish the protection of trademarks under the TRIPS Agreement, in the same way as registration of GIs at the Community level. As a consequence, it claims that the Regulation is inconsistent with Article 2.1 ("incorporating Articles 10*bis*(1) and 10*ter*(1) of the Paris Convention (1967)"), Articles 16.1, 41.1, 41.2, 41.3 and/or 42 of the TRIPS Agreement. It submits that these claims are independent of its other claims.[632]

7.733 The European Communities responds that these claims are dependent on the substantive claims and are equally unfounded.[633]

(b) Consideration by the Panel

7.734 These claims concern Article 5(5) of the Regulation, which provides that, in certain circumstances, an EC member State may "on a transitional basis only, grant on the national level a protection in the sense of the present Regulation" for GIs pending a decision on registration by the Commission.

7.735 The Panel recalls once again that, in its preliminary ruling of 5 April 2004, it assured the European Communities that "it is fully entitled to know the arguments of Australia during the course of the proceedings. Those arguments must be set out and may be clarified in Australia's submissions."[634]

7.736 Australia has cited a series of numbered provisions of the TRIPS Agreement and provided narrative text that paraphrases those provisions, but it has set out little in the way of supporting arguments. It has not explained whether Article 5(5) grants EC member States authority to continue to apply national legislation, what is the nature or content of that protection, how it can diminish trademark protection "in the same way" as the protection granted by registration under the Regulation nor how this is alleged to violate enforcement obligations in Part III of the TRIPS Agreement. Therefore, it is not clear why Australia considers that the Regulation should ensure that decisions of EC member States should be taken with proper regard to the provisions of the TRIPS Agreement. Accordingly, Australia has not made a prima facie case in support of its claim.

---

631 European Communities' first written submission, paras. 357-389, 393-397.

632 Australia's first written submission, paras. 149-150; rebuttal submission, paras. 162-165.

633 European Communities' first written submission, paras. 407-408.

634 See para. 40 of the 5 April 2004 preliminary ruling set out in para. 7.2 of this report.

5. Claims concerning individual registrations

(a) Main arguments of the parties

7.737 Australia claims, for reasons related to the amendment of the Regulation in April 2003, violations of the national treatment obligations in Articles 2(1) and 2(2) of the Paris Convention as incorporated by Article 2.1 of the TRIPS Agreement, and in Article 3.1 of the TRIPS Agreement, the obligation in Article 2.1 of the TRIPS Agreement to comply with Articles 1 through 12 and 19 of the Paris Convention (1967), and the obligation in Article 1.3 of the TRIPS Agreement to accord the treatment provided for in the TRIPS Agreement to the nationals of other Members.[635]

7.738 Australia notes that as of April 2003, more than 120 GIs had been registered under the Regulation according to a procedure which granted a right of objection to persons resident or established in an EC member States but not to nationals of other WTO Members not resident or established in an EC member State. The amendment inserted Article 12d which grants a right of objection to persons resident or established in WTO Members, but did not provide any right of objection to GIs already registered or adjust the period for lodgement of objections to applications which were pending.[636]

7.739 Australia also notes that as of April 2003, more than 480 GIs had been registered under a simplified procedure under the former Article 17 which granted a right of objection to EC member States but not to the nationals of other WTO Members. The amendment repealed Article 17 but did not grant a right of objection to nationals of other WTO Members in respect of GIs already registered or affect the continuing registrations in any other way.[637]

7.740 In response to a question from the Panel, Australia indicated that it seeks relief in respect of existing registration for which the European Communities did not comply with Articles 16.1, 22.2, 41.1, 41.2, 41.3 and 42 of the TRIPS Agreement and Article III:4 of the GATT 1994.[638] It submits that its claims under these provisions, as well as its claims under Article 2.1 of the TRIPS Agreement, "incorporating" Articles 10*bis* and 10*ter* of the Paris Convention (1967), and Article 24.5 of the TRIPS Agreement, encompass the registration of 480 GIs under the simplified procedure.[639] However, it does not challenge any specific individual registration.

7.741 The European Communities responds that the individual registrations themselves are not in violation of national treatment obligations. Australia's claim is based exclusively on the argument that no right of objection was available to third country nationals under the Regulation prior to its amendment. The rules governing the procedure leading up to the adoption of the measure are not the same as the measure itself. It is not clear how an individual registration that grants protection to a specific GI could grant less favourable treatment to third country nationals.[640] Moreover, under the simplified procedure, there was no right of objection to European Communities residents *or* third country residents.[641]

7.742 The European Communities considers it important to remark that Australia is seeking a retroactive remedy that it could not have obtained had it attacked the measure while it was still in force. It submits that it is universally accepted that Article 19.1 of the DSU signifies that the recommendations of panels and the Appellate Body are prospective, not retrospective, in nature. Even if Australia had challenged the Regulation

---

[635] Australia's first written submission, paras. 189 and 194.

[636] Australia's first written submission, paras. 184-188.

[637] Australia's first written submission, paras. 190-193.

[638] Australia's response to Panel question No. 92.

[639] Australia's comment on the EC response to Panel question No. 163.

[640] European Communities' first written submission, paras. 158-161, 171.

[641] European Communities' first written submission, para. 172; rebuttal submission, paras. 186-190.

before it was amended, it could not have claimed that the European Communities undo all the registrations already carried out or reopen a possibility of objection against such registrations or provide compensation.[642]

7.743 The European Communities considers that Australia's claims under provisions other than the national treatment provisions were raised after its first written submission and without any supporting arguments. In any case, these claims relate to objection procedures, which are optional under the TRIPS Agreement and unrelated to the treatment of products under GATT 1994.[643]

(b) Consideration by the Panel

7.744 The Panel notes that these claims concern individual registrations effected under the former Article 17 of the Regulation, which has been repealed, and under Article 6 of the Regulation, which remains in effect.

7.745 With respect to individual registrations effected under the former Article 17 of the Regulation, the Panel recalls its ruling in paragraph 7.17 that it will make findings with respect to prior versions of the Regulation where they serve some useful purpose in reaching conclusions with respect to measures within its terms of reference, including individual registrations, that are currently in force.

7.746 The simplified procedure under the former Article 17 of the Regulation granted no right of objection. Article 7 provides for objections, but the former Article 17(2) provided that Article 7 "shall not apply" under the simplified procedure. Australia directs our attention to a judgement of the European Court of Justice, concerning protection of the name "Feta," which made reference to Article 17(2). However, the Panel notes that the findings of the Court in that judgement do not suggest that a right of objection under Article 7 applied under the simplified procedure.[644]

7.747 The Panel noticed that the initial registrations under Article 17 in 1996 recited provisions of the Regulation that concerned prior trademark rights.[645] In response to a question from the Panel, the European Communities explains that this was an implicit reference to "Bayerisches Bier" which was not registered at that time "[b]ecause of the concerns raised by the owners of the trademarks at issue and by some Member States."[646] On the basis of that statement alone, Australia asserts that "[c]learly, there was indeed a mechanism available to at least some EC trademark right holders to make their objections known in the context of the decision-making process provided by Article 15 of Regulation No. 2081/92."[647] However, Australia has not been any more specific concerning this mechanism.[648] Therefore, Australia has not demonstrated the first premise of its national treatment claim with respect to individual registrations effected under the former Article 17, which was that there was a difference in the procedures or opportunities for objections themselves.

7.748 With respect to individual registrations effected under Article 6 of the Regulation, Article 7(3) provides a prior right to submit statements of objections to EC member States to persons resident or established within the European Communities. The European Communities amended the Regulation in April 2003 by inserting Article 12d, which provides a right to submit statements of objections to the authorities of other WTO Members to persons resident or established in those other WTO Members. Therefore, with respect to registrations effected under Article 6, there *was* previously a difference in the objection procedures. However, Australia does not challenge the procedures for objections as they stood prior to the April 2003 amendment. It

---

642 European Communities' first written submission, paras. 162-169, 171; rebuttal submission, paras. 179-185 and 191-196.

643 European Communities' rebuttal submission, paras. 171-173; response to Panel question No. 163.

644 *Denmark, Germany and France v Commission*, joined Cases C-289/96, C-293/96 and C-299/96 [1999] ECR I-01541: see Australia's first written submission, para. 191 and Exhibit COMP-11. The Panel refers to para. 92 of the findings of the Court.

645 Commission Regulation (EC) No. 1107/96 set out in Exhibit COMP-3a.

646 European Communities' response to Panel question No. 144.

647 Australia's comment on the EC response to Panel question No. 163.

648 Australia's national treatment claims under the TRIPS Agreement with respect to the regulatory procedure under Article 15 are considered at paragraphs 7.390 to 7.402 above.

challenges individual registrations effected under the Regulation, including all those effected prior to that amendment, which remain in effect. It does not challenge any specific individual registration.[649]

7.749 The Panel observes that the act of registration, and the omission of not allowing objections from foreign residents, both occurred in the past, prior to the date of establishment of the Panel. The provisions of the Regulation which provided for these acts and omissions have been amended and no longer exist as they did at the time of the registrations. However, the individual registrations, in terms of the legal protection which flows from those registrations in accordance with Article 13 of the Regulation, constitute subject matter which continues to exist. Therefore, the TRIPS Agreement is applicable to them.[650]

7.750 Nevertheless, Australia has not demonstrated how individual registrations, as opposed to the procedures under which they were granted, either under the former Article 17 or the current Article 6, are inconsistent with the European Communities' obligations under the TRIPS Agreement, either in respect of national treatment or any of the other obligations that that agreement lists, because it effectively asserts the identity of the past act of registration and the presently existing subject matter. The continuing individual registrations are the subject of Australia's claims here, but Australia does not submit any evidence relating to them, either individually or as a group, other than the circumstances surrounding the act of registration, and the fact that they remain in force.

7.751 Therefore, in view of the finding in paragraph 7.750 and, additionally with respect to individual registrations under Article 17, the findings in paragraph 7.747, the Panel concludes that Australia has failed to make a prima facie case in support of its claims with respect to individual registrations.

6. *Claim under Article 1.1 of the TRIPS Agreement*

(a) *Main arguments of the parties*

7.752 Australia claims that, as a consequence of the Regulation's inconsistencies with various provisions of the TRIPS Agreement, the European Communities has failed to comply with Article 1.1 of the TRIPS Agreement.[651] This claim does not address a separate aspect of the Regulation but Australia does seek confirmation that a WTO Member is obliged to give effect to the provisions of the TRIPS Agreement before it is able to offer more extensive protection for one particular category of intellectual property right.[652]

7.753 The European Communities responds that these claims are dependent on the substantive claims and are equally unfounded.[653]

---

649 The Panel asked Australia to clarify the form of the recommendations which it seeks in respect of individual registrations. Australia did not identify any specific individual registrations. Instead, it replied that "Australia seeks rulings and recommendations to the degree necessary to establish the extent to which the EC's actions in registering—and thus providing ongoing protection to—more than 600 EC-defined GIs were inconsistent with the EC's obligations under the covered agreements at the time at which those EC—defined GIs were registered, thus enabling those continuing registrations to be brought into conformity with the EC's obligations under the covered agreements." The Panel also asked Australia whether it sought relief in respect of individual registrations in respect of their continuing inconsistency with trademark rights to be conferred under Article 16.1 of the TRIPS Agreement and, if so, to list the individual registrations. It replied that "Australia is not able to say which individual registrations may have constituted a denial of rights to trademark right holders ... or to another party with a legitimate interest under any of the cited provisions. With due respect, however, nor can the EC legitimately say that its actions have not resulted in a denial of rights required to have been granted or made available under the TRIPS Agreement ...." See Australia's responses to Panel questions Nos. 91 and 93.

650 This is consistent with the approach of the Appellate Body to patents granted prior to the date of application of the TRIPS Agreement in *Canada – Patent Term*, at para. 69.

651 Australia's first written submission, paras. 153, 189, 194, 206.

652 Australia's response to Panel question No. 82.

653 European Communities' first written submission, paras. 405-406.

(b) Consideration by the Panel

7.754 Article 1.1 of the TRIPS Agreement provides as follows:

> 1. Members shall give effect to the provisions of this Agreement. Members may, but shall not be obliged to, implement in their law more extensive protection than is required by this Agreement, provided that such protection does not contravene the provisions of this Agreement. Members shall be free to determine the appropriate method of implementing the provisions of this Agreement within their own legal system and practice.

7.755 The Panel notes that the first sentence creates an obligation for Members to give effect to the provisions of the TRIPS Agreement and the second sentence recognizes Members' freedom to implement more extensive protection, subject to a condition. After the expiry of the transitional arrangements in Articles 65 and 66 (and 70.8 and 70.9), as applicable, a Member is obliged to give effect to the provisions of the Agreement with respect to each category of intellectual property right, irrespective of whether it implements more extensive protection in the same or another category of intellectual property right.

7.756 The Panel notes that Australia's claim under Article 1.1 is a consequential claim and considers that further findings on it would not provide any additional contribution to a positive solution to this dispute. The Panel exercises judicial economy with respect to this claim.

7. Consequential claims

(a) Main arguments of the parties

7.757 Australia claims that the Regulation is inconsistent with Article 65.1 of the TRIPS Agreement, which obliged the European Communities to apply the provisions of the TRIPS Agreement no later than 1 January 1996, because the actions alleged in its other claims constitute contraventions of the European Communities' obligations under the TRIPS Agreement.[654]

7.758 Australia claims that the European Communities has not complied with Article XVI:4 of the WTO Agreement.[655] as a consequence of the Regulation's inconsistency with various provisions of the TRIPS Agreement, GATT 1994 and the TBT Agreement, and of the European Communities' failure to observe its obligations pursuant to Articles 1.1, 2.1 and 65.1 of the TRIPS Agreement.

7.759 The European Communities responds that these claims are dependent on the substantive claims and are equally unfounded.[656]

(b) Consideration by the Panel

7.760 The Panel notes that these are consequential claims and considers that findings on them would not provide any additional contribution to a positive solution to this dispute. Therefore, the Panel exercises judicial economy with respect to these claims.

---

[654] Australia's first written submission, paras. 207-208.

[655] Australia's first written submission, paras. 266-267.

[656] European Communities' first written submission, paras. 502-503.

VIII. CONCLUSIONS AND RECOMMENDATION

8.1 In light of the findings set out in this report, the Panel concludes as follows:

From Section A of the findings:

(a) the measures and claims in Australia's request for establishment of a panel did not fail to meet the requirements of Article 6.2 of the DSU that it identify the specific measures at issue and provide a brief summary of the legal basis of the complaint sufficient to present the problem clearly;

(b) the claims under Article 2(2) of the Paris Convention (1967) are within the Panel's terms of reference;

(c) the claim under Article 4 of the Paris Convention (1967), as incorporated by Article 2.1 of the TRIPS Agreement and, consequently, under Article 24.5 of the TRIPS Agreement, is outside the Panel's terms of reference;

(d) the claim under Article 41 in conjunction with Articles 43, 44, 45, 46, 48 and 49 of the TRIPS Agreement is outside the Panel's terms of reference;

From Section B of the findings:

(e) Australia has made a prima facie case that the equivalence and reciprocity conditions in Article 12(1) of the Regulation apply to the availability of protection for GIs that refer to geographical areas located in third countries outside the European Communities, including WTO Members and the European Communities has not succeeded in rebutting that case;

(f) the Regulation is inconsistent with Article 3.1 of the TRIPS Agreement:

(i) with respect to the equivalence and reciprocity conditions, as applicable to the availability of protection;

(ii) with respect to the application procedures, insofar as they require examination and transmission of applications by governments; and

(iii) with respect to the objection procedures, insofar as they require verification and transmission of objections by governments;

(g) Australia has not made a prima facie case in support of its claims that the Regulation is inconsistent with Article 3.1 of the TRIPS Agreement and with Article 2(1) of the Paris Convention (1967) as incorporated by Article 2.1 of the TRIPS Agreement:

(i) with respect to the equivalence and reciprocity conditions, as allegedly applicable to objections; or

(ii) with respect to the regulatory committee;

(h) the Regulation does not impose a requirement of domicile or establishment inconsistently with Article 2(2) of the Paris Convention (1967) as incorporated by Article 2.1 of the TRIPS Agreement:

(i) with respect to the availability of protection for GIs;

(ii) with respect to the application procedures; or

(iii) with respect to the objection procedures;

(i) the Regulation is inconsistent with Article III:4 of GATT 1994:

(i) with respect to the equivalence and reciprocity conditions, as applicable to the availability of protection; and

(ii) with respect to the application procedures, insofar as they require examination and transmission of applications by governments, and these requirements are not justified by Article XX(d) of GATT 1994;

(j) Australia has not made a prima facie case in support of its claims that the Regulation is inconsistent with Article III:4 of GATT 1994 with respect to the regulatory committee;

(k) Australia has not made a prima facie case in support of its claim that the Regulation is inconsistent with Article 2.1 of the TBT Agreement with respect to the labelling requirement;

From Section C of the findings:

(l) Article 2.2 of the TBT Agreement is inapplicable to the inspection structures requirements, read together with Article 4 of the Regulation, and the Panel rejects Australia's claim;

From Section D of the findings:

(m) the Regulation is inconsistent with Article 16.1 of the TRIPS Agreement with respect to the coexistence of GIs with prior trademarks but this is justified by Article 17 of the TRIPS Agreement. In this respect:

(i) Article 24.3 of the TRIPS Agreement is inapplicable; and

(ii) Article 24.5 of the TRIPS Agreement is inapplicable;

(n) Australia has not made a prima facie case in support of its claims that the Regulation is inconsistent with Article 16.1 of the TRIPS Agreement with respect to the right of objection of trademark owners;

From Section E of the findings:

(o) the Panel rejects Australia's claim under Article 22.2 of the TRIPS Agreement;

(p) Australia has not made a prima facie case in support of its claims that the Regulation is inconsistent with Article 10*bis* and 10*ter* of the Paris Convention (1967) "as incorporated in the TRIPS Agreement;"

(q) the Panel rejects Australia's claims under 41.1, 41.2, 41.3 and 42 of the TRIPS Agreement (except as noted at paragraph 8.1(d));

(r) Australia has not made a prima facie case in support of its claims with respect to transitional national protection; and

(s) Australia has not made a prima facie case in support of its claims with respect to individual registrations.

8.2 The Panel exercises judicial economy with respect to Australia's claims under:

(a) Article 2(1) of the Paris Convention (1967), as incorporated by Article 2.1 of the TRIPS Agreement (except as noted at paragraph 8.1(g))

(b) Article 16.1 of the TRIPS Agreement (with respect to the presumption of confusion);

(c) Articles 1.1 and Article 65.1 of the TRIPS Agreement;

(d) Article III:4 of GATT 1994 (except as noted in paragraph 8.1); and

(e) Article XVI:4 of the WTO Agreement.

8.3 Under Article 3.8 of the DSU, in cases where there is an infringement of the obligations assumed under a covered agreement, the action is considered prima facie to constitute a case of nullification or impairment. The Panel concludes that, to the extent that the Regulation as such is inconsistent with the covered agreements, it has nullified or impaired benefits accruing to Australia under these agreements.

8.4 In light of these conclusions, the Panel recommends pursuant to Article 19.1 of the DSU that the European Communities bring the Regulation into conformity with the TRIPS Agreement and GATT 1994.

8.5 The Panel suggests, pursuant to Article 19.1 of the DSU, that one way in which the European Communities could implement the above recommendation with respect to the equivalence and reciprocity conditions, would be to amend the Regulation so as for those conditions not to apply to the procedures for registration of GIs located in other WTO Members which, it submitted to the Panel, is already the case. This suggestion is not intended to diminish the importance of the above recommendation with respect to any of the Panel's other conclusions.

EUROPEAN COMMUNITIES – PROTECTION OF TRADEMARKS AND GEOGRAPHICAL INDICATIONS FOR AGRICULTURAL PRODUCTS AND FOODSTUFFS – COMPLAINT BY AUSTRALIA

WT/DS290/R/ADD.1
REPORT OF THE PANEL

ADDENDUM

This addendum contains Annex A to the Report of the Panel to be found in document WT/DS290/R. Annex B can be found in Add.2 and Annexes C and D can be found in Add.3.

ANNEX A

SUBMISSIONS BY AUSTRALIA

ANNEX A-1

COMMENTS BY AUSTRALIA ON THE REQUEST BY THE EUROPEAN COMMUNITIES FOR A PRELIMINARY RULING REGARDING THE PANEL'S JURISDICTION UNDER ARTICLE 6.2 OF THE DSU

(15 March 2004)

TABLE OF CONTENTS

TABLE OF CASES REFERRED TO IN THIS REQUEST

Short Title	**Full Title**
US – Carbon Steel	*United States – Countervailing Duties on Certain Corrosion-Resistant Carbon Steel Flat Products from Germany*, Report of the Appellate Body, WT/DS213/AB/R.
EC – Bananas	*European Communities – Regime for the Importation, Sale and Distribution of Bananas*, Report of the Appellate Body, WT/DS27/AB/R.
Guatemala – Cement I	*Guatemala – Anti-Dumping Investigation Regarding Portland Cement from Mexico*, Report of the Appellate Body, WT/DS60/AB/R.
Korea – Dairy	*Korea – Definitive Safeguard Measure on Imports of Certain Dairy Products*, Report of the Appellate Body, WT/DS98/AB/R.
Thailand – H-Beams	*Thailand – Anti-Dumping Duties on Angles, Shapes and Sections of Iron or Non-Alloy Steel and H-Beams from Poland*, Report of the Appellate Body, WT/DS122/AB/R.
Canada – Wheat	*Canada – Measures Relating to Exports of Wheat and Treatment of Imported Grain*, Preliminary Ruling of the Panel, WT/DS276/12.

I. INTRODUCTION

1. The EC has requested that the Panel issue a preliminary ruling that Australia's request for the establishment of a panel does not meet the requirements of Article 6.2 of the *Understanding on the Rules and Procedures Governing the Settlement of Disputes* (the "DSU"). Arguments put forward by the EC in support of its request are without merit. Australia has explicitly identified the specific measure at issue and provided a brief summary of the legal basis of the complaint sufficient to present the problem clearly. Consequently, Australia's request for the establishment of a panel in this dispute fully complies with the requirements of DSU Article 6.2. Australia submits that, in the circumstances of this dispute, the EC is effectively asking the Panel to find that DSU Article 6.2 requires a complaining party to provide a summary of its legal argument in its panel establishment request. Such a finding would not be consistent with the terms of DSU Article 6.2 being given their ordinary meaning in light of the object and purpose of the DSU.

II. THE REQUIREMENTS OF DSU ARTICLE 6.2

2. DSU Article 6.2 requires, in relevant part, that the request for the establishment of a panel "identify the specific measures at issue and provide a brief summary of the legal basis of the complaint sufficient to present the problem clearly."

3. In *US – Carbon Steel*, the Appellate Body recapped and clarified its previous findings in relation to DSU Article 6.2. The Appellate Body said in that dispute:

> 125. There are ... two distinct requirements, namely identification of *the specific measures at issue*, and the provision of a *brief summary of the legal basis of the complaint* (or the *claims*). Together, they comprise the "matter referred to the DSB," which forms the basis for a panel's terms of reference under Article 7.1 of the DSU.[...]
>
> 126. The requirements of precision in the request for the establishment of a panel flow from the two essential purposes of the terms of reference. First, the terms of reference define the scope of the dispute. Secondly, the terms of reference, and the request for the establishment of a panel on which they are based, serve the *due process* objective of notifying the parties and third parties of the nature of a complainant's case.[...] When faced with an issue relating to the scope of its terms of reference, a panel must scrutinize carefully the request for establishment of a panel "to ensure its compliance with both the letter and the spirit of Article 6.2 of the DSU."[...]
>
> 127. ... [C]ompliance with the requirements of Article 6.2 must be demonstrated on the face of the request for the establishment of a panel. Defects in the request for the establishment of a panel cannot be "cured" in the subsequent submissions of the parties during the panel proceedings.[...] Nevertheless, in considering the sufficiency of a panel request, submissions and statements made during the course of the panel proceedings, in particular the first written submission of the complaining party, may be consulted in order to confirm the meaning of the words used in the panel request and as part of the assessment of whether the ability of the respondent to defend itself was prejudiced.[...] Moreover, compliance with the requirements of Article 6.2 must be determined on the merits of each case, having considered the panel request as a whole, and in the light of attendant circumstances.[...]
>
> ...
>
> 130. ... [A]lthough the listing of treaty provisions allegedly violated is always a *necessary* "minimum prerequisite" for compliance with Article 6.2, whether such a listing is *sufficient* to

> constitute a "brief summary of the legal basis of the complaint sufficient to present the problem clearly" within the meaning of Article 6.2 will depend on the circumstances of each case, and in particular on the extent to which mere reference to a treaty provision sheds light on the nature of the obligation at issue.[...] ...[1] *(emphases in original)*

4. Notwithstanding that the EC has cited several potentially relevant statements by the Appellate Body from *EC – Bananas*, *Guatemala – Cement I*, *Korea – Dairy*, *Thailand – H-Beams* and *US – Carbon Steel*,[2] the EC's choice of Appellate Body statements is selective. In particular, nowhere in its submission does the EC cite the full text of the Appellate Body's statement at paragraph 127, or the statement at paragraph 130, of *US – Carbon Steel*.

5. The relevant requirements for compliance are encapsulated in the statement by the Appellate Body: "... compliance with the requirements of Article 6.2 must be demonstrated on the face of the request for the establishment of a panel. ... [C]ompliance ... must be determined <u>on the merits of each case</u>, <u>having considered the panel request as a whole</u>, and <u>in the light of attendant circumstances</u>"[3] *(emphasis added)*.

III. AUSTRALIA'S PANEL REQUEST IDENTIFIES THE "SPECIFIC MEASURE AT ISSUE" AS REQUIRED BY DSU ARTICLE 6.2

6. DSU Article 6.2 requires that the request for establishment of a panel "identify the specific measures at issue." The Panel in *Canada – Wheat* has stated that the ordinary meaning of the phrase "identify the specific measures at issue" is "to establish the identity of the precise measures at issue."[4]

7. Australia's panel establishment request establishes the identity of the precise measure at issue in this dispute, and therefore conforms to the requirements of DSU Article 6.2. As set out in the fourth paragraph of Australia's request, the specific measure at issue is composed of three principal elements: (1) Council Regulation No. 2081/92 itself; (2) any amendments to that Regulation; and (3) related implementing and enforcement measures. That all three elements constitute the specific measure at issue is confirmed by the second sentence in that paragraph: "[t]he EC measure lays down <u>and</u> implements rules on the protection of designations of origin and geographical indications for agricultural products and foodstuffs, excluding wines and spirits." This statement is in fact an adaptation of Article 1.1 of Regulation No. 2081/92, a copy of the current version of which has been provided by the EC as Exhibit EC-1.

A. REGULATION NO. 2081/92

8. Australia agrees that what can be considered a "specific measure" will depend on the circumstances of the particular case, and in particular on the characteristics of the measure in question.[5]

9. Here, a legislative instrument establishes an integrated regulatory framework to govern a defined package of issues. Thus, nomination of that instrument alone is in this dispute sufficient to establish the identity of the specific measure at issue within the meaning of DSU Article 6.2 and to encompass all of the provisions of that legislative instrument within the scope of the specific measure at issue. The complexity of a legislative instrument does not preclude the nomination of that instrument as such or of the regime which it governs as the specific measure at issue within the meaning of DSU Article 6.2. Indeed, the EC itself acknowledges that "name, number, or date of adoption of the act" can identify the "specific measure at issue."[6]

---

[1] *US – Carbon Steel*, paragraphs 125-130.

[2] EC Request for a Preliminary Ruling, paragraphs 7-13.

[3] *US – Carbon Steel*, paragraph 127.

[4] *Canada – Wheat*, paragraph 14.

[5] EC Request for a Preliminary Ruling, paragraph 17.

[6] EC Request for a Preliminary Ruling, paragraph 17.

10. Regulation No. 2081/92 is not a circumstance where identifying a legislative instrument is not sufficient. It is not a "miscellaneous issues" legislative instrument covering a broad range of activities. Neither is it a legislative instrument establishing a regulatory framework governing a range of measures intended to be applied in the context of a broad spectrum of activities. If it established a comprehensive tax regime, for example, it is possible that a complaining party's failure to identify the specific provision(s) could legitimately be said in some circumstances not to establish the precise identity of the measure at issue.

11. The EC itself does not seem to have considered that DSU Article 6.2 requires explicit linkages between the detailed provisions of the measure(s) at issue and the provisions of the WTO Agreement in its own panel establishment requests. For example, the EC's panel requests in *US – Anti-Dumping Act of 1916*[7], *US – FSC*[8], *Indonesia – Autos*[9] and *Canada – Autos*[10] did not make such linkages.

12. The EC argues that "[t]he unspecific reference to 'Regulation 2081/92' made in the Panel requests does not permit the EC to understand which specific aspects among those covered by Regulation 2081/92 the complainants intend to raise in the context of the present proceedings."[11] However, to apply DSU Article 6.2 in a way that requires explicit linkages between the detailed provisions of the measure at issue and the provisions of the WTO Agreement in a panel establishment request could have a range of immediate potential effects. It could preclude claims based on the general design and architecture of a measure, such as national treatment claims based on arguments of systemic bias. Complaining parties could be required to provide a summary of their legal arguments in the panel establishment request in the event of a claim based on a measure's design and architecture, and possibly in respect of other claims, else the linkages could be argued not to have been sufficiently identified. Moreover, in such a case, a failure to identify even one provision of the measure in the panel establishment request could void the panel's mandate, an outcome which Australia considers would be totally at odds with the intent of the DSU generally and of Article 6.2 in particular. The EC's argument is not sustainable given that DSU Article 6.2 requires that panel establishment request provide a "brief summary of the legal basis of the complaint sufficient to present the problem clearly," not a summary of the legal argument.

B. ANY AMENDMENTS TO REGULATION NO. 2081/92

13. As the EC has not challenged the inclusion of amendments to Regulation No. 2081/92 in the specific measure at issue, Australia assumes the EC does not dispute that they form part of the specific measure at issue.

C. RELATED IMPLEMENTING AND ENFORCEMENT MEASURES

14. Read in context, the phrase "related implementing and enforcement measures" is specific. It clearly and precisely identifies actions connected to the implementation and enforcement of Regulation No. 2081/92 as being part of the measure at issue in this dispute.

15. The phrase brings within the scope of this dispute any actions—whether regulatory, administrative or judicial—for which Regulation No. 2081/92 constitutes the legislative basis, that is, any measures which are applied within the legal framework of Regulation No. 2081/92. The EC's isolated analysis of the word "related"

---

[7] *United States – Anti-Dumping Act of 1916*, Request for the Establishment of a Panel by the European Communities, WT/DS136/2.

[8] *United States – Tax Treatment for "Foreign Sales Corporations,"* Request for the Establishment of a Panel by the European Communities, WT/DS108/2.

[9] *Indonesia – Certain Measures Affecting the Automobile Industry*, Request for the Establishment of a Panel by the European Communities, WT/DS54/6.

[10] *Canada – Certain Measures Affecting the Automotive Industry*, Request for the Establishment of a Panel by the European Communities, WT/DS142/2.

[11] EC Request for a Preliminary Ruling, paragraph 22.

is misleading.[12] As the EC itself concedes,[13] the phrase "enforcement and implementing measures" narrows the measures at issue to those that implement and/or enforce Regulation No. 2081/92.

16. Neither DSU Article 6.2—nor any other provision of the DSU—limits the number of actions that may constitute the measure(s) at issue. The fact that there are by now 640 geographical indications or designations of origin registered under Regulation No. 2081/92,[14] or that implementation and enforcement may occur through a mix of legislative or administrative means at Community and Member State level or for some aspects through judicial review,[15] does not preclude those actions forming part of the specific measure at issue in this dispute.

17. By arguing that the phrase "related implementing and enforcement measures," read in the context of Australia's panel establishment request in this dispute, is not sufficiently specific, the EC is effectively asking the Panel to find that DSU Article 6.2 requires a complaining party: to provide a "statement of available evidence" in the sense of Articles 4.2 and 7.2 of the *Agreement on Subsidies and Countervailing Measures*; to provide a list of exhibits; and/or to inform the EC—through the panel establishment request—whether Australia is intending to pursue legal argument based on all elements of the measure. DSU Article 6.2 requires none of these things.

18. Australia notes that the EC itself has on a number of occasions considered that similar language was sufficiently specific to identify the precise measures at issue, for example, "any other implementing measures,"[16] "other relevant documents,"[17] "any implementing measures thereof and all other related measures,"[18] "any implementing decrees and other regulations,"[19] and "any implementing measures taken thereunder."[20]

D. CONCLUSION

19. The specific measure at issue is composed of Council Regulation No. 2081/92, any amendments to that Regulation, and related implementing and enforcement measures. Australia submits that EC arguments that Australia's identification of the specific measure at issue in this dispute is insufficiently specific are without merit and do not provide a basis for a finding by the Panel that Australia has not identified the specific measure at issue.

IV. AUSTRALIA'S PANEL REQUEST PROVIDES "A BRIEF SUMMARY OF THE LEGAL BASIS OF THE COMPLAINT SUFFICIENT TO PRESENT THE PROBLEM CLEARLY" AS REQUIRED BY DSU ARTICLE 6.2

20. The Appellate Body has said:

> ... whether ... a listing *[of treaty provisions allegedly violated]* is sufficient to constitute a "brief summary of the legal basis of the complaint sufficient to present the problem clearly"

---

[12] EC Request for a Preliminary Ruling, paragraph 28.

[13] EC Request for a Preliminary Ruling, paragraphs 29-32.

[14] EC Request for a Preliminary Ruling, paragraph 32.

[15] EC Request for a Preliminary Ruling, paragraph 30.

[16] *Canada – Certain Measures Affecting the Automotive Industry*, Request for the Establishment of a Panel by the European Communities, WT/DS142/2.

[17] *United States – Definitive Safeguard Measures on Imports of Certain Steel Products*, Request for the Establishment of a Panel by the European Communities, WT/DS248/12.

[18] *United States – Tariff Increases on Products from the European Communities*, Request for the Establishment of a Panel by the European Communities, WT/DS39/2.

[19] *Korea – Measures Affecting Trade in Commercial Vessels*, Request for the Establishment of a Panel by the European Communities, WT/DS273/2.

[20] *Indonesia – Certain Measures Affecting the Automobile Industry*, Request for the Establishment of a Panel by the European Communities, WT/DS54/6.

within the meaning of Article 6.2 will depend on the circumstances of each case, and in particularly on the extent to which mere reference to a treaty provision sheds light on the nature of the obligation at issue.[...] ...[21]

21. The EC has characterised this and other relevant Appellate Body statements as "the identification of the treaty provisions alleged to have been violated is a necessary, but not a sufficient condition under Article 6.2 DSU"[22] *(emphasis in original)*. This is not an accurate characterisation of the relevant Appellate Body statements because it suggests that such identification is always insufficient. In fact, as the above quotation demonstrates, the Appellate Body has said that whether such identification is sufficient will depend on the circumstances of the case.

22. The issue before the Panel is whether Australia's request for the establishment of a panel provides "a brief summary of the legal basis of the complaint sufficient to present the problem clearly" as required by DSU Article 6.2. "Basis" is defined as "the foundation" and "[a] thing on which anything is constructed and by which its constitution or operation is determined; ... a determining principle; a set of underlying or agreed principles."[23] Thus, DSU Article 6.2 requires that a request for the establishment of a panel set out the legal principles that underpin the complaint sufficient to present the problem clearly.

23. The six claims set out in Australia's panel establishment request provide a brief summary of the legal basis of the complaint sufficient to present the problem clearly. Notwithstanding that those claims might restate the essential elements of the relevant provisions of the WTO Agreement, that reference is sufficient in this dispute to shed light on the nature of the obligations at issue in relation to the specific measure at issue.

A. THE LEGAL BASES OF AUSTRALIA'S CLAIMS ARE CLEAR

24. The EC alleges that Australia's use of the term "and/or" makes unclear the legal bases of Australia's claim in relation to Articles 41 and 42 of the *TRIPS Agreement*. The expression "and/or" in fact applies to all of the provisions cited. This is not idiomatic Australian linguistic usage. Australia notes, for example, the usage of "and/or" in the context of three or more options in a number of WTO panel and Appellate Body reports.[24] Thus, consistent with common linguistic usage of the expression "and/or," Australia's claim is that the EC measure diminishes, or lessens, the legal protection for trademarks under the *TRIPS Agreement*, contrary to the provisions cited, considered individually and collectively.[25] The use of the expression "and/or," understood in its common usage, does not make the legal bases of Australia's claim unclear.

25. The EC also alleges that the legal bases of Australia's claim in relation to Articles 10, 10*bis* and 10*ter* of the Paris Convention, in conjunction with Article 2 of the *TRIPS Agreement*, are unclear.[26] The EC argues that these provisions of the Paris Convention are complex, being divided into various subparagraphs and imposing numerous distinct obligations. Irrespective of the accuracy of the EC's portrayal of those provisions, Australia's claim is that the EC measure diminishes the legal protection for trademarks under the *TRIPS Agreement*, contrary to the cited provisions. Thus, Australia's claim is that the EC measure diminishes the legal

---

[21] *US – Carbon Steel*, paragraph 130.

[22] EC Request for a Preliminary Ruling, paragraph 37.

[23] *The New Shorter Oxford English Dictionary*, Ed Lesley Brown, Clarendon Press, Oxford, 1993, Vol. 1, page 188.

[24] For example: *EC – Measures Affecting Asbestos and Asbestos-Containing Products*, Report of the Panel, WT/DS135/R, paragraph 3.83; *Argentina – Safeguard Measures on Imports of Footwear*, Report of the Panel, WT/DS121/R, paragraph 8.298; *Argentina – Measures Affecting the Export of Bovine Hides and the Import of Finished Leather*, Report of the Panel, WT/DS155/R, paragraphs 2.43, 8.138 and 11.6; *Canada – Certain Measures Affecting the Automotive Industry*, Report of the Panel, WT/DS139/R, WT/DS142/R, paragraph 6.1022; *EC – Anti-Dumping Duties on Malleable Cast Iron Tube or Pipe Fittings from Brazil*, Report of the Panel, WT/DS219/R, paragraph 7.335; and *US – Definitive Safeguard Measures on Imports of Certain Steel Products*, Report of the Appellate Body, WT/DS248/AB/R & others, paragraph 484.

[25] Australia notes that the EC seems to have understood the usage of the expression "and/or" in relation to Australia's claims under Article 2 of the *TBT Agreement*.

[26] EC Request for a Preliminary Ruling, paragraph 58.

protection for trademarks under the *TRIPS Agreement*, contrary to all aspects of those cited provisions. The EC has not offered any argument as to why this can not or should not be clearly understood from the claim.

B. AUSTRALIA'S CLAIMS SATISFY THE LEGAL STANDARD ESTABLISHED BY DSU ARTICLE 6.2

26. The EC seems to be alleging in relation to Australia's claim concerning the legal protection for trademarks under the *TRIPS Agreement* that Australia has not provided "a meaningful description of the claim."[27] However, DSU Article 6.2 does not require such a description: it requires a "brief summary of the legal basis of the complaint sufficient to present the problem clearly." In the circumstances of the present dispute, Australia's statement that the EC measure diminishes the protection for trademarks under the *TRIPS Agreement* contrary to the cited provisions meets this requirement. Australia has clearly set out the legal principle underpinning its claim as required by DSU Article 6.2.

27. Similarly, DSU Article 6.2 does not require Australia to set out in its panel establishment request precisely how it believes the EC measure violates fundamental national treatment and most favoured nation principles under GATT 1994, the *TRIPS Agreement* and the *TBT Agreement*.[28] The obligation on Australia is to provide a brief summary of the legal basis, or the legal principles, of the complaint sufficient to present the problem clearly, which Australia has done. It is not credible that the language used in Australia's panel establishment request does not provide to the EC a brief summary of the fundamental principles of national treatment and most favoured nation sufficient to present the problem clearly.

28. Equally, DSU Article 6.2 does not require Australia to set out in its panel establishment request precisely how it believes the EC measure has been prepared, adopted and/or applied with the effect of creating unnecessary obstacles to trade contrary to Article 2.2 of the *TBT Agreement*.[29] Australia notes, however, that the EC is also effectively alleging that Australia has provided too much information because Australia has informed the EC of its intention to demonstrate that the EC measure is inconsistent with provisions of the TBT Agreement. [30] Whether Point 1 of Annex 1 to the *TBT Agreement* "impose*[s]* any obligations which could have been violated by the EC" [31] will of course be for the Panel to determine as part of its consideration of the substantive aspects of the dispute in response to arguments put forward by Australia and the EC.

29. In relation to Australia's claims under TRIPS Articles 22.2[32], and 63.1 and 63.3[33], Australia notes that the EC does not allege that it is unable to comprehend the legal basis of the complaint, that is, the legal principles at issue in the claims, from the information provided. Rather, it alleges that "the claim is not comprehensible,"[34] and "Australia fails to explain in which way Regulation 2081/92 is not applied in a transparent way."[35] DSU Article 6.2 requires that Australia's panel establishment request "provide a brief summary of the legal basis of the complaint sufficient to present the problem clearly." This Australia has done.

C. DSU ARTICLE 6.2 DOES NOT REQUIRE A COMPLAINING PARTY TO INCLUDE A SUMMARY OF ITS LEGAL ARGUMENT IN ITS PANEL ESTABLISHMENT REQUEST

30. The EC has put forward many arguments in support of its Request for a Preliminary Ruling. In every case, however, the conclusion seems inescapable that these arguments are motivated by the EC's desire to have

---

[27] EC Request for a Preliminary Ruling, paragraph 61, referring to paragraphs 46-48.

[28] EC Request for a Preliminary Ruling, paragraph 61, referring to paragraphs 44-45, and paragraphs 62-64.

[29] EC Request for a Preliminary Ruling, paragraph 62.

[30] EC Request for a Preliminary Ruling, paragraph 63.

[31] *Ibid.*

[32] EC Request for a Preliminary Ruling, paragraph 61, referring to paragraph 49.

[33] EC Request for a Preliminary Ruling, paragraph 61, referring to paragraph 51.

[34] EC Request for a Preliminary Ruling, paragraph 49.

[35] EC Request for a Preliminary Ruling, paragraph 61.

the Panel find that DSU Article 6.2 requires that a complaining party provide a summary of its legal argument in its panel establishment request.

31. DSU Article 6.2 requires that a complaining party provide a "brief summary of the legal basis of the complaint sufficient to present the problem clearly." This was confirmed by the Appellate Body when it said: "Article 6.2 of the DSU requires that the *claims*, but not the *arguments*, must all be specified sufficiently in the request for the establishment of a panel in order to allow the defending party and any third parties to know the legal basis of the complaint" *(emphasis in original).*[36]

32. Australia submits that it has met its obligations under DSU Article 6.2. EC arguments that Australia's panel request does not provide "a brief summary of the legal basis of the complaint sufficient to present the problem clearly" are without merit and do not provide a basis for such a finding by the Panel.

V. THE EC HAS NOT SUFFERED SERIOUS PREJUDICE TO ITS ABILITY TO DEFEND ITSELF

33. Australia's request for the establishment of a panel fully complies with the requirements of DSU Article 6.2: it identifies the specific measures at issue and provides a brief summary of the legal basis of the complaint sufficient to present the problem clearly.

34. However, in the event the Panel considers that DSU Article 6.2 technically requires more information than is provided in Australia's panel establishment request, the Panel would also need to consider if it should address whether the EC's ability to defend its interests has been prejudiced.

35. Should the Panel decide to examine whether the EC's ability to defend its interests has been prejudiced, Australia recalls that in *Korea – Dairy* the Appellate Body said:

> ... we consider that whether the mere listing of the articles claimed to have been violated meets the standard of Article 6.2 must be examined on a case-by-case basis. In resolving that question, we take into account whether the ability of the respondent to defend itself was prejudiced, given the actual course of the panel proceedings, by the fact that the panel request simply listed the provisions claimed to have been violated.
>
> ...
>
> In assessing whether the European Communities' request met the requirements of Article 6.2 of the DSU, we consider that, in view of the particular circumstances of this case and in line with the letter and spirit of Article 6.2, the European Communities' request should have been more detailed. However, Korea failed to demonstrate to us that the mere listing of the articles asserted to have been violated has prejudiced its ability to defend itself in the course of the Panel proceedings. Korea did assert that it had sustained prejudice, but offered no supporting particulars in its appellant's submission nor at the oral hearing. We, therefore, deny Korea's appeal relating to the consistency of the European Communities' request for the establishment of a panel with Article 6.2 of the DSU.[37]

36. The EC alleges that Australia has prevented the EC from preparing its defence in a timely manner, thereby causing serious prejudice to the EC.[38]

---

[36] *EC – Bananas*, paragraph 143.

[37] *Korea –Dairy*, paragraphs 127-131.

[38] EC Request for a Preliminary Ruling, paragraph 74.

37. The EC argues that it is prejudiced by an alleged lack of clarity in Australia's request for the establishment of a panel. "As a defending party, the EC has a right to know what the case is which it will have to defend. This information must be contained in the Panel request" and "... the ambiguity of the Panel request is such that the EC is ... not sure of the case which the United States and Australia are bringing before the Panel. As a consequence, the EC has been seriously hampered in its efforts to prepare its defence" [39] *(emphases added)*.

38. The EC's argument is premised in part on statements by the Appellate Body in *Thailand – H-Beams* when the Appellate Body said in relevant part: "Article 6.2 of the DSU calls for sufficient clarity with respect to the legal basis of the complaint, that is, with respect to the 'claims' that are being asserted by the complaining party.[...] A defending party is entitled to know what case it has to answer, and what violations have been alleged so that it can begin preparing its defence.[...] ..."[40]

39. However, the EC argument overlooks that the Appellate Body clarified those statements in its later report in *US – Carbon Steel* when it said that "the terms of reference, and the request for the establishment of a panel on which they are based, serve the due process objective of notifying the parties and third parties of the nature of a complainant's case" [41] *(emphasis added)*.

40. Further, and in any event, in *Thailand – H-Beams*, the Appellate Body referred to a responding party "*[beginning to prepare]* its defence"[42] *(emphasis added)*. A request for establishment of a panel pursuant to DSU Article 6.2 does not provide the basis for a responding party's preparation of its defence, as the EC asserts. Indeed, such an interpretation would render meaningless the provisions of the DSU, for example, Article 12.4, concerning written submissions in panel proceedings. The EC will have the opportunity to present its defence in its written and oral presentations to the Panel, for which it has been granted the maximum three week period of preparation time envisaged under the Working Procedures at Appendix 3 to the DSU. Moreover, the EC implicitly admits when it subsequently says "... the EC cannot be expected to wait for the first written submission of the complainants to start preparing its defence"[43] *(emphasis added)* that DSU Article 6.2 does not provide the basis for a responding party's preparation of its defence.

41. Accordingly, DSU Article 6.2 does not bestow on a responding party "a right to know what the case is which it will have to defend" or provide that "[t]his information must be contained in the Panel request."[44] Nor has the Appellate Body suggested that DSU Article 6.2 provides such a right or sets out such a requirement. The EC has had all the information that DSU Article 6.2 provides that it should have to begin preparing its defence, and has had this information since Australia's initial panel establishment request. As a consequence, the EC's argument that it is prejudiced by the lack of clarity in Australia's panel request is not sustainable.

42. The EC also argues that the alleged lack of clarity in Australia's panel request is not acceptable from the point of view of the EC's rights of due process. However, the issue for the Panel is whether Australia's panel establishment request complies with DSU Article 6.2. There is no requirement for the Panel to consider whether DSU Article 6.2 in itself provides adequate due process rights to a responding party.

43. Australia notes too the EC's statement at footnote 25 of its Request that "[t]he EC does consider it necessary, in the present case, to take a position as to whether the requirement of prejudice in Article 6.2 DSU constitutes an additional requirement to those set out in Article 6.2 DSU." Australia submits that, since Australia's panel establishment request fully complies with the requirements of DSU Article 6.2, the EC has not

---

[39] EC Request for a Preliminary Ruling, paragraphs 67-68.

[40] *Thailand – Anti-Dumping Duties on Angles, shapes and Sections of Iron or Non-Alloy Steel and H-Beams from Poland*, Report of the Appellate Body, WT/DS122/AB/R, paragraph 88.

[41] *US – Carbon Steel*, paragraph 126.

[42] *Thailand – H-Beams*, paragraph 88.

[43] EC Request for a Preliminary Ruling, paragraph 69.

[44] EC Request for a Preliminary Ruling, paragraph 67.

been prejudiced as a defendant. There is thus no need for the Panel to consider this issue in the context of this dispute. Should, however, the Panel consider it necessary to consider the issue, Australia reserves the right to put forward further argument on this issue in its First Written Submission.

44. In conclusion, the EC is clearly aware of the specific measure at issue in this dispute and the legal basis of the complaint. Australia submits that the EC's allegation that Australia has prevented the EC from preparing its defence in a timely manner, thereby causing serious prejudice to the EC, is without foundation.

VI. THE EC'S REQUEST FOR A PRELIMINARY RULING

45. As the Panel has indicated its intention to issue a preliminary ruling in response to the EC's Request, Australia does not offer any comment on procedural issues associated with the EC's Request.

VII. THE PANEL SHOULD FIND THAT AUSTRALIA'S PANEL REQUEST COMPLIES WITH DSU ARTICLE 6.2

46. EC arguments in support of its Request for a Preliminary Ruling that Australia's request for the establishment of a panel does not meet the requirements of DSU Article 6.2 are without merit. Australia's panel establishment request in this dispute fully satisfies the requirements of DSU Article 6.2 as these have been clarified by the Appellate Body, most recently in *US – Carbon Steel*. Australia has clearly identified the specific measure at issue and provided a brief summary of the legal basis of the complaint to the standard required by DSU Article 6.2. There are thus no deficiencies in Australia's panel establishment request.

47. However, should the Panel find that Australia's panel establishment request requires more information and then decide to consider whether the EC's ability to defend itself has been prejudiced, Australia submits that the EC has not substantiated its claim that any deficiencies in the panel establishment request have resulted in serious prejudice to the EC as a defendant.

48. Accordingly, the substantive basis of the EC's Request for a Preliminary Ruling should be denied in full.

ANNEX A-2

FIRST WRITTEN SUBMISSION OF AUSTRALIA

(23 April 2004)

TABLE OF CONTENTS

(iv) The EC measure does not grant to the owner of a registered trademark – in the event of a likelihood of confusion between a registered trademark and a proposed EC-defined GI – the exclusive right required to be granted by Article 16.1 of the TRIPS Agreement

D. THE EC MEASURE UNJUSTIFIABLY ENCUMBERS THE USE OF A TRADEMARK IN THE COURSE OF TRADE WITH SPECIAL REQUIREMENTS, CONTRARY TO ARTICLE 20 OF THE TRIPS AGREEMENT

E. THE EC MEASURE DOES NOT ASSURE EFFECTIVE PROTECTION AGAINST UNFAIR COMPETITION, CONTRARY TO ARTICLE 2.1 OF THE TRIPS AGREEMENT INCORPORATING ARTICLE 10BIS(1) OF THE PARIS CONVENTION (1967)

F. THE EC MEASURE DOES NOT ASSURE APPROPRIATE LEGAL REMEDIES TO REPRESS EFFECTIVELY ACTS REFERRED TO IN ARTICLE 10BIS OF THE PARIS CONVENTION (1967), CONTRARY TO ARTICLE 2.1 OF THE TRIPS AGREEMENT INCORPORATING ARTICLE 10TER(1) OF THE PARIS CONVENTION (1967)

G. THE EC MEASURE DOES NOT MAKE AVAILABLE TO TRADEMARK RIGHT HOLDERS CIVIL JUDICIAL PROCEDURES CONCERNING THE ENFORCEMENT OF THEIR INTELLECTUAL PROPERTY RIGHTS, CONTRARY TO ARTICLE 42 OF THE TRIPS AGREEMENT

H. THE PROCEDURES CONCERNING THE ENFORCEMENT OF TRADEMARK RIGHTS MADE AVAILABLE BY THE EC MEASURE ARE INCONSISTENT WITH ARTICLE 41.2 OF THE TRIPS AGREEMENT

(i) The EC measure does not make available fair and equitable procedures for the enforcement of intellectual property rights, contrary to Article 41.2 of the TRIPS Agreement

(ii) The procedures for the enforcement of trademark rights made available by the EC measure are unnecessarily complicated and entail unwarranted delays, contrary to Article 41.2 of the TRIPS Agreement

I. DECISIONS ON THE REGISTRATION OF EC-DEFINED GIS UNDER THE EC MEASURE ARE NOT BASED ONLY ON EVIDENCE IN RESPECT OF WHICH TRADEMARK RIGHT HOLDERS WERE OFFERED THE OPPORTUNITY TO BE HEARD, CONTRARY TO ARTICLE 41.3 OF THE TRIPS AGREEMENT

J. THE EC HAS NOT ENSURED THE AVAILABILITY UNDER ITS LAW OF ENFORCEMENT PROCEDURES AS SPECIFIED IN PART III OF THE TRIPS AGREEMENT SO AS TO PERMIT EFFECTIVE ACTION AGAINST ANY ACT OF INFRINGEMENT OF TRADEMARK RIGHTS AS REQUIRED BY ARTICLE 41.1 OF THAT AGREEMENT

K. THE EC MEASURE DIMINISHES THE LEGAL PROTECTION FOR TRADEMARKS IN RESPECT OF DECISIONS BY EC MEMBER STATES TO GRANT TRANSITIONAL NATIONAL PROTECTION, CONTRARY TO ARTICLES 2.1 (INCORPORATING ARTICLES 10BIS(1) AND 10TER(1) OF THE PARIS CONVENTION (1967)), 16.1, 41.1, 41.2, 41.3 AND/OR 42 OF THE TRIPS AGREEMENT

L. THE EC HAS NOT GIVEN EFFECT TO THE PROVISIONS OF THE TRIPS AGREEMENT OR COMPLIED WITH THE SPECIFIED PROVISIONS OF THE PARIS CONVENTION (1967), CONTRARY TO ARTICLES 1.1 AND 2.1 OF THE TRIPS AGREEMENT

M. CONCLUSION

VII. THE EC MEASURE IS INCONSISTENT WITH ARTICLES 1.1 AND 22.2 OF THE TRIPS AGREEMENT

A. IN RESPECT OF EC-DEFINED GIS, THE EC MEASURE DOES NOT PROVIDE THE LEGAL MEANS FOR INTERESTED PARTIES TO PREVENT MISLEADING USE OR USE WHICH CONSTITUTES UNFAIR COMPETITION, CONTRARY TO ARTICLE 22.2 OF THE TRIPS AGREEMENT

B. THE EC HAS NOT GIVEN EFFECT TO THE PROVISIONS OF THE TRIPS AGREEMENT AS REQUIRED BY ARTICLE 1.1 OF THAT AGREEMENT

VIII. THE EC MEASURE IS INCONSISTENT WITH ARTICLE III:4 OF GATT 1994 AND ARTICLES 1.1 AND 1.3, 2.1 (INCORPORATING ARTICLE 2 OF THE PARIS CONVENTION (1967)) AND 3.1 OF THE TRIPS AGREEMENT

A. THE EC MEASURE ACCORDS TO THE PRODUCTS OF ANOTHER WTO MEMBER TREATMENT LESS FAVOURABLE THAN THAT IT ACCORDS TO LIKE PRODUCTS OF NATIONAL ORIGIN, CONTRARY TO ARTICLE III:4 OF GATT 1994

(i) The relevant requirements of Article III:4 of GATT 1994

(ii) The EC measure relates to imported and domestically produced "like products" within the meaning of Article III:4 of GATT 1994

(iii) The EC measure is a law affecting the internal sale or offering for sale of imported products which are like products to products of EC origin within the meaning of Article III:4 of GATT 1994

(iv) EC-defined GIs for imported products are accorded less favourable treatment than EC-defined GIs for like domestic products, contrary to Article III:4 of GATT 1994

(v) An EC-defined GI from another WTO Member may only be registered in the EC in respect of an imported like product if that other WTO Member deems the requirements of Regulation No. 2081/92#3 to be satisfied, thus according less favourable treatment to imported products contrary to Article III:4 of GATT 1994

(vi) The EC measure as a whole accords less favourable treatment to imported products bearing an EC-defined GI than to like domestic products bearing an EC-defined GI, contrary to GATT Article III:4

B. THE EC MEASURE DOES NOT ACCORD NATIONAL TREATMENT IN THE PROTECTION OF INTELLECTUAL PROPERTY, CONTRARY TO ARTICLES 1.1 AND 1.3, 2.1 (INCORPORATING BY REFERENCE ARTICLE 2 OF THE PARIS CONVENTION (1967)) AND 3.1OF THE TRIPS AGREEMENT

(i) The relevant requirements of Articles 1.1 and 1.3, 2.1 and 3.1 of the TRIPS Agreement and Article 2 of the Paris Convention (1967)

(ii) A right of objection was available to persons resident or established in an EC Member State that was not available to other WTO Member nationals in respect of the registration of more than 120 EC-defined GIs under the normal registration process, contrary to Articles 1.1 and 1.3, 2.1 (incorporating Article 2 of the Paris Convention (1967)) and 3.1 of the TRIPS Agreement

(iii) A right of objection was available to persons resident or established in an EC Member State that was not available to other WTO Member nationals in respect of the registration of more than 480 EC-defined GIs under the simplified registration process, contrary to Articles 1.1 and 1.3, 2.1 (incorporating Article 2 of the Paris Convention (1967)) and 3.1 of the TRIPS Agreement

(iv) The EC measure as a whole does not accord national treatment to non-EC nationals, contrary to Articles 1.1 and 1.3, 2.1 (incorporating Article 2 of the Paris Convention (1967)) and 3.1 of the TRIPS Agreement

IX. ARTICLE 65.1 OF THE TRIPS AGREEMENT DOES NOT EXCUSE INCONSISTENCIES WITH THE EC'S OBLIGATIONS UNDER THAT AGREEMENT

X. THE EC MEASURE IS INCONSISTENT WITH ARTICLE 2.1 AND 2.2 OF THE TBT AGREEMENT

A. THE EC MEASURE IS IN PART A TECHNICAL REGULATION WITHIN THE MEANING OF ANNEX 1 TO THE TBT AGREEMENT

(i) Definition of a "technical regulation"

(ii) The EC measure applies to an identifiable product or group of products

(iii) The EC measure lays down product characteristics or their related process and production methods, including the applicable administrative provisions

(iv) The EC measure mandates compliance with product characteristics or their related process and production methods, including the applicable administrative provisions

B. THE EC MEASURE ACCORDS TO PRODUCTS IMPORTED FROM THE TERRITORY OF ANY WTO MEMBER TREATMENT LESS FAVOURABLE THAN THAT ACCORDED TO LIKE PRODUCTS OF NATIONAL ORIGIN, CONTRARY TO ARTICLE 2.1 OF THE TBT AGREEMENT

(i) The relevant requirements of the TBT Agreement

(ii) The EC measure concerns both imported and domestically produced "like products" within the meaning of Article 2.1 of the TBT Agreement

(iii) The EC measure provides "less favourable" treatment to like imported and domestically produced products within the meaning of Article 2.1 of the TBT Agreement

C. THE EC MEASURE HAS BEEN PREPARED, ADOPTED AND/OR APPLIED WITH THE EFFECT OF CREATING UNNECESSARY OBSTACLES TO INTERNATIONAL TRADE, BEING MORE TRADE-RESTRICTIVE THAN NECESSARY TO FULFIL A LEGITIMATE OBJECTIVE, TAKING ACCOUNT OF THE RISKS NON-FULFILMENT WOULD CREATE, CONTRARY TO ARTICLE 2.2 OF THE TBT AGREEMENT

(i) The relevant requirements of the TBT Agreement

(ii) The EC measure pursues a legitimate objective within the meaning of Article 2.2 of the TBT Agreement

(iii) The EC measure fulfils, or is capable of fulfilling, its legitimate objective within the meaning of Article 2.2 of the TBT Agreement

(iv) The EC measure is more trade restrictive than necessary to fulfil its legitimate objective, taking account of the risks non-fulfilment would create, contrary to Article 2.2 of the TBT Agreement

D. CONCLUSION

XI. AS A CONSEQUENCE, THE EC HAS NOT COMPLIED WITH ITS OBLIGATIONS UNDER ARTICLE XVI:4 OF THE WTO AGREEMENT

XII. CONCLUSION

TABLE OF CASES CITED IN THIS SUBMISSION

Short Title	Full Title
US – Section 211 Appropriations Act	*United States – Section 211 Omnibus Appropriations Act of 1998*, Report of the Appellate Body, WT/DS176/AB/R, 2 January 2002
US – Section 337	*United States – Section 337 of the Tariff Act of 1930*, GATT Panel Report, adopted 7 November 1989, BISD 36S/345
Korea – Beef	*Korea – Measures Affecting Imports of Fresh, Chilled and Frozen Beef*, Report of the Appellate Body, WT/DS161/AB/R, WT/DS169/AB/R, 11 December 2000
EC – Asbestos	*European Communities – Measures Affecting Asbestos and Asbestos-Containing Products*, Report of the Appellate Body, WT/DS135/AB/R, 12 March 2001
EC – Bananas	*European Communities – Regime for the Importation, Sale and Distribution of Bananas*, Report of the Appellate Body, WT/DS27/AB/R, 9 September 1997
US – FSC (Article 21.5)	*United States – Tax Treatment for "Foreign Sales Corporations,"* Recourse to Article 21.5 of the DSU by the European Communities, Report of the Appellate Body, WT/DS108/AB/RW, 14 January 2002
EC – Sardines	*European Communities – Trade Description of Sardines*, Report of the Appellate Body, WT/DS231/AB/R, 26 September 2002

OTHER SOURCES CITED IN THIS SUBMISSION

Short Title	Full Title
Bodenhausen	*Guide to the Application of the Paris Convention for the Protection of Industrial Property as Revised at Stockholm in 1967*, Professor, G H C Bodenhausen, BIRPI, 1969, WIPO reprint 1991, Geneva
Gervais	*The TRIPS Agreement: Drafting History and Analysis*, Daniel Gervais, Sweet & Maxwell, London, 1998
OED	*The New Shorter Oxford English Dictionary*, Ed. Lesley Brown, Clarendon Press, Oxford, 1993

I. OVERVIEW

1. This dispute concerns the regime established by the European Communities (EC) for the registration and protection of geographical indications—or GIs—for agricultural products and foodstuffs on a Community-wide basis. The dispute does not concern the registration and/or protection of GIs for wines or spirits.

2. Council Regulation (EEC) No. 2081/92 *on the protection of geographical indications and designations of origin for agricultural products and foodstuffs* ("Regulation No. 2081/92") established the regulatory framework that governs the complex EC regime. In addition to Council Regulation No. 2081/92, there is a long list of subsidiary regulations at Community level.[1] Regulation No. 2081/92 expressly requires EC Member States to perform some specific activities and authorises the Member States to perform other actions at their discretion. EC Member State national courts and the European Court of Justice enforce the protection of GIs afforded by Regulation No. 2081/92.

3. Since its adoption in 1992, Regulation No. 2081/92 itself has been substantially amended on two occasions: in 1997, relating principally to transitional issues arising from the proposed registration of geographic terms under Regulation No. 2081/92; and more extensively in 2003, in part "to guarantee that the Community registration procedure is available" to WTO Members meeting conditions of reciprocity and equivalence[2]. Further, GIs have been continuously registered under the regime since registrations commenced in 1996.

4. The *Agreement on Trade-Related Aspects of Intellectual Property Rights* ("the *TRIPS Agreement*" or "TRIPS") expressly recognises geographical indications as a category of intellectual property. In this dispute, Australia is not contesting the EC's right:

- to register and/or protect GIs as intellectual property;
- to implement in its law more extensive protection for GIs than is required to be provided by the *TRIPS Agreement*;
- to limit that more extensive protection to GIs that meet a more rigorous attributive test than is required by the *TRIPS Agreement*, while protecting GIs that otherwise conform with the definition at TRIPS Article 22.1 through individual EC Member State legislation; or
- not to offer more extensive protection at the Community level to GIs which conform only to the basic definition of a GI at TRIPS Article 22.1.

5. However, the EC is providing that more extensive protection for GIs in a way that contravenes other provisions of the *TRIPS Agreement*, as well as provisions of the *General Agreement on Tariffs and Trade 1994* ("the GATT 1994" or "GATT"), of the *Agreement on Technical Barriers to Trade* ("the *TBT Agreement*" or "TBT") and, as a consequence, of the *Marrakesh Agreement Establishing the World Trade Organization* ("the *WTO Agreement*").

6. Specifically, the EC is failing to provide the level of protection of trademarks expressly required to be conferred pursuant to various provisions of the *TRIPS Agreement*, including because the EC regime:

- denies to the owner of a *registered* trademark the exclusive right to prevent all third parties not having the owner's consent from using in the course of trade identical or similar signs for goods

[1] These are listed in Annex 1 to this Submission.

[2] Regulation No. 692/2003, preambular clause 9, Exhibit COMP-1.h.

which are identical or similar to those in respect of which the trademark is registered where such use would result in a likelihood of confusion, contrary to TRIPS Article 16.1;

- denies to the owner of a *registered* trademark a presumption of a likelihood of confusion in case of use of an identical sign for identical goods, contrary to TRIPS Article 16.1;

- denies to nationals of other WTO Members effective protection against unfair competition and appropriate legal remedies to repress effectively all acts of unfair competition, contrary to TRIPS Article 2.1 incorporating Articles 10*bis*(1) and 10*ter*(1) of the *Paris Convention for the Protection of Industrial Property* ("the Paris Convention (1967)" or "Paris"); and

- denies to nationals of other WTO Members enforcement *procedures* so as to permit effective action against any act of infringement of a trademark right, and associated procedural and due process rights, contrary to TRIPS Articles 41 and 42.

7. Similarly, the EC's failure to provide at Community level the legal means for interested parties to prevent—in respect of a GI registered, or proposed to be registered, under the EC regime—misleading use or use which constitutes an act of unfair competition is contrary to TRIPS Article 22.2.

8. In relation to the registration of GIs under the regime, the EC fails to provide national treatment:

- to the products of other *WTO* Members, contrary to GATT Article III:4 as well as TBT Article 2.1; and

- in the protection of intellectual property, contrary to TRIPS Articles 2.1 (incorporating Paris Article 2) and 3.1.

9. Further, the EC regime comprises a technical regulation that is more restrictive than necessary to fulfil a legitimate objective, taking account of the risks non-fulfilment would create, contrary to TBT Article 2.2.

10. Australia reiterates that it is not contesting the EC's right to offer more extensive protection to GIs than is required to be offered pursuant to the *TRIPS Agreement*. However, if this right is to be exercised at the Community level, so too should the interconnected obligations be fulfilled at the Community level. Australia submits that, if the EC is to offer "one-stop" Community level registration of GIs for either EC nationals or products, it must also, for example, offer a "one-stop" Community level means: for interested parties to prevent, in respect of that GI registration, any use which constitutes an act of unfair competition within the meaning of Paris Article 10*bis*, consistent with the requirement of Paris Article 10*ter*; for trademark right holders to exercise their rights in respect of the registration of GIs under the regime; and for the registration of a GI from another WTO Member. Requiring trademark owners to initiate separate legal proceedings in up to 25 national courts to exercise the rights required to be bestowed on them under the *TRIPS Agreement* as these relate to a GI registered, or proposed to be registered, under the "one-stop" Community level EC regime is, in Australia's view, fundamentally at odds with the object and purpose of the *TRIPS Agreement*.

11. For the reasons set out in detail in this Submission, Australia submits that the Panel should find that the EC regime for the registration and protection of GIs is inconsistent with the EC's obligations pursuant to the *TRIPS Agreement*, GATT 1994, the *TBT Agreement* and the *WTO Agreement*.

II. INTRODUCTION

A. PROCEDURAL HISTORY

12. On 17 April 2003, Australia requested consultations with the EC pursuant to Article 4 of the *Understanding On Rules Governing the Settlement of Disputes* (DSU), Article XXII of the GATT 1994, Article 64 of the *TRIPS Agreement*, and Article 14 of the *TBT Agreement* relating to the protection of trademarks and to the registration and protection of geographical indications for foodstuffs and agricultural products in the EC.[3] Australia's request followed an earlier similar request for consultations from the United States to the EC.[4] Argentina, Bulgaria, Chinese Taipei, Colombia, Cyprus, Czech Republic, Hungary, Malta, Mexico, New Zealand, Romania, Slovak Republic, Slovenia, Turkey and the United States requested to be joined in the consultations requested by Australia.[5]

13. Consultations between Australia and the EC, and between the United States and the EC, were held jointly in Geneva on 27 May 2003, but failed to resolve the dispute.

14. On 21 July 2003, Australia requested the Dispute Settlement Body (DSB) to establish a panel pursuant to Articles 4.7 and 6 of the DSU, Article XXIII of GATT 1994, Article 64 of the *TRIPS Agreement* and Article 14 of the *TBT Agreement*.[6] The United States similarly requested establishment of a panel.[7]

15. On 2 October 2003, the DSB agreed that a single panel should be established pursuant to Article 9.1 of the DSU with standard terms of reference.[8] The terms of reference of the Panel are:

> To examine, in the light of the relevant provisions of the covered agreements cited by the United States in document WT/DS174/20 and by Australia in document WT/DS290/18, the matters referred to the DSB by the United States and Australia in those documents, and to make such findings as will assist the DSB in making the recommendations or in giving the rulings provided for in those agreements.

16. Argentina, Brazil, Canada, China, Chinese Taipei, Colombia, Guatemala, India, Mexico, New Zealand, Norway, Turkey and the United States reserved rights as third parties to the dispute.

B. TERMINOLOGY USED IN THIS SUBMISSION

17. Article 1.1 of Regulation No. 2081/92 states that the Regulation "lays down rules on the protection of designations of origin and geographical indications" of specified agricultural products and foodstuffs other than wines and spirits. However, the distinction between a designation of origin and a geographical indication within the meaning of the Regulation is not germane to Australia's claims in this dispute. Thus, throughout this Submission, except where specifically indicated otherwise, Australia will use the expressions:

> "*GI*" to refer to a geographical indication generally;
>
> "*EC-defined GI*" to refer to both a designation of origin and a geographical indication as these are defined and used in Regulation No. 2081/92;

---

[3] WT/DS290/1.

[4] WT/DS174/1 and WT/DS174/1/Add.1.

[5] WT/DS290/11, WT/DS290/3, WT/DS290/16, WT/DS290/13, WT/DS290/5, WT/DS290/4, WT/DS290/12, WT/DS290/2, WT/DS290/10, WT/DS290/8, WT/DS290/14, WT/DS290/15, WT/DS290/7, WT/DS290/9 and WT/DS290/6 respectively.

[6] WT/DS290/18.

[7] WT/DS174/20.

[8] WT/DSB/M/156, pages 6-8.

"*TRIPS-defined GI*" to refer to a geographical indication as this is defined in TRIPS Article 22.1; and

"*Indication of source*" to refer to an indication of source within the meaning of Paris Article 1(2). While the Paris Convention (1967) does not expressly define an indication of source, "indications of source are generally understood to include all ... signs used to indicate that a product ... originates in a given country or group of countries, region or locality."[9] Thus, both an EC-defined GI and a TRIPS-defined GI are categories of indications of source.

18. Regulation No. 2081/92 has been amended on several occasions. Substantive amendments relevant to Australia's claims and arguments in this dispute were introduced in Council Regulations (EC) No. 535/97 of 17 March 1997[10] and No. 692/2003 of 8 April 2003[11]. To identify the appropriate version of Regulation No. 2081/92, throughout this Submission Australia will, except where indicated otherwise, use the terminology:

"*Regulation No. 2081/92*" to refer to the Regulation in a broad sense or in relation to provisions that have not been amended since the Regulation originally entered into force;

"*Regulation No. 2081/92#1*" to refer to the Regulation as originally adopted and in force from 24 July 1993;

"*Regulation No. 2081/92#2*" to refer to the Regulation as amended by Council Regulation (EC) No. 535/97 of 17 March 1997 with effect from 28 March 1997; and

"*Regulation No. 2081/92#3*" to refer to the Regulation as amended by Council Regulation (EC) No. 692/2003 of 8 April 2003 with effect from 24 April 2003.

19. Other terminology and abbreviations used in this Submission are:

"*Commission*" to refer to the European Commission;

"*Committee of EC Member State representatives*" to refer to the decision-making process established by Article 15 of Regulation No. 2081/92#1 and amended by Council Regulation (EC) No. 806/2003 of 14 April 2003 *adapting to Decision 1999/468/EC the provisions relating to committees which assist the Commission in the exercise of its implementing powers laid down in Council instruments adopted in accordance with the consultation procedure (qualified majority)*[12];

"*Official Journal*" for the *Official Journal of the European Communities*; and

"*Register*" for the *Register of protected designations of origin and protected geographical indications* provided for by Article 6.3 of Regulation No. 2081/92.

---

[9] *Bodenhausen*, page 23.

[10] Exhibit COMP-1.e.

[11] Exhibit COMP-1.h.

[12] Exhibit COMP-1.i. A copy of Council Decision 1999/468/EC of 28 June 1999 *laying down the procedures for the exercise of implementing powers conferred on the Commission* is at Exhibit COMP-8.

III. FACTUAL DESCRIPTION OF THE MEASURE

A. THE MEASURE AT ISSUE

20. The measure at issue in this dispute ("the EC measure") is the EC's regime for the registration and protection of EC-defined GIs on a Community-wide basis, comprising:

- Council Regulation (EEC) No. 2081/92 of 14 July 1992 *on the protection of geographical indications and designations of origin for agricultural products and foodstuffs*;
- amendments to that Regulation;[13] and
- actions to implement and enforce that Regulation, including:
  - Commission Regulation (EEC) No. 2037/93 of 27 July 1993 as amended;[14]
  - Commission Regulation (EC) No. 1107/96 of 12 June 1996 as amended;[15]
  - Commission Regulation (EC) No. 2400/96 of 17 December 1996 as amended;[16]
  - by EC Member States to implement Regulation No. 2081/92 at national level, in particular, actions by Member States to grant transitional national protection pursuant to Article 5.5 of Regulation No. 2081/92#2; and
  - judicial decisions relating to the enforcement of Regulation No. 2081/92, for example:
    - Judgment of the European Court of Justice of 16 March 1999, Joined Cases C-289/96, C-293/96 and C-299/96, concerning the registration of "Feta" (the "Feta judgment");[17] and
    - Order of the Court of First Instance (Fifth Chamber) of 30 January 2001, Case T-215/00, concerning the geographical indication "Canard à foie gras du Sud-Ouest (the "Canard judgment").[18]

21. Regulation No. 2081/92 establishes the regulatory framework for the regime. Since being adopted in 1992, the Regulation has been substantially amended on two occasions. In particular, Regulation No. 2081/92#3 contains several amended and new provisions.

22. Further, under Regulation No. 2081/92#3, natural mineral and spring waters were removed from the list of products for which EC-defined GI registration and protection is available, while other products—including pasta and wool—were added. In addition, the scope of the Regulation was enlarged to include wine vinegars.[19]

---

[13] Exhibit COMP-1.a comprises, for the convenience of the Panel, an unofficial consolidated copy **prepared by the complaining parties** of Regulation No. 2081/92 showing all amendments to date. Regulation No. 2081/92 and all amendments to date are shown in Annex 1 and supported by COMP-1.

[14] Regulation No. 2037/93 and all amendments to date are shown in Annex 1 and supported by Exhibit COMP-2.

[15] Regulation No. 1107/96 and all amendments to date are shown in Annex 1 and supported by Exhibit COMP-3.

[16] Regulation No. 2400/96 and all amendments to date are shown in Annex 1 and supported by Exhibit COMP-4.

[17] Exhibit COMP-11.

[18] Exhibit COMP-12.

[19] Regulation No. 692/2003, Articles 1.1 and 1.16 and Annexes I and II, Exhibit COMP-1.h. For the approximately 30 mineral and spring water GIs already included in the Register, there is a transitional period until 31 December 2013 after which date these names will no longer be included in the Register.

23. The following sections describe the principal features of Regulation No. 2081/92 including, where appropriate, as these have been amended.

B. THE PROTECTION AFFORDED TO EC-DEFINED GIS BY REGULATION NO. 2081/92

24. There is no distinction in the protection afforded to a designation of origin and a geographical indication as these are defined in the Regulation. Under Article 13.1, a registered EC-defined GI "... shall be protected against:

(a) any direct or indirect commercial use of a name registered in respect of products not covered by the registration insofar as those products are comparable to the products registered under that name or insofar as using the name exploits the reputation of the protected name;

(b) any misuse, imitation or evocation, even if the true origin of the product is indicated or if the protected name is translated or accompanied by an expression such as 'style', 'type', 'method', 'as produced in', 'imitation' or similar;

(c) any other false or misleading indication as to the provenance, origin, nature or essential qualities of the product, on the inner or outer packaging, advertising material or documents relating to the product concerned, and the packing of the product in a container liable to convey a false impression as to its origin;

(d) any other practice liable to mislead the public as to the true origin of the product.

..."

C. DEFINITION OF A DESIGNATION OF ORIGIN AND A GEOGRAPHICAL INDICATION ("EC-DEFINED GI")

25. Article 2.2(a) defines a *designation of origin* as: "... the name of a region, a specific place or, in exceptional cases, a country, used to describe an agricultural product or a foodstuff: originating in that region, specific place or country, and the quality or characteristics of which are essentially or exclusively due to a particular geographical environment with its inherent natural and human factors, and the production, processing and preparation of which take place in the defined geographical area."

26. Article 2.2(b) defines a *geographical indication* as: "... the name of a region, a specific place or, in exceptional cases, a country, used to describe an agricultural product or a foodstuff: originating in that region, specific place or country, and which possesses a specific quality, reputation or other characteristics attributable to that geographical origin and the production and/or processing and/or preparation of which take place in the defined geographical area."

D. GENERIC NAMES

27. Article 3.1 provides that "[n]ames that have become generic may not be registered ...."

E. PRODUCT SPECIFICATION

28. Under Article 4, to be eligible to use an EC-defined GI, an agricultural product or foodstuff must comply with a product specification, including: a description of the principal physical, chemical, microbiological and/or organoleptic characteristics of the product or the foodstuff; the details bearing out the link with the geographical environment or the geographical origin within the meaning of an EC-defined GI; and

details of the inspection structures to ensure that products bearing an EC-defined GI meet the requirements of the product specification.

F. INSPECTION STRUCTURES

29. Under Article 10.1, EC Member States are required to ensure that inspection structures are in place, with the function of "ensur*[ing]* that agricultural products and foodstuffs bearing a protected name meet the requirements laid down in the specifications."

G. NORMAL REGISTRATION PROCESS FOR EC-DEFINED GIS FROM WITHIN THE EC

30. Under Article 5, a group may apply for registration of an EC-defined GI in respect of agricultural products or foodstuffs which it produces or obtains. The registration application must include the product specification, and be forwarded to the EC Member State in which the geographical area is located. The EC Member State must forward the application, including the product specification, to the Commission if it considers that the application complies with the Regulation.

31. Under paragraphs 1-4 of Article 6, the Commission has six months to verify whether the application includes all of the particulars required by the product specification. If the Commission concludes the "name" qualifies for protection, it is to publish the application details and, "if necessary, the grounds for its conclusions," in the Official Journal. "If no statement of objections is notified to the Commission," the "name" is entered in the Register and the entry notified in the Official Journal. Regulation No. 2081/92#3 amended Article 6.1 to require the Commission to "make public any application for registration *[of an EC-defined GI]*, stating the date on which the application was made."

32. Under Article 7, an EC Member State may object to the proposed registration of the "name" within six months of publication of the application in the Official Journal. If a statement of objection is admissible, "... the Commission shall ask the Member States concerned to seek agreement among themselves ...." If the Members States concerned agree, the Commission publishes the entry of the "name" in the Register in the Official Journal. If the Member States concerned do not agree, "the Commission shall take a decision *[in the Committee of EC Member State representatives]* having regard to traditional fair practice and of the actual likelihood of confusion." If the Commission decides to enter the "name" in the Register, it is to publish that fact in the Official Journal.

33. More than 140 EC-defined GIs have been registered pursuant to the normal registration process, and registrations are ongoing. The list of EC-defined GIs registered pursuant to this process is published in Commission Regulation (EC) No. 2400/96 as amended.[20]

H. HOMONYMS OF EXISTING REGISTERED EC-DEFINED GIS

34. Under Article 6.6 of Regulation No. 2081/92#3, if an application is made to register a homonym of an existing registered EC-defined GI, whether from an EC Member State or another WTO Member: "the Commission may request the opinion of the *[Committee of EC Member State representatives]*."

I. RIGHT OF OBJECTION TO THE PROPOSED REGISTRATION OF AN EC-DEFINED GI UNDER THE NORMAL REGISTRATION PROCESS

35. Under Article 7.3, "[a]ny legitimately concerned natural or legal person may object to the proposed registration *[by the Commission]* by sending a duly substantiated statement to the competent authority of the *[EC]* Member State in which he resides or is established."

---

[20] Exhibit COMP-4.

J. GROUNDS OF OBJECTION TO THE PROPOSED REGISTRATION OF AN EC-DEFINED GI UNDER THE NORMAL REGISTRATION PROCESS

36. Under Article 7.4 of Regulation No. 2081/92#1, "[a] statement of objection shall be admissible only if it: either shows non-compliance with the *[the definition of an EC-defined GI]*, or shows that the proposed registration of a name would jeopardize the existence of an entirely or partly identical name or trade mark or the existence of products which are legally on the market at the time of publication of this regulation in the *[Official Journal]*, or indicates the features which demonstrate that the name whose registration is applied for is generic in nature" *(emphasis added)*.

37. Article 7.4 was amended in Regulation No. 2081/92#2 so that the second ground for admissibility of an objection to a proposed registration of an EC-defined GI became "that the registration of the name proposed would jeopardize the existence of an entirely or partly identical name or of a mark or the existence of products which have been legally on the market for at least five years preceding the date of the publication *[of the application for registration in the Official Journal]*" *(emphasis added)*.

K. SIMPLIFIED REGISTRATION OF EC-DEFINED GIS ALREADY LEGALLY PROTECTED OR ESTABLISHED BY USAGE WITHIN EC MEMBER STATES

38. Under Article 17 of Regulation No. 2081/92#1, EC Member States had six months to inform the Commission "which of their legally protected names or ... which of their names established by usage they wish*[ed]* to register pursuant to this Regulation. ... [T]he Commission shall register the names ... which comply with *[the definition of an EC-defined GI]* and *[the product specification requirements]*. *[There is no objection process]*. However, generic names shall not be added."

39. However, in the Minutes of the Council Meeting that adopted Regulation No. 2081/92#1, the Council and the Commission stated that "where there are agricultural products or foodstuffs already being legally marketed ..., it has been provided for any Member States to object to the registration under the provisions of Article 7 of the regulation."[21]

40. More than 480 EC-defined GIs were registered pursuant to this simplified registration process. The list of EC-defined GIs registered under the simplified process is published in Commission Regulation (EC) No. 1107/96 as amended.[22]

41. Article 17 was repealed in Regulation No. 2081/92#3. "However, the provisions of *[Article 17]* shall continue to apply to registered names or to names for which a registration application was made by the procedure provided for in Article 17 before *[Regulation No. 2081/92#3]* entered into force."[23]

L. REGISTRATION OF AN EC-DEFINED GI RELATING TO THE TERRITORY OF ANOTHER WTO MEMBER

42. Article 12 provides:

> 1. Without prejudice to international agreements, this Regulation may apply to an agricultural product or foodstuff from a third country provided that:

---

[21] The Feta judgment, Exhibit COMP-11.

[22] Exhibit COMP-3.

[23] Article 1.15 of Regulation No. 692/2003, Exhibit COMP-1.h. Consistent with that provision, Regulation Nos 828/2003 of 14 May 2003 (Exhibit COMP-3.d) and 1571/2003 of 5 September 2003 (Exhibit COMP-3.e), for example, amended the product specifications of names entered in the Register pursuant to Article 17 of Regulation No. 2081/92#1.

- the third country is able to give guarantees identical or equivalent to *[the product specification requirement]*,
- the third country concerned has inspection arrangements equivalent to those laid down *[in the Regulation]*,
- the third country concerned is prepared to provide protection equivalent to that available in the Community to corresponding agricultural products for *[sic]* foodstuffs coming from the Community.

2. If a protected name of a third country is identical to a Community protected name, registration shall be granted with due regard for local and traditional usage and the practical risks of confusion.

Use of such names shall be authorised only if the country of origin of the product is clearly and visibly indicated on the label.

43. Article 12.1 was amended in Regulation No. 2081/92#3 to add the requirement that "the third country concerned has … a right to objection equivalent to *[that]* laid down in this Regulation."

M. PROCEDURE FOR APPLICATIONS FOR REGISTRATION OF AN EC-DEFINED GI RELATING TO THE TERRITORY OF ANOTHER WTO MEMBER

44. An application process for the registration of a "name" from another WTO Member was introduced in Regulation No. 2081/92#3. A new Article 12.3 provided: "[t]he Commission shall examine, at the request of the country concerned, and *[in the Committee of EC Member State representatives]* whether a third country satisfies the equivalence conditions and offers guarantees *[of the conditions for registration of third country GIs]* as a result of its national legislation. Where the Commission decision is in the affirmative, the procedure set out in Article 12a shall apply."

45. Article 12a was inserted in Regulation No. 2081/92#3 to provide:

1. … [I]f a group or a natural or legal person … in a third country wishes to have a name registered under this Regulation it shall send a registration application to the authorities in the country in which the geographical area is located. Applications must be accompanied by *[the product specification]* for each name. …

2. If the third country … deems the requirements of this Regulation to be satisfied it shall transmit the registration application to the Commission accompanied by:

(a) a description of the legal provisions and the usage on the basis of which the designation of origin or the geographical indication is protected or established in the country,

(b) a declaration that *[the inspection structures]* are established on its territory, and

(c) other documents on which it has based its assessment.

46. Article 12b was inserted in Regulation No. 2081/92#3 to provide:

1. The Commission shall verify within six months whether the registration request sent by the third country contains all the necessary elements and shall inform the country concerned of its conclusion.

If the Commission:

(a) concludes that the name satisfies the conditions for protection, it shall publish the application *[for objections]* ... Prior to publication the Commission may ask the *[Committee of EC Member State representatives]* for its opinion;

(b) concludes that the name does not satisfy the conditions for protection, it shall decide, after consulting the country having transmitted the application, in *[the Committee of EC Member State representatives]* not to proceed with publication *[for objections]*.

...

3. ... Where one or more objections are admissible the Commission shall adopt a decision *[in the Committee of EC Member State representatives]* after consulting the country which transmitted the application, taking account of traditional and fair usage and the actual risk of confusion on Community territory. If the decision is to proceed with registration the name shall be entered in the *[Register]* and published ...

4. If the Commission receives no statement of objection it shall enter the name(s) in question in the *[Register]* and publish the name(s) ...

N. RIGHT OF OBJECTION TO THE PROPOSED REGISTRATION OF AN EC-DEFINED GI RELATING TO THE TERRITORY OF ANOTHER WTO MEMBER

47. Article 12b.2 was inserted in Regulation No. 2081/92#3 to provide that, within six months of the date of publication of an application for registration of an EC-defined GI relating to a geographical location in the territory of another WTO Member, any natural or legal person from an EC Member State or a WTO Member with a legitimate interest may object to the application. Where the objection comes from another WTO Member, "Article 12d ... shall apply."

48. Article 12d of Regulation No. 2081/92#3 provides in relevant part: "any natural or legal person that has a legitimate interest and is from a WTO member country or a third country recognised under the procedure provided for in Article 12(3) may object to the proposed registration by sending a duly substantiated statement to the country in which it resides or is established, which shall transmit it ... to the Commission."

O. GROUNDS OF OBJECTION TO THE PROPOSED REGISTRATION OF AN EC-DEFINED GI RELATING TO THE TERRITORY OF ANOTHER WTO MEMBER

49. Under Articles 12b and 7.4 of Regulation No. 2081/92#3 read together, the grounds of objection to the registration of an EC-defined GI relating to a geographical location in the territory of another WTO Member are the same whether the objection comes from an EC Member State or another WTO Member: "[a] statement of objection shall be admissible only if it: either shows non-compliance with the definition *[of an EC-defined GI]*, shows that the registration of the name proposed would jeopardize the existence of an entirely or partly identical name or of a mark or the existence of products which are legally on the market for at least five years preceding the date of publication *[inviting objections]*, or indicates the features which demonstrate that the name whose registration is applied for is generic in nature." The criteria must be demonstrated with regard to EC territory.

P. RIGHT OF OBJECTION BY NON-EC NATIONALS TO THE PROPOSED REGISTRATION OF AN EC-DEFINED GI FROM WITHIN THE EC

50. Article 12d.1 was inserted in Regulation No. 2081/92#3 to provide: "[w]ithin six months of the date of *[publication of an application for registration of a "name" from within the EC]*, any natural or legal person that has a legitimate interest and is from a WTO member country or a third country recognised under the procedure provided for in Article 12(3) may object to the proposed registration ...."

Q. GROUNDS OF OBJECTION BY NON-EC NATIONALS TO THE PROPOSED REGISTRATION OF AN EC-DEFINED GI FROM WITHIN THE EC

51. Under Articles 12d.2 and 7.4 of Regulation No. 2081/92#3 read together: "[a] statement of objection shall be admissible only if it: either shows non-compliance with the definition *[of an EC-defined GI]*, shows that the registration of the name proposed would jeopardise the existence of an entirely or partly identical name or of a mark or the existence of products which are legally on the market for at least five years preceding the date of publication *[inviting objections]*, or indicates the features which demonstrate that the name whose registration is applied for is generic in nature." The criteria must be demonstrated with regard to EC territory.

R. PROCESS OF OBJECTION BY OTHER WTO MEMBER NATIONALS TO THE REGISTRATION OF AN EC-DEFINED GI FROM WITHIN THE EC OR FROM ANOTHER WTO MEMBER OR THIRD COUNTRY

52. Under Articles 12b.2 and 12d.1 of Regulation No. 2081/92#3 read together, a person "from a WTO Member country or a third country recognised under the procedure provided for in Article 12(3)" with a legitimate interest may object to the proposed registration of an EC-defined GI—whether concerning a geographical locality within an EC Member State, another WTO Member or a third country—"by sending a duly substantiated statement to the country in which it resides or is established, which shall transmit it ... to the Commission."

S. THE RELATIONSHIP BETWEEN EC-DEFINED GIS AND TRADEMARKS

53. Article 14 of Regulation No. 2081/92#1 provided in relevant part:

> 1. Where a designation of origin or geographical indication is registered in accordance with this Regulation, the application for registration of a trade mark corresponding to one of the situations *[against which an EC-defined GI is protected]*[24] and relating to the same type of product shall be refused, provided that the application for registration of the trade mark was submitted after the date of the publication *[of the application for registration of the "name"]*.
>
> Trademarks registered in breach of the first subparagraph shall be declared invalid.
>
> This paragraph shall also apply where the application for registration of a trademark was lodged before the date of publication of the application for registration *[of the "name"]*, provided that that publication occurred before the trademark was registered.
>
> 2. With due regard for Community law, use of a trade mark corresponding to one of the situations *[against which an EC-defined GI is protected]* which was registered in good faith before the date on which application for registration of a designation of origin or geographical indication was lodged may continue notwithstanding the registration of a designation of origin or geographical indication, where there are no grounds for invalidity or revocation of the trade mark ....

---

[24] See paragraph 24 above.

54. Preambular clause (11) to Regulation No. 692/2003 states:

> Article 24(5) of the TRIPS Agreement applies not only to trademarks registered or applied for but also those to which rights have been acquired through use before a specified date, notably that of protection of the name in the country of origin *[sic]*. Article 14(2) *[of the Regulation]* should therefore be amended: the reference date now specified should be changed to the date of protection in the country of origin or of submission of the application for registration of the geographical indication or designation of origin, depending on whether the name falls under Article 17 or the *[sic]* Article 5 ...; also, in Article 14(1) ... the reference date should become the date of application instead of the date of first publication.

55. Thus, Article 14.1 is amended in Regulation No. 2081/92#3 so that, where a proposed trademark corresponds to one of the situations against which an EC-defined GI is protected for the same type of product, the reference date for the determination of whether that trademark may be registered becomes the date of application to the Commission for the registration of an EC-defined GI rather than the date of first publication by the Commission.

56. Article 14.2 is amended in Regulation No. 2081/92#3 to provide as follows:

> With due regard to Community law, a trademark the use of which engenders one of the situations indicated in Article 13 and which has been applied for, registered, or established by use, if that possibility is provided for by the legislation concerned, in good faith within the territory of the Community, before either the date of protection in the country of origin or the date of submission to the Commission of the application for registration of the designation of origin or geographical indication may continue to be used notwithstanding the registration of a designation of origin or geographical indication, provided that no grounds for its invalidity or revocation exist as specified by Council Directive 89/104/EEC of 21 December 1988 to approximate the laws of the Member States relating to trade marks[...] and/or Council Regulation (EC) No 40/94 of 20 December 1993 on the Community trade mark[...].

T. TRADEMARKS OF REPUTATION AND RENOWN

57. Under Article 14.3, "*[an EC-defined GI]* shall not be registered where, in the light of a trademark's reputation and renown and the length of time it has been used, registration is liable to mislead the consumer as to the true identity of the product."

U. THE COMMITTEE OF EC MEMBER STATE REPRESENTATIVES

58. Under Article 15 of Regulation No. 2081/92, the Commission is to be assisted by a committee composed of the representatives of the EC Member States and chaired by the representative of the Commission. The Commission representative is to submit a draft of the measures to be taken. The committee is to deliver its opinion on the draft by weighted majority voting, and the chair may not vote. The Commission shall adopt the measures envisaged if the measures accord with the committee's opinion. If the measures do not accord with the committee's opinion, or if the committee does not deliver an opinion, the Commission is to submit a proposal to the Ministerial Council, which shall act by a qualified majority. If the Ministerial Council does not act within three months of the Commission submitting a proposal, the Commission shall adopt the proposed measure.[25]

---

[25] Article 15 of Regulation No. 2081/92#1 was amended by Regulation No. 806/2003 of 14 April 2003. See paragraph 19 above. The amendments to Article 15 introduced by Regulation No. 806/2003 do not affect Australia's claims and arguments in this dispute.

V. TRANSITIONAL NATIONAL PROTECTION

59. Under Article 5.5 of Regulation No. 2081/92#2, an EC Member State may grant transitional national "protection in the sense of the present Regulation" to a proposed EC-defined GI. "Such transitional national protection shall cease on the date on which a decision on registration under this Regulation is taken."

IV. SUMMARY OF AUSTRALIA'S LEGAL CLAIMS

60. The EC measure diminishes the legal protection for trademarks under the *TRIPS Agreement*, as it:

- prejudices the eligibility of an application for registration of a trademark, contrary to TRIPS Article 24.5;
- does not grant to the owner of a registered trademark the exclusive right to prevent all third parties not having the owner's consent from using in the course of trade identical or similar signs for goods which are identical or similar to those in respect of which the trademark is registered where such use would result in a likelihood of confusion, contrary to TRIPS Article 16.1;
- does not presume a likelihood of confusion in case of use of an identical sign for identical goods, contrary to TRIPS Article 16.1;
- unjustifiably encumbers the use of a trademark in the course of trade with special requirements, contrary to TRIPS Article 20;
- does not assure to WTO Member nationals effective protection against unfair competition, contrary to Paris Article 10*bis*(1);
- does not assure to WTO Member nationals appropriate effective legal remedies to repress acts of unfair competition, contrary to Paris Article 10*ter*(1);
- does not make available to trademark right holders civil judicial procedures concerning the enforcement of their intellectual property rights, contrary to TRIPS Article 42;
- makes available procedures concerning the enforcement of trademark rights which are not fair and equitable, and which are unnecessarily complicated and entail unwarranted delays, contrary to TRIPS Article 41.2;
- does not ensure that decisions on the registration of an EC-defined GI are based only on evidence in respect of which trademark right holders were offered the opportunity to be heard, contrary to TRIPS Article 41.3; and
- does not ensure the availability under its law of enforcement procedures as specified in Part III of the *TRIPS Agreement* so as to permit effective action against any act of infringement of trademark rights, contrary to TRIPS Article 41.1.

61. The EC measure does not provide at Community level the legal means for interested parties to prevent misleading use of an EC-defined GI or use which constitutes an act of unfair competition in relation to a trademark, contrary to TRIPS Article 22.2.

62. The EC measure does not accord national treatment to the products of other WTO Members, contrary to GATT Article III:4 as well as TBT Article 2.1, or in the protection of intellectual property, contrary to TRIPS Article 2.1, incorporating by reference Paris Article 2, and TRIPS Article 3.1.

63. The EC measure is more trade restrictive than necessary to fulfil a legitimate objective, taking account of the risks non-fulfilment would create, contrary to TBT Article 2.2.

64. As a consequence, the EC:

- has not complied with Paris Articles 10*bis* and 10*ter*, contrary to TRIPS Article 2.1;
- has not given effect to the provisions of the *TRIPS Agreement*, contrary to TRIPS Article 1.1; and
- has not ensured the conformity of its laws, regulations and administrative procedures with its obligations as provided in the annexed Agreements, contrary to Article XVI:4 of the *WTO Agreement*.

65. Australia reserves the right to pursue its claim that the EC measure does not accord immediately and unconditionally to the nationals and/or products of each WTO Member any advantage, favour, privilege or immunity granted to the nationals and/or products of any other WTO Member, contrary to TRIPS Article 4, GATT Article I:1 and/or TBT Article 2.1, in the event that:

- the EC is applying Community-wide protection to EC-defined GIs for foodstuffs and agricultural products from another WTO Member; or
- the EC begins to apply Community-wide protection to EC-defined GIs for foodstuffs and agricultural products from another WTO Member.

66. Similarly, Australia reserves the right to pursue its claim that the EC measure is not applied in a transparent manner, contrary to TRIPS Articles 63.1 and 63.3, should the EC in fact have in place criteria and/or guidelines for the purposes of making assessments and/or determinations under various provisions of Regulation No. 2081/92.

V. PRELIMINARY ISSUES

A. AN EC-DEFINED GI IS GENERALLY A TRIPS-DEFINED GI WITHIN THE MEANING OF ARTICLE 22.1 OF THE TRIPS AGREEMENT

67. Article 22.1 of the *TRIPS Agreement* defines geographical indications for the purposes of the *TRIPS Agreement* as "indications which identify a good as originating in the territory of a Member, or a region or locality in that territory, where a given quality, reputation or other characteristic of the good is essentially attributable to its geographical origin."

68. A "designation of origin" under Regulation No. 2081/92 must be an actual geographic name used to describe an agricultural product or foodstuff, which must originate in the place identified by the geographic name. The quality or characteristics of the agricultural product or foodstuff must be essentially or exclusively due to a particular geographical environment, and the production, processing and preparation of the agricultural product or foodstuff must occur in the place identified by the geographic name.

69. A "geographical indication" under Regulation No. 2081/92 must be an actual geographic name used to describe an agricultural product or foodstuff, which must originate in the place identified by the geographic name. A specific quality, reputation or other characteristics must be attributable to that geographical origin, and production, processing and/or preparation of the agricultural product or foodstuff must occur in the place identified by that geographic name.

70. Thus, both a "designation of origin" and a "geographical indication," as these are defined by Regulation No. 2081/92, would normally fall within the definition of a "geographical indication" set out in TRIPS Article 22.1. Each constitutes at a minimum an indication "which identif*[ies]* a good as originating in the territory of a Member, or a region or locality in that territory, where a given quality, reputation or other characteristic is essentially attributable to its geographical origin."

VI. THE EC MEASURE IS INCONSISTENT WITH ARTICLES 1.1, 2.1 (INCORPORATING ARTICLES 10BIS AND 10TER OF THE PARIS CONVENTION (1967)), 16.1, 20, 24.5, 41 AND/OR 42 OF THE TRIPS AGREEMENT

A. THE RELEVANT REQUIREMENTS OF THE TRIPS AGREEMENT AND OF THE PARIS CONVENTION

(i) Article 16.1 of the TRIPS Agreement

71. TRIPS Article 16.1[26] expressly affords to the owner of a registered trademark an exclusive right, that is, a right not possessed or enjoyed by anyone else, to stop or impede all third parties not having the owner's consent from using that sign: (1) in the course of trade; (2) in respect of identical or similar signs for goods or services identical or similar to those in respect of which the trademark is registered; and (3) where such use would likely be confusing. Further, in case of use of an identical sign for identical goods, Article 16.1 provides that a likelihood of confusion is to be presumed.

72. The exclusive right to be granted to the owner of a registered trademark is qualified by TRIPS Article 17[27], which allows any WTO Member to provide limited[28] exceptions to the rights conferred by a trademark. The provision cites fair use of descriptive terms to illustrate possible exceptions, and also requires that such exceptions take account of the legitimate interests of the trademark owner and of third parties. One commentator has said: "[f]air use of descriptive terms might include indications for the purpose of mere identification or information, such as bona fide use of a person's name, address or pseudonym, or a geographical name, or an exact indication concerning ... origin ...."[29]

(ii) Article 20 of the TRIPS Agreement

73. TRIPS Article 20[30] establishes that no WTO Member may, unjustifiably, impede or restrain use of a trademark in the course of trade by special requirements and provides illustrative examples of such special requirements: use with another trademark; use in a special form; or use in a manner detrimental to the trademark's capacity to distinguish the goods or services of one undertaking from those of other undertakings. Thus, if any WTO Member imposes special requirements on the use of a trademark in the course of trade, those special requirements must be justifiable.

---

[26] Article 16.1 of the *TRIPS Agreement* provides as follows:
The owner of a registered trademark shall have the exclusive right to prevent all third parties not having the owner's consent from using in the course of trade identical or similar signs for goods or services which are identical or similar to those in respect of which the trademark is registered where such use would result in a likelihood of confusion. In case of the use of an identical sign for identical goods or services, a likelihood of confusion shall be presumed. The rights described above shall not prejudice any existing prior rights, nor shall they affect the possibility of Members making rights available on the basis of use.

[27] Article 17 of the *TRIPS Agreement* provides as follows:
Members may provide limited exceptions to the rights conferred by a trademark, such as fair use of descriptive terms, provided that such exceptions take account of the legitimate interests of the owner of the trademark and of third parties.

[28] *OED*, Vol. 1, page 1592, defines "limited" as "fixed," "confined within definite limits" or "restricted in scope."

[29] *Gervais*, page 112.

[30] Article 20 of the *TRIPS Agreement* provides as follows:
The use of a trademark in the course of trade shall not be unjustifiably encumbered by special requirements, such as use with another trademark, use in a special form or use in a manner detrimental to its capability to distinguish the goods or services of one undertaking from those of other undertakings. This will not preclude a requirement prescribing the use of the trademark identifying the undertaking producing the goods or services along with, but without linking it to, the trademark distinguishing the specific goods or services in question of that undertaking.

(iii) Article 24.5 of the TRIPS Agreement

74. TRIPS Article 24.5[31] defines the boundaries of the range of possible actions open to a WTO Member to implement measures relating to TRIPS-defined GIs in relation to trademarks. TRIPS Article 24.5 provides in relevant part that:

- measures adopted to implement Section 3 of Part II of the *TRIPS Agreement* cannot adversely affect the entitlement of an application made in good faith for the registration of a trademark on the basis that the trademark is identical with, or similar to, a TRIPS-defined GI;

- measures adopted to implement Section 3 of Part II of the *TRIPS Agreement* cannot adversely affect the legality of a trademark registered in good faith on the basis that the trademark is identical with, or similar to, a TRIPS-defined GI; and

- measures adopted to implement Section 3 of Part II of the *TRIPS Agreement* cannot adversely affect the right to use a trademark to which rights have been acquired through use on the basis that the trademark is identical with, or similar to, a TRIPS-defined GI.

(iv) Article 10bis of the Paris Convention

75. Under Paris Article 10*bis*(1)[32] as incorporated by TRIPS Article 2.1, a WTO Member is obliged "to assure to nationals of *[WTO Members]* effective protection against unfair competition." Paris Article 10*bis*(2) defines an act of unfair competition as "[a]ny act of competition contrary to honest practices in industrial or commercial matters." The reference to "honest practices" includes practices established in international trade.[33]

---

[31] Article 24.5 of the *TRIPS Agreement* provides as follows:

Where a trademark has been applied for or registered in good faith, or where rights to a trademark have been acquired through use in good faith either:

(a) before the date of application of these provisions in that Member as defined Part VI: or

(b) before the geographical indication is protected in its country of origin;

measures adopted to implement this Section shall not prejudice eligibility for or the validity of the registration of a trademark, or the right to use a trademark, on the basis that such a trademark is identical with, or similar to, a geographical indication.

[32] Article 10*bis* of the Paris Convention provides as follows:

(1) The countries of the Union are bound to assure to nationals of such countries effective protection against unfair competition.

(2) Any act of competition contrary to honest practices in industrial or commercial matters constitutes an act of unfair competition.

(3) The following in particular shall be prohibited:

1. all acts of such a nature as to create confusion by any means whatever with the establishment, the goods, or the industrial or commercial activities, of a competitor;

2. false allegations in the course of trade of such a nature as to discredit the establishment, the goods, or the industrial or commercial activities, of a competitor;

3. indications or allegations the use of which in the course of trade is liable to mislead the public as to the nature, the manufacturing process, the characteristics, the suitability for their purpose, or the quantity, of the goods.

[33] *Bodenhausen*, page 144, states: "[t]his criterion is not limited to honest practices existing in the country where protection against unfair competition is sought. The judicial or administrative authorities of such country will therefore also have to take into account honest practices established in international trade."

(v) Article 10ter of the Paris Convention

76. Under Paris Article 10*ter*[34] as incorporated by TRIPS Article 2.1, a WTO Member is required "to assure to nationals of *[WTO Members]* appropriate legal remedies effectively to repress all the acts referred to in *[Paris Article 10bis]*."

(vi) Article 41 of the TRIPS Agreement

77. TRIPS Article 41[35] establishes general obligations for WTO Members in matters concerning the enforcement of intellectual property rights "so as to permit effective action against any act of infringement of intellectual property rights covered by this Agreement ...." These general obligations include, pursuant to TRIPS Article 41.1, to have available to right holders enforcement procedures as set out in Part III of the *TRIPS Agreement*, including civil judicial procedures concerning the enforcement of intellectual property rights, expeditious remedies to prevent infringements, and remedies which constitute a deterrent to further infringements. Pursuant to TRIPS Article 41.2, such procedures are to be fair and equitable, may not be unnecessarily complicated or costly and may not entail unreasonable time limits or unwarranted delays. Pursuant to TRIPS Article 41.3, decisions on the merits of a case are to be based only on evidence in respect of which parties to the proceeding were offered the opportunity to be heard. Pursuant to TRIPS Article 41.4, parties to a proceeding are to have an opportunity for review by a judicial authority of at least the legal aspects of initial judicial decisions on the merits of a case.

---

[34] Article 10*ter* of the Paris Convention provides as follows:

(1) The countries of the Union undertake to assure to nationals of other countries of the Union appropriate legal remedies effectively to repress all the acts referred to in Articles 9, 10, and 10bis.

(2) They undertake, further, to provide measures to permit federations and associations representing interested industrialists, producers, or merchants, provided that the existence of such federations and associations is not contrary to the laws of their countries, to take action in the courts or before the administrative authorities, with a view to the repression of the acts referred to in Article 9, 10, and 10bis, in so far as the law of the country in which protection is claimed allows such action by federations and associations of that country.

[35] Article 41 of the *TRIPS Agreement* provides as follows:

1. Members shall ensure that enforcement procedures as specified in this Part are available under their law so as to permit effective action against any act of infringement of intellectual property rights covered by this Agreement, including expeditious remedies to prevent infringements and remedies which constitute a deterrent to further infringements. These procedures shall be applied in such a manner as to avoid the creation of barriers to legitimate trade and to provide for safeguards against their abuse.

2. Procedures concerning the enforcement of intellectual property rights shall be fair and equitable. They shall not be unnecessarily complicated or costly, or entail unreasonable time-limits or unwarranted delays.

3. Decisions on the merits of a case shall preferably be in writing and reasoned. They shall be made available at least to the parties to the proceeding without undue delay. Decisions on the merits of a case shall be based only on evidence in respect of which parties were offered the opportunity to be heard.

4. Parties to a proceeding shall have an opportunity for review by a judicial authority of final administrative decisions and, subject to jurisdictional provisions in a Member's law concerning the importance of a case, of at least the legal aspects of initial judicial decisions on the merits of a case. However, there shall be no obligation to provide an opportunity for review of acquittals in criminal cases.

5. It is understood that this Part does not create any obligation to put in place a judicial system for the enforcement of intellectual property rights distinct from that for the enforcement of law in general, nor does it affect the capacity of Members to enforce their law in general. Nothing in this Part creates any obligation with respect to the distribution of resources as between enforcement of intellectual property rights and the enforcement of law in general.

(vii) Article 42 of the TRIPS Agreement

78. TRIPS Article 42[36] obliges WTO Members to make available to right holders "civil judicial procedures" for matters touching on or relating to the enforcement of any intellectual property right covered by the Agreement. Having regard to the ordinary meaning of the words in context, TRIPS Article 42 requires a WTO Member to make available court or other legal processes: in particular, such procedures may not be political.[37] In addition, TRIPS Article 42 expressly provides for certain rights which are to be granted to right holders under such judicial procedures, such as representation by independent legal counsel, and to substantiate their claims and to present relevant evidence.

(viii) Articles 1.1 and 2.1 of the TRIPS Agreement

79. TRIPS Article 1.1[38] obliges WTO Members to give effect to the provisions of the Agreement. It provides that Members may introduce more extensive protection for intellectual property than required by the Agreement, but only if that more extensive protection does not otherwise conflict with or infringe any provisions of the Agreement.

80. TRIPS Article 2.1[39] obliges WTO Members to comply with Articles 1 through 12, and Article 19, of the Paris Convention (1967).

B. THE EC MEASURE PREJUDICES THE ELIGIBILITY OF AN APPLICATION FOR REGISTRATION OF A TRADEMARK, CONTRARY TO ARTICLE 24.5 OF THE TRIPS AGREEMENT

81. Article 14.1 of Regulation No. 2081/92#1 required that, where an EC-defined GI was registered, an application for registration of a trademark for the same type of product as that bearing the EC-defined GI corresponding to a situation against which a registered EC-defined GI was protected under the Regulation was to be refused (or a subsequent trademark registration invalidated) if:

- the application for registration of the trademark was lodged after the date of first publication by the Commission of the application for registration of the EC-defined GI; or

- the application for registration of the trademark was lodged before the date of first publication by the Commission of the application for registration of the EC-defined GI but that publication occurred before the trademark was registered.

82. Article 14.1 of Regulation No. 2081/92#3 requires that, where an application for registration of a trademark for the same type of product as a registered EC-defined GI corresponds to a situation against which a

---

36 Article 42 of the *TRIPS Agreement* provides as follows:
Members shall make available to right holders[footnote omitted] civil judicial procedures concerning the enforcement of any intellectual property right covered by this Agreement. Defendants shall have the right to written notice which is timely and contains sufficient detail, including the basis of the claims. Parties shall be allowed to be represented by independent legal counsel, and procedures shall not impose overly burdensome requirements concerning mandatory personal appearances. All parties to such procedures shall be duly entitled to substantiate their claims and to present all relevant evidence. The procedure shall provide a means to identify and protect confidential information, unless this would be contrary to existing constitutional requirements.

37 *OED*, Vol.1, page 408, defines "civil" in relevant part as: "9. Of law, a legal process, etc.: not criminal, political, or (formerly) ecclesiastical; relating to private relations between members of a community."

38 Article 1.1 of the *TRIPS Agreement* provides as follows:
Members shall give effect to the provisions of this Agreement. Members may, but shall not be obliged to, implement in their law more extensive protection than is required by this Agreement, provided that such protection does not contravene the provisions of this Agreement. Members shall be free to determine the appropriate method of implementing the provisions of this Agreement within their own legal system and practice.

39 Article 2.1 of the *TRIPS Agreement* provides as follows:
In respect of Parts II, III and IV of this Agreement, Members shall comply with Articles 1 through 12, and Article 19, of the Paris Convention (1967).

registered EC-defined GI is protected under the Regulation, that application is to be refused (or a subsequent registration invalidated) if that application is made after an application for registration of an EC-defined GI has been lodged with the Commission. The date an application for registration of an EC-defined GI is lodged with the Commission thus became in all circumstances the decisive date for determining whether a trademark for the same type of product which involves a situation against which a registered EC-defined GI is protected may be registered.

83. Regulation Nos 2081/92#1 and 2081/92#3 are "measures adopted to implement this Section" within the meaning of TRIPS Article 24.5, establishing a regime for the protection of GIs as contemplated by Section 3 of Part II of the *TRIPS Agreement.*

84. Further, Article 14.1 of Regulation Nos 2081/92#1 and 2081/92#3 applies to a situation in which an application for registration of a trademark concerns the same type of product for which an EC-defined GI is later registered and use of the trademark will give rise to a situation against which an EC-defined GI is otherwise protected under Article 13.1 of the Regulation. Under Article 13.1, an EC-defined GI is protected, *inter alia*, against "any … commercial use of a name registered in respect of products not covered by the registration in so far as those products are comparable to the products registered under that name …." Thus, the situations against which products bearing a registered EC-defined GI are protected include situations in which the trademark being applied for is identical with, or similar to, a TRIPS-defined GI within the meaning of TRIPS Article 24.5.

85. However, Paris Article 4, and in particular paragraph B of that provision,[40] incorporated by TRIPS Article 2.1, requires that a WTO Member afford a right of priority of six months in respect of an application for registration of a trademark for which an application for registration had previously been filed in another WTO Member. Thus, having regard to the provisions of Paris Article 4, where a trademark has been applied for in another WTO Member and an application for registration of that trademark within the EC is made consistently with the provisions of Paris Article 4, the later registration by the EC of an EC-defined GI cannot by itself constitute a basis for refusing that application for—or invalidating—the registration of a trademark. Such a trademark application or registration can only be refused or invalidated for other valid reasons consistent with the EC's domestic legislation and relevant WTO obligations, for example, because use of that trademark in the EC market would be misleading.

86. Article 14.1 of Regulation No. 2081/92#1 did not afford the right of priority in respect of an application for registration of a trademark previously filed in another WTO Member required to be granted by Paris Article 4 where that trademark is identical with or similar to an EC-defined GI which is later registered. By not doing so, Article 14.1 of Regulation No. 2081/92#1 prejudiced, or adversely affected,[41] the eligibility for registration of a trademark for which an application had been made in good faith, contrary to TRIPS Article 24.5.

87. Similarly, Article 14.1 of Regulation No. 2081/92#3 does not afford the right of priority in respect of an application for registration of a trademark previously filed in another WTO Member required to be granted

[40] Article 4 of the Paris Convention (1967) provides in relevant part:

A.— (1) Any person who has duly filed an application … for the registration … of a trademark, in one *[WTO Member]* … shall enjoy, for the purpose of filing in *[other WTO Members]*, a right of priority during the periods hereinafter fixed.

…

B.— Consequently, any subsequent filing in any of the other *[WTO Members]* before the expiration of the periods referred to above shall not be invalidated by reason of any acts accomplished in the interval, in particular, another filing … or the use of the mark, and such acts cannot give rise to any third-party right or any right of personal possession. Rights acquired by third parties before the date of the first application that serves as the basis for the right of priority are reserved in accordance with the domestic legislation of each *[WTO Member]*.

C.—(1) The periods of priority referred to above shall be … six months for … trademarks.

(2) These periods shall start from the date of filing of the first application; …

…

[41] *OED*, Vol. II, p.2333. In the context of its usage in Article 24.5, "prejudice" is defined as "affect adversely or unfavourably; injure or impair the validity of (a right, claim, etc)."

by Paris Article 4 where that trademark is identical with or similar to an EC-defined GI which is later registered. By not doing so, Article 14.1 of Regulation No. 2081/92#3 continues to prejudice, or adversely affect, the eligibility for registration of a trademark for which an application has been made in good faith, contrary to TRIPS Article 24.5.

C. THE EC MEASURE DOES NOT GRANT THE OWNER OF A REGISTERED TRADEMARK THE RIGHTS REQUIRED TO BE GRANTED BY ARTICLE 16.1 OF THE TRIPS AGREEMENT

(i) The EC measure does not provide for an objection from the owner of a registered trademark to be admissible in the event of a likelihood of confusion between a registered trademark and a proposed EC-defined GI, contrary to Article 16.1 of the TRIPS Agreement

88. TRIPS Article 16.1 sets out the minimum right required to be conferred on the owner of a registered trademark: the exclusive right to prevent all third parties not having the owner's consent from using in the course of trade identical or similar signs for goods or services which are identical or similar to those in respect of which the trademark is registered where such use would result in a likelihood of confusion. TRIPS Article 16.1 also expressly provides a presumption of a likelihood of confusion in case of use of an identical sign for identical goods or services. Yet that right can only be exercised when the owner of a registered trademark has a means through which to pursue it.

89. Under Article 7.4 of Regulation No. 2081/92#1, a statement of objection to the proposed registration of an EC-defined GI from within the EC "shall be admissible only if it" shows non-compliance with the definition of an EC-defined GI, "shows that the proposed registration of a name would jeopardize the existence of an entirely or partly identical name or trade mark or the existence of products which are legally on the market at the time of publication of this regulation in the *[Official Journal]*," or shows that the proposed name is generic in nature (*emphases added*).

90. Under Article 7.4 of Regulation No. 2081/92#2, which remains in effect, a statement of objection to the proposed registration of an EC-defined GI from within the EC "shall be admissible only if it" shows non-compliance with the definition of an EC-defined GI, "shows that the registration of the name proposed would jeopardize the existence of an entirely or partly identical name or of a mark or the existence of products which have been legally on the market for at least five years preceding the date of publication of *[the application for registration of the name]*," or shows that the proposed name is generic in nature (*emphases added*).

91. In addition, in accordance with Articles 12b.3 and 12d.2 of Regulation No. 2081/92#3, the provisions of Article 7.4 of Regulation No. 2081/92#2 determine the admissibility of statements of objection:

- in respect of applications for the registration of an EC-defined GI relating to a geographical location in the territory of another WTO Member; and
- from nationals of other WTO Members in respect of applications for the registration of EC-defined GIs from within the EC.

However, requiring that the existence of an entirely or partly identical trademark be jeopardised imposes conditions for the enjoyment of rights required to be conferred by the *TRIPS Agreement* not contemplated by or otherwise justified under the *TRIPS Agreement* or any other provision of the *WTO Agreement.*

92. The EC measure does not ensure the admissibility of an objection from the owner of a registered trademark on the grounds that a proposed EC-defined GI would constitute use of an identical or similar sign for identical or similar goods that would result in a likelihood of confusion. As a consequence, the EC measure did not—and does not—provide a right required to be granted to the owner, contrary to TRIPS Article 16.1.

(ii) The EC measure does not provide for a presumption of a likelihood of confusion in the case of use of an identical sign for identical goods, contrary to Article 16.1 of the TRIPS Agreement

93. As noted above,[42] TRIPS Article 16.1 establishes a presumption of a likelihood of confusion in the case of use of an identical sign for identical goods. The EC measure does not implement this presumption, contrary to that provision.

(iii) The EC measure does not ensure – in the event of a likelihood of confusion between a registered trademark and a proposed EC-defined GI – that an objection from the owner of a registered trademark is considered by the Committee of EC Member State representatives, contrary to Article 16.1 of the TRIPS Agreement

94. As well as not ensuring the admissibility of an objection from the owner of a registered trademark seeking to enforce rights required to be conferred under TRIPS Article 16.1,[43] the EC measure does not ensure that an objection from the owner of a registered trademark will be considered by the ultimate decision-maker, being the Committee of EC Member State representatives.

95. The Court of First Instance of the European Court of Justice has found, in respect of Regulation No. 2081/92#1 and 2081/92#2:

> ... Article 7(1) of Regulation No 2081/92 grants only to the Member States the right to raise objections to registration before the Commission. ... [U]nder Article 7(3) ... any legitimately concerned natural or legal person may ... object to the proposed registration ... by sending a ... statement to ... the Member State in which he resides or is established. That provision does not require the Member State concerned to forward to the Commission the objection thus stated to it, but merely to take the necessary measures to consider the objection ...[44]

96. The Court of First Instance further found that the Commission "may not consider an objection communicated to it by any person other than a Member State."[45]

97. These provisions were not amended in Regulation No. 2081/92#3, and the Court's findings concerning the interpretation to be applied to Article 7 of the Regulation remain valid. Thus, the owner of a registered trademark resident or established in an EC Member State must send "a duly substantiated statement to the competent authority of the Member State in which he resides or is established" (Article 7.3). However, as found by the Court, there is no obligation on the EC Member State concerned to forward the statement of objection to the Commission, and the Commission "may not consider an objection communicated to it by any person other than a Member State."

98. In addition, in accordance with Articles 12b.2 and 12d.1 of Regulation No. 2081/92#3, the owner of a registered trademark resident or established in another WTO Member must send "a duly substantiated statement to the country in which it resides or is established, which shall transmit it ... to the Commission." Consistent with the rationale of the findings of the Court of First Instance in the Canard judgment, there is no obligation, nor indeed can there be in such circumstances, on another WTO Member government to forward an objection to the Commission. At the same time, Regulation No. 2081/92#3 does not empower the Commission to consider an objection communicated to it by any person other than an EC Member State, or another WTO Member government or third country meeting the equivalence and reciprocity conditions established by Article 12 of Regulation No. 2081/92#3.

---

[42] See paragraph 88 above.

[43] See paragraph 92 above.

[44] The Canard judgment, Exhibit COMP-12, paragraph 45.

[45] The Canard judgment, Exhibit COMP-12, paragraph 50.

99. Whether an objection is from the owner of a registered trademark who is resident or established in either an EC Member State or another WTO Member, however, that objection must be received by the Commission in order to be considered by the Committee of EC Member State representatives. Ensuring that an objection from the owner of a registered trademark is considered by the ultimate decision maker is essential to such an owner being able to exercise the rights required to be conferred by TRIPS Article 16.1. Yet the EC measure fails to ensure that an objection from the owner of a registered trademark is considered by the Committee of EC Member State representatives. Thus, the EC measure has not granted—and does not grant—the rights required to be granted to such owners by TRIPS Article 16.1, contrary to that provision.

(iv) The EC measure does not grant to the owner of a registered trademark – in the event of a likelihood of confusion between a registered trademark and a proposed EC-defined GI – the exclusive right required to be granted by Article 16.1 of the TRIPS Agreement

100. Article 14.2 of Regulation No. 2081/92#1 provided that a trademark registered in good faith before the date on which an application for registration of an EC-defined GI was lodged and whose use involved one of the situations against which an EC-defined GI was protected under the Regulation could continue to be used "notwithstanding the registration of *[an EC-defined GI]*."

101. Article 14.2 of Regulation No. 2081/92#3 provides that a trademark which has been applied for, registered, or established by use in good faith within the territory of the Community before either the date of protection in the country of origin or the date an application to the Commission for protection of an EC-defined GI and whose use involves one of the situations against which an EC-defined GI is protected under the Regulation can continue to be used "notwithstanding the registration of *[an EC-defined GI]*."

102. The EC measure establishes a presumption of co-existence between an existing trademark and a later registered EC-defined GI. The Regulation presumes co-existence by providing

- for the continued use of a registered trademark (Regulation No. 2081/92#1) or a trademark (Regulation No. 2081/92#3) "notwithstanding the registration of *[an EC-defined GI]*" (Article 14.2); and

- that the only ground to refuse an application for the registration of an EC-defined GI that otherwise complies with the requirements of the Regulation is where, because of a trademark's reputation and renown and the length of time it has been used, consumers are likely to be misled as to the true identity of the product (Article 14.3).

103. However, nothing in the *TRIPS Agreement*—whether in Section 3 of Part II of the Agreement, or elsewhere—justifies a WTO Member's failure to grant to the owner of a registered trademark the exclusive right required to be granted by TRIPS Article 16.1: to prevent all third parties not having that owner's consent from using in the course of trade identical or similar signs for goods which are identical or similar to those in respect of which the trademark is registered where such use would result in a likelihood of confusion.

104. The Appellate Body has previously found that had the negotiators of a covered agreement intended to permit WTO Members to act inconsistently with a provision of another covered agreement, they would have said so explicitly.[46] Australia submits that such reasoning is even more compelling when considered in the context of a single covered agreement. Had the negotiators of the *TRIPS Agreement* intended that the exclusive rights required to be conferred on the owner of a registered trademark under TRIPS Article 16.1 could be negated or otherwise limited by another provision of that same covered agreement, they would have expressly said so. Indeed, the negotiators did precisely that in TRIPS Article 17. It is therefore inconceivable to Australia

[46] *EC – Bananas*, paragraph 157.

that the provision of Section 3 of Part II of the *TRIPS Agreement*—which do not contain any express provisions allowing the exclusive right required to be granted to the owner of a registered trademark under TRIPS Article 16.1 to be negated or otherwise limited—could nevertheless be interpreted in such a way as to permit such negation or other limitation.

105. Together with TRIPS Articles 22.3 and 23.2, TRIPS Article 24.5 defines the boundary between a WTO Member's right to implement measures relating to TRIPS-defined GIs and its obligation to afford protection to trademarks. TRIPS Article 24.5 expressly provides that where a trademark has been registered in good faith, measures adopted to implement Section 3 of Part II of the *TRIPS Agreement* "shall not prejudice ... the validity of the registration of a trademark ... on the basis that such a trademark is identical with, or similar to, a *[TRIPS-defined GI]*." Thus, where a trademark is registered in good faith before measures adopted to implement Section 3 of Part II of the *TRIPS Agreement* that could otherwise have prevented that trademark's registration are in place, the validity of that registration cannot be prejudiced or adversely affected on the basis that it is identical or similar to a TRIPS-defined GI.

106. Further, TRIPS Article 24.5 does not in any way require or permit any negation or other limitation of the exclusive right required to be conferred on the owner of that registered trademark pursuant to TRIPS Article 16.1. The owner's exclusive right to prevent all unauthorised use of identical or similar signs for identical or similar goods that would result in a likelihood of confusion cannot be affected by measures adopted by a WTO Member to implement Section 3 of Part II of the *TRIPS Agreement.*

107. The regime of co-existence established by Article 14.2 of Regulation No. 2081/92 negates or repudiates the exclusive right required to be granted by TRIPS Article 16.1 to the owner of a registered trademark to prevent all unauthorised use of an identical or similar sign for identical or similar goods that would result in a likelihood of confusion. The EC measure is therefore contrary to TRIPS Article 16.1.

D. THE EC MEASURE UNJUSTIFIABLY ENCUMBERS THE USE OF A TRADEMARK IN THE COURSE OF TRADE WITH SPECIAL REQUIREMENTS, CONTRARY TO ARTICLE 20 OF THE TRIPS AGREEMENT

108. Regulation No. 2081/92#1 effectively required co-existence of an existing registered trademark and a later registered EC-defined GI. Similarly, Regulation No. 2081/92#3 effectively requires the co-existence of a trademark—whether registered or established through use—and a later registered EC-defined GI.[47]

109. TRIPS Article 20 provides, in part, that the use of a trademark in the course of trade shall not be unjustifiably encumbered—or burdened without good cause—by special requirements, such as use in a manner detrimental to its capability to distinguish the goods or services of one undertaking from those of other undertakings. In today's world of transboundary markets and marketing, the potential economic value of a trademark which is capable of distinguishing the goods or services of one undertaking from those of other undertakings is greater than ever. Thus, TRIPS Article 20 establishes a requirement that a WTO Member may not without good cause impose conditions on the use of a trademark such that there is a risk of the trademark's distinctiveness, and thus its economic value, being eroded. Further, TRIPS Article 20 applies to both registered and unregistered trademarks.[48]

110. By requiring co-existence of a trademark and a later registered EC-defined GI that consists of or contains an identical or similar sign for identical or similar goods notwithstanding a likelihood of confusion,[49] the EC measure has the effect of diminishing the distinctiveness, and hence the economic value, of an affected trademark. Requiring a trademark to be used in a market place where there exists the use of identical or similar signs for identical or similar goods that would result in a likelihood of confusion (such as a co-existent EC-defined GI) encumbers or burdens the use of a trademark "in a manner detrimental to its capability to

[47] See paragraph 102 above.

[48] See, for example, *Gervais*, page 116.

[49] See paragraph 102 above.

distinguish the goods ... of one undertaking from those of other undertakings" within the meaning of TRIPS Article 20.

111. Moreover, encumbering use of a trademark through a requirement of co-existence or concurrent use with an identical or similar EC-defined GI for identical or similar goods is neither required nor permitted by the provisions of Section 3 of Part II of the *TRIPS Agreement*, and in particular TRIPS Article 24.5. It is thus not justified by good cause within the meaning of TRIPS Article 20.

112. Accordingly, the EC measure unjustifiably encumbers by special requirements use of a trademark in the course of trade in a manner detrimental to its capability to distinguish the goods of one undertaking from those of other undertakings, contrary to TRIPS Article 20.

E. THE EC MEASURE DOES NOT ASSURE EFFECTIVE PROTECTION AGAINST UNFAIR COMPETITION, CONTRARY TO ARTICLE 2.1 OF THE TRIPS AGREEMENT INCORPORATING ARTICLE 10BIS(1) OF THE PARIS CONVENTION (1967)

113. Under Paris Article 10*bis*(1) as incorporated by TRIPS Article 2.1, a WTO Member is obliged to provide to nationals of WTO Members effective protection against unfair competition. Having regard to the broad scope of Paris Article 1(2), the obligation to provide protection against unfair competition under Paris Article 10*bis*(1) must include effective protection of trademarks from acts relating to indications of source as well as effective protection of indications of source from acts relating to trademarks.

114. Regulation No. 2081/92 establishes a Community-wide system of registration and protection of EC-defined GIs that provides effective protection from acts of unfair competition, including in relation to later trademark applications, within the Community. However, the Regulation does not provide a Community-wide system of effective protection of trademarks from acts of unfair competition arising from the later registration of EC-defined GIs under the Regulation.

115. Accordingly, the EC measure is inconsistent with the EC's obligation pursuant to Paris Article 10*bis*(1), as incorporated by TRIPS Article 2.1, to assure to nationals of WTO Members effective protection against unfair competition.

F. THE EC MEASURE DOES NOT ASSURE APPROPRIATE LEGAL REMEDIES TO REPRESS EFFECTIVELY ACTS REFERRED TO IN ARTICLE 10BIS OF THE PARIS CONVENTION (1967), CONTRARY TO ARTICLE 2.1 OF THE TRIPS AGREEMENT INCORPORATING ARTICLE 10TER(1) OF THE PARIS CONVENTION (1967)

116. Paris Article 10*ter*(1) as incorporated by TRIPS Article 2.1 requires that a WTO Member assure to nationals of WTO Members appropriate legal remedies to repress effectively all acts of unfair competition referred to in Paris Article 10*bis*. Those legal remedies include legal remedies to repress acts of unfair competition against trademarks arising from acts involving indications of source.

117. Notwithstanding that Regulation No. 2081/92 establishes a system of Community-wide registration and protection of EC-defined GIs, it does not provide for appropriate legal remedies to repress effectively at a Community-wide level acts of unfair competition, including against trademarks, arising from the registration or the proposed registration of an EC-defined GI.

118. Accordingly, the EC measure is inconsistent with the EC's obligations pursuant to Paris Article 10*ter*(1), as incorporated by TRIPS Article 2.1, to assure to nationals of WTO Members appropriate legal remedies to repress effectively acts of unfair competition referred to in Paris Article 10*bis*.

G. THE EC MEASURE DOES NOT MAKE AVAILABLE TO TRADEMARK RIGHT HOLDERS CIVIL JUDICIAL PROCEDURES CONCERNING THE ENFORCEMENT OF THEIR INTELLECTUAL PROPERTY RIGHTS, CONTRARY TO ARTICLE 42 OF THE TRIPS AGREEMENT

119. The obligation established by TRIPS Article 42 is straightforward. A WTO Member is required to "make available to right holders civil judicial procedures concerning the enforcement of any intellectual property right covered by this Agreement." Having regard to the ordinary meaning of the words, civil judicial procedures are court or other legal processes normally presided over by a judge: they may not be political or administrative processes.[50] Such an interpretation is supported as well by the provisions of TRIPS Articles 43-48, which refer to authorities to be granted to the "judicial authorities."

120. That civil judicial procedures for the enforcement of an intellectual property right covered by the *TRIPS Agreement* are required to be court or other legal processes presided over by a judge is confirmed when considered in light of footnote 4 to TRIPS Article 23.1 concerning TRIPS-defined GIs for wines and spirits. Footnote 4 provides that "[n]otwithstanding the first sentence of Article 42, WTO Members may, with respect to these obligations, instead provide for enforcement by administrative action." Thus, in accordance with footnote 4, WTO Members may enforce intellectual property rights relating to TRIPS-defined GIs for wines and spirits by administrative action. However, by the absence of a qualifying reference in TRIPS Article 42 in the same terms as footnote 4, it is clear that TRIPS Article 42 requires WTO Members to provide for the enforcement of other covered intellectual property rights only through a court or other legal process.

121. In addition, TRIPS Article 42 expressly provides for certain rights to be granted to parties under the civil judicial procedures, such as the right to be represented by independent legal counsel, and to substantiate claims and to present relevant evidence.

122. Regulation No. 2081/92 does not provide to trademark right holders civil judicial procedures at the Community level for the enforcement of their intellectual property rights *vis-à-vis* the registration of EC-defined GIs. The Committee of EC Member State representatives—which decides both applications for the registration of an EC-defined GI and the enforcement of the rights of a trademark owner in relation to a proposed EC-defined GI—consists of officials from EC Member State agencies responsible for implementing Regulation No. 2081/92 at national level. And, if necessary, the enforcement of the rights of a trademark owner in relation to the proposed registration of an EC-defined GI is ultimately decided by EC Member State Ministers responsible for domestic agriculture policies and programs or the Commission's Directorate-General for Agriculture. Further, Article 7.5 of Regulation No. 2081/92 expressly provides that where an objection is admissible, "the Commission shall ask the Member States concerned to seek agreement among themselves ...." None of these processes are civil judicial procedures.

123. That Regulation No. 2081/92 does not provide civil judicial procedures as required was essentially confirmed in the Canard judgment when the Court of First Instance of the European Court of Justice found that "Article 7(1) ... grants only to the Member States the right to raise objections to registration before the Commission" and that the Commission "may not consider an objection communicated to it by any person other than a Member State."[51]

124. Further, even if a trademark right holder is successful in having its objection considered by the Committee of EC Member State representatives,[52] Regulation No. 2081/92 does not provide a right to be

[50] *OED*, Vol.1, defines:
"civil" in relevant part as "Of law, a legal process, etc; not criminal, political, or (formerly) ecclesiastical; relating to private relations between member of a community" (page 408); and
"judicial" in relevant part as "Of or pertaining to proceedings in a court of law; of or pertaining to the administration of justice; resulting from or fixed by a judgement in court. Of law: enforced by secular judges and tribunals" (page 1459).

[51] The findings of the Court of First Instance remain valid as the provisions of Article 7 of Regulation No. 2081/92 on which the Court based its findings were not amended by Regulation No. 2081/92#3. See paragraph 95 above.

[52] See paragraphs 92 and 99 above.

represented by independent legal counsel before that Committee, or a right to substantiate claims or to present relevant evidence.

125. Accordingly, Regulation No. 2081/92 does not make available to trademark right holders civil judicial procedures concerning the enforcement of a covered intellectual property right, or the right to be presented by independent legal counsel, or the right to substantiate their claims or to present relevant evidence, contrary to TRIPS Article 42.

H. THE PROCEDURES CONCERNING THE ENFORCEMENT OF TRADEMARK RIGHTS MADE AVAILABLE BY THE EC MEASURE ARE INCONSISTENT WITH ARTICLE 41.2 OF THE TRIPS AGREEMENT

(i) The EC measure does not make available fair and equitable procedures for the enforcement of intellectual property rights, contrary to Article 41.2 of the TRIPS Agreement

126. TRIPS Article 41.2 requires in relevant part that "[p]rocedures concerning the enforcement of intellectual property rights shall be fair and equitable." Even if the Panel does not accept Australia's claim that the EC measure is inconsistent with TRIPS Article 42 (and instead finds that the EC measure does make available to trademark right holders civil judicial procedures for the enforcement of their rights), Australia submits that the enforcement procedures made available are not fair and equitable.

127. An objection by a trademark right holder resident or established in an EC Member State is first dealt with by the EC Member State agencies responsible for implementing Regulation No. 2081/92 at a national level.[53]

128. Many of those EC Member State agencies are also responsible for making the initial assessment of applications for the proposed registration of an EC-defined GI and for implementing domestic agricultural policies and programs within the EC Member States, of which Regulation No. 2081/92 forms an integral part. Australia submits that EC Member State agencies with either or both such roles are likely to have an interest in supporting and promoting the proposed registration of a geographic term from within that EC Member State as an EC-defined GI.

129. Yet it is with those very EC Member State agencies that a statement of objection from a trademark right holder resident or established in an EC Member State may have to be lodged. Further, the EC measure does not require an EC Member State to forward that statement of objection to the Commission for consideration by the Committee of EC Member State representatives, "but merely to take the necessary measures to consider the objection."[54]

130. Australia submits that requiring or permitting an objection that aims to protect the interests of a trademark right holder to be lodged with an agency that is likely to have an interest in supporting and promoting the registration of an EC-defined GI is a procedure that is neither fair nor equitable.

131. If an EC Member State agency does forward a statement of objection from a trademark right holder to the Commission, it is then considered by the Committee of EC Member State representatives. Yet that Committee comprises delegates of the same EC Member State agencies which are likely to have an interest in supporting and promoting the proposed registration of EC Member State geographic terms as EC defined GIs.

132. Thus, a situation exists in which the enforcement of the rights of a trademark owner in relation to the proposed registration of an EC-defined GI is decided—whether at officials or Ministerial level, or ultimately by the Commission's Directorate-General for Agriculture—by the very Member States and their agencies which:

---

[53] See Exhibit AUS-01 for the full list of EC Member State agencies, downloaded from http://www.europa.eu.int/comm/agriculture/foodqual/protec/national/index_en.htm (last visited 20 April 2004).

[54] See paragraph 95 above.

(1) considered that a proposed geographical name meets the requirements of Regulation No. 2081/92; and (2) must presumably therefore support the application in the Committee of EC Member State representatives. Australia submits that this is a procedure that is neither fair nor equitable within the meaning of TRIPS Article 41.2 insofar as trademark right holders are concerned.

133. In addition, Article 7.5 of Regulation No. 2081/92 expressly provides that where an objection is admissible, "the Commission shall ask the Member States concerned to seek agreement among themselves ..." in the first instance. Australia submits that, at the very least, the possibility of "deal-making" between EC Member States irrespective of the interests of a trademark right holder cannot be excluded in such circumstances. Once again, such process is neither fair nor equitable within the meaning of TRIPS Article 41.2 insofar as trademark right holders are concerned.

134. A trademark right holder who is not resident or established in an EC Member State is in no better situation. Such a trademark right holder must rely upon the goodwill of another WTO Member government, which has no obligation or incentive in the matter, to forward its statement of objection to the Commission. Even if such a trademark right holder's statement of objection is forwarded to the Commission, it faces the generally deficient situation already outlined in respect of statements of objection from trademark right holders resident or established in an EC Member State. In addition, a trademark right holder not resident or established in an EC Member State faces the additional hurdle of not having a national representative on the Committee of EC Member State representatives to speak for its interests.

135. Australia submits that the process for enforcement of a trademark right provided by the EC measure for a right holder not resident or established in an EC Member State is not a fair and equitable procedure. The EC measure requires any objection to be considered by a group of representatives that are likely to have an interest in the registration of the proposed EC-defined GI at issue as well as interests corresponding to the national interests of the EC Member States. In such circumstances, the possibility of bias in favour of both the proposed EC-defined GI and the interests of EC Member States cannot be seen to be excluded. Australia further submits that the possibility of bias against the interests of a trademark right holder is even stronger where an objection concerns a proposed EC-defined GI relating to a geographical location within an EC Member State and the trademark right holder is not an EC national.

136. The process provided by the EC measure for the consideration of the rights of trademark holders resident or established in the EC gives rise to real and significant questions concerning the potential for conflicts of interest in the Committee of EC Member State representatives. The EC measure thus does not provide fair and equitable procedures for the enforcement of trademark right as required by TRIPS Article 41.2.

(ii) The procedures for the enforcement of trademark rights made available by the EC measure are unnecessarily complicated and entail unwarranted delays, contrary to Article 41.2 of the TRIPS Agreement

137. TRIPS Article 41.2 requires in relevant part that procedures for the enforcement of intellectual property right not be unnecessarily complicated or entail unwarranted delays.

138. Even if the EC measure is not considered to be inconsistent with TRIPS Article 42, requiring that statements of objection from trademark right holders be lodged through the competent authority of an EC Member State or through another WTO Member government adds unjustifiable complexity and delay to the process of exercising the rights required to be granted to trademark right holders under the *TRIPS Agreement*. If a trademark has been registered or rights to a trademark have been acquired through use within the territory of the EC, the owner of that trademark has rights within the EC that do not directly concern either an EC Member State government or any other WTO Member government. There is no good reason why another government need be involved, but by doing so the EC measure adds complexity and delay to the process of exercising trademark rights within the EC. Further, in the case of a non-EC national not resident or established in an EC Member State, the very fact of having to make a request to another WTO Member government exacerbates the

complexity and delay associated with exercising a trademark right, even if that government is willing and able to act on behalf of that trademark owner.

139. The preambular provisions of the *TRIPS Agreement* expressly recognise that intellectual property rights are private rights. As such, making the ability of a right holder to exercise or enforce such rights dependent on the willingness and/or ability of an otherwise unconcerned government to act is not supported by good cause and thus cannot be justified.

140. Accordingly, Regulation No. 2081/92 does not make available to trademark right holders procedures for the enforcement of intellectual property rights which are not unnecessarily complicated or entail unwarranted delays, contrary to TRIPS Article 41.2.

I. DECISIONS ON THE REGISTRATION OF EC-DEFINED GIS UNDER THE EC MEASURE ARE NOT BASED ONLY ON EVIDENCE IN RESPECT OF WHICH TRADEMARK RIGHT HOLDERS WERE OFFERED THE OPPORTUNITY TO BE HEARD, CONTRARY TO ARTICLE 41.3 OF THE TRIPS AGREEMENT

141. TRIPS Article 41.3 requires that decisions on the merits of a case "be based only on evidence in respect of which parties were offered the opportunity to be heard."

142. The Court of First Instance of the European Court of Justice has found that, under Regulation No. 2081/92#1 and 2081/92#2, only EC Member States have the right to raise objections to registration before the Commission, and that the Commission "may not consider an objection communicated to it by any person other than a Member State."[55] The Court's decision confirmed that decisions on the registration of EC-defined GIs could be made without the Commission necessarily having to provide to trademark right holders the opportunity to be heard. Further, the Court's findings concerning the meaning of Article 7 of the Regulation remain valid, as the provisions of Article 7 were not amended by Regulation No. 2081/92#3.

143. Regulation No. 2081/92#3 introduced a right of objection for trademark right holders who were resident or established in another WTO Member. However, by requiring pursuant to Articles 12b.2(a) and 12d.1 of the Regulation that such trademark right holders lodge their objections with the government of that other WTO Member, the Regulation does not guarantee to such holders the right to communicate their objections to the Commission. In such circumstances, the EC measure does not guarantee that the Committee of EC Member State representatives makes decisions based only on evidence in respect of which a concerned trademark right holder was offered the opportunity to be heard.

144. Accordingly, because the EC measure does not ensure that:

- a trademark right holder's objections will always be admissible in the event of a likelihood of confusion between a registered trademark and a proposed EC-defined GI;[56] or

- a trademark right holder's objections will be considered by the Committee of EC Member State representatives;[57]

the EC measure does not ensure that decisions on the merits of a case, that is, whether to register an EC-defined GI, are based only on evidence in respect of which any holder of a trademark right in part or all of the territory of the EC was offered the opportunity to be heard, contrary to TRIPS Article 41.3.

---

[55] See paragraph 95 above.

[56] See paragraph 92 above.

[57] See paragraph 99 above.

J. THE EC HAS NOT ENSURED THE AVAILABILITY UNDER ITS LAW OF ENFORCEMENT PROCEDURES AS SPECIFIED IN PART III OF THE TRIPS AGREEMENT SO AS TO PERMIT EFFECTIVE ACTION AGAINST ANY ACT OF INFRINGEMENT OF TRADEMARK RIGHTS AS REQUIRED BY ARTICLE 41.1 OF THAT AGREEMENT

145. TRIPS Article 41.1 requires WTO Members to "ensure that enforcement procedures as specified in this Part are available under their law so as to permit effective action against any act of infringement of intellectual property rights covered by this Agreement, including expeditious remedies to prevent infringements and remedies which constitute a deterrent to further infringements."

146. TRIPS Article 41 is the first provision of Part III of the *TRIPS Agreement* headed "Enforcement of Intellectual Property Rights. Part III comprises five Sections as follows:

- Section 1 "General Obligations:" comprising Article 41 itself;
- Section 2 "Civil and Administrative procedures and Remedies:" comprising
  - Article 42 "Fair and Equitable Procedures,"
  - Article 43 "Evidence,"
  - Article 44 "Injunctions,"
  - Article 45 "Damages,"
  - Article 46 "Other Remedies,"
  - Article 47 "Right of Information,"
  - Article 48 "Indemnification of the Defendant,"
  - Article 49 "Administrative Procedures;"
- Section 3 headed "Provisional Measures:" comprising Article 50;
- Section 4 headed "Special Requirements Related to Border Measures:" comprising
  - Article 51 "Suspension of Release by Customs Authorities,"
  - Article 52 "Application,"
  - Article 53 "Security or Equivalent Assurance,"
  - Article 54 "Notice of Suspension,"
  - Article 55 "Duration of Suspension,"
  - Article 56 "Indemnification of the Importer and of the Owner of the Goods,"
  - Article 57 "Right of Inspection and Information,
  - Article 58 "Ex Officio Action,"
  - Article 59 "Remedies,"

  - Article 60 "De Minimis Imports;"

  and

- Section 5 headed "Criminal Procedures:" comprising Article 61.

147. Thus, TRIPS Article 41.1 establishes an obligation on WTO Members to make available—in respect of any act of infringement of intellectual property rights encompassed by the *TRIPS Agreement*—the enforcement procedures set out in Part III of that Agreement. However, Regulation No. 2081/92 does not make available to right holder civil judicial procedures concerning the enforcement of any intellectual property right covered by this Agreement as required by TRIPS Article 42. Even if the Panel were to consider that the EC measure is consistent with TRIPS Article 42, Regulation No. 2081/92 establishes the Committee of EC Member State representatives as the ultimate decision-making body for the enforcement of trademark rights in the circumstances covered by that Regulation, but does not grant that Committee the authority:

- as required by and consistent with TRIPS Article 43, to order the production of evidence by an opposing party;
- as required by and consistent with TRIPS Article 44, to order a party to desist from an infringement;
- as required by and consistent with TRIPS Article 45, to order an infringer to pay damages to a trademark right holder;
- as required by and consistent with TRIPS Article 46, to order that goods found to be infringing be disposed of outside the channels of commerce; and
- as required by and consistent with TRIPS Article 48, to order indemnification of the defendant.

148. As a consequence of the EC measure's failure:

- to provide fair and equitable procedures for the enforcement of a trademark holder's rights in relation to the registration of an EC-defined GI under the EC measure as required by TRIPS Article 41.2;
- to ensure that procedures for the enforcement of a trademark holder's rights in relation to the registration of an EC-defined GI under the EC measure are not unnecessarily complicated or do not entail unwarranted delays as required by TRIPS Article 41.2;
- to provide that decisions on the merits of a case involving the proposed registration of an EC-defined GI shall be based only on evidence in respect of which any holder of a trademark right in part or all of the territory of the EC was offered the opportunity to be heard as required by TRIPS Article 41.3;
- to make available to trademark right holders civil judicial procedures at the Community level concerning the enforcement of an intellectual property right covered by the *TRIPS Agreement*, as required by TRIPS Article 42;
- to provide to trademark right holders the right to be represented by independent legal counsel in any enforcement proceedings, to substantiate their claims and to present all relevant evidence, as required by TRIPS Article 42;

- to provide to judicial authorities the authority required to be conferred on them by TRIPS Articles 43, 44, 45, 46, 48 and 49 in respect of the enforcement of trademark rights vis-à-vis the proposed registration of an EC-defined GI;

the EC has not ensured that enforcement procedures as specified in Part III of the *TRIPS Agreement* are available under its law so as to permit effective action at the Community level against any act of infringement of intellectual property rights covered by the Agreement, contrary to TRIPS Article 41.1.

K. THE EC MEASURE DIMINISHES THE LEGAL PROTECTION FOR TRADEMARKS IN RESPECT OF DECISIONS BY EC MEMBER STATES TO GRANT TRANSITIONAL NATIONAL PROTECTION, CONTRARY TO ARTICLES 2.1 (INCORPORATING ARTICLES 10BIS(1) AND 10TER(1) OF THE PARIS CONVENTION (1967)), 16.1, 41.1, 41.2, 41.3 AND/OR 42 OF THE TRIPS AGREEMENT

149. In the same way that the EC measure diminishes the legal protection for trademarks under the *TRIPS Agreement* in respect of the registration of EC-defined GIs at Community level, the EC measure diminishes the legal protection for trademarks under the *TRIPS Agreement* in respect of decisions by EC Member States to grant transitional national protection pursuant to Article 5.5 of Regulation No. 2081/92#2.

150. Under Article 5.5 of Regulation No. 2081/92#2, an EC Member State "may, on a transitional basis only, grant on the national level a protection in the sense of the present Regulation" to proposed EC-defined GIs from that Member State. However, while providing for a Member State to grant transitional national protection pending the outcome of the application for registration of an EC-defined GI at the Community level, the Regulation does not ensure that such decisions are made by a Member State with proper regard to the relevant provisions of the *TRIPS Agreement*. As a consequence, the Regulation does not, in respect of such decisions, require a Member State:

- to grant to the owner of a registered trademark the exclusive right to prevent all third parties not having the owner's consent from using in the course of trade identical or similar signs for goods which are identical or similar to those in respect of which the trademark is registered where such use would result in a likelihood of confusion or to establish a presumption of a likelihood of confusion in case of the use of an identical sign for identical goods, contrary to TRIPS Article 16.1;

- to assure effective protection against unfair competition as required by Paris Article 10*bis*(1) or to assure appropriate legal remedies to repress effectively acts of unfair competition as required by Paris Article 10*ter*(1), contrary to TRIPS Article 2.1;

- to make available to trademark right holders civil judicial procedures concerning the enforcement of their intellectual property rights, contrary to TRIPS Article 42;

- to make available fair and equitable procedures for the enforcement of intellectual property rights, contrary to TRIPS Article 41.2;

- to make available procedures for the enforcement of an intellectual property right which are not unnecessarily complicated or which do not entail unwarranted delays, contrary to TRIPS Article 41.2;

- to make decisions on the grant of transitional national protection which are based only on evidence in respect of which parties to a proceeding were offered the opportunity to be heard, contrary to TRIPS Article 41.3; and

- to ensure the availability under EC Member State laws of enforcement procedures as specified in Part III of the *TRIPS Agreement* so as to permit effective action against any act of infringement of intellectual property rights covered by that Agreement, contrary to TRIPS Article 41.1.

L. THE EC HAS NOT GIVEN EFFECT TO THE PROVISIONS OF THE TRIPS AGREEMENT OR COMPLIED WITH THE SPECIFIED PROVISIONS OF THE PARIS CONVENTION (1967), CONTRARY TO ARTICLES 1.1 AND 2.1 OF THE TRIPS AGREEMENT

151. As a consequence of its failure to comply with Paris Articles 10*bis*(1) and 10*ter*(1) in respect of decisions to register EC-defined GIs at the Community level and in respect of decisions by EC Member States to grant transitional national protection, the EC measure is inconsistent with Article 2.1 of the *TRIPS Agreement*.

152. Similarly, as a consequence of the EC measure's inconsistency with Articles 2.1 (incorporating by reference Paris Articles 10*bis*(1) and 10*ter*(1)), 16.1, 20, 24.5, 41.1, 41.2, 41.3 and/or 42 in respect of decisions to register EC-defined GIs at the Community level and in respect of decisions by EC Member States to grant transitional national protection, the EC has failed to give effect to the provisions of the *TRIPS Agreement*, as required by Article 1.1 of that Agreement.

M. CONCLUSION

153. The EC measure establishes a regime for the registration and protection of EC-defined GIs that systematically undermines and/or fails to protect adequately the rights required by the *TRIPS Agreement* to be granted in respect of trademarks. The EC measure diminishes legal protection for trademarks by:

- prejudicing the eligibility of an application for registration of a trademark, contrary to TRIPS Article 24.5;

- not granting to the owner of a registered trademark the rights required to be granted by TRIPS Article 16.1, contrary to that provision;

- not establishing a presumption of likelihood of confusion in the case of use of an identical sign for identical goods, contrary to TRIPS Article 16.1;

- unjustifiably encumbering the use of a trademark in the course of trade with special requirements, contrary to TRIPS Article 20;

- not assuring effective protection against unfair competition as required by Paris Article 10*bis*(1) and not assuring appropriate legal remedies to repress effectively acts referred to in Paris Article 10*bis* as required by Paris Article 10*ter*(1), contrary to TRIPS Article 2.1;

- not making available to trademark right holders civil judicial procedures concerning the enforcement of their intellectual property rights, contrary to TRIPS Article 42;

- not making available fair and equitable procedures for the enforcement of intellectual property rights, contrary to TRIPS Article 41.2;

- making the limited procedures which are available for the enforcement of intellectual property rights unnecessarily complicated and subject to unwarranted delays, contrary to TRIPS Article 41.2;

- making decisions on the registration of EC-defined GIs which are not based only on evidence in respect of which parties to a proceeding were offered the opportunity to be heard, contrary to TRIPS Article 41.3;

- not ensuring the availability under its law of enforcement procedures as specified in Part III of the *TRIPS Agreement* so as to permit effective action against any act of infringement of intellectual property rights covered by that Agreement, contrary to TRIPS Article 41.1;

- not ensuring that EC Member State decisions to grant transitional national protection under Article 5.5 of Regulation No. 2081/92#2 accord with the EC's obligations under TRIPS Articles 2.1 (incorporating Paris Articles 10*bis*(1) and 10*ter*(1)), 16.1, 41.1, 41.2, 41.3 and 42;

- not giving effect to the provisions of the Paris Convention (1967), contrary to TRIPS Article 2.1; and

- not giving effect to the provisions of the *TRIPS Agreement*, contrary to TRIPS Article 1.1.

VII. THE EC MEASURE IS INCONSISTENT WITH ARTICLES 1.1 AND 22.2 OF THE TRIPS AGREEMENT

A. IN RESPECT OF EC-DEFINED GIS, THE EC MEASURE DOES NOT PROVIDE THE LEGAL MEANS FOR INTERESTED PARTIES TO PREVENT MISLEADING USE OR USE WHICH CONSTITUTES UNFAIR COMPETITION, CONTRARY TO ARTICLE 22.2 OF THE TRIPS AGREEMENT

154. Article 22.2[58] of the *TRIPS Agreement* requires a WTO Member to provide, "in respect of geographical indications," that is, "as concerns" [59] TRIPS-defined GIs, legal channels for interested parties to prevent use which misleads the public as to the geographical origin of a good or use which constitutes an act of unfair competition within the meaning of Paris Article 10*bis*. The obligation is not limited to actions to protect TRIPS-defined GIs, but extends to any situation that concerns TRIPS-defined GIs, including a situation involving the proposed registration of an EC-defined GI that potentially constitutes an act of unfair competition within the meaning of Paris Article 10*bis*.

155. Regulation No. 2081/92 establishes a Community-wide regime for the registration and protection of EC-defined GIs. However, the EC measure does not provide—as concerns those same EC-defined GIs—legal channels for interested parties to prevent on a Community-wide basis any use of those EC-defined GIs which would mislead the public as to the geographical origin of a good or any use which would constitute an act of unfair competition within the meaning of Paris Article 10*bis*. The EC measure is thus inconsistent with TRIPS Article 22.2.

B. THE EC HAS NOT GIVEN EFFECT TO THE PROVISIONS OF THE TRIPS AGREEMENT AS REQUIRED BY ARTICLE 1.1 OF THAT AGREEMENT

156. As a consequence of the EC measure's inconsistency with Article 22.2 of the *TRIPS Agreement*, the EC has failed to give effect to the provisions of that Agreement as required by TRIPS Article 1.1.

---

[58] Article 22.2 of the *TRIPS Agreement* provides as follows:
In respect of geographical indications, Members shall provide the legal means for interested parties to prevent:
(a) the use of any means in the designation or presentation of a good that indicates or suggests that the good in question originates in a geographical area other than the true place of origin in a manner which misleads the public as to the geographical origin of the good;
(b) any use which constitutes an act of unfair competition within the meaning of Article 10bis of the Paris Convention (1967).

[59] *OED*, Vol. 2, page 2565.

VIII. THE EC MEASURE IS INCONSISTENT WITH ARTICLE III:4 OF GATT 1994 AND ARTICLES 1.1 AND 1.3, 2.1 (INCORPORATING ARTICLE 2 OF THE PARIS CONVENTION (1967)) AND 3.1 OF THE TRIPS AGREEMENT

A. THE EC MEASURE ACCORDS TO THE PRODUCTS OF ANOTHER WTO MEMBER TREATMENT LESS FAVOURABLE THAN THAT IT ACCORDS TO LIKE PRODUCTS OF NATIONAL ORIGIN, CONTRARY TO ARTICLE III:4 OF GATT 1994

(i) The relevant requirements of Article III:4 of GATT 1994[60]

157. In *Korea – Beef*, the Appellate Body said:

> For a violation of Article III:4 to be established, three elements must be satisfied: that the imported and domestic products at issue are "like products;" that the measure at issue is a "law, regulation, or requirement affecting their internal sale, offering for sale, purchase, transportation, distribution, or use;" and that the imported products are accorded "less favourable" treatment than that accorded to like domestic products.[61]

158. In *EC – Asbestos*, the Appellate Body said:

> ... *[The approach for analyzing "likeness"]* has ... consisted of employing four general criteria in analyzing "likeness:" (i) the properties, nature and quality of the products; (ii) the end-uses of the products; (iii) consumers' tastes and habits—more comprehensively termed consumers' perceptions and behaviour—in respect of the products; and (iv) the tariff classification of the products.[...] ...[62]

159. In *EC – Bananas*, the Appellate Body said:

> ... The ordinary meaning of the word "affecting" implies a measure that has "an effect on," which indicates a broad scope of application. This interpretation is ... reinforced by the conclusions of previous panels that the term "affecting" in the context of Article III of the GATT is wider in scope than such terms as "regulating" or "governing."[...] [63]

160. In *Korea – Beef*, the Appellate Body said: "[w]hether or not imported products are treated 'less favourably' than like domestic products should be assessed ... by examining whether a measure modified the *conditions of competition* in the relevant market to the detriment of imported products"[64] *(emphasis in original)*. Further, in *US – FSC (Article 21.5)*, the Appellate Body said: "[t]he examination of whether a measure involves 'less favourable treatment' of imported products within the meaning of Article III:4 of the GATT 1994 must be grounded in close scrutiny of the 'fundamental thrust and effect of the measure itself'.[...] This examination ... must be founded on a careful analysis of the contested measure and of its implications in the marketplace. At the same time, however, the examination need not be based on the *actual effects* of the contested measure in the marketplace" [65] *(emphasis in original)*.

---

[60] Article III:4 of GATT 1994 provides:
The products of the territory of any contracting party imported into the territory of any other contracting party shall be accorded treatment no less favourable than that accorded to like products of national origin in respect of all laws, regulations and requirements affecting their internal sale, offering for sale, purchase, transportation, distribution or use. ...

[61] *Korea – Beef*, paragraph 133.

[62] *EC – Asbestos*, paragraph 101.

[63] *EC – Bananas*, paragraph 220.

[64] *Korea – Beef*, paragraph 137.

[65] *US – FSC (Article 21.5)*, paragraph 215.

(ii) The EC measure relates to imported and domestically produced "like products" within the meaning of Article III:4 of GATT 1994

161. As set out in Article 1.1 of Regulation No. 2081/92#3, EC-defined GIs may be registered and protected in respect of any: agricultural products intended for human consumption referred to in Annex I to the Treaty establishing the European Community; foodstuffs referred to in Annex I to the Regulation; and other agricultural products referred to in Annex II of the Regulation. From within these products, only wine products and spirit drinks are excluded from the scope of the Regulation (as GI registration and protection for wine products and spirit drinks is provided for under separate legislation). Further, in accordance with Article 12.1, the Regulation "may apply to an agricultural product or foodstuff from a third country ...."

162. However, the products in respect of which an EC-defined GI may be registered remain subject to the provisions of Article III:4 of GATT 1994. Thus, within the meaning of GATT Article III:4, for example: imported apples and pears would be like products to "Savoie" apples and pears; imported oysters would be like products to "Whitstable" oysters; imported olive oils would be like product to the many olive oils for which an EC-defined GI has been registered; and imported trout would be like product with "Black Forest" trout.[66]

(iii) The EC measure is a law affecting the internal sale or offering for sale of imported products which are like products to products of EC origin within the meaning of Article III:4 of GATT 1994

163. Council Regulation No. 2081/92, including as amended, provides the integrated regulatory framework for the measure at issue in this dispute. Pursuant to Article 249 of the Treaty Establishing the European Community, "[a] regulation shall have general application. It shall be binding in its entirety and directly applicable in all Member States."[67] Thus, Regulation No. 2081/92 is a law within the meaning of Article III:4 of GATT 1994.

164. Further, the EC measure affects the internal sale and/or offering for sale of imported products which are like products to domestically produced products within the meaning of GATT Article III:4 in at least two ways. Firstly, if an EC-defined GI from another WTO Member is to benefit within the EC domestic market from the Community-wide protection made available by Regulation No. 2081/92 and/or from the esteem purportedly attached to foodstuffs or agricultural products with an identifiable geographical origin[68], then that EC-defined GI must be registered pursuant to the Regulation. Secondly, imported products being sold or offered for sale within the EC may not bear a registered EC-defined GI—whether from within the EC or from another WTO Member—even where that registered EC-defined GI is the common name for a product in the country of origin and/or in the course of trade.

(iv) EC-defined GIs for imported products are accorded less favourable treatment than EC-defined GIs for like domestic products, contrary to Article III:4 of GATT 1994

165. Article 12.1 of Regulation No. 2081/92#3 provides that the Regulation may apply to an agricultural product or foodstuff from another WTO Member if:

- "the *[WTO Member]* is able to give guarantees identical or equivalent to those referred to in Article 4 *[re product specification]*;"
- "the *[WTO Member]* concerned has inspection arrangements and a right to objection equivalent to those laid down in this Regulation;" and

---

66 See Regulation No. 1107/96 at Exhibit COMP-3.a.

67 A consolidated version of the Treaty is available on the Europa website at http://europa.eu.int/eur-lex/en/treaties/dat/EC_consol.pdf (last visited 21 April 2004).

68 See, for example the preambular paragraphs to Regulation No. 2081/92#1.

- "the *[WTO Member]* concerned is prepared to provide protection equivalent to that available in the Community to corresponding agricultural products for *[sic]* foodstuffs coming from the Community."

166. Article 12.1 of Regulation No. 2081/92#3 sets out a broad requirement for reciprocal protection to the level provided in the EC of any "corresponding" products of EC origin, although the precise meaning of the requirement is not clear to Australia. Australia notes that, in the French version of the Regulation, the reference in the final requirement of Article 12.1 is to "corresponding agricultural products or foodstuffs coming from the Community."[69] Australia assumes that the English version of the Regulation should read "or" instead of "for," having regard to the overall content and context of the Regulation. At the same time, Australia notes that the French version does not clarify the meaning of "corresponding" in relation to "agricultural products or foodstuffs coming from the Community." It is arguable that "corresponding" has a general effect, requiring reciprocal treatment for a wide range of products.

167. Ultimately, however, it is not necessary to determine the precise meaning of "corresponding" agricultural products of foodstuffs in the context of Article 12.1 of Regulation No. 2081/92#3. Having regard to the ordinary meaning of "corresponding"[70] and the context of its use, Australia believes it reasonable to assume that use of the expression "corresponding" products in Article 12.1 of the Regulation encompasses at least "like products" in the sense of GATT Article III:4. Thus, for example, an EC-defined GI from Australia for an apple is only able to be registered and protected under the Regulation if Australia is prepared to provide protection equivalent to that provided in the EC for all EC-defined GIs from within the EC for apples.

168. Thus, Article 12.1 of Regulation No. 2081/92#3 imposes on imported products distinct additional requirements to which domestic like products are not subject. Further, these additional requirements significantly modify the conditions of competition for imported products vis-à-vis domestic like products in the EC market. Unless another WTO Member is willing and able:

- to give identical or equivalent guarantees concerning the product specification;
- to have in place inspection arrangements and a right of objection equivalent to those laid down in the Regulation; and
- to grant protection equivalent protection to that available in the EC to corresponding products from the EC;

EC-defined GIs from that WTO Member are unable to be registered and protected for imported products under Regulation No. 2081/92#3 in the EC market.

169. In *US – Section 211 Appropriations Act*, the Appellate Body cited with approval the statement by the panel in *US – Section 337* that "while the likelihood of having to defend imported products in two fora is small, the existence of the possibility is inherently less favourable than being faced with having to conduct a defence in only one of these fora."[71]

170. Regulation No. 2081/92#3, however, imposes the reality—not just the possibility—of equivalence and reciprocity requirements for the registration and protection of EC-defined GIs for imported products additional

---

[69] The final requirement of Article 12.1 of the French version of Regulation No. 2081/92 reads in relevant part:
que le pays tiers concerné soit disposé à accorder une protection équivalente à celle existant dans la Communauté, aux produits agricoles ou aux denrées alimentaires correspondants provenant de la Communauté.

[70] *OED*, Vol.1, page 517, defines "corresponding" in relevant part as "[t]hat corresponds to something else; analogous, equivalent, proportional."

[71] *US – Section 211 Appropriations Act*, paragraph 263, referring to the panel report in *US – Section 337*, paragraph 5.18-9.

to those faced by like domestic products bearing an EC-defined GI. Using the words of the Appellate Body's findings in *Korea – Beef*,[72] Regulation No. 2081/92 categorically "modifie*[s]* the conditions of competition in the *[EC]* market to the detriment of imported products."

171. Accordingly, Regulation No. 2081/92#3 accords to the products of other WTO Members bearing an EC-defined GI less favourable treatment than that accorded to like domestic products bearing an EC-defined GI, contrary to GATT Article III:4.

(v) An EC-defined GI from another WTO Member may only be registered in the EC in respect of an imported like product if that other WTO Member deems the requirements of Regulation No. 2081/92#3 to be satisfied, thus according less favourable treatment to imported products contrary to Article III:4 of GATT 1994

172. Article 12a.2 of Regulation No. 2081/92#3 provides: "[i]f *[the WTO Member in whose territory the EC-defined GI is located]* deems the requirements of this Regulation to be satisfied it shall transmit the registration application to the Commission ...." Article 12.3 provides that "[t]he Commission shall examine, at the request of the *[WTO Member]* concerned, *[in the Committee of EC Member State representatives]* whether *[the WTO Member]* satisfies the equivalence conditions and offers guarantees within the meaning of paragraph 1 as a result of its national legislation." Articles 12.3 and 12a read together establish a requirement that the other WTO Member in which that EC-defined GI is located "pre-approve" each and every application for registration.

173. Through the operation of Articles 12a.2 and 12.3 read together, Regulation No. 2081/92#3 significantly modifies the conditions of competition for imported products vis-à-vis domestic like products in the EC market.[73] The Regulation imposes on products imported into the EC a distinct and additional requirement that another WTO Member "deems the requirements of *[the Regulation]* to be satisfied" before imported products bearing an EC-defined GI can benefit from Community-wide protection for that EC-defined GI under the Regulation. Again, having regard to the Appellate Body's findings in *US – Section 211 Appropriations Act*,[74] the additional hurdle to the registration of EC-defined GIs from another WTO Member—the requirement that the WTO Member in which the EC-defined GI is located deem that the requirements of Regulation No. 2081/92#3 have been met—is a reality, not just a possibility.

174. Any outward appearance of symmetry of treatment for applications for registration of an EC-defined GI from another WTO Member in fact masks a fundamentally different situation. The EC and its Member States have legally defined rights and obligations in relation to each other and to EC Member State nationals. Few other WTO Member governments have such legally defined relationships affecting the maintenance and enforcement of an intellectual property right expressly recognised as a private right by the *TRIPS Agreement*.

175. Regulation No. 2081/92 thus accords to the products of other WTO Members bearing an EC-defined GI less favourable treatment than that accorded to like domestic products bearing an EC-defined GI, contrary to GATT Article III:4.

(vi) The EC measure as a whole accords less favourable treatment to imported products bearing an EC-defined GI than to like domestic products bearing an EC-defined GI, contrary to GATT Article III:4

176. Regulation No. 2081/92#3 provides an integrated regulatory framework for the registration and protection of EC-defined GIs that systemically accords to imported products bearing an EC-defined GI less favourable treatment than that accorded to like domestic products bearing an EC-defined GI.

---

[72] See paragraph 160 above.

[73] *Korea – Beef*, paragraph 137, see paragraph 160 above.

[74] See paragraph 169 above.

177. From the outset, the registration of EC-defined GIs for imported products is subject to requirements additional to those that apply to the registration of EC-defined GIs for like domestic products. In addition to satisfying the Regulation's requirements concerning product specifications and inspection structures that apply to domestic like products, before imported products may benefit from registration of an EC-defined GI for a geographic location in another WTO Member, their producers and/or importers are subject to and/or must overcome:

- the EC's inability to state clearly what is required by Article 12 of Regulation No. 2081/92#3;
- the EC's inability to state the decision-making criteria that would govern the assessments required to be made under Article 12 of the Regulation;
- another WTO Member's willingness or ability even to consider offering guarantees identical or equivalent to those referred to in Article 4 of the Regulation;
- whether another WTO Member has in place inspection arrangements equivalent to those required by Article 10 of the Regulation;
- the EC's determination of whether another WTO Member provides a "right to objection" equivalent to that laid down in the Regulation;
- another WTO Member's willingness and/or ability "to provide protection equivalent to that available in the Community to corresponding agricultural products or foodstuffs coming from the Community;"
- another WTO Member's willingness and/or ability to consider and/or assess each application to register an EC-defined GI for a geographical location in that WTO Member; and
- finally and particularly, that the outcome of the application is to be determined through a process, that is, the Committee of EC Member State representatives, in which:
  - there is no representative or advocate for the registration of an EC-defined GI for an imported product; and
  - there is no requirement for procedural fairness, due process and/or transparency concerning that Committee's decision-making process.

178. Further, the disadvantage to imported products bearing an EC-defined GI from a geographic location in another WTO Member is cumulative. Each and every one of the additional requirements or barriers must be satisfied before an EC-defined GI for a geographical location in another WTO Member can be registered in respect of an imported product. Moreover, those additional requirements or barriers would normally be considered to constitute governmental functions beyond the ability of an individual producer to satisfy.

179. A careful analysis of the fundamental thrust and effect of the EC measure as a whole and of its implications in the marketplace[75] shows that the EC measure accords such unfavourable treatment to imported products bearing an EC-defined GI in comparison to like domestic products bearing an EC-defined GI that it is, in effect, not possible to register an EC-defined GI for an imported product under Regulation No. 2081/92 unless that other WTO Member in which the EC-defined GI originates also operates a similar system of registration and protection of EC-defined GIs.

---

[75] See paragraph 160 above.

180. Accordingly, the EC measure as a whole is inconsistent with the EC's obligations pursuant to Article III:4 of GATT 1994, as it does not accord to imported products bearing an EC-defined GI treatment no less favourable than that accorded to like domestic products bearing an EC-defined GI.

B. THE EC MEASURE DOES NOT ACCORD NATIONAL TREATMENT IN THE PROTECTION OF INTELLECTUAL PROPERTY, CONTRARY TO ARTICLES 1.1 AND 1.3, 2.1 (INCORPORATING BY REFERENCE ARTICLE 2 OF THE PARIS CONVENTION (1967)) AND 3.1OF THE TRIPS AGREEMENT

(i) The relevant requirements of Articles 1.1 and 1.3, 2.1 and 3.1 of the TRIPS Agreement and Article 2 of the Paris Convention (1967)

181. Under the relevant provisions of TRIPS Articles 1.1 and 1.3[76], 2.1[77] and 3.1[78] and Paris Article 2[79]:

- nationals of any WTO Member enjoy in all other WTO Members the advantages granted now or in the future by those other WTO Members to their own nationals. They have the same protection, and the same legal remedy against any infringement of their rights, provided that the conditions and formalities imposed upon nationals are complied with (Paris Article 2(1) read together with TRIPS Article 2.1[80]);

- no requirement as to domicile or establishment in the country where protection is claimed may be imposed upon nationals of other WTO Members (Paris Article 2(2) read together with TRIPS Article 2.1[81]);

- each WTO Member is to accord to the nationals of other WTO Members treatment no less favourable than that it accords to its own nationals with regard to the protection of intellectual property, subject only to the exceptions already provided in the Paris Convention (1967). "Protection" includes matters affecting the availability, acquisition, scope, maintenance and enforcement of intellectual property rights as well as those matters affecting the use of intellectual property rights specifically addressed in the *TRIPS Agreement* (TRIPS Article 3.1);

---

[76] Article 1 of the *TRIPS Agreement* provides in relevant part:

1. Members shall give effect to the provisions of this Agreement. ...

2. ...

3. Members shall accord the treatment provided for in this Agreement to the nationals of other Members.[...] In respect of the relevant intellectual property rights, the nationals of other Members shall be understood as those natural or legal persons that would meet the criteria for eligibility for protection provided for in the Paris Convention (1967) ...

[77] Article 2.1 of the *TRIPS Agreement* provides in relevant part:

In respect of Parts II, III and IV of this Agreement, Members shall comply with Articles 1 through 12, and Article 19, of the Paris Convention (1967).

[78] Article 3.1 of the *TRIPS Agreement* provides in relevant part:

Each Member shall accord to the nationals of other Members treatment no less favourable than that it accords to its own nationals with regard to the protection [Footnote 3] of intellectual property, subject to the exceptions already provided in ... the Paris Convention (1967) ...

Footnote 3: For the purposes of Articles 3 and 4, 'protection' shall include matters affecting the availability, acquisition, scope, maintenance and enforcement of intellectual property rights as well as those matters affecting the use of intellectual property rights specifically addressed in this Agreement.

[79] Article 2 of the *Paris Convention (1967)* provides in relevant part:

1. Nationals of any country of the Union shall, as regards the protection of industrial property, enjoy in all the other countries of the Union the advantages that their respective laws now grant, or may hereafter grant, to nationals; all without prejudice to the rights specially provided for by this Convention. Consequently, they shall have the same protection as the latter, and the same legal remedy against any infringement of their rights, provided that the conditions and formalities imposed upon nationals are complied with.

2. However, no requirement as to domicile or establishment in the country where protection is claimed may be imposed upon nationals of countries of the Union for the enjoyment of any industrial property rights.

[80] See also *US – Section 211 Appropriations Act*, paragraph 238.

[81] *Ibid.*

- each WTO Member is to accord the treatment provided for in the *TRIPS Agreement* to the nationals of other WTO Members (TRIPS Article 1.3); and

- each WTO Member is to give effect to the provisions of the *TRIPS Agreement* (TRIPS Article 1.1).

182. In *US – Section 211 Appropriations Act*, the Appellate Body said: "... the national treatment obligation *[has]* long been a cornerstone of the Paris Convention" as well as "of the world trading system that is served by the WTO."[82] The Appellate Body has not otherwise considered the meaning of Paris Article 2. However, one expert commentator has said:

> The *advantages* which the nationals of the countries of the Union may claim in any other member country consist in the application, without any discrimination, of the national law as applied to nationals of the country itself. ... [T]his means that no reciprocity of protection can be required by the States party to the Convention. ...[83] *(emphasis in original)*.

and

> For nationals of the countries of the Union, the question where they are domiciled or established is irrelevant. The fact that no establishment in the country where protection is claimed may be required does not however diminish the possibility of an obligation to exploit certain industrial property rights in such country.[84]

183. In *US – Section 211 Appropriations Act*, the Appellate Body went on to say: "[t]he Panel was correct in concluding that, as the language of Article 3.1 of the *TRIPS Agreement*, in particular, is similar to that of Article III:4 of the GATT 1994, the jurisprudence on Article III:4 of the GATT 1994 may be useful in interpreting the national treatment obligation in the *TRIPS Agreement*."[85] In *Korea – Beef*, the Appellate Body said: "[w]hether or not imported products are treated 'less favourably' than like domestic products should be assessed ... by examining whether a measure modified the *conditions of competition* in the relevant market to the detriment of imported products"[86] *(emphasis in original)*. Further, in *US – FSC (Article 21.5)*, the Appellate Body said: "[t]he examination of whether a measure involves 'less favourable treatment' of imported products within the meaning of Article III:4 of the GATT 1994 must be grounded in close scrutiny of the 'fundamental thrust and effect of the measure itself'.[...] This examination ... must be founded on a careful analysis of the contested measure and of its implications in the marketplace. At the same time, however, the examination need not be based on the *actual effects* of the contested measure in the marketplace"[87] *(emphasis in original)*.

(ii) A right of objection was available to persons resident or established in an EC Member State that was not available to other WTO Member nationals in respect of the registration of more than 120 EC-defined GIs under the normal registration process, contrary to Articles 1.1 and 1.3, 2.1 (incorporating Article 2 of the Paris Convention (1967)) and 3.1 of the TRIPS Agreement

184. For the normal registration process for an EC-defined GI, Article 7.3 of Regulation No. 2081/92 provides in relevant part: "[a]ny legitimately concerned natural or legal person may object to the proposed

[82] *US – Section 211 Appropriations Act*, paragraph 241.
[83] *Bodenhausen*, page 29.
[84] *Bodenhausen*, pages 31-32.
[85] *US – Section 211 Appropriations Act*, paragraph 242.
[86] *Korea – Beef*, paragraph 137.
[87] *US – FSC (Article 21.5)*, paragraph 215.

registration by sending a duly substantiated statement to the competent authority of the Member State in which he resides or is established" *(emphasis added)*.

185. Until Article 12d.1 of Regulation No. 2081/92#3 changed the situation, there was no right of objection to the proposed registration of an EC-defined GI for other WTO Member nationals who were not resident or established in an EC Member State. Indeed, the EC itself conceded this. The tenth recital to Regulation No. 692/2003 states in relevant part: "[t]he right of objection should be granted to WTO member countries' nationals with a legitimate interest on the same terms as laid down in Article 7.4 ..." *(emphasis added)*.

186. However, in granting a right of objection to other WTO Member nationals under Regulation No. 2081/92#3, the EC did so only in respect of new, and some then current, applications for registration of an EC-defined GI. For applications for registration of an EC-defined GI for which the six-month notification period required by Article 7.1 of the Regulation expired before 24 April 2003[88], nationals of other WTO Members not resident or established in an EC Member State still had no right of objection.

187. Yet, as at 24 April 2003, more than 120 EC-defined GIs[89] had been registered under the normal registration procedure in respect of which persons residing or established in an EC Member State had had a right of objection that was not available to other WTO Member nationals. Regulation No. 2081/92#3 did not provide any right of objection in respect of, or in any way affect the registration of, those more than 120 EC-defined GIs.

188. Further, in respect of then current applications for registration of an EC-defined GI, Regulation No. 2081/92#3 did not provide any adjustment of the six-month period for lodgement of objections under Article 7.1 of the Regulation. Nationals of other WTO Members who were not resident or established in an EC Member State had less than six months in which to lodge an objection against the proposed registration of an EC-defined GI from an EC Member State, while the full six-month period remained unaffected for EC Member State nationals.

189. Accordingly, the EC measure is inconsistent with the EC's obligations:

- pursuant to Paris Article 2(1) as incorporated by TRIPS Article 2.1. In respect of the registration under the normal registration process of more than 120 EC-defined GIs notified in Regulation No. 2400/96 as amended for which the period for lodging objections expired before 24 April 2003, the EC measure did not allow other WTO Member nationals not resident or established in an EC Member State to enjoy, as regards the protection of industrial property, the advantages that EC law granted to EC nationals. In particular, nationals of other WTO Members did not have the same legal remedy against infringement of their rights as EC nationals, even if the conditions and formalities imposed upon EC nationals were complied with, as the measure did not provide a means by which other WTO Member nationals could seek to protect any industrial property rights they may have held;

- pursuant to Paris Article 2(2), as incorporated by TRIPS Article 2.1. In respect of the registration under the normal registration process of more than 120 EC-defined GIs notified in Regulation No. 2400/96 as amended for which the period for lodging objections expired before 24 April 2003, the EC measure imposed on other WTO Members nationals a requirement as to domicile or establishment in the EC for the enjoyment of an industrial property right;

- pursuant to TRIPS Article 3.1. In respect of the registration under the normal registration process of more than 120 EC-defined GIs notified in Regulation No. 2400/96 as amended for which the

[88] The date Regulation No. 2081/92#3 came into effect.

[89] These are the registrations published in Regulation No. 2400/96 as amended, Exhibit COMP-4.

period for lodging objections expired before 24 April 2003, the EC measure accorded to other WTO Member nationals not resident or established in an EC Member State treatment less favourable than that accorded to EC nationals with regard to the protection of intellectual property. Unlike EC nationals for whom such a means was made available, the EC measure did not provide a means by which other WTO Member nationals who were not resident or established in an EC Member State could seek to enforce their intellectual property rights;

- pursuant to Paris Article 2(1), as incorporated by TRIPS Article 2.1, and pursuant to TRIPS Article 3.1. In respect of any registrations of EC-defined GIs notified in Regulation No. 2400/96 as amended where the six-month period for lodgement of objections under Article 7.1 of Regulation No. 2081/92 expired between 24 April and 22 October 2003 inclusive,[90] Regulation No. 2081/92#3 did not make any transitional provision in regard to the lodgement of objections by other WTO Member nationals not resident or established in an EC Member State in respect of such objection periods. Accordingly, the EC measure did not:

    - allow nationals of any WTO Member to enjoy, as regards the protection of industrial property, the advantages that EC law granted to EC nationals as required by Paris Article 2(1); and

    - accord to other WTO Member nationals treatment no less favourable than that accorded to EC nationals as required by TRIPS Article 3.1;

- pursuant to TRIPS Article 2.1 to comply with Paris Articles 1 through 12, and 19; and

- pursuant to TRIPS Article 1.3 to accord the treatment provided for in the *TRIPS Agreement* to the nationals of other WTO Members.

As a consequence, the EC has not complied with its obligation pursuant to TRIPS Article 1.1 to give effect to the provisions of the *TRIPS Agreement.*

(iii) A right of objection was available to persons resident or established in an EC Member State that was not available to other WTO Member nationals in respect of the registration of more than 480 EC-defined GIs under the simplified registration process, contrary to Articles 1.1 and 1.3, 2.1 (incorporating Article 2 of the Paris Convention (1967)) and 3.1 of the TRIPS Agreement

190. Article 17.1 of Regulation No. 2081/92#1 and #2 provided a simplified registration process for "names" which were already legally protected or established by usage in Member States. Further, Article 17.2 of the Regulation provided that: "Article 7 shall not apply."[91]

191. Notwithstanding the provisions of Article 17.2, the European Court of Justice has found:

> When adopting the basic regulation, the Council and the Commission stated in the minutes of the Council meeting … that 'where there are agricultural products or foodstuffs already being legally marketed before the making of the regulation which may be the subject of an

[90] See, for example, Official Journal notice 2002/C 291/02 of 26 November 2002, Exhibit AUS-02, concerning the proposed registration of the name "Torta del Casar."

[91] Article 7 of Regulation No. 2081/92 provides a right of objection to the proposed registration of an EC-defined GI to natural or legal persons who reside in or are established in an EC Member State.

application for registration, it has been provided for any Member States to object to the registration under the provisions of Article 7 of the regulation'. ...[92] *(emphasis added)*.

192. However, that right of objection was not provided to other WTO Member nationals not resident or established in an EC Member State.

193. Thus, as at 24 April 2003 when Regulation No. 2081/92#3 came into effect and Article 17 was repealed, more than 480 EC-defined GIs[93] had been registered under the simplified registration process in respect of which persons who were resident or established in an EC Member State had a right of objection that was not available to other WTO Member nationals. Regulation No. 2081/92#3 did not provide any right of objection to other WTO Member nationals in respect of the registration of those more than 480 EC-defined GIs. Nor did Regulation No. 2081/92#3 in any other way affect the continuing registration of those more than 480 EC-defined GIs and they remain in effect.

194. Accordingly, the EC measure is inconsistent with the EC's obligations:

- pursuant to Paris Article 2(1) as incorporated by TRIPS Article 2.1. In respect of the registration under the simplified registration process of more than 480 EC-defined GIs notified in Regulation No. 1107/96 as amended, the EC measure did not allow other WTO Member nationals not resident or established in an EC Member State to enjoy, as regards the protection of industrial property, the advantages that EC law granted to EC nationals. In particular, such WTO Member nationals did not have the same legal remedy against infringement of their rights as EC nationals, even if the conditions and formalities imposed upon EC nationals were complied with, as the EC measure did not provide a means by which other WTO Member nationals could seek to protect any industrial property rights they may have held;

- pursuant to Paris Article 2(2) as incorporated by TRIPS Article 2.1. In respect of the registration under the simplified registration process of more than 480 EC-defined GIs notified in Regulation No. 1107/96 as amended, the EC measure imposed on nationals of other WTO Members a requirement as to domicile or establishment in the EC for the enjoyment of an industrial property right;

- pursuant to TRIPS Article 3.1. In respect of the continuing registration under the simplified registration process of more than 480 EC-defined GIs notified in Regulation No. 1107/96 as amended, the EC measure accorded to other WTO Member nationals not resident or established in an EC Member State treatment less favourable than that it accorded to EC nationals with regard to the protection of intellectual property. Unlike EC nationals for whom such a means was made available, the EC measure did not provide a means by which other WTO Member nationals who were not resident or established in an EC Member State could seek to enforce their intellectual property rights;

- pursuant to TRIPS Article 2.1 to comply with Paris Articles 1 through 12, and 19; and

- pursuant to TRIPS Article 1.3 to accord the treatment provided for in the *TRIPS Agreement* to the nationals of other WTO Members.

---

[92] The Feta judgement, Exhibit COMP-11, paragraph 21.

[93] These are the registrations published in Regulation No. 1107/96 as amended, Exhibit COMP-3. Note that the registrations of an additional 31 EC-defined GIs for natural mineral waters and spring waters remain in effect until 31 December 2013 pursuant to Article 2 of Regulation No. 692/2003.

As a consequence, the EC has not complied with its obligation pursuant to TRIPS Article 1.1 to give effect to the provisions of the *TRIPS Agreement*.

(iv) The EC measure as a whole does not accord national treatment to non-EC nationals, contrary to Articles 1.1 and 1.3, 2.1 (incorporating Article 2 of the Paris Convention (1967)) and 3.1 of the TRIPS Agreement

195. In *US – FSC (Article 21.5)*, the Appellate Body found that "[t]he examination of whether a measure involves 'less favourable treatment' of imported products within the meaning of Article III:4 of the GATT 1994 must be grounded in close scrutiny of the 'fundamental thrust and effect of the measure itself'" and that "[t]his examination ... must be founded on a careful analysis of the contested measure and of its implications in the marketplace."[94]

196. Regulation No. 2081/92 provides an integrated regulatory framework for the registration and protection of EC-defined GIs that systematically accords to non-EC nationals less favourable treatment than that accorded to EC nationals in regard to the registration of an EC-defined GI from another WTO Member.

197. EC producers perceive clear competitive advantages attached to registration, and thus protection, of an EC-defined GI under Regulation No. 2081/92, evidenced by the more than 600 EC-defined GIs already registered, the ongoing processing of further applications[95] and by EC Member State support for the EC measure. Perceived advantages include protection against a registered name becoming generic, broad ranging protection including even against evocation of a registered EC-defined GI, as well as *ex officio* Community wide protection[96].

198. However, non-EC nationals seeking to register, and thus protect, an EC-defined GI in respect of a geographical location in the territory of another WTO Member pursuant to Regulation No. 2081/92 are not able to apply directly to the EC (whether to the Commission or another Community level body) to register an EC-defined GI. That is the case even if non-EC nationals can demonstrate full compliance with the requirements of Article 4 of the Regulation (the product specification), for example, through evidence of registration in another WTO Member as a certification trademark.

199. Unless the WTO Member government in whose territory the geographical location at issue is situated is able and willing to meet the equivalence and reciprocity conditions set out by Article 12.1 of Regulation No. 2081/92, non-EC nationals are not able to access the rights available to EC nationals.

200. Regulation No. 2081/92 also systematically accords to non-EC nationals less favourable treatment than that accorded to EC nationals relating to the enforcement of trademark rights. Further, the less favourable treatment applies in respect of both current and future registrations of EC-defined GIs.

201. The registrations of approximately 600 EC-defined GIs made before Regulation No. 2081/92#3 came into effect on 24 April 2003 and provided a right of objection to the proposed registration of an EC-defined GI to other WTO Member nationals not resident or established in the EC remain in effect. Yet to this day, the EC has not provided a means for nationals of other WTO Members not resident or established in an EC Member State to seek to exercise, or enforce, an intellectual property right potentially affected by those registrations. The pervasive less favourable treatment accorded to non-EC nationals not resident or established in an EC Member State is not excused by the fact that a few non-EC nationals resident or established in an EC Member State might have been able to seek to exercise, or enforce, any intellectual property rights they may have held in

---

[94] See paragraph 160 above.

[95] See, for example, Official Journal notice 2004/C 93/11 of 17 April 2004 concerning an application for registration of the name "Zafferano di San Gimignano."

[96] See, for example, WTO document IP/Q2/EEC/1 of 1 October 1997, Section II "Replies to Questions from New Zealand," part B of the EC's response to question 4.

relation to those proposed registrations. The national treatment obligation extends to all nationals of other WTO Members, not just those resident or established in an EC Member State.

202. That less favourable treatment to non-EC nationals is ongoing.

203. A non-EC national not resident or established in an EC Member State must lodge an objection to the proposed registration of an EC-defined GI through the government of the WTO Member in which it resides or is established. That requirement applies regardless of whether the EC-defined GI concerns a geographic location within an EC Member State or another WTO Member. Even if a non-EC national trademark right holder is able to have its objection considered by the Committee of EC Member States,[97] it faces the additional hurdle of not having a national representative on the Committee to speak for its interests.

204. Australia further understands Article 12d.1 of Regulation No. 2081/92#3 to impose the condition of recognition under Article 12.3 of the Regulation with regard to the equivalence and reciprocity requirements set out in Article 12.1 of the Regulation for the exercise of a right of objection by another WTO Member national. For the same reasons as set out in relation to Australia's claim under GATT Article III:4 above,[98] such requirements are distinct additional requirements to which EC nationals are not subject.

205. Moreover, notwithstanding any outward appearance of symmetry of treatment, the EC measure accords non-EC nationals less favourable treatment than that accorded to EC nationals in respect of the registration of an EC-defined GI from another WTO Member and in respect of the enforcement of trademark rights concerning the proposed registration of an EC-defined GI. The fact that the EC and its Member States have legally defined rights and obligations in relation to each other and to EC Member State nationals makes the registration and objection processes for EC nationals fundamentally different to those for non-EC nationals. Few other WTO Member governments have such legally defined relationships affecting the maintenance and enforcement of an intellectual property right, a right expressly recognised as a private right by the *TRIPS Agreement*.

206. Close scrutiny of the fundamental thrust and effect of the EC measure based on a careful analysis of the measure and of its implications in the marketplace, as suggested by the Appellate Body,[99] demonstrates that the EC measure as a whole fails to provide to non-EC nationals the equality of opportunity with regard to the protection of intellectual property that underpins the national treatment principle of the *TRIPS Agreement* and the Paris Convention (1967). Accordingly, Australia submits that the EC measure as a whole is inconsistent with the EC's obligations:

- pursuant to Paris Article 2(1) as incorporated by TRIPS Article 2.1, as it does not allow nationals of any other WTO Member to enjoy, as regards the protection of industrial property, the advantages or benefits that EC law grants to EC nationals;

- pursuant to Paris Article 2(2) as incorporated by TRIPS Article 2.1, as it sets out a requirement as to domicile or establishment for the enjoyment of an industrial property right;

- pursuant to TRIPS Article 3.1, as it does not accord to nationals of other WTO Members treatment no less favourable than that it accords to EC nationals with regard to the protection of intellectual property;

- pursuant to TRIPS Article 2.1 to comply with Paris Articles 1 through 12, and 19; and

---

[97] See paragraph 99 above.

[98] See paragraph 168 above.

[99] See paragraph 160 above.

- pursuant to TRIPS Article 1.3 to accord the treatment provided for in the *TRIPS Agreement* to the nationals of other WTO Members.

As a consequence, the EC has not given effect to the provisions of the *TRIPS Agreement*, contrary to TRIPS Article 1.1.

IX. ARTICLE 65.1 OF THE TRIPS AGREEMENT DOES NOT EXCUSE INCONSISTENCIES WITH THE EC'S OBLIGATIONS UNDER THAT AGREEMENT

207. Under Article 65.1[100] of the *TRIPS Agreement*, WTO Members were not required to apply the provisions of the *TRIPS Agreement* until 1 January 1996, that is, after a general period of one year following the date of entry into force of the *WTO Agreement* (which occurred on 1 January 1995). The EC does not qualify for an additional transitional period as it is not a developing country (TRIPS Articles 65.2 and 65.4) or an economy in transition (TRIPS Article 65.3). Nor is it a least developed country to which TRIPS Article 66.1 might apply. The EC was thus required to apply the provisions of the *TRIPS Agreement* not later than 1 January 1996.

208. The actions by the EC alleged in this submission constitute contraventions of the EC's obligations under the *TRIPS Agreement* after 1 January 1996. Accordingly, the transitional period provided for in TRIPS Article 65.1 does not operate to excuse the inconsistencies of the EC measure with the EC's obligations under TRIPS Articles 1.3, 2.1 (incorporating Paris Articles 2(1) and 2(2), 10*bis*(1) and 10*ter*(1)), 3.1, 16.1, 20, 22.2, 24.5, 41.1, 41.2, 41.3 and 42.

X. THE EC MEASURE IS INCONSISTENT WITH ARTICLE 2.1 AND 2.2 OF THE TBT AGREEMENT

A. THE EC MEASURE IS IN PART A TECHNICAL REGULATION WITHIN THE MEANING OF ANNEX 1 TO THE TBT AGREEMENT

(i) Definition of a "technical regulation"

209. TBT Annex 1.1 defines a "technical regulation" for the purposes of the *TBT Agreement* as a:

> [d]ocument which lays down product characteristics or their related processes and production methods, including the applicable administrative provisions, with which compliance is mandatory. It may also include or deal exclusively with terminology, symbols, packaging, marking or labelling requirements as they apply to a product, process or production method.

210. In *EC – Sardines*, the Appellate Body recapped the three criteria that a document must meet to fall within the definition of a "technical regulation:"

> ... *First*, the document must apply to an identifiable product or group of products. The *identifiable* product or group of products need not, however, be expressly *identified* in the document. *Second*, the document must lay down one or more characteristics of the product. These product characteristics may be intrinsic, or they may be related to the product. They may be prescribed or imposed in either a positive or a negative form. *Third*, compliance with the product characteristics must be mandatory. ...[101] *(emphases in original)*

---

[100] Article 65.1 of the *TRIPS Agreement* reads as follows:
Subject to the provisions of paragraphs 2, 3 and 4, no Member shall be obliged to apply the provisions of this Agreement before the expiry of a general period of one year following the date of entry into force of the WTO Agreement.

[101] *EC – Sardines*, paragraph 176.

(ii) The EC measure applies to an identifiable product or group of products

211. In *EC – Asbestos*, the Appellate Body found: "[a]lthough the *TBT Agreement* clearly applies to 'products' generally, nothing in the text of that Agreement suggested that those products need be named or otherwise *expressly* identified in a 'technical regulation'"[102] *(emphasis in original)*. In *EC – Sardines*, the Appellate Body elaborated: "the requirement that a 'technical regulation' be applicable to *identifiable* products relates to aspects of compliance and enforcement, because it would be impossible to comply with or enforce a 'technical regulation' without knowing to what the regulation applied"[103] *(emphasis in original)*.

212. The formal title of Regulation No. 2081/92 is "Council Regulation (EEC) No. 2081/92 on the protection of *[EC-defined GIs]* for agricultural products and foodstuffs." The preamble to Regulation No. 2081/92#1 states in relevant part that "the scope of this Regulation is limited to certain agricultural products and foodstuffs for which a link between product or foodstuff characteristics and geographical origin exist," while noting that the scope could be enlarged to encompass other products or foodstuffs. Further, Article 1.1 of the Regulation provides that the Regulation "lays down rules on the protection of *[EC-defined GIs]* of *[agricultural products and foodstuffs]*."

213. The EC measure applies to an identifiable group of products: it applies to agricultural products and foodstuffs in respect of which an EC-defined GI is registered and being protected, or in respect of which registration and protection of an EC-defined GI is being sought, pursuant to Regulation No. 2081/92.

(iii) The EC measure lays down product characteristics or their related process and production methods, including the applicable administrative provisions

214. In *EC – Asbestos*, the Appellate Body found that:

> ... the "characteristics" of a product include ... any objectively definable "features," "qualities," "attributes," or other "distinguishing mark" of a product. Such "characteristics" might relate ... to a product's composition, size, shape, colour, texture, hardness, tensile strength, flammability, conductivity, density or viscosity. In the definition of a "technical regulation" in Annex 1.1, the *TBT Agreement* itself gives certain examples of "product characteristics"—"terminology, symbols, packaging, marking or labelling requirements." ...[104]

215. The Appellate Body held that these examples indicate that "product characteristics" include not only features and qualities intrinsic to the product itself but also related "characteristics," such as the means of identification, the presentation and the appearance of a product. Finally, it noted that the language used in the TBT Annex 1.1 definition indicates that a "technical regulation" may be limited to only one or a few product characteristics.[105]

216. In addition to laying down product characteristics, the definition of a technical regulation in TBT Annex 1.1 includes a document which lays down "related processes and production methods, including the applicable administrative provisions." Therefore, a document which does not stipulate mandatory "product characteristics" *per se* but lays down mandatory related processes and/or production methods or their applicable administrative provisions may be a "technical regulation" for the purposes of the *TBT Agreement*.

---

[102] *EC – Asbestos*, paragraph 70.

[103] *EC – Sardines*, paragraph 185.

[104] *EC – Asbestos*, paragraph 67.

[105] *EC – Asbestos*, paragraph 67.

217. The meaning of "related processes and production methods, including the applicable administrative provisions" has not been considered by a WTO Panel or the Appellate Body. However, having regard to the ordinary meaning of the words in their context and in light of the object and purpose of the *TBT Agreement*, Australia submits that:

- a "process" may generally be considered as a regular sequence of actions directed at a specified purpose;[106]
- a "production method" may generally be considered as the way in which something is produced;[107] and
- "related" processes and production methods may generally be considered as processes and production methods which are connected to the product characteristics.

218. Accordingly, a technical regulation within the meaning of the *TBT Agreement* includes a document which may generally be considered to set out a regular sequence of actions directed at a specified purpose or the way in which something is produced and which is connected to one or more product characteristics.

219. The EC measure lays down product characteristics or their related processes within the meaning of the TBT Annex 1.1 definition in two ways.

220. Firstly, Article 12.2[108] of Regulation No. 2081/92 sets out a specific labelling requirement. It provides that use of EC-defined GIs from other WTO Members will only be authorised "if the country of origin of the product is clearly and visibly indicated on the label." To that extent, the EC measure is a document which "include[s] … labelling requirements as they apply to a product" within the meaning of a technical regulation as defined in TBT Annex 1.1.

221. Secondly, Articles 4, in particular Article 4.2(g), and 10 of Regulation No. 2081/92 read together require that EC Member States have in place inspection structures to ensure that agricultural products and foodstuffs bearing a protected name meet the requirements laid down in the product specification. Checking compliance with the criteria set out in product specifications is a regular sequence of actions directed at a specified purpose, that is, to determine whether a product complies with its product specification.[109] Further, by definition, the product specification requirements set out in Article 4.2 of the Regulation include product characteristics, in particular in sub-paragraphs (b) and (e). To the extent that Articles 4 and 10 of the Regulation read together set out a process related to product characteristics for agricultural products and foodstuffs, the EC measure is a technical regulation as defined in TBT Annex 1.1. Further, Article 12.1 of the Regulation extends the application of Articles 4 and 10 of the Regulation to agricultural products and foodstuffs from other WTO

---

106 *OED*, Vol.2, page 2364, defines "process" in relevant part as: "[a] thing that goes on or is carried on; a continuous series of actions, events, or changes; a course of action, a procedure; *esp.* a continuous and regular action or succession of actions occurring or performed in a definite manner; a systematic series of actions or operations directed to some end, as in manufacturing, printing, photography, etc."

107 *OED* defines:
"production" in relevant part as: "1. Something which is produced by an action, process, etc, a product. … 2. The action or an act of producing, making or causing something; the fact or condition of being produced. The process of being manufactured commercially, esp. in large quantities; the rate of this" (Vol.2, page 2367); and
"method" in relevant part as: "Procedure for attaining an object. … 2. A mode of procedure; a (defined or systematic) way of doing a thing, …" (Vol.1, page 1759).

108 Article 12.2 of Regulation No. 2081/92 provides as follows:
If a protected name of a third country is identical to a Community protected name, registration shall be granted with due regard for local and traditional usage and the practical risks of confusion.
Use of such names shall be authorized only if the country of origin of the product is clearly and visibly indicated on the label.

109 See paragraph 28 above.

Members as one of the conditions for the application of the Regulation to agricultural products and foodstuffs from other WTO Members.[110]

(iv) The EC measure mandates compliance with product characteristics or their related process and production methods, including the applicable administrative provisions

222. In *EC – Asbestos*, the Appellate Body noted that the definition of a technical regulation in TBT Annex 1.1 states that compliance with the product characteristics laid down in the document is mandatory: "[w]ith respect to products, a 'technical regulation' has the effect of *prescribing* or *imposing* one or more 'characteristics'—'features', 'qualities', 'attributes' or other 'distinguishing mark' " *(emphases in original)*.[111] The Appellate Body also found in *EC – Asbestos* that a measure should be examined as an "integrated whole," rather than being separated out into constituent elements, e.g. a prohibition and an exception.[112]

223. In Article 12.2 of Regulation No. 2081/92, the term "shall" shows that this condition meets the requirement in TBT Annex 1.1 of mandatory compliance: use of an EC-defined GI on an agricultural product or foodstuff from another WTO Member can be authorised only if the labelling requirement set out in Article 12.2 of the Regulation is met.

224. Similarly, the requirement to have in place inspection structures pursuant to Articles 4, 10 and 12.1 of the Regulation is mandatory. Unless these requirements are met, agricultural products or foodstuffs from another WTO Member are not able to be registered—and therefore protected—under the Regulation.

B. THE EC MEASURE ACCORDS TO PRODUCTS IMPORTED FROM THE TERRITORY OF ANY WTO MEMBER TREATMENT LESS FAVOURABLE THAN THAT ACCORDED TO LIKE PRODUCTS OF NATIONAL ORIGIN, CONTRARY TO ARTICLE 2.1 OF THE TBT AGREEMENT

(i) The relevant requirements of the TBT Agreement

225. TBT Article 2.1[113] requires in relevant part that, in their technical regulations, central government bodies of WTO Members provide to imported products treatment no less favourable than that accorded to like domestic products.

226. The concepts of "like product" and "treatment no less favourable" have been examined in many disputes under the GATT and the WTO in the context of obligations under the GATT 1947 and the GATT 1994. In *US – Section 211 Appropriations Act*, the Appellate Body said: "[t]he Panel was correct in concluding that, as the language of Article 3.1 of the *TRIPS Agreement*, in particular, is similar to that of Article III:4 of the GATT 1994, the jurisprudence on Article III:4 of the GATT 1994 may be useful in interpreting the national treatment obligation in the *TRIPS Agreement*."[114] The current situation is analogous to that examined by the Appellate Body in *US – Section 211 Appropriations Act*. Moreover, the *TBT Agreement* was negotiated to further the objectives of GATT 1994.[115] In addition, the TBT national treatment obligation in Article 2.1 follows closely GATT Articles III, reproducing the requirement of "treatment no less favourable than that

---

[110] In *EC – Asbestos* (paragraph 64), the Appellate Body said, in determining whether a measure is a technical regulation, "... the proper legal character of the measure at issue cannot be determined unless the measure is examined as a whole." Thus, specific provisions of Regulation No. 2081/92 that extend other provisions to apply to products from other WTO Members bearing protected names need to be examined as an integrated whole with those provisions.

[111] *EC – Asbestos*, paragraph 68. The Appellate Body reaffirmed this finding in *EC – Sardines*, at paragraph 176.

[112] *EC – Asbestos*, paragraph 64. The Appellate Body reaffirmed this finding in *EC – Sardines*, at paragraphs 192-193.

[113] Article 2.1 of the *TBT Agreement* provides that, with respect to their central government bodies:

Members shall ensure that in respect of technical regulations, products imported from the territory of any Member shall be accorded treatment no less favourable than that accorded to like products of national origin ...

[114] *US – Section 211 Appropriations Act*, paragraphs 242.

[115] See second preambular paragraph to the *TBT Agreement*.

accorded to like products." In Australia's view therefore, the previous consideration of GATT Article III:4 can properly be looked to for clarification of the national treatment obligation in TBT Article 2.1.

227. In *EC – Asbestos* the Appellate Body made the following statement about the term "like products" with regard to a GATT Article III:4 claim:

> As products that are in a competitive relationship in the marketplace could be affected through treatment of *imports* "less favourable" than the treatment accorded to *domestic* products, it follows that the word "like" in Article III:4 is to be interpreted to apply to products that are in such a competitive relationship. Thus, a determination of "likeness" under Article III:4 is, fundamentally, a determination about the nature and extent of a competitive relationship between and among products. ...[116] *(emphases in original)*

228. In *EC – Asbestos*, the Appellate Body also found that the conditions of the marketplace and the effect of measures on the competitive relationship between imported products and products of national origin is key to the "broad and fundamental purpose" of GATT Article III to avoid protectionist internal measures.[117] The Appellate Body said:

> The term "less favourable treatment" expresses the general principle, in Article III:1, that internal regulations "should not be applied ... so as to afford protection to domestic production." If there is "less favourable treatment" of the group of "like" imported products, there is, conversely, "protection" of the group of "like" domestic products. ...[118]

229. In *Korea – Beef*, the Appellate Body found: "[w]hether or not imported products are treated 'less favourably' than like domestic products should be assessed ... by examining whether a measure modified the *conditions of competition* in the relevant market to the detriment of imported products."[119] In *US – FSC (Article 21.5)*, the Appellate Body found: "[t]he examination of whether a measure involves 'less favourable treatment' of imported products within the meaning of Article III:4 of the GATT 1994 must be grounded in close scrutiny of the 'fundamental thrust and effect of the measure itself'.[...] This examination ... must be founded on a careful analysis of the contested measure and of its implications in the marketplace. At the same time, however, the examination need not be based on the *actual effects* of the contested measure in the marketplace."[120] *(emphases in originals)*

(ii) The EC measure concerns both imported and domestically produced "like products" within the meaning of Article 2.1 of the TBT Agreement

230. In the circumstances of the present dispute, it is sufficient for the Panel to consider the issues in the context of a general presumption of likeness.[121] As a type of TRIPS-defined GI, an EC-defined GI is an intellectual property right and does not affect the analysis of likeness of the underlying products. Thus, for example: imported apples and pears would be like products to "Savoie" apples and pears; imported oysters would be like products to "Whitstable" oysters; imported olive oils would be like products to the many olive

---

[116] *EC – Asbestos*, paragraph 99. The Appellate Body used the four criteria approach to determining likeness that has its origins in the Report of the Working Party on *Border Tax Adjustments* and has been followed since by panels and the Appellate Body in disputes including *Japan – Alcoholic Beverages* and *US – Gasoline*. These, which it stressed provide a "framework" for a case-by-case analysis of "likeness," are: (i) the properties, nature and quality of the products; (ii) the end-uses of the products; (iii) consumers' tastes and habits; and (iv) the tariff classification of the products (paragraphs 100-102).

[117] *EC – Asbestos*, paragraphs 96-98.

[118] *EC – Asbestos*, paragraph 100.

[119] *Korea – Beef*, paragraph 137.

[120] *US – FSC (Article 21.5)*, paragraph 215.

[121] Australia notes that, in the circumstances of this dispute, it is not necessary for the Panel to consider whether products which are like within the meaning of GATT Article III:4 will always be like within the meaning of TBT Article 2.1.

oils for which an EC-defined GI has been registered; and imported trout would be like product with "Black Forest" trout.[122]

231. In addition, where the geographical area is a region which encompasses territory in both an EC Member State and another WTO Member, agricultural products or foodstuffs produced in that geographic area could be exactly the same irrespective of the traversing border. Under Regulation No. 2081/92, it is the geographical area which by definition gives rise to the characteristics attributable to the product protected by the EC-defined GI. Logically, products produced within that geographical area—irrespective of the territory of which WTO Member in which they are produced—must also by definition be able to be like products.

232. Finally, Australia notes the overall context in which the labelling requirement established by Article 12.2 of Regulation No. 2081/92 occurs, which includes to "ensure fair competition between the producers of products bearing such *[EC-defined GIs]*.[123] To that end, the Regulation offers protection to registered EC-defined GIs against misuse and unfair competition, including misleading indication, evocation, unauthorised commercial use exploiting the reputation of the protected name "or any other practice likely to mislead the public as to the true origin of the product."[124] The notion of imitating a product in a way that would lead to unfair competition between that product and its legitimate counterpart would normally involve a high degree of similarity or "likeness."

233. Thus, the EC measure concerns both imported and domestically produced like products within the meaning of TBT Article 2.1.

(iii) The EC measure provides "less favourable" treatment to like imported and domestically produced products within the meaning of Article 2.1 of the TBT Agreement

234. Under Article 12.2 of Regulation No. 2081/92, use of a "protected name of a third country" "shall be authorized only if the country of origin of the product is clearly and visibly indicated on the label." The precise meaning of this provision is unclear.

235. Firstly, it is unclear whether the expression "such names" in the second sub-paragraph of Article 12.2 refers to an EC-defined GI relating to a geographical location in the territory of another WTO Member that is identical to a Community protected name or to *all* products from other WTO Members bearing an EC-defined GI. Australia understands this provision to mean that use within the EC on an imported product of an EC-defined GI relating to a geographical location in another WTO Member that is protected by that WTO Member and which is identical to an EC-defined GI that is already being protected within the EC may be authorised "only if the country of origin of the *[imported]* product is clearly and visibly indicated on the label." Where, however, the EC-defined GI that is already being protected is for a like product from within the EC, the EC product is not required to show the country of origin.

236. Secondly, the phrase "protected name of a third country" is ambiguous. Given the context of Article 12 of Regulation No. 2081/92 as a whole, however, Australia assumes that the phrase means an EC-defined GI relating to a geographical location in the territory of another WTO Member that is protected by that WTO Member.[125]

---

[122] Australia notes that the question of the extent to which cheeses are like products has not previously been the subject of a ruling by a GATT or WTO dispute settlement panel. Australia considers that there would be few, if any, imported cheeses which are not like products to EC domestic cheeses within the meaning of TBT Article 2.1, but does not consider it necessary for the Panel to make a finding on this precise issue to resolve the claims made in this dispute.

[123] Regulation No. 2081/92, preambular paragraphs.

[124] See paragraph 24 above.

[125] Australia notes two other possible meanings are: a "name" that is protected in another WTO Member as another form of intellectual property right; and the actual name of a WTO Member, for example, "Australia."

237. Irrespective of the precise meaning of a "protected name of a third country," however, Article 12.2 of Regulation No. 2081/92 imposes on an agricultural product or foodstuff from another WTO Member different treatment to that applicable to a domestically produced like product. For a "protected name of a third country" that is identical to a "Community protected name" to be used in the EC market, the country of origin of the imported good bearing the "protected name" must be clearly and visibly indicated on the label of that imported good, notwithstanding that there is no requirement for the corresponding domestically produced like product to clearly and visibly indicate a country of origin on its label.

238. Australia notes that differential treatment alone is not necessarily conclusive of less favourable treatment.[126]

239. In the broad range of circumstances potentially encompassed by Article 12.2 of Regulation No. 2081/92, however, there are likely to be situations where this labelling requirement modifies the conditions of competition between imported products and the like domestically produced products to the detriment of the imported products. For example, producers of a fresh fruit product such as an apple from another WTO Member could be required to incur extra expense to produce and attach a second label to that piece of fruit to comply with the Regulation. Thus, a prescriptive requirement that applies without exception to imported products but not to domestically produced like products will in some circumstances result in less favourable treatment being accorded to an imported product, contrary to TBT Article 2.1.

240. Even if Article 12.2 of the Regulation applies to all imported products bearing an EC-defined GI rather than only to those bearing an EC-defined GI that is identical to an EC-defined GI already being protected within the EC, it will still be inconsistent with TBT Article 2.1 for the reasons set out in the preceding paragraphs.

241. Accordingly, the EC measure accords less favourable treatment to imported products than to domestically produced like products, contrary to TBT Article 2.1.

C. THE EC MEASURE HAS BEEN PREPARED, ADOPTED AND/OR APPLIED WITH THE EFFECT OF CREATING UNNECESSARY OBSTACLES TO INTERNATIONAL TRADE, BEING MORE TRADE-RESTRICTIVE THAN NECESSARY TO FULFIL A LEGITIMATE OBJECTIVE, TAKING ACCOUNT OF THE RISKS NON-FULFILMENT WOULD CREATE, CONTRARY TO ARTICLE 2.2 OF THE TBT AGREEMENT

(i) The relevant requirements of the TBT Agreement

242. TBT Article 2.2[127] requires that, in respect of technical regulations, central government bodies of WTO Members ensure that those technical regulations are not prepared, adopted or applied with a view to or with the effect of creating unnecessary obstacles to international trade. To that end, technical regulations must not be more trade restrictive than necessary to fulfil a legitimate objective, taking account of the risks non-fulfilment would create.

243. Having regard to the text of TBT Article 2.2, Australia submits that for a technical regulation to be consistent with the provision, it must:

- pursue a "legitimate objective;"

[126] *Korea – Beef*, paragraph 135.

[127] Article 2.2 of the *TBT Agreement* provides that, with respect to their central government bodies:

Members shall ensure that technical regulations are not prepared, adopted or applied with a view to or with the effect of creating unnecessary obstacles to international trade. For this purpose, technical regulations shall not be more trade-restrictive than necessary to fulfil a legitimate objective, taking account of the risks non-fulfilment would create. Such legitimate objectives are, *inter alia*: … the prevention of deceptive practices … In assessing such risks, relevant elements of consideration are, *inter alia*: available scientific and technical information, related processing technology or intended end-uses of products.

- achieve—or be capable of achieving—that objective; and
- not be more trade restrictive than necessary to achieve that objective, taking account of the risks non-fulfilment would create.

A failure to comply with one or more of these elements would render a technical regulation inconsistent with TBT Article 2.2.

244. Read in the context of the object and purpose of the *TBT Agreement*, including as set out in the preamble to that Agreement, [128] the concepts and the tests set out in TBT Article 2.2 share characteristics with those applicable to the general exceptions of GATT Article XX, and in particular GATT Article XX(d)[129]. Such similarity is logical given that the *TBT Agreement* was expressly intended to further GATT objectives. WTO jurisprudence on GATT Article XX is therefore relevant and may thus provide a useful guide to the clarification of TBT Article 2.2.

245. In *EC – Asbestos*[130] and *Korea – Beef*[131], the Appellate Body addressed the "necessity test" in the context of GATT Article XX(b) and (d) respectively and cited with approval the standard set forth by the Panel in *United States – Section 337*:

> ... [A] contracting party cannot justify a measure inconsistent with another GATT provision as "necessary" in terms of Article XX(d) if an alternative measure which it could reasonably be expected to employ and which is not inconsistent with other GATT provisions is available to it.[132]

246. In *EC – Asbestos*, the Appellate Body recapped and summarised its findings in *Korea – Beef* in relation to GATT Article XX(d) thus:

> ... [O]ne aspect of the "weighing and balancing process ... comprehended in the determination of whether a WTO-consistent alternative measure" is reasonably available is the extent to which the alternative measure "contributes to the realization of the end pursued."[...] In addition, we observed in that case, that "[t]he more vital or important [the] common interests or values" pursued, the easier it would be to accept as "necessary" measures designed to achieve those ends.[...] In this case, the objective pursued by the measure is the preservation of human life and health through the elimination, or reduction, of the well-known, and life-threatening, health risks posed by asbestos fibres. The value pursued is both vital and important in the highest degree. The remaining question, then, is whether there is an

---

128 The second preambular paragraph of the *TBT Agreement* states:
Desiring to further the objectives of GATT 1994
The sixth preambular paragraph of the *TBT Agreement* states:
Recognizing that no country should be prevented from taking measures necessary to ensure the quality of its exports, or for the protection of human, animal or plant life or health, of the environment, or for the prevention of deceptive practices, at the levels it considers appropriate, subject to the requirement that they are not applied in a manner which would constitute a means of arbitrary or unjustifiable discrimination between countries where the same conditions prevail or a disguised restriction on international trade, and are otherwise in accordance with the provisions of this Agreement.

129 Article XX(d) of GATT 1994, headed "General Exceptions," provides as follows:
Subject to the requirement that such measures are not applied in a manner which would constitute a means of arbitrary or unjustifiable discrimination between countries where the same conditions prevail, or a disguised restriction on international trade, nothing in this Agreement shall be construed to prevent the adoption or enforcement by any contracting party of measures: ... necessary to secure compliance with laws or regulations which are not inconsistent with the provisions of this Agreement, including those relating to customs enforcement, ... the protection of patents, trade marks and copyrights, and the prevention of deceptive practices; ...

130 *EC – Asbestos*, paragraph 171.

131 *Korea – Beef*, paragraphs 165-166.

132 *United States – Section 337*, paragraph 5.26.

alternative measure that would achieve the same end and that is less restrictive of trade than a prohibition.[133]

(ii) The EC measure pursues a legitimate objective within the meaning of Article 2.2 of the TBT Agreement

247. Australia understands that the purpose being pursued by the EC measure is the implementation of matters concerning the availability, acquisition, scope, maintenance, use and/or enforcement of an intellectual property right expressly provided for by the *TRIPS Agreement* within the territory of the EC, and the prevention of associated deceptive practices. Australia does not contest that such purposes could constitute "legitimate objectives" within the meaning of TBT Article 2.2.

(iii) The EC measure fulfils, or is capable of fulfilling, its legitimate objective within the meaning of Article 2.2 of the TBT Agreement

248. Australia does not contest that the EC measure generally fulfils, or is capable of generally fulfilling, the legitimate objectives seemingly being pursued by the measure in respect of agricultural products and foodstuffs bearing an EC-defined GI.

(iv) The EC measure is more trade restrictive than necessary to fulfil its legitimate objective, taking account of the risks non-fulfilment would create, contrary to Article 2.2 of the TBT Agreement

249. As described previously,[134] Articles 4, 10 and 12.1 of Regulation No. 2081/92 read together require that another WTO Member have in place "inspection arrangements equivalent to those laid down in" the Regulation. Article 10.1 provides that "the function of *[the inspection structures]* shall be to ensure that agricultural products and foodstuffs bearing a protected name meet the requirements laid down in the *[product specification]*" and sets out the detailed requirements for the inspection structures. The precise meaning of "inspection arrangements" in Article 12.1 is not immediately clear given use of the expression "inspection structures" in Articles 4.2(g) and 10. However, Article 12a.2(b) expressly requires from another WTO Member "a declaration that the <u>structures provided for in Article 10</u> are established in its territory" *(emphasis added)*.

250. Accordingly, Australia understands that the requirement of Article 12.1 of Regulation No. 2081/92 for another WTO Member to have in place "inspection arrangements" is in fact a requirement to have in place the inspection structures required by Article 10 of the Regulation. Further, that requirement is absolute: it provides no leeway for regard to be had to the particular circumstances or the existing arrangements of another WTO Member.

251. Consistent with the requirement established by Regulation No. 2081/92, a producer in another WTO Member wishing to export to and market in the EC a product bearing an EC-defined GI registered and protected under Regulation No. 2081/92 cannot do so if that WTO Member does not have in place an inspection structure consistent with the requirements of Article 10 of the Regulation. Thus, the Regulation is restrictive of trade. It limits the opportunities for non-EC producers to be able to register an EC-defined GI under the Regulation to those cases where the imported products bearing a potentially eligible geographic term originate in WTO Members with such inspection structures in place. Producers in other WTO Members not having the same inspection structures in place are not able to benefit in trade from the protection afforded to products bearing registered EC-defined GIs under the Regulation.

---

[133] *EC – Asbestos*, paragraph 172.

[134] See paragraph 221 above.

252. Australia submits that the measure is more trade restrictive than necessary. By prescribing "inspection arrangements ... equivalent to those laid down in this Regulation," the Regulation mandates the type of structure or design for inspection that other WTO Members must have in place. In doing so, it essentially rules out the acceptability of other types of inspection mechanisms. The Regulation does not even leave open the possibility of verifying the adequacy of any existing inspection structures in other WTO Members before imposing an EC-type "model." The EC model is imposed regardless, even where the inspection structure required by Article 10 of the Regulation may be inappropriate having regard to the circumstances of another WTO Member.

253. For such a requirement to be necessary to fulfil the EC measure's legitimate objective, the EC would have to have determined that no other systems in any WTO Member could in any circumstances provide the same degree of assurance as the EC's system for compliance verification and/or enforcement, or for the prevention of deceptive practices.

254. Australia submits that such a determination is not sustainable: it creates a non-rebuttable presumption that all other such systems in place in other WTO Members are deficient in all circumstances compared to the EC's system. Thus, for example, the EC has determined that other WTO Members having in place a system of law that establishes a general prohibition on misleading and deceptive conduct in any commercial and/or food safety matters, administered by government agencies with wide-ranging investigative and enforcement powers, cannot provide the same effective level of assurance as the EC's system.

255. Further, the EC measure does not allow for the possibility of any inspection structure being unnecessary. There may, for example, be only one producer of an agricultural product or foodstuff that could qualify for registration of an EC-defined GI and who is the sole occupant of the geographical region where a good can physically be produced.[135]

256. Finally, the real problem of unauthorised use and/or deceptive practices concerning an EC-defined GI relating to a geographical locality in another WTO Member may actually occur in the EC itself involving goods from a third WTO Member. Imposing an inspection structure requirement on the WTO Member of production in such circumstances would be meaningless.

257. Australia recalls the factors discussed by the Appellate Body in determining questions of necessity in the GATT context, described above. In accordance with Appellate Body statements in *EC – Asbestos*, Australia submits that the EC measure is more trade restrictive than necessary because an alternative, less trade restrictive measure reasonably available to the EC exists that would achieve the objective of protecting EC-defined GIs in the EC.

258. TBT Article 2.2 requires in relevant part that "technical regulations shall not be more trade-restrictive than necessary to fulfil a legitimate objective, taking account of the risks non-fulfilment would create."

259. There may be risks that could result from non-fulfilment of the objective as described above. However, Australia submits that there are alternatives to the EC inspection structures that can achieve the legitimate objectives of the EC measure with the same degree of effectiveness. A legislative regime that prohibits misleading and deceptive commercial practices is one option. Such a regime could include an investigating authority that ensures that a product is marketed honestly, that is, that verifies its authenticity. This may operate in conjunction with food labelling laws, enforced by a food authority that, among other functions, ensures that foodstuffs comply with specifications. Such laws and systems which, in order to be enforced must have an inspection procedure in place, can address any risks created by non-fulfilment. The common law tort of passing off is another way through which the prevention of the misuse of IP rights is addressed. Industry certifications or self-regulation by producers are further possibilities.

---

[135] Even if there are only a limited number of producers, the inspection structure requirement could be meaningless if there is only a limited geographical region in a WTO Member in which a good can physically be produced.

260. Alone or in combination, there are alternatives that can ensure compliance with specifications to the same degree as the EC inspection structure model, thus serving as effectively the Regulation's legitimate objectives. Recognition of the equivalence of other systems that perform the function of ensuring that products meet specification requirements in other WTO Members would be a less trade restrictive alternative to imposing the EC-type regime on other WTO Members.

261. Australia submits that the EC measure is therefore more trade restrictive than necessary to fulfil a legitimate objective, taking account of the risks non-fulfilment would create.

D. CONCLUSION

262. The EC measure applies to an identifiable group or products. It lays down product characteristics or their related processes and production methods, including the applicable administrative provisions, with which compliance is mandatory, in respect of:

- the labelling requirement set out in Article 12.2 of Regulation No. 2081/92; and
- the requirement set out in Articles 4, 10 and 12.1 of Regulation No. 2081/92 to have in place inspection structures to ensure that agricultural products and foodstuffs bearing a protected name meet the product specification.

263. To the extent that the EC measure lays down product characteristics or their related processes and production methods, including the applicable administrative provisions, with which compliance is mandatory as defined in TBT Annex 1.1, it is a technical regulation for the purpose of the *TBT Agreement*.

264. To the extent that Article 12.2 of Regulation No. 2081/92 is a mandatory labelling provision that:

- applies to imported products, whether
    - imported products bearing a "protected name" that "is identical to a Community protected name," or
    - all imported products bearing a "protected name;"

and

- provides no discretion for a different labelling regime to apply when necessary to avoid less favourable treatment being accorded to imported products;

the EC measure is inconsistent with TBT Article 2.1.

265. To the extent that Articles 4, 10 and 12.1 of Regulation No. 2081/92 establish a mandatory requirement for another WTO Member to have in place in all circumstances an inspection structure as set out in Article 10 of the Regulation, the EC measure is more trade restrictive than necessary to fulfil a legitimate objective, taking account of the risks non-fulfilment would create, contrary to TBT Article 2.2.

XI. AS A CONSEQUENCE, THE EC HAS NOT COMPLIED WITH ITS OBLIGATIONS UNDER ARTICLE XVI:4 OF THE WTO AGREEMENT

266. Article XVI.4 of the *WTO Agreement* provides:

> Each Member shall ensure the conformity of its laws, regulations and administrative procedures with its obligations as provided in the annexed Agreements.

267. As a consequence of the EC measure's inconsistency with various provisions of the *TRIPS Agreement*, GATT 1994 and the *TBT Agreement* and of the EC's failure to observe its obligations pursuant to TRIPS Articles 1.1, 2.1 and 65.1, the EC has not ensured the conformity of its laws, regulations and administrative procedures with its obligations as provided in the annexed Agreements, contrary to Article XVI.4 of the *WTO Agreement*.

XII. CONCLUSION

268. Australia requests that the Panel find that the EC measure is inconsistent with the EC's obligations under:

- Articles 1.1, 1.3, 2.1 (incorporating Articles 2(1) and 2(2), 10*bis*(1) and 10*ter*(1) of the Paris Convention (1967)), 3.1, 16.1, 20, 22.2, 24.5, 41.1, 41.2, 41.3, 42 and 65.1 of the *TRIPS Agreement*;
- Article III:4 of GATT 1994;
- Articles 2.1 and 2.2 of the *TBT Agreement*; and
- Article XVI.4 of the *WTO Agreement*;

and that the European Communities should bring the EC measure into conformity with its obligations under the *WTO Agreement*, including in respect of the *TRIPS Agreement*, GATT 1994 and the *TBT Agreement*.

269. Australia further requests that the Panel find that, by being inconsistent with those provisions, the EC measure nullifies or impairs the benefits accruing to Australia under the *TRIPS Agreement*, GATT 1994, the *TBT Agreement* and the *WTO Agreement*.

ANNEX A-3

ORAL STATEMENT OF AUSTRALIA FIRST SUBSTANTIVE MEETING

(23 June 2004)

1. This is the first WTO dispute about those provisions of the TRIPS Agreement relating to TRIPS-defined GIs. Further, it is only the second dispute in which the provisions of the TRIPS Agreement on trademarks have been considered in detail.

2. As a consequence, this dispute has relevance for many commercial actors because of its potential impact on the economic value of their intellectual property rights. Further, many of these rights have been acquired against the background of more than 100 years of internationally agreed rules on trademarks.

3. The WTO dispute settlement system cannot re-write the covered agreements. In particular, we cannot attribute to the TRIPS Agreement rights and obligations which were not agreed during the Uruguay Round negotiations, notwithstanding that participants in those negotiations may have sought different outcomes.

4. Notwithstanding that there are some issues being considered for the first time in this dispute, at a fundamental, conceptual level this dispute is about four key issues. These become very clear when the EC measure is examined closely—and its practical application understood.

5. Firstly, is the EC treating the nationals and products of other WTO Members less favourably than it treats its own nationals and products? The answer is yes.

6. Secondly, with regard to registration and protection of EC-defined GIs, has the EC granted the rights in respect of trademarks it is obliged to grant by the TRIPS Agreement? It has not.

7. Thirdly, is the EC fully implementing its obligations concerning TRIPS-defined GIs? The answer is that it is not doing that either.

8. Finally, in implementing its regime for the registration and protection of EC-defined GIs, has the EC established certain requirements that are so restrictive that the EC has contravened the TBT Agreement? For anyone concerned with trying to meet the EC's requirements to register an EC-defined GI from another WTO Member, the answer is "yes."

9. Australia's claims and arguments in this dispute have been set out in detail in our First Written Submission. Australia will of course respond in detail in our written rebuttal submission to the arguments put forward by the EC in its First Written Submission.

10. My statement today will therefore focus on some threshold issues in this dispute: the measure at issue; the Panel's terms of reference; and the factual description of the measure. I will also recap some key legal arguments of Australia's First Written Submission taking account of some specific issues raised by the EC in its First Written Submission.

11. I now turn to the measure at issue in the dispute initiated by Australia. The measure at issue is essentially the EC regime for the protection of designations of origin and geographical indications for agricultural products and foodstuffs, for which Regulation 2081/92 provides the regulatory framework.

12. I want to emphasise that it is an EC measure that Australia is challenging. As the EC itself has stated: "the subject matter of the present dispute falls within the exclusive competence of the EC, and not of the Member States."[1]

13. The EC's arguments that versions of Regulation 2081/92 before the adoption of Regulation 692/2003 are outside the Panel's terms of reference[2] are without merit. The EC mischaracterises the measure at issue as set out in Australia's request for the establishment of a panel. The EC's argument equates the meaning of "[and] any amendments thereto (including ... Regulation ... 692/2003)" to "as amended by ... Regulation ... 692/2003," notwithstanding the plain language of Australia's panel request.

14. Australia is not seeking to analyse historical versions[3] of Regulation 2081/92 in a vacuum: it is seeking a remedy in respect of the 640 currently protected GIs that the EC is seeking to shield from the Panel's scrutiny.

15. Let me be quite clear on the terms of reference for this dispute. Australia has asked the Panel to determine—within the meaning of DSU Article 12.7—whether the EC measure is inconsistent with TRIPS Articles 25.4 and 41.1. To that end, the DSU permits the Panel to consider the EC measure's consistency with Paris Article 4 and TRIPS Articles 43-49 respectively. Indeed, such an examination is necessary for such a determination.

16. Australia also disagrees with the EC's argument that Paris Article 2.2 is outside the Panel's terms of reference in this dispute.[4] Paris Article 2.2 makes clear the point at which a WTO Member is no longer in compliance with its national treatment obligation under Paris Article 2.1. Thus, Paris Article 2.2 needs to be considered with Paris Article 2.1 as an integral aspect of a WTO Member's national treatment obligations, and was properly raised as an issue in Australia's panel request.

17. I turn now to some factual aspects of Regulation 2081/92.

18. The EC says that Australia misunderstands Article 12.1 of the Regulation.[5] The EC further says that Articles 12.1 and 12.3 do not apply to WTO Members.[6]

19. The EC's statement is extraordinary. The EC has consistently led other WTO Members to believe that Article 12.1 of Regulation 2081/92 applies to them. Confirmation of this can be seen in document IP/Q2/EEC/1 of 1 October 1997—the review of the EC's legislation on trademarks, geographical indications and industrial designs. In particular, I draw the Panel's attention to the EC's answers to the first question from India and the fourth question from New Zealand.

20. Further, in 2002, the EC was considering the changes to Regulation 2081/92 which were eventually adopted in Regulation 692/2003. An EU press release at the time said:

> ... [T]o improve protection of European quality products outside the EU ... non-EU countries ... would be invited to do so on a reciprocal basis. If a non-EU country introduced an equivalent system including the right of objection for the EU and the commitment to protect

---

[1] First Written Submission of the EC, paragraph 255.

[2] First Written Submission of the EC, paragraph 15.

[3] First Written Submission of the EC, paragraph 20.

[4] First Written Submission of the EC, paragraphs 36-42.

[5] First Written Submission of the EC, paragraph 65.

[6] First Written Submission of the EC, paragraph 66.

EU names on their territory, the EU would offer a specific procedure to register their products for the EU market.[7]

21. DSU Article 11 expressly provides that a panel should make an objective assessment of the facts of the case. An examination of textual provisions forming part of the measure before it is a proper exercise of the Panel's authority to assess the facts of the case. So too is consideration of whether the EC's explanation of those provisions is supported by the relevant texts.

22. Australia submits that the Panel should find that the EC's explanation is not supported by the texts of Articles 12 to 12d of Regulation 2081/92, and that Articles 12.1 and 12.3 must be considered to apply to agricultural products and foodstuffs from other WTO Members.

23. Australia further submits that the EC's advice that paragraphs 1 and 3 of Article 12 don't apply to WTO Members in effect constitutes an admission by the EC that the equivalence and reciprocity requirements of those provisions are inconsistent with the EC's WTO obligations.

24. The EC has sought to explain the decision-making process provided by Article 15 of Regulation 2081/92.[8] Australia submits that the EC's explanation of that process is not accurate. The plain language of Decision 1999/468 indicates that, in significant circumstances, the Commission cannot decide the matter without the consent of either the Committee or the Council, or until the Council has been unable to form an opinion for three months.

25. I turn now to the issue of country of origin labelling. The EC's explanation that the country of origin labelling requirement in Article 12.2 can apply to both the third country and EC names[9] is not convincing.

26. Australia submits that the Panel should find that the EC's explanation of the country of origin labelling requirement in Article 12.2 is not supported by the actual text of Article 12.2, particularly when read together with Article 6.6. As the EC admits,[10] the registration of an EC-defined GI from within the Community that is homonymous with an already registered name is governed by Article 6.6, not Article 12.2.

27. Australia notes the EC's statement that, in respect of the simplified registrations under the now repealed Article 17, the EC did not grant to the owner of a registered trademark within the territory of the EC the exclusive rights required to have been granted by TRIPS Article 16.1.[11]

28. I now turn to some of the key legal arguments that have been raised in this dispute.

29. As I noted earlier, Australia's claims in this dispute fall into four broad categories:

- the rights required to be granted by the EC in respect of trademarks;
- the EC's national treatment obligations;
- the EC's obligations concerning TRIPS-defined GIs; and
- the EC's obligations not to make technical regulations more trade restrictive than necessary.

---

[7] EU press release, IP/02/422, Brussels, 15 March 2002, to be submitted as Exhibit AUS-04.

[8] First Written Submission of the EC, paragraph 79-83.

[9] First Written Submission of the EC, paragraphs 87-88.

[10] First Written Submission of the EC, paragraph 89.

[11] First Written Submission of the EC, paragraphs 92-97.

30. For the purposes of brevity, instead of repeating the arguments made by the United States, I will instead note that Australia endorses those comments concerning the rights required to be granted in respect of trademarks. I make the following additional comments.

31. Australia will respond to the EC's arguments in detail in our written rebuttal. We want to emphasise, however, that Australia fully agrees that GIs are intellectual property rights covered by the TRIPS Agreement, and that the TRIPS Agreement establishes no hierarchy between trademarks and TRIPS-defined GIs as such.[12]

32. The real issue is whether the EC measure is inconsistent *at Community level* with TRIPS Article 16.1. Australia submits that the co-existence standard established by Regulation 2081/92 effectively deems the territory of the EC Member State of origin of the EC-defined GI to be synonymous with the territory of the EC as a whole. The co-existence standard ignores the principle of territoriality that has underpinned development of the international regime for the protection of intellectual property. As the Committee on Legal Affairs and the Internal Market of the European Parliament has noted, "to deprive a trademark owner of the exclusive right conferred by Community trademark law by obliging him to allow ... *[coexistence]* ... is tantamount to expropriation."[13] Further, such inconsistency cannot be justified by TRIPS Articles 24.5, 24.3 or 17.

33. Australia endorses the comments made by the United States concerning the EC's national treatment obligations under the TRIPS Agreement and GATT 1994, and offers the following additional comments.

34. The EC says that Australia has not claimed that Regulation 2081/92 violates the national treatment obligations of the TRIPS Agreement and the Paris Convention by requiring that applications be transmitted by the country in which the geographical area is located.[14] For the record, Australia has in fact clearly referred to this requirement in support of its claim that the measure as a whole does not accord national treatment to non-EC nationals.[15]

35. The EC also says that Australia has claimed that Regulation 2081/92 accords less favourable treatment because a non-EC right holder has no representative in the Article 15 decision-making process to speak for its interests.[16] For the record, Australia makes this argument in support of its claim that the measure as a whole does not accord national treatment to non-EC nationals.[17]

36. Australia has claimed that the EC breached its TRIPS Agreement and Paris Convention national treatment obligations by registering more than 120 EC-defined GIs under the normal registration process before 24 April 2003, because the EC did not provide non-EC nationals a right of objection. The registrations of those more than 120 EC-defined GIs—which in any case remain in force—clearly form part of the measure at issue in this dispute. The EC offers no explanation why making a right of objection to persons resident or established in the EC but not to other WTO Member nationals does not breach its national treatment obligations. Nor do the EC's arguments about retrospective remedies have any merit.

37. Finally, Australia notes that bringing the EC's measure into WTO conformity might not require "undoing" those registrations in the sense that Australia understands the EC to be meaning. The EC might, for example, be able to bring the registrations into conformity by providing for any right holders adversely affected by the registrations to be heard in a civil judicial proceeding, and/or to be justly compensated for any trademarks rights if unsuccessful in overturning particular registrations.

---

[12] *Ibid.*

[13] Report on the proposal for a Council regulation amending Regulation (EEC) No 2081/92 on the protect ion of geographical indications and designations of origin for agricultural products and foodstuffs, Committee on Agriculture and Rural Development, Exhibit COMP-14, page 35.

[14] First Written Submission of the EC, paragraph 127.

[15] First Written Submission of Australia, paragraphs 198-199 and 205.

[16] First Written Submission of the EC, paragraphs 153-155.

[17] First Written Submission of Australia, paragraph 203.

38. Australia does not argue that protection of TRIPS-defined GIs against misleading use or use which constitutes an act of unfair competition must be provided at any given territorial level.[18] What Australia does argue is that the EC must provide at Community level in respect of the Community level registration of EC-defined GIs the legal means for interested parties: to prevent misleading use of an EC-defined GI; and use which constitutes an act of unfair competition. This is particularly so given that Community law takes precedence over inconsistent Member State law.

39. I turn now to the TBT Agreement, which requires that technical regulations not result in less favourable treatment for imported products than for products of national origin. It also requires that technical regulations not be "more trade restrictive than necessary." Australia submits that aspects of the EC measure are inconsistent with both of these obligations.

40. Having regard to the findings of the Appellate Body in *EC – Asbestos* and *EC – Sardines*, Australia has shown that the EC measure is, in part, a "technical regulation" within the meaning of the TBT Agreement. To the extent that the EC measure sets out a mandatory labelling requirement—and sets out processes related to product characteristics—for agricultural products and foodstuffs eligible to bear a registered EC-defined GI, the measure applies to an identifiable group of products, sets out product characteristics, and requires mandatory compliance.

41. As the Appellate Body found in *Brazil – Desiccated Coconut*, the WTO Agreement was accepted by WTO Members as a single undertaking, and "all WTO Members are bound by all the rights and obligations in the WTO Agreement and its Annexes 1, 2 and 3." The Annexes of course include both the TBT Agreement and the TRIPS Agreement. Accordingly, a measure implementing matters concerning intellectual property rights is not necessarily excluded from the scope of the TBT Agreement.

42. The EC argues that Regulation 2081/92 itself "does not allow to identify" products which might be affected by Article 12.2.[19] Australia submits that the EC misunderstands the essential distinction made by the Appellate Body between products that are expressly identified on the one hand and those that are identifiable on the other.

43. Similarly, the EC's arguments that Article 12.2, and Articles 4 and 10 read together, do not set out product characteristics are not sustainable.[20] Labelling requirements are explicitly included within the scope of a "technical regulation." Australia submits that the EC's interpretation of Article 12.2, if correct, would render meaningless the concept of a label.[21] In addition, the EC argues that the purpose of Article 4(g)—read in conjunction with the inspection structure requirement of Article 10—is not to lay down product characteristics.[22] Regardless of the EC's intent, Articles 4 and 10 read together have the effect of establishing a process related to product characteristics within the definition of a technical regulation.

44. Finally, the EC's argument that the requirements concerning labelling, and concerning a process related to product characteristics, are not mandatory is not supported by the plain text of the provisions.

45. It remains Australia's claim that imported products bearing an EC-defined GI are treated less favourably than "like" domestic products in the circumstances in which Article 12.2 of Regulation 2081/92 applies.

---

[18] First Written Submission of the EC, paragraphs 401 and 415.

[19] First Written Submission of the EC, paragraph 447.

[20] First Written Submission of the EC, paragraphs 448-452 and 459-466 respectively.

[21] First Written Submission of the EC, paragraph 451.

[22] First Written Submission of the EC, paragraph 461.

46. Australia also maintains its claim that the EC measure is "more trade restrictive than necessary" because it obliges other WTO Members to have in place the same type of inspection structures as those mandated for the EC by Regulation 2081/92. The EC has failed to explain why other WTO Members' systems for compliance verification and/or enforcement, or for the prevention of deceptive practices, can never provide the EC's required degree of assurance.

47. There are many other issues that could be discussed in this statement. However, for the sake of brevity and given the processes ahead in this dispute, I will conclude Australia's statement at this point. I look forward to providing further detail through questions and answers, and in our written rebuttal statement.

ANNEX A-4

REPLIES BY AUSTRALIA TO QUESTIONS POSED BY THE PANEL AND THE EUROPEAN COMMUNITIES TO THE COMPLAINING PARTIES FOLLOWING THE FIRST SUBSTANTIVE MEETING

(8 July 2004)

1. To what extent is the Panel bound by the EC's interpretation of its own Regulation? **USA, AUS, EC**

The Panel is not bound by the EC's interpretation of Regulation No. 2081/92 to any extent.

In *EC – Hormones*, the Appellate Body said: "[s]o far as fact-finding by panels is concerned, ... the applicable standard is neither *de novo* review as such, nor 'total deference', but rather the 'unbiased assessment of the facts'."[1] This standard has been applied in all subsequent disputes (other than in those concerning the Anti-Dumping Agreement). Moreover, the EC itself said, in *Korea – Alcohol*, that "the 'deferential' standard of review ... finds no support in either the DSU or the GATT 1994."[2]
In *India – Patents*, India argued that the Panel should have given India the benefit of the doubt as to the status of the measure at issue under Indian domestic law. The Appellate Body found: "[i]t is clear that an examination of the relevant aspects of Indian municipal law ... is essential to determining whether India has complied with its obligations ... There was simply no way for the Panel to make this determination without engaging in an examination of Indian law. ... To say that the Panel should have done otherwise would be to say that only India can assess whether Indian law is consistent with India's obligations under the WTO Agreement. This, clearly, cannot be so."[3]

Australia submits that the obligation on the Panel in regard to the interpretation of Regulation No. 2081/92 includes an appraisal of whether the interpretation being put forward by the EC is supported by the text of the Regulation having regard to all relevant factors, including the plain text of the relevant provisions, explanations of the Regulation's applicability to other WTO Members previously offered by the EC, and the EC's failure to explain interpretive inconsistencies in its newly proffered interpretation.

2. Can the procedures under Articles 5 and 6 of Regulation (EC) No. 2081/92 apply to names of geographical areas located outside the EC? **EC**

3. Did the phrase "[w]ithout prejudice to international agreements" in Article 12(1) of Regulation (EC) No. 2081/92 predate the TRIPS Agreement? Did it refer to any specific agreements when it was adopted? Which agreements does it refer to now? Would it cover bilateral agreements for the protection of individual geographical indications? **EC**

4. Is it unusual that the text of Article 12(1) of Regulation (EC) No. 2081/92 covers only a small number of countries that are non-WTO Members, but the introductory phrase "[w]ithout prejudice to international agreements" covers the entire membership of the WTO? Why was this structure retained when the Regulation was amended in April 2003? **EC**

---

[1] *EC – Hormones*, Report of the Appellate Body, paragraph 22.

[2] *Korea – Taxes on Alcoholic Beverages*, Report of the Appellate Body, paragraph 68.

[3] *India – Patent Protection for Pharmaceutical and Agricultural Chemical Products*, Report of the Appellate Body, WT/DS50/AB/R, paragraphs 64-66.

5. In paragraph 8 of the US oral statement it is implied that the purpose of the phrase "[w]ithout prejudice to international agreements" in Article 12(1) of Regulation (EC) No. 2081/92 is to reserve the EC's flexibility to protect specific non-EC GIs through bilateral agreements. In the US view, in what way does the phrase apply to bilateral agreements? Please also explain on what basis the US draws the distinction between bilateral and other international agreements. **USA**

6. What meaning does Australia give to the phrase "[w]ithout prejudice to international agreements" in Article 12(1) of Regulation (EC) No. 2081/92? **AUS**

Within a different legal system and within a different context, this phrase could be read as a reference to ensuring the primacy of the WTO Agreement. However, in the context in which it is used Australia understands the phrase "without prejudice to international agreements" in Article 12.1 of Regulation No. 2081/92 was intended to allow for an international agreement—whether bilateral or plurilateral—to incorporate conditions different to those strictly required by Article 12.1. Australia further understands that the phrase does not—and was not intended to—incorporate the EC's obligations as a party to the WTO Agreement.

Australia's understanding of the phrase is based on the EC's earlier statements in TRIPS Council,[4] as well as statements by the Commission and by Committees of the European Parliament. Moreover, according to a presentation by an official of the European Commission at a WIPO National Seminar on the Protection of Trademarks and Geographical Indications in Beirut in March, 2003,[5] non-EU countries "can seek recognition for your country before the EU based on the fact that you have a system reciprocal to that of the EU. If your system protects GIs similarly (enforcement, level of protection), our registration system will be open to your GIs. You can conclude a bilateral agreement with the EU and all your GIs will be protected in Europe at once. EU authorities will take care of the defense *[sic]* of your GIs (as well)."[6]

Australia's understanding was reinforced by the EC's answer to a specific question on this very issue asked by Australia in our dispute settlement consultations.[7]

Further, in requesting the establishment of a panel, Australia expressly set out its understanding that Article 12.1 of Regulation No. 2081/92 established conditions of reciprocity and equivalence for the registration of EC-defined GIs from non-EC WTO Members.[8] Yet the EC did not seek to correct Australia's "misunderstanding" at either the 29 August or 2 October 2003 meetings of the DSB.

Moreover, Australia notes that the ECJ has found that: "... the WTO agreements are not in principle among the rules in the light of which the Court is to review the legality of measures adopted by the Community institutions ... It is only where the Community has intended to implement a particular obligation assumed in the context of the WTO, or where the Community measure refers expressly to the precise provisions of the WTO agreements, that it is for the Court to review the legality of the Community measure in question in the light of the WTO rules."[9]

The phrase "[w]ithout prejudice to international agreements" in Article 12.1 of Regulation No. 2081/92 pre-dates the entry into force of the WTO Agreement: the phrase therefore cannot have been intended to implement an obligation assumed in the context of that Agreement. Nor does the Community measure refer expressly to a

---

[4] For example, "Review of Legislation on Trademarks, Geographical Indications and Industrial Designs: European Communities," document IP/Q2/EEC/1.

[5] WIPO document WIPO /TM/BEY/ 03/11B, Exhibit AUS-05, attached.

[6] Exhibit AUS-05, Slide 15, attached.

[7] See question 12 of "Questions from Australia," Exhibit AUS-06, attached.

[8] WT/DSB/M/155, paragraph 74.

[9] Case C-93/02 P, *Biret International SA v. Council of the European Union*, Judgment of the ECJ of 30 September 2003, Exhibit AUS-07, attached.

precise provision of the WTO Agreement so as to enable Regulation 2081/92 to be considered in the light of a particular WTO obligation established by that provision.

Thus, the existing jurisprudence of the ECJ in fact precludes the EC's explanation that the phrase "[w]ithout prejudice to international agreements" enables the EC to apply Articles 12.1 and 12.3 of Regulation No. 2081/92 consistently with its WTO obligations.

7. Do the last sentence of Article 12(3) of Regulation (EC) No. 2081/92 and the first clause in Article 12a "[i]n the case provided for in Article 12(3)" limit the applicability of Article 12a? **EC**

8. Which references to a "third country" in Articles 12, 12a, 12b and 12d of Regulation (EC) No. 2081/92 include all WTO Members, and which do not? What, in the context of each reference, indicates what "third country" means? Why are different terms not used? **EC**

9. Why is it that only the rights of objection in Articles 12b(2)(a) and 12d(1) of Regulation (EC) No. 2081/92 mention a "WTO Member" or "WTO member country"? Is it relevant that Regulation (EC) No. 692/2003 explained, in its 10th recital, that in the matter of objections the provisions in question apply without prejudice to international agreements but, in its 9th recital, it explained that the protection provided by registration is open to third countries' names by reciprocity and under equivalence conditions? **EC**

10. Has the Commission recognized any countries under the procedure set out in Article 12(3) of Regulation (EC) No. 2081/92? Have any countries requested to be recognized under that procedure? **EC**

11. Has an application for registration under Regulation (EC) No. 2081/92 ever been made in respect of the name of a geographical area located outside the EC? If so, what happened? **EC**

12. Has any group or a natural or legal person interested in a geographical indication for agricultural products or foodstuffs originating in your territory ever sent a registration application to your authorities pursuant to Regulation (EC) No. 2081/92? If not, do you know the reason? **USA, AUS**

To the best of Australia's knowledge, it has not been sent such an application. As Australia noted in the first meeting of the parties with the Panel, Australia has not established any mechanism for identifying and/or receiving such information. Australia—consistent with the express preambular provision to the TRIPS Agreement—recognises intellectual property rights as private rights: in the absence of express commitments voluntarily entered into by Australia at international level which could require it to send such an application, Australia has not had any reason to seek such information. Further, Australian stakeholders would be aware, including because of previous statements by the EC, that they could not seek such registration given the reciprocity and equivalence conditions of Regulation No. 2081/92.

13. What discretion does the Commission enjoy in the application of Regulation (EC) No. 2081/92? **EC**

14. Please express your view on whether and to what extent the mandatory/discretionary distinction in GATT and WTO jurisprudence applies under the TRIPS Agreement. Would the nature of those TRIPS obligations which are not prohibitions but rather oblige Members to take certain actions, affect the application of the distinction? **USA, AUS, EC**

In *US – 1916 Anti-Dumping Act*, the Appellate Body considered that the reason it had to be possible to find legislation as such to be inconsistent with a GATT 1947 Contracting Party's obligations had been provided by the panel in the *United States – Superfund* dispute under GATT 1947.[10] The panel in that GATT dispute explained:

---

[10] *US – 1916 Anti-Dumping Act*, Report of the Appellate Body, paragraph 88, referring to *United States – Taxes on Petroleum and Certain Imported Substances ("United States – Superfund")*, adopted 17 June 1987, BISD 34S/136.

> [the provisions of the GATT 1947] are not only to protect current trade but also to create the predictability needed to plan future trade. That objective could not be attained if contracting parties could not challenge existing legislation mandating actions at variance with the General Agreement until the administrative acts implementing it had actually been applied to their trade.

Many of a WTO Member's obligations under the TRIPS Agreement are expressed in terms of the minimum standards of rights to be conferred and of processes to be made available in respect of categories of intellectual property. Thus, in some situations, it may be appropriate to apply in a different manner the Appellate Body's finding in the context of a covered Annex 1A agreement that "the relevant discretion, for purposes of distinguishing between mandatory and discretionary legislation, is a discretion vested in the *executive branch* of government"[11] *(emphasis in original)*. For example, Australia submits that the issue in the context of TRIPS Article 42 should more appropriately be considered to be whether a WTO Member has vested in its judiciary the authority to enforce intellectual property rights covered by the TRIPS Agreement.

Nevertheless, in Australia's view, the principles that underpinned the GATT panel's statement in *United States – Superfund* remain valid in the context of the TRIPS Agreement. In relation to the specified categories of intellectual property rights, the provisions of the TRIPS Agreement are intended to protect current rights and to create the predictability needed for the future protection of such rights. Further, that objective could not be achieved if WTO Members could not challenge the absence of mechanisms needed to attain the benefit of that protection in relation to a particular intellectual property right.

15. What would be the most authoritative statement of the interpretation of Regulation (EC) No. 2081/92? Is a statement by the EC delegation to this Panel legally binding on the European Communities? **EC**

16. Can the EC provide the Panel with any official statement predating its first written submission that names of geographical areas located in all WTO Members could be registered under Regulation (EC) No. 2081/92 without satisfying its equivalence and reciprocity conditions? **EC**

17. Is the EC's explanation of the availability of registration of foreign GIs under its system, set out in its written statement to the Council for TRIPS in September 2002, (IP/C/M/37/Add.1, para. 142 and Annex, pp. 77-85) consistent with the text of Articles 12-12c of the Regulation? Why did that written statement not qualify the position that the Regulation's equivalence and reciprocity conditions apply to foreign GIs, if they did not apply to WTO Members, to whom the statement was addressed? **EC**

18. Did the EC member States agree with the Commission's written statement to the Council for TRIPS in September 2002 with respect to the conditions attached to the registration of foreign GIs? How can the Commission ensure that the Council of Ministers will not prevent registration under the Regulation of the name of a geographical area located in a third country WTO Member because that Member does not satisfy the equivalence and reciprocity conditions of Article 12(1)? **EC**

19. Has a judicial authority ever ruled on the availability of protection provided by registration for third countries under Regulation (EC) No. 2081/92? If the Commission registered the name of a geographical area located in a third country WTO Member, could that registration be subject to judicial review because the area was located in a WTO Member that did not fulfil the equivalence and reciprocity conditions of Article 12(1) of the Regulation? **EC**

---

[11] *US – 1916 Anti-Dumping Act*, Report of the Appellate Body, paragraph 89.

20. With reference to paragraph 43 of the EC's oral statement, does the EC contest that equivalence and reciprocity conditions such as those under Article 12(1) and (3) of Regulation (EC) No. 2081/92, if applied to other WTO Members, would be inconsistent with the national treatment obligations in the TRIPS Agreement and/or Article III:4 of the GATT 1994? **EC**

21. If Switzerland, as a WTO Member, can apply for registration of its GIs under Regulation (EC) No. 2081/92 without satisfying equivalence and reciprocity conditions, what was the purpose of its joint declaration with the EC concerning GIs set out in Exhibit US-6 and mentioned in paragraph 119 of the US first written submission and paragraphs 243-244 of the EC's first written submission? **USA, AUS, EC**

Australia cannot speak for Switzerland, but notes that a paper by the Swiss Federal Institute of Technology Zurich concerning the protection of EC-defined GIs in Switzerland contains the following statement:

> *[Regulation No. 2081/92]* gave countries outside the European Community an opportunity to have their own products recognised and protected within the EC, provided those countries already had similar protection legislation in place[footnote 3].
>
> ---
>
> Footnote 3: Preamble to Regulation (EEC) 2081/92 of 14 July 1992.[12]

This statement indicates an understanding on the part of Switzerland that Regulation No. 2081/92 required that non-EC countries have in place at least a similar level of protection to that provided by Regulation No. 2081/92.

22. Are there any legal requirements or other provisions in EC or national laws which ensure that groups or persons entitled to apply for registration under Article 5 of Regulation (EC) No. 2081/92 are always, or usually, EC citizens or legal persons organized under the laws of the EC or an EC member State? What conditions have been laid down for natural or legal persons to be entitled to apply for registration pursuant to Article 5(1)? **USA, AUS, EC**

Australia is not aware of any legal requirements or other provisions in EC or national laws which ensure that groups or persons entitled to apply for registration under Article 5 of Regulation No. 2081/92 are always EC citizens or EC legal persons. At the same time, however, Australia notes the view of the EC that "geographical indications are the common patrimony of all the producers of a certain area, and ultimately of the entire population of that area."[13]

Having in mind the requirement of Article 5.4 that "[t]he application shall be sent to the *[EC]* Member State <u>in which the geographical area is located</u>," an individual non-EC citizen or legal person could normally only qualify to apply for registration pursuant to Article 5.1 as part of a group within the meaning of that provision. Australia submits that the effect of the requirement of Article 5.4—especially when interpreted in the light of the EC's view of the nature of a geographical indication—is that groups or persons entitled to apply for registration under Article 5 will almost always comprise EC citizens and/or legal persons.

23. How do you interpret the term "nationals" as used in Article 1.3, including footnote 1, and Articles 3.1 and 4 of the TRIPS Agreement and Article 2 of the Paris Convention (1967) in relation to this dispute? Do a Member's nationals necessarily include natural persons who are domiciled, or legal persons who have a real and effective industrial and commercial establishment, in that Member? **USA, AUS, EC**

---

[12] "The Protected Denomination of Origin and Geographical Indication Legislation in Switzerland: Institutional Aspects," Swiss Federal Institute of Technology Zurich, financed by the Office federal de l'éducation et de la science, November 1998, page 8, Exhibit AUS-07.

[13] First Written Submission of the EC, paragraph 307, 4th bullet point.

The 1900 Brussels Revision Conference of the Paris Convention unanimously agreed that Paris Article 2.1 applies to legal persons or entities, as well as to natural persons.[14] It was implicit in that decision that—for the purposes of the Paris Convention—a national in the context of a natural person was considered to be, and remains, a person who is a "national" of a state in accordance with that state's laws.

That decision of the parties to the Paris Convention continues to have effect in the context of the TRIPS Agreement through the provisions of TRIPS Article 1.3, which provides in relevant part: "[i]n respect of the relevant intellectual property right, the nationals of other Members shall be understood as those natural or legal persons that would meet the criteria for eligibility for protection provided for in the Paris Convention (1967) …." In any case, that decision continues to be relevant to a WTO Member's obligation to comply with Paris Article 2 through the operation of TRIPS Article 2.1.

Further, the intent of the negotiators in this regard is confirmed by Footnote 1 to TRIPS Article 1.3, which reflects recognition on the part of the negotiators of the TRIPS Agreement that the situation of a separate customs territory Member of the WTO required special consideration. Natural persons could not normally be a national of a separate customs territory in the sense of having the citizenship of that territory: thus a definition of a national that took account of expected circumstances in relation to a separate customs territory WTO Member was included.

In Australia's view, the term "nationals" as used in Article 1.3, including footnote 1, Articles 3.1 and 4 of the TRIPS Agreement and Paris Article 2 means:

- in the case of natural persons in accordance with the laws of the WTO Member of which nationality is claimed, either:

  - persons who possess the nationality of a state in accordance with that state's laws, and/or

  - persons who are domiciled or who have a real and effective industrial or commercial establishment in a separate customs territory WTO Member (as a proxy for the ordinary notion of nationality);

  and

- in the case of legal persons, such persons—whether companies, associations or other entities recognised in accordance with the laws of the WTO Member—who are domiciled or who are established in that WTO Member in accordance with the laws of the WTO Member of which nationality is claimed.

Thus, a WTO Member's nationals normally include natural persons who are domiciled, or legal persons who have a real and effective industrial and commercial establishment, in that Member. Australia notes, however, that these categories of persons would not always qualify as nationals.

24. In your view, which natural or legal persons can be considered "interested parties" in the sense of Article 22.2 of the TRIPS Agreement? Is Article 10(2) of the Paris Convention (1967) relevant? **USA, AUS, EC**

"Interested parties" in the sense of TRIPS Article 22.2 cannot be construed so narrowly so as to exclude the possibility of legal action in relation to any use of a TRIPS-defined GI which could constitute an act of unfair competition within the meaning of Paris Article 10*bis*. As provided by Paris Article 10*bis*.2, "[a]ny act of competition contrary to honest practices in industrial or commercial matters constitutes an act of unfair competition."

---

[14] *Bodenhausen*, page 27.

"[H]onest practices in industrial or commercial matters" within the meaning of Paris Article 10*bis*.2, however, includes the notion of honest practices established in international trade.[15] Thus, "interested parties" in the sense of TRIPS Article 22.2 must be capable of encompassing parties with an interest in honest practices in industrial or commercial matters in international trade.

Further, it cannot be presumed that legal action within the meaning of TRIPS Article 22.2 will only ever involve action to protect a TRIPS-defined GI against misleading use or use which constitutes an act of unfair competition. Having regard to the principle of territoriality and to developments in international trade over time, recognition of a TRIPS-defined GI—whether through registration or some other system—could in some circumstances result in misleading use or use which constitutes an act of unfair competition. For example, it is entirely possible that there are products which, while originally based on European production processes, have been further developed and refined outside the European country of origin and which have subsequently come to represent the "international" trading standard for that product: to register the original geographic name under Regulation No. 2081/92 in such circumstances—notwithstanding that the product may qualify for registration—could well constitute misleading use or use which constitutes an act of unfair competition within the meaning of TRIPS Article 22.2 even within the EC. This type of action is clearly contemplated by the text of TRIPS Article 22.2.

Thus, the categories of persons identified in Paris Article 10.2 could be "interested parties" within the meaning of TRIPS Article 22.2. On the other hand, "interested parties" within the meaning of TRIPS Article 22.2 must be able to include a broader spectrum of persons than just those categories. Moreover, Australia notes that the scope of Paris Article 10.2 concerns goods which use a false indication of the source of the goods or of the identity of the producer, manufacturer or merchant. That is, Paris Article 10.2 concerns acts which involve deceptive conduct. Misleading use or use which constitutes an act of unfair competition need not necessarily involve such deceptive conduct.

25. Is it appropriate to compare nationals who are interested in GIs that refer to areas located in different WTO Members in order to examine national treatment under the TRIPS Agreement? Why or why not? **USA, AUS, EC**

Yes.

The TRIPS Agreement is premised on the continuation of the principle of territoriality that has underpinned the development of the international intellectual property regime over the past 120 years and more. The TRIPS Agreement establishes minimum standards which each WTO Member must provide in respect of each category of intellectual property identified in the Agreement, but otherwise accords to a WTO Member a degree of discretion to determine matters concerning the availability, scope and use of intellectual property rights. Moreover, TRIPS Article 1.1 expressly provides that a WTO Member may implement in its law more extensive protection than is required to be provided by the TRIPS Agreement, provided that such protection does not otherwise contravene the Agreement.

However, the target, or "object," of the TRIPS Agreement—consistent with its title *"Agreement on Trade-Related Aspects of Intellectual Property Rights,"* and with TRIPS Article 1.3—is the "nationals of other Members." Further, in exercising the discretion permitted by the TRIPS Agreement, a WTO Member has an overarching obligation under TRIPS Article 3.1 to accord to the nationals of other WTO Members treatment no less favourable than that it accords to its own nationals with regard to the protection of intellectual property. That protection includes—but is not limited to—matters affecting the availability, acquisition, scope, maintenance and enforcement of intellectual property rights as well as those matters affecting the use of those rights specifically addressed in the TRIPS Agreement.

---

[15] See, for example, *Bodenhausen*, page 144, and "Model Provisions on Protection Against Unfair Competition," Articles and Notes presented by the International Bureau of WIPO, Geneva 1996, paragraph 1.02, Exhibit AUS-08, attached.

Moreover, the fact that GIs may refer to areas located in different WTO Members does not mean that the treatment accorded to persons seeking to benefit from the protection being offered by a WTO Member must be inherently different. Where a WTO Member offers more extensive protection for a category of intellectual property right than that required to be granted by the TRIPS Agreement, the treatment of the persons—whether natural or legal—seeking to benefit from that protection must still accord with that Member's national treatment—and most favoured nation—obligations.

26. If national treatment can be examined in relation to GIs in terms of the location of the geographical area to the territory of a Member, is it appropriate to examine national treatment in relation to any other intellectual property rights in terms of an attachment to a Member besides the nationality of the right holder? Why or why not? **USA, AUS, EC**

Australia is not contending that location may not in any circumstance be a relevant issue in relation to an intellectual property right—if that is the premise of this question. However, it is Australia's contention that the location of a geographical area is not a permissible basis to derogate from the EC's national treatment obligations in the context and circumstances of this dispute.

27. Can the Panel assume that it is likely that interested parties in relation to names of geographical areas located in a Member are nationals of that Member? Have the complainants attempted to gather data on the relative numbers of EC, and non-EC, interested parties in names of geographical areas located within, and outside, the EC that might be eligible for registration under Regulation (EC) No. 2081/92? Would such data be relevant? **USA, AUS**

If the term "interested parties" in this question is being used in the sense of persons with an interest in securing the registration of the name of a geographical area—whether from within or outside the EC—under Regulation No. 2081/92, Australia considers that the Panel can assume that such interested parties are likely to be nationals of the WTO Member in which the geographical area is located.

If, however, the term "interested parties" is being used in this question in the sense of TRIPS Article 22.2, in Australia's view the Panel cannot assume it likely that "interested parties" in relation to names of geographical areas located in a WTO Member are nationals of that Member: the context of TRIPS Article 22.2 necessitates a broader meaning be given to the phrase. See also Australia's response to Question 24 above.

Similarly, if the term "interested parties" is being used in this question in the sense of persons with an interest in preventing the registration of the name of a geographical area—whether because of the existence of trademark rights or because the name is considered to be generic or for some other reason—in Australia's view the Panel cannot assume it likely that "interested parties" in relation to the proposed registration of a name of a geographical area will be nationals of the WTO Member in which the geographical area is located.

Australia has not sought systematically to gather data on numbers of Australian "interested parties" in relation to the potential registration of names of geographical areas located within, and outside, the EC under Regulation No. 2081/92. Australia is, however, aware of potential "interested parties" within Australia in all three of the situations outlined above.

28. Do you have information on the numbers of EC nationals who are interested parties in relation to GIs protected in your territory for agricultural products and foodstuffs other than wines and spirits? **USA, AUS**

Australia does not have a system for the registration of GIs as a separate category of intellectual property other than for wines, and protection TRIPS-defined GIs is provided through a number of means.

Under the Australian Trade Marks Act, however, TRIPS-defined GIs for agricultural products or foodstuffs may be registered as certification trademarks. Pursuant to the provisions of that Act, for example, the terms "Stilton,"

"Grana Padano" and "Parmigiano Reggiano"—which are recognised EC-defined GIs under Regulation No. 2081/92—have been registered as certification trademarks in Australia.

Australia does not otherwise have any information on the numbers of EC nationals who may be "interested parties" in relation to the protection of GIs within Australia for agricultural products and foodstuffs other than wines and spirits.

29. The Japan – Alcoholic Beverages II, Korea – Alcoholic Beverages and Chile – Alcoholic Beverages disputes show that measures which are origin-neutral on their face can be inconsistent with Article III of GATT 1994. Is Regulation (EC) No. 2081/92 also open to challenge under Article 3.1 of the TRIPS Agreement despite its apparently national-neutral text? **EC**

30. In Article 2(1) of the Paris Convention (1967) as incorporated in the TRIPS Agreement by its Article 2.1, should the words "country of the Union" be read mutatis mutandis to refer to "WTO Member"? **USA, AUS, EC**

For matters relevant to this dispute, they can be.

However, notwithstanding that Australia itself has used the words "incorporated" and "WTO Member" as quick references to the obligations established by TRIPS Article 2.1 in relation to the Paris Convention and to "country of the Union" respectively in its First Written Submission, Australia notes that TRIPS Article 2.1 provides that WTO Members "shall comply with" Paris Article 2.1, rather than incorporating that provision.

31. What is the respective scope of the national treatment obligations in Article 2(1) of the Paris Convention (1967) and Article 3.1 of the TRIPS Agreement? Do they overlap? **USA, AUS, EC**

Paris Article 2.1 provides that nationals of any country of the Union shall enjoy in all other countries of the Union the "advantages" granted by those countries to nationals. On the other hand, TRIPS Article 3.1 provides that each WTO Member shall accord to the nationals of other Members "treatment" no less favourable than that it accords to its own nationals.

Australia notes that "treatment" encompasses a broader spectrum of action than "advantages," that is, the notion of "treatment" includes "advantages," but could also include disadvantages or costs. Further, having regard to the findings of the Appellate Body in *Korea – Beef*,[16] "treatment no less favourable" within the meaning of TRIPS Article 3.1 would not preclude formally different treatment by a WTO Member of its own nationals and the nationals of other WTO Members. Paris Article 2.1, on the other hand, requires a country of the Union to allow the nationals of all other countries of the Union to enjoy the same advantages as a country of the Union grants to its own nationals.

Thus, while there is an overlap between the obligations of Paris Article 2.1 and TRIPS Article 3.1, the obligations are not necessarily identical.

32. If Regulation (EC) No. 2081/92 grants different treatment to names, why does this amount to less favourable treatment to like products? What evidence is there of actual modification of conditions of competition? Would such evidence be relevant to a determination of less favourable treatment? **USA, AUS**

Imported products eligible to bear an EC-defined GI are treated less favourably than like domestic products eligible to bear an EC-defined GI because the imported products must overcome extra hurdles to the registration of a geographical name from another WTO Member as an EC-defined GI.[17] Further, Regulation No. 2081/92 as

[16] *Korea – Measures Affecting Imports of Fresh, Chilled and Frozen Beef*, Report of the Appellate Body, WT/DS161/AB/R, WT/DS169/AB/R, paragraph 137.

[17] First Written Submission of Australia, paragraphs 165-175.

a whole results in such cumulative and systemic less favourable treatment to the registration of a geographical name from another WTO Member as an EC-defined GI that it is, in effect, not possible to register an EC-defined GI for an imported product under the regulation unless that other WTO Member also operates a similar system of registration and protection of EC-defined GIs.[18]

In *US – Section 211*, the Appellate Body cited with approval the finding of the panel in the GATT dispute *US – Section 337* that: "... while the likelihood of having to defend imported products in two fora is small, the existence of the possibility is inherently less favourable than being faced with having to conduct a defence in only one of those fora." [19]

Regulation No. 2081/92, on its face, imposes the reality—not even just the likelihood—of extra "hurdles" to the registration—and thus protection—of an EC-defined GI for an imported product which do not apply to the registration—and thus protection—of an EC-defined GI for a like domestic product. Given the benefits of protection under the Regulation claimed by the EC, these extra hurdles significantly modify the conditions of competition for imported products vis-à-vis like domestic products.

33. Is there a public policy requirement specific to GIs which underlies the requirement that a group or person must send a registration application under Regulation (EC) No. 2081/92 to the EC Member State or authorities of a third country in which the geographical area is located, rather than directly to the Commission? **EC**

34. Is there a public policy requirement specific to GIs which underlies the requirement that a person wishing to object to a registration under Regulation (EC) No. 2081/92 must send an objection to the EC Member State or authorities of a third country in which he resides or is established, rather than directly to the Commission? **EC**

35. Has an objection to the registration of a name under Regulation (EC) No. 2081/92 ever been filed by a person from a third country? If so, what happened? **EC**

36. Has any person ever sent an objection to the registration of a name under Regulation (EC) No. 2081/92 to your authorities? If not, do you know the reason? If so, did your authorities transmit it to the EC Commission? **USA, AUS**

To the best of Australia's knowledge, it has not been sent such a statement of objection. As Australia noted earlier (question 12 above), it has not established any mechanism for identifying and/or receiving such information. Australia—consistent with the express preambular provision to the TRIPS Agreement—recognises intellectual property rights as private rights: in the absence of express commitments voluntarily entered into by Australia at international level which could require it to send such a statement of objection, Australia has not had any reason to seek such information.

37. Please indicate examples of other international arrangements, such as the Madrid Protocol, under which national governments cooperate by acting as agents or intermediaries in the protection of private rights. Which of these arrangements are established under international treaties and which under the legislation of one of the parties to the arrangement? Which are relevant to the matter before the Panel? **USA, AUS, EC**

Australia is not aware of any such arrangements that require cooperation by a national government in the absence of the express consent of that government to act in the capacity of agent or intermediary in the protection of private rights.

---

[18] First Written Submission of Australia, paragraphs 176-180.

[19] *United States – Section 211 Omnibus Appropriations Act of 1998*, Report of the Appellate Body, WT/DS176/AB/R, paragraph 263, referring to the report of the GATT panel in *United States – Section 337 of the Tariff Act of 1930*, adopted 7 November 1989, BISD 36S/345, paragraph 5.19.

38. If a group or person interested in a GI in your territory were to send an application for registration or objection to registration under Regulation (EC) 2081/92 to your authorities, would your Government be able and/or willing to transmit such an application to the EC Commission? If not, please explain why. **USA, AUS**

As a temporary measure pending the outcome of this dispute, Australia would most certainly send an objection to a proposed registration under Regulation No. 2081/92 to the EC Commission if the Australian Government were to become aware of such an objection. Longer term, however, Australia's view is that the EC has an obligation pursuant to the TRIPS Agreement to provide the means for intellectual property right holders to exercise their rights without intervention by another government.

Further, while Australia would certainly send an application for registration of an EC-defined GI from within Australia were the Australian Government to become aware of such an application, Australia could not state positively that it could meet the equivalence and reciprocity requirements of the Regulation, even as a temporary measure pending the outcome of this dispute. For example, it may be that Australia could not "provide protection equivalent to that available in the Community to corresponding agricultural products for *[sic]* foodstuffs coming from the Community" because of the existence of a trademark right in respect of a corresponding agricultural product or foodstuff, or because an EC-defined GI for a corresponding agricultural product or foodstuff is considered to be a generic term within the territory of Australia. Similarly, Australia may not have in place "inspection arrangements … equivalent to those laid down in this Regulation" for the product at issue. Thus, Australia may not have the ability to satisfy the requirements of the Regulation in some instances unless it were willing to provide a false certification, which it would not do.

39. Does an EC member State participate in decision-making on a proposed registration either in the Committee established under Article 15 of Regulation (EC) No. 2081/92 or in the Council of Ministers, where that EC member State transmitted the application or an objection to it to the Commission? Is the EC member State identified with the applicant or person raising the objection in any way? Are there any limits on the participation of the EC member State – for instance, can it object to an application which it transmitted? **EC**

40. How many applications to register names under Regulation (EC) No. 2081/92 have been considered by the Committee established under Article 15 of the Regulation or the Council of Ministers? **EC**

41. In paragraph 137 of your first written submission, you indicate that the term "such names" in the second sub-paragraph of Article 12(2) of Regulation (EC) No. 2081/92 is a reference to the first sub-paragraph of Article 12(2), and that this means that the requirement to indicate the country of origin applies where "a protected name of a third country is identical to a Community protected name." Please clarify the meaning of the following terms, as used in Article 12(2) of Regulation (EC) No. 2081/92:

(a) what is the meaning of the term "protected" in the phrase "a protected name of a third country"?

(b) does the phrase "a Community protected name" cover both names of geographical areas located in the EC as well as in third countries, registered under the Regulation?

(c) does the requirement to indicate the country of origin apply also where a name of a geographical area located in the EC is identical to a Community protected name (irrespective of whether this Community protected name is the name of a geographical area located in the EC or in a third country). **EC**

42. If Article 12(2) of Regulation (EC) No. 2081/92 applies to the registration of a name of a geographical area located in the EC that is identical to a name, already registered in the EC, of an area located in a third country, what is the difference in its scope compared to Article 6(6) of the Regulation? Why is it necessary to cover this situation in both provisions? **EC**

43 Where does Regulation (EC) No. 2081/92 provide for the registration of a name of a geographical area located in a third country WTO Member which is a homonym of an already registered name? Where does it provide for the registration of a name which is a homonym of an already registered name of a geographical area located in a third country WTO Member? **EC**

44. Can the EC provide the Panel with any official statement predating its first written submission that Article 12(2) of Regulation (EC) No. 2081/92 applies to names of geographical areas located in the EC and that Article 12(2) will be applied on the basis of the date of registration? **EC**

45. With respect to paragraph 135 of the EC's first written submission, could the Council of Ministers prevent a registration because the Commission applied Article 12(2) to names of geographical areas located in the EC on the basis of the date of registration? **EC**

46. Has a judicial authority ever ruled on the applicability of Article 12(2) of Regulation (EC) No. 2081/92? If the Commission applied Article 12(2) to the name of a geographical area located in the EC on the basis of the date of registration, could that action be subject to judicial review due to the fact that the area was located in the EC? **EC**

47. Are you aware of any GIs registered under Regulation (EC) No. 2081/92 that are identical or confusingly similar to Community protected trademarks owned by your own nationals? **USA, AUS**

No.

48. Would the United States pursue any claim in respect of Article 12(2) of Regulation (EC) No. 2081/92 if that provision only applies to identical names? **USA**

49. Do you seek separate rulings on the procedural aspects of Regulation (EC) No. 2081/92 or a ruling on the Regulation as a whole? For example, should the provision in Article 12(2) be examined in isolation, or would it be appropriate to adopt an approach like the Panel in Korea – Beef, which only examined a display sign requirement within its findings related to a system as a whole? **USA, AUS, EC**

DSU Article 3.7 provides in relevant part that: "[t]he aim of the dispute settlement mechanism is to secure a positive solution to a dispute." With that in mind, Australia requests that the Panel's findings be sufficiently detailed so as to facilitate a positive solution to the current dispute, including in respect of the procedural aspects at issue.

50. In paragraph 451 of its first written submission, the EC argues that labels which address the geographical origin of a product cannot be considered a technical regulation under the TBT Agreement, since they do not apply to a "product, process or production method." Why in the EC's view is the geographical origin of a product not related to that product or its process or production method? Does the coverage of the TBT Agreement with respect to labels depend on the content of the labels? **EC**

51. How should the term "like products" be interpreted under Article 2.1 of the TBT Agreement? If the labelling requirement in Article 12(2) of Regulation (EC) No. 2081/92 applies to situations where identical names arise between imported products and EC products, but does not apply to situations where identical names arise between two EC products, to what extent would this be a distinction between "like situations" rather than a distinction between "like products"? **AUS, EC**

In Australia's view, the TBT Agreement is—in part—an elaboration of the provisions of GATT Article III:4. Consequently—and having regard to the findings of the Appellate Body in *EC – Asbestos* concerning the meaning of "like products" in GATT Article III:4 and in the covered agreements more generally[20]—Australia considers that the meaning of "like products" in TBT Article 2.1 is substantively the same as in GATT Article III:4.

Australia notes that TBT Article 2.1 would not be applicable to situations involving identical names for two EC products. However, to the extent that Article 12.2 of Regulation No. 2081/92 mandates less favourable treatment for an imported product bearing a later registered EC-defined GI than that accorded to a domestic like product bearing an earlier registered EC-defined GI, it is inconsistent with the EC's obligation pursuant to TBT Article 2.1.

52. Does Australia allege that Article 12(2) of Regulation (EC) No. 2081/92 provides any less favourable treatment to imported products besides labelling costs? **AUS**

No.

53. The EC argues in paragraph 88 of its first written submission that Article 12(2) of Regulation (EC) No. 2081/92 is meant to be read in the following way: "whichever indication is registered later would normally be required to indicate the country of origin." If the EC interpreted Article 12(2) this way in practice, would this satisfy Australia, or would Australia also view this interpretation as providing less favourable treatment to imported products? **AUS**

If the EC were to interpret Article 12.2 of Regulation No. 2081/92 in the manner specified, this could be expected to overcome the provision's inconsistency with TBT Article 2.1.

Australia submits, however, that such an interpretation would be contrary to the plain text of Article 12.2 of the Regulation, which expressly relates to a situation where the later registered name is "a protected name of a third country." Further, as long as the provision is drafted in its current form, the EC is not bound to apply the interpretation it has offered, as the ECJ would enforce the specific terms of the Regulation were the EC's interpretation to be the subject of a legal action.

54. Article 12(2) of Regulation (EC) No. 2081/92 is designed to avoid "practical risks of confusion." How would the application of the country of origin label on the basis of a product's date of registration help avoid those risks of confusion? **EC**

55. Does the TRIPS Agreement apply as lex specialis as regards GATT 1994 and the TBT Agreement, with respect to a practical condition to differentiate homonymous or identical GIs on a label? Please comment in the light of Article 23.3 of the TRIPS Agreement, which is applicable to homonymous GIs for wines, and the national treatment obligation, which is applicable to GIs for other products. **USA, AUS, EC**

A special rule does not necessarily exclude the application of a general rule. Instead, two such rules may apply cumulatively, with the special rule prevailing only to the extent of any conflict between the two rules.

Australia notes that, in *Korea – Dairy Safeguard*, the Appellate Body cited with approval the Panel's statement that: "... the WTO Agreement is a 'Single Undertaking' and therefore all WTO obligations are generally cumulative and Members must comply with all of them simultaneously ... [...]," considering that this finding was supported by Article II:2 of the WTO Agreement on the integrated, binding nature of the WTO Agreement and its Annexes.[21] Indeed, the Appellate Body found further: "[i]t is important to understand that the WTO

[20] *European Communities – Measures Affecting Asbestos and Asbestos-Containing Products*, Report of the Appellate Body, WT/DS135/AB/R, paragraphs 84-100.

[21] *Korea – Definitive Safeguard Measure on Imports of Certain Dairy Products*, Report of the Appellate Body, WT/DS98/AB/R, paragraph 74.

Agreement is *one* treaty. ... [I]ntegral parts of that treaty ... are equally binding on all Members pursuant to Article II:2 of the WTO Agreement"[22] *(emphasis in original).*

Thus, in Australia's view, the issue of whether the TRIPS Agreement—or any particular provision of that Agreement—is *lex specialis* is not determinative unless and until there is shown to be a clear conflict between the TRIPS Agreement and another covered agreement, or between a specific provision of the TRIPS Agreement and a specific provision of another covered agreement.

Further, Australia does not believe there to be any conflict between TRIPS Article 23.3 on the one hand, and GATT and/or TBT national treatment provisions on the other hand. Australia does not see that a requirement to determine the practical conditions under which homonymous GIs will be differentiated from each other would necessarily involve a breach of a WTO Member's obligations. Indeed, the final clause of TRIPS Article 23.3 expressly refers to "the need to ensure equitable treatment of the producers concerned and that consumers are not misled." In Australia's view, had the negotiators of the TRIPS Agreement intended that TRIPS Article 23.3—or any other provision of the TRIPS Agreement—excuse compliance with a WTO Member's national treatment or MFN obligations under the GATT and/or TBT Agreement, they would have said so.

56. With reference to paragraphs 17-21 of the US oral statement, does the Panel need to consider the US arguments concerning the declaration under Article 12a(2) of Regulation (EC) No. 2081/92 and the inspections structures, if it reaches a conclusion on the applicability to WTO Members of the equivalence and reciprocity conditions in Article 12(1)? **USA**

57. Does the EC consider that it may apply equivalence and reciprocity conditions to WTO Members under Article 12a(2) or any other provision of Regulation (EC) No. 2081/92, even if Article 12(1) does not apply to them? **EC**

58. Please clarify whether your claim is that the requirement of the existence of an inspection structure as a condition for the registration of a GI is inconsistent with WTO obligations per se, or the particular inspection structures requirements under Regulation (EC) No. 2081/92, are inconsistent with the EC's WTO obligations. In the latter case, please specify in detail which aspects of the inspection structures required under the Regulation are inconsistent with the EC's WTO obligations. **USA, AUS**

Australia's claim is that the absolute requirement for an EC model inspection structure as a condition for the registration of an EC-defined GI—irrespective of the circumstances in the WTO Member in which the geographical area is located or of the circumstances of trade of a product bearing the name proposed to be registered—is inconsistent with the EC's obligations pursuant to TBT Article 2.2. Australia does not claim either that requiring some form of verification process that takes into account the particular circumstances of the WTO Member of origin of the agricultural product or foodstuff as a condition for the registration of an EC-defined GI is necessarily inconsistent with the EC's WTO obligations *per se*, or that there are any specific aspects of the required inspection structures that make it inconsistent with EC's WTO obligations.

59. Under what circumstances would the Commission consider the holder of a GI certification mark registered in another WTO Member to meet the requirements for inspection structures under Article 10 of Regulation (EC) 2081/92 (read together with Article 12a of that Regulation)? **EC**

60. Australia argues that the EC's inspection structures requirements are a technical regulation under the TBT Agreement (paragraphs 209-224 of its first written submission). Is there a dividing line under the TBT Agreement between a technical regulation and a conformity assessment procedure? If so, where does it lie? **AUS, EC**

---

[22] *Korea – Dairy Safeguard*, Report of the Appellate Body, paragraph 75.

It is Australia's claim that the absolute requirement for an EC model inspection structure as a condition for the registration of an EC-defined GI is a technical regulation. To the extent that Articles 4, in particular Article 4.2(g), and 10 of Regulation No. 2081/92 read together:

(i) apply to an identifiable product or group of products;

(ii) lay down a process related to product characteristics;

(iii) compliance with which is mandatory;

the EC measure is a technical regulation within the meaning of the TBT Agreement.

The dividing line between a technical regulation and a conformity assessment procedure is difficult to determine in the abstract. Australia notes, however, that it is the express and fundamental premise of TBT Articles 5-9 that the purpose of a conformity assessment procedure within the meaning of those provisions is to provide a positive assurance of conformity with a technical regulation or standard. Wherever the dividing line may lie—and Australia does not take a position on whether a technical regulation or standard and a conformity assessment procedure are necessarily mutually exclusive—a conformity assessment procedure requires at the very least a separate technical regulation or standard against which products are to be assessed. Does the EC contend that the product specification requirement set out in Article 4 of Regulation No. 2081/92 constitutes a technical regulation?

61. If the inspection structures are conformity assessment procedures, are the eligibility criteria for registration under Regulation (EC) No. 2081/92, against which conformity is assessed, technical regulations? **AUS, EC**

See response to question 60 above.

62. With respect to paragraph 259 of Australia's first written submission, can Australia provide examples of alternatives to the EC's inspection structures which would be less trade restrictive and achieve the same objective? **AUS**

As noted in response to questions 58 and 60 above, it is Australia's claim that the absolute requirement for an EC model "one size fits all" inspection structure as a condition for the registration of an EC-defined GI is a technical regulation that is inconsistent with the EC's obligations pursuant to TBT Article 2.2.

Having regard to the particular production circumstances of an agricultural product or foodstuff, an inspection structure that fails to meet the requirements of Article 10 of Regulation No. 2081/92—for example, one that engages staff as required rather than having qualified staff "permanently at *[its]* disposal"—could fulfil the objective of ensuring compliance with a product specification. In other circumstances, it may be that an inspection structure might not be necessary at all because of limitations—for example, geographical combined with a very small number of producers—on the production capacity of products from the territory of a WTO Member. In such circumstances, other means of ensuring compliance with the product specification, such as causes of action under the relevant WTO Member's law, may be sufficient to fulfil the legitimate objective being pursued. It may be that problems concerning the use of an EC-defined GI from a WTO Member arise in respect of products originating in a third WTO Member: a prescriptive EC model inspection requirement would not be of any benefit in such circumstances.

Otherwise, a WTO Member might have in place a system of laws providing a general prohibition on misleading and deceptive commercial practices: such laws and their accompanying enforcement mechanisms can cover misleading and deceptive practices, unfair competition consequences of misleading or deceptive use of GIs, and/or the prevention of abuse of the rights of IP rights-holders. The common law tort of passing off is another way by which the prevention of misuse of IP rights can be addressed. Industry certification and self-regulation by producers are further possibilities, as are food safety/labelling laws. Alone or in combination, these systems are alternatives that could—in some circumstances—provide the same effective level of assurance of compliance with a product specification as the EC model inspection structure.

Moreover, where these alternatives exist in another WTO Member, the requirement of the EC model inspection structure would constitute a requirement for a duplication of those existing mechanisms. As such, the EC requirement is more trade restrictive than necessary.

63. What does Article 14(2) of Regulation (EC) No. 2081/92 mean where it provides that a prior trademark "may continue to be used"? Can a trademark owner invoke the rights conferred by the trademark registration against the user of a GI used in accordance with its GI registration? **EC**

64. Does Article 14(2) of Regulation (EC) No. 2081/92 implement the provision in Article 24.5 of the TRIPS Agreement that measures adopted to implement the Section on GIs shall not prejudice "eligibility for or validity of the registration of a trademark, or the right to use a trademark" or does it only implement the provision that such measures shall not prejudice "the right to use a trademark"? **EC**

65. Does the scope of Article 14(2) of Regulation (EC) No. 2081/92, as drafted, include trademarks applied for or registered, or to which rights have been acquired, subsequent to both dates set out in Article 24.5(a) and (b) of the TRIPS Agreement? **EC**

66. Has Article 14(2) of Regulation (EC) No. 2081/92 ever been applied in a specific case? For example, what did the national courts finally decide in the Gorgonzola case, referred to in Exhibit US-17 and in footnote 140 to paragraph 163 of the US first written submission, after the order of the European Court of Justice? **EC**

67. Does Article 14(3) of Regulation (EC) No. 2081/92 affect the possibility of coexistence of GIs already on the register with prior trademarks, such as Gorgonzola? In these cases, is Article 14(3) relevant to the applicability of Article 14(2)? **EC**

68. Article 14(3) of Regulation (EC) No. 2081/92 mentions certain criteria. If these are not exhaustive, why does is it not expressly stated as in Articles 3(1), 4(2) and 6(6) of the Regulation? Do other criteria, such as similarity of signs and goods fall within "reputation and renown"? Is the criterion of "length of time [a trade mark] has been used" relevant to its liability to mislead if the trademark has not been used for a significant, or considerable, length of time? **EC**

69. Can the EC provide the Panel with any official statement predating its first written submission that application of the grounds for registration, invalidity or revocation of trademarks and Article 14(3) of Regulation (EC) No. 2081/92 will or should be applied in such a way as to render Article 14(2) inapplicable? **EC**

70. Do the EC member States agree with the Commission's submission to this Panel that the terms of Article 14(3) of Regulation (EC) No. 2081/92, if properly interpreted, are sufficient to prevent the registration of any confusing GIs? Could the EC member States apply national trademark laws in a way that made this impossible? Could the Council of Ministers prevent the application of Article 14(3) of the Regulation if proposed by the Commission in a specific case and apply Article 14(2)? **EC**

71. Has a judicial authority ever ruled on the interpretation of Article 14(3) of Regulation (EC) No. 2081/92? If Article 14(3) of the Regulation, the Community trademark regulation and national trademark laws were applied in such a way as to prevent the registration of GIs that were confusing with a prior trademark, could this be subject to judicial review? **EC**

72. The Panel notes the responses of Members to the Checklist of Questions in document IP/C/W/253/Rev.1 cited by the EC in footnote 150 of its first written submission, which show that there are diverse approaches taken by several Members to accommodate possible conflicts between GIs and prior trademarks. Would this mean that the TRIPS Agreement, in particular Article 24.5, allows for some degree of flexibility for individual WTO Members to implement their obligations? **USA, AUS**

The TRIPS Agreement does provide some degree of flexibility for individual WTO Members to implement their obligations. TRIPS Article 1.1 expressly provides that "Members shall be free to determine the appropriate method of implementing the provisions of this Agreement within their own legal system and practice." Consistent with that tenet, the heading of Part II of the TRIPS Agreement expressly refers to "Standards concerning the availability, scope and use of intellectual property rights."

On the other hand, TRIPS Article 24.5—read in context together with TRIPS Articles 16.1 and 1.1—does not provide for any flexibility in relation to pre-existing trademark rights to prevent confusing use. Indeed, the express purpose of TRIPS Article 24.5 is to protect such pre-existing rights.

73. Please supply a copy of the wine regulations referred to in paragraph 16 of the EC oral statement. **EC**

74. Which particular GIs did the EC protect under Regulation (EC) No. 2081/92 prior to 1 January 1995? Is Article 24.3 of the TRIPS Agreement relevant to any other GIs? **EC**

75. Which party bears the burden of proof in relation to:

(a) Article 24.5 of the TRIPS Agreement? In particular, does this relate to the scope of the obligation in Article 16.1? Does it create an exception for measures otherwise covered by Article 16.1? Or neither?

(b) Article 17 of the TRIPS Agreement? In particular, does this only permit exceptions to the rights conferred by a trademark, or does it also create an exception to the obligations imposed on Members? ***USA, AUS, EC***

In accordance with the Appellate Body's findings in *US – Woven Shirts and Blouses*[23] and as consistently applied in WTO dispute settlement since:

(a) a complaining party bears the burden of proof where a complaining party alleges a breach of obligations pursuant to TRIPS Article 24.5—otherwise, a responding party which relies on that provision to excuse or otherwise justify a measure's inconsistency with another provision bears the burden of proof;

- TRIPS Article 24.5 does not alter the scope of TRIPS Article 16.1. Rather, TRIPS Article 24.5 confirms the continued applicability of the rights granted by TRIPS Article 16.1 in the circumstances covered by TRIPS Article 24.5.

and

(b) a responding party bears the burden of proof in relation to TRIPS Article 17.

- In Australia's view, and having regard to previous dispute settlement findings relating to analogous TRIPS provisions concerning patents[24] and copyright[25], TRIPS Article 17 only permits a WTO Member to provide for limited exceptions to the rights conferred by a trademark.

---

[23] *United States – Measure Affecting Imports of Woven Wool Shirts and Blouses from India*, Report of the Appellate Body, WT/DS33/AB/R, page 14.

[24] *Canada – Patent Protection of Pharmaceutical Products*, Report of the Panel, WT/DS114/R.

[25] *United States – Section 110(5) of the US Copyright Act*, Report of the Panel, WT/DS160/R.

76. Article 24.5 of the TRIPS Agreement uses the phrases "validity of the registration of a trademark" and "the right to use a trademark." Please set out your interpretation of these phrases, in accordance with the general rule of treaty interpretation in Article 31 of the Vienna Convention on the Law of Treaties and, if appropriate, the supplementary means in Article 32. Please explain how you determine what is the relevant context. **USA, AUS, EC**

Relevant context for the interpretation of TRIPS Article 24.5 is provided particularly by the design and architecture of the TRIPS Agreement. TRIPS Article 24.5 is placed in Section 3, Part II, of the TRIPS Agreement, which is concerned with the "Geographical Indications" category of intellectual property rights. Moreover, TRIPS Article 24 is headed "International Negotiations: Exceptions." In Australia's view, in the absence of an express provision to the contrary, the exceptions set out in that Article can only be exceptions to the provisions of Section 3, Part II, on Geographical Indications.

Having regard to the ordinary meaning of the words in context and in light of the object and purpose of the TRIPS Agreement, to the provisions of Section 2, Part II, of the Agreement concerning Trademarks, and to the standards relating to the availability, scope and use of intellectual property rights set out in that Part, in Australia's view:

- the validity of the registration of a trademark refers to the ongoing legality of the good faith registration of a trademark.

  Thus, measures adopted to implement Section 3, Part II, of the TRIPS Agreement cannot prejudice, that is, affect adversely, such trademark registrations on the basis that the trademark is identical with, or similar to, a GI. In Australia's view, the legal bundle of rights contained in a validly registered trademark includes the exclusive right to prevent confusing use granted by TRIPS Article 16.1. As such, the obligation that a WTO Member "shall not prejudice ... the validity of the registration of a trademark" includes an obligation on a WTO Member not to act so as to undermine the exclusive right to prevent confusing use granted by TRIPS Article 16.1;

  and

- the right to use a trademark refers to the ongoing ability to use a trademark where rights to a trademark have been acquired through use in good faith.

  Thus, measures adopted to implement Section 3, Part II, of the TRIPS Agreement cannot prejudice, that is, affect adversely, such rights to use a trademark on the basis that the trademark is identical with, or similar to, a GI.

77. Article 24.5 of the TRIPS Agreement uses the phrase "right to use" a trademark. Why did the drafters not choose to state, for example, "exclusive rights" or "rights under Article 16.1"? Is that fact relevant to interpretation of the phrase "right to use" a trademark? **USA, AUS, EC**

As stated in response to question 76 above, Australia considers that the phrase "not prejudice ... the right to use a trademark" applies to trademarks acquired through use.

However, on any interpretation, the obligation to "not prejudice ... the validity of the registration of a trademark" clearly applies to registered trademarks, and therefore the obligation to provide the rights set out in TRIPS Article 16.1 remains applicable. The "exclusive right *[to prevent confusing use]*" or "rights under Article 16.1" are therefore already captured by the phrase "not prejudice ... the validity of the registration of a trademark." Whatever may have been the intention in including the phrase "right to use," it was clearly separate from, and in addition to, the exclusive right to prevent confusing use required to be granted in respect of registered trademarks under TRIPS Article 16.1.

78. With reference to paragraph 58 of the US oral statement, Article 24.5 of the TRIPS Agreement refers to trademarks; certain Members implement GI obligations through collective and certification marks; Article 25.2 refers to more than one category of intellectual property, as does Article 4 of the IPIC Treaty as incorporated by Article 35 of the TRIPS Agreement. Therefore, must the provisions dealing with each category of intellectual property covered in Part II of the TRIPS Agreement be restricted to one Section? Can the rights conferred by a category of intellectual property and an exception to them appear in different Sections of Part II? **USA, AUS**

In Australia's view, the customary principles of interpretation of public international law considered together with the design and architecture of the TRIPS Agreement would not support the view that obligations and exceptions in relation to any given category of intellectual property right covered by Part II of the TRIPS Agreement would appear in any Section other than the one dealing with that category of intellectual property right without an express, unequivocal statement to the contrary. Accordingly, an obligation and related exception would not appear in different Sections without an express, unequivocal statement to that effect.

79. Is there a conflict between Articles 16.1 and 22.3 of the TRIPS Agreement? How may a Member avoid or resolve any potential conflict? **USA, AUS**

Australia does not consider that TRIPS Article 16.1 and 22.3 are in conflict. For example, Australian trademark law expressly provides, at section 61, that the registration of a trademark may be opposed on the basis that the proposed trademark contains or consists of a false GI.

In rare circumstances and having regard to the principle of territoriality, it is possible that a registered trademark could become misleading over time. For example, because of advances in communication, the relevant public within the territory of a WTO Member may come to be aware that a term included in a trademark is in fact a TRIPS-defined GI for a product from elsewhere and thus be misled as to the true place of origin. TRIPS Article 22.3 recognises the possibility of such a situation and provides a means to resolve such a conflict.

80. Are any exceptions permitted to exclusive trademark rights under your domestic law for concurrent registrations, honest concurrent use or comparative advertising? If so, are these limited to other trademarks? Can they cover GIs? **USA, AUS**

Subsections 44(3) and (4) provide for concurrent trademark registration in cases of honest concurrent use, and prior and continuous use.

Section 122 of the Australian Trade Marks Act provides a number of exceptions from the rights granted to trademark right holder. These exceptions include:

- the good faith use of a person's name or place of business, or the good faith use of the name or place of business of a predecessor in business;
- the good faith use of a sign to indicate kind, quality, quantity, intended purpose, value, geographical origin, or some other characteristic, of goods or services, or the time of production of goods or of the rendering of services;
- use for the purposes of comparative advertising;
- exercising a right to use a trademark given to the person under the Act; and
- where a court is of the opinion that registration would be obtained if applied for. (This opinion would be based on evidence of use.)

However, the exception for use of a sign to indicate geographical origin does not create an exception for a TRIPS-defined GI. In fact, section 6 of the Australian Trade Marks Act expressly defines a GI in terms closely mirroring TRIPS Article 22.1. Moreover, where the Act refers to a GI as an intellectual property right, it does so explicitly. Thus, for example, section 61 of the Act expressly provides for the rejection of an application for registration of a trademark that contains or consists of a false GI.

81. Please cite any authority for the proposition that a Member must comply with a particular WTO obligation through a single measure applicable throughout its territory. Is your claim concerning an "EC-wide" level of protection based on the fact that the EC's member States are also WTO Members? **AUS**

Australia has not contended—and does not contend—that a WTO Member must comply with a particular WTO obligation through a single measure applicable throughout its territory. Rather, Australia contends that, while the EC can choose to offer more extensive protection of EC-defined GIs at the Community level, the EC must also ensure that it does not breach its TRIPS obligations in doing so. Given the EC legal system, and the terms of Regulation No. 2081/92 and of other EC and EC Member State law, the EC has effectively implemented a TRIPS right—at Community level—without also effectively implementing at the same level the concurrent TRIPS obligations.

82. If the Panel were to uphold the complainants' claims under Article 16.1 of the TRIPS Agreement, how would conclusions with respect to the claims under Articles 1.1, 22.2, 24.5, 41.1, 41.2, 41.3 and 42, and under Articles 10bis(1) and 10ter(1) of the Paris Convention (1967) provide an additional contribution to a positive solution to this dispute? **USA, AUS**

Other than in respect of TRIPS Article 1.1, Australia's claims concerning the registration of EC-defined GIs pursuant to Regulation No. 2081/92 generally address specific, separate aspects of the EC measure:

- in relation to TRIPS Article 16.1, it is Australia's claim that the EC measure does not grant to the owner of a registered trademark the rights required to be granted by that provision: thus, the claim concerns registered trademarks;

- Australia's claim in relation to TRIPS Article 24.5 is that the EC measure prejudices the eligibility of an application for registration of a trademark by denying a right of priority required to be granted by Paris Article 4: thus, the claim concerns an application for registration of a trademark;

- the situations covered by TRIPS Article 22.2 do not necessarily involve trademark rights: for example, a term may have become a generic product description in international trade before it was protected in its country of origin;

- Australia's claims in relation to TRIPS Articles 41.1, 41.2, 41.3 and 42 concern the EC's obligations to ensure the availability of procedures for the enforcement of an intellectual property right under EC law so as to permit effective action against an infringement; and

- Paris Article 10*bis*.1 deals with the issue of unfair competition, which is not otherwise dealt with in the TRIPS Agreement except "in respect of geographical indications" in TRIPS Article 22.2. A WTO Member's obligation to comply with Paris Article 10*bis*.1 includes the obligation to protect trademarks against unfair competition from a GI. The obligation in Paris Article 10*ter*.1 therefore ensures that a country of the Union/WTO Member actually provides the mechanisms necessary to assure protection against unfair competition in any guise.

Australia's claim under TRIPS Article 1.1 does not, of course, address a separate aspect of the EC measure. It does, however, seek confirmation that a WTO Member is obliged to give effect to the provisions of the TRIPS

Agreement before it is able to offer more extensive protection for one particular category of intellectual property right.

83. If the Panel were to reject the complainants' claims under Article 16.1 of the TRIPS Agreement, would there be any scope for it to uphold the claims under Articles 1.1, 22.2, 24.5, 41.1, 41.2, 41.3 and 42, and under Articles 10bis(1) and 10ter(1) of the Paris Convention (1967)? **USA, AUS**

Yes. Please see answer to question 82 above.

84. Are the procedures raised in the United States' claims under Article 22.2 of the TRIPS Agreement governed by Part IV of the TRIPS Agreement? If so, can they also be governed by Part II? **USA**

85. Are the procedures raised in Australia's claims under Articles 41 and 42 of the TRIPS Agreement governed by Part IV of the TRIPS Agreement? If so, can they also be governed by Part III? **AUS**

In the event that the Panel should consider that the decision-making process provided by Article 15 of Regulation 2081/92 does provide a means for the owner of a registered trademark to enforce rights required to be granted by TRIPS Article 16.1, it is Australia's view that the decision-making process constitutes an enforcement process in respect of such trademark rights governed by Part III of the TRIPS Agreement: Part IV of that Agreement is not applicable.

86. Article 4 the Paris Convention (1967) creates no right of priority for indications of source. Does this indicate that they are irrelevant for the purposes of the right of priority? **AUS, EC**

Yes.

87. What is the significance of the EC's statement that the complainants' claims are "theoretical"? Does the EC suggest that this affects the Panel's mandate or function in any way? **EC**

88. Please clarify the form of the recommendations which Australia seeks in respect of versions of Regulation (EC) No. 2081/92 prior to its most recent amendment, as distinct from registrations effected under them. Please cite to the dispute settlement rules and procedures of the covered agreements under which this form of recommendation is requested. **AUS**

In relevant part:

- DSU Article 3.7 provides: "[t]he aim of the dispute settlement mechanism is to secure a positive solution to a dispute;"

- DSU Article 11 provides: "[t]he function of panels is to assist the DSB in discharging its responsibilities under this Understanding and the covered agreements. Accordingly, a panel should make … an objective assessment of the facts of the case and the applicability of and conformity with the relevant covered agreements …;"

- DSU Article 12.7 provides: "… the report of a panel shall set out the findings of fact, the applicability of relevant provisions and the basic rationale behind any findings and recommendations that it makes;" and

- DSU Article 19.1 provides: "[w]here a panel or the Appellate Body concludes that a measure is inconsistent with a covered agreement, it shall recommend that the Member concerned[…] bring the measure into conformity with that agreement[…]."

The measure at issue in this dispute includes the registrations—and protection in perpetuity—of more than 600 EC-defined GIs pursuant to processes that were inconsistent with the EC's obligations pursuant to the TRIPS Agreement and the GATT 1994. Australia seeks rulings and recommendations from the Panel in respect of earlier versions of Regulation No. 2081/92 to the degree necessary to establish the extent to which the EC's actions in registering those EC-defined GIs were inconsistent with the EC's obligations under the covered agreements, and therefore the extent to which the protection afforded those registrations continues in perpetuity the EC's violation of its obligations.

89. Is there a notion of estoppel in WTO dispute settlement which applies where a Member refrains from raising claims in relation to a measure until after it is amended? **EC**

90. Does Australia challenge registrations of geographical indications, or procedures leading up to such registrations or to refusal of such registrations, that took place prior to 1 January 1996? If so, please explain how Article 70 of the TRIPS Agreement applies to these measures. **AUS**

The first registrations of EC-defined GIs under Regulation 2081/92 did not occur until the adoption of Regulation No. 1107/96 of 12 June 1996.[26] Thus TRIPS Article 70 has no applicable to these measures.

91. Please clarify the form of the recommendations which Australia seeks in respect of individual registrations. Please cite to the dispute settlement rules and procedures of the covered agreements under which this form of recommendation is requested. **AUS**

Please see response to question 88 above.

Australia seeks rulings and recommendations from the Panel to the degree necessary to establish the extent to which the EC's actions in registering—and thus providing ongoing protection to—more than 600 EC-defined GIs were inconsistent with EC's obligations under the covered agreements at the time at which those EC-defined GIs were registered, thus enabling those continuing registrations to be brought into conformity with the EC's obligations under the covered agreements.

92. Does Australia seek relief in respect of existing individual registrations for reasons related to rights of objection? How many such registrations were made under the former Article 17 of the Regulation? How many under Article 6? Does Australia seek relief in respect of any other aspect of procedures leading up to existing individual registrations? Please cite to any previous GATT or WTO panel report which has made such a recommendation. Please explain why such a recommendation would be appropriate in this dispute if the Panel upheld Australia's claim. **AUS**

Please see responses to questions 88 and 91 above.

Approximately 480 EC-defined GIs were registered under the process provided by the now repealed Article 17 of Regulation No. 2081/92. Australia understands the number of registrations pursuant to Article 6 of Regulation No. 2081/92 now stands at approximately 160.

Australia seeks "relief" in respect of existing registrations of more than 600 EC-defined GIs for which the EC did not:

- grant to the owners of registered trademarks the rights required to be granted by TRIPS Article 16.1;

[26] Exhibit COMP-3.a.

- provide to interested parties the legal means to prevent misleading use or use which constitutes an act of unfair competition within the meaning of Paris Article 10bis as required by TRIPS Article 22.2;
- grant the enforcement procedures required to be made available under TRIPS Articles 41.1, 41.2, 41.3 and 42; or
- observe its national treatment obligations pursuant to TRIPS Article 3.1, Paris Article 2 and GATT Article III:4.

Australia is not aware of a similar factual situation arising in another dispute. That said, Australia does not believe that what it is seeking is unusual. Once the Panel has determined which aspects of the EC measure are WTO inconsistent, it is open to the EC to determine the action necessary to bring its measure into conformity. It may be possible for the EC to do this by providing to persons adversely affected by the registrations access to a civil judicial proceeding vested—in respect of registrations of EC-defined GIs pursuant to Regulation No. 2081/92—with the authority required to be made available by Part III of the TRIPS Agreement or with the authority to hear and determine claims pursuant to TRIPS Article 22.2. Alternatively, it may be possible for the EC to bring some registrations into conformity through the provision of just compensation for any trademark rights unable to be otherwise remedied. Ultimately, it may be that a few registrations of EC-defined GIs might have to be revoked, although Australia notes that such action is normally prospective in effect.

93. Does Australia seek relief in respect of individual registrations in respect of their continuing inconsistency with trademark rights to be conferred under Article 16.1 of the TRIPS Agreement? If so, please list these individual registrations. **AUS**

Australia seeks relief in respect of the continuing protection of individual EC-defined GIs whose registrations were made inconsistently with the EC's obligations under the covered agreements, including because of the EC's failure to grant to the owner of a registered trademark the rights required to be granted by TRIPS Article 16.1.

Australia is not able to say which individual registrations may have constituted a denial of rights to trademark right holders—which are expressly recognised by the TRIPS Agreement as private rights—or to another party with a legitimate interest under any of the cited provisions. With due respect, however, nor can the EC legitimately say that its actions have not resulted in a denial of rights required to have been granted or made available under the TRIPS Agreement, as it has never provided the means to enable such issues to be tested.

It may be possible, therefore, having regard to the answer to question 92 above, to "implement" any adverse findings by the Panel via the provision of such means. This may lead to few, or to many, of the individual registrations being contested.

QUESTIONS POSED BY THE EUROPEAN COMMUNITIES TO THE COMPLAINING PARTIES

1. ***Australia:*** *Could you please give details of any case where the authorities of the Member States have declared inadmissible an objection for the reasons alleged under Claim 21 (Australia's FWS, paras. 88-92)*

Australia has not claimed that an EC Member State has declared inadmissible an objection made to it. Whether an individual EC Member State has declared an objection to be inadmissible in a particular case is irrelevant.

Rather, Australia has claimed that Regulation No. 2081/92 as such does not ensure the admissibility of a statement of objection from the owner of a registered trademark on the grounds that a proposed EC-defined GI would constitute use of an identical or similar sign for identical or similar goods that would result in a likelihood of confusion.[27] As the Court of First Instance said in the Canard Judgment: "[n]o provision in Article 7 of Regulation 2081/92 authorises the Commission to consider an objection notified to it by anyone other than a Member State."[28] As the Court has confirmed that the Regulation does not ensure that a statement of objection from any person—let alone a trademark right holder—is admissible, the Regulation as such denies to the owner of a registered trademark the exclusive right to prevent unauthorised confusing use in relation to an EC-defined GIs registered under the Regulation, contrary to the EC's obligation to grant such a right pursuant to TRIPS Article 16.1.

2. ***Australia:*** *Could you please give details of any application for the registration of a trademark that has been refused for the reasons alleged under Claim 24 (Australia's FWS, paras. 81-87).*

Australia has not claimed that the EC has refused an application in the circumstances covered by Australia's claim that the EC measure is inconsistent with the EC's obligations pursuant to TRIPS Article 24.5. Rather, Australia claims that Regulation No. 2081/92 as such does not provide—and never has provided—the right of priority required to be granted pursuant to Paris Article 4 in relation to the registration of an EC-defined GI under the Regulation.

3. ***United States:*** *The EC understands that the regulations of the US Alcohol and Tobacco Tax and Trade Board, and more specifically Section 27 CFR 4.39(i), provide for the co-existence of geographical indications for wine and some earlier trademarks, under certain conditions.*

(a) Is this understanding correct?

(b) If so, how does the United States reconcile this form of co-existence with the interpretation of Articles 16.1 and 24.5 of the TRIPS Agreement that it has put forward in this dispute?

4. ***Australia:*** *The EC understands that Australia's Wine and Brandy Corporation Act 1980 (the "WBC Act") prohibits the use of a registered geographical indication for wine which does not originate in the area covered by the geographical indication. The EC further understands that no exception to this prohibition is provided with respect to prior trademarks.*

(a) Is this understanding correct?

(b) If so, how does Australia reconcile this prohibition on the use of earlier trademarks with the interpretation of Articles 16 and 24.5 of the TRIPS Agreement that it has advanced in this dispute?

---

[27] First Written Submission of Australia, paragraph 92.

[28] The Canard Judgment, Exhibit COMP-12, paragraph 45.

The WBC Act provides that it is an offence to sell, export or import wine with a false or misleading description and presentation. The description and presentation of a wine is false if, *inter alia*, it includes the name of a registered GI and the wine did not originate in the country, region or locality in relation to which the GI is registered. All GIs that are protected under the WBC Act notwithstanding prior trademark rights are protected with the consent of the owners of those trademarks. Consent by a trademark owner not to use a trademark in the course of trade is a very different issue to the denial by a WTO Member of rights required to be granted to trademark owners pursuant to the TRIPS Agreement.

5. ***Australia:*** *The EC further understands that the Geographical Indications Committee set up by the WBC Act has announced that*

> *The GIC will not determine a geographical indication where there is an exclusive trademark using the name which is the same or similar to the trademark, without the approval of the trademark owner.*

(a) Is this policy still in place?

Yes.

(b) What is the legal basis for this policy? Has the GIC the authority to derogate from the WBC Act?

Under Regulation 25 of the WBC Act, when determining a GI, the Committee is not prohibited from having regard to any other relevant matters. Relevant matters include the existence of a prior trademark using a name which is the same as or similar to the proposed GI as well as the trademark owner's consent to the determination of the GI as proposed.

(c) Does this policy apply also with the respect to the registration of foreign geographical indications?

Foreign GIs other than those registered pursuant to a bilateral agreement (such as the Agreement between Australia and the European Community on Trade in Wine) are determined by the Australian Wine and Brandy Corporation under subsection 8(2)(ad) of the WBC Act. The Australian Wine and Brandy Corporation is developing administrative procedures for the determination of such foreign GIs. Nonetheless, the provisions of the WBC Act allow for the inclusion in such procedures of a policy similar to that applied by the GIC regarding the existence of prior trademark rights in relation to a name which is the same as or similar to a proposed foreign GI.

Once registered, all GIs—whether Australian or foreign—are given equal protection under the WBC Act.

(d) If so, does it apply also when the trademark was registered after 1 January 1996 and after the date of protection of the geographical indication in the country of origin?

AND

(e) If so, how does Australia reconcile this policy with the terms of Article 24.5 of the TRIPS Agreement?

An application for registration of a GI under the WBC Act is considered on its merits, having regard to the principle of territoriality.

6. ***Australia:***

(a) Are the registration and opposition procedures before Australia's Trade Mark Office "enforcement procedures" within the meaning of Part III of the TRIPS Agreement?

The registration and opposition procedures before the Trade Mark Office of IP Australia are part of a broader system whereby trademark right holders can enforce their rights as granted by section 20 of the Australian Trade Marks Act. To the extent that the registration and opposition procedures before the Trade Mark Office provide a means for a trademark right holder to enforce his/her trademark rights, those procedures may be characterised as "enforcement procedures" within the meaning of Part III of the TRIPS Agreement. Further, all decisions concerning registration and opposition in relation to a trademark application are reviewable *de novo* in the Federal Court of Australia.

(b) Is Australia's Trade Mark Office a "judicial body"?

No.

(c) Are the registration and opposition procedures before Australia's Trade Mark Office "judicial procedures" within the meaning of Article 42 of the TRIPS Agreement?

Australia does not consider the registration and opposition procedures before the Trade Mark Office of IP Australia to be "judicial procedures" within the meaning of TRIPS Article 42. However, all decisions concerning registration and opposition in relation to a trademark application are reviewable *de novo* in the Federal Court of Australia, which are judicial procedures within the meaning of TRIPS Article 42.

(d) Does Australia's Trade Mark Office have the authority to order the remedies provided in Articles 44, 45 and 46 of the TRIPS Agreement?

The Federal Court of Australia has the authority to order remedies within the meaning of TRIPS Articles 44-46.

7. ***United States:***

(a) Are the registration and opposition procedures before the US Patent and Trademark Office ("PTO") "enforcement procedures" within the meaning of Part III of the TRIPS Agreement?

(b) Is the US PTO a "judicial body"?

(c) Are the registration and opposition procedures before the US PTO "judicial procedures" within the meaning of Article 42 of the TRIPS Agreement?

(d) Does the US PTO have the authority to order the remedies provided in Articles 44, 45 and 46 of the TRIPS Agreement?

8. ***Australia and the United States:***

(a) Would it be possible under your domestic law for an EC national who owns an Australia/US trademark to claim before the Australian/US courts that another trademark has been registered by Australia's Trade Mark Office / the US PTO in violation of Article 16.1 of the TRIPS Agreement, even where it is not contested that such registration is in conformity with all the relevant provisions of your domestic trademark law?

A decision to register a trademark is reviewable *de novo* by the Federal Court of Australia. Thus, it would be possible for an EC national who owns an Australian trademark to claim before that court that another trademark has been registered by the Trade Marks Office of IP Australia in violation of the exclusive rights to use a trade mark and to authorise other persons to use that trademark granted by section 20 of the Australian Trade Marks Act, which implements Australia's obligations pursuant to TRIPS Article 16.1,[29] even where it is not contested that the later registration is in conformity with all the relevant provisions of the Act.

> *(b) If not, is it your position that your domestic law is inconsistent with Part III of the TRIPS Agreement, because it does not provide "judicial civil procedures" in order to "enforce" Article 16.1?*

Not applicable.

*9. **Australia:** The WBC Act set up a register of geographical indications. While the WBC Act lays down the conditions and procedures for the registration of Australian geographical indications, it does not appear to provide any conditions or procedures for the registration of foreign geographical indications.*

> *(a) Can foreign geographical indications be registered under the WBC Act?*

Yes. Foreign GIs can be determined and registered under the WBC Act pursuant to subsections 8(2) and 40ZD(2) respectively.

> *(b) If so, what are the relevant conditions and procedures for the registration of foreign geographical indications?*

Pursuant to the provisions of subsection 8(2)(ad) of the WBC Act, applications for the registration of foreign GIs (other than those registered pursuant to a bilateral agreement with Australia) can be received from either individuals or foreign countries. Administrative procedures for the determination of such foreign GIs are currently being developed by the Australian Wine and Brandy Corporation.

Foreign GIs protected under bilateral agreements with Australia are registered under subsection 40ZD(2) of the WBC Act in accordance with the provisions of the bilateral agreement.

> *(c) Has any foreign geographical indication been registered under the WBC Act, other than those registered pursuant to a bilateral agreement?*

No foreign GIs have been registered under the WBC Act other than those registered pursuant to a bilateral agreement. Nor have any applications to register such GIs been received.

*10. **Australia and the United States:** Have Australia and the United States ever been requested to transmit an application for the registration, under Regulation 2081/92, of a geographical indication relating to an area located in their territory? If yes, what action have they taken?*

To the best of Australia's knowledge, it has not been requested to "transmit"[30] such an application. Stakeholders would be aware that Regulation No. 2081/92 requires reciprocal and equivalent treatment of EC-defined GIs for corresponding agricultural products or foodstuffs, which Australia is not obliged to provide.

*11. **Australia and the United States:** Have Australia and the United States ever been requested to transmit a statement of objection to the registration, under Regulation 2081/92, of a geographical indication? If yes, what action have they taken?*

---

[29] The provisions of international agreement do not have direct effect in Australian law.

[30] It is unclear to Australia whether the EC is using the word "transmit" in the sense of Article 12a.2 of Regulation No. 2081/92, or simply in the sense of acting as a postbox to onforward an application.

To the best of Australia's knowledge, it has not been requested to "transmit" [31] such a statement of objection. As Australia noted before the Panel, Australia has not established any mechanism for identifying and/or receiving such information. Australia—consistent with the express preambular provision to the TRIPS Agreement—recognises intellectual property rights as private rights: in the absence of express commitments voluntarily entered into by Australia at international level which could require it to "transmit" such a statement of objection, Australia has not had any reason to systematically assemble such information.

With the growing list of agricultural products and foodstuffs for which registration—and thus protection—of EC-defined GIs is available under Regulation No. 2081/92, an increased number of stakeholders want to ensure that they can safeguard their intellectual property rights within the EC both now and into the future. This may in the future include seeking that the Australian Government "transmit" an objection on their behalf.

12. ***United States:*** *How many US geographical indications for products falling under the scope of Regulation 2081/92 are protected in the United States?*

13. ***Australia:*** *How many Australian geographical indications for products falling under the scope of Regulation 2081/92 are protected in Australia?*

Australia does not have a system for the registration of GIs as a separate category of intellectual property right other than for wines. Protection of TRIPS-defined GIs for other products is provided through a number of means.

However, Australia is a large agricultural producer with many high quality production regions. Given the growing list of agricultural products and foodstuffs for which registration—and thus protection—may be sought under Regulation No. 2081/92, Australia believes that there are a significant number of Australian terms that producers could seek to have registered—and thus protected—under the Regulation for the purposes of export into the EC.

[31] Again, it is unclear to Australia whether the EC is using the word "transmit" in the sense of Article 12d.1 of Regulation No. 2081/92, or simply in the sense of acting as a postbox to onforward an objection.

ANNEX A-5

WRITTEN REBUTTAL SUBMISSION OF AUSTRALIA

(22 July 2004)

TABLE OF CONTENTS

(iv) Article 24.3 of the TRIPS Agreement is irrelevant to the matters at issue

(v) The requirement for co-existence of a pre-existing trademark right and an EC-defined GI cannot be justified by Article 17 of the TRIPS Agreement

(vi) The EC measure does not ensure that an objection from the owner of a registered trademark is admissible or that such an objection is considered through the Article 15 decision-making process, contrary to Article 16.1 of the TRIPS Agreement

(vii) Conclusion

B. IN RESPECT OF THE REGISTRATION OF AN EC-DEFINED GI, THE EC MEASURE DOES NOT PROVIDE A PRESUMPTION OF A LIKELIHOOD OF CONFUSION IN THE CASE OF USE OF AN IDENTICAL SIGN FOR IDENTICAL GOODS, CONTRARY TO ARTICLE 16.1 OF THE TRIPS AGREEMENT

C. IN RESPECT OF THE REGISTRATION OF AN EC-DEFINED GI, THE EC MEASURE PREJUDICES THE VALIDITY OF AN APPLICATION FOR THE REGISTRATION OF A TRADEMARK BY FAILING TO GRANT THE RIGHT OF PRIORITY REQUIRED TO BE GRANTED UNDER ARTICLE 4 OF THE PARIS CONVENTION, CONTRARY TO ARTICLE 24.5 OF THE TRIPS AGREEMENT

D. IN RESPECT OF THE REGISTRATION OF AN EC-DEFINED GI, THE EC MEASURE DOES NOT ASSURE TO WTO MEMBER NATIONALS EITHER EFFECTIVE PROTECTION AGAINST UNFAIR COMPETITION OR APPROPRIATE LEGAL REMEDIES TO REPRESS ACTS OF UNFAIR COMPETITION, CONTRARY TO ARTICLE 2.1 OF THE TRIPS AGREEMENT "INCORPORATING" ARTICLES 10BIS(1) AND 10TER(1) OF THE PARIS CONVENTION (1967)

E. IN RESPECT OF THE REGISTRATION OF AN EC-DEFINED GI, THE EC MEASURE IS INCONSISTENT WITH ARTICLES 41.1, 41.2, 41.3 AND 42 OF THE TRIPS AGREEMENT

(i) Introduction

(ii) In respect of the registration of an EC-defined GI, the EC measure does not make available to trademark right holders civil judicial procedures concerning the enforcement of their intellectual property rights, contrary to Article 42 of the TRIPS Agreement

(iii) In respect of the registration of an EC-defined GI, the EC measure provides procedures which are not fair and equitable, and which are unnecessarily complicated and entail unwarranted delays, contrary to Article 41.2 of the TRIPS Agreement

(iv) In respect of the registration of an EC-defined GI, the EC measure does not ensure that decisions are based only on evidence in respect of which trademark right holders were offered the opportunity to be heard, contrary to Article 41.3 of the TRIPS Agreement

(v) In respect of the registration of an EC-defined GI, the EC measure does not ensure the availability under EC law of enforcement procedures as specified in Part III of the TRIPS Agreement so as to permit effective action against any act of infringement or trademark rights, contrary to Article 41.1 of the TRIPS Agreement

F. IN RESPECT OF DECISIONS BY EC MEMBER STATES TO GRANT TRANSITIONAL NATIONAL PROTECTION TO A PROPOSED EC-DEFINED GI, THE EC MEASURE DIMINISHES THE LEGAL PROTECTION FOR TRADEMARKS, CONTRARY TO ARTICLES 2.1 ("INCORPORATING" ARTICLES 10BIS(1) AND 10TER(1) OF THE PARIS CONVENTION (1967)), 16.1, 41.1, 41.2, 41.3 AND/OR 42 OF THE TRIPS AGREEMENT

G. CONCLUSION

VIII. THE EC MEASURE DOES NOT PROVIDE THE LEGAL MEANS FOR INTERESTED PARTIES TO PREVENT MISLEADING USE OR USE WHICH CONSTITUTES AN ACT OF UNFAIR COMPETITION IN RESPECT OF GEOGRAPHICAL INDICATIONS PROPOSED TO BE REGISTERED UNDER REGULATION NO. 2081/92

IX. THE EC MEASURE DOES NOT ACCORD TO NATIONALS OR PRODUCTS OF EACH WTO MEMBER TREATMENT NO LESS FAVOURABLE THAN THAT IT ACCORDS TO ITS OWN NATIONALS OR TO LIKE PRODUCTS OF DOMESTIC ORIGIN

A. THE REQUIREMENT FOR THE INVOLVEMENT OF ANOTHER WTO MEMBER GOVERNMENT CONSTITUTES LESS FAVOURABLE TREATMENT UNDER THE EC MEASURE

B. IN RESPECT OF PRODUCTS BEARING—OR ELIGIBLE TO BEAR—AN EC-DEFINED GI, THE EC MEASURE ACCORDS TO THE PRODUCTS OF OTHER WTO MEMBERS TREATMENT LESS FAVOURABLE THAN THAT IT ACCORDS TO LIKE PRODUCTS OF NATIONAL ORIGIN, CONTRARY TO ARTICLE III:4 OF GATT 1994

C. IN RESPECT OF APPLICATIONS FOR—OR OBJECTIONS TO—THE REGISTRATION OF AN EC-DEFINED GI, THE EC MEASURE DOES NOT ACCORD NATIONAL TREATMENT TO NATIONALS OF OTHER WTO MEMBERS, CONTRARY TO ARTICLES 2.1 ("INCORPORATING" ARTICLE 2 OF THE PARIS CONVENTION (1967)) AND 3.1 OF THE TRIPS AGREEMENT

D. CONCLUSION

X. THE EC MEASURE IS, IN PART, A TECHNICAL REGULATION THAT ACCORDS LESS FAVOURABLE TREATMENT TO IMPORTED PRODUCTS THAN TO LIKE DOMESTIC PRODUCTS AND CREATES UNNECESSARY OBSTACLES TO INTERNATIONAL TRADE, BEING MORE TRADE-RESTRICTIVE THAN NECESSARY TO FULFIL A LEGITIMATE OBJECTIVE, TAKING ACCOUNT OF THE RISKS NON-FULFILMENT WOULD CREATE

A. THE EC MEASURE IS, IN PART, A TECHNICAL REGULATION WITHIN THE MEANING OF ANNEX 1.1 OF THE TBT AGREEMENT

(i) Article 12.2 – and Articles 4 and 10 read together – of Regulation No. 2081/92 apply to an identifiable product or group of products

(ii) Article 12.2 – and Articles 4 and 10 read together – of Regulation No. 2081/92 mandate compliance with product characteristics or their related processes and production methods

(iii) Article 12.2 – and Articles 4 and 10 read together – of Regulation No. 2081/92 lay down product characteristics or their related processes and production methods

(iv) Conclusion

B. IN RESPECT OF PRODUCTS BEARING—OR ELIGIBLE TO BEAR—AN EC-DEFINED GI, THE EC MEASURE ACCORDS TO THE PRODUCTS OF OTHER WTO MEMBERS TREATMENT LESS FAVOURABLE THAN THAT IT ACCORDS TO LIKE PRODUCTS OF NATIONAL ORIGIN, CONTRARY TO ARTICLE 2.1 OF THE TBT AGREEMENT

C. IN RESPECT OF PRODUCTS BEARING—OR ELIGIBLE TO BEAR—AN EC-DEFINED GI, THE EC MEASURE IS MORE TRADE RESTRICTIVE THAN NECESSARY TO FULFIL A LEGITIMATE OBJECTIVE, TAKING ACCOUNT OF THE RISKS NON-FULFILMENT WOULD CREATE, CONTRARY TO ARTICLE 2.2 OF THE TBT AGREEMENT

D. CONCLUSION

XI. AS A CONSEQUENCE, THE EC HAS NOT ENSURED THE CONFORMITY OF ITS LAWS, REGULATIONS AND ADMINISTRATIVE PROCEDURES WITH ITS WTO OBLIGATIONS

TABLE OF CASES CITED IN THIS SUBMISSION

Short Title	Full Title
Chile – Price Band System	*Chile – Price Band System and Safeguard Measures Relating to Certain Agricultural Products*, Report of the Appellate Body, WT/DS/AB/R, 23 September 2002
Argentina – Footwear Safeguard	*Argentina – Safeguard Measures on Imports of Footwear*, Panel Report, WT/DS121/R, 25 June 1999
EC – Hormones	*EC Measures Concerning Meat and Meat Products (Hormones),* Report of the Appellate Body, WT/DS26/AB/R, WT/DS48/AB/R, 16 January 1998
Guatemala – Cement II	*Guatemala – Definitive Anti-Dumping Measures on Grey Portland Cement from Mexico*, Panel Report, WT/DS156/R, 24 October 2000
EEC – Bananas I	*EEC – Member States' Import Regimes for Bananas*, DS32/R , GATT Panel Report, not adopted
US – Homestyle Copyright	*United States – Section 110(5) of the US Copyright Act*, Panel Report, WT/DS160/R, 15 June 2000
Canada – Pharmaceutical Products	*Canada – Patent Protection of Pharmaceutical Products*, Panel Report, WT/DS114/R, 17 March 2000
US – Woven Shirts and Blouses	*United States – Measures Affecting Imports of Woven Wool Shirts and Blouses from India*, WT/DS33/AB/R, Report of the Appellate Body, adopted 23 May 1997
Korea – Beef	*Korea – Measures Affecting Imports of Fresh, Chilled and Frozen Beef,* Report of the Appellate Body, WT/DS161/AB/R, WT/DS169/AB/R, 11 December 2000
US – Shrimp	*United States – Import Prohibition of Certain Shrimp and Shrimp Products,* Report of the Appellate Body, WT/DS58/AB/R, 12 October 1998
US – Gasoline	*United States – Standards for Reformulated and Conventional Gasoline,* Report of the Appellate Body, WT/DS2/AB/R, 29 April 1996
EC – Asbestos	*European Communities – Measures Affecting Asbestos and Asbestos-Containing Products*, Report of the Appellate Body, WT/DS135/AB/R, 12 March 2001
EC – Sardines	*European Communities – Trade Description of Sardines,* Report of the Appellate Body, WT/DS231/AB/R, 26 September 2002
Japan – Alcoholic Beverages II	*Japan – Taxes on Alcoholic Beverages,* Report of the Appellate Body, WT/DS8/AB/R, WT/DS10/AB/R, WT/DS11/AB/R, 4 October 1996
US – CDSOA	*United States – Continued Dumping and Subsidy Offset Act of 2000,* Report of the Appellate Body, WT/DS217/AB/R, WT/DS234/AB/R, 16 January 2003
Korea – Dairy Safeguard	*Korea – Definitive Safeguard Measure on Imports of Certain Dairy Products,* Report of the Appellate Body, WT/DS98/AB/R, 14 December 1999

OTHER SOURCES CITED IN THIS SUBMISSION

Short Title	Full Title
OED	*The New Shorter Oxford English Dictionary*, Ed. Lesley Brown, Clarendon Press, Oxford, 1993
Bodenhausen	*Guide to the Application of the Paris Convention for the Protection of Industrial Property as Revised at Stockholm in 1967*, Professor G H C Bodenhausen, BIRPI, 1969, WIPO reprint 1991, Geneva
Gervais	*The TRIPS Agreement: Drafting History and Analysis*, Daniel Gervais, Sweet & Maxwell, London, 1998

INTRODUCTORY REMARKS

1. Council Regulation (EEC) No. 2081/92 ("Regulation No. 2081/92") established a regime for the registration—and ongoing protection across the territory of the Community—of designations of origin and geographical indications as these were defined by the EC ("EC-defined GIs"). To date, approximately 640 EC-defined GIs have been registered under Regulation No. 2081/92—and thus attract the protection in perpetuity that flows from such registration.

2. Yet more than 600 of these EC-defined GIs were registered as a result of processes which were contrary to the EC's obligations pursuant to the:

- *Agreement on Trade-Related Aspects of Intellectual Property Rights* ("the TRIPS Agreement" or "TRIPS"), including to the extent that the *TRIPS Agreement* requires compliance with provisions of the Paris Convention (1967) ("Paris");
- *General Agreement on Tariffs and Trade 1994* ("the GATT 1994" or "GATT"); and/or
- *Agreement on Technical Barriers to Trade* ("the TBT Agreement" or "TBT");

and, as a consequence, to the EC's obligations pursuant to the *Marrakesh Agreement Establishing the World Trade Organization* ("the WTO Agreement").

3. Moreover, the EC measure[1] remains in violation of the EC's WTO obligations in a variety of ways.

4. As Australia set out in its First Written Submission, Australia is not contesting the EC's right to register and protect EC-defined GIs as intellectual property.[2] Nor does Australia assert that the EC is required to provide protection of EC-defined GIs at either Community or EC Member State level.

5. However, Australia does contest whether—in respect of the registration of an EC-defined GI—the EC has provided the rights that it is obliged to provide to a trademark right holder or other interested party. Given that Community law takes primacy over EC Member State law in the event of a conflict, there is no effective legal right enabling a trademark right holder or other interested party to challenge particular infringing actions—even leaving aside the issue of having to seek redress in up to 25 national courts individually.

6. The stated intention of Regulation No. 2081/92 was to give protection to terms under "a Community approach" based on the system of "registered designations of origin" introduced by "certain Member States."[3] That intention was initially given effect in the simplified registration process provided by the now repealed Article 17 of the Regulation, under which approximately 480 terms that were already protected or established by usage in individual EC Member States were "fast tracked" on to the Community Register. The only basis on which the "fast track" registration of a term that was otherwise considered to meet the definition of an EC-defined GI could be opposed was that the term was generic.

7. In transposing the protection of EC-defined GIs from the EC Member State to the Community level, however, the EC did not take account of any trademark rights existing within the territory of another EC Member State. Instead, the EC in effect "deemed" the territory of the EC Member State of origin of the EC-

---

[1] As set out in the First Written Submission of Australia (paragraph 20), the measure at issue in this dispute ("the EC measure") is the EC's regime for the registration and protection of EC-defined GIs on a Community-wide basis, comprising:

- Regulation No. 2081/92 of 14 July 1992;
- amendments to that Regulation; and

actions to implement and enforce that Regulation, including actions by the Commission, by the EC Member States and judicial decisions.

[2] First Written Submission of Australia, paragraph 4.

[3] Regulation No. 2081/92 as originally adopted, sixth and seventh recitals, Exhibit COMP-1.d.

defined GI to be the territory of the Community, and overrode—in effect, expropriated—any trademark rights in that term that may have existed in any other EC Member State. Moreover, that same situation continues to exist in respect of registrations of new EC-defined GIs.

8. The EC's action in overriding trademark rights in other EC Member States in relation to the fast track registration of EC-defined GIs is particularly noticeable when compared to the treatment of EC Member State-based trademark rights under the Community Trademark Regulation.[4] Article 8 of that Regulation expressly provides to the proprietor of an earlier trademark, including the proprietor of an earlier trademark registered in an EC Member State, the right to oppose a Community trademark application.

9. Contrary to the EC's assertion that there is no hierarchy between TRIPS-defined GIs and trademarks[5] under the *TRIPS Agreement*, it is in fact the EC that has established a system that clearly grants primacy to EC-defined GIs at the expense of the rights required to be conferred in respect of pre-existing trademarks.

10. The EC asserts that Australia's claims are "purely theoretical."[6] There is, of course, no requirement that Australia demonstrate actual trade effects to be able to initiate a dispute and Australia has chosen not to identify specific commercial interests potentially affected by the EC measure. That said, Australia, Australian producers and Australian intellectual property right holders most definitely do have specific commercial—and systemic—interests potentially affected by the EC measure. Moreover, the EC cannot say that its measure has not adversely affected the nationals or products of other WTO Members: it has not provided the legal avenues by which the issues raised in this dispute can be effectively tested.

11. The EC asserts that the purported theoretical nature of Australia's claims "has implications for the Panel's assessment of whether such claims are well-founded."[7] Australia notes in response to this extraordinary statement that Article 3.8 of the *Dispute Settlement Understanding* ("the DSU") expressly provides: "[i]n cases where there is an infringement of the obligations assumed under a covered agreement, the action is considered *prima facie* to constitute a case of nullification or impairment." The Panel's function is as set out in DSU Article 11—"to make an objective assessment of the matter before it."

I. TERMINOLOGY USED IN THIS SUBMISSION

12. Throughout this Submission, Australia will continue to use the terminology used in its First Written Submission.

13. Thus, except where a different meaning is expressly noted, Australia will continue to use the following expressions in the sense indicated:

- "*GI*" to refer to a geographical indication in a general sense;
- "*EC-defined GI*" to refer to both a designation of origin and a geographical indication as these are defined and used in Regulation No. 2081/92;[8]
- "*TRIPS-defined GI*" to refer to a geographical indication as this is defined in TRIPS Article 22.1;
- "*Indication of source*" to refer to an indication of source within the meaning of Paris Article 1(2). Both an EC-defined GI and a TRIPS-defined GI are categories of indications of source;

[4] Exhibit COMP-7.

[5] First Written Submission of the EC, paragraph 294.

[6] EC's Response to Question 87 from the Panel following the first substantive meeting, paragraph 223.

[7] EC's Response to Question 87 from the Panel following the first substantive meeting, paragraph 224.

[8] Australia notes the view of the EC—at paragraph 46 of its First Written Submission—that both designations of origin and geographical indications within the meaning of Regulation No. 2081/92 are geographical indications as defined in TRIPS Article 22.1.

– "*Commission*" to refer to the European Commission;

– "*Official Journal*" for the *Official Journal of the European Communities*;

– "*Register*" for the *Register of protected designations of origin and protected geographical indications* provided for by Article 6.3 of Regulation No. 2081/92;

– "*Regulation No. 2081/92*" to refer to the Regulation in a broad sense or in relation to provisions that have not been amended since the Regulation originally entered into force;

– "*Regulation No. 2081/92#1*" to refer to the Regulation as originally adopted and in force from 24 July 1993;

– "*Regulation No. 2081/92#2*" to refer to the Regulation as amended by Council Regulation (EC) No. 535/97 of 17 March 1997 with effect from 28 March 1997; and

– "*Regulation No. 2081/92#3*" to refer to the Regulation as amended by Council Regulation (EC) No. 692/2003 of 8 April 2003 with effect from 24 April 2003.

14. In view of the explanations provided by the EC in its First Written Submission, however, Australia will use the phrase "Article 15 decision-making process" in lieu of the phrase "Committee of EC Member State representatives" in this Submission. In any case, Australia addresses this issue in more detail in Part IV.C of this Submission.

II. THE MEASURE AT ISSUE

A. VERSIONS OF REGULATION NO. 2081/92 NO LONGER IN FORCE

15. The EC argues that versions of Regulation No. 2081/92 which were no longer in force at the time of the Panel's establishment are not within the scope of the Panel's terms of reference.[9]

16. The EC's argument is without merit. It is premised on an inaccurate characterisation of the terms of Australia's panel establishment request that seeks to transform Australia's reference to the amendments introduced by Regulation No. 692/2003 from an illustrative to an exhaustive or exclusive basis. The EC's argument ignores the plain language of that request by equating the meaning of "*[and]* any amendments thereto (including … Regulation … No. 692/2003)" to "as amended by … Regulation … No. 692/2003."

17. The EC has not even attempted to argue that the registrations of those more than 600 EC-defined GIs were consistent with the EC's WTO obligations. The EC's whole defence of those registrations is that they were made pursuant to versions of Regulation No. 2081/92 which are no longer in force, and therefore cannot be within the Panel's terms of reference. Yet the EC's arguments ignore that, notwithstanding that earlier versions of Regulation No. 2081/92 may no longer be in force, those more than 600 registrations made pursuant to earlier versions of Regulation No. 2081/92 continue in effect—and the registered terms are protected in perpetuity.

18. In reality, the EC is seeking to shield from the Panel's scrutiny—and from the consequences of findings of WTO inconsistency—the registrations, and ongoing protection, of more than 600 EC-defined GIs pursuant to processes that were inconsistent with the EC's obligations under the TRIPS Agreement and GATT 1994. The EC is—in effect—asking the Panel to find that WTO-inconsistent implementation actions by WTO Members pursuant to short-lived statutory frameworks are beyond the reach of the WTO dispute settlement

[9] First Written Submission of the EC, paragraph 15.

system. In Australia's view, such an interpretation of the covered agreements would be fundamentally at odds with the object and purpose of the *WTO Agreement* and the covered agreements generally, and the *Dispute Settlement Understanding* in particular.

19. Moreover, the EC is asking the Panel to make such a finding notwithstanding the potential availability of prospective remedies to bring the WTO-inconsistent EC measure into conformity, for example, by providing access for trademark right holders to civil judicial proceedings and/or by providing for just compensation for any trademark rights adversely affected by the registration—and ongoing protection—of an EC-defined GI. Even if revocation—as distinct from invalidation—were ultimately to be required in a few cases, such action would only need to have prospective effect.

B. AMENDMENTS TO THE EC MEASURE AFTER PANEL ESTABLISHMENT

20. The EC argues that a number of amendments to the EC measure made after 2 October 2003, the date of the Panel's establishment by the DSB, are not within the Panel's terms of reference.[10]

21. In *Chile – Price Band System*, the Appellate Body considered a situation in which an amendment to the measure at issue was enacted after the Panel had been established and while the Panel was engaged in assessing the measure. The Appellate Body considered that the amendment in question "*[did]* not change the price band system into a measure *different* from the price band system that was in force before the Amendment"[11] *(emphasis in original)*. Further, the Appellate Body expressly cited with approval the finding of the Panel in *Argentina – Footwear Safeguard*, in which the Panel "decided to examine *modifications* made to the measure in issue *during* the panel proceedings, on the ground that the modifications in question did:

> ... not constitute entirely new safeguard measures in the sense that they were based on a different safeguard investigation, but are instead modifications of the legal form of the original definitive measure, which remains in force in substance and which is the subject of the complaint[...] (emphasis in original).[12]

22. The Appellate Body's findings in *Chile – Price Band System* are particularly pertinent to the current dispute. None of the amendments identified by the EC, including the amendment relating to the accession of ten new Member States to the EC, in any way "change the essence" of the EC measure in the sense that the EC measure was—and remains—a measure concerning the availability, acquisition, scope, maintenance, use and/or enforcement within the territory of the EC of an intellectual property right expressly provided for by the *TRIPS Agreement*, and the prevention of associated deceptive practices.[13]

23. The EC measure remains essentially the same notwithstanding the amendments to the measure made since 2 October 2003: none of the amendments changed the essence of the measure and, accordingly, those amendments form part of the measure at issue in this dispute.

---

[10] First Written Submission of the EC, paragraphs 21-25.

[11] *Chile – Price Band System*, paragraph 137.

[12] *Chile – Price Band System*, paragraph 138.

[13] Australia notes that, in its First Written Submission, the EC itself describes Regulation No. 2081/92 as prescribing a procedure "for the registration of geographical indications" (paragraph 160), as "a procedure for the acquisition of another intellectual property right" (paragraph 327) and as laying down "an administrative procedure for the acquisition of geographical indications via a system of registration" (paragraph 359).

III. TERMS OF REFERENCE

A. ARTICLE 4 OF THE PARIS CONVENTION AND ARTICLES 43, 44, 45, 46, 48 AND 49 OF THE TRIPS AGREEMENT

24. Australia wishes to state unambiguously that it has not asked that the Panel find—within the meaning of DSU Article 12.7—that the EC measure is inconsistent with Paris Article 4 or with TRIPS Articles 43, 44, 45, 46, 48 or 49.[14]

25. However, the DSU does not preclude the Panel from considering the fact of a measure's inconsistency with other obligations established by the covered agreements in its assessment of the WTO consistency of a measure with specified provisions of the covered agreements. Indeed, an evaluation of a measure's inconsistency with certain provisions as an issue of fact—whether or not these provisions are specified as part of the legal basis of a complaint within the meaning of DSU Article 6.2—can be a necessary pre-condition for establishing a violation of another, specified provision. Australia notes that in *EC – Hormones*, the Appellate Body said:

> Panels are inhibited from addressing legal claims falling outside their terms of reference. However, nothing in the DSU limits the faculty of a panel freely to use arguments submitted by any of the parties—or to develop its own legal reasoning—to support its own findings and conclusions on the matter under its consideration. A panel might well be unable to carry out an objective assessment of the matter, as mandated by Article 11 of the DSU, if in its reasoning it had to restrict itself solely to arguments presented by the parties to the dispute. ...[15]

B. ARTICLE 2(2) OF THE PARIS CONVENTION

26. The EC also argues that Paris Article 2(2) is outside the Panel's terms of reference in this dispute. The EC argues that Paris Article 2(2) is not concerned with national treatment but with a prohibition on the imposition of requirements as to domicile or establishment, and was therefore not "raised" in Australia's panel request.[16] Australia disagrees.

27. In Australia's view, the word "however" at the beginning of Paris Article 2(2) is properly understood in the sense of "in spite of." Thus, in spite of the fact that, under Paris Article 2(1), a country of the Union / WTO Member may impose in its domestic law a condition of domicile or establishment on its own nationals for the protection of an industrial property right, it may not do so in respect of nationals of other countries of the Union / WTO Members.[17] Moreover, this interpretation is consistent with the apparent intent of the parties to the Paris Convention when Paris Article 2(2) was amended to include the word "however."[18] The use of "however" at the start of Paris Article 2(2) therefore establishes a direct and express linkage between the provisions of that paragraph and the provisions of the preceding Paris Article 2(1).

28. Paris Article 2(2) defines the boundary of permissible action in relation to domicile or establishment in the application of the national treatment obligation established by Paris Article 2(1). When a WTO Member conditions the enjoyment of advantages with respect to the protection of industrial property within the meaning of Paris Article 2(1) for nationals of countries of the Union—and thus on nationals of WTO Members—on a requirement of domicile or residence, that WTO Member is no longer in compliance with its national treatment

---

[14] First Written Submission of the EC, paragraphs 26-35.

[15] *EC – Hormones*, paragraph 61.

[16] First Written Submission of the EC, paragraphs 36-42.

[17] *OED*, Vol.1, page 1272, defines relevant meanings of "however" as: "[f]or all that, nevertheless, notwithstanding; but; *arch.* however much, notwithstanding that. Used in qualifying a whole cl. or sentence."

[18] *Bodenhausen*, page 31.

obligation under Paris Article 2(1). Paris Article 2(2) is thus an integral aspect of a WTO Member's national treatment obligations under the Paris Convention as "incorporated" into the *WTO Agreement*, and was properly raised in Australia's panel establishment request.

IV. THE MEANING OF REGULATION NO. 2081/92

A. RULES OF INTERPRETATION OF EC LAW

29. The EC has said: "... the objective assessment of the facts requires establishing the meaning that the act will normally have within the legal order of the WTO Member in question. This means that the interpretation should be guided by the rules of interpretation customary in the legal order of such member, and taking account of the legal context of the measure in the domestic law of the Member."[19]

30. Australia notes that the European Court of Justice ("the ECJ") has held: "... in interpreting a provision of Community law it is necessary to consider its wording, its context and its aims."[20] This rule has been reaffirmed in a number of subsequent cases, including in an ECJ judgment of September 2003, when the ECJ held: "in interpreting a provision of Community law it is necessary to consider not only its wording but also the context in which it occurs and the aims of the rules of which it forms part."[21]

31. Thus, notwithstanding that the context and aims of provisions of Community law are key elements of the ECJ's interpretive rules, so too is the wording of a provision.

B. REGISTRATION OF AN EC-DEFINED GI RELATING TO THE TERRITORY OF ANOTHER WTO MEMBER

32. The EC says that Australia has misunderstood relevant provisions of Regulation No. 2081/92 and that the registration of an EC-defined GI from another WTO Member is not subject to the conditions of reciprocity and equivalence set down in Article 12 of Regulation No. 2081/92#3.[22]

33. Almost since the inception of the WTO, the EC has explicitly said that Article 12.1 of Regulation No. 2081/92 applies to WTO Members who wish to take advantage of the higher level of protection offered by the Regulation.[23]

34. In March 2002, the EC was considering the changes to Regulation No. 2081/92 that were eventually adopted in Regulation No. 692/2003. In a press release dated 15 March 2002,[24] the European Commission said:

---

[19] EC Response to Question 1 from the Panel to the parties, paragraph 6.

[20] ECJ judgment: *Bosphorus Hara Yollari Turizm ve Ticaret AS v Minister for Transport, Energy and Communications and others*, case C-84/95, [1996] ECR I-3953, paragraph 11, Exhibit AUS-10, attached.

[21] ECJ judgment: *Freistaat Sachsen and Volkswagen AG and Volkswagen Sachsen GmbH v Commission of the European Communities*, joined cases C-57/00 P and C-61/00 P, paragraph 133, Exhibit AUS-11, attached.

[22] First Written Submission of the EC, paragraphs 65-69.

[23] For example, in 1997, in the review of the EC's legislation on trademarks, geographical indications and industrial designs by the WTO TRIPS Council, the EC said:

Question from India: How far is Article 12 of Council Regulation 2081/92/EEC in compliance with the TRIPS Agreement? Please particularly explain how: ... having inspection arrangements equivalent to Article 10 can be a requirement for non-Members of the EC, when this is not a requirement under the TRIPS Agreement? ...

EC response: It is important to stress that, in general, conditions provided in Article 12 of Regulation 2081/92/EEC are only required when a bilateral agreement is concluded between the EC and a WTO Member. This means that it only occurs when two parties voluntarily wish higher level of protection ("ex officio") than this *[sic]* provided under the TRIPS Agreement. So, this is not a compulsory condition but another option that can be used when systems are equivalent, in particular conditions under Article 4 (specifications) and Article 10 (inspection).[23] *(emphasis added)*

The EC responded in similar terms to a question from New Zealand. (WTO document IP/Q2/EEC/1 of 1 October 1997, Part II, EC's reply B.2 to Question 4 from New Zealand.)

[24] Press release IP/02/422, Exhibit AUS-04, lodged with Australia's Oral Statement to the first substantive meeting of the parties with the Panel.

> ... [T]he proposal aims at full implementation of the TRIPS agreement[...] and improve *[sic]* protection for geographical indications. To comply with the Commission's obligations as set out in the TRIPS Agreement, the following amendments to Regulation (EEC) No. 2081/92 are proposed:
>
> - The right of objection to registrations is extended to WTO member country nationals with a right and a legitimate interest within EU territory. This gives WTO member country nationals the same right as EU Member State nationals to object to registrations of products within 6 months of their publication in the Official Journal of the European Communities;
>
> - Beyond mere TRIPS consistency, the Commission proposes important amendments designed to promote the EU system denominations of origin as a model to the rest of the world. The driving idea behind is the wish to improve protection of European quality products also outside the EU. As the EU cannot force non-EU countries to do so, they would be invited to do so on a reciprocal basis. If a non-EU country introduced an equivalent system including the right of objection for the EU and the commitment to protect EU names on their territory, the EU would offer a specific procedure to register their products for the EU market; *(emphases added)*

35. In September 2002, in a discussion in the TRIPS Council on issues related to the extension of the protection of GIs provided for in TRIPS Article 23 to products other than wines and spirits, the EC representative said in a written statement annexed to the Minutes of that Council meeting: "... I would like to address one issue that is raised regarding the fact that the EU register for GIs on foodstuffs does not allow the registration of foreign GI *[sic]* unless it is determined that a third country has an equivalent or reciprocal system of GI protection"[25] *(emphasis added)*. In other words, the EC statement was expressly premised on the fact that the EC did not allow the registration of foreign GIs unless a third country has an equivalent or reciprocal system of GI protection. There was no qualification in that statement that the limitation on the registration of foreign GIs did not apply to GIs from WTO Members, notwithstanding that the statement was being made to the TRIPS Council, the very body charged with overseeing the functioning of the *TRIPS Agreement* under Article IV:5 of the *WTO Agreement*.

36. In November 2002, the Committee on Agriculture and Rural Development of the European Parliament issued its Report on the amendments being proposed to Regulation No. 2081/92. That Report was expressly premised on the understanding that:

> The Commission is proposing a special procedure for registering products originating in third countries on the Community market. In return, third countries will, in accordance with the reciprocity principle, have to afford equivalent protection to protected Community names. Moreover, in order that products from third countries can be recognised at EU level, the third countries concerned must be able to give guarantees equivalent to those required in the Union.[26] *(emphases added)*

37. In March 2003, an official of the European Commission at a WIPO National Seminar on the Protection of Trademarks and Geographical Indications in Beirut said non-EU countries "can seek recognition for your country before the EU based on the fact that you have a system reciprocal to that of the EU. If your system

---

25 WTO document IP/C/M/37/Add.1 of 8 November 2002, page 79.

26 Report on the proposal for a Council regulation amending Regulation (EEC) No. 2081/92 on the protection of geographical indications and designations of origin for agricultural products and foodstuffs (COM(2002) 139—C5-0178/2002—2002/0066(CNS))," Committee on Agriculture and Rural Development, 6 November 2002, Exhibit COMP-14, page 20.

protects GIs similarly (enforcement, level of protection), our registration system will be open to your GIs. You can conclude a bilateral agreement with the EU and all your GIs will be protected in Europe at once."[27]

38. Yet the EC would have the Panel believe that—up until now—everyone has misunderstood the Regulation, notwithstanding:

- the plain language of Regulation No. 2081/92 itself;
- repeated statements by appointed representatives of the European Communities;
- the plain language of a press release from the European Commission itself concerning the express intent of the very amendments which the EC now relies on to argue that that Regulation No. 2081/92 is being misunderstood;
- the apparent understanding of the Committee of the European Parliament with primary authority concerning the subject matter of the express intent of the amendments which the EC now relies on to argue that Regulation No. 2081/92 is being misunderstood;

  and
- the plain language of the explanation for the amendment to Article 12 of Regulation No. 2081/92 provided in recital (9) to Regulation No. 692/2003 that: "[t]he protection provided by registration under Regulation ... No 2081/92 is open to third countries' names by reciprocity and under equivalence conditions as provided for in Article 12 of that Regulation. That Article should be supplemented so as to guarantee that the Community registration procedure is available to the countries meeting those conditions"
  - that is, one of the express aims of the amendments in 2003 to Article 12 of the Regulation was to guarantee that the Community registration procedure is available to countries that meet the reciprocity and equivalence conditions;

39. In purported support of its contention, the EC points[28] to a document: (a) which was issued after the panel in this dispute was established by the DSB; (b) which was issued by an entity other than the EC; (c) which carries an express disclaimer that it has been prepared under the WTO Secretariat's own responsibility; and (d) which—on the previous page—clearly states that reciprocity and equivalence are conditions for registration of foreign GIs in the EC. The EC also points to a statement made in the TRIPS Council on 16 June 2004—some eight months following the establishment of the panel in this dispute—and for which, at the time of writing, there is no official WTO record.[29]

40. In claiming that Australia has misunderstood Regulation No. 2081/92, however, the EC offers no explanations of its earlier statements, or of how so many of its own appointed representatives could have offered the same—consistently incorrect—explanations of the provisions of the Regulation, or of how such a wide range of interested observers could also have similarly misunderstood the Regulation. The EC does not explain why it did not use the opportunity of either the 29 August 2003 or the 2 October 2003 DSB meetings to

---

[27] "Geographical Indications and Trademarks: Harmony of Conflict," Presentation by Mrs Susanna Perez Ferreras, Administrator, Industrial Property Unit, European Commission, Brussels, at the WIPO National Seminar on the Protection of Trademarks and Geographical Indications, Beirut, March 2003, published as WIPO document WIPO /TM/BEY/ 03/11B, Exhibit AUS-05, Slide 15 (lodged with Australia's replies to questions posed by the Panel to the parties to the dispute following the first substantive meeting with the parties).

[28] Response of the European Communities to Question 16 from the Panel after the first substantive meeting, referring to WTO document IP/C/W/253/Rev.1.

[29] Indeed, Australia notes that there may not even be an official record of the EC's statement published by the time of the second substantive meeting of the parties with the Panel.

correct Australia's misunderstanding, given that Australia expressly referred to the requirements for reciprocity and equivalence in making its request for the establishment of a panel at the DSB of 29 August 2003.[30]

41. In particular, the EC has not explained why the European Commission's press release of 15 March 2002 that specifically addressed the aims of the proposed amendments to Regulation No. 2081/92 which were eventually adopted in Regulation No. 692/2003, and the recitals to Regulation No. 692/2003 itself, should not be accorded at least equal—if not greater—weight than "statements made by the EC in the course of the Panel proceedings *[which]* should also be taken into account."[31]

42. Moreover, the EC—in responding to question 15 from the Panel following the first substantive meeting with the parties to the dispute—did not address the ECJ's judgment in *Biret International* concerning the relevance of the EC's WTO obligations in implementing a Community measure.[32] In that judgment, the ECJ found: "... the WTO agreements are not in principle among the rules in the light of which the Court is to review the legality of measures adopted by the Community institutions ... It is only where the Community has intended to implement a particular obligation assumed in the context of the WTO, or where the Community measure refers expressly to the precise provisions of the WTO agreements, that it is for the Court to review the legality of the Community measure in question in the light of the WTO rules."[33]

43. The EC has said:

> At the time that Regulation 2081/92 was adopted, the GATT was one of the agreements to which the "without prejudice" clause applied. Moreover, at the time that Regulation 2081/92 was adopted, the TRIPS Agreement was in the final phases of its negotiation. It was therefore the objective that the "without prejudice" clause should also apply to the TRIPS and other WTO agreements resulting from the Uruguay Round.[34]

44. However, Regulation No. 2081/92#1 made no reference to the *General Agreement on Tariffs and Trade 1947* ("the GATT 1947") in either its recitals or in its operative provisions. Nor did it make any references—in either its recitals or its operative provisions—to the *TRIPS Agreement* or the *WTO Agreement* more generally. Further, Regulation No. 2081/92#3 makes no reference to the *WTO Agreement* in its operative provisions. Thus, consistent with established ECJ jurisprudence, the Regulation could not have been intended to implement a particular obligation assumed in the context of either the *GATT 1947 or the WTO Agreement.*[35]

45. Regulation No. 692/2003, however, did make references to the *WTO Agreement* in its recitals. Those references are a generic description of the *TRIPS Agreement* in recital (8), a specific reference to TRIPS Article 22 in recital (10), and a specific reference to TRIPS Article 24.5 in recital (11).

46. Having regard to the ECJ's findings in *Biret International*, the generic description of the *TRIPS Agreement* in recital (8) would seem to be irrelevant to the proper interpretation of the provisions of Regulation No. 2081/92, including the phrase "[w]ithout prejudice to international agreements" at the beginning of Article 12.1 of the Regulation, as recital (8) does not show an intent to implement a particular obligation assumed in the context of the WTO. In the alternative, recital (8) could only inform the proper interpretation of the provisions of Regulation No. 2081/92 in regard to the EC's obligations pursuant to the *TRIPS Agreement*: it

---

[30] WTO document WT/DSB/M/155, paragraph 74.

[31] Response of the European Communities to Question 16 from the Panel after the first substantive meeting, paragraph 40.

[32] Case C-93/02 P, *Biret International SA v. Council of the European Union*, Judgment of the ECJ of 30 September 2003, Exhibit AUS-07 (lodged with Australia's replies to questions posed by the Panel to the parties ot the dispute following the first substantive meeting with the parties).

[33] *Ibid*, paragraphs 52-53.

[34] Response of the European Communities to Question 3 from the Panel after the first substantive meeting, paragraph 12.

[35] Response of the European Communities to Question 3 from the Panel after the first substantive meeting, paragraph 12.

could not be considered to show an intent to implement particular obligations assumed in the context of the WTO in regard to the other covered agreements, including the *GATT 1994*.

47. On the other hand, having regard to the ECJ's findings in *Biret International*, the specific references to TRIPS Article 22 in recital (10) and to TRIPS Article 4.5 in recital (11) would seem to be directly relevant to the proper interpretation of the respective specified provisions of Regulation No. 2081/92. Further, Australia notes that the findings of the ECJ in the cases cited by the EC in its response to question 15 from the Panel after the first substantive meeting would seem to have been consistent with the ECJ's findings in *Biret International*, in that the relevant WTO provisions were expressly identified in the Community measures at issue in those cases.

48. Australia submits that the EC has not disproved the factual premise informing Australia's claims that the registration of an EC-defined GI from another WTO Member is subject to the conditions of reciprocity and equivalence set out in paragraphs 1 and 3 of Article 12 of Regulation No. 2081/92#3. The EC's counterarguments are not sustainable on the basis of the meaning, context and aims of those provisions in accordance with the rules of interpretation of EC law.

49. Further, Australia submits that the EC has not disproved the associated factual premise informing Australia's claims that Articles 12a to 12d of Regulation No. 2081/92 only distinguish between nationals of WTO Members and nationals of other third countries where the express language of those provisions so provides.

C. ARTICLE 15 DECISION-MAKING PROCESS

50. The EC argues that Australia has consistently misrepresented the decision-making process applicable to Regulation No. 2081/92 pursuant to Article 15 of the Regulation.[36] However, Australia questions whether the EC's description of that process is entirely accurate.

51. As the EC itself acknowledges,[37] under Article 5.3 of Decision 1999/468,[38] the Commission can adopt a measure "[i]f the measure is in accordance with the opinion of the Committee" composed of representatives of the EC Member States. Moreover, Article 5.4 of that Decision states in relevant part: "[i]f the measures envisaged are not in accordance with the opinion of the committee, or if no opinion is delivered, the Commission shall ... submit to the Council a proposal relating to the measures to be taken ...."

52. The express language of Articles 5.3 and 5.4 of Decision 1999/468 indicates that the Commission may only decide a matter required to be referred to the Committee composed of representatives of the EC Member States <u>with the consent of that Committee</u>. If that consent is not forthcoming, the matter must be referred to the EC's Council of Ministers.

53. Under Article 5.6 of Decision 1999/468, once a matter has been referred to the EC's Council of Ministers, the Commission is only able to decide a matter if, after a period of three months, the Council has neither adopted nor indicated its opposition to a proposed measure.

54. The express language of Decision 1999/468 indicates that the Commission cannot decide a matter without the consent of either the Committee or the Council, or until the Council has been unable to form an opinion for three months. Moreover, this does not require exceptional circumstances—simply disagreement. Thus, the EC's statements that "[u]nder the Regulation, decisions with respect to the registration of

---

[36] First Written Submission of the EC, paragraph 79.

[37] First Written Submission of the EC, paragraph 82.

[38] Council Decision of 28 June 1999 laying down the procedures for the exercise of implementing powers conferred on the Commission (1999/468/EC), Exhibit COMP-8.

geographical indications are in principle taken by the Commission,"[39] "[o]nly exceptionally, if the measure is not in accordance with the opinion of the Committee, may the matter be referred to the Council of Ministers,"[40] and "the decision-maker under the Regulation is the Commission, or exceptionally the Council of Ministers"[41] do not accurately convey the full consequence of the decision-making process under Regulation No. 2081/92.

55. Notwithstanding that the Committee does not exercise formal decision-making authority, it must agree with the Commission's proposed decision before the Commission can formally take that decision. Alternatively, the Commission may only formally decide a matter in the absence of express approval or disapproval from the Council of Ministers. Indeed, Australia notes that the final preambular recital to Regulation No. 1107/96—which authorised the first registrations of EC-defined GIs under Regulation No. 2081/92 by the simplified procedure set out in the now repealed Article 17—expressly states:

> [w]hereas the vote in the Committee provided for in Article 15 of Regulation ... No. 2081/92 resulted in no opinion; whereas, in the absence of an opinion and in accordance with that Article, the Commission forwarded a proposal to the Council for it to act on a qualified majority within three months; whereas, given that the Council did not act within that period, the proposed measures should be adopted by the Commission.[42]

56. In accordance with the decision-making processes applicable to Regulation No. 2081/92 pursuant to Article 15 of the Regulation, the Committee composed of representatives of the EC Member States or the Council of Ministers has to agree with the Commission's proposed decision. Alternatively, the Council of Ministers may disagree with the Commission's proposed decision. Only if the Council of Ministers is unable to form an opinion may the Commission adopt the proposed measure notwithstanding objections from a number of EC Member States.[43] In fact, Australia notes that the EC's own information[44] shows that almost half of the EC-defined GIs registered to date have been registered by the Commission only following the failure of the Council of Ministers to form an opinion on the Commission's proposals. This does not suggest only "exceptional" referrals to the Council.[45]

57. This process is applicable to many decisions under Regulation No. 2081/92, including:

- all decisions concerning objections to the proposed registration of an EC-defined GI, irrespective of
    - whether the name is from within the EC or from another WTO Member
        - although in respect of a proposed name from an EC Member State, the decision-making process does not apply if the EC Member State of origin and an objecting EC Member State are able to reach agreement between themselves (Article 7.5 of the Regulation),

      or
    - whether the objection comes from a national of the EC or of another WTO Member;

[39] First Written Submission of the EC, paragraph 80.

[40] First Written Submission of the EC, paragraph 82.

[41] First Written Submission of the EC, paragraph 83.

[42] Australia notes that similar wording appears in recital (39) to Regulation No. 1829/2002 concerning the name "Feta." Exhibit COMP-3.b refers.

[43] That is, from at least a number of EC Member States that had earlier been sufficient to form a "blocking minority" to the adoption of the proposed measure by the Commission.

[44] Exhibit EC-28.

[45] First Written Submission of the EC, paragraph 82.

- whether a third country satisfies—within the meaning of Article 12.3 of the Regulation—the reciprocity and equivalence conditions of Article 12.1 of the Regulation; and
- if the Commission concludes that a name proposed by either an EC Member State or another WTO Member does not qualify for protection, the decision not to proceed with publication of the application (Articles 6.5 and 12b.1(b) of the Regulation)—which publication also constitutes publication for the purpose of inviting objections.

58. In addition, the Commission may consult the EC Member States through the Article 15 decision-making process on other issues—for example, under Articles 6.5 and 12b.1(a), before publishing the details of an application for registration of an EC-defined GI.

59. Australia submits that the EC has not disproved the factual premise informing Australia's claims that the Committee composed of EC Member State representatives and/or the Council of (EC Member States) Ministers participate in the decision-making process applicable under Regulation No. 2081/92. Confirmation of this factual premise is provided by the dispute concerning the name "Feta,"[46] which is ongoing,[47] and by the number of EC-defined GIs which were registered by the Commission following the failure of the Council of Ministers to form an opinion.[48]

D. PROTECTION OF HOMONYMOUS EC-DEFINED GIS

60. Article 12.2 of Regulation No. 2081/92 provides as follows:

> If a protected name of a third country is identical to a Community protected name, registration shall be granted with due regard for local and traditional usage and the practical risks of confusion.
>
> Use of such names shall be authorized only if the country of origin of the product is clearly and visibly indicated on the label.

61. According to the EC:

- "the second subparagraph does not concern third country names in general, but only homonyms"[49]
  - by which Australia understands the EC to say that a name that is "identical to" another name is a "homonym" of that other name;
- "'such names' applies both to third country protected names and to Community protected names;"[50]
- "[i]n the case of identical names, the requirement to indicate the country of origin can apply both to the third country name and the Community name. In practice, this would mean that whichever indication is registered later would normally be required to indicate the country of origin. Where a Community indication is registered after an identical third country indication, the Community indication would therefore be required to indicate the country of origin;"[51]

---

[46] See Exhibits COMP-3.b and COMP-11.

[47] See Danish Dairy Board statement of 10 January 2003, Exhibit AUS-12, attached.

[48] Exhibit EC-28.

[49] First Written Submission of the EC, paragraph 87.

[50] First Written Submission of the EC, paragraph 88.

[51] First Written Submission of the EC, paragraph 88.

- "whether a protected name is a 'Community name' or a 'third country name' within the meaning of Regulation 2081/92 depends on where the geographical area to which the geographical indication is related is located;"[52]

- "the requirement in Article 12.2 can apply both to geographical indications from a third country or from the EC, depending on which name has been protected earlier[...];"[53]

- "[b]oth in 'protected name of a third country' and in 'Community protected name', 'protected' in principle means 'protected under Regulation 2081/92'. However, the provision also applies where protection under Regulation 2081/92 is sought for a protected name from a third country;"[54] and

- in response to a question from the Panel as to whether the requirement to indicate the country of origin applies also where a name of a geographical area located in the EC is identical to a Community protected name (irrespective of whether this Community protected name is the name of a geographical area located in the EC or in a third country), the EC said: "[n]o. 'Community protected name' covers only protected names of areas located in the EC. Moreover, the provision applies only to protected names."[55]

62. Thus, on the basis of the EC's explanations, Article 12.2 of Regulation No. 2081/92 applies in all situations involving identical EC-defined GIs where one of those names concerns a geographical area within the EC and the other concerns a geographical area in another WTO Member.

63. However, the express basis of Article 12.2 is that there is already an EC-defined GI being protected under Regulation No. 2081/92: "[i]f a protected name of a third country is identical to a Community protected name." "[A] protected name of a third country" cannot be "identical to," that is, the same as, a "Community protected name" unless there is already a "Community protected name" in existence. Thus, contrary to the EC's explanations, having regard to its meaning, context and aims, Article 12.2 indicates that it can only apply to situations where there is already a "Community protected name" and the "protected name of a third country" is the later name to be registered.

64. Moreover, elsewhere in Regulation No. 2081/92, the word "Community" is used consistently in the sense of the territory of the Community as a whole. For example, it is used in "Community provisions" in Articles 1.2 and 4.2(i), "Community protection" in Article 2.1, "Community laws" in Article 3.1, "Community trade" in Article 5.5, "the Community" in Article 12.1, "the territory of the Community" in Articles 12b.3, 12d.2 and 14.2. Its use in Article 12.2 in the sense put forward by the EC, that is, in the sense of EC-defined GIs relating to geographical areas within the EC, would constitute the only use of "Community" in that sense in the Regulation, and would in fact seem to be inconsistent with the express function of the Regulation as set out in Article 2.1: "Community protection of *[EC-defined GIs]* shall be obtained in accordance with the Regulation."

65. Australia submits that the term "Community protected name" in fact refers to an EC-defined GI that is already being protected under Regulation No. 2081/92, irrespective of whether that name relates to a geographic area within the Community or in another WTO Member. As the EC itself acknowledges,[56] an application for the registration of an EC-defined GI from within the territory of the EC that "concerns a homonym of an already registered name from the European Union or a third country recognised in accordance with the procedure in Article 12.3" is governed by Article 6.6 of Regulation No. 2081/92.

---

[52] First Written Submission of the EC, paragraph 138.

[53] First Written Submission of the EC, paragraph 446.

[54] Response of the European Communities to Question 41(a) from the Panel after the first substantive meeting, paragraph 108.

[55] Response of the European Communities to Question 41(c) from the Panel after the first substantive meeting, paragraph 110.

[56] First Written Submission of the EC, paragraph 89.

66. Thus, Article 12.2 of Regulation No. 2081/92 should properly be considered to govern an application for the registration of an EC-defined GI from another WTO Member that meets the conditions of reciprocity and equivalence established by Article 12.1 of the Regulation where that EC-defined GI is homonymous with an EC-defined GI that is already being protected under the Regulation, irrespective of whether the earlier name relates to a geographical area within the EC or in another WTO Member. Article 6.6 of the Regulation is the parallel provision governing an application for the registration of an EC-defined GI from within the EC that is homonymous with an EC-defined GI that is already being protected under the Regulation, irrespective of whether the earlier name relates to a geographical area within the EC or in another WTO Member.

67. Australia submits that the EC has not disproved the factual premise informing Australia's claims that Article 12.2 of Regulation No. 2081/92 governs an application for the registration of an EC-defined GI relating to a geographical area in another WTO Member that is identical to an EC-defined GI—whether relating to a geographical area in an EC Member State or in another WTO Member—that is already being protected within the EC pursuant to the Regulation. The EC's counterarguments are not sustainable having regard to the meaning, context and aims of those provisions in accordance with the rules of interpretation of EC laws.

E. CONCLUSION

68. DSU Article 11 sets out the functions of a panel, and expressly provides that a panel should make an objective assessment of the facts of the case. As the EC itself says, that requires that the Panel establish the meaning that Regulation No. 2081/92 would normally have within the EC's own legal order.

69. Australia submits that the Panel should find that the explanations put forward by the EC of the meanings of the provisions of Regulation No. 2081/92 concerned with the registration of an EC-defined GI relating to the territory of another WTO Member, the Article 15 decision-making process and the protection of homonymous EC-defined GIs are not consistent with the meaning that Regulation No. 2081/92 would normally have within the EC's own legal order having regard to the rules of interpretation applied by the ECJ.

70. Thus, Australia noted with particular interest the Panel's question whether a statement by the EC delegation to the Panel is legally binding on the EC, and the relevant part of the EC's response:

> ... [T]he statements made by the agents of the European Commission before the Panel commit and engage the European Communities.
>
> However, it should also be noted that where the statements of the European Communities regard the interpretation of Regulation 2081/92, these statements concern an issue of fact. ... Their purpose is ... to clarify the existing legal situation in European Community law. Their intention is not to create new legal obligations in public international or in Community law.
>
> This being said, the EC does not consider that its statements before the Panel are without legal significance. ... It is not conceivable to the European Commission that it would, in the interpretation or application of the Regulation, take a different approach to the one it has set out before the Panel.[57] *(emphases added)*

71. The EC expressly concedes that statements made by EC representatives before the Panel regarding the interpretation of Regulation No. 2081/92 are not intended to create new legal obligations in Community law. The statements of EC representatives before the Panel cannot therefore be relied upon by the Panel to counteract conclusions concerning the meaning of the provisions of Regulation No. 2081/92 as a result of the Panel's objective assessment of the facts of the case pursuant to the Panel's obligation under DSU Article 11. Even if the statements by EC representatives before the Panel were the only basis on which to determine how Regulation No. 2081/92 were to apply, given the number of conflicting statements made by various EC

[57] Response of the European Communities to Question 15 from the Panel after the first substantive meeting, paragraphs 29-31.

representatives, WTO Members could not have any assurance of how the Regulation would be interpreted by the EC at the conclusion of the Panel's proceedings. On the other hand, should the EC apply the provisions of the Regulation in the manner it has set out, any challenge to the EC's actions to implement the Regulation would be heard before the ECJ, which would have to consider the meaning of the provisions of the Regulation in accordance with its normal rules of interpretation of Community law, that is, considering the wording, context and aims of the provisions at issue. Further, if it is open to the ECJ to look to statements made by EC representatives before the Panel, would it not also be open to the ECJ to look at statements made by other senior EC representatives and entities in other contexts?

72. Consequently, only formal amendments of the provisions of Regulation No. 2081/92 could ensure their interpretation in a manner consistent with the EC's WTO obligations.

V. ESTOPPEL

73. In its First Written Submission, the EC has several times argued that Australia would be estopped from making certain claims.[58] Moreover, according to the EC:

> According to Article 3.10 of the DSU, the participants in dispute settlement procedures under the DSU are bound by an obligation of good faith. The principle of estoppel is similarly based on the notion of good faith. Accordingly, the EC considers that the notion of estoppel is applicable in the context of WTO dispute settlement."[59]

74. The EC's statement is extraordinary. According to the EC's logic, estoppel forms part of the principles of the WTO dispute settlement system merely because estoppel exhibits characteristics similar to aspects of that system. This is a flawed argument.

75. DSU Article 3.10 does not affect the right of a WTO Member to bring a particular claim. Rather, DSU Article 3.10 deals with good faith participation in and observance of WTO dispute settlement procedures. It could not provide the basis for a claim of estoppel, assuming for the sake of argument that such a claim could be made.

76. Although the principle of estoppel may be grounded in the general principle of good faith (as noted by the International Court of Justice in the *Gulf of Maine Case*[60]), this does not mean that a WTO Member may rely on the principle of estoppel to defeat a claim brought by another WTO Member. Nor is the principle of estoppel imported into the *WTO Agreement* by the reference in DSU Article 3.2 to the customary rules of interpretation of public international law: estoppel is not a customary rule of interpretation.

77. The principle of estoppel has been raised in earlier disputes. However, it has never been applied by a panel in determining a claim before it and there are no Appellate Body findings on the issue.

78. In *Guatemala – Cement II*, Guatemala argued that Mexico's failure to object immediately to a delay in a required notification by Guatemala gave rise to an estoppel, although Guatemala did not identify a provision of a covered agreement as supporting its reliance on the principle of estoppel. The Panel in that dispute considered that:

---

[58] See, for example, paragraph 344.

[59] EC response to Question 89 from the Panel following the first substantive meeting with the parties, paragraph 227.

[60] 1984 ICJ Reports, page 305, paragraph 130.

> [e]stoppel is premised on the view that where one party has been induced to act in reliance on the assurances of another party, in such a way that it would be prejudiced were the other party later to change its position, such a change in position is "estopped," that is precluded.[61]

79. The Panel did not find it necessary to determine whether a WTO Member could rely on the principle of estoppel, as it held that "Mexico was under no obligation to object immediately to the violations" it alleged before the Panel.[62] The Panel went on to hold that, as Mexico had:

> ... raised its claims at an appropriate moment under the WTO dispute settlement procedures, Guatemala could not have reasonably relied upon Mexico's alleged lack of protest to conclude that Mexico would not bring a WTO complaint.[63]

80. Australia notes that the Panel in *Guatemala – Cement II* held that the fact that a WTO Member does not complain about a measure at a given point in time cannot by itself deprive that WTO Member of its right to initiate a dispute at some later point in time. The lack of complaint does not create an estoppel.

81. Further, in *EEC – Bananas I*, the Panel rejected an EC argument that the complaining parties' silence regarding the GATT inconsistent banana import regimes at issue resulted in the complaining parties being estopped from making such claims. The Panel noted that "[e]stoppel could only result from the express, or in exceptional circumstances, implied, consent of the complaining parties."[64] Applying this standard the Panel found that "[t]he mere inaction of the contracting parties could not in good faith be interpreted as an expression of their consent to release the EEC from its obligations under Part II of the GATT."[65]

82. Australia submits that the rationale of the Panel in *EEC – Bananas I* is equally applicable in the current case. Australia has never consented—either explicitly or implicitly—to the EC's unilateral imposition of WTO-inconsistent requirements for action on the part of Australia. Thus, not having sought a DSU process earlier cannot be interpreted as an expression of Australia's consent to release the EC from its obligations under the *TRIPS Agreement*—or indeed under any of the other covered agreements. To allow the EC's arguments to stand would lead to the perverse outcome of requiring WTO Members to hurry to dispute settlement for fear of otherwise losing their rights.

83. Even if the principle of estoppel is applicable to WTO dispute settlement—which Australia does not concede—it would not operate to prevent Australia from initiating this dispute or from pursuing any claims as part of that dispute.

VI. THE REGISTRATION AND ENFORCEMENT OF TRADEMARKS IN AUSTRALIA

84. In its First Written Submission, the EC makes a number of incorrect and/or confusing references to the situation concerning the registration and enforcement of trademarks in Australia.[66] The Australian trademark regime is not the measure at issue in this dispute, and the EC's references to it are irrelevant. Nevertheless, to ensure accuracy in the record, Australia notes the following points.

85. Australia's Trade Marks Act 1995 is administered by the Trade Marks Office, a part of IP Australia. Initial decisions relating to an application for registration of a trademark are made within the Trade Marks Office. Those initial decisions are appellable within the Trade Marks Office.

---

[61] *Guatemala – Cement II*, paragraph 8.23.

[62] *Guatemala – Cement II*, paragraph 8.24.

[63] *Guatemala – Cement II*, paragraph 8.24.

[64] *EEC – Bananas I*, paragraph 361.

[65] *EEC – Bananas I*, paragraph 363.

[66] See, for example, paragraph 365.

86. However, neither the Trade Marks Office nor IP Australia is a judicial body within the meaning of Part III of the *TRIPS Agreement*. All decisions by the Trade Marks Office concerning registration and opposition in relation to a trademark application are reviewable *de novo* by the Federal Court of Australia.

87. Thus, the situation concerning the registration and enforcement of trademarks in Australia cannot be compared to the situation concerning the registration and enforcement of an EC-defined GI under Regulation No. 2081/92. The situation in Australia is more akin to that applying in relation to the Community Trademark Regulation,[67] which is administered by the EC's Office for Harmonisation in the Internal Market (OHIM). The Community Trademark Regulation provides for an initial decision-making level and internal appeal at OHIM in respect of the registration of a trademark, with all actions for infringement of trademark rights being heard *de novo* by designated Community trademark courts.

VII. THE EC MEASURE DIMINISHES THE LEGAL PROTECTION FOR TRADEMARKS IN WAYS NOT PERMITTED BY THE TRIPS AGREEMENT

88. In its First Written Submission,[68] Australia claimed that the EC measure is inconsistent with the EC's obligations pursuant to the *TRIPS Agreement* because—in respect of the registration of EC-defined GIs—the EC measure diminishes the legal protection for pre-existing trademarks in ways not permitted by the *TRIPS Agreement*. In particular, the EC measure:

- does not grant to the owner of a registered trademark the exclusive right to prevent all third parties not having the owner's consent from using in the course of trade identical or similar signs for goods which are identical or similar to those in respect of which the trademark is registered where such use would result in a likelihood of confusion, contrary to TRIPS Article 16.1;

- does not provide for a presumption of a likelihood of confusion in the case of use of an identical sign for identical goods, contrary to TRIPS Article 16.1;

- prejudices the validity of an application for the registration of a trademark by failing to grant the right of priority required to be granted under Paris Article 4, contrary to TRIPS Article 24.5;

- does not assure to WTO Member nationals either effective protection against unfair competition or appropriate effective legal remedies to repress acts of unfair competition as required by Paris Articles 10*bis*(1) and 10*ter*(1), contrary to TRIPS Article 2.1;

- does not make available to trademark right holders civil judicial procedures concerning the enforcement of their intellectual property rights, contrary to TRIPS Article 42;

- provides procedures concerning the enforcement of trademark rights which are not fair and equitable, and which are unnecessarily complicated and entail unwarranted delays, contrary to TRIPS Article 41.2;

- does not ensure that decisions on the registration of an EC-defined GI are based only on evidence in respect of which trademark right holders were offered the opportunity to be heard, contrary to TRIPS Article 41.3;

- does not ensure the availability under its law of enforcement procedures as specified in Part III of the *TRIPS Agreement* so as to permit effective action against any act of infringement of trademark rights, contrary to TRIPS Article 41.1; and

[67] Exhibit COMP-7.

[68] First Written Submission of Australia, paragraphs 88-107

- in respect of decisions by EC Member States to grant transitional national protection to a proposed EC-defined GI, does not ensure that such decisions are made by an EC Member State with proper regard to the rights required to be granted to trademark rights holders in accordance with the EC's obligations pursuant to the *TRIPS Agreement*.

89. Australia also claimed that, as a consequence of the EC's failure to comply with the provisions of Paris Articles 10*bis*(1) and 10*ter*(1) in respect of the registration of EC-defined GIs and in respect of decisions by EC Member States to grant transitional national protection, the EC measure is inconsistent with TRIPS Article 2.1.

90. Australia further claimed that, as a consequence of the EC measure's inconsistency with TRIPS Article 2.1 ("incorporating" by reference Paris Articles 10*bis*(1) and 10*ter*(1)), 16.1, 24.5, 41.1, 41.2, 41.3 and/or 42 in respect of the registration of EC-defined GIs and in respect of decisions by EC Member States to grant transitional national protection, the EC has failed:

- to give effect to the provisions of the *TRIPS Agreement* as required by Article 1.1 of that Agreement;

- to accord the treatment provided for in the *TRIPS Agreement* to the nationals of other WTO Members as required by Article 1.3 of that Agreement.

A. IN RESPECT OF THE REGISTRATION OF AN EC-DEFINED GI, THE EC MEASURE DOES NOT GRANT TO THE OWNER OF A REGISTERED TRADEMARK THE EXCLUSIVE RIGHT TO PREVENT CONFUSINGLY SIMILAR OR IDENTICAL USE OF A SIGN FOR SIMILAR OR IDENTICAL GOODS, CONTRARY TO ARTICLE 16.1 OF THE TRIPS AGREEMENT

(i) That Regulation No. 2081/92 does not allow the registration of confusing new trademarks is irrelevant to the claim at issue

91. In the factual circumstances that underpin Australia's claim, the trademark rights already exist within the territory of the EC under EC Member State law: the trademark rights pre-date the application for registration of an EC-defined GI and possibly also the adoption of Regulation No. 2081/92 itself. Indeed, they could pre-date the adoption of Community Trademark Directive[69]. Thus, that Regulation No. 2081/92 and the Community Trademark Directive—or indeed the Community Trademark Regulation[70]—might now operate, individually and/or collectively, to prevent the future acquisition of new trademark rights in geographical names does not mean that such trademark rights do not already exist within the EC. Indeed, the "Bavaria" trademark registered in Denmark referred to in Regulation No. 1347/2001[71] is just such an example.

92. Australia notes that the EC acknowledges the possibility of such a situation when it says: "... it is extremely unlikely that the situation described by Australia will ever present itself in practice"[72] *(emphasis added)*. In reality, the EC cannot say that such trademark rights do not exist because it has not provided—and still does not provide—to any such right holders the effective legal avenues to challenge an application for the registration of an EC-defined GI. However large or small the number of such trademarks may be, the EC is obliged by the express provisions of TRIPS Article 16.1 to grant to the owners of those trademarks the exclusive right to prevent in the course of trade confusing use of an identical or similar sign for identical or similar goods.

---

[69] First Council Directive of 21 December 1988 *to approximate the laws of the Member States relating to trade marks* (89/104/EEC), Exhibit COMP-6.

[70] Council Regulation (EC) No. 40/94 of 20 December 1993 *on the Community trade mark*, Exhibit COMP-7.

[71] Exhibit EC-9.

[72] First Written Submission of the EC, paragraph 323.

(ii) Article 24.5 of the TRIPS Agreement does not envisage co-existence of TRIPS-defined GIs and pre-existing trademarks

93. Article 24.5 is placed in Section 3, Part II, of the *TRIPS Agreement*, which is concerned with the "Geographical Indications" category of intellectual property rights. Moreover, TRIPS Article 24 is headed "International Negotiations: Exceptions." In Australia's view, paragraph 5 of Article 24 is one of the "exceptions" provided by that Article. Further, in the absence of an express provision to the contrary, the exceptions set out in that Article can only be exceptions to the provisions of Section 3, Part II, of the *TRIPS Agreement* concerning Geographical Indications.

94. By definition, an "exception" is something that does not follow an established rule.[73] Thus, in respect of the universe of trademark rights that fall within TRIPS Article 24.5—that is, in respect of "pre-existing" trademark rights—the rules otherwise established by Section 3, Part II, of the *TRIPS Agreement* do not apply to the extent that they would prejudice, that is, adversely affect, the relevant trademark rights on the basis of being identical or similar to a TRIPS-defined GI. Conversely, had it been intended that the rights required to be granted to the owner of a registered trademark under TRIPS Article 16.1 should not apply in relation to the later registration of a TRIPS-defined GI, this would have been stated expressly in an exception within Section 2, Part II, of the *TRIPS Agreement.*

95. The EC argues at length that TRIPS Article 24.5 envisages the co-existence of GIs and pre-existing trademarks.[74] In doing so, however, the EC mischaracterises or ignores Australia's arguments, and indeed ignores the provisions of the *TRIPS Agreement* and of its own legislation. At other times,[75] the EC's arguments seem to be premised on a view that TRIPS Article 24.5 governs conflicts involving the future acquisition of trademark rights and GIs. As Australia does not make such claims or arguments, it simply notes that such arguments by the EC are irrelevant to the matter at issue.

96. Australia has not claimed—and does not claim—that TRIPS Article 16.1 requires that "trademarks must prevail over later geographical indications."[76] Rather, Australia has argued: "[t]ogether with TRIPS Articles 22.3 and 23.2, TRIPS Article 24.5 defines the boundary between a WTO Member's right to implement measures relating to TRIPS-defined GIs and its obligation to afford protection to trademarks,"[77] a statement with which the EC apparently agrees.[78]

97. The EC argues that WTO Members "are entitled to provide more extensive protection for geographical indications, in accordance with Article 1.1 of the TRIPS Agreement."[79] Indeed, they are—a point expressly recognised by Australia when it said that it was not contesting the EC's right "to register and/or protect GIs as intellectual property; *[or]* to implement in its law more extensive protection for GIs than is required to be provided by the *TRIPS Agreement*."[80]

98. However, the EC has ignored the remaining clause of that sentence in TRIPS Article 1.1: "provided that such protection does not contravene the provisions of this Agreement." Thus, more extensive protection of GIs by the EC cannot be implemented in such a way as to contravene any *TRIPS Agreement* provisions, including those concerned with trademark rights. The EC's argument that TRIPS Article 24.5 allows a WTO

---

[73] *OED*, Vol.1, page 872, defines "exception" in relevant part as "1 The action of excepting … something from a group, the scope of a proposition, etc.; the state or fact of being so excepted. 2 A … thing which is excepted; *esp.* a particular case … that does not follow some general rule or to which a generalization is not applicable. Foll. by *to* …"

[74] First Written Submission of the EC, paragraphs 294-311.

[75] For example, First Written Submission of the EC, paragraph 307.

[76] First Written Submission of the EC, paragraph 297.

[77] First Written Submission of Australia, paragraph 105.

[78] First Written Submission of the EC, paragraphs 298-300.

[79] First Written Submission of the EC, paragraph 300.

[80] First Written Submission of Australia, paragraph 4.

Member to prejudice rights of a trademark owner not referred to in that Article is therefore not sustainable.[81] TRIPS Article 24.5 imposes an obligation on a WTO Member to ensure that the implementation of Section 3, Part II, of the *TRIPS Agreement* does not prejudice specific rights attaching to the universe of pre-existing trademark rights covered by that provision on the basis being identical or similar to a TRIPS-defined GI.

99. The EC argues that Article 14.2 of Regulation No. 2081/92 is fully consistent with "the right to use a trademark" provided by TRIPS Article 24.5, the trademark owner's right to use being "one of the two basic rights of the trademark owner, together with the right to prevent other persons from using that sign[...]."[82] However, no provision of Section 2, Part II, of the *TRIPS Agreement* obliges a WTO Member to grant to a trademark right holder a "right to use a trademark." Moreover, if the EC's view of the proper interpretation of the rights of a trademark owner provided by the *TRIPS Agreement* is that such a right is so inherent in a trademark that an express statement to that effect is not required, then by its own admission the Community Trademark Regulation and Directive are inconsistent with the EC's TRIPS obligations as they do not in fact grant a right to use a trademark within the Community or require an EC Member State to grant such a right.[83]

100. In any case, in Australia's view[84] the better interpretation of TRIPS Article 24.5 is that the phrase "the right to use a trademark" only applies to trademarks to which rights have been acquired through use. The *TRIPS Agreement* does not contain any obligation to grant exclusive rights in respect of trademarks to which the rights have been acquired through use, notwithstanding that TRIPS Article 16.1 recognises that a WTO Member can choose to grant rights on that basis. It could be entirely consistent with a WTO Member's obligations pursuant to the *TRIPS Agreement* to provide a non-exclusive right to use a trademark to which rights have been acquired through use. Were TRIPS Article 24.5 to have used the phrase "exclusive right to use a trademark," it would have been presuming that trademark rights acquired through use would always be exclusive rights, which need not be the case. Further, were TRIPS Article 24.5 to have used the phrase "rights under TRIPS Article 16.1," it would have been presuming that trademark rights acquired through use would always be the same as those required to have been granted in respect of a registered trademark: again this need not be the case.

101. Should the Panel consider that the phrase "the right to use a trademark" applies to the universe of pre-existing trademark rights covered by TRIPS Article 24.5 as distinct from trademark rights acquired on the basis of use, it remains the fact that the obligation that a WTO Member "shall not prejudice ... the validity of the registration of a trademark" applies to registered trademarks within that universe of pre-existing trademark rights. Accordingly, a WTO Member's "measures adopted to implement this Section" cannot prejudice the

---

[81] Given the EC's assertions concerning the consistency of the Australian Wine and Brandy Corporation Act with the arguments put forward by Australia in this dispute (First Written Submission of the EC, footnote 152) and notwithstanding that the provisions of the Australian Wine and Brandy Corporation Act are not at issue in this dispute, Australia notes that all Australian TRIPS-defined GIs protected under that Act notwithstanding prior trademark rights are protected with the consent of the owners of those trademarks (see Australia's replies to questions 4, 5 9 from the EC to the complaining parties following the first substantive meeting with the Panel). It is not possible to compare the circumstances of this dispute to a situation in which a WTO Member has adopted a different balance of intellectual property rights as a consequence of voluntary agreement among all potentially affected right holders.

[82] First Written Submission of the EC, paragraph 303.

[83] Article 9.1 of Council Regulation (EC) No. 40/94 of 20 December 1993 on the Community trade mark, Exhibit COMP-7, provides as follows (Articles 5.1 and 5.2 of First Council Directive of 21 December 1988 to approximate the laws of the Member States relating to trade marks (89/104/EEC), Exhibit COMP-6, provide similarly):

A Community trade mark shall confer on the proprietor exclusive rights therein. The proprietor shall be entitled to prevent all third parties not having his consent from using in the course of trade:

(a) any sign which is identical with the Community trade mark in relation to goods or services which are identical with those for which the Community trade mark is registered;

(b) any sign where, because of its identity with or similarity to the Community trade mark and the identity or similarity of the goods or services covered by the Community trade mark and the sign, there exists a likelihood of confusion on the part of the public; the likelihood of confusion includes the likelihood of association between the sign and the trade mark;

(c) any sign which is identical with or similar to the Community trade mark in relation to goods or services which are not similar to those for which the Community trade mark is registered, where the latter has a reputation in the Community and where use of that sign without due cause takes unfair advantage of, or is detrimental to, the distinctive character or the repute of the Community trade mark.

[84] First Written Submission of Australia, paragraph 74, and Australia's reply to Questions 76 and 77 posed by the Panel to the parties following the first substantive meeting with the parties.

validity of the registration of those trademarks by removing the exclusive right of the owners of those registered trademarks to prevent confusing use.

(iii) Article 14.3 of Regulation No. 2081/92 does not allow the registration of a confusing – as distinct from a misleading – EC-defined GI to be refused

102. The EC also argues that Article 14.3 of Regulation No. 2081/92 allows the registration of a "confusing" EC-defined GI to be refused.[85] Article 14.3 of the Regulation provides:

> *[An EC-defined GI]* shall not be registered where, in the light of a trade mark's reputation and renown and the length of time it has been used, registration is liable to mislead the consumer as to the true identity of the product. *(emphases added)*

103. The reason that "Australia *[did]* not even attempt to interpret the terms of Article 14.3"[86] is, of course, that Article 14.3 of Regulation No. 2081/92 does not concern use that is liable to confuse the consumer of a good that will bear the proposed EC-defined GI that is the same as a trademark. Article 14.3 of the Regulation concerns use that is liable to mislead the consumer of a good that will bear the proposed EC-defined GI that is the same as a trademark.[87] Article 14.3 of the Regulation—by its plain language—also requires that the issue of whether use of an EC-defined GI would mislead the consumer be determined in the light of a trademark's reputation, renown and the length of time it has been used.

104. Firstly, "misleading" establishes a stricter evidentiary standard than "confusing." The ordinary meaning of "confusing" is "perplexing, bewildering."[88] Thus, TRIPS Article 16.1 grants to the owner of a registered trademark the exclusive right to prevent use of similar or identical sign for similar or identical goods where such use would perplex or bewilder the consumer as to the source undertaking of the goods. The ordinary meaning of "misleading," on the other hand, is "[t]hat leads someone astray, that causes error; imprecise, confusing, deceptive."[89] Although "misleading" might in some contexts be synonymous with "confusing," its use in the context of TRIPS Articles 22.2 and 22.3—use which misleads the public as to origin—makes clear that the ordinary meaning of "misleading" in context of those provisions is use which "leads someone astray or that causes error." In other words, misleading use in the sense of TRIPS Articles 22.2 and 22.3 is use which positively provokes an error on the part of a consumer. At the same time, TRIPS Articles 22.2 and 22.3 serve to confirm that the standard of "confusing" use established by TRIPS Article 16.1 is a separate standard to that of "misleading" use.

105. The context and aim of Article 14 of Regulation No. 2081/92 indicate that "misleading" in the sense of Article 14.3 has a similar meaning to "misleading" in TRIPS Articles 22.2 and 22.3, that is, that an EC-defined GI will not be registered where, in the light of a trademark's reputation and renown and the length of time it has been used, registration of the EC-defined GI is liable to cause an error on the part of the consumer as to the true identity of the product.

106. Thus, there is a category of applications for registration of an EC-defined GI—those whose use of a sign would be confusing, but not necessarily misleading—which are excluded by the express terms of Article 14.3 of Regulation No. 2081/92. Further, in respect of this category, neither the Regulation nor any other

[85] First Written Submission of the EC, paragraph 286.

[86] First Written Submission of the EC, paragraph 287.

[87] Moreover, contrary to the EC's statement (at footnote 140 of its First Written Submission), recital (3) to Regulation No. 1347/2001 (Exhibit EC-9) concerning the registration of "Bayerisches Bier" as an EC-defined GI expressly provides: "... it was considered ... that registration of the name 'Bayerisches Bier' was not likely to mislead the consumer as to the true identity of the product. Consequently, the geographical indication 'Bayerisches Bier' and the trade mark 'Bavaria' are not in the situation referred to in Article 14.3 of Regulation ... No. 2081/92" *(emphasis added)*.

[88] *OED*, Vol.1, page 477.

[89] *OED*, Vol. 1, page 1791.

provision of EC law grants to the owner of a registered trademark the rights required to be granted by TRIPS Article 16.1 with respect to the registration of an EC-defined GI.

107. Secondly, the express terms of Article 14.3 of Regulation No. 2081/92 require that the EC determine whether registration of a name as an EC-defined GI would be misleading having regard to a trademark's reputation, renown and the length of time it has been used. Yet TRIPS Article 16.1 requires that a WTO Member grant to the owner of a registered trademark the exclusive right to prevent unauthorised use in the course of trade of identical or similar signs for identical or similar goods "where such use would result in a likelihood of confusion." That right is not in any way qualified with regard to reputation and renown and/or length of time a trademark has been in use. Thus, applications for registration of an EC-defined GI whose use of a sign would be misleading for reasons other than a trademark's reputation and renown and length of time in use again constitute a category in respect of which neither Article 14.3 of the Regulation—or any other provision of EC law—grants to the owner of a registered trademark the rights required to be granted by TRIPS Article 16.1.

108. For the owners of registered trademarks which do not meet the tests expressly established by Article 14.3 of Regulation No. 2081/92 in regard to whether registration of an EC-defined GI would be liable to mislead the consumer as to the true identity of the product in the light of a trademark's reputation and renown and the length of time it has been used, neither the Regulation—nor any other provision of EC law—grants to them the rights required to have been granted to them by the EC pursuant to TRIPS Article 16.1.

109. Thus, Article 14.2 and 14.3 of Regulation No. 2081/92 read together result in a situation in which—unless the registration of an EC-defined GI is liable to mislead the consumer as to the true identity of the product in the light of a trademark's reputation and renown and the length of time that trademark has been used—an earlier registered trademark and a later registered EC-defined GI must co-exist in the marketplace. Regulation No. 2081/92 simply does not provide for the refusal of the registration of an EC-defined GI that is <u>confusingly</u> similar or identical to a registered trademark where that EC-defined GI would not be liable to <u>mislead</u> the consumer as to the true identity of the product.

110. Moreover, the application of those provisions of Regulation No. 2081/92 in the "Bayerisches Bier" case is fully consistent with Australia's interpretation. Recital (3) of Regulation No. 1347/2001[90] sets out that it was considered that registration of the EC-defined GI "Bayerisches Bier" would not be misleading in relation to the existence of the name "Bavaria" as a trademark pursuant to Article 14.3 of Regulation No. 2081/92. Recital (4) of Regulation No. 1347/2001 then provides: "[t]he use of certain trademarks, for example, ... 'Bavaria' ... may continue <u>notwithstanding</u> the registration of the geographical indication 'Bayerisches Bier' as long as they fulfil the conditions provided for in Article 14.2 of Regulation ... No. 2081/92" *(emphasis added)*. Having found that registration of "Bayerisches Bier" as an EC-defined GI would not be liable to mislead the consumer as to the true identity of the product within the meaning of Article 14.3 of Regulation No. 2081/92, the EC then considered that the trademark "Bavaria" could continue to be used "notwithstanding"—that is, in spite of—the registration of "Bayerishes Bier" as an EC-defined GI. The EC simply did not consider whether registration of "Bayerisches Bier" as an EC-defined GI would nevertheless constitute confusing use in relation to the trademark "Bavaria."

(iv) Article 24.3 of the TRIPS Agreement is irrelevant to the matters at issue

111. The EC argues that, irrespective of whether co-existence of EC-defined GIs and pre-existing trademarks is consistent with TRIPS Article 24.5, the EC is required to maintain such co-existence by virtue of TRIPS Article 24.3. TRIPS Article 24.3 provides:

---

[90] Exhibit EC-9.

> In implementing this Section, a Member shall not diminish the protection of geographical indications that existed in that Member immediately prior to the date of entry into force of the WTO Agreement. *(emphases added)*

112. The "protection of geographical indications that existed in" the EC as of 31 December 1994[91] within the meaning of TRIPS Article 24.3 is the protection provided by Article 13.1 of Regulation No. 2081/92. Article 13.1 of the Regulation begins: "[r]egistered names shall be protected against …." Article 14.2 of Regulation No. 2081/92 is in the nature of an exception to that protection in respect of a trademark which fulfils the conditions laid down in Article 14.2.[92]

113. Australia is not seeking an assessment in this dispute about the "level of" protection granted to a registered EC-defined GI pursuant to Article 13.1 of the Regulation. Rather, Australia is challenging the processes by which a property right in an EC-defined GI is acquired under Regulation No. 2081/92—and the EC's failure to observe its WTO obligations in respect of those processes. Indeed, the EC has several times described the Regulation in such terms, for example, as prescribing a procedure "for the registration of geographical indications," as "as procedure for the acquisition of another intellectual property right," and as laying down "an administrative procedure for the acquisition of geographical indications via a system of registration."[93]

114. Removing the co-existence standard found in Article 14.2 of Regulation No. 2081/92 would not "diminish the protection of geographical indications" within the meaning of TRIPS Article 24.3. Accordingly, TRIPS Article 24.3 does not require the system of co-existence to be maintained.

115. Further, and in any case, it is Australia's view that "the protection of geographical indications" in TRIPS Article 24.3 encompasses protection actually extended to specific TRIPS-defined GIs, not merely the regime that was in place. In the context of the EC measure, this would mean that the protection actually extended to registered EC-defined GIs as of 31 December 1994 could not be diminished. However, as of that date, no EC-defined GIs were registered pursuant to Regulation No. 2081/92. The first registrations were made pursuant to Regulation No. 1107/96 of 12 June 1996.[94] Once again, TRIPS Article 24.3 does not require the system of co-existence to be maintained.

116. Finally, and again in any case, TRIPS Article 24.3 relates only to the implementation of "this Section," that is, to Section 3, Part II, of the *TRIPS Agreement* concerning Geographical Indications. The obligation to grant to the owner of a registered trademark the exclusive right to prevent confusing similar or identical use of a sign for similar or identical goods—the obligation with which the EC's requirement for co-existence is inconsistent—arises from TRIPS Article 16.1, which is in Section 2, Part II, of the *TRIPS Agreement*. TRIPS Article 24.3 does not shield the EC from implementing its obligations pursuant to provisions of the *TRIPS Agreement* other than those contained in Section 3, Part II, of that Agreement.

117. Accordingly, for all of the reasons set out above, TRIPS Article 24.3 does not require the system of co-existence to be maintained.

(v) The requirement for co-existence of a pre-existing trademark right and an EC-defined GI cannot be justified by Article 17 of the TRIPS Agreement

118. The EC argues in the alternative that, if Article 14.3 of Regulation No. 2081/92 does not prevent the registration of a confusing EC-defined GI and assuming further that co-existence of a pre-existing registered

---

91 In Australia's view, "the date of entry into force of the WTO Agreement" within the meaning of TRIPS Article 24.3 is 1 January 1995. Australia assumes that the EC's reference to 31 December 1995 in paragraph 314 of its First Written Submission is a typographical error.

92 The seventh recital to Regulation No. 1107/96, Exhibit COMP-3.a, and Recital (4) to Regulation No. 1347/2001, Exhibit EC-9.

93 First Written Submission of the EC, paragraphs 160, 327 and 359 respectively.

94 Exhibit COMP-3.a.

trademark and an EC-defined GI is neither consistent with TRIPS Article 24.5 nor required in the case of the EC by TRIPS Article 24.3, such co-existence would be justified under TRIPS Article 17.[95]

119. TRIPS Article 17 has not been the subject of detailed findings in any previous dispute. However, the analogous provisions concerning the patent and copyright provisions of the *TRIPS Agreement* have been considered in previous disputes and thus provide some guidance to the proper interpretation of TRIPS Article 17. TRIPS Article 30 concerning "Exceptions to Rights Conferred" in respect of patents was examined in *Canada – Pharmaceutical Products*. TRIPS Article 13 concerning "Limitations and Exceptions" in respect of copyright and related rights was examined in *US – Homestyle Copyright*.

120. In *US – Homestyle Copyright*, the Panel expressly found that the burden of proof rested on the responding party "to establish that any exception or limitation is applicable and that the conditions, if any, for invoking such exception are fulfilled."[96] Australia submits:

- firstly, that the burden of proof in relation to TRIPS Article 17 in this dispute lies similarly with the EC as the responding party "to establish that any exception or limitation is applicable and that the conditions, if any for invoking such exception are fulfilled;"[97] and

- secondly, that the EC has not met that burden of proof.

121. In the event that the Panel should consider that the EC has in fact met its burden of proof, Australia submits the following arguments in rebuttal for the Panel's consideration.

122. TRIPS Article 17 permits a WTO Member to provide for "limited exceptions"—or small diminutions—to trademark rights, measured by the extent to which the exclusive rights granted by TRIPS Article 16.1 or to which other trademark rights are curtailed.[98] Those limited exceptions must take account of both the legitimate interests of the trademark owner and the legitimate interests of third parties. Thus, any limited exceptions must consider, from both legal and normative societal perspectives, the interests of both the trademark owner and third parties in light of the objectives that underlie the protection of trademark rights.[99] That said, "third parties are by definition parties who have no legal right at all in being able to perform the tasks excluded by *[the relevant IP]* rights."[100]

123. Moreover, the requirements are cumulative, each being a separate and independent requirement that must be satisfied.[101] Thus, for TRIPS Article 17 to be applicable, the exception must: be limited; take account of the legitimate interests of the trademark owner; and take account of the legitimate interests of third parties.

124. An exception that allows co-existence with a pre-existing trademark in every case in which an EC-defined GI is registered cannot be considered "limited" within the terms of TRIPS Article 17. Further, if TRIPS Article 24.5 does not permit co-existence, such an exception under TRIPS Article 17 would—in effect—render TRIPS Article 24.5 meaningless.

---

[95] First Written Submission of the EC, paragraphs 315-319. Australia also notes the EC's comment in relation to the provisions of the Australian Trade Marks Act concerning use of a sign to indicate the geographical origin of goods (at footnote 154 of the EC's First Written Submission). The exception under the Act for use of sign to indicate the geographical origin of goods (section 122(1)(b)(i)) does not create an exception for a TRIPS-defined GI. Section 6 of the Act in fact expressly defines a GI in terms closely mirroring the terms of TRIPS Article 22.1. Moreover, where the Act refers to a GI as an intellectual property right, it does so expressly. Thus, for example, section 61 of the Act expressly provides for the rejection of an application for registration of a trademark that contains or consists of a false GI.

[96] *US – Homestyle Copyright*, Panel Report, paragraph 6.13.

[97] Australia notes that the EC seems to agree that it bears the burden of proof in relation to TRIPS Article 17: Response of the European Communities to Question 75(b) from the Panel after the first substantive meeting, paragraph 199.

[98] *Canada – Pharmaceutical Products*, Panel Report, paragraphs 7.30-7.31.

[99] *US – Homestyle Copyright*, Panel Report, paragraph 6.224.

[100] *Canada – Pharmaceutical Products*, Panel Report, paragraph 7.68.

[101] *Canada – Pharmaceutical Products*, Panel Report, paragraph 7.20.

125. Moreover, an exception that allows co-existence with a pre-existing trademark in every case in which an EC-defined GI is registered denies the exclusive right to prevent confusingly similar or identical use required to be granted pursuant to TRIPS Article 16.1 and protected pursuant to TRIPS Article 24.5. Such an exception cannot therefore be considered to "take account of the legitimate interests of the owner of the trademark."

126. Thus, even without considering what might be the legitimate interests of third parties needing to be taken into account, the EC argument cannot satisfy the requirements of TRIPS Article 17.

127. Moreover, having regard to the text of TRIPS Article 17 and to the design and architecture of the *TRIPS Agreement* generally, Australia submits that TRIPS Article 17 neither permits—nor was intended to permit—a general release from a WTO Member's obligation to grant the basic right attached to a registered trademark in the event of acquisition of another type of intellectual property right without some express recognition of that fact.

(vi) The EC measure does not ensure that an objection from the owner of a registered trademark is admissible or that such an objection is considered through the Article 15 decision-making process, contrary to Article 16.1 of the TRIPS Agreement

128. Australia submits that, in respect of the registration of an EC-defined GI pursuant to the EC measure, the EC does not make available to trademark right holders civil judicial procedures concerning the enforcement of an intellectual property right, contrary to the EC's obligations under TRIPS Article 42.[102]

129. Further and in any case, Australia submits that to the extent that the Article 15 decision-making process pursuant to Regulation No. 2081/92 constitutes the initial and only means through which a trademark right holder can seek to exercise the trademark rights required to be granted by the *TRIPS Agreement* in relation to the registration of an EC-defined GI, the EC measure does not ensure that an objection from the owner of a registered trademark is admissible or that such an objection is considered pursuant to the Regulation's Article 15 decision-making process.

130. The EC argues in response that TRIPS Article 16.1 does not confer a right of objection on trademark owners and that in any case Australia's arguments are factually incorrect.[103]

131. While TRIPS Article 16.1 may not confer a "right of objection" in express terms, such a right is nevertheless necessary to allow exercise of the right that is expressly required by that provision to be granted to the owner of a registered trademark: the exclusive right to prevent in the course of trade confusing use of an identical or similar sign for identical or similar goods. To say that a TRIPS Article 16.1 right does not necessitate a right of objection to the proposed acquisition of another category of intellectual property right is tantamount to saying that a trademark owner may not take the only means available to prevent a confusing use of that intellectual property right from day one: that the only avenue through which trademark rights could be enforced by the owner of a registered trademark is through judicial procedures—assuming that the right holder has effective access to such procedures—after the alleged confusing use has already begun. Australia does not believe that such a view is sustainable.

132. The EC argument overlooks that, to the extent that the Article 15 decision-making process constitutes the only means through which the owner of a registered trademark can seek to exercise the rights required to be granted to that owner pursuant to TRIPS Article 16.1 in respect of the registration of an EC-defined GI, the Article 15 decision-making process is an enforcement procedure that is subject to the EC's obligations pursuant to Part III of the *TRIPS Agreement*. The only means by which the owner of a registered trademark can seek to

---

[102] See Part VII.E.ii below.

[103] First Written Submission of the EC, paragraphs 325-344.

invoke that enforcement procedure in respect of the registration of an EC-defined GI is through the right of objection provided by Regulation No. 2081/92.

133. Further, in arguing that Australia's arguments are factually incorrect,[104] the EC has once again overlooked the meaning, context and aims of the provisions of Regulation No. 2081/92 at issue and the actual arguments made by Australia. The express criterion for the admissibility of a statement of objection from the owner of a registered trademark pursuant to Article 7.4 of Regulation No. 2081/92 is if it "shows that registration of the name proposed would jeopardize the existence ... of a mark." "[J]eopardise the existence"[105] establishes a far more rigorous standard than a "likelihood of confusion." For a statement of objection to show that the existence of a trademark would be jeopardised, the statement of objection would have to show that the very being of that trademark would be threatened. The grounds of objection in Article 7.4 of Regulation No. 2081/92 are too narrow to allow the owner of a registered trademark to exercise the right required to have been granted to him/her by TRIPS Article 16.1.

134. The EC also argues that "[w]hile Member states are not required to transmit the statements objections *[sic]*, their decisions are not discretionary and may be subject to judicial review under the national law of each Member State." Yet the EC does not explain how the possibility of judicial review of a procedural deficiency under an EC Member State's national law grants to the owner of a registered trademark the rights required to be granted pursuant to TRIPS Article 16.1 in respect of the registration of an EC-defined GI under Regulation No. 2081/92. Further, the EC does not even attempt to reconcile this statement with its advice before the Panel during the first substantive meeting with the parties to the dispute that Community law takes primacy over EC Member State law in the event of a conflict. It seems that—in the EC's view—the possibility of judicial review of a procedural deficiency at EC Member State level—an action, moreover, which could not in any case invalidate the Community level registration of an EC-defined GI pursuant to Regulation No. 2081/92—is sufficient to fulfil the EC's obligation pursuant to TRIPS Article 16.1. Such an argument by the EC is not sustainable.

(vii) Conclusion

135. The EC has not rebutted the *prima facie* case made by Australia that, in respect of the registration of an EC-defined GI, the EC measure does not grant to the owner of a registered trademark the exclusive right to prevent confusingly similar or identical use of a sign for similar or identical goods.

136. Moreover, Australia notes the express provision of TRIPS Article 1.3 that the object of the treatment provided for in the *TRIPS Agreement* is nationals. However, in Australia's view, a degree of care is needed to ensure that a too literal interpretation of the *TRIPS Agreement* does not result in unjustifiable discrimination on the basis of the type of intellectual property at issue. The treatment of nationals cannot be considered in a vacuum divorced from context: the protection of intellectual property rights generally.

B. IN RESPECT OF THE REGISTRATION OF AN EC-DEFINED GI, THE EC MEASURE DOES NOT PROVIDE A PRESUMPTION OF A LIKELIHOOD OF CONFUSION IN THE CASE OF USE OF AN IDENTICAL SIGN FOR IDENTICAL GOODS, CONTRARY TO ARTICLE 16.1 OF THE TRIPS AGREEMENT

137. TRIPS Article 16.1 requires that a WTO Member grant to the owner of a registered trademark the evidentiary presumption of a likelihood of confusion in the event of use of an identical sign for identical goods. It would of course be open to a WTO Member to provide in its domestic law for that presumption to be rebuttable in defined circumstances.

[104] First Written Submission of the EC, paragraphs 341-344.

[105] *OED*, Vol.1, defines "jeopardize" as "Put into jeopardy, endanger, put at risk" (page 1444) and "existence" in relevant part as "2 The fact or state of existing; actual possession of being. b Continued being; *spec.* continued being as a living creature, life, esp. under adverse conditions" (page 882).

138. The EC argues that a WTO Member is not required to reproduce the presumption explicitly in its domestic law.[106] Even if that is the case, however, the provisions of Regulation No. 2081/92 do not grant to the "registering authority"—and thus ultimately to the EC courts—the necessary discretion to apply the presumption.[107]

139. The EC argues too that the situation would be extremely unlikely ever to present itself in practice.[108] Even if this were true, it is irrelevant: even if there is only one registered trademark within the whole of the territory of the EC that meets this criterion, the EC must grant to that trademark owner the evidentiary presumption of a likelihood of confusion in respect of the proposed registration of an EC-defined GI.

140. Finally, the EC "considers that none of the registered geographical indications falls within *[the]* situation" of being identical to any earlier registered trademark used for identical goods.[109] In reality, however, the EC simply does not know, because it has not provided the means for an owner of a registered trademark to claim the presumption in respect of the registration of an EC-defined GI.

141. The EC has not rebutted the *prima facie* case made by Australia that, in respect of the registration of an EC-defined GI pursuant to Regulation No. 2081/92, the EC does not provide to the owner of a registered trademark a presumption of a likelihood of confusion in the case of use of an identical sign for identical goods, contrary to TRIPS Article 16.1.

C. IN RESPECT OF THE REGISTRATION OF AN EC-DEFINED GI, THE EC MEASURE PREJUDICES THE VALIDITY OF AN APPLICATION FOR THE REGISTRATION OF A TRADEMARK BY FAILING TO GRANT THE RIGHT OF PRIORITY REQUIRED TO BE GRANTED UNDER ARTICLE 4 OF THE PARIS CONVENTION, CONTRARY TO ARTICLE 24.5 OF THE TRIPS AGREEMENT

142. Australia argued in straightforward terms in its First Written Submission that the EC measure does not grant—in respect of the registration of an EC-defined GI—the right of priority required to be granted by Paris Article 4 and that, as a consequence, the EC measure prejudices eligibility of an application for registration of a trademark made in good faith, contrary to TRIPS Article 24.5. As the EC acknowledges, the Paris Convention does not provide for a similar right of priority in respect of indications of source.[110] The EC has responded to an argument that Australia has not made.[111] The EC has not rebutted the *prima facie* case made by Australia.

D. IN RESPECT OF THE REGISTRATION OF AN EC-DEFINED GI, THE EC MEASURE DOES NOT ASSURE TO WTO MEMBER NATIONALS EITHER EFFECTIVE PROTECTION AGAINST UNFAIR COMPETITION OR APPROPRIATE LEGAL REMEDIES TO REPRESS ACTS OF UNFAIR COMPETITION, CONTRARY TO ARTICLE 2.1 OF THE TRIPS AGREEMENT "INCORPORATING" ARTICLES 10BIS(1) AND 10TER(1) OF THE PARIS CONVENTION (1967)

143. The EC argues that Australia's claims are "insufficiently argued and difficult to understand."[112] In fact, Australia's claims are straightforward: in respect of the registration of an EC-defined GI, the EC measure does not assure to WTO Member nationals either effective protection against unfair competition or appropriate legal remedies to repress such acts, contrary to TRIPS Article 2.1 "incorporating" Paris Articles 10*bis*(1) and 10*ter*(1).

144. Paris Article 10*bis*(2) provides that an act of unfair competition is "any act of competition contrary to honest practices in industrial or commercial matters." "[H]onest practices in industrial or commercial matters"

---

[106] First Written Submission of the EC, paragraph 322.

[107] See Part VII.A.iii above.

[108] First Written Submission of the EC, paragraph 323.

[109] First Written Submission of the EC, paragraph 324.

[110] EC Response to Question 86 from the Panel following the first substantive meeting, paragraph 222.

[111] First Written Submission of the EC, paragraphs 354-356.

[112] First Written Submission of the EC, paragraph 399.

within the meaning of Paris Article 10*bis*(2), however, include the notion of honest practices established in international trade.[113] Thus, to comply with its obligation pursuant to Paris Article 10*bis*(1), a WTO Member must assure to nationals of other WTO Members effective protection against unfair competition that permits account to be taken of honest practices established in international trade.

145. It cannot be presumed that "effective protection against unfair competition" within the meaning of Paris Article 10*bis*(1) will only ever involve protection of a TRIPS-defined GI. It may be that, having regard to the principle of territoriality and to developments in international trade over time, recognition of a TRIPS-defined GI could constitute an act of unfair competition within the meaning of Paris Article 10*bis*(2).

146. It is irrelevant that the EC might not understand how the use of a registered EC-defined GI—even if the registration of that EC-defined GI was otherwise consistent with the EC's obligations pursuant to the *TRIPS Agreement*—could constitute an act of unfair competition within the meaning of Paris Article 10*bis*(2) and thus invoke the EC's obligation pursuant to Paris Article 10*bis*(1). It is also irrelevant that the use of registered EC-defined GIs "remains subject to the EC legislation on labelling and misleading advertising, as well as to the law of the EC Member States on unfair competition."[114] As the EC itself indicates elsewhere,[115] there is no Community "law" in the sense of a Regulation with Community level effect in relation to labelling and misleading advertising in any case. Moreover and in any event, as the EC indicated before the Panel, Community law takes primacy over EC Member State law in the event of a conflict: therefore an EC measure cannot be overturned by an EC Member State measure in any event.

147. In respect of the registration of an EC-defined GI, the provisions of Paris Articles 10*bis*(1) and 10*ter*(1) require that the EC provide to the nationals of other WTO Members "effective protection against unfair competition" and "appropriate legal remedies effectively to repress all the acts referred to in Articles … 10*bis*." The EC does not in fact comply with those requirements and it has not rebutted Australia's *prima facie* case that, by failing to comply with those requirements, the EC has not complied with the requirements of TRIPS Article 2.1.

E. IN RESPECT OF THE REGISTRATION OF AN EC-DEFINED GI, THE EC MEASURE IS INCONSISTENT WITH ARTICLES 41.1, 41.2, 41.3 AND 42 OF THE TRIPS AGREEMENT

(i) Introduction

148. The EC argues[116] that Australia's claims are unfounded because Part III of the TRIPS Agreement does not apply to Regulation No. 2081/92. The EC states that Regulation No. 2081/92 lays down an administrative procedure for the acquisition of EC-defined GIs via a system of registration, that the Regulation does not purport to regulate the procedures for enforcing trademark rights and that the consequence of Australia's argument is that intellectual property rights would always have to be conferred by a judicial body in accordance with judicial procedures.

149. Once again, the EC misunderstands and/or mischaracterises the basis of Australia's claims.

150. Australia has not contested—and does not contest—matters concerning the enforcement of trademark rights generally, whether those trademark rights exist at Community or at EC Member State level. However,

---

[113] See, for example, *Bodenhausen*, page 144, and WIPO's "Model Provisions on Protection Against Unfair Competition," Exhibit AUS-09.

[114] First Written Submission of the EC, paragraph 400.

[115] First Written Submission of the EC, paragraph 434.

[116] First Written Submission of the EC, paragraphs 357-365.

Australia notes that—pursuant to Article 159 of Regulation No. 40/94[117]—*"[the EC Trademark]* Regulation shall not affect … Regulation … No. 2081/92 on the protection of geographical indications and designations of origin for agricultural products and foodstuffs …, and in particular Article 14 thereof." Thus, matters concerning the enforcement of trademark rights in respect of the registration of an EC-defined GIs are specifically excluded from the scope of Regulation No. 40/94. Moreover, they were so excluded from the time that Regulation No. 40/94 was adopted. On the other hand, the Community trademark Directive[118] makes no mention of Regulation No. 40/94 because there is no need: as the EC has itself said before the Panel, Community law takes primacy over EC Member State law in the event of a conflict.

151. Thus neither Community trademark law nor EC Member State trademark law provide the means to enforce trademark rights in respect of the registration of an EC-defined GI.

(ii) In respect of the registration of an EC-defined GI, the EC measure does not make available to trademark right holders civil judicial procedures concerning the enforcement of their intellectual property rights, contrary to Article 42 of the TRIPS Agreement

152. Irrespective of whether the Article 15 decision-making process provided by Regulation No. 2081/92 is an administrative procedure in relation to the acquisition of an intellectual property right in an EC-defined GI,[119] the EC measure does not provide—in relation to the registration of an EC-defined GI—access to civil judicial procedures within the meaning of TRIPS Article 42 for the enforcement of the trademark rights required to be granted under TRIPS Article 16.1. The fact that a decision to register an EC-defined GI pursuant to Regulation No. 2081/92 may be subject to judicial review on points of law does not satisfy the requirement of TRIPS Article 42. The EC has not rebutted Australia's *prima facie* case in respect of this claim.

153. Further and in any case, even if the Article 15 decision-making process provided by Regulation No. 2081/92 is presumed to be an administrative procedure in relation to the acquisition of an intellectual property right in an EC-defined GI, to the extent that that decision-making process constitutes the only means through which a trademark right holder can seek to exercise the trademark rights required to have been granted by the EC pursuant to TRIPS Article 16.1 in relation to the registration of an EC-defined GI, the Article 15 decision-making procedure is an enforcement procedure subject to the EC's obligations pursuant to Part III of the *TRIPS Agreement.*

(iii) In respect of the registration of an EC-defined GI, the EC measure provides procedures which are not fair and equitable, and which are unnecessarily complicated and entail unwarranted delays, contrary to Article 41.2 of the TRIPS Agreement

154. Again, the EC misunderstands and/or mischaracterises the basis of Australia's claims. Australia has not said that it can "be assumed those agencies, or their officials, are 'likely' to breach systematically those duties."[120]

155. TRIPS Article 41.2 requires that "[p]rocedures concerning the enforcement of intellectual property rights shall be fair and equitable." In other words, there is an express obligation on the EC to ensure the

---

[117] Exhibits COMP-7.a, 7.b.i and 7.b.ii. The text of what is now Article 159 of Regulation No. 40/94 was originally numbered as Article 142 (Exhibit COMP-7.a). However, it was renumbered as Article 159 pursuant to Article 1.5 of Regulation No. 1992/2003 (Exhibit COMP-7.b.i).

[118] First Council Directive of 21 December 1988 to approximate the laws of the Member States relating to trade marks (89/104/EEC), Exhibit COMP-6.a.

[119] Australia does not take a position on this issue at this time, noting that it requires consideration of a broad range of matters—including the nature and status of the European Communities' membership of the WTO, the shared competence of the EC and its Member States in matters covered by the *TRIPS Agreement* (in accordance with ECJ Opinion No. 1/94) and whether the Article 15 decision-making process provided by Regulation No. 2081/92 is in fact an inter-governmental process—and that resolution of the issue is not necessary to allow the Panel to make appropriate findings.

[120] First Written Submission of the EC, paragraph 381.

impartiality of its procedures for the enforcement of intellectual property rights. Moreover, Article 5.5 of Regulation No. 2081/92 expressly envisages situations involving agreement between EC Member States without regard to any affected trademark rights. It is thus the case that the possibility of bias in favour of the proposed EC-defined GI cannot be seen to be excluded.

156. The EC argues that the procedures provided in Regulation No. 2081/92 are not unnecessarily complicated, or entail unwarranted delays.[121] Firstly, the EC argues that it would still be necessary for the Commission to request the assistance of the EC Member State in order to verify the relevant facts. Secondly, the EC argues that another WTO Member is estopped from making such a claim should it decline to act in accordance with the requirements imposed by the Regulation, notwithstanding that the WTO Member never consented to act in accordance with the requirements imposed by the Regulation to begin with.[122] Under neither argument, however, does the EC address the implications of the express recognition in the preambular clauses of the *TRIPS Agreement* that intellectual property rights are private rights: that, for example, a WTO Member is required to confer on the owner of a registered trademark a particular set of rights and make available the means to enforce those rights without needing to act through a government.

157. To the extent that the Article 15 decision-making process is considered to provide a means for the enforcement of a trademark right required to have been granted in accordance with the EC's obligations pursuant to TRIPS Article 16.1 in relation to the registration of an EC-defined GI, the EC has not rebutted Australia's *prima facie* case in respect of these claims.

(iv) In respect of the registration of an EC-defined GI, the EC measure does not ensure that decisions are based only on evidence in respect of which trademark right holders were offered the opportunity to be heard, contrary to Article 41.3 of the TRIPS Agreement

158. To the extent that the Article 15 decision-making process is considered to provide a means for the enforcement of a trademark right required to have been granted in accordance with the EC's obligations pursuant to TRIPS Article 16.1 in relation to the registration of an EC-defined GI, the EC has not rebutted Australia's *prima facie* case in respect of this claim.

(v) In respect of the registration of an EC-defined GI, the EC measure does not ensure the availability under EC law of enforcement procedures as specified in Part III of the TRIPS Agreement so as to permit effective action against any act of infringement or trademark rights, contrary to Article 41.1 of the TRIPS Agreement

159. The EC asserts that TRIPS Article 41.1 "is an introductory provision, which does not impose any obligation by itself" and continues "Australia appears to agree ...."[123] Again, the EC misunderstands Australia's claims and arguments.

160. Contrary to the EC's assertion, TRIPS Article 41.1 imposes a very clear and explicit obligation that WTO Members "shall ensure that enforcement procedures as specified in this Part are available under their law ...." Consistent with normal interpretive principles, WTO Members have a positive duty to make certain that the enforcement procedures specified in Part III of the TRIPS Agreement are available under their law for the purpose specified.

161. Thus, in respect of the registration of an EC-defined GI, a finding by the Panel that the EC measure is inconsistent with any of TRIPS Articles 41.2, 41.3 or 42—or should the Panel otherwise consider that the EC measure does not comply with any of TRIPS Articles 43, 44, 45, 46, 48 or 49—would consequentially require a separate finding of inconsistency with TRIPS Article 41.1.

---

[121] First Written Submission of the EC, paragraphs 384-386.

[122] Australia has addressed the issue of estoppel and its relevance in this dispute in more detail above.

[123] First Written Submission of the EC, paragraph 367.

F. IN RESPECT OF DECISIONS BY EC MEMBER STATES TO GRANT TRANSITIONAL NATIONAL PROTECTION TO A PROPOSED EC-DEFINED GI, THE EC MEASURE DIMINISHES THE LEGAL PROTECTION FOR TRADEMARKS, CONTRARY TO ARTICLES 2.1 ("INCORPORATING" ARTICLES 10BIS(1) AND 10TER(1) OF THE PARIS CONVENTION (1967)), 16.1, 41.1, 41.2, 41.3 AND/OR 42 OF THE TRIPS AGREEMENT

162. The EC says: "[t]his claim is entirely dependent on the previous claims submitted by Australia under the above listed provisions."[124]

163. Nowhere in Australia's First Written Submission has Australia indicated that its claim is "entirely dependent" on Australia's other claims. Indeed, Australia's claims in respect of decisions by EC Member States to grant transitional national protection to a proposed EC-defined GI are independent of Australia's other claims and are based on the express provision of Article 5.5 of Regulation No. 2081/92—and the absence of other provisions requiring EC Member States to grant to trademark right holders the rights required to be granted to them by the *TRIPS Agreement* in respect of a decision to grant transitional national protection.

164. In any case, Australia notes that the implicit assumption of the EC's statement—"[s]ince those claims are unfounded, so is this claim"[125]—is that if Australia's other claims are properly founded, then so is this claim as a matter of course.

165. The EC has not rebutted the *prima facie* case made by Australia in respect of decisions to grant transitional national protection to a proposed EC-defined GI.

G. CONCLUSION

166. The EC has not rebutted the *prima facie* case made by Australia that the EC measure diminishes the legal protect for trademarks in ways not permitted by the *TRIPS Agreement*, contrary to Articles 2.1 ("incorporating" Articles 10bis(1) and 10ter(1) of the Paris Convention (1967)), 16.1, 24.5, 41.1, 41.2, 41.3 and/or 42 of the *TRIPS Agreement* and, as a consequence, to Articles 1.1 and 1.3 of that Agreement.

167. Australia does not contest that the EC may choose to implement in its law more extensive protection than it is required to do by the *TRIPS Agreement*. However, that discretion is subject to the proviso that "such protection does not contravene the provisions of the *TRIPS Agreement*." Thus, the discretion offered by TRIPS Article 1.1 is a conditional discretion: it applies only to the extent that a WTO Member offering more extensive protection does so in a manner that does not contravene the provisions of the *TRIPS Agreement*. The EC measure does not meet that condition.

VIII. THE EC MEASURE DOES NOT PROVIDE THE LEGAL MEANS FOR INTERESTED PARTIES TO PREVENT MISLEADING USE OR USE WHICH CONSTITUTES AN ACT OF UNFAIR COMPETITION IN RESPECT OF GEOGRAPHICAL INDICATIONS PROPOSED TO BE REGISTERED UNDER REGULATION NO. 2081/92

168. The EC asserts that Australia's arguments in relation to this claim are "obscure."[126] Nevertheless, the EC then sets out a categorical statement as to what it considers to be the meaning of TRIPS Article 22.2, but without any argument to show that its view is supported by the actual text of TRIPS Article 22.2 in accordance with normal interpretive provisions.[127]

[124] First Written Submission of the EC, paragraph 408.
[125] First Written Submission of the EC, paragraph 408.
[126] First Written Submission of the EC, paragraph 411.
[127] First Written Submission of the EC, paragraph 412.

169. Australia's claim is straightforward: in respect of the registration of an EC-defined GI, the EC does not provide the legal means for interested parties to prevent use which misleads the public as to the geographical origin of a good or use which constitutes an act of unfair competition within the meaning of Paris Article 10*bis*. The obligation established by TRIPS Article 22.2 extends to any situation that concerns TRIPS-defined GIs: it is not "concerned exclusively with the protection of geographical indications," and a trademark right holder is not necessarily excluded from being a potential "interested party" within the meaning of TRIPS Article 22.2.[128]

170. As Australia has previously stated,[129] Paris Article 10*bis*(2) provides that an act of unfair competition is "any act of competition contrary to honest practices in industrial or commercial matters." "[H]onest practices in industrial or commercial matters" within the meaning of Paris Article 10*bis*(2), however, include the notion of honest practices established in international trade.[130] It may be that, having regard to the principle of territoriality and to developments in international trade over time, registration and ongoing protection of a TRIPS-defined GI could constitute an act of unfair competition within the meaning of Paris Article 10*bis*(2). For example, it is entirely possible that there are products which, while originally based on a European production process, have been further developed and refined outside the European country of origin and which have subsequently come to represent the "international" trading standard for that product: to register the original geographic name under Regulation No. 2081/92 in such circumstances—notwithstanding that the product may qualify for registration—could well constitute misleading use or use which constitutes an act of unfair competition within the meaning of Paris Article 10*bis*, even within the EC. Yet the EC does not provide any effective legal avenue through which such issues can be tested.

171. To comply with its obligation pursuant to TRIPS Article 22.2 in respect of the registration of an EC-defined GI, a WTO Member must provide the legal means for interested parties to prevent misleading use or use which constitutes an act of unfair competition within the meaning of Paris Article 10*bis*. The EC cannot rely on EC Member State unfair competition law in this regard because, as the EC explained before the Panel, Community law takes primacy over EC Member State law in the event of a conflict.

IX. THE EC MEASURE DOES NOT ACCORD TO NATIONALS OR PRODUCTS OF EACH WTO MEMBER TREATMENT NO LESS FAVOURABLE THAN THAT IT ACCORDS TO ITS OWN NATIONALS OR TO LIKE PRODUCTS OF DOMESTIC ORIGIN

172. In its First Written Submission, Australia claimed that the EC measure is inconsistent with the EC's national treatment obligations pursuant to GATT Article III:4,[131] and TRIPS Articles 2.1 ("incorporating" the provisions of Paris Article 2) and 3.1.[132]

A. THE REQUIREMENT FOR THE INVOLVEMENT OF ANOTHER WTO MEMBER GOVERNMENT CONSTITUTES LESS FAVOURABLE TREATMENT UNDER THE EC MEASURE

173. The EC indicates a number of times that it does not consider the requirement established in Regulation No. 2081/92 for involvement by another WTO Member government in the process of acquisition or enforcement of an intellectual property right to constitute less favourable treatment.[133]

174. Australia expressly endorses and adopts Canada's clear and succinct portrayal of the issues concerning the relationship between WTO Members, the EC, the EC Member States and nationals raised by the EC's

[128] First Written Submission of the EC, paragraph 412.

[129] See Part VII.D above.

[130] See, for example, *Bodenhausen*, page 144, and WIPO's "Model Provisions on Protection Against Unfair Competition," Exhibit AUS-09.

[131] First Written Submission of Australia, paragraphs 157-180.

[132] First Written Submission of Australia, paragraphs 181-206.

[133] See, for example, First Written Submission of the EC, paragraphs 128-129, 145-146 and 207.

argument.[134] In particular, Australia would like to highlight Canada's statement that, having regard to the EC's explanation that "the subject matter of the present dispute falls within the exclusive competence of the EC, and not of the Member States"[135]:

> ... the EC Regulation is the equivalent of a national measure, and that any functions carried out by EC Member States for the purposes of implementing the EC Regulation are carried out as sub-national units of the EC. ...[136]

175. In respect of matters concerning the registration of an EC-defined GI under Regulation No. 2081/92, it is treatment at EC level ("the national level") which determines whether the EC has met its national treatment obligation under each of the *TRIPS Agreement*, *GATT 1994* and the *TBT Agreement*. As Australia pointed out in its First Written Submission,[137] any outward appearance of symmetry of treatment in fact masks a fundamentally different situation. It is a supposed symmetry—or equality—of treatment that is in fact premised on other WTO Members being "sub-national" units of the EC.

176. Thus, wherever the EC relies on an assertion of ensuring "equal treatment"[138] of EC and non-EC nationals and products as a defence to a claim of a national treatment violation, the EC has not rebutted the *prima facie* case made by Australia.

B. IN RESPECT OF PRODUCTS BEARING—OR ELIGIBLE TO BEAR—AN EC-DEFINED GI, THE EC MEASURE ACCORDS TO THE PRODUCTS OF OTHER WTO MEMBERS TREATMENT LESS FAVOURABLE THAN THAT IT ACCORDS TO LIKE PRODUCTS OF NATIONAL ORIGIN, CONTRARY TO ARTICLE III:4 OF GATT 1994

177. The EC's major defence to Australia's claim is that Regulation No. 2081/92 "does not impose a condition of reciprocity and systemic equivalence for the registration of geographical indications from other WTO Members."[139] Together with the EC's attempted explanations that the requirements of paragraphs 1 and 3 of Article 12 of Regulation No. 2081/92#3 do not apply to other WTO Members,[140] these statements in effect constitute an admission by the EC that the equivalence and reciprocity conditions of those provisions are inconsistent with the EC's WTO obligations.

178. Thus, to the extent that the Panel considers that the EC's explanations of the meaning of Articles 12.1 and 12.3 of Regulation No. 2081/92 are not sustainable on the basis of the meaning, context and aims of those provisions in accordance with the rules of interpretation of EC law, the EC has not rebutted the *prima facie* case made by Australia.

179. Moreover, should the Panel consider that Article 12.2 of Regulation No. 2081/92 does not constitute a technical regulation within the meaning of Annex 1.1 of the *TBT Agreement*,[141] Australia notes that Article 12.2 nevertheless accords treatment less favourable to imported products bearing—or eligible to bear—an EC-defined GI than that accorded to like products of EC origin bearing—or eligible to bear—an EC-defined GI, inconsistently with GATT Article III:4. In the circumstances in which it applies, Article 12.2 mandates that the imported like product bearing the later, or second, registered EC-defined GI also carry a country of origin label. On the other hand, Article 6.6 does not mandate such a requirement where the later, or second, registered EC-defined GI is a like product of domestic origin.

---

[134] Third Party Oral Statement of Canada, paragraphs 11-17.

[135] First Written Submission of the EC, paragraph 255.

[136] Third Party Oral Statement of Canada, paragraph 15.

[137] See, for example, paragraph 174.

[138] See, for example, First Written Submission of the EC, paragraphs 129, 146 and 207.

[139] First Written Submission of the EC, paragraph 203.

[140] First Written Submission of the EC, paragraph 66.

[141] See Parts X.A and X.B below.

180. The EC seems—in the alternative—to be invoking GATT Article XX(d) as a justification in respect of at least some of Australia's GATT Article III:4 claim.[142]

181. However, despite the fact that it bears the burden of proof in invoking such a defence,[143] the EC has not attempted to show that Regulation No. 2081/92 could be justified under GATT Article XX(d). Australia notes that the findings of the Appellate Body in the *Korea – Beef*, *US – Shrimp* and *US – Gasoline* disputes provide guidance as to the tests which would have to be met for an affirmative defence pursuant to GATT Article XX(d) to be available to the EC:

- firstly, for the measure at issue to be provisionally justified, that the measure is designed "to secure compliance with laws or regulations which are not inconsistent with the provisions of" *GATT 1994*, and that the measure is "necessary" to secure such compliance; and
- secondly, further appraisal of the measure under the chapeau of GATT Article XX.

C. IN RESPECT OF APPLICATIONS FOR—OR OBJECTIONS TO—THE REGISTRATION OF AN EC-DEFINED GI, THE EC MEASURE DOES NOT ACCORD NATIONAL TREATMENT TO NATIONALS OF OTHER WTO MEMBERS, CONTRARY TO ARTICLES 2.1 ("INCORPORATING" ARTICLE 2 OF THE PARIS CONVENTION (1967)) AND 3.1 OF THE TRIPS AGREEMENT

182. In its attempt to rebut Australia's claims under these provisions, the EC has repeatedly ignored or confused the basis of Australia's claims. For example, the EC asserts that Australia has made "no attempt to establish that Regulation 2081/92 discriminates between nationals of the EC and nationals of other WTO members"[144] *(emphases in original)*. On the other hand, 10 of the first 11 of the EC's own headings to describe the claims being made—including those by Australia—include the word "national," "rightholder" and/or "person."

183. Once again, the EC relies primarily on the defence that the EC does not apply conditions of reciprocity and equivalence to the registration of an EC-defined GI from another WTO Member. Thus, to the extent that the Panel considers that the EC's explanations of the applicability of Articles 12.1 and 12.3 of Regulation No. 2081/92 are not sustainable on the basis of the meaning, context and aims of those provisions having regard to the rules of interpretation of EC law, the EC has not rebutted the *prima facie* case made by Australia.

184. However, Australia notes the surprising statements by the EC that the conditions for the registration of EC-defined GIs under Regulation No. 2081/92 do not depend on nationality[145] and that "[w]hether the area to which a geographic *[sic]* indication is related is located inside the EC or outside is in no way linked to the question of the nationality of the producers of the product concerned."[146] The reality is that persons with an interest in securing the registration of the name of a geographical area as an EC-defined GI will overwhelmingly be nationals of the WTO Member in which that geographical area is located. Accordingly, Australia expressly endorses and adopts New Zealand's very clear and concise explanation of why the EC's interpretation would render meaningless a WTO Member's national treatment obligation:

> If the EC's interpretation of 'nationals' were to prevail, then even if the EC Regulation provided that only geographical indications located in the EC could be registered, the national treatment obligations would not be violated: in theory, the nationals of any country could live in the EC and register EC geographical indications. But this would mean that persons interested in registering geographical indications located outside the EC would not be able to do so. They would be disadvantaged in the EC market. ... [A]ccepting the EC's interpretation

[142] First Written Submission of the EC, paragraphs 190 and 224-226.

[143] *US – Woven Shirts and Blouses*, Appellate Body Report, page 14.

[144] First Written Submission of the EC, paragraph 110.

[145] First Written Submission of the EC, paragraphs 123-126.

[146] First Written Submission of the EC, paragraph 125.

of 'nationals' would gut the national treatment obligation under the *TRIPS Agreement* of any value with respect to geographical indications.[147]

185. Further, the EC argues that the Panel should reject Australia's claim of a violation of the EC's TRIPS and Paris Convention national treatment obligations in respect of the registration of more than 120 EC-defined GIs under the normal registration process. The EC's arguments concerning versions of Regulation No. 2081/92 no longer in force and registrations made thereunder which continue in effect are addressed in Part II.A of this Submission above. The EC also asserts—without any supporting argument—that the individual registrations of those more than 120 EC-defined GIs were not in violation of the EC's national treatment obligations. The EC makes this assertion notwithstanding: that a right of objection was available to EC nationals in respect of these more than 120 EC-defined GIs that was not available to nationals of other WTO Members; and the express statement of the intent of Regulation No. 692/2003 in Recital (10) to grant a right of objection to nationals of other WTO Members on the same terms as the right available to EC nationals.148 The EC has not rebutted the *prima facie* case made by Australia.

D. CONCLUSION

186. The EC has not rebutted the *prima facie* case made by Australia that the EC measure is inconsistent with the EC's national treatment obligations pursuant to GATT Article III:4 and TRIPS Articles 2.1 ("incorporating" the provisions of Paris Article 2) and 3.1.

187. Further, as a consequence of the EC measure's inconsistency with TRIPS Articles 2.1 ("incorporating" by reference Paris Article 2) and 3.1 in respect of the registration of EC-defined GIs, the EC measure is inconsistent with the EC's obligations pursuant to Articles 1.1 and 1.3 of the *TRIPS Agreement.*

X. THE EC MEASURE IS, IN PART, A TECHNICAL REGULATION THAT ACCORDS LESS FAVOURABLE TREATMENT TO IMPORTED PRODUCTS THAN TO LIKE DOMESTIC PRODUCTS AND CREATES UNNECESSARY OBSTACLES TO INTERNATIONAL TRADE, BEING MORE TRADE-RESTRICTIVE THAN NECESSARY TO FULFIL A LEGITIMATE OBJECTIVE, TAKING ACCOUNT OF THE RISKS NON-FULFILMENT WOULD CREATE

188. In its First Written Submission, Australia claimed that, to the extent that Article 12.2 of Regulation No. 2081/92 is a mandatory labelling provision that applies to imported products bearing—or eligible to bear—an EC-defined GI that is identical to an EC-defined GI from within the EC already registered under the Regulation for a like domestic product and provides no discretion for the EC to apply the provision in such a way as to avoid less favourable treatment to the imported product, the EC measure is a technical regulation that is inconsistent with TBT Article 2.1.

189. Further, Australia claimed that, to the extent that Articles 4, 10 and 12.1 of Regulation No. 2081/92 establish a mandatory requirement for another WTO Member to have in place in all circumstances an inspection structure consistent with the requirements of Article 10 of the Regulation, the EC measure is a technical regulation that is more trade restrictive than necessary to fulfil a legitimate objective, taking account of the risks non-fulfilment would create, contrary to TBT Article 2.2.

A. THE EC MEASURE IS, IN PART, A TECHNICAL REGULATION WITHIN THE MEANING OF ANNEX 1.1 OF THE TBT AGREEMENT

190. As set out by both Australia and the EC,[149] the Appellate Body has found that the definition of a "technical regulation" in TBT Annex 1.1 establishes three criteria. Australia has argued that Article 12. 2—and

147 Third Party Oral Statement of New Zealand, paragraph 9.

148 Exhibit COMP-1.h.

149 First Written Submission of Australia, paragraphs 209-224, and First Written Submission of the EC, paragraph 442.

Articles 4 and 10 read together—of Regulation No. 2081/92 are technical regulations in accordance with the TBT Annex 1.1 definition. In response, the EC argues that none of the three criteria are met with respect to Article 12.2 of the Regulation and, in the case of Articles 4 and 10 of the Regulation, the EC argues that two of the criteria are not met and does not address the third criterion.[150]

(i) Article 12.2 – and Articles 4 and 10 read together – of Regulation No. 2081/92 apply to an identifiable product or group of products

191. The EC argues that Article 12.2 of Regulation No. 2081/92 applies only to cases of homonymous protected *names* from the EC and another WTO Member and that the Regulation does not allow identification of *products* affected by the requirement in Article 12.2.[151] Australia does not contest that Article 12.2 of Regulation No. 2081/92 applies only to a specific class of protected names. These names, however, do not exist in isolation, but with regard to specific agricultural products or foodstuffs for which the homonymous names have been registered. Therefore, the EC's argument that Article 12.2 applies only to names, and not to the underlying product that those names identify, is not sustainable.

192. The EC argues that "[t]he Regulation does not allow to identify the products *[sic]* which might be affected by this requirement. Accordingly, Article 12.2 does not apply to identifiable products."[152] In *EC – Asbestos*, the Appellate Body said: "... nothing in the text of *[the TBT Agreement]* suggests that those products need be named or otherwise *expressly* identified in a 'technical regulation'." [153] *(emphasis in original)* The Appellate Body affirmed that finding in *EC – Sardines* and added: "... a product does not necessarily have to be mentioned *explicitly* in a document for that product to be an *identifiable* product. *Identifiable* does not mean expressly identified."[154] *(emphases in original)* Article 12.2 of Regulation No. 2081/92 does not expressly identify any product. Nonetheless, it does apply to identifiable products: any imported product bearing—or eligible to bear—an EC-defined GI that is identical to an EC-defined GI already being protected within the EC under Regulation No. 2081/92. This is the precise distinction made by the Appellate Body.

193. Australia notes that the EC did not address the question of whether Articles 4 and 10 of Regulation No. 2081/92 read together apply to an identifiable product or group of products.

194. The EC has not rebutted Australia's *prima facie* case that Article 12.2—and Articles 4 and 10 read together—of Regulation No. 2081/92 apply to an identifiable product or group of products within the meaning of the definition of a technical regulation in TBT Annex 1.1.

(ii) Article 12.2 – and Articles 4 and 10 read together – of Regulation No. 2081/92 mandate compliance with product characteristics or their related processes and production methods

195. The EC argues[155] that Article 12.2—and Articles 4 and 10 read together—of Regulation No. 2081/92 are not mandatory. The EC argues—and Australia does not dispute—that registration of an EC-defined GI under the Regulation is not a precondition for the marketing of a product in the EC. Similarly, the EC argues—and Australia does not dispute—that compliance with Articles 12.2—and Articles 4 and 10 read together—is not mandatory for placing a product on the market in the EC.

196. However, registration under Regulation No. 2081/92 is mandatory for trading an imported product eligible to bear an EC-defined GI under the same competitive conditions as those afforded a product of EC origin for which an EC-defined GI has been registered. As the EC has said, "Article 12.2 is a condition for the

[150] First Written Submission of the EC, paragraphs 443-468.

[151] First Written Submission of the EC, paragraphs 445-447.

[152] First Written Submission of the EC, paragraph 447.

[153] *EC – Asbestos*, paragraph 70.

[154] *EC – Sardines*, paragraph 180.

[155] First Written Submission of the EC, paragraphs 453-457 and 467-468.

registration of a geographical indication,"[156] and "[t]he existence of inspection structures constitutes a condition for registration."[157] Without registration, an imported product does not benefit from protection against unauthorised use of an EC-defined GI, nor does it benefit from the reputation of superior quality engendered by registration of an EC-defined GI under the Regulation.

197. Accordingly, the EC has not rebutted Australia's *prima facie* case that Article 12.2—and Articles 4 and 10 read together—of Regulation No. 2081/92 mandate compliance with product characteristics or their related processes and production methods for those products bearing—or eligible to bear—an EC-defined GI.

(iii) Article 12.2 – and Articles 4 and 10 read together – of Regulation No. 2081/92 lay down product characteristics or their related processes and production methods

198. The EC states that Article 12.2 of Regulation No. 2081/92 "does not contain a specific labelling requirement for any specific product" but rather that it "sets out merely the conditions under which a geographical indication will be registered in a situation where there are homonyms from the EC and a third country."[158] Australia notes that the two statements are not mutually exclusive: indeed, one of the conditions is a labelling requirement.

199. The EC asserts that Article 12.2 of Regulation No. 2081/92 does not itself impose a labelling requirement, but that "the requirement to indicate the country of origin will be among the labelling details which must be indicated in the product specification" required in accordance with Article 4.2(h) of the Regulation.[159] This argument is not sustainable. Article 12.2 of the Regulation, and in particular its second sentence—"[u]se of such names shall be authorised only if the country of origin of the product is clearly and visibly indicated on the label"—clearly imposes a labelling requirement on an imported product bearing—or eligible to bear—an EC-defined GI which is identical to an EC-defined GI which has already been registered under the Regulation. This requirement is unaffected by the existence elsewhere in the Regulation of other labelling requirements.

200. The argument is unfounded on other grounds. A label within the meaning of Article 12.2 of Regulation No. 2081/92 is something that attaches to a product or to the packaging of a product to describe the content or nature of the product. The EC's argument that "the labelling requirement does not relate to a product"[160] is unsustainable: it renders the concept of a label meaningless.

201. The EC argues that Articles 4 and 10 read together do not lay down product characteristics because "the purpose of Article 4(g) *[sic]* in conjunction with Article 10 is not to lay down product characteristics, but to ensure conformity with the product specification."[161] However, the EC ignores the actual arguments made by Australia: that is, that a technical regulation within the meaning of the *TBT Agreement* includes a document which may generally be considered to set out a regular sequence of actions (that is, a process) directed at a specified purpose or the way in which something is produced and which is connected to one or more product characteristics.[162]

202. A measure may lay down related processes within the meaning of a technical regulation, even if it has a different or additional purpose. The purpose of itself is not conclusive of the proper characterisation of a measure. In *Japan – Alcoholic Beverages II* and in *US – CDSOA*, the Appellate Body considered issues concerning legislative intent. In each case, the Appellate Body considered that it was not necessary for the Panel

[156] First Written Submission of the EC, paragraph 456.

[157] EC response to Question 61 from the Panel following the first substantive meeting, paragraph 136.

[158] First Written Submission of the EC, paragraph 449.

[159] First Written Submission of the EC, paragraph 450.

[160] First Written Submission of the EC, paragraph 451.

[161] First Written Submission of the EC, paragraph 461.

[162] First Written Submission of Australia, paragraph 218, text in brackets added.

to inquire into the intent of the respective legislatures: the key determinant was whether the measures as applied were consistent with the relevant WTO obligations.[163]

203. The EC's argument that trademark laws, such as those implementing certification marks systems, do not appear so far to have been considered as falling under the *TBT Agreement*[164] is neither conclusive of, nor relevant to, the issue at hand. Assessing whether a measure is a technical regulation within the meaning of the *TBT Agreement* is a threshold issue for the application of that Agreement: it is not determinative of whether a WTO Member has violated its obligations under that Agreement. Moreover, the Appellate Body has several times noted the generally cumulative nature of a WTO Member's obligations, consistent with the integrated, binding nature of the *WTO Agreement* pursuant to Article II.2 of that Agreement.[165]

204. Accordingly, the EC has not rebutted Australia's *prima facie* case that Article 12.2—and Articles 4 and 10 read together—of Regulation No. 2081/92 lay down product characteristics or their related processes and production methods.

(iv) Conclusion

205. The EC has not rebutted Australia's *prima facie* case that, in respect of imported products bearing—or eligible to bear—an EC-defined GI, the EC measure in relevant part applies to an identifiable product or group of products, lays down product characteristics or their related processes, and mandates compliance. The EC measure is therefore, in relevant part, a technical regulation within the meaning of TBT Annex 1.1.

B. IN RESPECT OF PRODUCTS BEARING—OR ELIGIBLE TO BEAR—AN EC-DEFINED GI, THE EC MEASURE ACCORDS TO THE PRODUCTS OF OTHER WTO MEMBERS TREATMENT LESS FAVOURABLE THAN THAT IT ACCORDS TO LIKE PRODUCTS OF NATIONAL ORIGIN, CONTRARY TO ARTICLE 2.1 OF THE TBT AGREEMENT

206. Australia claims that, to the extent that Article 12.2 of Regulation No. 2081/92 is a mandatory labelling provision that applies to imported products bearing—or eligible to bear—an EC-defined GI, it is a technical regulation that accords less favourable treatment to imported products than to like domestic products, contrary to TBT Article 2.1.

207. Once again, the EC has overlooked or confused the arguments put forward by Australia. In fact, Australia did not argue that "the jurisprudence concerning Article III GATT can simply be transposed to Article 2.1 TBT Agreement, for instance with respect to the likeness of products,"[166] notwithstanding that the EC itself has sought to transpose its arguments under GATT Article III:4 in seeking to rebut Australia's claim of a national treatment violation under the *TBT Agreement.*[167] Rather, Australia suggested—consistent with previous findings of the Appellate Body—that "previous consideration of GATT Article III:4 can properly be looked to for clarification of the national treatment obligation in TBT Article 2.1."[168]

208. In any case, in the context of the present dispute, it is sufficient to consider the issue of like product within the context of TBT Article 2.1 in terms of basic agricultural products such as apples or pears bearing—or eligible to bear—an EC-defined GI. Australia submits that, notwithstanding the EC's assertion concerning the "important structural differences" between the *TBT Agreement* and *GATT 1994*,[169] an apple from Australia

---

[163] *Japan – Alcoholic Beverages II*, pages 27-28, and *US – CDSOA*, paragraph 259.

[164] First Written Submission of the EC, paragraph 465.

[165] See, for example, *Korea – Dairy Safeguard*, paragraph 75.

[166] First Written Submission of the EC, paragraph 473.

[167] First Written Submission of the EC, paragraph 470.

[168] First Written Submission of Australia, paragraph 226.

[169] First Written Submission of the EC, paragraph 474.

bearing—or eligible to bear—an EC-defined GI is like product to an apple from within the EC bearing—or eligible to bear—an EC-defined GI.

209. The EC argues that Article 12.2 of Regulation No. 2081/92 "does not treat foreign and EC geographical indications differently."[170] As set out in Part IV.D above, the EC's explanations of the meaning of Article 12.2 of the Regulation are not sustainable. In circumstances where an application for the registration of an EC-defined GI relates to an area in another WTO Member and is identical to an existing registered EC-defined GI relating to an area within the EC, Article 12.2 mandates that the product bearing the later, or second, registered EC-defined GI also carry a country of origin label. Conversely, Article 6.6 of the Regulation does not mandate this requirement in circumstances where the later, or second, registered EC-defined GI is also from within the EC.

210. The EC argues that marks of origin are not subject to the national treatment obligation of TBT Article 2.1 because they are governed by GATT Article IX, which imposes an MFN obligation only.[171] The EC argues that if Article 12.2 of Regulation No. 2081/92 is a technical regulation, "this should not have the effect of rendering the specific provision of Article IX:1 GATT useless."[172]

211. Australia recognises that *GATT 1994* and the *TBT Agreement* have different purposes and orientations. Indeed, Australia notes that the Appellate Body said in *EC – Asbestos*: "... although the *TBT Agreement* is intended to 'further the objectives of GATT 1994', it does so through a specialised legal regime that applies solely to a limited class of measures. For these measures, the *TBT Agreement* imposes obligations on Members that seem to be *different* from, and *additional* to, the obligations imposed on Members under the GATT 1994"[173] *(emphases in original).*

212. Having regard to those findings of the Appellate Body, even if the effect of GATT Article IX is to impose only an MFN obligation with regard to marks of origin and therefore to exclude the application of GATT Article III, Australia submits this does not mean that *TBT Agreement* obligations (such as that contained in TBT Article 2.1) do not apply to measures concerning marks of origin if those measures are "technical regulations."

213. Finally, Australia notes that the *General interpretive note to Annex 1A* of the *WTO Agreement* provides that, in the event of conflict between a provision of *GATT 1994* and a provision of another Annex 1A Agreement, the latter will prevail to the extent of the conflict. The EC suggests that, if Article 12.2 of Regulation No. 2081/92 is considered to be a technical regulation and thus subject to a national treatment obligation under the *TBT Agreement*, GATT Article IX:1 would be rendered "useless." Australia submits that any such conflict is governed by the *General interpretive note*: to the extent that GATT Article IX:1 conflicts with a national treatment obligation in another Annex 1A agreement, the obligation in the latter agreement will prevail. The existence of GATT Article IX:1 cannot be used to deny the applicability of TBT Article 2.1 to a technical regulation dealing with marks of origin.

214. Accordingly, the EC has not rebutted the *prima facie* case made by Australia.

C. IN RESPECT OF PRODUCTS BEARING—OR ELIGIBLE TO BEAR—AN EC-DEFINED GI, THE EC MEASURE IS MORE TRADE RESTRICTIVE THAN NECESSARY TO FULFIL A LEGITIMATE OBJECTIVE, TAKING ACCOUNT OF THE RISKS NON-FULFILMENT WOULD CREATE, CONTRARY TO ARTICLE 2.2 OF THE TBT AGREEMENT

215. The EC makes a number of arguments in response to Australia's claim under TBT Article 2.2.

---

170 First Written Submission of the EC, paragraph 476.

171 First Written Submission of the EC, paragraph 481.

172 First Written Submission of the EC, paragraph 481.

173 *EC – Asbestos*, paragragh 80.

216. The EC says that the existence of inspection structures is only required with respect to the specific product for which protection is sought.[174] Australia notes that it has not contested this issue.

217. The EC says that Regulation No. 2081/92 does not determine the specific design of the inspection structures.[175] Yet Article 10.3 of the Regulation expressly provides that inspection structures "must ... have permanently at their disposal the qualified staff and resources necessary to carry out inspection of agricultural products and foodstuffs bearing a protected name." In Australia's view, a requirement that such an inspection structure "must" have permanently at its disposal the "necessary" qualified staff mandates a specific design feature: moreover, it mandates a specific design feature that does not admit of the possibility that use of temporary staff—for example, during harvest season—may be all that is necessary to provide the required level of assurance. In addition and in any case, Regulation No. 2081/92—whether through Article 10 or another provision—does not admit of the possibility that no inspection structure may be required at all in some circumstances.

218. Further, Article 12a.2(b) of Regulation No. 2081/92 requires that a WTO Member submit to the Commission, among other documents, a "declaration that the structures provided for in Article 10 are established on its territory." In Australia's view, this is a clear statement that a specific type of structure must be established, and that alternative mechanisms which may perform the same function but are not "inspection structures," e.g. systems of laws, are excluded. Thus, the express terms of the Regulation preclude any leeway insofar as the type of inspection structure required of another WTO Member is concerned.

219. The EC asserts that Australia's "real concern is not with the specific requirements for inspection structures set out in Regulation 2081/92, but rather that it considers that no inspection structures at all should be required."[176] Contrary to the EC's assertion, Australia has not contested—and does not contest—that some type of compliance verification mechanism may be necessary in most cases to ensure that a product bearing an EC-defined GI complies with its product specification.[177] Australia does argue, however, that the EC model "one size fits all" inspection structure model may not be the only mechanism by which the EC's required degree of assurance can be provided in all circumstances. Further, Australia argues that the EC measure does not allow for the possibility of any inspection structure being unnecessary. In this context, Australia notes the EC's puzzling argument that "a monopolistic situation might require inspections even more strongly."[178] Even if so, the EC has not explained why other consumer protection mechanisms could not provide the necessary degree of assurance. Nor has the EC explained how an EC model inspection structure would be necessary in all circumstances to prevent EC consumers being misled or deceived, for example, in the event that the misleading or deceptive conduct at issue concerns product from a third country.

220. The EC asserts that the inspection structure requirement is "necessary to achieve the legitimate objectives of Regulation 2081/92."[179] However, having regard to normal interpretive principles, for a measure to be "necessary" under TBT Article 2.2, no other, less restrictive, alternatives can exist. The EC has not explained why the alternative systems suggested by Australia—alone or in combination—could not in any circumstances provide the same degree of assurance as the EC's system for compliance verification and/or enforcement, or for the prevention of deceptive practices. Nor has the EC explained the basis for the effective underlying assumption that that all other such systems in place in other WTO Members are deficient in all circumstances compared to the EC's system.

---

[174] First Written Submission of the EC, paragraphs 486-487.

[175] First Written Submission of the EC, paragraphs 488-491.

[176] First Written Submission of the EC, paragraph 492.

[177] Indeed, Australian law provides for a verification mechanism to be a part of the requirements for registration of a certification trademark.

[178] First Written Submission of the EC, paragraph 497.

[179] First Written Submission of the EC, paragraph 500.

221. The EC has argued that the discretion given to the EC under TRIPS Article 1.1 to implement in its law more extensive protection than is required by the *TRIPS Agreement*, provided that such protection does not contravene the provisions of that Agreement, "cannot be limited on the basis of" TBT Article 2.2.[180] Yet the EC offers no argument in support of its view. The EC does not offer any explanation of how its view is consistent with the express provisions of the *TRIPS Agreement* or with the object and purpose of that Agreement, including as expressed in the first preambular clause that "measures and procedures to enforce intellectual property rights do not themselves become barriers to legitimate trade." Nor does the EC offer any explanation of how its view is consistent with the provisions of Article II.2 of the *WTO Agreement* in relation to the integrated, binding nature of the covered agreements.[181]

222. Australia notes that the EC has not contested Australia's contention that Articles 4, 10 and 12.1 of Regulation No. 2081/92 read together are trade restrictive because their effect is to limit the opportunities for products from other WTO Members otherwise eligible to bear an EC-defined GI to those cases where the imported product originates in a WTO Member that has an Article 10-type inspection structure in place.[182] Thus, Australia understands that the EC does not dispute this issue.

223. Further, the EC has not rebutted Australia's contention that Articles 4, 10 and 12.1 of Regulation No. 2081/92 are more trade restrictive than necessary because they establish an irrebuttable presumption that no other system that may exist in another WTO Member could in any circumstance provide the same degree of assurance as the EC-mandated inspection structure.[183] Nor has the EC rebutted Australia's contention that Articles 4, 10 and 12.1 of the Regulation do not allow for the possibility of any inspection structure being unnecessary.[184]

224. As a consequence, the EC has not rebutted the *prima facie* case made by Australia that—to the extent that Articles 4, 10, and 12.1 of Regulation No. 2081/92 mandate that another WTO Member have in place in all circumstances an inspection structure as set out in Article 10 of the Regulation—the EC measure is more trade restrictive than necessary to fulfil a legitimate objective, taking account of the risks non-fulfilment would create.

D. CONCLUSION

225. The fact that a measure is intended to implement an intellectual property right does not of itself remove that measure—or relevant aspects of that measure—from the scope of the *TBT Agreement*. The EC has not rebutted the *prima facie* case made by Australia that the EC measure is, in part, a technical regulation. Similarly, the EC has failed to rebut Australia's *prima facie* case that the EC measure—to the extent that it is a technical regulation—is inconsistent with the EC's obligations under TBT Articles 2.1 and 2.2.

XI. AS A CONSEQUENCE, THE EC HAS NOT ENSURED THE CONFORMITY OF ITS LAWS, REGULATIONS AND ADMINISTRATIVE PROCEDURES WITH ITS WTO OBLIGATIONS

226. The EC has not rebutted Australia's *prima facie* case that the EC measure at issue in this dispute is inconsistent with:

- Articles 2.1 ("incorporating" Articles 2, 10*bis*(1) and 10*ter*(1) of the Paris Convention (1967)), 3.1, 16.1, 22.2 24.5, 41.1, 41.2, 41.3 and/or 42 of the *TRIPS Agreement*;

[180] First Written Submission of the EC, paragraph 499.

[181] See Australia's response to Question 55 from the Panel following the first substantive meeting with the parties.

[182] First Written Submission of Australia, paragraph 251.

[183] First Written Submission of Australia, paragraphs 252-254.

[184] First Written Submission of Australia, paragraph 255.

- Article III:4 of the *GATT 1994*; and/or

- Articles 2.1 and/or 2.2 of the *TBT Agreement*.

227. As a consequence, the EC has not given effect to the provisions of the *TRIPS Agreement*, contrary to Articles 1.1 and 1.3 of that Agreement.

228. Further, as a consequence of its failure to comply with its obligations pursuant to the *TRIPS Agreement*, the *GATT 1994* and the *TBT Agreement*, the EC has not ensured the conformity of its laws, regulations and administrative procedures with its obligations as provided in the annexed Agreements, contrary to Article XVI.4 of the *WTO Agreement*.

229. Australia respectfully reiterates its request that the Panel make the findings referred to above, and recommend that the EC bring the EC measure into conformity with its WTO obligations. In addition, Australia reiterates its request that the Panel find that, by its inconsistency with the EC's WTO obligations, the EC measure nullifies or impairs the benefits accruing to Australia under the *TRIPS Agreement*, the *GATT 1994*, the *TBT Agreement* and the *WTO Agreement*.

ANNEX A-6

OPENING STATEMENT OF AUSTRALIA SECOND SUBSTANTIVE MEETING

(11 August 2004)

1. The EC has not rebutted the *prima facie* case made by Australia with respect to the inconsistencies of the EC's measure with the EC's WTO obligations. Instead, the EC has made a number of arguments that are unsubstantiated, incorrect, or simply irrelevant with regard to the actual claims and arguments put forward by Australia.

2. Our statement today will therefore recap some of the key elements of our claims and arguments, particularly to highlight areas where the EC has implicitly or explicitly accepted the validity of our arguments. We note that this statement forms a part of Australia's argumentation in this dispute—it is not intended as a summary of our entire case. Our case in total would include of course all the material we have submitted to the Panel directly, or via endorsement of arguments made by the US in this dispute.

THE MEANING OF REGULATION NO. 2081/92

3. The EC argues that "... due account must ... be taken of the meaning which is given to the measure in question by the authorities of the Member concerned."[1] In support of its argument, the EC says that the Panel in *US – Section 301* found that "considerable deference must be given to the explanations given by the Member concerned as to the meaning of its own measure."[2] In fact, the EC's characterisation of the Panel's findings in that dispute is not accurate. What the Panel actually said was that "... any Member can reasonably expect that considerable deference be given to its views on the meaning of its own law."[3] There is a considerable difference in the meaning of deference that must be given and deference that can be "reasonably expected."

4. In the *US – Section 301* dispute, the Panel found as it did on the basis of an interpretation of those provisions that was legally authoritative in domestic law. In the present case, however, the EC has no such legally authoritative interpretation of the meaning of the provisions at issue to offer to show that Australia's interpretation of the meaning of Regulation 2081/92 in accordance with the EC's own rules of interpretation is flawed.

5. Australia has demonstrated the proper meaning of the provisions of Regulation 2081/92 in the context of EC domestic law. Australia has demonstrated the meaning based on a consistent pattern of statements by authorised EC representatives over many years, including in the WTO TRIPS Council and in WIPO; an official public document issued by the European Commission on the express intent of the proposed amendments to Regulation 2081/92 eventually adopted in Regulation 692/2003; clear statements about the meaning of Regulation 2081/92 and of the intent of the proposed amendments on the part of the Committee of the European Parliament with primary responsibility for the subject matter; the express provisions of the preambular recitals to Regulation 692/2003 itself; the ECJ's rules of interpretation, under which it is necessary to consider wording, context and aims in interpreting provisions of Community law; and relevant ECJ jurisprudence.

6. The EC has not offered any explanation of the meaning of the provisions of Regulation 2081/92 in its domestic law that reconciles its latest view with these facts. On the other hand, the EC discusses in detail ECJ jurisprudence which addresses only some of the issues in this dispute—and which in any case:

---

[1] Second Written Submission of the EC, paragraph 8.

[2] Second Written Submission of the EC, paragraph 8.

[3] *United States – Sections 301-310 of the Trade Act of 1974*, Report of the Panel, WT/DS152/R, paragraph 7.18.

- is consistent with the wider ECJ jurisprudence identified by Australia; and
- does not invalidate the meaning of the provisions of the Regulation at issue as put forward by Australia.

7. The EC asks that the Panel—and the complaining parties—accord deference to its statements before the Panel on the meaning of Regulation 2081/92. At the same time, however, the EC admits that its statements have no legal significance in Community law.

8. The EC asks that the Panel—and the complaining parties—ignore all other statements by authorised EC representatives as to the proper meaning of Regulation 2081/92. In doing so, however, the EC offers no credible explanation as to:

- why the explanation it offers before the Panel as to the meaning of the Regulation is more authoritative than the explanations offered by other EC representatives or in an official European Commission press release;
- what would prevent the EC from reverting to those previous explanations of the meaning of the Regulation at some future time; or
- how other WTO Members can be assured that any future rejection of an application for the registration of an EC-defined GI would not be based on the application of Articles 12.1 and 12.3 of the Regulation to them.

9. The EC's arguments in reply are summed up in the statement that "… the Panel should not assume that the institutions of the EC, and in particular the European Court of Justice, will ignore WTO obligations in the interpretation and application of Regulation 2081/92."[4] No one is suggesting the ECJ will ignore the EC's WTO obligations. However, the Regulation itself and the ECJ's approach to interpretation as stated in its jurisprudence provides incontrovertible evidence that the EC's latest view of the Regulation is not sustainable.

TRADEMARKS

TRIPS ARTICLE 16.1

10. Australia has claimed that—in respect of the registration of an EC-defined GI—the EC measure diminishes the legal protection for trademarks, contrary to TRIPS Article 16.1. The EC measure does not grant to the owner of a registered trademark the exclusive right to prevent confusingly similar or identical use of a sign in the course of trade for similar or identical goods. Nor does the EC measure provide for a presumption of a likelihood of confusion in the case of use of an identical sign for identical goods. Moreover, to the extent that the Article 15 decision-making process constitutes the initial and only means through which the owner of a trademark can seek to exercise—in respect of the registration of an EC-defined GI—the trademark rights required to be granted by the TRIPS Agreement, the EC measure:

- does not ensure that an objection from a trademark owner is admissible in such circumstances; and
- does not ensure that such an objection from a trademark owner will be considered in the Article 15 decision-making process.

11. In response, the EC has asserted:

[4] Second Written Submission of the EC, paragraph 26.

- that Article 14.3 of Regulation 2081/92 prevents the registration of EC-defined GIs that would result in a likelihood of confusion with an earlier trademark; or
- that TRIPS Articles 17, 24.3 or 24.5 somehow justify the co-existence of TRIPS-defined GIs and earlier trademarks.

12. As Australia has addressed most of the EC's supporting arguments in its Written Rebuttal Submission, I will focus here on the arguments made by the EC in its Written Rebuttal Submission.

Article 14.3 of Regulation 2081/92

13. Regulation 2081/92 provides that an EC-defined GI shall not be registered where—in the light of a trademark's reputation and renown and the length of time it has been used—registration of that EC-defined GI "is liable to mislead the consumer as to the true identity of the product."

14. In Australia's view, the EC's attempts to suggest that Article 14.3 of the Regulation does what the EC says it does is an implicit admission by the EC that nowhere else does the Regulation even attempt to provide trademark right holders with the rights required to have been granted to them under TRIPS Article 16.1.

15. However, "mislead" is used in Article 14.3 in the sense of causing a consumer to mistake the true identity of the product, rather than as a synonym of "confuse" in the sense of causing a consumer to be puzzled about the true identity of the product. It is therefore simply not sustainable for the EC to argue that "mislead" and "confuse" mean the same thing.

16. The EC argues that Australia has misinterpreted Article 14.3 of Regulation 2081/92 and that Australia's reading of the provision "is unsupported by the ordinary meaning of its terms." The EC also argues that Australia's interpretation "is neither workable nor reasonable in practice and cannot be reconciled with the obligations imposed upon the EC authorities by other provisions of Regulation 2081/92."[5]

17. However, Australia's interpretation of Article 14.3 of the Regulation is fully consistent with the relevant rules of interpretation of EC law. It considers the wording, context and aims of the provision, in accordance with the ECJ's well-established case law. Although the EC claims that the ECJ would not ignore the EC's obligations, the ECJ itself has implemented a test that requires express reference to an international agreement or its provisions. But there is nowhere in the Regulation any reference to a precise provision of the TRIPS Agreement to indicate to the ECJ an intent to implement a particular obligation assumed in the context of the WTO or another international agreement. Further, Australia's interpretation of "mislead" is fully consistent with the interpretation of that word by the EC in the case of the registration of "Bayerisches Bier."[6]

18. Even if the EC's interpretation was correct, the immediate consequence is that it would render the reference in Article 14.2 to the grounds for revocation under the Community Trademark Directive and Regulation totally meaningless. In both cases, the relevant grounds for revocation are that, in consequence of its use, the trademark "is liable to mislead the public, particularly as to the ... geographical origin ...."[7] Yet elsewhere, both the Directive and the Regulation expressly grant to owner of a trademark the exclusive right to prevent use of a similar or identical sign for similar or identical goods where "there exists a likelihood of confusion on the part of the public."[8]

---

[5] Second Written Submission of the EC, paragraph 277

[6] Regulation No. 1347/2001, Recital (3), Exhibit EC-9.

[7] Directive 89/104/EEC, Article 12.2(b), Exhibit COMP-6, and Regulation No. 40/94, Article 50.1(c), Exhibit COMP-7.

[8] Directive 89/104/EEC, Article 5.1(b), Exhibit COMP-6, and Regulation No. 40/94, Article 9.1(b), Exhibit COMP-7.

19. A likelihood of confusion on the part of the public as elaborated by the ECJ in its case law[9] is a very different standard from conduct which positively causes a consumer to mistake the source of a product. Thus, the Community Trademark Directive and Regulation differentiate the meanings of "confuse" and "mislead." As a consequence, the reference to the revocation provisions of those instruments in Article 14.2 of Regulation 2081/92 imports that differentiation into that Regulation.

20. The EC also asserts that Australia's interpretation of the meaning of Article 14.3 "would lead to a result that is incompatible with" Articles 7.4 and 7.5(b) of Regulation 2081/92.[10] Again, however, the interpretation of Article 7.4—and consequently Article 7.5(b)—being put forward by the EC is premised on a meaning of the words "jeopardise the existence" that is simply not consistent with the meaning and context of those provisions.

21. The plain meaning of "jeopardize the existence … of a mark" in Article 7.4 of Regulation 2081/92 is to threaten the very being of that mark. Threatening the very being of a trademark is a very different standard for the admissibility of a statement of objection than the standard established by a likelihood of confusion.

22. As a final point, I choose not to take offence at being called crass and ignorant when it comes to the complexities of EC law as done by the EC this morning. I do question the EC's judgment in making such an allegation with respect to my fellow Australians—particularly when the EC has, including in the consultations, been unhelpful on the relevant issues. I will therefore briefly ask my colleague to say a few words about the various translations.

23. *English translation:* The EC asserts that Australia hasn't considered other linguistic versions of Regulation 2081/92, and that these shed light on the intention of the EC.[11] In fact, Australia had indeed noted the language used in the French and Spanish versions. The EC seems to have overlooked that the complaining parties submitted the French version of the Regulation as Common Exhibit 1.c. Moreover, Australia fails to understand how its argument is undermined by the Spanish version. Saying that the very being of a trademark must be adversely affected seems to us to be not much different to saying that the very being of a trademark must be threatened.

TRIPS Article 24.5

24. TRIPS Article 24.5 does not envisage the co-existence of TRIPS-defined GIs and earlier trademarks as argued by the EC. In accordance with TRIPS Article 24.5, where a trademark has been registered in good faith, a WTO Member's measures adopted to implement Section 3, Part II, of the TRIPS Agreement concerning GIs may not prejudice the validity of the registration of an existing trademark on the basis that the trademark is identical with or similar to a GI. In other words, a WTO Member's measures adopted to implement the TRIPS Agreement provisions concerning GIs may not adversely affect the legitimacy of a trademark's registration. Such measures may not provide for the validity of a trademark's registration to be prejudiced because the trademark contains or consists of a GI.

25. Because a WTO Member is prohibited from prejudicing the validity of the registration of a trademark in implementing the GIs provisions of the TRIPS Agreement, the necessary and logical consequence is that the rights required to be granted to the owner of a registered trademark under TRIPS Article 16.1 continue to attach to that trademark. Once a valid trademark is registered, exceptions to the rights required to be granted to the owner of that trademark under TRIPS Article 16.1 must accord with TRIPS Article 17, to which I will return shortly.

---

[9] See, for example, Opinion of Advocate General Jacobs, *Marca Mode v Adidas AB and Adidas Benelux BV*, paragraph 40, Exhibit US-12.

[10] Second Written Submission of the EC, paragraph 282.

[11] Second Oral Statement of the EC, paragraph 230.

26. To the extent that registration and/or use of an EC-defined GI would constitute confusingly similar or identical use of a sign for a similar or identical good, the owner of a registered trademark is required to be granted the exclusive right to prevent the registration and/or use of that EC-defined GI. Thus, TRIPS Article 24.5 does not envisage the co-existence of TRIPS-defined GIs and earlier registered trademarks.

TRIPS Article 24.3

27. TRIPS Article 24.3 does not require the EC to maintain the co-existence of EC-defined GIs and earlier trademarks as argued by the EC. Australia has responded to this argument in detail in its Rebuttal Submission.[12] In addition—in the circumstances of the measure at issue in this dispute—to the extent that TRIPS Article 24.3 might protect the geographical indications that existed within the EC on 31 December 1994, it would do so only in respect of the territories of those EC Member States which did protect the EC-defined GIs as at that date.

TRIPS Article 17

28. I noted earlier that—once a valid trademark is registered—exceptions to the rights required to be granted to the owner of that trademark under TRIPS Article 16.1 must accord with TRIPS Article 17.

29. The EC has already put forward a number of arguments in support of its contention that the requirement of Regulation 2081/92 for the co-existence of an EC-defined GI and a pre-existing trademark right is justified by TRIPS Article 17. Australia responded to these arguments in its Written Rebuttal Submission.[13]

30. The EC now argues as well that Article 14.3 of Regulation 2081/92 "would nonetheless prevent the registration of confusing geographical indications in those instances where the likelihood of confusion is greater."[14] Even leaving aside the issue of whether Article 14.3 applies in a situation of "confusing"—as distinct from "misleading"—use to which I referred earlier, the right required to be granted to the owner of a registered trademark under TRIPS Article 16.1 is not subject to a test of the degree of likelihood in relation to the likelihood of confusion. Rather, it is a right that applies in all circumstances of a likelihood of confusion.

31. The EC argues that the phrase "the fair use of descriptive terms" in TRIPS Article 17 includes a term used to indicate the place of origin of a product, which in turn includes any term used as an "indication of source" in the sense of the Paris Convention, which in turn includes both TRIPS and EC-defined GIs.[15]

32. However, the EC argument ignores the principle of territoriality that underpins the global regime for the protection of IP rights. It assumes that all indications of source, including TRIPS and EC-defined GIs, are immediately and universally recognised as such.

33. The EC argument also ignores that while GIs may be a "sub-set" of indications of source in the sense of the Paris Convention, they are—in accordance with TRIPS Article 22.1—a very particular sub-set. They don't simply identify or describe a good as originating in a geographic place. If that were all they did, IP protection would not be needed—nor would it be appropriate. This surely is precisely the distinction between a geographic term and a TRIPS-defined GI. TRIPS Article 22.1 says that a geographic term qualifies to be called a "geographical indication" in a specific situation. That situation is where the term signifies that a given quality, reputation or other characteristic of the good is essentially attributable to its geographical origin. This is not descriptive of the geographic origin, nor is it descriptive of the quality, reputation or other characteristic of the good that is essentially attributable to its geographical origin. It is much more than that: it signifies the causative link between geographical origin and some characteristic of the product.

---

[12] Australia's Written Rebuttal Submission, paragraphs 111-117.

[13] Australia's Written Rebuttal Submission, paragraphs 118-127.

[14] Second Written Submission of the EC, paragraph 337.

[15] Second Written Submission of the EC, paragraph 338.

34. Thus, TRIPS-defined GIs are not "descriptive terms" in the sense of TRIPS Article 17 that simply indicate the place of origin of a product. The EC's suggested interpretation would render meaningless the express requirement of TRIPS Article 22.1 that a TRIPS-defined GI indicate that a given quality, reputation or other characteristic of the good be essentially attributable to its geographical origin. Moreover, such an interpretation would be contrary to the principle of effectiveness in the interpretation of treaties that the Appellate Body has several times expressly recognised.[16]

35. Similarly, the EC's professed difficulty in understanding the provisions of the Australian Trade Marks Act[17] ignores the principle of territoriality. Bearing in mind that Australia's recognises IP rights as private rights, it is up to GI right holders from the EC—or anywhere else—to act to protect those rights in the territory of Australia. This can be done through the multiple opportunities provided by Australian law to oppose the registration of a trademark, or by seeking to invalidate or revoke such a registration in accordance with Australian law. If GI right holders do not make use of those opportunities, then a trademark right holder can legitimately seek to exercise the rights granted by Australian law to prevent confusing use of a TRIPS-defined GI.

36. Finally, the EC's view that the phrase "fair use of descriptive terms" in TRIPS Article 17 can encompass confusingly similar or identical use of TRIPS-defined GIs for similar or identical goods would also render meaningless the provisions of TRIPS Article 24.5, contrary to the principle of effectiveness in the interpretation of treaties.

The evidentiary presumption of a likelihood of confusion

37. Australia has addressed the EC's arguments—in respect of the registration of EC-defined GIs—concerning the evidentiary presumption of a likelihood of confusion required to be granted to the owner of a registered trademark in the case of use of an identical sign for identical goods in its Written Rebuttal.[18]

38. As a final point on this issue, Australia notes that the Community Trademark Directive and Regulation both expressly reproduce that evidentiary presumption.[19]

Conclusion

39. The EC has not rebutted the *prima facie* case made by Australia that—in respect of the registration of an EC-defined GI—the EC measure diminishes the legal protection for trademarks, contrary to TRIPS Article 16.1. The arguments put by the EC in response to Australia's claims are not sustainable. Either they do not accord with the actual provisions of Regulation 2081/92 having regard to rules of interpretation applicable to domestic EC legislation, or they are not supported by the relevant provisions of the TRIPS Agreement.

TRIPS ARTICLE 24.5

40. Australia has claimed that—in respect of the registration of an EC-defined GI—the EC measure diminishes the legal protection for trademarks, contrary to TRIPS Article 24.5. The EC measure prejudices eligibility of an application for registration of a trademark because Regulation 2081/92 does not afford the right of priority required to be afforded by Paris Article 4.

41. The EC asserts that Paris Article 4 "cannot be applied in order to determine whether an application is 'grandfathered' in accordance with Article 24.5."[20] However, the EC's argument ignores that—consistent with

---

[16] See, for example, *Korea – Dairy Safeguard*, Report of the Appellate Body, WT/DS98/AB/R, paragraph 80

[17] Second Written Submission of the EC, footnote 219.

[18] Australia's Written Rebuttal Submission, paragraphs 137-141.

[19] Directive 89/104/EEC, Article 5.1(a), Exhibit COMP-6, and Regulation No. 40/94, Article 9.1(a), Exhibit COMP-7.

[20] First Written Submission of the EC, paragraph 355.

TRIPS Article 2.1—it is obliged to comply with Paris Article 4. Thus, the EC's obligation to apply a right of priority to a trademark application in accordance with Paris Article 4 exists independently of its obligations under TRIPS Article 24.5.

42. It is not a case of applying Paris Article 4 "in order to determine whether an application is 'grandfathered' in accordance with Article 24.5" in the sense put forward by the EC. Rather, it is a case of whether, having given effect to its obligations—including those which arise from Paris Article 4—an application is "grandfathered" by TRIPS Article 24.5.

43. The EC has not rebutted Australia's *prima facie* case.

PARIS ARTICLES 10BIS(1) AND 10TER(1), AND TRIPS ARTICLE 2.1

44. Australia has claimed that—in respect of the registration of an EC-defined GI—the EC measure diminishes the legal protection for trademarks, contrary to Paris Articles 10*bis*(1) and 10*ter*(1) as "incorporated" by TRIPS Article 2.1. The EC measure does not assure effective protection of trademarks against unfair competition, and does not assure appropriate legal remedies to repress effectively such acts of unfair competition.

45. Trademarks are expressly recognised as a category of industrial property protected by the Paris Convention. Moreover, the provisions of Paris Articles 10*bis* and 10*ter* apply in respect of all of the industrial property rights protected by the Paris Convention.

46. The obligations established by Paris Articles 10*bis*(1) and 10*ter*(1) are straightforward, and WTO Members are required to comply with those obligations by the terms of TRIPS Article 2.1. Australia does not have to explain how the use of a registered EC-defined GI could constitute an act of unfair competition within the meaning of those provisions of the Paris Convention.[21] That would be determined by the body required to be empowered by the EC to consider such matters in the event that the holder of an industrial property right within the EC considered that such issues may be raised by the registration of an EC-defined GI.

47. The EC has not rebutted the *prima facie* case made by Australia.

TRIPS ARTICLES 41 AND 42

48. It is Australia's claim that—in respect of the registration of an EC-defined GI—the EC measure diminishes the legal protection for trademarks, contrary to TRIPS Articles 41 and 42. The EC measure does not make available to trademark right holders civil judicial procedures concerning the enforcement of their IP rights, contrary to TRIPS Article 42. Further, to the extent to which the Article 15 decision-making process constitutes the initial and only means through which a trademark right holder can seek to exercise the trademark rights required to have been granted under TRIPS Article 16.1, the EC measure:

- provides procedures which are not fair and equitable, and which are unnecessarily complicated and entail unwarranted delays, contrary to TRIPS Article 41.2; and
- does not ensure that decisions are based only on evidence in respect of which trademark right holders were offered the opportunity to be heard, contrary to TRIPS Article 41.3

49. As a consequence—in respect of the registration of an EC-defined GI—the EC measure does not ensure the availability under its law of enforcement procedures as specified in Part III of the TRIPS Agreement, contrary to TRIPS Article 41.1.

[21] First Written Submission of the EC, paragraph 399.

50. The EC has said: "[t]rademark owners have a right to challenge the validity of the registrations under Regulation 2081/92 also in those cases where no right of objection has been provided as part of the registration procedure."[22] In other words, according to the EC:

- firstly, there can be occasions when a right of objection to the proposed registration of an EC-defined GI is not provided to a trademark owner; and
- secondly, in that event, trademark owners have only the right to challenge the validity of the registration of an EC-defined GI in judicial proceedings: they do not have access to judicial proceedings to enforce their rights in a trademark.

51. By its own admission, the EC does not make available to trademark right holders civil judicial procedures concerning the enforcement of any IP right covered by the TRIPS Agreement, contrary to Article 42 of that Agreement.

52. Similarly, by its own admission, the EC does not make decisions on the merits of a case based only on evidence in respect of which parties were offered the opportunity to be heard, contrary to TRIPS Article 41.3.

53. The EC is obliged by Article 41.2 to provide procedures for the enforcement of IP rights which are fair and equitable. Inherent in that requirement is that such procedures must be seen to be fair and equitable to potential users of the procedures. The nature of the Article 15 decision-making process does not allow the possibility of bias in favour of the proposed EC-defined GI to be seen to be excluded. Thus, the EC has not rebutted Australia's *prima facie* case that the EC measure is inconsistent with TRIPS Article 41.2.

54. Further, the EC is obliged to ensure that procedures for the enforcement of IP rights are not unnecessarily complicated or entail unwarranted delays. The EC has yet to offer any valid justification for requiring a national of another WTO Member to forward an objection to the proposed registration of an EC-defined GI through the government of another WTO Member. The EC has not even attempted to justify the requirement that a statement of objection on the basis of a trademark right within the territory of the EC be lodged through another WTO Member government. The EC has not rebutted Australia's *prima facie* case that the EC measure is inconsistent TRIPS Article 41.2.

55. As a consequence of the EC measure's inconsistency with TRIPS Articles 41.2, 41.3 and 42 and in any case—including because the EC has not given effect to the provisions of TRIPS Articles 43, 44, 45, 46, 48 and 49—the EC has not ensured the availability of enforcement procedures in respect of the registration of an EC-defined GI against any act of infringement of IP rights covered by the TRIPS Agreement, contrary to TRIPS Article 41.1.

56. The EC has not rebutted Australia's *prima facie* case.

TRANSITIONAL NATIONAL PROTECTION BY EC MEMBER STATES

57. Australia also claims that the EC measure diminishes the legal protection for trademarks—contrary to TRIPS Articles 16.1, 41.1, 41.2, 41.3 and 42, and Paris Articles 10bis(1) and 10ter(1) as incorporated by TRIPS Article 2.1—in respect of EC Member State decisions to grant transitional national protection pursuant to Article 5.5 of Regulation 2081/92. Regulation 2081/92 does not ensure that such decisions by EC Member States take account of the EC's obligations pursuant to the TRIPS Agreement.

58. The EC has not rebutted Australia's *prima facie* case.

---

[22] Second Written Submission of the EC, paragraph 297.

NATIONAL TREATMENT

GATT ARTICLE III:4

59. Australia has claimed that—in respect of the registration of an EC-defined GI—the EC measure accords to the products of another WTO Member treatment less favourable than that it accords to like products of national origin, contrary to GATT Article III:4. The EC measure applies conditions of reciprocity and equivalence to the registration of an EC-defined GI for an imported like product. The EC measure requires that another WTO Member government endorse an application for the registration of an EC-defined GI for an imported like product. Finally, the EC measure as a whole accords less favourable treatment to the registration of an EC-defined GI for an imported like product.

60. In response, the EC has asserted that:

- Articles 12.1 and 12.3 of Regulation 2081/92 do not apply to other WTO Members: thus, the EC does not impose a condition of reciprocity and equivalence on the registration of an EC-defined GI from another WTO Member;
- the requirement that an application for registration of an EC-defined GI from another WTO Member be transmitted by the government of that WTO Member does not amount to less favourable treatment; and
- "Australia has argued that Regulation 2081/92 accords less favourable treatment in that there is an overall bias in the decision-making process."[23]

61. Australia noted with particular interest how the EC avoided answering the Panel's question as to whether the conditions of reciprocity and equivalence would be inconsistent with the EC's national treatment obligations under the TRIPS Agreement and GATT 1994 if applied to another WTO Member. Australia submits that the EC's failure to give a clear answer to this question in the circumstances of the measure at issue in this dispute, and its arguments in this dispute generally, must be viewed as an admission by the EC that applying such conditions would constitute a breach of those national treatment obligations.

62. Australia notes that the EC's rebuttal to this aspect of Australia's claim consists solely of the assertion that Articles 12.1 and 12.3 of Regulation 2081/92 do not apply to other WTO Members. Thus, to the extent that the Panel considers the EC's explanations of the proper interpretation of those provisions is not sustainable on the basis of the rules of interpretation of EC law, the EC has not rebutted Australia's *prima facie* case.

63. The EC refers to Australia's "remarkable" argument about the EC's failure to correct Australia's understanding of the proper interpretation of Article 12.1 of Regulation 2081/92.[24] Nonetheless, the EC once again ignores the fundamental point at issue. Why has the EC consistently stated or implied—before the panel stage of this dispute—that Article 12.1 did apply to WTO Members? If Australia's understanding of the proper meaning of the Regulation—and Article 12.1 in particular—was so wrong as a factual matter, why didn't the EC seek to correct Australia's understanding at the earliest opportunity?

64. Equally, the EC has not rebutted Australia's claim concerning the need for an application to be transmitted by another WTO Member government. The EC measure in effect requires other WTO Member governments to act as sub-national units of the EC. A superficial appearance of symmetry of treatment does not—in the circumstances of the EC measure—constitute treatment no less favourable within the meaning of GATT Article III:4.

---

[23] First Written Submission of the EC, paragraph 219.

[24] Second Written Submission of the EC, paragraph 89.

65. Finally, beyond mischaracterising an aspect of the claim, the EC has simply not responded to Australia's claim concerning the treatment afforded to imported products by the EC measure <u>as a whole</u>.

66. The EC is invoking Article XX(d) only in respect of Australia's claim concerning the requirement that an application for the registration of an EC-defined GI for an imported product be submitted through the government of the WTO Member in which the relevant geographical area is located.

67. In *Korea – Beef*, the Appellate Body indicated that determination of whether a measure is "necessary" within the meaning of Article XX(d) should be considered in the context of whether there is a WTO-consistent alternative measure available which a WTO Member could reasonably be expected to employ, or whether there is a less WTO-inconsistent alternative measure reasonably available.

68. Thus, in relation to the EC's requirement that another WTO Member government verify and submit an application for the registration of an EC-defined GI for an imported product: is there a WTO-consistent alternative measure reasonably available? Yes—the EC could simply leave it to the applicant to provide the required information. In addition—and in any case—the EC could <u>ask</u> for the cooperation of another WTO Member government after an application has been lodged should such cooperation be necessary to enable an application to be assessed. Is there a less WTO-inconsistent alternative measure reasonably available? Yes—once again, the EC could <u>ask</u> for the cooperation of another WTO Member government after an application has been lodged should such cooperation be necessary to assess an application.

69. Moreover, the EC has not even attempted to establish a *prima facie* case that the requirement for an application for the registration of an EC-defined GI for an imported product to be submitted through the government of the WTO Member in which the relevant geographical area is located is consistent with the <u>chapeau</u> of Article XX. A simple assertion[25] does not constitute a *prima facie* case. The EC has not met its burden of proof for the invocation of GATT Article XX(d).

70. In any case—should the Panel consider that the requirement for an application for the registration of an EC-defined GI for an imported product to be submitted through the government of the WTO Member in which the relevant geographical area is located is provisionally justified under paragraph (d) of Article XX—Australia submits that the requirement would constitute "unjustifiable discrimination between countries where the same conditions prevail" within the meaning of the chapeau. Once again, if the term is already "registered" or otherwise expressly protected under another WTO Member's law—whether as a GI or, for example, as a certification trademark—the information could just as readily be provided by the applicant as by another WTO Member government. Further, and in any case, Australia notes that in *US – Shrimp*, the Appellate Body found that a measure being applied in a way that "<u>require[d]</u> other WTO Members to adopt a regulatory program that *[was]* not merely <u>comparable</u>, but rather <u>essentially the same</u>" *(emphases in original)* was not justifiable within the meaning of the chapeau of Article XX[26]

71. The EC has not rebutted Australia's *prima facie* case in regard to GATT Article III:4. Indeed, having regard to paragraph 33 of the EC's Oral Statement this morning, the EC seems to agree that its measure does in fact breach its GATT Article III:4 obligations.

<u>PARIS ARTICLE 2 AND TRIPS ARTICLES 1.1 AND 1.3, 2.1 AND 3.1</u>

72. Australia claims that—in respect of the registration of, or objections to, an EC-defined GI—the EC measure does not accord national treatment in the protection of intellectual property, contrary to Paris Article 2 and TRIPS Articles 1.1 and 1.3, 2.1 and 3.1. In respect of the registration of more than 120 EC-defined GIs under the normal registration process, the EC measure provided a right of objection to persons resident or

[25] EC's Second Written Submission, paragraph 238.

[26] *US – Shrimp*, AB report, para. 163

established in an EC Member State that was not available to other WTO Member nationals. In addition, the EC measure as a whole does not accord national treatment to the nationals of other WTO Members.

73. In the *US – Section 211 Appropriations Act* dispute, the Appellate Body found that "... the jurisprudence on Article III:4 of the GATT 1994 may be useful in interpreting the national treatment obligation in the TRIPS Agreement."[27] In Australia's view, the general principles that underpin the "treatment no less favourable" standard of GATT Article III:4 were intended to apply in the context of TRIPS Article 3.1. Thus, each WTO Member is required to accord to the nationals of other WTO Members treatment no less favourable than the treatment it accords to its own nationals with regard to the protection of intellectual property.

74. In Australia's view, the obligation in TRIPS Article 3.1 could appropriately be considered in this dispute within the framework of the question: "does the treatment accorded by the EC measure modify the conditions of competition in the EC market to the detriment of nationals of other WTO Members with regard to the protection of intellectual property"?

75. Australia has addressed the EC's arguments in respect of the registration of more than 120 EC-defined GIs under the normal registration process in detail in its Written Rebuttal Submission. Did the treatment accorded by the EC measure modify the conditions of competition in the EC market to the detriment of other WTO Member nationals, who were able to object to the registration of these EC-defined GIs? Most assuredly, yes. There was simply no mechanism by which a national of another WTO Member who was not resident or established in an EC Member State could object to the proposed registration of an EC-defined GI.

76. The EC again relies on the assertion that Articles 12.1 and 12.3 of Regulation 2081/92 do not apply to other WTO Members. As in relation to GATT Article III:4, Australia submits that the EC must be viewed as having conceded that applying conditions of reciprocity and equivalence to the registration of an EC-defined GI from another WTO Member would breach the "treatment no less favourable" standard of TRIPS Article 3.1. Thus, to the extent that the Panel considers the EC's explanation of the proper interpretation of Regulation 2081/92 is not sustainable on the basis of the rules of interpretation of EC law, the EC has not rebutted Australia's *prima facie* case.

77. Equally, the EC has not rebutted Australia's claim concerning the need for an application or an objection to be transmitted by another WTO Member government. Requiring that another WTO Member government act as a "sub-national" government of the EC in respect to an EC measure is not—and indeed cannot be—"treatment no less favourable" to nationals of other WTO Members within the meaning of TRIPS Article 3.1. Given the express recognition by the TRIPS Agreement that IP rights are private rights, there is no basis in the Agreement to deny applicants for the registration of EC-defined GIs direct access to the EC as the WTO Member granting the IP right. Nor is there any basis in the Agreement to require that nationals of other WTO Members lodge objections to the registration of an EC-defined GI through another WTO Member government. Notwithstanding a superficial appearance of symmetry of treatment, the EC measure accords less favourable treatment to the nationals of other WTO Members with regard to the protection of intellectual property within the meaning of TRIPS Article 3.1.

78. Moreover, Australia notes the EC's assertion that the registration of the 480 EC-defined GIs under the simplified registration system is in any case outside the temporal scope of the TRIPS Agreement because of TRIPS Article 70.1. In the *Canada – Patent Term* dispute, the Appellate Body found that Article 70.1 applies where acts were done, carried out or completed before the date of application of the TRIPS Agreement for a Member.[28] As the registrations of those 480 EC-defined GIs were not done, carried out or completed before 1 January 1996, they are subject to all of the EC's obligations pursuant to the TRIPS Agreement.

---

[27] *US – Section 211 Appropriations Act*, Appellate Body report, paragraph 242.

[28] *Canada – Patent Term*, Report of the Appellate Body, paragraphs 54-55.

79. The EC has not rebutted Australia's *prima facie* case that the EC measure is inconsistent with Paris Article 2 as "incorporated" by TRIPS Article 2.1, as well as TRIPS Articles 1.1 and 1.3, and 3.1.

GEOGRAPHICAL INDICATIONS

TRIPS ARTICLE 22.2

80. It is Australia's claim that—in respect of the registration of an EC-defined GI—the EC measure does not provide the legal means for interested parties to prevent misleading use or use which constitutes an act of unfair competition within the meaning of Paris Article 10*bis*.

81. The EC's response[29] presupposes that the territory of the EC Member State of origin of an EC-defined GI and the territory of the EC itself are interchangeable. Indeed, some of the EC's own Member States have argued vigorously that the term "Feta" should not have been registered as an EC-defined GI because it has long been a generic term within those Member States.

82. In addition, the EC's response is premised on a mischaracterisation of Australia's arguments. Australia has not said that registration of a term as an EC-defined GI in territory A could be deemed misleading simply because the term has become generic in territory B.[30]

83. The EC disparages Australia's reliance on Bodenhausen, but ignores that the EC itself has elsewhere relied on that source.[31] The EC also ignores that Australia pointed as well to the WIPO Model Provisions on Protection Against Unfair Competition in support of its contention that Paris Article 10*bis* encompasses the notion of honest practices established in international trade.[32] In its turn, however, the EC offers no sources in support of its own interpretation of TRIPS Article 22.2.

84. Australia does not purport to say whether it may be that registration of any particular EC-defined GI would be misleading or would constitute an act of unfair competition within the meaning of Paris Article 10*bis* under TRIPS Article 22.2.

85. What is clear, however, is that the EC has an obligation to provide the legal means by which interested parties can seek to test such issues in relation to the registration of an EC-defined GI. It does not do so.

TRIPS ARTICLES 1.1 AND 2.1

86. As a consequence of the EC's failure to comply with Paris Articles 10*bis*(1) and 10*ter*(1) in respect of the registration of an EC-defined GI, the EC has not complied with TRIPS Article 2.1.

87. Further, and in any case, as a consequence of the EC's failure to comply with any of its obligations under the TRIPS Agreement in respect of the registration of an EC-defined GI—including in relation to decisions by EC Member States to grant transitional national protection—the EC has failed to give effect to the provisions of the TRIPS Agreement, contrary to TRIPS Article 1.1.

---

[29] Second Written Submission of the EC, paragraphs 381-393.

[30] Second Written Submission of the EC, paragraph 389.

[31] First Written Submission of the EC, footnote 46.

[32] Australia's reply to Question 24 from the Panel following the first meeting with the parties.

TBT

TBT ARTICLES 2.1 AND 2.2

88. Australia claims that the EC measure is a technical Regulation that is inconsistent with TBT Article 2.1 to the extent that Article 12.2 of Regulation 2081/92:

- is a mandatory labelling provision
- that applies to imported products bearing, or eligible to bear,
- an EC-defined GI that is identical to an EC-defined GI from within the EC already registered under the Regulation
- for a like domestic product and provides no discretion for the EC to apply the provision in such a way as to avoid less favourable treatment to the imported product.

89. Australia also claims that the EC measure is a technical Regulation that is more trade restrictive than necessary to fulfil a legitimate objective—taking account of the risks non-fulfilment would create—contrary to TBT Article 2.2, to the extent that Articles 4, 10 and 12.1 of Regulation 2081/92:

- establish a mandatory requirement
- for another WTO Member to have in place in all circumstances an EC-mandated inspection structure.

90. In reply, the EC sets out arguments that are irrelevant to Australia's claims.

91. Firstly, on the threshold question as to whether the Regulation is in part a technical regulation, with respect to Articles 4 and 10 of the Regulation, the EC alludes to other provisions of the TBT Agreement—those dealing with conformity assessment procedures—while only partially addressing Australia's arguments supporting its claim that those Articles read together constitute a technical regulation.

92. The question at issue is the following: has the EC rebutted Australia's claim that these provisions of the Regulation impose (i) product characteristics or related processes or a labelling requirement (ii) applying to identifiable products and (iii) with which compliance is mandatory? If the answer is no, the EC has not rebutted Australia's claim that these provisions constitute technical regulations. Any discussion of what might be a conformity assessment procedure under the Regulation—or of what might be the function of the inspection structure mandated by Article 10 of the Regulation—is irrelevant to this central question.

93. Secondly, with regard to Australia's claim pursuant to TBT Article 2.2, the EC confuses the issue by responding to claims Australia has not made. It asserts, wrongly, that Australia objects to the idea of inspection structures *per se*, preferring that there be no inspection structure at all. It then proceeds to elaborate on elements of the inspection structure required by Article 10, stating that Australia *"[has]* been unable to identify a single element in the requirements of Article 10 … that would be objectionable."[33]

94. Australia has not sought to identify objectionable elements in the inspection structure mandated by Article 10 because it is not that structure itself which is "objectionable." Let's be clear on what Australia does consider to be the "objectionable"—and WTO-inconsistent—feature of the EC regime. It is not one or more specific elements of the inspection structure provided for in Article 10. Nor is it the notion of a verification process for the authenticity of agricultural products bearing an EC-defined EC.

---

[33] Second Written Submission of the EC, paragraph 103.

95. It is the fact that the Article 10 type of inspection structure is imposed on other WTO Members, regardless of their existing inspection structures and/or other systems or mechanisms that perform the same function. If such a requirement were necessary, the EC would have had to determine that no other system in any WTO Member could in any circumstances provide the same degree of assurance as the EC's system for compliance verification and enforcement, or for the prevention of deceptive practices.

96. That is the issue here. The EC's repeated explanations of how its inspection structures work and how unobjectionable its features may be are irrelevant to this central point.

97. Australia submits that the EC has not rebutted Australia's claim that Regulation 2081/92 is in part a technical regulation. Similarly the EC has failed to rebut Australia's *prima facie* case that to the extent it is a technical regulation, the EC measure is inconsistent with TBT Articles 2.1 and 2.2.

98. I would like to make a final point in relation to the TBT Agreement. Australia noted with interest the EC's selective use of the Appellate Body's findings at paragraph 241 of its Oral Statement. The EC noted the Appellate Body's in the *EC – Asbestos* dispute that products to which a technical Regulation applies need not be expressly identified in order to be an "identifiable product." The EC then went on to say—and I quote: "[h]owever, the product should at least be identifiable on the basis of the document itself. This is not the case here …." If the EC had continued reading the Appellate Body report, it would have seen that—two paragraphs later the Appellate Body said: "although this prohibition against products containing asbestos applies to a large number of products, and although it is, indeed, true that the products to which this prohibition applies cannot be determined from the terms of the measure itself, it seems to us that the products covered by the measure are *identifiable*: all products must be asbestos free and products containing asbestos are prohibited."[34] Those further findings by the Appellate Body in that dispute are equally applicable here.

TRIPS ARTICLE 20

99. As a final point concerning the actual claims made by Australia—and with the benefit of the explanations of the EC measure now provided by the EC—I confirm that Australia withdraws its claim under TRIPS Article 20.

GENERAL ISSUES

100. I would also like to make some general comments about some of the EC's characterisations of issues raised by this dispute. I note that there are a number of statements and comments made by the EC in this dispute about international law, WTO dispute settlement and even Australia's intellectual property system. Australia does not agree with many of these, but in the interests of not being distracted from the main issues in the dispute, we have chosen not to engage in pointless debate. But there are some EC "red herrings" on which I feel I must comment for the record.

101. Firstly—having regard to the requirements of the DSU—Australia is not obliged to address each and every claim and to set out its complete case at each and every stage of the dispute. Nor is Australia obliged to demonstrate adverse trade effects from a measure it is complaining against. And it is for the complaining Member to judge whether dispute settlement action would be "fruitful" in accordance with DSU Article 3.7: the function of the Panel is to "make an objective assessment of the matter before it" in accordance with DSU Article 11.

102. Indeed, particularly after hearing the statement by the EC this morning, I would suggest that it looks like part of the Panel's work is going to require checking the EC's citations and sources very carefully, given that a number of them are misleading. I simply don't believe the EC's attempts at alleging differences between

[34] *EC – Asbestos*, Appellate Body Report, paragraph 72.

Australia and the US add anything to its arguments. There are no material differences anyway, and surely the EC is not suggesting that where Australia and the US agree, we are right and the EC accepts it is wrong?

103. Moreover, on the subject of citations and footnotes, Australia notes the EC's inclusion of substantive text in some footnotes which was not read. It is therefore unclear to Australia what constitutes the EC's Oral Statement.

104. Secondly, a superficial similarity between aspects of the complaining and responding parties' implementation measures does not constitute a defence for a challenged measure. It is rarely possible to consider the meaning of a legislative provision in isolation, a fact recognised by the EC in its own statement that the meaning of Regulation 2081/92 must be assessed within the legal order of the EC.[35] The EC's attempts to have the Panel examine Australia's measures implementing Australia's obligations under the TRIPS Agreement should be dismissed. For these reasons, Australia requests that the Panel reject Exhibits EC-67, EC-68, EC-78 and EC-79. They are not relevant to the measure at issue in Australia's complaint, and do not constitute rebuttal of arguments made by Australia. Australia is very willing to discuss its legislation should the Panel so wish. Ultimately, however, Australia's legislation is simply not relevant to this dispute. For the same reasons, Australia requests that the Panel also reject Exhibits EC-73 concerning Canadian legislation and EC-80 concerning New Zealand legislation.

105. Thirdly, the EC seems to be of the view that the territories of the EC and of its constituent Member States can be interchangeable for the purposes of some IP rights, and that geographical indications are granted some form of primacy as an IP right by the TRIPS Agreement. How else could an EC-defined GI that was not recognised as such in all of the EC's individual Member States be transformed overnight into a term protected throughout the territory of the EC without regard to the EC's other obligations under the TRIPS Agreement? Yet the territories of the EC and its constituent Member States are not interchangeable in any and all circumstances come what may. Nor does the TRIPS Agreement grant primacy to any particular IP right, whether a TRIPS-defined GI or a trademark.

106. Finally, the EC has expressly acknowledged that "... the subject matter of the present dispute falls within the exclusive competence of the EC, and not of the Member States."[36] The subject matter of this dispute—in respect of the complaint initiated by Australia and as set out in Australia's panel establishment request—is, in effect, the EC's regime for the registration and protection of EC-defined GIs.

107. Thus, the rights and obligations of a WTO Member under TRIPS Article 1.1 devolve directly onto the EC in its own right insofar as the subject matter in this dispute is concerned.

108. Moreover, pursuant to that Article, a WTO Member must unreservedly give effect to the provisions of the TRIPS Agreement—including the standards concerning the availability, scope and use for <u>all</u> categories of IP rights as set out in Part II of the Agreement. These, of course, include the standards established by the Agreement concerning the scope and use of trademarks. A WTO Member <u>may</u> implement more extensive protection than it is required to implement—but <u>only</u> if that more extensive protection is not in breach of the provisions of the TRIPS Agreement, including those concerning trademarks. Finally, while each and every WTO Member is able to decide for itself how to implement the provisions of the TRIPS Agreement, whether these constitute rights or obligations, it is not consistent with the EC's obligations to interpret the TRIPS Agreement in such a way that its internal legal order renders provisions of that Agreement meaningless insofar as the territory of the EC and/or its individual Member States is concerned.

---

[35] See, for example, Second Written Submission of the EC, paragraph 7.

[36] First Written Submission of the EC, paragraph 255.

CONCLUSION

109. While the EC has sought to complicate the issues before the Panel, I think at least three or four key issues are clearer as we go into this second meeting with you.

110. Firstly—in respect of the registration of an EC-defined GI—do trademark holders have a readily discernible and specific right under the Regulation as required to be provided to them under TRIPS Article 16.1? While the EC has sought to suggest that there is something resembling this within the Regulation, these arguments require a reinterpretation of key terms within intellectual property law, such as "confuse" versus "mislead." The EC has not provided any credible evidence even then that there is anything in the Regulation that provides for the security of this right. This clearly contrasts with its own specific Regulation and Directive in respect of trademarks which would otherwise apply—but for the system of protection of GIs under Regulation 2081/92—with respect to GIs registered pursuant to that Regulation. Consequently, the EC has not rebutted Australia's claims in this context.

111. Secondly, does Article 12.1 of the Regulation apply with respect to nationals of WTO Members? The EC has introduced little or no credible evidence, as opposed to unsubstantiated statements, that provides reassurance that it doesn't. Consequently, at least with respect to claims about reciprocity and equivalence, the EC is in breach of its national treatment obligations.

112. Thirdly, with respect to geographical indications themselves, the EC has argued that it provides for TRIPS Article 22.2 rights under EC Member State law. Again, a clear admission with respect to what is lacking under the Regulation itself. But again, the system of protection of GIs under Regulation 2081/92 and with respect to GIs registered pursuant to that Regulation disturbs what may otherwise be sufficient to meet the EC's obligations. Consequently, the EC has not rebutted Australia's claims in this context either.

113. Fourthly, the EC has not provided any credible argument why a measure cannot be examined under both the TBT Agreement and TRIPS, given they are part of the same agreement. By contrast, Australia has been mindful of findings of the Appellate Body on the integrated nature of the WTO Agreement. Further, Australia has shown why aspects of Regulation 2081/92 are subject to the TBT Agreement, and how the Regulation breaches obligations established by that Agreement.

114. For all these reasons, and those substantiated in our other statements and submissions, Australia submits that the EC measure is inconsistent with a number of the EC's WTO obligations.

ANNEX A-7

CLOSING STATEMENT OF AUSTRALIA SECOND SUBSTANTIVE MEETING

(12 August 2004)

Mr Chairman, Members of the Panel

Between the written argumentation and the two meetings with you, I believe that when you review all of the material that Australia has submitted, you will see that Australia's case is straightforward, succinct and thoroughly substantiated. And the EC can rest assured we have carefully considered our case and the implications.

Australia endorses all of the arguments put forward by the United States. Where there are differences between the complainants, these are a result of different understandings of the flawed measure at issue in this dispute, and, in any case, are not material differences.

I will therefore not go through our substantive claims and arguments again, except for two points.

The discussion on the ECJ this morning was interesting in the context of our claims under TRIPS Article 16.1 and Article 42. In particular, it is useful to compare the EC's answers with the Appellate Body discussion in *Canada – Patent Term*. At paragraph 92, where the Appellate Body was talking about the relevant right, it said that the right must be "a readily discernible and specific right, and it must be clearly seen as such."

With respect to GATT Article XX(d), in addition to the US's comments, we note the EC's attempt to shift the burden of proof regarding the chapeau to the complaining parties in its closing statement. The EC has clearly failed to meet its burden of proof for invoking a GATT Article XX(d) defence.

On the rest of the substance, I will not reopen all the debates, but obviously found much in the EC's closing statement that we disagree with.

I believe you will find little from the EC by way of substantiated rebuttal that addresses Australia's *actual* claims and arguments.

Instead, the EC has ignored our actual claims and arguments and adopted the tactic of insulting Australia. At the same time, the EC has directed its rebuttal to claims and arguments Australia has not made.

Further, it has variously claimed poor drafting, abandoned previous statements made by various EC entities and authorised representatives, or just ignored aspects of its own Regulation and legal system.

None of this constitutes rebuttal of Australia's *prima facie* case, however.

And none of this constitutes an excuse to try and get from the WTO Membership through the Regulation what the EC failed to get out of the Uruguay Round.

The obligations of the EC are clear, and the EC is not living up to these to the extent and as shown in Australia's submissions.

Thank you, Mr Chairman and Members of the Panel.

ANNEX A-8

REPLIES BY AUSTRALIA TO QUESTIONS POSED BY THE PANEL FOLLOWING THE SECOND SUBSTANTIVE MEETING

(26 August 2004)

I. TABLE OF CASES CITED IN THIS SUBMISSION

Short Title	Full Title
Korea – Beef	*Korea – Measures Affecting Imports of Fresh, Chilled and Frozen Beef,* Report of the Appellate Body, WT/DS161/AB/R, WT/DS169/AB/R, 11 December 2000
US – Section 211 Appropriations Act	*United States – Section 211 Omnibus Appropriations Act of 1998*, Report of the Appellate Body, WT/DS176/AB/R, 2 January 2002
Japan – Alcohol Taxes	*Japan – Taxes on Alcoholic Beverages,* Report of the Appellate Body, WT/DS8/AB/R, WT/DS10/AB/R, WT/DS11/AB/R, 4 October 1996
EC – Asbestos	*European Communities – Measures Affecting Asbestos and Asbestos-Containing Products*, Report of the Appellate Body, WT/DS135/AB/R, 12 March 2001
Korea – Dairy Safeguard	*Korea – Definitive Safeguard Measure on Imports of Certain Dairy Products,* Report of the Appellate Body, WT/DS98/AB/R, 14 December 1999
Canada – Patent Term	*Canada – Term of Patent Protection*, Report of the Appellate Body, WT/DS170/AB/R, 18 September 2000
India – Patents	*India – Patent Protection for Pharmaceutical and Agricultural Chemical Products*, Report of the Appellate Body, WT/DS50/AB/R, 19 December 1997

II. OTHER SOURCES CITED IN THIS SUBMISSION

Short Title	Full Title
OED	*The New Shorter Oxford English Dictionary*, Ed. Lesley Brown, Clarendon Press, Oxford, 1993

94. The Panel takes note that, in the EC's view, the specific conditions contained in Article 12(1) of Regulation (EC) No. 2081/92 do not apply to WTO Members because the introductory phrase "[w]ithout prejudice to international agreements" ensures that the WTO agreements prevail where there is a conflict with the Regulation (EC rebuttal, para. 55). Which precise EC obligations under the WTO agreements would be prejudiced by the application of those specific conditions to other WTO Members? In particular:

(a) would the EC's obligations under Article III:4 of GATT 1994 be prejudiced?

(b) would the EC's obligations under Article 3.1 of the TRIPS Agreement be prejudiced? If not, please explain the relevance of your reference to the fact that the TRIPS Agreement obliges WTO Members to provide protection to GIs in accordance with Section 3 of Part II and the general provisions and basic principles of the TRIPS Agreement (EC first written submission, paras 65-66). ***EC***

95. Can the EC provide the Panel with any official statement by the Commission or any other EC institution, that the application of conditions of reciprocity and equivalence, such as those under Article 12(1) of Regulation (EC) No. 2081/92, would be inconsistent with the EC's obligations under international agreements, in particular, the WTO Agreement? ***EC***

96. The EC has provided a revised Guide to Regulation (EC) No. 2081/92, dated August 2004 (Exhibit EC-64). Was this new version prepared in connection with this Panel proceeding? How is it relevant to the Panel's work if the Commission assumes no liability for its contents (see its cover page)? A new paragraph in the introduction (page 5) indicates that "the Commission reserves the right to amend procedures" and indicates the possibility of further possible revisions. Does this mean that the Guide could be changed back to the old version? ***EC***

97. The Panel takes note of the EC's responses to Panel questions nos. 16 and 17 and the EC's rebuttal, paras 79-86. Please explain in detail how the Commission's interpretation that Article 12(1) of Regulation (EC) No. 2081/92 does not apply to WTO Members is consistent with the statements in the EC responses in the TRIPS Council review of legislation to question No. 4 posed by New Zealand and the follow-up question posed by India on page 24 in IP/Q2/EEC/1 (cited in Australia's rebuttal, para. 33, fn. 23). ***EC***

98. Is it the EC's submission that the conditions in Article 12(1) of Regulation (EC) No. 2081/92 do not apply to WTO Members so that:

(a) WTO Member nationals may obtain GIs for areas located in all countries; or

(b) persons from all countries may obtain GIs for areas located in all WTO Members? ***EC***

99. The EC has referred to other Community legal acts in relation to the meaning of the phrase "without prejudice to international agreements" (EC rebuttal, paras 62-66). Please also refer to Regulation (EC) No. 2082/92 on certificates of specific character for agricultural products and foodstuffs, which was adopted with the Regulation at issue in this dispute. To what international agreements does the phrase "[w]ithout prejudice to international agreements" refer as used in Article 16 of that Regulation? ***EC***

100. In Regulation (EC) No. 753/2002 on wine (set out in Exhibit US-35), Articles 34-36 refer to "third countries," apparently to refer to both WTO and non-WTO Members. It expressly states wherever a "third country" is limited to, or excludes, WTO Members. Why was Regulation (EC) No. 2081/92 drafted in such a way that the meaning of "third country" in Articles 12 through 12d is not clearer each time it was used? Does the use of "WTO Member" together with "third country" in certain instances in Articles 12 through 12d of Regulation (EC) No. 2081/92 not suggest that the term "third country" excludes WTO Members in those articles? ***EC***

101. The Panel takes note of the parties' respective views on the meaning of "nationals" under the TRIPS Agreement and the Paris Convention. Without prejudice to those views, please explain in detail which nationals should be compared for the purposes of the TRIPS national treatment obligations, based on the text of the agreement.

Please refer to the quadrant in the third party submission of Chinese Taipei (para. 9). Both the EC and the US compare an EC national with rights to a GI located in the EC. On the US view, that national should be compared with a US national with rights to a GI located in the US. But on the EC view, that national should be compared with a US national with rights to a GI located in the EC. Would it be appropriate instead to compare all EC nationals with rights to GIs who might wish to register them under Regulation (EC) No. 2081/92, wherever the geographical areas are located, and compare them with all US nationals with rights to GIs who might wish to register them under the Regulation, wherever the geographical areas are located?

More generally, is there a principle in the TRIPS Agreement that all nationals of one WTO Member with rights to a particular category of intellectual property, such as GIs, should be compared with all nationals of other WTO Members with rights to the same category of intellectual property, unless the text of the agreement indicates that with respect to particular types of products or other sub-categories, they require particular treatment? ***USA, AUS, EC***

1. As set out by Chinese Taipei, there are four combinations of nationals and geographic areas that can be examined:

1. EC national, relevant geographical area located within the EC;
2. Non-EC national, relevant geographical area located within the EC;
3. EC national, relevant geographical area located outside the EC; and
4. Non-EC national, relevant geographical area located outside the EC.

2. Regardless of any other comparisons, it is appropriate, and necessary, to compare Category 1 with Category 4 for the purposes of determining whether there is a breach of the EC's national treatment obligations.

3. TRIPS Article 3.1 provides that nationals of other WTO Members shall be accorded treatment no less favourable than that accorded to a WTO Member's own nationals with regard to the protection of intellectual property. Protection is defined in that context as including "matters affecting the availability, acquisition, scope, maintenance and enforcement of intellectual property rights …."

4. At least one right at issue in this dispute is the right of a person to register an EC-defined GI to which that person has a valid claim. Clearly, under the EC measure, nationals (however defined) of a non-EC WTO Member, when seeking to register an EC-defined GI for a geographical area outside the EC (that is, Category 4 above) are treated less favourably than EC nationals seeking to register an EC-defined GI for a geographical area inside the EC (that is, Category 1 above).

5. There is nothing in the TRIPS Agreement or Paris Convention that enables or excuses such less favourable treatment for non-EC nationals.

102. Is it safe to assume that persons resident or established in one country to produce agricultural products or foodstuffs will be considered "nationals" of that country for the purposes of TRIPS? Why is it, or is it not, safe to assume that applicants for GIs under Regulation (EC) No. 2081/92 are "nationals" of the country where their GI is located, for the purposes of TRIPS? ***USA, AUS, EC***

6. As set out in response to question No. 101 above, there is clearly at least one category of non-EC nationals that is being treated less favourably than a category of EC nationals with regard to the protection of an EC-defined GI to which the respective nationals have a claim. It is therefore not necessary to make any

assumptions about the population of other categories, or to seek to characterise all persons in every WTO Member that may be seeking to register an EC-defined GI.

7. In any case, Australia notes that the Appellate Body in *Korea – Beef*, with regard to the national treatment obligation in GATT Article III:4 held that, notwithstanding the fact that the measure did not in and of itself result in less favourable treatment to imported products, the effect of the measure in that dispute was to treat imported products less favourably than domestic like products.[1] Similarly, in the present dispute, the overwhelming majority of applications for registrations related to geographical locations in other WTO Members will be made by nationals (however defined) of those Members. Thus, the effect of the EC measure is that the specific provisions and additional requirements of the measure for names relating to products originating outside of the EC will overwhelmingly apply to non-EC nationals.

103. The Panel takes note that the EC does not exclude entirely that "under certain circumstances, measures which are neutral on their face may nonetheless constitute less favourable treatment of foreign nationals" and that the EC believes that national treatment under TRIPS should not overlap with GATT 1994 (EC response to Panel question No. 29, paras 71 and 74). What other considerations are relevant to the assessment of de facto discrimination under TRIPS? What is the relevance, if any, of the fact that the TRIPS Agreement does not contain a general exceptions provision analogous to Article XX of GATT 1994? ***USA, AUS, EC***

8. The preambular clauses to the TRIPS Agreement expressly recognise "the need for new rules and disciplines concerning … the applicability of the basic principles of GATT 1994." As the Appellate Body has noted, the national treatment obligation is a "cornerstone of the world trading system that is served by the WTO."[2] The Appellate Body has found that: "… as the language of Article 3.1 of the *TRIPS Agreement*, in particular, is similar to that of Article III:4 of the *GATT 1994*, the jurisprudence on Article III:4 of the *GATT 1994* may be useful in interpreting the national treatment obligation in the *TRIPS Agreement*."[3] In *Korea – Beef*, the Appellate Body said: "[a]ccording 'treatment no less favourable' means … according *conditions of competition* no less favourable to the imported product than to the like domestic product."[4] *(emphasis in original)*

9. It was against that background that Australia suggested that the "treatment no less favourable" obligation in TRIPS Article 3.1 could appropriately be considered within the framework of the question: "does the treatment accorded by the EC measure modify the conditions of competition in the EC market to the detriment of nationals of other WTO Members with regard to the protection of intellectual property?."[5] In Australia's view, considering the obligation established by TRIPS Article 3.1 in that manner ensures that the basic national treatment principle that is a cornerstone of the world trading system applies in relation to the protection of intellectual property and in relation to nationals rather than to products. Further, and as a consequence, considering the obligation established by TRIPS Article 3.1 in that manner enables any factors which may constitute *de facto* discrimination within the meaning of TRIPS Article 3.1 to be properly assessed.

10. It is true that the TRIPS Agreement does not contain a mirror provision to GATT Article XX in the same way as, for example, GATS Article XIV. Unlike GATT 1947 and GATS at the time of their respective negotiations, the TRIPS Agreement was not a pioneering multilateral agreement for many of the IP rights it covers. Thus, it expressly recognises that multilateral regimes with broad adherence already existed—and continue to co-exist—for the protection of many of the IP rights to which it relates. Further, it recognises that, in accordance with those established multilateral regimes, IP rights are generally made available, acquired and enforced in accordance with the national laws of, and with respect to the territory of, a party to those regimes.

---

[1] *Korea – Beef*, paragraphs 142-148.

[2] *US – Section 211 Appropriations Act*, paragraph 241.

[3] *US – Section 211 Appropriations Act*, paragraph 242.

[4] *Korea – Beef*, paragraph 135.

[5] Second Australian Oral Statement, paragraph 74.

11. Reflecting the historical development of the international IP protection regime, the TRIPS Agreement—at Article 7—expressly recognises that the protection and enforcement of IP rights should take place "in a manner conducive to social and economic welfare," and—at Article 8.1—expressly provides that WTO Members "may, in formulating or amending their laws and regulations, adopt measures necessary to protect public health and nutrition ..., provided that such measures are consistent with the provisions of this Agreement." In other words, WTO Members may take account of legitimate public policy objectives and principles when establishing their national regimes for the protection of IP rights. Having incorporated legitimate public policy objectives and principles in its national regime, a WTO Member is obliged to apply such measures consistently with the provisions of the TRIPS Agreement. These include the national treatment and MFN obligations at TRIPS Articles 3.1 and 4 respectively, as well as the obligation to comply with the national treatment obligation of Paris Article 2. Once a WTO Member adopts measures for the protection of a category of an IP right, those measures apply equally to its own nationals and to the nationals of all other WTO Members.

12. Further, to the extent that a legitimate public policy objective may be specific to a particular category of IP right, the provisions of Part II of the TRIPS Agreement provide additional means for a WTO Member to prevent the acquisition of some categories of IP rights, for example, through TRIPS Articles 15.2 and 27.2 in respect of trademark and patent rights respectively, or to limit the scope of a category of IP right, for example, through TRIPS Articles 17 and 30 in respect of trademark and patent rights respectively. Indeed, TRIPS Article 27.2 expressly anticipates that a WTO Member may wish to adopt patentability exclusions on the basis of the necessity to protect human, animal or plant life or health or to avoid serious prejudice to the environment.

13. An overarching exceptions provision analogous to GATT Article XX is thus unnecessary.

14. Further, given the express provisions of TRIPS Articles 7 and 8, and of TRIPS Articles 15.2 and 17, and 27.2 and 30, the omission of an overarching exceptions provision analogous to GATT Article XX must be considered to have been deliberate. The absence of an analogous provision is, therefore, irrelevant to the assessment of the existence of *de facto* discrimination within the meaning of the national treatment obligation set out in TRIPS Article 3.1.

104. Please provide your interpretation of the term "separate customs territory" as used in footnote 1 to Article 1.3 of the TRIPS Agreement in accordance with the customary rules of treaty interpretation. What relevance can be drawn from the fact that the same term is used in Article XXVI of GATT 1994? ***USA, AUS, EC***

15. As a general matter, Australia notes that a "separate customs territory" within the meaning of TRIPS footnote 1 would normally be a customs territory that is distinct or detached from another customs territory.

16. Australia also notes that, in accordance with ECJ Advisory Opinion No. 1/94,[6] competence in the subjects covered by the TRIPS Agreement is shared between the EC and its Member States, with some matters being solely within the domain of the EC Member States. In relation to matters covered by the TRIPS Agreement, the customs territory of the EC will not always be the same as the individual territories of its constituent Member States. There may be occasions in relation to matters covered by the TRIPS Agreement when the "customs territor*[ies]*" of its Member States may be distinct from the "customs territory" of the EC itself. Moreover, in some matters covered by the TRIPS Agreement, for example, trademarks, rights can be acquired with respect to either the territory of the EC under the Community Trademark Regulation or the territory of a constituent Member State. This suggests that the respective customs territories are separate, that is, that the respective customs territories are distinct or detached from each other, in relation to such matters covered by the TRIPS Agreement.

---

[6] ECJ Advisory Opinion No. 1/94, Exhibit AUS-13.

17. In Australia's view, consideration of whether the EC would constitute a "separate customs territory" within the meaning of footnote 1 of the TRIPS Agreement would also require consideration of the nature of the EC's membership of the WTO more generally. That latter consideration would need to take account of many factors, including the provisions of Articles IX.1, XI.1, XII.1 and XIV of the WTO Agreement, as well as the Explanatory Notes to that Agreement. The terms of GATT Articles XXIV:2 and XXVI may secondarily provide some relevant context for that consideration, although they would not be determinative.

105. The Panel takes note of the EC's view that it is not a separate customs territory Member of the WTO within the meaning of footnote 1 to Article 1.3 of the TRIPS Agreement (EC rebuttal, para. 35).

(a) Which natural persons does the EC consider EC nationals for the purposes of TRIPS? Are they also nationals of EC member States?

(b) Which legal persons does the EC consider EC nationals for the purposes of TRIPS? Are they also nationals of EC member States? ***EC***

106. What are the nationalities of the applicants for GIs registered under Regulation (EC) No. 2081/92? Have there been any applicants who were not nationals of the EC member State in which the relevant GI was located? Please supply details of any that were not, and the relevant GIs. To the extent that you are aware of the nationality of persons other than the applicants who use a GI in accordance with its registration, please supply the same information. ***EC***

107. The Panel takes note of the examples of foreigners and foreign companies which have invested in Europe (EC rebuttal, para. 46 and Exhibits EC-36 to EC-39; EC second oral statement, para. 28 and Exhibits EC-61 to EC-63). Is the Larsen firm a French company? Have Suntory Limited, E & J Gallo and the Robert Mondavi family formed subsidiaries, joint ventures or other entities under the laws of France and Italy to invest in those wine estates? Did Sara Lee, Kraft Foods and Nestlé purchase companies formed under the law of an EC member State?

The Panel takes note that the EC argues that the possibility that these foreign nationals formed legal persons under the laws of an EC member State is not attributable to Regulation (EC) No. 2081/92 (EC second oral statement, para. 30). Is it appropriate to exclude such other factors from an examination of the WTO-consistency of the Regulation? Does the EC submit that the Panel should "pierce the corporate veil" and refer to ownership and control to determine nationality for the purposes of TRIPS? ***EC***

108. Article 13 of Regulation (EC) No. 2081/92 provides certain protection for registered names. Please explain the practical operation of this article with respect to products, including the types of orders which may be made under Article 13(1) and the consequences of Article 13(3). How would they affect imported products? How would they provide less favourable treatment to imported products? ***USA, AUS***

18. In response to referrals for preliminary rulings from courts of the EC Member States, the ECJ has made findings concerning the extent of protection afforded by Article 13.1 of Regulation No. 2081/92 in well-publicised cases concerning the registered names of "Prosciutto di Parma"[7] ("the Prosciutto judgment") and "Grana Padano"[8] ("the Grana Padano judgment").

- In the Prosciutto judgment, the ECJ found that "... the protection conferred by *[an EC-defined GI]* does not normally extend to operations such as slicing and packaging the product. Those operations are prohibited to third parties outside the region of production only if a condition to that effect is expressly provided for in the specification" (paragraph 94).

[7] "The Prosciutto judgment," Exhibit AUS-14.

[8] "The Grana Padano judgment," Exhbit AUS-15.

- In the Grana Padano judgment, the ECJ found:
  - "Article 4.1 ... makes eligibility to use *[an EC-defined GI]* subject to the product's compliance with a specification. Article 8 ... makes the affixing of the indication *[EC-defined GI]* on a product subject to its compliance with the regulation, and hence with the specification. Article 13 then determines the content of the uniform protection conferred on the registered name" (paragraph 76); and
  - "... Regulation No. 2081/92 must be interpreted as not precluding the use of *[an EC-defined GI]* from being subject to the condition that operations such as the grating and packaging of the product take place in the region of production, where such a condition is laid down in the specification" (paragraph 83).

19. In relation to Article 13.3 of Regulation No. 2081/92 and generic terms, "[i]n accordance with Article 3 ..., the generic nature of a name hindering its registration must be assessed with regard to the Community situation as a whole."[9]

20. In cases concerning the registered names "Parmigiano Reggiano"[10] ("the Parmesan judgment") and "Epoisses de Bourgogne"[11] ("the Chiciak judgment"), the ECJ has found:

- in the Parmesan judgment, that "... in the present case it is far from clear that the designation 'parmesan' has become generic" (paragraph 20), despite an earlier Opinion by Advocate General Ruiz-Jarabo Colmer ("the Canadene Opinion")[12] that the term "parmesan" had become generic (paragraph 35 and footnote 49, and paragraph 77).

- in the Chiciak judgment concerning the protection to be afforded to the constituent parts of a compound term, that: "... under the system of protection created by the 1992 regulation questions concerning the protection to be accorded to the various constituent parts of a name, and, in particular, the question whether a generic name or a constituent part protected against the practices referred to in Article 13 of the 1992 regulation may be concerned, are matters which fall for determination by the national court on the basis of a detailed analysis of the facts presented before it by the parties concerned" (paragraph 38).

21. Following the Parmesan judgment, the European Commission has initiated action in the ECJ against Germany for failure to protect the registered term "Parmigiano Reggiano" as required by Regulation No. 2081/92, because cheeses not made in accordance with the product specification for that term continue to be sold in Germany under the name "Parmesan." In reply, Germany has asserted that "Parmesan" is a generic name.[13]

22. In addition, Australia notes that the ongoing legal action in the ECJ concerning registration of the term "Feta" largely revolves around the issue of whether that term is generic.[14]

23. As relevant to the issues before the Panel, it is already clear from the terms of Article 13.1 of Regulation No. 2081/92—when read together with Articles 14.2 and 14.3 and in accordance with the rules of interpretation of EC law—that the owner of a registered trademark would not be able to prevent confusingly similar or identical use of a sign for similar or identical goods.

---

[9] Regulation No. 1347/2001, preambular Recital (5), Exhibit EC-9.

[10] "The Parmesan judgment," Exhibit AUS-16.

[11] "The Chiciak judgment," Exhibit AUS-17.

[12] "The Canadeane Opinion," Exhibit AUS-18.

[13] "The Parmesan press release, Exhibit AUS-19.

[14] See Common Exhibits COMP-3.b ("the Feta amendment") and COMP-11 ("the Feta judgment"), and Exhibit AUS-12.

24. Further, it is also clear that the protection afforded by Article 13.1 is able to be extended to any restrictive condition(s) included in the product specification mandated by Article 4 of the Regulation.

25. This situation is particularly detrimental to the objective of security and predictability in trade intended to be fostered by the WTO.

26. The situation concerning the term "parmesan" illustrates the uncertainty created as a consequence of the protection afforded by Article 13.1 of Regulation No. 2081/92. As far as Australia can ascertain, use of the word "parmesan" as a generic product descriptor in the territory of the EC is banned on the basis that the ECJ has found "it is far from clear that the designation 'Parmesan' has become generic." However, the ECJ's finding was made in a preliminary ruling relating to criminal proceedings in Italy, the EC Member State of origin of the registered term "Parmigiano Reggiano." If "parmesan" originally was the French translation of the term "Parmigiano Reggiano"[15]—an issue Australia does not contest in these proceedings—it logically follows that it would not have been a generic term within Italy: thus, no evidence would have been considered in the criminal proceedings in Italy, and thus referred to the ECJ. If use of what are considered in many parts of the world—including many EC Member States—to be generic product descriptors can be prevented within the territory of the EC on such a basis, on what other bases could such terms be prevented? Moreover, potential competitors have no way of knowing what terms may be considered to be translations of a registered—and thus protected—name.

27. The uncertainties created by the practical operation of Article 13.1 of Regulation No. 2081/92 and its application in situations involving generic terms partially inform Australia's claims concerning TRIPS Article 22.2 and Paris Articles 10*bis*(1) and 10*ter*(1) in respect of the registration of an EC-defined GI. Australia has not been able to identify any means within the EC's legal order by which a legitimately interested person—whether natural or legal, or a national of the EC or of another WTO Member—is assured of access to a court empowered to consider substantively an act of unfair competition contrary to honest practices in industrial or commercial matters, including in international trade, in respect of the registration of an EC-defined GI. The fact that Australia has not made a claim under GATT Article III:4 concerning less favourable treatment to imported products on the basis of Article 13.1 of the Regulation as well in this dispute is without prejudice to Australia's view of whether there are in fact grounds for such a claim.

109. Leaving aside the rights conferred by Article 13 of Regulation (EC) No. 2081/92, the complainants refer to the "intent and the effect of the Regulation," the "perceived" advantages of registration and the benefits "claimed by the EC" to be gained from protection under the Regulation (US first written submission, paras 61-62; Australia's first written submission, para. 197 and US and Australia's respective responses to Panel question No. 32). On what basis do the complainants argue that the aims and effects of the EC measure are relevant to ascertaining less favourable treatment within the meaning of Article III:4 of GATT 1994? ***USA, AUS***

28. Australia notes that its reference to the advantages of registration perceived by EC producers at paragraph 197 of its First Written Submission was in the context of its claim that the EC measure as a whole does not accord national treatment to non-EC nationals under TRIPS Article 3.1 and Paris Article 2. On the other hand, Panel question No. 32—and Australia's response—expressly referred to like products and thus, by implication, GATT Article III:4.

29. In examining a claim under GATT Article III:4 in *Korea – Beef*, the Appellate Body recalled its finding in *Japan – Alcohol Taxes* that:

> The broad and fundamental purpose of Article III is to avoid protectionism in the application of internal tax and regulatory measures. More specifically, the purpose of Article III "is to

[15] The Parmesan judgment, Exhibit AUS-16, paragraph 20.

> ensure that internal measures 'not be applied to imported or domestic products so as to afford protection to domestic production'."[...] Toward this end, Article III obliges Members of the WTO to provide equality of competitive conditions for imported products in relation to domestic products.[...] ...[16]

30. In this dispute, the effect of the EC measure taken as a whole is to afford protection to domestic production within the meaning of GATT Article III:4. This is consistent with the intent of the EC measure, in particular as expressed in the preambular recitals of Regulation No. 2081/92#1.[17] However, Australia notes that even if the Panel believes the <u>aim</u> of the Regulation is not to provide protection to domestic production, the <u>effect</u> is the critical determining factor.

31. Further, Australia recalls the findings of the Appellate Body in *US – Section 211 Appropriations Act* concerning the usefulness of GATT Article III:4 jurisprudence in interpreting the TRIPS Agreement national treatment obligation.[18]

32. It is these—now well-established—findings by the Appellate Body that provide the support for Australia's claims that Regulation No. 2081/92 specifically—and the EC measure as a whole—accord less favourable treatment to non-EC nationals and to imported products within the meaning of TRIPS Article 3.1 and GATT Article III:4 respectively.

110. Does the EC contest that, to the extent that Regulation (EC) No. 2081/92 provides GI protection for EC nationals and is a law affecting EC products, GI protection for other WTO Member nationals and imported products solely through other laws, such as labelling and unfair competition, would be less favourable treatment? ***EC***

111. Does the EC contest that national treatment and MFN obligations under TRIPS apply to TRIPS-plus protection, and apply to Regulation (EC) No. 2081/92 even to the extent that it does not merely implement the EC's obligations under Article 22? ***EC***

112. The Panel takes note that the Commission has not recognized any country under Article 12(3) of Regulation (EC) No. 2081/92 (EC response to Panel question No. 10, para. 22). Is the Commission obliged to recognize any country that satisfies the conditions set out in Article 12(1)? ***USA, AUS, EC***

33. No.

34. Article 12.1 of Regulation No. 2081/92 expressly provides that the Regulation "may" apply to an agricultural product or foodstuff from a "third country." Thus, even if the conditions set out in Article 12.1 are complied with by a WTO Member or other third country, the EC is not obliged to recognise that WTO Member or other third country under Article 12.3. (And if it does recognise a WTO Member or other third country, it must in any case do so in accordance with the terms of the Regulation.)

113. The EC argues that there must be a substantive difference between two provisions governing the registration of GIs in order for one to entail less favourable treatment (EC second oral statement, para. 40). What is a "substantive" difference in this sense? Does the EC allege that there is a de minimis standard for less favourable treatment under TRIPS or GATT 1994? Is a simple difference in language insufficient to establish different treatment? ***EC***

---

[16] *Korea – Beef*, paragraph 135, referring to *Japan – Alcohol Taxes*, pages 16-17.

[17] Common Exhibit COMP-1.d.

[18] *US – Section 211 Appropriations Act*, paragraph 242.

114. With respect to registration applications under Article 12a(2) of Regulation (EC) No. 2081/92, a third country must verify that the requirements of the Regulation are satisfied before it transmits the application:

(a) to what extent is this designed to confirm the protection of the GI in its country of origin in accordance with Article 24.9 of the TRIPS Agreement, and to what extent does it respond to other objectives?

(b) is this additional to the requirement that a registration application transmitted to the Commission must be accompanied by a description of the matters set out in Article 12a(2)(a)?

(c) does the Commission also examine whether the application satisfies the conditions for protection under Article 12b(1)(a)? How is this examination different from the verification by the third country? ***EC***

115. With respect to objections under Article 12b(2)(a) of Regulation (EC) No. 2081/92, what is an objection that "comes from a WTO Member"? With respect to objections under Article 12d(1) of the Regulation, what is the meaning of a person who "is from a WTO Member"? Do they both refer to the place of residence or establishment of the person who wishes to object? Must objections under both provisions be sent to the country in which the person resides or is established? ***EC***

116. To the extent that certain responsibilities under Articles 12a and 12d(1) of Regulation (EC) No. 2081/92 are borne by non-EC WTO Members:

(a) how is the EC satisfied that every other WTO Member has the authorization to carry them out? (Please refer to Brazil's response to Panel third party question No. 1) (EC second oral statement, paras 72-77).

(b) if other WTO Member governments lack authorization to carry them out, can they be carried out by the EC instead?

(c) to what extent does the EC <u>itself</u> accord no less favourable treatment to the nationals of other Members, and to what extent do other WTO Members share the implementation of that obligation? Can a Member delegate the implementation of WTO obligations to other Members with or without their prior consent?

(d) to what extent has the EC accorded certain treatment <u>to the nationals of other WTO Members</u> rather than to the governments of those other WTO Members? ***EC***

117. The Panel takes note of the EC's response to Panel question No. 8 concerning the meaning of "third country" and seeks clarification as to whether "third country" as used in Article 12(2) of Regulation (EC) No. 2081/92, includes WTO Members. If so, why does the "without prejudice" clause in Article 12(1) form part of the context of Articles 12(1) and (3) but not Article 12(2)? If not, where does the Regulation cover identical GIs from the EC and other WTO Members? ***EC***

118. The Panel takes note that, in Australia's view, the identical GI labelling requirement would not be inconsistent with Article 2.1 of the TBT Agreement if it was applied to both EC and imported products according to date of registration, not origin. (Australia's response to Panel question No. 53). Even if Article 12(2) does not apply to EC products as well as imported products, does the Commission have the discretion to apply the same requirement according to the date of registration to EC products under Article 6(6) in order to ensure that the identical labelling requirement is applied to the later GI irrespective of the origin of the products? ***USA, AUS, EC***

35. Australia notes that its response to Panel question No. 53 was in the context only of Article 12.2 of Regulation No. 2081/92 which—having regard to the rules of interpretation applicable to EC law—governs the registration of an EC-defined GI from another WTO Member where that name is identical to an existing Community protected name. Where the earlier protected name relates to a geographic area within the EC, Article 12.2 mandates that the imported product clearly and visibly indicate the country of origin on the label. In the situation covered by Article 12.2 which is the subject of Australia's claim, Article 6.6 has no relevance.

36. As set out in response to question No. 123 below, Article 12.2 of the Regulation mandates a means of distinguishing an imported product, rather than functioning as a mark of origin *per se*. Thus, Article 12.2 mandates less favourable treatment to imported products bearing—or eligible to bear—an EC-defined GI which is identical to an already registered EC-defined GI relating to a geographical area within the EC.

119. What is the difference, if any, in the meaning of the word "homonymous" as used in Article 6(6) of Regulation (EC) No. 2081/92 and "identical" as used in Article 12(2)? Why does the EC consider that homonyms are covered by the word "identical" in Article 12(2) (EC response to Panel question No. 43)? ***EC***

120. The Panel takes note of Australia's confirmation that the only less favourable treatment under the identical GIs labelling requirement is relabelling costs (Australia's response to Panel question No. 52). Would imported products have to be relabelled? Would existing marks of origin satisfy this requirement? What does "clearly and visibly indicated" mean? ***AUS, USA, EC***

37. Australia notes that the labelling costs that it referred to in its response to Panel question No. 52 could involve either re-labelling or additional labelling, depending on the circumstances. It is possible that in some cases existing labels may—coincidentally—meet the labelling requirement of Article 12.2 of Regulation No. 2081/92.

38. Having regard to the wording, context and aim of Article 12.2 of the Regulation, the "clearly and visibly indicated" standard would seem to require at a minimum that the label be noticeably evident in the same field of vision as the registered name and the *[EC-defined GI]* symbol (Article 8 of Regulation No. 2081/92 and Articles 5a and 5b of Regulation No. 2037/93[19]).

121. The Panel takes note that Australia refers to Article 6(6) of Regulation (EC) No. 2081/92 as the parallel provision to Article 12(2) (Australia's rebuttal, paras 65-66). Does Australia wish the Panel to address alleged discrimination arising from differences between these two provisions? What is the less favourable treatment? ***AUS***

39. Australia notes that paragraphs 65-66 of its Written Rebuttal Submission form part of Australia's argument concerning the proper interpretation of Article 12.2 of Regulation No. 2081/92 as an issue of fact. The proper interpretation of that provision—and of Article 6.6 of the Regulation—as an issue of fact forms the basis of Australia's claim that the EC measure accords less favourable treatment to imported products bearing—or eligible to bear—an EC-defined GI than to domestic like products bearing—or eligible to bear—an EC-defined GI, contrary to the EC's obligations under TBT Article 2.1. In that context, the labelling requirement can be expected to modify the conditions of competition to the detriment of the producers of the imported product bearing—or eligible to bear—an EC-defined GI in situations where a different, or additional, label is required to be produced and attached to a product because of the extra expense which will be incurred.[20]

---

19 Common Exhibit COMP-2.

20 Australia's First Written Submission, paragraphs 237-241.

122. Please refer to the phrase "labelling requirements as they apply to a product" as used in the definition of "technical regulation" in Annex 1.1 of the TBT Agreement.

> *(a) The EC argues that the "origin of a product is different from the product itself" (EC response to Panel question No. 50). However, as the EC acknowledges, the origin of a product may confer specific characteristics on it. This is consistent with the definitions of designation of origin and geographical indication in Article 2 of Regulation (EC) No. 2081/92, which provide that "the quality or characteristics of the product ... are essentially or exclusively due to a particular geographical environment ..." and that the product "possesses a specific quality, reputation or other characteristics attributable to that geographical origin ...." How then is the origin of a product entitled to bear a registered GI different from the product itself? **EC***
>
> *(b) What is the meaning of the words "as they apply to" as used in this part of the definition? Do they refer to the application of labelling requirements to the characteristics of a product, or to the product itself, or both? **AUS, EC***

40. TBT Annex 1.1 defines a "technical regulation" as follows:

> Document which lays down product characteristics or their related processes and production methods, include the applicable administrative provisions, with which compliance is mandatory. <u>It may also include or deal exclusively with terminology, symbols, packaging, marking or labelling requirements as they apply to a product, process or production method.</u> *(emphasis added)*

41. The plain reading of this provision indicates that the words "as they apply to" refer to a product (as opposed to the characteristics of a product).

42. Moreover, Australia's interpretation is consistent with the findings of the Appellate Body in *EC – Asbestos*, and confirmed in *EC – Sardines*, that according to the TBT Annex 1.1 definition labelling requirements are themselves an example of a product characteristic:

> The heart of the definition of a "technical regulation" is that a "document" must "lay down" ... "product *characteristics*." The word "characteristic" has a number of synonyms that are helpful in understanding the ordinary meaning of that word, in this context. Thus, the "characteristics" of a product include, in our view, any objectively definable "features," "qualities," "attributes" or other "distinguishing mark" of a product. Such "characteristics" might relate, *inter alia*, to a product's composition, size, shape, colour, texture ... In the definition of a "technical regulation" in Annex 1.1, the *TBT Agreement* itself gives certain examples of "product characteristics"—"terminology, symbols, packaging, marking or labelling requirements." These examples indicate that "product characteristics" include, not only features and qualities intrinsic to the product itself, but also related "characteristics," such as the means of identification, the presentation and the appearance of a product. ...[21] *(emphasis in original)*

*123. Does the requirement to display a country of origin on a label under Article 12(2) of Regulation (EC) No. 2081/92 constitute a mark of origin covered by Article IX of GATT 1994? **AUS, EC, USA***

43. Even if the labelling requirement established by Article 12.2 of Regulation No. 2081/92 is a mark of origin within the meaning of GATT Article IX, Article 12.2 is the means by which the EC measure compulsorily differentiates between a registered EC-defined GI on an imported product and a registered EC-defined GI on a domestic EC good, where the imported product bears the later registered EC-defined GI. As

[21] *EC – Asbestos*, paragraph 67.

such, Article 12.2 mandates a means of distinguishing an imported product, rather than functioning as a mark of origin *per se*.

44. Further, Australia's claims under the TBT Agreement are entirely unaffected even if GATT Article IX applies. The TBT Agreement, as noted by the Appellate Body in *EC – Asbestos*, imposes a specialised legal regime applying to measures within its scope. The Appellate Body found that these obligations "seem to be *different* from, and *additional* to" *(emphases in original)* the obligations imposed on Members under the GATT 1994.[22] Moreover, the Appellate Body has noted several times the generally cumulative nature of a WTO Member's obligations, consistent with the integrated, binding nature of the WTO Agreement pursuant to Article II.2 of that Agreement.[23] Thus, even if GATT Article IX:I does exclude marks of origin from the GATT Article III:4 national treatment obligation, it does not follow that TBT obligations—including the national treatment obligation in TBT Article 2.1—do not apply to marks of origin measures if those measures qualify as a "technical regulation."

124. The definition of "technical regulation" in Annex 1.1 of the TBT Agreement expressly encompasses "marking or labelling requirements as they apply to a product, process or production method." Are marks of origin and labels of origin covered by Article IX of GATT 1994 excluded from the scope of the TBT Agreement? Why did the negotiators not explicitly carve them out of its scope? Can a line be drawn between marks of origin that fall under the TBT Agreement and those that do not? What are the systemic consequences for marks of origin if they all fall within the scope of the TBT Agreement? ***AUS, EC, USA***

45. As noted in response to question No. 123 above, even if Article 12.2 of Regulation No. 2081/92 is covered by GATT Article IX, this does not exclude the simultaneous application of the TBT Agreement to the same provision. In Australia's view, it would be a perverse outcome if an agreement that was meant to "further the objectives of GATT 1994," and an agreement which prevails over the provisions of the GATT 1994 in the event of conflict, was made narrower in scope by having express provisions read out of that agreement.

46. The only line that has to be drawn is the line that already exists—the TBT Agreement applies to measures that it defines within its scope. This is exactly the same outcome as between the Agreement on Sanitary and Phytosanitary Measures and relevant GATT provisions, or the Agreement on Subsidies and Countervailing Measures and relevant GATT provisions.

47. As to the question of the systemic consequences marks of origin requirements falling under the TBT Agreement, Australia recalls that WTO obligations are generally cumulative[24] and that it is not uncommon for measures to fall under more than one WTO Agreement. This is consistent with the Appellate Body statement referred to in response to question No. 123 above that the TBT Agreement imposes a specialised legal regime applying to measures within its scope, and that these obligations "seem to be *different* from, and *additional* to" *(emphases in original)* the obligations imposed on Members under the GATT 1994.[25] Australia notes also that marks of origin requirements have not been excluded from the scope of other WTO Agreements: indeed, Article 1.2 of the Agreement on Rules of Origin expressly includes within its scope rules of origin used in the application of origin marking requirements under GATT Article IX. Whether all mark of origin requirements will fall under the scope of the TBT Agreement is an open question—there may be such requirements that are not in the form of measures covered by the TBT Agreement.

---

[22] *EC – Asbestos*, paragraph 80.

[23] See, for example, *Korea – Dairy Safeguard*, paragraphs 74-75.

[24] *Korea – Dairy Safeguard*, paragraphs 74-75.

[25] *EC – Asbestos*, paragraph 80.

125. To what extent would any less favourable treatment under Article 2.1 of the TBT Agreement have to be determined in light of the regulatory objective a Member is trying to pursue under Article 2.2? ***AUS, EC***

48. Australia understands that the "regulatory objective" referred to in the Panel's question is the legitimate public policy objective pursued via a technical regulation, as distinct from the intent of the legislators with regard to the specific application or treatment accorded by a measure to imported and domestic products.

49. Unlike TBT Article 2.2, TBT Article 2.1 makes no reference whatsoever to regulatory objectives. It simply establishes a national treatment obligation in respect of technical regulations, reproducing the GATT Article III:4 "treatment no less favourable" obligation. Moreover, Australia has previously noted that the TBT Agreement was negotiated to further the objectives of GATT 1994.[26] Australia has also previously noted the finding of the Appellate Body on the usefulness of jurisprudence on GATT Article III:4 in interpreting the national treatment obligation in another agreement.[27] Australia notes too the findings of the Appellate Body in *Japan – Alcohol Taxes*:

> ... It is not necessary for a panel to sort through the many reasons legislators and regulators often have for what they do and weigh the relative significance of those reasons to establish legislative or regulatory intent. If the measure is applied to imported or domestic products so as to afford protection to domestic production, then it does not matter that there may not have been any desire to engage in protectionism in the minds of the legislators or the regulators who imposed the measure. ...[28]

50. Against that background, it is Australia's view that the appropriate standard for determining any less favourable treatment within the meaning of TBT Article 2.1 is that set out by the Appellate Body in *Korea – Beef* when it found: "[w]hether ... imported products are treated 'less favourably' than like domestic products should be assessed ... by examining whether a measure modified the *conditions of competition* in the relevant market to the detriment of imported products."[29] *(emphasis in original)*

126. With respect to Article 10(3) of Regulation (EC) No. 2081/92:

(a) the first indent sets out certain requirements for designated inspection authorities and/or approved private bodies. Do these apply to all countries whose GIs are protected under the Regulation, including non-EC member States?

(b) the fifth indent appears to refer only to EC member States and third countries recognized pursuant to Article 12(3). Where does the Regulation refer to the applicable standard for WTO Members not recognized pursuant to Article 12(3), whose requirements private bodies must fulfil for approval purposes?

(c) the fifth indent refers to "[t]he equivalent standard or the applicable version of the equivalent standard." What equivalent standard has been established for GIs for areas located in WTO Members which do not satisfy the conditions of equivalence and reciprocity in Article 12(1)? What are the criteria for establishing that standard? Is it a matter of determining what is "equivalent" to standard EN 45011? Or is it a matter of determining what standard would fulfil the objectives of the Regulation in the light of each third country's own circumstances and conditions? ***EC***

127. Article 12a(2)(b) requires a declaration by a third country government that the structures provided for in Article 10 are established on its territory. Article 10(2) refers to inspection authorities and/or private bodies

---

26 See, for example, Australia's First Written Submission, paragraph 226.

27 *Ibid.*

28 *Japan – Alcohol Taxes*, pages 27-28.

29 *Korea – Beef*, paragraph 137.

approved for that person by the Member State and Article 10(3) provides that where they outsource they continue to be responsible vis-à-vis the Member State for all inspections. What is the exact nature of the role that third country governments must play in the creation and maintenance of the inspection structures that are called for under Article 10? ***EC***

128. In the goods area, it is not uncommon that importing country governments designate, or require the accreditation of, the bodies which exporters may use in the territory of the exporting country in order to determine compliance with product requirements. To what extent does the EC actually give the US and Australia more, rather than less, flexibility by allowing the US and Australian governments themselves to designate the bodies that may participate in the inspection process? Can the US and Australia elaborate on the reasons for which they consider governmental involvement problematic? ***USA, AUS***

51. Australia reiterates that it does not contest all requirements for an inspection structure *per se*, nor does it consider government involvement in such procedures necessarily to be problematic. Rather, Australia contests the EC measure's imposition of EC-mandated inspection structures on other WTO Members, regardless of any existing inspection structures and/or other systems or mechanisms that perform the same function as the EC-mandated inspection structures.

52. This requirement is, firstly, trade restrictive, because it restricts the opportunities for non-EC producers to register an EC-defined GI to cases where the products in question originate from Members with EC-mandated inspection structures in place. Secondly, the requirement is more trade restrictive than necessary. For such a requirement to be necessary within the meaning of TBT Article 2.2, the EC would have had to have determined that no other system in any WTO Member could in any circumstances provide the same degree of assurance as the EC's system for compliance verification and/or enforcement, or for the prevention of deceptive practices.

129. The Panel takes note of the US arguments on inspection structures (US rebuttal, paras 46-48 and 89-93; US second oral statement paras 21-27). What aspects of government involvement in inspection structures do you allege constitute less favourable treatment for foreign nationals? What aspects do you allege constitute less favourable treatment for imported products? Is there less favourable treatment where such structures already exist? ***USA***

130. Other than governmental involvement in the inspection structures, what aspects of the inspection structures do the US and Australia find problematic? ***USA, AUS***

53. Please see answer to question No. 128 above.

131. Which EC Directives govern conformity assessment to EC technical regulations in the goods area? To what extent do those Directives require foreign governmental involvement in the designation/approval of conformity assessment bodies, when mutual recognition agreements in the conformity assessment area do not already exist? ***EC***

132. The Panel takes note of the EC's examples of flexibility in the design of inspections structures (EC rebuttal, para. 104 and Exhibit EC-48). Do these examples all relate to the nature of the inspecting authority? Who determines what constitutes an appropriate inspection for each product, and on the basis of what criteria? ***EC***

133. The Panel takes note that Australia argues that the product specification requirements set out in Article 4(2) of Regulation (EC) No. 2081/92 include "product characteristics," in particular subparagraphs (b) and (e). (Australia's rebuttal, paras 197 and 204) If the inspection structures are designed to ensure that the product specifications under Article 4 of the Regulation are fulfilled, how can they be a technical regulation and not a conformity assessment procedure? ***AUS, EC***

54. The TBT Annex 1.1 definition of "technical regulation" includes, in addition to product characteristics, a document that lays down "related processes and production methods, including the applicable administrative provisions." Australia has argued[30] therefore that a document which does not stipulate mandatory product characteristics *per se* but lays down related processes that are mandatory is a "technical regulation" for the purposes of the TBT Agreement.

55. Having regard to the ordinary meaning of the words in their context, a mandatory requirement for the verification of compliance with product specifications to be carried out in a particular manner is a process related to product characteristics, and therefore corresponds to the TBT Annex 1.1 definition of a technical regulation. Thus, Articles 4 and 10 of Regulation No. 2081/92 read together constitute a technical regulation. The fact that these provisions read together address the issue of conformity does not change their nature as a technical regulation.

56. The EC argues that the difference between a technical regulation and a conformity assessment procedure is that one sets out product characteristics in abstract terms while the other is concerned with enforcement of such regulations in concrete cases.[31] However, this interpretation does not correspond to the Appellate Body's interpretation of the term "technical regulation," nor the definition of that term in the TBT Agreement. It ignores the express terms of the TBT Annex 1.1 definition that a technical regulation may lay down "related processes and production methods, including the applicable administrative provisions." Moreover, a technical regulation lays down mandatory product characteristics applicable to identifiable products: this does not imply a regulation that is "abstract."[32]

134. The Panel takes note of the EC's response to Panel question No. 61, in particular regarding the Panel's terms of reference. However, does the EC contest that a "conformity assessment procedure" within the meaning of the TBT Agreement assesses conformity with a "technical regulation" or "standard" within the meaning of the TBT Agreement? If not, then can the EC complete its analysis and explain whether the inspection structures of Regulation (EC) No. 2081/92 assess conformity with each individual product specification referred to in Article 4 of the Regulation for a registered name, and that those specifications therefore would constitute a "technical regulation" within the meaning of the TBT Agreement? ***EC***

135. The EC invokes Article XX(d) of GATT 1994 as a defence to the national treatment and MFN claims with respect to third country governments' verification and transmittal of applications, the identical GIs labelling requirement and inspection structures requirement. The EC alleges that these requirements are "necessary" to secure compliance with Regulation (EC) No. 2081/92 or to attain the legitimate objectives of the Regulation (EC rebuttal, paras 228-242, paras 263-265; EC second oral statement, paras 132-135):

(a) what is the "measure" necessary to secure compliance with laws or regulations within the meaning of Article XX(d) in each case? What are the laws and regulations with which each one secures compliance? Are the "measures" separate from the laws or regulations?

(b) can a measure that secures compliance with the "objectives" of a regulation, rather than a regulation itself, satisfy Article XX(d)?

(c) in what sense does each of these measures "secure compliance" with laws or regulations? Are they enforcement mechanisms?

(d) how are the laws and regulations with which each measure secures compliance not inconsistent with the GATT 1994? ***EC***

---

[30] Australia's First Written Submission, paragraphs 214-221.

[31] EC response to Question 60 from the Panel following the first meeting with the Panel, paragraph 133.

[32] *Ibid.*

136. With respect to the issue whether the measures are necessary to secure compliance, and without prejudice to the WTO-consistency of any alternative measures:

(a) is the requirement that a third country government verify applications "necessary" to secure compliance in cases where an applicant itself is able to prove that a GI is protected in its country of origin, for example, by submitting an authenticated copy of a registration certificate?

(b) is the requirement that a third country government verify applications "necessary" to secure compliance in cases where the third country has no registration system for GIs or where determinations that a GI is protected under unfair competition laws are only made by the judicial branch of government after litigation?

(c) is the requirement that a third country government transmit applications "necessary" to secure compliance in cases where an applicant itself is able to send an application to the Commission?

(d) why does a third country government need to verify whether the person objecting is resident or established in the third country? Why does the Commission need consult with the third country if the statement of objection is admissible? (EC response to Panel question No. 34).

(e) is the identical GIs labelling requirement "necessary" to secure compliance in cases where there is already a clear distinction in practice in the usual presentation of the relevant products without clearly and visibly displaying the country of origin?

(f) is the requirement that a third country government designate inspection authorities "necessary" to secure compliance in cases where the Commission could designate them in third countries (see US second oral statement, para. 53)?

(g) is the requirement that a third country government declare that inspection structures are established on its territory "necessary" to secure compliance in cases where an applicant could arrange for independent inspection structures to be put in place in respect of a specific product (see US second oral statement, para. 53)?

(h) how is the requirement that a private inspection body continues to be responsible vis-à-vis a third country government "necessary" to secure compliance in cases where the EC could conduct its own inspections of foreign GIs (see US second oral statement, para. 53)?

(i) how is the requirement that the inspection authorities and/or private bodies have permanently at their disposal staff and resources necessary to ensure that all products bearing GIs comply with the product specifications in their registrations? (see Australia's rebuttal submission, para. 217). ***EC***

137. The Panel takes note of the EC's view that Article 14(3) of Regulation (EC) No. 2081/92 allows its authorities to refuse or invalidate the registration of any confusing GIs (EC first written submission, para. 286; EC rebuttal, para. 270). The complainants do not agree (US second written submission, para. 166 and Australia's second written submission, para. 109). The following examples have been referred to in this proceeding:

(a) BAYERISCHES BIER and BAVARIA and HØKER BAJER?

(b) BUDEJOVICKÉ PIVO and BUDWEISER?

(c) GORGONZOLA and CAMBOZOLA?

Could these GIs be used in accordance with their registrations in a way that results in a likelihood of confusion with the respective trademark(s)? ***USA, AUS, EC***

57. Yes.

58. Statements by the EC that Article 14.3 of Regulation No. 2081/92 would permit the EC to refuse registration of an EC-defined GI on the basis of a likelihood of confusion are not sustainable when considered in light of the wording, context and aims of the provision as required by the rules of EC law (see response to question No. 149 below). Equally, the EC's statements that Article 14.3 of the Regulation permits the EC to invalidate registration of an EC-defined GI on the basis of a likelihood of confusion are unsustainable for the same reasons. Moreover, the EC has not sought to explain how a trademark owner would have standing to initiate legal action seeking invalidation of a registration of an EC-defined GI on the basis of a likelihood of confusion. These are particularly important issues given the express terms of Article 142 (now Article 159) of Regulation No. 40/94[33] and—in the case of the owner of a trademark registered in an EC Member State—the fact that Community law has primacy over EC Member State law in the event of a conflict.[34]

59. Even if Article 14.3 of the Regulation did permit the EC to refuse or invalidate the registration of an EC-defined GI on the basis of a likelihood of confusion, it would still be possible for the registered EC-defined GIs "Bayersiches Bier" and "Budějovické pivo" to be used in a way that results in a likelihood of confusion with the respective trademarks. Even within the EC Member States where the trademarks "Bavaria," "Høker Bajer" and "Budweiser" are registered, the protection afforded by Regulation No. 2081/92—in particular Article 13.1—makes clear that the owner of a registered trademark would not be able to prevent confusingly similar or identical use of a sign for similar or identical goods (see response to question No. 108 above). Moreover, even the EC's assertion that a trademark right holder could initiate infringement action is highly qualified: "... a court would be entitled to find, depending on the specific circumstances of each case, that the 'used sign' is different from the 'registered sign' and, therefore, not protected ..."[35] *(emphases added)*. Even where those trademarks are not registered in other EC Member States, each could still enjoy a reputation in the territories of those other States—particularly in adjoining States—which the EC-defined GI right holders could exploit through confusingly similar use of translations of the EC-defined GIs. The EC has not explained how, in such situations, the owners of those trademarks would be assured of the rights of a registered trademark owner to initiate infringement action, or of the standing to initiate legal action under other legal provisions, such as labelling, misleading advertising or unfair competition laws.[36]

60. In relation to the registered EC-defined GI "Gorgonzola," Australia understands that the trademark "Cambozola" was not considered to be a translation or a synonym of "Gorgonzola." Rather, it was considered to be a sign that deliberately sought to evoke "Gorgonzola," even though there was no likelihood of confusion.[37]

138. What is the meaning of the phrase "[w]ith due regard to Community law" in Article 14(2) of Regulation (EC) No. 2081/92? Which aspects of "Community law" are relevant? What is the meaning of the phrase "shall not affect [Regulation No. 2081/92] ... and in particular Article 14 thereof" in Article 142 of Regulation (EC) No. 40/94 on the Community trade mark? ***EC***

---

[33] Common Exhibit COMP-7.

[34] Australia's Closing Statement at the second substantive meeting with the Panel, referring to *Canada – Patent Term*, paragraph 92.

[35] EC's Second Written Submission, paragraph 302.

[36] Australia's Closing Statement at the second substantive meeting with the Panel, referring to *Canada – Patent Term*, paragraph 92.

[37] The Gorgonzola judgment, Exhibit EC-32, paragraph 26.

139. The Panel takes note of the EC's view that the owner of a trademark may not prevent the right holders of a registered GI from using the registered name on the grounds that such name is confusing (EC second oral statement, para. 181). Please confirm that as long as a GI remains registered and is used in accordance with its registration, a trademark owner may not enforce his trademark rights against that use either under the Regulation on the Community trademark or the national trademark laws of the member States. What legal provisions prevent the trademark owners exercising their rights against persons using a GI in accordance with its registration? ***EC***

140. Under what provision of Regulation (EC) No. 2081/92 does the registration of a GI give the right holder a positive right to use the GI? How is that right delimited? Does it include translations of the protected term? For example, what uses do the registrations of the four cheese GIs referred to in Exhibit US-52 permit? How far does that positive right extend before it can be challenged under labelling and misleading advertising laws? ***EC***

141. What is the legal basis for an action to invalidate a registration under Regulation (EC) No. 2081/92 on the grounds of confusion with a trademark? Is there any basis for an action to invalidate a GI registration in Regulation (EC) No. 40/94 on the Community trade mark? ***EC***

142. The Panel takes note of the EC's view that the owner of a concurrent trademark could challenge a decision to register a GI inconsistently with Article 14(3) of Regulation (EC) No. 2081/92 even after the GI has been formally registered (EC response to Panel question No. 67; EC rebuttal paras. 270 and 296). If a trademark owner applied to invalidate a GI registration under Article 14(3):

(a) is this a precondition to a trademark infringement action?

(b) is there any time-limit on such an invalidation action?

(c) is this possibility available where the GI is registered pursuant to an Act of Accession or otherwise without the normal application procedures?

(d) how would such an application for invalidation relate to the cancellation procedure in Article 11a of the Regulation? Are the grounds for cancellation in Article 11a exhaustive? ***EC***

143. The Panel takes note that the Council Decision to register BAYERISCHES BIER as a GI states that "[i]n view of the facts and information available, it was, however, considered that registration of [that name] was not liable to mislead the consumer as to the true identity of the product" (Exhibit EC-9, para. (3), cited in EC rebuttal, para. 287). Please detail what were the facts and information to which the Council referred in that Decision and how they were evaluated so that the Panel can see how the criteria in Article 14(3) were applied in that case. ***EC***

144. The Panel takes note that Commission Regulation (EC) No. 1107/96 (set out in Exhibit COMP-3a), which effected the registration of many individual GIs, recites Article 14(2) and (3) of Regulation (EC) No. 2081/92. How were Article 14(2) and (3) taken into account in the registration of those GIs? ***EC***

145. Please refer to Article 24.5 of the TRIPS Agreement and comment on the suggestion that:

(a) the phrase "shall not prejudice eligibility for or the validity of the registration of a trademark" merely creates an exception to the obligations in Articles 22.3 and 23.2 to refuse or invalidate the registration of trademarks; and

(b) the phrase "shall not prejudice ... the right to use a trademark" merely creates an exception to the obligations in Articles 22.2 and 23.1 to provide the legal means to prevent certain uses and does not create any positive right. ***USA, AUS, EC***

61. Australia does not consider that TRIPS Article 24.5 can be said merely to create an exception to the obligations in TRIPS Article 22.2, 22.3, 23.1 and/or 23.2. As Australia has said previously,[38] TRIPS Article 24.5—together with TRIPS Articles 22.3 and 23.2—defines the boundary between a WTO Member's right to implement measures relating to TRIPS-defined GIs and its obligation to afford protection to pre-existing trademark rights. In establishing that boundary, TRIPS Article 24.5 in effect also creates a positive right: that the specified trademark rights, for example, those required to have been granted in accordance with Paris Article 4, cannot be adversely affected by measures adopted to implement Section 3, Part II, of the TRIPS Agreement.

62. Australia has previously noted the principle of territoriality that underpins the global regime for the protection of IP rights.[39] Moreover, that has been the case for more than 100 years. Thus, pursuant to the provisions of Paris Article 6(1), "[t]he conditions for the filing and registration of trademarks shall be determined in each country of the Union by its domestic legislation." It was, in effect, the norm for parties to the Paris Convention to provide for the registration of a misleading trademark—that is, a trademark that positively provoked an error on the part of the consumer as to the source undertaking of the good—to be refused or invalidated *ex officio*. At the same time, whether a specific sign was misleading was determined in relation to the territory of that Paris Convention party: a sign could have been determined to be misleading in relation to the territory of country A but not of country B, and *vice versa*. As a consequence, registration and use as a trademark of a sign recognised as a GI in country A could have been determined to be misleading, while registration and use as a trademark of that same sign in country B could have been determined not to be misleading.

63. The TRIPS Agreement reinforces that situation, establishing a general obligation on a WTO Member to provide—as a minimum standard[40] in its domestic legal regime covering trademarks and TRIPS-defined GIs—that:

- use of a trademark that contains or consists of a TRIPS-defined GI and which misleads the public as to the true place of origin constitutes a ground for refusal or invalidation of that trademark; or

- in the case of wines and spirits, use of a trademark that contains or consists of a TRIPS-defined GI for wines or spirits not originating in the place indicated by the GI constitutes grounds for refusal or invalidation of that trademark.

64. In any case, the clauses quoted in the question cannot be considered in isolation from the previous phrase "measures adopted to implement this Section." Moreover, that phrase—and TRIPS Article 24.5 more generally—cannot be considered in isolation from the rights expressly required to be granted to the owner of a registered trademark pursuant to TRIPS Article 16.1 as well as the fact that, in accordance with the principle of territoriality, a WTO Member may make available to the owner of a trademark on the basis of use the exclusive right to prevent confusingly similar or identical use of a sign. Nor can the phrase "measures adopted to implement this Section"—and TRIPS Article 24.5 more generally—be considered in isolation from the right expressly accorded under TRIPS Article 1.1 to a WTO Member to implement in its law more extensive protection than required by the TRIPS Agreement, provided that such protection does not contravene the provisions of the Agreement.

146. The Panel takes note of the respective views of the EC and US on simultaneous exercise of rights with respect to use (EC rebuttal, para. 309 and US rebuttal, para. 119). Without prejudice to the EC's views on Article 24.5, would there be any practical conflict between the rights to prevent certain uses conferred under Articles 16.1 and 22.2 of TRIPS? Under what circumstances is it impossible for, simultaneously:

---

[38] See, for example, Australia's Written Rebuttal Submission, paragraph 96.

[39] See, for example, Australia's Second Oral Statement, paragraph 32.

[40] See heading of Part II of the TRIPS Agreement, covering both Trademarks and Geographical Indications.

(a) a trademark owner to prevent *uses* *of a sign where such use would result in a likelihood of confusion (under Article 16.1), and*

(b) a right holder in a GI to prevent *uses* *of an indication that are misleading with respect to the geographical origin of the product or which constitute unfair competition (under Article 22.2) except on the basis that the trademark is identical with, or similar to, the GI (under Article 24.5)?* ***USA, AUS, EC***

65. Australia has several times set out its view during the course of this dispute[41] that TRIPS Article 24.5—together with TRIPS Articles 22.3 and 23.2—defines the boundary between a WTO Member's right to implement measures relating to TRIPS-defined GIs and its obligation to afford protection to pre-existing trademark rights.

66. Thus, in Australia's view, the only relevance of TRIPS Article 22.2(a) to trademark rights would be in the context of the acquisition of new trademark rights. There would thus be no practical conflict in the application of TRIPS Articles 16.1 and 22.2(a).

67. Australia notes that a conflict between a trademark and a GI right usually arises because of the way in which the signs are being used and not because of their inherent nature. Thus, a trademark owner would be able to take action to prevent confusing use. In such a situation, a court would typically look at the nature and scope of any rights, the legitimate interests of the parties and the facts of the case. Regulation No. 2081/92—far from facilitating such an assessment consistent with the rights required to be granted to the owner of a registered trademark under TRIPS Article 16.1—prevents it irrespective of the circumstances.

147. Article 24.5 as finally agreed contains the phrase "measures adopted to implement this Section shall not prejudice eligibility for or the validity of the registration of a trademark, or the right to use a trademark." Please comment on the suggestion that during the Uruguay Round negotiations there was a disagreement as to whether the predecessor to this provision in the Brussels Draft should be made permissive rather than mandatory, and that the choice of this language was part of an effort to reach agreement on the issue of the mandatory / permissive nature of the provision. ***USA, AUS, EC***

68. Australia is not in a position to comment in these dispute settlement proceedings on the proposition set out in this question.

69. DSU Article 3.2, however, requires that the provisions of TRIPS Article 24.5—and indeed of the WTO Agreement as a whole—be clarified in dispute settlement proceedings in accordance with the customary rules of interpretation of public international law. Those interpretive rules have been found by the Appellate Body to be set out at Articles 31 and 32 of the Vienna Convention on the Law of Treaties.[42] Australia notes that the Appellate Body found in *India – Patents* that: "[t]he duty of a treaty interpreter is to examine the words of the treaty to determine the intentions of the parties. This should be done in accordance with the principles of treaty interpretation set out in Article 31 of the Vienna Convention."[43] *(emphasis added)*

148. What is the meaning of the phrase "where such use would result in a likelihood of confusion" as used in Article 16.1 of the TRIPS Agreement? How should such likelihood of confusion be assessed? How does the assessment differ from that under Article 14(3) of Regulation (EC) No. 2081/92? In particular:

(a) ow should the likelihood of confusion, and the liability to mislead the consumer, be assessed with respect to a mark to which rights have not been acquired on the basis of use?

[41] See, for example, Australia's Written Rebuttal Submission, paragraph 96.

[42] See, for example, *Japan – Alcohol Taxes*, pages 10-12.

[43] *India – Patents*, paragraph 45.

(b) as of what time should the likelihood of confusion, and the liability to mislead the consumer, be assessed?

*(c) are the trademark's reputation and renown and the length of time it has been used necessarily rele*vant to both analyses? **USA, AUS, EC**

70. The words "where such use would result in a likelihood of confusion" in TRIPS Article 16.1 have three key elements: "such use;" "would result;" and "a likelihood of confusion." Having regard to the normal rules of interpretation applicable to the WTO Agreement:

- "such use" refers to use of an identical or similar sign for goods or services which are identical or similar to those goods or services in respect of which the trademark is registered or in respect of which trademark rights have been acquired by use;

- "would result" means that such use will have the specified outcome or consequence if the use were to be allowed; and

- "a likelihood of confusion" means that there is a reasonable chance that consumers of the goods or services at issue would be puzzled or bewildered as to the source of the goods or services.

71. There are, in addition, two implicit premises: firstly, that there is—or is intended to be—active use of a trademark; and secondly, by the use of the words "would result," that the right to prevent confusingly similar or identical use of a sign necessarily encompasses pre-emptive action.

72. The likelihood of confusion is assessed having regard to the principle of territoriality. In general terms, it is assessed on the basis of a reasonable number of the relevant consuming public being caused to wonder as to the source of the products. Accordingly, in the context of the specific questions above (see also Australia's response to question No. 149 below):

(a) In respect of trademarks to which rights have not been acquired on the basis of use, how rights have been acquired does not affect the assessment of the likelihood of confusion *per se*. It is the prospective use of the second sign that is the issue. Although substantial use and renown of the trademark mean that a wider range of uses by other parties may cause the consumer to wonder as to the source of a good, reputation is not a prerequisite for a likelihood of confusion or for the exercise of the rights required to be granted under TRIPS Article 16.1. It is possible to cause confusion with a registered trademark even where it has little use and no reputation. This can occur both by virtue of the signs themselves or by the way in which the signs are used and presented. Moreover, even where trademark rights have been acquired through registration, such trademarks are used: this post-acquisition use also forms the context of any likelihood of confusion.

Similarly, how rights have been acquired does not affect the assessment of the liability to mislead the consumer. On the other hand, some degree of reputation would normally be required if a consumer is to be provoked into error in a purchase.

Moreover, having regard to its wording, context and aim, Article 14.3 of Regulation No. 2081/92 is premised on there being a distinction between confusing and misleading use.

(b) The likelihood of confusion and the liability to mislead the consumer may need to be assessed at several stages.

An initial assessment must be made as at the date of application for registration of a trademark. Further, this assessment should be informed—in accordance with a WTO Member's law—by the evidentiary presumption of a likelihood of confusion required to be granted to the owner of a registered trademark for use of an identical sign for identical goods under TRIPS Article 16.1. Where the second application relates to the registration of a GI, the initial assessment must be made as at the date of application for registration of the GI, again informed by the evidentiary presumption required to be granted to the owner of a registered trademark.

Subsequently, an assessment can be made at the time of use. An assessment at this time typically considers not only the later sign, but the nature of its use. It may be that the sign in and of itself would not result in a likelihood of confusion or be liable to mislead the consumer, but that over time the manner in which the sign is presented and used would have one or other of those outcomes.

The rights required to be granted under TRIPS Article 16.1 do not limit the rights of the owner of a registered trademark to be able to prevent confusing use of a sign. Those rights extend to all such use, and include use of an identical sign for identical goods (presumed to be confusing), of a misleading sign, or of a sign intended to deceive. Further, those rights apply both at the time of the initial application for registration of a later trademark or GI and at later stages of use, including in the case of changed circumstances which would result in a likelihood of confusion.

(c) The reputation and renown and the length of time a trademark has been used are not necessarily relevant to the assessment of a likelihood of confusion.

TRIPS Article 16.1 states that a likelihood of confusion is to be presumed in the case of use of an identical sign for an identical good. Clearly, reputation and renown and the length of time a trademark has been used are not relevant in such a situation.

Of course, in reality, the likelihood of confusion is a continuum. Where there is extensive use, reputation and/or renown and the signs are similar, these are relevant factors. However, it is possible to find that confusion is likely even though there is very little use and very little reputation and no renown. Equally, it is possible that renown can lessen the likelihood of confusion. Discerning consumers in a market where significant care in purchasing is the norm—for example, when purchasing a vehicle—would normally be more aware of slight differences in a sign.

On the other hand, where the assessment concerns whether a sign would be liable to <u>mislead</u> the consumer (as is required by Article 14.3 of Regulation No. 2081/92 in respect of an EC-defined GI), such factors as reputation, renown and extent of use would normally be highly relevant.

149. What are the differences between "confusion" and "misleads" as used in Articles 16.1 and 22.2 of the TRIPS Agreement, respectively? Do they have any bearing on the misleading standard under Article 14(3) of Regulation (EC) No. 2081/92? ***USA, AUS, EC***

73. Having regard to customary rules of interpretation:

- the ordinary meanings of "confusion" include "embarrassment," "perplexity," "disorder," and "the quality of being confused, indistinct or obscure;"[44] and

- the ordinary meanings of "misleading" are "[t]hat leads someone astray, that causes error; imprecise, confusing, deceptive."[45]

[44] *OED*, Vol.1, page 478.

74. "Confusion" in the sense of TRIPS Article 16.1 is use which would cause perplexity or bewilderment on the part of the consumer as to the source undertaking of the good. In other words, "confusion" concerns use which would cause the consumer to wonder about the source undertaking of the good.[46]

75. On the other hand, although "misleading" might in some contexts be synonymous with "confus*[ing]*," the wording of TRIPS Article 22.2—use which misleads the public as to the geographical origin of the good—makes clear that the ordinary meaning of "misleading" in the context of that provision is use which "leads someone astray or that causes error." In other words, misleading use in the sense of TRIPS Article 22.2 is use which positively provokes an error on the part of a consumer as to the geographical origin of the good.[47]

76. The wording, context and aim of Article 14.3 of Regulation No. 2081/92 confirm that "misleading" in the sense of Article 14.3 is similar to the meaning of "misleading" in the sense of TRIPS Article 22.2. Article 14.3 of the Regulation refers to a situation where "registration is liable to mislead the consumer as to the true identity of the product." In other words, "misleading" is used in the sense of Article 14.3 of causing the consumer to mistake the true identity of the product.

77. Indeed, the words "confusion" and "misleading" have been used throughout Regulation No. 2081/92 in the same sense as they have been used in TRIPS Articles 16.1 and 22.2. The word "confusion" is used in Articles 6.6, 7.5(b), 12.2, 12b.3 and 12d.3 of the Regulation in the sense of wondering about the source of the good. On the other hand, the word "misleading" is used throughout the Regulation—in Articles 3.2, 6.6, 13.1(c), 13.1(d) and 14.3—in the sense of an action which positively provokes an error on the part of a consumer.

78. Further, this distinction is shown even more clearly in the French version of the Regulation.[48] For every occurrence of "confusion" in the English version, the word "confusion" is used in the French version. On the other hand, for every occurrence of "mislead" or "misleading" in the English version of the Regulation, the French version uses the language: "induire le [public/consommateur] en erreur quant à la veritable origine du produit" (Articles 3.2, 13.1(d) and 14.3); "donne à penser à tort au public que les produits sont originaires d'un autre territoire" (Article 6.6); "induire en erreur les consommateurs" (Article 6.6); and "fallacieuse quant à la provenance, l'origine" (Article 13.1(c)).

79. Thus, notwithstanding EC arguments that Article 14.3 of Regulation No. 2081/92 would permit the registration of an EC-defined GI to be refused on the basis of a likelihood of confusion,[49] such an interpretation would not be sustainable having regard to the rules of interpretation of EC law. The word "misleading" in Article 14.3 of the Regulation establishes a stricter evidentiary standard than "confusion" as "confusion" is used elsewhere in the Regulation, in the same way that the word "misleading" in TRIPS Article 22.2 establishes a stricter evidentiary standard than the word "confusion" in TRIPS Article 16.1.

150. The United States refers to the possibility of informing "consumers about the origin of a product and its characteristics through the use of descriptive terms in a non-trademark sense without affirmatively confusing the consumer about the source of goods" (US response to Panel question No. 75(b)). Would the addition of such a requirement in Article 14 of Regulation (EC) No. 2081/92 in respect of either prior trademarks, later geographical indications, or both, satisfy the requirements of Article 16.1 of the TRIPS Agreement in the view of the United States? Or does the United States object to any later protection of a geographical indication that is confusingly similar to a prior trademark? ***USA***

---

45 *OED*, Vol.1, page 1791.

46 Australia's Written Rebuttal Submission, paragraph 104.

47 *Ibid.*

48 Common Exhibit COMP-1.c.

49 See, for example, the EC's Second Written Submission, paragraph 285.

151. Please comment on the suggestion that Article 24.3 of the TRIPS Agreement was inserted in the draft text in November 1991 to make it clear that the exceptions provisions in Section 3 of Part II could not be used as a justification for diminishing a Member's pre-existing protection of GIs. ***USA, AUS, EC***

80. As in the case of Question 147 above, Australia is not in a position to comment in these dispute settlement proceedings on the proposition set out in this question.

81. Again as in the case of Question 147 above, Australia notes the findings of the Appellate Body that "[t]he duty of a treaty interpreter is to examine the words of the treaty to determine the intentions of the parties."[50] *(emphasis added)*

152. If a Member is obliged to diminish the pre-existing protection of GIs in order to allow trademark owners to exercise their rights under Article 16.1 as against GIs, does that obligation not arise under Article 16.1 rather than "[i]n implementing this Section," as used in Article 24.3? ***EC***

153. Without prejudice to the EC's view that a GI confusingly similar to a trademark will not be registered, if one were registered nevertheless, in what way would this exception be "limited"? In particular, could the rights of the GI owner be limited in such a way as to minimize the likelihood of confusion? ***EC***

154. What, specifically, are "the legitimate interests of the owner of the trademark and of third parties" within the meaning of Article 17? How can legitimate interests be "taken into account" under Article 17 where they conflict with other relevant interests? ***USA, AUS, EC***

82. As set out in TRIPS Article 15.1, the purpose of a trademark is to distinguish the goods or services of one undertaking from those of other undertakings. A trademark serves to identify the source of a good or service, thus enabling consumers to be informed of the quality of that good or service having regard to its source. Therein lies the economic value of the trademark to its owner.

83. It is a legitimate interest of a trademark owner to maintain the economic value of the private property right in the trademark by maintaining the trademark's capacity to distinguish the owner's goods from the goods of others. A trademark owner does this through the exclusive right to prevent confusingly similar or identical use of a sign for similar or identical goods or services required to be granted to that trademark owner by a WTO Member under TRIPS Article 16.1. Any dilution of this capability damages the legitimate interest of the trademark owner. Confusing or misleading use of a sign may deprive the trademark owner of income. Moreover, confusing or misleading use of a sign may also result in a diminution of the reputation of a trademark if the infringing use involves goods or services of lesser quality. TRIPS Article 17 permits uses of signs as an exception to TRIPS Article 16.1 only where there is a small diminution of the capacity to distinguish a trademark owner's goods or services from those of other undertakings.[51]

84. Third parties within the meaning of TRIPS Article 17 would normally include consumers and other traders. Consumers have a legitimate interest in being able to purchase products they intended to purchase rather than products of which they have no knowledge. Other traders have a legitimate interest in being able to use signs that they need to use in order to describe or present their goods or services in the marketplace. Thus, TRIPS Article 17 expressly refers to fair use of descriptive terms. It is important to note, however, that "fair use of descriptive terms" does not encompass all use of a sign or class of descriptive terms: the use of the word "fair" expressly limits the manner in which a "descriptive term" may be used as an exception.

85. The legitimate interests of trademark owners can be "take[n] account of" within the meaning of TRIPS Article 17 by ensuring that such owners are able to prevent use that undermines the economic value of the trademark right. In particular, the legitimate interests of trademark owners require that they be able to prevent

[50] *India – Patents*, paragraph 45.

[51] Australia's Written Rebuttal Submission, paragraphs 121-127.

use that undermines the capacity of the sign to serve as a trademark and to prevent use that undermines the capacity of the sign to distinguish the goods or services of the owner from those of other undertakings. "Fair use of descriptive terms" cannot include use which does not take account of these legitimate interests of trademark owners.

86. The legitimate interests of others can be "take[n] account of" within the meaning of TRIPS Article 17 by ensuring that consumers are not given cause to wonder about the source of a good or service and that other traders are able to use terms they need to use to describe or present their goods or services. The latter requirement does not, however, mean that other traders are able to use a sign freely in the face of an existing trademark. It must be seen in terms of the manner in which other traders need to use the sign at issue. It is reasonable and fair for people to be able to use their actual address, or to be able to say "made in Australia." On the other hand, it is not reasonable or fair to use a term in a way that has a signifying function, rather than a purely descriptive one, if that use undermines the capacity of a trademark to function as a trademark, thus undermining its economic value. This is true even if the term has some descriptive connotation. Thus, TRIPS Article 17 balances the requirement of providing other traders with the terms they need to use with the requirement of ensuring that a trademark is able to distinguish the goods or services of one undertaking from those of other undertakings.

155. Does an exception to the exclusive right in Article 16.1 presuppose a certain degree of confusion? Does "fair use of descriptive terms" within the meaning of Article 17 include the use of a trademark to indicate source? ***USA, AUS***

87. TRIPS Article 17 permits a WTO Member to provide "limited exceptions"—or small diminutions—to the rights required to be granted under TRIPS Article 16.1.[52] Within those confines, an exception to the scope of the rights required to be conferred under TRIPS Article 16.1 presupposes the possibility of a minimal degree of confusion.

88. Further, and in any case, the essence of a TRIPS-defined GI—of which EC-defined GIs are generally a sub-set—is that it indicates a causative connection between a particular geographic origin and the nature, reputation or some other characteristic of the product. If a TRIPS-defined GI were purely descriptive, there would not be any need—or indeed basis—for an intellectual property right, and thus for Section 3, Part II, of the TRIPS Agreement.[53]

89. In relation to the second question above, an indication of source within the meaning of the Paris Convention describes the geographic origin of the product. Consistent with the express terms of TRIPS Article 15.1, a trademark does not do this: rather, it functions as a means of distinguishing the goods or services of one undertaking from those of other undertakings.

90. It is possible for a trademark to denote source as a secondary effect. Consider, for example, a hypothetical trademark "Sydney Monarch." Such a trademark could be distinctive for a whole range of goods or services, but consumers would normally assume some connection with Sydney. Certainly, "Sydney" is an indication of source and should not be used in a way to mislead. However, it would not be true to say that the whole trademark "Sydney Monarch" was being used primarily either as an indication of source (within the meaning of the Paris Convention) or as a descriptive term. Rather, the trademark must be taken as a whole and would be seen as functioning to distinguish the goods of one undertaking from those of others.

91. Equally, if there was already a trademark "Monarch" for similar or identical goods or services, a decision to allow the use of "Sydney Monarch" as a trademark (on the pretext that it was descriptive) would contravene each of the tests of TRIPS Article 17. It would not constitute a limited exception, because it would attack the essential distinguishing feature of the trademark "Monarch," thus undermining its economic value.

[52] Australia's Written Rebuttal Submission, paragraphs 121-127.

[53] Australia's Second Oral Statement, paragraphs 31-36.

Nor would allowing "Sydney Monarch" to be used in this context constitute "fair use of a descriptive term:" it reproduces the essential distinguishing feature of another trademark. Thus, although the word "Sydney" in such a trademark may have a geographic connotation, its use is not fundamentally as a descriptive term, and allowing use of such a trademark would not take account of the legitimate interests of the owner of the trademark "Monarch" and of third parties.

92. Trademarks are not merely descriptive, and cannot be considered "descriptive terms" within the meaning of TRIPS Article 17. In the same way, and for the same reasons, use of a GI cannot be said to be merely use of an indication of source within the meaning of the Paris Convention or to be use of a descriptive term within the meaning of TRIPS Article 17.

156. Why do the requirements in Article 17 differ from those in Articles 13, 26.2 and 30 of the TRIPS Agreement? How should their interpretation reflect those differences? ***USA, AUS, EC***

93. Australia notes that the nature of IP rights other than trademarks and GIs has not been the subject of detailed consideration in this dispute. Moreover, it is the EC that has argued that the differences in language between TRIPS Articles 13, 17 26.2 and 30 have significance. The EC therefore has the burden of proof in establishing a *prima facie* case to this effect, which Australia submits it has not done. However, should the Panel consider that the EC has met its burden of proof, Australia submits the following comments.

94. The differences in the texts of TRIPS Articles 13 concerning copyright and related rights, 17 concerning trademarks, 26.2 concerning industrial designs and 30 concerning patents reflect differences in the nature of each of those rights. Rights concerning copyright material include rights in relation to authoring, copying, using, adapting, arranging, altering and importing.[54] Rights concerning industrial designs include rights in relation to making, selling or importing.[55] Rights concerning patents include rights in relation to making, using, offering for sale, selling and/or importing.

95. The most immediate difference between the texts of the four provisions is that TRIPS Articles 13, 26.2 and 30 refer to "limitations or exceptions" or "limited exceptions" that do not "conflict with [a/the] normal exploitation" of the protected right or "unreasonably prejudice" the legitimate interests of concerned parties. Clearly, an exception must relate to the nature of the right. "Exploitation" is relevantly defined as the action or practice of utilising or taking advantage of something for one's own ends.[56] The word "exploitation" was clearly intended to reflect the broad nature of the rights required to be granted in relation to copyright, industrial designs and patents. Having regard to the ordinary meanings of the words,[57] "unreasonably prejudice" should be considered in the sense of exceptions that unfairly affect the interests of concerned parties. Again, the words clearly reflect the broad nature of the rights required to be granted in relation to those other IP rights.

96. Under the TRIPS Agreement, however, a trademark does not attract the same spectrum of rights as those other categories of IP rights: it attracts only the exclusive right to prevent confusingly similar or identical use for similar or identical goods. "Use" is relevantly defined—having regard to the context of Section 2, Part II, of the TRIPS Agreement generally and of TRIPS Article 15.1 in particular—in terms of the purpose served by the thing used.[58] A trademark is used for the purpose of distinguishing the goods or services of one

[54] Articles 9-15 of the Berne Convention.

[55] TRIPS Article 26.1.

[56] *OED*, Vol.1, pages 888 and 889, definitions of "exploit" and "exploitation" respectively.

[57] *OED*, Vol.2, relevantly defines "unreasonably" and "unreasonable" in the sense of "going beyond what is reasonably or equitable (page 3503) and "prejudice" as "[h]arm or injury to a person or thing that may result from a judgement or action, esp. one in which his or her rights are disregarded."

[58] *OED*, Vol.2, page 3531, definition of "use" as a noun, section IV.

undertaking from those of other undertakings. A trademark may be used for that purpose in respect of a very few or a very large number of goods or services emanating from a single undertaking.[59]

97. Thus, the nature of the right required to be granted by the TRIPS Agreement in respect of a trademark is very different to the other rights. Moreover, the provisions of TRIPS Article 17 need to be interpreted having full regard to the nature of the right actually accorded to a trademark. Thus, any exception must be limited. For example, "use of descriptive terms" must be "fair" having regard to the nature of the right required to be granted by Article 16.1. The legitimate interest of a trademark owner clearly includes the ability to use the sign as a trademark—that is, that the sign be able to distinguish the owner's goods or services from those of other undertakings. To this end, a small level of confusingly similar use of a sign could only be justified in situations where the legitimate interests of the trademark owner and of other parties could not reasonably be met in any other way.

98. Nonetheless, TRIPS Article 17 shares a common structure and purpose with TRIPS Articles 13, 26.2 and 30 and should be interpreted accordingly.[60] Each allows a WTO Member to provide limited exceptions—that is, small diminutions—to the particular rights required to be conferred for each category of IP right, while providing that those exceptions not undermine the essential nature of the IP right and give due weight to legitimate competing interests. The wording of TRIPS Article 17 differs from those of the analogous provisions for other categories of IP rights in recognition of the differing nature of a trademark right. However, those differences do not change the essential similarities of the provision. In particular, it is not consistent with TRIPS Article 17 to allow exceptions that are neither limited nor fair, or which fundamentally obviate the ability of a trademark to distinguish the goods or services of one undertaking from those of other undertakings.

157. The United States alleges that the EC does not provide legal means required under Article 22 of the TRIPS Agreement (see United States first written submission, paras 177-178; US rebuttal, para. 213). Do you claim that the EC fails to provide a legal means to prevent uses of indications in accordance with Article 22.2 because of alleged inadequacies in Regulation (EC) No. 2081/92 alone? Or do you allege that measures outside the Panel's terms of reference are also inadequate to fulfil that obligation? If the latter, on what evidence do you rely? ***USA***

158. The Panel notes the United States' submission that the Panel should find that "the EC GI Regulation" is inconsistent with Articles 16.1 and 22.2 of the TRIPS Agreement (US rebuttal, paras 166 and 217, respectively). However, why would it be appropriate to conclude that <u>a single measure</u>, rather than a <u>Member</u>, fails to comply with each obligation? If the EC or its member States adopted other measures which complied with Articles 16.1 and 22.2, could they fill the gaps in the alleged inconsistencies in Regulation (EC) No. 2081/92? ***USA***

159. May protection for designations of origin and geographical indications now be afforded in the EC <u>only</u> within the framework laid down by Regulation (EC) No. 2081/92? To what extent does the EC implement its obligations under Article 22.2 of the TRIPS Agreement through Regulation (EC) No. 2081/92 and to what extent through other measures (see EC first written submission, paras 433 and 434)? Are the other measures cited by the EC alone sufficient to fulfil its obligations under Article 22.2? ***EC***

[59] Australia notes too that differences in the nature of the various categories of IP rights are reflected as well in the varying nature of the provisions of the TRIPS Agreement concerning compulsory licensing of IP rights. TRIPS Article 21 expressly prohibits compulsory licensing of trademarks, while TRIPS Article 31 recognises the possibility in respect of patents. The TRIPS Agreement is silent on the issue, however, in respect of copyright and industrial designs, as well as in respect of GIs.

[60] See Australia's Written Rebuttal Submission, paragraphs 118-127.

160. To what extent does the EC implement its obligations under Article 22.2 of the TRIPS Agreement through Regulation (EC) No. 2081/92 and to what extent through other measures? Does the EC believe that the complainants should prove a negative, i.e. that no legal means required under Article 22.2 are available? Can a respondent simply argue that other measures, outside the Panel's terms of reference, fulfil an obligation, without proof of how those other measures fulfil that obligation? ***EC***

161. Australia refers to Article10bis(1) of the Paris Convention, "as incorporated by TRIPS Article 2.1" (Australia's first written submission, para. 75, also para. 268) and also submits that "Paris Article 10bis.1 deals with the issue of unfair competition, which is not otherwise dealt with in the TRIPS Agreement except 'in respect of geographical indications' in TRIPS Article 22.2" (response to Panel question No. 82). Please clarify whether Australia seeks a finding that the alleged inconsistency with Article 10bis is a violation of Article 2.1 or 22.2 of the TRIPS Agreement or both. ***AUS***

99. Australia makes two distinct claims involving Paris Article 10*bis*. Firstly, Australia claims that—in respect of the registration of an EC-defined GI—the EC measure diminishes the legal protection for trademarks, contrary to the EC's obligation pursuant to TRIPS Article 2.1 to comply with Paris Article 10*bis*. Secondly, Australia claims that—in respect of the registration of an EC-defined GI—the EC does not provide the legal means for interested parties to prevent use which constitutes an act of unfair competition within the meaning of Paris Article 10*bis*, contrary to TRIPS Article 22.2.

100. Australia confirms that it seeks distinct findings in respect of each of these claims.

162. How did Australia's reference to Article 24.5 of the TRIPS Agreement in its request for establishment of a panel put the EC on notice that Australia challenged Regulation (EC) No. 2081/92 in respect of Article 24.5 in conjunction with Article 4 of the Paris Convention (1967) as incorporated by Article 2.1 of the TRIPS Agreement? In Australia's view, to what extent could a respondent begin preparing its defence of this claim without knowing that it was based on the right of priority? ***AUS***

101. In accordance with TRIPS Article 24.5, the EC has an express obligation not to prejudice the eligibility for registration of a trademark on the basis that the trademark is identical with, or similar to, a GI. Separately, the EC has an express obligation to comply with the requirement of Paris Article 4 in respect of the right of priority for applications for registration of a trademark in accordance with TRIPS Article 2.1.

102. Australia's panel establishment request set out that Australia's claim was that the EC measure diminishes the legal protection for trademarks under the TRIPS Agreement, contrary *inter alia* to Article 24.5 of that Agreement. The obligation not to prejudice eligibility for the registration of a trademark is plain, even on a cursory reading of TRIPS Article 24.5. Given the express obligation on the EC to comply with Paris Article 4, it was clear that non-compliance with that provision would constitute prejudice to the eligibility for registration of a trademark, thereby diminishing the legal protection for trademarks under the TRIPS Agreement and thus falling within the terms of Australia's panel establishment request.

103. Australia remains conscious that DSU Article 6.2 requires that a complaining party's request for the establishment of a panel *inter alia* identify the specific measures at issue and provide a brief summary of the legal basis of the complaint sufficient to present the problem clearly, to enable the responding party to being preparing its defence. At the same time, however, Australia is of the view that some caution is needed in interpreting and applying this provision: it should not be interpreted and applied in such a way as to require that a complaining party have fully developed its argumentation for a dispute—in effect, to have prepared its first written submission—before lodging its panel establishment request.

163. The Panel takes note of Australia's and the EC's respective views on the applicability of Article 70.1 of the TRIPS Agreement to individual GI registrations (Australia's response to Panel question No. 90; EC rebuttal, para. 202). On 31 December 1995, at what stage of the procedure under the former Article 15 were the GIs later registered under Article 17? Did any individual GIs registered under Article 6 have an objection period that expired prior to 1 January 1996? ***EC***

164. In what way are the objectives and principles set out in Articles 7 and 8 of the TRIPS Agreement, and the considerations recited in the first paragraph of its preamble, relevant to the interpretation of the provisions of that agreement at issue in this dispute? ***USA, AUS, EC***

104. As Australia explained in response to question No. 103 above, the TRIPS Agreement provides that a WTO Member may incorporate legitimate public policy objectives and principles within its national measures to implement an IP right. However, once a WTO Member adopts measures for the protection of a category of IP right, those measures apply equally to its own nationals and to the nationals of all other WTO Members.

ANNEX A-9

COMMENTS OF AUSTRALIA ON THE EUROPEAN COMMUNITIES' REPLIES TO QUESTIONS POSED BY THE PANEL AND TO QUESTIONS POSED BY AUSTRALIA FOLLOWING THE SECOND SUBSTANTIVE MEETING

(2 September 2004)

INTRODUCTION

1. These comments supplement Australia's claims and arguments in this dispute, addressing issues newly raised in the EC's responses to questions from the Panel following the second substantive meeting with the parties. They should be read together with Australia's earlier submissions, statements and responses to questions. Australia's silence in relation to any issue raised in the EC's responses to questions should not be construed as signifying Australian agreement to the arguments made by the EC.

2. In its responses to the Questions from the Panel following the second substantive meeting, the EC has submitted as Exhibits extracts from the trademark legislation of a number of WTO Members not party to this dispute.[1] The EC itself has said: "... the objective assessment of the facts requires establishing the meaning that the act will normally have within the legal order of the WTO Member in question. This means that the interpretation should be guided by the rules of interpretation customary in the legal order of such member, and taking account of the legal context of the measure in the domestic law of the Member."[2]

3. Notwithstanding that the EC has raised the provisions of other WTO Members' trademark law and thus has the burden of proof—according to its own argument—of establishing the meaning of those provisions within the legal order of the WTO Member in question, it has not made any attempt to do so.

4. Australia requests that those Exhibits be excluded from the Panel's consideration of the EC's responses to Question Nos. 139 and 153.[3]

QUESTION NO. 96

5. The EC states that "... where an institution has adopted rules which are not legally binding, it may nevertheless not depart from such rules without giving the reasons which have led it to do so."[4] The implicit—but nevertheless unambiguous—premise of that statement is that an institution may depart from the rules it has adopted provided it gives reasons for doing so.

6. Australia notes too that the Guide to Regulation No. 2081/92 is in the nature of administrative guidance.[5] In *India – Patents*, the Appellate Body examined an analogous situation involving administrative

---

[1] Exhibits EC-93 (re Canada's Trade Mark Law), EC-94 (re Hong Kong's Trade Marks Ordinance), EC-95 (re India's Trade Marks Act), EC96 re New Zealand's Trade Marks Act), EC-97 (re Singapore's Trade Marks Act), EC-98 (re South Africa's Trade Marks Law), EC-104 (re Japan's Trademark Law), EC-105 (re Romania's Trade Marks Act) and EC-106 (re Iceland's Trade Marks Act).
In addition, Australia has already requested the exclusion of Exhibit EC-80 (re New Zealand legislation)—as well as Exhibit EC-73 (re Canadian legislation)—in its Second Oral Statement, paragraph 104. If, however, the Panel were to find that Exhibit EC-80 was admissible as an Exhibit to the EC's Second Oral Statement, Australia requests that—in any case—it be excluded from the Panel's consideration of the EC's answer to Question No. 153 as the EC has not established the meaning of that provision within New Zealand's legal order.

[2] EC Response to Question No. 1, paragraph 6.

[3] See also Australia's comment on the EC Responses to Question Nos. 137 and 139 below for a clear example of the dangers of considering provisions of other WTO Members' trademark laws in isolation.

[4] EC Response to Question No. 96, paragraph 9.

[5] The EC itself refers to the relevant section of the guide as "providing guidance to interested governments and applicants" (EC Response to Question No. 96, paragraph 7).

instructions that seemed to contradict mandatory provisions of the relevant legislation. However, the Appellate Body in that dispute was not persuaded that administrative instructions would prevail over the contradictory mandatory provisions of the Act at issue in the event of a legal challenge nor, as a consequence, that the administrative instructions provided a sound legal basis to preserve the IP rights at issue.[6]

7. Further, Australia notes that should the Panel consider that related implementing and enforcement actions adopted on or after 2 October 2003 are outside the Panel's terms of reference as argued by the EC, so too would be the Guide and the EC's 16 June 2004 TRIPS Council statement.

QUESTION NO. 97

8. Australia notes that the EC's response confusingly combines the situation concerning GIs as defined in TRIPS Article 22.1 ("TRIPS-defined GIs") with the situation concerning "designations of origin" and "geographical indications" as defined in Article 2.2 of Regulation No. 2081/92 ("EC-defined GIs").

9. Further, the EC's response fails to make clear the full context of its initial response to the question from New Zealand. The paragraph quoted by the EC was preceded by the following paragraphs:

> Council Regulation 2081/92/EEC sets out the procedure for the registration of geographical indications in the Community territory. The procedure contained in Articles 5, 6 and 7 is as follows:
>
> 1. A group of producers must submit a detailed application for registration to the competent authority of the Member State, in accordance with the conditions specified in the Regulation.
>
> 2. If the application is considered to be in conformity with the Regulation, it shall be referred to the Community authorities, who will verify that the conditions of the Regulation have been formally satisfied and will publish the application in the *Official Journal* to allow other parties the opportunity to raise objections.
>
> 3. If an objection is raised, the final decision on registration is taken by the Commission and Member States.

10. Thus, the reference to "the procedure followed by Community producers as outlined above ..., in accordance with the principle of national treatment" in the paragraph cited by the EC was in fact the procedure to be followed by "producers" of other WTO Members who wished to register an EC-defined GI from within the EC. The "principle of national treatment" referred to by the EC was in fact a reference to the principle of national treatment of <u>nationals</u> under the TRIPS Agreement.

11. Moreover, as the response to the question from India cited by the EC[7] makes clear:

> ... in general, conditions provided in Article 12 of *[the Regulation]* are only required when a bilateral agreement is concluded between the EC and a WTO Member. This means that it only occurs when two parties voluntarily wish higher level of protection ("ex officio") than this provided under the TRIPS Agreement. ...

---

[6] *India – Patent Protection for Pharmaceutical and Agricultural Chemical Products*, Report of the Appellate Body, WT/DS50/AB/R, paragraphs 69-70.

[7] EC Response to Question No. 97, paragraph 14.

12. In other words, the EC stated that if another WTO Member wishes to benefit from the higher level of protection made available under Regulation No. 2081/92, a bilateral agreement addressing the conditions provided for in Article 12 of the Regulation is required.

13. Further, the EC's response again fails to make clear the full context of the subsequent response to the follow up question from India. The extract quoted by the EC was preceded by the following statements:

> As a preliminary remark, the Community would like to underline that the protection of geographical indications foreseen in Article 22.2 of the TRIPS agreement is provided for in Council Directive 79/112/EEC *[concerning food labelling]* and Council Directive 84/450/EEC *[concerning misleading advertising]*. …
>
> The protection foreseen by these provisions under Community law and Member States' law is applicable to any WTO Member citizen without discrimination.
>
> (a) On the one hand, Council Regulation 2081/92/EEC provides for:
>
> (i) the "reputation" which is attributable to the name (geographical origin) (Article 2); and
>
> (ii) the product (which is covered by the geographical name) which complies with a specification (Article 4).
>
> This means that the Regulation has established a difference between the designation and the product.
>
> Both conditions are cumulative.
>
> On the other hand, to comply with a specification, it is important to guarantee a continuity and homogeneity of the product's characteristics which are necessary as a reference for the inspection bodies. This is essential also for the consumer.
>
> As a matter of fact, a geographical indication requires anyway that the product which is covered presents a defined description. If these conditions must be complied with by the producers established in the EC to obtain an *[EC-defined GI]*, they must also be complied with by the third country nationals, should they wish to obtain the same protection.
>
> (b) …

14. Thus, the clear message being conveyed by the EC when the full answer is considered in context was that Regulation No. 2081/92 was not concerned with the protection of TRIPS-defined GIs in the sense of TRIPS Article 22.2. Rather, the Regulation deals with products which have both a reputation and a product specification in the sense of Article 4 of the Regulation. If another WTO Member wishes to take advantage of the higher level of protection potentially available for such products under the Regulation, then that WTO Member must have in place a system equivalent to that in place in the EC, including in relation to the product specification and the inspection structure. The EC could not allow any other system because, if it did, EC producers would be discriminated against.

QUESTION NO. 101

15. The EC says it "does not consider the present case requires any comparison between nationals."[8] The EC has not sought to explain how its view is consistent with the express requirement of TRIPS Article 1.3, which provides that "Members shall accord the treatment provided for in this Agreement to the nationals of other Members."

QUESTION NOS. 103 AND 113

16. In responding to Question No. 103, the EC does not accept the express recognition of the applicability of the basic principles of GATT 1994 in the preamble to the TRIPS Agreement, or the finding of the Appellate Body in *US – Section 211 Appropriations Act* relating to the usefulness of the jurisprudence on GATT Article III:4 in interpreting the TRIPS national treatment obligation.[9] Yet in responding to Question No. 113, the EC nonetheless relies on a basic GATT principle and GATT jurisprudence in support of its argument.

17. Further, the EC now seems to be suggesting that GATT Article XX(d) could also excuse a breach of the TRIPS Agreement.[10] However, the EC has not even attempted to meet its burden of proof in relation to the potential applicability of GATT Article XX(d) to the TRIPS Agreement.

QUESTION NO. 106

18. The examples referred to by the EC at paragraph 54 both involve EC nationals.

QUESTION NOS. 114 AND 116

19. In responding to Question No. 116, the EC says[11] that because:

(a) all WTO Members are obliged to provide protection to TRIPS-defined GIs in accordance with TRIPS Article 22;

(b) the EC is not obliged to provide protection to TRIPS-defined GIs not protected in their country of origin in accordance with TRIPS Article 24.9; and

(c) any WTO Member should be able to state whether it protects a "GI" for which protection is sought in the EC;

then a WTO Member cannot:

(1) argue that it does not have "authority" to state whether a "GI" is protected in its territory; and

(2) at the same time claim that this "GI" should be protected in the EC.

20. Australia has not claimed in this dispute that the EC is not in compliance with its obligations under the TRIPS Agreement because a TRIPS-defined GI cannot be registered under Regulation No. 2081/92 if that TRIPS-defined GI does not also meet the definition of an EC-defined GI under Article 2.2 of that Regulation.

---

8 EC Response to Question No. 101, paragraph 22.

9 *United States – Section 211 Omnibus Appropriations Act of 1998*, Report of the Appellate Body, WT/DS176/AB/R, paragraph 242.

10 EC Response to Question No. 103, paragraph 36.

11 EC Response to Question No. 116(a), paragraph 74.

From the beginning, Australia has expressly recognised the EC's right to implement in its law more extensive protection for GIs than is required to be provided by the TRIPS Agreement.[12]

21. On the other hand, and in its responses to both Question Nos. 114 and 116, the EC totally ignores the implications of a situation where protection of an EC-defined GI is provided by other means, for example, through registration of a term as a certification trademark.[13] In addition, the EC argument that a WTO Member cannot say that it does not have authority to state whether a GI is protected within its territory[14] overlooks that—as in the Australian legal order, for example—in the absence of an explicit court judgment, no government agency might be able to be empowered to provide, with the necessary degree of assurance, the certification required by the EC.

22. Further, the EC's responses make clear that—one way or another—the EC will seek to ensure that its views on the registration and protection of EC-defined GIs prevail. The EC has conceded that the reciprocity and equivalence conditions of Article 12.1 of Regulation No. 2081/92 would be inconsistent with the EC's obligations under GATT Article III:4 if those conditions were to be applied to other WTO Members.[15] Yet having made that concession, the EC now seeks to have the Panel find that the EC can nonetheless require other WTO Members to participate in the implementation of a system of registration and protection of EC-defined GIs, even though that system is contrary to the EC's obligations pursuant to the WTO Agreement. The EC argues that if other WTO Members don't "cooperate"—in effect, adopt the EC's system—it is their own fault that nationals of those other WTO Members can't access the benefits of the EC's system.

23. At the same time, the EC does not explain how such a view might be in harmony with the express recognition in the preambular clauses of the TRIPS Agreement that IP rights are private rights. Nor does it explain how its requirements are consistent with the requirements of TRIPS Article 1.3 to "accord the treatment provided for in this Agreement to the nationals of other Members."

24. Further, notwithstanding its arguments that any interpretation of the TRIPS Agreement must consider the relevance of GATT Article XX(d),[16] the EC has not acknowledged the finding of the Appellate Body in *US – Shrimp* that a measure being applied in a way that "*require[d]* other WTO Members to adopt a regulatory program that *[was]* not merely *comparable*, but rather *essentially the same*" *(emphases in original)* was not justifiable under the chapeau of GATT Article XX.[17]

QUESTION NO. 122

25. The EC's attempts to make a conceptual distinction for the purpose of interpreting the mandatory labelling requirement in Article 12.2 of Regulation No 2081/92 between the origin of a product eligible to bear an EC-defined GI and the product itself are flawed. The origin of a product eligible to bear an EC-defined GI is inextricably linked to that product by virtue of the definitions set out in Article 2.2 of the Regulation. In addition, the notion of origin involves a product; a geographical location only becomes a geographical origin if there is something that has been produced in it. Australia submits therefore that when talking about the origin of a product (as opposed to simply a geographical location) eligible to bear an EC-defined GI, the EC's argument[18] that the labelling requirement applies to the origin of the product and not the product itself, does not make sense.

---

[12] Australia's First Written Submission, paragraph 4, second bullet point.

[13] See, for example, Australia's First Written Submission, paragraph 198.

[14] EC Response to Question No. 116(a), paragraph 74.

[15] EC Response to Question No. 94.

[16] See, for example, EC Response to Question No. 103, paragraph 36.

[17] *United States – Import Prohibition of Certain Shrimp and Shrimp Products*, Report of the Appellate Body, WT/DS58/AB/R, paragraph 163, referred to in Australia's Second Oral Statement, paragraph 70.

[18] First Written Submission of the EC, paragraph 451.

26. Australia would also like to point out that, contrary to the EC's suggestion,[19] Australia has not argued that the origin of a product is a product characteristic within the meaning of the definition of "technical regulation" in the TBT Agreement. Rather, Australia argues that the mandatory labelling requirement in Article 12.2 of Regulation No. 2081/92 for the specific products envisaged by that Article meets the definition of a "technical regulation" pursuant to the TBT Agreement.

QUESTION NO. 124

27. The EC's statement[20] that GATT Article IX:1[21] "exempts origin marking from national treatment obligations" is incorrect. GATT Article IX:1 imposes a positive obligation of no less favourable treatment vis-à-vis products of third countries (MFN obligation). It is silent on the issue of origin marking requirements in relation to the national treatment obligation in GATT Article III:4.

QUESTION NO. 125

28. The EC suggests that the Panel might have to consider whether GATT Article XX would be applicable within the context of the TBT Agreement. In Australia's view, had the drafters wished for the TBT Agreement to contain a direct reference to GATT Article XX, they would have included one. Instead, TBT Article 2.2, read in light of the preamble, which reproduces closely the chapeau of GATT Article XX, contains a similar "necessity" test to that in GATT Article XX.

29. In any case, these issues are outside the parameters of what the Panel needs to consider in determining whether Article 12.2 of Regulation No. 2081/92 accords less favourable treatment, contrary to TBT Article 2.1, to imported like products bearing—or eligible to bear—an EC-defined GI. Moreover, the EC bears the burden of proof for establishing any significance of GATT Article XX in the context of the TBT Agreement. The EC has not, however, met its burden: indeed, it has not presented any supporting arguments.

QUESTION NO. 134

30. Australia assumes that the first sentence of paragraph 119 of the EC's response was intended to read "any claim under the provision of Articles 5-9 TBT Agreement concerning inspection structures" as, as the EC itself says, Australia has made a claim under TBT Article 2.2.

31. Further, notwithstanding the EC's statement that "the essential question which the Panel needs to decide is whether these structures by themselves are a technical regulation,"[22] Australia's claim in relation to the inspection structure requirement is that Article 4, in particular Article 4.2(g), and Article 10 read together constitute the technical regulation.[23] Australia has not made a claim in relation to the inspection structure requirements of Article 10 of Regulation No. 2081/92 in isolation.

QUESTION NO. 135

32. Once again, the EC invokes its right—pursuant to TRIPS Article 1.1—to implement in its law more extensive protection than it is required by the TRIPS Agreement to grant,[24] without also acknowledging the conditionality of that right: "provided that such protection does not contravene the provisions of this Agreement."[25] Thus, even if Regulation No. 2081/92 might be a measure not inconsistent with the provisions of

[19] EC Response to Question No. 122, paragraph 91.

[20] EC Response to Question No. 124, paragraph 99.

[21] Australia assumes that the reference to Article XI:I is a typographical error.

[22] EC Response to Question No. 134, paragraph 119.

[23] Australia's First Written Submission, paragraphs 209-224.

[24] EC Response to Question No. 135, paragraph 130.

[25] Australia's Second Oral Statement, paragraph 108.

the GATT 1994 within the meaning of GATT Article XX(d)—an issue Australia does not concede—it would only be so to the extent that it was fully consistent with the EC's obligations pursuant to the TRIPS Agreement.

QUESTION NO. 136

33. Once again, the EC ignores the implications of a situation where protection of an EC-defined GI is provided through registration of a term as a certification trademark.[26]

34. And once again, the EC's response makes clear that—one way or another—the EC will seek to ensure that its views on the registration and protection of EC-defined GIs will prevail.

35. In the context of this question, the EC seeks to have the Panel accept the view that—when a WTO Member has a system of registration and protection similar to that of the EC—there is no problem. According to the EC's logic, a requirement for another WTO Member government to verify an application for registration of an EC-defined GI "would not seem burdensome" and "the impact on exports ... should be extremely small."[27] That the requirement—even in those situations—would not meet the necessity test of GATT Article XX(d) seems to have been overlooked by the EC.

36. Equally, the EC seeks to have the Panel accept the view that—when a WTO Member does not have a system of registration and protection similar to that of the EC—it is reasonable for the EC to seek to compel another WTO Member to act as a sub-national unit of the EC in any case.[28] In addition, the EC argument that other WTO Member governments must verify that applications comply with the requirements of Regulation No. 2081/92[29] overlooks that—as in the Australian legal order, for example—in the absence of an explicit court judgment, no government agency might be able to be empowered to provide, with the necessary degree of assurance, the certification required by the EC.

37. Even if <u>requiring</u> the cooperation of another WTO Member may be "an issue of timing and sequencing of the application process" in some cases,[30] the provisions of Regulation No. 2081/92 do not provide for the possibility that an applicant could demonstrate compliance with the requirements of Articles 2.2, 4 and 10 directly, for example, on the basis of registration as a certification trademark. Compelling the involvement of the government of another WTO Member in the application process does not meet the necessity test of GATT Article XX(d).[31]

38. The EC now says that "... Regulation 2081/92 does not require unnecessary levels of staff to be maintained throughout the year" and that "... since it is presumably not economic to establish and wind down an inspection body every year, in such a case it would be reasonable to entrust the function of inspections to a body which also carries out tasks other than inspections under Regulation 2081/92."[32] Article 10.3 of the Regulation expressly provides: "[d]esignated inspection authorities and/or approved private body <u>must</u> ... <u>have permanently at their disposal the qualified staff and resources</u> necessary to carry out inspection of agricultural products and foodstuffs bearing a protected name" *(emphasis added)*. Australia contests that Article 10.3—having regard to its wording, context and aims—may properly be interpreted in the manner now suggested by

---

26 See Australia's comment above on the EC Response to Question No. 116.

27 EC Response to Question No. 136(a), paragraph 134.

28 EC Response to Question No. 136(b), paragraphs 135-138.

29 EC Response to Question No. 136(a), paragraph 131.

30 EC Response to Question No. 136(c), paragraph 141.

31 Australia's Second Oral Statement, paragraphs 67-70.

32 EC Response to Question No. 136(f), paragraph 155.

the EC. Article 10.3 is clearly premised on the inspections being undertaken by an autonomous agency, the staff of which are permanently available to that agency.[33]

39. In any case, Australia's claim in relation to the EC's requirement to have in place in all circumstances an EC-mandated inspection structure has been made under TBT Article 2.2. In that context, the EC has not met its burden of proof to show that GATT Article XX(d) has any significance in the context of the TBT Agreement.[34]

40. Finally, Australia recalls that the EC has invoked GATT Article XX(d) only in respect of Australia's claim concerning the requirement that an application for the registration of an imported product be submitted through the government of the WTO Member in which the relevant geographical area is located. Moreover, the EC has not, at any stage in this dispute, attempted to establish a *prima facie* case that such a requirement is consistent with the chapeau of GATT Article XX.[35]

QUESTION NOS. 137 AND 139

41. The EC argues that Australia is requesting "a remedy against the confusing use of a registered geographical indications *[sic]* which many Members do not provide with respect to the infringement of a registered trademark by a latter *[sic]* registered trademark."[36] The EC points to the trademark provisions of a number of other WTO Members which it has set out in its response to Question No. 139.[37] Australia has already requested that the Panel exclude from consideration the provisions of other WTO Members' trademark laws.[38]

42. The inherent dangers of considering provisions of other WTO Members' trademark laws in isolation from their full context are amply demonstrated in the case of the Australian Trade Marks Act provision cited by the EC (section 122(1)(e)). That provision—when considered in the full context of the Act and in the legal order of Australia—excepts certain actions from infringing an earlier trademark right only where the prior right holder expressly consented to the co-existence, for example, in a licensing arrangement, or where the prior right holder failed to take the extensive opportunities provided under Australia law to prevent the acquisition of the later trademark right.

43. Notwithstanding the EC's assertions to the contrary, Australia is not requesting a remedy which it does not provide with respect to the infringement of a trademark right under its own domestic law.

QUESTION NOS. 143, 146, 148 AND 149

44. The EC's responses are premised on "confusion" and "mislead" being synonymous terms in the context of both TRIPS Article 16.1 and Article 14.3 of Regulation No. 2081/92. In support of its contention that "confusion" in the sense of TRIPS Article 16.1 is synonymous with "mislead" in the sense of Article 14.3 of the Regulation, the EC points to a WIPO publication. Further, the EC appears to be arguing that "mislead" in the context of TRIPS Article 22.2 is also synonymous with "confusion" in the sense of TRIPS Article 16.1.[39]

45. A WIPO publication cannot be determinative of the issue. Notwithstanding the obvious synergy between matters which fall within the purview of WIPO and matters covered by the TRIPS Agreement, the

---

[33] The implicit premise of Article 10.3 of Regulation No. 2081/92 is confirmed by the EC's subsequent statement (in paragraph 155) that: "... in such a case it would be reasonable to entrust the function of inspections to a body which also carries out tasks other than inspections under Regulation 2081/92."

[34] See Australia's comment above on the EC Response to Question No. 125.

[35] Australia's Second Oral Statement, paragraphs 66-70.

[36] EC Response to Question No. 137, paragraph 163.

[37] EC Response to Question No. 139, paragraph 170 and footnote 68.

[38] See Introduction above.

[39] EC Response to Question No. 149.

interpretation of the TRIPS Agreement is expressly reserved to the Ministerial Conference and the General Conference of the WTO in accordance with Article IX.2 of the WTO Agreement. Moreover, the WIPO publication quoted by the EC is not inconsistent with Australia's view of the proper interpretation of the notion of "a likelihood of confusion." As Australia has previously said, in reality the likelihood of confusion is a continuum.[40] The publication quoted by the EC simply defines one point in the continuum. It does not equate confusing to misleading, but rather suggests that if a particular use is confusing, it is likely also to mislead. Further, Australia notes that other WIPO publications explain the notion of "a likelihood of confusion" in different ways, for example:

> ... The basic test is whether the allegedly similar mark resembles the protected mark in such a way as to be *likely to confuse the average consumer* as to the source of the goods or services or as to the connection between the concurrent users of the similar marks, taking into account all the circumstances of the particular case. In other words, a mark is generally considered "confusingly similar" if it is so similar to the protected mark that a substantial number of average consumers are likely to be confused or misled as to the source of the goods or services sold under the similar mark, in the belief that such products or services originate from the same enterprise which owns and/or uses the protected mark (or that there is a "connection" between such enterprise and the enterprise using the similar mark, as, for example, in the case of a licensor and a licensee).[41]

46. Finally, as the Appellate Body found in *India – Patents*, "[t]he duty of a treaty interpreter is to examine the words of the treaty to determine the intentions of the parties"[42] *(emphasis added)*. It is the actual words of the TRIPS Agreement that determine a WTO Member's obligations pursuant to that Agreement.

QUESTION NO. 145

47. The EC says—in the context of a WTO Member enacting a measure permitted by TRIPS Article 15.2 to prevent registration of a GI as a trademark—that "if a trademark has been registered, or applied for, before either of the two dates mentioned in Article 24.5, the Member in question would be prohibited by virtue of Article 24.5 from invalidating that trademark on the ground that such trademark is identical or similar to a geographical indication."[43]

48. Australia notes, however, that the two dates mentioned in TRIPS Article 24.5 do not apply to a good faith application for, or registration of, a trademark.[44] In accordance with the normal usage of punctuation in the English language, had it been intended that the two dates apply to a trademark application or registration, there would have been a comma between the words "good faith" and "either." In the absence of a comma, the two dates are applicable only "where rights to a trademark have been acquired through use." Moreover, Australia notes that the French text of TRIPS Article 24.5 similarly does not apply the two dates to a trademark application or registration.

---

[40] Australian Response to Question No.148, paragraph 72(c).

[41] *The Role of Industrial Property in the Protection of Consumers*, WIPO, Geneva 1983, Exhibit AUS-20, paragraph 41.

[42] *India – Patent Protection for Pharmaceutical and Agricultural Chemical Products*, Report of the Appellate Body, WT/DS50/AB/R, paragraph 45.

[43] EC Response to Question No.145, paragraph 199, first bullet point.

[44] While section 61 of the Australian Trade Marks Act applies those two dates to applications for and registrations of trademarks also, it does so in the context of a higher level of protection of TRIPS-defined GIs consistent with the provisions of TRIPS Articles 1.1 and 15.2. Australia retains the right—consistent with its obligations under other provisions of the TRIPS Agreements—to diminish that level of protection if, with the passage of time, the application of that provision were to be shown to be unfair consistent with the principle of territoriality.

QUESTION NO. 148

49. The EC refers to Australia's request to register the term "Australia" as a GI under the Australia-EU bilateral agreement concerning trade in wine.[45] Australia notes that the bilateral agreement does not form part of the measure at issue in the dispute initiated by Australia. In any case, the term "Australia" on its own could not *per se* function as a trademark as it could not distinguish the goods or services of one undertaking from those of other undertakings.

QUESTION NO. 153

50. Once again, the inherent danger of considering provisions of other WTO Members' trademark laws in isolation from their full context is demonstrated in the case of the Australian Trade Marks Act provision cited by the EC (section 122(1)(b)(i)). That provision excepts certain actions from infringing an earlier trademark right where a sign is used to indicate the geographical origin of a good or service. When considered in the full context of the Act and in the legal order of Australia, and as previously explained by Australia[46] and notwithstanding the EC's seeming unwillingness to accept that explanation,[47] a sign used to indicate geographical origin within the meaning of section 122(1)(b)(i) does not include either a TRIPS- or an EC-defined GI. It simply means a sign to indicate a place from which the goods or services originate, irrespective of whether that place may also be a geographical indication within the meaning of TRIPS Article 22.1. Thus, for example, the right holders of the certification trademark "Stilton" in Australia could not automatically prevent good faith use of the phrase "Made in Stilton" to indicate the place from which another product originated.

51. Australia has already requested that the Panel exclude from consideration the provisions of other WTO Members' trademark laws.[48]

52. Finally, and in any case, the ECJ case law referred to by the EC[49] as supposedly supporting its view of the proper interpretation of an indication of geographical origin in the Community Trademark Directive and Regulation in fact concerned use of such an indication <u>as a trademark</u>. Further, it concerned a term that was expressly recognised as a geographic source of natural mineral waters under the relevant EC Directive. Moreover, Australia notes that the Explanatory Memorandum prepared by the European Commission concerning the proposed changes to Regulation No. 2081/92 which were eventually adopted in Regulation No. 692/2003 expressly referred to the problems revealed by applications for registration of mineral and spring waters as EC-defined GIs.[50] The case law referred to by the EC does not substantiate its argument.

QUESTION NOS. 159 AND 160 AND AUSTRALIAN QUESTION NOS. 2 AND 3

53. At no stage in this dispute has Australia claimed that "the additional protection afforded to registered geographical indications under Article 13.1 of Regulation No. 2081/92 ... could be 'an act of unfair competition'."[51] Rather, Australia has claimed that—in respect of the registration of an EC-defined GI—the EC does not provide the legal means for interested parties to prevent misleading use or use which constitutes an act of unfair competition within the meaning of Paris Article 10*bis*.[52]

---

[45] EC Response to Question No. 148, paragraph 220.

[46] Australian Response to Question No. 80 from the Panel.

[47] EC's Second Written Submission, footnote 219.

[48] See Introduction above.

[49] EC Response to Question No. 153, paragraphs 242-244 and footnote 99.

[50] *Proposal for a Council Regulation amending Regulation (EEC) No 2081/92 on the protection of geographical indications and designations of origin for agricultural products and foodstuffs*, Brussels, 15.03.2002, 2002/0066 (CNS), Exhibit US-20.

[51] EC Response to Question No. 159, paragraph 263.

[52] Australia's First Written Submission, paragraphs 154-155, and Australia's Second Oral Statement, paragraphs 80-85.

54. Further, Australia notes the inherent contradiction in the EC's responses to Question Nos. 159 and 160. On the one hand, it acknowledges that Australia has not claimed that "the other measures cited by the EC"—in its First Written Submission and in the responses of the EC and its Member States in the context of the TRIPS Article 24.2 review by the TRIPS Council—"are not sufficient to protect geographical indications that have not been registered Regulation 2081/92."[53] On the other hand, it argues that because Australia has not mentioned those other measures in the context of its claim in respect of the registration of an EC-defined GI—even though Australia does not contest the issue of whether those other measures are sufficient to meet the EC's obligations in respect of TRIPS-defined GIs more generally—Australia has improperly shifted the burden of proof to the EC.[54] The consequence of the EC's argument is that Australia should have analysed and demonstrated a negative, notwithstanding an express and unambiguous obligation on the EC to make available the legal means to prevent the uses set out in TRIPS Article 22.2.

55. Moreover, and in any case, Australia notes that the EC Responses to Australian Question Nos. 2 and 3 do not show that—in respect of the registration of an EC-defined GI—the EC assures access:

- by a trademark right holder to "appropriate legal remedies effectively to repress" acts of unfair competition within the meaning of Paris Article 10*bis* as required by Paris Article 10*ter*(1);

- by "interested parties" to "legal means ... to prevent" misleading use or use which constitutes an act of unfair competition within the meaning of TRIPS Article 22.2; or

- by a trademark right holder to "civil judicial procedures concerning the enforcement of any intellectual property right covered by this Agreement" within the meaning of TRIPS Article 42.

56. Firstly, "the Codorníu judgment" [55] did not address the rights of trademark holders generally. (It concerned a single trademark right holder who was able to show that its trademark registration pre-dated registration of the term at issue by some 65 years.[56]) Moreover, the EC admits this when it asserts that there are some circumstances where a trademark right holder will be able to show it is individually concerned.[57] Equally, this suggests that there will be circumstances where a trademark right holder will not meet this threshold requirement.

57. Secondly, even if—in accordance with the ECJ's judgement in *Commission of the European Communities v Jégo-Quéré & Cie SA*[58]—a trademark right holder or, in the context of TRIPS Article 22.2, an interested party were always able to initiate action to ensure review of the legality of acts of the institutions, "review of the legality of the acts of the institutions" does not necessarily extend to the exercise of rights required to have been granted to such persons pursuant to the EC's obligations under the TRIPS Agreement. "... [T]he WTO agreements are not in principle among the rules in the light of which the Court is to review the legality of measures adopted by the Community institutions ...."[59] Unless an obligation arising from the EC's membership of the WTO Agreement is incorporated in an act of an institution, a trademark right holder or interested party is not assured of the rights required to have been granted to that person under the TRIPS Agreement. Thus, for example, where the EC's breach of an obligation is by omission—such as in the case of

---

[53] EC Response to Question No. 159, paragraph 263.

[54] EC Response to Question No. 160, paragraph 265.

[55] *Codorníu SA v Council of the European Union* (Case C-309/89), [1994] ECRI-01853, Exhibit EC-111.

[56] The Codorníu judgment, paragraphs 21-22. Australia also notes that the term at issue—"cremant"—was considered to "*[refer]* primarily not to the origin but the method of manufacture" of the wine (paragraph 28).

[57] "... this does not mean necessarily that a trademark holder will never be able to show that it is individually concerned. In particular, a trademark holder could seek to rely on the Codorníu case law"[57] *(emphases added)*: EC Response to Australian Question No. 2, paragraph 9.

[58] Case C-263/02 P, Exhibit EC-113.

[59] See Australian Response to Question No. 6, referring to the Biret judgment, Exhibit AUS-07.

TRIPS Article 22.2 in respect of the registration of an EC-defined GI—there is no act of an institution whose legality can be reviewed.

58. Thirdly, notwithstanding the EC's argument that "Regulation 2081/92 and the other measures mentioned in its first submission apply cumulatively,"[60] Australia notes again that the other measures are specifically excluded (Article 142—now Article 159—of the Community Trademark Regulation) from applying to, or would not prevail over, the relevant rights granted by Regulation No. 2081/92.[61]

59. In *Canada – Patent Term*, the Appellate Body examined a claim concerning the obligation pursuant to TRIPS Article 33 to grant a term of patent protection of not less than 20 years. The Appellate Body found: "]t]he opportunity to obtain a twenty-year term must be a readily discernible and specific right ...."[62] The current situation is analogous: the opportunity to exercise the rights required to be granted to a person pursuant to the EC's obligations under the TRIPS Agreement must be readily discernible and specific.[63]

QUESTION NO. 163

60. The EC once again says: "... as a matter of fact, no objection procedure applied under the simplified procedure regardless of whether EC residents or foreign residents were involved."[64] However, the EC has also said: "[b]ecause of the concerns raised <u>by the owners of the trademarks</u> at issue and by some Member States, the EC institutions could not reach a decision with respect to *[the "Bayerisches Bier"]* name as of the time of the adoption of Regulation 1107/96"[65] *(emphasis added)*.

61. Clearly, there was indeed a mechanism available to at least some EC trademark right holders to make their objections known in the context of the decision-making process provided by Article 15 of Regulation No. 2081/92. How else could "the owners of the trademarks at issue" have made their concerns known?

62. Australia maintains its claim that a right of objection was available to persons resident or established in an EC Member State that was not available to other WTO Member nationals in respect of the registration of more than 480 EC-defined GIs under the simplified registration process, contrary to Articles 1.1 and 1.3, 2.1 ("incorporating" Article 2 of Paris Convention) and 3.1 of the TRIPS Agreement.[66] Further, and contrary to the EC's assertion,[67] the registrations of those 480 EC-defined GIs are encompassed by Australia's claims under TRIPS Articles 16.1,[68] 2.1 ("incorporating" Paris Articles 10*bis*[69] and 10*ter*[70]), 24.5,[71] 42,[72] 41.2,[73] 41.3[74] and 41.1,[75] as well as under TRIPS Articles 1.1 and 2.1.[76]

---

[60] EC Response to Question No. 159, paragraph 258. Australia understands the EC's reference to "other measures mentioned in its first submission" to mean those measures listed at paragraph 434 of that submission.

[61] See, for example, Australia's Written Rebuttal Submission, paragraphs 146 and 171.

[62] *Canada – Term of Patent Protection*, Report of the Appellate Body, paragraph 92

[63] See Australia's Closing Statement to the second meeting with the Panel.

[64] EC Response to Question No. 163, paragraph 271.

[65] EC Response to Question No. 144, paragraph 195.

[66] Australia's First Written Submission, paragraphs 190-194.

[67] EC Response to Question No. 163, paragraph 270.

[68] Australia's First Written Submission, paragraphs 88-107.

[69] Australia's First Written Submission, paragraphs 113-115.

[70] Australia's First Written Submission, paragraphs 115-118.

[71] Australia's First Written Submission, paragraphs 81-87.

[72] Australia's First Written Submission, paragraphs 119-125.

[73] Australia's First Written Submission, paragraphs 126-140.

[74] Australia's First Written Submission, paragraphs 141-144.

[75] Australia's First Written Submission, paragraphs 145-148.

[76] Australia's First Written Submission, paragraphs 151-152.

63. TRIPS Article 70.1 does not place the registrations of the 480 EC-defined GIs pursuant to Regulation No. 1107/96 outside the temporal scope of the TRIPS Agreement for any purpose. That any inconsistencies with the EC's obligations pursuant to the TRIPS Agreement may have arisen from acts of omission, or because the proposed list of names to be registered was already under consideration by a decision-making authority as at 1 January 1996 (the date of application of the TRIPS Agreement for the EC), does not excuse the EC from complying with any of its obligations pursuant to the TRIPS Agreements in respect of acts of registration of EC-defined GIs which took place after that date.

AUSTRALIAN QUESTION NOS. 2 AND 3

64. See Australia's comment on EC Responses to Question Nos. 159 and 160 above.

ANNEX A-10

COMMENTS OF AUSTRALIA ON THE REPLY OF THE WORLD INTELLECTUAL PROPERTY ORGANIZATION TO THE PANEL'S LETTER OF 9 JULY 2004

(28 September 2004)

Through this letter, I am conveying Australia's comments on the reply of the World Intellectual Property Organization ("WIPO") to the Panel's request of 9 July 2004. In that letter, the Panel requested factual information available to WIPO relevant to the interpretation of Article 2 of the Paris Convention for the Protection of Industrial Property (1967), and of any other provisions concerning the eligibility of natural or legal persons for protection under that Convention.

As a preliminary matter, Australia notes that none of the parties to the dispute have argued that interpretation of Paris Article 2 in accordance with the customary rules of interpretation of public international law, which have guided Australia's interpretive approach in this dispute, leaves the meaning of Paris Article 2 ambiguous or obscure or leads to a result which is manifestly absurd or unreasonable. Consequently, the Panel is not obliged to have recourse to supplementary means of interpretation, such as those contained in the records provided by WIPO.

Nevertheless, the records confirm that the interpretation of the Convention put forward by Australia in this dispute is fully consistent with the intent of the negotiators of the Convention.

The records show a clear intent on the part of the negotiators that Paris Article 2 should not permit any condition of domicile or establishment to be imposed on the nationals of other countries of the Union for the enjoyment, as regards the protection of industrial property, of the advantages that a country grants to its own nationals.

In addition, the Report of the Drafting Commission at the 1925 Revision Conference at The Hague expressly states, in relation to the provision that is now Article 2(2) of the Paris Convention, that:

> ... we put at the beginning *[of this sentence]* 'however' to show that this *[condition]* concerns a restriction on the rule, expressed in indent 1, of the reservation of fulfilment of the conditions and formalities imposed on nationals.

Accordingly, the records explicitly confirm the view of the relationship between paragraphs 1 and 2 of Article 2 of the Paris Convention put forward by Australia in its First Oral Statement (at paragraph 16) and in its Written Rebuttal Submission (at paragraphs 26-28). Paris Article 2(2) defines the boundary of permissible action in relation to conditions of domicile or establishment for nationals of other WTO Members in the application of the national treatment obligation established by Paris Article 2(1), and is an integral aspect of the national treatment obligation established by the Paris Convention with which a WTO Member is required to comply. Consequently, Paris Article 2(2) was properly raised in Australia's panel establishment request.

TABLES

TABLE I
OVERVIEW OF DISPUTE SETTLEMENT ACTIVITY

The following is a summary of dispute settlement activity from March 8 – 15, 2005. Included are any requests for consultation, requests for a panel, DSB establishment of a panel, circulation, appeal or adoption of a Panel Report, circulation or adoption of an Appellate Body Report, or termination/withdrawal of a panel request or consultations.

WT/DS174 European Communities – Protection of Trademarks and Geographical Indications for Agricultural Products and Foodstuffs
Complainant: United States
Action: On 15 March 2005, the Panel issued its Report.

WT/DS268 United States – Sunset Reviews of Anti-Dumping Measures on Oil Country Tubular Goods from Argentina
Complainant: Argentina
Action: On 15 March 2005, Argentina requested arbitration under Article 21.3(c) of the DSU.

WT/DS285 United States – Measures Affecting the Cross-Border Supply of Gambling and Betting Services
Complainant: Antigua and Barbuda
On 11 March 2005, the Appellate Body notified the DSB it would not be able to circulate its Report by Tuesday, 8 March 2005. It estimated that the Report will be circulated to WTO Members no later than Thursday, 7 April 2005.

WT/DS290 European Communities – Protection of Trademarks and Geographical Indications for Agricultural Products and Foodstuffs
Complainant: Australia
Action: On 15 March 2005, the Panel issued its Report.

TABLE II

MEMBER COUNTRIES – INVOLVEMENT IN DISPUTES

The following chart identifies Member Countries and their involvement in Disputes through March 15, 2005. Two columns adjacent to country listings list dispute numbers where the Member Country identified was either Complainant or Respondent. The total number of disputes in which a Member Country has participated in total, as a Complainant, and as a Respondent is listed in brackets.

MEMBER COUNTRY	COMPLAINANT		RESPONDENT	
Albania {0}	{0}		{0}	
Angola {0}	{0}		{0}	
Antigua and Barbuda {1}	{1}		{0}	
Argentina {24}	{9}	WT/DS35 WT/DS111 WT/DS207 WT/DS226 WT/DS263 WT/DS268 WT/DS272 WT/DS278 WT/DS293	{15}	WT/DS56 WT/DS77 WT/DS121 WT/DS123 WT/DS145 WT/DS155 WT/DS157 WT/DS164 WT/DS171 WT/DS189 WT/DS190 WT/DS196 WT/DS233 WT/DS238 WT/DS241
Armenia {0}	{0}		{0}	
Australia {16}	{7}	WT/DS35 WT/DS91 WT/DS169 WT/DS178 WT/DS217 WT/DS265 WT/DS290	{9}	WT/DS18 WT/DS21 WT/DS57 WT/DS106 WT/DS119 WT/DS126 WT/DS270 WT/DS271 WT/DS287
Austria {0}	{0}		{0}	
Bahrain {0}	{0}		{0}	
Bangladesh {1}	{1}	WT/DS306	{0}	

TABLE II – COUNTRIES

MEMBER COUNTRY	COMPLAINANT		RESPONDENT	
Barbados {0}	{0}		{0}	
Belgium {3}	{0}		{3}	WT/DS80 WT/DS127 WT/DS209
Belize {0}	{0}		{0}	
Benin {0}	{0}		{0}	
Bolivia {0}	{0}		{0}	
Botswana {0}	{0}		{0}	
Brazil {34}	{22}	WT/DS4 WT/DS69 WT/DS70 WT/DS71 WT/DS112 WT/DS154 WT/DS190 WT/DS208 WT/DS209 WT/DS216 WT/DS217 WT/DS218 WT/DS219 WT/DS222 WT/DS224 WT/DS239 WT/DS241 WT/DS250 WT/DS259 WT/DS266 WT/DS267 WT/DS269	{12}	WT/DS22 WT/DS30 WT/DS46 WT/DS51 WT/DS52 WT/DS65 WT/DS81 WT/DS116 WT/DS183 WT/DS197 WT/DS199 WT/DS229
Brunei Darussalem {0}	{0}		{0}	
Bulgaria {0}	{0}		{0}	
Burkina Faso {0}	{0}		{0}	
Burundi {0}	{0}		{0}	
Cambodia {0}	{0}		{0}	
Cameroon {0}	{0}		{0}	

MEMBER COUNTRY		COMPLAINANT		RESPONDENT
Canada {38}	{26}	WT/DS7 WT/DS9 WT/DS10 WT/DS18 WT/DS20 WT/DS35 WT/DS46 WT/DS48 WT/DS92 WT/DS114 WT/DS135 WT/DS137 WT/DS144 WT/DS153 WT/DS167 WT/DS180 WT/DS221 WT/DS234 WT/DS236 WT/DS247 WT/DS257 WT/DS264 WT/DS277 WT/DS292 WT/DS310 WT/DS311	{12}	WT/DS31 WT/DS70 WT/DS71 WT/DS103 WT/DS113 WT/DS117 WT/DS139 WT/DS142 WT/DS170 WT/DS222 WT/DS276 WT/DS321
Central African Republic {0}	{0}		{0}	
Chad {0}	{0}		{0}	
Chile {20}	{10}	WT/DS14 WT/DS97 WT/DS217 WT/DS227 WT/DS232 WT/DS238 WT/DS255 WT/DS261 WT/DS303 WT/DS326	{10}	WT/DS87 WT/DS109 WT/DS110 WT/DS193 WT/DS207 WT/DS220 WT/DS226 WT/DS228 WT/DS230 WT/DS278
China {2}	{1}	WT/DS252	{1}	WT/DS309
Colombia {5}	{4}	WT/DS78 WT/DS188 WT/DS228 WT/DS230	{1}	WT/DS181
Congo {0}	{0}		{0}	
Costa Rica {3}	{3}	WT/DS24 WT/DS185 WT/DS187	{0}	

TABLE II – COUNTRIES

MEMBER COUNTRY	**COMPLAINANT**		**RESPONDENT**	
Cotê d'Ivoire {0}	{0}		{0}	
Croatia {1}	{0}		{1}	WT/DS297
Cuba {0}	{0}		{0}	
Cyprus {0}	{0}		{0}	
Czech Republic {3}	{1}	WT/DS159	{2}	WT/DS148 WT/DS289
Democratic Republic of the Congo {0}	{0}		{0}	
Denmark {1}	{0}		{1}	WT/DS83
Djibouti {0}	{0}		{0}	
Dominica {0}	{0}		{0}	
Dominican Republic {2}	{0}		{2}	WT/DS300 WT/DS302
Ecuador {5}	{2}	WT/DS27 WT/DS237	{5}	WT/DS182 WT/DS191 WT/DS303
Egypt {4}	{0}		{4}	WT/DS205 WT/DS211 WT/DS305 WT/DS327
El Salvador {0}	{0}		{0}	
Estonia {0}	{0}		{0}	
European Communities {122}	{68}	WT/DS8 WT/DS15 WT/DS38 WT/DS39 WT/DS40 WT/DS42 WT/DS53 WT/DS54 WT/DS63 WT/DS66 WT/DS73 WT/DS75 WT/DS77 WT/DS79 WT/DS81 WT/DS85 WT/DS87 WT/DS88 WT/DS96 WT/DS98 WT/DS100 WT/DS107 WT/DS108	{54}	WT/DS7 WT/DS9 WT/DS12 WT/DS13 WT/DS14 WT/DS16 WT/DS17 WT/DS25 WT/DS26 WT/DS27 WT/DS48 WT/DS62 WT/DS69 WT/DS72 WT/DS104 WT/DS105 WT/DS114 WT/DS115 WT/DS124 WT/DS134 WT/DS135 WT/DS137 WT/DS140

MEMBER COUNTRY	COMPLAINANT	RESPONDENT
European Community (cont.)	WT/DS110 WT/DS116 WT/DS117 WT/DS118 WT/DS120 WT/DS121 WT/DS136 WT/DS138 WT/DS142 WT/DS145 WT/DS146 WT/DS147 WT/DS149 WT/DS150 WT/DS151 WT/DS152 WT/DS155 WT/DS157 WT/DS160 WT/DS165 WT/DS166 WT/DS176 WT/DS183 WT/DS186 WT/DS189 WT/DS193 WT/DS200 WT/DS212 WT/DS213 WT/DS214 WT/DS217 WT/DS225 WT/DS248 WT/DS262 WT/DS273 WT/DS279 WT/DS287 WT/DS294 WT/DS304 WT/DS314 WT/DS317 WT/DS319 WT/DS320 WT/DS321	WT/DS231 WT/DS141 WT/DS153 WT/DS154 WT/DS158 WT/DS172 WT/DS174 WT/DS209 WT/DS219 WT/DS223 WT/DS242 WT/DS246 WT/DS260 WT/DS263 WT/DS265 WT/DS266 WT/DS269 WT/DS283 WT/DS286 WT/DS290 WT/DS291 WT/DS292 WT/DS293 WT/DS299 WT/DS301 WT/DS307 WT/DS313 WT/DS315 WT/DS316 WT/DS326 WT/DS328
Fiji {0}	{0}	{0}
Finland {0}	{0}	{0}
France {2}	{0}	{2} WT/DS131 WT/DS173
Gabon {0}	{0}	{0}

TABLE II – COUNTRIES

MEMBER COUNTRY	COMPLAINANT		RESPONDENT	
Gambia {0}	{0}		{0}	
Georgia {0}	{0}		{0}	
Germany {0}	{0}		{0}	
Ghana {0}	{0}		{0}	
Greece {2}	{0}		{2}	WT/DS129 WT/DS125
Grenada {0}	{0}		{0}	
Guatemala {7}	{4}	WT/DS16 WT/DS27 WT/DS158 WT/DS220 WT/DS298	{2}	WT/DS60 WT/DS156
Guinea {0}	{0}		{0}	
Guinea Bissau {0}	{0}		{0}	
Guyana {0}	{0}		{0}	
Haiti {0}	{0}		{0}	
Honduras {6}	{6}	WT/DS16 WT/DS27 WT/DS158 WT/DS201 WT/DS300 WT/DS302	{0}	
Hong Kong, China {1}	{1}	WT/DS29	{0}	
Hungary {7}	{5}	WT/DS143 WT/DS148 WT/DS240 WT/DS256 WT/DS297	{2}	WT/DS35 WT/DS159
Iceland {0}	{0}		{0}	

MEMBER COUNTRY	COMPLAINANT		RESPONDENT	
India {33}	{16}	WT/DS19 WT/DS32 WT/DS33 WT/DS58 WT/DS34 WT/DS134 WT/DS140 WT/DS141 WT/DS168 WT/DS206 WT/DS217 WT/DS229 WT/DS233 WT/DS243 WT/DS246 WT/DS313	{17}	WT/DS50 WT/DS79 WT/DS90 WT/DS91 WT/DS92 WT/DS93 WT/DS94 WT/DS96 WT/DS120 WT/DS146 WT/DS149 WT/DS150 WT/DS175 WT/DS279 WT/DS304 WT/DS306 WT/DS318
Indonesia {7}	{3}	WT/DS123 WT/DS217 WT/DS312	{4}	WT/DS54 WT/DS55 WT/DS59 WT/DS64
Ireland {3}	{0}		{3}	WT/DS68 WT/DS82 WT/DS130
Israel {0}	{0}		{0}	
Italy {0}	{0}		{0}	
Jamaica {0}	{0}		{0}	
Japan {26}	{11}	WT/DS6 WT/DS51 WT/DS55 WT/DS64 WT/DS95 WT/DS139 WT/DS162 WT/DS184 WT/DS217 WT/DS244 WT/DS249 WT/DS322	{14}	WT/DS8 WT/DS10 WT/DS11 WT/DS15 WT/DS28 WT/DS42 WT/DS44 WT/DS45 WT/DS66 WT/DS73 WT/DS76 WT/DS147 WT/DS245 WT/DS323
Jordan {0}	{0}		{0}	
Kenya {0}	{0}		{0}	

MEMBER COUNTRY	COMPLAINANT		RESPONDENT	
Korea {25}	{13}	WT/DS89 WT/DS99 WT/DS179 WT/DS202 WT/DS215 WT/DS217 WT/DS251 WT/DS273 WT/DS296 WT/DS299 WT/DS301 WT/DS307 WT/DS323	{12}	WT/DS3 WT/DS5 WT/DS20 WT/DS40 WT/DS41 WT/DS75 WT/DS84 WT/DS98 WT/DS161 WT/DS163 WT/DS169 WT/DS312
Kuwait {0}	{0}		{0}	
Kyrgyz Republic {0}	{0}		{0}	
Latvia {0}	{0}		{0}	
Lesotho {0}	{0}		{0}	
Liechtenstein {0}	{0}		{0}	
Lithuania {0}	{0}		{0}	
Luxembourg {0}	{0}		{0}	
Macao, China {0}	{0}		{0}	
Macedonia	{0}		{0}	
Madagascar {0}	{0}		{0}	
Malawi {0}	{0}		{0}	
Malaysia {2}	{1}	WT/DS58	{1}	WT/DS1
Maldives {0}	{0}		{0}	
Mali {0}	{0}		{0}	
Malta {0}	{0}		{0}	
Mauritania {0}	{0}		{0}	
Mauritius {0}	{0}		{0}	

MEMBER COUNTRY	COMPLAINANT		RESPONDENT	
Mexico {26}	{15}	WT/DS16 WT/DS23 WT/DS27 WT/DS49 WT/DS60 WT/DS156 WT/DS158 WT/DS182 WT/DS191 WT/DS234 WT/DS280 WT/DS281 WT/DS282 WT/DS295 WT/DS325	{11}	WT/DS53 WT/DS101 WT/DS132 WT/DS203 WT/DS204 WT/DS216 WT/DS232 WT/DS284 WT/DS298 WT/DS308 WT/DS314
Moldova {0}	{0}		{0}	
Mongolia {0}	{0}		{0}	
Morocco {0}	{0}		{0}	
Mozambique {0}	{0}		{0}	
Myanmar {0}	{0}		{0}	
Namibia {0}	{0}		{0}	
Nepal {0}	{0}		{0}	
Netherlands/Netherlands Antilles {1}	{1}	WT/DS128	{0}	
New Zealand {6}	{6}	WT/DS35 WT/DS72 WT/DS93 WT/DS113 WT/DS177 WT/DS258	{0}	
Nicaragua {3}	{1}	WT/DS284	{2}	WT/DS188 WT/DS201
Niger {0}	{0}		{0}	
Nigeria {0}	{0}		{0}	
Norway {2}	{2}	WT/DS254 WT/DS328		{0}
Oman {0}	{0}		{0}	
Pakistan {5}	{2}	WT/DS58 WT/DS192 WT/DS327	{2}	WT/DS36 WT/DS107
Panama {2}	{2}	WT/DS105 WT/DS158	{0}	
Papua New Guinea {0}	{0}		{0}	

MEMBER COUNTRY	COMPLAINANT		RESPONDENT	
Paraguay {0}	{0}		{0}	
Peru {6}	{4}	WT/DS12 WT/DS227 WT/DS231 WT/DS272	{2}	WT/DS112 WT/DS255
Philippines {8}	{2}	WT/DS22 WT/DS61	{6}	WT/DS74 WT/DS102 WT/DS195 WT/DS215 WT/DS270 WT/DS271
Poland {4}	{3}	WT/DS122 WT/DS235 WT/DS289	{1}	WT/DS19
Portugal {1}	{0}		{1}	WT/DS37
Qatar {0}	{0}		{0}	
Romania {2}	{0}		{2}	WT/DS198 WT/DS240
Rwanda {0}	{0}		{0}	
Saint Kitts and Nevis {0}	{0}		{0}	
Saint Lucia {0}	{0}		{0}	
Saint Vincent and the Grenadines {0}	{0}		{0}	
Senegal {0}	{0}		{0}	
Sierra Leone {0}	{0}		{0}	
Singapore {1}	{1}	WT/DS1	{0}	
Slovak Republic {3}	{0}		{3}	WT/DS133 WT/DS143 WT/DS235
Slovenia {0}	{0}		{0}	
Solomon Islands {0}	{0}		{0}	
South Africa {2}	{0}		{2}	WT/DS168 WT/DS288
Spain {0}	{0}		{0}	
Sri Lanka {1}	{1}	WT/DS30	{0}	
Suriname {0}	{0}		{0}	
Swaziland {0}	{0}		{0}	
Sweden {1}	{0}		{1}	WT/DS86

MEMBER COUNTRY	COMPLAINANT		RESPONDENT	
Switzerland {4}	{4}	WT/DS94 WT/DS119 WT/DS133 WT/DS253	{0}	
Taiwan, Penghu, Kinmen, and Matsu {2} Separate Customs Territory of	{2}	WT/DS274 WT/DS318	{0}	
Tanzania {0}	{0}		{0}	
Thailand {12}	{11}	WT/DS17 WT/DS35 WT/DS47 WT/DS58 WT/DS181 WT/DS205 WT/DS217 WT/DS242 WT/DS283 WT/DS286 WT/DS324	{1}	WT/DS122
Togo {0}	{0}		{0}	
Trinidad and Tobago {2}	{0}		{2}	WT/DS185 WT/DS187
Tunisia {0}	{0}		{0}	
Turkey {9}	{2}	WT/DS211 WT/DS288	{7}	WT/DS29 WT/DS34 WT/DS43 WT/DS47 WT/DS208 WT/DS237 WT/DS256
Uganda {0}	{0}		{0}	
United Arab Emirates {0}	{0}		{0}	
United Kingdom {1}	{0}		{1}	WT/DS67
United States {168}	{79}	WT/DS3 WT/DS5 WT/DS11 WT/DS13 WT/DS16 WT/DS21 WT/DS26 WT/DS27 WT/DS28 WT/DS31 WT/DS35 WT/DS36 WT/DS37	{89}	WT/DS2 WT/DS4 WT/DS6 WT/DS24 WT/DS32 WT/DS33 WT/DS38 WT/DS39 WT/DS49 WT/DS58 WT/DS61 WT/DS63 WT/DS78

MEMBER COUNTRY	COMPLAINANT	RESPONDENT
United States (cont.)	WT/DS41	WT/DS85
	WT/DS43	WT/DS88
	WT/DS44	WT/DS89
	WT/DS45	WT/DS95
	WT/DS50	WT/DS97
	WT/DS52	WT/DS99
	WT/DS56	WT/DS100
	WT/DS57	WT/DS108
	WT/DS59	WT/DS111
	WT/DS62	WT/DS118
	WT/DS65	WT/DS136
	WT/DS67	WT/DS138
	WT/DS68	WT/DS144
	WT/DS74	WT/DS151
	WT/DS76	WT/DS152
	WT/DS80	WT/DS160
	WT/DS82	WT/DS162
	WT/DS83	WT/DS165
	WT/DS84	WT/DS166
	WT/DS86	WT/DS167
	WT/DS90	WT/DS176
	WT/DS101	WT/DS177
	WT/DS102	WT/DS178
	WT/DS103	WT/DS179
	WT/DS104	WT/DS180
	WT/DS106	WT/DS184
	WT/DS109	WT/DS186
	WT/DS115	WT/DS192
	WT/DS124	WT/DS194
	WT/DS125	WT/DS200
	WT/DS126	WT/DS202
	WT/DS127	WT/DS206
	WT/DS128	WT/DS212
	WT/DS129	WT/DS213
	WT/DS130	WT/DS214
	WT/DS131	WT/DS217
	WT/DS132	WT/DS218
	WT/DS158	WT/DS221
	WT/DS161	WT/DS224
	WT/DS163	WT/DS225
	WT/DS164	WT/DS234
	WT/DS170	WT/DS236
	WT/DS171	WT/DS239
	WT/DS172	WT/DS243
	WT/DS173	WT/DS244
	WT/DS174	WT/DS247
	WT/DS175	WT/DS248
	WT/DS195	WT/DS249
	WT/DS196	WT/DS250
	WT/DS197	WT/DS251
	WT/DS198	WT/DS252

MEMBER COUNTRY		COMPLAINANT		RESPONDENT
United States (cont.)		WT/DS199		WT/DS253
		WT/DS203		WT/DS254
		WT/DS204		WT/DS257
		WT/DS210		WT/DS258
		WT/DS223		WT/DS259
		WT/DS245		WT/DS262
		WT/DS260		WT/DS264
		WT/DS275		WT/DS267
		WT/DS276		WT/DS268
		WT/DS291		WT/DS274
		WT/DS305		WT/DS277
		WT/DS308		WT/DS280
		WT/DS309		WT/DS281
		WT/DS315		WT/DS282
		WT/DS316		WT/DS285
				WT/DS294
				WT/DS295
				WT/DS296
				WT/DS310
				WT/DS311
				WT/DS317
				WT/DS319
				WT/DS320
				WT/DS322
				WT/DS324
				WT/DS325
Uruguay {2}	{1}	WT/DS25	{1}	WT/DS261
Venezuela {3}	{1}	WT/DS2	{2}	WT/DS23
				WT/DS275
Zambia {0}	{0}		{0}	
Zimbabwe {0}	{0}		{0}	

TABLE III

TREATY PROVISIONS INTERPRETED

The following is a table of treaty provisions interpreted by the Dispute Settlement Decisions included within this volume. Treatment of the particular provision of the agreement will be found at the paragraph number indicated adjacent to the case citation.

GENERAL AGREEMENT ON TARIFFS AND TRADE

Article III – National Treatment

Paragraph 4 "treatment no less favourable"

WT/DS174/R European Communities – Trademarks and Geographical Indications – Complaint by the United States, 7.133, 7.136, 7.230

WT/DS290/R European Communities – Trademarks and Geographical Indications – Complaint by Australia, 7.183, 7.186, 7.266

Article XX – General Exceptions

Paragraph (d) "protection of patents, trademarks and copyrights"

WT/DS174/R European Communities – Trademarks and Geographical Indications – Complaint by the United States, 7.296

Paragraph (d) "to secure compliance"

WT/DS174/R European Communities – Trademarks and Geographical Indications – Complaint by the United States, 7.447

AGREEMENT ON TRADE-RELATED ASPECTS OF INTELLECTUAL PROPERTY RIGHTS

Article 1 – Nature and Scope of Obligations

Paragraph 4

WT/DS174/R European Communities – Trademarks and Geographical Indications – Complaint by the United States, 7.742-43

Footnote 1

WT/DS174/R European Communities – Trademarks and Geographical Indications – Complaint by the United States, 7.198

WT/DS290/R European Communities – Trademarks and Geographical Indications – Complaint by Australia, 7.234

Article 3 – National Treatment

Paragraph 1

WT/DS174/R European Communities – Trademarks and Geographical Indications – Complaint by the United States, 7.125, 7.148, 7.212, 7.413

WT/DS290/R European Communities – Trademarks and Geographical Indications – Complaint by Australia, 7.198, 7.248

Footnote 3

WT/DS174/R European Communities – Trademarks and Geographical Indications – Complaint by the United States, 7.329

WT/DS290/R European Communities – Trademarks and Geographical Indications – Complaint by Australia, 7.364

Article 4 – Most-Favoured Nation Treatment

WT/DS174/R European Communities – Trademarks and Geographical Indications – Complaint by the United States, 7.697

Article 8 – Principles

WT/DS174/R European Communities – Trademarks and Geographical Indications – Complaint by the United States, 7.209-210

WT/DS290/R European Communities – Trademarks and Geographical Indications – Complaint by Australia, 7.245-46

Part II – Standards Concerning the Availability, Scope and Use of Intellectual Property Rights

WT/DS174/R European Communities – Trademarks and Geographical Indications – Complaint by the United States, 7.598

WT/DS290/R European Communities – Trademarks and Geographical Indications – Complaint by Australia, 7.598

Article 16 – Rights Conferred

Paragraph 1

WT/DS174/R European Communities – Trademarks and Geographical Indications – Complaint by the United States, 7.602

WT/DS290/R European Communities – Trademarks and Geographical Indications – Complaint by Australia, 7.602

Article 17 – Exceptions

WT/DS174/R European Communities – Trademarks and Geographical Indications – Complaint by the United States, 7.647-48, 7.650, 7.662-64, 7.676-683

WT/DS290/R European Communities – Trademarks and Geographical Indications – Complaint by Australia, 7.647-48, 7.650, 7.662-64, 7.676-681

Article 22 – Protection of Geographical Indications

Paragraph 1

WT/DS174/R European Communities – Trademarks and Geographical Indications – Complaint by the United States, 7.682

WT/DS290/R European Communities – Trademarks and Geographical Indications – Complaint by Australia, 7.680

Paragraph 2

WT/DS174/R European Communities – Trademarks and Geographical Indications – Complaint by the United States, 7.742-43, 7.754

Article 24 – International Negotiations: Exceptions

Paragraph 5

WT/DS174/R European Communities – Trademarks and Geographical Indications – Complaint by the United States, 7.610, 7.615, 7.619

WT/DS290/R European Communities – Trademarks and Geographical Indications – Complaint by Australia, 7.39, 7.610, 7.615, 7.619

DISPUTE SETTLEMENT UNDERSTANDING

Article 6 – Panel Procedures

Paragraph 2 Request for Establishment

WT/DS174/R European Communities – Trademarks and Geographical Indications – Complaint by the United States, 7.2

WT/DS290/R European Communities – Trademarks and Geographical Indications – Complaint by Australia, 7.2

TABLE IV – BISD AND DISPUTE REFERENCES

The following table shows references to the Basic Instruments and Selected Documents (BISD), and GATT and WTO disputes made by panels and the Appellate Body in the reports in this volume. On the right is the location of the reference (noted by paragraph number) in the report.

WT/DS174/R; *European Communities – Protection of Trademarks and Geographical Indications for Agricultural Products and Foodstuffs – Complaint by the United States*

BISD	23S/127 *Income Tax Practices Maintained by Belgium*	*7.693*
BISD	36S/345 *United States Section 337 of the Tariff Act of 1930*	*7.183, 7.206, 7.227, 7.299, 7.494, 7.508*
BISD	37S/132 *European Economic Community – Regulation on Imports of Parts and Components*	*7.447*
BISD	41S/I/131 *United States Measures Affecting the Importation, Internal Sale and Use of Tobacco*	*7.706*
WTO DSD	WT/DS2/AB/R *United States – Standards for Reformulated and Conventional Gasoline*	*7.294, 7.443, 7.605*
WTO DSD	WT/DS8/AB/R *Japan – Taxes on Alcoholic Beverages*	*7.605*
WTO DSD	WT/DS18/AB/R *Australia – Measures Affecting Importation of Salmon*	*7.375*
WTO DSD	WT/DS26/AB/R, WT/DS48/AB/R *European Communities – Measures Concerning Meat and Meat Products (Hormones)*	*7.624*
WTO DSD	WT/DS27/AB/R *European Communities – Regime for the Importation, Sale and Distribution of Bananas*	*7.2, 7.208, 7.624*
WTO DSD	WT/DS31/AB/R *Canada – Certain Measures Concerning Periodicals*	*7.208, 7.227, 7.447*
WTO DSD	WT/DS34/R *Turkey – Restrictions on Imports of Textile and Clothing Products*	*7.624*
WTO DSD	WT/DS50/AB/R *India – Patent Protection for Pharmaceutical and Agricultural Chemical Products – Complaint by the United States*	*7.605, 7.751*

<u>WT/DS174/R</u> (Cont.)

WTO DSD WT/DS54/R, WT/DS55/R, WT/DS59/R, WT/DS64/R *Indonesia – Certain Measures Affecting the Automobile Industry*	*7.624*
WTO DSD WT/DS79/R *India – Patent Protection for Pharmaceutical and Agricultural Chemical Products – Complaint by the European Communities*	*7.55, 7.751*
WTO DSD WT/DS98/AB/R *Korea – Definitive Safeguard Measure on Imports of Certain Dairy Products*	*7.2, 7.25, 7.208*
WTO DSD WT/DS108/AB/RW *United States – Tax Treatment for "Foreign Sales Corporations – Recourse to Article 21.5 by the European Communities*	*7.136, 7.230*
WTO DSD WT/DS114//R *Canada – Patent Protection of Pharmaceutical Products*	*7.175, 7.645, 7.650, 7.663*
WTO DSD WT/DS121/AB/R *Argentina – Safeguard Measures on Imports of Footwear*	*7.208*
WTO DSD WT/DS122/AB/R *Thailand – Anti-Dumping Duties on Angles, Shapes and Sections of Iron or Non-Alloy Steel and H-Beams from Poland*	*7.2, 7.25*
WTO DSD WT/DS135/AB/R *European Communities – Measures Affecting Asbestos and Asbestos-Containing Products*	*7.181-82, 7.299, 7.449*
WTO DSD WT/DS136/AB/R, WT/DS162/AB/R *United States – Anti-Dumping Act of 1916*	*7.706*
WTO DSD WT/DS152/R *United States – Sections 301-310 of the Trade Act of 1974*	*7.98*
WTO DSD WT/DS160/R *United States – Section 110(5) of the US Copyright Act*	*7.645*
WTO DSD WT/DS161/AB/R, WT/DS169/AB/R *Korea – Measures Affecting Imports of Fresh, Chilled and Frozen Beef*	*7.136, 7.174, 7.206, 7.226, 7.230, 7.298, 7.447, 7.449*
WTO DSD WT/DS170/AB/R *Canada – Term of Patent Protection*	*7.744*
WTO DSD WT/DS176/AB/R *United States – Section 211 Omnibus Appropriations Act of 1998*	*7.133, 7.139, 7.215, 7.494*
WTO DSD WT/DS213/AB/R *United States – Countervailing Duties on Certain Corrosion-Resistant Carbon Steel Flat Products from Germany*	*7.2-3, 7.706*

WT/DS174/R (Cont.)

WT/DS290/R; *European Communities – Protection of Trademarks and Geographical Indications for Agricultural Products and Foodstuffs – Complaint by Australia*

INDEX

INDEX

MEASURES AT ISSUE

MEXICO

MOST-FAVORED NATION (MFN)

N

NATIONAL TREATMENT

NEW ZEALAND

P

PARIS CONVENTION

TRADEMARKS AND GEOGRAPHICAL INDICATIONS FOR PRODUCTS – AUSTRALIA

TRADEMARKS AND GEOGRAPHICAL INDICATIONS FOR PRODUCTS – UNITED STATES

World Trade Organization
Dispute Settlement Decisions

Bernan's Annotated Reporter

Volume 67-A
Decisions Reported
March 8–15, 2005

World Trade Organization
Dispute Settlement Decisions

Bernan's Annotated Reporter

Bernan Press
Lanham, Maryland, USA
James J. Patton, Editor

Printed by Automated Graphic Systems, Inc., White Plains, MD, USA, on acid-free paper that meets The American National Standards Institute Z39-48 standard.

BERNAN PRESS
4611-F Assembly Drive
Lanham, MD 20706-4391
(800) 274-4447 (301) 459-2255
Email: info@bernan.com
www.bernanpress.com

ISBN: 1-59888-000-4
ISSN: 1534-7559

TABLE OF CONTENTS

PREFACE

The WORLD TRADE ORGANIZATION DISPUTE SETTLEMENT DECISIONS: BERNAN'S ANNOTATED REPORTER series is intended to provide the user with comprehensive and efficient access to the decisions of the World Trade Organization's Dispute Settlement Body and its activities. Provided herein are the full text cases of all WTO Panels and of the Appellate Body.

Cases are set forth in chronological order, based on the date of the decision being reported. References to the disputes may be limited to the common name (i.e., *Japan – Alcohol*), or the Dispute Settlement reference number (i.e., WT/DS8/AB/R). Before each opinion, several additional features are offered. Each case has a front section that includes:

i. Title of case
ii. Parties
iii. Procedural history
iv. Summary of conclusions
v. Annotations
vi. Table of contents

The annotations recite significant legal determinations made by the Panel or Appellate Body in the course of its ruling. Each such annotation includes a paragraph reference, a principle, and a WTO treaty source document reference. An example follows:

7.70–7.72 **Allocation of quotas** [GATT, Article XIII.2(d)]

This indicates that on paragraphs 7.70–7.72 of the given case, the user will find a ruling or interpretation by the Panel (or Appellate Body) on quota allocation as regulated under the terms of the General Agreements on Tariffs and Trade, Article XIII.2(d). The principles used in reference to GATT provisions are based on the *GATT Guide to Law and Practice*, co-published by the World Trade Organization and Bernan.

Four tables follow the reported cases.

i. Overview of Dispute Settlement Activity
ii. Countries Involved in Disputes
iii. Treaty Provisions Interpreted
iv. BISD and Dispute References

The first two of these tables relate to dispute settlement activity generally under the auspices of the Dispute Settlement Body. Table I provides an update of disputes that have been acted upon during the time period covered within this volume. Noted along with dispute name and reference number are the complainant(s) and a brief description of the action that occurred. Also noted are connections between complaints where the same laws, regulations, or government practices are being disputed by more than one Member. Table II shows the distribution of dispute settlement activity to date by country. Herein, each country is listed with dispute reference citations noted as to whether the country was a complainant or a respondent.

The third and fourth tables refer only to the cases reported in this volume. Table III indicates which WTO agreements have been interpreted by the Panels and Appellate Body in the cases within this volume. Paragraph references are again provided, with the number indicating the location of the analysis of the given provision. Table IV is a table of references within the reports of this volume to other WTO and GATT materials, particularly decisions, protocols, announcements, and reports published in the Basic Instruments and Selected Documents (BISD) and WTO dispute settlement references.

Lastly, each volume includes a topical index. The index also provides reference to the cases by paragraph number.

*****

The goal of producing this series is to increase access to the World Trade Organization's Dispute Settlement system through the conveyance of its decisions in a comprehensive and accessible manner. Please submit any questions or remarks to the address on page iv, or by e-mail to info@bernan.com.

EUROPEAN COMMUNITIES – PROTECTION OF TRADEMARKS AND GEOGRAPHICAL INDICATIONS FOR AGRICULTURAL PRODUCTS AND FOODSTUFFS – COMPLAINT BY THE UNITED STATES

WT/DS174/R
REPORT OF THE PANEL

Complainant:	United States	
Respondent:	European Communities	
Third Parties:	Argentina	Australia
	Brazil	Canada
	China	Colombia
	Guatemala	India
	Mexico	New Zealand
	Chinese Taipei	
Reported:	March 15, 2005	

Procedural History

On 1 June 1999, the United States requested consultations with the European Communities.

The United States and the European Communities held consultations on 9 July 1999, and thereafter, but these consultations failed to resolve the dispute.

On 4 April 2003, the United States supplemented its earlier request with a request for additional consultations with the European Communities.

The United States and the European Communities held consultations pursuant to this supplemental request on 27 May 2003, but these consultations also failed to resolve the dispute.

On 18 August 2003, the United States requested the Dispute Settlement Body to establish a panel.

On 13 February 2004, the United States and Australia (in WT/DS290) requested the Director-General to determine the composition of the Panel.

On 23 February 2004, the Director-General accordingly composed the Panel.

Argentina, Australia (in respect of the United States' complaint), Brazil, Canada, China, Colombia, Guatemala, India, Mexico, New Zealand, the Separate Customs Territory of Taiwan, Penghu, Kinmen and Matsu (hereinafter referred to as "Chinese Taipei"), and Turkey reserved their rights to participate in the Panel proceedings as third parties.

The Panel met with the parties on 23-24 June 2004 and on 11-12 August 2004.

The Panel submitted its interim report to the parties on 16 November 2004.

EUROPEAN COMMUNITIES – TRADEMARKS AND GEOGRAPHICAL INDICATIONS – COMPLAINT BY THE UNITED STATES

The Panel submitted its final report to the parties on 21 December 2004.

Conclusions

- The Panel rules that the United States' request for establishment of a panel did not fail to identify the specific measures at issue in accordance with Article 6.2 of the DSU.

  - Article 22.1 of the TRIPS Agreement does not set out an obligation but rather a definition of a term which is used in other provisions set out in the United States' request. The reference to Article 22.1 and the corresponding narrative text in the request actually presents the problem more, rather than less, clearly because they explain that the United States will challenge the measures at issue under the relevant obligations on the basis of an alleged inconsistency with this definition;

  - Article 22.2 of the TRIPS Agreement contains an obligation regarding the use of a geographical indication in two circumstances, but the narrative text paraphrases the first one from Article 22.2(a). This clarifies that the obligation in this circumstance is the subject of a claim;

  - Article 41.1 of the TRIPS Agreement contains a general obligation which relates, on its face, to "enforcement procedures as specified in [Part III]." Several of those enforcement procedures are raised in the United States' request, namely those under Articles 41.2, 41.4, 42 and 44.1. This clarifies that the general obligation is the subject of a claim in relation to these procedures. The narrative text also states that the regulation at issue "does not provide adequate enforcement procedures;"

  - Article 41.2 of the TRIPS Agreement contains general obligations which relate to the operation of procedures concerning the enforcement of intellectual property rights. The requirements of each sentence of Article 41.2 are distinct but they are all closely related;

  - Article 42 of the TRIPS Agreement contains closely related obligations concerning fair and equitable procedures. The requirements of each sentence in Article 42 are distinct but they all set out specific features of fair and equitable civil judicial procedures concerning the enforcement of intellectual property rights;

  - the focus of the claims under Articles 41.1, 41.2 and 42 of the TRIPS Agreement is further clarified by the fact that the measures at issue deal with the subject of the protection of geographical indications and designations of origin, which does not impact all intellectual property rights covered by the Agreement, and the narrative text also refers to the protection of trademarks and geographical indications; and

  - Article I of the GATT 1994 contains four paragraphs, but the narrative text quotes only the first paragraph. This clarifies that the obligation in Article I:1 is the subject of a claim. The European Communities recognizes this treaty text.

- On the basis of the facts available, the Panel rules that the United States' request for establishment of a panel did not fail to provide a brief summary of the legal basis of the complaint sufficient to present the problem clearly in accordance with Article 6.2 of the DSU.

- The Panel rules that the claims under Article 2(2) of the Paris Convention (1967), as incorporated by Article 2.1 of the TRIPS Agreement, are within the Panel's terms of reference.

- The Panel concludes that the United States has made a prima facie case that the equivalence and reciprocity conditions in Article 12(1) of the Regulation apply to the availability of protection for GIs located in third countries, including WTO Members. In other words, the registration procedure in Articles 12a and 12b is not available for GIs located in third countries, including WTO Members, that do not satisfy the conditions in Article 12(1). The European Communities has not succeeded in rebutting that case.

- The Panel finds that the equivalence and reciprocity conditions modify the effective equality of opportunities with respect to the availability of protection to persons who wish to obtain GI protection under the Regulation, to the detriment of those who wish to obtain protection in respect of geographical areas located in third countries, including WTO Members. This is less favourable treatment.

- The United States has not challenged the criteria used by the European Communities to determine nationality. The Panel notes that these criteria appear to be the same as those used in public international law. Therefore, the Panel can use them to determine which persons are "nationals" under Article 3.1 of the TRIPS Agreement.

- The Panel accepts the European Communities' submission that it is not a "separate customs territory Member of the WTO" within the meaning of footnote 1 to the TRIPS Agreement, and finds that its nationals, for the purposes of the TRIPS Agreement, are not defined by that footnote.

- Even if the provisions of the Regulation are formally identical in the treatment that they accord to the nationals of other Members and to the European Communities' own nationals, this is not sufficient to demonstrate that there is no violation of Article 3.1 of the TRIPS Agreement. Whether or not the Regulation accords less favourable treatment to the nationals of other Members than it accords to the European Communities' own nationals should be examined instead according to the "effective equality of opportunities" with regard to the protection of intellectual property rights.

- Insofar as the Regulation discriminates with respect to the availability of protection between GIs located in the European Communities, on the one hand, and those located in third countries, including WTO Members, on the other hand, it formally discriminates between those persons who produce, process and/or prepare a product in accordance with a specification, in the European Communities, on the one hand, and those persons who produce, process and/or prepare a product in accordance with a specification, in third countries, including WTO Members, on the other hand.

- The Panel's preliminary conclusion is that, with respect to the availability of protection, the treatment accorded to the group of nationals of other Members is different from, and less favourable than, that accorded to the European Communities' own nationals.

- With respect to the equivalence and reciprocity conditions, as applicable to the availability of GI protection, the Regulation accords treatment to the nationals of other Members less favourable than that it accords to the European Communities' own nationals, inconsistently with Article 3.1 of the TRIPS Agreement.

- The Panel concludes that, with respect to the availability of protection, the Regulation does not impose a requirement as to domicile or establishment inconsistently with Article 2(2) of the Paris Convention (1967), as incorporated by Article 2.1 of the TRIPS Agreement.

- The Regulation sets down requirements concerning the use of certain names in the presentation for sale of agricultural products and foodstuffs. It is therefore a law or regulation affecting the internal sale and offering for sale of products within the meaning of Article III:4 of GATT 1994. This is not altered by the fact that the Regulation is also an intellectual property measure covered by the TRIPS Agreement since GATT 1994 and the TRIPS Agreement apply cumulatively.

- The Panel concludes that, with respect to the equivalence and reciprocity conditions, as applicable to the availability of protection, the Regulation accords less favourable treatment to imported products, inconsistently with Article III:4 of GATT 1994.

- The Panel concludes that, with respect to the application procedures, insofar as they require examination and transmission of applications by governments, the Regulation accords other WTO Member nationals less favourable treatment than it accords the European Communities' own nationals, inconsistently with Article 3.1 of the TRIPS Agreement.

- The Panel concludes that, with respect to the application procedures, insofar as they require examination and transmission of applications by governments, the Regulation accords less favourable treatment to imported products than domestic products, inconsistently with Article III:4 of GATT 1994.

- The Panel concludes that, with respect to the application procedures, insofar as they require examination and transmission of applications by governments, the Regulation accords less favourable treatment to imported products inconsistently with Article III:4 of GATT 1994, and these requirements are not justified by Article XX(d).

- Persons resident or established in third countries, including other WTO Members, who wish to object to applications for registration under the Regulation do not have a right in the objection procedures that is provided to persons in the European Communities. Objectors in third countries face an "extra hurdle" in ensuring that the authorities in those countries carry out the functions reserved to them under the Regulation, which objectors in EC member States do not face. Consequently, certain objections may not be verified or transmitted. Each of these considerations significantly reduces the opportunities available to other WTO Member nationals in matters affecting the acquisition of rights under the Regulation compared with those available to EC nationals. For this reason, the Regulation accords nationals of other WTO Members "less favourable treatment" within the meaning of Article 3.1 of the TRIPS Agreement.

- The Panel concludes that, with respect to the equivalence and reciprocity conditions, as allegedly applicable to objections, the United States has not made a prima facie case in support of its claims under Article 3.1 of the TRIPS Agreement or Article 2(1) of the Paris Convention (1967) as incorporated by Article 2.1 of the TRIPS Agreement.

- The Panel concludes that, with respect to the standing requirements for objections, the United States has not made a prima facie case in support of its claims.

- The Panel considers that the United States has not made a prima facie case in support of its claim with respect to objection procedures under Article III:4 of GATT 1994.

- The Panel concludes that, with respect to the allegedly prescriptive requirements for inspection structures, the United States has not made a prima facie case in support of its claim under Article 3.1 of the TRIPS Agreement.

- Applicants for GIs that refer to geographical areas located in third countries do not have a right in the availability of protection and application procedures that is provided to applicants for GIs that refer to geographical areas located within the European Communities. Applicants in third countries face an "extra hurdle" in ensuring that the authorities in those countries carry out the functions reserved to them under the Regulation, which applicants in EC member States do not face. Consequently, certain applications may be rejected. This significantly reduces the opportunities available to the nationals of other WTO Members in the availability and acquisition of rights under the Regulation below those available to the European Communities' own nationals. For this reason, the Regulation accords nationals of other WTO Members "less favourable treatment" within the meaning of Article 3.1 of the TRIPS Agreement than it accords the European Communities' own nationals.

- The Panel concludes that, with respect to the requirements of government participation in the inspection structures under Article 10, and the provision of the declaration by governments under Article 12a(2)(b), but in no other respects related to the inspection structures, the Regulation accords less favourable treatment to imported products than domestic products, inconsistently with Article III:4 of GATT 1994, and these requirements are not justified by Article XX(d).

- The Panel concludes that, with respect to the labelling requirement, the United States has not made a prima facie case in support of its claim under Article 3.1 of the TRIPS Agreement.

- The Panel considers that the European Communities has not rebutted the United States' prima facie case that Article 14(3) of the Regulation cannot prevent all situations from occurring in which a trademark would be subject to Article 14(2) and, hence, in which the Regulation would limit the rights of the owner of such a trademark.

- The Panel concludes that, under Article 16.1 of the TRIPS Agreement, Members are required to make available to trademark owners a right against certain uses, including uses as a GI. The Regulation limits the availability of that right for the owners of trademarks which are subject to Article 14(2). Article 24.5 of the TRIPS Agreement is inapplicable and does not provide authority to limit that right.

- The Panel interprets the phrase "the protection of geographical indications that existed in that Member immediately prior to the date of entry into force of the WTO Agreement" to mean the state of protection of GIs immediately prior to 1 January 1995, in terms of the individual GIs which were protected at that point in time. In the present dispute, the parties agree that no GIs were registered under the Regulation prior to 1 January 1995. Therefore, Article 24.3 is inapplicable.

- The Panel finds that the Regulation creates a "limited exception" within the meaning of Article 17 of the TRIPS Agreement.

- The Panel considers that the exception created by the Regulation takes account of the legitimate interests of the owner of the trademark within the meaning of Article 17.

- The Panel concludes that, with respect to the coexistence of GIs with prior trademarks, the Regulation is inconsistent with Article 16.1 of the TRIPS Agreement but, on the basis of the evidence presented to the Panel, this is justified by Article 17 of the TRIPS Agreement. Article 24.3 and Article 24.5 of the TRIPS Agreement are inapplicable.

- The MFN obligation in Article 4 of the TRIPS Agreement applies only to any advantage, favour, privilege or immunity "granted by a Member," in this case the European Communities. The United States has not shown how the differences in the treatment accorded to nationals of different Members are granted by the European Communities. Therefore, the Panel concludes that the United States has not made a prima facie case in support of its most favoured nation treatment claim.

- The Panel accepts the European Communities' explanation of what amount to its *sui generis* domestic constitutional arrangements that Community laws are generally not executed through authorities at Community level but rather through recourse to the authorities of its member States which, in such a situation, act *de facto* as organs of the Community, for which the Community would be responsible under WTO law and international law in general. Therefore, to the extent that advantages are granted under the Regulation, by the Community and EC member State authorities exercising powers under the Regulation, to the European Communities' own nationals, those advantages are not granted to "the nationals of any other country," within the meaning of Article 4 of the TRIPS Agreement.

- The United States chose to challenge only the Regulation, as amended, "and its related implementing and enforcement measures." It has not demonstrated that these alternative measures, which lie outside the Panel's terms of reference, are inadequate to provide GI protection to for interested parties nationals of other Members as required under Article 22.2 of the TRIPS Agreement. Therefore, it has not presented sufficient evidence to raise a presumption that the European Communities (as opposed to the Regulation) does not implement its obligations under Article 22.2. Accordingly, the Panel concludes that, with respect to the equivalence and reciprocity conditions and the examination and transmission of applications under the Regulation, the United States has not made a prima facie case that the European Communities has failed to implement its obligation under Article 22.2 of the TRIPS Agreement.

- In view of the findings at paragraphs **Error! Reference source not found.**, **Error! Reference source not found.** and **Error! Reference source not found.**, with respect to this claim, the Panel concludes that the United States has not made a prima facie case that the European Communities has failed to implement its obligation under Article 22.2 of the TRIPS Agreement.

- The United States asserts that the inspection structures requirements force Members to adopt a particular set of rules to implement the TRIPS Agreement, contrary to Article 1.1. The evidence does not, however, suggest that they are inconsistent with the freedom granted under the third sentence of Article 1.1.

Annotations

7.2 **Request for Establishment** [DSU, Article 6.2]

The Panel considers the ordinary meaning of the terms of the text in Article 6.2 of the DSU, read in their context and in the light of the object and purpose of the provision, to be quite clear. They require that a request for establishment of a panel "identify the specific measures at issue." They do not require the identification of the "specific aspects" of these "specific measures."

7.2 **Request for Establishment** [DSU, Article 6.2]

The Panel considers that the mere listing of provisions of the relevant covered agreements may not satisfy the standard of Article 6.2 of the DSU, for instance, where the listed provisions establish multiple obligations rather than one single, distinct obligation. However, where the multiple obligations are closely related and interlinked, a reference to a common obligation in the specific listed provisions should be sufficient to meet the standard of Article 6.2 of the DSU under certain circumstances in a particular case.

7.2 **Request for Establishment** [DSU, Article 6.2]

Article 6.2 of the DSU calls for sufficient clarity with respect to the legal basis of the complaint so as to enable a defending party to begin preparing its defence.

7.125 **National Treatment** [TRIPs, Article 3.1]

Two elements must be satisfied to establish an inconsistency with TRIPs Article 3.1: (1) the measure at issue must apply with regard to the protection of intellectual property; and (2) the nationals of other Members must be accorded "less favourable" treatment than the Member's own nationals.

7.133 **"treatment no less favourable"** [GATT, Article III.4]

The words 'treatment no less favourable' in paragraph 4 call for effective equality of opportunities for imported products in respect of the application of laws, regulations and requirements affecting the internal sale, offering for sale, purchase, transportation, distribution or use of products. This clearly sets a minimum permissible standard as a basis.

7.136 **"treatment no less favourable"** [GATT, Article III.4]

The examination of whether a measure involves 'less favourable treatment' of imported products within the meaning of Article III:4 of the GATT 1994 must be grounded in close scrutiny of the fundamental thrust and effect of the measure itself. This examination cannot rest on simple assertion, but must be founded on a careful analysis of the contested measure and of its implications in the marketplace. At the same time, however, the examination need not be based on the *actual effects* of the contested measure in the marketplace.

7.148 **National Treatment** [TRIPs, Article 3.1]

Whilst the TRIPS Agreement does not create obligations for a Member to accord treatment to its own nationals, it does refer to the treatment that each Member accords to its own nationals as the benchmark for its obligation to accord national treatment under Article 3.1, as well as under the other national treatment obligations incorporated by reference, including Article 2 of the Paris Convention (1967). To that extent, the way in which a Member defines its own nationals can also be subject to review for the purposes of determining conformity with its national treatment obligations under the TRIPS Agreement.

7.198 [TRIPs, footnote 1]

The text of the TRIPS Agreement contains a recognition that discrimination according to residence and establishment will be a close substitute for nationality.

7.209-210 **Principles** [TRIPs, Article 8]

Article 8 of the TRIPS Agreement sets out the principles of that agreement. These principles reflect the fact that the TRIPS Agreement does not generally provide for the grant of positive rights to exploit or use certain subject matter, but rather provides for the grant of negative rights to prevent certain acts. This fundamental feature of intellectual property protection inherently grants Members freedom to pursue legitimate public policy objectives since many measures to attain those public policy objectives lie outside the scope of intellectual property rights and do not require an exception under the TRIPS Agreement.

7.212 **National Treatment** [TRIPs, Article 3.1]

The fact that a general exceptions provision analogous to Article XX of GATT 1994 was not included in the TRIPS Agreement has no impact on its analysis of Article 3.1.

7.230 **"treatment no less favourable"** [GATT, Article III.4]

The "less favourable treatment" standard should be assessed under Article III:4 of GATT 1994 by examining whether the measures at issue modify the conditions of competition between domestic and imported products in the relevant market to the detriment of imported products. This examination must closely scrutinize the "fundamental thrust and effect of the measure itself" founded on a careful analysis of the contested measure and of its implications in the marketplace.

7.296 **"protection of patents, trademarks and copyrights"** [GATT, Article XX(d)]

Article XX, paragraph (d) refers to laws or regulations, including those relating to "the protection of patents, trade marks and copyrights, and the prevention of deceptive practices." However, the term "laws or regulations" is qualified by the phrase "not inconsistent with the provisions of this Agreement."

7.329 [TRIPs, footnote 3]

Procedures for the filing and examination of *applications* for registration are matters affecting the acquisition of intellectual property rights, within the scope of "protection" of intellectual property as clarified in footnote 3 of the TRIPS Agreement. Procedures for *objections* to such applications are related to the procedures for acquisition. Hence, opposition procedures are also matters "affecting" the acquisition of intellectual property rights which concern the "protection" of intellectual property, as clarified in footnote 3 to the TRIPS Agreement.

7.413 **National Treatment** [TRIPs, Article 3.1]

The treatment accorded *by other Members* to their own respective nationals is not relevant to this claim. The level of protection in the country of origin does not affect GI protection in the country where GI protection is sought under the TRIPS Agreement, except to the extent that a lack of GI protection in the country of origin provides a ground to *deny* GI protection in accordance with Article 24.9.

7.447 **"to secure compliance"** [GATT, Article XX(d)]

Measures that merely secure compliance with the objectives of a law or regulation, rather than with the laws or regulations themselves, do not fall within the purview of Article XX(d) of GATT 1994.

7.598 **Standards Concerning the Availability, Scope and Use of Intellectual Property Rights** [TRIPs, Part II]

Part II of the TRIPS Agreement contains minimum standards concerning the availability, scope and use of intellectual property rights. The first seven Sections of Part II contain standards relating to categories of intellectual property rights. Each Section sets out, as a minimum, the *subject matter* which is eligible for protection, the scope of the *rights conferred* by the relevant category of intellectual property and permitted *exceptions* to those rights.

7.602 **Rights Conferred** [TRIPs, Article 16.1]

The text of Article 16.1 stipulates that the right for which it provides is an "exclusive" right. This indicates that the right belongs to the owner of the registered trademark alone, who may exercise it to prevent certain uses by "all third parties" not having the owner's consent.

7.610 **International Negotiations: Exceptions** [TRIPs, Article 24.5]

There is no language in Article 24.5 of the TRIPS Agreement which would provide for the conferral of a right to use a trademark. Instead, it is a saving provision which ensures that "the right to use a trademark" is not prejudiced, or affected, by measures adopted to implement Section 3 of Part II. Irrespective of how the right to use a trademark arises, there is no obligation under Article 24.5 to confer it.

7.615 **International Negotiations: Exceptions** [TRIPs, Article 24.5]

The Panel considers that Article 24.5 creates an exception to GI protection—as reflected in the title of Article 24.

7.619 **International Negotiations: Exceptions** [TRIPs, Article 24.5]

It is inappropriate to imply in Article 24.5 *either* the right to prevent confusing uses *or* a limitation on the right to prevent confusing uses.

7.647-48 **Exceptions** [TRIPs, Article 17]

Article 17 expressly permits Members to provide limited exceptions to the rights conferred by a trademark, which include the right provided for in Article 16.1 of the TRIPS Agreement. Article 17 permits "limited exceptions." It provides an example of a limited exception, and is subject to a proviso that "such exceptions take account of the legitimate interests of the owner of the trademark and of third parties." The ordinary meaning of the terms indicates that an exception must not only be "limited" but must also comply with the proviso in order to satisfy Article 17. The example of "fair use of descriptive terms" is illustrative only, but it can provide interpretative guidance because, *a priori*, it falls within the meaning of a "limited" exception and must be capable of satisfying the proviso in some circumstances.

7.650 **Exceptions** [TRIPs, Article 17]

The meaning of the term "limited exceptions" as used in Article 17 should be equated to a minor derogation, one that does not undercut the body of rules from which it is made" where the exception must be narrow and permit only a small diminution of rights. The fact that the exception may affect only few trademarks or few trademark owners is irrelevant to the question whether it is limited. The issue is whether the exception to the *rights conferred by a trademark* is narrow.

7.662-64 **Exceptions** [TRIPs, Article 17]

The term "legitimate interests" of a trademark owner and third parties in the context of Article 17 must be defined as a normative claim calling for protection of interests that are 'justifiable' in the sense that they are supported by relevant public policies or other social norms. Every trademark owner has a legitimate interest in preserving the distinctiveness, or capacity to distinguish, of its trademark so that it can perform that function. This includes its interest in using its own trademark in connection with the relevant goods and services of its own and authorized undertakings. Taking account of that legitimate interest will also take account of the trademark owner's interest in the economic value of its mark arising from the reputation that it enjoys and the quality that it denotes.

7.676-81 **Exceptions** [TRIPs, Article 17]

Third parties for the purposes of Article 17 include consumers and persons using a GI in accordance with a geographical indication ("GI") registration. Third parties" for the purposes of Article 17 also include trademark licensees, but the legitimate interests of trademark licensees are, to a large extent, identified with those of the trademark owner, and can be taken into account at the same time. It is not clear how their interests could be taken into account as a separate issue.

7.682 **Exceptions** [TRIPs, Article 17]
Protection of Geographical Indications [TRIPs, Article 22.1]

The definition of a GI in Article 22.1 reflects a legitimate interest that a person may have in identifying the source and other characteristics of a good by the name of the place where it is from, if the name would serve that purpose. Nevertheless, as "legitimate interests," the interests of GI users as third parties within the meaning of Article 17 would be different from the legal protection provided for in Articles 22 and 23.

7.683 **Exceptions** [TRIPs, Article 17]

Although GIs are intellectual property rights, and not purely descriptive terms, the function of the terms in the example is analogous to a descriptive function of GIs and provides contextual support for the notion that the interest of GIs users in using a place name to indicate their products is "legitimate."

7.697 **Most-Favoured Nation Treatment** [TRIPs, Article 4]

The following two elements must be satisfied to establish an inconsistency with Article 4 of the TRIPS Agreement: (1) the measure at issue must apply with regard to the protection of intellectual property; and (2) the nationals of other Members are not "immediately and unconditionally" accorded any advantage, favour, privilege or immunity granted by a Member to the nationals of any other country.

7.742-43 **Nature and Scope of Obligations** [TRIPs, Article 1.3]
Protection of Geographical Indications [TRIPs, Article 22.2]

In order to determine whether a Member has implemented its obligation owed to other Members in Article 22.2, a Panel must examine whether it has provided the legal means required by that provision for interested parties who are nationals of other Members.

7.754 **Protection of Geographical Indications** [TRIPs, Article 22.2]

Article 22.2 does not provide for a right of objection to the registration of a GI. Although Article 15.5 provides for a right of objection to registration of a trademark, no provision in Part II of the TRIPS Agreement provides for objections to the registration of a GI.

EUROPEAN COMMUNITIES – PROTECTION OF TRADEMARKS AND GEOGRAPHICAL INDICATIONS FOR AGRICULTURAL PRODUCTS AND FOODSTUFFS – COMPLAINT BY THE UNITED STATES

WT/DS174/R
REPORT OF THE PANEL

TABLE OF CONTENTS

LIST OF ANNEXES

ANNEX A

SUBMISSIONS BY THE UNITED STATES

ANNEX B

SUBMISSIONS BY THE EUROPEAN COMMUNITIES

ANNEX C

ARGUMENTS OF THE THIRD PARTIES

ANNEX D

MISCELLANEOUS

TABLE OF CASES CITED IN THIS REPORT

Short Title	Full Case Title and Citation
Argentina – Footwear (EC)	Appellate Body Report, *Argentina – Safeguard Measures on Imports of Footwear*, WT/DS121/AB/R, adopted 12 January 2000, DSR 2000:I, 515
Australia – Salmon	Appellate Body Report, *Australia – Measures Affecting Importation of Salmon*, WT/DS18/AB/R, adopted 6 November 1998, DSR 1998:VIII, 3327
Belgium – Family Allowances	GATT Panel Report, *Income Tax Practices Maintained by Belgium*, adopted 7 December 1981, BISD 23S/127 and 28S/114
Brazil – Aircraft	Appellate Body Report, *Brazil – Export Financing Programme for Aircraft*, WT/DS46/AB/R, adopted 20 August 1999, DSR 1999:III, 1161
Canada – Patent Term	Appellate Body Report, *Canada – Term of Patent Protection*, WT/DS170/AB/R, adopted 12 October 2000, DSR 2000:X, 5093
Canada – Periodicals	Appellate Body Report, *Canada – Certain Measures Concerning Periodicals*, WT/DS31/AB/R, adopted 30 July 1997, DSR 1997:I, 449
Canada – Pharmaceutical Patents	Panel Report, *Canada – Patent Protection of Pharmaceutical Products*, WT/DS114/R, adopted 7 April 2000, DSR 2000:V, 2289
EC – Asbestos	Appellate Body Report, *European Communities – Measures Affecting Asbestos and Asbestos-Containing Products*, WT/DS135/AB/R, adopted 5 April 2001, DSR 2001:VII, 3243
EC – Bananas III	Appellate Body Report, *European Communities – Regime for the Importation, Sale and Distribution of Bananas*, WT/DS27/AB/R, adopted 25 September 1997, DSR 1997:II, 591
EC – Bananas III (US)	Panel Report, *European Communities – Regime for the Importation, Sale and Distribution of Bananas – Complaint by the United States*, WT/DS27/R/USA, adopted 25 September 1997, as modified by the Appellate Body Report, WT/DS27/AB/R, DSR 1997:II, 943
EC – Hormones	Appellate Body Report, *EC Measures Concerning Meat and Meat Products (Hormones)*, WT/DS26/AB/R, WT/DS48/AB/R, adopted 13 February 1998, DSR 1998:I, 135
EC – Sardines	Appellate Body Report, *European Communities – Trade Description of Sardines*, WT/DS231/AB/R, adopted 23 October 2002
EC – Tariff Preferences	Appellate Body Report, *European Communities – Conditions for the Granting of Tariff Preferences to Developing Countries*, WT/DS246/AB/R, adopted 20 April 2004.
EEC – Parts and Components	GATT Panel Report, *European Economic Community – Regulation on Imports of Parts and Components*, adopted 16 May 1990, BISD 37S/132
India – Patents (US)	Appellate Body Report, *India – Patent Protection for Pharmaceutical and Agricultural Chemical Products*, WT/DS50/AB/R, adopted 16 January 1998, DSR 1998:I, 9
India – Patents (US)	Panel Report, *India – Patent Protection for Pharmaceutical and Agricultural Chemical Products – Complaint by the United States*, WT/DS50/R, adopted 16 January 1998, as modified by the Appellate Body Report, WT/DS50/AB/R, DSR 1998:I, 41
India – Patents (EC)	Panel Report, *India – Patent Protection for Pharmaceutical and Agricultural Chemical Products – Complaint by the European Communities*, WT/DS79/R, adopted 22 September 1998, DSR 1998:VI, 2661
Indonesia – Autos	Panel Report, *Indonesia – Certain Measures Affecting the Automobile Industry*, WT/DS54/R, WT/DS55/R, WT/DS59/R, WT/DS64/R and Corr.1, 2, 3, and 4, adopted 23 July 1998, DSR 1998:VI, 2201

Short Title	Full Case Title and Citation
Japan – Alcoholic Beverages II	Appellate Body Report, *Japan – Taxes on Alcoholic Beverages*, WT/DS8/AB/R, WT/DS10/AB/R, WT/DS11/AB/R, adopted 1 November 1996, DSR 1996:I, 97
Korea – Dairy	Appellate Body Report, *Korea – Definitive Safeguard Measure on Imports of Certain Dairy Products*, WT/DS98/AB/R, adopted 12 January 2000, DSR 2000:I, 3
Korea – Various Measures on Beef	Appellate Body Report, *Korea – Measures Affecting Imports of Fresh, Chilled and Frozen Beef*, WT/DS161/AB/R, WT/DS169/AB/R, adopted 10 January 2001, DSR 2001:I, 5
Korea – Various Measures on Beef	Panel Report, *Korea – Measures Affecting Imports of Fresh, Chilled and Frozen Beef*, WT/DS161/R, WT/DS169/R, adopted 10 January 2001, as modified by the Appellate Body Report, WT/DS161/AB/R, WT/DS169/AB/R, DSR 2001:I, 59
Thailand – H-Beams	Appellate Body Report, *Thailand – Anti-Dumping Duties on Angles, Shapes and Sections of Iron or Non-Alloy Steel and H-Beams from Poland*, WT/DS122/AB/R, adopted 5 April 2001, DSR 2001:VII, 2701
Turkey – Textiles	Panel Report, *Turkey – Restrictions on Imports of Textile and Clothing Products*, WT/DS34/R, adopted 19 November 1999, as modified by the Appellate Body Report, WT/DS34/AB/R, DSR 1999:VI, 2363
US – 1916 Act	Appellate Body Report, *United States – Anti-Dumping Act of 1916*, WT/DS136/AB/R, WT/DS162/AB/R, adopted 26 September 2000, DSR 2000:X, 4793
US – Carbon Steel	Appellate Body Report, *United States – Countervailing Duties on Certain Corrosion-Resistant Carbon Steel Flat Products from Germany*, WT/DS213/AB/R and Corr.1, adopted 19 December 2002
US – Certain EC Products	Appellate Body Report, *United States – Import Measures on Certain Products from the European Communities*, WT/DS165/AB/R, adopted 10 January 2001, DSR 2001:I, 373
US – Corrosion-Resistant Steel Sunset Review	Appellate Body Report, *United States – Sunset Review of Anti-Dumping Duties on Corrosion-Resistant Carbon Steel Flat Products from Japan*, WT/DS244/AB/R, adopted 9 January 2004
US – FSC (Article 21.5 – EC)	Appellate Body Report, *United States – Tax Treatment for "Foreign Sales Corporations" – Recourse to Article 21.5 of the DSU by the European Communities*, WT/DS108/AB/RW, adopted 29 January 2002
US – Gasoline	Appellate Body Report, *United States – Standards for Reformulated and Conventional Gasoline*, WT/DS2/AB/R, adopted 20 May 1996, DSR 1996:I, 3
US – Section 110(5) Copyright Act	Panel Report, *United States – Section 110(5) of the US Copyright Act*, WT/DS160/R, adopted 27 July 2000, DSR 2000:VIII, 3769
US – Section 211 Appropriations Act	Appellate Body Report, *United States – Section 211 Omnibus Appropriations Act of 1998*, WT/DS176/AB/R, adopted 1 February 2002
US – Section 301 Trade Act	Panel Report, *United States – Sections 301-310 of the Trade Act of 1974*, WT/DS152/R, adopted 27 January 2000, DSR 2000:II, 815
US – Section 337	GATT Panel Report, *United States Section 337 of the Tariff Act of 1930*, adopted 7 November 1989, BISD 36S/345
US – Tobacco	GATT Panel Report, *United States Measures Affecting the Importation, Internal Sale and Use of Tobacco*, adopted 4 October 1994, BISD 41S/I/131

I. INTRODUCTION

1.1 On 1 June 1999, the United States requested consultations[1] with the European Communities pursuant to Article 4 of the Understanding on Rules and Procedures Governing the Settlement of Disputes ("DSU") and Article 64 of the Agreement on Trade-Related Aspects of Intellectual Property Rights ("TRIPS Agreement") (to the extent that it incorporates by reference Article XXIII of the General Agreement on Tariffs and Trade 1994 ("GATT 1994") regarding EC Council Regulation (EEC) No. 2081/92 of 14 July 1992 on the protection of geographical indications and designations of origin for agricultural products and foodstuffs, as amended. The United States and the European Communities held consultations on 9 July 1999, and thereafter, but these consultations failed to resolve the dispute.

1.2 On 4 April 2003, the United States supplemented its earlier request with a request for additional consultations[2] with the European Communities pursuant to Article 4 of the DSU, Article 64 of the TRIPS Agreement and Article XXII of the GATT 1994, regarding the protection of trademarks and geographical indications for agricultural products and foodstuffs in the European Communities pursuant to Regulation 2081/92, as amended, and its related implementing and enforcement measures ("Regulation 2081/92"). The United States and the European Communities held consultations pursuant to this supplemental request on 27 May 2003, but these consultations also failed to resolve the dispute.

1.3 On 18 August 2003, the United States requested the Dispute Settlement Body ("DSB") to establish a panel with standard terms of reference as set out in Article 7.1 of the DSU.[3] At its meeting on 2 October 2003, the DSB established a single Panel pursuant to the requests of the United States in document WT/DS174/20 and Australia in document WT/DS290/18, in accordance with Article 9 of the DSU (WT/DSB/M/156)[4]. At that meeting, the parties to the dispute also agreed that the Panel should have standard terms of reference. The terms of reference are, therefore, the following:

> To examine, in the light of the relevant provisions of the covered agreements cited by the United States in document WT/DS174/20 and Australia in document WT/DS290/18, the matter referred to the DSB by the United States and Australia in those documents, and to make such findings as will assist the DSB in making the recommendations or in giving the rulings provided for in those agreements.

1.4 On 13 February 2004, the United States and Australia requested the Director-General to determine the composition of the Panel, pursuant to paragraph 7 of Article 8 of the DSU.

1.5 On 23 February 2004, the Director-General accordingly composed the Panel as follows:

Chair:	Mr Miguel Rodríguez Mendoza
Members:	Prof. Seung Wha Chang Mr Peter Kam-fai Cheung

1.6 Argentina, Australia (in respect of the United States' complaint), Brazil, Canada, China, Colombia, Guatemala, India, Mexico, New Zealand, the Separate Customs Territory of Taiwan, Penghu, Kinmen and Matsu (hereinafter referred to as "Chinese Taipei"), Turkey and the United States (in respect of Australia's complaint) reserved their rights to participate in the Panel proceedings as third parties.

---

[1] WT/DS174/1.

[2].WT/DS174/1/Add.1.

[3] WT/DS174/20.

[4] WT/DS174/21 and Corr.1.

1.7 The Panel met with the parties on 23-24 June 2004 and on 11-12 August 2004. It met with the third parties on 24 June 2004.

1.8 The Panel submitted its interim report to the parties on 16 November 2004. The Panel submitted its final report to the parties on 21 December 2004.

II. FACTUAL ASPECTS

A. Measures at Issue

2.1 The measures at issue in this dispute are identified in the United States' request for establishment of a panel as Council Regulation (EEC) No. 2081/92 of 14 July 1992 on the protection of geographical indications and designations of origin for agricultural products and foodstuffs, as amended, and its related implementing and enforcement measures.

B. Procedural History

1. Preliminary ruling prior to the first written submissions

2.2 On 24 February 2004, the day after the Panel was composed and prior to the organizational meeting, the European Communities requested that the Panel issue a preliminary ruling that the United States' and Australia's respective requests for establishment of a panel were inconsistent with the requirements of Article 6.2 of the DSU. The European Communities considered it appropriate that the Panel issue a preliminary ruling before the first written submissions of the parties were due.

2.3 At the organizational meeting, the Panel sought the parties' views on appropriate procedures to deal with this request. The complainants did not object to filing written responses to the request for a preliminary ruling prior to their first written submissions but requested additional time for the filing of their first written submissions.

2.4 On 8 March 2004, the Panel adopted its working procedures and timetable, which indicated a date for the United States and Australia to file written responses to the European Communities' request for a preliminary ruling. They submitted their responses accordingly.

2.5 On 5 April 2004, the Panel issued a preliminary ruling, which is set out in full in Section VII:A of this report.

2.6 On 20 April 2004, the European Communities sent a letter to the Panel expressing its regret at the Panel's ruling and "reserving its right to raise issues of law regarding the interpretation of Article 6.2 of the DSU before the Appellate Body." In its letter, the European Communities asked the Panel to clarify the status of its preliminary ruling of 5 April 2004, in particular whether such ruling would be incorporated into the Panel's final reports and whether the findings contained in the ruling would be an integral part of the final reports.

2.7 On 23 April 2004, the Panel responded to the European Communities, advising that its preliminary ruling would be reflected in the Panel's final reports, as appropriate.

2.8 On 26 April 2004, the European Communities sent a second letter to the Panel indicating that it had understood from the Panel's previous response that the findings contained in the preliminary ruling of 5 April 2004 would be incorporated into the Panel's final reports and could, therefore, be appealed in the same way as any legal interpretation contained in these reports.

2.9 On 28 April 2004, the Panel responded again to the European Communities, advising that it had taken note of the European Communities' letter of 26 April 2004 and reiterating that its preliminary ruling would be reflected in its final reports, as appropriate.

2. Request for extension of time

2.10 On 9 March 2004, the European Communities requested that the Panel extend the period for it to submit its first written submission in view of the circumstances that (a) there were two cases brought by two complainants; (b) these cases did not appear to contain identical claims; and (c) these cases raised new and complex issues and involved a large number of claims. It also alleged that the timetable was unbalanced in favour of the complainants.

2.11 On 16 March 2004, the United States and Australia each responded to the European Communities' request, disagreeing with its assertions but not objecting to an extension of the period for the European Communities to submit its first written submission, provided that such extension would not affect the timeframe structure of the remainder of the timetable.

2.12 On 22 March 2004, the Panel revised its timetable, extending the time for the submission of the respondent's first written submission, without affecting the time between any of the subsequent steps as established in the original timetable.

3. Request for separate reports

2.13 On 3 March 2004, after the conclusion of the Panel's organizational meeting, the European Communities filed a request pursuant to Article 9.2 of the DSU that the Panel submit separate reports on the present dispute. On 8 March 2004 the Panel acknowledged receipt of such request. The complainants did not comment on this request.

2.14 On 23 April 2004, the Panel informed the parties that it would submit separate reports on this dispute, as requested by the European Communities.

2.15 At the second substantive meeting with the parties on 11-12 August 2004, the Panel invited the parties to comment on the way in which the Panel should submit separate reports. The Panel took note of the parties' views and confirmed the following facts: (a) the complainants have made similar, but not identical claims in this dispute; (b) the complainants have made separate written submissions and separate oral statements and submitted separate responses to questions, although they did submit 16 common exhibits with their respective first written submissions; (c) the complainants have not collectively endorsed the arguments made in one another's submissions although Australia, in its first oral statement, expressly endorsed certain comments made by the United States[5], and the United States, on occasions, cited information and arguments submitted by Australia in support of its arguments; and (d) although each complainant reserved its right to participate in the Panel proceedings as a third party in respect of the other's complaint, they did not exercise these rights. They both declined the opportunity given to them by the Panel to make a statement as a third party during the session with the third parties.

4. Request for factual information from the International Bureau of WIPO

2.16 On 9 July 2004, the Panel sent a letter to the International Bureau of WIPO requesting its assistance in the form of any factual information available to it relevant to the interpretation of certain provisions of the Paris Convention for the Protection of Industrial Property.[6] The parties were given the opportunity to comment.

---

[5] Australia also purported to endorse all arguments put forward by the United States in its closing statement at the second substantive meeting. This is considered in Section VII:A of the report on Australia's complaint (WT/DS290/R).

[6] Attached as Annex D-2 to this report.

2.17 The International Bureau's reply was received by the Panel and the WTO Secretariat on 14 September 2004. The Panel gave the parties an opportunity to submit comments on the reply by 28 September 2004. The parties submitted their comments accordingly.[7]

2.18 The factual information provided by the International Bureau consists of a note it prepared and five annexes containing excerpts from the Official Records of the various Diplomatic Conferences which adopted, amended or revised the provisions currently contained in Articles 2 and 3 of the Paris Convention (Stockholm Act of 1967)[8].

III. PARTIES' REQUESTS FOR FINDINGS AND RECOMMENDATIONS

A. United States

3.1 The United States requests that the Panel find that the measures at issue are inconsistent with the European Communities' obligations under:

(a) Articles 1.1, 3.1, 4, 16.1, 22.2, 41.1, 41.2, 41.4, 42, 44.1 and 65.1 of the TRIPS Agreement and, through its incorporation by Article 2.1 of the TRIPS Agreement, Article 2 of the Paris Convention (1967); and

(b) Articles I:1 and III:4 of GATT 1994.

3.2 The United States requests that the Panel recommend that the European Communities bring its measures into conformity with its obligations under the TRIPS Agreement and GATT 1994.

B. European Communities

3.3 The European Communities requests that the Panel:

(a) find that certain measures not yet adopted at the time the Panel was established, and the United States' claim under Article 2(2) of the Paris Convention (incorporated by Article 2.1 of the TRIPS Agreement), are outside the Panel's terms of reference; and

(b) reject all claims within the Panel's terms of reference.

IV. ARGUMENTS OF THE PARTIES

4.1 The arguments of the European Communities and the United States, as set out in their respective submissions (European Communities' request for a preliminary ruling, United States response to the European Communities' request for a preliminary ruling, first written submissions, written rebuttals, oral statements, responses to questions; comments on each other's responses; and comments on the factual information from the International Bureau of WIPO), are attached as Annexes A and B.

V. ARGUMENTS OF THE THIRD PARTIES

5.1 The arguments of those third parties that made submissions to the Panel (first written submissions, oral statements and/or responses to questions) are summarized and attached as Annex C.

---

[7] The submissions are attached to this report as Annexes A-10 and B-10.

[8] The International Bureau's Note, but not its annexes, are attached as Annex D-3 to this report.

VI. INTERIM REVIEW

6.1 On 16 November 2004, the Panel submitted its interim report to the parties. On 30 November 2004, the United States and the European Communities submitted written requests for review of precise aspects of the interim report. On 7 December 2004, the United States and the European Communities submitted written comments on each other's request for interim review.

6.2 The Panel has modified aspects of its report in light of the parties' comments where it considered appropriate, as explained below. The Panel has also made certain revisions and technical corrections for the purposes of clarity and accuracy. References to paragraph numbers and footnotes in this Section VI refer to those in the interim report, except as otherwise noted.

<u>incorporation of arguments by co-complainant</u>

6.3 The United States requests that the interim report reflect the fact that the United States incorporated information and arguments put forward by Australia with respect to the issue whether the conditions of equivalence and reciprocity apply to WTO Members, citing two references in its submissions and paragraph 2.15.

6.4 The Panel has noted these two particular references in footnote 73 and also corrected paragraph 2.15 of the final report.

<u>further comments on preliminary ruling</u>

6.5 The European Communities requests the deletion of paragraphs 7.3 to 7.8 as the conformity of a panel request with Article 6.2 of the DSU must be evaluated on the face of the panel request. In its view, references to discussions that take place in other fora, like those in the Council for TRIPS, are irrelevant for this purpose. The same reasoning applies to the letter from Commissioner Lamy to the USTR, which was only provided by the United States at the second substantive meeting. If it were of any relevance to Article 6.2, it could have been expected that the United States would have referred to it in its response to the request for a preliminary ruling, but it did not. Moreover, the letter is irrelevant for this question as it did not form part of the dispute settlement process.

6.6 The United States opposes this request. It believes that the preliminary ruling of 5 April 2004 stands on its own merits. But it also fails to see on what basis the European Communities objects to the Panel's description of facts confirming that, at the time of the panel request, the European Communities was aware of the legal basis for the panel request and that the summary of the legal basis of the compliant in that request was sufficient to present the problem clearly.

6.7 The Panel recalls that the European Communities made a request for a preliminary ruling the day after the Panel was composed in which it alleged defects in the panel request and submitted that it was appropriate that the Panel issue a preliminary ruling before the first written submissions of the parties were due. The Panel issued a preliminary ruling accordingly, in which it found that those allegations were unfounded on the face of the panel request and on the basis of the facts available to it at that time. That preliminary ruling sets out part of the basic rationale for the Panel's findings and recommendation in this dispute. Accordingly, in the course of making an objective assessment of the facts, the Panel does not disregard probative evidence relevant to that ruling submitted later in the course of the proceeding, other than the references to what took place during the consultations, which were without prejudice to the rights of the European Communities and other parties in these proceedings, in accordance with Article 4.6 of the DSU. The Panel has modified the relevant paragraphs, numbered 7.3 to 7.13 of the final report, to elaborate on the reasons for their inclusion. The relevance of the letter from Commissioner Lamy is discussed below.

letter from Commissioner Lamy

6.8 The European Communities requests the deletion of paragraph 7.79 as the letter from Commissioner Lamy to the USTR was provided only at the second substantive meeting and "the European Communities has had very little occasion so far to comment on this letter." Moreover, it was written in the context of the Doha Round negotiations and largely addresses questions relating to those negotiations. Even to the extent that it pronounces itself on certain aspects of the Regulation, it does not constitute an authoritative explanation of EC law and therefore does not form a sufficient basis for the Panel's findings regarding the content of the Regulation.

6.9 The United States opposes this request. Part of the issue before the Panel was the Commission's interpretation of whether the Regulation imposes equivalence and reciprocity conditions on WTO Members. A direct communication that it does, sent from the EC Trade Commissioner to the US Trade Representative, is plainly relevant. This is particularly true given that the European Communities had denied that its position on the issue had changed from that which it held prior to the dispute. In addition, the Panel cites the letter in a single sentence as further corroboration of a thorough Panel analysis. The United States recalls the European Communities' response to Panel question No. 15 that its own statements to the Panel regarding EC law are not authoritative explanations either so, under the European Communities' reasoning in its request for interim review, the Panel should also consider such statements to be irrelevant.

6.10 The Panel observes that the European Communities has taken the opportunity to comment on the letter in its request for interim review, and the Panel takes note of those comments. A full copy of the letter and its attachment was provided at the second substantive meeting. The European Communities had an opportunity to comment on the letter at that meeting and in its response to question No. 95, which specifically related to "any official statement by the Commission" as well as in its responses to six other questions relevant to the applicability of the equivalence and reciprocity conditions.

6.11 The Panel has already noted in the relevant paragraph that the letter provides further corroboration of the Panel's interpretation, so that it does not form the basis of any findings on its own. The letter is relevant for the following reasons: (a) it is from a member of the European Commission responsible for trade matters to the United States Trade Representative; (b) it states that the attachment contains a detailed analysis that covers certification marks *vis-à-vis* Doha Round issues "as well as a reply to [the USTR's] comments on EC Regulation 2081/92;" (c) the attachment specifically responds to the national treatment claim that is the subject of the Panel's examination in Section VII:B.1 of this report; and (d) it is recent. Therefore, the Panel has retained the paragraph, numbered 7.82 in the final report.

6.12 The Panel has also referred to Commissioner Lamy's letter in paragraph 7.733, as evidence in support of the European Communities' position under Article 22.2 of the TRIPS Agreement. The European Communities did not request review of that paragraph, which is numbered 7.750 in the final report, and the Panel has retained it also.

the phrase "[w]ithout prejudice to international agreements"

6.13 The European Communities requests the deletion of paragraphs 7.85 to 7.90 because it did not argue that the application of Article 12 of the Regulation would prejudice "the EC's obligations under the TRIPS Agreement." It quotes paragraph 66 of its first written submission and paragraph 43 of its first oral statement and asserts that "[t]hese statements do not contain any indication that the EC consider that its obligations under the TRIPS Agreement would be prejudiced by the application of Article 12 of Regulation 2081/92. Rather, the reference to the obligation to provide protection for geographical indications was clearly intended as a reference to the obligation of other WTO Members to provide protection. This is also what the EC explained in response to the Panel's Question No. 94(b)." The European Communities agrees that it is true that it did not provide an explicit response to Panel question No. 20 but it asserts that it did, however, address this point in response to

Panel question No. 94, in which it clarified that whereas the application of these conditions would not prejudice the European Communities' national treatment obligations under the TRIPS Agreement, it would prejudice its national treatment obligations under the GATT. Given this context, it comments that the Panel is wrong to read into the European Communities' submission a statement which the European Communities clearly did not make, and which contradicts the entire logic of the European Communities' submissions. In its view, by attempting to read admissions into the European Communities' submissions, the Panel effectively distorts these submissions. This is not compatible with the task of the Panel under Article 11 of the DSU, which is to make an objective assessment of the facts. The European Communities also requests the deletion of paragraph 7.200 for the same reason and because it is unnecessary to the legal analysis which precedes it.

6.14 The United States expresses surprise and disappointment that the European Communities would suggest that the Panel's assessment of the facts is non-objective, simply because the Panel has noted accurately the inconsistencies in the positions taken by the European Communities over the course of this dispute. The European Communities' sole basis for the deletion of six full paragraphs of Panel analysis is its disagreement with one part of one sentence in paragraph 7.86. The Panel's summary on this point is accurate, objective and fair and therefore the paragraphs should be retained. The United States notes that the European Communities admits that it avoided answering Panel question No. 20 but apparently seeks credit for answering Panel question No. 94. The United States recalls that the Panel has already made note of this response in paragraph 7.88.

6.15 The Panel takes note of the parties' comments and has carefully reviewed the European Communities' submissions, statements and responses to questions in this dispute, and confirms the following facts: (a) the interim report is consistent with the European Communities' own detailed analysis of the phrase "[w]ithout prejudice to international agreements" in its rebuttal submission; and (b) the European Communities repeatedly emphasized the importance of *its own* obligations in the interpretation of the equivalence and reciprocity conditions but there is no clear explanation on the record of this dispute as to how the obligations of *other* WTO Members would render the equivalence and reciprocity conditions under the European Communities' own Regulation inapplicable and the Panel declines to speculate. Therefore, the Panel has expanded and revised, rather than deleted, the relevant paragraphs, numbered 7.89 to 7.96 in the final report, and deleted paragraph 7.200 without affecting the preceding legal analysis.

6.16 The Panel takes note that, although the European Communities has now requested the deletion of most consideration of its own arguments concerning the phrase "[w]ithout prejudice to international agreements," this point is important to its defence and those arguments have not been withdrawn. Therefore, the Panel considers it important to address them as part of its objective assessment of the matter before it, in accordance with its function under Article 11 of the DSU.

<u>examination of applications for registration</u>

6.17 The European Communities requests the amendment of paragraph 7.262(b) to take account of the requirement in Article 12a(2)(a) of the Regulation that a third country must also transmit "a description of the legal provisions and the usage on the basis of which the designation of origin or the geographical indication is protected or established in the country," which is a question of the law of the third country, not Community law. It also comments that paragraph 7.272 should explain how the European Communities can implement Article 24.9 of the TRIPS Agreement with respect to such questions of foreign law, taking into account that the complainants have stated that such questions can be of high complexity and have indicated their unwillingness or inability to cooperate on such issues.

6.18 The United States considers that paragraph 7.262 should not be amended. The requirement that the European Communities wants to add is already described in the third step in that paragraph, which sets out the different requirements for third countries. The United States considers that the Panel's logical description would become "muddied" and confusing if part of the third step were collapsed into the second step. The United States also considers that the Panel should decline to offer further recommendations as to how the European

Communities should implement Article 24.9 of the TRIPS Agreement as the Panel's task is not to recommend how to implement provisions not part of its terms of reference. The United States also disagrees that it has indicated its unwillingness or inability to cooperate: it has challenged mandatory unilateral requirements, which is not a request for co-operation.

6.19 The Panel takes note of the European Communities' request and notes that the description of protection in the country of origin is already included in paragraph 7.262, numbered 7.268 in the final report, which is the logical place for it. The Panel considers it inappropriate to make further findings in this paragraph. The Panel's findings on transmission of applications already apply to all accompanying documents, including the description of protection in the country of origin. Further, this is an "as such" claim but Article 12a(2)(a) of the Regulation does not specify what form of description of protection in the country of origin would be acceptable, nor is there conclusive evidence on this point. In any event, Article 62 of the TRIPS Agreement would appear to be important in framing any recommendation on implementation, but it lies outside the Panel's terms of reference, as explained in paragraph 7.279 of the final report.

6.20 The Panel has also replaced the word "verification" in relation to applications for registration later in the report in order to be consistent with the use of the word "examination" used in the description of the application procedures and the consideration of the national treatment claim under the TRIPS Agreement. This does not imply that verification in the course of examination of applications is not covered by the Panel's conclusions with respect to examination.

Article XX(d) of GATT 1994

6.21 The United States suggested amendments to paragraphs 7.289 and 7.431 for clarity and accuracy concerning the alleged "laws and regulations not inconsistent with this Agreement" within the meaning of Article XX(d) of GATT 1994.

6.22 The European Communities responds that part of the drafting suggestion does not correctly represent its arguments and refers to its response to question No. 135(c) from the Panel. It requests that this argument be fully reflected in paragraph 7.289.

6.23 The Panel partly modified the paragraphs, numbered 7.297 and 7.446 in the final report, and reflected the arguments in the European Communities' responses to Panel questions Nos. 135(a), (b), (c) and (d) and addressed those arguments.

standard for private inspection bodies

6.24 The United States suggests the deletion from paragraph 7.405 of the phrase "the standard specified in the Regulation is based on an international standard" because this is a legal conclusion that must be based on a thorough analysis and which can have significant legal consequences, for instance, under Article 2.4 of the TBT Agreement and Article 3.1 of the SPS Agreement.

6.25 The European Communities opposes this suggestion because it was entirely appropriate for the Panel to consider whether the Regulation's requirements were based on an international standard, the United States did not make any claim under the TBT Agreement, and the United States never indicated prior to interim review that the ISO/IEC Guide at issue was not a relevant international standard, or that it saw any problems of substance with the content of this Guide.

6.26 The Panel does not take any view on whether the relevant ISO/IEC Guide is an international standard for the purposes of the TBT Agreement or the SPS Agreement and, for the avoidance of doubt, has amended paragraph 7.417 of the final report, based on its factual observations earlier in that sub-section.

marks of origin

6.27 The European Communities requests the deletion of point (b) of paragraph 7.496, with which it does not agree. The use of the words "made in" is not a specific requirement for a mark of origin in Article IX:1 of GATT 1994. It comments that it does not understand what is meant by indication in a pictorial manner nor by indication alongside the GI nor how this is relevant. Given the Panel's findings, it considers it unnecessary to reach a conclusion on this issue.

6.28 The United States suggests that paragraph 7.496(b) be retained as it is helpful to the resolution of the dispute for the Panel to summarize why, as a factual matter, an analysis of Article III:4, not Article IX, of GATT 1994 was appropriate.

6.29 The Panel has retained the paragraph, numbered 7.510 in the final report, because it is appropriate to explain why the European Communities' defence concerning marks of origin appears to be irrelevant to the preceding legal analysis. However, it has modified the point.

right to prevent the use of translations of registered GIs

6.30 The European Communities considers that it would be useful to recall in paragraph 7.504, for the sake of completeness, that under Article 13(1)(b) of the Regulation, GI holders do have a negative right to prevent the use of the registered name or names in translation.

6.31 The United States opposes this suggestion because paragraph 7.504 addresses the scope of the positive right of the GI holder under the Regulation, not what the GI holder can stop others from doing. Further, the negative right may cover a broad range of activities and is not limited to the use of so-called translations of GIs. With respect to the trademark claim in this dispute, the scope of the third party uses that the GI holder can prevent was never at issue because the European Communities concedes that, under Article 14(2) of the Regulation, the GI holder cannot stop trademark owners from using their valid trademarks in commerce.

6.32 The Panel has added a footnote to the paragraph, numbered 7.518 to clarify the scope of the positive right to use a GI with respect to translations and has also clarified the importance of the fact that a trademark may continue to be used under Article 14(2) of the Regulation. However, the Panel declines to amend the referenced paragraph as requested because the protection granted by Article 13 of the Regulation is already addressed elsewhere and it has not been shown to what extent Article 13(1)(b) covers translations.

exceptions in trademark legislation with respect to the use of GIs

6.33 The European Communities comments that the assertion in paragraph 7.545 to the effect that its trademark legislation provides no exceptions with respect to the use of geographical indications is factually incorrect, and refers to its response to Panel question No. 153 and, specifically, to Article 6.1(b) of the First Trademark Directive and Article 12(b) of the Community Trademark Regulation. Therefore, even where a trademark owner is allowed under the GI Regulation to enforce his rights under the First Trademark Directive or the Community Trademark Regulation with respect to the confusing use of a registered GI, he cannot prevent such use if it is "in accordance with honest practices in industrial or commercial matters."

6.34 The United States responds that the Panel's point is that the exception in the trademark legislation may be narrower than that in the GI Regulation. It considers that the Panel's meaning is clear and that any possible ambiguity might be removed by adding the word "unqualified" before exception. It also comments that the European Communities asserted before the Panel that the trademark owners cannot prevent GI holders from using a registered GI on the grounds that the use of the name is confusing *per se*.

6.35 The Panel takes note of the factual correction and has deleted the paragraph.

scope of a limited exception for GIs in translation

6.36 The European Communities suggests a redraft of paragraph 7.645 for the following reasons: (a) lest it imply that the European Communities agrees with the last sentence of paragraph 7.643; (b) in order to include all the relevant limitations to the exception in Article 14(2) of the Regulation relied upon by the Panel including "what is undoubtedly the most crucial one, namely that the trademark owner maintains the right to prevent any confusing uses by all parties except the GI holders;" and (c) because a registration under the Regulation may specify more than one linguistic version of the geographical indication and the last part of the second sentence of paragraph 7.645 may suggest otherwise.

6.37 The United States opposes the suggestion which it considers a significant redrafting of the Panel's factual conclusions as to the meaning of Article 14(2) of the Regulation. In its view, the European Communities' arguments are baseless and appear to represent an attempt to back away from factual findings that the European Communities itself repeatedly encouraged the Panel to make, as it asks the Panel to purge all references from paragraph 7.645 regarding translations of registered GIs. The United States provides some illustrative references of the European Communities' representations during the panel proceeding and suggests that the Panel consider repeating citations to them to avoid any misunderstandings. The United States considers that (a) paragraph 7.645 does not imply that the European Communities agrees with paragraph 7.643; (b) there is no legitimate purpose served by replacing a summary of the issue of curtailment of the right against all signs (removing references to translations) with a summary of the issue of curtailment of the right against all third parties, which has already been summarized at paragraph 7.642; and (c) it is clear that paragraph 7.645 addresses names "rendered differently in another language" from the name registered, and not names in other languages that are registered.

6.38 The Panel has taken careful note of the parties' comments and has amended the paragraph, numbered 7.659 in the final report, to track more closely the wording of the explanations in the European Communities' own submissions, and then made a finding on the basis of the terms of the legislation and those explanations. It has also added references in the succeeding paragraph and elsewhere to the limitation provided by certain directives which the European Communities explained during the proceeding.

conclusions

6.39 The European Communities requests that the Panel reflect in its conclusions its rejection of the US claim that the requirement of inspection structures as such constitutes a violation of national treatment obligations under the TRIPS Agreement and GATT 1994.

6.40 The United States opposes this request as the report does not contain a separate finding rejecting any claim that an inspection structure requirement "as such" violates national treatment obligations. No purpose is served by repeating reasoning that the Panel did not find persuasive.

6.41 The Panel has clarified that its findings that the United States did not make a prima facie case with respect to certain aspects of the inspection structures and has reflected this in its conclusions in paragraph 8.1. The Panel has also explained its reasons for exercising judicial economy in relation to Article 2(1) of the Paris Convention (1967), as incorporated by Article 2.1 of the TRIPS Agreement, reflected this in its conclusions in paragraph 8.1, and reflected all conclusions under that provision. The Panel has also added its conclusions from Section A of the findings to paragraph 8.1.

suggestion by the Panel on a way to implement its recommendation

6.42 The United States suggests that the Panel refrain from making a suggestion in paragraph 8.5 as to a way to implement the recommendation because (a) the European Communities is in a better position than either the Panel or the United States to determine the most appropriate way to implement the recommendations in the report; and (b) the simple clarification suggested by the Panel is not enough because, as the Panel correctly found (at paragraphs numbered 7.84 to 7.86 in the final report), the Regulation does not appear to have any procedures for the registration of GIs from WTO Members that do not satisfy the equivalence and reciprocity conditions.

6.43 The European Communities is surprised by the United States' suggestion as the United States had informed the Panel that it "would welcome any objective clarification" that these conditions do not apply, (as noted at paragraph 7.39 in the final report). The European Communities remarks that if the Regulation is clarified in the sense suggested by the Panel, this would necessarily also include a clarification that the appropriate procedures are available for the registration of geographical indications from other WTO Members. For these reasons, the European Communities requests that paragraph 8.5 not be deleted.

6.44 The Panel has modified its suggestion in paragraph 8.5 but, on the basis of the European Communities' remarks on interim review, considers it helpful to retain it.

other requests for review

6.45 The United States also requests modifications to paragraphs 7.28, 7.71, 7.72, 7.125, 7.400, 7.559 and 7.596 and footnotes 100 and 479 and makes some clerical observations. It suggests the addition of a general statement that where a party elaborates on a statement in later submission or answers to questions that citations to a submission are meant to be illustrative and not exhaustive. The Panel has modified its report accordingly.

6.46 The European Communities also requests the modification of paragraphs 7.407, 7.712 and 8.1. The Panel has modified those paragraphs and paragraphs 7.696 and 7.697 accordingly.

VII. FINDINGS

A. Preliminary Issues

1. *Consistency of panel requests with Article 6.2 of the DSU*

7.1 On 24 February 2004, the day after the Panel was composed and prior to the organizational meeting, the European Communities submitted a detailed request that the Panel issue a preliminary ruling that the United States' and Australia's respective requests for establishment of a panel were inconsistent with the requirements of Article 6.2 of the DSU. In accordance with the Panel's timetable, the United States and Australia submitted responses to the European Communities' request for a preliminary ruling.

7.2 On 5 April 2004, the Panel issued the following preliminary ruling.[9]

(a) Introduction

1. The European Communities is of the view that the requests for establishment of a panel in this matter do not meet the requirements of Article 6.2 of the DSU. It has requested that the Panel issue a preliminary ruling regarding this question.[10]

2. The United States is of the view that the European Communities' arguments in support of its request for a preliminary ruling that the United States' panel request does not meet the

---

[9] The preliminary ruling is reproduced with minor editorial changes.

[10] *(footnote original)* European Communities' request for a preliminary ruling dated 24 February 2004 ("EC request"), paras. 1, 2, 3 and 5. [Note: that request is attached as Annex B-1 to this final report]

requirements of Article 6.2 of the DSU are without merit. It submits that the Panel should reject that request.[11]

(...)[12]

4. Article 6.2 of the DSU provides as follows:

> 2. The request for the establishment of a panel shall be made in writing. It shall indicate whether consultations were held, identify the specific measures at issue and provide a brief summary of the legal basis of the complaint sufficient to present the problem clearly. In case the applicant requests the establishment of a panel with other than standard terms of reference, the written request shall include the proposed text of special terms of reference."

5. The European Communities alleges that the requests for establishment of a panel are inconsistent with the following requirements in Article 6.2:

(a) they fail to identify the specific measure at issue; and

(b) they do not provide a brief summary of the legal basis of the complaint sufficient to present the problem clearly.

6. The Panel will examine each of the requests for establishment of a panel as a whole on its face in the light of the parties' respective communications to the Panel to date and the relevant provisions of the covered agreements to assess its compliance with each of these requirements in the sections below.[13]

(b) United States' request for establishment of a panel[14]

(i). Identification of the specific measure at issue

7. The United States' request, in its first paragraph, refers to the following measure:

> EC Council Regulation (EEC) No 2081/92 of 14 July 1992 on the protection of geographical indications and designations of origin for agricultural products and foodstuffs, as amended.

8. The United States' request, in its second paragraph, identifies the following measures at issue:

> Regulation 2081/92, as amended, and its related implementing and enforcement measures ('Regulation 2081/92').

<u>Council Regulation (EEC) No. 2081/92, as amended</u>

9. The United States' request identifies a particular regulation by the name of the authority which adopted it, by its number, by its date of adoption and by its full title. It includes

[11] *(footnote original)* United States' response to EC request, dated 15 March 2004 ("US response"), para. 47. [Note: that response is attached as Annex A-1 to this final report]

[12] Note: paragraph 3 of the preliminary ruling dealt with Australia's request for establishment of a panel.

[13] *(footnote original)* This is consistent with the approach of the Appellate Body in *US – Carbon Steel* at para. 127 of its report.

[14] *(footnote original)* Document WT/DS174/20.

amendments of this regulation. This is a specific measure,[15] and the request has identified it. There is no doubt as to which specific measure is in issue, as the European Communities has itself demonstrated by annexing a consolidated text of the regulation to the request for a preliminary ruling.[16]

10. The European Communities argues that:

> The unspecific reference to Regulation 2081/92 made in the Panel requests does not permit the EC to understand *which specific aspects among those covered by Regulation 2081/92* the complainants intend to raise in the context of the present proceedings. (italics added)

11. The Panel considers the ordinary meaning of the terms of the text in Article 6.2 of the DSU, read in their context and in the light of the object and purpose of the provision, to be quite clear. They require that a request for establishment of a panel "identify the specific measures at issue." They do not require the identification of the "specific aspects" of these "specific measures."

"its related implementing and enforcement measures"

12. The United States' request identifies, in addition to the regulation as amended, "its related implementing and enforcement measures." The European Communities asserts that this phrase does not appear in the United States' request.[17] The Panel draws the European Communities' attention to the definition of "Regulation 2081/92" in the second paragraph of the request.[18] This phrase, as used in the United States' request, expressly refers to measures which implement and enforce Regulation (EEC) No. 2081/92, as amended. The word "related" is not used in isolation in the request.

13. The Regulation as amended itself expressly provides for the taking of particular types of decisions and actions and the adoption of rules of procedure for applying the Regulation. For example, Article 6 provides for the Commission to verify that registration applications include all the requisite particulars and, if it concludes that the name qualifies for protection, to publish certain details and, if no objection is notified, the name is entered in a register or, if the Commission concludes that the name does not qualify for protection, to decide not to proceed with the publication. Article 11a provides that the Commission may cancel the registration of a name. Article 12 provides for decisions by the Commission as to whether a third country satisfies the equivalence conditions and offers the requisite guarantees. Article 12b provides for the Commission, if it concludes that a name the subject of a registration request sent by a third country satisfies the conditions for protection, to publish certain details or, if it concludes that the name does not satisfy the conditions for protection, to decide not to proceed with publication. Article 16 provides for detailed rules for applying the Regulation to be adopted.[19] Those decisions, actions and rules, among others, implement the Regulation. The European Communities has indicated that the competent judicial and executive authorities enforce the Regulation.[20] In the

---

[15] *(footnote original)* In this respect, the Panel notes that the Appellate Body in *EC – Bananas III* (at para. 140 of its report) agreed with the Panel in that case that similar language in the following extract from a panel request sufficiently identified the specific measure at issue in accordance with Article 6.2 of the DSU: "a regime for the importation, sale and distribution of bananas established by Regulation 404/93 [...], and subsequent EC legislation, regulations and administrative measures, including those reflecting the provisions of the Framework Agreement on bananas, which implement, supplement and amend that regime."

[16] *(footnote original)* Exhibit EC-1 annexed to EC request, *supra* at 10. A list containing the names, numbers and dates of the amendments reflected in the consolidated text of the regulation can be found on page 1 of that document.

[17] *(footnote original)* EC request, *supra* at 10, para. 24, fn. 10.

[18] *(footnote original)* Quoted above at para. 8.

[19] *(footnote original)* Exhibit EC-1.

[20] *(footnote original)* EC request, *supra* at 10, para. 30.

Panel's view, this does not imply that there is any uncertainty as to which measures taken by those authorities implement and enforce the Regulation and which do not. All of the Regulation's implementing and enforcement measures form a group of specific measures which, although they may be a large group, are identified by the United States' request for establishment of a panel.[21]

14. For these reasons, on the basis of the facts available to us, the Panel rules that the United States' request for establishment of a panel did not fail to identify the specific measures at issue in accordance with Article 6.2 of the DSU.

(ii) A brief summary of the legal basis of the complaint sufficient to present the problem clearly

Preliminary remarks

15. The United States' request, in its third paragraph, sets out in narrative form alleged inconsistencies with the covered agreements, by quoting or paraphrasing the text of certain provisions of the covered agreements. The fourth paragraph begins with the words "Regulation 2081/92 appears to be inconsistent with:" and then sets out provisions of the covered agreements by number with which the United States alleges that the measures at issue are inconsistent.

16. It is clear on a plain reading of the request that the series of numbered provisions is not to be limited to what appears in the narrative text. The narrative text quotes or paraphrases some of these provisions which, in the Panel's view, illustrates and clarifies the alleged violations. In this regard, the Panel notes that the European Communities has conceded that it recognizes in the narrative text the treaty language of Articles 3 and 4 of the TRIPS Agreement and Articles I:1 and III:4 of the GATT 1994.[22]

17. The series of numbered provisions identifies every article of every covered agreement at issue and, where there are paragraphs within an article, it identifies every paragraph by number (with the exception of Article 2 of the Paris Convention, as incorporated by Article 2.1 of the TRIPS Agreement, and Article I of the GATT 1994).

Individual analyses

18. The Panel considers that the mere listing of provisions of the relevant covered agreements may not satisfy the standard of Article 6.2 of the DSU, for instance, where the listed provisions establish multiple obligations rather than one single, distinct obligation.[23] However, where the multiple obligations are closely related and interlinked, a reference to a common obligation in the specific listed provisions should be sufficient to meet the standard of Article 6.2 of the DSU under certain circumstances in a particular case.[24]

19. With these considerations in mind, the Panel now examines individual claims related to each provision listed by the United States in its request for establishment of a panel. The Panel notes that Articles 1.1, 2.1 (incorporating by reference Article 2 of the Paris Convention (1967)), 3.1, 4, 16.1, 20, 24.5, 41.4, 44.1, 63.1, 63.3 and 65.1 of the TRIPS Agreement and Article III:4 of the GATT 1994, which were enumerated in the United States' request, each contains either a single obligation or very closely related obligations. In addition, the Panel notes the following:

[21] *(footnote original)* See *supra* at 15.

[22] *(footnote original)* EC request, *supra* at 10, paras. 44 and 45.

[23] *(footnote original)* See the Appellate Body report on *Korea – Dairy*, para. 124.

[24] *(footnote original)* See the Appellate Body report on *Thailand – H-Beams*, para. 93.

(a) Article 22.1 of the TRIPS Agreement does not set out an obligation but rather a definition of a term which is used in other provisions set out in the United States' request. The reference to Article 22.1 and the corresponding narrative text in the request actually presents the problem more, rather than less, clearly because they explain that the United States will challenge the measures at issue under the relevant obligations on the basis of an alleged inconsistency with this definition;

(b) Article 22.2 of the TRIPS Agreement contains an obligation regarding the use of a geographical indication in two circumstances, but the narrative text paraphrases the first one from Article 22.2(a). This clarifies that the obligation in this circumstance is the subject of a claim;

(c) Article 41.1 of the TRIPS Agreement contains a general obligation which relates, on its face, to "enforcement procedures as specified in [Part III]." Several of those enforcement procedures are raised in the United States' request, namely those under Articles 41.2, 41.4, 42 and 44.1. This clarifies that the general obligation is the subject of a claim in relation to these procedures. The narrative text also states that the regulation at issue "does not provide adequate enforcement procedures;"

(d) Article 41.2 of the TRIPS Agreement contains general obligations which relate to the operation of procedures concerning the enforcement of intellectual property rights. The requirements of each sentence of Article 41.2 are distinct but they are all closely related;

(e) Article 42 of the TRIPS Agreement contains closely related obligations concerning fair and equitable procedures. The requirements of each sentence in Article 42 are distinct but they all set out specific features of fair and equitable civil judicial procedures concerning the enforcement of intellectual property rights;

(f) the focus of the claims under Articles 41.1, 41.2 and 42 of the TRIPS Agreement is further clarified by the fact that the measures at issue deal with the subject of the protection of geographical indications and designations of origin, which does not impact all intellectual property rights covered by the Agreement, and the narrative text also refers to the protection of trademarks and geographical indications; and

(g) Article I of the GATT 1994 contains four paragraphs, but the narrative text quotes only the first paragraph. This clarifies that the obligation in Article I:1 is the subject of a claim. The European Communities recognizes this treaty text.[25]

20. The European Communities further contends that it is entitled to know which provision or aspect of Regulation No. 2081/92 is supposed to violate certain obligations and in which way such a violation is deemed to occur. In the Panel's view, the European Communities is seeking the arguments, rather than just the claims, of the United States.[26] That being said, the Panel wishes to assure the European Communities that it is fully entitled to know the arguments of the United States *during the course of the proceedings*. Those arguments must be set out and may be clarified in the United States' submissions.[27] However, Article 6.2 of the DSU does not require those arguments to be set out in the request for establishment of a panel.[28]

---

[25] *(footnote original)* EC request, *supra* at 10, para. 45.

[26] *(footnote original)* See the Appellate Body report on *EC – Bananas III*, para. 141; *Korea – Dairy*, para. 139; and *US – Carbon Steel*, para. 173.

[27] *(footnote original) Ibid.*

[28] *(footnote original)* See the Appellate Body report on *Korea – Dairy*, para. 123.

21. The Panel notes that Article 6.2 of the DSU calls for sufficient clarity with respect to the legal basis of the complaint so as to enable a defending party to begin preparing its defence.[29] Our examination of the United States' request for establishment of a panel as a whole, in the light of the United States' and the European Communities' respective communications to the Panel to date and the relevant provisions of the covered agreements, leads us to believe that the request for establishment of a panel was sufficiently clear for the European Communities to begin preparing its defence.

22. For these reasons, on the basis of the facts available to us, the Panel rules that the United States' request for establishment of a panel did not fail to provide a brief summary of the legal basis of the complaint sufficient to present the problem clearly in accordance with Article 6.2 of the DSU.

(...)[30]

(d) Due process

43. The European Communities is also of the view that the "deficiencies" of the requests for establishment of a panel seriously prejudice its due process rights as a defending party, notably, to know the case it has to answer.[31]

44. The Panel recalls once again that Article 6.2 of the DSU calls for sufficient clarity with respect to the legal basis of the complaint so as to enable a defending party to begin preparing its defence.[32] In this respect, the Panel has found that the complainants' requests for establishment of a panel were sufficiently clear for the European Communities to begin preparing its defence.[33] Therefore, the Panel considers that it is not necessary to make a separate ruling on this issue, as presented by the European Communities in its request.[34]

45. The Panel is mindful of the due process rights of all parties in this proceeding. In this regard, it notes that the European Communities had a period of over four months after the establishment of the Panel prior to its constitution plus a period of over seven weeks prior to receipt of the complainants' first written submissions to begin preparing its case, and will have an additional period of four and a half weeks from receipt of the complainants' first written submissions to continue preparation of its own first written submission, which is in excess of the maximum period proposed in Appendix 3 to the DSU.

(e) Timeliness

46. The European Communities submitted its request for a preliminary ruling two days after the composition of the Panel. It also raised its concerns at the DSB meetings at which the requests for establishment of a panel were considered.[35]

---

[29] *(footnote original)* See the Appellate Body report on *Thailand – H-Beams*, para. 88.

[30] Note: paragraphs 23-42 of the preliminary ruling dealt with Australia's request for establishment of a panel.

[31] *(footnote original)* EC request, *supra* at 10, para. 4.

[32] *(footnote original)* See *supra* at 29.

[33] *(footnote original)* See para. 21.

[34] *(footnote original)* The Panel takes note that the European Communities stated that it does not take a position as to whether "the requirement of prejudice in Article 6.2 DSU" constitutes an additional requirement to those set out in Article 6.2 of the DSU: EC request, *supra* at 10, para. 66, fn. 25

[35] *(footnote original)* See the minutes of those meetings in documents WT/DSB/M/155, para. 75, and WT/DSB/M/156, para. 32, reproduced in Exhibits EC-2 and EC-3, respectively. The Panel takes note that the European Communities did not clearly raise any problem concerning the alleged failure of Australia's request to identify the specific measures at issue on those occasions.

47. The Panel therefore considers that the European Communities has raised its concerns in a timely manner.[36]

(f) Conclusion

48. In light of the foregoing, on the basis of the facts available to us, the Panel rules that the measures and claims in Australia's and the United States' respective requests for establishment of a panel did not fail to meet the requirements of Article 6.2 of the DSU that they identify the specific measures at issue and provide a brief summary of the legal basis of the complaint sufficient to present the problem clearly. [End of 5 April 2004 ruling]

7.3 The Panel stated expressly that its 5 April 2004 preliminary ruling was based on the facts available to it at that time.[37] In this final report, the Panel makes further findings on the sufficiency of the panel request, in light of submissions made later during the course of the panel proceeding. These submissions confirm the Panel's ruling as to the meaning of the words used in the panel request and the Panel's assessment that the ability of the respondent to defend itself was not prejudiced.[38]

7.4 First, the Panel recalls that the European Communities argued, in its request for a preliminary ruling, that:

> The unspecific reference to Regulation 2081/92 made in the Panel requests does not permit the EC to understand which specific aspects among those covered by Regulation 2081/92 the complainants intend to raise in the context of the present proceedings.[39]

7.5 The Panel ruled that Article 6.2 did not require the identification of the "specific aspects" of the specific measures at issue.[40] In any event, after consulting the parties' first written submissions, it is clear that the reference to "Regulation No. 2081/92, as amended" in the request for establishment of a panel did identify certain specific aspects among those covered by the Regulation that the complainant later raised, as follows:

(a) the United States' claims concerning national treatment (considered in Section VII:B of this report) are based on the differences between the two sets of registration and objection procedures set out in Regulation (EEC) No. 2081/92 (the "Regulation") in Articles 5 through 7 and 12 through 12d, respectively.[41] This is one of the principal features of the Regulation. It was clear from the request for establishment of a panel that the complainant intended to raise these aspects of the Regulation; and

(b) the United States' claim concerning the legal protection for trademarks (considered in Section VII:C of this report) is based on Article 14 of the Regulation. This provision is specifically devoted to that issue. It was clear from the request for establishment of a panel that the

[36] *(corrected footnote original)* This does not imply that these issues could not be raised later in the proceedings.

[37] See paras. 6, 14 and 48 of the preliminary ruling set out above.

[38] This is consistent with the approach of the Appellate Body in *US – Carbon Steel*, para. 127.

[39] Quoted at para. 10 of the preliminary ruling set out above.

[40] See para. 11 of the preliminary ruling set out above.

[41] To the extent that the claims concern the actions of EC member State authorities in the examination, verification and transmission of applications and objections, the European Communities expressly referred to these actions at para. 31 of its request for a preliminary ruling, attached as Annex B-1 to this report. It also informed the Panel during this proceeding that Community laws are generally not executed through authorities at Community level but rather through recourse to the authorities of its member States: see para. 7.98 below.

complainant intended to raise this article of the Regulation, as the European Communities itself confirmed in its request for a preliminary ruling[42].

7.6 Second, the Panel recalls that the European Communities submitted in its February 2004 request for a preliminary ruling that:

> In the present case, the ambiguity of the Panel request is such that the EC is, to this date, not sure of the case which the United States and Australia are bringing before the Panel. As a consequence, the EC has been seriously hampered in its efforts to prepare its defence.[43]

7.7 Specifically, with respect to the national treatment claims, it submitted as follows:

> [T]he US claim is limited to a paraphrasing of the treaty language of [Article 3 TRIPS and Article III:4 GATT]. The US claim does not permit to understand which provision or aspect of Regulation 2081/92 is supposed to violate the national treatment principle, and in which way such a violation is deemed to occur.[44]

7.8 The Panel's assessment was that the request for establishment of a panel was sufficiently clear for the European Communities to begin preparing its defence.[45] After consulting the European Communities' first written submission, and information submitted by the United States, the Panel is now aware that the European Communities had already presented in the Council for TRIPS in September 2002 a statement that responded specifically to the United States' argument that national treatment under the TRIPS Agreement applied to geographical indications. In that statement, the European Communities quoted the texts of Article 3 of the TRIPS Agreement and Article III:4 of GATT 1994 and argued that "[t]hose entitled to rights under TRIPS are nationals."

7.9 Further, in an attachment to a letter sent in January 2003 by Commissioner Lamy to the United States Trade Representative, under the heading "national treatment," the Commissioner referred *inter alia* to the equivalence and reciprocity conditions, the notion of "nationals" under the TRIPS Agreement, and the availability to U.S. nationals of protection for GIs located in the European Communities.[46] These arguments are also an important defence set out in the European Communities' first written submission, in which it is argued that "[t]he conditions for the registration of geographical indications do not depend on nationality."[47]

7.10 With respect to the claim concerning minimum standards of GI protection, the European Communities had submitted in its request for a preliminary ruling that:

> The United States alleges that Regulation 2081/92 'does not provide legal means for interested parties to prevent the misleading use of a geographical indication.' This claim is not

---

[42] The claim concerned coexistence under Article 14(2), subject to Article 14(3). The European Communities expressly referred to both, as well as Article 7(4), to which it referred in its defence, at paras. 47 and 61 of its request for a preliminary ruling, attached as Annex B-1 to this report. The only aspect of the Regulation which it raised in this respect in its request for a preliminary ruling, that it did not later raise in its defence, was Article 14(1): see Section VII:C of this report.

[43] European Communities' request, para. 68, *supra* at 10.

[44] *Ibid.*, para. 44.

[45] See para. 21 of the preliminary ruling set out above.

[46] Exhibit US-73, attachment, page 1. The Panel notes that this letter did not form part of the consultations under Article 4 of the DSU on the national treatment and MFN claims in this dispute, which the United States requested in April 2003 (WT/DS174/1/Add.1). The United States first submitted only a relevant page of the attachment to this letter, identifying it as a "Communication from the EC to the United States of January 16, 2003." The European Communities replied that it did not consider that "this document is attributable to the EC, and will not comment on it any further," (EC rebuttal, para. 84). The United States therefore submitted the full text of the letter and its attachment, which includes other matters relevant to geographical indications, including the issue of prior trademarks, on which the United States requested consultations in 1999 (WT/DS174/1).

[47] European Communities' first written submission, paras. 114 and 123-126.

> comprehensible to the EC. In its Article 13, Regulation 2081/92 contains detailed provisions regarding the protection of geographical indications. These provisions provide interested parties with the legal means to prevent the misleading use of a geographical indication. In the absence of further explanations, the EC fails to comprehend what is the claim that the United States is intending to establish.[48]

7.11 The Panel is now aware that, in the same letter, Commissioner Lamy had earlier confirmed to the United States Trade Representative that "US GIs cannot be registered in the EU" but argued that alternative measures besides the Regulation provided protection for U.S. GIs.[49] In light of these attendant circumstances, the allegation that "Regulation 2081/92 'does not provide legal means for interested parties to prevent the misleading use of a geographical indication'" should have been readily comprehensible to the European Communities.

7.12 These statements support the Panel's assessment that the relevant wording of the request for establishment of a panel was sufficiently clear for the European Communities to begin preparing its defence of the first national treatment claim and the claim under Article 22.2 of the TRIPS Agreement.[50]

7.13 Third, the Panel notes that, in any event, the United States' other claims (considered in Section VII:D of this report), brought under the provisions discussed in subparagraphs (a) through (g) of paragraph 19 of the preliminary ruling, were not pursued in such detail. The Panel has found no prima facie case or exercised judicial economy in respect of all these claims. This confirms the Panel's assessment that no prejudice has been caused to the rights of the respondent by these claims.

2. Measures adopted after the date of establishment of the Panel

(a) Main arguments of the parties

7.14 The United States and Australia submitted, as an exhibit, a copy of Commission Regulation (EC) No. 2400/96[51], which is effectively the register under Article 6 of Council Regulation (EEC) No. 2081/92. Individual designations of origin and geographical indications are added to the register by amending this Commission Regulation. The exhibit includes amendments made up until the time of the first written submissions in this proceeding, nine of which were adopted after the date of establishment of the Panel. Those nine amendments effected the registrations of 15 individual designations of origin and geographical indications.[52]

7.15 The United States and Australia also submitted, as an exhibit, an unofficial consolidated version of Council Regulation (EEC) No. 2081/92, which included amendments published in the Official Journal of the European Communities up until the date of establishment of the Panel.[53] The latest of these amendments is the Act of Accession of ten new EC member States. They also submitted, as an exhibit, an extract from that Act of Accession which provides for the registration of three Czech beer GIs under Article 17 of the Regulation.[54]

---

[48] European Communities' request, para. 49, attached as Annex B-1 to this report.

[49] Exhibit US-73, attachment, page 1, *supra* at 46. The relevant passage is quoted at para. 7.83 below.

[50] See also para. 6.7 above.

[51] Exhibit COMP-4b.

[52] Exhibit COMP-4b.viii to xvi. The 15 GIs are "Westlandse druif;" "Alcachofa de Benicarló" or "Carxofa de Benicarló;" "Marrone di San Zeno;" "Mantequilla de l'Alt Urgell y la Cerdanya" or "Mantega de l'Alt Urgell i la Cerdanya;" "Thüringer Leberwurst," "Thüringer Rotwurst," "Thüringer Rostbratwurst;" "Spressa delle Giudicarie;" "Fraise du Périgord;" "Queso de Valdeón;" "Ensaimada de Mallorca" or "Ensaimada mallorquina;" "Arbroath Smokies;" "Carciofo di Paestum;" "Farina di Neccio della Garfagnana;" "Agneau de Pauillac" and "Agneau du Poitou-Charentes."

[53] Exhibit COMP-1a.

[54] Exhibit COMP-3c. The Czech beer GIs are "Budějovické pivo," "Českobudějovické pivo" and "Budějovický měšt'anský var."

7.16 The United States indicates that it does not raise claims against the three Czech beer GIs but provides them as examples relevant to issues in dispute. Nevertheless, it submits that the Panel's findings could affect trademark rights in future disputes regarding allegedly infringing uses of these three GIs.[55]

7.17 The European Communities responds that these measures did not yet exist at the time the Panel was established and are therefore outside the terms of reference. In particular, it submits that the Act of Accession was subject to ratification, which was not completed on the date of establishment of the Panel, and did not enter into force until 1 May 2004.[56] However, it understands that the United States does not raise a claim concerning the registration of the three Czech beer GIs.[57]

(b) Main arguments of third parties

7.18 China argues that the wording of the request for establishment of a panel specified amendments to the Regulation and that, therefore, they are properly included in the Panel's terms of reference. The respondent received notice of the inclusion of amendments and had enough opportunity to respond to the complainant's case. It is irrelevant whether the amendments came into effect before or after the Panel was established.[58]

(c) Consideration by the Panel

7.19 The Panel begins by noting that Council Regulation (EEC) No. 2081/92 (referred to in this report as the "Regulation") has not been amended in any relevant respects during this panel proceeding. It was last amended in April 2003, prior to the date of the request for establishment of a panel. However, certain individual registrations were effected under the Regulation after the date of establishment of the Panel and prior to the date of the complainant's first written submission, and registrations continue to be made after that date.

7.20 The Panel notes that the United States does not challenge any individual registrations in this dispute. It is therefore unnecessary to rule on these measures. It suffices to note that individual registrations made after the date of the request for establishment of a panel can be among the best evidence of the way in which certain provisions of the Regulation itself, which are at issue, are interpreted and applied.[59] The Panel may therefore refer to them, as factual evidence, in the course of its assessment of the matter before it.[60]

3. Claims under Article 2(2) of the Paris Convention (1967), as incorporated by Article 2.1 of the TRIPS Agreement

(a) Main arguments of the parties

7.21 The United States claims that the Regulation imposes a requirement as to domicile or establishment in the European Communities on the availability of registration and the right to object to registrations contrary to Article 2(2) of the Paris Convention (1967) as incorporated by Article 2.1 of the TRIPS Agreement.[61] In its view, the requirement of commercial establishment in the European Union under the Regulation at issue is simply another aspect of the alleged denial of national treatment and the requirement in Article 2(2) of the Paris Convention (1967) is connected to and part of the obligation in Article 2(1). Its request for establishment of a

---

[55] United States' comments on EC response to Panel question No. 137.

[56] European Communities' first written submission, paras. 21-25.

[57] United States' rebuttal submission, paras. 291-292.

[58] Annex C, paras. 70-71.

[59] In fact, the European Communities itself has included one of these GIs in its exhibits: the 2002 publication of the application to register "Thüringer Leberwurst" is Exhibit EC-54.

[60] The Panel refers to the registration of the three Czech beer GIs submitted in an exhibit by the complainants (see para. 7.15 above) as evidence of the operation of Article 14(3) of the Regulation in paras. 7.573 and 7.669 below.

[61] United States' first written submission, paras. 84-85 and 91.

panel referred to "national treatment" and "Article 2" of the Paris Convention (1967), which include both paragraphs 1 and 2.[62]

7.22 The European Communities responds that these claims are outside the Panel's terms of reference because they relate to Article 2(2) of the Paris Convention (1967) which was not explicitly mentioned in the request for establishment of a panel. Article 2(2) prohibits the imposition of requirements as to domicile or establishment and is therefore different from, and additional to, the obligations resulting from the national treatment provision of Article 2(1).[63]

(b) Consideration by the Panel

7.23 The Panel notes that the United States' request for establishment of a panel refers in narrative form to the treatment of other nationals and products originating outside the European Communities and that provided to the European Communities' own nationals and products, and cites by number Article 2.1 of the TRIPS Agreement "incorporating by reference Article 2 of the Paris Convention" (1967). In its submissions to the Panel, the United States claims that certain aspects of the Regulation are inconsistent with both Article 2(1) and 2(2) of the Paris Convention (1967) as incorporated by Article 2.1 of the TRIPS Agreement.

7.24 The issue for the Panel is whether the reference to national treatment and to Article 2 of the Paris Convention (1967) is sufficient to present the legal basis of the complaint under Articles 2(1) and 2(2), or only Article 2(1).

7.25 The Panel considers that the mere listing of provisions of the relevant covered agreements may not satisfy the standard of Article 6.2 of the DSU, for instance, where the listed provisions establish multiple obligations rather than one single, distinct obligation.[64] However, where the multiple obligations are closely related and interlinked, a reference to a common obligation in the specific listed provisions should be sufficient to meet the standard of Article 6.2 of the DSU under certain circumstances in a particular case.[65]

7.26 Paragraph 1 of Article 2 of the Paris Convention (1967) expresses a national treatment obligation. Paragraph 2 prohibits local domicile or establishment requirements as a condition for the enjoyment of any industrial property rights. The texts of paragraphs 1 and 2 are linked by the use of the conjunction "[h]owever" which indicates that paragraph 2 restricts the rule of paragraph 1. Paragraph 2 in effect provides that certain conditions may not be imposed on foreign nationals, even if they are imposed on a country's own nationals.[66] Paragraph 3 also reserves or excepts certain conditions from the national treatment obligation, but by stating certain conditions which may be imposed on foreign nationals, even if they are not imposed on a country's own nationals. Read in context, all three paragraphs either establish a single obligation or are very closely related: paragraph 1 sets out an obligation to provide national treatment and paragraphs 2 and 3 limit that obligation.

7.27 Therefore, in the Panel's view, the references in the request for establishment of a panel to national treatment and to Article 2 of the Paris Convention (1967), which does not specify particular paragraphs, as incorporated by Article 2.1 of the TRIPS Agreement, is sufficient to explain the legal basis of the complaints under both paragraphs 1 and 2 of Article 2. Accordingly, the Panel rules that the claims under Article 2(2) of the

---

[62] United States' first oral statement, para. 27; rebuttal submission, paras. 80-83.

[63] European Communities' first written submission, paras. 36-42; second oral statement, paras. 112-117.

[64] See the Appellate Body report on *Korea – Dairy*, para. 124.

[65] See the Appellate Body report on *Thailand – H-Beams*, para. 93.

[66] A leading commentator explains the addition of the word "however" as follows: "Even when the conditions imposed upon nationals of a country include the stipulation that *those nationals* can claim protection of certain industrial property rights only if they are domiciled or established in the country, this same stipulation cannot be imposed upon *nationals of other countries* of the Union." in Bodenhausen, Professor G.H.C., *Guide to the Application of the Paris Convention for the Protection of Industrial Property*, United International Bureaux for the Protection of Intellectual Property (BIRPI) (1969) (reprinted 1991) ("Bodenhausen"), p. 31. [Emphasis in the original]

Paris Convention (1967), as incorporated by Article 2.1 of the TRIPS Agreement, are within the Panel's terms of reference.

4. Claim regarding objection procedures under GATT 1994

7.28 The European Communities indicates in its responses to questions after the second substantive meeting that, in its view, the United States has made a claim in relation to the objection procedures under the TRIPS Agreement but not under GATT 1994.[67] It does not indicate the reasons for its view.

7.29 The United States replies that it makes its claim in relation to the objection procedures under GATT 1994 as well, and refers to passages in its rebuttal submission.[68]

7.30 The parties do not dispute that the United States' claim with respect to objection procedures under GATT 1994 is within the Panel's terms of reference. Nor do they dispute that the United States' rebuttal submission clearly raises a claim in respect of the objection procedures under "the national treatment obligations of GATT 1994." However, the presentation of this claim after the first substantive meeting raises an issue of due process. The United States chose not to pursue this claim in its first written submission but later expected the European Communities to defend itself against an additional claim.

7.31 Normally, this would prejudice a respondent's ability to defend itself. However, the overlapping nature of the United States' claims with respect to different aspects of the same measure and the same type of obligation under different covered agreements is a feature of this dispute. The facts and arguments submitted in support of this claim in respect of the objection procedures under the national treatment obligations of GATT 1994 completely overlap with those in support of claims in respect of the objection procedures under the national treatment obligations in the TRIPS Agreement, and the application procedures under the national treatment obligation in Article III:4 of GATT 1994. This also serves to clarify that this claim is made under Article III:4.

7.32 The requirements of due process have been observed. The European Communities has responded to all the relevant facts and arguments in detail, as well as a question from the Panel concerning the justification of the objection procedures under Article XX(d) of GATT 1994, although it did not otherwise respond to this claim.

7.33 For all these reasons, the Panel will consider this claim.[69]

5. Request by a third party for a suggestion on ways to implement a recommendation

7.34 Mexico considers that "cochineal" should be removed from the list of products covered by the Regulation set out in its Annex II. As a third party, Mexico does not submit this as a claim, but requests that the Panel make a suggestion to this effect pursuant to the second sentence of Article 19.1 of the DSU. Mexico argues that there is no requirement that a request for such a suggestion must be forwarded by one of the parties and, if the Panel does not deem it appropriate to make such a specific suggestion, the same result would be achieved by a suggestion that the European Communities withdraw the Regulation.[70]

7.35 The Panel takes note of Mexico's request. The issue of the product coverage of the Regulation is not challenged by the claims in this dispute and is therefore outside the Panel's terms of reference. However, Mexico's attention is drawn to Article 10.4 of the DSU.

---

[67] See European Communities' response to Panel question No. 136(d).

[68] United States' comments on EC response to Panel question No. 136(d).

[69] See paras. 7.367 to 7.373 below.

[70] Annex C, paras. 115 and 117.

6. Order of analysis of claims

7.36 The claims in this dispute are made under the TRIPS Agreement and GATT 1994 and certain claims under each agreement relate to the same aspects of the measure at issue. There is no hierarchy between these two agreements which appear in separate annexes to the WTO Agreement. The parties have addressed claims under the TRIPS Agreement first in their submissions, which appears logical. Therefore, the Panel will follow that order of analysis in this report.

7.37 The Panel will consider the claims relevant to each aspect of the measure in turn. The following sections of the findings are organized as follows:

- Section B National treatment claims
- Section C Trademark claim
- Section D Other claims

B. National Treatment Claims

1. Availability of protection

(a) Do the conditions in Article 12(1) of the Regulation apply to WTO Members?

(i) main arguments of the parties[71]

7.38 The United States claims that GIs located in the territory of a WTO Member outside the European Union can only be registered under the Regulation if that Member satisfies the conditions in Article 12(1), which require it to adopt a system for GI protection that is equivalent to that in the European Communities and provide reciprocal protection to products from the European Communities.[72]

7.39 The United States argues that these conditions are clearly set out as requirements for registration of GIs in all third countries, including WTO Members, in Articles 12 and 12a of the Regulation. Article 12(1) does not suggest that WTO Members are excluded from its conditions and Article 12a sets out the sole process under the Regulation for the registration of non-EC GIs. If the conditions in Article 12(1) do not apply to WTO Members, then they may not be recognized under Article 12(3) and the Article 12a procedure is still not available for them. It argues that the European Communities had maintained in its public statements up until the time of its first written submission that the conditions did apply to WTO Members. It did not amend the conditions so that they would not apply to WTO Members when it amended the Regulation in April 2003. The United States would welcome any objective clarification that the conditions do not apply, but the clear language of the Regulation shows that they do. The introductory phrase "[w]ithout prejudice to international agreements" reserves flexibility to protect specific non-EC GIs through bilateral agreements.[73]

7.40 The United States argues that the Panel is not bound by the European Communities' interpretation of its own measure. It is not based on any published official notice, it runs counter to the terms of the Regulation and it does not appear to be authoritative or binding as a matter of EC law. It is a statement by the European

---

[71] The Panel's citations of parties' submissions in this report are not exhaustive. At times, parties' positions are elaborated in other submissions and responses to questions which are attached in full in Annexes A and B to this report.

[72] United States' first written submission, para. 22.

[73] United States' first oral statement, paras. 7-16; rebuttal submission, paras. 8 and 20-21; second oral statement, paras. 18-22. In this regard, the United States also makes a reference to Australia's first written submission and responses to Panel questions in a footnote to para. 8 of its rebuttal submission, and states that the United States "and Australia" have documented numerous cases of EC explanations of its views, in its comment on the EC response to Panel question No. 97.

Commission which does not prevent the European Council, the EC member States or individuals from contesting that interpretation before the Community courts.[74]

7.41 The European Communities responds that the conditions in Article 12(1) of the Regulation do not apply to geographical areas located in WTO Members. The introductory phrase of Article 12(1) provides that it applies "[w]ithout prejudice to international agreements"—which include the WTO agreements. This is made clear by the eighth recital of the April 2003 amending Regulation which took specific account of the provision of the TRIPS Agreement. WTO Members are obliged to provide protection to geographical indications in accordance with Section 3 of Part II and the general provisions and basic principles of the TRIPS Agreement. For this reason, Article 12(1) and 12(3) do not apply to WTO Members. Accordingly, the registration of GIs from other WTO Members is subject to exactly the same conditions as the registration of GIs from the European Communities.[75]

7.42 The European Communities argues that the procedure under Article 12a of the Regulation is not limited to the cases covered by Article 12(3). The term "third country" in Articles 12 through 12d does or does not include WTO Members depending on the wording, context and objectives of each specific provision. The evidence of prior statements by Community officials does not contradict the EC's interpretation in this Panel proceeding and more recent statements support it. The statements made by the agents of the European Commission before the Panel commit and engage the European Communities but their intention is not to create new legal obligations in public international or in Community law. They are made on behalf of the European Communities as a whole and not only the Commission. Community legislation must, so far as possible, be interpreted in a manner that is consistent with international law, in particular where its provisions are intended specifically to give effect to an international agreement concluded by the Community, as indicated by the phrase "[w]ithout prejudice to international agreements." An interpretation that limited that phrase to bilateral agreements would largely deprive it of its useful value.[76]

7.43 The European Communities does not consider that the Panel is "bound" by the EC's interpretation of its own measure. However, it submits that the Panel must take due account of the fact that the Regulation is a measure of EC domestic law and establish its meaning as a factual element. This means that: (1) the burden of proof is on the complainant to establish the meaning of the measure. Given that the claim in the present dispute is based on the measure *per se* and not as applied, the complainant must establish "beyond doubt" that the measure entails a violation; (2) in making an objective assessment of the facts and the interpretation of the measure, the Panel should be guided by the rules of interpretation customary in the EC's domestic legal order; and (3) it is the EC's authorities who must interpret and apply the measure and therefore its explanations must be given considerable deference.[77]

(ii) main arguments of third parties

7.44 Argentina asserts that the conditions of equivalence and reciprocity apply to GIs located in all third countries. It is unconvinced by the European Communities' explanation of its measure. If its intention had been to distinguish between WTO Members and other third countries, it could have done so more explicitly.[78]

7.45 Brazil asserts that the conditions of equivalence and reciprocity apply to GIs located in all third countries. It considers that the European Commission's interpretation of the phrase "without prejudice to international agreements" would not necessarily withstand scrutiny by a judicial body and is unlikely given that the provisions that refer to "third countries" would have been drafted with only a handful of non-WTO

[74] United States' response to Panel question No. 1 and rebuttal submission, para. 12.

[75] European Communities' first written submission, paras. 62-67; first oral statement, paras. 41-44; rebuttal submission, para. 52.

[76] European Communities' responses to Panel question Nos. 7, 8, 15 and 16; rebuttal submission, paras. 11, 58-60 and 71-87; second oral statement, paras. 45 and 50.

[77] European Communities' response to Panel question No. 1; second oral statement, paras. 5-7.

[78] Annex C, para. 17.

Members in mind. The reference in Article 12(2) indicates that third countries means all third countries outside the European Communities, although in Articles 12a(2) and 12d(1) it could mean non-WTO Members. The EC's interpretation could *a contrario* indicate a recognition that the equivalence and reciprocity conditions violate national treatment obligations in GATT 1994 and TRIPS.[79]

7.46 Canada considers that Article 12 of the Regulation, read in context with Articles 12a, 12b and 12d, cannot support the interpretation advanced by the European Communities. The ambiguous reference to "international agreements" is insufficient to counter their clear wording. There would not appear to be an alternative legal basis for filing applications for countries outside the European Communities besides Article 12 due to the wording of Article 12a(1). Articles 12b and 12d refer to "WTO Members" and "third countries" which suggests no differential application to "third countries" in Articles 12 and 12a. The European Communities indicated that Article 12 applied to all WTO Members in a statement in September 2002 to the Council for TRIPS.[80]

7.47 China argues that the European Communities' interpretation is not accompanied by any supporting evidence and that there is no regulatory language in the provisions to exclude expressly the application of these provisions to WTO Members. The preamble to the April 2003 amending Regulation refers specifically to WTO Members in relation to the right of objection, but does not exclude WTO Members from the equivalence and reciprocity conditions. Had the drafters intended that it should not apply, they would have inserted a clause to that effect in the preamble. The European Communities appears to have admitted that portions of Article 12, regarding product specifications and inspection, do apply to WTO Members.[81]

7.48 Colombia submits that, if the European Communities' interpretation of "without prejudice to international agreements" is correct, the Panel should recommend that it modify its legislation in such a way that that phrase acquires the scope and meaning that are assigned to it in the EC's first written submission.[82]

7.49 Mexico submits that the language of Article 12(1) of the Regulation is precise and unequivocal. Third countries must satisfy conditions of equivalence and reciprocity in order to receive the same protection as EC member States.[83]

7.50 New Zealand submits that the European Communities' interpretation of Article 12(1) and (3) and the phrase "without prejudice to international agreements" is novel and does not withstand close scrutiny. It runs counter to the usual meaning of that phrase and effectively admits that requiring nationals of WTO Members to satisfy the procedures in Article 12(1) and (3) would be contrary to WTO obligations. It is inconsistent with the wording of the Regulation itself and, if Article 12(3) does not apply to WTO Members, then the application procedure in Article 12a would not either. This is the first time that this interpretation has been raised by the European Communities. The alternative interpretation adopted by the complainant is consistent with the wording of the Regulation.[84]

7.51 Chinese Taipei asserts that the conditions of equivalence and reciprocity apply to GIs located in all third countries.[85]

---

[79] Annex C, paras. 23-24.
[80] Annex C, paras. 47-50.
[81] Annex C, para. 72.
[82] Annex C, para. 99.
[83] Annex C, para. 110.
[84] Annex C, paras. 126-128.
[85] Annex C, paras. 171-172.

(iii) consideration by the Panel

7.52 The first issue in this claim concerns the conditions for registration of GIs under the Regulation. It is not disputed that a GI located outside the European Communities has never been registered nor the subject of an application made under the Regulation.[86] Therefore, the provisions concerning the protection of such GIs have never been applied in a particular instance. However, the United States challenges this aspect of the Regulation "as such."

7.53 The parties agree that the conditions set out in Article 12(1) of the Regulation do not apply to the protection of GIs located within the territory of the European Communities. They disagree as to whether they apply to the protection of GIs located in other WTO Members. The United States claims that they do so apply, and it is not disputed that the European Communities never made a clear statement that these conditions did not so apply prior to this panel proceeding. However, the European Communities responds in its submissions to the Panel that the conditions only apply to third countries that are not WTO Members.

7.54 The European Communities' position, as expressed in its submissions to the Panel, has been welcomed in principle by the complainants and by two third parties[87]. If the United States were satisfied with this position, it would provide a positive solution to many of the national treatment claims in this dispute. However, the United States is not persuaded that the European Communities would be able to implement the position that it has presented to the Panel in light of the terms of the Regulation on its face, allegedly prior inconsistent statements by the European Communities to the Council for TRIPS, the Commission's Guide to the Regulation and elsewhere, and inconsistent statements made during this Panel proceeding by the European Communities.[88] Therefore, although the European Communities submits that the Regulation already is in conformity with its obligations, the Panel is obliged to proceed with its assessment of the national treatment claims based on Article 12(1) of the Regulation.

7.55 The fact that this is an "as such" challenge, and that the parties disagree sharply on whether the European Communities' interpretation of its own measure is correct, requires the Panel to conduct a detailed examination of the Regulation. In doing so, it examines the Regulation solely for the purpose of determining its conformity with relevant obligations under the WTO covered agreements.[89] Although the Regulation is part of the European Communities' domestic law, the parties agree that the Panel is not bound by the European Communities' interpretation of its provisions.[90] Rather, the Panel is obliged, in accordance with its mandate, to make an objective assessment of the meaning of the relevant provisions of the Regulation. In this context, the Panel is mindful that, objectively, a Member is normally well placed to explain the meaning of its own law. To the extent that either party advances a particular interpretation of a provision of the Regulation at issue, it bears the burden of proof that its interpretation is correct.

7.56 Turning to the Regulation, the Panel notes that it applies to the registration of "designations of origin" and "geographical indications," as defined.[91] For ease of reference, and without prejudice to their consistency with the definition of a geographical indication in Article 22.1 of the TRIPS Agreement, we shall refer to them both as "GIs" in this report, except where the context requires otherwise.

---

[86] See the parties' respective responses to Panel question Nos. 11 and 12 and third parties' comments in Annex C. For the sake of brevity, the Panel refers to a name that refers to a geographical area located in a Member as a GI located in that Member.

[87] See para. 7 of the United States' first oral statement, endorsed by Australia, first oral statement, para. 33, and summaries of arguments of Brazil and Canada, Annex C, paras. 24 and 47.

[88] United States' first oral statement, para. 8; rebuttal submission, para. 5.

[89] This was the approach of the Appellate Body in *India – Patents (US)*, paras. 65-68.

[90] Parties' respective responses to Panel question No. 1.

[91] The terms "designation of origin" and "geographical indication" are defined in Article 2(2) of the Regulation and they and the abbreviations "PDO" and "PGI" are found in Article 4 of the Regulation (Exhibits COMP-1b and EC-1). Detailed rules of application of the Regulation are found in Commission Regulation (EEC) No. 2037/93 (Exhibit COMP-2).

7.57 Certain facts are agreed. The parties agree that the Regulation contains two sets of detailed procedures for the registration of GIs for agricultural products and foodstuffs. The first procedure, in Articles 5 through 7, applies to the names of geographical areas located in the European Communities.[92] It has been part of the Regulation since its adoption in 1992, although it has been amended subsequently in certain respects. The second procedure, principally found in Articles 12a and 12b, applies to the names of geographical areas located in third countries outside the European Communities.[93] It was inserted in the Regulation in April 2003. A third procedure for registration of GIs protected under the national law of EC member States was formerly available under Article 17, but was deleted in April 2003. A fourth possibility is registration by means of an international agreement, discussed below.

7.58 The parties disagree as to whether the second of these procedures is subject to additional conditions found in Article 12(1) of the Regulation that do not apply to the first procedure. Article 12(1) provides as follows:

> 1. Without prejudice to international agreements, this Regulation may apply to an agricultural product or foodstuff from a third country provided that:
>
> - the third country is able to give guarantees identical or equivalent to those referred to in Article 4,
>
> - the third country concerned has inspection arrangements and a right to objection equivalent to those laid down in this Regulation,
>
> - the third country concerned is prepared to provide protection equivalent to that available in the Community to corresponding agricultural products or foodstuffs coming from the Community."

7.59 Article 12 has been part of the Regulation since its adoption in 1992, although it was amended in April 2003 by the insertion of the requirement of a right of objection equivalent to those laid down in the Regulation, when Article 12(3) and Articles 12a through 12d, including the second procedure described above, among other provisions, were inserted. It is not in dispute that many WTO Members, including the United States, do *not* satisfy the conditions set out in Article 12(1).

7.60 The factual issue for the Panel to decide is whether the conditions set out in Article 12(1) apply to the availability of protection for GIs located in WTO Members. In other words, the factual issue is whether the registration procedure in Articles 12a and 12b is available for GIs located in WTO Members that do not satisfy the conditions in Article 12(1).

7.61 The United States presents two types of evidence. The first is the text of the Regulation and the second consists of the European Communities' own statements concerning the Regulation prior to, and during, this Panel proceeding.

7.62 The Panel begins its analysis by reviewing the measure on its face.[94] The procedure in Articles 12a and 12b of the Regulation begins with the filing of an application under paragraph 1 of Article 12a and continues

---

[92] This is apparent from Article 5(4) of the Regulation which provides that "[t]he application shall be sent to the Member State in which the geographical area is located," and was confirmed by the European Communities in its response to Panel question No. 2. The European Communities also notes that Articles 12a and 12b refer to certain provisions in Articles 5 to 7 as well.

[93] This is apparent from Article 12a(1) of the Regulation which provides that "if a group of a natural or legal person ... in a third country wishes to have a name registered under this Regulation it shall send a registration application to the authorities in the country in which the geographical area is located," and was confirmed by the European Communities in its response to Panel question No. 2.

[94] This was the Appellate Body's approach to an "as such" claim in its report on *US – Corrosion-Resistant Steel Sunset Review*, at para. 168.

with its initial examination under paragraph 2. The text of paragraph 1 begins "[i]n the case provided for in Article 12(3)," which immediately limits the availability of the procedure according to the terms of Article 12(3). The text of paragraph 2 of Article 12a begins "[i]f the third country referred to in paragraph 1 deems ..." which confirms that this aspect of the procedure is limited in the same way as paragraph 1. Paragraph 1 of Article 12b sets out the next step in the same procedure and refers to the registration request sent by "the third country," which is the third country described in Article 12b(2).

7.63 Article 12(3) of the Regulation provides as follows:

> 3. The Commission shall examine, at the request of the country concerned, and in accordance with the procedure laid down in Article 15 whether a third country satisfies the equivalence conditions and offers guarantees within the meaning of paragraph 1 as a result of its national legislation. Where the Commission decision is in the affirmative, the procedure set out in Article 12a shall apply.

7.64 The case provided for in this paragraph is clear: it refers to a third country which satisfies the conditions in Article 12(1). The initial clause of Article 12a, as confirmed by the chain of cross-references in Articles 12a(2) and 12b(1), therefore limits the procedure in Articles 12a and 12b to such third countries. No other provision in Article 12a or 12b indicates that that procedure is available for the registration of GIs located in a third country which does not satisfy the conditions in Article 12(1), even if it is a WTO Member. This is consistent with Article 12b(2), which provides for objections in the same procedure, and expressly distinguishes between a "Member State of the European Union or a WTO member" and "a third country meeting the equivalence conditions of Article 12(3)." The implication is that a WTO Member is not necessarily a third country meeting those conditions.[95]

7.65 The only other provision in the Regulation which could indicate the possibility of registration of GIs located in a third country which does *not* satisfy the conditions in Article 12(1) is the introductory phrase of Article 12(1) itself, which prefaces the conditions with the clause "[w]ithout prejudice to international agreements." The European Communities concedes that the application of the conditions in Article 12(1) of the Regulation would prejudice its obligations under Article III:4 of GATT 1994 and submits to the Panel that, as a consequence, it would not apply those conditions to GIs located in WTO Members. Nevertheless, it does not follow that the procedure in Articles 12a and 12b is available for the registration of GIs located in WTO Members. That procedure is limited to third countries which satisfy the conditions in Article 12(1) and there is no other procedure in the Regulation available for WTO Members that do not satisfy those conditions. There is the possibility of protection pursuant to an international agreement, but no existing international agreement either incorporates the procedure under Articles 12a and 12b of the Regulation or contains an application and registration procedure for GIs located in all WTO Members. In particular, neither GATT 1994 nor the TRIPS Agreement contains any such procedure.

7.66 Other provisions in the Regulation may also shed light on this issue. Article 12d(1), which provides a right of objection to registration of GIs located in the European Communities, distinguishes twice between persons from "a WTO Member country or a third country recognized under the procedure provided for in Article 12(3)."[96] This expressly grants a right of objection to persons from WTO Members and is a further indication that where the Regulation refers to "a third country recognized under the procedure provided for in Article 12(3)" it does not include a WTO Member unless it has been recognized under that procedure.

7.67 Four other provisions also refer to "a third country recognized under the procedure provided for in Article 12(3)" (or analogous terms) without referring to a WTO Member: Article 5(5) on registration of GIs

---

[95] The second sentence of Article 12(3) provides that the procedure in Article 12a shall apply to third countries which the Commission decides satisfy the conditions in Article 12(1). This sentence alone does not exclude the possibility that the procedure might apply to other third countries which do not satisfy those conditions, but there is no other provision in the Regulation to that effect.

[96] This is considered in detail in para.7.349 below.

that straddle the external border of the European Communities, Article 6(6) on homonymous GIs, Article 10(3) on inspection structures and Article 13(5) on the coexistence of registered and unregistered GIs. The European Communities' view of Article 10(3) is that it includes WTO Members[97], and there seems to be no reason why the other three provisions should exclude WTO Members. These provisions seem to confirm that WTO Members are included in the term "third countries" and therefore require recognition under the procedure provided for in Article 12(3).

7.68 The preamble of the Regulation, which has contained the conditions in Article 12(1) more or less in their current form since the original version was adopted in 1992, sets out its justification. The 19th recital reads as follows:

> Whereas provision should be made for trade with third countries offering equivalent guarantees for the issue and inspection of geographical indications or designations of origin granted on their territory;[98]

7.69 The phrase "equivalent guarantees for the issue and inspection" of GIs is a clear reference to the conditions in Article 12(1). There is no recital referring to the possibility of GIs located in any other third countries which do not satisfy these conditions.

7.70 The preamble to the April 2003 amending Regulation, which modified Article 12 and inserted a detailed procedure for applications and objections from third countries in Articles 12a through 12d, sets out the justification for the amendments as follows:

> (8) The Agreement on Trade-Related Aspects of Intellectual Property Rights (TRIPS Agreement 1994, contained in Annex 1C to the Agreement establishing the World Trade Organisation contains detailed provisions on the existence, acquisition, scope, maintenance and enforcement of intellectual property rights.
>
> (9) The protection provided by registration under Regulation (EEC) No 2081/92 is open to third countries' names by reciprocity and under equivalence conditions as provided for in Article 12 of that Regulation. That Article should be supplemented so as to guarantee that the Community registration procedure is available to the countries meeting those conditions.
>
> (10) Article 7 of Regulation (EEC) No 2081/92 specifies how objections are to be made and dealt with. To satisfy the obligation resulting from Article 22 of the TRIPS Agreement it should be made clear that in this matter nationals of WTO member countries are covered by these arrangements and that the provisions in question apply without prejudice to international agreements, as provided for in Article 12 of the said Regulation. (...)[99]

7.71 Paragraph 8 recalls the subject-matter of the TRIPS Agreement without elaborating on its relevance to the Regulation. This clarifies the reference to Article 22 of the TRIPS Agreement in paragraph 10 but it is not clear whether it also relates to paragraph 9. In any event, on the European Communities' later interpretation, the TRIPS Agreement is not relevant to the WTO-consistency of the conditions provided for in Article 12, as referred to in paragraph 9. Rather, the European Communities submits that GATT 1994 ensures their WTO-consistency. GATT 1994 is not recited in the preamble.

---

[97] European Communities' responses to Panel question Nos. 126(a) and (b).

[98] Exhibits COMP-1b and EC-1.

[99] Exhibit COMP-1h.

7.72 Paragraph 9 contains no qualifier referring to WTO Members, which appears to confirm the position that the conditions in Article 12(1) apply to the availability of protection of GIs located in all third countries and that the registration procedure in Articles 12a and 12b is not available for GIs located in WTO Members that do not satisfy those conditions.

7.73 Paragraph 10 includes the phrase "without prejudice to international agreements, as provided for in Article 12," but it only relates to the right of objection granted to WTO Members' nationals. This is a clear reference to Articles 12b(2) and 12d(1), which were inserted by the amending Regulation. It can be noted that they are the only two provisions in the current version of the Regulation that expressly refer to a "WTO Member," where they also distinguish a WTO Member from a third country recognized under Article 12(3).

7.74 In the Panel's view, the meaning and content of these aspects of the Regulation, together with the amending Regulation, are sufficiently clear on their face for the United States to have discharged its burden of proof of establishing that, under the Regulation "as such," the availability of protection for GIs located in WTO Members is contingent upon satisfaction of the conditions set out in Article 12(1) and recognition by the Commission under Article 12(3).[100]

7.75 There is no supporting evidence of the meaning of these aspects of the Regulation in the form of an interpretation of the relevant provisions by the European Court of Justice or any other domestic court.[101] This is partly explained by the facts that no requests for registration of foreign GIs have been made under the Regulation and that Articles 12a through 12d were inserted only recently, in April 2003.

7.76 The United States also presents evidence consisting of various statements by executive authorities of the European Communities which contain interpretations of the Regulation. The Panel considers that such statements can be useful as, objectively, a WTO Member is normally well placed to explain the meaning of its own domestic law.[102] However, the usefulness of any particular statement will depend on its contents and the circumstances in which it was made. The Panel has weighed the evidence and considers that one statement in particular, in light of the clarity of its contents and the official capacity in which it was delivered, is highly relevant to the issue at hand.

7.77 In a lengthy statement to the Council for TRIPS in September 2002 (prior to the insertion of Articles 12a through 12d), the European Communities specifically responded to the following view expressed by a group of Members, including the United States:

> [U]nder the current EC regulations, the EC does not appear to provide protection for non-EC geographical indications (i.e., place names of other WTO Members), except on the basis of bilateral agreements, or if the EC has determined that a country has a system for geographical indications that is equivalent to the detailed system of the EC.[103]

7.78 The European Communities introduced the relevant part of its response as follows:

---

[100] The European Commission has not recognized any other country under this procedure: see European Communities' response to Panel question No. 10. It is not contested that the Commission cannot recognize a third country under Article 12(3) that does not satisfy the equivalence and reciprocity conditions.

[101] European Communities' response to Panel question No. 19.

[102] See para. 7.55 above.

[103] Communication from Australia, Canada, Guatemala, New Zealand, Paraguay, the Philippines and the United States (IP/C/W/360), para. 4.

> (...) I would like to address one issue that is raised regarding the fact that the EU register for GIs on foodstuffs does not allow the registration of foreign GI unless it is determined that a third country has an equivalent or reciprocal system of GI protection.[104]

7.79 The Panel notes that the European Communities was emphatic at that time that registration systems should primarily be aimed at domestic GIs and it quoted the legislation of several other WTO Members which allegedly do not register foreign GIs without an international agreement.[105] This statement by the European Communities in September 2002 to the Council for TRIPS therefore appears to support the United States' interpretation of the Regulation on its face.

7.80 The European Communities argues that the interpretation set forth in its September 2002 statement to the Council for TRIPS "is not incompatible with the text of Regulation 2081/92 as in force at the time it was made or with the statements of the EC in the present case." In its view, its intention at that time was not primarily to explain the EC system for the protection of geographical indications and its statement did not take account of amendments made in April 2003.

7.81 In the Panel's view, the European Communities' September 2002 statement was very clear in its interpretation of the relevant point of the Regulation. Further, nothing in the April 2003 amending Regulation appears to render that statement incompatible with the current version of the Regulation. In fact, the Panel's examination of the insertion of Article 12(3) and Articles 12a through 12d confirms that the conditions in Article 12(1) remain applicable on the same terms.

7.82 The United States also refers to the explanation of the amendments given by the European Commission at the time it proposed them, in March 2002. The Panel considers that this evidence corroborates the previous statement because of the clarity of its contents and the capacity in which it was made. In a press release, the Commission explained that, in order to comply with the TRIPS Agreement, it proposed to extend the right of objection to certain other WTO Member country nationals and further stated:

> Beyond mere TRIPS consistency, the Commission proposes important amendments designed to promote the EU system of denominations of origin as a model to the rest of the world. The driving idea behind is the wish to improve protection of European quality products also outside the EU. As the EU cannot force non-EU countries to do so, they would be invited to do so on a 'reciprocal basis'. If a non-EU country introduced an 'equivalent system' including the right of objection for the EU and the commitment to protect EU names on their territory, the EU would offer a specific protection to register their products for the EU market.[106]

The references to a reciprocal basis and an equivalent system are clear references to the conditions in Article 12(1) of the Regulation.[107]

7.83 The Panel notes that this interpretation is further corroborated by a letter from Commissioner Lamy to the United States Trade Representative in January 2003, as follows:

> While it is true that US GIs cannot be registered in the EU, this does not mean that they are not protected! Any US GI can:

---

[104] See the statement in the Annex to the minutes of that meeting in document IP/C/M/37/Add.1.

[105] *Ibid.*

[106] European Commission: "Food quality: Commission proposes better protection for geographical names" (Press Release Reference: IP/02/422), Brussels, 15 March 2002 set out in Exhibit US-22.

[107] The amendments effected are identical in this respect to those proposed. The Commission's explanatory memorandum to its Proposal for the amending Regulation also stated that "Article 12 applies the Regulation by reciprocity and under equivalence conditions to agricultural products or foodstuffs originating in a third country, without prejudice to international agreements," Brussels, 15 March 2002 set out in Exhibit US-20 at page 3.

(1) be registered as a certification trademark (...)

(2) get protection without registration by invoking before any tribunal in the EU Article 2(1) of Directive 2000/13 on labelling (...)

(3) invoke the unfair competition rules of the Member States (...)[108]

7.84 In its submissions to the Panel, the European Communities rejects that interpretation and submits that, due to the introductory phrase of Article 12(1) of the Regulation, "[w]ithout prejudice to international agreements," the conditions in Article 12(1) do not apply to the availability of protection for GIs located in WTO Members. It refers to a statement it made to the Council for TRIPS in June 2004 in the days before the first substantive meeting of this Panel[109] and a second edition of the Commission's Guide to the Regulation published in August 2004 in the days prior to the second substantive meeting of this Panel.[110] It advises that "[t]he guide was not prepared in connection with the Panel proceedings."[111]

7.85 The Panel recalls its reasoning in paragraph 7.65 above, and reiterates its view that, even if the phrase "[w]ithout prejudice to international agreements" had the effect of subjecting the conditions in Article 12(1) to the terms of GATT 1994 or the TRIPS Agreement, those agreements do not contain a procedure for applications and registration for GIs located in all WTO Members. WTO Members would still have to satisfy the conditions in Article 12(1) in order for their GIs to gain access to the procedure in Articles 12a and 12b.

7.86 The European Communities admits that this would be a "nonsensical result."[112] However, it is unable to provide a satisfactory explanation as to how this result could be avoided in light of the wording of Article 12a, which begins "[i]n the case provided for in Article 12(3)." The European Communities points out that Article 12(3) refers to the conditions in Article 12(1) and since, in its view, those conditions do not apply to WTO Members, the procedure in Article 12(3) and the reference in Article 12a do not apply to them either.[113]

7.87 The Panel agrees that Article 12(3) provides for a Commission decision on whether a third country satisfies the conditions in Article 12(1) and accepts that, if those conditions do not apply to a third country, there would be no relevant decision under Article 12(3). Yet this does not alter the text of Article 12a which applies "[i]n the case provided for in Article 12(3)." Article 12a does not appear, on its face, to apply to the registration of a GI located in a third country, including a WTO Member, which is not recognized under Article 12(3). For these reasons, the Panel is not persuaded that the European Communities' interpretation is correct.

7.88 It is not necessary for the purposes of this dispute to determine which are the precise international agreements covered by the phrase "[w]ithout prejudice to international agreements." It suffices to note that there is a plausible alternative interpretation that it refers to bilateral agreements under which the European Communities would protect specific GIs.[114] The European Communities does not exclude this, but argues that

---

[108] Exhibit US-73, attachment, page 1, *supra* at note 46.

[109] See the minutes of that meeting in IP/C/M/44, paras. 62-63, quoted in the European Communities' response to Panel question No. 16 prior to circulation and also set out in Exhibit EC-83. Responses given by the European Communities to questions posed by two other WTO Members in the TRIPS Council review of its legislation in 1996-1997, before the insertion of Articles 12a through 12d, are inconclusive on this issue as they contain no clear statement that equivalence and reciprocity conditions do not apply to the registration of GIs located outside the European Communities in countries without a bilateral agreement: see European Communities' response to Panel question No. 97.

[110] Exhibit EC-64.

[111] European Communities' response to Panel question No. 96.

[112] European Communities' second oral statement, para. 48.

[113] European Communities' response to Panel question No. 7.

[114] United States' first oral statement, para. 8.

there is no reason why *only* such specific agreements should be covered.[115] There are currently no such bilateral agreements for agricultural products and foodstuffs, although one has been foreshadowed in a joint declaration with Switzerland.[116]

7.89 In any event, the Panel is not persuaded by the European Communities' explanations during this Panel proceeding of the phrase "[w]ithout prejudice to international agreements" as used in Article 12(1) of the Regulation. At the first substantive meeting, in support of its first defence, it provided the following explanation of that phrase:

> (...) Such international agreements include the WTO Agreements. This is made clear by the 8th recital of Regulation 692/2003, which amended the procedures for the registration of non-EC geographical indications, and in this context took specific account of the provisions of the TRIPS.
>
> "WTO Members are obliged to provide protection to geographical indications in accordance with Section 3 of Part II and the general provisions and basic principles of the TRIPS Agreement. For this reason, Article 12 (1) and (3) of Regulation 2081/92 do not apply to WTO Members. (...)[117]

7.90 This explanation was also reflected in a June 2004 statement that the European Communities made to the Council for TRIPS[118] and the August 2004 edition of the Commission's Guide to the Regulation[119].

7.91 At the same time, the European Communities' second defence was that the conditions in Article 12(1) of the Regulation were not inconsistent with the national treatment obligations in the TRIPS Agreement, essentially because they discriminate according to the location of GIs and not according to the nationality of persons with rights in relation to GIs.[120]

7.92 It was not clear how these two defences could be reconciled. If the first defence implied that the conditions did not apply because they would prejudice the European Communities' national treatment obligations under the TRIPS Agreement, it would have contradicted the second defence that these conditions were not inconsistent with the national treatment obligations in the TRIPS Agreement. The Panel sought clarification from the European Communities by posing the question "does the EC contest that equivalence and reciprocity conditions such as those under Article 12(1) and (3) of Regulation (EC) No. 2081/92, if applied to other WTO Members, would be inconsistent with the national treatment obligations in the TRIPS Agreement and/or Article III:4 of the GATT 1994?." The European Communities declined to give a specific answer to the Panel's question and concluded as follows:

> As regards the specific conditions contained in Article 12 (1) of Regulation 2081/92, the EC has already confirmed that it does not apply these to WTO Members. For this reason, the EC

---

115 European Communities' rebuttal submission, para. 69.

116 European Communities' response to Panel question No. 21, and see the European Community—Switzerland Joint Declaration on the protection of geographical indications and designations of origin of agricultural products and foodstuffs, 21 June 1999, OJ L 144/350 at 366 set out in Exhibit US-6.

117 European Communities' first written submission, paras. 65-66. It reiterated this in its first oral statement, at para. 43, and confirmed it in its response to Panel question No. 3 adding as follows:
At the time that Regulation 2081/92 was adopted, the GATT was one of the agreements to which the 'without prejudice' clause applied. Moreover, at the time that Regulation 2081/92 was adopted, the TRIPS Agreement was in the final phases of its negotiation. It was therefore the objective that the 'without prejudice' clause should also apply to the TRIPS and other WTO agreements resulting from the Uruguay Round.

118 See the minutes of that meeting in document IP/C/M/44, paras. 62-63, cited in response to Panel question Nos. 16 and 95 and set out in Exhibit EC-83.

119 Set out in Exhibit EC-64.

120 European Communities' first written submission, paras. 123-126; first oral statement, paras. 46-47; rebuttal submission, para. 43.

considers that the question whether these conditions are inconsistent with the national treatment obligations of the TRIPS Agreement and the GATT does not arise.[121]

7.93 The United States then submitted that the European Communities had decided not to defend the conditions in Article 12(1) of the Regulation and that it had apparently conceded that any such requirement was contrary to national treatment and MFN obligations.[122]

7.94 The Panel again sought clarification at the second substantive meeting, by asking which precise obligations under an international agreement would be prejudiced by the application of the specific conditions in Article 12(1) of the Regulation to WTO Members. The European Communities responded that it was its obligations under Article III:4 of GATT 1994, but not Article 3.1 of the TRIPS Agreement, because the Regulation did not involve any discrimination between nationals. It later confirmed this in writing.[123] Therefore, to the extent that the European Communities' explanation of the phrase "[w]ithout prejudice to international agreements" as used in Article 12(1) of the Regulation relies on the TRIPS Agreement, the European Communities has expressly denied that the phrase refers to its own obligations and the Panel does not consider that possible explanation further.[124]

7.95 At this time, the European Communities' explanation of the phrase "[w]ithout prejudice to international agreements" as used in Article 12(1) of the Regulation relies on GATT 1994. In light of the European Communities' analysis that this phrase ensures that "should a conflict between the two acts or provisions occur, then the act or provision to which the 'without prejudice' reference is made prevails"[125], it is clear that this explanation depends on the view that the equivalence and reciprocity conditions are inconsistent with the European Communities' obligations under Article III:4 of GATT 1994. However, this is difficult to reconcile with the European Communities' earlier view that the question whether these conditions are inconsistent with the national treatment obligations of GATT does not arise, quoted at paragraph 7.92 above. It was also omitted from the earlier explanation that the conditions did not apply because of obligations under the TRIPS Agreement, quoted at paragraph 7.89 above. Further, the evidence submitted by the European Communities provides no additional support for this explanation, as the amending Regulation recites the TRIPS Agreement but not GATT 1994, and the evidence identified at paragraph 7.90 above also reflects the explanation quoted at paragraph 7.89 above.[126]

7.96 For all these reasons, the Panel is not persuaded by the European Communities' explanations of the phrase "[w]ithout prejudice to international agreements" as used in Article 12(1) of the Regulation.

7.97 The Panel takes note that there are various executive authorities involved in the implementation of the Regulation, including representatives of EC member States. Article 15 of the Regulation provides for a regulatory procedure under which the Commission shall be assisted by a regulatory committee composed of the representatives of the EC member States and chaired by the representative of the Commission, who does not vote. The representative of the Commission shall submit to the committee a draft of the measures to be taken. The committee shall deliver its opinion on the draft within a time-limit by qualified majority voting. The Commission shall adopt the measures envisaged if they are in accordance with the opinion of the committee. If the measures are not in accordance with the opinion of the committee, or if no opinion is delivered, the

---

[121] European Communities' response to Panel question No. 20.

[122] United States' rebuttal submission, paras. 3 and 9.

[123] European Communities' response to Panel question No. 94.

[124] In the same question, the Panel also sought clarification of the relevance of the reference to the TRIPS Agreement in the European Communities' first written submission, quoted at paragraph 7.89 above. The European Communities' response does not provide a clear explanation of the relationship between the obligations of WTO Members under the TRIPS Agreement and the applicability of the equivalence and reciprocity conditions under the EC's GI Regulation: see its response to question No. 94(b), second paragraph.

[125] European Communities' rebuttal submission, para. 55.

[126] The United States drew attention to the problems in reconciling the European Communities' submissions on this point in its comment on the EC response to Panel question No. 94.

Commission shall, without delay, submit to the Council a proposal relating to the measures to be taken and shall inform the European Parliament. The Council may act by qualified majority on the proposal within three months. If the Council indicates by qualified majority that it opposes the proposal, the Commission shall re-examine it. If the Council neither adopts the proposed measure nor indicates its opposition within three months, the Commission shall adopt the proposed measure.[127]

7.98 The European Communities' delegation to this panel proceeding confirms that the statements made by agents of the European Commission before the Panel commit and engage the European Communities.[128] It indicates that Community laws are generally not executed through authorities at Community level but rather through recourse to the authorities of its member States which, in such a situation, "act *de facto* as organs of the Community, for which the Community would be responsible under WTO law and international law in general."[129] The Panel accepts this explanation of what amounts to the European Communities' domestic constitutional arrangements and accepts that the submissions of the European Communities' delegation to this panel proceeding are made on behalf of all the executive authorities of the European Communities.[130]

7.99 The parties have presented evidence with respect to the approach that would be taken by the European Court of Justice if the executive authorities registered a GI that was not the subject of an international agreement and that was located in a third country that did not satisfy the conditions in Article 12(1) of the Regulation. The European Communities submits that, according to the settled case law of the European Court of Justice:

> Community legislation must, so far as possible, be interpreted in a manner that is consistent with international law, in particular where its provisions are intended specifically to give effect to an international agreement concluded by the Community.[131]

7.100 The Panel is not persuaded that it is possible to interpret the relevant aspects of the Regulation in the manner advanced by the European Communities in these proceedings, for the reasons already given. The Panel also notes that the basic Regulation does not indicate that its provisions are intended specifically to give effect to an international agreement concluded by the Community. Whilst the April 2003 amending Regulation recites the TRIPS Agreement, it would only seem to do so to justify extending the right of objection to nationals of WTO Members. In any case, the European Communities' later explanation is that the interpretation must take account of GATT 1994, which is not mentioned at all.

7.101 Article 11 of the DSU requires that "a panel should make an objective assessment of the matter before it, including an objective assessment of the facts of the case ...." In our view, our duty to make an *objective* assessment prohibits us from accepting the interpretation of the applicability of the conditions in Article 12(1) of the Regulation presented by the European Communities in this proceeding, for the reasons set out above.

7.102 Therefore, the Panel concludes that the United States has made a prima facie case that the equivalence and reciprocity conditions in Article 12(1) of the Regulation apply to the availability of protection for GIs

---

[127] Article 15 of the Regulation, set out in Exhibits COMP-1b and EC-1, Article 5 of Council Decision (EC) No. 1999/468 set out in Exhibit COMP-8 and the European Communities' first written submission, paras. 81-82. There have been instances where the Commission's draft measures have not been in accordance with the opinion of the Committee and where the Council of Ministers has adopted measures under the Regulation: see Exhibit EC-28.

[128] European Communities' responses to Panel questions Nos. 15 and 18.

[129] European Communities' second oral statement, para. 148.

[130] The delegation of the European Communities to the meetings with the Panel was composed of officials of the European Commission and delegates of certain EC member States. The European Communities indicated that its statements to the Panel "commit and engage the European Communities:" see response to Panel question No. 15. The Panel accepts that explanation, for the same reasons as those explained by the Panel in *US – Section 301 Trade Act*, at para. 7.123. See also, in this regard, paras. 7.269, 7.339, 7.450 and 7.725 of the present report.

[131] European Communities' response to Panel question No. 15 quoting Case C-341/95, *Bettati*, [1998] ECR I-4355, para. 20; which cited Case C-61/94, *Commission/Germany* [1996] ECR I-4006, para. 52, set out in Exhibits EC-13 and EC-14.

located in third countries, including WTO Members. In other words, the registration procedure in Articles 12a and 12b is not available for GIs located in third countries, including WTO Members, that do not satisfy the conditions in Article 12(1). The European Communities has not succeeded in rebutting that case.

7.103 The Panel has evaluated the European Communities' interpretation of the applicability of the equivalence and reciprocity conditions and not found it reflected in the text of the Regulation. Had this interpretation been reflected in the text of the Regulation, the Panel could have reached a different conclusion which would have rendered it unnecessary to continue with an examination of the consistency of those conditions with the provisions of the covered agreements.

(b) National treatment under the TRIPS Agreement

(i) main arguments of the parties

7.104 The United States claims that the Regulation is inconsistent with Article 3.1 of the TRIPS Agreement and Article 2(1) of the Paris Convention (1967), as incorporated by Article 2.1 of the TRIPS Agreement, because it imposes conditions of *reciprocity* and *equivalence* on the availability of protection. National treatment requires protection of the intellectual property of other Members' nationals regardless of how those other Members treat their own nationals. National treatment does not allow a Member to require that other Members adopt particular standards or procedural rules as a condition for protecting their nationals' intellectual property. This is underscored by Article 1.1 of the TRIPS Agreement which provides that Members are not obligated to select any particular means of implementation over another. There is a wide variety of mechanisms used to implement the GI obligations and one Member cannot require a particular method of implementation as a condition for protecting the GI rights of other Members' nationals.[132]

7.105 The United States argues that the conditions in Article 12(1) of the Regulation apply to *nationals* because EC nationals are permitted to register their home-based EC GIs but U.S. nationals (and nationals of most other WTO Members) are currently not able to register their home-based U.S. GIs.[133] The distinction between the location of a geographical area and the nationality of the right holder is not meaningful as right holders are overwhelmingly nationals of the place where their respective GIs are located. There is an obvious link and close relationship between the nationality of the persons who would seek GI protection for agricultural products and foodstuffs and the territory of the Member in which they are growing or producing such products, which is supported by data on the applicants for certification marks in the United States.[134] The European Communities is a "separate customs territory" within the meaning of footnote 1 to the TRIPS Agreement and, as such, its "nationals" are persons domiciled in its territory or legal persons who have a real and effective industrial and commercial establishment in its territory.[135] As a practical matter, any commercial entity growing agricultural products or processing foodstuffs in an EC member State will set up a legal entity under the laws of that EC member State for that purpose.[136] The Regulation protects indications of source, for which the relevant persons are "interested parties" defined in Article 10 of the Paris Convention (1967) to include any locally established producer, regardless of nationality.[137] The April 2003 amending Regulation itself equates nationals with persons resident and established in a Member with respect to the right of objection.[138]

7.106 The United States argues that the conditions in Article 12(1) of the Regulation accord neither the *same protection* nor *no less favourable treatment* to non-EC nationals because they are currently unable to register

[132] United States' first written submission, paras. 35, 42, 46, 48 and 49.

[133] United States' first written submission, paras. 59, 65 and 76. The United States also cites the GATT Panel report on *US – Malt Beverages* in support of an argument that it is not relevant that certain EC nationals with GIs based outside the EC might be faced with the same conditions because nationals of other WTO Members are entitled to the treatment accorded to the most-favoured EC nationals.

[134] United States' first oral statement, paras. 22-27; response to Panel question No. 27; rebuttal submission, para. 26.

[135] United States' response to Panel question No. 23; rebuttal submission, paras. 27-31.

[136] United States' response to Panel question No. 22; rebuttal submission, para. 32.

[137] United States' first written submission, paras. 38-39; rebuttal submission, para. 33.

[138] United States' second oral statement, para. 9.

their home-based GIs. The only way that they might be able to register home-based GIs in the European Communities is for their countries to grant reciprocal GI protection for agricultural products and foodstuffs from the European Communities and adopt an equivalent system of GI protection. The explicit purpose of the Regulation is to bestow significant commercial and competitive advantages through the registration of GIs, including higher profits, the right to use a label, rights to prevent uses by third parties, enforcement and guarantees against the GI becoming generic.[139] This amounts to a denial of "effective equality of opportunities" with respect to the protection of GIs.[140]

7.107 The United States argues that jurisprudence on Article III:4 of GATT 1994 offers useful guidance in the interpretation of Article 3.1 of the TRIPS Agreement. The broad and fundamental purpose of Article III is to avoid protectionism in the application of tax and regulatory measures. This is easily extrapolated to the TRIPS Agreement in which the national treatment obligation is intended to avoid protectionism with respect to the protection of intellectual property rights. Like the measures considered in previous disputes under Article III, the Regulation at issue in this dispute has a plain protective structure in that it systematically denies advantages to nationals producing in their country of nationality where that country does not satisfy the conditions of reciprocity and equivalence.[141]

7.108 The United States argues that the obligations in Article III:4 of GATT 1994 are separate from those in Article 3.1 of the TRIPS Agreement and Article 2 of the Paris Convention (1967) and that the European Communities must satisfy both sets of obligations.[142] The lack of a general exception like Article XX of GATT 1994 is not relevant to whether there is *de facto* discrimination under the TRIPS Agreement or to the interpretation of Article 3 of the TRIPS Agreement.[143]

7.109 The United States also claims that the Regulation imposes a requirement of establishment in the European Communities which is inconsistent with Article 2(2) of the Paris Convention (1967) because a foreign national can only register a GI for a product if he is producing or processing it in the European Communities.[144]

7.110 The European Communities responds that this claim must fail. Its first defence is that it does not, in fact, apply the conditions in Article 12(1) of the Regulation to geographical areas located in WTO Members. That defence has been considered in the previous sub-section.

7.111 The European Communities does not contest that national treatment under the TRIPS Agreement applies to more extensive protection granted in respect of intellectual property rights addressed in the TRIPS Agreement.[145]

7.112 The European Communities argues that the conditions in Article 12(1) of the Regulation do not depend on *nationality*. The Regulation sets out two procedures for registration: one for geographical areas located within the European Communities and one for those located outside the European Communities. Whether the geographical area is located within or outside the European Communities is in no way linked to the question of the nationality of the producers concerned.[146] This may concern the origin of the product but has nothing to do with the nationality of the producer, which is simply of no relevance for the registration of the GI.[147] There are no legal requirements which ensure that applicants for GIs for geographical areas located in the European

[139] United States' first written submission, paras. 58, 61 and 62; response to Panel question No. 31.

[140] United States' response to Panel question No. 101.

[141] United States' first written submission, paras. 69-75.

[142] United States' rebuttal submission, para. 42.

[143] United States' response to Panel question No. 103.

[144] United States' first written submission, paras. 84-85; rebuttal submission, paras. 84-86.

[145] European Communities' response to Panel question No. 111.

[146] European Communities' first written submission, paras. 123-126.

[147] European Communities' first oral statement, paras. 46-47; response to Panel question No. 106.

Communities are always, or usually, EC nationals.[148] There is no reason why a foreign national cannot produce products in accordance with a product specification in a GI registration located in the European Communities, and there are examples of foreign companies which have invested in the European Communities in this way.[149] If an applicant or user sets up a legal entity in the geographical area, that is simply a practical consequence of the fact that products must be produced in accordance with product specifications.[150] Nationality is determined by the laws of each State and is not simply a matter of domicile or establishment, which is highlighted by the specific rules in Article 3 of the Paris Convention (1967) and footnote 1 to the TRIPS Agreement which would otherwise be unnecessary.[151] The European Communities is not a "separate customs territory" within the meaning of footnote 1 to the TRIPS Agreement.[152] The meaning of "interested parties" in Article 10(2) of the Paris Convention (1967) is inapplicable in Article 22 of the TRIPS Agreement.[153] Nationality is not linked to the points of attachment but must be given a uniform meaning for all intellectual property rights.[154] The Regulation does not require any comparison of nationals because it does not contain any discrimination on the basis of nationality.[155]

7.113 The European Communities argues that the existence of different procedures which apply according to location of geographical areas is not sufficient to show *less favourable treatment* but rather there must be a substantive difference between those provisions which entails less favourable treatment. A measure would have to modify the conditions regarding the protection of intellectual property rights within the meaning of the TRIPS Agreement to the detriment of foreign nationals.[156]

7.114 The European Communities argues that the jurisprudence on Article III:2 of GATT 1994 is not relevant to the present dispute because of differences between paragraphs 2 and 4 of Article III and between Article III and Article 3.1 of the TRIPS Agreement. There is no general concept of discrimination common to all WTO agreements. There has never been a *de facto* application of Article 3.1 and the concept of conditions of competition is not easily transposable to the TRIPS Agreement. Whilst it may be possible under certain circumstances that measures which are neutral on their face accord less favourable treatment to nationals, the Panel should take account of the following: (1) the present case relates primarily to the origin of goods which is already dealt with more appropriately in the context of Article III:4 of GATT 1994, not the TRIPS Agreement; (2) *de facto* discrimination is a notion closely related to preventing circumvention of national treatment obligations, which does not exist when the specific issue is dealt with in other national treatment provisions, such as those of GATT; and (3) the national treatment provisions of GATT and the TRIPS Agreement should not systematically overlap. In addition, the TRIPS Agreement does not contain any provision corresponding to Article XX of GATT 1994 and it would not seem appropriate for a measure justified on the basis of Article XX to be found incompatible with the covered agreements on the basis of a *de facto* application of TRIPS national treatment.[157]

---

[148] European Communities' response to Panel question No. 22.

[149] European Communities' rebuttal submission, paras. 45-48; second oral statement, paras. 28-30; response to Panel question No. 106.

[150] European Communities' response to Panel question No. 107; second oral statement, paras. 29-30.

[151] European Communities' response to Panel question No. 23; rebuttal submission, paras. 37-40.

[152] European Communities' rebuttal submission, para. 35.

[153] European Communities' response to Panel question No. 24.

[154] European Communities' response to Panel question No. 26.

[155] European Communities' response to Panel question No. 101 and comments on that response.

[156] European Communities' second oral statement, paras. 39-41; response to Panel question No. 113.

[157] European Communities' response to Panel question No. 29; rebuttal submission, para. 49; second oral statement, paras. 33-37; response to Panel question No. 103.

(ii) main arguments of third parties

7.115 Brazil submits that the equivalence and reciprocity conditions in the Regulation are inconsistent with national treatment under Article 3.1 of the TRIPS Agreement. In most cases under the Regulation, discrimination according to geographical areas is discrimination between nationals.[158]

7.116 Canada submits that the equivalence and reciprocity conditions in the Regulation are inconsistent with national treatment under Articles 2.1 and 3.1 of the TRIPS Agreement. Discrimination on the basis of geographical area discriminates on the basis of nationality because of the "simple and incontestable" reality that EC nationals are likely to register for protection of GIs located in the European Communities and non-EC nationals are likely to register for protection of GIs located outside the European Communities. The explicit requirement that the physical production of a good that qualifies for a GI take place in the area indicated by the GI, means that an applicant for a GI located in the European Communities will, in all probability be a national of an EC member State. The treatment of "nationals" under the TRIPS Agreement extends *de jure* to geographical area.[159]

7.117 China considers that "nationals" within the meaning of the TRIPS Agreement includes natural persons who are domiciled, or legal persons who have a real and effective industrial and commercial establishment, in that Member.[160]

7.118 Colombia considers that any distinction that in any way identifies the GIs of the European Communities clearly entails a violation of national treatment obligations.[161]

7.119 India considers that the only valid interpretation of "treatment with regard to the protection " in Article 3.1 of the TRIPS Agreement is that no less favourable treatment to nationals of other WTO Members cannot be provided unless no less favourable treatment is also provided to the GIs for which they apply, whether located in the European Communities or in other WTO Members. The only available exceptions are found in Article 3.2.[162]

7.120 Mexico considers that the equivalence and reciprocity conditions prevent nationals of other WTO Members enjoying the protection afforded by the Regulation, which is contrary to the national treatment principle in Article 3.1 of the TRIPS Agreement.[163]

7.121 New Zealand submits that the term "nationals" clearly has a geographical connotation in the context of the TRIPS Agreement. Article 3 of the Paris Convention (1967) sets out a criterion for eligibility for protection to which the definition of "nationals" in Article 1.3 of the TRIPS Agreement refers. Footnote 1 to Article 1.3 of the TRIPS Agreement provides further support. The definition of an applicant in the Regulation includes persons according to their location. The most favourable treatment accorded to EC nationals should be compared with that received by WTO Member nationals. "Less favourable treatment" requires not only a difference in applicable laws but some disadvantage as a result of that difference. At worst, the difference means that the benefits of registration are entirely unavailable. At best, it means that other WTO Member nationals are subject to "extra hurdles" and disadvantaged. As a result, they do not have the same opportunities to protect their GIs through registration as do EC nationals. The individual's right to apply for protection is

---

[158] Annex C, paras. 23 and 34.

[159] Annex C, paras. 57-63.

[160] Annex C, para. 93.

[161] Annex C, para. 101.

[162] Annex C, para. 104.

[163] Annex C, para. 110.

conditioned on factors over which the applicant has no control. The advantages granted by registration include those under Article 13 and, according to the preamble, higher incomes.[164]

7.122 Chinese Taipei submits that the equivalence and reciprocity conditions violate the national treatment obligation in Article 3.1 of the TRIPS Agreement and Article 2(1) of the Paris Convention (1967). It recalls that national treatment under the TRIPS Agreement applies to "nationals" and that the European Communities compares EC nationals and non-EC nationals with GIs located in the European Communities. It treats them completely independently of EC nationals and non-EC nationals with GIs located outside the European Communities. This essentially is an argument that the European Communities can establish a separate set of rules for, and discriminate against, non-EC GIs as it wishes. Chinese Taipei submits that the Panel should examine whether any person, whether an European Communities or a non-EC national, with a GI, whether located in the European Communities or outside the European Communities, receives treatment less favourable than that accorded to an EC national with a GI located in the European Communities. Footnote 1 to the TRIPS Agreement applies to the European Communities as a separate customs territory.[165]

(iii) consideration by the Panel

national treatment obligations in the TRIPS Agreement

7.123 These claims are made under two national treatment obligations: one found in Article 3 of the TRIPS Agreement, which forms part of the text of that agreement, and the other found in Article 2 of the Paris Convention (1967) as incorporated by Article 2.1 of the TRIPS Agreement. The Panel will first consider the claim under Article 3.1 of the TRIPS Agreement.

7.124 Article 3.1 of the TRIPS Agreement provides as follows:

> 1. Each Member shall accord to the nationals of other Members treatment no less favourable than that it accords to its own nationals with regard to the protection of intellectual property, subject to the exceptions already provided in, respectively, the Paris Convention (1967), the Berne Convention (1971), the Rome Convention or the Treaty on Intellectual Property in Respect of Integrated Circuits. ... [footnote 3 omitted]

7.125 Two elements must be satisfied to establish an inconsistency with this obligation: (1) the measure at issue must apply with regard to the protection of intellectual property; and (2) the nationals of other Members must be accorded "less favourable" treatment than the Member's own nationals. The Panel will address each of these elements in turn. The parties do not agree on the meaning of "nationals" for the purposes of this claim. The Panel will therefore address that issue in the course of its consideration of the second element of this claim.

protection of intellectual property

7.126 The national treatment obligation in Article 3 of the TRIPS Agreement applies "with regard to the protection of intellectual property." Footnote 3 provides an inclusive definition of the term "protection" as used in Articles 3 and 4. It reads as follows:

> For the purposes of Articles 3 and 4, 'protection' shall include matters affecting the availability, acquisition, scope, maintenance and enforcement of intellectual property rights as well as those matters affecting the use of intellectual property rights specifically addressed in this Agreement.

7.127 Article 1.2 explains the term "intellectual property:"

---

[164] Annex C, paras. 130-132.

[165] Annex C, paras. 168-172.

> 2. For the purposes of this Agreement, the term 'intellectual property' refers to all categories of intellectual property that are the subject of Sections 1 through 7 of Part II.

7.128 Turning to the Regulation, Article 12(1) refers to how the Regulation "may apply," which is a reference to the *availability* of intellectual property rights in relation to "designations of origin" and "geographical indications," as defined in the Regulation. It is not disputed that "designations of origin" and "geographical indications," as defined in the Regulation, fall within the category of "geographical indications," the subject of Section 3 of Part II, and therefore part of a category of intellectual property within the meaning of Article 1.2 of the TRIPS Agreement.

7.129 Therefore, this claim concerns the "protection" of intellectual property, as clarified in footnote 3 to the TRIPS Agreement, within the scope of the national treatment obligation in Article 3 of that Agreement.

7.130 It is not necessary to show that the Regulation implements the minimum standards in Part II of the TRIPS Agreement for the purposes of these claims. National treatment is required with regard to the protection of intellectual property, even where measures provide a higher level of protection.

<u>less favourable treatment accorded to the nationals of other Members</u>

less favourable treatment

7.131 The Panel now examines the second element of this claim which is whether the nationals of other Members are accorded less favourable treatment than the European Communities' own nationals. It is useful to recall that Article 3.1 of the TRIPS Agreement combines elements of national treatment both from pre-existing intellectual property agreements and GATT 1994.[166] Like the pre-existing intellectual property conventions, Article 3.1 applies to "nationals," not products. Like GATT 1994, Article 3.1 refers to "no less favourable" treatment, not the advantages or rights that laws now grant or may hereafter grant, but it does not refer to likeness. This combination of elements is reflected in the preamble to the TRIPS Agreement which explains the purpose of the "basic principles" in Articles 3 and 4 (a term highlighted in the title of Part I) as follows:

> *Recognizing*, to this end, the need for new rules and disciplines concerning:
>
> (a) the applicability of the basic principles of GATT 1994 and of relevant international intellectual property agreements or conventions;

7.132 The "no less favourable" treatment standard set out in the first sentence of Article 3.1 of the TRIPS Agreement is subject to certain specific exceptions, some of them found in the pre-existing intellectual property conventions. None of the exceptions in Article 3.1 and 3.2 are relevant to this dispute.[167] Where these exceptions and limitations do not apply, the language of the basic obligation in the first sentence of Article 3.1 is very broad, referring to treatment that is "no less favourable."

7.133 We recall that the Panel in *US – Section 211 Appropriations Act*, in a finding with which the Appellate Body agreed[168], found that the appropriate standard of examination under Article 3.1 of the TRIPS Agreement is that enunciated by the GATT Panel in *US – Section 337*. That GATT Panel made the following findings on the "no less favourable" treatment standard under Article III:4 of GATT 1947:

---

[166] Three of these national treatment obligations are incorporated in the TRIPS Agreement itself: Article 2 of the Paris Convention (1967) (considered below at paras. 7.214 and following), Article 5 of the Berne Convention (1971) and Article 5 of the IPIC Treaty, which are incorporated by Articles 2.1, 9.1 and 35 of the TRIPS Agreement, respectively.

[167] Article 24.9 also provides that there shall be no obligation under this Agreement to protect GIs which are not or cease to be protected in their country of origin or which have fallen into disuse in that country.

[168] See the Panel report on *US – Section 211 Appropriations Act*, at paras. 8.131-8.133 and the Appellate Body report, at para. 258.

> The words 'treatment no less favourable' in paragraph 4 call for effective equality of opportunities for imported products in respect of the application of laws, regulations and requirements affecting the internal sale, offering for sale, purchase, transportation, distribution or use of products. This clearly sets a minimum permissible standard as a basis.[169]

7.134 Therefore, the Panel will examine whether the difference in treatment affects the "effective equality of opportunities" between the nationals of other Members and the European Communities' own nationals with regard to the "protection" of intellectual property rights, to the detriment of nationals of other Members.

7.135 The interpretation of the "no less favourable" treatment standard under other covered agreements may be relevant in interpreting Article 3.1 of the TRIPS Agreement, taking account of its context in each agreement including, in particular, any differences arising from its application to like products or like services and service suppliers, rather than to nationals.[170]

7.136 Under Article III:4 of GATT 1994, the Appellate Body in *US – FSC (Article 21.5 – EC)* has explained its approach to the examination of whether measures affecting the internal sale of *products* accord "treatment no less favourable" as follows:

> The examination of whether a measure involves 'less favourable treatment' of imported products within the meaning of Article III:4 of the GATT 1994 must be grounded in close scrutiny of the 'fundamental thrust and effect of the measure itself.' This examination cannot rest on simple assertion, but must be founded on a careful analysis of the contested measure and of its implications in the marketplace. At the same time, however, the examination need not be based on the *actual effects* of the contested measure in the marketplace.[171]

7.137 Similarly, in the present dispute, the Panel considers it appropriate to base its examination under Article 3.1 of the TRIPS Agreement on the fundamental thrust and effect of the Regulation, including an analysis of its terms and its practical implications. However, as far as the TRIPS Agreement is concerned, the relevant practical implications are those on opportunities with regard to the protection of intellectual property. The implications in the marketplace for the agricultural products and foodstuffs in respect of which GIs may be protected are relevant to the examination under Article III:4 of GATT 1994, considered later in this report.

7.138 The parties disagree on whether the equivalence and reciprocity conditions in Article 12(1) of the Regulation apply to GIs located in other WTO Members outside the European Communities. The Panel recalls its finding at paragraph 7.102 that they do so apply.

7.139 Although the parties disagree on whether the equivalence and reciprocity conditions in Article 12(1) of the Regulation discriminate in a manner inconsistent with the covered agreements, it is not disputed that those conditions accord less favourable treatment to persons with interests in the *GIs* to which those conditions apply.[172] The Panel considers that those conditions modify the effective equality of opportunities to obtain protection with respect to intellectual property in two ways. First, GI protection is not available under the

---

[169] GATT panel report in *US – Section 337*, at para. 5.11.

[170] In *US – Section 211 Appropriations Act*, the Panel considered that the jurisprudence on Article III:4 of GATT 1994 may be useful in interpreting Article 3.1 of the TRIPS Agreement due to the similarity of their language: see the Panel report at para. 8.129; Appellate Body report at para. 242.

[171] Appellate Body Report, *US – FSC (Article 21.5 – EC)*, para. 215, quoting reports in *Korea – Various Measures on Beef*, para. 142, and *Japan – Alcoholic Beverages II*, at 110.

[172] United States' first written submission, paras. 57-60. Note that the European Communities asserts only that the product specifications and inspection regimes for individual GIs do not constitute less favourable treatment. With respect to the equivalence and reciprocity conditions, it asserts that it does not apply them and that they do not depend on nationality, but *not* that they do not accord less favourable treatment where they apply: see its first written submission, paras. 113-126, and paras. 62-69. It also concedes that they constitute less favourable treatment for the purposes of Article III:4 of GATT 1994, but does not consider that the meaning of the phrase is necessarily the same as in Article 3.1 of the TRIPS Agreement: see its responses to Panel question Nos. 94(a) and 113.

Regulation in respect of geographical areas located in third countries which the Commission has not recognized under Article 12(3). The European Communities confirms that the Commission has not recognized any third countries. Second, GI protection under the Regulation may become available if the third country in which the GI is located enters into an international agreement or satisfies the conditions in Article 12(1). Both of those requirements represent a significant "extra hurdle" in obtaining GI protection that does not apply to geographical areas located in the European Communities.[173] The significance of the hurdle is reflected in the fact that currently no third country has entered into such an agreement or satisfied those conditions.

7.140 Accordingly, the Panel finds that the equivalence and reciprocity conditions modify the effective equality of opportunities with respect to the availability of protection to persons who wish to obtain GI protection under the Regulation, to the detriment of those who wish to obtain protection in respect of geographical areas located in third countries, including WTO Members. This is less favourable treatment.

nationals of other Members

7.141 The issue for the Panel is how the less favourable treatment accorded under the Regulation with respect to the availability of protection affects the treatment accorded to the nationals of other Members and that accorded to the European Communities' own nationals for the purposes of Article 3.1 of the TRIPS Agreement. Article 1.3 defines "nationals of other Members" in order to determine the persons to whom Members shall accord treatment, which includes national treatment.[174] It provides as follows:

> 3. Members shall accord the treatment provided for in this Agreement to the nationals of other Members. In respect of the relevant intellectual property right, the nationals of other Members shall be understood as those natural or legal persons that would meet the criteria for eligibility for protection provided for in the Paris Convention (1967), the Berne Convention (1971), the Rome Convention and the Treaty on Intellectual Property in Respect of Integrated Circuits, were all Members of the WTO members of those conventions. (...) [footnote 1 omitted]

7.142 In respect of the intellectual property rights relevant to this dispute, it is not disputed that the criteria for eligibility for protection that apply are those found in the Paris Convention (1967). Articles 2 and 3 of the Paris Convention (1967) provide how nationals and persons assimilated to nationals are to be treated. In the Panel's view, these are "criteria for eligibility for protection" for the purposes of the TRIPS Agreement.[175]

7.143 Articles 2 and 3 of the Paris Convention (1967) refer to "nationals" without defining that term. Article 3 of the Paris Convention (1967) provides for the assimilation of certain persons to nationals as follows:

> Nationals of countries outside the Union who are domiciled or who have real and effective industrial or commercial establishments in the territory of one of the countries of the Union shall be treated in the same manner as nationals of the countries of the Union.[176]

---

[173] This was also the approach of the Appellate Body in *US – Section 211 Appropriations Act* to an "extra hurdle" imposed only on foreign nationals: see para. 268 of its report.

[174] This can be contrasted with the detailed definitions in Article XXVIII of GATS of "natural person of another Member," "juridical person of another Member," "juridical person" and a juridical person "owned" or "controlled" by persons of a Member or "affiliated" with another person.

[175] Article 1.3 of the TRIPS Agreement also refers to the criteria for eligibility for protection in the Berne Convention (1971). It can be observed that the title inserted to facilitate identification of Article 3 of the Berne Convention (1971), which concerns authors who are nationals or assimilated to nationals, also refers to "Criteria of Eligibility for Protection." This is consistent with the Panel's view of the criteria in the Paris Convention (1967) for the purposes of the TRIPS Agreement.

[176] These are the same criteria at those used in footnote 1 to the TRIPS Agreement, set out at para. 7.154 below.

7.144 The rule in Article 3 of the Paris Convention (1967) only applies to nationals of countries *outside the Paris Union.* According to Article 1.3 of the TRIPS Agreement, these criteria shall be understood as if "all Members of the WTO" were members of that Convention. Therefore, for the purposes of the TRIPS Agreement, that rule of assimilation only applies to persons that are nationals of a country *that is not a WTO Member*. It does not apply to nationals of other WTO Members, such as the United States. Therefore, it does not mean that all persons who have a domicile or a real and effective industrial and commercial establishment in a WTO Member are necessarily nationals of that WTO Member for the purposes of the TRIPS Agreement.

7.145 Otherwise, the Paris Convention (1967) contains no common rules on the meaning of "nationals." It can be noted that the original Paris Convention of 1883 appeared to use the term "subjects and citizens" and "nationals" interchangeably. The phrase "subjects and citizens" was replaced with "nationals" in Articles 2 and 3 in the Hague Act of 1925 without, apparently, changing the scope of the Convention.[177]

7.146 A leading commentator on the Paris Convention (1967) explains the practice under that Convention as follows:

> With respect to *natural* persons, nationality is a quality accorded or withdrawn by the legislation of the State whose nationality is claimed. Therefore, it is only the legislation of that State which can define the said nationality and which must be applied also in other countries where it is invoked.
>
> With respect to *legal* persons, the question is more complicated because generally no 'nationality' as such is granted to legal persons by existing legislations. Where these legal persons are the State themselves, or State enterprises, or other bodies of *public status*, it would be logical to accord to them the nationality of their country. With regard to corporate bodies of *private status*, such as companies and associations, the authorities of the countries where application of the Convention is sought will have to decide on the criterion of 'nationality' which they will employ. This 'nationality' can be made dependent upon the law according to which these legal persons have been constituted, or upon the law of their actual headquarters, or even on other criteria. Such law will also decide whether a legal person or entity really exists. [original footnote omitted][178]

7.147 This is consistent with the position under public international law.[179] With respect to the meaning of "nationals of other Members" for the purposes of the TRIPS Agreement, WTO Members have, through Article 1.3 of the TRIPS Agreement, incorporated the meaning of "nationals" as it was understood in the Paris Convention (1967) and under public international law. With respect to natural persons, they refer first to the law of the Member of which nationality is claimed.[180] With respect to legal persons, each Member first applies its own criteria to determine nationality.

---

[177] Article 2 originally provided that "subjects and citizens" will enjoy the advantages granted to "nationals." As early as 1897, the Chair of the Brussels Diplomatic Conference commented that, in practice, the rights conferred on physical persons must belong equally to juridical persons and it seemed to be unanimously recognized that this was the scope of the Convention, see *Actes de Paris*, 1897, 3rd session, p. 196. "Subjects and citizens" was replaced with the word "nationals" at the 1925 Hague Diplomatic Conference because, in its brevity, it was considered more comprehensive, and was consistent with the terminology of the Convention: see *Actes de Paris*, 1925, report of drafting committee, p. 538.

[178] See Bodenhausen, *supra* at note 66, pp. 27-28.

[179] See, for example, A.A. Fatouros, "National Legal Persons in International Law" in R. Bernhardt (ed.), *Encyclopedia of Public International Law,* Volume III (1997) pp. 495-501; and I. Brownlie, *Principles of Public International Law* (5th edition, Oxford, 1998), p.426, submitted to the Panel by the European Communities in Exhibits EC-88 and EC-115, respectively.

[180] With respect to natural persons, the Panel also notes that a State may not be bound to recognize a grant of nationality if it does not represent a genuine connection between the natural person and the State granting the nationality: see the judgement of the International Court of Justice in the *Nottenbohm case (Liechtenstein v Guatemala)* (second phase), ICJ Reports (1955), 4.

7.148 The meaning of "nationals" under public international law is also relevant to the meaning of a Member's "own nationals." Whilst the TRIPS Agreement does not create obligations for a Member to accord treatment to its own nationals, it does refer to the treatment that each Member accords to its own nationals as the benchmark for its obligation to accord national treatment under Article 3.1, as well as under the other national treatment obligations incorporated by reference, including Article 2 of the Paris Convention (1967). To that extent, the way in which a Member defines its own nationals can also be subject to review for the purposes of determining conformity with its national treatment obligations under the TRIPS Agreement.

7.149 The European Communities has explained to the Panel that, with respect to natural persons, under the domestic law of the European Communities, any person who is a national of an EC member State is a citizen of the European Union and, accordingly, an EC national.[181] It has explained that, with respect to legal persons, the domestic law of the European Communities does not contain a specific definition of nationality, but nor does the domestic law of many other WTO Members.[182] However, the European Communities informs the Panel that any legal person considered a national under the laws of an EC member State would also be an EC national. The criteria used by the EC member States to determine the nationality of a legal person may vary and include criteria such as the place of incorporation and the place of the seat of the company or a combination of such criteria.[183]

7.150 The United States has not challenged the criteria used by the European Communities to determine nationality. The Panel notes that these criteria appear to be the same as those used in public international law.[184] Therefore, the Panel can use them to determine which persons are "nationals" under Article 3.1 of the TRIPS Agreement.

7.151 Turning to the Regulation, it is agreed that it does not, on its face, refer to "nationals." It refers to the location of geographical areas, or GIs. In theory, there may be foreign citizens or corporations who are entitled to use GIs located in the European Communities and obtain protection under the Regulation. The issue for the Panel is to determine the treatment accorded to the nationals of other Members and that accorded to the European Communities' own nationals, when such treatment depends on the location of GIs.

specific definitions of "nationals"

7.152 The United States argues that there are specific definitions of "nationals" applicable in this dispute, either of which would identify the nationality of persons with the location of GIs. The first specific definition would apply to the European Communities and the other would apply to GIs. The Panel finds that the following graphic, based on one set out in Chinese Taipei's third party submission, provides a useful framework for its analysis of this issue.

---

[181] Article 8 of the EC Treaty.

[182] Article 58 of the EC Treaty provides that companies or firms formed in accordance with the law of an EC member State and having their registered office, central administration or principal place of business within the European Community shall, for the purposes of Chapter 2 of the EC Treaty on the right of establishment, be treated in the same way as natural persons who are nationals of EC member States.

[183] European Communities' response to Panel question No. 105. It also referred to a criterion based on the nationality of controlling shareholders, but the evidence submitted in support does not appear to indicate that this is of relevance to corporate nationality under the TRIPS Agreement.

[184] See *supra* at note 179.

1. EC national with GI located in the EC	3. EC national with GI located outside the EC
2. Non-EC national with GI located in the EC	4. Non-EC national with GI located outside the EC

Graphic 1

7.153 The graphic depicts the four relevant possible combinations of nationality of persons and the location of a GI, each in a separate numbered quadrant. In terms of this graphic, the Panel's conclusion at paragraph 7.102 is that the conditions of reciprocity and equivalence in Article 12(1) of the Regulation apply to the persons in quadrants 3 and 4 only. There is therefore discrimination between the persons in quadrants 1 and 2, on the one hand, and those in quadrants 3 and 4, on the other hand.

7.154 The United States argues that a special regime to determine nationals applies to the European Communities as a separate customs territory Member of the WTO within the meaning of footnote 1 to Article 1.3 of the TRIPS Agreement. Footnote 1 provides as follows:

> Footnote 1: When 'nationals' are referred to in this Agreement, they shall be deemed, in the case of a separate customs territory Member of the WTO, to mean persons, natural or legal, who are domiciled or who have a real and effective industrial or commercial establishment in that customs territory.[185]

7.155 If the European Communities is a "separate customs territory Member of the WTO" within the meaning of footnote 1, references to its "nationals" in the TRIPS Agreement mean all persons, natural or legal, who are domiciled or who have a real and effective industrial or commercial establishment in the European Communities, irrespective of the citizenship of an individual or the nationality of a corporation under public international law. Persons who are entitled to a GI in a particular geographical area within the territory of the European Communities, may correspond to this definition of nationals, even if they are foreign citizens or corporations. This would conflate quadrants 1 and 2, to which conditions of reciprocity and equivalence do not apply, and require any comparison of treatment for the purposes of the national treatment obligation to be made with persons in either or both of quadrants 3 and 4, to whom those additional conditions do apply.

7.156 The European Communities submits that it is not a separate customs territory Member of the WTO.

7.157 The Panel notes that the term "separate customs territory" in the text of footnote 1 is qualified by the term "Member of the WTO." The parties refer us to certain interpretative guidance in the WTO Agreement as to the meaning of these terms.

7.158 The original Members of the WTO are described in Article XI:1 of the WTO Agreement as "[t]he contracting parties to GATT 1947 as of [1 January 1995], and the European Communities." This simply reflects the fact that the European Communities is the only original Member that was not a Contracting Party to GATT 1947, but does not address the issue whether or not it is a separate customs territory Member of the WTO. The voting rules in Article IX:1 of the WTO Agreement reflect the *sui generis* character of the European Communities among the Members of the WTO.

[185] These are the same criteria as those used in Article 3 of the Paris Convention (1967), set out at paragraph 7.143 above.

7.159 Accession of new Members to the WTO is possible under Article XII of the WTO Agreement, paragraph 1 of which refers to "[a]ny State or separate customs territory possessing full autonomy in the conduct of its external commercial relations and of the other matters provided for in this Agreement and the Multilateral Trade Agreements." It is not disputed that the European Communities is not a State, but it did not accede to the WTO under the terms of Article XII and the terms of that Article are therefore inapplicable to it.

7.160 The first explanatory note to the WTO Agreement only refers to countries and separate customs territories Members of the WTO.[186] The European Communities is not a country, but this note might not be relevant if all references to a "country" in the relevant agreements can be adequately understood in relation to the European Communities.[187]

7.161 The second explanatory note to the WTO Agreement provides guidance where an expression in that agreement and the multilateral trade agreements is qualified by the term "national" in the case of a "separate customs territory Member of the WTO."[188] Footnote 1 to the TRIPS Agreement is not within the scope of this explanatory note because it uses the word "national" as a noun and not as a qualifying expression. In any case, the explanatory note does not indicate if the European Communities is a separate customs territory Member of the WTO.

7.162 The Panel considers these provisions inconclusive as regards the question before it and must therefore interpret the term "separate customs territory Member of the WTO" according to the general rule of treaty interpretation. It is not disputed that the European Communities is a customs territory.[189] The key word appears to be "separate," which can be defined as follows:

> Put apart, disunite, part, (two or more persons or things, or one from another); detach, disconnect, *treat as distinct, (one thing)*; make a division between (two things). [emphasis added][190]

7.163 We highlight the definition "treat as distinct, (one thing)," given that a "separate customs territory Member of the WTO" is one thing, and the word "distinct" corresponds to the term used in that phrase in the French and Spanish versions, which are equally authentic.[191] It is not disputed that all Members of the WTO are separate, or distinct, from one another. Most Members that are not part of a customs union are a customs territory separate from other customs territories. The word "separate" would be redundant if this is all it meant. Logically, it must indicate a customs territory that is separate from another Member in some other way.

---

[186] The first explanatory note provides as follows:
"The terms 'country' or 'countries' as used in this Agreement and the Multilateral Trade Agreements are to be understood to include any separate customs territory Member of the WTO."

[187] For example, references in the covered agreements to "developing countries," "least-developed countries," "importing country," "exporting country," "third country" and "country of origin."

[188] The second explanatory note provides as follows:
"In the case of a separate customs territory Member of the WTO, where an expression in this Agreement and the Multilateral Trade Agreements is qualified by the term 'national', such expression shall be read as pertaining to that customs territory, unless otherwise specified."

[189] This is consistent with the definition of a "customs territory" for the purposes of GATT 1994 in Article XXIV:2.

[190] *The New Shorter Oxford English Dictionary* (1993).

[191] See the final clause of the WTO Agreement.

7.164 The context elsewhere in the WTO Agreement bears this out. The term "separate customs territory" is used in Article XXVI:5 of GATT 1994[192], which treats a separate customs territory as a territory for which a GATT Contracting Party, now a WTO Member[193], has international responsibility, and is distinguished from a metropolitan territory. It is also found in Article XXXIII of GATT 1994.[194]

7.165 The object and purpose of the TRIPS Agreement includes the conferral of intellectual property protection on the nationals of WTO Members. Footnote 1 is a deeming provision for the purposes of nationality. This confirms that the reason for the inclusion of footnote 1 was that separate customs territories do not confer nationality and, hence, a supplementary definition was required.

7.166 The European Communities does not form a separate part of the territory of a country. Rather, the territory of the European Communities is made up primarily of the territories in Europe, that is, where relevant, the metropolitan territories, of a group of countries, the number of which increased to 25 during this Panel proceeding.[195] It is neither a territory part of another country, nor a separate territory for which other WTO Members have international responsibility. The European Communities has informed the Panel that it has a citizenship for natural persons, and, generally speaking, treats legal persons organized under the laws of an EC member State as EC nationals under its domestic law, as described above.[196]

7.167 Therefore, the Panel accepts the European Communities' submission that it is not a "separate customs territory Member of the WTO" within the meaning of footnote 1 to the TRIPS Agreement, and finds that its nationals, for the purposes of the TRIPS Agreement, are not defined by that footnote. The Panel would like to stress that its finding is limited solely to footnote 1 of the TRIPS Agreement and is not intended to be a finding of general application for other covered agreements.

7.168 The United States also argues that the criteria for eligibility for protection in the Paris Convention (1967), as incorporated by Article 1.3 of the TRIPS Agreement, include Article 10(2) of the Paris Convention (1967). It argues that Article 10(2) sets out a specific criterion of eligibility of protection in respect of designations of origin and geographical indications, which defines the "nationals of other Members" in respect of those industrial property rights for the purposes of the TRIPS Agreement. Persons entitled to use a GI in a geographical area in a WTO Member outside the territory of the European Communities may correspond to this definition of nationals of other Members. This argument would conflate quadrants 3 and 4 in the graphic set out earlier, to which the conditions of reciprocity and equivalence apply, and require any comparison of treatment for the purposes of the national treatment obligation to be made with persons in either or both of quadrants 1 and 2, to whom those additional conditions do not apply.

---

[192] Article XXVI:5 provides as follows:

"(*a*) Each government accepting this Agreement does so in respect of its metropolitan territory and of the other territories for which it has international responsibility, except such separate customs territories as it shall notify to the Executive Secretary to the CONTRACTING PARTIES at the time of its own acceptance.

"(*b*) Any government, which has so notified the Executive Secretary under the exceptions in subparagraph (*a*) of this paragraph, may at any time give notice to the Executive Secretary that its acceptance shall be effective in respect of any separate customs territory or territories so excepted and such notice shall take effect on the thirtieth day following the day on which it is received by the Executive Secretary.

"(*c*) If any of the customs territories, in respect of which a contracting party has accepted this Agreement, possesses or acquires full autonomy in the conduct of its external commercial relations and of the other matters provided for in this Agreement, such territory shall, upon sponsorship through a declaration by the responsible contracting party establishing the above-mentioned fact, be deemed to be a contracting party." [footnotes omitted]

[193] Read in accordance with explanatory note 2(a) to GATT 1994.

[194] Article XXXIII provides as follows:

"A government not party to this Agreement, or a government acting on behalf of a separate customs territory possessing full autonomy in the conduct of its external commercial relations and of the other matters provided for in this Agreement, may accede to this Agreement, on its own behalf or on behalf of that territory, on terms to be agreed between such government and the CONTRACTING PARTIES. Decisions of the CONTRACTING PARTIES under this paragraph shall be taken by a two-thirds majority."

[195] Under Article 182 of the EC Treaty, the EC member States agree to associate with the Community the non-European countries and territories which have special relations with Denmark, France, the Netherlands and the United Kingdom listed in Annex II to the Treaty.

[196] European Communities' response to Panel question No. 105.

7.169 The United States observes that the GI obligations in Articles 22 and 23 of the TRIPS Agreement refer to the persons entitled to protection as "interested parties" and that Article 10(2) of the Paris Convention (1967) sets out persons who shall be deemed an "interested party" for the purposes of an obligation related to certain false indications. Article 10(2) refers *inter alia* to establishment in the locality or country falsely indicated. The United States argues that this provides guidance as to the persons who shall be deemed an "interested party" for the purposes of Articles 22 and 23 of the TRIPS Agreement and, hence, the national treatment obligation in Article 3.1.

7.170 The Panel accepts that an "interested party" is a person who is entitled to receive protection under Articles 22 and 23 of the TRIPS Agreement. However, in the Panel's view, Article 10(2) of the Paris Convention (1967) does not set out a criterion for eligibility for protection. Article 10(2) is a deeming provision for the term "interested party" used in Article 9(3) of the Paris Convention (1967), as made applicable under Article 10(1). Once a person has qualified as a national, Article 10(2) may provide guidance on whether that person may be treated as an interested party for the purposes of Articles 22 and 23 of the TRIPS Agreement. However, Article 10(2) does not set out a criterion for eligibility for protection under the Paris Convention (1967) for the purposes of Article 1.3 of the TRIPS Agreement.

7.171 Therefore, the Panel rejects the specific definitions of "nationals" advanced by the United States and confirms its finding at paragraph 7.150 as to the criteria that can be used to determine which persons are "nationals" for the purposes of Article 3.1 of the TRIPS Agreement, for the purposes of this dispute.

formally identical provisions

7.172 The issue for the Panel remains that of determining the treatment accorded to the nationals of other Members and to the European Communities' own nationals. On its face, the Regulation contains formally identical provisions vis-à-vis the nationals of different Members, with respect to the availability of GI protection.

7.173 It is well recognized that the concept of "no less favourable" treatment under Article III:4 of GATT 1994 is sufficiently broad to include situations where the application of formally identical legal provisions would in practice accord less favourable treatment. The GATT Panel in *US – Section 337*, which considered an intellectual property enforcement measure prior to the conclusion of the TRIPS Agreement, interpreted the "no less favourable" standard under Article III:4 as follows:

> On the one hand, contracting parties may apply to imported products different formal legal requirements if doing so would accord imported products more favourable treatment. On the other hand, it also has to be recognised that there may be cases where application of formally identical legal provisions would in practice accord less favourable treatment to imported products and a contracting party might thus have to apply different legal provisions to imported products to ensure that the treatment accorded them is in fact no less favourable.[197]

7.174 The Appellate Body in *Korea – Various Measures on Beef*, in a dispute concerning formally different treatment, quoted this passage and drew the conclusion that "[a] formal difference in treatment between imported and like domestic products is thus neither necessary, nor sufficient, to show a violation of Article III:4."[198] It then proceeded to apply the relevant standard of examination.

[197] GATT panel report in *US – Section 337*, para. 5.11.

[198] Appellate Body report on *Korea – Various Measures on Beef*, para. 137. This view is also consistent with the findings of the Appellate Body in its report on *EC – Bananas III* with respect to the phrase "treatment no less favourable" as used in the MFN obligation in relation to trade in services in Article II of GATS, at para. 233.

7.175 The Panel in *Canada – Pharmaceutical Patents* also considered that claims against both formal and practical discrimination are possible under the TRIPS Agreement, although that dispute concerned minimum standards of protection in Part II and not the basic principles in Part I.[199]

7.176 We consider that this reasoning applies with equal force to the no less favourable treatment standard in Article 3.1 of the TRIPS Agreement. In our view, even if the provisions of the Regulation are formally identical in the treatment that they accord to the nationals of other Members and to the European Communities' own nationals, this is not sufficient to demonstrate that there is no violation of Article 3.1 of the TRIPS Agreement. Whether or not the Regulation accords less favourable treatment to the nationals of other Members than it accords to the European Communities' own nationals should be examined instead according to the standard we set out at paragraph 7.134, namely, the "effective equality of opportunities" with regard to the protection of intellectual property rights. In this examination, we will follow the approach that we set out at paragraph 7.137, which focuses on the "fundamental thrust and effect" of the Regulation.

which nationals to compare?

7.177 The text of Article 3.1 expressly calls for a comparison when it provides that "[e]ach Member shall accord to the nationals of other Members treatment no *less* favourable *than* that it accords to its own nationals" (emphasis added). The question arises as to which nationals it is appropriate to compare.

7.178 The United States submits that the Panel should compare the treatment of a hypothetical EC national with a GI located in the European Communities, and the treatment of a hypothetical U.S. national with a GI located in the United States. This is a comparison of a person in quadrant 1 with a person in quadrant 4 in the graphic set out earlier.

7.179 The Panel recalls that the Regulation contains formally identical provisions vis-à-vis the nationals of different Members. In the absence of less favourable treatment based on a formal criterion of nationality, or a criterion that fully corresponds with nationality, the Panel is reluctant to compare a hypothetical national of one Member with a national of another Member simply because they both claim rights to the same category of intellectual property. This is a very low threshold with possibly unforeseen systemic implications for all intellectual property rights covered by the TRIPS Agreement.

7.180 The United States also submits that there is discrimination according to nationality on the basis of a comparison of the group of the European Communities' own nationals who wish to obtain GI protection under the Regulation, with the group of nationals of other WTO Members who wish to obtain GI protection under the Regulation. This is a comparison of the persons in both quadrants 1 and 3 with the persons in both quadrants 2 and 4 in the graphic set out earlier.

7.181 The Panel recalls that the standard of examination is based on "effective equality of opportunities." It follows that the nationals that are relevant to an examination under Article 3.1 of the TRIPS Agreement should be those who seek opportunities with respect to the same type of intellectual property in comparable situations.[200] On the one hand, this excludes a comparison of opportunities for nationals with respect to different categories of intellectual property, such as GIs and copyright. On the other hand, no reason has been advanced as to why the equality of opportunities should be limited *a priori* to rights with a territorial link to a particular Member.[201]

---

[199] Panel report on *Canada – Pharmaceutical Patents*, at paras. 7.100-7.105.

[200] The Appellate Body in *EC – Asbestos* adopted an analogous approach to the term "like" products in Article III:4 of GATT 1994, which it interpreted in terms of the competitive relationship between products: see its report at para. 99.

[201] See the European Communities' responses to Panel question Nos. 25, 101 and 103.

7.182 The Panel therefore considers it appropriate for the purposes of this claim to compare the effective equality of opportunities for the group of nationals of other Members who may wish to seek GI protection under the Regulation and the group of the European Communities' own nationals who may wish to seek GI protection under the Regulation. On this approach, there is no need to make a factual assumption that every person who wishes to obtain protection for a GI in a particular Member is a national of that Member.[202]

7.183 The European Communities disagrees with this approach. It argues that the concept of *de facto* discrimination should be limited to cases of circumvention of obligations, which is unnecessary in this dispute because of the applicability of the national treatment obligation under GATT 1994.[203]

7.184 The Panel is mindful of the need to ensure a harmonious interpretation of the national treatment obligation within the TRIPS Agreement itself as applied to different intellectual property rights. The fact that circumvention of that obligation may be prevented, uniquely, under GATT 1994 in certain cases concerning geographical indications, does not justify a different interpretation of Article 3.1 of the TRIPS Agreement from that which would be applicable to all other intellectual property rights, which do not have an inherent link to the territorial origin of a product. The Panel's interpretation preserves internal coherence in the interpretation of national treatment under the TRIPS Agreement.

comparison of treatment accorded to the nationals of other Members and that accorded to the European Communities' own nationals

7.185 Articles 5 through 7 of the Regulation set out a registration procedure for GIs that refer to a geographical area located within the territory of the European Communities.[204] Articles 12a and 12b set out a registration procedure for GIs that refers to geographical areas located in third countries, including WTO Members. The conditions in Article 12(1) only apply to the latter procedures and, hence, only to GIs that refer to geographical areas located in third countries.

7.186 There is a link between the location of a geographical area to which a GI refers and certain persons. Article 5(1) and 5(2) provides that the following persons may apply for registration of a GI:

> 1. Only a group or, subject to certain conditions to be laid down in accordance with the procedure provided for in Article 15[205], a natural or legal person, shall be entitled to apply for registration.

---

[202] The Panel notes that its approach based on the respective treatment accorded to groups (of nationals) is consistent with an approach based on the respective treatment accorded to groups (of products) contemplated by the Appellate Body in *EC – Asbestos*, in the context of the national treatment obligation in Article III:4 of GATT 1994:

"(...) A complaining Member must still establish that the measure accords to the group of 'like' *imported* products "less favourable treatment" than it accords to the group of 'like' *domestic* products. The term 'less favourable treatment' expresses the general principle, in Article III:1, that internal regulations 'should not be applied … so as to afford protection to domestic production'. If there is 'less favourable treatment' of the group of 'like' imported products, there is, conversely, 'protection' of the group of 'like' domestic products. However, a Member may draw distinctions between products which have been found to be 'like', without, for this reason alone, according to the group of 'like' *imported* products 'less favourable treatment' than that accorded to the group of 'like' *domestic* products. (...)" at para. 100.

[203] European Communities' rebuttal submission, para. 49; response to Panel question No. 29.

[204] This is reflected in the fact that under Article 5(4) an application under the procedures set out in Articles 5 through 7 shall be sent to the EC member State in which the geographical area is located but under Article 12a(1) an application under the procedures set out in Articles 12a and 12b shall be sent to the authorities in the country in which the geographical area is located. This was confirmed by the European Communities in its response to Panel question No. 2.

[205] The European Commission has laid down in Article 1 of Commission Regulation (EEC) No. 2037/93 that applications for registration pursuant to Article 5 of Regulation (EEC) No. 2081/92 may be submitted by a natural or legal person not complying with the definition in the second subparagraph of Article 5(1) in exceptional, duly substantiated cases where the person concerned is the only producer in the geographical area defined at the time the application is submitted.

For the purposes of this Article, 'Group' means any association, irrespective of its legal form or composition, of producers and/or processors working with the same agricultural product or foodstuff. Other interested parties may participate in the group.

2. A group or a natural or legal person may apply for registration only in respect of agricultural products or foodstuffs which it produces or obtains within the meaning of Article 2(2)(a) or (b).

7.187 These definitions of applicants cross-refer to the definitions of designations of origin and geographical indications in the Regulation in Article 2(2)(a) and (b), which provide as follows:

2. For the purposes of this Regulation:

(a) *designation of origin*: means the name of a region, a specific place or, in exceptional cases, a country, used to describe an agricultural product or a foodstuff:

– originating in that region, specific place or country, and

– the quality or characteristics of which are essentially or exclusively due to a particular geographical environment with its inherent natural and human factors, and the production, processing and preparation of which take place in the defined geographical area;

(b) *geographical indication*: means the name of a region, a specific place or, in exceptional cases, a country, used to describe an agricultural product or a foodstuff:

– originating in that region, specific place or country, and

– which possesses a specific quality, reputation or other characteristics attributable to that geographical origin and the production and/or processing and/or preparation of which take place in the defined geographical area.

7.188 Registration confers certain protection, but only agricultural products or foodstuffs that comply with a specification are eligible to "use" a registered GI. Article 4(2) sets out the minimum requirements which must be included in a product specification, which include *inter alia* "evidence that the agricultural product or the foodstuff originates in the geographical area," "a description of the method of obtaining the agricultural product or foodstuff and, if appropriate, the authentic and unvarying local methods" and "the details bearing out the link with the geographical environment or the geographical origin" (from items (d), (e) and (f), respectively). Any person, and not merely the applicant, that produces or obtains the products in accordance with the specification in the registration is entitled to use the GI.

7.189 These provisions create a link between persons, the territory of a particular Member, and the availability of protection. The definition of a "designation of origin" requires that the applicant and users must produce, process and prepare the products covered by a registration in the relevant geographical area, whilst the definition of a "geographical indication" requires that the applicant and users must carry out at least one, or some combination, of these three activities in the geographical area, and must do so in accordance with a specification.

7.190 Accordingly, insofar as the Regulation discriminates with respect to the availability of protection between GIs located in the European Communities, on the one hand, and those located in third countries, including WTO Members, on the other hand, it formally discriminates between those persons who produce, process and/or prepare a product in accordance with a specification, in the European Communities, on the one hand, and those persons who produce, process and/or prepare a product in accordance with a specification, in third countries, including WTO Members, on the other hand.

7.191 The Panel recalls its finding in paragraph 7.182 that it is appropriate for the purposes of this dispute to compare the treatment accorded to the group of nationals of other Members who may wish to seek GI protection under the Regulation and the group of the European Communities' own nationals, who may wish to seek GI protection under the Regulation.

7.192 The United States argues that there is an extremely close fit between a distinction based on where a legal person is established and producing agricultural products and foodstuffs, and a distinction based on nationality.[206]

7.193 The European Communities does not deny this. It relies on the fact that the Regulation itself contains no legal obstacle to foreign nationals taking advantage of EC geographical indications and disputes that any person who is producing a product must *necessarily* have the nationality of the place where the product is produced.[207] However, in the Panel's view, that is not dispositive of the issue.

7.194 The Panel agrees that the vast majority of natural and legal persons who produce, process and/or prepare products according to a GI specification within the territory of a WTO Member party to this dispute will be nationals of that Member. The fact that there may be cases where such a person does not qualify as a national—and none has been brought to its attention—does not alter the fact that the distinction made by the Regulation on the basis of the location of a GI will operate in practice to discriminate between the group of nationals of other Members who wish to obtain GI protection, and the group of the European Communities' own nationals who wish to obtain GI protection, to the detriment of the nationals of other Members. This will not occur as a random outcome in a particular case but as a feature of the design and structure of the system. This design is evident in the Regulation's objective characteristics, in particular, the definitions of "designation of origin" and "geographical indication" and the requirements of the product specifications. The structure is evident in the different registration procedures.

7.195 Complete data on the persons who have actually availed themselves of protection under the Regulation is not available. Any person who produces, processes and/or prepares a product according to the specification in a GI registration is entitled to use the GI. Data on the persons who have applied for, and obtained, protection under the Regulation and their respective addresses is available but their nationality is not recorded. However, there is no clear evidence that even a single person who has applied for or is entitled to use a registered GI is not one of the European Communities' own nationals.

7.196 Whilst certain of the European Communities' own nationals may wish to obtain protection for GIs located outside the European Communities as well, it cannot seriously be contested that the GIs for which nationals of other WTO Members would wish to obtain protection are overwhelmingly located outside the European Communities. This is supported by evidence presented by the United States showing that the nationality of certain French, German, Italian, Spanish and U.S. holders of certification marks for principally place names registered in the United States is that of the country in which the relevant geographical area is located.[208]

---

[206] United States' response to Panel question No. 102. Brazil and Canada expressed the same view: see Annex C, paras. 24 and 47.

[207] European Communities' comment on US responses to Panel question Nos. 102 and 103.

[208] Set out in Exhibit US-43. Some of these marks relate to wines which are not a product covered by the Regulation at issue. This does not imply any view as to whether certification marks are an adequate means of protecting GIs.

7.197 The European Communities presented evidence intended to show that certain foreign nationals have actually obtained protection under the Regulation. The Panel notes that all its examples consist of a foreign national, or a corporation incorporated under the laws of an EC member State, that acquired another corporation incorporated under the laws of an EC member State, which produces products entitled to GI protection.[209] Those subsidiary corporations obtaining the benefit of protection appear to be the European Communities' own nationals, according to a place of incorporation test. Evidence is not available on the place of their company seat but such cases appear to be rare. This evidence confirms, rather than contradicts, the link between the treatment accorded to GIs located in the European Communities and EC nationality.

7.198 The text of the TRIPS Agreement contains a recognition that discrimination according to residence and establishment will be a close substitute for nationality. The criteria set out in footnote 1 to the TRIPS Agreement are clearly intended to provide close substitute criteria to determine nationality where criteria to determine nationality as such are not available in a Member's domestic law. These criteria are "domicile" and "real and effective industrial or commercial establishment." They are taken from the criteria used for the assimilation of nationals in Article 3 of the Paris Convention (1967). It is clear that, in using these terms, the drafters of footnote 1 of the TRIPS Agreement chose terms that were already understood in this pre-existing intellectual property convention. Under Article 3 of the Paris Convention (1967), "domicile" is not generally understood to indicate a legal situation, but rather a more or less permanent residence of a natural person, and an actual headquarters of a legal person. A "real and effective industrial and commercial establishment" is intended to refer to all but a sham or ephemeral establishment.[210]

7.199 The object and purpose of the TRIPS Agreement depends on the obligation in Article 1.3 to accord the treatment provided for in the Agreement to the nationals of other Members, including national treatment under Article 3.1. That object and purpose would be severely undermined if a Member could avoid its obligations by simply according treatment to its own nationals on the basis of close substitute criteria, such as place of production, or establishment, and denying treatment to the nationals of other WTO Members who produce or are established in their own countries.

7.200 Further, the Panel recalls its finding at paragraph 7.182 and considers that Article 3.1 calls for a comparison of the effective equality of opportunities for the group of nationals of other Members who may wish to seek GI protection under the Regulation and the group of the European Communities' own nationals who may wish to seek GI protection under the Regulation. An objective assessment of that comparison cannot ignore the difference in treatment between quadrants 1 and 2 and quadrants 3 and 4 in the graphic set out earlier.

7.201 The Panel also notes that the close link between nationality, on the one hand, and residence and establishment, on the other, appears to be recognized in the Regulation itself. Article 12d of the Regulation accords a right of objection to persons, which the European Communities confirms is a reference to persons resident or established outside the European Communities, regardless of their nationality.[211] Yet the April 2003

---

[209] The evidence is as follows: Mr. Jens-Reidar Larsen, a Norwegian national, acquired a French cognac firm in 1928. Cognac is not a product covered by the Regulation at issue; Sara Lee Personal Products SpA, an Italian corporation under common control with Sara Lee Charcuterie SA, a French corporation belonging to the Sara Lee group, acquired Al Ponte Prosciutto SRL, an Italian corporation; Kraft Foods Group, which has an Italian subsidiary, acquired the business of Giovanni Invernizzi, an Italian, and partly sold it to Lactalis, a French dairy company with an Italian subsidiary; Nestlé sold Vismara, a salami firm, to an Italian company. The persons who acquired GI protection in these three examples may all be the European Communities' own nationals. The European Communities also refers to the website of a private beer label collector who disclaims accuracy but suggests that a Belgian company used to produce a beer with a German GI, possibly before the Regulation entered into force. The Panel considers this example unreliable. See Exhibits EC-36, EC-61, EC-62, EC-63 and EC-89 and the United States' response to Panel question No. 102.

[210] Bodenhausen, *supra* at note 66, p. 33, citing Ladas, *The International Protection of Industrial Property*, pp. 187-188, and Roubier, *Le Droit de la propriété industrielle I*, pp. 268-269. This is confirmed by the Official Records of the Paris Convention provided to the Panel by the International Bureau of WIPO and quoted in Bodenhausen, *ibid.*, p. 34.

[211] European Communities' first written submission, para. 142.

amending Regulation, which inserted Article 12d, explained that it granted the right of objection to the *nationals* of other WTO Members.[212]

7.202 The European Communities argues that any difference in treatment of the nationals of other Members is not attributable to the Regulation. In its view, if a person sets up a legal entity in the area where the GI is located, "[i]t is simply a practical consequence of the fact that products have to be produced in accordance with the product specification, which may require that an important part of the production process takes place in the geographical area concerned." It argues that if, for practical considerations related for instance to taxation or labour law, a person producing in conformity with a product specification chooses to set up a legal entity in the area where the geographical area is located, this is not related to the Regulation.[213]

7.203 The Panel considers that this constitutes part of the fundamental thrust and effect of the Regulation, including its practical implications, and that therefore it must be taken into account in assessing whether the Regulation accords less favourable treatment. Whilst the Regulation does not prevent a foreign national from producing goods within the territory of the European Communities which would be entitled to use a GI, the implications of its design and structure on the opportunities for protection are such that its different procedures will operate to accord different treatment to the European Communities' own nationals and to the nationals of other Members, to the detriment of the nationals of other Members.[214]

7.204 Accordingly, the Panel's preliminary conclusion is that, with respect to the availability of protection, the treatment accorded to the group of nationals of other Members is different from, and less favourable than, that accorded to the European Communities' own nationals.

defences based on systemic considerations

7.205 The European Communities argues that the interpretation of the national treatment obligations in the TRIPS Agreement and GATT 1994 should not lead to "systematic overlap" between them.

7.206 The Panel notes that the demonstration of less favourable treatment under each agreement remains a distinct exercise since national treatment under Article 3.1 of the TRIPS Agreement ensures effective equality of opportunities for nationals with regard to the protection of intellectual property rights, whereas national treatment under GATT 1994 ensures equality of conditions of competition between products.[215]

7.207 The European Communities also argues that one must take account of the absence in the TRIPS Agreement of a general exceptions provision analogous to Article XX of GATT 1994.

7.208 The Panel notes that there is no hierarchy between the TRIPS Agreement and GATT 1994, which appear in separate annexes to the WTO Agreement. The ordinary meaning of the texts of the TRIPS Agreement and GATT 1994, as well as Article II:2 of the WTO Agreement, taken together, indicates that obligations under the TRIPS Agreement and GATT 1994 can co-exist and that one does not override the other. This is analogous to the finding of the Panel in *Canada – Periodicals,* with which the Appellate Body agreed, concerning the respective scopes of GATS and GATT 1994.[216] Further, a "harmonious interpretation" does not require an interpretation of

---

[212] See paragraph 10 of the recitals to the April 2003 amending Regulation, set out in para. 7.70 above.

[213] European Communities' second oral statement, paras. 29-30; response to Panel question No. 107.

[214] Article 8a of the EC Treaty provides that every citizen of the European Union shall have the right to move and reside freely within the territory of the EC member States. Article 52 (in conjunction with Article 58) provides for the progressive abolition of restrictions on the freedom of establishment of nationals of an EC member State. These provisions remove obstacles to persons who wish to produce products according to a GI specification within the territory of the European Communities, but apply to the European Communities' own nationals only.

[215] See the Appellate Body report on *Korea – Various Measures on Beef*, paras. 137 and 144 and the GATT Panel report on *US – Section 337*, para. 5.11.

[216] Panel report on *Canada – Periodicals*, at para. 5.17; Appellate Body report on *Canada – Periodicals,* DSR 1997:I, 449, at 465.

one that shadows the contours of the other. It is well established that the covered agreements apply cumulatively and that consistency with one does not necessarily imply consistency with them all.[217]

7.209 More specifically, the Panel notes that Article 8 of the TRIPS Agreement sets out the principles of that agreement. Article 8.1 provides as follows:

> 1. Members may, in formulating or amending their laws and regulations, adopt measures necessary to protect public health and nutrition, and to promote the public interest in sectors of vital importance to their socio-economic and technological development, provided that such measures are consistent with the provisions of this Agreement.

7.210 These principles reflect the fact that the TRIPS Agreement does not generally provide for the grant of positive rights to exploit or use certain subject matter, but rather provides for the grant of negative rights to prevent certain acts. This fundamental feature of intellectual property protection inherently grants Members freedom to pursue legitimate public policy objectives since many measures to attain those public policy objectives lie outside the scope of intellectual property rights and do not require an exception under the TRIPS Agreement.

7.211 The scope of the national treatment obligation in Article 3.1 of the TRIPS Agreement also differs from that of the national treatment obligation in Article III:4 of GATT 1994, as it is subject to certain exceptions in Articles 3.1, 3.2 and 5, one of which is inspired by the language of Article XX of GATT 1994.[218] There is also a series of specific exceptions in the provisions relating to the minimum standards in Part II of the TRIPS Agreement and Part VII contains a provision on security exceptions analogous to Article XXI of GATT 1994, but none on general exceptions.

7.212 For all these reasons, in the Panel's view, the fact that a general exceptions provision analogous to Article XX of GATT 1994 was not included in the TRIPS Agreement has no impact on its analysis of Article 3.1.

<u>conclusion with respect to Article 3.1 of the TRIPS Agreement</u>

7.213 Therefore, the Panel concludes that, with respect to the equivalence and reciprocity conditions, as applicable to the availability of GI protection, the Regulation accords treatment to the nationals of other Members less favourable than that it accords to the European Communities' own nationals, inconsistently with Article 3.1 of the TRIPS Agreement.

<u>Article 2 of the Paris Convention (1967)</u>

7.214 The United States also makes claims under the national treatment obligation set out in Article 2 of the Paris Convention (1967). These claims are made under paragraphs 1 and 2 of that article, which provide as follows:

> (1) Nationals of any country of the Union shall, as regards the protection of industrial property, enjoy in all the other countries of the Union the advantages that their respective laws now grant, or may hereafter grant, to nationals; all without prejudice to the rights specially provided for by this Convention. Consequently, they shall have the same protection as the latter, and the same legal remedy against any infringement of their rights, provided that the conditions and formalities imposed upon nationals are complied with.

---

[217] See, for example, the Appellate Body report on *Argentina – Footwear (EC)*, para. 81; the Appellate Body report on *Korea – Dairy*, para. 74; and the Panel reports in *EC – Bananas III*, para. 7.160.

[218] Article 24.9 of the TRIPS Agreement also provides that there shall be no obligation under the TRIPS Agreement to protect geographical indications which are not or cease to be protected in their country of origin, or which have fallen into disuse in that country.

> (2) However, no requirement as to domicile or establishment in the country where protection is claimed may be imposed upon nationals of countries of the Union for the enjoyment of any industrial property rights.

7.215 The text refers to the "countries of the Union" for the purposes of identifying States which bear the obligation to accord national treatment under that provision. However, Article 2.1 of the TRIPS Agreement obliges WTO Members to comply with Articles 1 through 12, and Article 19, of that Convention.[219] Therefore, as a WTO Member, the European Communities owes obligations under Article 2 of the Paris Convention (1967), as incorporated by Article 2.1 of the TRIPS Agreement.

7.216 With respect to the claim under paragraph 1 of Article 2 of the Paris Convention (1967), as incorporated by Article 2.1 of the TRIPS Agreement, the Panel observes that, unlike Article 3.1 of the TRIPS Agreement, Article 2(1) of the Paris Convention (1967) refers to "the advantages that ... laws now grant, or may hereafter grant" and not to "no less favourable" treatment. Therefore, the Panel has not actually reached a conclusion on this claim. However, further findings on this claim would not provide any additional contribution to a positive solution to this dispute and are therefore unnecessary.

7.217 With respect to the claim under paragraph 2 of Article 2 of the Paris Convention (1967), as incorporated by Article 2.1 of the TRIPS Agreement, the Panel does not consider that the Regulation contains a requirement of domicile or establishment.[220] We have found that the design and structure of the Regulation will operate to ensure that persons who use a protected GI, located in the European Communities, will have a domicile or establishment within the territory of the European Communities. We have also found that the availability of protection for GIs located in third countries, including WTO Members, is dependent on whether the third country in which the GI is located satisfies the conditions of equivalence or reciprocity or enters into an international agreement with the European Communities. It is irrelevant to the protection of a GI located in a third country whether or not the person who seeks protection has a domicile or establishment in the European Communities.

7.218 Therefore, the Panel concludes that, with respect to the availability of protection, the Regulation does not impose a requirement as to domicile or establishment inconsistently with Article 2(2) of the Paris Convention (1967), as incorporated by Article 2.1 of the TRIPS Agreement.

(c) National treatment under GATT 1994

(i) main arguments of the parties

7.219 The United States claims that the Regulation is inconsistent with Article III:4 of GATT 1994 because it imposes conditions of *reciprocity* and *equivalence* on the benefits of registration. It argues that the Regulation applies to products from the European Communities and third countries which are *like products* because the only difference between products that do, and do not, benefit from registration without conditions of reciprocity and equivalence, is their origin in the European Communities or a third country.[221] It argues that the Regulation is a measure *affecting the internal sale, offering for sale, purchase, distribution or use* of the imported product because it governs the manner in which registered names can be used on products which are sold, offered for sale, purchased, distributed or used, it governs use of the logo which allegedly provides competitive advantages and it provides protection for products that qualify for registered GIs broad protections against competitive and disparaging uses and against their names becoming generic.[222]

---

[219] The Appellate Body report on *US – Section 211 Appropriations Act* also notes that the obligations of countries of the Paris Union under the Paris Convention (1967) are also obligations of WTO Members by virtue of Article 2.1 of the TRIPS Agreement, para. 125.

[220] The Panel recalls its findings at para. 7.198 above on the meaning of those terms as understood under Article 3 of the Paris Convention (1967).

[221] United States' first written submission, paras. 99-100.

[222] United States' first written submission, paras. 101-102.

7.220 The United States argues that the Regulation accords *less favourable treatment* to imported products because it does not permit registration of GIs on the same conditions as those for products from the European Communities but imposes substantial and often insurmountable additional conditions.[223] The Regulation is motivated by the European Communities' belief that producers of products with GI protection fare much better in the marketplace than those whose products do not have such protection.[224] Registration permits use of the GI and the logo and provides broad protection against competing and disparaging uses and against their names becoming generic.[225] The effects of registration, listed in Article 13(1) of the Regulation, authorize judicial and administrative authorities to issue orders preventing all other products from being promoted or sold accompanied by names or labels that fall within the scope of the registration. These include removal of terms that evoke the protected GI, which may be an important selling point for the imported product. Another effect of registration, mentioned in Article 13(3) of the Regulation, prevents names becoming generic and thereby losing their status as an identifier of source.[226] The Regulation itself indicates that both the intent and the effect of the Regulation is to provide competitive benefits to products that satisfy the registration criteria.[227]

7.221 The European Communities responds that the Regulation is fully compatible with Article III:4 of GATT 1994. It does not contest that products from the European Communities and from third countries falling under the scope of the Regulation may be *like products*, although it stresses that this alone does not preclude the European Communities from applying the conditions for registration to individual GIs.[228] It does not contest that the Regulation is a measure *affecting the internal sale* of products.[229]

7.222 The European Communities argues that the Regulation does not accord *less favourable treatment* to imported products because it does not apply the conditions in Article 12(1) to the registration of GIs from other WTO Members.[230] It concedes that the application of those conditions would prejudice its obligations under Article III:4 of GATT 1994.[231]

(ii) main arguments of third parties

7.223 Brazil argues the GATT—and WTO—underlying principle of national treatment would be completely voided of any meaning if it were made conditional on requirements of reciprocity and adoption of equivalent legislation.[232]

7.224 China argues that the different treatment accorded to GIs by the Regulation will amount to less favourable treatment if it is found to modify the conditions of competition under which like imported and EC products compete in the EC market to the disadvantage of imported products.[233]

7.225 New Zealand considers that the complainants have demonstrated all three elements constituting a violation of Article III:4 of GATT 1994. The only issue under debate is whether the Regulation confers "less

---

223 United States' response to Panel question No. 109.

224 United States' first written submission, para. 97.

225 United States' first written submission, paras. 103-105.

226 United States' response to Panel question No. 108.

227 United States' response to Panel question No. 32.

228 European Communities' first written submission, paras. 195-197.

229 European Communities' first written submission, para. 194.

230 European Communities' first written submission, para. 203; rebuttal submission, para. 212.

231 European Communities' response to Panel question No. 94.

232 Annex C, para. 25.

233 Annex C, para. 95.

favourable treatment" on imported products. As the same phrase is used in Article 3.1 of the TRIPS Agreement, all arguments raised under that claim apply equally here.[234]

(iii) consideration by the Panel

7.226 The Panel notes that the European Communities concedes that the conditions of equivalence and reciprocity in Article 12(1) of the Regulation, if applied to WTO Members, are inconsistent with Article III:4 of GATT 1994.[235] Given that the Panel has found that the Regulation "as such" imposes those conditions on the registration of GIs located in other WTO Members, there is no longer any defence before the Panel to the claim that, in this respect, the Regulation is inconsistent with Article III:4 of GATT 1994. It suffices to recall below that the essential elements of an inconsistency with Article III:4 are all met in this claim. These elements are the following: that the imported and domestic products at issue are "like products;" that the measure at issue is a "law, regulation, or requirement affecting their internal sale, offering for sale, purchase, transportation, distribution, or use;" and that the imported products are accorded "less favourable" treatment than that accorded to like domestic products.[236]

7.227 The Regulation sets down requirements concerning the use of certain names in the presentation for sale of agricultural products and foodstuffs.[237] It is therefore a law or regulation affecting the internal sale and offering for sale of products within the meaning of Article III:4 of GATT 1994. This is not altered by the fact that the Regulation is also an intellectual property measure covered by the TRIPS Agreement since GATT 1994 and the TRIPS Agreement apply cumulatively.[238]

7.228 The Regulation links the protection of the name of a product to the territory of a particular country.[239] In the case of "designations of origin," as defined in Article 2 of the Regulation, this is the place of production, processing and preparation of the product and, in the case of "geographical indications," as defined in Article 2 of the Regulation, this is the place of production, processing and/or preparation. It is not disputed that in most cases these criteria are sufficient to confer origin on the products. Given that the Panel has found that the protection of names of products from other WTO Members is contingent on satisfaction of certain conditions of equivalence and reciprocity that do not apply to the names of products from the European Communities, the Regulation formally discriminates between imported products and products of European Communities origin within the meaning of Article III:4 of GATT 1994.

7.229 The Regulation applies to the names of a wide class of products described in Article 1(1), which refers to the large number of agricultural products intended for human consumption referred to in Annex 1 to the EC Treaty as well as 13 additional types of agricultural products and foodstuffs listed in the annexes to the Regulation. The European Communities does not contest that there are, among this group, "like products" among the imported products and products of European Communities origin. The European Communities and other WTO Members produce the same types of covered agricultural products and foodstuffs with GIs that may be eligible for protection. Article 13(1)(a) of the Regulation provides that protection is provided against use of a name in respect of products "comparable to the products registered under that name." It is axiomatic that one

---

[234] Annex C, para. 141.

[235] European Communities' response to Panel question No. 94(a).

[236] These three elements are also set out in the Appellate Body report on *Korea – Various Measures on Beef* at para. 133.

[237] Article 1(1) of the Regulation provides that it "lays down rules on the protection of designations of origin and geographical indications of agricultural products ... and of ... foodstuffs ..." and Commission Regulation (EEC) No. 2037/93 sets out detailed rules on the application of the Regulation, including use of the PDO and PGI logos in the promotion of products (see Exhibit COMP-2). Article 13(1) of the Regulation sets out uses against which registered names are protected.

[238] The Panel recalls its comment on the order of analysis in para. 7.36 and its findings in para. 7.208, that there is no hierarchy between GATT 1994 and the TRIPS Agreement, which appear in separate annexes to the WTO Agreement. Further, an intellectual property measure was the subject of conclusions under Article III:4 of GATT 1947 in the GATT Panel report on *US – Section 337*. The Panel does not consider that the conclusion of the TRIPS Agreement reduced the scope of application of GATT: see, on the same point with respect to GATS, the Appellate Body report on *Canada – Periodicals*, DSR 1997:I, 449, at 465.

[239] Exceptionally, it may extend across a border of more than one country, see Articles 5(5) and 12a(1) of the Regulation.

must compare apples with apples and oranges with oranges. In this dispute, it is not contested that Tasmanian apples may be like *pommes de Savoie*[240] and Florida citrus may be like *cítricos valencianos*[241] for the purposes of Article III:4 of GATT 1994.

7.230 In our analysis of the question of "less favourable treatment," we follow the approach of the Appellate Body in *Korea – Various Measures on Beef* and *US – FSC (Article 21.5 – EC)* that this standard should be assessed under Article III:4 of GATT 1994 by examining whether the measures at issue modify the conditions of competition between domestic and imported products in the relevant market to the detriment of imported products. This examination must closely scrutinize the "fundamental thrust and effect of the measure itself" founded on a careful analysis of the contested measure and of its implications in the marketplace.[242]

7.231 The Regulation provides in Article 13 that registered GIs shall be protected against certain commercial uses and other practices. Registration provides the legal means to prevent the sale and offering for sale of products, including competitive products, where they use, imitate or evoke a registered GI, which is a substantive advantage conferred on products that comply with the GI registration. Registration does not grant a right to exclude competition, or deny the possibility of sale without a registered GI but, where products, including competitive products, bear an indication that falls within the protection granted by registration, they may be removed from sale. This is a substantive advantage that affects the conditions of competition of the relevant products.

7.232 The declared purposes of the Regulation set out in its preamble include the following, which links GIs to demand for products:

> Whereas, moreover, it has been observed in recent years that consumers are tending to attach greater importance to the quality of foodstuffs rather than to quantity; whereas this quest for specific products generates a growing demand for agricultural products or foodstuffs with an identifiable geographical origin;

7.233 Agricultural products and foodstuffs from the European Communities may obtain this advantage where they satisfy the eligibility criteria in the Regulation. Like products imported from WTO Members that the Commission has not decided meet the equivalence and reciprocity conditions in Article 12(1) of the Regulation—which is all of them—are not able to obtain that advantage and, hence, are accorded less favourable treatment. Products from WTO Members which can satisfy the equivalence and reciprocity conditions in Article 12(1) still face an "extra hurdle" in obtaining the advantage of registration since the Commission must decide that their country of origin meets those conditions—a step which is not required of like products from the European Communities. This is also less favourable treatment.

7.234 The United States cites other alleged advantages conferred by registration. It refers to the entitlement to use the indications "PDO" and "PGI" and a Community symbol or logo with products that comply with a registration.[243] The graphic manual annexed to the rules under the Regulation states *inter alia* that "[t]he logo will allow producers of food products to increase awareness of their products among consumers in the European Union;" that the logo provides producers with "a marketing tool;" and that, because of the logo, "products will inspire more confidence."[244] The United States also cites the preamble to the Regulation which refers to higher incomes for producers from the promotion of their products as one of the justifications for protection.

[240] Registered by Commission Regulation (EC) No. 1107/96, p. 13, Exhibit COMP-3a.

[241] Registered by Commission Regulation (EC) No. 865/2003, Exhibit COMP-4b.i.

[242] See the Appellate Body report on *Korea – Various Measures on Beef*, paras. 137 and 142; and also *US – FSC (Article 21.5 – EC)*, para. 215, quoted at para. 7.136 above.

[243] Under Article 8 of the Regulation and the detailed rules of application of the Regulation in Exhibit COMP-2.

[244] Exhibit COMP-2.

7.235 The European Communities does not contest that these are benefits of protection under the Regulation, and also refers to the right to use the designation and logo under Article 8 and the possibility of excluding others from use of the GI under Article 13.[245]

7.236 The United States submits a powerpoint presentation prepared by the European Commission which lists some random facts on the prices of certain products with protected names, the results of an opinion poll on consumer perceptions conducted by a group of nougat producers, and economic data contrasting cheese production in Franche-Comté and Emmental.[246] It is not clear to what extent the advantages illustrated in this data flow from the protection of the indications or from better marketing, increased advertising and superior product quality. In any event, in view of the significant competitive advantage conferred under Article 13 of the Regulation, it is unnecessary to determine the weight to be given to this evidence.

7.237 Lastly, the Panel notes that there is the possibility that a WTO Member could conclude an international agreement with the European Communities for the protection of specific GIs for its agricultural products and foodstuffs. It is not in dispute that this possibility would provide less favourable treatment to imported agricultural products and foodstuffs than the procedure for the registration of GIs provides for agricultural products and foodstuffs from the European Communities.

7.238 Therefore, the Panel concludes that, with respect to the equivalence and reciprocity conditions, as applicable to the availability of protection, the Regulation accords less favourable treatment to imported products, inconsistently with Article III:4 of GATT 1994.[247]

7.239 The European Communities has not asserted that, with respect to the availability of protection, the Regulation is justified by Article XX(d) of GATT 1994.[248]

2. *Application procedures*

(a) *Description of application procedures under Articles 5 and 12a of the Regulation*

7.240 The parties agree on the features of the application procedures under the Regulation. There are separate provisions setting out the procedures for applications for registration of GIs which apply according to the location of the GI.[249] Article 5 applies where the GI is located in an EC member State. Article 12a applies where the GI is located in a third country.

7.241 Article 5(4) and 5(5) provide, relevantly, as follows:

> 4. The application shall be sent to the Member State in which the geographical area is located.
>
> 5. The Member State shall check that the application is justified and shall forward the application, including the product specification referred to in Article 4 and other documents

---

[245] European Communities' rebuttal submission, para. 118.

[246] Exhibit US-44 cited in the United States' response to Panel question No. 32.

[247] This conclusion is without prejudice to the Panel's examination of the inspection structures required for registration, considered later in this report.

[248] See the European Communities' first written submission, paras. 224-225, in which it asserts Article XX(d) as a defence only in relation to Article 12a, in conjunction with Articles 4 and 10, of the Regulation. See also its rebuttal submission, paras. 228-242, and its second oral statement, paras. 132 and 135, in which it asserts Article XX(d) as a defence only with respect to inspections, application procedures and the labelling requirement. Despite broader references to the Regulation in its first written submission, para. 190, and first oral statement, para. 73, the European Communities did not provide any specific arguments in defence of the equivalence and reciprocity conditions under Article XX(d).

[249] For the sake of brevity, the Panel refers to a name that refers to a geographical area located in a Member as a GI located in that Member.

on which it has based its decision, to the Commission, if it considers that it satisfies the requirements of this Regulation. [...]

7.242 Article 12a(1) and 12a(2) provide, relevantly, as follows:

> 1. In the case provided for in Article 12(3), if a group or a natural or legal person as referred to in Article 5(1) and (2) in a third country wishes to have a name registered under this Regulation it shall send a registration application to the authorities in the country in which the geographical area is located. [...]
>
> 2. If the third country referred to in paragraph 1 deems the requirements of this Regulation to be satisfied it shall transmit the registration application to the Commission accompanied by:
>
> (a) a description of the legal provisions and the usage on the basis of which the designation of origin or the geographical indication is protected or established in the country,
>
> (b) a declaration that the structures provided for in Article 10 are established on its territory, and
>
> (c) other documents on which it has based its assessment."

7.243 After an application is forwarded by an EC member State or a third country, Articles 6(1) and 12b(1) of the Regulation oblige the Commission to verify whether the registration application includes all the requisite particulars and satisfies the conditions for protection. There are differences in the drafting of Articles 6(1) and 12b(1) which relate, respectively, to applications forwarded by EC member States and those transmitted by third countries, which the United States has not put in issue.

(b) National treatment under the TRIPS Agreement

(i) main arguments of the parties

7.244 The United States claims that the Regulation is inconsistent with Article 3.1 of the TRIPS Agreement and Article 2(1) of the Paris Convention (1967), as incorporated by Article 2.1 of the TRIPS Agreement, because application procedures do not allow applications for registration in respect of geographical areas located in third countries to be filed directly with the competent authorities in Europe. This is *less favourable treatment* because the Regulation provides the direct means for EC nationals to apply through their EC member States to the Commission, whilst non-EC nationals who wish to file an application for registration of a GI located in their own country must petition their government to apply on their behalf.[250] The Regulation does not accord equal treatment because third country governments only comply voluntarily whereas EC member States have a legal obligation to do so.[251]

7.245 The United States argues that it is irrelevant whether the Regulation accords equal treatment to other WTO Members and EC member States because the TRIPS Agreement requires that no less favourable treatment be accorded to nationals of WTO Members.[252] Intellectual property rights are private rights.[253]

---

[250] United States' first written submission, paras. 81-82; rebuttal submission, paras. 68 and 71.

[251] United States' rebuttal submission, para. 70.

[252] United States' first oral statement, paras. 30-31.

[253] United States' first oral statement, para. 37.

7.246 The United States argues that whilst it would probably not be too difficult to designate an office in the U.S. government to perform a purely ministerial act of transmitting documents to the Commission, it might be difficult for some Members and, in any event, the Regulation requires more than mere transmission of documents. Third country governments must *inter alia* determine that the application meets the Regulation's requirements and demonstrate how the GI is protected in its country of origin.[254] This is a substantial burden and involves an active role in the registration procedure in which the third country government must administer and enforce the Regulation on its own territory.[255] This is neither appropriate nor necessary and results in less favourable treatment.[256] Article 22.1 of the TRIPS Agreement does not require this.[257] Article 24.9 of the TRIPS Agreement does not justify this, because other systems of GI protection do not put the government in a better position than the right holder to provide information on protection in the country of origin.[258] This is a unilateral requirement that foreign governments verify compliance with the Regulation and not an example of international cooperation.[259]

7.247 The European Communities responds that this claim must fail. Its first defence is that the application procedures do not apply to nationality but according to the location of geographical areas. That defence has been considered above.

7.248 The European Communities argues that the application procedures do not accord *less favourable treatment* because the role of third country governments corresponds exactly to that of EC member States. The transmission of applications by governments in fact ensures equal treatment.[260] The authorities of third countries and EC member States are best placed to evaluate whether a GI fulfils the conditions for protection, which requires familiarity with a host of factors and may require knowledge of the market conditions in the country of origin. The evaluation of whether a GI is protected in the country of origin requires the implication of the authorities of the third country. Verification in a third country calls for respect for its sovereignty. Involvement of third country authorities facilitates cooperation during the registration process and should be of practical benefit to the applicant.[261]

7.249 The European Communities argues that the verification and transmission of an application are not overly burdensome for another WTO Member. Another WTO Member cannot invoke its own unwillingness to cooperate in the registration process in order to demonstrate a national treatment violation on the part of the European Communities.[262] There are many examples of international cooperation between governments in the protection of private rights including, in the field of intellectual property protection, such as the Madrid Protocol, the Lisbon Agreement and Article 6*quinquies*A(1) of the Paris Convention, and in the fields of certificates of origin, technical standards, conformity assessment, transport, fisheries and judicial cooperation. These examples illustrate that in an increasingly interdependent world, the effective protection of individual rights in cross-border situations inevitably engenders a need for cross-border cooperation.[263]

7.250 The European Communities does not want to impose obligations on third countries, but the protection of GIs located in the territory of third countries depends on their cooperation. This is partially mandated by the definition of a GI in Article 22.1 of the TRIPS Agreement, which requires verification of whether certain characteristics of a good are essentially attributable to its geographical origin. This is an obligation for all

---

[254] United States' first oral statement, para. 28 and response to Panel question No. 38. The third country government must also declare that the inspection structures are established on its territory. This is discussed in a later section of this report.

[255] United States' rebuttal submission, paras. 64-67.

[256] United States' rebuttal submission, para. 74.

[257] United States' second oral statement, para. 34.

[258] United States' second closing oral statement, para. 11-12.

[259] United States' second oral statement, para. 36; second closing oral statement, para. 13.

[260] European Communities' first written submission, para. 130.

[261] European Communities' response to Panel question No. 33; rebuttal submission, paras. 124-129.

[262] European Communities' first written submission, para. 131.

[263] European Communities' response to Panel question No. 37.

Members and should normally facilitate the examination of whether the name fulfils the criteria in the Regulation. The description of how a GI is protected in its country of origin reflects the provision in Article 24.9 of the TRIPS Agreement. Even where there is no specific registration system in the country of origin, that is still a TRIPS requirement for the European Communities and a matter of foreign law.[264] The transmission of the application by the same government is not a significant extra burden.[265]

(ii) main arguments of third parties

7.251 Argentina, Brazil, India, Mexico, New Zealand and Chinese Taipei all inform the Panel that they are not aware of any person ever having attempted to file with their respective authorities an application for registration under the Regulation.[266]

7.252 Argentina expresses uncertainty regarding the consistency of the application procedures with the characterization of intellectual property rights under the TRIPS Agreement, in that they require States to manage the registration of a GI instead of right holders who are private persons.[267]

7.253 Brazil argues that the application procedures require WTO Members to "pre-approve" applications before they forward them to the European Commission, which is a striking violation of the national treatment obligation in Article 3.1 of the TRIPS Agreement for two reasons: (1) this is an additional procedure for other WTO Members; and (2) the approval process must be conducted according to EC law, not the law of the other WTO Member.[268]

7.254 China argues that the provisions on verification and publication do not afford clarity. The procedures for EC member States and third countries are in parallel but are not the same in substance. The provisions on verification by, and transmission to, the Commission differ between the procedures which suggests that third countries must satisfy more than an EC member State.

7.255 Colombia expresses uncertainty as to whether the country of origin must in all cases provide a declaration under Article 12a(2) with a description of the legal provisions under which the GI is protected. This is, in practice, a condition which entails an evaluation of the system of GI protection in the country of origin contrary to Article 1.1 of the TRIPS Agreement.[269]

7.256 Mexico refers to cochineal as a practical example of the way in which Mexican producers would be required to go through specific procedures which EC nationals are not.[270]

7.257 New Zealand submits that, although the requirement to submit all applications through government applies equally to applications from EC member States and other WTO Member nationals, its effect is to disadvantage nationals from other WTO Members. EC nationals have an enforceable right that applications that satisfy the requirements of the Regulation are forwarded to the Commission. Submission of an application via an EC member State is essentially a formality. Other WTO Member nationals have no such enforceable right.[271]

---

[264] European Communities' rebuttal submission, paras. 131-134; response to Panel question No. 114.

[265] European Communities' rebuttal submission, para. 139.

[266] See their respective comments in Annex C at paras. 18, 32, 103, 118, 160 and 179.

[267] Annex C, paras. 2-15.

[268] Annex C, para. 27.

[269] Annex C, para. 99.

[270] Annex C, paras. 115-117.

[271] Annex C, paras. 136-137.

(iii) consideration by the Panel

7.258 These claims are made under Article 3.1 of the TRIPS Agreement and Article 2 of the Paris Convention (1967), as incorporated by Article 2.1 of the TRIPS Agreement. The Panel will first consider the claim under Article 3.1 of the TRIPS Agreement.

7.259 The Panel recalls that two elements must be satisfied to establish an inconsistency with this obligation: (1) the measure at issue must apply with regard to the protection of intellectual property; and (2) the nationals of other Members must be accorded "less favourable" treatment than the Member's own nationals. The Panel will address each of these elements in turn.

protection of intellectual property

7.260 This claim concerns procedures for filing and examination of applications for registration of "designations of origin and "geographical indications," as defined in the Regulation. They are referred to in this report, for the sake of brevity, as "application procedures."

7.261 The Panel recalls that the national treatment obligation in Article 3 of the TRIPS Agreement applies to the treatment accorded by a Member "with regard to the protection of intellectual property." Footnote 3 provides an inclusive definition of the term "protection" as used in Articles 3 and 4. It reads as follows:

> For the purposes of Articles 3 and 4, 'protection' shall include matters affecting the availability, acquisition, scope, maintenance and enforcement of intellectual property rights as well as those matters affecting the use of intellectual property rights specifically addressed in this Agreement.

7.262 Turning to the Regulation, procedures for the filing and examination of applications for registration are matters affecting the *acquisition* of intellectual property rights in relation to "designations of origin" and "geographical indications," as defined in the Regulation.

7.263 It is not disputed that "designations of origin" and "geographical indications," as defined in the Regulation, are a subset of "geographical indications," the subject of Section 3 of Part II, and therefore part of a category of intellectual property within the meaning of Article 1.2 of the TRIPS Agreement.

7.264 Therefore, this claim concerns the "protection" of intellectual property, as clarified in footnote 3 to the TRIPS Agreement, within the scope of the national treatment obligation in Article 3.1 of that Agreement.

less favourable treatment accorded to the nationals of other Members

7.265 The Panel recalls its findings:

(a) at paragraphs 7.185 to 7.190 as to the treatment accorded to the "nationals of other Members" under the Regulation by its treatment according to the location of GIs; and

(b) at paragraph 7.134 that under Article 3.1 of the TRIPS Agreement we must examine the "effective equality of opportunities" with regard to the protection of intellectual property rights and at paragraph 7.137 that in this examination we will focus on the "fundamental thrust and effect" of the Regulation.

7.266 The parties and third parties who responded to the Panel's question on this point all reported that they were not aware of any application for the registration of a name of an area located in a third country outside the

European Communities ever having been filed with the authorities of a third country.[272] However, the United States challenges the Regulation, in this respect, "as such."

7.267 The United States claims that the treatment accorded under the application procedures in Article 12a(1) and (2) is less favourable than that accorded under the applications procedures in Article 5(4) and (5). There is an apparent equivalence in the drafting of these provisions but the question is whether this would imply a modification of the effective equality of opportunities with regard to the protection of intellectual property.

7.268 The Panel notes that the initial steps in the application procedures can be broken down as follows.

(a) as a first step, *all* applicants are required to submit their application to the authorities in the country in which the geographical area is located. These will be authorities of an EC member State or a third country, depending on the case;

(b) as a second step, the authorities who receive an application consider whether the application is justified or satisfies the requirements of the Regulation. This involves a detailed examination of the application in accordance with the criteria in the EC Regulation, not the domestic law of the country where the application is filed; and

(c) as a third step, if the authorities who receive an application consider that the application is justified or satisfies the requirements of the Regulation, they forward or transmit it to the Commission. If the application concerns a geographical area located outside the European Communities, the authorities must also transmit a description of the protection of the GI in its country of origin, as well as a declaration concerning inspection structures.[273]

7.269 We recall the European Communities' explanation of its domestic constitutional arrangements, set out at paragraph 7.98, that Community laws are generally not executed through authorities at Community level but rather through recourse to the authorities of its member States which, in such a situation, "act *de facto* as organs of the Community, for which the Community would be responsible under WTO law and international law in general."[274] It follows that any application relating to a geographical area located in an EC member State is filed directly with a "*de facto* organ of the Community" which also carries out the initial examination. An application relating to a geographical area located in a third country cannot be filed directly, but must be filed with a foreign government. This is a formal difference in treatment.

7.270 Further, Article 5 of the Regulation provides for application procedures for GIs located in the European Communities. Paragraph 6 provides as follows:

> 6. Member States shall introduce the laws, regulations and administrative provisions necessary to comply with this Article.

7.271 An EC member State has an obligation to establish application procedures for the purposes of the Regulation. Under Community law, an EC member State has an obligation to examine an application and decide whether it is justified and, if it is justified, to forward it to the Commission. A group or person who

---

[272] However, the United States provided evidence from the Idaho Potato Commission that it could not obtain protection for its U.S. certification mark in the European Union. Its attorneys in three EC member States had advised that there were no steps it could take to stop use of the term "Idaho" by other companies in Europe: see testimony to the Committee on Agriculture in the U.S. House of Representatives of 22 July 2003, in response to Panel question No. 12, and reproduced in Exhibit US-38. The European Communities responds that this is based on a misperception of the content of the Regulation, that it does not contain evidence of an attempt to register a GI under the Regulation, and that it seems to relate more to the protection of trademarks than GIs: see its rebuttal submission, para. 85.

[273] For the purposes of this report, references to examination and transmission of "applications" include examination and transmission of these supporting documents. The declaration concerning inspection structures is considered later in this report.

[274] European Communities' second oral statement, para. 148.

submits an application in an EC member State may enforce these obligations through recourse to judicial procedures based on the Regulation. In contrast, a third country government has no obligation under Community law or any other law to examine an application or to transmit it or any other document to the Commission. A group or person who submits an application in a third country has no right to such treatment.

7.272 Therefore, applicants for GIs that refer to geographical areas located in third countries do not have a right in the application procedures that is provided to applicants for GIs that refer to geographical areas located in the European Communities. Applicants in third countries face an "extra hurdle" in ensuring that the authorities in those countries carry out the functions reserved to them under the Regulation, which applicants in EC member States do not face. Consequently, certain applications and requisite supporting documents may not be examined or transmitted. Each of these considerations significantly reduces the opportunities available to the nationals of other WTO Members in the acquisition of rights under the Regulation below those available to the European Communities' own nationals.

7.273 The European Communities submits that that "[t]he Regulation does not require anything that would be outside the scope of any WTO Member with a normally functioning government."[275] The Panel notes that, whilst a normally functioning government might have the capacity to carry out the first and third steps, it cannot be assumed that it would have the capacity to carry out the examination according to EC law required by the second step. WTO Members have no obligation to implement a system of protection for geographical indications comparable to that of the European Communities and there is no reason to believe that they would nevertheless have the capacity to carry out examinations of technical issues that involve interpretations of EC law. In this regard, we note that one third party in this Panel proceeding indicates that its authorities would be devoid of legal competence to perform this analysis.[276] Whilst a WTO Member that provided equivalent protection under its domestic law might presumably have the technical capacity, if not the legal competence, to perform this analysis, the provision of such equivalent protection forms part of the conditions under Article 12(1) of the Regulation. We have found that requirement, as a precondition to the availability of GI protection, to be inconsistent with the national treatment obligations in the TRIPS Agreement and GATT 1994.

7.274 In any event, even if any normally functioning government could perform these three steps, that would not alter the Panel's conclusion. The obligation to accord national treatment with respect to a measure of the European Communities is the obligation of the European Communities. This is highlighted in the text of Article 3.1 of the TRIPS Agreement under which "[e]ach Member" shall accord to the nationals of other Members no less favourable treatment.

7.275 In accordance with its domestic law, the European Communities is entitled to delegate certain functions under its measure to the authorities of EC member States. However, under the Regulation, the European Communities has purported to delegate part of this obligation to other WTO Members, who must carry out these three steps in the application procedures in order to ensure that no less favourable treatment is accorded to their respective nationals. To that extent, the European Communities fails to accord no less favourable treatment *itself* to the nationals of other Members.[277]

7.276 The Panel notes that the European Commission does not have the discretion to ensure that applications for GIs that refer to geographical areas located in third countries receive no less favourable treatment than those located in the European Communities because it has structured the Regulation in such a way that certain functions are completely outside its control.

---

[275] European Communities' rebuttal submission, para. 141; second oral statement, para. 142.

[276] See comments by Brazil in Annex C, para. 32.

[277] See further paras. 7.741 to 7.743 below.

7.277 The European Communities drew the Panel's attention to many examples of international cooperation in the protection of private rights, including in the field of intellectual property protection.[278] The Panel notes that under two of them, the Patent Cooperation Treaty and the Madrid Protocol, the possibility of filing an application with an office in the applicant's own country does not prevent the applicant filing an application directly in the another country. The Panel certainly does not intend to discourage international cooperation. However, in each of these examples, cooperation is provided in the framework of treaties in which contracting parties have voluntarily agreed to participate. In contrast, the Regulation is a domestic law adopted by one Member.

7.278 The Panel also confirms that nothing in these findings purports to diminish the rights of Members under Article 24.9 of the TRIPS Agreement, which provides, in essence, that there is no obligation under this Agreement to protect geographical indications which are not protected in their country of origin[279].

7.279 The Panel further confirms that the European Communities is entitled, under Article 62.1 of the TRIPS Agreement, to require that applicants comply with reasonable procedures and formalities that are consistent with the Agreement in order to prove that they meet the conditions of protection. However, Article 62 is outside the Panel's terms of reference.

7.280 The Panel recalls its finding at paragraph 7.212 that the fact that a general exceptions provision analogous to Article XX of GATT 1994 was not included in the TRIPS Agreement has no impact on its analysis of Article 3.1.

7.281 For the above reasons, the Panel concludes that, with respect to the application procedures, insofar as they require examination and transmission of applications by governments, the Regulation accords other WTO Member nationals less favourable treatment than it accords the European Communities' own nationals, inconsistently with Article 3.1 of the TRIPS Agreement.

7.282 In view of that conclusion, it is unnecessary to consider the consistency of the Regulation, with respect to the application procedures, with Article 2(1) of the Paris Convention (1967), as incorporated by Article 2.1 of the TRIPS Agreement.

(c) National treatment under GATT 1994

(i) main arguments of the parties

7.283 The United States claims that the Regulation is inconsistent with Article III:4 of GATT 1994 because an application for registration must be submitted by a WTO Member on behalf of its national. It reiterates its arguments in relation to the conditions of equivalence and reciprocity and Article III:4 of GATT 1994, it reiterates its arguments in relation to the application procedures and Article 3.1 of the TRIPS Agreement, and it adds that the application procedures deny the benefits of registration which accords less favourable treatment to imported products.[280] Products imported from Members, like the United States, which lack a mechanism to assess compliance under the Regulation, will be denied these benefits for reasons unrelated to the characteristics of the product itself, but for reasons related to the products' origin.[281]

7.284 The United States argues that the relevant aspects of the application procedures are not justified under Article XX(d) of GATT 1994. They do not satisfy paragraph (d) because they do not "secure compliance." At best, they solicit other Members' views but the decision on registration is made by the European Communities. Whether a product satisfies the Regulation's requirements is a legal judgement and has nothing to do with

---

278 See European Communities' response to Panel question No. 37, and Exhibits EC-20 through EC-27.

279 Nothing in these findings purports to diminish the rights of Members under Article 5 of the TRIPS Agreement either.

280 United States' first written submission, paras. 104(d) and 105; rebuttal submission, para. 95.

281 United States' second oral statement, para. 45.

compliance with the Regulation. These aspects shift the burden for assessing compliance from the European Communities onto other Members. The Regulation itself is not a law consistent with GATT 1994, which is the fundamental issue in this dispute. These aspects are not "necessary" to secure compliance because another Member's views or on-site checks will not always be required, by the EC's own admission. There is no reason why alternative measures are not reasonably available, such as allowing nationals to file applications directly with the European Communities, or establish by other means that a GI is protected in its country of origin.[282] These aspects do not satisfy the chapeau of Article XX because the European Communities favours countries that protect GIs the way it does, which arbitrarily and unjustifiably discriminates between countries where the same conditions apply.[283]

7.285 The European Communities responds that this claim must fail. It reiterates its arguments that the application procedures provide equal treatment, not less favourable treatment.[284]

7.286 The European Communities asserts that verification and transmission of applications by the government of the home country of the GI is justified by Article XX(d) of GATT 1994.[285] It argues that this is necessary to secure compliance with the Regulation itself, in particular, the definition of a GI, the product specifications, protection in the country of origin, establishment of the inspection structures and the requirement that only products that comply with a specification bear the PDO and PGI indications. It argues that the cooperation of the home government is indispensable for the implementation of the Regulation which, in particular, requires the evaluation of factual and legal questions which only the home country of the GI is in a position to carry out. These requirements for cooperation do not go beyond what is necessary for the implementation of the Regulation. The requirement of transmission follows naturally from the required intergovernmental cooperation and is not particularly burdensome for WTO Members. Article XX(d) does not exclude that the measures and the laws and regulations with which they secure compliance may be part of the same legal act. In addition, there is nothing which limits measures which secure compliance to *ex post* enforcement and excludes safeguards in the registration process. The Regulation is not inconsistent with GATT 1994 because it implements an obligation under Article 22 of the TRIPS Agreement and a higher level of protection permitted by Article 1.1. It is applied in a manner consistent with the chapeau of Article XX.[286]

7.287 The European Communities argues that, with respect to verification that the GI is protected in its country of origin, verification requires knowledge of local factors that typically only the country of origin will have and which may also require on-site checks. Submission of a registration certificate authenticated by the country of origin would normally provide sufficient evidence that the indication is protected in the country of origin. However, it is not an option for those Members which do not have a specific register, such as the United States. Verification by third country governments is particularly necessary where they do not have a specific register as evaluation of protection in the country of origin may be more difficult. It is not credible that the United States government would not be better qualified than the right holder or the European Communities. Transmission of applications by third country governments is an integral part of the application procedure and should not be viewed in isolation. It has no significant impact on trade in goods. It makes no difference whether the European Communities asks for cooperation from a third country government before or after an application is filed.[287]

282 United States' second oral statement, para. 55.

283 United States' second oral statement, para. 57 and comments on EC responses to Panel question Nos. 135 and 136.

284 European Communities' first written submission, para. 207; rebuttal submission, para. 218.

285 European Communities' rebuttal submission, paras. 237-239.

286 European Communities' rebuttal submission, paras. 237-239; responses to Panel question No. 135(a), (b) and (c) and 136(a).

287 European Communities' response to Panel question No. 136(b), (c) and (d).

(ii) main arguments by third parties

7.288 Argentina, Brazil, India, Mexico and Chinese Taipei inform the Panel that direct applications to register GIs located in third countries are possible under their respective national legislation.[288]

7.289 Brazil argues that the application procedures require WTO Members to "pre-approve" applications before they forward them to the European Commission, which is a striking violation of the national treatment obligation in Article 3.1 of the TRIPS Agreement.[289]

7.290 New Zealand considers that, as the same phrase "less favourable treatment" is used in Article III:4 as in Article 3.1 of the TRIPS Agreement, all arguments raised under that claim apply equally here. New Zealand does not consider that the measure can be justified as "necessary" within the meaning of Article XX(d) of GATT 1994. The Commission conducts its own six-month investigation of an application so that it is not necessary for applications to be passed through a third country government filter.[290]

(iii) consideration by the Panel

7.291 This claim concerns procedures for applications for registration under the Regulation. The Panel recalls its findings:

(a) at paragraph 7.227, that the Regulation is a law or regulation affecting the internal sale and offering for sale of products within the meaning of Article III:4 of GATT 1994;

(b) at paragraph 7.228 that the Regulation links the protection of the name of a product to the territory of a particular country and formally discriminates between imported products and products of European Communities origin within the meaning of Article III:4 of GATT 1994;

(c) at paragraph 7.229 that the European Communities does not contest that there are, among the group of products covered by the Regulation, "like products" among the imported products and products of European Communities origin;

(d) at paragraph 7.230, that under Article III:4 of GATT 1994 we must examine whether the measure modifies the conditions of competition between domestic and imported products and that in this examination we will focus on the "fundamental thrust and effect of the measure itself;"

(e) at paragraph 7.231 to 7.235 on the substantive advantage provided under Article 13 of the Regulation that affects the conditions of competition of the relevant products;

(f) at paragraphs 7.268 to 7.272 concerning the differences between the application procedures for GIs that refer to geographical areas located in EC member States and those located in third countries. These differences can result in some applications from third countries, including WTO Members, not being examined and transmitted to the Commission; and

(g) at paragraph 7.276 that the European Communities has no discretion in the implementation of the Regulation to ensure that all applications from third countries are transmitted to the Commission.

7.292 A failure to transmit an application would entail non-registration of GIs, which would lead to failure of the products from those third countries to obtain the benefits of registration set out in Article 13 of the

---

[288] See their respective comments in Annex C at paras. 18, 27, 103, 118 and 180.

[289] Annex C, para. 27.

[290] Annex C, paras. 141-143.

Regulation. Therefore, the Panel concludes that, with respect to the application procedures, insofar as they require examination and transmission of applications by governments, the Regulation accords less favourable treatment to imported products than domestic products, inconsistently with Article III:4 of GATT 1994.

7.293 The European Communities asserts that these procedures are justified by Article XX(d) of GATT 1994. As the party invoking this affirmative defence, the European Communities bears the burden of proof that the conditions of the defence are met.

7.294 Article XX provides exceptions for certain measures. The "measures" which the European Communities needs to justify at this point are the requirements of examination and transmission of applications for registration by governments under the Regulation. These apply to applications from both EC member States and third countries. However, it does not need to justify the less favourable treatment which denies applicants for GIs located in third countries the opportunity to file direct applications.[291]

7.295 Paragraph (d) of Article XX refers to "measures" falling within the following description:

> (*d*) necessary to secure compliance with laws or regulations which are not inconsistent with the provisions of this Agreement, including those relating to customs enforcement, the enforcement of monopolies operated under paragraph 4 of Article II and Article XVII, the protection of patents, trade marks and copyrights, and the prevention of deceptive practices;

7.296 The Panel takes note that paragraph (d) refers to laws or regulations, including those relating to "the protection of patents, trade marks and copyrights, and the prevention of deceptive practices." The Regulation provides for the protection of GIs and is an analogous law or regulation, as the European Communities points out.[292] However, the term "laws or regulations" is qualified by the phrase "not inconsistent with the provisions of this Agreement."

7.297 The European Communities argues that the requirements of examination and transmission of applications by governments secure compliance with the Regulation.[293] The Panel has found that the Regulation is inconsistent with the provisions of GATT 1994 for the reasons set out in this report. Therefore, the Regulation is not a law or regulation within the meaning of paragraph (d). In response to questions, the European Communities argued that these requirements secure compliance with a provision within the Regulation. However, if that provision could itself be a law or regulation within the meaning of paragraph (d), the European Communities did not demonstrate that it was "not inconsistent" with GATT 1994.[294]

7.298 The Panel also notes the use of the term "necessary" in paragraph (d). We recall the clarification of that term provided by the Appellate Body in *Korea – Various Measures on Beef*, as follows:

> We believe that, as used in the context of Article XX(d), the reach of the word 'necessary' is not limited to that which is 'indispensable' or 'of absolute necessity' or 'inevitable'. Measures which are indispensable or of absolute necessity or inevitable to secure compliance certainly fulfil the requirements of Article XX(d). But other measures, too, may fall within the ambit of

---

[291] This is consistent with the approach of the Appellate Body in *US – Gasoline*, according to which one must examine whether the relevant "measure," rather than the legal finding of less favourable treatment, falls within a paragraph of Article XX: see DSR 1996:I, 3, at 15.

[292] European Communities' rebuttal submission, para. 234.

[293] European Communities' first written submission, para. 226; rebuttal submission, para. 238.

[294] The European Communities argued that verification (and incidentally also the transmission) of applications by the government of the country of origin served the purpose of establishing whether the requirements of the Regulation for registration of GIs are satisfied and, accordingly, secured compliance with the requirement in Article 8 that the PDO, PGI and equivalent indications may appear only on products that comply with the Regulation. However, it only explained how the Regulation itself was, in its view, not inconsistent with GATT 1994: see its responses to Panel questions No. 135(a), (c) and (d).

> this exception. As used in Article XX(d), the term 'necessary' refers, in our view, to a range of degrees of necessity. At one end of this continuum lies 'necessary' understood as 'indispensable;' at the other end, is 'necessary' taken to mean as 'making a contribution to.' We consider that a 'necessary' measure is, in this continuum, located significantly closer to the pole of 'indispensable' than to the opposite pole of simply 'making a contribution to.' [footnote omitted][295]

7.299 The Appellate Body summed up its approach to the determination of whether a measure which is not "indispensable" may nevertheless be "necessary" within the meaning of Article XX(d) as a process of weighing and balancing a series of factors. It approved the approach of the GATT Panel in *US – Section 337* as a way in which to apply this process as follows:

> In our view, the weighing and balancing process we have outlined is comprehended in the determination of whether a WTO-consistent alternative measure which the Member concerned could 'reasonably be expected to employ' is available, or whether a less WTO-inconsistent measure is 'reasonably available.'[296]

7.300 The Panel will follow this approach.

7.301 The United States argues that the European Communities could reasonably be expected to allow applicants to file applications directly with its authorities without prior examination by third country governments, and that this is WTO-consistent. Many other WTO Members employ such a procedure.[297] It is not disputed that such a procedure would be WTO-consistent.

7.302 The European Communities submits that the cooperation of the government of the country where the GI is located is indispensable because the registration of GIs requires the evaluation of factual and legal questions which "only the home country of the GI is in a position to carry out."[298]

7.303 The Panel observes that Articles 6(2) and 12b(1) of the Regulation provide that the Commission makes the decision on whether the conditions are satisfied so as to warrant publication. It is not clear why an additional examination of the conditions by other governments is also required. Nor is it clear that a third country government is even able to conduct an examination according to the requirements, not of its own law, but of an EC Regulation. The European Communities has not explained why physical proximity or potential knowledge of certain questions in the country of origin implies a capacity to assess matters of EC law. Therefore, it is not clear to what extent examination by governments, including third country governments, contributes to securing compliance with the conditions for registration.

7.304 With respect to factual and legal questions that can, as part of the examination, be verified in the country of origin, the European Communities does not explain why the Regulation does not permit applicants to provide objective and impartial evidence that may verify their applications nor does it explain why the Commission cannot seek consent to carry out its own verifications. In its responses to the Panel's questions, the European Communities indicates that "typically" only the country of origin has the required knowledge of local factors and that verification "may" require on-site checks which the Commission cannot carry out in third countries without express consent.[299] The Panel considers that these responses constitute an admission that, in some cases, verification by third country governments is not necessary and that, if it sought and obtained

---

[295] Appellate Body report on *Korea – Various Measures on Beef*, para. 161.

[296] *Ibid.* para. 166. The Appellate Body also followed this approach to the word "necessary" as used in paragraph (b) of Article XX in *EC – Asbestos*, para. 172.

[297] See comments of Argentina, Brazil, India, Mexico, New Zealand and Chinese Taipei as third parties in Annex C, paras. 18, 28, 103, 118, 161 and 180.

[298] European Communities' rebuttal submission, para. 237.

[299] European Communities' response to Panel question No. 136(a).

consent, the Commission could conduct verifications itself. The European Communities has not demonstrated the factual premise of its defence that only the government of the country of origin is in a position to carry out the evaluation of these factual and legal questions. Therefore, the Panel does not need to consider further the requirement of examination by governments.

7.305 With respect to the transmission of applications, the European Communities is unable to explain why a procedure permitting applicants to file applications directly with its competent authorities would not permit an examination of whether an application for a GI in another WTO Member complies with the conditions in the Regulation. It submitted that transmission of applications by governments should not be viewed in isolation. Given that it has not established that examination by governments, including third country governments, is necessary, it has not established that transmission by them is necessary either.

7.306 Therefore, the Panel considers that the European Communities has not discharged its burden of proving that the requirements of examination and transmission of applications by governments is covered by paragraph (d) of Article XX. It is therefore unnecessary to consider the chapeau of Article XX.

7.307 For these reasons, the Panel concludes that, with respect to the application procedures, insofar as they require examination and transmission of applications by governments, the Regulation accords less favourable treatment to imported products inconsistently with Article III:4 of GATT 1994, and these requirements are not justified by Article XX(d).

3. Objection procedures

(a) Description of objection procedures under Articles 7, 12b and 12d of the Regulation

7.308 The parties agree on most features of the objection procedures under the Regulation. There are separate provisions setting out the procedures for objections to applications for registration of GIs which apply according to the location of the geographical area and the location of the person who wishes to file an objection. Article 7 applies where the geographical area and the person who wishes to file an objection are both located in EC member States. Article 12b applies where the geographical area is located in a third country. Article 12d applies where the geographical area is located in an EC member State and the person who wishes to file an objection is located in a third country.

7.309 Article 7(1) and 7(3) provide as follows:

> 1. Within six months of the date of publication in the *Official Journal of the European Communities* referred to in Article 6(2), any Member State may object to the registration.
>
> 3. Any legitimately concerned natural or legal person may object to the proposed registration by sending a duly substantiated statement to the competent authority of the Member State in which he resides or is established. The competent authority shall take the necessary measures to consider these comments or objection within the deadline laid down."

7.310 Article 12b(2) provides, relevantly, as follows:

> 2. Within six months of the date of publication as provided for in paragraph 1(a), any natural or legal person with a legitimate interest may object to the application published in accordance with paragraph 1(a) on the following terms:
>
> (a) where the objection comes from a Member State of the European Union or a WTO Member, Article 7(1), (2) and (3) or Article 12d respectively shall apply;

(b) where the objection comes from a third country meeting the equivalence conditions of Article 12(3), a duly substantiated statement of objection shall be addressed to the country in which the abovementioned natural or legal person resides or is established, which shall forward it to the Commission.

7.311 Article 12d(1) provides, relevantly, as follows:

> 1. Within six months of the date of the notice in the *Official Journal of the European Union* specified in Article 6(2) relating to a registration application submitted by a Member State, any natural or legal person that has a legitimate interest and is from a WTO member country or a third country recognised under the procedure provided for in Article 12(3) may object to the proposed registration by sending a duly substantiated statement to the country in which it resides or is established, which shall transmit it, made out or translated into a Community language, to the Commission.

7.312 Article 7(4) sets out the grounds for admission of objections. Articles 12b(3) and 12d(2) provide that the Commission shall examine the admissibility of objections in accordance with the criteria laid down in Article 7(4).

(b) National treatment under the TRIPS Agreement

(i) main arguments of the parties

7.313 The United States claims that the Regulation is inconsistent with Article 3.1 of the TRIPS Agreement and Article 2 of the Paris Convention (1967), as incorporated in Article 2.1 of the TRIPS Agreement, because the objection procedures accord less favourable treatment to non-EC nationals. It argues that the right of to object to registration of a GI is part of the protection of industrial property and of intellectual property because it is part of the ability to prevent others from using indications in a way that is misleading as to source.[300]

7.314 The United States argues that EC nationals have a *direct means to object* to registrations but non-EC nationals do not. Objections must be filed with the authorities of the third country or EC member State in which the objector resides or is established. The competent authority of an EC member State has an obligation under Article 7(3) of the Regulation to take the necessary measures. The authorities in the third country do not. They are responsible for *verification and transmission* of the objection. This represents an extra hurdle for non-EC nationals and less favourable treatment. It also constitutes a requirement of domicile or establishment inconsistent with Article 2(2) of the Paris Convention (1967).[301]

7.315 The United States argues that Article 12d of the Regulation limits the persons who may file objections to those resident or established in a country that satisfies the conditions of *equivalence* and *reciprocity*.[302]

7.316 The United States argues that Article 12d of the Regulation provides *standing to object* to non-EC nationals who have a "legitimate interest." Non-EC nationals are at a disadvantage because they are less likely to have a product on the EC market with a competing name due to the discrimination in availability of protection. Article 7(3) provides standing to object to EC nationals who are "legitimately concerned" which is a lower standard that makes it easier to object.[303] It cites dictionary definitions which show that "concern" is

[300] United States' first written submission, para. 87.

[301] United States' first written submission, paras. 89-91; second oral statement, paras. 40 and 43.

[302] United States' first written submission, para. 92; second oral statement, para. 39.

[303] United States' first written submission, paras. 93-94; first oral statement, para. 34.

broader than "interest." Article 12d was inserted by the April 2003 amending Regulation—if the standard were the same it would have been logical to use the same word.[304]

7.317 The European Communities responds that these claims must fail. The *verification and transmission* of an objection by a third country should not be particularly burdensome and does not amount to an "extra hurdle" for third country residents. A third country is not required to conduct a substantive verification under Article 7(4) the Regulation—which is clear from the wording of Article12d(2) that indicates that the criteria must be assessed in relation to the territory of the Community. Rather, the third country verifies whether the person objecting is indeed resident or established there. It could also be useful to have an official contact point if questions arise concerning the territory of the third country, it should be beneficial to the person objecting to deal directly with an authority in the third country and, if the objection is admissible, the third country is to be consulted before the Commission takes its decision on registration.[305]

7.318 The European Communities argues that Article 12d grants a right of objection to persons from WTO Members because the phrase "recognised under the procedure provided for in Article 12(3)" only applies to other third countries. The conditions of *equivalence* and *reciprocity* do not apply to WTO Members' right to object. Otherwise, the specific reference to "WTO Members" would be meaningless. This is also clear in Article 12b(2).[306] It also argues that Article 12d does not discriminate according to nationality but according to residence or establishment. It cannot simply be assumed that the reference to "nationals" in Article 3.1 of the TRIPS Agreement and Article 2 of the Paris Convention (1967) also applies to persons who are domiciled or established abroad, regardless of their nationality.[307]

7.319 The European Communities argues that the requirements for *standing to object* by persons from within the European Communities do not differ from those for persons from outside the European Communities. There is no substantive difference between the two expressions "legitimately concerned" and "legitimately interested." It cites a dictionary definition of "concerned" which includes "interested."[308]

(ii) main arguments of third parties

7.320 Argentina, India, Mexico, New Zealand and Chinese Taipei all inform the Panel that they are not aware of any person ever having attempted to file with their respective authorities an objection to registration under the Regulation.[309]

7.321 Brazil considers that the requirement to file objections with the country in which the objector resides or is established is an "unnecessarily complicated or costly" procedure in breach of Article 41.2 of the TRIPS Agreement. Brazil sees no necessity that would justify preventing private parties forwarding objections directly to the European Commission as many countries, including Brazil, allow for direct access for foreigners to object.[310]

7.322 Mexico argues that the Regulation is inconsistent with national treatment because it imposes conditions of reciprocity and prevents third country nationals filing objections directly with European authorities. Non-EC WTO Member nationals have an additional burden to involve their national authorities and

---

[304] United States' rebuttal submission, paras. 87-88; second oral statement, para. 42.

[305] European Communities' response to Panel question No. 34; rebuttal submission, paras. 155-159; second oral statement, paras. 89-94.

[306] European Communities' first written submission, paras. 73-75; first oral statement, para. 50; second oral statement, paras. 86-88.

[307] European Communities' first written submission, para. 142; first oral statement, para. 51.

[308] European Communities' first written submission, paras. 76-78 and 151; rebuttal submission, paras. 160-163.

[309] See their respective comments in Annex C at paras. 18, 103, 118, 160 and 179.

[310] Annex C, para. 28.

delegate to them the objection process. Mexico refers to cochineal as a practical example of the way in which Mexican producers would be required to go through specific procedures which EC nationals are not.[311]

7.323 New Zealand argues that the objection procedure can potentially result in an application for registration not proceeding. Not having the right to object is a loss of a valuable right of a producer to protect its intellectual property rights. Objections under the Regulation are subject to equivalence and reciprocity requirements: the distinction between WTO Members and other third countries in Article 12d(1) could have been made clear by inserting a comma or other words. Objections must also be submitted through governments. At worst, the benefits of the right to object are entirely unavailable to third country producers. As a result, the system virtually guarantees that no objections will be received from WTO Member nationals to applications for registration of GIs.[312]

(iii) consideration by the Panel

7.324 These claims concern procedures for filing and examination of objections to applications for registration of "designations of origin and "geographical indications," as defined in the Regulation. They are referred to in this report, for the sake of brevity, as "objection procedures."

7.325 The claims relate to three separate issues: (1) regarding verification and transmission; (2) regarding equivalence and reciprocity conditions; and (3) regarding standing requirements to raise an objection. The Panel will address these issues in turn.

7.326 These claims are made under Article 3.1 of the TRIPS Agreement and Article 2 of the Paris Convention (1967), as incorporated by Article 2.1 of the TRIPS Agreement. The Panel will first consider the claims under Article 3.1 of the TRIPS Agreement.

7.327 The Panel recalls that two elements must be satisfied to establish an inconsistency with this obligation: (1) the measure at issue must apply with regard to the protection of intellectual property; and (2) the nationals of other Members must be accorded "less favourable" treatment than the Member's own nationals. The Panel will address each of these elements in turn.

<u>verification and transmission</u>

protection of intellectual property

7.328 The Panel recalls that the national treatment obligation in Article 3 of the TRIPS Agreement applies to the treatment accorded by a Member "with regard to the protection of intellectual property." Footnote 3 provides an inclusive definition of the term "protection" as used in Articles 3 and 4:

> For the purposes of Articles 3 and 4, 'protection' shall include matters affecting the availability, acquisition, scope, maintenance and enforcement of intellectual property rights as well as those matters affecting the use of intellectual property rights specifically addressed in this Agreement.

7.329 The Panel recalls its finding at paragraph 7.262 that procedures for the filing and examination of *applications* for registration are matters affecting the acquisition of intellectual property rights, within the scope of "protection" of intellectual property as clarified in footnote 3 of the TRIPS Agreement. Procedures for *objections* to such applications are related to the procedures for acquisition, as recognized in the fourth paragraph of Article 62 (which uses the word "opposition") and the title of that article. Hence, opposition

[311] Annex C, para. 110.

[312] Annex C, paras. 139-140.

procedures are also matters "affecting" the acquisition of intellectual property rights which concern the "protection" of intellectual property, as clarified in footnote 3 to the TRIPS Agreement.

7.330 It is not disputed that "designations of origin" and "geographical indications," as defined in the Regulation, are a subset of geographical indications, the subject of Section 3 of Part II, and therefore part of a category of intellectual property within the meaning of Article 1.2 of the TRIPS Agreement.

7.331 Therefore, this claim concerns the "protection" of intellectual property, as clarified in footnote 3 to the TRIPS Agreement, within the scope of the national treatment obligation in Article 3.1 of that Agreement.

less favourable treatment accorded to the nationals of other Members

7.332 The United States claims that the procedures relating to verification and transmission of objections are inconsistent with the national treatment obligations under the TRIPS Agreement.

7.333 The Panel notes that, unlike the application procedures, the objection procedures do *not* concern the location of the geographical area to which the GI refers. Rather, they refer to the place where the objector resides or is established. The Panel recalls its findings at paragraphs 7.185 to 7.203 and considers, for the same reasons *a fortiori*, that the treatment accorded by the Regulation to persons resident or established in certain countries will, objectively, translate into treatment of persons with the nationality of those countries.

7.334 The Panel notes once again that the close link between nationality, on the one hand, and residence and establishment, on the other, appears to be recognized in the Regulation itself. Articles 12b(2)(a) and 12d(1) of the Regulation accord a right of objection to persons, which the European Communities confirms refers to persons resident or established outside the European Communities regardless of their nationality.[313] Yet the April 2003 amending Regulation, which inserted these provisions, explained that Article 12d granted the right of objection to the *nationals* of other WTO Members.[314]

7.335 The Panel recalls its finding at paragraph 7.134 that under Article 3.1 of the TRIPS Agreement we must examine the "effective equality of opportunities" with regard to the protection of intellectual property rights and at paragraph 7.137 that in this examination we will focus on the "fundamental thrust and effect" of the Regulation.

7.336 The parties and third parties who responded to the Panel's question on this point all reported that they were not aware of any objections to registration of GIs under the Regulation ever having been filed with the authorities of a third country.[315] However, the United States challenges the Regulation, in this respect, "as such."

7.337 The United States claims that the treatment accorded under the objection procedures in Articles 12b(2) and 12d(1) is less favourable than that accorded under the objection procedure in Article 7(3). There is an apparent equivalence in the drafting of these provisions but the question is whether this would imply a modification of the effective equality of opportunities with regard to the protection of intellectual property.

7.338 The Panel notes that the initial steps in the procedures for objections by private persons can be broken down as follows:

---

[313] European Communities' first written submission, para. 142.

[314] See paragraph 10 of the recitals to the April 2003 amending Regulation, set out in para. 7.70 above.

[315] However, the United States provided evidence from the U.S. Dairy Export Council and the National Milk Producers Federation that U.S. dairy producers and processors had been unable to prevent the registration as protected GIs in the European Union of a number of cheese types that they considered generic prior to registration: see letter dated 26 March 2004 to the Office of the United States Trade Representative, in response to Panel question No. 36, reproduced in Exhibit US-39. The European Communities responds that this is based on a misperception of the content of the Regulation: see its rebuttal submission, para. 85.

(a) as a first step, all objectors are required to submit their objection to the authorities in the country in which they reside or are established. These will be authorities of an EC member State or a third country, depending on the case; and

(b) as a second step, the authorities who receive an objection verify certain formal matters[316] and forward or transmit it to the Commission.

7.339 We recall the European Communities' explanation of what amounts to its domestic constitutional arrangements, set out at paragraph 7.98, that Community laws are generally not executed through authorities at Community level but rather through recourse to the authorities of its member States which, in such a situation, "act *de facto* as organs of the Community, for which the Community would be responsible under WTO law and international law in general."[317] It follows that any objection from a person in an EC member State is filed directly with a "*de facto* organ of the Community." An objection from a person in a third country cannot be filed directly, but must be filed with a foreign government. This is a formal difference in treatment.

7.340 An EC member State has an obligation under Community law to verify an objection and forward it to the Commission. A group or person who submits an objection in an EC member State may enforce these obligations through recourse to judicial procedures based on the Regulation. In contrast, a third country government has no obligation under Community law or any other law to receive an objection or to transmit it to the Commission. A group or person who submits an objection in a third country has no right to such treatment.

7.341 Therefore, persons resident or established in third countries, including other WTO Members, who wish to object to applications for registration under the Regulation do not have a right in the objection procedures that is provided to persons in the European Communities. Objectors in third countries face an "extra hurdle" in ensuring that the authorities in those countries carry out the functions reserved to them under the Regulation, which objectors in EC member States do not face. Consequently, certain objections may not be verified or transmitted. Each of these considerations significantly reduces the opportunities available to other WTO Member nationals in matters affecting the acquisition of rights under the Regulation compared with those available to EC nationals. For this reason, the Regulation accords nationals of other WTO Members "less favourable treatment" within the meaning of Article 3.1 of the TRIPS Agreement.

7.342 The European Communities submits that the requirement that statements of objection be transmitted by the country where the person is resident or established is not an unreasonable condition and that, if there is no objective reason for the third country government to refuse to cooperate, it is not the European Communities' rules which create an extra hurdle for third country residents.[318] The Panel recalls its finding at paragraph 7.274 that the obligation to accord national treatment with respect to a measure of the European Communities is the obligation of the European Communities. For the reason set out in paragraph 7.275 in relation to application procedures, the Panel considers that the European Communities has failed to accord no less favourable treatment *itself* to the nationals of other Members.[319]

7.343 The Panel confirms that the European Communities is entitled, under Article 62.4 of the TRIPS Agreement, to provide for procedures for objections that comply with the general principles in paragraphs 2 and 3 of Article 41. However, Article 62 is outside the Panel's terms of reference.

---

[316] The Panel takes note of the European Communities' position that it does not require third country governments to verify whether the objections are admissible, but it agrees that it does require them to verify certain formal matters: see European Communities' rebuttal submission, paras. 155-156.

[317] European Communities' second oral statement, para. 148.

[318] European Communities' rebuttal submission, para. 157.

[319] See further paras. 7.741 to 7.743 below.

7.344 The Panel recalls its finding at paragraph 7.212 that the fact that a general exceptions provision analogous to Article XX of GATT 1994 was not included in the TRIPS Agreement has no impact on its analysis of Article 3.1.

7.345 Therefore, the Panel concludes that, with respect to the objection procedures, insofar as they require the verification and transmission of objections by governments, the Regulation accords less favourable treatment to the nationals of other Members, inconsistently with Article 3.1 of the TRIPS Agreement.

Article 2 of the Paris Convention (1967)

7.346 In view of the conclusion at paragraph 7.345 with respect to the objection procedures, insofar as they require the verification and transmission of objections by governments, it is unnecessary to consider their consistency with Article 2(1) of the Paris Convention (1967), as incorporated by Article 2.1 of the TRIPS Agreement.

7.347 The Panel recalls its finding at paragraph 7.217 and, for the same reasons, concludes that, with respect to the opposition procedures, the Regulation does not impose a requirement of domicile or establishment inconsistently with Article 2(2) of the Paris Convention (1967), as incorporated by Article 2.1 of the TRIPS Agreement.

equivalence and reciprocity conditions

7.348 The United States claims that the right to file an objection under Article 12d(1) of the Regulation is limited to countries that satisfy the equivalence and reciprocity conditions in Article 12(1), based on a reading of the phrase "a WTO member country or a third country recognised under the procedure provided for in Article 12(3)" as if it read "a WTO member country recognised under the procedure provided for in Article 12(3) or a third country recognised under the procedure provided for in Article 12(3)." It is necessary for the Panel to make an objective assessment of the meaning of that phrase in this provision, although solely for the purpose of determining the European Communities' compliance with its WTO obligations.[320]

7.349 The Panel observes that this claim is based entirely on the absence of a comma. A reading of the text of Article 12d(1), set out in full at paragraph 7.311, shows that if there were a comma after the words "a WTO member country," it would be clear that it was separate from the following words "or a third country recognised under the procedure provided for in Article 12(3)." However, in the Panel's view, even without a comma, it is unlikely that the phrase "recognised under the procedure provided for in Article 12(3)" refers to both a "WTO member country" and a "third country" in this context. If that were the correct reading, then there would be no need to specify a "WTO member country" separately because, outside the European Communities, a "WTO member country" is necessarily a third country. There would be no need to refer specifically to a "WTO member country" if it was not distinguished in some way from any other third country. The difference must be that a third country is only included if it is recognized under the procedure provided for in Article 12(3) so that, consequently, this phrase would not apply to a "WTO member country." Indeed, the fact that there is no need for a WTO Member to obtain recognition under Article 12(3) for its residents to object seems to be precisely the reason that it is included. Therefore, the Panel's interpretation of Article 12d of the Regulation is that it does not apply conditions of equivalence and reciprocity to the right of objection for nationals of other WTO Members.

7.350 This is consistent with the fact that Article 12b(2), in which the format is clearer, creates a right of objection for WTO Member and other third country nationals but clearly indicates that recognition under the procedure in Article 12(3) does not apply to WTO Members in this respect. Further confirmation is provided by the recitals to the April 2003 amending Regulation. Those recitals explained the justification for the insertion of

---

[320] In this regard, the Panel recalls its comments at para. 7.55 above.

the right of objection in Articles 12b and 12d in terms of WTO Members, but limited the explanation of the equivalence and reciprocity conditions to the issue of protection provided by registration to foreign names.[321]

7.351 The European Communities confirms that the Panel's interpretation of this aspect of the Regulation is correct and submits undisputed evidence that since the entry into force of Article 12d(1), the publications of all applications for registration of a geographical indication specifically refer to the possibility for residents from WTO countries to object to the application.[322]

7.352 Therefore, based on this interpretation of Article 12d(1) of the Regulation, the Panel concludes that, with respect to the equivalence and reciprocity conditions, as allegedly applicable to objections, the United States has not made a prima facie case in support of its claims under Article 3.1 of the TRIPS Agreement or Article 2(1) of the Paris Convention (1967) as incorporated by Article 2.1 of the TRIPS Agreement.

standing requirements

7.353 The United States also claims that there is a difference in the requirements for standing to object under the Regulation, based on the difference between the words:

(a) "[a]ny legitimately concerned natural or legal person may object" in Article 7(3);

(b) "any natural or legal person with a legitimate interest may object" in Article 12b(2); and

(c) "any natural or legal person that has a legitimate interest ... may object," in Article 12d(1).

7.354 The requirement in Article 7(3) of the Regulation applies to persons who wish to file objections who reside or are established in the European Communities, whilst the requirements in Articles 12b(2) and 12d(1) apply to persons who wish to file objections who reside or are established in other WTO Members and third countries.

7.355 The United States' claims are based on the premise that a "legitimate interest" is a higher standard than "legitimately concerned."

7.356 The Panel notes that the Regulation, on its face, uses two different words in the standing requirements applicable to persons resident and established within or outside the European Communities. The word "interest" can be defined as follows:

> The fact or relation of having a share or concern in, or a right to, something, esp. by law; a right or title, esp. to (a share in) property or a use or benefit relating to property; (a) share *in* something.

7.357 The word "concern" can be defined as follows:

> Reference, respect, relation. Now *spec.* important relation, importance, interest (chiefly in *of concern (to)*).[323]

7.358 The difference between these two words is apparently minor, particularly since each appears in the definition of the other quoted above.

---

[321] Paragraphs 9 and 10 of the recitals to Council Regulation (EC) No. 692/2003 set out in Exhibit COMP-1h.

[322] European Communities' rebuttal submission, para. 152, attaching as an example the publication of the application to register "Lardo di Colonnata" dated 5 June 2003, set out in Exhibit EC-56.

[323] *The New Shorter Oxford English Dictionary* (1993).

7.359 The Regulation uses the same term "legitimate interest" in a related context where it refers to persons who may have access to applications filed with an EC member State in Article 7(2). It uses the more specific term "legitimate economic interest" where it refers to persons who may consult an application in Articles 7(2) and 12d(1), and contrasts it with "legitimate interest" in Article 7(2), which confirms that they have different meanings. However, there is nothing in the context that would suggest that there is a difference between a person with a "legitimate interest" and a "legitimately concerned" person.

7.360 It is pertinent to note that in many places the Regulation uses slightly different words or formulations to refer to an identical concept. For instance, it refers variously to "a third country recognised in accordance with the procedure in Article 12(3)," "[i]n the case provided for in Article 12(3);" "a third country meeting the equivalence conditions of Article 12(3);" "a third country recognised under the procedure provided for in Article 12(3)" in Articles 6(6), 12a(1), 12b(2)(b), 12d(1) and 13(5), respectively. There is no suggestion that these mean different things.

7.361 It is also pertinent to recall that Article 7(3) was adopted in 1992, but Articles 12b and 12d were drafted separately and inserted in April 2003. This may explain minor differences between them.

7.362 Even if the meaning of these provisions is different, it appears that the European Communities can apply them in the same manner. Indeed, the European Communities indicates to the Panel that it considers that these two terms have the same meaning and it confirms that the Commission would implement them in the same way. Further, if the Commission's interpretation was ever challenged, the institution with ultimate authority to interpret the measure is the European Court of Justice. We recall the European Communities' explanation of its domestic law set out at paragraph 7.99 that:

> Community legislation must, so far as possible, be interpreted in a manner that is consistent with international law, in particular where its provision are intended specifically to give effect to an international agreement concluded by the Community.[324]

7.363 We note that paragraph 10 of the recitals to the amending Regulation expressly states as follows:

> (10) (...) The right of objection should be granted to WTO member countries' nationals with a legitimate interest on the same terms as laid down in Article 7(4) of the said Regulation. (...)."[325]

7.364 This confirms that the difference in the wording of the standing requirements is not intended to create a lower standard for objectors resident or established in WTO Members outside the European Communities but rather that a person that has a "legitimate interest" and a "legitimately concerned" person should be interpreted in the same way.

7.365 Therefore, the Panel concludes that, with respect to the standing requirements for objections, the United States has not made a prima facie case in support of its claims under Article 3.1 of the TRIPS Agreement and Article 2(1) of the Paris Convention (1967), as incorporated by Article 2.1 of the TRIPS Agreement.

---

[324] See *supra* at note 131.

[325] Exhibit COMP-1h.

summary of conclusions regarding objection procedures and the TRIPS Agreement

7.366 In summary:

(a) with respect to the objection procedures, insofar as they require the verification and transmission of objections by governments, the Regulation accords the nationals of other Members less favourable treatment than the European Communities' own nationals inconsistently with Article 3.1 of the TRIPS Agreement;

(b) with respect to the objection procedures, the Regulation does not impose a requirement of domicile or establishment inconsistently with Article 2(2) of the Paris Convention (1967) as incorporated by Article 2.1 of the TRIPS Agreement;

(c) with respect to the equivalence and reciprocity conditions, as allegedly applicable to the objection procedures, the United States has not made a prima facie case in support of its claims; and

(d) with respect to the standing requirements for objections, the United States has not made a prima facie case in support of its claims.

(c) National treatment under GATT 1994

(i) main arguments of the parties

7.367 The United States claims that the Regulation is inconsistent with the national treatment obligations under GATT 1994 because it applies conditions of equivalence and reciprocity to the right of objection.[326]

7.368 The United States also claims that the requirement that WTO Members themselves become active participants and advocates for their nationals in analyzing and submitting GI registration applications and objections also amounts to less favourable treatment of non-EC products. This requirement is imposed unilaterally and is both burdensome and unnecessary and acts as an additional barrier to market access for non-EC goods.[327]

7.369 The European Communities does not respond to this claim, although it does submit that the right of objection does not affect the treatment of products under GATT 1994.[328] However, in response to a question from the Panel, it indicated that transmission of objections is necessary within the meaning of Article XX(d) of GATT 1994 because it has no significant impact on trade in goods and is a purely ministerial act which would not pose particular difficulties.[329]

(ii) consideration by the Panel

7.370 The Panel recalls its findings in paragraphs 7.30 to 7.33 that the United States presented this claim after the first substantive meeting but that, in the circumstances of this dispute, this had not prejudiced the European Communities' ability to defend itself. For that reason, the Panel decided to consider this claim.

7.371 The Panel recalls its finding at paragraph 7.349 that Article 12d of the Regulation does not apply conditions of equivalence and reciprocity to the right of objection for nationals of other WTO Members.

[326] United States' rebuttal submission, paras. 89-94.

[327] United States' rebuttal submission, para. 95.

[328] European Communities' rebuttal submission, para. 173 (in response to Australia's claim concerning individual registrations under the simplified procedure in the former Article 17 of the Regulation).

[329] European Communities' response to Panel question No. 136(d).

7.372 The Panel recalls its findings at paragraph 7.338 to 7.341 on the verification and transmission of objections under the Regulation. In the single paragraph of its rebuttal submission devoted to this aspect of the objection procedures and GATT 1994, the United States asserts, but does not demonstrate, that this treatment accorded to nationals amounts to less favourable treatment of products. The arguments concerning verification and transmission in earlier submissions relate to the application procedures only. The rebuttal submission does refer to the procedures for protection of GIs for "products," but that also apparently relates to application procedures only, not the objection procedures which are the subject of this claim.

7.373 The United States has not explained the link between the interests of a person who wishes to file an objection, and the conditions of competition between a product for which GI registration is granted and other products. The Panel declines to embark on an examination of the grounds for objection and speculate on the possible link between those and trade in goods, as it is unable to relieve the United States of the burden of proving all elements of its claim. Accordingly, the Panel considers that the United States has not made a prima facie case in support of its claim with respect to objection procedures under Article III:4 of GATT 1994.

4. Inspection structures

(a) Description of inspection structures (Articles 4, 10 and 12a of the Regulation)[330]

7.374 The condition in Article 12(1) of the Regulation that a "third country ... has inspection arrangements ... equivalent to those laid down in this Regulation" was considered earlier as one of the equivalence and reciprocity conditions. That is a per-country condition. The condition at issue here concerns the inspection structures required by Article 10 of the Regulation under the procedures for registration of individual GIs. This is, allegedly, a per-product requirement.

7.375 The Panel continues its examination in respect of this particular requirement, bearing in mind the aim of the dispute settlement mechanism, which is to secure a positive solution to a dispute[331], and the views of the Appellate Body in *Australia – Salmon* on the principle of judicial economy.[332] Were the Panel not to examine the claim with respect to the inspection structures requirements within the application procedures, its conclusion on the inspection structures condition in Article 12(1) would not enable the DSB to make sufficiently precise recommendations and rulings so as to allow for prompt compliance in order to ensure effective resolution of this dispute.

7.376 The Regulation provides that an application for registration of a GI must be accompanied by certain documents. The first is the product specification. Article 5(3) provides as follows with respect to an application to register a GI located within the European Communities:

> 3. The application for registration shall include the product specification referred to in Article 4.

7.377 Article 12a(1) of the Regulation provides as follows with respect to applications to register GIs located in third countries:

> 1. Applications must be accompanied by the specification referred to in Article 4 for each name.

7.378 With respect to the specification, Article 4 provides as follows:

---

[330] European Communities' first written submission, paras. 50-55; rebuttal submission, paras. 96-100.

[331] Article 3.7 of the DSU.

[332] Appellate Body report on *Australia – Salmon,* para. 223.

1. To be eligible to use a protected designation of origin (PDO) or a protected geographical indication (PGI) an agricultural product or foodstuff must comply with a specification.

2. The product specification shall include at least: (...)

(g) details of the inspection structures provided for in Article 10;

7.379 A specification refers to a particular product and the list of items that must be included in a product specification all appear to be product-specific.

7.380 Applications to register GIs located in third countries must also be accompanied by a declaration by a third country government. Article 12a(2)(b) of the Regulation provides for a third country to transmit to the Commission an application to register a GI located in its territory accompanied by:

(b) a declaration that the structures provided for in Article 10 are established on its territory.

7.381 This declaration is not required of an EC member State when it transmits to the Commission an application to register a GI located within the European Communities. However, EC member States have an obligation under Article 10 itself to ensure that inspection structures are in place. The European Communities confirms that the requirements are the same for EC member States and third countries.[333]

7.382 Article 10(1) explains that the function of inspection structures is "to ensure that agricultural products and foodstuffs bearing a protected name meet the requirements laid down in the specifications." Article 10(2) provides that an "inspection structure" may comprise one or more "designated inspection authorities and/or private bodies approved for that purpose" by the EC member State. Article 10(3) lays down requirements regarding the characteristics and duties of the inspection authorities and/or private bodies but not the product-specific requirements which appear in product specifications. We highlight the requirements for inspection authorities under Article 10(3) which are relevant to the claims below.

7.383 The characteristics of the inspection authorities and/or private bodies include the following:

> Designated inspection authorities and/or approved private bodies must offer adequate guarantees of objectivity and impartiality with regard to all producers or processors subject to their control and have permanently at their disposal the qualified staff and resources necessary to carry out inspection of agricultural products and foodstuffs bearing a protected name.

7.384 The inspection authorities and/or private bodies may outsource certain functions as follows:

> If an inspection structure uses the services of another body for some inspections, that body must offer the same guarantees. In that event, the designated inspection authorities and/or approved private bodies shall, however, continue to be responsible *vis-à-vis* the Member State for all inspections.

7.385 The applicable standards for private bodies are described as follows:

> As from 1 January 1998, in order to be approved by the Member States for the purpose of this Regulation, private bodies must fulfil the requirements laid down in standard EN 45011 of 26 June 1989.

---

[333] European Communities' response to Panel question No. 126(a).

> The standard or the applicable version of standard EN 45011, whose requirements private bodies must fulfil for approval purposes, shall be established or amended in accordance with the procedure laid down in Article 15.
>
> The equivalent standard or the applicable version of the equivalent standard in the case of third countries recognised pursuant to Article 12(3), whose requirements private bodies must fulfil for approval purposes, shall be established or amended in accordance with the procedure laid down in Article 15.

7.386 Standard EN 45011 sets out "General requirements for bodies operating product certification systems." It specifies general requirements that a third party operating a product certification system shall meet if it is to be recognized as competent and reliable. These include requirements relating to the certification body itself and its personnel; changes in the certification requirements; applications for, evaluation of, and decisions on, certification; surveillance; use of licences, certificates and marks of conformity; and complaints to suppliers. It applies for EC member States although the European Communities has not yet established the standard or the applicable version of that standard on the basis of Article 10(3) of the Regulation.

7.387 Standard EN 45011 is a European standard that takes over the text of ISO/IEC Guide 65:1996 prepared by the ISO Committee on Conformity Assessment (CASCO). The European Communities has not established an equivalent standard in the case of third countries, but the European Communities informs the Panel that ISO/IEC Guide 65:1996 is an example of such an equivalent international standard.[334]

7.388 The responsibilities of governments with respect to inspection structures are set out in Article 10(1) and (2).[335] Governments must ensure that inspection structures are in place by designating a public inspection authority and/or approving a private inspection body and then notify them to the Commission. Where the government designates a public inspection authority, it carries out inspections itself. Where the government approves a private inspection body, it must ascertain that the private body is capable of fulfilling its functions in accordance with Article 10(1) and meets the requirements of Article 10(3), set out above. The basic criterion for the approval process is that the private body can effectively ensure that products comply with a specification. After designation and/or approval, the government is responsible for continued monitoring that an approved private body continues to meet the requirements.[336]

(b) National treatment under the TRIPS Agreement

(i) main arguments of the parties

7.389 The United States claims that the inspection structures requirement is contrary to the national treatment obligations in the TRIPS Agreement, including that in the Paris Convention (1967). The United States submits that it is important to a resolution of this dispute that the Panel make a finding on this particular requirement, as otherwise the European Communities could remove Article 12(1) of the Regulation but impose equivalence by another name through the requirement under Article 12a(2)(b) that another WTO Member provide a declaration that inspection structures are established on its territory.[337]

7.390 The United States argues that the *government participation* by another WTO Member is inconsistent with national treatment under the TRIPS Agreement because a foreign applicant must petition its government to

---

[334] The European Communities supplied copies of EN 45011 and ISO/IEC Guide 65:1996 to the Panel in Exhibits EC-2 and EC-3, respectively. See European Communities' response to Panel question No. 126(c).

[335] Article 10(1) and (2) refers to EC member States but, in conjunction with Article 12a(2)(a), they also apply to the governments of third countries.

[336] Uncontested information provided by the European Communities in its responses to Panel question Nos. 127 and 132. See the United States' comments on those EC responses.

[337] United States' rebuttal submission, para. 48; response to Panel question No. 56.

provide a declaration under Article 12a(2)(b).[338] Even though the European Communities argues that the requirement for specific inspection structures accords equal treatment, in cases of formally different legal provisions, the respondent bears the burden of showing that, in spite of such differences, the less favourable treatment standard is met. The inspection structures do not accord equal treatment to EC and other WTO Member nationals because EC member States have an obligation to establish specific structures under the Regulation so that the EC national automatically has a qualifying inspection structure which other WTO Member nationals do not. Many WTO Members have no such inspection structures. Therefore, all EC nationals are in a position to satisfy the inspection structures requirement but nationals of other Members cannot satisfy this condition, at least where the WTO Member concerned has not established the EC inspection structures.[339] It is not clear on what basis a U.S. government authority would be in a position to assess that inspection structures are in place in its territory which would meet the requirements of the Regulation.[340]

7.391 The United States argues that the inspection structure requirements are highly *prescriptive* and go beyond simply assuring that products meet the product specifications. The issue is not which particular aspects of the inspection structures are objectionable. The issue is that, if a Member demands that other WTO Members establish the same particular inspection structures that it has chosen for itself as a precondition for granting TRIPS rights to nationals of other Members, it accords less favourable treatment. The United States does not disagree that the European Communities can require, as a condition of registration, that the applicant itself be in a position to control use of the GI and ensure that products bearing the GI are entitled to it. Intellectual property rights are private rights, so the applicant must be in a position to satisfy the requirements for protection and not have to depend on actions of government outside its control. The European Communities has overstated the flexibility in its requirements. Article 12a(2) refers to the structures provided for in Article 10, which refers to a "structure" under which particular bodies may be authorized to conduct inspections. This requires a broad inspection structure capable of inspecting all agricultural products and foodstuffs, not just the one which the applicant seeks to register. It imposes specific requirements that go far beyond what is necessary to ensure the integrity of a GI. The inspection authority must have staff "permanently at its disposal" and, if it is a private body, fulfil the requirements of a European standard and continue to be responsible vis-à-vis the EC member State for all inspections.[341] It is not possible to separate the requirement that the government establish particular inspection systems from other aspects of those systems.[342]

7.392 The United States also argues that, even if certain certification mark holders might qualify as inspection authorities, the Regulation still accords less favourable treatment to the nationals of other Members because (1) the governments of other Members must ensure compliance by providing the declaration under Article 12a(2)(b) and monitoring private inspection bodies; and (2) some other GI right holders who are able to assure the integrity of their GI, such as collective mark owners and common law GI owners, would be excluded. The United States is not challenging the European Communities' basic standard for what constitutes a GI, but it does assert that if a product meets that standard, the non-EC national should be able to register it under the Regulation, regardless of whether its home government has established the same inspection structures as the EC member States.[343]

7.393 The United States argues that the issue of what is *necessary* does not arise under the national treatment obligations in the TRIPS Agreement and the Paris Convention (1967). In any case, the inspection structures required by the Regulation are not necessary. There is no reason to assume that only the government, as

---

[338] United States' first written submission, para. 81; response to Panel question No. 56.

[339] United States' rebuttal submission, paras. 47-48; second oral statement, para. 25.

[340] United States' rebuttal submission, para. 64.

[341] United States' rebuttal submission, paras. 51-54; second closing oral statement, para. 10.

[342] United States' response to Panel question No. 130.

[343] United States' rebuttal submission, paras. 55-61.

opposed to the right holder, can sufficiently assure that products qualify for protection. It is not clear why the government, not the right holder, has to approve or authorize inspection structures.[344]

7.394 The European Communities responds that the requirement of inspection structures does not involve any less favourable treatment of foreign nationals. Indeed, it represents equal treatment.[345]

7.395 The European Communities denies that the Regulation imposes equivalence by another name because it requires inspection structures only for products for which protection is sought and on a product-specific basis.[346] It does not impose an EC-model because it merely requires that inspection structures must exist according to the general principles set out in Article 10. This leaves considerable flexibility in the design of the actual structures. In particular, it provides a choice between public and private elements. This flexibility is illustrated by the variety of structures notified by EC member States under Article 10(2). Public bodies are situated at the national, regional and local levels of government; frequently they are general public administrations dealing with many other policy issues besides inspections under the Regulation; private bodies may be commercial enterprises or not-for-profit and may engage in other activities besides inspections. The European Communities provides examples of two firms which provide inspections as a commercial service.[347]

7.396 The European Communities submits that a GI is less reliable and informative for consumers if its proper use is not ensured by an effective inspection regime. The function of inspection structures is to ensure that products bearing a protected name comply with the product specifications. They are inseparably linked with the object and purpose of the Regulation and their removal would undermine the EC's system of GI protection. In response to the suggested alternative of unfair competition laws, the European Communities does not contest that they may be one way of protecting GIs, but they could not provide an equivalent degree of GI protection as that achieved by the Regulation. For example, a producer would have to have recourse to legal action and could not rely on controls carried out by an inspection body. A consumer would only have the assurance that a competitor might take legal action against non-conforming products. This would also affect the value of the GI for producers and undermine confidence in the EC system. There would be a "free rider" problem if producers from third countries were able to benefit from the EC system without complying with inspection structures.[348]

(ii) main arguments of third parties

7.397 Argentina submits that the inspection structures requirements in the Regulation are inconsistent with the TRIPS Agreement. It notes that Article 4(h) [sic] of the Regulation refers to the inspection structures provided for in Article 10, which does not state what is the applicable criterion to identify these structures when the applicant is from a third country. Article 12 requires that a third country must have inspection arrangements equivalent to those laid down in the Regulation. This creates an obstacle which completely escapes the decision of a natural or legal person to accept the requirements of Article 4, given that the decision to create inspection structures is restricted to government and is not foreseen in all third countries. Even in those third countries which do have inspection structures, their structures might not satisfy the requirement of equivalence in Articles 10 and 12 of the Regulation.[349]

7.398 China notes that Article 10 of the Regulation sets out detailed provisions on inspection structures in EC member States but not for other WTO Members. Article 12a(2) requires a third country to transmit with an application a declaration that the structures provided for in Article 10 are established on its territory. The Commission determines whether the declaration satisfies the conditions of the Regulation. EC member States

[344] United States' second oral statement, paras. 27-29; comment on EC response to Panel question No. 127.

[345] European Communities' rebuttal submission, paras. 94-95.

[346] European Communities' rebuttal submission, paras. 96-98.

[347] European Communities' rebuttal submission, paras. 101-107.

[348] European Communities' rebuttal submission, paras. 109-121.

[349] Annex C, paras. 9-10.

are obliged to establish the Article 10 inspection structures and, hence, they are not obliged to guarantee them when they transmit an application and can reasonably expect no objection from the Commission to their designated authorities. It appears that WTO Members are required to establish an "equivalent standard" for private inspection bodies and possibly also for "designated inspection authorities" but there is no guidance as to what constitutes an equivalent standard as the European Communities has submitted ISO/IEC Guide 65:1996 only by way of example. China agrees with the European Communities that product specifications and inspection structures are essential to the value and quality of GIs, but does not find its argument that equivalence and reciprocity conditions apply only in these two respects and not as an outright requirement of a third country's overall system of GI protection.[350]

(iii) consideration by the Panel

7.399 These claims are brought under Article 3.1 of the TRIPS Agreement and Article 2 of the Paris Convention (1967) as incorporated by Article 2.1 of the TRIPS Agreement. The Panel will consider the claim under Article 3.1 of the TRIPS Agreement first.

7.400 The Panel recalls that two elements must be satisfied to establish an inconsistency with this obligation: (1) the measure at issue must apply with regard to the protection of intellectual property; and (2) the nationals of other Members must be accorded "less favourable" treatment than the Member's own nationals. The Panel will address each of these elements in turn.

<u>protection of intellectual property</u>

7.401 This claim concerns the inspection structures required in respect of particular products for which individual GIs are registered under the Regulation.

7.402 The Panel recalls that the national treatment obligation in Article 3 of the TRIPS Agreement applies to the treatment accorded by a Member "with regard to the protection of intellectual property." Footnote 3 provides an inclusive definition of the term "protection" as used in Articles 3 and 4. It reads as follows:

> For the purposes of Articles 3 and 4, "protection" shall include matters affecting the availability, acquisition, scope, maintenance and enforcement of intellectual property rights as well as those matters affecting the use of intellectual property rights specifically addressed in this Agreement.

7.403 Turning to the Regulation, inspection structures ensure that *products* meet the requirements in the specifications. Whatever else may be the legal character of those structures, it is clear that the specifications include details of the inspection structures and these must be included in, or accompany, all applications for registration. The declaration under Article 12a(2)(b) must also accompany applications to register GIs located in third countries. Therefore, under this Regulation, the inspection structures are a matter affecting the availability and acquisition of protection for GIs.

7.404 It is not disputed that "designations of origin" and "geographical indications," as defined in the Regulation, are a subset of "geographical indications," the subject of Section 3 of Part II, and therefore part of a category of intellectual property within the meaning of Article 1.2 of the TRIPS Agreement.

7.405 Therefore, this claim concerns the "protection" of intellectual property, as clarified in footnote 3 to the TRIPS Agreement, within the scope of the national treatment obligation in Article 3.1 of that Agreement.

[350] Annex C, paras. 84-91.

less favourable treatment accorded to the nationals of other Members

7.406 The Panel recalls its findings:

(a) at paragraphs 7.185 to 7.203 as to the treatment accorded to the "nationals of other Members" in this dispute; and

(b) at paragraph 7.134 that under Article 3.1 of the TRIPS Agreement we must examine the "effective equality of opportunities" with regard to the protection of intellectual property rights and at paragraph 7.137 that in this examination we will focus on the "fundamental thrust and effect" of the Regulation.

7.407 No application for registration of a GI located in a third country has ever been filed under the Regulation. However, the United States challenges the Regulation, in this respect, "as such."

7.408 The United States claims that the treatment accorded under the inspection structures requirements for GIs located in third countries is less favourable than that accorded under the inspection structures requirements for GIs located within the European Communities, based on two main aspects: the first relates to the allegedly prescriptive nature of the requirements and the second to the issue of government participation. We will take them up in that order.

allegedly prescriptive requirements for inspection structures

7.409 The Panel notes that the text of Article 10 contains virtually no formal difference between the requirements that apply to GIs located within the European Communities and those located in the territory of third countries. The same substantive requirements for the design of inspection structures apply to the protection of all GIs registered under the Regulation. There is a choice of public inspection authorities, private inspection bodies or both.[351] All authorities and bodies must offer adequate guarantees of objectivity and impartiality and all must have permanently at their disposal the qualified staff and resources necessary to carry out inspections. These requirements apply both to GIs located within the European Communities and to those located in third countries.

7.410 There is one formal difference in Article 10.[352] Paragraph 3 provides that private inspection bodies located in EC member States must fulfil the requirements laid down in standard EN 45011 and those located in third countries must fulfil the requirements laid down in an "equivalent" standard. The Panel notes that standard EN 45011 and ISO/IEC Guide 65:1996, which the European Communities informs us is an example of an equivalent international standard, have the same text and are basically identical. Therefore, this does not appear to amount to a substantive formal difference in Article 10(3). The provisions on public inspection authorities are identical.

7.411 The Panel recalls its finding at paragraph 7.176 that, even if the provisions of the Regulation are formally identical in the treatment that they accord to the nationals of other Members and to the European Communities' own nationals, this is not sufficient to demonstrate that there is no violation of Article 3.1 of the TRIPS Agreement. The question is whether this would imply a modification of the effective equality of opportunities with regard to the protection of intellectual property.

7.412 The United States argues that these provisions, in practice, accord less favourable treatment to the nationals of other Members who enjoy GI protection without inspection structures, or without inspection

[351] The European Communities provided a copy of a list published by the Commission of inspection structures notified by EC member States in accordance with Article 10(2) of the Regulation in OJ C 69, 18.3.2002, p.1, reproduced in Exhibit EC-48.

[352] Article 12a(2)(b), which contains a formal difference applicable to third countries only, is dealt with below.

structures that would satisfy Article 10 of the Regulation, in the territory of other WTO Members. Specifically, it asserts that certain holders of certification marks, collective marks and common law rights would not satisfy the requirements of Article 10(3) and standard EN45011, for instance, with respect to the independence of the inspection body from the producers.

7.413 The Panel recalls that the European Communities' obligation under Article 3.1 of the TRIPS Agreement is to accord no less favourable treatment to the nationals of other Members than it accords to its own nationals. The benchmark for the obligation is the treatment accorded *by the European Communities* to the European Communities' own nationals. The treatment accorded *by other Members* to their own respective nationals is not relevant to this claim. The level of protection in the country of origin does not affect GI protection in the country where GI protection is sought under the TRIPS Agreement, except to the extent that a lack of GI protection in the country of origin provides a ground to *deny* GI protection in accordance with Article 24.9.[353]

7.414 The Panel agrees with the European Communities that WTO Members are entitled to aim for objective assessment of product conformity, provided that they implement this objective in a WTO-consistent manner. The implication of the United States' argument would be to oblige the European Communities to recognize forms of protection granted by the United States. This would be a kind of reverse equivalence condition.

7.415 It is not contested that the European Communities would apply the same criteria for protection in Article 2, the same requirements for product specifications in Article 4 and the same inspection structures requirements in Article 10 to all applications for registration under the Regulation, both those in respect of GIs located within the European Communities, and those located outside the European Communities. It therefore appears to accord equal treatment. In any event, the Panel notes that Article 10 of the Regulation permits a certain degree of flexibility. Both public inspection authorities and private inspection bodies may be used.[354] The European Communities has also confirmed to the Panel that inspection bodies need not be established for the sole purpose of conducting inspections under Article 10 of the Regulation—public inspection authorities may be general public administrations dealing with public policy issues besides inspection under this Regulation whilst private inspection bodies may engage in a number of other activities.[355]

7.416 The United States objects, in particular, to the requirement in Article 10(3) of the Regulation that inspection bodies must have qualified staff permanently at their disposal. However, the European Communities responds that this may be interpreted flexibly. It submits that this requirement does not exclude the possibility of products for which the entire production process is confined to part of the year, and for which the need for inspection arises only or primarily during that time of the year. In such a case, it submits that the Regulation would not require unnecessary levels of staff to be maintained throughout the year.[356]

7.417 The Panel also notes that the standard specified in the Regulation has the same text and is basically identical to a guide emanating from the International Organization for Standardization and the International Electrotechnical Commission. Further, Article 10(3) permits an "equivalent," and not necessarily identical, standard for GIs located outside the European Communities, which may provide certain flexibility for GIs located outside the European Communities.

7.418 The United States has not referred to an alternative model of independent, objective and impartial assessment of product conformity which would clearly be refused recognition by the European Communities for reasons other than the requirements of government participation, discussed below.

[353] See also the consideration of the United States' claim under Article 1.1 of the TRIPS Agreement at paras. 7.762 to 7.767 below.

[354] The European Communities has provided a list of inspection structures notified by EC member States in accordance with Article 10(2) of the Regulation which shows a wide range of public inspection authorities and private inspection bodies. This list is reproduced in Exhibit EC-48.

[355] European Communities' rebuttal submission; paras. 105-106.

[356] European Communities' response to Panel question No. 136(f).

7.419 The United States also argues that the inspection structures requirements go beyond simply assuring that products meet the product specifications. This does not disclose a lack of national treatment.

7.420 Therefore, in view of the lack of evidence of different treatment, the Panel concludes that, with respect to the allegedly prescriptive requirements for inspection structures, the United States has not made a prima facie case in support of its claim under Article 3.1 of the TRIPS Agreement.

government participation in inspection structures

7.421 The Panel notes that the text of Article 10 of the Regulation, when read in conjunction with Article 12a(2)(b), contains a formal difference between the requirements that apply to GIs located within the European Communities and those located in third countries.

7.422 Article 10 obliges EC member States to ensure that inspection structures are in place. These require that the EC member States designate inspection authorities and/or approve private bodies for that purpose, and monitor them. Third country governments do not have these obligations under the Regulation. However, Article 12a(2)(b) requires that a third country government provide a declaration that the inspection structures are established on its territory together with an application to register a GI located in that territory. This is a condition in the application procedures.

7.423 The parties do not agree as to the content of this declaration. The United States alleges that it relates to the existence of inspection structures in respect of the full range of agricultural products and foodstuffs covered by the Regulation. The European Communities responds that it only applies with respect to particular products.

7.424 The Panel observes that the second equivalence requirement in Article 12(1) appears to relate to inspection structures for the full range of products, whilst the declaration in Article 12a(2)(a) is forwarded with an application for a particular product. Therefore, it appears that this declaration relates only to the inspection structures for a particular product. In any event, it is not disputed that it is only required to accompany applications to register GIs located outside the European Communities. This is a formal difference in treatment.

7.425 The requirement for a third country government to provide a declaration under Article 12a(2)(b) that the inspection structures are established on its territory and the obligation for an EC member State to establish inspection structures complement one another. Both are expressly intended to serve the same purpose of ensuring that agricultural products and foodstuffs bearing a protected name meet the requirements laid down in the specifications. Both depend on the government designating and/or approving, and monitoring, inspection structures.

7.426 An EC member State has an obligation to designate and/or approve, and monitor, inspection structures under the Regulation. In contrast, a third country government has no obligation under Community law to do so nor to provide the declaration under Article 12a(2)(a). Although the TRIPS Agreement contains obligations to protect GIs, it is not asserted that WTO Members have any obligation under that agreement to establish inspection structures such as those required under Article 10 of the Regulation.

7.427 A group or person who submits an application in a third country has no right to have inspection structures designated and/or approved, and monitored, by its own government, and has no right to the requisite declaration by its own government. Moreover, a group or person who submits an application in a third country cannot nominate inspection structures notified under the Regulation by an EC member State and dispense with the declaration by its own government. This is apparent from the terms of the declaration required under Article 12a(2)(b). It has also been confirmed by the European Communities.[357] A group or person who submits an application in a third country must use an inspection authority or private body notified by its own

[357] European Communities' responses to Panel question Nos. 131 and 136(f).

government. As a result, if the third country government does not designate and/or approve, and monitor, inspection structures and provide the declaration, the group or person cannot obtain protection under the Regulation.

7.428 Therefore, applicants for GIs that refer to geographical areas located in third countries do not have a right in the availability of protection and application procedures that is provided to applicants for GIs that refer to geographical areas located within the European Communities. Applicants in third countries face an "extra hurdle" in ensuring that the authorities in those countries carry out the functions reserved to them under the Regulation, which applicants in EC member States do not face. Consequently, certain applications may be rejected. This significantly reduces the opportunities available to the nationals of other WTO Members in the availability and acquisition of rights under the Regulation below those available to the European Communities' own nationals. For this reason, the Regulation accords nationals of other WTO Members "less favourable treatment" within the meaning of Article 3.1 of the TRIPS Agreement than it accords the European Communities' own nationals.

7.429 The Panel confirms that the European Communities is entitled, under Article 62.1 of the TRIPS Agreement, to require that applicants comply with reasonable procedures and formalities that are consistent with the Agreement in order to prove that they meet the conditions of protection. These might include requirements for applicants to demonstrate that they comply with standards of objective and impartial assessment of conformity. However, Article 62 lies outside the Panel's terms of reference.

7.430 The Panel recalls its finding at paragraph 7.212 that the fact that a general exceptions provision analogous to Article XX of GATT 1994 was not included in the TRIPS Agreement has no impact on its analysis of Article 3.1.

7.431 For these reasons, the Panel concludes that, with respect to the government participation required in the inspection structures under Article 10, and the provision of the declaration by governments under Article 12a(2)(b), the Regulation accords less favourable treatment to the nationals of other Members than to the European Communities' own nationals, inconsistently with Article 3.1 of the TRIPS Agreement.

7.432 The United States has not separately argued its claim under Article 2(1) of the Paris Convention (1967), as incorporated by Article 2.1 of the TRIPS Agreement with respect to the inspection structures requirements.[358] Accordingly, the Panel concludes that, in this respect, it has not made a prima facie case in support of its claim under that provision.

(c) National treatment under GATT 1994

(i) main arguments of the parties

7.433 The United States claims that the inspection structures requirement is contrary to Article III:4 of GATT 1994. It argues that the Regulation does not accord equal treatment because it conditions the granting of national treatment on another WTO Member adopting the same compliance structure as the European Communities. This is precisely the reciprocity and *equivalence* conditionality that the national treatment obligation was designed to avoid. An imported product from the U.S. that satisfies the definitions of a GI in the Regulation should receive no less favourable treatment than the domestic product that meets those definitions. However, the product imported from the U.S. is denied protection for reasons unrelated to the characteristics of the product.[359] They are like products.[360] The additional requirements that the European Communities imposes

[358] See United States' rebuttal submission, paras. 49 and 60, which refer to no less favourable treatment.

[359] United States' rebuttal submission, paras. 89-94.

[360] United States' second oral statement, paras. 47-48.

on other WTO Members, notably to establish specific inspection structures, are simply equivalence by another name and are designed to discourage the registration and protection of foreign GIs.[361]

7.434 The United States argues that the Regulation accords imported products less favourable treatment than domestic products because it requires substantial *government participation* by another WTO Member in the registration process. The government must make a declaration under Article 12a(2). It must establish particular inspection structures, approve inspection bodies, remain responsible for those bodies and satisfy all of the requirements for those bodies and structures as set forth in Article 10 of the Regulation.[362] It appears that the Regulation's approach is unprecedented as the European Communities declined to indicate any other area in which it requires foreign involvement in the designation/approval of conformity assessment bodies where mutual recognition agreements do not already exist.[363]

7.435 The United States argues that this less favourable treatment for imported products cannot be justified under Article XX of GATT 1994.[364] The European Communities has not discharged its burden of proof to show that the inspection structures are so justified.[365] The inspection structures do not appear to have any relationship to any of the product specification requirements in Article 4(2) of the Regulation and therefore do not "secure compliance" with them. The European Communities has not shown how the product specifications are not inconsistent with GATT 1994. The European Communities has not shown that the inspection structures are "necessary" and that there are no WTO-consistent alternatives. It is not clear at all that approval of, and responsibility for, inspection bodies by government rather than the right holder is even preferable, let alone necessary.[366] The European Communities argues that on-site checks "may also" be required which suggests that they are not necessary, and that government involvement is not necessary either. It is untrue that the European Communities cannot provide for on-site inspections outside the European Communities in the absence of a WTO agreement.[367] The inspection structures favour countries that protect GIs in the way that the European Communities does, which arbitrarily and unjustifiably discriminates between countries where the same conditions prevail, contrary to the chapeau of Article XX.[368]

7.436 The European Communities responds that this claim should be rejected. The Regulation is fully compatible with Article III:4 of GATT 1994 because the requirements imposed by Article 12a of the Regulation, in conjunction with Articles 4 and 10, do not provide less favourable treatment to imported like products. The European Communities must ensure that GIs from third countries comply with the conditions set out in the Regulation.[369] The European Communities refers to its arguments concerning inspection structures in relation to national treatment under the TRIPS Agreement: they represent equal, not unequal, treatment; they are not equivalence by another name; they do not impose an EC model of inspection structures and their existence is necessary for attaining the objectives of the Regulation.[370]

7.437 The European Communities submits, in the alternative, that the requirements imposed by Article 12a, in conjunction with Articles 4 and 10, with respect to individual GIs, are justified by Article XX(d) of GATT 1994. In particular, they are necessary to ensure that products which use a GI and benefit from GI protection conform to the definitions in Article 2(2) of the Regulation, which is itself fully consistent with GATT 1994.[371]

---

[361] United States' second oral statement, para. 49; comment on EC response to Panel question No. 136.

[362] United States' first written submission, paras. 104(d) and 107; response to Panel question No. 129.

[363] United States' comment on EC response to Panel question No. 131.

[364] United States' first written submission, para. 107; first oral statement, para. 38.

[365] United States' rebuttal submission, paras. 100-103.

[366] United States' second oral statement, paras. 53-57.

[367] United States' comment on EC response to Panel question No. 136.

[368] United States' second oral statement, para. 60.

[369] European Communities' first written submission, para. 204.

[370] European Communities' rebuttal submission, paras. 109-121 and 214-215.

[371] European Communities' first written submission, paras. 225-226.

Later, it argues that the inspection structures secure compliance with Articles 4(1) and 8 of the Regulation that a product must comply with a product specification and can only bear the PDO and PGI indications if they do so. Article XX(d) does not exclude that "measures necessary to secure compliance" and the "laws and regulations" with which they secure compliance may be part of the same legal act. The objectives of the Regulation may be relevant for establishing the meaning of the provisions with which compliance is secured.[372]

7.438 The European Communities refers to its arguments concerning inspection structures in relation to national treatment under the TRIPS Agreement: they are necessary for the attainment of the objectives of the Regulation by providing a high degree of assurance for producers and consumers that a product bearing a registered GI does, in fact, correspond to the required product specifications; a similar degree of protection could not be achieved through other means such as unfair competition laws; they do not go beyond what is necessary to attain the objectives of the Regulation but leave considerable flexibility in the design of the concrete structures. Moreover, they are not applied in a manner inconsistent with the chapeau of Article XX of GATT 1994.[373] It is necessary for the third country government to designate the inspection authority because the European Communities cannot designate them itself. Designation may require on-site inspections and audits outside the EC's territory. Inspections typically require a presence in or near the area where the GI is located. It is necessary for the bodies to remain responsible to the third country government as some form of public oversight is required to ensure objectivity and impartiality.[374]

7.439 The European Communities refers to the conformity assessment procedures foreseen in Article 6 of the TBT Agreement. Nothing in that agreement obliges Members simply to accept conformity assessment carried out by bodies of another Member. Article 6.1 of the TBT Agreement obliges Members to accept conformity assessment in other Members only under specific conditions, and recognizes that prior consultations may be necessary. Article 6.2 (sic) encourages Members to enter into negotiations for the mutual recognition of conformity assessment procedures. Article 6.4 encourages Members to permit participation of conformity assessment bodies located in the territories of other Members in their conformity assessment procedures but it is not a legal obligation to permit such participation. The United States has concluded a mutual recognition agreement which permits bodies designated by those countries to carry out conformity assessment with respect to EC standards and vice versa.[375] The United States has failed to explain why government involvement in designation of inspection bodies is problematic.[376]

(ii) consideration by the Panel

7.440 This claim concerns the inspection structures requirements for particular products. The Panel recalls its findings:

(a) at paragraph 7.227, that the Regulation is a law or regulation affecting the internal sale and offering for sale of products within the meaning of Article III:4 of GATT 1994;

(b) at paragraph 7.228 that the Regulation links the protection of the name of a product to the territory of a particular country and formally discriminates between imported products and products of European Communities origin within the meaning of Article III:4 of GATT 1994;

(c) at paragraph 7.229 that the European Communities does not contest that there are, among the group of products covered by the Regulation, "like products" among the imported products and products of European Communities origin;

---

[372] European Communities' response to Panel question No. 135.

[373] European Communities' rebuttal submission, paras. 232-236.

[374] European Communities' response to Panel question No. 136.

[375] European Communities' response to Panel question No. 131.

[376] European Communities' comment on United States' response to Panel question No. 128.

(d) at paragraph 7.230, that under Article III:4 of GATT 1994 we must examine whether the measure modifies the conditions of competition between domestic and imported products and that in this examination we will focus on the "fundamental thrust and effect of the measure itself;"

(e) at paragraph 7.231 to 7.235 on the substantive advantage provided under Article 13 of the Regulation that affects the conditions of competition of the relevant products;

(f) at paragraphs 7.409 and 7.410 on the lack of a substantive formal difference between the allegedly prescriptive requirements and at paragraphs 7.414 to 7.419 on the lack of evidence of different treatment accorded by those requirements;

(g) at paragraphs 7.426 and 7.427 concerning the differences between government participation in the inspection structure requirements which can result in some applications for registration of GIs located in third countries, but not those in EC member States, being rejected; and

(h) at paragraph 7.428 that rejection of an application would entail non-registration of GIs.

7.441 Non-registration of GIs would lead to a failure of the products from those third countries to obtain the benefits of registration set out in Article 13 of the Regulation. Therefore, the Panel concludes that:

(a) with respect to the allegedly prescriptive requirements for inspection structures, the United States has not made a prima facie case in support of its claim under Article III:4 of GATT 1994; but

(b) with respect to the requirements of government participation in the inspection structures under Article 10, and the provision of the declaration by governments under Article 12a(2)(b), the Regulation accords less favourable treatment to imported products than domestic products, inconsistently with Article III:4 of GATT 1994.

7.442 The European Communities asserts that the inspection structures requirements are justified by Article XX(d) of GATT 1994. As the party invoking this affirmative defence, the European Communities bears the burden of proof that the conditions of the defence are met.

7.443 At this point, the measures that the European Communities needs to justify are only the requirements for government participation in the designation and/or approval, and monitoring, of inspection structures, and the declaration by governments under Article 12a2(b).[377]

7.444 The Panel notes, once again, that paragraph (d) of Article XX refers to "measures" falling within the following description:

> (*d*) necessary to secure compliance with laws or regulations which are not inconsistent with the provisions of this Agreement, including those relating to customs enforcement, the enforcement of monopolies operated under paragraph 4 of Article II and Article XVII, the protection of patents, trade marks and copyrights, and the prevention of deceptive practices;

[377] The United States submits that the measures relevant to Article XX(d) are the measures that it alleges are inconsistent with GATT 1994 (United States' comments on EC responses to Panel question No. 135). However, the Panel has not found that the allegedly prescriptive requirements are inconsistent with GATT 1994 and, consequently, it only examines whether the government participation required in the inspection structures is justified under Article XX(d). The Panel does *not* examine whether the less favourable treatment that those requirements accord is justified under Article XX(d), consistently with the approach of the Appellate Body in *US – Gasoline*, DSR 1996:I, 3, at 15.

7.445 The Panel observes that paragraph (d) refers to measures necessary to "secure compliance." The Regulation states expressly in Article 10(1) that the function of the inspection structures is "to ensure that agricultural products and foodstuffs bearing a protected name meet the requirements laid down in the specifications." On its face, this appears to be an express confirmation that the inspection structures are intended to "secure compliance" with the product specifications.[378]

7.446 The Panel takes note that paragraph (d) refers to measures that secure compliance with laws or regulations, including those relating to "the protection of patents, trade marks and copyrights, and the prevention of deceptive practices." The Regulation provides for the protection of GIs and is an analogous law or regulation, as the European Communities points out.[379] However, the term "laws or regulations" is qualified by the phrase "not inconsistent with the provisions of this Agreement."

7.447 The European Communities submitted that the requirement of inspection structures is "necessary for the attainment of the objectives" of the Regulation.[380] The Panel agrees with previous panels that measures that merely secure compliance with the objectives of a law or regulation, rather than with the laws or regulations themselves, do not fall within the purview of Article XX(d) of GATT 1994 for the reasons explained by the GATT Panel in *EEC – Parts and Components*.[381]

7.448 The European Communities submits that the requirement of inspection structures is necessary to secure compliance with requirements in the Regulation.[382] The Panel has found that the Regulation is inconsistent with the provisions of GATT 1994 for the reasons set out in this report. Therefore, the Regulation is not a law or regulation within the meaning of paragraph (d). In response to questions, the European Communities argued that these requirements secure compliance with provisions within the Regulation. However, if those provisions could themselves be "laws or regulations" within the meaning of paragraph (d), the European Communities did not demonstrate that they were "not inconsistent" with GATT 1994.[383]

7.449 The Panel notes, once again, the use of the term "necessary" in paragraph (d) of Article XX and recalls the views of the Appellate Body in *Korea – Various Measures on Beef* set out at paragraph 7.298 above that, in this context, a necessary measure is "located significantly closer to the pole of 'indispensable' than to

---

[378] See further note 383 below. It is not clear to what extent the inspection structures secure compliance with the requirement in Article 4(1) of the Regulation, which refers to eligibility. Nor is it clear to what extent they cover use of the PDO, PGI and equivalent indications and, hence, secure compliance with Article 8 of the Regulation.

[379] European Communities' rebuttal submission, para. 234.

[380] European Communities' rebuttal submission, para. 232, citing paras 109-121. The European Communities agrees that the measure to be justified must secure compliance with the provisions of the law or regulation in question but that "the objectives of a regulation may be relevant for establishing the meaning of the provisions with which compliance is secured:" see its response to Panel question No. 135(b).

[381] See the Panel report on *Canada – Periodicals*, paras. 5.8-5.10; and Panel report on *Korea – Various Measures on Beef*, at para. 658; both citing the GATT Panel report on *EEC – Parts and Components* which included the following finding at para. 5.17:

"If the qualification 'to secure compliance with laws and regulations' is interpreted to mean 'to ensure the attainment of the objectives of the laws and regulations', the function of Article XX(d) would be substantially broader. Whenever the objective of a law consistent with the General Agreement cannot be attained by enforcing the obligations under that law, the imposition of further obligations inconsistent with the General Agreement could then be justified under Article XX(d) on the grounds that this secures compliance with the objectives of that law. This cannot, in the view of the Panel, be the purpose of Article XX(d): each of the exceptions in the General Agreement—such as Articles VI, XII or XIX—recognizes the legitimacy of a policy objective but at the same time sets out conditions as to the obligations which may be imposed to secure the attainment of that objective. These conditions would no longer be effective if it were possible to justify under Article XX(d) the enforcement of obligations that may not be imposed consistently with these exceptions on the grounds that the objective recognized to be legitimate by the exception cannot be attained within the framework of the conditions set out in the exception."

[382] European Communities' rebuttal submission, para. 234.

[383] The European Communities argued that the function of inspection structures is to secure compliance with the requirement in Article 4(1) of the Regulation that products bearing a protected name must comply with a product specification. Similarly, the requirement of inspection structures also secures compliance with the requirement in Article 8 of the Regulation that the PDO, PGI and equivalent indications may appear only on products that comply with the Regulation. However, it only explained how the Regulation itself was, in its view, not inconsistent with GATT 1994: see its responses to Panel questions No. 135(a), (c) and (d).

the opposite pole of simply 'making a contribution to'."[384] The Appellate Body summed up its approach to the determination of whether a measure which is not "indispensable" may nevertheless be "necessary" within the meaning of Article XX(d) as a process of weighing and balancing a series of factors. It approved the approach of the GATT Panel in *US – Section 337* that this process is "comprehended" in the determination of whether a WTO-consistent alternative measure which the Member concerned could "reasonably be expected to employ" is available, or whether a less WTO-inconsistent measure is "reasonably available."[385] The Panel will once again follow this approach.

7.450 We recall the European Communities' explanation of its domestic constitutional arrangements, set out at paragraph 7.98, that Community laws are generally not executed through authorities at Community level but rather through recourse to the authorities of its member States which, in such a situation, "act *de facto* as organs of the Community, for which the Community would be responsible under WTO law and international law in general."[386] In accordance with its domestic law, the European Communities is entitled to delegate certain functions under its measure to the authorities of EC member States. However, it is unable to explain adequately why it is necessary for all governments, including third country governments, to designate inspection authorities, approve private inspection bodies, and monitor them, and for third country governments to provide a declaration that they do so, for the purposes of securing compliance with an EC Regulation.

7.451 The European Communities is entitled under GATT 1994 to pursue the objectives set out in Article 10(3) of the Regulation of ensuring that inspection structures are objective and impartial with regard to all producers or processors subject to their control, which might require assessment by a neutral entity. It is not obliged to accept a producer's or supplier's declaration of conformity.

7.452 The European Communities may also be correct, in many cases, that it cannot designate or approve bodies located outside its territory itself because it is unable to ascertain and continuously monitor whether those bodies are capable of fulfilling their functions and meeting the requirements in Article 10(1) and (3), set out above.[387] It is not obliged to enter into mutual recognition agreements, although we note that it has recognized numerous conformity assessment bodies designated by other countries, including the United States, in other sectors.[388]

7.453 However, at the same time, the European Communities does not allow the products of other WTO Members to be inspected by its own designated authorities and approved bodies. A group or person who submits an application in a third country must use an inspection structure located in the territory of that country. Such a group or person cannot use an inspection structure notified by an EC member State. The European Communities requires that each government, including third country governments, participate in the inspection structures for products originating in its own territory. Yet we note that, in other areas such as technical regulations, its own designated authorities and approved bodies are open to exporters for assessment of conformity with technical regulations.[389]

7.454 The United States has indicated that the normal practice in conformity assessment is that an importing country imposes its own inspection requirements in its own territory, as necessary, to ensure that imported

---

[384] Appellate Body report on *Korea – Various Measures on Beef*, para. 161.

[385] *Ibid.*, para. 166. The Appellate Body also followed this approach to the word "necessary" as used in paragraph (b) of Article XX in *EC – Asbestos*, para. 172.

[386] European Communities' second oral statement, para. 148.

[387] European Communities' responses to Panel question Nos. 131 and 136(f).

[388] See European Communities' response to Panel question No. 131.

[389] The European Communities has explained its conformity assessment system to the TBT Committee as follows: "In respect of the Global Approach, which was relevant to conformity assessment, the fundamental point was that the manufacturer (or his authorised representative in the case of imported goods) was responsible for conformity. There was an effort to limit the number of different types of conformity assessment procedures to a reasonably small range (these were referred to as "modules" in the Global Approach). In most cases, the manufacturer was aided by a Notified Body (a certification body—or conformity assessment body) and there was an element of choice in that the manufacturer could chose any Notified Body." See document G/TBT/M/33/Add.1, para. 117.

products meet applicable requirements. It submits that it is unusual that the conformity assessment bodies of the European Communities, as the importing country, cannot be used for imported products under the Regulation.[390] The United States has also explained that, even in those instances in which inspection of manufacturing facilities is required, for instance, with respect to pharmaceutical manufacturing facilities, such inspections are primarily carried out by the administering authorities of the importing country. The exporting country government itself is not required to establish and be responsible for inspection systems.[391]

7.455 The combination of the absence of recognized inspection structures in third countries, and the fact that notified bodies in the European Communities are not available to applicants for GIs located in third countries, effectively excludes the products of third countries from the benefits of protection granted under the Regulation. This is a consequence of the requisite government participation in inspection structures under the Regulation.

7.456 The European Communities has not explained why the conditions of protection and the general requirement that a product bearing a registered GI must comply with a product specification, for which it requires every government to designate its own bodies, distinguish the GI Regulation from other areas, such as technical regulations, where it permits exporters to use notified bodies within the European Communities, where it seeks permission to conduct inspections in exporting countries or where it sometimes recognizes bodies located outside its territory, through mutual recognition agreements or accreditation.

7.457 The European Communities has referred to the contents of a product specification required under Article 4(1) of the Regulation, in particular, the detailed description of the raw materials and methods and processes according to which a product is obtained.[392] On the basis of these items, it argues that "inspection structures ... may involve on-site inspections at the place of production."[393] The United States argues that there is little or no relationship between the product specifications and the inspection structures.[394]

7.458 The Panel notes that the Regulation requires that the product specifications for each product include the items to which the European Communities refers.[395] However, the European Communities has not explained how and to what extent compliance with them cannot be assessed through reporting requirements or through an inspection of the physical characteristics of products on import by designated bodies located within the European Communities. The Panel accepts that there might be a reason why compliance with these specific requirements must be assessed in the place of production outside the European Communities' territory and that, in these cases, it may be reasonable for the European Communities, as an importing country, to expect certain cooperation from exporting country governments, in particular with respect to information related to the production methods of an agricultural product or foodstuff, in accordance with the provisions of covered agreements.

7.459 However, the European Communities has not explained why the cooperation that it requires from third country governments must take the form of establishing a mandatory inspection structure in which the government plays a central role. It confirms that governments, including third country governments, must carry out inspections to ensure compliance with product specifications in an EC GI registration, or ascertain that a private inspection body can effectively ensure that products comply with the specification and remain responsible for continued monitoring that the private body meets the requirements of the Regulation and, where

[390] See the European Communities' comment on responses to Panel question No. 128, in which it confirms that the inspection bodies will be located on the territory of the country of origin of the GI.

[391] United States' comments on EC responses to Panel question No. 136(f).

[392] The European Communities provides examples of product specifications for "Pruneaux d'Agen," "Melons du Haut Poitou," "Dorset Blue Cheese" and "Thüringer Leberwurst" in Exhibits EC-51 through EC-54.

[393] European Communities' rebuttal submission, paras 112-113 in relation to the same aspect of the Regulation with respect to national treatment under the TRIPS Agreement. See also its response to Panel question No. 136(f).

[394] United States' comment on EC response to Panel question No. 135.

[395] Article 4(2)(b), (d) and (e) of the Regulation, respectively.

they are third country governments, provide declarations that they have done so.[396] It asserts, but has not demonstrated, that "[o]nly through some form of public oversight can it be ensured that the inspection body will at all times carry out its functions duly and appropriately in accordance with the requirements of the Regulation."[397] However, in response to a question from the Panel, it was unable to identify any EC Directives governing assessment of conformity to EC technical regulations in the goods area that require third country government participation in the designation and approval of conformity assessment bodies.[398] It has not explained what aspect of GI protection distinguishes it from these other areas and makes it necessary to require government participation, including third country government participation, to the extent that it does.

7.460 The European Communities argues that it does not itself have the inspection bodies that are needed to conduct inspection outside its territory. It also notes that the costs of inspection must be borne by the producer as stipulated in Article 10(7) of the Regulation. It argues that if it were to carry out inspections of imported products bearing a GI, this would result in less favourable treatment for products of domestic origin.[399] The Panel's findings do not imply that the European Communities must establish inspection bodies outside its territory nor that it cannot continue to require producers to bear the costs. The Panel sees these issues as separate from the extent of government participation in inspections required by the Regulation.

7.461 For these reasons, the Panel considers that there are alternative measures available to the European Communities which it could reasonably be expected to employ and which are not inconsistent with GATT 1994 to ensure that products using a registered GI comply with their specifications.

7.462 Therefore, the Panel considers that the European Communities has not discharged its burden of proving that government participation in the designation, approval and monitoring of inspection structures, and the provision of a declaration by governments concerning these matters, is covered by paragraph (d) of Article XX. It is therefore unnecessary to consider the chapeau of Article XX.

7.463 For these reasons, the Panel concludes that, with respect to the requirements of government participation in the inspection structures under Article 10, and the provision of the declaration by governments under Article 12a(2)(b), but in no other respects related to the inspection structures, the Regulation accords less favourable treatment to imported products than domestic products, inconsistently with Article III:4 of GATT 1994, and these requirements are not justified by Article XX(d).

5. *Labelling requirement*

(a) *Factual aspects of the labelling requirement in Article 12(2) of the Regulation*

(i) *text of Article 12(2) of the Regulation*

7.464 This claim concerns a labelling requirement in the second indent of Article 12(2) of the Regulation. The parties disagree sharply on the meaning and scope of this provision, read in its context. Therefore, the Panel will begin by quoting Article 12(2) in full before turning to the factual arguments of the parties.

> 2. If a protected name of a third country is identical to a Community protected name, registration shall be granted with due regard for local and traditional usage and the practical risks of confusion.
>
> Use of such names shall be authorized only if the country of origin of the product is clearly and visibly indicated on the label.

---

[396] This information was provided by the European Communities in its responses to Panel question Nos. 127 and 132 and not contested. See the United States' comments on EC responses.

[397] European Communities' response to Panel question No. 136(g).

[398] European Communities' response to Panel question No. 131.

[399] European Communities' response to Panel question No. 136(h).

(ii) *main arguments of the parties*

7.465 The United States claims that this labelling requirement applies to any use of a GI in connection with products from other WTO Members. It notes that this requirement appears as an unlabelled paragraph within Article 12, which addresses GIs located in third countries in general, and not just those that are identical to GIs located in the European Communities. However, it pursues this claim even if it applies only to GIs identical to a GI located in the European Communities.[400]

7.466 The United States claims that this labelling requirement only applies to third country GIs, not the GI located in the European Communities with which they are identical. It argues that this requirement does not address the conditions of registration of GIs located in the European Communities. There is simply no basis for reading this as applying also to GIs located in the European Communities.[401]

7.467 The United States argues that there is nothing in Article 6(6) of the Regulation that would permit the Commission to import the requirement of Article 12(2) into the registration of a GI located in the European Communities. Under Article 6(6), an EC GI that gives rise to a "clear distinction in practice" with a homonymous prior registered GI would have to be registered without indicating the country of origin on the label of products. Under Article 12(2), a third country GI must be accompanied by the country of origin.[402]

7.468 The European Communities responds that the second subparagraph of Article 12(2) only applies to the GIs in the situation referred to in its first subparagraph. It only applies in cases of identical or homonymous names and not to third country names in general.[403] It confirms that there have been no cases in which this provision has been applied in practice.[404]

7.469 The European Communities argues that "such names" in the second subparagraph refers to both "a protected name of a third country" and a "Community protected name," so that the requirement to indicate the country of origin can apply to both the third country name and the Community name. In practice, this would mean that whichever indication is registered later would normally be required to indicate the country of origin.[405] In both these terms, "protected" means, in principle, "protected under Regulation 2081/92" but "the provision also applies where protection is sought for a protected name from a third country." "Community protected name" covers only protected names of geographical areas located in the European Communities.[406] Article 12(2) covers both a situation where a third country GI is a homonym of an EC GI already on the register, as well as an EC GI which is a homonym of a third country GI already on the register.[407] "Such names" is written in the plural which clearly indicates that the requirement can relate to both the EC and third country GIs.[408] Nothing in the wording of the provision prevents it applying to GIs from both third countries and the European Communities.[409] Even if "Community protected name" referred to EC and third country names already on the register, "protected name of a third country" should be interpreted to include names protected in

400 United States' first written submission, para. 25; rebuttal submission, paras. 76 and 97.

401 United States' first oral statement, para. 35; response to Panel question No. 48; rebuttal submission, paras. 77 and 98; second oral statement, para. 38.

402 United States' response to Panel question No. 118.

403 European Communities' first written submission, paras. 88 and 133; rebuttal submission, para. 144; second oral statement, para. 80.

404 European Communities' response to Panel question No. 44.

405 European Communities' first written submission, paras. 88, 134-135 and 211; rebuttal submission, para. 145.

406 European Communities' response to Panel question No. 41.

407 European Communities' response to Panel question No. 43.

408 European Communities' rebuttal submission, para. 147.

409 European Communities' second oral statement, para. 81.

a third country, whether or not from the European Communities or a third country.[410] In the European Communities' view, Article 12(2) has no specific link with Article 12(1).[411]

7.470 The European Communities argues that, in cases of homonymous GIs from the European Communities, the last indent of Article 6(6) also requires a clear distinction in practice between them which would normally, in practice, require the indication of the country of origin.[412] The only reason why the last indent of Article 6(6) does not explicitly require the indication of the country of origin is that this provision deals with a wider set of conflicts than Article 12(2).[413] There is no difference between the word "homonymous" in Article 6(6) and "identical" in Article 12(2) as the English definitions of those words are synonymous and the French and Spanish versions use the same term in both provisions.[414] Article 6(6) deals with a wider set of conflicts than Article 12(2), such as homonyms from within the European Communities, homonyms from within the same third country or different third countries.[415] Article 6(6) simply refers to "protected names" from the European Communities and a third country, without specifying which of these is the one the subject of an application and which is already on the register.[416]

7.471 The European Communities argues that "clearly and visibly indicated" must be evaluated in each specific case from the point of view of what a normally attentive consumer can easily notice and not be induced in error as to the origin of the product.[417]

(iii) consideration by the Panel

7.472 The Panel begins by noting that the second indent of Article 12(2) of the Regulation expressly sets out a requirement that concerns what is indicated on "the label" of a product. Therefore, for the sake of brevity, the Panel refers to it as "the labelling requirement."[418] The labelling requirement has not been applied in practice. However, the United States challenges this aspect of the Regulation "as such."

7.473 The meaning of the various terms in the second indent of Article 12(2) is essential to a resolution of this claim. Therefore, it is necessary for the Panel to make an objective assessment of the meaning of this provision, although solely for the purpose of determining the European Communities' compliance with WTO obligations.[419]

7.474 The parties disagree on the scope of the labelling requirement. The United States argues that it applies to all GIs from third countries, like the wider context in Article 12, which applies to all GIs from third countries that satisfy the conditions in paragraph 1 and are recognized as equivalent under paragraph 3. The European Communities responds that it applies only to identical or homonymous GIs, consistent with the immediate context in paragraph 2 of Article 12.

7.475 The Panel observes that the scope of the labelling requirement is indicated by its subject: "[u]se of such names." "Such" is a demonstrative adjective that refers to something previously specified, which expressly requires an examination of the context. The context indicates that "such names" refers to the subject of the previous indent, which is eligible GIs from third countries that are identical to a Community protected name.

---

[410] European Communities' second oral statement, para. 82.

[411] European Communities' response to Panel question No. 117.

[412] European Communities' first written submission, para. 89; response to Panel question No. 118.

[413] European Communities' first written submission, para. 479.

[414] European Communities' response to Panel question No. 119.

[415] European Communities' response to Panel question No. 42.

[416] European Communities' rebuttal submission, para. 146.

[417] European Communities' response to Panel question No. 120.

[418] The use of this term does not prejudge whether this is a "labelling requirement" as used in Annex 1.1 of the TBT Agreement.

[419] In this regard, the Panel recalls its comments at para. 7.55.

This is confirmed by the content of the two indents: the first refers to practical risks of confusion, and the second imposes a requirement that a detail be clearly and visibly indicated, which appears to be a specific requirement that addresses the more general consideration in the first. Whilst it is possible to look back further in the context and read the phrase "[u]se of such names" as referring to the names or GIs in the preceding paragraph 1, such a reading is, in our view, constrained. We note that the position of paragraph 2 near the beginning of Articles 12 through 12d might suggest that it is a more general provision, but its position can perhaps be explained by the fact that it is one of the two original provisions on GIs from third countries that predate the insertion of Articles 12(3) and 12a through 12d. The European Communities has confirmed that "such names" refers to the previous indent, which covers only identical GIs. On the basis of the text of the provision, which has not been applied, the Panel agrees.

7.476 The parties disagree on the meaning of "such names" even if it only refers to "identical" GIs.[420] The United States argues that it refers to the subject of the previous indent, which is "a protected name of a third country" that is identical to a Community protected name. The European Communities responds that it refers not only to "a protected name of a third country" which is identical, but also to the "Community protected name" with which it is identical.

7.477 The Panel considers, once again, that, "such names" refers to the subject of the previous indent, which is eligible GIs from third countries that are identical to a Community protected name. Although the term "a Community protected name" also appears in the previous indent, its registration is not in issue. It appears that the first indent relates only to the registration of GIs from a third country. The second indent attaches a condition to that registration which, logically, only applies to the use of GIs from a third country.

7.478 This reading is confirmed by the wider context in Articles 12 through 12b which relates only to the registration of GIs from third countries. The registration of GIs located within the European Communities is dealt with in Articles 5 through 7. A provision permitting objections to such registrations from persons in third countries was inserted in Article 12d in April 2003. It would be a very special reading if the second indent of Article 12(2) were the sole provision in the scheme of Articles 12 through 12b that attached a condition to registration of GIs located within the European Communities, which is unlikely, given that context. The Panel takes note that the term "such names" is in the plural, unlike "a protected name of a third country" which is in the singular. However, the qualifier "such names" is linked to "the product" which is in the singular, so that the plural form is not determinative of the issue before us.

7.479 Therefore, the Panel concludes that Article 12(2), including the labelling requirement in the second indent, refers only to the registration and use of a GI from a third country that is identical to a "Community protected name." It appears that this refers to a GI that is already registered under the Regulation, as no party has suggested a reason why it would matter for this requirement where the prior GI was located, as long as it was identical.

7.480 The Panel also notes that the first indent of Article 12(2) contains language almost identical to that found in Article 6(6) of the Regulation. Both refer to registration of names "with due regard for local and traditional usage and the actual risk [or practical risks] of confusion." However, Article 6(6) applies to an application to register a GI located *within the European Communities* which "concerns a homonym of an already registered name from the European Union or a third country recognised in accordance with the procedure in Article 12(3)." Unlike the second indent of Article 12(2), the last tiret of Article 6(6) sets out the following requirement:

---

[420] The Panel notes that, whilst the English version of the Regulation uses the word "identical" in Article 12(2), two other official versions of the Regulation use words corresponding to the English word "homonymous:" these are *homonyme* in the French version and *homónima* in the Spanish version. The Panel assumes that the meaning of the different versions of the text can be reconciled, and uses the word "identical" in relation to Article 12(2) in the English version of this report in such a sense. See further para. 7.492 below.

"[T]he use of a registered homonymous name shall be subject to there being a clear distinction in practice between the homonym registered subsequently and the name already on the register, having regard to the need to treat the producers concerned in an equitable manner and not to mislead consumers."

7.481 The Panel will revert to the parallel in the construction of the requirements in Articles 12(2) and 6(6) in its consideration of this claim.

(b) National treatment under the TRIPS Agreement

(i) main arguments of the parties

7.482 The United States claims that the Regulation accords less favourable treatment to third country nationals than to EC nationals because Article 12(2) imposes a requirement on the registration of GIs located in third countries that does not apply to GIs located in the European Communities, inconsistently with the national treatment obligations in the TRIPS Agreement.[421] It provides that the third country GI must be burdened by a clear and visible indication of the country of origin on the label, which is a violation of national treatment obligations. This is in the nature of a qualifier that detracts from the value of the GI by implying that it is something other than the "true" GI. There is also the issue of labelling costs, although that will depend on how particular imported products are labelled in the first place. This remains an additional burden on foreign nationals that is not faced by EC nationals. The United States does not believe that existing marks of origin requirements in the European Communities would satisfy this requirement.[422]

7.483 The European Communities argues that Article 12(2) of the Regulation does not discriminate between nationals because it applies according to the location of geographical areas, not nationality.[423] It can relate to both EC and third country GIs. Application of the requirement to indicate the country of origin to the later registered GI is the only feasible option because, according to Article 4(2)(h), the specifications of the GI already on the register will include specific labelling details which it is not easy to amend.[424] The European Communities does not see in which way a requirement to indicate truthfully the origin of a product constitutes less favourable treatment.[425]

(ii) consideration by the Panel

7.484 This claim is brought under Article 3.1 of the TRIPS Agreement. The Panel recalls that two elements must be satisfied to establish an inconsistency with this obligation: (1) the measure at issue must apply with regard to the protection of intellectual property; and (2) the nationals of other Members must be accorded "less favourable" treatment than the Member's own nationals.

<u>protection of intellectual property</u>

7.485 This claim concerns the labelling requirement in respect of a limited subset of GIs that may be registered under the Regulation. Footnote 3 provides an inclusive definition of the term "protection" as used in Articles 3 and 4. It reads as follows:

For the purposes of Articles 3 and 4, 'protection' shall include matters affecting the availability, acquisition, scope, maintenance and enforcement of intellectual property rights as

[421] United States' first written submission, para. 68.

[422] United States' response to Panel question No. 120.

[423] European Communities' first written submission, paras. 137-138.

[424] European Communities' rebuttal submission, para. 147.

[425] European Communities' second oral statement, para. 83.

well as those matters affecting the use of intellectual property rights specifically addressed in this Agreement.

7.486 Turning to the Regulation, the labelling requirement relates to the "use" of an identical GI on a product. Whatever else may be the legal character of this requirement, through its inclusion in the provisions of Article 12, which sets out the conditions on which the Regulation may apply to GIs located in third countries, it attaches a specific condition to registration of certain GIs. Therefore, under this Regulation, the labelling requirement is a matter affecting the acquisition of protection for GIs.[426]

7.487 It is not disputed that "designations of origin" and "geographical indications," as defined in the Regulation, are a subset of "geographical indications," the subject of Section 3 of Part II, and therefore part of a category of intellectual property within the meaning of Article 1.2 of the TRIPS Agreement.

7.488 Therefore, this claim concerns the "protection" of intellectual property, as clarified in footnote 3 to the TRIPS Agreement, within the scope of the national treatment obligation in Article 3 of that Agreement.

<u>less favourable treatment accorded to the nationals of other Members</u>

7.489 The Panel recalls its findings:

(a) at paragraphs 7.185 to 7.203 as to the treatment accorded to the "nationals of other Members" in this dispute; and

(b) at paragraph 7.134 that under Article 3.1 of the TRIPS Agreement we must examine the "effective equality of opportunities" with regard to the protection of intellectual property rights and at paragraph 7.137 that in this examination we will focus on the "fundamental thrust and effect" of the Regulation.

7.490 The United States claims that the treatment accorded under the labelling requirement for GIs located in third countries, including WTO Members, is less favourable than that accorded to GIs located within the European Communities.

7.491 The Panel has found at paragraph 7.479 that the labelling requirement only applies to GIs from third countries that are identical to a Community protected name. This is a narrow circumstance.

7.492 The Panel notes that Articles 12(2) and 6(6) share almost identical language that indicates that the purpose of each provision is to minimize actual, or practical, risks of confusion between the use of two registered identical or homonymous GIs. An obvious difference in the English version is that Article 12(2) uses the word "identical" and Article 6(6) uses the word "homonymous." However, two other official versions of the Regulation use the same word in both provisions (*homonyme* in French and *homónima* in Spanish). The Panel assumes that the meaning of the different versions of the text can be reconciled, and that, therefore, the words in Articles 12(2) and 6(6) can have the same meaning in English as well.

7.493 Both requirements are mandatory, providing that use "shall" be authorized only if a particular condition is met or "shall" be subject to a particular condition. However, there is a formal difference in that Article 12(2) states the condition expressly that "the country of origin of the product is clearly and visibly indicated on the label." In contrast, Article 6(6) states the condition in terms of factors that "a clear distinction in practice between the homonym registered subsequently and the name already on the register, having regard to the need to treat the producers concerned in an equitable manner and not to mislead consumers."

---

[426] It can be noted that the second indent of Article 12(2) is not the only provision of the Regulation which refers to "use." Article 4 of the Regulation refers to "use" of a GI by a product in accordance with a specification, which includes labelling under Article 4(h) and which, according to Articles 5(3) and 12a(1), is part of the application for registration.

7.494 In light of the applicable standard of examination set out at 7.489(b), the Panel does not consider that the mere fact that nationals of other Members and the European Communities' own nationals are subject to different legal provisions is in itself conclusive in establishing an inconsistency with Article 3.1 of the TRIPS Agreement.[427]

7.495 The European Communities explains that this difference between the wording of the relevant provisions is due to the fact that Article 6(6) applies to a wider class of GIs. For example, it could apply to identical GIs located in different EC member States, as well as to a GI within the European Communities identical to a GI located in a third country, which Article 12(2) cannot.

7.496 The essential point is that nothing in the text appears to prevent the European Communities implementing the two requirements in the same manner where an application is made to register a GI, whether located within the European Communities or in a third country, that is identical to a prior registered GI. It appears that the wording of Article 6(6) permits the European Communities to apply the same condition found in the text of Article 12(2) so that both requirements would be applied according to which GI was registered later in time, irrespective of the nationality of the applicant or user or the location of the GI. The European Communities has confirmed to the Panel that the clear distinction in practice would normally require the indication of the country of origin.[428]

7.497 The United States has not provided any evidence that the formal difference in the wording of the two requirements leads to any difference in treatment nor that it accords any different treatment to the nationals of other Members. It has not provided evidence that, where the European Commission applies the same condition under the labelling requirement in Article 12(2) and the last tiret of Article 6(6), that such a practice would not survive a legal challenge before the European Court of Justice.

7.498 The Panel recalls the European Communities' submission that, according to the settled case law of the European Court of Justice, "Community legislation must, so far as possible, be interpreted in a manner that is consistent with international law."[429]

7.499 Therefore, for the above reasons, in particular the confirmation by the European Communities that the clear distinction in practice under Article 6(6) would normally require the indication of the country of origin, the Panel concludes that, with respect to the labelling requirement, the United States has not made a prima facie case in support of its claim under Article 3.1 of the TRIPS Agreement.

(c) National treatment under GATT 1994

(i) main arguments of the parties

7.500 The United States claims that the Regulation accords less favourable treatment to imported products than to EC products because Article 12(2) imposes a requirement on the registration of GIs located outside the European Communities that does not apply to GIs located in the European Communities, inconsistently with Article III:4 of GATT 1994.[430]

7.501 The United States argues that this requirement provides that the third country GI must be burdened by a clear and visible indication of the country of origin on the label, which is a violation of national treatment obligations. This is in the nature of a qualifier that detracts from the value of the GI by implying that it is something other than the "true" GI. There is also the issue of labelling costs, although that will depend on how

---

[427] See also the GATT Panel report on *US – Section 337,* at para. 5.11, regarding the no less favourable treatment standard, cited with approval by the Appellate Body in *US – Section 211 Appropriations Act,* para. 264.

[428] European Communities' first written submission, para. 479; response to Panel question No. 118.

[429] See *supra* at note 131.

[430] United States' first written submission, para. 106.

particular imported products are labelled in the first place. This remains an additional burden on imported products that is not faced by EC products. The United States does not believe that existing marks of origin requirements in the European Communities would satisfy this requirement.[431]

7.502 The United States does not consider that this is a general country of origin requirement as described in Article IX of GATT 1994 but rather is a special rule triggered by the fact that a third country product is characterized as a GI and is intended to encumber the third country GI itself. There is nothing in Article IX that exempts such a requirement from the obligation to provide no less favourable treatment to imported products.[432]

7.503 The United States argues that the European Communities has not made a prima facie case under Article XX(d) of GATT 1994 and has failed to make any showing that the requirement that third country GIs be identified with a country of origin is necessary to ensure compliance with a WTO-consistent law or regulation. In any case, the less favourable treatment under the Regulation cannot be justified under that provision.[433] The fact that the requirement is not mandatory for EC GIs under Article 6(6) of the Regulation is an admission that the requirement is not "necessary."[434]

7.504 The European Communities responds that this claim is unfounded. Article 12(2) of the Regulation does not accord less favourable treatment but rather treats EC and imported products alike.[435]

7.505 The European Communities argues that Article III:4 is not applicable. Marks of origin are dealt with in Article IX of GATT 1994, which contains an MFN obligation but not a national treatment obligation. This omission implies that Members are free to impose country of origin marking requirements only with respect to imported products and not domestic products.[436]

7.506 The European Communities argues, in the alternative, that the requirement to indicate the country of origin is justified by Article XX(d) of GATT 1994. It serves the purpose of achieving a clear distinction in practice between homonymous GIs and prevents consumer confusion. Article 12(2) achieves this in the least intrusive way by requiring that the GI registered later, which is typically the one less known to the consumer, be the one for which the country of origin must be indicated. This complies with paragraph (d) and the chapeau of Article XX.[437]

(ii) consideration by the Panel

7.507 This claim concerns the labelling requirement in Article 12(2) of the Regulation "as such." The Panel recalls its findings:

(a) at paragraph 7.227, that the Regulation is a law or regulation affecting the internal sale and offering for sale of products within the meaning of Article III:4 of GATT 1994;

(b) at paragraph 7.228 that the Regulation links the protection of the name of a product to the territory of a particular country and formally discriminates between imported products and products of European Communities origin within the meaning of Article III:4 of GATT 1994;

---

431 United States' response to Panel question No. 120.

432 United States' first oral statement, para. 35; rebuttal submission, para. 99; response to Panel question No. 122.

433 United States' first oral statement, para. 38; second oral statement, para. 59.

434 United States' comment on EC response to Panel question No. 136.

435 European Communities' first written submission, para. 212.

436 European Communities' first written submission, paras. 213-217.

437 European Communities' first oral statement, para. 73; rebuttal submission, paras. 240-242.

(c) at paragraph 7.229 that the European Communities does not contest that there are, among the group of products covered by the Regulation, "like products" among the imported products and products of European Communities origin;

(d) at paragraph 7.230, that under Article III:4 of GATT 1994 we must examine whether the measure modifies the conditions of competition between domestic and imported products and that in this examination we will focus on the "fundamental thrust and effect of the measure itself;" and

(e) at paragraph 7.479 that the labelling requirement only applies to identical GIs.

7.508 In light of the applicable standard of examination set out at 7.507(d), the Panel does not consider that the mere fact that imported products are subject to legal provisions that are different from those applying to products of national origin is in itself conclusive in establishing inconsistency with Article III:4.[438] However, the Panel recalls its findings:

(a) at paragraph 7.496 concerning the differences in the wording of Articles 12(2) and 6(6) of the Regulation; and

(b) at paragraph 7.497 that the United States has not provided any evidence that the formal difference in the wording of the requirements in the second indent of Article 12(2) and the last tiret of Article 6(6) leads to any difference in treatment.

7.509 Therefore, for the above reasons, in particular the confirmation by the European Communities that the clear distinction in practice under Article 6(6) would normally require the indication of the country of origin, the Panel concludes that, with respect to the labelling requirement, the United States has not made a prima facie case in support of its claim under Article III:4 of GATT 1994.

7.510 As for the European Communities' argument that this labelling requirement cannot be subject to the national treatment obligation in Article III:4 of GATT 1994 due to the terms of Article IX of GATT 1994 on marks of origin, it suffices to note that the labelling requirement is part of the Regulation, which is a law or regulation affecting the internal sale and offering for sale of products within the meaning of Article III:4 of GATT 1994. In any event, it has not been shown that this is, in fact, a requirement to display a mark of origin.[439]

7.511 However, in view of our finding at paragraph 7.509 that the United States has not made a prima facie case in support of this claim, it is unnecessary for the purposes of this dispute to reach a definitive view on these questions, and the Panel's views do not imply any view on the relationship of Articles III:4 and IX:1 of GATT 1994.

C. Trademark Claim

1. *The relationship between GIs and prior trademarks*

(a) *Introduction*

7.512 The United States claims that the Regulation is inconsistent with Article 16.1 of the TRIPS Agreement because it does not ensure that a trademark owner may prevent uses of GIs which would result in a likelihood of confusion with a prior trademark.[440] Its claim only concerns valid prior trademarks, not trademarks liable to

---

[438] See also the GATT Panel report on *US – Section 337,* at para. 5.11.

[439] For example, the GATT CONTRACTING PARTIES Recommendation of 21 November 1958 on marks of origin, para. 5, "Countries should accept as a satisfactory marking the indication of the name of the country of origin in the English language introduced by the words 'made in':" BISD 7S/30. That example shows that a mark of origin can be different from the labelling requirement at issue.

[440] United States' first written submission, para. 170.

invalidation because they lack distinctiveness or mislead consumers as to the origin of goods.[441] It does not dispute that GIs that are identical or similar to trademarks may be used, but only to the extent that they do not result in a likelihood of confusion with respect to prior trademarks.[442]

7.513 The European Communities responds that this claim is unfounded for several reasons: (1) Article 14(3) of the Regulation, in fact, prevents the registration of GIs, use of which would result in a likelihood of confusion with a prior trademark; (2) Article 24.5 of the TRIPS Agreement provides for the "coexistence" of GIs and prior trademarks; (3) Article 24.3 of the TRIPS Agreement requires the European Communities to maintain "coexistence;" and (4) in any event, Article 14(2) of the Regulation would be justified as a limited exception under Article 17 of the TRIPS Agreement.[443]

7.514 For the sake of brevity, the Panel uses the term "coexistence" in this report to refer to a legal regime under which a GI and a trademark can both be used concurrently to some extent even though the use of one or both of them would otherwise infringe the rights conferred by the other. The use of this term does not imply any view on whether such a regime is justified.

7.515 The Panel will begin its examination of this claim by describing Article 14(2) of the Regulation and how the Regulation can, in principle, limit the rights of the owner of a trademark subject to Article 14(2) against the use of a GI. We will then assess whether Article 14(3) of the Regulation prevents a situation from occurring in which a trademark would be subject to Article 14(2). If Article 14(3) cannot prevent that situation from occurring, we will proceed to examine whether Article 16.1 of the TRIPS Agreement requires Members to make available to trademark owners the right to prevent confusing uses of signs, even where the signs are used as GIs. If it does, we will consider whether Article 24.5 provides authority to limit that right and, if Article 24.5 does not, conclude our examination by assessing whether Article 17 or Article 24.3 of the TRIPS Agreement permits or requires the European Communities to limit that right with respect to uses of signs used as GIs.

(b) Description of Article 14(2) of the Regulation

7.516 Article 13 of the Regulation sets out the protection conferred by registration of a GI under the Regulation. Paragraph 1 provides for the prevention of certain uses of the GI and other practices. These are negative rights to prevent, essentially, uses which are misleading as to the origin of a product or otherwise unfair.

7.517 Under the European Communities' domestic law, it is considered that the Regulation impliedly grants the positive right to use the GI in accordance with the product specification and other terms of its registration to the exclusion of any other sign. The European Communities explains, and the United States does not contest, that under the European Communities' domestic law, this positive right is implicit in several provisions, including Article 4(1), which refers to eligibility to use a protected designation of origin or a protected geographical indication; Article 8, which provides that the indications PDO and PGI and equivalent national indications may appear only on agricultural products and foodstuffs that comply with the Regulation; and Article 13(1)(a) which provides protection for registered names against direct or indirect commercial use on certain conditions. Without this positive right, in the European Communities' view, the protection granted by Article 13 would be "meaningless." Accordingly, under the European Communities' domestic law, that positive right prevails over the rights of trademark owners to prevent the use of a sign that infringes trademarks.[444]

7.518 A registered GI may be used together with other signs or as part of a combination of signs but the registration does not confer a positive right to use any such other signs or combination of signs or to use the

---

[441] United States' first oral statement, paras. 42-43.

[442] United States' rebuttal submission, para. 183.

[443] European Communities' first written submission, paras. 268-273.

[444] Confirmed in the European Communities' response to Panel question No. 139.

name in any linguistic versions not entered in the register.[445] Therefore, the registration does not affect the right of trademark owners to exercise their rights with respect to such uses.[446]

7.519 Article 14 of the Regulation governs the relationship of GIs and trademarks under Community law. Paragraph 1 deals with later trademarks. It provides for the refusal of trademark applications where use of the trademark would infringe the rights in a GI already registered under the Regulation. This, in effect, ensures that a registered *GI prevails over a later trademark.*

7.520 Paragraph 2 of Article 14 deals with prior trademarks. It provides as follows:

> 2. With due regard to Community law, a trademark the use of which engenders one of the situations indicated in Article 13 and which has been applied for, registered, or established by use, if that possibility is provided for by the legislation concerned, in good faith within the territory of the Community, before either the date of protection in the country of origin or the date of submission to the Commission of the application for registration of the designation of origin or geographical indication, may continue to be used notwithstanding the registration of a designation of origin or geographical indication, provided that no grounds for its invalidity or revocation exist as specified by Council Directive 89/194/EEC of 21 December 1998 to approximate the laws of the Member States relating to trade marks and/or Council Regulation (EC) No 40/94 of 20 December 1993 on the Community trade mark. [footnotes omitted]

7.521 This is an exception to Article 13, as it provides for the continued use of a prior trademark even though use of that trademark would conflict with the rights conferred by registration of a GI under the Regulation. It prevents the exercise of rights conferred by registration of a GI against the continued use of that particular prior trademark and is an express recognition that, in principle, *a GI and a trademark can coexist* under Community law. It is intended to implement Article 24.5 of the TRIPS Agreement.[447]

7.522 Article 14(2) only applies:

(a) with respect to the GI, where a particular indication satisfies the conditions for protection, including the definitions of a "designation of origin" or a "geographical indication," and is not subject to refusal on any grounds, including those in paragraph 3 of Article 14 (discussed below);

(b) with respect to the trademark, where a particular sign has already been applied for, registered, or established by use in good faith and there are no grounds for its invalidity or revocation; and

(c) where use of that trademark would infringe the GI registration.

---

[445] The European Communities explains that "[t]he positive right extends only to the linguistic versions that have been entered into the register" in its response to Panel question No. 140; see also its rebuttal submission, paras. 288 and 293; response to Panel question No. 137 and comment on US response to that question. A different "linguistic version" means a translation which renders the name differently. Some GIs are registered in more than one linguistic version: see, for example, the second, fourth and eleventh GIs set out *supra* at note 52.

[446] Under Community law, those rights would become meaningless if there was no positive right to use the registered GI. See European Communities' rebuttal submission, para. 301; responses to Panel question Nos. 139 and 140 (but contrast its comment on Australia's response to Panel question No. 137).

[447] Paragraph 11 of the recitals to the April 2003 amending Regulation explained that the dates referred to in Article 14(2) should be amended in line with Article 24.5 of the TRIPS Agreement: see Exhibit COMP-1h. Article 14(2) has been interpreted once by the European Court of Justice, in Case C-87/97, *Consorzio per la tutela del frommagio Gorgonzola v Käserai Champignon Hofmeister GmbH & Co Kg* [1999] ECR I-1301, concerning the trademark CAMBOZOLA for cheese and the GI "Gorgonzola." The opinion of the Advocate-General was submitted by the United States in Exhibit US-17 and the judgement of the Court was submitted by the European Communities in Exhibit EC-32.

7.523 The scope of Article 14(2) is confined temporally to those trademarks applied for, registered or established by use either before the GI is protected in its country of origin or before the date of submission to the Commission of an application for GI registration.

7.524 The text of Article 14(2) begins with the introductory phrase "[w]ith due regard to Community law." This refers, among other things, to the Community Trademark Regulation and the First Trademark Directive[448], both of which provide that trademark registration confers the right to prevent "all third parties" from certain uses of "any sign," including uses where there exists a likelihood of confusion.[449] This corresponds to the right provided for in Article 16.1 of the TRIPS Agreement.

7.525 However, Article 159 of the Community Trademark Regulation, as amended[450], provides as follows:

> This Regulation shall not affect Council Regulation (EEC) No. 2081/92 on the protection of geographical indications and designations of origin for agricultural products and foodstuffs of 14 July 1992, and in particular Article 14 thereof. [original footnote omitted]

7.526 This ensures that the rights conferred by a trademark registration against "all third parties" and uses of "any sign" do not prevail over a third party using a registered GI in accordance with its registration. It does not limit the rights conferred by a trademark registration against any other third party.[451] The same applies to trademarks protected under the national laws of the EC member States: due to the principle of the primacy of Community legislation, a trademark owner's rights cannot prevail over a third party using a GI registered under the Regulation in accordance with its registration. The rights conferred by a trademark registration against other third parties are not affected.

7.527 Accordingly, the trademark owner's right provided by trademark legislation in the implementation of Article 16.1 of the TRIPS Agreement, in principle, cannot be exercised against a person who uses a registered GI in accordance with its registration where the trademark is subject to Article 14(2) of the Regulation.

7.528 The phrase "[w]ith due regard to Community law" also refers to other legislation, such as labelling and misleading advertising legislation, which qualify the right to continue use of a trademark under Article 14(2). Conversely, the same legislation allows persons, including trademark owners, to take action against certain uses of a registered GI which are not covered by the GI registration.[452]

7.529 Paragraph 3 of Article 14 provides as follows:

> 3. A designation of origin or geographical indication shall not be registered where, in the light of a trade mark's reputation and renown and the length of time it has been used, registration is liable to mislead the consumer as to the true identity of the product.

7.530 This is a condition for the registration of a GI, as it provides for the refusal of registration of a GI that is liable to mislead the consumer as to the true identity of the product in light of certain factors relevant to a prior trademark. This, in effect, provides that *a prior trademark may prevail* over a later application for GI registration under certain conditions.

---

[448] European Communities' response to Panel question No. 138. The "Community Trademark Regulation" refers to Council Regulation (EC) No. 40/94 on the Community trade mark, as amended by Council Regulation (EC) No. 1992/2003 and Council Regulation (EC) No. 422/2004, set out in Exhibit COMP-7. The "First Trademark Directive" refers to the First Council Directive 89/104/EEC to approximate the laws of the member States relating to trade marks, set out in Exhibit COMP-6.

[449] Article 9 of the Community Trademark Regulation and Article 5 of the First Trademark Directive.

[450] Article 142 of the original Council Regulation (EC) No. 40/94 was renumbered Article 159 by Article 156(5) of Council Regulation (EC) No. 1992/2003.

[451] European Communities' first written submission, para. 317; response to Panel question No. 76; rebuttal submission, para. 336.

[452] European Communities' response to Panel question No. 140.

7.531 The European Communities argues that Article 14(3) of the Regulation, together with the criteria for registrability of trademarks applied under EC law, prevent the registration of a GI, use of which would result in a likelihood of confusion with a prior trademark. The United States disagrees. The Panel will consider this factual issue below.

(c) Article 14(3) of the Regulation
(i) main arguments of the parties

7.532 The United States submits that the Panel's task is to make an objective assessment of the facts, including with respect to the meaning of Article 14(3) of the Regulation. It argues that the European Communities' interpretation is irreconcilable with the way in which the terms included in this provision have been interpreted in other provisions.

7.533 The United States argues that it is no defence that the number of trademarks deprived of the right provided for in Article 16.1 of the TRIPS Agreement may be small (a fact that it does not concede). Trademarks can incorporate certain geographical elements. If that geographical name subsequently qualifies for GI protection under the Regulation, it will inhibit the ability of the trademark owner from preventing confusing uses. Non-geographical names can be registered as GIs under the Regulation. There are actual examples of geographical names registered as trademarks in the European Communities without distinctiveness acquired through use.[453]

7.534 The United States argues that Article 14(3) is the sole provision in the Regulation that addresses the confusing use of registered GIs vis-à-vis trademarks and it does not satisfy the obligations under Article 16.1 of the TRIPS Agreement. Article 16.1 provides a right owed to the owner of any valid registered trademark but Article 14(3) of the Regulation is limited to a subset of trademarks by its reference to "a trade mark's reputation and renown and the length of time it has been used." There is no guidance in the Regulation with respect to this standard.[454] A seminar presentation by an EC official in March 2004 characterized this as a requirement of "long use" and the Commission Guide to the Regulation also explains Article 14 without referring to likelihood of confusion.[455] The criteria in Article 14(3) are different from, and more restrictive than, those in Article 16.1. Had the Regulation been intended to implement Article 16.1, why did it use language not found in Article 16.1 that was plainly more restrictive?[456] The United States refers to the opinion of the Committee on Legal Affairs and the Internal Market of the European Parliament on the Commission's proposal to insert the current text of Article 14(2). That Committee had proposed an addition to Article 14(2) which would have subjected the Regulation to the right to bring proceedings for trademark infringement but this was not accepted by the Commission.[457]

7.535 The United States argues that the threshold prerequisites of reputation, renown, and length of time used are factors generally used to determine the scope of protection given to "well-known" or "famous" trademarks under Article 6*bis* of the Paris Convention (1967) and Articles 16.2 and 16.3 of the TRIPS Agreement. They correspond to the factors used for this purpose in the Joint Recommendation Concerning Provisions on the Protection of Well-Known Marks adopted by the Assembly of the Paris Union and the General Assembly of

---

[453] United States' rebuttal submission, paras. 167-170; second oral statement, paras. 74-75.

[454] The United States' first written submission refers to a trademark that has been used for a "long" time and has "considerable" reputation and renown: see paras. 158-159. Its first oral statement refers to trademarks of a "certain" reputation or "particular" renown, and used for "any" length of time: see para. 52.

[455] Exhibits US-23 and US-24.

[456] United States' rebuttal submission, paras. 143-144.

[457] United States' first written submission, paras. 166-169. The Opinion (document 2002/0066(CNS) dated 10 September 2002) is reproduced in Exhibit US-21 and attached to the Report of the Committee on Agriculture and Rural Development (document A5-0375/2002 dated 6 November 2002) reproduced in Exhibit COMP-14. The United States also cites certain statements by the Advocate-General of the European Court of Justice and the European Commission that Article 14(2) envisages "coexistence" of registered GIs with a valid prior trademark. This issue has been considered at para. 7.521.

WIPO in 1999.[458] A statement of Ministerial reasoning in Hungary indicated that its rule on the protection of a prior well-known mark corresponds to the ground for refusal of a GI registration in Article 14(3) of the Regulation. The Community Trademark Regulation and Trademark Directive refer to "reputation" in their provisions on rights to prevent confusing uses of signs on dissimilar goods. The interpretation of that factor by the European Court of Justice and the practice of the Office for Harmonization in the Internal Market indicate at the very least uninterrupted use for a considerable number of years.[459] "Reputation" is not relevant in assessing likelihood of confusion in all cases, such as identical signs for identical goods. A trademark registered in only one EC member State without reputation, renown, or length of time of use would also fail the standard in Article 14(3) of the Regulation.[460]

7.536 The United States argues that Article 14(3) does not provide a right to the "owner of a trademark," as required by Article 16.1, but merely authorizes the EC authorities to decline registration of a GI in limited circumstances. Intellectual property rights are private rights.[461] Article 14(3) does not afford a right to prevent uses as the trademark owner cannot necessarily tell, at the time of registration of the GI, whether its subsequent use will be confusing. For example, a GI may be used in a "trademark like manner," in translation or in a manner that emphasizes certain of its aspects or letters in a way that causes a likelihood of confusion.[462] The product specifications do not always limit the way in which GIs are used so that it is not always evident what use will be protected by registration.[463] In litigation pending in an EC member State, a Czech brewer has argued that registration grants the right to use the disputed names in translations. In other proceedings in an EC member State and outside the European Communities, one of the Czech beer GIs registered under the Regulation was considered confusingly similar to the trademark BUDWEISER.[464] The Czech beer GIs also show that registration is also possible outside the established procedures in the Regulation, such as through an accession treaty, in a manner that precludes objections based on Article 14(3) or any other provision.[465]

7.537 The United States argues that if an action can be brought under Article 230 of the EC Treaty for annulment of a registration, EC rules require it to be brought within two-months of the publication of the registration. Actual confusing uses of a registered GI may not become apparent within two-months and Article 16.1 of the TRIPS Agreement does not permit any such expiration. Referrals under the preliminary ruling procedure in Article 234 of the EC Treaty are also subject to the two-month deadline if the trademark owner could have challenged the registration under Article 230.[466] Even the European Communities does not assert that all trademark owners would have the opportunity to challenge a registration after the two-month deadline under Article 230. Registrations pursuant to accession protocols do not appear to be subject to challenge at all.

7.538 The United States argues that Articles 7(4) and 14(3) of the Regulation must be read cumulatively. If Articles 7(4) and 14(3) were both applied to all trademarks, the phrase "reputation and renown and length of time used" would be read out of Article 14(3). Articles 7(5)(b) and 14(3) must also be read cumulatively. If Article 14(3) is interpreted in the light of Article 7(5)(b), it still only applies to trademarks that satisfy the factors in Article 14(3). In any case, Article 7(5)(b) only applies where EC member States are unable to

---

[458] The Joint Recommendation is reproduced in Exhibit US-58.

[459] United States' rebuttal submission, paras. 146-152.

[460] United States' second oral statement, para. 85.

[461] United States' first written submission, para. 54; rebuttal submission, para. 136.

[462] United States' first oral statement, paras. 54-55; rebuttal submission, para. 131.

[463] United States' second oral statement, para. 78. The United States provides copies of the applications for the following registered GIs: "Timoleague Brown Pudding," "Lausitzer Leinöl," "Kanterkaas," "Kanternagelkass," "Kanterkomijnekass" and "Newcastle Brown Ale." The summaries of product specifications show labelling requirements that are either "PGI" or the protected terms themselves. These are reproduced in Exhibit US-77.

[464] United States' response to Panel question No. 137.

[465] United States' response to Panel question No. 67.

[466] United States' rebuttal submission, paras. 138-140; second oral statement, para. 83.

agree.[467] Article 7(4) is insufficient to implement Article 16.1 of the TRIPS Agreement in the registration procedure because the European Communities does not consider that Article 16.1 confers a right of objection. In any case, there is no right of objection under the Article 17 procedure or where GIs are registered through an act of accession. The United States also argues that it is insufficient because it is not available on a non-discriminatory basis. This argument has been considered earlier.[468]

7.539 The United States argues that Community law on labelling, advertising and unfair competition do not offer trademark owners the standard of protection required by Article 16.1 of the TRIPS Agreement. For example, a right to prevent injurious, deceptive advertising is no substitute for the right to prevent confusing uses of an identical or similar sign.[469]

7.540 The European Communities argues that, as a factual matter, the risk of registration of a GI confusingly similar to a prior trademark is very limited due to the criteria for registrability of trademarks applied under EC law. Moreover, Article 14(3) of the Regulation, if properly interpreted, is sufficient to prevent the registration of any confusing GIs.[470] The complainant bears the burden of proving that its interpretation of Article 14(3) is the only reasonable one and that the European Communities' interpretation is not reasonable or that the provision is being applied in a manner which results in the registration of confusing GIs.[471]

7.541 The European Communities argues that the criteria for the registrability of trademarks limit *a priori* the possibility of conflicts between GIs and earlier trademarks. Geographical names are primarily non-distinctive and, as such, are not apt for registration as trademarks. Their use may also be deceptive insofar as they are used for goods that do not originate in the location that they designate. Under EC law, they may only be registered as a trademark where the geographical name is not currently associated, and it can reasonably be assumed that it will not be associated in the future, with the product concerned; or where the name has acquired distinctiveness through use.[472]

7.542 The European Commission considers that the criteria listed in Article 14(3) of the Regulation are not exhaustive, so that other relevant criteria may be taken into account in order to assess whether the registration of the GI will result in a likelihood of confusion, such as the similarity between the signs or between the goods concerned. The likelihood of confusion will depend to a large extent on the degree of distinctiveness which the trademark has acquired through use. A trademark consisting of a GI, which has never been used or has no reputation or renown, should not have been registered in the first place because it would lack the required distinctiveness.[473] The length of time a trademark has been used does not limit Article 14(3) to cases where the trademark has been used for a long time as it is conceivable that a trademark which has been used for a relatively short period of time may have become strongly distinctive through other means, e.g. publicity.[474]

7.543 The European Communities submits that reputation, renown, and length of time of use are not threshold prerequisites under Article 14(3) of the Regulation but are criteria for assessing whether the GI is misleading. They are relevant for the purposes of establishing likelihood of confusion even where a trademark is not a "well-known" mark. Reputation functions as a threshold pre-requisite in the context of the "anti-dilution" provisions in the Community Trademark Regulation and the Trademark Directive but that would not be justified in a situation involving signs for similar goods. There is no credible evidence that it functions this way under Article 14(3): the presentation cited by the United States is oversimplified and has no legal

[467] United States' rebuttal submission, paras. 160-164.

[468] United States' rebuttal submission, para. 137.

[469] United States' second oral statement, para. 81.

[470] European Communities' first written submission, paras. 275-277.

[471] European Communities' first written submission, para. 292; rebuttal submission, paras. 271-276.

[472] European Communities' first written submission, paras. 278-285; rebuttal submission, para. 270.

[473] European Communities' first written submission, paras. 286-291.

[474] European Communities' response to Panel question No. 68.

authority; the Commission's Guide to the Regulation repeats verbatim the working of Article 14(3) and alludes to other cases of conflicts in Article 13(1); and the provision of Hungary's law cited by the United States does not implement the Regulation.[475]

7.544 The European Communities informs the Panel that the only instance in which Article 14(3) has been applied was the registration of "Bayerisches Bier" as a GI. There was no suggestion that this decision was based on the fact that the trademarks concerned were not famous enough or had not been used for long enough. The complainants have not identified an example of a GI which gives rise to a likelihood of confusion with an earlier trademark. Registration covers only the term in the specification and not its translations into other languages unless the term is the same in translation. The three Czech beer GIs also contain a unique endorsement that they apply "without prejudice to any beer trademark or other rights existing in the European Union on the date of accession."[476]

7.545 The European Communities argues that Article 14(3) requires the EC authorities to refuse registrations and does not allow for a margin of discretion. It can be invoked before the courts after registration of a GI, including in trademark infringement proceedings brought against a user of a GI. This applies to registrations under the ordinary procedure in Article 6 or the "fast-track" procedure in Article 17. A trademark owner may raise the invalidity of the measure before the courts under the preliminary ruling procedure in Article 234 of the EC Treaty. Depending on the factual circumstances of each case, a trademark owner may also have standing to bring an action in annulment under Article 230 of the EC Treaty, if a GI registration were considered to affect adversely specific substantive trademark rights. A two-month time limit applies to the action in annulment and, in specific circumstances, may also apply to the preliminary ruling procedure.[477] Under both procedures, judicial review is available on points of fact and law. The cancellation procedure is set out in Article 11a of the Regulation and the grounds mentioned in Articles 11 and 11a are exhaustive.[478]

7.546 The European Communities notes that Article 7(4) of the Regulation provides that an objection is admissible if it "shows that the registration of the name proposed would jeopardize the existence ... of a mark." It argues that this language is broad enough to encompass any instance of likelihood of confusion with any mark. Logically, Article 14(3) must permit registration to be refused in such cases. Article 7(5)(b) refers expressly to a decision having regard to the "likelihood of confusion."[479]

7.547 The European Communities argues that, in principle, a GI which has been found not to be confusing *per se* following the assessment required by Article 14(3) should not subsequently give rise to confusion.[480] In its view, GIs and trademarks can be presented in a similar fashion. Whether or not a particular sign falls within the scope of a particular GI registration is a factual question to be resolved by the courts on a case-by-case basis.[481]

7.548 The European Communities argues that Community law provides the means to prevent use of a registered GI in a confusing manner. Failure to comply with the product specifications in the registration may lead to cancellation. The right conferred by registration does not extend to other names or signs not in the registration. Registration does not cover translations. A presentation of a GI in a mutilated or deformed manner may be deemed different from the registered sign and not protected. Use of a GI is subject to the Community

---

475 European Communities' second oral statement, paras. 163-172.

476 European Communities' rebuttal submission, paras. 286-293; response to Panel question No. 142.

477 European Communities' responses to Australia's question Nos. 2 and 3 after the second substantive meeting.

478 European Communities' responses to Panel question Nos. 67 and 142; rebuttal submission, paras. 294-297; second oral statement, paras. 174-179.

479 European Communities' first written submission, para. 336; response to Panel question No. 68; rebuttal submission, paras. 282-285.

480 European Communities' response to Panel question No. 137.

481 European Communities' second oral statement, paras. 182-184.

directives on labelling, presentation and advertising of foodstuffs and on misleading advertising and the EC member States' unfair competition laws.[482]

7.549 The European Communities argues that few, if any, Members provide a remedy to prevent confusing use of a registered trademark without first obtaining cancellation, invalidation or revocation of the trademark registration. In the same way, Community law does not provide a remedy to prevent use of a registered GI on the grounds that it is confusing, although the trademark owner may request a judicial ruling that the GI registration is invalid on those grounds.[483]

(ii) main arguments of third parties

7.550 Argentina, Brazil, India and Mexico indicated, in response to a question from the Panel, that they were not aware of any GIs registered under the Regulation that were identical or confusingly similar to a trademark owned by their respective nationals and protected in the European Communities.[484]

7.551 Brazil argues that Article 16.1 of the TRIPS Agreement deals with trademarks in general and not only with those referred to in the narrow terms of Article 14(3) of the Regulation, which refers to the trademark's reputation, renown, and the length of time it has been used, and its liability to mislead the consumer as to the true identity of the product.[485]

7.552 New Zealand argues that Article 14(3) conditions the rights of a prior registered trademark owner on certain factors, such as reputation, renown and length of time of use, for which there is no basis in Article 16.1 of the TRIPS Agreement.[486]

7.553 Chinese Taipei argues that Article 14(3) of the Regulation only prevents the registration of a trademark if it fulfils the conditions of reputation, renown and length of time of use. This provision negates the right granted to trademark owners pursuant to Article 16.1 of the TRIPS Agreement.[487]

(iii) consideration by the Panel

7.554 The United States does not take issue in this dispute with trademarks protected later in time than a GI. Therefore, there is no need to consider Article 14(1) of the Regulation. Moreover, it does not take issue in this dispute with the *dates* for establishing which trademarks are considered earlier than a GI under Article 14(2) of the Regulation. Therefore, there is no need to consider that issue either.

7.555 The United States challenges coexistence under the Regulation "as such." It relies on the fact that Article 14(2) of the Regulation, on its face, can apply to certain trademarks and, when it does, the Regulation will limit the right of the owner of such a trademark against the use of a GI.[488]

7.556 The parties largely agree on the factual implications, in principle, of the application of Article 14(2). It allows the continued use of a trademark on certain conditions but, at the same time, the Regulation confers a positive right to use a GI which prevents the owner of a trademark from exercising the right conferred by that

---

[482] European Communities' rebuttal submission, paras. 298-303; response to Panel question No. 63.

[483] European Communities' second oral statement, para. 181; response to Panel question No. 139.

[484] See their comments in Annex C at paras. 19, 37, 106 and 120.

[485] Annex C, para. 29.

[486] Annex C, paras. 148-152.

[487] Annex C, para. 178.

[488] Although Article 14(2) of the Regulation is drafted as an exception to GI protection in Article 13, it is not disputed that in most of the situations described in Article 13, in which Article 14(2) applies, the use of the GI would otherwise constitute infringement of the trademark. If Article 14(3) were able to prevent the registration of any GI, use of which could otherwise constitute a trademark infringement, Article 14(2) would be redundant in all of these situations.

trademark against a person who uses a registered GI in accordance with its registration. The particular right of a trademark owner at issue is the right to prevent uses of a sign that would result in a likelihood of confusion, which is discussed in paragraphs 7.598 to 7.603 below.

7.557 The European Communities' first defence is that Article 14(3) can prevent the registration of any GI which would subject a prior trademark to Article 14(2), where the GI could be used in a manner that would result in a likelihood of confusion. This is a factual issue for the Panel to decide. This involves matters of interpretation of an EC Regulation which forms part of the European Communities' domestic law. It is necessary for the Panel to make an objective assessment of the meaning of this provision, although solely for the purpose of determining the European Communities' compliance with its WTO obligations.[489]

7.558 As a preliminary remark, the Panel does not consider that this defence is necessarily contradicted by the European Communities' other defences that it is fully entitled and even required under the TRIPS Agreement to apply its coexistence regime, regardless of whether a GI would otherwise infringe the rights in a prior trademark. However, given that this is the European Communities' view of its rights and obligations under the TRIPS Agreement, it would seem coincidental if Article 14(3) of the Regulation could operate in a way that a GI would never, in fact, otherwise infringe the rights in a prior trademark.

7.559 Turning to the text of Article 14(3) of the Regulation, the Panel's first observation is that it requires GI registration to be refused where it would be "liable to mislead the consumer as to the true identity of the product." This is limited to liability to mislead as to a single issue, and not with respect to anything else.

7.560 The Panel's second observation is that Article 14(3) specifically prohibits GI registration "in light of a trade mark's reputation and renown and the length of time it has been used." It is clear that these factors must all be taken into account in the application of Article 14(3). It is difficult to imagine how Article 14(3) could be applied without some consideration of the similarity of the signs and goods as well.[490] However, even if these factors are not exhaustive, and even if they do not require strong reputation, wide renown and long use, they indicate that the scope of Article 14(3) is limited to a subset of trademarks which, as a minimum, excludes trademarks with no reputation, renown or use. Article 14(3) does not prevent the registration of a GI on the basis that its use would affect any prior trademark outside that subset.

7.561 The Panel's third observation on the text of Article 14(3) is that it does not refer to use (of the GI) or to likelihood or to confusion, when other provisions of the Regulation do. Articles 7(5)(b), 12b(3) and 12d(3) permit refusal of a GI registration "having regard to" or "taking account of" factors including the "actual likelihood of confusion" and the "actual risk of confusion."[491] This indicates that the standard in Article 14(3) that registration would "mislead the consumer as to the true identity of the product" is intended to apply in a narrower set of circumstances than the trademark owner's right to prevent use that would result in a likelihood of confusion.[492]

7.562 For these reasons, the Panel considers that the United States has made a prima facie case that Article 14(3) of the Regulation cannot prevent all situations from occurring in which Article 14(2) would, in fact, limit the rights of a trademark owner.

---

[489] In this regard, the Panel recalls its comments at para. 7.55.

[490] Article 14(3) presupposes the applicability of Article 13, which requires a consideration of the similarity of the goods and signs.

[491] Articles 7(5)(b) and 12d(3) do not apply to GIs located in third countries. To the extent that they apply to GIs located in the European Communities, they only apply in limited circumstances where there is an admissible objection from an EC member State, other than the one which transmitted the application, or a third country, and they do not provide that the actual likelihood or risk of confusion is an absolute ground for refusal.

[492] The TRIPS Agreement does not define the terms "likelihood of confusion" and "mislead the public as to the geographical origin." These terms define the scope of protection provided for in Articles 16.1 and 22.2 of the TRIPS Agreement and apply in a very wide range of factual situations. Therefore, the Panel considers it inappropriate to embark on a detailed interpretation of these or similar terms unless necessary for the purposes of the resolution of the dispute, which is not the case here.

7.563 Consistent with this view, it can be noted that the European Communities specifically rejected a proposal by a Committee of the European Parliament to amend Article 14(2) so as to subject it to the trademark owners' rights when Article 14 was amended in April 2003.[493] This at least suggests that Article 14(3) was considered different from a blanket protection of trademark rights.

7.564 The European Communities has submitted that the United States' interpretation of Article 14(3) would conflict with Article 7(4), which provides that a statement of objection shall be admissible *inter alia* if it shows that the proposed GI registration would jeopardize the existence of a mark. It asserts that this language encompasses any instance of likelihood of confusion between the proposed GI and a prior trademark.[494] It has not explained why the text does not set forth the likelihood of confusion standard, when the following provision of the Regulation in Article 7(5)(b) does. The contrast is marked. Article 7(5)(b) sets out a procedure to reach agreement in cases where an objection is admissible, which appears to indicate that it contains a lower standard than the ground for objection in Article 7(4).

7.565 The European Communities has submitted that the criteria for registrability of a trademark limit *a priori* the risk of GIs being confused with a prior trademark, but it does not submit that they completely eliminate that risk. The evidence shows that signs eligible for protection as GIs can and have been registered as trademarks in the Community.[495] The European Communities has not shown that the criteria for registrability of trademarks can anticipate adequately a situation in which a GI could be used in a way that results in a likelihood of confusion with a trademark, wherever Article 14(3) of the Regulation does not provide for refusal of registration of a GI. Those criteria and Article 14(3) would have to offset each other in every case. However, Article 14(2) and (3) apply to trademarks that are already protected. They cannot apply to signs which do not satisfy the trademark registrability criteria, either because they are geographical names or for whatever other reason, and have been refused registration, are subject to invalidation or are otherwise unprotected. These signs are filtered out before Article 14 of the GI Regulation comes into play. Given that Article 14(3) applies to a subset of protected trademarks, those to which it does *not* apply have by definition already satisfied the trademark registrability criteria.

7.566 There is also the question of how Article 14(3) can protect a trademark owner's right to prevent uses which occur subsequent to GI registration. In response to a question from the Panel as to whether Article 14(3) could be invoked if use of the GI would otherwise infringe the trademark *subsequent* to GI registration, the European Communities submitted that it could.[496] The parties then made various submissions on this point, based on which the Panel makes the following observations:

(a) the Regulation does not refer to invalidation under Article 14(3). It sets out cancellation procedures in Articles 11 and 11a, the grounds for which do not appear to relate to the improper application of Article 14(3). If invalidation procedures are possible, it would be as a matter of general Community law under the EC Treaty;

(b) Article 230 of the EC Treaty provides a procedure for a direct challenge to the validity of a Community measure before the Court of First Instance of the European Communities on the condition that the applicant "is directly and individually concerned" by the measure. It is not submitted by any party that all trademark owners can satisfy that condition. Further, this procedure

[493] The Committee proposal is set out in Exhibits COMP-14 and US-21.

[494] European Communities' response to Panel question No. 68; rebuttal submission, paras. 282-285.

[495] For example, the following are registered Community trademarks: CALABRIA for pasta; DERBY for milk and chocolate based products; WIENERWALD for prepared meals, condiments and other goods and services. Extracts of registrations are reproduced in Exhibits US-74, US-75 and US-76, respectively.

[496] European Communities' response to Panel question No. 67; see also its rebuttal submission, paras. 270 and 296. The Panel's findings do not imply any view on whether a requirement to seek GI invalidation as a condition precedent to obtaining relief against trademark infringement would be consistent with the enforcement obligations under the TRIPS Agreement.

is subject to a two-month time limit which could render it unavailable to certain trademark owners who did satisfy that condition[497];

(c) Article 234 of the EC Treaty provides a procedure for an indirect challenge to a Community measure under which a court of an EC member State can refer a question to the European Court of Justice for a preliminary ruling. This procedure could be invoked in a trademark infringement proceeding to obtain invalidation of a GI registration. It is not clear in what circumstances this procedure is available to a trademark owner who could have invoked the Article 230 procedure. The procedure under Article 234 would only be available where the court of the EC member State considered the question of validity of the GI necessary to resolve the trademark infringement action. In any case, the decision not to refuse a registration under Article 14(3) of the Regulation would be interpreted in the preliminary ruling as at the time of that decision, and not at the time of the subsequent allegedly infringing use[498]; and

(d) Article 14(3) may not be applicable in all cases as it is not clear whether GIs registered in accordance with the terms of an Act of Accession to the European Union (there are three such GIs) can be invalidated on the basis of that provision.[499]

7.567 In light of these observations, the Panel considers that there is no evidence to show that it is possible to seek invalidation of a GI registration under Article 14(3) in *all* cases in which use of a GI would otherwise be found to infringe a prior trademark. In those cases where it is not possible, it would be necessary for the owner of a prior trademark to be able to anticipate, at the time of the proposed GI registration, all subsequent uses of the proposed GI that would result in a likelihood of confusion. There is no reason to believe that this is possible. The evidence submitted to the Panel shows that GI registrations under the Regulation simply refer to names without limiting the way in which they are used. Indeed, it became apparent in the course of the proceedings that what the United States regards as "trademark-like use" is, in the European Communities, considered perfectly legitimate use as a GI.[500]

7.568 The European Communities has submitted that the food labelling and misleading advertising directives and unfair competition laws of the EC member States also prevent confusing uses. We understand, and the European Communities does not deny, that this is only possible where the use is not in accordance with the GI registration. In any event, the scope of the directives is narrower than that of the GI Regulation and the standards which they apply are different from the right of a trademark owner to prevent use which would result in a likelihood of confusion, for the following reasons:

(a) the food labelling directive only applies to the labelling of foodstuffs to be delivered as such to the ultimate consumer and certain aspects relating to the presentation and advertising thereof. It provides that "labelling and methods used must not be such as could mislead the purchaser to a material degree, particularly ... as to the characteristics of the foodstuff and, in particular, as to its

[497] United States' comment on EC response to Panel question No. 142 and Exhibits US-99 and US-100; European Communities' second oral statement, para. 177.

[498] United States' comment on EC response to Panel question No. 142 and Exhibits US-100 and US-101; European Communities' second oral statement, para. 178.

[499] See European Communities' response to Panel question No. 142(c) and contrast the United States' comment on that response and Exhibit US-101.

[500] The United States submitted copies of the packaging of cheeses bearing the GIs "Esrom," "Bitto," "Bra" and "Tomme de Savoie" in Exhibit US-52. The European Communities submitted the approved specifications for these GIs in Exhibits EC-99 through EC-102. See the European Communities' response to Panel question No. 140 and the United States' comment on that response.

nature, identity, properties, composition, quantity, durability, origin or provenance, method of manufacture or production"[501]; and

(b) the misleading advertising directive applies to "any advertising which in any way, including presentation, deceives or is likely to deceive the persons to whom it is addressed or whom it reaches and which, by reason of its deceptive nature is likely to affect their economic behaviour or which, for those reasons, injures or is likely to injure a competitor."[502]

7.569 The unfair competition laws of the EC member States apply subject to the terms of registration under the Regulation, due to the primacy of Community law. It is not clear to what extent these laws apply in addition to the Regulation but, to the extent that they do, they use various standards, some of which require deception, which is narrower than confusion, and some of which appear only to apply the misleading standard which is embodied in the Regulation itself.[503]

7.570 The United States also refers to specific cases in which the Regulation has been applied in support of its claim, as set out in the following paragraphs.

7.571 Article 14(3) of the Regulation has only been applied once. This was the case of "Bayerisches Bier," which was registered as a protected geographical indication in 2001 subject to the proviso that the use of certain prior trademarks, for example, BAVARIA and HØKER BAJER, was permitted to continue under Article 14(2). The GI refers to a beer and the trademarks are registered in respect of beer. The GI and the trademarks are, respectively, the words "Bavaria" or "Bavarian Beer" rendered in the German, English and Danish languages. Upon its registration, the EC Council concluded that the GI would not mislead the public as to the identity of the product, which is the standard embodied in Article 14(3) of the Regulation.[504]

7.572 The United States alleges that the GI "Bayerisches Bier" could be used in a manner that would result in a likelihood of confusion with these prior trademarks.[505] In response to a direct question from the Panel, the European Communities did not deny this specific allegation. It only responded that "in principle" a name registered following the assessment required by Article 14(3) "should not give rise to confusion when used subsequently" and submitted that "in practice" this may happen only when the registered name is used together with other signs or as part of a combination of signs. This was a conspicuous choice of words because in the same response it commented in detail on two other specific cases which it considered irrelevant to the dispute.[506]

7.573 The United States also alleges that three Czech beer GIs, "Budějovické pivo," "Českobudějovické pivo" and "Budějovický měšt'anský var" could be used in a manner that would result in a likelihood of

---

501 Articles 1 and 2(1)(a)(i) of Directive 2000/13/EC of the European Parliament and of the Council on the approximation of the laws of the Member States relating to the labelling, presentation and advertising of foodstuffs, referred to in the European Communities' responses to Panel question No. 63, fn 38; United States' comments on EC response to Panel question No. 140, fn. 74, and reproduced in Exhibit EC-30.

502 Article 2(2) of Council Directive 84/450/EEC relating to the approximation of the laws, regulations and administrative provisions of the Member States concerning misleading advertising, referred to in European Communities' responses to Panel question No. 63, fn 39, United States' comments on EC response to Panel question No. 140, fn. 74, and reproduced in Exhibit EC-31.

503 See information supplied by the European Communities and some of its member States to the Council for TRIPS in the review under Article 24.2 of the TRIPS Agreement, document IP/C/W/117/Add.10, reproduced in Exhibit EC-29. The European Communities did not supply information on the unfair competition laws of its ten new member States.

504 Council Regulation (EC) No. 1347/2001 reproduced in Exhibits US-41 and EC-9.

505 See the United States' response to Panel question No. 137.

506 The European Communities submitted twice that the EC Council had concluded that the registration of this GI would not lead to a likelihood of confusion with these prior trademarks but this is different from the EC Council's conclusion as stated in the decision on registration. The European Communities later indicated in response to a question from the Panel that the EC Council's conclusion was that the signs were not sufficiently similar to mislead the public, which is closer to the wording of the conclusion as stated in the decision, but not necessarily a likelihood of confusion: see European Communities' first written submission, para. 288, fn. 140; rebuttal submission, para. 287; and responses to Panel questions Nos. 137 and 143 and compare Council Regulation (EC) No. 1347/2001 reproduced in Exhibits US-41 and EC-9 and the Commission Guide to the Regulation (August 2004 edition, p. 12) in Exhibit EC-64.

confusion with the prior trademarks BUDWEISER and BUD, registered in respect of beer.[507] The evidence shows that a court in a non-EC WTO Member found a reasonable probability that a substantial number of persons would be confused if the marks BUDEJOVICKY BUDVAR depicted in a special script, and BUDWEISER and BUD, were used together in relation to beer in a normal and fair manner and in the ordinary course of business, particularly the mark BUD.[508] However, courts in two other non-EC WTO Members found that the use of "Budìjovický Budvar" on specific beer labels did not give rise to a likelihood of confusion with the trademarks BUDWEISER and BUD, registered in respect of beer.[509] In response to a direct question from the Panel, the European Communities did not deny that these GIs could be used in a manner that would result in a likelihood of confusion with these prior trademarks. Instead, it pointed to an endorsement on the three GI registrations that they apply "without prejudice to any beer trademark or other rights existing in the European Union on the date of accession."[510] This might imply that it accepts a likelihood of confusion, but considers that there are other means besides Article 14(3) to deal with that. It also argued that these GIs were outside the terms of reference but the United States expressly clarified that it referred to them only as evidence in support of its claim and did not challenge these individual registrations in this panel proceeding.[511]

7.574 There appears to be an inconsistency between the European Communities' position that Article 14(3) of the Regulation, in practice, prevents the registration of GIs, use of which would result in a likelihood of confusion with a prior trademark, and its decision to avoid contesting that there may be circumstances in which the four specific GIs referred to above could be used which would not result in a likelihood of confusion with these specific prior trademarks.

7.575 For the above reasons, the Panel considers that the European Communities has not rebutted the United States' prima facie case that Article 14(3) of the Regulation cannot prevent all situations from occurring in which a trademark would be subject to Article 14(2) and, hence, in which the Regulation would limit the rights of the owner of such a trademark.

7.576 The Panel will now proceed to examine whether the TRIPS Agreement requires Members to make available to trademark owners rights against the use of GIs.

(d) Relationship between protection of GIs and prior trademarks under the TRIPS Agreement

(i) main arguments of the parties

7.577 The United States argues that the ordinary meaning of the terms used in Article 16.1 show that the rights to prevent certain uses are exclusive, are valid against all third parties and cover identical or similar signs, including GIs.[512]

7.578 The United States argues that the context shows that the TRIPS Agreement explicitly clarifies the relationship among individual rights in GIs and trademarks, where there is a need. For instance, Article 22.3 explicitly provides for the refusal or invalidation of trademark registrations that contain or consist of a GI, in certain circumstances. In contrast, Article 24.5 does not explicitly set out an exception to trademark rights but

---

507 The evidence indicates that these trademarks are registered in at least two EC member States and rights to them appear to have been acquired through use in another EC member State: see Exhibits US-53, Section 3.6; US-51, para. 26; and US-82.

508 Judgement of the High Court of South Africa in *Budweiser Budvar National Corporation v Anheuser-Busch Corporation*, dated 3 December 2003, reproduced in Exhibit US-82.

509 Judgement of the Federal Court of Australia in *Anheuser-Busch, Inc. v Budìjovický Budvar, Národní Podnik,* [2002] FCA 390 (dated 5 April 2002); judgement of the Court of Appeal of New Zealand in *Anheuser Busch Incorporated v Budweiser Budwar National Corporation & Ors* [2002] NZCA 264 (dated 19 September 2002) reproduced in Exhibits EC-117 and EC-118, respectively.

510 European Communities' rebuttal submission, paras. 286-293; response to Panel question No. 142.

511 United States' response to Panel question No. 137 and European Communities' comment on that response. See the Panel's comments on individual registrations at para. 7.20.

512 United States' first written submission, paras. 137-140.

only creates an exception to GI protection.[513] Compromises between rights to exclude, including simultaneous uses of identical place names, are spelt out in the text. For instance, Article 23.3 provides for homonymous GIs for wines. There is no explicit provision for simultaneous use of a GI and a prior trademark where use of the GI would be inconsistent with the rights under Article 16.1.[514]

7.579 The United States submits that Article 24.5 is clearly titled as an exception to GI protection. It protects certain grandfathered trademarks but is not an exception to trademark protection.[515] It does not create any positive rights.[516] The phrase "validity of the registration of a trademark" must be read in connection with the legal authority accorded by trademark registration, which is the right provided under Article 16.1, in addition to rights under domestic law. Trademark registration is virtually meaningless without the associated rights under Article 16.1. The drafting history shows that the predecessor of Article 24.5 in the Brussels Draft set out a simple prohibition against invalidation of registration. This became a requirement that Members not even "prejudice" the validity of the registration which is a more stringent requirement.[517] The obligations not to prejudice the "right to use a trademark" would include an obligation with respect to both registered trademarks and trademarks to which rights are acquired through use. If the owner cannot exclude confusing uses of identical or similar signs, the owner's ability to use the trademark for its purpose is severely prejudiced. The corresponding provision in the Brussels Draft did not refer to the right to use.[518]

7.580 The United States emphasizes the exclusivity of the rights provided for in Article 16.1. Exclusivity has been recognized as the core of a trademark right by the European Court of Justice and the United States Supreme Court.[519] A trademark can only fulfil its role of identifying an undertaking or the quality of goods if it is exclusive.[520] This is confirmed by Article 15.1.[521]

7.581 The United States argues that there is no conflict between Articles 16.1 and 22. It is possible to comply simultaneously with both.[522] A conflict may occur between right holders in an individual trademark and an individual GI, but this is not a conflict between obligations in the TRIPS Agreement.[523] If a trademark misleads consumers as to the origin of goods, its registration should be refused or invalidated.[524] Articles 16.1 and 22.3 can both be implemented in a way that gives each its full scope. They should be interpreted in a way that does not presume a conflict. If a trademark is misleading, its registration may be refused or invalidated. As long as the registration remains valid, it must provide the owner with the right to exclude others from confusing uses.[525]

7.582 The United States argues that the European Communities bears the burden of proof in relation to Article 24.5 because it asserts that provision as an affirmative defence to the claim under Article 16.1.[526]

7.583 The European Communities responds that this claim is unfounded.[527] The TRIPS Agreement recognizes trademarks and GIs as intellectual property rights on the same level, and confers no superiority to

513 United States' first written submission, paras. 141-142; first oral statement, para. 58.

514 United States' first written submission, para. 143.

515 United States' first oral statement, para. 59; second oral statement, para. 88.

516 United States' response to Panel question No. 145.

517 United States' first oral statement, para. 65; response to Panel question Nos. 76, 145 and 147.

518 United States' response to Panel question No. 76.

519 United States' first written submission, paras. 145-150.

520 United States' first oral statement, para. 67.

521 United States' rebuttal submission, para. 174; response to Panel question No. 76.

522 United States' response to Panel question No. 146.

523 United States' second oral statement, para. 71.

524 United States' response to Panel question No. 146.

525 United States' response to Panel question No. 79.

526 United States' response to Panel question No. 75(a); rebuttal submission, para. 173.

527 European Communities' first written submission, para. 269-273.

trademarks over GIs. The provisions of Section 3 of Part II on GI protection are not "exceptions" to the provision of Article 16.1 on trademark rights. The criteria for registrability of trademarks limit *a priori* the possibility of conflicts between GIs and trademarks but conflicts may arise. Article 16.1 does not address this issue. Rather, the boundary between GIs and trademarks is defined by Article 24.5 which provides for coexistence with earlier trademarks. Article 24.5 must be read with Article 22.3 and Article 23.2 which also provide protection to GIs vis-à-vis trademarks.[528] Section 2 of Part II cannot be applied without having regard to Section 3.[529]

7.584 The European Communities argues that Article 24.5 has two implications: (1) with respect to grandfathered trademarks (or applications): (a) Members are not allowed to prejudice the validity of the registration (or the eligibility of the application or the right to use the trademark), but (b) Members may prejudice other rights of the trademark owner, including in particular the right to prevent others from using the sign of which the trademark consists; and (2) with respect to other trademarks (or applications), Members may prejudice any right.[530]

7.585 The European Communities argues that the ordinary meaning of the word "prejudice" used in all three official versions includes the notion of "judge beforehand" but only the word in the English version includes the notion of "cause injury, damage or harm."[531] The phrase "validity of the registration" does not necessarily imply that the registration must confer exclusive rights vis-à-vis all third parties. The fact that the owner cannot prevent use of the same or a similar sign by the GI right holder does not mean that the registration is set aside. The phrase "the right to use a trademark" refers to the basic right of the trademark owner to use the trademark, whether it has been acquired through registration or use.[532] It is the right to use a sign, which is different from the right to prevent others from using the same or a similar sign. If that right were inherent in the term "validity of the registration," it would have been superfluous to refer to the "right to use a trademark" as well. If that right had been intended, the drafters would have referred to the "exclusive right to use a trademark." If that right were inherently exclusive, it would have been superfluous to provide in Article 16.1 that the owners of trademarks shall have exclusive rights. The drafting history shows that the Brussels Draft referred to the continued use of a GI as a trademark, which envisaged coexistence, in a separate provision from the predecessor to Article 24.5. Its transfer to Article 24.5 in the final version did not alter its meaning or purpose.[533]

7.586 The European Communities argues that Article 24.5 is drafted in mandatory terms and imposes self-standing obligations which go beyond those in Section 2 of Part II. This may be illustrated by the case of a Member which provides for the refusal or invalidation of registration of a trademark in terms broader than those in Article 22.3, or which prohibits the use of any trademark acquired by use in terms broader than those in Article 22.2. Both would be consistent with Section 2 of Part II but Article 24.5 would prevent either applying to prior trademarks. This would be an obligation arising exclusively under Article 24.5.[534]

7.587 The European Communities argues that if Article 24.5 did not allow coexistence, the protection of GIs provided under Section 3 of Part II would become pointless whenever there is a grandfathered trademark. The phrase "measures adopted to implement this Section" assumes that Members will continue to protect GIs notwithstanding the existence of grandfathered trademarks. Coexistence may not be a perfect solution to resolve conflicts between different types of intellectual property rights but there is no such perfect solution.[535] It is not an unusual solution, since coexistence is envisaged in Articles 23.2 (with respect to a GI and a trademark that is

---

[528] European Communities' first written submission, paras. 294-300.

[529] European Communities' rebuttal submission, paras. 306-307.

[530] European Communities' first written submission, para. 301.

[531] European Communities' comment on US response to Panel question No. 145.

[532] European Communities' first written submission, para. 305; response to Panel question No. 76.

[533] European Communities' response to Panel question No. 76; rebuttal submission, paras. 327-328.

[534] European Communities' response to Panel question No. 145.

[535] European Communities' first written submission, para. 307; response to Panel question No. 77.

not misleading), 23.3, 24.3 (where pre-existing protection provided for coexistence) 24.4 and 16.1 (vis-à-vis existing prior rights).[536] Article 24.5 embodies a compromise. The European Communities and other participants agreed to make it mandatory on the understanding that the trademark owners would have the right to use the trademark but not the right to exclude use by GI right holders.[537]

7.588 There is no "conflict" between Articles 16.1 and 22.3 but there is a potential "conflict" between Articles 16.1 and 22.2(a), and possibly 23.1. Article 22.2 confers on GI right holders the right to prevent certain uses of trademarks, which may conflict with the right of the trademark owner under Article 16.1 to prevent certain uses of signs. The simultaneous exercise of both rights would lead to a situation where neither the trademark owner nor the GI right holders could use the sign in question. Neither would be able to fulfil its purpose. This conflict is resolved by Articles 22.3, 23.2 and 24.5.[538]

7.589 The European Communities argues that only the object and purpose of the treaty as a whole is relevant to the general rule of treaty interpretation. To the extent that the exclusivity of a trademark is an object and purpose of the TRIPS Agreement, it submits that exclusivity is as essential to a GI or even more essential, because the choice of a GI is not arbitrary, unlike a trademark, and the establishment of a GI takes longer than a trademark.[539]

7.590 The European Communities argues that the complainant bears the burden of proof that a measure falls within the scope of the obligations provided in Article 16.1. Article 24.5 is not an exception but defines the boundary between the obligations in Article 16.1 and a Member's right to implement GI protection. It does not provide an exemption from an obligation but places a limit on the measures that Members must or may take when implementing GI protection under Section 3 of Part II. It confers a right to use a trademark, a right which owners of trademarks acquired through use do not have under Article 16.1 because rights the basis of use are optional under Article 16.1. It notes that the United States stated a claim under Article 24.5 in its request for establishment of a panel.[540]

(ii) main arguments of third parties

7.591 Argentina argues that coexistence is inconsistent with Articles 16.1 and 22.3 of the TRIPS Agreement. Article 24.5 sets out a cut-off date different from the one in the Regulation and does not provide for the possibility of limiting the trademark owner's right as the Regulation does. Article 24.4 determines the boundaries for alternatives available to Members in the implementation of measures relating to GI protection and its link to trademarks.[541]

7.592 Brazil argues GIs which are identical to trademarks are likely to create confusion and, consequently, may affect the value of trademarks. Article 16.1 of the TRIPS Agreement provides for a right that covers the use of any sign, and not only that of a trademark, which might cause confusion. The possibility of coexistence between a trademark and a GI is only acceptable in terms of Articles 24.5 and 16.1, read in conjunction, which mean that the use of a GI and the need to protect it must not be at the expense of both trademark owners and consumers, which may undermine the value of a trademark contrary to the "exclusive rights" of a trademark owner under Article 16.1.[542]

---

[536] European Communities' first written submission, para. 308; response to Panel question No. 76.

[537] European Communities' response to Panel question No. 147.

[538] European Communities' rebuttal submission, paras. 308-310; response to Panel question No. 146.

[539] European Communities' response to Panel question No. 76.

[540] European Communities' response to Panel question No. 75; rebuttal submission, paras. 312-315.

[541] Annex C, para. 5.

[542] Annex C, para. 30.

7.593 Colombia argues that, under the TRIPS Agreement, no form of protection is superior to another. Therefore, the Regulation cannot deny the right of the trademark owner under Article 16.1 of the TRIPS Agreement. Such denial constitutes a clear violation of WTO obligations.[543]

7.594 Mexico argues that the exclusive right in Article 16.1 of the TRIPS Agreement is severely nullified by Article 14(2) of the Regulation as it permits coexistence between a prior registered trademark and a later GI. The European Communities' explanation that coexistence is not the perfect solution is an inadequate justification but a recognition of inconsistency. By ignoring the "first in time, first in right" rule, the Regulation not only contravenes Article 24.5 of the TRIPS Agreement but also a recognized general principle of law.[544]

7.595 New Zealand argues that Article 16.1 of the TRIPS Agreement provides for a right against "all third parties." Despite an appearance of conflict between the rights in Articles 16.1 and 22.2, each must be read to the fullest extent permissible without conflicting with the other. Article 24.5 is a provision that resolves conflict by compromising this exclusivity, but in all other cases, the rights provided for in Articles 16.1 and 22.2 must both be upheld. Article 14(2) of the Regulation excludes users of a registered GI from the scope of "all third parties" against whom a trademark owner should be able to exercise rights, and is inconsistent with Article 16.1.[545]

7.596 Chinese Taipei argues that Articles 16.1 and 22.2 of the TRIPS Agreement must be given their full scope in a manner that would not cause conflict. The Regulation creates precisely such a conflict, rendering Article 16.1 inutile, as the right of trademark owners under that article is negated by coexistence under Article 14(2) of the Regulation. The result is the creation of a hierarchy in which GIs have a superior status than trademarks, which is not contemplated by the TRIPS Agreement.[546]

(iii) consideration by the Panel

7.597 The Panel will now proceed to examine whether the TRIPS Agreement requires Members to make available to trademark owners rights against the use of GIs. This involves two steps: first, we examine the right of trademark owners provided for in Article 16.1 of the TRIPS Agreement and then we continue by examining whether Article 24.5 provides authority to limit that right.

Article 16.1 of the TRIPS Agreement

7.598 Part II of the TRIPS Agreement contains minimum standards concerning the availability, scope and use of intellectual property rights. The first seven Sections of Part II contain standards relating to categories of intellectual property rights. Each Section sets out, as a minimum, the *subject matter* which is eligible for protection, the scope of the *rights conferred* by the relevant category of intellectual property and permitted *exceptions* to those rights.

7.599 Although each of the Sections in Part II provides for a different category of intellectual property, at times they refer to one another[547], as certain subject matter may be eligible for protection by more than one category of intellectual property. This is particularly apparent in the case of trademarks and GIs, both of which are, in general terms, forms of distinctive signs. The potential for overlap is expressly confirmed by Articles

543 Annex C, para. 102.

544 Annex C, para. 114.

545 Annex C, paras. 148-151.

546 Annex C, para. 178.

547 For instance, Article 25.2 of the TRIPS Agreement refers to more than one category of intellectual property, as does Article 4 of the IPIC Treaty, as incorporated by Article 35 of the TRIPS Agreement.

22.3 and 23.2, which provide for the refusal or invalidation of the registration of a trademark which contains or consists of a GI.[548]

7.600 Section 2 of Part II provides for the category of trademarks. Article 15.1 sets out the definition of the subject matter which is capable of constituting a trademark. These are signs that satisfy certain criteria. Article 16.1 sets out a right which must be conferred on the owner of a registered trademark, and which may also be acquired on the basis of use, as follows:

> 1. The owner of a registered trademark shall have the exclusive right to prevent all third parties not having the owner's consent from using in the course of trade identical or similar signs for goods or services which are identical or similar to those in respect of which the trademark is registered where such use would result in a likelihood of confusion. In case of the use of an identical sign for identical goods or services, a likelihood of confusion shall be presumed. The rights described above shall not prejudice any existing prior rights, nor shall they affect the possibility of Members making rights available on the basis of use.

7.601 The right which must be conferred on the owner of a registered trademark is set out in the first sentence of the text. There are certain limitations on that right which relate to use in the course of trade, the signs, the goods or services for which the signs are used and those with respect to which they are registered and the likelihood of confusion. The ordinary meaning of the text indicates that, basically, this right applies to use in the course of trade of identical or similar signs, on identical or similar goods, where such use would result in a likelihood of confusion. It does not specifically exclude use of signs protected as GIs.

7.602 The text of Article 16.1 stipulates that the right for which it provides is an "exclusive" right. This must signify more than the fact that it is a right to "exclude" others, since that notion is already captured in the use of the word "prevent." Rather, it indicates that this right belongs to the owner of the registered trademark alone, who may exercise it to prevent certain uses by "all third parties" not having the owner's consent. The last sentence provides for an exception to that right, which is that it shall not prejudice any existing prior rights. Otherwise, the text of Article 16.1 is unqualified.

7.603 Other exceptions to the right under Article 16.1 are provided for in Article 17 and possibly elsewhere in the TRIPS Agreement. However, there is no implied limitation vis-à-vis GIs in the text of Article 16.1 on the exclusive right which Members must make available to the owner of a registered trademark. That right may be exercised against a third party not having the owner's consent on the same terms, whether or not the third party uses the sign in accordance with GI protection, subject to any applicable exception.

<u>Article 24.5 of the TRIPS Agreement</u>

7.604 The parties have referred to Article 24.5 of the TRIPS Agreement. This appears in Section 3 of Part II, which provides for the category of GIs.[549] Article 24.5 provides as follows:

> 5. Where a trademark has been applied for or registered in good faith, or where rights to a trademark have been acquired through use in good faith either:
>
> (a) before the date of application of these provisions in that Member as defined in Part VI; or
>
> (b) before the geographical indication is protected in its country of origin;

[548] Articles 22.3 and 23.2, respectively.

[549] Section 3 of Part II consists of three articles: Articles 22, 23 and 24. Article 23 concerns only GIs for wines and spirits, which are not covered by the Regulation. Nevertheless, the meaning of that article is important in understanding Section 3 in general and Article 24 in particular. The Panel therefore refers to it in its examination, where that is helpful.

measures adopted to implement this Section shall not prejudice eligibility for or the validity of the registration of a trademark, or the right to use a trademark, on the basis that such a trademark is identical with, or similar to, a geographical indication.

7.605 The Panel must interpret this provision, like all other provisions of the covered agreements relevant to this dispute, in accordance with the customary rules of interpretation of public international law, as required by Article 3.2 of the DSU. For present purposes, this means the general rule of treaty interpretation contained in Article 31 of the Vienna Convention on the Law of Treaties. This requires an interpretation in good faith in accordance with the ordinary meaning to be given to the terms in their context and in the light of the object and purpose of the agreement. Recourse may be had to supplementary means of interpretation in accordance with Article 32 of that Convention.[550]

7.606 Commencing with the terms of the provision, we observe that Article 24.5 consists of a single sentence, of which the subject is "measures adopted to implement this Section." Article 24.5 appears in Section 3 of Part II of the TRIPS Agreement. Therefore, the reference to "this Section" is a reference to Section 3.[551]

7.607 The principal verb in Article 24.5 is "shall not prejudice." There are various definitions of the verb "prejudice" used in the three authentic language versions of the TRIPS Agreement.[552] The ordinary meaning of the verb "prejudice" in English can be defined as "affect adversely or unfavourably; injure or impair the validity of (a right, claim, etc.)." The latter part of this definition appears particularly apposite in this context since it refers to a right or claim, and the objects of the verb in Article 24.5 are legal rights. However, the European Communities emphasizes that the verbs used in the French and Spanish versions, *préjuger* and *prejuzgar* respectively, correspond to the modern English verb "prejudge." The Panel notes that this is an archaic sense of the English verb "prejudice" now analogous to its use in the phrase "without prejudice." Other usages of the English verb "prejudice" in the TRIPS Agreement outside Article 24 have been rendered differently in the French and Spanish versions, which are equally authentic,[553] to capture the sense of adverse effect or injury, so that that sense should not be read into Article 24.5. Nevertheless, the essence of all these definitions is that the provision does not affect certain other rights. The Panel's task in this dispute is to determine the applicability of Article 24.5. For that purpose, it suffices to note that the verb "shall not prejudice" denotes that the measures that are the subject of that provision shall not affect certain other rights.

7.608 The United States argues that the word "prejudice" connotes additional protection for trademark rights under Article 24.5. However, the Panel notes that the word "prejudice" is relatively common in all three versions of the TRIPS Agreement and the phrase "shall not prejudice" or "shall in no way prejudice" occurs three other times in the English version, including once in another exception in Article 24, and once in relation to prior rights in Article 16.1 itself.[554] Read in context, "prejudice" simply appears to be a word which the drafters used to indicate that a particular measure shall not affect certain other rights, including prior rights.

7.609 The objects of the principal verb in Article 24.5 are "the eligibility for or the validity of the registration of a trademark" and "the right to use a trademark." The context indicates the relevance of these rights in Article 24.5. The choice of words "the eligibility for or the validity of the registration of a trademark" reflects the fact that these are the aspects of trademark protection which might otherwise be prejudiced by the

---

[550] See, for example, the Appellate Body report on *US – Gasoline*, DSR 1996:I, 3, at 16; Appellate Body report on *Japan – Alcoholic Beverages II*, DSR 1996:I, 97, at 104; and Appellate Body report on *India – Patents (US)*, paras. 45-46.

[551] The parties referred to the text above and below subparagraphs (a) and (b) as a *chapeau* and a *chaussette*. The Panel attaches no importance to the allegedly sartorial format of the paragraph.

[552] *The New Shorter Oxford English Dictionary* (1993); *Le Nouveau Petit Robert: Dictionnaire de la langue française* (June 2000) and *Diccionario de la Lengua Española*, 21st edition, (1992).

[553] See the final clause of the WTO Agreement.

[554] The phrase "shall in no way prejudice" appears in all three versions in Article 24.8, and "shall not prejudice" appears in Articles 16.1 and 53.2 in the English version. The phrase "without prejudice" appears in Articles 10.2, 40.3, 50.6, 57 and 59, and the word "prejudice" appears in the exception clauses in Articles 13, 26.2 and 30 (and Article 27.2 in the English version), and also in Article 63.4.

obligations to "refuse or invalidate the registration of a trademark" and that "registration of a trademark ... shall be refused or invalidated" in Articles 22.3 and 23.2. In the same way, the choice of the words "the right to use a trademark" reflects the fact that this is the aspect of trademark protection which would otherwise be prejudiced by the obligations to provide the legal means to prevent certain uses in Articles 22.2 and 23.1.[555]

7.610 The European Communities asserts that the words "the right to use a trademark" provide for an additional positive right to use a trademark. However, in the Panel's view, the verb "shall not prejudice" is not capable of supporting this interpretation. It does not provide for the conferral of new rights on trademark owners or GI holders, but provides that the specifically mentioned rights shall not be affected by the measures that are the subject of the provision. If the drafters had intended to grant a positive right, they would have used positive language. Indeed, Article 14(2) of the Regulation (which was adopted prior to the end of the TRIPS negotiations) expressly provides that "a trademark ... may continue to be used" under certain conditions. In contrast, there is no language in Article 24.5 of the TRIPS Agreement which would provide for the conferral of a right to use a trademark. Instead, it is a saving provision which ensures that "the right to use a trademark" is not prejudiced, or affected, by measures adopted to implement Section 3 of Part II. Irrespective of how the right to use a trademark arises, there is no obligation under Article 24.5 to confer it.[556]

7.611 Even if the TRIPS Agreement does not expressly provide for a "right to use a trademark" elsewhere, this does not mean that a provision that measures "shall not prejudice" that right provides for it instead. The right to use a trademark is a right that Members may provide under national law.[557] This is the right saved by Article 24.5 where it provides that certain measures "shall not prejudice ... the right to use a trademark."[558]

7.612 The context in other paragraphs of Article 24 confirms the Panel's interpretation of "the eligibility for or the validity of the registration of a trademark" and "the right to use a trademark," as used in paragraph 5. Other exceptions in that article also refer to the implications of these two types of protection. Paragraph 4 refers to "continued and similar *use* of a particular [GI] ... identifying wines and spirits;" paragraph 7 refers to "any request made under this Section in connection with the *use* or *registration of a trademark*;" and paragraph 8 refers to "the right of any person to *use*, in the course of trade, that person's name."

7.613 There is no reason to limit the "right to use a trademark" to trademarks acquired through use due to the optical symmetry between, on the one hand, the passive subjects of the first relative clause: "a trademark

---

[555] The order of these two exceptions in Article 24.5 reverses the order of the types of protection in relation to *uses* and in relation to *registration of a trademark* in Article 22.2 and 22.3 and in Article 23.1 and 23.2. However, it can be observed that the exceptions followed the same order as the corresponding rights in paragraphs 1 and 2 of the GI exceptions provision in the Brussels Draft, which were the predecessors of Article 24.4 and 24.5 in the final version. Draft paragraph 1 referred to a GI that had been "used," "including use as a trademark," and draft paragraph 2 only referred to "action to refuse or invalidate registration of a trademark:" see document MTN.TNC/W/35/Rev.1 dated 3 December 1990 entitled "Draft Final Act Embodying the Results of the Uruguay Round of Multilateral Trade Negotiations—Revision," the so-called "Brussels Draft." The phrase "including use as a trademark" was later deleted from paragraph 1, and prior trademark issues, including the right to use a trademark, were dealt with in Article 24.5 in the final version, in that order.

[556] The European Communities raises the issue of a Member that provides additional GI protection beyond that which is required by Article 22, in support of its view that Article 24.5 imposes self-standing obligations. It argues that in this situation Article 24.5, not Article 22 nor Section 2, would prohibit that Member from invalidating or denying protection to prior trademarks inconsistent with that additional protection. In the Panel's view, this overlooks the subject of Article 24.5 which is "measures adopted to implement ... Section [3]." To the extent that measures implement GI protection beyond that which is required by Article 22 for products other than wines and spirits they are, by definition, not measures adopted to implement Section 3 and Article 24.5 is irrelevant to them. It has not been argued by any party that the Regulation is not such a measure. See European Communities' response to Panel question No. 145 and United States' comment on that response.

[557] This is confirmed in WIPO publications, including *Introduction to Trademark Law & Practice, The Basic Concepts, A WIPO Training Manual* (1993), pp. 51-52, and *WIPO Intellectual Property Handbook: Policy, Law and Use*, (June 2001) at p. 82, cited by the European Communities in its rebuttal submission, para. 324 and its response to Panel question No. 76. See, for example, Australia's Trade Marks Act 1995, Section 20(1)(a), reproduced in Exhibit EC-58.

[558] Article 16.1 of the TRIPS Agreement only provides for a negative right to prevent all third parties from using signs in certain circumstances. Article 15.3 permits Members to make registrability depend on use and Article 19.1 permits Members to require use in order to maintain a registration, which might imply a right to use the trademark, but any such right is subject to the general law. Article 20 does not preclude a requirement prescribing the use of a trademark in a certain way.

applied for ... in good faith," "a trademark ... registered in good faith" and "rights to a trademark ... acquired through use in good faith" and, on the other hand, the active objects of the principal verb: "eligibility for ... the registration of a trademark," "the validity of the registration of a trademark" and "the right to use a trademark." The operative parallel is between the rights which shall not be prejudiced and the types of GI protection which would otherwise prejudice them.

7.614 Therefore, according to their ordinary meaning read in context, the terms "shall not prejudice," "the eligibility for or the validity of the registration of a trademark" and "the right to use a trademark," as used in paragraph 5 of Article 24, indicate the creation of exceptions to the obligations to provide two types of GI protection in Section 3. Both these types of protection could otherwise affect the rights identified in paragraph 5. Indeed, the refusal or invalidation of the registration of a trademark has no other function but to extinguish the eligibility for or the validity of the registration of a trademark. Paragraph 5 ensures that each of these types of protection shall not affect those rights.

7.615 Accordingly, the Panel considers that Article 24.5 creates an exception to GI protection—as reflected in the title of Article 24.

7.616 Both parties submit that Article 24.5 implies certain things. The United States argues that the term "validity of the registration" impliedly refers to all the rights which flow from registration, including the right to prevent uses that would result in a likelihood of confusion. In contrast, the European Communities argues that the use of the more specific language in Article 24.5 in fact implies a limitation on the trademark owner's right to exclude use.[559]

7.617 As to the United States' argument, the Panel notes the contrast between the use of the specific terms "eligibility for or the validity of the registration" in Article 24.5, rather than simply "existing prior rights," which is the language used in the last sentence of Article 16.1. The use of language such as "existing prior rights" would have clearly preserved the right to prevent certain uses without any need for implication. The more specific language used in Article 24.5 does not, which suggests that Article 24.5 does not impliedly preserve that right. However, this does not mean that Article 24.5 authorizes Members to prejudice that right. Members may prejudice that right if there is another provision that obliges or permits them to do so.

7.618 As to the European Communities' argument, the Panel considers that it is difficult to sustain an argument that a limitation which is allegedly implied can prevail over an obligation in a WTO covered agreement which is express. It is evidently the position under the European Communities' domestic law that an implied positive right to use a registered GI prevails over the negative right of a prior trademark holder to prevent confusing uses.[560] However, such an interpretation of the TRIPS Agreement is not possible without a suitable basis in the treaty text. The text of Article 24.5 expressly preserves the right to use a trademark—which is *not* expressly provided for in the TRIPS Agreement—and is silent as to any limitation on the trademark owner's exclusive right to prevent confusing uses of signs—which *is* expressly provided for in the TRIPS Agreement—when the sign is used as a GI.

7.619 Accordingly, the Panel's preliminary conclusion is that it is inappropriate to imply in Article 24.5 *either* the right to prevent confusing uses *or* a limitation on the right to prevent confusing uses.

7.620 The ordinary meaning of the terms in their context must also be interpreted in light of the object and purpose of the agreement. The object and purpose of the TRIPS Agreement, as indicated by Articles 9 through 62 and 70 and reflected in the preamble, includes the provision of adequate standards and principles concerning the availability, scope, use and enforcement of trade-related intellectual property rights. This confirms that a

[559] European Communities' first written submission, para. 301; response to Panel question No. 147.

[560] That position may be evidenced by, among other things, the express provision in Article 159 of the Community Trademark Regulation that it shall not affect the GI Regulation and in particular Article 14 thereof. There is no such provision in Section 2 of Part II of the TRIPS Agreement on trademarks that refers to Section 3 of Part II on GIs.

limitation on the standards for trademark or GI protection should not be implied unless it is supported by the text.

7.621 The standards of protection in Part II of the Agreement and, hence, the procedures for their enforcement under Part III, could be undermined by systematic conflicts between the standards for different categories of intellectual property available to different parties but applied to the same subject matter. This is particularly apparent in the case of trademarks and GIs due to the similarity of the subject matter eligible for protection by those two categories of intellectual property and the fact that the rights in respect of uses are indifferent as to whether the infringing subject matter is protected by another category of intellectual property. The subject matter eligible for protection overlaps whilst the rights conferred by each category intersect.

7.622 The European Communities submits that this is a conflict resolved by Article 22.3 (and Article 23.2) by effectively giving priority to the GI.[561] The Panel agrees that Articles 22.3 and 23.2 can resolve conflicts with *later* trademarks but they do not resolve conflicts with prior trademarks that meet the conditions set out in Article 24.5.

7.623 Both the United States and the European Communities agree that the simultaneous exercise of two negative rights to prevent uses provided for in Articles 16.1 and 22.2 (and 23.1) can lead to a conflict between different private parties who wish to use an individual sign as a trademark and as a GI. The European Communities sees this potential for conflict as a matter which should be avoided in the interpretation of the TRIPS Agreement. The United States distinguishes this from a conflict between Members' obligations under the Agreement, and argues that the need for a harmonious interpretation of the Agreement does not require the treaty interpreter to resolve potential conflicts between private parties.

7.624 The Panel notes that the parties do not dispute that *Members* may comply simultaneously with both obligations in the TRIPS Agreement. They do not allege that there are conflicting provisions in the treaty itself.[562] The general rule of treaty interpretation requires us to interpret the treaty in accordance with the ordinary meaning to be given to its terms in their context in the light of its object and purpose. The Panel has had recourse to supplementary means of interpretation, in particular a draft text, in order to confirm the meaning resulting from the application of the general rule of treaty interpretation, which has not left the meaning ambiguous or obscure or led to a result which is manifestly absurd or unreasonable. We would not adopt an approach in treaty interpretation that produced a result that might, on one view, further the object and purpose of the Agreement, but which is not supported by the ordinary meaning to be given to its terms in their context. The following statement by the Appellate Body in *EC – Hormones* appears apposite:

> The fundamental rule of treaty interpretation requires a treaty interpreter to read and interpret the words actually used by the agreement under examination, not words the interpreter may feel should have been used.[563]

7.625 Therefore, the Panel concludes that, under Article 16.1 of the TRIPS Agreement, Members are required to make available to trademark owners a right against certain uses, including uses as a GI. The Regulation limits the availability of that right for the owners of trademarks which are subject to Article 14(2). Article 24.5 of the TRIPS Agreement is inapplicable and does not provide authority to limit that right.

7.626 The European Communities raises two other defences that, in this respect, the Regulation is justified by exceptions found in Articles 24.3 and 17 of the TRIPS Agreement. The Panel will consider each of these in turn.

---

[561] European Communities' response to Panel question No. 146.

[562] In this respect, the Panel recalls the findings in the Panel reports on *Indonesia – Autos* at para 14.28; *Turkey – Textiles* at paras. 9.92-9.95; and *EC – Bananas III* at paras. 7.151-7.163.

[563] Appellate Body report on *EC – Hormones*, para. 181.

(e) Article 24.3 of the TRIPS Agreement

(i) main arguments of the parties

7.627 The United States argues that Article 24.3 of the TRIPS Agreement is an exception with respect to the implementation of the GI Section of the Agreement and does not impose any exception to the obligation to provide trademark rights under Article 16.1. The EC's interpretation would create a major and permanent exception to the trademark Section of the TRIPS Agreement which would require a Member to apply all aspects of its pre-TRIPS GI regime to all GIs—including those registered after 1 January 1996—so that the Member would never fully implement the rights granted to trademark owners by Article 16.1.[564] The "protection" of GIs, within the meaning of Article 24.3, could just as easily mean protection as it relates to individual GIs as it could mean the general scope or level of protection overall.[565]

7.628 The European Communities argues that it is required to maintain coexistence of GIs and earlier trademarks by Article 24.3 of the TRIPS Agreement, which is a standstill obligation that prohibits Members from diminishing the level of GI protection that existed at the time of entry into force of the WTO Agreement. The Regulation provided for coexistence in Article 14(2) immediately prior to the entry into force of the WTO Agreement. If the European Communities allowed the owners of prior registered trademarks to prevent the use of later GIs, this would diminish the protection of GIs contrary to Article 24.3.[566] The standstill obligation applies to the general level of protection of GIs available in a Member on 1 January 1995 rather than the protection of individual GIs registered or applied for on that date. The relevant verb, "existed," appears in the singular in the French and Spanish versions, which indicates that it refers to the whole phrase "protection of geographical indications" rather than the plural noun "geographical indications." It is an additional obligation, not an exception. It refers to GI protection, which expressly includes protection vis-à-vis trademark rights in Articles 22.3, 23.2 and 24.5. Those provisions limit the trademark obligations under Article 16.1, as does Article 24.3.[567] Article 24.3 applies "[i]n implementing this Section." The Section includes Article 24.5, which prevents Members from invalidating and prohibiting the use of grandfathered trademarks.[568]

(ii) main arguments of third parties

7.629 New Zealand informs the Panel that no GIs were registered under the Regulation prior to the entry into force of the TRIPS Agreement. In any case, Article 24.3 is qualified by the phrase "[i]n implementing this Section" and does not justify a breach of the Section on trademarks.[569]

(iii) consideration by the Panel

7.630 The Panel now considers the European Communities' argument that it is required to maintain coexistence of GIs and earlier trademarks by Article 24.3 of the TRIPS Agreement. That provision reads as follows:

> 3. In implementing this Section, a Member shall not diminish the protection of geographical indications that existed in that Member immediately prior to the date of entry into force of the WTO Agreement.

---

[564] United States' first oral statement, paras. 70-73.

[565] United States' rebuttal submission, para. 197.

[566] European Communities' first written submission, paras. 272, 312-314.

[567] European Communities' response to Panel question No. 74.

[568] European Communities' response to Panel question No. 152.

[569] Annex C, para. 158.

7.631 Article 24.3 appears in Section 3 of Part II of the TRIPS Agreement. The reference to "this Section" is therefore a reference to Section 3, which sets out standards for the protection of GIs. The "date of entry into force of the WTO Agreement" was 1 January 1995.

7.632 The scope of Article 24.3 is limited by the introductory phrase "[i]n implementing this Section." It does not apply to measures adopted to implement provisions outside Section 3. Trademark owners' rights, which Members must make available in the implementation of Article 16.1, are found in Section 2. Therefore, Article 24.3 is inapplicable.

7.633 Turning to the ordinary meaning of the terms used in the rest of the provision, the principal verb is "shall not diminish." This indicates that this is a standstill provision, and that it is mandatory. The parties do not agree on the meaning of the object of that verb, which is the phrase "the protection of geographical indications" as qualified by the final relative clause. In the English version of the text, that phrase could refer either to "the protection of GIs" as a whole, or to "the protection" of individual GIs. In the French and Spanish versions, which are equally authentic[570], the verb "existed" in the relative clause is in the singular, which indicates that the "protection of geographical indications" must be interpreted as a whole. It is unclear in all three versions whether this refers to the legal framework or system of protection in a Member that existed immediately prior to 1 January 1995, or to the state of GI protection in a Member that existed at that time in terms of the individual rights which were protected.

7.634 If Article 24.3 referred to a system of protection in a Member, this would have two important consequences. First, as a mandatory provision, it would prevent a Member which had a system that granted a higher level of protection than that provided for in the TRIPS Agreement from implementing the same minimum standards of protection as other Members, even if it wished to do so. For example, in the European Communities, Article 14 of the Regulation entered into force in 1993 but was amended in April 2003 in respect of trademark rights acquired through use.[571] To the extent that those amendments diminished the general level of protection of GIs under the European Communities' system, they would be inconsistent with Article 24.3 on its own view.

7.635 Second, a standstill provision for a system of protection would exclude from the scope of Section 3 not only individual rights already in force under that system as at the date of entry into force of the WTO Agreement, but also rights subsequently granted under that system in perpetuity. This would be a sweeping exclusion which would grow, rather than diminish, in importance, as an increasing number of GIs were protected under the prior legislation. The Panel is reluctant to find such an exclusion in the absence of any clear language to that effect, and none has been drawn to its attention. In this respect, it can be noted that the TRIPS Agreement *does* contain an exclusion for a type of system (in respect of phonograms) in Article 14.4 but it is optional, it clearly refers to a "system" and it is subject to a proviso against abuse. Article 24.3 contains none of these features.

7.636 For these reasons, the Panel interprets the phrase "the protection of geographical indications that existed in that Member immediately prior to the date of entry into force of the WTO Agreement" to mean the state of protection of GIs immediately prior to 1 January 1995, in terms of the individual GIs which were protected at that point in time. In the present dispute, the parties agree that no GIs were registered under the Regulation prior to 1 January 1995. Therefore, Article 24.3 is inapplicable.

7.637 For all the reasons set out above, the Panel concludes that Article 24.3 is inapplicable.

---

570 See the final clause of the WTO Agreement.

571 See Council Regulation (EC) No. 692/2003, Article 13 and paragraph 11 of the recitals, set out in Exhibit COMP-1h.

(f) *Article 17 of the TRIPS Agreement*

(i) *main arguments of the parties*

7.638 The United States argues that the European Communities has not shown that Article 14(2) constitutes a limited exception within the meaning of Article 17 of the TRIPS Agreement. The United States interprets a "limited exception" to connote an exception which makes only a small diminution of the rights in question. The blanket inability of trademark owners to prevent confusing uses is not "limited" because it does not involve a small diminution of rights and there is no limit on the number of potential users of a registered GI. United States trademark law, to which the European Communities referred, allows fair use of descriptive terms *otherwise than as a mark*, i.e. in a non-distinctive sense, and calls for a case-by-case analysis. The EC GI Regulation does neither. Even if geographical names are descriptive terms, the Regulation allows registration of some non-geographical names. Even if Article 14(3) of the Regulation prevents registration of well-known marks, these are a narrow subset of all trademarks and, in any case, the analysis must be conducted for each trademark individually. Article 17 presupposes a certain degree of likelihood of confusion for a particular trademark but not the unlimited degree permitted by the Regulation.[572]

7.639 The United States argues that the "legitimate interests of the owner of the trademark" could be the owner's interest in the economic value of the rights the trademark confers. The Regulation places no limits on the manner in which a GI can be used which could, in most cases, destroy the economic value of the trademark. It is not tailored in any way to the legitimate interests of a particular trademark owner. The largest set of "third parties" are consumers, and also trademark licensees. It should be possible to inform consumers about the origin of a product and its characteristics through the use of descriptive terms in a non-trademark sense without confusing the consumer about the source of the goods. Allowing confusing use of a GI harms the interests of consumers. Labelling, misleading advertising and unfair competition laws are irrelevant because they simply add prohibitions and do not affect whether a particular use is a trademark infringement.[573]

7.640 The European Communities argues that, in the alternative, the coexistence of GIs and earlier trademarks would be justified under Article 17 of the TRIPS Agreement. It considers that Article 17 is an exception to the obligations in Article 16 and that previous panels have taken the view that the burden of invoking similar exceptions was on the respondent. It accepts that it bears the burden of proof. Article 14(2) of the Regulation is a "limited exception" because it only allows use by those producers who are established in the geographical area on products that comply with the specification. The trademark owner retains the exclusive right to prevent use by any other persons. Coexistence falls within the example of "fair use of descriptive terms" because GIs are descriptive terms, even where they consist of a non-geographical name, and their use to indicate the true origin of goods and the characteristic associated with that origin is "fair."[574]

7.641 The European Communities argues that the legitimate interests of the trademark owner and of third parties are taken into account because Article 14(3) of the Regulation would prevent the most significant cases of confusion, and legislation on labelling, misleading advertising and unfair competition still applies. The legitimate interests of the trademark owner are less than full enjoyment of all exclusive rights under Article 16.1 of the TRIPS Agreement. The legitimate interests of third parties include the interests of producers who use GIs as well as consumers. GIs inform consumers about the origin of products and take account of the interests of third parties in that way. Article 17 of the TRIPS Agreement does not require the avoidance of all likelihood of confusion, otherwise it would be superfluous, nor does it require confusion to be confined to that which is strictly necessary, which would render the example of "fair use of descriptive term" irrelevant. Article 17 calls for a balancing of different interests which, in the present dispute, requires that account should be taken of the

---

[572] United States' rebuttal submission, paras. 198-201, 205-207; second oral statement, paras. 100 and 102; responses to Panel question Nos. 154 and 155; comments on EC responses to Panel question Nos. 153 and 156.

[573] United States' rebuttal submission, paras. 202-205 and 209-210.

[574] European Communities' first written submission, paras. 315-318; rebuttal submission, paras. 333-338, 348-350; responses to Panel question No. 75(b).

fact that trademarks are arbitrary and much easier to create than GIs and GIs are collective rights and also serve a public interest of informing consumers.[575]

(ii) main arguments of third parties

7.642 Argentina, Brazil, India, Mexico and New Zealand indicated, in response to a question from the Panel, that they provide certain exceptions to exclusive trademark rights. Examples included honest concurrent use, prior use in good faith, comparative advertising, uses for spare parts and certain non-commercial fair uses.[576]

7.643 New Zealand also argues that coexistence is not a "limited" exception within the meaning of Article 17 of the TRIPS Agreement because it excludes an entire group of producers from the trademark owner's right to prevent confusing uses, which is a major exception.[577]

(iii) consideration by the Panel

introduction

7.644 The Panel will now consider the European Communities' argument that its particular regime of coexistence between GIs and prior trademarks is justified under Article 17 of the TRIPS Agreement. The European Communities defends its regime of coexistence "as such," not as applied. Therefore, our consideration of this defence focuses almost entirely on the terms of the measure and its potential effects, rather than any actual effects. Nevertheless, we will refer to the few examples of how the GI Regulation has been applied with respect to prior trademarks, where that is instructive.

7.645 The United States submits that the European Communities, as the party asserting that its measure is covered by the exception in Article 17, bears the burden of proving that assertion. The European Communities does not contest this position.[578] Therefore, the Panel will follow this approach in the present dispute.

7.646 Article 17 provides as follows:

Exceptions

> Members may provide limited exceptions to the rights conferred by a trademark, such as fair use of descriptive terms, provided that such exceptions take account of the legitimate interests of the owner of the trademark and of third parties."

7.647 Article 17 expressly permits Members to provide limited exceptions to the rights conferred by a trademark, which include the right provided for in Article 16.1 of the TRIPS Agreement. The Panel has already found that the Regulation limits the availability of the right provided for in Article 16.1. Therefore, to the extent that it satisfies the conditions in Article 17, this limitation will be permitted under the TRIPS Agreement.

---

575 European Communities' first written submission, para. 319; rebuttal submission, paras. 339-347; responses to Panel question Nos. 153 and 154; comment on US response to Panel question No. 154.

576 See Annex C.

577 Annex C, para. 159.

578 All parties note that it was the approach of two previous panels to exceptions provisions in Part II of the TRIPS Agreement: see Panel reports on *US – Section 110(5) Copyright Act*, para. 6.239; and *Canada – Pharmaceutical Patents*, para. 7.16. This approach was not contested in those disputes and was adopted without discussion, although the Panel in *Canada – Pharmaceutical Patents* observed that a respondent cannot demonstrate that no legitimate interest of a patent owner has been prejudiced until it knows what claims of legitimate interests can be made by the complainant. Similarly, the weight of legitimate third party interests cannot be fully appraised until the legitimacy of the patent owner's legitimate interests, if any, are defined: see para. 7.60 of its report. These practical problems also apply in disputes under Article 17. In this regard, the Panel recalls the distinction between the rights and obligations owed by WTO Members to one another under the covered agreements, and the rights conferred by Members on nationals by individual intellectual property rights under the TRIPS Agreement. The burden of proof in WTO dispute settlement between Members relates to the first set of rights and obligations and not to the fact that a provision creates exceptions to the rights to be conferred by Members on the nationals of other Members.

7.648 Article 17 permits "limited exceptions." It provides an example of a limited exception, and is subject to a proviso that "such exceptions take account of the legitimate interests of the owner of the trademark and of third parties." The ordinary meaning of the terms indicates that an exception must not only be "limited" but must also comply with the proviso in order to satisfy Article 17. The example of "fair use of descriptive terms" is illustrative only, but it can provide interpretative guidance because, *a priori*, it falls within the meaning of a "limited" exception and must be capable of satisfying the proviso in some circumstances. Any interpretation of the term "limited" or of the proviso which excluded the example would be manifestly incorrect.

7.649 The structure of Article 17 differs from that of other exceptions provisions to which the parties refer. It can be noted that Articles 13, 26.2 and 30 of the TRIPS Agreement, as well as Article 9(2) of the Berne Convention (1971) as incorporated by Article 9.1 of the TRIPS Agreement, also permit exceptions to intellectual property rights and all contain, to varying degrees, similar language to Article 17. However, unlike these other provisions, Article 17 contains no reference to "conflict with a [or the] normal exploitation," no reference to "unreasonabl[e] prejudice" to the legitimate interests" of the right holder or owner, and it not only refers to the legitimate interests of third parties but treats them on par with those of the right holder. It is also the only one of these provisions which contains an example. Further, Article 17 permits exceptions to trademark rights, which differ from each of the intellectual property rights to which these other exceptions apply. Therefore, whilst it is instructive to refer to the interpretation by two previous panels of certain shared elements found in Articles 13 and 30, it is important to interpret Article 17 according to its own terms.

<u>limited exceptions</u>

7.650 The first issue to decide is the meaning of the term "limited exceptions" as used in Article 17. The United States interprets this in terms of a small diminution of rights. The European Communities does not disagree with this approach. The Panel agrees with the views of the Panel in *Canada – Pharmaceutical Patents*, which interpreted the identical term in Article 30, that "[t]he word 'exception' by itself connotes a limited derogation, one that does not undercut the body of rules from which it is made."[579] The addition of the word "limited" emphasizes that the exception must be narrow and permit only a small diminution of rights. The limited exceptions apply "to the rights conferred by a trademark." They do not apply to the set of all trademarks or all trademark owners. Accordingly, the fact that it may affect only few trademarks or few trademark owners is irrelevant to the question whether an exception is limited. The issue is whether the exception to the *rights conferred by a trademark* is narrow.

7.651 There is only one right conferred by a trademark at issue in this dispute, namely the exclusive right to prevent certain uses of a sign, provided for in Article 16.1. Therefore, it is necessary to examine the exception on an individual "per right" basis. This is a legal assessment of the extent to which the exception curtails that right. There is no indication in the text of Article 17 that this involves an economic assessment, although economic impact can be taken into account in the proviso. In this regard, we note the absence of any reference to a "normal exploitation" of the trademark in Article 17, and the absence of any reference in Section 2, to which Article 17 permits exceptions, to rights to exclude legitimate competition. Rather, they confer, *inter alia*, the right to prevent uses that would result in a likelihood of confusion, which can lead to the removal of products from sale where they are marketed using particular signs, but without otherwise restraining the manufacture, sale or importation of competing goods or services.

7.652 The right provided for in Article 16.1 contains several elements and an exception could, in principle, curtail the right in respect of any of them. We recall these elements in the text of that provision as follows:

> The owner of a registered trademark shall have the exclusive right to prevent *all third parties* not having the owner's consent from using in the course of trade *identical or similar signs* for

579 Panel report on *Canada – Pharmaceutical Patents*, para. 7.30.

goods or services which are identical or similar to those in respect of which the trademark is registered where such use would result in *a likelihood of confusion.* [emphasis added]

7.653 In principle, an exception could curtail the right of the owner in respect of the third parties concerned, or with respect to the identity or the similarity of the signs or the goods or services concerned or with respect to the degree of likelihood of confusion, or some combination of these. There may be other possibilities as well. The overriding requirement is that the exception must be "limited" and it must also satisfy the proviso, considered below. These elements provide a useful framework for an assessment of the extent to which an exception curtails the right provided for in Article 16.1.

7.654 The example in the text, "fair use of descriptive terms," provides guidance as to what is considered a "limited exception," although it is illustrative only. Fair use of descriptive terms is inherently limited in terms of the sign which may be used and the degree of likelihood of confusion which may result from its use, as a purely descriptive term on its own is not distinctive and is not protectable as a trademark. Fair use of descriptive terms is *not* limited in terms of the number of third parties who may benefit, nor in terms of the quantity of goods or services with respect to which they use the descriptive terms, although implicitly it only applies to those third parties who would use those terms in the course of trade and to those goods or services which those terms describe. The number of trademarks or trademark owners affected is irrelevant, although implicitly it would only affect those marks which can consist of, or include, signs that can be used in a descriptive manner. According to the text, this is a "limited" exception for the purposes of Article 17.

7.655 Turning to the Regulation, it curtails the trademark owner's right in respect of certain goods but not all goods identical or similar to those in respect of which the trademark is registered. It prevents the trademark owner from exercising the right to prevent confusing uses of a sign for the agricultural product or foodstuff produced in accordance with the product specification in the GI registration. We recall that, according to Article 2(2) of the Regulation, which is set out above at paragraph 7.187, those goods must all be produced, processed and/or prepared in the region, specific place or, in exceptional cases, country, the name of which is used to describe them. Goods that are not from that geographical area may not use the GI. Further, according to Article 4 of the Regulation, all products using a GI must comply with a product specification. Products that do not so comply may not use the GI even if they are from the geographical area. The trademark owner's right against all other goods is not curtailed. We note that there is no limit in terms of the quantity of goods which may benefit from the exception, as long as they conform to the product specification. However, this cannot prevent the limitation on rights of owners of trademarks subject to Article 14(2) from constituting a limited exception for the purposes of Article 17, as fair use of descriptive terms implies no limit in terms of quantity either, and the text indicates that it is a limited exception for the purposes of Article 17. The quantity of goods which benefits from an exception may be related to the curtailment of the rights to prevent the acts of making, selling or importing a product, but these are not rights conferred by a trademark.

7.656 The Regulation curtails the trademark owner's right against certain third parties, but not "all third parties." It prevents the trademark owner from exercising the right to prevent confusing uses against persons using a registered GI on a good in accordance with its registration. This is a limitation on the third parties who may benefit from the exception. The trademark owner's right is not curtailed with respect to any other third parties.[580]

7.657 The Regulation curtails the trademark owner's right in respect of certain signs but not all signs identical or similar to the one protected as a trademark. It prevents the trademark owner from exercising its right

[580] The United States refers to a case of trademark infringement in which the German Federal Supreme Court held that the concurrent use by Fiat of the SL trademark owned by Mercedes-Benz could put at risk the very existence of that trademark. note that, in coming to its decision, the Court observed that "it could be expected that other vehicle manufacturers might soon follow the defendant's example." See United States' rebuttal submission, para. 173, fn. 167 and Exhibit US-67. The opportunity for all other potential competitors to use a trademark does not arise under the GI Regulation as it only permits use of a GI in accordance with its registration, including the product specifications.

to prevent use of an indication registered as a GI in accordance with its registration. We recall our finding in paragraph 7.518 that the GI registration does not confer a positive right to use any other signs or combination of signs nor to use the name in any linguistic versions not entered in the register . The trademark owner's right is not curtailed against any such uses. If the GI registration prevented the trademark owner from exercising its rights against these signs, combinations of signs or linguistic versions, which do not appear expressly in the GI registration, it would seriously expand the exception and undermine the limitations on its scope.

7.658 Under the Regulation, once a GI has been registered and a trademark is subject to the coexistence regime under Article 14(2), set out above at paragraph 7.520, the GI may, in principle, be used without regard to the likelihood of confusion that it may cause. However, the Regulation refers to the likelihood or risk of confusion, with a given mark, which would result from use as a GI of an identical or similar sign, in Articles 7(5)(b), 12b(3) and 12d(3), in relation to the decision on whether to register a GI where an objection is admissible. Article 7(4) and, hence, Article 12b(3), provide a ground for objection where registration would jeopardize the existence of a mark, and Article 14(3) provides a ground for refusal of registration which refers to the trademark's reputation and renown and the length of time it has been used. These factors are relevant to the likelihood of confusion which could result from subsequent use of the GI. We recall our finding in paragraph 7.521 that Article 14(2) is an exception to Article 13, which presupposes a consideration of the similarity of the signs and goods as well. They are essential to an analysis of a likelihood of confusion. Whilst Articles 7(4), 12b(3) and 14(3) do not specifically refer to the concept of likelihood of confusion between a GI and a trademark subject to the exception in Article 14(2), they, together with Articles 7(5)(b), 12b(3) and 12d(3) can ensure that, in cases where the likelihood of confusion is relatively high, the exception simply does not apply.

7.659 The United States submitted that Article 14(2) eliminates the trademark owner's right, granting the owner only the right to continue to use the trademark. However, the European Communities has emphasized that the trademark owner retains the right to prevent the use of a name registered as a GI by any person in relation to any goods which originate in a different geographical area or which do not comply with the specifications[581], and that the positive right to use the GI extends only to the linguistic versions that have been entered in the register and not to other names or signs which have not been registered[582]. Accordingly, on the basis of the terms of the GI Regulation and of the Community Trademark Regulation, and the explanation of them provided by the European Communities, the Panel finds that not only may the trademark continue to be used, but that the trademark owner's right to prevent confusing uses, is unaffected except with respect to the use of a GI as entered in the GI register in accordance with its registration. In view of these limitations, the scope of the exception in Article 14(2) falls far short of that which the United States initially claimed.[583]

7.660 Furthermore, the European Communities has explained that the use of a name registered as a GI is subject to the applicable provisions of the food labelling and misleading advertising directives so that the ways in which it may be used are not unlimited.[584]

7.661 For the above reasons, the Panel finds that the Regulation creates a "limited exception" within the meaning of Article 17 of the TRIPS Agreement.

[581] European Communities' first written submission, para. 317; rebuttal submission, para. 336; responses to Panel question Nos. 76 and 153.

[582] European Communities' rebuttal submission, paras. 288, 293 and 301; responses to Panel question Nos. 63, 137 and 140; and comment on US response to Panel question No. 137.

[583] See United States' first oral statement, para. 75. The United States appears to acknowledge that the GI registration does not extinguish the trademark owner's rights against other third parties, although it alleges that use of the GI will affect the distinctiveness of the trademark: see United States' second oral statement, para. 101. The Panel considers that issue in relation to the proviso to Article 17.

[584] European Communities' first written submission, para. 319; response to Panel question No. 153.

the proviso to Article 17

7.662 Limited exceptions must satisfy the proviso that "such exceptions take account of the legitimate interests of the owner of the trademark and of third parties" in order to benefit from Article 17. We must first establish what are "legitimate interests." Read in context, the "legitimate interests" of the trademark owner are contrasted with the "rights conferred by a trademark," which also belong to the trademark owner. Given that Article 17 creates an exception to the rights conferred by a trademark, the "legitimate interests" of the trademark owner must be something different from full enjoyment of those legal rights. The "legitimate interests" of the trademark owner are also compared with those of "third parties," who have no rights conferred by the trademark. Therefore, the "legitimate interests," at least of third parties, are something different from simply the enjoyment of their legal rights. This is confirmed by the use of the verb "take account of," which is less than "protect."

7.663 We agree with the following view of the Panel in *Canada – Pharmaceutical Patents*, which interpreted the term "legitimate interests" of a patent owner and third parties in the context of Article 30 as follows:

> To make sense of the term 'legitimate interests' in this context, that term must be defined in the way that it is often used in legal discourse—as a normative claim calling for protection of interests that are 'justifiable' in the sense that they are supported by relevant public policies or other social norms.[585]

In our view, this is also true of the term "legitimate interests" of a trademark owner and third parties in the context of Article 17.

7.664 The legitimacy of some interest of the trademark owner is assumed because the owner of the trademark is specifically identified in Article 17. The TRIPS Agreement itself sets out a statement of what all WTO Members consider adequate standards and principles concerning trademark protection. Although it sets out standards for legal rights, it also provides guidance as to WTO Members' shared understandings of the policies and norms relevant to trademarks and, hence, what might be the legitimate interests of trademark owners. The function of trademarks can be understood by reference to Article 15.1 as distinguishing goods and services of undertakings in the course of trade. Every trademark owner has a legitimate interest in preserving the distinctiveness, or capacity to distinguish, of its trademark so that it can perform that function. This includes its interest in using its own trademark in connection with the relevant goods and services of its own and authorized undertakings. Taking account of that legitimate interest will also take account of the trademark owner's interest in the economic value of its mark arising from the reputation that it enjoys and the quality that it denotes.

7.665 Turning to the Regulation, the evidence shows that the owner's legitimate interest in preserving the distinctiveness, or capacity to distinguish, of its trademark can be taken into account in various ways. Article 7(4) of the Regulation provides that a statement of objection shall be admissible *inter alia* if it shows that the registration of the proposed GI would "jeopardize the existence ... of a mark." This requires GI registration to be refused.

7.666 Article 14(3) also requires the refusal of GI registration in light of a trademark's reputation and renown and the length of time it has been used, if a particular condition is fulfilled. This addresses the distinctiveness, or capacity to distinguish, of prior trademarks and can ensure that, in cases where trademark owners' legitimate interests would be most likely to be affected, the exception in Article 14(2) simply does not apply.

7.667 In the one instance in which Article 14(3) has been applied, the European Communities informs the Panel that its authorities:

---

585 Panel report on *Canada – Pharmaceutical Patents*, para. 7.69.

> [T]ook account of the submissions made by the interested parties and by some Member States, as well as of the discussions which took place within the Committee. The main facts taken into consideration were the similarity of the signs; the similarity of the products, having regard to the production methods and organoleptic properties; the date of registration of the trademark; the recognition of the trademark in the different EC member States, having regard in particular to the level of exports; and the labeling practices of the trademark and the proposed geographical indication.[586]

7.668 This indicates to the Panel that Article 14(3) of the Regulation was, in fact, applied to take account *inter alia* of the legitimate interest of the trademark owners to protect the distinctiveness of their respective marks.

7.669 In the other instance to which the parties refer, the registration of the three Czech beer GIs contains an endorsement that they apply "without prejudice to any beer trademark or other rights existing in the European Union on the date of accession."[587] Although the European Communities has confirmed that such an endorsement is unique and it has not explained in what other circumstances such an endorsement might be possible, this example does show that, at least in this case, not only the legitimate interests of trademark owners, but also their rights, have been taken into account.

7.670 Where Articles 7(4) and 14(3) of the Regulation are unavailable, and a trademark is subject to Article 14(2), there remains the possibility that its distinctiveness will be affected by the use of the GI. We do not consider this fatal to the applicability of Article 17 given that, as a provision permitting an exception to the exclusive right to prevent uses that would result in a likelihood of confusion, it presupposes that a certain degree of likelihood of confusion can be permitted. In the light of the provisions of Articles 7(4) and 14(3), we are satisfied that where the likelihood of confusion is relatively high, the exception in Article 14(2) will not apply. In any event, even where the exception does apply, Article 14(2) expressly provides that the trademark may continue to be used, on certain conditions.

7.671 We also note that the proviso to Article 17 requires only that exceptions "take account" of the legitimate interests of the owner of the trademark, and does not refer to "unreasonabl[e] prejudice" to those interests, unlike the provisos in Articles 13, 26.2 and 30 of the TRIPS Agreement and Article 9(2) of the Berne Convention (1971) as incorporated by Article 9.1 of the TRIPS Agreement. This suggests that a lesser standard of regard for the legitimate interests of the owner of the trademark is required.

7.672 The United States submits that Article 17 of the TRIPS Agreement requires a case-by-case analysis and that a blanket exception *a priori* does not take into account the legitimate interests of trademark owners. The Panel observes that Articles 7(4) and 14(3) of the Regulation do require a case-by-case analysis at the time of a decision on GI registration and, even though they do not require a case-by-case analysis at the time of subsequent use, nothing in the text of Article 17 indicates that a case-by-case analysis is a requirement under the TRIPS Agreement. Whilst it may be true that in the United States the doctrine of "fair use" is applied by courts on a case-by-case basis, we do not consider that this is necessarily implied in the use of those words in the TRIPS Agreement.[588]

---

[586] European Communities' response to Panel question No. 143. Although there is no supporting evidence, all of the considerations cited by the European Communities correspond to factors set out in Articles 13 and 14(3) of the Regulation.

[587] European Communities' rebuttal submission, paras. 286-293; response to Panel question No. 142.

[588] If there were any doubt on this point, can observe that this language in Article 17 was proposed in the TRIPS negotiations by the European Communities and Austria, and was not apparently intended to reflect the United States' practice: see "Synoptic tables setting out existing international standards and proposed standards and principles," prepared by the GATT Secretariat at the request of the Negotiating Group on Trade-related Aspects of Intellectual Property Rights, including trade in counterfeit goods, (document MTN.GNG/NG11/W/32/Rev.2 dated 2 February 1990, p. 51)

7.673 The Panel notes that there may be situations where, in order to take account of the legitimate interests of the owner of a trademark and third parties, practical conditions may be required to distinguish the goods with the trademark from those using the GI and to distinguish the respective undertakings.

7.674 For these reasons, the Panel considers that the exception created by the Regulation takes account of the legitimate interests of the owner of the trademark within the meaning of Article 17. This finding is confirmed by responses to a question from the Panel which revealed that, of over 600 GIs registered under the Regulation over a period of eight years, the complainants and third parties are unable to identify any that, in their view, could be used in a way that would result in a likelihood of confusion with a prior trademark, with four exceptions. Three of these are the Czech beer GIs, the registration of which is subject to the endorsement set out above. The only remaining example is "Bayerisches Bier," in respect of which the complainants have not shown an example of actual likelihood of confusion with a prior trademark.

7.675 We will now consider whether the exception created by the Regulation takes account of the legitimate interests of third parties.

7.676 The parties to this dispute agree that "third parties" for the purposes of Article 17 include consumers. The function of a trademark is to distinguish goods and services of undertakings in the course of trade. That function is served not only for the owner, but also for consumers. Accordingly, the relevant third parties include consumers.[589] Consumers have a legitimate interest in being able to distinguish the goods and services of one undertaking from those of another, and to avoid confusion.

7.677 Turning to the Regulation, Article 14(3) expressly addresses consumers, by providing for the refusal of GI registration where "registration is liable to mislead the consumer as to the true identity of the product." In the one instance in which Article 14(3) has been applied, the European Communities informs the Panel that:

> In essence, it was concluded that, although the products were similar, the signs were not sufficiently similar to mislead the public, having regard to the degree of recognition of the trademark in the different Member States.[590]

7.678 This indicates to the Panel that Article 14(3) of the Regulation was, in fact, applied to take account *inter alia* of the legitimate interests of consumers.

7.679 The Panel also observes, once again, that a name can only be registered as a GI where it is used to describe an agricultural product or a foodstuff. It is a precondition to GI registration that some consumers do, in fact, understand that the GI refers to the product from that geographical area with particular qualities or characteristics, which means that they do not consider that it indicates the trademark owner's goods.

7.680 The United States submits that the "third parties" for the purposes of Article 17 include trademark licensees. This may be correct, but the legitimate interests of trademark licensees are, to a large extent, identified with those of the trademark owner, and can be taken into account at the same time. It is not clear how their interests could be taken into account as a separate issue.

7.681 The European Communities submits that "third parties" for the purposes of Article 17 include persons using a GI in accordance with a GI registration. The Panel agrees. Article 17 permits an exception to the rights conferred by a trademark which include, according to Article 16.1, a right to prevent "all third parties" from using certain signs. The basis of the complainant's claim is that those third parties include GI users. It is logical that, if GI users are included in the third parties subject to the trademark owner's right, they are also included in the third parties taken into account in assessing the availability of an exception to that right.

---

[589] This is confirmed by the reference in Article 16.2 to "the relevant sector of the public," in relation to well-known trademarks.

[590] European Communities' response to Panel question No. 143.

7.682 The legitimacy of the interests of GI users is reflected in the TRIPS Agreement itself, to which all WTO Members have subscribed. Under Section 3 of Part II, all WTO Members agree to provide certain protection to GIs, although they remain free to determine the appropriate method of implementing those provisions in accordance with Article 1.1. The definition of a GI in Article 22.1 reflects a legitimate interest that a person may have in identifying the source and other characteristics of a good by the name of the place where it is from, if the name would serve that purpose. Nevertheless, as "legitimate interests," the interests of GI users as third parties within the meaning of Article 17 would be different from the legal protection provided for in Articles 22 and 23.

7.683 The Panel recalls that the example contained in Article 17 itself of "fair use of descriptive terms" provides some guidance as to what may satisfy its proviso. Its use of the word "fair" and the nature of descriptive terms illustrate a public policy concern that certain terms should be available for use under certain conditions. Although GIs are intellectual property rights, and not purely descriptive terms, the function of the terms in the example is analogous to a descriptive function of GIs and provides contextual support for the notion that the interest of GIs users in using a place name to indicate their products is "legitimate."

7.684 Turning to the Regulation, Article 2(2) provides that a "designation of origin" or a "geographical indication" "means the name of a region, a specific place or, in exceptional cases, a country, used to *describe* an agricultural product or a foodstuff ..." (emphasis added). There are additional conditions relevant to the origin and quality, reputation or characteristics of the product. Further, the European Communities has confirmed that use of a GI remains subject to the requirements of the food labelling and misleading advertising directives which prohibit certain misleading and deceptive uses.[591] These considerations support the view that the interests of GI users of which the Regulation takes account are "legitimate."

7.685 Article 13 of the Regulation sets out the protection conferred by GI registration. In providing such protection, the Regulation not only "takes account" of this legitimate interest, it also provides legally enforceable rights.

7.686 For these reasons, the Panel considers that the exception created by the Regulation takes account of the legitimate interests of third parties within the meaning of Article 17.

7.687 On the basis of the evidence presented to the Panel, which is necessarily limited given that Article 14(3) of the Regulation has only been applied once, and for all of the above reasons, the Panel concludes that the European Communities has succeeded in raising a presumption that the exception created by the Regulation to the trademark owner's right provided for in Article 16.1 of the TRIPS Agreement is justified by Article 17 of the TRIPS Agreement. The United States has not succeeded in rebutting that presumption.

7.688 Therefore, the Panel concludes that, with respect to the coexistence of GIs with prior trademarks, the Regulation is inconsistent with Article 16.1 of the TRIPS Agreement but, on the basis of the evidence presented to the Panel, this is justified by Article 17 of the TRIPS Agreement. Article 24.3 and Article 24.5 of the TRIPS Agreement are inapplicable.

D. Other Claims

1. *MFN treatment claims*

(a) *Availability of protection: MFN treatment under the TRIPS Agreement*

(i) *main arguments of the parties*

7.689 The United States claims that the Regulation is inconsistent with the most-favoured-nation obligations in Article 4 of the TRIPS Agreement "and the Paris Convention" because it imposes conditions of *reciprocity* and *equivalence* on the availability of protection. None of the exceptions in Article 4 permit reciprocity in

---

[591] See *supra* at note 482 and European Communities' first written submission, para. 319; response to Panel question No. 153.

relation to the protection of geographical indications. It cites the GATT panel report in *Belgium – Family Allowances* in which entitlement to an advantage for imported goods made conditional upon the system of family allowances in the exporting Member was found inconsistent with the MFN treatment obligation in GATT. The Regulation does not immediately and *unconditionally* accord the same advantages with respect to availability of protection that it accords to EC nationals. Nationals of WTO Members that satisfy those conditions are accorded more favourable treatment than nationals of WTO Members that do not. The conditions are placed on third country governments but deny rights to third country nationals.[592]

7.690 The United States draws attention to a joint declaration by the European Community and Switzerland for the mutual protection of GIs to be incorporated in a bilateral agreement. However, it challenges the Regulation "as such." The terms of the Regulation prevent the European Commission from determining that all WTO Members satisfy the conditions in Article 12(1): some may satisfy those conditions but others do not. The Regulation cannot be administered in such a way that will treat nationals of all WTO Members as favourably as each other and as favourably as EC nationals. The availability of registration is conditioned on a country-by-country basis. If the Commission refused to apply the Regulation to all third countries, this would theoretically ensure equal treatment but would be inconsistent with the national treatment obligation. In any case, the Regulation does not appear to permit the Commission to refuse to apply it to all third countries.[593]

7.691 The European Communities responds that this claim must fail. It argues that it does not, in fact, apply the conditions in Article 12(1) of the Regulation to geographical areas located in WTO Members.[594] It also argues that the conditions on availability of protection do not apply to nationality but according to the location of geographical areas.[595] These defences were considered in paragraphs 7.52 to 7.103 above.

7.692 The European Communities argues that the joint declaration of the European Community and Switzerland is irrelevant to this dispute because it is merely a political declaration stating the intention of the parties to incorporate, at a later stage, provisions on the protection of GIs in an agreement on trade in agricultural products, which has not yet occurred. It argues that the conditions in Article 12(1) of the Regulation are the same for all third countries which fall under that provision.

7.693 In the absence of a decision under Article 12(3) of the Regulation, Article 12 does not confer any advantage on a third country. It notes that, in GATT panel reports in both *Belgium – Family Allowances* and *EEC – Imports of Beef from Canada*, violations were found after the respondents had actually granted advantages to certain third countries. In response to a question from the Panel, it indicated that if the conditions in Article 12(1) are fulfilled, the Commission will normally recognize the country in question but Article 12(1) creates no legal "obligation" as against the third country. This follows from the wording in Article 12(1) that "this Regulation may apply."[596]

7.694 The European Communities does not contest that MFN treatment under the TRIPS Agreement applies to more extensive protection granted in respect of intellectual property rights addressed in the TRIPS Agreement.[597]

---

[592] United States' first written submission, paras. 117-122; rebuttal submission, para. 104; second oral statement, para. 60.

[593] United States' rebuttal submission, paras. 107-108; first oral statement, para. 36; second oral statement, para. 64.

[594] European Communities' first written submission, paras. 231-234. From an abundance of caution, the European Communities also stated its view that the product-specific conditions for the registration of individual GIs are examined for each product individually and do not discriminate according to nationality or product origin: see its first written submission, paras. 235-238.

[595] European Communities' first written submission, paras. 241-247.

[596] European Communities' first written submission, paras. 239-245; first oral statement, para. 79; second oral statement, para. 139; response to Panel question No. 112.

[597] European Communities' response to Panel question No. 111.

(ii) main arguments of third parties

7.695 Mexico submits that the Regulation violates the MFN treatment obligation in Article 4 of the TRIPS Agreement. Article 12(1) of the Regulation prescribes treatment which discriminates among third countries to the detriment of those which do not satisfy the conditions of reciprocity.[598]

7.696 Chinese Taipei submits that the Regulation violates the MFN treatment obligation in Article 4 of the TRIPS Agreement. Having granted protection to the nationals of a WTO Member who hold GIs located in the territory of that Member, the Regulation denies the same advantage to the nationals of other Members who hold GIs located in other territories.[599]

(iii) consideration by the Panel

7.697 This claim is made under the MFN treatment obligation in Article 4 of the TRIPS Agreement, which provides, relevantly, as follows:

> With regard to the protection of intellectual property, any advantage, favour, privilege or immunity granted by a Member to the nationals of any other country shall be accorded immediately and unconditionally to the nationals of all other Members.

7.698 The following two elements must be satisfied to establish an inconsistency with this obligation: (1) the measure at issue must apply with regard to the protection of intellectual property; and (2) the nationals of other Members are not "immediately and unconditionally" accorded any advantage, favour, privilege or immunity granted by a Member to the nationals of any other country. The Panel will consider each of these elements in turn.

<u>protection of intellectual property</u>

7.699 The MFN treatment obligation in Article 4 of the TRIPS Agreement applies "with regard to the protection of intellectual property." Footnote 3 provides an inclusive definition of the term "protection" as used in Articles 3 and 4, which is quoted at paragraphs 7.126 above.

7.700 The Panel recalls its findings at paragraphs 7.128 and 7.129 of this report that the conditions of reciprocity and equivalence in Article 12(1) of the Regulation are matters affecting the availability of intellectual property rights, in relation to "designations of origin" and "geographical indications," as defined in the Regulation, which are part of a category of intellectual property within the meaning of Article 1.2 of the TRIPS Agreement.

7.701 Therefore, this claim concerns the "protection" of intellectual property, as clarified in footnote 3 to the TRIPS Agreement, within the scope of the MFN treatment obligation in Article 4 of that Agreement.

7.702 It is not necessary to show that the Regulation implements the minimum standards in Part II of the TRIPS Agreement for the purposes of these claims. MFN treatment applies to the protection of intellectual property, even where measures provide a higher level of protection. Indeed, MFN treatment under the TRIPS Agreement generally only has an independent application where a Member grants to the nationals of any other country a level of protection that is higher than it grants to its own nationals and higher than the minimum standards laid down in the TRIPS Agreement.

---

[598] Annex C, para. 111.

[599] Annex C, paras. 173-176.

any advantage, favour, privilege or immunity granted by a Member to the nationals of any other country

7.703 The Panel recalls its conclusion at paragraph 7.102 that the United States has made a prima facie case that the registration procedure in Articles 12a and 12b of the Regulation is not available for GIs located in third countries, including WTO Members, that do not satisfy the conditions in Article 12(1). As a result, the Panel found that GI protection is not available under the Regulation in respect of geographical areas located in third countries which the Commission has not recognized under Article 12(3), although GI protection under the Regulation may become available if the third country in which the GI is located enters into an international agreement or satisfies the conditions in Article 12(1).

7.704 This constitutes an "advantage, favour, privilege or immunity" granted by the European Communities with regard to the protection of intellectual property. It is subject to the satisfaction of the equivalence and reciprocity conditions, or the conclusion of an international agreement, or both, which indicates that it is not accorded "immediately and unconditionally."

7.705 However, that is not sufficient to demonstrate an inconsistency with Article 4 of the TRIPS Agreement, as it must be shown that the advantage, favour, privilege or immunity is granted by a Member "to the nationals of any other country." It is unnecessary for the purposes of this claim to re-examine the issue of how the Regulation discriminates according to nationality, considered in Section VII:B of this report, because the European Commission has not recognized *any* other country as satisfying the conditions under Article 12(1) under the procedure in Article 12(3). However, the United States challenges the Regulation "as such."

7.706 The Panel notes that various GATT and WTO panels have applied the so-called "mandatory/discretionary distinction" as an analytical tool for evaluating claims brought against legislation "as such."[600] Although the Appellate Body has not yet pronounced generally upon its continuing relevance or significance, it has observed that its importance may vary from case to case and it has cautioned against the application of this distinction in a mechanistic fashion.[601]

7.707 Turning to the Regulation at issue in this dispute, the United States accepts that, theoretically, a refusal to apply the Regulation to *any* third country would ensure that no advantage, favour, privilege or immunity would be granted to the nationals of any third country within the meaning of Article 4 of the TRIPS Agreement, although it would be inconsistent with the European Communities' national treatment obligations under Article 3.[602] However, the United States submits that, where the conditions in Article 12(1) of the Regulation are satisfied, "it appears that the Commission would have to make an affirmative decision to that effect."[603]

7.708 The European Communities does *not* indicate that the Commission would exercise any discretion in an MFN-consistent manner by refusing to recognize any third country but expressly states that if the conditions in Article 12(1) of the Regulation are fulfilled the Commission *will* normally recognize the country in question. Its primary defence is that the conditions in paragraph 1 and the recognition procedure in paragraph 3 do not apply to WTO Members, which we have found in Section VII:B of this report is not the case.

7.709 In these circumstances, the Panel considers it appropriate to recall that, in view of its conclusion at paragraph 7.213 above, even if the Commission can refuse to recognize all third countries under the procedure in Article 12(3), this would necessarily be inconsistent with its national treatment obligation under Article 3.1 of the TRIPS Agreement. Given that the Panel has already found that the Regulation is inconsistent with that

---

600 Appellate Body report on *US – 1916 Act*, paras. 61 and 88, citing the GATT Panel report on *US – Tobacco* at para. 118.

601 *US – Corrosion-Resistant Steel Sunset Review*, para. 93.

602 United States' rebuttal submission, para. 108. It is also clear that the application of the Regulation to *all* third countries would also be consistent with MFN treatment. However, it is not disputed that, to the extent that the conditions apply, the Commission cannot recognize *all* third countries.

603 United States' response to Panel question No. 112.

obligation, a further conclusion on the MFN obligation would provide no additional positive contribution to a solution to this dispute. Therefore, the Panel exercises judicial economy with respect to this claim.

(b) Availability of protection: MFN treatment under GATT 1994

(i) main arguments of the parties

7.710 The United States claims that the Regulation is inconsistent with Article I:1 of GATT 1994 because it applies conditions of *equivalence* and *reciprocity* to the benefits of registration. It reiterates its arguments from its national treatment claim under Article III:4 that the Regulation applies to *like products* and is a measure affecting internal sale etc. and argues that, therefore, it is a *matter referred to in paragraph 4 of Article III* within the meaning of Article I:1 of GATT 1994. It reiterates its arguments concerning less favourable treatment of imported products and argues that these are significant *advantages* granted to products imported from a third country that are not immediately and *unconditionally* accorded to the products of all other Members.[604]

7.711 The European Communities responds that there is no violation of Article I:1 of GATT 1994. It reiterates its arguments in relation to MFN treatment under TRIPS that it does not, in fact, apply the conditions in Article 12(1) of the Regulation to geographical areas located in WTO Members; and that the conditions in Article 12(1) of the Regulation are the same for all third countries which fall under that provision.[605]

(ii) consideration by the Panel

7.712 The Panel notes that Article I:1 of GATT 1994 provides, relevantly, as follows:

> ... with respect to all matters referred to in paragraphs 2 and 4 of Article III,* any advantage, favour, privilege or immunity granted by any contracting party to any product originating in or destined for any other country shall be accorded immediately and unconditionally to the like product originating in or destined for the territories of all other contracting parties.

7.713 The Panel recalls its finding at paragraph 7.227 that the Regulation is a law or regulation affecting the internal sale and offering for sale of products within the meaning of Article III:4 of GATT 1994. It therefore falls within the "matters referred to in paragraphs 2 and 4 of Article III" as that phrase is used in Article I:1.

7.714 The Panel also recalls its finding at paragraph 7.229 that the Regulation discriminates on its face among products and that the European Communities does not contest that there are, among this group, "like products" among the imported products and products of European Communities origin, for the purposes of Article III:4 of GATT 1994. Protection under the Regulation is provided against use of a name in respect of products "comparable to the products registered under that name." In the Panel's view, this is sufficient basis to conclude that there are "like products" among the imported products of other countries including WTO Members for the purposes of Article I:1 of GATT 1994.

7.715 The Panel also recalls its finding at paragraph 7.704, that the advantage of availability of protection is not accorded "immediately and unconditionally."

7.716 However, in view of the Panel's conclusion at paragraph 7.238 above, even if the Commission can refuse to recognize all third countries under the procedure in Article 12(3), this would necessarily be inconsistent with the national treatment obligation in Article III:4 of GATT 1994. Given that the Panel has

---

[604] United States' first written submission, paras. 123-127.

[605] European Communities' first written submission, paras. 261 and 263. From an abundance of caution, the European Communities also stated its view that the product-specific conditions for the registration of individual GIs are examined for each product individually and do not discriminate according to nationality or product origin. As such, there is no violation of Article I:1 of GATT 1994 and, in the alternative, they are justified under Article XX(d): see its first written submission, paras. 262, 265-266.

already found that, in this respect, the Regulation is inconsistent with that obligation, a further conclusion with respect to the European Communities' MFN treatment obligation would provide no additional positive contribution to a solution to this dispute. Therefore, the Panel chooses to exercise judicial economy with respect to this claim.

(c) Application and objection procedures

(i) main arguments of the parties

7.717 The United States submits that the Regulation "is inconsistent with the most-favoured nation obligation of the TRIPS Agreement for the same reasons that it is inconsistent with the national treatment obligation of the TRIPS Agreement."[606] It argues that nationals of other WTO Members can register their home-based GIs if they are from a country which agrees to substantial participation in administering and enforcing the Regulation on behalf of its nationals.[607] There is no room for the Commission to determine that all WTO Members satisfy the conditions of the Regulation. Some Members might be able to prosecute applications successfully on behalf of their nationals but others cannot.[608] The United States also argues that the right to object is subject to WTO Members' satisfaction of conditions of *equivalence* and *reciprocity*.[609] For these reasons, the Regulation does not immediately and *unconditionally* accord to nationals of all WTO Members the advantages accorded to EC nationals.[610]

7.718 The European Communities does not respond specifically to this claim in relation to the right to object.[611] However, in its description of the Regulation it argues that Article 12d grants a right of objection to persons from WTO Members because the phrase "recognised under the procedure provided for in Article 12(3)" only applies to other third countries. The conditions of *equivalence* and *reciprocity* do not apply to WTO Members to the right to object. Otherwise, the specific reference to "WTO Members" would be meaningless. This is also clear in Article 12b(2).[612]

(ii) consideration by the Panel

7.719 The Panel recalls its findings at paragraphs 7.262 and 7.329 that the application and objection procedures under the Regulation are matters affecting the acquisition of intellectual property rights, in relation to "designations of origin" and "geographical indications," as defined in the Regulation, which are part of a category of intellectual property within the meaning of Article 1.2 of the TRIPS Agreement. Therefore, these claims concern the "protection" of intellectual property, as clarified in footnote 3 to the TRIPS Agreement, within the scope of the MFN treatment obligation in Article 4 of that Agreement.

7.720 The Panel recalls its finding at paragraph 7.352 that the procedure for recognition of third countries under Article 12(3) of the Regulation does not apply to WTO Members with respect to objection procedures.

7.721 The Panel has not found that there is any difference in the application and objection procedures under Articles 12b and 12d of the Regulation regarding the nationals of different WTO Members. Any differences that arise in practice would appear to depend on the actions of various other WTO Member governments. However, the MFN obligation in Article 4 of the TRIPS Agreement applies only to any advantage, favour, privilege or immunity "granted by a Member," in this case, the European Communities. The United States has not shown how the differences in the treatment accorded to nationals of different Members are granted by the European

[606] United States' first written submission, para. 118.

[607] United States' rebuttal submission, para. 104.

[608] United States' first written submission, para. 117, fn. 102; rebuttal submission, para. 107.

[609] United States' rebuttal submission, para. 104.

[610] United States' rebuttal submission, para. 104.

[611] European Communities' first written submission, paras. 227-256.

[612] European Communities' first written submission, paras. 73-75; first oral statement, para. 50; second oral statement, paras. 86-88.

Communities. Therefore, the Panel concludes that the United States has not made a prima facie case in support of this claim.

(d) Execution of the Regulation by authorities of EC member States

(i) main arguments of the parties

7.722 The United States argues that nationals of EC member States—which are WTO Members in their own right—are accorded more favourable treatment than nationals of WTO Members outside the European Communities. EC member States are not excused from this obligation by the fact that they are acting pursuant to an EC Regulation. Measures of EC member States are within the terms of reference because the request for establishment of a panel specifies not only the Regulation but also "its related implementation and enforcement measures."[613]

7.723 The European Communities argues that EC member States do not grant "advantages" within the meaning of the MFN treatment obligation because the Regulation is a Community measure adopted to harmonize Community law and the European Communities is an original Member of the WTO in its own right. The European Communities is the respondent in this Panel proceeding and claims of violations by EC member States cannot be raised. In any event, the United States has not identified any measures of EC member States.[614]

(ii) consideration by the Panel

7.724 The Panel observes that in this claim the United States asserts, in effect, that nationals of EC member States are "nationals of any other country" within the meaning of Article 4 of the TRIPS Agreement, quoted at paragraph 7.697 above. This, in turn, depends on the interpretation that each EC member State constitutes "any other country" within the meaning of Article 4 of the TRIPS Agreement.

7.725 The Panel recalls its finding at paragraph 7.150 as to which persons are the European Communities' own nationals. The Panel also recalls its findings at paragraph 7.98 that it has accepted the European Communities' explanation of what amount to its *sui generis* domestic constitutional arrangements that Community laws are generally not executed through authorities at Community level but rather through recourse to the authorities of its member States which, in such a situation, "act *de facto* as organs of the Community, for which the Community would be responsible under WTO law and international law in general."[615] Therefore, to the extent that advantages are granted under the Regulation, by the Community and EC member State authorities exercising powers under the Regulation, to the European Communities' own nationals, those advantages are not granted to "the nationals of any other country," within the meaning of Article 4 of the TRIPS Agreement.

7.726 Therefore, the Panel rejects this claim, to the extent that it is based on the execution of the Regulation by the authorities of EC member States.

7.727 The Panel wishes to confirm that it has accepted the European Communities' explanation as to the way in which Community laws are executed not only for this MFN claim but also for the national treatment claims[616]. This has repercussions for the European Communities' defences to those other claims, in particular concerning the application and objection procedures, as noted at paragraphs 7.269 and 7.339 of this report. The Panel has applied this explanation of the way in which Community laws are executed in a consistent manner to all relevant claims in this dispute.

---

613 United States' first written submission, para. 121; first oral statement, para. 37; rebuttal submission, paras. 110-113; second oral statement, para. 65.

614 European Communities' first written submission, paras. 249-255; rebuttal submission, paras. 252-256; second oral statement, paras. 145-149.

615 European Communities' second oral statement, para. 148.

616 See para. 7.98 above.

7.728 Finally, the Panel notes that the United States has also referred to the Paris Convention (1967), which does not contain a MFN treatment obligation. There is no need to consider this further.

7.729 In summary, with respect to the MFN treatment claims:

(a) under Article 4 of the TRIPS Agreement:

(i) with respect to the availability of protection, the Panel exercises judicial economy;

(ii) with respect to the application and objection procedures, the United States has not made a prima facie case in support of its claim; and

(iii) with respect to the execution of the Regulation by the authorities of EC member States, the Panel rejects the claim; and

(b) under Article I:1 of GATT 1994, the Panel exercises judicial economy.

2. Minimum standards of GI protection
(a) Main arguments of the parties

7.730 The United States claims that the Regulation is inconsistent with Article 22.2 of the TRIPS Agreement because it does not provide interested parties in other WTO Members which do not satisfy the *equivalence and reciprocity conditions*, including inspection structures, the legal means to protect their GIs on a uniform basis throughout the territory of the European Communities. Article 2 of the Regulation provides that GIs for certain products "shall be obtained" in accordance with the Regulation and does not appear to permit GI protection through other means.[617] Once a complainant presents a prima facie case that a measure is inconsistent with a WTO obligation, the respondent then bears the burden to rebut that case by showing that there is no inconsistency, which may include demonstrating that other domestic measures eliminate the alleged inconsistency. If there were other measures somewhere in the legal system of the European Communities or its member States that compensated for the inconsistencies in the Regulation, the United States submits that the European Communities would have and should have come forward with them, but that it has failed to do so.[618]

7.731 The United States also claims that the Regulation is inconsistent with Article 22.2 of the TRIPS Agreement because interested parties in other WTO Members must depend on their respective governments to intercede on their behalf in the *verification and transmission of applications*.[619]

7.732 The United States also claims that the Regulation is inconsistent with Article 22.2 of the TRIPS Agreement with respect to *objections* because (1) persons who wish to object to the registration of a GI cannot do so directly[620]; (2) the Regulation does not permit persons in other WTO Members which do not satisfy the equivalence and reciprocity conditions the right to object[621]; (3) persons who wish to object to the registration of a GI must have a legitimate interest or a legitimate economic interest in the European Communities, but an interested party can be any producer or seller established in the region falsely indicated as the source in a given territory[622]; and (4) the grounds for objection based on a prior trademark in Article 7(4) of the Regulation are narrower than the rights required to be made available under Article 22.2 of the TRIPS Agreement. A registered GI could be misleading. Registration grants an affirmative right to use, which cannot be prevented after

---

617 United States' first written submission, paras. 171-176; rebuttal submission, paras. 212 and 216.

618 United States' response to Panel question No. 158.

619 United States' first written submission, paras. 177-178; rebuttal submission, para. 213.

620 United States' first written submission, para. 179; rebuttal submission, para. 213.

621 United States' first written submission, para. 180.

622 United States' first written submission, para. 181; rebuttal submission, para. 214.

registration, so that the right of objection to registration must be available to all interested parties.[623] The United States confirms that it does not make any claim under Part IV of the TRIPS Agreement but that a measure can violate both Parts II and IV.[624]

7.733 The European Communities responds that the conditions of *equivalence and reciprocity* do not apply to WTO Members.[625] In any event, even if all the United States' arguments were correct, the European Communities would still comply with Article 22.2 of the TRIPS Agreement because the Regulation is not the only means made available by the European Communities and its member States in order to prevent the acts mentioned in Article 22.2. Specifically, additional means of protection are provided in the foodstuffs labelling, misleading advertising and trademarks directives, and the implementing legislation of the EC member States, the Community Trademark Regulation and the unfair competition laws of the EC member States. These laws have been notified under the TRIPS Agreement and identified in responses to questions in the TRIPS Council review under Article 24.2 of the TRIPS Agreement. These various measures and the Regulation apply cumulatively. They are sufficient to implement the European Communities' obligation under Article 22.2 of the TRIPS Agreement and are outside the Panel's terms of reference. [626] The complainants were well aware of the existence of these other measures. Had they been of the view that they were insufficient to comply with Article 22.2 they could and should have mentioned them in their panel requests. They cannot shift the burden of proof to the respondent simply by asserting that the respondent provides no means of implementation.[627]

7.734 The European Communities submits that the *transmission of applications* is a modality of the registration process. The United States has not shown that it is unreasonable and inconsistent with Article 62.1 of the TRIPS Agreement. Such a claim would be outside the Panel's terms of reference.[628]

7.735 The European Communities submits that Article 22.2 does not confer a *right to object* to the registration of a GI. Even if it did, (1) the rights conferred under Article 22.2 can be made subject to compliance with reasonable procedures and formalities, and transmission through governments is neither excessive nor unreasonable; (2) the conditions of reciprocity and equivalence do not apply to the right of objection; (3) although persons who wish to object must have an economic interest in the European Communities, this does not require them to establish or do business within the European Communities; (4) there are grounds for objection under Article 7(4) and it does not see what other acts of unfair competition could arise from the valid registration of a GI.[629] The European Communities agrees that a procedure for the acquisition of an intellectual property right may violate both Parts I and IV, and both Parts II and IV, of the TRIPS Agreement, but Article 22.2 does not regulate expressly the right of opposition and it may not be assumed that this derogates from the generally applicable rules under Part IV.[630] Further, registration of a GI is not a "use" covered by Article 22.2.[631]

(b) Consideration by the Panel

(i) introduction

7.736 The Panel begins by recalling that the United States, in its request for establishment of a panel, cited Article 22.2 of the TRIPS Agreement in the series of numbered provisions and, in the narrative text, paraphrased the text of subparagraph (a) of Article 22.2. It was clear on a plain reading of the request that the

---

623 United States' first written submission, para. 182; rebuttal submission, paras. 215-216; second oral statement, para. 69.

624 United States' response to Panel question No. 84.

625 European Communities' first written submission, paras. 422-423.

626 European Communities' first written submission, paras. 421, 433-436; response to Panel question No. 159.

627 European Communities' response to Panel question No. 162.

628 European Communities' first written submission, paras. 424-426.

629 European Communities' first written submission, paras. 427-432.

630 European Communities' rebuttal submission, paras. 395-397.

631 European Communities' rebuttal submission, para. 398.

series of numbered provisions was not to be limited to what appeared in the narrative text, even though it did not paraphrase subparagraph (b) of Article 22.2.[632] It is unnecessary for the purposes of this report to distinguish further between subparagraphs (a) and (b) as our findings apply with equal force to both.

7.737 Article 22.2 of the TRIPS Agreement provides as follows:

> 2. In respect of geographical indications, Members shall provide the legal means for interested parties to prevent:
>
> (a) the use of any means in the designation or presentation of a good that indicates or suggests that the good in question originates in a geographical area other than the true place of origin in a manner which misleads the public as to the geographical origin of the good;
>
> (b) any use which constitutes an act of unfair competition within the meaning of Article 10*bis* of the Paris Convention (1967).

7.738 The term "geographical indications" is defined in Article 22.1 of the TRIPS Agreement. It is not disputed that registered "designations of origin" and registered "geographical indications," as defined in the Article 2(2) of the Regulation, are a subset of "geographical indications" as defined in Article 22.1 and therefore relevant to the European Communities' implementation of Article 22.2.

(ii) equivalence and reciprocity conditions; examination and transmission of applications

7.739 The Panel recalls its conclusion in paragraphs 7.213, 7.238, 7.281 and 7.307 that the equivalence and reciprocity conditions in Article 12(1) of the Regulation, and the procedures for examination and transmission of applications, are inconsistent with the European Communities' national treatment obligations. Now we must consider whether they also deny the legal means that Article 22.2 of the TRIPS Agreement requires the European Communities to provide for interested parties who are nationals of other Members.

7.740 The Panel recalls its findings:

(a) at paragraph 7.102 that the United States has made a prima facie case that, due to the applicability of the equivalence and reciprocity conditions in Article 12(1) of the Regulation, the registration procedure in Articles 12a and 12b is not available for GIs located in third countries, including WTO Members, that do not satisfy those conditions; and

(b) at paragraph 7.272 that a group or person who submits an application in a third country has no right to have its application examined or transmitted to the Commission where its Member government does not examine and transmit the application.

7.741 Article 22.2 of the TRIPS Agreement imposes an obligation on Members. The obligation is owed to other Members, as the TRIPS Agreement creates rights and obligations between WTO Members. In this regard, it can be noted that the dispute settlement system of the WTO serves, *inter alia* to preserve the rights and obligations of *Members* under the covered agreements (emphasis added).[633] However, a particularity of the TRIPS Agreement is that the assessment of the conformity of measures with Members' obligations generally requires an assessment of the manner in which they confer rights or protection on private parties.

---

[632] See paras. 15-19 of the Panel's preliminary ruling set out in para. 7.2 above.

[633] See Article 3.2 of the DSU.

7.742 Article 1.3 provides that "Members shall accord the treatment provided for in this Agreement to the nationals of other Members." That includes the protection provided for in Article 22.2, which obliges Members to provide legal means for "interested parties." The interested parties must qualify as "nationals of other Members" in accordance with the criteria referred to in Article 1.3. These persons can be private parties, which is reflected in the fourth recital of the preamble to the agreement, which reads "*[r]ecognizing* that intellectual property rights are private rights."

7.743 Therefore, in order to determine whether the European Communities has implemented its obligation owed to other Members in Article 22.2, the Panel must examine whether it has provided the legal means required by that provision for interested parties who are nationals of other Members.

7.744 Naturally, the treatment that Members are obliged to accord under the TRIPS Agreement is not limited to the bundle of rights conferred on individuals by the grant of an intellectual property right. Whilst Article 22.2 sets out protection conferred by a GI, Article 16.1 sets out rights conferred by a trademark and other provisions in each of the Sections of Part II set out the rights conferred by other categories of intellectual property, these represent a subset of the treatment that Members are obliged to accord under the TRIPS Agreement. All of the obligations of Members considered in this report, including the obligations to accord national treatment and MFN treatment, form part of the treatment to be accorded under the TRIPS Agreement, but only the exclusive rights provided for the owner of a trademark and the legal means for interested parties considered in Sections VII:C and D:2 of this report constitute rights or protection conferred on a person by an intellectual property right.[634]

7.745 Turning to the Regulation, we note that it makes protection available, in the sense that it provides legal means to protect GIs. However, those legal means have *not* been provided to interested parties with respect to GIs located in a third country, including a WTO Member, that does not satisfy the equivalence and reciprocity conditions, and the government of which does not examine and transmit an application. These interested parties include persons who are "nationals of other Members" within the meaning of Article 1.3 of the TRIPS Agreement. Further, to the extent that the legal means may be provided to interested parties with respect to such GIs, the Regulation alone does not provide them, because protection is contingent on satisfaction of conditions and execution of certain functions by governments of third countries. Therefore, the Panel concludes that the United States has made a prima facie case in support of its claim that *the Regulation* does not make available the legal means to interested parties in accordance with Article 22.2 of the TRIPS Agreement.

7.746 However, the obligation under Article 22.2 is placed on *the European Communities*, not on the Regulation. The TRIPS Agreement creates positive obligations in Parts II and III to accord protection according to certain minimum standards, in addition to the prohibitions against discrimination found in the basic principles under Part I. In accordance with Article 1.1, the European Communities is free to determine the appropriate method of implementing the provisions of the Agreement within its own legal system and practice. It is not obliged to ensure that this particular Regulation implements Article 22.2 where it has other measures that do so.

7.747 The United States has challenged the Regulation only, and not other means by which the European Communities may have implemented Article 22.2. In doing so, the United States has complied with the requirement of Article 6.2 of the DSU that it "identify the specific measures at issue" and has not challenged any and all unspecified measures which the European Communities might have. Yet proof of the treatment accorded by that one specific measure may be inadequate to demonstrate that a Member has not implemented a positive obligation to accord certain treatment.

7.748 The United States submits that the Regulation is an exclusive means of implementation of Article 22.2, at least for agricultural products and foodstuffs, due to the terms of its Article 2(1), which provides as follows:

---

[634] The Panel is aware of the Appellate Body's comments in *Canada – Patent Term*, at para. 56, but confirms the distinction between national treatment and MFN treatment, which must be accorded to the nationals of other Members, and the rights or protection which must be conferred on interested parties in respect of GIs, as intellectual property rights, for the reasons explained in this report.

Community protection of designations of origin and of geographical indications of agricultural products and foodstuffs shall be obtained in accordance with this Regulation.

7.749 This provision ensures that "designations of origin" and "geographical indications," as defined in Article 2(2) of the Regulation, which are registered for agricultural products and foodstuffs under the Regulation, are protected under the Regulation at the Community level. However, it is not clear that this provision ensures that protection is exclusively available under the Regulation. It may simply reflect the matters set out in the eleventh recital in the preamble which refers to the pre-existing "diversity in the national practices for implementing registered designations of origin and geographical indications" and states that "a Community approach should be envisaged." This does not indicate that the Regulation is exclusive, particularly for GIs that are not registered under it, which presently appears to include all GIs of the nationals of other Members.

7.750 The European Communities submits that it implements Article 22.2 through other measures besides the Regulation, including the foodstuffs labelling and misleading advertising directives and implementing legislation of the EC member States. It identified the foodstuffs labelling directive and other measures prior to the Panel proceeding as part of the Community's implementation of the GI provisions of the TRIPS Agreement in a review in the Council for TRIPS and in a letter from Commissioner Lamy to the United States Trade Representative in January 2003[635] and it also listed them in its first written submission and first oral statement. It also referred to unfair competition laws of EC member States.[636] These other means of protection, while not specifically providing for the protection of GIs, prohibit business practices which can involve the misuse of GIs. A broad range of laws of this nature have been referred to by many Members, including the United States, in their implementation of the provisions of Section 3 in the review conducted in the Council for TRIPS under Article 24.2 of the TRIPS Agreement.[637]

7.751 Nevertheless, the United States chose to challenge only the Regulation, as amended, "and its related implementing and enforcement measures." It has not demonstrated that these alternative measures, which lie outside the Panel's terms of reference, are inadequate to provide GI protection to for interested parties nationals of other Members as required under Article 22.2 of the TRIPS Agreement. Therefore, it has not presented sufficient evidence to raise a presumption that the European Communities (as opposed to the Regulation) does not implement its obligations under Article 22.2. Accordingly, the Panel concludes that, with respect to the equivalence and reciprocity conditions and the examination and transmission of applications under the Regulation, the United States has not made a prima facie case that the European Communities has failed to implement its obligation under Article 22.2 of the TRIPS Agreement.[638]

(iii) objections

7.752 The United States also bases its claim under Article 22.2 of the TRIPS Agreement on four arguments that relate to the rights of persons who wish to object to a GI registration, the fourth of which concerns the grounds for objection available to trademark owners.

7.753 The Panel notes that Article 22.2 is found in Part II of the TRIPS Agreement, which sets out minimum standards concerning the availability, scope and use of intellectual property rights. The first seven Sections of

---

[635] Exhibit US-73, attachment, page 1, *supra* at note 46.

[636] Responses to the Checklist of questions received from the European Communities in the TRIPS Council "Review under Article 24.2 of the application of the provisions of the section of the TRIPS Agreement on geographical indications," document IP/C/W/117/Add.10, dated 26 November 1998, set out in Exhibit EC-29. European Communities' first written submission, para. 434; first oral statement, para. 35.

[637] See document IP/C/W/253/Rev.1, pp. 6-8.

[638] The Panel's findings are limited to the circumstances of this particular dispute and do not imply that a respondent can avoid a finding of inconsistency with an affirmative obligation to implement protection simply by asserting that alternative measures outside the Panel's terms of reference implement its obligations. It can be noted that in previous disputes which also involved an obligation to provide particular "means" under the TRIPS Agreement, the Panels and the Appellate Body referred to alternative measures which allegedly implemented the obligation, but it was not contested that the alternative measures lay outside the terms of reference: see the reports in *India – Patents (US) and (EC)* (documents WT/DS50/R; WT/DS50/AB/R and WT/DS79/R).

Part II contain standards relating to categories of intellectual property rights. Each Section provides for a different category of intellectual property, although at times they refer to one another, setting out, as a minimum, the subject matter which is eligible for protection, the scope of the rights conferred by the relevant category of intellectual property and permitted exceptions to those rights. Section 2 provides for trademarks. Article 22.2 is located in Section 3, which provides for the category of GIs. Whilst the provisions on protection of GIs affect the protection of trademarks, as expressly recognized in Articles 22.3 and 23.2, Section 3 does not provide for trademark protection, except to the extent that trademark systems are used to protect GIs.

7.754 Article 22.2 does not provide for a right of objection to the registration of a GI. Although Article 15.5 provides for a right of objection to registration of a trademark, no provision in Part II of the TRIPS Agreement provides for objections to the registration of a GI.

7.755 Therefore, the Panel rejects the United States' arguments in support of this claim insofar as they relate to objections to GI registration, including objections by trademark owners.

7.756 There are provisions on the acquisition and maintenance of intellectual property rights, including GIs, in Article 62. These specifically refer to related *inter partes* procedures such as opposition, revocation and cancellation, in paragraph 4, which is cross-referenced in paragraph 5, where a Member's law provides for such procedures. The opportunity or right to object forms part of an opposition procedure. However, Article 62 lies outside the Panel's terms of reference.

7.757 The Panel also recalls its finding at paragraph 7.352 that the equivalence and reciprocity conditions do not apply to the right of objection by persons resident or established in WTO Members. The United States' second argument relating to objections in support of its claim under Article 22.2 is unfounded for this reason as well.

(iv) conclusion with respect to Article 22.2 of the TRIPS Agreement

7.758 In view of the findings at paragraphs 7.751, 7.755 and 7.757, with respect to this claim, the Panel concludes that the United States has not made a prima facie case that the European Communities has failed to implement its obligation under Article 22.2 of the TRIPS Agreement.

3. Claims under Part III of the TRIPS Agreement

(a) Main arguments of the parties

7.759 The United States claims that the Regulation is inconsistent with Articles 41.1, 41.2, 41.4, 42 and 44.1 of the TRIPS Agreement because it denies the owner of a registered trademark the right provided for in Article 16.1 of the TRIPS Agreement, and because it does not, with respect to a GI, provide the rights provided for in Article 22.2 of the TRIPS Agreement.[639] It requests a finding that the enforcement obligations of the TRIPS Agreement apply to the Regulation to the extent that it makes unavailable to right holders the requisite enforcement procedures and remedies.[640]

7.760 The European Communities responds that these claims are unfounded because Part III of the TRIPS Agreement does not apply to the Regulation. The Regulation lays down an administrative procedure for the acquisition of GIs via a system of registration and does not purport to regulate enforcement procedures, which are the subject of Part III of the TRIPS Agreement.[641]

---

[639] United States' first written submission, paras. 184-188; rebuttal submission, para. 218.

[640] United States' rebuttal submission, para. 219.

[641] European Communities' first written submission, paras. 357-386, 390-397.

(b) Consideration by the Panel

7.761 These claims are made under the obligations with respect to enforcement procedures found in Part III of the TRIPS Agreement. The obligations in Part III are applicable to acts of infringement of geographical indications by virtue of the use of the term "intellectual property" in Part III and the definition of "intellectual property" in Article 1.2. However, the United States' claims are dependent on its claims concerning the minimum standards in Part II of the Agreement, specifically Articles 16.1 and 22.2. Given that the Panel has ruled on the claims under Articles 16.1 and 22.2, further findings on the claims under Part III would not provide any additional contribution to a positive solution to this dispute. Therefore, the Panel exercises judicial economy with respect to these claims.[642]

4. *Claim under Article 1.1 of the TRIPS Agreement*

(a) Main arguments of the parties

7.762 The United States claims that the inspection structures requirements force Members to adopt a particular set of rules to implement the TRIPS Agreement, contrary to Article 1.1. Protection is conditioned on the existence of inspection structures that the European Communities unilaterally decides are *equivalent* to those in the European Communities.[643] The United States does not challenge the EC inspection system itself, it challenges whether the European Communities can unilaterally require that other WTO Members adopt its system.[644]

7.763 The European Communities responds that the requirement of inspection structures is consistent with Article 1.1 of the TRIPS Agreement because it exclusively concerns GI protection in the European Communities and not other Members' systems of protection.[645]

(b) Consideration by the Panel

7.764 Article 1.1 of the TRIPS Agreement provides as follows:

> 1. Members shall give effect to the provisions of this Agreement. Members may, but shall not be obliged to, implement in their law more extensive protection than is required by this Agreement, provided that such protection does not contravene the provisions of this Agreement. Members shall be free to determine the appropriate method of implementing the provisions of this Agreement within their own legal system and practice.

7.765 To the extent that this claim concerns the equivalence and reciprocity conditions in Article 12(1) of the Regulation, which condition the treatment accorded to the nationals of other Members on the system of protection in those other Members, the Panel has made abundant findings in Section VII:B of this report.

7.766 To the extent that this claim concerns the inspection structures requirement for particular products, the Panel recognizes that these requirements may require inspections to take place not only within the European Communities but also within the territory of other WTO Members, for example, where the specifications concern production processes or other matters not related to the physical characteristics of the product itself. The evidence before the Panel does not disclose that these inspections concern other WTO Members' system of protection but, rather, only compliance with the product specifications, which are a feature of the European Communities' system of protection.

---

[642] In this respect, see the United States' responses to Panel question Nos. 82 and 83.

[643] United States' first written submission, paras. 59, 64.

[644] United States' second oral statement, para. 30.

[645] European Communities' rebuttal submission, para. 100.

7.767 Therefore, the evidence does not suggest that they are inconsistent with the freedom granted under the third sentence of Article 1.1. For this reason, the Panel rejects this claim.[646]

5. *Claim under Article 65.1 of the TRIPS Agreement*

(a) *Main arguments of the parties*

7.768 The United States claims that the Regulation is inconsistent with Article 65.1 of the TRIPS Agreement, which obliged the European Communities to apply the provisions of the TRIPS Agreement by 1 January 1996, because it is still inconsistent with several provisions of the Agreement.[647]

7.769 The European Communities responds that this claim is dependent on the substantive claims and is equally unfounded.[648]

(b) *Consideration by the Panel*

7.770 The Panel notes that this is a consequential claim and considers that a finding on it would not provide any additional contribution to a positive solution to this dispute. Therefore, the Panel exercises judicial economy with respect to this claim.

VIII. CONCLUSIONS AND RECOMMENDATION

8.1 In light of the findings set out in this report, the Panel concludes as follows:

From Section A of the findings:

(a) the measures and claims in the United States' request for establishment of a panel did not fail to meet the requirements of Article 6.2 of the DSU that it identify the specific measures at issue and provide a brief summary of the legal basis of the complaint sufficient to present the problem clearly;

(b) the claims under Article 2(2) of the Paris Convention (1967) are within the Panel's terms of reference;

From Section B of the findings:

(c) the United States has made a prima facie case that the equivalence and reciprocity conditions in Article 12(1) of the Regulation apply to the availability of protection for GIs that refer to geographical areas located in third countries outside the European Communities, including WTO Members, and the European Communities has not succeeded in rebutting that case;

(d) the Regulation is inconsistent with Article 3.1 of the TRIPS Agreement:

  (i) with respect to the equivalence and reciprocity conditions, as applicable to the availability of protection for GIs;

---

[646] This conclusion refers only to the United States' claim under Article 1.1 of the TRIPS Agreement and is without prejudice to the Panel's conclusion at paragraph 7.431 that certain aspects of the inspection structures requirements are inconsistent with Article 3.1 of the TRIPS Agreement. Those aspects contravene the provisions of the Agreement within the meaning of the proviso in the second sentence of Article 1.1.

[647] United States' first written submission, paras. 189-190.

[648] European Communities' first written submission, paras. 502-503.

(ii) with respect to the application procedures, insofar as they require examination and transmission of applications by governments;

(iii) with respect to the objection procedures, insofar as they require verification and transmission of objections by governments; and

(iv) with respect to the requirements of government participation in the inspection structures under Article 10, and the provision of the declaration by governments under Article 12a(2)(b);

(e) the United States has not made a prima facie case in support of its claim that the Regulation is inconsistent with Article 3.1 of the TRIPS Agreement:

(i) with respect to the equivalence and reciprocity conditions, as allegedly applicable to objections;

(ii) with respect to the standing requirements for objections;

(iii) with respect to the allegedly prescriptive requirements for inspection structures; or

(iv) with respect to the labelling requirement;

(f) the United States has not made a prima facie case in support of its claim that the Regulation is inconsistent with Article 2(1) of the Paris Convention, as incorporated by Article 2.1 of the TRIPS Agreement:

(i) with respect to the equivalence and reciprocity conditions, as allegedly applicable to objections;

(ii) with respect to the standing requirements for objections; or

(iii) with respect to the inspection structures;

(g) the Regulation does not impose a requirement of domicile or establishment inconsistently with Article 2(2) of the Paris Convention (1967) as incorporated by Article 2.1 of the TRIPS Agreement:

(i) with respect to the availability of protection for GIs; or

(ii) with respect to the objection procedures;

(h) the Regulation is inconsistent with Article III:4 of GATT 1994:

(i) with respect to the reciprocity and equivalence conditions, as applicable to the availability of protection for GIs;

(ii) with respect to the application procedures, insofar as they require examination and transmission of applications by governments, and these requirements are not justified by Article XX(d) of GATT 1994; and

(iii) with respect to the requirements of government participation in the inspection structures under Article 10, and the provision of the declaration by governments under Article 12a(2)(b), and these requirements are not justified by Article XX(d) of GATT 1994;

(i) the United States has not made a prima facie case in support of its claims that the Regulation is inconsistent with Article III:4 of GATT 1994:

(i) with respect to the equivalence and reciprocity conditions, as allegedly applicable to objections;

(ii) with respect to the objection procedures, insofar as they require verification and transmission of objections by governments;

(iii) with respect to the allegedly prescriptive requirements for inspection structures; or

(iv) with respect to the labelling requirement;

From Section C of the findings:

(j) the Regulation is inconsistent with Article 16.1 of the TRIPS Agreement with respect to the coexistence of GIs with prior trademarks but this is justified by Article 17 of the TRIPS Agreement. In this respect:

(i) Article 24.3 of the TRIPS Agreement is inapplicable; and

(ii) Article 24.5 of the TRIPS Agreement is inapplicable;

From Section D of the findings:

(k) the United States has not made a prima facie case in support of its claim under Article 4 of the TRIPS Agreement, with respect to the application and objection procedures;

(l) the Panel rejects the United States' claim under Article 4 of the TRIPS Agreement , with respect to the execution of the Regulation by the authorities of EC member States;

(m) the United States has not made a prima facie case that the European Communities has failed to implement its obligation under Article 22.2 of the TRIPS Agreement; and

(n) the Panel rejects the United States' claim that the Regulation is inconsistent with Article 1.1 of the TRIPS Agreement.

8.2 The Panel exercises judicial economy with respect to the United States' claims under:

(a) Article 2(1) of the Paris Convention (1967), as incorporated by Article 2.1 of the TRIPS Agreement (except as noted at paragraph 8.1(f));

(b) Article 4 of the TRIPS Agreement, (except as noted at paragraph 8.1(k) and (l));

(c) Articles 41.1, 41.2, 41.4, 42, 44.1 and 65.1 of the TRIPS Agreement; and

(d) Article I:1 of GATT 1994.

8.3 Under Article 3.8 of the DSU, in cases where there is an infringement of the obligations assumed under a covered agreement, the action is considered prima facie to constitute a case of nullification or impairment. The Panel concludes that, to the extent that the Regulation as such is inconsistent with the covered agreements, it has nullified or impaired benefits accruing to the United States under these agreements.

8.4 In light of these conclusions, the Panel recommends pursuant to Article 19.1 of the DSU that the European Communities bring the Regulation into conformity with the TRIPS Agreement and GATT 1994.

8.5 The Panel suggests, pursuant to Article 19.1 of the DSU, that one way in which the European Communities could implement the above recommendation with respect to the equivalence and reciprocity conditions, would be to amend the Regulation so as for those conditions not to apply to the procedures for registration of GIs located in other WTO Members which, it submitted to the Panel, is already the case. This suggestion is not intended to diminish the importance of the above recommendation with respect to any of the Panel's other conclusions.

EUROPEAN COMMUNITIES – PROTECTION OF TRADEMARKS AND GEOGRAPHICAL INDICATIONS FOR AGRICULTURAL PRODUCTS AND FOODSTUFFS

COMPLAINT BY THE UNITED STATES

WT/DS174/R/ADD.1
REPORT OF THE PANEL

ADDENDUM

This addendum contains Annex A to the Report of the Panel to be found in document WT/DS174/R. Annex B can be found in Add.2 and Annexes C and D can be found in Add.3.

ANNEX A

SUBMISSIONS BY THE UNITED STATES

ANNEX A-1

UNITED STATES' RESPONSE TO THE EUROPEAN COMMUNITIES' REQUEST FOR A PRELIMINARY RULING

(15 March 2004)

TABLE OF CONTENTS

EUROPEAN COMMUNITIES—TRADEMARKS AND GEOGRAPHICAL INDICATIONS—COMPLAINT BY THE UNITED STATES

I. INTRODUCTION

1. The European Communities ("EC") offers no legitimate basis for its request for a preliminary ruling ("EC Request") that the US panel request in this dispute fails to meet the requirements of Article 6.2 of the *Understanding on the Rules and Procedures Governing the Settlement of Disputes* ("DSU"). To the contrary, as required by Article 6.2, the US panel request properly "identif[ies] the specific measures at issue and provide[s] a brief summary of the legal basis of the complaint sufficient to present the problem clearly."

2. The EC would, in contrast, have this Panel require the identification, not of the "specific measures," but of the specific *aspects* or parts of the measures that the United States intends to raise in this proceeding. The EC would also have this Panel read into Article 6.2 another requirement that is not there and that the Appellate Body has specifically rejected: a requirement that the United States summarize the specific legal arguments to be presented in the first US submission. The Appellate Body in *EC Bananas*[1] has already rejected the suggestion that a complaining party must summarize its legal arguments in the panel request, and this Panel should do so as well.

II. STATEMENT OF FACTS

3. The United States requested formal dispute settlement consultations with the EC concerning "the protection of trademarks and geographical indications for agricultural products and foodstuffs," and, in particular, Regulation 2081/92, as amended,[2] almost five years ago, on June 1, 1999.[3] The United States and the EC held a first set of consultations on July 9, 1999. In its request, the United States stated that Regulation 2081/92 "does not provide national treatment with respect to geographical indications, and does not provide sufficient protection to pre-existing trademarks that are similar or identical to a geographical indication." At no time during this first set of consultations did the EC suggest it did not understand the legal basis for the US complaint.

4. Indeed, over the course of the following four years, numerous consultations were held between representatives of the United States and of the EC concerning, in detail, what the United States perceived to be inconsistencies between Regulation 2081/92 and the WTO obligations of the European Communities.[4]

5. On April 4, 2003, the United States requested additional consultations with the EC which, *inter alia,* specified that Regulation 2081/92, as amended, and its related implementing and enforcement measures appeared to be inconsistent with the national treatment and most favored nation ("MFN") obligations of the *Agreement on Trade-Related Aspects of Intellectual Property Rights* ("TRIPS Agreement"), with respect to nationals, and the *General Agreement on Tariffs and Trade 1994* ("GATT 1994"), with respect to goods.[5] On May 19, the United States submitted detailed questions to the EC in advance of consultations that were held on May 27, 2003, which, as noted above, addressed issues that are the subject of the panel request.[6] Again, at no

---

[1] Report of the Appellate Body, *European Communities – Regime for the Importation, Sale and Distribution of Bananas*, WT/DS27/AB/R, adopted September 25, 1997 ("*EC Bananas*").

[2] Council Regulation (EEC) No 2081/92 of 14 July 1992 on the protection of geographical indications and designations of origin for agricultural products and foodstuffs.

[3] WT/DS174/1.

[4] Letter from Joseph Papovich to Joao Pacheco, dated June 6, 2001, incorporating 20 questions concerning Regulation 2081/92 (Exhibit US-1); Letter from Joseph Papovich to Joao Pacheco, dated August 21, 2001, attaching additional 15 questions (Exhibit US-2); Letter from Steve Kho to Jean-Jacques Boufflet, dated May 19, 2003, enclosing 36 questions for purposes of the May 27, 2003, consultations, and addressing, among other issues relative to Regulation 2081: national treatment, most favored nation treatment, exclusivity of trademarks, implementing regulations and enforcement, availability of legal means for interested parties to prevent misleading uses of geographical indications, transparency, and definitions of geographical indications (Exhibit US-3). These documents from the consultations are relevant because they show that the EC is not in the dark, as it claims to be, concerning problems with respect to Regulation 2081/92. The claims in this dispute, however, are as set forth in the US panel request.

[5] WT/DS290/1 /Add.1.

[6] *See* Exhibit US-3.

time during this last set of consultations did the EC even suggest it did not understand the legal basis for the US complaint.

6. The May 27th consultations also failed to resolve the matter. Consequently, on August 18, 2003, the United States requested the establishment of a panel, specifically identifying Regulation 2081/92, as amended, and its related implementing and enforcement measures, and providing a brief summary of the legal basis of the complaint. That summary consisted of both a narrative and a specific citation to particular paragraphs of the TRIPS Agreement and the GATT 1994.

III. THE REQUIREMENTS OF DSU ARTICLE 6.2

7. Article 6.2 of the DSU requires, in relevant part, that a request for the establishment of a panel:

> identify the specific measures at issue and provide a brief summary of the legal basis of the complaint sufficient to present the problem clearly.

8. The EC Request contains a number of quotations from Appellate Body and panel reports, in particular from *Korea Dairy*[7] and *EC Bananas,* that explain this provision and emphasize its role and importance in dispute settlement. It has entirely missed, however, one aspect of these reports which is critical to the issue now before this Panel: the key distinction between the *claims*—which must be included in the panel request—and the *arguments* in support of those claims—which need not be included. As the Appellate Body explained in *EC Bananas*:

> In our view, there is a significant difference between the *claims* identified in the request for the establishment of a panel, which establish the panel's terms of reference under Article 7 of the DSU, and the *arguments* supporting those claims, which are set out and progressively clarified in the first written submissions, the rebuttal submissions and the first and second panel meetings with the parties.[8]

9. Furthermore, and contrary to the EC's argument at paragraph 37 of its preliminary ruling request, the Appellate Body in *EC Bananas* made clear that a panel request may adequately state a claim if the request simply cites the pertinent provision of the WTO agreement:

> We accept the Panel's view that it was sufficient for the Complaining Parties to list the provisions of the specific agreements alleged to have been violated without setting out detailed arguments as to which specific aspects of the measures at issue relate to which specific provisions of those agreements.[9]

10. The Appellate Body confirmed this reading in *Korea Dairy*. In that dispute, the problem with the panel request was that it cited too broadly to Article XIX of the GATT 1994 and various articles of the *Agreement on Safeguards*, all of which contained numerous sub-articles, so that it was difficult to determine which specific

---

[7] Report of the Appellate Body, *Korea – Definitive Safeguard Measure on Imports of Certain Dairy Products*, WT/DS98/AB/R, adopted January 12, 2000 ("*Korea Dairy*").

[8] *EC Bananas*, para. 141.

[9] *Id.*

obligations in those provisions were at issue.[10] The US panel request in this dispute, by contrast, cites to specific provisions of the WTO agreements at issue, and cannot be said to suffer a similar defect.

11. The EC also fails to note that *even if* a panel request is insufficiently detailed "to present the problem clearly," the Panel is not automatically deprived of jurisdiction over the matter. Rather, the Panel must examine, based on the "particular circumstances of the case," whether the defect has prejudiced the ability of the responding party to defend itself. As the Appellate Body explained in *Korea Dairy*:

> In assessing whether the European Communities' request met the requirements of Article 6.2 of the DSU, we consider that, in view of the particular circumstances of this case and in line with the letter and spirit of Article 6.2, the European Communities' request should have been more detailed. However, Korea failed to demonstrate to us that the mere listing of the articles asserted to have been violated has prejudiced its ability to defend itself in the course of the Panel proceedings. Korea did assert that it had sustained prejudice, but offered no supporting particulars in its appellant's submission nor at the oral hearing. We, therefore, deny Korea's appeal relating to the consistency of the European Communities' request for the establishment of a panel with Article 6.2 of the DSU.[11]

12. Therefore, in evaluating claims regarding whether a panel request "presents the problem clearly," the Panel must consider the particular circumstances of the dispute, including whether the responding party has been prejudiced.

13. The EC asserts that, inconsistently with Article 6.2, the US panel request neither (1) identifies the specific measures at issue, nor (2) provides a brief summary of the legal basis of the complaint sufficient to present the problem clearly, and that the EC has thereby been seriously prejudiced. As detailed in the sections that follow, the EC is wrong on all counts.

IV. THE EC'S ASSERTION THAT THE US PANEL REQUEST DOES NOT IDENTIFY THE "SPECIFIC MEASURES AT ISSUE" IS INCORRECT

A. IN CITING REGULATION 2081/92, THE US PANEL REQUEST HAS IDENTIFIED THE "SPECIFIC MEASURES AT ISSUE"

14. The EC argues that specifically citing a particular EC regulation is not "sufficiently specific to permit an identification of the 'specific measure [*sic*: measures] at issue'."[12] The EC argues that the complainants should have identified which specific aspects of Regulation 2081/92 they intend to raise, and claims that "it would have easily been possible for the complainants to provide more specific references to individual provisions of Regulation 2081/92."[13] This argument is groundless, for several reasons.

---

[10] The Appellate Body explained:
In the present case, we note that the European Communities' request for a panel, after identifying the Korean safeguard measure at issue, listed Articles 2, 4, 5 and 12 of the Agreement on Safeguards and Article XIX of the GATT 1994. Article XIX of the GATT 1994 has three sections and a total of five paragraphs, each of which has at least one distinct obligation. Articles 2, 4, 5 and 12 of the Agreement on Safeguards also have multiple paragraphs, most of which have at least one distinct obligation. The Agreement on Safeguards in fact addresses a complex multi-phased process from the initiation of an investigation, through evaluation of a number of factors, determination of serious injury and causation thereof, to the adoption of a definitive safeguard measure. Every phase must meet with certain legal requirements and comply with the legal standards set out in that Agreement.
Korea Dairy, para. 129.

[11] *Id.*, para. 131.

[12] EC Request, paras. 14—15. The EC quotes Article 6.2 as requiring identification of a single "measure" at issue, whereas Article 6.2 refers to the "measures" at issue.

[13] EC Request, para. 22. The EC Request does not question the inclusion of amendments to Regulation 2081/92 as part of the measures at issue in the US panel request. The United States therefore assumes that whether the inclusion of amendments is sufficiently specific under Article 6.2 is not at issue.

15. First, Article 6.2 requires that the complaining party identify the "specific measures at issue" in its panel request, and the United States has done precisely that in identifying EC Regulation 2081/92, in its entirety. There is nothing in Article 6.2 which limits the right of complaining parties to choose the measures they wish to challenge, and previous disputes have covered a broad range of measures.[14] This, in itself, is grounds for rejecting the EC request.

16. Second, the EC suggests that identifying EC Regulation 2081/92, which addresses the protection of geographic indications and designations of origin for agricultural products and foodstuffs, is analogous to identifying the entire civil code of another Member.[15] EC Regulation 2081/92, however, is not like a civil code. Unlike a civil code, which addresses a broad range of subject matter, including, for example, marriage, adoption, labor, property, contracts and other obligations, and antitrust, EC Regulation 2081/92 addresses one specific subject , *i.e.*, the rules for the protection of designations of origin and geographical indications for certain agricultural products and foodstuffs. Indeed, while it is true, as the EC notes, that EC Regulation 2081/92 includes several articles, they all relate to this one subject, and in fact all of these articles are relevant to the US claims in this dispute.

17. Third, the EC offers an "illustrative list" of supposedly distinct "topics" in Regulation 2081/92. Apart from the fact that Article 6.2 includes no requirement that specific "topics" within a measure be identified,[16] Regulation 2081/92 is an integrated whole: Article 12a, for instance, which concerns applications for third country geographical indications, contains specific cross-references to Articles 4, 5, 12, and 15, which in turn cross-reference Articles 2, 4, and 6. And, of course, other articles, *e.g.,* addressing definitions, objective, and scope, are implicitly incorporated. Taking into account the integrated nature of EC Regulation 2081/92, the United States chose, in exercising the broad discretion afforded it under Article 6.2, to identify the whole Regulation as the "specific measures at issue."

18. Fourth, the EC quotes from a number of disputes in which the sufficiency of panel requests under Article 6.2 was considered, but does not point to any in which the Appellate Body or a panel found that identifying a particular law or regulation as a measure, without identifying particular articles of the law or regulation, is insufficient. For instance, in *EC Bananas*, both the panel and the Appellate Body found a request sufficient when it referred to "a regime for the importation, sale and distribution of bananas established by Regulation 404/93 and subsequent EC legislation, regulations and administrative measures ... which implement, supplement and amend that regime."[17] Indeed, the issue in prior disputes regarding the identification of measures at issue has generally been whether Article 6.2 requires a citation to a particular law or regulation, or whether simply describing the measure without citation is specific enough. On that particular question, the panel in *Canada Wheat*, the only dispute cited by the EC on this issue, noted that it is desirable but unnecessary for panel requests to "specify measures of general application—*i.e.*, laws and regulations—by name, date of

---

[14] *See, e.g., United States – Measures Affecting the Cross-Border Supply of Gambling and Betting Services ("United States Gambling")*, Request for Establishment of a Panel by Antigua and Barbuda, WT/DS285/2, in which the cited measures included a range of code sections and constitutional provisions for all 50 US states and several US territories.

[15] EC Request, para. 18.

[16] The EC apparently does not believe itself obligated to identify specific topics within a measure in other disputes; *e.g., United States – Tax Treatment for "Foreign Sales Corporations,"* WT/DS108 ("*US FSC*"), where the measures identified were sections 921-927 of the US Internal Revenue Code and related measures. The cited statutory provisions alone consisted of seven sections with numerous sub-parts, taking up more than 20 pages of the EC's first exhibit. Further, in *Canada – Measures Relating to Exports of Wheat and Treatment of Imported Grain*, WT/DS276/12, Preliminary Ruling circulated July 21, 2003 ("*Canada Wheat*"), in which the EC is a third party, the EC stated, at paragraphs 15-16 of its June 4, 2003, comments, that the US identification of "the Canada Grain Act and Canadian grain regulations," without referencing specific articles, was sufficient to satisfy the requirements of Article 6.2.

[17] *EC Bananas*, para. 140.

adoption, etc."[18] In this dispute, by contrast, the US panel request specifically cites Regulation 2081/92 and the EC is arguing that even this "desirable," although unnecessary, form of identification is insufficient. In short, the EC is seeking to dramatically increase the level of specificity required under Article 6.2 in this proceeding without any textual or other basis, simply to suit its immediate interest in this dispute.

19. For the reasons above, the US reference to Regulation 2081/92 constitutes an identification of the specific measures at issue, as required by Article 6.2.

B. IN IDENTIFYING REGULATION 2081/92 "AND ITS RELATED IMPLEMENTING AND ENFORCEMENT MEASURES," THE US PANEL REQUEST IDENTIFIED THE "SPECIFIC MEASURES AT ISSUE"

20. The EC argues that Australia's identification of "related implementing and enforcement measures" falls short of the Article 6.2 requirement to identify the "specific measures at issue." The EC asserts, at footnote 10, that the US panel request does not include a reference to "related implementing and enforcement measures." This is incorrect. In paragraph 2 of its panel request, the United States defines the measures at issue—Regulation 2081/92, as amended—to include its related implementing and enforcement measures. Be that as it may, the EC has not challenged this aspect of the US panel request, even after it was pointed out at the March 3 organizational meeting that the United States used precisely the same formulation as Australia. Under these circumstances, it is unclear on what basis the EC continues to maintain its complaint about the Australian panel request.

21. In any case, the EC's argument with respect to Australia's panel request is wrong and ill-founded. The EC claims that "related" is a vague term and that many laws and regulations might be considered "related." It also claims that many laws and regulations may be necessary to implement and enforce the regulation. Therefore, the EC professes ignorance of what measures are at issue. This argument is disingenuous. The Australian panel request does not refer to unknown "related implementing and enforcement" measures. It refers to a specific regulation providing for the protection of geographical indications in the EC and <u>its</u> related implementing and enforcement measures. The identification of these measures is specified through the reference to its relationship to Regulation 2081/92, *i.e.*, those measures that enforce and implement Regulation 2081/92. As noted above, the Appellate Body found less specific language to be adequate in *EC Bananas*: "a regime for the importation, sale and distribution of bananas established by Regulation 404/93 and subsequent EC legislation, regulations and administrative measures ... which implement, supplement and amend that regime."[19] The EC itself adopted a similar approach in *US FSC* when it identified the measures as "sections 921—927 of the Internal Revenue Code and related measures establishing special tax treatment for 'Foreign Sales Corporations'."[20]

22. Finally, the EC is in a poor position to be pleading that the "related implementing and enforcement measures" are not specified. In trying to understand these measures fully during the course of consultations almost one year ago, the very first category of information the United States and Australia requested from the EC was with respect to "Implementing Regulations." In particular, the United States asked for a list of "all EC rules, regulations or other measures implementing or related to EC Regulation 2081/92" and copies of all such "relevant measures." In addition, the United States asked several specific questions about relevant member State implementing regulations, including those related to member State inspection structures, and asked for copies of

---

[18] Preliminary Ruling of the Panel, *Canada – Measures Relating to Exports of Wheat and Treatment of Imported Grain*, WT/DS276/12, circulated on July 21, 2003 (*"Canada Wheat")*, para. 19:

We note that the United States' panel request refers to "laws" and "regulations," yet does not specify the relevant laws and regulations by name, date of adoption, etc. We consider that it is desirable for Members to be as specific as possible in identifying measures of general application, including by indicating their name and date of adoption. However, by its terms, Article 6.2 does not require that panel requests explicitly specify measures of general application—*i.e.*, laws and regulations—by name, date of adoption, etc. Therefore, we consider that the fact that the United States has not specified the relevant laws or regulations by name, date of adoption, etc. does not necessarily render the panel request inconsistent with Article 6.2.

[19] *EC Bananas*, para. 140.

[20] WT/DS108/2, July 9, 1998.

all such relevant measures. The EC was utterly unresponsive to this request during the consultations, and never provided citations to a single implementing measure in response to this request, despite numerous opportunities to do so. Article 4.10 of the DSU states that Members will engage in dispute settlement procedures in good faith in an attempt to resolve the dispute. More specifically, Article 4.3 of the DSU obliges the Members to enter into consultations in good faith. Given the failure of the EC itself to identify Regulation 2081/92's implementing and enforcement measures by citation, this Panel should require no more specificity of the United States than the EC was willing to offer the United States.

23. The EC, in arguing that the identification of "related implementation and enforcement measures" is unspecific, refers to the preliminary ruling in *Canada Wheat*, where, in paragraphs 20 and 24, the panel found that, "in the absence of an explicit identification, sufficient information must be provided in the request for establishment of the panel itself that effectively identifies the precise measures at issue."[21] The *Canada Wheat* panel found there was not sufficient information where the panel request contained contradictory references which obscured the content and meaning of the "laws and regulations" referred to in the request.[22] However, that panel also found that a similarly broad reference to "actions" was clear, in context, because the request stated that these actions related to "purchases or sales involving wheat exports."[23]

24. In this dispute, there are no contradictory references, and there is no uncertainty as to the content or the nature of the "implementing and enforcement measures" at issue: they are the implementing and enforcement measures that are "related" to Regulation 2081/92, on the protection of geographical indications and designations of origin for agricultural products and foodstuffs.

25. In summary, both the Australian and the US panel requests specifically identify the "implementing and enforcement measures" at issue in this dispute, consistent with Article 6.2.

V. CONTRARY TO THE EC'S ALLEGATIONS, THE US PANEL REQUEST PROVIDES A BRIEF SUMMARY OF THE LEGAL BASIS OF THE COMPLAINT SUFFICIENT TO PRESENT THE PROBLEM CLEARLY

A. THE US PANEL REQUEST PROVIDES A BRIEF SUMMARY OF THE LEGAL BASIS OF THE COMPLAINT SUFFICIENT TO PRESENT THE PROBLEM CLEARLY

26. The United States does provide a brief summary of the legal basis of the complaint sufficient to present the problem clearly, as required by Article 6.2. It both lists the specific provisions of the TRIPS Agreement and the GATT 1994 alleged to be violated, and provides, in addition, a brief textual explanation of the basis of the complaint.

1. Citations to specific WTO agreement provisions

27. The Appellate Body has made clear on several occasions, directly contrary to the EC's assertion in paragraph 37 of its request, that a panel request may adequately summarize the legal basis of the complaint under Article 6.2 by simply citing the pertinent provisions of the WTO Agreement.[24] The EC cites *Korea Dairy*, in which the Appellate Body stated that there may be circumstances in which a "listing of treaty articles would not satisfy the standard of Article 6.2."[25] But in that proceeding the articles cited had multiple paragraphs, many of which had their own distinct obligations: for instance, the panel request cited Article XIX of the GATT

---

[21] EC Request, paras 25 and 26.

[22] *Canada Wheat,* para. 24.

[23] *Canada Wheat,* para. 26.

[24] *E.g., EC Bananas*, para. 141; *Korea Dairy*, para 124.

[25] *Korea Dairy*, para. 124, cited in EC Request, para. 36. The EC's conclusion, at paragraph 37, that identification of the treaty provisions "is a necessary, but not sufficient condition under Article 6.2 DSU" (emphasis in original) is a patently incorrect reading of *Korea Dairy.*

1994, containing three sections and five paragraphs, each with at least one distinct obligation, and Article 12 of the Safeguards Agreement, which spans two pages and contains 11 paragraphs.[26]

28. By contrast, the US panel request in this dispute lists 17 specific provisions of the TRIPS Agreement and two specific provisions of the GATT 1994. Where an article consisted of more than one paragraph, the US panel request specifically identified the particular paragraph number.[27] Generally, each of these paragraphs consists of a single obligation. Unlike in the case of *Korea Dairy*, there are no circumstances in this dispute that would render citation to the relevant specific provision of the WTO agreement insufficient under Article 6.2.

2. Narrative description

29. Moreover, the US panel request does not rest solely on specific citation to particular WTO obligations. It also includes a brief narrative description of the legal basis for the complaint, adding clarity to the summary. For instance, it summarizes that, in the view of the United States, Regulation 2081/92 does not provide national or most favored nation treatment to goods or nationals of other WTO Members, and that Regulation 2081/92 diminishes legal protection for trademarks (with a specific illustrative reference to the right to prevent confusing uses of an identical or similar sign and adequate protection against invalidation). It also states, as a brief summary of the legal basis of the complaint, in conjunction with specifically cited WTO agreement provisions, that Regulation 2081/92 does not provide the legal means for interested parties to prevent the misleading use of a geographical indication, defines geographical indications in a manner inconsistent with the TRIPS Agreement, is not sufficiently transparent, and does not provide for adequate enforcement procedures. Contrary to the EC's argument at paragraph 42 of its request, there is no requirement under Article 6.2 that each part of the narrative be specifically linked to particular WTO provisions, nor does the EC point to any disputes in which this was required.

30. As stated above, the citation to specific WTO obligations in the US panel request is sufficient to summarize the legal basis for the complaint under Article 6.2. The narrative is an additional description of the legal basis. Therefore, there is no legitimate foundation in this dispute for the EC to assert that the US panel request violated the second prong of Article 6.2.

3. Attendant circumstances

31. In addition to (1) the specific citation to WTO obligations, which alone is a sufficient summary of the legal basis of the complaint, and (2) the narrative description, which additionally describes the legal basis, the attendant circumstances surrounding this panel request make clear that the panel request's summary of the legal basis of the complaint is sufficient and presents the problem clearly. The Appellate Body, in *Korea Dairy*, clarified that the sufficiency of the panel request can be judged in light of these circumstances.[28]

32. There is a long history of consultations in this dispute. The United States requested formal consultations on June 1, 1999, and the first set of consultations was held almost five years ago, on July 9, 1999, and continued through the last set of formal consultations on May 27, 2003. As noted earlier, and as set forth in further detail below, as a result of these consultations it is abundantly clear that the EC understands the legal basis of the US complaint.

B. THE EC'S REAL CRITICISM OF THE US PANEL REQUEST IS THAT IT DOES NOT SET FORTH THE US ARGUMENTS, WHICH IS NOT REQUIRED BY ARTICLE 6.2

33. Previous panels and the Appellate Body have been very careful to distinguish between the claims that must be made in a panel request under Article 6.2—*i.e.*, the brief summary of the legal *basis* for the complaint

---

[26] *Korea Dairy*, para. 124.

[27] Except for GATT 1994 Article I, which consists of one paragraph followed by several exceptions.

[28] *Korea Dairy*, para. 124.

sufficient to present the problem clearly—and the *arguments* supporting those claims. The claims must be set forth in the panel request. The arguments do not. As the Appellate Body stated in *EC Bananas:*

> We accept the Panel's view that it was sufficient for the Complaining Parties to list the provisions of the specific agreements alleged to have been violated without setting out detailed arguments as to which specific aspects of the measures at issue relate to which specific provisions of those agreements. In our view, there is a significant difference between the *claims* identified in the request for the establishment of a panel, which establish the panel's terms of reference under Article 7 of the DSU, and the *arguments* supporting those claims, which are set out and progressively clarified in the first written submissions, the rebuttal submissions and the first and second panel meetings with the parties.[29]

34. In this dispute, the EC is not faulting the United States for failing to set out the legal *basis* for the complaint. It is faulting the United States, incorrectly, for not including its *arguments* in support of that basis.[30]

35. With respect to national treatment, for example, the EC complains that the US panel request does not specify which provision or aspect of Regulation 2081/92 violates the EC's national treatment obligations, and "in which way such a violation is deemed to occur."[31] This is precisely what the Appellate Body in *EC Bananas* found was not required. The United States will lay out in detail the specific ways in which Regulation 2081/92 fails to provide national treatment to non-EC nationals and non-EC goods, but will do so in its submissions, as part of its arguments supporting the claim that Regulation 2081/92 denies national treatment to non-EC nationals and goods.[32]

36. In other words, the legal basis for the complaint, made clear in the US panel request, is that the EC's regulation for the protection of certain geographical indications is inconsistent with specific national treatment obligations in the TRIPS Agreement, the Paris Convention, and the GATT 1994. The detailed arguments as to how specific aspects of Regulation 2081/02 are inconsistent with these obligations will be the subject of the arguments to be presented in future US submissions.

37. Similarly, with respect to MFN treatment, the EC complains that the panel request does not specify which provision of Regulation 2081/92 violates MFN obligations, how such a violation occurs, which WTO Members are being denied favorable treatment, what this more favorable treatment is, and how it is conferred. Such detailed explanations and argumentation clearly go beyond the requirements for a brief summary of the legal basis for the complaint pursuant to Article 6.2, and instead fall squarely into the category of arguments in

---

[29] *EC Bananas*, para. 141.

[30] In criticizing the specificity of the "measures" under Article 6.2, the EC argues incorrectly that the lack of citation to individual provisions of Regulation 2081/92 "does not permit the EC to understand which specific aspects among those covered by Regulation 2081/92 the complainants intend to raise . . ." EC Request, para. 22 (emphasis added). Article 6.2 requires an identification of the specific measures at issue; it does not require identification of the specific "aspect" of the measures. In fact, the EC's argument appears to be confusing the Article 6.2 requirement that the measures be identified with the requirement that the legal basis be summarized (*i.e.*, the claims). Even with respect to the claims, however, the Appellate Body specifically rejected this argument in the paragraph of *EC Bananas* quoted above. This issue is discussed in further detail in this section, but suffice it to say that the EC cannot fairly claim to be in the dark about what aspects of Regulation 2081/92 are at issue. *See, e.g.,* footnote 32 below.

[31] EC Request, para. 44.

[32] The claims are clear from the US panel request. But, in addition, the EC cannot fairly claim to be unaware of the problem presented, in light of the long history of consultations. For instance, several of the questions put to the EC in consultations question why non-EC nationals cannot register their own geographical indications for originating products, and why they are faced with various problematic provisions in Regulation 2081/92 that do not apply to EC nationals. *See, e.g.*, May 19, 2004, Consultation Questions, questions 7-25 (Exhibit US-3); indeed, the EC Request itself attaches, as EC Exhibits 2 and 3, the minutes of the DSB meetings in which the United States described some of the specific problems with Regulation 2018/92, including with respect to national and most favored nation treatment, among other issues. EC Exhibit 2, para. 72; EC Exhibit 3, paras. 28 and 29.

support of the claim that the regulation does not provide most favored nation treatment with respect to goods and nationals of WTO Members.[33]

38. With respect to "legal protection for trademarks," the EC acknowledges that Regulation 2081/92 addresses the issue of conflicts between trademarks and geographical indications in three paragraphs of Article 14, and in Article 7(4), all of which can and do have significant negative implications for trademark rights provided for under the TRIPS Agreement.[34] The EC further claims that Regulation 2081/92 provides "specific solutions" to the various conflicts between trademarks and geographical indications.[35] By engaging in the substance of the US claims in such detail in its preliminary ruling request, it is obvious that the US summary of the legal basis of the complaint was sufficient to present the problem clearly.[36] The EC's desire to "understand which specific problems the United States wishes to raise" is a request for argumentation that is appropriate for the first submission, but not for a panel request, a point that the EC has itself noted in other disputes.[37]

39. With respect to Regulation 2081/92's failure to "provide legal means for interested parties to prevent the misleading use of a geographical indication," the EC claims that Regulation 2081/92 contains detailed provisions regarding the protection of registered geographical indications that do provide such means. Again, the EC is interested in engaging in argumentation regarding the US claims, prior to the US first submission. And again, that the United States did not provide such argumentation in its panel request is not a violation of Article 6.2.

40. With respect to the differences between Regulation 2081/92's definition of "geographical indication" and that in the TRIPS Agreement, the EC is disingenuous to argue that the United States does not explain the differences between the two definitions. The TRIPS Agreement definition is in Article 22.1 of the TRIPS Agreement; the Regulation definition is in Article 2.2(b) of Regulation 2081. The differences between them are obvious, and speak for themselves. As for the nature of the breach, this is properly a subject for arguments in the submissions of the parties. Again, however, it is disingenuous for the EC to argue that it does not understand the US claim. As the United States explained to the EC during consultations, the TRIPS Agreement contains obligations to protect geographical indications, as defined in the TRIPS Agreement, yet Regulation 2081/92, which is how "Community protection of ... geographical indications of agricultural products and food stuffs shall be obtained," offers protection to an apparently different category of geographical indications. Differences in coverage therefore raise obvious questions of consistency with TRIPS Agreement obligations.[38]

41. The EC arguments with respect to transparency and enforcement procedures suffer from the same defects: the EC is attempting to engage in argumentation on the substance of the claims—for instance, asserting that Regulation 2081/92 is transparent, and faulting the United States for not detailing how it is not transparent—instead of trying to make out a case that the legal basis is not sufficiently summarized.

---

[33] With respect to this issue, too, the EC cannot fairly claim to be in the dark. Several questions were raised in consultations about why nationals and products of some WTO Members—*i.e.*, those that have a system of geographical indication protection that is equivalent to the EC system—have rights and receive protections that other WTO Members do not. *See, e.g.*, May 19, 2004, Consultation Questions, questions 7-25 (Exhibit US-3); EC Exhibit 2, para. 72; EC Exhibit 3, paras. 28-29.

[34] EC Request, paras 46-48.

[35] Yet it is these "solutions," among other things, that are at issue, particularly in light of the exclusive right of the registered trademark holder, under Article 16.1 of the TRIPS Agreement, to prevent the use of an identical or similar sign that is likely to confuse.

[36] Note also the detailed discussions that occurred on this subject at the consultations. *See, e.g.*, May 19, 2004, Consultation Questions, "Article 14—Exclusivity of Trademarks," questions 29-36, and "Article 13" , questions 27—28 (Exhibit US-3).

[37] In *United States Gambling*, the EC itself criticized the US request for an Article 6.2 preliminary ruling in its October 24, 2003, comments, arguing at paragraph 16 that the issue raised by the United States "was strictly connected with the substance of the case, which is legally and factually rather complex" and, therefore, "not suited for adjudication through a summary preliminary ruling proceeding brought under article 6.2 of the DSU." Further, the EC criticized Korea's preliminary ruling request in *Korea – Measures Affecting Trade in Commercial Vessels*, WT/DS273, characterizing Korea's objections to the panel request as "an ill-fated attempt to have the Panel make findings on substantive legal issues that should be at issue during the regular Panel phase, not at the preliminary stage."

[38] *See, e.g.*, May 19, 2004, Consultation Questions, "Definition of GIs," questions 4—6 (Exhibit US-3).

42. The above are examples of how the EC, in alleging that the US panel request does not "provide a brief summary of the legal basis of the complaint sufficient to present the problem clearly," is in fact arguing that the United States has not adequately set out its *arguments* in support of those claims. It is clear from the face of the panel request, particularly in light of the attendant circumstances of the consultations, that the US panel request does provide a sufficient brief summary of the legal basis of the complaint that presents the problem clearly.

VI. THE US PANEL REQUEST DOES NOT PREJUDICE THE ABILITY OF THE EC TO DEFEND ITSELF

43. The EC argues that the Appellate Body has "attached importance" to the question of whether a responding Party has suffered prejudice as a result of any deficiencies with respect to Article 6.2. More to the point, however, in *Korea Dairy*, the Appellate Body denied Korea's Article 6.2 claim *in toto* because, although it had asserted prejudice, Korea offered no supporting particulars.[39]

44. The EC's argument that it is prejudiced by the US panel request is nothing more than a restatement of its argument, refuted above, that the request is insufficiently detailed with respect to actual arguments to support the legal basis of the complaint. In light of the Appellate Body's reasoning in *Korea Dairy*, such a mere restatement is plainly insufficient to establish prejudice. If lack of detail in the panel request automatically meant "prejudice," there would be no need for a "prejudice" analysis. Even if the EC had succeeded in demonstrating that the US panel request does not meet the requirements of DSU Article 6.2, which it has not, the EC has offered nothing to suggest that it has been prejudiced.

45. The EC argues, at paragraph 71, that the United States made a similar "prejudice" argument in *US Lamb*,[40] and states that the same standard should be applied in the present case.[41] Of course, if this Panel does adopt the same standard as in the *US Lamb* dispute, it will reject the EC's request, consistent with the *US Lamb* panel's rejection of the US argument and its finding that the panel request in *US Lamb* was consistent with Article 6.2.[42]

46. The EC speculates, at paragraph 73 of its request, that either both co-complainants are conspiring to leave the EC in the dark, or both are unsure of the case they are intending to bring. The truth is more mundane: Article 6.2 requires only a brief summary of the legal *basis* for the complaint sufficient to present the problem clearly. It does not, as explained above, require a preview of the *arguments* that will be submitted later during the course of the panel proceedings.

VII. CONCLUSION

47. For the reasons stated above, the EC's arguments in support of its request for a preliminary ruling that the US panel request does not meet the requirements of Article 6.2 are without merit. Accordingly, the Panel should reject that request.

---

[39] *Korea Dairy*, para 131.

[40] Report of the Panel, *United States – Safeguard Measures on Imports of Fresh, Chilled or Frozen Lamb Meat from New Zealand and Australia*, WT/DS178/R, adopted May 16, 2001 ("*US Lamb*").

[41] EC Request, para. 72.

[42] *US Lamb*, para. 5.53.

ANNEX A-2

FIRST WRITTEN SUBMISSION OF THE UNITED STATES

(23 April 2004)

TABLE OF CONTENTS

B. THE EC'S GI REGULATION IS INCONSISTENT WITH THE EC'S OBLIGATIONS TO PROVIDE MOST FAVORED NATION TREATMENT

1. **The EC GI Regulations is inconsistent with the EC's most favored nation obligations with respect to other WTO Member's nationals under the TRIPS Agreement**
   (a) The TRIPS Agreement requires that any advantage, favor, privilege or immunity granted to nationals of any other country be accorded immediately and unconditionally to the nationals of all other WTO Members
   (b) The EC GI Regulation grants significant advantages, favors, privileges, and immunities to nationals of some countries that it does not accord at all to nationals of WTO Members
2. **The EC GI Regulation is inconsistent with the EC's most favored nation obligations with respect to goods of other WTO Members under the GATT 1994**
   (a) Article I:1 of the GATT 1994 requires that any advantage, favor, privilege, or immunity granted to any product originating in any other country be accorded immediately and unconditionally to the like product originating in the territories of all other WTO Members
   (b) The EC GI Regulation grants significant advantages, favors, privileges, and immunities to agricultural products and foodstuffs originating in some countries that it does not accord to like products originating in the territories of all WTO Members

C. THE EC GI REGULATION IS INCONSISTENT WITH THE EC'S OBLIGATIONS UNDER ARTICLE 16.1 OF THE TRIPS AGREEMENT

1. **Introduction**
2. **The US argument in light of the relationship between trademark rights and GI rights**
3. **Article 16.1 of the TRIPS Agreement requires Members to provide the owners of registered trademarks with the exclusive right to prevent all third parties from using identical or similar signs resulting in a likelihood of confusion**
   (a) Ordinary meaning of the terms in Article 16.1
   (b) The context of the terms in Article 16.1
   (c) The object and purpose of the TRIPS Agreement with respect to Article 16.1
   (d) Conclusion with respect to the meaning of Article 16.1
4. **Contrary to Article 16.1 of the TRIPS Agreement, the EC GI Regulation does not permit owners of registered trademarks to exercise their Article 16.1 exclusive rights to prevent confusing uses**
   (a) The text of the EC GI Regulation makes clear that owners of registered trademarks are not permitted to exercise their Article 16.1 rights
   (b) The EC's explanations of the GI Regulation and the circumstances surrounding its coming into force confirm that the GI Regulation prevents owners of registered trademarks from exercising their Article 16.1 rights
5. **Conclusion with respect to the GI Regulation's inconsistency with Article 16.1**

D. THE EC GI REGULATION IS INCONSISTENT WITH ARTICLE 22.2 OF THE TRIPS AGREEMENT

E. THE EC GI REGULATION IS INCONSISTENT WITH THE EC'S ENFORCEMENT OBLIGATIONS UNDER THE TRIPS AGREEMENT

F. THE EC GI REGULATION IS INCONSISTENT WITH ARTICLE 65.1 OF THE TRIPS AGREEMENT

V. CONCLUSION

TABLE OF REPORTS

Short Form	Full Citation
Belgian Family Allowances	GATT Panel Report, *Belgian Family Allowances,* BISD 1S/59, adopted 7 November 1953.
Canada – Patent Term	Panel Report, *Canada – Term of Patent Protection,* WT/DS170/R, adopted 12 October 2000.
Canada – Autos	Panel Report, *Canada – Certain Measures Affecting the Automotive Industry,* WT/DS139/R, WT/DS142/R, adopted 19 June 2000, as modified by the Appellate Body Report.
Canada – Autos	Appellate Body Report, *Canada – Certain Measures Affecting the Automotive Industry,* WT/DS139/AB/R, WT/DS142/AB/R, adopted 19 June 2000.
Chile – Alcohol	Panel Report, *Chile – Taxes on Alcoholic Beverages,* WT/DS87/R, WT/DS110/R, adopted 12 January 2000, as modified by the Appellate Body Report.
Chile – Alcohol	Appellate Body Report, *Chile – Taxes on Alcoholic Beverages,* WT/DS87/AB/R, WT/DS110/AB/R, adopted 12 January 2000.
EC – Asbestos	Appellate Body Report, *EC – Measures Affecting Asbestos and Asbestos Containing Products,* WT/DS135/AB/R, adopted 16 April 2001.
EEC – Parts and Components	GATT Panel Report, *EEC – Regulations on Imports of Parts and Components,* BISD 37S/132, adopted 16 May 1990.
EC – Sardines	Appellate Body Report, *EC–Trade Description of Sardines,* WT/DS231/AB/R, adopted 23 October 2003.
India – Autos	Panel Report, *India–Measures Affecting the Automotive Sector*, WT/DS/146/R, WT/DS175/R, adopted 5 April 2002.
Indonesia – Autos	Panel Report, *Indonesia–Certain Measures Affecting the Automobile Industry,* WT/DS54/R, WT/DS55/R, WT/DS59/R, WT/DS64/R, adopted 23 July 1998.
Italian Agricultural Machinery	GATT Panel Report, *Italian Discrimination Against Imported Agricultural Machinery,* L/833 BISD, 7S/60, adopted 23 October, 1958.
Japan – Alcohol	Appellate Body Report, *Japan – Taxes on Alcoholic Beverages,* WT/DS8/AB/R, WT/DS10/AB/R, adopted 1 November, 1996.
Korea – Alcohol	Appellate Body Report, *Korea – Taxes on Alcoholic Beverages,* WT/DS75/AB/R, WT/DS84/AB/R, adopted 17 February 1999.
Korea – Beef	Appellate Body Report, *Korea – Measures Affecting Imports of Fresh, Chilled and Frozen Beef,* WT/DS161/AB/R, WT/DS169/AB/R, adopted 10 January 2001.
US – FSC (Article 21.5–EC)	Panel Report, *United States – Tax Treatment for "Foreign Sales Corporations" – Recourse to Article 21.5 of the DSU by the European Communities,* WT/DS108/RW, adopted 19 January 2002.
US – Malt Beverages	GATT Panel Report, *United States – Measures Affecting Alcoholic and Malt Beverages,* DS23/R, BISD 39S/206, adopted 19 June 1992.
US – Section 211	Panel Report, *United States – Section 211 Omnibus Appropriations Act of 1998,* WT/DS176/R, adopted 1 February 2002, as modified by the Appellate Body Report.
US – Section 211	Appellate Body Report, *United States – Section 211 Omnibus Appropriations Act of 1998,* WT/DS176/AB/R, adopted 1 February 2002.
US – Section 337	GATT Panel Report, *United States – Section 337 of the Tariff Act of 1930*, BISD 36S/345, adopted 7 November 1989.

European Communities—Trademarks and Geographical Indications—Complaint by the United States

I. INTRODUCTION

1. The EC's Geographical Indications ("GI") Regulation[1] sets up a regime for the protection of geographical indications in order to realize and maximize what it considers to be substantial benefits for those producing and selling qualified agricultural products and foodstuffs in the EC. Unfortunately, the Regulation suffers from significant defects. First, while making these benefits easily available to EC nationals and products, it erects very significant—indeed, nearly insurmountable—barriers against many non-EC nationals and products.

2. Second, and importantly for all owners of registered trademarks—both US and European—the GI Regulation grants this protection at the expense of trademark rights that the EC is specifically obliged to guarantee under the TRIPS Agreement.[2]

3. The EC must, under the TRIPS Agreement, offer certain protections for geographical indications. It is not, however, permitted to do so in a manner that discriminates against non-EC nationals and products, nor is it permitted to do so at the expense of its TRIPS Agreement obligations with respect to trademarks.

4. This submission details how the EC's GI Regulation is inconsistent with the TRIPS Agreement and the GATT 1994[3] because of its discrimination against non-EC nationals and products. It is inconsistent with the national treatment obligations of the TRIPS Agreement and the Paris Convention,[4] both of which require national treatment as to "nationals" of other WTO Members. It is also inconsistent with the national treatment obligations of the GATT 1994 with respect to products from other WTO Members. Further, the GI Regulation is inconsistent with the obligation to provide most favored nation ("MFN") treatment with respect to nationals of other WTO Members, under the TRIPS Agreement, and with respect to products of other WTO Members, under the GATT 1994.

5. Next, and directly contrary to the express obligations of the TRIPS Agreement with respect to trademarks, the EC's GI Regulation denies the owner of a registered trademark his exclusive right to prevent all third parties from using similar or identical signs for goods or services that are identical or similar to those covered by the trademark registration—including geographical indications—where such use would result in a likelihood of confusion. For example, the owner of a registered trademark must, under the TRIPS Agreement, be able to take action against another producer selling an identical product, labeled with an identical name (protected as a geographical indication after the trademark registration), on the same shelf as the trademarked product. That owner cannot take such action under the EC GI Regulation.

6. Finally, as detailed further below, the EC GI Regulation fails to provide interested parties with the legal means to protect their geographical indications, as required by the TRIPS Agreement.

7. Consequently, the EC GI Regulation is also inconsistent with obligations under the TRIPS Agreement to enforce intellectual property rights.

---

[1] i..*e.*, the measure at issue in this dispute: Council Regulation (EEC) No. 2081/92 of July 14, 1992 on the protection of geographical indications and designations of origin for agricultural products and foodstuffs, as amended, and its related implementing and enforcement measures. In this submission, references to the "GI Regulation" or the "EC GI Regulation" are references to this measure, which includes both Regulation 2081 and its related implementing and enforcement measures. References to particular articles of the GI Regulation are references to Regulation 2081/92 itself, as most recently amended, provided as Exhibit COMP-1.b.

[2] *Agreement on* Trade-*Related Aspects of Intellectual Property Rights.*

[3] *General* Agreement *on Tariffs and Trade (1994).*

[4] *Paris Convention for the Protection of Industrial Property*, done at Paris, March 20, 1883, as revised at Brussels, December 14, 1990, at Washington, June 2, 1911, at The Hague, November 6, 1925, at London, June 2, 1934, at Lisbon, October 31, 1958, and at Stockholm, July 14, 1967. References to the Paris Convention are, unless otherwise indicated, to the Stockholm Act of this Convention (1967). The Paris Convention Article 2 national treatment obligation is incorporated into the TRIPS Agreement by Article 2.1 of the TRIPS Agreement.

II. PROCEDURAL HISTORY

8. On June 1, 1999, the United States requested consultations with the EC, pursuant to Article 4 of the DSU[5] and Article 64 of the TRIPS Agreement regarding the GI Regulation.[6] Consultations were held on July 9, 1999, and thereafter, but failed to resolve the dispute.

9. On April 4, 2003, the United States supplemented its request for consultations with a request for additional consultations with the EC pursuant to Article 4 of the DSU, Article 64 of the TRIPS Agreement, and Article XXII of the GATT 1994.[7] The Government of Australia also requested consultations with the EC, and joint consultations were held on May 27, 2003, which also failed to resolve the dispute. Consequently, on August 18, 2003, the United States requested the establishment of a panel, with standard terms of reference.[8] Australia also filed a request for the establishment of a panel, with standard terms of reference, on the same day.[9] At the meeting of the WTO Dispute Settlement Body ("DSB") on October 2, 2003, the DSB established a single panel pursuant to Article 9.1 of the DSU, with standard terms of reference, to examine the US and Australian complaints.[10]

10. The panel was composed on February 23, 2004.[11]

11. On March 3, 2004, the EC requested that the Panel issue separate panel reports with respect to the complaints filed by Australia and the United States, pursuant to Article 9.2 of the DSU. On April 23, 2004, the Panel confirmed that it would submit separate reports on this dispute.

III. FACTS

12. The EC GI Regulation lays down the rules for the protection of geographical indications of agricultural products and foodstuffs intended for human consumption throughout the member States of the EC.[12] It provides, in Article 2(1), that Community protection for geographical indications of agricultural products and foodstuffs shall be obtained in accordance with the Regulation, and establishes a comprehensive system for the registration and protection of GIs, as well as for objecting to the registration of GIs.

13. According to its preamble, the GI Regulation is a response to a consumer market that is increasingly willing to pay premium prices for agricultural products and foodstuffs with an identifiable geographic origin. For those producers able to register such designations of origin at the member State level, according to the preamble, this enables producers of qualifying products to secure higher incomes. The EC GI Regulation recognizes this benefit for qualifying products and producers and extends this benefit in a uniform manner throughout the EC.

14. Under the GI Regulation, a geographical indication is defined as the name of a region, a specific place or, in exceptional cases, a country, used to describe an agricultural product or a foodstuff:

---

[5] *Understanding on Rules and* Procedures *Governing the Settlement of Disputes.*

[6] WT/DS174/1 (June 1, 1999).

[7] WT/DS174/1/Add.1 (April 4, 2003).

[8] WT/DS174/20 (August 19, 2003).

[9] WT/DS290/18 (August 19, 2003).

[10] *Dispute Settlement Body: Minutes of Meeting Held on 2 October 2003*, WT/DSB/M/156, circulated November 10, 2003, para. 33.

[11] WT/DS174/21; WT/DS290/19 (February 24, 2004).

[12] Article 1(1) of the GI Regulation. Exhibit COMP 1.b. To avoid confusion, this submission will refer to countries that are part of the European Communities as "member States," as distinguished from WTO Members.

(a) originating in that region, specific place or country, and

(b) which possesses a specific quality, reputation, or other characteristics attributable to that geographic origin and the production and/or processing and/or preparation of which take place in the defined geographical area.[13]

15. In order to use a protected geographic indication, a product must comply with the relevant specification, as provided for in Article 4(2) of the GI Regulation.[14]

Registration

16. Under Article 5 of the GI Regulation, a person or a group of producers and processors may apply for a geographical indication—*i.e.*, a qualifying "name"—with respect to the products which they "produce or obtain" by sending the application to "the Member State in which the geographical area is located."

17. Thus, under Article 5, only persons or groups producing or obtaining products in the EC may file an application for a GI registration, and only products "produced or obtained" in the EC may be the subject of the registration.

18. The application must be accompanied by a "product specification" that includes information, not just on the product itself, but on how it is produced, as well as the details of the government inspection structures in place to ensure compliance with the specifications.[15] To summarize the details provided in Article 4 of the GI Regulation, the product specification must include, at a minimum:

(a) name of the product, including the GI

(b) description of the product and its physical, chemical, microbiological and/or organoleptic characteristics

(c) definition of the geographical area

(d) evidence that the product originates in the geographical area

(e) description of the method of obtaining the product and information concerning packaging, if the group making the request determines and justifies that the packaging must take place in the geographic area

(f) details bearing out the link with the geographical environment or origin

(g) details of inspection structures required by Article 10 of the GI Regulation (Article 10 contains detailed rules concerning inspection structures that the government must maintain in order to register a GI, and requires that any private inspection body approved by a member State must comply with EC standard EN 45011. This standard does not appear to be available from public

---

[13] Article 2(2)(b) of the GI Regulation. The GI Regulation also applies to a narrower category of geographical source indications, *i.e.*, "designations of origin," defined in Article 2(2)(b). The distinction between the broader category of "geographical indications" and the narrower category of "designations of origin" is not relevant for purposes of this submission, since the GI Regulation applies equally to both. Therefore, the United States will refer in this submission to both categories collectively as "geographical indications" or "GIs." Further, there are obvious differences between "geographical indications" as defined in the EC GI Regulation and "geographical indications" as defined in the TRIPS Agreement. The use of the same term to describe both in this submission is not meant to imply that the definition in the EC GI Regulation is consistent with the definition in the TRIPS Agreement.

[14] Article 4(1) of the GI Regulation.

[15] Article 4(2) of the GI Regulation.

sources,[16] and the United States is unaware of any "equivalent" standard approved for non-EC countries, referenced in Article 10(3)).

(h) specific labeling details

(i) requirements laid down by EC or member State provisions.

19. Under Article 5(5) of the GI Regulation, the EC member State is required to forward the application to the EC Commission, if the application satisfies the requirements of the GI Regulation.

20. After verification that the application for registration meets the formal requirements of the GI Regulation, and assuming the application withstands objections, if any, the geographical indication is entered in the "Register of protected designations of origin and protected geographical indications" maintained by the Commission and published in the Official Journal of the European Communities.[17]

21. Article 12(1) states that the GI Regulation "may apply" to agricultural products or foodstuffs from other WTO Members—*i.e.*, producers and processors in another WTO Member may apply to register the GI associated with products in that Member—only if that WTO Member:

(a) can give guarantees identical or equivalent to those referred to in Article 4 (*i.e.*, with respect to the product specifications and inspection procedures required by the EC);

(b) has inspection arrangements and a right to objection equivalent to those laid down in the EC GI Regulation for EC GIs; and

(c) is prepared to provide protection equivalent to that available in the EC to agricultural products and foodstuffs from the EC (*i.e.*, offers reciprocal treatment to EC products).

22. In other words, in order to benefit from the GI Regulation, a WTO Member must adopt a system for GI protection that is equivalent to that in the EC, that is, a system (i) under which the WTO Member can provide guarantees equivalent to those in the GI Regulation that its GI products meet the EC product specifications in Articles 4 and 10 of the GI Regulation, (ii) providing objection rights equivalent to those in the GI Regulation, (iii) providing for internal inspection structures equivalent to those in the EC, and (iv) providing GI protection to EC products that is equivalent to that available in the EC. Further, these conditions require "reciprocity:" the EC will register and protect GIs associated with products from another WTO Member only if that WTO Member provides "equivalent" GI protection in its own territory to "corresponding" products from the EC.

23. Under Article 12(3), upon request of the WTO Member concerned, the EC examines whether a WTO Member satisfies the above conditions "as a result of its national legislation." Only if it does so is registration and protection available in the EC under the GI Regulation for products from that WTO Member.

24. Article 12a sets out application procedures for producers and processors from other WTO Members satisfying these conditions of equivalency and reciprocity. It requires those producers and processors to submit an application to the "authorities" in the relevant WTO Member, and requires the WTO Member, before submitting the application, to "consult" with any EC Member State that has a geographical area or a traditional name connected to that area with the same name as is in the application.[18] It also requires the WTO Member to determine whether the application satisfies the requirements of the GI Regulation. It then requires the WTO

---

[16] The United States tried unsuccessfully to obtain this standard from public sources, although it appears that it may be available for purchase from national members of the European Committee for Standardization. *See, e.g.*, http://www.cenorm.be/cenorm/standards_drafts/index.asp

[17] Article 6(4) of the GI Regulation.

[18] It is not clear how third country officials become aware that such a situation exists.

Member to describe the basis for protection of the GI in that WTO Member, and declare that it has in place the same inspection structures required of EC member States. Next, the WTO Member is instructed to forward the application and accompanying documentation to the Commission.

25. Article 12(2) requires that any use of a geographical indication in connection with products of other WTO Members can be authorized only if the country of origin "is clearly and visibly indicated on the label."[19] There is no similar requirement with respect to products of EC member States.

Objections

26. "Legitimately concerned" natural or legal persons that reside or are established in a member State of the EC may object to a proposed registration under Article 7(3) of the GI Regulation. Only persons who can demonstrate a "legitimate economic interest," however, are authorized to consult the application.[20] Statements of objection are admissible[21] if they demonstrate that a proposed registration (a) does not qualify for protection pursuant to the Regulation (*e.g.*, for failure to meet the definition of geographical indication in the GI Regulation); (b) would "jeopardize the existence of an entirely or partly identical name or of a mark or the existence of products which have been legally on the market for at least five years" prior to publication of the application; or (c) is of a generic name.[22] The person objecting must file the statement of objection with the member State in which that person is resident or established. That member State then may object to the registration within six months of publication of the application.[23]

27. By contrast, under Articles 12b and 12d, just as in the case of registration, it appears that persons from another WTO Member can object to an application for GI registration only if that WTO Member satisfies the conditions of equivalency and reciprocity laid down under Article 12. Further, they may not submit their objections directly to an authority in the EC, such as the Commission or even to an EC member State, which is required to evaluate the objections pursuant to the GI Regulation and has a long-established internal mechanism for working with the Commission on these matters. Rather, they must submit their objection to the WTO Member in which they reside or are established, which then is supposed to decide whether to forward the objection to the Commission. In addition, only a person from a third country that has a "legitimate interest" may object to a registration, and only those with a "legitimate economic interest" are authorized to consult the application.[24] This is in contrast to objections from persons resident or established in an EC member State, who need only be "legitimately concerned."[25]

Scope of protection

28. The very broad scope of protection for registered geographical indications is set out in Article 13(1) of the GI Regulation, which states that

> Registered names shall be protected against the following:
>
> (a) any direct or indirect commercial use of a name registered in respect of products not covered by the registration in so far as those products are comparable to the products registered under the name or insofar as using the name exploits the reputation of the protected name;

[19] It is unclear under the Regulation whether this applies to all third country GIs.

[20] Article 7(2) of the GI Regulation.

[21] It appears from the context of Article 7 of the GI Regulation that this means that the objection is eligible for consideration by the EC Commission.

[22] Article 7(4) of the GI Regulation.

[23] Articles 7(1) and 7(2) of the GI Regulation.

[24] Article 12d(1) of the GI Regulation.

[25] Article 7(3) of the GI Regulation.

(b) any misuse, imitation or evocation, even if the true origin of the product is indicated or if the protected name is translated or accompanied by an expression such as 'style', 'type', 'method', 'as produced in', 'imitation' or 'similar';

(c) any other false or misleading indication as to the provenance, origin, nature or essential qualities of the product, on the inner or outer packaging, advertising material or documents relating to the product concerned, and the packing of the product in a container liable to convey a false impression as to origin;

(d) any other practice liable to mislead the public as to the true origin of the product.

29. Article 13(2) also provides that protected names may not become generic, *i.e.,* become the "common name" of an agricultural product or foodstuff.[26]

30. In addition, only products qualified to use a registered GI may include the official EC "GI" symbol or logo on its labels, packaging, and advertising materials.[27]

31. Finally, Article 14 specifically addresses trademarks in the context of GIs. Article 14(2) provides that if the use of certain prior trademarks "engenders one of the situations indicated in Article 13," they "may continue to be used notwithstanding the registration of" a geographical indication. The GI Regulation fails to provide the owner of a valid prior trademark the right to prevent the use of a GI that results in a likelihood of confusion with respect to the trademark.

IV. THE EC GI REGULATION IS INCONSISTENT WITH THE EC'S OBLIGATIONS UNDER THE TRIPS AGREEMENT AND THE GATT 1994

A. THE EC GI REGULATION IS INCONSISTENT WITH THE EC'S OBLIGATIONS TO PROVIDE NATIONAL TREATMENT

32. The EC GI Regulation is inconsistent with two different national treatment obligations under the WTO Agreements. The first is the obligation to provide national treatment with respect to the *nationals* of other WTO Members under Article 3.1 of the TRIPS Agreement, and, through its incorporation by Article 2.1 of the TRIPS Agreement, Article 2 of the Paris Convention. The second is the obligation to provide national treatment with respect to the *products* of other WTO Members, under Article III of the GATT 1994. This section addresses each of these inconsistencies separately below. Section A.1 immediately below addresses the GI Regulation's inconsistencies with the national treatment obligations of the TRIPS Agreement and the Paris Convention. Section A.2 then addresses the GI Regulation's inconsistencies with the national treatment obligations of the GATT 1994.

1. The EC GI Regulation is inconsistent with the EC's national treatment obligations with respect to nationals of other WTO Members under the TRIPS Agreement and the Paris Convention

(a) The national treatment obligation under the TRIPS Agreement and the Paris Convention

(i) Introduction

33. The national treatment obligation has been a standard element in intellectual property agreements for over 120 years, dating from 1883, when the Paris Convention was first concluded.[28] The Appellate Body called

---

[26] *See* Article 3(1) of the GI Regulation.

[27] Article 5a of Commission Regulation (EEC) No. 2037/93 of 27 July 1993, laying down detailed rules of application of Council Regulation (EEC) No. 2081/92 on the protection of geographical indications and designations of origin for agricultural products and foodstuffs ("Commission Regulation 2037/93"). Exhibit COMP-2.a.

it a "fundamental principle of the world trading system"[29] and noted that the framers of the TRIPS Agreement not only incorporated the national treatment obligations of the Paris Convention directly into the TRIPS Agreement, but also saw fit, in addition, to include an additional provision on national treatment in the TRIPS Agreement. "Clearly," the Appellate Body concluded, "this emphasizes the fundamental significance of the obligation of national treatment to their purposes in the TRIPS Agreement."[30] The Appellate Body continued:

> Indeed, the significance of the national treatment obligation can hardly be overstated. Not only has the national treatment obligation long been a cornerstone of the Paris Convention and other international intellectual property conventions. So, too, has the national treatment obligation long been a cornerstone of the world trading system that is served by the WTO.
>
> As we see it, the national treatment obligation is a fundamental principle underlying the TRIPS Agreement, just as it had been in what is now the GATT 1994.[31]

34. There is a considerable body of GATT and WTO dispute settlement reports that have considered the national treatment obligation in Article III of the GATT 1994. But there has been only one dispute raising the national treatment obligation in the context of the TRIPS Agreement and the Paris Convention.[32] Therefore, this dispute represents only the second time that the TRIPS Agreement and Paris Convention obligations with respect to this "fundamental principle of the world trading system" will be clarified.

(ii) Article 2 of the Paris Convention

<u>The ordinary meaning of the terms in Article 2 of the Paris Convention</u>

35. Article 2.1 of the TRIPS Agreement directly incorporates many provisions of the Paris Convention, including the national treatment obligation in Article 2 of the Paris Convention:

> Nationals of any country of the Union shall, as regards the protection of industrial property, enjoy in all the other countries of the Union the advantages that their respective laws now grant, or may hereafter grant, to nationals; all without prejudice to the rights specifically provided for by this Convention. Consequently, they shall have the same protection as the latter, and the same legal remedy against any infringement of their rights, provided that the conditions and formalities imposed upon nationals are complied with.

36. Article 2(2) of the Paris Convention specifies, in addition, that no requirement of domicile or establishment shall be imposed on nationals of other Members as a prerequisite for the enjoyment of any industrial property right.

37. In the Paris Convention, "industrial property" is understood "in its broadest sense."[33] "Protection of Industrial property," for which Members must provide national treatment, includes, among its "objects," trademarks, indications of source or appellations of origin, and the repression of unfair competition,[34] and applies specifically to agricultural industries and all manufactured and natural products.[35]

---

[28] *See* Gervais, Daniel, *The TRIPS Agreement: Drafting History and Analysis*, Sweet & Maxwell (2nd Edition, 2003) , p. 98. Exhibit US-1.

[29] Appellate Body Report, *US – Section 211,* para. 233.

[30] Appellate Body Report, *US – Section 211*, paras. 239-240.

[31] Appellate Body Report, *US – Section 211*, paras. 241-242.

[32] i.*e., US – Section 211.*

[33] Article 1(1) of the Paris Convention.

[34] Article 1(2) of the Paris Convention.

[35] Article 1(3) of the Paris Convention. Examples given include grain, fruit, cattle, mineral waters, beer, flowers, and flour.

38. The protection of "indications of source" is clarified in Article 10 of the Paris Convention, which provides that remedies be made available to "interested parties" against goods bearing false indications as to their source. "Interested party" includes any producer of goods located in the locality falsely indicated as the source (or located in the region where such locality is situated) or any producer located "in the country where the false indication of source is used."[36] Similarly, Article 10*bis*, which addresses unfair competition, requires Members to assure nationals of all other Members effective protection against unfair competition, which includes "indications or allegations the use of which in the course of trade is liable to mislead the public as to the nature, the manufacturing process, the characteristics, the suitability for their purpose, or the quantity, of the goods."

39. Therefore, with respect to the Paris Convention, national treatment "as regards the protection of industrial property" includes national treatment as regards the right of all interested parties, regardless of nationality, to prevent false indications that certain goods come from the region in which those interested parties produce goods or that the goods possess certain characteristics.[37] Further, this protection with respect to indications of source and unfair methods of competition is not limited to situations in which the region falsely indicated as the source is in the territory in which the false indication is used. Rather, it includes situations where that region—in which interested parties produce goods—is outside that territory (*e.g.*, a region in the territory of another Paris Convention Member).[38] It is this protection, which concerns false indications of source and unfair methods of competition in relation to any region in which interested parties are producing goods, that is subject to the national treatment obligation. Of course, a Member may impose substantive and procedural requirements for obtaining this protection on interested parties. But whatever requirements are in place with respect to indications of source and unfair methods of competition, they have to provide the same advantages to non-nationals as they do to nationals.

40. This is clear from the language of the national treatment obligation itself, in Article 2(1) of the Paris Convention, which provides that, as regards the protection of indications of source and unfair competition, among other industrial property:

> Nationals of any country of the Union shall ... enjoy in all the other countries of the Union the advantages that their respective laws now grant, or may hereafter grant, to nationals ... Consequently, they shall have the same protection as the latter, and the same legal remedy against any infringement of their rights.

41. The ordinary meaning of these terms is that, whatever advantages a Member grants to its own nationals with respect to the industrial property rights at issue, must also be granted to the nationals of other Members. This obligation does not dictate the substance or procedures of a Member's laws on intellectual property. It requires only that, whatever a Member's substantive rules or procedures—such as those of the EC's GI system, with its particular processes—they must result in the same advantages for nationals of other Members.

<u>Relationship between Article 2(1) of the Paris Convention and conditioning national treatment on reciprocity and equivalence</u>

42. The ordinary meaning of the national treatment obligation speaks for itself: a Member cannot deny to other nationals advantages that it grants to its own nationals with respect to indications of source and unfair competition. However, there are two specific concerns underlying this obligation that are relevant to this dispute. First is the concern that "reciprocity" must not be a condition for protecting the industrial property of other Members' nationals: a Member must treat nationals of other Members at least as well as it treats its own,

---

[36] Article 10(2) of the Paris Convention.

[37] *See* Articles 10 and 10*bis*(3) of the Paris Convention.

[38] Article 10 of the Paris Convention defines "interested parties" as including <u>both</u> producers in the locality falsely indicated as the source, <u>and</u> those in the country where the false indication of source is used.

regardless of the treatment accorded by the other Members to their own or other nationals.[39] The second is that a Member may not require that other Members adopt particular substantive or procedural rules as a condition for protecting the intellectual property rights of the nationals of those Members (*i.e.*, "equivalence").[40]

(iii) Article 3.1 of the TRIPS Agreement

43. As the Appellate Body recently noted, the importance of national treatment in the TRIPS Agreement is reflected in the fact that the framers of the WTO Agreement not only incorporated the long-standing national treatment obligation in the Paris Convention directly into the TRIPS Agreement, but they also added additional TRIPS Agreement-specific provisions that build on the Paris Convention national treatment obligations.[41]

44. Article 3.1 of the TRIPS Agreement requires a WTO Member to "accord to the nationals of other Members treatment no less favourable than that it accords to its own nationals with regard to the protection of intellectual property."[42] In that provision, "the term intellectual property refers to all categories of intellectual property that are the subject of Sections 1 through 7 of Part II"[43] of the TRIPS Agreement, which includes the categories "trademarks" (section 2) and "geographical indications" (section 3). "Protection" is broad in meaning, and includes "matters affecting the availability, acquisition, scope, maintenance and enforcement of intellectual property rights as well as those matters affecting the use of intellectual property rights specifically addressed in this Agreement."[44] The ordinary meaning of Article 3.1, therefore, signifies a broad obligation for the EC to accord non-EC nationals no less favorable treatment than it accords its own nationals with respect to the availability, acquisition, scope, maintenance and enforcement of rights in geographical indications, as well as to those matters affecting the use of geographical indications that are the subject of the TRIPS Agreement.

45. Under the TRIPS Agreement, these rights include the right, with respect to geographical indications, for "interested parties" to have the legal means to prevent the use of designations on a good that mislead the public as to the geographic origin of the good. Similarly to the Paris Convention, this includes the right of all interested parties, regardless of nationality, to prevent uses in *one* Member that, *inter alia*, mislead the public into thinking that a good comes from the geographic region of the interested parties in *another* Member. This reading is reinforced by the definition of "geographical indications" in the TRIPS Agreement as "indications which identify a good as originating in the territory of a Member, or a region or locality in that territory. . ." . Therefore, the national treatment obligation under the TRIPS Agreement is that, whatever treatment a Member accords to its own nationals with respect to the rights in geographical indications, it must accord treatment at

---

[39] *See, e.g.*, Bodenhausen, G.H.C., *Guide to the Application of the Paris Convention for the Protection of Industrial Property*, United International Bureau for the Protection of Intellectual Property (BIRPI) (1969) (reprinted (World Intellectual Property Organization) 1991), p. 12 (citing "the very important basic rule of the Convention," a principle which means that each Member must apply to nationals of other Members "the *same treatment as it gives to its own nationals*, without being allowed to require reciprocity." Emphasis in original.) Exhibit US-2.

[40] The importance of these conclusions was made clear at the very first negotiating session for the Paris Convention in 1880, where the concept of national treatment in intellectual property rights was born. In the welcoming remarks for that first session, the French Minister for Agriculture and Commerce stated that the Conference could not achieve a complete international treaty of industrial property because of the difficulty of unifying national laws. He concluded that the Conference should, therefore, strive to find the means to constitute a union which, without encroaching on domestic legislation, would assure national treatment and lay down a number of uniform general principles. *Actes de Paris*, 1880, pp. 14—17, at p. 16 (emphasis added). Exhibit US-3. In the negotiations on the national treatment provision, the French negotiator who had prepared the initial draft emphasized that, in order to be acceptable, the convention would have to respect the internal legislation of all contracting parties to the extent possible, and to restrict it to an obligation to extend national treatment to foreigners. *Actes de Paris*, 1880, pp. 33 (emphasis added). Exhibit US-3. In the course of that discussion, the national treatment obligation was clarified by the deletion of the word "reciproquement" from the original draft. *Id.*, pp. 39-45. Exhibit US-3. And indeed, in subsequent revisions to this provision, several proposals to include a reciprocity element in the obligation found no support and were withdrawn. For instance, a proposal by the United States to provide for the right to impose upon nationals of the other countries the fulfillment of conditions imposed on its nationals by those countries found no support and was withdrawn. *Actes de La Haye*, 1925, pp. 413-415 (First Sub-Committee). Exhibit US-4.

[41] Appellate Body Report, *US – Section 211*, paras. 239-240.

[42] Footnote omitted.

[43] Article 1.2 of the TRIPS Agreement.

[44] Article 3, fn. 3, of the TRIPS Agreement.

least as favorable to nationals of other WTO Members. This does not necessarily dictate how a Member provides for geographical indication protection, and does not prevent a Member from imposing substantive and procedural rules with respect to that protection. However, it does require that, whatever those rules are, they do not result in less favorable treatment of other Members' nationals.[45]

46. As in the case of the Paris Convention national treatment obligation, implicit in the TRIPS Agreement national treatment obligation is a prohibition on conditioning the treatment of other Members' nationals on reciprocity or on other Members having a specific domestic regime of protection. Indeed, the national treatment obligation is a recognition that, despite the many substantive and procedural obligations in the TRIPS Agreement, not all aspects of the protection of intellectual property rights are subject to specific obligations, and that the TRIPS Agreement does not represent or require a complete harmonization of the Members' intellectual property laws. The obligation is that, whatever the rules are for a Member's own nationals, including with respect to aspects not harmonized by the TRIPS Agreement, they must treat other Members' nationals at least as favorably.

47. The context of the TRIPS Agreement national treatment obligation supports this reading. Article 3.1 is in Part I of the TRIPS Agreement, entitled "General Provisions and Basic Principles." The specific obligations with respect to each of the categories of intellectual property are set out in Part II: "Standards Concerning the Availability, Scope and Use of Intellectual Property Rights." But the obligations specific to each of the seven categories of intellectual property in Part II do not cover all procedural and substantive aspects of protecting those intellectual property rights. For this reason, Article 3.1 is a general provision enunciating a basic principle underlying the obligations that follow in Part II that, whatever the rules are with respect to the protection of the seven categories of intellectual property—even with respect to those rules that are not subject to specific obligations—they must not result in treatment for other Members' nationals that is less favorable than that accorded one's own nationals.

48. Further, another "general provision and basic principle" is in Article 1.1, which specifically emphasizes that Members "shall be free to determine the appropriate method of implementing" the TRIPS Agreement. This provision recognizes that there are different ways to implement the obligations of the TRIPS Agreement and that Members are not obligated to select any particular means of implementation over another. Article 1.1 also permits Members to implement more extensive protection than is required by this Agreement, but specifically requires that any such more extensive protection not contravene the provisions of the Agreement. Therefore, whatever means of implementation or extent of protection a Member chooses under the TRIPS Agreement, it must not treat other Members' nationals less favorably than one's own nationals. This safeguard is critical, especially in the area of geographic indications, in which there is an acknowledged wide variety of mechanisms used to implement the obligations.[46]

49. Article 1.1 of the TRIPS Agreement as a whole underscores the conclusion already apparent from the ordinary meaning of Article 3.1 that a Member may not condition protection of GI rights on other Members having an equivalent system of protection: where the TRIPS Agreement itself provides the freedom for Members to determine the appropriate method of implementing its provisions, a particular Member cannot undercut this right by requiring a particular method of implementation as a condition of protecting GI rights. Again, this principle is especially significant in the area of geographical indications, where there is a wide variety of methods for implementing the TRIPS Agreement obligations.

50. With respect to national treatment in the context of goods, under Article III of the GATT 1994, as one panel noted, determinations as to whether imported "like products" are being discriminated against must be

---

[45] Indeed, as stated in its preamble, one object and purpose of the TRIPS Agreement is to provide adequate standards and principles concerning the availability, scope and use of trade-related intellectual property rights. GI rights are particularly "trade-related" to the extent they relate to the protection in one Member's territory of GIs indicating an area in another Member's territory.

[46] *See, e.g.*, "Document SCT/6/3 Rev. on Geographical Indications: Historical Background, Nature of Rights, Existing Systems for Protection and Obtaining Protection in Other Countries," World Intellectual Property Organization (WIPO) Document SCT/8/4 (April 2, 2002) (Exhibit US-5); "The Definition of Geographical Indications," WIPO Document SCT/9/4 (October 1, 2002) (Exhibit COMP-16).

made "in the light of the purpose of Article III, which is to ensure that internal taxes and regulations 'not be applied to imported or domestic products so as to afford protection to domestic production'. The purpose of Article III is not to harmonize the internal taxes and regulations of contracting parties, which differ from country to country."[47] The same is true for the national treatment provision in the TRIPS Agreement.

51. The underlying principle for the national treatment obligation was illustrated recently in *US – Section 211*. In that dispute, the panel recognized that, although the TRIPS Agreement contained obligations on the kinds of signs that must be eligible to be trademarks, it did not contain obligations with respect to who was the legitimate "owner" of a trademark under domestic law. The particular ownership rules for trademarks—like many substantive and procedural rules on intellectual property—were left to the domestic legislation of the Members. After expressing concern about the potential for abuse through arbitrary national legislation on ownership, the panel noted that the TRIPS Agreement "is not without safeguards against potential abuse," specifically noting that "Articles 3 and 4 of the Agreement require a Member to accord national and most-favoured-nation treatment to the nationals of other Members."[48] In other words, the panel, affirmed by the Appellate Body, found that the TRIPS Agreement had not harmonized or imposed specific trademark ownership rules, but that the national treatment and most-favored-nation obligations provided the necessary safeguards against abuse in those areas where the TRIPS Agreement did not provide specific obligations.

(iv) Conclusion with respect to Article 2 of the Paris Convention and Article 3.1 of the TRIPS Agreement

52. In sum, the right with respect to indications of source, unfair competition, and geographical indications in the Paris Convention and the TRIPS Agreement includes the right of interested parties with respect to designations that mislead the public in a given territory into thinking that a good comes from the region in which the interested party is established and produces goods, and, in the case of geographical indications under the TRIPS Agreement, that the good possesses the qualities, reputation, or other characteristic of products coming from that geographic area. This right applies whether or not the interested party is established and producing goods in the territory of the Member in which the misleading use is occurring. It is this right in geographical indications and indications of source that is subject to the national treatment obligation: whatever requirements a Member has may not result in less favorable treatment for other Members' nationals.

53. Moreover, the EC has an obligation under the TRIPS Agreement and the Paris Convention to treat non-EC nationals at least as well as EC nationals in all matters pertaining to the availability, acquisition, maintenance, and enforcement of rights in both non-EC and EC geographical indications and other types of indications of source, including with respect to the ability of non-EC nationals to register and protect the indications of source and geographical indications of goods they produce in their country of nationality from misleading and unfair uses in the EC. These national treatment provisions prohibit making the availability, acquisition, maintenance, and enforcement of these rights for nationals of other Members contingent on "reciprocity" by other Members. Further, these national treatment provisions prohibit making the availability, acquisition, maintenance, and enforcement of rights for nationals of other Members contingent on those other Members having a particular system of protection themselves. Indeed, especially with respect to geographical indications, where there are numerous accepted methods among the WTO Members of offering GI protection, there is no requirement in the TRIPS Agreement that a Member adopt a particular system of GI protection.[49] Nor can a single Member impose such a requirement as a prerequisite for other Members' nationals to receive protection. A Member cannot, through the selective withholding of rights from another Member's nationals, obtain concessions from other Members that it was unable to achieve at the negotiating table in the TRIPS Agreement. To the contrary, the national treatment obligation is clear: in all matters pertaining, *inter alia*, to the availability, acquisition, enforcement and maintenance of rights in geographical indications located in the territory of WTO Members, non-EC nationals must be accorded treatment at least as favorable as EC nationals.

[47] *US – Malt Beverages*, para. 5.25. Emphasis added.

[48] Panel Report, *US – Section 211*, para. 8.57.

[49] *See, e.g.*, WIPO Document SCT/8/4 (Exhibit US-5) and WIPO Document SCT/9/4 (Exhibit COMP-16).

54. The EC GI Regulation fails flatly to meet this obligation.

55. In sections b and c below, the United States describes in a unitary fashion how the EC GI Regulation is inconsistent with the national treatment obligations of the TRIPS Agreement and the Paris Convention. As discussed above, however, there is a distinction between the relevant rights in the Paris Convention and those in the TRIPS Agreement. "Protection of Industrial property" under the Paris Convention has as its object "indications of source or appellations of origin and the repression of unfair competition," and so requires protection against direct or indirect use of a false indication of geographic source that may, *inter alia*, mislead the consumer as to the characteristics of the goods. The TRIPS Agreement also covers indications of geographic source where they rise to the level of "geographical indication" as defined in Article 22.1 of the TRIPS Agreement—*i.e.,* where "a given quality, reputation, or other characteristic of the good is essentially attributable to that origin." The GI Regulation's rules with respect to geographical indications are also rules with respect to indications of source and unfair methods of competition. As such, they are subject both to the national treatment obligation of the Paris Convention, which requires national treatment with respect to indications of source and unfair methods of competition, and to the national treatment obligation of the TRIPS Agreement, which requires national treatment with respect to GIs in particular.

56. For ease of reading, therefore, in sections b and c below, when reference is made to the national treatment obligation with respect to GIs, it is understood to mean a reference to the TRIPS Agreement national treatment obligation with respect to GIs, as well as the Paris Convention national treatment obligation with respect to designations of origin and unfair competition.

(b) Non-EC nationals are accorded less favorable treatment than EC nationals under the GI Regulation with respect to the registration and protection of geographical indications.

(i) Introduction

57. The EC GI Regulation is entirely inconsistent with the national treatment obligations of the Paris Convention and the TRIPS Agreement. Indeed, it specifically conditions GI protection on reciprocity and equivalence, two conditions that the national treatment obligation was specifically intended to prohibit. Further, it runs directly contrary to the freedom that Members have under Article 1.1 of the TRIPS Agreement to determine the appropriate method of implementing the TRIPS Agreement. To summarize the details presented further below, the explicit purpose of the GI Regulation is to bestow numerous significant commercial and competitive advantages on those entitled to register and use geographical indications, including higher profits, a coveted label, the ability to stop others from a wide variety of uses, including the use of words that even "evoke" the geographical indication, broad enforcement in all EC Member States (both by government authorities on their own initiative, as well as by right holders), and guarantees against their registered name becoming generic, among other significant benefits. These advantages are available immediately and uniformly throughout the EC, which the EC itself recognizes is a significant advantage over attempting to seek protection separately under the different laws of each of the EC member States (even assuming that this is possible).

58. Yet these advantages are not made available on the same terms to the nationals of all other Members. EC nationals are permitted to register their home-based EC geographical indications, and obtain all of the considerable competitive advantages touted by the EC, but US nationals (and nationals of most other WTO Members) are currently not able to register their home US geographical indications, and therefore cannot get any of the benefits of EC-wide GI protection summarized above. This is plainly inconsistent with the EC's obligations under the TRIPS Agreement and Paris Convention to treat US and other WTO Member nationals at least as well as EC nationals with respect to the protection of rights in geographical indications.

59. Further, taking the United States as an example, the only way that US nationals might in the future be able to register US-based GIs, and thus obtain the same EC-wide GI protection for their US-based GIs as EC nationals have for their EC-based GIs, is for the United States to (a) reciprocally grant equivalent GI protection

for agricultural products and foodstuffs coming from the EC;[50] and (b) adopt a system for protecting geographical indications that the EC unilaterally decides is equivalent to that in the EC, including equivalent inspection and objection systems. As discussed above, such requirements are directly contrary, not only to the letter of the national treatment obligation, but also to its specific objective of prohibiting the conditioning of national treatment on reciprocity and equivalency. Further, it forces Members to adopt a particular set of rules to implement the TRIPS Agreement, contrary to Article 1.1 of the TRIPS Agreement. Instead of recognizing that there are many different ways to fulfill the TRIPS Agreement obligations on GIs, the EC is in effect telling the United States that its nationals will not be able to register their US-based GIs in the EC and receive EC-wide protection for those GIs—as EC nationals are permitted to do with respect to their EC-based GIs—unless the United States adopts a system for GI protection that the EC judges is equivalent to the EC system. In addition, only if the United States agrees, through this EC-mandated system, to offer reciprocal protection to EC products, will the EC allow US nationals protection with respect to their U.S-based GIs comparable to what EC nationals already receive with respect to their EC-based GIs.

60. These conditions simply cannot stand up in the face of the national treatment obligations of the TRIPS Agreement and the Paris Convention.

(ii) The EC GI Regulation accords less favorable treatment to non-EC Nationals with respect to registration and consequent protection

61. The preamble to the EC GI Regulation specifies that its major objective is to bestow a competitive benefit on producers of products with registered GIs, recognizing that:

(a) empirically, consumers are tending to attach greater importance to the quality of foodstuffs, generating a growing demand for agricultural products or foodstuffs with an identifiable origin;

(b) experience in the EC member States has been that agricultural products or foodstuffs with a registered and identifiable origin have proven successful for producers of those products, who have thus been able to secure higher incomes in return for improved quality; and

(c) in light of the diversity of national practices with respect to registered GIs, a uniform approach will ensure "fair competition between the producers" of registered GI products.

62. The specific advantages bestowed on producers of registered GI products are laid out in the GI Regulation, including:

(a) The ability to register their GIs in the official EC-wide "Register of protected designations of origin and protected geographical indications."[51]

(b) The right to use the protected geographical indication throughout the EC market on products that qualify for the GI.[52]

(c) The right to use an official EC "symbol" or "logo" informing the consumer that the product is a registered GI.[53] As the relevant EC regulation explains, "[t]he logo will allow producers of food products to increase awareness of their products among consumers in the European Union... The presence of this logo is a genuine guarantee for all European consumers, making it clear that the special nature of this product lies in its geographical origin. Because of this, products will inspire

[50] Article 12(1) of the GI Regulation.

[51] Articles 6(1)—6(4) of the GI Regulation.

[52] Article 4(1) of the GI Regulation.

[53] Article 5a of Commission Regulation 2037/93, p. 5. Exhibit COMP-2.a.

more confidence. As producers, the logo provides you which [*sic*] a marketing tool. You will be able to put the logo on the labels or packaging of your products, and also use it in your advertising."[54]

(d) A broad right to have that registered GI protected throughout the EC, both automatically, at the initiative of government authorities, as well as through private rights of action,[55] against a broad range of competing and disparaging uses.[56]

(e) Protection from having the registered GI become generic (which causes the geographic indication to lose its value).[57]

Non-EC National are accorded less favorable treatment with respect to the registration and protection of their non-EC-based GIs than EC nationals are with respect to their EC-based GIs

63. Plainly, the GI Regulation offers significant advantages and favorable treatment to producers of qualifying products with respect to the availability, acquisition, scope, maintenance, and enforcement of rights in GIs, as well as matters affecting the use of GIs. Unfortunately for US producers of quality products from US regions, these considerable advantages with respect to rights in GIs are available only for producers and processors in the EC. Article 5(3) requires that the application for the registration of a GI be "sent to the member State in which the geographical area is located." US producers of quality products from US geographical areas, therefore, cannot even file a registration application, because their GI does not refer to a region in the EC.

64. The only avenue available to US nationals to apply for GI protection with respect to their US-based GIs is in Article 12, which provides that the GI Regulation may apply to goods from third countries, including WTO Members, but only if that WTO Member satisfies certain conditions. First, that WTO Member must adopt a system for GI protection that is equivalent to that in the EC, that is, a system (i) under which the WTO Member can provide guarantees equivalent to those in the GI Regulation that its GI products meet the EC product specifications in Articles 4 and 10 of the GI Regulation, (ii) providing objection rights equivalent to those in the GI Regulation, (iii) providing for internal inspection structures equivalent to those in the EC,[58] and (iv) providing GI protection to EC products that is equivalent to that available in the EC. The required inspection structures, described under Article 10 of the GI Regulation, must satisfy numerous specific requirements, including, if private bodies are responsible, compliance with requirements laid down in other European standards.[59] Second, any such WTO Members must offer reciprocity: the EC will register and protect products from another WTO Member only if that WTO Member is "prepared to provide protection equivalent to that available in the Community to corresponding agricultural products for [*sic.* "or"] foodstuffs coming from the Community."

65. In other words, a US national is not able to acquire, does not have available to him, and is unable to enforce, the same rights to his US-based GIs as EC nationals have with respect to their EC-based GIs, unless the United States (1) harmonizes its GI protection system to that of the EC (and, therefore drops its current system of protection through the certification and collective mark system and creates two separate GI protection systems, one specific to GIs, the other trademark-based); and (2) offers reciprocity with respect to European products.

---

54 Annex II of Commission Regulation 2037/93. Exhibit COMP-2.a.

55 Review under Article 24.2 of the Application of the Provisions of the Section of the TRIPS Agreement on Geographical Indications, Responses to the Checklist of Questions, Addendum, WTO Council for Trade-Related Aspects of Intellectual Property Rights, IP/C/W/117/Add.10, March 26, 1999 ("Article 24.1 Review"), Responses of the EC to Questions in Document IP/C/B nos. 1, 34, and 35.

56 Article 13 of the GI Regulation.

57 Article 13(3) of the GI Regulation.

58 Article 12(1) of the GI Regulation.

59 Article 10 of the GI Regulation.

66. These requirements of equivalency and reciprocity by a WTO Member as a condition of granting GI rights to nationals of that Member are inconsistent with, and indeed, directly contrary to, the national treatment obligations of the TRIPS Agreement and the Paris Convention.

67. This reading of the national treatment obligation is not unique to geographical indications. For instance, in the area of trademarks, there are, in general, two recognized systems for providing trademark protection among WTO Members. The EC bases trademark ownership on registration; the United States generally bases trademark ownership on use.[60] The TRIPS Agreement is designed to accommodate both systems, and neither is preferred.[61] Yet the TRIPS Agreement does contain an obligation, in Article 15, to make certain signs eligible for registration as trademarks. It also requires, in Article 16.1, that the owner of a registered trademark be provided with specified exclusive rights to prevent certain uses of similar or identical signs. The EC could not, consistent with its national treatment obligations, withhold from US nationals the ability to register signs or to prevent confusing uses, simply because the US system of trademark protection is different from that of the EC. Nor could it refuse to allow US nationals to register a trademark in the EC or to exercise its trademark rights unless the United States agreed to permit EC nationals to base their US trademark ownership on registration in the United States, rather than use, contrary to the US system of trademark protection. In the area of trademarks, as in the area of geographical indications, the EC simply cannot condition intellectual property protection for a WTO Member's nationals on that WTO Member (1) adopting an EC-equivalent system of protection and (2) offering reciprocal protection to EC products or nationals. As discussed above, both of these conditions on making intellectual property protection available to US nationals—equivalency and reciprocity—are inconsistent with the EC's national treatment obligations. This is as true in the area of geographical indications as it is the in area of trademarks.

68. Finally, even if a non-EC national succeeds in registering his home-based GI in the EC, he is still faced with treatment that is less favorable than that accorded his EC national counterpart. Under Article 12(2) of the GI Regulation, a name registered by such a non-EC national will be authorized "only if the country of origin of the product is clearly and visibly indicated on the label." There is no such requirement with respect to the use of name by an EC national with respect to his EC-based GI.

<u>The national treatment obligation in the context of goods is instructive as to the GI Regulation's inconsistency with the national treatment obligations of the TRIPS Agreement and Paris Convention</u>

69. This conclusion is also consistent with a long line of adopted dispute settlement rulings and recommendations with respect to national treatment in the area of goods under the GATT 1994. The Appellate Body noted in *US – Section 211* that the national treatment obligation is a fundamental principle underlying the TRIPS Agreement, just as it was in what is now the GATT 1994.[62] The Appellate Body noted further that the language of Article 3.1 of the TRIPS Agreement is similar to that of Article III:4 of the GATT 1994, and stated that "the jurisprudence on Article III:4 may be useful in interpreting the national treatment obligation in the TRIPS Agreement."[63] Indeed, one object and purpose of the TRIPS Agreement is to establish new rules and disciplines "concerning the applicability of the basic principles of GATT 1994."[64] As the Appellate Body itself has noted, national treatment is one of these principles.[65]

70. The dispute settlement history under Article III of the GATT 1994 does in fact offer some useful guidance for this dispute. Both the Appellate Body and panels have repeatedly established that "[t]he broad and

---

[60] *E.g.,* Appellate Body Report, *US – Section 211*, para. 199.

[61] Note, *e.g.,* that Article 16.1, providing rights with respect to registered trademarks, states that those rights shall not "affect the possibility of Members making rights available on the basis of use." *See also US – Section 211*, paras. 188, 199.

[62] Appellate Body Report, *US – Section 211*, para. 242.

[63] Appellate Body Report, *US – Section 211*, para. 242.

[64] Second paragraph, preamble, TRIPS Agreement.

[65] Appellate Body Report, *US – Section 211*, para. 242.

fundamental purpose of Article III [the national treatment obligation] is to avoid protectionism in the application of tax and regulatory measures"[66] Of course, the national treatment obligation in the GATT 1994 applies to products and that in the TRIPS Agreement and the Paris Convention applies to nationals. But the general principle is easily extrapolated: the national treatment obligation is intended to avoid protectionism with respect to the protection of intellectual property rights.

71. To this end, in the goods context under Article III, the Appellate Body has stated that it will examine objectively the underlying criteria used in a measure, its structure and its overall application to ascertain whether it is applied in a way that affords protection to domestic products.[67] According to the Appellate Body, the protective application of a measure "can most often be discerned from the design, the architecture, and the revealing structure of a measure."[68] In the dispute *Japan – Alcohol*, such factors as the magnitude of dissimilar taxation between a primarily Japanese-produced white spirit, shoju, and a primarily imported white spirit, vodka, was considered evidence of a protective application.

72. Similarly, in the dispute *Korea – Alcohol*, the Appellate Body affirmed the panel's finding of a violation of national treatment in Korea's low taxes on soju and high taxes on other types of alcohol. The Appellate Body noted with approval the Panel's explanation that "[t]here is virtually no imported soju, so the beneficiaries of this structure are almost exclusively domestic producers."[69] In other words, the structure of the tax—although the rates were not expressly based on the origin of the product—was such that the high taxes were imposed almost exclusively on imported products.

73. In *Chile – Alcohol*, the Appellate Body found that, even though Chile's tax structure was based on objective criteria—*i.e.,* higher taxes were imposed on beverages with higher alcohol content, and lower taxes on beverages with lower alcohol content—there was a violation of national treatment because the lower tax rate ended at the point where most domestic products were found, and the higher tax rate began at the point where most imports were found.[70]

74. In this dispute, applying the principles found in adopted dispute settlement rulings and recommendations with respect to GATT Article III, the GI Regulation's protective structure is plain. The GI Regulation specifically recognizes the significant advantages it is granting, then systematically denies these advantages to nationals producing in their country of nationality when that country does not adopt EC-style rules and promise reciprocal treatment.

75. Similarly, just as the substantial difference between the tax rates on imported products and domestic products was evidence of the protective nature of the measure in the *Alcohol* disputes, the substantial difference in treatment between EC-based GIs and non-EC-based GIs—one can be registered and protected on an EC-wide basis, and the other cannot—is evidence of the protective nature of the GI Regulation.

76. In addition, the national treatment obligation with respect to goods under Article III of the GATT 1994 has been found to require "treatment of imported products no less favourable than that accorded to the most-favoured domestic products."[71] In this dispute, by analogy, the treatment accorded to the most favored EC nationals is the ability directly to register and protect GI products that they produce or obtain in their country of nationality under Article 5 of the GI Regulation. By contrast, non-EC nationals producing or obtaining products in their country of nationality are faced with additional conditions, under Article 12, amounting to less favorable treatment. It is not relevant that certain EC nationals—*i.e.*, those producing or obtaining products outside the EC—might be faced with these same conditions. Non-EC nationals are entitled, not to the less favorable

---

[66] Appellate Body Report, *Japan – Alcohol*, page 16, *citing US – Section 337.*

[67] Appellate Body Report, *Japan – Alcohol*, page 29.

[68] *Id.*

[69] Appellate Body Report, *Korea – Alcohol*, para. 150, *citing* the panel report, para. 10.101.

[70] Appellate Body Report, *Chile – Alcohol*, para. 66.

[71] *US – Malt Beverages*, paras. 5.17, 5.33 (emphasis added).

treatment accorded some EC nationals, but to the treatment accorded the most favored EC nationals. This is the treatment accorded to EC nationals who can register and protect GI products they produce in their country of nationality.

The GI Regulation's TRIPS-inconsistent conditions for permitting the registration and protection of GIs may be viewed as "extra hurdles" faced by non-EC nationals

77. The Appellate Body has been clear that a measure is inconsistent with national treatment if it imposes an "extra hurdle" on non-EC nationals that is not imposed on EC nationals.[72] As discussed above, the requirements imposed by the GI Regulation on non-EC nationals as a condition of national treatment are not merely an "extra hurdle:" they are themselves directly inconsistent with the national treatment obligation. However, they also can be viewed as "extra hurdles" imposed on non-EC nationals, albeit "extra hurdles" that are themselves inconsistent with national treatment.

78. The EC GI Regulation plainly imposes a number of "extra hurdles" on non-EC nationals who wish to have their home-based GIs registered and protected under the GI Regulation and achieve the same protection as is accorded to EC nationals with respect to their EC-based GIs. This registration and protection goes to the availability, acquisition, maintenance, and enforcement, among other matters, of GI rights in the EC.

79. Article 22.2 of the TRIPS Agreement requires Members to provide the legal means for interested parties to prevent misleading uses of GIs and any use constituting an act of unfair competition under Article 10*bis* of the Paris Convention. The GI Regulation does provide the direct legal means for persons established in the EC to apply for registration and have their EC-based GIs protected on an EC-wide basis.[73] By contrast, non-EC nationals hoping to have their non-EC based GIs registered and protected face a number of additional hurdles. First, and perhaps most significantly, under Article 12(1) of the GI Regulation, that national would have to convince its government to adopt an EC-equivalent system of GI protection (including extensive inspection systems and the like), to offer reciprocal GI treatment to EC agricultural products and foodstuffs, and to take actions necessary to convince the EC, under Article 12(3), that its GI protection system and offer of reciprocity satisfy the EC's requirements. To achieve protection, the WTO Member would have to actually take all of these steps, with all of the additional time, effort, and expense that this entails. An EC national seeking to register its own EC-based GI does not have to do any of this to register and have protected its GIs on an EC-wide basis.

80. Indeed, as a practical matter, non-EC nationals do not have the legal means to have their non-EC-based GIs registered and protected under the GI Regulation, and do not have any sure way of obtaining those legal means. These interested parties simply are not in a position, either to establish a full EC-style GI system in their home country, or to provide reciprocal treatment.

81. Second, even where this hurdle does not exist—where the EC has determined that the GI protection system of a WTO Member is equivalent to the EC system and where that Member offers reciprocal treatment to EC products—the non-EC national still faces an extra hurdle not faced by EC nationals. Unlike his EC-based counterpart, a non-EC national seeking protection for his home-based GI cannot apply for registration directly to the competent authorities in Europe. Rather, he must petition his government to apply on his behalf. That non-EC Member may have neither the infrastructure nor the inclination to satisfy the stringent EC requirements with respect to that application, which includes an independent analysis of whether the application meets the EC's standards, possible consultations with EC Member States, the development and submission of the legal provisions and the usage on which the GI status is based, a declaration that the full EC-compliant inspection structures exist in that WTO Member, and any other documents on which that Member's assessment was based.[74]

---

[72] Appellate Body Report, *US – Section 211*, paras 260-268.

[73] *E.g.*, Articles 5 and 6 of the GI Regulation.

[74] Articles 12(1) and 12(2) of the GI Regulation.

82. In other words, the GI Regulation has in place procedures, directly applicable to EC nationals and member States, under which EC nationals can apply through their member States to the Commission to have their GIs registered and protected on an EC-wide basis. There are no such procedures in place with respect to an application from a non-EC national producing products outside the EC. An EC national has the infrastructure and the regulations in place that allow him to register his EC-based GI directly with his member State. A non-EC national has no such infrastructure or regulations, and must depend on the WTO Member of which he is a national to first put such procedures in place.

83. For these reasons, in addition to those mentioned above, non-EC nationals are not being accorded treatment as favorable as that granted EC nationals under the GI Regulation with respect to the protection of geographical indications, under Article 3.1 of the TRIPS Agreement. And they are not enjoying all the advantages being granted to EC nationals with respect to their indications of source or with respect to unfair competition, under Article 2(1) of the Paris Convention. They certainly do not have the "same protection" as EC nationals or the "same legal remedy against infringement of their rights" with respect to indications of source or unfair competition.

The EC GI Regulation requires non-EC nationals to become established in the EC as a condition of obtaining GI protection, contrary to Article 2 of the Paris Convention

84. In addition, permitting only GIs located in the EC to be registered and protected is inconsistent with the Paris Convention prohibition on requiring domicile or establishment as a condition of enjoying intellectual property rights. As discussed above, Article 2(1) of the Paris Convention requires Members to permit nationals of other Members to enjoy the advantages "that their respective laws now grant, or may hereafter grant," to their own nationals. Paris Convention Article 2(2) provides, in addition, that the Member where protection is claimed—in this dispute, the EC—may not impose any "requirement as to domicile or establishment" in that Member on nationals of other Members "for the enjoyment of any industrial property rights." As discussed above, "industrial property" is understood broadly under the Paris Convention, and includes indications of source or appellations of origin, including GIs.

85. The EC GI Regulation imposes an obvious requirement of establishment in the EC as a condition of enjoying rights with respect to indications of origin. It may be possible under the GI Regulation for a US national to register and protect a geographical indication located in the EC, even though he cannot, absent the conditions noted above, do so with respect to his US-based GIs. Therefore a US national might be able to register and protect a GI only if he is producing a product that qualifies for that geographical indication in the EC. Further, he can only claim rights under the GI Regulation with respect to products produced in the EC. Therefore, in order to enjoy rights related to indications of source provided for under the GI Regulation, he must produce or obtain agricultural products or foodstuffs in the EC, and to do this he must have some form of investment or business establishment in the territory of the EC. This requirement that he establish himself in the EC as a precondition to obtain protections with respect to indications of source and unfair competition, is directly prohibited by Article 2(2) of the Paris Convention.

86. In sum, the EC GI Regulation accords less favorable treatment to non-EC nationals than to EC nationals with respect to the registration and consequent protection of GIs. It is for this reason, inconsistent with Article 2 of the Paris Convention and Article 3.1 of the TRIPS Agreement.

(c) The EC GI Regulation accords less favorable treatment to non-EC nationals with respect to opportunity to object to the registration of GIs

87. It is not only in the registration of GIs that the GI Regulation is inconsistent with national treatment obligations. The GI Regulation also lays out rules to permit natural or legal persons to object to the registration

of a GI.[75] The ability to object to the registration of a GI falls within the scope of "protection of intellectual property" under Article 3.1 of the TRIPS Agreement and "protection of industrial property" under Article 2(1) of the Paris Convention, with respect to which national treatment must be provided because the ability to object is part of the ability to prevent others from using indications in a way that is misleading as to source. Further, the right to object is necessary to the ability to acquire, maintain, or enforce intellectual property rights and to prevent misleading indications of source.[76]

88. The GI Regulation's provisions with respect to the ability to object to the registration of GIs accord less favorable treatment to non-EC nationals than to EC nationals in several respects.

89. First, the provisions for objecting to the registration of GIs mirror those for registering GIs in several respects, and therefore suffer from the same national treatment defects as those described above with respect to registration. For instance, under the GI Regulation, EC nationals can object to a registration directly by submitting their objection to the member State in which they reside or are established.[77] Under Article 7(3), "[t]he competent authority *shall* take the necessary measures to consider these comments or objections within the deadlines laid down."[78] The EC member States are then instructed to collaborate in determining how to respond to the objection, or to otherwise refer to the Commission for a final decision.

90. By contrast, non-EC nationals cannot submit their objection directly to the competent authorities in the EC, but must request that their own country transmit the objection.[79] That country may or may not have an appropriate mechanism to process the objection, and may or may not be inclined to transmit the objection, for its own political or other reasons. By contrast, EC member States have certain obligations under the EC GI Regulation with respect to the processing of objections, and there is an infrastructure in place in the EC to process those objections. As discussed above, the Appellate Body has been clear that a Member's measure is inconsistent with national treatment obligations if it imposes an extra hurdle on other Members' nationals that is not imposed on the Member's own nationals.[80] This is one of those "extra hurdles" to GI protection that non-EC nationals face, and is, therefore, a violation of national treatment.

91. Further, this additional hurdle also corresponds to a "requirement as to domicile or establishment," which is a prohibited condition for the enjoyment of rights under Article 2(2) of the Paris Convention. EC persons can submit objections to the member State in which they reside or are established, knowing that those objections will be considered in accordance with the GI Regulation. By contrast, persons not resident or established in the EC are not accorded the same or "no less favorable" treatment, simply because they are not resident or established in the EC.

92. Moreover, Article 12d limits the persons who can object to a registration application submitted by an EC member State to persons from "a WTO member country or a third country recognized under the procedure provided for in Article 12(3)" *i.e.*, satisfying the conditions of equivalency and reciprocity described in the previous section. Just as conditioning registration of US-based GIs on equivalency and reciprocity is impermissible under the national treatment obligations of the TRIPS Agreement and the Paris Convention, so, too, is conditioning the right to object to a registration on equivalency and reciprocity. Therefore, the analysis provided in the previous section with respect to registration and EC-wide protection is equally applicable to objections.

---

[75] Articles 7, and 12b(2) and 12d of the GI Regulation.

[76] *See, e.g.*, Article 7(4) of the GI Regulation, in which the grounds for objection include where the GI would "jeopardize the existence of an entirely or partly identical name or of a mark" in the EC.

[77] Article 7(3) of the GI Regulation.

[78] Emphasis added.

[79] Articles 12b.2 and 12d.1 of the GI Regulation.

[80] *See, e.g.*, Appellate Body Report, *US – Section 211*, para. 264; *US – Section 337*, para. 5.19.

93. Finally, the EC GI Regulation allows only non-EC nationals with a "legitimate interest" to object to a GI registration application, and provides further that only those with a "legitimate economic interest" may consult the application for the GI. One of the grounds for objecting to the registration of a name under Article 7(4) is that the registration would jeopardize the existence of an entirely or partly identical name or the existence of products which have been legally on the market for at least five years. Since the GI Regulation grants more favorable treatment to EC nationals than to non-EC nationals with respect to the registration and EC-wide protection of GIs in the first place, EC nationals are similarly more favored than non-EC nationals with respect to the ability to object, because they are in a better position than non-EC nationals to have a "legitimate interest" or a "legitimate economic interest" with respect to competing names in the EC. Non-EC nationals face an extra hurdle with respect to having a name that could be jeopardized by the registration of a GI.

94. Further, unlike a non-EC national, who must have a "legitimate interest" or a "legitimate economic interest" in order to object to the registration of a GI, an EC national wishing to object under Article 7(3) of the GI Regulation may do so if he is "legitimately concerned." It would appear that the requirement that one be "legitimately concerned" is a lower standard than the requirement that one have a "legitimate interest," making it easier for an EC national to object to a registration than a non-EC national.

95. For all of these reasons, the GI Regulation's provisions with respect to objections to a GI registration are inconsistent with the national treatment obligations of the TRIPS Agreement and the Paris Convention.

2. The EC GI Regulation is inconsistent with the EC's national treatment obligations with respect to goods of other WTO Members under the GATT 1994

96. Article III:4 of the GATT 1994 requires Members to accord no less favorable treatment to products originating in the territory of other Members than it accords to like products of national origin "with respect to all laws, regulations and requirements affecting their internal sale, offering for sale, purchase, transportation, distribution or use." The Appellate Body has noted that Article III:4 should be interpreted in light of Article III:1, which provides that the Members recognize that these laws, regulations and internal requirements "should not be applied to imported or domestic products so as to afford protection to domestic production." The result, according to the Appellate Body, is that Article III obligates Members "to provide *equality of competitive conditions* for imported products in relation to domestic products."[81] So, as the Appellate Body has concluded in prior disputes, the fundamental question of whether there is a violation of Article III of the GATT 1994 is answered "by examining whether a measure modifies the conditions of competition in the relevant market to the detriment of imported products."[82]

97. The answer to this question with respect to the EC GI Regulation is a resounding "yes." The EC GI Regulation is primarily intended to permit products that qualify for a registered geographical indication to gain substantial competitive advantages, in terms of prices, profits and market share, over their conventional counterparts that do not so qualify. The EC's motivation behind promulgating the GI Regulation is the strong belief that producers of products accorded GI protection fare much better in the marketplace than producers of products not accorded GI protection, and that restrictions on access to GI status and the provision of EC-wide protection for those GIs will enhance this profitability.[83] So, it is flatly inconsistent with Article III:4 to make this favorable GI status available under the GI Regulation to products of EC origin if those products meet certain requirements and specifications, but to make it unavailable to products of other WTO Members unless additional requirements are met: *i.e.*, unless those Members can prove to the satisfaction of the EC Commission that they (1) have a GI system that is equivalent to the EC's; (2) provide reciprocal GI protection to EC products, and (3) are willing and able to intervene at the EC Commission on behalf of its nationals. It is obvious

---

[81] Appellate Body Report, *Japan – Alcohol*, p. 16 (emphasis added).

[82] Appellate Body Report, *Korea – Beef*, para. 135, quoting *Japan – Alcohol*, pp. 16-17.

[83] Preamble, GI Regulation.

from the structure and architecture of the EC GI Regulation that it treats imported products less favorably than domestic products, and that it shifts the competitive conditions dramatically in favor of EC products.

98. The paragraphs that follow will establish that each of the elements of an Article III.4 violation is met.

(a) The imported and domestic products are "like"

99. Both the Appellate Body and panels have been clear that, where there is a general measure of general application (*i.e.*, not directly regulating specific products), the issue with respect to "like product" is not whether particular traded products are "like," but rather whether the measures makes distinctions between products based solely on origin.[84] As the Appellate Body has noted, the term "like product" in Article III:4 of the GATT 1994 "is concerned with competitive relationships between and among products."[85] The issue is whether any formal differentiation in treatment between an imported and a domestic product could be based upon the fact that the products are different—*i.e.,* not like—rather than on the origin of the products involved.[86]

100. In the case of the GI Regulation, the only difference between the products that may benefit from GI registration and protection—products from the EC—and those that may not so benefit on similarly favorable terms—products from other WTO Members—is their origin. Consequently, it is clear that the EC agricultural products and foodstuffs that are eligible for GI registration under one set of criteria and the non-EC agricultural products and foodstuffs that are only eligible if they satisfy an additional set of criteria are like products for purposes of Article III:4.

(b) The GI Regulation affects the "internal sale, offering for sale, purchase, transportation, distribution or use" of the imported product

101. Under Article III:4, Members have a national treatment obligation "with respect to all laws, regulations and requirements affecting the internal sale, offering for sale, purchase, transportation, distribution or use" of imported products of the territory of any other Member. This is a broad formulation, and a number of GATT and WTO dispute settlement reports have noted that the term "affecting" goes beyond measures that "directly" govern the conditions of sale or purchase, so as to cover measures which might "adversely modify the conditions of competition between domestic and imported products."[87]

102. The GI Regulation does exactly this. As discussed more fully in the "Facts" section III and in section IV.A.1.b above, the GI Regulation governs the manner in which registered names can be used—and not used—on products that are sold, offered for sale, purchased, distributed or used. It governs the use of the special EC GI symbol, or logo, on labels, packaging and advertising for certain products, throughout the EC marketplace that, according to the EC, provides consumer with a guarantee of quality and geographical origin with respect to

---

[84] *See* Panel Report, *US – FSC (Article 21.5 – EC)*, paras. 8.133 (Finding it unnecessary "to demonstrate the existence of actually traded like products in order to establish a violation of Article III:4" when a measure makes distinctions "between imported and domestic products" that are "solely and explicitly based on origin." *See also* Panel Report, *India – Autos*, para 7.174 (when origin is "the sole criterion distinguishing the products, it is correct to treat such products as like products within the meaning of Article III:4.")

[85] Appellate Body Report, *EC – Asbestos*, para. 103. *See also* discussion of *Alcohol* disputes in section IV.A.1.b.ii(2) above.

[86] Panel Report, *US – FSC (Article 21.5 – EC),* para. 8.132.

[87] *Eg.*, Panel Report, *India – Autos*, para. 7.196 ("Under GATT and WTO jurisprudence, the term 'affecting' has consistently been defined broadly. In particular, it has been well established that it implies a measure that has 'an effect on' and this indicates a broad scope of application" (*citing to Italy – Agricultural Machinery*, BISD 7S/60, para. 12.) *See also* Panel Report, *Canada – Autos*, para. 10.80 (This term therefore goes beyond laws and regulations which *directly* govern the conditions of sale or purchase to cover also "any laws or regulations which might adversely modify the conditions of competition between domestic and imported products."); Panel Report, *US – FSC (Article 21.5 – EC)*, at paras 8.139, 8.144 ("We agree with the views expressed in previous GATT and WTO panel reports that Article III:4 applies also to measures in the form of conditions that must be satisfied in order to obtain an 'advantage' from the government ... Furthermore, the terms 'law, regulation or requirement affecting…' in Article III:4 are general terms that have been interpreted as having a broad scope" [footnotes omitted].) Indeed, in *US – Section 337*, the panel found that a law enforcing intellectual property rights with respect to imported products was a measure "affecting" internal sale of imported products.

those products, and provides the EC producer increased profits and market share.[88] It allows the products that qualify for the registered GI name numerous and very broad protections against other competitive and disparaging uses of the GI associated with the product, including protection by government authorities on their own initiative, as well as protection requested by private parties.[89] And it provides protection against the geographical indication of the product becoming generic.[90] The GI Regulation is, therefore, a law or regulation "affecting [the] internal sale, offering for sale, purchase, transportation, distribution or use" of imported products.

(c) The imported product is accorded "less favorable treatment" than the domestic like product

103. The Appellate Body has stated that "[t]he term 'less favorable treatment' expresses the general principle, in Article III:1, that internal regulations 'should not be applied ... so as to afford protection to domestic production.' If there is 'less favourable treatment' of the group of 'like' imported products, there is, conversely, 'protection' of the group of 'like' domestic products."[91]

104. It could not be clearer that the EC GI Regulation accords imported products less favorable treatment than domestic products. Agricultural products and foodstuffs from another WTO Member will not be accorded the same favorable treatment under the GI Regulation as like products from the EC:

(a) unless that WTO Member has an internal system of GI protection that is equivalent to that in the EC;

(b) unless that WTO Member is prepared to offer reciprocity of GI protection to EC agricultural products and foodstuffs;

(c) unless a WTO Member is prepared itself to apply to the EC for an affirmative decision with respect to the above points; and

(d) unless, with respect to a particular application for a GI, that WTO Member is willing and able to submit an application to the EC on behalf of its national, certifying to the presence of EC-equivalent and mandated inspection structures and other requirements.

105. Imposing these requirements as a condition of according imported products as favorable treatment as domestic like products is contrary to the Article III:4 national treatment obligation, which requires that such treatment be accorded unconditionally.[92] Further, for imported products from WTO Members whose system of GI protection does not match that of the EC and which cannot meet the EC's requirements with respect to reciprocity, among other requirements, the less favorable treatment is obvious, and has been discussed in detail above. To summarize, even where such products produced outside the EC qualify as GIs under the definition provided in the GI Regulation, because of their reputation or other characteristics, they cannot, unlike their "like" counterparts produced in the EC:

(a) be registered in the official EC-wide "Register of protected designations of origin and protected geographical indications;"[93]

(b) use a registered geographical indication throughout the EC market;[94]

---

[88] Preamble of the GI Regulation; Regulation 2037/93 (Exhibit COMP-2.a).

[89] Article 13(1) of the GI Regulation.

[90] Article 13(3) of the GI Regulation.

[91] Appellate Body Report, *EC – Asbestos*, para 100.

[92] See, e.g., *Belgian Family Allowances*, in which a Belgian provision exempting from certain charges products from countries requiring family allowance benefits was found inconsistent with MFN (and likely) national treatment obligations.

[93] Articles 6(1)—6(4) of the GI Regulation.

(c) include on the packaging, label, or advertising the official EC "symbol" or "logo" informing the consumer that the product is a registered GI;[95]

(d) receive the broad protections throughout the EC provided to registered products, both on the government's own initiative and through private rights of action, against an extremely broad range of competing and disparaging uses;[96] or

(e) be protected from having their geographic name become generic (which causes the geographical indication to lose its value).[97]

106. Further, even where the EC does permit imported products to be registered and protected, that imported product is still faced with treatment that is less favorable than that accorded its EC counterpart. Under Article 12(2) of the GI Regulation, a registered name can be used in connection with imported products "only if the country of origin of the product is clearly and visibly indicated on the label." There is no such requirement with respect to the use of name on a product of EC-origin.

107. In sum, the EC GI Regulation accords less favorable treatment to imported products than it does to like products of national origin in respect of laws, regulations and requirements affecting their internal sale, offering for sale, purchase, transportation, distribution, or use. Consequently, it is inconsistent with EC's obligations under Article III:4 of the GATT 1994. Nor can this less favorable treatment for imported products be justified under any of the exceptions provided under Article XX of the GATT 1994.

B. THE EC'S GI REGULATION IS INCONSISTENT WITH THE EC'S OBLIGATIONS TO PROVIDE MOST FAVORED NATION TREATMENT

108. Just as was the case with respect to national treatment, the EC GI Regulation is also inconsistent with two different most-favored-nation obligations under the WTO Agreements, the first with respect to *nationals* of WTO Members under Article 4 of the TRIPS Agreement, and the second with respect to the *products* of other WTO Members, under Article I:1 of the GATT 1994. This section addresses each of these inconsistencies separately below. Section B.1 immediately below addresses the GI Regulation's inconsistencies with the MFN obligations of the TRIPS Agreement. Section B.2 then addresses the GI Regulation's inconsistencies with the MFN obligations of the GATT 1994.

1. The EC GI Regulations is inconsistent with the EC's most favored nation obligations with respect to other WTO Member's nationals under the TRIPS Agreement

(a) The TRIPS Agreement requires that any advantage, favor, privilege or immunity granted to nationals of any other country be accorded immediately and unconditionally to the nationals of all other WTO Members

109. As the Appellate Body recently confirmed, the most favored nation obligation is as significant and as fundamental to the world trading system as the national treatment obligation:

---

[94] Article 4(1) of the GI Regulation.

[95] Article 5a of Regulation 2037/93. Exhibit COMP-2.a. As Annex II of this regulation explains, "[t]he logo will allow producers of food products to increase awareness of their products among consumers in the European Union... The presence of this logo is a genuine guarantee for all European consumers, making it clear that the special nature of this product lies in its geographical origin. Because of this, products will inspire more confidence. As producers, the logo provides you which [*sic*] a marketing tool. You will be able to put the logo on the labels or packaging of your products, and also use it in your advertising." (Emphasis added.)

[96] Article 13 of the GI Regulation.

[97] Article 13(3) of the GI Regulation.

> Like the national treatment obligation, the obligation to provide most-favoured-nation treatment has long been one of the cornerstones of the world trading system. For more than fifty years, the obligation to provide most-favoured nation treatment in Article I of the GATT 1994 has been both central and essential to assuring the success of a global rules-based system for trade in goods. Unlike the national treatment principle, there is no provision in the Paris Convention (1967) that establishes a most-favoured-nation obligation with respect to rights in trademarks or other industrial property. However, the framers of the *TRIPS Agreement* decided to extend the most-favoured nation obligation to the protection of intellectual property rights covered by the Agreement. As a cornerstone of the world trading system, the most-favoured-nation obligation must be accorded the same significance with respect to intellectual property rights under the TRIPS Agreement that it has long been accorded with respect to trade in goods under the GATT. It is, in a word, fundamental.[98]

110. Indeed, the MFN obligation is, if anything, even more explicit in its rejection of conditions such as reciprocity and equivalent internal systems than is the national treatment obligation.

111. Article 4 of the TRIPS Agreement, the MFN obligation, provides that:

> With regard to the protection of intellectual property, any advantage, favour, privilege or immunity granted by a Member to the nationals of any other country <u>shall be accorded immediately and unconditionally</u> to the nationals of all other Members.

112. The phrase "with regard to the protection of intellectual property" is the same phrase as appears in the national treatment obligation, and refers, *inter alia,* to the rights of nationals in matters pertaining to the availability, acquisition, scope, maintenance, and enforcement of rights in their geographical indications, as well as those matters affecting the use of geographical indications addressed in the TRIPS Agreement, *i.e.*, with respect to their ability to protect their geographical indications from misleading uses and unfair acts of competition. The strong language that all advantages must be accorded "immediately and unconditionally to nationals of all other Members" emphasizes that this MFN provision prohibits making the availability, acquisition, maintenance, and enforcement of these rights to nationals of other Members contingent on (a) "reciprocity" by other Members *vis-à-vis* EC nationals; or on (b) the other Members having a particular system of protection themselves.

113. The context of these terms confirms this reading. Within the framework that establishes strong MFN obligations for the protection of intellectual property, Article 4 also sets forth a limited number of particular advantages, favors, privileges, or immunities, which, may, extraordinarily, be exempted from this obligation. Notably, Article 4(b) specifically exempts from this obligation any advantage, favor, privilege or immunity granted in accordance with the *Berne Convention for the Protection of Literary and Artistic Works (1971)* and the *International Convention for the Protection of Performers, Producers of Phonograms and Broadcasting Organizations (1961)*("Rome Convention") that authorize a Member to depart from the general national treatment rule under those conventions. Certain provisions of these copyright and related right conventions permit that treatment accorded nationals be a function not of national treatment, but of the treatment accorded in another country—*i.e.*, that a Member may in specific cases make the extent of protection for copyrighted works or the subject matter of related rights depend on the extent of protection in the country of origin of the work, instead of granting the same extent of protection to all nationals. Other specific exemptions from the MFN obligation, particularly in the area of copyright and related rights, are laid out in Article 4.[99]

114. By contrast, there is no exemption for advantage, favors, privileges, or immunities granted with respect to rights in geographical indications. The context of the terms in Article 4 therefore confirms that "reciprocity" is clearly prohibited with respect to GIs.

---

[98] Appellate Body Report, *US – Section 211*, para. 297.

[99] *See also* Gervais, pp. 105—110.

115. Further, adopted dispute settlement reports under Article I of the GATT 1994 (MFN in the goods context) provide guidance with respect to this obligation. The GATT panel in *Belgian Family Allowances* found a violation of Article I:1 based on Belgium's measure conditioning a benefit to imported goods—in that case, an exemption from a levy collected on purchases of products—on the adoption by the exporting Member of a system requiring companies to provide family allowance benefits to its employees that meets specific requirements.[100] The panel found that the exemption was inconsistent with Article I (and possibly Article III) because "it introduced a discrimination between countries having a given system of family allowances and those which had a different system or no system at all, and made the granting of the exemption dependent on certain conditions."[101]

116. In sum, the immediate and unconditional requirement in the MFN obligation to accord the same advantages, privileges, favors, or immunities to all nationals of WTO Members with respect to GIs does not permit Members to condition those advantages on an individual Member having a particular protection system or being prepared to offer reciprocity.

(b) The EC GI Regulation grants significant advantages, favors, privileges, and immunities to nationals of some countries that it does not accord at all to nationals of WTO Members

117. As discussed above with respect to national treatment, the EC GI Regulation grants numerous and significant advantages, favors, privileges, and immunities to the nationals of any third country with respect to their home-based GIs, as long as that country (a) has a GI protection system equivalent to that of the EC; and (b) provides protection to EC nationals that is equivalent to that available in the EC with respect to agricultural products and foodstuffs. Further, these advantages, favors, privileges, and immunities are available only if that third country is willing and able to convince the EC that it satisfies the EC's requirements with respect to the protection of GIs, and, with respect to applications for the registration of GIs, is willing and able to advocate on behalf of its national *vis-à-vis* the EC.[102] None of these advantages, favors, privileges, or immunities are available to nationals producing in their country of nationality, where that country is not willing or able to satisfy these requirements.

118. Consequently, the EC GI Regulation is inconsistent with the most-favored-nation obligation of the TRIPS Agreement for the same reasons that it is inconsistent with the national treatment obligation of the TRIPS Agreement. With respect to the registration and EC-wide protection of GIs, as well as the right to object to the registration of GIs, the GI Regulation conditions the protection of intellectual property rights for a WTO Member's nationals on equivalency and reciprocity, and it imposes additional hurdles on nationals of some WTO Members that are not imposed on Members of other WTO Member nationals. With respect to the latter point, a national from a WTO Member that already has in place a system of GI protection that is equivalent to the EC's system—recall, however, that there are many ways of implementing GI obligations, including that used by the EC—is not faced with the hurdle of developing a new GI protection system. A national from other WTO Members, such as the United States, by contrast, faces this considerable hurdle.[103]

119. Indeed, the GI Regulation is inconsistent with the MFN obligations of the TRIPS Agreement in two respects. First, as among non-EC WTO Members, nationals from WTO Members that satisfy the EC's conditions of reciprocity and equivalency are accorded more favorable treatment than nationals from those WTO Members that do not. In this connection, for example, the EU has signed a joint declaration on the

---

[100] *Belgian Family Allowances*, paras. 3, 8.

[101] *Belgian Family Allowances*, paras. 3, 8.

[102] The actions required of WTO Members with respect to GI applications and objections are detailed in the discussion on national treatment, and will not be repeated here.

[103] In *US – Section 211*, para. 314, the Appellate Body incorporated and applied the "additional hurdle" analysis used in analyzing the national treatment claim in its analysis of the MFN claim.

protection of geographical indications and designations of origin of agricultural products and foodstuffs with Switzerland, which states that:

> The European Community and Switzerland (hereinafter referred to as "the Parties") hereby agree that the mutual protection of designations of origin (PDOs) and geographical indications (PGIs) is essential for the liberalization of trade in agricultural products and foodstuffs between the Parties ... The Parties shall provide for provisions on the mutual protection of PDOs and PGIs to be incorporated in the Agreement on trade in agricultural products on the basis of equivalent legislation, as regards both the conditions governing the registration of PDOs and PGIs and the arrangements on controls.[104]

120. Nationals of a WTO Member that does not meet the EC's conditions, by contrast, cannot expect to have their home-based GIs registered and protected.

121. Second, each of the EC member States is also a WTO Member. Therefore, under Article 4 of the TRIPS Agreement, any advantage, favor, privilege, or immunity granted by an EC member State to a national of another EC member State must be accorded immediately and unconditionally to the nationals of all non-EC WTO Members. Yet, under the GI Regulation, for all of the reasons described in the section of this submission on national treatment, an EC member State grants more favorable treatment to nationals from other EC member States than it accords to nationals from non-EC WTO Members, with respect to the protection of GIs.

122. In sum, in these two respects, the GI Regulation accords advantages, favors, privileges, and immunities to nationals of some countries that it does not accord to nationals of other WTO Members, despite the Article 4 requirement to accord them "immediately and unconditionally to the nationals of all other Members."

2. The EC GI Regulation is inconsistent with the EC's most favored nation obligations with respect to goods of other WTO Members under the GATT 1994

(a) Article I:1 of the GATT 1994 requires that any advantage, favor, privilege, or immunity granted to any product originating in any other country be accorded immediately and unconditionally to the like product originating in the territories of all other WTO Members

123. Article I:1 of the GATT 1994 provides that:

> with respect to all matters referred to in paragraphs 2 and 4 of Article III, any advantage, favour, privilege or immunity granted by any contracting party to any product originating in or destined for any other country shall be accorded immediately and unconditionally to the like products originating in or destined for the territories of all other contracting parties.[105]

124. "Matters referred to in paragraphs 2 and 4 of Article III" include, with respect to imported products, "laws, regulations, and requirements affecting their internal sale, offering for sale, purchase, transportation, distribution or use." As discussed above in the context of national treatment, the GI Regulation is such a measure.

125. Further, the "like products" requirement is satisfied in the case of the EC GI Regulation, because, as discussed in the context of national treatment, the GI Regulation makes distinctions based solely on the origin of the product.

---

[104] Agreement between the European Community and the Swiss Confederation on trade in agricultural products—Final Act—Joint Declarations, including Joint Declaration on the protection of geographical indications and designations of origin of agricultural products and foodstuffs, OJ L 114 , April 30, 2002, p. 366. Exhibit US-6.

[105] Reference to Notes and Supplementary Provisions in Annex I omitted.

126. Therefore, Article I:1 of the GATT 1994 requires that any advantage, favor, privilege, or immunity granted by the EC GI Regulation to agricultural products and foodstuffs originating in any country be accorded, immediately and unconditionally to the agricultural products and foodstuffs originating in the territories of all other WTO Members.

(b) The EC GI Regulation grants significant advantages, favors, privileges, and immunities to agricultural products and foodstuffs originating in some countries that it does not accord to like products originating in the territories of all WTO Members

127. The EC GI Regulation does not satisfy the requirements of Article I:1 of the GATT 1994. Rather, the Regulation grants significant advantages, favors, privileges and immunities to products from a third country only if that country (a) has a GI protection system equivalent to that of the EC and (b) provides protection to EC nationals that is equivalent to that available in the EC with respect to agricultural products and foodstuffs. These significant advantages, favors, privileges, and immunities have been detailed elsewhere, and include the ability to be marketed as a quality product of identifiable geographic origin, the right to be marketed with a coveted EC GI symbol, protection, including at the authorities' own initiative, against a broad range of competing uses of the product's geographical indication, and protection against the geographic indication becoming generic (and thus losing its value). These are all advantages, favors, privileges, and immunities that are granted to the products of third countries that meet the conditions of reciprocity and equivalent GI systems, as determined by the EC. The Regulation does not accord these advantages, favors, privileges, and immunities to the products of any third country that does not meet these conditions, despite the Article I:1 requirement to accord them "immediately and unconditionally to the nationals of all other Members." Rather, it accords them to imported goods "subject to conditions with respect to the situation or conduct of"[106] WTO Members, discriminating against like products based on the origin of the product. Further, it imposes an "extra hurdle" on imported goods from some WTO Members that it does not impose on imported goods from other WTO Members, as detailed in the preceding sections.

128. This conclusion is in accord with GATT and WTO dispute settlement reports going back to the earliest days of the GATT. A GATT panel in *Belgian Family Allowances* found a violation of Article I:1 based on an exemption from a fee that was available only with respect to products from countries that required its companies to offer a specific family allowance benefit that satisfied requirements of Belgian law. That panel found that the fee exemption "would have to be granted unconditionally to all other contracting parties."[107]

> The consistency or otherwise of the system of family allowances in force in the territory of a given contracting party with the requirements of the Belgian law would be irrelevant in this respect, and the Belgian legislation would have to be amended insofar as it introduced a discrimination between countries having a given system of family allowances and those which had a different system or no system at all, and made the granting of the exemption dependent on certain conditions.[108]

129. Similarly, in this dispute, the GI Regulation "introduce[s] a discrimination between countries having a given system of [GI protection] and those which ha[ve] a different system." Consequently, for all of the reasons above, the GI Regulation is inconsistent with Article I:1 of the GATT 1994. Further, this discrimination is not excused by any of the exceptions under Article XX of the GATT 1994.

---

[106] Panel Report, *Canada – Autos*, para. 10.23.

[107] *Belgian Family Allowances*, para. 3.

[108] *Belgian Family Allowances*, para. 3.

C. THE EC GI REGULATION IS INCONSISTENT WITH THE EC'S OBLIGATIONS UNDER ARTICLE 16.1 OF THE TRIPS AGREEMENT

1. Introduction

130. Article 16.1 of the TRIPS Agreement requires Members to give owners of registered trademarks the exclusive right to prevent confusing uses of similar or identical signs by all third parties:

> The owner of a registered trademark shall have the exclusive right to prevent all third parties not having the owner's consent from using in the course of trade identical or similar signs for goods or services which are identical or similar to those in respect of which the trademark is registered where such use would result in a likelihood of confusion. In case of the use of an identical sign for identical goods or services, a likelihood of confusion shall be presumed.

131. Contrary to this obligation, and as explained in detail below, the EC GI Regulation fails to provide the owner of a valid prior registered trademark with the exclusive right to prevent all third parties (including those entitled to use a registered GI) from using identical or similar signs (including GIs) that result in a likelihood of confusion.[109] This shortcoming is directly inconsistent with the EC's obligations under Article 16.1 of the TRIPS Agreement.

2. The US argument in light of the relationship between trademark rights and GI rights

132. In many ways, GIs and trademarks serve the same function, in that they both are "source" indicators and can therefore serve as indicators of quality. They both aim to prevent consumers from being misled or confused as to whether the goods they buy possess the anticipated qualities and characteristics.[110] Moreover, they both may take a similar physical form, prominently displayed on labels and in advertising materials. On the one hand, trademarks indicate the source of goods as a particular undertaking (*e.g.*, a producer or group of producers).[111] On the other hand, geographical indications indicate the source of the goods as a particular geographic area, where a quality, reputation, or other characteristic of the good is essentially attributable to that origin. Both forms of intellectual property are aimed at distinguishing goods so that the consumer can make informed judgments about the goods they buy.

133. In addition, the TRIPS Agreement bestows each with a certain degree of exclusivity. Both trademark owners and GI owners[112] have the right to exclude others from certain uses of signs or indications. The right for trademark owners under Article 16.1 of the TRIPS Agreement is the right to exclude all others (including those entitled to use a registered GI) from using identical or similar signs (including GIs) for the same or similar goods in a way that results in a likelihood of confusion as to the source of the goods. Under Article 22.2 of the TRIPS Agreement, the right for GI owners is to prevent uses (including of trademarks) that mislead the consumer as to the geographic origin of the goods or constitute an act of unfair competition.[113] There is nothing

---

[109] In fact, even in a case where the GI is presented as a sign that is identical to a registered trademark and is being used for an identical good (where, under the TRIPS Agreement, a likelihood of confusion is presumed), under the GI Regulation, the owner of the registered trademark is powerless to prevent that sign from being used in the course of trade.

[110] And, indeed, among the varied means of satisfying the TRIPS Agreement obligations with respect to geographical indications, a number of WTO Members have chosen to protect geographical indications through their trademark system, notably through the use of certification marks and collective marks. *See* WIPO Document SCT/8/4 (Exhibit US-5) and WIPO Document SCT/9/4 (Exhibit COMP-16).

[111] *See* Article 15.1 of the TRIPS Agreement.

[112] i.*e.*, the collective body of authorized users of the GI.

[113] In addition, Article 22.3 of the TRIPS Agreement provides that Members must refuse or invalidate the registration of a trademark consisting of a GI that misleads the public as to the true origin of the product . Note also that Article 23.2 of the TRIPS Agreement provides for the refusal or invalidation of certain trademarks for wine and spirits that contain or consist of a geographical indication. Since the GI Regulation does not apply to wine and spirits, however, this provision is not directly relevant to this dispute.

inconsistent in these two obligations, and each should be given its full scope in a manner that does not bring them into conflict.[114]

134. With the distinctions and similarities between these two categories of intellectual property rights in mind, the United States argues in this dispute that the EC GI Regulation is inconsistent with Article 16.1 of the TRIPS Agreement because, under the EC GI Regulation, owners of prior registered trademarks cannot prevent all third parties from using identical or similar signs on the same or similar goods for which the trademark is registered, even where there is a likelihood that the consumer will be confused. Under Article 14(2) of the GI Regulation, the best that the owner of a valid prior registered trademark can hope for is the ability to continue using its trademark, but without the ability to exercise the exclusive right that lies at the heart of his trademark right. This is inconsistent with Article 16.1 of the TRIPS Agreement.

135. The United States is concerned in this dispute with the trademark rights provided owners of valid prior trademarks under Article 16.1 of the TRIPS Agreement. For example, as stated at the outset of this submission, under Article 16.1, the owner of a registered trademark has to be able to take action against another producer selling an identical product, labeled with an identical name (protected as a geographical indication after the trademark registration), on the same shelf as the trademark owner's trademarked product. The GI Regulation does not allow him to do this. The United States is not arguing that trademarks that "mislead the public as to the true place of origin" of the underlying goods in a given territory must be registered and provided Article 16.1 rights in that territory.[115] Rather, the US argument is narrow in focus, but critical: where a valid prior registered trademark exists, the owner of that trademark must, under Article 16.1, be able, through judicial proceedings or otherwise, to prevent all third parties from using a GI when the trademark owner can demonstrate that the GI is identical or similar to the trademark for identical or similar goods, and is used in a manner that is likely to confuse the consumer as to the source of the goods. As discussed below, the EC GI Regulation is inconsistent with this obligation.

136. In section 3 below, the United States describes the obligation to provide an exclusive right to prevent confusing uses under Article 16.1 of the TRIPS Agreement and explains why the exclusive right to prevent confusing uses is the essence of the trademark rights under the TRIPS Agreement. Section 4 then describes how the EC GI Regulation is inconsistent with this Article 16.1 obligation.

3. Article 16.1 of the TRIPS Agreement requires Members to provide the owners of registered trademarks with the exclusive right to prevent <u>all</u> third parties from using identical or similar signs resulting in a likelihood of confusion

(a) Ordinary meaning of the terms in Article 16.1

137. Article 16.1 provides that:

> The owner of a registered trademark shall have the exclusive <u>right to prevent all third parties</u> not having the owner's consent from using in the course of trade identical or similar signs for goods or services which are identical or similar to those in respect of which the trademark is registered where such use would result in a likelihood of confusion. In case of the use of an identical sign for identical goods or services, a likelihood of confusion shall be presumed.[116]

---

[114] As recognized by the panel in *Indonesia – Autos*, para 14.28, "in public international law there is a presumption against conflict," which "is especially relevant in the WTO context since all WTO agreements ... were negotiated at the same time, by the same Members and in the same forum." Footnotes omitted. Of course individual GIs that are identical or similar to trademarks may, however, "conflict" in the sense that the GI may be confusing consumers.

[115] *See* Article 22.3 of the TRIPS Agreement. Further, under Article 22.2 of the TRIPS Agreement, with respect to GIs, interested parties must be provided the legal means to prevent uses that mislead the public as to the geographical origin of the good.

[116] Emphasis added.

138. The ordinary meaning of the terms in Article 16.1 confirms the breadth and strength of the rights that must be accorded owners of registered trademarks. "Prevent" means to "[s]top, hinder, avoid," and "[c]ause to be unable to do ... something."[117] "All" means the "entire number of" and "without exception."[118] "Exclusive" means "[n]ot admitting of the simultaneous existence of something; incompatible" and "[o]f a right, privilege, quality, etc.; possessed or enjoyed by the individual(s) specified and no others."[119]

139. Further, the ordinary meaning of Article 16.1 shows that geographical indications are included among the "signs" whose use an owner of a registered trademark must be able to prevent. "Sign" has a broad meaning, as indicated in Article 15.1 of the TRIPS Agreement, which includes as particular examples of signs "words, including personal names, letters, numerals, figurative elements, and combinations of colours." The ordinary meaning of "sign" confirms this broad meaning: a "mark, symbol or device used to represent something or distinguish the object on which it is put;" "an *indication* or suggestion of a present state, fact, quality, etc."[120] Similarly, "indication," which is part of the TRIPS Agreement Article 22.1 definition of "geographical indication" is "something that indicates or suggests; a *sign*, a symptom, a hint."[121] In short, the fact that "sign" is a broad term, and specifically includes an "indication," along with the fact that the ordinary meaning of "indication" includes a "sign," confirms that geographical indications are signs, the confusing use of which owners of registered trademarks must be able to prevent under Article 16.1.[122]

140. The ordinary meaning of the terms in Article 16.1, therefore, confirms that the owner of a registered trademark must, under Article 16.1, have the *exclusive* right to stop

> *all* third parties (*i.e.,* the entire number of third parties, without exception, including third parties producing products that use a GI),
>
> from using in the course of trade *identical or similar signs* (*i.e.,* including identical or similar geographical indications, that is, "indications" that identify a good as originating in a particular geographic area where "a given quality, reputation, or other characteristic of [that] good is essentially attributable to " that geographic area) for goods or services which are identical or similar to those in respect of which the trademark is registered,
>
> where such use would result in a likelihood of confusion.

(b) The context of the terms in Article 16.1

141. The context of Article 16.1 confirms the ordinary meaning of these terms. Where there is a need to clarify the relationship among individual rights in geographical indications and trademarks, the TRIPS Agreement does so explicitly. For instance, Article 22.3 of the TRIPS Agreement provides that protection of a geographical indication requires that a Member "refuse or invalidate the registration of a trademark" in certain

---

[117] The New Shorter Oxford English Dictionary (4th ed 1993), p. 2348 (Exhibit US-7).

[118] The New Shorter Oxford English Dictionary (4th ed 1993), p. 52 (Exhibit US-7).

[119] The New Shorter Oxford English Dictionary (4th ed 1993), p. 875 (Exhibit US-7).

[120] The New Shorter Oxford English Dictionary (4th ed 1993), p. 2858 (Exhibit US-7).

[121] The New Shorter Oxford English Dictionary (4th ed 1993), p. 1348 (Exhibit US-7).

[122] Notwithstanding the GI Regulation, the EC's own Community Trademark Regulation reflects this. Article 4 of that regulation defines a trademark to "consist of any signs" and the preamble states that the function of a trade mark is to "guarantee the trade mark as an indication of origin." Council Regulation (EC) No. 40/94 of 20 December 1993 on the Community Trademark, OJ L 11, January 14, 1994, p. 1 ("Regulation 40/94 on the Community Trademark"). *See also* Article 2 of the First Council Directive of 21 December 1988 to approximate the laws of the Member States relating to registered trademarks (89/104/EEC), OJ L 40, February 2, 1989, p. 1. Exhibits COMP-6 and COMP-7.a.

specific instances where the trademark consists of or includes a geographical indication and its use would mislead the consumer as to the origin of the goods.[123]

142. The Appellate Body has made clear, *e.g.,* in *EC – Sardines*, that any exception to an obligation must be explicitly set out in the text of the Agreement.[124] Indeed, where the TRIPS Agreement negotiators meant to specify an exception to, or a limit on, geographical indication and trademark rights, they did so explicitly. Article 24.5, for example, is an exception to the protection of geographical indications[125] that specifies that a Member's measures to protect geographical indications under the TRIPS Agreement shall not prejudice eligibility for or the validity of the registration of a trademark, or the right to use a trademark. It applies to trademarks that were applied for or registered, or whose rights have been acquired through use either before January 1, 1996,[126] or before the geographical indication is protected in its country of origin. In other words, where implementation of the GI provisions of the TRIPS Agreement might otherwise have prejudiced "eligibility for or the validity of the registration ... or the right to use a trademark"—and Article 23.2, which requires the invalidation of wine and spirit trademark registrations that contain or consist of wine or spirit GIs, might be an example of such a case—Article 24.5 would prevent that result for, or would "grandfather," those trademarks covered by its terms.

143. Similarly, when a conflict between rights to exclude must result in a compromise, the TRIPS Agreement negotiators were also careful to spell this out. For instance, because GIs are a specific type of sign linked to geographic origin, the TRIPS Agreement contemplates some instances where two identically named places exist and therefore where two similar geographical indications may be used simultaneously under conditions set by the Members. Article 23.3 of the TRIPS Agreement provides for the situation where two different GIs for wine have the same name: "homonymous geographical indications." Article 23.3 provides that "protection shall be accorded to each indication," but that "[e]ach Member shall determine the practical conditions under which the homonymous indications in question will be differentiated from each other, taking into account the need to ensure equitable treatment of the producers concerned and that consumers are not misled." No such provision exists allowing Members to permit continued use of a GI that is identical or similar to a valid prior registered trademark that would result in a likelihood of confusion, in the face of an infringement challenge by the trademark owner.

144. In sum, the ordinary meaning of the terms in Article 16.1, confirmed by their context, demonstrates that owners of registered trademarks must be given the exclusive right to prevent all third parties, including those authorized to use GIs, from using in the course of trade similar or identical signs, including geographical indications, for goods or services that are identical or similar to those covered by the trademark registration, where such use would result in a likelihood of confusion.

---

123 Article 22.3 of the TRIPS Agreement requires the refusal or invalidation of a trademark registration "which contains or consists of a geographical indication with respect to goods not originating in the territory indicated, if use of the indication in the trademark for such goods in that Member is of such a nature as to mislead the public as to the true place of origin." This reflects principles that were already included in the domestic trademark law of WTO Members. *See, e.g.,* Regulation 40/94 on the Community Trademark, Article 7(1)(g) ("The following shall not be registered: ... trademarks which are of such a nature as to deceive the public, for instance as to the ... geographical origin of the goods or services") (Exhibit COMP-7.a); First Council Directive 89/104/EEC Article 3(1)(g) ("The following shall not be registered or if registered shall be liable to be declared invalid: ... trademarks which are such a nature as to deceive the public, for instance as to the ... geographical origin of the goods or services.") (Exhibit COMP-6). The principle these provisions reflect is not a superiority of geographical indications over trademarks, but a desire to protect the public or consumers from being misled.

124 Appellate Body Report, *EC – Sardines*, paras. 201—208.

125 Article 24, in section 3 of the TRIPS Agreement—"Geographical Indications"—is entitled "International Negotiations; Exceptions." It should be noted here that Article 17 of the TRIPS Agreement contains a general provision that permits Members to provide "limited exceptions" to the rights conferred by a trademark, such as fair use of descriptive terms, but any such limited exceptions "must take account of the legitimate interests of the owner of the trademark and of third parties." The EC GI Regulation does not qualify as a "limited" exception, because there is no limit placed on the permitted uses of registered GIs that are identical or similar to prior valid registered trademarks. Further, the GI Regulation does not take into account the legitimate interest of the trademark owner.

126 Article 24.5 specifies the date of application of the TRIPS Agreement provisions, which, for the European Communities, is January 1, 1996.

(c) The object and purpose of the TRIPS Agreement with respect to Article 16.1

145. Further, Article 16.1 must also be read in light of the object and purpose of the TRIPS Agreement, and specifically with respect to Article 16.1 and its grant of exclusive rights. The Appellate Body in *US – Section 211* emphasized the importance of the exclusive nature of these rights, finding that Article 16.1 confers on the owner of "registered trademarks an internationally agreed minimum level of 'exclusive rights' that all WTO Members must guarantee in their domestic legislation," and that these exclusive rights "protect the owner against infringement of the registered trademark by unauthorized third parties."[127]

146. Indeed, EC jurisprudence, like that of the United States, recognizes that trademark exclusivity—the right of the owner of a registered trademark to prevent the use of a similar or identical sign that would result in a likelihood of confusion—is the core of a trademark right. For example, Advocate General Jacobs of the European Court of Justice stated in the *Hag-II* case that:

> A trademark can only fulfil that role [*i.e.,*to identify the manufacturer and to guarantee quality] if it is exclusive. Once the proprietor is forced to share the mark with the competitor, he loses control over the goodwill associated with the mark. The reputation of his own goods will be harmed if the competitor sells inferior goods. From the consumer's point of view, equally undesirable consequences will ensue, because the clarity of the signal transmitted by the trademark will be impaired. The consumer will be confused and misled.[128]

147. These principles have been consistently followed by the European Court of Justice, which held, for instance, in *Bristol-Myers Squibb v. Paranova A/S*, that:

> As the Court has recognized on many occasions, the specific subject matter of a trademark is in particular to guarantee to the owner that he has the exclusive right to use that trademark ...[129]

148. As detailed below, the GI Regulation is an abrupt deviation from this jurisprudence in the EC. Maintenance of the principle underlying this jurisprudence would benefit nationals of all WTO members that are trademark owners in the EC—including nationals of the EC.

149. That the exclusivity of a trademark owner's right is the core of trademark rights has similarly been emphasized by the US Supreme Court. The Court held in 1916 that "the right to use a trademark is recognized as a kind of property, of which the owner is entitled to the exclusive enjoyment to the extent that it has actually been used."[130] That early judgment was fully endorsed in the 1999 decision in *College Savings Bank v. Florida Prepaid Postsecondary Education Expense Board*, in which the Court stated that "[t]he hallmark of a protected property interest is the right to exclude others. That is one of the most essential sticks in the bundle of rights that are commonly characterized as property."[131]

---

[127] Appellate Body Report, *United States – Section 211*, para. 186.

[128] Advocate General's Opinion in Case C-10/89, *SA CNL-Sucal NV v. HAG GFAG,* delivered on 13 March 1990 [1990] ECR I-3711, at para. 19. Exhibit US-8.

[129] C-427/93, *Bristol-Myers Squibb and others v. Paranova*, [1996] ECR I-3457, at para. 44 (Exhibit US-9); *see also* Advocate General's Opinion in Case C-517/99, *Merz & Krell GmbH & Co. KG*, delivered on 18 January 2001, [2001] ECR I- 6959, at paras 31, 42 ((Exhibit US-10); C-349/95, *Frits Loendersloot and George Ballantine & Son Ltd.*, [1997] ECR I-6227, at para. 24 ((Exhibit US-11); Advocate General's Opinion in Case C-425/98—*Marca Mode CV. v. ADIDAS AG and ADIDAS Benelux B.V.*, delivered on 27 January 2000, [2000] ECR I-4861, at para. 34 (Exhibit US-12).

[130] US Supreme Court, *Hamilton-Brown Show Co. v. Wolf Brothers & Co.*, 240 US 251, 272 (1916). Exhibit US-13.

[131] US Supreme Court, *College Savings Bank v. Florida Prepaid Postsecondary Education Expense Board*, 527 US 666, 667 (1999). Exhibit US-14.

150. In sum, Article 16.1 enshrines a principle of trademark protection recognized in the jurisprudence of both the United States and the EC, and imposes an obligation on Members that reflects the vital importance to trademark owners of exclusivity in the use of their trademarks.

(d) Conclusion with respect to the meaning of Article 16.1

151. In light of the clear obligation under Article 16.1, contained in the ordinary meaning of its terms, in their context, and in light of the object and purpose of the TRIPS Agreement, it is plain that the owner of a registered trademark must be given the exclusive right to prevent all third parties, including those authorized to use GIs, from using in the course of trade similar or identical signs, including geographical indications, for goods or services that are identical or similar to those covered by the trademark registration, where such use would result in a likelihood of confusion.

4. Contrary to Article 16.1 of the TRIPS Agreement, the EC GI Regulation does not permit owners of registered trademarks to exercise their Article 16.1 exclusive rights to prevent confusing uses

(a) The text of the EC GI Regulation makes clear that owners of registered trademarks are not permitted to exercise their Article 16.1 rights

152. The EC GI Regulation denies owners of registered trademarks their right under Article 16.1 of the TRIPS Agreement to prevent confusing uses of similar or identical signs.

153. Article 4(1) of the EC GI Regulation provides that an agricultural product or foodstuff that complies with the specification filed with a GI registration—and only that product—is eligible to use a protected geographical indication, *i.e.*, the name of a qualifying region, specific place, or country.[132] Article 13 of the GI Regulation provides that names registered under that Regulation "shall be protected against" a broad range of uses or practices by those not authorized to use the name under the GI Regulation.

154. By contrast, nothing in the GI Regulation provides that the use of the GI can be limited in any way by the owner of a valid prior registered trademark who wishes to exercise his exclusive right under Article 16.1 of the TRIPS Agreement—that is, the right to prevent the use of a geographical indication in a manner that is likely to confuse the consumer as to the source of a product identified with the earlier trademark. Nor is there any discretion provided under the EC GI Regulation to prevent or limit uses of EC-registered GIs by qualified GI users, except in the case of a homonymous use.[133]

155. To the contrary, Article 14 of the EC GI Regulation reinforces that owners of registered trademarks are denied their rights under Article 16.1 of the TRIPS Agreement. Most obvious is Article 14(2), which addresses the situation of a trademark right that predates the GI right,[134] but where the use of the trademark creates one of the situations against which registered GI names are to be protected under Article 13 of the GI Regulation—*e.g.*, the prior registered trademark "evokes" the later-registered GI name, in the terminology of Article 13. Under Article 16.1 of the TRIPS Agreement, if the use of the later GI in connection with identical or similar goods is likely to confuse the consumer as to the producer of the goods, then the owner of the registered trademark should have the exclusive right to prevent that confusing use by the GI owner. The EC GI Regulation should reflect this.

156. The EC GI Regulation, however, takes a very different approach. Far from providing that the owner of a prior registered trademark has the right to prevent confusing uses, as is required by Article 16.1, the GI Regulation, <u>as a narrow exception</u> to the general GI right to prevent a broad range of uses, simply permits the

---

[132] Article 2.2(b) of the GI Regulation (definition of "geographical indication").

[133] Article 6(6) of the GI Regulation.

[134] Under the EC GI Regulation, this is a trademark that acquires rights (by application, registration, or, where permitted, by use) before either (1) a GI registration application has been submitted to the EC; or (2) the GI is protected in its country of origin.

registered trademark holder to keep using his trademark "notwithstanding" the later GI registration. To be precise, Article 14(2) provides that such a trademark that predates the GI registration "may continue to be used notwithstanding the [later] registration of a ... geographical indication." (Emphasis added.)

157. In other words, Article 14(2) specifically envisions that, even in cases where use of a GI raises a likelihood of confusion within the meaning of Article 16.1 of the TRIPS Agreement, the product that is marketed and labeled with that GI can be sold alongside a similar or the same product that has been marketed and labeled with an identical or similar valid prior registered trademark. The owner of the trademark will have no ability to exercise his TRIPS Agreement Article 16.1 rights to prevent any confusing use by the later-registered GI. As discussed above, however, the right to use a trademark without the right to exclude others from confusing uses would mean practically nothing, since the whole purpose and value of a trademark is to be able to distinguish one company's goods from the goods of other companies; without the ability to stop confusing uses, this value is eliminated. As Advocate General Jacobs of the European Court of Justice wrote, a trademark's role can be fulfilled "only if it is exclusive. Once the proprietor is forced to share the mark with the competitor, he loses control over the goodwill associated with the mark... From the consumer's point of view, equally undesirable consequences will ensue, because the clarity of the signal transmitted by the trademark will be impaired. The consumer will be confused and misled."[135]

158. Article 14(3), the sole provision in the EC GI Regulation that addresses the confusing use of registered GIs *vis-à-vis* trademarks, underscores the limited impact that trademarks can have on GIs under the GI Regulation. Article 14(3) provides that a GI shall not be registered "where, in the light of a trade mark's reputation and renown and the length of time it has been used, registration is liable to mislead the consumer as to the true identity of the product."[136] In other words, under the EC GI Regulation, trademark rights are fully respected only where the trademark has been used for a long time, and has considerable "reputation and renown." There is no guidance in the GI Regulation with respect to this standard.

159. The exclusive right under Article 16.1 to prevent confusing uses, however, is not limited to owners of long-standing trademarks of reputation and renown, however this is interpreted. Rather, it is an exclusive right the Members must provide to all owners of valid prior registered trademarks, regardless of time of use, or of the trademark's reputation and renown.

160. In light of the EC GI Regulation, the EC trademark rules give no comfort that trademark owners' Article 16.1 rights will be respected. The EC trademark rules[137] generally provide for the rights required by Article 16.1 of the TRIPS Agreement. However, the EC Trademark Regulation, for example—which provides for a multinational trademark right across the EC—specifically undercuts these rights with respect to confusing geographical indications by stating, at Article 142, that the Trademark Regulation "shall not affect" the EC GI Regulation (which in parallel provides for a multinational GI right across the EC), and "in particular Article 14 thereof." Moreover, by operation of law, trademark law rights under the laws of the EC member States cannot contradict the provisions of EC regulations, including the Trademark Regulation and the GI Regulation. Article 249 of the Treaty Establishing the European Community states that a regulation "shall be binding in its

---

[135] *Hag II*, para. 19. Exhibit US-8.

[136] Emphasis added.

[137] Council Regulation (EC) No 40/94 of 20 December 1993 on the Community Trademark ("Regulation 40/94 on the Community Trademark") and the First Council Directive of 21 December 1988 to approximate the laws of the Member States relating to registered trademarks (89/104/EEC). Exhibits COMP-7.a and COMP-6.

entirety and directly applicable in all [m]ember States."[138] Consequently, if there is a conflict between domestic trademark law and the EC GI Regulation, the EC GI Regulation prevails.[139]

161. In sum, under the EC GI Regulation, those who qualify to use a GI with respect to particular products have a right to use that GI, even if that use results in a likelihood of confusion with respect to a prior registered trademark. The best that the trademark holder can hope for, under these circumstances, is continued use of his trademark on his own goods in the course of trade. But as the jurisprudence quoted above points out, the right to use a registered trademark means nothing if the owner of that trademark cannot exercise his exclusive right to prevent the use of the same or similar signs on the same or similar goods that is likely to result in confusion. For this reason, Article 16.1 of the TRIPS Agreement requires Members to provide these exclusive rights in respect of <u>all</u> third parties.

(b) The EC's explanations of the GI Regulation and the circumstances surrounding its coming into force confirm that the GI Regulation prevents owners of registered trademarks from exercising their Article 16.1 rights

162. In various published explanations of the GI Regulation, the EC has emphasized the right of GI owners to use the GI and the fact that conflicting trademarks will only be able to be used alongside such GIs, provided that the trademarks remain valid. This confirms the above reading of the text that, under the GI Regulation, the best the trademark holder can hope for is to be able to continue to use his trademark alongside the confusing GI.

163. For instance, Advocate General Jacobs of the European Court of Justice has explained that "Article 14(2) is designed to allow a prior trademark to co-exist with a subsequently registered conflicting designation of origin provided that the trade mark was registered in good faith."[140] Advocate General Jacobs concluded that, in light of a subsequently registered geographical indication, the "use of the name" protected by a registered trademark can "be allowed to continue pursuant to Article 14(2) of the regulation," but only if the additional requirements of Article 14(2) have been met.[141] In addition, a publication of the European Commission opines that the TRIPS Agreement only provides that a valid prior trademark will "exist alongside the" later-registered identical or similar geographical indication.[142] Indeed, the EC has specifically characterized the relationship between a geographical indication and a previously registered trademark in this situation as "coexistence," and states that ."... the TRIPs [Agreement] ... clearly envisages coexistence."[143]

164. Moreover, the EC has explained to the TRIPS Council that once a geographical indication is registered pursuant to the GI Regulation, "everybody who meets the established criteria has the right to use the

---

[138] Consolidated Version of the Treaty Establishing the European Community, Article 249. Exhibit US-15.

[139] *See, e.g.*, Judgment of the European Court of Justice in *Simmenthal II*, in which the Court stated as follows:

[I]n accordance with the principle of the precedence of Community law, the relationship between provisions of the Treaty and directly applicable measures of the institutions on the one hand and national law of the Member States on the other is such that those provisions and measures not only by their entry into force render automatically inapplicable any conflicting provision of current national law but—in so far as they are an integral part of, and take precedence in, the legal order applicable in the territory of each of the Member States—also preclude the valid adoption of new national legislative measures to the extent to which they would be incompatible with Community provisions.

Case 106/77, *Amministrazione delle Finanze dello Stato v. Simmenthal SpA*, [1978] ECR 629, at para. 17. Exhibit US-16.

[140] Opinion of Advocate General's Opinion in Case C-87/97, *Consorzio per la Tutela del Formaggio Gorgonzola v. 1. Käserei Champignon Hofmeister GmbH & Co. KG, Heising, Germany 2. Eduard Bracharz Gesellschaft mbH, Vienna, Austria*, delivered on December 17, 1998, para. 51. Exhibit US-17. The advocates general assist the European Court of Justice by providing "reasoned opinions on the cases brought before the court," opinions that the judges consider when drafting the ultimate ruling. *See* "European Union institutions and other bodies, The Court of Justice," <http://europa.eu.int/institutions/court/index_en.htm>. Exhibit US-18.

[141] *Id.*, para. 58.

[142] TRIPS Agreement—Geographical Indications, Official Publication of the European Commission, p. 23. Exhibit US-19.

[143] European Commission, Directorate General Trade, Report to the Trade Barriers Regulation Committee, TBR Proceedings concerning Canadian practices affecting Community exports of *Prosciutto di Parma*, p. 35 (1999). Exhibit COMP-13.

geographical indication."[144] There was no suggestion of any limitation on that right with respect to any prior registered trademark owners. Further, in the proposal that ultimately led to an amendment to the EC GI Regulation in April 2003,[145] the Commission explained that Article 14 offers a trademark no more than the "possibility of co-existence."[146]

165. Thus, far from offering any comfort that the GI Regulation preserves Article 16.1 trademark rights, these numerous explanations confirm the opposite conclusion.

166. This conclusion is even further buttressed by the unfortunately ill-fated attempt by the European Parliament to address the problem created by denying trademark owners their exclusive right to prevent confusing uses of signs under EC law. The Committee on Legal Affairs and the Internal Market of the European Parliament was critical of Article 14(2) of the GI Regulation for the very reasons identified in this submission: under Article 14(2), trademark owners lose their right to prevent all third parties from using a similar or identical sign that results in a likelihood of confusion. That Committee stated:

> To deprive a trademark owner of the exclusive right conferred by Community trademark law by obliging him to allow a similar designation of origin or geographical indication, such as is likely to cause confusion, to coexist with the trademark is tantamount to expropriation. Given that the regulation makes no provision to compensate trademark owners, such expropriation would constitute illegal confiscation.[147]

167. The proposed amendment by the Committee on Legal Affairs would have added the following language, in relevant part, to the end of Article 14(2):

> This Regulation shall be without prejudice to the right accorded under the laws of the Member States and/or Council Regulation (EEC) No 40/94 of 20 December 1993 on the Community trade mark to bring proceedings for infringement of the right embodied in a trade mark conforming to the conditions set out in the first sentence of this paragraph on account of the use of a designation of origin or geographical indication subsequent to that trade mark, be it under the civil, administrative, or criminal law of the Member States.[148]

168. This proposed amendment would have incorporated the substantive disciplines of EC trademark law into the GI Regulation, thereby providing for the ability of trademark owners to exercise their exclusive rights. In particular, the amendment would have provided for the rights of the owner of a valid prior registered trademark to prevent the use of a similar or identical geographical indication when such use would result in a likelihood of confusion with the trademark.

169. Unfortunately, the amendment was not adopted, and the defect in the EC GI Regulation remains in place.

---

[144] Review Under Article 24.2 of the Application of the Provisions of the Section of the TRIPS Agreement on Geographical Indications, Responses to the Checklist of Questions, Addendum, Council for Trade-Related Aspects of Intellectual Property Rights, IP/C/W/117/Add.10 (26 March 1999), p. 13 (EC response to question 36). The EC has also explained that "a geographical indication must be used [in order to maintain rights]." *Id.* at p. 12 (response to question 30).

[145] Council Regulation (EC) No 692/2003 of 8 April 2003 amending Regulation 2081/92, OJ L 99, July 14, 2003, p. 1. Exhibit COMP-1.h.

[146] Proposal for a Council Regulation amending Regulation (EEC) No. 2081/92 on the protection of geographical indications and designations of origin for agricultural products and foodstuffs, presented by the Commission of the European Communities, 2002/0066 (Brussels, March 15, 2002), p. 4. Exhibit US-20.

[147] Opinion of the Committee on Legal Affairs and the Internal Market for the Committee on Agriculture and Rural Development on the proposal for a Council regulation amending Regulation (EEC) No 2081/92 on the protection of geographical indications and designations of origin for agricultural products and foodstuffs, European Parliament, 2002/0066(CNS) (10 September 2002), p. 14. Exhibit US-21. *See also* Exhibit COMP-14.

[148] Exhibit US-21, at pp. 13-14.

5. Conclusion with respect to the GI Regulation's inconsistency with Article 16.1

170. To conclude, TRIPS Article 16.1 requires that owners of registered trademarks have the exclusive right to prevent confusing uses by others. The EC GI Regulation does not permit owners of registered trademarks to exercise those rights. Therefore, the EC GI Regulation is inconsistent with the EC's obligations under Article 16.1 of the TRIPS Agreement.

D. THE EC GI REGULATION IS INCONSISTENT WITH ARTICLE 22.2 OF THE TRIPS AGREEMENT

171. Article 22.2 of the TRIPS Agreement requires that "[i]n respect of geographical indications, Members shall provide the legal means for interested parties to prevent:

> (a) the use of any means in the designation or presentation of a good that indicates or suggests that the good in question originates in a geographic area other than the true place of origin in a manner which misleads the public as to the geographic origin of the good;
>
> (b) any use which constitutes an act of unfair competition within the meaning of Article 10*bis* of the Paris Convention (1967).

172. As discussed above in the context of national treatment, Article 22.2 requires WTO Members to provide these legal means directly to all "interested parties," a requirement that is not met by simply providing such means to WTO Members at the government-to-government level.

173. "Interested parties" is not defined in the TRIPS Agreement, but Article 10 of the Paris Convention, concerning false indications of geographical source, provides useful context that an "interested party" includes a producer or seller established in the region falsely indicated as the source. As discussed in the national treatment context, this includes producers or sellers in regions located outside the territory of the country where the false indication of source is being used.

174. The EC GI Regulation does not provide the legal means required by Article 22.2 to interested parties in at least two respects. First, as discussed above, interested persons with GIs outside the EC do not have the legal means to register and protect their own GIs—that is, those GIs in their country of origin—on an EC-wide basis under the GI Regulation. They therefore do not have the legal means under the GI Regulation to prevent misleading uses under Article 22.2(a) or acts of unfair competition under Article 22.2(b) of the TRIPS Agreement "[i]n respect of geographical indications."

175. It is important to recall that Article 2(1) of the GI Regulation specifies that "Community protection of designations of origin and of geographical indications of agricultural products and foodstuffs shall be obtained in accordance with this Regulation."[149] The broad protections laid out in Article 13 of that Regulation appear to encompass those that are required by Article 22.2 of the TRIPS Agreement. And, in fact, some interested parties—those with geographical indications located in the EC—do have the legal means to protect their GIs against misleading uses and acts of unfair competition through the registration process.

176. But for interested parties with geographical indications located outside the EC, the legal means to protect their GIs on a uniform basis throughout the territory of the EC are theoretically available only if the WTO Member in which their products are produced adopts an EC-specified system of GI protection and offers reciprocal treatment to EC goods.[150] With respect to interested parties in other WTO Members that do not satisfy these requirements, therefore, the EC GI Regulation fails to provide any legal means whatsoever to prevent misleading uses or unfair acts of competition on an EC-wide basis.

---

[149] Emphasis added.

[150] Article 12 of the GI Regulation.

177. Further, even if that Member adopted the appropriate system and offered reciprocity to the EC, the interested party would continue to depend on its Member government to intercede on its behalf and consult with any affected EC member State, make a determination that the interested party's application meets the requirements of the GI Regulation, certify to the Commission that it has the proper protection system and inspection structure in place, and transmit the application to the Commission.[151] Therefore, the EC GI Regulation does not provide the legal means to prevent misleading uses on an EC-wide basis to "interested parties" from all WTO Members.

178. Thus, an interested party from a Member that does not have an EC-equivalent system and that does not offer reciprocity does not have the legal means required by Article 22.2 of the TRIPS Agreement. Further, there is nothing that this interested party can do to obtain the "legal means" guaranteed him under the TRIPS Agreement, because it is not in a position, either to establish a full EC-style GI system in his home country, or to provide reciprocal treatment. In addition, even if such a system were in place, the interested party would need to rely on its own government to act on an application, which that government may or may not have the infrastructure or the political inclination to do. Consequently, the GI Regulation provides a possible method—and one that is highly intrusive and costly—only for other Members to obtain Article 22.2 protection on behalf of interested parties in their territory. It does not provide those legal means directly to those interested parties, as required by Article 22.2.

179. Moreover, there is a separate and possibly more serious concern with respect to interested parties' ability to object to the registration of GIs under the EC GI Regulation. As discussed above in the context of national treatment, the ability to object to a registration is an important element of the legal means required to prevent misleading uses and acts of unfair competition under Article 22.2 of the TRIPS Agreement. This is because once a GI is registered and protected, there appears to be no ability to prevent or limit its use through the EC,[152] even if it is or becomes misleading or confusing. In spite of this, interested parties from third countries cannot object directly to the registration of a GI. Rather, they must request their government to do so.[153] However, their government may or may not have the infrastructure or the inclination to present the objection to EC officials. Making the exercise of private rights contingent on actions of government entities outside the right holder's control fails to provide legal means to exercise a private right, as required by Article 22.2 of the TRIPS Agreement.

180. Further, Article 12d limits the persons who can object to an application for registration submitted by an EC member State to persons from "a WTO member country or a third country recognized under the procedure provided for in Article 12(3)," *i.e.*, satisfying the conditions of equivalency and reciprocity described earlier in this submission. It appears that interested parties from WTO Members who do not satisfy the conditions of equivalency and reciprocity may not object to the registration of a GI, and therefore do not have the legal means to prevent misleading uses required by Article 22.2 of the TRIPS Agreement.

181. In addition, the GI Regulation provides, under Articles 7, 12b and 12d that only those with a "legitimate interest" or a "legitimate economic interest" have a right to object. As discussed above, the Paris Convention provides that an interested party can be any producer or seller established in the region falsely indicated as the source in a given territory, which may be different from the region in which the false indication is being used. To the extent that the GI Regulation's requirement means that the person must have an economic interest in the EC, it is inconsistent with the TRIPS Agreement obligation to make legal means available to all "interested parties" and not just those established or doing business in the EC.

182. Finally, the possible grounds for objection—that the registration of the name "would jeopardize the existence of an entirely or partly identical name or of a mark or the existence of products which have been

---

151 Article 12 of the GI Regulation.

152 Recall that this is an EC Regulation, which is immediately applicable in all EC member States.

153 Articles 12b and 12d of the GI Regulation.

legally on the market for at least five years"[154]—is unduly restrictive and does not provide legal means to object to a registration in order to prevent "the use of any means in the designation or presentation of a good that indicates or suggests that the good in question originates in a geographic area other than the true place of origin in a manner which misleads the public as to the geographic origin of the good" or " any use which constitutes an act of unfair competition within the meaning of Article 10*bis* of the Paris Convention (1967)."

183. Consequently, the EC GI Regulation fails to provide the required legal means to interested parties as required by Article 22.2.

E. THE EC GI REGULATION IS INCONSISTENT WITH THE EC'S ENFORCEMENT OBLIGATIONS UNDER THE TRIPS AGREEMENT

184. Part III of the TRIPS Agreement—"Enforcement of Intellectual Property Rights"—contains a broad range of obligations with respect to the enforcement of intellectual property rights covered by the Agreement, which includes trademark rights and rights in geographical indications. As described in section IV.C of this submission, the EC GI Regulation denies the owner of a registered trademark its Article 16.1 exclusive right to prevent all third parties from using the same or similar signs for identical or similar goods as those for which the trademark is registered where such use would result in a likelihood of confusion. Further, the EC GI Regulation does not, with respect to GIs, provide the required legal means to interested parties to prevent misleading uses or acts of unfair competition. Therefore, as summarized below, that Regulation is also inconsistent with numerous TRIPS Agreement obligations to enforce intellectual property rights.

185. Article 41.1 requires that enforcement procedures be available to permit effective action against any act of infringement of intellectual property rights, and expeditious remedies to deter further infringements. In contrast, under the EC GI Regulation, an owner of a registered trademark does not have any procedures available to him to take action against infringement of his trademark by a registered GI, and has no remedies available to him to deter such further infringements. The same is true of interested parties with GIs based in territories other than the EC.

186. Article 41.2 requires that enforcement procedures be fair and equitable, and not be unnecessarily complicated or costly, or entail unreasonable time-limits or unwarranted delays. Article 41.4 requires the opportunity for judicial review. Neither of these obligations are satisfied with respect to owners of registered trademarks trying to enforce their Article 16.1 rights *vis-à-vis* a confusing GI or to interested parties with GIs based in territories other than the EC.

187. Article 42 requires that civil judicial procedures concerning the enforcement of "any intellectual property right" be made available to rightholders. Article 44.1 requires that judicial authorities have the authority to issue orders to desist from infringement. As detailed in this submission, no such procedures or injunctions are available to owners of registered trademarks *vis-à-vis* confusing signs that are registered as GIs. And no such procedures or injunctions are available to holders of rights in GIs located in WTO Members that do not satisfy the equivalency and reciprocity requirements of the GI Regulation.

188. Consequently, the EC GI Regulation is inconsistent with the TRIPS Agreement obligations to enforce intellectual property rights, including Articles 41.1, 41.2, 41.4, 42, and 44.1.

F. THE EC GI REGULATION IS INCONSISTENT WITH ARTICLE 65.1 OF THE TRIPS AGREEMENT

189. Under Article 65.1 of the TRIPS Agreement, the EC was obligated to apply the provisions of the TRIPS Agreement as of one year after the date of entry into force of the WTO Agreement, *i.e.*, one year after January 1, 1995, or as of January 1, 1996.

---

[154] Article 7(4) of the GI Regulation.

190. As demonstrated in this submission, the EC GI Regulation is still inconsistent with several provisions of the TRIPS Agreement, and consequently also violates Article 65.1 of the TRIPS Agreement.

V. CONCLUSION

191. For the foregoing reasons, the United States requests that the Panel find that the EC GI Regulation is inconsistent with the EC's obligations under the TRIPS Agreement and the GATT 1994, and to recommend that the EC bring its measure into conformity with those obligations.

ANNEX A-3

ORAL STATEMENT OF THE UNITED STATES FIRST SUBSTANTIVE MEETING

(23 June 2004)

1. Good morning, Mr. Chairman and members of the Panel. We have asked that you review the EC's GI Regulation—after five years of fruitless consultations—because it presents two major problems seriously affecting the rights of all WTO Members.

2. The Regulation sets up what the EC has characterized as a powerful system for registering and protecting geographical indications for agricultural products and foodstuffs sold in the substantial EC market. According to the EC, this system bestows significant commercial benefits on those persons and products able to qualify for protection. The EC has claimed that this system allows qualifying EC products to command higher prices in the EC market and to compete favorably based on quality. Indeed, so commercially meaningful is this GI protection that, in the eyes of the EC, it helps make it politically feasible to reduce or eliminate the EC's agricultural subsidies.

3. The problem is that the Regulation denies equal access to this powerful system of protection for *non-EC* nationals and products. Specifically, the Regulation puts in place a mandatory legal structure that directly allows only EC nationals to register and protect their GIs for EC products. Non-EC nationals, by contrast, cannot apply at all, unless their government has adopted a system of GI protection that (1) mirrors the EC's and (2) provides reciprocal protection to EC products—in other words, the "equivalence" and "reciprocity" requirements. Further, the non-EC national, unlike the EC national, can neither apply for, nor object to, a GI registration directly. Rather, the non-EC national—unlike the EC national—can only hope that his government will voluntarily put procedures in place to process objections according to EC standards and will be willing to try to convince the EC that (1) the government's GI protection system satisfies the EC's requirements and that (2) the particular GI should be registered.

4. As we detailed in our first submission, these aspects of the GI Regulation—the requirement of reciprocity and equivalence and the requirement for government-level intervention—discriminate in favor of EC nationals and products and against the nationals and products of other WTO Members. Further, with respect to countries that do happen to have an EC-equivalent system of GI protection, the GI Regulation discriminates in favor of nationals and products of those countries and against the nationals and products of WTO Members that do not have such a system. In other words, the EC's GI Regulation violates the national treatment and MFN obligations of the TRIPS Agreement, the Paris Convention, and the GATT 1994. For some of these same reasons, the GI Regulation does not provide the legal means required under the TRIPS Agreement for the protection of geographical indications.

5. Further, the GI Regulation grants these significant protections to EC nationals and products at the expense of rights that the EC is obligated to provide to owners of registered trademarks under the TRIPS Agreement. The TRIPS Agreement requires that WTO Members provide to the owners of registered trademarks the *exclusive* right to prevent confusing uses of similar or identical signs by *all third parties*. But under the GI Regulation, registered GIs are immune from the exercise of this right. Under the GI Regulation, if a person is using a GI that consists of the same or similar signs as a prior registered trademark—and does so in a manner that causes confusion with the trademark—the owner of the registered trademark is powerless to prevent that use. All that owner can do is continue to use his trademark in commerce, watching as the ability of that trademark to distinguish his goods is eroded away. This situation is simply not permitted by the TRIPS Agreement.

6. My oral statement this morning will focus on the two principal issues outlined above, although I will also briefly touch on other arguments raised by the EC. In sum, despite its denials and arguments to the contrary, the EC's first submission confirms the WTO inconsistencies noted above in every respect.

National Treatment/MFN

Requirements of Equivalence and Reciprocity

7. With respect to the lack of national and MFN treatment in the EC's GI Regulation, there are a few key questions that this Panel must examine. First, and astonishingly, the EC now claims that WTO Members do not have to satisfy the equivalence and reciprocity requirements. Yet, these requirements are clearly set out as preconditions for registering *all* third country GIs in Articles 12 and 12a of the EC GI Regulation. According to the EC, those requirements would "prejudice" the WTO Agreements, under Article 12(1). The United States is, of course, pleased that the EC has finally acknowledged that these requirements are inconsistent with WTO obligations.

8. Nevertheless, we remain skeptical. Article 12(1) of the GI Regulation clearly says that the Regulation may apply to products from a third country only if that country meets certain conditions, among them equivalence and reciprocity. These requirements apply with respect to GIs from *any* third country. There is no exclusion for WTO Members in Article 12(1), even though WTO Members are specifically mentioned in other parts of the Regulation. Therefore, there is every reason to believe that Article 12(1) means what it says. Of course, the EC reserves its flexibility to protect specific non-EC GIs through bilateral agreements, so Article 12(1) also states that it is "without prejudice to international agreements." But there is nothing in Article 12(1) to suggest that WTO Members are excluded from its requirements.

9. Further, Article 12a of the Regulation sets out the sole process under the GI Regulation for registering non-EC GIs. But Article 12a provides such a procedure only for countries that have satisfied the requirements of Article 12(1). Article 12a(1) says that a *third country fulfilling the conditions of Article 12(1)* may send a registration application to the Commission. Article 12a(2) describes what the *third country referred to in Article 12(1)* must do to apply for a GI registration on behalf of its nationals. If, as the EC suggests, Article 12(1) does not apply to WTO Members, Article 12a also does not apply to WTO Members, with the consequence that there is *no system whatsoever* under the GI Regulation for registering GI products from WTO Members. The EC has asserted that certain of the "third country" procedures in Article 12a apply to WTO Members, but that other references to "third countries," inexplicably, exclude WTO Members. There is simply no basis in the Regulation for picking and choosing which provisions apply to WTO Members and which do not.

10. Not only that, but until recently, the EC itself claimed that WTO Members *do* have to satisfy the reciprocity and equivalence requirements. We have held over five years of consultations, focused to a significant degree on the WTO-consistency of the reciprocity and equivalence requirements. *Not once* in those five years did the EC mention that these requirements do not apply to WTO Members.

11. To the contrary, the EC's clearly articulated view—at least prior to last month in this proceeding—was that (1) agricultural products from a WTO Member are not eligible for GI registration in the EC unless that Member satisfies the reciprocity and equivalence requirements; and (2) the United States, for one, does not satisfy those requirements, and so its nationals cannot register their US GIs.

12. We note, for instance, the written submission of the EC to the TRIPS Council, in September 2002, in which the EC, in describing its GI Registration system in the context of TRIPS obligations discussed the "fact that the EU register for GIs on foodstuffs does not allow the registration of foreign GI unless it is determined that a third country has an equivalent or reciprocal system of GI protection."[1] Or its statement in that same

[1] IP/C/M/37/Add.1, p. 79.

document that GI "registration systems should be primarily aimed at the identification of *domestic* GIs."[2] Likewise, its admission that the EC GI procedure requiring EU member States to verify that products meet the GI definition is "ill-adapted to foreign GIs."[3]

13. In addition, there are a number of statements from EC officials in connection with the amendments to the EC GI Regulation last year that emphasize the importance to the EC of requiring reciprocity and equivalence as a condition of registering GIs from non-EU countries. This is touted as a means of encouraging the adoption of the EC GI protection system abroad.[4] The references are to "non-EU" countries, not "non-WTO Members."

14. This Regulation has been in place and enforced for almost 12 years. In that time, according to the EC itself, over 640 EC geographical indications have been registered.[5] How many third country GIs have been registered? To our knowledge, none. This is not too surprising, since, at least up until last month, the EC has been confirming to WTO Members the plain meaning of the GI Regulation—that their nationals may as well not even apply for a GI unless the WTO Member is prepared to convince the Commission that it has a GI system that is equivalent to the EC's system and that offers reciprocal treatment to EC products. The EC has in effect been demanding that WTO Members adopt its system of GI protection, thereby trying to extract from its trading partners through the GI Regulation what it could not get during the Uruguay Round negotiations.

15. And now the EC wants this Panel to find that the exact opposite is true, despite the presence of the same GI Regulation language—"without prejudice to international agreements"—that has been in place for almost 12 years and despite the explanations provided by the EC itself during five years of consultations and in several other fora—simply because the EC is now, for purposes of this dispute, saying so. The EC amended this regulation last year with respect to some aspects of registration and objection, but, notably, left this language regarding equivalence and reciprocity untouched.[6]

16. With all due respect, this Panel should examine very thoroughly the factual basis for the EC's newfound—and unsupported—interpretation of its Regulation. If the EC can objectively establish that no requirements of reciprocity and equivalence apply to WTO Members—despite the clear language to the contrary—this clarification will be welcome. But mere assertions by the EC for purposes of this dispute are insufficient. To the contrary, the plain meaning of the Regulation, supported by the repeated assertions of the EC itself to WTO Members, demonstrate the contrary.

Equivalence by another name

17. Further, even if the Panel were to agree with the EC that Article 12(1) does not apply to WTO Members and that there is an alternative registration process for WTO Members somewhere in the GI Regulation, the EC nonetheless admits that Article 12a(2) requires WTO Members to submit a declaration that certain specific inspection structures are "established" on its territory.

> (Parenthetically, as I noted a moment ago, Article 12a(2) applies *only* to third countries that have been deemed to satisfy the requirements of reciprocity and equivalence under Article 12(3), an article that the EC now says does not apply to WTO Members. So it is not clear on what basis this Article applies to WTO Members at all, under the EC's new interpretation. But, assuming for the sake of argument that it does,)

---

[2] *Id.*, p. 80 (emphasis added).

[3] *Id.*, p. 80.

[4] *See, e.g.*, "Food quality: Commission proposes better protection for geographical names," IP/02/422, Brussels, March 15, 2002. Exhibit US-22. *See also* Exhibit US-20, p. 3; Exhibit COMP-14, pp. 20, 21, 23.

[5] *See* www.europa.eu.int/comm/agriculture/publi/capleaflet/cap_en.htm.

[6] *See* Council Regulation (EC) No 692/2003 of 8 April 2003 amending Regulation 2081/92, OJ L 99, July 14, 2003, p. 1. Exhibit COMP-1.h.

This requirement for inspection structures is tantamount to a requirement of equivalence, the same requirement that the EC itself appears to admit is WTO-inconsistent.

18. The purported function of the required "inspection structures," which are also required of EC member States under Article 10, is to ensure that any agricultural product or foodstuff bearing a protected name complies with the relevant specification.[7] Under Article 10, the inspection authorities of a country must have permanent qualified staff and resources "necessary to carry out inspection of agricultural products and foodstuffs bearing a protected name." One of the requirements of Article 10 is that if the inspection body establishes that an agricultural product bearing a protected name does not meet the criteria in the specification, it must take all necessary steps to ensure that the EC GI Regulation is complied with.

19. So, in order for its nationals to qualify for GI protection, a WTO Member must establish an inspection structure with the authority and the resources to enforce the EC's GI Regulation and to ensure that any agricultural product or foodstuff bearing a protected name qualifies for that name.

20. Although the EC calls this requirement a product "specification," as if it were related solely to whether the product itself qualifies to be a geographical indication, this is not really a product "specification" in the usual sense. Instead, it is a requirement that WTO Members adopt the same bureaucratic structures related to the protection of GIs as the EC has. But other WTO Members have the freedom under the TRIPS Agreement to set up a system that is different from the EC's for protecting GIs, and the EC cannot make protection of GIs conditional on other Members' adopting an EC-style system. The United States, for one, has not adopted the EC's approach to protecting GIs, and does not necessarily require an EC-style inspection structure. This fact, however, should not prevent US nationals from obtaining GI protection in the EC on the same basis as EC nationals.

21. In brief, the EC's requirement that the United States establish EC-style inspection structures to enforce GIs is simply equivalence by another name: The EC will not protect the GIs of US nationals unless the United States establishes the same inspection structures, with the same responsibilities and resources, that are required of EC member States. The EC has apparently recognized that it cannot require equivalence from WTO Members as a condition for protecting their GIs. For the same reason, it cannot require WTO Members to establish EC-style inspection structures to enforce GIs as a precondition.

The GI Regulation discriminates against certain nationals

22. The EC claims that its GI Regulation discriminates based on the *location* of the geographical area covered by the GI, and not on the basis of *nationality.*[8] This razor-thin distinction is not meaningful, and is certainly not a basis on which to determine whether fundamental TRIPS Agreement obligations are being respected. To the question, "whose GI rights are overwhelmingly connected to agricultural products and foodstuffs obtained or produced in the United States," the answer is obviously, "nationals of the United States." To the question, "whose are overwhelmingly connected to products produced in the EC," the answer is, equally obviously, "EC nationals." No one can be under any illusion that, in providing one set of requirements for agricultural products grown in the EC and a more burdensome set for agricultural products grown outside the EC, non-EC nationals are being treated less favorably than EC nationals with respect to the protection of their geographical indications. One might just as easily argue that a regulation directed at large white birds with long necks swimming in Lac Leman is not directed at swans, or that a regulation directed at birds that quack has nothing to do with ducks. Rights in GIs, perhaps to a greater extent than other forms of intellectual property, are inherently related to the territory of the national.

23. A US national growing a special onion in a particular region in the Southeast United States is, under the TRIPS Agreement, entitled to obtain geographical indication protection for his product on terms that are at

[7] Article 10(1) of the EC GI Regulation.

[8] *E.g.*, EC First Written Submission, para. 125.

least as favorable to those accorded to, for example, French nationals for their products. That US national, who has perhaps built up the quality and reputation of his product over many years, is simply not in the same position as a similarly situated French national in France to apply for, register and protect his GIs in the EC. Nor does he have any means of obtaining the same treatment as his French counterpart. He can't simply move his farm to France and qualify for GI protection, because the reputation and quality of his product is connected with its geographic area in the United States. It is simply not enough for the EC to assert that the location of the geographic area has nothing to do with nationality: this US person cannot protect his GI in the EC under the GI Regulation *because* of his US location. Further, if previous WTO dispute resolution findings with respect to national treatment in the goods area provide any guidance, US nationals are entitled to the best treatment granted to any EC national, which is the treatment granted the EC national with a GI in the EC.

24. To highlight the problem further, the Panel should recall that, under the TRIPS Agreement and the Paris Convention, "nationals" of a Member include legal persons who have a commercial establishment in that Member. So, if the US national at issue is a corporation or partnership running an onion farm in the United States, the only way that it could get the same treatment as a French national would be for it to establish a farm growing onions in the EC. But this is tantamount to a requirement that the farm move or expand its commercial establishment to the EC, which would mean that it would qualify under the TRIPS Agreement as an EC national.

25. In other words, as applied to legal persons such as a farm, "national" treatment for US nationals is available under the GI Regulation only if the US national *becomes an EC national.* (Of course, such a move would eliminate the ability to register the foreign GI, as the goods would no longer have a quality, reputation, or other characteristics essentially attributable to their location.)

26. This requirement subverts the whole purpose of the national treatment requirement. The EC is supposed to give national treatment to nationals of the United States, not give national treatment to any US national who agrees to become an EC national. Yet, this is the practical effect of the EC's restrictive definition of "national treatment" and "most favored nation treatment."

27. It is also one reason that the EC is wrong to argue that the US "national treatment" claim does not include Article 2, paragraph 2 of the Paris Convention. This paragraph of the Article 2 national treatment provision prohibits requiring establishment in the country where protection is claimed as a condition of enjoying rights. In this instance, the GI Regulation's requirement for a commercial establishment in Europe as a precondition to claiming the same rights as nationals is simply another aspect of its denial of national treatment to nationals of other WTO Members, a claim clearly within this Panel's terms of reference.

Requirement that the WTO Members intervene on behalf of their nationals

28. As the US first submission stated, another way the EC GI Regulation denies national and MFN treatment, and also fails to provide legal means for interested parties to protect GIs, is its requirement that a non-EC national's *government* take action in order for its *national* to protect its GI rights. For GI registration applications, the WTO Member government has to determine that the application meets the EC GI Regulation's requirements, has to demonstrate to the EC how the GI is protected in that country, and has to demonstrate that it has established the necessary "inspection structures," discussed earlier. And this is assuming, for the sake of argument, that the WTO Member does not also have to convince the Commission that it has satisfied the requirements of equivalence and reciprocity. Even for objections to GI applications, the WTO Member has to process that objection and present it to the Commission. The non-EC interested party has no ability to do that himself directly.

29. Now, the EC has a glib response to this argument: "The United States should not invoke its unwillingness to cooperate," says the EC, "to demonstrate a national treatment violation by the EC." This response avoids the issue. The issue is not whether the United States itself is willing to, as the EC puts it, "cooperate" with the EC's GI registration process. The issue is whether, under the GI Regulation, a non-EC

national has the same direct means to register his GI in the EC or to object to the registration of a GI in the EC, as does the EC national. He does not: the non-EC national has to go through a non-EC government that, unlike EC member States, is under no obligation to process GI registration applications or objections.

30. The EC tries to sell this requirement as "equal" treatment, because EC nationals must also apply to their member State governments for registrations and objections, and EC member States also have to have inspection structures in place. But this is a false "equality." The EC can, and in the GI Regulation does, impose substantive and procedural requirements on its member States. The GI Regulation, therefore, directly provides the means in the EC for EC nationals to register their GIs and to object to the registration of GIs. The TRIPS national treatment requirements are not satisfied by imposing the same requirements on WTO Members as the EC imposes on its member States. The TRIPS requirement is that the *nationals* of WTO Members are entitled to treatment at least as favorable as that accorded to EC nationals.

31. In sum, the GI Regulation provides the direct means, through mandatory enforceable rules imposed on its member States, and through the infrastructure and bureaucracy established under the European Union, for EC nationals to register their GIs and to object to the registration of GIs. A non-EC national, by contrast, does not have those means, but must hope that its government will voluntarily put in place the necessary rules, regulations and infrastructure to process EC GI applications and objections, and will advocate to the Commission on behalf of its nationals.

32. This does not provide equal treatment to non-EC nationals, and it does not provide non-EC interested parties with the legal means to protect GIs.

33. As the US and EC first submissions demonstrate, the issues we have just discussed cut across a number of the US claims, and demonstrate how, despite the EC's arguments to the contrary, the EC GI Regulation denies national treatment and most-favored nation treatment with respect to both the nationals and the products of other WTO Members, and fails to provide the legal means to protect GIs. Before moving on to the trademark issue, we do want to respond briefly to a number of the EC's arguments that are specific to particular claims.

Responses to other arguments

34. First, the GI Regulation says that any EU national who is "legitimately concerned" may object to a GI registration, while non-EC nationals must have a "legitimate interest" in order to object. The EC responds that there is no difference between the two standards. The United States submits to you, however, that a person may be "concerned" without his concern rising to the level of a "legitimate interest." The "legitimate interest" standard for non-EC nationals was introduced just last year; if the EC meant for the standard to be the same, why not use the same words? The EC has not sustained its burden of rebutting the presumption that this amounts to less favorable treatment.

35. Second, with respect to the special rule that non-EC GIs must be accompanied by a country of origin indication on its label, the EC claims that this rule applies to both EC and non-EC products, and that, in any case, country of origin marking requirements can never give rise to a national treatment violation. The provision at issue, however, is in Article 12(1), which deals exclusively with the authorization of non-EC GIs, not EC GIs. In addition, this provision is not a general country of origin requirement as described in Article IX of the GATT 1994; rather, it is a special rule that is triggered by the fact that a third country product is characterized as a GI, and is intended to encumber the non-EC GI itself.

36. Third, the EC argues that there is no MFN violation because the GI Regulation has not yet been applied to discriminate among WTO Members. But the United States is challenging this measure on its face, not any particular application of the measure. The fact is that Articles 12(1) and 12a of the GI Regulation are designed purely to favor nationals from countries that have an EC-style GI protection system, including inspection structures, and to disfavor nationals from countries that don't. This is contrary to MFN obligations.

37. The EC also argues that its member States are entitled to treat other nationals from the EC more favorably than nationals from other WTO Members, because they are doing so pursuant to an EC regulation. But each EC member State has an obligation to provide MFN treatment *vis-a-vis* nationals of *all* other WTO Members. That they may be acting pursuant to an EC regulation does not excuse them from this obligation.

38. Fourth, the EC claims that the less favorable treatment provided non-EC products is excused by Article XX(d) of the GATT 1994. The EC has not made out a *prima facie* case that this is so, but has merely asserted it. This Panel should reject this argument on that basis alone. The GI Regulation does not satisfy the requirements of Article XX(d): it is not necessary to ensure compliance with laws or regulations that are not inconsistent with the GATT 1994.

39. Finally, the EC claims that the enforcement obligations of the TRIPS Agreement do not apply to the GI Regulation, because that Regulation deals only with the acquisition and enforcement of intellectual property, and not with enforcement. This is incorrect. The TRIPS Agreement requires enforcement procedures to permit effective action against any act of infringement of the covered intellectual property rights. The GI Regulation prevents trademark owners, for instance, from enforcing their Article 16.1 rights with respect to registered GIs. This is plainly inconsistent with the obligation to provide such enforcement.

Trademark Rights

40. We would like to spend the balance of our time discussing the trademark right issue. We start by noting that, within a span of just a few pages, the EC's submission states that: (1) there is no hierarchy between GIs and trademarks; (2) the United States is trying to establish a hierarchy of trademarks over GIs; and (3) the proper balance is to provide GIs with rights superior to trademarks: that is, that TRIPS permits GIs to prejudice "*any right*" of trademark owners, with the only exception being certain grandfathered trademarks that can be "used" in commerce but that are deprived of the critical ability to exclude confusing uses by all others.[9] Interestingly, the EC derives this far-reaching ability to prejudice all trademark rights from, of all places, an article providing for exceptions, not to trademark rights, but to GI rights.

41. The EC's assertions notwithstanding, the United States agrees that there is no hierarchy between trademarks and GIs. In fact, the United States took great pains in its first submission to make it clear that is important to give *all* of the TRIPS provisions their full scope. There is no inconsistency between the obligation to provide trademark owners with the right to exclude uses by all others of signs that are likely to confuse consumers, on the one hand, and the obligation to give interested parties the ability to prevent misleading uses of GIs, on the other. The issue is not whether one form of intellectual property is "superior" to another, as the EC claims, but how to provide the rights set forth in the TRIPS Agreement in a manner that gives full affect to all of its provisions.

42. In other words, the EC's characterizations of the US position are wrong. We'd like to emphasize certain basic points that set the relationship between trademarks and GIs in context. First, trademarks that lack distinctiveness or that mislead consumers as to the origin of goods may, under the TRIPS Agreement and the Paris Convention, be refused registration. If they are registered, such marks may be subject to invalidation. The EC's concerns on this score, therefore, are misplaced. The United States was clear in its first submission that this dispute concerns valid prior trademarks, not trademarks that are subject to invalidation under the TRIPS Agreement and the Paris Convention.[10]

43. Second, despite the EC's suggestions to the contrary, it is not the position of the United States that a trademark owner will necessarily succeed in an action against a GI owner. For example, if a trademark owner brings an infringement action against the user of a similar or identical GI, the trademark owner might not be

---

[9] EC First Written Submission, para. 301.

[10] *E.g.*, US First Written Submission, para. 135.

able to prove that the particular use of the GI would result in a likelihood of confusion. Or the GI owner might be able to show that the trademark is subject to invalidation.

44. With this understanding as a backdrop, let us now respond briefly to the EC's arguments with respect to trademark rights.

Article 14(3) of the EC GI Regulation

45. The EC appears to argue that, under the GI Regulation, owners of registered trademarks do not need the Article 16.1 right to exclude all others from confusing uses of their signs, for two reasons. First, the EC argues that it is unlikely that any trademarks would be registered that could be confused with a GI (*i.e.*, the risk of confusion is "limited").[11] Second, the EC argues that Article 14(3) allows it to prevent the registration of all geographical indications that are confusing *vis-a-vis* certain trademarks.

46. But neither of these arguments addresses the main point, which is that the TRIPS Agreement requires that the owner of a registered trademark be able to exclude all others from the confusing use of identical or similar signs. And that the EC GI Regulation does not accord or even accommodate that right with respect to registered GIs.

47. The EC's argument, in essence, is to concede that owners of registered trademarks are being deprived of their TRIPS Agreement rights, but to claim that they do not *need* those rights, because Article 14(3) of the EC GI Regulation ensures that confusing GIs will not be registered in the first place.

48. This is not good enough, nor is it true. The TRIPS Agreement requires that trademark owners be given a certain exclusive right, and the EC cannot legitimately respond that the right can be withheld because it is unnecessary.

49. Moreover, it is untrue that the Article 16.1 right to exclude is unnecessary. First, the EC argues that few trademarks that contain or consist of a GI are registrable, and that the United States is therefore making much ado about nothing. Even if the Panel accepts the unsupported assertion that the number of trademarks affected is small, however, it is beyond dispute that those registered trademarks—whatever their number—must be accorded Article 16.1 rights. It is no defense to a WTO violation to claim that the number of specific rights affected is small.

50. In addition, however, it is simply untrue that valid registered trademarks cannot incorporate certain "geographical" elements. Take the hypothetical example of an EC registered trademark, "Luna," used in connection with cheese. Assume that the residents in the small town of Luna, Spain, start making cheese after the "Luna" mark was registered. If that cheese subsequently qualifies for GI protection, it would be eligible for registration as a GI, and, once registered, the owners of the "Luna" trademark would be powerless to stop the rightholders of the "Luna" GI from using the "Luna" name in a way that confuses the consumer. This is simply not a result permitted by Article 16.1 of the TRIPS Agreement. This is only a hypothetical, admittedly, but in fact there are thousands of registered trademarks around the world that incorporate or happen to sound like geographical names.

51. Second, contrary to the EC's arguments, Article 14(3) of the GI Regulation does not satisfy the obligations under Article 16.1 of the TRIPS Agreement. Article 14(3), the Panel will recall, allows the EC to reject GI registrations where, in the light of a trademark's reputation and renown and the length of time it has been used, the GI registration is liable to mislead the consumer as to the identity of the product.

52. This standard does not satisfy the TRIPS Agreement obligations for several reasons. To begin, it applies criteria that are different from and more restrictive than Article 16.1. Article 16.1 requires that the owner

[11] EC First Written Submission, para. 275.

of a registered trademark have the exclusive right to prevent all uses of identical or similar signs that result in a likelihood of confusion. This is not a right reserved solely to registered trademarks of a certain reputation or of any particular renown, nor is there any requirement under Article 16.1 that the trademark be used for any length of time. Article 16.1 articulates a right that is owed under the TRIPS Agreement to the owner of *any* valid registered trademark. Article 14(3), by contrast, comes into play only where there exists a trademark with a reputation, renown, and history of use.

53. Now, the EC implies that Article 14(3) actually permits the EC to block registration of a GI whenever there is a likelihood of confusion with a registered trademark, regardless of use, reputation or renown of the trademark. But that is not what Article 14(3) says: Article 14(3) clearly requires reputation, renown and use for some period of time. The EC not only confirms this reading in paragraph 290 of its submission, it has also confirmed this obvious meaning in its public explanations of its regulation outside of this meeting room. Thus, although the EC criticizes the United States in this room for characterizing Article 14(3) as requiring "long use," the EC itself uses the phrase "used for a long time" in describing the requirements of Article 14(3) outside this room, as our Exhibit US-23 shows.[12]

54. In any event, Article 14(3) does not, as required by Article 16.1 of the TRIPS Agreement, provide the *trademark owner* with the right to prevent confusing uses. It merely authorizes the *EC* to decline registration of a GI in limited circumstances. These are two different things. Moreover, Article 14(3) does not afford the trademark owner the right to ensure that no *uses* of that GI will result in a likelihood of confusion. Thus, even if Article 14(3) accorded rights to trademark owners rather than just authority to the EC, the trademark owner would not necessarily be able to tell, at the time of registration of the GI, whether the use of the GI will be confusing. For example, a registered GI may unexpectedly be used in translation, or in a manner that emphasizes certain aspects or letters of the geographical name, in a way that causes a likelihood of confusion with respect to a registered trademark.

55. Take the EC's own example of the GI "Bayerisches Bier," which the Commission decided to register despite concerns raised under Article 14(3) that it could confuse the consumer in relation to the "Bavaria" trademark in Holland. The Commission may have well been right that the reputation and renown of those trademarks were not such that the *registration* of the GI "Bayerisches Bier" is liable to mislead the consumer as to the identity of the product. But, once that GI is registered, how does the Commission ensure that the GI is not used in Holland, perhaps translated as "Bavaria Beer"—perhaps using signs similar or identical to those of the "Bavaria" trademark—in a manner that results in a likelihood of confusion? If the use of a GI confuses the consumer, shouldn't the trademark owner have the ability to prevent that use? TRIPS Article 16.1 says yes. The EC GI Regulation says no.

56. In short, the decision under Article 14(3) on whether to register a GI is distinct from the ability of a registered trademark owner to exercise its TRIPS Article 16.1 rights once it is registered. The EC cannot invoke the former to implement the latter.

TRIPS Article 24.5

57. The EC next argues that TRIPS Article 24.5 defines the boundary between trademarks and GIs, and that it specifically permits the EC to prejudice the Article 16.1 right of prior trademark owners—that is, the exclusive right to prevent all third parties from using identical or similar signs in a manner that results in a likelihood of confusion.[13]

58. But the EC is wrong. Article 24.5 is merely an exception to the obligation to protect GIs. Just as there are exceptions to patent obligations in the patent section of TRIPS (Article 30, in Section 5), exceptions to copyright obligations in the copyright section of TRIPS (Article 13, in Section 1), exceptions to trademark

---

[12] *See also* Exhibit US-24.

[13] EC First Written Submission, paras. 298, 301.

obligations in the trademark section of TRIPS (Article 17, in Section 2), there also exist exceptions to GI obligations in the GI section of TRIPS (Article 24, in Section 3). Each of these articles, including Article 24, is explicitly labeled "exceptions," and they are exceptions only to the obligations arising in the section in which they are found.

59. Article 24.5, therefore, is an exception to the scope of protection for GIs, an exception that protects certain grandfathered trademarks. It provides that measures adopted to implement the GI section of TRIPS "shall not prejudice eligibility for or the validity of the registration of a trademark, or the right to use a trademark," on the basis that the trademark is identical or similar to a geographical indication. The plain meaning of this provision is that, in whatever respect the implementation of the GI section of TRIPS might otherwise prejudice the registration, eligibility for registration, or the use of a grandfathered trademark, Article 24.5 will prevent that result. The EC's argument, by contrast, transforms a provision that plainly *protects* certain grandfathered trademarks into a provision that empowers it to *prejudice* trademarks.

60. The EC's reading appears to hinge on the Article 24.5 obligation that GI measures not prejudice the "right to use the trademark." The EC argues that the GI Regulation permits the continued "use" of the trademark in commerce, and therefore does not prejudice the "right to use the trademark," satisfying the Article 24.5 requirement. But the EC ignores two important facts.

61. First, Article 24.5 also contains a separate obligation not to prejudice the eligibility for or the validity of the registration of trademarks. The EC seems to think that this is a mere technical requirement that is satisfied by simply maintaining a registration on the books. But under the TRIPS Agreement, "registration" of a trademark means something very specific: the owner of a registered trademark has a certain right to exclude all others from the use of confusingly similar signs. Where, under Article 24.5, a Member cannot prejudice the validity of a trademark registration, the registration remains valid and the rights that go with that registration under Article 16.1 remain in force. In this way, Article 16.1 provides a sword to registered trademark owners, while Article 24.5 shields against anything in the GI section that could adversely affect grandfathered trademarks.

62. Article 24.5 cannot be read so as to require only that a name appear on the list of registered trademarks, but that all rights connected with that registration can be denied. Without the associated rights, "registration" is virtually meaningless.

63. Second, the EC seems to read the Article 24.5 obligation not to prejudice the right to use a trademark as affirmative permission to prejudice the Article 16.1 right to exclude all others from confusing uses. But the fact that the TRIPS negotiators included *both* a prohibition on prejudicing uses *and* a prohibition on prejudicing registration, does not mean that the rights associated with registration are to be ignored.

64. The November 1990 "Brussels Draft" of the TRIPS Agreement contained a predecessor to the current Article 24.5 requiring that registrations of grandfathered trademarks not be refused or invalidated. It made no mention of "use" of the trademarks.[14] This obligation, taken alone, means that registered trademarks remain registered and therefore benefit from their Article 16.1 rights. A reading that the trademarks remain registered but are deprived of all of the rights of registration would make no sense. Subsequently, the negotiators added an *additional* requirement that the use of such trademarks should also not be prejudiced on the grounds that they are similar to a GI. It is this *additional* obligation that the EC is now using to assert that the *only* trademark right preserved under Article 24.5 is the right to use the trademark in commerce, and that Article 24.5 no longer preserves the right to exclude all others. In other words, the EC is reading the language that *clarifies* and *adds* to the protection for grandfathered trademarks as a *denial* of the key protection given specifically to grandfathered trademarks: the right to exclude.

---

[14] See Exhibit US-25.

65. In addition, during this same period, the negotiators tightened the requirement not to "refuse or invalidate" trademark registrations up to a requirement not to even "prejudice" the validity of such registrations or the right to use the trademark. This emphasizes further that the negotiators were increasing the protection of grandfathered trademarks, not reducing it.

66. The EC's interpretation, therefore, simply makes no sense from the ordinary meaning of the text, and is contradicted by the negotiating history.

67. Further, the EC's interpretation of these terms is inconsistent with their context. When Article 24.5 refers to the "right to use a trademark," the Panel should keep in mind that a trademark is "used" by its owner—how?—to distinguish his goods from the goods of others. If that owner is not able to exclude all others from using confusingly similar signs—*i.e.*, to maintain the distinctiveness of his trademark as a source-identifier—his ability to use the trademark to distinguish his goods is severely prejudiced. As recognized by Advocate General Jacobs of the European Court of Justice in HAG II,[15] a trademark can only fulfill its role of identifying the manufacturer and guaranteeing quality if it is exclusive: the exclusive right of trademark owners to prevent confusing uses is the core of the trademark right.[16] As the EC itself suggests, the TRIPS Agreement negotiators knew how to draft a provision that required some accommodation between the rights of different right holders, for instance, in the area of two homonymous wine GIs. Article 24.5 is not such a provision.

68. The EC questions why certain wine labeling regulations in the United States appear to permit grandfathered trademarks to co-exist with later geographical indications. Although this question is not relevant, as this dispute involves neither wine nor US regulations, suffice it to say that, even where the wine labeling regulations permit the use of terms that may be similar to trademarks, US courts have confirmed that the trademark owner fully retains his exclusive right to prevent confusing uses of his signs.

Article 24.3 of the TRIPS Agreement

69. Having failed to show that Article 14(3) of the GI Regulation provides TRIPS Article 16.1 rights to trademark owners, and having failed to show that Article 24.5 of the TRIPS Agreement permits the EC to prejudice those rights freely, the EC next argues that Article 24.3 of the TRIPS Agreement *requires* the EC to deprive trademark owners of their Article 16.1 rights. According to the EC, this is because Article 24.3 requires that, in implementing protections for GIs, a Member may not diminish the protection of GIs that existed before the TRIPS Agreement entered into force. Therefore, according to the EC, Article 24.3 requires the EC to maintain "co-existence of geographical indications and earlier trademarks."[17]

70. This view is misguided. To begin, as in the case of Article 24.5, Article 24.3 is an exception with respect to the implementation of the *GI* section of the TRIPS Agreement. It is not an exception to the implementation of the trademark obligations. The meaning of Article 24.3 is that GIs should be protected in accordance with the GI section of the TRIPS Agreement, but that the protection provided those GIs should not diminish the protections for GIs that existed when the TRIPS Agreement came into force. Article 24.3 does not impose any such exceptions on the obligation to provide trademark rights under Article 16.1.

71. Under the EC's interpretation, Article 24.3 would create a major and permanent exception to the *trademark section* of the TRIPS Agreement. It would require a Member to apply all aspects of a pre-TRIPS GI regime to all GIs—including those registered after January 1, 1996—even though this means that the Member would *never* fully implement the rights granted trademark owners by Article 16.1.

72. The Panel should recall that the TRIPS Agreement text, and Article 24.3 in particular, was essentially agreed to by December 1991, three years before the WTO Agreement came into force. The EC GI Regulation

---

[15] Exhibit US-9.

[16] Exhibit US-9.

[17] EC First Written Submission, para. 312.

entered into force a year and a half later, on June 5, 1993. Under the EC's expansive reading of Article 24.3—that is, requiring a freezing of GI protection systems regardless of *any* WTO obligation (and not just the GI obligations)—a Member could have put in place a GI "protection" regime that exempted GI owners from the copyright and patent disciplines, or, indeed, any other WTO obligations, and then pointed to Article 24.3 as a broad exception to those obligations.

73. Plainly, this reading is incorrect. Article 24.3 is an exception to the implementation of protections for GIs, not an exception to the implementation of trademark—or other WTO—obligations.

Article 17 of the TRIPS Agreement

74. Finally, the EC argues that, as permitted by Article 17 of the TRIPS Agreement, the GI Regulation constitutes a limited exception to trademark protection—the fair use of descriptive terms—that takes account of the legitimate interests of the owner of the trademark and of third parties.

75. The EC's assertions would be more credible if the EC had not specifically *rejected* a proposed amendment to Article 14(2) of the GI Regulation that would have clarified that the trademark rules on "fair use" exceptions apply to GIs.[18] But this amendment was rejected in favor of the much broader "exception" provided for under the GI Regulation. A limited exception to trademark protection, such as that provided by a "fair use" exception, takes account of the legitimate interests of the trademark owner and of third parties on a case-by-case basis, depending on the manner in which a descriptive term is used. For example, it should be possible to inform consumers about the origin of a product and its characteristics through the use of descriptive terms in a non-trademark sense without affirmatively confusing the consumer about the source of the goods. It is possible simultaneously to protect the legitimate interests of the consumer, the GI owner and the trademark owner. The GI Regulation makes no such distinctions, however, but simply offers a broad immunity against actions by trademark owners, based purely on whether a particular GI has been registered. Further, with respect to the scope of the so-called "exception," the GI Regulation entirely eliminates the trademark holder's right to prevent confusing uses by all others, which is the whole core of his legitimate interest. This is not a limited exception and it does not take into account the legitimate interests of the owner of the trademark or, indeed, of the consumer. Consequently, the EC GI Regulation does not satisfy the requirements of Article 17 of the TRIPS Agreement.

Conclusion

76. Mr. Chairman, members of the Panel, this concludes the oral presentation of the United States this morning. We thank you for your attention and, indeed, for your willingness to serve on this Panel to review the important issues presented by this dispute. We look forward to our further discussions this afternoon and tomorrow.

---

[18] *See* Exhibit US-21.

ANNEX A-4

REPLIES BY THE UNITED STATES TO QUESTIONS POSED BY THE PANEL AND THE EUROPEAN COMMUNITIES TO THE COMPLAINING PARTIES FOLLOWING THE FIRST SUBSTANTIVE MEETING

(8 July 2004)

Q1. To what extent is the Panel bound by the EC's interpretation of its own Regulation? ***USA, AUS, EC***

Response:

1. The Panel is not bound by the EC's interpretation of the GI Regulation. The Panel is charged under Article 11 of the DSU with making "an objective assessment of the matter before it, including an objective assessment of the facts of the case ..." Therefore, as the Appellate Body has emphasized, for instance, in *India – Patents (US)*,[1] panels often must make a detailed examination of the domestic law of a Member in order to assess the conformity of that law with WTO obligations.[2] In this capacity, the Panel is a finder of fact: the Panel should "establish the meaning" of municipal law, "as a factual element," to "check whether these factual elements constitute conduct" contrary to WTO law.[3] The party asserting the inconsistency—in this dispute, the United States and Australia—has the initial burden of setting out evidence and arguments sufficient to demonstrate the inconsistency; if that burden is met, it is up to the responding party—the EC—to bring forth evidence and arguments to disprove the claim.

2. In conducting the analysis of municipal law, panels and the Appellate Body have stated expressly that "we are not bound to accept the interpretation [of municipal law] presented by the [responding Member]."[4] In *India – Patents (US)*, the Appellate Body pointed out that if the panel were obliged to accept the interpretation of municipal law offered by India in that dispute, the consequence would be that "only India can assess whether Indian law is consistent with India's obligations under the WTO Agreement. This, clearly, cannot be so."[5] In that dispute, India's explanation for certain "contradictions" in its municipal law was rejected by the panel and the Appellate Body.[6] Further, for panels to accept uncritically the responding Member's interpretation of its own municipal law would preclude them from making their own "objective assessment" of the matter, including the "factual element" of municipal law.[7]

3. Although panels are not bound by the interpretation offered by a responding Member of its own legislation, the panel in *US – Section 301* suggested that the responding Member "can reasonably expect that considerable deference be given to its views on the meaning of its own law."[8] However, in making an objective assessment, panels must critically review the interpretation offered, as they would critically review any other

---

[1] Appellate Body Report, *India – Patent Protection for Pharmaceutical and Agricultural Chemical Products ("India – Patents (US) ,"* WT/DS50/AB/R, adopted 16 January 1998), para. 66 ("It is clear that an examination of the relevant aspects of Indian municipal law...is essential to determining whether India has complied with its obligations under Article 70.8(a). There was simply no way for the Panel to make this determination without engaging in an examination of Indian law.")

[2] *See also* Appellate Body Report, India—Patents (US) "), para. 67; Appellate Body Report, *United States – Anti-Dumping Measures on Certain Hot-Rolled Steel Products from Japan ("US – Hot-Rolled Steel ")*, WT/DS184/AB/R, adopted 23 August 2001, para. 200; panel report, *United States – Sections 301-310 of the Trade Act of 1974 ("US – Section 301 Trade Act ")*, WT/DS152/R, adopted 27 January 2000, para. 7.18; Panel Report, *United States – Anti-Dumping Act of 1916 – Complaint by the European Communities ("US – 1916 Act (EC) ")*, WT/DS136/R and Corr.1, adopted 26 September 2000, as upheld by the Appellate Body Report, WT/DS136/AB/R, WT/DS162/AB/R, paras. 6.48-6.50.

[3] Panel Report, *US – Section 301 Trade Act*, para. 7.18.

[4] Panel Report, *US – Section 301 Trade Act*, para. 7.19.

[5] Appellate Body Report, *India – Patents (US)*, para. 66.

[6] Appellate Body Report, *India – Patents (US)*, para. 70.

[7] See Panel Report, *US – 1916 Act (EC)*, para. 6.48.

[8] Panel Report, *US – Section 301 Trade Act*, para. 7.19

evidence pertaining to the facts. In that respect, panels should weigh the circumstances carefully and determine what credibility to ascribe to the interpretation offered.

4. In some circumstances, the interpretation may be the result of other legal instruments that pre-date the dispute. Thus, the panel in *US – Section 301* accorded particular credibility to the interpretation given by the United States to its law because that interpretation was reflected in an authoritative statement of administrative action ("SAA"), issued by the President prior to the dispute, and approved by the US Congress.[9]

5. In this dispute, by contrast, the question is perhaps not how much weight to give to the EC's interpretation, but which of the conflicting interpretations to take into account: that consistently provided to WTO Members in the years leading up to the EC's first written submission in this proceeding, or that provided for the very first time in the EC's first written submission.

6. Related to this question are the questions of the Panel to the EC concerning whether the Commission's interpretation of Regulation No. 2081/92 is "binding on the European Communities" (question 15); what would be the most authoritative statement of the interpretation of the Regulation in European Community law (question 15); and whether the EC member States and the Council are bound by the Commission's interpretation of the Regulation (question 70).

7. As these questions also bear on the weight that the Panel should give to the Commission's interpretation of this measure in this dispute, the United States would like to offer its views on these questions.

8. According to Article 220 of the EC Treaty, the Court of Justice of the European Communities ("ECJ") and the Court of First Instance are responsible for "ensuring that in the interpretation and application" of EC law "the law is observed."[10] The Court has interpreted this provision to mean that it is the "ultimate interpretive authority in relation to the EC Treaty."[11] The ECJ is the highest court of EC law, and only its interpretation of the EC GI Regulation would be binding on the institutions and member States of the EC. Although it is true that in many, if not all, WTO Members, the highest authority for interpretation of a domestic law is the courts, there are particular aspects of the EC system that are distinct from other Members' systems and that are relevant to the Panel's consideration of the evidence in this dispute.

9. For instance, the EC Treaty specifically envisages that the Commission may incorrectly interpret or apply EC law, and the Treaty lays down judicial procedures for action to be taken against the Commission (Articles 230 and 232 of the EC Treaty). This underscores that, in EC law, the Commission's interpretation of EC law does not appear to have any special authority under EC law itself and may in fact be wrong.

10. A good example of this is the so-called "comfort letters" issued by the Commission in the exercise of its powers in the field of competition law. Where commercial parties notify an agreement to the Commission seeking an exemption under Article 81(3) of the EC Treaty, the Commission may respond through an informal "comfort letter." This letter expresses the opinion of the Commission on the interpretation and application of EC competition laws. The letter binds the Commission. However, if the agreement is challenged in a national court, the national court is not bound by the Commission opinion. Indeed, according to the ECJ, the national court is not even obliged to take the Commission opinion into account, although it "may" do so.[12]

---

[9] *See* Panel Report, *US – Section 301 Trade Act*, paras. 7.111 and 7.112.

[10] The EC Treaty provisions discussed in this response are included as Exhibit US-26.

[11] EU Law (2nd edition), Craig and De Burca, p. 30. Exhibit US-27. *See also* the ECJ's Opinion 1/91 on the Draft European Free Trade Agreement, [1991] I-ECR 6079, para. 35, where the ECJ explains that, "in the allocation of responsibilities defined in the Treaties," it has the "exclusive jurisdiction" for ensuring that "the law is observed." Exhibit US-28. In the ECJ's Opinion 1/92, also on the Draft European Free Trade Agreement, [1992] I-2821, para. 22, the ECJ states that its decisions are "binding" in the Community legal order, pursuant to Article 220 of the EC Treaty (formerly Article 164). Exhibit US-29.

[12] Bellamy & Child, European Community Law of Competition (5th edition, Roth), para. 10-028, citing Case 99/79 *Lancome v. Etos* [1980] ECR 2511. Exhibit US-30.

11. In the same vein, in proceedings before the ECJ, the Commission generally submits a brief. However, the Commission's brief carries no greater weight before the ECJ than a brief submitted by a private party, or by one of the other Community institutions or an EC member State. In many cases, the ECJ does not even accept the Commission's interpretation of provisions of Community law.

12. Therefore, it follows that the interpretation of the EC GI Regulation offered by the Commission to the Panel in this dispute (particularly in light of the fact that this interpretation contradicts all previous interpretations provided by the EC) is not binding upon the European Communities. It is no more than the opinion of the Commission and has no special authority.

13. The significance of this fact for this Panel might be illustrated by an example. Assume that, in applying its interpretation of the GI Regulation, the Commission grants an application for registration of a GI for a product from a WTO Member that has not received approval pursuant to Article 12(3) of the GI Regulation. The Commission would, by that act, have failed to apply the provisions of Articles 12 and 12a, which state that an application can only be entertained from only those third countries that have received approval under Article 12(3). In other words, the Commission would have registered a GI in circumstances where the Council had legislated that no GI should be registered.

14. In that case, the Commission's act would be open to challenge before the ECJ by any member State or by the Council or European Parliament, under Article 230 of the EC Treaty. Further, natural or legal persons that are directly and individually concerned by the decision could also challenge the Commission's act. In those proceedings, the Commission's interpretation of the Regulation would not be binding upon the ECJ. To the contrary, the ECJ could reach the view that the Commission was not entitled to disregard the requirements in Article 12(1) and 12(3).

15. In that regard, the ECJ has already ruled that "the WTO agreements are not in principle among the rules in the light of which the Court is to review the legality of measures adopted by the Community institutions."[13] In other words, the ECJ would not entertain the Commission's argument that it was entitled to disregard the terms of the Regulation in order to comply with WTO law. Instead, the ECJ will apply EC legislation even if that legislation is WTO-inconsistent.[14]

16. The only exception to this appears to be where the EC legislation "intended to implement a particular obligation assumed in the context of the WTO agreements, or where the Community measure refers expressly to the precise provisions of the WTO agreements."[15] In that event, the ECJ will examine whether EC legislation is consistent with the WTO obligations it seeks to implement. However, even in that case, the ECJ would not allow the Commission simply to disregard provisions of a Regulation. The Commission must apply the legislation. If the Commission considered that the legislation was WTO-inconsistent it could have challenged the Council's adoption of the legislation before the ECJ under Article 230 of the EC Treaty.

17. The Panel should also be aware that, according to Article 211 of the EC Treaty, the Commission has a responsibility in EC law for ensuring that the EC Treaty and secondary legislation "are applied." In that respect, if the Commission takes the view that an EC member State or another institution has failed to respect EC law, the Commission may bring proceedings to the ECJ under Articles 226, 230 or 232 of the EC Treaty. However, the Commission's responsibility under Article 211 does not confer any special status upon the Commission's interpretation of EC law. The other institutions, and the Member States, can and do take different views from

---

[13] Case C-93/02 P, *Biret International SA v. Council of the European Union*, judgment of 30 September 2003, para. 52. Exhibit US-31.

[14] *See* Case C-149/96, *Portuguese Republic v. Council of the European Union*, judgment of 23 November 1999, paras. 49—52. Exhibit US-32. Portugal argued that a Council decision concerning market access for textiles from Pakistan was contrary to Community law as it was inconsistent with WTO law. The ECJ declined to examine the WTO law arguments and held that the Council decision could not be challenged for these reasons. The ECJ found that the arguments on WTO law were "unfounded," without any substantive inquiry. In essence, the ECJ has already accepted, therefore, that Council legislation may well be WTO-inconsistent and must still be applied in the EC legal order.

[15] *Biret International SA*, para. 53. Exhibit US-31.

the Commission as to the meaning of EC law. At the end of the day, it is for the ECJ to ensure that "the law is observed," according to Article 220.

18. For all these reasons, the Panel should not accord any particular deference to the Commission's most recent interpretation of the GI Regulation, newly minted for purposes of this dispute, taken alone. This new interpretation does not appear to be based on any published official notice; it appears to run counter to the terms of the Regulation; and does not appear to be authoritative or binding as a matter of EC law. Further, as discussed above, the United States has substantial concerns that the EC's interpretation would not stand up to ECJ review.

Q2. Can the procedures under Articles 5 and 6 of Regulation (EC) No. 2081/92 apply to names of geographical areas located outside the EC? ***EC***

Q3. Did the phrase "[w]ithout prejudice to international agreements" in Article 12(1) of Regulation (EC) No. 2081/92 predate the TRIPS Agreement? Did it refer to any specific agreements when it was adopted? Which agreements does it refer to now? Would it cover bilateral agreements for the protection of individual geographical indications? ***EC***

Q4. Is it unusual that the text of Article 12(1) of Regulation (EC) No. 2081/92 covers only a small number of countries that are non-WTO Members, but the introductory phrase "[w]ithout prejudice to international agreements" covers the entire membership of the WTO? Why was this structure retained when the Regulation was amended in April 2003? ***EC***

Q5. In paragraph 8 of the US oral statement it is implied that the purpose of the phrase "[w]ithout prejudice to international agreements" in Article 12(1) of Regulation (EC) No. 2081/92 is to reserve the EC's flexibility to protect specific non-EC GIs through bilateral agreements. In the US view, in what way does the phrase apply to bilateral agreements? Please also explain on what basis the US draws the distinction between bilateral and other international agreements. ***USA***

Response:

19. The "without prejudice" language recognizes that international agreements may lay down specific GI rules (*i.e.*, either directly specifying GI protection for specific names or specifying procedures and requirements for protecting GIs from the parties to that agreement). In such an event, the specific regime established in the international agreement will be applied directly.

20. As context and by way of background, the EC has sought and granted protection to specific geographical indications in bilateral agreements with individual countries. Such provisions are contained, for instance, in the EC's agreement in the wine sector with Canada, Chile, and South Africa, among others, in which EC-wide GI protection is granted to specific GI terms listed in those agreements under specific procedures.[16] And, indeed, the basic EC wine regulation, Council Regulation (EC) 1493/1999, provides that imported wines bearing a geographical indication may be eligible for the EC's protection and control scheme for geographical indications "subject to reciprocity."[17] Further, the EC's wine labeling regulation, containing rules for applying Regulation 1493, makes the use of GIs for wine from third countries subject to a requirement

[16] *See, e.g.*, Agreement between Canada and the European Community on Trade in Wines and Spirit Drinks, Articles 10 and 11 ("In implementation of paragraphs 1 and 2, after receiving an official application by diplomatic note from Canada justifying that the names in paragraph 1 are geographical indications, the Community shall take the necessary steps to have the names listed in Annex III (b) protected by the competent authorities responsible for enforcement so that any wines incorrectly presented or described with a protected Canadian geographical indication are not placed on, or are withdrawn from, the market"). Exhibit US-33. *See also* Agreement Between the European Community and the Republic of South Africa on Trade in Wine,
http://europa.eu.int/eur-lex/pri/en/oj/dat/2002/l_028/l_02820020130en00040105.pdf;

[17] Council Regulation (EC) No. 1493/1999 of 17 May 1999, OJ L 179, 14.7.1999, page 1, Annex VII (G)(4). Exhibit US-34.

that they not give rise to confusion with the geographical indication of "another imported wine included in the lists in agreements concluded between the Community and third countries." [18]

21. In other words, in this area, the EC provides certain general rules for the use of GIs from third countries, but makes those rules subject to specific agreements that the EC has reached with certain third countries with respect to protection of specific GIs.

22. Similarly, in the non-wine context, the Joint Declaration included in the bilateral agreement between Switzerland and the EC "on the protection of geographical indications and designation or origin of agricultural products and foodstuffs" specifically anticipates special rules concerning both the registration of Swiss GIs and the inspection structures to be required of Switzerland:

> [t]he Parties shall provide for provision on the mutual protection of PDOs and PGIs to be incorporated in the Agreement on trade in agricultural products on the basis of equivalent legislation, as regards both the conditions governing the registration of PDOs and PGIs and the arrangement on controls.

23. Thus, to provide for the likelihood that these "conditions governing [PDO and PGI] registration" and the "arrangement on controls" will not necessarily mimic exactly the conditions and inspection structures required in the EC GI Regulation, the GI Regulation states that the conditions and inspection structures required of third countries in the GI Regulation are "[w]ithout prejudice to international agreements," such as that negotiated with Switzerland.

24. There are other examples of bilateral agreements to which the "without prejudice" language would appear to apply. For instance, there are bilateral agreements for the protection of specific GIs between member States of the EC and third countries, such as those between Austria and the Czechoslovak Republic and between Portugal and the Czechoslovak Republic on the protection of specific Czech GIs.[19] As the Supreme Court of Justice in Portugal noted in a case involving the latter agreement, the language of the GI Regulation—"[w]ithout prejudice to international agreements"—is aimed at excluding from "its field of application the third countries which are parties in agreements entered into with member States."[20] There are other bilateral and plurilateral agreements involving member States on GIs. Examples are provided in WTO document, IP/C/W/85/Add.1, 2 July 1999, Overview of Existing International Notification and Registration Systems for Geographical Indications Relating to Products Other Than Wines and Spirits, (Note by the Secretariat). As discussed above, certain of these agreements provide GI protection for specific names (examples include the Austria / Czechoslovak agreement that protects a list of named GIs) and the (plurilateral) Stresa Convention,[21] which protects a large number of names of cheeses.

25. In addition, the EC is also seeking more specific agreements on GIs. For instance, Article 46(4) of the Cotonou Agreement states that the EC, its member States and the ACP countries may enter into agreements on the protection of "geographical indications for products of particular interest" to the parties. The EC is also

---

[18] Article 36(3) of Commission Regulation (EC) No. 753/2002 of 29 April 2002, laying down certain rules for applying Council Regulation (EC) No. 1493 as regards the description, designation, presentation and protection of certain wine sector products, OJ L 118, 4.5.2002, p. 1. Exhibit US-35.

[19] *See* Case C-216/01, *Budejovicky Budvar v. Rudolf Ammersin*, judgment of 18 November 2003, paras. 70 and 71 (where the French government asserted that the "without prejudice" language preserved the protections offered by the Austrian-Czechoslovak Agreement; the ECJ did not have to address that assertion, however, since the case was decided on other grounds). At the time of the dispute, the Czech Republic, a successor State to the Czechoslovak Republic, was not a member State of the European Union and was, therefore, a third country for these purposes. Exhibit US-36.

[20] Exhibit US-37.

[21] Signed on 1 June 1951 and entered into force on 12 July 1953. To date the contracting parties are Austria, Denmark, France, Italy, The Netherlands, Norway and Switzerland.

engaged in negotiations with China on a bilateral agreement on GIs. (see http://europa.eu.int/comm/external_relations/china/intro/sect.htm).

26. In the context of all of these specific bilateral and plurilateral agreements, the "without prejudice" language allows the Commission to apply the specific GI protection regimes established by international agreements independently of the Regulation. For instance, if the EC concludes an agreement with a third country to provide GI protection for named agricultural products from that country, there is no need to use the registration procedures in the Regulation. The Commission can simply insert the names concerned in the register on the basis of the newly established international regime and the "without prejudice" language in the GI Regulation.

27. Similarly, if an international agreement were to lay down special procedures governing the registration of GIs for products from particular third countries, the Regulation would not prevent the Commission from applying these procedures directly, even though they are different from the procedures in the Regulation.

28. In these cases, the international agreement would be applied directly without need for implementing rules. In short, instead of applying the Regulation, the Commission would apply specific rules laid down in the agreement that deal with the particular fact situation. And the Commission would derive authority for its act directly from the international regime to which it specifically applies, displacing the general rules in the EC GI Regulation.

29. In the case of the national treatment obligation in the TRIPS Agreement, by contrast, there is no specific international registration regime for the Commission to apply. The Commission does not even purport to be applying an international regime of any kind. Instead, the Commission appears to acknowledge that it is applying the Community registration regime. However, apparently because of the requirements of the national treatment obligation in the TRIPS Agreement, the Commission now says it has to apply the Community regime differently from the regime the Council adopted.

30. The Commission is, therefore, purporting to apply a regime that is not provided for either in an international agreement or in Community law. In short, there are no specific rules in an international agreement to apply; instead, the Commission now purports to be taking it upon itself to modify the Community general rules.

31. But the "without prejudice" language does not authorize the Commission to apply rules that have no legal basis whatsoever, be it in international law or Community law. Furthermore, in general Community law, as the United States understands it, the Commission does not enjoy the legal authority to modify or refuse to apply a Council Regulation. Only the Council can modify its own Regulation.

32. Accordingly, the Commission appears to have no legal authority to receive GI applications for products from a third country unless the third country has requested, and been granted, approval by the Commission, pursuant to Article 12(3) of the Regulation.

33. With respect to the Panel's question about whether these agreements are necessarily "bilateral," the EC has generally sought reciprocal treatment, which implies that in general such agreements are bilateral. But the United States notes that the EC is also negotiating agreements in the wine sector with Mercosur, which would probably be characterized as plurilateral, and also notes the example of the Stresa Convention, discussed above, which is also plurilateral. It is, of course, possible for a multilateral agreement to provide for specific procedures and conditions for registering and protecting certain GIs of all parties to the agreement, as the EC has negotiated on a bilateral basis and plurilateral basis in the past. But, for the reasons mentioned above, the WTO Agreement is not such an agreement.

Q6. What meaning does Australia give to the phrase "[w]ithout prejudice to international agreements" in Article 12(1) of Regulation (EC) No. 2081/92? ***AUS***

Q7. Do the last sentence of Article 12(3) of Regulation (EC) No. 2081/92 and the first clause in Article 12a "[i]n the case provided for in Article 12(3)" limit the applicability of Article 12a? ***EC***

Q8. Which references to a "third country" in Articles 12, 12a, 12b and 12d of Regulation (EC) No. 2081/92 include all WTO Members, and which do not? What, in the context of each reference, indicates what "third country" means? Why are different terms not used? ***EC***

Q9. Why is it that only the rights of objection in Articles 12b(2)(a) and 12d(1) of Regulation (EC) No. 2081/92 mention a "WTO Member" or "WTO member country"? Is it relevant that Regulation (EC) No. 692/2003 explained, in its 10th recital, that in the matter of objections the provisions in question apply without prejudice to international agreements but, in its 9th recital, it explained that the protection provided by registration is open to third countries' names by reciprocity and under equivalence conditions? ***EC***

Q10. Has the Commission recognized any countries under the procedure set out in Article 12(3) of Regulation (EC) No. 2081/92? Have any countries requested to be recognized under that procedure? ***EC***

Q11. Has an application for registration under Regulation (EC) No. 2081/92 ever been made in respect of the name of a geographical area located outside the EC? If so, what happened? ***EC***

Q12. Has any group or a natural or legal person interested in a geographical indication for agricultural products or foodstuffs originating in your territory ever sent a registration application to your authorities pursuant to Regulation (EC) No. 2081/92? If not, do you know the reason? ***USA, AUS***

Response:

34. As the United States explained to the Panel during its first meeting, there is no office established within the US Government for processing applications for GI registrations in the EC; nor is the United States in a position to assess whether any such application would meet the requirements of the EC GI Regulation, as that regulation requires.[22] Therefore it is not clear to whom such an application would be sent.

35. However, after consulting various agencies in the US Government, it does not appear that any applications have been submitted, although there have been discussions with private sector stakeholders about the lack of access to the EC GI system. The United States is not privy to all of the reasons that a person with a US-based GI would not file an application. However, as illustrated by the case of the Idaho Potato Commission, which protects "Idaho Potatoes" as a certification mark in the United States, such rightholders recognize that it would be futile to apply, because the United States does not satisfy the GI Regulation's equivalence and reciprocity requirements.

36. In testimony presented to the Committee on Agriculture in the US House of Representatives on July 22, 2003, a representative of the Idaho Potato Commission testified that, in order to achieve GI protection under the GI Regulation, the country seeking GI protection for its nationals has to show that it "has essentially adopted the EU system for protecting GI's. This puts the EU in the position of evaluating the laws of another WTO Member, and then making a determination that their system for protecting GI's is reciprocal to the laws of the EU."[23] Testifying that "the existing US certification mark system is not, in the view of the EU, sufficient," he concluded that there was no way for US agricultural producers to achieve such protection. He further stated that "the attorneys we have retained in the EU to investigate and advise us of any recourse that

[22] Article 12a(2) of the GI Regulation.

[23] *See* Exhibit US-38, at p. 352.

might be available to us have all reached the same conclusions: the EU system has simply shut us out. We are powerless to protect our name in the EU, but EU nationals are free to register and use our name."[24]

37. As far as the United States is aware, the situation of the Idaho Potato Commission is not unique, and its view of the situation, which has been set out in public statements, is shared by many relevant stakeholders in the United States. For instance the US Dairy Export Council and the National Milk Producers Federation have also complained to the US Government that, absent EC-equivalent legislation in the United States, US persons are not eligible to register their GIs in the EU.[25]

38. Further, neither the Idaho Potato Commission nor any other US stakeholder would have received contrary information from the US Government. To the contrary, as discussed in the US first written submission, the EC has made clear on numerous occasions, including during five years of consultations, that the United States would have to satisfy the conditions of reciprocity and equivalence to have US-based GIs registered, and that the United States does not satisfy those conditions. Indeed, responding on January 16, 2003, to the US concern about conditioning the availability of GI registration on equivalence and reciprocity, *the EC specifically wrote that "it is true that US GIs cannot be registered in the EU,"* but claimed that other avenues for protection (*e.g.*, member State unfair competition rules) were available.[26]

39. In other words, the lack of applications appears to result from the success of the EC GI Regulation in erecting barriers to those applications.

Q13. What discretion does the Commission enjoy in the application of Regulation (EC) No. 2081/92? ***EC***

Q14. Please express your view on whether and to what extent the mandatory/discretionary distinction in GATT and WTO jurisprudence applies under the TRIPS Agreement. Would the nature of those TRIPS obligations which are not prohibitions but rather oblige Members to take certain actions, affect the application of the distinction? ***USA, AUS, EC***

Response:

40. In this dispute, the EC has argued, at para. 12 of its oral statement[27]

> In order to substantiate their claim, the complainants should have established that Regulation 2081/92 mandates necessarily the registration of later confusing geographical indications. In turn, this would have required them to show that Article 14(3) cannot be interpreted in a manner which allows the registering authority to refuse the registration of confusing geographical indications. At the very least, the complainants should have established that, in practice, Article 14(3) is being interpreted and applied in a manner which results in a consistent pattern of registrations of confusing geographical indications. The complainants have proved none of this. Indeed, they have not even attempted to do so. As mentioned, their complaint is purely theoretical. The Panel, therefore, should conclude that, as a matter of fact, the complainants' claim would be unfounded even on their own interpretation of Article 16.1 of the TRIPS Agreement.

41. This is not a proper application of the mandatory/discretionary analysis. Article 16.1 of the TRIPS Agreement requires Members to provide owners of registered trademarks with certain exclusive rights to prevent confusing uses of signs, including GIs. A WTO Member cannot decline to provide this right,

---

[24] Exhibit US-38 at p. 353.

[25] *See* Letter from US Dairy Export Council and the National Milk Producers Federation to the Office of the United States Trade Representative, dated March 26, 2004. Exhibit US-39.

[26] *See* Exhibit US-40.

[27] *See also*, EC First Written Submission, paras. 277 and 292.

guaranteed by the TRIPS Agreement, on the grounds that the *owner* of the registered trademark is unlikely to need it in light of how the *EC* might apply Article 14(3). Yet, that is just what the EC is arguing. Further, Article 14(3) cannot substitute entirely for this right. First, Article 14(3) applies only in the case of possible confusion with trademarks "in light of a trade mark's reputation and renown and the length of time it has been used." By contrast, Article 16.1 rights are required regardless of the reputation, renown, or length of time of use of the registered trademark. More significant, however, Article 14(3) cannot substitute entirely for TRIPS Article 16.1 rights because it is not possible to determine with certainty at the time of registration whether the use of a GI will likely result in confusion with a registered trademark, as such a determination is made on a case-by-case basis, and may require an evaluation of the use of the GI in the marketplace.

42. Simply stated, the EC cannot provide the required exclusive rights to owners of registered trademarks under TRIPS Article 16.1 by invoking the unrealistic hope that the EC authorities will make the exercise of those rights unnecessary through the use of Article 14(3) of the GI Regulation. The EC is incorrect in stating that to establish its TRIPS Article 16.1 claim, the United States "would need to prove that Regulation 2081/92 mandates necessarily the registration of confusing geographic indications."[28] The issue is not whether the EC has the legal discretion to grant or deny the registration of GIs when there is the possibility of confusion with any trademark (although the EC does not have such discretion.). The issue is whether the EC is providing *owners* of registered trademarks with the rights required by Article 16.1.

43. Thus, in the context of this dispute, a breach has been established through the failure of the EC to provide the right in question in its municipal law. The mandatory/discretionary analysis is not required in this particular instance. This is not to say, however, that it might not be relevant in other TRIPS Agreement contexts, including where the TRIPS Agreement obliges Members to take certain actions. For example, if a Member maintains a measure which affirmatively precludes the Member's authorities from taking required actions, under a mandatory/discretionary analysis, the measure would mandate a breach of the TRIPS Agreement obligation.

44. Finally, the EC has no basis for alleging that a challenge to the EC GI Regulation requires a showing of a "consistent pattern" of registering confusing GIs. As described above, the EC is obligated to provide a right in its municipal law, and it is not. Nevertheless, the United States notes that in the one invocation of Article 14(3) cited by the EC, the Commission decided to register the name Bayerisches Bier as a GI, notwithstanding having been informed of a trademark ("Bavaria") used for beer that included that name (apparently in translation).[29] This specific application of the Regulation does not give the United States much confidence that Article 14(3) fulfills the Article 16.1 rights of registered trademark owners.

Q15. What would be the most authoritative statement of the interpretation of Regulation (EC) No. 2081/92? Is a statement by the EC delegation to this Panel legally binding on the European Communities? ***EC***

Response:

See response to question 1.

Q16. Can the EC provide the Panel with any official statement predating its first written submission that names of geographical areas located in all WTO Members could be registered under Regulation (EC) No. 2081/92 without satisfying its equivalence and reciprocity conditions? ***EC***

Response:

45. *See* Exhibit US-40, in which, in a communication to the United States, the EC confirmed that US GIs "cannot be registered in the EU." *See also* Exhibit US-44 (slide 14/15).

---

[28] EC First Written Submission, para. 277.

[29] See Exhibit US-41.

Q17. Is the EC's explanation of the availability of registration of foreign GIs under its system, set out in its written statement to the Council for TRIPS in September 2002, (IP/C/M/37/Add.1, para. 142 and Annex, pp. 77-85) consistent with the text of Articles 12-12c of the Regulation? Why did that written statement not qualify the position that the Regulation's equivalence and reciprocity conditions apply to foreign GIs, if they did not apply to WTO Members, to whom the statement was addressed? ***EC***

Q18. Did the EC member States agree with the Commission's written statement to the Council for TRIPS in September 2002 with respect to the conditions attached to the registration of foreign GIs? How can the Commission ensure that the Council of Ministers will not prevent registration under the Regulation of the name of a geographical area located in a third country WTO Member because that Member does not satisfy the equivalence and reciprocity conditions of Article 12(1)? ***EC***

Q19. Has a judicial authority ever ruled on the availability of protection provided by registration for third countries under Regulation (EC) No. 2081/92? If the Commission registered the name of a geographical area located in a third country WTO Member, could that registration be subject to judicial review because the area was located in a WTO Member that did not fulfil the equivalence and reciprocity conditions of Article 12(1) of the Regulation? ***EC***

Q20. With reference to paragraph 43 of the EC's oral statement, does the EC contest that equivalence and reciprocity conditions such as those under Article 12(1) and (3) of Regulation (EC) No. 2081/92, if applied to other WTO Members, would be inconsistent with the national treatment obligations in the TRIPS Agreement and/or Article III:4 of the GATT 1994? ***EC***

Q21. If Switzerland, as a WTO Member, can apply for registration of its GIs under Regulation (EC) No. 2081/92 without satisfying equivalence and reciprocity conditions, what was the purpose of its joint declaration with the EC concerning GIs set out in Exhibit US-6 and mentioned in paragraph 119 of the US first written submission and paragraphs 243-244 of the EC's first written submission? ***USA, AUS, EC***

Response:

46. While the United States cannot speak for Switzerland, in the view of the United States, if there were *no* requirement for equivalence and reciprocity in the GI Regulation, as the EC maintains, it would make little sense for Switzerland to agree to "mutual protection" of GIs "on the basis of equivalent legislation." In effect, Switzerland would be agreeing to more onerous requirements than would be required under the GI Regulation. By contrast, such an agreement would be useful if it meant that Switzerland did not have to meet the equivalence and reciprocity requirements in the GI Regulation.

Q22. Are there any legal requirements or other provisions in EC or national laws which ensure that groups or persons entitled to apply for registration under Article 5 of Regulation (EC) No. 2081/92 are always, or usually, EC citizens or legal persons organized under the laws of the EC or an EC member State? What conditions have been laid down for natural or legal persons to be entitled to apply for registration pursuant to Article 5(1)? ***USA, AUS, EC***

Response:

47. Under Article 5 of the GI Regulation, only an association of producers and/or processors working with the same agricultural product or foodstuff may apply for a GI registration; Article 2 of Commission Regulation (EEC) No 2037/93 of 17 July 1993[30] permits applications by a group of individuals without legal personality where national law treats such a group as a legal person. Under Article 5.2, "[a] group or a natural or a legal

[30] Laying down detailed rules of application of Council Regulation (EEC) no 2081/92 on the protection of geographical indications and designations of origin for agricultural products and foodstuffs, OJ L 185, 28.7.1993, p. 5 (Exhibit COMP-2.a).

person may apply for registration only in respect to agricultural products or foodstuffs which it produces or obtains" within a particular region. Therefore, with respect to applications for GIs referring to regions within the EC, it would appear to follow that those entitled to submit an application for EC-based GIs include legal persons under member State national law that produce or process products in a particular region of that member State; in other words, such applicants are, generally legal persons under the laws of the EC or the EC member State. Indeed, as a practical matter, any commercial entity growing agricultural products or processing foodstuffs in a member State of the EC will set up a legal entity under the laws of that member State for that purpose.

48. Of course, Article 12a, provides for applications from "a group or a natural or legal person as referred to in Article 5(1) and 5(2) in a third country" that satisfies the equivalence and reciprocity conditions, so the same considerations apply with respect to applicants from qualifying third countries: "legal persons" in such a third country producing or obtaining product in that third country may also be able to submit an application for their GIs.

Q23. How do you interpret the term "nationals" as used in Article 1.3, including footnote 1, and Articles 3.1 and 4 of the TRIPS Agreement and Article 2 of the Paris Convention (1967) in relation to this dispute? Do a Member's nationals necessarily include natural persons who are domiciled, or legal persons who have a real and effective industrial and commercial establishment, in that Member? ***USA, AUS, EC***

Response:

49. Article 1.3, footnote 1, specifies that "nationals" of a WTO Member that is a separate customs territory, such as the EC, means "persons, natural or legal, who are domiciled or who have a real and effective industrial or commercial establishment in that customs territory." This is a definition that applies to the TRIPS Agreement as a whole, so it is a definition that also applies to Articles 3.1 and 4 of the TRIPS Agreement. Thus, for instance, under Article 3.1, the EC has an obligation to accord nationals of other Members treatment no less favorable than it accords natural or legal persons who have a real and effective industrial or commercial establishment in the EC. Further, under Article 2 of the Paris Convention, "nationals" refers to both natural and legal persons,[31] and, under Article 3, persons that are not nationals of a Paris Union member country, but that are domiciled or that have a real and effective industrial or commercial establishment in the territory of one of the member countries, are also treated as nationals of that member country.

Q24. In your view, which natural or legal persons can be considered "interested parties" in the sense of Article 22.2 of the TRIPS Agreement? Is Article 10(2) of the Paris Convention (1967) relevant? ***USA, AUS, EC***

Response:

50. "Interested parties" is not defined in the TRIPS Agreement, but the ordinary meaning of the term under TRIPS Article 2.2 would include a party that has an interest in the subject matter of the geographical indication. Article 10(2) of the Paris Convention, which concerns similar subject matter to TRIPS Agreement Article 22 of the TRIPS Agreement (including false indications of geographical source), provides useful context that an "interested party" includes producers or sellers of the relevant goods that are either established and producing in the region falsely indicated as the source, or established and producing in the country where the false indication of source is used. Article 10 is relevant in this respect notably because it is one of the Paris Convention provisions specifically incorporated into the TRIPS Agreement by Article 2.1.[32]

---

[31] Bodenhausen, p. 27. Exhibit US-2.

[32] *See* Gervais, page 193 (The definition of interested party in Article 10(2) "is useful and may be used to interpret the expression "interested party" used in Article 22(2)). Exhibit US-42.

Q25. Is it appropriate to compare nationals who are interested in GIs that refer to areas located in different WTO Members in order to examine national treatment under the TRIPS Agreement? Why or why not? ***USA, AUS, EC***

Response:

51. GIs are by nature related to geographic territory. An analysis of national treatment requires comparing the treatment of different nationals with respect to the protection of their intellectual property. Therefore it is appropriate to compare the treatment of domestic nationals with respect to the protection of their home-based GIs to the treatment of foreign nationals with respect to the protection of their home-based GIs. In addition, as a practical matter, and particularly in the agricultural sector, which is intrinsically tied to the land, a measure that provides less favorable treatment to products originating in certain WTO Members also provides less favorable treatment to the nationals of that Member.

Q26. If national treatment can be examined in relation to GIs in terms of the location of the geographical area to the territory of a Member, is it appropriate to examine national treatment in relation to any other intellectual property rights in terms of an attachment to a Member besides the nationality of the right holder? Why or why not? ***USA, AUS, EC***

Response:

52. National treatment obligations should be analyzed on a case-by-case basis, based on the measure at issue, as well as on the particular type of intellectual property right; broad conclusions in the absence of a particular issue are difficult to formulate accurately. However, the United States notes that footnote 1 to Article 1.3 of the TRIPS Agreement defines "national" throughout the Agreement not in terms of nationality, but in terms of where a person is domiciled or where a person has a real and effective industrial or commercial establishment. Further, in Article 1.3, "nationals" of other Members include persons meeting certain criteria for protection under other international agreements. In the case of copyright, as an example, non-nationals that would be treated as nationals for purposes of protection under the Berne Convention would include non-nationals whose works are first published in a member country (Berne Convention, Article 3), or persons with "habitual residences" in such a country. Similarly, under the Rome Convention, there are points of attachment that are broader than mere nationality, including where a phonogram was first fixed, or where a performance took place, or where a broadcast originated.

53. Geographical indications may be different from other forms of intellectual property in the degree to which they are related to the territories of the Parties, but finding points of attachment that go beyond mere "nationality" in a technical sense is not unusual.

Q27. Can the Panel assume that it is likely that interested parties in relation to names of geographical areas located in a Member are nationals of that Member? Have the complainants attempted to gather data on the relative numbers of EC, and non-EC, interested parties in names of geographical areas located within, and outside, the EC that might be eligible for registration under Regulation (EC) No. 2081/92? Would such data be relevant? ***USA, AUS***

Response:

54. Any meaningful and realistic appraisal of whether a measure provides less favorable treatment to nationals with respect to geographical indications would take into account that nationals have an interest in GIs in the country of their nationality, particularly with respect to agricultural products and foodstuffs. Therefore, a measure that provides less favorable treatment of, for instance, agricultural products from the United States would provide less favorable treatment to the US nationals that produce them.

55. Further, since the EC's requirements have discouraged anyone from applying for GI registration with respect to GIs in the United States, it is not possible to determine whether, for instance, there are any French nationals who would, in the absence of the barriers in the EC GI Regulation, seek to register a US-based GI in the EC.

56. In addition, as further support for this obvious link, the United States conducted a search for certification mark applications by French, German, Spanish and Italian nationals. As the Panel is aware, the United States protects geographical indications through certification marks (although certification marks can include subject matter that goes beyond "geographical indications" as defined in the TRIPS Agreement or the EC GI Regulation). The results are attached as Exhibit US-43, and show that nationals of a country typically register names that refer to geographical areas from the territory of their nationality. For example, the certification mark applications and registrations from French nationals include names of French geographic origin, and not names of US origin. The same is true of applications from German, Italian, and Spanish nationals. Similarly, Exhibit 43 includes a sample search of US entities with registered certification marks referring to selected food products, which shows that those entities are interested in geographical areas in the United States.

57. However, in the view of the United States, such data, while they might be obvious, are not necessary, because of the obvious link between the natural and legal persons who would seek GI protection for agricultural products and foodstuffs and the territory of the Member in which they are growing or producing such products.

Q28. Do you have information on the numbers of EC nationals who are interested parties in relation to GIs protected in your territory for agricultural products and foodstuffs other than wines and spirits? ***USA, AUS***

Response:

58. The information with respect to certification marks filed by various EC nationals, described in response to question 27, would suggest that EC nationals have an interest primarily in GIs referring to regions in their country of nationality. In addition, however, interested parties would also include those who are likely to be damaged by the registration of a GI—*e.g.*, an EC national using a generic term on a product exported to the United States, where there is an application at the USPTO to make that term proprietary. The United States has no way to know the number of EC nationals who are interested parties in this sense, but notes that any such parties are free to object to, or request cancellation of, the registration of a certification mark.

Q29. The Japan – Alcoholic Beverages II, Korea – Alcoholic Beverages and Chile – Alcoholic Beverages disputes show that measures which are origin-neutral on their face can be inconsistent with Article III of GATT 1994. Is Regulation (EC) No. 2081/92 also open to challenge under Article 3.1 of the TRIPS Agreement despite its apparently national-neutral text? ***EC***

Q30. In Article 2(1) of the Paris Convention (1967) as incorporated in the TRIPS Agreement by its Article 2.1, should the words "country of the Union" be read mutatis mutandis to refer to "WTO Member"? ***USA, AUS, EC***

Response:

59. Article 2.1 of the TRIPS Agreement requires WTO Members to "comply" with, *inter alia*, Article 2(1) of the Paris Convention, which imposes obligations with respect to the treatment of "[n]ationals of any country of the Union." Therefore, "country of the Union" should be read *mutatis mutandis* to refer to "WTO Member." The United States notes, however, that it is a WTO Member as well as a "country of the Union," so that its nationals are owed national treatment by the EC regardless of the interpretation of this phrase.

Q31. What is the respective scope of the national treatment obligations in Article 2(1) of the Paris Convention (1967) and Article 3.1 of the TRIPS Agreement? Do they overlap? ***USA, AUS, EC***

Response:

60. The national treatment obligations of the Paris Convention apply with respect to the protection of industrial property as defined in the Paris Convention. Those of the TRIPS Agreement apply to the protection of intellectual property as defined in the TRIPS Agreement. There is substantial overlap in these protections, but they are not entirely co-extensive.

61. With respect to the national treatment obligation itself, the scope of the obligation is slightly different in the Paris Convention compared to the TRIPS Agreement—notably, the Paris Convention requires that the "same protection" be granted to nationals of other Members as is granted to a Member's own nationals, whereas the TRIPS Agreement requires "no less favourable" treatment. However, the United States does not believe that this difference in scope is relevant for purposes of this dispute, as the treatment provided by the EC is neither the "same" nor "no less favorable." Similarly, the United States does not believe that the difference between other nationals enjoying the advantages of one's own nationals (Paris Convention Article 2(1)) and other nationals being accorded treatment "no less favourable" than that accorded one's own nationals (TRIPS Agreement Article 3.1) is significant in this dispute, since the EC GI Regulation complies with neither standard.

Q32. If Regulation (EC) No. 2081/92 grants different treatment to names, why does this amount to less favourable treatment to like products? What evidence is there of actual modification of conditions of competition? Would such evidence be relevant to a determination of less favourable treatment? ***USA, AUS***

Response:

62. Through the registration and protection of GIs for certain products, the GI Regulation bestows numerous significant competitive advantages on those products, which are detailed in the GI Regulation itself.[33] But access to this system of GI protection is not available to products of non-EC origin on as favorable a basis. The issue is not granting different treatment to "names" as such, but rather granting favorable treatment for products whose names qualify for a particular status that brings with it competitive advantages. The EC itself in its GI Regulation indicates that products that benefit from GI protection show enhanced profitability; indeed, that is the very reason for the Regulation. In addition, the EC has provided specific evidence of this competitive advantage, in presentations aimed at demonstrating the value of its GI registration system.[34]

63. With respect to the issue of "like product," both the Appellate Body and panels have been clear that, where there is a measure of general application (*i.e.*, not directly regulating specific products), the relevant "like product" consideration is not whether particular traded products are "like," but rather whether the measure at issue makes distinctions between products based solely on origin.[35] As the Appellate Body has noted, the term "like product" in Article III:4 of the GATT 1994 "is concerned with competitive relationships between and among products."[36] The issue is whether

[33] *See* US First Written Submission at paras. 104-107.

[34] *E.g.*, "Geographical Indications: An Opportunity for Japanese Specialty Products," Tokyo—Osaka, 10-12 March 2004 (showing pricing differentials for GI vs comparable non-GI products). Exhibit US-44.

[35] *See* Panel Report, *US – FSC (Article 21.5 – EC)*, paras. 8.133 (Finding it unnecessary "to demonstrate the existence of actually traded like products in order to establish a violation of Article III:4" when a measure makes distinctions "between imported and domestic products" that are "solely and explicitly based on origin.") *See also* Panel Report, *India – Autos*, para 7.174 (when origin is "the sole criterion distinguishing the products, it is correct to treat such products as like products within the meaning of Article III:4.")

[36] Appellate Body Report, *EC – Asbestos*, para. 103. See also discussion of *Alcohol* disputes in section IV.A.1.b.ii(2) of US First Written Submission.

> any formal differentiation in treatment between an imported and a domestic product could be based upon the fact that the products are different—*i.e.*, not like—rather than on the origin of the products involved.[37]

64. In the case of the GI Regulation, the only difference between the products that may benefit from GI registration and protection—products from the EC—and those that may not so benefit on similarly favorable terms—products from other WTO Members—is their origin. Consequently, the EC agricultural products and foodstuffs that are eligible for GI registration under one set of criteria and the non-EC agricultural products and foodstuffs that are eligible only if they satisfy an additional set of criteria are like products for purposes of Article III:4.

65. The EC GI Regulation itself offers evidence that both the intent and the effect of the Regulation is to provide competitive benefits on qualifying products. Further, however, the Regulation, on its face, provides for a lack of equality of competitive conditions between domestic products, on the one hand, and imported products on the other, by providing for numerous competitive advantages on qualifying products and by imposing barriers to access to those advantages on imported products. Panels in previous disputes, in analyzing "less favourable treatment," have examined the lack of equality of competitive conditions provided in the measure itself, without reliance on an actual demonstrated impact in the marketplace. *E.g., US – Section 337*[38]; *US – Gasoline*[39]. Therefore, evidence of an "actual" modification of competitive conditions in the marketplace is not required. Indeed, the Appellate Body in US – *FSC (Article 21.5)* stated that

> The examination of whether a measure involves "less favourable treatment" of imported products within the meaning of Article III:4 of the GATT 1994 must be grounded in close scrutiny of the "fundamental thrust and effect of the measure itself." This examination cannot rest on simple assertion, but must be founded on a careful analysis of the contested measure and of its implications in the marketplace. At the same time, however, **the examination need not be based on the actual effects of the contested measure in the marketplace.**"[40]

Q33. Is there a public policy requirement specific to GIs which underlies the requirement that a group or person must send a registration application under Regulation (EC) No. 2081/92 to the EC Member State or authorities of a third country in which the geographical area is located, rather than directly to the Commission? ***EC***

Q34. Is there a public policy requirement specific to GIs which underlies the requirement that a person wishing to object to a registration under Regulation (EC) No. 2081/92 must send an objection to the EC Member State or authorities of a third country in which he resides or is established, rather than directly to the Commission? ***EC***

Q35. Has an objection to the registration of a name under Regulation (EC) No. 2081/92 ever been filed by a person from a third country? If so, what happened? ***EC***

Q36. Has any person ever sent an objection to the registration of a name under Regulation (EC) No. 2081/92 to your authorities? If not, do you know the reason? If so, did your authorities transmit it to the EC Commission? ***USA, AUS***

---

[37] Panel Report, *US – FSC (Article 21.5 – EC)*, para. 8.132

[38] *United States – Section 337 of the Tariff Act of 1930*, Panel Report, adopted 7 November 1989, BISD 36S/345, para. 5.11.

[39] *United States – Standard for Reformulated and Conventional Gasoline*, Panel Report, WT/DS2/R, adopted 20 May 1996, as modified by Appellate Body Report, WT/DS2/AB/R.

[40] *United States – Tax Treatment for "Foreign Sales Corporations,"* Appellate Body Report, WT/DS108/AB/RW, adopted 29 January 2002, para. 215 (emphasis added).

Response:

66. As in the case of registrations, no US government agency has established regulations or procedures to receive, process, or transmit objections to the registration of names under the EC GI Regulation. Therefore, US persons have no means of raising objections within the meaning of Article 12b of the EC GI Regulation. After consulting with agencies to which such objections might have been presented, the United States is not aware of any formal objections being presented to it to be processed by the United States in accordance with the EC GI Regulation.

67. It is a matter of public record, however, that there are a considerable number of US stakeholders that are negatively impacted by the registration of GIs in the EC, but who did not have the means to present their concerns or objections to the EC Commission. The United States attaches, as Exhibit US-39, a letter from US Dairy Export Council and the National Milk Producers Federation to the Office of the United States Trade Representative, dated March 26, 2004, which states that because of the discriminatory nature of the GI Regulation, "dairy producers and processors have been unable to prevent the registration as protected GIs in the EU of a number of cheese types that had clearly become generic names before their registration." This interferes with their ability to use food names that they have developed over a large number of years.

68. In addition, the EC has apparently registered three names from the Czech Republic as part of the accession protocol of the Czech Republic to the European Union.[41] The registration of these names is of concern to a US stakeholder, but the United States is aware of no available means for that stakeholder to object to the registration. Under Article 7 of the GI Regulation, an objection is based on a review of the application for registration of a name and the product specification that accompanies the application. In the case of these three names, there was no application for registration, and, as far as the United States is aware, no product specification. Indeed, repeated requests for a copy of any proposed product specification for these names have been rebuffed by the EC. Nor, as far as the United States is aware, was any application for registration made public by the EC under Article 6(1) and (2) of the GI Regulation. In sum, it appears that these names have been registered without any ability to object to them. Nor was there an ability to object to other names registered as GIs upon accession of new EC member States, or upon adoption of Regulation 2081/92. This is significant, since of the 612 GIs registered in the EC, 487, or 80 percent, were registered in this way.[42]

Q37. Please indicate examples of other international arrangements, such as the Madrid Protocol, under which national governments cooperate by acting as agents or intermediaries in the protection of private rights. Which of these arrangements are established under international treaties and which under the legislation of one of the parties to the arrangement? Which are relevant to the matter before the Panel? ***USA, AUS, EC***

Response:

69. There are a number of examples in which parties have voluntarily come together to mutually agree to facilitate the protection of private rights. Under the Madrid Protocol, the United States, like other Contracting Parties, agrees to provide a mechanism for US trademark owners to file an international application through the United States Patent and Trademark Office (" USPTO") that is then forwarded to WIPO, which sends the application to the national office of the Contracting Parties in which the applicant requested an extension of protection. This Protocol is a mechanism of mutual convenience for trademark owners to which the United States and other countries voluntarily agreed: instead of having to file applications in numerous countries, the trademark owner files one application, which is then forwarded to those countries (which, then process the application according to their domestic trademark law). This is not an example in which one WTO Member is requiring that trademark applications from nationals of another WTO Member be submitted to that Member, reviewed for compliance with the <u>other</u> Member's trademark law, and then transmitted along with a

[41] These three names were provided as Exhibit COMP-3.c, paras. 18(a)-(b).

[42] The 487 GIs registered in this way are recorded in Commission Regulation 1107/96, as amended (Exhibit COMP-3(a)). The 125 remaining registered GIs are recorded in Commission Regulation 2400/96, as amended (Exhibit COMP-4(a)).

demonstration that particular protection and enforcement regimes are in place in the territory of the national making the application.

70. Similarly, the Patent Cooperation Treaty (PCT) provides for a filing mechanism in which a patent applicant can file an international patent application with the patent office of the PCT Contracting State in which they reside, eventually enter national stage processing of the patent application, and thereby effectively apply for patent protection for an invention in each of the relevant Contracting States. Under the PCT, the applicant may obtain a non-binding search and examination of the application, but the final determination on patentability is made by, and under the national law of, each of the designated Contracting Parties. Once again, this is an agreed mechanism for the mutual convenience of the Contracting Parties' nationals: it is not a case of one WTO Member unilaterally requiring another Member to assess or ensure compliance with the first Member's patent laws, or to demonstrate the existence of any particular protection or enforcement mechanism within its territory.

71. Another example in the patent area is the Budapest Treaty, which provides that Contracting States allowing or requiring the deposit of microorganisms as part of a patent application shall recognize the deposit of a microorganism with any international deposit authority. As part of this treaty, the Contracting Parties also agree to a set of requirements with respect to those deposits. Again, this is not the case of one WTO Member requiring another Member to assess whether the deposit complies with the first Member's laws. To the contrary, the Contracting Parties have mutually agreed to a set of requirements with respect to these deposits. And again, there is no unilateral requirement that the other Member demonstrate to the first Member that it has put into place a particular protection or enforcement mechanism within its territory.

72. These examples are relevant for several reasons. First, they facilitate, rather than hinder, the ability of foreign nationals to seek intellectual property rights in the territories of other Treaty Members. Second, they recognize the validity of the underlying intellectual property right—as created in the territory of any Treaty Member. In other words, no Treaty Member is obligated to meet the standards of another Treaty Member to ensure that its nationals are eligible to seek and obtain protection in the territories of other Treaty Members. Further, in none of these agreements were WTO Members unilaterally imposing particular protection or enforcement regimes on another Member. Rather, recognizing that private parties seek protection for their private rights directly under the laws of the Member in which protection is sought, these agreements provide voluntary mechanisms for facilitating the pursuit of such protection.

Q38. If a group or person interested in a GI in your territory were to send an application for registration or objection to registration under Regulation (EC) 2081/92 to your authorities, would your Government be able and/or willing to transmit such an application to the EC Commission? If not, please explain why. ***USA, AUS***

Response:

73. As an initial matter, the important question is not the willingness of the United States to transmit an application or objection, but whether, by requiring Members to do so the EC is making legal means available to all interested parties and is according no less favorable treatment to all US nationals than it provides to EC nationals. As noted above, where "Member to Member" interactions exist, they are generally established as the result of a negotiated treaty—not as the result of the unilateral requirements of one Member.

74. This said, from a practical point of view, in the case of the United States, it would probably not be difficult to designate an office in the US government to perform a purely ministerial act of transmitting registration applications and objections to the EC. However, this fact alone is not particularly relevant, for several reasons. First, the fact that the United States may be able to set up such an office does not mean that all WTO Members would be in a similar position from a resource point of view. Nationals of countries who cannot are effectively barred from access to the EC system. Second, the fact that the United States would likely be willing to transmit all such documents does not mean that all WTO Members would. It may well be that, in order to avoid aggravating already difficult negotiations with the EC over GIs, for instance, other WTO

Members would hesitate transmitting a controversial or politically sensitive registration application or objection.

75. Perhaps more significant, the EC GI Regulation does not simply require the transmission of applications and objections. Putting aside the fact that a WTO Member must first satisfy equivalence and reciprocity requirements under Article 12(3) of the GI Regulation before it can even apply for a GI Registration, Article 12a(2) of the GI Regulation would require the United States to (1) make a determination that the requirements of the GI Regulation are satisfied; (2) provide a description of the legal provisions and usage on the basis of which the geographical indication is protected or established in the United States; (3) make a declaration that the full inspection structures for agricultural products and foodstuffs are established in the United States (*i.e.*, the same inspection structures required of EC member States); and submit other documentation that would support the application. Aside from the fact that these are requirements that go beyond mere "transmission," it is not even clear on what basis a US government authority would be in a position to assess whether the application meets the requirements of the EC GI Regulation. Similar questions arise with respect to whether a person has standing under the GI Regulation to object to a GI registration, or whether the objection is sufficiently substantiated.

Q39. Does an EC member State participate in decision-making on a proposed registration either in the Committee established under Article 15 of Regulation (EC) No. 2081/92 or in the Council of Ministers, where that EC member State transmitted the application or an objection to it to the Commission? Is the EC member State identified with the applicant or person raising the objection in any way? Are there any limits on the participation of the EC member State – for instance, can it object to an application which it transmitted? ***EC***

Q40. How many applications to register names under Regulation (EC) No. 2081/92 have been considered by the Committee established under Article 15 of the Regulation or the Council of Ministers? ***EC***

Q41. In paragraph 137 of your first written submission, you indicate that the term "such names" in the second sub-paragraph of Article 12(2) of Regulation (EC) No. 2081/92 is a reference to the first sub-paragraph of Article 12(2), and that this means that the requirement to indicate the country of origin applies where "a protected name of a third country is identical to a Community protected name." Please clarify the meaning of the following terms, as used in Article 12(2) of Regulation (EC) No. 2081/92:

(a) what is the meaning of the term "protected" in the phrase "a protected name of a third country"?

(b) does the phrase "a Community protected name" cover both names of geographical areas located in the EC as well as in third countries, registered under the Regulation?

(c) does the requirement to indicate the country of origin apply also where a name of a geographical area located in the EC is identical to a Community protected name (irrespective of whether this Community protected name is the name of a geographical area located in the EC or in a third country). ***EC***

Q42. If Article 12(2) of Regulation (EC) No. 2081/92 applies to the registration of a name of a geographical area located in the EC that is identical to a name, already registered in the EC, of an area located in a third country, what is the difference in its scope compared to Article 6(6) of the Regulation? Why is it necessary to cover this situation in both provisions? ***EC***

Q43. Where does Regulation (EC) No. 2081/92 provide for the registration of a name of a geographical area located in a third country WTO Member which is a homonym of an already registered name? Where does it provide for the registration of a name which is a homonym of an already registered name of a geographical area located in a third country WTO Member? ***EC***

Q44. Can the EC provide the Panel with any official statement predating its first written submission that Article 12(2) of Regulation (EC) No. 2081/92 applies to names of geographical areas located in the EC and that Article 12(2) will be applied on the basis of the date of registration? ***EC***

Q45. With respect to paragraph 135 of the EC's first written submission, could the Council of Ministers prevent a registration because the Commission applied Article 12(2) to names of geographical areas located in the EC on the basis of the date of registration? ***EC***

Q46. Has a judicial authority ever ruled on the applicability of Article 12(2) of Regulation (EC) No. 2081/92? If the Commission applied Article 12(2) to the name of a geographical area located in the EC on the basis of the date of registration, could that action be subject to judicial review due to the fact that the area was located in the EC? ***EC***

Q47. Are you aware of any GIs registered under Regulation (EC) No. 2081/92 that are identical or confusingly similar to Community protected trademarks owned by your own nationals? ***USA, AUS***

Response:

76. Those stakeholders with the strongest direct interest in trademark rights have a substantial concern that registered GIs can and will give rise to confusion with trademarks in the marketplace, and that the trademark owner would be powerless to prevent such use. Trademark owners see a real threat in the GI Regulation. In this connection the United States would like to share with the Panel a written comment that the United States received on March 26, 2004, before this Panel was composed, from the International Trademark Association (INTA), which is attached as Exhibit US-45. INTA describes itself as a 126-year-old not-for-profit organization of more than 4000 members from more than 150 countries and the largest organization in the world dedicated solely to the interests of trademark owners. INTA expresses its concern, on behalf of its members, that the forced "coexistence" between trademarks and confusingly similar GIs in the GI Regulation, "which introduces consumer confusion into the marketplace and impairs the substantial investment made by trademark owners, is incompatible with the fundamental rules of exclusivity of the prior right as endorsed in Article 16 of the TRIPS Agreement and is highly discriminatory against trademarks."

77. In addition, there are three registered geographical indications, set out in paragraph 18 of Annex II of the Czech Republic's Act of Accession (included as Exhibit COMP-3.c) that present concerns. The names are Budejovické pivo, Ceskobudejovické pivo and Budejovický mešt'anský var.

78. Based on these registrations, a Czech producer has claimed entitlement to use the names "Budweiser Budvar," "Budweis," and "Budbräu" on Czech beer sold in Sweden. In trademark infringement proceedings pending before the Swedish courts, a US company holding prior valid registered Swedish trademarks for the names BUDWEISER, BUD and BUDWEISER KING OF BEERS has brought trademark infringement claims against the Czech producer, arguing that use by the Czech producers of "Budweiser Budvar," "Budweis," and "Budbräu" on Czech beer sold in Sweden raises a likelihood of confusion. In its defense, the Czech producer has argued that the GI registration recorded in paragraph 18 of Annex II of the Czech Republic's Act of Accession includes the right to use the registered GIs (Budejovické pivo, Ceskobudejovické pivo and Budejovický mešt'anský var) in translation, and that "Budweiser Budvar," "Budweis," and "Budbräu" constitute German translations of one or another of the three registered GIs.

79. Additionally, as noted at paragraph 50 of the United States' oral statement, there are many registered trademarks around the world that incorporate or sound like geographical names, which could give rise to a likelihood of confusion. For example, FARO is a registered Community Trademark used in connection with coffee and tea.[43] If the residents in the town of Faro, Portugal, begin to produce coffee or tea, and these products are registered pursuant to the GI Regulation, then the owner of the registered Community Trademark will be

[43] EC OHIM Application No. 000957100 (Registered March 24, 2000). Exhibit US-46.

unable to prevent the rightholders of the Faro GI from using the Faro name in a manner that causes a likelihood of consumer confusion.

Q48. Would the United States pursue any claim in respect of Article 12(2) of Regulation (EC) No. 2081/92 if that provision only applies to identical names? ***USA***

Response:

80. Yes. Although the United States submits that Article 12(2) appears to apply to all protected names of a third country, that provision is inconsistent with the national treatment obligations even if it applies only to third country names that are identical to protected EC name. In effect, under such a reading of Article 12(2) in the case of identical names, it is the third country GI, and not the EC GI, that must be burdened by a clear and visible indication of the country of origin on the label. This is a violation of national treatment obligations.

Q49. Do you seek separate rulings on the procedural aspects of Regulation (EC) No. 2081/92 or a ruling on the Regulation as a whole? For example, should the provision in Article 12(2) be examined in isolation, or would it be appropriate to adopt an approach like the Panel in Korea – Beef, which only examined a display sign requirement within its findings related to a system as a whole? ***USA, AUS, EC***

Response:

81. The United States is seeking specific findings on each of the aspects of the EC GI Regulation it has raised, in order to assist in securing a positive result in this dispute.

Q50. In paragraph 451 of its first written submission, the EC argues that labels which address the geographical origin of a product cannot be considered a technical regulation under the TBT Agreement, since they do not apply to a "product, process or production method." Why in the EC's view is the geographical origin of a product not related to that product or its process or production method? Does the coverage of the TBT Agreement with respect to labels depend on the content of the labels? ***EC***

Q51. How should the term "like products" be interpreted under Article 2.1 of the TBT Agreement? If the labelling requirement in Article 12(2) of Regulation (EC) No. 2081/92 applies to situations where identical names arise between imported products and EC products, but does not apply to situations where identical names arise between two EC products, to what extent would this be a distinction between "like situations" rather than a distinction between "like products"? ***AUS, EC***

Q52. Does Australia allege that Article 12(2) of Regulation (EC) No. 2081/92 provides any less favourable treatment to imported products besides labelling costs? ***AUS***

Q53. The EC argues in paragraph 88 of its first written submission that Article 12(2) of Regulation (EC) No. 2081/92 is meant to be read in the following way: "whichever indication is registered later would normally be required to indicate the country of origin." If the EC interpreted Article 12(2) this way in practice, would this satisfy Australia, or would Australia also view this interpretation as providing less favourable treatment to imported products? ***AUS***

Q54. Article 12(2) of Regulation (EC) No. 2081/92 is designed to avoid "practical risks of confusion." How would the application of the country of origin label on the basis of a product's date of registration help avoid those risks of confusion? ***EC***

Q55. Does the TRIPS Agreement apply as lex specialis as regards GATT 1994 and the TBT Agreement, with respect to a practical condition to differentiate homonymous or identical GIs on a label? Please comment in the light of Article 23.3 of the TRIPS Agreement, which is applicable to homonymous GIs for wines, and the national treatment obligation, which is applicable to GIs for other products. ***USA, AUS, EC***

Response:

82. WTO Members must comply with each of the obligations that apply with respect to homonymous or identical GIs—whether the TRIPS Agreement, GATT 1994, or the TBT Agreement. Where the TRIPS Agreement provides, for instance, in Article 23.3 that Member should determine the practical conditions under which homonymous wine indications will be differentiated from each other, such differentiation should not result in less favorable treatment of nationals of other WTO Members with respect to the protection of GIs, and should not result in less favorable treatment of products from other WTO Members. As the Appellate Body has made clear on several occasions, different treatment is not necessarily less favorable treatment.

Q56. With reference to paragraphs 17-21 of the US oral statement, does the Panel need to consider the US arguments concerning the declaration under Article 12a(2) of Regulation (EC) No. 2081/92 and the inspections structures, if it reaches a conclusion on the applicability to WTO Members of the equivalence and reciprocity conditions in Article 12(1)? ***USA***

Response:

83. Yes, the Panel should consider the US argument with respect to the required declaration and the inspection structures regardless of its findings with respect to the applicability to WTO Members of the equivalency and reciprocity conditions. The reason is that if the Panel finds that the GI Regulation requires WTO Members to comply with the reciprocity and equivalence conditions specified in the Regulation (rejecting the unsupported opinion of the Commission), and further finds that these conditions are inconsistent with WTO obligations, the EC could simply amend the regulation to remove these conditions in Article 12(1), with the result that the equivalence requirement imposed through the inspection structure requirement in Article 12a(2) might remain. It is important to a resolution of this dispute, therefore, that the Panel make a finding as to the EC requirement that the United States adopt the same inspection structures as are required of EC member States.

84. In addition, the arguments concerning the declaration and the inspection structures are also relevant to the argument that requiring the intercession of the US government is itself inconsistent with national treatment and with Article 22.2 of the TRIPS Agreement, which is separate from the argument that requiring reciprocity and equivalence is inconsistent with national treatment obligations.

Q57. Does the EC consider that it may apply equivalence and reciprocity conditions to WTO Members under Article 12a(2) or any other provision of Regulation (EC) No. 2081/92, even if Article 12(1) does not apply to them? ***EC***

Q58. Please clarify whether your claim is that the requirement of the existence of an inspection structure as a condition for the registration of a GI is inconsistent with WTO obligations per se, or the particular inspection structures requirements under Regulation (EC) No. 2081/92, are inconsistent with the EC's WTO obligations. In the latter case, please specify in detail which aspects of the inspection structures required under the Regulation are inconsistent with the EC's WTO obligations. ***USA, AUS***

Response:

85. Dictating that a Member have a particular inspection structure to (1) enforce agricultural product and foodstuff GIs in general in the United States, and (2) ensure compliance with the requirements of the EC GI Regulation, is itself inconsistent with the EC's WTO obligations. Such a unilateral requirement by the EC is not related to the question of whether the product for which GI protection is sought in the EC qualifies for that protection under the specifications submitted under the GI Regulation for that product. Indeed, the particular method chosen by another WTO Member to enforce GI rules in its territory is not relevant to such a determination.

Q59. Under what circumstances would the Commission consider the holder of a GI certification mark registered in another WTO Member to meet the requirements for inspection structures under Article 10 of Regulation (EC) 2081/92 (read together with Article 12a of that Regulation)? ***EC***

Q60. Australia argues that the EC's inspection structures requirements are a technical regulation under the TBT Agreement (paragraphs 209-224 of its first written submission). Is there a dividing line lies under the TBT Agreement between a technical regulation and a conformity assessment procedure? If so, where does it lie? ***AUS, EC***

Q61. If the inspection structures are conformity assessment procedures, are the eligibility criteria for registration under Regulation (EC) No. 2081/92, against which conformity is assessed, technical regulations? ***AUS, EC***

Q62. With respect to paragraph 259 of Australia's first written submission, can Australia provide examples of alternatives to the EC's inspection structures which would be less trade restrictive and achieve the same objective? ***AUS***

Q63. What does Article 14(2) of Regulation (EC) No. 2081/92 mean where it provides that a prior trademark "may continue to be used"? Can a trademark owner invoke the rights conferred by the trademark registration against the user of a GI used in accordance with its GI registration? ***EC***

Q64. Does Article 14(2) of Regulation (EC) No. 2081/92 implement the provision in Article 24.5 of the TRIPS Agreement that measures adopted to implement the Section on GIs shall not prejudice "eligibility for or validity of the registration of a trademark, or the right to use a trademark" or does it only implement the provision that such measures shall not prejudice "the right to use a trademark"? ***EC***

Q65. Does the scope of Article 14(2) of Regulation (EC) No. 2081/92, as drafted, include trademarks applied for or registered, or to which rights have been acquired, subsequent to both dates set out in Article 24.5(a) and (b) of the TRIPS Agreement? ***EC***

Q66. Has Article 14(2) of Regulation (EC) No. 2081/92 ever been applied in a specific case? For example, what did the national courts finally decide in the Gorgonzola case, referred to in Exhibit US-17 and in footnote 140 to paragraph 163 of the US first written submission, after the order of the European Court of Justice? ***EC***

Q67. Does Article 14(3) of Regulation (EC) No. 2081/92 affect the possibility of coexistence of GIs already on the register with prior trademarks, such as Gorgonzola? In these cases, is Article 14(3) relevant to the applicability of Article 14(2)? ***EC***

Response:

86. In the view of the United States, Article 14(3) does not affect the possibility of "coexistence" of GIs already on the register with prior trademarks. The EC argues that "geographical names" are generally not distinctive and, therefore, not often apt for registration as trademarks.[44] This argument attempts to minimize the violation of TRIPS Article 16.1 by arguing that few trademarks that contain or consist of a GI are registrable, and thus that there will rarely be a conflict between a trademark that contains or consists of a GI and an identical or similar GI. Even if the Panel were to accept that the potential set of trademarks is small, however, those trademarks that are validly registered would potentially fall in the category of trademarks subject to "coexistence" under Article 14(2).

[44] *E.g.*, EC First Written Submission, para. 279.

87. As the United States stated at the first meeting,[45] Article 14(3) of the GI Regulation does not entirely satisfy the obligations under Article 16.1 of the TRIPS Agreement. First, Article 16.1 articulates a right that is owed under the TRIPS Agreement to the owner of any valid registered trademark, while Article 14(3) comes into play (and does so only through action by the EC) only where there exists a trademark with a reputation, renown, and history of use. Second, it is not necessarily possible, at the time of registration of the GI, for the trademark owner to know from the GI registration itself whether the use of the GI will be confusing. For example, a registered GI may unexpectedly be used in translation, or in a manner that emphasizes certain aspects or letters of the geographical name, in a way that causes a likelihood of confusion with respect to a registered trademark. By the time a registered trademark owner realizes that a registered GI is being used in a manner that causes a likelihood of confusion with respect to the trademark, however, it may be too late to challenge the registration under Article 14(3). Third, as explained in the US response to Question 36, GIs may be registered outside the scope of the established procedures under the GI Regulation, such as through an accession treaty, in a manner that precludes any objections based on Article 14(3) or any other provision of the GI Regulation.

Q68. Article 14(3) of Regulation (EC) No. 2081/92 mentions certain criteria. If these are not exhaustive, why does is it not expressly stated as in Articles 3(1), 4(2) and 6(6) of the Regulation? Do other criteria, such as similarity of signs and goods fall within "reputation and renown"? Is the criterion of "length of time [a trade mark] has been used" relevant to its liability to mislead if the trademark has not been used for a significant, or considerable, length of time? ***EC***

Q69. Can the EC provide the Panel with any official statement predating its first written submission that application of the grounds for registration, invalidity or revocation of trademarks and Article 14(3) of Regulation (EC) No. 2081/92 will or should be applied in such a way as to render Article 14(2) inapplicable? ***EC***

Q70. Do the EC member States agree with the Commission's submission to this Panel that the terms of Article 14(3) of Regulation (EC) No. 2081/92, if properly interpreted, are sufficient to prevent the registration of any confusing GIs? Could the EC member States apply national trademark laws in a way that made this impossible? Could the Council of Ministers prevent the application of Article 14(3) of the Regulation if proposed by the Commission in a specific case and apply Article 14(2)? ***EC***

Q71. Has a judicial authority ever ruled on the interpretation of Article 14(3) of Regulation (EC) No. 2081/92? If Article 14(3) of the Regulation, the Community trademark regulation and national trademark laws were applied in such a way as to prevent the registration of GIs that were confusing with a prior trademark, could this be subject to judicial review? ***EC***

Q72. The Panel notes the responses of Members to the Checklist of Questions in document IP/C/W/253/Rev.1 cited by the EC in footnote 150 of its first written submission, which show that there are diverse approaches taken by several Members to accommodate possible conflicts between GIs and prior trademarks. Would this mean that the TRIPS Agreement, in particular Article 24.5, allows for some degree of flexibility for individual WTO Members to implement their obligations? ***USA, AUS***

Response:

88. The TRIPS Agreement does allow for a certain amount of flexibility in implementing obligations. As Article 1.1 of the TRIPS Agreement states, "Members shall be free to determine the appropriate method of implementing the provisions of this Agreement within their own legal system and practice."

89. However, Article 1.1 is equally clear that Members are to give effect to the provisions of the TRIPS Agreement, and that Members may implement more extensive protection than is required provided that such

[45] See Oral Statement by United States, paras. 51-55.

protection does not contravene the provisions of the Agreement. One such provision that may not be contravened is Article 16.1. A Member must, under Article 16.1, grant trademark owners the right to exclude all others from using identical or similar signs that result in a likelihood of confusion. Similarly, a Member must observe its obligations under Articles 22.2 and 22.3. As the United States explains in response to question 79, there is nothing inconsistent or mutually exclusive about these obligations. In determining what "flexibility" to grant WTO Members, the Panel should adopt an interpretation that gives each provision its full scope, in light of the presumption in public international law against conflict between obligations.[46]

90. Further, the United States notes that the referenced document discusses conflicts between trademarks and GIs in general terms, and generally with respect to the issue of whether a GI will be registered. It does not, however, address a key question that is before the Panel: regardless of whether a GI is registered or not, does the trademark owner retain his Article 16.1 rights to prevent uses of similar or identical signs that give rise to a likelihood of confusion. The EC essentially argues that Article 22 supersedes Article 16.1 in importance (although the EC also supports the contrary argument by saying that—under TRIPS—GI rights do not supercede trademark rights; thus it is not entirely clear what the EC's actual position is), and then supports this argument by suggesting that the US wine labeling system provides for "co-existence." The issue, however, is the right of trademark owners to prevent confusing uses of his signs. Under US law, consistent with the requirements of Article 16.1 of the TRIPS Agreement, the United States provides the legal means for the owners of registered trademarks to prevent infringing uses of signs. *See also* response to question 3 from the European Communities.

Q73. Please supply a copy of the wine regulations referred to in paragraph 16 of the EC oral statement. ***EC***

Q74. Which particular GIs did the EC protect under Regulation (EC) No. 2081/92 prior to 1 January 1995? Is Article 24.3 of the TRIPS Agreement relevant to any other GIs? ***EC***

Q75. Which party bears the burden of proof in relation to:

> *(a) Article 24.5 of the TRIPS Agreement? In particular, does this relate to the scope of the obligation in Article 16.1? Does it create an exception for measures otherwise covered by Article 16.1? Or neither?*

Response:

91. Since the EC is arguing that Article 24.5 is an affirmative defense to the US claims that the GI Regulation is inconsistent with the EC's obligations under Article 16.1 of the TRIPS Agreement (that is, that Article 24.5 is an exception to Article 16.1), it is the EC, as the party asserting the defense, that bears the burden of proof. As the Appellate Body noted in *Japan – Apples*, "although the complaining party bears the burden of proving its case, the responding party must prove the case it seeks to make in response."[47]

92. The United States notes, however, that, in its view, Article 24.5 is not an exception to the obligations in Section 2: Trademarks, which includes Article 16.1; rather it is an exception to the obligations in Section 3: Geographical Indications. See also Response to question 78 below.

> *(b) Article 17 of the TRIPS Agreement? In particular, does this only permit exceptions to the rights conferred by a trademark, or does it also create an exception to the obligations imposed on Members?* ***USA, AUS, EC***

[46] Panel Report, *Indonesia – Autos*, para. 14.28.

[47] Para. 154.

Response:

93. As the party asserting that its GI Regulation falls within the Article 17 exception, it is the EC, as the party asserting the defense, that bears the burden of proof. As the Appellate Body noted in *Japan – Apples*, "although the complaining party bears the burden of proving its case, the responding party must prove the case it seeks to make in response."[48]

94. Article 17 of the TRIPS Agreement permits Members to provide limited exceptions to the rights conferred by a trademark, such as fair use of descriptive terms. However, the Members, in providing for such exceptions to trademark rights, must ensure that they are limited, and must ensure that any such exceptions take account of the legitimate interests of the owner of the trademark and of third parties. Indeed, as the United States explained in its oral statement, the exception to Article 16.1 rights in the EC GI Regulation is not limited and it does not take into account the legitimate interests of the trademark owner or of third parties. As the United States noted in its oral statement, at paragraph 75, it is possible to inform consumers about the origin of a product and its characteristics through the use of descriptive terms in a non-trademark sense without affirmatively confusing the consumer about the source of the goods. It is possible in this sense simultaneously to protect the legitimate interests of the consumer, the GI owner and the trademark owner. The GI Regulation makes no such distinctions, but simply offers a broad immunity from a finding of trademark infringement based purely on whether a particular GI has been registered.

95. Article 14(2) of the GI Regulation, which the EC asserts meets the strict requirements of Article 17 of the TRIPS Agreement, automatically and in every case (according to its terms) divests a trademark owner of its right to prevent use of an identical or similar registered GI in a way that raises a likelihood of confusion. This is so even if the trademark owner could demonstrate that the particular use of the GI at issue does not qualify as "fair use of [a] descriptive term[]." Under Article 14(2), the EC adopts an irrebutable presumption that a registered GI's use will, in all cases, without consideration of the particular circumstances, constitute "fair use of descriptive terms." In the view of the United States, this is not a limited exception.

96. Finally, even under the EC's own interpretation of TRIPS Article 17, the EC fails to acknowledge that non-geographic names are subject to registration under Article 2(3) of the GI Regulation (*e.g.*, Feta). Nothing in the EC's interpretation explains how the Article 17 fair use exception applies to non-geographic names.

Q76. Article 24.5 of the TRIPS Agreement uses the phrases "validity of the registration of a trademark" and "the right to use a trademark." Please set out your interpretation of these phrases, in accordance with the general rule of treaty interpretation in Article 31 of the Vienna Convention on the Law of Treaties and, if appropriate, the supplementary means in Article 32. Please explain how you determine what is the relevant context. ***USA, AUS, EC***

Response:

"validity of the registration of a trademark"

97. As the United States explained in paragraphs 61-62 of its oral statement, the prohibition on prejudicing the "validity of the registration of a trademark," within the meaning of Article 24.5, requires Members to provide Article 16.1 rights to the trademark owner at issue. If a trademark remains registered, then, under Article 16.1, the owner of that registered trademark must be given its Article 16.1 rights.

98. The ordinary meaning of validity is "[t]he quality of being (esp. legally) valid,"[49] where "valid" refers to something "[p]ossessing legal authority" or "legally acceptable or binding."[50] Registration means "[t]he

---

[48] Para. 154.

[49] New Shorter Oxford English Dictionary, p. 3541. Exhibit US-47.

[50] New Shorter Oxford English Dictionary, p. 3541. Exhibit US-47.

action of registering or recording,"[51] and to "register" means to "[f]ormally enter or cause to be entered ... in a particular register."[52] Therefore, under the ordinary meaning of these terms, the "validity of the registration" refers to the possession of legal authority accorded by virtue of the entrance of a trademark in a register. Thus, the meaning of "validity of the registration of a trademark" must be read in connection with the legal authority accorded by trademark registration, which is the right provided for in Article 16.1, in addition to rights under domestic law. Article 16.1 demonstrates the clear link between registration and the legal authority that must be accorded the trademark owner by the registration—the right to prevent all others from using a similar or identical sign that causes a likelihood of confusion. Trademark registration is virtually meaningless without the associated Article 16.1 rights.

99. Moreover, as the United States has explained in its oral statement,[53] TRIPS negotiating history reveals that the language of Article 24.5 evolved from a simple prohibition against invalidation of registration (in the Brussels Draft) to a requirement that Members not even "prejudice" the validity of the trademark registration.[54] This is a more stringent requirement, as the ordinary meaning of the term "prejudice" is "injury, damage, harm,"[55] while the earlier version simply prevented complete eradication of the mark. Thus, the addition of the word "prejudice" means that Article 24.5 protects more than just the removal of a trademark from the register, as the EC argues. At a minimum, it must prevent Members from eliminating the core right of a trademark registration—the Article 16.1 right to prevent all others from confusing use.

100. Article 15.1 of the TRIPS Agreement also provides relevant context, as it requires that the only signs "capable of constituting a trademark" are signs that are "capable of distinguishing the goods or services of one undertaking from those of other undertakings." Without the ability to exercise the Article 16.1 rights to prevent all others from confusing uses, the trademark may lose this ability to distinguish, and therefore may no longer be "capable of constituting a trademark."

101. Thus, the loss of the ability to distinguish goods or services certainly prejudices the "validity of the registration of a trademark."

"the right to use a trademark"

102. Beginning with the ordinary meaning, "right" refers to "[t]he standard of permitted and forbidden activity."[56] "Use" is defined as the "application or conversion to some purpose."[57] Thus, the ordinary meaning of "prejudice ... the right to use" is the harm or damage to the permitted or forbidden activity associated with application of a trademark to its purpose. From the context provided by Articles 15.1 and 16.1, the purpose of a trademark is to allow its owner to distinguish the owner's goods from the goods of others. Under Article 15.1, any sign or combination of signs capable of distinguishing the goods or services of one undertaking from those of another must be capable of constituting a trademark. Under Article 16.1, the owner of a registered trademark must "have the exclusive right to prevent all third parties ... from using in the course of trade identical or similar signs for goods or services which are identical or similar to those in respect of which the trademark is registered where such use would result in a likelihood of confusion." Further, Article 16.1 provides that this obligation does not affect the possibility of making rights available on the basis of use.

103. A contextual consideration in interpreting this phrase is that the chapeau to Article 24.5 refers to certain trademarks "applied for or registered," and the chaussette states that measures shall not prejudice "eligibility for or the validity of the registration of a trademark;" further, the chapeau also refers to certain

[51] New Shorter Oxford English Dictionary, p. 2529. Exhibit US-47.

[52] New Shorter Oxford English Dictionary, p. 2528. Exhibit US-47.

[53] Oral Statement of the United States, paras. 64-65, Exhibit US-25.

[54] Exhibit US-25.

[55] New Shorter Oxford English Dictionary, p. 2333. Exhibit US-47.

[56] New Shorter Oxford English Dictionary, p. 2598. Exhibit US-47.

[57] New Shorter Oxford English Dictionary, p. 3531. Exhibit US-47.

trademarks whose rights "have been acquired through use," and the chaussette refers correspondingly to the obligation not to prejudice the "right to use" a trademark. Contextually, particularly considering that Article 16.1 specifically anticipates Members making trademark rights (*e.g.*, the right to exclude others) available based on use, there is support for an interpretation that the "right to use a trademark" refers, at least in part, to the right provided for under a Member's national law to acquire and continue to maintain trademark rights through use. In this way, both phrases in this question—the "validity of the registration of a trademark" and the "right to use a trademark" refer to the right of the owner of the trademark to exclude others from using similar signs (*i.e.*, to be able to distinguish his goods from the goods of others), and the requirement of Article 24.5 is not to prejudice this right to exclude others.

104. There is support for this reading in the negotiating history. The predecessor provision to Article 24.5, Article 24.2 of the Brussels Draft, of November 1990, contained only an obligation not to take action to refuse or invalidate the registration of certain trademarks, with no reference to use. By the time of the Dunkel Draft, a year later, in December 1991, the inclusion of trademarks "acquired through use" in the chapeau appears at the same time as the obligation in the chaussette not to prejudice the "right to use a trademark."

105. However, "the right to use a trademark" is not specifically limited in the text to trademarks whose rights are acquired through use (although it would appear to include such trademarks). Rather the obligation not to prejudice the right to use a trademark—to harm or damage the permitted or forbidden activity associated with application of a trademark to its purpose—would include an obligation with respect both to registered and non-registered trademarks not to damage the ability to use the trademark to distinguish the goods of the owner from the goods of others. In this sense, too, not prejudicing the right to use the registered trademark means not prejudicing the ability of the owner of the registered trademark to use his trademark to distinguish his goods from the goods of others. Plainly, if the owner cannot exclude others from confusing uses of identical or similar signs, the owner's ability to use the trademark for its purpose is severely prejudiced.

Q77. Article 24.5 of the TRIPS Agreement uses the phrase "right to use" a trademark. Why did the drafters not choose to state, for example, "exclusive rights" or "rights under Article 16.1"? Is that fact relevant to interpretation of the phrase "right to use" a trademark? ***USA, AUS, EC***

Response:

106. As suggested in the response to question 76, the phrase "right to use a trademark" references trademarks whose rights are "acquired through use," as set out in the Article 24.5 chapeau, and also the right to use a trademark for its purpose, *i.e.*, to distinguish the trademark owner's goods from the goods of others. It accurately describes the scope of the exception to GI protection. A reference to "exclusive right to use" would have been confusing, because the specific "exclusive right" in Article 16.1 is the right to exclude, not the right to use *per se*.[58] A simple reference to "exclusive rights," without the reference to use, would have been duplicative of the obligation not to prejudice the validity of the trademark, and also would not have clearly addressed the issue of trademarks acquired through use. Finally, simply referring to the "rights under Article 16.1" would also have been confusing, because there are three sets of rights described in Article 16.1: the right to exclude others from confusing uses, in the first sentence; "existing prior rights" in the first half of the third sentence; and the "rights" made available by Members on the basis of use, in the second half of the third sentence.

[58] With respect to patents, Article 28 uses the word "exclusive" is a similar manner.

Q78. With reference to paragraph 58 of the US oral statement, Article 24.5 of the TRIPS Agreement refers to trademarks; certain Members implement GI obligations through collective and certification marks; Article 25.2 refers to more than one category of intellectual property, as does Article 4 of the IPIC Treaty as incorporated by Article 35 of the TRIPS Agreement. Therefore, must the provisions dealing with each category of intellectual property covered in Part II of the TRIPS Agreement be restricted to one Section? Can the rights conferred by a category of intellectual property and an exception to them appear in different Sections of Part II? ***USA, AUS***

Response:

107. As the United States has noted, Article 24.5 is a clearly-labeled "exception" to the protection of geographical indications in Part II, Section 3 of the TRIPS Agreement. It is not an exception to trademark protection, which appears in Part II, Section 2.

108. The United States would not extrapolate the interpretation of this specific provision to a broad conclusion that the provisions dealing with each category of intellectual property covered in Part II of the TRIPS Agreement must be restricted to its own section. Provisions that appear in one section of Part II, but that explicitly address rights related to another section of Part II, must, of course, be given effect. By contrast, the United States does not believe that a clearly-labeled "exception" to the scope of protection for a right defined in one section can be considered an "exception" to the scope of protection for a different right defined in another section.

109. In other words, a provision listed under the heading "exception" in a particular section logically carries with it the strong presumption that it is an exception to the scope of protection for the right defined in the section in which it appears. An "exception" excepts or "exempts" something from "the scope of a proposition."[59] The "scope of the proposition" in a given section of Part II of the TRIPS Agreement must refer to the scope of protection accorded by the provisions of that section. Thus, an "exception" to the geographical indication section (Section 3) is an exception to the obligations with respect to geographical indications under that section. This would appear particularly to be the case where, as here, each section of Part II of the TRIPS Agreement has its own exception provision.

110. By contrast, in the case of "transitional arrangements," which appear in an individual "Part" of the TRIPS Agreement, the logical presumption is that the provisions are not limited to any one part or section unless otherwise indicated. Suppose, instead, that each section of Part II of the TRIPS Agreement had its own individual section entitled "transitional arrangements." The presumption in that case would be that the transitional arrangements apply to each individual section, whether it be for trademarks, patents, copyrights, etc. This is the way in which the "exceptions" have been drafted.

111. The Appellate Body has interpreted provisions based on their place in the overall structure of the covered agreement at issue, giving careful consideration to the headings or titles of the sections in which the provisions appear. In *Canada – Dairy*, the Appellate Body stated that:

> A strong presumption arises that the language which is inscribed in a Member's Schedule under the heading, "Other terms and Conditions," has some *qualifying* or *limiting* effect on the substantive content or scope of the concession or commitment.[60]

112. This is equally true of a heading "exceptions." An "exception" provision to the geographical indications section should therefore be interpreted to limit the protection otherwise granted to geographical indications.

---

[59] New Shorter Oxford English Dictionary at p. 872 (see definitions of "except" and "exception"). Exhibit US-47.

[60] *Canada – Measures Affecting the Importation of Milk and the Exportation of Dairy Products*, WT/DS103/AB/R (adopted 27 October 1999), para. 134 (emphasis in original).

113. Apart from the placement of Article 24.5 in Section 3 of Part II, the United States has also noted that Article 24.5 does not substantively provide an exception to the scope of protection for trademarks set out in Article 16.1. The exceptions to the trademark rights are explicitly provided for in Article 17. Rather, it provides a "shield" against anything in the GI Section that could adversely affect grandfathered trademarks.

Q79. Is there a conflict between Articles 16.1 and 22.3 of the TRIPS Agreement? How may a Member avoid or resolve any potential conflict? ***USA, AUS***

Response:

114. The United States does not believe there is a conflict between Articles 16.1 and 22.3 of the TRIPS Agreement. The obligations are not mutually exclusive and both can be implemented by a Member in a way that gives each its full scope. As the United States noted at paragraph 133 of its first written submission and paragraphs 41-42 of its oral statement, the TRIPS Agreement contains obligations to provide trademark and GI owners the right to exclude others from certain uses of signs or indications. The right for trademark owners, under Article 16.1, is the right to exclude all others from using identical or similar signs in a way that results in a likelihood of confusion. Under Article 22.3, trademarks that mislead consumers in a given territory as to the origin of goods should be refused registration or, if they are registered, subject to invalidation. Both of these provisions can and should be interpreted in a way that does not presume a conflict between them, based on the presumption in public international law against conflict.[61] If a trademark is misleading to consumers in a given territory, it may be refused registration. If registered, however, and if it is not subject to invalidation, it must provide its owner the legal basis to exclude others within the territory from the confusing use of identical or similar signs.

Q80. Are any exceptions permitted to exclusive trademark rights under your domestic law for concurrent registrations, honest concurrent use or comparative advertising? If so, are these limited to other trademarks? Can they cover GIs? ***USA, AUS***

Response:

115. The United States provides for several defenses to trademark infringement actions. Sections 33(b)(5) and (6) of the Lanham Act provide for what might be called honest concurrent use of two trademarks, but it should be emphasized that in the United States, concurrent use is allowed only to the extent that the marks are used in commerce in two different geographic areas within the United States. To allow for concurrent use of the two marks in the same area by two different owners would likely cause consumer confusion as to the source of the goods.

116. Section 33(b)(5) specifically refers to a situation where prior common law rights have been established in a particular limited area that conflict with a later federally registered trademark. This can lead to a court-ordered "concurrent use" of the two marks, but—as mentioned above—in different geographic areas within the United States.[62] Section 33(b)(6) refers to a situation where a registered mark owner charges that an earlier

---

[61] As recognized by the Panel in *Indonesia – Autos*, at para. 14.28, "in public international law there is a presumption against conflict," which "is especially relevant in the WTO context since all WTO agreements," including all the provisions of the TRIPS Agreement, "were negotiated at the same time, by the same Members and in the same forum."

[62] 15 USC §1115(b)(5), Section 33(b)(5) of the Lanham Act, reads: "That the mark whose use by a party is charged as an infringement was adopted without knowledge of the registrant's prior use and has been continuously used by such party or those in privity with him from a date prior to (A) the date of constructive use of the mark established pursuant to section 7(c), (B) the registration of the mark under this Act if the application for registration is filed before the effective date of the Trademark Law Revision Act of 1988, or (C) publication of the registered mark under subsection (c) of section 12 of this Act: Provided, however, That this defense or defect shall apply only for the area in which such continuous prior use is proved…."

registered mark infringes the later registered mark and the court can order concurrent use registrations. Again, such concurrent use would only be allowed in different geographic areas in the United States.[63]

117. In the United States, these rules cover GIs, since GIs are also protected in the United States through the certification and collective mark system.

118. In addition, Section 33(b)(4) of the Lanham Act provides for a defense based on fair use of descriptive terms, *e.g.*, the use of an individual's name or a descriptive term including of geographic origin.[64] The descriptive terms that are covered by the "fair use" defense cannot be used as trademarks, *i.e.*, to distinguish the goods of one undertaking from those of other undertakings. The trademark in a descriptive term attaches only to the specialized, secondary meaning that a word has acquired, and not to its original, primary descriptive context. The fair use defense gives practical force to that distinction by protecting the public's right to continue using the primary descriptive value of words and thus to use that aspect of a word that falls outside the scope of the trademark. The central purpose of the fair use defense, in other words, is to protect the particular descriptive usages that are not covered by the trademark and thus are not, by definition, infringing uses.

119. In any case, "fair use" requires a case-by-case determination of entitlement to the limited exception, upon challenge by a trademark owner. For example, in *Schafer Co. v. Innco Management Corp.*, 797 F.Supp. 477 (E.D. N.C. 1992), aff'd 995 F.2d 1064 (4th Cir. 1993), the owner of the SOUTH OF THE BORDER trademark (associated with a theme park located south of the border between North Carolina and South Carolina) challenged the use by a motel owner of the words "Border Exit" and "South of Border Exit" on highway billboards that directed drivers to the motel. In defense, the motel owner raised the fair use defense, based on the fact that "South of the Border" is generally known as the name of the town surrounding and including the trademark owner's theme park.

120. The court first described the limits of the fair use exception under US law as follows:

> [The user invoking fair use] must adapt and design his usage of the geographical term so as not to cause a likelihood of customer confusion.[65]

Then, with respect to the particular use of "Border Exit," the court proceeded to examine the facts of the particular case at issue, in the following manner:

> The phrase "Border Exit" accurately describes the location of the exit--Exit 1, either A or B--which travelers must take to reach defendant's motel. It does not purport to serve as a symbol of defendant's establishment or services. Nor does it in any way suggest to the traveling public that defendant's establishment is somehow connected with plaintiffs' establishment.
>
> Moreover, defendant has adapted its design and usage of "Border" so as not to confuse the traveling public. First, "Border" modifies "Exit," a geographical term, rather than a service defendant provides. Second, the visual depiction of "Border" on defendant's billboards does not resemble the visual depiction of "Border" on any of plaintiffs' billboards. Finally, prominently displayed on the left half of each of defendant's billboards is defendant's

---

[63] 15 USC §1115(b)(6), Section 33(b)(6) sets forth another defense to infringement: "That the mark whose use is charged as an infringement was registered and used prior to the registration under this Act or publication under subsection (c) of section 12 of this Act of the registered mark of the registrant, and not abandoned: Provided, however, that this defense or defect shall apply only for the area in which the mark was used prior to such registration or such publication of the registrant's mark…."

[64] 15 USC §1115(b)(4), Section 33(b)(4) of the Lanham Act, sets forth the defenses to a claim of infringement that include: "that the use of the name, term, or device charged to be an infringement is a use, otherwise than as a mark, of the party's individual name in his own business, or of the individual name of anyone in privity with such party, or of a term or device which is descriptive of and used fairly and in good faith only to describe the goods or services of such party, or their geographic origin…."

[65] *Schafer Co. v. Innco Management Corp.*, 797 F.Supp. at 481 (internal citations omitted).

> tradename "Family Inns of America" and its logo. Nothing in the record suggests that defendant's use was anything other than a good-faith attempt to point travelers on I-95 in its direction, and § 1154(b)(4) permits defendant to do that without infringing upon plaintiffs' mark.[66]

Similarly, the court found that the use of "South of Border" on the exit signs also constituted fair use.[67]

121. Under the law of the United States, the defense of "comparative advertising" is a form of the defense of fair use. Comparative advertising is advertising that compares the relative qualities of competitive goods or services. As long as a competitor's trademark is used fairly and in good faith and only to describe or make reference to the goods or services of the trademark owner, such fair use in the form of comparative advertising will be available as a defense. This unauthorized use of a competitor's trademark can occur so long as the advertising does not contain misrepresentations or create a likelihood that purchasers will be confused as to source, identity, or sponsorship of the advertiser's product.

Q81. Please cite any authority for the proposition that a Member must comply with a particular WTO obligation through a single measure applicable throughout its territory. Is your claim concerning an "EC-wide" level of protection based on the fact that the EC's member States are also WTO Members? ***AUS***

Q82. If the Panel were to uphold the complainants' claims under Article 16.1 of the TRIPS Agreement, how would conclusions with respect to the claims under Articles 1.1, 22.2, 24.5, 41.1, 41.2, 41.3 and 42, and under Articles 10bis(1) and 10ter(1) of the Paris Convention (1967) provide an additional contribution to a positive solution to this dispute? ***USA, AUS***

Response:

122. Whether the Panel agrees or disagrees with the United States with respect to its Article 16.1 claim, conclusions with respect to the other US claims—in particular the claim under Article 22.2 that legal means are not being made available to interested parties and the failure to provide enforcement procedures related to such means—would assist the Parties in understanding the actions that the EC would need to take to bring its measure into conformity with its WTO obligations.

Q83. If the Panel were to reject the complainants' claims under Article 16.1 of the TRIPS Agreement, would there be any scope for it to uphold the claims under Articles 1.1, 22.2, 24.5, 41.1, 41.2, 41.3 and 42, and under Articles 10bis(1) and 10ter(1) of the Paris Convention (1967)? ***USA, AUS***

Response:

123. Yes, the United States believes, for instance, that whether or not the GI Regulation is inconsistent with the EC's obligations under Article 16.1, the EC must nevertheless provide the legal means under Article 22.2 for interested parties to prevent the uses described in that Article, and must provide enforcement procedures with respect to those rights.

Q84. Are the procedures raised in the United States' claims under Article 22.2 of the TRIPS Agreement governed by Part IV of the TRIPS Agreement? If so, can they also be governed by Part II? ***USA***

Response:

124. Article 22.2, in Part II of the TRIPS Agreement, requires that Members provide interested parties with the legal means to prevent certain uses, *inter alia*, of certain signs and indications. If those means are not

---

[66] *Schafer Co. v. Innco Management Corp.*, 797 F.Supp. at 481 (internal citations omitted).

[67] *Schafer Co. v. Innco Management Corp.*, 797 F.Supp. at 481, 482.

provided, and the United States submits they are not, then there is an inconsistency with Article 22.2. It should be noted that fulfilling this obligation may or may not result in the acquisition or maintenance of intellectual property rights, *e.g.*, in the case of the ability to object to a registration.

125. It may also be true that procedures for acquiring and maintaining intellectual property, such as GIs, are inconsistent with Part IV, for instance, because, under Article 62.2 of the TRIPS Agreement, the registration process does not result in a registration being granted in a reasonable period of time. But the United States is not raising any such claims under Part IV in this dispute.

126. It does not appear that a claim of inconsistency would have to come within the scope of Part IV or of Part II, and cannot come within the scope of both. Notably, Article 62.1, which permits Members to require compliance with reasonable procedures and formalities, provides that such procedures and formalities must be consistent with the provisions of the TRIPS Agreement. This language plainly envisions that a measure can violate both Article 62.1 and other provisions of the TRIPS Agreement, including those in Part II.

Q85. Are the procedures raised in Australia's claims under Articles 41 and 42 of the TRIPS Agreement governed by Part IV of the TRIPS Agreement? If so, can they also be governed by Part III? ***AUS***

Q86. Article 4 the Paris Convention (1967) creates no right of priority for indications of source. Does this indicate that they are irrelevant for the purposes of the right of priority? ***AUS, EC***

Q87. What is the significance of the EC's statement that the complainants' claims are "theoretical"? Does the EC suggest that this affects the Panel's mandate or function in any way? ***EC***

Q88. Please clarify the form of the recommendations which Australia seeks in respect of versions of Regulation (EC) No. 2081/92 prior to its most recent amendment, as distinct from registrations effected under them. Please cite to the dispute settlement rules and procedures of the covered agreements under which this form of recommendation is requested. ***AUS***

Q89. Is there a notion of estoppel in WTO dispute settlement which applies where a Member refrains from raising claims in relation to a measure until after it is amended? ***EC***

Q90. Does Australia challenge registrations of geographical indications, or procedures leading up to such registrations or to refusal of such registrations, that took place prior to 1 January 1996? If so, please explain how Article 70 of the TRIPS Agreement applies to these measures. ***AUS***

Q91. Please clarify the form of the recommendations which Australia seeks in respect of individual registrations. Please cite to the dispute settlement rules and procedures of the covered agreements under which this form of recommendation is requested. ***AUS***

Q92. Does Australia seek relief in respect of existing individual registrations for reasons related to rights of objection? How many such registrations were made under the former Article 17 of the Regulation? How many under Article 6? Does Australia seek relief in respect of any other aspect of procedures leading up to existing individual registrations? Please cite to any previous GATT or WTO panel report which has made such a recommendation. Please explain why such a recommendation would be appropriate in this dispute if the Panel upheld Australia's claim. ***AUS***

Q93. Does Australia seek relief in respect of individual registrations in respect of their continuing inconsistency with trademark rights to be conferred under Article 16.1 of the TRIPS Agreement? If so, please list these individual registrations. ***AUS***

QUESTIONS POSED BY THE EUROPEAN COMMUNITIES TO THE COMPLAINING PARTIES

To Australia

Question 1

Could you please give details of any case where the authorities of the Member States have declared inadmissible an objection for the reasons alleged under Claim 21 (Australia's FWS, paras. 88-92)

Question 2

Could you please give details of any application for the registration of a trademark that has been refused for the reasons alleged under Claim 24 (Australia's FWS, paras. 81-87).

To the United States

Question 3

The EC understands that the regulations of the US Alcohol and Tobacco Tax and Trade Board, and more specifically Section 27 CFR 4.39(i), provide for the co-existence of geographical indications for wine and some earlier trademarks, under certain conditions.

(a) *Is this understanding correct?*

(b) *If so, how does the United States reconcile this form of co-existence with the interpretation of Articles 16.1 and 24.5 of the TRIPS Agreement that it has put forward in this dispute?*

Response:

127. The United States notes that the US wine labeling regulations are not part of this Panel's terms of reference; indeed, this dispute involves neither US measures nor wine products. With this caveat, under the regulations of the US Alcohol and Tobacco Tax and Trade Bureau ("TTB"), TTB authorizes the use of the names of certain viticultural areas on wine labels. However, there is nothing in this authorization that deprives the trademark owner of his right to pursue an infringement action against uses of that name that create a likelihood of confusion with respect to that trademark. *See, e.g., Sociedad Anonima Vina Santa Rita v. US Dept. of the Treasury,* 193 F.Supp.2d 6 (D.D.C. 2001) ("Of course, it is entirely possible or, indeed, likely that wineries will eventually produce labels bearing the Santa Rita Hills AVA designation. If Plaintiff concludes that any of those labels infringes on its trademark, Plaintiff is fully entitled to bring suit under the Lanham Act against the entity that has developed the label. In other words, the ATF's approval of the Santa Rita Hills AVA does not affect Plaintiff's right to pursue trademark claims against individual wineries if and when those wineries use labels that infringe or dilute Plaintiff's mark.") (Exhibit US-48).

To Australia

Question 4

The EC understands that Australia's Wine and Brandy Corporation Act 1980 (the "WBC Act") prohibits the use of a registered geographical indication for wine which does not originate in the area covered by the geographical indication. The EC further understands that no exception to this prohibition is provided with respect to prior trademarks.

(a) *Is this understanding correct?*

(b) *If so, how does Australia reconcile this prohibition on the use of earlier trademarks with the interpretation of Articles 16 and 24.5 of the TRIPS Agreement that it has advanced in this dispute?*

Question 5

The EC further understands that the Geographical Indications Committee set up by the WBC Act has announced that

> *The GIC will not determine a geographical indication where there is an exclusive trademark using the name which is the same or similar to the trademark, without the approval of the trademark owner.*

(a) *Is this policy still in place?*

(b) *What is the legal basis for this policy? Has the GIC the authority to derogate from the WBC Act?*

(c) *Does this policy apply also with the respect to the registration of foreign geographical indications?*

(d) *If so, does it apply also when the trademark was registered after 1 January 1996 and after the date of protection of the geographical indication in the country of origin?*

(e) *If so, how does Australia reconcile this policy with the terms of Article 24.5 of the TRIPS Agreement?*

To Australia

Question 6

(a) *Are the registration and opposition procedures before Australia's Trade Mark Office "enforcement procedures" within the meaning of Part III of the TRIPS Agreement?*

(b) *Is Australia's Trade Mark Office a "judicial body"?*

(c) *Are the registration and opposition procedures before Australia's Trade Mark Office "judicial procedures" within the meaning of Article 42 of the TRIPS Agreement?*

(d) *Does Australia's Trade Mark Office have the authority to order the remedies provided in Articles 44, 45 and 46 of the TRIPS Agreement?*

To the United States

Question 7

(a) *Are the registration and opposition procedures before the US Patent and Trademark Office ("PTO") "enforcement procedures" within the meaning of Part III of the TRIPS Agreement?*

(b) *Is the US PTO a "judicial body"?*

(c) *Are the registration and opposition procedures before the US PTO "judicial procedures" within the meaning of Article 42 of the TRIPS Agreement?*

(d) *Does the US PTO have the authority to order the remedies provided in Articles 44, 45 and 46 of the TRIPS Agreement?*

Response:

128. The United States fails to see the relevance of these questions to the dispute at hand. Notably, none of the procedures or authorities of the USPTO are included within this Panel's terms of reference. Nevertheless, as explained at the first meeting, certain aspects of the procedures of the USPTO could be regarded as part of the enforcement procedures available to US rightholders who believe that they are likely to be damaged by the registration of a mark or the continued registration of a mark. For instance, a petitioner who successfully cancels a registration at the USPTO can take the registration to a federal court to get an injunction against infringing use. Further, among the procedures available at the USPTO are proceedings before administrative law judges and the Trademark Trial and Appeal Board ("TTAB"), which are quasi-judicial.

To Australia and the United States

Question 8

(a) *Would it be possible under your domestic law for an EC national who owns an Australia/US trademark to claim before the Australian/US courts that another trademark has been registered by Australia's Trade Mark Office/ the US PTO in violation of Article 16.1 of the TRIPS Agreement, even where it is not contested that such registration is in conformity with all the relevant provisions of your domestic trademark law?*

Response:

129. With the caveat that this Panel's terms of reference do not include US measures, any person likely to be damaged by the registration or continued registration of a mark at the USPTO may request cancellation of the registration at the USPTO or in a federal court and would cite grounds under US law for such a request.

(b) *If not, is it your position that your domestic law is inconsistent with Part III of the TRIPS Agreement, because it does not provide "judicial civil procedures" in order to "enforce" Article 16.1?*

Response:

130. No, because where a trademark owner's rights are being infringed—where another person is using in commerce identical or similar signs for goods or services that are related to those in respect of which the trademark is registered in a manner that creates a likelihood of confusion—the trademark owner can enjoin that infringement and obtain damages, costs, and lost profits. Further, a trademark owner with superior rights, either under common law or in a prior registration, may obtain cancellation of a later registered trademark either through a federal court (where the true owner can also receive an injunction as well as damages) or through the USPTO. This answer is provided with the caveat that this Panel's terms of reference do not include any US measures.

To Australia

Question 9

The WBC Act set up a register of geographical indications. While the WBC Act lays down the conditions and procedures for the registration of Australian geographical indications, it does not appear to provide any conditions or procedures for the registration of foreign geographical indications.

(a) *Can foreign geographical indications be registered under the WCB Act?*

(b) *If so, what are the relevant conditions and procedures for the registration of foreign geographical indications?*

(c) *Has any foreign geographical indication been registered under the WCB Act, other than those registered pursuant to a bilateral agreement?*

To Australia and the United States

Question 10

Have Australia and the United States ever been requested to transmit an application for the registration, under Regulation 2081/92, of a geographical indication relating to an area located in their territory? If yes, what action have they taken?

Response:

131. Please see the US response to Panel questions 12 and 36.

Question 11

Have Australia and the United States ever been requested to transmit a statement of objection to the registration, under Regulation 2081/92, of a geographical indication? If yes, what action have they taken?

Response:

132. Please see the US response to Panel questions 12 and 36.

To the United States

Question 12

How many US geographical indications for products falling under the scope of Regulation 2081/92 are protected in the United States?

Response:

133. The United States is unclear as to the relevance of this question. If the EC is implying that there are no geographical indications in the United States that would fall within the scope of the GI Regulation, on what basis does the EC make this implication?

To Australia

Question 13

How many Australian geographical indications for products falling under the scope of Regulation 2081/92 are protected in Australia?

ANNEX A-5

SECOND WRITTEN SUBMISSION OF THE UNITED STATES

(22 July 2004)

TABLE OF CONTENTS

B. THE REQUIREMENT THAT NON-EC PRODUCTS BE ENCUMBERED BY A COUNTRY OF ORIGIN INDICATION ON THE LABEL IS INCONSISTENT WITH THE NATIONAL TREATMENT OBLIGATIONS OF THE GATT 1994

C. THE EC HAS PRESENTED NO INFORMATION WHATSOEVER THAT THE INCONSISTENCIES WITH GATT 1994 ARTICLE III:4 ARE EXCUSED BY ARTICLE XX(D) OF THE GATT 1994

V. THE EC GI REGULATION IS INCONSISTENT WITH THE MFN OBLIGATIONS OF THE TRIPS AGREEMENT AND THE PARIS CONVENTION

A. MFN OBLIGATIONS WITH RESPECT TO THE NATIONALS OF NON-EC WTO MEMBERS

B. MFN OBLIGATIONS OF EC MEMBER STATES WITH RESPECT TO NATIONALS OF ALL OTHER NON-EC WTO MEMBERS

VI. THE EC GI REGULATION IS INCONSISTENT WITH THE MFN OBLIGATIONS OF THE GATT 1994

VII. THE EC GI REGULATION IS INCONSISTENT WITH THE EC'S OBLIGATIONS UNDER ARTICLE 16.1 OF THE TRIPS AGREEMENT

A. INTRODUCTION

B. ARTICLE 14(3) OF THE EC GI REGULATION DOES NOT SATISFY THE EC'S OBLIGATIONS UNDER ARTICLE 16.1 OF THE TRIPS AGREEMENT

1. Even if the EC's reading of Article 14(3) of the EC GI Regulation were correct, Article 14(3) is not a substitute for the rights accorded trademark owners under Article 16.1 of the TRIPS Agreement

(a) TRIPS Article 16.1 addresses *uses*, while Article 14(3) of the EC Regulation addresses only *registration*

(b) TRIPS Article 16.1 grants rights to *trademark owners*, while Article 14(3) of the EC Regulation empowers the *EC authorities*

2. Article 14(3) of the EC GI Regulation neither requires nor permits the EC authorities to deny registration of all confusing geographical indications.

C. THE EC'S ASSERTION THAT FEW TRADEMARKS THAT CONTAIN OR CONSIST OF A GEOGRAPHICAL INDICATION ARE REGISTRABLE IS INCORRECT AND IRRELEVANT

D. ARTICLE 24.5 OF THE TRIPS AGREEMENT IS NOT AN EXCEPTION TO THE RIGHTS ACCORDED TO TRADEMARKS

E. ARTICLE 24.3 OF THE TRIPS AGREEMENT DOES NOT PERMIT OR MANDATE THE EC'S VIOLATION OF ARTICLE 16.1 OF THE TRIPS AGREEMENT

F. THE EC HAS NOT SHOWN THAT THE GI REGULATION'S TREATMENT OF TRADEMARKS CONSTITUTES A LIMITED EXCEPTION WITHIN THE MEANING OF ARTICLE 17 OF THE TRIPS AGREEMENT

VIII. THE EC GI REGULATION IS INCONSISTENT WITH ARTICLE 22.2 OF THE TRIPS AGREEMENT

IX. THE EC GI REGULATION IS INCONSISTENT WITH THE ENFORCEMENT PROVISIONS OF THE TRIPS AGREEMENT

X. CONCLUSION

TABLE OF REPORTS

Short Form	Full Citation
Belgian Family Allowances	GATT Panel Report, *Belgian Family Allowances,* BISD 1S/59, adopted 7 November 1953.
Canada – Patent Protection	Panel Report, *Canada – Term of Patent Protection,* WT/DS170/R, adopted 12 October 2000.
Canada – Dairy	Appellate Body Report, *Canada – Measures Affecting the Importation of Milk and the Exportation of Dairy Products,* WT/DS103/AB/R, WT/DS113/AB/R, adopted 27 October 1999.
EEC – Beef	GATT Panel Report, *European Economic Community – Imports of Beef from Canada,* L/5099-28S/92, adopted 10 March 1981.
Indonesia – Autos	Panel Report, *Indonesia – Certain Measures Affecting the Automobile Industry,* WT/DS54/R, WT/DS55/R, WT/DS59/R, WT/DS64/R, adopted 23 July 1998.
Japan – Apples	Appellate Body Report, *Japan – Measures Affecting the Importation of Apples,* WT/DS245/AB/R, adopted 10 December 2003.
Korea – Beef	Appellate Body Report, *Korea – Measures Affecting Imports of Fresh, Chilled and Frozen Beef,* WT/DS161/AB/R, WT/DS169/AB/R, adopted 10 January 2001.
Turkey - Textiles	Panel Report, *Turkey – Restrictions on Imports of Textile and Clothing Products,* WT/DS34/R, adopted 19 November 1999.
US – Section 110(5)	Panel Report, *United States – Section 110(5) of the U.S. Copyright Act,* WT/DS160/R, adopted 27 July 2000.
US – Section 211	Appellate Body Report, *United States – Section 211 Omnibus Appropriations Act of 1998,* WT/DS176/AB/R, adopted 1 February 2002.
US - Section 301	Panel Report, *United States – Sections 301-310 of the Trade Act of 1974,* WT/DS152/R, adopted 27 January 2000.
US - Shirts and Blouses	Appellate Body Report, *United States – Measure Affecting Import of Woven Wool Shirts and Blouses from India,* WT/DS33/AB/R, adopted 23 May 1997.
US - Superfund	GATT Panel Report, *United States – Taxes on Petroleum and Certain Imported Substances,* L/6175-34S/136, adopted 17 June 1987.
US – Section 337	GATT Panel Report, *United States – Section 337 of the Tariff Act of 1930,* BISD 36S/345, adopted 7 November 1989.

I. INTRODUCTION

1. Apparently motivated by a desire to benefit the rural economy in the EC—particularly in "less favoured or remote" areas[1]—by increasing the income of farmers and retaining the rural population in these areas, the EC has established what it believes to be a powerful system for protecting geographical indications for agricultural products and foodstuffs produced in the EC. This is a system of protection that, according to the EC itself, bestows significant competitive and commercial benefits on those persons and products able to qualify for protection: it increases the prices of qualifying products and increases the income for persons producing and selling those products.

2. Unfortunately, this substantial benefit to the EC rural economy—and the EC's agricultural products and farmers—comes at the expense of *non*-EC products and persons, which face substantial barriers to accessing this system of protection; it also comes at the expense of trademark right-holders, whose trademark rights, guaranteed under the TRIPS Agreement, are severely curtailed. Consequently, the instrument of this benefit—the EC GI Regulation[2]—is inconsistent with a number of fundamental obligations of the TRIPS Agreement and the GATT 1994—including obligations with respect to national treatment, most favored nation treatment ("MFN") and trademark rights, among others—as set forth in the first written submission of the United States.[3]

3. At this point in the proceeding, the issues have been somewhat narrowed and sharpened, and this second submission will reflect that fact. Notably, as discussed further below, the EC has decided not to defend the GI Regulation's requirements that third countries adopt the EC GI protection system and offer reciprocal protection to EC agricultural products as a condition to obtaining protection in the EC for its GIs. Apparently conceding that any such requirement is contrary to national treatment and most favored nation ("MFN") obligations, the EC has, instead, denied that these requirements apply to WTO Members. Consequently, the only real issue for the Panel to decide is whether these requirements do apply to WTO Members.

4. Therefore, this submission will first address, in section II below, the fact that these WTO-inconsistent obligations do apply to WTO Members, and the US concerns—heightened by the EC's response to the Panel questions— that the European Court of Justice ("ECJ") would, if presented with this question, so find. This submission will then address, in sections III through VI, the other aspects of the EC GI Regulation—*i.e.*, those aspects that the EC admits apply to WTO Members—that are inconsistent with the national treatment and MFN obligations of the EC under the TRIPS Agreement, the Paris Convention, and the GATT 1994. Section VII will then discuss how, in light of the US arguments and the EC's responses, the GI Regulation denies trademark owners the rights that they are required to have under Article 16.1 of the TRIPS Agreement to prevent all confusing uses of identical or similar signs. Section VIII will discuss the GI Regulation's failure to make required legal means available to interested parties to prevent misleading uses with respect to geographical indications, as required by Article 22.2 of the TRIPS Agreement. Finally, section IX will discuss the EC GI Regulation's denial of the enforcement procedures and remedies required by the TRIPS Agreement.

II. "RECIPROCITY" AND "EQUIVALENCE" REQUIREMENTS OF ARTICLE 12(1) OF THE EC GI REGULATION

5. In this section the United States discusses briefly the reciprocity and equivalence requirements imposed under Article 12(1) of the EC GI Regulation on all third countries whose nationals hope to gain access

[1] EC GI Regulation, second "whereas" clause.

[2] *i.e.*, the measure at issue in this dispute: Council Regulation (EEC) No. 2081/92 of July 14, 1992, on the protection of geographical indications of origin for agricultural products and foodstuffs, as amended, and its related implementing and enforcement measures. In this submission, as in the first submission, references to particular provisions of the GI Regulation are references to Regulation 2081/92 itself, as most recently amended, provided as Exhibit COMP-1-b.

[3] Submitted April 23, 2004 ("US First Written Submission").

to the EC GI registration system. As the United States explained in its first written submission,[4] these conditions are inconsistent with the EC's national treatment and MFN obligations under the TRIPS Agreement, the Paris Convention, and the GATT 1994. The sections that follow below will separately discuss the other aspects of the EC GI Regulation that are inconsistent with these obligations. The reason for this division is that, unlike other aspects of the EC GI Regulation, the EC does not appear to contest that the conditions of reciprocity and equivalence in Article 12(1)of the GI Regulation, if imposed on WTO Members, would be inconsistent with the EC's national treatment and MFN obligations. Also unlike the other aspects of the GI Regulation that are inconsistent with the EC's national treatment and MFN obligations, the EC denies that the Article 12(1) reciprocity and equivalence conditions are applicable to WTO Members. Therefore, the only open question with respect to these equivalence and reciprocity requirements appears to be whether the EC GI Regulation, in fact, imposes these requirements on WTO Members.[5] While the United States would be delighted to find that these requirements are not applicable to WTO Members, we do not see how the EC's claims in this proceeding can be reconciled with the text of the EC measure nor with the EC's position prior to this proceeding.

6. Regardless of the Panel's findings on this issue, however, it would assist in the resolution of this dispute to review and make separate findings on whether, in addition to the Article 12(1) reciprocity and equivalence conditions, other aspects of the GI Regulation, detailed further in the sections that follow, are inconsistent with the national treatment and MFN obligations of the EC under the TRIPS Agreement, the Paris Convention, and the GATT 1994. Therefore, the United States will not discuss the substance of the Article 12(1) conditions of reciprocity and equivalence further in the sections that follow, but simply refers back to its first submission and its oral statement at the first Panel meeting.

7. Before discussing the inconsistency with national treatment and MFN obligations of other aspects of the GI Regulation, however, the United States would like to emphasize that the EC's answers to the Panel's questions following the first meeting make it even more clear that these conditions of reciprocity and equivalence are, in fact, imposed on all third countries, including WTO Members.[6]

8. Notably, in response to the Panel's second question, the EC confirmed that the registration procedures in Articles 5 and 6 apply only to geographical areas in the EC, and that they apply with respect to geographical areas outside the EC *only* to the extent that there are "references to specific sections of Article 5 and 6" in Articles 12a and 12b (concerning registration of and objection to third country GIs, respectively).[7] The *only* such reference in Article 12a (third country registration) is to the ability of legal persons referred to in Article 5(1) and (2) to register a GI "in the case provided for in Article 12(3)." The only "case" provided for in Article 12(3) is where the Commission determines affirmatively that the equivalence conditions and guarantees required of third countries under 12(1) are satisfied. Therefore, either the Commission *does* make such a determination for WTO Members, in which case Article 12a applies, or it does *not* make such a determination,

---

[4] US First Written Submission, paras. 33-129.

[5] The United States has presented substantial information and arguments that the equivalence and reciprocity conditions that are imposed on all third countries seeking to have their GIs registered and protected in the EC (or whose nationals seek to object to a GI registration) are inconsistent with the national treatment and MFN obligations of the TRIPS Agreement, the Paris Convention, and the GATT 1994. The EC's only response has been to deny that the EC GI Regulation imposes any such obligation on WTO Members "because WTO Members have to protect GIs under the TRIPS Agreement." First Written Submission of the European Communities, submitted May 25, 2004 ("EC First Written Submission"), para. 116. The EC has presented no information or arguments to rebut the US argument that such conditions are inconsistent with those Agreements. To the contrary, the EC argues only that those conditions are inapplicable to WTO Members because of the requirements of the TRIPS Agreement. The United States recalls that these conditions apply both with respect to the ability to register and protect GIs, and with respect to the ability to object to the registration of GIs, although the exact text of the GI Regulation is different with respect to registrations, on the one hand, and objections, on the other. Therefore, separate findings with respect to each may be appropriate.

[6] The United States recalls that this reading of the EC GI Regulation is supported by the text of the Regulation in light of EC law, and was, in fact, the EC's consistent reading of this Regulation, up until its first written submission in this proceeding. *See* US First Written Submission, paras. 32-129, US Responses to Panel Questions, paras. 1-39, US Oral Statement of the United States at the First Substantive Meeting of the Panel ("US Oral Statement"), paras 7-16, and Australia's First Written Submission, Responses to Panel Questions.

[7] EC Responses to Panel Questions, para. 9.

in which case there is no procedure for registration available for products from other WTO Members. Plainly, the absence of any procedures whatsoever to register and protect GIs located in the territory of WTO Members provides even a clearer case of less favorable treatment than imposing conditions of reciprocity and equivalence. Either way, there is a violation of national treatment and MFN obligations.

9. Further, it is significant that the EC avoided the Panel's question 20 concerning whether the Article 12(1) conditions, if applied to WTO Members, would be inconsistent with the TRIPS Agreement or the GATT 1994.[8] If the EC's position is that these conditions are *not* inconsistent with these agreements, then it is simply not possible to read the language "without prejudice to international agreements" as exempting WTO Members from the conditions in Article 12(1). If it is the EC's position that these conditions are <u>are</u> inconsistent with the WTO agreements, the EC should say so.

10. Other aspects of the EC's responses to the Panel's questions reinforce the US concerns that, under the EC GI Regulation, the conditions of equivalence and reciprocity apply to WTO Members, and that the ECJ would so read the Regulation.

11. First, the EC itself admits that its interpretation in this dispute lacks legal force. Indeed, the Commission goes so far as to state that the Commission's "intention is not to create new legal obligations in public international or in Community law."[9] The significance of its statements, according to the EC is that they are "public" and "it is not conceivable ... that [the Commission] would, in the interpretation or application of the Regulation, take a different approach to the one it has set out before the Panel."[10]

12. But the EC's argument responds to only part of the concern. As the United States has explained, the Commission's statement does not prevent the Council, the 25 member States or individuals from contesting the Commission's application of the Regulation, in granting GI status, before the Community courts under Article 230 of the Treaty.[11] For this reason, it is misleading to assert that "the individual views of the EC Members [*sic*] States are [not] relevant for the interpretation of Regulation 2081/92."[12] Under Article 230 of the Treaty, each member State has a right to challenge any legal act of the Commission. This would include the act of registering a GI for a product originating in a "third country" which has not received approval from the Commission pursuant to Article 12(3) of the Regulation.

13. The EC refers the Panel to the ECJ judgment in *Petrotub* for the proposition that the ECJ "may take account of statements which the Commission has made on behalf of the European Community in the WTO."[13] The *Petrotub* case is both instructive and worrisome, for two reasons. First, in that case, which involved the imposition of antidumping duties on imports—a measure that is subject to the disciplines of the WTO Anti-Dumping Agreement, the Commission argued that it was not required under EC antidumping rules to state the reasons for discarding a particular method of calculating antidumping duties.[14] In propounding this interpretation of the EC antidumping rules, however, the Commission was directly contradicting an earlier

[8] EC Responses to Panel Questions, para. 49.

[9] EC Responses to Panel Questions, para. 30.

[10] EC Responses to Panel Questions, para. 31.

[11] US Responses to Panel Questions, para. 14.

[12] EC Responses to Panel Questions para. 173.

[13] EC Response to Panel Questions, para. 38; Case 76/00 P. *Petrotub*, judgment of 9 January 2003, para. 15 (Exhibit EC-17).

[14] *Petrotub*, para. 47.

communication to the WTO Anti-Dumping Committee, in which it explained to WTO Members that such explanations *would* be provided.[15]

14. In other words, in the *Petrotub* case, the Commission took a position before the ECJ that *directly contradicted* the Commission's assurances to WTO Members on the interpretation and application of EC law. Furthermore, the Commission and Council *opposed* efforts by the appellants to have the ECJ rely on these earlier representations, claiming, *inter alia*, that they were "irrelevant."[16] This case, therefore, hardly inspires confidence that the Commission will consider itself bound to interpretations presented to WTO Members.

15. Second, although in the *Petrotub* case, the ECJ held that it could take Commission statements to WTO Members into account, there are two important caveats relevant to this proceeding. First, nothing obliges the ECJ to take these statements into account. Further, and more important, the Commissions statements were not afforded any special status in EC law. Rather, the ECJ used the statements only as confirmation of the ECJ's interpretation of the EC's basic antidumping duty regulation.[17]

16. In this connection, an important part of the Commission's argument to the Panel is that the ECJ will interpret EC law consistently with international law and, therefore, consistently with the TRIPS Agreement.[18] However, the ECJ provides a "consistent interpretation" of EC law and international law *only if that is possible*, according to the terms of the EC law in question. As the ECJ has stated repeatedly, "Community legislation must, *so far as possible*, be interpreted in a manner that is consistent with international law".[19] If a consistent interpretation is not "possible", the ECJ will apply EC law alone.[20] In that event, the ECJ would disregard any assurances given by the Commission to a Panel because these assurances would be inconsistent with a proper interpretation of EC law.

17. In the *Petrotub* case, for instance, the ECJ had to decide whether a measure imposing an antidumping duty was required to include a statement of reasons explaining why a particular method had not been used to calculate a dumping margin. The WTO Anti-Dumping Agreement explicitly required such an explanation, but the basic EC antidumping regulation did not. However, Article 253 (formerly Article 190) of the EC Treaty requires that all EC regulations "shall state the reasons on which they are based". In these circumstances, the ECJ could provide a mutually consistent interpretation of Article 253 of the EC Treaty, the EC basic antidumping regulation, and the Anti-Dumping Agreement. The ECJ held that:

> Once Article 2.4.2 [of the Anti-Dumping Agreement] is transposed by the Community, the specific requirement to state reasons laid down by that provision *can be considered to be subsumed under the general requirement imposed by the Treaty* for acts adopted by the institutions to state the reasons on which they are based.[21] (Emphasis added.)

---

[15] Communication from the EC Commission, dated 15 February 1996, G/ADP/W/301. The communication was a response to question posed by Hong Kong, China (G/ADP/W/95); Japan (G/ADP/W/88); Korea (G/ADP/W/132); Singapore (G/ADP/W/145); and, Malaysia (G/ADP/W/107). The thrust of these questions was an apparent inconsistency between Article 2(11) of the EC basic anti-dumping regulation and Article 2.4.2 of the Anti-Dumping Agreement on the extent of the requirement to state reasons for the failure to apply symmetrical methods in calculating dumping margins. Japan expressly asked: "Although no explanation is required under Article 2.11 of the [EC] Regulation, *can the EC guarantee that it will give an explanation* for [using *asymmetrical* methods that compare] weighted average normal value with individual export price in accordance with Article 2.4.2 of the [Anti-Dumping Agreement]?" The EC responded that "*any departure from the [symmetrical] methods will be explained both to the parties concerned and in regulations imposing anti-dumping measures.*" (Emphasis added).

[16] *Petrotub*, para. 48.

[17] *Petrotub*, para. 59.

[18] *E.g.*, EC Responses to Panel Questions, para. 33.

[19] See the passages quoted from the ECJ in the EC Responses to Panel Questions, paras. 35 and 36.

[20] See C-149/96, *Portuguese Republic v. Council of the European Union*, judgment of 23 November 1999, paras. 49—52. (Exhibit US-32). *See also*, footnote 14 of the US Responses to Panel Questions.

[21] *Petrotub*, para. 58.

18. Thus, the consistent interpretation of EC and WTO law involved no more than the application of general rules already contained in the EC Treaty.[22]

19. In the case of Article 12 of the EC GI Regulation, by contrast, a consistent interpretation of EC and WTO law can only be achieved by disregarding the terms of the Regulation and applying a registration procedure that has no legal basis in either EC law or WTO law. In these circumstances, it does not appear "possible", under EC rules of interpretation, to arrive at the Commission's reading of the Regulation on the basis of a mutually consistent construction of EC and WTO law.[23]

20. The plain text of Articles 12(3) and 12a(1) of the EC GI Regulation state that the EC is entitled to register a GI for a product from a third country only if that country has received approval from the Commission pursuant to Article 12(3). Nonetheless, apparently to comply with the national treatment obligation in the TRIPS Agreement, the Commission now proposes to disregard this explicit requirement.

21. But if it does so, there is no registration procedure at all in the EC GI Regulation for WTO Members. And the EC cannot rely on the TRIPS Agreement, based on the "without prejudice to international agreements" language, because there is no registration procedure in the TRIPS Agreement that the Commission can apply. The only option for the Commission is to apply a novel registration procedure to WTO Members that is not laid down in either international law or Community law—or indeed anywhere else.

22. It does not appear that there is any support in EC law, including the EC GI Regulation, either for disregarding the express terms of the Regulation or for substituting a registration procedure for WTO Members that has no legal basis. Therefore, it would not appear "possible" for the ECJ to give effect to the Commission's non-binding assurances concerning the EC GI Regulation.

23. In sum, in the absence of convincing legal authority to the contrary, the United States submits that this Panel should find that the Article 12(1) conditions of reciprocity and equivalence apply to all third countries, including WTO Members, and that these conditions are inconsistent with the national treatment and MFN obligations of the TRIPS Agreement, the Paris Convention, and the GATT 1994.

III. THE EC GI REGULATION IS INCONSISTENT WITH THE NATIONAL TREATMENT OBLIGATIONS OF THE TRIPS AGREEMENT AND THE PARIS CONVENTION

24. Apart from denying that the Article 12(1) conditions of reciprocity and equivalence apply to WTO Members, discussed immediately above, the EC has several specific responses to the US arguments that the EC GI Regulation provides less favorable treatment to non-EC nationals than it does to EC nationals with regard to the protection of intellectual property rights. Each section below identifies a US argument with respect to the national treatment obligations of the TRIPS Agreement and the Paris Convention, and then specifically responds to the EC position with respect to that argument.

A. THE EC GI REGULATION DISCRIMINATES BASED ON NATIONALITY

25. The EC admits that there are separate registration procedures—*i.e.,* two different "tracks"—under the GI Regulation for producers and processors producing or obtaining products in the EC, on the one hand (*i.e.*, Articles 5 and 6 of the GI Regulation) and producers and processors producing or obtaining products outside the

---

[22] The *Hermes* case relied upon by the EC in paragraph 35 of its responses to Panel questions, if anything, reinforces this position, since it emphasized that, in some circumstances, EC member State national rules should be applied "as far as possible" in light of the TRIPS Agreement. In addition, however, that case did not involve Community legislation.

[23] *See, further,* US Responses to Panel Questions, paras. 26–32.

EC, on the other (*i.e.*, Articles 12 and 12a of the GI Regulation).[24] (Similarly, there are two tracks for objecting to registrations, depending on whether the objector is a "natural or legal person ... from a WTO Member or a third country recognized under the procedure provided for in Article 12(3)" (Article 12d), or whether, by contrast, the objector resides or is established in an EC member State.) The EC argues, however, that these two different tracks are based on the *location* of the GI, and not the *nationality* of the GI rightholder.[25] According to the EC, this distinction concerns the origin of the product but "has nothing to do with the nationality of the producer"[26] so the GI Regulation does not discriminate between EC and non-EC nationals, and is therefore not inconsistent with the national treatment obligations of the TRIPS Agreement and the Paris Convention.

26. As the various submissions of the complainants and all of the third parties suggest, there are many reasons that the EC's facile distinction between "national" and "location" does not withstand scrutiny. In the case of geographical indications, it is simply not possible or realistic to ignore the close relationship between the geographical area that gives rise to the GI right and the nationality of the rightholder. It is clear from the design, structure and architecture of the GI Regulation that the EC provides less favorable treatment to nationals of non-EC Members than to EC nationals.

27. First, under both the TRIPS Agreement and the Paris Convention there is a connection between where a person is domiciled or established and its nationality.[27] Article 1.3, footnote 1, states, for instance that, for purposes of the TRIPS Agreement, "nationals" of a separate customs territory Member of the WTO means "persons, natural or legal, who are domiciled or who have a real and effective industrial or commercial establishment in that customs territory." It would appear, then, that this provision would apply to the EC, among other WTO Members. As applied to the EC, for instance, this would mean that the EC's obligation under Article 3.1 of the TRIPS Agreement is to accord to nationals of other Members treatment no less favorable than it accords to persons who are domiciled or who have a real and effective industrial or commercial establishment in the EC. An initial question, therefore, is whether, in the GI Regulation, a distinction is being made between persons that have a real and effective industrial or commercial establishment in the EC (or who are domiciled there), and persons who do not—*e.g.*, persons whose commercial establishment or domicile is in another WTO Member. If so, the EC GI Regulation is, in fact, making a distinction between nationals of the EC, on the one hand, and nationals of other WTO Members, on the other.

28. As mentioned above, the EC admits that there are two different tracks under the GI Regulation for producers and processors producing or obtaining products in the EC, on the one hand, and producers and processors producing or obtaining products outside the EC, on the other. Given that, to qualify for GI registration, a product must satisfy strict requirements linking quality, reputation, or other characteristics of the product to the geographic area, any producer or processor producing or obtaining such a product in the EC would, under any reasonable definition, have to have a "real and effective commercial establishment" in the EC.

29. Thus, the distinct "tracks" for GI registration provided in the GI Regulation do, in fact, provide for different treatment for EC nationals compared to non-EC nationals. The only way for a person who is a non-EC national by virtue of a real and effective commercial establishment in another WTO Member to register for a GI under Articles 5 and 6 of the GI Regulation—the domestic track—is for that person to establish a real and effective industrial or commercial establishment that produces or obtains products in a geographic area *in the EC*, In other words, the only way for a non-EC national to receive treatment no less favorable than EC nationals is, in effect, to become an EC national within the meaning of the TRIPS Agreement.

---

[24] *See, e.g.,* EC First Written Submission, paras. 56-78 (Sections headed "D. The registration of geographical indications relating to an area located in the EC; E. The registration of geographical indications relating to an area located outside the EC; F. Objections from persons resident or established in the EC; and G. Objections from persons resident or established outside the EC.")

[25] *E.g.*, EC First Written Submission, para. 125.

[26] EC Oral Statement, para. 47.

[27] *See* US Response to Panel Questions, para. 49.

30. Therefore, it appears that, by definition, the only persons who can apply for GI registration under Articles 5 and 6 of the GI Regulation—the domestic track—are EC nationals, and that the solution for any non-EC national who wishes to take advantage of the domestic track is, in effect, to become an EC national. Plainly, the two separate tracks for registering GIs in the GI Regulation are directly linked to the nationality of the person seeking the registration and GI protection afforded by that registration.

31. The national treatment problem is equally apparent when viewed from the point of view of nationals of non-EC WTO Members. Such persons may well be nationals of those non-EC WTO Members purely because of their commercial establishment there, producing agricultural products.[28] Such persons—who are nationals of a non-EC WTO Member by virtue of their establishment in that Member producing agricultural products—are obviously relegated to the "foreign" track of GI Registration by virtue of that nationality.

32. In addition, any legal person producing or obtaining agricultural products and foodstuffs in a country will, as a practical and perhaps legal matter, become a juridical person of that country. Any such legal person established in a non-EC WTO Member producing agricultural products and foodstuffs in that Member is also relegated to the "foreign track" for GI registrations. And he is relegated to that foreign track because of where he has set up a legal status to enable him to produce such products, and therefore due to his status as a national of a non-EC WTO Member. Plainly, in this sense, the EC GI Regulation discriminates according to whether a producer of a GI product is an EC national or not.

33. Second, Article 1.3 of the TRIPS Agreement provides that "the nationals of other Members shall be understood as those natural or legal persons that would meet the criteria for eligibility for protection provided in the Paris Convention (1967)." As the US discussed in its first written submission, in the context of protection against false indications of source, Article 10 of the Paris Convention provides that "an interested party" includes any producer engaged in production of goods that is established in the locality falsely indicated as the source of goods. This underscores the strong linkage between the persons claiming protection and the territories in which the geographical indications are established.

34. Moreover, Paris Convention Article 3 provides that nationals outside the Paris Union shall be treated as nationals of countries of the Union if they "are domiciled or who have real and effective industrial or commercial establishments in the territory of one of the countries of the Union." Therefore, even a non-WTO Member national who has a real and effective industrial or commercial establishment in a WTO Member must be treated as national of that WTO Member, and provided no less favorable treatment than EC nationals. The EC GI Regulation also creates a separate track for GI registrations for any such person with a real and effective industrial or commercial establishment producing GI products in a non-EC WTO Member.

35. In all of these respects, the EC GI Regulation creates separate tracks for the registration and protection of GIs that is intimately intertwined with the nationality of the person seeking the protection.

36. Finally, it is obvious that any regulation that provides for separate tracks for registering and protecting GIs that refer to regions outside the EC, on the one hand, and those that refer to regions in the EC, on the other, is creating distinct tracks for non-EC nationals and EC nationals. This is particularly true in the agricultural sector, where nationals involved in agricultural production—particularly of products that have developed over many generations a special reputation and characteristics linked to the region—overwhelmingly have an interest in GIs in the country of their nationality.[29] A significant part of the value of a GI is its strong link to the region and history of the producers in that region: the attraction of French GI CHAOURCE for cheese, for instance, is that it takes its name from the market town of Chaource and is allegedly the most famous artisanal cheese from the Champagne region of France. It has been produced by local farmers since the 14th century, who still use traditional techniques today. Similar considerations would apply to for products in the United States or

[28] For example, at least in cases covered by Article 1.3, fn 1.

[29] *See, e.g., US* Response to Panel Questions, para. 57, and Exhibit US-43, indicating that nationals generally have an interest in GIs referring to the territories of their nationality.

elsewhere. As the EC itself has noted, "geographical indications are the common patrimony of all the producers of a certain area, and ultimately of the entire population of that area."[30] Similarly, EC Trade Commissioner Lamy, in a speech last year, described the benefits of geographical indication protection as follows:

> the geographical indication is a kind of collective "mark" of the farmers and craftsmen of a region. It guarantees that the use of a name will remain attached to a region *and to the community* that saw its birth.[31]

Similarly, as mentioned before, the preamble to the EC GI Regulation cites the "considerable" benefit to the rural economy by "improving the incomes of farmers and by *retaining the rural population* in these areas."

37. In this light, claiming that distinctions based on location of the geographical region in question has no relation to the nationality of the person producing the product, in the context of geographical indications, simply fails to recognize the reality of geographical indications.

38. The United States recalls that the *US – Section 337* panel specifically considered and rejected an argument that is similar to that presented by the EC in this dispute. In that dispute, the panel was reviewing whether the section 337 "procedures" for determining patent infringement with respect to imported products fell within the scope of Article III:4 of the GATT, *i.e.*, laws, regulations and requirements affecting the internal sale of imported products.[32] The panel considered whether these procedures, which applied to "persons", not to "goods", nevertheless fell within the scope of the Article III:4 prohibitions on discrimination against imported goods. Interestingly, the EC itself argued in that case that "[t]here was no justification in the wording of Article III:4 for exempting from its application the rules of procedures of tribunals. <u>Any such interpretation would enable contracting parties to take away, by openly discriminatory procedural rules applied to imports, almost all the benefits conferred by GATT.</u>"[33] The panel agreed, reasoning that:

> Nor could the applicability of Article III:4 be denied on the ground that most of the procedures in the case before the Panel are applied to persons rather than products, since the factor determining whether persons might be susceptible to Section 337 proceedings or federal district court procedures is the source of the challenged products, that is whether they are of United States origin or imported.[34]

39. Of course, this dispute, unlike *US – Section 337*, includes claims of discrimination as to nationals under the TRIPS Agreement as well as claims of discrimination as to goods under the GATT 1994. But nothing in *US – Section 337* would suggest that the GI Regulation should not be found to be inconsistent with both sets of obligations. Indeed, in that case, even though GATT Article III:4 addresses discriminatory treatment of products, the *Section 337* panel stated that "most of the procedures ... are applied to persons rather than to products", acknowledging that those procedures involving goods directly concerned, for the most part, persons.

40. One should also consider, as apparently did the panel in *United States – Section 337*, the consequences of finding that a regulation that does not literally and specifically discriminate purely according to nationality does not violate the national treatment obligations of the TRIPS Agreement and the Paris Convention. A WTO Member could discriminate against certain patent applications, based on where the application was first filed—for instance, subjecting all patents first filed abroad to higher fees. One should therefore beware of the EC's narrow interpretation of the national treatment obligation under the TRIPS Agreement and the Paris

---

[30] First Written Submission of the EC, paragraph 307, 4th bullet point.

[31] SPEECH/03/292 Pascal Lamy EU Trade Commissioner Creation of the Organisation Geographical Indications Network (ORIGIN) Brussels, June 11, 2003 (emphasis added). Exhibit US-49.

[32] *US – Section 337*, para. 5.10.

[33] *US – Section 337*, para. 3.10.

[34] *US – Section 337*, para. 5.10.

Convention, which could have the effect of rendering of little value an obligation that the Appellate Body has called "a fundamental principle of the world trading system"[35]

41. The EC has suggested in its responses to the Panel's questions that somehow the fact that there is a national treatment obligation under GATT 1994 with respect to goods means that the national treatment obligation under the TRIPS Agreement should be more narrowly interpreted than it would be in the absence of such an obligation.[36] For instance, the EC cautions against "systematic overlap."[37] Similarly, the EC implies that, since the GI Regulation does not literally and specifically provide for different treatment according to the "nationality" of the rightholder, the Panel should focus on whether the formulation actually used in the GI Regulation was an attempt to "circumvent" the national treatment obligation.[38] Specifically, the EC contends that, because Article III of the GATT 1994 covers discrimination based on a product's origin, there is no issue of "circumvention" in this case, implying that this means that only a literal, express discrimination against other WTO nationals would violate the national treatment obligations under the TRIPS Agreement and the Paris Convention. These arguments are wrong.

42. First, the obligations under Article III:4 of the GATT 1994 are separate from those of Article 3.1 of the TRIPS Agreement and Article 2 of the Paris Convention, and the EC has an obligation to satisfy both sets of obligations. If there is a violation of national treatment under Article III:4 of the GATT 1994—and the United States contends that there is—this does not mean that there is not also a violation of the national treatment obligations under the TRIPS Agreement and the Paris Convention. Indeed, in this case, there is a violation of both obligations. Further, the existence of an obligation under Article III:4 of the GATT 1994 does not automatically mean that the scope of the obligation under the TRIPS Agreement is narrower than it otherwise would be, and the EC has offered no basis for such a position. Finally, while attempts to "circumvent" the national treatment obligation may be relevant to whether a provision is inconsistent with that obligation, the issue in this dispute is not "circumvention", but rather, regardless of whether or not the GI Regulation literally uses the term "national", whether the GI Regulation accords less favorable treatment to non-EC nationals. In short, there is no basis for adopting a narrow interpretation of this fundamental TRIPS Agreement obligation.

43. The EC also states in its first written submission that the panel in *Indonesia – Autos* "cautioned against reading Article 3.1 TRIPS so as to apply to matters not directly related to the equal treatment of nationals."[39] But in that dispute, the panel was considering whether any measures of support not related to intellectual property—such as subsidies or customs tariffs—might give rise to a *de facto* violation of Article 3.1 of the TRIPS Agreement. This dispute, by contrast, concerns an intellectual property measure that does not provide the same access to the protection of intellectual property rights to non-EC nationals as it does to EC nationals. The issues in these two disputes are not at all comparable.

44. The EC GI Regulation makes a similar distinction between those who can object to the registration of a GI: Article 7(3) explicitly provides one track for persons who reside or are established in an EC member States; Article 12d explicitly provides another track for natural or legal persons of a WTO Member, whose objections are send to the country in which they reside or are established. Just as in the case of registrations, these two tracks—domestic and foreign—distinguish between nationals of the EC, on the one hand, and nationals of non-EC WTO Members, on the other.

45. In sum, despite the EC's overly narrow and baseless interpretation of one of the most basic and fundamental obligations in the TRIPS Agreement, the Panel should find that the EC GI Regulation provides for different treatment for EC nationals, on the one hand, and non-EC nationals, on the other.

---

[35] Appellate Body Report, *US – Section 211*, para. 233.

[36] EC Responses to Panel Questions, paras. 72-74.

[37] EC Responses to Panel Questions, para. 73.

[38] EC Responses to Panel Questions, para. 73.

[39] EC First Written Submission, para 109.

B. THE EC GI REGULATION ACCORDS LESS FAVORABLE TREATMENT TO NATIONALS OF ALL NON-EC WTO MEMBERS THAT HAVE NOT ESTABLISHED EC-STYLE INSPECTION STRUCTURES

1. Requiring that WTO Member nationals demonstrate the existence of inspection structures that their governments have not established accords less favorable treatment to those nationals than to EC nationals

46. Under Articles 10 and 12a(2)(b) of the GI Regulation a WTO Member must establish specific inspection structures in its territory in order for its nationals to register and protect their GIs under the GI Regulation. The EC argues that the requirement for specific inspection structures in the country in which the GI is located is "equal" not "less favorable" treatment, because the EC also requires its member States to have those same inspection structures.[40] To paraphrase the panel report in *US – Section 337*, where there are differences in the legal provisions applying to non-EC nationals, on the one hand, and EC nationals, on the other, "given that the underlying objective is to guarantee equality of treatment, it is incumbent on the contracting party applying differential treatment to show that, in spite of such differences, the no less favourable treatment standard" is met.[41]

47. The EC has not shown that this standard is met. To the contrary, the requirement for specific inspection structures does not amount to "equal treatment" of non-EC nationals, because nothing in the TRIPS Agreement or elsewhere requires WTO Members to establish the specific inspection structures required by the EC. And, indeed, as discussed further below, many WTO Members, because of the way they choose under the TRIPS Agreement to protect geographical indications, have no such inspection structures. EC member States, by contrast, are required under the EC GI Regulation to establish such structures.[42] Therefore, while EC nationals are all in a position to satisfy the "inspection structure" condition of the GI Regulation and can therefore register and protect their GIs, non-EC nationals cannot satisfy this condition—at least where the WTO Member concerned has not established the EC inspection structures—and are precluded from registering and protecting their GIs.

48. Therefore, requiring that a non-EC national demonstrate that his government has established the same specific inspection structures as EC member States provides less favorable treatment to that non-EC national than is provided to EC nationals. Simply stated, the national from a WTO Member that has not established such inspection structures is precluded from registering his GI in the EC. The United States submitted substantial information and arguments in its first written submission showing that a WTO Member cannot, consistent with the TRIPS Agreement and the Paris Convention, require that another WTO Member establish an equivalent system of GI protection as a precondition to granting GI protection to nationals of that WTO Member. The EC responded that WTO Members do not have to satisfy that condition, apparently because such a condition would be contrary to the TRIPS Agreement. But the requirement for specific inspection structures is merely equivalence by another name, and therefore also inconsistent with the TRIPS Agreement and the Paris Convention.

2. The EC inspection structure requirements are highly prescriptive, and go beyond simply assuring that the GI products meet the specifications

49. During the first Panel meeting, the EC suggested that the requirements for the inspection structures under Articles 10 and 12a of the EC GI Regulation were not unduly prescriptive, and the EC complained several times that complainants had not specified *which* particular aspects of the inspection structures were objectionable. The pertinent issue, however, is not which aspects of the EC-mandated inspection systems are objectionable, but rather whether the EC can, consistent with the TRIPS Agreement, demand of WTO Members

---

[40] *E.g.*, EC First Written Submission, para. 121.

[41] *United States – Section 337*, para 5.11 (emphasis added). That panel report was discussing the no less favorable treatment standard of Article III of the GATT, but the same principle would apply to the no less favorable standard of the TRIPS Agreement.

[42] Article 10 of the EC GI Regulation.

the establishment of the same particular inspection structures that the EC has chosen for itself as a precondition for granting TRIPS rights to that Member's nationals.[43] It cannot, because to do so is to accord less favorable treatment to nationals of WTO Members who have the right to choose the appropriate method of implementing its TRIPS obligations, and have not chosen such particular inspection systems to implement their obligations with respect to GIs.

50. The United States does not disagree that the EC can require, as a condition of registration, that a GI applicant assure that he is in a position to control the use of the GI, ensuring that products bearing the GI are entitled to it. Many countries require such assurances. If, once registered, the owner of the collective or certification mark is unable to control the use of the mark, the mark is subject to cancellation.[44] Similarly, as WIPO has noted, some WTO Members protect geographical indications through collective marks, in which a group of producers, for instance, in a particular geographical area, jointly own the mark and are entitled to use it.[45] Indeed, the EC has itself likened GI protection to protection offered by collective marks.[46] The requirements for registering a collective mark commonly include submitting the names of the persons entitled to use the mark, the conditions for membership in the organization, and the conditions for using the mark.[47]

51. These requirements for registering certification marks and collective marks appropriately reflect that intellectual property rights are private rights[48] and that the owner of those rights are in the best position to ensure that the marks are used in a manner consistent with their specifications. More important, these are requirements that the person seeking protection is in a position to satisfy, unlike the EC GI Regulation's requirement that the government, not the person seeking protection, establish and be responsible for particular inspection structures. Such requirements that are within the power of the rightholder himself to satisfy do not present the same problems as requirements imposed, not on the rightholder, but on his government.

52. The EC has suggested in its responses to the Panel's questions that the specific requirements for inspection structures are flexible. But the EC has overstated this flexibility. First, the EC states at paragraph 129 of its responses to the Panel's questions that "[t]he EC merely requires that the conditions of Regulation 2081/92 regarding product specifications and inspections are met as regards the specific product for which protection is sought." This implies that an inspection structure that is limited to ensuring compliance with the particular specifications for the individual GI for which registration is sought satisfies the Article 12a(2) requirement. This impression is encouraged by the EC's further response to the Panel at paragraph 131 that "it is not excluded" that the holder of a certification mark outside the EC could function as an inspection structure "[i]f the holder is not itself a producer or processor, and is independent of them... Otherwise, it would be

---

[43] The United States wonders if the EC would take the same position with respect to other intellectual property rights. For example, would the EC agree that a Member could require the EC to adopt specific inspection or other controls procedures before the Member would protect a trademark, copyright, or patent of an EC national?

[44] *E.g.,* UK Trade Marks Act of 1994, Schedule 2, Article 6 reads: "(1) An applicant for registration of a certification mark must file with the registrar regulations governing the use of the mark. (2) The regulations must indicate who is authorised to use the mark, the characteristics to be certified by the mark, how the certifying body is to test those characteristics and to supervise the use of the mark, the fees (if any) to be paid in connection with the operation of the mark and the procedures for resolving disputes. Further requirements with which they regulations have to comply may be imposed by rules." Exhibit US-50.

[45] WIPO Document SCT/8/4 (Exhibit US-5) and WIPO Document SCT/9/4 (Exhibit COMP-16).

[46] "The geographical indication is a kind of collective 'mark' of the farmers and craftsmen of a region." SPEECH/03/292 Pascal Lamy EU Trade Commissioner Creation of the Organisation Geographical Indications Network (ORIGIN) Brussels, June 11, 2003. Exhibit US-49.

[47] *E.g.*, EC Regulation 40/94, Article 64(2) "In derogation from Article 7(1)(c), signs or indications which may serve, in trade, to designate the geographical origin of the goods or services may constitute Community collective marks within the meaning of paragraph 1." OHIM Examination Guidelines on Community Collective Marks, Section 11.5.1 "An applicant for a collective mark must submit regulations governing its use." Section 11.5.2 "The regulations must specify: a) the name of the applicant's organisation and the address of its office; b) the object of the organisation; c) the bodies authorized to represent the organisation; d) conditions for membership; e) the persons authorized to use the mark; f) if there are conditions for use of the mark, including sanctions, these must be included; and g) if the mark designates the geographical origin of the goods or services, authorization for any person whose goods or services originate in the geographical area concerned to become a member of the organization." *See* discussion above for relevant US regulations.

[48] TRIPS Agreement preamble, third "*Recognizing*" clause.

necessary to establish an independent inspection structure which offers the necessary guarantees of independence and impartiality."

53. This response ignores two facts. First, Article 12a(2) specifically requires a declaration by the WTO Member that the "structures provided for in Article 10 are established in its territory". The structures provided for in Article 10 require inspection structures that ensure that agricultural products and foodstuffs bearing a protected name meet the requirements laid down in specifications. This is a requirement for a broad inspection structure capable of performing this function for all agricultural products and foodstuffs. A certification or collective mark holder, by contrast, would only ensure compliance with his particular mark. Second, Article 10 requires much more than a general "guarantee of independence and impartiality." Rather it imposes specific requirements that go far beyond what is necessary to assure the integrity of the geographical indication. It requires that the inspection authority have qualified staff and resources "permanently at their disposal" to carry out inspections. The inspection authority must be able to take steps "necessary to ensure that [the GI Regulation] is complied with;"[49] if the inspection authority is a private body, it must fulfill the requirements of a European standard for inspection authorities (standard EN 45011), and must "continue to be responsible *vis-a-vis* the EC member State[50] for all inspections."

54. In sum, and contrary to the EC's responses to the Panel, it does not appear that, under the GI Regulation, a certification mark holder would satisfy the requirements for an inspection structure under the EC GI Regulation. And yet, as discussed above, that certification mark holder would satisfy the requirements imposed upon it by a WTO Member that protects geographical indications through a certification mark system.

55. But even if certain certification mark holders might qualify as inspection authorities under the EC GI Regulation, the requirement that the WTO Members establish the EC inspection structures still provides less favorable treatment to non-EC nationals, for two reasons.

56. First, the EC GI Regulation does not merely require assurances that the specifications in the GI application will be complied with and that there are rules to ensure that compliance.[51] Rather, it requires that the government of the WTO Member itself assure that compliance. This is clear from the GI Regulation's requirement, under Articles 10 and 12a, that it is the WTO Member concerned that must declare to the EC that the Article 10 inspection structures are established in its territory, and from the requirement that private inspection bodies continue to be responsible to the WTO Member for all inspections.[52] But other WTO Members may not have a system where they are directly involved in the inspections, or where the private inspection authorities are "responsible" *vis-a-vis* the government for all inspections. Rather, as noted above, some WTO Members rely on a system in which the certification or collective mark holders themselves ensure that a certification or collective mark is being used in conformity with the terms of its issuance. The nationals of any such WTO Members are thus unable, under the GI Regulation, to register and protect their GIs in the EC.

57. Second, although an inspection authority that is completely independent of the producers and directly responsible to the government is one way assure that the specifications for the GI are met, but it is not the only way. The EC's recent response that certification mark owners might qualify as Article 10 inspection authorities—because they themselves do not produce the subject product—would appear to exclude other GI rightholders who are able to assure the integrity of their GI. One example is collective mark owners, who may

---

49 This is a broader responsibility than simply ensuring that the products meet the specifications, and would appear to include the enforcement of the GI rights provided for in Article 13 of the EC GI Regulation.

50 A requirement that the United States assumes should be read as a reference to the relevant WTO Member.

51 As discussed above, such a requirement is common with respect to applications for certification and collective marks, both in the United States and in the EC.

52 Article 10(3) of the EC GI Regulation.

both own a mark protecting a geographical indication, and police compliance with that mark.[53] Collective marks can be owned collectively by all producers in a particular region, and so are a good fit for protecting geographical indications.[54] Under the EC's own analysis, however, it would appear that, in the absence of a separate additional inspection structure as to the specific product, directly responsible to the US Government, collective owners of a GI in the United States would not be able to register their GI in the EC. Yet collective mark owners have as much of an interest in protecting the integrity of their mark as certification mark owners. While collective mark owners may not have a separate and independent inspection structure responsible to the government, they do generally have a rules for admission to the collective organization, the members of which are then authorized to use the mark upon admission (and compliance with the rules for the use of the mark). There is no reason that such a system should be considered *a priori* inadequate to qualify for an EC GI Registration.

58. Further, the United States is not alone in its requirements for collective marks. The EC Trademark Directive allows the registration by EC member States of terms that designate the geographical origin of the goods as both guarantee or certification marks *and* as collective marks.[55] In addition, since the Paris Convention requires the protection of collective marks, and since, as WIPO has noted, many WTO Members protect GIs through collective marks, it would appear that the same requirements that ensure the integrity of collective marks should assure the integrity of registered GIs. In other words, it should be sufficient under the EC GI Regulation that the owner of the collective mark can show that the product meets the definition of GI in Article 2 of the EC GI Regulation and can give appropriate assurances that he exercises control over the use of the mark of the goods produced to ensure compliance with the standards of the collective.

59. Nor are the examples of certification and collective marks exhaustive. In the United States and other WTO Members, common law GI owners—that is, those owners that have acquired rights in GIs through use, as well as those GI owners protecting their GIs through unfair trade statutes—may also have their own internal quality control system that ensures adequate control over the use of the GI.

60. In sum, the EC cannot require a WTO Member to establish and enforce an EC-style inspection structure as a precondition to that WTO Member's nationals being able to register and protect GIs in Europe. Such a requirement is inconsistent with the EC's WTO obligation to provide non-EC nationals treatment no less favorable than that accorded its own nationals, and is at odds with the status of GIs as private rights.

61. It is worth highlighting that the United States is not challenging in this dispute the EC basic standard for what constitutes a GI. The US position is that if a product meets that standard—*i.e.*, is an agricultural product or foodstuff originating in a region outside the EC which possesses a specific quality, reputation or other characteristics attributable to that geographic origin—the non-EC national should be able to register and protect it in the EC under the GI Regulation, regardless of whether his home government has established the same inspection structures as the EC member States.

62. In brief, the EC's requirement that the United States establish EC-style inspection structures to enforce GIs is simply equivalence by another name: the EC will not protect the GIs of US nationals unless the United States establishes the same inspection structures, with the same responsibilities and resources, that are required of EC member States. But other WTO Members have the freedom under the TRIPS Agreement to set up a system that is different from the EC's for protecting GIs, and the EC cannot make protection of GIs conditional

---

[53] In the United States, for instance, the Lanham Act provides that the owner of a certification mark cannot use the mark on goods, but only for advertising (anti-use by owner rule). In contrast, the owner of a collective mark is not barred from using the collective mark as a trademark for goods. "… [T]he collective itself may also use the same mark as a trademark for the goods covered by the collective trademark or service mark. See TMEP §1305. The 'anti-use by owner' rule of §4 of the Trademark Act, 15 US C. §1054 does not apply to collective marks." TMEP 1303.01.

[54] See Footnote 43, SPEECH/03/292 Pascal Lamy EU Trade Commissioner Creation of the Organisation Geographical Indications Network (ORIGIN) Brussels, June 11, 2003.

[55] Article 15 of the First Council Directive of 21 December 1988 to approximate the laws of the Member States relating to registered trademarks (89/104/EEC), OJ L 40, February 2, 1989, p. 1. Exhibit COMP-7.a.

on other Members' adopting an EC-style system. The United States, for one, has not adopted the EC's approach to protecting GIs, and does not require an EC-style inspection structure. This fact, however, should not prevent US nationals from obtaining GI protection in the EC on the same basis as EC nationals.

C. THE EC GI REGULATION ACCORDS LESS FAVORABLE TREATMENT TO NATIONALS OF ALL OTHER WTO MEMBERS THAT DO NOT OR CANNOT EVALUATE AND PROCESS EC GI REGISTRATION APPLICATIONS OR OBJECTIONS AND ADVOCATE TO THE EC ON BEHALF OF ITS NATIONALS

63. Two things have become apparent in connection with the EC GI Regulation's requirement that only WTO Members, and not their nationals, are able to submit GI registration applications and objections to the EC. (This is in contrast to the situation for EC nationals, for whom the GI Regulation provides a direct means to submit applications and objections). First, this requirement imposes a significant burden on the WTO Member involved—a burden that many may be unable to assume—resulting in a lack of access to the EC GI system by their nationals. Second, this requirement for national government intervention is both unwarranted and unnecessary. The result is that nationals of non-EC WTO Members are unnecessarily denied the same access to the EC GI system that EC nationals have.

1. The EC GI Regulation imposes a significant burden on other WTO Members to administer and enforce the Regulation

64. With respect to the first point, it is plain that, under the GI Regulation, WTO Members must play a substantial and active role in trying to convince the EC to accept the GI registration applications and objections of its nationals, submitting themselves to the EC's authority and committing themselves to administer and enforce the EC GI Regulation in their territory. With respect to GI registration applications, Article 12a(2) of the GI Regulation would require the United States to (1) make a determination that the requirements of the GI Regulation are satisfied; (2) provide a description of the legal provisions and usage on the basis of which the geographical indication is protected or established in the United States; (3) make a declaration that the full inspection structures for agricultural products and foodstuffs are established in the United States (*i.e.*, the same inspection structures required of EC member States); and (4) submit other documentation that would support the application. The United States notes that this is not a simple matter, because it is not even clear on what basis a US government authority would be in a position to assess whether the application meets the requirements of the EC GI Regulation.

65. Nevertheless, in response to the Panel's question, the EC made clear that this obligatory evaluation of an EC GI registration application by the WTO Member would require substantial work and expertise. In explaining why the EC GI Regulation required that WTO Members evaluate the EC GI applications, the EC stated:

> 80. First, the evaluation of whether a name fulfils the conditions for protection as a geographical indication requires familiarity with a host of geographical, natural, climatic and cultural factors specific to the geographical area in question. Moreover, knowledge of the market conditions in the country of origin may also be required, e.g. in order to establish whether the product in question has a particular reputation. Like in the case of applications from Member State, it is the third country's authorities which are best placed to evaluate such factors... .
>
> 81. Second, the evaluation of the application may require the assessment of legal questions arising under the law of the country where the area is located. In particular, Article 12a of the Regulation requires the application to be accompanied by a description of the legal provisions and the usage on the basis of which the geographical indication is protected or established in the third country. The Commission cannot unilaterally resolve such issues pertaining to the law of a third country, which therefore necessarily require the implication of the authorities of the third country.

> 82. Third, the involvement of the third country government appears called for also out of respect for the sovereignty of the third country. The assessment of whether an application meets the requirements of the Regulation, in particular concerning the link with the geographical area, requires in-depth knowledge of the conditions related to this area, as well as the possibility to verify on the spot the relevant claims made in the application. It would not be possible for the European Commission to carry out such inspections on the territory of the third country without the agreement or involvement of the third country.
>
> 83. Fourth, the involvement of the third country government also facilitates the cooperation of the authorities of the Community and of the third country throughout the registration process. If doubts or question arise during the registration process, the European Commission may need a contact point in the third country to which it can address itself. Moreover, the Regulation foresees that the third country which has transmitted the application must be consulted at certain stages of the procedure before the Commission can take a decision (cf. Articles 12b [1] [b]; 12b [3]).
>
> 84. Fifth, the involvement of the third country authorities should also be beneficial to the applicant. Regulation 2081/92 effectively enables the applicant to discuss, prepare, file, and where necessary refine and amend his application directly with the authorities where the geographical area is located. Since these authorities are more familiar with the area in question, this should help speed up the registration process. Moreover, frequently these authorities may be geographically closer to the applicant and may speak the applicant's language, which may also be a further benefit to the applicant.[56]

66. By its own admission, the EC is placing a substantial burden on other WTO Members to administer and enforce the EC's GI Regulation—and the EC will not register the GI of any national whose home government does not agree to shoulder this burden. Indeed, it would appear that the EC is envisioning not so much the transmission of an application as it is an in-depth analysis of whether the EC GI Regulations requirements are met—including on-site verifications—and, significantly, on-going discussions or negotiations with the EC throughout the process concerning whether the registration applications would be accepted. The EC made a similar point with respect to the need for WTO Members to process objections to GI registrations on behalf of its nationals.[57]

67. This process resembles more the submission of one government to another government's unilateral assertion of authority it does an application for protection, or an objection, from a private GI rightholder. It is also very different from EC and member State rules concerning the filing of applications for collective and certification marks, which do not require any government involvement at all on behalf of the applicant.[58]

68. In any case, a national from a WTO Member that does not have a mechanism for undertaking all that the EC is requiring with respect to applications and objections does not have access to the EC registration system for protecting GIs or for objecting to GIs. By contrast, an EC national seeking to have his home-based GI protected or to object to a GI registration has a pre-established mechanism for doing so through the EC GI Regulation, which requires EC member States to process such applications and objections.

69. In sum, the EC GI Regulation accords less favorable treatment to non-EC nationals than it accords to EC nationals with respect to the protection of geographical indications.

---

[56] EC Responses to Questions of the Panel, paras. 82-84.

[57] EC Response to Questions of the Panel, para. 87.

[58] *See* discussion under section III.B.2 above.

70. The EC has responded that this is equal treatment, not less favorable treatment, because EC nationals also have to send registration applications and objections through their member States.[59] The United States recalls again that it is up to the EC to demonstrate that different procedures applied to non-EC nationals as compared to EC nationals do not amount to "less favorable treatment."[60] In fact, the EC's assertion of "equality" is incorrect, because, just as in the case of inspection structures, EC member States are required by the GI Regulation to process the applications and the objections, and so EC nationals are directly provided the ability to register their GIs and object to the registration of GIs. Other WTO Members have no such obligation—under the TRIPS Agreement or elsewhere—and therefore the GI Regulation accords less favorable treatment for the nationals of those Members that do not "comply" with the EC GI Regulation.

71. The EC has also responded that any WTO Member's "unwillingness" to "cooperate" means that any resulting less favorable treatment is due to "their own attitude", and not to the GI Regulation.[61] With all due respect, the EC has provided the direct means for its own nationals to apply for the registration of GIs and to achieve EC-wide protection of those GIs. It has also provided the direct means for its nationals to object to the registration of GIs. It has provided none of this for non-EC nationals. To the contrary, it has erected enormous barriers to those nationals—effectively requiring unilaterally that other WTO Members administer and enforce the EC GI Regulation which, the EC's protestations notwithstanding[62] impose a considerable burden on those WTO Members, and is not required by any WTO Agreement.

72. The national treatment violation is, therefore, not due to the US "attitude", or the "attitude" of all other WTO Members that have not "complied" with the unilateral requirements of the EC, but rather to the barriers erected against non-EC WTO Member nationals in the GI Regulation.

2. The GI Regulation's requirement for extensive WTO Member involvement is unwarranted and unnecessary

73. With respect to the second point noted above, it is simply untrue that the extensive involvement of WTO Members is necessary or even appropriate in the process of either registering a GI or objecting to the registration of a GI. In the case of the United States, where GIs for agricultural products and foodstuffs are protected through collective marks and certification marks, the US government does not have any specialized knowledge or expertise that would render it better qualified than the rightholder, or, indeed, the EC, to make representations as to whether the specifications submitted by the rightholder meet the requirements of the EC GI Regulation. Indeed, to the contrary, it would seem that the EC, and not the United States Government, would be in a position to make that determination, particularly, for instance, with respect to whether a US GI has a reputation in the EC market. The GI applicant in the United States knows best the characteristics of his product that render it eligible for protection under the GI Regulation, and knows best what specifications under Article 4 of the GI Regulation his product meets. The EC should assess whether those specifications submitted by the applicant meet the EC's GI Regulation requirements on their own merits, without the intercession or intermediation of the United States Government. Indeed, this is precisely what the United States does in considering whether to register a certification or collective mark referring to a geographic area—including, significantly, registration applications received from EC nationals referring to areas in the EC. The USPTO relies on the declarations and representations of the certification or collective mark holder and relies on competitors in the marketplace to challenge the registration if the owner fails to uphold the standards provided

---

[59] *E.g.*, EC First Written Submission, para. 129.

[60] See *US – Section 337*, para. 5.11.

[61] EC Response to Questions of the Panel, para. 55.

[62] *E.g.*, EC First Written Submission, para. 130.

for in the registration.[63] This is also the practice of other jurisdictions which accept certification marks and collective marks for registration and which protect geographical indications through such marks.

74. In sum, it is neither appropriate nor necessary for the EC GI Regulation to require that other WTO Members administer and enforce the GI Regulation, and the condition that those Members do so results in less favorable treatment being accorded to their nationals than to the nationals of the EC.

D. THE REQUIREMENT THAT NON-EC GEOGRAPHICAL INDICATIONS—BUT NOT EC GEOGRAPHICAL INDICATIONS—BEAR A COUNTRY OF ORIGIN MARKING PROVIDES LESS FAVORABLE TREATMENT TO NON-EC NATIONALS THAN TO EC NATIONALS WITH REGARD TO THE PROTECTION OF GEOGRAPHICAL INDICATIONS.

75. The United States has argued that Article 12(2) of the EC GI Regulation imposes a special rule that non-EC GI names can be authorized only if the country of origin is visibly indicated on the label. The EC's two responses and the US rebuttals are as follows.

76. First, the EC argues that this requirement applies only where a third country name is identical to an EC name.[64] The United States notes, however, that this requirement for a country of origin indication, although it appears in Article 12(2) after a discussion of identical names, is set apart as a separate, albeit unnumbered, paragraph under Article 12, which addresses third country GIs in general. Thus, it appears to relate to all third country GIs, and not just to third country GIs that are identical to EC GIs.

77. Second, the EC claims that this rule applies to both EC and non-EC products equally. The United States notes, however, that the provision at issue falls under Article 12, which relates to the conditions of registration of non-EC GIs, not of EC GIs. The United States notes further that there appears to be no support in the text of the Regulation for the EC's assertion that the country of origin requirement applies to whichever GI—EC or third country—is registered later in time. That provision appears, rather, to be directed solely at the authorization of third country GIs. Therefore, if a third country GI is registered first, and then an application for an identical EC name is received, it is not clear on what basis the EC authorities would refer to Article 12 at all to determine under what conditions the EC name can be authorized.

78. Consequently, the requirement that non-EC geographical indications—but not EC geographical indications—bear a country of origin marking results in less favorable treatment of non-EC nationals than of EC nationals with regard to the protection of geographical indications

E. THE EC GI REGULATION REQUIRES DOMICILE OR ESTABLISHMENT IN THE EC AS A CONDITION FOR THE ENJOYMENT OF GI RIGHTS, CONTRARY TO THE OBLIGATION OF ARTICLE 2(3) OF THE PARIS CONVENTION

79. For those nationals from WTO Members who do not comply with the requirements of the EC GI Regulation, the only way to enjoy their intellectual property rights with respect to geographical indications is to become established or domiciled in the EC, and therefore to qualify directly to object to the registration of GIs under Article 7(3) of the GI Regulation, or to produce or obtain the products (for which they seek GI protection) in the EC. This is contrary to its Paris Convention obligation under Article 2(2) not to impose any requirement as to domicile or establishment in the EC "for the enjoyment of industrial property rights." The EC has two responses: first, a technical one that this plain violation is outside the Panel's terms of reference, so the Panel

---

[63] For example, the US Trademark Act provides that "any person who believes that he is or will be damaged...by the registration of a mark" may file a petition to cancel the registration of a mark. A certification mark registration may be challenged on the "ground that the registrant (A) does not control, or is not able legitimately to exercise control over, the use of such mark, or (B) engages in the production or marketing of any goods or services to which the certification mark is applied, or (C) permits the use of the certification mark for purposes other than to certify, or (D) discriminately refuses to certify or to continue to certify the goods or services of any person who maintains the standards or conditions which such mark certifies." 15 US C. Section 1064(5).

[64] *E.g.*, EC First Written Submission, para. 133.

cannot consider it.[65] Second, that a requirement that a legal person produce or obtain a product in the EC is not a requirement of "establishment" in the EC. Further, the EC apparently argues—somewhat surprisingly—that the requirement that, in order for a person to object to a registration under Article 7 of the GI Regulation, he must apply to the member State in which he "resides or is established"[66] is also not a requirement of "domicile or establishment."[67] Both of these arguments are baseless.

1. Article 2(2) of the Paris Convention is within the Panel's terms of reference

80. The US panel request contained both a statement that the GI Regulation failed to accord national treatment to non-EC nationals and a specific reference to Article 2 of the Paris Convention, a reference that plainly includes both paragraphs 1 and 2 of Article 2.[68] Neither paragraph uses the precise term "national treatment", but both together define that obligation. The non-establishment requirement of Article 2(2) follows immediately after Article 2(1), linked by the word "however", which indicates that what follows is connected to and part of the obligation in Article 2(1). Article 2(1) specifically provides that the same advantages must be provided to other nationals as to one's own nationals; and Article 2(2) specifies that a Member may not require domicile or establishment as a condition for the enjoyment of industrial property rights.

81. The link between these two paragraphs and their importance to "national treatment" is emphasized by this very proceeding. As the United States argued in its first submission, requiring an effective establishment in the EC as a precondition to obtaining GI protection is tantamount to a requirement that, in order to receive national treatment, a legal person must, in effect, become an EC national. In other words, the GI Regulation's requirement for a commercial establishment in Europe as a precondition to claiming the same rights as nationals is simply another aspect of its denial of national treatment to nationals of other WTO Members, a claim clearly within this Panel's terms of reference.

82. In addition, the United States notes that the entirety of Article 2 of the Paris Convention—not just Article 2(1)—is provided an annotated title "National Treatment for Nationals of the Countries of the Union" in the WIPO-published versions of the Convention. Finally, one of the main thrusts of the US complaint against the EC GI Regulation is that, to receive GI protection under the Regulation, persons have to set up a legal entity producing or obtaining products *in the EC*. Legal entities producing or obtaining products outside the EC are denied access to this system (barring compliance with substantial requirements by the WTO Member concerned). It can hardly be a surprise to the EC that the United States is claiming, as one aspect of its violation of national treatment obligations, that the EC is requiring establishment in the EC, in violation of Article 2(2) of the Paris Convention.

83. In short, because both the narrative description and the specific citation to Paris Convention Article 2 in the US Panel request include the obligations in Article 2(2), and because the EC clearly was aware of the nature of the US complaint, and could not have suffered any prejudice, the US claims under Article 2(2) are entirely within this Panel's terms of reference.

2. Nationals of WTO Members who do not comply with the EC GI Regulation's requirements must be domiciled or established in the EC in order to enjoy the GI rights provided under the EC GI Regulation

84. The EC's responses to this argument miss the mark. With respect to eligibility for registering GIs, the EC's primary argument is to claim, with no analysis or conclusion, that the "business establishment" in the EC, *inter alia*, growing agricultural products in the EC, would not "appear to constitute 'an establishment' within the

[65] EC First Written Submission, para. 42.

[66] EC GI Regulation, Article 7(3).

[67] EC First Written Submission, paras. 188-189.

[68] WT/DS174/20, August 19, 2003.

meaning of Article 2.2 of the Paris Convention."[69] The United States submits that, to the contrary, and the EC's unsupported assertion notwithstanding, a requirement to establish a business producing or obtaining agricultural products and foodstuffs in the EC is a requirement of "establishment" in the EC. Indeed, as discussed above in section II.A ("The EC GI Regulation discriminates based on nationality"), the EC's requirement appears to be tantamount to a requirement that the non-EC national—with a real and effective commercial establishment producing agricultural products in a non-EC WTO Member—set up a real and effective commercial establishment in the EC as a condition for taking advantage of the "domestic" track for GI Registration.

85. The EC also claims that the US is in effect arguing that geographical indications should be protected even if the products in question do not originate in the area in question.[70] This is untrue. What the United States is arguing is that the EC cannot require that the geographical area to be protected be *in the EC.* Yet, for any national from a WTO Member that does not comply with the GI Regulation's requirements, that is precisely what the EC is requiring.

86. Finally, with respect to the right of objection, the EC claims that the GI Regulation simply *allows* persons from other WTO Members to object to registrations.[71] This response misses the point. Nationals from WTO Members who do not assess objections from their nationals for compliance with the GI Regulation *must* reside or become established in the EC in order to object under the Article 7 objection procedures.[72] This is plainly a requirement of domicile of establishment in the EC for the enjoyment of an industrial property right.

F. THE EC GI REGULATION IMPOSES ADDITIONAL REQUIREMENTS ON NON-EC NATIONALS DESIRING TO OBJECT TO THE REGISTRATION OF A GI THAT ARE MORE BURDENSOME THAN THOSE IMPOSED ON EC NATIONALS

87. In addition to the above inconsistencies with the EC's national treatment obligations, the US first written submission explained that, while non-EC nationals must have a "legitimate interest" under Article 12d in order to object to the registration of an EC-based GI, an EC national wishing to object under Article 7(3) may do so if it is merely "legitimately concerned".[73] In addition, because the GI Regulation accords more favorable treatment to EC nationals than to non-EC nationals with respect to the registration and protection of GIs, it is harder for non-EC nationals than EC nationals to have a "legitimate interest" or a "legitimate economic interest" that would serve as grounds for objection under 12d.

88. The EC's sole response to this claim[74] is that there is no difference between the two standards. The United States submits, however, that a person may be "concerned" without his concern rising to the level of a "legitimate interest". An "interest", as a noun, generally implies some right to property or to a use or benefit relating to property. "Concerned" by contrast, is broader, and encompasses "interested, involved, troubled, anxious, showing concern."[75] The "legitimate interest" standard for non-EC nationals was introduced in April 2003. If the standard were the same as "legitimately concerned" it would have been logical to use the same words to describe it, instead of words that state a more restrictive standard. In the face of this plain difference in language, the EC has not sustained its burden of rebutting the presumption that this amounts to less favorable treatment of non-EC nationals.

---

[69] EC First Written Submission, para. 181.

[70] EC First Written Submission, para. 186.

[71] EC First Written Submission, para. 189.

[72] EC GI Regulation, Article 7(3).

[73] US First Written Submission, para. 93-94.

[74] EC First Written Submission, para. 151.

[75] *New Shorter Oxford English Dictionary* (Fourth Edition, 1993), pp. 467 ("concerned") and 1393 ("interest").

IV. THE EC GI REGULATION IS INCONSISTENT WITH THE NATIONAL TREATMENT OBLIGATIONS OF THE GATT 1994

A. THE EC GI REGULATION'S REQUIREMENTS THAT OTHER WTO MEMBERS ESTABLISH SPECIFIC INSPECTION STRUCTURES AND BECOME ACTIVE PARTICIPANTS AND ADVOCATES IN PROSECUTING ITS NATIONALS' GI REGISTRATIONS AND OBJECTIONS ACCORDS LESS FAVORABLE TREATMENT TO NON-EC PRODUCTS THAN IT DOES TO EC PRODUCTS.

89. In its first written submission, the United States showed that the EC GI Regulation was inconsistent with the EC's obligation under Article III:4 of the GATT 1994 to accord no less favorable treatment to products originating in the territory of other Members than it accords to like products of national origin. The EC does not contest that the imported products are "like" domestic products,[76] and does not contest that the EC GI Regulation is a measure that falls within the scope of Article III:4.[77] The only issue, therefore, is whether the EC GI Regulation accords imported products "less favorable treatment" than that accorded to the like domestic products.[78]

90. The EC contends that it does not, for the same reasons that it does not accord "less favorable treatment" to nationals of other WTO Members under the TRIPS Agreement: (1) there is no reciprocity and equivalence requirement for WTO Members; and (2) the requirement for inspection structures and the requirement that WTO Members themselves process GI registration applications and objections constitutes "equal" not "less favorable" treatment for products of non-EC origin.[79] The first of these arguments has been addressed above, and will not be addressed separately here.

91. The EC's argument that the treatment accorded non-EC products is "equal" to that accorded EC products is not correct. First, that the EC has chosen to establish particular inspection structures in the EC in order to ensure that EC producers comply with the EC GI Regulation does not mean that it is "equal treatment" of like products to impose the requirement for the same inspection structures on other WTO Members. To the contrary; to do so is to condition the granting of GATT 1994 Article III:4 rights on the WTO Member in question adopting the same compliance structure as the EC. This is precisely the "reciprocity" and "equivalence" conditionality that the national treatment obligation was designed to avoid.

92. A product from the United States that meets the requirements of the GI Regulation—that is, an agricultural product or foodstuff originating in a region of the United States which possesses a specific quality, reputation or other characteristics attributable to that geographic origin—must, under Article III:4 of the GATT 1994, be accorded no less favorable treatment than an EC product that meets those requirements. But under the GI Regulation, an EC product that qualifies for protection due to characteristics attributable to its origin can be registered and protected under the EC GI system. By contrast, a US product that similarly qualifies for registration and protection due to characteristics attributable to its origin is denied registration and protection in the EC. This is *not* because the product itself does not possess the necessary characteristics related to its origin. Rather, it is because the United States has not established the EC-mandated inspection structures.

93. In other words, a qualifying EC-origin product can be registered and protected under the EC GI Regulation, while a US product that is "like" that EC product in every respect is denied access to that system. And, of course, the consequence of registration and protection—denied the US product but granted the EC like product—is all of the competitive advantages and benefits bestowed on GI products under the EC system.[80]

---

[76] EC First Written Submission, para. 195.

[77] EC First Written Submission, para. 194.

[78] *See* Appellate Body Report, *Korea – Various Measures on Beef*, para. 133.

[79] *See* EC First Written Submission, para. 207; First Oral Statement, paras. 71 and 45.

[80] These benefits were detailed in the US First Written Submission, *e.g.*, at paras. 28-30 and 61-62, and will not be repeated here.

94. The United States submits that this amounts to treatment of non-EC products that is significantly less favorable than treatment accorded EC products, contrary to Article III:4 of the GATT 1994.

95. Second, and similarly, the requirement that WTO Members themselves become active participants and advocates for their nationals in analyzing and submitting GI registration applications and objections also amounts to less favorable treatment of non-EC products. As just discussed, a US product that meets the requirements of the EC GI Regulation should be eligible to be registered and protected under that Regulation. The requirement that the WTO Member have substantial participation in this process—a requirement imposed unilaterally by the EC and not otherwise required by any WTO agreement—is both burdensome and unnecessary, and acts as an additional barrier to non-EC goods seeking access to the EC GI system. This is not a barrier faced by EC goods, because the EC GI Regulation itself mandates authorities in the EC to process applications and objections.

B. THE REQUIREMENT THAT NON-EC PRODUCTS BE ENCUMBERED BY A COUNTRY OF ORIGIN INDICATION ON THE LABEL IS INCONSISTENT WITH THE NATIONAL TREATMENT OBLIGATIONS OF THE GATT 1994

96. The United States has argued that Article 12(2) of the EC GI Regulation imposes a special rule that non-EC GI names can be authorized only if the country of origin is visibly indicated on the label. The EC's three responses and the US rebuttals are as follows.

97. First, the EC argues that this requirement applies only where a third country name is identical to an EC name.[81] As above, the United States notes, however, that this requirement for a country of origin indication, although it appears in Article 12(2) below a discussion of identical names, is set apart as a separate, albeit unnumbered, paragraph under Article 12, which addresses third country GIs in general. Thus, it appears to relate to *all* third country GIs, and not just to third country GIs that are identical to EC GIs.

98. Second, the EC claims that this rule applies to both EC and non-EC products equally. Again, as above, the United States notes that the provision at issue falls under Article 12, which relates to the conditions of registration of non-EC GIs, not of EC GIs. The United States notes further that there appears to be no support in the text of the Regulation for the EC's assertion that the country of origin requirement applies to whichever GI—EC or third country—is registered later in time. That provision appears, rather, to be directed solely at the authorization of third country GIs, regardless. If a third country GI is registered first, and then an application for an identical EC name is received, it is not clear on what basis the EC authorities would refer to Article 12 to determine under what conditions the EC name can be authorized.

99. Finally, the EC argues, in effect, that a special country of origin labeling requirement cannot be inconsistent with national treatment obligations, because Article IX:1 of the GATT 1994 contains only an MFN obligation, and not a specific national treatment obligation, with respect to "marking requirements". But the EC's argument ignores the fact that the EC GI Regulation does not contain a general "marking requirement" for goods. Rather, it is a special rule that is triggered by the fact that a third country product is being authorized to use a protected GI name, and is intended to encumber the non-EC GI, while not so encumbering the EC GI. The United States does not believe that, under these circumstances, the EC is exempt from its obligation to provide no less favorable treatment to non-EC products.

C. THE EC HAS PRESENTED NO INFORMATION WHATSOEVER THAT THE INCONSISTENCIES WITH GATT 1994 ARTICLE III:4 ARE EXCUSED BY ARTICLE XX(D) OF THE GATT 1994

100. The United States presented information and arguments showing that the EC GI Regulation is inconsistent with the EC's national treatment obligations under Article III:4 of the GATT 1994. In addition to its general denials that there is less favorable treatment of non-EC products, the EC has also suggested, in a

[81] EC First Written Submission, para. 137.

conclusory fashion, that any such inconsistency would be excused by Article XX(d) of the GATT 1994.[82] As the party asserting that its GI Regulation falls within the scope of the Article XX exceptions, it is the EC, as the party asserting the defense, that bears the burden of proof. As the Appellate Body noted in *Japan – Apples*, "although the complaining party bears the burden of proving its case, the responding party must prove the case it seeks to make in response."[83] The Appellate Body also noted in *United States – Shirts and Blouses*, page 14, that:

> the burden of proof rests upon the party, whether complaining or defending, who asserts the affirmative of a particular claim or defence. If that party adduces evidence sufficient to raise a presumption that what is claimed is true, the burden then shifts to the other party, who will fail unless it adduces sufficient evidence to rebut the presumption." (footnotes omitted)

101. The EC's entire submission to this Panel with respect to Article XX(d) is that

> The requirements at issue are necessary in order to ensure that only those products which conform to the definition of geographical indications contained in Article 12(2) of Regulation 2081/92, which is itself fully consistent with the GATT, benefit from the protection afforded to geographical indications by Regulation 2081/92.[84]

102. But this is little more than an imprecise paraphrasing of Article XX(d) itself. There is no explanation of, or information concerning, how the WTO Member's significant involvement in the GI Registration application process—including the declarations that the WTO Member must make to the EC—or its involvement in the "objection" process is "necessary" to "secure compliance" with WTO-consistent laws or regulations, which is the limited basis on which Article XX(d) permits an exception to GATT 1994 obligations. Nor has the EC explained how the particular inspection structures it is requiring as a precondition to the registration of non-EC GIs are "necessary to ensure [such] compliance". Successfully proving the entitlement to this exception to GATT 1994 obligations involves much more than a conclusory statement, which provides neither the United States nor the Panel a foundation on which to base any analysis whatsoever of the EC's affirmative defense to a GATT violation.

103. The United States does not see anything in Article XX(d) that would excuse the EC from its GATT 1994 obligations, and the EC has not provided any information or evidence that it does. Therefore, this Panel should find that the EC GI Regulation's inconsistency with the GATT 1994 is not excused by Article XX(d) of the GATT 1994.

V. THE EC GI REGULATION IS INCONSISTENT WITH THE MFN OBLIGATIONS OF THE TRIPS AGREEMENT AND THE PARIS CONVENTION

A. MFN OBLIGATIONS WITH RESPECT TO THE NATIONALS OF NON-EC WTO MEMBERS

104. The United States argued in its first written submission that the EC GI Regulation's inconsistencies with the MFN obligations of the TRIPS Agreement and the Paris Convention derived from the same conditions for GI protection imposed on WTO Members that give rise to inconsistencies with the national treatment obligation under the TRIPS Agreement and the Paris Convention. That is, the nationals of any country that satisfies the GI Regulations requirements with respect to

[82] EC First Written Submission, para. 226.

[83] Appellate Body Report, para. 154.

[84] EC First Written Submission, para. 226.

- reciprocity and equivalence

- specified inspection structures, and

- the substantial participation in administering and enforcing the EC GI Regulation on behalf of its nationals

can register and protect their home-based GIs and can object to the registration of GIs. Any national of a WTO that does not satisfy these requirements, by contrast, cannot do so. Consequently, the EC GI Regulation does not "immediately and unconditionally" accord to nationals of all WTO Members the advantages, favors, privileges, or immunities accorded to EC nationals. In addition to the arguments refuted in the "national treatment" section above, the EC protests that it has not yet applied this Regulation to benefit the nationals of qualifying countries.[85]

105. But the lack of third country GI registrations under the GI Regulation does not mean that it is immune from challenge. The EC cites several disputes in which there was a discriminatory application of a law, implying that this is a requirement to challenge a measure on MFN grounds[86] but ignores that there are, equally, disputes in which a discriminatory measure had not yet been applied, but was nonetheless found inconsistent with obligations. In one such dispute, *United States – Superfund*, the panel explained that the obligations in that dispute:

> are not only to protect current trade but also to create the predictability needed to plan future trade. That objective could not be attained if contracting parties could not challenge existing legislation mandating actions at variance with the General Agreement until the administrative acts implementing it had actually been applied to their trade.

The United States has not, in fact, challenged any particular application of the GI Regulation on MFN grounds; rather it is challenging this aspect of the EC GI Regulation on its face.

106. The fact is that the conditions for protection described above—conditions that are necessarily determined on a country-by-country basis—reward nationals of those individual countries that agree to adopt EC structures and systems for protecting geographical indications and that agree to administer and enforce the EC GI Regulation in their territory. Nationals from those countries receive as favorable treatment as EC nationals. Nationals from countries that do not so agree are precluded from accessing the EC GI Regulation protection system.[87] In this connection, the EC's quotation of the *Canada – Autos* panel report,[88] discussing why not all non-product-related condition are *per se* inconsistent with Article I:1 of the GATT 1994 is not relevant.

107. There is no room under the EC GI Regulation for the Commission to determine that all WTO Members satisfy the conditions of the GI Regulation. Some WTO Members may have the EC-style inspection structures, others do not; some WTO Members might be able to prosecute GI registration applications successfully on behalf of their nationals, and others cannot. There is nothing that the EC can do in administering the EC GI Regulation that will treat nationals of all WTO Members as favorably as each other and as favorably as EC nationals.

108. In other words, *any* application of the EC GI Regulation to a third country would result in a failure to accord MFN treatment to nationals of all third country WTO Members. The Commission has no ability to

---

[85] EC First Written Submission, paras. 239-245.

[86] EC First Written Submission, para. 242, citing *EEC – Imports of Beef from Canada* and *Belgian Family Allowances*.

[87] As discussed above in the context of "national treatment," the GI Regulation discriminates on the basis of nationality. *See* Section III.A above.

[88] EC First Written Submission, para. 237.

avoid this result under the Regulation. And, of course, the refusal to apply the GI Regulation to other third countries at all—which is theoretically one way of assuring equal treatment among nationals of all third country WTO Members—would be inconsistent with the national treatment obligation. In any case, the GI Regulation does not appear to permit the Commission to refuse to apply the GI Regulation to all third countries.

109. Accordingly, even in the absence of a specific application to any third country, the EC GI Regulation is inconsistent with the MFN obligations of the GI Regulation.

B. MFN OBLIGATIONS OF EC MEMBER STATES WITH RESPECT TO NATIONALS OF ALL OTHER NON-EC WTO MEMBERS

110. The United States also argued that, since each of the EC member States is also a WTO Member in its own right, each member State has an obligation to accord to non-EC nationals the same advantages, favors, privileges, and immunities accorded to nationals of other EC member States. That is, any benefits France provides to German nationals must also be provided to US nationals. By requiring that, for instance, France accord advantages to German nationals that it does not accord to US nationals, the EC GI Regulation is inconsistent with the MFN obligation under the TRIPS Agreement. The GI Regulation does this, for instance, by requiring that France recognize and enforce GIs that are registered by German nationals, but does not require, or even permit, France to provide the same recognition to US GIs, since they cannot be registered under the GI Regulation in the first place.

111. The EC's response to this argument, aside from responses already addressed in the context of national treatment, is not clear.[89] The EC appears to be arguing that, in requiring its member States to accord advantages to nationals of other EC member States that they do not accord to nationals of other WTO Members, the EC *itself* is not according advantages to "any other country", and so the EC member States are exempted from the MFN obligation. The EC also states that the measure at issue is an EC measure, not a member State measure.[90]

112. But the EC ignores two important facts. First, in this dispute, the United States defined the measure—the EC GI Regulation—as Regulation 2081/92 *and its related implementation and enforcement measures.*[91] Therefore, any related implementation and enforcement measures—including those of EC member States—are included within the Panel's terms of reference. Consequently, the Panel can and should review whether the measures that EC member States must take to implement and enforce the EC GI Regulation—measures that accord advantages, favors, privileges and immunities to nationals of other EC member States—accord those same advantages, favors, privileges, and immunities to WTO Members that are not EC member States.

113. Second, the EC cannot reasonably claim that whether an EC member State is complying with its MFN obligations depends on whether or not it is implementing EC regulations or its own. The only question under Article 4 of the TRIPS Agreement is whether the WTO Member concerned is granting the same advantages, favors, privileges and immunities to other WTO Members as it grants to its own nationals. If not, there is a violation of the MFN obligation, and it does not matter *why* or pursuant to what *requirement* the WTO Member is discriminating against nationals of other WTO Members. An EC member State cannot avoid its MFN obligations simply by claiming that it is discriminating pursuant to an EC regulation.

VI. THE EC GI REGULATION IS INCONSISTENT WITH THE MFN OBLIGATIONS OF THE GATT 1994

114. In its first written submission, the United States argued that the EC GI Regulation was inconsistent with Article I:1 of the GATT 1994, because, in a manner similar to that presented in *Belgian Family Allowances*, the GI Regulation introduces a discrimination between countries having a given system of GI

[89] *See* EC First Written Submission, paras. 252—256.

[90] EC First Written Submission, para. 255.

[91] WT/DS174/20.

protection and having the ability to successfully advocate on behalf of their nationals with respect to the registration of GIs and objections to GIs.[92] The EC's responses to this argument are the same as those presented in connection with other issues described above: (1) There is no condition of reciprocity and equivalence for WTO Members; (2) The conditions for registration are not discriminatory; and (3) The GI Regulation has not yet been applied to products from third countries.[93]

115. As the United States has already responded to these arguments above, it will not repeat those arguments here.

116. Finally, as is the case with its response to the national treatment claim with respect to goods, the EC has failed to present any explanation whatsoever of how Article XX(d) of the GATT 1994 might excuse this inconsistency with the Article 1:1 MFN obligation.

VII. THE EC GI REGULATION IS INCONSISTENT WITH THE EC'S OBLIGATIONS UNDER ARTICLE 16.1 OF THE TRIPS AGREEMENT

A. INTRODUCTION

117. As the United States has shown in its first written submission and oral statement, Article 16.1 of the TRIPS Agreement requires that owners of registered trademarks be given the exclusive right to prevent *all* third parties from using similar or identical signs, including geographical indications, for identical or similar goods, where such use would result in a likelihood of confusion.[94] The United States has also shown that the EC GI Regulation is inconsistent with this obligation because, as the EC acknowledges,[95] *even if* the owner of a prior valid registered trademark can prove that use of an identical or similar registered geographical indication raises a likelihood of confusion, it cannot prevent that use.

118. Specifically, as Article 14(2) of the EC GI Regulation demonstrates, even in cases where use of a registered geographical indication gives rise to a likelihood of confusion within the meaning of Article 16.1 of the TRIPS Agreement, the product that is marketed and labeled with that geographical indication can be sold alongside a similar or the same product that has been marketed and labeled with an identical or similar valid prior registered trademark. The owner of the trademark will have no ability to exercise its Article 16.1 rights to prevent any confusing use by the later-registered geographical indication. As the United States has emphasized in its previous submissions to the Panel, the "exclusive right ... to prevent" confusing uses in Article 16.1 is critical to trademark owners. Without this right to exclude *all* others from confusing uses, owning a trademark would mean practically nothing, since the purpose and value of a trademark is to be able to distinguish one company's goods from the goods of other companies. Without the ability to stop confusing uses, this value is eliminated.

119. At this stage of the proceedings, and contrary to the EC's arguments, it should be clear that under the US interpretation of the relevant provisions of the TRIPS Agreement, no one form of intellectual property right is superior to another. The EC position appears to be that a GI will always take precedence over a trademark. By contrast, the US interpretation does not require any "hierarchy" between trademarks and geographical indications. Rather, under the US interpretation, each TRIPS Agreement provision is given its full scope, and both trademarks and geographical indications are granted their respective spheres of exclusivity. Under Article 16.1 of the TRIPS Agreement, a trademark owner is given the exclusive right to exclude uses by all others of similar or identical signs that are likely to confuse consumers within a given territory. Under Article 22.2 and 22.3 of the TRIPS Agreement, interested parties in geographical indications are granted the right to prevent the use of signs that mislead consumers within a given territory about the origin of goods.

---

[92] US First written Submission, paras. 127-129.

[93] EC First written submission, paras. 260-264.

[94] US First Written Submission, paras. 130-170; US Oral Statement, paras. 40-75.

[95] EC First Written Submission, paras. 302-307; EC Responses to Questions, para. 141.

There is no "conflict" between these provisions. The provisions are not mutually exclusive; "simultaneous compliance with the obligations" of these provisions is not "impossible" in any sense.[96]

120. The EC is simply wrong that under the US interpretation, trademarks that "lack ... distinctiveness,"[97] or trademarks that constitute "illegitimate uses" of geographical indications, will prevail over geographical indications. The United States has made it clear that if a trademark is not distinctive, or if it is "illegitimate" because it misleads consumers in a particular country about the origin of goods, then the TRIPS Agreement and the Paris Convention provide that it should not be registered.[98] If for some reason it is registered, it is subject to invalidation.[99]

121. The EC is also wrong to argue that under the US interpretation, the exclusivity of trademarks is valued over the exclusivity of geographical indications,[100] that the United States is supporting the "superiority of trademarks over geographical indications,"[101] and that, in the United States' view, trademarks "must prevail over later geographical indications."[102] The United States accepts—and nothing in its interpretation suggests otherwise—that in any given case, a trademark owner bringing an infringement claim against the user of a geographical indication might not succeed on the merits. For example, the trademark owner might not be able to prove that the particular use of the geographical indication would result in a likelihood of confusion. Or the interested party in the geographical indication might be able to show that the trademark is subject to invalidation.

122. Under the EC GI Regulation, however, *even if* the owner of a prior valid registered trademark can prove, consistent with TRIPS Article 16.1, that use of an identical or similar registered geographical indication confuses consumers, and *even if* the interested party in the geographical indication fails to show, consistent with TRIPS Article 22.3, that the trademark misleads consumers with respect to origin, the trademark owner *still* cannot prevent the continued use of that geographical indication in a manner that results in a likelihood of confusion. The very best that the trademark owner can hope for in this situation is the ability to continue selling products with its trademark affixed, but deprived of its ability to distinguish the goods of the trademark owner. The trademark owner cannot exercise its right to prevent confusing use of the geographical indication.

123. This is inconsistent with Article 16.1. In *United States – Section 211*, the Appellate Body emphasized the importance of the exclusive nature of trademark rights, finding that Article 16.1 confers on the owners of "registered trademarks an internationally agreed minimum level of 'exclusive rights' that all WTO Members

---

96 Panel Report, *Turkey – Textiles*, para. 9.92. *See also* Panel Report, *Indonesia – Autos*, para. 14.28 ("[I]n public international law there is a presumption against conflict," which is "especially relevant in the WTO context since all WTO agreements ... were negotiated at the same time, by the same Members and in the same forum." (footnotes omitted)).

97 EC First Written Statement, paras. 289, 291.

98 TRIPS Articles 22.3, 15.1; Paris Convention Article 6*quinquies*B.

99 TRIPS Article 22.3; Paris Convention Article 6*quinquies*B. For this reason, the EC is wrong to argue, at paragraph 307 of its first written submission, that the United States is proposing "rigid application of the first-in-time rule." As previously noted, the United States is concerned in this dispute with the rights accorded only to prior valid registered trademarks. Assuming that the trademark registration is valid, the United States finds it curious that the EC, also in paragraph 307, argues that priority is not appropriate "to resolve conflicts ... between trademarks and geographical indications, because they are distinct intellectual property rights, each with its own characteristics." *See also* EC Oral Statement, para. 15. The ECJ appears to disagree. Advocate General Tizzano recently issued an opinion stating that "[le] principe de la primauté du titre antérieur d'exclusivité ... représente un des fondements du droit des marques et, d'une façon plus générale, de tout le droit de la propriété industrielle." ("[The] principle of the priority of a preceding exclusive right ... is one of the basic principles of trademark law and, more generally, of all intellectual property law.") The Advocate General concluded (at paragraphs 102 and 119 of his Opinion) that the principle of priority should be applied to resolve conflicts between trademarks and trade names and that trade or commercial names, like geographical indications, are "distinct" from trademarks. Advocate General Tizzano's Opinion in Case C-245/02, *Anheuser-Busch Inc. v. Budejovický Budvar, národní podnik*, delivered 29 June 2004. Exhibit US-51 includes official versions of the Opinion in French and Finnish, along with an unofficial English translation (from the Finnish).

100 EC First Written Submission, paras. 271, 274; EC Responses to Questions, para. 215.

101 EC First Written Submission, para. 295.

102 EC First Written Submission, para. 297.

must guarantee in their domestic legislation"—rights that "protect the owner against infringement of the registered trademark by unauthorized third parties."[103]

124. In contrast, the EC argues in this dispute that "[t]he fact that the owner of a registered trademark cannot prevent the use of the same or a similar sign by the right holders of a geographical indication does not mean that the registration of the trademark is, for that reason alone, 'set aside', or 'overthrown' or that it is without 'legal strength' or 'efficacy'."[104] But even the EC jurisprudence recognizes that the core of a trademark right is the right of an owner of a trademark to prevent the use of a similar or identical sign that would result in a likelihood of confusion.[105]

125. The EC is correct that "co-existence"—meaning the ability of a trademark owner to do nothing more than to continue selling products with its trademark affixed, without the Article 16.1 right to prevent infringing uses of similar or identical signs—"may not be a perfect solution to resolve conflicts between different types of intellectual property rights."[106] More significant, however, it is a solution that is inconsistent with Article 16.1. It presumes that the simultaneous compliance with the obligations in Articles 16.1, 22.2 and 22.3 is impossible, and as such reads a conflict into complementary provisions of the TRIPS Agreement where there is none.

B. ARTICLE 14(3) OF THE EC GI REGULATION DOES NOT SATISFY THE EC'S OBLIGATIONS UNDER ARTICLE 16.1 OF THE TRIPS AGREEMENT

126. The EC argues, in effect, that owners of registered trademarks in the EC or its member States do not need the Article 16.1 right to prevent all uses of similar or identical geographical indications that raise a likelihood of confusion, because Article 14(3) of the GI Regulation "says that the registration of a geographical indication shall be refused if it is likely to lead to confusion with a trademark."[107] (At other points, however, the EC argues that the TRIPS Agreement does not provide for the exclusivity of prior valid trademarks with respect to conflicting geographical indications.[108])

127. Article 14(3) provides that:

> A designation of origin or geographical indication shall not be registered where, in the light of a trade mark's reputation and renown and the length of time it has been used, registration is liable to mislead the consumer as to the true origin of the product.

128. Article 14(3) does not satisfy the EC's obligations under Article 16.1 of the TRIPS Agreement, for at least two reasons. First, even if, for the sake of argument, this Panel were to accept the reading of Article 14(3) offered by the EC, the "protection" offered trademark owners is not sufficient to satisfy Article 16.1 of the TRIPS Agreement. Article 16.1 requires that *registered trademark owners* be given the right to prevent confusing *uses* of identical or similar signs, and not just that *government authorities* be given the authority to prevent the *registration* of confusing signs. Second, Article 14(3) does not permit the EC to refuse registration of all geographical indications that raise a likelihood of confusion with any similar or identical trademark. As is evident from the text of Article 14(3), it applies only with respect to a certain subset of valid registered trademarks—trademarks with a certain reputation, renown, and that have been used for a certain length of time.

---

[103] Appellate Body Report, *United States – Section 211*, para. 186.

[104] EC Responses to Questions, para. 204.

[105] *See, e.g.*, Advocate General Jacobs' Opinion in Case C-10/89, *SA CNL-Sucal NV v. HAG GFAG*, delivered 13 March 1990, [1990] ECR I-3711, para. 19 (Exhibit US-8) ("A trademark can only fulfil that role [*i.e.*, to identify the manufacturer and to guarantee quality] if it is exclusive. Once the proprietor is forced to share the mark with the competitor, he loses control over the goodwill associated with the mark. The reputation of his own goods will be harmed if the competitor sells inferior goods. From the consumers' point of view, equally undesirable consequences will ensue, because the clarity of the signal transmitted by the trademark will be impaired. The consumer will be confused and misled.").

[106] EC First Written Submission, para. 307.

[107] EC Responses to Questions, para. 155.

[108] EC Responses to Questions, paras. 200-221.

129. The United States addresses these two reasons in turn, below.

1. Even if the EC's reading of Article 14(3) of the EC GI Regulation were correct, Article 14(3) is not a substitute for the rights accorded trademark owners under Article 16.1 of the TRIPS Agreement

130. The EC asserts that Article 14(3) requires the EC to reject registration of a geographical indication if the registration is likely to lead to confusion with a trademark. Article 16.1 requires that the *owner* of a registered trademark have the exclusive right to prevent all *uses* of identical or similar signs that result in a likelihood of confusion. Even if the EC's reading of Article 14(3) is accurate, it does not satisfy Article 16.1 of the TRIPS Agreement, in two ways.

(a) TRIPS Article 16.1 addresses *uses*, while Article 14(3) of the EC Regulation addresses only *registration*

131. Even according to the EC's reading, Article 14(3) does not afford a trademark owner the right to ensure that no *uses* of a geographical indication, once registered, will result in a likelihood of confusion. This is an important distinction, because a trademark owner is not necessarily able to know, from the registration of a geographical indication alone, whether *use* of the registered geographical indication will raise a likelihood of confusion. This is because a trademark owner cannot know, from the registered name on its own, precisely how it will be used. For example, a registered geographical indication may be used in ways that cannot be anticipated, such as in a trademark-like manner or in translation, in a manner that causes a likelihood of confusion with respect to a registered trademark. The scope of permitted uses of a name registered as a geographical indication may be broader than the name, as such, that is registered.

132. In an apparent attempt to diffuse this concern, the EC states that

> a trademark owner may use its trademark rights in order to prevent the right holders of a geographical indication from using confusingly *any other names or other signs* (e.g. graphic signs) in conjunction with, or in place of, the name registered as a geographical indication. In other words, the right holders of a geographical indication only have a positive right to use *the name registered* as a geographical indication.[109]

133. But this distinction is not as straightforward as the EC suggests. The United States attaches as Exhibit US-52 four pictorial depictions of the packaging for products sold under geographical indications registered in the EC, and the accompanying product specifications. It should be noted that the product specifications do not limit the way in which the geographical indications are used, and the pictorial depictions demonstrate that the name is often used in a trademark-like fashion. Determining what exactly will constitute use of "the name registered," therefore, is not always evident from the name that is registered alone. To know whether "the name registered" raises a likelihood of confusion, in many cases, a trademark owner needs to see the registered name in use.[110]

134. The issue of translations also raises the question of what limits are imposed on, and what is encompassed by, use of "the name registered." The United States has referred to two examples. The United States has noted three registered geographical indications set out in the Czech Republic's Act of Accession:

[109] EC Responses to Questions, para. 142 (emphasis added).

[110] This is not to say, however, that a geographical indication cannot be found confusingly similar to a prior valid trademark at the time of registration, for instance, in cases where both the signs and the goods are identical. In such cases, Article 16.1 of the TRIPS Agreement requires that the likelihood of confusion be presumed. However, not all confusing uses can be foreseen at the time of registration; therefore, the trademark owner must be provided the right to prevent confusing uses in the market as they arise.

Budejovické pivo, Ceskobudejovické pivo and Budejovický mešťanský var.[111] In trademark infringement proceedings pending before the Swedish courts, a Czech brewer has argued that registration grants the right to use these three names in translation. Specifically, it asserts that the German translation of the three registered geographical indications include "Budweiser Budvar," "Budweis," and "Budbräu."[112] The United States has also cited to the registered geographical indication "Bayerisches Bier," which the Commission decided to register despite concerns raised under Article 14(3) that if used in translation, it could confuse the consumer in relation to the "Bavaria" trademark in Holland.[113] ("Bayer," the root of "Bayerisches," is translated into English as "Bavaria"—the suffix "isches" is the adjective form of "bayer".)

135. The text of Article 16.1 is clear—the owner of a registered trademark must be granted the right to prevent *uses* of similar or identical signs that raise a likelihood of confusion. The practical reason behind this requirement is equally clear from the examples cited above—in many cases, unless or until the registered geographical identification is actually used, neither the EC authorities nor the trademark owner will always know whether there is a likelihood of confusion. Even accepting the EC's reading of Article 14(3) on its face, the trademark owner is not afforded the right guaranteed under Article 16.1

(b) TRIPS Article 16.1 grants rights to *trademark owners*, while Article 14(3) of the EC Regulation empowers the *EC authorities*

136. Even under the EC's reading, Article 14(3) does not provide the *trademark owner* with the right to prevent confusing uses, as is required by Article 16.1 of the TRIPS Agreement. According to the EC, it merely requires the *EC authorities* to decline registration of a geographical indication in some circumstances. The trademark owner does not control this process—a factor critical to an owner's Article 16.1 rights. As stated in the preamble to the TRIPS Agreement, "intellectual property rights are private rights," and control over them by private owners is crucial.

137. The EC suggests that the trademark owner has two ways of asserting its Article 16.1 rights in the registration process. First, the EC refers to the "right" of a trademark owner to object to the registration of a geographical indication, pursuant to Article 7(4) of the EC GI Regulation.[114] This so-called "right" is insufficient to implement the Article 16.1 obligations. The United States has shown that, in fact, US nationals do not enjoy the "right" to object to registration of a geographical indication on a non-discriminatory basis. Moreover, even if they did, it is apparently the EC's own view that the right of objection is *not* part of the Article 16.1 right to prevent confusing uses.[115] In addition, as the United States noted in its responses to questions, nearly 80 percent of the geographical indications registered in the EC to date, including, most recently, names registered *via* accession protocols, were exempt from the objection procedures included in the EC GI Regulation.[116] In these circumstances, trademark owners will find no comfort in the EC's assertion of the "right" of objection as a sufficient substitute for Article 16.1 rights.

138. Second, the EC notes that if a trademark owner considers that the Commission has registered a geographical indication that raises a likelihood of confusion, the owner can challenge the Commission's failure

---

[111] Exhibit COMP-3.c (Annex II, para. 18).

[112] Copies of the Czech brewer's brief to the Swedish court, in Swedish and as unofficially translated to English, are included in Exhibit US-53. The relevant passage is at paragraphs 4-6 of Section 3.2 The EC has not indicated in these proceedings, or in the Swedish domestic court proceedings discussed above, whether use of a registered GI in translation constitutes a permitted use of that GI.

[113] US Oral Statement, para. 55.

[114] The EC states that a statement of objection "shall" be admissible if it demonstrates that "'the registration of the name proposed would jeopardize the existence of a mark.'" EC Responses to Questions, para. 160, *quoting* the EC GI Regulation, Article 7(4).

[115] EC First Written Submission, paras. 326 ("Article 16.1 does not confer a right of objection."), 327 (Article 16.1 does not grant to the trademark owners a right to formulate objections in the framework of a procedure for the acquisition of another intellectual property right, whether it is a trademark or a different right such as geographical indication."), and 427 ("[T]he EC considers that the right to formulate objections to the registration of another intellectual property rights is not inherent in the exclusive rights conferred to trademark rights holders by Article 16.1.").

[116] US Responses to Questions, para. 68.

properly to apply Article 14(3) before the "courts."[117] The United States presumes that the EC is referring to a challenge to the validity of a registration before the EU courts. Under Article 230 of the EC Treaty,[118] a natural or legal person that is "directly and individually concerned" by a registration can challenge the validity of the registration before the Court of First Instance ("CFI"), with an appeal to the European Court of Justice ("ECJ").[119] The very important qualification, however, is that under Article 230, the case must be brought *within two months of publication of the registration.*[120]

139. But actual confusing uses may not become apparent within two months, and Article 16.1 permits no such "expiration" of the Article 16.1 rights. Indeed, aware of this two-month window, a potential user of a registered geographical indication would be well-advised to preserve the registration from challenge by waiting until the two-month period has tolled to begin particular uses of the geographical indication that would arguably raise a likelihood of confusion with respect to a registered trademark.

140. At that stage, after the two-month period has expired, the trademark owner's only option would be to bring an infringement challenge against confusing use of the identical or similar geographical indication.[121] But as the EC has confirmed,[122] even if the owner of a prior valid registered trademark can prove that use of an identical or similar geographical indication raises a likelihood of confusion, it will not be able to prevent use of the geographical indication. The most the trademark owner can hope for is the continued ability to sell products with its trademark affixed, without the ability to prevent confusing use of the geographical indication.

141. For all of these reasons, the ability to challenge the registration of a geographical indication is no substitute for Article 16.1 rights. Article 16.1 of the TRIPS Agreement grants rights to *trademark owners* to prevent particular *uses* of identical or similar signs, and imposes no two-month time limit on the exercise of that right. For as long as the trademark is valid and registered, Article 16.1 grants the owner the right to prevent uses of identical or similar signs that raise a likelihood of confusion.

2. Article 14(3) of the EC GI Regulation neither requires nor permits the EC authorities to deny registration of all confusing geographical indications.

142. The EC asserts that Article 14(3) "says that the registration of a geographical indication shall be refused if it is likely to lead to confusion with a trademark."[123] But Article 14(3) does not say this. It says that a geographical indication "shall not be registered where, in the light of a trade mark's reputation and renown and the length of time it has been used, registration is liable to mislead the consumer as to the true origin of the product."

---

[117] EC Responses to Questions, paras. 153, 181.

[118] Exhibit US-26.

[119] The concept of "directly and individually concerned" is narrowly applied, as confirmed recently by the ECJ in C-50/00, *Union de Pequenos Agricultores v Council* (25 July 2002). Exhibit US-54.

[120] This deadline has been enforced strictly. *See, e.g.*, Case T-85/97, *Horeca-Wallonie v. Commission*, order of 20 November 1997 (Exhibit US-55); Case T-12/90, *Bayer AG v. Commission*, Case C-195/91 P, *Bayer A.G. v Commission* [1994] ECR 1-5619 (Exhibit US-56).

[121] The United States will later in this submission rebut assertions by the EC (EC Responses to Questions, para. 31) that the interpretation of Article 14(3) it offers to the Panel is the same interpretation that it has adopted and will continue to support in proceedings before the ECJ. At this point, the United States merely observes that once the two-month period to challenge the validity of the geographical indication registration expires, the Commission will no longer be there, and its allegedly helpful interpretation of Article 14(3) will no longer be relevant, to help trademark owners as they turn to national courts to resolve infringement claims regarding confusing uses of the registered geographical indications.

[122] EC First Written Submission, paras. 302-307; EC Responses to Questions, para. 141.

[123] EC Responses to Questions, para. 155. The EC has alternatively asserted that Article 14(3) merely "*allows* the registering authorities to refuse the registration of any confusing geographical indications," and that under Article 14(3) it is "*possible* to reject" an application for registration of a geographical indication that jeopardizes the existence of a mark. EC First Written Submission, para. 286 (emphasis added); EC Responses to Panel Questions, para. 160 (emphasis added). As discussed above, neither of these positions is correct. But the United States would note that Article 14(3) is an even poorer substitute for Article 16.1 rights if it permits the registration of confusing GIs.

143. Setting aside the point made above that TRIPS Article 16.1 accords trademark owners the right to prevent *uses* of identical or similar geographical indications, and not only *registration* of such geographical indications, it is clear that Article 14(3) applies criteria that are different from and more restrictive than Article 16.1. Article 16.1 rights are not reserved solely to registered trademarks of a certain reputation or particular renown. Nor is there any requirement under Article 16.1 that the trademark be used for any length of time. Article 16.1 articulates a right that is owed under the TRIPS Agreement to the owner of any valid registered trademark.

144. Had the EC wished to adopt a provision that "says that the registration of a geographical indication shall be refused if it is likely to lead to confusion with a trademark," it could have done so. According to the EC, "at the time that Regulation 2081/92 was adopted, the TRIPS Agreement was in the final phases of its negotiation," and the EC's "objective" was to track what would become its TRIPS obligations in the Regulation.[124] Why, in those circumstances, did the EC not simply include the Article 16.1 "likelihood of confusion" language in Article 14(3) of Regulation 2081/92? Why, instead, did it include language in Article 14(3) about a trademark's "reputation and renown and the length of time it has been used"—language that is not found in Article 16.1 and that is plainly more restrictive than the Article 16.1 standard?

145. The obvious answer is that the EC has limited the circumstances in which a geographical indication will be denied registration to those instances in which a trademark's "reputation and renown and the length of time it has been used" make the geographical indication "liable to mislead the consumer as to the true identity of the product."[125] These criteria—"reputation and renown and the length of time ... used"—cannot be threshold *prerequisites* that the owner of a prior valid registered trademark must invoke to prevent confusing uses by identical or similar signs. Even assuming that Article 16.1 can be entirely fulfilled by denying registration of confusing geographical indications, Article 14(3) of the GI Regulation makes the availability of those rights contingent on the trademark possessing "reputation and renown and ... use[]." TRIPS Article 16.1, however, requires only that the trademark be validly registered for the owner to avail itself of its rights.

146. Article 14(3)'s "reputation and renown" language limits the applicability of the provision to a certain class of trademarks, whereas TRIPS Article 16.1 places no limits on the class of registered trademarks that are granted the exclusive right to exclude others. In fact, the threshold prerequisites of reputation, renown, and length of time used are factors generally used to determine the scope of protection to give to "well-known" or "famous" trademarks, under Article 6*bis* of the Paris Convention, and Articles 16.2 and 16.3 of the TRIPS Agreement. Article 16.2 refers specifically to criteria such as "knowledge of the trademark" and knowledge "obtained as a result of the promotion of the trademark." The word "knowledge" in Article 16.2 means, among other things, "familiarity gained by experience."[126] The "familiarity" part of this definition would appear to encompass the "reputation and renown" criteria of Article 14(3), while "gained by experience" tracks the "length of time ... used" criterion in Article 14(3).

147. The threshold prerequisites included in Article 14(3)—"reputation and renown and the length of time ... used"—also track the factors for determining whether a trademark is well-known that are recorded in

---

[124] EC Responses to Panel Questions, para. 12.

[125] The EC states that since "it would be impossible to evaluate the likelihood of confusion on the basis of only" the two criteria listed in Article 14(3), the Commission must be able to consider other criteria relevant to a determination of likelihood of confusion. *See* EC Responses to Panel Questions, para. 156. The more logical implication, however, contrary to the EC's statement, is that Article 14(3) does not embody the "likelihood of confusion" standard, at least with respect to all but a certain category of marks. Moreover, the EC cites to the "Bayerisches Bier" example—in which the EC decided to register "Bayerisches Bier" as a geographical indication, despite objections from the owner of the trademark BAVARIA that the registration would raise a likelihood of confusion—as "consistent with" the interpretation of Article 14(3) offered in this dispute. EC Responses to Questions, para. 170. See also EC First Written Submission, para. 288 (footnote 140). But this decision does not, in fact, confirm the EC's interpretation of Article 14(3) for the purposes of this dispute. The Council's decision (provided as Exhibit EC-9) does *not* say that the Council took into account factors other than the reputation, renown and length of use of the trademark in reaching its decision to register the geographical indication. All it says is that "[i]n view of the facts and information available, it was ... considered that registration of the name ... was not liable to mislead the consumer as to the true identity of the product." This does not in any way confirm that the EC's interpretation of Article 14(3) is that applied in practice.

[126] *New Shorter Oxford English Dictionary* (Fourth Ed. 1993), pg. 1503. Exhibit US-57.

Article 2(1)(b) of the Joint Recommendation Concerning Provisions on the Protection of Well-Known Marks, adopted by the Paris Union Assembly and the WIPO General Assembly.[127] Among the factors to be considered are the "degree of knowledge or recognition" of the mark, the "duration" of any "use" of the mark, and the "duration" of any registrations of the mark. These factors correspond to the prerequisites included in Article 14(3) of the GI Regulation The repeated references in the WIPO Joint Recommendation to the "duration" of "use" or of "registrations" corresponds to the "length of time ... used" prerequisites in Article 14(3). Similarly, the reference to the "degree of knowledge or recognition" corresponds to the "reputation and renown" prerequisites in Article 14(3).

148. As further evidence of the meaning of Article 14(3), in the process of bringing its laws into conformity with the EC GI Regulation upon accession to the EU earlier this year, Hungary adopted amendments to its Law on the Protection of Trademarks and Geographical Indications that demonstrate its understanding that Article 14(3) tracks the factors for determining whether a trademark is well-known. In particular, Section 45(1)(c) of the amended Hungarian law reads as follows:

> a geographical indicator identical with or similar to a previous trademark if, with regard to the awareness, reputation or duration of the presence of the trademark in the market, the use thereof may result in the misleading of consumers in respect of the origin of the goods,
>
> ...
>
> shall be excluded from protection.[128]

The statement of ministerial reasoning accompanying Section 45 provides as follows:

> The rule on the protection of a prior *well-known mark* corresponds to the relative ground for refusal contained in Section 14(3) of EC Regulation 2081/92 on the protection of geographical indications and designations or origin for agricultural products and foodstuffs.[129]

149. Thus, Hungary, an EC member State that—presumably in consultation and negotiation with the EC—recently amended its law to make it consistent with the GI Regulation, also considers that the prerequisites in Article 14(3) block the registration of a geographical indication that is confusing *only with respect to* an identical or similar *well-known* trademark.[130] Article 14(3) does not extend the "likelihood of confusion" standard from TRIPS Article 16.1 to *all* valid registered trademarks; rather, it considers only a certain subset of trademarks that appear to correspond to the definition of well-known marks.

150. Finally, insight into the meaning of the prerequisites included in Article 14(3) can be drawn from use of those criteria in EC law and jurisprudence. "Reputation," one of the prerequisites in Article 14(3), is required by the EC Trademark Regulation and Trademark Directive to secure heightened protection against uses

---

[127] Exhibit US-58.

[128] An English language version of Section 45 is provided as Exhibit US-59. An English language version of the predecessor to Section 45 (Section 106), before amendments aimed at implementing EC Regulation 2081/92 were adopted, is provided separately, as Exhibit US-60. The predecessor to section 45 (section 106) appears to have been consistent with Article 16.1 of the TRIPS Agreement.

[129] Emphasis added. An English language version of the ministerial reasoning accompanying the amendments is included as Exhibit US-61.

[130] This evidence also demonstrates that contrary to the EC's response to question 70 from the Panel (paras. 172-174), the EC member States *do not agree with* the Commission's submission to the Panel that the terms of Article 14(3) are sufficient to prevent the registration of *all* confusing GIs.

of confusing identical or similar signs on *dissimilar* goods.[131] The requirements for a trademark to be considered as having a "reputation" were set out by the ECJ in *Chevy*.[132] In *Chevy*, the ECJ held that "reputation" requires that the trademark satisfy a *knowledge threshold requirement*, or in other words that it enjoy a certain degree of knowledge amongst the public.[133] The Court stated that the degree of knowledge must be considered to be reached when the trademark is known by a *significant part* of the public concerned.[134] In examining whether this condition is fulfilled, the Court stated that a national court must take into account, in particular, the market share held by the trademark, the intensity, geographical extent and duration of its use, and the size of the investment made by the undertaking promoting it.[135]

151. The "duration of use" required to qualify for status as a trademark of "reputation" under the ECJ's test in *Chevy* is particularly relevant to Article 14(3), which also requires that to secure refusal of registration of a confusing geographical indication, a trademark must have been "used" for some "length of time."

152. Although it undertakes a case-by-case analysis, the Office for Harmonization in the Internal Market (Trade Marks and Designs) ("OHIM") has found that use of a trademark in the market for 45 years (HOLLYWOOD)[136], 50 years (PLANETA)[137] or more than 100 years (OLYMPIC)[138] offers a strong indication of reputation. Further guidance on the prerequisite of "length of time ... used" in Article 14(3) can be derived from the EC Wine Regulation.[139] The Wine Regulation contains a grandfathering clause for well-known trademarks.[140] The holder of a well-known registered brand name for a wine may continue to use that brand name if the brand name was registered at least 25 years before the official recognition of the geographical name and has been used without interruption. At the very least, these sources indicate that the prerequisite of "length of time ... used" in Article 14(3) of EC Regulation 2081/92 requires uninterrupted use for a considerable number of years.

153. Thus, even assuming that Article 16.1 can be fulfilled by denying registration of confusing geographical indications, Article 14(3) of the EC GI Regulation, by requiring that the trademark possess "reputation and renown" and "length of time ... used," requires considerably more than that the trademark be validly registered for the owner to avail itself of TRIPS Article 16.1 rights.

154. This is inconsistent with Article 16.1 of the TRIPS Agreement. Article 16.1 accords rights to *all* registered trademarks, regardless whether they have acquired a "reputation and renown," and regardless whether they have been "used" for any "length of time" whatsoever. Therefore—and setting aside the critical point that TRIPS Article 16.1 accords trademark owners the right to prevent *uses* of identical or similar geographical indications, and not only *registration* of those signs—Article 14(3) is insufficient to satisfy the EC's obligations under Article 16.1.

---

[131] *See* Council Regulation (EC) No 40/94 of 20 December 1993 on the Community trade mark, as amended, Articles 8(5), 9(1)(c) (Exhibit COMP-7.a); First Council Directive of 21 December 1988 to approximate the laws of the Member States relating to trade marks (89/104/EEC), as amended, Articles 4(3), 4(4)(a), 5(2) (Exhibit COMP-6.a). Similarly, Article 14(3) of the EC GI Regulation is not limited to the denial of registration for a geographical indication proposed for use on products similar to those associated with a trademark of reputation, renown and some length of use. Article 14(1) of Regulation 2081/92, for example, includes such a limitation, but Article 14(3) does not. Exhibit COMP-1.b.

[132] Case C-375/97, *General Motors Corp. v. Yplon SA* ("Chevy"), judgment of 14 September 1999. Exhibit US-62.

[133] *Id.*, para. 22.

[134] *Id.*, para. 26.

[135] *Id.*, para. 27.

[136] OHIM Resolution 105/1999 (available in French only), pgs. 4-5. Exhibit US-63.

[137] OHIM Resolution 2/2000 (available in Spanish only), pg. 11. Exhibit US-64.

[138] OHIM Resolution 81/2000, pg. 8. Exhibit US-65.

[139] Council Regulation No. (EC) 1493/1999 of 17 May 1999 on the common organisation of the market in wine. See Annexes VII(F)(2) and VIII(H)(2) thereto, in connection with Article 47(2)(e). Exhibit US-66.

[140] In Annexes VII(F)(2) and VIII(H)(2) thereto, in connection with Article 47(2)(e).

155. It is also important to note that—like the EC's novel reading of Article 12(1) of its GI Regulation—these proceedings mark the first time in which the EC has asserted that Article 14(3) "says that the registration of a geographical indication shall be refused if it is likely to lead to confusion" with any registered trademark, and not just trademarks that hold reputation and renown and have been used for some length of time.[141] As recently as March 2004, in a "Guide to Community Regulations," the Commission explained Article 14(3) in the following terms:

> As a general rule, under the EU regime, the registration of a conflicting trademark does not prevent registration of the geographical name. *Only in one circumstance*, referred to in Article 14.3, is the application to register the geographical name refused. This is if, in the light of the trademark's reputation and renown and the length of time it has been used, registration of a geographical name would be liable to mislead the consumer as to the true identity of the product. *In all other cases*, the name can be registered *notwithstanding the existence of the registered trademark.*[142]

156. The United States has added italicized emphasis to demonstrate that outside the context of these proceedings, the Commission considers that Article 14(3) does not "say[] that the registration of a geographical indication shall be refused if it is likely to lead to confusion" with any registered trademark.[143] Instead, the Commission considers that Article 14(3) will apply and the registration denied "[o]nly in one circumstance"—where there is a trademark that possesses the requisite reputation and renown and length of time used. In contrast, "[i]n all other cases," the registration will be granted, "notwithstanding the existence of the registered trademark."

157. Outside of these proceedings, therefore, the Commission's guidance on the EC GI Regulation is that the general rule ("all other cases" apart from "one circumstance") involving "the existence of the registered trademark"—*i.e.*, all cases not involving a registered trademark that possesses the requisite reputation and renown and length of time used—is that Article 14(3) will *not* apply, and that the registration will be approved "notwithstanding" the registered trademark. Thus, although the EC here argues that "[i]t is not conceivable to the European Commission that it would, in the interpretation or application of the Regulation, take a different approach to the one it has set out before the Panel,"[144] it appears that the Commission has itself already adopted one interpretation or application of Article 14(3) before the Panel, and a different interpretation or application (one that has the merit of being consistent with the text of Article 14(3)) when not before the Panel.

158. Nor is this dispute unique in that regard. As discussed above in section II, in the *Petrotub* case at the ECJ, the Commission's assertions to the ECJ concerning the requirements of EC law *directly contradicted* the assurances it had given WTO Members the year before. Further, as discussed above, when the appellants sought to rely on those assurances at the ECJ, the Commission opposed the request, deeming them "irrelevant".[145]

159. In the light of what it termed the "irrelevant" assurances given to WTO Members, and the attempt to exclude the assurances from EC court proceedings, the Commission's assurances to this Panel on the meaning of Article 14(3) of the EC GI Regulation hardly inspire confidence. The text of Article 14(3) speaks for itself,

---

141 EC Responses to Questions, para. 155.

142 Guide to Community Regulations, "Protection of Geographical Indications, Designations of Origin and Certificates of Specific Character for Agricultural Products and Foodstuffs" (Working Document of the Commission Services issued by the European Commission Directorate-General for Agriculture, March 2004), pg. 23 (emphasis added). Exhibit US-24.

143 EC Responses to Questions, para. 155 (emphasis added).

144 EC Responses to Questions, para. 31.

145 Case 76/00 P. *Petrotub*, judgment of 9 January 2003, para 15 (Exhibit EC-17).

and, in the absence of specific convincing legal authority to the contrary, that is the reading the Panel should adopt for the purposes of this dispute.[146]

160. The EC also argues that unless Article 14(3) of the EC GI Regulation is interpreted to require the EC to refuse registration of any geographical indication that raises a likelihood of confusion with respect to an identical or similar trademark, Article 7(4) of the Regulation would be rendered "pointless."[147] Article 7(4) provides that "[a] statement of objection shall be admissible only if it ... shows that the registration of the name proposed would jeopardize the existence of ... a mark ..." According to the EC, unless Article 14(3) is read to encompass the likelihood of confusion standard, the Regulation would admit an objection on grounds that could not ultimately serve as the basis to refuse registration.

161. To begin, as the EC notes, Article 7(4) addresses what a trademark owner must establish to have its objection admitted. However, even if Article 14(3) were to be interpreted in light of Article 7(4), as the EC seems to suggest, the two provisions would still have to be interpreted *cumulatively*. Thus, the standard in Article 14(3) (requiring rejection of proposed registrations that are "liable to mislead" with respect to a well-known mark) would be interpreted in light of the admissibility standard in Article 7(4) (allowing admissibility of objections to proposed registrations that would "jeopardize the existence" of a mark). In the EC's view, together these two standards would "encompass[] any instance of likelihood of confusion ..."[148] But to apply this combined Article 7(4)/Article 14(3) standard to *all* trademarks, as opposed to only those trademarks with "reputation and renown" and "use" for some "length of time," would not amount to a *cumulative* interpretation of Articles 7(4) and 14(3). Rather, it would read the phrase "reputation and renown and the length of time used" limitation out of Article 14(3) altogether. For the Panel to accept such a reading would not amount to an "objective assessment of the facts of the case," as is required by Article 11 of the *DSU*.[149]

162. Finally, the EC suggests that where the EC member States have been unable to agree on whether to register a geographical indication that has been the subject of an objection by a trademark owner, Article 7(5)(b) of the EC GI Regulation overrides Article 14(3), and calls on the Commission "to adopt a decision having regard to the 'likelihood of confusion' between the proposed geographical indication and *any* other marks."[150] This argument should be rejected, for two reasons.

163. First, and as noted above with respect to Article 7(4), even under the EC's construction, Article 7(5)(b) applies cumulatively with Article 14(3). Thus, even if Article 7(5)(b) means that in some instances, the standard in Article 14(3) ("liable to mislead") would be interpreted in light of the standard in Article 7(5)b ("likelihood of confusion"), the combined standard would not apply for all trademarks. It would only apply with respect to those trademarks with "reputation and renown" and "use." Thus, it would not satisfy TRIPS Article 16.1, which extends protection to all trademarks.

164. Second, even if the EC's interpretation regarding the interaction between Articles 7(5)(b) and 14(3) is correct, Article 7(5)(b), by its own terms, applies only in those situations in which the EC member States are unable to agree. In all other situations, Article 14(3), which provides for the refusal of registration only where a trademark meets the criteria of reputation, renown and length of time used, would apply alone.

[146] For example, the panel in *US – Section 301* accorded particular credibility to the interpretation given by the United States to its law because that interpretation was reflected in an authoritative statement of administrative action ("SAA"), issued by the President prior to the dispute, and approved by the US Congress. See US Responses to Questions, para. 4, citing Panel Report, *US – Section 301 Trade Act*, paras. 7.111 and 7.112.

[147] EC Responses to Questions, para. 160.

[148] EC Responses to Panel Questions, para. 169. The EC simply answers that the "liable to mislead" standard and the "jeopardize the existence" standard "encompass[] any instance of likelihood of confusion."

[149] *See* US Responses to Questions, para. 1.

[150] EC Responses to Questions, para. 162.

165. For all of these reasons, the Panel should reject the EC's assertion that the owners of prior valid registered trademarks do not need the rights guaranteed by Article 16.1 of the TRIPS Agreement, since Article 14(3) of the GI Regulation "says that the registration of a geographical indication shall be refused if it is likely to lead to confusion with a trademark."[151] Even if Article 14(3) could be interpreted in this way, as noted earlier, it would be insufficient to satisfy the terms of TRIPS Article 16.1, which grants to *trademark owners* the right to prevent *uses* of confusing identical or similar geographical indications. In any event, the interpretation of Article 14(3) offered by the EC in these proceedings is not supported by the text of the provision, and is irreconcilable with the interpretation of the provision offered by the EC outside the bounds of this dispute. Article 14(3) merely empowers the EC authorities to refuse registration of a geographical indication that, on its face, is misleading with respect to trademarks that enjoy reputation, renown and use.

166. Thus, Article 14(3) will not stop registration of *all* geographical indications that may be used in a confusing manner with respect to identical or similar valid registered trademarks. And use of those confusing geographical indications that are registered is immune from the reach of TRIPS Article 16.1. By virtue of the EC GI Regulation, even if the owner of a prior valid registered trademark can prove that use of an identical or similar geographical indication that has been registered raises a likelihood of confusion, it cannot prevent continued use of that geographical indication in a manner that results in a likelihood of confusion. This is inconsistent with the obligations of Article 16.1 of the TRIPS Agreement.

C. THE EC'S ASSERTION THAT FEW TRADEMARKS THAT CONTAIN OR CONSIST OF A GEOGRAPHICAL INDICATION ARE REGISTRABLE IS INCORRECT AND IRRELEVANT

167. In its first written submission and its responses to the Panel's questions, the EC asserts that few trademarks that contain or consist of a geographical indication will be distinctive and therefore registrable. According to the EC, it will therefore only be the rare occasion in which a conflict would arise between a valid registered trademark and a registered geographical indication.[152] As the United States noted in its oral statement,[153] the United States is concerned with those trademarks that contain or consist of a geographical indication that are in fact registrable and validly registered, however few their number. The owners of those trademarks must be accorded their Article 16.1 rights.

168. Moreover, the United States does not concede that the number of trademarks containing or consisting of a geographical indication that are registrable is necessarily small. First, under Article 2(3) of the EC GI Regulation, non-geographical names are subject to registration as geographical indications. Even if the EC believes that a trademark containing or consisting of a geographical name would not qualify as distinctive, it presumably cannot easily extend that argument to trademarks that contain or consist of a non-geographic name.

169. Second, it is simply untrue that valid registered trademarks cannot incorporate certain "geographical" elements. The United States has cited to the hypothetical example of a trademark for LUNA, in connection with cheese, and potential registration of a geographical indication for use on cheese produced in Luna, Spain.[154] The United States has also cited to the example of FARO, a registered Community trademark for coffee and tea, and potential registration of a geographical indication for use on coffee produced in Faro, Portugal.[155]

170. Thus, valid registered trademarks containing or consisting of a geographical indication exist, and there is no evidence whatsoever that they are few in number. Even if the number of such trademarks were small, however, the owners of all valid registered trademarks must be granted their TRIPS Article 16.1 rights. Under the EC GI Regulation, by contrast, the very best these trademark owners can hope for is the ability to continue

---

[151] EC Responses to Questions, para. 155.

[152] EC First Written Submission, paras. 275, 278-285; EC Responses to Questions, para. 176.

[153] US Oral Statement, para. 49.

[154] US Oral Statement, para. 50.

[155] US Responses to Questions, para. 79.

selling products with their trademarks affixed. The trademark owners cannot exercise the right to prevent uses of identical or similar geographical indications, even if those uses confuse consumers.

D. ARTICLE 24.5 OF THE TRIPS AGREEMENT IS NOT AN EXCEPTION TO THE RIGHTS ACCORDED TO TRADEMARKS

171. As a defense against the claim that the GI Regulation is inconsistent with the EC's Article 16.1 obligations, the EC asserts that Article 24.5 of the TRIPS Agreement specifically allows for the type of "co-existence" of GIs and trademarks established by the GI Regulation.[156] The United States has demonstrated that the EC's interpretation is incorrect for multiple reasons, among them that Article 24.5 is a clearly-labeled exception to the obligation to protect GIs in Part II, Section 3 of the TRIPS Agreement.[157] An "exception" excepts or "exempts" something from the "scope of a proposition", which in this case is the scope of protection accorded to geographical indications.[158] The Appellate Body has interpreted provisions based on similar considerations of their place in the overall structure of the covered agreement at issue, including consideration of the headings or titles of sections.[159]

172. Accordingly, Article 24.5 provides an exception to the protection of GIs that shields certain trademarks; it is not an exception to the trademark obligations under Article 16.1 of the TRIPS Agreement. The EC acknowledges that "Article 24.5 is not an 'exception' to Article 16.1"[160], but nevertheless advocates an interpretation of Article 24.5 that places it in that position. The EC's reasoning attempts to transform a provision that *protects* certain grandfathered trademarks into a provision that empowers it to prejudice trademarks.

173. Because the EC is attempting to use Article 24.5 as an affirmative defense to the violation of Article 16.1 by the GI Regulation, the EC bears the burden of proof on this issue.[161] This follows from the Appellate Body's guidance in *Japan-Apples* that "although the complaining party bears the burden of proving its case, the responding party must prove the case it seeks to make in response."[162] Despite the EC's implication to the contrary,[163] the fact that the United States referred to Article 24.5 in its panel request does not change this burden, especially since the United States has made clear through its first written submission that it is not necessary for the Panel to even consider Article 24.5 to find a violation of Article 16.1, as Article 24.5 is an exception to GI protection, not trademark protection.[164] Nevertheless, in light of the EC's reliance on Article 24.5 as a defense to the claim that the EC GI Regulation is inconsistent with Article 16.1, the United States has provided a detailed interpretation of Article 24.5 consistent with the international customary rules of treaty interpretation, considering the ordinary meaning of the provision, its context, and the object and purpose of the Agreement.[165] This analysis demonstrates that the statement in Article 24.5 that Members shall not implement the GI section in a manner that "prejudice[s] ... the validity of the registration of a trademark" requires that owners of grandfathered trademarks continue to be accorded their Article 16.1 rights to prevent all others, including GI right holders, from confusing uses.[166] Specifically, the ordinary meaning of "validity of the registration of a trademark" refers to the possession of legal authority accorded by virtue of the entrance of a

[156] EC First Written Submission, paras. 294-309; EC Response to Panel Question 76.

[157] US Oral Statement, paras. 57-58; US Response to Panel Question 78.

[158] See US Response to Panel Question 78, at para. 59, *citing New Shorter Oxford English Dictionary* (Fourth Ed. 1993), p. 872.

[159] See Appellate Body Report, *Canada – Dairy*, para. 134 ("A strong presumption arises that the language which is inscribed in a Member's Schedule under the heading, 'Other terms and Conditions', has some *qualifying* or *limiting* effect on the substantive content or scope of the concession or commitment."); US Responses to Panel Question 78, paras. 111-112.

[160] EC Response to Panel Question 75, para. 197.

[161] *See* US Response to Panel Question 75, paras. 91-92.

[162] Para. 154.

[163] EC Response to Panel Question 75, para. 198.

[164] *See, e.g.*, US First Written Submission, para. 142.

[165] US Oral Statement, paras. 57-67; US Response to Panel Question 76.

[166] US Response to Panel Question 76, paras. 97-99.

trademark in a register. As the legal authority accorded by trademark registration is defined in Article 16.1, it follows that the validity of a trademark registration will be "prejudiced" or damaged if a Member fails to allow the trademark owner to prevent all others from confusing uses.

174. Moreover, Article 15.1 of the TRIPS Agreement clarifies that if a sign is not capable of "distinguishing the goods or services of one undertaking from those of other undertakings"—either inherently or through use—then it cannot constitute or function as a trademark, as it is not considered "protectable subject matter". The denial of the right to prevent confusing uses of the trademark prejudices the ability to establish and maintain the trademark's ability to distinguish goods of one enterprise from those of another and thereby prejudices its capability of "constituting a trademark."[167] This is another way in which depriving a trademark owner of his right to prevent confusing uses of similar or identical signs would prejudice the "validity of the registration of a trademark."

175. Indeed, the EC adopted this very view when it argued that the grounds for determining the admissibility of objections to a GI registration under Article 7(4) of the GI Regulation—that it would "jeopardize the existence ... of a mark"—"encompasses any instance of likelihood of confusion between the proposed geographical indication and an earlier trademark."[168] If, according to the EC, allowing confusing uses would "jeopardize the existence ... of a mark", then allowing confusing uses, contrary to Article 16.1 of the TRIPS Agreement, would also appear to "prejudice ... the validity of the registration of a trademark" under Article 24.5. [169]

176. The United States has also explained that the additional prohibition against "prejudice ... [of] the right to use a trademark" refers to the harm or damage to the permitted or forbidden activity associated with the application of a trademark to its purpose.[170] Based on the context of Articles 15.1 and 16.1 of the TRIPS Agreement, the purpose of a trademark is to allow its owner to distinguish the owner's goods from the goods of others, which requires that trademarks accord their owners the right to prevent all others from uses that would cause a likelihood of confusion.[171] Thus, the "right to use" the trademark for its purposes encompasses the right to exclude others from using the trademark.

177. The EC would convert an *additional* restriction on measures to implement the GI section of the TRIPS Agreement—that the GI not prejudice the right to use a trademark—into a *reduction* in the protection of trademarks. For the EC, Article 24.5 means that the measures *can* prejudice the basic right of the trademark

[167] For example, when considering the case of the "SL" trademark owned by Mercedes-Benz, and the concurrent use by Fiat of that same sign, the German Federal Supreme Court stated that concurrent use by others of Mercedes' "SL" mark could put at risk the very existence of Mercedes' SL mark. Federal Supreme Court (Bundesgerichtshot), Decision 06.12.1990—Case No. 1 ZR 297/88 ("SL"), published in IIC 1992 Heft 02, 286. ("Of more importance is, however, another aspect, which may determine not merely the reputation, but also the very existence of the plaintiff's trademark... [I]t could be expected that other vehicle manufacturers might soon follow the defendant's example [of concurrently using the trademark without permission]... . [A]s a result, ... the mark SL would not merely be impaired but its essential function as the distinctive sign of the goods would be threatened, and in the long term its very existence would be at risk.") Exhibit US-67.

[168] EC Response to Panel Question 68, para. 160.

[169] If a trademark is deemed invalid, and removed from a register in jurisdictions in which ownership is determined by registration, it can be said that it no longer exists, in particular in the ability of its owner to exclude all third parties from using it. Moreover, "prejudice" and "jeopardize" have virtually identical meanings. The definition of "prejudice" is "injury, damage, **harm**" (*New Shorter Oxford English Dictionary* (Fourth Ed. 1993), p. 2333.), while the definition of "jeopardize" is "put into jeopardy, endanger, put at risk," and "jeopardy" refers to "risk of loss, **harm**" (*New Shorter Oxford English Dictionary* (Fourth Ed. 1993), p. 1444.) Exhibit US-68.

[170] US Response to Panel Question 76, para. 102.

[171] The Appellate Body in *US – Section 211* emphasized the importance of the exclusive nature of these rights, finding that Article 16.1 confers on the owner of "registered trademarks an internationally agreed minimum level of 'exclusive rights' that all WTO Members must guarantee in their domestic legislation," and that these exclusive rights "protect the owner against infringement of the registered trademark by unauthorized third parties." Appellate Body Report, *United States – Section 211*, para. 186. *See also* Advocate General's Opinion in Case C-10/89, *SA CNL-Sucal NV v. HAG GFAG*, delivered on 13 March 1990 [1990] ECR I-3711, at para. 19 ("A trademark can only fulfil that role [*i.e.*, to identify the manufacturer and to guarantee quality] if it is exclusive. Once the proprietor is forced to share the mark with the competitor, he loses control over the goodwill associated with the mark. The reputation of his own goods will be harmed if the competitor sells inferior goods. From the consumer's point of view, equally undesirable consequences will ensue, because the clarity of the signal transmitted by the trademark will be impaired. The consumer will be confused and misled."). Exhibit US-8.

owner to prevent confusing uses of similar or identical signs that result in a likelihood of confusion with respect to the trademark. There is simply nothing in Article 24.5 that would support such a conclusion.

178. Even if one were to resort to the negotiating history (and under the customary rules of interpretation reflected in the *Vienna Convention*, one would not normally have recourse to negotiating history), as the United States has already noted,[172] the progress made between the Brussels draft and the Dunkel draft show that the language of Article 24.5 evolved from a simple prohibition against invalidation or denial of registration (in the Brussels Draft) to a requirement that Members not even "prejudice" the validity of the registration of the trademark. Further, this prohibition on prejudice was extended to cover common law trademarks, and a prohibition against prejudicing the right to use a trademark—on grounds of similarity with a GI—was added. Nowhere in this negotiating history—in which the scope of protection for certain trademarks was steadily increased—is there any indication of an intention to permit the emasculation of the very heart of the trademark right.

179. The EC's *Vienna Convention* analysis of Article 24.5 is seriously flawed. Starting with the ordinary meaning, the EC inexplicably begins with the curious statement that "A 'trademark' is not a right", referring to Article 15.1 of the TRIPS Agreement for support.[173] Apparently, the EC makes this statement in order to justify its argument that the word "trademark" should be understood without regard to the trademark's inherent rights. But this is incorrect. Article 15.1 explains the types of "signs" that are *capable* of constituting a trademark. In fact, the title of Article 15 is "Protectable Subject Matter", indicating what signs may be capable of functioning as trademarks if they meet the criteria in TRIPS Article 15, *i.e.*, the ability to distinguish goods, as well as any statutory criteria under national law. Of course, a simple "sign" is not a right. The term APPLE is merely a word in the public domain that identifies a type of fruit. But once the term APPLE is used as a source indicator and a quality guarantee for computers, it functions as a trademark. Furthermore, once a sign is registered as a trademark, Article 16.1 specifically states that a trademark accords to its owner certain "exclusive rights". Thus, the EC's conclusion that "the 'right to use a trademark' is the right to use a sign" is unsupported by the ordinary meaning of "trademark".

180. The EC attempts to support its "ordinary meaning" interpretation of the phrase "right to use a trademark" by reference to a WIPO publication that, according to the EC, breaks down the "right to use the trademark" into two entirely separate elements—"the right to use the trademark" and "the right to exclude others from using the mark", where the former relates to the right to place the trademark on labels, packaging, etc.[174] These statements are irrelevant and misleading. Not only would a WIPO publication not be part of the "context" of the WTO agreements for purposes of a *Vienna Convention* type of analysis, WIPO was not even purporting to interpret the ordinary meaning of "right to use" in the context of Article 24.5 of the TRIPS Agreement. Moreover, the EC appears to take these quotes out of context. In the two publications cited by the EC for the same concept[175], WIPO explains as follows:

> A trademark is any sign that individualizes the goods of a given enterprise and distinguishes them from the goods of its competition. This definition comprises two aspects, *which are sometimes referred to as the different functions of the trademark, but which are, however, interdependent, and for all practical purposes should always be looked at together.*[176]

181. WIPO also states in both publications that "[i]t follows from the mark's basic function of distinguishing the goods of its owner from those of others that he must be able to object to the use of

---

[172] US Responses to Panel Questions, paras. 99, 104; US Oral Statement, paras. 64-65.

[173] EC Response to Panel Question 76, at para. 200.

[174] EC Response to Panel Question 76, paras. 201-202.

[175] *See* EC First Written Submission, para. 303, n. 146; EC Response to Panel Question 76, paras. 201-202.

[176] WIPO, Introduction to Intellectual Property Theory and Practice (Kluwer 1997), p. 184 (emphasis added) (Exhibit US-69); WIPO, Introduction to Trademark Law & Practice: The Basic Concepts, A WIPO Training Manual (1993), pp. 9-10 (emphasis added) (Exhibit US-70).

confusingly similar marks in order to prevent consumers and the public in general from being misled. This is the *essence of the exclusive right* afforded to the trademark owner by registration."[177] Reading these two statements together, it is clear that WIPO considers that the right to affirmatively use a trademark (*i.e.*, to "individualize the goods of a given enterprise"), and the right to exclude all others from confusing uses (*i.e.*, to "distinguish [goods] from the goods of its competition"), are "interdependent, and for all practical purposes should always be looked at together."[178] The EC, however, ignores the interdependence of these two concepts, thereby contradicting WIPO's own understanding that they should always be considered together.

182. As for the protection in Article 24.5 against measures that "prejudice ... the validity of the registration of a trademark", the EC has explained that a trademark is either valid or invalid[179], thereby entirely ignoring the important effect of the word "prejudice" detailed by the United States, a word that was specifically added by the drafters after the Brussels draft.

183. In examining the context, the EC repeatedly refuses to address the fact that Article 24.5 is a clearly-labeled "exception" to the GI section.[180] Instead, the EC argues that the interpretation by the United States would result in a situation in which GI protection would be virtually meaningless, as GI owners would be "prohibited ... from even using that indication."[181] The EC apparently misunderstands the scope of the rights accorded to trademark owners by Article 16.1, which provides the right to prevent all uses that "result in a likelihood of confusion." Pursuant to the proper interpretation of Article 24.5, GIs that are identical or similar to trademarks can indeed be used in an affirmative way, but only to the extent that they do not result in a likelihood of confusion with respect to grandfathered trademarks.

184. Rather than addressing the negotiating history of Article 24.5 on its own terms, the EC purports to interpret Article 24.5 based on the negotiating history of an entirely different provision—Article 24.4.[182] Article 24.4 provides an exception to Article 23 of the TRIPS Agreement, by grandfathering certain uses of geographical indications for wines and spirits, by persons other than that GI right holders, that would otherwise be prohibited pursuant to Article 23 of the TRIPS Agreement. In its current form, Article 24.4 does not refer to trademarks.

185. Although, as pointed out by the EC, it is true that the precursor to Article 24.4 specifically referred to trademarks, it did so only as a subset of the broader category of geographical indications "used with regard to goods originating outside the territory of the PARTY ... by nationals or domiciliaries of another PARTY."[183] Unlike with Article 24.5 and its predecessors, trademark rights were not the focus of Article 24.4. The phrase "including [use] as a trademark" simply pointed to an example of the type of sign that might be affirmatively used. Thus, in this context, it was logical to address the affirmative right to use signs or indications on labels, advertising, etc., as the non-trademark owners in the broad group of users addressed by the provision likely had no intellectual property rights at all to address. The EC, however, somehow finds the possibility for co-existence of trademarks and geographical indications where none existed, in an early version of Article 24.4 that mentions trademarks only in passing. Moreover, as a clearly-marked exception to GI protection, there was nothing in the provision that would diminish the protection required by Article 16.1.

---

[177] WIPO, Introduction to Intellectual Property Theory and Practice (Kluwer 1997), p. 205 (emphasis added) (Exhibit US-69); WIPO, Introduction to Trademark Law & Practice: The Basic Concepts, A WIPO Training Manual (1993), p. 52 (emphasis added) (Exhibit US-70).

[178] WIPO, Introduction to Intellectual Property Theory and Practice (Kluwer 1997), p. 184 (emphasis added) (Exhibit US-69); WIPO, Introduction to Trademark Law & Practice: The Basic Concepts, A WIPO Training Manual (1993), pp. 9-10 (emphasis added) (Exhibit US-70).

[179] EC Answer to Question 76, paras. 203-204.

[180] EC Answer to Question 76, paras. 212-213.

[181] EC Response to Question 76, para. 212.

[182] EC Response to Question 76, paras. 216-219.

[183] Gervais, *The TRIPS Agreement – Drafting History and Analysis*, Excerptions from the Brussels Draft, Paragraph 1 (Prior Version of Article 24.4), pages 201-2. Exhibit US-71.

186. Despite the EC's explanation to the contrary, the removal of the specific reference to trademarks in the Dunkel draft did not appear to have any practical effect on Article 24.4. The drafters likely decided that there was no need to specifically mention the use of a GI as a trademark, given that it is already implied by reference to "continued and similar use of a particular geographical indication", where that affirmative use of a trademark was simply one of a number of types of uses. It follows that if the affirmative use of a GI by others, whether or not any intellectual property rights were involved, is grandfathered, then affirmative use of a trademark must also be grandfathered. Why should trademarks be at a *disadvantage* to users who have no intellectual property rights at all. Thus, the reference to trademarks in the prior version of Art. 24.4 was simply superfluous, as there is no reason to believe that affirmative use of trademarks is now excluded from its scope.

187. In addition, however, even if the added prohibition in Article 24.5 on prejudicing the "right to use" a trademark includes the affirmative right to use the trademark in connection with goods, this *added* prohibition does not *eliminate* or *reduce* the prohibition on prejudicing the right to exclude others from using identical or similar signs. Contrary to the EC's claims,[184] there is nothing duplicative about protecting both the trademark owner's right to exclude others from using identical or similar signs and protecting that owner's right to use the trademark in commerce. To the contrary, including both protections ensures that the implementation of the GI obligations does not prejudice the trademarks falling under Article 24.5.

E. ARTICLE 24.3 OF THE TRIPS AGREEMENT DOES NOT PERMIT OR MANDATE THE EC'S VIOLATION OF ARTICLE 16.1 OF THE TRIPS AGREEMENT

188. The EC argues that Article 24.3 of the TRIPS Agreement *requires* the EC to deprive trademark owners of their Article 16.1 rights. In doing so, however, the EC is forced to ignore critical elements of the ordinary meaning of the provision, as well as its context and the object and purpose of the TRIPS Agreement. In particular, the EC entirely ignores the first four words of Article 24.3.

189. Article 24.3 begins with the phrase "In implementing this Section", and then proceeds to detail what a Member shall not do "In implementing this Section". The EC's reading of Article 24.3, in addition to ignoring the fact that it is a clearly-marked exception to GI protection, transforms the language "In implementing this *Section*" into "In implementing this Agreement." As detailed herein, these have two very different meanings.

190. The phrase "this Section" refers to Part II, Section 3 of the TRIPS Agreement—the GI section. It follows that Article 24.3 does not establish any limitations on what Members must do in implementing *other* sections of the TRIPS Agreement, such as the trademark or copyright sections. For example, Article 24.3 does *not* say that "In implementing *the trademark section* (Section 2), a Member shall not diminish the protection of geographical indications ...".

191. Indeed, with respect to the GI Regulation, in implementing the trademark section of the TRIPS Agreement and Article 16.1 thereof, the EC was in fact *required* to amend the GI Regulation in order to comply with the obligations of that Section. Pursuant to Article 1.1 of the TRIPS Agreement, Members are permitted to implement more extensive protection than required by the TRIPS Agreement, "provided that such protection does not contravene the provisions of this Agreement." The United States has shown that the extensive protection provided to GIs by the GI Regulation does, in fact, contravene the provisions of the TRIPS Agreement—specifically, Article 16.1. As detailed above, Article 24.3 does not provide an exception to a Member's obligations under Article 16.1.

192. As detailed in the oral statement of the United States, the EC misconstrues Article 24.3 to create a major and permanent exception to not just the trademark section, but to every other section of the TRIPS Agreement. Under the EC's interpretation, a Member has an obligation to apply all aspects of a pre-TRIPS GI regime to all GIs—including those registered after 1 January 1996—even though that means that the Member will never, for instance, fully implement the rights granted trademark owners by Article 16.1. To illustrate, the

[184] EC Responses to the Panel's Questions, para. 207.

EC's reading would mean that a country acceding to the WTO could permanently avoid the results of its TRIPS negotiations on trademark protection by introducing a "co-existence" regime the day before its accession took effect. Indeed, a Member could have introduced a GI protection system under which all similar trademarks, regardless of when registered, had to be invalidated, regardless of any other WTO obligation. This would have provided a road map for Members to avoid the disciplines of the TRIPS Agreement, as the TRIPS Agreement text, and Article 24.3 in particular, was essentially agreed to by December 1991, three years before the WTO Agreement came into force.[185]

193. Under the EC's expansive reading of Article 24.3—requiring a freezing of GI protection systems regardless of *any* WTO obligation (and not just the GI obligations)— a Member could put in place a GI "protection" regime that exempted GI owners from the copyright and patent disciplines, or, indeed, any other WTO obligations, and then point to Article 24.3 as a broad exception to those obligations. Contrary to the customary rules of treaty interpretation, this would permanently render redundant parts of the TRIPS Agreement, and would lead to manifestly absurd results.[186] For instance, a WTO Member could deny copyright protection to any film that used the word "parmesan" in connection with any product other than the product qualifying in the EC for that name, and claim that Article 24.3 granted an exception to copyright protection.

194. The EC responds that Article 24.3 is limited in scope because it relates only to measures that "diminish the *protection* of geographical indications", where protection should be narrowly defined in such a way that it relates to trademarks, but not to patents or copyrights (or, presumably, any other WTO rights and obligations).[187] The EC states that "[i]n order to 'protect' geographical indications it is not necessary, for example, to limit patent rights or copyrights."[188] But Article 24.3 is not limited to measures that are "necessary" to protect geographical indications: by the EC's reading, it simply creates a broad exception for any protection provided to GIs.

195. Even if Article 24.3 applied only to measures "necessary" to protect GIs, however, the EC has not explained why—and there is no evidence that—"protection of geographical indications" makes it "necessary" to eliminate Article 16.1 trademark rights for trademarks that are not misleading or otherwise subject to invalidation pursuant to the GI Section (Section 3) of the TRIPS Agreement.

196. Finally, the EC contends that the phrase "protection of geographical indications that existed" in Article 24.3 applies to systems of protection, rather than to the protection of individual geographical indications.[189] In support, the EC states that "existed" modifies the term "protection", rather than the term "geographical indications", and further points out that "geographical indications" is not premised with the word "the." At best, the EC has demonstrated that the text is ambiguous as to whether the emphasis is on "protection" or "geographical indications." For example, although the EC contends that the absence of the word "the" prior to the term "geographical indications" indicates that it does not refer to individual geographical indications, the Spanish version does, in fact, premise the phrase "indicaciones geográficas" with the word "las" (Spanish for "the"). The use of the word "existía" does not take away from this important fact. Similarly, in the French version, the word "des" means "of *the*" in English.

197. Moreover, it is not determinative that the subject of the verb "existed" is "protection", and not "geographical indications." "Protection" could just as easily mean protection as it relates to individual geographical indications, as it could mean the general scope or level of protection overall. Indeed, it is important to note that Article 24.3 does not refer to the "scope of protection" or "level of protection," which is inherent in the EC's interpretation.

---

[185] The GI Regulation entered into force a year and a half later, on June 5, 1993

[186] Vienna Convention, Article 32(b).

[187] EC Response to Panel Question 74, para. 196.

[188] EC Response to Panel Question 74, para. 196.

[189] EC Response to Panel Question 74, paras. 187-193.

F. THE EC HAS NOT SHOWN THAT THE GI REGULATION'S TREATMENT OF TRADEMARKS CONSTITUTES A LIMITED EXCEPTION WITHIN THE MEANING OF ARTICLE 17 OF THE TRIPS AGREEMENT

198. The EC argues that "co-existence"—by which it means the inability of a trademark owner to prevent infringing uses of identical or similar geographical indications—constitutes recourse to the "fair use of descriptive terms" limited exception included in Article 17 of the TRIPS Agreement.[190] The EC implies that there is support for this proposition based on the fact that US law includes a "fair use of descriptive terms" exception.[191] The United States notes that US law with respect to this dispute is irrelevant, but the way in which the issue was raised is instructive for the Panel and for that reason, the United States will address the reference.

199. The EC is correct that the US Lanham Act provides for "the use of a term ... otherwise than as a mark ... of a term ... which is descriptive and used fairly and in good faith only to describe the goods ... of such party, or their geographical origin."[192] There are two critical differences, however, between US law and the EC's apparent view of TRIPS Article 17. US law requires that the alleged infringer relying on the fair use defense must be able to show that he or she is using the term "otherwise than as a mark."[193] Because a "mark" functions as a distinctive identifier of a source of goods coming from a particular undertaking, the use of a term in commerce as such a distinctive source identifier that infringes the prior trademark would not be allowed, in US law, under the fair use defense. To be allowed under US law, the use must be in a non-trademark sense, or in other words, in a non-distinctive sense.[194]

200. The second critical difference between US law and the EC's apparent view of Article 17 is that US law calls for a case-by-case analysis of whether the particular use of a sign at issue in a given case is in fact "fair use of a descriptive term", with an examination of whether the use is in a non-trademark sense, whether there is good faith use, and other factors.[195] The EC, by contrast, apparently considers that every use of a registered geographical indication that is similar or identical to a registered trademark is automatically "fair use of a descriptive term," by virtue of the simple fact that the geographical indication has been registered.

201. The United States has explained that a blanket inability of trademark owners to prevent confusing uses of registered GIs does not constitute a "limited exception" within the meaning of Article 17 of the TRIPS Agreement.[196] The same phrase in TRIPS Article 30 has been interpreted by the panel in *Canada – Patent Protection* "to connote a narrow exception—one which makes only a small diminution of the rights in question."[197] With respect to the exception to patent rights (*i.e.*, Article 30), the panel agreed with the

---

[190] EC First Written Submission , para. 318. While agreeing that it has the burden of demonstrating that the EC GI Regulation satisfies the limited trademark exception in Article 17, the EC fails to meet that burden. EC Response to Panel Question 75, para. 199.

[191] EC First Written Submission, para. 318 (note 154).

[192] Section 33(b)(4) of the US Lanham Act (15 USC 1115(b)(4)). Exhibit EC-6.

[193] 15 US C. Section 1115(b)(4).

[194] Because GIs are intellectual property rights for purposes of the TRIPS Agreement, they are not merely descriptive terms, as the EC claims, or they would not be protectable. They are protectable under the TRIPS Agreement because they are indicators of geographic origin where a given reputation, quality or other characteristic is essentially attributable to that geographic origin—something more than just a mere place name. Therefore, if used as a GI—which under US law means used as a mark or indicator of source or some other characteristic other than merely a place name—they are not "descriptive" terms.

[195] The GI Regulation would similarly have called for a case-by-case analysis, had the EC not specifically rejected a proposed amendment by the Committee on Legal Affairs and the Internal Market of the European Parliament that would have incorporated the substantive disciplines of trademark law, including the fair use exception, into the GI Regulation. *See* US Oral Statement, at para. 75, citing Opinion of the Committee on Legal Affairs and the Internal Market for the Committee on Agriculture and Rural Development on the proposal for a Council regulation amending Regulation (EEC) No 2081/92 on the protection of geographical indications and designations of origin for agricultural products and foodstuffs, European Parliament, 2002/0066(CNS) (10 September 2002), pp. 13-14. Exhibit US-21.

[196] US Oral Statement, paras. 74-75.

[197] Panel Report, *Canada – Patent Protection*, para. 7.30. Although the panel, in *Canada – Patent Protection*, was interpreting Article 30 of the TRIPS Agreement, it noted that all of the exception clauses in the TRIPS Agreement (Articles 13, 17, 26.2 and 30) were derived from the same model—Article 9(2) of the Berne Convention for the Protection of Literary and Artistic Works. *Id.* at para. 7.71 n. 420.

argument presented by the EC in that case that the term "'limited' is to be measured by the extent to which the exclusive rights of the patent owner have been curtailed."[198]

202. TRIPS Article 17 further provides that exceptions must "take account of the *legitimate interests of the owner of the trademark*."[199] In interpreting the phrase "legitimate interests" with respect to TRIPS Article 13, in the copyright context, the *US – Section 110(5)* panel found that one way to look at "legitimate interests is the economic value of the exclusive rights conferred" by the intellectual property right on its holder.[200] Moreover, Article 17 provides that the limited exception must take account of the interests "of third parties." Among such third parties are consumers that are likely to be confused by the use of a sign, including of a geographical indication, that is identical or similar to a registered trademark.

203. Applying this analysis, the inability of a trademark owner to prevent a competitor from using an identical or similar sign in the course of trade could, in most cases, destroy the economic value of the trademark by severely curtailing the "economic value of the exclusive rights conferred." The GI Regulation places no limits on the manner in which a geographical indication can be used. Instead, the Regulation calls for simultaneous use of trademarks and conflicting registered GIs without taking "account of the legitimate interests of the owner of the trademark and of third parties."

204. A limited exception to trademark protection, such as that provided by a "fair use of descriptive terms" exception should take into account the legitimate interests of the trademark owner and of third parties. It should be possible to inform consumers about the origin of a product and its characteristics through the use of descriptive terms in a non-trademark sense without affirmatively confusing the consumer about the source of the goods. It is possible simultaneously to protect the legitimate interests of the consumer, the GI owner, and the trademark owner.

205. The EC also argues that with "co-existence," there is only a "limited" exception because the trademark owner's Article 16.1 rights are violated "only" by those qualified to use the GI.[201] However, providing protection to trademark owners against all but "one" type of use (*i.e.*, use of geographical indications in any way), as the EC proposes, does not provide for a limited exception. The blanket "exception" granted by the EC is in no sense "limited" or tailored whatsoever to the legitimate interests of the particular trademark owner involved. Furthermore, there are no limits on the number of potential GI right holders for each individual GI. Under the EC's proposed "limited" exception, a trademark owner may be forced to allow concurrent use by tens, hundreds, or even thousands of GI right holders that cause a likelihood of confusion with respect to the trademark.

206. The United States also notes that even under the EC's own interpretation of Article 17, the EC fails to acknowledge that non-geographic names are subject to registration under Article 2(3) of the GI Regulation (*e.g.*, Feta). The EC has not explained how the Article 17 fair use exception could apply to non-geographic terms.

207. Finally, the EC asserts that the GI Regulation takes into account the legitimate interests of the trademark owner and of third parties in three ways.[202] First, the EC states as follows:

> [E]ven if Article 14(3) of Regulation 2081/92 does not avoid completely the registration of confusing trademarks, it would at the very least prevent the most significant cases of confusion, in the interest of both the trademark owner and the consumers.

---

198 *Id.*, para. 7.31.

199 Emphasis added.

200 Panel Report, *US – Section 110(5)*, para. 6.227.

201 EC Responses to Panel Questions, para. 317.

202 EC Responses to Panel Questions, para. 319.

208. In other words, the EC appears to be arguing that diminishing Article 16.1 rights for all trademarks other than well-known marks constitutes a "limited exception". But well-known marks constitute a narrow subset of all trademarks protected by Article 16.1. And Article 17 addresses "limited exceptions to the rights conferred by a trademark", implying an analysis for each trademark, rather than general exceptions to a broad class of trademarks (in this case, all trademarks that are not well-known). As noted above, this is in sharp contrast to the EC GI Regulation, which offers a blanket exception that is not limited to the legitimate interests of the particular trademark owner involved.

209. Next, the EC states that geographical indications serve to provide valuable information to consumers, and thereby "take account of the legitimate interests ... of third parties." This statement is incorrect. This dispute concerns the very situation in which a registered GI is used in a manner likely to result in confusion *vis-a-vis* a prior trademark. This will harm the interests of consumers, contrary to the claims of the EC, as they will purchase products that they do not intend to purchase because of confusion over the name.

210. Lastly, the EC states that the legitimate interests of trademark owners and third parties are taken into account by EC legislation, because use of the registered GI is subject to EC legislation on labeling and misleading advertising, and by member State laws on unfair competition. Here the EC does not even pretend to consider the interests of trademark owners or of third parties in the manner required by TRIPS Article 17. Instead of taking into consideration the legitimate interests of the owner of "the" trademark that may be subject to fair use—as required by Article 17—the EC proposes a blanket exception to a broad class of trademarks (here, all prior, registered trademarks that co-exist with registered GIs). The fact that certain acts that constitute trademark infringement may also be subject to prohibition under other EC or member State legislation is simply not relevant to a determination as to whether the infringement of a given trademark by a given use is subject to the fair use defense.

211. In sum, the EC is far from sustaining its burden of proving that the EC GI Regulation falls within the "limited exceptions" permitted under Article 17.

VIII. THE EC GI REGULATION IS INCONSISTENT WITH ARTICLE 22.2 OF THE TRIPS AGREEMENT

212. As the United States stated in its first written submission, the EC GI Regulation fails in several respects to provide the required legal means to interested parties with respect to geographical indications.[203] First, as discussed above, because the GI Regulation imposes requirements of equivalence and reciprocity and requires certain inspection structures of the WTO Members in which the relevant geographical area is found, it does not make the legal means available to all interested parties to protect their GIs, or to object to the registration of misleading GIs. The EC's only response is that there are no conditions of reciprocity and equivalence imposed on WTO Members.[204] The EC makes no response with respect to the requirement for inspection structures. The United States submits that these conditions do exist and that they mean that interested parties in non-EC WTO Members do not have the required legal means to protect their GIs or to object to the registration of misleading GIs.

213. Similarly, the United States argued that the requirement that nationals of non-EC WTO Members cannot apply for registration and protection, or object to a GI registration directly, but must rely on the active participation and involvement of their home government is also a failure to provide the required legal means.[205] The EC's only response is that this is a "reasonable procedure and formality" under Article 62.1 of the TRIPS Agreement. With all due respect, that is beside the point. Many nationals of non-EC WTO Members are simply unable to meet the conditions for registration or objection, because of factors that are out of their control. These interested parties do not have the legal means to register and protect their GIs, or to object to the

[203] Paras. 171-183.

[204] EC First Written Submission, para. 423.

[205] US First Written Submission, para. 177.

registration of a GI, because the EC has failed to provide those legal means to them. This failure is inconsistent with Article 22.2 of the TRIPS Agreement.

214. The United States also argued that the GI Regulation appears to require an economic interest in the EC as a prerequisite to filing an objection,[206] whereas Article 22.2 of the TRIPS Agreement provides that legal means must be provided to all interested parties, including those with an economic interest outside the EC. The EC's response is to deny that there is any such requirement. The United States requests, therefore, that if the Panel agrees that there is such a requirement, that the Panel make a finding that it is inconsistent with Article 22.2.

215. Finally, the US argued that, whereas Article 22.2 obligates the EC to provide interested parties with the legal means to prevent misleading uses of geographical indications, the GI Regulation only permits objections on the grounds that the registration would " jeopardize the existence of an entirely or partly identical name or of a mark or the existence of products which have been legally on the market for at least five years."[207] Plainly, a registered name might be misleading without necessarily satisfying the high standard for objections in the GI Regulation, so these grounds are narrower than permitted under Article 22.2. The EC counters that such a name would not be registered if it were misleading.[208] But this argument ignores the fact that it is the interested parties who should be provided the legal means to prevent such uses under Article 22.2, a requirement that cannot be satisfied by a conclusory and baseless statement that no "misleading" geographical indications would be registered in the first place.

216. Finally, the EC notes, at paragraph 433 - 436 of its first written submission, that the EC GI Regulation is not the only means to protect geographical indications, that there are various labeling, advertising, trademark, and unfair competition laws that achieve the same purpose. But this argument ignores two facts. First, with respect to the registration of GIs, according to Article 2(1) of the GI Regulation, the GI Regulation specifies that EC protection of geographical indications of agricultural products and foodstuffs "shall be obtained in accordance with this Regulation." It does not appear to permit EC protection of geographical indications to be obtained through other means. Second, with respect to objections to GI registrations, once a GI is registered on an EC-wide basis, there appears to be little opportunity for a interested party to prevent the uses of that GI under the national laws of EC member States or under EC or national trademark rules. Indeed, the EC has not provided any evidence to support its defense that other EC laws meet the EC's obligations under Article 22.2. Without such evidence, the EC's defense can only be seen as a concession that the GI Regulation does not meet the requirements of Article 22.2.

217. Consequently, the Panel should find that the EC GI Regulation is inconsistent with Article 22.2 of the TRIPS Agreement.

IX. THE EC GI REGULATION IS INCONSISTENT WITH THE ENFORCEMENT PROVISIONS OF THE TRIPS AGREEMENT

218. The United States explained, in paragraphs 184 - 188 of its first written submission, that the EC GI Regulation is inconsistent with various TRIPS Agreement requirements to enforce intellectual property rights, because it denies trademark owners their Article 16.1 rights and fails to provide interested parties with the required legal means to prevent misleading uses of geographical indications or acts of unfair competition. Consequently, with respect to these infringements of intellectual property rights, the GI Regulation fails to make fair and equitable enforcement procedures or judicial review available (Articles 41.1, 41.2 and 41.4), including civil judicial procedures (Article 42), and fails to provide injunctive relief (Article 44.1).

[206] US First Written Submission, para. 181.

[207] US First Written Submission, para. 182.

[208] EC First Written Submission, para. 432.

219. The thrust of the EC's response is that the enforcement obligations of the TRIPS Agreement do not apply to the GI Regulation— that the GI Regulation is a procedure for the acquisition of intellectual property rights, not for enforcement.[209] But the United States submits that, if a measure makes unavailable to rightholders the required enforcement procedures and remedies to prevent and deter infringements of covered intellectual property rights, that measure is inconsistent with the obligation under TRIPS to make such procedures and remedies available. The United States requests the Panel to so find with respect to the EC GI Regulation.

X. CONCLUSION

220. For the reasons set forth in this second submission, as well as the reasons set forth in the US first written submission, the US oral statement at the first Panel meeting, and in the answers to the Panel's questions, the United States requests that the Panel find that the EC GI Regulation is inconsistent with the EC's obligations under the TRIPS Agreement and the GATT 1994, and to recommend that the EC bring its measure into conformity with those requirements.

[209] EC First Written Submission, paras. 358 *et seq.*

ANNEX A-6

OPENING STATEMENT OF THE UNITED STATES SECOND SUBSTANTIVE MEETING

(11 August 2004)

1. Good afternoon, Mr. Chairman and members of the Panel. We brought this dispute because the EC GI Regulation provides significant commercial benefits to products and persons receiving GI status under the Regulation, but imposes prohibitive barriers to access to these benefits on non-EC products and persons. The GI Regulation has both the design and the effect of protecting EC agricultural products and persons against competition from non-EC products and persons. Let's not forget that, after 12 years, there is not a single non-EC GI registered under the GI Regulation. Not one. By contrast, there are over 600 registered GIs for EC products and persons. Further, these substantial benefits are provided at the expense of owners of prior registered trademarks: those owners are supposed to have certain rights associated with their trademarks under the TRIPS Agreement. The EC GI Regulation eviscerates those rights—rights that are critical to the trademark owner—in favor, again, of those EC products and persons who receive GI protection. Although this violation of trademark rights is a claim separate from that of national treatment, it is consistent with the approach of the EC Regulation to protect its agricultural production, especially as agricultural subsidies are reduced or eliminated.

2. The first meeting of this Panel and the submissions of the EC have, if anything, confirmed our worst fears. Some of the violations of the WTO agreements are so extreme that the EC can defend the Regulation only by denying that it says what it says. Whole provisions in the Regulation are ignored, and whole new provisions are added, based on nothing except the EC's "assurances" during these proceedings of what the Regulation means, despite the fact that these "assurances" are contrary to both the text of the Regulation and to what the EC has consistently said to everyone—including complainants—outside this room in the past 12 years. This effective rewriting of the Regulation is based, in part, on the EC's assertions that the EC and the ECJ would never read any provision of the Regulation as inconsistent with the WTO Agreement, regardless of what the Regulation actually says. Such an assertion is nothing short of remarkable.

3. It is the job of this Panel, not of the EC, to clarify the nature of the WTO obligations and to make an objective assessment of the facts of this dispute, including the meaning of the EC GI Regulation. Contrary to the EC's hope, it is not the US burden to show that the US reading of the EC GI Regulation is the only "reasonable" one. It is our burden to make a *prima facie* case that the Regulation means what it says, which we have done on the face of the Regulation in the light of EC law. It was then up to the EC to present evidence rebutting that meaning. In this, the EC has failed. Although the EC hopes to hide behind a so-called "considerable deference" defense, the plain truth is that it is unable to come forward with a domestic authoritative legal instrument—such as that found in the Section 301 dispute—supporting the EC's new found reading of the Regulation. Further, if neither the ECJ nor the EC member States give "considerable deference" to the Commission's interpretation of its Regulation, it is hard to see how this Panel should have confidence that the ECJ would agree with the EC's interpretation. In short, there is no basis for the EC's newly created defense.

4. The United States would, in fact, welcome positive evidence, beyond the EC's mere hopes that the ECJ might in the future agree with its assertions in this dispute, that would support a finding that the WTO-inconsistent provisions in the GI Regulation do not apply to WTO Members. However, on the evidence currently before the Panel, the United States simply has no confidence that the EC's new reading of its Regulation is the correct one, or that the ECJ would so find.

5. One other preliminary comment. I ask the Panel to look closely at what the EC provided in its second submission with respect to the relevance of the WTO agreements to the interpretation of EC regulations. It has

provided some scholarly opinions that the WTO agreements should not be ignored, and encouraging WTO-consistent interpretations of EC Regulations. But there is nothing in that submission to suggest that, in the case of this Regulation, the Commission's invention of new procedures for WTO Members is a "possible" reading of a Regulation that on its face requires reciprocity and equivalence for all third countries.

6. This oral statement is divided into three parts. The first discusses the national treatment and MFN violations under the TRIPS Agreement, the Paris Convention, and the GATT 1994. The second discusses the Regulation's violation of the GI obligations in the TRIPS Agreement—Article 22.2—and of the enforcement obligations. The final section discusses the GI Regulation's violation of trademark rights under Article 16.1 of the TRIPS Agreement.

National Treatment/MFN

"nationals"

7. With respect to national treatment and MFN obligations under the TRIPS Agreement and the Paris Convention, a threshold question appears to be whether the Regulation treats non-EC nationals differently from EC nationals. The EC admits there are two tracks for registering a GI—a "domestic" track for persons established and producing GI products in the EC, and a "foreign" track for persons established and producing GI products outside the EC. But, according to the EC, these two separate tracks correspond to a difference in the origin of the product and of the GI, not a difference in the "nationality" of the producer. The EC further claims that "establishment" and "nationality" are two completely separate concepts, and that less favorable treatment based on where a person is established does not translate into less favorable treatment of nationals.

8. With all due respect, the EC's position is contrary to principles of treaty interpretation, does not reflect reality, and would render the national treatment obligation a virtual nullity. We, along with Australia and numerous third parties, have set out our position and concerns in our various written submissions on this issue, and I will not repeat all of those arguments now.

9. But I do want to highlight a few issues concerning the EC's overly narrow and restrictive interpretation of the national treatment requirement. First, this interpretation is contrary to the EC's own analysis in support of the GI Regulation. In arguing that the two separate GI Regulation "tracks" for objecting to a GI Registration are not based on nationality, the EC stated that "Article 7(3) of Regulation 2081/92 refers to persons which are resident or established in the EC, regardless of their nationality. Similarly, Article 12d(1) refers to persons resident or established outside the EC, regardless of their nationality."[1] But Article 12d was added to the Regulation just last year, and the EC justified that amendment as follows, and I quote, "[t]o satisfy the obligation resulting from Article 22 of the TRIPS Agreement it should be made clear that in this matter *nationals* of WTO member countries are covered by these arrangements."[2] The EC went on to say that "[t]he right of objection should be granted to WTO member countries' *nationals* with a legitimate interest on the same terms as laid down in Article 7(4) of the said Regulation."[3] Thus, the EC itself equates where a person is from, *i.e.*, where that person is resident or established, with their nationality: before last year, there was one "domestic" track for persons "resident or established" in the EC, which the EC admitted did not make objections available to WTO Members' nationals. The EC then added an additional "foreign" track last year for persons "resident or established" outside the EC, to adequately cover "nationals" of WTO Member countries. The distinction in the two tracks for the registration of GIs is similar to that for objections—the track that applies depends on where the person is established and producing GI products—and likewise draws a distinction based on EC nationals, on the one hand, and non-EC nationals, on the other.

1 EC First Written Submission, para. 142.

2 Council Regulation No. 692/2003 of April 8, 2003, p. 2. Exhibit Comp-1h.

3 Council Regulation No. 692/2003 of April 8, 2003, p. 2. Exhibit Comp-1h.

10. Second, the EC has said that the "foreign track" conditions of equivalence and reciprocity do not apply to WTO Members. According to the EC, this is because those conditions apply "without prejudice to international agreements", and, to avoid a conflict between those conditions and the national treatment obligations of the TRIPS Agreement, the conditions are eliminated such that the TRIPS Agreement prevails.[4]

11. Yet, by arguing that the reciprocity and equivalence conditions must be eliminated for WTO Members in order to respect the national treatment obligation, the EC obviously considers that those conditions result in less favorable treatment of nationals of other WTO Members. The EC cannot, then, credibly argue the contrary: that conditions that depend on the origin of the product and of the GI do not result in different, and less favorable, treatment of nationals seeking to register GIs for those products.

12. Further, although the EC would like to engage in a detailed discussion of whether "establishment" in a country always results in a person being a "national" of that country, this is not the point. It is beyond dispute that, at least for some WTO Members, including separate customs unions, a real and effective establishment makes a person a "national" of that WTO Member. Creating a separate track in the GI Regulation for such persons results in different treatment of those persons.

13. In addition, we have made clear that the EC GI Regulation effectively requires that, in order to register a GI on the same basis as an EC national, a non-EC national must produce a qualifying product in the EC. Requiring that a person be established in a country before being able to claim equal access to a system of intellectual property protection is a denial of national treatment. This is clear from Article 2(2) of the Paris Convention, which specifically prohibits conditioning the enjoyment of industrial property rights on establishment or domicile. But more than that, if such a requirement were permitted, what would stop the United States from providing that only those with domiciles or establishments in the United States can register trademarks, or file patent applications, in the United States? We, like the EC, could well argue that EC nationals are being treated the same as US nationals, since both have to be established in the United States to register a trademark, and neither can do so if they are domiciled or established in the EC. But this could hardly be considered to be national treatment. The EC argues that "with the growing appreciation and knowledge of agricultural products and foodstuffs protected by geographical indications" the current lack of foreign companies producing qualifying products in the EC will change.[5] Although this may in fact be true, if companies are unable to obtain GI protection any other way except to abandon their existing GIs, and instead establish themselves in the EC and create a new EC GIs, this is little solace to US nationals now producing qualifying products in the United States, who are already entitled to as favorable treatment as their European counterparts.

14. Finally, from a practical point of view, it cannot be open to serious question that it is US nationals that have an interest in U.S.-based GIs and EC nationals that have an interest in EC-based GIs. In the United States, for instance, approximately 99% of agricultural land is owned by US nationals, and only 1% is owned by non-US nationals.[6] The EC itself, unable to provide a single example of a US national owning an EC-based GI, can only speculate that this situation may change as the value of GIs associated with European products becomes recognized.[7] A GI system that provides less favorable treatment to agricultural products and GIs located outside the EC than inside the EC does provide less favorable treatment to non-EC nationals than to EC nationals. While it is true, as the EC points out, that like Mr. Larsen of Cognac fame, a non-EC national <u>can</u> move to France, <u>can</u> buy a French company producing cognac, marry a French national and raise a family in France, we submit that <u>requiring</u> him to do so in order to register his GI on the same basis as EC nationals is hardly according him as favorable treatment as EC nationals.

---

[4] EC Second Written Submission, paras. 55-56.

[5] EC Second Written Submission, para. 48.

[6] Agricultural Resources and Environmental Indicators: Land ownership and farm structure, Economic Research Service, United States Department of Agriculture, July 2002, Chapter 1.3, p. 7. Available at www.ers.usda.gov/publications. Exhibit US-72.

[7] EC Second Written Submission, para. 48.

15. The EC this morning provided several supposed examples of non-EC companies taking advantage of EC GIs. But, looking at the actual exhibits, it appears that these examples concern companies incorporated in EC member States. I am not sure on what basis the EC claims that these are foreign nationals claiming EC-based GIs.

16. By the way, the EC appears to be using Larsen Cognac House as an example of a non-EC national claiming an EC-based GI. I'm curious to know whether Larsen Cognac House, which has apparently produced cognac in France since 1926, is not an EC national, or whether, in fact, Mr. Larsen set up a legal entity that is an EC national before claiming GI status for his product.

17. In its oral statement this morning, the EC claimed that the scope of the national treatment obligation under the TRIPS Agreement was limited because of the national treatment provisions provided under Article III of the GATT 1994. There is nothing unusual, however, about both obligations applying to the same measure. The EC's view that Article III cuts into and narrows the national treatment obligation under the TRIPS Agreement is incorrect and has no basis in the Vienna Convention rules of treaty interpretation.

Reciprocity and Equivalence

18. With respect to the issue of reciprocity and equivalence, at this point, I can only repeat that the GI Regulation on its face sets out only two tracks for registering GIs: one for registering products and GIs originating in the EC and one for registering products and GIs originating in all other countries, *i.e.*, "third countries". Article 12(1) of the GI Regulation clearly says that all third countries hoping to benefit from the Regulation have to have a GI protection system that is equivalent to that in the EC and have to offer reciprocal protection to EC products. The EC says that these conditions do not apply to WTO Members, because to do so would be in violation of the WTO agreements (and to this we agree). Further, beyond the question of whether the WTO agreements must be considered in interpreting EC regulations, the GI Regulation does not provide any procedures for registering GIs from WTO Members. And neither does the TRIPS Agreement, which simply spells out general obligations. Thus, even if the reciprocity and equivalence requirements do not apply to WTO Members, nationals of WTO Members would still not be able to register their GIs because no procedures exist for this to occur.

19. The EC provides several examples of agreements containing language similar to the "without prejudice" language of Article 12(1) of the GI Regulation. But in each of those cases, there is a simple requirement in the regulation or directive that can be directly supplanted by a specific contrary obligation in the international agreement. For instance, if the requirement for local ownership in the air carrier regulation conflicts with an international agreement imposing a different ownership requirement, the specific ownership provision in the international agreement can simply be applied. Consistent with these examples, the registration procedures and conditions in Articles 12(1) and 12a could be made inoperative by virtue of specific registration provisions for GIs in an international agreement. By contrast, the GI Regulation provides a track for registering GIs that is specifically limited to third countries satisfying the reciprocity and equivalence conditions. If a third country does not satisfy those conditions, there is no registration procedure in the GI Regulation, and there is nothing in the TRIPS Agreement to fill that void.

20. The United States provided examples of the kind of agreements that would give proper meaning to the "without prejudice" clause, for instance, agreements that provide for protection for specific GIs, which would then not be prejudiced by the GI Regulation's requirements. This included an agreement with Switzerland that specifically anticipated protection of specific GIs. The EC's only response is to deny that any of those agreements fall within the scope of the "without prejudice" language. In the case of Switzerland, the EC protests that there is no such specific protection *yet.* Now, even assuming that the EC's response is correct, however, it is beside the point. The EC apparently concedes that such specific agreements protecting GIs were and are anticipated, and that any such agreements would have to be exempt from the requirements of the GI Regulation. The "without prejudice" language would thus make sense with respect to any such agreements.

21. The EC also goes to great pains to distance itself from its many past representations to the WTO Membership that the conditions of reciprocity and equivalence apply to WTO Members—even invoking the confidentiality of consultations to shield its previous interpretation of this Regulation. But the plain facts are that the EC has publicized this interpretation widely, and that this consistent interpretation is directly contradicted for the first time by the EC's first submission in this dispute. The EC even goes so far as to deny authorship of the January 16, 2003, communication sent to the United States confirming that US GIs cannot be registered because the United States does not satisfy the reciprocity and equivalence requirements. The United States emphasizes that this document does no more than confirm what the United States was repeatedly told during consultations. But, in response to the denials of the EC, the United States notes that this document was included in a January 16, 2003, communication from Trade Commissioner Pascal Lamy to Ambassador Robert Zoellick. Although much of the letter and attachment are not relevant to this dispute, they are attached as Exhibit US-73 for the Panel's consideration.

22. Before closing on the subject of reciprocity and equivalence, I want to emphasize that, if it were clear that, contrary to the text of the GI Regulation and contrary to the repeated representations of the EC—both public and private—the EC GI Regulation does not impose any conditions of reciprocity and equivalence on WTO Members, the United States would welcome such a factual finding by the Panel. However, for all of the reasons that we have set out in our various submissions, we have substantial concerns that these conditions do apply to WTO Members and that the ECJ would so find.

Requirement for equivalent inspection structures

23. I would like to move on to one specific aspect of the EC's requirement of equivalence that the EC does not deny applies to WTO Members: the requirement for the establishment of equivalent inspection structures. Contrary to the EC's claims, the United States made plain from the beginning of this dispute its view that the specific requirement for equivalent inspection structures was inconsistent with the national treatment obligations of the TRIPS Agreement and the Paris Convention.[8]

24. And, indeed, this requirement does provide "less favorable" treatment to non-EC nationals. Under the GI Regulation, EC member States are required to ensure that inspection structures are in place on their territories, and are required to approve all inspection authorities and/or private bodies that make up the inspection structures.[9] All such bodies must be responsible to the member State.[10] Therefore, any EC national wishing to register a GI automatically has, by virtue of the EC GI Regulation itself, a qualifying inspection structure established by his member State. Thus it can obtain protection for its EC GI. A non-EC national, by contrast, can satisfy the GI Regulation's inspection requirements only if *his* sovereign government (1) has ensured the establishment of these same inspection structures, as dictated by Article 10 the EC GI Regulation; (2) has specifically approved particular inspection bodies that must also be approved by the EC; and (3) assumes responsibility for those inspection bodies, as required by the EC. If his government has not established such structures and approved such bodies, that non-EC WTO national cannot register and protect his GI in the EC. Needless to say, unlike member States, other WTO Members have no obligations under the EC Regulation. That non-EC national is therefore being treated less favorably than the EC national as regards the protection of his geographical indications because, in order to obtain protection for his non-EC GI, he must convince his government to subject itself to the EC through the EC GI Regulation, and dedicate government resources to establish a GI system exactly like the EC's.

25. The EC has emphasized the supposed extreme flexibility of this inspection structure requirement, implying that a US national hoping to register his GI in the United States could satisfy this requirement by simply hiring a private commercial company that provides inspection services.[11] But it is not as simple as that.

---

[8] *E.g.*, US First Written Submission, para. 64.

[9] EC GI Regulation, Article 10(1) and (2).

[10] EC GI Regulation, Article 10(3).

[11] EC Second Written Submission, para. 107.

The EC Regulation does not simply require that a non-EC national contract with a commercial inspection service, even one of those identified by the EC in Exhibits EC-49 and EC-50 as companies authorized to carry out inspections under the EC GI Regulation.

26. No, to satisfy the EC GI Regulation, the *government* of the non-EC national must ensure that structures are in place and must approve the particular inspection bodies and take responsibility for their inspections. If that *government* has not done so, its nationals are precluded from protection in the EC. In short, the GI Regulation requires extensive foreign government involvement; no non-EC national can on its own meet the requirements of the GI Regulation.

27. The EC's response is to argue at some length that the EC Regulation's requirement that other WTO Members establish inspection structures is "necessary" to attain the objectives of the GI Regulation.[12] But the issue before the Panel under the national treatment obligations of the TRIPS Agreement and the Paris Convention is whether non-EC nationals are treated at least as favorably as EC nationals with regard to the protection of geographical indications. Since they are not treated as favorably, the GI Regulation is inconsistent with these obligations. The question of whether the requirement is "necessary" simply does not enter into the analysis at all: Nothing in the text excuses less favorable treatment simply because a Member deems the violation "necessary". And since there is no basis in the TRIPS Agreement or the Paris Convention for the EC's novel "necessary" test, the Panel should simply reject this request. If anything, a "necessary" analysis is only relevant in this dispute with respect to the EC's GATT Article XX affirmative defense, and I will discuss this in due course.

28. But even though there is no "necessary" test in the TRIPS and Paris provisions at issue, I don't want to leave the Panel with the impression that the GI Regulation's requirement that non-EC WTO Members establish, approve, and be responsible for particular inspection structures is necessary. It is not. There is simply no reason to assume that only the *government* of the rightholder, as opposed to the rightholder himself, can sufficiently assure the EC that the products claiming GI status qualify for that status. And it is not clear why it is the government of the rightholder, and not the government whose regulation it is, that has to approve or authorize inspection structures. It is interesting that, in arguing that the EC inspection structures are "necessary", the EC cites the example of the US regulations concerning organic food, which require that any farmer seeking to claim that his products are organic must have his farm inspected by a certifying agent. Of course, this dispute does not concern any US measures, and organic labeling is not a private intellectual property right, as are geographical indications. But since the EC raised it, the Panel should be aware that in the case of US organic labeling regulations, the USDA maintains a list of certifying agents, including those able to conduct inspections in the EU, that any farmer in Europe can simply call directly and satisfy the US regulations. There is no unilateral US requirement for foreign government involvement, intervention, or allocation of resources. The same is *not* true of a non-EC national who wishes to apply to register his GI in Europe. He is simply foreclosed unless his government establishes, approves and takes responsibility for the inspection structures specified in Article 10.

29. Indeed, how would the EC react if the United States, as a condition of protecting EC GIs in the United States, required the EC to establish a specific inspection structure system designed by the United States? Suppose further that the inspection structure required by the United States is incompatible with the inspection system the EC has established for its GIs. Would the EC still consider the unilateral imposition of inspection requirements on other WTO Members appropriate? Perhaps more to the point, this Panel may wish to consider the impact of numerous WTO Members imposing their own different inspection system requirements on all other WTO Members as a condition to protecting foreign GIs. A WTO Member wanting its nationals to benefit from GI protection in the territories of these WTO Members would potentially have to establish every one of these distinct inspection systems in its territory, which—needless to say—would be impossible and unworkable. Yet that would be the result if the EC were to succeed in arguing that it is WTO-consistent for one Member to

[12] *E.g.*, EC Second Written Submission, paras. 109 *et seq.*

unilaterally require foreign governments to establish a particular inspection structure in order for their nationals to obtain protection for their GIs.

30. The EC implied this morning that the United States and Australia are asking the EC to somehow lower its standards for GIs from the United States and Australia. I emphasize, to the contrary, that the product standards that US nationals have to meet in order to obtain GI protection are not at issue. But the inspection structures required by the EC are not related to the product characteristics that qualify them for GI protection. In addition, this dispute is not about what is wrong with the EC inspection system itself. Rather, the issue is whether the EC can unilaterally require other WTO Members to adopt the EC's system. The inspection system may be fine for the EC; this does not justify the EC's imposing it on us.

Requirement that the non-EC WTO Member itself assess and verify whether the requirements of the EC GI Regulation are met and that the non-EC WTO Member advocate for registration on behalf of its nationals

31. A similar response can be made with respect to the requirement that the non-EC WTO Member itself assess and verify whether its nationals have satisfied the EC GI Regulation's requirements, and advocate for registration on behalf of its nationals. As in the case of inspection structures, an EC national has the direct means under the GI Regulation to register and protect his GIs. A non-EC national from a country that is not in a position to assess and verify that the requirements of the EC GI Regulation are satisfied does not have any ability to do so. Again, it is worth noting that, as the EC itself has specified, what is required is a substantial dedication of expertise and resources by the non-EC WTO Member government. Unlike EC nationals, non-EC nationals cannot on their own take advantage of pre-established infrastructure to register their non-EC GIs.

32. The EC's response, again, is that what it calls "cooperation" is "necessary" and "indispensable"[13] to the registration process. And again, as in the case of inspection structures, whether so-called "cooperation" is "necessary" or "indispensable" is not relevant to the national treatment issue before the Panel under the TRIPS Agreement and the Paris Convention. The only issue for the Panel is whether there is less favorable treatment. The EC's apparent excuse that less favorable treatment is necessary or indispensable is simply without basis.

33. But even so, as noted earlier, the EC's arguments that its requirements for so-called "cooperation" ring hollow.[14] The EC has not been able to show that, for instance, the United States Government is in the best position to evaluate whether the specifications provided by the rightholder are sufficiently established, or that it is only the US Government, and not the rightholder, that is capable of providing the elements necessary to show the rightholder's entitlement to a GI registration. Further, "facilitating cooperation" with the WTO Member is no excuse: it is the very unilateral imposition of requirements on non-EC WTO Members—under the guise of forced "cooperation"—that we find unnecessary. Moreover, the EC's argument that this requirement is "beneficial to the applicant"—who can "discuss, prepare, file, and where necessary refine and amend his application directly with the authorities where the geographical area is located"[15] emphasizes both the burden being placed on the WTO Member and the lack of its necessity—that it may be "beneficial to the applicant" does not equate to it being "necessary."

34. The EC's second submission, at paras. 130-142, makes a number of additional points in support of its contention that there is nothing wrong with requiring other sovereign governments to assess and verify whether an application satisfies the requirements of the GI Regulation. First, it is of course incorrect to assert that this is "partially mandated"—whatever that means—by the definition of a GI in the TRIPS Agreement.[16] Nothing in TRIPS Article 22.1 requires this, fully or partially. Furthermore, the EC is requiring that the WTO Member assess whether the EC Regulation requirements are satisfied, not whether the TRIPS Agreement obligations are satisfied.

---

[13] *E.g.*, EC Second Written Submission, paras. 124 *et seq.*

[14] EC Second Written Submission, paras. 124 *et seq.*

[15] EC Second Written Submission, para. 129.

[16] EC Second Written Submission, para. 132.

35. Second, the so-called "numerous" examples in which governments have agreed to cooperate can in no way be interpreted as licence for one WTO Member to unilaterally force another WTO Member to "cooperate". And despite the EC's claims to the contrary, the TRIPS Agreement does not permit such coercion: to the contrary, it requires no less favorable treatment for nationals of other WTO Members.

36. Third, the EC's citation to the *US – Gasoline* dispute as an example of where "cooperation" between countries may be necessary is instructive, but not for the reasons urged by the EC. In that dispute, the Appellate Body was questioning why, in establishing certain refinery-specific baselines for foreign refiners, the United States Environmental Protection Agency could not have adapted "procedures for verification of information found in US antidumping duty laws."[17] As the EC knows, those procedures involve having the foreign company submit information to the US Government, and having the US *Government* conduct an on-site verification of those data. The desired "cooperation" in that case was, therefore, permitting the US auditors to conduct an audit at the foreign refinery. It was not a unilateral requirement that the foreign government itself assess and verify compliance with US laws, which is the so-called "cooperation" that the EC has in mind in the EC GI Regulation. More fundamentally, the requirement at issue in US – *Gasoline* was analyzed in the context of GATT Article XX—that is, there was a breach of Article III, and the only issue was whether it was justified under Article XX.

37. Finally, the EC claims that simple transmittal of a registration application is not difficult and that the United States should not raise difficulties that other WTO Members might have meeting this requirement. But, as the EC itself admits, and contrary to what we heard this morning in the EC's oral statement, the EC's requirement goes beyond a simple ministerial act. It requires a thorough assessment and verification of whether an application meets the requirements of the GI Regulation. Further, the issue is not how difficult this requirement is to satisfy, but whether the EC is justified in imposing it. Consequently, it is misleading and irrelevant to assert that "any WTO Member with a normally functioning government should be able to carry out such an act"[18]—a quotation that was repeated this morning in the EC oral statement. First, this is untrue, as I just discussed. Second, if what is required *were* a simple ministerial act of transmission, then there is an obvious question as to why it is necessary, in light of the fact that intellectual property rights are private rights, for direct applications for protection in one country to be transmitted through the government of another country.

Country of origin marking requirement for non-EC GIs

38. I want to include a brief word on the EC's response concerning the country of origin marking requirement for non-EC GIs. The EC claims, contrary to the plain meaning of the Regulation, that that requirement applies, not to foreign GIs, but to whichever GI is registered later. The provision in question—Article 12(2)—is a provision directed purely at the conditions for authorizing the use of *non-EC* GIs. There is simply no basis for reading this as applying to *EC-based* GIs. I point this out as yet another example of the EC attempting to rewrite the Regulation on the grounds that it must be interpreted consistently with the WTO Agreement, regardless of the actual text.

Objections

39. I'd like to turn briefly to the failure to provide national treatment under the TRIPS Agreement with respect to the ability to object to the registration of GIs. The EC reads the GI Regulation as giving a right of objection to persons "from a WTO Member", on the one hand, and from "a third country recognized under the procedures provided for in Article 12(3)" (*i.e.*, countries satisfying the reciprocity and equivalence conditions), on the other. The EC claims that this distinction makes clear that the conditions of reciprocity and equivalence do not apply with respect to nationals from WTO Members, but only with respect to nationals from "other"

[17] EC Second Written Submission, para. 136, *citing* Appellate Body Report, US – *Gasoline*, p. 26.

[18] EC Second Written Submission, para. 141.

countries. The United States, by contrast, believes that the correct reading of the phrase "recognized under the procedures provided for in Article 12(3)" is that it applies both to WTO Members *and* to other third countries. I will not repeat our detailed arguments here, but would simply note that the EC's reading only emphasizes even more the weakness of the EC's argument with respect to the registration of GIs. According to the EC, this language in the objection provisions distinguishes between WTO Members and other third countries; yet such an argument only makes the failure to make any such distinction in the registration provisions all the more evident.

40. With respect to the GI Regulation's requirement that the WTO Member, and not its national, assess and submit any objections to a GI registration, I refer to the comments I made earlier concerning the similar requirement for registrations: under this requirement EC nationals have a direct means to object to registrations, while nationals from non-EC countries that do not process objections under the EC GI Regulation do not.

41. The EC's responses to this point are a bit curious. On the one hand, the EC claims that a WTO Member does not have to do anything other than transmit the objection, dismissing the notion that the EC is imposing any real requirements on other WTO Members. On the other hand, the EC claims that the WTO Member does have to verify where the objecting person is resident or established, and claims to need a "contact" in the government to address "questions relating to the territory of the third country".[19] It would appear that, in fact, more is required than a purely ministerial act of transmission. And, of course, the whole point is that the US national should not have to jump the extra hurdle of convincing the US Government to submit his objection for him. It is circular to claim that this is necessary because the US Government has to verify that he is a US national.

Legitimate interest

42. Finally, with respect to objections, the United States noted in its second submission that, before last year's amendments, only a "legitimately concerned" EC national could object to a GI registration.[20] The EC specifically amended the regulation last year to give WTO Members' nationals the right to object, yet it deliberately added a different and facially higher standard—one implying some property interest—for those WTO nationals: they have to have a "legitimate interest".[21] The United States showed in its second written submission that this is a different and higher standard, and the EC has not sustained its burden of showing that this higher standard does not amount to less favorable treatment for non-EC nationals.

Requirement of domicile or establishment

43. As mentioned earlier, in order to register GIs and object to the registration of GIs on the same basis as EC nationals, a non-EC national has to become established or domiciled in the EC. Further, for those non-EC nationals whose governments do not satisfy the EC's requirements, for instance, with respect to inspection structures, the only way to enjoy their GI rights is to become established in the EC. Contrary to the EC's second submission, this is not about the EC's ability to ensure that the product originates in the geographical region indicated. And it is not about allowing persons established outside the EC to object. This is about not imposing hurdles on persons established outside the EC such that, in order to enjoy their intellectual property rights, they have to establish themselves in the EC. The EC GI Regulation plainly does this, and so is inconsistent with Article 2(2) of the Paris Convention.

National treatment under the GATT 1994

44. Our first submission discussed in detail how the conditions of reciprocity and equivalence imposed on WTO Members are inconsistent also with national treatment obligations under the GATT 1994. And we have

[19] EC Second Written Submission, para. 156.

[20] Article 7(3) of the GI Regulation.

[21] Article 12d of the GI Regulation.

also discussed in detail the issue of whether the conditions of reciprocity and equivalence apply to WTO Members. I won't discuss that issue further here, except to recall that the EC has presented no arguments that these conditions are consistent with the GATT 1994 national treatment obligations, and to recall that the EC itself claims that these conditions conflict with the WTO agreements. That is the basis for their view that the "without prejudice" language in Article 12(1) eliminates these requirements for WTO Members. Accordingly, the Panel should find that these conditions are inconsistent with the national treatment obligations of the GATT 1994.

45. With respect to the other issues which I have also discussed above: the requirement for specific inspection structures and the requirement that other WTO Members assess and verify whether GI applications satisfy the requirements of the EC GI Regulation, the EC, in its second submission, simply refers back to its arguments with respect to national treatment under the TRIPS Agreement and the Paris Convention. Notably, the EC states that these requirements are also imposed on EC products, so they constitute "equal", not "less favorable", treatment.

46. This curt dismissal of this claim is interesting, because the EC itself argues that the EC GI Regulation does not discriminate according to nationality, but according to the origin of the product. Furthermore, the EC has justified its highly technical and overly narrow interpretation of the TRIPS Agreement national treatment obligation based on the fact that the GATT disciplines also cover this situation. In addition, it is the EC that has emphasized the differences between the GATT national treatment obligations and the TRIPS Agreement national treatment obligations.

47. Therefore, we should take some care with this argument. Treatment between EC products and non-EC products is clearly not "equal." Article III:4 of the GATT 1994 then requires that products from outside the EC be accorded treatment that is no less favorable than that accorded "like products of national origin." As the Appellate Body has noted, "like" means "[h]aving the same characteristics or qualities"[22] and has been analyzed in past disputes based on the characteristics of the products themselves, *i.e.,* physical properties, ability to serve the same end uses, consumer perceptions of whether the products serve the same end uses, and the tariff classification of the product.[23]

48. In the context of this dispute, therefore, the issue is whether an imported product that has characteristics qualifying it for GI status under the GI Regulation is treated at least as favorably as an EC product that has those characteristics. The answer is no. The imported product will be denied the benefits of the GI Regulation in the EC market, not because of any deficiency in the product itself, but because of a "failure" of the country of origin to establish an EC-style inspection system. These benefits will also be denied where the government of the country of origin—for instance, the United States—does not have a mechanism to take on the EC's job to assess whether a product meets the EC's requirements. This has nothing to do with the characteristics of the product itself. Favorable treatment is denied to "like" products for reasons related to the product's origin.

49. Further, this Panel should not ignore that the preamble to the Regulation emphasizes the importance of the production, manufacture, and distribution of agricultural products and foodstuffs to the European economy, and emphasizes the intended role of the Regulation in promoting products having certain characteristics, which "could be of considerable benefit to the rural economy, in particular to less-favoured or remote areas" in the EC. In this connection, it is hard to ignore that, of the over 600 registered GIs in Europe, exactly zero are for products produced outside the EC. And this, 12 years after the Regulation was implemented. In addition, although the EC argues now that its active advertisement of the reciprocity and equivalence requirements were not authoritative, it cannot be denied that the EC effectively sent a message discouraging any GI applications from countries not satisfying those requirements. The effect of this discouragement is plain to see. Finally, the additional requirements that the EC admits imposing on WTO Members—notably, to establish specific

[22] *EC – Asbestos*, para. 90, *citing* New Shorter Oxford English Dictionary.

[23] *EC – Asbestos*, para. 101.

inspection structures and to assess and verify whether GI applications meet the EC GI Regulation's requirements—are simply equivalence by another name, and are similarly designed to discourage the registration and protection of foreign GIs.

50. In sum, the GI Regulation is inconsistent with the national treatment obligations of the GATT 1994.

Article XX(d) of the GATT 1994

51. But I should note that, even more than in the case of the TRIPS Agreement national treatment obligation, the EC second submission contains virtually no arguments about whether the EC GI Regulation affords less favorable treatment to imported products than to domestic "like" products. Instead—just as in the case of the TRIPS Agreement national treatment discussion—the EC devotes the bulk of its presentation to justify why, in spite of the obligations, the various requirements of the EC GI Regulation are necessary or indispensable to the GI Regulation's objectives. So, let me respond to the EC's argument that the GI Regulation is covered by the Article XX(d) exception to the GATT 1994 obligations.

52. It is unfortunate that the EC has only just now, in its second written submission, spelled out its arguments on Article XX(d). Up until that submission, the EC failed to provide anything beyond the most conclusory statements on Article XX(d). It was a little amusing to hear this morning the EC's claim that the United States has not responded at all to these arguments, in light of the fact that we just received them, and that this statement is the first opportunity to respond. So, let me turn to them now.

53. The United States submits that the EC is far from meeting its burden, even at this late hour. Article XX(d) requires that the EC demonstrate that the measure that is inconsistent with the GATT 1994 (1) is designed to "secure compliance" with laws or regulations that are not inconsistent with the GATT 1994; and (2) is "necessary" to ensure such compliance. The EC's arguments fail on both counts.

54. With respect to the requirement for inspection structures, the EC, at paragraph 232, merely summarizes and cross references its statement that the "requirement of inspection structures is necessary for the attainment of the objectives of Regulation 2081/92."[24] And that a "similar degree of protection could not be achieved through other means."[25] But the standard in Article XX(d) is whether the GATT-inconsistent measure "is necessary to *secure compliance*" with a GATT-consistent law or regulation, not whether it is necessary to "attain the objectives" of the GATT-inconsistent law itself. The EC has not identified the GATT-consistent law or regulation for which the inspection structures are designed to ensure compliance, and has not described how they secure compliance with that law or regulation.

55. Further, the EC has not shown that the inspection structure requirements are "necessary" to ensure any such compliance. The Appellate Body in *Korea – Various Measures on Beef* considered that, in the context of Article XX(d), "necessary" is "located significantly closer to the pole of 'indispensable' than to the opposite pole of merely 'making a contribution to'."[26] In *EC – Asbestos*, citing *Korea – Various Measures on Beef*, the Appellate Body emphasized that the more vital the objective pursued, the easier it would be to accept a measure as "necessary", implying that, where the objective is not, for instance, the preservation of human life or health, a stricter standard for "necessary" may be appropriate.[27] Which is, of course, the case here. Finally, a measure is surely not "necessary" to ensure compliance if an alternative, WTO-consistent measure which the WTO Member could reasonably be expected to employ is available to it. And as noted earlier, the EC has not met its burden of demonstrating that there exists no such alternatives.

---

[24] EC Second Written Submission, para. 232.

[25] EC Second Written Submission, para. 233.

[26] Appellate Body Report, *Korea – Various Measures on Beef*, para. 161.

[27] Appellate Body Report, *EC – Asbestos*, para. 172, *citing Korea – Various Measures on Beef*, para. 162.

56. In fact, to the contrary, the EC itself offered the example of the US organics regulation, in which a non-US farmer hoping to use the "organic" label in the United States simply contacts a certifying agent approved, not by his home government, but by the US Department of Agriculture. The EC also provided the example in US – *Gasoline*, in which the Appellate Body suggested that the regulator—in that dispute the US EPA—conduct its own audit of the foreign firms. And, as the United States discussed in its second submission, the EC itself, in the context of collective marks, does not require the home government of the rightholder to establish specific inspection structures. As the Appellate Body has said, these other, less restrictive measures, are relevant as evidence that the WTO-inconsistent measures are not "necessary".[28]

57. It is not at all clear that having a WTO Member government approve and have responsibility for inspection bodies—as opposed to, for instance, the private rightholder, such as the certification mark holder—is even a preferable way of achieving the objective of the GI Regulation, let alone that it is "necessary" to do so. And, even so, what the EC should have shown is not that the WTO-inconsistent measure is "necessary" to the objective of the Regulation, but rather that it necessary to ensure compliance with a law or regulation that is not WTO-inconsistent.

58. Similarly, with respect to the requirement that the WTO Member assess and verify that the GI application of its nationals meets the EC GI Regulation's requirements and the requirement that the WTO Member advocate in favor of the registration on behalf of its nationals, the EC has not indicated how this requirement "secures compliance" with a WTO-consistent law or regulation. To the contrary, the EC has only argued that this requirement is "indispensable for the implementation" of the EC GI Regulation.[29] This is not the same as demonstrating that there is a WTO-consistent regulation, and that the otherwise WTO-inconsistent requirements imposed on Member are necessary to ensure compliance with that regulation, two demonstrations that are necessary to prove entitlement to the Article XX(d) exception. And indeed, far from being even "indispensable for the implementation" of the EC GI Regulation, at best, from the EC's perspective, this requirement shifts the burden of analyzing the application from the EC—where it belongs—to other WTO Members. Further, as discussed earlier, there is no reason that alternative measures—for instance, allowing the nationals to apply for GI registration directly to the EC—are not reasonably available to the EC.

59. The EC similarly fails to make any showing that the requirement that foreign GIs be identified with a country of origin is necessary to ensure compliance with a WTO-consistent law or regulation.

60. Finally, the EC simply asserts, with no information, no argument, that the chapeau to Article XX is also satisfied: that is, that these WTO-inconsistent requirements are not applied in a manner which would constitute a means of arbitrary or unjustifiable discrimination between countries where the same conditions prevail or a disguised restriction on trade. But, to the contrary, these measures mean that any country that protects GIs in the same manner as the EC—with EC-style inspection structures and with legal mechanisms for assessing whether the requirements of the GI Regulation are satisfied—may obtain registration and protection of its GIs. Those WTO Members that do not have such systems cannot obtain such protection. These are countries where the same conditions prevail, but, because the EC favors countries that protect GIs the way it does, the EC arbitrarily and unjustifiably discriminates between them.

61. In sum, the EC has not shown that the WTO-inconsistent measure at issue satisfies the requirements of the Article XX(d) exception.

MFN Treatment

62. I would like to shift over to the US arguments with respect to most favored nation treatment under the TRIPS Agreement and the Paris Convention. The EC GI Regulation grants advantages, favors, privileges and immunities to nationals from third countries that satisfy the EC's conditions of reciprocity and equivalence: *e.g.*,

[28] *See* Appellate Body Report, *Korea – Beef*, paras 168-170.

[29] EC Second Written Submission, para. 237.

they can have their GIs registered and protected in the EC. Even the EC concedes this, at least with respect to non-WTO third countries. In addition, the EC GI Regulation grants those advantages, favors, privileges and immunities to nationals of WTO Members that have established EC-style inspection systems and systems to assess and verify whether GI applications meet the EC GI Regulation's requirements, while denying those advantages, favors, privileges and immunities to nationals of WTO Members that have not. Consequently, the EC GI Regulation fails to accord those advantages, favors, privileges and immunities "immediately and unconditionally" to nationals of all other Members, as required by Article 4 of the TRIPS Agreement.

63. The EC's response is that the imposition of non-discriminatory conditions on nationals is not a violation of MFN treatment.[30] But it bears emphasizing that these are not conditions that the EC is placing on *nationals*, such that the nationals, without discrimination, are in a position to satisfy the conditions. Rather, these conditions are being placed on the government. The national is being denied his GI rights because of the system that his home government has in place—or does not have in place—with respect to GIs.

64. The EC also claims that it has not yet granted any benefit to any non-EC third country, so that there can be no MFN violation. Although the lack of any registration of a third country GI is certainly instructive with respect to whether national treatment is being provided, it is also apparent that whether to accept GI applications from third countries is made on a country-by-country basis: either a country has the appropriate EC-mandated mechanisms in place or it does not, and access to the EC GI regime is granted based on meeting this condition. This is thus a failure on the face of the Regulation to provide MFN treatment with respect to nationals from all WTO Members.

65. The United States has also noted that—as WTO Members in their own right—each member State of the EC also has an MFN obligation with respect to all other WTO Members, and that by according advantages, favors, privileges and immunities to nationals of other EC member States that are not immediately and unconditionally accorded to nationals of all other WTO Members through their implementation of the EC GI Regulation, the EC member States are acting inconsistently with those MFN obligations. The EC's sole response is that this is an EC measure, not a member State measure. But this response ignores two facts: first, the Panel's terms of reference include any implementation and enforcement measures, which include those taken at the member State level. Second, member States are not exempted from their MFN obligation simply because they are "required" to act inconsistently with those obligations by an EC regulation. France, for instance, is prohibited by WTO obligations from granting advantages to German nationals that are not granted to US nationals. That obligation does not disappear simply because the EC "requires" France to do that. The EC's argument at paragraphs 148-149 of its oral statement is extraordinary. The EC states that EC member States are WTO Members, yet claims that they have no MFN obligations. But either EC member States are WTO Members or they are not. Their MFN obligations do not disappear simply because the measure at issue includes an EC regulation. We suggest, therefore, that the Panel take a close look at the EC's argument on this issue.

GATT 1994 MFN obligations

66. With respect to the GI Regulation's violations of the GATT 1994 MFN obligations, I will simply refer back to our earlier submissions and comments, and note that this obvious discrimination against products of certain WTO Members cannot be justified as "necessary" to "secure compliance" with a WTO-consistent law or regulation under Article XX(d).

Enforcement

67. With respect to the fact that the EC GI Regulation denies enforcement procedures and remedies that are required under Part III of the TRIPS Agreement, the EC's response in its second submission is interesting. Most of the EC's discussion appears to be directed at the intellectual property regimes of the United States and

[30] EC Second Written Submission, paras. 249-250.

Australia, which are both irrelevant and outside this Panel's terms of reference. The United States can only conclude that the EC wants to divert attention from the measure that *is* before this Panel: the EC GI Regulation.

68. As to a substantive response, the EC's principle argument seems to be that the GI Regulation does not prevent the trademark owner from bringing an infringement action against a rightholder of a geographical indication.[31] But the point is that the trademark owner cannot prevent confusing uses of the GI, so he does not have the means to enforce his trademark or to obtain remedies against infringement.

Article 22.2 of the TRIPS Agreement

69. The United States argued in detail in its first submission how the GI Regulation failed to make the required legal means available to interested parties to prevent certain uses in respect of geographical indications. It does not provide the legal means for interested parties outside the EC to register and protect GIs, and, critically, it does not provide the legal means for interested persons—other than governments—to object to the registration of a GI, which is effectively the only way to prevent certain uses of terms that are proposed as registered GIs. The EC's sole response is that "registration" is not "use" and therefore it is not necessary to provide for the right of objection. But this does not address the failure to provide the legal means to register GIs at all. And, with respect to objections, it ignores the fact that, under the GI Regulation, once a GI is registered, the rightholder has an affirmative right to use that GI. For the interested party who does not have the legal means to object, the game is lost when the GI he would have objected to is registered. The United States submits, therefore, that the EC GI Regulation is inconsistent with the obligations of Article 22.2 of the TRIPS Agreement.

Trademark Rights

General comment

70. I turn now to our claim under TRIPS Article 16.1. Article 16.1 obligates the EC to give owners of registered trademarks the exclusive right to prevent all confusing uses of similar or identical signs, including GIs. In direct contrast to this obligation, the EC acknowledges that, under its GI Regulation, *even if* the owner of a prior valid registered trademark can prove use of an identical or similar registered GI results in a likelihood of confusion, it cannot prevent continued use of that GI.[32] Not only is this contrary to the obligation in Article 16.1 of the TRIPS Agreement, it also undermines what Appellate Body findings and US and EC jurisprudence all agree is the core of a trademark owner's right under Article 16.1.[33]

71. The United States believes that each provision of the TRIPS Agreement must be given its full scope, and our arguments have reflected this. Both trademarks and GIs are granted a sphere of exclusivity. The EC is correct that a "conflict" may occur between an individual trademark and an individual GI.[34] But this is not a "conflict" between trademark and GI *obligations* placed on the EC; it is merely a "conflict" between rightholders. The rights of those rightholders, and the ways in which to resolve any "conflicts" between those rights, are set out in the TRIPS Agreement. Specifically, where the owner of a prior valid registered trademark is confronted with use of a similar or identical GI, Article 16.1 empowers the owner of the trademark to prevent any use of the GI that is likely to confuse consumers within a given territory. And where a GI owner is confronted with a similar or identical trademark, that trademark is subject to invalidation under Article 22.3 if it misleads the public in a given territory about the origin of the goods.

---

[31] EC Second Written Submission, para. 360.

[32] EC First Written Submission, paras. 302-307; EC Responses to Questions, para. 141.

[33] *See* US First Written Submission, paras. 145-149, citing Appellate Body Report, *United States – Section 211*, para. 186; US Supreme Court, *College Savings Bank v. Florida Prepaid Postsecondary Education Expense Board*, 527 US 666. 667 (1999) (Exhibit US-14); Advocate General Jacobs' Opinion in Case C-10/89, *SA CNL-Sucal NV v. HAG GFAG*, delivered 13 March 1990, [1990] ECR I-3711, para. 19 (Exhibit US-8).

[34] EC Second Written Submission, para. 309.

72. In other words, there is no "conflict" between the obligations placed upon *the EC*, as a signatory to the WTO Agreement, by TRIPS Articles 16.1 and 22.[35] It is not "impossible" in any sense for the EC to "simultaneous[ly] compl[y]" with those provisions by providing both trademark and GI owners with the means to enforce the sphere of exclusivity granted them by Articles 16.1 and 22.[36]

73. The EC has five responses to the US arguments in its second submission: first, that there are no (or few) valid registered trademarks that could be similar or identical to registered GIs; second, that Article 14(3) of the GI Regulation prevents the registration of GIs that can give rise to confusing uses *vis-a-vis* trademarks (so there is no need for Article 16.1 rights); third, that Article 24.5 *permits* the EC to eliminate Article 16.1 trademark rights; fourth, that Article 24.3 *requires* the EC to eliminate Article 16.1 trademark rights; and, finally, that the GI Regulation's broad grant of immunity to all who qualify to use a GI is a "limited exception" permitted by Article 17 of the TRIPS Agreement.

Article 14(3) of the GI Regulation

Trademarks Containing or Consisting of Geographical Elements

74. The EC's first defense is to claim that, *vis-a-vis* GIs registered in the EC, trademark owners do not need their Article 16.1 rights in the EC, since, in the EC's view, few trademarks that contain or consist of a GI will be registrable. Therefore, the EC sees little risk that a registered GI will raise a likelihood of confusion with respect to a prior valid registered trademark. There are two responses to this argument. First, although the EC has not presented any evidence that the number of vulnerable trademarks is small, the number of marks is irrelevant. The owner of every valid registered trademark is entitled to its Article 16.1 rights. Further, however, it is a fact that valid registered trademarks can indeed consist of or incorporate "geographical" elements. In our first submission, we offered the hypothetical example of a trademark for LUNA, in connection with cheese, and the potential registration of a GI for cheese produced in Luna, Spain.[37] We had not submitted the example of a cheese produced on the moon, but we accept that the EC altered the hypothetical this morning. The EC's somewhat irrelevant, yet revealing, response is that the town of Luna does not exist "in Spain, or in any other Spanish speaking country, whether large or small."[38] The EC concludes that EC trademark officials would likely register "Luna" as a fanciful name. In fact, Luna is a town in Spain, and even has a website.[39] But the EC's glib response indicates, in fact, how easy it is for a geographical term to be registered as part of a trademark, even for EC officials trying to avoid such registrations. We found after midnight last night as we were preparing this oral statement, that there are quite a few LUNA trademarks registered in Europe. We did not have time to create an exhibit, but we suggest that you search "Luna" on the OHIM database and see for yourself. Since the EC is uncomfortable with hypotheticals, other potential examples include: CALABRIA, a registered Community Trademark for pasta,[40] and a region in Italy; DERBY, a registered Community Trademark for milk products,[41] and a city in the UK; and WIENERWALD, a registered Community Trademark for meat, vegetables and milk products,[42] and a region in Austria.

75. One of the EC's arguments this morning was that trademarks incorporating geographical elements can only be registered if they have acquired secondary meaning. Contrary to this argument, *none* of the three registrations discussed above was based on acquired distinctiveness. And we saw no evidence of acquired

---

[35] EC Second Written Submission, para. 309.

[36] *See* Panel Report, *Turkey – Textiles*, para. 9.92. *See also* Panel Report, *Indonesia – Autos*, para. 14.28.

[37] US First Oral Statement, para. 50; US Second Written Submission, para. 169.

[38] EC Second Written Submission, para. 290 (note 179).

[39] www.lunavirtual.net.

[40] EC OHIM Trademark No. 001575240. Exhibit US-74.

[41] EC OHIM Trademark No. 001305929. Exhibit US-75.

[42] EC OHIM Trademark No. 000229534. Exhibit US-76.

distinctiveness in connection with any of the "Luna" trademarks. Therefore, we suggest that the Panel take the EC's assertions this morning with more than a grain of salt.

76. In sum, validly registered trademarks that consist of or incorporate geographical elements exist, whether or not the origin of the trademark was geographical. In any event, the EC's argument ignores the potential for further conflict between prior registered trademarks and the registration as GIs of non-geographic names, under Article 2(3) of the Regulation.

Article 14(3) of the GI Regulation cannot substitute for TRIPS Article 16.1 rights

77. Second, the EC states that "Article 14(3) of Regulation 2081/92 provides the necessary means to trademark owners ... to prevent or invalidate the registration of *any* confusing geographical indications."[43] Even if the EC is offering an accurate reading of Article 14(3)—a point I will come back to later—this provision is not a substitute for Article 16.1. Article 16.1 requires WTO Members to grant rights to *trademark owners* to prevent particular *uses* of identical or similar GIs. Article 14(3), in contrast, merely permits the *EC authorities* to deny *registration* of GIs in some circumstances.

78. These are two critical distinctions and two critical ways in which Article 14(3) falls short of what is required by Article 16.1. It is not necessarily possible for a trademark owner—or, for that matter, the EC authorities—to know, on the face of an application for GI *registration*, if a GI will be *used* in a way that raises a likelihood of confusion with respect to a trademark.[44] The EC asserts that the product specifications submitted with a GI application will include "specific labeling details" that definitively limit the way in which the GI will be used.[45] Let me first note that 80 percent of GIs were registered upon accession of new EC member States, or upon adoption of the GI Regulation, and for many of those, product specifications are not even published in the EC's Official Journal. Even when product specifications are published, however, the Panel will note from Exhibit US-77 that the "specific labeling details"are not that specific at all. The "labeling" requirement for the registered GI "Lausitzer Leinöl," for example, reads, plain and simply, "Lausitzer Leinöl". The same goes for the registered GI "Kanterkass, Kanternagelkaas, Kanterkomijnekaas". The "labeling" requirements for the registered GIs "Timoleague brown pudding" and "Newcastle Brown Ale" read simply "PGI". These demonstrate that a trademark owner will not necessarily know at the time of registration how the GI will be used or if that use will be confusing.

79. This morning, in paragraphs 181-184 of its oral statement, we heard a bit of a shift in the EC's position. The EC now admits that GIs in the EC are used in much the same way as trademarks, that is, in a promotional way, to distinguish goods. And since the EC expects GIs to be used just like trademarks, the EC appears to be asking what is wrong with this trademark-like use of GIs, and why should the EC be concerned that the trademark owner may not be able to stop the use of such GIs if they are confusing. After, all, the EC argues, this trademark-like use is "legitimate." The problem, of course, is that under TRIPS Article 16.1, trademark owners have a right to prevent confusing uses of their signs, including GIs. "Legitimacy" is irrelevant. Under the EC system, trademark owners are powerless to prevent such confusing uses. We submit to the Panel that this is contrary to TRIPS Article 16.1.

80. Another particular issue regarding use of a registered GI that could arise frequently within the EC—a union with 20 official languages—is use of the GI in translation. Use in translation—which would not be apparent from the GI application itself—could cause confusion with a prior valid registered trademark. The EC appears to suggest, but avoids stating definitively, that the scope of protected use of a registered GI excludes the right to use the registered name as translated into other EC languages.[46] The question that has not been

---

[43] EC Second Written Submission, para. 270.

[44] US First Oral Statement, para. 54; US Responses to Questions, para. 87; US Second Written Submission, paras. 131-135.

[45] EC Second Written Submission, para. 300.

[46] EC Second Written Submission, paras. 288, 293, 301.

answered is: "Does the registration of a term under the EC GI Regulation give the rightholder a positive right to use that term as translated into other EC languages?"

81. Nor, as the EC asserts,[47] do labeling, advertising and unfair competition laws offer trademark owners the standard of protection required by TRIPS Article 16.1 to prevent certain uses. Under these laws, the trademark owner (along with the general population) is granted other rights, but not the specific rights guaranteed by Article 16.1. For instance, and using one of the EC's own examples,[48] the fact that a trademark owner might be able to stop *injurious*, *deceptive* advertising is no substitute for being able to prevent confusing uses of identical or similar signs.

82. It is also critical that even under the EC view, Article 14(3) enables or requires the *EC authorities* to deny GI registrations in some circumstances. By its express terms, however, TRIPS Article 16.1 grants rights to *trademark owners*. This is important because as noted in the TRIPS preamble, "intellectual property rights are private rights ..." And trademark owners, whose direct interests are at stake—and not government officials—are in the best position to identify confusing uses. While the United States welcomes efforts by the EC *authorities* to prevent registration of GIs that conflict with prior registered trademarks, even to the limited extent this is permitted by the GI Regulation, Article 14(3) cannot be sufficient, on its face, to satisfy the requirements of TRIPS Article 16.1, which are directed to *trademark owners*.

83. The EC now suggests that any trademark owner can challenge the validity of the GI registration before the EU Court of First Instance or, potentially, in infringement proceedings in EC member State courts, based on the EC's erroneous application of Article 14(3).[49] The implication is that this ability to challenge the registration on the basis of Article 14(3) permits the trademark owner to prevent confusing uses of his signs, as required by Article 16.1. But this is not accurate, first, because any such challenge must be brought *within two months of publication of the registration*.[50] This deadline has been very strictly enforced.[51] After two months, even if a trademark owner can prove that a use of a similar or identical registered GI results in a likelihood of confusion, it will not be able to challenge the registration. So, any confusing uses that arise after this deadline—and the savvy GI holder would be well advised to be cautious in the use of his GI during that time—cannot give rise to any challenge to the registration. In addition, it does not appear that GI registrations adopted via accession protocols are challengeable, for instance, even within the two-month time period.[52] Further, challenges to a GI registration by trademark owners in the EC member State courts will similarly be barred for those trademark owners who could have challenged the validity of the registration within the two-month deadline under Article 230 of the EC Treaty.[53] We find it fascinating that in its oral statement the EC referred to challenging the validity of registrations without mentioning these deadlines at all. Further, the EC appears to suggest that there are no deadlines for "referrals" to the ECJ under Article 234, yet neglects to note that even in the case of referrals, the registration may not be cancelled after the two-month deadline if the trademark owner could have challenged the registration under Article 230.

84. In any event, objections and challenges to GI registrations would be evaluated based on the substantive standard of Article 14(3), which is more restrictive than the standard required by TRIPS Article 16.1. The EC completely rewrites Article 14(3) when it claims that Article 14(3) "says that the registration of a geographical indication shall be refused if it is likely to lead to confusion with a trademark."[54] On its face, Article 14(3) limits the circumstances in which a GI will be denied registration to those instances in which a trademark's "reputation

[47] EC Second Written Submission, para. 303.

[48] EC Second Written Submission, para. 303.

[49] EC Responses to Questions, paras. 153, 181; EC Second Written Submission, para. 296.

[50] US Second Written Submission, para. 138.

[51] *See* citations included at US Second Written Submission, para. 138 (note 120).

[52] European Court of Justice Cases 31/86 and 35/86, *LAISA v Council*, [1988] ECR 2285.

[53] Case C-239/99, *Nachi Europe v. Hauptzollamt Krefeld*, [2001] ECR I-1197; Case C-188/92, *TWD Textilwerke Deggendorf v. Germany*, [1994] ECR I-833. Exhibit US-78.

[54] EC Responses to Questions, para. 155.

and renown and the length of time it has been used" make the GI "liable to mislead the consumer as to the true identity of the product." The EC has said that "the content of Regulation 2081/92 must be evaluated on the face of the measure."[55] We agree. And that is why the EC's reinvention of that provision should be rejected.

85. There was a discussion this morning about the role that reputation may play in the confusion analysis. The EC implies that reputation is always a factor in the confusion analysis, but, if you look even at the sources cited by the EC, it is plain that reputation is a factor in some instances—in the case of dissimilar goods, for instance—but not all. For instance, in the case of identical signs for identical goods, "reputation" would not enter into the analysis at all. Further, we encourage the Panel to consider the case of the owner of a registered trademark, perhaps with rights in only one EC member State, whose trademark is registered, but has no reputation, renown or length of time of use. Article 14(3) would not prevent the EC-wide registration of a GI that is confusing vis-a-vis that trademark. And would the trademark owner realistically be able to challenge in court a Commission decision to register that GI, in light of Article 14(3)'s requirement that the Commission consider the GI registration in light of the trademark's reputation, renown and length of time of use? Yet, that trademark owner is entitled to his Article 16.1 rights, despite the lack of reputation, renown, or use. In sum, Article 14(3) simply does not provide those rights required by TRIPS Article 16.1.

86. The EC predictably relies on the supposed "substantial deference" it is due in interpreting the Regulation, but any deference simply cannot ignore the plain meaning of the Regulation. The EC cannot simply substitute TRIPS-consistent language that it wishes were there. Equally predictable, since the EC is stretching the meaning of Article 14(3) beyond the breaking point, is the EC's assertion that the United States must prove that the actual language of Article 14(3) is "the only reasonable interpretation" of that provision and that any interpretation contrary to the TRIPS Agreement is "impossible."[56] To the contrary, this Panel's job is to make an objective assessment of the facts, including with respect to the meaning of Article 14(3). The United States has presented compelling evidence of what Article 14(3) means. The EC has failed to rebut this evidence. Indeed, the reading of Article 14(3) offered by the EC ignores the text of the provision. And, in what has become somewhat of a recurring theme in this dispute, the EC's interpretation is a complete departure from the definitive guidance offered by the Commission on the meaning of Article 14(3) outside of this dispute, as recently as March 2004.[57] (We note parenthetically that we were at first embarrassed to learn from the EC's oral statement this morning that we have been citing out-dated guidelines, from four months ago. Then we looked at the exhibit, and realized that the new guidelines had only been issued last week. But in any case the relevant language on Article 14(3) is unchanged in the revised guidelines.). The EC's interpretation is irreconcilable with the way in which the terms included in Article 14(3)—reputation, renown and length of use—have been interpreted by WIPO and the Paris Union,[58] as well as by the ECJ and OHIM.[59] It is contrary to the understanding of Article 14(3) expressed by EC member States.[60] And even if the EC is offering a new view of what Article 14(3) means, we note that the Commission admits that it cannot here commit the EC to "new legal obligations."[61] We have no assurances that at some later date, if the Commission's reading comes back to haunt it before the ECJ, it will feel free to disown that reading.[62] For these reasons, the Panel should reject the EC's novel reading of Article 14(3), and further find that even if that reading were correct, the provision would not be an adequate substitute for Article 16.1 rights.

---

[55] EC Second Written Submission, para. 79.

[56] EC Second Written Submission, para. 274-275.

[57] Guide to Community Regulations, "Protection of Geographical Indications, Designations of Origin and Certificates of Specific Character for Agricultural Products and Foodstuffs" (Working Document of the Commission Services issued by the European Commission Directorate-General for Agriculture, March 2004), p. 23. Exhibit US-24.

[58] US Second Written Submission, paras. 146-147.

[59] US Second Written Submission, paras. 150-152.

[60] US Second Written Submission, para. 148-149.

[61] EC Responses to Questions, para. 30.

[62] US Second Written Submission, paras. 158-159, addressing the ECJ's judgment in *Petrotub*.

87. It is worth noting before I move on to Article 24.5 that the EC's first response to the trademark owner's lack of ability to prevent confusing uses is that "[t]hese concerns are largely theoretical". This repeated refrain of the EC ignores the fact that there is no requirement to challenge a specific application of a measure. That a measure denies TRIPS Agreement rights to trademark owners is enough.

Article 24.5 of the TRIPS Agreement

88. I would like now to turn to the EC's argument that Article 24.5 of the TRIPS Agreement permits diminished protection of registered trademarks. I just want to underscore initially that Article 24.5 says only what measures adopted to implement the GI Section of TRIPS may *not* do *vis-a-vis* certain trademarks; it does not say what they *can* do. By its own terms, it does not *permit* the elimination of any trademark rights. Further, its context is as an "exception" to GI obligations, not as an exception to Article 16.1 obligations. It is curious, therefore, that this provision would be used to justify the non-fulfillment of *Article 16.1* obligations.

89. And, indeed, the EC concludes its Article 24.5 argument at paragraph 199 of its oral statement by stating that, "If the drafters deemed necessary to specify in Article 24.5 that the implementation of protection for geographical indications shall not prejudice the most basic right of the owner of a registered trademark ('the right to use it'), but not the right to exclude others from using it, the *clear implication* is that they did not intend to prevent Members from limiting the exercise of the latter right in order to allow the use of a geographical indication in co-existence with a grandfathered trademark."[63] In other words, the strongest support that the EC can muster for its interpretation of Article 24.5—an interpretation that creates an enormous exception to Article 16.1 obligations—is a negative implication. This is a slim reed indeed on which to base an exception to such a fundamental obligation.

90. Our position has been set out in our various written submissions. Briefly, the prohibition against "prejudice ... [of] the validity of the registration of a trademark" preserves the trademark owner's Article 16.1 rights.[64] This interpretation is supported by the fact that a trademark registration will be "prejudiced" or damaged if a Member fails to allow the trademark owner to prevent all others from confusing uses, given that the ordinary meaning of "validity of the registration of a trademark" refers to the possession of legal authority accorded by virtue of the entrance of a trademark in a register. This legal authority is defined in Article 16.1. Moreover, because the denial of the right to prevent confusing uses also prejudices the establishment and maintenance of the trademark's ability to distinguish goods of one enterprise from those of another, this prejudices its capability of "constituting a trademark" within the meaning of TRIPS Article 15.1, and thereby further prejudices the trademark's validity.

91. Further, the additional prohibition in Article 24.5 against "prejudice ... [of] the right to use a trademark", also encompasses the Article 16.1 right to prevent all confusing uses of similar or identical signs.[65] The interpretation of Article 24.5 presented by the United States, based on the ordinary meaning of the terms, in context, and in light of the object and purpose of the TRIPS Agreement, is confirmed by the negotiating history of Article 24.5, which reveals a progressive evolution in favor of protecting grandfathered trademarks, including through introduction of a reference to common law trademarks at the same time that the phrase "right to use" was added.[66] By contrast, as we have stated in our submissions, the EC misreads the text and disregards its context by interpreting the prohibition on a GI's prejudicing "the right to use a trademark" (on the basis that is it similar to a geographical indication) as an *affirmative right, again by implication, to prejudice the specific right accorded trademark owners under Article 16.1 to exclude all others from confusing uses of identical or similar signs.* In support, the EC also proposes a far-fetched reading of the negotiating history for an entirely different provision (Article 24.4).[67] Even if the EC's interpretation of "right to use" were correct—that is, that it

[63] Emphasis added.

[64] US Second Written Submission, paras. 173-175.

[65] US Second Written Submission, para. 176.

[66] US Responses to Panel Question 76, paras. 102-105.

[67] US Second Written Submission, paras. 177-187.

refers only to affixing certain signs to goods—the fact that the right to use those signs should not be prejudiced on the basis of their similarity with GIs has no bearing on the other obligation in Article 24.5: the obligation not to prejudice the validity of trademark registrations.

92. I want to emphasize that in its oral statement the EC refers once again to a trademark owner's right to affix a sign. Article 24.5 does not, however, talk about not prejudicing the right to *affix signs* to goods; it talks about not prejudicing the right to *use a trademark* on certain grounds. Trademarks have certain legal rights associated with them, as reflected in both Articles 16.1 and 15.1. The purpose of a trademark is to distinguish the goods of one manufacturer from the goods of another. Signs are just signs. The EC's interpretation ignores this plain text of Article 24.5 and its context.

93. The EC asserts that Article 24.5 is a provision that defines "the boundary between the protection of trademarks and the protection of geographical indications."[68] This is only partially correct. As an exception to the GI section, it defines only *one of several* boundaries—*i.e.*, it limits the scope of GI protection *vis-à-vis* certain grandfathered trademarks. Article 17, the exception to the trademark section, defines another boundary, by limiting the scope of trademark protection. The EC's understanding of the role of Article 24.5 is inconsistent with the context of an Agreement that includes separate exceptions for trademark protection and for GI protection.

94. With respect to the fact that Article 24 is entitled "international negotiations; exceptions", the EC now seems to argue that the context of Article 24.5—specifically, its placement among "exception" provisions under a heading entitled "exceptions"—is irrelevant with respect to Article 24.5, although the EC acknowledges that it is meaningful for Articles 24.6, 24.7, 24.8, and 24.9, and presumably would not deny that Articles 24.1 and 24.2 relate to international negotiations.[69] The EC implies that the placement of Article 24.5 as part of Article 24 was a drafting error despite the fact that the drafters correctly positioned other provisions. There is simply no evidence to support this contention.

95. Finally, the EC apparently contends that Article 24.5 accords additional rights to trademarks that are not provided by Article 16.1, and that it therefore cannot be regarded as an exception to GI protection.[70] Now, it is not at all clear how Article 24.5 accords additional rights to trademarks, since it simply limits the ability of GIs to prejudice trademarks. But even if it did, this does not take away from the fact that Article 24.5, by its own terms, acts as a shield for certain trademarks against GIs, and contains no provisions for limiting trademark rights. There is no rule that a provision that recognizes one right, such as with respect to trademarks, cannot be an exception to a separate obligation, such as with respect to GIs. To the contrary. Article 24.8, for example, limits GI protection in light of a person's right to use their own name, even though use of a person's name is not a form of intellectual property protected elsewhere in the TRIPS Agreement.

Article 24.3 of the TRIPS Agreement

96. With respect to the EC's claim that Article 24.3 requires the EC to maintain in place any violation of Article 16.1 that existed as of the entry into force of the TRIPS Agreement, the EC declines to provide any further arguments in its second written submission. We have already responded to the EC's argument that Article 24.3 mandates the maintenance of any system of GI protection, regardless of how contrary it is to other WTO obligations. In particular, the United States has explained that Article 24.3, like Article 24.5, is an exception to the protection of geographical indications (not trademarks) and that, by its introductory clause (*i.e.*, "In implementing *this Section")*, it limits only actions taken to implement the GI section of the TRIPS Agreement, and has no effect on other sections.[71] The EC, by contrast, implies that the "exception" heading for

[68] EC Second Written Submission, para. 314.

[69] EC Second Written Submission, paras. 313-314.

[70] EC Second Written Submission, para. 315.

[71] US Second Written Submission, paras. 188-190.

Article 24 is apparently the result of a drafting mistake[72]—and not part of the context of the provision— and inexplicably reads "in implementing *this Section*" to mean "in implementing *this Agreement*".

97. Moreover, given that the TRIPS Agreement was essentially unchanged between December 1991 and the time it entered into force three years later, the EC's interpretation of Article 24.3 would lead to the absurd result that a Member could have put in place a measure protecting GIs but containing blatant violations of numerous WTO obligations in the TRIPS Agreement and elsewhere, and then simply claim that Article 24.3 prevents the WTO-inconsistent measure from being modified. This is not what the provision says, is not consistent with its context, and could not have been what the Members intended. Indeed, a more logical reading of the text is that the reference to "diminish the protection of geographical indications that existed" in Article 24.3 is a reference to protection that existed with respect to individual GIs, rather than to entire systems of GI protection.[73] This interpretation is confirmed not just by the ordinary meaning, but also by the absurd ramifications that would result if the phrase were interpreted to apply to systems of protection.

98. Contrary to the EC's arguments, any measures taken to protect GIs at the expense of other WTO rights before the effective date of the TRIPS Agreement would not reflect bad faith, since Article 24.3, at least under the EC's reading, would specifically anticipate such measures.

Article 17 of the TRIPS Agreement

99. The EC maintains that the failure of the GI Regulation to accord owners of prior valid registered trademarks their "exclusive right to prevent all third parties" from confusing uses of identical or similar GIs, is a "limited exception" justified by TRIPS Article 17.[74] Indeed, the EC asserts that a system that allows Members "to define in advance ... the conditions for the application of an exception" has the "advantage of providing greater legal certainty to all parties involved, including the trademark owners."[75] The United States does not dispute that Article 14(2) of the GI Regulation provides a great degree of legal certainty—as the trademark owner will *always certainly* be unable to exercise its Article 16.1 rights *vis-à-vis* registered GIs.

100. If a blanket exception, requiring trademark owners to sell their products alongside the products of an *unlimited* number of producers using identical or similar signs in a confusing manner, is considered "limited", then the United States fails to understand how the EC accords "limited" a meaning providing any protection at all to a trademark. The phrase "limited exceptions", used in the context of TRIPS Article 30, was interpreted by the *Canada – Patent Protection* panel to "connote a narrow exception—one which makes only a small diminution of the rights", where "limited" was "measured by the extent to which the exclusive rights of the patent owner have been curtailed."[76] In this dispute, the EC has pointed to no true limits on the exception to the exclusive rights that trademark owners must tolerate under the GI Regulation. In fact, under the GI Regulation, the trademark owner is unable to assert its Article 16.1 rights during an *unlimited* period of time, and against an *unlimited* number of producers and products.

101. The EC's response that the trademark owner retains the right to prevent non-GI holders from confusing uses of similar or identical signs[77] is not relevant to the fact that they have already been subject to an unlimited exception. After all, diminution of the trademark owner's right to exclude can result in the loss of trademark

[72] EC Second Written Submission, para. 313 ("Article 24.3 is clearly not an exception"); EC Responses to Panel Question 74, para. 191.

[73] US Second Written Submission, para. 196-197.

[74] EC Second Written Submission, paras. 336-338.

[75] EC Second Written Submission, para. 346.

[76] Panel Report, *Canada-Patent Protection*, paras. 7.30-7.31. *See* US SWS, para. 201 and note 197.

[77] EC Second Written Submission, para. 336.

rights.[78] Nothing in the GI Regulation prevents the possibility of a total loss of trademark rights—a result that obviously cannot be considered "a small diminution of the rights in question."[79]

102. While TRIPS Article 17 contemplates some curtailment of the rights granted in Part II, Section 2 of the TRIPS Agreement, the language of Article 17 emphasizes that this curtailment for any particular trademark should be limited. Article 17 permits "limited exceptions to the rights conferred by *a* trademark"; it does not permit virtually unlimited exceptions to the rights of a limited *number* of trademarks. Thus, Article 17 permits limited exceptions to the rights conferred by a trademark, such that, as explained by the *Canada – Patent Protection* panel in the patent context, "the extent of the acts unauthorized by the right holder that are permitted by [the exception] will be small and narrowly bounded."[80] This is precisely the type of limited exception that would now be in place had the EC accepted a proposed amendment by a committee of Parliament that would have incorporated the substantive disciplines of trademark law, including the fair use exception thereof, into the GI Regulation.[81] But this amendment was rejected.

103. The EC also points to the specific reference in Article 17 to "fair use of descriptive terms" as a specified type of "limited exception", and argues that "[i]f 'fair use' of an indication of source qualifies as a 'limited exception' ... so must be, *a fortiori*, the fair use of a geographical indication registered under Regulation 2081/92."[82] As an initial matter, we note that a "descriptive" term is one that is "characterized by description", where description refers to "[a] detailed account of a ... thing."[83] Registered GIs, by contrast, are a form of intellectual property, with associated rights, that are not merely "descriptive." They are source indicators that represent "a quality, reputation or other characteristic of the good [that] is essentially attributable to its geographical origin." The EC cannot fairly assert, therefore, that all registered GIs can, without exception, be considered merely "descriptive".

104. Further, the EC's argument highlights its erroneous understanding that every use of a registered GI, regardless of the extent to which it affects the rights of a trademark, must be considered "fair" simply because the GI is registered. Indeed, the EC did not provide an interpretation of the phrase "fair use". This is probably because "fair" refers to use that is "just", "equitable, impartial."[84] In the copyright context, for example, "[f]air use involves a balancing process by which a complex of variables determine whether other interests should override the rights of the creators."[85] The EC fails to explain how a blanket and *unlimited* exception to Article 16.1 rights for owners of all trademarks that are similar or identical to registered GIs can, in every situation, be considered "just" or "equitable", or how trademark owners are accorded the benefit of a "balancing process". After all, the "fair use" must be a "limited exception".

105. Finally, the EC has not demonstrated that the GI Regulation takes into account the "legitimate interests" of third parties or of the trademark owner. For example, by diminishing the trademark owner's Article 16.1 rights, the GI Regulation results in consumer confusion, which is certainly not in their "legitimate interests". Nor are the legitimate interests of a trademark owner respected through a blanket exception that benefits GI right holders without any regard for the trademark owner.

---

[78] *See* US Second Written Submission, para. 167 and note 167, citing German Federal Supreme Court, Decision 06.12.1990—Case No. 1 ZR 297/88 ("SL"). (Exhibit US-67).

[79] Panel Report, *Canada-Patent Protection*, para. 7.30.

[80] Panel Report, *Canada-Patent Protection*, para. 7.45.

[81] *See* US First Oral Statement, at para. 75, citing Opinion of the Committee on Legal Affairs and the Internal Market for the Committee on Agriculture and Rural Development on the proposal for a Council regulation amending Regulation (EEC) No 2081/92 on the protection of geographical indications and designations of origin for agricultural products and foodstuffs, European Parliament, 2002/0066(CNS) (10 September 2002), pp. 13-14. Exhibit US-21.

[82] EC Second Written Submission, para. 338.

[83] The New Shorter Oxford English Dictionary, p. 644. Exhibit US-79.

[84] The New Shorter Oxford English Dictionary, p. 907. Exhibit US-79.

[85] Black's Law Dictionary (Abridged Sixth Edition 1991), p. 415. Exhibit US-80.

Conclusion

106. Before I conclude, I want to note that, as we listened to the oral statement of the EC this morning, we found that in most paragraphs in which the EC discusses a US argument or an exhibit, the EC's characterizations were inaccurate or misleading. For example, the EC implies that Hungary's ministerial reasoning with respect to its GI law has no relation to the EC GI Regulation, because that law applies only to products not covered by the EC GI Regulation. But the fact is that Hungary had to change its law upon accession to render it consistent with the EC GI Regulation and, in doing so, made clear that Article 14(3) provides protection to well-known marks. That reasoning, therefore, is directly pertinent to the EC GI Regulation and not in the least irrelevant. Similarly, the EC claims that its GI Regulation guidelines merely "repeat[] verbatim the wording of Article 14(3)" and therefore does not support the U.S.'s reading of that article. But this is untrue. In fact, the guidelines emphasize that conflicting trademarks do not prevent the registration of GIs "as a general rule"; that Article 14(3) represents the "only" circumstance in which this is not true; and that "in all other cases, the name can be registered notwithstanding the existence of the registered trademark." While this explanation is entirely consistent with any good-faith reading of Article 14(3), it is not in any sense a verbatim repetition.

107. You will be happy to hear, in light of the hour, that we considered, but rejected, the idea of rebutting each of the EC's misrepresentations paragraph by paragraph. Instead, we simply want to point out this aspect of the EC statement to the Panel, note several examples, both here and earlier in our statement, and strongly suggest that the Panel examine the source material—and not just the representations in the oral statements of the parties—as they consider the parties' arguments.

108. To conclude, as I said at the outset, we brought this dispute—after five years of fruitless consultations—because the EC GI Regulation provides significant commercial benefits to products and persons receiving GI status under the Regulation, but imposes prohibitive barriers to access to these benefits on non-EC products and persons. It also provides those significant benefits to EC persons and products at the expense of owners of prior registered trademarks, who are supposed to have certain rights associated with their trademarks under the TRIPS Agreement. We therefore ask that the Panel find that the EC GI Regulation is inconsistent with the EC's obligations under the TRIPS Agreement, the Paris Convention, and the GATT 1994, as set out in our written submissions and oral statements in this proceeding.

109. Thank you very much for your attention and for your hard work in analyzing the claims and arguments of the Parties in this dispute. We would be happy to answer any questions the Panel may have.

ANNEX A-7

CLOSING STATEMENT OF THE UNITED STATES SECOND SUBSTANTIVE MEETING

(12 August 2004)

1. Thank you, Mr. Chairman and members of the Panel. We appreciate your hard work over the past two days.

2. As the EC suggested in its closing statement, it is true that this case has become fairly complicated, although it started off fairly simple and straightforward. Our legal claims were based on a simple problem: An EC GI Regulation that benefits EC persons and products to the detriment of non-EC persons and products and to the detriment of trademark rights. The EC GI Regulation purports to provide significant economic and competitive benefits for persons and products receiving GI status, but then effectively reserves those benefits to EC persons and products, erecting prohibitive barriers to access to those benefits for non-EC persons and products, and protecting EC persons and products from competition from non-EC persons and products.

3. This relatively simple case became complicated because the EC, in order to defend itself against rather straight-forward WTO inconsistencies, threw one complicating factor after another into the mix. It is difficult to try to explain that the Regulation does not mean what it says, and that is where the complications come in. For instance, for the EC to defend against our claims, the meaning of the Regulation had to be seriously contorted so that, for instance, a relatively straightforward and WTO-inconsistent requirements of equivalence and reciprocity has to, somehow, be read out of the Regulation. Where it is clear that the EC GI Regulation prevents trademark owners from exercising rights guaranteed by Article 16.1 of the TRIPS Agreement, the EC has to explain somehow why trademark owners have no need of those rights—when, of course, they do—and has to devote long, complicated arguments to explaining how the Regulation blocks the registration of any and all confusing GIs, when in fact, by its own terms, it does not and cannot. The EC also has to try to explain how numerous and vague unfair trade statutes, labeling requirements, deceptive advertising rules and the like somehow make up for the lack of Article 16.1 rights. They, of course, do not, but attempting to explain that they do is complicated. That is why this relatively straightforward case has become complicated.

4. I will divide my closing remarks into two general categories—national treatment/MFN, and trademark rights.

National Treatment/MFN

5. On the issue of reciprocity and equivalence in Article 12(1) of the GI Regulation, there is obviously a disagreement between the complainants and the respondent on the facts, that is, on the meaning of the GI Regulation. The EC claims that it is entitled to "considerable deference", a standard that is not in any WTO agreement or any dispute settlement report. The EC's apparent hope is that the Panel will not make factual findings based on the evidence, but will simply adopt wholesale the EC's interpretation of the Regulation. But it is the task of this Panel to make an objective assessment of the facts concerning this measure and what it means. The Panel must determine if there is a solid evidentiary basis for a factual finding that reciprocity and equivalence conditions do not apply to non-EC WTO Members, and that, in fact, there is a mechanism in the GI Regulation for registering and protecting GIs of other WTO Members without those conditions. As the United States has said before, and I will repeat again today, the United States would welcome a finding based on authoritative domestic legal instruments that the GIs of other WTO Members can be registered without the WTO Members satisfying those conditions. But, on the basis of the evidence that we have seen, we have no confidence that this is the case, or that the European Court of Justice would agree with the EC's interpretation in this dispute.

6. With respect to whether the GI Regulation discriminates against nationals, the EC has effectively argued that, somehow—because of the special nature of the TRIPS national treatment requirement, and because there is also a GATT Article III national treatment requirement with respect to goods—unless a measure literally and specifically states the word "national" in connection with less favorable treatment, there can be no TRIPS national treatment violation. Although the Regulation itself does not use the word "national", it does everything but. And, indeed, the preamble to last year's amendments *does* use that word in admitting that the distinctions made in the Regulation are based on nationality. Without repeating all of the details we have argued elsewhere, the distinctions made in the Regulation between the EC track and the non-EC track for GI Registrations (and objections) correspond extremely closely, if not exactly, to nationality. Simply stated, non-EC nationals are on a different track than EC nationals, and that non-EC different track provides much less favorable treatment than the EC track.

7. Does the differential treatment also correspond to the origin of the product? Yes, it does. There is an overlap. And this overlap may well be more pronounced in the case of geographical indications than in the case of other forms of intellectual property rights. But the fact that the GI Regulation discriminates against non-EC products, should not and does not detract from the fact that it also provides less favorable treatment of non-EC nationals as well. There is absolutely no basis in any principle of treaty interpretation that would justify a narrow, technical reading of the TRIPS Agreement national treatment obligation, simply because the measure is also covered by the GATT 1994 Article III national treatment obligations. GATT Article III is simply not an excuse for whittling down the TRIPS Agreement national treatment obligation to virtually nothing.

8. The EC argument that the less favorable treatment is based on where a person is established and producing GI products and not on that person's nationality simply does not hold up. Nor does the EC's claim, which we just heard in the EC's closing statement, that the "foreign" and "domestic" registration tracks are simply a matter of "drafting" differences. The simply truth is that, because of the two "tracks", EC nationals have direct means to avail themselves of GI protections in the EC, and non-EC nationals do not.

Inspection Structures

9. With respect to the unilateral imposition of inspection structures on other WTO Members, the EC would like the issue to be "what is wrong with the EC's inspection structure system?" So, the EC jumped gleefully on my statement yesterday that their inspection system is "fine". What I meant was that it was fine for the EC. What we object to, and what is contrary to the WTO agreements, is imposing that particular structure on us as a precondition to our products and persons receiving GI status in the EC. What if we, too, established a inspection system for protection of GIs in the United States, and then imposed that inspection system on the EC as a condition to protecting EC GIs? What if the inspection system that we imposed were incompatible with the EC's system? What if all of the WTO Members did the same thing: developing particular inspection systems for themselves and requiring other WTO Members to adopt the same systems? How many competing and incompatible inspection structures can one WTO Member establish in its territory before its entire system becomes unworkable? That is one reason that the issue is not "what is wrong with the EC inspection system", but "why is the EC justified in imposing that system on other WTO Members."

10. Further, the EC says that its inspection structure is product-specific. This statement is misleading and inaccurately dismisses the broad scope of the requirement in Article 10 of the GI Regulation, which requires that an inspection <u>structure</u> be established by the WTO Member, and that, under that structure, particular inspection <u>bodies</u> may be authorized to conduct inspections. Further, these inspection structure requirements have nothing to do with whether the <u>products</u> satisfy the substantive criteria of the Regulation; we are not in this dispute challenging the requirements that a product must meet in order to claim GI status.

Government Involvement

11. We have already explained why it is WTO-inconsistent for the EC to require other WTO Members to assess whether GI applicants comply with the requirements of the EC GI Regulation and to do the EC's work for it. During this meeting, and for the first time to this degree, the EC focuses on TRIPS Article 24.9, which provides that Members need not protect GIs not protected in the country of origin. The EC uses this provision to support its proposition that the TRIPS Agreement itself permits the EC to require that other WTO Members assess the GI applications of its nationals and transmit those applications to the EC. According to the EC, only the WTO Member government, and not the individual rightholder, is in a position to show that the GI is protected in the country of origin.

12. But we ask the Panel to consider this argument carefully. The EC's assertion is perhaps true if a WTO Member has an EC-style GI protection system, with a central list of protected GIs maintained by the government. But, as indicated by several WIPO publications we have cited in this proceeding, WTO Members protect GIs in a number of ways, including through certification or collective marks, unfair trade statutes, and the like. Further, some WTO Members have common law certification and collective mark systems, in which the marks are not maintained on any central register. For all of these Members, perhaps unlike the EC, the government is not in a better position than the rightholder to provide information that the GI is protected in its country of origin. Therefore, implicit in the EC's argument—and in the requirement that the WTO Member government and not the rightholder show that the GI is protected in the country of origin—is the assumption that, in order to have their GIs protected in the EC, other WTO Members must have a system of GI protection that is similar to the EC system. This requirement is a "back-door" way of imposing an EC-style system of GI protection on other WTO Members.

13. Further, the EC characterizes its requirement that other WTO Members process GI applications as "cooperation". I know why they call it "cooperation": who can be against cooperation? But this is not cooperation. The EC is forcing other sovereign WTO Members to subject themselves to the EC's requirements and forcing other WTO Members to do the EC's job for it, as a condition of receiving GI status for its persons and products. That is not cooperation.

Article XX(d) of the GATT 1994

14. The EC's second submission contains the EC's only substantive argument on Article XX(d) of the GATT 1994. It went on for several pages; clearly some work went into it. Yet, the EC's argument was that the WTO-inconsistent requirements alleged by the United States are necessary for the "attainment of the objectives" of the Regulation or "indispensable for the implementation" of the Regulation. But we have to be much more rigorous than this when considering whether a Member has satisfied the strict conditions for an exception to basic WTO obligations. An examination of previous disputes discussing these exceptions—such as *Korea – Beef*—shows the level of rigor and analysis that is appropriate for this analysis. In brief, the requirement under the GATT 1994 Article XX(d) is that a WTO-inconsistent measure must be "necessary to secure compliance" with a WTO-consistent law or regulation. This requirement cannot be glossed over or swept under the carpet. It is simply irrelevant under GATT 1994 Article XX that a measure is necessary for the objectives of a regulation, or indispensable to the implementation of a regulation. It must be necessary to secure compliance with a WTO-consistent regulation.

15. I heard a brief conclusion in the EC's closing statement that these requirements are necessary to ensure that a product meets the specifications. But it is not clear that the specifications are a regulation, or in what sense the specifications—if they are the regulation the EC has in mind—are WTO-consistent. In short, the EC has not even made a credible attempt to support its case for entitlement to an Article XX(d) exception, because it has not even shown that the WTO-inconsistent requirements secure compliance with a WTO-consistent regulation. And, of course, we have already described in our oral and written submissions why these requirements are not in any sense "necessary".

Trademarks

16. While our claims with respect to trademarks are separate from our national treatment and MFN claims, the theme is the same: through GI registration, the EC gives its nationals protection against the trademark rights of all trademark owners under the TRIPS Agreement, including non-EC nationals.

17. Several points in our discussions today are worth highlighting. Notably, the EC continues to maintain that, presumably in satisfaction of his TRIPS Article 16.1 rights, the trademark owner has full rights to challenge and cancel a GI registration, by alleging inconsistency with Article 14(3) of the Regulation. We are not sure that this "right", if available, is responsive. But since we had a considerable amount of new discussion of this issue during this meeting, some comments are in order. First, Article 16.1 requires that the trademark owner be able to prevent confusing uses of a GI. Cancellation of an entire GI might or might not be necessary to do this. It seems wholly unrealistic, for instance, that the owner of a trademark in one EC member State would be able to convince the ECJ that an entire EC-wide GI should be cancelled, simply to avoid a particular confusing use in his local market. In this case, particularly, the supposed opportunity to "cancel" a registration is an inadequate substitute for the ability to prevent confusing uses.

18. Second, the EC had initially suggested to the Panel that a trademark holder could challenge the registration directly, presumably under Article 230 of the EC Treaty. In response, we pointed out that any such challenge would have to be made within two months from the registration, and that, after that point, the trademark owner would be powerless to challenge the registration, even through an "indirect" challenge in EC member State courts. The EC now responds, contrary to its earlier suggestions, that trademark owners might not be able to satisfy the "directly and individually concerned" standing requirement for challenging the registration under Article 230, raising the possibility that some trademark owners might be able to challenge the registration after the two-month deadline expires. At least in the case of identical signs for identical goods, it would seem that the trademark owner *would* be directly and individually concerned. But not even the EC is claiming that *no* trademark owners would be considered directly and individually concerned. Therefore, even under the EC's approach, not all trademark owners would have the opportunity to challenge the registration after the two-month deadline (and, indeed, it may be that none would have that opportunity). Consequently, it cannot reasonably be asserted that no trademark owners will be barred from challenging GI registrations after two months. Third, those trademark owners, if any, not prevented from challenging the registration after the two-month deadline expires, would not be entitled to a referral to the ECJ, which is in the discretion of the courts. Finally, it appears that none of the GI registrations pursuant to accession protocols is subject to challenge at all.

19. And in any case, the substantive standard that would be applied by the court under Article 14(3) is more strict than that required under TRIPS Article 16.1. Article 14(3) provides for the rejection of a GI Registration where it is likely to mislead the consumer in light of the trademark's reputation, renown and length of time used. That is not the standard under Article 16.1, which only requires confusion. The EC says that the confusion analysis always involves the consideration of renown, but that is not true. For example, where there are identical signs for identical goods, reputation, renown, and length of time will be irrelevant.

Article 24.5 of the TRIPS Agreement

20. The EC points to the supposed difference between the United States and Australia regarding Article 24.5 with respect to the Article 24.5 phrase "right to use a trademark". Regardless of whether this is true, however, there is no difference with respect to the main issue: that Article 24.5 says that measures to implement the GI section shall not prejudice the eligibility for or the validity of the registration of a trademark, and that Article 16.1 requires that owners of such registered trademarks have certain rights. Further, even if the EC is right that Article 24.5 prevents Members from prejudicing the right to put "signs" on goods, this does not give license *to* prejudice rights guaranteed under Article 16.1 to prevent confusing uses of signs. We urge the Panel to be very careful not to read away important Article 16.1 rights through a negative implication, particularly one arising from a misreading of Article 24.5.

Article 24.3 of the TRIPS Agreement

21. We find it extraordinary that the EC complains that our reading of Article 24.3 would mean that trademark owners have more rights after the TRIPS Agreement comes into force than they had before the TRIPS Agreement came into force. That is the whole point of Article 16.1 of the TRIPS Agreement. That's why we signed the TRIPS Agreement. In contrast, the EC says that whatever GI protections were in place when the TRIPS Agreement came into effect cannot be changed, regardless of whether they are consistent with other TRIPS Agreement or WTO obligations. This reading is not supported by the text and is not what the negotiators intended. Further, we do not understand the EC's point that our reading of Article 24.3 discriminates against those with registration systems in place on the date the TRIPS Agreement came into force. Article 24.3 does not identify any particular system for the protection of GIs. That provision merely says that whatever protection was provided to GIs—regardless of system—cannot be diminished in implementing the GI section of TRIPS.

Article 17 of the TRIPS Agreement

22. Under Article 17, there is a difference between using a place name to describe a product and using a GI in a trademark sense to differentiate and encourage consumers to buy the product. Use of a GI in a promotional sense by an unlimited number of people, over an unlimited amount of time and for nearly unlimited uses cannot be justified as a limited exception under Article 17. Further, this, by definition, allows consumers to be confused, which is not in the interest of either trademark owners or consumers.

Conclusion

23. We sincerely thank the Panel. We know this has been a long and complicated two days, and that we have generated a lot of paper over the course of this dispute. But I do agree with the EC that these past two days have elucidated many issues. While the EC and we still do not agree on many issues, we at least have a better sense of where we disagree. Thank you.

ANNEX A-8

REPLIES BY THE UNITED STATES TO QUESTIONS POSED BY THE PANEL FOLLOWING THE SECOND SUBSTANTIVE MEETING

(26 August 2004)

Q94. The Panel takes note that, in the EC's view, the specific conditions contained in Article 12(1) of Regulation (EC) No. 2081/92 do not apply to WTO Members because the introductory phrase "[w]ithout prejudice to international agreements" ensures that the WTO agreements prevail where there is a conflict with the Regulation (EC rebuttal, para. 55). Which precise EC obligations under the WTO agreements would be prejudiced by the application of those specific conditions to other WTO Members? In particular:

(a) would the EC's obligations under Article III:4 of GATT 1994 be prejudiced?

(b) would the EC's obligations under Article 3.1 of the TRIPS Agreement be prejudiced?

If not, please explain the relevance of your reference to the fact that the TRIPS Agreement obliges WTO Members to provide protection to GIs in accordance with Section 3 of Part II and the general provisions and basic principles of the TRIPS Agreement (EC first written submission, paras.65-66). ***EC***

Q95. Can the EC provide the Panel with any official statement by the Commission or any other EC institution, that the application of conditions of reciprocity and equivalence, such as those under Article 12(1) of Regulation (EC) No. 2081/92, would be inconsistent with the EC's obligations under international agreements, in particular, the WTO Agreement? ***EC***

Q96. The EC has provided a revised Guide to Regulation (EC) No. 2081/92, dated August 2004 (Exhibit EC-64). Was this new version prepared in connection with this Panel proceeding? How is it relevant to the Panel's work if the Commission assumes no liability for its contents (see its cover page)? A new paragraph in the introduction (page 5) indicates that "the Commission reserves the right to amend procedures" and indicates the possibility of further possible revisions. Does this mean that the Guide could be changed back to the old version? ***EC***

Q97. The Panel takes note of the EC's responses to Panel questions nos. 16 and 17 and the EC's rebuttal, paras. 79-86. Please explain in detail how the Commission's interpretation that Article 12(1) of Regulation (EC) No. 2081/92 does not apply to WTO Members is consistent with the statements in the EC responses in the TRIPS Council review of legislation to question No. 4 posed by New Zealand and the follow-up question posed by India on page 24 in IP/Q2/EEC/1 (cited in Australia's rebuttal, para. 33, fn. 23). ***EC***

Q98. Is it the EC's submission that the conditions in Article 12(1) of Regulation (EC) No. 2081/92 do not apply to WTO Members so that:

(a) WTO Member nationals may obtain GIs for areas located in all countries; or

(b) persons from all countries may obtain GIs for areas located in all WTO Members? ***EC***

Q99. The EC has referred to other Community legal acts in relation to the meaning of the phrase "without prejudice to international agreements" (EC rebuttal, paras. 62-66). Please also refer to Regulation (EC) No. 2082/92 on certificates of specific character for agricultural products and foodstuffs, which was adopted with the Regulation at issue in this dispute. To what international agreements does the phrase "[w]ithout prejudice to international agreements" refer as used in Article 16 of that Regulation? ***EC***

Q100. In Regulation (EC) No. 753/2002 on wine (set out in Exhibit US-35), Articles 34-36 refer to "third countries", apparently to refer to both WTO and non-WTO Members. It expressly states wherever a "third country" is limited to, or excludes, WTO Members. Why was Regulation (EC) No. 2081/92 drafted in such a way that the meaning of "third country" in Articles 12 through 12d is not clearer each time it was used? Does the use of "WTO Member" together with "third country" in certain instances in Articles 12 through 12d of Regulation (EC) No. 2081/92 not suggest that the term "third country" excludes WTO Members in those articles? ***EC***

Q101. The Panel takes note of the parties' respective views on the meaning of "nationals" under the TRIPS Agreement and the Paris Convention. Without prejudice to those views, please explain in detail which nationals should be compared for the purposes of the TRIPS national treatment obligations, based on the text of the agreement.

Please refer to the quadrant in the third party submission of Chinese Taipei (para. 9). Both the EC and the US compare an EC national with rights to a GI located in the EC. On the US view, that national should be compared with a US national with rights to a GI located in the US. But on the EC view, that national should be compared with a US national with rights to a GI located in the EC. Would it be appropriate instead to compare all EC nationals with rights to GIs who might wish to register them under Regulation (EC) No. 2081/92, wherever the geographical areas are located, and compare them with all US nationals with rights to GIs who might wish to register them under the Regulation, wherever the geographical areas are located?

More generally, is there a principle in the TRIPS Agreement that all nationals of one WTO Member with rights to a particular category of intellectual property, such as GIs, should be compared with all nationals of other WTO Members with rights to the same category of intellectual property, unless the text of the agreement indicates that with respect to particular types of products or other sub-categories, they require particular treatment? ***USA, AUS, EC***

Response:

1. As the United States understands it, the quadrants referenced by the Panel refer generally to four situations that might arise with respect to nationals and the protection of geographical indications: (1) an EC national claiming rights to a GI that refers to a territory in the EC ("EC-based GI"); (2) a non-EC national claiming rights to an EC-based GI; (3) an EC national claiming rights in a non-EC-based GI; and (4) a non-EC national claiming rights in a non-EC-based GI. Graphically, this is presented in four quadrants as follows:

GI: EC National: EC 1	GI: Non-EC National: EC 3
2 GI: EC National: Non-EC	4 GI: Non-EC National: Non-EC

2. As the Panel notes, in explaining the national treatment inconsistency, the United States has often illustrated the problem by comparing the treatment accorded in quadrant 1—that accorded EC nationals claiming rights in EC-based GIs—to the treatment accorded in quadrant 4—that accorded non-EC nationals asserting rights in non-EC GIs. Because of the close link between a GI and the territory to which it refers,[1] and a similarly close link between a territory and one's nationality, it stands to reason that discrimination based on the territory to which the GI refers effectively results in discrimination based on nationality. This is reflected in the comparison between the treatment accorded in quadrant 1 to the treatment accorded in quadrant 4.

3. This said, and addressing the Panel's question, it is appropriate to compare the treatment accorded to all EC nationals seeking to protect GIs, regardless of location, to all non-EC nationals seeking to protect GIs, regardless of location, as suggested by the Panel. This comparison arrives at the same result as that argued by the United States. The text of Article 3.1 of the TRIPS Agreement requires the EC to accord to the nationals of non-WTO Members "treatment no less favorable than that it accords to its own nationals with regard to the protection of intellectual property." The question presented by the text, therefore, is whether the EC accords any treatment to non-EC nationals with regard to the protection of rights in geographical indications that is less favorable than that accorded to any EC nationals. In other words, is any treatment accorded to any non-EC nationals in quadrants 2 and 4 less favorable than that accorded to any EC nationals in quadrants 1 and 3?

4. This question can be refined somewhat, because the most favorable treatment accorded to EC nationals—and that accorded to most, if not all, EC nationals—is in quadrant 1. That is because, as the EC itself admits, the EC nationals in quadrant 2 (those claiming GIs outside the EC), may face the same obstacles as non-EC nationals claiming GIs outside the EC. Therefore, the treatment in quadrant 1 is the benchmark—the national treatment—against which treatment of non-EC nationals must be measured. If treatment accorded to any non-EC nationals—in quadrants 2 or 4— is less favorable than that accorded to any nationals in quadrant 1, then there is a violation of the national treatment obligations. It does not matter whether some EC nationals—those in quadrant 3, to the extent there are any—are also treated less favorably than the EC nationals in quadrant 1. The issue is whether non-EC nationals are accorded less favorable treatment than that accorded EC nationals, not whether some EC nationals are also unable to get that same best treatment as other EC nationals.[2]

5. As the Panel notes, the EC relies on the existence of quadrant 2 to claim that some non-EC nationals are accorded the same treatment as EC nationals. But the fact that some non-EC nationals (however few in number) might be accorded the same treatment as EC nationals in quadrant 1 does not detract from the fact that,

---

[1] As the United States has noted previously, GIs are unique among intellectual property rights in its close link to territories and borders. *See, e.g.*, US Response to Panel questions 24-27 (July 8, 2004).

[2] In this connection, as the United States pointed out in its first written submission, at paragraph 76, the national treatment obligation with respect to goods under Article III of the GATT 1994 has been found to require "treatment of imported products no less favorable than that *accorded to the most-favoured domestic products.*" *US – Malt Beverages*, paras. 5.17, 5.33 (emphasis added). Furthermore, the United States pointed out in the first written submission, by analogy, that the treatment accorded to *the most favored EC nationals* is that accorded in quadrant 1. *See US – Section 211*, where the Appellate Body found that "as the language of Article 3.1 of the TRIPS Agreement, in particular, is similar to that of Article III:4 of the GATT 1994, the jurisprudence on Article III:4 of the GATT 1994 may be useful in interpreting the national treatment obligation in the TRIPS Agreement." (para. 242).

compared to the non-EC nationals in quadrant 4, there is less favorable treatment. A national treatment breach is not cured simply because *some* non-EC nationals may be treated the same as EC nationals, or because *some* EC nationals may be treated worse than others. That there are situations—in this case, an overwhelming number—in which the treatment accorded to non-EC nationals is less favorable than that accorded to EC nationals is sufficient to establish a national treatment breach.[3]

6. A similar analysis would apply with respect to the Paris Convention national treatment obligation in Article 2(1), which provides similarly that "[n]ationals of any country of the Union shall, as regards the protection of industrial property, enjoy in all other countries of the Union the advantages that their respective laws now grant, or may hereafter grant, to nationals ..."

7. The Appellate Body has found less favorable treatment of other WTO Member nationals under Article 3 of the TRIPS Agreement based on the denial of "effective equality of opportunities" to those nationals. In the context of GIs, "effective equality of opportunities" for non-EC nationals requires that persons in quadrant 4 be accorded treatment as favorable as that accorded to persons in quadrant 1. The EC GI Regulation denies such treatment. Consider the simple example of two sets of nationals, one group of EC nationals in France claiming GI rights with respect to their cheese in a particular region in southeastern France, and one group of Swiss nationals claiming GI rights to their cheese over the border in a particular region of Switzerland. By providing a ready avenue for the French nationals to register and protect their cheese GI in the EC, but making it considerably more difficult, if not impossible, for those Swiss nationals to register and protect their comparable cheese GI, the EC is plainly denying "effective equality of opportunities" for those Swiss nationals and according those Swiss nationals less favorable treatment with regard to the protection of intellectual property than it is according the French nationals.

8. With respect to the Panel's more general question, the text of the TRIPS Agreement is clear that the Article 3.1 analysis requires comparisons of treatment based solely on nationality with respect to "a particular category of intellectual property."[4] Moreover, nothing in the text of the TRIPS Agreement suggests that comparisons be made with respect to *both* nationality *and* "a particular type of products or other sub-categories." One could read the EC's argument as suggesting just such an analysis, *i.e.*, quadrant 1 (EC nationals with EC-based GIs) can be compared only with quadrant 2 (non-EC nationals with EC-based GIs), not with quadrant 4 (non-EC nationals with non-EC-based GIs). Yet there is simply no basis, textual or otherwise, to limit the national treatment obligation under TRIPS to this or any other sub-category of a particular intellectual property. The same is true for a TRIPS Article 4 analysis.

[3] Similarly, the panel in *US – Section 337* concluded that "the 'no less favorable' treatment requirement of Article III:4 has to be understood as applicable to each *individual case of imported products*. The Panel rejected any notion of balancing more favorable treatment of some imported products against the less favorable treatment of other imported products. If this notion were accepted, it would entitle a contracting party to derogate from the no less favourable treatment obligation in one case, or indeed in respect of one contracting party, on the ground that it accords more favourable treatment in some other case, or to another contracting party. *Such an interpretation would lead to great uncertainty about the conditions of competition between imported and domestic products and thus defeat the purposes of Article III.*" Panel Report, *US – Section 337*, para. 5.14 (emphasis added).

[4] To suggest that one make comparisons based on nationality with respect to *different* intellectual properties (e.g., treatment of national A with respect to patents compared to treatment of national B with respect to copyrights) is not only illogical, but is also inconsistent with the text and context of TRIPS Article 3. For instance, the second sentence of Article 3.1 refers to limitations to the national treatment obligation when comparing treatment of nationals with respect to related rights. The same is true for TRIPS Article 4, in which subparagraphs (b) and (c) of Article 4 refers to exceptions to the MFN obligation when comparing treatment of nationals with respect to copyright and related rights. Thus the text and context of both Articles 3 and 4 make clear that any analyses under these provisions requires comparisons of treatment based on nationality with respect to "a particular category of intellectual property."

Q102. Is it safe to assume that persons resident or established in one country to produce agricultural products or foodstuffs will be considered "nationals" of that country for the purposes of TRIPS? Why is it, or is it not, safe to assume that applicants for GIs under Regulation (EC) No. 2081/92 are "nationals" of the country where their GI is located, for the purposes of TRIPS? ***USA, AUS, EC***

Response:

9. As an initial point, as illustrated above in response to question 101, it is not critical for the Panel to make a factual assumption that all persons producing GI products in a country are nationals of that country. Indeed, it is undisputed that the EC GI Regulation on its face provides for different treatment of persons depending on which quadrant set out in response to question 101 they fall in.[5] Further, it is clear that, under the GI Regulation, there is less favorable treatment accorded to non-EC nationals in quadrant 4 than is accorded to EC nationals in quadrant 1. Consequently, there is a breach of national treatment obligations on the face of the EC GI Regulation, whether or not one makes assumptions concerning all persons producing GI products in a country

10. This said, applicants for a GI Registration are groups of producers and/or processors, natural persons and legal persons that apply for registration with respect to agricultural products or foodstuffs that they produce or obtain within a specific geographic area.[6] In order to produce or process agricultural products and foodstuffs in a particular geographic area, such persons will be established in that area and will have to set up a legal person under the laws of the country in which they are established and producing agricultural products and foodstuffs.[7]

11. Therefore, to the question whether it is safe to assume that such persons, established and producing agricultural products and foodstuffs in a country, are "nationals" of that country for purposes of the national treatment obligation of the TRIPS Agreement and the Paris Convention, the answer is, generally, yes. First, any real and effective commercial or industrial establishment in a separate customs territory WTO Member would, under Article 1.3, footnote 1, of the TRIPS Agreement, be a national of that WTO Member. Second, persons established and producing agricultural products and foodstuffs in any WTO Member that confers nationality on the basis of such establishment would necessarily be nationals of that WTO Member. Third, under Article 3 of the Paris Convention, even a national from a non-Paris Union country is treated as a national for national treatment purposes if it has a real and effective commercial establishment in a Paris Union country. Fourth, as the EC has itself noted, for legal persons, a country's "nationals" are often defined in terms of where that company is incorporated. As the EC has itself unwittingly illustrated in its examples of so-called non-EC nationals taking advantage of EC GIs, companies established and producing agricultural products and foodstuffs

---

[5] Moreover, the EC has not argued, as indeed it cannot, that there are no persons falling in quadrant 4.

[6] Articles 5(1), 5(2) and 12a(1) of the GI Regulation.

[7] See Article 2, Regulation 2037/93, which states: "Where national law treats a group of persons without legal personality as a legal person, the said group of individuals shall be authorized to submit an application." Exhibit Comp.-2a.

in a country generally become incorporated in that country and are therefore nationals of that country.[8] Finally, and as context, the United States notes that nationals are defined in Article 1.3 of the TRIPS Agreement to include natural or legal persons that would meet the criteria for eligibility of protection provided for in the Paris Convention. Article 10 of the Paris Convention defines "interested parties" in indications of source as including those natural or legal entities engaged in production of goods established either in the locality falsely indicated as the source, or in the country where the false indication of source is used.

12. In other words, it will generally follow as a legal matter that those established and producing agricultural products and foodstuffs in a Member are nationals of that Member; it also generally follows as a practical matter. In fact, the United States is unaware of any GI registrations granted to applications from a non-EC national for the protection of an EC GI. Nor has the EC provided any such examples. Instead, as noted above, the EC has simply provided examples of situations in which non-EC nationals have some involvement in companies that *are* EC nationals producing EC GI-protected products. Further, as the United States has pointed out, US agricultural land is held almost exclusively by US nationals.[9]

13. Finally, as noted previously, there is an extremely close fit between a distinction based on where a legal person is established and producing agricultural products and foodstuffs and a distinction based on nationality. The Panel therefore should find that, by discriminating against those established and producing products outside the EC, the GI Regulation discriminates against non-EC nationals.

Q103. The Panel takes note that the EC does not exclude entirely that "under certain circumstances, measures which are neutral on their face may nonetheless constitute less favourable treatment of foreign nationals" and that the EC believes that national treatment under TRIPS should not overlap with GATT 1994 (EC response to Panel question No. 29, paras.71 and 74). What other considerations are relevant to the assessment of de facto discrimination under TRIPS? What is the relevance, if any, of the fact that the TRIPS Agreement does not contain a general exceptions provision analogous to Article XX of GATT 1994? ***USA, AUS, EC***

Response:

14. The United States understands the question as referring to the fact that the two different "tracks" for registering GIs—the "domestic track" under Article 5 and the "foreign track" under Article 12 and 12a—do not literally use the words "EC national" and "non-EC national" to describe those using each track; and that, similarly, the two separate objection procedures also do not use the words "national" but refer to persons "from

[8] The EC has cited several purported examples of non-EC nationals claiming rights in EC-based GIs. However, these examples confirm the contrary proposition. In its oral statement at the second meeting, at paragraph 8, the EC cited the examples of Sara Lee, Kraft Foods, and Nestle. In the "Sara Lee" example, it is apparent from the EC's own Exhibit EC-61 that the transactions did not involve non-EC nationals. Exhibit EC-61 contains the decision of the Commission not to oppose, *inter alia*, the acquisition of Al Ponte Prosciutto, S.R.L. by Sara Lee Personal Products, S.p.A. The EC states in its oral statement that "Sara Lee, a large US multinational, acquired Al Ponte Prosciutto, which produces Prosciutto di Parma," citing to Exhibit EC-61. This is incorrect. Al Ponte Prosciutto was not acquired by Sara Lee Corporation, the US parent company of the Sara Lee group. As Exhibit EC-61 states, Al Ponte Prosciutto was acquired by Sara Lee Personal Products, S.p.A., an Italian corporation under common control with Sara Lee Charcuteria SA, a French corporation. As a legal matter, all companies involved in the transaction were EC companies and, thus, EC nationals. The "Kraft Foods" example involves, according to Exhibit EC-62, a company founded in Italy in 1908 by Giovanni Invernizzi. Nothing suggests that this company is not Italian. In 1985, his son sold the company to Kraft Foods Group, which has an Italian subsidiary. In 2003, the business of Giovanni Invernizzi's Italian company was partly sold to Lactalis, a French dairy company, again with an Italian subsidiary. Nothing suggests that the Italian company somehow became a US national at any point in these transactions. Similarly, with respect to the "Nestle" example, nothing in Exhibit EC-63 suggests that the salami firm Vismara, owned by Nestle, and sold to another Italian company, was not a company incorporated in Italy and an Italian national. Similarly, the EC cited in its second submission, paragraph 46, the example of a Norwegian, Mr. Larsen, who founded Larsen Cognac House in 1926. As Exhibit EC-36 notes, Mr. Larsen bought the small firm of Cognac Joseph Gautier and his son took over the firm which, by then, operated under the name Larsen. The firm's website indicates that the firm is a French corporation (a societe anonyme) domiciled in Cognac, France. Similarly, the other examples provided by the EC of companies in the wine sector—a sector not covered by the EC GI Regulation—do not support the EC's view with respect to any non-EC nationals claiming rights in EC-based GIs.

[9] US Opening Oral Statement at Second Meeting, para. 14.

a WTO Member" and persons "resident or established" in a WTO Member. Hence, the measure is arguably "neutral" on its face.

15. As an initial point, it is worth underscoring again that, although the EC GI Regulation does not use the word "national", it does provide for different treatment of persons depending on which quadrant set out in response to question 101 they fall in. Further, there is less favorable treatment accorded to non-EC nationals in quadrant 4 than is accorded to EC nationals in quadrant 1. Consequently, there is a breach of national treatment obligations, despite the lack of specific references to "nationals".

16. Of course, whether there is *de facto* discrimination depends on the particular measure and the facts involved. In the context of this particular dispute, among the additional factors relevant to finding inconsistency with the national treatment and MFN obligations under the TRIPS Agreement and the Paris Convention—despite the lack of the word "national" in connection with the discrimination in the EC GI Regulation—are that:

> (1) As discussed above, it is apparent from the measure itself that there is a very close fit—and often a complete identity—between the criteria for who qualifies for the "domestic track" versus who qualifies for the "foreign track" and EC nationals versus non-EC nationals. Although the GI Regulation does not use the terms "EC national" and "non-EC national", it does everything but. The same is true of the two tracks for objections: indeed, as the US second oral statement noted, the EC itself stated in the preamble to the amendment to the GI Regulation last year that the additional track for persons resident or established in other WTO Members was necessary in order to provide the right of objection to other WTO Members' "nationals".[10] Further, that there may not be a perfect fit—*i.e.,* that some situations might fall within quadrants 2 and 3 in the response to question 101—does not detract from the national treatment violation.
>
> (2) Indeed, from a practical point of view, it is hard to construct a closer fit between the distinctions drawn in the GI Regulation and "nationality". One possibility would have been for the EC GI Regulation literally to discriminate based on nationality. But this would have presented practical difficulties, because the EC has asserted that, under the TRIPS Agreement, the nationality of a person is determined according to the law of the country whose nationality is being claimed. Therefore, a literal distinction in the GI Regulation between EC nationals, on the one hand, and non-EC nationals, on the other, would have required reliance, not on rules set out in the GI Regulation itself, but on the laws of the various non-EC countries. By contrast, making distinctions based on where the person is established and producing agricultural products and foodstuffs—as the GI Regulation does—avoids reliance on the laws of non-EC countries, while nonetheless making distinctions corresponding to nationality.
>
> (3) There is a close connection between geographical indications, geographic regions, and the persons established in those regions[11]—a reputation for products from those regions often builds up over hundreds of years. For this reason, among others, it is obvious that, for instance, French nationals have an interest in claiming rights to French-based GIs, and US nationals have an interest in claiming rights to U.S.-based GIs. This fact is intrinsic to the very nature of the GI itself. Predictably, it is also born out by factual indications that for instance, in the United States, nationals have an interest in GIs

---

[10] US Opening Oral Statement at Second Meeting, para. 9.

[11] As the EC itself has noted, "geographical indications are the common patrimony of all the producers of a certain area, and ultimately of the entire population of that area." First Written Submission of the EC, paragraph 307, 4th bullet point. Similarly, EC Trade Commissioner Lamy, in a speech last year, described the benefits of geographical indication protection as follows:

the geographical indication is a kind of collective "mark" of the farmers and craftsmen of a region. It guarantees that the use of a name will remain attached to a region and to the community that saw its birth.

SPEECH/03/292 Pascal Lamy EU Trade Commissioner Creation of the Organisation Geographical Indications Network (ORIGIN) Brussels, June 11, 2003 (emphasis added). Exhibit US-49. Similarly, as mentioned in other US submissions, the preamble to the EC GI Regulation cites the "considerable" benefit to the rural economy by "improving the incomes of farmers and by retaining the rural population in these areas."

of their own nationality[12] and that agricultural land is 99% owned by US nationals.[13] Equally predictably, the only examples the EC can come up with in rebuttal are apparent examples of *EC nationals* with some non-EC connections taking advantage of EC GIs.[14] Therefore, discrimination against those with rights in non-EC GIs equates to discrimination against non-EC nationals.

(4) After 12 years, there is not a single non-EC-based GI that is registered in the EC, compared to over 600 EC-based GIs. Of the over 600 EC-based GIs, the EC to date has not been able to identify a single GI applicant who is not an EC national (even though it, and not the United States, has access to all of the relevant registration information).

(5) The Appellate Body has been clear in the analogous context of other national treatment obligations in the WTO agreements that the national treatment obligation covers both *de jure* and *de facto* discrimination. One reason is that, if the obligation were only *de jure*, circumventing the obligations would be easy.[15] Therefore, the Appellate Body has been clear about the need for a meaningful analysis of *de facto* discrimination, not just *de jure* discrimination. This is not to say, however, contrary to the EC's claims, that evidence of actual circumvention is necessary to justify a finding of *de facto* discrimination, or that the existence of Article III GATT 1994 obligations means that a *de facto* analysis under the TRIPS national treatment obligation is unnecessary. To the contrary, the Appellate Body has been clear in finding that, in the absence of *express* language limiting the analysis to *de jure* discrimination, national treatment obligations are *de facto* obligations:[16] a Member cannot avoid these obligations by formally neutral language.

17. As for the notion that the existence of Article III of the GATT 1994 somehow eliminates the possibility of a *de facto* breach of TRIPS Article 3, this is plainly wrong. Article III of the GATT 1994 concerns less favorable treatment of products based on origin, whereas TRIPS Article 3 concerns less favorable treatment of persons regarding intellectual property protection based on nationality. In the case of GIs, there is a strong link between persons claiming rights and the goods with respect to which the rights are claimed. According to Article 22 of the TRIPS Agreement, GI rights derive solely from the existence of *goods* that have a "quality, reputation or other characteristic" attributable to its territory of origin. Thus, a GI right does not exist in the abstract; it exists solely in connection with goods. To attempt, as the EC does, to divorce the acquisition of the right from the good that is the subject matter of the right overlooks this feature of the right. Indeed, given this fundamental aspect of GIs, the EC GI Regulation thus discriminates against both the goods identified by a GI and persons with rights to or interest in those GIs. The EC is wrong to complain about "overlap": the Regulation simply breaches more than one WTO obligation.

18. The lack of a general exception like Article XX of the GATT 1994 is not relevant to whether there is *de facto* discrimination under the TRIPS Agreement or to the interpretation of Article 3 of the TRIPS Agreement. It is, however, relevant to the fact that Article III of the GATT 1994 and Article 3 of the TRIPS Agreement are two separate obligations. The TRIPS Agreement contains general "security exceptions" (Article 73), just as the GATT 1994 contains "security exceptions" in Article XXI. Article 3.2 of the TRIPS Agreement also contains limited exceptions to national treatment as provided for in the Paris Convention, using language directly analogous to parts of Article XX(d). This shows that the drafters were able to incorporate Article XX type approaches where they deemed warranted. That there are no general Article XX exceptions to TRIPS obligations can only be regarded as deliberate. And while the lack of such exceptions has no impact on how to interpret the fundamental national treatment obligation (much less should its absence be read to adopt a

[12] *See* Response of the United States to Panel Question 27 (July 8, 2004), para. 55; Exhibit US-43.

[13] Exhibit US-72; US Opening Oral Statement at Second Meeting, para. 14.

[14] *See* response to question 104 above, note 8.

[15] Appellate Body Report, *EC – Bananas*, para. 233; Appellate Body Report, *Canada – Autos*, para. 142.

[16] Appellate Body Report, *EC – Bananas*, para. 233. It is important to note that, by arguing that evidence of actual circumvention is necessary for a determination of de facto violation, the EC is only confusing the *de jure – de facto* distinction with the "as such"—"as applied" distinction.

narrow reading of this obligation), it does confirm that any defense the EC might present under GATT Article XX(d) with respect to GATT violations is not transferrable to violations under the TRIPS Agreement.

19. As the United States has stated on several occasions, the Panel should not be concerned by the potential overlap between the TRIPS Agreement and the GATT 1994. Indeed, particularly with respect to geographical indications, such overlap is to be expected. Any such overlap, however, does not affect the analysis of discrimination against nationals under the TRIPS Agreement. A measure may be simultaneously covered by several covered agreements—*e.g.*, the TBT Agreement and Article III of the GATT 1994—without the obligations of each agreement being narrowed thereby.

20. As a final note, it should be no surprise that the GI Regulation is inconsistent with the EC's national treatment obligations under the TRIPS Agreement and the Paris Convention, considering that the GI Regulation itself evidences a specific intention in its preamble to protect EC agricultural production and populations in rural areas in the EC. Further, such a breach of national treatment is entirely consistent with the EC's long-standing public statements—both to the complainants and third parties to this dispute and to the WTO Membership at large—that GI protection would be made available only to those Members with equivalent GI systems and offering reciprocal protection to EC products. In the case of the GI Regulation, the WTO breach established by the Regulation itself is fully supported by and entirely consistent with the protectionist structure of the GI Regulation.

Q104. Please provide your interpretation of the term "separate customs territory" as used in footnote 1 to Article 1.3 of the TRIPS Agreement in accordance with the customary rules of treaty interpretation. What relevance can be drawn from the fact that the same term is used in Article XXVI of GATT 1994? ***USA, AUS, EC***

Response:

21. The United States would like to emphasize as an initial matter that it is beyond dispute that this footnote defines nationals for at least some WTO Members, and that for those Members, it is plain that any discrimination based on where a legal person has a real and effective industrial or commercial establishment is based on nationality. Thus the EC GI Regulation discriminates based on nationality when it explicitly discriminates in favor of EC nationals and against legal persons with a real and effective industrial or commercial establishment in those separate customs territory Members of the WTO.

22. In response to the Panel's question, however, under the customary rules of treaty interpretation "[a] treaty shall be interpreted in good faith in accordance with the ordinary meaning to be given to the terms of the treaty in their context and in the light of its object and purpose".[17] A general interpretation of the phrase "separate customs territory" starts with the ordinary meaning of the word "territory", which indicates that the term refers to a defined geographical area. The word "customs" indicates that the territory in question is defined by reference to a unique customs regime applicable in that territory. The United States notes, as part of the context for interpreting the term, that Article XXIV:2 of the GATT 1994 defines a "customs territory" in similar terms. It states that a "a customs territory shall be understood to mean any territory with respect to which *separate* tariffs or other regulations of commerce are maintained for a substantial part of the trade of such territory with other territories." (Emphasis added).

23. The factor that distinguishes one customs territory from another is the maintenance of "separate tariffs or other regulations of commerce". "Separateness" is, therefore, an intrinsic feature of a "customs territory". As the EC correctly points out, this means that every customs territory is "separate" from every other customs territory. Indeed, most WTO Members are customs territories that are "separate" from the customs territory of most other WTO Members. However, the term as used in footnote 1 of the TRIPS Agreement refers not to "separate customs territories" generally, but to a "separate customs territory Member of the WTO." For this

[17] These rules are reflected in Article 31(1) of the Vienna Convention on the Law of Treaties.

reason, the United States agrees with the EC that the term "separate customs territory Member of the WTO" in footnote 1 of the TRIPS Agreement does not encompass every "customs territory". Indeed, Article XXVI:5 of the GATT 1994 is useful to demonstrate the type of distinction that footnote 1 of the TRIPS Agreement is making. Article XXVI:5 refers to a separate customs territory for which a GATT contracting party has responsibility and has singled out <u>not</u> to be covered by that contracting party's acceptance of the GATT 1994. These separate customs territories would clearly <u>not</u> be a separate customs territory "Member" of the WTO.

24. In footnote 1, the reference to "a separate customs territory *Member* of the WTO" describes a particular *category of WTO Members* and seeks to distinguish this category of WTO Members from some other category of WTO Members. The key to the distinction between the two categories is that WTO Members in the sub-category covered by footnote 1 are all "separate customs territory Members". In identifying the other category of WTO Members from which the Members covered by footnote 1 are distinguished, the United States turns to context. As part of the context, the United States observes that Article XII of the *Marrakesh Agreement Establishing the World Trade Organization* ("Marrakesh Agreement" or "WTO Agreement") lays down rules on accession as a Member of the WTO. The opening clause of Article XII defines which legal entities may become WTO Members. It states:

> *Any State or separate customs territory possessing full autonomy in the conduct of its external commercial relations* and of the other matters provided for in this Agreement and the Multilateral Trade Agreements may accede to this Agreement ...

25. Article XII, therefore, confirms the two categories of WTO Members. First, there are "States". The second category of Members consists of separate customs territories with full autonomy over external commercial relations and of other matters provided for in the Marrakesh Agreement.

26. There is nothing in footnote 1 that suggests that the expression "separate customs territory possessing full autonomy in the conduct of its external commercial relations" should apply solely to only *certain* separate customs territories fulfilling the autonomy requirements, such as territories that form a sub-part of a State. Instead, the text of Article XII covers "any" autonomous separate customs territories, without qualification. Such separate customs territories may, therefore, form a sub-part of a State or comprise some or all of the territory of several States. The issue is simply whether the territory possesses full autonomy in the conduct of its external commercial relations and of the other matters provided for in the Marrakesh Agreement.

27. In that respect, the United States observes that the EC is not a "State"; however, the EC is a "separate customs territory possessing full autonomy in the conduct of its external commercial relations". The United States, therefore, believes that the EC is a "separate customs territory Member of the WTO" rather than a State Member of the WTO for purposes of footnote 1 of the TRIPS Agreement.

28. The United States notes, though, that the EC did not accede to the WTO pursuant to Article XII of the Marakesh Agreement. Rather, the EC was an original Member of the WTO explicitly covered by Articles XI:1 and XIV of the Agreement. The EC's intention to be an original member was known during the negotiation of the Marrakesh Agreement. Article IX:1 and other provisions of the Marrakesh Agreement recognize that the EC would be a WTO member. Articles XI:1 and XIV do not distinguish between States and separate customs territories, as there was no need for these categories in determining rules for original membership of the WTO. Instead, original membership was reserved for GATT contracting parties. There was only a single exception to this and that was for the European Communities. Thus, in Articles XI:1 and XIV there was no need to describe a class or category to which the EC belonged. Instead, the EC could be identified by name as the sole original WTO Member that was not a GATT contracting party. This does not mean, though, that the EC is not a separate customs territory Member of the WTO.

29. In particular, there is nothing in the text of Articles XI:1, XII, or XIV to suggest that the original WTO Members do not fall within one of the two categories of WTO Member described in Article XII, namely States or fully autonomous separate customs territories. To the contrary, all the original WTO Members fit easily into

one or the other group of Members. It would, in any event, be curious to interpret Article XII in such a way that an original WTO Member could not qualify to become a WTO Member.

30. Accordingly, the United States submits that Article XII confirms the interpretation of TRIPS footnote 1 that there are two categories of WTO Member—States and fully autonomous separate customs territories.

31. This interpretation is also confirmed by how footnote 1 is used. Article 1.3 defines "nationals" for the purposes of the TRIPS Agreement. In that provision, "nationals" are defined by reference to the scope of protection afforded under various international conventions on intellectual property. In each of these WIPO-administered conventions, protection is afforded to persons possessing the nationality of a country. Not all WTO Members grant nationality, however; *see, e.g.,* GATS Article XVIII(k)(ii)(1). For that reason, the TRIPS Agreement has to have two definitions of "nationals". The first definition, in the main text of Article 1.3, applies to Members that can confer nationality, as provided for in the list of WIPO-administered conventions, including the Paris Convention. The second definition, in footnote 1, applies to separate customs territory WTO Members that cannot so confer nationality.

32. The EC acknowledges that it cannot grant nationality as it argues that, in its view, EC nationals are nationals of an EC member State. However, as just explained, the TRIPS Agreement provides only two definitions of "nationals". There is no third option for the EC along the lines the EC envisages. The EC must fall within one or other of the definitions applicable to the categories of WTO Member identified in TRIPS Article 1.3 and in Article XII of the WTO Agreement, and it clearly does not fall within the definition reserved for States.

33. The absurd consequence of the EC's view that it is not a separate customs territory for purposes of the TRIPS Agreement, is that the EC has no nationals, and, therefore, has no national treatment obligations. Such an interpretation of the TRIPS Agreement, rendering *inutile* for one WTO Member the fundamental obligation of national treatment, must be rejected, since it is contrary to customary principles of interpretation of public international law.

34. The drafting history confirms the United States' view. First, an "Informal Note by the Secretariat", of 7 December 1992, states that the term "national" in various draft texts "entails a lack of precision, and could engender legal uncertainty, with regard to the legal position of separate customs territories Members of the MTO." A number of proposals were made for resolving these difficulties. Among them was the addition of text to the draft TRIPS Agreement.

35. In the TRIPS Agreement, there was a proposal to amend a footnote that had been proposed in the Brussels draft of the Agreement. That draft included an early version of footnote 1 that applied solely to "Hong Kong". The Secretariat Note proposed extending the footnote generally to "separate customs territory Member[s] of the MTO". Again, the reason for this proposal was to resolve the legal difficulty stemming from the fact that certain Members cannot confer nationality and, therefore, the definition of "national" in Article 1.3 would not apply to them. The final text of footnote 1 is based closely on the proposal in the Secretariat Note.

36. Additional support for this view of the negotiating history comes from Daniel Gervais' commentary on the drafting history. Gervais states that "[a] footnote was added to deal with *customs territories which may be WTO Members without being states*, and hence unable to join WIPO-administered treaties."[18] This statement again identifies the two categories of WTO Membership. The text and context of footnote 1 of the TRIPS Agreement, in light of the object and purpose of the TRIPS Agreement to "reduce distortions and impediments to international trade, ... to promote effective and adequate protection of intellectual property rights, and to ensure that measures and procedures to enforce intellectual property rights do not themselves become barriers to

[18] Gervais, The TRIPS Agreement, Drafting History and Analysis (Second Edition). Sweet and Maxwell, London, 2003, p. 88. As Gervais notes, post-TRIPS WIPO Treaties allow certain intergovernmental organizations to adhere, but this was not true of the WIPO treaties referenced in Article 1.3 of the TRIPS Agreement with respect to the definition of "nationals."

legitimate trade ..." for all WTO Members (State or non-State),[19] therefore, support the view that footnote 1 applies to the EC, a separate customs territory WTO Member. Moreover, pursuant to Article 32 of the Vienna Convention, the negotiating history confirms this interpretation.

Q105. The Panel takes note of the EC's view that it is not a separate customs territory Member of the WTO within the meaning of footnote 1 to Article 1.3 of the TRIPS Agreement (EC rebuttal, para. 35).

> *(a) Which natural persons does the EC consider EC nationals for the purposes of TRIPS? Are they also nationals of EC member States?*
>
> *(b) Which legal persons does the EC consider EC nationals for the purposes of TRIPS? Are they also nationals of EC member States?* ***EC***

Q106. What are the nationalities of the applicants for GIs registered under Regulation (EC) No. 2081/92? Have there been any applicants who were not nationals of the EC member State in which the relevant GI was located? Please supply details of any that were not, and the relevant GIs. To the extent that you are aware of the nationality of persons other than the applicants who use a GI in accordance with its registration, please supply the same information. ***EC***

Q107. The Panel takes note of the examples of foreigners and foreign companies which have invested in Europe (EC rebuttal, para. 46 and Exhibits EC-36 to EC-39; EC second oral statement, para. 28 and Exhibits EC-61 to EC-63). Is the Larsen firm a French company? Have Suntory Limited, E & J Gallo and the Robert Mondavi family formed subsidiaries, joint ventures or other entities under the laws of France and Italy to invest in those wine estates? Did Sara Lee, Kraft Foods and Nestlé purchase companies formed under the law of an EC member State?

The Panel takes note that the EC argues that the possibility that these foreign nationals formed legal persons under the laws of an EC member State is not attributable to Regulation (EC) No. 2081/92 (EC second oral statement, para. 30). Is it appropriate to exclude such other factors from an examination of the WTO-consistency of the Regulation? Does the EC submit that the Panel should "pierce the corporate veil" and refer to ownership and control to determine nationality for the purposes of TRIPS? ***EC***

Q108. Article 13 of Regulation (EC) No. 2081/92 provides certain protection for registered names. Please explain the practical operation of this article with respect to products, including the types of orders which may be made under Article 13(1) and the consequences of Article 13(2). How would they affect imported products? How would they provide less favourable treatment to imported products? ***USA, AUS***

Response:

37. The United States does not fully understand this question, as Article 13(1) does not refer to "orders". In addition, the United States understands that the reference to Article 13(2) should be to Article 13(3). The United States assumes that this question refers to any orders, including by EC member State institutions, that may be used to protect registered names as provided in Article 13.

38. With this understanding, products whose names the EC registers under the GI Regulation benefit from numerous competitive advantages that have been detailed in the US submissions, oral statements and answers to questions. These advantages include the ability to be distinguished in the market-place—through an EC-sanctioned mechanism— as products with special characteristics or other qualities attributable to their geographical origin. Those products—and only those products— may also be accompanied by an official EC

---

[19] *See* first paragraph of the preamble of the TRIPS Agreement.

"symbol" or "logo" informing the consumer that the product is a registered GI.[20] As the relevant EC regulation explains

> [t]he logo will allow producers of food products to increase awareness of their products among consumers in the European Union... The presence of this logo is a genuine guarantee for all European consumers, making it clear that the special nature of this product lies in its geographical origin. Because of this, products will inspire more confidence. As producers, the logo provides you which [*sic*] a marketing tool. You will be able to put the logo on the labels or packaging of your products, and also use it in your advertising.[21]

39. Further, the registered names of those products are reserved for the use of those registered products, and, indeed, other products will be barred from being accompanied by any name that even evokes the registered name, even if there is no risk of consumers being misled.[22] Those products whose names are registered under the GI Regulation are protected in the marketplace against a broad range of competing uses of names or descriptions, which are laid out in Article 13. Consequently, the kinds of orders that might be issued pursuant to Article 13(1), and more particularly by judicial and administrative authorities in EC member States that implement Article 13, would be to prevent all other products from being promoted—or sold accompanied by names or labels—using the names or words that are deemed to fall within the scope of protection offered by Article 13(1).

40. But imported products do not have access to this system of protection on the same terms as EC products. Indeed, as presented by the United States throughout this dispute, the EC GI Regulation erects prohibitive barriers to access to this system of GI protection for non-EC products. Thus, imported products are affected in at least two ways. First, they, unlike their EC-origin "like" counterparts, cannot benefit from the coveted registered GI status, cannot use the official "logos" and cannot benefit from the competitive advantages that the EC GI Regulation bestows on GI products. This amounts to less favorable treatment of imported products compared to their "like" EC counterparts.

41. Second, the imported products are at an affirmative competitive disadvantage *vis-a-vis* their European competition in cases where any name, product description, or descriptive labeling that is an important selling point for the imported product is deemed to fall within the ambit of "protection" afforded to the protected EC product under Article 13(1). Thus, under Article 13(1), an EC member State judicial or administrative body might issue an order that an imported cheese product be stripped of any mention of a recognized descriptive term for that cheese because it is deemed "evocative" of the name of the protected EC cheese. In sum, due to the lack of ability to object to the registration of the EC product's name, and the lack of ability of the imported product to benefit from the protections of registration itself, this situation, too, amounts to less favorable treatment of imported products.

42. The consequence of Article 13(3) of the GI Regulation is to enhance this competitive edge bestowed on products that benefit from GI status. The names used to promote and sell imported products that do not benefit from GI status—names which might communicate a special characteristic of the product—could become generic, meaning that they could become the "common name" for the product, thereby losing their status as a source identifier.[23] Names of products benefitting from GI status cannot lose this status. This also means that an imported product might be blocked from being identified using what would normally be a "generic" description for the product, essentially reserving to the GI product generic terms that accurately describe a product to the consumer. The inability to identify imported goods to consumers by their common name—reserving that name to particular GI products—accords less favorable treatment to those goods.

---

[20] Article 5a of Commission Regulation 2037/93, p. 5. Exhibit COMP-2.a.

[21] Annex II of Commission Regulation 2037/93. Exhibit COMP-2.a.

[22] Article 13(b) of the GI Regulation.

[23] Article 3(1) of the GI Regulation.

Q109. Leaving aside the rights conferred by Article 13 of Regulation (EC) No. 2081/92, the complainants refer to the "intent and the effect of the Regulation", the "perceived" advantages of registration and the benefits "claimed by the EC" to be gained from protection under the Regulation (US first written submission, paras.61-62; Australia's first written submission, para. 197 and US and Australia's respective responses to Panel question No. 32). On what basis do the complainants argue that the aims and effects of the EC measure are relevant to ascertaining less favourable treatment within the meaning of Article III:4 of GATT 1994? ***USA, AUS***

Response:

43. The United States is not using the "aim and effects" of the EC measure to determine whether there is less favorable treatment under Article III:4 of the GATT 1994. The less favorable treatment accorded imported products is apparent from the measure itself, and the obligation is fully articulated in Article III:4. However, as the United States has noted throughout this proceeding, the EC itself emphasizes the significant competitive and other advantages being bestowed on persons and products that can benefit from GI protection under the GI Regulation, yet both the EC (in public and private statements to WTO Members) and the Regulation itself make clear that there are substantial—often insurmountable—obstacles to non-EC persons and products benefitting from these competitive and other advantages. Further, the preamble to the Regulation highlights the role of the Regulation in promoting EC products with certain characteristics, which are of "considerable benefit" to the EC rural economy and highlights the importance of the role that production, manufacture and distribution of agricultural products and foodstuffs play in the Community economy. The EC has noted that GI protection for its products and persons are particularly important as agricultural subsidies are phased out. And of course, not a single non-EC-based GI has ever been registered, compared to the over 600 EC-based GIs that have been registered. Taken together, this evidence is a virtual admission by the EC that the EC GI Regulation does not provide the same access to these benefits to non-EC products and nationals as it provides to EC nationals and products. Further, this evidence helps clarify the factual question of the meaning of the various provisions of the EC GI Regulation, and how it operates.

44. In light of this evidence, it should come as little surprise that the EC GI Regulation is in breach of the EC's national treatment obligations under the TRIPS Agreement, the Paris Convention, and the GATT 1994, a legal conclusion that is apparent from the EC GI Regulation itself. More generally, the United States notes that, as the Appellate Body has said, "[t]he broad and fundamental purpose of Article III is to avoid protectionism in the application of internal tax and regulatory measures.[24] The Appellate Body has also noted that Article III:1, in which the Members recognize that internal regulations and requirements such as those at issue here "should not be applied to imported or domestic products so as to afford protection to domestic production" informs and provides part of the context of all of Article III.

Q110. Does the EC contest that, to the extent that Regulation (EC) No. 2081/92 provides GI protection for EC nationals and is a law affecting EC products, GI protection for other WTO Member nationals and imported products solely through other laws, such as labelling and unfair competition, would be less favourable treatment? ***EC***

Q111. Does the EC contest that national treatment and MFN obligations under TRIPS apply to TRIPS-plus protection, and apply to Regulation (EC) No. 2081/92 even to the extent that it does not merely implement the EC's obligations under Article 22? ***EC***

Q112. The Panel takes note that the Commission has not recognized any country under Article 12(3) of Regulation (EC) No. 2081/92 (EC response to Panel question No. 10, para. 22). Is the Commission obliged to recognize any country that satisfies the conditions set out in Article 12(1)? ***USA, AUS, EC***

---

[24] Appellate Body Report, *Japan – Alcohol*, p. 16.

Rsesponse:

45. It appears that the Commission is so obliged. Article 12(3) of the GI Regulation requires the Commission, upon request, to examine whether a third country satisfies the conditions set out in Article 12(1), *i.e.*, "[t]he Commission *shall* examine..." Where those conditions are satisfied, it appears that the Commission would have to make an affirmative decision to that effect, and that, following that decision, the registration procedures set out in Article 12a "shall apply."

Q113. The EC argues that there must be a substantive difference between two provisions governing the registration of GIs in order for one to entail less favourable treatment (EC second oral statement, para. 40). What is a "substantive" difference in this sense? Does the EC allege that there is a de minimis standard for less favourable treatment under TRIPS or GATT 1994? Is a simple difference in language insufficient to establish different treatment? ***EC***

Q114. With respect to registration applications under Article 12a(2) of Regulation (EC) No. 2081/92, a third country must verify that the requirements of the Regulation are satisfied before it transmits the application:

(a) to what extent is this designed to confirm the protection of the GI in its country of origin in accordance with Article 24.9 of the TRIPS Agreement, and to what extent does it respond to other objectives?

(b) is this additional to the requirement that a registration application transmitted to the Commission must be accompanied by a description of the matters set out in Article 12a(2)(a)?

(c) does the Commission also examine whether the application satisfies the conditions for protection under Article 12b(1)(a)? How is this examination different from the verification by the third country? ***EC***

Q115. With respect to objections under Article 12b(2)(a) of Regulation (EC) No. 2081/92, what is an objection that "comes from a WTO Member"? With respect to objections under Article 12d(1) of the Regulation, what is the meaning of a person who "is from a WTO Member"? Do they both refer to the place of residence or establishment of the person who wishes to object? Must objections under both provisions be sent to the country in which the person resides or is established? ***EC***

Q116. To the extent that certain responsibilities under Articles 12a and 12d(1) of Regulation (EC) No. 2081/92 are borne by non-EC WTO Members:

(a) how is the EC satisfied that every other WTO Member has the authorization to carry them out? (Please refer to Brazil's response to Panel third party question No. 1) (EC second oral statement, paras. 72-77).

(b) if other WTO Member governments lack authorization to carry them out, can they be carried out by the EC instead?

(c) to what extent does the EC itself accord no less favourable treatment to the nationals of other Members, and to what extent do other WTO Members share the implementation of that obligation? Can a Member delegate the implementation of WTO obligations to other Members with or without their prior consent?

(d) to what extent has the EC accorded certain treatment to the nationals of other WTO Members rather than to the governments of those other WTO Members? **EC**

Q117. The Panel takes note of the EC's response to Panel question No. 8 concerning the meaning of "third country" and seeks clarification as to whether "third country" as used in Article 12(2) of Regulation (EC) No. 2081/92, includes WTO Members. If so, why does the "without prejudice" clause in Article 12(1) form part of the context of Articles 12(1) and (3) but not Article 12(2)? If not, where does the Regulation cover identical GIs from the EC and other WTO Members? ***EC***

Q118. The Panel takes note that, in Australia's view, the identical GI labelling requirement would not be inconsistent with Article 2.1 of the TBT Agreement if it was applied to both EC and imported products according to date of registration, not origin. (Australia's response to Panel question No. 53). Even if Article 12(2) does not apply to EC products as well as imported products, does the Commission have the discretion to apply the same requirement according to the date of registration to EC products under Article 6(6) in order to ensure that the identical labelling requirement is applied to the later GI irrespective of the origin of the products? ***USA, AUS, EC***

Response:

46. There is nothing in Article 6(6) that would permit the Commission to import the requirement of Article 12(2) into Article 6(6). In Article 6(6), the requirement is that the use of registered homonymous name "be subject to there being a clear distinction in practice between the homonym registered subsequently and the name already on the register", subject to certain equitable requirements. Consequently, the proposed use of an EC-based homonym that gives rise to such a "clear distinction in practice"—and does so without using an indication of country of origin—would have to be registered. By contrast, a non-EC-based homonym that similarly gives rise to a "clear distinction in practice" without using an indication of country of origin, would, nevertheless, under Article 12(2), have to accompanied by a country of origin.

Q119. What is the difference, if any, in the meaning of the word "homonymous" as used in Article 6(6) of Regulation (EC) No. 2081/92 and "identical" as used in Article 12(2)? Why does the EC consider that homonyms are covered by the word "identical" in Article 12(2) (EC response to Panel question No. 43)? ***EC***

Q120. The Panel takes note of Australia's confirmation that the only less favourable treatment under the identical GIs labelling requirement is relabelling costs (Australia's response to Panel question No. 52). Would imported products have to be relabelled? Would existing marks of origin satisfy this requirement? What does "clearly and visibly indicated" mean? ***AUS, USA, EC***

Response:

47. The requirement of Article 12(2) that GIs for imported products, but not for domestic products, must be accompanied by a clear and visible indication of country of origin on the label is not simply a labeling cost issue. This requirement provides less favorable treatment to non-EC nationals and products in part because the non-EC GI, unlike the EC GI, is being burdened by an additional labeling requirement that is in the nature of a qualifier that detracts from the value of the GI—that is, in the case of two homonymous GIs, the EC-based GI will be known purely by that GI, while the non-EC product's homonymous GI will be qualified by a country of origin, implying that it is something other than the "true" GI. Whether the imported products have to be "relabelled" or not would, of course, depend on how the products were first labeled. The fact remains that this requirement constitutes an additional burden on foreign products and foreign GI holders that is not faced by EC products and GI holders. The United States does not believe that existing marks of origin requirements in the EC would satisfy this requirement. "Clearly and visibly indicated" means, in the US view, that the consumer is made aware that this GI has a stature that is different from EC-based GIs.

Q121. The Panel takes note that Australia refers to Article 6(6) of Regulation (EC) No. 2081/92 as the parallel provision to Article 12(2) (Australia's rebuttal, paras. 65-66). Does Australia wish the Panel to address alleged discrimination arising from differences between these two provisions? What is the less favourable treatment? ***AUS***

Q122. Please refer to the phrase "labelling requirements as they apply to a product" as used in the definition of "technical regulation" in Annex 1.1 of the TBT Agreement.

(a) *The EC argues that the "origin of a product is different from the product itself" (EC response to Panel question No. 50). However, as the EC acknowledges, the origin of a product may confer specific characteristics on it. This is consistent with the definitions of designation of origin and geographical indication in Article 2 of Regulation (EC) No. 2081/92, which provide that "the quality or characteristics of the product ... are essentially or exclusively due to a particular geographical environment ..." and that the product "possesses a specific quality, reputation or other characteristics attributable to that geographical origin ...". How then is the origin of a product entitled to bear a registered GI different from the product itself?* ***EC***

(b) *What is the meaning of the words "as they apply to" as used in this part of the definition? Do they refer to the application of labelling requirements to the characteristics of a product, or to the product itself, or both?* ***AUS, EC***

Q123. Does the requirement to display a country of origin on a label under Article 12(2) of Regulation (EC) No. 2081/92 constitute a mark of origin covered by Article IX of GATT 1994? ***AUS, EC, US***

Response:

48. Article 12(2) of the GI Regulation is not a general country of origin marking requirement: it is a specific labeling requirement imposed with respect to geographical indications which, as discussed above in response to question 120, burdens non-EC GIs to the disadvantage of non-EC products and persons. This requirement is above and beyond any other general country of origin marking requirement that may apply to all agricultural products and foodstuffs, and the EC has not argued that the requirements of Article 12(2) are met through any general country of origin marking requirements. Contrary to the EC's claims, there is nothing in Article IX of the GATT 1994 that exempts such a requirement imposed with respect to GIs from national treatment obligations under Article III of the GATT 1994.

Q124. The definition of "technical regulation" in Annex 1.1 of the TBT Agreement expressly encompasses "marking or labelling requirements as they apply to a product, process or production method". Are marks of origin and labels of origin covered by Article IX of GATT 1994 excluded from the scope of the TBT Agreement? Why did the negotiators not explicitly carve them out of its scope? Can a line be drawn between marks of origin that fall under the TBT Agreement and those that do not? What are the systemic consequences for marks of origin if they all fall within the scope of the TBT Agreement? ***AUS, EC, USA***

Response:

49. In this dispute, the United States is not challenging any EC general mark or label of origin requirements. Presumably the EC general mark or label of origin requirements would already apply separately to the types of products that may bear geographical indications, and the application of these requirements would be independent of the geographical indication. As a result, this dispute does not present the systemic questions posed in the Panel's question and the United States is not seeking that the Panel make findings with regard to this area. Rather, this dispute involves a specific requirement imposed on imported products in connection with the use of geographical indications. The specific requirement is an additional requirement for non-EC products to be able to use a geographical indication that does not apply to EC products. The additional requirement is all the more confusing since geographical indications by their very nature concern indicating the particular geographical origin of products. The EC requirements for labeling geographic indications are mandatory labeling requirements that come within the scope of the TBT Agreement.

Q125. To what extent would any less favourable treatment under Article 2.1 of the TBT Agreement have to be determined in light of the regulatory objective a Member is trying to pursue under Article 2.2? ***AUS, EC***

Q126. With respect to Article 10(3) of Regulation (EC) No. 2081/92:

(a) the first indent sets out certain requirements for designated inspection authorities and/or approved private bodies. Do these apply to all countries whose GIs are protected under the Regulation, including non-EC member States?

(b) the fifth indent appears to refer only to EC member States and third countries recognized pursuant to Article 12(3). Where does the Regulation refer to the applicable standard for WTO Members not recognized pursuant to Article 12(3), whose requirements private bodies must fulfil for approval purposes?

(c) the fifth indent refers to "[t]he equivalent standard or the applicable version of the equivalent standard". What equivalent standard has been established for GIs for areas located in WTO Members which do not satisfy the conditions of equivalence and reciprocity in Article 12(1)? What are the criteria for establishing that standard? Is it a matter of determining what is "equivalent" to standard EN 45011? Or is it a matter of determining what standard would fulfil the objectives of the Regulation in the light of each third country's own circumstances and conditions? ***EC***

Q127. Article 12a(2)(b) requires a declaration by a third country government that the structures provided for in Article 10 are established on its territory. Article 10(2) refers to inspection authorities and/or private bodies approved for that person by the Member State and Article 10(3) provides that where they outsource they continue to be responsible vis-à-vis the Member State for all inspections. What is the exact nature of the role that third country governments must play in the creation and maintenance of the inspection structures that are called for under Article 10? ***EC***

Q128. In the goods area, it is not uncommon that importing country governments designate, or require the accreditation of, the bodies which exporters may use in the territory of the exporting country in order to determine compliance with product requirements. To what extent does the EC actually give the US and Australia more, rather than less, flexibility by allowing the US and Australian governments themselves to designate the bodies that may participate in the inspection process? Can the US and Australia elaborate on the reasons for which they consider governmental involvement problematic? ***USA, AUS***

Response:

50. The starting point with respect to regulatory requirements for products in the goods area is generally that the imported product must undergo the same procedures to determine compliance with regulatory requirements in the importing country as do the domestic products of the importing country. Normally this will mean that the imported product will be inspected in the importing country. However, Article 6 of the TBT Agreement provides for the acceptance of the results of conformity assessment procedures in other countries. In keeping with Article 6, the importing country may, as the Panel suggests, accept the results of conformity assessment procedures conducted in the exporting country, and for this purpose may designate conformity assessment bodies in the territory of the exporting country, enter into mutual recognition agreements, or permit conformity assessment bodies in another Member to participate in their own conformity assessment procedures.

51. The EC GI Regulation, by contrast, does not make its inspection process available to imported products at all. This presents an immediate national treatment problem. And it does not compensate for this deficiency by designating bodies in the territory of the exporting country that can determine compliance with the EC's requirements. The requirements of the EC GI Regulation are, therefore, very different from those that are not uncommon in the goods area, and favor domestic products over foreign products.

52. In addition, there is a significant difference between imposing requirements on persons hoping to have their GIs registered and protected in the EC, on the one hand, and imposing requirements—including particular domestic inspection structures— on their sovereign governments, on the other. The former situation is anticipated with respect to the protection of intellectual property rights, which, as the TRIPS Agreement explicitly recognizes, are private rights. The United States has noted that both it and the EC, for instance, require that collective mark owners satisfy certain requirements in order to register their marks. The imposition of requirements on rightholders is also reflected in the nature of the national treatment and MFN obligations in the TRIPS Agreement and the Paris Convention, which require no less favorable treatment of *nationals* with regard to the protection of intellectual property rights, and not no less favorable treatment of *WTO Members*.

53. By contrast, imposing a requirement on sovereign *WTO Members* to put in place certain inspection structures dictated by the EC as a condition for their *nationals* to obtain protection for their GIs in the EC accords less favorable treatment to those nationals than to EC nationals. EC nationals have the direct means, provided under the GI Regulation itself, in light of the already established infrastructure of the European Union, to register and protect their GIs. Non-EC nationals do not, and can only achieve those means if their governments decide to adopt the EC-style inspection structures.[25]

54. Therefore, it also cannot be said, as between two systems:

(a) one in which the rightholder is itself in a position to satisfy the requirements of the GI Regulation directly; and

(b) one in which the US government is required to put in place certain inspection structures, approve inspection bodies within that structure, and have the inspection bodies be responsible to the US government for those inspections—all of which must satisfy the EC's idea of an appropriate inspection structure, as set out in Article 10 of the EC GI Regulation;

that the *latter* system affords the US government more "flexibility" than the former.

55. The same considerations apply with respect to the obligations under Article III of the GATT 1994, for the reasons elaborated in the US submissions and oral statements. If a WTO Member does not or cannot establish the EC-dictated inspection structures under Article 10 of the GI Regulation, a product from that WTO Member that has all the necessary product-specific characteristics attributable to origin required by the EC GI Regulation will nevertheless *not* be accorded GI status, while its corresponding EC "like" product *will* be accorded that status. This constitutes less favorable treatment of like products.

56. Two other points are worth noting. First, the EC is not allowing the US and Australian governments themselves to designate the bodies that may participate in the inspection process. This would be a different case if the EC imposed requirements on the rightholder, but then "allowed" the United States under the Regulation to facilitate the rightholder's ability to satisfy those requirements. But the GI Regulation does not "allow" the United States to do so; it requires that the United States establish certain inspection structures, to approve inspection bodies under that structure, and to remain responsible for those inspection bodies; and all of

---

[25] It is worth recalling once again that while the EC attempts to label the requirement that foreign sovereign countries establish EC-like inspection structures as a "product-specific requirement," this is inaccurate. The EC's requirement has nothing to do with the product and whether a particular product meets the EC substantive criteria for GI status. Instead, an inspection structure must be established by a foreign government if any product from that country is to be protected in the EC under the GI Regulation. This is a requirement of all products seeking protection in the EC. The EC attempts to confuse the distinction between a substantive product-specific requirement (*e.g.*, that an indication identify a good originating in a territory where a given quality, reputation or other characteristic is attributable to that territory) and this overarching procedural requirement by claiming that different inspection bodies might be used to determine compliance of different products with these product-specific requirements. It should be clear to all, however, that these inspection bodies are not the inspection structures themselves (rather, they make up a part of a structure), nor are the bodies a part of the product-specific requirements (rather, they merely determine whether such requirements are met).

these structures and bodies must conform to the EC's idea of what a good inspection structure is, as required by Article 10 of the EC GI Regulation.

57. Second, the EC is not permitting the United States to make its own determination as to the sufficiency of the inspection structures and the inspection bodies instead of the EC doing so. Setting aside the question of whether the United States' participation is optional (it is not), the EC is in no sense shifting the ability to designate appropriate inspection bodies from the EC to the United States. Although the EC GI Regulation requires the United States Government to establish the EC's inspection structures and to designate inspection bodies that satisfy the EC's requirements, this is only the threshold requirement for presenting an application under Article 12a of the GI Regulation. The EC then, under Article 12b of the Regulation, makes its own determination as to whether the request "contains all of the necessary elements".

58. In other words, having forced other sovereign WTO Members to themselves meet the requirements of the Article 10 inspection structures, the EC reserves to itself the power to decide that those inspection structures, including any inspection bodies approved by the WTO Member, are inadequate. The EC is in no sense, therefore, "allowing the US and Australian governments themselves to designate the bodies that may participate in the inspection process". By retaining ultimate authority to approve or reject another sovereign country's decisions, it is clear the EC is not providing flexibility, but is instead unilaterally attempting to subordinate sovereign countries to its authority with respect to GI protection. While the EC is able to do this with respect to the EC member States, it has no basis for doing this with other sovereign countries of the world. In this connection, the United States wonders if the EC would accept if the United States required the EC to adopt a particular inspection structure in order to have its GIs protected in the United States. An approach of "dueling inspection requirements" could very quickly cause any system for GIs to break down.

59. The United States refers to its oral statements at the second meeting and to its first and second submissions for further details concerning why requiring that other WTO Members establish particular inspection structures is not appropriate and is in no sense "necessary".

Q129. The Panel takes note of the US arguments on inspection structures (US rebuttal, paras. 46-48 and 89-93; US second oral statement paras. 21-27). What aspects of government involvement in inspection structures do you allege constitute less favourable treatment for foreign nationals? What aspects do you allege constitute less favourable treatment for imported products? Is there less favourable treatment where such structures already exist? ***USA***

Response:

60. Requiring that WTO Members establish particular inspection structures, approve inspection bodies, remain responsible for those bodies, and satisfy all of the requirements for those bodies and structures as set forth in Article 10 of the GI Regulation—all as a precondition for nationals to protect their GIs in the EC and for non-EC products to benefit from GI status—results in less favorable treatment for non-EC nationals and non-EC products.

61. It does not matter, from the perspective of the national treatment obligation, whether some countries may have EC-compliant inspection structures in place. The fact that some nationals and products may have overcome the significant extra barriers to entry put in place by the EC does not mean that those significant extra barriers no longer constitute "less favorable treatment" of non-EC nationals compared to EC nationals. Further, the fact that some countries can meet the EC's requirements means that their nationals and products are being granted advantages, favors, privileges, and immunities that are not being accorded to nationals and products of all WTO Members, which is a breach of MFN obligations.

Q130. Other than governmental involvement in the inspection structures, what aspects of the inspection structures do the US and Australia find problematic? ***USA, AUS***

Response:

62. Because of the nature of the obligation in Article 10 for inspection structures, it is not possible to separate the requirement that the government establish particular inspection systems from other aspects of the inspection systems. As the United States has said, however, it is appropriate for the EC to require assurances with respect to the integrity of the geographical indication, and both the EC and the US, among other WTO Members, have such requirements, for instance, with respect to collective marks.

Q131. Which EC Directives govern conformity assessment to EC technical regulations in the goods area? To what extent do those Directives require foreign governmental involvement in the designation/approval of conformity assessment bodies, when mutual recognition agreements in the conformity assessment area do not already exist? ***EC***

Q132. The Panel takes note of the EC's examples of flexibility in the design of inspections structures (EC rebuttal, para. 104 and Exhibit EC-48). Do these examples all relate to the nature of the inspecting authority? Who determines what constitutes an appropriate inspection for each product, and on the basis of what criteria? ***EC***

Q133. The Panel takes note that Australia argues that the product specification requirements set out in Article 4(2) of Regulation (EC) No. 2081/92 include "product characteristics", in particular subparagraphs (b) and (e). (Australia's rebuttal, paras.197 and 204) If the inspection structures are designed to ensure that the product specifications under Article 4 of the Regulation are fulfilled, how can they be a technical regulation and not a conformity assessment procedure? ***AUS, EC***

Q134. The Panel takes note of the EC's response to Panel question No. 61, in particular regarding the Panel's terms of reference. However, does the EC contest that a "conformity assessment procedure" within the meaning of the TBT Agreement assesses conformity with a "technical regulation" or "standard" within the meaning of the TBT Agreement? If not, then can the EC complete its analysis and explain whether the inspection structures of Regulation (EC) No. 2081/92 assess conformity with each individual product specification referred to in Article 4 of the Regulation for a registered name, and that those specifications therefore would constitute a "technical regulation" within the meaning of the TBT Agreement? ***EC***

Q135. The EC invokes Article XX(d) of GATT 1994 as a defence to the national treatment and MFN claims with respect to third country governments' verification and transmittal of applications, the identical GIs labelling requirement and inspection structures requirement. The EC alleges that these requirements are "necessary" to secure compliance with Regulation (EC) No. 2081/92 or to attain the legitimate objectives of the Regulation (EC rebuttal, paras.228-242, paras.263-265; EC second oral statement, paras.132-135):

(a) what is the "measure" necessary to secure compliance with laws or regulations within the meaning of Article XX(d) in each case? What are the laws and regulations with which each one secures compliance? Are the "measures" separate from the laws or regulations?

(b) can a measure that secures compliance with the "objectives" of a regulation, rather than a regulation itself, satisfy Article XX(d)?

(c) in what sense does each of these measures "secure compliance" with laws or regulations? Are they enforcement mechanisms?

(d) how are the laws and regulations with which each measure secures compliance not inconsistent with the GATT 1994? ***EC***

Q136. With respect to the issue whether the measures are necessary to secure compliance, and without prejudice to the WTO-consistency of any alternative measures:

(a) is the requirement that a third country government verify applications "necessary" to secure compliance in cases where an applicant itself is able to prove that a GI is protected in its country of origin, for example, by submitting an authenticated copy of a registration certificate?

(b) is the requirement that a third country government verify applications "necessary" to secure compliance in cases where the third country has no registration system for GIs or where determinations that a GI is protected under unfair competition laws are only made by the judicial branch of government after litigation?

(c) is the requirement that a third country government transmit applications "necessary" to secure compliance in cases where an applicant itself is able to send an application to the Commission?

(d) why does a third country government need to verify whether the person objecting is resident or established in the third country? Why does the Commission need consult with the third country if the statement of objection is admissible? (EC response to Panel question No. 34).

(e) is the identical GIs labelling requirement "necessary" to secure compliance in cases where there is already a clear distinction in practice in the usual presentation of the relevant products without clearly and visibly displaying the country of origin?

(f) is the requirement that a third country government designate inspection authorities "necessary" to secure compliance in cases where the Commission could designate them in third countries (see US second oral statement, para. 53)?

(g) is the requirement that a third country government declare that inspection structures are established on its territory "necessary" to secure compliance in cases where an applicant could arrange for independent inspection structures to be put in place in respect of a specific product (see US second oral statement, para. 53)?

(h) how is the requirement that a private inspection body continues to be responsible vis-à-vis a third country government "necessary" to secure compliance in cases where the EC could conduct its own inspections of foreign GIs (see US second oral statement, para. 53)?

(i) how is the requirement that the inspection authorities and/or private bodies have permanently at their disposal staff and resources necessary to ensure that all products bearing GIs comply with the product specifications in their registrations? (see Australia's rebuttal submission, para. 217). ***EC***

Q137. The Panel takes note of the EC's view that Article 14(3) of Regulation (EC) No. 2081/92 allows its authorities to refuse or invalidate the registration of any confusing GIs (EC first written submission, para. 286; EC rebuttal, para. 270). The complainants do not agree (US second written submission, para. 166 and Australia's second written submission, para. 109). The following examples have been referred to in this proceeding:

(a) BAYERISCHES BIER and BAVARIA and HØKER BAJER?
(b) BUDEJOVICKÉ PIVO and BUDWEISER?
(c) GORGONZOLA and CAMBOZOLA?

Could these GIs be used in accordance with their registrations in a way that results in a likelihood of confusion with the respective trademark(s)? ***USA, AUS, EC***

Response:

63. Before addressing this question, the United States would like to emphasize that the issue identified by the Panel in the question is only one aspect of the inability of 14(3) of the GI Regulation to substitute for the exclusive rights required by Article 16.1 of the TRIPS Agreement. As the Panel notes, the United States indeed disagrees that Article 14(3) allows the EC authorities to refuse or invalidate the registration of any confusing GIs.[26] But even if Article 14(3) does so allow, it still does not satisfy the requirements of TRIPS Article 16.1. While Article 16.1 grants *trademark owners* the right to prevent confusing *uses* of identical or similar GIs, Article 14(3) merely empowers *the EC authorities* to deny *registration* of GIs in some circumstances.[27]

64. The Panel asks whether three registered GIs "could ... be used in accordance with their registrations in a way that results in a likelihood of confusion with the respective trademarks." The short answer to the Panel's question is "yes." However, as the United States has emphasized in this dispute, neither the EC nor the owners of the trademarks cited by the Panel will necessarily know from a GI registration alone to what uses the GI will be put or whether those uses will result in a likelihood of confusion with a trademark. That question depends on what uses an individual GI rightholder employs, and the perceptions of consumers in a given territory with respect to those uses.

65. First, the EC has asserted that the registered name can only be used in accordance with the "specific labelling details" included in a product specification.[28] The United States does not have access to the product specifications for any of the three GIs cited by the Panel. In fact, despite repeated requests to the EC,[29] the United States has not been given a copy of the product specification for the GI included in item (b) to the Panel's question. (In any event, as the United States has demonstrated,[30] the "specific labelling details" included in product specifications do not necessarily offer much guidance regarding limits on uses of the GI.)

66. Second, the EC has clarified that registration of a GI gives an owner the right to use the GI in a "trademark-like manner."[31] In and of itself, nothing in the TRIPS Agreement prevents such a use. The United States has no objection to the use of a GI in a trademark-like fashion, featured prominently on a label, because GIs are valuable source identifiers and quality indicators—like trademarks. However, the TRIPS Agreement does not allow a GI to be used in a trademark-like fashion if prior valid trademark rights exist in that territory and consumers would likely be confused with respect to those trademarks. Further, the fact that a GI registration gives the owner the right to use the GI in a trademark-like fashion highlights that the scope of permitted uses is not as simply characterized as, in the EC's words, "use [of] the name registered as a geographical indication."[32] Indeed, to the contrary, it raises the specter of GIs being used in a way that could raise a likelihood of confusion with a trademark. The EC stated in its oral statement at the second meeting, at paragraph 184, that:

---

[26] *See* US Oral Statement at First Meeting, paras. 52-53; US Second Written Submission, paras. 142-166; US Opening Oral Statement at Second Meeting, paras. 84-86; US Closing Statement at Second Meeting, para. 19.

[27] *See* US Oral Statement at First Meeting, paras. 54-55; US Responses to Questions, para. 87; US Second Written Submission, paras. 130-141; US Opening Oral Statement at Second Meeting, paras. 77-83; US Closing Statement at Second Meeting, paras. 17-18.

[28] EC Second Written Submission, para. 300.

[29] *See* US Responses to Questions, para. 68.

[30] US Opening Oral Statement at Second Meeting, para. 78, and Exhibit US-77.

[31] EC Oral Statement at Second Meeting, para. 184.

[32] EC Second Written Submission, para. 301.

> EC consumers are familiar with the use of geographical indications for foodstuffs. They value them as much as trademarks when making their purchasing decisions, if not more, and expect them to be used in what the United States calls "trademark-like" fashion.

67. In this connection, the United States points out that the EC itself explains the trademark owner's possible rights in very qualified terms: "a court would be entitled to find, depending on the specific circumstances of each case, that the 'used sign' is different from the 'registered sign' and, therefore, not protected under Regulation 2081/92."[33] The "possibility" that a trademark owner may be able to show that the use is not "protected" by the EC GI Regulation is a far cry from his ability to prevent all confusing uses of similar signs, whether or not "protected", which is what Article 16.1 of the TRIPS Agreement requires.

68. Third, it appears that the registration of a term under the EC GI Regulation gives the rightholder a positive right to use that term as translated into other EC languages, and the EC has not provided any information or arguments to the contrary.[34] For example, as the United States has already noted,[35] in trademark infringement proceedings pending before the Swedish courts, a Czech brewer has argued that registration grants the right to use the registered GIs "Budejovické pivo," "Ceskobudejovické pivo," and "Budejovický mešt'anský var" in alleged translation, including as "Budweiser Budvar," "Budweis," and "Budbräu."[36] Similarly, the United States has noted that the root of the registered GI "Bayerisches Bier," when translated into English, is "Bavaria."[37] In some EC member States in which the name BUDWEISER, BUD or BAVARIA are registered as a prior valid trademark, use of the registered GIs as so translated might confuse consumers, and the trademark owners would need their TRIPS Article 16.1 rights to prevent those uses. Notably, in allowing the registration of "Bayerisches Bier" the Commission did not state that the GI could not be used in translation, which would have been an obvious response to the concern that use of the GI could result in confusion with the "Bavaria" trademark.

69. Fourth, whether the use of a registered GI results in a likelihood of confusion in the country in which an identical or similar trademark is registered will depend on the perceptions and response of consumers in that country. In some countries, consumer surveys could show that particular uses of the GIs listed in the Panel's question are confusing with respect to the trademarks listed in the Panel's question. Under Article 16.1, rather than seeking rejection or cancellation of a GI registration on an EC-wide basis, the owner of an identical or similar prior valid trademark registered in an EC member State is entitled to prevent particular "uses" of the GI that confuse consumers in that member State. In such a situation, rejection or cancellation of the GI registration on an EC-wide basis—the only option even arguably available under Article 14(3)—may be neither appropriate nor necessary.[38] Of course, rejection or cancellation of GIs that are *prime facie* confusing is also appropriate: the point is that rejection or cancellation of a GI registration cannot be the only option open to trademark

---

[33] EC Second Written Submission, para. 302.

[34] The EC has stated that a GI registration "covers only the term ... and not its translations to other languages." EC Second Written Submission, paras. 288, 293. Separately, the EC has stated that "the right holders of a geographical indication have a positive right to use the name registered as a geographical indication," and that "that right does not extend to other names or signs which have ... not been registered." EC Second Written Submission, para. 301. However, the EC has not joined these two concepts, and does not definitively state that the "positive right to use the name registered" excludes the right to use the name as it is translated (accurately, of course) into other EC languages.

[35] US Second Written Submission, para. 134.

[36] *See* Exhibit US-53 (paras. 4-6, Section 3.2). The United States reiterates that the GI included in item (b) of the Panel's question was registered via the Czech accession protocol to the EU. Validity of the registration was and is not subject to challenge based on Article 14(3) of the EC GI Regulation (even under the EC's reading of that provision). Even if the Panel accepts the EC's reading of Article 14(3), the provision does not serve as a substitute for TRIPS Article 16.1 rights with respect to GIs registered pursuant to accession protocols. See US Closing Statement at Second Meeting, para. 18.

[37] US Second Written Submission, para. 134.

[38] The United States also notes that the ability of a trademark owner to challenge a registration on the basis of Article 14(3) is extremely limited, and in many cases—such as for GIs registered pursuant to accession treaties or for "directly and individually concerned" trademark owners outside of the 2-month time period following registration of the GI—does not exist at all. *See* US Second Written Submission, paras. 138-140; US Opening Oral Statement at Second Meeting, para. 83; US Closing Statement at Second Meeting, para. 18.

owners, since Article 16.1 offers trademark owners the right to prevent confusing "uses" of identical or similar signs.

70. The United States notes two examples in which actual likelihood of confusion has been found between terms similar to those included in item (b) of the Panel's question. First, a South African court confirmed the decision of the Tribunal of the Registrar of Trademarks to refuse the registration of trademark applications for BUDEJOVICKÝ BUDVAR, following opposition brought by the owners of prior trademarks BUDWEISER and BUD. The decision explains that the average South African consumer would tend to abbreviate BUDEJOVICKÝ BUDVAR to the first syllable, BUD, since the whole mark is difficult to pronounce. At the same time, the decision held that BUDWEISER is often shortened to BUD. Consequently, the decision acknowledged a likelihood of confusion between BUDEJOVICKÝ BUDVAR and prior trademarks BUDWEISER and BUD.[39] Similarly, in Italy, in a decision that pre-dated the Czech Protocol of Accession to the EU and the registration of the GI listed in item (b) of the Panel's question, the Italian distributors of the defendant involved in the South Africa case was enjoined from using any designation with the words "Budweiser" or "Bud", because of rights associated with the complainant's two prior trademarks, BUDWEISER and BUD.[40]

71. In sum, the United States submits that there are myriad ways in which registered GIs can be used in a manner that raises a likelihood of confusion with a registered trademark, and that those uses will not necessarily be apparent from the registration itself.

Q138. What is the meaning of the phrase "[w]ith due regard to Community law" in Article 14(2) of Regulation (EC) No. 2081/92? Which aspects of "Community law" are relevant? What is the meaning of the phrase "shall not affect [Regulation No. 2081/92] ... and in particular Article 14 thereof" in Article 142 of Regulation (EC) No. 40/94 on the Community trade mark? ***EC***

Q139. The Panel takes note of the EC's view that the owner of a trademark may not prevent the right holders of a registered GI from using the registered name on the grounds that such name is confusing (EC second oral statement, para. 181). Please confirm that as long as a GI remains registered and is used in accordance with its registration, a trademark owner may not enforce his trademark rights against that use either under the Regulation on the Community trademark or the national trademark laws of the member States. What legal provisions prevent the trademark owners exercising their rights against persons using a GI in accordance with its registration? ***EC***

Q140. Under what provision of Regulation (EC) No. 2081/92 does the registration of a GI give the right holder a positive right to use the GI? How is that right delimited? Does it include translations of the protected term? For example, what uses do the registrations of the four cheese GIs referred to in Exhibit US-52 permit? How far does that positive right extend before it can be challenged under labelling and misleading advertising laws? ***EC***

Q141. What is the legal basis for an action to invalidate a registration under Regulation (EC) No. 2081/92 on the grounds of confusion with a trademark? Is there any basis for an action to invalidate a GI registration in Regulation (EC) No. 40/94 on the Community trade mark? ***EC***

---

[39] Judgment of the High Court of South Africa, Case No. A9/03, *Budweiser Budvar National Corporation v Anheuser-Busch Corporation*, 3 December 2003. Exhibit US-81. *See also* Decision of the Tribunal of the Registrar of Trademarks of South Africa, Case No. 96/17026-29, *Budweiser Budvar National Corporation v Anheuser-Busch Corporation*, 22 October 2002. Exhibit US-82.

[40] Order of the Court of Milan, First Civil Division, Docket No. 464/02. Exhibit US-83. The defendant's distributor consequently turned to the use of CZECHVAR in Italy.

Q142. The Panel takes note of the EC's view that the owner of a concurrent trademark could challenge a decision to register a GI inconsistently with Article 14(3) of Regulation (EC) No. 2081/92 even after the GI has been formally registered (EC response to Panel question No. 67; EC rebuttal paras.270 and 296). If a trademark owner applied to invalidate a GI registration under Article 14(3):

(a) is this a precondition to a trademark infringement action?

(b) is there any time-limit on such an invalidation action?

(c) is this possibility available where the GI is registered pursuant to an Act of Accession or otherwise without the normal application procedures?

(d) how would such an application for invalidation relate to the cancellation procedure in Article 11a of the Regulation? Are the grounds for cancellation in Article 11a exhaustive? ***EC***

Q143. The Panel takes note that the Council Decision to register BAYERISCHES BIER as a GI states that "[i]n view of the facts and information available, it was, however, considered that registration of [that name] was not liable to mislead the consumer as to the true identity of the product" (Exhibit EC-9, para. (3), cited in EC rebuttal, para. 287). Please detail what were the facts and information to which the Council referred in that Decision and how they were evaluated so that the Panel can see how the criteria in Article 14(3) were applied in that case. ***EC***

Q144. The Panel takes note that Commission Regulation (EC) No. 1107/96 (set out in Exhibit COMP-3a), which effected the registration of many individual GIs, recites Article 14(2) and (3) of Regulation (EC) No. 2081/92. How were Article 14(2) and (3) taken into account in the registration of those GIs? ***EC***

Q145. Please refer to Article 24.5 of the TRIPS Agreement and comment on the suggestion that:

(a) the phrase "shall not prejudice eligibility for or the validity of the registration of a trademark" merely creates an exception to the obligations in Articles 22.3 and 23.2 to refuse or invalidate the registration of trademarks; and

(b) the phrase "shall not prejudice ... the right to use a trademark" merely creates an exception to the obligations in Articles 22.2 and 23.1 to provide the legal means to prevent certain uses and does not create any positive right. ***USA, AUS, EC***

Response:

72. The United States agrees with the proposition that Article 24.5 is an exception to the provisions of Part II, Section 3 of the TRIPS Agreement. As such, Article 24.5 preserves certain trademark rights *vis-à-vis* geographical indications. The two "suggestions" appear to be consistent with this understanding.[41]

73. With respect to suggestion (a), it appears that the reference in Article 24.5 to the "eligibility for or the validity of the registration of a trademark" logically includes an exception to the obligations under Articles 22.3

[41] The United States notes that even if this interpretation of Article 24.5 would seem to protect trademarks that are misleading as to geographic origin, this effect is mitigated by certain limitations in Article 24.5. For instance, there is a requirement that trademarks subject to the Article 24.5 exception must be applied for, registered, or acquired through use "in good faith." Further, the exception in Article 24.5 prohibits prejudicing certain trademarks "on the basis that such a trademark is identical with, or similar to, a geographical indication." For purposes of this dispute, in any event, the United States' arguments are directed at those TRIPS Article 16.1 rights associated with valid trademarks, and not with the effect of Regulation 2081/92 on trademarks that are misleading as to geographic origin. *See* US First Written Submission, para. 135 ("The United States is not arguing that trademarks that 'mislead the public as to the true place of origin' of the underlying goods in a given territory must be registered and provided Article 16.1 rights in that territory.").

and 23.2 to invalidate or refuse registration of certain trademarks. Indeed, Articles 22.3 and 23.2 are the only provisions of the GI section that speak directly to refusal of registration or invalidation of trademarks.[42] Suggestion (a) demonstrates that Article 24.5 has no effect on the exclusive rights granted to valid trademarks (because Articles 22.3 and 23.2 likewise have no effect on the exclusive rights granted to *valid* trademarks) and is therefore fully consistent with the US views in this dispute.

74. In addition, however, as argued previously by the United States, the prohibition on "prejudic[ing] eligibility for or the validity of the registration of a trademark" is not limited to situations where the choice is simply between registration, on the one hand, and total loss (or absence) of registration, on the other. Otherwise, the word "prejudice" would not be given meaning. In fact, the inclusion of the word "prejudice" suggests that the phrase "prejudice eligibility for or the validity of the registration of a trademark" protects trademarks against something more than immediate invalidation or refusal. As previously explained by the United States, this phrase further emphasizes that owners of trademarks covered by Article 24.5 are accorded the Article 16.1 right to prevent all others from confusing uses, given that the legal authority accorded by trademark registration is defined by Article 16.1, and that denial of the right to prevent all confusing uses could diminish the ability of the trademark owner to distinguish his goods, within the meaning of Article 15.1.[43] The importance of the word "prejudice" is further confirmed by the fact that it was specifically added by the drafters after the Brussels draft.[44] Thus, while the United States agrees that "prejudice eligibility for or the validity of the registration of a trademark" provides an exception to the obligations under Articles 22.3 and 23.2, it may also protect trademarks within its scope from implementation of the GI section that would diminish a trademark owner's Article 16.1 rights.

75. Similarly, as for suggestion (b), the United States agrees that the phrase "shall not prejudice ... the right to use a trademark" in Article 24.5 creates an exception to the obligations in the GI section, including those in Articles 22.2 and 23.1 to prevent certain uses, and does not create any positive rights. Again, suggestion (b) also demonstrates that Article 24.5 has no effect on the exclusive rights granted to valid trademarks (because Articles 22.2 and 23.1 likewise have no effect on the exclusive rights granted to valid trademarks), and is fully consistent with the US views in this dispute.

76. But, given that the core use and value of a trademark comes from the Article 16.1 exclusive right to prevent all others from confusing uses, the United States has explained that this phrase also provides an exception to any implementation of the GI section that diminishes Article 16.1 protection for the covered trademarks.[45] This follows from the ordinary meaning of "prejudice ... the right to use a trademark", which refers to the harm or damage to the permitted or forbidden activity associated with the application of a trademark to its purpose.[46] Based on the context of Articles 15.1 and 16.1 of the TRIPS Agreement, this purpose is to allow a trademark's owner to distinguish his goods from the goods of all others, which requires that trademark registrations accord their owners the right to prevent all others from uses that would cause a likelihood of confusion.[47]

77. Significantly, these suggested readings of Article 24.5 contradict the EC's position that, by negative implication, Article 24.5 gives permission to Members to strip covered trademarks of their Article 16.1 rights.[48]

---

[42] However, the United States is not able to conclude that Article 24.5 is "merely" or "only" an exception to these Articles, as the text of Article 24.5 refers to measures adopted to implement the GI section, and not only to specific articles.

[43] US Second Written Submission, paras. 173-174.

[44] *See* US Responses to Panel Questions, paras. 99, 104; US Oral Statement at First Meeting, paras. 64-65.

[45] *See* US Second Written Submission, para. 176.

[46] US Second Written Submission, para. 176.

[47] *Id.*

[48] *See, e.g.,* the EC summation of its Article 24.5 argument in its oral statement at paragraph 199:

If the drafters deemed necessary to specify in Article 24.5 that the implementation of protection for geographical indications shall not prejudice the most basic right of the owner of a registered trademark ("the right to use it"), but not the right to exclude others from using it, *the clear implication* is that they did not intend to prevent Members from limiting the exercise of the latter right in order to allow the use of a geographical indication in co-existence with a grandfathered trademark. (Emphasis added.)

Q146. The Panel takes note of the respective views of the EC and US on simultaneous exercise of rights with respect to use (EC rebuttal, para. 309 and US rebuttal, para. 119). Without prejudice to the EC's views on Article 24.5, would there be any practical conflict between the rights to prevent certain uses conferred under Articles 16.1 and 22.2 of TRIPS? Under what circumstances is it impossible for, simultaneously:

(a) a trademark owner to prevent uses of a sign where such use would result in a likelihood of confusion (under Article 16.1), and

(b) a right holder in a GI to prevent uses of an indication that are misleading with respect to the geographical origin of the product or which constitute unfair competition (under Article 22.2) except on the basis that the trademark is identical with, or similar to, the GI (under Article 24.5)? ***USA, AUS, EC***

Response:

78. The EC posits that there is a "conflict" between TRIPS Articles 16.1 and 22.2 because "[t]he simultaneous exercise" of a trademark that is misleading with respect to origin, and an identical or similar GI that raises a likelihood of confusion with respect to the trademark, "would lead to a situation where neither the trademark owner nor the right holders of the geographical indication could use the sign in question."[49]

79. This is incorrect. As the United States has already noted,[50] the EC is confusing a "conflict" that may indeed occur between an individual trademark and an individual GI, and a "conflict" that does not in any way occur between the *obligations placed on the EC* by Articles 16.1 and 22. As the United States explained, it is in no way "impossible" for the EC to "simultaneous[ly] compl[y]" with the obligations in Articles 16.1 and 22;[51] there is, therefore, no "conflict" between those obligations.

80. The Panel's question appears to be directed at the situation presented by a "conflict" between an individual trademark and an individual GI. The TRIPS Agreement sets out rules specifying the way in which this "conflict" would be resolved. As the United States has explained,[52] if a trademark misleads consumers as to the origin of goods, as the Panel posits in part (b) of its question, the TRIPS Agreement and the Paris Convention provide that it should not be registered.[53] The trademark will not, therefore, be accorded the right to prevent the confusing uses of a similar or identical GI, as the Panel posits in part (a) of its question, since it will not be registered. As the United States has also explained,[54] if such a trademark is nonetheless registered, it is subject to invalidation.[55] In other words, the facts envisioned by the Panel in part (b) of its question would serve as a defense to the infringement claim brought by the trademark owner in part (a) of the question.

81. How a conflict between particular rightholders is resolved will depend on the particular facts of the case and on the application of municipal law in the WTO Member in which the case is brought. In the view of the United States, given the different standards for trademark rights and GI rights, it is unlikely that there would be an irresolvable conflict between those two rightholders. But this Panel is not called upon to resolve all such disputes prospectively in this proceeding. That is a matter for the decision-makers in the WTO Member before which the particular dispute is brought. What is important here is that the municipal law in that WTO Member is consistent with that Member's TRIPS obligations. Those obligations include providing Article 16.1 TRIPS

[49] EC Second Written Submission, para. 309.

[50] US Opening Oral Statement at Second Meeting, paras. 71-72.

[51] *See* Panel Report, *Turkey – Textiles*, para. 9.92. *See also* Panel Report, *Indonesia – Autos*, para. 14.28.

[52] US Oral Statement at First Meeting, para. 42; US Second Written Submission, para. 120.

[53] TRIPS Articles 22.3, 15.1, and 15.2; Paris Convention Articles 9, 10, 10*bis* and 6*quinquies*B.

[54] *See* US First Written Submission, para. 135; US Oral Statement at First Meeting, para. 42; US Responses to Questions, para. 114; US Second Written Submission, paras. 119-121; US Opening Oral Statement at Second Meeting, para. 71.

[55] TRIPS Articles 22.3, 15.1 and 15.2; Paris Convention Articles 9, 10, 10*bis,* and 6*quinquies*B.

Agreement rights to trademark owners in situations encompassed by the EC GI Regulation, where signs used as a GI result in a likelihood of confusion with a pre-existing trademark.

Q147. Article 24.5 as finally agreed contains the phrase "measures adopted to implement this Section shall not prejudice eligibility for or the validity of the registration of a trademark, or the right to use a trademark". Please comment on the suggestion that during the Uruguay Round negotiations there was a disagreement as to whether the predecessor to this provision in the Brussels Draft should be made permissive rather than mandatory, and that the choice of this language was part of an effort to reach agreement on the issue of the mandatory / permissive nature of the provision. ***USA, AUS, EC***

Response:

82. As an initial matter, the United States recalls that Article 24.5 should be interpreted in good faith in accordance with the ordinary meaning of its terms, in their context and in the light of the object and purpose of the TRIPS Agreement. Customary rules of interpretation provide a very limited role for negotiating history, and for good reason. For example, in the case of the TRIPS Agreement, as the Panel is undoubtedly aware, there is no comprehensive, official negotiating history. There were numerous discussions, drafts, and memoranda between and among various WTO Members, both before and after the Brussels Ministerial in late 1990, many unrecorded or for which there are no agreed minutes or official documents. Accordingly, many would not fairly be considered useful as "negotiating history." Nevertheless, the evolution of the drafts does suggest that there were two opposing views about whether what is currently Article 24.5 should allow Members, at their discretion, to protect certain trademarks vis-à-vis geographical indications or should require Members to protect those trademarks. As the United States has explained, the evolution of Article 24.5 revealed a progression in favor of stronger and clearer protection for covered trademarks. In addition to the change from a permissive to a mandatory provision, the United States has also explained that, as negotiations progressed, the term "prejudice" was introduced, and the specific mention of the "right to use" a trademark was also integrated.[56] All of these modifications served to increase the protection accorded to trademarks pursuant to Article 24.5.

83. It follows that the negotiating history confirms the interpretation that Article 24.5 does not diminish the rights accorded trademarks, as the EC alleges, but that it instead provides a shield for covered trademarks that would otherwise be affected by implementation of the GI section. This history provides no support for the EC's argument that Article 24.5, by negative implication, authorizes Members to strip covered trademarks of their Article 16.1 rights.[57]

84. In addition, the predecessor to Article 24.5 in the Brussels draft stated that "A Party *shall not* take action to refuse or invalidate [covered trademarks.]"[58] This provision, however, was entirely in brackets, indicating a lack of agreement with respect to that obligation, which provided for mandatory protection of covered trademarks. What emerged from the discussions among the Members subsequent to the Brussels Ministerial was a text that retained the mandatory nature of the protection of covered trademarks, but instead of the broad formulation— "A Party shall not"—the final text states that "measures adopted to implement [the GI] Section shall not prejudice ...", clarifying that this obligation was directed, not at any and all measures of a Party, but at those adopted to implement the GI Section of the TRIPS Agreement. Thus, the suggestion that the final language resolved a difference among the Members as to the mandatory or discretionary nature of the obligation in Article 24.5 is not inconsistent with how Article 24.5 appears to have evolved.

---

[56] *See* US Responses to Panel Question 76, paras. 102-105.

[57] *See, e.g.*, the EC summation of its Article 24.5 argument in its oral statement at the second Panel meeting, at paragraph 199:

If the drafters deemed necessary to specify in Article 24.5 that the implementation of protection for geographical indications shall not prejudice the most basic right of the owner of a registered trademark ("the right to use it"), but not the right to exclude others from using it, *the clear implication* is that they did not intend to prevent Members from limiting the exercise of the latter right in order to allow the use of a geographical indication in co-existence with a grandfathered trademark. (Emphasis added.)

[58] *See* Gervais, The TRIPS Agreement, Drafting History and Analysis (Second Edition). Sweet and Maxwell, London, 2003, p. 133 (emphasis added).

Q148. What is the meaning of the phrase "where such use would result in a likelihood of confusion" as used in Article 16.1 of the TRIPS Agreement? How should such likelihood of confusion be assessed? How does the assessment differ from that under Article 14(3) of Regulation (EC) No. 2081/92? In particular:

(a) how should the likelihood of confusion, and the liability to mislead the consumer, be assessed with respect to a mark to which rights have not been acquired on the basis of use?

(b) as of what time should the likelihood of confusion, and the liability to mislead the consumer, be assessed?

(c) are the trademark's reputation and renown and the length of time it has been used necessarily relevant to both analyses? ***USA, AUS, EC***

Response:

(a) how should the likelihood of confusion, and the liability to mislead the consumer, be assessed with respect to a mark to which rights have not been acquired on the basis of use?

85. The ordinary meaning of the term "confusion," from Article 16.1, includes "failure to distinguish."[59] The ordinary meaning of "likelihood" includes "that looks as if it would happen, be realized or prove to be what is alleged or suggested; probable; to be reasonably expected."[60] Thus, under the ordinary meaning of Article 16.1, a "likelihood of confusion" arises where it is reasonably expected that a trademark owner will no longer be able to distinguish his goods from identical or similar goods labeled with an identical or similar sign.

86. To further inform this interpretation, the United States discusses the factors commonly used in EC law and member State jurisprudence to assess likelihood of confusion, in response to question 148(c), below. As the Panel is aware, the "likelihood of confusion" standard was applied by countries in national law well in advance of the negotiation and conclusion of the TRIPS Agreement.

87. The United States is not aware of any judicial interpretation of the "liable to mislead" standard in Article 14(3). Article 14(3) has been applied by the EC administering authorities only once. In that case, the Council simply determined that "[i]n view of the facts and information available, it was ... considered that registration of the name 'Bayerisches Bier' was not liable to mislead the consumer as to the true identity of the product."[61] The Council's decision offers no insights into the factual elements informing its application of the "liable to mislead" standard in Article 14(3).

88. EC trademark law suggests that the "likelihood of confusion" standard is different from the "liable to mislead" standard. The EC Trademark Regulation and Trademark Directive differentiate between the two standards. Article 50.1(c) of the Trademark Regulation and Article 12.2(b) of the Trademark Directive provide for revocation of a trademark where it is "liable to mislead the public, particularly as to ... geographical origin ..."[62] In contrast, Article 9.1(b) of the Trademark Regulation and Article 5.1(b) of the Trademark Directive grant trademark owners the exclusive right to prevent use of a similar or identical sign for similar or identical goods where "there exists a likelihood of confusion on the part of the public."[63] Accepting that "liable to mislead" in Article 14(3) actually means "likelihood of confusion" would require the Panel to overlook the objective fact that those standards are expressly differentiated in EC trademark law. In addition, as discussed further below in response to question 149, use of the term "mislead" in the GI Regulation itself indicates that that term has a different meaning from "confusion" in the sense of Article 16.1.

---

59 *New Shorter Oxford English Dictionary* (Fourth Ed. 1993), pg. 478. Exhibit US-84.

60 *New Shorter Oxford English Dictionary* (Fourth Ed. 1993), pg. 1588. Exhibit US-84.

61 Council Regulation (EC) No 1347/2001, para. 3. Exhibit EC-9.

62 Regulation No 40/94, Article 50.1(c), Exhibit COMP-7; Directive 89/104/EEC, Article 12.2(b), Exhibit COMP-6.

63 Regulation No 40/94, Article 9.1(b), Exhibit COMP-7; Directive 89/104/EEC, Article 5.1(b), Exhibit COMP-6.

(b) as of what time should the likelihood of confusion, and the liability to mislead the consumer, be assessed?

89. Likelihood of confusion should be assessed at the time the allegedly confusing use arises. Article 16.1 enables a trademark owner to prevent particular "uses" that are confusing. As a matter of context, therefore, whether likelihood of confusion arises should be based on consumers' perceptions and response at the time the allegedly confusing use arises. While the United States does not object to the opportunity to assess whether a GI, at the time of application for registration, likely confuses consumers within a country in which the trademark is registered, TRIPS Article 16.1 requires that the trademark owner also be permitted to prevent consumer confusion that arises because of and at the time of particular uses of the GI.

90. Article 14(3) of the EC GI Regulation is relevant to the EC authorities' decision to register a GI. Thus, it appears to the United States that the determination whether a GI is misleading with respect to a trademark that enjoys reputation, renown and length of use would be made at the time of application to register the GI. In the "Bayerisches Bier" case—the only time Article 14(3) has been applied—the determination that the GI was not misleading with respect to prior valid registered trademarks was evidently made by the Council at the time of application for registration of the GI.

(c) are the trademark's reputation and renown and the length of time it has been used necessarily relevant to both analyses?

91. In this dispute, the EC asserts that the references to reputation, renown and use are included in Article 14(3) merely because they are factors used to judge whether a GI raises a likelihood of confusion with respect to a prior registered trademark. The EC notes that in EC and other Members' laws, reputation, renown and length of use are relevant to the determination of likelihood of confusion.[64] While reputation, renown and length of use might indeed be considered to determine whether a likelihood of confusion arises in certain cases, these factors are often, in many other cases, irrelevant to whether there is a likelihood of confusion under Article 16.1, as illustrated by the many EC cases described further below.[65]

92. In contrast, Article 14(3), by its own terms, expressly requires that trademarks enjoy reputation, renown and use to block registration of a GI. In other words, Article 14(3) *requires* that these elements be present and considered in determining whether to refuse a GI Registration—under Article 14(3), they are always relevant and, in fact, necessary. The Commission's Guide to Regulation 2081/92 confirms this fact. The Guide emphasizes that the "general rule" is that "the registration of a conflicting trademark does not prevent registration of the geographical name."[66] According to the Commission, departure from this general rule to deny registration of a GI occurs "only in one circumstance"—where the express terms of Article 14(3) have been met, or in other words, when the trademark satisfies the three prerequisites of reputation, renown and length of use.[67] "In all other cases," the EC authorities revert to the "general rule" and register the GI, "notwithstanding the existence of the registered trademark."[68]

---

[64] EC Oral Statement at Second Meeting, paras. 166-169.

[65] Moreover, even without reviewing any EC cases, it should be evident that Article 16.1 requires a presumption of "likelihood of confusion," without regard to reputation, renown, or length of time used, in the case of identical signs used for identical goods.

[66] Guide to Community Regulations, "Protection of Geographical Indications, Designations of Origin and Certificates of Specific Character for Agricultural Products and Foodstuffs" (Working Document of the Commission Services issued by the European Commission Directorate-General for Agriculture, August 2004), pg. 24. Exhibit EC-64; Guide to Community Regulations, "Protection of Geographical Indications, Designations of Origin and Certificates of Specific Character for Agricultural Products and Foodstuffs" (Working Document of the Commission Services issued by the European Commission Directorate-General for Agriculture, March 2004), pg. 23. Exhibit US-24. The United States notes that while the Commission made certain self-serving amendments, during the course of these proceedings, to the description of Article 12(1) ultimately included in the August 2004 version of the Guide, it made no amendments to the description of Article 14(3), which remains unchanged from the March 2004 version of the Guide.

[67] Guide to Community Regulations, August 2004, pg. 24. Exhibit EC-64.

[68] Guide to Community Regulations, August 2004, pg. 24. Exhibit EC-64.

93. In other words, establishing reputation, renown and use are not merely part of the EC authorities' inquiry, under Article 14(3), into whether the GI raises a likelihood of confusion with respect to a prior, identical or similar trademark. Rather, for a prior valid registered trademark to block registration of an identical or similar GI, the trademark *must* enjoy reputation, renown and use, because Article 14(3) requires that a decision on GI registration be made "in the light of" these factors. According to the Commission, this is the "one circumstance" in which the GI registration will be denied.[69]

94. Limiting Article 16.1 rights to owners of those trademarks that satisfy the requirements of reputation, renown and length of use may be appropriate in one context—when determining whether to extend the heightened scope of protection associated with well-known trademarks. Well-known trademarks are protected against certain uses of identical or similar signs, even when used on *dissimilar* goods or services.[70]

95. For a trademark to be considered "well-known" and accorded this heightened protection, it must satisfy the following criteria, under TRIPS Article 16.2: "knowledge of the trademark" by the public, including knowledge "obtained as a result of the promotion of the trademark."

96. The ordinary meaning of these terms is instructive. The ordinary meaning of the term "well-known" is "known to many, widely or generally known, famous," and "intimately or thoroughly known."[71] The elements of "fame," as well as "wide" and "general" knowledge, accord well with the EC's reference to "reputation and renown," in Article 14(3). Moreover, the ordinary meaning of the term "knowledge," as used in TRIPS Article 16.2, is, among other things, "familiarity gained by experience."[72] The "familiarity" part of this definition accords with the "reputation and renown" criteria in Article 14(3). Additionally, familiarity with a trademark is most likely "gained by experience" if the trademark is actually used, which corresponds to the "length of use" requirement in Article 14(3).

97. Thus, while it may be appropriate to limit the heightened protection for well-known trademarks to those trademarks that enjoy reputation, renown and use, a trademark need not satisfy those prerequisites to secure the rights guaranteed by TRIPS Article 16.1.[73]

98. Outside the context of well-known trademarks, this is certainly the case in EC and member State law. EC[74] and member State[75] [76] courts, as well as OHIM,[77] routinely find a likelihood of confusion *without the*

---

[69] Guide to Community Regulations, August 2004, pg. 24. Exhibit EC-64.

[70] *See* TRIPS Articles 16.2, 16.3.

[71] *New Shorter Oxford English Dictionary* (Fourth Ed. 1993), pg. 3655. Exhibit US-84.

[72] *New Shorter Oxford English Dictionary* (Fourth Ed. 1993), pg. 1503. Exhibit US-57.

[73] The United States takes no position on whether Article 14(3) of the EC GI Regulation is consistent with TRIPS Articles 16.2 and 16.3, or Article 6*bis* of the Paris Convention. For the purposes of this dispute, the United States simply observes that Article 14(3) evokes well-established standards for well-known trademarks.

[74] *See, e.g.*, Case T-129/01, *Budmen/Bud*, 3 July 2003, paras. 56, 42-59 (Owner of prior trademark BUD opposed registration of BUDMEN for identical goods (clothing and footwear). CFI specifically found that BUD did not enjoy reputation for the goods at issue, but nonetheless concluded that a likelihood of confusion arose, based principally on the fact that the public might believe that products designated with BUDMEN formed part of a new range of products marketed by the owner of BUD.); Case T-10/03, *Conforflex/Flex*, 18 February 2004, paras. 52, 40-62 (Owner of prior trademark FLEX opposed registration of CONFORFLEX for identical goods (furniture). CFI rejected evidence submitted by the owner of FLEX regarding reputation of prior trademark, but nonetheless concluded that a likelihood of confusion arose, due to the identity of the goods and the close conceptual similarity of the signs at issue.); Case T-99/01, *Mystery/Mixery*, 15 January 2003, paras. 35, 36-48 (Owner of prior trademark MIXERY unable to establish enhanced distinctiveness based on use of its trademark, or reputation, but CFI nonetheless upheld OHIM's decision to deny registration of MYSTERY, based upon a likelihood of confusion due to the similarity of both the signs and the goods (beer and beverages containing beer).); Case T-6/01, *Matratzen Markt* Concord/Matratzen, 23 October 2002, paras. 28-48 (CFI found likelihood of confusion, without treating the question of reputation or use of prior trademark MATRATZEN, when reviewing OHIM's decision to deny registration of MATRATZEN MARKT CONCORD. CFI based its decision on the similarity of the goods (textiles and furniture), and the similarity of the signs, in particular inclusion of the element "Matratzen" in both signs.); Case T-104/01, *Fifties/Miss Fifties*, 23 October 2002, paras. 30-50 (CFI found likelihood of confusion, without any discussion of reputation or use of prior trademark MISS FIFTIES, when reviewing OHIM's decision to deny registration of FIFTIES. CFI's decision was based solely on the similarity of both the goods (clothing) and the signs at issue.). CFI decisions are available, using the case number as a search term, at http://europa.eu.int/jurisp/cgi-bin/form.pl?lang=en.

[75] *See* Judgment of the Court of Appeals of Munich, *ArtDeco vs Deco Art*, 6 June 2002, GRUR-RR 2003, pgs. 169-170 (Court considered registration of DECOART for perfumes and cosmetics as confusingly similar to prior trademark ARTDECO for similar and identical goods. Court found that the two trademarks ARTDECO and DECOART were confusingly similar, because the meaning/concept of the two marks was similar, but expressly left open question whether prior mark enjoyed a wider scope of protection because of prior use, basing its decision solely on the assumption that this was not the case, and that prior mark was of average distinctiveness only.) (English excerpt and German version at Exhibit US-85); Judgment of the Federal Patent Court, *Aproma vs Artproma*, 2 October 2002 as published in PAVIS PROMA database (Court considered two trademarks APROMA and ARTPROMA as confusingly similar, since the services at issue (advertising, marketing and consultancy services) were identical or at least very similar, and the sound of the two marks was similar. Court held that prior trademark was of only average distinctiveness, since it had neither been shown that it enjoyed a wider scope of protection due to widespread prior use, nor that distinctiveness had been weakened, either through third party use of similar marks, or because the designation was descriptive.) (English excerpt and German version at Exhibit US-86); Judgment of the Federal Patent Court, *7hils vs. Stihl*, 1 August 2000 as published in PAVIS PROMA database (Court considered use of trademark 7HILS for identical or closely similar goods (motor and chain saws, and agricultural machines) to be confusingly similar to prior trademark STIHL, given a high degree of graphic and phonetic similarity between the signs. Court expressly held that likelihood of confusion existed not only with respect to goods for which prior mark had acquired a reputation, *but also with respect to those goods for which reputation was not established.*) (English excerpt and German version at Exhibit US-87); Judgment of the Court of Appeals of Cologne, *Fiorini vs Fioccini*, 13 September 2002, GRUR-RR 2003, pg. 71 et seq., at pg. 72 (Court considered trademark FIOCCINI to be confusingly similar to prior trademark FIORINI, based exclusively on a comparison of the signs at issue and the goods at issue. Court held that the goods (pasta) were identical, and that to exclude a likelihood of confusion in such a situation, the two signs would have to have been, but were not, considerably different. Court dealt expressly with the question whether prior trademark, FIORINI, enjoyed a wider scope of protection because of alleged widespread prior use, but determined that an extended scope of protection was unwarranted, since reputation and extended prior use had not been properly presented to the court, let alone proven.) (English excerpt and German version at Exhibit US-88); Judgment of the Federal Patent Court, *AGCO vs. ARCO*, 23 July 2002, as published in PAVIS PROMA database (Court found that high degree of phonetic similarity between trademark AGCO and prior trademark ARCO raised a likelihood of confusion with respect to use on similar goods (toys), simply assuming that prior trademark had ordinary distinctiveness, and without addressing reputation or use.) (English excerpt and German version at Exhibit US-89); Judgment of the Hamburg Court of Appeals, *Cellofit vs Cellvit*, 26 June 2003, GRUR-RR 2004, pgs. 5-7 (Court held that use of trademark CELLVIT on identical or closely similar goods (pharmaceutical products) raised a likelihood of confusion with respect to prior trademark CELLOFIT (although a likelihood of confusion was not found with respect to use of CELLVIT on less similar goods such as adhesive tape, beauty care products and cosmetics), without addressing reputation or use of the prior trademark, and with finding that prior trademark was of regular to weak distinctiveness.) (English excerpt and German version at Exhibit US-90); Judgment of the Cologne Court of Appeals, *Team is Money vs T-is Money*, 7 June 2002, GRUR-RR 2002, pgs. 290-293 (Court found that use of term "T-is money" raised a likelihood of confusion with respect to prior trademark TEAM IS MONEY, since both signs were used for identical services (telecommunications), both were pronounced similarly, and both alluded to slogan "time is money." Reputation and use of prior trademark played no part in court's decision.) (English excerpt and German version at Exhibit US-91); Judgment of the German Federal Supreme Court, *Flâminger*, 28 May 1998, GRUR 1998, pgs. 930-932 (Owner of prior trademark sought to enjoin use of confusingly similar sign featuring an allegedly geographically descriptive term. Court upheld decision to block registration of the confusingly similar term FLÄMINGER as part of a word/device mark, on the basis that it was confusingly similar to prior trademark FÄLINGER, even though prior trademark enjoyed no reputation, no renown and no lengthy prior use, and despite the fact that the word FLÄMINGER referred to the Eastern German region of Fläming.) (English excerpt and German version at Exhibit US-92);

trademark owner having established that the trademark enjoys reputation, renown or use. In fact, it is fair to say that in most standard cases arising in EC and member State courts, reputation, renown and use are not at issue. Only where the trademark and the allegedly infringing sign are somewhat "less similar" does the trademark owner appeal to reputation to help establish likelihood of confusion and entitlement to a broader scope of protection. In the more common case, the court makes a judgment regarding the likelihood of confusion based simply on a comparison of the similarity of the two signs and the similarity of the goods or services at issue.

99. The United States makes one final point regarding the relevance of "reputation" to the determination of likelihood of confusion in EC law. As noted in the United States' second written submission, only those provisions of the EC Trademark Regulation and Trademark Directive concerning heightened protection against uses of confusing identical or similar signs on *dissimilar* goods make specific reference to the need to establish "reputation."[78] If, as the EC asserts in this dispute, reputation is also necessary to prove likelihood of confusion with respect to identical or similar signs on *identical or similar* goods, it would seem to render void or redundant the considered references to "reputation" included in the Trademark Regulation and the Trademark Directive. Such a finding would not be consistent with an objective assessment of the facts.

Q149. What are the differences between "confusion" and "misleads" as used in Articles 16.1 and 22.2 of the TRIPS Agreement, respectively? Do they have any bearing on the misleading standard under Article 14(3) of Regulation (EC) No. 2081/92? ***USA, AUS, EC***

---

[76] Judgment of the UK High Court of Justice, *Origins Natural Resources Inc v. Origin Clothing Limited*, 17 November 1994, pg. 284 (Court found likelihood of confusion with respect to use of a similar sign on identical goods even where the registered trademark had never been used. Where trademark has not been used, court simply assumed that it would come into use at some stage, "in a normal and fair manner in relation to the goods for which it is registered," and undertook a comparison "mark to mark," concluding that "[o]ne cannot reasonably expect the public to distinguish between" registered trademark (ORIGINS) and similar sign (ORIGIN) when used on identical goods.) (Exhibit US-93); Judgment of the UK High Court of Justice, Chancery Division, *British Sugar Plc v. James Robertson & Sons Ltd*, January-February 1996, pg. 293 (Court reiterated test that if prior mark had not been used, court would assume that it would come into use at some stage, in a normal and fair manner in relation to the goods for which it is registered, and went on to make a "mark to sign" comparison.) (Exhibit US-94); Judgment of the UK High Court of Justice, Chancery Division, *Wagamama Ltd v. City Centre Restaurants Plc and Another*, July-August 1995, pgs. 731-732 (Court reiterated test that if prior mark had not been used, court would assume that it would come into use at some stage, in a normal and fair manner in relation to the goods for which it is registered, and went on to make a "mark to mark" comparison.) (Exhibit US-95); Decision of the Appointed Person, *React Trade Mark*, 29 June 1999, pg. 288 (lines 13-19) (Tribunal noted that evidence relating to use of prior mark was withdrawn, and that comparison was simply made on basis of "the degree of visual, aural and conceptual similarity" with the allegedly infringing sign, assuming notional, fair use of the prior mark) (Exhibit US-96); Decision of the Appointed Person, *Balmoral Trade Mark*, 18 August 1998, pg. 300 (lines 7-8) (Tribunal held that prior trademark "need not have reputation" to enjoin use of similar or identical signs that raise a likelihood of confusion under Article 5(2) of the Trade Marks Act (corresponding to Article 4(1)(b) of the EC Trademarks Directive)). Exhibit US-97.

[77] See OHIM Board of Appeal, Case R 433/2002-3, *Tei-Fu/Tai-Fun*, 11 December 2002, paras. 32-43, 31, 28 (Board found that trademark TEI-FU raised a likelihood of confusion with respect to prior trademark TAI-FUN, based on the similarity of the goods covered, and the close phonetic and graphic similarity of the signs. Board reached this conclusion despite express findings that no evidence had been submitted regarding use of prior trademark, and that owner had not established any particular distinctiveness of prior trademark.) (http://oami.eu.int/LegalDocs/BoA/2002/en/R0433_2002-3.pdf); OHIM Board of Appeal, Case R 49/2002-4, *Foris/Fortis*, 17 March 2003, paras. 7-16 (Board found a likelihood of confusion between prior trademark FORTIS and trademark FORIS, based solely on identity of the services at issue and the close similarity of the signs, without any discussion of prior trademark's reputation or use.) (http://oami.eu.int/LegalDocs/BoA/2002/en/R0049_2002-4.pdf); OHIM Board of Appeal, Case R 987/2002-1, *Zelecta/Zelletra*, 4 February 2004, paras. 24-30 (Board found that trademark ZELECTA raised a likelihood of confusion with respect to prior trademark ZELLETRA, based solely on identity of the goods (and, for one category of goods, the similarity of those goods), and the close phonetic and visual similarity of the signs, without any finding that prior trademark enjoyed reputation or use.) (http://oami.eu.int/LegalDocs/BoA/2002/en/R0987_2002-1.pdf).

[78] US Second Written Submission, para. 150 (note 131), *citing* Council Regulation (EC) No 40/94 of 20 December 1993 on the Community trade mark, as amended, Articles 8(5), 9(1)(c) (Exhibit COMP-7.a); First Council Directive of 21 December 1988 to approximate the laws of the Member States relating to trade marks (89/104/EEC), as amended, Articles 4(3), 4(4)(a), 5(2) (Exhibit COMP-6.a).

Response:

100. The ordinary meaning of the term "confusion," from Article 16.1, includes "failure to distinguish."[79] The ordinary meaning of the term "mislead," from Article 22.2, includes "cause to have an incorrect impression or belief" and "lead or guide in the wrong direction."[80] As Australia has argued,[81] these two terms, in their context, are distinguishable. When Article 22.2 speaks of preventing uses that "mislead[ ] the public as to the geographical origin of the good," it speaks of uses that lead the public to believe, incorrectly, that the origin of the good is other than its true place of origin. When Article 16.1 accords a trademark owner the right to prevent uses that "would result in a likelihood of confusion," it speaks to uses that undermine the ability of the owner to distinguish its goods from those goods using an identical or similar sign.[82]

101. Additional context points to distinctions between the two standards. The standard in Article 16.1 is whether the uses of an identical or similar sign would result in a "*likelihood* of confusion," while the standard in Article 22.2 is whether uses of that sign "mislead[ ] the public." Under Article 16.1, a trademark owner need only show that confusion will *likely* result. In contrast, under Article 22.2, an interested party must show that the public is actually misled.

102. The Panel's second question is whether the "likelihood of confusion" and "misleads the public" standards in TRIPS Articles 16.1 and 22.2 have any bearing on the "liable to mislead the consumer" standard in Article 14(3) of the EC GI Regulation. Although both Article 14(3) of the EC GI Regulation and TRIPS Article 22.2 use the term "mislead," there is no specific indication in the Regulation that Article 14(3) was modeled on Article 22.2. In fact, the Article 22.2 standard seems rather to have been adopted by the EC in Article 13(1)(d) of the Regulation. (The "misleading" standard included in TRIPS Article 22.3 is similarly tracked in Article 50.1(c) of the Trademark Regulation and Article 12.2(b) of the Trademark Directive.[83])

103. Virtually the only common term used in Article 14(3) and TRIPS Article 16.1 is the word "trademark." The United States does not therefore see any indication that Article 14(3) was drafted with any regard for the standard in Article 16.1, or that Article 16.1 has any bearing on the reading to be given Article 14(3). The EC has appropriately used the "likelihood of confusion" standard in its internal legislation in connection with WTO obligations: that is the specific standard adopted in Article 9.1(b) of the Trademark Regulation and Article 5.1(b) of the Trademark Directive.[84] A fair inference can be drawn that when the EC meant to use the likelihood of confusion standard, it did so expressly.

104. The word "mislead" appears to be used throughout the EC GI Regulation in the sense of affirmatively leading the public to believe something about the product that is not true, *e.g.*, that the product comes from a place other than the true place of origin.[85] This is in contrast to the term "confusion", which appears generally to be used in the Article 16.1 sense of a failure or inability to distinguish.[86] This distinction also appears in the equally authentic French versions of the GI Regulation, which renders "confusion" as "confusion", but renders "mislead" as a more affirmative act of leading the public to believe something untrue.[87] This distinction

---

[79] *New Shorter Oxford English Dictionary* (Fourth Ed. 1993), pg. 478. Exhibit US-84.

[80] *New Shorter Oxford English Dictionary* (Fourth Ed. 1993), pg. 1791. Exhibit US-84.

[81] *See* Australian Oral Statement at Second Meeting, para. 15.

[82] The EC Court of First Instance has stated that "the likelihood that the public might believe that the goods or services in question come from the same undertaking or, as the case may be, economically-linked undertakings, constitutes a likelihood of confusion." Case T-388/00, ILS/ELS, 23 October 2002, para. 44. Exhibit US-98.

[83] Regulation No 40/94, Article 50.1(c), Exhibit COMP-7; Directive 89/104/EEC, Article 12.2(b), Exhibit COMP-6.

[84] Regulation No 40/94, Article 9.1(b), Exhibit COMP-7; Directive 89/104/EEC, Article 5.1(b), Exhibit COMP-6.

[85] *See, e.g.,* Articles 3.2, 6.6, 13.1(c), 13.1(d), and 14(3) of the EC GI Regulation.

[86] *See, e.g.,* Articles 6.6, 7.5(b), 12(2), 12b(3) and 12d(3) of the EC GI Regulation.

[87] *E.g.,* "induire le [public/consommateur] en erreur quant à la veritable origine du produit" (Articles 3(2), 13(1)(d) and 14(3)); "donne à penser à tort au public que les produits sont originaires d'un autre territoire" (Article 6.6); "induire en erreur les consommateurs" (Article 6.6); and "fallacieuse quant à la provenance, l'origine" (Article 13.1(c).

strongly suggests, as a factual matter, that "liable to mislead" in the sense of Article 14(3) cannot be read as meeting the "likelihood of confusion" standard of Article 16.1.

105. Further, as the United States has explained elsewhere,[88] the reference in Article 14(3) to trademarks with reputation, renown and some length of use is consistent with the definition of well-known or famous marks offered in TRIPS Articles 16.2 and 16.3, as well as Article 6*bis* of the Paris Convention. Similarly, the prerequisites in Article 14(3) track the factors for determination whether a trademark is well-known that are recorded in Article 2(1)(b) of the Joint Recommendation Concerning Provisions on the Protection of Well-Known Marks, adopted by the Paris Union Assembly and the WIPO General Assembly.[89] Additionally, in adopting recent amendments to its laws upon accession to the EC, an EC member State characterized its understanding that Article 14(3) tracks the factors for determining whether a trademark is well-known.[90] Moreover, the EC Trademark Regulation and Trademark Directive similarly refer to "reputation" as a prerequisite for the heightened protection associated with well-known marks.[91]

Q150. The United States refers to the possibility of informing "consumers about the origin of a product and its characteristics through the use of descriptive terms in a non-trademark sense without affirmatively confusing the consumer about the source of goods" (US response to Panel question No. 75(b)). Would the addition of such a requirement in Article 14 of Regulation (EC) No. 2081/92 in respect of either prior trademarks, later geographical indications, or both, satisfy the requirements of Article 16.1 of the TRIPS Agreement in the view of the United States? Or does the United States object to any later protection of a geographical indication that is confusingly similar to a prior trademark? ***USA***

Response:

106. It would appear that the particular inconsistencies with Article 16.1 identified by the United States in this dispute might be addressed if the GI Regulation were to incorporate the substantive disciplines of EC trademark law into Article 14(2), or elsewhere in the Regulation. In fact, as the United States has explained, the Committee on Legal Affairs and the Internal Market of the European Parliament proposed just such an amendment.[92] This proposal would have added the following language to Article 14(2):

> This Regulation shall be without prejudice to the right accorded under the laws of the Member States and/or Council Regulation (EEC) No 40/94 of 20 December 1993 on the Community trade mark to bring proceedings for infringement of the right embodied in a trade mark conforming to the conditions set out in the first sentence of this paragraph on account of the use of a designation of origin or geographical indication subsequent to that trade mark, be it under the civil, administrative, or criminal law of the Member States.[93]

This language would address these inconsistencies with Article 16.1, assuming that it fully maintains and incorporates the substantive rights of exclusivity of prior trademarks, consistent with Article 16.1 of the TRIPS Agreement. As the United States understands it, this amendment would allow trademark owners to exercise

---

[88] US Second Written Submission, para. 146.

[89] US Second Written Submission, para. 147.

[90] US Second Written Submission, paras. 148-149. The EC asserts that the amended provision of Hungarian law cited by the United States in Exhibit US-59 "applies to products not covered by Regulation 2081/92." EC Oral Statement at Second Meeting, para. 172 (tiret 3). This rebuttal is beside the point. The important point is that in the Hungarian government's view, Article 14(3) applies to "well-known mark[s]." *See* Exhibit US-61. The EC had previously asserted that the EC member States agree with its position, in this dispute, that Article 14(3) denies registration to GIs that mislead with respect to all trademarks. EC Responses to Questions, paras. 172-174. Exhibit US-61 demonstrates that the EC's assertion is untrue, and that some member States agree that Article 14(3) denies registration only to those GIs that mislead with respect to well-known trademarks.

[91] US Second Written Submission, para. 150.

[92] US Second Written Submission, para. 166.

[93] Exhibit US-21, at pp. 13-14.

their TRIPS Article 16.1 rights, but would also provide for fair use and other exceptions pursuant to EC and member State trademark laws, consistent with TRIPS Article 17.

107. Finally, the United States again notes that it is difficult to understand how "fair use of descriptive terms" might apply to registered GIs (pursuant to Article 2(3) of the GI Regulation) that are not geographic names (*e.g.*, Feta).

Q151. Please comment on the suggestion that Article 24.3 of the TRIPS Agreement was inserted in the draft text in November 1991 to make it clear that the exceptions provisions in Section 3 of Part II could not be used as a justification for diminishing a Member's pre-existing protection of GIs. ***USA, AUS, EC***

Response:

108. The United States agrees that Article 24.3 is an exception to Part II, Section 3 of the TRIPS Agreement. As the United States has explained, this is evident both from the heading to Article 24 ("International Negotiations; Exceptions"), as well as the introductory clause that limits its scope to actions taken "[i]n implementing this Section".[94]

109. Given that the other exceptions in Article 24 constitute an important part of Part II, Section 3, it is reasonable to read "In implementing this Section" as incorporating measures taken to implement the other exceptions, when such measures could diminish the protection of individual GIs that existed in that Member prior to entry into force of the WTO Agreement. However, the ordinary meaning of the phrase "In implementing this Section" is not *limited* to implementation of Article 24, but would seem to also apply, where appropriate, to measures taken to implement aspects of other provisions of the GI section that could diminish the protection of individual GIs protected prior to entry into force of the WTO Agreement.

110. Nevertheless, the Panel's suggestion regarding Article 24.3 is not only consistent with a textual and contextual interpretation of Article 24.3 as an exception to the obligations in the GI section. It also directly contradicts the EC's views that (1) Article 24.3 is not an exception (despite clear language and context to the contrary) and (2) it in fact imposes an additional obligation on the EC not to modify its GI protection system in any way, despite its inconsistencies with the trademark obligations under the TRIPS Agreement.

Q152. If a Member is obliged to diminish the pre-existing protection of GIs in order to allow trademark owners to exercise their rights under Article 16.1 as against GIs, does that obligation not arise under Article 16.1 rather than "[i]n implementing this Section", as used in Article 24.3? ***EC***

Q153. Without prejudice to the EC's view that a GI confusingly similar to a trademark will not be registered, if one were registered nevertheless, in what way would this exception be "limited"? In particular, could the rights of the GI owner be limited in such a way as to minimize the likelihood of confusion? ***EC***

Q154. What, specifically, are "the legitimate interests of the owner of the trademark and of third parties" within the meaning of Article 17? How can legitimate interests be "taken into account" under Article 17 where they conflict with other relevant interests? ***USA, AUS, EC***

Response:

111. An "interest" is defined as "[t]he fact or relation of having a share or concern in, or a right to, something, esp. by law" or "[t]he relation of being involved or concerned as regards potential detriment or (esp.) advantage."[95] "Legitimate" refers to "[g]enuine", "[c]onformable to, sanctioned or authorized by, law or

94 US Second Written Submission, paras. 189-190.

95 *New Shorter Oxford English Dictionary* (Fourth Ed. 1993), pg. 1393. Exhibit US-84.

principle"; "normal, regular, conformable to a recognized standard type."[96] Thus, a "legitimate" interest arises when a party has a concern that is recognized either by law, or by other types of normative standards.[97]

112. Article 17 does not specifically list the types of "legitimate interests of the owner of the trademark and of third parties" that must be taken into account when providing limited exceptions. Immediate context, however, provides important guidance.

113. The largest and most obvious set of third parties affected by trademarks are consumers who make decisions in the marketplace based on their association of a trademark with a product. When Article 16.1 provides rights to trademark owners to prevent uses that "would result in a likelihood of confusion", the "confusion" that is avoided is confusion on the part of consumers who are making purchasing decisions based on trademarks. Therefore, "legitimate interests of ... third parties", under Article 16.1, includes the interests of consumers not to be confused by signs. Anything that results in a likelihood of confusion for consumers is not in their legitimate interests. Moreover, consumers benefit from a strong trademark system, generally, as trademarks encourages fair competition among producers and provide valuable information to consumers about the particular products that they are purchasing.

114. Another type of relevant third party consists of those parties that have licenses to affirmatively use a trademark, or to exclude others from using the mark. This is evident from Article 16.1, which refers to "all third parties *not having the owner's consent*", and which implies that third parties with the trademark owner's consent have the right to use identical or similar signs. It is also evident from TRIPS Article 21, which refers to licensing of trademarks. The legitimate interest of the licensees are tied directly to those of the trademark owner, as their license agreements are accorded value as a result of the Article 16.1 rights accorded to the trademark owner (or licensed to the licensee).

115. As for the "legitimate interests of the owner of the trademark", such interests are also evident from the context provided by Articles 16.1 and 15.1 of the TRIPS Agreement. Trademark owners have a legitimate interest in exercising their exclusive right to prevent all others from confusing use, as this maintains the value of the trademark, and preserves the investments made to promote the trademark and associated products to the public in a territory (*i.e.*, through advertising, etc.).[98] In other words, trademark owners have a legitimate interest in preventing competitors from inducing consumers to buy competing products based not on the quality of the competing product, but instead on an inaccurate belief that they are buying the product associated with the trademark. In addition to harming consumers, this reduces the economic value of the trademark, and the profits of the trademark owner's business.

116. This consideration is consistent with the analysis of the *US – Section 110(5)* panel which, when interpreting the phrase "legitimate interests of the right holder" in the context of the copyright section, explained as follows:

> In our view, one—albeit incomplete and thus conservative—way of looking at legitimate interests is the economic value of the exclusive rights conferred by copyright on their holders. It is possible to estimate in economic terms the value of exercising, e.g., by licensing, such rights. That is not to say that legitimate interests are necessarily limited to this economic value.[99]

Similarly, the "legitimate interests of the owner of the trademark" encompasses the interests in preserving the economic value of the exclusive rights conferred by a trademark.

---

[96] *New Shorter Oxford English Dictionary* (Fourth Ed. 1993), pg. 1563. Exhibit US-84.

[97] *See* Panel Report, *US – Section 110(5)*, para. 6.224.

[98] *See infra* Response to Question 155, regarding the extent to which these exclusive rights could be limited pursuant to Article 17 of the TRIPS Agreement.

[99] Panel Report, *US – Section 110(5)*, para. 6.227.

117. Moreover, a trademark owner has a legitimate interest in ensuring that its trademark continues to be capable of distinguishing the goods or services of its undertaking from those of other undertakings, within the meaning of Article 15.1. If others are able to dilute the value of the trademark by using it on their products without the consent of the trademark owner, then this diminishes the capability of the sign to distinguish its goods or services, and may even result in total loss of the trademark.[100]

118. With respect to the relationship among the legitimate interests, it seems that the interests of the trademark owners, licensees, and consumers do not conflict at all, as they all benefit from enforceable Article 16.1 rights, which preserve the value of the trademark for the trademark owner and licensee, at the same time that they prevent confusion of the consumers. This is quite different from the patent context, for example, where the short term interests of the consumers (to purchase cheaper products) may differ from the short term interests of the patent holder (to profit from the invention and recover the associated research and development expenses).

119. To the extent that "legitimate interests ... of third parties" include the interests of producers in providing information to consumers about the geographical origin of the product, or in using a purely descriptive term, and the corresponding interests of consumers in receiving such information, these interests may also be taken into account, but only to the extent that they "provide limited exceptions to the rights conferred by a trademark" and do not require ignoring the legitimate interests of the trademark owner, pursuant to Article 17. As the United States has explained, the phrase "limited exception" refers to "a narrow exception - one which makes only a small diminution of the rights", where "limited", is "measured by the extent to which the exclusive rights" of a trademark have been curtailed.[101]

120. By contrast, as the United States has detailed elsewhere, the blanket exception to trademark rights in Article 14(2) of the GI Regulation is not a "limited exception" and does not take into account the interests of anyone other than producers of certain agricultural products in the EC who have rights to use a registered GI. Under the EC's interpretation of TRIPS Article 17, all uses of a registered GI are automatically entitled to the "fair use" exception, no matter what the facts of the particular case at hand (*i.e.*, whether the use is fair, the term is descriptive, or the legitimate interests of the trademark owner are considered), by simple virtue of registration alone. It is an exception that harms consumers, as they will purchase products that they do not intend to purchase because of confusion over the name.

Q155. Does an exception to the exclusive right in Article 16.1 presuppose a certain degree of confusion? Does "fair use of descriptive terms" within the meaning of Article 17 include the use of a trademark to indicate source? ***USA, AUS***

Response:

121. As the United States explained in its second oral statement, TRIPS Article 17 does contemplate some curtailment of the rights granted in Part II, Section 2 of the TRIPS Agreement, but the provision explicitly states that such curtailment for any given trademark must be limited.[102] Given that Article 17 refers to limited exceptions to the "rights conferred by a trademark", and Article 16 (including Articles 16.1, 16.2, and 16.3) defines the "Rights Conferred", it is logical that Article 17 presupposes a certain degree of likelihood of confusion for a particular trademark within the meaning of Article 16.1. By its very terms, however, Article 17, unlike the GI Regulation, does not permit virtually unlimited exceptions, simply because those exceptions relate to the rights of a limited *number* of trademarks.[103] Nor does Article 17 permit the unlimited degree of

---

[100] US Opening Oral Statement at Second Meeting, para. 90; US Second Written Submission, para. 174.

[101] US Opening Oral Statement at Second Meeting, para. 100, quoting Panel Report, *Canada – Patent Protection*, paras. 7.30-7.31. *See infra* US Response to Question 155.

[102] US Opening Oral Statement at Second Meeting, para. 102.

[103] US Opening Oral Statement at Second Meeting, para. 102.

likelihood of confusion allowed by the GI Regulation. Finally, with specific textual references to the rights conferred by "a" trademark and the legitimate interests of the owner of "the" trademark, Article 17 does not permit automatic entitlement to an exception, without consideration, for example, of whether the "use" at issue is "fair," or the "terms" at issue are "descriptive."

122. As noted above, under the EC's interpretation of TRIPS Article 17, uses of a registered GI are automatically entitled to the "fair use" exception, by simple virtue of registration alone. The EC has failed to explain, nor can it, how a blanket exception, requiring trademark owners to sell their products alongside the products of an *unlimited* number of producers using identical or similar GIs, for an *unlimited* amount of time, and with an *unlimited* degree of consumer confusion, is a "limited exception".

123. With respect to the Panel's question about whether "fair use of descriptive terms" within the meaning of Article 17 includes the use of a trademark to indicate source, the answer is No. As the United States explained during its second oral statement, a "descriptive" term is one that is "characterized by description", where description refers to "[a] detailed account of a ... thing." Trademarks are a form of intellectual property, with associated rights, that are not merely "descriptive." According to TRIPS Article 15.1, for example, only those signs that are "capable of distinguishing the goods or services of one undertaking from those of other undertakings" may constitute a trademark. Thus, trademarks are not merely descriptive and can not be considered "descriptive terms" within the meaning of Article 17.

Q156. Why do the requirements in Article 17 differ from those in Articles 13, 26.2 and 30 of the TRIPS Agreement? How should their interpretation reflect those differences? ***USA, AUS, EC***

Response:

124. Beginning with the text of the provisions themselves, Article 17, the trademark exception, states:

> Members may provide limited exceptions to the rights conferred by a trademark, such as the fair use of descriptive terms, provided that such exceptions take account of the legitimate interests of the owner of the trademark and of third parties.

125. Article 13, the copyright exception, states:

> Members shall confine limitations or exceptions to exclusive rights to certain special cases which do not conflict with a normal exploitation of the work and do not unreasonably prejudice the legitimate interests of the right holder.

126. Article 26.2, the industrial design exception, states:

> Members may provide limited exceptions to the protection of industrial designs, provided that such exceptions do not unreasonably conflict with the normal exploitation of protected industrial designs and do not unreasonably prejudice the legitimate interests of the owner of the protected design, taking account of the legitimate interests of third parties.

127. Article 30, the patent exception, states:

> Members may provide limited exceptions to the exclusive rights conferred by a patent, provided that such exceptions do not unreasonably conflict with a normal exploitation of the patent and do not unreasonably prejudice the legitimate interests of the patent owner, taking account of the legitimate interests of third parties.

128. The first apparent difference between the latter three exceptions and Article 17 is the reference in Articles 13, 26.2 and 30 to "normal exploitation." Exceptions to copyright may not conflict with "a normal

exploitation of the work"; exceptions to industrial design protection may not "unreasonably conflict with the normal exploitation" of the design; and exceptions to patent rights may not "unreasonably conflict with a normal exploitation of the patent". This difference is based on the difference in the nature of the intellectual property right. Copyrighted works, industrial designs, and patents are all subject to "exploitation" by the rightholder by, for example, including the protected work, industrial design, or invention in a product for use or sale—or licensing others to do so. It is possible for exceptions to rights to conflict either not at all (copyrights) or not unreasonably (industrial designs and patents) with "a normal exploitation". Further, exceptions might conflict with an "exploitation" of the copyright, industrial design or patent, without conflicting with a "normal" exploitation, which implies a normative standard for what is "normal".[104]

129. By contrast, a trademark owner is provided the exclusive right to prevent uses of signs that cause a likelihood of confusion with respect to the trademark. That right is not subject to "exploitation" in the same sense as the "exploitation" of a copyrighted work, protected industrial design, or patented invention. Unlike in other intellectual property areas, therefore, Article 17 does not permit exceptions that would conflict with *any* exploitation of the trademark—normal or not—and does not permit reasonable conflicts with "a normal exploitation", because any conflict with trademark rights goes to the heart of the trademark owner's legitimate interest. Therefore, there is no need for Article 17 to provide for exceptions that conflict with an "exploitation" of the trademark.

130. Similarly, Articles 13, 26.2, and 30 permit exceptions that "do not unreasonably prejudice the legitimate interests of the" intellectual property right holder. Article 17, by contrast, requires that any exceptions "take account of the legitimate interests of the owner of the trademark." This, too, is explained by the differences in the intellectual property rights concerned. A WTO Member might permit businesses to make performances of copyrighted works through "homestyle" audio equipment because it had been shown that copyright owners did not derive much revenue from such use, and thus the use did not unreasonably prejudice the legitimate interests of the copyright holder. A WTO Member might permit persons other than the patent holder to make drugs covered by a patent, purely for the purpose of obtaining market approval for the drug, so that it can be sold once the patent expires, again without prejudicing the legitimate interests of the patent holder. By contrast, the very ability of a trademark owner to distinguish goods using his trademark is significantly compromised if that trademark owner cannot stop confusing uses of his signs—that is, if there are signs in the marketplace that are likely to cause confusion. So, for the same reason that the language "does not [unreasonably] conflict with the normal exploitation" of a trademark is not included in Article 17—because any conflict with the trademark undermines the trademark right entirely—the standard of "unreasonably prejudice" the rights of the owner is not included - because any uses of signs likely to cause confusion with a mark will prejudice the owner's interests. In order to "take account" of the trademark owner's legitimate interests in being able to use his trademark to distinguish goods, likelihood of confusion must be avoided to the maximum extent possible, and where likelihood of confusion is necessary—because of the competing interests concerned—such likelihood of confusion should be limited to that which is strictly necessary to serve the particular competing interest in the case.[105]

131. Indeed, reinforcing this view of the trademark obligation, in contrast to the obligations with respect to other intellectual property rights, Article 21 of the TRIPS Agreement provides that "compulsory licensing of trademarks shall not be permitted." By contrast, there is no such provision with respect to copyrights, industrial designs, or patents.

---

[104] The Panel in *Canada – Patent Protection of Pharmaceutical Products* explained that the term "normal" as used in Article 30, "can be understood to refer either to an empirical conclusion about what is common within a relevant community, or to a normative standard of entitlement. The Panel concluded that the word 'normal' was being used in Article 30 in a sense that combined the two meanings." Panel Report, *Canada – Patent Protection of Pharmaceutical Products*, para 7.54.

[105] As noted in the US response to question 155, to be "limited," an exception cannot apply automatically and in all cases, without an analysis of the particular competing interests at issue.

132. With respect to the interests of third parties, Articles 26.2 and 30 are virtually identical to Article 17, as all require the exceptions to take "account of the legitimate interests of third parties." Article 13, by contrast, does not specifically refer to the interests of third parties. Again, this difference demonstrates the simple proposition that third party interests must specifically be considered when providing exceptions to trademarks, industrial designs, and patents, but that this is not an explicitly-stated requirement for copyright exceptions in the TRIPS Agreement.

133. Finally, another difference between the other three exceptions is that Article 17 refers specifically to "fair use of descriptive terms", as an example of the types of permitted limited exceptions. As the reference to "fair use" is introduced by the phrase "such as", this is not the only permitted limited exception. The fact that Articles 13, 26.2, and 30 do not contain specific examples of exceptions does not provide any relevant information about how Article 17 should be interpreted.

Q157. The United States alleges that the EC does not provide legal means required under Article 22 of the TRIPS Agreement (see United States first written submission, paras.177-178; US rebuttal, para. 213). Do you claim that the EC fails to provide a legal means to prevent uses of indications in accordance with Article 22.2 because of alleged inadequacies in Regulation (EC) No. 2081/92 alone? Or do you allege that measures outside the Panel's terms of reference are also inadequate to fulfil that obligation? If the latter, on what evidence do you rely? ***USA***

Response:

134. The United States' claim that the EC does not provide the legal means required under Article 22 of the TRIPS Agreement is based on inadequacies in the EC GI Regulation. As the United States has pointed out in its submissions and oral statements, the EC GI Regulation provides *the* means for obtaining Community protection of geographical indications of agricultural products and foodstuffs (Article 2(1) of the GI Regulation). And it fails to provide those means to all interested parties, as required by Article 22. Further, by providing *the* vehicle for obtaining Community-wide protection for geographical indications, and then failing to provide rights of objection to interested parties, it has failed to provide any mechanism at all for interested parties to protect against misleading uses with respect to a GI that has been registered: once a GI has been registered, those who might have objected are powerless to prevent misleading uses with respect to those GIs. The EC has suggested that other, unspecified, member State laws and Community rules make up for these deficiencies in the GI Regulation, but it has not sustained its burden of refuting the US *prima facie* case. To the contrary, the EC declined an invitation from the Panel to provide such information.

Q158. The Panel notes the United States' submission that the Panel should find that "the EC GI Regulation" is inconsistent with Articles 16.1 and 22.2 of the TRIPS Agreement (US rebuttal, paras.166 and 217, respectively). However, why would it be appropriate to conclude that a single measure, rather than a Member, fails to comply with each obligation? If the EC or its member States adopted other measures which complied with Articles 16.1 and 22.2, could they fill the gaps in the alleged inconsistencies in Regulation (EC) No. 2081/92? ***USA***

Response:

135. The drafters of the DSU chose to refer to "measures" being inconsistent with the covered agreements. For example, Article 19.1 of the DSU refers to the situation where "a panel or the Appellate Body concludes that a measure is inconsistent with a covered agreement."[106] The United States has followed this convention.

136. The EC may have a number of options to implement DSB recommendations and rulings that its GI Regulation is inconsistent with the EC's WTO obligations, and the United States is not attempting to prejudge what those options are at this point in the dispute nor which option the EC should choose.

---

[106] See also for example Articles 3.7 and 21.5.

137. If the Panel's question is directed at *current* measures that may fill the gaps, in any dispute, of course, it is theoretically possible that there are other measures, of which the complainant is unaware and which it did not cite, that eliminate or counteract any alleged inconsistency identified by the complainant. For example, a law cited in a panel request may have been overturned by a later law. Or, in identifying burdens placed on foreign products in one regulation, the complainant may have been unaware of another regulation placing the identical burdens on domestic products (although, ideally, such omissions would have been elucidated in consultations). In such a case, once the complainant has presented a *prima facie* case that a measure is inconsistent with a WTO obligation, it is the respondent that then has the burden to rebut that *prima facie* case by presenting facts and arguments showing that there is no inconsistency. Such facts and arguments may very well include other domestic measures, not cited by the complainant, that demonstrate that any alleged inconsistency is eliminated. This would then constitute the respondent's affirmative defense (it is the respondent that is in the best position to come forward with such information about its own domestic law). However, if the respondent fails to do this—*i.e.*, if it fails to overcome the *prima facie* case presented by the complainant—then the panel must make findings in favor of the complainant.

138. In this dispute, for instance, in response to claims that the GI Regulation deprives trademark owners of their Article 16.1 rights, the EC has merely presented excerpts of a few other laws—such as unfair advertising laws—that they claim "fill in the gap" left by the GI Regulation. Of course, the United States has explained that, since the standards in those laws are much more stringent than those in Article 16.1, they in no way provide trademark owners with their Article 16.1 rights. But the point with respect to the Panel's question is that, if there were other measures somewhere in EC legal system or in those of its member States that compensated for the WTO inconsistencies in the GI Regulation, the EC would have and should have come forward with them. But in fact, if there are any such measures, the EC failed to present them to the United States during five years of consultations. And they failed to do so during the entire course of this proceeding. Indeed, at the first Panel meeting, the United States recalls that the Panel specifically invited the EC to present information to support its vague allegations that other, unspecified EC and EC member State laws and regulations might make up for the apparent WTO inconsistencies in the EC GI Regulation. The EC declined to do so, implying that it was the responsibility of the United States to show that there were no such laws or regulations.[107]

139. But the consequences of this approach would be to require the complainant to show that (1) a particular measure is inconsistent with WTO obligations <u>and</u> (2) there is no other measure anywhere throughout the legal system of the respondent that compensates for this WTO-inconsistent measure. Such a requirement would be tantamount to requiring a complainant to cite in its consultation and panel requests the entire body of the respondent's law as the measures at issue. Needless to say, putting such a burden on the complainant to "prove the negative" is inappropriate and unworkable.

Q159. May protection for designations of origin and geographical indications now be afforded in the EC only within the framework laid down by Regulation (EC) No. 2081/92? To what extent does the EC implement its obligations under Article 22.2 of the TRIPS Agreement through Regulation (EC) No. 2081/92 and to what extent through other measures (see EC first written submission, paras. 433 and 434)? Are the other measures cited by the EC alone sufficient to fulfil its obligations under Article 22.2? ***EC***

---

[107] The United States also reminds the Panel that, contrary to the EC's arguments, the United States does not have the burden of proving that its reading of the GI Regulation is "the only reasonable interpretation" (EC Second Written Submission, para. 275) or the "only correct one" (EC Oral Statement at the Second Panel Meeting, para. 5), or that a WTO-consistent interpretation of the regulation is "impossible" (EC Second Written Submission, para. 274). Nor can the EC simply rely on "considerable deference" to immunize it from claims of WTO-inconsistency. (EC Second Written Submission, para. 273). Rather, the United States has the burden of presenting information and arguments that the EC Regulation means what it says sufficient to make a *prima facie* case of a WTO-inconsistency. It is then up to the EC to present information and arguments to rebut that *prima facie* case.

Q160. To what extent does the EC implement its obligations under Article 22.2 of the TRIPS Agreement through Regulation (EC) No. 2081/92 and to what extent through other measures? Does the EC believe that the complainants should prove a negative, i.e. that no legal means required under Article 22.2 are available? Can a respondent simply argue that other measures, outside the Panel's terms of reference, fulfil an obligation, without proof of how those other measures fulfil that obligation? ***EC***

Q161. Australia refers to Article10bis(1) of the Paris Convention, "as incorporated by TRIPS Article 2.1" (Australia's first written submission, para. 75, also para. 268) and also submits that "Paris Article 10bis.1 deals with the issue of unfair competition, which is not otherwise dealt with in the TRIPS Agreement except 'in respect of geographical indications' in TRIPS Article 22.2" (response to Panel question No. 82). Please clarify whether Australia seeks a finding that the alleged inconsistency with Article 10bis is a violation of Article 2.1 or 22.2 of the TRIPS Agreement or both. ***AUS***

Q162. How did Australia's reference to Article 24.5 of the TRIPS Agreement in its request for establishment of a panel put the EC on notice that Australia challenged Regulation (EC) No. 2081/92 in respect of Article 24.5 in conjunction with Article 4 of the Paris Convention (1967) as incorporated by Article 2.1 of the TRIPS Agreement? In Australia's view, to what extent could a respondent begin preparing its defence of this claim without knowing that it was based on the right of priority? ***AUS***

Q163. The Panel takes note of Australia's and the EC's respective views on the applicability of Article 70.1 of the TRIPS Agreement to individual GI registrations (Australia's response to Panel question No. 90; EC rebuttal, para. 202). On 31 December 1995, at what stage of the procedure under the former Article 15 were the GIs later registered under Article 17? Did any individual GIs registered under Article 6 have an objection period that expired prior to 1 January 1996? ***EC***

Q164. In what way are the objectives and principles set out in Articles 7 and 8 of the TRIPS Agreement, and the considerations recited in the first paragraph of its preamble, relevant to the interpretation of the provisions of that agreement at issue in this dispute? ***USA, AUS, EC***

Response:

140. The first paragraph of the preamble, and Articles 7 and 8, of the TRIPS Agreement are potentially relevant to the extent they provide context for interpreting the provisions offered by the parties, or to the extent they point to the object and purpose of the TRIPS Agreement. And, indeed, the first paragraph to the preamble to the TRIPS Agreement is instructive, as it reflects the desire of the Members "to reduce distortions and impediments to international trade" and "to ensure that measures and procedures to enforce intellectual property rights do not themselves become barriers to legitimate trade." The United States has already discussed the relevance of this provision to interpreting footnote 1 to Article 1.3 of the TRIPS Agreement in response to question 104. In addition, however, in interpreting the provisions of the TRIPS Agreement that the United States argues are breached by the EC GI Regulation, the Panel should be mindful of the object and purpose of the TRIPS Agreement, as reflected in this preamble, as contrasted with the obvious distortions, impediments, and barriers to international trade introduced by the EC GI Regulation.

141. By contrast, the United States does not believe that Articles 7 and 8 of the TRIPS Agreement contribute significantly to an understanding of the TRIPS provisions at issue. Likewise, the EC has also not provided arguments with respect to these provisions.

ANNEX A-9

COMMENTS OF THE UNITED STATES ON THE EUROPEAN COMMUNITIES' REPLIES TO QUESTIONS POSED BY THE PANEL AND TO QUESTIONS POSED BY AUSTRALIA FOLLOWING THE SECOND SUBSTANTIVE MEETING

(2 September 2004)

1. The United States is providing comments below on the responses of the European Commission ("EC") to the second set of questions presented by the Panel and Australia on August 13, 2004. The question numbers used as headings are the questions presented to the EC by the Panel, and the paragraph numbers, if any, at the beginning of each comment refer to the paragraph number of the EC response. The United States has incorporated its comments on the EC's responses to the questions of Australia in the comments on the EC's responses to the questions of the Panel. The United States has not commented on all responses, nor has it commented on all aspects of the responses that are addressed. Silence should not be construed as agreement. With respect to many questions, the EC responses raise the same points that the EC has argued previously and that the United States has already addressed in the course of this dispute (including in its own responses to the second set of Panel questions).

Question 94

2. Two comments are in order. First, the EC again admits in paragraph 1 that the reciprocity and equivalence requirements in Article 12(1) of the GI Regulation conflict with the EC's obligations under Article III:4 of the GATT 1994.[1] Since Article 12(1) contains the requirement for equivalent inspection structures, the United States does not see the basis for the EC's claim that the requirement for EC-equivalent protection is inconsistent with Article III:4 and yet the requirement for EC-equivalent inspection structures is not.[2]

3. Second, despite the EC's equivocations, the fact is that the EC claimed in its first submission—and still claims in its most recent official Guide of one month ago[3]– that the *obligations of the TRIPS Agreement* rendered the equivalency and reciprocity requirements inapplicable to WTO Members. Further, in its responses to Panel questions, the EC specified that the "without prejudice" language referred to *both* the TRIPS Agreement *and* the GATT 1994.[4] And in its second submission, the EC clarified that the introductory phrase "without prejudice to international agreements" means that the provisions that follow are inapplicable to the extent they *conflict* with an international agreement.[5] The EC also specified immediately afterward in that same submission that the "without prejudice" language prevents any conflict with the national treatment obligations of the TRIPS Agreement and the GATT 1994, by rendering equivalency and reciprocity requirements inapplicable to WTO Members.[6] Yet, as the EC has perhaps only recently come to see, the EC's own argument necessarily means that the reciprocity and equivalence conditions of the GI Regulation provide less favorable treatment to non-EC nationals than to EC nationals. This directly contradicts the EC's separate argument that the EC GI Regulation has nothing to do with discrimination against "nationals". Now that it has become apparent that the EC's earlier arguments constitute an admission that the GI Regulation *does* accord different

[1] *See* EC Second Written Submission, para. 55, in which the EC states that when regulatory provisions are preceded by the "without prejudice to international agreements" language, this means that the international agreement prevails when there is a "conflict" between the regulatory provision and the international agreement.

[2] Article 12(1), foreshadowing the requirements in Article 12a(2), imposes the condition of "inspection arrangements ... equivalent to those laid down in this Regulation."

[3] Exhibit EC-64, page 18

[4] EC Responses to First Set of Panel Questions (July 8, 2004), paras. 12-13.

[5] EC Second Written Submission, para. 55

[6] EC Second Written Submission, para. 56.

treatment to non-EC nationals than to EC nationals, the EC is trying to back away from those earlier arguments (as it has with respect to its own consistent interpretation of its Regulation). But the truth is found in the EC's own assessment of its own Regulation before the ramifications of that assessment became apparent: the GI Regulation does, in fact, accord different, and less favorable, treatment to non-EC nationals than it accords to EC nationals.

Question 95

4. It appears clear from the EC's response that, prior to the EC's first written submission in this dispute, neither the EC nor any EC institution expressed any view to anyone that the conditions of reciprocity and equivalence do not apply to WTO Members because those conditions are inconsistent with the EC's WTO obligations.

Question 96

5. The EC's answer speaks for itself, although the United States would note that even if the Commission did consider the "guide"—which is not a measure within this Panel's terms of reference—to be internally binding, it would not, even in the EC's view, be binding on any EC member States or other EC institutions, such as, most notably, the European Court of Justice ("ECJ"). Consequently, this "guide" offers no comfort that the ECJ would uphold the Commission's strained and non-textual interpretation of the GI Regulation.

Question 97

6. The United States confesses that it does not see how any of the quoted documents support the EC's apparent view that it "confirmed [in TRIPS Council] that there were no conditions of equivalence or reciprocity."[7] By contrast, the United States and Australia have documented numerous cases in which, in describing the GI Regulation to WTO Members, the conditions of equivalency and reciprocity were prominently mentioned, with no disclaimer that these conditions did not apply to the WTO Members to whom the descriptions were addressed.

7. Further, the Panel should recall that, whatever shades of nuance the EC now seeks to have the Panel read into general communications to the WTO Members over the years, the EC specifically confirmed in writing the US understanding that its GIs could not be registered because the United States did not satisfy the GI Regulation's conditions of equivalence and reciprocity.[8]

8. Finally, while the EC communications to other WTO Members in the TRIPS Council do nothing to dispel the conclusion that the conditions of reciprocity and equivalence apply to WTO Members, they do shed light on the issue of national treatment under the TRIPS Agreement. In the very excerpt quoted and relied upon by the EC from the official EC responses to questions from India, the EC itself described the Regulation as making a distinction between producers established in the EC, on the one hand, and "third country *nationals*", on the other. The EC was attempting to characterize the treatment as equal—"to avoid discrimination"—but was not disguising the fact that the two tracks for GI registration corresponded to nationality:

In order to obtain the same protection (Article 13 of the Regulation), if it must be complied with by the producers established in the EC, *it must also be complied with by the third country nationals, to avoid discrimination.*[9]

---

[7] EC Response to Second Set of Panel Questions, para. 15.

[8] *See* US Opening Oral Statement at the Second Panel Meeting, para. 21; Exhibit US-73, unnumbered p.4: "While it is true that US GIs cannot be registered in the EU . . .".

[9] IP/Q2/EEC1, p. 23, cited at EC Response to Second Set of Panel Questions, para. 15 (emphasis added).

9. Further, lest there be any doubt as to the EC's view of its own GI Regulation, the EC specifically stated that providing protection to GIs in respect of products from third countries was required by the national treatment obligation of the TRIPS Agreement:

> Article 12 of Council Regulation 2081/92/EEC provides for the same protection in respect of products from third countries which meet those requirements. *Therefore, nationals from other WTO Members are afforded treatment "no less favorable" than Community nationals, as required by Article 3 of the TRIPS Agreement.*[10]

The paragraph that immediately follows makes the same statements with respect to the MFN obligation under Article 4 of the TRIPS Agreement. The quoted passages from the EC's response to New Zealand are in a similar vein.[11]

Question 100

10. The United States submits that, within a single measure and as between related measures, the calculated use of different words and phrases would normally reflect that a difference in meaning is intended.

Question 101

11. The United States finds it interesting that, in response to a claim that a measure accords less favorable treatment to non-EC nationals than to EC nationals—in direct breach of the TRIPS Agreement and Paris Convention national treatment obligations—the EC is asking the Panel simply not to make "any comparison between nationals." The purported ground is that the Regulation does not contain any discrimination on the basis of nationality.

12. But the TRIPS Agreement requires that non-EC nationals be accorded treatment no less favorable than that accorded to EC nationals with regard to the protection of intellectual property. That the EC would now ask the Panel not to even compare treatment of EC versus non-EC nationals in a measure that concerns protection of intellectual property is itself probative of what the EC believes such a comparison—which is mandated by the very nature of the obligation—would show. And, as discussed above, it is contrary to the EC's communications in the TRIPS Council, which specifically *invited* such a comparison in the mistaken belief that the discrimination with respect to non-EC nationals did not amount to less favorable treatment.[12]

13. Another reading of the EC's response is that the EC believes that, since the GI Regulation does not state literally that EC "nationals" are accorded one treatment and that non-EC "nationals" are accorded lesser treatment, the measure is *per se* non-discriminatory, and any further analysis is therefore unnecessary. As the United States has set forth in detail in its comments on Panel question 103 below, and its own responses to Panel question 103, this is simply untrue, and is contrary to findings of the Appellate Body in, for instance, *US Bananas* and *Canada – Autos*.

14. Further, it is simply untrue as a factual matter that "the only relevant element to which the Regulation refers is the location of the area to which the geographical indication is related." The Regulation specifically limits the ability to apply to register a GI, and thereby to obtain rights in the GI, to persons producing or obtaining the products in the relevant geographical area. Further, it is the persons established and producing the products in the relevant area that are the intellectual property rightholders whose rights are protected by the TRIPS Agreement and the Paris Convention. Finally, the right of objection is expressed purely in terms of

---

[10] *Id.* Emphasis added.

[11] *E.g.*, EC Response to Second Set of Panel Questions, para. 12 ("the procedure followed by Community producers as outlined above must be followed, in accordance with the principle of national treatment.")

[12] *See* US comment to EC question 97 response.

where the person is resident or established, and where that person is "from", which the EC itself specifically characterized in last year's amendments to the EC GI Regulation as corresponding to the person's nationality.[13]

15. As the United States notes above in its comment on the response to question 97, the EC itself, in communications in the TRIPS Council, characterized the requirements of the GI Regulation as applying to EC producers, on the one hand, and third country "nationals" on the other. Further, in those same communications, the EC itself asserted that, *because* the GI Regulation provides GI protection "in respect of products from third countries which meet [the requirements of Article 12]", "*[t]herefore, nationals* from other WTO Members are afforded treatment 'no less favourable' *than Community nationals*, as required by Article 3 of the TRIPS Agreement."

Question 103

16. In response to the Panel's question concerning considerations relevant to the Panel's assessment of *de facto* discrimination, the EC takes two tacks. The first is to draw various distinctions between the national treatment obligation in the GATT 1994 and the national treatment obligation in the TRIPS Agreement and the Paris Convention. This is apparently an attempt to create as much distance as possible between this dispute and the considerable body of panel and Appellate Body findings in the goods context that would lead the Panel to find a breach of national treatment with respect to intellectual property rights in this dispute. But while there are certainly distinctions between the national treatment obligation under Article III of the GATT and the national treatment obligation under Article 3 of the TRIPS Agreement and Article 2 of the Paris Convention, the Appellate Body itself stated in *US – Section 211* that the national treatment obligation is a fundamental principle underlying the TRIPS Agreement, just as it was in what is now the GATT 1994.[14] The Appellate Body noted further that the language of Article 3.1 of the TRIPS Agreement is similar to that of Article III:4 of the GATT 1994, and stated that "the jurisprudence on Article III:4 may be useful in interpreting the national treatment obligation in the TRIPS Agreement."[15] Indeed, one object and purpose of the TRIPS Agreement is to establish new rules and disciplines "concerning the applicability of the basic principles of GATT 1994."[16] As the Appellate Body itself has noted, national treatment is one of these principles.[17]

17. The United States also notes that the EC itself supported this view in the dispute *US – Section 211*. Before the Appellate Body, the EC argued breaches of national treatment under the TRIPS Agreement by pointing to findings in a dispute involving the national treatment obligation with respect to goods under Article III:4, *US – Section 337*.[18] Further, at the panel stage of that dispute, the EC argued that:

> the language of Article 3.1 of the TRIPS Agreement on "National treatment" is based on Article III(4) of the General Agreement on Tariffs and Trade ("GATT"). However, while national treatment in GATT attaches to goods - not to the respective owners of the goods - it attaches under TRIPS to the person of the right holder. This modified "attachment" *is systematically linked to the territorial character of intellectual property rights. In the EC view, the vast jurisprudence on Article III(4) of GATT, under the GATT dispute settlement system as well as under the WTO dispute settlement system, may give valuable insight for the interpretation of Article 3.1 of the TRIPS Agreement*. In any event, the basic feature contained in Article 3.1 of the TRIPS Agreement would appear to be straight forward. *A WTO Member cannot treat a national of another WTO Member in relation to an intellectual*

---

[13] *See US Opening Oral Statement at Second Panel Meeting*, para. 9; Council Regulation (EC) 693/2003 of 8 April 2003, p. 2. Exhibit Comp-1h.

[14] Appellate Body Report, *US – Section 211*, para. 242.

[15] Appellate Body Report, *US – Section 211*, para. 242.

[16] Second paragraph, preamble, TRIPS Agreement.

[17] Appellate Body Report, *US – Section 211*, para. 242.

[18] *See* Appellate Body Report, *US – Section 211*, para. 48.

> *property right which its IPR system offers less favourably than it treats its own nationals in relation to such an intellectual property right.*[19]

18. Further, the EC states at paragraph 27 that "so far, Article 3.1 of the TRIPS Agreement has never been applied on a *de facto* basis." What the EC apparently means is that no TRIPS dispute thus far has involved *de facto* discrimination. This is true, since this is only the third dispute in which a breach of national treatment under TRIPS has been alleged, and only the second in which it is a significant issue. What the EC seems to imply, however, is that there should *be* no *de facto* analysis, and that national treatment in the goods area is not instructive with respect to any *de facto* analysis in the TRIPS context.

19. But this implication is wrong, and is contrary to the Appellate Body's instruction in *US – Section 211* that such findings may well be useful. Incidentally, in a dispute involving a breach of most favored nation treatment obligations under the *General Agreement on Trade in Services* ("GATS")—which, like the TRIPS Agreement, contains national treatment and MFN obligations based on treatment of *persons* instead of *goods*—the Appellate Body specifically looked for guidance to MFN findings in the goods area.[20] Citing *European Economic Community - Imports of Beef from Canada*,[21] in which the panel found *de facto* discrimination, the Appellate Body found that the MFN obligation with respect to treatment accorded certain *persons* under the GATS Agreement "should be interpreted to include *de facto*, as well as *de jure*, discrimination."[22] Also relevant in this context, the Appellate Body interpreted the "person-based" MFN obligation as including *de facto* discrimination in part because the language did not exclude such an interpretation, stating that

> The obligation imposed by Article II [the MFN obligation] is unqualified. The ordinary meaning of this provision does not exclude *de facto* discrimination. Moreover, if Article II was not applicable to *de facto* discrimination, it would not be difficult -- and, indeed, it would be a good deal easier in the case of trade in services, than in the case of trade in goods -- to devise discriminatory measures aimed at circumventing the basic purpose of that Article.[23]

20. In analyzing the national treatment obligation under the TRIPS Agreement, the Appellate Body specifically endorsed an approach that asked whether there is differential treatment of nationals and whether that treatment "could be considered to provide a less favourable treatment to nationals of other Members as it denies *effective equality of opportunities*" to those nationals.[24] It is therefore relevant for this Panel to ask, for instance, whether the EC GI Regulation, with respect to French nationals claiming GI rights in a French cheese and US nationals claiming GI rights in a US cheese, is denying "effective equality of opportunities" to those US nationals. In this context, the EC's argument that the TRIPS Agreement national treatment obligation would always require that the treatment of pharmaceutical patent holders be compared to the treatment of motor vehicle part patent holders is irrelevant for purposes of this dispute.

21. Finally, it is untrue that the complainants have focused in this dispute purely on discrimination based on the origin of the goods, and not on discrimination between nationals.[25] The United States will not reiterate all of its arguments here, but only notes that there is a strong link between the nationality of the person able to apply for GI registration/protection, and whether that person can take advantage of the "domestic track" for

---

19 Panel Report, *US – Section 211*, para. 4.108 (emphasis added).

20 Appellate Body Report, *EC – Bananas*, paras. 232—233.

21 Adopted 10 March 1981, BISD 28S/92, paras. 4.2-4.3.

22 *EC – Bananas*, para. 233.

23 *Id.*, para. 233. *See also* Appellate Body Report, *Canada – Autos*, in which the Appellate Body, citing its findings in *EC – Bananas*, reversed the panel and found that, despite the lack of express language, whether subsidies were contingent on the use of domestic over foreign goods should be determined on a *de facto*, and not just *de jure*, basis. It is also interesting to note that in that dispute, the EC was arguing in favor of a *de facto* analysis of the MFN obligations in the GATS. Appellate Body Report, *Canada – Autos*, para. 175.

24 Appellate Body Report, *US – Section 211*, para. 258 (emphasis added).

25 EC's Response to Second Set of Panel Questions, para. 32.

registration or is relegated to the "foreign"track for registration under the GI Regulation. The EC has also confirmed in the TRIPS Council that what it believes to be equal treatment with respect to producers of non-EC based GI is required by the national treatment obligation of the TRIPS Agreement.[26]

22. The EC's second tack in responding to the Panel's question concerning *de facto* discrimination is to conjure a false "conflict" between the obligations under the GATT Article III and TRIPS Agreement Article 3.1. As the United States has already noted, however, there is nothing unusual about a measure being covered by two different sets of obligations, and there is nothing about this situation that requires anything other than the normal approach to the interpretation of the agreement provisions. More particularly, there is nothing in this situation that presents any kind of "conflict." Certainly, nothing in this situation would support narrowing the obligations in one or the other of the agreements at issue. Further, the United States reiterates that the lack of a general Article XX exception in the TRIPS Agreement—but the specific inclusion of particular exceptions in Article 3.2, based on the Paris Convention and on language similar to Article XX(d)—can only be regarded as deliberate.

Questions 104-105

23. The United States refers to its response to Panel's question 104, concerning the interpretation of "separate customs territory Member of the WTO", and offers only the following comments on the EC's response. First, there is nothing in the word "separate" that suggests that the term "customs territory Member of the WTO" (which "separate" modifies), can only mean a subpart of a country. The word "separate" can, and in context does, just as equally mean separate from other WTO Members (*i.e.*, the EC as a WTO Member "separate" from its EC member States, who are also WTO Members), and "separate" in the sense of "separate" from "country" Members of the WTO. There is no question that the EC's customs territory is "separate" from that of France, or Italy, or any of the other 23 member States—it is a distinct customs territory that is separate from that of the countries that make up the EC. Indeed, it would be odd to think that a customs union was not intended to create a customs territory separate from that of its constituent Members. Indeed it is clear from Article XXIV:8(a) of the GATT 1994 that a customs union creates a "separate" customs territory since it defines a customs union as the "substitution of a single customs territory for two or more customs territories." The single customs territory is "separate" and distinct from the two or more customs territories for which it substitutes.

24. Second, although the EC Treaty has a concept of EC "citizenship" as applied to natural persons, it does not confer any nationality itself, and does not contain any concept of "nationality" as applied to legal persons. Further, what the EC itself may consider to be "nationals" and what are considered "nationals" under the WIPO administered treaties listed in Article 1.3 of the TRIPS Agreement—which apply only to countries, and not to entities like the EC—are two different things.

Question 106

25. The United States has presented to the Panel substantial information and argument demonstrating that, particularly in the area of agricultural products and foodstuffs, it is *EC* nationals that claim rights in *EC-based* GIs, and *non-EC* nationals that claim rights in *non-EC-based* GIs. Consequently, a regulation that discriminates based on where a person is established producing GI products discriminates based on nationality.[27] Four months after the United States submitted its first submission to this effect, on April 23, 2004, the EC has not been able to present a single example of a non-EC national claiming rights in an EC-based GI (*i.e.*, quadrant 2 of China Taipei's model in the US response to Panel question 101). This is in spite of the fact that it is the EC, and not the United States, that has the best access to the relevant information and the relevant private and public

[26] EC Response to Second Set of Panel Questions, para. 15; *See* US comment above on EC response to question 97, above.

[27] The United States has also argued that it is not critical to a finding of a breach of national treatment under the TRIPS Agreement that the Panel find, as a matter of fact that there are no non-EC nationals claiming rights to EC-based GIs, or EC nationals claiming rights to non-EC GIs. *See* US Response to Panel Questions 101-103.

sector stakeholders who would know. If there were such persons, the EC would certainly have informed the Panel and the complainants.

26. In other words, not only are there no non-EC-based GIs registered under the EC GI Regulation—compared to over 600 EC-based GIs—but there is also no indication whatsoever that any non-EC national has been able to become a rightholder in any EC-based registered GI. Effectively, non-EC GI rightholders have simply been shut out by the requirements of the EC GI Regulation.[28]

27. Further, the EC appears to concede, at paragraph 51, that there is no further information available that would shed any additional light on this question. Therefore the information presented to the Panel demonstrates that the EC GI Regulation distinguishes based on nationality and accords less favorable treatment to non-EC nationals than it accords to EC nationals.

28. As a final point, the EC claims "at the outset" that the Panel is wrong to focus on the nationality of the GI "applicant", since, according to the EC, the "conditions for applicants are a procedural modality of the application process" and the applicant is not identical with the rightholder. This is wrong. Under the GI Regulation, the applicant is a group or a natural or legal person that applies to register the agricultural products or foodstuffs "*which it produces or obtains*". Article 5(2) of the GI Regulation. It is clear that the applicant is the GI rightholder for that product. It is thus perfectly appropriate to inquire into the nationality of that person, as the Panel has done.

Question 107

29. The EC again appears to claim that, simply because the GI Regulation does not use the word "national" (which is the only reasonable way to understand the EC's conclusory mantra that the Regulation "does not involve any discrimination on the basis of nationality"), it cannot breach national treatment obligations. The EC behaves as if the legal and practical requirement that a legal person become a "national" in order to establish itself in the EC producing agricultural products and foodstuffs is a mere accident or coincidence, and thus irrelevant. But practical and legal considerations—primarily on the face of the GI Regulation, but also in conjunction with other legal and practical factors—mean that EC nationals can have their GIs registered and protected under the GI Regulation, while non-EC nationals cannot. Such a situation spells out a breach of national treatment under the TRIPS Agreement and the Paris Convention.

Question 112

30. For the reasons submitted in its response to this question, there *is* a requirement under the GI Regulation to recognize any country that satisfies the conditions in Article 12(1) of the GI Regulation, contrary to the EC's response.

Question 114

31. *Paragraph 68.* The United States notes that, contrary to the implications of the EC, Article 12a(2)(a) requires the WTO Member to determine whether a GI application satisfies the requirements of the GI Regulation, not of the TRIPS Agreement; this is not a determination of whether the GI falls under the definition of a GI under Article 22.1 of the TRIPS Agreement. There are obvious differences between the definition of a GI in the GI Regulation and the definition in the TRIPS Agreement, and the GI Regulation imposes a host of requirements that have no relation to the TRIPS Agreement definition of a GI.[29]

---

[28] Although the EC cites two examples of one EC member State national owning companies in another EC member State, there is no indication that, even in those cases, the producing companies were not incorporated in the EC member State in which they are established.

[29] *E.g.*, Articles 2(3)-2(6), 3(2), 4, 5(1), and 10, to name but a few GI Regulation requirements that are not related to the TRIPS definition of a GI.

32. *Paragraph 69.* In this response, the EC confirms the US argument in response to the Panel's question 128, that the EC is not simply allowing other WTO Members to determine whether the GI Regulation requirements, including inspection structures, are satisfied. Rather, having required other WTO Members to establish inspection structures and to determine whether the GI Regulation's requirements are met, the EC unilaterally reserves to itself the overriding power to decide whether the WTO Member's determination is right or wrong.

Question 115

33. The EC confirms that, for purposes of objections under the Regulation, the person that is "from a WTO Member country" is the same as the person who is "resident or established in the WTO Member country." In turn, this is the same person that the EC itself describes as the "national" of the WTO Member who had to be granted the right to object in order to comply with the TRIPS Agreement.[30] The United States does not see how the EC can maintain that the person resident or established in a WTO Member is considered a "national" of that Member for purposes of objections, but that the same person established and producing a product in that same WTO Member is not a "national" of that WTO Member when it comes to submitting applications for GI protection. Particularly since the EC maintained the exact opposite—that such a person *is* a national of that WTO Member—when trying to justify the TRIPS-consistency of the GI Regulation in TRIPS Council.[31]

Question 116

34. The United States notes the EC's indifference to whether other WTO Members have the legal competence to determine whether the requirements of the EC's GI Regulation are satisfied, and reiterates its view that it is not clear on what basis other WTO Members can deem or not deem that the requirements of other WTO Members' laws are met. This is a separate question from whether it is necessary that the WTO Member itself, rather than the rightholder, demonstrate that a GI is protected in the country of origin.[32] The United States also reiterates that, contrary to the assertions of the EC, what the GI Regulation requires is not a determination of whether a GI applicant meets the TRIPS Agreement definition of a GI; rather, Article 12a(2) of the GI Regulation requires on its face that the WTO Member determine that all of the GI Regulation's requirements are met.

35. Finally, the United States notes that the EC here, and not for the first or last time[33] in this proceeding, mischaracterizes the United States as having acknowledged that what the EC characterizes as the "transmission" of GI applications and objections are "purely ministerial": they are not, as even the EC acknowledges in its responses to the Panel's questions.[34] In the passage that the EC incorrectly and repeatedly seizes upon, the United States was responding to a specific hypothetical Panel question that "from a practical point of view ... it would probably not be difficult to designate an office in the US government to perform *a purely ministerial act* of transmitting registration applications and objections to the EC."[35] But, as the United States made plain in the following paragraph of the same response, what the GI Regulation requires is far from a "purely ministerial act". Therefore, the EC errs in claiming that the United States regards the EC GI Regulation's requirements as a purely ministerial act.

---

[30] *See US* Opening Oral Statement at Second Panel Meeting, para. 9; Council Regulation (EC) 693/2003 of 8 April 2003, p. 2. Exhibit Comp-1h.

[31] *See* US comment to EC response to Panel question 97, above.

[32] *See* US comment to EC response to Panel Question 136, *infra.*

[33] This mischaracterization is repeated a number of times in the EC's responses.

[34] *E.g.,* paragraph 139 of the EC Response to the Second Set of Panel Questions, in which the EC says that "by transmitting the application, the government of the country of origin certifies that it deems the requirements of Article 12a(2) [which, *inter alia*, requires a determination that all the requirements of the GI Regulation have been met] to be fulfilled."

[35] US Response to First Set of Panel Questions, para. 74 (emphasis added).

36. *Paragraph 77.* As discussed below in the US comments with respect to questions 135 and 136, the EC has provided no convincing reason why the EC cannot itself assess whether the requirements of the EC GI Regulation have been met, on the basis of information provided by the rightholder.

37. *Paragraphs 78-80.* The United States submits that unilaterally forcing other WTO Members to establish particular inspection structures and to determine whether a GI application meets the requirements of the EC GI Regulation is, in no sense of the word, "cooperation".

Question 120

38. If the EC is correct that current country of origin marking requirements satisfy the requirements of Article 12(2) of the GI Regulation, then it is not clear what Article 12(2) adds or why a specific provision burdening non-EC GI products is necessary.

Question 126

39. *Paragraph 103.* The United States submits that the distinctions drawn by the EC with respect to when "third countries" includes WTO Members and when it does not are not supported by the very text of the Regulation itself.

Question 127

40. The United States notes that this response emphasizes the burden being placed on other WTO Members with respect to the establishment of particular inspection structures, without any indication of why it is necessary that the WTO Member itself establish such structures, as the Panel's question asks.

Question 131

41. The Panel asks a direct question: whether any EC Directives "require foreign involvement in the designation/approval of conformity assessment bodies, when mutual acceptance agreements in the conformity assessment area do not already exist." In response, the EC discusses and provides examples of cases in which importing countries have agreed to allow conformity assessment bodies in the territory of another WTO Member to assess conformity with the importing country's regulations. But the EC fails to address the Panel's question, because the approach taken by the GI Regulation is apparently unprecedented as well as WTO-inconsistent. The United States submits that there is a substantial difference between an importing WTO Member allowing another WTO Member, as an option, to designate conformity assessment bodies on its own territory to assess conformity with regulations of the importing country (or a mutual agreement to that effect), and a WTO Member unilaterally requiring other WTO Members to establish particular inspection structures as a condition of meeting the importing country's regulatory requirements.

Questions 135 and 136 [EC's Article XX(d) Affirmative Defense]

42. A few initial comments are appropriate with respect to the Article XX(d) issue. Apparently for tactical reasons, the EC decided to present virtually no information or arguments with respect to its GATT 1994 Article XX(d) affirmative defense until its second submission on July 22, 2004. This meant that the United States' first opportunity to respond to the EC's Article XX(d) arguments was in its oral statement at the second Panel meeting. In that oral statement, the United States presented a full response to the EC's arguments, demonstrating that the EC had failed even to argue most of the elements required by Article XX(d):[36] the EC did not argue that the measures at issues were "to secure compliance" with laws or regulations (instead arguing generally only their relation to the "objectives" of the EC GI Regulation and to its "implementation"), and did not identify the "laws or regulations" with which the measures were supposedly designed to secure compliance

[36] US Opening Oral Statement at Second Panel Meeting, paras. 51-61.

that were consistent with the GATT 1994. Further, the United States demonstrated that the GATT-inconsistent measures were not "necessary" in any sense, showing that there are other measures reasonably available to the EC (indeed, showing that the EC itself had identified such measures in attempting to show that its GATT-inconsistent measures had some parallels with other measures used by the EC, the United States and other WTO Members).

43. Finally, in response to the EC's unsupported single-sentence assertion that its GATT 1994-inconsistent measures met the requirements in the chapeau to Article XX(d), the United States argued that these measures are applied in a manner which constitutes a means of arbitrary or unjustifiable discrimination between countries where the same conditions prevail or a disguised restriction on trade. As the United States explained, the requirements of the GI Regulation mean that any country that protects GIs in the same manner as the EC—with EC-style inspection structures and with legal mechanisms for assessing whether the requirements of the GI Regulation are satisfied—may obtain registration and protection of its GIs. Those WTO Members that do not have such systems cannot obtain such protection. These are countries where the same conditions prevail, but, because the EC favors countries that protect GIs the way it does, the EC arbitrarily and unjustifiably discriminates between them.

44. The Panel's questions 135 and 136 are designed to extract from the EC the arguments and information that it should have presented, but failed to present, as its affirmative defense. As discussed further below, the EC continues to fail to show that it qualifies for the Article XX(d) exception with respect to the issues raised by the Panel. But to the extent that open questions remain with respect any of these issues, the United States submits that the Panel should be cognizant that it was the EC's burden to present convincing information and arguments that its WTO-inconsistent measures are nonetheless justified by an Article XX(d) exception. There may be many unanswered questions and incomplete arguments in the EC's responses to the Panel's questions, and the cost of not making the Article XX(d) arguments clear at this stage must, in the US view, be borne by the EC.

45. Further, the United States notes that the EC has presented no information or argument whatsoever—not in any closing oral statement at the second Panel meeting, and not even in response to the Panel's questions—to rebut the US arguments that its GATT-inconsistent measures do not satisfy the requirements of the *chapeau* to Article XX(d)—that is, that they are applied in a manner that which would constitute a means of arbitrary or unjustifiable discrimination between countries where the same conditions prevail or a disguised restriction on trade. Since the EC has failed even to attempt to rebut these arguments, and keeping in mind the Appellate Body's instruction that panels may not make a case for a party,[37] the United States requests that the Panel find that the EC has failed to show that its GATT-inconsistent measure satisfies the requirements of Article XX(d).

Question 135 [Article XX(d)'s requirement that the measure be a "measure to secure compliance with laws or regulations which are not inconsistent with the provisions of [the GATT 1994]."]

46. *Paragraph 122.* The relevant "measures" for which the Panel should assess compliance with Article XX(d) are the requirements of the GI Regulation that the United States alleges are inconsistent with the GATT 1994. These include the reciprocity and equivalence requirements of the GI Regulation, as well as the requirements that WTO Members assess compliance of GI applications with the EC GI Regulation and certify certain information to the EC concerning the application and concerning the WTO Member's GI protection system, and that the WTO Members satisfy various EC requirements related to inspection structures. These heavy burdens placed on WTO Members, which have been set out in detail in the US submissions, oral statements, and responses to questions in this dispute, are not simply "verification" and "transmission" of GI applications, as suggested by the EC.

[37] *See* Appellate Body Report, Japan—Measures Affecting Agricultural Products ("Japan—Agricultural Products"), WT/DS76/AB/R, adopted 19 March 1999, para. 129 (stating that it is the complainant's burden to make a *prima facie* case, and that a panel is not entitled to "make the case for the complaining party.")

47. *Paragraph 125.* The EC states that the function of the inspection structures is to secure compliance with the requirement in Article 4(1) of the GI Regulation that products bearing a protected name comply with a "product specification" (and the similar requirement in Article 8 of the GI Regulation). But the contents of the "product specification" are listed in Article 4(2) of the GI Regulation, and it is not clear how the requirement for specific "inspection structures" relate to securing compliance with those specifications. Specifically, and considering each of the "product specifications" in Article 4(2) of the GI Regulation, the requirement for inspection structures does not appear to have any relation to securing compliance with

(a) the name of the product—which would appear to simply be a fact allowing the product to be registered

(b) a description of the physical characteristics of the product—which should be verifiable from an examination of the product itself upon importation: either the product has the characteristics or it does not (and, in any case, those characteristics would not be more readily verified through on-site inspections than through other means)

(c) definition of the geographic area—which is just a definition and not susceptible to "inspection"

(d) evidence that the product originates in the area—either there is or is not evidence that the product originates in an area; the evidence can be evaluated upon application, and inspection structures could not be considered to "secure compliance" with such evidence

(e) description of method of obtaining the product—to the extent this is relevant for particular names, it would seem that this factor would be reflected in the product itself, considering that the Article 2(2) definition concerns "quality or characteristics" of the product.

(f) link between geography and the product—again, there either is or is not a link between the two: inspection structures will not "secure compliance" with such a link

(g) details of inspection structures—it is non-sensical to require inspection structures to secure compliance with inspection structures

(h) specific labeling details—like the "name", this simply reveals how the product will be labeled; inspection structures will not secure compliance with these details

(i) any other requirements—it is not clear how inspection structures would secure compliance with these unspecified requirements

48. In sum, contrary to the EC's arguments, there appears to be little or no relationship between the "product specifications" in Article 4(2) and the "inspection structures" that the EC claims are designed to "secure compliance" with those specifications. Indeed, with respect to several "specifications" it is not even clear what "securing compliance" means. To the extent the concept of "securing compliance" is relevant at all with respect to the Article 4(2) "specifications"—for instance, how does one secure compliance with a "name" or a "geographic area"—the inspection structures do not appear at all suited to securing any such compliance. The United States submits that the EC has not sustained any burden of showing that the requirement for inspection structures "secures compliance" with the specifications.

49. Further, although the EC argues that the inspection structure requirement is to "secure" compliance with the "product specifications", it does not show how the "product specifications" constitute "laws or regulations which are not inconsistent" with the GATT 1994, which Article XX(d) requires. For instance, the

"product specifications" include details of required inspection structures, which the United States has shown is GATT-inconsistent.

50. *Paragraph 126.* The EC states that "verification (and incidentally also the transmission)" of the application by the country of origin serve the purpose of establishing whether the requirements of the GI Regulation are satisfied. But regardless of whether this is the purpose, having the WTO Member assess whether an application meets the EC GI Regulation's requirements, and requiring the WTO Member to transmit the application to the EC, along with other documents and declarations required under Article 12a(2) of the GI Regulation, do not "secure compliance" with the GI Regulation. At best, such requirements solicit the WTO Member's view as to whether, in the case of a particular applicant, an applicant meets the standards set in the EC GI Regulation and require the communication of that view to the EC (however irrelevant, since it is the EC, and not the WTO Member, that makes the determination as to whether a GI will be registered). Whether or not a particular product satisfies the legal requirements of the EC GI Regulation—and therefor may be registered and protected in the EC—is a legal judgement based on the facts presented as applied to the legal provisions of the GI Regulation. It has nothing to do with whether a product or the applicant is "complying" with the Regulation. So, neither aspect of this measure— neither the so-called "verification" (actually an assessment of whether the Regulation's requirements are met under Article 12a(2)), nor "incidentally also the transmission"—have anything to do with "securing compliance", as required by GATT Article XX(d).

51. *Paragraph 127.* The EC claims that the requirement that foreign GIs be burdened with a country of origin label "secures compliance" with the requirement that foreign GIs may only be granted with due regard for local and traditional usage and the practical risks of confusion. The EC also claims that this requirement secures compliance with the requirement that only qualifying products may use a "GI" label. With respect to the first point, it is, in part, the very fact that *foreign* GIs, and not *domestic* GIs, have to bear the burden of removing risks of confusion that give rise to the WTO breach in the first place. This labeling requirement is not, therefore, in any sense securing compliance with a WTO-consistent regulation. To the contrary, it is making the discriminatory nature of the requirement more concrete. As to the second point, the United States fails to see any relation between this country of origin labeling requirement and the requirement that a product comply with the Regulation in order to bear a protected GI. Further, this requirement does not satisfy the requirement in the *chapeau* to GATT Article XX(d) that the GATT-inconsistent measure not be "applied in a manner which would constitute a means of arbitrary or unjustifiable discrimination between countries where the same conditions prevail, or a disguised restriction on international trade." EC member States, as well as other WTO Members, are all equally situated with respect to making sure that the consumer is able to distinguish between GI products. Therefore it is arbitrary and unjustifiable to require that only non-EC GIs bear the burden bearing the distinctive country of origin label.

52. *Paragraphs 128-129.* While the EC is correct that Article XX(d) refers to measures to secure compliance, and not "enforcement mechanisms" *per se*, it is plain that the WTO-inconsistent requirements of the EC GI Regulation are neither "enforcement mechanisms" nor measures "to secure compliance". Rather they appear to be part of a process intended to assess whether applications from non-EC GI holders should be accepted—a process that creates enormous burdens for foreign GIs—that is not justified under Article XX(d).

53. *Paragraph 130.* The EC's argument is circular. The EC claims that the GI Regulation itself is the WTO-consistent regulation with which the WTO-inconsistent requirements noted above are designed to secure compliance. But the EC GI Regulation itself is not consistent with the WTO—that is what this dispute is about. Therefore, despite the Panel's direct question, it is still unclear as to what WTO-consistent "laws or regulations" the WTO-inconsistent requirements of the EC GI Regulation are supposed to ensure compliance.

Question 136 [Whether the measures are "necessary" to ensure compliance].

54. *Paragraph 131.* The EC has referred to its requirements under Article 12a(2)—that other WTO Members assess whether applications from their nationals meet the requirements of the EC GI Regulation, provide a description of the legal basis for protection of the GI in the country of origin, file a declaration that the

EC-mandated inspection structures are established on their territory, and submit all other relevant documents—simply as "verification", presumably to minimize the appearance of the extent of the responsibility being placed on other WTO Members by the EC. But EC reacts with some alarm at the Panel's suggestion that what is at stake is simple "verification" that the GI at issue is protected in its country of origin. Therefore, the EC responds to the Panel's question by attempting to justify broader Article 12a(2) requirements, not just those related to whether the GI is protected in its country of origin.

55. But none of the EC's responses show that the requirements of Article 12a(2) are "necessary" in any sense. The EC says that assessment of whether the application complies with the requirements of the EC GI Regulation—that is, not only the requirement that it be protected in the country of origin, but the substantive requirements, concerning, *e.g.*, whether the product possesses the required characteristics—requires local knowledge, which "typically" only the country of origin will have. It is not clear whether knowledge of local conditions *is* necessary, but even if it is, the EC itself only believes that the country of origin will "typically" have such information. The GI Regulation leaves no option for countries that do not have such information. The EC's own justification is thus a virtual admission that the WTO Member itself will not necessarily have more or better information than other parties (for instance the rightholder). Further, the EC claims that on-site checks "may also" be required, which the EC could not carry out without consent of the country of origin. But this answer suggests that such on-site inspections are not necessary under the GI Regulation. If so, it is unclear what remains of the EC's argument that the involvement of the WTO Member is "necessary" on the basis of on-site inspections that themselves are *not* necessary. Further, whether the WTO Member consents or not to the EC's on-site checks is not at issue: the GI Regulation does not anticipate or even permit such an option. If it did, this would be another matter. Consequently, there is no basis for finding that the Article 12a(2) requirements are in any sense "necessary".

56. The United States notes in this connection that, even in the case of measures to protect human or animal life or health falling within the scope of the *Agreement on the Application of Sanitary and Phytosanitary Measures* ("SPS Agreement"), the SPS Agreement states that where such a measure "specifies control at the level of production, the Member in whose territory the production takes place shall provide the necessary assistance to facilitate such control and the work of the controlling authorities."

57. *Paragraph 133.* In essence, the Panel asks why the GI Regulation cannot provide an opportunity to the rightholder itself to show that his GI is protected in the country of origin. The EC's non-response is that it does not appear that a US rightholder would be able to present an "authenticated certificate of registration." But this response is irrelevant, and demonstrates a bias against non-EC systems of GI protection. There is no reason that the GI Regulation could not permit other, equally valid methods for the rightholder to establish that his GI is protected in the country of origin. The assumed absence of a particular document is no excuse to deny to the rightholder the opportunity to prove entitlement to registration and protection in other ways (ways that WTO Members other than the EC currently use to effectively protect GIs).

58. *Paragraphs 135 - 138.* Referring to Article 24.9 of the TRIPS Agreement—allowing WTO Members not to protect GIs that are not protected in their country of origin—the EC claims that absence of an EC-style specific GI registration system in other WTO Members makes it "particularly necessary" that the relevant WTO Member "verify" the GI application, in particular showing that the GI is protected in the country of origin. But, to the contrary, it is the widespread existence of those non-registration systems among the WTO Membership that makes it important to impose this requirement on the rightholder, not the WTO Member itself. In the absence of a central registration system, it is the rightholder, not the government, that will be in the best position to provide the legal provisions and the usage on the basis of which his GI is protected in the country of origin. For instance, it is the rightholder, not the government, who will know whether there has been a judicial decision upholding protection of his GI. It is the rightholder, not the government, who can provide information on the usage of his GI in the country of origin.

59. The United States suggests that the Panel be particularly wary of this line of reasoning from the EC, as it amounts to a "back-door" method of imposing the EC's system of GI protection on other WTO Members as a

condition of providing GI protection. As the United States has explained elsewhere, the TRIPS Agreement specifically provides leeway to WTO Members in implementing their obligations. Article 1.1 states that "Members shall be free to determine the appropriate method of implementing the provisions of this Agreement within their own legal system and practice." The need for this freedom is particularly obvious in the area of GIs, where there is a broad variety of methods of providing protection.[38] Yet, the EC GI Regulation, by requiring the WTO Member, instead of the rightholder, to show that the GI is protected in the country of origin, essentially requires WTO Members to adopt a centralized system similar to the registration system adopted by the EC, nullifying Article 1.1 of the TRIPS Agreement unilaterally. Members that do not have an EC-style system—but that protect GIs through, for instance, unfair trade statutes or common law certification mark systems—are not in as good a position as the rightholder to demonstrate that the GI is protected, and yet are penalized under the EC GI Regulation. Indeed, the EC itself recognizes that it is penalizing systems for GI protection that are different from the EC system, when it admits, at paragraph 135, that persons with GIs from WTO Members that do not protect GIs through an EC-like GI-specific registration system may find it more difficult to meet the EC's requirements.

60. The Panel should also consider the full consequences of the EC's argument. The EC claims that, in addition to the registration system for GIs, it also protects GIs through unfair trade laws and laws against deceptive advertising. The United States wonders whether the EC would be satisfied if the United States refused to allow EC nationals to file applications for GI certification marks for certain names or to use unfair trade laws with respect to those names unless the EC could show that those specific names were registered as GIs in Europe. Yet that is exactly what the EC is requiring of other WTO Members in the GI Regulation.

61. *Paragraphs 139-141.* The EC has no real response to the question of why it is necessary for the WTO Member, instead of the rightholder, to "transmit" the GI application, other than to claim, incorrectly, that the United States admits that this would be a "purely ministerial act" and that "it would not appear to have a significant impact on imports". But, as the United States made perfectly plain in the very response that the EC repeatedly and incorrectly cites,[39] what the EC GI Regulation requires is not a purely ministerial act of transmission: to the contrary, the EC GI Regulation imposes substantial requirements on WTO Members with respect to GI applications of its nationals.[40] Further, the EC even admits, in paragraph 139 of its response, that "by transmitting the application, the government of the country of origin certifies that it deems the requirements of Article 12a(2) [which, *inter alia*, requires a determination that all the requirements of the GI Regulation have been met] to be fulfilled." What the EC has failed to answer is the key question asked by the Panel: why is it necessary for the WTO Member, instead of the rightholder to submit the application?

62. *Paragraphs 142-144.* The EC offers no answer whatsoever to the Panel's direct question of why it is "necessary" for WTO Members to transmit objections to the EC, other than to claim that it is purely ministerial (which, despite the EC's mischaracterization of the US responses to the Panel questions, it is not), and that it "does not have any significant impact on trade in goods." But the issue under Article XX(d) of the GATT 1994 is whether the measure is "necessary to secure compliance" with a WTO-consistent law or regulation, not whether the EC believes that the requirement will have a significant trade impact or whether it is "purely ministerial". Indeed, panels and the Appellate Body have emphasized that a breach of Article III:4 of the GATT 1994 does not require a showing of an actual trade impact.[41] If this is the best the EC can do to meet its

---

[38] *See, e.g.*, "Document SCT/6/3 Rev. on Geographical Indications: Historical Background, Nature of Rights, Existing Systems for Protection and Obtaining Protection in Other Countries," World Intellectual Property Organization (WIPO) Document SCT/8/4 (April 2, 2002) (Exhibit US-5); "The Definition of Geographical Indications," WIPO Document SCT/9/4 (October 1, 2002) (Exhibit COMP-16).

[39] As noted above, the United States responded to a specific hypothetical Panel question that "from a practical point of view ... it would probably not be difficult **to designate an office in the US government to perform *a purely ministerial act* of transmitting registration applications and objections to the EC." (Para. 74. Emphasis added.)** But, as the United States made plain in the following paragraph of the same response, what the GI Regulation requires is far from the "purely ministerial act" . Therefore, the EC is wrong to claim that the United States regards the EC GI Regulation's requirements as a purely ministerial act.

[40] US Response to First Set of Panel Questions, para. 75.

[41] *See* US Response to First Panel Questions, para. 65, *citing, US – Gasoline, US – Section 337, US – FSC (Article 21.5).*

Article XX(d) burden, the EC's non-response only adds weight to the conclusion that such a requirement is not necessary.

63. The United States also notes that, the EC's statement to the contrary notwithstanding, the United States has included deficiencies in the GI Regulation's right of objection as a part of its arguments under the GATT 1994.[42]

64. *Paragraph 145.* Article 6(6) of the GI Regulation, which applies to EC-based GIs, only requires that there be a "clear distinction in practice" between the two EC-based homonyms, without any specific requirement of country of origin labeling. This is an admission in the GI Regulation itself that a requirement for country of origin labeling is not "necessary", since it apparently is unnecessary with respect to EC-based GIs.

65. *Paragraphs 146-149.* The EC has presented no reasons why it could not itself designate inspection bodies in the United States or conduct its own inspections. The EC suggests that, somehow, because such inspections may require on-site audits and inspections, these options are not possible. But the United States does not see why either of those options is inconsistent with the possible need for on-site inspections or audits.

66. The Panel did not ask why the EC does not itself conduct the inspections, but the EC nevertheless volunteers that any such option would require the agreement of the WTO Member concerned. But this does not appear to present any impediment to the EC itself conducting its own inspections in relation to the requirements of its own Regulation. The EC offers no suggestion that Members would object to such inspections. Indeed, the EC's citation to the WTO Antidumping and SCM Agreements[43] confirms the groundlessness of the EC's objections. It is true that the Antidumping and SCM Agreements provide rules related to on-site verifications in the exporting country of information provided to the importing country's antidumping and countervailing duty administrators. However, those agreements did not provide the "right" to carry out those verifications. Long before these agreements were in place, both the EC and the United States conducted such on-site verifications in the exporting country as part of antidumping and countervailing duty investigations. The only thing that changed as a result of the Antidumping and SCM Agreements is that those verifications were subjected to certain disciplines. Consequently, it is simply untrue that, in the absence of a specific WTO agreement, the EC cannot provide for on-site inspections outside of the EC.

67. Finally, it is equally untrue that the EC GI Regulation requirements are fully compatible with the practices of the parties in the field of conformity assessment, as asserted by the EC. The United States does not see the relevance of the EC's reference to its response to Panel question 127, but the United States is aware of the normal practice that importing countries impose their own inspection requirements in the territory of the importing country, as necessary, to ensure that imported products meet any applicable requirements. *See* US Response to Second Set of Panel Questions, paragraphs 50-51. Even where on-site inspections of manufacturing facilities are required, as is the case, for instance, with respect to pharmaceutical manufacturing facilities, such on-site inspections are primarily carried out by the administering authorities of the importing country. In addition, consistent with the TBT Agreement, an importing party may agree to accept the results of conformity assessment procedures conducted in the exporting country, and may designate conformity assessment bodies in that territory for that purpose.[44] However, this is very different from a situation in which the exporting WTO Member is required to establish inspection structures as dictated by the importing country, as is required under the GI Regulation.

68. *Paragraph 152.* Again, the EC offers no reason that WTO Members themselves must establish specific inspection structures, instead of permitting the rightholder to provide the necessary assurances, including through independent inspections. The EC merely asserts, with no reason or justification, that

[42] *See, e.g.,* US Second Written Submission, paras. 89-95.

[43] Agreement on Implementation of Article VI of the General Agreement on Tariffs and Trade 1994 and Agreement on Subsidies and Countervailing Measures, respectively.

[44] *See* US Response to Second Set of Panel Question, para. 50.

inspection bodies can only carry out their functions "through some form of public oversight." But this is a conclusion without reasons, and is insufficient to demonstrate that such a requirement is "necessary".

69. *Paragraph 153.* As above, the EC offers no reason why it could not itself conduct any necessary inspections or designate bodies that could. It is of course, irrelevant that EC producers may have to pay for inspections; nothing would prevent requiring appropriate payment from non-EC producers.

70. *Paragraphs 154-155.* In these paragraphs, the EC is simply attempting to back away from the rigid inspection requirements imposed on non-EC WTO Members that are plainly set out in Article 10 of the EC GI Regulation.

Overview of Comments to Trademark Questions 137-156

71. To assist the Panel in considering the specific US comments on each of the EC responses with respect to trademark rights, which are set out further below, the United States believes it useful to present the following initial overview of those comments.

72. The United States argues that the GI Regulation deprives the owner of a registered trademark of its ability to prevent third parties from using identical or similar signs in a manner that results in a likelihood of confusion, as required by Article 16.1. The EC essentially acknowledges that the GI Regulation is inconsistent with TRIPS Article 16.1 when, at paragraph 166 of its responses, it states that it "can confirm that a trademark owner cannot prevent the holders of a registered geographical indication from using the name or names registered under Regulation 2081/92 on the grounds that the use of such name or names is confusing per se with an earlier trademark." This is a clear admission that the GI Regulation is inconsistent with Article 16.1. In its defense, the EC then justifies this departure from the requirements of Article 16.1 in four ways:

- Article 14(3) of the GI Regulation prevents registration of GIs that are confusingly similar to prior registered trademarks, thereby preserving the Article 16.1 rights of trademark owners.

- TRIPS Article 24.5 allows for the coexistence of a GI with an earlier registered trademark.

- TRIPS Article 24.3 prevents the EC from implementing the protections of TRIPS Article 16.1 because it would "diminish the protection of geographical indications that existed in that Member immediately prior to the date of entry into force of the WTO Agreement."

- TRIPS Article 17 allows for the elimination of the TRIPS Article 16.1 rights as a "limited exception."

73. None of these explanations is sufficient to justify departure from the strict requirements of TRIPS Article 16.1.

EC GI Regulation Article 14(3)

74. The EC's reliance on Article 14(3) as a rough substitute for a trademark owner's Article 16.1 rights is misplaced in several respects. In sum, even if the EC's reading of Article 14(3) is correct, the provision does not grant trademark owners the right to prevent "use[s] in the course of trade" of identical or confusingly similar signs. Importantly, however, the EC's reading of Article 14(3) is incorrect, and inconsistent with how the provision has been interpreted by the EC outside the confines of this dispute.

75. As the United States has shown, merely enabling the EC authorities to deny registration of a GI that is identical or confusingly similar to a valid prior registered trademark is not sufficient. In its comments, the United States demonstrates that not all (and in fact not many) trademark owners will be entitled to challenge before EC or member State courts the failure by the EC authorities to use Article 14(3) to deny registration of

particular GIs. For example, GIs registered via accession treaties are not subject to invalidation pursuant to Article 14(3), and therefore any trademarks with which such GIs are confusingly similar are not provided Article 16.1 rights.

76. Additionally, Article 16.1 requires Members to grant trademark owners the right to prevent "us[es] in the course of trade" that result in a likelihood of confusion with respect to their trademarks. The EC's reliance on Article 14(3) presupposes that a trademark owner will necessarily be able to know, at the time of registration, every way in which a GI rightholder will use the registered name, and how consumers in any given territory in the EC will perceive that use. The United States has shown that a trademark owner will not necessarily so know. Nonetheless, the EC makes clear that to enjoy its Article 16.1 rights, the owner of a trademark in one member State can not simply seek to enjoin "use[s] in the course of trade" of an identical or similar GI that confuse consumers in that one member State, but must first invalidate the GI on an EC-wide basis, on a showing that consumers EC-wide are confused (presuming, incorrectly, that Article 14(3) includes a "likelihood of confusion" standard).[45] Thus, even if the EC's reading of Article 14(3) were correct, it would not constitute an adequate substitute for Article 16.1 rights.

77. Moreover, and putting these points aside, the EC's argument that Article 14(3) is essentially a "likelihood of confusion" standard is simply not supportable. The plain wording of Article 14(3) demonstrates that it requires a different standard from likelihood of confusion: Article 14(3) enables the EC authorities to deny registration of a GI where the GI would "mislead the consumer" with respect to a prior trademark, in light of that trademark's reputation, renown and length of time of use. The "likelihood of confusion" standard and the "mislead the consumer" standard are clearly distinguished elsewhere in EC law, and the use of one over the other in the EC GI Regulation is not accidental.

78. Finally, the EC Guide to the GI Regulation confirms that Article 14(3) grants authority to deny registration "only in one circumstance"—when faced with a prior valid trademark that enjoys reputation, renown and use. While the EC argues that the reference in Article 14(3) to reputation, renown and use are merely shorthand references to a few of the factors involved in a likelihood of confusion analysis, the United States has shown that in EC and member State law and jurisprudence, those three elements are not necessary to find a likelihood of confusion. They are, however, prerequisites to the denial of registration for a GI, under Article 14(3). In the EC's view, these prerequisites in Article 14(3) even override the presumption, in TRIPS Article 16.1, that use of an identical sign on identical goods raises a likelihood of confusion. The EC goes so far as to state that a trademark owner cannot enjoin use of an identical GI on identical goods, unless it can show that the trademark has been used and is known to the public in the EC.[46]

Article 24.5

79. The EC continues to argue that Article 24.5 is not an exception to GI protection, despite the fact that (1) by its very terms, Article 24.5 limits the protection of GIs *vis-à-vis* trademarks, thereby constituting an exception to GI protection (and not to trademark protection); and (2) Article 24.5 is a part of Article 24, which is labeled "international negotiations; exceptions". As an exception, Article 24.5 acts as a shield for covered trademarks against GIs, and contains no provisions for limiting trademark rights. The EC's reliance on Article 24.5, apparently by negative implication, as allowing for coexistence of trademarks and conflicting GIs denies the drafters' ability to specifically provide for coexistence when coexistence is intended.

Article 24.3

80. By its terms, Article 24.3 has no place in a discussion as to whether the obligations of Article 16.1 are met. It is telling that the EC failed to answer the direct question from the Panel as to whether an obligation to diminish the pre-existing protection of GIs in order to allow trademark owners to exercise their rights under

[45] *See* Exhibit US-73, pg. 6 (the EC "examines consumer confusion ... with respect to the whole European public.").

[46] EC Responses to Questions following the Second Panel Meeting, para. 220.

Article 16.1 would arise under Article 16.1 or the GI section. The Panel's question derives from the fact that TRIPS Article 24.3 prevents diminishment of protection for GIs that could be caused by "implementing this Section", referring to Part II, Section 3 of the TRIPS Agreement. It follows that any diminishing of GI protection that could arise by virtue of implementation of another section of the TRIPS Agreement, including the trademark section, is not prohibited by Article 24.3.

<u>Article 17</u>

81. The immunity provided to GI owners for the use of registered GIs is far from being a "limited exception" to the Article 16.1 trademark rights under Article 17 of the TRIPS Agreement. The EC GI Regulation in fact provides for a blanket, or unlimited, exception to the protections of Article 16.1. The EC seems to defend the exception as being "limited" because it would only be an exception in a limited number of cases. That is not what is required by Article 17: it must be a limited exception even if it is an exception with respect to only one trademark.

82. Further, the GI Regulation does not take into account the interests of anyone other than producers of certain agricultural products. In responding to the question as to what the "legitimate interests of the owner of the trademark" are, the EC begins with the remarkable statement that "[a] trademark which has never been used or which is virtually unknown ... could be easily replaced without significant prejudice to the owner." This reveals an utter failure to take into account the interests of the trademark owner, much less the population of consumers who would undoubtedly be confused by having, for example, identical terms used on identical products side-by-side on the grocery store shelves.

83. Lastly, the EC's defense of the GI Regulation implies that all uses of registered GIs must be automatically entitled to the "fair use" exception by simple virtue of registration alone, without considering the facts of a particular case or whether such "use" is actually "fair". Especially given that non-geographic terms can be registered pursuant to the GI Regulation, it is difficult to understand how all uses of a registered GI can be unequivocally deemed "fair". One problem is that the GI Regulation provides blanket rights to use the GI rather than considering each particular use on a case-by-case basis, as is the case under the trademark laws of the EC and other jurisdictions the EC references in its responses. The EC offers the possibility that a trademark owner may resort to particular labeling and misleading advertising laws, as well as member State unfair competition laws. But even if recourse to such laws were possible, they do not consider the interests of trademark owners in the manner required by TRIPS Article 17; they may be sufficient to meet the general obligations of Article 10*bis* of the Paris Convention, but they are not sufficient to meet the specific trademark obligations under the TRIPS Agreement.

84. US comments with respect to each of the EC's responses to Panel questions follows.

Question 137

85. As it has throughout this dispute, the EC ignores fundamental problems with its argument that Article 14(3) serves as an adequate substitute for TRIPS Article 16.1. As the United States has frequently noted, Article 14(3) merely enables the *EC authorities* to deny *registration* of a GI. Moreover, the EC is enabled by Article 14(3) to do so "only in one circumstance"—when faced with a prior valid trademark that enjoys reputation, renown and use.[47] In contrast, TRIPS Article 16.1 requires the EC to grant *trademark owners* the right to prevent confusing "*use[s] in the course of trade*" of identical or similar signs. Nor are Article 16.1 rights limited only to those trademarks that enjoy reputation, renown and use.

---

[47] Guide to Community Regulations, "Protection of Geographical Indications, Designations of Origin and Certificates of Specific Character for Agricultural Products and Foodstuffs" (Working Document of the Commission Services issued by the European Commission Directorate-General for Agriculture, August 2004), pg. 24. Exhibit EC-64.

86. The EC's response to the Panel's question can be distilled down to two related statements. First, the EC states that under Article 14(3) of the EC GI Regulation, "the EC authorities will refuse a proposed geographical indication *[if it] is anticipated* that, when used in what the United States calls 'trademark-like fashion', it will result in a likelihood of confusion."[48] Similarly, the EC asserts that "[i]n principle, a name which has been found not to be confusing *per se* following the assessment required by Article 14(3) should not give rise to confusion when used subsequently."

87. Putting this "principle" to the test, however, demonstrates the critical error in the EC's assertion that Article 14(3) adequately substitutes for TRIPS Article 16.1 rights. The EC asserts that if a GI is not *per se* confusingly similar to a prior valid registered trademark at the time the GI is registered, then it is impossible that unanticipated uses that raise a likelihood of confusion could subsequently arise.

88. The fact is, however, that confusing uses not foreseen at the time of application for, and registration of, a GI can arise. As the United States has explained, a trademark owner will not necessarily know, at the time of registration, what uses a GI rightholder will employ, or how consumers in a particular territory will perceive those uses. This is so for several reasons, two of which the United States addresses below.

89. First, the United States has shown that product specifications—*if* available for review by trademark owners[49]—do not necessarily contain the "specific labelling details" that the EC asserts will offer definitive and circumscribed guidance on those uses of the GI that may arise and would be permitted or specifically prohibited.[50] Even if a product specification did include "specific labelling details" limiting the presentation of the sign on a product label, it is evident that the manner in which a GI is presented on a product label, on the one hand, and how that GI is marketed or promoted, on the other hand, can be two very different things. Labeling details included in a product specification have no necessary bearing on how the GI is used in marketing or promotion of the sign.[51]

90. Second, the EC acknowledges that a GI registration gives authorized users the right to use the registered term in a manner that is considerably more than merely descriptive.[52] Under the TRIPS Agreement, this is perfectly acceptable, as long as such use does not breach other provisions of the Agreement. The United States does not in any way, as the EC seeks to imply,[53] suggest otherwise. This point simply illustrates that the range of uses that a rightholder in a GI registered in the EC is authorized to employ is not necessarily readily apparent at the time of registration. It also demonstrates that there is not nearly as clear a distinction as the EC implies between use of the sign registered, which it says is authorized, and use of "other names,"[54] which it says is not authorized. Nor is it, as the EC suggests, a simple matter of distinguishing between the sign registered and "deformed, mutilated or otherwise manipulated" use of that sign.[55] The EC's acknowledgment that a GI rightholder is entitled to use the term in a "trademark-like" fashion shows that the universe of potential and authorized uses of the sign registered is not a finite concept, and is certainly not evident at the time of registration. If uses that would confuse consumers in a particular territory with respect to an identical or similar prior registered trademark arise at some later date, Article 16.1 grants the owner of that trademark the right to enjoin them. Article 14(3) does not.

---

48 EC Responses to Questions following the Second Panel Meeting, para. 161 (emphasis added).

49 The United States notes that in many instances, the product specifications are withheld or otherwise not available. US Responses to Questions following the Second Panel Meeting, para. 65.

50 *See* US Opening Oral Statement at Second Meeting, para. 78, and Exhibit US-77.

51 It is possible that the labeling details included in a product specification might speak more generally about marketing of the product in general, such as the Bitto product specification included in Exhibit EC-99. However, as the Panel will note, other product specifications, including those in Exhibits EC-101 and US-77, do not always include such limits.

52 *See* EC Oral Statement at Second Meeting, para. 184; EC Responses to Questions following the Second Panel Meeting, para. 161.

53 EC Oral Statement at Second Meeting, paras. 161, 180.

54 *See* EC Responses to Questions following the Second Panel Meeting, para. 167.

55 EC Responses to Questions following the Second Panel Meeting, para. 162.

91. The United States makes one final observation on the EC's response. Oddly, the EC repeats its assertion that three GIs registered pursuant to the Czech Republic's Act of Accession to the EU are "outside the Panel's terms of reference."[56] As the Panel is aware, the United States is challenging the consistency of the EC GI Regulation itself with TRIPS Article 16.1. It has not raised claims against the three Czech GIs.[57]

92. Although it is clear that a complainant need not show actual application of a measure in contravention of an obligation, much of the EC's first written submission was devoted to its view that the US and Australian claims under TRIPS Article 16.1 are "purely theoretical."[58] According to the EC, this is either because trademarks containing or consisting of geographical elements lack distinctiveness and are as such not registrable (thus making the possibility of conflicts with identical or similar registered GIs unlikely), or because Article 14(3) would prevent the registration of any GI that raises a likelihood of confusion with a prior registered trademark.

93. To demonstrate that its claims were not "purely theoretical," the United States, in response to a request from the Panel to disclose the names of any registered GIs that are identical or confusingly similar to EC trademarks, offered several examples,[59] including the three Czech GIs.[60] The United States noted that the rightholders in the three GIs are asserting a right, based on the registration, to use these three names in translation,[61] in a way that has in some jurisdictions been found to raise a likelihood of confusion with respect to prior valid registered trademarks.[62]

94. Moreover, the United States has noted that Article 14(3), which the EC has asserted provides protection for *all* prior registered trademarks against registration of confusingly similar GIs, does not in fact protect all such trademarks. In its comments on the EC response to question 142, below, the United States shows how significant numbers of trademarks and trademark owners will not be accorded any rights under Article 14(3). As one example, the United States has noted that GIs (like the three Czech GIs) registered *via* acts of accession are immune from challenges to their validity on the basis of Article 14(3), even if they are identical or confusingly similar to prior registered trademarks.[63]

95. Thus, it is not relevant whether the three Czech GIs, or the other examples cited by the United States, are within the Panel's terms of reference. The United States has used those GIs as illustrations of the manner in which the EC GI Regulation operates and the scope of protection granted by registration under the Regulation, and as a means of rebutting erroneous factual assertions made by the EC about its law in the course of this dispute. They are relevant to the Panel's "objective assessment of the facts of the case," within the meaning of Article 11 of the DSU. Moreover, to the extent that the Panel's findings address the rights that should be accorded trademark owners *vis-à-vis* particular uses of identical or similar GIs on identical or similar goods and services, those findings would be relevant to trademark rights in future disputes regarding infringing uses of those example GIs.

---

[56] EC Responses to Questions following the Second Panel Meeting, para. 157. *See also* EC Second Written Submission, para. 292.

[57] Of course, as noted below, the Panel's findings could affect trademark rights in future disputes regarding infringing uses of these GIs.

[58] EC First Written Submission, para. 277

[59] US Responses to Questions following the First Panel Meeting, para. 79; US Second Written Submission, para. 169; US Oral Statement at Second Panel Meeting, para. 74.

[60] US Responses to Questions following the First Panel Meeting, paras. 77-78. *See also US* Second Written Submission, para. 134; US Responses to Questions following the Second Panel Meeting, para. 68.

[61] Exhibit US-53.

[62] US Responses to Second Set of Panel Questions, para. 70, Exhibits US-81 through US-83. As a result, the EC's statement that "the United States does not argue that any of [the three Czech names] gives rise to a likelihood of confusion with the name 'Budweiser'" is in error. *See* EC Responses to Questions following the Second Panel Meeting, para. 157.

[63] See US Closing Statement at Second Panel Meeting, para. 18; US Responses to Questions following the Second Panel Meeting, para. 68 (note 36).

Question 138

96. The United States submits that the phrase "[w]ith due regard to Community law" in Article 14(2) of the EC GI Regulation, also refers to the provision in Article 142 of Regulation (EC) No. 40/92, which the EC describes as meaning that the relationship between trademarks and GIs is controlled by the GI Regulation.

Question 139

97. Paragraph 166 of the EC's response essentially constitutes an admission that the GI Regulation is inconsistent with TRIPS Article 16.1:

> The EC can confirm that a trademark owner cannot prevent the holders of a registered geographical indication from using the name or names registered under Regulation 2081/92 on the grounds that the use of such name or names is confusing *per se* with an earlier trademark.

98. Article 16.1 grants trademark owners the right to enjoin uses of identical or similar GIs that raise a likelihood of confusion. The EC denies trademark owners that right, and thus violates Article 16.1.

99. The EC continues, in paragraph 167, to state that two factors qualify the right to use the registered GI. First, the EC states that "the right to use the registered name does not confer a right to use other names not covered by the registration, or to use the registered name together with other signs or as part of a combination of signs."[64] As the United States noted in its comment on the EC response to question 137, however, a distinction between use of the sign registered, and use of "other signs," simply begs the question of what uses of the registered sign are authorized. The EC has noted that registration confers the right to use a GI in a manner that is considerably more than merely descriptive. Specifically, the EC has stated that registration confers the right to use the GI in a "trademark-like sense."[65] While this is in principle perfectly legitimate under the TRIPS Agreement, it demonstrates that potential uses of the GI are broad, and that the owner of an identical or similar prior registered trademark will not necessarily be aware of all potential uses at the time of registration—much less which of those uses will be considered confusingly similar by consumers in a given territory. Therefore, as required by Article 16.1, the owner needs the opportunity to enjoin those uses "in the course of trade" as they arise.

100. Second, the EC states that labeling, misleading advertising, and unfair competition laws qualify the right to use a registered GI. However, those laws are not adequate substitutes for Article 16.1 rights. The EC does not argue that those laws permit a trademark owner to enjoin use of identical or similar signs that raise a "likelihood of confusion."

101. In paragraph 169, the EC states that registration of a GI "establishes a legal presumption that the use of that name as a geographical indication does not give rise *per se* to a likelihood of confusion with an earlier trademark . . ." The EC continues, stating that "[i]n order to be able to exercise its trademark rights the trademark owner must rebut first that legal presumption by invalidating the registration of the geographical indication." The legal basis to do so, according to the EC, is found in Article 14(3) of the GI Regulation.

102. Under TRIPS Article 16.1, however, the owner of a registered trademark has the right to enjoin confusing uses of identical or similar signs. Nothing in Article 16.1 suggests that this right is contingent on the owner first rebutting any presumption created by the subsequent registration of a confusingly similar sign under the EC GI Regulation. (In fact, Article 16.1 includes a presumption that operates in precisely the opposite manner implemented by the EC in the GI Regulation. With respect to uses of identical signs on identical goods or services, Article 16.1 presumes that the competing sign raises a likelihood of confusion.)

---

[64] EC Responses to Questions following the Second Panel Meeting, para. 167.

[65] *See* EC Oral Statement at Second Panel Meeting, para. 184; EC Responses to Questions following the Second Panel Meeting, para. 161.

103. Nor is there anything in Article 16.1 that requires the trademark owner to first "invalidate" any intellectual property rights associated with the similar sign before enjoining a use of that sign that confuses consumers in a given territory. As the United States has previously observed, under Article 16.1, rather than seeking invalidation of a GI registration on an EC-wide basis, the owner of an identical or similar prior trademark registered in one EC member State is entitled to prevent particular "uses" of the GI that confuse consumers in that member State.[66] The EC has previously stated that to invalidate a GI on an EC-wide basis, the owner of a trademark would need to prove that consumers are confused "with respect to the whole European public."[67]

104. For these reasons, invalidating a GI registration under the standard included in Article 14(3) involves a considerably higher showing than would be required simply to enjoin particular uses "in the course of trade" that confuse consumers in a particular member State, under Article 16.1 (or rather, as implemented in EC law, under Article 5 of the EC Trademark Directive).[68] Article 14(3) is not, therefore, an adequate substitute for Article 16.1.

105. The EC notes, in paragraphs 163 and 170, that some WTO Members may require the owner of a prior registered trademark to first invalidate a later similar or identical trademark before pursuing an infringement claim against the latter mark. The United States' claims in this dispute involve the consistency of the EC GI Regulation alone with TRIPS Article 16.1. Other Members' measures are not at issue in this dispute.

106. The United States also notes, however, that the provisions of other Members' laws cited in footnote 68 to the EC's response are not analogous to Article 14(3). In those instances, the grounds for invalidating a later-in-time trademark are the same as the grounds for establishing infringement with respect to an earlier-in-time trademark.[69] As noted in paragraph 163 of the EC's response, the grounds for invalidating the later-in-time mark are that it is confusingly similar to an earlier-in-time mark, which is of course also the standard for establishing infringement, under national laws implementing TRIPS Article 16.1.

107. The grounds included in Article 14(3) for invalidation of a GI, however, are not the same as the grounds for establishing infringement with respect to a prior registered trademark. Indeed, as noted above, the national trademark laws cited to by the EC include precisely the Article 16.1 standard as the basis for determining whether a trademark should be registered over an earlier trademark. The grounds included in Article 14(3) and 16.1 differ in two important respects.

---

[66] US Responses to Questions following the Second Panel Meeting, para. 69; US Closing Statement at Second Meeting, para. 17.

[67] Exhibit US-73, pg. 6.

[68] The United States also reiterates that while Article 16.1 provides rights to owners of all registered trademarks, Article 14(3) provides those rights only to owners of trademarks that enjoy reputation, renown and use. *See* Guide to Community Regulations, "Protection of Geographical Indications, Designations of Origin and Certificates of Specific Character for Agricultural Products and Foodstuffs" (Working Document of the Commission Services issued by the European Commission Directorate-General for Agriculture, August 2004), pg. 24. Exhibit EC-64.

[69] As is a consistent theme in this case, the EC tells only part of the story—leaving the Panel with an incomplete and misleading picture of relevant law and legal principles. All of the countries whose laws are cited to in footnote 68 of the EC's response are members of the Commonwealth and have historical ties to the United Kingdom. Hence, the law of the United Kingdom is representative of the general approach taken to this matter by the countries whose laws are cited to by the EC. As noted in the excerpt of the United Kingdom's Trade Marks Act 1994 cited to by the EC (Section 11(1)), the provision is subject to Section 47 of that Act on declaration of invalidity of registration. Section 47(2) provides that "[t]he registration of a trade mark may be declared invalid on the ground ... that there is an earlier trade mark in relation to which the conditions set out in section 5(1), (2) or (3) obtain." Section 5(1) and (2) read as follows:
(1) A trade mark shall not be registered if it is identical with an earlier trade mark and the goods or services for which the trade mark is applied for are identical with the goods or services for which the earlier trade mark is protected.
(2) A trade mark shall not be registered if because— (a) it is identical with an earlier trade mark and is to be registered for goods or services similar to those for which the earlier trade mark is protected, or(b) it is similar to an earlier trade mark and is to be registered for goods or services identical with or similar to those for which the earlier trade mark is protected, there exists a likelihood of confusion on the part of the public, which includes the likelihood of association with the earlier trade mark.
Section 47(6) then provides that "[w]here the registration of a trade mark is declared invalid to any extent, the registration shall to that extent be deemed never to have been made."

108. First, and as noted above, in determining whether to deny registration under Article 14(3), the EC "examines consumer confusion ... with respect to the whole European public."[70] In contrast, in determining whether use of a similar sign raises a likelihood of confusion with respect to a trademark registered in one EC member State, courts determine whether consumers in that member State are confused. The EC Trademark Regulation provides for relative grounds of refusal of a Community trademark application in Article 8. The owner of an earlier trademark may file an opposition (Article 42) or invalidation action (Article 52) against the registration of a confusingly similar Community trademark. Article 8(1)(b) provides: Upon opposition by the proprietor of an earlier trade mark, the trade mark applied for shall not be registered:

> if because of its identity with or similarity to the earlier trade mark and the identity or similarity of the goods or services covered by the trade marks there exists a likelihood of confusion on the part of the public *in the territory in which the earlier trade mark is protected*; the likelihood of confusion includes the likelihood of association with the earlier trade mark." (emphasis added)

109. The EC Trademark Regulation itself therefore provides that the likelihood of confusion must be assessed with regard to the territory in which the earlier trademark is protected. According to Article 8 (2) of the Trademark Regulation, an earlier trademark is not only an earlier Community trademark, but also includes a trademark registered in an EC member State. Hence, assessing whether a likelihood of confusion exists between a trademark application and an earlier trademark registered in an EC member State requires an examination of whether a likelihood of confusion exists with regard to the public in that particular member State.[71]

110. Second, as the United States has previously demonstrated, Article 14(3) does not include the "likelihood of confusion" standard applied in infringement cases. Rather, Article 14(3) adopts a "mislead the consumer" standard. As noted in paragraph 104 of the US responses to the Panel's questions, the words "mislead" and "confusion" have different meanings—the former used in the EC GI Regulation in the sense of affirmatively leading the public to believe something about the product that is not true, and the latter used in Article 16.1 in the sense of a failure or inability to distinguish.

111. Moreover, as noted in paragraph 88 of the US responses to the Panel's questions, the EC Trademark Regulation and Trademark Directive differentiate between the two standards.[72] Accepting that "liable to mislead" in Article 14(3) actually means "likelihood of confusion" would require the Panel to overlook the objective fact that those standards are expressly differentiated in EC trademark law.

---

[70] Exhibit US-73, pg. 6.

[71] *See, e.g.*, Case T-99/01, *Mystery/Mixery*, 15 January 2003, para. 37 ("In this case, given that beverages in Class 32 are everyday consumer items and that the earlier mark on which the opposition is based is registered and protected in Germany, the relevant public by reference to which the likelihood of confusion must be assessed is composed of average consumers in that Member State."); Case T-104/01, *Fifties/Miss Fifties*, 23 October 2002, para. 29 ("In this case, given the nature of the goods concerned (denim clothing) which are everyday consumer items, and the fact that the earlier mark on which the opposition is based is registered and protected in Spain, the targeted public by reference to which the likelihood of confusion must be assessed is composed of average consumers in Spain."); Case T-10/03, *Conforflex/Flex*, 18 February 2004, para. 39 ("In this case, given the nature of the goods concerned, namely items of bedding and bedroom furniture, which are everyday consumer items, and the fact that the earlier marks are registered and protected in Spain, the target public with reference to which the likelihood of confusion must be assessed is composed of average consumers in Spain."). These decisions, which were similarly cited in footnote 74 to the US Responses to Questions following the Second Panel Meeting, are available at http://europa.eu.int/jurisp/cgi-bin/form.pl?lang=en. *See also* OHIM Board of Appeal, Case R 433/2002-3, *Tei-Fu/Tai-Fun*, 11 December 2002, para. 26 ("The assessment of whether the public will either confuse the marks in competition or make a connection between the proprietors of those signs and confuse them, given the existence in the market of the mark applied for and the earlier trade mark, must therefore be carried out from the perspective of the relevant public in Germany because of the fact that the opposition is grounded on a national trade mark registration in this Member State.") (also cited by the United States, at footnote 77, and available at: http://oami.eu.int/LegalDocs/BoA/2002/en/R0433_2002-3.pdf.

[72] *Compare* Article 50.1(c) of EC Regulation 40/94 *with* Article 9.1(b) of that same measure. Exhibit COMP-7. *Compare also* Article 12.2(b) of EC Directive 89/104/EEC with Article 5.1(b) of that same measure. Exhibit COMP-6.

Question 140

112. In paragraphs 177-178, and Exhibits EC-99 through EC-102, the EC offers "approved specifications" for four cheeses referred to in Exhibit US-52.[73] The United States makes several observations.

113. The Panel had asked the EC "what uses ... the registrations ... permit." The EC has not answered the Panel's question. Labeling specifications do not necessarily dictate or limit how or in what ways the GI may be marketed or promoted, as the United States has already noted in its comment on the EC response to question 137.

114. Moreover, the "labeling details" included in the specifications do not offer much guidance to a trademark owner trying to figure out whether, at the time of registration, the GI could one day be used in a manner that raises a likelihood of confusion. The specification for Esrom, for example (Exhibit EC-101) merely states that the label "must *contain*" particular words. It does not say that the label must consist of those words and only those words. The specification does not state that the label may not also include other words or signs, in addition to those that the label "must contain." The labeling details for Bra (Exhibit EC-102) are also not specific, and merely state that "the product must be marketed with the label of the relevant manufacturers' consortium." There are no limits placed on what that label can contain or consist of; there is no guidance regarding how to determine what the "relevant" manufacturers' consortia are, or any depiction of what their GI might look like in use on a consortium's label. Even more dramatic are the product specifications included in Exhibit US-77, which contain nothing more than a name or the word "PGI."

115. In none of these instances would the owner of a similar or identical trademark be able to tell, from the registration and product specification itself, that the rightholder is authorized to use the registered GI in the manner displayed in the pictorial depictions included in Exhibit US-52. The simple point is that until the registered GI is used, the trademark owner will not necessarily know how it will be used, or if it will confuse consumers in a particular territory. For this reason alone, Article 14(3) is not an adequate substitute for TRIPS Article 16.1.

116. The Panel has asked the EC how far the positive right to use a registered GI extends "before it can be challenged under labeling and misleading advertising laws." Whatever the threshold, one thing is clear—the EC has not established that EC and member State labeling and misleading advertising laws, as well as unfair competition laws, include the same "likelihood of confusion" standard contained in TRIPS Article 16.1.[74]

117. To illustrate where the threshold falls, the EC refers to the Bayerisches Bier case, and states as follows:

> [I]f the holder of a geographical indication which has a right to use a certain name (say "Bayerisches Bier") were to use it in a manner which imitates the label or the packaging of the products of a trademark ("Bavaria"), this could be considered as a breach of the laws on labeling and unfair competition, even if the constituent elements of the label or the packaging, other than the trademark itself, were not covered by any intellectual property rights.[75]

118. This example entirely misses the United States' point. The owner of the BAVARIA trademark has the right, under Article 16.1, to enjoin any use of a sign similar to "Bavaria" that raises a likelihood of confusion for consumers in a given territory. The trademark owner's right is not limited to the ability to enjoin uses of a label or packaging that is similar to that included on its products. Rather, it has the right, under Article 16.1, to enjoin

---

[73] The United States offered specifications received from the EC authorities for these four cheeses, in Exhibit US-52. Exhibits EC-99 through EC-102 contain additional pages, some of which are historical in nature and which appear to speak to production methods, rather than offering guidance on the manner in which the sign registered can or must be used.

[74] Those standards are in fact different from the "likelihood of confusion" standard included in TRIPS Article 16.1. *See, e.g.*, the standards included in paragraph 143 (and notes 38-40) of the EC Responses to Questions Following the First Panel Meeting.

[75] EC Responses to Questions following the Second Panel Meeting, para. 181.

use of any identical or similar sign—a word, for example—that raises a likelihood of confusion. As the EC makes clear with its example, EC and member State labeling and misleading advertising laws, as well as unfair competition laws, do not provide this right. Instead, they provide the right to prevent "imitating" uses not of the sign itself, but of the sign in conjunction with other elements or other elements of the labeling or packaging that do not necessarily include the sign at all.

119. The examples cited in paragraph 182 of the EC's response make a similar error. According to the EC, EC and member State labeling and misleading advertising laws, or unfair competition laws, would prohibit use of a GI "used together with other signs or statements that suggested or indicated that the geographical indication is in fact the trademark of a producer." Again, the right in Article 16.1 is to enjoin use of an identical or similar sign, as such, that raises a likelihood of confusion.

Question 142

120. The United States' comments on the EC's response to this question also include comments on the EC's related responses to questions 2 and 3 from Australia.

121. The EC has asserted that if the owner of a prior registered trademark considers that the EC has registered an identical or similar GI that raises a likelihood of confusion with respect to the trademark, the owner can challenge the validity of the GI registration, on the basis of Article 14(3) of the EC GI Regulation. The EC asserts that this is a sufficient substitute for the right, under TRIPS Article 16.1, to enjoin confusing uses of identical or similar signs.

122. To begin, the United States has demonstrated that Article 14(3) does not embody the "likelihood of confusion" standard required by TRIPS Article 16.1 (*see, e.g.*, the United States' comment on the EC's response to question 139, above). Moreover, requiring a trademark owner to seek invalidation of a confusingly similar registered GI, rather than granting the owner the right to enjoin only those "uses" of the GI that confuse consumers in a particular territory, is inconsistent with Article 16.1 (*see* the United States' comment on the EC's response to question 139, above). Additionally, Article 14(3) is not available to owners of trademarks that do not enjoy reputation, renown and use. The Commission's Guide to Regulation 2081/92 unequivocally confirms this reading.[76]

123. For these reasons alone, Article 14(3) does not serve as an adequate substitute for Article 16.1 rights.

124. For the sake of argument, however, the United States would like to leave these threshold points aside. Even so, however, for the ability to challenge the validity of a GI under Article 14(3) to serve as an adequate substitute for Article 16.1, the ability to challenge must be available to *owners of all valid registered trademarks*, because Article 16.1 provides rights to owners of <u>*all*</u> valid registered trademarks.

125. The ability to challenge the validity of a registered GI on the basis of Article 14(3), however, is not available to owners of all valid registered trademarks. To demonstrate this in graphic terms, the United States includes as Exhibit US-99 and US-100 two flowcharts. Exhibit US-99 is a flowchart for challenges to the validity of a GI registration brought directly to the Court of First Instance, pursuant to Article 230 of the EC Treaty. Exhibit US-100 is a flowchart for challenges to the validity of a GI registration brought to EC member State courts and then referred to the European Court of Justice ("ECJ"), pursuant to Article 234 of the EC Treaty.

126. These flowcharts demonstrate that many trademark owners will not be able to challenge the validity of a GI registration either in a case brought directly to the CFI, pursuant to Article 230 of the EC Treaty, or in a

---

[76] Guide to Community Regulations, "Protection of Geographical Indications, Designations of Origin and Certificates of Specific Character for Agricultural Products and Foodstuffs" (Working Document of the Commission Services issued by the European Commission Directorate-General for Agriculture, August 2004), pg. 24. Exhibit EC-64.

case brought to a member State court and referred to the ECJ, under Article 234.[77] The shaded boxes in the charts represent categories of trademark owners for which Article 14(3) would provide no opportunity to challenge the validity of a registered GI. These trademark owners would be denied the opportunity to challenge the validity of a GI for reasons that are not relevant grounds for denying an owner its rights under TRIPS Article 16.1. Exhibit US-101 provides a detailed explanation of the flow charts and of the inability of many trademark owners to challenge GI registrations under the EC Treaty.

127. The United States makes one brief comment on the EC's response to question 142(d). The EC has often stated that Article 14(3), supplemented by other provisions of the EC GI Regulation, provide grounds for cancellation of a GI registration on the basis that the GI is identical or confusingly similar to a prior trademark. Yet, in its response to question 142(d) (at paragraph 189), the EC states that the "grounds for cancellation mentioned in Articles 11 and 11a are *exhaustive*."[78] The grounds for cancellation included in Articles 11 and 11a do not address cancellation based on likelihood of confusion with a registered trademark.

Question 143

128. The United States simply notes that the EC offers absolutely no documentary support for its assertion[79] that the Council, in considering the relevance of Article 14(3) in the Bayerisches Bier, considered factors other than whether valid prior registered trademarks for BAVARIA enjoyed reputation, renown and use.

Question 145

129. The United States and the EC agree that the coverage of Article 24.5 is not necessarily limited to the specific articles mentioned in the Panel's question (*i.e.*, Articles 22.2, 22.3, 23.1, and 23.2).[80] The agreement between the United States and EC, however, appears to end there.

130. The EC continues to argue that Article 24.5 is not an exception to GI protection, this time with the qualifier that Article 24.5 is not a "genuine exception" like those in Articles 24.4, 24.6, 24.7, and 24.8.[81] While the EC points to nothing in Article 24 of the TRIPS Agreement that supports a distinction between "genuine exceptions" and other, presumably "non-genuine" exceptions, the United States notes that the EC now apparently includes Article 24.4 as a "genuine exception", while at the same time leaving Article 24.9 off the list, in contrast to its second written submission, where Articles 24.6-24.9 (but not Article 24.4) were considered exceptions by the EC.[82] These unsupported and rapidly-changing characterizations of clearly-labeled exceptions to GI protection in Article 24 do nothing to contradict the understanding derived from an analysis of Article 24.5 based on the ordinary meaning of the terms, in their context, in light of the object and purpose of the TRIPS Agreement. Through such an analysis, the United States has demonstrated, in part, that (1) by its very terms, Article 24.5 limits the protection of GIs *vis-à-vis* trademarks, thereby constituting an exception to

[77] The United States notes that over the period 1999-2003, EC member State courts referred a total of 8 intellectual property cases to the ECJ, pursuant to Article 234. These statistics are available in the ECJ's annual reports, titled "Statistics of Judicial Activity of the Court of Justice," at http://curia.eu.int/en/instit/presentationfr/index.htm. In each annual report, the statistics are maintained in Table 11, in the column "References for a preliminary ruling."

[78] Emphasis added.

[79] EC Responses to Questions following the Second Panel Meeting, para. 191.

[80] EC Response to Panel Question 145, para. 197; US Response to Panel Question 145, note 42.

[81] EC Responses to Panel Question 145, para. 198.

[82] EC Second Written Submission, para. 314.

GI protection; and (2) Article 24.5 is a part of Article 24, which is labeled "international negotiations; exceptions", and it is undisputed that Article 24.5 does not relate to "international negotiations."[83]

131. The EC states that Article 24.5 "imposes self-standing [positive] obligations with respect to the protection of trademarks" and therefore is not an "exception" to GI protection.[84] As the United States has explained, Article 24.5 does not accord self-standing rights to trademarks, since it simply limits the ability of GIs to prejudice trademarks.[85] The two examples presented by the EC in paragraph 199 of their response to the panel's question confirm this interpretation, as they demonstrate instances in which Article 24.5 limits the scope of GI protection *vis-à-vis* trademarks; they do not demonstrate that Article 24.5 creates self-standing obligations with respect to trademarks.

132. The EC's examples also do not provide any clarity and, if anything, argue against the proposition, put forward by the EC, that Article 24.5 "imposes self-standing [positive] obligations with respect to the protection of trademarks" and therefore is not an "exception" to GI protection.[86] The EC presents a hypothetical in which a "Member's trademark law provides that a trademark including or consisting of a geographic indication shall not be registered or, if registered, shall be invalidated."[87] They then state that while such a provision—if there were one—would go beyond what is *required* by Article 22.3 and that the obligation not to invalidate such a trademark is only found in Article 24.5. But Article 24.5 protects certain trademarks that might otherwise be prejudiced in certain defined ways by "measures adopted to implement" Section 3 of Part II of the TRIPS Agreement. Quite simply, the provision in a Member's trademark law postulated by the EC—to the extent it exists in an any WTO Member—would not appear to be a measure adopted to implement Article 22.3 of the TRIPS Agreement. Further, that article requires more than mere identity of the trademark and geographical indication—in particular it requires that the use of the indication in the trademark be "of such a nature as to mislead the public as to the true place of origin." Whether the example put forward by the EC is otherwise consistent with Article 15.2 of the TRIPS Agreement or Articles *6quinquies,* 9, 10, and 10*bis* is another question. The point is that the EC's example is simply irrelevant to the interpretation of Article 24.5.

133. Similarly, the second example offered by the EC[88] is irrelevant to the interpretation of Article 24.5. The EC sets up an example that provides for a prohibition of the use of a trademark that is identical or similar to a subsequently recognized geographical indication in a manner that "goes beyond the obligation found in Article 22.2." Again, it does not appear that the EC is hypothesizing a measure "adopted to implement" Section 3 of Part II of the TRIPS Agreement within the meaning of Article 24.5. Whether such a provision would be otherwise constrained by Article 15.2 or Articles *6quinquies,* 9, 10, or 10*bis* of the Paris Convention is not an

---

[83] *See* US Opening Statement at Second Meeting, para. 94; US Second Written Submission, paras. 171-173; US Response to Panel Question 78, paras. 107-113. The Appellate Body has interpreted provisions based in part on their place in the overall structure of the covered agreement at issue, giving careful consideration to the headings or titles of the sections in which the provisions appear. *See* Appellate Body Report, *Canada-Dairy*, para 134 ("A strong presumption arises that the language which is inscribed in a Member's Schedule under the heading, 'Other terms and Conditions', has some *qualifying* or *limiting* effect on the substantive content or scope of the concession or commitment."); *See also* Appellate Body Report, *Definitive Safeguard Measures on Imports of Circular Welded Carbon Quality Line Pipe from Korea*, paras. 80-82, fn. 171; Appellate Body Report, *US – Definitive Safeguards on Measures of Imports of Certain Steel Products*, paras. 337-338; Appellate Body Report, *Argentina – Safeguard Measures on Footwear*, para. 93; Appellate Body Report, *Korea – Definitive Safeguard Measure on Imports of Certain Dairy Products*, para. 86.

[84] EC Responses to Panel Question 145, para. 200.

[85] US Opening Statement at Second Meeting, para. 95.

[86] EC Responses to Panel Question 145, para. 200.

[87] The EC states that this is not a hypothetical example, citing to Section 61 of Australia's Trademark Act 1995. Once again, the EC creates a false impression by telling only part of the story. It is true that Section 61(1) of Australia's Trade Marks Act 1995 provides that the "registration of a trade mark in respect of particular goods (*relevant goods*) may be opposed on the ground that the trade mark contains or consists of a sign that is a geographical indication for goods (*designated goods*) ... " What the EC fails to mention is that Section 61, as its title clearly indicates, applies to trademarks "containing or consisting of **a false geographical indication.**" Further, its specific terms limit its application to goods " originating in: (a) a country, or in a region or locality in a country, other than the country in which the relevant goods originated; or (b) a region or locality in the country in which the relevant goods originated other than the region or locality in which the relevant goods originated."

[88] EC Responses to Panel Question 145, para. 199.

issue before this Panel, however. It is sufficient to observe that the examples put forward by the EC have no basis in fact and are irrelevant to the interpretation of Article 24.5.

134. Article 24.5, by its own terms, acts as a shield for covered trademarks against GIs, and contains no provisions for limiting trademark rights. There is no rule that a provision that recognizes one right, such as with respect to trademarks, cannot be an exception to a separate obligation, such as with respect to GIs. To the contrary. Article 24.8, for example, limits GI protection in light of a person's right to use their own name, even though use of a person's name is not a form of intellectual property protected elsewhere in the TRIPS Agreement; Article 24.8 would, in this sense, clearly offer "additional protection" to the name that is not provided elsewhere in the TRIPS Agreement. Such protection, like the protection for trademarks illustrated in the examples presented in paragraph 199 of the EC's response, "does not result" from any provision of the TRIPS Agreement other than the "exception" provision. The EC has now stated twice that Article 24.8 is an exception (or "genuine" exception) to GI protection, although in view of the fact that it appears to recognize a positive right, the United States would not be surprised if the EC changed its mind on this point.

135. The EC also repeats its contention that Article 24.5 "defines in a comprehensive manner the boundary" between GIs and trademarks.[89] The United States has already explained why this is incorrect.[90] While Article 24.5 does define *a* boundary between GIs and trademarks, it is not *the only* boundary. By limiting the scope of GI protection *vis-à-vis* certain (but not all) trademarks, Article 24.5 certainly constitutes one boundary. Article 17, the exception to the trademark section, defines another boundary, by limiting the scope of trademark protection. The EC's understanding of the role of Article 24.5 as a "comprehensive" boundary is inconsistent with the context of an Agreement that includes separate exceptions for trademark protection and GI protection.[91]

Question 146

136. As a means of justifying the "co-existence" of prior registered trademarks with later, identical or confusingly similar registered GIs, the EC repeats its assertion that the simultaneous exercise of the two GI and trademark rights cited in the Panel's question "would lead to a situation where neither the trademark owner nor the right holders of the geographical indications could use the sign which is the subject matter of their respective right."[92]

137. Yet, later in its response, the EC acknowledges that the "conflict" between the two individual rights "is resolved by Article 22.3 (and 23.2), which provides for the invalidation of the trademark, thereby effectively giving priority to the geographical indication."[93] Thus, it appears that the EC concedes that there is no "conflict" between the rights at issue (much less any conflict between the obligations imposed on the EC by the relevant TRIPS provisions).

138. The United States is uncertain about the meaning of the final sentence of the EC's response, which reads as follows:

---

[89] EC Responses to Panel Question 145, para. 201.

[90] *See, e.g.*, US Opening Statement at Second Meeting, para. 93.

[91] *See* US Responses to Panel Question 78, paras. 107-113.

[92] EC Responses to Questions following the Second Panel Meeting, para. 204. *See also* EC Second Written Submission, para. 309.

[93] EC Responses to Questions following the Second Panel Meeting, para. 206. In its own response to question 146, the United States similarly stated that the "conflict" between the two rights would likely be resolved, under TRIPS Article 22.3, by denying registration of the misleading trademark (or, if registered, by making it subject to invalidity). US Responses to Questions following the Second Panel Meeting, paras. 78-81.

> This "rule of conflict", however, does not apply to "grandfathered trademarks", as defined in Article 24.5, which are subject to a different rule, as explained in the response to the preceding question.[94]

The United States simply observes, as it has previously,[95] that Article 24.5 includes, for example, a requirement that trademarks subject to the Article 24.5 exception must be applied for, registered, or acquired through use "in good faith." Further, the exception in Article 24.5 prohibits prejudicing certain trademarks "on the basis that such a trademark is identical with, or similar to, a geographical indication."[96] Finally, Article 24.5 applies only to "measures adopted to implement this Section."[97]

Question 147

139. The EC argues that the addition of the phrase "the right to use a trademark" during the negotiating history of Article 24.5 reflects a "compromise" that "grandfathered" trademarks should not be accorded their Article 16.1 rights, but only the right to affirmative use of the mark on labels, advertising, etc. The United States has already explained in great detail, and will not repeat here, why the EC's statement is incorrect and unsupported by an interpretation of the phrase "prejudice ... the right to use a trademark" according to the customary rules of treaty interpretation.[98]

140. By contrast, as the United States explained in its response to Question 147, the evolution of Article 24.5 is entirely consistent with the suggestion that the inclusion of language clarifying that Article 24.5 applied only with respect to "measures adopted to implement [the GI] Section", was part of the compromise arrived at in agreeing that Article 24.5 would be a mandatory provision.

Questions 148 and 149

141. It would be contrary to all of the evidence in this dispute to accept the EC's assertion that:

> The assessment made by the EC authorities under Article 14(3) is analogous to the assessment carried out by the EC trademark authorities in order to establish whether the use of a later trademark will give rise to likelihood of confusion with an earlier trademark. When applying Article 14(3), the registering authorities, or the courts, as applicable, must take into account all relevant factors, including in particular the similarity of goods and signs. As explained, length of use, reputation and renown are mentioned expressly in Article 14(3) because geographical indications, when used as trademarks, are primarily descriptive and non-distinctive.[99]

142. The EC cannot simply substitute TRIPS-consistent language that it wishes were included in Article 14(3). The United States has presented compelling evidence of what Article 14(3) means, and the EC has failed to rebut that evidence.

---

[94] EC Responses to Questions following the Second Panel Meeting, para. 206.

[95] US Responses to Questions following the Second Panel Meeting, para. 72 (note 41).

[96] Moreover, for purposes of this dispute, the United States' arguments are directed at those TRIPS Article 16.1 rights associated with valid trademarks, and not with the effect of Regulation 2081/92 on trademarks that are misleading as to geographic origin. *See* US First Written Submission, para. 135 ("The United States is not arguing that trademarks that 'mislead the public as to the true place of origin' of the underlying goods in a given territory must be registered and provided Article 16.1 rights in that territory.").

[97] Any other measures must, of course, be otherwise consistent with the TRIPS Agreement and the Paris Convention.

[98] *See, e.g.*, US Responses to Panel Question 145, para. 76; US Second Written Submission, paras. 176-181; US Response to Panel Question 76, para. 102.

[99] EC Responses to Questions following the Second Panel Meeting, para. 215.

143. The EC's reading of Article 14(3) ignores the text of the provision. The plain text of the provision requires denial of registration for a GI if it is "liable to mislead the consumer," and not if it raises a "likelihood of confusion," which is the term used in TRIPS Article 16.1. Equating the "liable to mislead" standard with the "likelihood of confusion" standard in Article 16.1, would not be consistent with this evidence, because it ignores the distinct use of those two standards elsewhere in EC law.[100]

144. The EC's reading also ignores the limited scope of Article 14(3), which is by its own terms relevant only when a trademark enjoys reputation, renown and use. The EC's reading represents a complete departure from what it has termed "highly relevant"[101] guidance offered by the Commission on the meaning of Article 14(3) outside the bounds of this dispute, as recently as August 2004. The Commission's Guide to Regulation 2081/92 states, in unequivocal terms, that "only in one circumstance"—when the trademark enjoys reputation, renown and use—will the EC apply Article 14(3) to deny registration of a similar or identical GI.[102] "In all other cases," the EC applies its "general rule," which is that the GI is registered, "notwithstanding the existence of the registered trademark."[103]

145. The EC's reading of Article 14(3) is also irreconcilable with the way in which the prerequisites included in Article 14(3)—reputation, renown and use—have been interpreted by WIPO and the Paris Union, as well as by the ECJ and OHIM.[104] Each of these entities has attached particular significance to these terms, as prerequisites for the heightened protection extended to well-known or famous marks.

146. The EC's reading is, in addition, contrary to the understanding of Article 14(3) expressed by EC member States, which consider that the provision speaks to "well-known mark[s]."[105]

147. Finally, the EC's reading is also contrary to the EC Trademark Regulation and Trademark Directive, which refer to "reputation" solely as a prerequisite for the heightened protection associated with well-known marks.[106]

148. For all of these reasons, Article 14(3) does not even enable the EC authorities to deny registration of any GI that is identical or confusingly similar to any prior valid registered trademark—much less provide the right to trademark owners to enjoin confusing uses of such GIs, if registered. Article 14(3) is not an adequate substitute for TRIPS Article 16.1 rights.

149. Nor do Articles 7(4) and 7(5)(b) of the EC GI Regulation transform Article 14(3) into an adequate substitute for TRIPS Article 16.1 At paragraph 222 of its response, the EC repeats its assertion that Articles 7(4) and 7(5)(b) modify the meaning of Article 14(3), requiring the EC to deny registration of not just GIs that are "liable to mislead," as Article 14(3) reads, but also GIs that raise a "likelihood of confusion" with respect to all trademarks (not just those of reputation, renown and use). Articles 7(4) and 7(5)(b) simply do not do this.

---

[100] The EC Trademark Regulation and Trademark Directive differentiate between the two standards. Article 50.1(c) of the Trademark Regulation and Article 12.2(b) of the Trademark Directive provide for revocation of a trademark where it is "liable to mislead the public, particularly as to ... geographical origin . . ." Regulation No 40/94, Article 50.1(c), Exhibit COMP-7; Directive 89/104/EEC, Article 12.2(b), Exhibit COMP-6.In contrast, Article 9.1(b) of the Trademark Regulation and Article 5.1(b) of the Trademark Directive grant trademark owners the exclusive right to prevent use of a similar or identical sign for similar or identical goods where "there exists a likelihood of confusion on the part of the public." Regulation No 40/94, Article 9.1(b), Exhibit COMP-7; Directive 89/104/EEC, Article 5.1(b), Exhibit COMP-6.

[101] EC Responses to Questions following the Second Panel Meeting, para. 8.

[102] Guide to Community Regulations, "Protection of Geographical Indications, Designations of Origin and Certificates of Specific Character for Agricultural Products and Foodstuffs" (Working Document of the Commission Services issued by the European Commission Directorate-General for Agriculture, August 2004), pg. 24. Exhibit EC-64.

[103] *Id.*

[104] US Second Written Submission, paras. 147, 150-152.

[105] US Second Written Submission, paras. 148-149. *See also US* Responses to Questions following the Second Panel Meeting, para. 105 (note 90).

[106] US Second Written Submission, para. 150.

150. As the United States has previously noted,[107] even if Articles 7(4) and 7(5)(b) augment Article 14(3) and change the "liable to mislead" standard to a "likelihood of confusion" standard,[108] that standard would still apply only to trademarks that enjoy reputation, renown and use. To conclude otherwise would be to read the words "reputation and renown and length of time it has been used" out of Article 14(3). We have also noted that even if Article 7(5)(b) somehow turns the "liable to mislead" standard from Article 14(3) into a "likelihood of confusion" standard, Article 7(5)(b) only applies, by its own express terms, in situations in which the EC member States have been unable to reach agreement on whether to grant an objection made by, for example, a trademark owner. If the member States agree on whether to grant the trademark owner's objection (pursuant to Article 7(5)(a)), it is unclear how Article 7(5)(b) could have any relevance to Article 14(3), let alone modify it to include a "likelihood of confusion" standard. In those situations, trademark owners affected by Article 14(3) would still face the "liable to mislead" standard (and, of course, would only benefit if their trademarks enjoyed reputation, renown and use); Article 14(3) would not substitute for TRIPS Article 16.1 for all of these trademark owners.

151. The United States also recalls that Article 7(4) is a provision that states under what circumstances an objection raised by a trademark owner should be admitted.[109] One ground is whether the GI would "prejudice the existence of ... a mark." The EC has argued that this must serve as grounds not only for admitting an objection, but also for granting the objection and denying registration of the GI with respect to <u>all trademarks</u>, because otherwise, there would be no point in admitting the objection in the first place. The United States does not find it at all unusual, however, to admit more objections than will ultimately be successful. The EC's view, in fact, implies that unless <u>every</u> objection that is admitted is successful, with the GI registration denied in <u>every</u> case in which an objection arises and is admitted, Article 7(4) will have no meaning. This is not necessary to give Article 7(4) meaning. The United States notes the express statement by the ECJ that "the fact that an objection is admissible under [Article 7(4)] does not prevent the registration applied for from being finally granted."[110]

152. It is also important to note that the EC's assertion that reputation, renown and use are "relevant in all cases" involving an evaluation against the "likelihood of confusion" standard is plain and simply untrue.[111] In lengthy string cites included as footnotes 74-77 of its response to question 148, the United States offered many decisions in which OHIM, the CFI and EC member State courts found a likelihood of confusion, without addressing whether the prior trademark at issue enjoyed reputation, renown and use. In some of those cases, OHIM, the CFI and the EC member State courts expressly held that the prior trademark for which a likelihood of confusion was found did not enjoy reputation, renown and/or use—a fact that would have precluded the EC from stopping the registration of a confusing GI under Article 14(3) of the GI Regulation. While reputation, renown and use might be relevant in some cases, *e.g.*, where the prior trademark and the allegedly infringing sign are somewhat less similar, OHIM and the courts routinely find a likelihood of confusion *without the trademark owner having established that the trademark enjoys reputation, renown or use*. In other words, establishing reputation, renown and use are not, as the EC asserts, merely part of the EC authorities' inquiry, under Article 14(3), into whether the GI rises a likelihood of confusion with respect to a prior, identical or similar mark.

---

[107] US Second Written Submission, paras. 160-164.

[108] The United States does not understand precisely how Article 7(4) does this, since it does not even refer to "likelihood of confusion."

[109] US Second Written Submission, para. 161.

[110] Case C-289/96, *Kingdom of Denmark, Federal Republic of Germany and French Republic v Commission*, [1999] ECR I-1541, para. 93. Available at http://europa.eu.int/jurisp/cgi-bin/form.pl?lang=en. Moreover, in that case, the ECJ was reviewing claims that a GI was generic, under the factors in Article 3(1) of the EC GI Regulation, and therefore not registrable. Article 3(1), unlike Article 14(3), specifically directs the Commission to take into account "the relevant national or Community laws," which the ECJ found included Article 7(4) of the GI Regulation itself. *Id.*, paras. 95, 102. Article 14(3) does not include any such requirement, and it is not therefore clear why Article 7(4) should be considered at all to modify the meaning and application of Article 14(3).

[111] EC Responses to Questions following the Second Panel Meeting, para. 219.

153. Nor is it true, as the EC implies at paragraphs 210 -214, that reputation, renown, and use are always part of the "likelihood of confusion" analysis of other WTO Members. Of course, WTO Member practices are irrelevant to a review of the WTO-consistency of the measure at issue in this dispute. Even so, however, it is plain from the EC's own quotations from the laws of other WTO Members that reputation, renown, and use are among the factors that might come into play in a "likelihood of confusion" analysis by various WTO Members. But not even in the materials cited by the EC are their presence required to find a likelihood of confusion. This is in stark contrast to Article 14(3) of the GI Regulation.

154. As it argued previously in this dispute,[112] the EC again argues that trademarks containing or consisting of geographical elements lack distinctiveness and are as such not registrable.[113] The EC states that those trademarks should be registered only if they have acquired distinctiveness through use.[114] The EC reasons that since trademarks containing or consisting of geographical elements will be registered only if they have acquired distinctiveness through use, consumers are unlikely to confuse such a trademark with an identical or similar GI unless the trademark has been used.[115] The EC's implication appears to be that it is entirely appropriate, under Article 16.1, for Article 14(3) to limit denial of registration for a GI to situations in which an identical or similar prior trademark has been used.

155. The EC's analysis is wrong. As the Panel will recall, the United States has offered several examples of registered Community Trademarks that contain or consist entirely of geographical place names.[116] In fact, the Community Trademark registrations for each of these trademarks expressly state that there was no showing of acquired distinctiveness through use.

156. Moreover, the United States has in fact provided a decision in which a court found a likelihood of confusion in the very situation envisioned by the EC. In the *Fläminger* case, the German Federal Supreme Court upheld a decision to block registration of the term FLÄMINGER as part of a word/device mark, on the basis that it was confusingly similar to a prior trademark, FÄLINGER. The court so held, despite the fact that the word Fläminger referred to the Eastern German region of Fläming, and even though the prior trademark was a "fanciful" name, enjoyed no reputation and had not achieved acquired distinctiveness through use.[117]

157. Finally, paragraph 220 of the EC's response illustrates with remarkable clarity why Article 14(3) is an inadequate substitute for TRIPS Article 16.1. In the EC's hypothetical, the EC states that where a prior trademark AUSTRALIA for wine has not been used, the public would not be misled and, therefore, if applied for, the GI "Australia" would presumably be registered. Under Article 16.1, likelihood of confusion would be *presumed* in this case, given that the later sign is identical and is to be used on identical goods. Under Article 14(3), however, the GI would be registered nonetheless. If Article 14(3) is to serve as an adequate substitute for TRIPS Article 16.1, it must, at the very least, lead to denial of registration of the GI in this situation. The EC's admission that the GI would be registered is a clear indication that Article 14(3) does not serve as an adequate substitute for Article 16(1).

Question 151

158. The EC states that if Article 24.3 is considered to be an exception to the exception provisions in Article 24, then "Members could not rely upon Article 24.5 as a 'justification' to diminish the [p]re-existing

---

[112] *See* EC First Written Submission, paras. 275, 278-285; EC Responses to Questions following First Panel Meeting, para. 176.

[113] EC Responses to Questions following the Second Panel Meeting, para. 219.

[114] *Id.*

[115] *Id.*

[116] US Responses to Questions following the First Panel Meeting, para. 79 (and Exhibit US-46); US Second Written Submission, para. 169; US Oral Statement at Second Panel Meeting, para. 74 (and Exhibits US-74 through US-76). The registrations in the cited exhibits include a field entitled "Acquired distinctiveness" (which is followed by "No" in each of the examples provided).

[117] Judgment of the German Federal Supreme Court, *Fläminger*, 28 May 1998, GRUR 1998, pgs. 930-932. Exhibit US-92.

protection of geographical indications."[118] It is not clear, however, how Article 24.5 would lead to diminishing of the protection of individual GIs protected under the EC GI Regulation that existed prior to entry into force of WTO Agreement, since it only protects certain trademarks from prejudice arising from measures adopted to implement the GI section of the TRIPS Agreement. The United States notes that there were no GIs protected under the EC GI Regulation prior to January 1, 1995. Moreover, as the United States has explained, Article 24.3 does not establish limitations on what Members must do in implementing other sections of the TRIPS Agreement - such as in the trademark and copyright sections.[119]

Question 152

159. The EC's failure to answer the Panel's direct question is significant. The Panel's question derives from the fact that TRIPS Article 24.3 prevents diminishment of protection for GIs that could be caused by "implementing this Section", referring to Part II, Section 3 of the TRIPS Agreement.[120] It follows that any diminishing of GI protection that could arise by virtue of implementation of another section of the TRIPS Agreement, including the trademark section, is not prohibited by Article 24.3.

160. The EC's response that "[o]n the complainants' own interpretation of Article 24.5, the obligation to diminish protection would arise from the obligation imposed by Article 24.5 and not from Article 16.1", is simply wrong, and an attempt to avoid answering a direct and important question from the Panel. If the maintenance of GI protection violates the exclusive rights of owners of prior valid trademarks to prevent all others from using signs that result in a likelihood of confusion, then this constitutes a breach of Article 16.1 of the TRIPS Agreement. (The EC in fact acknowledges that under the EC GI Regulation, "a trademark owner cannot prevent the holder of a registered geographical indication from using the name or names registered under Regulation 2081/92 on the grounds that the use of such name or names is confusing *per se* with an earlier trademark."[121])

161. Indeed, the United States emphasizes, once again, that it has not made an affirmative claim against the EC GI Regulation based on TRIPS Article 24.5. The US claim is, and always has been, based on a violation of TRIPS Article 16.1. It is the EC that has raised TRIPS Article 24.5 in its own defense.[122] Thus, the United States does not understand how, at this point in the proceedings, the EC could be under the erroneous impression that "[o]n the complainants' own interpretation of Article 24.5, the obligation to diminish protection would arise from the obligation imposed by Article 24.5 and not from Article 16.1."

Question 153

162. The United States has explained on numerous occasions why the blanket exception to trademark rights in Article 14(2) of the GI Regulation is not a "limited exception" and does not take into account the interests of anyone other than producers of certain agricultural products in the EC who have rights to use a registered GI. Instead, for a given trademark, Article 14(2) allows for an unlimited number of users of registered GIs to create an unlimited degree of likelihood of confusion with respect to the trademark, and to do so for an unlimited period of time.[123] Under the EC's interpretation of TRIPS Article 17, all uses of a registered GI are automatically entitled to the "fair use" exception, no matter what the facts of the particular case at hand (*i.e.*, whether the use is fair, the term is descriptive, or the legitimate interests of the particular trademark owner are considered), by simple virtue of registration alone.

---

118 EC Response to Panel Question 151, para. 228.

119 US Second Written Submission, para. 190.

120 *See* US Opening Statement at Second Meeting, para. 96; US Second Written Submission, paras. 188-190.

121 EC Response to Question 139, para. 166.

122 *See* US Response to Question 75, para. 91.

123 *See, e.g.*, US Opening Statement at Second Panel Meeting, para. 100.

163. While the national trademark laws cited by the EC all allow descriptive uses that might otherwise infringe a trademark, such uses are subject to the proviso that they be in accordance with honest practice in industrial or commercial matters or consistent with fair practice. A determination as to whether such a proviso is met under trademark law requires a case-by-case analysis to determine if a particular use is "fair" in accordance with national law and within the meaning of TRIPS Article 17. In contrast, the EC provides for a blanket, limitless exception to trademark rights through operation of Article 14(2) of the EC GI Regulation.

164. In its response to Question 153, the EC again attempts to justify its treatment of trademarks as permissible under TRIPS Article 17. First, the EC states that the exception created by the GI Regulation is "limited" because the trademark owner "retains the right to prevent the use of the name by *any* person in relation to *any* goods which originate in a different geographical area or which do not comply with the specifications."[124] As the United States has explained, whether the trademark owner retains the right to prevent parties that are not rightholders in registered GIs from confusing uses of similar or identical signs does not change the fact that the trademark owner has already been subject to an unlimited exception, especially when considered the potential detrimental effect on the trademark rights.[125]

165. The EC states that the potential uses of GIs permitted by the GI Regulation are "narrower than the potential universe of uses of other descriptive terms, such as indications of source", and that this consideration is important because "Australia and the United States appear to concede that the use of those terms would qualify for an exception under Article 17."[126] With this statement, the EC now reads the word "fair" out of the phrase "fair use of descriptive terms". The United States has never stated or "conceded" that *any* use of descriptive terms would qualify for an exception under Article 17. Pursuant to the terms of Article 17, only *fair* use of descriptive terms is permitted.

166. Now, considering that the EC also reads "descriptive terms" in a way that fails to give meaning to "descriptive"[127], it is apparent that the EC is reading Article 17 to allow the "use of terms", regardless of the type of use or the type of term, and regardless of the effect on trademark owners, despite the fact that Article 17 speaks to "*fair* use of *descriptive* terms", requires that the exceptions be "limited", and further requires that the trademark owner's legitimate interests be taken into account.

167. Next, the EC disputes that Article 17 requires that an exception to trademark rights "minimizes" the "likelihood of confusion."[128] The EC argues that a requirement to minimize the likelihood of confusion would lead to a situation where the interests of third parties would not be taken into account, or otherwise balanced with the interests of the trademark owner. This is incorrect. By permitting a limited exception in the first place, the legitimate interests of third parties are already being taken into account. In other words, if there were no legitimate third party interests militating in favor of allowing an exception to trademark rights, then no such exception would be permitted. After all, it is certainly not in the legitimate interests of the trademark owner to agree to an exception to his right. Once it has been determined that an exception is appropriate because it takes into account certain third party interests, then the remainder of Article 17 demonstrates that the exception must be limited, including through the specific reference to "*limited* exceptions", the requirement to take account of the legitimate interests of the trademark owner, and the example requiring "*fair* use of *descriptive* terms." Given that the core trademark right is provided in Article 16.1, a "limited" exception refers to an exception that results in a limited degree of likelihood of confusion with respect to the trademark. As detailed previously, "limited exception" refers to "a narrow exception—one which makes only a small diminution of the rights", where "limited" is "measured by the extent to which the exclusive rights" of a trademark have been curtailed.[129]

---

[124] EC Response to Question 153, para. 231.

[125] US Opening Statement at Second Panel Meeting, para. 101.

[126] EC Response to Question 153, para. 230.

[127] US Opening Statement at Second Meeting, para. 103.

[128] EC Response to Question 153, para. 232.

[129] US Response to Panel Question 154, para. 119; US Opening Statement at Second Meeting, para. 100, quoting Panel Report, *Canada – Patent Protection*, paras. 7.30-7.31.

168. The EC also tries to minimize the effect of Article 14(2) of the GI Regulation on trademarks by stating that, even under the reading of the United States, Article 14(3) prevents registration for certain GIs that are misleading with respect to a certain category of trademarks (*i.e.*, those that enjoy reputation, renown and use).[130] The United States has explained, however, that this does not qualify as a "limited" exception within the meaning of Article 17. Article 17 permits "limited exceptions to the rights conferred by *a* trademark", not unlimited exceptions to the rights of a limited *number* of trademarks, as the EC's interpretation suggests.[131]

169. The EC again raises its labeling and misleading advertising laws, as well as member State unfair competition laws, as evidence that the exception to Article 16.1 rights is "limited".[132] As a threshold matter, national laws in the EC governing labeling, misleading advertising, and unfair competition, cannot prevent the use of a geographical indication registered under the GI Regulation. Under the principle of the superiority of EC law, a national court would not have the authority to stop the use of a right granted by Regulation 2081/92 based on national law.

170. Further, even if applicable, the United States has explained that such laws do not even pretend to consider the interests of trademark owners in the manner required by TRIPS Article 17.[133] These laws have nothing to do with the right of trademark owners to defend their mark from infringement within the meaning of TRIPS Article 16.1. The fact that certain acts that constitute trademark infringement may also, coincidentally, be subject to prohibition under other EC or member State legislation is simply not relevant to a determination whether the infringement of a given trademark by a given use constitutes a limited exception to the rights of a given trademark owner.

171. In fact, if the EC's argument were to be accepted, then a Member could simply ignore the obligations of the trademark section of the TRIPS Agreement in their entirety, and instead argue that implementation of Article 10*bis* of the Paris Convention, alone, satisfies the obligations of TRIPS Article 16.1, when read in conjunction with TRIPS Article 17. Article 10*bis* requires countries of the Paris Union to provide, for example, "effective protection against unfair competition", defined as "[a]ny act of competition contrary to honest practices in industrial or commercial matters." While it is true that a number of the exceptions to trademark laws cited by the EC, including the EC's own Trademark Directive and Regulation, similarly require that such exceptions accord with "honest practices in industrial or commercial matters", they all do so in the context of trademark law. By contrast, EC misleading advertising and labeling laws, and Member state unfair competition laws, are entirely disconnected from the protection of individual trademark rights. Recourse to such laws is available to anyone, regardless of whether they are owners of registered trademarks. Again, while the substantive standards of the EC misleading advertising and member State unfair competition laws may, perhaps, be consistent with the requirements of Article 10*bis* of the Paris Convention, they do not satisfy the specific obligations of the trademark section of the TRIPS Agreement. Thus, the EC's arguments, more than just ignoring "fair" in the phrase "fair use", or "limited" in the phrase "limited exceptions", now seem to replace the entire trademark section of the TRIPS Agreement with Article 10*bis* of the Paris Convention to justify any and all harm to trademark rights imposed by the GI Regulation. This is not permitted, for it does not "give effect to the provisions of [the TRIPS] Agreement", as required by TRIPS Article 1.1, and treats an entire section of the TRIPS Agreement as being redundant with the Paris Convention.[134]

---

[130] EC Response to Question 153, para. 234.

[131] US Opening Statement at Second Meeting, para. 102; US Second Written Submission, paras. 208-209.

[132] EC Response to Question 153, paras. 235-239.

[133] US Second Written Submission, para. 210.

[134] *See* Panel Report, *India – Patents*, WT/DS50/R, para. 7.53 ("The TRIPS Agreement is different from other covered agreements in that most of its provisions require Members to take positive action ... In situations where it is necessary for a Member to give effect to such positive action, a failure to provide the executive with the required authority constitutes a breach of the Agreement ... ."). *See also* Appellate Body Report, *Canada-Dairy*, para. 133 ("[T]he task of the treaty interpreter is to ascertain and give effect to a legally operative meaning for the terms of the treaty. The applicable fundamental principle of *effet utile* is that a treaty interpreter is not free to adopt a meaning that would reduce parts of a treaty to redundancy or inutility.")

172. Moreover, the generalized unfair competition laws and misleading advertising laws cited by the EC are not somehow "equivalent to" the requirements generally stipulated in the exceptions provided in the trademark law of many Members, because the EC measures, unlike the exceptions to trademark law, are entirely disconnected from the confines of trademark law, itself.[135] For example, in a typical trademark infringement case, the trademark owner has the burden to demonstrate that a certain use causes a likelihood of confusion (or, alternatively, that the presumption for identical signs for identical goods is appropriate). Once the trademark owner presents a *prima facie* case of infringement, the burden shifts to the accused infringer to demonstrate that such use is justified by a limited exception, such as fair use. By contrast, when a registered trademark owner brings a trademark infringement case against the likely confusing use of a registered GI in the EC, the user of the registered GI can stop the proceedings before the court even begins to consider likelihood of confusion by simply showing, at the outset of the proceedings, that the GI is registered and used pursuant to the GI Regulation. In such a situation, it would be useless for the trademark owner to demonstrate trademark infringement, because, as the EC has confirmed, pursuant to the GI Regulation, "a trademark owner cannot prevent the holder of a registered geographical indication from using the name or names registered under Regulation 2081/92 on the grounds that the use of such name or names is confusing *per se* with an earlier trademark."[136] Thus, during the course of trademark infringement proceedings, the GI user never has the burden to show, for example, that use of the GI constitutes "fair use" or qualifies as a limited exception. Once the GI user shows that the GI is registered, the trademark owner automatically loses, even if it can demonstrate infringement.

173. In fact, rather than placing the burden on the GI rightholder to prove its entitlement to a limited exception under Article 17, the EC would place the burden on the trademark owner to demonstrate that a particular use of the registered GI is *not* limited, or does not take account of the legitimate interests of the trademark owner, in the sense that the use violates member State unfair competition laws, or EC labeling and misleading advertising laws. As described above, this is at odds with the course of trademark infringement proceedings in a system where the exceptions to trademark law are connected to the trademark law, itself, and it is also at odds with the TRIPS Agreement.

174. Under the EC's reasoning, after the trademark infringement case is dismissed based simply on the fact that the allegedly infringing use is that of a registered GI, the trademark owner would then have to bring a separate claim or case against use of the GI for misleading advertising or unfair competition. But the ability to bring such a case does not satisfy the requirements of TRIPS Articles 16 and 17, as it does not accord any rights specifically to the trademark owner. To this effect, the obligation in TRIPS Article 42 for Members to "make available to right holders civil judicial procedures *concerning the enforcement of any intellectual property right covered by this Agreement*" provides relevant context.[137] Recourse to misleading advertising law, or unfair competition law, simply does not "concern[ ] the enforcement of . . .", trademark rights. It concerns something entirely different, namely the enforcement of Article 10*bis* of the Paris Convention. Moreover, TRIPS Article 44.1 relates to injunctions for "infringement of an intellectual property right", while TRIPS Article 45.1 speaks to "the authority to order the *infringer* to pay the *right holder* damages adequate to compensate for the injury the right holder has suffered because of an infringement of that person's intellectual property rights."[138] By contrast, a claim pursuant to EC misleading advertising laws or Member state unfair competition laws does not relate to "infringers" or "right holders".

Questions 154 and 156

175. The EC begins with the surprising assertion that "[a] trademark which has never been used or which is virtually unknown ... could be easily replaced without significant prejudice to the owner."[139] The EC's belief

[135] EC Response to Question 153, paras. 240-241.

[136] EC Response to Question 139, para. 166.

[137] Emphasis added; footnote omitted.

[138] Emphasis added.

[139] EC Response to Question 154, para. 245.

that a trademark owner would not suffer "significant prejudice" if the owner of a "virtually unknown" trademark were forced to replace his trademark reflects the EC's complete disregard for certain classes of trademarks and a fundamental misunderstanding of the commercial realities confronting trademark registrants and users. A company will make significant investments in the creation of a trademark and in the development of the product and its advertising prior to product launch—that is prior to it being known in the market. Such investments can be considerable—in particular for small and medium sized enterprises that develop a local market in one EC Member State and seek protection for the trademark and develop the markets (and knowledge of the trademark among consumers) subsequently in other EC Member States. For the EC to say that a trademark under such circumstances "could be easily replaced" exhibits an utter lack of understanding of how products and services are developed and brought to market in Europe, and the role that trademarks play in that complex and costly endeavor. While the EC's understanding may be consistent with the treatment that the GI Regulation accords registered trademarks, it is not consistent with the treatment accorded trademarks under the TRIPS Agreement.

176. As the United States has explained previously, TRIPS Article 17 states that Members may provide "limited exceptions to the rights conferred by *a trademark*." It does not allow unlimited exceptions to a certain class of trademarks, even for trademarks that the EC considers "virtually unknown". What the EC might consider "unknown" trademarks are accorded the same protection under Article 16.1 as trademarks that the EC would consider "known"; similarly, they are granted the same treatment under Article 17 as trademarks that are known.

177. The EC's limited view of trademark rights is emphasized by its implication, at paragraphs 246-247, that a trademark owner does not have a legitimate interest that is reflected in Articles 15.1 and 16.1 of the TRIPS Agreement—a legitimate interest in preventing competitors from inducing consumers to buy competing products based not on the quality of the competing product, but instead on the mistaken belief that they are buying the product associated with the trademark. While it may be true that "legitimate interest" does not coincide exactly with "legal interest"—as the panel in *Canada – Pharmaceutical Patents* noted, third parties may have a legitimate interest without having a legal interest under the TRIPS Agreement[140]– the trademark owner's legitimate interest in preventing others from using identical or similar signs in a manner that results in a likelihood of confusion is undeniable.

178. Consistent with the US response to Panel Question 154, however, the EC correctly identifies two categories of third parties with relevant legitimate interests—namely, producers who aim to provide information to consumers about the geographical origin of the product, and consumers who benefit from such information.[141] The EC suggests, in paragraph 251 of its response to Panel Question 154, several factors that may be considered in determining whether a degree of likelihood of confusion may be appropriate, such as instances "where the geographical indication enjoys more recognition than the trademark."[142] Yet, the unlimited exception to trademark rights created by the GI Regulation does not allow for any such considerations of individual geographical indications or trademarks. Instead, it provides a blanket exception to trademark rights, and allows for an unlimited degree of confusion, over an unlimited period of time, with respect to an unlimited number of GI users, based on the simple fact that the use is of a registered GI. Consideration of whether a "geographical indication enjoys more recognition than the trademark", just as any other individualized consideration, plays no part in this blanket exception.

179. In reviewing the terms of Article 17, the EC states that "all that is required by Article 17 is that Members 'take account of' the different interests at issue", including those of the trademark owner and third parties.[143] Of course, this is not "all that is required by Article 17." Before reaching the analysis of whether the "legitimate interests" are taken into account, it must first be determined, pursuant to Article 17, that the

[140] Panel Report, *Canada – Pharmaceutical Patents,* para. 7.68.

[141] US Response to Question 154, para. 119.

[142] EC Response to Question 154.

[143] EC Response to Question 154, para. 252.

exception is "limited." This is a distinct requirement. As detailed previously, "limited exception" refers to "a narrow exception—one which makes only a small diminution of the rights", where "limited", is "measured by the extent to which the exclusive rights" of a trademark have been curtailed.[144] Thus, the EC errs when it states that "Article 17 puts on an equal level all the interests involved."[145]

180. The EC presents, in paragraph 253 of its response to Panel Question 154, a list of reasons why it apparently believes that GIs are superior to trademarks -- reasons that have absolutely no basis in the TRIPS Agreement but that may explain some of the motivations behind the EC's breaches of TRIPS Article 16. For example, the EC implies that GIs are superior to trademarks because they "serve a public interest", as opposed to trademarks, which they allege have only "a commercial function."[146] Yet, the TRIPS Agreement, itself, demonstrates that trademarks do, in fact, serve a public interest by providing consumers with valuable information and allowing them to "distinguish[] the goods or services of one undertaking from those of other undertakings", without a likelihood of confusion.[147] Indeed, as the United States pointed out in its first written submission,[148] EC jurisprudence recognizes the important public interest role that exclusive protection for trademarks plays. In this respect, Advocate General Jacobs of the European Court of Justice stated in the *Hag-II* case, that:

> A trademark can only fulfil that role if it is exclusive. Once the proprietor is forced to share the mark with the competitor, he loses control over the goodwill associated with the mark. The reputation of his own goods will be harmed if the competitor sells inferior goods. From the consumer's point of view, equally undesirable consequences will ensue, because the clarity of the signal transmitted by the trademark will be impaired. The consumer will be confused and misled.[149]

181. The United States has already set forth, in its own detailed response to Panel question 156, the underlying reasons for the differences in the language of the various exceptions to intellectual property protection in the TRIPS Agreement.

182. With respect to the EC's contention that "it is beyond dispute that the requirements of Article 17 are substantially less stringent than those of [TRIPS Articles 13, 26.2 and 30]",[150] the United States would like to reiterate that such a conclusion stems from an incorrect reading of Article 17. In particular, contrary to the EC's interpretation, the United States has explained that Article 17 makes no reference to "normal exploitation" of a trademark because a trademark right (*i.e.*, the exclusive right to prevent uses of signs that cause a likelihood of confusion with respect to a trademark) is simply not subject to exploitation in the same sense as the "exploitation" of a copyrighted work, protected industrial design, or patented invention.[151] Unlike in other intellectual property areas, therefore, Article 17 does not permit exceptions that would conflict with any exploitation of the trademark—normal or not—and does not permit reasonable conflicts with a "normal exploitation", because any conflict with the trademark rights goes to the heart of the trademark owner's legitimate interest. Therefore, there is no need for Article 17 to provide for exceptions that conflict with an "exploitation" of the trademark.

183. Likewise, Article 17 does not include the language regarding "unreasonabl[e] prejudice [to] the legitimate interests of the" intellectual property right holder referred to in other exceptions because of the

---

[144] US Response to Panel Question 154, para. 119; US Opening Statement at Second Meeting, para. 100, quoting Panel Report, *Canada – Patent Protection*, paras. 7.30-7.31.

[145] EC Response to Question 154, para. 252.

[146] EC Response to Question 154, para. 253.

[147] TRIPS Articles 15.1 and 16.1.

[148] US First Written Submission, para. 146.

[149] Case C-10/89 *SA CNL-Sucal NV v. HAG GFAG,* opinion delivered on 13 March 1990, European Court reports 1990 I-3711, at para 19.

[150] EC Response to Question 156, para. 257.

[151] US Response to Panel Question 156, para. 129.

fundamental differences in the intellectual property rights concerned. By contrast to patents and copyrights, where one can point to examples in which certain limited exceptions do not unreasonably prejudice the legitimate interests of the right holder, the very ability of a trademark owner to distinguish goods using his trademark is significantly compromised if that trademark owner cannot stop confusing uses of his signs.[152] As a result, the standard of "unreasonably prejudice" the rights of the owner is not included, because any uses of signs likely to cause confusion with a mark will prejudice the owner's interests. Thus, the absence of such language certainly does not demonstrate that Article 17 is "substantially less stringent" than that of other exceptions to TRIPS obligations.

Questions 159-160

184. Contrary to the EC's argument, the United States is not arguing that the GI Regulation excludes the application of other measures to designations of origin and geographical indications. The United States detailed its arguments at paragraphs 171-183 of its first written submission. For instance, Article 2(1) of the EC GI Regulation provides that the GI Regulation is the means of achieving "Community protection" of GIs, but fails to provide legal means under that Regulation to all interested parties. Further, and perhaps more significant, by not permitting all interested persons to object to a GI registration, the GI Regulation fails to provide the legal means to those persons to prevent misleading uses vis-a-vis the registered GI. The EC has suggested that other laws are available to protect GIs in the EC, but has not shown that these other laws overcome the deficiencies on the face of the GI Regulation, particularly keeping in mind that EC regulations take precedence over EC member State laws.

Question 164

185. The United States agrees with the EC that TRIPS Article 7 seems to be of limited relevance to this dispute, as it relates to the role of TRIPS rules in promoting technological innovation and technology transfer.[153]

186. The EC asserts that the EC GI Regulation is a measure that promotes the public interest in a sector of vital importance to the EC's socio-economic and technological development, within the meaning of TRIPS Article 8.1. The EC has not demonstrated, however, that requiring prior valid registered trademarks to "coexist" with later registered GIs—by depriving trademark owners of their Article 16.1 rights— is "necessary" to promote this public interest, as required by Article 8.1. In any event, the EC can maintain this "coexistence" only to the extent that it is "consistent with the provisions of" the TRIPS Agreement, within the meaning of Article 8.1. As the United States has shown, however, this is an impossible task for the EC, since "coexistence" is fundamentally inconsistent with TRIPS Article 16.1.

---

[152] US Response to Panel Question 156, para. 130.

[153] EC Responses to Questions following the Second Panel Meeting, para. 273.

ANNEX A-10

COMMENTS OF THE UNITED STATES ON THE REPLY OF THE INTERNATIONAL BUREAU OF WIPO TO THE PANEL'S LETTER OF 9 JULY 2004

(28 September 2004)

1. As provided in item 3(k) of the Panel's "Further Revised Timetable for Panel Proceedings", the United States is providing comments below on the reply of the World Intellectual Property Organization ("WIPO") to the Panel's letter of July 9, requesting available factual information relevant to the interpretation of certain provisions of the Paris Convention (in particular, Article 2, related to national treatment).

2. The factual information provided by WIPO consists of excerpts from WIPO's official records of various diplomatic conferences that adopted, amended, or revised provisions currently contained in Articles 2 and 3 of the Paris Convention (Stockholm Act, 1967). As a preliminary matter, the United States notes that, under customary rules of interpretation of international public law, reflected in Article 31 of the *Vienna Convention on the Law of Treaties*, a treaty must be interpreted in good faith in accordance with the ordinary meaning to be given to the terms of the treaty in their context and in the light of its object and purpose. Throughout this dispute, the United States has applied this approach to interpreting the TRIPS Agreement and Paris Convention provisions at issue in this dispute. Supplemental means of interpretation, including the preparatory work of the treaty and the circumstances of its conclusion, may only be used for a limited purpose: to confirm the meaning resulting from the application of the general rule of interpretation, or to determine the meaning when that interpretation leaves the meaning ambiguous or obscure, or leads to a result which is manifestly absurd or unreasonable.[1]

3. No party to this dispute has argued that the terms of Articles 2 and 3 of the Paris Convention are ambiguous or obscure. Instead, the materials presented by WIPO confirm the interpretation of the Paris Convention presented by the United States in this dispute, applying the customary rules of interpretation of public international law. Indeed, the materials provide useful emphasis in at least two respects.

4. First, the materials confirm that, in adopting Article 2 and its predecessors, the negotiators were keenly aware that, as concerns the protection of industrial property, a Member would have to provide the same advantages to nationals of other Members as it provides to its own nationals, *regardless* of the domestic laws or regulations in those other Members relating to intellectual property. It was clear to the negotiators that, under Article 2, a Member would not be able to condition the protection of industrial property provided to another Member's nationals on that other Member itself having a particular system of protection (or indeed, any system)

[1] *See Vienna Convention on the Law of Treaties*, Article 32.

or having a particular set of substantive or procedural rules in place.[2] Thus, in the example that recurs in the WIPO materials, the United States would have to allow all Member national inventors 17 years of patent protection, with minimal fees and no exploitation requirement, even though other Members imposed significant fees for such protection, provided substantially shorter patent terms, and required exploitation.[3] The delegate from France, who made the initial proposal for Article 2 in 1880, insisted on the importance of providing the same advantages to the nationals of other Members as one provides to one's own nationals, regardless of the protections provided in those other Members, and his successor at the Hague Conference reiterated the same points in 1925, when the national treatment provision of the Paris Convention was last amended.[4] That conference rejected suggestions that the regime be changed to compensate for the perceived problem of requiring that a Member's nationals benefit from strong protections in another Member, even though the first Member does not provide the same protections.[5]

5. A second, and related, issue is that, throughout the negotiations, there was an emphasis on the fact that, under the national treatment obligation, Members were not obliged to change their substantive law, or to put in place legal regimes that they did not currently have.[6] It simply required that whatever regime was in place be applied equally to nationals of other Members. For instance, specifically in connection with the national treatment obligation with respect to indications of source, the Belgian representative clarified that the Paris Convention did not obligate Belgium to have a particular legal regime in place for indications of source, but only that, whatever the regime, it would apply even-handedly to all nationals.[7] And it was the expectation that Belgian nationals would receive the same treatment in another Union Member as that Member's nationals, *regardless* of the lack of a particular protection regime in Belgium.

6. These two points are significant because they stand in contrast to the EC GI Regulation. As the United States has described in greater detail in its submissions, oral statements, and answers to Panel questions, the EC will not register and protect the home-based GIs of another Member's nationals unless that Member itself—not the national claiming the right, but the Member—satisfies certain requirements. Among those requirements are that the Member concerned establish an EC-style inspection system for GIs, and that the Member itself demonstrate that the GI is protected in the Member (a requirement that accommodates well Members with an EC-style GI registration system, but presents significant obstacles for Members that protect GIs in other ways). The Member must also be able to assess whether an application for GI registration from one of its nationals satisfies the requirements of the EC GI Regulation, which requires an infrastructure and decision-making

---

[2] As the United States noted in its first submission, citing the same materials as have now been provided by WIPO, the importance of this principle was made clear at the very first negotiating session for the Paris Convention in 1880, where the concept of national treatment in what was to become the Paris Convention was first introduced. In the welcoming remarks for that first session, the French Minister for Agriculture and Commerce stated that the Conference could not achieve a complete international treaty of industrial property because of the difficulty of unifying national laws. He concluded that the Conference should, therefore, strive to find the means to constitute a union which, <u>without encroaching on domestic legislation</u>, would assure national treatment and lay down a number of uniform general principles. Paris Diplomatic Conference (1880/1883), pp. 14-17, at p. 16 (emphasis added). Also provided as Exhibit US-3. In the negotiations on the national treatment provision, the French negotiator who had prepared the initial draft emphasized that, in order to be acceptable, the convention <u>would have to respect the internal legislation of all contracting parties to the extent possible</u>, and to restrict itself to an obligation to extend national treatment to foreigners. Paris Diplomatic Conference (1880/1883), p. 33 (emphasis added). Also provided as Exhibit US-3. In the course of that discussion, the national treatment obligation was <u>clarified by the deletion of the word "reciproquement"</u> from the original draft. *Id.*, pp. 39-45. Also provided as Exhibit US-3. And indeed, in subsequent revisions to this provision, several proposals to include a reciprocity element in the obligation found no support and were withdrawn. For instance, a proposal by the United States to provide for the right to impose upon nationals of the other countries the fulfillment of conditions imposed on its nationals by those countries found no support and was withdrawn. Hague Revision Conference (1925), pp. 413-415 (First Sub-Committee). Also provided as Exhibit US-4.

[3] *E.g.*, Brussels Revision Conference (1897/1900), pp. 95-97, 143-144, 195-196.; Hague Revision Conference (1925), pp. 413-415. *See also* Paris Diplomatic Conference (1880/1883), pp. 33-45, clarifying that the national treatment approach should be acceptable to countries, like The Netherlands and Switzerland, that do not protect patents under their national law, because they would not have to treat foreigners better than their own citizens.

[4] Paris Diplomatic Conference (1880/1883), pp. 14-17; Hague Revision Conference (1925), p. 414.

[5] *See* Hague Revision Conference (1925), pp. 413-415 (First Sub-Committee). Also provided as Exhibit US-4.

[6] *See* note 2, *supra.*

[7] Brussels Revision Conference (1897/1900), p. 246.

capability similar to that possessed by the EC and the EC member States (which also must make that assessment under the GI Regulation). As the United States has pointed out in this dispute, these are effectively requirements that, as a condition of obtaining intellectual property protection in the EC for their nationals, other WTO Members adopt aspects of a GI regime that are similar to what the EC has chosen to adopt. In contrast, as reflected in the materials provided by WIPO, the negotiators of the Paris Convention intended that such intellectual property protections be made available to all nationals of Members *regardless* of the internal laws and regulations of those Members and, in particular, *without* a requirement that those Members adopt particular systems of protection.[8]

7. Indeed, it is also revealing that, in the many pages provided by WIPO, there is considerable discussion of the requirements that Members could impose on foreign *nationals* in order for them to receive the same advantages as domestic nationals. By contrast, there is no discussion that the United States could see concerning any requirements that could be imposed on *other Members* as a condition of their nationals receiving the benefits of intellectual property protections, aside, of course, from the requirement to become a Member of the Union.[9] This, too, is consistent with the views of the United States in this proceeding, based on the customary rules of interpretation of public international law: it is the *nationals* of other Members, not the Members themselves, to whom national treatment is owed. The EC GI Regulation denies this treatment to non-EC nationals when it imposes conditions that the non-EC national himself cannot meet, but for which he must rely on his government.

8. In sum, the United States reiterates its positions, set forth in its submissions, oral statements, and responses to Panel questions, that the EC GI Regulation is inconsistent with the EC's national treatment obligations under the TRIPS Agreement and the Paris Convention, as properly interpreted using general rules of treaty interpretation, and submits that the materials provided by WIPO confirm and reinforce this interpretation and the inconsistencies of the EC GI Regulation.

---

[8] Further, at this point it almost goes without saying that the EC's explicit conditions of reciprocity and equivalence in Article 12(1) of the GI Regulation are directly contrary to what the negotiators of the Paris Convention either drafted or intended to draft. Indeed, even the EC has abandoned any defense that these conditions are consistent with national treatment.

[9] Indeed, even if a country did not join the Union, however, its nationals could be eligible for national treatment under Article 3 of the Paris Convention, if they had a real and effective commercial or industrial establishment in the territory of a country of the Union.

EUROPEAN COMMUNITIES – PROTECTION OF TRADEMARKS AND GEOGRAPHICAL INDICATIONS FOR AGRICULTURAL PRODUCTS AND FOODSTUFFS – COMPLAINT BY THE UNITED STATES

WT/DS174/R/ADD.2
REPORT OF THE PANEL

ADDENDUM

This addendum contains Annex B to the Report of the Panel to be found in document WT/DS174/R. Annex A can be found in Add.1 and Annexes C and D can be found in Add.3.

ANNEX B

SUBMISSIONS BY THE EUROPEAN COMMUNITIES

ANNEX B-1

EUROPEAN COMMUNITIES' REQUEST FOR A PRELIMINARY RULING

(24 February 2004)

TABLE OF CONTENTS

Short Title	Full Case Title and Citation of Case
Canada – Wheat	Preliminary Ruling of the Panel, *Canada – Measures Relating to Exports of Wheat and Treatment of Imported Grain*, WT/DS276/12, circulated on 21 July 2003
EC – Bananas III	Appellate Body Report, *European Communities – Regime for the Importation, Sale and Distribution of Bananas*, WT/DS27/AB/R, adopted 25 September 1997
Guatemala – Cement I	Appellate Body Report, *Guatemala – Anti-Dumping Investigation Regarding Portland Cement from Mexico*, WT/DS60/AB/R, adopted 25 November 1998
Korea – Dairy	Appellate Body Report, *Korea – Definitive Safeguard Measure on Imports of Certain Dairy Products*, WT/DS98/AB/R, adopted 12 January 2000
Thailand – H-Beams	Appellate Body Report, *Thailand – Anti-Dumping Duties on Angles, Shapes and Sections of Iron or Non-Alloy Steel and H-Beams from Poland*, WT/DS122/AB/R, adopted 5 April 2001
US – Carbon Steel from Germany	Panel Report, *United States – Countervailing Duties on Certain Corrosion-Resistant Carbon Steel Flat Products from Germany*, WT/DS213/R and Corr.1, adopted 19 December 2002 Appellate Body Report, *United States – Countervailing Duties on Certain Corrosion-Resistant Carbon Steel Flat Products from Germany*, WT/DS213/AB/R, adopted 28 November 2002
US – FSC	Appellate Body Report, *United States – Tax Treatment for "Foreign Sales Corporations,"* WT/DS108/AB/R, adopted 20 March 2000
US – Lamb	Panel Report, *United States – Safeguard Measures on Imports of Fresh, Chilled or Frozen Lamb Meat from New Zealand and Australia*, WT/DS177/R, WT/DS178/R, adopted 16 May 2001

I. INTRODUCTION

1. The European Communities (hereinafter "the EC") is of the view that the requests for the establishment of the Panel made by Australia (hereinafter: Australian request)[1] and by the United States (hereinafter: United States request)[2] do not meet the requirements of Article 6.2 of the Dispute Settlement Understanding (DSU).

2. The Panel requests fail to identify the specific measure at issue in the present dispute. Moreover, the Panel requests do not provide a brief summary of the legal basis of the complaint sufficient to present the problem clearly.

3. The respect of the requirements of Article 6.2 DSU is an essential precondition for the jurisdiction of a Panel. Where a complaining party has failed to clearly set out its claim in accordance with Article 6.2 DSU, the Panel does not have jurisdiction.

4. Moreover, the deficiencies of the Panel requests seriously prejudice the due process rights of the EC as a defending party. As a defending party, the EC is entitled to know the case it has to answer. The Panel requests in the present case do not meet the minimum requirements necessary for ensuring a fair and orderly conduct of the dispute settlement proceedings.

5. Given these fundamental concerns, the EC requests that the Panel issue a preliminary ruling regarding Article 6.2 DSU.

II. THE REQUIREMENTS OF ARTICLE 6.2 DSU

6. Article 6.2 DSU sets out the following minimum requirements with which any Panel request must comply:

> The request for the establishment of a panel shall be made in writing. It shall indicate whether consultations were held, identify the specific measures at issue and provide a brief summary of the legal basis of the complaint sufficient to present the problem clearly.

A. THE CONTENT AND PURPOSE OF ARTICLE 6.2 DSU

7. In *Korea – Dairy*, the Appellate Body held that Article 6.2 of the DSU imposes four separate requirements:[3]

> When parsed into its constituent parts, Article 6.2 may be seen to impose the following requirements. The request must: (i) be in writing; (ii) indicate whether consultations were held; (iii) identify the specific measures at issue; and (iv) provide a brief summary of the legal basis of the complaint sufficient to present the problem clearly. In its fourth requirement, Article 6.2 demands only a summary—and it may be a brief one—of the legal basis of the complaint; but the summary must, in any event, be one that is "sufficient to present the problem clearly." It is not enough, in other words, that "the legal basis of the complaint" is summarily identified; the identification must "present the problem clearly."

8. The objective and purpose of Article 6.2 of the DSU is to guarantee a minimum measure of procedural fairness throughout the proceedings. This is of particular importance to the defendant, who must rely on the Panel request in order to begin preparing its defense. Similarly, WTO Members who intend to participate as

[1] Request of 18 August 2003, WT/DS290/18.

[2] Request of 18 August 2003, WT/DS174/20.

[3] Appellate Body Report, *Korea –Dairy*, para. 120.

third parties must be informed of the subject-matter of the dispute. This underlying rationale of Article 6.2 DSU has been explained by the Appellate Body in *Thailand – H-Beams*:[4]

> Article 6.2 of the DSU calls for sufficient clarity with respect to the legal basis of the complaint, that is, with respect to the "claims" that are being asserted by the complaining party. A defending party is entitled to know what case it has to answer, and what violations have been alleged so that it can begin preparing its defence. Likewise, those Members of the WTO who intend to participate as third parties in panel proceedings must be informed of the legal basis of the complaint. This requirement of due process is fundamental to ensuring a fair and orderly conduct of dispute settlement proceedings.

B. THE PANEL MUST NOT ASSUME JURISDICTION IN RESPECT OF CLAIMS THAT HAVE NOT BEEN ESTABLISHED IN ACCORDANCE WITH ARTICLE 6.2 DSU

9. Moreover, the respect of the requirements of Article 6.2 DSU is of crucial importance for properly establishing the jurisdiction of the Panel. As the Appellate Body has confirmed in *US – Carbon Steel*, the panel request forms the basis of the panel's terms of reference under Article 7.1 of the DSU:[5]

> There are, therefore, two distinct requirements, namely identification of *the specific measures at issue*, and the provision of a *brief summary of the legal basis of the complaint* (or the *claims*). Together, they comprise the "matter referred to the DSB," which forms the basis for a panel's terms of reference under Article 7.1 of the DSU.

10. For this reason, a strict respect of the requirements of Article 6.2 DSU is essential for the orderly conduct of dispute settlement proceedings under the DSU. As the Appellate Body has clearly stated in *EC – Bananas*, Panels must therefore verify carefully that the conditions or Article 6.2 DSU are fulfilled:[6]

> As a panel request is normally not subjected to detailed scrutiny by the DSB, it is incumbent upon a panel to examine the request for the establishment of the panel very carefully to ensure its compliance with both the letter and the spirit of Article 6.2 of the DSU. It is important that a panel request be sufficiently precise for two reasons: first, it often forms the basis for the terms of reference of the panel pursuant to Article 7 of the DSU; and, second, it informs the defending party and the third parties of the legal basis of the complaint.

11. Accordingly, the present Panel must verify carefully that the Panel request meet the requirements of Article 6.2 DSU. The Panel must not assume jurisdiction over any claim that has not been set out in accordance with Article 6.2 DSU.

C. THE REQUIREMENTS OF ARTICLE 6.2 DSU MUST BE EVALUATED ON THE FACE OF THE PANEL REQUEST

12. In *EC – Bananas*, the Appellate Body has clarified that the claims, which are set out in the panel request, must be distinguished from the subsequent arguments of the parties in support of their claim. Consequently, the Appellate Body has held that a faulty Panel request cannot be subsequently "cured" by the written submission of the parties:[7]

> We do not agree with the Panel that "even if there was some uncertainty whether the panel request had met the requirements of Article 6.2, the first written submissions of the

[4] Appellate Body Report, *Thailand – H Beams*, para. 88 (emphasis added). Similarly Appellate Body Report, *US – Carbon Steel*, para. 126.

[5] Appellate Body Report, *US – Carbon Steel*, para. 125. Similarly, Appellate Body Report, *Guatemala – Cement*, para. 72.

[6] Appellate Body Report, *EC – Bananas III*, para. 142 (emphasis added). Similarly also Appellate Body Report, *US – Carbon Steel*, para. 126.

[7] Appellate Body Report, *EC – Bananas III*, para. 143.

> Complainants 'cured' that uncertainty because their submissions were sufficiently detailed to present all the factual and legal issues clearly." Article 6.2 of the DSU requires that the *claims*, but not the *arguments*, must all be specified sufficiently in the request for the establishment of a panel in order to allow the defending party and any third parties to know the legal basis of the complaint. If a *claim* is not specified in the request for the establishment of a panel, then a faulty request cannot be subsequently "cured" by a complaining party's argumentation in its first written submission to the panel or in any other submission or statement made later in the panel proceeding.

13. As a consequence, the only basis on which to establish whether a Panel request is in conformity with the requirements of Article 6.2 is the text of the request itself. This has been confirmed by the Appellate Body in *United States – Carbon Steel*:[8]

> As we have said previously, compliance with the requirements of Article 6.2 must be demonstrated <u>on the face of the request</u> for the establishment of a panel. Defects in the request for the establishment of a panel cannot be "cured" in the subsequent submissions of the parties during the panel proceedings.

III. THE PANEL REQUESTS FAIL TO IDENTIFY THE "SPECIFIC MEASURE AT ISSUE"

14. Both Panel requests identify the measure at issue as Council Regulation (EEC) No. 2081/92 on the protection of geographical indications and designations of origin for agricultural products and foodstuffs, as amended (hereinafter: Regulation 2081/92). Moreover, the Australian request, in its fourth paragraph, defines the "EC measure" as also including "related implementing and enforcement measures." In the view of the EC, these references are insufficient in order to define the "specific measure at issue," as required by Article 6.2 DSU.

A. THE REFERENCES TO REGULATION 2081/92 ARE NOT SUFFICIENTLY SPECIFIC

15. The EC considers that the references to Regulation 2081/92 are not sufficiently specific to permit an identification of the "specific measure at issue" in the present dispute.

16. The EC would like to stress that Article 6.2 DSU requires not only the identification of a "measure," but of the "<u>specific</u> measure at issue." The wording of Article 6.2 DSU is different from that of Article 4.4 DSU, which provides that consultation requests must identify "the measures at issue." As the Panel in *Canada – Wheat* has convincingly explained, this difference in wording is intentional, and must be given meaning:[9]

> Having regard to the relevant context of Article 6.2 of the DSU, we note Article 4.4 of the DSU, which deals with the contents of requests for consultations. It states in relevant part that "any request for consultations shall give the reasons for the request, including identification of the measures at issue." Notably, Article 4.4 omits the term "specific" in referring to the "measures at issue." We believe that this difference in language is not inadvertent and must be given meaning. Indeed, in our view, this difference in language supports the view that requests for consultations need not be as specific and as detailed as requests for establishment of a panel under Article 6.2 of the DSU. As a corollary, in our view, this relevant context bears out the importance of the term "specific" as it appears in Article 6.2.

17. In the view of the EC, what can be considered a "specific measure" will depend on the circumstances of the particular case, and in particular on the characteristics of the measure in question. Where a measure is of a relatively simple character, or where it is clear from the circumstances of the case which aspect of the measure

---

[8] Appellate Body Report, *United States –Carbon Steel*, para. 127 (emphasis added).

[9] Preliminary Ruling by the Panel, *Canada – Wheat*, para. 15.

is contested, it may be sufficient to refer to the measure as a whole and identify it by name, number, or date of adoption.

18. However, such a reference to a "measure" as a whole may not always be sufficient to establish the "specific measure at issue." This is the case, in particular, where the measure in question is a complex legislative text. For instance, it would not seem conceivable to the EC that a WTO member would refer, in a request for the establishment of a Panel, simply to the Civil Code of another member, without specifying which specific provision is at issue in the dispute. Accordingly, in the case of complex legislative measures, it will not be sufficient to refer to the measure as a whole, but it will be necessary to identify the specific provisions or sections of the measure which are at issue.

19. In the present case, Regulation 2081/92 is a measure with establishes the legal framework for the protection of geographical indications and designations of origin for agricultural products and foodstuffs in the European Community. The text of Regulation 2081/92, as most recently amended by Council Regulation (EC) no. 806/2003 of 14 April 2003, is attached as Exhibit EC–1.

20. The EC does not propose to describe in detail the content of Regulation 2081/92 in the context of the present request for a preliminary ruling. However, the EC believes that even a cursory study of Regulation 2081/92 will confirm that this regulation is a complex piece of legislation in the field of the protection of intellectual property. As is typical for such legislation, Regulation 2081/92 deals with a host of issues relating to all aspects of the protection of geographical indications and designations of origin for agricultural products and foodstuffs.

21. The text of Regulation 2081/92 extends over 15 pages, including two annexes. The operational provisions of Regulation 2081/92 are contained in 22 Articles, each of which in turn is subdivided into numerous further paragraphs and sections. These articles deal with a host of widely differing issues. Purely for illustrative purposes, and without any claim to being exhaustive or particularly detailed, the following topics are dealt with in Regulation 2081/92:

- The objective and scope of application of the regulation (Article 1);
- definitions (Article 2);
- exclusion from registration of names, and in particular the issue of generic names (Article 3);
- product specifications (Article 4);
- the right to apply for registrations and the procedure for applications (Article 5);
- the procedures for registration of geographical indications and related issues; the issue of homonymous names (Article 6);
- objections to registrations (Article 7);
- conditions for the use of geographical indications and designations of origin (Article 8);
- the amendment of product specifications (Article 9);
- inspection procedures (Article 10);
- procedures in case product specifications are not respected (Article 11);
- cancellation of protected names (Article 11a);
- the application of the regulation to agricultural products and foodstuffs from third countries (Article 12);
- the application procedure for the protection of third country geographical indications (Article 12a);
- the registration procedure for the protection of third country geographical indications (Article 12b);
- the amendment of the product specifications for third country geographical indications (Article 12c);
- objections to the registration of geographical indications emanating from third countries (Article 12d);

- the protection of registered names (Article 13);
- certain questions regarding the relationship between geographical indications and trademarks (Article 14);
- the Committee assisting the Commission (Article 15);
- implementing rules (Article 16);
- entry into force (Article 18).

22. The unspecific reference to "Regulation 2081/92" made in the Panel requests does not permit the EC to understand which specific aspects among those covered by Regulation 2081/92 the complainants intend to raise in the context of the present proceedings. This appears particularly objectionable given the fact that it would have been easily possible for the complainants to provide more specific references to individual provisions of Regulation 2081/92.

23. For these reasons, the EC submits that the references to "Regulation 2081/92" do not meet the requirement of the identification of the "specific measure at issue" in Article 6.2 DSU.

B. THE REFERENCES TO "RELATED IMPLEMENTING AND ENFORCEMENT MEASURES" ARE NOT SUFFICIENTLY SPECIFIC

24. In the fourth paragraph of its Panel request, Australia has referred to "related implementing and enforcement measures" as part of the "EC measure."[10] The EC is of the view that this blanket reference to "related implementing and enforcement measures" falls short of the requirement to identify the "specific measure at issue" in Article 6.2 DSU.

25. The requirement to identify the "specific measure at issue" means that if the measure is not already identified beyond reasonable doubt through elements such as name, number, or date of adoption of the act, then the Panel request must at the very least contain the necessary information which enables the Panel, the defendant, and the third parties to establish <u>with full certainty</u> which is the specific measure at issue in the present dispute. This has been convincingly stated by the Panel in *Canada – Wheat*:[11]

> We consider that in the absence of an explicit identification of a measure of general application by name, as in the present case, sufficient information must be provided in the request for establishment of a panel itself that effectively identifies the precise measures at issue. Whether sufficient information is provided on the face of the panel request will depend, as noted above, on whether the information provided serves the purposes of Article 6.2, and in particular its due process objective, as well as the specific circumstances of each case, including the type of measure that is at issue.

26. As the Panel in *Canada – Wheat* also explained, due process does not allow the complainant to shift the burden of identifying the specific measures under challenge to the defendant:[12]

> Due process requires that the complaining party fully assume the burden of identifying the specific measures under challenge. In the present case, the panel request effectively shifts part of that burden onto Canada as the responding party, inasmuch as it leaves Canada little choice, if it wants to begin preparing its defence, but to undertake legal research and exercise

[10] In this context, the EC notes that whereas the United States amended request for consultations (WT/DS174/1/Add.1), in its second paragraph, included a reference to "related implementing and enforcement measures," such a reference no longer appears in the Panel request, which, in its third and fourth paragraph, refers exclusively to "Regulation 2081/92." Accordingly, the EC understands that the United States Panel request extends only to Regulation 2081/92.

[11] Preliminary Ruling by the Panel, *Canada – Wheat*, para. 20.

[12] Preliminary Ruling by the Panel, *Canada – Wheat*, para. 24.

judgement in order to establish the precise identity of the laws and regulations implicated by the panel request.

27. The Australian request falls entirely short of these requirements. The Australian request contains no elements to identify the "measures" at issue, other than they are "related" and that they are supposed to be "enforcement or implementing measures."

28. The statement that the measures are "related" is so vague that it does not permit any meaningful narrowing-down of the measures in question. In fact, a whole range of legislative and other measures might be considered to be "related" in some way to the present dispute, including trademark and other intellectual property legislation, unfair competition laws, law on food labelling and food marketing, or consumer protection laws. Moreover, such laws may exist at the level of both the European Community and its Member States.

29. Similarly, the reference to "enforcement or implementing measures" does not provide the required precision with respect to the definition of the specific measure at issue. Since Regulation 2081/92 is a complex piece of intellectual property legislation, there is very large number of different measures that are necessary for its implementation and enforcement.

30. First of all, implementation may occur through legislative measures, for instance through the adoption of "detailed rules" on the basis of Article 16 of Regulation 2081/92. More importantly, implementation and enforcement may require measures of the executive, for instance concerning the transmission of applications or objections, the decision to register or to cancel geographical indications, or to amend specifications, etc. Finally, implementation and enforcement is also a responsibility of the judiciary, which is responsible for the judicial review of the actions of the Community and Member States authorities in the application of Regulation 2081/92.

31. Moreover, it should be noted that the implementation of Regulation 2081/92 is not only the responsibility of the Community, but also that of its Member States, who, for instance, are responsible for the transmission of applications and objections regarding the registration of geographical indications to the Commission. Therefore, Member States also may have to adopt implementing rules, and take decisions which are subject to judicial review by national courts.

32. Finally, it should be noted that the measures which have been taken for implementing or enforcing Regulation 2081/92 are of a very high number. To take only one figure, the EC has by now registered 640 geographical indications or designations of origin. The EC would consider it inconceivable that each one of these registrations would be the subject of the present dispute settlement proceedings simply because of the blanket reference to "implementing and enforcement measures."

33. For these reasons, the EC submits that the reference to "related implementing and enforcement measures" in the Australian request fails to identify the "specific measure at issue."

IV. THE PANEL REQUESTS DO NOT CONTAIN A BRIEF SUMMARY OF THE LEGAL BASIS OF THE COMPLAINT

34. The Panel requests in the present case do not only fail to identify the specific measure at issue. They also fail to include a brief summary of the legal basis of the complaint.

A. THE BRIEF SUMMARY OF THE LEGAL BASIS OF THE COMPLAINT

35. Article 6.2 DSU requires that a request for the establishment of a Panel must contain a "brief summary of the legal basis of the complaint sufficient to present the problem clearly."

36. As the Appellate Body has stated in *EC – Bananas*, there is a distinction between the claims, which must be contained in the Panel request, and the arguments supporting these claims, which are set out in the subsequent submissions of the Parties.[13] However, in *Korea – Dairy*, the Appellate Body has also clarified that the mere listing of provisions claimed to have been violated may not be sufficient for the purposes of Article 6.2 DSU:[14]

> Identification of the treaty provisions claimed to have been violated by the respondent is always necessary both for purposes of defining the terms of reference of a panel and for informing the respondent and the third parties of the claims made by the complainant; such identification is a minimum prerequisite if the legal basis of the complaint is to be presented at all. But it may not always be enough. There may be situations where the simple listing of the articles of the agreement or agreements involved may, in the light of attendant circumstances, suffice to meet the standard of *clarity* in the statement of the legal basis of the complaint. However, there may also be situations in which the circumstances are such that the mere listing of treaty articles would not satisfy the standard of Article 6.2. This may be the case, for instance, where the articles listed establish not one single, distinct obligation, but rather multiple obligations. In such a situation, the listing of articles of an agreement, in and of itself, may fall short of the standard of Article 6.2.

37. In the concrete case, the Appellate Body was primarily concerned with the question of whether a reference to a provision in a WTO agreement may be sufficient when such provision contains multiple obligations. However, the findings of the Appellate Body are of a more general importance. First, the Appellate Body held that the precise identification of the WTO provisions alleged to have been violated is always required under Article 6.2 DSU. Second, the Appellate Body has also stated that the identification of treaty provisions may not be enough to state the problem clearly. In other words, the identification of the treaty provisions alleged to have been violated is a necessary, but not a sufficient condition under Article 6.2 DSU.

38. It is this second element which is of particular interest in the present case. Article 6.2 DSU does not require complainants to "to list the treaty provisions alleged to have been violated." Rather, it obliges complainants to provide a "brief summary of the legal basis of the complaint sufficient to present the problem clearly." The reference to treaty provisions is only one element of the "legal basis of the complaint," which must also include other factual and legal elements necessary to present the problem clearly.

B. THE PANEL REQUESTS FAIL TO "PRESENT THE PROBLEM CLEARLY"

39. In the view of the EC, the Panel requests do not establish the problem clearly in accordance with Article 6.2 DSU. Even a cursory examination of the Panel requests will show that the "summary of the legal basis of the complaint" provided in them is in fact limited to vague listings of articles and some narrative text which, in general, is limited to restating the language of the treaty provision in question. As the EC will show, by adopting such a minimalist approach, both the United States and the Australian request fail to present the problem clearly in accordance with Article 6.2 DSU.

1. The United States request

40. The United States request is drafted in an extremely minimalist way. The "claims" of the United States seem to be contained in the third paragraph of the United States request. In this short paragraph, the United States appears to raise seven claims with respect to Regulation 2081/92. In particular, the United States claims that Regulation 2081/92:

[13] Appellate Body Report, *EC – Bananas III*, para. 141.

[14] Appellate Body Report, *Korea – Dairy*, para. 124.

- does not provide the same treatment to other nationals and products originating outside the EC that it provides to the EC's own nationals and products (**claim 1**);
- does not accord immediately and unconditionally to the nationals and products of each WTO Member any advantage, favour, privilege or immunity granted to the nationals and products of other WTO Members (**claim 2**);
- diminishes the legal protection for trademarks (including to prevent the use of an identical or similar sign that is likely to confuse and adequate protection against invalidation) (**claim 3**);
- does not provide legal means for interested parties to prevent the misleading use of a geographical indication (**claim 4**);
- does not define a geographical indication in a manner that is consistent with the definition provided in the TRIPS Agreement (**claim 5**);
- is not sufficiently transparent (**claim 6**);
- and does not provide adequate enforcement procedures (**claim 7**).

(a) The United States request does not indicate the legal bases of the claims

41. The United States request does not provide any indication of a legal basis for each of these claims. The only reference to substantive WTO provisions is contained in the fourth paragraph of the Panel request, which states that Regulation 2081/92 appears to be inconsistent with "TRIPS Agreement Articles 1.1, 2.1 (incorporating by reference Article 2 of the *Paris Convention for the Protection of Industrial Property* (Paris Convention (1967)), 3.1, 4, 16.1, 20, 22.1, 22.2, 24.5, 41.1, 41.2, 41.4, 42, 44.1, 63.1, 63.3, 65.1" as well as "Articles I and III:4 of the GATT 1994."

42. This long list of WTO provisions, however, is in no way correlated with the individual claims raised in the third paragraph of the United States request. On the other hand, it is not conceivable that each of the claims of the United States would be based on all the provisions mentioned in the fourth paragraph of the United States request. The result is a total lack of clarity regarding the legal bases of the United States' claims. By not even identifying the provisions of the WTO agreements which it considers to underlie each of its claims, the US falls short of the minimum requirements for the brief summary as established by the Appellate Body in *Korea – Dairy*.[15]

(b) The United States claims are unclear

43. The absence of a sufficient summary of the legal bases of the United States claims can also be demonstrated for each of the claims set out in the third paragraph of the United States request.

44. As regards the **first claim**, the United States is alleging that Regulation 2081/92 "does not provide the same treatment to other nationals and products originating outside the EC that it provides to the EC's own nationals and products." This claim would appear to be a reference to the principle of national treatment, as contained in Article 3 TRIPS and Article III:4 GATT. However, the US claim is limited to a paraphrasing of the treaty language of these two provisions. The US claim does not permit to understand which provision or aspect of Regulation 2081/92 is supposed to violate the national treatment principle, and in which way such a violation is deemed to occur. This does not constitue a summary of the legal basis of the claim sufficient to present the problem clearly.

45. In its **second claim**, the United States claims that Regulation 2081/92 "does not accord immediately and unconditionally to the nationals and products of each WTO Member any advantage, favour, privilege or immunity granted to the nationals and products of other WTO Members." This claim seems to be a reference to the principle of most favoured nation treatment, as contained in Article 4 TRIPS and Article I:1 GATT. However, as the first claim, this claim is limited to the paraphrasing of the language of treaty provisions,

[15] Appellate Body Report, *Korea – Dairy*, para. 124.

without any indication of which provision of Regulation 2081/92 is supposed to constitute the violation, and how such a violation occurs. More specifically, the United States request does not indicate which are the "other WTO members" who are supposed to enjoy more favourable treatment, what constitutes this "more favourable treatment," and how it is conferred.

46. As regards the **third claim**, the United States alleges that Regulation 2081/92 "diminishes the legal protection for trademarks." Unfortunately, the United States does not provide any further explanation as to why it considers that Regulation 2081/92 diminishes the "legal protection of trademarks." In the view of the EC, this does not constitute a meaningful description of the claim. The claim is made no clearer by the cryptic parenthesis "including to prevent the use of an identical or similar sign that is likely to confuse and adequate protection against invalidation," which the United States has added to its claim. Moreover, this parenthesis would seems to indicate that there might be other aspects diminishing the legal protection for trademarks, without however indicating what these aspects are.

47. The absence of a brief summary of the third claim is further compounded by the absence of any specific references to the provisions of Regulation 2081/92. It is certainly correct that Regulation 2081/92 contains various provisions also concerning trademarks. For instance, Article 14.1 of the Regulation concerns the conditions under which the registration of a trademark conflicting with a geographical indication will be refused or invalidated. Article 14.2 deals with situations of coexistence between trademarks and geographical indications. Article 14.3 provides for situations where, in the light of a trademark's reputation, renown, and length of time of use, registration of a geographical indication shall be refused. Finally, the existence of trademarks is mentioned as a possible ground for objection in Article 7 (4) of Regulation 2081/92.

48. In other words, Regulation 2081/92 deals with conflicts between trademarks and geographical indications in a number of different constellations, and provides for specific solutions for each of these. The United States request, by merely referring to the "legal protection of trademarks," does not enable the EC to understand which specific problems the United States wishes to raise in this respect.

49. In its **fourth claim**, the United States alleges that Regulation 2081/92 "does not provide legal means for interested parties to prevent the misleading use of a geographical indication." This claim is not comprehensible to the EC. In its Article 13, Regulation 2081/92 contains detailed provisions regarding the protection of registered geographical indications. These provisions provide interested parties with the legal means to prevent the misleading use of a geographical indication. In the absence of further explanations, the EC fails to comprehend what is the claim that the United States is intending to establish.

50. In its **fifth claim**, the United States claims that Regulation 2081/92 does not define a geographical indication in a manner that is consistent with the definition provided in the TRIPS Agreement. First of all, the United States does not explain what are the differences in the definition of geographical indications between the TRIPS Agreement and Regulation 2081/92. Moreover, there is no conceivable legal basis for the US claim. It is certainly true that Article 22.1 TRIPS contains a definition of geographical indications. However, this definition is explicitly made "for the purposes of this Agreement," and in particular for the subsequent provisions setting out the substantive obligations with respect to the protection of geographic indications. In contrast, Article 22.1 does not contain any independent obligation to "define" a geographical indication in any particular way. It is therefore irrelevant under the TRIPS Agreement how the legislation of a WTO Member "defines" a geographical indication, provided that the Member affords geographical indications the necessary protection as required in the provisions of the TRIPS Agreement. In the view of the EC, the United States fails therefore to set out a claim in this respect.

51. In its **sixth claim**, the United States pretends that Regulation 2081/92 "is not sufficiently transparent." Once again, this claim is incomprehensible to the EC. Regulation 2081/92 is a legislative measure adopted by the Council of the European Union, and published in the Official Journal of the European Union. The EC notes that unlike Australia, the United States refers to the transparency of the Regulation, rather than that of its application. The EC does not understand, however, how a legislative measure such as Regulation 2081/92 can

be said not to be "sufficiently transparent." In any case, the US request fails to state in which respect Regulation 2081/92 is supposed not to be "sufficiently transparent."

52. Finally, in its **seventh claim**, the United States claims that Regulation 2081/92 "does not provide adequate enforcement procedures." In the view of the EC, this claim is devoid of all clarity. The United States request neither indicates what, in its view, would be "adequate enforcement procedures," nor in which way Regulation 2081/92 falls short of providing such procedures. Moreover, the United States request does not identify what is the right to be enforced, an in particular whether it is talking about the enforcement of geographical indications or of trademarks.

53. Overall, the EC considers that the United States request fails both to identify the specific measure at issue, and to set out the claims of the United States. The compounded effect of these deficiencies is a Panel request of such vagueness and ambiguity that the EC is not capable to understand which is the case that the United States would like it to answer. For these reasons, the Panel must reject the US request as being incompatible with Article 6.2 DSU.

2. The Australian request

54. The Australian request is marked by deficiencies similar to those of the United States request.

55. The claims of Australia appear to be contained in the fifth paragraph of the Australian request. In this paragraph, Australia claims that Regulation 2081/92 (which, according to Australia, also includes its "related measures"):

- diminishes the legal protection for trademarks under the TRIPS Agreement, contrary to Articles 1, 2 (incorporating by reference Articles 6*quinques*(B), 10, 10*bis* and 10*ter* of the Paris Convention (1967)), 16, 20, 24.5, 41 and/or 42 of the TRIPS Agreement (**claim 1**);

- does not accord immediately and unconditionally to the nationals and/or products of each WTO Member any advantage, favour privilege or immunity granted to the nationals of any other WTO Member, contrary to Articles 1 and 4 of the TRIPS Agreement and/or Article I:1 of GATT 1994 (**claim 2**);

- does not accord to nationals and/or products of each WTO Member treatment no less favourable than that it accords to its own nationals and/or like products of national origin, contrary to Articles 1, 2 (incorporating by reference Article 2 of the Paris Convention (1967)) and 3.1 of the TRIPS Agreement and/or Article III:4 of GATT 1994 (**claim 3**);

- does not provide the legal means for interested parties to prevent misleading use of a geographical indication and/or to prevent any use of a geographical indication which constitutes an act of unfair competition within the meaning of Article 10bis of the Paris Convention (1967), contrary to Articles 1 and 22.2 of the TRIPS Agreement (**claim 4**);

- is not applied in a transparent manner, contrary to Articles 1, and 63.1 and 63.3 of the TRIPS Agreement (**claim 5**);

- is a technical regulation within the meaning of Annex 1 to the TBT Agreement, does not accord to products imported from the territory of any WTO Member treatment no less favourable than that accorded to like products of national origin and/or to like products originating in any other country, and/or has been prepared, adopted and/or applied with the effect of creating unnecessary obstacles to trade, being more trade-restrictive than necessary to fulfil a legitimate objective, taking account of the risks non-fulfilment would create, contrary to Articles 2.1 and 2.2 of the TBT Agreement (**claim 6**).

(a) The legal bases of the claims indicated in the Australian request are in some cases unclear

56. The structure of the Australian request differs from that of the United States in that Australia does indicate, for each of the claims it makes, the provision of the WTO agreements which it considers violated. However, even these listings lack, in some instances, the precision required by the Appellate Body in *Korea – Dairy*.[16]

57. In its first claim, Australia is referring to "Article 41 and/or 42 of the TRIPS Agreement. However, Article 41 TRIPS Agreement is a complex provision subdivided into a number of paragraphs, which contains a number of different obligations.[17] The same also applies for Article 42 TRIPS Agreement, which, although set out in one paragraph, also comprises several sentences establishing distinct obligations for WTO Members. Finally, the EC does not understand the "and/or" which seems to indicate that Articles 41 and 42 TRIPS are somehow alternative obligations.

58. Also in its first claim, Australia refers, in conjunction with Article 2 TRIPS Agreement, to Articles 10, 10*bis* and 10*ter* of the Paris Convention. Once again, these articles of the Paris Convention are complex provisions subdivided into various paragraphs, and imposing numerous distinct obligations.

59. Accordingly, the EC considers that the references to Articles 41 and 42 TRIPS Agreement, and to Articles 10, 10*bis* and 10*ter* of the Paris Convention do not meet the minimum requirements of specificity under Article 6.2 DSU.

(b) The Australian claims are unclear

60. However, even where the Australian request lists correctly the provisions of the WTO agreements, this indication of treaty provisions is not sufficient for the purposes of Article 6.2 DSU. This is due to the fact that the narrative description of the claims, as in the case of the United States request, is limited to the paraphrasing of the text of treaty provisions, or is so excessively vague that it does not permit to understand the substance of Australia's claims.

61. Since most of Australia's claims are similar to those of the United States, reference can be made to what has been said about the United States request. Australia's **claim 1** is almost identical to the United States claim 3,[18] and similarly fails to meet the requirements of Article 6.2 DSU.[19] Australia's **claim 2** is similar to US claim 2, and Australia's **claim 3** is similar to US claim 1. Like the US claims, Australia's claims 2 and 3 are limited to the restatement of language already contained in treaty provisions, and therefore encounter the same objections.[20] Australia's **claim 4** corresponds to the fourth claim of the United States, so that reference can be made to what has been said in this respect.[21] Finally, **claim 5** corresponds to United States claim 6, with the sole difference that Australia refers to the transparency of the "application of Regulation 2081/92," rather than that of the Regulation itself. However, since Australia fails to explain in which way Regulation 2081/92 is not applied in a transparent way, its claim fails to meet the requirements of Article 6.2 DSU for the same reasons as the United States claim.[22]

---

[16] Appellate Body Report, *Korea – Dairy*, para. 124. For the full quotation, see above para. 36.

[17] It is useful to note that the United States request refers only to Articles 41.2 and 41.4 TRIPS.

[18] The only difference is that the Australian request does not contain the cryptic parenthesis included in the United States request.

[19] Supra para. 46 to 48.

[20] Supra para. 44 to 45.

[21] Supra para. 49.

[22] Supra para. 51.

62. The only claim of Australia which finds no equivalent in the United States request is **claim 6**, by which Australia raises certain claims under the TBT Agreement, namely that Regulation 2081/92 "is a technical regulation within the meaning of Annex 1 to the TBT Agreement, does not accord to products imported from the territory of any WTO Member treatment no less favourable than that accorded to like products of national origin and/or to like products originating in any other country, and/or has been prepared, adopted and/or applied with the effect of creating unnecessary obstacles to trade, being more trade-restrictive than necessary to fulfil a legitimate objective, taking account of the risks non-fulfilment would create, contrary to Articles 2.1 and 2.2 of the TBT Agreement."

63. As to the first element of this claim, namely whether Regulation 2081/92 is a "technical regulation" within the meaning of Annex 1 to the TBT Agreement, the EC considers that this cannot constitute an admissible claim, since Point 1 of Annex 1 to the TBT Agreement, which defines the term "technical regulation" for the purposes of the TBT Agreement, does not impose any obligations which could have been violated by the EC.[23]

64. As regards the claims that Regulation 2081/92 does not accord to products imported from the territory of any WTO Member treatment no less favourable than that accorded to like products of national origin and/or to like products originating in any other country, and/or has been prepared, adopted and/or applied with the effect of creating unnecessary obstacles to trade, these claims merely seem to restate language which is contained in Article 2.1 and 2.2 of the TBT Agreement, without however providing any indication of how Regulation 2081/92, and which provision thereof, violates these obligations. For the same reasons as Australia's claims 2 and 3, claim 6 therefore fails to meet the requirements of Article 6.2 DSU.

65. In conclusion, both the United States and the US request fail to contain a brief summary of the legal basis of the claims, as required by Article 6.2 DSU. Both request do not "present the problem clearly." For the reasons set out above, the EC considers that both the Australian and the US Panel requests fail to meet the requirements of Article 6.2 DSU.

V. THE DEFICIENCIES OF THE PANEL REQUESTS RESULT IN SERIOUS PREJUDICE FOR THE EUROPEAN COMMUNITY AS A DEFENDANT

66. As has been stated above, the requirements of Article 6.2 DSU also serve to protect the due process rights of the defending party in dispute settlement proceedings under the DSU.[24] As a consequence, the Appellate Body has, when considering the requirements of Article 6.2 DSU, attached importance to the question of whether the defending party has suffered prejudice as a result of the deficiencies of a panel request.[25]

67. In the present case, the EC considers it clear that it is prejudiced by the lack of clarity of the United States and Australian request. As a defending party, the EC has a right to know what the case is which it will have to defend. This information must be contained in the Panel request.

68. In the present case, the ambiguity of the Panel request is such that the EC is, to this date, not sure of the case which the United States and Australia are bringing before the Panel. As a consequence, the EC has been seriously hampered in its efforts to prepare its defence.

69. This situation is not acceptable from the point of view of the due process rights of the EC. Dispute settlement proceedings under the DSU are subject to very strict deadlines. As a consequence, the EC cannot be expected to wait for the first written submission of the complainants to start preparing its defence. Rather, the

[23] Cf. also the discussion of United States claim 5 (supra para. 50).

[24] Supra note 4.

[25] Appellate Body Report, *Korea – Dairy*, para. 131; Appellate Body Report, *Thailand – H Beams*, para. 95. The EC does consider it necessary, in the present case, to take a position as to whether the requirement of prejudice in Article 6.2 DSU constitutes an additional requirement to those set out in Article 6.2 DSU.

time between the submission of the panel request and the constitution of the Panel is used by both complaining and defending parties for the preparation of their case.

70. The strict respect of Article 6.2 DSU is also necessary to ensure a level playing field for the complaining and defending parties. Since the complainants have the initiative in dispute settlement, they can take all the time necessary to prepare their case before the introduction of the panel request. In contrast, the defendant can begin preparing its case only once he has received a notice of the case in accordance with Article 6.2 DSU.

71. The EC notes that the United States has, as a defending party, frequently criticised Panel requests for not respecting the requirements of Article 6.2 DSU, and has requested preliminary rulings on this question.[26] In the present context, the EC considers it useful to quote from the United States' submissions before the Panel in *US – Lamb*:[27]

> The insufficiency of the Panel requests has seriously prejudiced the United States in the preparation of its defense. It prevented the United States from knowing the true nature of the claims being made against the U.S. measure and placed the United States in the position of merely guessing which of the many obligations in these several articles might be at issue in this review. This severely limited the ability of the United States to begin the task of preparing its defense. The dispute resolution process is intended to be a relatively speedy process. Central to such a speedy process is the requirement that claims be clearly stated at the required time. The failure of a complaining party to do so prejudices the responding party and undercuts the fairness of the entire process. It effectively stacks the deck against the responding party.

72. The EC does not consider that different standards should be applied in the present case. The EC would also like to recall that Article 3.10 DSU requires Members to engage in dispute settlement procedures in good faith. As the Appellate Body has underlined in *US – FSC*, this obligations applies also to the complainants:[28]

> This pervasive principle requires both complaining and responding Members to comply with the requirements of the DSU (and related requirements in other covered agreements) in good faith. By good faith compliance, complaining Members accord to the responding Members the full measure of protection and opportunity to defend, contemplated by the letter and spirit of the procedural rules.

73. The EC does not wish to speculate about what are the reasons for the deficient drafting of the Panel requests. In particular, the EC does not know whether this drafting reflects a conscious choice on the side of the complainants to leave the EC in the dark about their prospective case, or whether the complainants simply were unsure of the case that they were intending to bring. Whatever the explanation may be, the Panel requests in their current form would provide the complainants with a maximum flexibility in terms of their subsequent litigation strategy, and oblige the EC to defend itself against a moving target. This is not in accordance with the requirement of due process underlying Article 6.2 DSU.

74. By keeping their panel requests excessively vague, the United States and Australia have prevented the EC from preparing its defence in a timely manner. They have thereby caused serious prejudice to the EC.

---

[26] Panel Report, *US – Lamb*, para. 5.5; Panel Report, *US – Carbon Steel*, para. 4.1-4.2.

[27] Panel Report, *US – Lamb*, para. 5.5

[28] Appellate Body Report, *US – FSC*, para. 166.

VI. THE DEFICIENCIES OF THE PANEL REQUESTS HAVE BEEN RAISED BY THE EC IN A TIMELY MANNER, AND MUST BE ADDRESSED WITHOUT DELAY

75. In considering the requirements of Article 6.2 DSU, the Appellate Body has held that the respect of the conditions of this provision is of a fundamental nature, and may be examined at any stage in the proceedings.[29]

76. At the same time, the Appellate Body has attached importance to the fact that the parties should bring procedural deficiencies to the attention of the Panel at the earliest possible opportunity.[30] This requirement was justified by the Appellate Body in *US – FSC* on the basis of the principle of good faith, which pervades dispute settlement proceedings under the DSU:[31]

> Article 3.10 of the DSU commits Members of the WTO, if a dispute arises, to engage in dispute settlement procedures "in good faith in an effort to resolve the dispute." This is another specific manifestation of the principle of good faith which, we have pointed out, is at once a general principle of law and a principle of general international law. This pervasive principle requires both complaining and responding Members to comply with the requirements of the DSU (and related requirements in other covered agreements) in good faith. By good faith compliance, complaining Members accord to the responding Members the full measure of protection and opportunity to defend, contemplated by the letter and spirit of the procedural rules. The same principle of good faith requires that responding Members seasonably and promptly bring claimed procedural deficiencies to the attention of the complaining Member, and to the DSB or the Panel, so that corrections, if needed, can be made to resolve disputes. The procedural rules of WTO dispute settlement are designed to promote, not the development of litigation techniques, but simply the fair, prompt and effective resolution of trade disputes.

77. The present request for a preliminary ruling is in full accordance with these requirements established by the Appellate Body. The EC has raised the objection regarding the compatibility of the Panel requests with Article 6.2 DSU at the first possible occasion, namely at the meeting of the Dispute Settlement Body (DSB) on 29 August 2003, at which the requests were discussed for the first time.[32] At this meeting, the EC explicitly called upon the United States and Australia to submit new panel requests compatible with Article 6.2 DSU. Since the complainants failed to do so, the EC repeated its concerns at the second meeting of the DSB on 2 October 2003, and reserved its rights to raise the issue during the Panel proceedings.[33]

78. In the view of the EC, the deficiencies of the Panel requests are such that they will affect the entire subsequent proceedings. In particular, if the Panel requests are not amended, the scope of the present dispute will remain entirely unclear. This will have as an inevitable consequence that the submissions of the parties will have to deal not only with issues of substance, but also with the scope of the claims of the complainants. Moreover, it would be regrettable for the Parties to engage in pleadings on the substance of the dispute, only for the Panel requests to be found insufficient in the Panel report or by the Appellate Body. For these reasons, and in order to safeguard the proper conduct of the present dispute settlement proceedings, the EC considers it appropriate for the Panel to issue a preliminary ruling regarding Article 6.2 DSU.

79. This would also be in line with the ruling of the Appellate Body has *EC – Bananas,* in which the Appellate Body held that questions regarding the respect of Article 6.2 DSU should be decided early in panel proceedings, without causing prejudice or unfairness to any party or third party.[34]

---

[29] Appellate Body Report, *US – Carbon Steel*, para. 123.

[30] Appellate Body Report, *Thailand – H Beams*, para. 95; Appellate Body Report, *US – Carbon Steel*, para. 123.

[31] Appellate Body Report, *US – FSC*, para. 166.

[32] Minutes of the Meeting of the Dispute Settlement Body of 29 August 2003, WT/DSB/M/155, para. 75 (Exhibit EC-2).

[33] Minutes of the Meeting of the Dispute Settlement Body of 2 October 2003, WT/DSB/M/156, para. 32 (Exhibit EC-3).

[34] Appellate Body Report, *EC – Bananas III*, para. 144.

80. The EC would like to clarify that it remains committed to a speedy resolution of the present dispute. For this reason, the EC would not consider it inappropriate for the Panel to suggest to the complaining parties to introduce a new Panel request in full compliance with Article 6.2 DSU. The EC would like to note that such a course of action has recently been taken by a Panel in another dispute.[35]

VII. CONCLUSION

81. For the reasons set out above, the EC respectfully requests that the Panel find that the panel requests do not meet the requirements of Article 6.2 DSU.

82. Given the importance of the jurisdictional issues raised in the present request, the EC considers it appropriate that the Panel issue a preliminary ruling on this matter before the first written submissions of the Parties are due.

---

[35] Cf. Preliminary Ruling by the Panel, *Canada – Wheat*, para. 65. In this case, the United States indeed introduced a new Panel request (WT/DS276/9). The dispute then continued to be heard before the Panel originally established after the first Panel request.

ANNEX B-2

FIRST WRITTEN SUBMISSION OF THE EUROPEAN COMMUNITIES

(25 May 2004)

TABLE OF CONTENTS

2. **Claims 1: Non-EC nationals are accorded less favorable treatment than EC nationals with respect to the registration of geographical indications through the application of a condition of reciprocity and equivalence**
   (a) The EC does not apply a condition of reciprocity and equivalence for the registration of geographical indications from other WTO members
   (b) The conditions for the registration of individual geographical indications do not constitute less favourable treatment
   (c) The conditions for the registration of geographical indications do not depend on nationality
3. **Claim 2: Regulation 2081/92 violates the national treatment obligations under the TRIPS and the Paris Convention by requiring that applications must be transmitted by the country in which the geographical area is located**
4. **Claim 3: Non-EC nationals are accorded less favorable treatment than EC nationals with respect to the requirement to indicate the country of origin for homonymous geographical indications**
   (a) Article 12(2) of Regulation 2081/92 does not apply to all geographical indications, but only to homonyms
   (b) The requirement to indicate the country of origin for homonymous geographical indications from the EC and third countries does not constitute less favourable treatment
   (c) Article 12(2) of Regulation 2081/92 does not discriminate between nationals
5. **Claim 4: Regulation 2081/92 accords less favourable treatment to non-EC nationals by subjecting the right to object to the registration of geographical indications to conditions of reciprocity and equivalence**
6. **Claim 5: Regulation 2081/92 accords less favourable treatment to non-EC nationals by requiring their own country to transmit the objection**
7. **Claim 6: Regulation 2081/92 accords less favourable treatment to non-EC nationals by requiring non-EC national to have a "legitimate interest" to object to the registration of geographical indications**
8. **Claim 7: Regulation 2081/92 accords less favourable treatment because a non-EC rightholder has no "representative" in the regulatory committee to "speak for him"**
9. **Claim 8: A right of objection was available to persons resident or established in an EC Member State that was not available to other WTO Member nationals in respect of the registration of more than 120 geographical indications under the normal registration process**
   (a) Australia's claim relates to a measure which was no longer in force at the time of establishment of the Panel, and which is therefore not within the terms of reference of the Panel
   (b) The individual registrations are not in violation of national treatment obligations
   (c) Australia is seeking to obtain a retroactive remedy it could not have obtained had it attacked the measure while it was still in force.
10. **Claim 9: A right of objection was available to persons resident or established in an EC Member State that was not available to other WTO Member nationals in respect of the registration of more than 480 EC-defined GIs under the simplified registration process**

B. PROHIBITED REQUIREMENT OF DOMICILE OR ESTABLISHMENT(ARTICLE 2.1 TRIPS IN CONJUNCTION WITH ARTICLE 2.2 PARIS CONVENTION)

1. **Claim 10: Regulation 2081/92 requires non-EC nationals to become established in the EC as a condition for registering geographical indications**
   (a) Geographical indications relating to an area located in a WTO country can be registered under Regulation 2081/92
   (b) The right to register a geographical indication does not depend on domicile or establishment
   (c) Article 2.2 Paris Convention does not exclude measures which ensure that a product originates in the geographical area to which a protected geographical indication is related

(i) *Registrability of geographical names as trademarks*
(ii) *Article 14(3) of Regulation 2081/92*
(iii) *Provisional conclusion*

(b) Article 24.5 envisages the co-existence of GIs and earlier trademarks
(c) The EC is required to maintain the co-existence of geographical indications and earlier trademarks by Article 24.3
(d) In any event, the co-existence of geographical indications and earlier trademarks would be justified under Article 17 of the TRIPS Agreement

2. Claim 20: Regulation 2081/92 does not provide for a presumption of a likelihood of confusion in the case of use of an identical sign for identical goods

3. Claim 21: Article 7(4) of Regulation 2081/92 is inconsistent with Article 16.1 of the TRIPS Agreement because it limits the grounds of objection

(a) Article 16.1 of the TRIPS Agreement does not confer a right of objection
(b) Australia has misread Article 7(4) of Regulation 2081/92

4. Claim 22: Regulation 2081/92 does not ensure that objections from trademark owners will be considered by the Committee

B. CLAIM 23: BY REQUIRING THE CO-EXISTENCE OF A REGISTERED GEOGRAPHICAL INDICATION AND AN EARLIER TRADEMARK, ARTICLE 14(2) ENCUMBERS UNJUSTIFIABLY THE USE OF THE TRADEMARK, CONTRARY TO ARTICLE 20 OF THE TRIPS AGREEMENT

C. CLAIM 24: ARTICLE 14(1) OF REGULATION 2081/92 IS INCONSISTENT WITH ARTICLE 24.5 OF THE TRIPS AGREEMENT BECAUSE IT DOES NOT AFFORD THE RIGHT OF PRIORITY PROVIDED IN ARTICLE 4 OF THE PARIS CONVENTION

D. ARTICLES 41.1, 41.2, 41.3, 41.4, 42, 43, 44.1, 45, 46, 48 AND 49 OF THE TRIPS AGREEMENT

1. General Considerations

2. Claim 25: Regulation 2081/92 is inconsistent with Article 41.1 of the TRIPS Agreement

3. Claim 26: Regulation 2081/92 is inconsistent with Article 41.2 of the TRIPS Agreement

(a) The procedures provided in Regulation 2081/92 are neither inequitable nor unfair
(b) The procedures provided in Regulation 2081/92 are not unnecessarily complicated and do not entail unwarranted delays

4. Claim 27: Regulation 2081/92 is inconsistent with Article 41.3 of the TRIPS Agreement

5. Claim 28: Regulation 2081/92 is inconsistent with Article 41.4 of the TRIPS Agreement

6. Claim 29: Regulation 2081/92 is inconsistent with Article 42 of the TRIPS Agreement

E. CLAIM 30: REGULATION 2081/92 IS INCONSISTENT WITH ARTICLE 10*BIS* (1) AND 10*TER* (1) OF THE PARIS CONVENTION

F. CONSEQUENTIAL CLAIMS

1. Claim 31: Regulation 2081/92 is inconsistent with Article 2.1 of the TRIPS Agreement

2. Claim 32: Regulation 2081/92 is inconsistent with Article 1.1 of the TRIPS Agreement

3. Claim 33: The transitional national protection provided by the Member States is inconsistent with Articles 2.1, 16.1, 41.1, 41.2, 41.3 and/or 42 of the TRIPS Agreement

VII. THE EC MEASURE IS CONSISTENT WITH THE OBLIGATION TO PROVIDE PROTECTION TO GEOGRAPHICAL INDICATIONS UNDER ARTICLE 22.2 OF THE TRIPS AGREEMENT

1. **Claim 34: Regulation 2081/92 is inconsistent with Article 22.2 of the TRIPS Agreement**
2. **Claim 35: Regulation 2081/92 is inconsistent with Article 1.1 of the TRIPS Agreement because it is inconsistent with Article 22.2**
3. **Claim 36: Regulation 2081/92 is inconsistent with Article 22.2 TRIPS**
   (a) Regulation 2081/92 provides to interested parties of other WTO Members the means to prevent the acts mentioned in Article 22.2
      (i) Reciprocity and equivalence conditions
      (ii) The requirement that the application must be transmitted by the Government
      (iii) The right of objection
   (b) The EC and its Member States provides to interested parties of other WTO Members other means to prevent the acts mentioned in Article 22.2

VIII. REGULATION 2081/92 IS CONSISTENT WITH OBLIGATIONS UNDER THE TBT AGREEMENT

A. REGULATION 2081/92 IS NOT A TECHNICAL REGULATION

1. **General**
2. **Article 12(2) of Regulation 2081/92 is not a technical regulation**
   (a) Article 12(2) does not apply to identifiable products
   (b) Article 12(2) does not lay down product characteristics
   (c) Article 12(2) of Regulation 2081/92 is not mandatory
3. **Articles 4 and 10 of Regulation 2081/92 are not a technical regulation**
   (a) Articles 4 and 10 do not lay down product characteristics
   (b) Articles 4 and 10 are not mandatory

B. CLAIM 37: ARTICLE 12(2) OF REGULATION 2081/92 IS INCOMPATIBLE WITH ARTICLE 2.1 OF THE TBT AGREEMENT

1. **General**
2. **Article 12(2) of Regulation 2081/92 does not apply to all geographical indications, but only to homonyms**
3. **The requirement to indicate the country of origin for homonymous geographical indications from the EC and third countries does not constitute less favourable treatment**
4. **National treatment obligations do not apply to requirements to mark the country of origin**

C. CLAIM 38: ARTICLES 4, 10, AND 12 (1) OF REGULATION 2081/92 ARE INCOMPATIBLE WITH ARTICLE 2.2 OF THE TBT AGREEMENT

1. **The existence of inspection structures is only required with respect to the specific product for which protection is sought**
2. **The Regulation does not determine the specific design of the inspection structures**
3. **The existence of inspection structures is necessary to achieve the legitimate objectives of Regulation 2081/92**

IX. CLAIM 39, 40: THE EC MEASURE IS COMPATIBLE WITH ARTICLE 65.1 TRIPS AND ARTICLE XVI:4 WTO

X. CONCLUSION

Table of WTO and GATT cases referred to in this submission

Short Title	Full Case Title and Citation of Case
Argentina – Textiles and Apparel	Panel Report, *Argentina – Measures Affecting Imports of Footwear, Textiles, Apparel and Other Items*, WT/DS56/R, adopted 22 April 1998, as modified by the Appellate Body Report, WT/DS56/AB/R, DSR 1998:III, 1033
Australia – Automotive Leather	Panel Report, *Australia – Subsidies Provided to Producers and Exporters of Automotive Leather*, WT/DS126/R, adopted 16 June 1999, DSR 1999:III, 951
Belgian Family Allowances	GATT 1947 Panel Report, *Belgian Family Allowances*, adopted on 7 November 1952, 1S/59
Canada – Autos	Panel Report, *Canada – Certain Measures Affecting the Automotive Industry*, WT/DS139/R, WT/DS142/R, adopted 19 June 2000, as modified by the Appellate Body Report, WT/DS139/AB/R, WT/DS142/AB/R, DSR 2000:VII, 3043
EEC – Beef from Canada	GATT 1947 Panel Report, *European Economic Community – Imports of Beef from Canada*, adopted on 10 March 1981, 28S/92
EC – Asbestos	Appellate Body Report, *European Communities – Measures Affecting Asbestos and Asbestos-Containing Products*, WT/DS135/AB/R, adopted 5 April 2001
EC – Sardines	Appellate Body Report, *European Communities – Trade Description of Sardines*, WT/DS231/AB/R, adopted 23 October 2002
India – Autos	Panel Report, *India – Measures Affecting the Automotive Sector*, WT/DS146/R, WT/DS175/R and Corr.1, adopted 5 April 2002
India – Patents (US)	Appellate Body Report, *India – Patent Protection for Pharmaceutical and Agricultural Chemical Products*, WT/DS50/AB/R, adopted 16 January 1998, DSR 1998:I, 9
Indonesia – Autos	Panel Report, *Indonesia – Certain Measures Affecting the Automobile Industry*, WT/DS54/R, WT/DS55/R, WT/DS59/R, WT/DS64/R and Corr.1, 2, 3, and 4, adopted 23 July 1998, DSR 1998:VI, 2201
Japan – Film	Panel Report, *Japan – Measures Affecting Consumer Photographic Film and Paper*, WT/DS44/R, adopted 22 April 1998, DSR 1998:IV, 1179
Korea – Dairy	Appellate Body Report, *Korea – Definitive Safeguard Measure on Imports of Certain Dairy Products*, WT/DS98/AB/R, adopted 12 January 2000, DSR 2000:I, 3
Korea – Various Measures on Beef	Appellate Body Report, *Korea – Measures Affecting Imports of Fresh, Chilled and Frozen Beef*, WT/DS161/AB/R, WT/DS169/AB/R, adopted 10 January 2001
Norway – Trondheim Bridge	Panel report under the 1979 Agreement on Government Procurement, *Norway – Procurement of Toll Collection Equipment for the City of Trondheim*, GPR/DS.2/R, adopted 13 May 1992
US – Tuna	GATT 1947 Panel Report, *United States – Restrictions on Imports of Tuna*, DS21/R, 3 September 1991, 39S/155, not adopted
US – Certain EC Products	Appellate Body Report, *United States – Import Measures on Certain Products from the European Communities*, WT/DS165/AB/R, adopted 10 January 2001
US – Gasoline	Panel Report, *United States – Standards for Reformulated and Conventional Gasoline*, WT/DS2/R, adopted 20 May 1996, as modified by the Appellate Body Report, WT/DS2/AB/R, DSR 1996:I, 29
US – Section 211 Appropriations Act	Appellate Body Report, *United States – Section 211 Omnibus Appropriations Act of 1998*, WT/DS176/AB/R, adopted 1 February 2002
US – Wool Shirts and Blouses	Appellate Body Report, *United States – Measure Affecting Imports of Woven Wool Shirts and Blouses from India*, WT/DS33/AB/R and Corr.1, adopted 23 May 1997, DSR 1997:I, 323

GLOSSARY

Commission, EC Commission	Commission of the European Communities
Committee	Committee of representatives of the Member States referred to in Article 15 of Council Regulation 2081/92
Community Trademark Regulation	Council Regulation (EC) No 40/94, of 20 December 1993, on the Community Trademark, as amended on the date of establishment of the Panel
Council, EC Council	Council of the European Union
Court of Justice, European Court of Justice	Court of Justice of the European Communities
DSU	Understanding on Rules and Procedures Governing the Settlement of Disputes
EC	European Communities
GATT	General Agreement on Tariffs and Trade 1994
FWS	First Written Submission
GI	Geographical indication
Member States, EC Member States	Member States of the European Union
Official Journal	Official Journal of the European Union
Paris Convention	Stockholm Act of the Paris Convention for the protection of Industrial property, of 14 July 1967
Regulation 2081/92, Regulation	Council Regulation (EEC) No 2081/92 of 14 July 1992 on the protection of geographical indications and designations of origin for agricultural products and foodstuffs, as amended on the date of establishment of the Panel
SCM Agreement, SCM	Agreement on Subsidies and Countervailing Duties
Trademarks Directive	First Council Directive 89/104, of 20 December, on the Community Trademark, as amended on the date of establishment of the Panel
TBT Agreement, TBT	Agreement on Technical Barriers to Trade

TRIPS Agreement, TRIPS	Agreement on Trade-Related Aspects of Intellectual Property Rights
US	United States
WTO	World Trade Organization
WTO Agreement	Marrakesh Agreement Establishing the World Trade Organization

I. INTRODUCTION

1. This submission provides the response of the European Communities to the first written submissions filed by Australia and the United States on 25 May 2004.

2. Section II raises a number of issues in connection with the terms of reference of the Panel.

3. Section III sets out the content of Regulation 2081/1992 to the extent relevant for the present dispute and corrects a number of errors and misrepresentations made by the complainants in their first written submissions.

4. Section IV addresses the various claims submitted by the complainants to the effect that certain requirements of Regulation 2081/92 are incompatible with the national treatment obligations under Article 3.1 of the TRIPS Agreement, Article 2.1 of the Paris Convention and Article III:4 of the GATT, as well as with the prohibition on requirements of domicile or establishment in Article 2.2 of the Paris Convention.

5. Section V addresses the United States' claims that some of those requirements are incompatible with the most-favoured-nation obligations under Article 4 of the TRIPS Agreement and Article I:1 of the GATT.

6. Section VI deals with the complainants' various claims to the effect that Regulation 2081/92 diminishes the legal protection of trademarks, thereby violating Articles 16.1, 20 and 24.5 of the TRIPS Agreement, as well as certain provisions of Part III of that Agreement, and Articles 10*bis* and 10*ter* of the Paris Convention.

7. Section VII responds to the claims that the EC does not comply with the obligation to provide protection to geographical indications under Article 22.2 of the TRIPS Agreement.

8. Finally, Section VIII deals with the claims raised by Australia that Regulation 2081/92 is incompatible with certain provisions of the TBT Agreement.

9. For ease of reference, the EC has grouped and numbered sequentially the claims submitted by the complainants. In each case, the EC has indicated which of the complainants has made the claim, and referred to the paragraphs of the first submission where the claim is made.

II. TERMS OF REFERENCE

10. The present Panel has been established by the DSB on 2 October 2003 with standard terms of reference in accordance with Article 7.1 of the DSU.[1] These terms of reference define the Panel's scope of jurisdiction. As the Appellate Body has explained in *India – Patents (US)*, a panel cannot consider claims which are not within its terms of reference:[2]

> The jurisdiction of a panel is established by that panel's terms of reference, which are governed by Article 7 of the DSU. A panel may consider only those claims that it has the authority to consider under its terms of reference. A panel cannot assume jurisdiction that it does not have. In this case, Article 63 was not within the Panel's jurisdiction, as defined by its terms of reference. Therefore, the Panel had no authority to consider the alternative claim by the United States under Article 63.

---

[1] Cf. WT/DS174/21, WT/DS290/19, para. 2. As the EC has set out in its request for a preliminary ruling made on 24 February 2004, it considers that the panel requests of the United States and of Australia are not in compliance with the requirements of Article 6.2 DSU. The EC reserves the right to raise this issue in the context of an appeal.

[2] Appellate Body Report, *India – Patents (US)*, para. 92.

11. In its first written submission, Australia is referring to versions of Regulation 2081/92 which were no longer in force at the time the Panel's terms of reference were established. Moreover, the complainants have referred to a number of measures that were not yet in existence at the time the Panel was established. In the view of the EC, only measures which were in force at the time that the Panel was established are within the terms of reference of the Panel.

12. Moreover, Australia and the United States raise a number of claims which are not identified in their requests for the establishment of the Panel. Such claims not identified in the panel requests are not within the jurisdiction of the Panel.

A. THE MEASURE AT ISSUE

1. Versions of Regulation 2081/92 no longer in force at the time the Panel was established

13. In its first written submission, Australia (but not the United States)[3] has referred to several versions of Regulation 2081/92 no longer in force. It has numbered these versions #1 to #3, reflecting various subsequent amendments of Regulation 2081/92.[4]

14. Throughout its submission, Australia refers repeatedly to these different versions of Regulation 2081/92. In particular, Australia claims that no right of objection was available to persons not resident or established in the EC "until Article 12d (1) of Regulation No 2081/92#3 changed the situation."[5] Similarly, Australia refers to the fact that "Article 17.1 of Regulation No 2081/92#1 and #2 provided for a simplified registration process for certain names which were already legally protected or established by usage in the Member States."[6]

15. These references to versions of Regulation No. 2081/92 which were no longer in force at the time the present Panel was established are not within the scope of the Panel's terms of reference. This already flows from Australia's request for the establishment of the Panel,[7] which is the basis for the Panel's terms of reference. In its Panel request, Australia referred to "Council Regulation (EEC) No 2081/92 of 14 July 1992 [...] and any amendments thereto" as "the EC measure." Australia's request did not make it clear that Australia intended to challenge as the "EC measure" several versions of the same measure resulting from subsequent amendments over time.

16. Moreover, as the Panel in *India – Autos* recalled, a " WTO Panel is generally competent to consider measures in existence at the time of its establishment."[8] Accordingly, in WTO practice, Panels have declined to examine measures which were no longer in force at the time the Panel was established. In *US – Gasoline*, the Panel explained the legal situation as follows:[9]

> The Panel observed that it had not been the usual practice of a panel established under the General Agreement to rule on measures that, at the time the panel's terms of reference were fixed, were not and would not become effective. In the 1978 *Animal Feed Protein* case, the Panel ruled on a discontinued measure, but one that had terminated after agreement on the panel's terms of reference. In the 1980 *Chile Apples* case, the panel ruled on a measure terminated before agreement on the panel's terms of reference; however, the terms of

[3] The United States has referred to Regulation 2081/92 "as most recently amended" (US FWS, footnote 1).

[4] Australia's FWS, para. 18.

[5] Australia's FWS, para. 185 (emphasis added).

[6] Australia's FWS, para. 190 (emphasis added).

[7] WT/DS290/18.

[8] Panel Report, *India – Autos*, para. 7.26.

[9] Panel Report, *US – Gasoline*, para. 6.19; similarly, Panel Report, *Japan – Film*, para. 10.58; Panel Report, *Argentina – Textiles and Apparel*, para. 6.15.

reference in that case specifically included the terminated measure and, it being a seasonal measure, there remained the prospect of its reintroduction. In the present case, the Panel's terms of reference were established after the 75 percent rule had ceased to have any effect, and the rule had not been specifically mentioned in the terms of reference. The Panel further noted that there was no indication by the parties that the 75 percent rule was a measure that, although currently not in force, was likely to be renewed. Finally, the Panel considered that its findings on treatment under the baseline establishment methods under Articles III:4 and XX (b), (d) and (g) would in any case have made unnecessary the examination of the 75 percent rule under Article I:1. The Panel did not therefore proceed to examine this aspect of the Gasoline Rule under Article I:1 of the General Agreement.

17. In the present case, there are no specific reasons which could justify an examination of versions of Regulation 2081/92 no longer in force. From its adoption in 1992 to the establishment of the Panel, Regulation 2081/92 has been amended six times.[10] Australia has arbitrarily chosen certain points in time to reflect versions of Regulation 2081/92 going as far back as 1997 or 1993.

18. The same applies also with respect to Australia's reference to the version of Regulation 2081/92 as applicable before its amendment by Regulation 692/2003 of 8 April 2003.[11] In accordance with its Article 2.1, Regulation 692/2003 entered into force on 24 April 2003, i.e. before the present Panel was established. The EC has no intention to repeal Regulation 692/2003, or to remove the changes introduced by it. Therefore, Regulation 2081/92 as applicable prior to its amendment by Regulation 692/2003 is not within the scope of the Panel's terms of reference.

19. Moreover, as the Appellate Body has recalled in *US – Shirts and Blouses*, the purpose of Panel proceedings under the DSU is the settlement of concrete disputes between the parties:[12]

> Given the explicit aim of dispute settlement that permeates the *DSU*, we do not consider that Article 3.2 of the *DSU* is meant to encourage either panels or the Appellate Body to "make law" by clarifying existing provisions of the *WTO Agreement* outside the context of resolving a particular dispute. A panel need only address those claims which must be addressed in order to resolve the matter in issue in the dispute.

20. An analysis of historical versions of Regulation 2081/92 is not useful for the purposes of settling the present dispute. Accordingly, the EC submits that the measure at issue in the present dispute is Regulation 2081/92 as in force at the time the Panel was established. A consolidated version of Regulation 2081/92 as in force on 2 October 2003 is provided by the EC as Exhibit EC-1.

2. Measures not yet adopted at the time the Panel was established

21. The complainants have referred to a number of measures which had not yet been adopted at the time the Panel was established.

22. In Exhibits COMP-4b (viii) – (xvi), the complainants are referring to a number of amendments to Commission Regulation 2400/96 adopted between 11 November 2003 and 5 April 2004. These measures did not yet exist at the time the Panel was established, and are therefore outside its terms of reference.

23. Moreover, the complainants have prepared a "consolidated unofficial version" of Regulation 2081/92, which they provide as Exhibit COMP-1a. The complainants state that this consolidated unofficial version incorporates amendments made by the Act of Accession of Cyprus, Czech Republic, Estonia, Hungary, Latvia,

---

[10] See consolidated version of Regulation 2081/92, Exihibit EC-1, p. 1.

[11] Exhibit COMP-1i.

[12] Appellate Body Report, *US – Shirts and Blouses*, p. 22.

Lithuania, Malta, Poland, Slovakia, and Slovenia. Moreover, the complainants have also provided an extract from the Act of Accession as Exhibit COMP-3c.

24. In accordance with Article 2.3 of the Treaty of Accession, of which the Act of Accession is an integral part, the Treaty of Accession had to be ratified by all Member States of the European Union and by the acceding countries. At the time the Panel was established, the process of ratification was still ongoing. The Act of Accession entered into force only on 1 May 2004. Accordingly, the Act of Accession was not yet adopted at the time the Panel was established, and is therefore not within the scope of the Panel's terms of reference.

25. Accordingly, the EC submits that measures which had not yet been adopted at the time the Panel was established are not within the Panel's terms of reference.

B. CLAIMS

26. In its first written submission, Australia has raised claims under Article 4 of the Paris Convention, and Articles 43 to 49 of the TRIPS Agreement. None of these claims is referred to in Australia's request for the establishment of the Panel.[13]

27. Moreover, both Australia and the United States have made claims according to which the EC measure imposes a requirement of domicile or residence for the enjoyment of intellectual property rights contrary to Article 2.2 of the Paris Convention. No such claim was raised in the panel requests of the complainants.[14]

1. Australia's claim under Article 4 of the Paris Convention

28. In its first written submission, Australia alleges that Regulation 2081/92 is incompatible with Article 4 of the Paris Convention, incorporated by Article 2.1 TRIPS, which requires that a WTO member afford a right of priority of six months in respect of an application for registration of a trademark for which an application for registration had previously been filed in another WTO member.[15]

29. However, Australia's panel request does not refer to Article 4 of the Paris Convention. Australia can also not argue that its reference to Article 2.1 of the TRIPS Agreement, which requires Members to comply with Articles 1 through 12 and Article 19 of the Paris Convention, is sufficient to bring Article 4 of the Paris Convention within the scope of the Panel's terms of reference. The incorporated provisions of the Paris Convention contain numerous distinct obligations, which need to be referred to specifically in order to meet the requirements of Article 6.2 of the DSU.[16] In fact, Australia's panel request specifies alongside the reference to Article 2.1 of the TRIPS Agreement a number of other provisions of the Paris Convention alleged to be violated. However, Article 4 of the Paris Convention is not among the provisions alleged to have been violated in Australia's panel request.

30. Therefore, the EC considers that Australia's claim regarding Article 4 of the Paris Convention is outside the terms of reference of the Panel.

2. Australia's claim under Articles 43 to 49 of the TRIPS

31. In its first written submission, Australia has claimed that the EC measure has failed "to provide the judicial authorities the authority required to be conferred on them by TRIPS Articles 43, 44, 45, 46, 48 and 49 in respect of the enforcement of trademark rights vis-à-vis the proposed registration of an EC-defined GI."[17]

---

[13] WT/DS290/18.

[14] WT/DS290/18; WT/DS174/20.

[15] Australia's FWS, para. 85.

[16] Appellate Body Report, *Korea – Dairy*, para. 124.

[17] Australia's FWS, para. 148.

32. However, Articles 43 to 49 TRIPS Agreement are not mentioned in Australia's panel request. In its panel request (fifth paragraph, first bullet point), Australia has alleged that the EC measure diminishes the legal protection of trademarks, and has referred in this respect to Articles 41 and 42 TRIPS. However, Articles 43 through 49 of the TRIPS Agreement contain distinct obligations which are separate from and additional to those contained in Articles 41 and 42.

33. Australia cannot argue that a reference to the specific provisions of Articles 43 to 49 TRIPS was made redundant by its reference to Article 41 TRIPS. Article 41 is an introductory provision contained in the first section, entitled "General Obligations," of Part III. It sets out general obligations and principles to be respected by the Parties in the application of Part III.

34. More specifically, Article 41.1 is a purely introductory provision which does not create separate legal obligations. The fact that Article 41.1 TRIPS refers to the "enforcement procedures as specified in this Part" cannot mean that a reference to Article 41.1 TRIPS would be sufficient to bring all the provisions of Part III within the terms of reference of the Panel. Otherwise, it could be argued that a simple reference to Article 1.1 TRIPS is sufficient to bring all provisions of the TRIPS Agreement within the scope of a panel's jurisdiction, or that a reference to Article XVI:4 WTO would bring all provisions of the covered agreements within the scope of a panel's jurisdiction. Such an interpretation would be manifestly incompatible with the requirements for panel requests contained in Article 6.2 DSU.

35. Accordingly, the EC considers that Australia's claim under Articles 43 to 49 of the TRIPS is outside the terms of reference of the Panel.

3. The claims regarding Article 2.2 of the Paris Convention

36. In its first written submission, the United States has argued that with respect to the registration of foreign geographical indications, Regulation 2081/92 imposes a requirement as to domicile or establishment contrary to Article 2.2 of the Paris Convention.[18] The United States has made a claim based on Article 2.2 of the Paris Convention also with respect to the conditions under which foreign nationals can object to the registration of geographical indications.[19]

37. Australia has made a similar claim based on Article 2.2 of the Paris Convention with respect to the alleged unavailability of a right of objection to foreign right holders prior to the amendment of Regulation 2081/92 by Regulation 692/2003.[20]

38. Article 2.1 and 2.2 of the Paris Convention are drafted as follows:

> (1) Nationals of any country of the Union shall, as regards the protection of industrial property, enjoy in all the other countries of the Union the advantages that their respective laws now grant, or may hereafter grant, to nationals; all without prejudice to the rights specially provided for by this Convention. Consequently, they shall have the same protection as the latter, and the same legal remedy against any infringement of their rights, provided that the conditions and formalities imposed upon nationals are complied with.

[18] US FWS, para. 84.

[19] US FWS, para. 89.

[20] Australia's FWS, para. 189, second bullet point; para. 194, second bullet point. As the EC has already set out above, these claims relate to a measure which is no longer in force, and are therefore in any case outside the terms of reference of the present panel.

(2) However, no requirement as to domicile or establishment in the country where protection is claimed may be imposed upon nationals of countries of the Union for the enjoyment of any industrial property rights.

39. Article 2.1 of the Paris Convention is concerned with national treatment. In contrast, Article 2.2 prohibits the imposition of requirements as to domicile or establishment. This obligation is different and additional to the obligations resulting from the national treatment provision of Article 2.1 Paris Convention. This is also made clear by the term "however," which indicates that Article 2.2 goes beyond what is provided in Article 2.1.

40. This view also seems to be shared by the complainants. In its first written submission, the United States has argued that the EC measure "is directly prohibited by Article 2(2) of the Paris Convention."[21] Similarly, Australia has referred to the EC's obligations pursuant to Article 2(2) of the Paris Convention.[22]

41. However, in their panel requests, the complainants have merely referred to an alleged failure of the EC measure to provide national treatment. They have not raised any issue regarding the imposition of a requirement as to domicile or establishment contrary to Article 2.2 of the Paris Convention.

42. For this reason, the EC submits that the US and Australian claims under Article 2.2 of the Paris Convention are outside the terms of reference of the Panel.

III. FACTS

43. The measure at issue in the present dispute is Council Regulation 2081/1992 on the protection of geographical indications and designations of origin for agricultural products and foodstuffs, as in force at the date of establishment of the Panel. A consolidated version of this Regulation is provided in Exhibit EC-1.

44. In this section, the EC will set out the content of Regulation 2081/1992 relevant for the present dispute. In this context, the EC will also correct a number of errors and misrepresentations that are contained in the first written submissions of the complainants with respect to the content of Regulation 2081/1992.

A. THE DEFINITION OF GEOGRAPHIC INDICATIONS

45. Regulation 2081/92 lays down rules on the protection, within the European Community, of designations of origin and geographical indications for agricultural products and foodstuffs. Article 2(2) of the Regulation defines the terms "designation of origin" and "geographical indication" as follows:[23]

(a) *designation of origin*: means the name of a region, a specific place or, in exceptional cases, a country, used to describe an agricultural product or a foodstuff:

- originating in that region, specific place or country, and
- the quality or characteristics of which are essentially or exclusively due to a particular geographical environment with its inherent natural and human factors, and the production, processing and preparation of which take place in the defined geographical area;

---

[21] US FWS, para. 85.

[22] Australia's FWS, para. 189, 194.

[23] Further specific aspects of these definitions are set out in paragraphs 3 to 7 of Article 2.

(b) *geographical indication:* means the name of a region, a specific place or, in exceptional cases, a country, used to describe an agricultural product or a foodstuff:

- originating in that region, specific place or country, and

- which possesses a specific quality, reputation or other characteristics attributable to that geographical origin and the production and/or processing and/or preparation of which take place in the defined geographical area.

46. The distinction between designations of origin and geographical indications depends on how closely the product is linked to the geographical area in which it originates. However, both designations of origin and geographical indications within the meaning of Regulation 2081/92 are geographical indications as defined in Article 22.1 TRIPS Agreement.

47. Under Regulation 2081/92, designations of origin and geographical indications are subject to identical rules as regards their registration and protection. For this reason, wherever the EC, in the present submission, refers to geographical indications within the meaning of Regulation 2081/92, this reference shall also include designations of origin.

B. PRODUCT SPECIFICATIONS

48. In accordance with Article 4 (1) of Regulation 2081/92, in order to be eligible to use a geographical indication, an agricultural product must comply with a product specification. The purpose of this requirement is to ensure that the agricultural product marketed using a particular geographical indication in fact originates in the area to which the indication is related, and possesses the specific quality, reputation or other characteristics which justify the protection of the geographical indication.

49. Regulation 2081/92 does not itself define the product specifications with which a particular product must comply. Rather, in accordance with Article 5 (3) of Regulation 2081/92, the product specifications must be contained in the application for registration of a geographical indication. Article 4 (2) of the Regulation defines the elements with which a product specification must comply:

The product specification shall include at least:

(a) the name of the agricultural product or foodstuffs, including the designation of origin or the geographical indication;

(b) a description of the agricultural product or foodstuff including the raw materials, if appropriate, and principal physical, chemical, microbiological and/or organoleptic characteristics of the product or the foodstuff;

(c) the definition of the geographical area and, if appropriate, details indicating compliance with the requirements in Article 2 (4);

(d) evidence that the agricultural product or the foodstuff originates in the geographical area, within the meaning of Article 2(2) (a) or (b), whichever is applicable;

(e) a description of the method of obtaining the agricultural product or foodstuff and, if appropriate, the authentic and unvarying local methods as well as information concerning the packaging, if the group making the request determines and justifies that the packaging must take place in the limited geographical area to safeguard quality, ensure traceability or ensure control;

(f) the details bearing out the link with the geographical environment or the geographical origin within the meaning of Article 2(2)(a) or (b), whichever is applicable;

(g) details of the inspection structures provided for in Article 10;

(h) the specific labelling details relating to the indication PDO or PGI, whichever is applicable, or the equivalent traditional national indications;

(i) any requirements laid down by Community and/or national provisions.

C. INSPECTION STRUCTURES

50. As has been explained, each protected geographical indication has to comply with a product specification. However, a geographical indication is less reliable and informative for consumers if its proper use is not ensured by an effective inspection regime. For this reason, Article 10(1) of Regulation 2081/92 provides that EC Member States shall ensure that inspection structures are in place, the function of which shall be to ensure that agricultural products and foodstuffs bearing a protected name meet the requirements laid down in the specifications.

51. Article 10 does not regulate all details of such inspection structures. In particular, Article 10(2) provides that an inspection structure "may comprise one or more designated inspection authorities and/or private bodies." It thereby leaves the Member State a choice between public and private elements in the design of the inspection bodies.

52. Article 10(3) further provides that designated inspection authorities and/or approved private bodies "must offer adequate guarantees of objectivity and impartiality with regard to all producers or processors subject to their control and have permanently at their disposal the qualified staff and resources necessary to carry out inspection of agricultural products and foodstuffs bearing a protected name."

53. Further, the third subparagraph of Article 10(3) provides that in order to be approved by the Member States, private bodies must fulfil the requirements laid down in standard EN 45011 of 26 June 1989, which sets out general requirements for bodies operating product certification systems. A copy of this standard, which is available from CEN/CENELEC, is provided as Exhibit EC-2.

54. It should be noted that compliance with standard EN 45011 is only required for bodies to be approved by the EC Member States. In accordance with the last subparagraph of Article 10(3), for bodies located outside the Community, compliance with equivalent international standards will be sufficient. An example for an equivalent international standard is ISO/IEC Guide 65:1996 (E), a copy of which is provided as Exhibit EC-3.

55. In accordance with Article 4(2)(g) of Regulation 2081/92, details of the inspection structure applicable must be included in the product specification, which is part of any application for registration of a geographical indication.

D. THE REGISTRATION OF GEOGRAPHICAL INDICATIONS RELATING TO AN AREA LOCATED IN THE EC

56. Articles 5 and 6 of Regulation 2081/92 set out the procedure for the registration of geographical indications which relate to a geographical area located in the European Community.

57. In accordance with Article 5(4) of Regulation 2081/92, the application shall be sent to the EC Member State in which the geographical area is located. In accordance with Article 5(5), the Member State shall check that the application is justified and, if it considers that the application fulfils the requirements of the Regulation,

shall forward the application, including the product specification and all other relevant documents to the EC Commission.

58. This involvement of the Member State in the registration process is crucial for the proper implementation of the Regulation. In fact, Member States are particularly well placed to examine the admissibility of applications relating to geographical areas located on their territory.

59. Within six months of the receipt of the application, the EC Commission shall verify, by means of a formal investigation, whether the registration application includes all the particulars provided for in Article 4 of the Regulation. If, after this examination, the Commission concludes that the name qualifies for protection, it shall publish a notice in the Official Journal of the European Union containing among others the name of the applicant, the name of the product, and the main points of the application (Article 6(2) of the Regulation).

60. If no statement of objection is notified to the Commission in accordance with Article 7 of the Regulation, the name shall be entered in the register of protected names kept by the Commission (Article 6(3) of the Regulation). The name entered in the register shall be published in the Official Journal (Article 6.4 of the Regulation).

61. If, in the light of the investigation provided for in Article 6(1) of the Regulation, the Commission concludes that the name does not qualify for protection, it shall decide, in accordance with the procedure provided for in Article 15 of the Regulation, not to proceed with the registration of the name.

E. THE REGISTRATION OF GEOGRAPHICAL INDICATIONS RELATING TO AN AREA LOCATED OUTSIDE THE EC

62. Regulation 2081/92 also applies to geographical indications relating to areas located outside the EC. For this purpose, the Regulation lays down rules relating to the registration of such geographical indications from outside the EC which closely parallel the provisions applicable to geographical indications from inside the EC.

63. The purpose of these specific rules, some of which were introduced by Regulation 692/2003, is to facilitate the registration of non-EC geographical indications while at the same time ensuring that geographical indications from outside the EC correspond to the definition of a geographical indication.

64. The United States and Australia have claimed that Regulation 2081/92 allows the registration of geographical indications from other WTO members only under the condition of "reciprocity and equivalence."[24] In support of this contention, they have relied on Article 12(1) of the Regulation, which provides as follows:

> Without prejudice to international agreements, this Regulation may apply to an agricultural product or foodstuff from a third country provided that:
>
> – the third country is able to give guarantees identical or equivalent to those referred to in Article 4,
>
> – the third country concerned has inspection arrangements and a right to objection equivalent to those laid down in this Regulation,
>
> – the third country concerned is prepared to provide protection equivalent to that available in the Community to corresponding agricultural products for foodstuffs coming from the Community.

---

[24] US FWS, para. 22; Australia's FWS, para. 170.

65. However, this interpretation is based on a misunderstanding of the Regulation. Article 12(1) of Regulation 2081/92 clearly provides that it applies "without prejudice to international agreements." Such international agreements include the WTO Agreements. This is made clear by the 8th recital of Regulation 692/2003,[25] which amended the procedures for the registration of non-EC geographical indications, and in this context took specific account of the provisions of the TRIPS.

66. WTO Members are obliged to provide protection to geographical indications in accordance with Section 3 of Part II and the general provisions and basic principles of the TRIPS Agreement. For this reason, Article 12(1) and (3) of Regulation 2081/92 do not apply to WTO Members. This distinction between WTO countries and other third countries is also found in other provisions of the Regulation, for instance in Article 12(2)(a) and (b) and in Article 12d(1), both concerning objections from outside the EC.

67. Accordingly, the registration of a geographical indication relating to an area located in the territory of another WTO Member does not require that the Commission examines whether the conditions set out in Article 12(1) of the Regulation are fulfilled. Rather, the procedure for the registration of third country geographical indications can be immediately applied. The applicant shall therefore send the registration application to the authorities in the country in which the geographical area is located (Article 12a(1) of the Regulation). Like applications for registration of EC geographical indications, applications must be accompanied by the specification referred to in Article 4.

68. According to Article 12a(2), if the third country deems that the requirements of the Regulation are satisfied, it shall transmit the registration application to the Commission accompanied by the following:

(a) a description of the legal provisions and the usage on the basis of which the designation of origin or the geographical indication is protected or established in the country,

(b) a declaration that the structures provided for in Article 10 are established on its territory, and

(c) other documents on which it has based its assessment.

69. Article 12b regulates the further procedure for the registration of the geographical indication in a way which corresponds closely to the procedure set out in Article 6 for the registration of geographical indications from inside the EC.[26]

F. OBJECTIONS FROM PERSONS RESIDENT OR ESTABLISHED IN THE EC

70. Within six months of the date of publication of the application in the Official Journal, the Member State may object to the registration. Article 7(2) of the Regulation provides that Member States shall ensure that all persons who can demonstrate a legitimate economic interest are authorised to consult the application. Pursuant to Article 7(3) of the Regulation, any legitimately concerned natural or legal person may object to a proposed registration by sending a duly substantiated statement to the competent authority of the Member State in which he resides or is established, who shall transmit the objection to the Commission.

71. According to Article 7 (4) of the Regulation, a statement of objection shall be admissible only if it:

either shows non-compliance with the conditions referred to in Article 2,

– shows that the registration of the name proposed would jeopardize the existence of an entirely or partly identical name or of a mark or the existence of products which have

[25] Exhibit COMP-1h.

[26] See above paragraph 59 et seq.

been legally on the market for at least five years preceding the date of the publication provided for in Article 6(2).

– or indicates the features which demonstrate that the name whose registration is applied for is generic in nature.

72. Where a statement of objection is admissible, the Commission shall proceed in accordance with Article 7(5):

> Where an objection is admissible within the meaning of paragraph 4, the Commission shall ask the Member States concerned to seek agreement among themselves in accordance with their internal procedures within three months. If:
>
> (a) agreement is reached, the Member States in question shall communicate to the Commission all the factors which made agreement possible together with the applicant's opinion and that of the objector. Where there has been no change to the information received under Article 5, the Commission shall proceed in accordance with Article 6(4). If there has been a change, it shall again initiate the procedure laid down in Article 7;
>
> (b) no agreement is reached, the Commission shall take a decision in accordance with the procedure laid down in Article 15, having regard to traditional fair practice and of the actual likelihood of confusion. Should it decide to proceed with registration, the Commission shall carry out publication in accordance with Article 6(4).

G. OBJECTIONS FROM PERSONS RESIDENT OR ESTABLISHED OUTSIDE THE EC

73. Article 12d(1) of Regulation 2081/92 provides a right of objection to persons not resident or established in the EC. Article 12d(1) is drafted as follows:

> Within six months of the date of the notice in the *Official Journal of the European Union* specified in Article 6(2) relating to a registration application submitted by a Member State, any natural or legal person that has a legitimate interest and is from a WTO member country or a third country recognised under the procedure provided for in Article 12(3) may object to the proposed registration by sending a duly substantiated statement to the country in which it resides or is established, which shall transmit it, made out or translated into a Community language, to the Commission. Member States shall ensure that any person from a WTO member country or a third country recognised under the procedure provided for in Article 12(3) who can demonstrate a legitimate economic interest is authorised to consult the application.

74. Australia and the US have claimed that this right of objection is subject to the condition that the individual concerned is from a country which is recognised as fulfilling the conditions of Article 12(1) of the Regulation.[27] This is wrong. Article 12d(1) of the Regulation refers to any person that "is from a WTO Member or a third country recognised under the procedure provided for in Article 12(3)." The phrase "recognised under the procedure provided for in Article 12(3)" only refers to third countries other than WTO Members. Otherwise, the specific reference to WTO Members would be meaningless. WTO Members are therefore not subject to the procedure of Article 12(3) applicable to other third countries.

75. This is also clear in Article 12b(2) of the Regulation, which concerns objections against applications for registration of geographical indications relating to an area outside the EC. As regards WTO Members,

[27] US FWS, para. 27, 92; Australia's FWS, para. 204.

Article 12b(2)(a) simply provides that Article 12d shall apply; whereas Article 12b(2)(b) requires for persons resident or established in third countries that the requirements of Article 12(3) must be met.

76. In accordance with Article 12d(2), the conditions for the admissibility of objections from outside the EC are those laid down in Article 7(4) for objections from inside the EC. The admissibility conditions and the further procedure with respect to objections from outside the EC do not differ from those applicable to objections from inside the EC.

77. The United States has nonetheless seen a difference in the fact that whereas under Article 7(3) of the Regulation, only persons who are "legitimately concerned" may object to an application, under Article 12d, persons from outside the EC must have a "legitimate interest."[28] According to the US, "it would appear" that the requirement to be "legitimately concerned" is a lower standard than that one has a "legitimate interest."[29]

78. This assumption of the United States is wrong. There is no substantive difference between the two expressions "legitimately concerned" and "legitimately interested." The New Shorter Oxford English Dictionary defines "concerned" as: "<u>interested</u>, involved, troubled, anxious, showing concern."[30] In other words, "interested" and "concerned" are synonyms. The terminological difference raised by the United States is therefore without any substantive relevance, and does not imply a different standard applicable to persons resident or established outside the EC.

H. DECISION-MAKING PROCEDURES UNDER THE REGULATION

79. In its first written submission, Australia has consistently misrepresented the decision-making process applicable under Regulation 2081/92. In particular, it has referred to the "Committee of EC Member States representatives" as the "decision-making process established by Article 15 of Regulation 2081/92."[31] Consequently, it has repeatedly referred to decisions taken according to the procedure set out in Article 15 of the Regulation as decisions taken "in the Committee of EC Member States representatives."[32] Finally, Australia has referred to the Committee of EC Member States as the "ultimate decision-maker" under the Regulation.[33]

80. These statements are based on a misconception of the decision-making process under the Regulation, and have the effect of exaggerating the role of the Committee. Under the Regulation, decisions with respect to the registration of geographical indications are in principle taken by the Commission. In certain cases, for instance where a statement of objection has been received or the Commission considers that a name does not qualify for protection, the Commission must act in accordance with the procedure in Article 15 of the Regulation.[34] Article 15 provides the following:

> 1. The Commission shall be assisted by a committee.
>
> 2. Where reference is made to this Article, Articles 5 and 7 of Decision 1999/468/EC shall apply.
>
> The period laid down in Article 5(6) of Decision 1999/468/EC shall be set at three months.
>
> 3. The Committee shall adopt its Rules of Procedure.

---

[28] US FWS, para. 26-27.

[29] US FWS, para. 94.

[30] New Shorter Oxford English Dictionary, 1993, Vol. 1, p. 467 (emphasis added).

[31] Australia's FWS, para. 19.

[32] E.g. Australia's FWS, para. 32, 44, 46,

[33] Australia's FWS, para. 94.

[34] Cf. Article 6(5), 7(5), 12b(1)(b), 12d(3) of the Regulation.

81. Decision 1999/468[35] is a decision which lays down, on a general level, the procedures for the exercise of implementing powers which the Council may delegate to the Commission in application of Article 202 of the EC Treaty. The procedure which is applicable under Regulation 2081/92 is the regulatory procedure set out in Article 5 of Decision 1999/468.

82. According to Article 5(1) of Decision 1999/468, the Commission is assisted by a Committee composed of representatives of the Member States. In accordance with Article 5(2) of the Decision, the Commission shall submit to the Committee a draft of the measures to be taken. If the measure is in accordance with the opinion of the Committee, the Commission adopts the Measures (Article 5(3) of the Decision). Only exceptionally, if the measure is not in accordance with the opinion of the Committee, may the matter be referred to the Council of Ministers (Article 5(4) of the Decision). In this case, the following procedure applies (Article 5(5) of the Decision):

> The Council may, where appropriate in view of any such position, act by qualified majority on the proposal, within a period to be laid down in each basic instrument but which shall in no case exceed three months from the date of referral to the Council.
>
> If within that period the Council has indicated by qualified majority that it opposes the proposal, the Commission shall re-examine it. It may submit an amended proposal to the Council, re-submit its proposal or present a legislative proposal on the basis of the Treaty.
>
> If on the expiry of that period the Council has neither adopted the proposed implementing act nor indicated its opposition to the proposal for implementing measures, the proposed implementing act shall be adopted by the Commission.

83. Consequently, the decision-maker under the Regulation is the Commission, or exceptionally the Council of Ministers. The Committee assists the Commission, but does not take decisions; it may, however, achieve that a proposal is referred to the Council of Ministers.

I. THE PROTECTION OF GEOGRAPHICAL INDICATIONS

84. According to Article 13(1) of the Regulation, a name registered under the regulation shall be protected against:

> Registered names shall be protected against:
>
> (a) any direct or indirect commercial use of a name registered in respect of products not covered by the registration in so far as those products are comparable to the products registered under that name or insofar as using the name exploits the reputation of the protected name;
>
> (b) any misuse, imitation or evocation, even if the true origin of the product is indicated or if the protected name is translated or accompanied by an expression such as 'style', 'type', 'method', 'as produced in', 'imitation' or similar;
>
> (c) any other false or misleading indication as to the provenance, origin, nature or essential qualities of the product, on the inner or outer packaging, advertising material or documents relating to the product concerned, and the packing of the product in a container liable to convey a false impression as to its origin;

[35] Exhibit EC-4.

(d) any other practice liable to mislead the public as to the true origin of the product.

J. INDICATION OF THE COUNTRY OF ORIGIN FOR HOMONYMOUS GEOGRAPHICAL INDICATIONS

85. In their first written submission, the United States has claimed that Article 12(2) requires that any use of a geographical indication in connection with products of other WTO Members can be authorized only if the country of origin "is clearly and visibly indicated on the label," and that there is no similar requirement with respect to products of EC Member States.[36]

86. This interpretation is based on a misunderstanding of Article 12(2) of the Regulation. This provision is drafted as follows:

> If a protected name of a third country is identical to a Community protected name, registration shall be granted with due regard for local and traditional usage and the practical risks of confusion.
>
> Use of such names shall be authorized only if the country of origin of the product is clearly and visibly indicated on the label.

87. It follows clearly from the structure of this provision that the reference to "such names" in the second subparagraph of Article 12(2) is a reference to the names mentioned in the first subparagraph, i.e. identical protected names from a third country and the Community. In other words, the second subparagraph does not concern third country names in general, but only homonyms.

88. Moreover, it should be noted that the reference to "such names" applies both to third country protected names and to Community protected names. In the case of identical names, the requirement to indicate the country of origin can apply both to the third country name and the Community name. In practice, this would mean that whichever indication is registered later would normally be required to indicate the country of origin. Where a Community indication is registered after an identical third country indication, the Community indication would therefore be required to indicate the country of origin.

89. Finally, it should be noted that in case of homonymous names from the EC, the last indent of Article 6(6) of the Regulation also requires "a clear distinction in practice" between the two homonyms. Where the two homonyms are from different Member States, this may in practice require the indication of the country of origin.

K. GEOGRAPHICAL INDICATIONS AND TRADEMARKS

90. The relationship between geographical indications and trademarks is regulated in Article 14 of the Regulation, which is drafted as follows:

> 1. Where a designation of origin or geographical indication is registered under this Regulation, any application for registration of a trademark that is for a product of the same type and use of which will engender one of the situations indicated in Article 13 shall be refused if made after the date of submission to the Commission of the application for registration of the designation of origin or geographical indication.
>
> Trademarks registered in breach of the first subparagraph shall be invalidated.

[36] US FWS, para. 25. Australia rightly assumed that this provision only applies to homonyms (Australia's FWS, para. 235).

2. With due regard to Community law, a trademark the use of which engenders one of the situations indicated in Article 13 and which has been applied for, registered, or established by use, if that possibility is provided for by the legislation concerned, in good faith within the territory of the Community, before either the date of protection in the country of origin or the date of submission to the Commission of the application for registration of the designation of origin or geographical indication, may continue to be used notwithstanding the registration of a designation of origin or geographical indication, provided that no grounds for its invalidity or revocation exist as specified by Council Directive 89/104/EEC of 21 December 1998 to approximate the laws of the Member States relating to trade marks and/or Council Regulation (EC) No 40/94 of 20 December 1993 on the Community trade mark.

3. A designation of origin or geographical indication shall not be registered where, in the light of a trade mark's reputation and renown and the length of time it has been used, registration is liable to mislead the consumer as to the true identity of the product.

L. SIMPLIFIED REGISTRATION OF GEOGRAPHICAL INDICATIONS PRIOR TO THE ENTRY INTO FORCE OF REGULATION 692/2003

91. In its first written submission, Australia has also made certain claims regarding the simplified registration procedure according to Article 17 of Regulation 2081/92 as applicable until the entry into force of Regulation 692/2003.

92. As the Commission has already set out, these claims relate to a measure no longer in force at the time the Panel was established, and are therefore outside the terms of reference of the present Panel.[37] However, since certain of the factual claims made by Australia in this respect are factually wrong, the EC would like to take the opportunity to correct them.

93. In its first written submission, Australia claims that under the simplified procedure, a right of objection was available to persons resident or established in the EC, which was not available to persons from outside the EC.[38] In support of its thesis, it relies in particular on a declaration of the Commission and the Council quoted in the *Feta* judgment of the European Court of Justice.[39]

94. Australia's interpretation is unfounded. Article 17, as applicable until the entry into force of Regulation 692/2003, provided as follows (emphasis added):

> Within six months of the entry into force of the Regulation, Member States shall inform the Commission which of their legally protected names or, in those Member States where there is no protection system, which of their names established by usage they wish to register pursuant to this Regulation.
>
> In accordance with the procedure laid down in Article 15, the Commission shall register the names referred to in paragraph 1 which comply with Articles 2 and 4. Article 7 shall not apply. However, generic names shall not be added.

95. Article 17(2) thus provided clearly that Article 7, which laid down the right of objection, did not apply in the simplified procedure. This was explicitly confirmed by the European Court of Justice in the *Feta* judgment:[40]

---

[37] See above, para. 13 et seq.

[38] Australia's FWS, para. 39, 191-192.

[39] The declaration was quoted in para. 21 of the Court's judgment (Exhibit COMP-11).

[40] Paragraph 92 of the Judgment (Exhibit COMP-11; emphasis added).

> Second, as the Commission itself pointed out in its defence in Case C-293/96, it must be noted that, even though Article 17(2) of the basic regulation expressly provides that Article 7 thereof is not applicable in the simplified registration procedure, a registration under that procedure also presupposes that the names conform with the substantive requirements of that regulation. In the absence of express provisions to the contrary, there is no possibility, under the simplified procedure, of names being registered which do not fulfil the substantive conditions for registration under the normal registration procedure.

96. Furthermore, the declaration of the Council and the Commission referred to by the Court of Justice did not concern the simplified procedure of Article 17. The declaration read in relevant part as follows:[41]

> The Council and the Commission further declare that where there are agriculture products or foodstuffs already being legally marketed before the making of this Regulation which may be the subject of an application for registration, it has been provided for any Member States to object to the registration under the provisions of Article 7 of the Regulation [...].

97. This declaration simply referred to the situation envisaged in the second indent of Article 7(4) of Regulation 2081/92, in which a statement of objection will be admissible. This declaration did in no way refer to the simplified procedure foreseen in Article 17. Nor did the European Court of Justice, as shown above, deduce from this declaration that a right of objection applied in the context of the simplified procedure.

98. In accordance with the clear wording of Article 17(2) of Regulation as applicable until the entry into force of Regulation 692/2003, the right of objection did not apply in the context of the simplified procedure.

IV. REGULATION 2081/92 IS COMPATIBLE WITH NATIONAL TREATMENT OBLIGATIONS, AND DOES NOT IMPOSE A REQUIREMENT OF DOMICILE OR ESTABLISHMENT

99. In their first written submissions, the complainants have claimed that Regulation 2081/92:

- is incompatible with the national treatment obligation of the TRIPS and the Paris Convention (Article 3.1 TRIPS and Article 2.1 TRIPS in conjunction with Article 2.1 Paris Convention);
- establishes a requirement of domicile or establishment prohibited by the Paris Convention (Article 2.1 TRIPS in conjunction with Article 2.2 Paris Convention);
- is incompatible with the national treatment obligation of Article III:4 GATT.

100. The EC will discuss the claims under each of these provisions in turn.

A. NATIONAL TREATMENT UNDER THE TRIPS AGREEMENT (ARTICLE 3.1 TRIPS AND ARTICLE 2.1 TRIPS IN CONJUNCTION WITH ARTICLE 2.1 PARIS CONVENTION)

101. Under the TRIPS Agreement, the obligation to provide national treatment with regard to the protection of intellectual property is set out in two different provisions. First, Article 3.1 TRIPS provides as follows:

> Each Member shall accord to the nationals of other Members treatment no less favourable than that it accords to its own nationals with regard to the protection of intellectual property, subject to the exceptions already provided in, respectively, the Paris Convention (1967), the

[41] Exhibit EC-5.

> Berne Convention (1971), the Rome Convention or the Treaty on Intellectual Property in Respect of Integrated Circuits. In respect of performers, producers of phonograms and broadcasting organizations, this obligation only applies in respect of the rights provided under this Agreement. Any Member availing itself of the possibilities provided in Article 6 of the Berne Convention (1971) or paragraph 1(b) of Article 16 of the Rome Convention shall make a notification as foreseen in those provisions to the Council for TRIPS.

102. Moreover, Article 2.1 TRIPS integrates into the TRIPS Agreement the national treatment provision contained in Article 2.1 of the Paris Convention. Article 2.1 of the Paris Convention reads as follows:

> Nationals of any country of the Union shall, as regards the protection of industrial property, enjoy in all the other countries of the Union the advantages that their respective laws now grant, or may hereafter grant, to nationals; all without prejudice to the rights specially provided for by this Convention. Consequently, they shall have the same protection as the latter, and the same legal remedy against any infringement of their rights, provided that the conditions and formalities imposed upon nationals are complied with.

103. Since both obligations are expressed in similar terms, the EC shall discuss the claims made by the complainants under both provisions jointly.

1. General remarks

104. Both Article 3.1 TRIPS and Article 2.1 Paris Convention oblige WTO Members to treat nationals of other Member no less favourably than their own nationals with respect to the protection of intellectual property rights. In *US – Section 211,* the Appellate Body has underlined the fundamental significance of the national treatment obligation within the context of the TRIPS.[42] In its first written submission, the United States has recalled this fundamental importance of the national treatment obligation under the TRIPS.[43] The EC agrees.

105. However, the EC considers it equally important to understand the correct scope and meaning of the national treatment provisions of the TRIPS and the Paris Convention. Article 3.1 TRIPS provides that each Member shall accord to the nationals of other Members treatment no less favourable than that it accords to its own nationals. Similarly, Article 2.1 of the Paris Convention provides that nationals of any country of the Union shall, as regards the protection of industrial property, enjoy in all the other countries of the Union the advantages that their respective laws now grant, or may hereafter grant, to nationals. Accordingly, the national treatment obligation under the TRIPS aims at an equality of treatment between nationals.[44]

106. This reference to nationals is of fundamental importance in the application of the national treatment provision under the TRIPS. This is illustrated by the findings of the Panel in *Indonesia – Cars*. In this case, the United States had argued that the Indonesian system put the United States companies in a position that, if they were successful in becoming a partner in the National Car Programme, they would be unlikely to use in Indonesia the mark normally used ("global" mark) on the vehicle marketed as a "national motor vehicle" in Indonesia, for fear of creating confusion. The Panel rejected this claim referring explicitly to the fact that no evidence had been brought to support the conclusion that the Indonesian system constituted discrimination between nationals:[45]

> We do not accept this argument for the following reasons. First, no evidence has been put forward to refute the Indonesian statement that the system, in requiring a new, albeit

[42] Appellate Body Report, *United States – Section 211*, para. 241.

[43] US FWS, para. 33.

[44] Daniel Gervais, *The TRIPS Agreement, Drafting History and Analysis*, (Sweet & Maxwell, 1998), p. 48.

[45] Panel Report, *Indonesia – Cars*, para. 14.271 (emphasis added). The United States is therefore wrong to claim that *US – Section 211* has been the only dispute concerning the national treatment obligation in the context of the TRIPS Agreement (US FWS, para. 34).

> Indonesian-owned, trademark to be created, applies equally to pre-existing trademarks owned by Indonesian nationals and foreign nationals. Second, if a foreign company enters into an arrangement with a Pioneer company, it would do so voluntarily, with knowledge of any consequent implications for its ability to maintain pre-existing trademark rights [...].

107. The emphasis put by the TRIPS Agreement on nationals is not accidental. In Article 3.1 TRIPS and 2.1 Paris Convention, national treatment is provided "with regard to the protection of intellectual property." Intellectual property rights are held by natural and legal persons.[46] It is therefore entirely consistent with the object and purpose of the national treatment provision of TRIPS that national treatment be granted between nationals.

108. In this regard, the national treatment obligation of the TRIPS differs fundamentally from national treatment in the GATT. Article III:4 of the GATT provides that "the products of the territory of any contracting party imported into the territory of any other contracting party shall be accorded treatment no less favourable than that accorded to like products of national origin." Accordingly, unlike Article 3.1 TRIPS and 2.1 Paris Convention, Article III:4 GATT prescribes national treatment between goods, not between nationals.

109. The Panel in *Indonesia – Autos* in fact cautioned against reading Article 3.1 TRIPS so as to apply to matters not directly related to the equal treatment of nationals:[47]

> In considering this argument, we note that any customs tariff, subsidy or other governmental measure of support could have a "de facto" effect of giving such an advantage to the beneficiaries of this support. We consider that considerable caution needs to be used in respect of "de facto" based arguments of this sort, because of the danger of reading into a provision obligations which go far beyond the letter of that provision and the objectives of the Agreement. It would not be reasonable to construe the national treatment obligation of the TRIPS Agreement in relation to the maintenance of trademark rights as preventing the grant of tariff, subsidy or other measures of support to national companies on the grounds that this would render the maintenance of trademark rights by foreign companies wishing to export to that market relatively more difficult.

110. The United States and Australia fail to acknowledge this fundamental difference between the national treatment obligations of the TRIPS and the GATT.[48] In their first written submissions, they make no attempt to establish that Regulation 2081/92 discriminates between nationals of the EC and nationals of other WTO members.

111. As the EC will show, Regulation 2081/92 does not discriminate between EC nationals and nationals of other WTO members.

112. Moreover, the EC will show for each of the claims raised that, even if Regulation 2081/92 applied differently to foreign and EC nationals, it could not be considered as providing less favourable treatment.

---

[46] On the definition of nationality in this respect, cf. Bodenhausen, Guide to the Application of the Paris Convention for the Protection of Industrial Property, p. 27-28 (1968).

[47] Panel Report, *Indonesia – Autos*, para. 14.723 (emphasis added).

[48] This is all the more striking since the US, when discussing the most-favored-nation obligation under the TRIPS and the GATT, did distinguish between treatment of nationals and treatment of products (US, FWS, para. 108).

2. Claims 1: Non-EC nationals are accorded less favorable treatment than EC nationals with respect to the registration of geographical indications through the application of a condition of reciprocity and equivalence

113. The US and Australia have claimed that by subjecting the registration of geographic indications from other WTO members to "conditions of reciprocity and equivalence," Regulation 2081/92 violates the national treatment provisions of Article 3.1 TRIPS and 2.1 Paris Convention.[49]

114. This claim is wrong for the following reasons:

- The EC does not apply a condition of reciprocity and equivalence for the registration of geographical indications from other WTO members;
- The conditions for the registration of individual geographical indications do not constitute less favourable treatment;
- The conditions for the registration of geographical indications do not depend on nationality.

(a) The EC does not apply a condition of reciprocity and equivalence for the registration of geographical indications from other WTO members

115. The United States and Australia have alleged that Article 12(1) of Regulation 2081/92 subjects the registration of foreign geographical indications to a condition of "reciprocity and equivalence." In particular, the United States has argued that in order to ensure the protection of geographical indications relating to areas in other WTO Members, the EC requires them to (a) reciprocally grant equivalent GI protection for agricultural products and foodstuffs coming from the EC and (b) adopt a system for protecting geographical indications that the EC unilaterally decides is equivalent to that in the EC, including equivalent inspection and objection systems.[50]

116. As the EC has already set out previously, this claim is factually incorrect.[51] WTO Members must provide adequate protection of geographical indications in accordance with the TRIPS Agreement. For this reason, Article 12(1) of Regulation 2081/92, which applies only subject to international agreements, does not apply to other WTO Members.[52]

117. Accordingly, the EC does not condition the registration of geographical indications relating to the territory of another WTO Member to the condition that it reciprocally grant equivalent protection for agricultural products and foodstuffs coming from the EC and that it adopts a system for protecting geographical indications equivalent to that in the EC.

(b) The conditions for the registration of individual geographical indications do not constitute less favourable treatment

118. However, the EC would like to clarify that whereas it does not require equivalence as regards the system of protection of geographical indications, it does require that the product specifications and inspection regimes with regard to specific geographical indications from third countries meet the conditions of Regulation

---

[49] US FWS, para. 57 et seq. It appears that Australia has also attempted to raise the same claim, albeit in less clear form (Australia's FWS, para. 199).

[50] US FWS, para. 59.

[51] Above para. 62 et seq.

[52] Above para. 62 et seq.

2081/92. For this reason, any application for a geographical indication relating to an area in a third country must be accompanied by a product specification, and must indicate that the necessary inspection procedures exist.[53]

119. It is not entirely clear to the EC whether the complainants are also challenging these GI-specific requirements. The EC notes, however, that in its submission, the United States has frequently referred to the notion of "equivalence" without any further qualification, and has claimed that the national treatment obligation was specifically intended to prohibit such a condition.[54]

120. In case the complainants should also challenge these GI-specific requirements, the EC would like to clarify that it considers that this interpretation would be erroneous. Article 3.1 TRIPS and 2.1 Paris Convention oblige WTO Members to provide "treatment no less favourable" to the nationals of other WTO Members; they do no oblige WTO Members to provide treatment more favourable.

121. As the EC has also explained, the objective of the product specification and the inspection regimes foreseen in Regulation 2081/92 is to ensure that the products meet the requirements that can be expected from products marketed using the protected name.[55] These considerations apply to protected names from the EC and from third countries alike. Therefore, the requirement in Regulation 2081/92 of an assurance that the product specifications regarding a foreign geographical indication are respected is not less favourable treatment, but equal treatment.

122. Accordingly, any claim regarding a violation of the national treatment provisions of Article 3.1 TRIPS and 2.1 Paris Convention through the conditions for the registration of individual geographic indications would be unfounded.

(c) The conditions for the registration of geographical indications do not depend on nationality

123. As the EC has set out, Article 3.1 TRIPS and 2.1 Paris Convention require equal treatment, as regards the protection of intellectual property, between nationals. However, the conditions and procedures contained in Regulation 2081/92 for the registration of geographical indications do not depend on nationality.

124. As the EC has explained above, the conditions and procedures for the registration of geographical indications relating to an area located in the EC are set out in Article 5 and 6 of Regulation 2081/92.[56] In contrast, the conditions and procedures for the registration of geographical indications relating to an area located in another WTO Member are contained in Article 12a and 12b of the Regulation.[57]

125. Whether the area to which a geographic indication is related is located inside the EC or outside is in no way linked to the question of the nationality of the producers of the product concerned. Protection of a geographical indication relating to an area located in the EC is obtained in accordance with Article 5 and 6 of the Regulation, even if the producers in question are foreign nationals. Inversely, protection for a geographical indication located outside the EC must be obtained in accordance with Articles 12a and 12b of Regulation 2081/92, even if the producers in question are EC nationals. In both situations, the same also applies if certain producers are EC nationals, and others are not.

126. Accordingly, Regulation 2081/92 does not distinguish between EC nationals and other nationals. For this reason also, the claim must fail.

---

[53] Cf. above para. 68.

[54] Cf. e.g. US FWS, para. 57.

[55] Above para. 48 et seq., 50 et seq.

[56] See above para. 56 et seq.

[57] See above para. 62.

3. Claim 2: Regulation 2081/92 violates the national treatment obligations under the TRIPS and the Paris Convention by requiring that applications must be transmitted by the country in which the geographical area is located

127. The United States (but not Australia) has claimed that Regulation 2081/92 violates the national treatment obligations under the TRIPS and the Paris Convention by requiring that applications must be transmitted by the country in which the geographical area is located.[58] The United States has argued that this requirement implies an "extra hurdle" for foreign nationals which is not faced by EC nationals. In particular, the United States has invoked the possibility that the third country concerned might have "neither the infrastructure nor the inclination" to process and transmit the application.

128. The EC submits that this claim must fail. First, the question which government must transmit the application in accordance with Article 6 or Article 12a of the Regulation does not depend on nationality, but on the question where the geographic area in question is located.[59] Accordingly, Regulation 2081/92 does not differentiate on the basis of nationality.

129. Second, the Regulation does not constitute less favourable treatment for third country nationals. The role of third country governments provided for in Article 12a of the Regulation corresponds exactly to that of EC Member States where geographical indications relating to an area located in the EC are concerned. As the EC has set out above, this involvement of the Member State or third country concerned in the registration process is crucial, as the government of the country concerned is particularly well placed to examine the admissibility of applications relating to geographical areas located on its territory. Accordingly, the condition that an application relating to an area located in a third country is transmitted by the government in question does not amount to "less favourable treatment," but in fact ensures equal treatment.

130. The references by the US to an absence of "infrastructure" or "inclination" on the part of the third country are not convincing. The verification and transmission of an application for registration of a geographical indication are not overly burdensome for another WTO Member. As regards "inclination," the EC finds it remarkable that the United States would invoke its own unwillingness to cooperate in the registration process in order to demonstrate a national treatment violation on the part of the EC.

131. Accordingly, the claim that Regulation 2081/92 violates the national treatment obligations under the TRIPS and the Paris Convention by requiring that applications must be transmitted by the country in which the geographical area is located is unfounded.

4. Claim 3: Non-EC nationals are accorded less favorable treatment than EC nationals with respect to the requirement to indicate the country of origin for homonymous geographical indications

132. The United States (but not Australia) has claimed that the requirement contained in Article 12(2) of Regulation 2081/92 to indicate the country of origin constitutes a violation of national treatment provisions under the TRIPS and the Paris Convention.[60] This claim is unfounded for the following reasons:

- Article 12(2) of Regulation 2081/92 does not apply to all geographical indications, but only to homonyms;
- the requirement to indicate the country of origin for homonymous geographical indications from the EC and third countries does not constitute less favourable treatment;

---

[58] US FWS, para. 81.

[59] Cf. above para. 123 et seq.

[60] US FWS, para. 68. Australia has made a similar claim under Article 2.1 of the TBT Agreement, which will be discussed below (cf. Australia's FWS, para. 234).

- Article 12(2) of Regulation 2081/92 does not discriminate between nationals.

(a) Article 12(2) of Regulation 2081/92 does not apply to all geographical indications, but only to homonyms

133. The United States has claimed that Article 12(2) of Regulation 2081/92 provides that use of all foreign geographical indications require the indication of the country of origin. As the EC has already clarified,[61] this claim of the United States is based on a misunderstanding. The second subparagraph of Article 12(2) only relates to the situation of the first subparagraph where "a protected name of a third country is identical to a Community protected name." Accordingly, there is no need to examine whether a requirement to indicate the country of origin for all foreign geographical indications would be compatible with national treatment obligations.

(b) The requirement to indicate the country of origin for homonymous geographical indications from the EC and third countries does not constitute less favourable treatment

134. Since it has misunderstood the meaning of Article 12(2) of the Regulation 2081/92, the United States has not indicated whether it considers the requirement to indicate the country of origin discriminatory also when only applying to homonymous names from the EC and a third country. Should the United States have intended to make such an argument, then it would be manifestly unfounded.

135. Article 12(2) in fact does not only apply to third country names, but also to Community names. As the EC has explained, it therefore may require the indication of the country of origin for both EC and third country names, depending on which geographical indication has been protected earlier.[62] Accordingly, Article 12(2) of Regulations treats geographical indications from the EC and third countries alike.

136. Accordingly, Article 12(2) of Regulation 2081/92 is entirely compatible with the national treatment obligations of the TRIPS and the Paris Convention.

(c) Article 12(2) of Regulation 2081/92 does not discriminate between nationals

137. The second subparagraph of Article 12(2) of Regulation 2081/92 provides that the use of "such names" is authorized only if the country of origin is clearly and visibly indicated on the label. As the EC has set out above,[63] "such names" is a reference to the first subparagraph of Article 12(2). Accordingly, the requirement to indicate the country of origin applies where "a protected name of a third country is identical to a Community protected name."

138. As the EC has already set out in response to Claim 1, whether a protected name is a "Community name" or a "third country name" within the meaning of Regulation 2081/92 depends on where the geographical area to which the geographical indication is related is located. It has nothing to do with nationality. Accordingly, Article 12(2) does not imply any discrimination between nationals.[64]

139. For all these reasons, the claim should be rejected.

---

[61] Above para. 85.

[62] Above para. 88.

[63] Above para. 87.

[64] The EC would point out that if national treatment under the TRIPS were considered as applying also to discrimination between goods, then the relationship between the provisions of the TRIPS on national treatment and Article IX:1 of the GATT would become an issue (on the relationship between Article III:4 and IX:1 GATT, see below para. 213 et seq.).

5. Claim 4: Regulation 2081/92 accords less favourable treatment to non-EC nationals by subjecting the right to object to the registration of geographical indications to conditions of reciprocity and equivalence

140. The United States and Australia have claimed that only nationals from WTO member countries recognised in accordance with Article 12(3) of Regulation 2081/92 as fulfilling the conditions of reciprocity and equivalence may object to registrations of geographical indications in accordance with Article 12d of the Regulation.[65]

141. This is factually wrong. As the EC has already set out,[66] Article 12d(1) of Regulation 2081/92 gives a right to object to any person that "is from a WTO Member or a third country recognised under the procedure provided for in Article 12(3)." It is clear from this explicit reference to WTO Members that WTO Members are not subject to the procedure of Article 12(3) applicable to other third countries. The same applies also under Article 12.b.2 with respect to objections against the registration of geographical indications from outside the EC.

142. The claim is also legally unfounded. Article 3.1 TRIPS and 2.1 of the Paris Convention relate only to equal treatment between nationals. However, Article 7(3) of Regulation 2081/92 refers to persons which are resident or established in the EC, regardless of their nationality. Similarly, Article 12d(1) refers to persons resident or established outside the EC, regardless of their nationality. It should also be noted that conditions regarding domicile or establishment are the subject of Article 2.2 Paris Convention, on the basis of which the complainants have formulated separate claims.[67]

143. Accordingly, this claim should be dismissed.

6. Claim 5: Regulation 2081/92 accords less favourable treatment to non-EC nationals by requiring their own country to transmit the objection

144. The United States and Australia have claimed that Regulation 2081/92 accords less favourable treatment to non-EC nationals by requiring their own country to transmit the objection.[68]

145. First, it must once again be remarked that Article 12d(2) applies not to nationals, but to persons resident or established in a third country. Accordingly, Regulation 2081/92 does not accord different treatment on the basis of nationality.

146. Second, the treatment accorded to persons resident or established in the Community and persons resident or established in the EC is exactly identical. For persons resident or established in the Community, Article 7 requires that the statement of objection shall be submitted to the EC Member State where the person is resident or established, who shall transmit the objection to the Commission. For persons resident or established in a third country, Article 12d(1) provides that the statement shall be submitted to the third country of residence or establishment, which shall transmit it to the Commission. Accordingly, Regulation 2081/92 does not apply unequal, but equal treatment.

147. The United States has argued that the third country might not have "the appropriate mechanism to process the objection, or may or may not be inclined to transmit the objection, for its own political reasons."[69] Similarly, Australia has argued that third countries "have no legally defined relationship" regarding such objections.[70]

---

[65] United States FWS, para. 92; Australia's FWS, para. 204.

[66] Above para. 73 et seq.

[67] See above Section II.B.3 and below Section IV.B.

[68] US, FWS, para. 90; Australia's FWS, para. 205.

[69] US, FWS, para. 90.

[70] Australia's FWS, para. 205.

148. These objections are unconvincing. First, it does not appear that a particularly demanding infrastructure is required for processing and transmitting a statement of objection. Second, the complainants cannot rely on their own unwillingness to cooperate in the transmission of a statement of objection in order to demonstrate a violation of national treatment obligations on the part of the EC.

149. Accordingly, Regulation 2081/92 does not accord less favourable treatment to non-EC nationals by requiring their own country to transmit the objection.

7. Claim 6: Regulation 2081/92 accords less favourable treatment to non-EC nationals by requiring non-EC national to have a "legitimate interest" to object to the registration of geographical indications

150. The United States (but not Australia) has claimed that Article 12d(1) Regulation 2081/92 accords less favourable treatment to non-EC nationals by requiring non-EC nationals to have a "legitimate interest" to object to the registration of geographical indications.[71]

151. As the EC has shown, there is no substantive difference between the term "legitimate interest" used in Article 12d(1) of Regulation 2081/92 and the term "legitimately concerned" in Article 7(3). Rather, "legitimately concerned" and "legitimately concerned" are synonymous expressions.

152. Since the claim is based on a misunderstanding of the Regulation, it does not need to be discussed any further.

8. Claim 7: Regulation 2081/92 accords less favourable treatment because a non-EC rightholder has no "representative" in the regulatory committee to "speak for him"

153. Australia (but not the United States) has argued that Regulation 2081/92 accords less favourable treatment because a non-EC rightholder has no "representative" in the regulatory committee to "speak for him."[72]

154. This claim is manifestly unfounded. First, Australia has not correctly understood the decision-making process under the Regulation. As the EC has set out,[73] the decision-maker under the Regulation is the Commission, or exceptionally the Council. The Committee merely assists the Commission, and may exceptionally achieve that a proposal is referred to the Council. In no case does it take decisions itself. Moreover, Member States representatives on the Committee do not speak for particular rightholders, but represent the respective EC Member State.

155. Secondly, Australia's claim to have a representative on the regulatory committee is not reasonable. The public authorities of a WTO Member must be presumed to administer their duties properly and fairly. This is independent of the nationality of the civil servants and employees working for such authorities. The EC also notes that there are no "EC representatives" in the public authorities and agencies of Australia. The EC does not assume that Australia would want to suggest that for this reason, Australian authorities cannot be assumed to correctly implement their WTO obligations with respect to the EC.

---

[71] US, FWS, para. 93-94.

[72] Australia's FWS, para. 203.

[73] Above, para. 79 et seq.

9. Claim 8: A right of objection was available to persons resident or established in an EC Member State that was not available to other WTO Member nationals in respect of the registration of more than 120 geographical indications under the normal registration process

156. Australia has claimed that there is a violation of national treatment in the fact that a right of objection was available to persons resident or established in an EC Member State that was not available to other WTO Member nationals in respect of the registration of more than 120 geographical indications under the normal registration process.[74] This claim must fail for the following reasons:

- Australia's claim relates to a measure which was no longer in force at the time of establishment of the Panel, and which is therefore not within the terms of reference of the Panel;
- the individual registrations are not in violation of national treatment obligations;
- Australia is seeking to obtain a retroactive remedy it could not have obtained had it attacked the measure while it was still in force.

(a) Australia's claim relates to a measure which was no longer in force at the time of establishment of the Panel, and which is therefore not within the terms of reference of the Panel

157. Australia's claim relates to Regulation 2081/92 as in force until 8 April 2003, when Regulation 692/2003 entered into force. It therefore relates to a measure which was no longer in force at the time of establishment of the Panel. Accordingly, as the EC has set out above, this measure is therefore not within the terms of reference of the Panel.[75]

(b) The individual registrations are not in violation of national treatment obligations

158. In its submission, Australia has also argued that "in respect to the registration under the normal registration process of more than 120 EC-defined GIs" before Regulation 2081/92 was amended by Regulation 692/2003, the "EC measure" accorded less favourable treatment to foreign nationals. With this claim, Australia seems to suggest that the individual registrations of geographical indications which were carried out prior to the entry into force of Regulation 692/2003 somehow violate the national treatment obligations under the TRIPS and the Paris Convention.

159. This claim of Australia's is unfounded. Australia has made no plausible case that the 120 registrations in question in any way violate the national treatment obligations under the TRIPS and the Paris Convention.

160. Australia's claim is based exclusively on the argument that no right of objection was available to third country-nationals under Regulation 2081/92 before its amendment by Regulation 692/2003. However, this claim relates to Regulation 2081/92 as applicable before its amendment, and the procedure it prescribed for the registration of geographical indications. The rules governing the procedure leading up to the adoption of a measure are not the same as the measure itself.

161. In contrast, Australia has advanced no arguments in support of its claim that the individual registrations are incompatible with national treatment obligations. It is submitted that Australia is unable to do so. Each individual registration grants protection to a specific geographical indication relating to a specific geographical area. It is not clear to the European Community how such a registration could be considered to grant less favourable treatment to third-country nationals.

---

[74] Australia's FWS, para. 184 et seq.

[75] See above Section II.A.1.

(c) Australia is seeking to obtain a retroactive remedy it could not have obtained had it attacked the measure while it was still in force.

162. In addition, the EC considers it important to remark that Australia's claim, if directed against the individual registrations, has considerable implications for the dispute settlement system set up by the DSU. In fact, with its claim, Australia is seeking to obtain a retroactive remedy that it could not even have obtained had it attacked Regulation 2081/92 before it was amended by Regulation 692/2003.

163. According to Article 19.1 DSU, where a panel or the Appellate Body concludes that a measure is inconsistent with a covered agreement, it shall recommend that the Member concerned "bring the measure into conformity with that agreement." It is universally accepted that this signifies that recommendations of panels and the Appellate Body are prospective, not retrospective in nature.[76] This has also been confirmed by the Appellate Body in *US – Certain EC Products*:[77]

> We note, though, that there is an obvious inconsistency between the finding of the Panel that "the 3 March Measure is no longer in existence" and the subsequent recommendation of the Panel that the DSB request that the United States bring its 3 March Measure into conformity with its WTO obligations. The Panel erred in recommending that the DSB request the United States to bring into conformity with its WTO obligations a measure which the Panel has found no longer exists.

164. Reference can also be made to the findings of the GATT Panel in *Norway – Trondheim Bridge*, which clearly stated that GATT remedies were not retroactive:[78]

> The Panel then turned its attention to the recommendations that the United States had requested it to make. In regard to the United States' request that the Panel recommend that Norway take the necessary measures to bring its practices into compliance with the Agreement with regard to the Trondheim procurement, the Panel noted that all the acts of non-compliance alleged by the United States were acts that had taken place in the past. The only way mentioned during the Panel's proceedings that Norway could bring the Trondheim procurement into line with its obligations under the Agreement would be by annulling the contract and recommencing the procurement process. The Panel did not consider it appropriate to make such a recommendation. Recommendations of this nature had not been within customary practice in dispute settlement under the GATT system and the drafters of the Agreement on Government Procurement had not made specific provision that such recommendations be within the task assigned to panels under standard terms of reference. Moreover, the Panel considered that in the case under examination such a recommendation might be disproportionate, involving waste of resources and possible damage to the interests of third parties.

165. The Panel went on to emphasise that these considerations were in no way specific to government procurement, but were of a general nature:[79]

> In considering this argument, the Panel was of the view that situations of the type described by the United States were not unique to government procurement. Considerable trade damage could be caused in other areas by an administrative decision without there necessarily being any GATT inconsistent legislation, for example in the areas of discretionary licensing,

---

[76] Australia itself has argued in favour of the prospective character of WTO remedies even in regard to Article 4.7 SCM Agreement; cf. Panel Report, *Australia – Automotive Leather (Article 21.5 – US)*, para. 6.14.

[77] Appellate Body, *US – Certain EC Products*, para. 81.

[78] Panel Report, *Norway – Trondheim Bridge*, para. 4.17.

[79] Panel Report, *Norway – Trondheim Bridge*, para. 4.23.

technical regulations, sanitary and phytosanitary measures and subsidies. Moreover, there had been cases where a temporary measure contested before the GATT had been lifted before a Panel had been able to report.

166. In the present case, even if Australia had challenged a violation of national treatment before Regulation 2081/92 was amended by Regulation 692/2003, it could therefore not have claimed that the EC undo all the registrations already carried out, or that it reopen a possibility of objection against such registrations.

167. Australia has also argued that when Regulation 692/2003 entered into force, it should have reopened a full objection period in respect to all geographical indications for which applications were pending.[80] This argument shows even more clearly the retroactive character of Australia's claims. If the period of objection had already fully or partially run out for EC residents, then claims based on national treatment would not have given a retroactive right to reopen an objection period for non-EC residents.

168. By formulating its claim not against the terminated measure but against the acts which are derived from it, Australia is effectively trying to circumvent the principle that WTO remedies are not retroactive in nature. For this reason also, Australia's claim must be rejected.

169. For all the reasons set out above, Australia's claim must be rejected.

10. Claim 9: A right of objection was available to persons resident or established in an EC Member State that was not available to other WTO Member nationals in respect of the registration of more than 480 EC-defined GIs under the simplified registration process

170. Finally, Australia also claims that a right of objection was available to persons resident or established in an EC Member State that was not available to other WTO Member nationals in respect of the registration of more than 480 EC-defined GIs under the simplified registration procedure.[81] In this respect, Australia refers to the simplified registration procedure provided for in Article 17 of Regulation 2082/92 until its amendment through Regulation 2081/92.

171. With this claim, Australia is once again trying to obtain a retrospective remedy for a measure which is not within the terms of reference of the Panel, and which it did no challenge while it was still in force. All arguments that have been set out in respect of the Claim 8 therefore apply here as well.

172. Moreover, Australia's claim is factually wrong. As the EC has already set out, there was no right of objection for EC residents under the simplified procedure.[82] The fact that there was no right of objection for third-country residents therefore did not constitute a violation of national treatment obligations.

173. Australia's claims must therefore be rejected.

B. PROHIBITED REQUIREMENT OF DOMICILE OR ESTABLISHMENT(ARTICLE 2.1 TRIPS IN CONJUNCTION WITH ARTICLE 2.2 PARIS CONVENTION)

174. The complainants have also raised certain claims under Article 2.1 TRIPS in conjunction with Article 2.2 Paris Convention. Article 2.2 Paris Convention, which prohibits subjecting the enjoyment of intellectual property rights to a condition of domicile or establishment, is a separate and distinct obligation from Article 2.1 of the Paris Convention.

---

[80] Australia's FWS, para. 188.

[81] Australia's FWS, para. 190 et seq.

[82] Supra para. 91 et seq.

175. As the EC has set out, the complainant's claims under Article 2.2 Paris Convention are not within the Panel's terms of reference.[83] This notwithstanding, the EC will hereafter briefly refute certain erroneous arguments made in this respect by the complainants.

1. Claim 10: Regulation 2081/92 requires non-EC nationals to become established in the EC as a condition for registering geographical indications

176. The United States (but not Australia) has argued that Regulation 2081/92 requires non-EC nationals to become established in the EC as a condition for registering geographical indications.[84] This claim is unfounded for the following reasons:

- Geographical indications relating to an area located in a WTO country can be registered under Regulation 2081/92;
- The right to register a geographical indication does not depend on domicile or establishment;
- Article 2.2 Paris Convention does not exclude measures which ensure that a product originates in the geographical to which a protected geographical indication area is related.

(a) Geographical indications relating to an area located in a WTO country can be registered under Regulation 2081/92

177. The United States has based its claim on the assumption that a US national cannot register a geographical indication relating to an area in the United States.[85] The United States claim therefore seems to be based on its assumption that the registration of geographical indications relating to an area outside the EC is possible only if conditions of reciprocity and equivalence of protection systems are fulfilled.

178. As the EC has already explained, the registration of geographical indications relating to an area located in anther WTO Member does not depend on the fulfilment of such conditions.[86] Any geographical indication relating to an area in another WTO Member can be registered if it fulfils the conditions set out in the Regulation.

179. Accordingly, there is no requirement as to domicile or establishment for the registration of geographical indications relating to an area located in a third country. Already for this reason, the United States claim must fail.

(b) The right to register a geographical indication does not depend on domicile or establishment

180. The United States has argued further that a US national could not register a geographical indication relating to an area located in the EC without "having some form of investment or business establishment in the EC."[87]

181. This assumption of the United States is wrong. First of all, not any form of investment or "business establishment" would appear to constitute "an establishment" within the meaning of Article 2.2 of the Paris Convention.

---

[83] See above Section II.B.3.
[84] US FWS, para. 84.
[85] US FWS, para. 85.
[86] Above para. 62 et seq.
[87] US FWS, para. 85.

182. Second, in order for a name to qualify as a geographical indication under Regulation 2081/92, it must "possess a specific quality, reputation or other characteristics attributable to that geographical origin and the production and/or processing and/or preparation of which take place in the defined geographical area."[88]

183. Accordingly, the Regulation does not require that a producer be domiciled or established in the EC. It merely requires that the production, processing or preparation, alternatively or cumulatively, must take place in the defined geographical area. What specific activities of production, processing, or preparation must take place in the specific area will depend on the specifications for the product in question. It cannot be assumed, however, that these specifications will necessarily require a producer to be domiciled or established in the geographical area in question.

(c) Article 2.2 Paris Convention does not exclude measures which ensure that a product originates in the geographical area to which a protected geographical indication is related

184. Moreover, if the argument of the United States were accepted, it would have the effect of rendering the protection of geographical indications as defined in the TRIPS impossible.

185. According to Article 22.1 TRIPS, a geographical indication identifies "a good as originating in the territory of a Member, or a region or locality in that territory, where a given quality, reputation or other characteristic of the good is essentially attributable to its geographical origin." Thus, the definition of a geographical indication in the TRIPS presupposes that the good in question has an identifiable geographical origin.

186. The definition in Regulation 2081/92 that the production and/or processing and/or preparation must take place in the defined geographical area implements this requirement of an identifiable geographical origin. The argument of the United States that this constitutes a requirement of "domicile or establishment" incompatible with Article 2.2 of the Paris Convention is equivalent to saying that a geographical indication should be protected even if the products in question do not originate in the area to which the geographical indication relates.

187. Such an interpretation is incompatible with Article 22.1 TRIPS, and must also for this reason be rejected.

2. Claim 11: Regulation 2081/92 requires non-EC nationals to become established in the EC as a condition for objecting

188. The United States has argued that the fact that Regulation 2081/92 requires the home country of third country nationals to transmit the statement of objection constitutes a requirement of residence or domicile contrary to Article 2.2 of the Paris Convention.[89]

189. This claim is manifestly unfounded. Article 12d(1) of Regulation 2081/92 explicitly allows persons from other WTO countries who are resident or established in third countries to object to registrations. It merely requires that, in close parallelism with the situation for EC residents, the statement of objection be transmitted by the third country in which the person is resident. This procedural modality does not constitute a "requirement of domicile or establishment" for the enjoyment of an industrial property right. Accordingly, this claim must be rejected.

---

[88] Article 2.2 (b) of the Regulation. As has been noted above para. 46, a closer link with the geographical area is required for designations of origin. However, since the procedures for registration and protection of designations of origin are identical to those for geographical indications, the EC will refer only to the latter.

[89] US FWS, para. 91. Australia has raised Article 2.2 Paris Convention in the context of its claims with respect to Regulation 2081/92 as applicable before it was amended by Regulation 692/2003 (Australia's FWS, paras. 189, 194). Like the claims raised under Article 3.1 TRIPS and 2.1 Paris Convention, these claims are outside the terms of reference of the Panel, and therefore need not be considered further (cf. above Section II.A.1).

C. NATIONAL TREATMENT UNDER ARTICLE III:4 GATT

190. The complainants have raised a number of claims alleging that Regulation 2081/92 is incompatible with the national treatment obligation contained in Article III:4 GATT. In this section, the EC will show that Regulation 2081/92 is fully compatible with Article III:4 GATT. In the alternative, the EC considers that the EC measure is justified by Article XX (d) GATT.

1. The regulation 2081/92 is not incompatible with Article III:4 GATT

191. The national treatment obligation contained in Article III:4 GATT provides as follows:

> The products of the territory of any contracting party imported into the territory of any other contracting party shall be accorded treatment no less favourable than that accorded to like products of national origin in respect of all laws, regulations and requirements affecting their internal sale, offering for sale, purchase, transportation, distribution or use. The provisions of this paragraph shall not prevent the application of differential internal transportation charges which are based exclusively on the economic operation of the means of transport and not on the nationality of the product.

192. As the EC will show, Regulation 2081/92 is entirely compatible with this obligation.

(a) General remarks

193. In *Korea – Various Measures on Beef*, the Appellate Body explained that for a violation of Article III:4 to be established, three elements must be satisfied:[90]

> For a violation of Article III:4 to be established, three elements must be satisfied: that the imported and domestic products at issue are "like products;" that the measure at issue is a "law, regulation, or requirement affecting their internal sale, offering for sale, purchase, transportation, distribution, or use;" and that the imported products are accorded "less favourable" treatment than that accorded to like domestic products.

194. The EC does not contest that Regulation 2081/92 is a measure affecting the internal sale of products. However, it considers that some general remarks are necessary on the first and the third condition, namely that products at issue must be "like products," and that the imported products must be accorded "less favourable treatment" than like domestic products.

(i) Like products

195. The EC does not contest that products from third countries falling under the scope of Regulation 2081/92 may be "like" EC products which fall under the scope of that Regulation.

196. The EC would also like to stress, however, that the question of whether products are "like" for the purposes of Article III:4 GATT must be separated from the question of whether the conditions for the registration of individual geographic indications are fulfilled. In the following passage in its first written submission, Australia seems to be merging these two issues:[91]

---

[90] Appellate Body Report, *Korea – Various Measures on Beef*, para. 133.

[91] Australia's FWS, para. 162.

> However, the products in respect of which an EC-defined GI may be registered remain subject to the provisions of Article III:4 of GATT 1994. Thus, within the meaning of GATT Article III:4, for example: imported apples and pears would be like products to "Savoie" apples and pears; imported oysters would be like products to "Whitstable" oysters; imported olive oils would be like product to the many olive oils for which an EC-defined GI has been registered; and imported trout would be like product with "Black Forest" trout.

197. Once again, the EC has no problem in accepting that apples or oysters from Australia may be "like" apples or oysters from the EC. However, the EC would like to remark that this does not mean that the EC cannot apply the conditions for the registration of geographic indications, as long as these conditions do not result in less favourable treatment for imported products.

198. The fact that a domestic measure may distinguish between "like" products without for that reason alone according less favorable treatment, was also explicitly confirmed by the Appellate Body in *EC – Asbestos*:[92]

> We recognize that, by interpreting the term "like products" in Article III:4 in this way, we give that provision a relatively broad product scope—although no broader than the product scope of Article III:2. In so doing, we observe that there is a second element that must be established before a measure can be held to be inconsistent with Article III:4. Thus, even if two products are "like," that does not mean that a measure is inconsistent with Article III:4. A complaining Member must still establish that the measure accords to the group of "like" *imported* products "less favourable treatment" than it accords to the group of "like" *domestic* products. The term "less favourable treatment" expresses the general principle, in Article III:1, that internal regulations "should not be applied ... so as to afford protection to domestic production." If there is "less favourable treatment" of the group of "like" imported products, there is, conversely, "protection" of the group of "like" domestic products. However, a Member may draw distinctions between products which have been found to be "like," without, for this reason alone, according to the group of "like" *imported* products "less favourable treatment" than that accorded to the group of "like" *domestic* products. [...].

(ii) Less favourable treatment

199. In *Korea – Various Measures on Beef*, the Appellate Body has defined the meaning of "less favourable treatment" as follows:[93]

> We observe, however, that Article III:4 requires only that a measure accord treatment to imported products that is "no less favourable" than that accorded to like domestic products. A measure that provides treatment to imported products that is *different* from that accorded to like domestic products is not necessarily inconsistent with Article III:4, as long as the treatment provided by the measure is "no less favourable." According "treatment no less favourable" means, as we have previously said, according *conditions of competition* no less favourable to the imported product than to the like domestic product.

200. The Appellate Body continued as follows:[94]

> A formal difference in treatment between imported and like domestic products is thus neither necessary, nor sufficient, to show a violation of Article III:4. Whether or not imported products are treated "less favourably" than like domestic products should be assessed instead

---

[92] Appellate Body Report, *EC – Asbestos*, para. 100.

[93] Appellate Body Report, *Korea – Various Measures on Beef*, para. 135.

[94] Appellate Body Report, *Korea – Various Measures on Beef*, para. 137.

by examining whether a measure modifies the *conditions of competition* in the relevant market to the detriment of imported products.

201. As the EC will show, Regulation 2081/92 does not modify the conditions of competition to the detriment of imported products.

(b) Claim 12: Regulation 2081/92 accords less favourable treatment as regards the conditions for registration of foreign geographical indications

202. The complainants have claimed that Regulation 2081/92 accords less favourable treatment as regards the conditions for registration of foreign geographical indications by imposing conditions of reciprocity and equivalence.[95]

203. As the EC has already stated above, Regulation 2081/92 does not impose a condition of reciprocity and systemic equivalence for the registration of geographical indications from other WTO Members.[96] Accordingly, it does not apply less favourable treatment to products from other WTO Members.

204. As it has already done in response to the claims under the national treatment provisions of the TRIPS and the Paris Convention,[97] the EC would like to recall, however, that whereas it does not require other WTO Members to have an equivalent system for the protection of geographical indications, it must ensure that indications from third countries comply with the conditions set out in Regulation 2081/92. However, in this respect, the EC treats products from the EC like it treats products from other WTO Members.

205. The claim that Regulation 2081/92 accords less favourable treatments as regards the conditions for registration of foreign geographical indications by imposing conditions of reciprocity and equivalence must therefore be dismissed.

(c) Claim 13: Regulation 2081/92 accords less favourable treatment as regards the requirement that the application must be transmitted by the government of the third country

206. The complainants have argued that Regulation 2081/92 accords less favourable treatment as regards the requirement that the application must be transmitted by the government of the third country.[98]

207. As the EC has already set out above with respect to the national treatment obligations under the TRIPS and the Paris Convention,[99] the role of third country governments provided for in Article 12a of the Regulation corresponds exactly to that of EC Member States where geographical indications relating to an area located in the EC are concerned. Accordingly, the condition that an application relating to an area located in a third country is transmitted by the government in question does not amount to "less favourable treatment," but in fact ensures equal treatment. Moreover, Australia and the United States cannot invoke their own unwillingness to cooperate in the application process in order to argue that Regulation 2081/92 constitutes less favourable treatment for their own nationals.

208. Accordingly, this claim is equally unfounded.

---

[95] US FWS, para. 104; Australia's FWS, para. 165 et seq.

[96] See above, para. 62.

[97] Above para. 113 et seq.

[98] US FWS, para. 104(d); Australia's FWS, para. 172 et seq.

[99] Above para. 127 et seq.

(d) Claim 14: Regulation 2081/92 accords less favourable treatment as regards the requirement to indicate the country of origin

209. The United States (but not Australia) has argued that Regulation 2081/92 accords less favourable treatments as regards the requirement to indicate the country of origin.[100]

210. This claim is unfounded for the following reasons:

- Article 12(2) of Regulation 2081/92 does not apply to all geographical indications, but only to homonyms;
- The requirement to indicate the country of origin for homonymous geographical indications from the EC and third countries does not constitute less favourable treatment;
- Article IX:1 of the GATT is a *lex specialis* to Article III:4 GATT; national treatment obligations therefore do not apply to requirements to mark the country of origin.

(i) Article 12(2) of Regulation 2081/92 does not apply to all geographical indications, but only to homonyms

211. As the EC has already set out in response to the United States' corresponding claim under the TRIPS Agreement, Article 12(2) of Regulation 2081/92 does not apply to all geographical indications, but only to homonyms.[101] Accordingly, there is no requirement to indicate the country of origin for all foreign geographical indications.

(ii) The requirement to indicate the country of origin for homonymous geographical indications from the EC and third countries does not constitute less favourable treatment

212. As the EC has also already explained, Article 12(2) does not only apply to third country names, but applies on equal terms to Community names.[102] Accordingly, Article 12(2) treats foreign and EC goods alike.

(iii) Article IX:1 of the GATT is a lex specialis to Article III:4 GATT; national treatment obligations therefore do not apply to requirements to mark the country of origin

213. Finally, it should be noted that marks of origin are dealt with in Article IX of the GATT. Article IX:1 provides as follows:

> Each contracting party shall accord to the products of the territories of other contracting parties treatment with regard to marking requirements no less favourable than the treatment accorded to like products of any third country.

214. It is noteworthy that Article IX GATT contains, with respect to marks of origin, exclusively an obligation to provide most-favoured nation treatment. It does not contain an obligation to also provide national treatment. This has been confirmed by the GATT Panel in *US – Tuna*:[103]

> The Panel noted that the title of Article IX is 'Marks of Origin' and its text refers to marking of origin of imported products. The Panel further noted that Article IX does not contain a

[100] US FWS, para. 106. Australia has made a similar claim under Article 2.1 of the TBT Agreement, which will be discussed below (cf. Australia's FWS, para. 234).
[101] Above para. 133.
[102] Above para. 134.
[103] Panel Report, *US – Import Restrictions on Tuna*, para. 5.41.

> national-treatment but only a most-favoured-nation requirement, which indicates that this provision was intended to regulate marking of origin of imported products but not marking of products generally. The Panel therefore found that the labelling provisions of the DPCIA did not fall under Article IX:1.

215. This omission in Article IX:1 cannot be regarded as accidental. If the GATT had meant to also impose a national treatment obligation with respect to marks of origin, it would have been natural to include such an obligation in Article IX. Alternatively, Article IX could have remained silent on the issue of national and most-favoured nation treatment, in which case the general obligations contained in Articles I and III of the GATT would have applied.

216. By laying down an obligation only to provide most-favoured nation treatment and not also national treatment, Article IX implies that WTO members are free to impose country of origin marking only with respect to imported products and not to domestic products. This understanding is also confirmed by a report of a GATT working party:[104]

> The Working Party considered that the question of additional marking requirements, such as an obligation to add the name of the producer or the place of origin or the formula of the product, should not be brought within the scope of any recommendation dealing with the problem of marks of origin. The point was stressed that <u>requirements going beyond the obligation to indicate origin would not be consistent with the requirements of Article III, if the same requirements did not apply to domestic producers of like products</u>.

217. For these reasons, Article III:4 is not applicable to requirements to indicate the country of origin for an imported product.

218. For all the reasons set out, the EC submits that the United States claim must be rejected.

(e) Claim 15: Regulation 2081/92 accords less favourable treatment due to an overall bias in the decision-making process

219. Australia has argued that Regulation 2081/92 accords less favourable treatment in that there is an overall bias in the decision-making process due to the alleged fact:[105]

> that the outcome of the application is to be determined through a process, that is, the Committee of EC Member State representatives, in which:
>
> - there is no representative or advocate for the registration of an EC-defined GI for an imported product; and
> - there is no requirement for procedural fairness, due process and/or transparency concerning that Committee's decision-making process.

220. First of all, this claim is based on a misunderstanding of the decision-making process under the Regulation. As the EC has already explained, the decision-maker under the Regulation is the Commission, or exceptionally the Council.[106] The Committee merely assists the Commission, and may exceptionally achieve that a proposal is referred to the Council.

---

[104] L/595, adopted on 17 November 1956, 5S/102, 105-106, para. 13 (emphasis added).

[105] Australia's FWS, para. 177.

[106] Above, para. 79.

221. Secondly, as the EC has already argued, Australia's claim to a have representative on the regulatory committee is manifestly unfounded.[107]

222. Finally, the Australian statement that there is "no requirement for procedural fairness, due process and/or transparency" concerning the decision-making process of the Committee is completely unsupported by fact.

223. For these reasons, the Australian claim must be rejected.

2. The measure would be justified under Article XX (d) GATT

224. As explained, it is unclear to the EC whether the complainants claim that the requirements imposed by Article 12a, in conjunction with Articles 4 and 10, of Regulation 2081/92 with respect to the registration of each specific geographical indication are as such incompatible with Article III:4 of the GATT. The EC has shown that those requirements do not provide less favourable treatment to imported like products and, therefore, are consistent with that provision.

225. In the event that the complainants were to claim that such requirements are inconsistent with Article III:4 of the GATT, and should the Panel find that they afford less favourable treatment to imported products, the EC submits in the alternative that such requirements would be justified under Article XX(d) of the GATT.

226. More specifically, the EC submits that the requirements at issue are necessary in order to ensure that only those products which conform to the definition of geographical indications contained in Article 2(2) of Regulation 2081/92, which is itself fully consistent with the GATT, benefit from the protection afforded to geographical indications by Regulation 2081/92.

V. REGULATION 2081/92 IS COMPATIBLE WITH THE OBLIGATION TO PROVIDE MOST-FAVOURED-NATION TREATMENT

227. The United States (but not Australia)[108] has claimed that Regulation 2081/92 is incompatible with the obligation to provide most-favoured-nation treatment under Article 4 TRIPS and Article I:1 GATT. The EC will discuss the United States claims under both provisions separately.

A. ARTICLE 4 TRIPS

228. The United States has made two claims under the most-favoured-nation provision of Article 4 TRIPS:

- As among non-EC WTO Members, nationals from WTO Members that satisfy the EC's conditions of reciprocity and equivalency are accorded more favourable treatment than nationals from those WTO Members that do not;

- under Regulation 2081/92, an EC Member State grants more favourable treatment to nationals from other EC Member States than it accords to nationals from non-EC WTO Members.

[107] Above, para. 155.

[108] Australia has not made any claim in this respect, but has reserved the "right to pursue such a claim" in the event that the EC "is applying" or "begins to apply Community-wide protection to EC-defined GIs for foodstuffs and agricultural products from another WTO Member" (Australia's FWS, para. 65).

1. Claim 16: As among non-EC WTO Members, nationals from WTO Members that satisfy the EC's conditions of reciprocity and equivalency are accorded more favourable treatment than nationals from those WTO Members that do not

229. The United States has claimed that nationals from WTO Members that satisfy the EC's conditions of reciprocity and equivalency are accorded more favourable treatment than nationals from those WTO Members that do not.[109]

230. This claim is unfounded for the following reasons:

- the EC does not apply a condition of reciprocity and equivalence for the registration of geographical indications from other WTO members;
- the conditions for the registration of individual geographical indications from third countries are not discriminatory;
- Article 12 of Regulation 2081/92 does not grant any advantage, favour, privilege or immunity to any other country;
- the conditions for the registration of geographical indications do not depend on nationality.

(a) The EC does not apply a condition of reciprocity and equivalence for the registration of geographical indications from other WTO members

231. Article 4 TRIPS requires that "with regard to the protection of intellectual property, any advantage, favour, privilege or immunity granted by a Member to the nationals of any other country shall be accorded immediately and unconditionally to the nationals of all other Members."

232. As the EC has already explained, it does not apply a condition of reciprocity and equivalence to the registration of geographical indications from other WTO Members.[110] Accordingly, geographical indications relating to an area located in another WTO country can be registered under Regulation 2081/92 in accordance with Article 12a and 12b of Regulation 2081/92.

233. In contrast, the conditions of Article 12(1) and 12(3) are applicable for the registration of geographical indications from third countries which are not WTO Members. Moreover, it should be recalled that Article 4 TRIPS does not require that benefits are extended to third countries which are not WTO Members.

234. Accordingly, Regulation 2081/92 does not treat nationals of other WTO Members less favourable than those of other third countries.

(b) The conditions for the registration of individual geographical indications from third countries are not discriminatory

235. As in respect of the claims regarding national treatment, the EC is not sure whether the United States also challenges the product-specific conditions for the registration of geographical indications from third countries.

236. However, if it does, such a claim would have to be regarded as unfounded. The conditions for the registration of individual geographical indications, and in particular the requirement of a product specification

---

[109] US FWS, para. 119.

[110] Above para. 62 et seq.

and the existence of inspection structures, do not discriminate on the basis of nationality or product origin. Moreover, they are examined for each product individually.

237. In this context, it is useful to recall the Panel report in *Canada – Autos*, which stated that most-favoured nation treatment does not exclude subjecting advantages to conditions, as long as these conditions are non-discriminatory:[111]

> In this respect, it appears to us that there is an important distinction to be made between, on the one hand, the issue of whether an advantage within the meaning of Article I:1 is subject to conditions, and on the other, whether an advantage, once it has been granted to the product of any country, is accorded "unconditionally" to the like product of other Members. An advantage can be granted subject to conditions without necessarily implying that it is not accorded "unconditionally" to the like product of other Members. More specifically, the fact that conditions attached to such an advantage are not related to the imported product itself does not necessarily imply that such conditions are discriminatory with respect to the origin of imported products. We therefore do not believe that, as argued by Japan, the word "unconditionally" in Article I:1 must be interpreted to mean that making an advantage conditional on criteria not related to the imported product itself is *per se* inconsistent with Article I:1, irrespective of whether and how such criteria relate to the origin of the imported products.

238. Accordingly, the application of the conditions for the registration of individual geographical indications from other WTO Members is not incompatible with most-favoured-nation principles.

(c) Article 12 of Regulation 2081/92 does not grant any advantage, favour, privilege or immunity to any other country

239. Second, Article 12 of Regulation 2081/92 does not involve the granting of any advantage to a third country.[112]

240. Article 12(1) of Regulation 2081/92 provides the conditions under which the Regulation may apply to a third country which is not a WTO Member. In accordance with Article 12(3) of the Regulation, the Commission must examine whether the conditions in Article 12(1) are fulfilled. The conditions set out in Article 12(1) are the same for all third countries which fall under this provision. In the absence of a decision under Article 12(3) of the Regulation, Article 12 does not confer any advantage onto a third country.

241. In support of its claim, the United States has referred to the GATT Panel Report in *Belgian Family Allowances*.[113] However, this Panel report does not support the proposition of the United States. In this case, Belgium had in fact granted an exception from a certain levy to a number of third countries.[114] This resembled the situation in *EEC – Imports of Beef from Canada*, where the Panel found as follows:[115]

> The Panel further found that exports of like products of other origin than that of United States were in effect denied access to the EEC market considering that the only certifying agency authorized to certify the meat described in Article 1(1)(d), listed in Annex II of the

[111] Panel Report, *Canada – Autos*, para. 10.24.

[112] The EC notes that Australia seems to share this view, since it reserves to make a claim in regard to most-favoured-nation treatment only in the event that the EC "is applying" or "begins to apply Community-wide protection to EC-defined GIs for foodstuffs and agricultural products from another WTO Member" (Australia's FWS, para. 65).

[113] US FWS, para. 115.

[114] Panel Report, *Belgian Family Allowances*, para. 3.

[115] Panel Report, *EEC – Imports of Beef from Canada*, paras. 4.2–4.3.

> Commission Regulation, was a United States agency mandated to certify only meat from the United States.
>
> (b) The Panel further found that the mention "Beef graded USDA 'choice', or 'prime' automatically meets the definition above" could accord an advantage to products of United States' origin in so far as other like products were not mentioned in the same manner. The Panel found, however, that only the practical application of the Commission Regulation would make it possible to judge whether this mention in itself was inconsistent with Article I of the General Agreement.
>
> 4.3 The Panel concluded that Commission Regulation (EEC) No. 2972/79 and its Annex II, in their present form had the effect of preventing access of "like products" from other origin than the United States, thus being inconsistent with the most-favoured-nation principle in Article I of the General Agreement.

242. In both cases, it was the granting of concrete advantages to <u>specific countries</u> which led the Panels to find a violation of the most-favoured-nation principle. This is fundamentally different from the situation under Article 12 of Regulation 2081/92, which merely provides for the conditions under which Regulation 2081/92 may apply to geographical indications from third countries which are not WTO members.

243. The United States has also referred to a Joint Declaration of the European Community and Switzerland made on occasion of the signature of the Agreement between the European Community and Switzerland on Trade in Agricultural Products.[116] This declaration reads in full as follows:[117]

> The European Community and Switzerland (hereinafter referred to as "the Parties") hereby agree that the mutual protection of designations of origin (PDOs) and geographical indications (PGIs) is essential for the liberalisation of trade in agricultural products and foodstuffs between the Parties. The <u>incorporation of provisions relating thereto in the bilateral Agreement on trade in agricultural products is a necessary addition</u> to Annex 7 to the Agreement on trade in wine-sector products, and in particular Title II thereof, which provides for the mutual protection of the names of such products, and to Annex 8 to the Agreement on the mutual recognition and protection of names of spirit drinks and aromatised wine-based drinks.
>
> The Parties shall provide for provisions on the mutual protection of PDOs and PGIs to be incorporated in the Agreement on trade in agricultural products on the basis of equivalent legislation, as regards both the conditions governing the registration of PDOs and PGIs and the arrangements on controls. <u>The incorporation of those provisions should take place on a date which is acceptable to both Parties</u>, and not before Article 17 of Council Regulation (EEC) No 2081/92 has been fully applied as regards the Community as constituted at present. <u>In the meantime, the Parties shall keep each other informed of their work in this area while taking legal constraints into account</u>.

244. This declaration is merely a political declaration stating the intention of the parties to incorporate, at a later stage, provisions on the protection on geographical indications into the Agreement on Trade in Agricultural Products. No such provisions have so far been incorporated into the Agreement between the EC and Switzerland. This declaration is therefore irrelevant for the purposes of the present dispute.

245. Accordingly, Article 12 of Regulation 2081/92 does not grant any advantage, favour, privilege or immunity to any other country.

---

[116] US FWS, para. 119.

[117] Exhibit US-6 (emphasis added).

(d) The conditions for the registration of geographical indications do not depend on nationality

246. Finally, as the United States has recognised itself,[118] Article 4 TRIPS establishes a most-favoured-nation obligation as regards the treatment of nationals, whereas Article I:1 GATT establishes a most-favoured-nation obligation with respect to products. As the EC has set out above, this difference between the TRIPS and the GATT is not accidental, but results from the different object and purpose of both agreements.[119]

247. Furthermore, as the EC has already set out with respect to the claims regarding national treatment under the TRIPS, whether a geographical indication can be registered under Regulation 2081/92 does not depend in any way on nationality.[120] In particular, Articles 12a and 12b govern the registration of geographical indications where the area to which the indication is related is located outside the EC, and this irrespective of the nationality of producers. This means that where a geographical indication from a third country is protected under the Regulation, this protection also extends to producers which are nationals of other third countries.

248. For all the reasons set out above, the United States claim must be rejected.

2. Claim 17: Under Regulation 2081/92, an EC Member State grants more favourable treatment to nationals from other EC Member States than it accords to nationals from non-EC WTO Members

249. The United States has claimed that under Regulation 2081/92, an EC Member State grants more favourable treatment to nationals from other EC Member States than it accords to nationals from non-EC WTO Members.[121]

250. In the view of the EC, this argument must fail already because under Regulation 2081/92, geographical indications from third countries which are WTO Members are protected on the same terms as geographical indications from other Member States.[122]

251. Secondly, as the EC has already set out, the conditions for the registration of geographical indications do not depend on nationality.[123] Accordingly, the EC is not discriminating between third-country nationals on the basis of nationality.

252. Finally, it should be noted that Article 4 TRIPS requires WTO Members to extend to other Members the advantages, favours, privileges or immunities that they grant to "the nationals of <u>any other country</u>." However, through Regulation 2081/92, the EC is not granting an advantage to the national of "any other country."

253. Regulation 2081/92 is a measure which the EC has adopted on the basis of its own competences, and which applies throughout the EC. In accordance with Articles IX:1 and XIV:1 of the WTO Agreement, the European Community is an original member of the WTO. Measures with which the EC harmonises the law inside the European Community can therefore not regarded as granting advantages to "other countries."

254. The fact that the EC Member States are also Members to the WTO[124] is irrelevant in this respect. The measure at issue is a Regulation adopted by the EC. It is not a measure of the Member States. Accordingly, it cannot be said that through Regulation 2081/92, Member States are granting one another "advantages."

---

[118] US FWS, para. 108.

[119] Above para. 104.

[120] Above para. 123 et seq.

[121] US FWS, para. 121.

[122] Above para. 134 et seq.

[123] Above, para. 137.

255. Finally, since the measure at issue is an EC measure, the subject matter of the present dispute falls within the exclusive competence of the EC, and not of the Member States. The United States has accepted this by correctly bringing the present dispute settlement proceedings against the EC. It can therefore not now raise a claim assuming a violation of most-favoured-nation-obligations on the part of the EC Member States.

256. Accordingly, this claim of the United States must be rejected.

B. CLAIM 18: BY SUBJECTING THE REGISTRATION OF THIRD-COUNTRY GEOGRAPHICAL INDICATIONS TO CONDITIONS OF RECIPROCITY AND EQUIVALENCE, THE EC MEASURE IS INCONSISTENT WITH THE MOST-FAVOURED-NATION OBLIGATION UNDER THE ARTICLE I:1 GATT

257. The United States has argued that by subjecting the registration of third-country geographical indications to conditions of reciprocity and equivalence, the EC measure is inconsistent with the most-favoured-nation obligation under Article I:1 GATT.[125]

1. Article I:1 GATT is not violated

258. Contrary to the claim of the United States, there is no violation of Article I:1 GATT.

259. Article I:1 GATT requires in relevant part that "[...] with respect to all matters referred to in paragraphs 2 and 4 of Article III, any advantage, favour, privilege or immunity granted by any contracting party to any product originating in or destined for any other country shall be accorded immediately and unconditionally to the like product originating in or destined for the territories of all other contracting parties."

260. As the EC has already set out with respect to Article 4 TRIPS, Regulation 2081/92 does not involve any less favourable treatment of WTO members compared to other third countries.

261. First of all, the EC does not apply a condition of reciprocity and equivalence for the registration of geographical indications from other WTO members, which can therefore be registered as geographical indications under the conditions set out in Regulation 2081/92.[126]

262. Secondly, as the EC has also explained, the conditions for the registration of geographical indications from third countries are not discriminatory.[127]

263. Finally, as the EC has also set out, Article 12 of Regulation 2081/92 does not grant any advantage, favour, privilege or immunity, but merely sets out the conditions under which geographical indications from third countries other than WTO members may be registered.[128]

264. For these reasons, Regulation 2081/92 is not incompatible with Article I:1 GATT.

2. The EC measure would be justified under Article XX (d) GATT

265. It is unclear to the EC whether the complainants claim that the requirements imposed by Article 12a, in conjunction with Articles 4 and 10, of Regulation 2081/92 with respect to the registration of each specific geographical indication are as such incompatible with Article I:1 of the GATT. As shown above, the EC considers that those requirements are fully consistent with Article I:1 of the GATT.

---

[124] US FWS para. 121.

[125] US FWS para. 127 et seq.

[126] Above para. 231 et seq.

[127] Above para. 235 et seq.

[128] Above para. 239 et seq.

266. In the event that the complainants were to claim that such requirements are inconsistent with Article I:1 of the GATT, and should the Panel find that they are inconsistent with that provision, the EC submits in the alternative that such requirements would be justified under Article XX(d) of the GATT, for the same reasons already advanced in connection with the complainants' claim under Article III:4 of the GATT.

VI. REGULATION 2081/92 DOES NOT DIMINISH THE LEGAL PROTECTION OF TRADEMARKS

267. The complainants have raised a number of claims to the effect that Regulation 2081/92 diminishes the legal protection of trademarks. The EC will show hereunder that these claims are unfounded.

A. ARTICLE 16.1 OF THE TRIPS AGREEMENT

1. Claim 19: Article 14(2) of Regulation 2081/92 is inconsistent with Article 16.1 of the TRIPS Agreement in that it allows the co-existence of geographical indications and earlier registered trademarks

268. The complainants claim that Article 14(2) of Regulation 2081/92 is inconsistent with Article 16.1 of the TRIPS Agreement in that it allows the "co-existence" of a registered geographical indication and a prior similar or identical registered trademark for similar or identical goods, which results in a likelihood of confusion. [129]

269. As will be shown in this section, this claim is unfounded for several reasons.

270. First, this claim is based on a misunderstanding of the relevant provisions of Regulation 2081/92. Contrary to the complainants' assumption, Article 14(3) of Regulation 2081/92 prevents the registration of geographical indications that would result in a likelihood of confusion with an earlier trademark. Thus, as a matter of fact, the situation alleged by the complainants does not even arise.

271. Second, the exclusivity conferred upon the trademark owners by Article 16.1 of the TRIPS Agreement is without prejudice to the protection that Members are entitled to accord to geographical indications in accordance with Part II, Section 3, of the TRIPS Agreement. The boundary between a Member's right to protect geographical indications and its obligation to protect trademarks is defined by Article 24.5 of the TRIPS, which provides for the co-existence of geographical indications and earlier trademarks. Article 14(2) of Regulation 2081/92 is fully consistent with Article 24.5.

272. Third, irrespective of whether the co-existence of geographical indications and earlier trademarks is permitted by Article 24.5, the EC is required to maintain such co-existence by virtue of Article 24.3 of the TRIPS Agreement, a "stand-still" provision that prohibits Members from diminishing the level of protection of GIs that existed at the time of entry into force of the WTO Agreement.

273. Finally, even assuming that Article 14(2) of Regulation 2081/92 were *prima facie* inconsistent with Article 16.1, it would be justified as a "limited exception" to the trademark owner's exclusive rights under Article 17 of the TRIPS Agreement.

(a) Regulation 2081/92 does not allow the registration of confusing trademarks

274. The exclusivity conferred by Article 16.1 of the TRIPS Agreement is not absolute. That provision does not grant to the owner of a registered trademark a right to prevent any possible use of the same or a similar sign, but only its use for identical or similar goods, "where such use would result in a likelihood of confusion."

---

[129] Australia's FWS, paras. 100-107. US FWS, paras. 130-170.

275. As will be shown below, because of the criteria of registrability applied under EC trademark law, the risk of confusion between trademarks and geographical indications is very limited *a priori*. To the extent that those criteria do not preclude such possibility, the problem is addressed adequately by Article 14(3) of Regulation 2081/92, which provides that

> A designation of origin or geographical indication shall not be registered where, in the light of a trademark's reputation and renown and the length of time it has been used, registration is liable to mislead the consumer as to the true identity of the product.

276. The complainants have erroneously characterized Article 14(3) as a "narrow exception."[130] As explained below, the terms of Article 14(3), if properly interpreted, are sufficient to prevent the registration of any confusing geographical indications.

277. According to their own interpretation of Article 16.1 of the TRIPS Agreement, in order to establish a violation of that provision, the complainants would need to prove that Regulation 2081/92 mandates necessarily the registration of confusing geographical indications. The complainants have failed to do so. Indeed, the complainants have not even shown that the actual application of Regulation 2081/92 has resulted occasionally in the registration of confusing geographical indications. As of the date of establishment of this Panel, the EC authorities had registered more than 600 geographical indications. The complainants have not alleged, let alone proved, that any of those geographical indications has resulted in a likelihood of confusion with any prior registered trademark. The complainant's claim is purely theoretical and, as will be shown below, unfounded.

(i) Registrability of geographical names as trademarks

278. The purpose of a trademark is to distinguish the goods or services of one undertaking from those of other undertakings. A sign that cannot fulfil this function, i.e. a sign which is not "distinctive," cannot be registered as a trademark. Thus, Article 15.1 of the TRIPS Agreement provides that

> Any sign, or any combination of signs, capable of distinguishing the goods or services of one undertaking from those of other undertakings, shall be capable of constituting a trademark.[131]

279. Geographical names are primarily "non-distinctive" and, as such, non apt for registration as trademarks.[132] For example, the name "Australia," if used as a trademark by an undertaking, would not allow to distinguish the goods of that undertaking from those of any other Australian undertaking selling the same or similar products. Moreover, the use of geographical names as trademarks may be deceptive in so far as they are used for goods which do not originate in the location designated by that name. For example, the name "Australia," if used as a trademark for US goods, could mislead the consumers as regards the origin of the goods.

---

[130] US FWS, para. 158.

[131] Similarly, Article 6*quinquies* B (2) of the Paris Convention (1967) provides that the registration of trademarks may be denied "when they are devoid of any distinctive character."

[132] Article 6*quinquies* B of the Paris Convention (1967) provides that trademarks may be denied registration when

2. … they consist exclusively of signs or indications which may serve, in trade, to designate the … place of origin;
3. when they are … of such a nature as to deceive the public.

280. For the above reasons, the registration of geographical names as trademarks is subject to restrictions in all countries.[133] Broadly speaking, it is permitted only in two situations: first, where consumers would not expect the goods to be produced in that place; and, second, where the name has become distinctive through use. In other words, when, as a result of its continued use by an undertaking, the geographical name acquires a "secondary meaning," so that consumers do not associate it with a geographical location but instead with the undertaking in question.[134] This possibility is expressly envisaged in the second sentence of Article 15.1 of the TRIPS Agreement, which provides that

> Where signs are not inherently capable of distinguishing the relevant goods or services, Members may make registrability depend on distinctiveness acquired through use.

281. Like in other jurisdictions, in the EC the registration of geographical names as trademarks is permitted only exceptionally. Article 3.1 of the Trademarks Directive provides that the following shall not be registered or, if registered, shall be liable to be declared invalid:

> (b) trade marks which are devoid of any distinctive character;
>
> (c) trade marks which consist exclusively of signs or indications which may serve, in trade, to designate ... the geographical origin;
>
> (g) trade marks which are of such nature as to deceive the public, for instance as to the ... geographical origin of the goods...[135]

282. The European Court of Justice has held that:

> under Article 3(1)(c) of the Directive, the competent authority must assess whether a geographical name in respect of which application for registration as a trade mark is made designates a place which is currently associated in the mind of the relevant class of persons with the category of goods concerned, or whether it is reasonable to assume that such an association may be established in the future.[136]

283. By way of exception to letters (b) and (c) of Article 3.1 (but not to letter (g)), Article 3.3 of the Trademarks Directive provides that geographical names that are primarily non-distinctive may be registered where they have become distinctive through use:

---

[133] Section 2 of the US Lanham Act prohibits the registration of trademarks that, when used in connection with the goods of the applicant, are "primarily geographically descriptive," unless they have become distinctive through use, or "primarily geographically deceptively misdescriptive" (15 USC. 1052 (e) and (f)). (Exhibit EC-6).
Similarly, Australia's Trade Marks Act of 1995 prohibits the registration of trademarks that are not "inherently adapted to distinguish goods or services" unless they have become distinctive through use. Trademarks that are not "inherently adapted to distinguish goods or services" include "trade marks that consist wholly of a sign that is ordinarily used to indicate: (a) the ... geographical origin... " (Section 41(6) Note 1 (a)) (Exhibit EC-7)

[134] A well known example of trademark consisting of a geographical name which has become distinctive through use in some countries is "Budweiser." After much litigation in the United States, it was deemed to have acquired secondary meaning in that country, so that it could be registered as a trademark. See Albrecht Conrad, "The Protection of Geographical Indications in the TRIPS Agreement," 86 *The Trademark Reporter*, p.43.

[135] Similarly, Article 7(1) of the Community Trademark Regulation provides that:
The following shall not be registered:
(b) trade marks which are devoid of any distinctive character;
(c) trademarks which consist exclusively of signs or indications which may serve, in trade, to designate the...geographical origin of the goods or service;
...
(g) trade marks which are of such a nature as to deceive the public, for instance as to the ... geographical origin of the goods or service;

[136] Judgement of the European Court of Justice of 4 May 1999, C-108/97 and C-109/97, *Chiemsee*, ECR [1999] I-2779, para. 37. (Exhibit EC-8).

> A trademark shall not be refused registration or be declared invalid in accordance with paragraph 1 (b), (c) or (d) if , before the date of application for registration and following the use which has been made of it, it has acquired a distinctive character.[137]

284. In sum, under EC law, the registration of a geographical name as a trademark is possible only in the following circumstances:

- where the geographical name is not currently associated, and it can be reasonably assumed that it will not be associated in the future, with the product concerned; or

- where the name has acquired distinctiveness through use.

285. In principle, any geographical name which qualifies, or may reasonably qualify in the future, as a "designation of origin" or a "geographical indication" within the meaning of Article 2(2) of Regulation 2081/92, will not fall within the first situation. Thus, it may be concluded that, in practice, a geographical indication, or a geographical name with the potential to become a geographical indication, may not be validly registered as a trademark unless it has become distinctive through use.

(ii) Article 14(3) of Regulation 2081/92

286. The complainants' claim is based on an unwarrantedly narrow interpretation of Article 14(3) of Regulation 2081/92. When properly interpreted, that provision allows the registering authorities to refuse the registration of any confusing geographical indications.

287. Australia does not even attempt to interpret the terms of Article 14(3). For its part, the United States declares it to be a "narrow exception" [138] after a cursory analysis. Moreover, the United States reaches that conclusion by reading into Article 14(3) additional requirements which are not stated in that provision. Thus, according to the United States, this provision would exclude the registration of a geographical indication "only where the trademark has been used for *a long time* and has a *considerable* reputation or renown."[139] Neither of those two qualifications is provided in Article 14(3).

288. Article 14(3) has been applied only once by the EC authorities since Regulation 2081/92 came into force.[140] It has never been interpreted by the European Court Justice or by the courts of the Member States. This confirms that, as explained above, the criteria for the registrability of trademarks ensure that the potential for conflicts between trademarks and geographical indications is indeed very limited.

289. The EC Commission considers that the criteria listed in Article 14(3) are not limitative. The registering authority may take into account also other relevant criteria in order to assess whether the registration of the geographical indication will result in a likelihood of confusion. For example, it is obvious that the degree of similarity between the signs or between the goods concerned is always relevant in assessing the likelihood of confusion between two signs for goods. Nevertheless, given that geographical names are primarily non-distinctive as trademarks, the two criteria specified in Article 14(3) will often be of particular relevance in practice. It is for that reason, and not because they are the only relevant criteria, that the registering authorities are directed expressly to consider those two criteria.

---

[137] Similarly, Article 7 (3) of the Community Trademark Regulation provides that
Paragraph 1(b), (c) and (d) shall not apply if the trade mark has become distinctive in relation to the goods or services for which registration is required in consequence of the use which has been made of it.

[138] US FWS, para. 158.

[139] Ibid.

[140] In that case, the EC Council concluded that the registration of the GI "Bayerisches Bier" was not likely to lead to confusion with the existing trademarks "Bavaria" and "Hoker Bajer;" Council Regulation (EC) No 1347, of 28 June 2001, OJ (2001) L 182. (Exhibit EC-9).

290. It is well-established that the more distinctive the trademark the greater the likelihood that consumers will confuse another sign with that trademark[141]. As explained above, geographical names are primarily non-distinctive. Thus, the degree of distinctiveness and, consequently, the likelihood that it may be confused with a geographical indication will depend to a large extent on the degree of distinctiveness which the trademark has acquired through use. In turn, the basic criteria to measure such acquired distinctiveness are the length of time during which the trademark has been used and the extent of the reputation or renown acquired as a result of such use.

291. Consumers are unlikely to confuse a geographical indication with a trademark that has never been used and/or has no reputation or renown simply because the signs and/or the goods concerned are similar. In fact, as explained above, a trademark consisting of a geographical indication, which has never been used or which has no reputation or renown, should not have been registered in the first place because it would lack the required distinctiveness.

(iii) Provisional conclusion

292. In order to substantiate their claim that Article 14(2) of Regulation 2081/92 is inconsistent with Article 16.1 of the TRIPS Agreement, the complainants should have established that Regulation 2081/92 mandates necessarily the registration of later confusing geographical indications. In turn, this would have required them to show that Article 14(3) cannot be interpreted in a manner which allows the registering authorities to refuse the registration of confusing geographical indications, or, at the very least, that, in practice, Article 14(3) is being interpreted and applied in a manner which results in the registration of confusing geographical indications. The complainants have proved neither.

293. Therefore, the Panel should conclude that, as a matter of fact, the complainants' claim is unfounded even on their own interpretation of Article 16.1 of the TRIPS Agreement. In any event, as discussed below, that interpretation is incorrect.

(b) Article 24.5 envisages the co-existence of GIs and earlier trademarks

294. The complainants' claim rests on a misconception of the relationship between trademarks and geographical indications, as well as between Article 16.1 and Part II, Section 3, of the TRIPS Agreement. The TRIPS Agreement recognises geographical indications as intellectual property rights, on the same level as trademarks. It confers no superiority to trademarks over geographical indications. Nor are the provisions of Part II, Section 3, "exceptions" to Article 16.1. There is no hierarchy between them.

295. In an attempt to establish the superiority of trademarks over geographical indications, the complainants emphasise that exclusivity is an essential feature of trademarks. It is, of course, correct that trademarks are exclusive rights. But from this it does not follow that trademarks must prevail over geographical indications. Geographical indications are also exclusive rights, because their basic purpose, like that of trademarks, is to distinguish the goods from a certain source. The fact that geographical indications are collective rights does not render their exclusivity less indispensable. If any producer of cheese could use the term "Roquefort," the geographical indication "Roquefort" could not fulfil its distinctive function and would be deprived of its economic value.

296. As explained above, the criteria for the registrability of trademarks limit *a priori* the possibility of conflicts between geographical indications and trademarks. However, to the extent that geographical indications may exceptionally be validly registered as trademarks, there may arise conflicts between the exclusivity of those two types of intellectual property rights. The question before the Panel is, therefore, how to resolve those conflicts.

---

[141] Judgement of the European Court of Justice of 11 November 1997, C – 251/95, *Sabel*, para. 24. (Exhibit EC-10).

297. Article 16.1 does not address this issue. More specifically, and contrary to the complainants' claims, Article 16.1 contains no provision to the effect that trademarks must prevail over later geographical indications. The complainants argue that the right conferred by Article 16.1 to the trademark owner in order to prevent the confusing use of identical or similar "signs" for identical or similar goods applies also with respect to later geographical indications, because geographical indications are "signs." True, geographical indications consist of a special type of "sign:" words or other signs with a geographical connotation. But they are more than mere "signs." They are a distinct intellectual property right, with a specific subject matter and a specific function, different from those of trademarks, which Members are entitled to protect under their domestic laws and which, indeed, they are required to protect under Part II, Section 3, of the TRIPS Agreement.

298. The boundary between geographical indications and trademarks is not defined in Article 16.1, but instead in Article 24.5 of the TRIPS Agreement. Therefore, the WTO consistency of Article 14(2) of Regulation 2081/92 must be determined in relation to that provision, and not with respect to Article 16.1.

299. Article 24.5 provides that

> Where a trademark has been applied for or registered in good faith, or where rights to a trademark have been acquired through use in good faith either:
>
> (a) before the date of application of these provisions in that member as defined in Part VI; or
>
> (b) before the geographical indication is protected in its country of origin;
>
> measures adopted to implement this Section shall not prejudice eligibility for or the validity of the registration of a trademark, or the right to use a trademark, on the basis that such trademark is identical with, or similar to, a geographical indication.

300. Article 24.5 must be read together with Articles 22.3[142] and 23.2[143], which require that the registration of trademarks must be refused or invalidated in certain situations. Those two provisions, however, do not exhaust the protection afforded to geographical indications vis-à-vis trademarks. Right holders of geographical indications can invoke also Articles 22.2[144] and 23.1[145] in order to prevent the use of a trademark (whether registered or non-registered) in the circumstances described in those provisions. In addition, in implementing

---

[142] Article 22.3 of the TRIPS Agreement provides that:

A Member shall, *ex officio* if its legislation so permits, or at the request of an interested party, refuse or invalidate the registration of a trademark which contains or consists of a geographical indication with respect to goods not originating in the territory indicated, if use of the indication in the trademark for such goods in that Member is of such nature as to mislead the public as to the true place of origin.

[143] Article 23.2 of the TRIPS Agreement provides that:

The registration of a trademark for wines which contains or consists of a geographical indication identifying wines or for spirits which contains or consists of a geographical indication identifying spirits shall be refused or invalidated, *ex officio* if a Member's legislation so permits or at the request of an interested party, with respect to such wines or spirits not having this origin.

[144] Article 22.2 of the TRIPS Agreement provides that:

In respect of geographical indications, Members shall provide the legal means for interested parties to prevent:

(a) the use of any means in the designation or presentation of a good that indicates or suggests that the good in question originates in a geographical area other than the true place of origin in a manner which misleads the public as to the geographical origin of the good;

(b) any use which constitutes an act of unfair competition within the meaning of Article 10*bis* of the Paris Convention (1967).

[145] Article 23.1 of the TRIPS Agreement provides that:

Each Member shall provide the legal means for interested parties to prevent use of a geographical indication identifying wines for wines not originating in the place indicated by the geographical indication in question or identifying spirits for spirits not originating in the place indicated by the geographical indication in question, even where the true origin of the goods is indicated or the geographical indication is used in translation or accompanied by expressions such as "kind," "type," "style," "imitation" or the like. [footnote omitted]

Part II, Section 3, Members are entitled to provide more extensive protection for geographical indications, in accordance with Article 1.1 of the TRIPS Agreement.

301. Article 24.5 has two implications:

- with respect to grandfathered trademarks (or applications for trademarks), Members are not allowed to *prejudice* the validity of the registration (or the eligibility of the application) or the "right to use the trademark," but they may *prejudice* other rights of the trademark owner, including in particular the right to prevent others from using the sign of which the trademark consists.

- with respect to other trademarks (or applications for trademarks), Members may prejudice *any* right.

302. Regulation 2081/92 implements Part II, Section 3, of the TRIPS Agreement. The rule of conflict between geographical indications and trademarks defined in Article 25.4 has been transposed by Articles 14(1) and 14(2) of Regulation 2081/92. Article 14(1) maintains the eligibility of the applications and the validity of the registrations "grandfathered" by Article 24.5. In turn, Article 14(2) preserves the right of the owners of "grandfathered" trademarks to continue to use their trademarks concurrently with the geographical indications.

303. Article 14(2) of Regulation 2081/92 is fully consistent with Article 24.5, which provides that Members shall not prejudice "the right to use a trademark." That phrase alludes to the owner's right to use the sign of which the trademark consists, which is one of the two basic rights of the trademark owner, together with the right to prevent other persons from using that sign.[146] If the drafters had meant to exclude the co-existence of trademarks and geographical indications, they would have provided instead that Members shall not prejudice "the *exclusive* right to use a trademark."

304. Furthermore, if Article 24.5 did not allow co-existence, the protection of geographical indications provided under Part II, Section 3, would become pointless whenever there is a grandfathered trademark. Indeed, why protect a geographical indication against illegitimate uses by third parties if the legitimate users cannot use it themselves? Yet, Article 24.5 assumes that Members will continue to protect geographical indications ("...measures adopted to implement this Section shall not prejudice..."), notwithstanding the existence of "grandfathered" trademarks. If the drafters' intention had been to prohibit the use of geographical indications concurrently with grandfathered trademarks, they would have excluded completely the applicability of Part II, Section 3, with respect to the geographical indications concerned, rather than providing that the implementation of that Section shall not prejudice "the right to use the trademark."

305. Australia has suggested[147] that the phrase "the right to use a trademark" alludes exclusively to the trademark rights acquired through use, to which reference is made in the introductory phrase of Article 24.5. However, if so, it would have been more logical to say that the measures taken to implement Sections 3 "shall not prejudice ... the trademark rights acquired through use," rather than that they "shall not prejudice ... the right to use a trademark." Australia confuses the mode of acquisition of the trademark rights (use or registration) with one of the basic rights of the trademark owner (irrespective of whether the trademark rights have been acquired through use or registration), i.e. the right to use the trademark.

306. Moreover, trademark rights acquired through use are also, as a general rule, exclusive within the boundaries of the area in which they have been used. Article 16.1 of the TRIPS Agreement recognises expressly

---

[146] WIPO's "Introduction to Intellectual Property, Theory and Practice" (Kluwer, 1997), aptly describes the rights arising from trademark registration as follows (para. 9.147):
The registered owner has the exclusive right to use the trademark. This short definition of the specific subject matter of trademark right encompasses two things: the right to use the trademark and the right to exclude others from using it.

[147] Australia's FWS, para. 74.

the right of Members to make available trademark rights, including exclusive rights, on the basis of use. In view of that, there is no good reason why Article 24.5 should provide for the co-existence of geographical indications and non-registered trademarks, but prohibit the co-existence of geographical indications and registered trademarks, which would be the anomalous consequence of Australia's interpretation.

307. Co-existence may not be a perfect solution to resolve conflicts between different types of intellectual property rights. But then there is no such perfect solution. Co-existence is preferable to a rigid application of the first-in-time rule, which is what the complainants are proposing. That rule is generally appropriate to resolve conflicts between trademarks, but not between trademarks and geographical indications, because they are distinct intellectual property rights, each with its own characteristics. In particular, the following differences make inappropriate the strict application of that principle to conflicts between geographical indications and trademarks:

- trademarks are much easier to create than geographical indications. Trademarks can be acquired almost instantaneously, simply by an "intent to use" or by the mere lodging of an application with a registration system. In contrast, the creation of a geographical indication requires to establish first a "link" between the name and certain product characteristics, which may require years. Indeed, as is often the case in the EC, such link is the result of centuries of tradition. Thus, the first-in-time principle would provide an unfair advantage to trademark owners;

- trademarks are arbitrary, with the consequence that there is a virtually unlimited choice of trademarks. By choosing deliberately a geographical name as a trademark, an undertaking accepts the risk that the same sign may be used concurrently as a geographical indication. In contrast, geographical indications are "necessary" in the sense that the range of names used to designate a certain geographical is limited *a priori* by well established usage. Right holders of geographical indications may not easily change the name given by the public to the geographical area where they are located. For that reason, it is much more difficult to find an alternative geographical indication than it is to find an alternative trademark;

- geographical indications serve to inform consumers that the product originates in a certain area and has certain characteristics linked to that origin. Trademarks only guarantee the identity of the undertaking that markets the product. Thus, in addition to having a commercial function, geographical indications serve a public interest, which deserves additional protection.

- geographical indications are the common patrimony of all the producers of a certain area, and ultimately of the entire population of that area, which may potentially qualify for the right to use the geographical indication. It would be unfair to deprive that population from the use of a geographical indication for the exclusive benefit of an individual trademark owner, who may or may not have contributed to the development of the geographical indication, simply because he happened to register that name first as a trademark.

308. The co-existence of intellectual property rights is by no means an unusual solution for resolving conflicts between intellectual property rights, including between trademarks. Indeed, several other provisions of the TRIPS Agreement provide for co-existence:

- Article 23.3 provides for co-existence between homonymous geographical indications for wines;[148]

---

[148] Article 23.3 of the TRIPS Agreement provides that:
In the case of homonymous geographical indications for wines, protection shall be accorded to each indication, subject to the provisions of paragraph 4 of Article 22. Each Member shall determine the practical conditions under which the homonymous indications in questions will be differentiated from each other, taking into account the need to ensure equitable treatment of the producers concerned and that consumers are not misled.

- Article 24.4 permits, under certain circumstances, that the nationals or residents of one Member continue to use a geographical indication of another Member in co-existence with the users of that Member;[149]

- Article 16.1 itself provides that the exclusivity of registered trademarks "shall not prejudice any existing prior rights."

309. The co-existence of different types of intellectual property rights, and in particular between geographical indications and trademarks, is provided also in the law of other Members.[150]

310. Remarkably, the United States itself provides for the co-existence of geographical indications and earlier trademarks with respect to wines. Specifically, the regulations of the US Alcohol and Tobacco Tax and Trade Board (the "TTB") provide that a brand name of viticultural significance (including the name of US approved viticultural areas) may not be used unless 1) the wine meets the appellation of origin requirements for the geographical area concerned; or 2) the brand name is used in accordance with a "certificate of label approval" issued prior to 1 July 1986.[151]

311. In other words, under the TTB Regulations, the existence of a registered trademark including a geographical name (e.g. "Rutherford Vintners") does not prevent the subsequent recognition and use of that name as a geographical indication ("Rutherford"), which is what would be required by the interpretation of Article 16.1 of the TRIPS Agreement put forward by the United States in this dispute. Quite to the contrary, the use of the earlier trademark is prohibited, subject to a very limited temporal exception, with a narrower scope than that of Article 24.5 of the TRIPS Agreement. Furthermore, grandfathered trademarks are allowed to co-exist with the later geographical indications, provided only that they are used in accordance with special labelling requirements. The United States should explain why this solution to the conflicts between geographical indications and earlier trademarks, which is undoubtedly a sensible one, must be deemed compatible with the TRIPS Agreement when US geographical indications for wines are at stake, but not in the case of EC geographical indications for other products.[152]

(c) The EC is required to maintain the co-existence of geographical indications and earlier trademarks by Article 24.3

312. Irrespective of whether the co-existence of geographical indications and earlier trademarks is consistent with Article 24.5, the EC is required to maintain such co-existence by virtue of Article 24.3 of the TRIPS Agreement, which provides that

> In implementing this Section, a Member shall not diminish the protection of geographical indications that existed in that Member immediately prior to the date of entry into force of the WTO Agreement.

---

[149] Article 24.4 of the TRIPS Agreement provides that:
Nothing in this section shall require a Member to prevent continued and similar use of a particular geographical indication of another Member identifying wines or spirits in connection with goods or services by any of its nationals or domiciliaries who have used that geographical indication in a continuous manner with regard to the same or related goods or services in the territory of that Member either (a) for at least 10 years preceding 15 April 1994 or (b) in good faith preceding that date.

[150] See "Review under Article 24.2 of the Application of the Provisions of the Section of the TRIPS Agreement on Geographical Indications—Summary of the Responses to the Checklist of Questions," IP/C/W/253/Rev.1, 24 November 2003, paras. 149-150.

[151] 27 CFR 4.39 (i). (Exhibit EC-11).

[152] The lack of consistency appears to be even more blatant in the case of Australia. The Wine and Brandy Corporation Act prohibits the use of a registered GI for wine which does not originate in the area covered by the GI. No exception is provided with respect to prior trademarks. Australia can hardly complain about the fact that the EC allows the co-existence of GIs with earlier trademarks grandfathered under Article 24.5, when it prohibits the use of those trademarks, unless the wine originates in the area designated by the GI. (Sections 40 D-F). (Exhibit EC -12).

313. Article 24.3 is in the nature of a "stand still" obligation. It requires Members to maintain at least the level of protection of geographical indications that they applied immediately prior to the entry into force of the WTO Agreement, where such level is higher than the level of protection required by Part II, Section 3, of the TRIPS Agreement.[153]

314. Regulation 2081/92 was adopted on 14 July 1992 and entered into force on 14 July 1993. As of 31 December 1995, i.e. the day before the entry into force of the WTO Agreement, Article 14(2) of Regulation 2081/92 provided for the co-existence of geographical indications and earlier trademarks. If the EC were to allow now the owners of prior registered trademarks to prevent the use of later geographical indications, as demanded by the complainants, it would be diminishing the protection of geographical indications, contrary to the obligation imposed upon the EC by Article 23.4

(d) In any event, the co-existence of geographical indications and earlier trademarks would be justified under Article 17 of the TRIPS Agreement

315. Assuming that 14(3) of Regulation 2081/92 did not prevent the registration of confusing geographical indications, and assuming further that the co-existence of geographical indications and earlier registered trademarks were neither consistent with Article 24.5 of the TRIPS Agreement nor, in the case of the EC, required by Article 24.3 of the TRIPS Agreement, the EC submits in the alternative that such co-existence would be justified under Article 17 of the TRIPS Agreement.

316. Article 17 states that:

> Members may provide limited exceptions to the rights conferred by a trademark, such as fair use of descriptive terms, provided that such exceptions take account of the legitimate interests of the owner of the trademark and of third parties.

317. Article 14(2) is a "limited exception" because it allows the concurrent use of the geographical name registered as a trademark only by those producers who are established in the geographical area designated by the geographical indication and who, furthermore, comply with the relevant product specifications and other requirements for using the geographical indication. The trademark owner retains the exclusive right to prevent the use of that name by any other persons.

318. Moreover, Article 17 mentions expressly as an example of "limited exception" the "fair use of descriptive terms." Geographical indications are "descriptive terms."[154] The use of a geographical indication in order to indicate the true origin of the goods and the characteristic associated to that origin is certainly a "fair" use of that descriptive term.

319. Finally, the legitimate interests of the trademark owner and of third parties are "taken into account" in several ways:

- even if Article 14(3) of Regulation 2081/92 did not avoid completely the registration of confusing trademarks, it would at the very least prevent the most significant cases of confusion, in the interest of both the trademark owner and the consumers;

---

[153] See e.g. Daniel Gervais, *The TRIPS Agreement, Drafting History and Analysis*, (Sweet & Maxwell, 1998), p. 135.

[154] The trademark laws of both the United States and Australia provide that the use of a term registered as a trademark to indicate the origin of goods does not constitute an infringement of the trademark.

Section 33(b)(4) of the US Lanham Act (15 USC 115 (b) (4))(Exhibit EC-6) provides the following defence against a claim of infringement of the exclusive right of a trademark owner:

That the use of a term ... charged to be an infringement is a use, otherwise than as mark ... of a term ... which is descriptive and used fairly and in good faith only to describe the goods ... of such party, or their geographical origin.

In turn, Section 122(1) (b)(i) of Australia's 1995 Trade Mark Law provides that a person does not infringe a registered trade mark when "the person uses a sign in good faith to indicate the ... geographical origin ... of goods." (Exhibit EC-7).

- moreover, the concurrent use of the geographical indications is subject to the generally applicable EC legislation on labelling and misleading advertising, as well as to the laws of the Member States on unfair competition;

- finally, geographical indications serve to inform consumers about the origin of the products and their characteristics and, therefore, "take account of the interests of third parties" also in that way.

2. Claim 20: Regulation 2081/92 does not provide for a presumption of a likelihood of confusion in the case of use of an identical sign for identical goods

320. Australia claims that Regulation 2081/1992 is inconsistent with Article 16.1 of the TRIPS Agreement because it does not "implement" the presumption of a likelihood of confusion in the case of use of an identical sign for identical goods.[155]

321. The EC's response to Claim 19 disposes also of this claim. However, for the sake of completeness, the EC would like to add the following comments.

322. First, contrary to what Australia appears to suggest, Members are not required to reproduce explicitly the presumption of Article 16.1 in their domestic law. It may be sufficient if their domestic law leaves to the registering authority, or to the courts, the necessary discretion to apply the presumption and, in practice, the presumption is complied with.[156]

323. Second, it is extremely unlikely that the situation described by Australia will ever present itself in practice. In the first place, as explained above, the criteria for the registrability of trademarks limit a *priori* the possibility to register as a trademark a name which is identical to that of a geographical indication or of a potential geographical indication. Moreover, the definition of "geographical indication" in Regulation 2081/92, together with the requirement to comply with certain product specifications, would normally have the consequence that the goods covered by a registered geographical indication are not identical to other goods. In any event, should the situation arise, Article 14(3) would allow the registering authority to refuse the registration of a proposed geographical indication, if necessary to implement the presumption.

324. Finally, Australia's complaint is, once again, purely theoretical. Australia has not alleged, let alone proved that any of the more than 600 registered geographical indications is identical to any earlier registered trademark used for identical goods. The EC considers that none of the registered geographical indications falls within that situation.

3. Claim 21: Article 7(4) of Regulation 2081/92 is inconsistent with Article 16.1 of the TRIPS Agreement because it limits the grounds of objection

325. Australia (but not the United States) claims that Article 7(4) of Regulation 2081/92 is inconsistent with Article 16.1 of the TRIPS Agreement[157] because it does not allow trademark owners to object to the registration of a proposed geographical indication where there is likelihood of confusion, but only where the proposed geographical indication would "jeopardize the existence of an entirely or partly identical trademark."

326. This claim is unfounded, both as a matter of law, because Article 16.1 does not confer a right of objection, and as a matter of fact, because Article 7(4) of Regulation 2081/92 does not limit the grounds of objection in the manner alleged by Australia.

---

[155] Australia's FWS, para. 93.

[156] Thus, for example, the EC understands that the US trademark laws do not restate the presumption, but the US authorities are satisfied that the criteria usually applied in order to appreciate the likelihood of confusion between trademarks are sufficient to meet the presumption.

[157] Australia's FWS, paras. 88-92.

(a) Article 16.1 of the TRIPS Agreement does not confer a right of objection

327. Article 16.1 does not grant to the trademark owners a right to formulate objections in the framework of a procedure for the acquisition of another intellectual property right, whether it is a trademark or a different right such as geographical indication.

328. Article 16.1 regulates exclusively the substantive content of the rights conferred to the trademark owners. It does not address the procedural means to exercise those rights, which are regulated elsewhere in the TRIPS Agreement. Thus, the possibility to raise objections to the registration of another intellectual property right is addressed in Article 62.4, with respect to all intellectual property rights in general, and in Article 15.5, with respect specifically to trademarks.

329. Article 62.4, which is included in Part IV of the TRIPS Agreement, dealing specifically with the "Acquisition and Maintenance of Intellectual Property Rights and Related *Inter Partes* Procedures," provides that

> Procedures concerning the acquisition or maintenance of intellectual property rights and, where a Member's law provides for such procedures, administrative revocation and *inter partes* procedures such as opposition, revocation and cancellation, shall be governed by the general principles set out in paragraphs 2 and 3 of Article 41.[158]

330. In turn, Article 15.5 provides that Members "may afford an opportunity for the registration of a trademark to be opposed."[159]

331. The above quoted provisions make it clear that Members are not required to grant a right of opposition to the trademark owners with respect to the acquisition of another intellectual property right.

332. Moreover, contrary to Australia's assertions, the right to formulate objections is not necessary to "exercise" effectively the substantive right conferred by Article 16, if final registration decisions are subject to judicial review, as they should under Article 62.5 of the TRIPS Agreement.

333. Since Article 16.1 does not confer to the trademark owners the right to formulate objections with respect to the registration of a geographical indication, the fact that Article 7(4) of Regulation 2081/92 limits the possible grounds of objection cannot be inconsistent with Article 16.1.

(b) Australia has misread Article 7(4) of Regulation 2081/92

334. In any event, Australia's claim is based on a misreading of Article 7(4) of Regulation 2081/92. The text in force of that Article provides in relevant part as follows:

> A statement of objection shall be admissible only if it:
>
> ...
>
> – shows that the registration of the name proposed would jeopardize the existence of an entirely or partly identical name or of a mark ...[160]

[158] Emphasis added.

[159] Emphasis added.

[160] Emphasis added.

335. The term "entirely or partially identical" qualifies only the term "name," and not the term "mark." Thus, an objection is admissible if the proposed name "would jeopardize the existence of the mark," regardless of whether the mark is "entirely or partially identical." This is confirmed by the other linguistic versions of the Regulation, including the French and the Spanish ones, which read as follows:

> Pour être recevable, toute déclaration d'opposition doit :
>
> ...
>
> – ... démontrer que l'enregistrement du nom proposé porterait préjudice a l'existence d'une dénomination totalement ou partiellement homonyme ou d'une marque ...
>
> Para que sea admitida, toda declaración de oposición deberá:
>
> ...
>
> – ...demostrar que el registro del nombre propuesto perjudicaría la existencia de una denominación total o parcialmente homónima o de una marca...

336. The ground provided in Article 7(4), i.e. that the proposed name "would jeopardize ("porterait préjudice" in French, "perjudicaría" in Spanish) the existence of a mark" is broad enough to encompass the likelihood of confusion between the proposed name and the trademark.

337. Australia appears to have been confused by the English version of the text in force until the amendment introduced by Council Regulation 806/2003, which read as follows:

> A statement of objection shall be admissible only if it:
>
> ...
>
> – shows that the registration of the name proposed would jeopardize the existence of an entirely or partly identical name or trade mark ...

338. However, no consequences can be attributed to the omission of the term "of a" before the term "trade mark," which appears to have been a translation error. Indeed, the other linguistics versions in force until the said amendment, including the French and the Spanish, were identical on this point to the text currently in force in those versions.

4. Claim 22: Regulation 2081/92 does not ensure that objections from trademark owners will be considered by the Committee

339. Australia (but not the United States) claims that Regulation 2081/92 is inconsistent with Article 16.1 because it does not ensure that an objection from the owner of a registered trademark is considered by the Committee[161], which Australia characterizes as "the ultimate decision maker."

340. For the reasons explained in the response to Claim 3, Article 16.1 does not confer a right of objection to the trademark owners. Therefore, the procedures laid down in Regulation 2081/92 with a view to organize the exercise of such right cannot be inconsistent with Article 16.1.

341. In any event, Australia's allegations are incorrect as a matter of fact.

---

[161] Australia's FWS, paras. 94-99.

342. First, as explained above,[162] the Commission, or the Council, and not the Committee is "the ultimate decision-maker" under the Regulation.

343. Second, Regulation 2081/92 entrusts to the authorities of the Member States the task of receiving and examining the objections because they are generally better placed to ascertain and assess the relevant facts. While Member States are not required to transmit the statements objections, their decisions are not discretionary and may be subject to judicial review under the national law of each Member State.

344. Third, the authorities of other WTO Members enjoy complete discretion in order to decide whether or not to forward the objections to the EC Commission. Thus, Australia would be estopped from complaining that the refusal by the Australian authorities to transmit a statement of objections to the EC Commission would infringe the trademark rights of its own nationals in the EC. The same would be true of any other WTO Member.

B. CLAIM 23: BY REQUIRING THE CO-EXISTENCE OF A REGISTERED GEOGRAPHICAL INDICATION AND AN EARLIER TRADEMARK, ARTICLE 14(2) ENCUMBERS UNJUSTIFIABLY THE USE OF THE TRADEMARK, CONTRARY TO ARTICLE 20 OF THE TRIPS AGREEMENT

345. Australia (but not the United States) claims that by requiring the co-existence of a an existing trademark and a later geographical indication, Article 14(2) of Regulation 2081/92 "encumbers unjustifiably" the use of the trademark, thereby violating Article 20 of the TRIPS Agreement.[163]

346. Article 20 of the TRIPS provides that

> The use of a trademark in the course of trade shall not be unjustifiably encumbered by special requirements, such as use with another trademark, use in a special form or use in a manner detrimental to its capability to distinguish the goods or services of one undertaking from those of other undertakings. This will not preclude a requirement prescribing the use of the trademark identifying the undertaking producing the goods or services along with, but without linking it to, the trademark distinguishing the specific goods or services in question of that undertaking.

347. Australia has misunderstood the purpose and, as result, also the scope of Article 20. That provision is not concerned with the issue of exclusivity (i.e. *who* has the right to use a sign), which, as between trademarks, is dealt with exhaustively by Article 16. Instead, Article 20 addresses the distinct issue of which requirements may be imposed upon the trademark right holder with respect to the use of *his* own trademark (i.e, *how* to use a trademark").

348. On Australia's interpretation Article 20 would overlap, and potentially conflict, with Article 16. For example,

- Article 16.1 allows the use of a later similar trademark for similar goods, provided that it does not result in "likelihood of confusion." Yet, on Australia's theory, the use of that trademark would still be prohibited under Article 20 if it "encumbered unjustifiably" the use of the earlier trademark, for example by "diminishing its distinctiveness;"

- Article 16.1 provides that the exclusivity of registered trademarks is without prejudice of existing prior rights. Yet, on Australia's interpretation, the exercise of such prior rights could still be prohibited if it "encumbered unjustifiably" the use of a later trademark;

[162] See above Section II. H.

[163] Australia's FWS, paras. 108-112.

- Article 16 allows the use of identical or similar signs for different goods, except as provided in Article 16.3. On Australia's interpretation, however, such use could be prohibited by Article 20 whenever it "encumbers unjustifiably" the use of another trademark.

349. The three examples of "special requirements" included in the first sentence confirm that Article 20 does not address the issue of exclusivity:

- the first example ("use with another trademark") refers to the requirement that an undertaking uses, in addition to its own trademark, another trademark for the same goods, and not to the use of a trademark in coexistence with another trademark used by a different undertaking for its own goods. A typical example is the requirement to use a foreign trademark together with the trademark of a domestic producer.[164]

- the second example ("use in a special from") is, by its owns terms, concerned exclusively with the *form* in which the trademark may be used, rather than with the issue of who has the right to use it. It concerns, for example, the requirements affecting the affixing of the trademark.[165]

- as regards the third example ("in *a manner* detrimental to the capability to distinguish the goods or services, etc."), on which Australia places particular emphasis, the term "in a manner" confirms that the requirement must relate to the "way," "method" or "mode"[166] in which the trademark is used by each trademark owner, rather than to the issue of exclusivity.

350. Article 14(2) of Regulation 2081/192 limits the exclusive right of the trademark right holder to prevent the use of the trademark by others, by providing for the co-existence of a geographical indication, but imposes no "requirement" with respect to *how* the trademark owner may use its own trademark. Since Article 14(2) imposes no requirements falling within the scope of Article 20 of the TRIPS Agreement, it cannot be inconsistent with that provision.

351. In any event, as shown in the response to Claim 19, co-existence is consistent with the relevant EC's obligations under the TRIPS Agreement and, therefore, would not be "unjustified."

C. CLAIM 24: ARTICLE 14(1) OF REGULATION 2081/92 IS INCONSISTENT WITH ARTICLE 24.5 OF THE TRIPS AGREEMENT BECAUSE IT DOES NOT AFFORD THE RIGHT OF PRIORITY PROVIDED IN ARTICLE 4 OF THE PARIS CONVENTION

352. Australia (but not the United States) claims that Article 14(1) of Regulation 2081/92 violates Article 25.4 of the TRIPS Agreement because it does not afford the right of priority in respect of an application for registration of a trademark previously filed in another WTO Member provided in Article 4 of the Paris Convention (1967).[167]

353. As explained in Section II,[168] the EC considers that this claim is outside the terms of reference because it is entirely dependent on a supposed violation of Article 4 of the Paris Convention (1967), which was not mentioned in Australia's panel request.

354. In any event, Australia's claim is insufficiently argued and difficult to understand.

---

[164] See Daniel Gervais, *The TRIPS Agreement, Drafting History and Analysis* (Sweet and Maxwell, 1998), p. 116. See also Eleanor.K. Meltzer, "TRIPS and Trademarks, or GATT got your tongue?" (1993) 83 *The Trademark Reporter*, pp. 18-37, p. 29.

[165] Daniel Gervais, *op.cit.*, p. 117.

[166] New Shorter Oxford English Dictionary, 1993, Vol. I, p. 1687.

[167] Australia's FWS, paras. 81-87.

[168] See above paras. 28-30.

355. Australia appears to be arguing that, in accordance with Article 4 of the Paris Convention (1967), an application for a trademark that was filed in Member X up to six months prior to one of the two dates mentioned in Article 24.5 of the TRIPS Agreement would have the effect of bringing within the scope of the protection provided by Article 24.5 any subsequent application made after those dates in Member Y. That interpretation, however, would be incorrect, because it relies on the legal consequences of Article 24.5 in order to establish that certain facts fall within the scope of that provision. In other words, Australia's interpretation of Article 24.5 already anticipates the result of such interpretation.

356. Article 24.5 requires to afford the priority right of Article 4 of the Paris Convention (1967) to those applications that are "grandfathered" by virtue of that provision, i.e. to the applications filed before the date of entry into force of the WTO Agreement (1 January 1996) or before the date of protection of the GI in its country of origin. But Article 4 of the Paris Convention (1967) cannot be applied in order to determine whether an application is "grandfathered" in accordance with Article 25.4. For that purpose, the only relevant date is the actual date of filing in the Member applying the implementing measures. When that date is taken into account, Article 14(1) of Regulation 2081/1992 is fully consistent with Article 24.5 of the TRIPS Agreement.

D. ARTICLES 41.1, 41.2, 41.3, 41.4, 42, 43, 44.1, 45, 46, 48 AND 49 OF THE TRIPS AGREEMENT

1. General Considerations

357. Australia and the United States claim that Regulation 2081/92 is inconsistent with numerous provisions of Part III of the TRIPS Agreement because it does not afford to trademark right holders the enforcement rights stipulated in those provisions.

358. The EC considers that these claims are unfounded because Part III of the TRIPS Agreement does not apply to Regulation 2081/92.

359. Regulation 2081/92 lays down an administrative procedure for the acquisition of geographical indications via a system of registration. It does not purport to regulate the procedures for enforcing trademark rights, which are provided instead in the trademark laws, and related civil and criminal procedural laws, of the EC and of its Member States. Those laws, which have been notified to the WTO, are not within the terms of reference of the Panel.

360. The TRIPS Agreement draws a clear distinction between, on the one hand, the procedures for the "enforcement" of intellectual property rights, which are provided in Part III, and, on the other hand, the "procedures for the acquisition and maintenance of intellectual rights and related *inter partes* procedures," which are addressed in Part IV. The procedures provided in Regulation 2081/92 for the registration of geographical indications at issue in this dispute fall clearly within the second category and are subject exclusively to Part IV, and not to Part III.

361. The purpose of Part III is expressed in Article 41.1 which provides that

> Members shall ensure that enforcement procedures as specified in this part are available under their law so as to permit effective action against any act of infringement of intellectual property rights covered by this Agreement, including expeditious remedies to prevent infringements and remedies which constitute a deterrent to further infringements.

362. The granting of an intellectual property right in accordance with the domestic law of each Member is not an "infringement" and, therefore, is not subject to Part III of the TRIPS Agreement. Further, the subsequent use of a validly granted intellectual property right in conformity with the domestic laws of a Member is also not an "infringement."

363. For the purposes of Part III, the existence of an "infringement" must be established with respect to the applicable domestic law implementing Part II of the TRIPS Agreement, and not in relation to Part II itself. In other words, an act which is consistent with a Member's domestic law, such as the use of a validly registered geographical indication, is not an "infringement" for the purposes of Part III, even if the domestic law is inconsistent with Part II. Indeed, requiring Members to provide "enforcement" procedures against acts that are consistent with their own domestic laws, but are inconsistent with Part II, would be as much as requiring them to give direct effect to the WTO Agreement in their domestic legal order.

364. In addition, applying the provisions of Part III to the procedures for the acquisition of intellectual property rights, such as those regulated in Regulation 2081/1992, would render redundant many of the provisions of Part IV and give rise to conflicts between Part III and Part IV.

365. Moreover, it would have unacceptable results for most Members, as illustrated by the complainants' claims. It would mean, for example, that intellectual property rights would have to be conferred always by a judicial body in accordance with judicial procedures, rather than by an administrative body in accordance with administrative procedures, as is currently the case in most Members, including Australia and the United States. The EC does not believe, for instance, that the complainants' own systems of registration of trademarks, which are operated by an administrative body, would comply with the provisions of Part III.

2. Claim 25: Regulation 2081/92 is inconsistent with Article 41.1 of the TRIPS Agreement

366. Both Australia and the United States claim that Regulation 2081/92 is inconsistent with Article 41.1 of the TRIPS Agreement[169].

367. Article 41.1 of the TRIPS Agreement is an introductory provision, which does not impose any obligation by itself. Australia appears to agree because it argues that the measure is inconsistent with Article 41.1 "as a consequence of"[170] the fact that it is inconsistent with Articles 41.2, 41.3, 42, 43, 44, 45, 46, 48 and 49. As explained in Section II, the EC considers that Articles 43, 44, 45, 46, 48 and 49 are outside the terms of reference of the Panel, because they were not mentioned in Australia's panel request. Australia's claims under Articles 41.2, 41.3 and 42 will be addressed here below.

368. The United States submits no arguments in support of this claim.[171]

3. Claim 26: Regulation 2081/92 is inconsistent with Article 41.2 of the TRIPS Agreement

369. Both Australia and the United States claim that Regulation 2081/92 is inconsistent with Article 41.2 of the TRIPS Agreement[172] because

- it does not make available to trademark owners "fair and equitable procedures" for objecting to the registration of geographical indications;
- the objection procedures are "unnecessarily complicated" and "entail unwarranted delays."

370. For the reasons explained above, the EC considers that Article 41.2, like the rest of Part III of the TRIPS Agreement, does not apply to the procedures for the acquisition of intellectual property rights, which are instead subject exclusively to the provisions of Part IV. In the case of Article 41.2, this is made clear by Article 62.4 of the TRIPS Agreement, which provides that

---

[169] Australia's FWS 145-148. US FWS, para. 185.

[170] Australia's FWS, para. 148.

[171] US FWS, para. 185.

[172] Australia's FWS, paras. 126-136. US FWS, para. 186.

> The procedures concerning the acquisition or maintenance of intellectual property rights and, where a Member's law provides for such procedures, administrative revocation and *inter partes* procedures such as opposition, revocation and cancellation, shall be governed by the general principles set out in paragraphs 2 and 3 of Article 41.

371. The cross-reference to "the *general principles* set out in paragraphs 2 and 3 of Article 41" would have been superfluous if Article 41 could be applied, as such, to the procedures for the registration of an intellectual property right.

372. Neither Australia nor the United States have claimed in their panel requests that Regulation 2081/92 is inconsistent with Article 62.4, which is, therefore, outside the terms of reference of the Panel.

373. In any event, as shown below, the complainants' allegations are unfounded as a matter of fact.

(a) The procedures provided in Regulation 2081/92 are neither inequitable nor unfair

374. The accusation that a Member acts in an "unfair and inequitable" manner is a very serious one. One could expect that such an accusation would be made against another Member only after careful consideration and on the basis of indisputable evidence.

375. Yet, the United States does not even bother to provide argument, let alone evidence, in support of its claim under Article 41.2.[173]

376. For its part, Australia alleges that the objection procedures provided for in Regulation 2081/92 are neither fair nor equitable because

- objections must be lodged with an agency "that is *likely* to have an interest in supporting and promoting the registration of EC-defined GIs;"[174]
- objections must be considered by a Committee comprised of "delegates of the same EC Member States agencies which are *likely* to have an interest in supporting and promoting the proposed registration of EC Member State geographic terms as defined GIs"[175]
- "trademark right holders not resident in the EC face the additional hurdle of not having a national representative in the Committee."[176]

377. Australia concludes that "in such circumstances, the *possibility of bias* in favour of both the proposed EC-defined GI and the interests of EC Member States *cannot be seen to be excluded*."[177]

378. At the outset, the EC would submit that the mere fact that the "possibility of bias cannot be seen to be excluded" cannot be sufficient to establish a violation of Article 41.2. Instead, it would need to be shown that the procedures at issue are positively unfair and inequitable. In any event, Australia has not met even the very low standard which it has set forth itself.

379. To begin with, Australia's allegations are fraught with factual errors. Australia repeats, once again, the mistake of considering that the Committee is the decision-making body. Moreover, it is also incorrect to

[173] US FWS, para. 186.

[174] Australia's FWS, para. 130. Emphasis added.

[175] Ibid., para.131. Emphasis added.

[176] Ibid., para. 134.

[177] Ibid., para. 135. Emphasis added.

describe the members of the Committee as "delegates" of the national agencies in charge of applying Regulation 2081/92.[178] The members of the Committee represent the Member States, and not specific agencies.

380. Even more crucially, Australia's allegations of "possibility of bias" are not based on actual fact, but on mere speculations about the "likely" conduct of public agencies and their officials. Those speculations are baseless and, indeed, offensive.

381. Neither the agencies of the Member States responsible for the administration of Regulation 2081/92, nor the officials employed by such agencies, are under any instructions to "promote" the registration of "their" geographical indications at the expense of the rights of trademark holders, whether they are EC nationals or foreigners. To the contrary, they are under a statutory duty to apply Regulation 2081/92 in an objective and unbiased manner. In the absence of compelling evidence, which Australia has not provided, it cannot be assumed that those agencies, or their officials, are "likely" to breach systematically those duties.

382. Surely, Australia would agree that Australia's own trademark office, and the officials of that agency, are not "likely" to be biased in favour of registering trademarks requested by Australian nationals over the objections of EC's right holders of geographical indications. Australia would also agree that the fact that the EC or its Member States are not "represented" in the decision making bodies of Australia's trade mark office does not render the procedures before that office "unfair" and "inequitable." Again, in the absence of any compelling evidence to the contrary, which Australia has not provided, it cannot be assumed that the agencies of the EC Member States, and their officials, will behave differently from Australia's own agencies and officials.

(b) The procedures provided in Regulation 2081/92 are not unnecessarily complicated and do not entail unwarranted delays

383. Again, the United States has not submitted any argument in support of this claim.[179]

384. The thrust of Australia's claim is that the requirement to lodge the statement of objection with the authorities of the Member State or the WTO member of residence "adds unjustifiable complexity and delay" to the enforcement of trademark rights.[180]

385. Australia's complaint is unfounded. As explained, Regulation 2081/92 entrusts the examination of objections to the Member States because they are closer to the facts and better equipped to ascertain and assess them. Even if objections were lodged directly with the EC Commission, it would still be necessary for the EC Commission to request the assistance of the authorities of the Member States in order to verify the relevant facts. Thus, it is very doubtful that centralising the submission of objections at the Commission level would add simplicity or speed to the procedures.

386. The same is true as regards the statements of objections filed with another WTO Member, in particular when they relate to the registration of a geographical indication from that WTO Member. Moreover, each WTO Member has complete discretion in order to decide whether or not to transmit an objection to the EC Commission. If they wished, the Australian authorities could limit themselves to forward immediately to the EC Commission any objection that they receive. This can hardly be described as an "unnecessarily complicated" formality or as an "unwarranted delay." Once again, Australia cannot plead its own unwillingness to forward the statement, or its failure to do so expeditiously, in order to claim that this requirement adds unjustified complexity or delay.

---

[178] Ibid., para. 131.

[179] US FWS, para. 186.

[180] Australia's FWS, para. 138.

4. Claim 27: Regulation 2081/92 is inconsistent with Article 41.3 of the TRIPS Agreement

387. Australia (but not the United States) claims that Regulation 2081/92 is inconsistent with Article 41.3 of the TRIPS Agreement in that the registration decisions are not "based only on evidence on which parties were offered the opportunity to be heard." Specifically, Australia alleges that Regulation 2081/92 does not ensure that the Committee will consider the objections lodged with the Member States. [181]

388. Like the rest of Part III of the TRIPS Agreement, Article 41.3 does not apply to the procedures for the acquisition of intellectual property rights, which are instead subject to the provisions of Part IV. This is made clear, once again, by Article 62.4 of the TRIPS Agreement, which makes a cross-reference to the *general principles* stated in paragraph 3 of Article 41. As mentioned, Australia did not state in its panel request Article 62.4, which is, therefore, outside the terms of reference of the Panel.

389. In any event, Australia's factual allegations under this heading are incorrect. (See above the responses to Claims 21 and 22)

5. Claim 28: Regulation 2081/92 is inconsistent with Article 41.4 of the TRIPS Agreement

390. The United States (but not Australia) claims that the measure is inconsistent with Article 41.4 because "owners of registered trademarks trying to enforce their Article 16.1 rights vis-à-vis a confusing GI or interested parties with GIs based in other territories other than the EC" are not provided an opportunity for review by a judicial authority. [182]

391. Again, the United States limits itself to assert this claim, but does not submit any argument in order to support it.

392. In any event, Article 41.4 of the TRIPS Agreement does not apply with respect to the procedures for the acquisition of intellectual property rights. As discussed below, Article 62.5 of the TRIPS Agreement provides that final administrative decisions in those procedures shall be subject to judicial review. The United States, however, has not mentioned this provision in its panel request. In any event, registration decisions under Regulation 2081/92 are subject to judicial review.

6. Claim 29: Regulation 2081/92 is inconsistent with Article 42 of the TRIPS Agreement

393. The complainants claim that Regulation 2081/92 is inconsistent with Article 42 because it does not provide to trademark right holders civil judicial procedures for the enforcement of their rights vis-à-vis the registration of geographical indications. [183]

394. The valid registration of a geographical indication in accordance with Regulation 2081/92 does not constitute an "infringement" of trademark rights for purposes of Part III. Accordingly, there is no obligation under Article 42 to provide judicial procedures for "enforcing" those rights against the registration of a geographical indication.

395. As explained, Regulation 2081/92 lays down an administrative procedure for the acquisition of geographical indication rights via a system of registration As such, it is subject to Part IV of the TRIPS Agreement, and not to Part III. Unlike Part III, Part IV does not require to provide judicial procedures. In most countries, including the United States and Australia, registration procedures are administrative in nature.

---

[181] Australia's FWS, paras. 141-144.

[182] US FWS, para. 187.

[183] Australia's FWS, paras. 119-125. US FWS, para. 187.

396. While Part IV does not require to provide judicial procedures, it requires that final decisions in administrative procedures must be subject to judicial review. Thus, Article 62.5 states that

> Final administrative decisions in any of the procedures referred to under paragraph 4 shall be subject to review by a judicial or quasi judicial authority. However, there shall be no obligation to provide an opportunity for such review of decisions in cases of unsuccessful opposition or administrative revocation, provided that the grounds for such procedures can be the subject of invalidation.

397. Consistent with Article 62.5, the final decisions on registration reached under Regulation 2081/92 are subject to judicial review. Likewise, the decisions of the Member States authorities with regard to *inter alia* objections may be subject to judicial review under their national laws. In any event, neither the United States nor Australia have stated in their panel requests any claim under Article 65.2, which is therefore outside the terms of reference.

E. CLAIM 30: REGULATION 2081/92 IS INCONSISTENT WITH ARTICLE 10*BIS* (1) AND 10*TER* (1) OF THE PARIS CONVENTION

398. Australia (but not the United States) claims that Regulation 2081/92 is inconsistent with Article 10*bis* (1) of the Paris Convention (1967)[184] because "it does not provide a Community wide system of effective protection of trademarks from acts of unfair competition arising from the later registration of EC-defined GIs under the Regulation."[185]

399. This claim is insufficiently argued and difficult to understand. Australia does not explain how the use of a registered geographical indication, which is otherwise consistent with the TRIPS Agreement, and in particular with Articles 24.5 and 16, could constitute an act of unfair competition within the meaning of Article 10*bis* (1).

400. In any event, the use of registered geographical indications remains subject to the EC legislation on labelling and misleading advertising, as well as to the laws of the EC Member States on unfair competition. That legislation is not within the terms of reference of the Panel.

401. Australia suggests that the violation would arise from the fact that there is no Community wide system of protection.[186] However, there is no basis in Article 10*bis* (1), or anywhere else in the Paris Convention (1967) for the proposition that the protection against unfair competition must be provided at any given territorial level.[187]

402. Australia's claim under Article 10*ter* (1)of the Paris Convention (1967)[188] is based on the same allegations as the claim under Article10*bis* (1) and is equally unfounded for the same reasons.

F. CONSEQUENTIAL CLAIMS

1. Claim 31: Regulation 2081/92 is inconsistent with Article 2.1 of the TRIPS Agreement

403. Australia claims that, because Regulation 2081/92 is inconsistent with Articles 10*bis* (1) and 10*ter* (1) of the Paris Convention (1967), it is also inconsistent with Article 2.1 of the TRIPS Agreement.[189]

---

[184] Australia's FWS, paras. 113-118.

[185] Australia's FWS, para. 114.

[186] Australia's FWS, para. 114.

[187] Australia is a federal state. Surely, Australia would agree that Article 10*bis* (1) does not require it to change the constitutional allocation of powers between the Commonwealth and the State and Territory Governments.

[188] Australia's FWS, para. 117.

404. This claim is entirely dependent on the previous claims under Articles 10*bis* (1) and 10*ter* (1) of the Paris Convention. Both claims are unfounded and, as a consequence, so is this claim.

2. Claim 32: Regulation 2081/92 is inconsistent with Article 1.1 of the TRIPS Agreement

405. Australia claims that because Regulation 2081/92 is inconsistent with Articles 2.1, 16.1, 20, 24.5, 41.1, 41.2, 41.3 and/ or 42 of the TRIPS Agreement it is also inconsistent with Article 1.1 of the TRIPS Agreement.[190]

406. The EC has shown that Australia's claims under those provisions are without merit. Therefore, Australia's claim under Article 1.1 is likewise unfounded.

3. Claim 33: The transitional national protection provided by the Member States is inconsistent with Articles 2.1, 16.1, 41.1, 41.2, 41.3 and/or 42 of the TRIPS Agreement

407. Australia (but not the United States) claims that the transitional protection that Member States are entitled to provide under Article 5(5) of Regulation 2081/92 pending a registration decision is inconsistent with Articles 2.1 (incorporating Articles 10*bis* (1) and 10*ter* (1) of the Paris Convention (1967)) 16.1, 41.1, 41.2, 41.3 and/or 42 of the TRIPS Agreement.[191]

408. This claim is entirely dependent on the previous claims submitted by Australia under the above listed provisions. Since those claims are unfounded, so is this claim.

VII. THE EC MEASURE IS CONSISTENT WITH THE OBLIGATION TO PROVIDE PROTECTION TO GEOGRAPHICAL INDICATIONS UNDER ARTICLE 22.2 OF THE TRIPS AGREEMENT

409. Australia[192] and the United States[193] have submitted very different claims under this heading. The EC will address them separately here below.

1. Claim 34: Regulation 2081/92 is inconsistent with Article 22.2 of the TRIPS Agreement

410. Australia claims that [194]

> Regulation No. 2081/92 establishes a Community-wide regime for the registration and protection of EC-defined GIs. However, the EC measure does not provide –as concerns those same EC-defined GIs—legal channels for interested parties to prevent on a Community-wide basis any use of those EC-defined GIs which would mislead the public as to the geographical origin of a good or any use which would constitute an act of unfair competition within the meaning of Paris Article 10 bis.

411. Once again, this claim is insufficiently argued. Here below, the EC will provide a provisional answer based on its limited understanding of Australia's rather obscure arguments.

---

[189] Australia's FWS, para. 151.
[190] Australia's FWS para. 152.
[191] Australia's FWS, paras. 149-150.
[192] Australia's FWS, paras. 154-155.
[193] US FWS, paras. 171-183.
[194] Ibid., para. 155.

412. First, the EC considers that Article 22.2 of the TRIPS Agreement is concerned exclusively with the protection of geographical indications. It cannot be invoked by a trademark right holder in order to prevent the use a geographical indication which supposedly infringes its trademark right, which is what Australia appears to be suggesting.

413. Second, Regulation 2081/92 only allows the use of a geographical indication in connection with goods that originate in the geographical area designated by that geographical indication. The EC fails to see how the use of a validly registered geographical indication, which is otherwise consistent with the TRIPS Agreement, could possibly mislead the public as to the geographical origin of the goods. In fact, the registration of the geographical indication seeks to avoid precisely that result.

414. Third, the EC also fails to understand how the registration or the use of a geographical indication consistently with the EC domestic laws, as well as with all other provisions of the TRIPS Agreement, including Articles 24.5 and 16, could ever constitute an act of unfair competition within the meaning of Article 10*bis* of the Paris Convention (1967). Australia has not explained it. In any event, the use of registered geographical indications remains subject to the EC legislation on labelling and misleading advertising, as well as to the laws of the Member States on unfair competition. That legislation is not within the terms of reference of the Panel.

415. Finally, Australia suggests that the violation would arise from the fact that there is no Community-wide system of protection. However, there is no basis in Article 22.2, or anywhere else in the TRIPS Agreement, for the proposition that protection must be provided at any particular territorial level.

2. Claim 35: Regulation 2081/92 is inconsistent with Article 1.1 of the TRIPS Agreement because it is inconsistent with Article 22.2

416. Australia claims that, because Regulation 2081/92 is inconsistent with Article 22.2 of the TRIPS Agreement, it is also inconsistent with Article 1.1.[195]

417. This claim is entirely consequential on Claim 21. Since there is no violation of Article 22.2, there is also no violation of Article 1.1.

3. Claim 36: Regulation 2081/92 is inconsistent with Article 22.2 TRIPS

418. The United States claims that Regulation 2081/92 is inconsistent with Article 22.2 because it fails to provide to "interested parties" established outside the EC the means to prevent the acts specified in that provision.[196]

419. The United States cites the following reasons:

- the registration of geographical indications is subject to the conditions of equivalence and reciprocity;
- the applications for registration of geographical indications must be made by the foreign governments;
- the right to lodge an objection against a registration is subject to certain restrictions.

---

[195] Australia's FWS, para. 156.

[196] US FWS, paras. 171-183.

420. As shown below, the reasons mentioned by the United States are either incorrect, as a matter of EC law, or irrelevant under WTO law. Therefore, Regulation 2081/92 implements adequately the EC's obligations under Article 22.2 also with respect to the "interested parties" of other WTO Members.

421. In any event, the EC recalls that Regulation 2081/92 is not the only means made available by the EC and its Member States to the "interested parties" of other WTO Members in order to prevent the acts mentioned in Article 22.2. Therefore, even assuming that the US arguments with respect to Article 2081/92 were correct, the EC would still comply with its obligations under Article 22.2.

(a) Regulation 2081/92 provides to interested parties of other WTO Members the means to prevent the acts mentioned in Article 22.2

(i) Reciprocity and equivalence conditions

422. In support of its claim, the United States has claimed that the registration of geographical indications is subject to conditions of "reciprocity and equivalence."

423. As the EC has already stated before,[197] this claim is factually not correct. Article 12(1), to which the United States has referred, is not applicable to WTO Members. Accordingly, the United States' claim under Article 22.2 TRIPS is equally unfounded.

(ii) The requirement that the application must be transmitted by the Government

424. The United States has also referred to the fact that the application for registration of a geographical indication must be transmitted by the government of the country in which the relevant area is located.

425. As the EC has already set out, this requirement is a modality of the registration process which equally applies to applications from Member States and from third countries, i.e. concerns the procedure for the acquisition of an intellectual property right. According to Article 62.1 TRIPS, Members may require, as a condition of the acquisition or maintenance of intellectual property rights provided for under Sections 2 through 6 of Part II, compliance with reasonable procedures and formalities.

426. The United States has not shown that the requirement of transmission by the third country government is an unreasonable procedural requirement. In any event, such a claim would be a claim under Article 62.1 TRIPS. Since the United States has not referred to this provision in its Panel request, such a claim would be outside the Panel's terms of reference.

(iii) The right of objection

427. As explained above in response to Claim 21, the EC considers that the right to formulate objections to the registration of another intellectual property right is not inherent in the exclusivity rights conferred to trademark rights holders by Article 16.1. For the same reasons, the EC submits that Article 22.2 does not confer to "interested parties" a right to object to the registration of a geographical indication under Regulation 2081/92.

428. In any event, the US arguments are unfounded.

429. First, the exercise of the rights conferred by Article 22.2, like that of other intellectual property rights, can be made subject to compliance with reasonable procedures and formalities.[198] The requirement that statements of objections must be channelled through the authorities of other WTO Members is equivalent to the requirement imposed on EC residents. It is neither excessive nor unreasonable. Indeed, the authorities of other

[197] See above paras. 62-69.

[198] Cf. Articles 62.1 and 41.2 of the TRIPS Agreement.

WTO Members enjoy complete discretion to decided whether or not to transmit an objection. If the US authorities wished, they could limit themselves to forward immediately any objection that they receive. Furthermore, the United States would be estopped from pleading that, because of its own willingness to forward a statement of objections to the EC Commission, US nationals are deprived from the means of protection required by Article 22.2.[199]

430. Second, as explained in the factual part, the United States has misread Article 12d of Regulation 2081/92.[200] The requirement that the country must have been recognized under Article 12(3) does not apply to WTO Members.

431. Third, Articles 12b (2) and 12d (1) of Regulation 2081/92 require a "legitimate interest" as a condition for objecting to the registration of a geographical indication. However, this term does not, in accordance with its ordinary meaning, require that the person concerned must have an economic interest "in the EC" in the sense that it must be "established" or "do business" within the EC.[201]

432. Fourth, a name which is misleading as to the origin of the product would fail to comply with the requirements of Article 2 (the first ground of objection under Article 7(4)).[202] The EC fails to see what "acts of unfair competition," in addition to those already covered by the existing grounds of objection, could arise from the valid registration of a geographical indication under Regulation 2081/92.[203] The United States has specified none.

(b) The EC and its Member States provides to interested parties of other WTO Members other means to prevent the acts mentioned in Article 22.2

433. Regulation 2081/92 is not the only means made available by the EC and its Member States to interested parties established both in the EC and in other WTO Members in order to prevent the acts mentioned in Article 22.2.

434. Specifically, additional means of protection are provided in:

- Directive 79/112 on the labelling, presentation and advertising of foodstuffs[204] and implementing legislation of the Member States;
- Directive 84/450 on misleading advertising[205] and implementing legislation of the Member States;
- the Trademarks Directive and implementing legislation of the Member States;
- the Community Trademark Regulation;
- unfair competition laws of the Member States.

---

199 US FWS, para. 179.

200 US FWS, para. 180.

201 US FWS, para. 181.

202 US FWS, para. 182.

203 Ibid.

204 Directive 2000/13/EC of the European Parliament and of the Council, of 20 March 2000, on the approximation of the laws of the member States relating to the labelling, presentation and advertising of foodstuffs, OJ (2000) L 109/29.

205 Council Directive 84/450/EEC of 10 September 1984 relating to the approximation of the laws, regulations and administrative provisions of the Member States concerning misleading advertising, OJ (1984) L 250/17.

435. The United States is aware of the above measures, which were specified in the responses provided by the EC and its Member States in the context of the review under Article 24.2 of the TRIPS Agreement[206] and have been notified to the WTO.

436. The means of protection provided by the above measures are sufficient to implement the EC's obligation under Article 22.2. In any event, these measures are outside the terms of reference of the Panel.

VIII. REGULATION 2081/92 IS CONSISTENT WITH OBLIGATIONS UNDER THE TBT AGREEMENT

437. Australia (but not the United States) has raised two claims under the TBT Agreement:

- that Article 12(2) of Regulation 2081/92 is incompatible with Article 2.1 of the TBT Agreement (claim 37);[207]

- that Articles 4 and 10 of Regulation 2081/92 are incompatible with Article 2.2 of the TBT Agreement (claim 38).[208]

438. Hereafter, the EC will first show that the provisions of Regulation 2081/92 referred to by Australia cannot be regarded as technical regulations within the meaning of Articles 2.1 and 2.2 TBT Agreement. Subsequently, the EC will show that in any event, Australia's claims under Article 2.1 and 2.2 TBT Agreement are unfounded.

A. REGULATION 2081/92 IS NOT A TECHNICAL REGULATION

439. Australia has argued that Regulation 2081/92 is in part a technical regulation within the meaning of Annex 1 to the TBT Agreement.[209] In this respect, it has referred on the one hand to Article 12(2) of Regulation 2081/92, and on the other hand to Article 4, in particular 4 (2) (g), and 10 of Regulation 2081/92.[210] As the EC will show, none of these provisions constitutes a technical regulation within the meaning of the TBT Agreement.

1. General

440. Articles 2.1 and 2.2 of the TBT Agreement impose obligations on WTO Members with respect to "technical regulations." As the Appellate Body has explained in *EC – Asbestos*, whether the measure is a technical regulation is therefore a threshold issue which determines whether the obligations contained in Article 2 TBT Agreement are applicable.[211]

441. Point 1 of Annex 1 to the TBT Agreement defines a technical regulation as follows:

> Document which lays down product characteristics or their related processes and production methods, including the applicable administrative provisions, with which compliance is mandatory. It may also include or deal exclusively with terminology, symbols, packaging, marking or labelling requirements as they apply to a product, process or production method.

---

[206] IP/C/W/117/Add. 10, 26 March 1999.

[207] Australia's FWS, para. 234 et seq.

[208] Australia's FWS, para. 249 et seq.

[209] Australia's FWS, para. 209 et seq.

[210] Australia's FWS, paras. 219–221.

[211] Appellate Body Report, *EC – Asbestos*, para. 59 ; similarly Appellate Body Report, *EC – Sardines*, para. 175.

442. As the Appellate Body has stated in *EC – Sardines*, there are three criteria which must be fulfilled cumulatively in order for a measure to be considered a technical regulation:[212]

> We interpreted this definition in *EC – Asbestos*. In doing so, we set out *three criteria* that a document must meet to fall within the definition of "technical regulation" in the *TBT Agreement*. *First*, the document must apply to an identifiable product or group of products. The *identifiable* product or group of products need not, however, be expressly *identified* in the document. *Second*, the document must lay down one or more characteristics of the product. These product characteristics may be intrinsic, or they may be related to the product. They may be prescribed or imposed in either a positive or a negative form. *Third*, compliance with the product characteristics must be mandatory. As we stressed in *EC – Asbestos*, these three criteria are derived from the wording of the definition in Annex 1.1.

2. Article 12(2) of Regulation 2081/92 is not a technical regulation

443. Contrary to the view of Australia, Article 12(2) of Regulation 2081/92 is not a technical regulation within the meaning of the TBT Agreement.

(a) Article 12(2) does not apply to identifiable products

444. First of all, Article 12(2) of Regulation 2081/92 does not apply to identifiable products.

445. Australia has argued that Regulation 2081/92 applies to agricultural products and foodstuffs, and that these are identifiable products.[213] However, the EC would like to recall that the requirement to indicate the country of origin contained in the second subparagraph of Article 12(2) applies only to the names in the situation referred to in the first subparagraph of Article 12(2).[214]

446. Accordingly, the requirement of Article 12(2) does not apply to all agricultural products and foodstuffs for which a registration is obtained under Regulation 2081/92, but only to cases of homonymous protected names from the EC and a third country. Moreover, as the EC has also explained, the requirement in Article 12(2) can apply both to geographical indications from a third country or from the EC, depending on which name has been protected earlier.[215]

447. The Regulation itself does not allow to identify the products which might be affected by this requirement. Accordingly, Article 12(2) does not apply to identifiable products.

(b) Article 12(2) does not lay down product characteristics

448. Second, Article 12(2) does not lay down product characteristics. Australia has argued that Article 12(2) "sets out a specific labelling requirement" falling within the meaning of a technical regulation as defined in Annex 1 to the TBT Agreement.[216]

449. Australia overlooks that Article 12(2) does not contain a specific labelling requirement for any specific product. Article 12(2) sets out merely the conditions under which a geographical indication will be registered in a situation where there are homonyms from the EC and a third country. The requirement to indicate the country of origin will be a condition for the registration of the geographical indication for which protection is sought later.

---

[212] Appellate Body Report, *EC – Sardines*, para. 176.

[213] Australia's FWS, para. 231.

[214] Above para. 85 et seq.

[215] Above, para. 88.

[216] Australia's FWS, para. 220.

450. However, it is not Article 12(2) TBT Agreement itself which imposes a labelling requirement. The application for the registration of any geographical indication, whether from the EC or a third country, must be accompanied by a product specification. In accordance with Article 4 (2) (h) of Regulation 2081/92, the product specification shall contain the specific labelling details relating to the geographical indication. In the situation envisaged by Article 12(2), the requirement to indicate the country of origin will be among the labelling details which must be indicated in the product specification.

451. Moreover, it must be noted that the definition of "technical regulation" in Annex 1 to the TBT Agreement encompasses labelling requirements only "as they apply to a product, process or production method." In the present case, the labelling requirement does not relate to a product, process, or its production method, but merely to its geographic origin. As the EC has already set out,[217] this question of origin marking is covered by the special disciplines of Article IX GATT.

452. Accordingly, Article 12(2) does not lay down product characteristics within the meaning of the definition of a technical regulation.

(c) Article 12(2) of Regulation 2081/92 is not mandatory

453. Finally, Article 12(2) does not impose a requirement with which compliance is mandatory.

454. Regulation 2081/92 establishes a system for the registration and protection of geographical indications. The possibility to apply for registration of a geographical indication is a right, not an obligation. In particular, registration under Regulation 2081/92 is not a precondition for the marketing of products.

455. Article 4(1) of Regulation 2081/92 provides that in order to be eligible to use a geographical indication, a product "must comply with a specification." However, it is important to note that this compliance refers only to the specifications in Article 4(2), not to the Regulation itself.

456. Similarly, Article 12(2) is a condition for the registration of a geographical indication. Since the registration process is voluntary, compliance with Article 12(2) is not a mandatory condition for the placing of products on the market.

457. For all the reasons set out above, Article 12(2) of Regulation 2081/92 is not a technical regulation within the meaning of the TBT Agreement.

3. Articles 4 and 10 of Regulation 2081/92 are not a technical regulation

458. Contrary to the view of Australia, Articles 4 and 10 of Regulation 2081/92 are not a technical regulation within the meaning of the TBT Agreement.

(a) Articles 4 and 10 do not lay down product characteristics

459. First of all, Article 4 and 10 of Regulation 2081/92 do not lay down product characteristics.

460. Article 4(g), to which Australia has referred specifically, provides merely that the product specification shall include the details of the inspection procedures provided for in Article 10. Article 10 provides the basic criteria with which such inspection structures must comply. These provisions cannot be regarded as laying down product characteristics.

---

[217] Above 213.

461. First, Article 10(1) defines that the function of inspection structures is "to ensure that agricultural products and foodstuffs bearing a protected name meet the requirements laid down in the specifications." Accordingly, the purpose of Article 4(g) in conjunction with Article 10 is not to lay down product characteristics, but to ensure conformity with the product specification.

462. However, the TBT Agreement makes a clear distinction between measures laying down product characteristics, and measures ensuring conformity with technical regulations. Articles 2 to 4 of the TBT Agreement deal with technical regulations and standards, whereas Articles 5 to 9 of the TBT Agreement are concerned with the assessment of conformity with technical regulations and standards. Point 3 of Annex 1 to the TBT Agreement defines a conformity assessment procedure as follows:

> Any procedure used, directly or indirectly, to determine that relevant requirements in technical regulations or standards are fulfilled.

463. Even if the product specification were to be considered a technical regulation, the inspection structure ensuring conformity with the specification would not be a technical regulation, but a conformity assessment procedure. Accordingly, Australia's claim regarding the inspection procedure does not concern a technical regulation, and accordingly does not fall under Article 2 TBT Agreement. Rather, Australia's claim would appear to fall, depending on the nature of the conformity assessment body involved, under Articles 5 to 9 of the TBT Agreement. However, since Australia did not refer to these provisions in its Panel request, any such claim would be outside the terms of reference of the present Panel.

464. Second, Article 4 of Regulation 2081/92 does not lay down product characteristics. Article 4(2) simply sets out the requirements with which a product specification must comply in order to permit the registration of a geographical indication. Article 4 (2) does not itself set out the product characteristics for specific products; rather, these characteristics are contained in the application for registration of a geographical indication in accordance with Article 5 (3) of the Regulation.

465. Moreover, it is not exceptional that the definition of product characteristics is required as a condition for the acquisition of certain intellectual property rights. In particular, the system of certification marks which used by certain countries requires that products bearing the mark comply with certain product characteristics.[218] However, it does not appear that such trade mark laws have so far been considered as falling under the TBT Agreement.

466. Accordingly, Article 4 in conjunction with Article 10 of Regulation 2081/92 cannot be regarded as laying down product characteristics.

(b) Articles 4 and 10 are not mandatory

467. As the EC has already explained, Regulation 2081/92 establishes a system for the registration and protection of geographical indications which is voluntary. The requirement that inspection structures must exist is a necessary requirement for the registration of geographical indications. However, this registration is not a precondition for the placing of products on the market.

468. For these reasons, Articles 4 and 10 of Regulation 2081/92 are not a technical regulation within the meaning of the TBT Agreement.

---

[218] Cf. e.g. US Trademark Act, 15 US § 1127 (Exhibit EC-6).

B. CLAIM 37: ARTICLE 12(2) OF REGULATION 2081/92 IS INCOMPATIBLE WITH ARTICLE 2.1 OF THE TBT AGREEMENT

469. Australia has claimed that Article 12(2) of Regulation 2081/92 is incompatible with Article 2.1 of the TBT Agreement.[219] As the EC has already explained, Article 12(2) of the Regulation is not a technical regulation, and Article 2.2 TBT Agreement is therefore not applicable.

470. Alternatively, the EC considers that Article 12(2) is fully compatible with Article 2.1 of the TBT Agreement. In this respect, the EC can also refer to the response the EC has already given to the United States' claims 3 and 14, regarding Article 12(2) with respect to the national treatment provisions of the GATT and the TRIPS.

1. General

471. Article 2.1 TBT Agreement contains a national treatment provision applicable to goods in respect of technical regulations. The provision is drafted as follows.

> Members shall ensure that in respect of technical regulations, products imported from the territory of any Member shall be accorded treatment no less favourable than that accorded to like products of national origin and to like products originating in any other country.

472. There is so far no WTO jurisprudence on this provision. For the reasons set out below, the EC does not consider it necessary to define, in the present context, the meaning of each of the elements of Article 2.1 TBT Agreement.

473. However, the EC would also like to recall that each provision of a covered agreement must be interpreted within the specific context of that agreement. For this reason, the EC does not agree with Australia that the jurisprudence concerning Article III GATT can simply be transposed to Article 2.1 TBT Agreement, for instance with respect to the likeness of products.[220]

474. Such an approach would overlook that there are important structural differences between the GATT and the TBT Agreement. In particular, there is no provision corresponding to Article XX of the GATT in the TBT Agreement. These structural differences between the two agreements must be taken into account when interpreting the requirements of Article 2.1 TBT Agreement.

2. Article 12(2) of Regulation 2081/92 does not apply to all geographical indications, but only to homonyms

475. As the EC has already set out, Article 12(2) merely sets out the conditions under which a geographical indication will be registered in a situation where there are homonyms from the EC and a third country. The requirement to indicate the country of origin will be a condition for the registration of the geographical indication for which protection is sought later.[221]

476. Accordingly, Article 12(2) does not treat foreign and EC geographical indications differently; on the contrary, it treats them exactly alike. Accordingly, there is no violation of the national treatment obligation in Article 2.1 TBT Agreement.

---

219 Australia's FWS, para. 234 et seq.

220 Australia's FWS, para. 226.

221 Above para. 88.

3. The requirement to indicate the country of origin for homonymous geographical indications from the EC and third countries does not constitute less favourable treatment

477. Australia has argued that a violation of Article 2.1 exists to the extent that a requirement to indicate the country of origin does not exist in the case of two homonyms from the EC.[222]

478. This claim is equally unfounded. First of all, such a difference of treatment would also affect EC geographical indications, which are equally covered by Article 12(2), and therefore not be an issue of national treatment. In addition, the relevant point of comparison in this case would be the treatment of two homonyms within Australia; however, this is not a question which falls within the responsibility of the EC.

479. Moreover, Article 6(6) of Regulation 2081/92 requires "a clear distinction in practice" also where conflicts between homonyms arise within the EC. As the EC has explained, where the two homonyms are from different Member States, this may in practice require the indication of the country of origin.[223] The only reason why the last indent of Article 6 (6) does not explicitly require the indication of the country of origin is that this provision deals with a wider set of conflicts than Article 12(2). In particular, Article 6(6) also applies to conflicts between homonyms from the same EC Member State. In such a situation, the indication of the country of origin would not be a meaningful way of achieving the necessary "clear distinction."

480. Accordingly, Article 12(2) of Regulation 2081/92 is compatible with Article 12(1) TBT Agreement.

4. National treatment obligations do not apply to requirements to mark the country of origin

481. Finally, it must be recalled that marks of origin are specifically dealt with in Article IX:1 of the GATT, which excludes the applicability of the national treatment obligation under Article III:4 GATT.[224] Should Article 12(2) of Regulation 2081/92 be considered as a technical regulation, then this should not have the effect of rendering the specific provision of Article IX:1 GATT useless. Accordingly, in this case, the national treatment obligation contained in Article 2.1 TBT Agreement could not apply to origin marking requirements.

482. In conclusion, Article 12(2) of Regulation 2081/92 is not incompatible with Article 2.1 TBT Agreement.

C. CLAIM 38: ARTICLES 4, 10, AND 12 (1) OF REGULATION 2081/92 ARE INCOMPATIBLE WITH ARTICLE 2.2 OF THE TBT AGREEMENT

483. Australia has claimed that Articles 4, 10, and 12(1) of Regulation 2081/92 are incompatible with Article 2.2 of the TBT Agreement.[225] Article 2.2 is drafted as follows:

> Members shall ensure that technical regulations are not prepared, adopted or applied with a view to or with the effect of creating unnecessary obstacles to international trade. For this purpose, technical regulations shall not be more trade-restrictive than necessary to fulfil a legitimate objective, taking account of the risks non-fulfilment would create. Such legitimate objectives are, *inter alia:* national security requirements; the prevention of deceptive practices; protection of human health or safety, animal or plant life or health, or the environment. In assessing such risks, relevant elements of consideration are, *inter alia:* available scientific and technical information, related processing technology or intended end-uses of products.

---

[222] Australia's FWS, para. 235.

[223] Above para. 89.

[224] Above para. 213.

[225] Australia's FWS, para. 249 et seq.

484. Australia has explicitly recognised that Regulation 2081/92 pursues a legitimate objective, and is capable of fulfilling its legitimate objective.[226] However, Australia argues that Article 4, 10, and 12(1) of Regulation 2081/92 read together require that another WTO Member have in place "inspection arrangements equivalent to those laid down" in the Regulation, and that this is more trade-restrictive than necessary to fulfil the legitimate objective.

485. As the EC has already explained, the provision of Regulation 2081/92 regarding inspection structures do no constitute a technical regulation, and therefore do not fall under Article 2.2 of the TBT Agreement. In any case, the EC considers that the requirements regarding inspection structures are not more trade-restrictive than necessary, and this for the following reasons:

- the existence of inspection structures is only required with respect to the specific product for which protection is sought;
- the Regulation does not determine the specific design of the inspection structures;
- the existence of inspection structures is necessary to achieve the legitimate objectives of Regulation 2081/92.

1. The existence of inspection structures is only required with respect to the specific product for which protection is sought

486. In support of its claim, Australia has referred also to Article 12(1) of Regulation 2081/92. However, as the EC has explained, Article 12(1) is not applicable to WTO Members.[227]

487. Accordingly, the registration of a geographical indication from another WTO country does not require the existence of equivalent inspection structures for all products in that country. Rather, Article 12a, 10 and 4(2)(g) require the existence of equivalent inspection structures only with respect to the specific product for which protection is sought.

2. The Regulation does not determine the specific design of the inspection structures

488. Australia has argued that Article 10(1) of Regulation 2081/92 sets out the "detailed requirements" for the inspection structures, and claimed that the Regulation "provides no leeway for regard to be had to the particular circumstances or the existing arrangements of another WTO Member."[228] Similarly, Australia has argued that the Regulation imposes an "EC model," and rules out the acceptability of other types of inspection mechanisms.[229]

489. These allegations are wrong. As the EC has explained, Regulation 2081/92, and in particular Article 10 thereof, provides considerable flexibility as to the specific design of inspection structures.[230] Article 10 limits itself to setting out the basic functions and principles applicable to inspection bodies, without regulating their design in detail. Moreover, Articles 10(2) specifically allows a choice between public and private elements in the design of the inspection bodies. Finally, for bodies outside the EC, Article 10 does not mandate compliance with EC standards, but also allows compliance with equivalent international standards.

---

[226] Australia's FWS, paras. 247–248.

[227] Above, para. 62.

[228] Australia's FWS, paras. 249–250.

[229] Australia's FWS, para. 252.

[230] Above para. 50 et seq.

490. Accordingly, Australia's allegation that Regulation 2081/92 "leaves no leeway" for the design of inspection structures is unsupported by fact. Indeed, Australia does not explain what specific problems it has with the principles and objectives set out in Article 10 of Regulation 2081/92. Moreover, it does not give any example for "other types of inspection mechanisms" which would be excluded by Regulation 2081/92.

491. Accordingly, Australia fails to show that the requirements relating to inspection structures are more trade-restrictive than necessary.

3. The existence of inspection structures is necessary to achieve the legitimate objectives of Regulation 2081/92

492. Indeed, it appears from Australia's submission that its real concern is not with the specific requirements for inspection structures set out in Regulation 2081/92, but rather that it considers that no inspection structures at all should be required.[231]

493. However, this argument of Australia must be rejected. The legitimate objective of Regulation 2081/92 is the protection of geographical indications. Geographical indications within the meaning of Article 22.1 TRIPS relate to goods that have "a given quality, reputation or other characteristic" essentially attributable to their geographical origin.

494. The objective of the inspection procedures foreseen in Regulation 2081/92 is to ensure that products using a protected geographical indication do comply with the product specifications, and therefore have the "quality, reputation or other characteristic" which justifies this protection.

495. The existence of such inspection procedures is beneficial both to consumers and to producers. Through the existence of inspection regimes, consumers have a higher degree of assurance that a product using a specific geographic indication will indeed comply with their expectations. This in turn will increase the value of the geographical indication, and thereby benefit the producers which produce in accordance with the product specifications.

496. The EC notes that as regards certification marks, the United States has also recognised that some form of control of the proper use of the name may be necessary, and that this cannot be simply left to the user of the mark:[232]

> When a geographic term is used as a certification mark, two elements are of basic concern: first, preserving the freedom of all persons in the region to use the term and, second, preventing abuses or illegal uses of the mark which would be detrimental to all those entitled to use the mark. <u>Normally a private individual is not in the best position to fulfill these objectives satisfactorily.</u> The government of a region would be the logical authority to control the use of the name of the region. The government, either directly or through a body to which it has given authority, would have power to preserve the right of all persons and to prevent abuse or illegal use of the mark.

497. Australia has argued that inspection structures might not be necessary where there is only one producer, for instance where there is only one occupant of the geographical area where the good can be produced.[233] The EC does not agree with this argument. Even where there is only one producer, the expectations of consumers should still be protected. In fact, a monopolistic situation might require inspections even more strongly then where several producers produce a good protected by a geographical indication.

---

[231] Australia's FWS, para. 255 et seq.

[232] IP/C/W/117/Add.3, p. 10, 1 December 1998 (emphasis added).

[233] Australia's FWS, para. 254.

498. Australia has also argued that other systems of protection of geographical indications might achieve the same objective, and has referred in particular to the application of unfair competition law. The EC does not consider this convincing. The EC does not contest that Members are free to implement Article 22 TRIPS through different systems of protection. This follows explicitly from Article 1.1 TRIPS, according to which Members shall be free to determine the appropriate method of implementing the provisions of the Agreement within their own legal system.

499. However, Article 1.1 TRIPS also provides that Members may implement in their law more extensive protection than is required by the TRIPS, provided that such protection does not contravene the provisions of the TRIPS. By establishing a specific system for the protection of geographical indications, the EC has established a system which grants more extensive protection, in respect of geographical indications, both to consumers and producers. This discretion left to the EC under Article 1.1 TRIPS cannot be limited on the basis of Article 2.2 TBT Agreement.

500. The requirements regarding inspection structure are an indispensable part of the EC system for the protection of geographical indications. It is therefore necessary to achieve the legitimate objectives of Regulation 2081/92.

501. Accordingly, Regulation 2081/92 is fully compatible with Article 2.2 TBT Agreement.

IX. CLAIM 39, 40: THE EC MEASURE IS COMPATIBLE WITH ARTICLE 65.1 TRIPS AND ARTICLE XVI:4 WTO

502. The United States has claimed that the EC has not fulfilled its obligations under Article 65.1 TRIPS.[234] Similarly, Australia has claimed that the EC has not complied with its obligations under Article XVI:4 WTO.[235]

503. Both claims are dependent on substantive claims discussed above. Since these claims are unfounded, the consequential claims under Article 65.1 TRIPS and XVI:4 WTO are equally unfounded.

X. CONCLUSION

504. For the reasons set out in this submission, the EC requests the Panel:

- to find that the claims and the measures specified in Section II are outside its terms of reference;
- to reject all the claims within its terms of reference.

---

[234] US FWS, para. 190.

[235] Australia's FWS, para. 267.

ANNEX B-3

ORAL STATEMENT OF THE EUROPEAN COMMUNITIES FIRST SUBSTANTIVE MEETING

(23 June 2004)

Mr Chairman, distinguished Members of the Panel,

1. The European Communities (the "EC") welcomes this opportunity to submit its views in this dispute. The EC has provided a comprehensive response to the complainants' claims in its first written submission. In this statement we will limit ourselves to outline briefly our main arguments.

2. I will first recall a number of objections raised by the EC in connection with the coverage of the terms of reference of the Panel. I will then address the complainants' claims that Regulation 2081/92 diminishes the legal protection of trademarks, contrary to Articles 16, 20, 24.5 and several provisions of Part III of the TRIPS Agreement. I will then turn to the complainants' claims that the EC measure is inconsistent with the obligation to protect geographical indications under Article 22.2 of the TRIPS Agreement.

3. Following that, my colleague, Mr Martenczuk, will discuss the claim that Regulation 2081/92 is inconsistent with the national treatment obligations under the GATT and the TRIPS Agreement. He will then respond to the US claims that Regulation 2081/92 is inconsistent with the obligation to provide most-favoured nation treatment under those two agreements. To conclude, he will address Australia's claims that Regulation 2081/92 is inconsistent with the TBT Agreement.

I. TERMS OF REFERENCE

4. At the outset, we would like to stress that the Panel should consider only those claims which are properly within its terms of reference.

5. First of all, certain claims of Australia, in particular those regarding the right of objection, concern versions of Regulation 2081/92 which had already been repealed at the time that the Panel was established. In addition, the complainants have also referred to certain measures which were not yet adopted at the time that the Panel was established. The EC has submitted that such measures which were no longer, or not yet, in existence at the time when the Panel was established are not within the terms of reference of the Panel.

6. Moreover, a number of claims raised by the complainants in their first written submissions are based on WTO provisions that were not cited in their panel requests. For this reason, the Australian claims made under Article 4 of the Paris Convention and Articles 43 to 49 of the TRIPS Agreement are outside the Panel's terms of reference. The same is true of the complainants' claims under Article 2.2 of the Paris Convention.

II. REGULATION 2081/92 DOES NOT DIMINISH THE LEGAL PROTECTION OF TRADEMARKS

7. The Complainants have raised numerous claims (we have counted as many as fourteen) to the effect that the registration of geographical indications under Regulation 2081/92 diminishes the legal protection of trademarks. The complainants' arguments could suggest to the Panel that the registration of confusing geographical indications is a frequent occurrence in the EC, which should be a cause of immediate and serious concern to all WTO Members. That suggestion is totally unfounded.

8. As of the date of establishment of this Panel, the EC authorities had registered more than 600 geographical indications. The complainants have never alleged that any of those geographical indications has resulted in a likelihood of confusion with any prior registered trademark, let alone with a trademark owned by a US or by an Australian national. The complainants' claims, all fourteen of them, are purely theoretical. They are based on supposed "systemic" concerns. Those concerns, however, have not prevented the complainants from enacting in their own statute books legislation which is less protective of the rights of trademark owners than the EC measure that they attack in this dispute.

A. ARTICLE 16.1 OF THE TRIPS AGREEMENT

1. The issue of "co-existence"

9. Both Australia and the United States claim that Article 14(2) of Regulation 2081/92 is inconsistent with Article 16.1 of the TRIPS Agreement in that it allows the "co-existence" of a later confusing geographical indication and a prior registered trademark.

10. As we have shown, this claim is unfounded for several reasons.

11. First, this claim is wrong as a matter of fact. Because of the registrability criteria provided under EC trademark law, the risk of confusion between trademarks and geographical indications is very limited. To the extent that there subsists any such risk, the problem is addressed adequately by Article 14(3) of Regulation 2081/92. The complainants have mischaracterized that provision. Article 14(3) is not a "narrow exception." The terms of Article 14(3), if properly interpreted, are sufficient to prevent the registration of any confusing geographical indications.

12. In order to substantiate their claim, the complainants should have established that Regulation 2081/92 mandates necessarily the registration of later confusing geographical indications. In turn, this would have required them to show that Article 14(3) cannot be interpreted in a manner which allows the registering authority to refuse the registration of confusing geographical indications. At the very least, the complainants should have established that, in practice, Article 14(3) is being interpreted and applied in a manner which results in a consistent pattern of registrations of confusing geographical indications. The complainants have proved none of this. Indeed, they have not even attempted to do so. As mentioned, their complaint is purely theoretical. The Panel, therefore, should conclude that, as a matter of fact, the complainants' claim would be unfounded even on their own interpretation of Article 16.1 of the TRIPS Agreement.

13. Second, in any event, the complainants' interpretation of Article 16.1 is wrong as a matter of law. The complainants' claim rests on a misconception of the relationship between trademarks and geographical indications. The TRIPS Agreement recognises geographical indications as intellectual property rights, on the same level as trademarks. It confers no superiority to trademarks over geographical indications. Nor are the provisions of Part II, Section 3, "exceptions" to Article 16.1. There is no hierarchy between them. In an attempt to establish the superiority of trademarks over geographical indications, the complainants have emphasised the exclusivity of trademarks. But from this it does not follow that trademarks must prevail over geographical indications. Geographical indications are also exclusive rights.

14. The boundary between a Member's right to protect geographical indications and its obligation to protect trademarks is not established in Article 16.1. It is defined in Article 24.5 of the TRIPS Agreement. Article 14(2) of Regulation 2081/92 is fully consistent with Article 24.5, which provides that Members shall not prejudice "the right to use a trademark." Had the drafters meant to exclude the co-existence of trademarks and later geographical indications, they would have provided instead that Members shall not prejudice "the *exclusive* right to use a trademark." Furthermore, if Article 24.5 did not allow co-existence, the protection of geographical indications would become pointless whenever there is a grandfathered trademark. Indeed, why protect a geographical indication against illegitimate uses by third parties if the legitimate users cannot use it themselves? Yet, Article 24.5 envisages such protection even in the presence of grandfathered trademarks.

15. Co-existence may not be a perfect solution, but then there is no such perfect solution. Co-existence is, nonetheless, a more reasonable solution than a rigid application of the first-in-time rule, because when comparing trademarks and geographical indications one is not comparing apples with apples. Trademarks and geographical indications are distinct intellectual property rights, each with a different subject matter and a different function. Moreover, the co-existence of intellectual property rights is by no means an unusual solution. Several other provisions of the TRIPS Agreement provide expressly for co-existence. The same is true of the law of other Members, including the United States itself.

16. The following example, drawn from the US own practice, illustrates the unreasonable consequences of the interpretation put forward by the complainants in this dispute. Napa Valley is a famous geographical indication for wine. Prior to its official recognition by the US authorities, the term "Napa" had been registered as part of several trademarks, some of which were not used for wine originating in that region. On the complainants' interpretation, the owners of those trademarks should be entitled to prevent the winemakers of Napa Valley from using that term in order to describe the origin and the characteristics of their wine. This result would be manifestly inequitable. And, indeed, the US authorities seem to agree. The applicable regulations reserve the term "Napa Valley" exclusively for the wine originating in that region. By way of exception, prior trademarks including that name are allowed to "co-exist" with that geographical indication, subject to certain labelling requirements. This solution is similar to that provided under Regulation 2081/92. The EC, therefore, fails to understand why the United States has considered it necessary to bring this claim against Regulation 2081/92.

17. <u>Third</u>, irrespective of whether the co-existence of geographical indications and earlier trademarks is envisaged by Article 24.5 of the TRIPS Agreement, the EC is required to maintain such co-existence by virtue of Article 24.3, a "stand-still" provision that prohibits Members from diminishing the level of protection of geographical indications that existed at the time of entry into force of the WTO Agreement.

18. <u>Finally</u>, even assuming that Article 14(2) of Regulation 2081/92 were *prima facie* inconsistent with Article 16.1, it would be justified as a "limited exception" to the trademark owner's exclusive rights under Article 17 of the TRIPS Agreement.

2. Article 16.1 does not confer a right of objection

19. Australia (but not the United States) also claims that Regulation 2081/92 is inconsistent with Article 16.1 of the TRIPS Agreement in that it restricts the grounds on which trademark owners may object to the registration of a geographical indication and does not ensure that objections from trademark owners are considered by the Committee.

20. These claims are based on a mistaken premise. Contrary to Australia's assumption, Article 16.1 does not confer to trademark owners a right of objection. The wording of Article 15.5 and 62.4 of the TRIPS Agreement is unequivocal in this respect. Members may, but are not required to, make available opposition procedures. In any event, as a matter of fact, Article 7(4) of Regulation 2081/92 does not limit the grounds of objection in the manner alleged by Australia. Nor is it correct that the Committee is the "ultimate decision-maker" under Regulation 2081/92. Furthermore, while Member States are not required to forward all objections to the Commission, their decisions are not discretionary and may be subject to judicial review.

B. ARTICLE 20 OF THE TRIPS AGREEMENT

21. Australia (but not the United States) claims that, by requiring the co-existence of an existing trademark and a later geographical indication, Article 14(2) of Regulation 2081/92 "encumbers unjustifiably" the use of the trademark, thereby violating Article 20 of the TRIPS Agreement.

22. As we have shown, Australia has misunderstood the purpose and the scope of Article 20. That provision is not concerned with the issue of exclusivity (i.e. *who* has the right to use a sign). Instead, Article 20 addresses the distinct issue of which requirements may be imposed upon the trademark right holder with respect to the use of *his* own trademark. As described in our first written submission, on Australia's interpretation, Article 20 would overlap and conflict with Article 16. The three examples of "special requirements" included in its first sentence confirm beyond doubt that Article 20 does not address the issue of exclusivity.

C. ARTICLE 24.5 OF THE TRIPS AGREEMENT

23. Australia (but, again, not the United States) claims that Article 14(1) of Regulation 2081/92 is inconsistent with Article 24.5 of the TRIPS Agreement because it does not afford the right of priority provided in Article 4 of the Paris Convention (1967).

24. As the EC has already explained, Article 4 of the Paris Convention was not identified in Australia's Panel request and is therefore outside the terms of reference. Moreover, this claim is insufficiently argued and difficult to understand. In so far as the EC understands it, Australia's claim is patently flawed. Article 24.5 requires to afford the priority right of Article 4 of the Paris Convention (1967) to those applications that are "grandfathered" by virtue of that provision. But Article 4 of the Paris Convention (1967) cannot be applied in order to determine whether an application is "grandfathered."

D. PART III OF THE TRIPS AGREEMENT

25. Australia and the United States claim that Regulation 2081/92 is inconsistent with numerous provisions of Part III of the TRIPS Agreement because it does not afford to trademark right holders the enforcement rights stipulated in those provisions.

26. These claims are unfounded because Part III of the TRIPS Agreement does not apply to Regulation 2081/92.

27. Regulation 2081/92 lays down an administrative procedure for the acquisition of geographical indications via a system of registration. It does not purport to regulate the procedures for enforcing trademark rights. Those procedures are provided in the trademark laws, and related civil and criminal procedural laws, of the EC and of its Member States. Those laws are not within the terms of reference of the Panel.

28. The TRIPS Agreement draws a clear distinction between, on the one hand, the procedures for the "enforcement" of intellectual property rights, which are provided in Part III, and, on the other hand, the "procedures for the acquisition and maintenance of intellectual rights and related *inter partes* procedures," which are dealt with in Part IV. The procedures provided in Regulation 2081/92 fall clearly within the second category and are subject exclusively to Part IV, and not to Part III.

29. The granting of an intellectual property right in accordance with the domestic law of each Member is not an "infringement" and, therefore, is not subject to Part III of the TRIPS Agreement. The subsequent use of a validly granted intellectual property right in conformity with the domestic laws of a Member is also not an "infringement." Requiring Members to provide judicial "enforcement" procedures against acts that are consistent with their own domestic laws, but are inconsistent with Part II of the TRIPS Agreement, would be as much as requiring them to give direct effect to the WTO Agreement in their domestic legal order. The EC would be surprised if the complainants agreed with that proposition.

30. Furthermore, applying the provisions of Part III to the procedures for the acquisition of intellectual property rights, such as those regulated in Regulation 2081/1992, would render redundant many of the provisions of Part IV and give rise to conflicts between Part III and Part IV.

31. Moreover, it would have unacceptable results for most Members. It would mean, for example, that intellectual property rights would have to be conferred always by a judicial body in accordance with judicial procedures, rather than by an administrative body in accordance with administrative procedures, as is currently the case in most Members, including Australia and the United States. The EC does not believe, for instance, that the complainants' own systems of registration of trademarks, which are operated by an administrative body, would comply with the provisions of Part III.

III. THE EC MEASURE IS CONSISTENT WITH THE OBLIGATION TO PROVIDE PROTECTION TO GEOGRAPHICAL INDICATIONS UNDER ARTICLE 22 OF THE TRIPS AGREEMENT

32. Australia and the United States have submitted very different claims under this heading.

33. Australia's claims are, once again, insufficiently argued and difficult to understand. Australia suggests that the alleged violation would arise from the fact that there is no "Community-wide system of protection" outside Regulation 2081/92. However, there is no basis in Article 22.2, or anywhere else in the TRIPS Agreement, for the proposition that protection must be provided at any particular territorial level. Again, the EC would be surprised if it were the considered view of Australia, a federal state, that the WTO Agreement may affect the constitutional allocation of competencies within Members.

34. For its part, the United States claims that Regulation 2081/92 is inconsistent with Article 22.2 because it fails to provide to "interested parties" established outside the EC the means to prevent the acts specified in that provision. As we have shown in our first written submission, the grounds alleged by the United States are either incorrect, as a matter of EC law, or irrelevant under WTO law.

35. In any event, Regulation 2081/92 is not the only means made available by the EC and its Member States. Additional means of protection are provided in:

- Directive 2000/13/EC on the labelling, presentation and advertising of foodstuffs and implementing legislation of the Member States;
- Directive 84/450 on misleading advertising and implementing legislation of the Member States;
- the Trademarks Directive and implementing legislation of the Member States;
- the Community Trademark Regulation; and
- the unfair competition laws of the Member States.

36. The United States was aware of the above measures, which were specified in the responses provided by the EC and its Member States in the context of the review under Article 24.2 of the TRIPS Agreement and have been notified to the WTO.

37. The means of protection provided by these measures are sufficient in themselves to implement the EC's obligation under Article 22.2. In any event, they are outside the terms of reference of the Panel.

IV. REGULATION 2081/92 IS COMPATIBLE WITH NATIONAL TREATMENT OBLIGATIONS, AND DOES NOT IMPOSE A REQUIREMENT OF DOMICILE OR ESTABLISHMENT

38. The complainants have raised a large number of claims alleging that Regulation 2081/92 is incompatible with national treatment obligations under the TRIPS Agreement or under the GATT, and with the prohibition on requirements of domicile or residence in Article 2.2 of the Paris Convention.

39. As the EC has shown in its written submission, these claims are unfounded both in fact and in law. In particular, many of the claims of the complainants seem to be based on misunderstandings of the content of Regulation 2081/92. The EC will now briefly recall its main arguments regarding the most salient of these claims.

A. NATIONAL TREATMENT UNDER THE TRIPS AGREEMENT

1. The conditions for the registration of geographical indications from third countries

40. The complainants have argued that Regulation 2081/92 violates the national treatment obligation of the TRIPS Agreement by imposing a condition of reciprocity and equivalence for the registration of geographical indications relating to areas located outside the EC.

41. At the outset, the EC would like to point out that neither complainant has identified an example where the EC has refused to register a geographical indication from the United States or Australia—or from any other WTO Member, for that matter—on account of conditions of reciprocity and equivalence. In fact, there has never been an application for registration of a geographical indication from the United States or Australia. Like many other claims in the present dispute, it appears therefore that this claim is purely theoretical in nature.

42. More importantly still, the claim is based on a misinterpretation of the Regulation. As the EC has set out in its first written submission, the EC does not impose conditions of reciprocity and equivalence on the registration of geographical indications from other WTO Members. Article 12 (1) of Regulation 2081/92, on which the complainants have based their arguments, clearly applies "without prejudice to international agreements," including the WTO Agreements.

43. This important element of Article 12 (1) has been completely ignored by the complainants. Under the TRIPS Agreement, WTO Members are obliged to provide protection to geographical indications. This is why the EC does not apply conditions of reciprocity and equivalence to other WTO Members. Moreover, other provisions of Regulation 2081/92, in particular those regarding the right of objection, similarly distinguish the situation of WTO Members from that of other third countries. Accordingly, it should be clear that WTO Members are not in the same situation as other third countries with respect to the registration of geographical indications relating to areas on their territory.

44. Accordingly, the registration of geographical indications from other WTO Members is subject to exactly the same conditions as the registration of geographical indications from the EC. As the EC has confirmed in its written submission, this means that geographical indications must comply with the same requirements regarding product specifications as geographical indications from the EC. Moreover, just like for EC indications, there must be inspection structures in place that ensure that the products comply with the product specifications for the specific geographical indication in question.

45. In their written submission, the complainants have not made clear whether they also consider these product-specific requirements to be in violation of national treatment obligations. In case they intended such a challenge, the EC would like to affirm that this would be manifestly unfounded. The very definition of a geographical indication is that products must have a certain quality, reputation, or other characteristics attributable to their geographical origin. The regulation simply intends to ensure that products using a protected

name indeed comply with these requirements, and it does so in a way which does not distinguish between domestic and foreign products. The application of these product-specific conditions does therefore not constitute less favourable, but indeed equal treatment.

46. As a final point, the EC would like to recall that Article 3.1 TRIPS Agreement, just like Article 2.1 of the Paris Convention, requires national treatment as between nationals, i.e. natural or legal persons. National treatment under the TRIPS Agreement therefore differs in an important respect from Article III:4 GATT, which requires national treatment as between foreign and domestic products. It is striking that in their written submissions, the complainants do not acknowledge this important difference, and indeed provide no indication of how they consider that Regulation 2081/92 discriminates between nationals.

47. Contrary to the assumption of the complainants, the conditions for registration of geographical indications do not depend on nationality. The regulation contains parallel procedures for the registration of geographical indications, depending on whether the area to which the indication is related is located inside or outside the EC. This is a question which may concern the origin of the product, but which has nothing to do with the nationality of the producer. The nationality of the producers is simply of no relevance for the registration of geographical indications. Accordingly, for this reason also, the Regulation cannot be said to discriminate between EC and non-EC nationals.

48. For all these reasons, the conditions for registration of geographical indications are fully compatible with national treatment obligations.

2. The right of objection

49. The complainants have also claimed that Regulation 2081/92 violates the national treatment obligation under the TRIPS Agreement by subjecting the right to object to a registration to conditions of reciprocity and equivalence.

50. Once again, this claim is based on an incorrect interpretation of Regulation 2081/92. As the EC already has set out, Article 12d (1) of Regulation 2081/92 gives a right to object to any person that "is from a WTO Member or a third country recognised under the procedure provided for in Article 12 (3)." It is therefore clear that WTO Members are not subject to the procedure of Article 12 (3) applicable to other third countries. The same applies also under Article 12b (2) with respect to objections against the registration of geographical indications from outside the EC.

51. Moreover, the claim is also legally unfounded. Once again, the complainants fail to establish that there is discrimination between nationals. Article 12d (1) of the Regulation refers to persons resident or established outside the EC, regardless of their nationality. It cannot simply be assumed that the reference to "nationals" in the national treatment provisions of the TRIPS Agreement also applies to persons who are domiciled or established abroad, regardless of their nationality. In fact, conditions regarding domicile or establishment are the subject of Article 2.2 Paris Convention, on the basis of which the complainants have formulated separate claims. It is not clear to the EC how these claims are consistent with the complainant's apparent view that Article 3.1 TRIPS Agreement and 2.1 of the Paris Convention also provide for national treatment between domestic and foreign residents.

3. The transmission of applications and objections

52. The complainants have argued that the requirement that applications for the registration of geographical indications must be transmitted by the government of the country where the geographical area is located, constitutes a violation of national treatment obligations. Moreover, they have raised the same claim also with respect to the transmission of statements of objection.

53. The EC considers this claim to be unfounded. First of all, the requirement of transmission through governmental channels applies to domestic and foreign geographical indications alike. Accordingly, the Regulation cannot be said to discriminate between nationals, nor between foreign and domestic geographical indications.

54. More importantly still, governments fulfil an important role in the registration process. It is clear that the government in whose territory the geographical area is located to which a geographical indication relates, is better placed than any other to verify the admissibility of applications relating to such an area. It is rather striking to the EC that the complainants seem to consider that the protection in one country of a geographical indication related to an area located in the territory of another country could be achieved without any cooperation between the two countries concerned. Moreover, it does not appear that the responsibilities of governments in the transmission of applications and objections are unduly burdensome or difficult for another WTO Member to fulfil.

55. In fact, as the complainants themselves have indicated in their written submission, the real problem is essentially their absence of "inclination" to cooperate in the process. However, this unwillingness to cooperate is not attributable to the Community, but is the choice of the complainants. The complainants should therefore not be permitted to label as less favourable treatment by the EC a situation that would exclusively be due to their own attitude.

4. Indication of the country of origin for homonymous names

56. The United States has argued that Article 12 (2) of Regulation 2081/92 provides less favourable treatment to nationals because it requires in certain circumstances the indication of the country of origin.

57. Once again, this claim is theoretical in nature, and is moreover based on a misinterpretation of the Regulation. First of all, it should be relatively clear that Article 12 (2) is not a provision which requires the origin labelling of protected products generally, but is a provision which applies only in very specific circumstances, namely where there are identical protected names from the EC and a third country.

58. Secondly, the provision, when understood properly, in no way discriminates between foreign and domestic geographical indications, let alone nationals. It simply requires that the country of origin be indicated in order to avoid confusion and to achieve a clear distinction in practice. Logically, this requirement will normally be applied to whichever name is protected later, regardless of whether this is the EC or the foreign indication. Accordingly, Article 12 (2) of the Regulation treats foreign and domestic products exactly alike.

5. The historical claims of Australia

59. Australia has formulated a number of claims also regarding the alleged absence of a right of objection under Regulation 2081/92 before it was amended through Regulation 692/2003, which entered into force on 8 April 2003.

60. The EC finds it astonishing to have to defend itself against claims which are formulated essentially in the past tense. The objective of WTO dispute settlement is to solve actual disputes and to achieve compliance with WTO obligations. It is not the object of WTO dispute settlement to dwell on historical grievances, whether real or perceived. As the EC has already stated, it therefore considers that Australia's claims relating to measures no longer in force at the time of the Panel's establishment are outside the Panel's terms of reference.

61. However, since Australia has raised these historical claims, the EC nonetheless would like to take the opportunity to correct the historical facts. Australia has referred to the simplified procedure which used to be provided for in Article 17 of Regulation 2081/92, and has claimed that under this procedure, a right of objection was available to EC residents which was not available to foreign residents. This claim is historically incorrect. As the EC has set out in its first written submission, under Article 17 of Regulation 2081/92, the right of

objection was explicitly excluded. Therefore, there existed no possibility for objection, regardless of whether the person in question was an EC or a foreign resident. Australia's claims of unequal treatment are already for this reason deprived of any historical basis.

62. The EC notes furthermore that in its submission, Australia appears to have made its national treatment claims not just with respect to the Regulation itself, but also with respect to the over 600 registrations of individual geographical indications carried out until the entry into force of Regulation 692/2003. In the view of the EC, this apparent attempt to invalidate the individual registrations is devoid of all legal basis. The registrations of the individual indications are not in violation of national treatment obligations. In reality, Australia is simply attacking the procedure that was set out in Regulation 2081/92 until its amendment through Regulation 692/2003, but which it did not challenge when it was still in force.

63. Moreover, Australia seems to forget that WTO remedies are not retroactive. Even if it had challenged Regulation 2081/92 before it was amended through Regulation 692/2003, all it could have achieved would have been the amendment of that particular measure. It could not have claimed the cancellation of the hundreds of geographical indications already registered. It seems to the EC that not having attacked Regulation 2081/92 before it was amended, Australia can certainly not claim more now than it could have claimed then.

B. PROHIBITED REQUIREMENT OF DOMICILE OR ESTABLISHMENT

64. The United States has claimed that the conditions for registration of geographical indications amount to a requirement of domicile or establishment prohibited by Article 2.2 of the Paris Convention. As the EC has already mentioned, this claim was not identified in the Panel requests, and is therefore outside the terms of reference of the Panel. Moreover, as the EC has also set out, this claim also fails on its merits.

65. In a first alternative, the United States has argued that Regulation 2081/92 imposes a requirement of domicile or establishment because it prevents a US national from registering a geographical indication relating to an area located in the US. Quite apart from the question of whether this has anything to do with domicile or establishment, the EC has already confirmed that geographical indications relating to areas in the US can be registered under Regulation 2081/92. Therefore, this claim must fail.

66. Presumably conscious of this weakness, the United States has also tried an alternative formulation of this claim. In this formulation, Regulation 2081/92 imposes a requirement of domicile or establishment because a US national could not register a geographical indication relating to an area located in the EC without some form of investment or business establishment in the EC.

67. This claim already does not do justice to the content of Regulation 2081/92. Faithful to Article 22.1 of the TRIPS Agreement, Regulation 2081/92 requires that in order to qualify for protection as a geographical indication, the product in question must possess characteristics attributable to that geographical origin and that "the production and/or processing and/or preparation" of the product must take place in the defined geographical area. Nowhere does the Regulation, nor indeed Article 22.1 of the TRIPS Agreement, impose a requirement of domicile or establishment.

68. Moreover, the implications of the United States claim are worth noting. The United States seems to believe that a US national should be allowed to register a geographical indication relating to an area in the EC regardless of whether this producer or his products have any link with that area. Taken to its logical consequence, this view of the United States would entirely undermine the protection of geographical indications as foreseen in the TRIPS Agreement. The EC regrets to have to say that this claim casts some doubt on how seriously the United States takes the conditions for the protection of geographical indications.

69. Finally, both complainants have also alleged that the conditions for objecting to the registration of geographical indications impose a requirement of domicile or establishment. These claims seem to be based on

the assumption that residents of WTO Members cannot object under the Regulation. As the EC has already stated, that is not so. Accordingly, this claim is unfounded.

C. NATIONAL TREATMENT UNDER ARTICLE III:4 GATT

70. The complainants have raised a number of their national treatment claims also under the GATT, namely as regards the conditions of registration, the transmission of applications, and the labelling of homonymous geographical indications.

71. As the EC has already set out, none of these elements of Regulation 2081/92 constitute less favourable treatment, regardless of whether one refers to nationals or to goods. The EC will therefore not restate its arguments in this respect, which equally apply to Article III:4 GATT.

72. The EC would merely signal one additional question regarding the issue of origin labelling, which the Panel would have to consider should it come to the conclusion that, contrary to the EC's submission, Article 12 (2) of the Regulation does involve discrimination between domestic and foreign products. When they argue that there is a violation of national treatment under the GATT of other agreements, the complainants seem to have forgotten the existence of Article IX GATT, which is, however, the specific provision in WTO law concerning origin marking. Remarkably, Article IX:1 GATT does specifically contain a most-favoured nation rule in respect of origin marking, but does not contain a national treatment rule. If Article IX:1 GATT is to have any useful meaning at all, then it must be that it contains a specific—and exclusive—set of disciplines for origin marking. Accordingly, national treatment obligations would not seem to apply to origin marking.

73. As a final point on national treatment under the GATT, and only in case the Panel should come to the conclusion that Regulation 2081/92 does entail a difference in treatment between domestic and foreign products, the EC considers that the challenged elements of Regulation 2081/92 are justified by Article XX (d) GATT. All relevant aspects of the Regulation, and in particular the conditions for the registration of geographical indications, are necessary to secure compliance with the conditions for the registration and protection of geographical indications.

74. In conclusion, Regulation 2081/92 is therefore compatible with national treatment obligations under the GATT.

V. REGULATION 2081/92 IS COMPATIBLE WITH THE OBLIGATION TO PROVIDE MOST-FAVOURED-NATION TREATMENT

75. The United States has also claimed that Regulation 2081/92 is incompatible with the obligation to provide most-favoured-nation treatment under the TRIPS Agreement and under the GATT. In this respect, the US has claimed that a) the EC discriminates among non-EC WTO Members by imposing conditions of reciprocity and equivalence and b) that the EC Member States grant each other more favourable treatment than they accord to non-EC WTO Members.

A. THE EC DOES NOT DISCRIMINATE AMONG WTO MEMBERS

76. The first of these US MFN claims is already clearly unfounded in fact and in law.

77. First of all, the US claim is based on the assumption that the EC applies a condition of reciprocity and equivalence to WTO Members. As the EC has already stated, it does not apply such a condition to WTO members. Therefore, WTO Members are treated as well as any other in respect of the conditions of registration of geographical indications.

78. Second, the conditions which the Regulation requires to be fulfilled for registration, notably the requirement of product specifications and inspection structures, apply without discrimination to all foreign products. Accordingly, they cannot be argued to be incompatible with most-favoured-nation principles.

79. Third, even if Article 12 (1) of Regulation 2081/92 did apply to WTO Members, which it does not, it is worth pointing out that this provision does not yet confer any advantage on any third country. It merely sets out the abstract conditions for rendering the Regulation applicable to non-WTO third countries. These conditions do not distinguish between third countries, and can therefore not be said to confer an advantage on any particular country.

80. Finally, as regards most-favoured-nation treatment under the TRIPS Agreement, it should be recalled that unlike Article I:1 GATT, Article 4 TRIPS requires discrimination between nationals, not between products. However, Regulation 2081/92 does not refer to nationality, but to the question of where the geographical area is located. As the EC has said already, this may have something do with the origin of the product, but it has nothing to do with the nationality of the producer.

81. For all these reasons, this claim of the United States should be rejected.

B. REGULATION 2081/92 DOES NOT INVOLVE THE GRANTING OF ADVANTAGES BETWEEN MEMBER STATES

82. The second claim of violation of Article 4 TRIPS Agreement by the United States is a rather curious one. In essence, the United States is arguing that "through Regulation 2081/92," EC Member States are granting "each other" advantages, which are not available to other WTO Members, and are thereby violating Article 4 TRIPS.

83. In the view of the EC, this claim is entirely unfounded. To begin with, as the EC has already set out, the conditions for the registration of geographical indications do not discriminate between geographical indications from the EC and from WTO countries. Accordingly, the EC does not understand which are the specific advantages which the US claims are being withheld from it.

84. Moreover, Article 4 TRIPS refers to advantages which are granted to the "nationals of another country." Regulation 2081/92 does not grant any advantage to nationals of "another country." The EC is a founding member of the WTO. When it adopts a measure which harmonises the law within the EC, it does therefore neither grant its Member States any advantages, nor do its Member States grant each other advantages.

85. As the United States knows perfectly well, Regulation 2081/92 is a measure of the EC. This is why the United States has correctly brought this case against the EC, and not against its Member States. The US claim that "through Regulation 2081/92," Member States are granting each other advantages is therefore entirely artificial and in contradiction with the United States' own actions in the present dispute settlement proceedings.

VI. REGULATION 2081/92 IS CONSISTENT WITH OBLIGATIONS UNDER THE TBT AGREEMENT

86. Australia has alleged that Regulation 2081/92 is inconsistent with the TBT Agreement in two respects: first, it has claimed that the requirement to indicate the country of origin in Article 12 (2) of the Regulation is inconsistent with Article 2.1 TBT Agreement; and second, it has claimed that Articles 4 and 10 of Regulation 2081/92 are incompatible with Article 2.2 TBT Agreement to the extent that the require they existence of inspection structures.

A. REGULATION 2081/92 IS NOT A TECHNICAL REGULATION

87. Article 2 of the TBT Agreement applies only to technical regulations. The claims raised by Australia under the TBT Agreement must fail already because none of the provisions of Regulation 2081/92 challenged by Australia constitutes a technical regulation within the meaning of the TBT Agreement.

1. Article 12 (2) of Regulation 2081/92 is not a technical regulation

88. As the EC has already set out in its written submission, Article 12 (2) is not a technical regulation within the meaning of the TBT Agreement.

89. First of all, Article 12 (2) does not apply to all agricultural products and foodstuffs covered by the Regulation, but only to products in the specific situation envisaged in the provision, namely where a protected name from the EC is identical to a protected name from a third country. Accordingly, Article 12 (2) does not apply to identifiable products.

90. Moreover, Article 12 (2) does not lay down product characteristics. First of all, the provision does not itself lay down how any specific product should be labelled. As the EC has set out in its written submission, where the situation envisaged in Article 12 (2) occurs, the labelling requirement will normally be part of the product specifications. In addition, the indication of the country of origin does not constitute a labelling requirement as it applies "to a product, process or production method."

91. Finally, it should also be noted that the possibility for registration under Regulation 2081/92 is a right, but is not a condition for marketing of products in the EC. The registration process is entirely voluntary. Accordingly, Regulation 2081/92 cannot be held to lay down product characteristics with which compliance is mandatory.

2. Articles 4 and 10 of Regulation 2081/92 are not a technical regulation

92. With its claim regarding Articles 4 and 10 of Regulation 2081/92, Australia is challenging the requirement that inspection structures must exist. As follows from Article 10(1) of Regulation 2081/92, the objective of inspection structures is to ensure that agricultural products and foodstuffs bearing a protected name meet the requirements laid down in the specification.

93. As the EC has set out in its first written submission, this requirement of the existence of inspection structures cannot be regarded as constituting a technical regulation. Under the TBT Agreement, a technical regulation is a measure which lays down product characteristics. The TBT Agreement carefully distinguishes technical regulations from conformity assessment procedures, which are used to determine whether the requirements contained in technical regulations are met. Whereas technical regulations are dealt with in Articles 2 and 3 of the TBT Agreement, the WTO obligations regarding conformity assessment procedures are set out separately in Articles 5 to 9 of the TBT Agreement.

94. Even if the product specifications, with which the inspection structures must ensure conformity, were to be regarded as a technical regulation, then the inspection structure itself could still not be regarded as a technical regulation falling under Article 2 of the TBT Agreement. Rather, it would have to be regarded as a conformity assessment procedure falling under Articles 5 to 9 of the TBT Agreement. However, Australia has not referred to these provisions in its panel request, so that such a claim would be outside the terms of reference of the panel.

95. For this reason, Articles 4 and 10 of Regulation 2081/92 cannot be regarded as technical regulation falling under Article 2 of the TBT Agreement.

B. ARTICLE 12 (2) OF REGULATION 2081/92 IS NOT INCOMPATIBLE WITH ARTICLE 2.1 OF THE TBT AGREEMENT

96. Australia has claimed that the requirement to indicate the country of origin in Article 12 (2) of Regulation 2081/92 violates the national treatment provision in Article 2.1 TBT Agreement. In the view of the EC, even if the Panel came to consider that Article 12 (2) constitutes a technical regulation, this claim would have to fail.

97. As the EC has said earlier, Article 12 (2) does not treat EC and foreign geographical indications differently. It merely requires that where there are identical protected names from the EC and from a third country, the country of origin must be indicated. This requirement may affect the EC or the third country geographical indication, whichever is registered later. There is therefore perfect equality of treatment between domestic and foreign geographic indications.

98. Australia has criticised the fact that Article 6 (6) of Regulation 2081/92 does not contain the same requirement as regards identical geographical indications from within the EC. In the view of the EC, this comparison is not pertinent. First of all, the EC does not see how Australian products can be disadvantaged by the way in which conflicts between homonyms from within the EC are being resolved. Moreover, it should be noted that Article 6 (6) deals with a larger set of potential conflicts than Article 12 (2). In particular, it also may concern conflicts between geographical indications from within the same Member State. It is therefore not surprising that the provision requires a "clear distinction in practice," rather than requiring the indication of the country of origin in all cases.

C. ARTICLES 4, 10, AND 12 (1) OF REGULATION 2081/92 ARE NOT INCOMPATIBLE WITH ARTICLE 2.2 OF THE TBT AGREEMENT

99. Finally, even if the Panel considered that Articles 4 and 10 constituted a technical regulation, there would be no violation of Article 2.2 TBT Agreement.

100. Article 2.2 TBT Agreement provides that technical regulation must not be more trade-restrictive than necessary to fulfil a legitimate objective. The EC submits that the requirement that inspection procedures must exist to ensure that products bearing a protected name comply with the product specifications is necessary to fulfil the legitimate objectives of Regulation 2081/92.

101. The legitimate objective of the inspection procedures foreseen in Regulation 2081/92 is to ensure that products using a protected geographical indication do comply with the product specifications, and therefore have the "quality, reputation or other characteristics" which justify this protection. The existence of such inspection procedures is beneficial both to consumers and to producers.

102. The existence of such inspection structures is also in no way disproportionate to this objective. First of all, as the EC has set out in its written submission, Article 10 of Regulation 2081/92 limits itself to fixing the general principles, and leaves a maximum of flexibility as regards the specific design of the inspection procedures. Despite its complaints that Article 10 is unduly restrictive and obliges other WTO Members to follow an "EC model," Australia has not actually explained what specific type of inspection structures it envisages which would be ruled out by Article 10 of Regulation 2081/92.

103. In reality, Australia's argument seems to be that the existence of inspection structures should be required at all. However, this does not seem to be compatible with the objectives of Regulation 2081/92 regarding the protection of geographical indications. In fact, Australia does not take into account the specific nature of geographical indications, which are defined as having a specific quality, reputation, or characteristics attributable to their geographical origin. It is therefore entirely appropriate that the EC provides for mechanisms which ensure that products marketed bearing a geographical indication do in fact comply with these requirements.

104. Whether there are also, as Australia argues, other systems of protection which may achieve the objective of protecting geographical indications in accordance with Article 22 TRIPS is not the question. Article 1.1 TRIPS explicitly allows each WTO member the freedom to determine how to implement the provisions of the Agreement within their legal system. Moreover, Article 1.1 also allows the WTO Members to provide more extensive protection than required by the Agreement. This is indeed what the EC has done in Regulation 2081/92. However, it would not be acceptable for third country geographical indications to take advantage of this extensive protection without complying with the same requirements as an EC indication. This would in fact not result in equal treatment, but in more favourable treatment for foreign products.

105. Accordingly, Australia's claim under Article 2.2 TBT Agreement must be rejected.

*

* *

106. Thank you for your attention. This concludes our statement. We look forward to answering any questions that the Panel may wish to ask.

ANNEX B-4

REPLIES BY THE EUROPEAN COMMUNITIES TO QUESTIONS POSED BY THE PANEL FOLLOWING THE FIRST SUBSTANTIVE MEETING

TABLE OF WTO CASES REFERRED TO IN THE RESPONSES

Short Title	Full Case Title and Citation
Canada – Autos	Appellate Body Report, *Canada – Certain Measures Affecting the Automotive Industry*, WT/DS139/AB/R, WT/DS142/AB/R, adopted 19 June 2000, DSR 2000:VI, 2995
Canada – Pharmaceutical Patents	Panel Report, *Canada – Patent Protection of Pharmaceutical Products*, WT/DS114/R, adopted 7 April 2000, DSR 2000:V, 2295
EC – Asbestos	Appellate Body Report, *European Communities – Measures Affecting Asbestos and Asbestos-Containing Products*, WT/DS135/AB/R, adopted 5 April 2001
EC – Bananas III	Appellate Body Report, *European Communities – Regime for the Importation, Sale and Distribution of Bananas*, WT/DS27/AB/R, adopted 25 September 1997, DSR 1997:II, 591
India – Patents (US)	Appellate Body Report, *India – Patent Protection for Pharmaceutical and Agricultural Chemical Products*, WT/DS50/AB/R, adopted 16 January 1998, DSR 1998:I, 9
US – Corrosion-Resistant Steel Sunset Review	Appellate Body Report, *United States – Sunset Review of Anti-Dumping Duties on Corrosion-Resistant Carbon Steel Flat Products from Japan*, WT/DS244/AB/R, adopted 9 January 2004.
US – Section 110(5) Copyright Act	Panel Report, *United States – Section 110(5) of the US Copyright Act*, WT/DS160/R, adopted 27 July 2000, DSR 2000:VIII, 3769
US – Section 211 Appropriations Act	Panel Report, *United States – Section 211 Omnibus Appropriations Act of 1998*, WT/DS176/R, adopted 1 February 2002, as modified by the Appellate Body Report, WT/DS176/AB/R
US – Section 211 Appropriations Act	Appellate Body Report, *United States – Section 211 Omnibus Appropriations Act of 1998*, WT/DS176/AB/R, adopted 1 February 2002
US – Section 301 Trade Act	Panel Report, *United States – Sections 301-310 of the Trade Act of 1974*, WT/DS152/R, adopted 27 January 2000, DSR 2000:II, 815

Question 1

To what extent is the Panel bound by the EC's interpretation of its own Regulation?

1. Regulation 2081/92, which is the measure at issue in the present proceedings, is an act of EC domestic law. As the Appellate Body has held in *India – Patents*, domestic law may constitute evidence of compliance or non-compliance with international obligations.[1] Accordingly, as the Appellate Body has held, a Panel may be required to determine the meaning of an act of domestic law in order to establish whether such act is compatible with WTO obligations.[2]

2. The Panel's approach to the interpretation of Regulation 2081/92 should therefore be governed by Article 11 of the DSU, according to which the Panel must make "an objective assessment of the facts of the

[1] Appellate Body Report, *India – Patents*, para. 65.

[2] Appellate Body Report, *India – Patents*, para. 66.

case." Accordingly, the EC does not consider that the Panel is "bound" by the EC's interpretation of Regulation 2081/92.

3. However, the EC would like to underline that in making an objective assessment of the facts, and in particular of the meaning of Regulation 2081/92, the Panel must take due account of the fact that Regulation 2081/92 is a measure of EC domestic law. It can therefore not "interpret" Regulation 2081/92, but rather must establish the meaning of its provisions as factual elements. In this context, reference can be made to the approach described by the Panel in *US – Section 301*:[3]

> In this case, too, we have to examine aspects of municipal law, namely Sections 301-310 of the US Trade Act of 1974. Our mandate is to examine Sections 301-310 solely for the purpose of determining whether the US meets its WTO obligations. In doing so, we do not, as noted by the Appellate Body in *India – Patents (US)*, interpret US law "as such," the way we would, say, interpret provisions of the covered agreements. We are, instead, called upon to establish the meaning of Sections 301-310 as factual elements and to check whether these factual elements constitute conduct by the US contrary to its WTO obligations. The rules on burden of proof for the establishment of facts referred to above also apply in this respect.
>
> It follows that in making factual findings concerning the meaning of Sections 301-310 we are not bound to accept the interpretation presented by the US. That said, any Member can reasonably expect that considerable deference be given to its views on the meaning of its own law.

4. It follows from this approach that there are considerable differences between the interpretation of the WTO agreements by a Panel, and the establishment of the meaning of a challenged act of domestic law by a Panel. First of all, as a question of fact, the rules regarding the burden of proof must apply. Accordingly, the burden of proof for establishing that Regulation 2081/92 as the measure at issue has a particular meaning is on the complainants, not on the EC.

5. This is particularly important in the case of *per se* challenges against measures which have so far not been applied by the authorities of a Member. In such a case, a Member should not be held in violation of its WTO obligations unless it is established beyond doubt that the measure in fact entails the violations alleged by the complainants.

6. Second, the establishment of the meaning of an act of domestic law is not governed by the customary principles of interpretation of international law. Rather, the objective assessment of the facts requires establishing the meaning that the act will normally have within the legal order of the WTO Member in question. This means that the interpretation should be guided by the rules of interpretation customary in the legal order of such member, and taking account of the legal context of the measure in the domestic law of the Member.

7. Third, even though a Panel is not bound by the interpretation of a WTO Member of it own measure, due account must be taken of the fact that it is the authorities of this Member which must interpret and apply the measure in the domestic legal order. Therefore, as the Panel set out in *US – Section 301*, the explanations given by such Member of the meaning of its own measure must be given considerable deference.

8. This deference accorded to the author of a domestic act is also illustrated in Panel practice. When establishing the meaning of domestic measures, Panels have regularly relied on statements and explanations given by the defending party in the course of the proceedings. This is the case for instance in *US – Section 301*, where the Panel relied to an important extent on statements made by the United States as regards the interpretation and application of the challenged measure.[4] The same was also the case in *Canada –*

[3] Panel Report, *US – Section 301*, para. 7.18 (footnotes omitted).

[4] Panel Report, *US – Section 301*, para. 7.125.

Pharmaceutical Patents, where the Panel relied on assurances given by Canada during the proceedings.[5] Similarly, in *US – Section 211*, the Panel relied on a US response given to the Panel in order to establish the meaning of the challenged measure.[6]

Question 2

Can the procedures under Articles 5 and 6 of Regulation (EC) No. 2081/92 apply to names of geographical areas located outside the EC?

9. The procedures set out in Articles 5 and 6 of Regulation 2081/92 in principle apply only to names related to geographical areas located inside the EC. The corresponding procedures for geographical indications related to geographical areas located outside the EC are contained in Articles 12a and 12b. However, these provisions also contain a number of references to specific sections of Articles 5 and 6, which to this extent are applicable to the registration of geographical indications from outside the EC.

Question 3

Did the phrase "[w]ithout prejudice to international agreements" in Article 12(1) of Regulation (EC) No. 2081/92 predate the TRIPS Agreement? Did it refer to any specific agreements when it was adopted? Which agreements does it refer to now? Would it cover bilateral agreements for the protection of individual geographical indications?

10. The phrase "[w]ithout prejudice to international agreements" was already contained in Article 12(1) of Regulation 2081/92 as originally adopted in 1992.

11. The phrase "without prejudice to international agreements" is not in any way limited to particular specific agreements or types of agreements. Accordingly, this phrase applies both to multilateral and to bilateral agreements. Moreover, the phrase does not just apply to agreements in force at the time the Regulation was adopted, but also to agreements which were adopted subsequently.

12. At the time that Regulation 2081/92 was adopted, the GATT was one of the agreements to which the "without prejudice" clause applied. Moreover, at the time that Regulation 2081/92 was adopted, the TRIPS Agreement was in the final phases of its negotiation. It was therefore the objective that the "without prejudice" clause should also apply to the TRIPS and other WTO agreements resulting from the Uruguay Round.

13. The importance of the WTO Agreements, and notably of the TRIPS Agreement, for the interpretation and application of Regulation 2081/92 was reconfirmed by Regulation 692/2003,[7] the 8th recital of which prominently refers to the obligations resulting from the TRIPS Agreement.

Question 4

Is it unusual that the text of Article 12(1) of Regulation (EC) No. 2081/92 covers only a small number of countries that are non-WTO Members, but the introductory phrase "[w]ithout prejudice to international agreements" covers the entire membership of the WTO? Why was this structure retained when the Regulation was amended in April 2003?

14. The EC does not consider this as unusual. First, the EC would like to point out that out of the 191 current Members of the United Nations, 48 are not Members of the WTO, including certain important countries

---

5 Panel Report, *Canada – Pharmaceutical Patents*, para. 7.99.

6 Panel Report, *US – Section 211*, para. 8.69.

7 Exhibit COMP 1h.

such as Russia. Therefore, even though this group has been shrinking since the establishment of the WTO, the EC does not consider this number as "small."

15. It is also not surprising that the fundamental structure of Article 12 was not changed. When proposing to amend an act of the Council, it is a concern for the Commission to preserve the Council act to the extent that it does not require amendment. Therefore, the Commission proposal will frequently limit itself to those amendments which are strictly speaking necessary, and will leave those provisions the amendment of which is not necessary untouched.

Question 7

Do the last sentence of Article 12(3) of Regulation (EC) No. 2081/92 and the first clause in Article 12a "[i]n the case provided for in Article 12(3)" limit the applicability of Article 12a?

16. No. The last sentence of Article 12 (3) of Regulation 2081/92 merely provides that where the Commission decision provided for in this provision is in the affirmative, the procedure set out in Article 12a shall apply. This does not mean that the procedure in Article 12a cannot apply in other cases.

17. As regards the reference in Article 12a (1) to Article 12 (3), the EC would like to point out that Article 12 (3) refers to the conditions set out in Article 12(1). As the EC has confirmed, by virtue of the "without prejudice" clause, these conditions do not apply to WTO Members. Accordingly, since the procedure in Article 12 (3) is inapplicable to WTO Members, so is the reference to this provision in Article 12a (1).

Question 8

Which references to a "third country" in Articles 12, 12a, 12b and 12d of Regulation (EC) No. 2081/92 include all WTO Members, and which do not? What, in the context of each reference, indicates what "third country" means? Why are different terms not used?

18. Whether the term "third country" includes WTO Members or not must be established on the basis of the wording, context, and objectives of the specific provision in question. In Article 12(1) of Regulation 2081/92, this context includes the "without prejudice" clause. Accordingly, as the EC has explained, the references to "third countries" in Article 12(1) do not include WTO Members. The same applies where a provision refers to a "third country meeting the equivalence conditions of Article 12(3)" (Article 12b[2][b]) or a "third country recognised under the procedure provided for in Article 12(3)" (Article 12d[1]), or where a provision specifically distinguishes between third countries and WTO Members. Where this is not the case, as for instance in Article 12a(1) or Article 12b(1), the reference to third countries may also include WTO Members.

Question 9

Why is it that only the rights of objection in Articles 12b(2)(a) and 12d(1) of Regulation (EC) No. 2081/92 mention a "WTO Member" or "WTO member country"? Is it relevant that Regulation (EC) No. 692/2003 explained, in its 10th recital, that in the matter of objections the provisions in question apply without prejudice to international agreements but, in its 9th recital, it explained that the protection provided by registration is open to third countries' names by reciprocity and under equivalence conditions?

19. This is due to the differences in the structure of Article 12 on the one hand, and of Articles 12b and 12d, on the other. Article 12 contains the introductory clause "without prejudice to international agreements," which made it possible not to specifically single out the position of WTO Members in the text of the provision. Articles 12b and 12d do not contain such a clause, so that it was necessary to differentiate between WTO Members and other third countries.

20. The 10th recital of Regulation 692/2003 confirms this interpretation by stating that the objective of the amendment of the provisions regarding objections was "that it should be made clear that in this matter nationals of WTO member countries are covered by these arrangements and that the provisions in question apply without prejudice to international agreements." In order words, the distinction between WTO Members and third countries was intended to have exactly the same function as the without prejudice clause in Article 12(1) of Regulation 2081/92. Given this common objective of ensuring compatibility with WTO obligations, the differences in drafting technique between Articles 12(1) and 12b and 12d appear secondary.

21. As regards the 9th recital, this recital refers to the reciprocity and equivalence conditions "as provided for in Article 12" of Regulation 2081/92. This reference of course includes the "without prejudice" clause of Article 12(1). Accordingly, the 9th recital does not concern WTO Members.

Question 10

Has the Commission recognized any countries under the procedure set out in Article 12(3) of Regulation (EC) No. 2081/92? Have any countries requested to be recognized under that procedure?

22. No (to both questions).

Question 11

Has an application for registration under Regulation (EC) No. 2081/92 ever been made in respect of the name of a geographical area located outside the EC? If so, what happened?

23. No.

Question 13

What discretion does the Commission enjoy in the application of Regulation (EC) No. 2081/92?

24. Whether the provisions of the Regulation leave the Commission a discretion or not, and the extent of such discretion, will depend on the wording of each particular provision conferring powers on the Commission. Where such provisions provide that the Commission "shall" take a certain action, the Commission would normally be obliged to take such action. Where the Regulation provides that the Commission "may" take a certain action, then the Commission would normally enjoy a discretion as to whether to take such action or not. In any case, the Commission is bound to respect and apply the terms of the Regulation.

Question 14

Please express your view on whether and to what extent the mandatory/discretionary distinction in GATT and WTO jurisprudence applies under the TRIPS Agreement. Would the nature of those TRIPS obligations which are not prohibitions but rather oblige Members to take certain actions, affect the application of the distinction?

25. The relevance of the distinction between "mandatory" and "discretionary" measures under the TRIPS Agreement is the same as under the other WTO Agreements.

26. As clarified by the Appellate Body in *United States – Carbon Steel (Japan)*[8], panels are not required, as a preliminary jurisdictional matter, to examine whether the challenged measure is "mandatory." Rather, this issue is relevant as part of the panel's assessment of whether the measure is, as such, inconsistent with particular obligations. Accordingly, whether or not the distinction between "discretionary" and "mandatory" measures is

[8] Appellate Body Report, *United States – Carbon Steel (Japan)*, para. 89

"relevant" under the TRIPS Agreement will depend on the specific obligations imposed by each provision at issue.

27. That the distinction between "discretionary" and "mandatory" measures may be relevant also under the TRIPS Agreement is illustrated by *United States – Section 211*, where the Appellate Body recalled such distinction and concluded that the panel had applied it correctly.[9]

Question 15

What would be the most authoritative statement of the interpretation of Regulation (EC) No. 2081/92? Is a statement by the EC delegation to this Panel legally binding on the European Communities?

28. According to Article 220 (1) of the EC Treaty, it is the European Court of Justice which ensures that in the interpretation and application of the Treaty the law is observed. This judicial function of the Court of Justice also applies to acts of the Community institutions adopted on the basis of the Treaty. Accordingly, the highest judicial authority competent to interpret the meaning of Regulation 2081/92 is the European Court of Justice.

29. The European Commission represents the European Community in the proceedings before the Panel. Accordingly, the statements made by the agents of the European Commission before the Panel commit and engage the European Communities.

30. However, it should also be noted that where the statements of the European Communities regard the interpretation of Regulation 2081/92, these statements concern an issue <u>of fact</u>. These statements are made in order to assist the Panel in its function to make an objective assessment of the facts. Their purpose is therefore to clarify the existing legal situation in European Community law. Their intention is not to create new legal obligations in public international or in Community law.

31. This being said, the EC does not consider that its statements before the Panel are without legal significance. In this context, the EC is aware that its submissions to the Panel will be public as part of the final report to the Panel. It is not conceivable to the European Commission that it would, in the interpretation or application of the Regulation, take a different approach to the one it has set out before the Panel.

32. As regards the approach to be taken by the European Court of Justice, the European Commission considers it important to underline that the European Court of Justice has shown a consistently high degree of awareness and respect for the international obligations of the European Communities.

33. According to the settled case law of the Court of Justice, Community legislation must, so far as possible, be interpreted in a manner that is consistent with international law, in particular where its provision are intended specifically to give effect to an international agreement concluded by the Community.[10]

34. As one scholar of Community law has observed in a recent book on the external relations law of the European Communities, the principle of consistent interpretation has been particularly important with respect to GATT and WTO law: "The EU Courts have never hesitated to make use of consistent interpretation for the purpose of applying GATT and WTO law."[11]

35. As regards specifically the TRIPS Agreement, the Court for instance has held as follows:[12]

---

[9] Appellate Body Report, *United States – Section 211*, para. 258.

[10] Case C-61/94, *Commission/Germany*, [1996] ECR I-4006, para. 52 (Exhibit EC-13); C-341/95, *Bettati*, [1998] ECR I-4355, para. 20 (Exhibit EC-14).

[11] Piet Eeckhout, *External Relations of the European Union*, Oxford University Press, p. 315 (2004).

[12] Case C-53/96, *Hermès*, [1998] ECR I-3603, para. 28 (Exhibit EC-15); confirmed in C-300/98 and 392/98, *Dior*, [2000] ECR I-1344, para. 47 (Exhibit EC-16).

> It is true that the measures envisaged by Article 99 and the relevant procedural rules are those provided for by the domestic law of the Member State concerned for the purposes of the national trade mark. However, since the Community is a party to the TRIPs Agreement and since that agreement applies to the Community trade mark, the courts referred to in Article 99 of Regulation No 40/94, when called upon to apply national rules with a view to ordering provisional measures for the protection of rights arising under a Community trade mark, are required to do so, as far as possible, in the light of the wording and purpose of Article 50 of the TRIPs Agreement.

36. The Court of Justice will be particularly prone to take into account the international obligations of the Community where the Community legislative act itself indicates that it is intended to implement obligations of international law. For instance, in a recent judgment, the Court held that, on the basis of a recital in the Community Anti-Dumping Regulation, the duty to provide an explanation contained in Article 2.4.2 of the AD Agreement had to apply also in the context of the application of the Community Regulation:[13]

> However, where the Community intended to implement a particular obligation assumed in the context of the WTO, or where the Community measure refers expressly to precise provisions of the agreements and understandings contained in the annexes to the WTO Agreement, it is for the Court to review the legality of the Community measure in question in the light of the WTO rules (see, in particular, Portugal v Council, paragraph 49).
>
> The preamble to the basic regulation, and more specifically the fifth recital therein, shows that the purpose of that regulation is, inter alia, to transpose into Community law as far as possible the new and detailed rules contained in the 1994 Anti-dumping Code, which include, in particular, those relating to the calculation of dumping, so as to ensure a proper and transparent application of those rules.
>
> It is therefore established that the Community adopted the basic regulation in order to satisfy its obligations arising from the 1994 Anti-dumping Code and that, by means of Article 2(11) of that regulation, it intended to implement the particular obligations laid down by Article 2.4.2 of that code. To that extent, as is clear from the case-law cited in paragraph 54 of the present judgment, it is for the Court to review the legality of the Community measure in question in the light of the last-mentioned provision.
>
> In that regard, it should be recalled that Community legislation must, so far as possible, be interpreted in a manner that is consistent with international law, in particular where its provisions are intended specifically to give effect to an international agreement concluded by the Community (see, in particular, Case C-341/95 Bettati [1998] ECR I-4355, paragraph 20).

37. The interpretation of Article 12 of Regulation 2081/92 which the EC has set out before the Panel is therefore in full accordance with the principles of interpretation applied on a constant basis by the European Court of Justice.

38. In addition, it also useful to know that the Court of Justice may take account of statements which the Commission has made on behalf of the European Community in the WTO. For instance, in the judgement just cited, the Court of Justice referred in support of its interpretation to a assurances given by the European Commission to the secretariat of the WTO Committee on Anti-Dumping Practices:[14]

---

[13] Case C-76/00 P, *Petrotub*, [2003] ECR I-79, para. 54–57 (Exhibit EC-17).

[14] Case C-76/00 P, *Petrotub*, [2003] ECR I-79, para. 59 (Exhibit EC-17).

> Such an interpretation coincides in essence with the international assurances given in the communication of 15 February 1996 from the Commission to the secretariat of the WTO Committee on Anti-Dumping Practices, according to which the explanation referred to in Article 2.4.2 of the 1994 Anti-dumping Code will be given directly to the parties and in regulations imposing anti-dumping duties.

Question 16

Can the EC provide the Panel with any official statement predating its first written submission that names of geographical areas located in all WTO Members could be registered under Regulation (EC) No. 2081/92 without satisfying its equivalence and reciprocity conditions?

39. In the context of the review under Article 24.2 TRIPS, the EC explained that the reciprocity requirement applied without prejudice to international agreements.[15] Moreover, in the meeting of the TRIPS Council of 16 June 2004, the EC was asked to clarify whether it applied conditions of reciprocity and equivalence to other WTO Members. The EC provided the following response to this question:[16]

> EC Regulation No 2081/92 applies to geographical indications relating to areas located inside as well as outside the EC. For this purpose, the Regulation lays down rules relating to the registration of geographical indications from outside the EC which closely parallel the provisions applicable to geographical indications from inside the EC. The purpose of these specific rules, some of which were recently introduced by Regulation No. 692/2003, is to facilitate the registration of non-EC geographical indications while at the same time ensuring that geographical indications from outside the EC correspond to the definition of a geographical indication.
>
> As to the conditions which must be fulfilled for registration to take place, some WTO Members have considered, on the basis of Article 12(1) of Regulation No 2081/92, that registration of geographical indications from outside the EC is possible in only under conditions of "reciprocity and equivalence." However, Article 12(1) of Regulation No. 2081/92 provides that it applies "without prejudice to international agreements" including the TRIPs Agreement. Since WTO Members are obliged to provide protection to geographical indications in accordance with the TRIPS Agreement, the reciprocity and equivalence conditions mentioned in Article 12(1) of Regulation 2081/92 do not apply to WTO Members.
>
> In other words, the EC GI register is open to GIs from other WTO Members, and registration of such GIs may take place on the same substantive conditions which apply to registration of GIs from EC Member States.

40. Moreover, the EC would like to remark that this question concerns evidence regarding the interpretation of Regulation 2081/92 as in force at the time of establishment of the Panel. Regarding a question of admissible evidence, the EC does not consider that only evidence which predates the date of its first written submission in the present proceedings is relevant. For this reason, for instance, the statements made by the EC in the course of the Panel proceedings should also be taken into account.

[15] IP/C/W/253/Rev.1, p. 27 (Exhibit EC-18).

[16] The EC's statement should be reflected in due course in the minutes of the TRIPS Council.

Question 17

Is the EC's explanation of the availability of registration of foreign GIs under its system, set out in its written statement to the Council for TRIPS in September 2002, (IP/C/M/37/Add.1, para. 142 and Annex, pp. 77-85) consistent with the text of Articles 12-12c of the Regulation? Why did that written statement not qualify the position that the Regulation's equivalence and reciprocity conditions apply to foreign GIs, if they did not apply to WTO Members, to whom the statement was addressed?

41. The EC considers that the written statement to the TRIPS Council is not incompatible with the text of Regulation 2081/92 as in force at the time it was made or with the statements of the EC in the present case.

42. The EC would like to remark, however, that this statement is of limited relevance for the present case. It was made in the context of the negotiations for the extension of protection under Article 23 TRIPS to products other than wines and spirits. The intention of the statement was therefore not primarily to explain the EC system for the protection of geographical indications. In addition, the statement was made in 2002, and therefore does not take into account the amendments made by Regulation 692/2003.

Question 18

Did the EC member States agree with the Commission's written statement to the Council for TRIPS in September 2002 with respect to the conditions attached to the registration of foreign GIs? How can the Commission ensure that the Council of Ministers will not prevent registration under the Regulation of the name of a geographical area located in a third country WTO Member because that Member does not satisfy the equivalence and reciprocity conditions of Article 12(1)?

43. It is the European Commission which represents the European Communities within the WTO. Where appropriate, the European Commission consults with the competent instances of the Council. The position of individual Member States is therefore of no relevance in the present proceedings.

44. Like the Commission, the Council of Ministers is bound to apply the terms of Regulation 2081/92. Like the Commission, it is bound to give effect to the wording "without prejudice to international agreements," and to take account of the Community's international obligations under the WTO Agreements.

Question 19

Has a judicial authority ever ruled on the availability of protection provided by registration for third countries under Regulation (EC) No. 2081/92? If the Commission registered the name of a geographical area located in a third country WTO Member, could that registration be subject to judicial review because the area was located in a WTO Member that did not fulfil the equivalence and reciprocity conditions of Article 12(1) of the Regulation?

45. Community courts can only rule on an issue when concrete cases are brought before them. Since no request for registration has ever been made in respect of a geographical indication from a third country, no judicial authority has ever had the occasion to rule on the availability of protection provided by registration for third countries under Regulation 2081/92.

46. The registration of the name of a geographical indication, whether from a third country or from within the EC, takes the form of a regulation of the Commission. The condition under which such a regulation can be challenged before the European Court of Justice are set out in Article 230 of the EC Treaty, which reads as follows:

> The Court of Justice shall review the legality of acts adopted jointly by the European Parliament and the Council, of acts of the Council, of the Commission and of the ECB, other

than recommendations and opinions, and of acts of the European Parliament intended to produce legal effects vis-à-vis third parties.

It shall for this purpose have jurisdiction in actions brought by a Member State, the European Parliament, the Council or the Commission on grounds of lack of competence, infringement of an essential procedural requirement, infringement of this Treaty or of any rule of law relating to its application, or misuse of powers.

The Court of Justice shall have jurisdiction under the same conditions in actions brought by the Court of Auditors and by the ECB for the purpose of protecting their prerogatives.

Any natural or legal person may, under the same conditions, institute proceedings against a decision addressed to that person or against a decision which, although in the form of a regulation or a decision addressed to another person, is of direct and individual concern to the former.

The proceedings provided for in this Article shall be instituted within two months of the publication of the measure, or of its notification to the plaintiff, or, in the absence thereof, of the day on which it came to the knowledge of the latter, as the case may be.

47. The question of the validity of EC regulations may also become an issue in proceedings before the courts of the Member States. According to Article 234 of the EC Treaty, national courts are obliged to refer questions concerning the validity of EC regulations to the European Court of Justice for a preliminary ruling. Such preliminary rulings are legally binding upon the national courts. Article 234 of the EC Treaty provides:

The Court of Justice shall have jurisdiction to give preliminary rulings concerning:

(a) the interpretation of this Treaty;

(b) the validity and interpretation of acts of the institutions of the Community and of the [European Central Bank];

(c) the interpretation of the statutes of bodies established by an act of the Council, where those statutes so provide.

Where such a question is raised before any court or tribunal of a Member State, that court or tribunal may, if it considers that a decision on the question is necessary to enable it to give judgment, request the Court of Justice to give a ruling thereon.

Where any such question is raised in a case pending before a court or tribunal of a Member State against whose decisions there is no judicial remedy under national law, that court or tribunal shall bring the matter before the Court of Justice.

Question 20

With reference to paragraph 43 of the EC's oral statement, does the EC contest that equivalence and reciprocity conditions such as those under Article 12(1) and (3) of Regulation (EC) No. 2081/92, if applied to other WTO Members, would be inconsistent with the national treatment obligations in the TRIPS Agreement and/or Article III:4 of the GATT 1994?

48. First of all, the EC considers that this question may be too broad to be answered in abstract terms. Since different things may be understood by "conditions of reciprocity and equivalence," an answer can only be

given on a case by case basis. This is aptly illustrated by the United States' reference to the EC's requirement of inspection structures as "equivalence by another name."[17] As the EC has already indicated during the first meeting with the Panel, it emphatically considers that this requirement is not inconsistent with the national treatment obligations of the TRIPS Agreement or the GATT.

49. As regards the specific conditions contained in Article 12(1) of Regulation 2081/92, the EC has already confirmed that it does not apply these to WTO Members. For this reason, the EC considers that the question whether these conditions are inconsistent with the national treatment obligations of the TRIPS Agreement and the GATT does not arise.

Question 21

If Switzerland, as a WTO Member, can apply for registration of its GIs under Regulation (EC) No. 2081/92 without satisfying equivalence and reciprocity conditions, what was the purpose of its joint declaration with the EC concerning GIs set out in Exhibit US-6 and mentioned in paragraph 119 of the US first written submission and paragraphs 243-244 of the EC's first written submission?

50. The bilateral agreement envisaged in the declaration represents an alternative approach to the protection of geographical indications to the direct registration under Regulation 2081/92. Compared to the registration on a case-by-case basis, a bilateral agreement would have the advantage that protection of the parties' geographical indications would be obtained in one single act. Moreover, possible controversial issues, for instance regarding generic names, homonyms, or registrations concerning cross-border areas, could be resolved in a non-contentious way.

51. However, the declaration is without prejudice to the possibility of applying for protection of Swiss geographical indications under Regulation 2081/92. Accordingly, the envisaged agreement merely represents an alternative approach to protection which does not exclude direct applications under Regulation 2081.

52. Finally, as the EC has already said in its first written submission, it would like to recall that the declaration is merely a political text, and that so far no such agreement has been concluded.

Question 22

Are there any legal requirements or other provisions in EC or national laws which ensure that groups or persons entitled to apply for registration under Article 5 of Regulation (EC) No. 2081/92 are always, or usually, EC citizens or legal persons organized under the laws of the EC or an EC member State? What conditions have been laid down for natural or legal persons to be entitled to apply for registration pursuant to Article 5(1)?

53. There are no such requirements.

54. The conditions subject to which a natural or legal person shall be entitled to apply for registration are set out in Article 1 of Commission Regulation 2037/93,[18] which reads as follows:

> Applications for registration pursuant to Article 5 of Regulation (EEC) No 2081/92, may be submitted by a natural or legal person not complying with the definition laid down in the second subparagraph of paragraph 1 of that Article in exceptional, duly substantiated cases where the person concerned is the only producer in the geographical area defined at the time the application is submitted.
>
> The application may be accepted only where:

[17] Oral Statement of the US at the first substantive meeting of the Panel, para. 17.

[18] Exhibit COMP-2.

(a) the said single person engages in authentic and unvarying local methods; and

(b) the geographical area defined possesses characteristics which differ appreciably from those of neighbouring areas and/or the characteristics of the product are different.

2. In the case referred to in paragraph 1, the single natural or legal person who has submitted the application for registration shall be deemed to constitute a group within the meaning of Article 5 of Regulation (EEC) No 2081/92.

55. These conditions define only the conditions under which a natural or legal person, as opposed to a group as defined in the second subparagraph of Article 5 (1) of Regulation 2081/92, may apply for registration. As can be seen, these conditions have nothing to do with nationality.

Question 23

How do you interpret the term "nationals" as used in Article 1.3, including footnote 1, and Articles 3.1 and 4 of the TRIPS Agreement and Article 2 of the Paris Convention (1967) in relation to this dispute? Do a Member's nationals necessarily include natural persons who are domiciled, or legal persons who have a real and effective industrial and commercial establishment, in that Member?

56. As regards the definition of nationals in Article 3.1 and 4 of the TRIPS Agreement and Article 2.1 of the Paris Convention, a distinction must be made between natural and legal persons. For natural persons, a national is any person who holds the nationality of the State in question in conformity with the legislation of such state. As regards legal persons, the question of nationality depends on the law of the state in question, which may use criteria such as the law of incorporation, headquarters, or other criteria. The legal situation has been summed up by Bodenhausen in his commentary to Article 2.1 of the Paris Convention as follows:[19]

> In deciding the question who are such nationals, account has to be taken of the fact that the Convention can also apply to *legal persons or entities*, so that a distinction must be made between the nationality of *natural* and *legal* persons, respectively.
>
> With respect to *natural* persons, nationality is a quality accorded or withdrawn by the legislation of the State whose nationality is claimed. Therefore it is only the legislation of that State which can define the said nationality and which must be applied also in other countries where it is invoked.
>
> With respect to *legal* persons, the question is more complicated because generally no "nationality" as such is granted to legal persons by existing legislations. Where these legal persons are the States themselves, or State enterprises, or other bodies of *public status*, it would be logical to accord to them the nationality of their country. With regard to corporate bodies of *private status*, such as companies and associations, the authorities of the countries where application of the Convention is sought will have to decide on the criterion of "nationality" which they will employ. This "nationality" can be made dependent upon the law according to which these legal persons have been constituted, or upon the law of their actual headquarters, or even on other criteria. Such law will also decide whether a legal person or entity really exists.

57. Natural persons who are merely domiciled in a State, but are not nationals of that state, are not "nationals" within the meaning of the national treatment provisions of the TRIPS Agreement and the Paris Convention. Similarly, legal persons who have a real and effective industrial and commercial establishment in a

[19] Bodenhausen, Guide to the Application of the Paris Convention for the Protection of Industrial Property, p. 27-28 (1968).

State, but do not fulfil the conditions for nationality of such state, are not nationals of such state. Domicile and establishment can therefore not simply be equated with "nationality" within the meaning of the national treatment provisions of the TRIPS Agreement and the Paris Convention.

58. That nationality on the one hand, and domicile or establishment on the other hand, are not identical concepts also follows from the context of the Paris Convention. First of all, if all persons domiciled or established in a particular State were its nationals, then the separate prohibition on conditions of domicile or establishment in Article 2.2 of the Paris Convention would be devoid of all useful purpose.

59. More importantly still, Article 3 of the Paris Convention enlarges the national treatment obligation to "nationals of countries outside the Union who are domiciled or who have real and effective industrial or commercial establishments in the territory of one of the countries of the Union." This provision would be completely unnecessary if all residents of a member of the Union were in any event to be considered as its nationals, and therefore benefited from national treatment under Article 2.1 of the Paris Convention. Article 3 of the Paris Convention therefore clearly illustrates that the Paris Convention, and similarly also the corresponding provisions of the TRIPS Agreement, regard nationality as a concept different from domicile or residence.

60. Finally, this is also illustrated by footnote 1 to Article 1.3 of the TRIPS Agreement. This footnote defines nationals, in the case of a separate customs territory which is a WTO Member, to mean persons natural or legal who are domiciled or who have a real and effective industrial or commercial establishment in that customs territory. This definition was necessary since separate customs territories are not states, and therefore normally do not have "nationals." Thus, the criterion of residence or establishment is used here as a replacement for the criterion of nationality, which cannot apply to separate customs territories. In turn, this special definition for custom territories would have been unnecessary had this been already the normal meaning of "nationality." Once more, footnote 1 to Article 1.3 proves that nationality and residence or establishment are not identical concepts under Articles 3.1 and 4 TRIPS and 2.1 Paris Convention.

Question 24

In your view, which natural or legal persons can be considered "interested parties" in the sense of Article 22.2 of the TRIPS Agreement? Is Article 10(2) of the Paris Convention (1967) relevant?

61. The notion of "interested parties" must be defined in relation to the intellectual property rights that Article 22.2 seeks to protect. Article 22.2 is included in Section 3 of Part II of the TRIPS Agreement dealing with "Geographical Indications" and is entitled "Protection of geographical indications." Moreover, the introductory phrase of Article 22.2 provides that the obligation set out in that provision apply "in respect of geographical indications." Accordingly, for purposes of Article 22.2, "interested parties" are those which can claim an interest in the protection of a geographical indication, and not of other intellectual property rights, such as, for example, a conflicting trademark.

62. The definition of "interested parties" in Article 10(2) of the Paris Convention does not apply to Article 10bis, which is the only provision of the Paris Convention referred to in Article 22.2 of the TRIPS Agreement. Nor should Article 10bis be extrapolated by way of contextual interpretation to Article 22.2. Article 10bis is concerned with false "indications of source," a notion which is much broader than that of geographical indications, as defined in Article 22.1 of the TRIPS Agreement.

63. Without prejudice to the above, the EC recalls that Regulation 2081/92 grants to "any legitimately concerned legal or natural person"[20] the right to object to the registration of a geographical indication. The EC considers that this wording is broad enough to encompass all "interested parties," as defined in Article 10bis of the Paris Convention.

---

[20] Cf. Article 7(4). Equivalent wording is used in Articles 12b(2) and 12d(1), which confer a right of objection to any legal or natural person with a "legitimate interest."

Question 25

Is it appropriate to compare nationals who are interested in GIs that refer to areas located in different WTO Members in order to examine national treatment under the TRIPS Agreement? Why or why not?

64. The EC is not entirely certain that it understands the meaning of the phrase "nationals who are interested in GIs that refer to areas located in different WTO Members" in the present context. However, the EC would like to recall that national treatment under the TRIPS requires a comparison as between domestic and foreign nationals who are otherwise in the same situation.

Question 26

If national treatment can be examined in relation to GIs in terms of the location of the geographical area to the territory of a Member, is it appropriate to examine national treatment in relation to any other intellectual property rights in terms of an attachment to a Member besides the nationality of the right holder? Why or why not?

65. The EC would once again like to stress that the term "nationality" in Articles 3.1 and 4 TRIPS and 2.1 Paris Convention is not linked to an attachment to the territory of a Member.

66. Moreover, the EC would like to stress that the term "national" must be given a uniform meeting regardless of which intellectual property right is concerned. It is incontestable that in accordance with Article 22.1 TRIPS, geographical indications are characterised by a link with a particular geographical area. However, this link, which is an inherent part of the definition of a geographical indication, provides no justification for defining the term "national" in Articles 3.1 and 4 TRIPS and 2.1 Paris Convention differently when geographical indications are concerned.

Question 29

The Japan – Alcoholic Beverages II, Korea – Alcoholic Beverages and Chile – Alcoholic Beverages disputes show that measures which are origin-neutral on their face can be inconsistent with Article III of GATT 1994. Is Regulation (EC) No. 2081/92 also open to challenge under Article 3.1 of the TRIPS Agreement despite its apparently national-neutral text?

67. The EC notes that the disputes *Japan – Alcoholic Beverages II, Korea – Alcoholic Beverages* and *Chile – Alcoholic Beverages* all concerned tax measures which were found to be incompatible with Article III:2 of the GATT.

68. The EC considers that this jurisprudence concerning the interpretation of Article III:2 of the GATT is not relevant for the present dispute. Article III:2 GATT is a provision dealing specifically with national treatment as regards internal taxes or other internal charges. As the Appellate Body has stated in *EC – Asbestos*, there are important textual and structural differences between Articles III:2 and III:4 of the GATT. Accordingly, the Appellate Body found for instance that the term "like products" in Article III:4 GATT could not be interpreted in the same way as the same term in the first sentence of Article III:2 GATT.[21]

69. These findings of the Appellate Body confirm that national treatment provisions cannot simply be assumed to have the same scope and meaning, but must be interpreted on the basis of their specific wording and context. If this already applies between two paragraphs of Article III GATT, even more caution is necessary when attempting to transpose national treatment principles from one agreement to another.

[21] Appellate Body Report, *EC – Asbestos*, para. 94-96.

70. As the Panel in *Canada – Pharmaceutical Patents* has convincingly explained, there is therefore no general concept of discrimination which would be common to all WTO Agreements. Rather, the meaning of each provision prescribing equal treatment must be established on the basis of the precise legal text in issue:[22]

> In considering how to address these conflicting claims of discrimination, the Panel recalled that various claims of discrimination, *de jure* and de facto, have been the subject of legal rulings under GATT or the WTO. These rulings have addressed the question whether measures were in conflict with various GATT or WTO provisions prohibiting variously defined forms of discrimination. As the Appellate Body has repeatedly made clear, each of these rulings has necessarily been based on the precise legal text in issue, so that it is not possible to treat them as applications of a general concept of discrimination. Given the very broad range of issues that might be involved in defining the word "discrimination" in Article 27.1 of the TRIPS Agreement, the Panel decided that it would be better to defer attempting to define that term at the outset, but instead to determine which issues were raised by the record before the Panel, and to define the concept of discrimination to the extent necessary to resolve those issues.

71. The EC would suggest that such a case-specific approach would also be appropriate in the present case. In this context, the EC would not exclude entirely that under certain circumstances, measures which are neutral on their face may nonetheless constitute less favourable treatment of foreign nationals. However, the EC would suggest that when considering whether Regulation 2081/92 involves discrimination as between nationals within the meaning of Article 3.1 TRIPS and 2.1 of the Paris Convention, the Panel should also take account of the following considerations:

72. First, Article 3 TRIPS refers to nationals. This specific reference, which differs from Art III:4 GATT, must be given meaning. For this reason, it should not be argued that because a measure involves discrimination on the basis of the origin of a good, or of domicile and establishment, it also constitutes de facto discrimination of nationals, since such discrimination is already covered by Article III:4 GATT, or Article 2.2 of the Paris Convention.

73. Second, the Appellate Body has held repeatedly that *de facto* discrimination is a notion intended to prevent circumvention of national treatment obligations.[23] Such a risk does not exist if a specific issue is already dealt with in other national treatment provisions, such as those of the GATT.

74. Third, the national treatment provisions of the TRIPS and the GATT should not systematically overlap. The Panel must also take account the different legal context of the provisions, which are contained in different agreements. For example, the Panel would have to consider whether Articles XX and XXIV GATT, which are available as defenses against national treatment claims under the GATT, could also apply under the TRIPS Agreement. This is an issue of major systemic implications, which should be taken into account in the interpretation of the national treatment provisions of the TRIPS Agreement.

Question 30

In Article 2(1) of the Paris Convention (1967) as incorporated in the TRIPS Agreement by its Article 2.1, should the words "country of the Union" be read mutatis mutandis to refer to "WTO Member"?

75. Yes.

---

[22] Panel Report, *Canada – Pharmaceutical Patents*, para. 7.98 (footnotes omitted).

[23] Cf. Appellate Body Report, *EC – Bananas III*, para. 233; Appellate Body Report, *Canada – Autos*, para. 142.

Question 31

What is the respective scope of the national treatment obligations in Article 2(1) of the Paris Convention (1967) and Article 3.1 of the TRIPS Agreement? Do they overlap?

76. The scope of the national treatment obligations in Article 2(1) of the Paris Convention (1967) and Article 3.1 of the TRIPS Agreement must be derived from the precise wording of those provisions. Given the closely parallel wording of the two provisions, it appears to the EC that they overlap to a considerable extent.

Question 33

Is there a public policy requirement specific to GIs which underlies the requirement that a group or person must send a registration application under Regulation (EC) No. 2081/92 to the EC Member State or authorities of a third country in which the geographical area is located, rather than directly to the Commission?

77. The requirement that a group or person must send a registration application to the EC Member State or authorities of a third country in which the geographical area is located reflects the important role that Member States or third country authorities play in the registration process under Regulation 2081/92.

78. According to Article 5 (5) of Regulation 2081/92, the Member State shall check that the application is justified and shall forward the application, including the product specification referred to in Article 4 and other documents on which it has based its decision, to the Commission. In a recent judgment, the European Court of Justice has explained that this role of Member States is due in particular to the detailed knowledge of Member States in respect of geographic indications relating to their territory:[24]

> It follows that the decision to register a designation as a PDO or as a PGI may only be taken by the Commission if the Member State concerned has submitted to it an application for that purpose and that such an application may only be made if the Member State has checked that it is justified. That system of division of powers is attributable particularly to the fact that registration assumes that it has been verified that a certain number of conditions have been met, which requires, to a great extent, detailed knowledge of matters particular to the Member State concerned, matters which the competent authorities of that State are best placed to check.

79. These same considerations are also underlying the requirement in Article 12a (2) of the Regulation, according to which the third country must verify that the requirements of the Regulation are verified before it transmits the application. Indeed, the need for an involvement of the national authorities appears even more compelling when the application concerns a geographical indication from a third country rather than from a Member State.

80. First, the evaluation of whether a name fulfils the conditions for protection as a geographical indication requires familiarity with a host of geographical, natural, climatic and cultural factors specific to the geographical area in question. Moreover, knowledge of the market conditions in the country of origin may also be required, e.g. in order to establish whether the product in question has a particular reputation. Like in the case of applications from Member State, it is the third country's authorities which are best placed to evaluate such factors. In contrast, the European Commission is less likely to be familiar with such factors than in the case of an area in a Member State. Moreover, the evaluation may also require knowledge of the language of the third country in question, which the authorities of the European Community may not have.

81. Second, the evaluation of the application may require the assessment of legal questions arising under the law of the country where the area is located. In particular, Article 12a of the Regulation requires the

---

[24] Case C-269/99, *Karl Kühne*, [2001] ECR I-9517, para. 53 (Exhibit EC-19).

application to be accompanied by a description of the legal provisions and the usage on the basis of which the geographical indication is protected or established in the third country. The Commission cannot unilaterally resolve such issues pertaining to the law of a third country, which therefore necessarily require the implication of the authorities of the third country.

82. Third, the involvement of the third country government appears called for also out of respect for the sovereignty of the third country. The assessment of whether an application meets the requirements of the Regulation, in particular concerning the link with the geographical area, requires in-depth knowledge of the conditions related to this area, as well as the possibility to verify on the spot the relevant claims made in the application. It would not be possible for the European Commission to carry out such inspections on the territory of the third country without the agreement or involvement of the third country.

83. Fourth, the involvement of the third country government also facilitates the cooperation of the authorities of the Community and of the third country throughout the registration process. If doubts or question arise during the registration process, the European Commission may need a contact point in the third country to which it can address itself. Moreover, the Regulation foresees that the third country which has transmitted the application must be consulted at certain stages of the procedure before the Commission can take a decision (cf. Articles 12b [1] [b]; 12b [3]).

84. Fifth, the involvement of the third country authorities should also be beneficial to the applicant. Regulation 2081/92 effectively enables the applicant to discuss, prepare, file, and where necessary refine and amend his application directly with the authorities where the geographical area is located. Since these authorities are more familiar with the area in question, this should help speed up the registration process. Moreover, frequently these authorities may be geographically closer to the applicant and may speak the applicant's language, which may also be a further benefit to the applicant.

Question 34

Is there a public policy requirement specific to GIs which underlies the requirement that a person wishing to object to a registration under Regulation (EC) No. 2081/92 must send an objection to the EC Member State or authorities of a third country in which he resides or is established, rather than directly to the Commission?

85. Article 12d(1) requires any natural or legal person that has a legitimate interest and is from a WTO Member Country to transmit a duly substantiated statement to the country in which it resides or is established, which shall transmit it to the Commission.

86. It is to be noted that under this provision, the third country is not required to verify the admissibility of the objection on the basis of the criteria laid down in Article 7(4) of the Regulation. Accordingly, the transmission of such applications does not require the same degree of verification as the transmission of applications for registration, and should therefore not be particularly burdensome for third countries.

87. Despite this somewhat less important role of third countries in the transmission of statements of objection, some degree of involvement of the third country government remains necessary. First, it is necessary to verify whether the person objecting is indeed resident or established in the third country, which is only possible for the authorities of that country. Second, it is not excluded that in the further procedure, questions relating to the territory of the third country might arise, in which case it is useful for there to be an official contact point in the third country. Third, it should also be beneficial to the person making the objection to be able to deal directly with an authority in the country where it is resident or established. Finally, if a statement of objection is admissible, Article 12d (3) provides that the third country which has transmitted the statement of objection is to be consulted before the Commission takes its decision.

Question 35

Has an objection to the registration of a name under Regulation (EC) No. 2081/92 ever been filed by a person from a third country? If so, what happened?

88. No.

Question 37

Please indicate examples of other international arrangements, such as the Madrid Protocol, under which national governments cooperate by acting as agents or intermediaries in the protection of private rights. Which of these arrangements are established under international treaties and which under the legislation of one of the parties to the arrangement? Which are relevant to the matter before the Panel?

89. There are a large number of examples in international law and practice in which national governments cooperate by acting as agents or intermediaries in the protection of private rights. Given the limited time available, the EC will limit itself to providing some examples drawn from a number of different sectors.

90. As referred to by the Panel, a first example is already provided by Article 2 (2) of the Protocol to the Madrid Agreement concerning the international registration of trademarks (Exhibit EC-20), which reads as follows:

> The application for international registration (hereinafter referred to as "the international application") shall be filed with the International Bureau through the intermediary of the Office with which the basic application was filed or by which the basic registration was made (hereinafter referred to as "the Office of origin"), as the case may be.

91. Similar examples where the protection of an intellectual property right requires action of the home country of the right holder can also be found in other agreements. For instance, Article 6 quinquies A (1) of the Paris Convention provides that Members of the Union may require, before registering a trademark duly registered in the country of origin, a certificate of registration in the country of origin, issued by the competent authority.

92. Similarly, Article 5(1) of the Lisbon Agreement for the Protection of Appellations of Origin (Exhibit EC-21) provides that applications for the registration of appellations of origin must be requested by the offices of the countries of the Special Union:

> The registration of appellations of origin shall be effected at the International Bureau, at the request of the Offices of the countries of the Special Union, in the name of any natural persons or legal entities, public or private, having, according to their national legislation, a right to use such appellations.

93. Such examples for requirements for cooperation between governmental authorities can also be found outside the area of intellectual property protection. For instance, the Specific Annex on Origin to the International Convention on the Simplification and Harmonisation of Customs Procedures (Kyoto Convention) provides that in certain cases, a certificate of origin issued by the competent authorities of the country of origin may be required.[25] Moreover, the Specific Annex also provides that in certain cases, the customs authorities of the importing party may request the competent authorities of the party where the certificate of origin has been established to carry out controls.[26]

---

[25] Specific Annex K to the Kyoto Convention, pts. 2 to 5, 9-12 (Exhibit EC-22).

[26] Appendix III to Specific Annex K to the Kyoto Convention, pt. 3 (Exhibit EC-22).

94. Further examples can be found in the field of technical standards and conformity assessment. For instance, the EC has concluded mutual recognition agreements with both the United States and Australia. Under these agreements, the parties mutually recognize the results of conformity assessment carried out by conformity assessment bodies recognized under the agreement. Each party designates its conformity assessment bodies to be recognized under the agreement.[27] Moreover, each party remains responsible for monitoring the conformity assessment bodies which it has designated.[28]

95. Similar arrangements can be found in the field of transport. According to Article 31 of the Chicago Convention on International Civil Aviation (Exhibit EC-25), every aircraft engaged in international navigation shall be provided with a certificate of airworthiness issued or rendered valid by the State in which it is registered. Similarly, according to Article 32 of the Chicago Convention, the pilot of every aircraft and the other members of the crew of every aircraft engaged in international civil aviation shall be provided with certificates of competency and licences issued or rendered valid by the State in which the aircraft is registered.

96. Another example can be drawn from the field of fisheries. In accordance with Article 62 of the UN Convention on the Law of the Sea, bilateral agreements may give other states access to fishing resources in the exclusive economic zone of a coastal state. However, the applications for fishing licenses must usually be transmitted by the authorities of the fishing state to those of the coastal state. By way of example, reference can be made to the Annex of the bilateral fisheries agreement between the European Community and Mozambique (Exhibit EC-26), which provides the following:

> The procedure to be followed in applying for and issuing licences authorising Community vessels to fish in Mozambican waters shall be as follows:
>
> (a) for each vessel, the European Commission, acting via its representative in Mozambique and through the agency of its delegation in that country, shall submit to the Mozambican authorities a licence application drawn up by the vessel owner wishing to carry on fishing activities under this Agreement; the application shall be submitted no later than 25 days before the start of the validity period mentioned therein. Applications shall be made using the forms provided for this purpose by Mozambique, specimens of which are given in Appendix 1 for tuna seiners and longliners, and in Appendices 1 and 2 for freezer bottom trawlers. They shall be accompanied by proof of payment of the advance payable by the vessel owner;

97. Finally, examples can also be found in the field of judicial cooperation in civil and commercial matters. For instance, Article 3 of the Hague Convention on the Service Abroad of Judicial and Extrajudicial Documents in Civil or Commercial Matters (Exhibit EC-27) provides as follows:

> The authority or judicial officer competent under the law of the State in which the documents originate shall forward to the Central Authority of the State addressed a request conforming to the model annexed to the present Convention, without any requirement of legalisation or other equivalent formality.

98. Finally, the EC would like to recall that it is a common feature of customary international law that states act on behalf of their nationals and their rights and interest. This is most clearly recognized in the institution of diplomatic protection, on the basis of which states may raise claims against other states on the basis of injury suffered by the national of the claiming state.[29]

---

[27] Cf. Article 7 of the Agreement with the United States (Exhibit EC-23); Article 5 of the Agreement with Australia (Exhibit EC-24).

[28] Cf. Article 10 of the Agreement with the United States (Exhibit EC-23); cf. also Article 8 of the Agreement with Australia (Exhibit EC-24).

[29] Cf. Diplomatic Protection of Foreign Nationals, in: Encyclopaedia of Public International Law, Vol. 1, p. 1067 (1992).

99. That fact that most of the examples above are drawn from international agreements does not diminish their relevance for the present case. Rather, these examples illustrate that in an increasingly interdependent world, the effective protection of individual rights in cross-border situations inevitable engenders a need for cross-border cooperation.

100. The EC considers that the examples quoted above are merely a fraction of the cases where intergovernmental cooperation occurs in the cross-border protection of individual rights. The EC reserves the right to elaborate further on this question in the later stages of the procedure. However, at this stage, the EC would like to remark that the Panel should be mindful that the claims of the complainants may have implications that go far beyond the present case.

Question 39

Does an EC member State participate in decision-making on a proposed registration either in the Committee established under Article 15 of Regulation (EC) No. 2081/92 or in the Council of Ministers, where that EC member State transmitted the application or an objection to it to the Commission? Is the EC member State identified with the applicant or person raising the objection in any way? Are there any limits on the participation of the EC member State – for instance, can it object to an application which it transmitted?

101. The Committee assisting the Commission in accordance with Article 15(1) of Regulation 2081/92 is composed of representatives of all Member States. This includes also the Member State which has transmitted the application or the statement of objection.

102. As the EC has already explained in its first written submission,[30] the constitution of regulatory committees is a typical modality under which the Council of Ministers delegates regulatory powers to the European Commission. Regulatory committees such as the one foreseen in Article 15(1) of Regulation 2081/92 are therefore an integral part of the Community's constitutional system.

103. When fulfilling their functions under Regulation 2081/92, a Member State is in no way identified with the applicant or the person raising the objection. In verifying the applications or statements of objection, the Member State must correctly, impartially and objectively apply the terms of the Regulation. Similarly, when exercising its role in the Committee, the Member States must be guided by the terms of the Regulation, and not act as a representative of any individual applicant or objecting person.

104. It should be noted that already when examining the admissibility of an application, the Member State must take into account all objections from within its own country, and resolve these before transmitting the application. The situation envisaged in the last sentence of the question can therefore not occur. This has been clarified in a recent judgment of the European Court of Justice:[31]

> In this connection, it should be observed that it follows from the wording and the scheme of Article 7 of Regulation No 2081/92 that a statement of objection to a registration cannot come from the Member State which has applied for the registration and that the objection procedure established by Article 7 of that regulation is not therefore intended to settle disputes between the competent authority of the Member State which has applied for registration of a designation and a natural or legal person resident or established in that Member State.

[30] EC, FWS, paras. 79 to 83.

[31] Case C-269/99, *Karl Kühne*, [2001] ECR I-9517, para. 55 (Exhibit EC-19).

Question 40

How many applications to register names under Regulation (EC) No. 2081/92 have been considered by the Committee established under Article 15 of the Regulation or the Council of Ministers?

105. Under the simplified procedure foreseen in Article 17 of Regulation 2081/92 as applicable until its amendment through Regulation 692/2003, the consultation of the Committee was required in all cases. A number of these applications were also, for various reasons, referred to the Council.

106. As regards the normal procedure, out of 171 applications, only a small number (10) have been considered by the Committee. Non of these cases was referred to the Council.

107. For the convenience of the Panel, the EC submits as Exhibit EC-28 a table which sets out in more detail the different cases of consultation of the Committee and referral to the Council.

Question 41

In paragraph 137 of your first written submission, you indicate that the term "such names" in the second sub-paragraph of Article 12(2) of Regulation (EC) No. 2081/92 is a reference to the first sub-paragraph of Article 12(2), and that this means that the requirement to indicate the country of origin applies where "a protected name of a third country is identical to a Community protected name." Please clarify the meaning of the following terms, as used in Article 12(2) of Regulation (EC) No. 2081/92:

(a) what is the meaning of the term "protected" in the phrase "a protected name of a third country"?

108. Both in "protected name of a third country" and in "Community protected name," "protected" in principle means "protected under Regulation 2081/92." However, the provision also applies where protection under Regulation 2081/92 is sought for a protected name from a third country.

(b) does the phrase "a Community protected name" cover both names of geographical areas located in the EC as well as in third countries, registered under the Regulation?

109. No. "Community protected name" covers only protected names of areas located in the EC.

(c) does the requirement to indicate the country of origin apply also where a name of a geographical area located in the EC is identical to a Community protected name (irrespective of whether this Community protected name is the name of a geographical area located in the EC or in a third country).

110. No. "Community protected name" covers only protected names of areas located in the EC. Moreover, the provision applies only to protected names.

Question 42

If Article 12(2) of Regulation (EC) No. 2081/92 applies to the registration of a name of a geographical area located in the EC that is identical to a name, already registered in the EC, of an area located in a third country, what is the difference in its scope compared to Article 6(6) of the Regulation? Why is it necessary to cover this situation in both provisions?

111. Article 12(2) is a specific provision dealing with certain cases of conflicts between homonyms which may arise between Community and third country protected names. Article 6(6) is a more general provision dealing with a wider set of conflicts, and notably conflicts between homonyms from within the Community, but

including also conflicts involving third country names not yet resolved by Article 12(2), for instance between names from within the same third country, or between third countries.

Question 43

Where does Regulation (EC) No. 2081/92 provide for the registration of a name of a geographical area located in a third country WTO Member which is a homonym of an already registered name? Where does it provide for the registration of a name which is a homonym of an already registered name of a geographical area located in a third country WTO Member?

112. As regards the first question, if the already registered name is a name from the Community, this situation would be covered by Article 12(2) of Regulation 2081/92. As regards the second question, if the name to be registered is from the Community, this situation would equally be covered by Article 12(2).

Question 44

Can the EC provide the Panel with any official statement predating its first written submission that Article 12(2) of Regulation (EC) No. 2081/92 applies to names of geographical areas located in the EC and that Article 12(2) will be applied on the basis of the date of registration?

113. No. The EC would like to remark that since there have been no cases of application of Article 12(2) so far, the EC has not felt a need to make official statements as regards the application of this provision.

Question 45

With respect to paragraph 135 of the EC's first written submission, could the Council of Ministers prevent a registration because the Commission applied Article 12(2) to names of geographical areas located in the EC on the basis of the date of registration?

114. No. As the Commission, the Council is bound by law to apply the terms of Regulation 2081/92.

Question 46

Has a judicial authority ever ruled on the applicability of Article 12(2) of Regulation (EC) No. 2081/92? If the Commission applied Article 12(2) to the name of a geographical area located in the EC on the basis of the date of registration, could that action be subject to judicial review due to the fact that the area was located in the EC?

115. Since Article 12(2) has never been applied, no judicial authority has ever had the occasion to interpret this provision.

116. Any Commission decision regarding the registration of a geographical indication can be the subject of judicial review under the conditions to which the EC has referred in its response to Question 19.[32]

[32] Above para. 46 et seq.

Question 49

Do you seek separate rulings on the procedural aspects of Regulation (EC) No. 2081/92 or a ruling on the Regulation as a whole? For example, should the provision in Article 12(2) be examined in isolation, or would it be appropriate to adopt an approach like the Panel in Korea – Beef, which only examined a display sign requirement within its findings related to a system as a whole?

117. In accordance with Article 3.7 of the DSU, the purpose of the present proceedings is to secure a positive solution to the dispute. In the view of the EC, securing a positive solution to the dispute requires the Panel to address all the claims which have been raised by the complainants with respect to particular aspects of Regulation 2081/92.

118. Moreover, Article 19.1 of the DSU provides that where a Panel concludes that a measure is inconsistent with a covered agreement, it shall recommend the Member concerned to bring the measure in conformity. The Panel's recommendations are the basis for implementation in accordance with Article 21 of the DSU. In order to enable the Member to properly implement the Panel's recommendations, it is therefore essential that a Panel's recommendation be as specific and clear as possible.

119. For this reason, if the Panel came to the conclusion that certain aspects of Regulation 2081/92 are inconsistent with a covered agreement, it would be necessary that these aspects be specifically identified in the Panel's conclusions and recommendations in order to enable the EC to duly implement the report.

Question 50

In paragraph 451 of its first written submission, the EC argues that labels which address the geographical origin of a product cannot be considered a technical regulation under the TBT Agreement, since they do not apply to a "product, process or production method." Why in the EC's view is the geographical origin of a product not related to that product or its process or production method? Does the coverage of the TBT Agreement with respect to labels depend on the content of the labels?

120. First of all, the EC would like to recall that Article 12(2) is not a labelling requirement, but merely sets out the conditions under which geographical indications can be registered in the case of homonymous protected names from the EC and from a third country.

121. Second, it is clear that the origin of a product is not a "process or production method." The question can therefore only be whether the indication of the country of origin is a labelling requirement as it relates to a product. However, it seems to the EC that the origin of a product is different from the product itself.

122. Of course, the origin of a product may confer specific characteristics or a reputation on it, which may entitle it for protection as a geographical indication. However, these issues are already covered in the TRIPS, and do therefore not need to be addressed by the TBT Agreement. Moreover, as the EC has already remarked, the question of origin marking is already covered by the special disciplines of Article IX GATT.[33]

---

[33] EC FWS, paras. 450-451.

Question 51

How should the term "like products" be interpreted under Article 2.1 of the TBT Agreement? If the labelling requirement in Article 12(2) of Regulation (EC) No. 2081/92 applies to situations where identical names arise between imported products and EC products, but does not apply to situations where identical names arise between two EC products, to what extent would this be a distinction between "like situations" rather than a distinction between "like products"?

123. The EC agrees that Article 2.1 TBT Agreement requires a comparison between like products, not between "like situations." In the view of the EC, Australia has not shown that homonymous products from within the EC covered by Article 6 (6) of the Regulation would in any sense be "like" a third country product which is covered by Article 12(2) of the Regulation. Accordingly, Australia has failed to establish any claim under Article 2.1 TBT Agreement.

124. Moreover, the EC considers that under Australia's argument, the two situations are not even like. In fact, the comparable situation to two homonymous EC GIs protected under Regulation 2081/92 would be that of two homonymous Australian GI's protected under Australian law. This is obviously not a situation which can give rise to discrimination between Australian and EC products. In fact, as the EC has already stated, it does not understand how Australian products could be affected by the way in which conflicts between homonymous names from within the EC are resolved.

125. Since Australia has in any case failed to establish a case under Article 2.1 TBT Agreement, the EC considers that the Panel does not need to resolve the meaning of the expression "like products" in Article 2.1 TBT Agreement. As the EC has already said in its first written submission, this is an issue of considerable legal complexity, which could not be resolved simply through transposition of jurisprudence on Article III:4 GATT, but rather would also have to take the structural differences between the TBT Agreement and the GATT into account.[34]

Question 54

Article 12(2) of Regulation (EC) No. 2081/92 is designed to avoid "practical risks of confusion." How would the application of the country of origin label on the basis of a product's date of registration help avoid those risks of confusion?

126. Typically, the geographical indication which is registered first will have been marketed under that name longer, and will therefore already be known by consumers. Inversely, the geographical indication which is registered later will have been used less long, and will be less known by consumers. It is therefore in line with consumer expectations to require appropriate labelling for the indication registered later. This solution also takes into account the fact that the older geographical indication is already registered, and that the terms of its protection can therefore no longer easily be amended.

Question 55

Does the TRIPS Agreement apply as lex specialis as regards GATT 1994 and the TBT Agreement, with respect to a practical condition to differentiate homonymous or identical GIs on a label? Please comment in the light of Article 23.3 of the TRIPS Agreement, which is applicable to homonymous GIs for wines, and the national treatment obligation, which is applicable to GIs for other products.

127. The EC would agree that Article 23.3 TRIPS must be considered as a *lex specialis* with respect to the practical conditions to differentiate homonymous or identical GIs on a label. Under this provision, the practical conditions for differentiation of homonymous indications will be determined by each Member, taking into

[34] EC FWS, para. 474.

account the need to ensure equitable treatment of the producers concerned and that consumers are not misled. This constitutes an exhaustive set of disciplines for this issue, which exclude the application of the national treatment provisions of the GATT and the TBT Agreement.

128. It is noteworthy that the TRIPS Agreement does not contain a corresponding provision for homonymous geographical indications for products other than wines. Therefore Members must decide whether and how to accord protection to homonymous geographical indications on the basis of the general provisions of Section 3, and notably of Article 22.4 of the TRIPS Agreement. This indicates that Member enjoy a greater degree of discretion as to how to resolve conflicts between homonyms for products other than wines. This further confirms the view of the EC that the national treatment provisions of the GATT, the TRIPS and the TBT Agreement should not be held to apply to Article 2(2) of Regulation 2081/92.

Question 57

Does the EC consider that it may apply equivalence and reciprocity conditions to WTO Members under Article 12a(2) or any other provision of Regulation (EC) No. 2081/92, even if Article 12(1) does not apply to them?

129. No. The EC merely requires that the conditions of Regulation 2081/92 regarding product specifications and inspections are met as regards the specific product for which protection is sought.

Question 59

Under what circumstances would the Commission consider the holder of a GI certification mark registered in another WTO Member to meet the requirements for inspection structures under Article 10 of Regulation (EC) 2081/92 (read together with Article 12a of that Regulation)?

130. The EC understands that the question of the Panel relates to a certification mark which protects the use of a name which would qualify for protection as a geographical indication under Regulation 2081/92.

131. Any inspection structure must comply with the conditions set out in Article 10 of Regulation 2081/92. According to Article 10 (2) of Regulation 2081/92, the inspection structures must offer adequate guarantees of objectivity and impartiality with regard to all producers or processors subject to their control. The answer to the question would therefore depend on how the holder of the certification mark is related to the producers or processors in question. If the holder is not itself a producer or processor, and is independent of them, then it would not seem excluded that it could also function as an inspection structure. Otherwise, it would be necessary to establish an independent inspection structure which offers the necessary guarantees of independence and impartiality.

Question 60

Australia argues that the EC's inspection structures requirements are a technical regulation under the TBT Agreement (paragraphs 209-224 of its first written submission). Is there a dividing line lies under the TBT Agreement between a technical regulation and a conformity assessment procedure? If so, where does it lie?

132. In the view of the EC, the dividing line follows clearly from the definitions in points 1 and 3 of Annex 1 to the TBT Agreement. According to point 1 of Annex 1, a technical regulation "lays down product characteristics." According to point 3, a conformity assessment procedure ensures that "relevant requirements in technical regulations [...] are fulfilled."

133. In other words, technical regulation set down product characteristics in general and abstract terms. Conformity assessment procedures verify the compliance of concrete products with such requirements. In yet

other words, the difference is the one between abstract regulation and the enforcement of regulations in concrete cases.

134. In accordance with Article 10(1) of Regulation 2081/92, inspection structures ensure that agricultural products and foodstuffs bearing a protected name meet the requirements laid down in the specifications. In other words, inspection procedures ensure the compliance of concrete products with the abstract specifications. On the basis of the definitions set out above, there should therefore be no doubt that the requirements regarding inspection structures concern a conformity assessment procedure.

Question 61

If the inspection structures are conformity assessment procedures, are the eligibility criteria for registration under Regulation (EC) No. 2081/92, against which conformity is assessed, technical regulations?

135. As a preliminary point, the EC would like to remark that the only claim which Australia has raised with respect to the eligibility criteria for registration under Regulation 2081/92 concerns Article 12(2), i.e. the provision regarding homonymous protected names from the EC and third countries. The Panel does therefore not need to the address the question of whether other eligibility criteria contained in the Regulation might constitute technical regulations.

136. Furthermore, the EC notes that it is wrong to suggest that "conformity is assessed against" the eligibility criteria for registration. The existence of inspection structures constitutes a condition for registration. Accordingly, inspection structures do not ensure that the criteria for the eligibility of registration are met; they ensure that concrete products bearing a protected name comply with the product specifications.

137. In reality, the eligibility criteria for registration have nothing to do with technical regulations. They do not lay down characteristics for specific products, but apply for all geographical indications for which protection is sought under the Regulation. Accordingly, the Regulation, and in particular its eligibility criteria for registration, do no lay down product characteristics. Rather, they require the definition of product specifications as part of the application process. However, "requiring the definition of product characteristics" (by the applicant) is not the same thing as "laying down product characteristics."

138. Quite remarkably, Australia has characterised Regulation 2081/92 as "establishing a process related to product characteristics."[35] However, as the EC has already had the occasion to remark at the first meeting with the Panel, a measure "establishing a process related to product characteristics" is not the same thing as a measure actually laying down product characteristics.

139. Are the very most, the question could therefore be asked whether the individual product specifications for specific protected names constitute technical regulations. However, the EC notes that Australia has made no claims with respect to any particular specifications, and that this issue is therefore outside the terms of reference of the Panel.

Question 63

What does Article 14(2) of Regulation (EC) No. 2081/92 mean where it provides that a prior trademark "may continue to be used"?

140. Article 14(2) of Regulation 2081/92 is an exception to Article 13(1) of the same regulation, which provides that registered geographical indications shall be protected against certain practices, including certain uses of trademarks. Article 14(2) allows trademark owners to continue to use their trademarks in relation to

[35] Oral Statement by Australia at the First Panel hearing, para. 43.

goods which do not comply with the requirements of the geographical indication, in circumstances where such use would be prohibited by Article 13(1).

Can a trademark owner invoke the rights conferred by the trademark registration against the user of a GI used in accordance with its GI registration?

141. Article 14(2) of Regulation 2081/92 does not confer to a trademark owner the right to prevent the use of the name, as such, that has been registered as a geographical indication by the right holders of such indication. That would render meaningless the registration of that name as a geographical indication and the protection attached to such registration by Article 13(1).

142. On the other hand, and contrary to what is erroneously assumed by the United States[36], a trademark owner may use its trademark rights in order to prevent the right holders of a geographical indication from using confusingly any other names or other signs (e.g. graphic signs) in conjunction with, or in place of, the name registered as a geographical indication, which are not covered by such registration. In other words, the right holders of a geographical indication only have a positive right to use the name registered as a geographical indication. That right does not extend to other names or signs which have been not been registered. If the use of such unregistered names or signs leads to likelihood of confusion with the same or a similar sign which is the subject of a valid trademark it may be prevented by the owner of that trademark.

143. Furthermore, while the right holders of a geographical indication have a positive right to use the registered name, this does not mean that they are allowed to use it in any possible manner. As explained[37], the name registered as a geographical indication must be used in accordance with the generally applicable provisions of Directive 2000/13 on the labelling, presentation and advertising of foodstuffs[38] and of Directive 84/450 on misleading advertising[39], as well as with the unfair competition laws of the Member States.[40]

Question 64

Does Article 14(2) of Regulation (EC) No. 2081/92 implement the provision in Article 24.5 of the TRIPS Agreement that measures adopted to implement the Section on GIs shall not prejudice "eligibility for or validity of the registration of a trademark, or the right to use a trademark" or does it only implement the provision that such measures shall not prejudice "the right to use a trademark"?

144. As explained in the EC's First Written Submission (paragraph 302), Article 14(1) of Regulation 2081/92 maintains the eligibility of the applications and the validity of the registrations grandfathered by Article 24.5 of the TRIPS Agreement, while Article 14(2) preserves the right of the owners of grandfathered trademarks to continue to use their trademarks concurrently with a registered geographical indication.

---

[36] US Oral Statement paras. 54-55.

[37] EC's First Submission, para. 319. See also the responses of the EC and its Member States to the review under Article 24.2 of the TRIPS Agreement contained in document IP/C/W/117/Add10 (Exhibit EC-29).

[38] Exhibit EC-30. See in particular Article 2.1, which provides that

The labelling and methods used must not: (a) be such as could mislead the purchaser to a material degree, particularly: (i) as to the characteristics of the foodstuff and, in particular, as to its ... origin or provenance ...

[39] Exhibit EC-31. Article 2.2 of the Directive defines "misleading advertising" as

"any advertising which in any way, including presentation, deceives or is likely to deceive the person to whom it is addressed or whom it reaches and which, by reason of its deceptive nature, is likely yoto affect their economic behaviour or which, for those reasons, injures or is likely to injure a competitor."

Article 3 provides that in determining whether advertising is misleading account shall be taken *inter alia* of information concerning the geographic or commercial origin of the goods and of the rights of the advertiser, including ownership of commercial, industrial and intellectual property rights.

[40] References to the relevant laws of the Member States are found in their responses to the review under Article 24.2 of the TRIPS Agreement. (Exhibit EC-29)

Question 65

Does the scope of Article 14(2) of Regulation (EC) No. 2081/92, as drafted, include trademarks applied for or registered, or to which rights have been acquired, subsequent to both dates set out in Article 24.5(a) and (b) of the TRIPS Agreement?

145. This question does not appear to be relevant to resolve the issues before the Panel, since the complainants have not made any claim to the effect that the temporal criteria laid down in Article 14(2) of Regulation 2081/92 would be somehow inconsistent with those of Article 24.5 of the TRIPS Agreement. Were the complainants to raise any such claim at this stage of the proceedings, it would have to be considered outside the terms of reference of the Panel.

146. In any event, Article 14(2) is fully consistent with Article 24.5 of the TRIPS Agreement. Any trademark applied for, or established by use, before 1 January 1996, but after the date of application for a registered geographical indication, could not be deemed to have been so "in good faith."

147. Furthermore, the complainants have not alleged, let alone proved, that the registration of any of the geographical indications that were applied for before 1 January 1996, which constitute a closed category, has resulted or will result in a likelihood of confusion with any of the trademarks that were applied for, registered, or established by use before 1 January 1996, but after the date of the application for the geographical indication, which also constitute a closed category.

Question 66

Has Article 14(2) of Regulation (EC) No. 2081/92 ever been applied in a specific case? For example, what did the national courts finally decide in the Gorgonzola case, referred to in Exhibit US-17 and in footnote 140 to paragraph 163 of the US first written submission, after the order of the European Court of Justice?

148. Article 14(2) of Regulation 2081/92 does not have to be "applied" by the registering authorities. Rather, it sets out the legal consequences that follow from a decision providing for the registration of a proposed geographical indication.

149. The "Cambozola"[41] case mentioned in the question remains so far the only instance where Article 14(2) has been interpreted by the European Court of Justice. In essence, the issues in dispute in that case were whether the use of the trademark "Cambozola" fell within one of the situations listed under Article 13(1) and, if so, whether the conditions laid down in Article 14(2) for allowing the continued use of that trademark were met.

150. The European Court of Justice concluded that the use of the trademark "Cambozola" might be deemed to evoke the registered geographical indication "Gorgonzola" and, therefore, fall within the scope of Article 13(1)(b), even if the true origin was indicated in the package. As regards the question of whether the trademark "Cambozola" could continue to be used in accordance with Article 14(2) the Court ruled that

> ... It is for the national court to decide whether, on the facts, the conditions laid down in Article 14(2) of Regulation No 2081/92 allow use of an earlier trademark to continue notwithstanding the registration of the protected designation of origin 'Gorgonzola', having regard in particular to the law in force at the time of registration of the trade mark, in order to determine whether such registration could have been made in good faith, on the basis that use of a name such as 'Cambozola' does not, per se, constitute an attempt to deceive the consumer.

[41] Judgement of the European Court of Justice of 4 March 1999, Case C- 87/97, *Consorzio per la tutela del Fromaggio Gorgonzola v. Kaeserai Champignon Hofmeister GmbH & Co. KG, Eduard Bracharz GMbH.* (Exhibit EC-32).

151. Following the Judgement of the European Court of Justice, the Supreme Court of Austria ruled that the trademark "Cambozola" had been registered in good faith and was not affected by any ground of invalidity and, therefore, in accordance with Article 14(2), could continue to be used concurrently with the registered geographical indication "Gorgonzola."[42]

152. The EC Commission is not aware of any other decisions of the courts of the Member States where Article 14(2) has been interpreted.

Question 67

Does Article 14(3) of Regulation (EC) No. 2081/92 affect the possibility of coexistence of GIs already on the register with prior trademarks, such as Gorgonzola? In these cases, is Article 14(3) relevant to the applicability of Article 14(2)?

153. Article 14(3) remains relevant even after a geographical indication has been formally registered. The owner of a concurrent trademark (e.g. "Cambozola") could challenge before the courts the decision to register the geographical indication by claiming that the decision is inconsistent with Article 14(3).

Question 68

Article 14(3) of Regulation (EC) No. 2081/92 mentions certain criteria. If these are not exhaustive, why does is it not expressly stated as in Articles 3(1), 4(2) and 6(6) of the Regulation?

154. At the outset, it is useful to recall the wording of Article 14(3) of Regulation 2081/92:

> A designation of origin or geographical indication shall not be registered where, in the light of trade mark's reputation and renown and the length of time it has been used, registration is liable to mislead the consumer as to the true origin of the product.

155. Thus, contrary to what has been claimed by the complainants, Article 14(3) does not say that the registering authority shall refuse the registration of a geographical indication only if it gives rise to a likelihood of confusion with a trademark which is famous and has been used for a long period of time. Rather, Article 14(3) says that the registration of a geographical indication shall be refused if it is likely to lead to confusion with a trademark, "in light of" the trademark's reputation and renown and the length of time that it has been used.

156. In other words, the length of use and reputation/renown of the trademark are not separate "requirements"[43], additional to the likelihood of confusion, for the application of Article 14(3). Rather, they are criteria for establishing the existence of a likelihood of confusion. From the fact that the Commission must consider those two criteria when assessing the likelihood of confusion, it does not follow *a contrario* that it cannot consider also other criteria. Indeed, as explained below, in practice it would be impossible to evaluate the likelihood of confusion on the basis of only those two criteria.

157. As explained[44], Article 14(3) directs expressly the registering authority to consider the length of use and the reputation and renown of earlier trademarks because those criteria will generally be decisive in order to establish the likelihood of confusion, given that geographical names are primarily non-distinctive, and not because only the likelihood of confusion with famous marks that have been used for a long time is deemed relevant.

---

[42] Austrian Supreme Court (Oberster Gerichtshof), Case 40625/01 G, Judgement of 7 October 2001.

[43] US Oral Statement, para. 53.

[44] EC's FWS, paras. 278-291.

158. If Article 14(3) does not mention expressly the similarity of goods and signs, it is simply because those criteria are always relevant to establish the likelihood of confusion between two signs and must necessarily be taken into account. Indeed, as discussed below, neither the length of use nor the reputation and renown of a trademark can be assessed meaningfully without taking into account the degree of similarity of the goods and signs. Moreover, it must be recalled that the application of Article 14(3) presupposes the applicability of Article 13(1) and that, in order to determine whether the use of a trademark falls within one of the situations listed under Article 13(1), it is necessary to consider the similarity of goods and signs.

159. Furthermore, the interpretation of Article 14(3) made by the complainants would lead to a result which conflicts and cannot be reconciled with the obligations imposed upon the EC institutions by Articles 7(4) and 7(5)(b).

160. Article 7(4) provides that a statement of objection shall be admissible, *inter alia*, if it shows that "the registration of the name proposed would jeopardize the existence of a mark."[45] This language encompasses any instance of likelihood of confusion between the proposed geographical indication and an earlier trademark. If Article 14(3) only required the refusal of a proposed geographical indication where it gives rise to likelihood of confusion with a famous trademark used for a long time, as claimed by the complainants, the admissible grounds of objection would have been limited to the cases where one such mark is likely to be jeopardized. Article 7(4), however, refers to all trademarks, without any distinction or qualification. It would be pointless to admit an objection on certain grounds if, in any event, it were not possible to reject the application on such grounds.

161. Further confirmation is provided by Article 7(5)(b), which provides that where an objection is admissible, and no agreement is reached among the Member States concerned,

> the Commission shall take a decision in accordance with the procedure laid down in Article 15, having regard to traditional fair practice and likelihood of confusion.[46]

162. Thus, Article 7(5)(b) requires the Commission to adopt a decision having regard to the "likelihood of confusion" between the proposed geographical indication and *any* other marks. There is no basis in Article 7(5)(b) for the proposition that only the likelihood of confusion with famous marks used for a long time must be taken into account by the Commission.

Do other criteria, such as similarity of signs and goods fall within "reputation and renown"?

163. As suggested by the question, the criteria mentioned expressly in Article 14(3) cannot be applied without taking into account at the same time the degree of similarity between the goods and signs concerned, which must, therefore, be deemed implicit in Article 14(3).

164. The mere fact that a trademark enjoys reputation and renown and that it has been used for a long time is not sufficient to establish that a geographical indication will be confused with that trademark, if the two signs are not similar. For example, it is beyond dispute that "Coca-Cola" is a trademark that enjoys a formidable reputation and renown and has been used for a long time. Yet, it would be absurd to pretend that, as a result, the EC public is likely to confuse the geographical indication "Jijona" with the trademark "Coca-Cola," given the lack of similarity between the two signs.

---

[45] Articles 12b(3) and 12d(2) provide, respectively, that the criteria of Article 7(4) shall apply also with respect to the admissibility of objections to the registration of foreign geographical indications and of objections from outside the EC to EC geographical indications.

[46] Similar language is found in Articles 12b(3) and12d(3) with regard to the registration of geographical indications from other WTO Members and third countries and to the registration of EC geographical indications, following an objection from outside the EC, respectively.

165. Similar considerations can be made with respect to the similarity of goods. For example, a geographical indication for cheese may be less likely to be confused with a trademark that enjoys great reputation and renown with respect to shoes than with a trademark for cheese even if it has less renown and reputation. Similarly, the length of time during which a trademark has been used must be determined in relation to a given category of goods. To continue with the same example, a geographical indication for cheese may be less likely to be confused with a trademark for shoes that has been used for decades than with a relatively recent trademark for cheese.

166. The above examples illustrate that the likelihood of confusion between two signs cannot be properly established by considering only the length of use and the reputation/renown of one of them, but must take into account necessarily the similarity of the goods and signs concerned. An interpretation of Article 14(3) which prevented the registering authority from considering the similarity of goods and signs would be neither reasonable, nor workable, and cannot be correct. It must be concluded, therefore, that the criteria mentioned in Article 14(3) do not purport to be exhaustive.

Is the criterion of "length of time [a trade mark] has been used" relevant to its liability to mislead if the trademark has not been used for a significant, or considerable, length of time?

167. Article 14(3) requires the registering authority to consider the length of time during which a trademark has been used. The reason why this criterion must be considered is because, as a general rule, the longer a trademark has been used, the more distinctive it will be, and, as result, the more likely that a proposed geographical indication may be confused with it.

168. However, contrary to what has been argued by the complainants, Article 14(3) does not say that the registering authority must refuse the registration of a geographical indication only if it has been shown that the trademark has been used for a long time. It is conceivable that a trademark which has been used for a relatively short period of time may, nevertheless, have become strongly distinctive through other means (e.g. publicity), so as to make it likely that the proposed geographical will be confused with it.

Question 69

Can the EC provide the Panel with any official statement predating its first written submission that application of the grounds for registration, invalidity or revocation of trademarks and Article 14(3) of Regulation (EC) No. 2081/92 will or should be applied in such a way as to render Article 14(2) inapplicable?

169. The EC institutions have not issued any general interpretative "statement" of Article 14(3) of Regulation 2081/92. The same is true of all the other provisions of Regulation 2081/92. Indeed, unlike in other jurisdictions, it is relatively unusual for the EC authorities to issue any such general interpretative statements with respect to the EC legislative acts.

170. As mentioned in the EC's First Written Submission[47], Article 14(3) of Regulation 2081/92 has been applied only once by the EC institutions. The interpretation made in that case is consistent with the interpretation advanced by the EC in this dispute. The Council concluded that there was no likelihood of confusion with earlier trademarks "in view of the facts and information available." There is no suggestion in the Council decision that it was considered that there was no likelihood of confusion because the trademarks concerned were not famous enough or had not been used for a sufficiently long time.

171. The EC wishes to clarify that it is not the EC's position that its trademark legislation, together with Article 14(3) of Regulation 2081/92, "render Article 14(2) inapplicable." Rather, the EC's position is that its trademark legislation, together with Article 14(3), prevent the registration of geographical indications that result in a likelihood of confusion with pre-existing trademarks, which is the only type of confusion envisaged in

[47] EC's FWS, para. 288.

Article 16.1 of the TRIPS Agreement. Article 14(2) applies to other situations not involving that type of confusion where, in accordance with Article 13(1) of Regulation 2081/92, the right holders of a registered geographical indication would be entitled, in principle, to prevent the use of an earlier trademark.

Question 70

Do the EC member States agree with the Commission's submission to this Panel that the terms of Article 14(3) of Regulation (EC) No. 2081/92, if properly interpreted, are sufficient to prevent the registration of any confusing GIs?

172. The EC recalls that the submissions to the Panel are made on behalf of the European Communities, and not of the EC Commission.

173. The EC also recalls that Regulation 2081/92 is a measure of the European Community and not of its Member States. Therefore, in principle, only the views of the EC institutions, and not the individual views of the EC Members States, are relevant for the interpretation of Regulation 2081/92.

174. In any event, the Member States of the EC are aware of the legal interpretations stated in the EC submission. They have expressed no objections or reservations.

Could the EC member States apply national trademark laws in a way that made this impossible?

175. This question is unclear to the EC. The EC fails to see how the Member States could, through the application of their national trademark laws, prevent a correct application of Article 14(3) of Regulation 2081/92.

176. In any event, the EC Member States are required under EC law to apply their trademark laws consistently with all the relevant provisions of EC law, including in particular the Trademark Directive. For the reasons explained by the EC in its First Written Submission, the registrability criteria provided in the Trademark Directive limit *a priori* the risk of conflicts between trademarks and geographical indications. The complainants have not been able to identify one single case where a registered geographical indication has resulted in a likelihood of confusion with a trademark registered by the authorities of the Member States under their national trademark laws. This confirms that, in practice, Member States apply those laws consistently with the interpretation advanced by the EC in this dispute.

Could the Council of Ministers prevent the application of Article 14(3) of the Regulation if proposed by the Commission in a specific case and apply Article 14(2)?

177. In principle, the Commission is not required to submit proposals to the Council. Rather, the Commission must request the opinion of the Committee in accordance with Article 15 of Regulation 2081/92 before adopting a decision granting or refusing a registration. If the Committee gives a negative opinion, the Commission must submit a proposal to the Council, which may, acting by qualified majority, adopt it or indicate its opposition within a certain period of time. The Council could oppose a proposal from the Commission to refuse a registration on the basis of Article 14(3) if it considers that the conditions provided in that Article are not met.

Question 71

Has a judicial authority ever ruled on the interpretation of Article 14(3) of Regulation (EC) No. 2081/92?

178. As noted in the EC's First Written Submission (para. 288) Article 14(3) of Regulation (EC) No. 2081/92 has never been interpreted by the European Court of Justice or by the courts of the Member States.

Once again, this confirms that, as explained by the EC, the criteria for the registrability of trademarks ensure that the potential for conflicts between trademarks and geographical indications is very limited.

179. As explained above[48], according to well-established case law of the European Court of Justice, EC law must be interpreted, to the extent possible, in a manner that ensures its consistency with the WTO Agreement, in particular where it is intended specifically to give effect to that agreement. This principle of interpretation must be observed also by the other EC institutions and by the courts of the Member States when interpreting EC law.

180. Moreover, as also explained[49], the European Court of Justice takes account of the assurances regarding the interpretation of EC law given by the EC Commission on behalf of the European Communities in international fora, such as the WTO.

If Article 14(3) of the Regulation, the Community trademark regulation and national trademark laws were applied in such a way as to prevent the registration of GIs that were confusing with a prior trademark, could this be subject to judicial review?

181. A decision refusing the registration of a proposed geographical indication on the grounds provided in Article 14(3) of Regulation 2081/92 can be challenged before the courts, just like any other decision refusing or granting the registration of a proposed geographical indication.

182. Likewise, the decisions of the trademark authorities of the Member States or of the Office for Harmonisation in the Internal Market to refuse the registration of a trademark on the grounds provided in letters (b), (c) or (g) of Article 3.1 of the Trademarks Directive, or in letters (b), (c) or (g) of Article 7.1 of the Community Trademark Regulation, respectively, are also subject to judicial review.

Question 73

Please supply a copy of the wine regulations referred to in paragraph 16 of the EC oral statement.

183. The wine regulations referred to in paragraph 16 of the EC's First Oral Statement are the same mentioned in paragraphs 310-311 of the EC's First Written Submission. A copy of the relevant provisions of those regulations has been supplied as Exhibit EC-11, together with the EC's First Written Submission.

Question 74

Which particular GIs did the EC protect under Regulation (EC) No. 2081/92 prior to 1 January 1995?

184. The registration of a geographical indication under Regulation 2081/92 produces effects vis-à-vis concurrent trademarks from the date of application (cf. Article 14(1) of Regulation 2081/92). Of the 658 geographical indications currently registered, 487 were applied for prior to 1 January 1995.

185. Furthermore, many of the geographical indications registered or applied for under Regulation 2081/92 were already protected at the Member State level prior to 1 January 1995.

Is Article 24.3 of the TRIPS Agreement relevant to any other GIs?

186. Yes. Article 24.3 requires to maintain the level of protection of geographical indications available on 1 January 1995, rather than the protection of the particular geographical indications that were registered, or applied for on that date.

---

[48] Response to Question 15.

[49] Ibid.

187. On the interpretation suggested in the question, Article 24.3 would impose obligations only upon those Members which protect geographical indications via a system of registration, or another system involving the recognition *ex ante* of geographical indications, but not where protection is provided through other systems (e.g. unfair competition laws or generally applicable consumer protection regulations that apply indistinctly to any geographical indications).

188. For example, assume that, before 1 January 1995, a Member had legislation in place prohibiting the use of *any* geographical indications for products of a different origin, even when the geographical indication is used together with terms such as "type," "kind," etc. On the interpretation suggested in the question, after 1 January 1995, that Member would be free to repeal such legislation with respect to products other than wine and spirits, even though this would clearly "diminish the protection of geographical indications."

189. Moreover, the above result would be at odds with the principle established in Article 1.1 of the TRIPS Agreement, according to which Members are free to determine the appropriate method of implementation of their WTO obligations. Members cannot be said to be "free" to choose the method of implementation of Section 3 of Part II, if choosing a certain method has the consequence of subjecting them to stricter obligations under Article 24.3.

190. The United States has argued that the meaning of Article 24.3 is that "the protection provided to those GIs should not diminish the protections (sic) for the GIs that existed when the TRIPS Agreement came into force."[50]

191. This proposition is difficult to understand. Providing protection to geographical indications cannot, as a matter of simple logic, "diminish" such protection. Rather the existing protection of geographical indications may be "diminished" as a result of the implementation of the limitations to the protection of geographical indications provided in Section 3 of Part II, including in particular those stipulated in Article 24.5 in order to maintain certain rights of the owners of grandfathered trademarks.

192. Moreover, the US interpretation has no textual basis in the wording of Article 24.3, which reads as follows:

> In implementing this section, a Member shall not diminish the protection of geographical indications that existed in that Member immediately prior to the date of entry into force of the WTO Agreement.

193. First, Article 24.3 alludes to the "protection of geographical indications," and not to the "protections" in the plural form, as argued by the United States. Moreover, the term "geographical indications" is not preceded by the word "the." This indicates that the drafters had in mind the general level of protection available in each Member. Second, the term "existed" refers to the word "protection" and not to the "geographical indications." It is not required, therefore, that the geographical indications "existed," or *a fortiori* that they had been specifically recognised as such, as of the date of entry into force of the WTO Agreement. This is made clear by the Spanish and the French versions, which read as follows, respectively:

> Al aplicar esta Sección, ningún Miembro reducirá la protección de las indicaciones geográficas que **existía** en él inmediatamente antes de la fecha de entrada en vigor del Acuerdo sobre la OMC. [emphasis added]

> Lorsqu'il mettra en oeuvre la présente section, un Membre ne diminuera pas la protection des indications géographiques qui **existait** dans ce Membre immédiatement avant la date d'entrée en vigueur de l'Accord sur l'OMC. [emphasis added]

[50] US Oral Statement, para. 70.

194. The United States also argues that Article 24.3 is an "exception" with respect to the "implementation of the GI Section of the TRIPS Agreement" and not an "exception to the implementation of the trademark obligations."[51] This argument is specious. In the first place, Article 24.3 is not an "exception" to the protection of geographical indications, because it does not exempt Members from the obligations provided under Section 3 of Part II. Rather, it adds a supplementary obligation. Second, the "protection" of geographical indications includes "protection" vis-à-vis the exercise of trademark rights. Indeed, Section 3 of Part II provides expressly for such type of protection in Articles 22.3, 23.2 and 24.5. Those provisions operate as limitations to the "trademark obligations" under Article 16.1. Article 24.3 provides for another limitation to those "trademarks obligations."

195. The objective of Article 24.3 is to maintain the balance between the protection of geographical indications and that of trademarks that existed in each Member at the entry into force of the WTO Agreement. If, prior to that date, a Member provided protection vis-à-vis trademarks going beyond that required by Section 3 of Part II, it is required to continue do so after that date. For example, if prior to 1 January 1995 a Member provided generally the type of protection required by Article 23.2 for wines and spirits with respect to all products, it must continue to do so after that date, whether or not a certain geographical indication had been specifically recognised as such before that date.

196. Finally, the United States argues that the EC interpretation would allow Members to derogate from "*any* WTO provision."[52] This is simply not true. Article 24.3 requires Members to depart from other WTO provisions only to the extent necessary to maintain the existing "protection" of geographical indications. In order to "protect" geographical indications it is not necessary, for example, to limit patent rights or copyrights.[53] On the other hand, as mentioned, it is beyond question that "protecting" geographical indications may require to limit trademark rights.

Question 75

Which party bears the burden of proof in relation to:

> *(a) Article 24.5 of the TRIPS Agreement? In particular, does this relate to the scope of the obligation in Article 16.1? Does it create an exception for measures otherwise covered by Article 16.1? Or neither?*

197. Article 24.5 is not an "exception" to Article 16.1. Rather, it defines the boundary between a Member's right to implement protection for geographical indications and its obligation to protect trademarks under Article 16.1.[54] The burden of proving that a measure falls within the scope of the obligations provided in Article 16.1 is on the complainants.

198. The EC notes that, while the United States now argues that Article 24.5 is an "exception"[55], in its panel request it has stated a claim under that provision. Similarly, Australia cited Article 24.5 in its panel request and has made a claim under that provision in its First Written Submission.[56]

---

[51] Ibid.

[52] Ibid., para. 72.

[53] Ibid.

[54] Australia's FWS, para. 105.

[55] US Oral Statement, para. 58.

[56] Australia's FWS, paras. 81-87.

(b) Article 17 of the TRIPS Agreement? In particular, does this only permit exceptions to the rights conferred by a trademark, or does it also create an exception to the obligations imposed on Members?

199. Article 17 allows Members to provide limited exceptions to the rights which they are obliged to confer upon the owner of trademark by virtue of Article 16. To that extent, it is an exception to the obligations imposed upon Members by Article 16. The function of Article 17 is similar to that of Articles 13 and 30. Previous panels have taken the view that the burden of invoking those provisions and of proving that the relevant conditions for their applicability were met was on the defendant.[57]

Question 76

Article 24.5 of the TRIPS Agreement uses the phrases "validity of the registration of a trademark" and "the right to use a trademark." Please set out your interpretation of these phrases, in accordance with the general rule of treaty interpretation in Article 31 of the Vienna Convention on the Law of Treaties and, if appropriate, the supplementary means in Article 32. Please explain how you determine what is the relevant context.

The ordinary meaning

200. A "trademark" is not a right. It is a sign which may be the subject of a right. Thus, Article 15.1 of the TRIPS Agreement provides in relevant part that

> Any sign, or any combination of signs, capable of distinguishing the goods or services of one undertaking from those of other undertakings, shall be capable of constituting a trademark.

201. Therefore, the "right to use a trademark" is the right to use a sign. That right is different from, and does not include the right to prevent others from using the same or a similar sign. According to WIPO[58], typically the owner of a registered trademark has an "exclusive right to use the trademark," which "encompasses two things:"

- the "right to use the trademark" and
- the "right to exclude others from using the mark."

202. In turn, according to WIPO the "right to use a trademark" means the following:[59]

> It means first the right of the owner of the mark to affix it on goods, contains, packaging, labels, etc. or to use it in any other way in relation to the goods for which it is registered.
>
> It means also the right to introduce the goods to the market under the trademark.

203. The term "validity" alludes to something which is "valid," which in turn means something "having legal strength or force, executed with proper formalities, incapable of being rightfully overthrown or set aside."[60] The opposite of "valid" is "invalid," which means "having no force, efficacy, or cogency, esp. in law."[61]

---

[57] See Panel Report, *United States – Section 110(5) of the Copyright Act*, paras. 6.9-6.16; and Panel Report, *Canada – Patent Protection of Pharmaceutical Products*, para. 7.16.

[58] WIPO, *Introduction to Trademark Law & Practice, The Basic Concepts, a WTO Training Manual*, Geneva 1993, p.51

[59] Ibid.

[60] Black's Law Dictionary, West Publishing Co., St. Paul, Minn., 1990.

[61] The New Shorter Oxford English Dictionary, Ed. Lesley Brown, Clarendon Press, Oxford 1993.

204. In order to be "valid," the registration of a trademark does not necessarily have to confer exclusive rights vis-à-vis all third parties. The fact that the owner of a registered trademark cannot prevent the use of the same or a similar sign by the right holders of a geographical indication does not mean that the registration of the trademark is, for that reason alone, "set aside," or "overthrown" or that it is without "legal strength" or "efficacy."

205. The US interpretation of Article 24.5 fails to give meaning to the phrase "the right to use the trademark." If the exclusive right to use a trademark were already inherent in the term "validity of the registration," it would have been superfluous to provide in Article 24.5 that the implementation of Section 3 of Part II shall not prejudice "the right to use the trademark."

206. The United States asserts that the phrase "the right to use a trademark" *clarifies* and *adds* to the protection of grandfathered trademarks already provided by the other terms of Article 24.5.[62] However, as a matter of simple of logic, that phrase cannot do both things simultaneously. Either it *adds* an obligation, or it *clarifies* those obligations already provided by the other terms of Article 24.5.

207. If the phrase "the right to use a trademark" *adds* new obligations, it would mean that, as argued by the EC, the "validity" of a registration does not confer *per se* the exclusive right to use a trademark. Moreover, the United States does not explain how it can reconcile its position that Article 24.5 is an "exception" with the view that Article 24.5 confers to the trademark owners *additional* rights which they do not have under Article 16.

208. On the other hand, if the purpose of the phrase "the right to use a trademark" is to *clarify* the obligations provided by the other terms of Article 24.5, then why did the drafters not use *clear* wording to that effect, such as, for example, that the implementation of Section 3 of Part II is without prejudice to "the *exclusive* right to use the trademark" or to "the rights conferred by Article 16.1"?

209. The United States also argues that the EC's interpretation would allow to "deny all the rights connected with registration" and would render it "meaningless."[63] This is simply not true. It must be emphasised, once again, that, on the EC's interpretation, the trademark owner retains the right to prevent all others parties from using the trademark.

210. For its part, Australia has suggested[64] that the phrase "the right to use a trademark" alludes exclusively to the trademark rights acquired through use, to which reference is made in the introductory phrase of Article 24.5. However, if so, it would have been more logical to say that the measures taken to implement Sections 3 "shall not prejudice ... the trademark rights acquired through use," rather than that they "shall not prejudice ... the right to use a trademark." Australia confuses the mode of acquisition of the trademark rights (use or registration) with one of the basic rights of the trademark owner (irrespective of whether the trademark rights have been acquired through use or registration), i.e. the right to use the trademark.

211. Moreover, trademark rights acquired through use are also, as a general rule, exclusive within the boundaries of the area in which they have been used. Article 16.1 of the TRIPS Agreement recognises expressly the right of Members to make available exclusive trademark rights on the basis of use. In view of that, there is no good reason why Article 24.5 should provide for the co-existence of geographical indications and non-registered trademarks, but prohibit the co-existence of geographical indications and registered trademarks, which would be the anomalous but necessary consequence of the complainants' interpretation.

---

62 US Oral Statement, para. 64.

63 Ibid.

64 Australia's FWS, para. 74.

The context

212. Article 24.5 is included in Section 3 of Part II, the purpose of which is to provide a minimum of protection to geographical indications. Such protection is subject to limitations in order to accommodate other intellectual property rights. However, it would be a paradoxical result if Article 24.5 were interpreted in such a way that, far from providing any protection to the legitimate right holders of a geographical indication, it prohibited them from even using that indication.

213. As already explained by the EC, co-existence is by no means an unusual solution. It is envisaged by several other provisions of Section 3, of Part II, and not just by Article 23.3, contrary to what is argued by the United States. Furthermore, co-existence is envisaged even where it may lead to some confusion. For example:

- Article 23.2 allows co-existence of a geographical indication for wines or spirits and a trademark consisting or including such geographical indication if used for wines and spirits originating in the area to which the geographical indication relates. *A priori*, the risk that consumers may confuse that geographical indication with the trademark may be the same as when the products covered by the trademark do not originate in that area. Nevertheless, co-existence is allowed because it does not mislead consumers as to the true geographical origin of the products;

- Co-existence may arise as well from Article 24.3, when the protection of geographical indications existing before the date of entry into force of the WTO Agreement provided for such co-existence (see the response to Question 74 above);

- Finally, co-existence is envisaged also by Article 24.4, which provides that a Member may allow "continued and similar" use of a geographical indication for wines or spirits of another Member by its nationals or domiciliaries who have used it before 1 April 1994 in good faith or for at least 10 years preceding that date, regardless of whether this gives rise to confusion with the products of the other Member that are entitled to use that geographical indication.

Object and purpose

214. In its First Written Submission, the United States stressed that Article 16.1 had to be interpreted "in the light of the object and purpose of the TRIPS Agreement, and specifically with respect to Article 16.1 and its grant of exclusive rights."[65]

215. It must be recalled, however, that, under Article 31 of the *Vienna Convention*, only the object and purpose of the treaty as a whole is relevant. To the extent that granting exclusivity to trademark owners is one of the objects and purposes of the TRIPS Agreement, so is affording exclusivity to the right holders of geographical indications. As explained, exclusivity is as essential to geographical indications as to trademarks. Indeed, it could be argued that exclusivity is even more important in the case of geographical indications because the choice of geographical indications, unlike the choice of trademarks, is not arbitrary, and because it takes longer to establish a geographical indication.[66]

Drafting history

216. The United States has argued that the predecessor to the current Article 24.5 included in the so-called Brussels Draft made no reference to the right to use the trademark.[67] However, such reference was included in the predecessor to the current Article 24.4, which provided as follows:[68]

---

[65] US FWS, para. 145.

[66] EC's FWS, paras. 295 and 307.

[67] US Oral Statement, para. 64.

[68] Reproduced in Daniel Gervais, "The TRIPS Agreement, Drafting History and Analysis," Sweet and Maxwell, 1998, p. 133.

> Where a geographical indication of a PARTY has been used with regard to goods originating outside the territory of the PARTY in good faith and in a widespread and continuous manner by nationals or domiciliaries of another PARTY, **including as a trademark**, before the date of application of these provisions in the other PARTY as defined in Article [65] below, nothing in this Agreement shall prevent such continued use of the geographical indication by those nationals or domiciliaries of the said other PARTY. [emphasis added]

217. The scope of the above draft provision overlapped, as far as trademarks are concerned, with the predecessor to Article 24.5, which read as follows:[69]

> A PARTY shall not take action to refuse or invalidate registration of a trademark first applied for or registered:
>
> (a) before the date of application of those provisions in that PARTY as defined in Article [65] below;
>
> (b) before the geographical indication is protected in its country of origin;
>
> on the basis that the trademark is identical with, or similar to, a geographical indication.

218. The reference in the predecessor to Article 24.4 to the continued use of the geographical indications as trademarks indicates that the authors of the Brussels Draft envisaged the co-existence of trademarks and geographical indications of other Members. Such co-existence, however, would be rendered impossible by the US reading of the predecessor to Article 24.5, which would confer to the owners of the trademarks covered by the predecessor to Article 24.4 an exclusive right to use the geographical indication.

219. In the final text of the agreement, the reference to the "use of trademarks" was deleted from the predecessor to Article 24.4 and added to Article 24.5, but it has the same meaning and purpose as when it was included in Article 24.4.[70]

Question 77

Article 24.5 of the TRIPS Agreement uses the phrase "right to use" a trademark. Why did the drafters not choose to state, for example, "exclusive rights" or "rights under Article 16.1"? Is that fact relevant to interpretation of the phrase "right to use" a trademark?

220. As suggested in the question, if the drafters had intended to preserve the right of the owners of the grandfathered trademarks to prevent the use of the geographical indication, they would have used express language to that effect.

221. Furthermore, if Article 24.5 did not allow co-existence, the protection of geographical indications provided under Part II, Section 3, would become pointless whenever there is a grandfathered trademark. Indeed, why protect the intellectual property rights of the holders of geographical indications against illegitimate uses by third parties if the right holders cannot use it themselves? Yet, Article 24.5 assumes that Members will

[69] Ibid.

[70] Several reasons may explain why the reference to the use of trademarks was deleted from Article 24.4 and added to Article 24.5. First, unlike its predecessor in the Brussels Draft, Article 24.4 applies to wines and spirits only. Second, the temporal criteria for the application of Article 24.4 were changed and differ from those of Article 24.5. Third, unlike its predecessor in the Brussels Draft, Article 24.4 applies only to the use of geographical indications by nationals and domiciliaries of the Member concerned. Finally, from a systematic point of view, it is more logic to group in the same Article all the provisions concerning the relationship between geographical indications and earlier trademarks.

continue to protect geographical indications ("...measures adopted to implement this Section shall not prejudice..."), notwithstanding the existence of "grandfathered" trademarks. If the drafters' intention had been to prohibit the use of geographical indications concurrently with grandfathered trademarks, they would have excluded completely the applicability of Part II, Section 3, with respect to the geographical indications concerned, rather than providing that the implementation of that Section shall not prejudice "the right to use the trademark."

Question 86

Article 4 the Paris Convention (1967) creates no right of priority for indications of source. Does this indicate that they are irrelevant for the purposes of the right of priority?

222. The fact that the Paris Convention does not provide for a right of priority in respect of indications of source (including appellations of origin) suggests that the parties to the Paris Convention were of the view that conflicts between indications of source and other industrial property rights should not be resolved according to the first-in-time principle.

Question 87

What is the significance of the EC's statement that the complainants' claims are "theoretical"? Does the EC suggest that this affects the Panel's mandate or function in any way?

223. The fact that the claims raised by the complainants are purely theoretical cast doubts on whether the complainants have a genuine interest in bringing this dispute. The EC, nevertheless, is not suggesting that the Panel's jurisdiction is affected by the complainants' apparent lack of genuine interest. In particular the EC does not consider it necessary to request the Panel to rule on whether the complainants have acted consistently with Article 3.7 of the DSU.

224. If the EC has insisted that the complainants' claims are often theoretical it is because this has implications for the Panel's assessment of whether such claims are well-founded. In particular, in some cases the fact that the complainants' claims are theoretical confirms that they are based on a misinterpretation of the measures in dispute.

225. For example, the fact that the complainants have not been able to identify any single registered geographical indication which gives rise to likelihood of confusion with any prior trademark confirms that, as argued by the EC, the criteria for registrability of trademarks, together with Article 14(3) of Regulation 2081/92, prevent the registration of confusing geographical indications.

226. Similarly, to mention but another example, the fact that Australia has not been able to provide any evidence that the EC authorities have rejected statements of objection for the reasons mentioned by Australia under Claim 21[71] confirms that Article 7(4) does not provide for the limitation of the grounds of objection alleged by Australia.

Question 89

Is there a notion of estoppel in WTO dispute settlement which applies where a Member refrains from raising claims in relation to a measure until after it is amended?

227. According to Article 3.10 of the DSU, the participants in dispute settlement procedures under the DSU are bound by an obligation of good faith. The principle of estoppel is similarly based on the notion of good

---

[71] Australia's FWS, paras. 89-92.

faith. Accordingly, the EC considers that the notion of estoppel is applicable in the context of WTO dispute settlement.

228. However, the EC considers that the Panel may not have to rely on the notion of estoppel in the present case. As the EC has set out already in its first written submission, it considers that the Panel does not have jurisdiction to hear claims which are directed at measures which were no longer in force at the time the Panel was established.[72] Similarly, as regards the individual registrations, even if these were considered to be within the terms of reference of the Panel, the EC has already set out that these registrations in now way violate the principle of national treatment.[73]

229. Since the claims which Australia has raised are either manifestly inadmissible or unfounded, the EC does not consider it necessary to rely on the notion of estoppel at this stage. However, the EC is ready to return to this issue at a later stage should the Panel consider it necessary.

---

[72] EC FWS, para. 13 et seq.

[73] EC FWS, para. 156 et seq.

ANNEX B-5

SECOND WRITTEN SUBMISSION OF THE EUROPEAN COMMUNITIES

(22 July 2004)

TABLE OF CONTENTS

(c) The requirement that the application be transmitted by the country on whose territory the area is located is not unreasonable

5. Claim 3: Non-EC nationals are accorded less favorable treatment than EC nationals with respect to the requirement to indicate the country of origin for homonymous geographical indications

6. Claim 4: Regulation 2081/92 accords less favourable treatment to non-EC nationals by subjecting the right to object to the registration of geographical indications to conditions of reciprocity and equivalence

7. Claim 5: Regulation 2081/92 accords less favourable treatment to non-EC nationals by requiring their own country to transmit the objection

(a) The complainants are not required to verify the admissibility of objections, but merely to transmit the objection

(b) The transmission of objections is not an unreasonable requirement

8. Claim 6: Regulation 2081/92 accords less favourable treatment to non-EC nationals by requiring non-EC national to have a "legitimate interest" to object to the registration of geographical indications

9. Claim 7: Regulation 2081/92 accords less favourable treatment because a non-EC rightholder has no "representative" in the regulatory committee to "speak for him"

10. Claim 8: A right of objection was available to persons resident or established in an EC Member State that was not available to other WTO Member nationals in respect of the registration of more than 120 geographical indications under the normal registration process

(a) The legal basis of Australia's claim is unclear, and keeps shifting

(b) Australia's claims regarding old versions of Regulation 2081/92 are outside the terms of reference of the Panel

(c) Australia's claims are moot and therefore not within the terms of reference of the Panel

(d) Australia has not shown that the individual registrations are in violation of national treatment obligations

(e) There is no legal basis for the recommendations suggested by Australia

11. Claim 9: A right of objection was available to persons resident or established in an EC Member State that was not available to other WTO Member nationals in respect of the registration of more than 480 EC-defined GIs under the simplified registration process

B. PROHIBITED REQUIREMENT OF DOMICILE OR ESTABLISHMENT (ARTICLE 2.1 TRIPS IN CONJUNCTION WITH ARTICLE 2.2 PARIS CONVENTION)

1. Claim 10: Regulation 2081/92 requires non-EC nationals to become established in the EC as a condition for registering geographical indications

2. Claim 11: Regulation 2081/92 requires non-EC nationals to become established in the EC as a condition for objecting

C. NATIONAL TREATMENT UNDER ARTICLE III:4 GATT

1. The regulation 2081/92 is not incompatible with Article III:4 GATT

(a) Claim 12: Regulation 2081/92 accords less favourable treatment as regards the conditions for registration of foreign geographical indications

(b) Claim 12bis: Regulation 2081/92 violates the national treatment obligations under the GATT by requiring the existence of inspection structures with respect to the specific product for which protection is requested

(c) Claim 13: Regulation 2081/92 accords less favourable treatment as regards the requirement that the application must be transmitted by the government of the third country

(d) Claim 14: Regulation 2081/92 accords less favourable treatment as regards the requirement to indicate the country of origin

(e) Claim 15: Regulation 2081/92 accords less favourable treatment due to an overall bias in the decision-making process

2. The measure would be justified under Article XX(d) GATT

(a) The requirement of inspection structures is justified by Article XX(d) GATT (Claim 12bis)

(b) The requirement that the application must be verified and transmitted by the government where the area is located is justified by Article XX(d) GATT (Claim 13)
(c) The requirement to indicate the country of origin for homonymous geographical indications is justified by Article XX(d) GATT (Claim 14)

IV. REGULATION 2081/92 IS COMPATIBLE WITH THE OBLIGATION TO PROVIDE MOST-FAVOURED-NATION TREATMENT

A. ARTICLE 4 TRIPS

1. Claim 16: As among non-EC WTO Members, nationals from WTO Members that satisfy the EC's conditions of reciprocity and equivalency are accorded more favourable treatment than nationals from those WTO Members that do not

2. Claim 17: Under Regulation 2081/92, an EC Member State grants more favourable treatment to nationals from other EC Member States than it accords to nationals from non-EC WTO Members

B. CLAIM 18: BY SUBJECTING THE REGISTRATION OF THIRD-COUNTRY GEOGRAPHICAL INDICATIONS TO CONDITIONS OF RECIPROCITY AND EQUIVALENCE, THE EC MEASURE IS INCONSISTENT WITH THE MOST-FAVOURED-NATION OBLIGATION UNDER THE ARTICLE I:1 GATT

1. Article I:1 GATT is not violated

2. The EC measure would be justified under Article XX(d) GATT

V. REGULATION 2081/92 DOES NOT DIMINISH THE LEGAL PROTECTION OF TRADEMARKS

A. ARTICLE 16.1 OF THE TRIPS AGREEMENT

1. Claim 19: Article 14(2) of Regulation 2081/92 is inconsistent with Article 16.1 of the TRIPS Agreement in that it allows the co-existence of geographical indications and earlier registered trademarks

(a) Article 14(3) of Regulation 2081/92
(i) Registrability of geographical names as trademarks
(ii) Standard of evidence for establishing the meaning of Article 14(3)
(iii) The Complainants have misinterpreted Article 14(3)
(iv) There is no evidence that Article 14(3) has been applied in accordance with the complainants' interpretation
(v) Article 14(3) confers enforceable rights to the trademark owners
(vi) EC law provides means to prevent confusing uses of a registered geographical indication

(b) Article 24.5 of the TRIPS Agreement
(i) Relationship between Section 3 of Part II and Article 16.1
(ii) The meaning of "the right to use a trademark"

(c) Article 24.3 of the TRIPS Agreement

(d) Article 17 of the TRIPS Agreement
(i) The scope of the exception is "limited"
(ii) The exception "takes account" of the interests of the trademark owners
(iii) Article 17 applies to non-geographical names

2. Claim 20: Regulation 2081/92 does not provide for a presumption of a likelihood of confusion in the case of use of an identical sign for identical goods

3. Claim 21: Article 7(4) of Regulation 2081/92 is inconsistent with Article 16.1 of the TRIPS Agreement because it limits the grounds of objection

4. Claim 22: Regulation 2081/92 does not ensure that objections from trademark owners will be considered by the Committee

B. CLAIM 23: BY REQUIRING THE CO-EXISTENCE OF A REGISTERED GEOGRAPHICAL INDICATION AND AN EARLIER TRADEMARK, ARTICLE 14(2) ENCUMBERS UNJUSTIFIABLY THE USE OF THE TRADEMARK, CONTRARY TO ARTICLE 20 OF THE TRIPS AGREEMENT

Table of WTO cases referred to in this submission

Short Title	Full Case Title and Citation of Case
Canada – Autos	Panel Report, *Canada – Certain Measures Affecting the Automotive Industry*, WT/DS139/R, WT/DS142/R, adopted 19 June 2000, as modified by the Appellate Body Report, WT/DS139/AB/R, WT/DS142/AB/R, DSR 2000:VII, 3043
EC – Sardines	Appellate Body Report, *European Communities – Trade Description of Sardines*, WT/DS231/AB/R, adopted 23 October 2002
EC – Hormones	Appellate Body Report, *EC Measures Concerning Meat and Meat Products (Hormones)*, WT/DS26/AB/R, WT/DS48/AB/R, adopted 13 February 1998, DSR 1998:I, 135
Korea – Various Measures on Beef	Appellate Body Report, *Korea – Measures Affecting Imports of Fresh, Chilled and Frozen Beef*, WT/DS161/AB/R, WT/DS169/AB/R, adopted 10 January 2001
US – Gasoline	Appellate Body Report, *United States – Standards for Reformulated and Conventional Gasoline*, WT/DS2/AB/R, adopted 20 May 1996, DSR 1996:I, 3
US – Section 301 Trade Act	Panel Report, *United States – Sections 301-310 of the Trade Act of 1974*, WT/DS152/R, adopted 27 January 2000, DSR 2000:II, 815

GLOSSARY

Commission, EC Commission	Commission of the European Communities
Committee	Committee of representatives of the Member States referred to in Article 15 of Council Regulation 2081/92
Community Trademark Regulation	Council Regulation (EC) No 40/94, of 20 December 1993, on the Community Trademark, as amended
Council, EC Council	Council of the European Union
Court of Justice, European Court of Justice	Court of Justice of the European Communities
DSU	Understanding on Rules and Procedures Governing the Settlement of Disputes
EC	European Communities
GATT	General Agreement on Tariffs and Trade 1994
FOS	First Oral Statement
FWS	First Written Submission
GI	Geographical indication
Member States, EC Member States	Member States of the European Union
Official Journal	Official Journal of the European Union
Paris Convention	Stockholm Act of the Paris Convention for the protection of Industrial property, of 14 July 1967
Regulation 2081/92, Regulation	Council Regulation (EEC) No 2081/92 of 14 July 1992 on the protection of geographical indications and designations of origin for agricultural products and foodstuffs, as amended on the date of establishment of the Panel
SCM Agreement, SCM	Agreement on Subsidies and Countervailing Duties
Trademarks Directive	First Council Directive 89/104, of 20 December, on the Community Trademark, as amended
TBT Agreement, TBT	Agreement on Technical Barriers to Trade
TRIPS Agreement, TRIPS	Agreement on Trade-Related Aspects of Intellectual Property Rights
US	United States
WTO Agreement	Marrakesh Agreement Establishing the World Trade Organization

I. INTRODUCTION

1. This submission provides the rebuttal of the European Communities to the arguments made by the complainants at the first meeting with the Panel of 23-24 June 2004, as well as in their responses to the questions from the Panel and from the EC of 8 July 2004. The EC has addressed some of those arguments as part of its own responses to the Panel's questions. In order to avoid unnecessary repetitions, the EC will refer to those responses where appropriate.

2. In the following section, the EC will first discuss some horizontal issues concerning the objective assessment of the content of Regulation 2081/92. In the following sections, the EC will comment on the arguments of the complainants claim by claim, following the structure already used in the EC's first written submission.

II. THE OBJECTIVE ASSESSMENT OF THE CONTENT OF REGULATION 2081/92

3. The EC has already set out the content of Regulation 2081/92 in its first written submission.[1] In the present submission, the EC refers to this general presentation. Where the complainants have contested the interpretation of particular provisions of Regulation 2081/92, the EC will respond to these arguments in the discussion of the specific claims raised by the complainants.

4. In the present section, the EC would like to address two horizontal issues which are essential for the objective assessment of the content of Regulation 2081/92 by the Panel:

- the proper approach to the interpretation of Regulation 2081/92 as a measure of EC domestic law;
- the importance of WTO law and obligations for the interpretation of Regulation 2081/92 in the EC legal order.

A. THE PROPER APPROACH TO THE INTERPRETATION OF REGULATION 2081/92 AS A MEASURE OF EC DOMESTIC LAW

5. In its response to the first question asked by the Panel after the first substantive hearing, the EC has set out how it believes the Panel should approach the interpretation of Regulation 2081/92.[2]

6. As the EC has already stated, the meaning of Regulation 2081/92 is, for the purposes of the present dispute, a question of fact. Accordingly, the burden of proof for establishing that Regulation 2081/92 has a particular meaning rests on the complainants. This means that it is the complainants, not the EC, who must show that Regulation 2081/92 has in fact the meaning which they allege it has.

7. Since the interpretation of Regulation 2081/92 as a measure of EC domestic law is a question of fact, it follows that Panel must not "interpret" the meaning of Regulation 2081/92 as it would interpret provisions of the WTO Agreement. Rather, the Panel must, accordance with Article 11 DSU, proceed to an objective assessment of the meaning of this Regulation within the legal order of the EC.

8. For the purposes of this objective assessment, it is essential that the Panel take into account the legal context of the measure within the legal order of the Member concerned. For this reason, due account must also be taken of the meaning which is given to the measure in question by the authorities of the Member concerned.

---

[1] EC FWS, para. 43 et seq.

[2] EC Response to Panel's Question No. 1, para. 1 et seq.

As the Panel in *US – Section 301* has held, for this reason, considerable deference must be given to the explanations given by the Member concerned as to the meaning of its own measure.[3]

9. In their responses to the questions of the Panel, the United States and Australia have failed to correctly appreciate these principles. First of all, it appears that the United States attempts to shift the burden of proof as regards the content of Regulation 2081/92 to the EC.[4] However, this burden of proof is on the complainants; and as the EC will set out in its discussion of the individual claims Australia and the United States do not provide sufficient evidence to demonstrate that the provisions of the Regulation do indeed have the meaning which they allege.

10. More importantly still, the United States and Australia fail to give due weight to the fact that Regulation 2081/92 is a measure of EC domestic law. This is illustrated by the incorrect statements of the United States and Australia as regards the interpretation of the Regulation 2081/92 by the Court of Justice. As the EC will set out in greater detail in the next section, these statements entirely fail to appreciate the relevance of WTO law and obligations for the interpretation of Regulation 2081/92 in the EC legal order.

11. Particularly striking in this context is the contention of the United States that the "Commission's interpretation" before the Panel should not be granted "any particular deference."[5] First of all, the EC would like to stress that the US is incorrect to refer to the "Commission's" statements or interpretations. As the US is well aware, the European Communities as a Member of the WTO is represented by the European Commission. Accordingly, the statements made by the EC representatives before the Panel are made on behalf of the European Communities as a whole, and not on behalf of the European Commission or any other institution of the EC.

12. For this reason, the US comments regarding the weight of the Commission's opinions with respect to other institutions within the EC legal order[6] are without any relevance for evaluating the statements made by the EC before the Panel. In addition, the US statements in this regard are partially incorrect, and give a tilted picture of the institutional system of the EC.

13. For instance, the United States refers to the practice of complaint letters in the field of competition law.[7] The EC does not see the relevance of this example for the present dispute. That the Commission's comfort letters, which are not intended to be binding, are not binding on national courts, is not particularly surprising. What the US fails to mention, in contrast, is that despite their not being binding, such letters are usually respected. As one author has put it in a recent publication on competition law: "Furthermore, it is likely that a national court, although not formally bound by a comfort letter, would be strongly influenced by it."[8]

14. Similarly, the EC wonders what is the basis for the US statement that before the Court of Justice, the Commission's brief "carries no greater weight than a brief submitted by a private party," and that "in many cases, the ECJ does not even accept the Commission's interpretation."[9] This statement already disregards that in accordance with Article 211 EC Treaty, the Commission is responsible "to ensure that the provision of this Treaty and the measures taken by the institutions pursuant thereto are applied." In other words, the EC is not just "any other private party," but is the guardian of the EC Treaty.

---

[3] Panel Report, *US – Section 301*, para. 7.18. Full quotation cf. EC Response to Panel's Question No. 1, para. 3.

[4] US Response to Panel's Question No. 1, para. 1.

[5] US Response to Panel's Question No. 1, para. 18.

[6] US Response to Panel's Question No. 1, para. 8 et seq.

[7] Cf. US Response to Panel's Question No. 1, para. 10.

[8] R. Whish, *Competition Law*, 5th edition (2003), p. 167 (Exhibit EC-33).

[9] US Response to Panel's Question No. 1, para. 11.

15. This is also reflected by the fact that unlike a private party, the Commission may intervene in any proceedings pending before the Court of Justice to which it is not itself a party.[10] Similarly, it may present observations with respect to all requests for preliminary rulings.[11] The Commission exercises this right to intervene and present observations systematically, and in the great majority of cases, its observations are followed by the Court.

16. Finally, the complainants fail to accord a reasonable degree of deference to the statements of the EC as regards its own measure. In its oral statement in the first hearing, the United States has stated that a clarification that the EC does not apply conditions of reciprocity and equivalence to other WTO Members "will be welcome."[12] However, its comments give the opposite impression. Indeed, the EC is wondering from whom the US is hoping to receive the desired clarification, if not from the representatives of the European Communities.[13]

17. In conclusion, the Panel should, in its approach to Regulation 2081/92, take due of account of the character of this measure as a measure of EC domestic law, and give due weight to the explanation which are furnished by the European Communities in this respect.

B. THE IMPORTANCE OF WTO LAW AND OBLIGATIONS FOR THE INTERPRETATION OF REGULATION 2081/92 IN THE EC LEGAL ORDER

18. A particular point with respect to which the United States and Australia fail to appreciate the proper legal context of Regulation 2081/92 is the importance of WTO law and obligations for the interpretation of the Regulation. This issue is of particular importance regarding the claims that the EC applies conditions of "reciprocity and equivalence" to the registration of geographical indications from other WTO Members, and the EC will return to it in this context. However, it is also a horizontal question, on which the EC would therefore offer a number of general observations.

19. In its response to Question 15 of the Panel, the EC has already set out in detail, citing concrete examples from the case law, how the European Court of Justice takes into account the obligations arising from international agreements, in particular the WTO Agreements, in the interpretation and application of acts of Community law.[14]

20. The United States and Australia have entirely ignored this case law, and have rather superficially limited themselves to stating that according to the European Court of Justice, the WTO Agreements do not have direct effect, and are not in principle among the rules in the light of which the Court of Justice is to review the legality of measures adopted by the Community institutions.[15] In support of this statement, the complainants have relied on two judgements of the Court of Justice, namely the judgements in case C-149/96, *Portugal/Council*, and in Case C-93/02 P, *Biret.*[16]

21. This presentation of the importance of WTO law within the EC legal order is incorrect. First of all, the cases referred to by the complainants are not relevant for the present context. Both judgments concerned the conditions under which the legality of a Community measure could be challenged under EC law because of incompatibilities with WTO law. This question has nothing to do with the present case. In the present case, the

---

[10] Article 40 (1) of the Statute of the European Court of Justice.

[11] Article 23 (2) of the Statute of the European Court of Justice.

[12] US FOS, para. 16.

[13] The EC also notes that in its comments on the Panel's draft letter to WIPO, which it transmitted by e-mail to the Secretariat on 9 July 2004, Australia warns against "inappropriate interpretative analysis on the part of the International Bureau of WIPO of those countries' legislation and intentions." The EC wonders why Australia insists on deference as regards the legislation of WIPO Members, but would not want the Panel to afford any deference as regards the interpretation of EC legislation.

[14] EC Response to Panel's Question No. 15, para. 28 et seq.

[15] US Response to Panel's Question No. 1, para. 15–16; Australian response to Question 6.

[16] Exhibits US-31 and US-32.

question is not whether Regulation 2081/92 could be challenged before the European Court of Justice for alleged inconsistencies with WTO law; the question is how Regulation 2081/92 must be interpreted taking into account the international obligations of the EC, and given the references to these international obligations which it contains.

22. In fact, the complainants fail to appreciate that WTO law is important in more than one way in the EC legal order. As one scholar of Community law has observed, one of the most important openings for WTO law in the legal order of the EC is the principle of that EC law must be interpreted in line with the EC's international obligations:[17]

> As a consequence, WTO compliant interpretation could result in the most effective means to judicially enforce, in the absence of specific measures of transformation, WTO law into the Community legal order. This is not the least reinforced by the weight the Panel in its Report on Section 301 on the US Trade Act has put on the option of WTO conform interpretation.

23. In fact, the European Court of Justice consistently strives to interpret EC legal measures in accordance with the EC's international obligations. As the EC has already set out, there are numerous examples where the European Court of Justice has taken account of and applied international obligations, including the WTO agreements, in the interpretation of EC law.[18]

24. As one commentator, now a Judge of the European Court of Justice, has observed, the judgement in case C-149/96, *Portugal/Council*, does not have the effect of rendering WTO law irrelevant under Community law:[19]

> The judgment in *Portugal v. Council* does not render the WTO Agreements irrelevant under Community law. First of all, they may have what has been called "indirect" effect, implying an obligation for domestic courts to *interpret* national law in the light of WTO law. In *Hermès*, the Court of Justice made the following finding:
>
>> It should be stressed at the outset that, although the issue of the direct effect of Article 50 of the TRIPs Agreement has been argued, the Court is not required to give a ruling on that question, but only to answer the question of *interpretation* submitted to it by the national court so as to enable that court to *interpret Netherlands procedural rules in the light of that article.* (emphasis added)
>
> Apart from this "indirect" effect, the Court in an infringement case has held that, because of the "primacy" of international agreements over provisions of secondary Community legislation, such provisions "must," so far as is possible, be interpreted in a manner that is consistent with those agreements" (the agreement in question was a GATT Agreement). In the same case, the Court confirmed that EU Member States are called upon to respect the GATT Agreements and can in the interest of uniform application of these Agreements throughout the EU be brought before the Court of Justice in infringement proceedings.

25. Accordingly, the misgivings that the complainants voice regarding the approach which the European Court of Justice, or other institutions of the EC, might take to the interpretation of Regulation 2081/92 are misplaced. This is particularly so where, as in the case of Article 12(1) of Regulation 2081/92, the EC measure specifically provides that it applies "without prejudice to international agreements."

---

[17] Stefan Griller, *Enforcement and Implementation of WTO Law in the European Union*, in Breuss/Griller/Vranes (ed.), The Banana Dispute, p. 247, 270 (2003) (Exhibit EC-34).

[18] EC Response to Panel's Question No. 15, para. 33–38.

[19] Allan Rosas, Case note, 37 CMLR 797, 814 (2000) (Exhibit EC-35).

26. For these reasons, the Panel should not assume that the institutions of the EC, and in particular the European Court of Justice, will ignore WTO obligations in the interpretation and application of Regulation 2081/92.

III. REGULATION 2081/92 IS COMPATIBLE WITH NATIONAL TREATMENT OBLIGATIONS, AND DOES NOT IMPOSE A REQUIREMENT OF DOMICILE OR ESTABLISHMENT

27. The EC has already responded in its first written submission to the claims raised by the complainants as regards the alleged violation of the national treatment provisions of the TRIPS and the GATT, as well as the prohibition on conditions of residence and domicile in Article 2.2 of the Paris Convention.[20] Hereunder, the EC will add a number of further observations on these claims in response to the statements made by the complainants during the first hearing and in their responses to the Panel's questions.

A. NATIONAL TREATMENT UNDER THE TRIPS AGREEMENT (ARTICLE 3.1 TRIPS AND ARTICLE 2.1 TRIPS IN CONJUNCTION WITH ARTICLE 2.1 PARIS CONVENTION)

28. As in its first written submission, the EC will first turn to the claims made in respect of the national treatment provisions of the TRIPS and the Paris Convention.

1. The Meaning and Scope of National Treatment under the TRIPS Agreement

29. Already in its first written submission, the EC has pointed out the importance of giving a proper interpretation to the national treatment provisions of Article 3.1 TRIPS Agreement, and similarly of Article 2.1 of the Paris Convention. In particular, the EC has stressed that unlike national treatment under the GATT, which concerns products, national treatment under the TRIPS Agreement is concerned with the treatment of nationals.[21]

30. In their responses to the questions of the Panel, the complainants offer interpretations of Article 3.1 TRIPS Agreement which do not correspond to the wording of the provision. Since this is a horizontal question underlying all the claims brought by the complainants under the national treatment provisions of the TRIPS and the Paris Convention, the EC will offer here some general remarks on the interpretations made by the complainants.

(a) The meaning of "national"

31. In its response to Question 23 of the Panel, the EC has explained that for natural persons, a national is any person who holds the nationality of the State in question in conformity with the legislation of such state. As regards legal persons, the question of nationality similarly depends on the law of the state in question, which may use criteria such as the law of incorporation, headquarters, or other criteria.[22] In the view of the EC, nationality is a distinct concept from domicile or establishment. Accordingly, the EC is of the view that it cannot be assumed that a Members State's nationals necessarily include natural persons who are domiciled, or legal persons who have a real and effective industrial and commercial establishment, in that Member.

32. In their responses to the Panel, the United States and Australia have argued the contrary. However, the legal grounds on which they base this view are unclear to the EC.

---

[20] EC FWS, para. 101 et seq.

[21] EC FWS, para. 104 et seq.

[22] EC Response to Panel's Question No. 23, para. 56 et seq.

33. In its responses, the United States seems to have relied primarily on footnote 1 to Article 1.3 of the TRIPS Agreement, which defines the notion of national for the purposes of a "separate customs territory." This reliance by the US on footnote 1 is misplaced.

34. In its response to Question 52, the United States alleges that "footnote 1 to Article 1.3 of the TRIPS Agreement defines 'national' throughout the Agreement not in terms of nationality, but in terms of where a person is domiciled or where a person has a real and effective industrial or commercial establishment."[23] This statement is misleading. Footnote 1 does not define the term "national" for all purposes of the Agreement, but only as regards separate customs territories. As the EC has already remarked, this definition in fact demonstrates that for all cases other than separate customs territories, nationality does not depend on domicile or establishment.[24]

35. Attempting another variant of its argument, the United States seems to suggest that the EC is a separate customs territory, to which footnote 1 to Article 1.3 of the TRIPS Agreement should apply.[25] The EC is not quite sure whether this is a drafting error, or meant to be a serious argument. In the latter case, the EC would be interested to know from what other customs territory the EC is supposed to be "separate."[26] It seems that if the EC is a separate customs territory, so are the United States, Australia, and in fact all WTO Members. Obviously this cannot be the correct meaning of "separate customs territory" in footnote 1 to Article 1.3 TRIPS Agreement.

36. Australia's responses on this point are no less unclear. In its responses, Australia first states that nationals are in the case of natural persons, "persons who possess the nationality of a State," and in regard to legal persons, persons "who are domiciled or established in that WTO Member in accordance with the laws of the WTO Member of which nationality is claimed." However, then Australia goes on to conclude that "nationals normally include natural persons who are domiciled or legal persons who have a real and effective industrial and commercial establishment in that Member." Australia notes further "that these categories of person would not always qualify as nationals."

37. In the view of the EC, these responses obscure the question. The question is not who is "normally" included among nationals, but the question who is a national. Contrary to the views of the complainants, "nationality" is a distinct concept, which is different from questions of domicile or establishment.

38. This is particularly obvious in the case of natural persons. National laws do not "normally" confer nationality simply on the basis of residence or establishment. Similarly, a national does not normally lose his or her nationality simply because of residence abroad.

39. The situation in this respect is not fundamentally different for legal persons. Even if the criteria which national laws use may vary, typically nationality is not simply attributed on the basis that a legal person is established in a particular country. The EC would note that if this criterion were sufficient, this could lead to situation where e.g. multinationals companies would be nationals of a very large number of countries.

40. In the view of the EC, this would not be a reasonable definition of nationality. This is why other criteria, such as notably the law of incorporation, are used.[27] The EC notes that its views in this respect coincide with those expressed by Canada in its responses to a Question of the Panel.[28]

---

[23] US Response to Panel's Question No. 26, para. 52.

[24] EC Response to Panel's Question No. 23, para. 60.

[25] US Response to Panel's Question No. 23, para. 49 (referring to "a separate customs territory, such as the EC").

[26] In passing, the EC would note that unlike in the case of a a separate customs territory, there is a citizenship of the European Union. Cf. 17 of the EC Treaty, which provides that every person holding the nationality of a Member State shall be a citizen of the Union.

[27] In this respect, reference can be made to Article 48(1) of the EC Treaty, which provides as follows: "Companies or firms formed in accordance with the law of a Member State and having their registered office, central administration or principal place of business within the Community shall, for the purposes of this Chapter, be treated in the same way as natural persons who are nationals of Member States."

41. Accordingly, the Panel should conclude that the term "national" in Article 3.1 TRIPS Agreement and Article 2.1 Paris Convention does not necessarily include persons who are domiciled or established in a particular WTO Member.

(b) The conditions for applications and objections do not depend on nationality

42. On the basis of this understanding, the EC is of the view that the claims of the complainants raised in respect of Regulation 2081/92 do not involve any difference in treatment on the basis of nationality.

43. As the EC has already set out in its first submission, the parallel procedures for the registration of geographical indications depend exclusively on where the area is located to which the geographical indication is related. The conditions for registration do not therefore depend on nationality.[29] Similarly, the procedures for objecting to the registration of a geographical indication do not distinguish between nationals, but depend on where the objecting person is domiciled or established.[30] The fact that there are different provisions setting out parallel procedures does not entail any discrimination, but simply is necessary to take account of the need to involve the governments of the Member States or of the third country, respectively.

44. The EC notes that in their responses to the Panel, the complainants seem to recognise that Regulation 2081/92 does not contain any distinctions on the basis of nationality. Rather, the complainants seem to be basing themselves on the notion that US and Australian nationals would more "likely" be affected by the alleged violations than EC nationals.[31]

45. First of all, the EC would note that the complainants do not provide any factual basis for these claims. Even though it may be true that persons producing in a specific geographical area may frequently be nationals of the state where the area is located, this is not inevitably so. Indeed, there is no reason why a US or Australian national could not produce products in accordance with the product specifications of an EC GI.

46. Indeed, in the area of wines and spirits, investment by foreign nationals in protected geographic names is a common phenomenon. By way of example, the EC can refer to the story of Jens-Reidar Larsen, a Norwegian national who is the founder of the Larsen Cognac House in Cognac, France (extract from Exhibit EC-36):

> The Larsen firm was founded in 1926 by Jens-Reidar Larsen, a young Norwegian, who arrived in Bordeaux in 1919. He settled shortly afterwards in Cognac, charmed by the inimitable atmosphere of the small Charentes town and there, discovered the refinement of its famous eau-de-vie. Having become a fine connoisseur, and driven by an innate business insight, he bought the small firm of Cognac Joseph Gautier. He then launched his own "Larsen" brand which soon prospered on Scandinavian markets, particularly in Norway. Having married a native of Cognac, he had a son who took over the Larsen firm and made the brand prosper around the world.

47. Similar examples of foreign companies, including from the United States or Japan, investing in wine or spirits estates in France, Italy, or German can be seen in Exhibits EC-37 to EC-39.

48. The EC sees no reason why the example of Mr. Larsen could not be followed by a US or Australian national who devotes himself to the making of Roquefort or Stilton cheese, or of other agricultural products and

---

[28] Response of Canada to Panel's Question No. 6 to the third parties, para. 2–5.

[29] EC FWS, para. 123 et seq.

[30] EC FWS, para. 142.

[31] Cf. US Response to Panel's Question No. 27, para. 54-55, where the US refers to the possibility of an EC national being prevented by Regulation 2081/92 from registering a US GI in the EC; Australia's Response to Question 27.

foodstuffs protected under Regulation 2081/92.[32] That such examples may not yet be as common for agricultural products and foodstuffs covered by Regulation 2081/92 as they are for wines and spirits has nothing to do with any restrictions imposed by that Regulation. Rather, it is the result of the fact that wines and spirits are high-value products, which have been traded for a long time, and where international investment accordingly has a long tradition. However, the EC is convinced that with the growing appreciation and knowledge of agricultural products and foodstuffs protected by geographical indications, this may change, and foreign nationals may indeed begin to produce such products in accordance with the product specifications.

49. Moreover, as the EC has already explained in its response to Question 29 of the Panel,[33] the present case is not one which implies a "*de facto*" discrimination between nationals within the meaning of the TRIPS Agreement. As the EC has set out, *de facto* discrimination is a notion which is closely related to preventing circumvention of national treatment obligations.[34] However, the concerns that the complainants have raised, in particular the application procedure, are linked primarily to the origin of the goods. Such issues regarding the treatment of goods are dealt with more appropriately in the context of the GATT, and not of the TRIPS Agreement. Similarly, conditions of residence and requirement are dealt with in Article 2.2 of the Paris Convention, on the basis of which the complainants have made separate claims.

50. For the reasons set out, the claims do not fall under the scope of Article 3.1 TRIPS and 2.1 Paris Convention.

2. Claim 1: Non-EC nationals are accorded less favorable treatment than EC nationals with respect to the registration of geographical indications through the application of a condition of reciprocity and equivalence

51. The US and Australia have claimed that by subjecting the registration of geographic indications from other WTO members to "conditions of reciprocity and equivalence," Regulation 2081/92 violates the national treatment provisions of Article 3.1 TRIPS and 2.1 Paris Convention.

52. In its submissions to the Panel, the EC has repeatedly confirmed that it does not apply such conditions to other WTO Members.[35] Accordingly, this claim of the complainants is without factual basis. However, the complainants have expressed scepticism about the EC's interpretation.[36] Hereunder, the EC will show that such scepticism is unwarranted.

(a) The complainant's interpretation is incompatible with the plain wording of Regulation 2081/92

53. First of all, the interpretation given by the complainants of Regulation 2081/92 is incompatible with the plain wording of Regulation 2081/92. Article 12(1) of the Regulation states clearly that it applies only "without prejudice to international agreements." Accordingly, the conditions of reciprocity and equivalence set out in Article 12(1) are applied only without prejudice to international agreements.

54. The formula "without prejudice to" is a common occurrence in EC legislation. In a drafting manual for EC legislation, the meaning of the expression "without prejudice to ... " is defined as "without affecting ...," "independently of ...," "leaving intact ...."[37]

---

[32] As a matter of fact, the EC believes that there probably are examples of non-EC nationals who produce products in the EC bearing names protected under Regulation 2081/92. However, since nationality of the producer is not a relevant criterion for protection under Regulation 2081/92, the EC does not have specific information about the nationality of such producers.

[33] EC Response to Panel's Question No. 29, para. 67 et seq.

[34] Cf. EC Response to Panel's Question No. 29, para. 73-74.

[35] EC FWS, para. 65 et seq, 115 et seq.; EC FOS, para. 42.

[36] US FOS, para. 16; Australia's FOS, para. 19.

[37] Manual of Precedents for Acts Established within the Council of the European Communities, 3rd edition, p. 135 (1990) (Exhibit EC-40).

55. In other words, the effect of such "without prejudice" clauses is to isolate and protect the act or provision to which reference is made from the effect of the act or provision in which the reference is contained. In other words, should a conflict between the two acts or provisions occur, then the act or provision to which the "without prejudice" reference is made prevails.

56. According to the submissions of the complainants, the application of conditions of reciprocity and equivalence to WTO Members conflicts with the national treatment obligations of the TRIPS Agreement and the GATT. However, Article 12(1) precisely prevents such a conflict by stating that it applies "without prejudice" to international agreements.

57. Accordingly, on the basis of the plain wording of the Regulation, the conditions of reciprocity and equivalence do not apply to WTO Members. Rather, as the EC has already explained in its response to Question 7 of the Panel, an application for registration of a geographical indication from a WTO Member may be made directly under Article 12a of Regulation 2081/92.[38]

(b) The without prejudice clause requires that the WTO Agreements be taken into account

58. The EC's interpretation of the plain meaning of Article 12(1) of the Regulation is further confirmed by the legal context of the Regulation in the EC domestic legal order.

59. As the EC has already explained, an important principle in the jurisprudence of the Court of Justice is that the legal acts of the institutions should be interpreted in line with the international obligations of the European Communities.[39] On this basis, the EC does not see how the European institutions, and in particular the European Court of Justice, could avoid taking into account the EC's obligations under the WTO agreements. The fears and doubts which the complainants have expressed in this context as regards the possible approach that could be taken by the Commission, the Council of Ministers, or the European Court of Justice, are exaggerated and based an insufficient understanding of the relationship between EC law and WTO law.

60. Quite on the contrary, the EC believes that on the basis of the wording of Regulation 2081/92, there would be a considerable risk of a successful legal challenge if the Community institutions rejected an application for the registration of a geographical indication from another WTO member with the argument that such WTO Member does not fulfil the conditions of Article 12(1) of the Regulation. The wording "without prejudice to international agreements" clearly requires the institutions to take into account and apply international agreements, including the WTO Agreements. In such a situation, the Community institutions would be violating Community law if they applied Regulation 2081/92 in a way that prejudices the WTO Agreements. This is confirmed also by the jurisprudence of the Court of Justice, which has held that where a Community measure is intended to implement a particular obligation, or where the Community measure refers explicitly to the precise provisions of the WTO Agreements, the Court may review the legality of EC measures in the light of WTO obligations.[40] In the case of Article 12(1) of Regulation 2081/92, the measure not only "implements" or refers" to obligations of WTO law, but provides that it shall be "without prejudice." This is a stronger formulation than the one relied on by the Court in previous cases where it reviewed the compatibility of Community measures with WTO law, and therefore requires even more strongly that WTO obligations be taken into account.

61. The plain wording of the Regulation, in particular when interpreted in the light of the principles of interpretation of Community law, clearly confirms the interpretation given by the EC.

---

[38] EC Response to Panel's Question No. 7, para. 16-17.

[39] Supra para. 18. Cf. also EC Response to Panel's Question No. 15, para. 32 et seq.

[40] Case C-70/87, *Fediol*, [1989] ECR 1781, para. 19–22 (Exhibit EC-41); Case C-69/89, *Nakajima* [1991] ECR I-2069, para. 30–32 (Exhibit EC-42); Case C-93/02 P, *Biret*, Judgment of 30 September 2003, para. 53 (Exhibit US-31).

(c) It is not uncommon for Community legal acts to apply "without prejudice to international agreements"

62. It may also be useful for the Panel to know that there is nothing unusual about the fact that a Community legal act would apply "without prejudice to international agreements." In fact, analogous provisions can be found in numerous Community legislative acts drawn from various sectors.

63. For instance, Article 22.4 of Regulation 1784/2003 on the common market organisation in cereals provides that it applies "having regard to the obligations arising from agreements concluded in accordance with Article 300 of the Treaty."[41] Similar provisions were introduced into a number of Regulations in the agricultural field by Council Regulation EC 3290/94 of 22 December 1994 on the adjustments and transitional arrangements required in the agricultural sector resulting from the Uruguay Round agreements.[42]

64. Article 4(2) of Regulation 2407/92 on licensing of air carriers provides as follows:[43] "Without prejudice to agreements and conventions to which the Community is a contracting party, the undertaking shall be owned and continue to be owned directly or through majority ownership by Member States and/or nationals of Member States."

65. Article 3 of Council Regulation 1356/96 on transport of persons and goods on Community rivers reads as follows:[44] "This Regulation shall not affect the rights of third-country operators under the Revised Convention for the Navigation of the Rhine (Mannheim Convention), the Convention on Navigation on the Danube (Belgrade Convention) or the rights arising from the European Community's international obligations."

66. Article 12(1) of Directive 2003/86 on the right to family reunification reads as follows:[45] "Without prejudice to international obligations, where family reunification is possible in a third country with which the sponsor and/or family member has special links, Member States may require provision of the evidence referred to in the first subparagraph."

(d) The "without prejudice" clause was not intended to apply only to bilateral agreements, or to agreements which contain "specific rules" on geographical indications

67. In its oral statement, the US has argued that the "without prejudice" clause in Article 12(1) of the Regulation applies only to bilateral, but not to multilateral agreements.[46] In response to the questions of the Panel, the complainants now seem to argue that the "without prejudice" clause covers certain "specific" agreements concerning the protection of geographical indications, but not the obligations under the WTO Agreements.[47]

68. Neither the former nor the latter distinction has any basis in the wording of Article 12(1) of the Regulation. Article 12(1) simply refers to "international agreements." It does not distinguish between bilateral and multilateral agreements. Neither does it distinguish between agreements which lay down "specific rules" for the protection of geographical indications, and others which do not.

69. The EC would note the suggestion that the "without prejudice" clause should only apply to agreements which set out specific rules by "either directly specifying GI protection for specific names or specifying procedures and requirements for protecting GIs from the parties to that agreement" is not consistent with the wording and context of Article 12(1). Whereas it is not excluded that such specific agreements might be

---

[41] Exhibit EC-43 (emphasis added).

[42] Exhibit EC-44.

[43] Exhibit EC-45 (emphasis added).

[44] Exhibit EC-46# (emphasis added).

[45] Exhibit EC-47 (emphasis added).

[46] US FOS, para. 8.

[47] US Response to Panel's Question No. 5, para. 19; Australian response to Question 6.

covered by the "without prejudice" clause, there is no reason why only such specific agreements should be covered.

70. Similarly, the fact that in the context of the TRIPS Agreement, "there is no specific international registration regime for the Commission to apply," to quote another US argument,[48] does not prevent the application of the "without prejudice" clause to the WTO Agreements. Moreover, the EC does not understand where the US would draw the line between "specific" and "unspecific" agreements. After all, the WTO Agreements, and in particular the TRIPS Agreement, also contain rules concerning the protection of geographical indication. To the extent that they contain rules applicable to geographical indications, the EC does not see why they should not be covered by the "without prejudice" clause.

71. The EC would like to point out that the interpretation made by the complainants would largely deprive the "without prejudice" clause of its useful value. In order to counter this argument, the United States has attempted to give a number of examples of agreements which it believes fall under the "without prejudice" clause. However, the United States' examples prove the opposite, since not a single of the agreements to which it refers in fact fall under this clause.

72. As a first example, the United States refers to bilateral agreements in the field of wines.[49] However, it follows clearly from Article 1 (1), second subparagraph, of Regulation 2081/92, that the Regulation does not apply to wine-sector products. Since the Regulation does not apply to wines, bilateral agreements concerning geographical indications for wines are hardly a pertinent example.

73. As a second example, the United States once again refers to the joint declaration to the Agreement on Trade in Agriculture between Switzerland and the EC.[50] Similarly, the US refers to Article 46 (4) of the Cotonou Agreement, according to which the Community and the ACP countries "may consider the conclusion of agreements aimed at protecting trademarks and geographical indications, and to "ongoing negotiations between the EC and China."[51] In all these respects, the EC would simply like to remark that no such agreement has so far been negotiated with any of the parties mentioned. Political statements of intent or interest do not constitute examples of application of the "without prejudice" clause.

74. Finally, the US is also referring to agreements between the EU Member States and third countries as a possible example for the application of the "without prejudice" clause.[52] This is wrong. The reference to "international agreements" in Article 12(1) of the Regulation applies only to international agreements concluded by the Community.

75. This follows simply from the fact that there are no bilateral agreements of Member for the protection of geographical indications which could be covered by the "without prejudice" clause. Agreements concerning the protection of geographical indications fall under the exclusive competence of the EC. The only agreements which may be legally maintained by Member States in this field are such which the Member State concluded before it became an EU member, or before the EC competence became exclusive. However, this situation is explicitly covered by Article 307 of the EC Treaty, which reads as follows:

> The rights and obligations arising from agreements concluded before 1 January 1958 or, for acceding States, before the date of their accession, between one or more Member States on the one hand, and one or more third countries on the other, shall not be affected by the provisions of this Treaty.

---

[48] US Response to Panel's Question No. 5, para. 29.

[49] US Response to Panel's Question No. 5, para. 20.

[50] US Response to Panel's Question No. 5, para. 22.

[51] US Response to Panel's Question No. 5, para. 25.

[52] US Response to Panel's Question No. 5, para. 24.

> To the extent that such agreements are not compatible with this Treaty, the Member State or States concerned shall take all appropriate steps to eliminate the incompatibilities established. Member States shall, where necessary, assist each other to this end and shall, where appropriate, adopt a common attitude.
>
> In applying the agreements referred to in the first paragraph, Member States shall take into account the fact that the advantages accorded under this Treaty by each Member State form an integral part of the establishment of the Community and are thereby inseparably linked with the creation of common institutions, the conferring of powers upon them and the granting of the same advantages by all the other Member States.

76. Since the only possible agreements of Member States which may still remain in force are covered by Article 307 EC Treaty, there is no need to apply the "without prejudice" clause to such agreements. Contrary to the view of the United States, the recent judgment of the European Court of Justice in Case C-216/01, *Budejovicky Budvar*, proves this point. In this case, which concerned an agreement between Austria and Czechoslovakia concluded in 1976, i.e. before either country became a Member of the EU, the Court did not base itself on the "without prejudice" clause, but on Article 307 EC Treaty:[53]

> In the light of the foregoing, the answer to the third and fourth questions must be that the first paragraph of Article 307 EC is to be interpreted as permitting a court of a Member State, subject to the findings to be made by that court having regard inter alia to the criteria set out in this judgment, to apply the provisions of bilateral agreements such as those at issue in the main proceedings, concluded between that State and a non-member country and according protection to a name from the non-member country, even where those provisions prove to be contrary to the Treaty rules, on the ground that they concern an obligation resulting from agreements concluded before the date of the accession of the Member State concerned to the European Union. Pending the success of one of the methods referred to in the second paragraph of Article 307 EC in eliminating any incompatibilities between an agreement predating that accession and the Treaty, the first paragraph of that article permits that State to continue to apply such an agreement in so far as it contains obligations which remain binding on that State under international law.

77. Accordingly, one is left with the perplexing result that the US is unable to quote a single example of an agreement to which the "without prejudice" clause would apply, but at the same time denies that it applies to the Agreements to which according to its own submissions it should certainly apply, namely the WTO agreements. This is hardly an interpretation which gives its full useful meaning to the "without prejudice" clause.

(e) The evidence adduced by the complainants is neither pertinent nor conclusive

78. The complainants have alleged that the interpretation made by the EC of Article 12(1) of Regulation 2081/92 in the present proceedings is not in accordance with the interpretation given by the EC previously. In support of this argument, the complainants cite a number of presentations and other documents made by officials of European Institutions.

79. As a general remark, the EC would like to recall that in principle, the content of Regulation 2081/92 must be evaluated on the face of the measure. Of course, it is not excluded to take into account authoritative statements made on behalf of the European Communities as regards the interpretation of Regulation 2081/92. In contrast, statements made by officials of the European institutions in the course of presentations or slide shows cannot be assumed to necessarily reflect the opinion of the European Communities, and to correctly represent the content of Community law.

[53] Judgment of 18 November 2003, Case C-216/01, *Budejovicky Budvar*, para. 173 (Exhibit US-36).

80. With this caveat, the EC would like to offer the following comments on the "evidence" advanced by the complainants:

81. The US has referred to an EC press release concerning Regulation 2081/92.[54] It is true that this press release did not refer to the "without prejudice language," and the implications it had for WTO countries. However, this was simply due to the fact that this part of Article 12(1) of Regulation 2081/92 had not been amended. It should also be kept in mind that press releases are typically short documents, which are not intended to give a comprehensive explanation of the content of a complex legislative measure.

82. In its oral statement, the US has referred to a slide show given on 10-12 March 2004.[55] Quite apart from the evidentiary value of such a slide show, the EC would remark that this slide show simply seems to contain a literal reproduction of Article 12(1), including the "without prejudice" language. The EC does not see what conclusions the US could draw from this slide show.

83. In its responses to the Panel, Australia has similarly referred to a slide show given in Beirut in March 2003.[56] However, this presentation was made before and clearly directed at a Lebanese public. Since Lebanon is not a WTO Member, the EC does not see what should follow from this presentation for the purposes of the present dispute.

84. In its responses to the Panel, the US has referred to a "communication" which it claims to have received from the EC on January 16, 2003.[57] The corresponding exhibit consists of one single page of text, apparently taken from a longer document, and indicates neither the date, the title, the author nor the addressee of the document. Accordingly, the EC does not consider that this document is attributable to the EC, and will not comment on it any further.

85. In its responses to the Panel's questions, the US has referred to complaints raised on the part of certain US industries regarding the application of Regulation 2081/92.[58] However, these industry statements are based on misperceptions of the content of Regulation 2081/92, and are not pertinent evidence as to its proper interpretation. Moreover, none of the industries concerned in fact seem to have attempted to register a geographical indication under Regulation 2081/92, so that the complaints are largely theoretical. Finally, the EC notes that the concerns expressed on behalf of the Idaho Potato Commission seem to be related, to the extent that the EC understands them, more to the protection of trademarks in the EC than to the registration of geographical indications.[59]

86. Finally, in its responses to the Panel's questions, Australia has also referred to the EC responses to the questions of Australia during the consultations.[60] In this regard, the EC would like to recall that according to Article 4.6 of the DSU, consultations are confidential, and cannot therefore be relied on as evidence in subsequent panel proceedings. Moreover, the EC did not give any answers during the consultations which are inconsistent with its submissions before the Panel.

87. In conclusion, the complainants have not adduced evidence which contradict the interpretation of Regulation 2081/92 set out by the EC in the present proceedings.

---

[54] US FOS, para. 13; Exhibit US-22.

[55] Exhibit US-23.

[56] Australian response to Question 6, and Exhibit 5 thereto.

[57] US Response to Panel's Question No. 12, para. 38, and Exhibit US-40.

[58] US Response to Panel's Question No. 12, para. 36.

[59] Cf. Exhibit US-38, p. 353.

[60] Australia's Response to Panel's Question No. 6.

(f) The EC is not belated in having corrected the complainants' misunderstanding

88. Finally, Australia has reproached the EC for not having corrected Australia's understanding of Article 12(1) of Regulation 2081/92 at the DSB meetings of 29 August or 2 October 2003, at which the Panel requests were considered.[61]

89. The EC considers this argument to be remarkable. Quite apart form the fact that there is certainly no obligation for a defendant to present its arguments already at the meeting of the DSB, it should be recalled that the panel requests of both Australia and the United States did not contain any reference to Article 12(1) of the Regulation, nor to "conditions of reciprocity and equivalence." In fact, as the EC stated already at the meeting of the DSB, and as it still believes, the Panel requests did not set out in sufficient detail the claims of the complainants, and did therefore not comply with Article 6.2 DSU. In its response to the EC's request for a preliminary ruling on this issue, Australia argued that Article 6.2 DSU "does not require Australia to set out in its panel establishment request precisely how it believes the EC measure violates fundamental national treatment and most favoured nation principles."[62]

90. The EC finds it hard to believe that Australia would first deliberately withhold its arguments from the EC until its first written submission, and then reproach the EC for not having responded to its arguments already at the meeting of the DSB. It rather appears to the EC that this is a consequence of the deficient drafting of Australia's panel request, for which it cannot blame the EC.

3. Claim 1bis: Regulation 2081/92 violates the national treatment obligations under the TRIPS Agreement by requiring the existence of inspection structures with respect to the specific product for which protection is requested

91. In its first written submission, the United States had broadly criticised the EC for applying conditions of "reciprocity and equivalence" to the registration of geographical indications from other WTO Members. As the EC has stated in its first written submission, it was not clear whether the United States also intended to challenge the conditions for the registration of individual geographical indications, and notably the requirement that inspection structures must exist with respect to the product concerned.[63]

92. In its Oral Statement before the Panel, the United States has claimed that the requirement of the existence of inspection procedures amounts to a requirement of "equivalence by another name."[64] Moreover, in its response to Question 58 of the Panel, the United States now claims that the requirement that a Member "have a particular inspection structure [...] is itself inconsistent with WTO obligations."[65]

93. The EC therefore understands that the United States is raising a separate claim as regards the compatibility of the requirement of inspection structures with national treatment obligations.[66] As the EC will show, this claim of the United States is unfounded for the following reasons:

- The requirement of inspection structures represents equal, not unequal treatment;
- The requirement of inspection structures does not require "equivalence by another name;"
- Regulation 2081/92 does not impose an "EC model" of inspection structures;

---

[61] Australia's Response to Panel's Question No. 6.

[62] Comments of Australia on the EC Request, para. 27.

[63] EC FWS, para. 119.

[64] US FOS, para. 17–21.

[65] US Response to Panel's Question No. 58, para. 85. Cf. also US Response to Question 56, para. 83.

[66] The EC recalls that Australia has not raised such a claim under the national treatment provisions of the TRIPS Agreement or of the GATT, but has made a similar claim under Article 2.2 of the TBT Agreement.

- The existence of inspection structures is necessary for attaining the objectives of Regulation 2081/92.

(a) The requirement of inspection structures represents equal, not unequal treatment

94. First of all, since the United States is making its claim under the national treatment provisions of the TRIPS Agreement and the GATT, the EC would like to recall that the requirement of inspection procedures in Regulation 2081/92 does not involve any less favourable treatment of foreign nationals or goods.

95. As the EC has already explained in its first written submission, the requirement of inspection structures does apply to geographical indications from the EC and from third countries alike.[67] Accordingly, it does not involve less favourable treatment of foreign nationals or products, but indeed equal treatment.

(b) The requirement of inspection structures does not require "equivalence by another name"

96. The United States has attempted to cast doubt on this conclusion by arguing that "the EC's requirement that the United States establish EC-style inspection structures to enforce GIs is simply equivalence by another name."[68] Similarly, in its response to the Question 58 of the Panel, the United States has argued that the requirement of inspection structures "is not related to the question of whether the product for which GI protection is sought in the EC qualifies for that protection." The US goes on to add that "the particular method chosen by another WTO Member to enforce GI rules in its territory is not relevant to such a determination."[69]

97. These statements are simply incorrect. As the EC has already set out in its first written submission, as regards applications for registration from other WTO Members, Regulation 2081/92 requires the existence of inspection structures only with respect to the particular product for which protection is sought.[70]

98. Article 12a(2)(b) of the Regulation requires that the application for the registration of a geographical indication from a third country be accompanied by a declaration that the inspection structures provided of in Article 10 of the Regulation are established on its territory. This requirement is part of the application process leading to the registration of the individual geographical indication. It is clear from the provision that this condition is, like those contained in Article 12a(2)(a) and (c), applied on a product-specific basis.

99. Accordingly, the United States' claim that through its requirement of inspection structures, the EC is imposing on other WTO Members "the particular method chosen by them to enforce GI rules in their territory" is without foundation. The EC recognises the freedom granted by Article 1.1 of the TRIPS Agreement to each WTO Member to decide how to implement protection of geographical indications in its legal system.

100. The requirement of inspection structures does not relate to the question of how geographical indications are protected in the United States. It exclusively concerns the question of how a particular geographical indication can be protected <u>in the EC</u>. Accordingly, the United States is wrong to claim that the EC's requirement of inspection structures some constitutes a condition of "equivalence by another name."

(c) Regulation 2081/92 does not impose an "EC model" of inspection structures

101. The United States has referred to "EC-style inspection structures," and has argued that the United States should not be required to adopt "the same inspection structures as are required of Member States."[71] In the same vein, Australia has referred to "the absolute requirement for an EC model 'one size fits all'."[72]

---

[67] EC FWS, para. 121.

[68] US FOS, para. 21.

[69] US Response to Panel's Question No. 58, para. 85.

[70] EC FWS, para. 118.

102. These statements have no basis in the text of Regulation 2081/92. Regulation 2081/92 does not prescribe a particular "EC model" of inspection structures. The Regulation merely requires that inspection structures must exist, and in its Article 10 sets out the general principles with which such inspection structures must comply.

103. The EC notes that despite the explicit questions of the Panel, both the United States and Australia have been unable to identify a single element in the requirements of Article 10 of Regulation 2081/92 that would be objectionable.[73] In the view of the EC, this is hardly surprising given the content of Article 10 of the Regulation. In fact, Article 10 is far from establishing any kind of "model" inspection structure. For instance, Article 10 (3) sets out general principles such as that inspection bodies must offer adequate guarantees of objectivity and impartiality, and must have the qualified staff and resources at their disposal to carry out their functions. The EC hardly sees what could be objectionable about these principles. For the rest, as the EC has already explained in its first written submission, Article 10 allows a considerable flexibility in the design of the actual inspection structures.[74] In particular, it leaves the choice between public and private elements in the design of the inspection structures.

104. This considerable flexibility in the design of inspection structures is also illustrated by EC practice in the application of Article 10. For the information of the Panel, the EC attaches a list of inspection structures notified by the EC Member States in accordance with Article 10 (2) of Regulation 2081/92 (Exhibit EC-48). As a cursory examination of this list will show, the practices regarding inspection structures vary considerable from Member State to Member State, and within Member States. First of all, inspection structures are almost evenly divided between public and private bodies. Whereas in some Member States, public bodies are more prevalent, other Member States seem to prefer private bodies, and some use both, depending on national traditions and other considerations.

105. As regards public bodies, there is also considerable variety. Inspection bodies can be situated at national, regional, or even local level. Frequently, they are general public administrations dealing with many public policy issues besides inspections under Regulation 2081/92. In other cases, their only task may be such inspections.

106. The same variety of designs can also be observed in respect of private bodies. Frequently, such private bodies may be commercial enterprises; however, not-for-profit bodies can also be found. Private inspection bodies may engage in a large number of activities besides inspections under Regulation 2081/92; however, in other cases, bodies may be dedicated only to carrying out such activities.

107. As regards commercial enterprises carrying out inspections under Regulation 2081/92, the EC would like to give the example of two firms which are authorised to carry out inspections for a number of geographical indications under Regulation 2081/92 (Exhibits EC-49 and EC-50). As can be seen from the descriptions attached, both firms engage, besides inspections under Regulation 2081/92, in a vast number of professional activities in the field of agriculture, food, and sanitation, including sanitary inspections, inspections under organic labelling programmes, or food safety inspections of factories, hotels and retail premises. In other words, an inspection structure may also be a service which can be procured commercially. It would appear to the EC that there must be firms which could provide comparable services in the United States or Australia, if it was decided to have recourse to private firms for the purposes of inspections under Regulation 2081/92.

---

[71] US FOS, para. 21; US Response to Panel's Question No. 56, para. 83.

[72] Australia's Response to Panel's Question No. 62.

[73] US Response to Panel's Question No. 58, para. 85; Australia's Responses to Panel's Question No. 58 and to Panel's Question No. 62.

[74] EC FWS, para. 488 et seq.

108. Overall, it should have become clear that Article 10 of Regulation 2081/92 in no way imposes an "EC model." On the contrary, there are many different ways to satisfy the requirement of Regulation 2081/92 that an inspection structure must exist.

(d) The existence of inspection structures is necessary for attaining the objectives of Regulation 2081/92

109. Indeed, it seems to the EC that the real concern of the complainants, as expressed in particular by Australia, is not so much the specific "model" of inspection structure which Regulation 2081/92 requires, but rather that no inspection structures should be required at all.[75]

110. However, the existence of inspection structures is inseparably linked with the object and purpose of Regulation 2081/92. Removing the requirement of inspection structures would therefore undermine the system of protection of geographical indications established by Regulation 2081/92.

111. It should be recalled that in accordance with Article 4(1), to be eligible to use a protected geographical indication, an agricultural product or foodstuff must comply with a product specification. For the information of the Panel, and purely for purposes of illustration, the EC attaches to its submission the applications setting out the product specifications for the following products:

- Pruenaux d'Agen (Exhibit EC-51)
- Melons du Haut Poitou (Exhibit EC-52)
- Dorset Blue Cheese (Exhibit EC-53)
- Thüringer Leberwurst (Exhibit EC-54)

112. The product specifications are set out in point 4 of each application. As can be seen from the applications, which are the basis of the registrations, for each product, the specifications contain a detailed description of the raw materials and of the methods and processes according to which the product is obtained. Compliance with these specifications is essential since it is these materials, methods and processes which will confer on the product in question the specific quality, reputation or other characteristics attributable to its geographic origin which justify the protection of the geographical indication.

113. In accordance with Article 10(1) of Regulation 2081/92, it is the function of inspection structures to ensure that agricultural products and foodstuffs bearing a protected name shall meet the requirements laid down in the specifications. The inspection structures are based on continuous control, and may involve on-site inspections at the place of production. In this way, inspection structures provide a high degree of assurance that products bearing a protected name do indeed comply with the product specifications.

114. Australia has suggested that the same degree of protection might also be achieved through other systems of protection of geographical indications, and has in particular referred to the application of unfair competition law.[76] Whereas the EC does not contest that unfair competition laws may be one way of protecting geographical indications in accordance with Article 22.2 TRIPS Agreement, the EC does not believe that such laws could provide an equivalent degree of protection of geographical indications to that achieved by Regulation 2081/92.

115. This can be illustrated with the example of a producer of a protected product who wants to defend himself against unfair competition from another producer marking a similar product using the same protected

---

[75] In its Response to the Panel's Question No. 62, Australia for instance speculates about the circumstances in which an inspection structure might "not be necessary at all."

[76] Australia's Response to Panel's Question No. 62.

name. Under a system based on unfair competition law, this producer will have to prove in court that his competitor is producing using materials, methods or processes which are not compatible with the use of the protected name, or is not producing in the required geographic area. This in turn may require knowledge about the materials, methods or processes employed by the competitor which may be difficult to ascertain.

116. In contrast, Article 10(4) of Regulation 2081/92 provides that where an inspection body establishes that a product marketed using a protected name does not comply with the product specifications, it shall take the necessary steps to ensure that the specifications are complied with. Accordingly, the producer does not have to investigate the facts himself, and accept the considerable litigation risk in pursuing unfair competitors. Rather, the producer can rely on the controls carried out by the inspection body, and be thereby be assured that any competitor using the name will indeed comply with the specifications. It is clear that in this way, the Regulation provides a higher degree of protection than the simple application of unfair competition laws.

117. The requirement of inspection structures is equally beneficial to consumer. For consumers, it will, at least at the time of purchase, be very difficult to ascertain that product bearing a protected name is indeed complying with the required specifications. The only assurance that a system based on the application of unfair competition laws can provide to the consumer is the possibility that some competitor might (or might not) pursue unfair competitors through the courts. It is clear that this is a far lower degree of assurance than that provided by Regulation 2081/92. This in turn will also affect the value of the geographical indication for producers.

118. Accordingly, if a product from third countries were entitled to benefit from protection under Regulation 2081/92 without having to comply with inspection structures, this would effectively allow third country a free ride on the EC system. Third countries would be able to use the same designation and logo as EC products, and like EC producers would benefit from the possibility of excluding others from the use of the geographical indication in accordance with Article 13 of the Regulation, without however at the same time providing the same assurances as EC geographical indications. This would create two classes of protected geographical indications, and undermine confidence in the protection of geographical indications on the part of both producers and consumers.

119. The EC would like to remark that the US itself has variously recognised the need for inspection structures. The EC has already pointed out that according to the US authorities' opinion, use of certification marks may require some public involvement to insure the proper use of such a mark.[77] Another pertinent example in the present context is the US National Organic Program run by the US Department of Agriculture. The applicable US regulations (Exhibit EC-55) provide that a person wanting to obtain or maintain organic certification must be certified by a "certifying agent," to whom he must submit an annual organic production plan (Exhibit EC-55, §205.400). It is also provided that the certifying agent must conduct an initial on-site inspection, and annual inspections thereafter (Exhibit EC-55, §205.403). The conditions for accreditation of certifying agents are described in the regulations in terms not dissimilar to those of Article 10 of Regulation 2081/92. In particular, it is required that the certifying agent must have sufficient experience, adequately trained personnel, and must prevent conflicts of interest (Exhibit EC-55, § 205.501 [a] [1], [4], and [11]).

120. The EC assumes that the objective of certification and accredited certifying agents under the US Organic Production Program is to prevent that products are marketed as organic which do not comply with the requirements of the program, and in this way to protect the expectations of producers and consumers. These objectives are comparable to those underlying the requirement of inspection structures in Regulation 2081/92. However, if the logic of the complainants were followed, it would appear that the conditions of the US National Organic Program are unnecessary, and unduly trade restrictive, because the application of unfair competition laws should be sufficient to prevent any such abuses. The EC wonders why what is acceptable in the case of the US National Organic Program should not be acceptable in the case of Regulation 2081/92.

---

[77] EC FWS, para. 496.

121. In conclusion, the requirement of inspection structures is an integral part of the EC's system of protection of geographical indications. With this system, the EC obtains, in full compliance with Article 1.1 TRIPS Agreement, a higher degree of protection of geographical indications than other Members may have chosen to do. The requirement of inspection structures does not involve discrimination between EC and foreign products, let alone nationals. Accordingly, the US claim should be rejected.

4. Claim 2: Regulation 2081/92 violates the national treatment obligations under the TRIPS and the Paris Convention by requiring that applications must be transmitted by the country in which the geographical area is located

122. The United States has claimed that Regulation 2081/92 violates the national treatment obligations under the TRIPS and the Paris Convention by requiring that applications must be transmitted by the country in which the geographical area is located. Australia has made no such claim under the TRIPS Agreement, but has raised similar claims under Article III:4 GATT.

123. In the view of the EC, these claims are unfounded. As the EC has already explained in its first written submission, the requirement that applications must be transmitted by the country in which the geographical area is located does not constitute less favourable, but indeed equal treatment.[78] As the EC has also set out in its responses to the questions to the Panel, the cooperation of the country in which the geographical area is located is indispensable for the protection of the geographical indications relating to such an area.[79] Moreover, as the EC has also explained, the role of the third country government corresponds to the cooperation required from Member States in the implementation of Regulation 2081/92.[80]

(a) The cooperation of the country on whose territory the area is located is indispensable for the implementation of Regulation 2081/92

124. As the EC has already set out in response to the Panel's Question 33, the cooperation of the third country on whose territory the geographical area is located is an indispensable element of the registration process. The EC considers it useful to recall here once again the basic need for cooperation between the home country of the geographical indication and the country of registration.

125. First, the evaluation of whether a name fulfils the conditions for protection as a geographical indication requires familiarity with a host of geographical, natural, climatic and cultural factors specific to the geographical area in question. Moreover, knowledge of the market conditions in the country of origin may also be required, e.g. in order to establish whether the product in question has a particular reputation. Like in the case of applications from Member States, it is the third country's authorities which are best placed to evaluate such factors. In contrast, the European Commission is less likely to be familiar with such factors than in the case of an area in a Member State. Moreover, the evaluation may also require knowledge of the language of the third country in question, which the authorities of the European Community may not have.

126. Second, the evaluation of the application may require the assessment of legal questions arising under the law of the country where the area is located. In particular, Article 12a of the Regulation requires the application to be accompanied by a description of the legal provisions and the usage on the basis of which the geographical indication is protected or established in the third country. This reflects Article 24.9 of the TRIPS Agreement, according to which there shall be no obligation to protect geographical indications which are not or cease to be protected in their country of origin, or which have fallen into disuse in that country. Clearly, the Commission cannot unilaterally resolve such issues pertaining to the law of a third country, which therefore necessarily require the implication of the authorities of the third country.

---

[78] EC FWS, para. 87 et seq.

[79] EC Response to Panel's Question No. 33, para. 80 et seq.

[80] EC Response to Panel's Question No. 33, para. 77 et seq.

127. Third, the involvement of the third country government appears called for also out of respect for the sovereignty of the third country. The assessment of whether an application meets the requirements of the Regulation, in particular concerning the link with the geographical area, requires in-depth knowledge of the conditions related to this area, as well as the possibility to verify on the spot the relevant claims made in the application. It would not be possible for the European Commission to carry out such inspections on the territory of the third country without the agreement or involvement of the third country.

128. Fourth, the involvement of the third country government also facilitates the cooperation of the authorities of the Community and of the third country throughout the registration process. If doubts or questions arise during the registration process, the European Commission may need a contact point in the third country to which it can address itself. Moreover, the Regulation foresees that the third country which has transmitted the application must be consulted at certain stages of the procedure before the Commission can take a decision (cf. Articles 12b [1] [b]; 12b [3]).

129. Fifth, the involvement of the third country authorities should also be beneficial to the applicant. Regulation 2081/92 effectively enables the applicant to discuss, prepare, file, and where necessary refine and amend his application directly with the authorities where the geographical area is located. Since these authorities are more familiar with the area in question, this should help speed up the registration process. Moreover, frequently these authorities may be geographically closer to the applicant and may speak the applicant's language, which may also be a further benefit to the applicant.

(b) The requirement that the application be verified by the country on whose territory the area is located is not unreasonable

130. On the basis of the considerations above, it appears indispensable that the country where the geographical area is located be involved in the verification of applications for the protection of geographical indications relating to its territory. Independent of whether the area is located in a third country or a Member State, this involvement is a necessary element of the application process.

131. Contrary to the allegations of the complainants, this has nothing to do with whether the United States and Australia are under an obligation to cooperate with the EC or not. Obviously, the EC does not pretend that it could impose obligations on the United States or Australia by adopting internal measures. However, the essential point is not that the EC wants to impose obligations on third countries, but rather that it depends on the cooperation of those third countries for the protection of geographical indications related to their territory.

132. It should be noted that this cooperation is partially mandated by the TRIPS Agreement itself. Article 22.1 TRIPS specifically requires that a good using a geographical indication must have a given quality, reputation or other characteristics essentially attributable to its geographical origin. As the EC has already explained, the verification of whether these conditions are fulfilled can be done by no one better than by the country of origin of the indication. Accordingly, the need for cooperation is not created by the EC, but results directly from the definition of a geographical indication in the TRIPS Agreement.

133. Similarly, Article 12a of the Regulation requires the application to be accompanied by a description of the legal provisions and the usage on the basis of which the geographical indication is protected or established in the third country. This directly reflects the provision of Article 24.9 of the TRIPS Agreement, according to which there is no obligation to protect geographical indications which are not protected in their country of origin. Whether this condition is fulfilled clearly depends on legal questions under the law of the country of origin of the geographical indication. It is unreasonable for the complainants to expect that the EC should resolve such questions of US or Australian law.

134. The fact that unlike the EC, the US or Australia do not have a specific registration system for the protection of geographical indications is no counterargument. The EC appreciates that in the absence of such a

dedicated registration system, it may be more difficult to determine whether a geographical protection is protected in its country of origin. However, the fact remains that Article 24.9 TRIPS Agreement requires that it must be protected, and that this is a question of US or Australian law. It is simply unreasonable for the complainants to argue that because this may be a difficult question of Australian or US law, the EC should find the answer by itself.

135. As the EC has also shown in its responses to the Panel's Question 37, there are numerous examples in international practice where cooperation between governments is necessary for the protection of private rights and interests.[81] Contrary to the views of the complainants,[82] it is not a decisive difference that these examples are drawn from international agreements. First of all, there is an agreement between the parties, namely the TRIPS Agreement. As the EC has shown, the conditions for applications in Regulation 2081/92 reflect the conditions for the protection of geographical indications in the TRIPS Agreement.

136. Moreover, it is simply a matter of fact that the protection of geographical indications related to the territory of the United States or Australia has a link to those territories, and that therefore the cooperation of those governments is inevitable. In fact, in *US – Gasoline*, the Appellate Body specifically recognised that there may be situations were cooperation between WTO Members as territorial sovereigns is necessary to facilitate trade:[83]

> There are, as the Panel Report found, established techniques for checking, verification, assessment and enforcement of data relating to imported goods, techniques which in many contexts are accepted as adequate to permit international trade—trade between territorial sovereigns—to go on and grow. The United States must have been aware that for these established techniques and procedures to work, cooperative arrangements with both foreign refiners and the foreign governments concerned would have been necessary and appropriate. At the oral hearing, in the course of responding to an enquiry as to whether the EPA could have adapted, for purposes of establishing individual refinery baselines for foreign refiners, procedures for verification of information found in US antidumping laws, the United States said that "in the absence of refinery cooperation and the possible absence of foreign government cooperation as well," it was unlikely that the EPA auditors would be able to conduct the on-site audit reviews necessary to establish even the overall quality of refineries' 1990 gasoline. From this statement, there arises a strong implication, it appears to the Appellate Body, that the United States had not pursued the possibility of entering into cooperative arrangements with the governments of Venezuela and Brazil or, if it had, not to the point where it encountered governments that were unwilling to cooperate.

137. In the present case, however, it is the complainants who have explicitly declared their unwillingness to cooperate in the protection of their own geographical indications. The EC considers that this is not an admissible way of showing that the EC Regulation constitutes less favourable treatment for US or Australian nationals. To the extent that Regulation 2081/92 requires cooperation from the complainants which is reasonable and necessary, it cannot be held to constitute less favourable treatment for the nationals of these countries.

---

[81] EC Response to Panel's Question No. 37, para. 89 et seq.

[82] Cf. US Response to Panel's Question No. 37, para. 69, 72; Australia's Response to Panel's Question No. 37 (referring to the absence of « express consent »).

[83] Appellate Body Report, *US – Gasoline*, p. 26.

(c) The requirement that the application be transmitted by the country on whose territory the area is located is not unreasonable

138. Similarly, the requirement that the application must be transmitted by the country on whose territory the area is located cannot be regarded as unreasonable, and does not constitute an extra hurdle constituting discrimination of US or Australian nationals.

139. First of all, the requirement that the application be transmitted by the third country government simply reflects the important role played by such governments in the verification process. It does not appear that for a government that has verified the application conditions, the transmission of the application would constitute a significant extra burden. Moreover, the transmission by the government also ensures that the Commission has a contact point to which it can address any questions it might have regarding the application.

140. In fact, in its response to Question 38 of the Panel, the United States has explicitly recognised that "it would probably not be difficult to designate an office in the US government to perform a purely ministerial act of transmitting registration applications and objections to the EC."[84] The EC agrees with this statement. Accordingly, the EC understands that the United States claim relates essentially to the requirement of cooperation regarding the verification of the conditions for registration, and not to the requirement of transmission by the government.

141. The EC in fact considers that it would be rather odd for the United States or Australia to argue that they are not able to designate an office to transmit an application for registration of a geographical indication. In order to escape the apparent difficulty of this argument, the US is arguing that even if it were willing and able to transmit such applications, other WTO Members might not be similarly willing and able.[85] This argument is unfounded. First of all, the Panel is dealing with a dispute between the US and the EC. The EC does not understand why it should be of concern to the US whether and how other WTO Members cooperate with the EC in the protection of geographical indications relating to their territory. Moreover, as the US has said itself, the transmission of an application as a purely ministerial act is not one of particular difficulty. In fact, any WTO Member with a normally functioning government should be able to carry out such an act.

142. Accordingly, the claim that Regulation 2081/92 violates the national treatment obligations under the TRIPS and the Paris Convention by requiring that applications must be transmitted by the country in which the geographical area is located is unfounded.

5. Claim 3: Non-EC nationals are accorded less favorable treatment than EC nationals with respect to the requirement to indicate the country of origin for homonymous geographical indications

143. The United States has claimed that the requirement contained in Article 12(2) of Regulation 2081/92 to indicate the country of origin constitutes a violation of national treatment provisions under the TRIPS and the Paris Convention, whereas Australia has made a similar claim only under Article 2.1 TBT Agreement.

144. As the EC has set out in its first written submission, this claim is unfounded.[86] First of all, contrary to the view that the US still seems to maintain,[87] it is clear form the wording of the provision that the second subparagraph of Article 12(2) of Regulation 2081/92 does not apply to all geographical indications, or all foreign geographical indications, but only to the names in the specific situation of the first subparagraph, i.e. homonymous geographical indications from the EC and a third country.

[84] US Response to Panel's Question No. 38, para. 74.

[85] US Response to Panel's Question No. 38, para. 74.

[86] EC FWS, para. 132 et seq.

[87] US Response to Panel's Question No. 48, para. 80.

145. Second, as the EC has also explained, Article 12(2) in fact does not only apply to third country names, but also to Community names. It therefore may require the indication of the country of origin for both EC and third country names, depending on which geographical indication has been protected earlier. Accordingly, Article 12(2) of Regulations treats geographical indications from the EC and third countries alike.

146. In its oral statement, Australia has contested the EC's interpretation of Article 12(2) of the Regulation, and has relied in particular on a comparison with Article 6.6 of the Regulation. However, the EC believes that such a comparison in fact shows that the EC's interpretation is correct. Unlike Article 6 (6), the first subparagraph of Article 12(2) of Regulation 2081/92 simply refers to "protected names" from the EC and a third country, without specifying which of these names is the one for which registration is sought, and which is the one which is already protected. Moreover, Article 12(2), second subparagraph, explicitly states that the requirement to indicate the country of origin applies to "such names." The use of the plural in this provision clearly indicates that the requirement can relate both to the EC name and to the third country name.

147. The EC would also remark that its interpretation is the only one which is feasible in the context of the registration system established by Regulation 2081/92. In order to be legally binding, the requirement to indicate the country of origin would normally be included in the product specifications, which, in accordance with Article 4(2)(h) of Regulation 2081/92, also include specific labelling details. However, once a geographical indication is registered, it not easily possible to amend this registration to impose such labelling details. For this reason, unless registration for two homonymous geographical indications is sought simultaneously, Article 12(2) will inevitably have to apply to the geographical indication which is registered later.

148. Finally, it should also be recalled that Community law is to be interpreted to the extent possible in accordance with the Community's international obligations.[88]

149. For all these reasons, the claim should be rejected.

6. Claim 4: Regulation 2081/92 accords less favourable treatment to non-EC nationals by subjecting the right to object to the registration of geographical indications to conditions of reciprocity and equivalence

150. The United States and Australia have claimed that only nationals from WTO member countries recognised in accordance with Article 12(3) of Regulation 2081/92 as fulfilling the conditions of reciprocity and equivalence may object to registrations of geographical indications in accordance with Article 12d of the Regulation.

151. As the EC has already set out in its first written submission,[89] and as it has further explained in its responses to the questions of the Panel,[90] the claim is based on a misunderstanding of the Regulation. Article 12d (1) of Regulation 2081/92 gives a right to object to any person that "is from a WTO Member or a third country recognised under the procedure provided for in Article 12(3)." It is clear from this explicit reference to WTO Members that WTO Members are not subject to the procedure of Article 12(3) applicable to other third countries. The same applies also under Article 12.b.2 with respect to objections against the registration of geographical indications from outside the EC.

152. In fact, since the entry into force of Regulation 692/2003, the publications of all applications for registration of a geographical indication specifically refer to the possibility of residents from WTO countries to object to the application. As an example, the EC can refer to the publication of the application for the

---

[88] Above Section II.B.

[89] EC FWS, para. 140.

[90] EC Response to Panel's Question No. 8, para. 18, 19.

registration of a geographical indication for "Lardo di Colonnata," which was published in the Official Journal on 6 June 2003. The introductory sentence of this publication reads as follows (Exhibit EC-56; emphasis added):

> This publication confers the right to object to the application pursuant to Articles 7 and 12(d) of the abovementioned Regulation. Any objection to this application must be submitted via the competent authority in a Member State, <u>in a WTO member country</u> or in a third country recognised in accordance with Article 12(3) within a time limit of six months from the date of this publication. The arguments for publication are set out below, in particular under 4.6, and are considered to justify the application within the meaning of Regulation (EEC) No 2081/92.

153. The EC notes that the complainants have not submitted any detailed arguments on this point in response to the EC's submision. Accordingly, this claim should be dismissed.

7. Claim 5: Regulation 2081/92 accords less favourable treatment to non-EC nationals by requiring their own country to transmit the objection

154. The United States and Australia have claimed that Regulation 2081/92 accords less favourable treatment to non-EC nationals by requiring their own country to transmit the objection. This claim is equally unfounded. As the EC has already explained, this requirement applies equally to persons resident or established in the EC or in third countries. The attempts of the complainants to show that somehow, this requirement constitutes an "extra hurdle" for third country residents amounting to less favourable treatment fail.

(a) The complainants are not required to verify the admissibility of objections, but merely to transmit the objection

155. In its responses to the questions of the Panel, the United States seems to assume that before transmitting a statement of objection, it must verify that the objection is admissible on the basis of the criteria contained in Article 7(4) of the Regulation.[91] As it has already explained in its responses to the Panel, the EC would like to confirm that this is not so.[92] In fact, the second sentence of Article 12d(2) of Regulation 2081/92 states clearly that the conditions of Article 7(4) must be assessed in relation to the territory of the Community. This is why, unlike in the case of applications for registration, which require an assessment in relation to the territory and law of a third country, the Regulation does not require that these conditions be verified by the third country concerned.

156. This having been said, and as the EC already explained in its responses to the Panel's questions,[93] some degree of involvement of the third country government remains necessary. First, it is necessary to verify whether the person objecting is indeed resident or established in the third country, which is only possible for the authorities of that country. Second, it is not excluded that in the further procedure, questions relating to the territory of the third country might arise, in which case it is useful for there to be an official contact point in the third country. Third, it should also be beneficial to the person making the objection to be able to deal directly with an authority in the country where it is resident or established. Finally, if a statement of objection is admissible, Article 12d(3) provides that the third country which has transmitted the statement of objection is to be consulted before the Commission takes its decision.

[91] US Response to Panel's Question No. 38, para. 75.

[92] EC Response to Panel's Question No. 34, para. 86.

[93] EC Response to Panel's Question No. 34, para. 85 et seq.

(b) The transmission of objections is not an unreasonable requirement

157. The requirement that statements of objection be transmitted by the country where the objecting person is resident or established does not appear to be an unreasonable condition which could amount to an "extra hurdle" for third country residents.

158. As the United States has itself acknowledged in its response to Question 38 of the Panel, "it would probably not be difficult to designate an office in the US government to perform a purely ministerial act of transmitting registration applications and objections to the EC."[94] If this is not particularly difficult, then the question arises why the United States would refuse to transmit such objections. However, if there is not objective reason for this refusal to cooperate, then the complainants can also not pretend that it is the EC's rules which amount to extra hurdles for their residents. Similarly, as the EC has already explained in response to the United States claim regarding the transmission of applications, the US can not invoke the attitude which other WTO Members might or might not take in respect of the requirements of Regulation 2081/92.[95]

159. Accordingly, this claim should be dismissed.

8. Claim 6: Regulation 2081/92 accords less favourable treatment to non-EC nationals by requiring non-EC national to have a "legitimate interest" to object to the registration of geographical indications

160. The United States (but not Australia) has claimed that Article 12d (1) of Regulation 2081/92 accords less favourable treatment to non-EC nationals by requiring non-EC nationals to have a "legitimate interest" to object to the registration of geographical indications.

161. In its first written submission,[96] the EC has shown that there is no substantive difference between the term "legitimate interest" used in Article 12d (1) of Regulation 2081/92 and the term "legitimately concerned" in Article 7 (3). Rather, it results from simple consultation of the New Shorter Oxford English Dictionary that "legitimately concerned" and "legitimately interested" are synonymous expressions.

162. In its Oral Statement, the United States has raised the question why, if the standard is the same, the Regulation uses different words, and has claimed that the EC has "failed to rebut the presumption" that this amounts to less favourable treatment.[97] First of all, the burden of proof for showing that there is a difference in standard is on the US, not on the EC. Second, the fact that words are different does not yet create a presumption that such a difference in wording entails a difference in treatment, let alone less favourable treatment. Third, the EC considers that by referring the US to a standard dictionary of English, according to which "concerned" and "interested" are synonyms, it should have been shown that there is indeed no difference in treatment. As regards finally the question why the same language was not chosen, the EC would remark that WTO dispute settlement is concerned with the enforcement of rights and obligations under the WTO Agreement. Its objective is not to criticise the legal drafting of internal measures of a Member when such drafting question have no impact on the WTO rights of any Member.

163. Accordingly, this claim should also be rejected.

---

[94] US Response to Panel's Question No. 38, para. 74.

[95] Above para. 141.

[96] EC FWS, para. 78, 150-152.

[97] US FOS, para. 34.

9. Claim 7: Regulation 2081/92 accords less favourable treatment because a non-EC rightholder has no "representative" in the regulatory committee to "speak for him"

164. Australia has argued that Regulation 2081/92 accords less favourable treatment because a non-EC rightholder has no "representative" in the regulatory committee to "speak for him."

165. Already in its first written submission, the EC has set out that this claim is patently unfounded.[98] The EC notes that Australia has not so far responded to the EC's arguments.

166. However, at this stage the EC would like to add that this claim is in remarkable contradiction with Australia's claims regarding the requirements of transmission of applications and objections. As the EC has explained, these requirements also permit the Commission to take into account the views of the third country government concerned. Moreover, certain provisions of the Regulation require that the third country government which has transmitted an application or objection must be consulted before the Commission decides on such an application or objection.[99] However, Australia has argued that it does not wish to cooperate at all in the transmission of objections and applications. The EC finds it highly contradictory that Australia should on the one hand refuse any cooperation in the protection of its geographical indications in the EC, and then on the other hand complain that it is not sufficiently heard and does not have a "representative" on a Committee composed of representatives of the Member States.

167. Accordingly, not only should this claim be dismissed, but it also casts doubt on the consistency of Australia's arguments regarding its role in the protection of the geographical indications related to its territory.

10. Claim 8: A right of objection was available to persons resident or established in an EC Member State that was not available to other WTO Member nationals in respect of the registration of more than 120 geographical indications under the normal registration process

168. Australia has claimed that there is a violation of national treatment in the fact that a right of objection was available to persons resident or established in an EC Member State that was not available to other WTO Member nationals in respect of the registration of more than 120 geographical indications under the normal registration process.[100] As the EC has set out already in its first written submission, this historic claim of Australia must fail. First, it relates to a measure which was no longer in force at the time of establishment of the Panel, and which is therefore not within the terms of reference of the Panel. Second, the individual registrations, even if considered to be within the Panel's terms of reference, are not in violation of national treatment obligations.[101]

169. The EC notes that the Panel has posed a number of specific questions regarding Australia's claims relating to past versions of Regulation 2081/92 (Questions 88 and 90 to 93). In the view of the EC, Australia's responses demonstrate that its claims are unfounded.

(a) The legal basis of Australia's claim is unclear, and keeps shifting

170. As a preliminary point, the EC would like to recall that so far, Australia had raised its claims concerning the absence of a right of objection under previous versions of Regulation 2081/92 under the national treatment provisions of the TRIPS Agreement and the Paris Convention.[102]

---

[98] EC FWS, para. 153–155.

[99] Above para. 128, 156.

[100] Australia's FWS, para. 184 et seq.

[101] EC FWS, para. 156 et seq.

[102] Australia's FWS, para. 184, para. 190.

171. To its astonishment, the EC notes that in its response to the Panel's question 92, Australia alleges that the absence of a right of objection under previous versions of Regulation 2081/92 constitutes a violation not only of national treatment obligations under the TRIPS Agreement and the Paris Convention, but also of Article 16.1 TRIPS, Article 22.2 TRIPS in conjunction with Article 10bis of the Paris Convention, Articles 41.1, 41.2, 41.3, and 42 TRIPS, and Article III:4 GATT.

172. The EC considers that in its responses, Australia is raising new claims, which it did not raise in its first written submission. The EC notes also that Australia does not offer any arguments in support of its claims. The EC considers therefore that the Panel should not consider these claims.

173. In addition, the EC has already explained in its first written submission that *inter partes* procedures such as objection procedures are covered by Article 62.4 TRIPS Agreement, which makes it optional whether to provide for such procedures. Accordingly, there is no obligation on Members to provide for objection procedures.[103] Already for this reason, the claims under Articles 16.1, 22.2, 41.1, 41.2, 41.3 and 42 TRIPS are unfounded. Moreover, as regards the reference to Article III:4 GATT, the EC does not see how a provision concerning a right of objection to the registration of a geographical indication is related to the treatment of <u>products</u>.

(b) Australia's claims regarding old versions of Regulation 2081/92 are outside the terms of reference of the Panel

174. Australia's claim relates to Regulation 2081/92 as in force until 8 April 2003, when Regulation 692/2003 entered into force. In its first written submission, the EC has already pointed out that the terms of reference of the Panel include only measures which were in existence at the time that the Panel was established.[104]

175. In its oral statement, Australia has argued that that the reference in its Panel request to Regulation 2081/92 "and any amendments thereto" should not be read as Regulation 2081/92 "as amended by."[105] It appears from these statements that Australia maintains that any version of Regulation 2081/92 which applied at any point in time, even if no longer in force at the time the Panel was established, is nonetheless within the terms of reference of the Panel. The EC does not understand what could possibly be the justification for such an approach, which condemns Panels to examine historical facts which may have no relevance for current legal dispute. In any case, the EC submits that Australia's interpretation of its Panel request is so unusual that it would have had to make its intention to also attack historical versions of the Regulation much clearer in its Panel request.

176. The EC notes that this also seems to have been the understanding of the Panel. In its preliminary ruling issued on 5 April 2004, the Panel argued that "[t]here is no doubt as to which specific measure is in issue, as the European Communities has itself demonstrated by annexing a <u>consolidated text</u> of the regulation to the request for a preliminary ruling."[106] By referring to "consolidated text," the Panel made it clear that like the EC, it understood Australia's request to refer only to Regulation 2081/92 at the time the Panel was established, and not to older versions no longer in force.

177. The EC notes that Australia does not seem to be entirely sure of its own interpretation. Already in its oral statement, Australia has indicated that "it is not seeking to analyse historical versions of Regulation 2081/92 in a vacuum."[107] In its response to Question 88 of the Panel, Australia indicates that it "seeks rulings and recommendations from the Panel in respect of earlier versions of Regulation 2081/92 to the

---

[103] EC FWS, para. 327 et seq., para. 357 et seq.

[104] EC FWS, para. 13 et seq., para. 157.

[105] Australia FOS, para. 13.

[106] Preliminary Ruling of 5 April 2004, para. 24.

[107] Australia FOS, para. 14.

degree necessary to establish the extent to which the EC's actions in registering those EC-defined GIs were inconsistent with the EC's obligations."[108] The EC considers that these ambiguous submissions of Australia create a total confusion as to whether in Australia's view the measures at issue are also the historical versions of Regulation 2081/92 or not.

178. Overall, the Panel should conclude that the historical versions were not identified in the Panel request, and already for this reason are not within the Panel's terms of reference.

(c) Australia's claims are moot and therefore not within the terms of reference of the Panel

179. In any event, even if the historical versions had been clearly referred to in the Panel request, it is not up to Australia to enlarge the Panel's terms of reference in a way that runs counter to the object and purpose of the DSU.

180. As the EC has already recalled in its first written submission, the object and purpose of dispute settlement in accordance with Article 3.3 DSU is the settlement of concrete disputes between the parties, and to induce compliance with WTO obligations.[109] It does not serve as a mechanism for investigating historical violations. This is why according to constant case law under the DSU, Panels are competent to consider measures in force at the time of their establishment, and not measures which have already ceased to exist.[110]

181. This limitation to actual and current disputes is not unique to the DSU, but is in fact a general principle of international dispute settlement. For instance, in the case concerning *Border and Transborder Armed Actions (Nicaragua v. Honduras)*, the International Court of Justice stated that "the critical date for determining the admissibility of an application is the date on which it is filed."[111] Similarly, in the *Nuclear Tests* Case, the International Court of Justice stated that "[t]he Court, as a court of law, is called upon to resolve <u>existing</u> disputes between States."[112]

182. In the case concerning the *Northern Cameroons*, the International Court of Justice specifically refused to rule on a question regarding the interpretation of a trusteeship agreement which had expired after the application was filed, but before the Court rendered its judgment. The Court explained its decision as follows:[113]

> Moreover the Court observes that if in a declaratory judgment it expounds a rule of customary law or interprets a treaty which remains in force, its judgment has a continuing applicability. But in this case there is a dispute about the interpretation and application of a treaty—the Trusteeship Agreement—which has now been terminated, is no longer in force, and there can be no opportunity for a future act of interpretation or application of that treaty in accordance with any judgment the Court might render.

183. Interestingly, the International Court of Justice in its judgment explicitly noted that this did not mean that the trusteeship agreement could no longer have any legal effects, for instance as regards property rights which might have been obtained in accordance with the trusteeship agreement:[114]

---

[108] Australia's Response to Panel's Question No. 88.

[109] EC FWS, para. 19.

[110] EC FWS, para. 16.

[111] *Border and Transborder Armed Actions (Nicaragua v. Honduras), Jurisdiction and Admissibility,* Judgment of 20 December 1988, I.C.J. Reports 1988, p. 69.

[112] *Nuclear Tests (Australia vs. France)*, Judgment of 20 September 1974, I.C.J. Reports 1974, para. 253 (emphasis added).

[113] *Northern Cameroons (Cameroon v. United Kingdom)*, Preliminary Objections, Judgment of 2 December 1963, I.C.J. Reports 1963, p. 37.

[114] *Northern Cameroons (Cameroon v. United Kingdom)*, Preliminary Objections, Judgment of 2 December 1963, I.C.J. Reports 1963, p. 34.

> Looking at the situation brought about by the termination of the Trusteeship Agreement from the point of view of a Member of the United Nations, other than the Administering Authority itself, it is clear that any rights which may have been granted by the Articles of the Trusteeship Agreement to other Members of the United Nations or their nationals came to an end. This is not to say that, for example, property rights which might have been obtained in accordance with certain Articles of the Trusteeship Agreement and which might have vested before the termination of the Agreement, would have been divested by the termination.

184. In the present case, the Australian claims did not become moot during the Panel proceedings; rather, they were already moot when Australia made its Panel request. The fact that Regulation 2081/92 before its amendment through Regulation 692/2003 did not provide for a right of objection is a fact entirely in the past. As a situation in the past, it is not possible for any dispute settlement procedures to undo this historical fact.

185. For this reason also, the Australian claim is outside the Panel's terms of reference.

(d) Australia has not shown that the individual registrations are in violation of national treatment obligations

186. Presumably aware of these difficulties, Australia has argued that the measure at issue also includes the registrations of the "600 EC-defined GIs" which were carried out until the Panel was established.

187. The EC has already indicated that it does not believe that the individual registrations were identified in sufficient detail in Australia's Panel request.[115] However, even if the Panel, on the basis of its Preliminary Ruling issued on 5 April 2004, should consider that the individual registrations are within the Panel's terms of reference, Australia still fails to make any case that these individual registrations are in violation of the national treatment obligations under the TRIPS Agreement or the Paris Convention.

188. This follows clearly from Australia's response to Question 93 of the Panel, in which Australia concedes that it is "not able to say which individual registrations may have constituted a denial of rights to trademark holders." However, if this is so, then the EC seriously wonders what is the basis of Australia's claim that there is a violation not only of national treatment obligations under the TRIPS Agreement and the Paris Convention, but also of Article 16.1 TRIPS, Article 22.2 TRIPS in conjunction with Article 10bis of the Paris Convention, Articles 41.1, 41.2, 41.3, and 42 TRIPS, and Article III:4 GATT.

189. In the same response, Australia continues with the statement that "nor can the EC legitimately say that its actions have not resulted in a denial of rights." In this respect, the EC would like to recall that the burden of proving its claim is on Australia, not on the EC. In the view of the EC, Australia entirely fails in discharging this burden of proof.

190. Finally, the EC would recall that Australia's claim is based on a violation of national treatment obligations. In this respect, as the EC has already said in its first written submission, even if an individual registration might conceivable violate trademark rights, it is not clear how an individual registration could violate national treatment principles.[116] Australia forgets that the individual registrations and Regulation 2081/92 are separate measures. Therefore, even if an older version of Regulation 2081/92 had contained a violation of national treatment principles by not providing for a right of objection, this does not mean that individual registrations based on such a version also violate national treatment principles.

(e) There is no legal basis for the recommendations suggested by Australia

191. Finally, the EC would also like to comment on the recommendations suggested by Australia.

[115] EC Request for a Preliminary Ruling, para. 32.

[116] EC FWS, para. 161.

192. In its response to Question 92 of the Panel, Australia suggests that the EC might implement any recommendation e.g. by providing persons adversely affected with access to a "civil judicial proceeding," through the provision of "just compensation" for trademark owners whose rights have been infringed, or through the revocation of "a few registrations of EC-defined GIs."

193. The EC sees no legal basis for these suggestions. According to Article 19.1 of the DSU, a Panel shall recommend to the Member concerned to bring its measure into conformity with its WTO obligations. As the EC has set out in its first written submission, this implies that WTO remedies are prospective, not retrospective.[117]

194. Accordingly, if a Panel had found that Regulation 2081/92 violated national treatment obligations by not providing for objection procedures, the way to implement such a finding for the EC would have been to amend Regulation 2081/92 accordingly. The EC would not have been obliged to reopen the registration procedures for already registered geographical indications, nor would it have been obliged to provide compensation or to cancel such trademarks. Accordingly, the EC cannot be under an obligation to do so now.

195. In its Response to Question 92, Australia has also indicated that it cannot cite any precedents where a Panel has made comparable recommendation because "Australia is not aware of a similar factual situation in another dispute." The EC considers that given over 300 disputes which have been dealt with by the dispute settlement system to date, this by itself is already an indication that Australia's claim is not in line with WTO law and practice.

196. In conclusion, this claim of Australia should be rejected.

11. Claim 9: A right of objection was available to persons resident or established in an EC Member State that was not available to other WTO Member nationals in respect of the registration of more than 480 EC-defined GIs under the simplified registration process

197. Finally, Australia also claims that a right of objection was available to persons resident or established in an EC Member State that was not available to other WTO Member nationals in respect of the registration of more than 480 EC-defined GIs under the simplified registration procedure.[118] In this respect, Australia refers to the simplified registration procedure provided for in Article 17 of Regulation 2082/92 until its amendment through Regulation 692/2003.

198. With this claim, Australia is once again trying to obtain a retrospective remedy for a measure which is not within the terms of reference of the Panel, and which it did no challenge while it was still in force. All arguments that have been set out in respect of Claim 8 therefore apply here as well.

199. Moreover, Australia's claim is factually wrong. As the EC has already set out in its first written submission, there was no right of objection for EC residents under the simplified procedure.[119] The fact that there was no right of objection for third-country residents therefore did not constitute a violation of national treatment obligations.

200. Finally, Australia's claim also falls outside the temporal scope of application of the TRIPS Agreement. In accordance with Article 70.1 of the TRIPS Agreement, the Agreement does not give rise to obligations in respect of acts (or omissions) which occurred before the date of application of the Agreement for the Member in question. In accordance with Article 65.1 of the TRIPS Agreement, the date of application for the EC was 1 January 1996.

---

[117] EC FWS, para. 162 et seq.

[118] Australia's FWS, para. 190 et seq.

[119] EC FWS, para. 91 et seq., para. 172.

201. In accordance with Article 17.1 of Regulation 2081/92 as originally adopted, Member States had to inform the Commission of the names for which protection was sought under this provision within six months of the entry into force of the Regulation. Since the Regulation entered, in accordance with its Article 18, into force on 24 July 1993, the Member States had to request protection at the latest by 24 January 1994. If the Community had been obliged to provide objection procedures to the registration of these geographical indications, it is at this date that it should have opened them. However, at this date, the TRIPS Agreement was not yet in force, let alone applicable to the EC.

202. In its response to Question 90 of the Panel, Australia has argued that Article 70.1 TRIPS is inapplicable since the first registration under Regulation 2081/92 did not occur until the adoption of Regulation 1107/96 of 12 June 1996. This argument is erroneous. By the time the registration occurs, objection procedures are no longer meaningful. Accordingly, objection procedures have to be provided before. The natural date for opening these procedures, had there been an obligation to do so, would have been the expiration of the time limit provided for in Article 17.1 of Regulation 2081/92, i.e. at the latest on 24 January 1994. However, at this time, the TRIPS Agreement did not yet apply.

203. For all these reasons, Australia's claims must be rejected.

B. PROHIBITED REQUIREMENT OF DOMICILE OR ESTABLISHMENT (ARTICLE 2.1 TRIPS IN CONJUNCTION WITH ARTICLE 2.2 PARIS CONVENTION)

204. The complainants have also raised certain claims under Article 2.1 TRIPS in conjunction with Article 2.2 Paris Convention. As the EC has set out in its first written submission, the complainant's claims under Article 2.2 Paris Convention are not within the Panel's terms of reference.[120] Moreover, the EC has shown in its first written submission that these claims are unfounded.

1. Claim 10: Regulation 2081/92 requires non-EC nationals to become established in the EC as a condition for registering geographical indications

205. The United States (but not Australia) has argued that Regulation 2081/92 requires non-EC nationals to become established in the EC as a condition for registering geographical indications.[121] As the EC has set out in its first written submission, this claim is unfounded for the following reasons:

- Geographical indications relating to an area located in a WTO country can be registered under Regulation 2081/92;
- The right to register a geographical indication does not depend on domicile or establishment;
- Article 2.2 Paris Convention does not exclude measures which ensure that a product originates in the geographical to which a protected geographical indication area is related.

206. So far, the United States has not responded in substance to the EC's arguments. Accordingly, the EC can refer to what it has already said in its first written submission.[122]

[120] EC FWS, para. 36 et seq.
[121] US FWS, para. 84.
[122] EC FWS, para. 176 et seq.

2. Claim 11: Regulation 2081/92 requires non-EC nationals to become established in the EC as a condition for objecting

207. The United States has argued that the fact that Regulation 2081/92 requires the home country of third country nationals to transmit the statement of objection constitutes a requirement of residence or domicile contrary to Article 2.2 of the Paris Convention.[123]

208. As the EC has explained in its first written submission, this claim is manifestly unfounded.[124] Article 12d(1) of Regulation 2081/92 explicitly allows persons from other WTO countries who are resident or established in third countries to object to registrations. Accordingly, this claim must be rejected.

C. NATIONAL TREATMENT UNDER ARTICLE III:4 GATT

209. The complainants have raised a number of claims alleging that Regulation 2081/92 is incompatible with the national treatment obligation contained in Article III:4 GATT. As the EC has already shown in its first written submission,[125] Regulation 2081/92 is fully compatible with Article III:4 GATT. In the alternative, the EC submits that the measure is justified by Article XX(d) GATT.

1. The regulation 2081/92 is not incompatible with Article III:4 GATT

210. So far, the complainants have not specifically responded to the EC's arguments concerning the claims under Article III:4 GATT. Accordingly, the EC can generally refer to what it has said in its first written submission. In addition, it can also refer to its remarks in the present submission regarding the parallel claims made under the national treatment provisions of the TRIPS Agreement.

(a) Claim 12: Regulation 2081/92 accords less favourable treatment as regards the conditions for registration of foreign geographical indications

211. The complainants have claimed that Regulation 2081/92 accords less favourable treatment as regards the conditions for registration of foreign geographical indications by imposing conditions of reciprocity and equivalence.[126]

212. As the EC has already stated in its first written submission,[127] and confirmed in the present submission,[128] Regulation 2081/92 does not impose a condition of reciprocity and equivalence for the registration of geographical indications from other WTO Members. Accordingly, it does not apply less favourable treatment to products from other WTO Members.

213. The claim that Regulation 2081/92 accords less favourable treatments as regards the conditions for registration of foreign geographical indications by imposing conditions of reciprocity and equivalence must therefore be dismissed.

---

[123] US FWS, para. 91. Australia has raised Article 2.2 Paris Convention in the context of its claims with respect to Regulation 2081/92 as applicable before it was amended by Regulation 692/2003 (Australia's FWS, para. 189, 194), which are in any event outside the Panel's terms of reference.

[124] EC FWS, paras. 188–189.

[125] EC FWS, para. 190 et seq.

[126] US FWS, para. 104; Australia's FWS, para. 165 et seq.

[127] EC FWS, para. 62 et seq., 202 et seq.

[128] Above para. 51 et seq.

(b) Claim 12bis: Regulation 2081/92 violates the national treatment obligations under the GATT by requiring the existence of inspection structures with respect to the specific product for which protection is requested

214. As the EC has noted above, the US has now clarified that it considers the requirement of inspection structures with respect to specific products for which protection is sought constitutes a violation of national treatment obligations. The EC assumes that the United States is raising this claim also under the national treatment provisions of the GATT.

215. The EC considers that as under the national treatment obligations of the TRIPS, this claim is also unfounded under Article III:4 GATT. In this respect, the EC can refer to its arguments regarding Claim 1bis under the TRIPS Agreement.[129]

216. Accordingly, this claim should also be rejected.

(c) Claim 13: Regulation 2081/92 accords less favourable treatment as regards the requirement that the application must be transmitted by the government of the third country

217. The complainants have argued that Regulation 2081/92 accords less favourable treatment as regards the requirement that the application must be transmitted by the government of the third country.[130]

218. As the EC has already set out above with respect to Claim 2, the role of third country governments provided for in Article 12a of the Regulation corresponds exactly to that of EC Member States where geographical indications relating to an area located in the EC are concerned. Accordingly, the condition that an application relating to an area located in a third country is transmitted by the government in question does not amount to "less favourable treatment," but in fact ensures equal treatment. Moreover, the EC has also explained that the cooperation of the home country of a geographical indication is indispensable for the protection of a geographical indication in the EC.[131]

219. Accordingly, this claim is equally unfounded.

(d) Claim 14: Regulation 2081/92 accords less favourable treatment as regards the requirement to indicate the country of origin

220. The United States (but not Australia) has argued that Regulation 2081/92 accords less favourable treatments as regards the requirement to indicate the country of origin.[132]

221. As the EC has already set out in its first written submission, this claim is unfounded for the following reasons:[133]

- Article 12(2) of Regulation 2081/92 does not apply to all geographical indications, but only to homonyms;

- The requirement to indicate the country of origin for homonymous geographical indications from the EC and third countries does not constitute less favourable treatment;

---

[129] Above, para. 91.

[130] US FWS, para. 104 (d); Australia's FWS, para. 172 et seq.

[131] Above, para. 122.

[132] US FWS, para. 106. Australia has made a similar claim under Article 2.1 of the TBT Agreement (cf. Australia's FWS, para. 234).

[133] EC FWS, para. 209.

- Article IX:1 of the GATT is a *lex specialis* to Article III:4 GATT; national treatment obligations therefore do not apply to requirements to mark the country of origin.

222. To the extent that the complainants have responded to the first and second of the EC's arguments, the EC can refer to what it is replied above in respect of claim 3.[134]

223. In response to the EC's third argument relating to Article IX:1 GATT, the United States in its oral statement has argued that Article 12(2) of Regulation 2081/92 "is not a general country of origin requirement as described in Article IX of the GATT 1994."[135] The EC does not consider this objection to be justified. Article IX GATT is entitled "Marks of Origin." Article IX:1 GATT establishes a most-favoured nation rule "with regard to marking requirements." The article contains no distinction between "general requirements," which would apply to all products, and "specific requirements," which would apply only to specific products or groups of products.

224. Accordingly, Article 12(2) of Regulation 2081/92 is an origin marking requirement falling under Article IX:1 GATT. For this reason, national treatment obligations do not apply to this requirement.

225. For all the reasons set out, the EC submits that the United States claim must be rejected.

(e) Claim 15: Regulation 2081/92 accords less favourable treatment due to an overall bias in the decision-making process

226. Australia has argued that Regulation 2081/92 accords less favourable treatment in that there is an overall bias in the decision-making process.[136] As the EC has already set out in its first submission, this claim is confused and insufficiently reasoned.[137] So far, Australia has not further substantiated its claim.[138] Accordingly, the EC sees no need to discuss this claim any further.

227. For these reasons, the Australian claim must be rejected.

2. The measure would be justified under Article XX(d) GATT

228. The EC considers that if the Panel were to find that Regulation 2081/92 does involve less favourable treatment of foreign goods by requiring the existence of inspection structures, the transmission and verification of applications by the third country government, and the indication of the country of origin for homonymous geographical indications, this less favourable treatment would be justified by Article XX(d) GATT.

229. According to Article XX(d) GATT, a measure otherwise incompatible with the GATT will be justified under the following conditions:

> Subject to the requirement that such measures are not applied in a manner which would constitute a means of arbitrary or unjustifiable discrimination between countries where the same conditions prevail, or a disguised restriction on international trade, nothing in this Agreement shall be construed to prevent the adoption or enforcement by any contracting party of measures:

---

[134] Above, para. 143.

[135] US FOS, para. 35.

[136] Australia's FWS, para. 177.

[137] EC FWS, para. 219 et seq.

[138] In para. 24 of its FOS, Australia has argued that the EC's description of the decision-making process is "not accurate." The EC does not understand in what respect its description is "not accurate." The EC also does not understand what is the relevance of the discussion of the Community's comitology procedures for the present case.

[...]

(*d*) necessary to secure compliance with laws or regulations which are not inconsistent with the provisions of this Agreement, including those relating to customs enforcement, the enforcement of monopolies operated under paragraph 4 of Article II and Article XVII, the protection of patents, trade marks and copyrights, and the prevention of deceptive practices;

[...]

230. In *Korea – Various Measures on Beef*, the Appellate Body held that paragraph (d) of Article XX contained the following two requirements.[139]

> For a measure, otherwise inconsistent with GATT 1994, to be justified provisionally under paragraph (d) of Article XX, two elements must be shown. First, the measure must be one designed to "secure compliance" with laws or regulations that are not themselves inconsistent with some provision of the GATT 1994. Second, the measure must be "necessary" to secure such compliance. A Member who invokes Article XX(d) as a justification has the burden of demonstrating that these two requirements are met.

231. The Appellate Body continued to define the term "necessary" in Article XX(d) as follows:[140]

> We believe that, as used in the context of Article XX(d), the reach of the word "necessary" is not limited to that which is "indispensable" or "of absolute necessity" or "inevitable." Measures which are indispensable or of absolute necessity or inevitable to secure compliance certainly fulfil the requirements of Article XX(d). But other measures, too, may fall within the ambit of this exception. As used in Article XX(d), the term "necessary" refers, in our view, to a range of degrees of necessity. At one end of this continuum lies "necessary" understood as "indispensable;" at the other end, is "necessary" taken to mean as "making a contribution to." We consider that a "necessary" measure is, in this continuum, located significantly closer to the pole of "indispensable" than to the opposite pole of simply "making a contribution to."

(a) The requirement of inspection structures is justified by Article XX(d) GATT (Claim 12bis)

232. The EC has already explained above that the requirement of inspection structures is necessary for the attainment of the objectives of Regulation 2081/92.[141] In particular, the EC has explained that the requirement of inspection structures provides a high degree of assurance for producers and consumers that a product bearing a protected name does in fact correspond to the required product specifications.

233. Moreover, the EC has shown that a similar degree of protection could not be achieved through other means. In particular, the EC has explained that the application of unfair competition law would not result in the same degree of protection of geographical indications.[142] Moreover, the EC has also explained that the requirement of inspection structures does not go beyond what is necessary for the attainment of the objectives of the Regulation, and in particular leaves considerable flexibility in terms of the design of the concrete structures.[143]

---

139 Appellate Body Report, *Korea – Various Measures on Beef*, para. 157.

140 Appellate Body Report, *Korea – Various Measures on Beef*, para. 161.

141 Above, para. 109 et seq.

142 Above, para. 114 et seq.

143 Above, para. 101 et seq.

234. Accordingly, the requirement of inspection structures is necessary to secure compliance with Regulation 2081/92, which is a measure not incompatible with the provisions of the GATT. In this context, the EC notes that the protection of intellectual property rights and the prevention of deceptive practices is an objective explicitly referred to in Article XX(d) GATT.

235. Moreover, the requirement of inspection structures is not applied in a manner which would constitute a means of arbitrary or unjustifiable discrimination between countries where the same conditions prevail. Similarly, it is not a disguised restriction on international trade.

236. Accordingly, the requirement of inspection structures is in any event justified under Article XX(d) GATT.

(b) The requirement that the application must be verified and transmitted by the government where the area is located is justified by Article XX(d) GATT (Claim 13)

237. As the EC has already set out above, the cooperation of the government of the country where the geographical indication is located is indispensable for the implementation of Regulation 2081/92.[144] The EC has explained, in particular, that the registration of geographical indications requires the evaluation of factual and legal questions which only the home country of the geographical indication is in a position to carry out. Moreover, the EC has also explained that the requirements for cooperation do not go beyond what is necessary for the implementation of Regulation 2081/92.[145] As regards specifically the requirement that the application be transmitted by the government of the home country, the EC has explained that this follows naturally from the required intergovernmental cooperation, and is not particularly burdensome for any WTO Member.[146]

238. Accordingly, the requirement of verification and transmission of applications by the government of the home country of the geographical indication is necessary to secure compliance with Regulation 2081/92, which is a measure not incompatible with the provisions of the GATT. Moreover, the requirement of verification and transmission of applications by the government of the home country of the geographical indication is not applied in a manner which would constitute a means of arbitrary or unjustifiable discrimination between countries where the same conditions prevail. Similarly, it is not a disguised restriction on international trade.

239. Accordingly, the requirement of verification and transmission of applications by the government of the home country of the geographical indication is in any event justified under Article XX(d) GATT.

(c) The requirement to indicate the country of origin for homonymous geographical indications is justified by Article XX(d) GATT (Claim 14)

240. Finally, the EC has already indicated that the requirement to indicate the country of origin for homonymous geographical indications serves the purpose of achieving a clear distinction in practice between homonymous geographical indications.[147] In this way, it prevents that consumers are confused by homonymous geographical indications. As the EC has also explained, Article 12(2) achieves this in the least intrusive way by requiring that the indication which is registered later, and which is therefore typically the one less known to the consumer, be the one for which it is required to indicate the country of origin.[148]

241. Accordingly, the requirement to indicate the country of origin for homonymous geographical indications is necessary to secure compliance with Regulation 2081/92, which is a measure not incompatible

---

[144] Above para. 124 et seq.

[145] Above para. 130 et seq

[146] Above para. 138 et seq

[147] EC FWS, para. 479.

[148] Above para. 143.

with the provisions of the GATT. Moreover, the requirement to indicate the country of origin for homonymous geographical indications is not applied in a manner which would constitute a means of arbitrary or unjustifiable discrimination between countries where the same conditions prevail. Similarly, it is not a disguised restriction on international trade.

242. Accordingly, the requirement to indicate the country of origin for homonymous geographical indications is in any event justified under Article XX(d) GATT.

IV. REGULATION 2081/92 IS COMPATIBLE WITH THE OBLIGATION TO PROVIDE MOST-FAVOURED-NATION TREATMENT

243. The United States (but not Australia) has claimed that Regulation 2081/92 is incompatible with the obligation to provide most-favoured-nation treatment under Article 4 TRIPS and Article I:1 GATT. As it has done in its first written submission, the EC will discuss the United States claims under both provisions separately.

A. ARTICLE 4 TRIPS

244. The United States has made two claims under the most-favoured-nation provision of Article 4 TRIPS:

- As among non-EC WTO Members, nationals from WTO Members that satisfy the EC's conditions of reciprocity and equivalency are accorded more favourable treatment than nationals from those WTO Members that do not;

- under Regulation 2081/92, an EC Member State grants more favourable treatment to nationals from other EC Member States than it accords to nationals from non-EC WTO Members.

1. Claim 16: As among non-EC WTO Members, nationals from WTO Members that satisfy the EC's conditions of reciprocity and equivalency are accorded more favourable treatment than nationals from those WTO Members that do not

245. The United States has claimed that nationals from WTO Members that satisfy the EC's conditions of reciprocity and equivalency are accorded more favourable treatment than nationals from those WTO Members that do not.

246. In its first written submission, the EC has explained that this claim is unfounded for the following reasons:[149]

- the EC does not apply a condition of reciprocity and equivalence for the registration of geographical indications from other WTO members;

- the conditions for the registration of individual geographical indications from third countries are not discriminatory;

- Article 12 of Regulation 2081/92 does not grant any advantage, favour, privilege or immunity to any other country;

- the conditions for the registration of geographical indications do not depend on nationality.

[149] EC FWS, para. 228 et seq.

247. The EC notes that the United States has made almost no arguments in defence of this claim. Accordingly, the EC can largely refer to what is has already set out in its first written submission.

248. The EC notes, however, that the United States claim appears to be parallel to its Claim 1, according to which the EC violates its national treatment obligations under the TRIPS Agreement by applying "conditions of reciprocity and equivalence" to other WTO Members.[150] As the EC has already explained in detail in response to Claim 1, it does not apply such conditions to other WTO Members.[151] Accordingly, the United States claim must fail already for this reason.

249. In its oral statement, the United States has also claimed that there is a violation of most-favoured nation treatment because Regulation 2081/92 favours nationals of countries "that have an EC-style GI protection system, <u>including inspection structures</u>."[152] The EC would like to underline that this is wrong. As the EC has already explained in response to Claim 1bis, as regards geographical indications from WTO Members, the requirement of inspection structures is evaluated with respect to the specific product for which protection is sought.[153] Accordingly, Regulation 2081/92 does not impose a requirement that a "WTO Member" must have particular inspection structures. Rather, the requirement of inspection structures applies purely on a product-specific basis, and without regard to the country of origin of the product. As the Panel in *Canada – Autos* has said, such non-discriminatory conditions are not a violation of most-favoured nation treatment.[154]

250. Finally, the United States has claimed that Regulation 2081/92 involves the granting of an advantage within the meaning of Article 4 TRIPS because Articles 12 (1) and 12a are "designed" to favour national from countries that have an EC-style protection system.[155] Even if the United States' interpretation of these provisions were correct, which it is not, then the Regulation 2081/92 would not involve the granting of an advantage to any specific country. Rather, as the EC has already explained,[156] Article 12 merely sets out the conditions under which the Regulation may apply to a third country which is not a WTO Member. Accordingly, in the absence of a decision under Article 12(3) of the Regulation, Article 12 does therefore not confer any advantage onto any specific third country.

251. For all the reasons set out, the United States claim must be rejected.

2. Claim 17: Under Regulation 2081/92, an EC Member State grants more favourable treatment to nationals from other EC Member States than it accords to nationals from non-EC WTO Members

252. The United States has claimed that under Regulation 2081/92, an EC Member State grants more favourable treatment to nationals from other EC Member States than it accords to nationals from non-EC WTO Members.[157]

253. In its first written submission, the EC has already explained that this claim is fundamentally flawed.[158] The EC is an original member of the WTO. Measures with which the EC harmonises the law inside the EC are not measures through which the Member States grant "each other" advantages. That Regulation 2081/92 is a measure of the Community, and not of the Member States, is also reflected in the fact that the United States has correctly brought the present dispute against the EC, and not against its Member States. Accordingly, the EC

[150] Above para. 51.
[151] Above para. 51.
[152] US FOS, para. 36 (emphasis added).
[153] Above, para. 96.
[154] Panel Report, *Canada – Autos*, para. 10.24 (full quotation in EC FWS, para. 237).
[155] US FOS, para. 36.
[156] EC FWS, para. 239 et seq.
[157] US FWS, para. 121.
[158] EC FWS, para. 249 et seq.

does not comprehend why, in the context of this dispute with the EC concerning an EC measure, the United States is now alleging a violation of WTO obligations by the EC Member States.

254. So far, the United States has not been able to provide an explanation for its claim. In its Oral Statement, the US has merely argued that each Member State is under the obligation to provide MFN, and argued "that the fact that they may be acting pursuant to an EC regulation does not excuse them from this obligation."

255. The EC does not understand what the United States means when it says that Member States are "acting pursuant to an EC Regulation." Undoubtedly, the Member States have certain responsibilities in the implementation and execution of Regulation 2081/92. However, the EC does not see that these functions give rise to any particular MFN violation, nor has the United States identified any such violations.

256. As regards the real concern of the United States, namely the alleged application of conditions of reciprocity and equivalence and the requirement of inspection structures, these result –supposing that the erroneous interpretations of the United States of Regulation 2081/92 were correct—not from any actions of the Member States, but from the text of EC Regulation 2081/92. Accordingly, the claim that Member States are granting each other advantages, or granting other third countries advantages, is devoid of all foundation.

257. Accordingly, this claim of the United States must be rejected.

B. CLAIM 18: BY SUBJECTING THE REGISTRATION OF THIRD-COUNTRY GEOGRAPHICAL INDICATIONS TO CONDITIONS OF RECIPROCITY AND EQUIVALENCE, THE EC MEASURE IS INCONSISTENT WITH THE MOST-FAVOURED-NATION OBLIGATION UNDER THE ARTICLE I:1 GATT

258. The United States has argued that by subjecting the registration of third-country geographical indications to conditions of reciprocity and equivalence, the EC measure is inconsistent with the most-favoured-nation obligation under Article I:1 GATT.[159]

1. Article I:1 GATT is not violated

259. Contrary to the claim of the United States, there is no violation of Article I:1 GATT.

260. Since the United States has so far not made any specific arguments in response to the EC's first written submission, the EC can refer to what it has said in its first written submission.[160]

261. The EC can also refer to its arguments in response to Claim 16, concerning a violation of national treatment principles under the TRIPS Agreement,[161] which apply also in the present context. In particular, the EC would like to point out once more that the requirement of inspection structures applies on a product-specific basis, and does in no way involve discrimination on the basis of the origin of the product.

262. For these reasons, Regulation 2081/92 is not incompatible with Article I:1 GATT.

2. The EC measure would be justified under Article XX(d) GATT

263. For the sake of completeness, the EC would like to remark that should the Panel nonetheless come to the conclusion that the requirement of inspection structures somehow involves discrimination between third countries, the EC would consider that this requirement is justified under Article XX(d) GATT.

---

[159] US FWS para. 127 et seq.

[160] EC FWS, para. 258 et seq.

[161] Above para. 245.

264. In relation to the claims regarding a violation of Article III:4 GATT, the EC has already explained that the requirement of inspection structures is necessary for the attainment of the legitimate objectives of Regulation 2081/92.[162] These considerations apply not only to the claim under Article III:4 GATT, but also to the claim under Article I:1 GATT.

265. Accordingly, the requirement of inspection structures is in any event justified by Article XX(d) GATT.

V. REGULATION 2081/92 DOES NOT DIMINISH THE LEGAL PROTECTION OF TRADEMARKS

A. ARTICLE 16.1 OF THE TRIPS AGREEMENT

1. Claim 19: Article 14(2) of Regulation 2081/92 is inconsistent with Article 16.1 of the TRIPS Agreement in that it allows the co-existence of geographical indications and earlier registered trademarks

(a) Article 14(3) of Regulation 2081/92

266. The United States, but not Australia, addressed the EC's arguments based on Article 14(3) of Regulation 2081/92 in its First Oral Statement. The EC has provided a comprehensive response to the US counter-arguments as part of its replies to the Panel's questions Nos. 63 to 71, to which the Panel is referred. In this section the EC will elaborate on those replies and provide comments on the responses given by the United States to the Panel's Questions Nos. 14 and 67.

(i) Registrability of geographical names as trademarks

267. In its First Written Submission, the EC explained that geographical terms are primarily "non-distinctive" and, for that reason, their registration as trademarks is permitted only exceptionally.[163] More specifically, the EC explained that, under the Trademark Directive and the Community Trademark Regulation, as interpreted by the European Court of Justice, the registration of a geographical term is permitted only in the following circumstances:[164]

- where the geographical name is not currently associated, and it can be reasonably assumed that it will not be associated in the future, with the product concerned; or
- where the name has acquired distinctiveness through use.

268. The United States does not dispute this. Yet it suggests that, in practice, the registration as trademarks of geographical terms which qualify, or may potentially qualify, as geographical indications is a frequent occurrence. As discussed below, however, the United States provides no evidence of this, other than a few hypothetical examples.

269. In addition, the United States seeks to misrepresent the EC position by attributing to the EC arguments which the EC has not made. Thus, the EC has not argued that the criteria for the registrability of trademarks are sufficient in themselves to prevent the registration of later confusing geographical indications. In particular, the EC has never said that "valid registered trademarks cannot incorporate certain geographical elements."[165] Indeed, if so, it would have been unnecessary to include Article 14(3) in Regulation 2081/92. Nor is it the EC's

[162] Above para. 232.

[163] EC FWS paras. 278-285.

[164] Ibid., para. 284.

[165] US FOS, para. 50.

position that the violation of Article 16.1 of the TRIPS claimed by the complainants should be tolerated because "the number of specific rights affected is small."[166] The EC is not seeking to "minimize the violation of Article 16.1."[167]

270. To be clear, the EC's position is that there is no violation of Article 16.1, even on the complainants' interpretation of that provision. First, the criteria for the registrability of trademarks limit *a priori* the possibility of conflicts between geographical indications and earlier trademarks. Second, to the extent that any such conflict arises, Article 14(3) of Regulation 2081/92 provides the necessary means to trademark owners in order to prevent or invalidate the registration of *any* confusing geographical indications. Finally, the provisions of Regulation 2081/92, together with other provisions of EC law and the unfair competition laws of the Member States, provide the necessary means to ensure that, in practice, registered geographical indications are not misused so as to create confusion.

(ii) Standard of evidence for establishing the meaning of Article 14(3)

271. The United States argues that the EC has made an improper application of the "mandatory/discretionary analysis."[168] This criticism is misplaced because the EC is not relying on that distinction. The EC is not arguing that Article 14(3) complies with Article 16.1 of the TRIPS Agreement because it gives "discretion" to the EC authorities in order to decide whether or not to refuse the registration of a confusing geographical indication. Article 14(3) is a "mandatory" provision in the sense that it imposes an unqualified obligation upon the EC authorities to refuse any proposed geographical indication that gives rise to the situation described in that provision.

272. The EC's statement quoted by the United States does not relate to the distinction between "mandatory" and "discretionary" legislation, but instead to the issue of what is the appropriate standard of evidence in order to establish the meaning of Article 14(3).

273. The complainants' claim is premised on a certain reading of Article 14(3), which is contested by the EC. The interpretation of Article 14(3) is a matter of EC law and must be treated as a factual issue by the Panel. The complainants bear the burden of proving that Article 14(3) has the meaning which they have asserted in this dispute. In order to do so, it is not enough for them to show that their reading of Article 14(3) is a reasonable interpretation of that provision. As explained above, the EC's own views on the meaning of Article 14(3) must be given "considerable deference." For that reason, the complainants must show not only that their interpretation is reasonable but, in addition, that the EC's interpretation of Article 14(3) is not a reasonable one.

274. Furthermore, Article 14(3) must be interpreted in accordance with the relevant rules of interpretation of EC law. This means, in particular, that, in accordance with well-established case law of the European Court of Justice, the complainants must prove that is impossible to interpret Article 14(3) in a manner that is consistent with the EC's obligations under Article 16.1 of the TRIPS Agreement, as the complainants understand such obligations.

275. Unless the complainants can show that their reading of Article 14(3) is, on the basis of the terms of that provision, the only reasonable interpretation, they would have to prove that, as a matter of fact, Article 14(3) is being applied in practice by the EC authorities in accordance with the complainants' interpretation of that provision, as demonstrated, for example, by the decisions of the EC authorities that apply Article 14(3) or by a consistent pattern of registration of confusing geographical indications.

276. As discussed below, the complainants have failed to show that their interpretation of Article 14(3) is the only reasonable interpretation of that provision. And they have not even attempted to prove that their

[166] Ibid., para. 49.

[167] US Response to Panel's Question No. 67.

[168] US Response to Panel's Question No. 14.

reading of Article 14(3) is, in practice, the interpretation effectively applied by the EC authorities. Therefore, the Panel should conclude that this claim is unfounded, as a matter of fact, even on the complainants' own interpretation of Article 16.1 of the TRIPS.

(iii) The Complainants have misinterpreted Article 14(3)

277. Far from being the only reasonable interpretation of the terms of Article 14(3), the complainants' reading of that provision is unsupported by the ordinary meaning of its terms. Furthermore, the complainants' interpretation is neither workable nor reasonable in practice and cannot be reconciled with the obligations imposed upon the EC authorities by other provisions of Regulation 2081/92.

278. The complainants' claim is based on the false premise that Article 14(3) applies only to a special sub-category of trademarks, namely those which have been used "for a long time" and which, in addition, are famous. Thus, for example, the United States argues that Article 14(3) "only comes into play where there exists a trademark with reputation, renown and history of use."[169] But this is not what Article 14(3) says.

279. The length of use and reputation/renown of the trademark are not separate "requirements"[170] for the application of Article 14(3), distinct from, and additional to the likelihood of confusion. Rather, they are criteria for assessing the existence of a likelihood of confusion. From the fact that the EC Commission must consider those two criteria in order to establish the existence of a likelihood of confusion, it does not follow *a contrario* that any other criteria must be deemed irrelevant for that purpose.

280. As explained[171], Article 14(3) directs expressly the registering authority to consider the length of use and the reputation and renown of earlier trademarks because those criteria will generally be decisive in order to establish the likelihood of confusion, given that geographical names are primarily non-distinctive when used as trademarks.

281. If Article 14(3) does not mention expressly the similarity of goods and signs, it is simply because those criteria are always relevant for a determination of likelihood of confusion. The likelihood of confusion between two signs cannot be meaningfully established by considering only the length of use and the reputation/renown of one of them. The analysis must take into account necessarily the similarity of the goods and signs concerned, which must therefore be deemed implicit in Article 14(3). As shown by the EC, an interpretation of Article 14(3) which prevented the registering authority from considering the similarity of goods and signs would be neither reasonable, nor workable, and cannot be correct.[172]

282. Moreover, the interpretation of Article 14(3) made by the complainants would lead to a result which is incompatible with the terms of Articles 7(4) and 7(5)(b) of Regulation 2081/92.

283. Article 7(4) provides that a statement of objection shall be admissible, *inter alia*, if it shows that "the registration of the name proposed would jeopardize the existence of a mark."[173] This language encompasses *any* instance of likelihood of confusion between the proposed geographical indication and *any* earlier trademark. If Article 14(3) required the refusal of a proposed geographical indication only where it gives rise to a likelihood of confusion with a trademark which is famous and which has been used for a long time, as claimed by the complainants, the admissible grounds of objection would have been limited to the cases where one such trademark is likely to be jeopardized. Article 7(4), however, refers to all trademarks, without any distinction or

[169] US FOS, para. 52.

[170] US FOS, para. 53.

[171] EC FWS, paras. 278-291.

[172] EC Response to Panel's Question No. 68.

[173] Articles 12b(3) and 12d(2) provide, respectively, that the criteria of Article 7(4) shall apply also with respect to the admissibility of objections to the registration of foreign geographical indications and of objections from outside the EC to EC geographical indications.

qualification. It would be pointless to admit an objection on certain grounds if, in any event, it were not possible to reject the application on such grounds.

284. Consistent with Article 7(4), Article 7(5)(b) provides that where an objection is admissible,

> the Commission shall take a decision in accordance with the procedure laid down in Article 15, having regard to traditional fair practice and likelihood of confusion.[174]

285. Thus, Article 7(5)(b) requires the Commission to adopt a decision having regard to the "likelihood of confusion" between the proposed geographical indication and *any* trademark, and not just with those trademarks which are famous and which have been used for a long time.

(iv) There is no evidence that Article 14(3) has been applied in accordance with the complainants' interpretation

286. Since the complainants have failed to show that their reading of the terms of Article 14(3) is the only reasonable interpretation of that provision, they should prove that, *de facto*, Article 14(3) is being applied by the EC authorities in accordance with that interpretation. The complainants have not even attempted to do so.

287. Article 14(3) of Regulation 2081/92 has been applied only once by the EC institutions, in a case where it was alleged that the proposed geographical indication "Bayerisches Bier" was likely to be confused with the existing trademarks "Bavaria" and "Hoker Bajer."[175] The interpretation of Article 14(3) made in that case is consistent with the interpretation put forward by the EC in this dispute. The EC Council concluded that there was no likelihood of confusion with the trademarks in question "in view of the facts and information available." There is no suggestion in the Council decision that this conclusion was reached because the trademarks concerned were not famous enough or had not been used for a sufficiently long time.

288. The United States now suggests that the Council decision to register the geographical indication "Bayerisches Bier" was flawed because that term is likely to be confused with the trademarks at issue when used in translation.[176] This criticism is unfounded because the registration covers only the term "Bayerisches Bier" and not its translations to other languages. Moreover, even if the decision in the "Bayerisches Bier" case had been based on an erroneous factual assessment, that would not contradict the EC's interpretation of Article 14(3).[177]

289. In response to a question from the Panel[178], neither the complaining parties nor any of the third parties have been able to identify even one single geographical indication, of the more than 600 registered under Regulation 2081/92, which gives rise to a likelihood of confusion with an earlier trademark.

290. Instead, the United States refers to purely hypothetical examples, which have no probative value whatsoever with respect to the actual interpretation of Article 14(3) made by the EC authorities.[179]

---

[174] Similar language is found in Articles 12b (3) and12d(3) with regard to the registration of geographical indications from other WTO Members and third countries and to the registration of EC geographical indications, following an objection from outside the EC, respectively.

[175] Council Regulation (EC) 1347/2001, of 28 June 2001 (Exhibit EC-9).

[176] US Response to Panel's Question No. 44.

[177] Furthermore, the US suggestion that *any* possible use of the term "Bayerisches Bier" would create *per se* a likelihood of confusion with the trademarks "Bavaria" and "Bajer Hoker" is difficult to reconcile with the US position, as the EC understands it, that the use of geographical indications for wines recognised in the United States such as "Rutherford" or "Santa Rita Hills" does not lead *per se* to a likelihood of confusion with virtually identical earlier trademarks such as "Rutherford Vintners" or "Santa Rita," respectively, but needs to be examined on case-by-case basis with respect to particular uses. See US Response to EC's Question No. 3.

[178] Panel's Question No. 47 to Australia and the United States and Panel's Question No. 9 to third parties.

291. The United States also refers to a case pending before the Swedish courts, where a a US company claims that the use by Czech producers of beer of the names "Budweiser Budwar," "Budweis" and "Budbräu" infringe its trademarks for the names "Budweiser," "Bud" and "Budweiser King of Beers."[180]

292. The EC understands that the United States is not raising a claim concerning the registration of the geographical indications Budějovické pivo, Českobudějovické pivo and Budějovický měšt'anský var" at this stage of the proceedings. Were the United States to raise that claim, the EC would object that the claim is clearly outside the terms of reference of the Panel, given that the process of ratification of the Treaty of Accession providing for the registration of those names had not been completed yet at the time of establishment of this Panel.[181]

293. In any event, the EC recalls that the registration under Regulation 2081/92 only covers the terms Budějovické pivo, Českobudějovické pivo and Budějovický měšt'anský and not any alleged translations of those terms to other languages. The EC understands that the United States is not suggesting that the use of those names is *per se* likely to result in a likelihood of confusion with the above mentioned trademarks of the US producer concerned.

(v) Article 14(3) confers enforceable rights to the trademark owners

294. The United States argues that, even if the EC's reading of Article 14(3) were correct, that provision "merely authorizes the EC to decline registration of a GI"[182], but does not accord rights to the trademark owners.

295. The United States is wrong again. The EC authorities are required, and not simply authorized, to refuse the registration of a geographical indication. Article 14(3) provides that the registration "shall not be registered" and, therefore, leaves no margin of discretion to the Commission in order to register the proposed geographical indication where the conditions set out in Article 14(3) are met.

296. Furthermore, Article 14(3) confers judicially enforceable rights to the owners of trademarks. If a trademark owner considers that the EC authorities have registered a geographical indication in violation of Article 14(3) it is entitled to challenge the validity of such registration before the courts, including in the framework of the infringement proceedings brought against the user of the geographical indication under the Community Trademark Regulation or the trademark law of the Member States.

297. The United States argues that some geographical indications have been registered in accordance with special procedures that do not provide for a right of objection, such as the so-called "fast track" procedure

---

179 The examples cited by the United States are:

1) the hypothetical conflict between the hypothetical trademark "Luna" for cheese and the hypothetical geographical indication "Luna" for a hypothetical cheese produced in a hypothetical Spanish small town called "Luna." (US FOS, para. 50). There is no town in Spain, or in any other Spanish speaking country, whether big or small, called "Luna." For Spanish speakers, "Luna" is the name of the only satellite of the planet Earth, which is as an unlikely place for producing cheese as the planet "Mars" for producing chocolate bars. In view of that, EC trademark officials would be likely to register "Luna" as a purely fanciful name. But, for the same reason, it is unlikely that such trademark would enter into conflict with a subsequent geographical indication.

2) the hypothetical conflict between the trademark "Faro" for coffee and tea and a hypothetical geographical indication "Faro" for the hypothetical coffee and tea grown in the Portuguese town of Faro. (US Response to Panel's Question No. 47). To the best of the EC's knowledge, no tea or coffee has ever been grown in Faro. Indeed, it is doubtful that either coffee or tea can be grown commercially in Faro, given the prevailing climatic conditions. Therefore, the town of Faro is unlikely to be associated by consumers with those products. Even if, as an effect of global warming, coffee and tea became one day a speciality of the town of Faro, the registration of the hypothetical geographical indication would still have to be refused if it led to confusion with the earlier trademark "Faro" in accordance with Article 14(3).

180 US Response to Panel's Question 47.

181 EC FWS, paras. 21-25.

182 US FOS, para. 54. See also US Responses to Panel's Questions Nos. 14 (at para. 41) and 67 (at para. 87).

provided in the former Article 17 of Regulation 2081/92.[183] As explained by the EC[184], however, neither Article 16.1 nor Article 22.2 of the TRIPS Agreement requires to grant a right of objection with respect to the registration of geographical indications. All that is required by the TRIPS Agreement is that the final registration decision be subject to judicial review.[185] Trademark owners have a right to challenge the validity of the registrations under Regulation 2081/92 also in those cases where no right of objection has been provided as part of the registration procedure. [186]

(vi) EC law provides means to prevent confusing uses of a registered geographical indication

298. The United States goes on to argue that, even if Article 14(3) prevents the registration of confusing geographical indications, it does not provide means to prevent that a registered geographical indication will be used subsequently in a confusing manner. Specifically, the United States has argued that[187]

> ...even if Article 14(3) accorded rights to trademark owners rather than just authority to the EC, the trademark owner would not necessarily be able to tell, at the time of registration of the GI, whether the use of the GI will be confusing. For example, a registered GI may unexpectedly be used in translation, or in a manner that emphasizes certain aspects or letters of the geographical name, in a way that causes a likelihood of confusion with respect to a registered trademark.

299. These concerns are largely theoretical and, in any event, unfounded.

300. First, the product specifications to be submitted with the application for registration must include "the specific labelling details" relating to the geographical indication.[188] Those specifications may be subject to objections in accordance with Article 7(4) and are taken into account for the purposes of the determination required by Article 14(3) and of the final decision provided in Article 7(5)(b). Any change of the labelling specifications must be approved by the EC authorities.[189] Failure to comply with the specifications may lead to the cancellation of the registration.[190]

301. Second, the right holders of a geographical indication have a positive right to use the name registered as a geographical indication. But that right does not extend to other names or signs which have been not been registered. If the use of such unregistered names or signs leads to a likelihood of confusion with the same or a similar sign which is the subject of a valid trademark, it can be challenged judicially by the trademark owner under the Community Trademark Regulation or the trademark laws of the Member States, as applicable.

---

[183] US Response to Questions No. 6 (at para. 68) and 67 (at para. 87).

[184] EC FWS, paras. 327-333 and para. 427.

[185] Cf. Article 62.5 of the TRIPS Agreement.

[186] The EC notes that, unlike Australia, the United States did not claim in its First Written Submission that the lack of an adequate right of objection with respect to the registration of a geographical indication under Regulation 2081/92 is inconsistent with Article 16.1 of the TRIPS Agreement. It is unclear to the EC whether the United States is raising this claim at this stage.
In any event, the EC would note that, under US law, trademark owners do not seem to have a right to challenge *ex post* before the courts the validity of the recognition of a geographical indication for wines on the grounds that it infringes their trademark rights, let alone a right to object in advance to such recognition. See *Sociedad Anonima Viña Santa Rita v. US Dept. of the Treasury*, 193 F. Supp. 2d 6 (D.D.C 2001) ("The Court finds that an entity with a non-geographic interest in a particular name is not empowered, under the Lanham Act, to contest the ATF's recognition of a distinct geographic region that bears that name.") (Exhibit US–48, at. p. 13). In view of this, the United States can hardly complain about the fact that trademark owners have not been recognised a right of objection with respect to the registration of some geographical indications under Regulation 2081/92.

[187] US FOS, para. 54

[188] Cf. Article 4(2)(h) of Regulation 2081/92.

[189] Cf. Article 9 of Regulation 2081/92.

[190] Cf. Articles 11(4) and 11a of Regulation 2081/92.

302. Third, in so far as a right holder of a registered geographical indication were to present the registered name in a mutilated or deformed manner so as to imitate an earlier trademark, which is what the United States appears to be suggesting, a court would be entitled to find, depending on the specific circumstances of each case, that the "used sign" is different from the "registered sign" and, therefore, not protected under Regulation 2081/92.

303. Furthermore, while the right holders of a geographical indication have a positive right to use the registered name, this does not mean that they are allowed to use it in any conceivable manner. As explained[191], the use of a name registered as a geographical indication is subject to the applicable provisions of

- Directive 2000/13 on the labelling, presentation and advertising of foodstuffs[192], and in particular Article 2(1)(a), which provides that

  the labelling and methods used must not be such as could mislead to the purchaser to a material degree, particularly:

  (i) as to the characteristics of the product and, in particular, as to ... its origin or provenance

  [...]

  For the purposes of this Directive, "labelling" is defined as:

  > any words, particulars, trade marks, brand name, pictorial matter or symbol relating to a foodstuff and placed on any packaging, document, notice, label, ring or collar accompanying or referring to such foodstuff.

  Article 2(1)(a) also applies to:

  > (a) the presentation of foodstuffs, in particular their shape, appearance or packaging, the packaging materials used, the way in which they are arranged and the setting in which they are displayed;
  >
  > (b) advertising.[193]

- Directive 84/450 on misleading advertising[194], which is defined as:

  any advertising which in any way, including presentation, deceives or is likely to deceive the person to whom it is addressed or whom it reaches and which, by reason of its deceptive nature, is likely to affect their economic behaviour or which, for those reasons, injures or is likely to injure a competitor.[195]

- the unfair competition laws of the Member States.[196]

---

[191] EC's First Submission, para. 319. See also the responses of the EC and its Member States to the review under Article 24.2 of the TRIPS Agreement contained in document IP/C/W/117/Add.10 (Exhibit EC-29).

[192] Exhibit EC–30.

[193] Article 2(3).

[194] Exhibit EC–31.

[195] Article 2(2).

[196] References to the relevant laws of the Member States are found in their responses to the review under Article 24.2 of the TRIPS Agreement. (Exhibit EC-32).

(b) Article 24.5 of the TRIPS Agreement

304. The EC has addressed the arguments made by the United States with respect to Article 24.5 in its First Oral Statement as part of the EC's responses to the Panel's Questions Nos. 76 and 77, to which the Panel is referred. Here below, the EC will provide its comments with respect to some issues raised by the complainants' responses to the Panel's Questions Nos. 75 to 79.

(i) Relationship between Section 3 of Part II and Article 16.1

305. In response to the Panel's Question No.79, both Australia and the United States argue that there is no "conflict" between Articles 16.1 and 22.3 because Members may, in accordance with Article 15.2, refuse or invalidate the registration of any trademark that would be misleading as to the place of origin of the goods and in practice most Members do so. This is, of course, correct and has never been disputed by the EC.

306. It remains, however, that, as matter of law, neither Article 15.2 nor any other provision of Section 2 of Part II requires Members to refuse or invalidate the trademarks that are misleading as to the place of origin of the goods. Such obligation arises exclusively from Article 22.3. This shows that, contrary to what is suggested by the complainants, the provisions of Section 3 of Part II do impose restrictions on the protection of trademarks, and not just on the protection of geographical indications, and, therefore, that Section 2 of Part III cannot be applied without having regard to Section 3.

307. That Section 3 limits the protection of trademarks is made even clearer by Article 23.2, which requires Members to refuse or invalidate trademarks for wines and spirits which could, and in practice would, have been validly registered in most Members before the entry into force of the WTO Agreement. As a result, both Australia and the United States, like many other Members, had to amend their trademark laws in order to implement Article 23.2.

308. While, for the reasons explained, there is no "conflict" between Articles 16.1 and 22.3, there is a potential "conflict" between Article 16.1 and Article 22.2(a), which requires Members to provide legal means for interested parties to prevent

> the use of any means in the designation or presentation of a good that indicates or suggests that the good in question originates in a geographical area other than the true place of origin in a manner which misleads the public as to the geographical origin of the goods.

309. The "means" referred to in Article 22.2(a) may include the use of a geographical indication as a trademark, whether registered or established through use. Thus, Article 22.2 confers to the right holders of a geographical indication the right to prevent the use of any trademark which misleads the public as to the origin of the goods. This right may conflict with the right of the owner of a trademark under Article 16.1 to prevent the use of any sign that results in a likelihood of confusion with its trademark. The simultaneous exercise of both rights would lead to a situation where neither the trademark owner nor the right holders of the geographical indication could use the sign in question. A similar conflict may arise between Articles 16.1 and 23.1.

310. The above described conflict between Articles 16.1, on the one hand, and Article 22.2 and 23.1, on the other hand, was resolved by the drafters of the TRIPS Agreement through the application of the rules contained din Articles 22.3, 23.2 and 24.5, which together define the boundary between the protection that Members must or may provide to trademarks under Section 2 of Part III and the protection which Members must or may provide to geographical indications under Section 3 of Part III.

311. In response to the Panel's Question No. 75, the United States makes the unsupported assertion that[197]

---

[197] US Response to Question No. 75, para. 91.

the EC is arguing that Article 24.5 is an affirmative defence to the US claims that the GI Regulation is inconsistent with the EC's obligations under Article 16.1 of the TRIPS Agreement (that is that Article 24.5 is an exception to Article 16.1).

312. This is a gross misrepresentation of the EC's position. The EC has never argued that Article 24.5 is an "exception" to Article 16.1, let alone an "affirmative defence."

313. Although Article 24.5 is part of Article 24, which is entitled "International Negotiations: Exceptions," it is not an exception in the same sense as, for example, Article XX of the GATT.[198] The Appellate Body has cautioned against characterizing a measure as an exception simply because it is referred as such in the agreement. This caution applies *a fortiori* in the present case, given that the term "exception" is not used in the text of Article 24.5 itself, or in another provision that refers specifically to Article 24.5, but only in the title of Article 24, an article consisting of many distinct and heterogeneous provisions, not all of which can be considered as "exceptions" or concerned with "international negotiations." For example, Article 24.3 is clearly not an exception. To the contrary, it imposes additional obligations upon Members.

314. Unlike paragraphs 6 to 9 of Article 24, Article 24.5 does not provide an exemption from an obligation, of which Members may or may not avail themselves. Instead, Article 24.5 places a limit on the measures that Members must or may take in order to protect geographical indications when implementing Section 3 of Part II. As explained, by doing so, Article 25.4 defines the boundary between the protection of trademarks and the protection of geographical indications. The EC has submitted that the protection provided to geographical indications under Article 14(2) of Regulation 2081/92 is within the limits defined in Article 24.5. It is for the United States and Australia, as the complaining parties, to show that, in fact, such protection goes beyond those limits and is inconsistent with Article 16.1.

315. The US position that Article 24.5 is an "exception" to the obligations provided in Section 3 of Part II, which, therefore, cannot affect the scope of the obligations imposed by Article 16.1 is contradicted by the fact that Article 24.5 confers to the owners of trademarks established by use rights which they do not have under Article 16.1. The last sentence of Article 16.1 reserves "the possibility of Members making trademark rights available on the basis of use," but it does not require them to do so. Members are free to decide whether or not to grant such rights and, if so, to limit or withdraw them at will. Yet, one of the consequences of Article 24.5 is that, in implementing protection for geographical indications, Members must not prejudice "the right to use" a grandfathered trademark acquired through use. Thus, Article 24.5 imposes upon Members an obligation with respect to the protection of trademarks which they do not have under Article 16.1.

(ii) The meaning of "the right to use a trademark"

316. In response to the Panel's Questions Nos. 76 and 77, Australia and the United States have provided different and contradictory interpretations of the phrase "the right to use a trademark."

317. Australia says that the phrase "the right to use a trademark" applies only to the trademarks acquired through use and not to registered trademarks. Australia does not say whether "the right to use a trademark" includes also the right to prevent others from using the trademark, as claimed by the United States. Instead, Australia suggests the Panel need not reach that question.

318. Australia's reading of the phrase "the right to use a trademark" raises obvious problems. First, it cannot be reconciled with the ordinary meaning of the term "trademark," which includes all trademarks, whether registered or acquired through use. Moreover, as used throughout the TRIPS Agreement, the term

---

[198] See Appellate Body Report, *EC – Hormones*, para. 104, where the Appellate Body held that the burden of proof with respect to Article 3.3 of the *SPS Agreement* was on the complaining party, even though that provision was described as an exception in Article 3.1. See also Appellate Body Report, *EC – Sardines*, para. 275, where the Appellate Body ruled that the last part of Article 2.4 of the *TBT Agreement* was not an affirmative defence even though it is introduced by the term "except."

"trademark" includes both types of trademarks (for example, in the title of Section 2 of Part III). When the drafters intended to distinguish between registered trademarks and trademarks acquired through use they did so expressly, like in Article 16.1 or in Article 21.[199]

319. In its First Written Submission, Australia suggested that the phrase "the right to use a trademark" is linked to the reference made in the chapeau of Article 24.5 to the situation where "rights to a trademark have been acquired through use." But, as already noted in the EC's First Written Submission, in that case it would have been more logical to say in the chausette that implementation "shall not prejudice ... the rights to a trademark acquired through use." Australia's argument confuses the mode of acquisition of the trademark with one of the basic rights attached to any trademark, whether registered or established by use.

320. Furthermore, by arguing that the phrase "the right to use a trademark" refers exclusively to the trademarks acquired through use, and not contesting that such phrase does not include the right to prevent others from using the trademark, Australia appears to be conceding that Article 24.5 provides for the co-existence of geographical indications with earlier trademark acquired through use. Australia does not explain why co-existence should be allowed in that case, but not with respect to registered trademarks, given that Article 16.1 reserves the right of Members to grant trademark rights, including exclusive rights, on the basis of use.

321. For its part, the United States, following a contorted reasoning, concludes that the phrase "the right to use a trademark" has simultaneously three different meanings:

- first, it would be a reference to the trademarks whose rights are acquired through use;[200]
- second, it means the "the right to use *per se*" the trademark;[201]
- third, it would mean also "the right to exclude others from using similar signs."[202]

322. The EC has already commented upon the first meaning and agrees with the second meaning.

323. The view that the phrase "the right to use a trademark" includes the right to exclude others from using the trademark cannot be reconciled with the meaning of that phrase in ordinary language or in the particular context of intellectual property law.

324. For example, WIPO's Trademark Manual says that the "the registered owner has the exclusive right to use the trademark," which encompasses two things: "the right to use the trademark" and "the right to exclude others from using the mark."[203]

325. Similarly, to mention but another example, Section 20 of Australia's Trade Marks Act 1995 (which is entitled "Rights given by registration of trade mark") provides in relevant part that

> (1) If a trade mark is registered, the registered owner of the trademark has, subject to this Part, the *exclusive* rights:
>
> (a) to use the trade mark;

---

199 Contradicting Australia's position, the United States says that (Response to Question No. 76, para. 105):
"the right to use a trademark" is not specifically linked in the text to trademarks whose rights are acquired through use (although it would appear to include such trademarks).

200 US Response to the Panel's Question No. 76, para. 103.

201 US Response to the Panel's Question No. 77, para. 106.

202 US Response to the Panel's Question No. 76, para. 103.

203 WIPO, "Introduction to Trademark Law & Practice, The Basic Concepts, A WIPO Training Manual," Geneva 1993, pp. 51–52 (Exhibit EC-57).

(b) to authorise other persons to use the trade mark;

(2) The registered owner of trade mark has *also* the right to obtain relief under this Act if the trade mark has been infringed.

[...][204]

326. By implication, Australia's Trade Marks Act 1995 recognises that the right to use a trademark is not necessarily "exclusive" and that "the right to use a trademark" is different from the right to prevent others from infringing the trademark.[205]

327. The United States itself refers to what it calls "the right to use *per se*"[206], thus acknowledging implicitly that, in its ordinary meaning, the phrase "the right to use a trademark" does not include the right to exclude others from using the trademark. In spite of this, the United States seeks to stretch the meaning of the phrase "the right to use the trade mark" by resorting to an interpretation based on the "purpose" of a trademark.[207] It is beyond dispute that, as argued by the United States, the purpose of a trademark is to distinguish the goods from a certain source and that, in order to achieve that purpose, the right to use a trademark *should* be exclusive. But from this it does not follow logically that "the right to use a trademark" is inherently exclusive. In practice, the right to use a trademark is not always exclusive. Indeed, if the "right to use a trademark" were inherently exclusive, it would have been superfluous to provide in Article 16.1 that the owners of registered trademarks shall have exclusive rights. Also, on the US interpretation, any rights granted to the owners of unregistered trademarks on the basis of use would have to be exclusive. While this may be generally the case, there is no obligation under the TRIPS Agreement to do so.

328. As suggested by the Panel's Question No. 77, if the drafters had intended to preserve the right of the trademark owners to exclude all others, including the right holders of a protected geographical indication, from using the trademark, they would have used express language to that effect, such as "shall not prejudice ... the exclusive right to use the trademark" or "the rights conferred to the trademark owners under Article 16.1" The explanations given by the United States in its response to this question are unconvincing:

- the United States says that reference to "exclusive right to use" would have been "confusing"[208], because the "specific exclusive right in Article 16.1 is the right to exclude, not the right to use *per se*."[209] As shown above, however, the phrase "exclusive right to use" is of common usage in the intellectual property law field, including in the trademark laws of both Australia and the United States. Moreover, the right to exclude all others from using the trademarks is but the corollary of the exclusivity of the owner's right to use it. There is no contradiction or confusion.

- the United States also says that a reference to "the rights conferred under Article 16.1" would have been "confusing" because Article 16.1 describes three sets of rights.[210] Yet, the US position, as the EC understands it, is that Article 24.5 leaves unaffected each of those three sets of rights. Thus, the suggested formula would have described accurately the result sought by the United States.

---

[204] Exhibit EC -58. [Emphasis added].

[205] The term "exclusive right to use a trademark" is used also in the US Lanham Act. See e.g. Section 1115, which is entitled "Registration on principal register as evidence of exclusive right to use a mark; defenses). (Exhibit EC–6).

[206] US Response to the Panel's Question No. 77, para. 106.

[207] US Response to the Panel's Question No. 76, para. 102.

[208] US Response to the Panel's Question No. 77, para. 106.

[209] Ibid.

[210] Ibid.

329. Australia has suggested that the Panel need not concern itself with the meaning of "the right to use a trademark."[211] The EC disagrees. And apparently so does the United States. The two phrases need to be interpreted together because they are part of the same obligation and impart meaning to each other.

330. If the phrase "right to use the trademark" means what it says, rather than the "right- to-use-a-trademark-and-in-addition-to-exclude-all-others-from-using-it," as argued by the United States, it would confirm the EC's reading of the phrase "the validity of the registration." If the drafters deemed necessary to specify that the implementation of protection for geographical indications shall not prejudice one of the two basic rights of the owner of a registered trademark (the right to use it), but not the other (the right to exclude others from using it), the clear implication is that they did not intend to prevent Members from limiting the latter right in order to allow the use of a geographical indication in co-existence with a grandfathered trademark. Hence the US insistence that the phrase the "right to use a trademark" includes also the right to exclude others. Because Australia, apparently, does not share this interpretation, it is forced to argue instead that the phrase "the right to use a trademark" does not apply at all to registered trademarks and need not be considered by the Panel.

(c) Article 24.3 of the TRIPS Agreement

331. The EC has argued that, regardless of whether the co-existence of geographical indications and earlier trademarks is permitted by Article 24.5, it is required to maintain such co-existence by virtue of the stand-still provision contained in Article 24.3.[212]

332. Australia has not responded to this argument. The United States addressed it in its Oral Statement.[213] The EC has responded comprehensively to the US arguments in its reply to the Panel's Question No. 74, to which the Panel is referred.

(d) Article 17 of the TRIPS Agreement

333. The EC has argued in the alternative that, even if Regulation 2081/92 were found to be *prima facie* inconsistent with Article 16.1 of the TRIPS Agreement in that it allows the co-existence of a registered geographical indication with an earlier trademark, such co-existence would be justified under Article 17 of the TRIPS Agreement.[214]

334. Australia has not addressed this defence. Here below, the EC will respond to the counter-arguments made by the United States in its Oral Statement[215] and in response to the Panel's Question No. 75.

(i) The scope of the exception is "limited"

335. The United States contends that Regulation 2081/92 does not provide a "limited exception" because its scope is too broad:[216]

> Further, with respect to the scope of the so-called "exception," the GI Regulation entirely eliminates the trademark holder's right to prevent confusing uses by all others, which is the core of its legitimate interest.

336. This is plainly wrong as a matter of fact. Regulation 2081/92 does not "eliminate the trademark holder's right to prevent confusing uses by *all* others." Article 14(2) of Regulation 2081/92 allows the

[211] Australia's Response to the Panel's Question No. 77.
[212] EC FWS, paras. 312-314.
[213] US FOS, paras. 69-73.
[214] EC FWS, paras. 315-319.
[215] US FOS, paras. 74-75.
[216] US FOS, para. 75.

concurrent use as a geographical indication of a name registered as a trademark only in relation to products which originate in the area designated by the registered geographical indication and which, in addition, comply with all the relevant product specifications and other requirements for using the registered geographical indication. The trademark owner retains the exclusive right to prevent the confusing use of that name by *any* person in relation to *any* products which do not qualify for the use of the registered geographical indication.

337. Moreover, Article 14(3) of Regulation 2081/92 restricts even further the scope of the exception. Even if the complainants' interpretation of Article 14(3) were correct and that provision did not prevent the registration of all confusing geographical indications, it would nonetheless prevent the registration of confusing geographical indications in those instances where the likelihood of confusion is greater, because the trademarks are particularly distinctive, and may cause a greater prejudice to the trademark owners, because of the reputation and renown of the trademark.[217]

338. Article 17 mentions expressly as an example of limited exception "the fair use of descriptive terms." The notion of "descriptive terms" includes *inter alia* any term used to indicate the place of origin of a product.[218] In other words, it includes any term used as an "indication of source" in the sense of the Paris Convention. Geographical indications are a subset of the category of indications of source. The universe of potential users of a geographical indication registered under Regulation 2081/92 is narrower than that of the universe of potential users of an indication of source which does not qualify as a geographical indication, because the products bearing a registered geographical indication must comply with certain product specifications and other requirements, while an indication of source may be used by any product of that origin. If "fair use" of an indication of source qualifies as as a "limited exception," as the United States appears to concede, so must be, *a fortiori*, the fair use of a geographical indication registered under Regulation 2081/92.[219]

---

[217] This may be contrasted with the situation under US law, where the risk of likelihood with an existing trademark is *never* considered a relevant ground for not recognising a geographical indication for wines. See *Sociedad Anonima Viña Santa Rita v. US Dept. of the Treasury*, 193 F. Supp. 2d 6 (D.D.C 2001) (Exhibit US–48). Hence the recognition of geographical indications such as "Rutherford" or "Santa Rita Hills," despite the existence of virtually identical earlier trademarks such as "Rutherford Vintners" and "Santa Rita," respectively. Instead, trademark owners are forced to bring infringement suits against each particular use of the geographical indication. Once again, EC law is more protective of the rights of trademark owners than US law.

[218] In the United States, the courts have considered that recognised geographical indications for wine are descriptive terms. See *Sociedad Anonima Viña Santa Rita v. US Dept. of the Treasury*, 193 F. Supp. 2d 6 (D.D.C 2001) (Exhibit US–48):

As the ATF aptly explains in its opposition, "AVA designations differ from trademark because a trademark is used to convey to the consumer the identity of the manufacturer or producer of the good whereas the AVA is used to describe the geographical origin of the good and can be used by many wineries." … Thus, by approving the Santa Rita Hills AVA, the ATF has not developed any name or mark of its own. Rather, the ATF has simply taken the step of recognizing its viticultural singularity and confirming the boundaries that encompass the region.

[219] The EC finds it difficult to understand the explanation provided by Australia in its Response to the Panel's Question No. 80 to the effect that the exception provided under Section 122 of the Australian Trade Marks Act (Exhibit EC-7) with respect to the "good faith use" of a sign used "to indicate the geographic origin" of a product does not apply with respect to a "TRIPS-defined GI," because Section 6 (Exhibit EC-59) of that Act defines expressly the notion of "geographical indication." In the EC's respectful view, this is an obvious *non-sequitur*. Section 6 defines a geographical indication as follows:

in relation to goods originating in a particular country or in a region or locality of that country, means a sign recognised in that country as a sign indicating that the goods: (a)originated in that country, region or locality; and (b)have a quality, reputation or other characteristic attributable to their geographical origin.

Thus, it is plain that the term "signs used to indicate the geographical origin of goods" used in Section 122 includes any sign falling within the category of geographical indications as defined in Section 6.

Although, as noted by Australia, Section 61 (Exhibit EC-60) provides for the rejection of an application for the registration of a trademark that contains or consists of a geographical indication, this is subject to exceptions, including one which purports to implement Article 24.5 of the TRIPS Agreement. As a result, Australia's reading of Section 6 would have the manifestly absurd consequence that geographical indications, which would be entitled in principle to protection under the TRIPS Agreement, could not be used under the "good faith use" exception, while other indications of source, which are not geographical indication and are not entitled to protection under Section 3 of Part II of the TRIPS Agreement, would qualify for that exception.

(ii) The exception "takes account" of the interests of the trademark owners

339. The United States argued in its First Oral Statement that Article 14(2) of Regulation 2081 is not covered by Article 17 because[220]

> It should be possible to inform consumers about the origin of a product and its characteristics through the use of descriptive terms in a non-trademark sense without affirmatively *confusing* the consumer about the source of the goods.

340. The United States has repeated again the same argument literally in its response to the Panel's Question No. 75.[221] Its precise meaning, however, still remains unclear to the EC.

341. This argument suggests that the United States considers that an exception may not be justified under Article 17 unless it avoids any likelihood of confusion with the trademark. Thus, the United States appears to be importing into Article 17 the interpretation made by the US courts of the "fair use" exception provided under US trademark law. According to that interpretation, as restated in the US response to the Panel's Question No. 80:[222]

> The user invoking fair use must adapt and design his usage of the geographical indication so as not to cause a likelihood of consumer confusion.

342. This interpretation of the US "fair use" exception cannot be transposed to Article 17 because it would render that provision inoperative and superfluous. Article 17 is an exception to Article 16.1, which does not come into play unless there is a *prima facie* violation of the exclusive rights conferred by Article 16.1. If the use of a geographical indication does not result in a likelihood of confusion with an earlier registered trademark, there is no violation of Article 16.1 and, therefore, no need to invoke Article 17. The application of Article 17 presupposes necessarily that the excepted uses give rise to a likelihood of confusion with the trademark. Requiring as a condition for the application of Article 17 that the excepted uses must not result in a likelihood of confusion with the trademark would render that provision wholly redundant.

343. Alternatively, the US argument could be understood as meaning that, in order to be justified under Article 17, the likelihood of confusion must be confined to the strictly necessary. However, the wording of Article 17 provide no basis for such narrow interpretation. Article 17 includes no "necessity" test, unlike other exceptions in the TRIPS Agreement (for example, Articles 3.2, 27.2, 39.3 and 73(b)) or in other WTO Agreements (for example, Article XX (a), (b) and (d) of the GATT).[223] All that is required by Article 17 is that the exception "takes account" of the legitimate interests of the trademark owner and of third parties.

344. The language of Article 17 may be contrasted also with that of Articles 13, 26.2 and 30 of the TRIPS Agreement, which provide that exceptions "shall not unreasonably prejudice" the interests of the right holder. This is a more stringent requirement than simply "taking account"[224] of the interests of the right holders, which nevertheless falls short of a "necessity" requirement.

345. The United States also argues that the exception invoked by the EC is not justified under Article 17 because it fails to[225]

---

[220] US FOS, para. 75. Emphasis added.

[221] At para. 94.

[222] At para. 120.

[223] In *US – Gasoline*, pp. 14-19, the Appellate Body chastised the panel for reading a necessity requirement into Article XX(g) which, unlike other exceptions included in Article XX, does not use the term "necessary."

[224] Articles 26.2 and 30 of the TRIPS Agreement distinguish between the interests of the right holders, which must not be "unreasonably prejudiced" and the interests of third parties, which must be simply "taken account of."

[225] US FOS, para. 75

take account of the interests of the trademark owners and of third parties on a case-by-case basis, depending on the manner in which a descriptive term is used.

346. Once again, the United States is importing into Article 17 conditions from its own trademark law which have no basis in that provision. Article 17 provides that the exception must "take account" of the interests of trademark owners and third parties. It does not prescribe any particular method to do so. Members may choose to define an exception in very broad terms and leave to their courts wide discretion in order to apply it on a case-by-case basis, as appears to be the US own preference.[226] But Members may as well choose to define in advance with greater precision the conditions for the application of an exception in its laws or regulations, in a manner which leaves less discretion to the implementing authorities. This method is arguably less flexible than the method advocated by the United States. But it has the advantage of providing greater legal certainty to all the parties involved, including the trademark owners, and is not incompatible *per se* with Article 17.

347. In any event, as a matter of fact, the US objections are unwarranted. As explained above at paragraphs 299-303 the concerns expressed by the United States with respect to certain particular misuses of a registered geographical indication are largely theoretical and can be addressed appropriately under Regulation 2081/92 and complementary legislation. Even if the remedies against those particular misuses available under EC law were not deemed sufficient in order to comply with Article 16.1, they would be sufficient to consider that the interests of the trademark owners and third parties are appropriately taken into account for the purposes of Article 17.

(iii) Article 17 applies to non-geographical names

348. Finally, the United States contends that "nothing in the EC's interpretation explains how the Article 17 fair use exception applies to non-geographic names."[227]

349. The EC fails to understand the pertinence of this argument. The reasoning developed by the EC applies indistinctly to all geographical indications, regardless of whether they consist of a geographical or a non-geographical names, because all of them serve identical purpose. They identify a product as originating in a certain geographical location to which consumers associate a given quality, reputation or other characteristic.[228]

350. There is nothing in Article 17 which excludes non-geographical names from its scope. In particular, the term "descriptive terms" may include any term which serves to describe the origin of goods, and the product characteristics associated to such origin, regardless of whether it is a geographical name.

2. Claim 20: Regulation 2081/92 does not provide for a presumption of a likelihood of confusion in the case of use of an identical sign for identical goods

351. Australia has submitted no further arguments.

3. Claim 21: Article 7(4) of Regulation 2081/92 is inconsistent with Article 16.1 of the TRIPS Agreement because it limits the grounds of objection

352. Australia has submitted no further arguments.

---

[226] As explained above, under US law, trademark owners may not challenge before the courts the validity of the decision recognising a geographical indication for wines on the grounds that it infringes their trademark rights. Instead, they are forced to bring individual suits against each particular infringing use. In contrast, Article 14(3) of Regulation 2081/92 allows trademark owners to prevent *a priori* the registration of any proposed geographical indication that results in a likelihood of confusion with an earlier trademark. This limits considerably the risk of subsequent infringing uses, since they are limited to the misuse of a name which is not confusing *per se*.

[227] US Response to the Panel's Question No. 75, at para. 96.

[228] Cf. Article 22.1 of the TRIPS Agreement.

353. The EC notes that, in response to a question from the EC, Australia has been unable to identify any case where the EC authorities have limited the grounds of objection under Article 7(4) of Regulation 2081/92 in the manner alleged by Australia.[229] This confirms the EC's interpretation of that provision.

4. Claim 22: Regulation 2081/92 does not ensure that objections from trademark owners will be considered by the Committee

354. Australia has submitted no further arguments.

B. CLAIM 23: BY REQUIRING THE CO-EXISTENCE OF A REGISTERED GEOGRAPHICAL INDICATION AND AN EARLIER TRADEMARK, ARTICLE 14(2) ENCUMBERS UNJUSTIFIABLY THE USE OF THE TRADEMARK, CONTRARY TO ARTICLE 20 OF THE TRIPS AGREEMENT

355. Australia has submitted no further arguments.

C. CLAIM 24: ARTICLE 14(1) OF REGULATION 2081/92 IS INCONSISTENT WITH ARTICLE 24.5 OF THE TRIPS AGREEMENT BECAUSE IT DOES NOT AFFORD THE RIGHT OF PRIORITY PROVIDED IN ARTICLE 4 OF THE PARIS CONVENTION

356. Australia has submitted no further arguments, even though the EC had requested Australia to clarify this claim.

357. The EC notes that, in response to a question from the EC, Australia has not been able to identify even one single application for a trademark that falls within the situation that Australia alleges under this claim.[230]

D. ARTICLES 41.1, 41.2, 41.3, 41.4, 42, 43, 44.1, 45, 46, 48 AND 49 OF THE TRIPS AGREEMENT

1. General Considerations

358. In response to the Panel's Question No. 85, Australia appears to concede that Parts III and IV of the TRIPS Agreement cannot be applied cumulatively to the same procedures:

> In the event that the Panel should consider that the decision-making process provided by Article 15 of Regulation 2081/92 does provide a means for the owner of a registered trademark to enforce rights required to be granted by TRIPS Article 16.1, it is Australia's view that the decision-making process constitutes an enforcement process in respect of such trademark rights governed by Part III of the TRIPS Agreement: Part IV is not applicable.

359. The registration procedure laid down in Regulation 2081/92, including the objection procedure, is not a means to "enforce" the rights of the trademark owners. Article 16.1 of the TRIPS Agreement confers to the owner of a registered trademark the exclusive right to prevent all third parties from *using* identical or similar signs for identical or similar good where such use would result in a likelihood of confusion

360. The registration of geographical indication does not amount to the *use* of that geographical indication and does not infringe *per se* any rights of the trademarks owner.[231] Such infringement may result only from the

---

[229] Australia's Response to the EC's Question No. 1.

[230] Australia's Response to the EC's Question No. 2.

subsequent *use* of the registered geographical indication by one of the right holders. Regulation 2081/92 does not prevent trademark owners from bringing infringement proceedings under the applicable provisions of trademark law against a right holder of a geographical indication, if and when it *uses* the geographical indication, in the context of which trademark owners can invoke that the registration is invalid or that the particular use (or misuse) of the geographical indication is not covered by Regulation 2081/92.

361. The EC notes that, in response to questions posed by the EC, Australia has conceded that

- Australia's Trade Marks Office is not a judicial body;[232]
- the procedures before Australia's Trade Marks Office are not "judicial procedures" within the meaning of Article 42 of the TRIPS Agreement;[233]
- Australia's Trade Marks Office does not have the authority to order the remedies provided in Articles 44, 45 and 46.[234]

362. Despite the above, Australia maintains that the registration and opposition procedures before Australia's Trade Marks Office may be characterised as "enforcement procedures" within the meaning of Part III of the TRIPS Agreement.[235] However, if so, it would follow that Australia's registration and opposition procedures for trademarks are subject to Part III and not to Part IV. Furthermore, it would mean that those procedures are in clear violation of Part III, and in particular of Articles 42, 44, 45 and 46.

363. Australia appears to consider that there is no such violation because the decisions of the Trade Marks Office are reviewable by the Federal Court of Australia.[236] But the requirement to provide for such judicial review is contained in Part IV and not in Part III (cf. Article 62.5). Furthermore, the EC has explained repeatedly that the registration decisions under Regulation 2081/92 and the decisions of the authorities of the Member States with respect to the statements of objections are also subject to review by the courts, which can order the remedies provided in Part III. In view of that, Australia should explain why the EC's procedures for the registration of geographical indications are inconsistent with Part III, but Australia's own procedures for the registration of trademarks are not.

364. The United States does not answer to the questions whether the USPTO is a judicial body and whether the procedures before the USPTO are judicial procedures, although it seem to concede that they are not by saying that some of them are "quasi-judicial."[237] The United States also says that "certain aspects of the procedures of the USPTO could be regarded as part of the enforcement procedures available to US right holders."[238] For example, according to the United States, a petitioner could take a cancellation decision of the USPTO to a federal court to get an injunction.[239] But the same is true of Regulation 2081/92. If a trademark owner objects successfully to the registration of a geographical indication, it could take the decision rejecting the registration to a Member State court to get an injunction against an infringing use.

---

[231] The US courts have followed a similar reasoning in order to deny to trademark owners the right to contest judicially the validity of the decision to recognise a geographical indication for wines on the grounds that it infringes their trademark rights. See *Sociedad Anonima Viña Santa Rita v. US Dept. of the Treasury*, 193 F. Supp. 2d 6 (D.D.C 2001) (Exhibit US–48) ("While the Bureau has recognized an AVA under the name "Santa Rita Hills" it has not used, imitated, or copied the name at all. Because such conduct is a necessary element of an infringement claim … the Court finds that the ATF's decision does not, in and of itself, contravene Plaintiff's trademark rights").

[232] Australia's Response to the EC's Question No. 6 b).

[233] Australia's Response to the EC's Question No. 6 c).

[234] Australia's Response to the EC's Question No. 6 d).

[235] Australia's Response to the EC's Question No. 6 a).

[236] Australia's Response to the EC's Question No. 6 a).

[237] US Response to the EC's Question No. 7.

[238] Ibid.

[239] Ibid.

365. In its First Written Submission, the EC argued that, for the purposes of Part III, the existence of an "infringement" must be determined in relation to the domestic law implementing Part II and not to Part II itself. Otherwise, Members would be required to give "direct effect" to the provisions of Part II. In connection with this argument the EC asked the following question to the complainants:[240]

> Would it be possible under domestic law for an EC national who owns an Australian/US trademark to claim before the Australia/US courts that another trademark has been registered by Australia's Trademark Office/the US PTO in violation of Article 16.1 of the TRIPS Agreement, even where it is not contested that such registration is in conformity with all the relevant provisions of your domestic trademark law?

366. The United States has responded evasively:

> ... any person likely to be damaged by the registration or continued registration of a mark at the USPTO may request cancellation of the registration at the USPTO or in a federal court and would cite grounds under US law for such request.

367. The EC understands that the "grounds under US law" mentioned in the above response do not include the violation of Article 16.1. The EC assumes, therefore, that the United States agrees that there is no obligation under Part III to provide "enforcement procedures" against the infringement of Article 16.1 as such, but only against the infringement of those provisions of domestic law that purport to implement Article 16.1, irrespective of their consistency with Article 16.1.

368. For its part, Australia answered as follows:

> A decision to register a trademark is reviewable *de novo* by the Federal Court of Australia. Thus, it would be possible for an EC national who owns an Australian trademark to claim before that court that another trademark has been registered by the Trade Marks Office of IP Australia in violation of the exclusive rights to use a trademark and to authorise other persons to use the trademark granted by section 20 of the Australian Trade Marks Act, which implements Australia's obligations pursuant to TRIPS Article 16.1, even where it is not contested that the latter registration is in conformity with all the relevant provisions of the Act.

369. The EC does not understand this response, which appears to be contradictory. How could the EC owner of the Australian trademark "A" claim that the registration of the Australian trademark "B" infringes section 20 without contesting that the registration of trademark "B" is in conformity "with all the relevant provisions of the Act"? In a footnote to this response Australia confirms that "the provisions of international agreements do not have direct effect in Australian law." Thus, the EC understands that the owner of trademark "A" could not claim that, although trademark "B" has been registered in conformity with section 20, the registration of trademark "B" should be cancelled because it breaches Article 16.1. The EC assumes that, in view of this, Australia would agree that the situation described in the question would not give rise *per se* to a violation of Part III of the TRIPS Agreement, irrespective of the question whether section 20 is consistent with Article 16.1 of the TRIPS Agreement.

2. Claim 25: Regulation 2081/92 is inconsistent with Article 41.1 of the TRIPS Agreement

370. Neither Australia nor the United States have submitted any further arguments.

---

[240] EC's Question to the complainants No. 8.

3. Claim 26: Regulation 2081/92 is inconsistent with Article 41.2 of the TRIPS Agreement

371. Neither Australia nor the United States have submitted any further arguments.

372. The EC notes, nevertheless, that, in the context of another claim, the United States has conceded that:[241]

> in the case of the United States, it would probably not be difficult to designate an office in the US Government to perform a purely ministerial act of transmitting a registration ... objections to the EC.

373. As explained by the EC[242], the action described in the US response is all that is required from the governments of other WTO Members under the objection procedure. The US admission confirms that, contrary to Australia's allegations[243], the requirement to lodge objections with the governments of other WTO Members does not "add unjustifiable complexity and delay."

4. Claim 27: Regulation 2081/92 is inconsistent with Article 41.3 of the TRIPS Agreement

374. Australia has submitted no further arguments.

5. Claim 28: Regulation 2081/92 is inconsistent with Article 41.4 of the TRIPS Agreement

375. The United States has made no further arguments.

6. Claim 29: Regulation 2081/92 is inconsistent with Article 42 of the TRIPS Agreement

376. See above the comments under "General Considerations."

E. CLAIM 30: REGULATION 2081/92 IS INCONSISTENT WITH ARTICLE 10*BIS* (1) AND 10*TER* (1) OF THE PARIS CONVENTION

377. Australia has submitted no further arguments.

F. CONSEQUENTIAL CLAIMS

1. Claim 31: Regulation 2081/92 is inconsistent with Article 2.1 of the TRIPS Agreement

378. Australia has made no further arguments.

2. Claim 32: Regulation 2081/92 is inconsistent with Article 1.1 of the TRIPS Agreement

379. Australia has conceded that this claim is entirely dependent on other claims.[244]

3. Claim 33: The transitional national protection provided by the Member States is inconsistent with Articles 2.1, 16.1, 41.1, 41.2, 41.3 and/or 42 of the TRIPS Agreement

380. Australia has made no further arguments.

---

[241] US Response to the Panel's Question No. 38, para. 74.

[242] EC Response to the Panel's Question No. 34, para. 86.

[243] Australia's FWS, para. 138.

[244] Australia's Response to the Panel's Question No. 82.

VI. THE EC MEASURE IS CONSISTENT WITH THE OBLIGATION TO PROVIDE PROTECTION TO GEOGRAPHICAL INDICATIONS UNDER ARTICLE 22.2 OF THE TRIPS AGREEMENT

1. Claim 34: Regulation 2081/92 is inconsistent with Article 22.2 of the TRIPS Agreement

381. In its First Written Submission, Australia stated this claim as follows:[245]

> Regulation No. 2081/92 establishes a Community-wide regime for the registration and protection of EC-defined GIs. However, the EC measure does not provide –as concerns those same EC-defined GIs—legal channels for interested parties to prevent on a Community-wide basis any use of those EC-defined GIs which would mislead the public as to the geographical origin of a good or any use which would constitute an act of unfair competition within the meaning of Paris Article 10 bis.

382. The EC noted that this claim was insufficiently argued and difficult to understand. As discussed below, after one hearing and a round of questions and answers, this claim remains as obscure, if not more, as in Australia's First Written Submission.

383. The above quoted passage suggested that the alleged violation would arise from the absence of Community-wide system of protection. The EC noted in its First Written Submission that there is no basis in Article 22.2, or anywhere else in the TRIPS Agreement, for the proposition that protection must be provided at any particular territorial level. The Panel seemed to share the EC's perplexity because it asked Australia to "cite any authority for the proposition that a Member must comply with a particular WTO obligation through a single measure applicable throughout its territory." Australia has responded this question as follows:[246]

> Australia has not contended –and does not contend—that a WTO Member must comply with a particular WTO obligation though a single measure applicable throughout its territory. Rather, Australia contends that, while the EC can choose to offer more extensive protection of EC-defined GIS at the Community level, the EC must also ensure that it does not breach its TRIPS obligations in doing so. Given the legal EC system, and the terms of Regulation No. 2081/92 and of other EC and Member States law, the EC has effectively implemented a TRIPS right –at Community level- without also effectively implementing at the same level the concurrent TRIPS obligation.

384. The EC wishes to put on record that it still fails to understand the grounds for Australia's claim. In particular, the EC does not know what are the "concurrent TRIPS obligations" that the EC should have implemented at Community level, rather than at Member State level. In addition, the EC notes that Australia does not answer the Panel's question, because it does not cite any authority for the proposition that WTO rights and "concurrent obligations" should be implemented at the same level. The EC is not aware of any such authority.

385. In its First Written Submission, the EC noted that it failed to see how the use of a validly registered geographical indication, which is otherwise consistent with the TRIPS Agreement, could possibly mislead the public as to the geographical origin of the goods. The EC also observed that it failed to understand how the registration or the use of a geographical indication consistently with the EC domestic laws, as well as with all other provisions of the TRIPS Agreement, including Articles 24.5 and 16, could ever constitute an act of unfair competition within the meaning of Article 10*bis* of the Paris Convention (1967).

---

245 Ibid., para. 155.

246 Australia's response to the Panel's Question No. 81.

386. In response to the Panel's Question No. 24 concerning the meaning of the term "interested parties" in Article 22.2 Australia provides an "example" of the type of "uses" which it has in mind:

> For example, it is entirely possible that there are products which, while originally based on European processes, have subsequently come to represent the "international" trading standard for that product: to register the original geographic name under regulation No. 2081/92 in such circumstances—notwithstanding that the product qualify for registration—could well constitute misleading use or use which constitutes an act of unfair competition within the meaning of TRIPS Article 22.2 even within the EC. This type of action is clearly contemplated by the text of Article 22.2.

387. Later, in response to the Panel's Question No. 82, Australia states what appears to be a condensed version of the same "example:"

> the situations covered by TRIPS Article 22.2 do not necessarily involve trademark rights: for example, a term may have become a generic product description in international trade before it was protected in its country of origin.

388. It is unclear to the EC whether these "examples" are provided simply in order to illustrate Australia's interpretation of the notion of "interested parties" or purport to be claims on their own. The EC surmises that Australia does not dare to state them more openly as claims because it realises that they are as provocative as ill-founded.

389. First, the EC does not understand, and Australia does not explain, how the use of a term which in the territory of Member "A" is not a "generic" product description but a "geographical indication" within the meaning of Article 22.1 (i.e. a term which "identifies the origin" of the product) could be deemed "misleading" for the purposes of Article 22.2(a) when used in relation to goods of the origin designated by the geographical indication, simply because the same term has become "generic" in the territory of Member "B."

390. Second, Article 22.2 is concerned with the protection of geographical indications as defined in Articled 22.1. Article 22.2(b) applies to unfair competition acts against the right holders of geographical indications and not to supposed unfair competition acts against other parties arising from the legitimate use of geographical indications.

391. Third, in any event, the conduct described by Australia cannot be deemed an act of unfair competition by any reasonable standard. Australia cites no authority for its interpretation, except a quotation from Bodenhausen's treatise to the effect that the notion of "honest practice in industrial or commercial matters" within the meaning of Article 10bis.2 of the Paris Convention includes "honest practices established in international trade."[247] The EC submits that the exercise of a right conferred by a WTO Member in order to comply with its obligations under the TRIPS Agreement is not a "dishonest practice" in international trade. In particular, where such right is exercised in order to avoid that the public of that WTO Member be mislead as to the origin of the products. In other words, in order to prevent a genuine act of unfair competition.

392. Moreover, Australia's interpretation would create a conflict between Article 22.2(a), which requires Members to provide means to protect the geographical indications of other Members, unless they have become "generic" in *their* own territory[248], and Article 22.2(b), which, on Australia's construction, would require them to provide means to prevent the use of geographical indications that are "generic" in the territory of *other* Members. Indeed, Australia's interpretation would create a conflict *within* Article 22.2(b) itself, because, as mentioned, the fact of using a term which is a geographical indication in the territory of one Member in relation to products that do not have that origin is an act of unfair competition.

---

[247] Australia's Response to Question No. 24.

[248] Cf. Article24.9 of the TRIPS Agreement.

393. Finally, Article 22.2(b) applies to "uses." The registration of a geographical indication is not a "use" and cannot be *per se* an act of unfair competition. Rather the alleged act of unfair competition would result from the subsequent use of a geographical indication. Regulation 2081/92 does not exclude the application of the laws on unfair competition of the Member States. To the extent that the conduct described by Australia could ever be considered as an act of unfair competition, the use of a registered geographical indication would be caught by those laws, which are all based on the relevant provisions of the Paris Convention. Those laws are not within the terms of reference of the Panel.

2. Claim 35: Regulation 2081/92 is inconsistent with Article 1.1 of the TRIPS Agreement because it is inconsistent with Article 22.2

394. Australia concedes that this claim is entirely dependent on its claim under Article 22.2 of the TRIPS.[249]

3. Claim 36: Regulation 2081/92 is inconsistent with Article 22.2 TRIPS

395. In its response to the Panel's Question No. 84, the United States argues that the fact that opposition procedures are regulated specifically in Part IV does not exclude the possibility that the lack of adequate objection procedures may be inconsistent as well with Article 22.2.

396. The United States argues that Article 62.1 envisions that the procedures for the acquisition of an intellectual property right can violate both Part IV and other provisions of the TRIPS Agreement, including Part II. This is correct. For example, it is beyond question that those procedures may violate Articles 3 and 4. In addition, some provisions of Part II lay down special procedural rules. For example, Article 15.5 provides that "Members may afford an opportunity for the registration of a trademark to be opposed."

397. Unlike Article 15.5, Article 22.2 does not regulate expressly the right of opposition. In the absence of any such express rules in Article 22.2 or elsewhere in Section 3 of Part II, it may not be assumed that the drafters' intention was to derogate from the generally applicable rules contained in Part IV.

398. Moreover, Article 22.2 requires to provide "means" to prevent certain "uses." The registration of a geographical indication is not a "use" of a geographical indication. For that reason, in order to comply with Article 22.2 it is not necessary to provide for a right of objection to the registration of a geographical indication. Article 22.2 does not even require to provide for the possibility to challenge directly before the courts the registration decision. In order to comply with Article 22.2 it may be sufficient if a Members provide for the possibility to bring infringement proceedings against a particular "use" prohibited by Article 22.2, in the context of which the plaintiff may challenge the validity of the registration, if necessary. EC law does provide for such possibility.

VII. REGULATION 2081/92 IS CONSISTENT WITH OBLIGATIONS UNDER THE TBT AGREEMENT

399. Australia (but not the United States) has raised two claims under the TBT Agreement:

- that Article 12(2) of Regulation 2081/92 is incompatible with Article 2.1 of the TBT Agreement (Claim 37);[250]
- that Articles 4 and 10 of Regulation 2081/92 are incompatible with Article 2.2 of the TBT Agreement (Claim 38).[251]

---

[249] Australia's Response to the Panel's Question No. 82.

[250] Australia's FWS, para. 234 et seq.

400. In its first written submission, the EC has shown that the provisions of Regulation 2081/92 referred to by Australia cannot be regarded as technical regulations within the meaning of Articles 2.1 and 2.2 TBT Agreement.[252] Moreover, the EC has shown that in any event, Australia's claims under Article 2.1 and 2.2 TBT Agreement are unfounded.[253]

A. REGULATION 2081/92 IS NOT A TECHNICAL REGULATION

401. At this stage, Australia has provided very little in response to the EC's arguments. In particular, in the view of the EC, Australia has failed to show that the provisions of Regulation 2081/92 which it challenges do indeed constitute a technical regulation falling under Article 2 of the TBT Agreement.

1. Article 12(2) of Regulation 2081/92 is not a technical regulation

402. Contrary to the view of Australia, Article 12(2) of Regulation 2081/92 is not a technical regulation within the meaning of the TBT Agreement. In its first written submission, the EC has set out that Article 12(2) does not apply to identifiable products, does not lay down product characteristics, and is not a mandatory requirement.[254] Moreover, in response to Question 50 of the Panel, the EC explained that the requirement to indicate the origin of the product is not a "labelling requirement as it applies to a product, process or production method" within the meaning of Annex 1, Point 1, to the TBT Agreement.[255]

403. For all these reasons, Article 12(2) of Regulation 2081/92 is not a technical regulation within the meaning of the TBT Agreement.

2. Articles 4 and 10 of Regulation 2081/92 are not a technical regulation

404. Contrary to the view of Australia, Articles 4 and 10 of Regulation 2081/92 are not a technical regulation within the meaning of the TBT Agreement.

405. In its first written submission, the EC has explained that by requiring the existence of inspection structures, Articles 4 and 10 of Regulation 2081/92 do not lay down product characteristics, and therefore cannot be regarded as a technical regulation within the meaning of Point 1 of Annex 1 to the TBT Agreement.[256] The EC stressed that the objective of the requirement of inspection structures was to ensure that the product specifications are complied with. Accordingly, even if, for the sake of argument, it were accepted that these product specifications are a technical regulation or a standard, then the inspection structures would constitute a conformity assessment procedure within the meaning of Point 3 of Annex 1 to the TBT Agreement, but not a technical regulation. Accordingly the applicable provisions would be Articles 5 to 9 of the TBT Agreement, and not Articles 2 to 4 thereof.

406. In response to Question 60 of the Panel, Australia has claimed that the dividing line between a technical regulation and a conformity assessment procedure is "difficult to determine in the abstract." The EC does not agree. As the EC has set out in its response to the same question,[257] the dividing line is perfectly clear, and follows from the definitions contained in Points 1 and 3 of Annex 1 to the TBT Agreement. According to Point 1 of Annex 1, a technical regulation "lays down product characteristics." According to Point 3, a conformity assessment procedure ensures that "relevant requirements in technical regulations or standards are

---

251 Australia's FWS, para. 249 et seq.

252 EC FWS, para. 439 et seq.

253 EC FWS, para. 469 et seq.

254 EC FWS, para. 443 et seq.

255 EC Response to Panel's Question No. 50, para. 120.

256 EC FWS, para. 458 et seq.

257 EC Response to Panel's Question No. 60, para. 132-134.

fulfilled." In application of these definitions, it should be clear that the requirement of inspection structures is not a technical regulation.

407. In its response to Question 60, Australia has raised the question whether the EC contends that the "product specifications requirement set out in Article 4 of the Regulation" constitutes a technical regulation. The EC certainly does not contend that the requirement that a geographical indication must correspond to certain product specifications constitutes a technical regulation. This requirement is merely a condition for the registration of geographical indications, i.e. of an intellectual property right, and does not itself constitute a technical regulation.

408. A different question would be whether individual product specifications laid down for particular geographical indications are technical regulations. The EC does not believe so. However, the Panel does not need to address this issue, since Australia has not raised any specific claims with respect to specific product specifications. It is sufficient to note that even if, for the sake of hypothesis, Australia's thesis were accepted that somehow product specifications are technical regulations, still the requirement of inspection structures would not constitute a technical regulation.

409. For these reasons, the requirement of inspection structures set out in Articles 4 and 10 of Regulation 2081/92 does not constitute a technical regulation within the meaning of the TBT Agreement.

B. CLAIM 37: ARTICLE 12(2) OF REGULATION 2081/92 IS INCOMPATIBLE WITH ARTICLE 2.1 OF THE TBT AGREEMENT

410. Australia has claimed that Article 12(2) of Regulation 2081/92 is incompatible with Article 2.1 of the TBT Agreement.[258]

411. As the EC has set out in its first written submission, Article 12(2) is fully compatible with Article 2.1 of the TBT Agreement.[259] In particular, the EC has explained that Article 12(2) of Regulation 2081/92 applies to domestic and foreign geographical indications in a non-discriminatory fashion, since it requires in fact the indication of the country of origin for the homonymous geographical indication which is protected later, irrespective of whether this is the EC or the third country indication.

412. The EC notes that in its response to Question 53 of the Panel, Australia has indicated that if interpreted in this way, Article 12(2) would not be incompatible with Article 2.1 TBT Agreement. However, Australia voices doubts as to whether the interpretation set out by the EC is correct. As the EC has already explained above in response to Claim 3, these doubts are unfounded.[260]

413. Accordingly, Article 12(2) of Regulation 2081/92 is not incompatible with Article 2.1 TBT Agreement.

C. CLAIM 38: ARTICLES 4, 10, AND 12 (1) OF REGULATION 2081/92 ARE INCOMPATIBLE WITH ARTICLE 2.2 OF THE TBT AGREEMENT

414. Australia has claimed that Articles 4, 10, and 12 (1) of Regulation 2081/92 are incompatible with Article 2.2 of the TBT Agreement.[261]

415. Australia's claims in this respect are similar to those which the United States now is raising under the national treatment provisions of the TRIPS Agreement and the GATT (Claims 1bis and 12bis). In response to

---

[258] Australia's FWS, para. 234 et seq.

[259] EC FWS, para. 469 et seq.

[260] Above para. 143.

[261] Australia's FWS, para. 249 et seq.

Claim 1bis, the EC has already set out in detail that the requirement of inspection structures is necessary for the attainment of the objectives of Regulation 2081/92, and is not more trade-restrictive than necessary for the fulfilment of these purposes. These arguments apply also to the Australian claim made under Article 2.2 TBT Agreement. Accordingly, the EC refer to its defence to Claim 1bis in this respect.[262]

416. Accordingly, Regulation 2081/92 is fully compatible with Article 2.2 TBT Agreement.

VIII. CLAIM 39, 40: THE EC MEASURE IS COMPATIBLE WITH ARTICLE 65.1 TRIPS AND ARTICLE XVI:4 WTO

417. The United States has claimed that the EC has not fulfilled its obligations under Article 65.1 TRIPS.[263] Similarly, Australia has claimed that the EC has not complied with its obligations under Article XVI:4 WTO.[264]

418. Both claims are dependent on substantive claims discussed above. Since these claims are unfounded, the consequential claims under Article 65.1 TRIPS and XVI:4 WTO are equally unfounded.

IX. CONCLUSION

419. For the above reasons, the EC reiterates the conclusions stated in its First Written Submission.

[262] Above, para. 91.

[263] US FWS, para. 190.

[264] Australia's FWS, para. 267.